A cool tool is ...

Anything useful
That increases learning
Empowers individuals
Does work that matters
Is either the best
Or the cheapest
Or the only thing that works.

Cool Tools
A Catalog of Possibilities

By Kevin Kelly

Produced by Camille Hartsell

© 2013 by Kevin Kelly. All rights reserved.

Published by KK★, an imprint of Cool Tools Lab

Distributed in the United States by Publishers Group West and in Canada by Publishers Group Canada.

Library of Congress Cataloging-in-Publication Data

Kelly, Kevin, 1952-

Cool tools : a catalog of possibilities / Kevin Kelly.

p. cm.

Includes index

ISBN-13: 978-1-940689-00-5 (trade paperback)

1. Implements, utensils, etc. -- Catalogs. 2. Handicraft -- Equipment and supplies -- Catalogs. 3. Appropriate technology -- Catalogs. 4. Technology and civilization.

TS199.C66 2013   2013916271

Printed in Hong Kong   First edition, fifth printing

www.kk.org

KK★

All those KKs signed throughout this book are by me, Kevin Kelly. Writing reviews of cool tools is my obsession. I speak, blog, and write non-fiction books for my living. My most recent big-idea book is entitled *What Technology Wants*. It's about the very long-term trends in techology and about technology's uplifting role in our lives. If you want to know what technology means, I offer a theory, with stories. Two decades earlier I wrote a book about how technology is becoming life-like (entitled *Out of Control*), and a decade ago I wrote a book about the new economics of information (*New Rules for the New Economy*). Besides big ideas, I am a photographer of small things and vanishing traditions in Asia. The art-book publisher Taschen published my collection of exotic Asia scenes as *Asia Grace*, now out of print. I try to funnel all my magazine writings (*Wired*, *New York Times*, etc.), interviews, presentations, travels, new projects, and biographical notes onto my website, kk.org. My personal logo of KK★ is a small nerdy joke. The asterick is a computerese symbol that means "all and anything else." So all and anything else I do I include on my site. My homepage links to all my books and my previous startups like the Quantified Self and True Films, and all my current projects. There's more there about me than you'll want to know. My email has been public since I first logged online in 1982. To save you the trouble of googling it, here it is: kk@kk.org. For better or worse I read all my mail and answer most. You can follow me @kevin2kelly on social spaces, where I have an uneven presence.

-- KK

Are You Missing?

People move, and don't tell us! We tried very hard to contact every person who submitted a published review on the Cool Tools website that was reprinted in this book (all reviews here first appeared online), but we have a long list of folks whose email we have is now defunct. It's been 10 years in some cases so we don't blame anyone. If you see a review you wrote in this book and we haven't contacted you, send us your current email. We have a thank you gift for you. Email to editor@cool-tools.org.

The people who made this book

To put this gigantic book together required many souls. The text was written by a thousand readers of Cool Tools whose names appear in the signatures of the reviews. The chief producer of this book was Camille Hartsell. Camille did everything that needed done. She hired proofers and artists, engineered the workflow, created the spreadsheets, prepared the first draft of the book, and even designed some pages. The book would simply not have happened without her. In addition to

Camille Hartsell delivers justice at Comic-Con as Nightshade.

her excellent craftmanship and energy, she brought unwavering cheerfulness to the long project. When the final PDF leaves for the printer she is planning to celebrate by delivering a baby, her first.

Josko Kirigin explains a Space Elevator in an impromptu classroom.

Josko Kirigin, a friend of Camille, oversaw the lion's share of updating ordering information and placing items into our layouts. He worked remotely in the shadow of cyberspace, quietly but wholly dependable.

The other souls contributing to this book also worked remotely. At first it was only me. Cool Tools began in 2000 as a private email list to a small circle of my friends. I reviewed each tool myself and emailed my reviews to friends weekly. My friends began sending back reviews of their favorite tools, which I edited and sent out with my reviews. After 2 years or so, I started to post all the reviews on a blog as well. I did this for 4 more years, until I hired help. The

Charles Platt makes his own hats.

Steven Leckart training to be a chef at Benihana

first guest editor was author Charles Platt, an active fan of the site. I had worked with Charles at *Wired*; he was one of my favorite writers. Charles gathered and edited reviews for four months as a temporary editor.

Our first permament editor, Steven Leckart, came from the research desks at *Wired*. Steven oversaw Cool Tools for the next two and a half years. Steven shaped Cool Tools into a reliable daily source of goodness, and later edited our first ebook, before moving onto his own book writing. We found the next chief of the site, Elon Schoenholz, through a solicitation to our readers. Elon was a jack of all trades, and a photographer practicing in LA. Elon

Elon Schoenholz hiking with his kids using the Kelty Pathfinder backpack he recommends.

Oliver Hulland finishes foraging with a 17-pound Giant Polypore.

Mark Frauenfelder has harvested 25 pounds of backyard honey with only one sting.

Camille checks proofs under the watch of the Styrobot.

edited Cool Tools with great intelligence and diligence for two years. We worked by email; I still haven't met him in person. When Elon went back to photography full time, we discovered Oliver Hulland, another fan of the site. I first spoke to Oliver Hulland over Skype as he traveled in China. Oliver has many passions, including spelunking, EMT, and traveling. He remotely edited CT for three years. Just when Oliver started his medical school, Mark Frauenfelder took the helm of editorship. Mark had worked as an editor with me at *Wired* in the 90s, and later went on to start one of the very first blogs ever. (Mark was the one who introduced me to blogs.) His bOING bOING blog grew to become one of the most popular destinations on the web. Later Mark became the founding editor at *MAKE* magazine. Mark now partners with me in running the Cool Tools website.

Out in cyberspace reside our artists and proofers. We hired three designers working remotely through the free-lance sites, Odesk and Elance (see page 376). I have not met Carla Green, Laura Fortin, or Mary Alderdice but I was incredibly impressed by their fast and handsome design work. Hatem Kahil from Turkey prepared our images. We hired a whole gang of freelancers on Elance to proof the book in two days: Marcia Abramson, Apryl Duncan, Alicia Haque, Amber Raden, Sam Severn. Tywen Kelly and Laura Fortin helped in proofing QR codes. The cover was designed by me; the artwork is by the graphic artist Matt W. Moore.

World headquarters for production of the book is my studio in Pacifica, California, where Camille and I work non-remotely. We benefit by the long work tables and

two-story library that line the walls of the studio. Meetings with our distant colleagues are conducted on Google Hangouts. Just out the window over Camille's desk, we get a street-level view of the chickens chasing each other in the afternoon sun.

-- KK

Photo credits from the beginning: Trevor Hartsell, Kim Loda, Rudy Rucker, Jonathan Snyder. Kristyna Solawetz, Carla Sinclair, Kevin Kelly, Camille Hartsell.

The Tool Revolution

Tools are the revolution. New tools create new visions, new possibilities. New tools are the source of all progress.

At the same time old tools continue to improve, making it easier to make things. Making things is what makes us human; the more we make, the more human we become.

The book is full of tools, most of which are not-digital, but are as physical as a hammer and anvil. Digital tools are wonderful, but they obsolete within minutes, and are not worth tracking on paper. So we don't feature very many apps or gizmos, preferring to focus on more tangible tools. Additionally, as our collective attention is swallowed by the digital realm, there's been a dawning realization that behind the virtual worlds stand an immense physical infrastructure of generators, roads, power towers, as well as buildings, vehicles, shelters, and so on. They all need to be designed, built, and improved, and in many ways contain the real frontier for innovation. Whereas previously, making big things required institutional or corporate assistance, new tools such as some highlighted in this book enable individuals and small groups to make great stuff,

A third industrial revolution is stirring -- the Maker era. In this era the digital is embodied by the physical, producing a hybrid of intense virtuality embedded in high-tech physicality, a new matrix for civilization. The skills for this accelerated era lean toward the agile and decentralized. Therefore tools recommended here are aimed at small groups, decentralized communities, the do-it-yourselfer, and the self-educated. That means you. The empowered individual or small group that wants to create something. These possibilities cataloged here will help makers become better makers. These are tools to make us better humans.

--KK

Two tools the same size, both revolutionary in their time. One you could make in a weekend with practice. The other no individual, no matter how skilled, could make alone. Each is a doorway into the new. Image from Matt Ridely's Rational Optimist.

Every tool is an opportunity. You don't need to buy it. Just explore where it can take you.

Anatomy of a Review

Major benefit of the tool.

Proper name of the tool.

Where to get the item if it is not available on Amazon.

Model or version number.

QR code

Street price (What you can expect to pay).

The cheapest perfect thing
Obtainium 3000
$1 Model 3000 internetstore.com

This is where we tell you why this thing is so great and wonderful, and why you should believe us. Also, we may tell you who the tool is best suited for, and maybe some disadvantages it may have.

Review written by user of tool, edited by us.

-- KK

Author of review, in this case, Kevin Kelly.

▪ If it is a book, a few excerpts will give you a sense of the tenor of the books and also teach you a few nuggets.

Examples from a book.

▪ This symbol indicates the excerpts are not continuous in the book.

Those QR codes

QR codes are hyperlinks on paper. Use your smartphone to scan one and it will take you to a link on the web. You need to load a QR app onto your phone. Tap the app, scan the code on the tool review, and it will instantly load the precise web page where you can purchase the tool -- or at least bring you to its source. There are dozens of free QR readers; Scan is one with versions for iPhone and Android.

A tip: If two QR codes are near each other in a review try to isolate one by rotating your phone 90 degrees.

How To Use This Book

You don't need most of the tools in this book. The purpose of these reviews is not to entice you to buy more stuff, but to alert you to the possibilities they contain. Often knowing that a specific tool is available can 1) encourage you to try a new task yourself, 2) inspire a new way of doing an old chore, 3) give you an idea of something no one has ever made before, or 4) reside in your mind for future use.

Should you really want to get your hands on one of these tools, the QR code (square bar code) next to each item will point your smart phone to the website where it can be purchased. (See explanation above right for details.) Or you can search for the source given in blue text. Of course, used tools can be found on Craigslist and eBay. But many tools can be rented for a fee (see p. 30). Renting is a good way to try something first. Most tools can also be borrowed from a friend. Friends, by definition, share interests and often have tools to share. In a few places around the country you can borrow tools from a Tool Lending Library (see p. 32). Lastly, an increasing number of subscription-based workshops that are stocked with the latest of every tool for use by members are opening up around the US (see p. 29). The point is, you don't need to own things. Access trumps ownership.

Books can be tools, too. Books have never been cheaper. You can often find used version of books for pennies on Amazon (plus a fixed cost of shipping). Libraries are discarding perfectly good books. Despite this discarding, check your local library because most areas have extensive inter-library loan programs, which means they'll get you a copy somehow.

The QR code listed near each item often resolves into a link on Amazon where you can purchase the item. On the rare cases where Amazon does not carry the item, we list an alternative retail site, or the manufacturer. We list Amazon first for several reasons: 1) They carry almost everything, so we can list one source; 2) They are utterly reliable, fast, and often the cheapest. We may have no personal experience with alternative sources; 3) They offer additional customer reviews which you can double check for confirmation; 4) They give us a fractional percentage of the sale price which is how we pay for the website. (This reasoning is expanded in the FAQ, p.5.)

Every submitted tool review goes through a fairly extensive process of evaluation. If it comes from an author new to us, we sniff out any possible conflicts of interest to make sure the recommendation is authentic, personal, and not a shill for a company. We also look at forums around the web for confirming evidence that this tool is indeed cool. We check popular review sites for additional confirmation of "bestness." Sometimes we google the review to make sure it is not being recycled, a red flag. And we study the reviews on Amazon carefully. No product will have a perfect score, so over the years we've learned how to "read" the reviews, to interpret the inevitable bad reviews. And then the review itself is edited in collaboration with the author to make sure it is clear and decisive. We are good but not perfect. After all that work you still have to figure out if this tool is exactly what you need.

Prices change rapidly, and models go out of date quickly. We've done our best to update every item for this book, but their accuracy is highly perishable. If you find an item's link is stale, look around for similar models. Generally items improve. If you don't like Amazon it is easy enough to google alternative sources for items, or to track it to your favorite retailer.

Over the past decade a lot of the reviews in this book have been written by me; some have been crafted by the editors hired by me, and most have been written by knowledgable readers of the Cool Tools website. With very few exceptions the tools recommended were purchased by the reviewers themselves, and are as impartial as we can make them. We really believe that these are the best.

-- KK

Updates: On the Blog

The approximately 1,500 recommendations included here are written by folks who've personally used the items reviewed. If you have experience with something better, please send us your expertise. Tell us about a cool tool that should be included here, yet is not. Be sure to explain what benefits it brings and why it should be included. Send it to editor@cool-tools.org. If we are encouraged enough to tackle a second edition of the book, your addition will improve it. Any reviews we publish we pay $25.

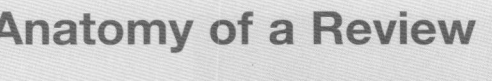

But whether or not we dare make a second edition, we'll continue to publish one rave review per day on the Cool Tools blog. All the 1,500 reviews in this book first appeared on this blog. Each day we introduce one new useful, uncommon tool that will open up possibilities. Readers can join a discussion where each tool is evaluated, and the Cool Tools site offers a forum where you can ask the community for your own tool requests. Wait, there's more! Starting with the release of this book, we'll also be organizing regional Meetups for Show & Tell evenings. Come and demo your favorite cool tools with others in your hometown.

ask
COOLTOOLS
Recently Asked
Has anyone used this hard drive upgrade kit?
What should you do to choose the perfect right bulb?
AM Radio Headset
Super pogo sticks?

Of course we have a twitter following as well: @cool_tools. And a hashtag: #cooltools. Google+ circle: Cool Tools.

This book is simply a snapshot of the ongoing process online, where the heart of the community that produced it resides. The Cool Tools site is the best way to keep updated with new tools, corrections, and better tools than the ones printed here.

The url is www.cool-tools.org. Join us!

-- KK

Origins

This book began with a simple idea: I wanted to give my three kids a box of tools when they left home. The box (a plastic storage crate) would contain essential handyman tools needed for everyday chores, as well as a set of other uncommon "cool" tools that I've found crucial in my own endeavors. I imagined including a few really great how-to-books and DVDs that would enlarge their sense of what could be done with the tools. I soon found out that only a few of the items I choose would actually fit in the crate. I had to leave out a lot. So the principal item I decided to include in their box was a book -- a book pointing to all the great tools beyond the box. This is the book you are now reading. It took me ten years to put it together, but it includes so much more than the box could hold. As I assembled it I began to think of the book as a catalog of possibilities, a self-education of the sort my kids would not get in school.

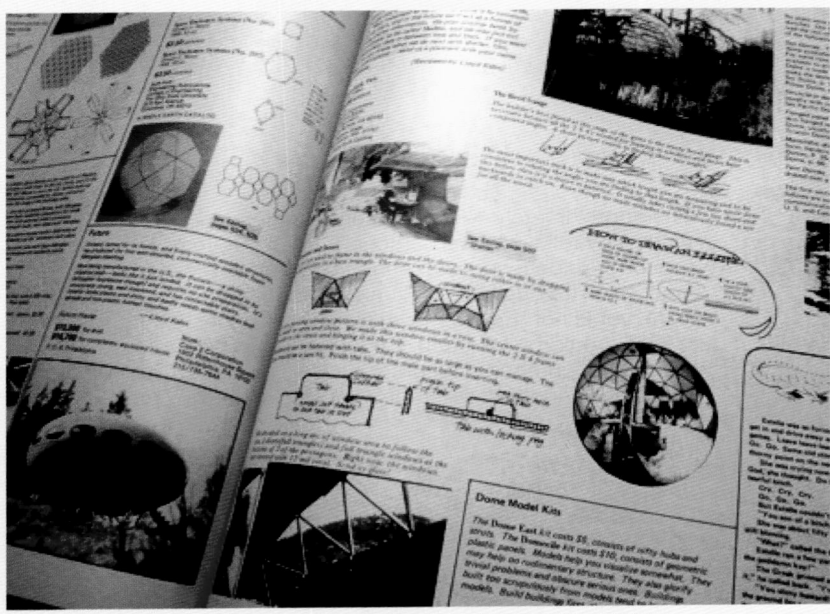

Look familar? Cool Tools is blantant ripoff of this book, both in spirit and style.

In fact this best of cool tools book would be a replica of a legendary book first published 45 years ago: The *Whole Earth Catalog*. Created in 1968 by a 23-year-old Stewart Brand, the *Catalog* was his selection of the best tools that would fit into a small store built into a truck. Brand drove his truck store to the new hippy communes eager to do everything themselves. "Here's a tool that will make drilling a well, or grinding flour, easier," Brand would tell them pointing it out in his catalog of recommended tools. But his best selling tool was the catalog itself, annotated by him, featuring tools that didn't fit into his truck. Soon Brand ditched the truck and began publishing accumulatively

WHOLE EARTH CATALOG

access to tools

Fall 1968
$5

larger versions of his tool catalog. He sold them by mail, and eventually he printed millions of them.

I was one of those million readers. I first came across the *Whole Earth Catalog* in my last year of high school. It opened me up. Its pages featured possibilities far outside the cultural confines of suburban New Jersey. As we said back then, it blew my mind. You mean anyone can learn to raise bees, or build their own house, or travel to Japan, or start their own business? From the Catalog I learned to do all those things, and did them, but more importantly, I learned to invent my own life. With the implicit encouragement of the *Whole Earth Catalog*, I dropped out of college, roamed Asia with a camera, and started my own businesses. But the only job I ever really want to do, was to work on the *Catalog*.

Through the usual indirect coincidences that shape our lives, I eventually got my first real job working at the *Whole Earth Catalog* in 1984, based along the houseboat community in Sausalito, California. I was 32 and in heaven. With the team I conceived and produced an *Essential Whole Earth Catalog*, a digest version of

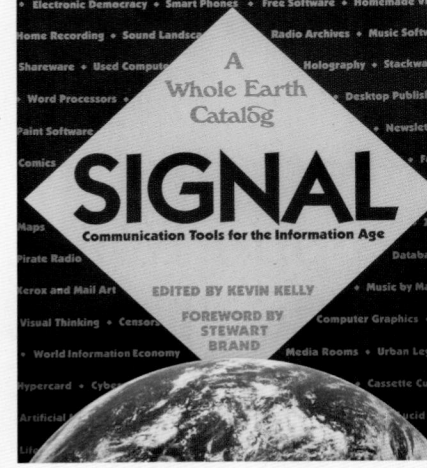

the great compendium, and several other specialty versions, as well as the *Catalog*'s quarterly supplements. In 1988 I produced a *Whole Earth Catalog* of "communication tools for the information age" called *SIGNAL*, which in some ways foreshadowed a startup I was involved in four years later: *Wired* magazine.

Then the World Wide Web came along in the 1990s. It turns out the heart of the *Whole Earth Catalog* was networking. The Whole Earth Catalog was a community network run on newsprint. We took reader-generated content, and with minimal editing and maximum cheapness, rapidly broadcasted the best stuff back to the readers, without advertising. Nowadays that's called digital peer-to-peer user generated content; it's valued at billions of dollars.

But that's what we always wanted: an electronic version of the Catalog that was ceaselessly being updated by the readers themselves, with immediate links to where you can get stuff, and no boundaries on our enthusiasm. That's of course, exactly what the web birthed, but on a scale way beyond our shack on the waterfront in Sausalito. Once the WWW took off, the paper *Catalog* died. It felt like you didn't need a slow paper nexus if you had the whole web.

But evaluating a broad spectrum of tools -- defined as anything useful -- was too valuable a service to let go. Opinions were cheap and plentiful on the web, but informed, useful, comparative reviews were rare. So I continued the mission on my own as a free online web-based blog. I called it Cool Tools, and I used the same format as *Whole Earth Catalog*:

1) Run enthusiastic reviews submitted by readers.

2) Only publish positive recommendations; skip the negative.

3) No teasers; review only things easily available to anyone now.

4) Provide current access information.

5) Keep the recommendations short and useful.

So every week day for the next 10 years, Cool Tools published a rave review of a new tool from someone who used and loved it. It was finally the *Whole Earth Catalog* on the web. Where it belonged.

But as good as it was on the web, after 10 years the sprawling tangle of tools needed

Stewart Brand just arriving from Morocco in the desert of Burning Man, 1999.

pruning and a better navigation through its abundance. It needed a handy interface, better context, a way to profitably browse, and more encouragement to make your own associations between ideas. In short, it needed to be on paper. Back on paper from where it came. In a huge oversized book! As big and thick as the *Whole Earth Catalog* in its day! I'll subtitle it, *A Catalog of Possibilities*.

In the spirit of Stewart Brand's *Catalog*, this one too is self-published. Instead of using the 1970s cool tools of an IBM Selectric typesetter and a Polaroid instant camera employed by young hippies, I used off-the-shelf consumer software and crowdsourced hired help. (More about the tools used on next page and p. 376.) I self-publish mostly to ramp up the rapid peer-to-peer benefits but in part to escape the mainstreaming impulses professional publishers can't help "recommending." I can assure you this book would not be what it is if I had gone through a New York publisher.

The author in 1987 working on one of the first Macintosh computers at the Whole Earth Catalog, showing his face scanned with the first Apple Scanner.

Self-published or not, it's crazy to make a book on dead trees in 2013. There will be no Kindle or tablet version. This thing is heavy, costly to ship. But it is totally exciting as well. You can judge for yourself if it works. If you really want electrons all the material that appears in this book is on the web as well, where you'll get better search and instant access.

But finally I can now put a meta-book into the box of tools for my kids. It just fits in. And since I've finished making it for them (in the end that is truly why I made it), you may find it useful as well. If you have suggestions about how to make it better, let me know.

-- KK

No, no, you're not thinking; you're just being logical. - Niels Bohr

Tools Used to Make this Book

InDesign -- The current industry standard for book layout and design. Very powerful, but like most Adobe products, it is so complex you'll need a refresher course on its functions in between projects.

Google Docs -- A free cloud-based doc program we used for text, workflow, spreadsheets, tracking files, accessible to anyone in the group.

QR Creator -- This cool custom app made by Dean Putney turned each review item's url links into QR codes of the exact size we wanted.

Epson Workforce Printer -- We printed out reams and reams of proofs and could only afford to do so because we had it modified for bulk inks by Cobra Inks (see p. 345).

Post-it Tags -- These removable color flags ready in their handy tiny dispenser are the perfect things to dog-ear select book passages.

Photoshop -- So versatile it's hard to get away from. We used its image processing to remove backgrounds, tweak images, and occasionally create visuals.

Acrobat Pro -- We use this to compress the book into a standard form to send to the printer. Also we use its OCR function to extract text files from scans of book pages.

DropBox -- The only way we could move large design files with their attendent images to so many makers in so many places in the world was by having everything stored in the cloud on Dropbox. We used the pro versions in order to claim all the storage space we needed. Worth the small fees for everyone. (See p. 368)

Google Hangouts -- Better than Skype, especially with more than two attendees, weekly Hangouts were our staff meetings. It's free too.

Epson Flatbed Scanner -- Old style scanner used to capture book illustrations.

ScanSnap -- This Fuji marvel will bulk scan a huge stack of documents in a few minutes. (See p. 360). We used it to scan and then send marked up pages back to the designers for revisions.

CrashPlan -- You have to be paranoid and dogmatic about backups. In addition to local backups we back up to the cloud mindlessly with Crashplan. (See p. 369).

Library -- We borrow books from our local library, we have a multi- thousand volume library, and we order books from Amazon weekly. Physical books have never been cheaper, and will never be as cheap in the future.

40 years of using, collecting, and reviewing how-to books has gone into this two-story library. The cat-walk is made from plexiglass recycled from a used bank window.

My Electronic Tools

My electronic tools change so fast, most are not worth reviewing individually. Here is what I employ as of September 2013.

In my office I use a Mac G5 Quad Core tower with 2, (yes 2!), huge Cinema screens. One screen is set up at standing desk height, the other for me sitting on a huge rubber ball. I alternate between them during the day. I have 16 gigs RAM in the Mac and I keep 15 huge apps open all at once, a bad habit I can't seem to break. Plugged into it is a Logitech web cam for videoconferencing. When videoconferencing I use a Plantronics USB headset for better audio quality.

My main software suite, in the order they appear on my dock: Postbox (mail), Chrome (browser), SpamSeive (excellent spam filter), Apple Address book, Lightroom (main photo app), Word, Powerpoint, Evernote, MarsEdit (for blogging on Wordpress), Easycrop (quick cropping of photos), and during this project, InDesign, Photoshop and Adobe Bridge. As I mentioned, all of these will usually be opened together all day, every day.

I travel with a lovely, cheery, tiny 11-inch Mac Air, which I love. It is synced to my Mac Tower using Dropbox and Google Drive. I use a first-gen 3G Kindle as well. I carry an iPhone 5, but I am not a big chat or text person. I rarely use it.

On my desk is a Wacom Graphite tablet for drawing, an ancient Panasonic 2-line phone, a Radio Shack headset (the only way to talk on a phone), a Transcend USB Card Reader, and a Zoom recorder for recording interviews.

In my WiseWalker travel bag with 16 pockets I have a pair of Bose 15 noise canceling earphones for airplane flights, which I will wear even while I sleep onboard, a tiny AAA LED flashlight, and a Lumix pocket camera. When I am presenting a talk I carry a Mac VGA dongle to connect my Air to the projector and a Logitech wireless mouse for advancing slides remotely; this works perfectly.

In my boring Toyota minivan, I have a Garmin Nuvi and plug my iPhone into an audio jack, filled with podcasts and audio books. That's where I get most of my "reading" done.

When I am seriously photographing I use a Lumix FZ150, with its awesome 24x optical zoom, the equivalent of something like a 400mm lens for film. It's light and compact. Does stereo HD video as well. I can't be bothered with an SLR, because I carried two of those heavy film versions everyday for years and it was a supreme drag. I'll never go back to film. *-- KK*

FAQ

Why didn't you review my favorite tool?

There are a lot of holes in this catalog. Most of the tools here were recommended and reviewed by other readers. We missed a lot of good stuff because we did not know about it. You may know far more about a particular subject than most of our readers. Maybe you are a scuba enthusiast, or an avid treasure hunter, or you raise fish for food -- none of which we covered. If you use and love a tool we have not included here please let us know about it. Tell us what the tool allows you to do and why it is superior. Emphasize its benefits rather than list its features. We pay $25 for each review we use and will send you a copy of the book version.

The information in this book is -- by definition -- nearly obsolete as soon as it is printed. That's the inherent problem with paper books. You should assume actual prices will be higher than printed prices. Recommended great tools may have been discontinued (happens all the time). Consider the tools reviewed here as starting points -- as possibilities for further exploration. If a recommended product is out of production, check for similar models. Names often change for a newer version of an item.

The best way to submit a correction is to supply an alternative.

Will there be another edition?

Don't know. Depends on how many readers submit better tools. The best way to encourage us to make another edition is to send us a rave review of a tool you love, a resource you cherish, a how-to book you can recommend -- particularly in an area we have overlooked. At the very least we'll publish it in the Cool Tools website, which is where all the tools here were first published. ◄Follow this QR code to a page to submit your suggestion.

Why do you list Amazon for almost everything?

In case it is not clear, we don't directly sell or provide the items recommended here. We only point to where you can get them. Many of the QR codes in this book refer to Amazon in part because almost everything is available on Amazon. There are other reasons:

Amazon usually has the best price. Not always but usually. This is a reader-oriented book. We don't care about vendors, retailers, wholesalers, or advertisers. Our main focus is trying to find the best source from the users' point of view. We provide Amazon as the select source when they have the best or comparable price for the product. And usually they do. If we see another source with significantly better prices, we will list that.

However, we also have a self-interest in using Amazon. When you click one of the QR codes in this book it often takes you to an Amazon page. If you purchase that item on that visit, Cool Tools collects a tiny fee from Amazon. (It gets nothing if you don't purchase, and we don't have that kind of relationship with other vendors.) This fractional income helps pay for the work of producing the book.

But the most important reason we generally list Amazon is because they are the most reliable and convenient. Whenever we list a small-time source we are taking a chance that their delivery will not be reliable, or their return policy not good, or their shipping charges excessive, or spam policy stupid, or whatever. Sadly, we've guessed wrong on a number of products in the past, where we had to pick a small vendor with no experience, only to hear from readers that that source was not reliable. In the spirit of Cool Tools, with reviews that are written by people who have actually used things, we like to provide sources that we have actually used. Amazon is not the only source we have used, but combined with the reasons above, we have generally found it to be the most reliable for most users.

In addition we personally find other users' reviews on Amazon to be very helpful, and often more numerous than on other sites (if other sites have any reviews at all), and therefore there is yet another bonus to providing the Amazon link first. (Yes, there is a feedback loop wherein the more folks that use Amazon, the more attractive it becomes. That's the new economy.)

Finally, these days it is so easy to google any of the hundreds of other shopping comparison sites to find alternative online sources for things that you don't need us to list them. We simply can't do as good a job in finding them as they do.

To sum up, we list Amazon because it is a convenience for most readers. Think of it as the place to start looking. You can see what a good price is that you should expect to pay, you can read the reviews, you can see the specs all laid out, you can see similar products. If all those meet your approval you can buy in one-click. If you care to patronize alternative sources, you are now better informed to do so.

In our experience this is how most people shop already. It's rare someone buys something from another source without first checking on Amazon just to get a baseline. We provide this initial link for that baseline.

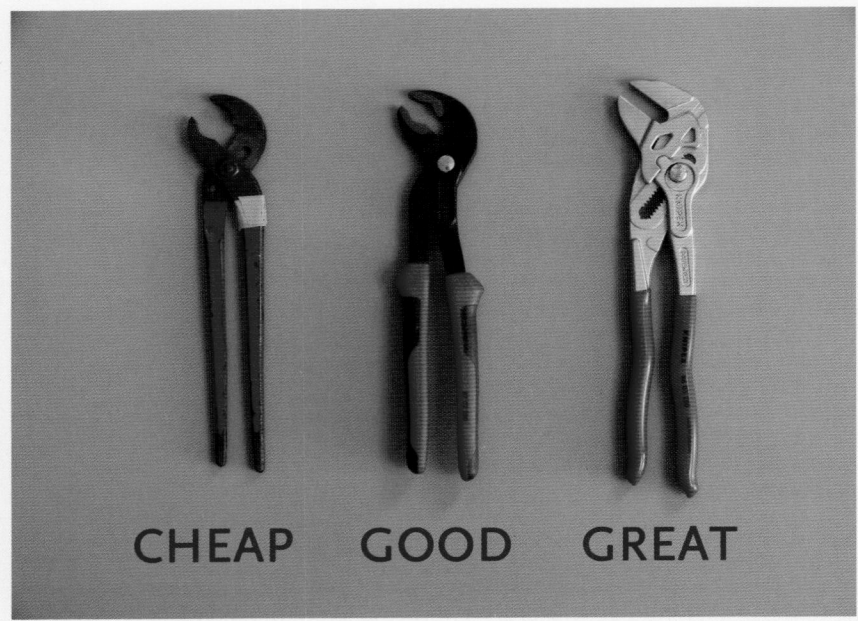

CHEAP GOOD GREAT

Tool Shopping Strategies

For fifty years I've been trying out tools of all kinds, mostly being thrifty, outfitting my studio and workshops with equipment, stocking our large household, making stuff as big as houses and as small as electronics, splurging on obscure hobbies, tracking gear for my kid's enthusiasms, and all the while writing tool reviews. Here's what I know about buying tools. (This philosophy informs this book.)

Cool Tools recommends four different types of tools:

The best tool made

The highest common quality tool

The cheapest possible tool

The tool you did not know about

The standard advice for a tool-buyer is to always purchase the highest quality tool available because, the argument goes, in the long run you'll have no regrets and the premium item will pay for itself. That's not generally true. Purchasing the best possible tool is neither always optimal nor doable.

The Best

It makes sense to buy the best tool available in cases where the tool type is well-proven, has few moving parts, and is general purpose. So when it comes to screwdrivers, hammers, clamps, pens, ladders, stuff like that, go for the best! These tools won't go out of fashion, they are inherently stable in design, probably won't wear out, and have multiple uses. Might as well get the best. For these I am happy to spend money on a few good ones.

It also makes sense to buy the best when you know what the best is. If you are using a tool every day, or even every week, or your income requires the tool, you'll educate yourself on what capabilities are essential, and you'll eventually require dependability. In these cases you will want to have the best possible model.

But most tools these days are not stable in design, they have many moving parts, they are not income related, and are more specialized. In these cases I have found it best to grow into quality.

Good Deal!

BENEFITS

PRICE

The Highest Common

To grow into quality my advice is to buy the "highest common denominator" tool at first. This is the cheapest decent quality version. It's about the quality you can find at Costco. It is not the rock bottom cheapest, but a mid-range that will allow you to use the tool long enough to decide whether you need to graduate to a higher quality.

Often — in fact very often — this mid-level highest common denominator quality is sufficient for occasional use. If you are not sewing every week, a Costco-level sewing machine is good enough. Ditto for the occasional use battery charger, or camp lantern; all you need is good enough. When you find yourself sewing more, camping more, woodworking more, then you can step up to the premium.

However, at Cool Tools we don't review a lot of tools in this category because this kind of quality needs no recommendation. For the average tool there is a very simple formula: the more money you spend the better quality. This can be summarized in this graph. Each dot is a model with a different price and quality point.

Durability, usability, the number of features, etc. increase as the cost increases. It's an even slope; no one brand or model of that tool usually stands out. For instance, right now cordless power drills follow this line. At the bottom you get a simple model for cheap; at the top you get a premium model for dear. Because every drill falls on this line, with no drill uncommonly better for the price, there is no reason to highlight one particular cordless drill in this book. Most tools are like this. No one model stands heads above the other; you merely get what you pay for. (Any jumping off the line are a great deal.) Just follow the price to get either the best, or the bargain — or head to a place with a limited selection of highest common stuff like Costco and shop there. However, Costco has a very narrow range of things they are selling at any one time so you'll need to rely on reviews.

The Cheapest Possible

There are at least 5 perfectly good reasons to buy the rock bottomest cheapo tool that will actually work:

1) You just want to try it out, have no idea whether you'll use it more than once and can't find a way to borrow or rent one (see Tool Lending Library).

2) It's all you can afford.

3) It'll be used by a community, or kids, or in settings where its care cannot be guaranteed.

4) You want to modify or enhance it.

5) It's in a fast moving field with high obsolescence

This last reason is important, and one of the best arguments against paying a lot for the very best tools. In highly technologically-driven fields, the "best" can be bettered every 3 months by new models and revolutionary innovations. For instance the best camera or laptop today will be second best in a few months. In two years, you might have trouble selling it. As a tool category becomes more innovative, rates of obsolescence increase. It makes more sense to aim for the low end — unless your job depends on it.

I think of aiming for the low end in a fast changing line of gear as Time-Shifting Value Strategy. Here's how this strategy works. Let's say I am buying a low-end orbital sander or super light tent. While that cheap sander or tent is many times inferior to the best model today, it is at least as good as the best model from 10 years ago. In other words, for the same cheap price I can buy the top of the line model from yesteryear. That's a bargain! All those cool features the magazines were drooling over before are now in my hands. I just pretend I am working in 2002! A simple mind-switch and now I am dazzled by what the cheapo tool taken from the future can do. Another way of thinking about this is that instead of considering tools to be a line of varying quality with ascending prices — $50, $75, $100 — think of them as being top-of-the-line models with ascending dates — 2002, 2007, 2012. Just pick a date you want to work in.

Note this caveat: Cheap comes in two flavors. There is a bad kind of cheap which means the tool does not do its intended job, or that it fails quickly. Its failure is subjective, but all too real. This kind of cheap tool does no one any good. I urge you to avoid them. But the good kind of cheap is a sturdy tool that provides only basic functions. It may be a bit slower, or heavier to hold, or it may lack many refinements — but it works okay for at least a sensible number of times. This is the kind of cheap tool worth considering. To distinguish between the two kinds of cheapness you'll need some reviews (see below).

The Tool You Did Not Know About

The coolest tools here are those tools that are relatively unknown. The tool may be familiar to experts, or only used in a specialized field. Like, a tool for sailmakers, or for opening watchcases. Or it may be so unique that it has no competitors (I'm thinking of the Griphoist hand winch). Or it may be so full of features that it falls off the standard price/benefits line for competing tools. The cost of these tools is not as important as the fact that they exist. They are often the only things that will do the job well. Many of these are the types of tools you don't need to buy ever — but just knowing they exist is a power that can steer you to other tools, or even other achievements, projects, and designs.

Like most areas of our life today this state is subject to churn. The tool no one knows about this year may become the cliche only a year later. When I started Cool Tools 13 years ago Garmin automobile GPS, Proton pocket LED lights, and Netflix were novelties, one-of-a-kind gems; now they hardly need to be mentioned because they are one of many. In only a few years many of the unique tools reviewed here now will become the norm. Assume the half-life of any innovation is about 5 years.

Reviews

To discern between good cheap and bad cheap, you need reviews. Once I hone in on a potential tool, I spend a lot of time checking out the reviews on both Amazon and other retailers, as well as the enthusiasts' blogs. The enthusiast blogs and forums will have very detailed dissections, but I often find them too obsessive and lost in the details. In a sense they know too much. But occasionally you can find a roundup review that will point out what is best. (For a suggestion of some enthusiast review blogs see Best Review Sites, p. 12-13.) At the other extreme the reviews on Amazon often don't know enough. Few reviewers have any experience with competing models or brands, or previous incarnations and older models. They gush over what they just bought, and are impressed by anything that works. Studies have shown reviewers have an uncritical bias to 5-star reviews. These 5-stars are useful only when their sum outpaces, or overhangs, the normal distribution curve, indicating something out of the ordinary. If there are as many 1- and 2-stars as 4- and 5s, that is a no-go.

5 star	29	5 star	1,830	5 star	82
4 star	11	4 star	216	4 star	4
3 star	4	3 star	50	3 star	6
2 star	4	2 star	35	2 star	7
1 star	2	1 star	75	1 star	54
Decent		**Outstanding!**		**Loser**	

The Acquisition Sequence

In summary, here's my checklist for buying tools:

I like to borrow, or rent a tool first, or to at least see it in action with my own eyes. That gives me some idea of what the tool wants. Is it forgiving, delicate, fussy, or idiot-proof? Sometimes having it accessible for rent or borrow is all I need.

If renting or borrowing is not practical, I'll consider purchasing either a cheap one or a mid-level highest common version. This is a hard decision to make and depends on a complicated equation that entails predicting how often I'll use it, how robust it is, and how fast it will become obsolete. Usually my answer is the cheapest good one; occasionally the highest common one is better.

In those cases where I pursue a craft, I'll check out the premium tools, and upgrade if the improvements seem substantial. Occasionally I'll go right to the best if it is a tool that is general purpose, or stable in design, and will last a lifetime. I confess I don't have many of these, but of the few ultimate tools I do own, they bring me great joy.

-- KK

How to declutter your life

It's All Too Much

$12 Peter Walsh, 2007, 230 p.

I to moved California hauling a lot of boxes still unopened from at least two previous purges of epic proportions. Sound at all familiar?

It's All Too Much is a terrific book that inverts the typical approach to dealing with existential kipple. Rather than helping you find new places and novel ways to "organize" all your crap, author Peter Walsh encourages you to explore why you ever kept all that junk in the first place. Does it reflect a fantasy waistline or a long-abandoned career? What about this "priceless" relic of a late loved one that's been sitting in a moldy trash bag for 10 years? Be honest: what place do these things have in the life that you imagine for yourself? Because, if the stuff you accumulate isn't actively helping get you closer to a life you truly want, then it's getting in the way, and it needs to go. Period.

The biggest change in attitude this book made in my life was to teach me not to generate false relevance by "organizing" stuff I don't want or will never need. Organization is what you do to stuff that you need, want, or love – it's not what you do to get useless stuff out of sight or to manufacture makebelieve meaning. For me, this is about the opposite of organizing; it means disinterring every sarcophagus of crap in my house and, item by item, evaluating whether it's making my family's life better today. And if some heirloom really is precious to me, can I find a better home for it than a shelf in the back of my garage?

You can't believe how emotionally complex this process is for a craphound like me, but once I get started, it's completely exciting – the illusion that all this junk is making me happy melts away with every scrap of paper or broken piece of equipment I can get out of the way.

That's been this book's revelation for me: this is about calculating the very real cost that clutter incurs every day, then deciding what you can tolerate _not_ doing about it. The mindless junk of your past crowds out opportunities and sets pointless limitations. Move out the junk, and you create room for the rest of your life. Ultimately, it's not just a question of tidying your house; it's a question of liberating your heart.

-- Merlin Mann

Merlin Mann's review above turned me onto this fantastic book. We've rethought our household because of it. We were reminded that life is not about stuff; it's about possibilities, which the right tools can enable. For a world of expanding stuff, this book is the necessary anti-stuff tool. If you are reading Cool Tools, you need to read this. It will help you distinguish between that which is fabulous for you personally and that which is just more junk to organize. I've learned so much from the author that I've excerpted it generously in the hope that even if you don't read the book, you'll glean a bit of its wisdom.

-- KK

•

Imagine the life you want to live. I cannot think of a sentence that has had more impact on the lives of people I have worked with. … When clutter fills your home, not only does it block your space, but it also blocks your vision.

•

You need space to live a happy, fruitful life. If you fill up that space with stuff for "the next house," your present life suffers. Stop claiming your house is too small. The amount of space you have cannot be changed — the amount of stuff you have can.

•

I know it sounds strange, but if you start by focusing on the clutter, you will never get organized. Getting truly organized is rarely about "the stuff."

This is the bottom line: If your stuff and the way it is organized is getting you to your goals… fantastic. But if it's impeding your vision for the life you want, then why is it in your home? Why is it in your life? Why do you cling to it? For me, this is the only starting point in dealing with clutter.

•

If it's taken you ten years or more to accumulate your mess, it's impossible to make it disappear overnight. Letting go is a learning process. You might need to start slowly, and it may take time to discover that not having things makes your life better, not worse.

•

Most things that you save for the future represent hopes and dreams. But the money, space, and energy you spend trying to create a specific future are wasted. We can't control what tomorrow will bring. Those things we hoard for an imaginary future do little other than limit our possibilities and stunt our growth. When I urge you to get rid of them, I'm not telling you to discard your hopes and dreams. It's actually quite the opposite. Because if you throw out the stuff that does a rather shabby job of representing your hopes and dreams, you actually create room to make dreams come true.

•

It's easy to accumulate things, but hard to let go. Trust me–if you always add and never subtract, you will eventually bury yourself. You need to set limits, and the limits are easy to create. They are determined by the amount of space you have, your priorities and interests, and the agreements you make with other members of your household.

Clutter takes over. One thing that constantly surprises me is that regardless of the amount of clutter in a home, the homeowners often express some surprise at it being there — almost as though someone filled their home with stuff while they were away on vacation! People freely admit that it is their stuff, but in the next breath they tell me they are confounded by how it got that way.

You own your possessions. What you have is yours, or is in your case. It's your responsibility. It's your doing.

•

Get rid of the trash to make room for the treasures. Let the things that are important take center stage.

•

In my experience, close to half of what fills a kitchen has not seen the light of day in the last twelve months. Face facts: If you haven't used an item in the last year, it is highly unlikely that you really need it or that you are going to ever get enough use from it to justify it cluttering up your home. Take the plunge and get rid of it!

If you're tempted to keep something because it was expensive, remember the difference between value and cost. Value is what something is worth. You spent a lot of money on it. To throw it away would mean admitting that the money was wasted. Now you need to think about the cost. What is it costing you to keep this item? How much space? How much energy?

•

There are only three options for each and every item you come across in this, your initial purge:

1) Keep. This is the stuff that you want to stay in your home. You use it all the time. It's crucial to the life you want to live. Or (let's be honest) you don't really use it, but can't bear to part with it just now.

2) Trash. Remember that every bag you fill is space you've created to live and love your life. Everything you decide to throw away is a victory. Make it a competition to see who can fill more trash bags.

3) Out the door. So you've had trouble getting rid of stuff because it's "valuable"? Well, here's your chance to either make a little money or let someone put it to real use. The items that go into the "out the door" zone are items that you are either going to sell–a yard sale, on consignment, or even online–or you are going to donate to a charitable organization. Other items here include things that are being returned to their rightful owners or to someone who has a real use for that item. Once in this pile, the item never comes back into your home.

•

Instead of "Why don't you put your tools away?" ask "What is it that you want from this space?"

Instead of "Why do we have to keep your grandmother's sewing kit?" ask "Why is that important to you? Does it have meaning?"

Instead of "There's no room for all of your stuff in there," say "Let's see how we can share this space so that it works for both of us."

Instead of "Why do you have to hold on to these ugly sweaters your dad gave you?" ask "What do these sweaters make you think of or remind you of?"

Instead of "I don't understand how you can life with all of this junk," ask "How do you feel when you have to spend time in this room?"

•

Mementos are not memories. Just because it was a gift does not mean you must keep it forever. If it is important, then keep it in a condition that shows that it is important.

•

When the purpose of the room is lost, clutter inevitably follows.

•

Put your relationship first. Preserve your sense of peace. Enhance your sleep. Find another place for it. Even if you live in a studio apartment, you must create a separate, sacred space for your bedroom. Put up a screen or a curtain. Use a bookshelf to create a wall if you can't afford to have one built. This is too important to ignore.

•

When it comes to clothes, it is seldom an issue of not enough space–there is never enough space. The real issue is simply too much stuff, and that's where we need to look for the solution to the clothing clutter.

•

Every single time I help organize someone's closet, I find clothing that still has the original sales tags on it, clothing that has never been worn. When I ask about it, the response is always the same: "It was such a bargain, I couldn't pass it up!" A Bargain. It's hanging in the closet, unworn. Please explain to me how exactly that is a bargain? If you have unworn clothes that have been in your closet longer than six months, you should either give them to a worthwhile charity or sell them online where they will fetch the best price. Get them out of the closet and clear some space for the things you love and wear.

•

Reality check — Giving to charities

Goodwill receives a billion pounds of clothing every year. Ultimately, they use less than half of the clothing they get. Clothing is cheap, and the cost of sorting, cleaning, storing, and transporting the clothes is higher than their value. If you wouldn't give an article to a family member, it's probably not good enough for charity. Sure, it's great to get the tax deduction and it makes you feel like you didn't waste money buying the clothes, but if you're truly charitable, be sensitive to the needs of the organization. Charities aren't dumping grounds for your trash. Talk to your local charities or visit www.charitynavigator.org. Find out what they can most use. Although giving to charities is a great way to get stuff out of your house, it's far better not to let stuff into your house.

•

Reality check — Collections

It's a collection if:

- it's displayed in a way that makes you proud and shows that you value and honor it.
- looking at it brings you pleasure.
- you enjoy showing it to others.
- it is not an obsession that is damaging your relationships.
- it is not buried under other clutter.
- it doesn't get in the way of living the life you wish you had.

•

Holiday in/out

Remember the In/Out Rule — you don't want more to come in than goes out. But holidays tend to be one-way. Items come in, in, in! What goes out? Now's the time to examine your haul and see what items of equivalent size and use can go.

•

My job may be all about organization and decluttering, but I cannot say enough times that it is not about "the stuff." I have been in more cluttered homes than I can count, and the one factor I see in every single situation is people whose lives hinge on what they own instead of who they are. These people have lost their way. They no longer own their stuff–their stuff owns them. I am convinced that this is more the norm than the exception in this country. At some point, we started to believe that the more we own, the better off we are. In times past and in other cultures, people believe that one of the worst things that can happen is for someone to be possessed., to have a demon exercise power over you. Isn't that what being inundated with possession is– being possessed?

Good Enough

The satisficing approach to shopping

Costco

$55 yearly membership Costco

Costco is the Ur warehouse club store. They have a decent choice of one model for each type of product, but at jaw-dropping prices.

My allegiance to Costco is a running joke between me and Stewart Brand. He finds it funny that I buy almost everything I can there. Let's see, I recently got a fine leather jacket I wear all the time ($89), a DVD player, batteries by the score, an okay digital camera, and real Vermont maple syrup by the gallon ($12).

Costco has become my personal shopper. I do some research, then I buy what they sell. Like all discount chains they have professionals working full time looking for deals/quality. But what I like about Costco is their niche — which is my niche. They consistently find a bargain in the "highest common denominator" bracket. What they seem to aim for, and what I am happy with, is the highest quality common quality. Not the very best, not the cheapest, and not mediocre either, but a good brand-name bargain in the high middle. They consistently deliver a great price on a very popular and competent item. It's neither optimization (the top model with the most features), nor is it minimization (cheapest per feature) nor plain thriftiness. Rather Costco aims for some sort of consumer satisficing, to use Herb Simon's term: a high quality that is just good enough, but at a low-end price.

They make shopping easy by eliminating the tyranny of non-essential choice. You don't have to waste cycles trying to scrutinize similar models or brands. They do that for you: "here's the good enough one you need" they say. The typical Wal-Mart store will have 80,000 unique stock items; the typical Costco will have only 3,500.

Costco has a reputation for bulk food items, but many of these are slow perishables, and many items are not that bulky. Since we have a large household, their food prices are simply too inexpensive to ignore; we buy 25 lb. sacks of flour and rice for almost nothing per pound. Milk in 2 gallon cartons, eggs by the 18, fruit by the crate, drinks on pallets, etc. We get our eyeglasses and contacts there. And car tires! It's crazy to think about getting tires anywhere else in town. Plus they increasingly have great tools, and if you are willing to adopt the satisficing mode they excel in, you can get the best deals on electronic gizmos like walkie talkies, refrigerators, vacuums, kitchen gear, office furniture and so on. If the store sells gasoline, they price it a dime cheaper per gallon than anywhere else in town. Some of their best deals are one-offs; items that appear briefly and then are gone forever: over the years I've seen fantastic (not corny) authentic stain glass windows for cheap, great wet suits, new hot tubs about half off, and I kid you not, funeral caskets (where I would hope "good enough" would suffice).

One other thing about Costco which they don't advertise. They will take any item (except computers) back any time. People do abuse this, but it makes shopping there a no brainer.

-- KK

Old-fashioned tool resource

Lehman's Non-Electric Catalog

$3, or free w/any order Lehman's

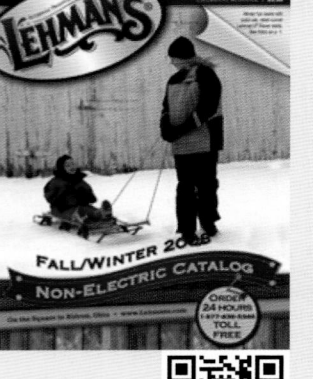

Lehman's is a 50-year-old company in Ohio's Amish country, with a unique bunch of well-made, carefully selected and useful tools for "sustainable" living. Emphasis is on cooking, homesteading, farming, gardening, and doing things for yourself. Country living for sure, but some of this could appeal to urbanites who want to bring some country into the city. Kitchen equipment, canning supplies, copper kettles, cheese-making supplies, grain grinders, toboggans, kerosene lanterns, axes, water pumps. A large selection of wood-burning stoves, as well as cookstoves. Old-time farming and gardening tools (for old-time skills still viable)-on and on. Most of their items are USA-made.

The hard copy (172 pp. catalog) is way better than the electronic version. If you're into this stuff, and/or you live in the country, you'll end up reading it like a book. We've had their catalogs around for over 30 years and I still find myself leafing through one from time to time.

-- Lloyd Kahn

Pump it up, adjust fuel valve, and light. Solid stainless steel tank and stem. Solid forged brass burner disassembles easily for maintenance and cleaning.

Use with any 10" glass shade
Burns Coleman fuel. Fuel is volatile!
19"H, 1/4"OD tank, 4 lb

An air pump is required but not included with lamp. This way you can buy as many lamps as you need but only one pump.

Note: This lamp can be dangerous and difficult to operate. Eliminate fuel leaks by occasionally tightening parts. Adequate ventilation required.

The Elmira Fireview™ cookstove brings the old-world coziness of the fire and the modern convenience of gas cooking into your kitchen. Choose the features that suit your needs: enjoy the incomparable warmth and pleasure of wood cooking; make meals faster and keep your kitchen cooler on hot summer days with optional high-output gas burners; or, extend your prep area with the optional work surface. A large viewing window (standard on every Fireview™ stove) lets you enjoy the dramatic display of the fire while quickly and easily fine-tuning the flame for perfect cooking temperatures every time.

Black porcelain finish with nickel trim
Spacious 3.0 cu ft oven
Warming cabinet
1.7 cu ft firebox with large viewing area
Optional work surface adds 1' of space or gas side burners
Made in Canada

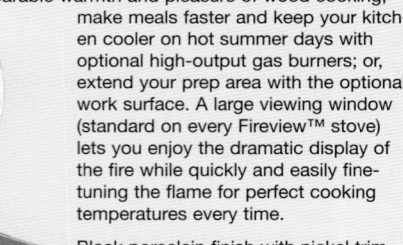

The Elmira Woodstove is exempt from EPA regulations and is legal for sale in most of the USA. However, it is not legal for sale in the state of Washington.

Source for old-fashioned Amish clothes and goods

Gohn Bros.

Free Catalog Gohn Bros.

For Amish goods, you can hardly do better than the incomparable Gohn Brothers. They're the real old school. Need diaper pins, buggy robes or, oddly, LA Gear High Top Leather shoes? The Gohns got 'em. Probably their most well-known items are the broadfall drop-front work pants and old fashioned colonial shirts, which are popular with the Revolutionary and Civil War re-enactment people. No web store, as you might expect, but call or write for a catalog.

-- Edward J. Murphy

Remembering forgotten tools

Low-tech Magazine

Free Low-tech Magazine

This web based magazine publishes a lushly illustrated and researched article every few months highlighting a technology from the past that is no longer used, but could still be very useful. The articles, in describing the history of tools, is a valuable tool in itself.

Some recent examples include Gas Bag Vehicles, Human Powered Cranes, and Hoffman Kilns.

-- Stephen Balbach

One engine operated up to 45 pumps in different locations, each up to a mile away. Power was transmitted by means of wooden rods or steel cables that moved back and forth, snaking through the landscape.

The system was so efficient that an engine used for pumping an oil well could operate a whole cluster of pump jacks. The technology, which still operates in a handful of small oil fields, could also work with renewable energy sources, and shows great potential for efficient small-scale energy use.

Nothing is more complex than the unknown, for it masquerades as the unknowable. - Mark O. Martin

1987 25' Chris Craft Amerosport 250 Cabin Cruiser (14022645)

Currently	$607.00 USD
Item ID #	14022645
Quantity	1
Start	8/20/2013 9:22:52

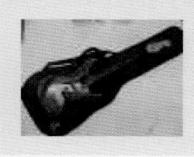

Yamaha Electric Guitar – Stained Wood Body (14002389)

Currently	$56.00 USD
Item ID #	14002389

Thrift store eBay
Goodwill Online Auctions
Goodwill Online Auctions

Thrift store hunting isn't just a pastime. It can be an honest living. Finding and flipping used goods for profit has been the main source of income for one of my friends for more than a decade. Though picking through racks of clothing, bins of electronics and boxes of watches — or trolling eBay and Craigslist — can be fruitful, another weekend-thrifter friend also swears by Goodwill's online auction site, which features 18,000 items daily that have been handpicked by several stores nationwide. You're getting access to the cream of the crop, but not every storeworker knows the value of what they have or how to describe it — and every bidder doesn't necessarily know either (the market for vintage Levi's has become so lucrative that people try to pass off faux-jeans to less-discerning eBayers).

Whether you're looking to join the flip economy or you enjoy stumbling on old, rare, cheap stuff, Goodwill's site is a great resource. Here's a bit of what I found recently (followed by current bids): Kodak Colorburst 50 Polaroid ($4.99), Ronco Rhinestone & Stud Setter ($5), Harley-Davidson Men's Boots – size 11 ($11), Nintendo 64 System ($15), Hohner Student IV Accordion w/Case ($9.59), and a Minolta Hi-Matic F 35mm ($8).

Warning: Shipping can be expensive. Also, items are purchased 'as is' and cannot be returned.

-- Steven Leckart

Stuff for free
Freecycle
Free Freecycle Network

The worldwide Freecycle Network is a grassroots movement of people who are giving (& getting) stuff for free in their own towns. Each local group is run by a local volunteer moderator (them's good people). Membership is free. To sign up, find your city on the Freecycle website. Can't find your city? It takes about ten minutes to start your own (click on "Start your own" for instructions). One rule: everything posted must be free. Whether it's a chair, a fax machine, piano, or an old door to be given away, it wants to be free!

-- Verdean Ackerson

A very cool service. In my neighborhood (the peninsula coast south of San Francisco) the following free items were recently listed: camper shell, mirror, working computer monitor, rusty motorcycle, linoleum remnant...

-- KK

Global Amazon shopping
Pricenoia
Free Pricenoia

This little site is an international Amazon stores comparison engine.

Amazon has 6 stores in the world: USA, UK, Germany, France, Canada and Japan. A lot of products are offered in all the stores, or many of them. Well, prices vary A LOT between stores. If you are from the US, you can get cheaper products from Canada (music, DVDs) or UK (import music mainly). If you are from somewhere else, it's even better! People tend to think that the best store to order from is the nearest one. Well, that's absolutely false. Europeans can usually get stuff cheaper from the US (including shipping) than from any other European store. And for other countries, this site shows you many Amazon stores to check and it sure can have nice surprises.

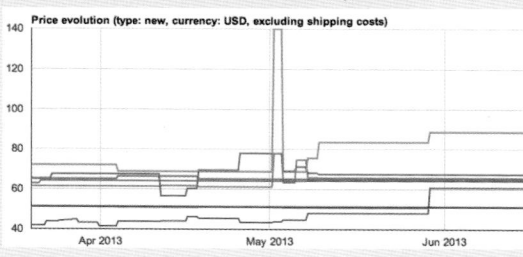

The site gets prices, puts them in your currency and then adds shipping cost to your country (looks like they get it from your IP).

Pricenoia has a couple of nice add-ons. A bookmarklet that lets you compare prices when you are looking at a product page at Amazon, and a graph of the price evolution over time for every product in every store.

A great tool for the holiday season, and a good reference for the rest of the year!

-- Leon C.

Impossible to find on the web site
Amazon's 800 number

On average I've ordered from Amazon once a week for the last 15 years or so. Not just books, but power tools, toys, kitchen stuff, the whole lot. Given the volume of my orders I think their customer service is super great; it sets the gold standard for other companies. No other merchant online or offline has provided the ease and accuracy of ordering as Amazon does. Still, in my experience there are occasionally glitches that their email-bots can't deal with, usually entailing a minor billing snafu. In these rare cases you need Amazon.com's almost-secret real-person customer service telephone number. You won't find it on their website. I once got it by calling 800 directory assistance. In any case, they make it hard to find because a call costs Amazon more, so you should jot down these numbers for those special moments when only a human will do:

1.866.216.1072 (Toll free, US and Canada)

1.206.266.2992 (Outside US and Canada)

-- KK

Amazon price tracker
CamelCamelCamel
Free CamelCamelCamel

This site allows you to track price history and has price drop and price watch alerts. Ever since I discovered it a few weeks ago, I've looked at it before I bought anything on Amazon just to make sure I was at or near a historical low. The price charts are intuitive, and allow you to see highs and lows for the past year, 6 months, 3 months, 1 month. You can set your tracker to include just Amazon.com, 3rd party sellers, or Used. The best part? It's absolutely free.

If you need something immediately, there's not a whole lot this can do for you. But, for example, I've had my eye on the MEElectronics M9P headphones. It's currently $15. Hopping on CamelCamelCamel, I can see that historically, it has run at about $23 until early December, took a dive to $15, a dip all the way down to $10 earlier this month, then popped back up to $15. I don't want to pay 50% more than what it was a few weeks ago, so I'll set up the Tracker to notify me by e-mail when it gets back down to $10.

While I've found some bugs, such as hours-behind updating, and while I wish it incorporated shipping costs, it's still allowed me to save cash. More than that, I learned a long time ago I get a great deal of satisfaction from knowing I got a great deal.

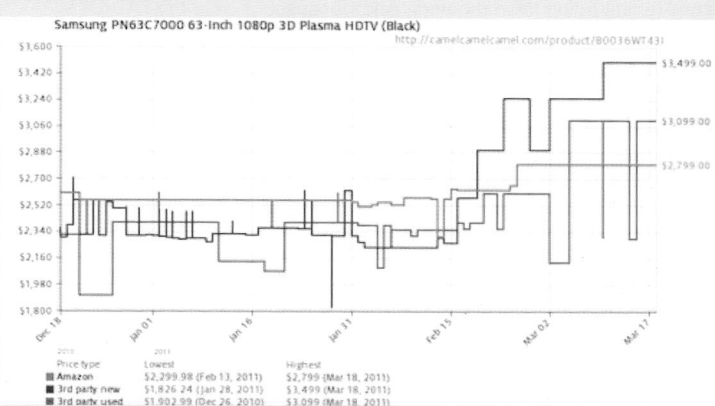

CamelCamelCamel give me the data I need. If used car salesmen could hand you data-rich, neutral third-party charts like this every time they told you you were getting a steal, it'd go a long way to negating that sleazy image.

Alas, we can only dream, as it only covers Amazon.com and Newegg, BestBuy, BackCountry and Zzounds.com through sister-sites.

-- Doug Wong

Access to human help
Get Human
Free Get Human

When you need a problem-solving human on the phone, try these numbers and their short cuts. This is the best list I've seen of 800 numbers with humans at the other end. Even better are the voice mail short cuts for each number that take you to the warm brain the quickest. Searchable with cntrl-F.

-- KK

NetFlix	F	888-638-3549	Press 0 at each prompt.
Netscape	F	866-541-8233	Press 000.
NetZero	F	866-841-1442	Press #### at each prompt, ignoring messages.
Overstock.com	F	800-843-2446	Press 0 at each prompt, ignoring messages.
PayPal	F	888-221-1161	Press 0 at each prompt, ignoring messages. See also.
SBC DSL support	F	877-722-3755	Say "sales".
Sprint Broadband Direct	F	888-996-0001	Press 00.
Target Online	F	800-591-3869	Press 1; don't press or say anything, ignoring messages.

Computers are useless. They can only give you answers. - Pablo Picasso

9

Warranties

Extended Warranty Evaluation

The sales pitch for an extended warranty is simple: pay some extra money now to extend the manufacture's 90-day warranty another 3 years to save on expensive repairs later. For most appliances an extended warranty is a rip-off. The cost of this insurance rarely pays for itself. Either the device keeps working till just after the warranty period, or the cost of the warranty extension exceeds the cost of replacing the unit. Either way, the money made by selling

uneconomical extended warranties is a major source of profit for retailers. That is why they are selling it: because on average most devices don't break during this period. Therefore, the wisdom of the smart shopper: skip the extended warranty.

There are a few exceptions to this rule. At this particular moment in technology, there are 3 major devices that seem particularly repair-prone and problematic, with frequent failures within their first 3 years, and with high costs of repair. According to a study by the independent Consumer Reports (August 2011), those three are: personal computers, refrigerators and zero-turn-radius riding lawn mowers. And because of their frequent failure across brands the insurance of an extended warranty is justified in their cases.

But not all extended warranties (EW) are the same. You can purchase an EW from the manufacturer, from the retailer selling the device, from a third party, or from your credit card company. And different issuers have different selling points.

In the personal computer realm, the best deal is Apple's. As 25-year Apple fans we automatically figure in the cost of AppleCare's 3-year EW for any device we purchase from them. Sad to say, we frequently need it. Happy to say, their service is great. We take the ailing unit to a local Genius Bar, and they swap out what's broken and make it right. Over the years we'd had screens, keyboards, drives, motherboards, power supply, all repaired for no extra costs over the EW. And that is not to mention the great real-human phone support help for any kind of software related questions.

Refrigerators are a different matter. Almost everybody has one, and newer models (particular those with ice makers) can be very complex. In the past few months, we needed to purchase our first new refrigerator. Even our plumber told us that the EW was worth getting for a refriger-

ator. But what kind? Sears offered one plan. Home Depot another. Visa, our credit card company offered another if we used their card. Square Trade offered third-party service. With the help of Camille Hartsell, we researched all the plans to see which had the best deal using a new LG refrigerator as a test case.

The short answer is that like many other industries, when you get behind the curtain there are really only a few major players. Most retailers and card companies outsource their extended warranty programs to a few industry giants, who rebrand their service, and then outsource the actual repairs to local companies. But because there are so many brands involved in this transaction it is very hard to assign credit or blame when things don't work out. If you read the feedback in forums on refrigerator repairs most unhappy customers aren't making the distinction between the manufacturer of the appliance, or the retail seller of it, or the company selling the EW, or the actual company supplying the repair technicians who come to your house. Those are four different companies for one experience for the customer.

What I found in warranty repair is that the competency of the local service branch probably plays more of a difference in customer satisfaction than anything else, but was the least consistent. If the local agency did a poor job fixing a problem, customers would naturally blame LG, or Panasonic, or GE for crappy quality and service. It is hard to judge the service quality in an EW, but it is essentially the same as the quality of a regular warranty repair — that is dependent on local crews — and this is important — who often service all the different manufacturers. The Maytag man is unusual because most of the others repair technicians are contracted out and work on all brands.

So the choice of EW providers comes down to price and plan. All the policies we examined include a "No Lemon" clause — if three of the same repairs are made in a 12 month period and a fourth becomes necessary, they will replace the unit, and most of them share the same long list of exclusions. Of all the policies, Visa's was the shortest and least specific. Its instructions on claim processing seemed the most lengthy (to report a problem, they mail you a claims form, you get an estimate and return that claim form, once it's approve, the claim can proceed).

Most 4- to 5-year service plans cost about 20% of the purchase price. Except Home Depot; they charge a flat fee of $100 for a 4-year extended contract on refrigerators (on a large one that's only 4%). It begins when the 1-year manufacturer's warranty ends, so I went with them for our extended warranty on a new fridge. I now have 5 years of service for $100, which seems like reasonable insurance.

-- KK

User Manual First

In the old days (before the web) you could not read the operating manual or instructions for an appliance, device, or tool until you got it home and unpacked it. Getting the manual was considered one of the benefits of purchasing the product. In fact, you had to purchase extra copies if you lost the original, or wanted to check it out. It was often only later when you finally had the box opened that you discovered a) it did not permit the function you bought it for, or b) it was a quarter inch smaller than it looked and so didn't fit, or c) it was incompatible with the accessoriess set you already had, or d) it had no manual!

Those days are gone. You can find a PDF version of the manual for most products on the web if you search hard enough. It is not as easy as it should be, but the smarter manufacturers make it easy to download the specs of whatever they sell.

That leads to this new rule: **get the manual first, before you buy.**

For a large home remodel I had to purchase a pile of new appliances, lights, plumbing fixtures, hardware, materials, gadgets, and some tools. I instituted a "Manual First, Buy Later" policy, and it had immediate positive effects. Once I identified a possible candidate for purchase, I would google for its manual. Equally important as finding the operating instructions and basic specs, is to get hold of the installation instructions. There are few sites that aggregate manuals and specs of major lines, but often I would wind up at the manufacturer's site. There I would download the PDF and read it carefully. That's where you find out its precise dimensions, its actual power needs,

I was heartened to see that even the professionals do this. Here is a snapshot of our plumber "at work" in the bathroom. He has his tablet opened to an installation PDF, and his phone is googling a help number for questions brought up by specs in the PDF.

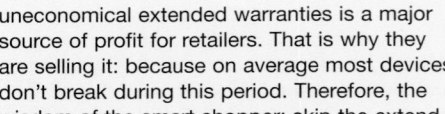

its exact connections, its real compatibility. I lost count of the number of inappropriate bad purchases I avoided by studying the manual and specs first.

What baffles me are the clueless manufacturers who still don't put their installation and operating manuals online in 2012. (I'm thinking of you, LG.) The main result of this process is simply fewer surprises. Less returns, better integration.

Locating any particular item's installation and operating specs is still not as easy as it should be. Amazon could make it the norm to have the full spec PDF for every item they sell, or Google could try to algorithmically sort them out, or some clever aggregator could centralize them all. But for now it is worth seeking them out first, and purchase later.

-- KK

Tips

Use permanent marker to put purchase dates on your air filters and fire alarm batteries. We put the purchase dates on the back of all our appliances, too.

-- Akaladybug

If you are researching a product or thing, add "vs" after the name when searching. Google helpfully offers in autocomplete to find related items. For example, if you are considering a Black and Decker product, Google for "Black and Decker vs" and Google will suggest "craftsman", "ryobi", and "dewalt" - these are likely the most popular competitors.

-- Joshua Schachter

Most public libraries have online reservation systems. I haven't browsed the library shelves in months. Anytime I see an interesting title now I jump over to the library's web site and reserve it if possible. I get up to 25 books/CDs in my queue at any given time, and quite often it's full. I just head to the library periodically and there's always something or other waiting for me with my name on it.

-- Mike Lietz

I must confess I owe Martha Stewart for this one: All my power cords, other computer cables, phone cables, power-strips, and even the DSL modem and the wireless router are contained in a wire basket (from Hold Everything or Pottery Barn or Ikea or something) which is hung from the bottom of the desk by four screw hooks. Leaves plenty of room to stretch my legs without the fear of yanking out a cord or kicking a power switch with my feet.

-- Charles Kiblinger

I would strongly suggest adding tie-wraps or zip ties to any bicycle repair set. They can hold a whole lot of things in place when screws get lost... I'm speaking here as an avid cyclist (I do about 2 to 3000 kilometers every year, most in vacations).

-- Michiel Kemeling

If we are to survive through a long future, we must stay in contact with our long past. - Freeman Dyson

Exceptional Warranties

What happens when a great tool ceases to function? Do you just throw it away and buy a new one? Given how expensive this can be it is often a better investment to find a company that stands behind their product for life.

This kind of commitment is admirable in any company and deserves to be rewarded. So we asked our readers to recommend companies with stellar customer service, lifetime warranties, and a commitment to their products. Companies listed in alphabetical order.
-- *Oliver Hulland*

ALLIED INTERNATIONAL

I received an 105-piece screwdriver/ratchet set made by Allied when I signed up for my bank account in 1992. Since then the ratchet has failed twice (one time because my brother took it apart and couldn't figure out how to get it back together and the other because the little bearing that holds the bits in popped out) both times Allied sent me a replacement. I asked to buy a replacement adapter for the socket pieces because I lost mine and they said "sir we will replace any part that isn't working and if you lost it, it obviously isn't working". -- Austin Morgan

blue sky

My excellent Blue Sky EXO monitor system (aka "Really Nice Computer Speakers") stopped working in January 2009. Pascal Sijen, a founder of the company, handled my service call personally and shipped a replacement amp module free of charge. He made sure I knew how to install it and was exceedingly courteous and helpful every step of the way. A recent support call to Blue Sky showed it was no fluke; excellent customer care is still the norm there. -- Andrew S.

BUCK KNIVES

Return the faulty product and it will be replaced. They were no longer making the Model 360 Buck tool I had, but they still sent me a replacement. -- Adam

Columbia

I wore a fantastic pair of Columbia boots trekking in Bhutan. Sometime later the sole started to separate from the boot. I called Columbia, emailed them a photo and they sent me a new pair right away. That's the kind of company I want to support. -- Rick True

COSTCO WHOLESALE

Costco has a fantastic lifetime return policy that has unfortunately been abused by many. The updated policy sets a 90-day limit for returns on high-end electronics, but almost everything else you can purchase in store is covered. -- Oliver Hulland

CourierWare

Courierware Messenger Bags, in Boston, has a lifetime guarantee on their sturdy, simple Cordura bags. If the stitching, hardware, or fabric gives, they will repair it and return it for free. I've been very pleased, and have used one of their bags daily for the last fifteen years (although I did have to send it back to get the strap restitched once). --Cofax

CRAFTSMAN

I got the advice from my dad in the 1980s, who got the advice from his dad in the 1950s, to always buy Craftsman tools, because as long as you keep them (don't lose them), you'll never have to buy that tool again. So I bought a set of small, special purpose pliers; fairly soon after one of them broke right in my hand. Just as my dad said, Sears made an immediate, no questions asked, no receipt needed replacement. -- Jeff J.

CROSS

I had a 14 yr-old gold plated "standard" Cross Pen. Used it enough that the gold plating was pitting. Eventually the mechanism started to slip, so I sent it back. They not only replaced the pen, they re-engraved my name on it! "Lifetime" warranty evidently means something to some companies. -- Dave

eagle creek

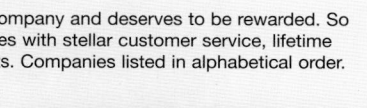

Eagle Creek makes travel- and business-related things. Back in January of 1998, I bought a roll-on suitcase of theirs, the Switchback Plus. As I travel a lot, this suitcase was used a lot. About five years ago, the wheels wore out, so I shipped my suitcase to Eagle Creek. They replaced the wheels and axle and shipped my suitcase back. Then about three years ago, a buckle broke on the bag; again I shipped it to them and again they repaired my suitcase and sent it back to me. -- Tim

Eastern Mountain Sports

They have a lifetime return policy; as the sales guy who sold me my winter jacket explained, "You can bring it back after 30 years and get a full refund or exchange, no questions asked." I asked him how they could possibly find that policy sustainable, and he said "My instructions are not to just sell you something; my instructions are to try and find customers for life." -- Rain N.

EASTPAK

Eastpak is a manufacturer of backpacks. They offer a 30 year warranty. We bought two for our twins when they entered high school. High school students carry an unbelievably heavy load of books every day, and they have to cram the backpack to bursting. Sure enough, the main zipper on one of them parted. I called the company. They paid for the shipping both ways - and here's what I like the best - they repaired the zipper instead of just replacing it. One less backpack in the landfill.

Eddie Bauer

Eddie Bauer has a great policy for their backpacks and bags. Anytime one breaks or wears out, you can apply the full purchase price of the bag toward a new one. As a result, I've been a loyal Eddie Bauer backpack customer for well over a decade. -- Steve

FILSON

Filson out of Seattle has one of the best customer service departments I have ever had the pleasure of dealing with. They have a lifetime, unconditional guarantee, and will repair or replace any item regardless of age or condition. Bonus: custom hemming and custom orders. They have been around for more than 100 years, still produce their products in Seattle, and are generally wonderful. --TET

FISKARS

On more than one occasion, I've written to Fiskars about a garden tool that I had beaten up and broken, asking about replacement parts. Each time, although they had no parts to offer, they told me to send in proof that I had the tool (in one case, I sent them a digital photo), and they sent me a replacement. -- Rich Morin

KOHL'S

Some will scoff, but Kohls has astonishing return policy and is CHEAP if you shop the sales. Basically, lifetime exchange even if you don't have a receipt! Money back no questions asked if you do! Example, bought an Arrow dress shirt on sale there, button blew out, four months later swap out no questions. Plus, they are nice. --JCW

L.L.Bean

My parents recently returned a set of 10-year-old luggage to LL Bean because of malfunctioning zippers. Customer service credited them the full purchase price within minutes. Needless to say, my parents are life-time LL Bean customers. -- Oliver Hulland

LANDS' END

When a half-dozen dress shirts started showing unusual wear after 18 months (they usually last me 5+ years), they were replaced with brand new shirts in a higher-quality line at no cost, although I was only requesting a partial credit.-- Faba

LE CREUSET

Le Creuset will replace any piece of cookware, no matter how long you've had it, no matter how chipped or cracked. -- P. Bickart

LEATHERMAN

Leatherman offers a truly stellar service. Having been heavily overused for inappropriate DIY tasks my Blast finally failed on a Rosemary bush. I sent the tool to Leatherman along with a description of my idiocy. They wordlessly replaced not only the tool but the missing screwdriver - tact and service together. -- Tim

Lee Valley

I once broke a watering can and was shocked when I returned it asking for repair parts and they replaced it no questions asked. All their tools come with a lifetime warranty. -- J. Vanduren

Marmot

Marmot has excellent customer service and they stand behind their products. After using a Gore-Tex shell for several years it started leaking and they were happy to replace it with a new one after it failed their leak test. --Dean

MOUNTAIN EQUIPMENT

I bought a Gore-Tex jacket there 10 years ago, finally the waterproof seam liners came unglued. I brought it back and - even better than giving me a new one - they repaired it. Less waste, and I get to keep the jacket I love. --Smith

MOUNTAIN HARDWEAR

I would give extra kudos to Mountain Hardwear - both my wife and I have fleece jackets that we wear regularly from them and when the fleece broke down they have replaced them at no cost to us even though it is expected that the longer you wear fleece the more it will break down. They also replaced my favorite softshell that had a shredded sleeve from a feral dog - I just wanted to buy a replacement sleeve when I contacted them (wife is an epic sewing master, so I figured she could swap out sleeves). But their policy pays off. -- Josh

NORDSTROM

There's never been a better guarantee; I save all my Nordstrom receipts knowing that if a pair of jeans so much as frays, years later I can return them for the full price in cash. No questions asked. I spend my money there for a reason. Every single thing there is covered by a lifetime return policy. -- Tarah Wheeler Van Vlack

ORVIS

My brothers have taken back numerous fly fishing poles that they've abused or misused and have always gotten replacements as good or better than what they returned. --Justin

Otter Box

They sent a replacement for a leaky box without even asking for the original back. -- Mark Adkins

patagonia

Yvon Chouinard's company honors an Iron-Clad Guarantee. Simply call customer service or drop into a store in order to get your product repaired or replaced. -- Oliver Hulland

PELICAN

Pelican--makers of awesome waterproof cases especially beloved by video and photo types--had a lifetime replacement guarantee. I toured the facility about a decade ago and was impressed by the pile of damaged cases that had been returned for replacement. Many of them were obviously well used and well aged and damaged by the user. No problem. Free replacement. That impressed me. -- Bill

REI

The legendary no questions asked return policy is one of the biggest reasons why I shop at REI. It gives me the confidence to try out new tools, and is well worth the slight premium you pay over other online retailers. -- Oliver Hulland

RED OXX MFG, INC.

Red Oxx soft-side luggage, duffles, packs etc. Made in America with an unconditional lifetime warranty - they suggest you put their products in your will. -- Austin

SHIMANO

My broken fishing rod was replaced with a new one of the latest design for nothing more than the cost of sending in the broken one. My fishing reel full of sand was replaced with a brand new one for the normal cost of their cleaning ($25) after they determined it couldn't be properly cleaned. They even wound my expensive fishing line onto the new reel. Shimano does have some low-end, low-price fishing products that don't come with a lifetime warranty, but if you invest in the ones that do, I'm sure you will be very happy with their service. -- Jason

SHURE

They replaced a set of headphones at no charge when one earpiece broke two years after I bought them -- without needing to see a warranty. Moreover, they replaced them with their newer (improved) equivalent model rather than the original. Customer service was *extremely* helpful throughout, no quibbles whatsoever. I'd recommend them at the drop of a hat to anyone. -- Tim Barrass

SUREFIRE

Surefire flashlights. They cost more than your average flashlight but the warranty is lifetime and their service is the best I've ever experienced. Even if you pick one up used (not the original owner) they still take care of you. -- Chris G.

VICTORINOX

Victorinox (Swiss Army Knives) needs my mention as well. I have had the same Swiss Army Knife and carried it in my pocket for over 30 years now. However, after 12 years or so my knife was really beat up with one of the plastic sides off, the scissors messed up, and of course the toothpick/tweezers lost. I love this knife but finally decided it just wasn't very useful as it was and so sent it back to Victorinox but with a note about how much it meant to me. I was sure they would just send me a replacement. However, they didn't and they actually repaired the old knife which I am convinced has to have cost them many times as much effort and I am SO appreciative. -- Aaron Fuegi

Civilization advances by extending the number of important operations which we can perform without thinking of them. - Alfred North Whitehead 11

Best Review Sites

Best of Review Sites

Scattered through the web are sleepless enthusiasts who have much to say about new stuff in their field. They load their enthusiasm and opinions into review sites.

There are two kinds of review sites: ones run by know-it-all individuals, and ones powered by a community of users. The advantage of a single voice is that — at their best — they make outright comparative recommendations. For instance, "I've seen everything and this is best." The downside is that individuals, even those who don't sleep, have trouble keeping up with an expanding or fast-moving field with tons of new gear.

The advantage of the second kind of review site -- one built on peer reviews -- is that the collective can keep up with constant change; the weakness of peer reviews, however, is that each individual of the group often has narrow experience and no sense of what else is out there. This is the chief weakness of Amazon reviews; they judge too much on an item's own merits and not on how it compares with similar products or substitutes. Clear contextual recommendations are scarce.

What I want from a review site is an informed judgement based on both the wisdom of the crowd and the judgement of an individual. Ideally I'd like a very smart friend online who can give a single word answer about what you should buy: "Get this," they would say. The wider the range of uses, the more choices in models, and the faster the innovation in that area, the harder -- and more valuable -- it is to get a definite answer.

My model of the ideal review site then, is one built on a broad base of user reviews, plus a field of experts conducting uniform and comparative reviews. The ideal site ends up with decisive recommendations of what to get. I have not yet seen a perfect site. What doesn't work for me is a site sporting a vast matrix of all products and their features, or a site recommending a few products – ones that they happen to also sell, or a site with evaluations of gear they happen to get free from cooperative manufacturers, or heaven forbid, a site that has a few feeble reviews and is supported by a zillion ads.

There are some wonderful review sites. I found the following to be useful. For the most part they have: useful, specific recommendations, a minimal ad environment, no primary connection to sales, a means to extract recommendations and not just feature lists, and users with enough experience to indicate how tools compare to others like it. I've ranked these "best of reviews sites" from 1 to 5 stars, listed here in descending usefulness to me.

– KK

Backpacking Light

★★★★☆

Not just any backpacking but ultra-lightweight hiking. Gear here is only considered worthy if it does its job and weighs less than the previous champ. More and more gear is going radically featherweight. Rather than a user forum, this site is a magazine. Reviews are primarily written by an editorial staff. The reviews are thorough, nerdy, informative and extensive. A subscription of $25/year is required to read them in detail (summaries are free). I found them useful enough that I have a lifetime subscription. Great stuff and well-worth the price if you are dedicated to losing pounds.

How I use it: For formal reviews of the latest and greatest innovation in backpacking gear.

Mountain Bike Review

★★★★★

Mountain bike gear reviewed by mountain bikers. Lots of forums, classified ads, and plenty of hard-hitting user reviews based on experience. A wonderful addition are thousands of bike trails reviewed by users. All-in-all a fantastic review site; one of the best!

How I use it: The first stop for advice on anything mountain bike related.

Digital Photography Review

★★★★★

This is one of the first online review sites, and by now the best known. New models of digital cameras and printers are vetted with systematic, technically rigorous, scientifically fair and precise testing. Products are compared to previous models. No aspect of a camera is left untested. DPReview deserves its reputation as *the* place to keep up with the incredible swift moving frontier of digital media. In fact for most photographers this site has rendered photography magazines as superfluous. The site also boasts extremely active discussion boards for the die-hard enthusiast, and really great buyers' guides. I wish there was a site like this for every vocation.

How I use it: I troll for the latest and greatest by checking out which models are used as the comparison standard (a sign its the one I want) and dipping into the chat boards.

Find a Scope

★★★★☆

An opinionated single-author site which reviews, guides, and advises you how to select a home telescope. He does a commendable job in covering the major brands of commercial telescopes, and bless his heart, he does a great job in comparing them in context of each other. He's really good at explaining what value and dangers lie in bargain scopes. He even tells you which telescopes to avoid.

How I use it: To get a first-class orientation and specific recommendations of good scopes.

Backpack Gear Test

★★★★☆

Nerds on this large site conduct extremely thorough, if not obsessive, testing and documenting of every type of gear needed for camping and hiking -- including pet hiking! While many reviews are written by enthusiasts who bought their own gear, most are based on free samples donated by gear companies. Like many detailed gear sites, this one lacks comparative awareness — how this pack compares to all other packs. Evaluations are markedly ignorant of other stuff. There is no rating scale either, or even a "best of" hint. But the gear gets tons of hours of testing and evaluation, so its very useful.

How I use it: When I have a candidate item that I want to get great detailed user feedback on.

Bent Rider

★★★★☆

A marvelous review site for recumbent bicycles. Rather than offer an endless list of features, the reviewers on this site attempt to make a judgement about the value of the bike in context of other bikes they have known. There is a good buyer's guide that puts different makes in relation to each other.

How I use it: When I was shopping for a recumbent bike this was the place I hung out for the real scoop. It also has some of the best info and reviews of regular bike gear.

Two Wheeling Tots

★★★★☆

It's a little bit niche, but the owners are wonderfully thorough. They review with good judgement bikes for kids, bike seats for kids, helmets, bike trailers, tandems, and everything else concerning bicycles and kids. They are incredibly instructional, organized, and impartial. What a great service.

How I use it: It's my first stop for the larger world of bikes.

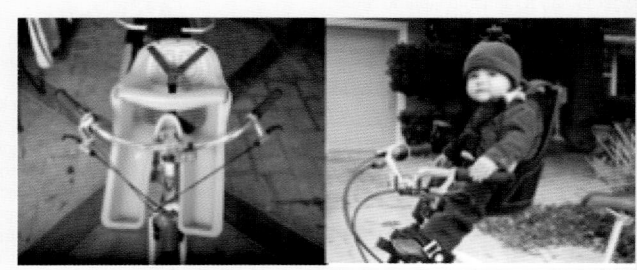

All creativity is an extended form of a joke. - Alan Kay

Telescope Review Site
☆☆☆

More comprehensive than Find a Scope, this review site is less comparative. It's aimed more at the hard-core telescope enthusiast who already owns more than one scope, and less at the ordinary buyer looking for "the right one." Still, the reviews (also all by obsessive one guy) are informative and complete. He's written up detail reports on 140 different telescopes, and has good shopping advice.

How I use it: For second opinions on a potential telescope, and to see what is new.

LED Light Review
☆☆☆

This site keeps up with the fast moving field of LED lighting in the home. They review new LED lights (one per week!) with the same attention you might give a new electronic gadget -- because in fact that's what these bulbs are. Lots of unpacking and detailed accounts of features. More overviews would be helpful.

How I use it: Since I am in the process of changing over all our lights to LEDs I monitor this for new bargains.

Boardgame Geek
☆☆☆

Every board game ever made is dissected, analyzed and rated on this most geeky website. Fierce opinions are stated. It is a deep world, and many who enter never return the same.

How I use it: I don't, but any gamer will.

Equipped to Survive
☆☆☆

Serious reviews of the serious gear of medical aid and search and rescue missions, as well as individual survival tools. This site considers low tech first aid kits and high tech location beacons and everything in between. As far as I can tell all reviews are written by one obsessed and highly informed guy, and his crusade is operated as a non-profit. While these reviews are not searchable in a comparative way, the summaries are excellent and extremely helpful for potential buyers.

How I use it: As a one-stop reality check for any tool related to first aid and survival.

Pattern Review
☆☆☆

Sewing patterns -- which are not reviewed anywhere else I know of -- are rated for clarity, ease of use, and design in this extremely helpful user site. They also rate sewing machines and other sewing gear. All around its a very sharing site, with great user content.

How I use it: I check out the sewing machine recommendations.

Wise Heat
☆☆☆

User reviews of wood stoves and other alternative heating sources. This is one of those areas it is hard to get comparative reviews on, but these user reviews are better than none.

How I use it: It's a good starting point when shopping for a stove.

Trusted Reviews
☆☆

A team of geeks review computer hardware and peripherals. No attempt is made to be comparative or comprehensive -- but they do cover a lot of gear, from game consoles to projectors. They tend to review the newest stuff — but at least they review it, unlike most sites featuring new gadgets.

How I use it: When I am hunting for a particular gadget.

One Bag
☆☆

One guy's reviews and tips for traveling gear and resources. I pretty much agree with his selections and you won't find such good advice in a more compact form. However, this is not a proper review site since actual reviews of specific brands of luggage or whatnot are rare.

How I use it: I stop by every now and then to hunt for a well-worn cool travel tool.

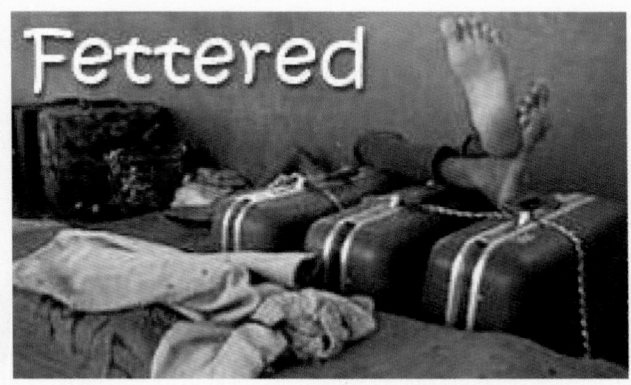

Everything USB
☆

Since you can find a USB-powered version of almost anything we are talking lots of gear and most computer peripherals: Obvious ones like USB flash storage , but also nonobvious ones like digital cameras, and the whimsical ones like USB powered coffee makers. There are no formal reviews here, but busy user forums dispense chat on USB products and USB tutorials, and there is a very handy comparative shopping matrix, which offers some relief in deciding which model of a USB device is best. These days they also cover bluetooth devices, too.

How I use this: For good reviews of offbeat gadgets..

Garden Tool Review
☆

A good start with intelligent, single voice, comparative reviews of more than one tool at once. But additions come slow, so there is not a lot of material so far. The chore is sorely needed: evaluating garden tools.

How I use it: I inspect it when researching a garden tool.

Missing?

Did I miss your favorite review site? Let me know about it and I'll share it with others. -- KK

Meta review site
Consumer Search
Free Consumer Search

Consumer Search isn't a review site per se but rather a metareview site, similar to Rottentomatoes.com. They spend the time running around the net, digging up reviews of items, rate those reviews on objectivity and completeness, then correlate them all.

It's not as up-to-date as I'd like it, nor does it cover every item that I'd like to buy. Nevertheless, it's always worth a quick driveby when considering any item over $100.

-- Joshua Keroes

Many Cool Tool readers alerted me to this fantastic supermarket of comparative reviews. They do all the hard work I wish I had time to do for Cool Tools. For each kind of consumer product (say bread machines, or roller skates) Consumer Search aggregates all the reviews that appear elsewhere on the web, and then extracts and unifies the results. Their final report is pretty comprehensive, although quality varies according to topic: The entry on home furnaces is (not surprisingly) thin compared to say, home sound systems. When they are good, they are very good.

-- KK

Reliable tool recommendations
Taunton's Yearly Tool Guide
$10 2013 Tool Guide Taunton

This special annual issue published by jointly Fine Homebuilding and Fine Woodworking magazines gives in-depth, comparative reviews of several hundred tools. The two sister magazines of Taunton Press roundup all the tool reviews that have appeared in their pages during the past year. They'll test a bunch of jigsaws, or portable table saws, or T-squares, and then give you smart recommendations for the best one to get.

Their selection of candidates for each tool is wide, fairly unbiased by freebies or advertisers, and just not stuck on the newest things; they'll include older models as well. I've used their annual Guide to find and choose a number of great tools for my toolbox. This year's list includes deep reviews of the best routers, miter saws, shop mats, hole saws, paint brushes, bench-top lathes, cordless nailers, and many more. ("201 tools tested" they claim on the cover.)

I like their sensibility — stressing function over looks, reliability over fancy features, and I have come to trust their judgments. Generally if they recommend something as good, it is. I especially value the non-power tools they review, such as the best first aid "tools" for injuries on a worksite in this issue. Their reviews are is the same spirit as Cool Tools, but they go much deeper and are more thorough.

These annuals are so good I even recommend the past few year's versions, since building tools don't change that fast.

-- KK

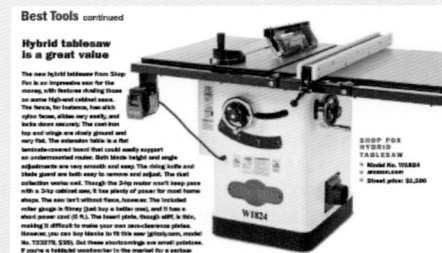

How-to video rentals
SmartFlix
SmartFlix

SmartFlix will rent you nearly seven thousand How-To DVDs in English. Subjects range from construction techniques (tile laying, cabinet making, timber framing), outdoor activities (kayaking, archery), and self-help, to such specialties as welding, lock-picking, and primitive fire-making.

The quality of the instruction varies tremendously. Some DVDs are smart and effective, some aren't. Some are old, some brand new. All come from various publishers. The SmartFlix site smartly provides customer reviews (although not all DVDs have reviews). I have found the reviews tend to be generous; I mentally deduct one star from the ratings.

It's amazing what you can learn from how-to books and videos. Most of my livelihood skills I learned this way, out of school and without teachers. A great book or video can equal, or at least compliment, an okay teacher. Through years of watching instructional videos, I've found I need to view them more than once. First I watch before I do anything; then I review parts in the midst of doing; and lastly I watch it again after I'm done, when I finally understand what they were trying to say. You to rent these videos for one week (it should be longer).

Renting these DVDs is not as cheap as using Netflix, but they are nearly as handy with their postage-paid mail-back carton and clear website. The cost is $10 per rental for a week, which works out to about half or a third or more of what buying them would be. None of these how-to's are available on Netflix, and no where else are they gathered together with such easy search, ordering, and evaluation.

-- KK

Scheduled, discounted delivery
Amazon Subscribe & Save
Up to 15% off with 5 or more subscriptions Amazon

I started using Amazon Subscribe & Save for ECGc (Green Tea) supplements initially out of frustration with my local health food store. They'd be out, only have small quantity options, pricing was all over the place.

Now a couple bottles ship to me every couple months at a good price, with free shipping even without Prime. I get an email in advance so I can skip a shipment, and I can also do an emergency "ship now" if I run out unexpectedly.

I've since gradually started putting other regular consumables into the Subscribe & Save queue to save money, time and effort.

-- Richard Viets

Best of the best for homes
The Sweethome

The Sweethome seeks out the best in household products and appliances. Using a research formula similar to its sister site, the Wirecutter, its writers scour the web for published reviews by other publications or reader forums and then compile their own meta-review of what is "best" . In fact, Sweethome is the site most similar to Cool Tools, except Sweethome authors may never actually use the item they recommend. However, their recommendations are generally reliable and always helpful. I use them often.

-- KK

The Best Dutch Oven

Meta-review site for gadgets
The Wirecutter
Free The Wirecutter

Like Cool Tools, The Wirecutter is a website that only points to stuff worth knowing about. Specifically, consumer electronics in most every major category: laptops, cameras, TVs, tablets, smartphones, etc. Unlike Cool Tools, they don't post reviews based on experience. Instead, they're written by knowledgeable gadget writers who have surveyed the field, read all the review and comment threads, and talked to experts to make an educated judgment call. There's no jargony hairsplitting. No biased fanboyism. No product bashing. Only: "Here's the one you want."

All reviews feature labels like "What I'd get," "Good Enough" or "The Wi-Fi Router You Want." The reviews themselves are succinct and clear enough for a layperson — which brings me to how I use the site…

Being labeled a "gadget guy" is both a blessing and a curse. It's an ego boost to receive emails from friends and family asking for my input before any purchases. But I'll let you in on a little secret: I don't know everything about everything. Of course, I do know how to read between the lines (and hype) and search for a solid recommendation. That's exactly what The Wirecutter does. Hence, it's now the first site I turn to before recommending anything to anyone, including myself.

This week, I bought a portable bluetooth speaker for our kitchen. I settled on the Jawbone JAMBOX, which I actually reviewed for Wired one year ago. I do know that space pretty well, but hadn't been following it closely. So I assumed something better had come along. I was wrong. Go figure.

-- Steven Leckart

A FAST AND RELIABLE EXTERNAL HARD DRIVE
HITACHI'S G-TECHNOLOGY G-DRIVE

The Best Dutch Oven

Bargain tools
Harbor Freight Catalog

Free Harbor Freight

Both a web presence and a store chain with a mail order catalog, Harbor Freight imports really inexpensive machine, automotive and wood-working tools from the People's Republic of China. It's the first place to go for tools which are needed for one project but you don't anticipate a huge use for afterwards. They also have beguiling assortments of clamps, safety equipment, cast-ers and consumables. Not everything smacks of first rate quality but the tools generally are sturdier than the lightweight offerings from the likes of Black and Decker, and still significantly cheaper.

-- Thayer G.

The ultimate hardware store
McMaster-Carr Online Catalog

Free Online Catalog McMaster-Carr

The best way to describe McMaster is to say that they carry everything you need to build anything. Items that you could normally only order through fac-tory distributors, or materials that could only be ordered in large quantities, are easily available in any size and quan-tity, no matter how small. (No minimum order, either!) Their prices are excellent and they tend to only carry good mer-chandise. Amazingly, when I order stuff at 5:30 p.m., it arrives the next morning with their normal shipping. Their catalog has long been difficult to get because you had to be a reasonably sized busi-ness with a Dun and Bradstreet number and established credit to have them mail it to you. But now that they have added an online service, everyone can easily order from them with a credit card.

-- Alexander Rose

▲ **Quantum Storage Wire Shelving System with 25 Clear Bins — 6-Shelf Unit, 36in.W x 12in.D x 36in.H, Model# WR-36-1236-102CL**

$300

Quantum Storage all purpose complete bin system provides high-density storage with easy visibility to stored contents. Clear view polypropylene shelf bins are tough, durable and economical. Features wide hop-per front, label holder and multiple grips. Shelf rack is made of chrome steel and holds up to 800 lbs. per shelf.

SEARS

Free Online Catalog Sears

Free tool-drooling
Sears Tool Catalog

On a recent trip to Sears, I was happily surprised to see a thick catalog near the checkout. I hadn't realized the Sears Tool Catalog is still in print, still available for free, and just about as big as the old Radio Shack catalogs I used to get.

It's not just Craftsman tools in here. They have all of your professional brands inside, and some wicked tools you can't find at a brick-and-mortar Sears. Woodworking tools are well-represented. Mechanics tools are, too, as you'd expect, including SK tools and some small specialty brands; also shop equipment, even some boots and cloth-ing. Sears has also recently made major upgrades to what it's calling its interactive catalog.

-- Christopher Wanko

Heavy-duty stuff
Northern Tool

Free Online and Print Catalogs Northern Tool

Northern Tool is an emporium for heavy-duty tools of every variety. This is your source for all cool things belonging in the barn, the garage, the warehouse, the basement, the workshop, or the maintenance yard. Their catalog offers some 10,000 tools and parts, with an astound-ing selection that makes the big box hardware retailers look empty. I find it is worth inspecting their wares every now and then just to see what kind of new tools and materials are available in the world. In addition to their website, they also print a big fat paper catalog, ideal for inspired browsing.

They are so good with finding cool new stuff that we are including a whole bunch of sample tools from their pages. I have not used any of these, so I am not recommending them per se, except as examples of what is available from this catalog.

-- KK

NORTHERN® TOOL + EQUIPMENT

▲ **NorthStar Trencherman Backhoe — 270cc Honda GX Engine**

$5,500

The NorthStar® Trencherman Backhoe is built bigger, heavier and stronger for amazing digging power — over 4400 lbs. of ripping force at the bucket. Easily towed to any jobsite, with 16 1/2in. x 8in. tires, and a 3500-lb. capacity 2in. coupler.

NPower Wind Turbine — 400 Watt, Marine Grade ▶

$500

The NPower™ 400 Watt Wind Turbine efficiently harnesses wind energy 24/7. AC output at the wind turbine body ensures you keep the most pos-sible power over long distances from generator to batteries. High-quality marine-grade coating and construction provides versatility in both land or sea environments. Begins to supply power at a low 5.6 MPH wind speed, so even if the wind dies down, your power won't. 400 Watt max power is reached at 28 MPH wind speed.

◀ **Q Standard Belt-Drive Drum Fan — 48in., 1 1/2 HP, 19,500 CFM Model# 10248**

$380

This two-speed Q Standard Belt-Drive Drum Fan features a 4-blade design for even airflow.

▲ **Northern Industrial Machinery Mover — 13,200-Lb. Capacity, 360° Rotation**

$120

Easy and safe transport of heavy machinery and household appliances. Smooth movement and 360° rotation improves work efficiency and safety. Sold as singles.

▲ **Northern Industrial Hand Press Pump**

$33

Needs no gas or electric power to draw well water. Simple, durable hand pump is engineered to last. Old-time styling 19 1/2ft. suction head.

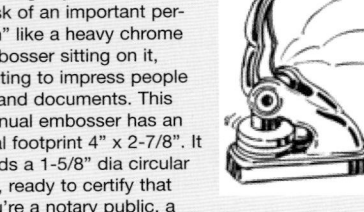

Nerdy bargains
American Science & Surplus

Following behind the juggernaut of high-tech industry is a trail of odd bits and stray leftovers. This surplus is a tinkerer's delight. One legendary source of cheap parts, weird stuff, cheap knockoffs, and plain junk is American Science & Surplus. They sell "closeouts, inventory overruns, mis-manufactures, and items whose time has not come. When a surplus item is gone, it is gone." It's the ultimate hacker's mail-order junk store.

They don't take themselves too seriously, either, often belittling the scrap they are selling. The items are illustrated with crude sketches on yellow newsprint paper in their crowded 95-page paper catalog. It's a cornucopia of irresistible bargains. Science fair motors! Chemistry kits! Craft tools. I dare you to open it without finding something you have to have. (AS&S's rustic tone is part of their "crazy cheap" schtick. On their website, in addition to the doodles you can also click to see a photo of an item as well.) While funny, their descriptions are always honest, and the stuff delivered will be entirely usable. More so than most catalogs, the bulk of the items listed are inspirational: " Oh, I could do that!" Prices are, as they say, incredible.

If you "make different," click here.

-- KK

Press Your Point

Nothing says "This is the desk of an important person" like a heavy chrome embosser sitting on it, waiting to impress people — and documents. This manual embosser has an oval footprint 4" x 2-7/8". It holds a 1-5/8" dia circular die, ready to certify that you're a notary public, a petty bureaucrat with delusions of grandeur, or just someone who likes really elegant-looking return addresses on your envelope flaps. You provide the removable dies, ordering them from your local full-service stationery store.

EMBOSSER

Giant Sucker

Huge black soft rubbery suction cup, 4-3/4" dia with a handle molded onto the back. Made in Taiwan, the French and English labeling suggests it was destined for use as a dent puller or glass carrier. Which is fine if you have dents to pull and glass to carry. If not, use it as a noninvasive and or temporary hanging device in locales where such features are desirable, such as hotel rooms, boat hulls, windows, and the sides of fine antiques (Grandmothers excepted). It is really powerful!!

GIANT SUCTION CUP

Got A Horse Of A Different Color?

Recycle old crayons. Now you can finally color him, with custom colors from the Crayola Crayon Maker. You get the machine and (24) mix-and-match colors. (You've already got that whole box of broken crayons and leftover nubs the kids keep digging through!) Just start melting and molding completely new crayons. There are even (18) sheets of labels included, in which to wrap the new ones. The Crayon Maker measures 9-5/8" tall x 7-3/8" wide x 9-5/8" deep, with a 6-foot power cord and a power switch. It uses a 60W candelabra bulb (not included). It turns off automatically if it's tipped, and the lid locks until the crayons are cool, but it's still for ages 8+ only. UL.

CRAYOLA® CRAYON MAKER

Chinex?

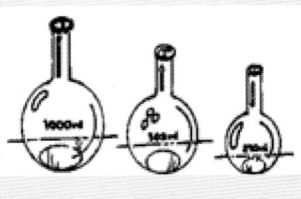

Rejoice, we have finally found a source of reasonably priced boro-silicate lab glassware.
This is the kind of glass in the trade marked Pyrex(tm) and Kimax(tm) labware. The stuff you can put right over the flame of the Bunsen burner, or directly onto the hot plate. This stuff is imported from China, and is considered student grade, which is good enough for anything but the most exotic applications. We have beakers, test tubes, graduated cylinders and flasks. Compare the prices below and you will see that they are around half the U.S. equivalent. Call us for larger quantity prices.

BEAKER, 50ML, 250ML, 600ML

Better Grade Dental Tools

A variety of shapes and ugliness, but unbroken tips. Some single ended, some double.. Super for all manner of hobbyism, save do-it-yourself-dentistry. Excellent price in today's weakened dollar market. All stainless steel.

DENTAL TOOLS

Genuine aviation surplus
Boeing/Pratt & Whitney Surplus Sales

Boeing Recovery and Surplus Sales
Pratt & Whitney Surplus

I weld, build, and purposely tangle myself up in lots of computers/servers. I discovered two surplus stores that not only provide material fuel for all of the aforementioned activities but at a great discount no less. Both stores are open to the public and offer everything from large precision machinery to fiber optic cables to airplane leather by the roll (!). I spotted a Herman Miller Eames molded office chair at the Boeing store (sold tag on it) while I was walking out with my $15 in purchases, an IBM M-series (clickety) keyboard, and a portable DIGITAL anti-static electronics workspace circa 1970. If you are a grade school science teacher with a dwindling budget for demonstration instruments, or an art teacher in need of found objects for your class on sculpture or still life drawing, these places might be useful. Perhaps you're just in need of milling equipment, pneumatic tools, safes, drafting tables, powered work carts, or raw sheets of aluminum, mild and stainless steel, titanium even. It's there if you ask. Oscilloscopes are often for sale at less than $50. I recently acquired another Sun Microsystems Ultra-x, which was one too many, and I saw that the laser printers which I ought to have bought instead were on sale for $10 that day.

Too good to be true? Sometimes. While there are online listings, there is no online purchasing so one is bound by geography and you have to go often as the good stuff rapidly departs. Take your time on a nice day to explore both the inside hanger and outside lots for things. Bring a truck and some friends to help you move the stuff. The large equipment goes quickly and the electronic and computers/peripherals are usually untested. Drill bits and calipers are plane- and submarine-building size, though great candidates for creative adaptive reuse reincarnations into your latest robotics project. The best finds are sometimes boxes of widgets that, when asked what they are, the staff smirk, shrug, and tell you they can't remember. Respect that most of the people there, at P&W certainly, seem to know what everything is to insure that the stuff gets priced accordingly and, more importantly, to make sure nothing whose purpose was previously classified, is marked or misplaced.

The Boeing store is the larger of the two and Pratt & Whitney is only open 3 days a week. I'm sure there are more of these shops around but I've only just found these.

-- Shin Ae

There are indeed other great surplus stores. Ebay is great for everything, but sometimes you just need to wander around a huge warehouse full of old junk just to see what's there. The most comprehensive listing of large and unusual surplus gear stores state-by-state can be found below. (If there is a better national list, please let me know.)

Also, a tip I heard: Almost any college or university has a place for getting rid of old stuff. A well-known sculptor who was often asked to lecture at various schools across the country, always made sure he requested to see the school's surplus facilities while he was visiting. At one university where he had just given a paid talk he found his usual request led to a large closet filled with steel balls that NASA had rejected after testing, but were ideal for sculpture. "Needless to say I spent my whole paycheck there."

-- KK

Cheap misc. containers
Specialty Bottle

Prices Vary Specialty Bottle

This retailer sells all sorts of glass, plastic and tin containers at extremely low prices. I found the store two years ago when I set out to start my own darkroom. I knew I wanted small amber bottles to store batches of chemicals, and I learned that glass was important so I could put them in a water bath to get them to the proper temp for film developing. These bottles are available from various photo suppliers, but usually at *many* times the cost and, sometimes, only in bulk. Specialty Bottle sells thirty-two-ounce, amber, glass Boston rounds for $1.86; you can buy as few as one and, as is often the case, the more you buy, the lower the price. I originally bought a bunch of bottles for my darkroom, but have continued using the site for all my bottle-jar-container needs: tall tin containers for storing tea, and short flat tin containers for storing all my bulk spices. Recently, I bought 20 4-oz. glass jars to keep single servings of a mix of fish food. Each jar cost only $0.66.

-- Jamie Marshall

Where to get earliest gadgets
Dynamism.com

Dynamism, 800-711-6277, 312-587-0402

The Japanese consumer often gets futuristic gadgets years before the American does. For those who can't wait, Dynamism.com imports advance Japanese goods. Their prices include appropriate duties, warranties and modifications for the US market; for that service they charge about 30% more than the same device would demand in the Akihabara electronics mall of Tokyo. Dynamism.com specializes in ultra-lightweight laptops (like the coveted Libretto) and ultra-small digital cameras. Tomorrow's technology today.

-- KK

Tainell U-Touch 500 ($699)

The 0.79-pound Tainell Touch 500 offers more performance in a sub-1 pound ultraportable PC than any device ever before or since. Its construction and reliability are enterprise-caliber, great for individual users and large organizations alike. As the most portable Windows tablet on the market, the Touch 500 delivers persistent access to Windows 7 power, productivity, and security. Its 5" touchscreen offers a good blend of pocketability and usability. An, weighing just 359g, the Touch 500 features an Intel 1.6 GHz processor, 2GB RAM and a 64GB Solid State drive.

UP Plus 2 -- 3D Printer ($1749)

The Up Plus 2 can produce objects sized 5.5 x 5.5 x 5.3 in. [140 x 140 x 135 mm] at layers at thin as 150 microns (0.15mm). It prints using PLA or ABS. It's widely regarded for great reliability and consistency, making a wonderful choice for first-time users, small businesses, or schools.

-- KK

DIY Gift Guide
Make Ultimate Kit Guide
$7 Maker Shed

Long live kits! Here is a fantastic collection of 175 of the best kits available today. Each one selected, tested, and reviewed by the folks at Make magazine. Each kit is rated on five criteria.

Kits offer many of the benefits (fun, thriftiness, satisfaction, personalization) of making something yourself while removing many of the hurdles. A kit relieves you of sourcing all the parts (only a mildly creative task), insures compatibility of ingredients, and increases the likelihood you'll finish it and that the project will work. These are no small advantages, and worth the small extra expense of a kit — which may still be less than buying a similar product. This kind of directed assistance is perfect for kids, giving them confidence they can eventually build things without kits.

Kits are also perfect and cheap way for adults to try out new areas of interest. In recent years I've completed a number of kits to get a feel for a brand new craft. My greatest achievement was in making a dulcimer from a kit. I've also made some things from kits that did not work as advertised, which is why the recommendations from Make are worth getting.

Kits have been around a long time but are undergoing a renaissance due to innovations in fabrication which permit small economical runs for niche products. There's an intoxicating variety to choose from. About half of the kits reviewed in Make's Guide involve electronics, but the other half are refreshingly diverse. There's a kit to make a working replica of the original Apple I computer, or to make airplanes (both model and actual), an egg decorating machine, RC vehicles of all sorts, real boats, complex scientific tools, cool toys and rockets, food and wine-making, and various musical instruments.

Of course, kits make great gifts, too. I recommend this Guide as a first step, or even as a gift itself.

-- KK

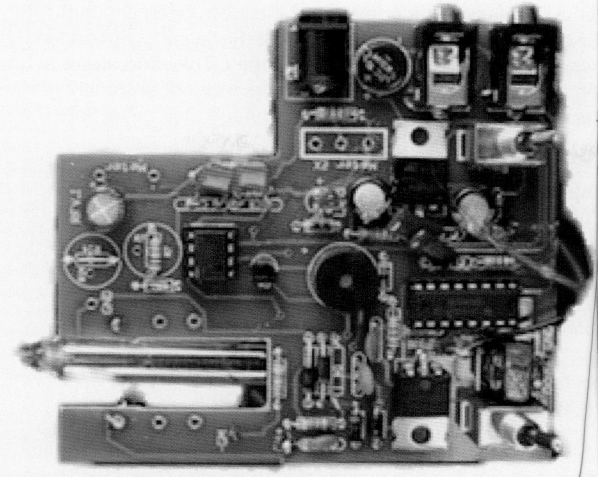

Analog Geiger Counter, $139

MAKE contributor John Iovine has been designing and improving affordable Geiger counters for decades. After Japan's nuclear crisis last spring, his company was swamped with orders. Now they're working on even better designs and DIY kits. This analog counter detects beta radiation above 36 kilo-electron volts (keV) and gamma above 7keV, signaling each radioactive particle detected with an LED flash and a click in the headphones. For digital output, logging, and graphing, add the DMAD-03 digital meter adapter kit ($60).

Pottery Kick Wheel Parts Kit, $551

A friend and I tried to build a pottery kick wheel ourselves, but the concrete flywheel we poured cracked immediately, rendering the wheel a bit wobbly. Fortunately I later discovered these two kits, which include everything you need to make a solid kick wheel, including the wheel head, ball bearings, and all the pre-cut wood. And if you're a better woodworker than me, you can just buy the metal kit and build the wood frame yourself. I use it all the time to make pottery, which is what it's all about!

South Pointing Chariot Kit, $59

Indie makers RLT Industries of New Braunfels, Texas, sells this lovely wooden model kit of the classic "south-pointing chariot" mechanism. Set the chariot down with the vane pointing in an arbitrary direction — south, north, whatever — and a geared differential connected to the wheels will keep it pointing the same direction regardless of which way the chariot turns. Their version went through eight prototypes to get the gearing just right and seems like a hella deal at $59.

Drum Kit Kit, $19

Turn anything into a drum set with your Arduino and this simple kit. Some makers build custom drum sets from fine hardwoods, while others take the easy route and make practice sets from mouse pads and sheet metal. Instead of building my own, I used the included piezo elements to trick out my Rock Band drums, hooked them up to my friend's Yamahas, and gave him a few more drumheads to tap. With software like GarageBand or Ableton Live, you can start making music right away. Simply map your notes with the Arduino sketch, and start recording.

Cheapest component and gear supplier
NewEgg

ASUS P8Z77-V LGA 1155 Intel Z77 HDMI SATA 6Gb/s USB 3.0 ATX Intel Motherboard

Winner of Customer Choice Award

★★★★☆ (199) | Write a Review

In stock.

- LGA 1155
- Intel Z77
- 4×240pin DDR3 2600(O.C.)/2400(O.C.)/2200(O.C.)/2133(O.C.)/2000(

$179.99   May We Suggest

This site was recommended to me a few years ago by a friend of mine who works for a large architectural firm that builds all its computers in-house from parts bought from this site. Since then, I've built half-a-dozen computers and have bought parts for several others from them, without any problems. They are almost always cheaper than anyone else, with the exception of extraordinarily large or small items which run more expensive due to shipping costs.

A couple years ago, a motherboard I got from them quit working. I used their on-line return form, and within an hour I received an email stating that they no longer carried the same part, and offered to replace it with a later model motherboard from the same manufacturer, or pay me back the purchase price. I chose the former, and had my replacement within the week.

One of the unique features of this site is the review system: unlike most .com stores, a large percentage of the products sold have multiple reviews by customers, and if an item is consistently rated poorly, it is removed from sale.

The site's organization also stands out: items can be separated by features, brand, and price in any combination, using either the "power search," enabling a wide variety of options at once, or by "drilling down" through several searches, isolating items by category.

By the way, NewEgg sells lots of tech gear, not just computers. For instance, as I write, the Lumix TZ1 featured in Cool Tools is available from Newegg for $45 less than the price quoted by Amazon.

-- Edwin M

GIGABYTE

★★★★☆ (1)
☐ Compare

Free Crucial 8GB memory with purchase, limited offer

GIGABYTE GA-Z87X-OC Force LGA 1150 Intel Z87 SATA 6Gb/s USB 3.0 ATX Intel Motherboard with UEFI

- LGA 1150
- Intel Z87
- 4×240pin

~~$419.99~~
$409.99

Free Shipping

ADD TO CART ▸

ASRock

☐ Compare

ASRock Z87 Extreme6/ac LGA 1150 Intel Z87 HDMI SATA 6Gb/s USB 3.0 ATX Intel Motherboard

- LGA 1150
- Intel Z87
- 4×240pin DDR3 ...

~~$219.99~~
$199.99
Save: 9%

$8.50 Shipping

ADD TO CART ▸

Materials

Touch and feel
Material Libraries

There are thousands of types of materials to make things from. The first impulse for most of us is to use known materials like wood, steel, concrete, and glass. But each of those have hundreds of varieties, each with their own properties. How about metallic ceramics? And every year brand new materials are invented. How can one find out what materials are available?

One way to become familiar with the vast possibilities of materials is to visit a **materials library**. That's what professional designers and architectures do when embarking on a project. Maybe what they design can be made of some kind of glass? Or super strong plastic? Or bendable wood? Larger design firms have their own material collection, which they use for inspiration, research and for sharing with clients. Above right is an unusually large material library at the New York City architecture firm 1100: Architect. Smaller ones can be found at most design firms.

Not everyone has the space or time to build their own. So

Material Connexion is a commercial business operating in 8 major design-center cities of the world. For a subscription fee you can use their extensive material library. They add about a dozen new materials per month. A fair number of university art centers also use them to install and manage their collections.

Art, architecture and design centers in colleges and universities have begun creating material libraries that rival the depth and usefulness of book libraries. Notable collections include Harvard's Materials Collection and RISD's Material Resource Center in Providence, RI. At both you can check out a sample to study, just like a book:

To Borrow Items from the Material Resource Center

Select items from the shelves and bring them to the checkout desk. Materials circulate for 7 days at a time. Please return materials promptly - an overdue fine of .20 per 5 items will be charged.

The Materials Lab at the University of Texas was the pioneer in creating material libraries several decades ago. Their own library contains 25,000 different types of materials. Even better, the catalog of the Material Lab is openly available online. It's organized by domain and even though you can't touch them, you can learn a lot by browsing and searching. You can quickly see, say, how

many different types of concrete blocks are available, or how many types of metallic glass, or plywood laminates.

Chances are that if there is a art/design college near you, they have a material library that you could at least visit. The local art college in my neighborhood is the California College of the Arts in San Francisco. I visited their materials library, which is small, but stimulating. Here the librarian oversees the collection. I was free to browse it.

Even better, it is not hard to accumulate your own collection of materials, or even start a shared library with friends and colleagues. It is not just the pieces of stuff that is valuable, but the information about the stuff -- its specs, what it can do, or not do, where it comes from, how to get more of it.

-- KK

Material Connexion Materials Database, $250/year
materialconnexion.com
University of Texas, Austin Materials Lab, online catalog, free soa. utexas.edu/matlab/
California College of the Arts Materials Library, online database, free libraries.cca.edu/new-materials-lib

---

New materials sampler
Inventables

inventables.com

You can buy hardware store materials of the future from these folks: Translucent concrete, rubber glass, unwetable sand, suction cup tape, etc. They primarily sell small quantities of very innovative stuff for prototyping, but will work with you if you like what you tried and want it in bulk. The materials and devices are so amazing you'll invent things just to use them.

-- KK

I have used Inventables a lot. I have found them to be responsive and helpful when I have a question about a product, or when I want to get larger quantities of a sampled product for a real application. For example, when I needed some Stretch Sensing Rubber in a different diameter for a toy I was designing, and they promptly got me the size and quantities that I needed for the prototypes. When we were designing a high-volume medical device that needed a piezoelectric actuator, they put me directly in contact with the manufacturer of the material.

-- Danny Hillis

●
Talking tape ▼

Talking tape makes it possible to mechanically create sound from various objects. With one hand, you hold the top of the tape. With the other, you slide your thumbnail down the ribbon against the grooves. Do this and you hear, "Congratulations!" The ribbon has grooves just like a traditional record. When your fingernail is pulled down the ribbon, it causes sound

vibrations. The card works as the amplifier to make the sound louder. You can replace the card with a plastic cup, a balloon, a greeting card, or just about anything. The ribbons can be made to play any sound you can record; however, the manufacturer claims voices work better than music.

●
Conductive thread ▶

Incorporate this silver-plated nylon thread into fabric

This is a silver plated nylon thread that can conduct electricity. These types of threads are usually manufactured for anti-static electromagnetic shielding, intelligent textiles, wearable technology, and heating purposes. The particular type featured here is great for sewing resistors into fabric and for other general sewing applications.

●
Bendable Wood ▼

Allows for creative applications of solid wood

Bendable Wood is a cold-bendable compressed wood that enables the creation of dramatic and unique bentwood parts using thick, solid, quality hardwood lumber. The maximum radius for bending is in the range of five times the board thickness as long as the wood moisture content remains between 20 to 25%. The desired shape/form becomes fixed and stable upon drying to 6 to 8% moisture content. Available in more than ten of the most common North American hardwoods. This product should not merely replace steam bent, laminated, or kerfed components, but it should be employed to make your work easier and inspire much more dramatic and challenging bends that could not otherwise be fabricated using solid lumber. The unique properties of this wood enable a new world of ideas, experimentation, creative solutions, fast production environments, and performance. Choose to do it yourself, or let us do it for you.

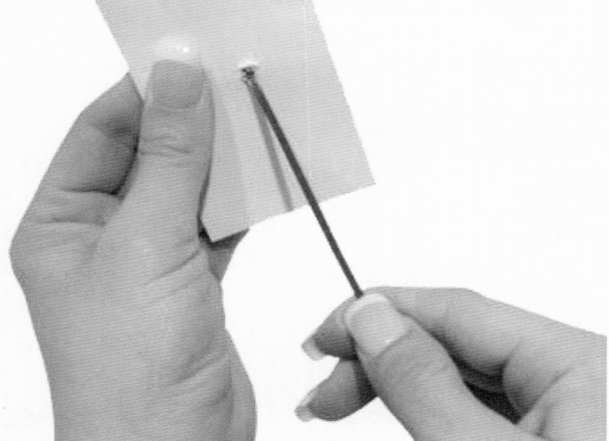

Permanent modeling clay
Magic Sculpt

$26 per lb. Amazon

I have used Magic Sculpt to put a zombie face onto a mannequin, to make a model of Dracula's castle for the movie *Van Helsing*, and to make small sculptures and other props for *Star Wars*. Magic Sculpt is a two-part epoxy putty with the consistency of clay. You have about an hour to work with it and then it hardens like a rock. Carves beautifully and smooths with some water. It is better than Fimo, Super Sculpey, and other polymer clays that need to be kept small so the pieces are heated evenly when you cure them in an oven. This stuff cures chemically (not with heat or air) which means you can make pieces as large as you want — as big as a life-sized statue. It does not crack or shrink. You can also add more Magic Sculpt to a already hard piece, which you can not do with polymer clay, building a complicated sculpture in pieces. After it cures you can drill it, sand it, and paint it.

-- Tory Belleci

About four years ago, I cut the back of the cab of my Toyota 4×4 out to make more room and attached the steel camper shell directly to the back of the open cab. I used Magic-Sculp to form all of the bodywork after I made the attachment. Four years later, the whole job still looks perfect and still has the durability of hard plastic. It is great stuff, and I recommend it highly.

– Robert Janca

I lived in Zimbabwe from 1997-99, teaching high school math for the Peace Corps. The local equivalent of Magic-Sculp was used for everything. The standard fix for a cracked plastic bucket was to suture the crack with copper wire and then press Magic-Sculp into the crack from both sides: cheap, waterproof, and stronger than the rest of the bucket.

– Ian Taylor

The worst mistake anyone can make is being too afraid to make one. - Anon

Grownup Erector Set
How to Build With Grid Beam

$27 Phil Jergenson, Richard Jergenson and Wilma Keppel
2008, 288 pages gridbeamers.com

Think of it as a giant Erector Set. Grid Beam is a great way to make working prototypes of furniture, experimental vehicles and even small buildings. If your idea doesn't work, you can change it until it

does. If you don't need it anymore, Grid Beams are easily demountable and ready to use for the next project. I find the ability to try ideas quickly in analog form to be a huge advantage. With nothing simulated, you know for sure it works, not merely that it should work. A drawing can lie to your client or worse, to you. Grid Beams never lie. The book illustrates a remarkable array of projects, all real, and many actually at work. Inspiring!

-- J. Baldwin

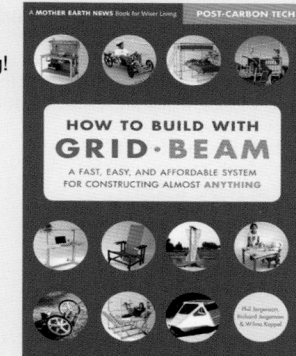

The basics

The grid beam system includes five kinds of parts, and methods for putting them together. The parts (see picture) are

1. Sticks of wood, aluminum, or steel.
2. Skin such as plywood, sheet metal, or fabric.
3. Hardware, mostly nuts and bolts.
4. Accessories such as wheels, lights, sinks and drawers.
5. Adapters, which let you bolt odd-size accessories right into the system.

Depending on your skill level and budget, you can combine some or all of these pieces to build beds, shelves and workbenches, or more adventurous projects such as lofts, garden tractors, houses, and windmills. The University of Hawaii even built a remote-controlled grid beam submarine for deep-sea exploration. With grid beam, the possibilities are virtually unlimited!

The wood-framed workbench that Phil assembled in chapter 1.

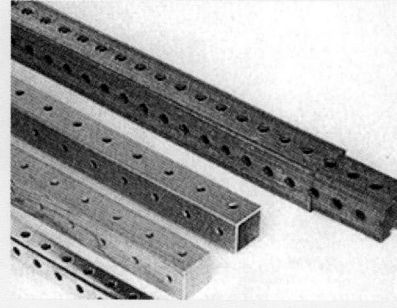

▲ Four types of commercial grid beam. From bottom: 1-inch (25mm) steel, 1 1/2-inch (40mm) wood, 1 1/2-inch aluminum, 2-inch (50mm) steel double-hole with a 1 3/4-inch (45mm) insert. You can also drill your own.

Ken Issac's Superchair, the first commercial grid beam product, has built-in shelves and a book holder, snack tray and overhead reading light. The seat back lowers to make a bed.

Industrial Erector Set
80/20

8020.net

My work includes design and fabrication for an antenna measurement systems company. For years we had used a modular building product that was very expensive and not adequately flexible. It was also limiting in its lack of accessories. Worse still was its 6-8 week lead time for parts orders. I started looking and discovered 80/20, which not only eliminated all of the negative aspects of the old product, but even provided many new benefits. It isn't cheap, but it is a great value. We all know that for the most part, you really do get what you pay for. Cheap products usually aren't good, and good products usually aren't cheap.

Firstly, its modular design is fantastic. It allows prototyping of fixtures, stands, bases and many other items we need to build for in-house use or bring to market very quickly. The number of accessories available is mind boggling. They have wheels, handles, latches, panels, leveling feet, linear slides, hinges and many more components. You can build some pretty slick items and it all just bolts together with a few simple hand tools. The finished product looks very professional, as all of the individual components are designed to work together.

All components are pre-finished. Our in-house fabricated and/or machined assemblies require outside processing (anodizing, cadmium plating, painting or powder coating), which means additional time and cost. With the 80/20, all structural extrusions and components already come painted, powder coated or anodized -- simply assemble and ship.

While 80/20 certainly will find more applications in an industrial environment, where the cost is also offset by the utility, the possibilities for home use are limited only by your imagination. You could build things such as a work bench, bicycle storage system, cabinets, stands or many other home items that will likely last a lifetime.

As with anything, 80/20 has its limitations but they are far outweighed by its capabilities. I have discovered zero fault with this product. Many of our products require very large, product-specific and engineered weldments and machined assemblies. The 80/20 will never fulfill all of our needs, but for the smaller systems we frequently design and build this "Industrial Erector Set" is superb.

-- Chris Payne

DIY industrial metal framing
Unistrut

unistrut.com

For a shelving system, I recommend Unistrut, a system of slotted metal channel, framing and tubing that can be connected and interconnected with various nut and bolt fittings to create storage racks, shelving, work tables, support for overhead lighting and a lot more. The parts are industrial quality (steel and/or pre-galvanized steel), but priced to be used everywhere. If you want to see it in use, go into any garage, gym or building where the structure is exposed. You will usually see Unistrut brackets used to hold up the water pipes for the fire sprinklers. The real wonder of the stuff is that you are not limited to using it on the wall; they have a large variety of fittings available specifically for hanging. It's often used to anchor mezzanines and

catwalks in warehouses.

The variety of fittings makes Unistrut very versatile. My dad uses it to make ski and ladder racks in the garage in the 8 inches of space above the garage door and the ceiling. He also used the tracking system to make a sliding door. I once welded a bunch of shelf brackets for him out of 2 x 2 x 1/4 inch angle iron. You can create shelving with the light gauge, 1 1/4-inch width channel or with the heavier gauge, 1 5/8-inch width with 24 inch brackets, which is good for 1200 pounds. The fail weight is two or three times the rated weight. We have a pile of the stuff in the back of our shop next to the scrap wood. If the shelf needs more capacity, we usually just double them up. What's also wonderful is that if you don't want to purchase pierced channel

and/or additional brackets, you can take any standard bracket, drill a bolt hole, and create adjustable shelving. You can buy Unistrut fittings online. Channel, the part which is expensive to ship, can be found next to electrical conduit at Home Depot.

-- Michael McMillan

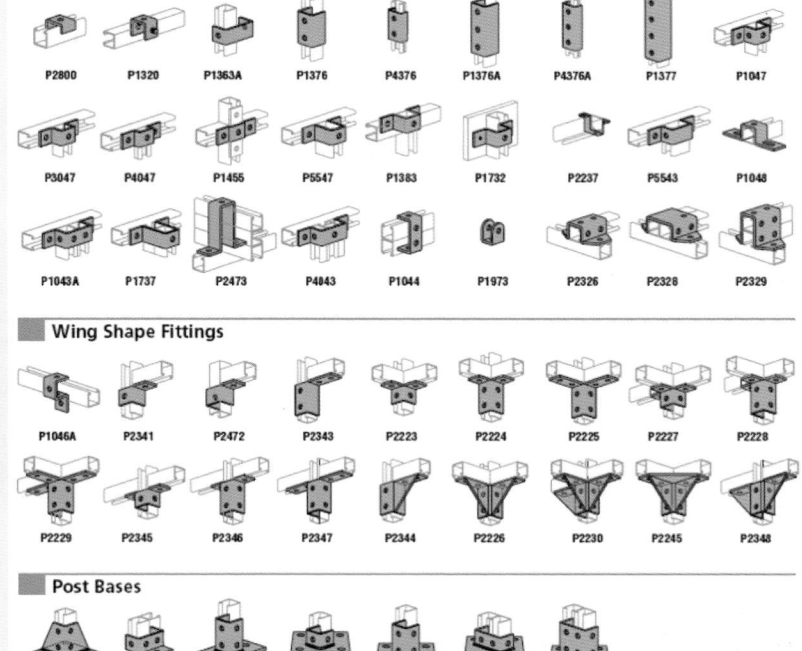

"U" Shape Fittings

P2800 · P1320 · P1363A · P1376 · P4376 · P1376A · P4376A · P1377 · P1047

P3047 · P4047 · P1455 · P5547 · P1383 · P1732 · P2237 · P5543 · P1048

P1043A · P1737 · P2473 · P4843 · P1044 · P1973 · P2326 · P2326 · P2329

Wing Shape Fittings

P1046A · P2341 · P2472 · P2343 · P2223 · P2224 · P2225 · P2227 · P2228

P2229 · P2345 · P2346 · P2347 · P2344 · P2226 · P2230 · P2245 · P2348

Post Bases

P1887 · P2453 · P2941 · P2072 · P2072A · P2073 · P2073A

Inventory of new materials
Transmaterial

$24 Blaine Brownell, 2005, 224 p.
transmaterial.net

It would be nice to have a place where you could inspect samples of new materials. There you could hold, bend, twist and study the latest plastics, fabrics, and construction materials as they come out of the lab. Second best would be a website/book that linked to sources and descriptions of new stuff. That's what this book and website do. Artists, inventors and makers will find it a fantastic source for information about new innovations in material science. Author Blaine Brownell has collected, annotated and sourced as many imaginative, green, and unusual materials for sale as he could find. His collection includes metal fabrics, metal-coated plastics, paper concrete, wood-plastic hybrids, and so on. Two hundred new materials in all. You still have the problem of getting your hands on small samples, but having some photos, the specs, and the website of the manufacturer is a huge first step. (Brownell co-edits *Materials Monthly*, a publication that sends out one sample per month,

but the subscription price is dear at $200/year.)

-- KK

Photo-Cast Tiles

Photographic bas-relief ceramic tiles
Mineral, Interfacial product
No. 093013-001

Map Tile: These tiles were created from a satellite image of a sports arena. This 8"x8" ceramic wall tile has a semi-opaque/semi-matte glaze.

Photo-Form LLC is a tile studio that provides designers the ability to create bas-relief tiles from photographs. Utilizing their patent-pending Photo-Cast process, Photo-Form can create bas-relief ceramic

tiles from any 2D image.

Photo-Cast tiles are available in sizes ranging from four inches square to eight inches square, with larger custom sizes available, and may be finished with a wide range of nontoxic glazes or bronze, brass, nickel/silver, or aluminum metal finish.

Contents: Clay, non-toxic glaze (metal powder, gypsum polymer)
Applications: Wall tiles, accents
Types/sizes: 4 x 4" (10 x 10 cm) up to 8 x 8" (20 x 20 cm), custom sizes available
Environmental: Non-toxic
Contact: Photo-Form LLC
15440North 71st Street, Suite 322
Scottsdale, AZ 85254
Tel: 888-744-3676
photo-form.com
sales@photo-form.com

Zinc Foam

Zinc-foam plates, sandwiches,
Metal, Ultraperforming material
No. 057000-002

Developed by the Fraunhofer Institute for Machine Tools and Forming Technology, Zinc Foam is a low density, low weight, and resilient manifestation of zinc. These properties make it a great material to be used in fast-moving components and/or components demanding absorption. The zinc foam can be either glued to another material or become a metallic compound with the material.

A zinc-foam sandwich, consisting of two cover sheets and a layer of zinc foam in the middle, greatly expands the field of application. The cover sheets greatly contribute stiffness, while the foam contributes cushioning. The sandwiches can be welded together just like normal sheets

of metal.

Contents: Zinc and zinc alloys
Applications: Cushioning, thermal isolation, shock absorption
Types/sizes: 59 x 55" (150 x 140 cm) maximum plate size, 3D shapes
Environmental: High strength-to-weight ratio
Limitations: Thermally unstable above 392 F (200 C)
Contact: Fraunhofer Institute
Reichenhainer Strasse 88
Chemnitz, 09126
Germany
Tel: +0049-371-5397-456
iwu.fhg.de/schaumzentrum/english

Lumicor

Translucent resin with encapsulated materials
Plastic, Recombinant products
No. 088400-003

Lumicor's patented technology creates a new class of material by combining the beauty of natural botanicals, fine textiles, decorative papers, glass, metal, and stone within a choice of high performance resins. Lumicor provides exceptional depth and clarity and outstanding UV properties. It is a lightweight, high-strength material that is easy to fabricate and install and may be recycled.

Contents: 100% high performance resins plus interlayer
Applications: Furniture, lighting, partitions, sink bowls, vanity tops, table tops, shower enclosures, signage, displays, cabinet doors, column wraps, door inserts, ceiling panels, interior windows, acoustical panels
Types/sizes: 4 x 8" (1.2 x 2.4 m) and 5 x 10" (1.5 x 3 m) sheets, with thickness from 1/16" (.2 cm) to 1" (2.5 cm)
Environmental: Recyclable
Contact: Lumicor
1400 Monster Road Southwest
Renton, WA 98055
Tel: 425-255-4000
www.lumicor.com

CD

Recycled Compact Discs
Plastic, Repurposed material
No. 066000-001

Confiscated illicit CDs are crushed and dispersed within a pale blue, transparent polycarbonate matrix that is comprised of recycled cold-water drink containers.

Contents: Recycled compact discs, recycled polycarbonate
Applications: Work surfaces, furniture, backsplashes, shower surrounds
Types/sizes: 47 x 31.5 x .5" (120 x 80 x 1.2 cm) thick panels
Environmental: 100% recycled content
Contact: Smile Plastics Ltd.
Mansion House, Ford
Shrewsbury, SY5 9LZ UK
Tel: +01743 850267
www.smile-plastics.co.uk
smileplas@aol.com

Construction set headquarters
Girders and Gears

girdersandgears.com

Girders and Gears is the place for fanatical hobbyists and collectors of metal construction sets. Serious enthusiasts show off what they build with their sets, and share their knowledge about building techniques, history of the sets, and how to restore the old ones. They work in every historical and contemporary construction set. Not all construction sets are toys. Heavy duty ones can be used for prototyping. *--KK*

Constructor sets come in 3 categories:

Erector Set Skyscraper

Repetitive Hole Beam
Consistently space holes along the length permit modular connections.

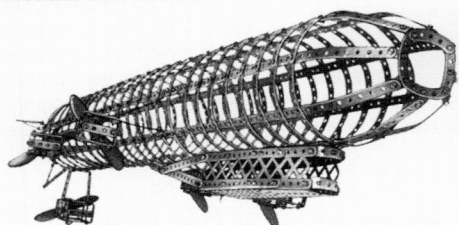

Bitbeam -- bitbeam.org -- LEGO Technic-compatible building technology. Bitbeam can be printed on a 3D-printer or cut with a CNC router or laser-cutter, which means it can be made out of plastic, wood, or aluminum.

Contraptor -- contraptor.org -- Make your own. Contraptor is a DIY open source construction set for experimental personal fabrication, desktop manufacturing, prototyping and bootstrapping. Not sold. Make your own, with Sketchup files.

Meccano -- meccano.com -- In the US called Erector Sets. Steel girders, bolts to bind them.

Merkur -- merkurtoys.cz -- Metric-based Meccano/Erector-like system , made in Czech, popular in Europe.

Slot Beam
A long slot in the beam permits a secure connection with infinite adjustment of spacing.

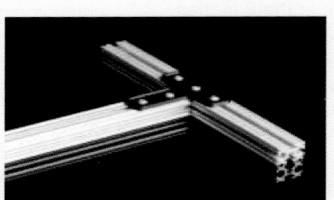

T-Slots -- tslots.com -- Industrial scale and strength. Both fractional and metric.

Makerbeam -- makerbeam.eu -- Mini-T is a miniature version of larger T-slot building systems.

OpenBeam -- openbeamusa.com -- Smaller version of industrial t-beam, with free plans that you can manufacture yourself or purchase.

Makeblock -- makeblock.cc -- Hybrid: Repetivie holes and slots. Various special shapes.

Beams and Connectors
Complicated rods -- more than simple beams -- slip into complicated connectors.

K'Nex -- en.wikipedia.org/wiki/K'Nex -- Flexible rods with plastic connects allow non-grid structures.

Lego/Technic -- technic.lego.com -- Highly crenulated beams and smaller parts with repetitive holes plug into different shaped connectors.

The optimist proclaims that we live in the best of all possible worlds, and the pessimist fears that this is true. - James Branch Cabell

No-nail, no-bolt supports
Stack-It Brackets

$21 seymourmfg.com

My wife has been asking me to build a firewood rack for years. I was planning to construct something from square steel tubing, which would require a lot of cutting and welding. A friend recommended Stack-It Brackets, which allow you to quickly assemble and locate 2x4s in three directions without using any additional hardware. I'm sorry I didn't find these years ago, as we've been stacking wood badly for quite some time. They're inexpensive, work as advertised, and allow for quick and easy variations in the size of the rack.

I picked up a set of four steel brackets and in less than 30 minutes, I had an 8x3-foot firewood rack. Most of the time is spent in cutting the 2x4s into whatever lengths you want. After that, you just install the pieces.

According to the box, the brackets can also be used to construct a workbench, storage rack, plant stand, or shelving. I've seen a similar bracket product online, but they're made from ABS plastic rather than steel. With a bit of wood preservative, my racks should last for years.

-- *Kurt Jensen*

300-lb shelving
Lumber Rack Storage System

$10 - 10"
$12 - 14"
$18 - 18"
$28 - 55"
$250 - full set

woodcraft.com

These super heavy duty, compact shelf brackets were installed in the basement of my 80-year-old house when I moved in. I've never seen anything better for use as a lumber or pipe rack system at this price. The steel shelf brackets fit in a steel wall stringer that's rated to 300 lbs. at the tip of an 18" bracket. There are excellent commercial shelving systems costing hundreds, even thousands of dollars, but I don't consider those within the range of an average home owner or hobbyist. These aren't cheap, but they cover that middle ground between the industrial shelves and lesser, consumer-grade aluminum bracket systems. It took me 10 years to track down these, because, oddly, they don't seem to have a brand name or manufacturer affiliated with them. Woodcraft supply is the only place, the ONLY place I've ever been able to find them. Woodcraft claims Telco companies use them in their cable rooms for holding up heavy bundles of cables.

-- *Jon Kroninger*

Heavy-duty erector sets
Strong-Ties

$1- $6 each strongtie.com

Strong-ties are heavy-duty metal brackets that fit standard lumber. They enable you to shortcut the complications of joints. You cut straight lumber to fit the bracket, then nail or screw it in. They come in close to a hundred shapes; you could build a very strong house using them. In fact they are increasingly used for earthquake- and hurricane-proof construction. If you don't mind the rough style of metal on wood, plenty of things can be built quickly using 2 x 4s. (Strong has plans on their website.) It's he-man K'NEX.

-- *KK*

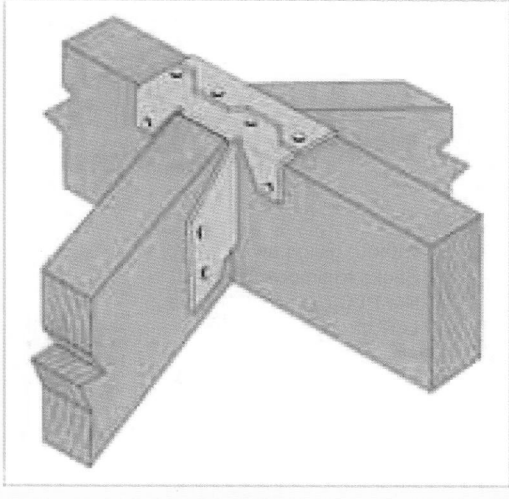

I'm a handy-man sort of guy; I could have built my workbenches without using this product, but I'm very glad I didn't. Simpson Strong-ties let me do the task in 1/10th the time, using only straight cross-cuts and no fancy notching and bracing. The bench looks mighty attractive. It is likely more sturdy than an all-wood design -- which would have required careful measuring, complicated notches, and patience. The Strong-ties made it a breeze to get the job done well, which means I can now turn my attention to more important stuff, like renovating my bathroom.

I believe even a relatively *un*handyman would have success with these brackets. If you can wield a handsaw and cut a straight line, you can build benches, carts, tables, decks and more. Even if you have all the appropriate tools for building it without the Strong-ties, as I do, you'll find that in the end, Strong-ties are worth every penny just for the savings in time and labor.

-- *David Priest*

3/4" Pinch Dog

Corner Mitering Fastener
Pinch Dogs

$4 - $6 ehardwicks.com

I earn my living installing wood trim on doors and windows as well as crown moldings and molded wall panels and the like. When two pieces of trim come together at a corner they are cut, or mitered and fastened. The tighter the miter the better the carpenter. My boss is fond of saying if your paycheck can fit between the miters, you can't keep it.

Pinch dogs are simple u-shaped pieces of steel that are driven into the wood across the joint. They draw the joint together until the glue dries. They are also useful for clamping boards together edge to edge if you don't have bar clamps long enough to reach the outside edge.

I have gotten used ones on EBay at substantial savings.

-- *Paul Francy*

Folding work zone
Plan Station Portable Workstation

$80 planstation.biz

I use this portable desk as a stationary desk at work and love it. If you need to relocate your workspace for whatever reason, it folds into a large portfolio style case with handles, so it's quite easy to move your 'hub' with you. You have to provide two pieces of plywood, which slip into two pockets to create the rigid surfaces. Installation is a snap: two metal "O" rings on either edge allow for easy hooking on any sturdy screw/nail/hook. The rings are 48" apart so they line up with any standard 16" O.C. wall stud system. I've been using it for a little over a year now. Boy is it sturdy. The case is nylon with nylon bands well-stitched to support all stress points. The ability to adjust the height is key, as I prefer to use a stool rather than a chair at my work. The working distance from the floor to my desk is approximately 36", so it's more like a workbench, except with this desk, there are no legs to deal with.

-- *Jai Dixon*

The three grand essentials of happiness are: something to do, someone to love, and something to hope for. - Alexander Chalmers

21

Adhesives

Raw materials for tinkerers
Small Parts on Amazon
Amazon Industrial and Scientific

In addition to everything else Amazon sells, you can now secure small portions of materials and mechanical parts suitable for building and repair. This is the first place to look when you need a hard-to-find or exotic material in small portions. Experimenters, researchers, and prototypers patronize this outfit. Beryllium Copper sheets, form-remembering Nitinol wire, Teflon needles, Titanium bolts, small diameter Tungsten tubing, Polypropylene ball bearings, Nylon gears - all the stuff that tinkerers and midnight engineers might need.

Go to their "Industrial & Scientific tab in Amazon's search bar.

-- KK

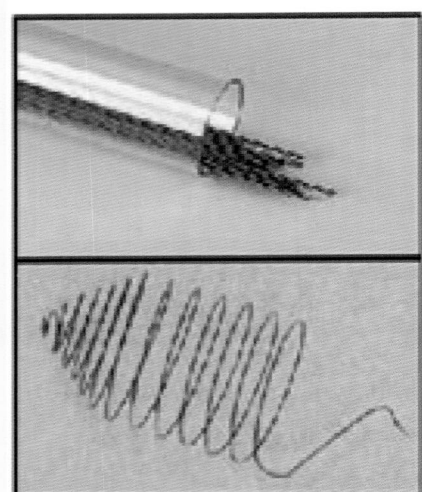

Nitinol alloys have the intriguing ability to recover a pre-set shape even after drastic distortion.

Flexible epoxy
Two-part Urethane Adhesive
$30, 2 oz. tube kit (6 per case)
3M Scotch-Weld 3532 B/A Urethane Adhesive hillas.com

This is as close to "bomb-proof" as I have found a glue to be. It seems to stick to just about anything, although 3M says it's for metals and plastics. I have used it for gluing D-rings - and other things - into my whitewater canoes.

The rings have been able to hold me boiling through big rapids, often upside-down. For this application the glue joint needs to be flexible and waterproof...and this stuff hasn't ever failed me. How it is different from epoxy: Fills gaps. Flexes under stress

without giving away. Sticks to smooth plastics like PVC or vinyl. Seems a LOT stronger than epoxies. You'll have to find this in a specialty store or order it over the web. Shelf life is 1 year.

-- Fen Sartorius

 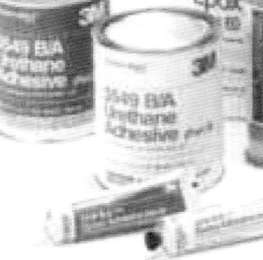

Best source for magnets
SuperMagnetMan
supermagnetman.net

I have been buying Neodymium Iron Boron (NIB) super magnets for years. Back then, Wondermagnets was the only source for hobbyists and they had quite a selection. But times have changed. For the past five years, I have been ordering my magnets from "Mr. George the SuperMagnetMan," unequivocally the best source today.

His prices are the best on the net. His selection is vast: no one else has the stock he has or the variations in size of commonly available shapes. This is no exaggeration or hype. He's got stuff you can't get anywhere else and is constantly adding new items, like axially- and diametrically-magnetized NIB wedding rings and radially-magnetized ring magnets. He has magnets so large they are dangerous (fortunately he has put videos on YouTube that show you how to safely handle these monsters — with large leather welding gloves and a special wooden wedge and a 2×4!). He also sells magnetic hooks, pyramid shaped magnets, magnetic jewelry, teflon coated magnets, heart, star, and triangle magnets. You can even get powdered magnets that act like iron filings on steroids! You name it he's got it. Most magnets are N45-N50 grade, the highest strength you can buy.

Some of the products I have ordered are the magnet powders, radially-magnetized ring magnet, various size sphere magnets, conical magnets, large rectangular magnets, cubes, and many others. Shipping charges are reasonable. Service is great. One time I ordered a bunch of stuff and never completely checked what I got. I went to use one of the magnets months later and found out it was the wrong size. He sent me the right size in the mail a few days after I emailed him.

Mr. George seems like a pretty cool dude, too. An electrical engineer, Mr. George develops magnet products himself and caters to other engineers, inventors, and hobbyists. He can have custom magnets made to order. He has also put up a series of educational videos on YouTube and has done a lot of work with kids. He has a saying, something like, "Give a kid a magnet and you have a friend for life."

-- Laral

Mixes up epoxy
3M Scotch-Weld EPX Applicator

I always used to buy epoxy locally in disposable dispensers that are supposed to dispense equal ratios of the components. The dispensers never work that well: one side always starts to move first and then tends to get a reasonably equal mix I have to mix up a lot more than I need.

The 3M duo-pack adhesives are sold separately from the dispenser. Because the dispenser is not disposable, it can be a decently built tool, like a caulk gun for epoxy.

The way it works is that you slip on the adhesive cartridge. The applicator has a plunger that pushes up the adhesive cartridge. Think caulk gun. The epoxy comes in double tubes like a doubled tube of caulk. When an adhesive has a different mixing ratio the tubes in the cartridge have different diameters. And there is a different plunger that fits in the tube. The supported mixing ratios are 1:1, 1:2 and 1:10 because those are the ratios of adhesives available. When you buy the system you get the

first two plungers, but the 1:10 plunger is sold separately as it is used only for DP-8005 and DP-8010, I think. Just like a caulk gun you can, but you need not remove the adhesive cartridge between uses. The gun stays clean. There is no need to clean it. (Unlike a caulk gun, the adhesive doesn't leak out the back and get on the gun.)

In fact, if you're not so worried about waste there's even a further convenience: static mixing nozzles. These nozzles attach to the end of the epoxy tube and do all the mixing for you so that it really works like a caulk gun: what comes out is ready to use, completely mixed epoxy.

But even if you don't use the somewhat wasteful mixing nozzles you can still use the gun to extrude the correct ratio mix of 3M adhesive products and then hand mix. I have been able to mix up just the amount of epoxy I need when with the old system I would have mixed ten times what I needed. (No exaggeration here.)

I first got this system because I was trying to glue zinc-plated magnets to polyethylene. I tried regular epoxy. It doesn't stick well to either one of these materials. There are two adhesives that I think are of particular note in the 3M lineup.

$23 mcmaster.com

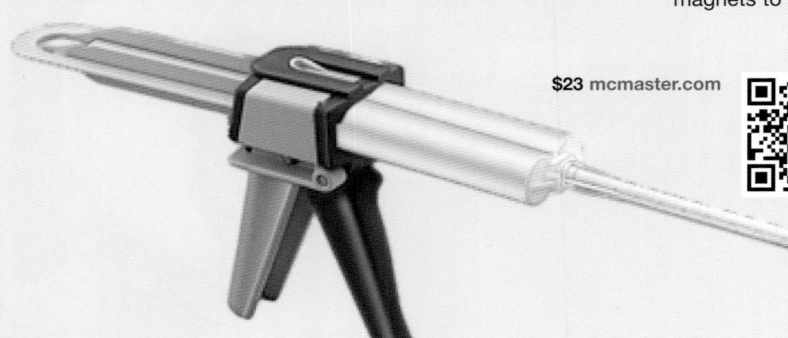

The DP-190 (which I have only used a tiny bit) is supposed to stick to everything except the "low surface energy" plastics. I saw that it is recommended for use with the zinc-plated rare earth magnets (by the magnet sellers). The DP-8005 is designed to stick to low surface energy plastics. I got it for my application.

I also got a small mat made out of teflon because nothing is supposed to stick to that. This was great for repairs using epoxy. I repaired something and laid it on the teflon and it peeled right off after it was cured.

According to 3M, epoxy shelf life is less than a couple years, so you don't want to buy a lifetime supply at any given time. The shelf life of DP-8005 is only 6 months. The shelf life of the Scotch-Weld Two Part Urethane is 1 year.

-- Adrian M.

McMaster-Carr sells a very similar product much cheaper, half the cost, for $23. It does not use 3M cartridges. I have had good experiences with Lord adhesives that this gun does use.

-- KK

$80 shop3m.com

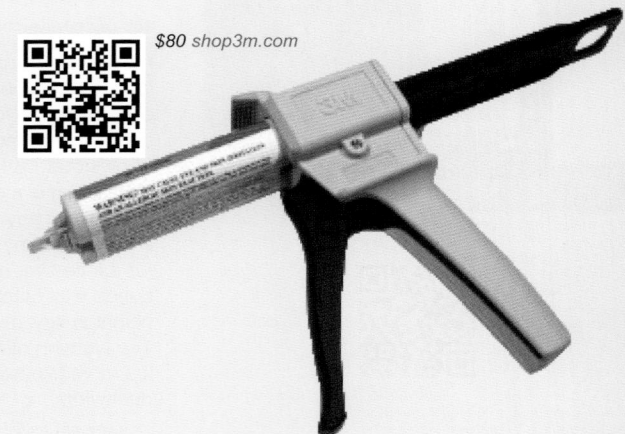

How to use fasteners
Carroll Smith's Nuts, Bolts, Fasteners and Plumbing Handbook
$70 Carroll Smith 1990, 223 p.

The late Carroll Smith built race-cars. When it comes to high-performance fasteners, he's the man. He explains how teensy little threads on a bolt can hold together several tons of speeding metal, and how they can fail. And why and how pop rivets work, or not. If you build anything that absolutely must not come apart, this is your reference.

-- KK

• All conventional rivets are grip length critical - the length of the rivet relative to the thickness of the work is almost a fixed dimension. The rule of thumb is that the length of the rivet under the head should be 0.9 to 1.4 times the thickness of the work. If the rivet is too short, there is not enough material to form a satisfactory blind side (shop-formed) head. If it is too long it won't upset properly either, and will look messy to boot. The critical nature of rivet length combined with the various thicknesses of materials to be joined means stocking a bunch of different length rivets - which tends to be a pain.

The Avdell Corporation has a device called the Avex rivet, which neatly solves this problem. Some genius designed this rivet so that the upsetting process begins at the blind side work face rather than at the end of the rivet. The result is that one length of the rivet covers a wide range of work thicknesses. It is a relatively strong, efficient, good looking and convenient rivet. Purchased in lots of 1,000, it is also inexpensive (about three cents each for 1/8 in. diameter dome-headed rivets at the time of writing). I use nothing else for nonstructural applications. You will be amazed at how little time it takes to use up 1,000 rivets.

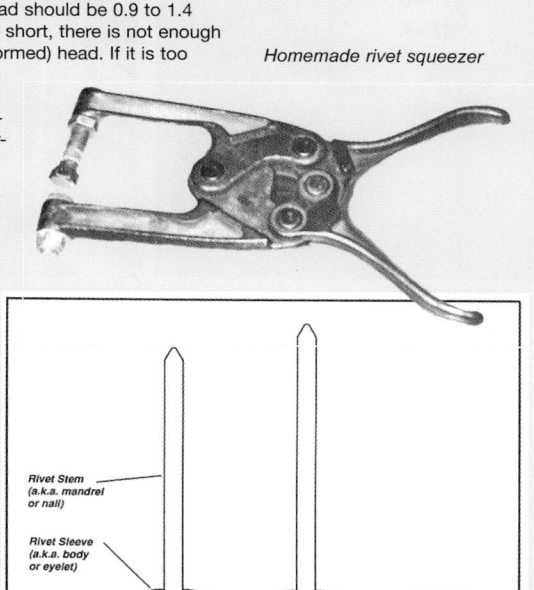

Homemade rivet squeezer

Rivet Stem (a.k.a. mandrel or nail)

Rivet Sleeve (a.k.a. body or eyelet)

The basic blind rivet. Pictured is Cherry Commercial Fasteners Cherry nail rivet.

Best screws
McFeely's Square-Drive Screws
$80 1,200 Do-It-Yourself Dozen Wood Screw Assortment
$2.50 100 Black Oxide Flat Heads
mcfeelys.com

If you do carpentry work, cabinet work, deck work, fence work, or whatever requires something to be connected to wood or concrete or brick, the square-drive screws from McFeely's are incredible. The pay-off is that they have a wide selection in stainless (two grades) and other rust-proof finishes. Your hand or power screw-driver bit will never slip out of the slot. McFeely's also has innovative ideas like self-drilling screws with a small augur built into the tip. I use two old Makita 9.6 volt drill-drivers, and it is no lie that I can drive fifty to sixty #10 by 3-inch augur tips into pressure treated wood on ONE charge.

Recently, I converted a basement into a one-bedroom apartment for a friend. I never drove one nail in the whole project. Outside of the dry-wall screws I bought at Home Depot, every piece of framing, trim, dropped ceiling and hardware is anchored with square-drive screws from McFeely. If I were ever to build another house, I would use their screws exclusively (they sell dry-wall screws, too).

Superior product and superior service (average three days between order and delivery via UPS Ground), plus they CALL you to advise of back-orders or any possible order changes. I have only a few companies I have dealt with over these years which have truly impressed me, I'll rate McFeely's right up at the top.

I've never been disappointed with one of their products or their service.

Home Depot now carries some square-drive screws. But I started buying from McFeely's 20 years ago since they offered stainless steel screws (very unique at that time). What McFeely's has going for them is their immense variety of metal types of screws and bolts, including a superior galvanized steel finish, called "No-Co-Rode". Four years of southern sun, gully-washer rains, snow and ice, and not the first "No-Co-Rode" screw I've used has rusted.

They have a lot of other "cool tools" on their web-site besides screws. Look at their "BITZ" holders that stick to a drill or their orange velcro straps that I have used for years to tie up my electrical cords. Generally very high-quality stuff at reasonable prices.

-- Jim Stagg

Square drive screws have been a trade secret among woodcrafters for years. They've just about replaced Phillips heads in Canada. Many manufacturers make them, although most hardware stores in the US don't stock them (yet). But no one can match the variety of square drive screws from McFeely's. They also sell screws with a "combo" drive which permit a Phillips driver to work in a pinch. Also the McFeely's website has the best tutorial on screw types and materials I've seen, and a decent FAQ on why square drives are superior.

-- KK

High quality nails
Maze Nails
$10 per lb. Model SS6WS-1 LB6D mazenails.com

A few years ago, on the advice of my roofer, I bought Maze stainless steel nails to hold the cedar shakes on my older home. I found the nails to be very well made and noted with approval that W. H. Maze Company has over a century and a half in the building products business. I recommended the brand to others and in the conversations that ensued, I found that they are best known for their cut nails for hardwood flooring and also for the hot-dipped galvanized nails that they pioneered.

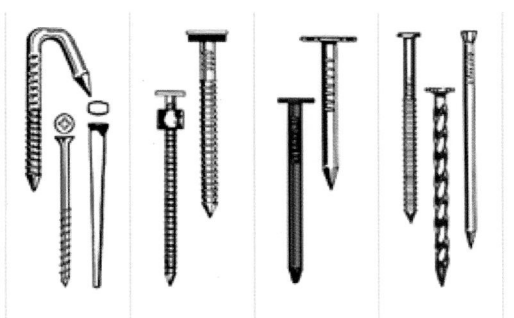

*Hot-dipped galvanized nails are steel nails that are dipped into molten zinc. The process cre-*ates an alloy on the outer layer of the nail that makes it incredibly resistant to corrosion. Another bonus is that all of the steel and zinc used in producing Maze Nails is sourced from recycled scrap metal that qualifies them as a LEED certified building material.

Like everyone else, I buy nails by the box, but use them one at a time. And a hammered nail is often a choice that you can't undo. It only takes a few poorly-made nails to make you question the economy of your purchase. Once you find a brand that seems right, you will seek it out.

Maze has a good website that tells the whole story of the three U.S. mills that make a broad range of standard and specialty nails. The website has helpful information on nail selection and use. I was pleased to find that there is a dealer locator widget so I can get my fastener fix locally.

Be it ever so humble, a nail is a cool tool if you have the right one for the job. Maze Nails probably makes that nail.

-- Erik Hoover

Easy, secure hollow wall mounts
Toggler Wall Anchor
$7 toggler.com

Over the years I have tried every type of wall anchor and toggle bolts on the market. The best product I have come across is the Toggler Hollow Wall Anchor. They are quick and easy to install and very strong. They work equally well in both drywall and plaster walls. These anchors are also translucent (many other anchors are color coded to designate size) which is nice if your object is small and doesn't cover the anchor completely, such as a coat hook. You can get a sample kit from their website.

-- Scott Darley

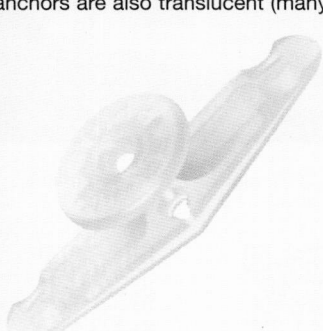

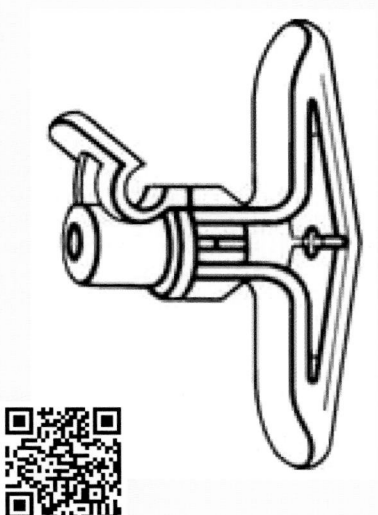

Revitalize loose screws
Mr. Grip
$3 Mr. Grip Screw Hole Repair doitbest.com

I work in an independent hardware store that carries a plethora of interesting items that Home Depot and Lowes will not. This tool is by far my favorite dohicky. It provides you with a way to keep a stripped out screw screwed in. Essentially Mr. Grips are little metal strips that are perforated much like the fine side of a cheese grater. If you cut off a strip as long as your screw, then fold it over like a taco, you can jam it down into the hole that has become stripped out. Simply run the screw back in next to the strip and, presto, the screw holds like new. Our bathroom door is held up with nothing but these. Works in metal, wood and even cheap particle board.

-- Brad Thompson

Clays

Non-fired sculpting clay
Sugru

$18, 10 5g-sachets, multiple colors Sugru

Sugru is a soft moldable material that reminds me of Fimo clay. But unlike Fimo, it does not have to be heated to cure. It air dries and is rubbery and sticks to anything. I used it to make a new button for my utility knife when the plastic one broke. I made bumpers for my cell phone. I put some on my tools so they would not roll off the table. I am still discovering ways to use the product.

-- Philip Lipton

This stuff comes in tiny pouches of different primary colors. You knead a bit with your hands until soft, then you apply it where you would like an additional grip, or stop, or section of repair. It's pretty sticky, can be worked like clay, but dries into a hard rubber. The photo shows a paring knife handle that was falling apart from years of dishwasher use. I coated the outside with Sugru and it now it feels great and is dishwasher proof. See Sugru's website for other ways it can be used.

-- KK

Better than clay
Sculpey

Artists know about this stuff. It's flexible polymer clay that hardens into rigid plastic after a spell in your kitchen oven. Bright steadfast colors. Or you can paint, drill, and polish it. Great for making toys, models, small sculptures, modern jewelry, and weird stuff -- anything that demands that colored plastic look. SuperSculpey is a translucent beige-colored (skin like) variety sold in bulk that dollmakers and Hollywood special effects swear by. Most good art suppliers will stock it.

-- KK

$11 1.75 lbs. / $140, 24 lbs. Sculpey

Figurine by Jenny Fields ▶

Stiff polymer clay
SuperSculpey Firm

$16, 1 lb. Sculpey

A few weeks ago, my 11-year old son and I decided to sculpt, so we got out SuperSculpey Firm polymer clay. After working with this newer style of Sculpey for a while, we decided it totally kicks ass on softer styles of Sculpey. Why? Because it doesn't flop over on its side when handled. And it's firm enough to keep its shape when carved. My son began making a tank. So I made a tank. We have yet to paint them.

The Sculpey brands are especially encouraging for beginners, yet professional artists depend on them as well. Pros ranging from vinyl toy artists to designers for film use it. Unlike normal clay, Sculpey hardly changes shape or size when baked, and hardening takes place quickly, at the relatively low temperatures of a convection oven (even a toaster oven will do).

Because of its polymer base, there's loads of fun techniques to try with Sculpey: like baking your sculpture for only half the allotted time. When you take it out of the oven, prematurely,

you'll find your little masterpiece has a soft, rubbery texture. In this state, it won't lose its shape and can be easily carved with a knife or a file. Have you cut too much away? Add a little more Sculpey and put it back in the oven, for more cooking!

-- Robyn Miller

Silver clay that becomes silver metal
Precious Metal Clay

$20, 6 grams Metal Clay Supply

Precious Metal Clay lets you make fine jewelry with little experience or equipment. It works like Fimo clay, except it is more crumbly because it contains powdered precious metal, such as silver, or gold. (It will also dry out faster.) The organic clay binding burns off when you fire it and you end up with pure fine silver or gold in the shape of the clay you made. If you have jewelry skills you can keep working it from there, soldering, shaping, etc.. Since I don't have much skill I just polish up my pieces or antique them with silver black. There's an implication that you have to fire PMC pieces in a kiln (that would be nice), but so far everything I've done I've fired myself on the kitchen floor with a basic propane torch.

All PMC shrinks significantly when fired. However since the shrinkage is proportional, jewlers use this shrinkage to produce very fine detail that would be difficult if you had to work at full size. PMC comes in various formulations with different shrinkage rates. The original PMC shrinks 30%, while PMC+ and PMC3 shrinks only 10%. (I've never tried using the torch on anything except silver PMC+ and PMC3 because I prefer the lower shrinkage of these.)

My one piece of advice about firing PMC with a pro-

pane torch: This stuff is very expensive (it's silver or gold, remember!) so take a small piece and sacrifice it to learn how to heat evenly first. It is very easy to overheat it which will melt the silver into a blob, which is bad. If you aren't sure if it's metal yet (it'll be whitish), pick it up with needle nose plier and drop it very gently on the metal surface you fired it on. It should make a satisfying metal-on-metal thunk. When I am feeling more flush, I'll find out if gold PMC can be fired this way.

-- Quinn Norton

Moldable plastic
Shapelock

Shapelock is "Ultra-High Molecular Weight Low Temperature Thermoplastic. Similar to nylon and polypropylene in toughness, except it's easy to work with and shape."

You get a bag of plastic pellets, put them in 160F water, and they phase change, becoming soft and moldable. If you don't let the water get too hot, when you take the plastic out, it's cool enough to shape with your hands.

When it cools down, it hardens into a strong, durable, paintable, machine-able white plastic. If you don't like what you made, you just put it in 160F water again and reshape it.

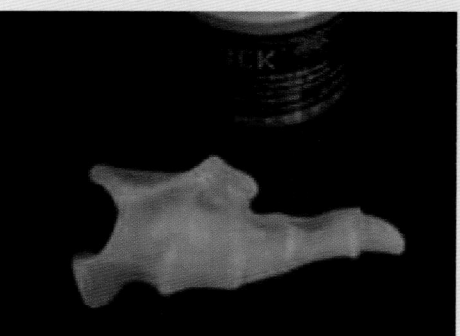

Great for making prototypes -- also fun to play with.

The same stuff, under a different name (Friendly Plastic), is available in larger quantities, at a slightly cheaper rate.

-- Patrick Tufts

$15, 250 grams Shapelock

$52, 793 grams Sculpt

Industrial-strength graffiti remover
Anti-Vandal Spray

$6, or $80 for a case of twelve 14 oz. cans Aervoe

Decent consumer solvents -- for say removing graffiti -- are pretty much unobtainable because of their abuse ("huffing") and paranoia about carcinogenicity. So I was very happy to run across this industrial-grade stuff in an urban San Francisco hardware store.

Not only does it tackle every kind of marker and paint graffiti, but it's perfect for those sticky removal situations like price tags and tree-sap-on-your-car that the consumer-grade citrus solvents still have trouble with. This stuff is also the perfect solution for those otherwise intractable remnants of double-sided foam tape: one shot of this and they rub right off with a paper towel.

It's a pretty potent blend of solvents (including MEK, toluene, and trichloroethylene). So you will want to use it in a ventilated place away from flames, and minimize your skin exposure, but it really does work better.

-- Jonathan Foote

Straw keeper
Hold-It

$5 for 2

I've used many different types of spray lubricants over the years, some good, some not so. One problem with all of them is I always lose the little straw that comes with them. Rubber bands always seem to dry out. Hold-it's hold the straw to the can. I haven't lost one yet. Fairly inexpensive as well- $4.99 for twelve. I've given some to friends, they love them as well.

-- Mark Phillips

General stick
Lexel Caulk

$6, 5 oz. Lexel

They call this stuff caulk, but I use it as a general purpose glue. It pretty much sticks anything to anything. It may not hold as strongly as epoxy, but for 90% of my attachment jobs it does the trick. Almost everything in my mobile illusions museum (shown above) is adhered with Lexel. It sticks better than silicone sealant and is not as obnoxious to work with.

Used it stick everything to everything.

-- Doug Payne

Adhesive Remover
Un-Du * Grip Solvent

This stuff is incredible. It essentially undoes any sticky sticker from any surface, and then totally evaporates leaving no mark. As an art teacher, I'd find that masking tape, for example, when left too long on the back of a displayed piece of artwork, was impossible to remove. Un-Du released its stickiness, and AMAZINGLY, after a few moments of evaporation, the masking tape reverts to it's original sticky state. The original ad for it demonstrated removing a piece of duct tape from a piece of toilet paper. BOTH were intact after a few seconds of application.

-- Duffy Franco

Un-du is nice but it's way overpriced. I buy the same thing but a quart at a time. It's called Grip Solvent and it's for regripping golf clubs. $5.69 for a quart instead of $9 for an ounce.

-- Rob

$15 Un-Du
amazon.com

$7 Grip Solvent
golfsmith.com

Unsticking stuff
Kroil

$10 Kano Labs

Kroil is an extremely effective penetrating lubricant. Almost every professional machine shop I've been in has a bottle of this sitting prominently beside the workbench. I first saw it about 8 years ago, and asked the mechanic why he used it. His words are the same I now say to those who ask me: It will unstick ANYTHING.

I frequently take apart antique machinery or general equipment. There is almost always rust, grime, burned grease, metal shavings, and the wear of decades that prevent me from separating bolts from nuts, pins from holes, or keeping sliding surfaces from doing anything BUT sliding. I've used every possible penetrating lubricant on the market. Some worked OK, but nothing really was "magic" until I found Kroil. Not many products make me laugh with glee. But the satisfying twist of an otherwise impossible-to-remove bolt or the turn of a shaft that was rusted solid now make me smile because of this little orange can.

Kroil doesn't work instantly. It takes between a few minutes and a few days (for extremely large bearing surfaces) to work its magic. I once let it sit for a week on a 300 pound flywheel that was being very stubborn, and it came right off.

Kroil is not for general lubrication purposes. It's very thin (which is part of how it works) and is not very sticky. But that's not the reason I use it; I use it to get things apart. Kroil has a weird creeping capability, it finds its way up and across metal surfaces like some sort of strange science fiction amoeba. After I use Kroil to separate things, I'll typically clean them completely (dip in mineral spirits) air-blast to remove residue, and then re-oil with a more permanent lubricant. The Kroil won't hurt anything if it stays, but I like to get a thicker material in everywhere to avoid having to fix the problem again in a few years.

It's somewhat hard to find in a retail setting. I've never seen it in a hardware store, but that doesn't mean some don't carry it. (The label on my bottle says "For industrial use only - not for retail sale" which is somewhat antiquated.) I typically get it directly from kanolabs.com, though eBay also might have some good deals. There are now several variants of Kroil including graphite and

silicone, but I stick with the old-fashioned stuff since I haven't read the data enough on the other mixtures to figure out if it's worth changing.

If someone asked me what critical items I'd want for my toolbox, this would be among them. It comes at an even higher value than general-purpose sprays like WD-40. Simply put, Kroil is the most useful lubricant I know of.

-- John Todd

A recent example of when I have used Kroil came when I bought an Ideal #3 Stencil machine on eBay, which is used for cutting out cardboard or paper letters and numbers for making paint stencils. I purchased the machine for $40, which is about 1/5th the normal price, because the machine was rusty and jammed.

I took the risk because I knew Kroil would work. Indeed, when I opened up the box, the rust was pretty severe. All of the vertical punch letters were rusted in place, and the dial didn't even spin at all to change letters. I liberally dosed all of the moving component interface areas I could see with Kroil, and then started to take it apart. After an hour or so of time, I was able to get all of the moving components back into fully operational condition after slowly working them through a few gritty and then progressively smoother cycles with the Kroil finding its way into the nooks and crannies.

Even the central shaft which was frozen solid with several hundred pounds of turning force, after two hours or so I was able to feel a little movement, and after another hour and some huffing and puffing I was able to get the assembly off the shaft.

Miscellaneous Aids

Quick weighing
Electro-Samson Hanging Scale
$75 Quick Supply

This hanging digital scale is great for weighing odd shaped things quickly. In our workshop we use it all the time for weighing bicycles, bags, components, things we invent, things we need to ship. Rather than drag the work to the scale, you bring this light scale to whereever you need it. You can easily grab hold of the scale in one hand. You hang the object from the bottom. For very heavy stuff, hook the scale on something solid. This one is ranges up to about 45 kilogram (99 pounds), detecting a minimum of 50 grams (.1 pound). It's perfect as an inexpensive general purpose "good enough" scale, especially for things that aren't compact. Also it's a fantastic baby scale if you wish to chart growth. Just put baby in a sling then weigh. There are smaller versions, too.

-- Saul Griffith

Plastic polishing compound
Novus Plastic Polish
$17 Novus Polish Kit, 3 8-oz bottles
novuspolish.com

I've found that Novus plastic polish works very well. I use it when cleaning and removing scratches from pinball machine parts and have had a lot of success polishing things ranging from cell phone displays to sunglasses.

There are three different compounds: #3 for dealing with big scratches, #2 for normal/light scratches, and #1 for a basic clean. #2 does the job for just about everything I've used it on. Available in 2-oz, 8-oz and half-gallon bottles. I've had 8-oz bottles of #1 and #2 that have lasted me several years of occasional use. I'd expect the half-gallon to last practically forever. Wonderful stuff.

-- Alex Mauer

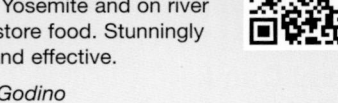

Robust, flexible multipurpose pails
Tubtrug Buckets
$20 26-liter faulks.co.uk

If you keep rigid, used 5 gallon spackle buckets with broken handles and cracked sides for odd jobs, you should recycle 'em and get these plastic buckets. They are molded in one piece with two integrated handles. The handles are large enough that they won't hurt your palms or break away. There are too many uses to list, but I got mine earlier this year and have mostly used them in the garden where I've moved a lot of dirt and mulch and some large plants. The units are strong enough to fill completely with dirt, at which point they are too heavy for me to carry alone. I was most impressed with the ease with which I moved a large rock, which required two of us to lift. Yet, the tubs, which wipe clean easy, are still flexible enough to form a pouring spout.

-- Jack Roosma

Converts buckets to air-tight containers
Gamma Seal Lid
$10 usplastic.com

This product turns an empty pail into a more useful item: a resealable pail that's strong enough for stacking and sitting. I started using the lids because I just wanted a seat for my fishing pail. It does more than that, though. Keeps everything inside nice and dry (like my camera). And when I'm done, it will seal up the fish I bring home with no fishy water getting out in my car. The lid has two parts: one snaps onto your pail and a gasket seals it tight. The second part is a removable screw in/out center piece also with a gasket for an air- and watertight seal. They fit 3.5 - 7-gallon pails. I happened upon them in the in the livestock section of my local Farm and Fleet store. So far, I have only used mine for fishing. However, I have purchased several more to use for storage around the house. Just need to get the pails. A local pool company sometimes throws out larger buckets, which I'm hoping to reuse.

-- Dave Friese

The Gamma Lid creates a useful object from trash and works with simplicity and perfection. A hammer and a bit of scrap wood can help secure the outer ring onto the rim of the bucket. After that, the inner disc-shaped lid threads neatly onto the outer ring, leaving you with a solid, easy-to-open, waterproof lid that can replace those pry-off tops that shred your fingertips. I have used these for about five years. You can get free, clean, food grade buckets at most large food store bakeries. At present, I store rice and bulk grains in them (a 20-lb. bag of rice fits nicely into a three-gallon bucket). I have also used them as a food bucket for a big wall climb in Yosemite and on river trips to store food. Stunningly simple and effective.

-- John Godino

Reusable wonder wax
Museum Wax
$7 Quakehold! 66111 2-Ounce Museum Wax quakehold.com

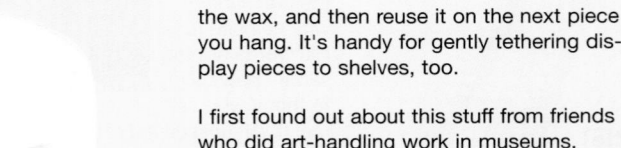

It's stickier and firmer than Play-Doh and comes off easier than Poster Putty. A little pinch of museum wax on the back of a frame stabilizes it, and holds its position firmly against a wall. Level your artwork and it'll stay level. If you rotate works on display at home, pull the framed art off the wall, remove the wax, and then reuse it on the next piece you hang. It's handy for gently tethering display pieces to shelves, too.

I first found out about this stuff from friends who did art-handling work in museums, where it is, in fact, used. Outside of the galleries, it's also a prime tool in the museum's photo studio. While on staff photographing artwork from the permanent collection of a Southern California museum, I was taught to use museum wax for shooting still-life work: Museum wax is just right for table-top photography of smaller objects, particularly to hold the object being photographed to its out-of-view support. Small dabs of museum wax are easily positioned to remain unnoticeable, and wipe clean off ceramic and glass surfaces without the need for solvents. It's a key tool for food stylists, too.

A little of this stuff goes a long way. It is reusable, and doesn't seem to dry out or lose it's tackiness. I still have a clump I was given many years ago.

-- Elon Schoenholz

Forever glue applier
Rockler Silicone Glue Brush
$12 rockler.com

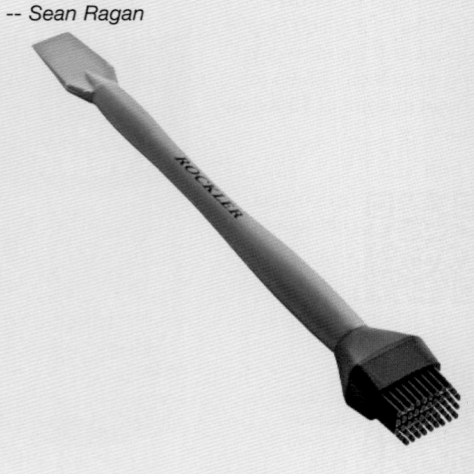

If, like me, you tend to use disposable foam brushes when gluing to save cleanup time, this silicon brush can be more environmentally responsible and, in the long run, cheaper option. Instead of throwing the brush away, you clean off the typical polyvinyl acetate-based wood glue, or white glue, by letting the glue dry into a blob on the brush. Unlike a natural or synthetic fiber brush, the solidified mass of glue doesn't stick in the silicone bristles: just flex them a bit, and the dried glue falls off and/or pulls out in a single clump. I didn't get a chance to test this, but they claim this works on fully-cured polyurethane construction adhesive (like Liquid Nails). I did try it on two-part epoxy, which cleans up surprisingly well. The hardened epoxy simply flakes off the bristles and falls or pulls out in clumps. Cyanoacrylate super glue does not want to come out and will ruin the brush. I tried using it for latex paint; it cleans up okay, but it doesn't paint that well.

-- Sean Ragan

Epoxy Putty
Henkel Solid Ribbon Epoxy
$6 2oz henkel.com

Epoxy putty is your standard two-component epoxy in concept, but like plasticene in initial consistency. You mix two strips by cutting an equal length of each and kneading them together with your fingers until it's even in color. Once it's kneaded, you mold it into shape with your fingers or the same kind of craft tools you would use on clay or plasticene. When it hardens, after about a half hour, it's like rock--you can pound it with a hammer with no apparent effect. I've used it to make handles for broken pocketknife blades, for fixing glasses (like this time), for temporary patches on water pipes, and for a variety of other repairs and odd tasks.

-- Clifton Royston

Two pennies: One for rice to give life. One for flowers to give meaning. - Chinese Proverb

Bootstrapping tools
Build Your Own Metal Working Shop Series

$8 The Charcoal Foundry David J. Gingery, 1983, 80 pages

Wouldn't it be cool if you could start with molten metal and make your own simple tools that made better more complex tools which make better tools, and so on, bootstrapping your way to a full workshop? You can. You start by making a foundry to pour molten scrap metal in the shapes you need, which you then use to make a milling machine and drill press, etc., each previous step enabling the next step until you have a full machine shop. That's the lessons of these books.

There is a bit of a "doomsday backup" to the idea of being able to restart civilization from scratch if you had to, but the late author David Gingery main purpose was to make significant metal working tools he could afford. Through a series of seven books he demonstrates how to do this. But even if you have no intention of making your own lathe, the first book in this series gives very good instructions for making your own foundry so you can melt and cast scrap aluminum or pot metal. You start with charcoal, a 5-gallon metal bucket, a fan, metal from the dump., and your own sand molds. Pouring hot liquid metal is a primeval thrill which can lead to all kinds of adventures.

-- KK

The more than 20 years of research and experimentation that precede this group of manuals was inspired by a statement by someone I've long forgotten: "The metal lathe is the only machine in the shop that can duplicate itself or any other machine in the shop." It followed then: If you have a lathe you can produce the rest of the needed equipment to make up a fully equipped machine shop. Of course my first problem was that I didn't have the lathe.

The theme of the idea is remarkably like the recipe of someones grandmother for chicken soup, which begins "First you get a chicken." Well, if you want to make chicken soup you'll have to buy a chicken. Or, lacking the necessary funds, you might steal one. You can't make a chicken, but you can build your own lathe, and with it you can produce the rest of the equipment to make up a full and practical machine shop.

The photo on the previous page is of the lathe that was built as this series of manuals was being prepared. ... All of the castings are made with the simple charcoal foundry, and the remainder of the parts are standard hardware items. The only power tool used was a 3/8" electric drill, and there was no custom machine work of any kind. The lathe can not only duplicate itself, it can actually build itself. All of the machine work was done on the machine itself as it progressed step by step. When it was complete I used it to build another just like it.

Index to DIY
Homemade Tools

Free homemadetools.net

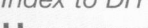

This website collects and points to how-to tutorials on the web by folks making their own tools. They range from simple hammers to complex lathes. The site is just a clearing house with not much of its own activity. The list of homemade tool instructions also vary in quality, but it's a great resource if you make your own tools — and you should.

-- KK

• It's always a temptation to "gussy" up a casting and include more in it than is really needed. In many cases it would be better to make two castings and bolt them together than to make a complicated casting in one piece.

•

The blast furnace.

Building The Furnace

This is simple work, very much like working with concrete or mortar. It is likely that you have much of what is needed on hand, and the remainder won't be hard to get. A clean 5 gallon metal pail, a piece of sheet metal about 18" X 30", some scraps of plywood, some wire and a roll of tape make up the body and form. Sand and fire clay are all you need for the lining, or you can purchase a castable refractory mix for the lining. Add an old vacuum cleaner or a hair dryer, a bag of charcoal and a pot for the metal and you are ready to go to work.

The Drill Press

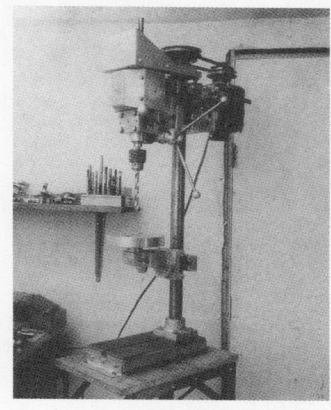

◄ You could buy a drill press easily, but that only takes money. What you really need is the still and knowledge you will gain from building one. I can think of no metal project that will expand your ability better than this one.

Book website, with helpful videos: gingerybooks.com

Arc Welding Gun
by Vintage Projects
tags: arc welder, welder

Assorted Anvil Tools
by METAL TWISTER
tags: anvil

Belt-Driven Hammer
by VÅgjund
tags: power hammer

Hand-tool making methods
The Complete Modern Blacksmith

$15 Alexander Weygers, 1997, 304 p.

I make my own tools occasionally. This book, written and drawn by Alexander Weyger, showed me how to make pliers, a sloyd knife, a tool handle using a drill press like a small lathe, and a way to make a ferrule for a tool handle -- just to name a few things. There is a lot of blacksmith related stuff in the book, but I didn't get into that part in great detail. He did show how to make a lot of Blacksmith tools, though.

-- David Keeler

This text (drawn from 3 thinner books created in the 1970s) is primary about bootstrapping new tools from simpler tools, often with high heat. It is brilliant for that.

-- KK

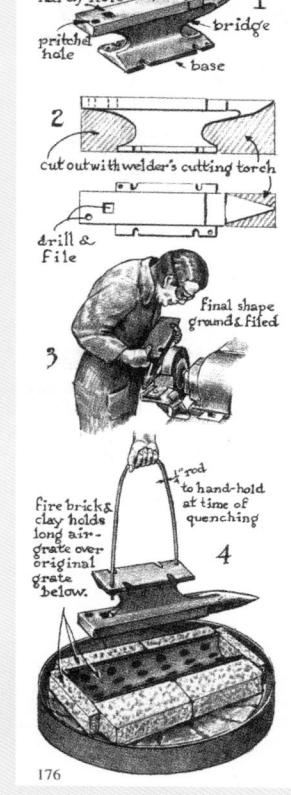

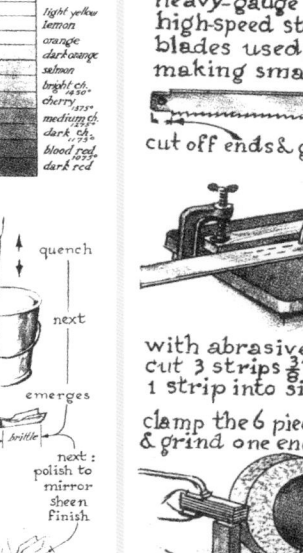
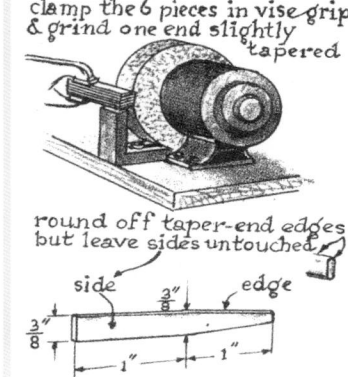

Workshop Setup

Three best guides
Building Workshops

Tools need a home. *Setting Up Shop* is the best guide I've found for designing a workshop. It focuses on the practical details that other workshop books tend to ignore like how to arrange the lighting, or set up dust collectors, design the placement of wiring, even determining the height of work surfaces. It got me thinking about aspects of a shop I had not considered before and helped me improve the plans for my shop. Its very thorough coverage of sound, light, air, and movement options makes it the most useful of the three books mentioned here.

Workshop Idea Book is a scrapbook of hundreds of tips and clever solutions for a shop discovered by others. It showcases a lot of storage suggestions, and ideas for arranging stuff, such as how to handle large sheets of materials. Think of it as a kind of great, well-curated Pinterest board for workshops.

Both of these books are biased to wood. A better version of either book would include metal and plastic working tools, which are ignored. This failing is somewhat countered by *The Workshop Book* which tours through a much larger variety of work places. It documents several workshops installed in trucks, or fit into apartments, or made portable with everything mounted on casters. I found the greater diversity of shops covered in this collection to be more useful to me since my shop is more general purpose.

The great designer's guide to creating a small-time prototype shop with laser cutters, 3D printers, solder stations, as well as drill presses and table saws, has not be written yet. In the meantime, these three idea books will get you started.

-- KK

$17 Setting Up Shop, Sandor Nagyszalanczy, 2006, 236p

$8 Workshop Idea Book, Andy Rae, 2007, 170p

$17 The Workshop Book, Scott Landis, 1998, 216p

From *Setting Up Shop*

▲ Three strategies for preventing long cords on portable power tools from ending up snarled and tangled are (left to right): Buy tools with detachable power cords, such as this Sawzall; fit each tool a short pigtail and plug it into an extension cord (using locking plugs) before using it; and refit existing power cords with tangle-resistant, self-retracting coil cords.

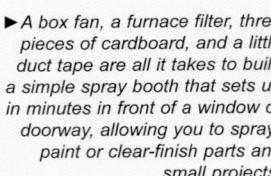

▶ A box fan, a furnace filter, three pieces of cardboard, and a little duct tape are all it takes to build a simple spray booth that sets up in minutes in front of a window or doorway, allowing you to spray-paint or clear-finish parts and small projects.

By setting tables to the same height and leveling them, a workpiece can pass over any or all of these machines.

Orienting Machines in a Line

By carefully coordinating the positions and table heights of stationary machines, you can reduce the amount of clearance between certain machines. For example, by placing machines such as a shaper/router table, oscillating-spindle sander or disc sander, and horizontal boring machine in line, then setting them up with all their tables level and at the same height, a long workpiece may rest or slide on an adjacent machine's table (as shown here). Such an arrangement allows you to handle large or long work without having to rely on outfeed tables or roller stands for support. For this same reason, it's a good idea to level the tabletops of benchtop tools that are in close proximity to one another.

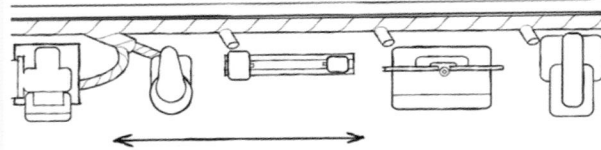

▲ Machine Layout against a Wall

Machines such as a bandsaw, drill press, router table, shaper, stationary sanders, lathe, joinery machines, and overarm routers are ideal to locate along a wall. Power and dust collection are easy to hook up.

From *Workshop Idea Book*

THREE SAWS IN ONE. For serious production work, two or more saws combined into one sawing station let you mill wood and cut joints without breaking down your setups. The three cabinet saws at Placeways Woodworking share a central shopbuilt table, which doubles as an auxiliary work surface.

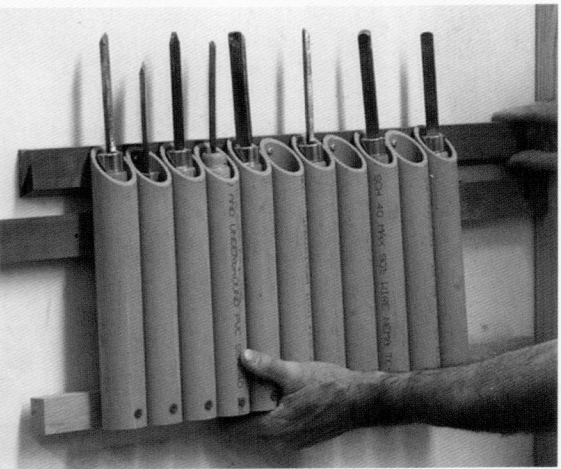

PLUGGED PIPES. Make good use of inexpensive PVC pipe to store lathe tools and make them portable as well. Doug Stowe's pipes are mounted to a French-cleat system on the wall and can be moved to the lathe when needed. The top of the pipes are cut at an angle to facilitate loading, and the bottoms are plugged with wood.

SHOPPING IN THE SHOP. A converted shopping cart makes a convenient rolling hardware station. For his cart, dubbed the "piercing pagoda," Gabe Aucott added a plywood top fitted with divided boxes to keep screws and other hardware neatly sorted and a staging platform at one end. Below, a large plywood box holds glue and other assembly tools.

From *The Workshop Book*

◀ By hanging two narrow doors within two larger doors, Martha Collins can create four different openings to accommodate movement of objects large or small.

▶ Years ago, when I worked in a shop without electricity, I had a hand-cranked grinder. It did the job, and I liked the slow speed, but I found it irritating to hold the tool with one hand and crank with the other. Fred Matlack converted his hand-cranked grinder to foot power by adding a rope and a hinged pedal. He gets the wheel going with the crank, then keeps it going with the pedal. The arrangement frees both hands to guide the tool.

▲ Two plywood cabinets flank the box of Lester Walker's Datsun Pickup truck. Walker, of Woodstock, New York, built one cabinet for woodworking tools and supplies and the other for camping equipment. On the road, the space between the two cabinets is covered with waterproof canvas and serves as a tent.

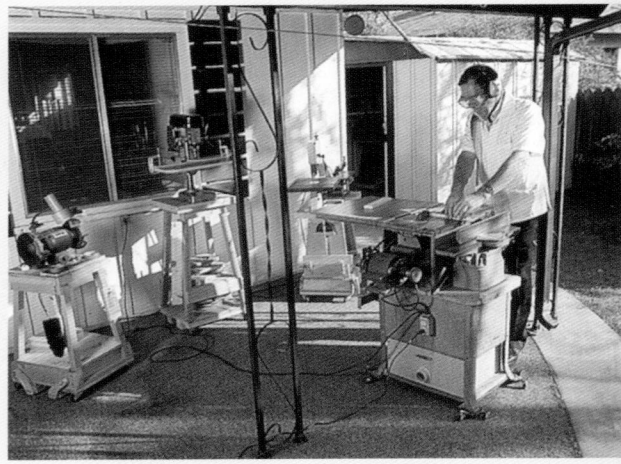

Donald Kinnaman packs the contents of an entire workshop into a 90-sq. ft. metal shed next to his Phoenix, Arizona, home. He rolls the machines he needs out onto the covered patio behind his house and goes to work.

Don't say yes. Be yes. - Anne Herbert

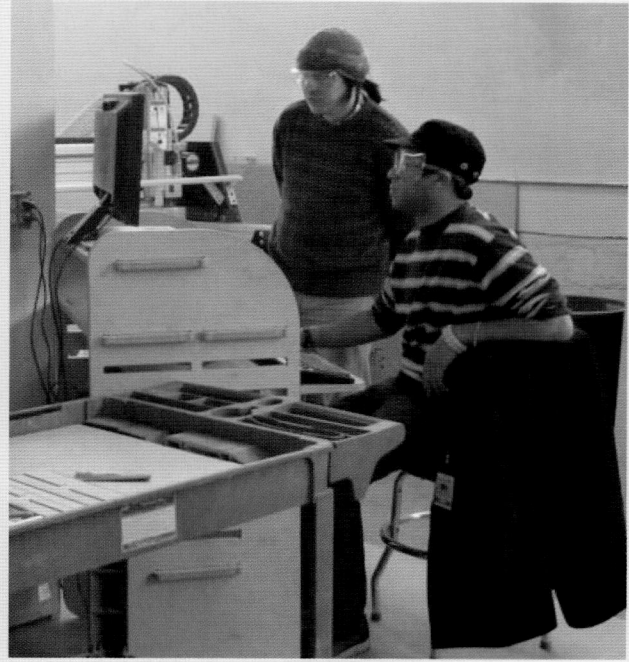

Working at the laser cutter control station.

Industrial tinkering space
TechShop

The idea is brilliant. Why should you purchase, maintain, and upgrade expensive shop tools that you might need only once in a while? It's a whole lot better to join a co-op that buys, houses, and upkeeps the gear. You pay rent to use it — a price that will be a lot less than the cost of purchase. The downside, of course, is that you need to travel to the TechShop, which can be inconvenient. I've found 3 types of folks using it: 1) Those who have tiny apartments and no tools, or tool space, of their own; this is their workshop. 2) Those who are working on a prototype, or a big art project, for a specific period of time; this is their lab and office. 3) Those who own a decent typical workshop but want occasional access to a laser cutter, or 3D printer; this is their luxury.

TechShop sells day passes, week passes, monthly passes, or yearly membership. They are currently in 6 US locations, with 3 more in progress, and are adding more each year.

-- KK

Wouldn't it be great to have a full machine shop at your disposal, with dozens of industrial tools also at your disposal, and all you have to do is contribute to the upkeep? TechShop is just that -- a membership-based fabrication and invention shop. I've been a member since before TechShop really even started, back when it was just some guys passing out flyers trying to gauge interest. For $100 a month, members can use any tool in the shop on which they've received training. MUCH cheaper than buying your own gear. The list of equipment is pretty extensive, too, and new items are arriving frequently (like a new hot-wire foam cutter).

I've spent the most time with the laser cutter and the plasma cutter, and a bit of time on the mill and lathes. The laser cutters are the best "deal" since even a novice can start building really intricate objects out of plastics quite rapidly, and the fact that the laser cutters simply "print" with a laser beam makes them the most approachable for people who want to work off-line and who come in just to cut materials. The plasma cutter is a bit more picky, and requires a jump up to a 'real' CNC computer, which is not difficult and is just as rewarding. One of the first things I did at TechShop was to build a gib key puller for

a particularly obstinate key on the flywheel of a 50+ year old diesel engine I'm restoring. The robotic plasma cutter made short work of cutting what would have been otherwise a difficult piece, and I learned basic CNC methods in the process. I've since progressed to fairly advanced CNC operation skills, which have been useful in more intricate object construction. I've used the lathe to finish off some custom valves, the laser cutter for cutting gasket material and making signs, and I'm itching to try the 3D material printer.

TechShop offers classes on their equipment, as well as general classes on various methods and skills. The safety classes are typically very good, focused on safety and basic operation of the equipment. Classes are required for any equipment as a 'basic' instruction set, though some equipment has advanced classes for better technique and more complex jobs. Classes typically cost between $20 and $30 dollars for the basic safety class, but that's still a bargain. This is just what I've been looking for, since most machine shop instruction I've seen has been terribly expensive, and has been geared for "lowest common denominator" instructions, which are typically agonizingly boring. The TechShop classes are taught for safety and rapid understanding to try to bring members to the point where they can start producing their own objects as quickly as possible. There is still going to be some trial and error, but the feedback loop is very short and it doesn't take long before you're comfortable and confident on the equipment. This is industrial arts instruction for people with a high level of clue.

Motorcycle customizers, automotive gearheads, robot war fanatics, electronics fabricators, modelmakers, metal benders, Burning Man artists, startup companies, mechanical engineering students: I've met all of these at TechShop, and I'm sure quite a few others that defy categorization. If you have any interest in making things, or modifying things, then TechShop is for you. Having spent years and a lot of dollars in outfitting my own shop, I can say that the TechShop concept beats anything I could possibly hope to have done on my own with the added benefit of the people that one meets at a shared space like TechShop.

While the tools and physical resources of TechShop are excellent, there is a hidden benefit to participating: the other members. The breadth of skills of the members and projects underway is perhaps the most impressive and fascinating part of TechShop. At any one time, there are a half-dozen people working on fantastic and innovative things, either as hobby projects or as budding startups who have found an inexpensive way to bootstrap themselves into prototyping a better mousetrap. Here's a word to the wise for smart venture capital folks: find a hobby that requires TechShop and spend some quality time in the building doing your project. You'll get amazing things done on your own project, and get to review a few hundred of the most clever projects happening as well as meet the working engineers that are often so difficult to find otherwise.

The downside to TechShop is that there are often waits for the laser cutters, since those are the most popular items in the shop. And, of course, if you are a "top-secret" inventor, you won't find much privacy -- plan on people being very interested in your project and asking lots of questions. There are also almost no places to store materials between visits -- pretty much everything needs to go home with you.

-- John Todd

$125 - Unlimited Monthly Access
$1400 - Unlimited Annual Access
$30+ - Classes

techshop.ws

4' x 8' CNC Metal Plasma Cutter

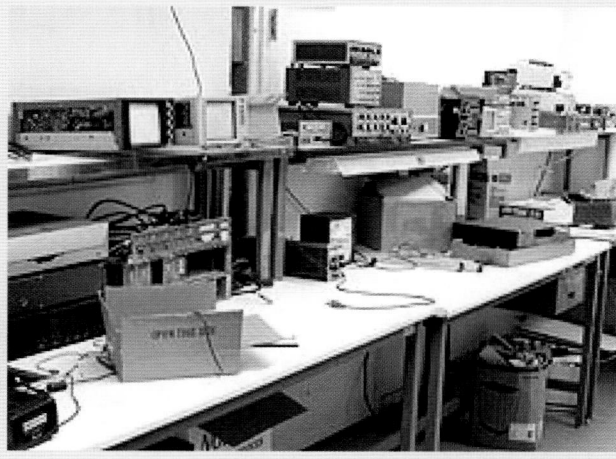

Electronics Laboratory

Band Saws & Presses

A plywood bench made using tools on the premises.

A cage of power tools.

Welding machines waiting to be used.

A work table with floating power cord, easily accessible from any side, but not in the way. The lockers are for members use.

Rental Tools

The right tools to rent
Tool Rental Know-How

The benefits of ownership are often overrated. Renting a tool can be a far smarter way to go than purchasing it. Renting can be far cheaper, and you'll get the latest version of the tool. You can try out a new-to-you tool. Maintenance is not your headache. For instance you don't have to store large tools, like a cement mixer. (You do have to return them!) Of course renting is particularly great for those tools you only need for a one-time job. How often do you need a wet saw, or a jackhammer?

But don't stop there. Most people are unaware of the vast variety of expert tools available for rental from any decent rental store. The choices are mind-boggling and inspiring. Many of these tools will make a tough job easy and smooth. I did a tile fireplace once only because I was able to rent that wet saw to cut through marble like butter.

Every year or so I walk through a large rental place just looking to see what's available. I come away with ideas like: why use a post hole digger for a fence line when you can rent an auger? Firewood time: rent log splitter, idle rest of the year. At a well-stocked rental store you can rent almost any tool you can think of: paper shredders, moisture meters, gas detectors, chimney brushes, sewer cameras, staple hammers, and so on. I'll try new things because I know I can rent the right tool.

Here is a small selection of tools you can rent. Most great rental centers seem regional. (Can anyone suggest a great national rental store?) I've given approximate rates per day as a guideline, but most will also rent per hour, or half day too.

-- KK

Rototiller

A mini horse and plow. Really useful when starting your garden area from sod. $85 per day.

Stump Grinder

No other way to remove a stump. The grinder swings back and forth, throwing off a huge pile of chips. Despite its power, slowly nibbling across the stump down to its roots (don't even think of using a chain saw) will take longer than you think. $125 per day.

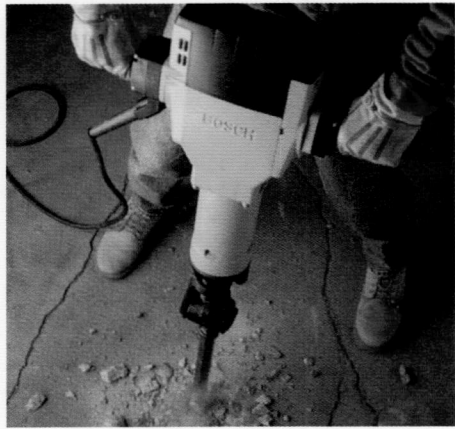

Electric Jack Hammer

This has one moving part: it. Will pulverize concrete, whether in a wall or on the floor. Not easy to handle, it will give you a workout. Even though it is electric, it still requires ear protection. $100 per day.

Heat Cannon

This is a mega heat gun. Used to hurry the drying of paint or sheet rock spackle. It eats lots of propane and oxygen – ventilation is a must. $135 per day.

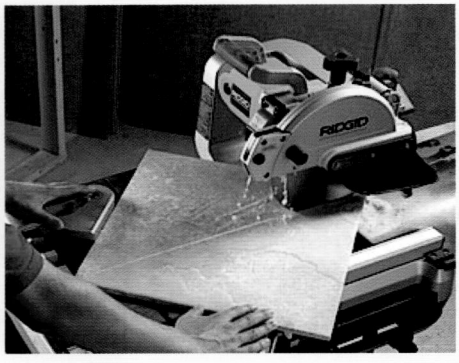

Wet Saw

An abrasive wheel lubricated by water hooked up to your garden house. Will easily and fairly accurately cut tile, pavers, concrete, stone, etc. Use outside if possible. $85 per day.

Carpet Dryer

When a flood soaks your wall-to-wall carpeting, you need to dry it out as fast as possible. Stick the "nose" of one of these under the yanked up edge and keep it running till everything dries out. You'll probably need more than one, and you'll need to have electric power on. $30 per day.

Mini Mortar Mixer

You don't need a full-sized cement mixer to do mortar jobs like laying brick or stone, or making stucco. $50 per day.

Steam Wallpaper Remover

Removing wall paper is an ugly mess, and hopefully only a once-in-your-lifetime job, but this makes it possible. $40 per day.

Ditch Witch

These walk-behind ditch diggers come in all sizes. The small ones will dig narrow trenches for irrigation and cables 12 to 18 inches deep; larger ones for larger or deeper pipes. Call 811 to make sure you ain't cutting through underground utilities. $280 per day.

Mini Excavator

Aaaah, so cute! This 3-foot wide excavator will go where its big brothers can't: through a gate, in between houses, onto landscaping, near foundations, into backyards. Its arm can reach out 13 feet and dig down 8 feet, and is strong enough to do minor earthwork. Some have a self-leveling cabin that really helps offset that paralyzing feeling on a slope that you are going to tip over. I recommend practicing before you get in close quarters. $275 per day.

Airless Paint Sprayer

Will lay paint or stain as fast as you can walk. Sucks the paint from its own 5-gallon bucket. You'll need long cords to feed its electric motor. $90 per day.

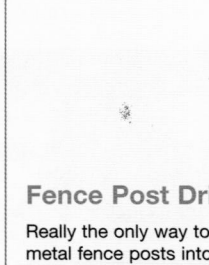

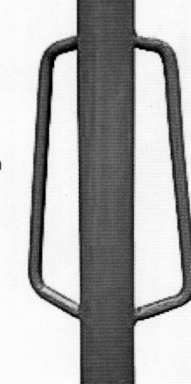

Fence Post Driver

Really the only way to bang metal fence posts into the ground. Lift up the weight with two hands, pull down hard over the post. It will employ muscles you have never used before. $13 per day. $80 per day.

I'm predicting what has already happened. - Marshall McLuhan

Hole Auger

Far superior when you have many post holes to dig. The two-person version is easiest to use – if you have a second person. It is heavy; the weight of the machine does the work.

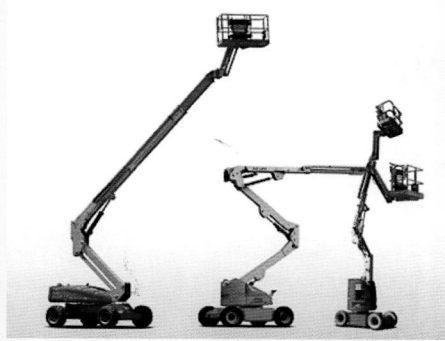

Boom Lift

For working on ceilings, signs, chimneys, roofs. May be cheaper than scaffolding if you have wheeled access. $280 per day.

Plumber's Snake

The industrial version of the little one in hardware stores. Powered by an electric motor, this will clean out your sewer drains, chewing up gunk and even roots. It's a do it yourself version of Roto-rooter. $90 per day.

Horizontal Drill

Drills under sidewalks, patios, even streets. You keep adding pipe sections to the front probe as you progress. How else are you going to get that wire under cement? Uses water pressure. $75 per day.

Piano Dolly

These two trucks sandwich an upright piano so that it can be rolled around without damaging its legs. $22 per day.

Electric Conveyor Belt

For schlepping rock, dirt, debris out of a basement or over a fence. The 12-inch width fits through even a tiny window. What a time saver! Can be maneuvered with two people and hooks up to a standard tow hitch. $250 per day.

Magnetic Sweeper

Construction has a nasty habit of seeding driveways with tire-eating nails, screws, and shrapnel. You sweep this thing over the pavement (or lawn) and it sucks up the nasties. A pull on the handle releases the ferrous bits. Good to do at least once after the contractors leave. $25 per day.

Wood Chipper

After a storm, after tree pruning, this will turn a pile of branches into compostable mulch. Not hard to use; you'll need a hitch to haul it. $225 per day.

Water Leak Detector

This electronic stethoscope listens for leaks in water pipes. Needs to be fairly close. $22 per day.

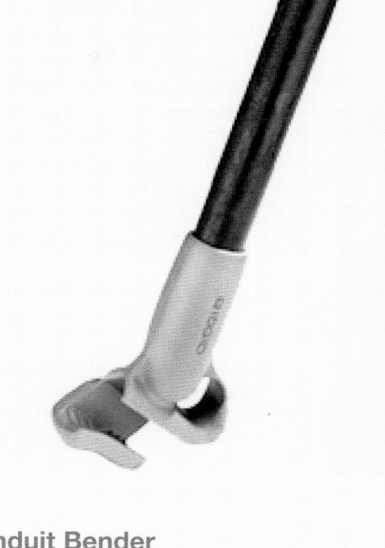

Conduit Bender

Bends electrical conduit cleanly. Cheap to rent. Get the right sized diameter for your pipe. $6 per day.

Brush Hog

Every now weeds take over a lot, along driveways, and you need to cut them down to size. Some models like this one will handle saplings 2 inches thick. $100 per day.

Log Splitter

Tow it to your trees. In one day two energetic workers can make a huge pile of firewood assisted by one of these. There are a thousand models out there; the better ones flip from vertical to horizontal to suit your site. $100 per day.

Carpet Stretchers

The secret tool for laying carpet, either new or after it has dried from being wet. Comes in either knee-powered, or lever operated. $30 per day.

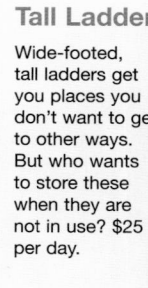

Tall Ladder

Wide-footed, tall ladders get you places you don't want to get to other ways. But who wants to store these when they are not in use? $25 per day.

Pipe Locator

Will locate buried pipes, which is no small feat if you've tried to do it by other means. $55 per day.

Post Puller

When you need to pull up old posts, this jack does the trick. $40 per day.

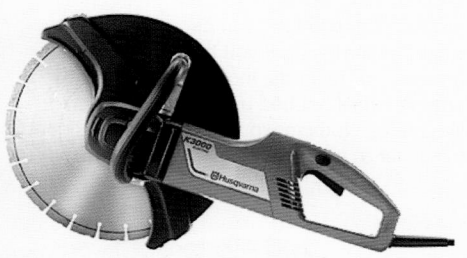

Concrete Cutoff Saw

Cut cement or asphalt! Electric or gas. For bigger jobs you can get a walk-behind variety. Either way you'll have to pay extra for blades since they wear out quickly. $100 per day.

Tool Lending

Borrowable Tools
Tool Lending Libraries

A decade ago some community librarians in California initiated a great idea: why not lend tools as well as books? The idea slowly spread to a couple of dozen other US towns, but the most active and well-stocked tool libraries are still in the Bay Area -- one in Berkeley and Oakland. (The San Francisco Tool Lending Library is no longer open, though there is some community support to bring it back.) The typical tool lending library offers basic hand tools, and a selection of garden,

landscaping and construction tools. The hot items with waiting lists are heavy duty power tools. The top four borrowings are: an electric jack hammer, a drain snake for clearing sewage lines, an electric weed wacker (the library only deals with electrical tools, no gas), and rotary impact drills. There are racks of shovels, rakes, stampers, crow bars, pliers, and the usual shop tools, but the Saws-alls, belt sanders, wet tile saws, and other not-so-often needed tools get the most rotation. Many of these occasional tools are what you might find at a tool rental shop; indeed anyone with a city library card -- including contractors -- can, and do, borrow tools for the maximum 3 days.

Lending tools, like planting trees, is unalloyed goodness. Tool Lending Libraries are a great idea that should be duplicated everywhere. The biggest cost is not the tools but the liability insurance for the power tools. Patrons are pretty good at returning things in good order -- they want to be able to use 'em again.

Check your local system to see if they have one up and running. If they don't, start one. If you live in the Bay Area head for one of the three below.

-- *KK*

 Oakland Tool Library

 Berkeley Tool Lending Library

---

How to borrow tools and keep friends

If people can trust you with their tools, there isn't a hell of a lot more they need to know about you. How trust is made:

* When you borrow the tool, have the owner check you out on it, even if you know it cold. This encourages the owner and insures you.

* Agree on a time it will be returned by. Return it by then.

* Return it to either the owner's hand or to the EXACT place you picked it up from.

* Use if carefully. If you break it, replace it immediately, preferably with a better one.

* When you're finished, service it. Clean it, sharpen it, oil it, fuel it, fix it. If you return someone's tool improved, they'll let you have anything they've got.

* If you make anyone loan you something out of guilt, you'll be sorry.

-- *Stewart Brand, The Whole Earth Catalog*

Sees through walls
Hilti PX-10 Transpointer

This tool is under-marketed, over-priced, and difficult to find, but once you've used it, you won't want to be without one. It solves a problem that nothing else on the market solves: making a drilled hole come out at the right place on the other side of a wall, and I mean a wall where getting to the other side requires a hike.

The PX-10 consists of two handheld units: a transmitter and a receiver. You put the transmitter on one side of the wall, then take the receiver to the other side. The receiver has four illuminated arrows that tell you which way to move it; when all four are lit, it's exactly lined up with the transmitter. There's even a hole in the center so you can make a pencil mark. It's also got a readout the tells you the wall thickness.

The manufacturer says the PX-10 works on walls from 5cm to 1.35m (>4 ft) thick, with a positioning accuracy of +/- 2mm per 200mm of wall thickness.

I bought mine in 2008 while working on a historic masonry building. To run a cable, we needed a hole through an exterior wall 14" thick, starting in an interior closet and exiting in a mortar joint, not in the adjacent brick. To get from one side to the other, you navigated a warren of interior hallways, descended two flights of stairs, and climbed up several levels of scaffolding. A single measurement with the Transpointer showed us where to drill... and the hole came out spot-on!

I've also used the PX-10 when installing thru-hull fittings in boats, otherwise a slow, nerve-wracking job (especially near the waterline). It works well for me, even when the hull is thinner than the nominal 5" minimum range. If you're working alone, the transmitter is light enough to stick onto a surface with adhesive putty, which comes with it.

I suspect this tool has a broader market than Hilti realizes; their marketing seems focused on contractors doing core-drilling in concrete. The $600 price tag is hard to stomach; I bought mine when it dropped, briefly, to $200. Perhaps they'll see the light again.

-- *Jeff Zurkow*

The Hilti Transpointer is hard to find, and very expensive. The Magnespot Extended Range Point Finder does a very similar thing, but costs $200. Still, at that price, it's more of a rental tool for most people. The Magnespot works with a high-powered magnet, which is a trick a DIYer can use for thin walls. -- *KK*

 $600 Hilti PX-10 Transpointer Hilti

 $210 Magnespot XR1000 Extended Range Reference Point Locator TechToolSupply

---

Rent it
Chain Pipe Cutter

$108 Amazon
Check your local tool rental shop for prices.

I'm a long-time tool-renter. It's a great way to go for all kinds of needs. Years ago I had to cut a 4" iron (not steel) pipe deep in a hole in my backyard. (The pipe led to a septic system that was supposed to be 18" underground, but was actually 6 feet underground.) I needed a clean cut, and iron has a way of shattering if you hit it wrong. I tried a variety of methods, including an abrasive cutting wheel hooked up to a circular-saw-like motor. Nothing worked. Then the resident old-timer at my local tool rental place recommended a chain cutter, similar to this one, though much more well-used.

It consists of a flexible chain that you wrap around the pipe and lock in place. Inside each link of the chain is a small circular cutting blade. Once locked in place, you use the handles to ratchet the chain tighter and tighter around the pipe. The circular blades provide even pressure from all sides, and within a few ratchets you hear a satisfying snick sound and your pipe is cut clean and even. This was definitely a cool tool, one that made an otherwise impossible situation ridiculously easy.

-- *Mike Sellers*

Rent it
Diamond Core Saw

Rental costs vary

If you happen to live in a brick house as I do, you are painfully aware of how difficult it is to change the layout of any feature that is part of the external wall. However, if you need to move your clothes dryer exhaust (or other round pipe), renting a diamond core saw makes for quick and easy work. Diamond saws are often horribly expensive (for obvious reasons) -- but renting one for only an hour would be enough time to make a wall into Swiss cheese. A typical hole takes a couple minutes at best, and is perfectly round and smooth -- not at all like the result one often gets with a hammer drill, masonry bits, and chisel -- it is well worth the trip to the rental office and fees. (And if you have neighbors with brick houses, be sure to ask them if they

need any neat holes in exchange for a few dollars/beers!)

I rented from a small local shop (which is sadly now defunct) in my neighborhood of Seattle, and paid $50 for 4 hours' use of a drill and bit. I just called "Pacific Rim Equipment Rental" where they unfortunately don't have half-day rates: it is $65 for the drill, and $35 for the bit. I would guess that many Home Depots that do tool rental would carry the drill and bit.

-- *Phil Evans*

Machines, pictured
The New Way Things Work
$23 David Macaulay, Neil Ardley, 1998, 400p

This illustration-rich book provides a peek under the hood of the mechanized world we inhabit. David Macaulay, with tech writer Neil Ardley, has that rare gift of technical understanding paired with an ability to convey complex concepts through visual imagery. Kids, parents, Lit. majors, curious people – all can learn, and laugh, from the interpretive drawings that fill this wonderful tome, granting insight into the workings of everything from twin-rotor helicopters to printing presses to self-winding watches and even modems.

Remember floppy discs? The 1998 edition of this book (the most current) does feature some dated material regarding digital technology. Still, it's an overwhelmingly relevant, educational reference — awe-inspiring because of Macaulay's talents as well as the achievements of human ingenuity on which his pictures shed light.

-- *Elon Schoenholz*

Drill Chuck

The chuck of a power drill has to grip very strongly as it rotates the drill, yet it must be possible to loosen or tighten the chuck by hand. A compact arrangement of bevel gears and levers does the trick. The key pinion is turned to rotate the collar of the chuck, which turns the screw inside the chuck to move the jaws in or out. the screw is set at an angle so the jaws open as they withdraw into the chuck, and close to grip the drill bit as they protrude from the chuck.

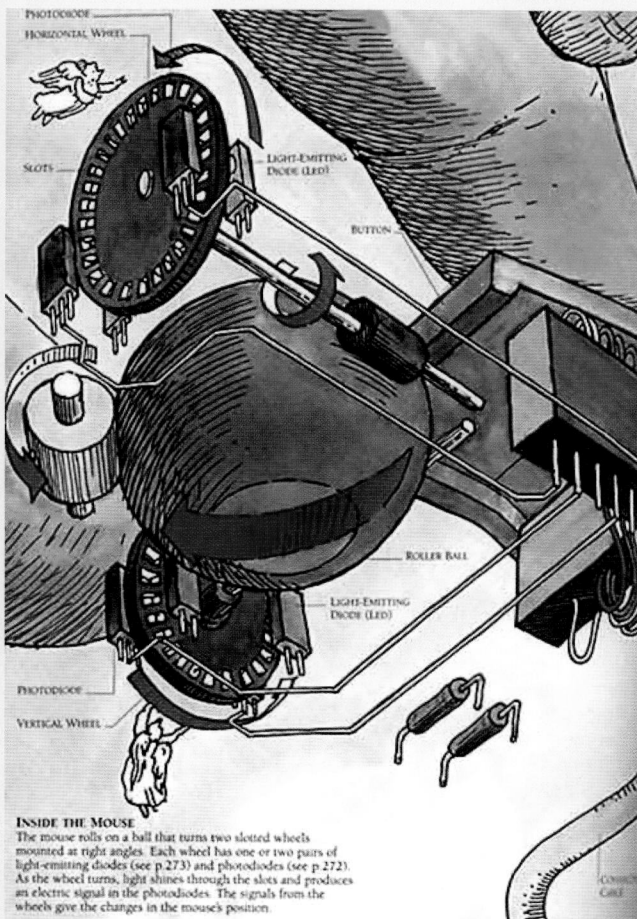

Inside the Mouse

The mouse rolls on a ball that turns two slotted wheels mounted at right angles. Each wheel has one or two pairs of light-emitting diodes and photodiodes. As the wheel turns, light shines through the slots and produces an electric signal in the photodiodes. The signals from the wheels give the changes in the mouse's position.

The Sewing Machine

The Feed-Dog: This moves the fabric forward. One train of cams and cranks moves the feed-dog forward and backward, while the other makes it rise and fall. Both are powered by a wheel driven by the electric motor, synchronizing their movements. The feed-dog rises and moves forward between stitches to shift the fabric and then dips and moves back.

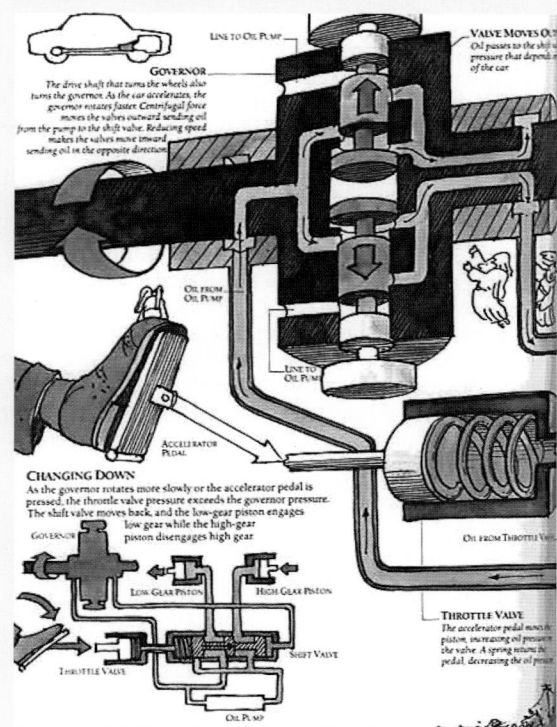
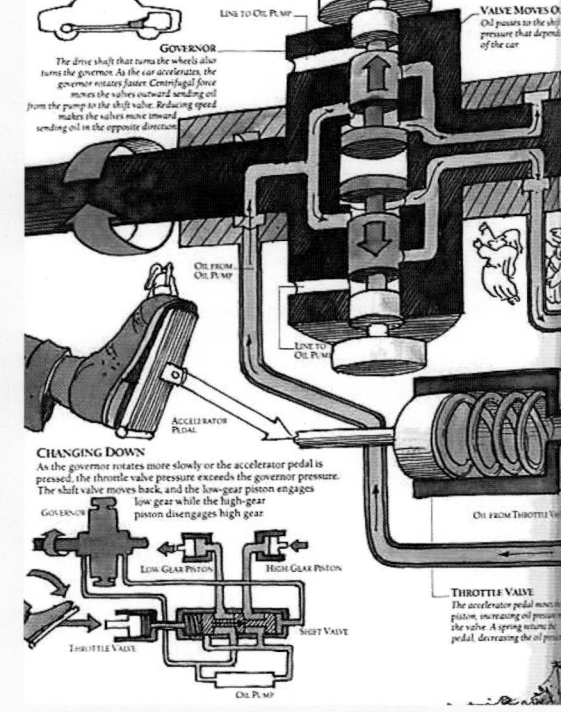

Automatic Transmission

Changing Down: As the governor rotates more slowly or the accelerator pedal is pressed, the throttle valve pressure exceeds the governor pressure. The shift valve moves back, and the low-gear piston engages low gear while the high-gear piston disengages high gear.

Ingenious but useless mechanical devices
Arthur Ganson Presents a Few Machines
$20 Arthur Ganson, 2004, 70 min.

A midnight engineer and MIT professor creates totally useless machines. They are exquisitely beautiful. They do a lot of nothing. At best they whir and click and shake. A genuine artist, he also has filmed his machines obliquely, only partially seen, behind a veil of mystery. You want to know how they work, what they do, how come? No answers. Only peeks at cool and useless machines in marvelous varieties and cleverness, turning, turning, turning. Utterly riveting, supremely inspiring, and very geeky. Show this at a party, and everyone stops transfixed.

-- *KK*

Catalog of possible mechanisms
507 Mechanical Movements
$8 Henry T. Brown, 2005, 128 p.

This book dates back to 1868. It's compendium of all kinds of clever ways levers, gears, cams, wheels and pulleys can be arranged to complete different kinds of actions. Say you want a knob on a BBQ rack to reserve a spindle's direction after 180 degrees, or you want to turn a motor's rotation into reciprocating back-and-forth motion in a toy you are designing. Or maybe you want two points to close up while two perpendicular points widen and vice versa. Here's where to find how to do this and 500 more examples. Artists, tinkerers and mechanical engineers have referred to this slim economical book ($7.50!) for a century. (There's even more devices, in greater sophistication and with more mathematical details in a 4-volume encyclopedia called *Ingenious Mechanisms for Designers and Engineers*, but it costs 20 times as much and is harder to decipher.) This simple one is perfect for makers and basement inventors, or anyone trying to make physical stuff move in interesting ways.

-- *KK*

Organizers

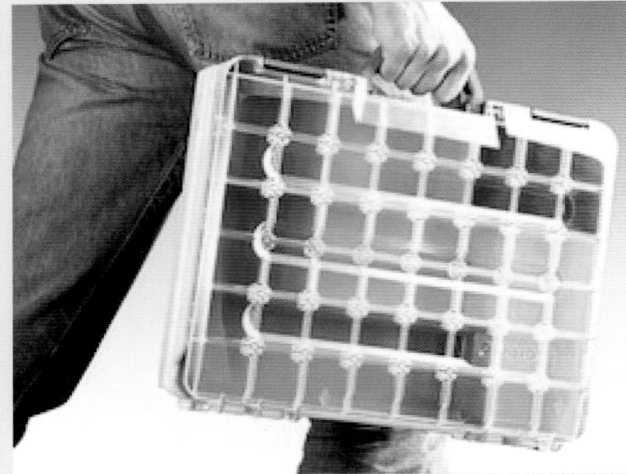

Ultimate smart-part organizer
Sortimo
$86 Sortimo

This is the ultimate sorting box system for small parts. I have a full hardware store's worth of stuff in my boxes mounted in a rack. Each drawer slips completely out of the rack. The top is clear so you can see what is inside of it, which I love. It's got compartments, but they're all self-registering in the bottom, so they are modular which means you can easily mix and match and rearrange them. They come in all different sizes and colors. Because of the clever design, the inserts are separated from each other, so nothing cross-pollinates.

You can pick up the case by the handle and carry it vertically without fear of the contents spilling inside. Lastly, one of the most difficult things about sorting boxes is that you need to bring them over to your work. But with the Sortimo, you merely lift out the handy compartment with the needed parts and bring that over to your bench and then take it back. It's really brilliant. The boxes are kind of spendy; A tray with inserts is about $60. But I'll have these for the rest of my life. I've never had one of these fail.

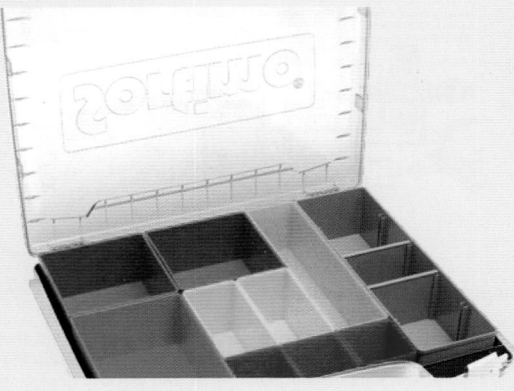

They are not so easy to find. Sortimo is a German company that actually builds these tool systems for ambulances and work vehicles in Europe. They have one US distributor who really hasn't worked very hard to get the word out. But I am constantly raving about them.

-- Adam Savage

This is a German product with a old-world shopping interface. You can't order directly online. You can download a PDF catalog --without prices. You select what you think you want and call the US distributor, who gives you a quote for your system. Most of their customers are companies who are outfitting fleets of trucks or other service vehicles. In fact, they have very cool rigs to hold their trays in different vehicles. --KK

Affordable parts organizer
Stanley Compartment Organizer

A cheaper alternative to the expensve and hard to find Sortimo are these Stanley Organizers. I bought a dozen of them for the same price as two Sortimos. They are sturdy and handy -- and hanve most of the advantages of Sortimo's compartments.

--KK

My favorite compartmented organizer is the Stanley 25-Removable Compartment Professional Organizer. The lid is clear but doesn't seem brittle, and the compartments are removable (nice if you want to grab one or two instead of the whole thing). Matching this, but deeper and with larger compartments, is the Stanley 10-Compartment Deep Professional Organizer, great for larger bolts and nuts.

Harbor Freight has a similar line – which I was about to say, isn't that much cheaper, but turns out, on sale it's about half as much. HF's version is a little deeper, meaning the two are not interchangeable – you can stick a Stanley compartment in the HF, but not vice versa. I use a flat file cabinet for tool storage (totally affordable at local used office furniture resellers, keep your eyes peeled) and the difference in height means Stanley just barely fits without scraping, where the HF causes the drawer to bind a bit.

Both systems stack well on one another. The other thing I like about the HF is that they have a half-sized model that still stacks well (one full sized organizer will stack fine on two half-sized placed next to each other).

The trade-off with removable compartments is some flexibility. For longer bolts or drill bits, I remove two or more compartments in a row and set them in the negative space created. The other plastic bins (held in place by

ridges on the lid) keep this space in one place.

Both types have handles that allow you to carry them, and the hinges, while plastic, have proven robust in use.

-- Taylor Bryant

$16 25 Removable Compartments
$23 10-Compartment, deep
Stanley Tools

Mobile tool chest
Pelican 0450
$520 Pelican

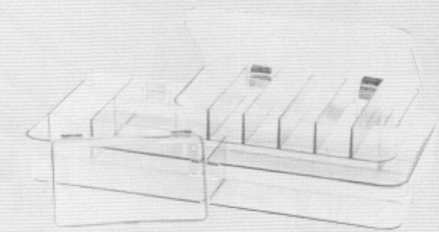

Before I decided to purchase this Pelican case, I did check out some other options. One that I considered was the Stanley FatMax 4-in-1 Mobile Work Station, but it isn't waterproof and doesn't seem as durable as the Pelican. While the Pelican tool chest is pricier than most of its competition, it has several features that have made it well worth the extra cost.

First off, it's virtually indestructible. No matter how rough I am with it or how often it gets banged up, it has not been damaged. The same is true, of course, for the tools tucked away safely inside. Secondly, I live in Southern Louisiana and our weather is often humid and wet; like all Pelican cases, this one's watertight and it ensures that my tools are kept safe from moisture and corrosion. The few times I've left the chest in the back of my truck in the rain everything inside the case stayed as dry as can be.

A variety of drawer configurations are available, including custom-made, and the drawers even extract for on-site mobility. This case isn't light -- about 40 pounds without tools -- however, the trolley handle and wheel system make it possible for me to move it around easily on my own.

-- Chris Catalanotto

Long life plastic boxes
Mighty Tuff Compartmented Boxes
$18 Flambeau

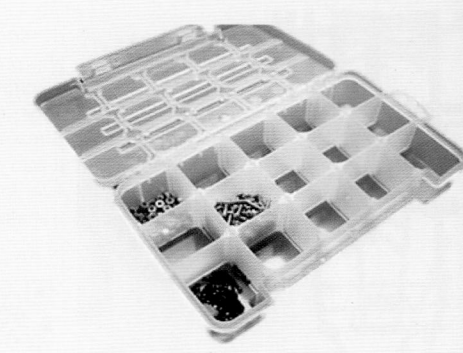

Small "tackle boxes" are well known to all, used far beyond fishing purposes. Also well known is how short their lifespans are, their plastic cracking or even shattering far sooner than we ever hope. Winter is death to these things.

It's the material, right? Over 20 years ago, I got a small Mighty Tuff box to carry fuses (for telecom work). I've still got it, and it's intact. A little yellower than it was new, but still clear and undamaged. I've got a lot more of them now, all kicking along nicely. They're simple, reliable and do their jobs as expected.

Can't expect more from a Cool Tool than that.

-- Wayne Ruffner

Curved-bottom organizer
Akro-Mils Small Parts Storage
$7 Small Akro-Mils

Working in industrial design, I constantly acquire small sets of parts to use for multiple clients and projects. I've tried using a variety of translucent plastic boxes to contain and organize these parts, but they've been flawed in a number of ways: the parts are difficult to pick out with your fingers; the small pieces migrate

from compartment to compartment; and finally, the latches break.

I think Akro-Mils has solved all of these problems with their cases. The latches span the

entire front side of the organizer, work well, and don't seem to break. The bottom of each compartment is curved on at least two sides to allow picking up those 0-80 screws, and the top has ridges that surround each divider to make it much less likely for the parts to jump out of their compartments. The two Akro-Mils organizers I have been using are the small (05-705) and the large (05-905). There's a medium available, too. I think I paid $4 and $7, respectively, which is about the same price as products with none of these features or durability.

-- Arthur Carr

To do great work one must be very idle as well as very industrious. - Samuel Butler

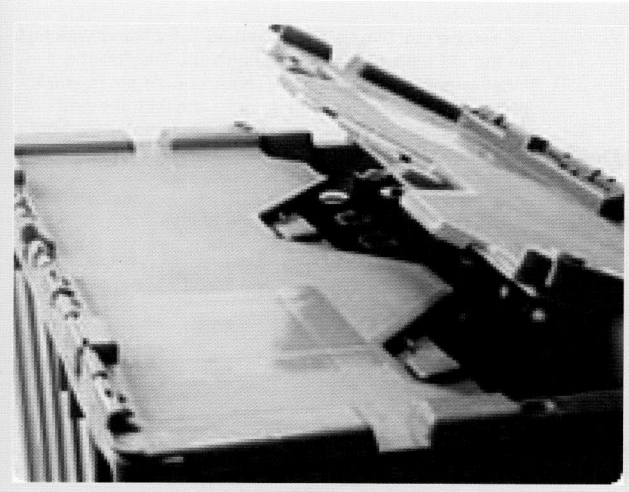

Heavy duty storage totes
Monoflo Nestable Totes
$20 16-gallons 12.5"H x 16.6"W x 27.2"L miworldwide.com

These Monoflo storage containers, most commonly seen in the back of grocery store delivery trucks, are the best solution I've found for moving, shipping, and storing stuff. Every other system I've used previously had a fatal flaw. In particular, the Rubbermaid and Sterilite totes I've tried all cracked, failed to stack well, and had lids (when I could find them) that never seemed to fit properly (especially if you came close to loading them to full capacity).

Manufactured here in the USA by Monoflo, a company that specializes in industrial storage and delivery solutions, these totes are really well made and far superior. Originally designed for light industry, they work just as well in domestic settings.

I own ten of the 16-gallon nestable totes. Five went to a project that required the distribution of kits filled with educational materials to local schools, and the other five I use at home for storage. While they aren't exactly a sight for sore eyes (I keep them tucked away when at home), everything else about them sings with utility.

They stack efficiently and safely (I've stacked all ten with weight inside and they barely budge when shoved). When empty, the two halves of the attached lid fall to the side allowing the containers to nest perfectly. They have reinforced holes moulded into the handles for zip ties that secure the lids shut when needed. Unlike others I've tried these crates don't buckle or crack when moving (I've filled one with as much water as I and a friend could lift, and it held fast). And despite being made of a hard plastic they are fairly comfortable to carry.

Speaking of which, they're made out of a high-density polyethylene resin (reminiscent of milk crates) that is far sturdier than alternatives like Rubbermaid. A testament to their durability came when I shipped them across country via FedEx (the heaviest weighing 80-lbs) and everyone arrived without failure; no cracks, chips, or broken hinges, despite what was clearly rough handling over a 3,000 mile journey.

Not everybody will love the criss-cross "multi-fingered" lids, but I find that they work well, stay closed when moving, and create a uniform flat surface for stacking. The biggest problem emerges when trying to access anything when the crates are stacked.

Overall, I have found the 16-gallon size to be perfect for my needs. Anymore, and they'd be so big I wouldn't be able to move them myself when fully loaded. And while they aren't the cheapest storage solution around at $15 a piece, I know they will last far longer than all the others I've tried. Highly recommended.

I believe they are eligible for a volume-discount and free ship-to-store at Ace Hardware.

-- Oliver Hulland

Mobile tool organizer
Nantucket Diddy Bagg
$170 nantucketbagg.com

I bought this bag about four years ago at a boat show, intending to use it as a home for tools on my sailboat. I ended up using it more as a transport than a permanent home for tools, in part because I liked it so much and found it so useful that I didn't want to be limited to using in solely on the boat.

I use it anytime I need to cart tools out of the shop for a project whether at the boat, in the house or farther afield. It holds a lot and the tools are protected. I end up making fewer trips back to the shop because it's quick, easy and safe to carry those tools that I'd otherwise

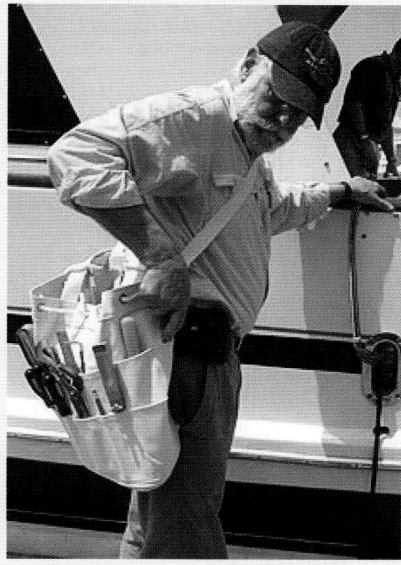

hesitate to take, but end up needing. I assembled a wine storage unit for a restaurant on the fourth floor of a mall, and it was really helpful to load the Diddy Bagg up and configure the straps so I could wear it like a backpack. It left both hands free for carrying other stuff.

A ditty bag is a traditional tool carrier for marine use. Unlike a hard toolbox, it fits just about anywhere and is less likely to ding your shin (or a pretty piece of varnished mahogany) if you bump into it. The Nantucket Diddy Bagg adds to the traditional bag's usefulness: It's larger, has lots of individual pockets for delicate tools (can safely carry a sharp chisel) and it's stiff enough to protect its contents.

The bag's outstanding features are its straps and zipper. The adjustable straps allow you to carry it in a variety of ways, including as a backpack, and the zipper allows you to lay the whole thing out flat for access or cleaning. You can even attach it to the wall as a permanent, yet portable, means of tool storage.

Its weaknesses are that it is really too big to be a perfect boater's ditty bag and

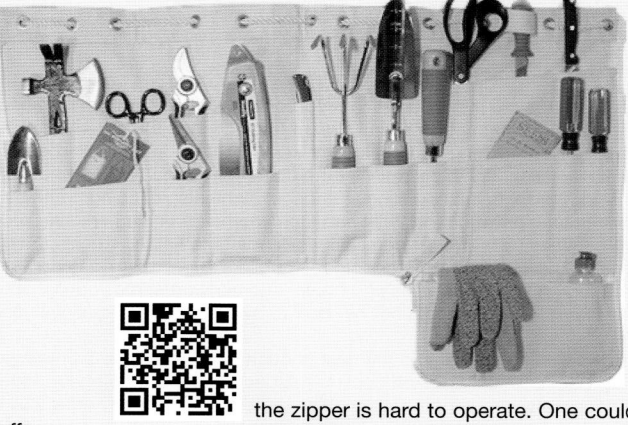

the zipper is hard to operate. One could wash the bag and soften the canvas, but it might eventually get too soft and not be sufficiently rigid to stand up when full. So I opt to live with a hard to operate zipper rather than risk a flaccid bag. I added leather pulls on the zipper, which helps, but it still requires a firm pull.

-- Quinn McKenna

For those looking for a more affordable alternative, Harbor Freight sells a Canvas Rigger Bag for $15 that serves a similar function, and it gets stellar reviews.

--Oliver Hulland

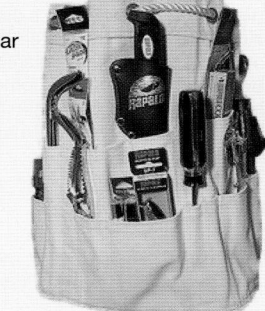

Forever storage for cheap
Plastic Storage Containers
$125 Sterilite (4-pack, 70-Quart bins)

Tuffcrates contico.com rubbermaidproducts.com

As an untidy person, I've found that the secret to an organized work spaces is to have lots of bins, boxes, drawers, tubs, and containers. A couple of each are not enough. You need scores of each size. The key is to not skimp on the numbers. The wonderful news is that plastic containers are getting cheap enough to buy in bulk . If you keep an eye out for sales you can get molded, lidded, durable containers for only few dollars a piece. I recently bought about 40 plastic stackable breadbox-size containers at IKEA for 99 cents apiece. I use them in my workshop and studio and kitchen pantry.

Suitable containers come in all sizes and shapes. Some of the cheapest these days are the 12-gallon Tuffcrates, with hinged lids. (There are larger versions but I find these unmanageable when full.) The 12-gallon laundry-basket sized guys swallow a nice pile of stuff. They are semi-transparent giving you a hint of what's inside. Empty they stack up compactly. Full, they stack up solidly five or six high. We store seasonal clothes, hobby materials, vacation gear, holiday decorations, old documents, and so on in a handy self-made wall in our basement. They are easy to move around, easy to get in and out of, pestproof and dustproof. They look fine too. Stored in basements and garages, we've had zero problem with mildew or mold or mice, which I cannot say about goods stored in cardboard boxes. I've seen Tuffcrates for sale as low as $3 a piece. Since they don't ever wear out; you could easily pass them onto the next generation. You simply can't have too many of them.

For more specialized storage I gravitate to Rubbermaid containers. They are often perfect for certain uses, but it's harder to find good discount deals on them; they are usually not cheap. I like the small stackable small-parts containers (#7747). They are book size (good), open fast and are indestructible - unlike a lot of tackle boxes. I use the smaller ones, about 6 inches square, called ActionPackers (#7874), for office supplies as well - all those paperclips, pins, and easily lost paraphernalia. Get at least a dozen. I thought at first that having uniform containers

would make finding things more difficult because you'd be without distinctive visual cues, but in fact labeling and standard holders speed up locating stuff.

Rubbermaid and others produce a whole line of containers called underbed containers, which slip into the underutilized - or at least under-organized - space under most beds. We've found no where else that stores giftwrapping paper as safely and conveniently; we keep a set of cutters and tape right in the wrap boxes. But I've recently discovered that these long sealed flat containers are also marvelous for storing maps, charts, blueprints and other rolled paper quite securely. The Rubbermaid versions come in regular (#2128) and the Jumbo (#2129) -- a full 42 inches long - which I prefer. They are also stackable.

I was in one of those discount stores the other day and I found a stockpile of shoebox-size containers for about $1.50/ piece. They are not as good as the Rubbermaids, because their lids slide off too easily, but I got a dozen and now they have brought order to the closet that holds our craft materials. A bigger size - larger than a breadbox but smaller than the Tuffcrates - took the chaos out of the Legos, Duo blocks, and Konexits toys.

Find a good deal, then pounce on a bunch. I've never gotten a set of containers that we haven't used sustainably. But I have bought one or two here and there that I haven't made much use of. You need a critical mass.

-- KK

Moving Heavy Stuff

Best come-along
Maasdam Pow'r Pull

$40 maasdam.com

Come-alongs are a must-have for country living. They're most often used to tug vehicles out of ditches and unsuccessful stream fordings, and to tighten fencing. I've also used mine for erecting and tightening large tents and canopies, pulling objects into and onto trucks, hoisting 350 lb carcasses for butchering, encouraging crunched automobile bodies back into proper shape, pulling stumps, straightening sagging barns back to verticality, moving large logs, turning trailers to face another direction, erecting pre-assembled 2x4 wall sections built on the floor, cinching loads onto flatbed trucks, dragging heavy boats up the ramp onto the dock or onto their trailers, erecting wind generators, extracting and installing engines in vehicles and boats. In other words, moving just about anything up to 2 tons. Come-alongs should not be used to move people, since a well-used cable can snap.

The Maasdam Pow'r Pull is the best (though not the cheapest) come-along you can buy. It is built better than knock-off copies -- especially the $19.95 ones -- in every way. There's an accessory wire gripper that enables the Maasdam (or any other pull tool) to tighten fences, clotheslines etc. I've beat the hell out of my 1969-model, and it has never failed. It will pull 2 tons. You can buy very expensive aluminum giant come-alongs from several firms, but the fine print with them sez that they are also 2-ton, so I don't see much point in them except they are beautiful and classy-looking. Any tool that carries a high load-ing should be of the very best quality, as failure can be deadly or at the least scary. The Maasdam is good stuff.

Hints for working with a come-along: Many folks loop a come-along's cable hook around an object and then hook it back onto the cable like a noose. This is very unsafe, as the hook will either cut or seriously damage the cable. Users should invest in a couple of suitable "Shackles" (any hardware or boat store) for such duty, and never hook anything directly to a come-along's cable. Hint for come-along use where there are no trees or objects to anchor it to: Bury your spare tire a couple feet down and hook to that. Come-alongs also need some sort of anchor for the mechanism. I keep a length of 3/8ths chain for that purpose.

-- J. Baldwin

How to move five tons
Johnson Bar, or Pry Truck

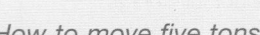

I have always had a penchant for large, heavy objects, and therefore long ago started to pay close attention to how to move things which had weights far past the threshold of "mere human" move-ability. Palette jacks are the first and foremost tool for moving such things, but there are seri-ous limitations with palette jacks in close quarters, or just getting a heavy load raised to the point where you can put a palette under it.

The "Johnson bar" (also known as pry truck, pry bar, mule, or wheeled steel lever) is a tool that solves those problems, and it has a host of other uses which you will discover. The pry truck is a miracle of sim-plicity and unbelievable strength. Moving a 1500-pound (680kg) lathe is child's play with one of these levers, and I have moved multi-ton steel shipping containers (empty) with them. With two levers (and two peo-ple) almost any large object can be shifted and moved into position or onto more con-venient conveyance (dollies, casters, or just onto steel pipe rollers.) Given two people, some time, and some shims, one can get large objects raised off the floor enough to slide a palette under with a palette jack or dollies. While it seems like this should remain in the realm of "industrial moving", I've found that I use it almost once a week for other odd jobs around the house, like levelling a shed, moving a palette of floor tiles in the basement, etc.

Unlike a floor jack that needs clearance, this can be put under things with only ~1/4" (~64mm) of gap between the floor and the object. It takes a few minutes of experimenta-tion, but one can learn very quickly how to move objects by levering them off the floor and then rotating the handle around it's axis to make objects move 4-6 inches (10cm-15cm) at a time.

Every time I use this tool, I wonder how I would have ever been able to do any mov-ing and transport task without it and I can't imagine not having one handy. Apologies to Archimedes: Give me a big enough lever on wheels and a place to stand, and I shall move the world.

There are several varieties and sources to purchase them. I have always used the wood-handled variety, however I can't imagine there's much of a difference between various models other than capacity. They're somewhat expensive, but I've never seen one on the "used" market -- I suspect once people have such a useful item, they only part with them during estate sales.

-- John Todd

$150-$200 Oak Lever Dollies 5,000 lbs. gilmorekramer.com

Better than a come-along or winch
Griphoist (Tirfor) Hand Winch

I don't know anything else non-explosive, that you can pick up with one hand, and that can move five tons one hundred feet -- with safety, precision, and astonishingly little work. Like many good tools the Tirfor is a thing of beauty, superbly designed and engineered. With 100 feet of cable (or more) its reach is much greater than a come-along, and this can often make all the difference. Its speed is much faster, too, not just the speed in mov-ing something (the lever is double-acting) but speed in setting up or moving the set-up around. Often when you need to move something, minutes if not seconds count. The action is precise. A come-along winds the cable upon itself, and often when the cable comes under ten-sion the cable wrap slips a bit. The resulting jerks can cause all kinds of problems in a situation where precise movement counts, and a sudden shift in load may cause failure somewhere else. Finally, the Tirfor has a much more effective (and safer) mechanism for smoothly *low-ering* a heavy load. Most (ratcheted) come-alongs are very poor at this.

--George Dyson

How to ...
Moving Heavy Things

$13 Jan Adkins 2004, 48 pages

Sooner or later, most people need to move something too heavy to lift or too awkward to handle. This little book presents the basic physics, tactics, and best moves. Lift that piano without fear of hernia. Get your truck out of the ditch without calling for help. Stand that 500 lb. 55-gallon drum up on end with a flick of the wrist. Here are the tools, knots, and safety precautions you'll need. The formulas and tables for calculating the capacities of ropes, chains and cables are here, too, all described in the proper lingo (e.g. "swigging" and "parbuckling " - very useful moves) and illustrated with the author's classy drawings. Long out of print, and really missed, this classic book is now avail-able again.

-- J. Baldwin

•
Precept Two: The Geezer Ploy

When the old fellows didn't have diesel cranes to pull their fat out of the fire, they were obliged to be fiendishly clever. Ask yourself how they would have set up for your problem in 1900, in 1800, 1700, and so forth.

•
Precept Five: Applied Sloth

As stated in the stagehand's axiom: "Never lift what you can drag, never drag what you can roll, never roll what you can leave." Creativity

---

In Europe these tools are known as Tirfor Hand Winches. In the US they are branded Griphoists. They do the work of motorized winches -- haul logs, or move stuck tractors, raise towers, and so on -- but with the deft-ness of a human hand. Because there is no ratchet or coil, a Griphoist permits very small adjustments, unlike either come-alongs or winches. The patented double grip mechanism of the Griphoist/Tirfor is considered so reliable that some versions of the unit are rated by the UL to be suitable for hoisting humans -- for instance in hoisting window-washers scaffolding. They come in models rated from 1500 pounds up to 8 tons.

--KK

$250 Pull All Griphoist $630 Super Pull All Griphoist Tractel

$333 3/4 Ton Rope Grip Puller Jet

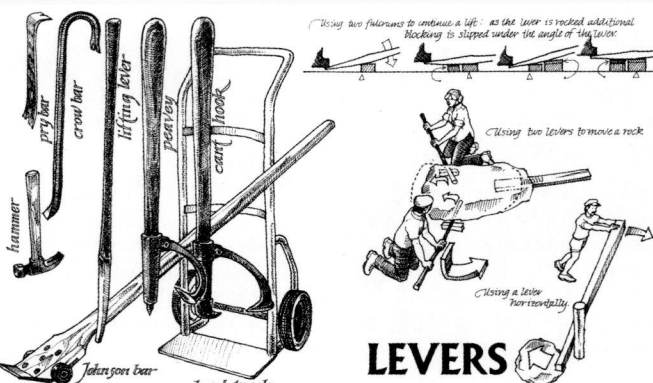

germinates in indolence, and the cleverest people are often the laziest: they are always looking for an easier way. The easiest way is often the simplest, most direct, and the best way.

This sloop is being launched from a beach far from cranes and highlifts, moving on rollers and track and using block & tackle to multiply the pull of a small car in reverse (its most powerful gear). The movers are securing their stationary block to a hefty anchor; ashore, a stationary anchor is called a dead man. Sometimes natural dead men aren't available and movers must dig or drill or rig one' The stump puller here is anchored by a well-protected tree. The ground has been dug out as much as possible, and exposed roots have been cut. The tackle has been rove to advantage, the pulling fall on the moving block, and the stump then should come out.

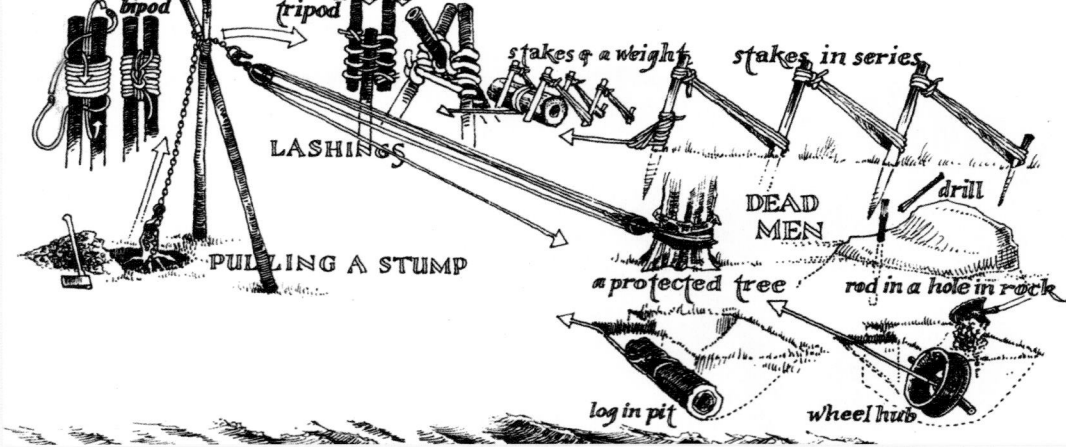

Moving up
Hi-Lift Jack
$101 48 inches Hi-Lift

When trying to move Very Large Objects don't forget the Hi-Lift Jack, still about 100 bucks and able to lift 7000 lbs 4 feet or more. After a flood moved a 60 ft. barn nearby, I moved it right back where it belonged with that jack, and a few pulls on a come-along. The Hi-Lift is great for extracting fence posts, too. While living on a nature preserve, I jacked out several miles of steel fence posts and dozens of big gate posts complete with concrete wad still stuck on using a Hi-Lift Jack. Also levelled our house, which was 6 inches out of level, one click per day, without breaking any windows. No problems. It's a big bad beast, but a good-'un. It can also serve as a high labor, low frequency log splitter (good upper body exercise)! You can buy wheels for it (but they'll only work on smooth hard surfaces)

and a neat "sheath" for stowing it theft-resistantly in or on your vehicle. However, as someone once told me: "Never let go of the handle while lowering the load or you'll EAT TEETH!" -- a worthwhile reminder for users of this pre-OSHA device.

The Hi-Lift comes in a number of lengths in either cast or steel. I like the cast model best, as it seems to be more durable in heavy use. The 60-incher is not rated to take a full load to 60 inches, and it is heavy enough to be damned awkward to carry around. The 48" is perfectly fine -- though no lightweight -- and the one I use.

-- J. Baldwin

Also called a farm jack or off-road jack. I have a Chinese version from Harbor Freight, really heavy duty, and only $50. --KK

Light dolly
Nylon Hand Truck
$40 30151 Flow Back Handle Truck
Milwaukee

Every household garage and homestead needs a hand truck. It's amazing how often you'll use it once you have one. Makes heavy and awkward things seem less so. I've hauled all kinds of weird stuff. Big tires can work outside in the yard, too. And you'll be a hero next time a friend needs to move. "Be sure to bring your hand truck," they say.

The truck I settled on is a light weight yet tough nylon model made by Harper, but I don't think the make matters much. (There is a similar one from Gleason.) Since it weighs only 22 pounds it's easy to toss in the trunk, yet it will handle weights greater than I can move (600 pounds). It has big fat balloon tires, stair glides (to ease going up or down stairs), and is just about indestructible. Given that it will outlive me, it's a bargain at $60.

You can get a cheap new metal one for $20. Since they are hard to kill, a hand truck is a great candidate for buying used.

-- KK

Collapsible hand truck
Magna Cart
$29 Welcom Products

One problem with a standard dolly is storing it within easy reach. It kind of hogs a closet. The Magna Cart is an ingenious solution to this storage challenge. It folds up flat and small enough to slip behind a desk, or under a desk, or in a car trunk, or even on the top shelf of a closet. Weighs only 7 pounds. Yet it is also rugged enough to haul 150 pounds, and unfolds in a second. And collapses again just as fast. Its wheels are large enough for paved surfaces. Reasonably priced. Very nifty, and very handy. (Magna makes a slightly larger wheeled version that carries 200 pounds which I have not used.)

-- KK

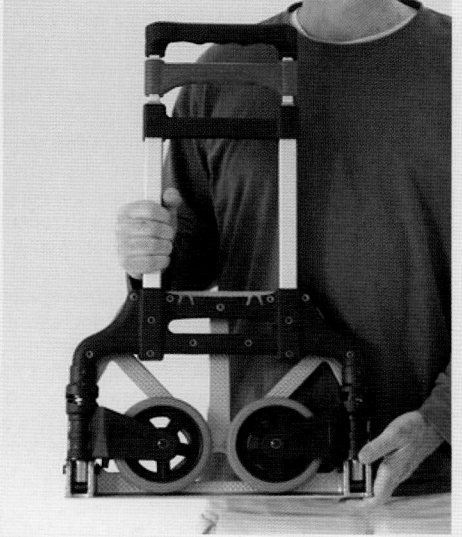

Foldable large-package hauler
Rock N Roller MultiCart R2 Micro
$110 Rock N Roller

What I find most useful and unique about this adaptable rolling cart is that it folds to a relatively compact size that I can easily fit into a normal car while being able to unfold and expand to carry a large number of boxes.

I like it better than the common folding dollies that have a lower load capacity and have only two wheels that only operate in an upright position. Being able to put into a long horizontal position allows the Rock N Roller carts to carry unusual loads that might not stack in a stable fashion on a typical upright dolly.

Rock N Roller offer this same design in multiple sizes.

-- Evan Goss

Instant long arms
Velstrap
$9 2" x 6 feet Amazon

This black nylon strap is used to carry hefty and unwieldy loads. It has a handle, a d-ring, and a lot of velcro on it, allowing you to cinch a load together and comfortably carry it. It's rated for 50 pounds, but I've used it for maybe 10 pounds more than that. I use it to carry stuff all in one trip which I'd never been able to managed without the strap. It's six feet long and 2 inches wide, and most of it is velcro, so I've not yet run out of strap or had so much extra I couldn't use it. It's great for things that are in bunches or are otherwise unwieldy. (It also allows you to say "unwieldy" a lot.) I actually got a load of packages at work today, and wished I'd had mine with me; I might go grab another one.

-- Jeremy Gllissen

Cheap huge tote bag
Ikea Tote Bag
$.60 Frakta Ikea stores

Ikea sells these near the cash register. They are large -- about 4 feet by 2 by 2, with two clever lengthened (short & long) handles, made of some nearly indestructible nylon-plasticy mesh fabric in Ikea blue. For a buck, they're amazing. We put a mess at

home, in the car, garden, garage. Great for dragging stuff from Sam's Club, or dirt in the garden, hauling firewood or just whenever you've a lot of loose stuff to move.

-- Vince Crisci

We use 'em. Lightweight, generously oversized, foldable, durable, and only 99 cents. What's not to like?

-- KK

Slide, don't lift
Furniture Sliders
$8 (8 pieces)

Moving Men Furniture Sliders are smooth frisbee-shaped polymer disks, either 7" or 3 1/2" in diameters, filled with a spongy material (they call it a special grip pad). They are an improvement on the "furniture coasters" my mother used to put under the sofa in that the special grip pad does really work, allowing you to move furniture easily. They work on carpet, though our experience has involved sliding things over berber and low-ply (we've never owned shag).

We have moved some pretty heavy furniture using them. You

might be able to slide an upright piano this way -- but I would leave moving a grand piano to the professionals.

These also work well for slipping under boxes on moving day.

-- Martin Schwimmer

Demolition

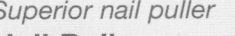

Cheap and Nearly Indestructible Carbon Steel Wrecker
Multipurpose Pry Bar

$4 10" Multipurpose Pry Bar Harbor Freight

I got one of these pry bars at a Harbor Freight about 10 years ago and have since gotten many more as gifts and spares. Their natural versatility is furthered by expendability (often on sale for $2.50).

I've used mine to pry off moulding, pry flooring slats tightly together, widen gaps too tight for a full crowbar, chisel old mortar off bricks, open paint cans, scrape paint, caulk, act as a spacer when decking, bang on various things, and pull nails in tight locations with its cat's paw.

It's a great general purpose abuse tool that fits in a small toolbox and won't worry you if chipped, bent, painted, greased, bespeckled with construction adhesive, or lost.

-- Evanda

Best Nail Puller
SharkGrip

$20 sharkcorp.com

I recently needed to remove several panels of particle board subflooring while preparing to install a hardwood floor. These panels were fastened with a gazillion ring-shanked nails, driven in by an overly enthusiastic pneumatic nail-gun operator. After much sweat and frustration with a conventional assortment of hammer claws, cat paws, and pry bars, I finally came across the magic tool. It's the Japanese manufactured SharkGrip Nail Puller. The tool very efficiently gets underneath the offending nail head and will even latch onto the nail's shank should the head shear off. It's available in various sizes and configurations.

-- Mike Pel

Demo specialist
Duckbill Deck Wrecker

$68 deckwrecker.com

I set out to replace the boards on our backyard deck this summer, and initially tried removing the old boards with a three-foot crowbar. The main problem was getting it between the deck board and the joist, so I could start prying. This required a hammer to drive it under the board. Then with a lot of effort, time and hammering I eventually removed one board. Clearly not the way to do the entire deck.

After some searching I discovered the Duckbill Deck Wrecker. This thing is a monster. It sits on the joist and has two legs that straddle the joist and slip under the board you're removing. With almost 4 1/2 feet of leverage it's easy to pry up the board, progressing along its length every one or two joists. You stand on the old section of deck and push the handle of the Duckbill up, thus prying up the old board in front of you. As far as other tools go, Mayhew's Cats Paw functions with a similar design, though without the rotating head. The Cats Paw has a little less leverage and costs a little more.

The first, outermost, board(s) must be removed some other way to expose enough joist so that the Duckbill can fit under a board. As you make your way closer to the house -- putting down new boards as you take old ones up -- eventually there isn't room to stand behind the Duckbill. At this point you remove the Duckbill head (it's pinned to the shaft and can be rotated 180°), turn it around and now you are standing on the new decking and pulling the handle of the Duckbill to remove the last few old boards.

I'm sure I will find some other uses for this thing, but even if it's only good for decks, it was well worth the money.

-- Jeff Scott

Hammer & pry bar for wrecking
FuBar Demolition Tool

$20 stanleyfubar.com

The FuBar is a single cast piece of high carbon steel that looks like a prettied up hammer. One end has a hammer and a tearing, armour-penetrating beak, while the opposite end has a conventional pry bar and nail puller. You can use it to drive nails, but what it really excels in is F'ing things up beyond recognition -- hence FuBar. You hit something with the axe-like end until it's weakened, then hit again, twist to pry, and CRUNCH!

Demolition is a very violent activity and from my experience FuBar can make it safer, as well as much faster. There's more control, fewer blows are needed, and less contact with the object being destroyed are required - which matters, because said object usually becomes a mass of sharp nails and wood early in the process, and the less you have to risk cuts and tetanus by getting close up, the better. It's also durable -- looks the same now as before I destroyed enough furniture to fill a pickup.

I have the smallest version, a 2.5-pound FuBar 2. I think you'd only want a larger FuBar if you were doing some very serious demolition.

-- Jonathan Coupe

Superior nail puller
Nail Puller

$33 Cooper Group 56 Nail Puller

$63 Bahco Nail Puller

Pry bar nail pullers will gouge a quite horrible crater in your material unless the nail is at the surface, or just the right size. With this one, on the other hand, I can extract a headless nail from more than a centimeter inside a beam. The wood was not unscratched of course, but since it was compressed rather than splintered, a bit of water can make it swell back up somewhat.

-- Gaute Amundsen

This design is not new. You can find antique nail pullers like this hundreds of years old. The sharp teeth of this tool are perfect for slicing into the wood, yanking out deep air-hammered nails, or finishing nails from a surface you care about. There are several different makes; none are cheap, but these last a lifetime.

-- KK

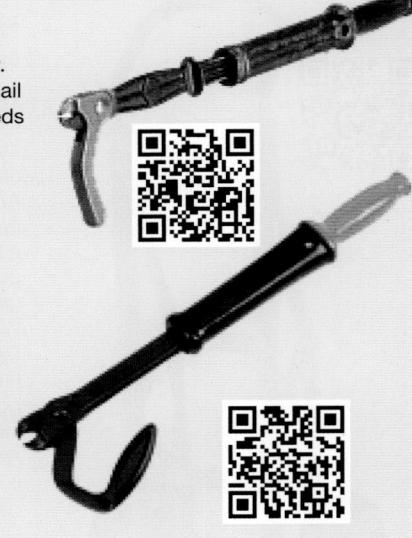

Tile remover
Spyder Scraper

$10 spyderproducts.com

Last year I removed some old vinyl tile from our dining room. Even with the help of a friend and a a heavy duty floor scraper, it took all afternoon. Some tiles popped up fine, but most stuck tenaciously and had to be pried up with a thin blade. Miserable.

The kitchen had the same tiles, and yesterday I cleared them all out by myself in about 30 minutes without breaking a sweat. The difference? A Spyder Scraper, which fits into any brand reciprocating saw.

It's not a complete solution alone, because it's hard to get the saw itself underneath the tiles as they peel up. Use the Spyder to loosen the edges, and then a long handled manual scraper to scoop up the tiles. When the manual scraper hits another tough edge, hit it with the Spyder again. Two people working together in this fashion should be able to clear 300 sq-ft in well under an hour.

I used the 4" blade; they also come in 2" and 6" for different purposes including removing tiles adhered with thinset. I wish I'd had one a couple of years ago when I redid the bathroom!

The Spyder Scraper attaches to any brand reciprocating saw.

-- Scott Noyes

Whatever tool you use, do what we used to do: buy a block of dry ice and put it briefly on each tile before removal (put it on the next tile while you work on the current one). The tiles shatter easily, the glue is rendered brittle, and removal is fast.

--John Jorsett

Shovel with leverage
Kodiak Roofer's Blade

$30 ames.com

This is designed for and sold as a roofing shingle removal shovel, but what it actually is is a shovel with teeth and a fulcrum. I bought it twelve years ago to strip my roof. It did the job then, and ever since I've used it for everything but stripping shingles. The teeth are good for cutting through and breaking up a variety of materials. The fulcrum maximizes prying leverage (and also reinforces the blade tip so as to not fold while prying).

What this is really great for is removing thick layers of ice or hard packed snow from pavement. The teeth do a great job of digging under and breaking up the layers, and the fulcrum often lets me pop large sections of a layer up in one piece.

-- Gary Puckett

Do-it-all steel bar
Hyde 9-1/2-inch Pry Bar Scraper

$9 hydetools.com

I've used this fantastic multi-use Hyde Pry Bar for 30 years. If my house were burning down I would grab it, along with my computer backup and photo albums.

I have scraped paint, removed nails without having to run to get another tool, pried things apart, scraped gum off the floor. It doesn't stay bent out of shape like other more cheaply built products, but instead springs back into position. It's also sharpenable. My son wants to inherit it.

-- Carol

The simplification of anything is always sensational. - G.K. Chesterton

Magnetic Stud Finder
Most accurate stud finder

$9 CH Hanson 03040 Magnetic Stud Finder Amazon

Using a magnet to find the hardware in studs is the most accurate way to find a stud. This simple, non-electric gizmo really works — much more consistently than other stud finders I've tried. You could make your own using a supermagnet, but this one comes ready to go with two large supermagnets mounted in an easy-to-hold device with a level. You swipe it around the wall till it pulls itself to a nail or screw underneath. Perpendicularly up/down is your stud. It's strong enough to work through baseboards. No batteries, lasts forever.

-- KK

Gorilla Gripper
Big panel moving

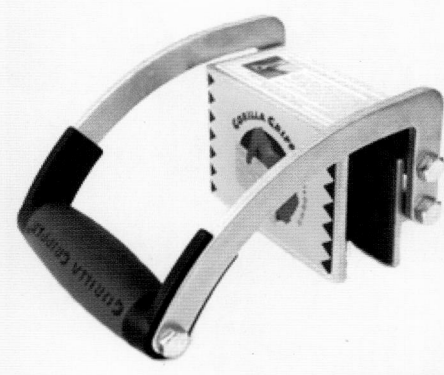

$40 Gorilla Gripper

I have the Stanley Panel Carry, but I greatly prefer the Gorilla Gripper, which works with panel widths from 3/8 to 1 1/8 inch. It is about six times more expensive, but it works significantly better for moving large panels.

The Stanley tool goes under the bottom edge of the sheet. This can be awkward if it's heavy material, such as plywood, and seems more likely to result in damaged corners. Using the Stanley holder, I had to bend my back at an awkward angle to pick up the sheet -- the length from the tray (where the bottom edge of the sheet rests) to the handle is too short. The Gorilla Gripper lifts from the top of the panel,

so there's less need to bend before lifting, and I can keep my back straight. Also, with the Gorilla Gripper it's easier to adjust your balance, since you don't have the friction of the material moving the tool from side to side.

-- Taylor Bryant

Free Hands Drywall Cleats
Drywall Construction Aid

$15 (for a three-pack) Freehand 2000

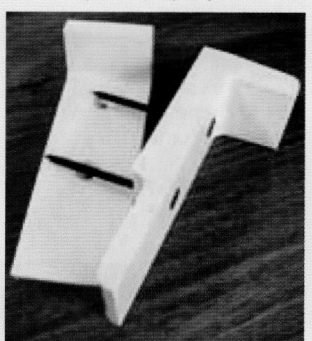

I'm finishing my basement and am in the drywall phase of this year-long solo project. After renting a 100 lb drywall lift for a weekend for $60 to get the largest ceiling panels positioned, I found Free Hands on the internet. They are simple plastic cleats which you screw into the studs or joists to provide a ledge to support an edge of the drywall while you position and screw it in place. I've been using them for all the rest of

the odd-sized and half-sheet drywall panels on the ceiling and all the panels on the walls. It takes about a minute to attach and remove the two cleats each time. The smooth plastic surfaces allow me to slide the drywall up onto the cleats and move the panel around until I get a precise fit. They're sturdy and inexpensive, and I'm making good progress with them. I could have made cleats out of scrap wood, but I really doubt they would have performed nearly as well as these. They've made one-person drywalling possible for me.

-- Malcolm MacDonald

Sand & Kleen Dustless Drywall Sanding
Dust-busting drywall sander

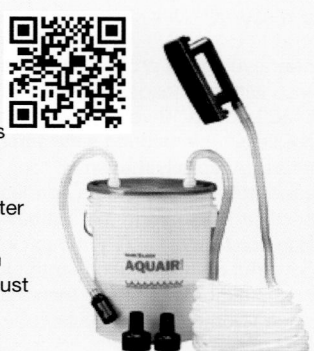

$55 Sand Kleen

Sanding drywall is messy and nasty — it's hard on both your tools and lungs. With this system the majority of the dust is sucked up right at the sanding pad. The sanding head, which uses standard sanding screens, is attached to a hose that runs to the Aquair Water Filter, a five gallon bucket that has a another hose you attach to a Shop-Vac (not provided). As you sand, the dust is sucked through 36 little holes on a pad attached to the sanding head. When the dust hits the water it goes into suspension, and doesn't reach (or ruin) the Shop-Vac. Note: after a good bit of use, you will need to change the water.

As a builder sometimes forced to live at the site (the horror!), I can say that this has made my life (and marriage) much less messy. Even if you're a homeowner and not a professional, this tool is especially useful, as drywall dust is incredibly pernicious. It can blow all over the house and settle everywhere. With this system, you can sand in the areas that you live in with significantly less clean up – and you won't even need a mask!

-- Doug Barnard

Setting Tile
Best how to tile

$9 Michael Byrne, 1995, 260 p.

Setting Tile is an excellent guide to any home tile project I can think of. (And most tiling of any kind.)

I checked this out of the local library when getting ready to tile a full bathroom floor and shower, and immediately ordered my own copy even before returning it. Not quite a reference, and shorter than a bible, but comprehensive and just wonderfully written, the author has a fantastic way to explain processes and tips that do not require multiple readings to fully apprehend (as in many how-to books). The information is presented logically, and is a pleasure to just read and learn. I have remodeled one bathroom before finding this book and one after. It saved

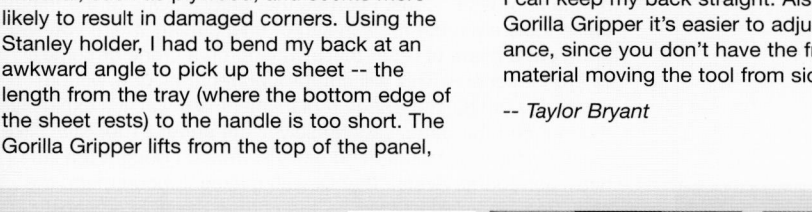

a lot of work and worry the second time around.

I also recommend the tile forums at johnbridge.com for great FAQs and friendly advice.

-- Dave Rudolph

▲ The biters are used to nibble away a waste area of tile, working from the outside toward the center of the cut. To produce a clean break, use a prying motion rather than attempting to cut entirely through the tile with each bite.

Unger Trim Scraper
Folding safety blade for cleaning glass

$8 (Trim10) Unger Global

I work in the beverage industry and use this scraper for removing stickers from cooler doors that other guys with pocket knives, razors, car keys, etc. couldn't budge. The Trim 10 has wide, super thin, very flexible blades about 4 inches long that really conform to the surface of the work. I find it picks up more material per stroke and gets down to the bottom of things better than a single-edge razor blade. The holder has a very elegant folding design that allows for safe, touchless blade changes and compact, safe transport -- a much smaller, flatter package than a lot of utility knives. The scraper comes in a nifty case that holds a few extra blades, which can be purchased separately. A modular handle is also available for heavier work, but I never need it. I get mine from a janitorial supply company in. I believe the scrapers are popular with window tint installers, too.

-- Christian Taylor

Drill Saw
Fastest sheetrock saw

$3 Harbor Freight

A cool tool. Unlike the usual drywall saw, this hand-tool is like a drill with a round grinding blade. The tip allows precise "drilling" into the drywall to start your cut. The rough round blade then allows cutting either straight or curvy lines. Very useful for the renovator. Nothing worse than mucking up a cut on a sheet that has a few cutouts required.

-- James Wagner

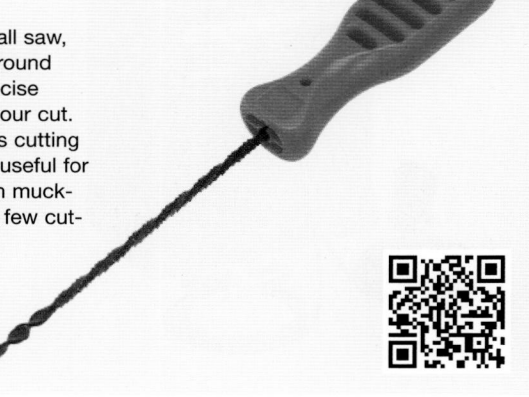

Live as if you were to die tomorrow. Learn as if you were to live forever. - Mahatma Gandhi

39

Shop Tools

The cordless shop
Makita Cordless System

$639 Makita 18-volt Cordless 7-Piece Combo Kit Amazon

Cordless tools have taken over our shop. The saw, drill, grinder, driver, cutter that we reach for first is the cordless one. The key to going cordless is to settle on one make so you can use the same set of batteries for all. Several big tool brands offer a cordless system, including Milwaukee and Dewalt. We choose the Makita 18v Lithium system because their drills and drivers were very light for how much torque they put out, are quite

small for getting into tight spaces, have a nice LED light on them and can be set down on their pommel. One quirk we have found about the Makita system is that you can run the lighter tools like drills on the small capacity lithium packs, but the larger tools only accept the large capacity 3 AH packs. I assume Makita does this because the draw on the larger tools will heat up the smaller packs. So we ended up always using the larger 3 AH packs as they work with all the tools and require less charging. It also simplifies your inventory. There's a slight difference in the attachment shape of their 18v Lithium batteries vs the older

18v NiCads, but if you have some of those you can this widget for getting your old 18v tools to work with the new Lithium batteries.

-- Alexander Rose

Cheap portable power saws
Ryobi Cordless Saws

$120 (reconditioned) ryobitools.com

Cordless power tools are obviously the way to go. I have a drill but what I really wanted was a portable cordless circular saw and sawzall. All instant cutting, no cords.

After eyeing the pro tool sections for years, I've finally got my wish with an inexpensive set of cordless tools from Ryobi. For $150 I got an 18 volt system with a cordless circular saw, a cordless reciprocating saw, a cordless drill/driver and two batteries. (A lamp is thrown in, too.) The driver is standard but the saws are a treat. I grab a cordless saw and charge out to the backyard, or garage without having to unwind a trailing extension cord. Zip, zap. Then back in their box. Neither tool is super powerful or industrial strength. Just zippy enough for weekend projects (nothing thicker than a 2 x 4), but cheap! Fine with me since I don't use them every day.

The battery charge lasted beyond my usual chores of cutting up plywood, rebar or pipe, and so on. I have not pushed them to their limits yet. I have an issue with the buttons on the reciprocating sawzall, but otherwise each tool is easy to handle. They yield astounding quality for the price.

The handiness of a cordless power saw, like all great tools, urges me to take on stuff I would otherwise not do.

-- KK

Light-duty arc welder
Lincoln Stick Welder

$400 Lincoln AC 225 stick welder K1170

I recommend the Lincoln for arc welding for one simple reason: It always works. I've used this welder for farm equipment repair and fabrication for more than 35 years with absolutely no problems. It's ideal for any light-duty work and just right for a weekend welder.

Its range is 40 to 225 amps, and for 85% of my work, I use it at 90 amps; there's plenty of range available. It's not cheap, but you'll likely end up disappointed in anything less. Wire feeds in this price range are almost useless. It does require 220 volt power, but welders that will operate on 110 power are generally a disappointment. You won't regret buying this one and your grandchildren won't wear it out.

-- Keith Carpenter

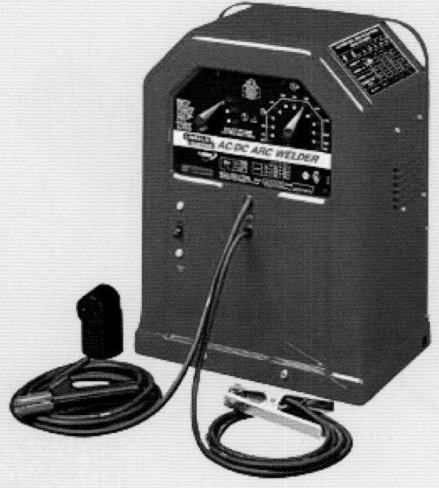

Super-fast material removal
Max Pedestal Disc Sander

$4,750 Factory New

Any serious shop should have a big stationary disc sander. All special-effects shops I know have one. Mine is a Max 16" diameter, three-phase, 220-volt pedestal stand disc sander. I've had a succession of little disc sanders and drum sanders from all the different manufacturers, but they don't compare. This is more than a sander; it's a cutter and shaper, too.

You can remove such fine degrees of material with great precision, and so fast, that it's almost like cutting. You can't do this on your belt sander. I have an electronic three-phase converter on mine, so I can't run it for more than 15 minutes, but I've never ever run it for a total of 15 minutes because it does everything I need it to do in about 30 seconds. You can do huge amounts of rapid shaping with it. Often, I'll cut something rough to an eight of an inch from the line on the band saw, and then do all of the finishing on this one. The sanding discs are attached with stickum. It's pretty much always one grit — 80 grit. These generally run in the several thousands of dollars; however, I picked this one up on Craigslist for $600. That's about as good a deal as you would find on one. I love this thing.

-- Adam Savage

Portable precise cutting
Port-a-Band

$320 Milwaukee 6232-6 6 Amp Portable Band Saw

I love portable band saws. Many tools that cut metal are super noisy and polluting. If you're cutting metal with a cutting wheel it will spray hot metal; it shrieks. The great thing about the Milwaukee Port-a-Band is that it cuts almost silently. There's no shaking. Zero. I can get my hands up really close to the cut; I can be precise. In fact, one of my favorite things to do with the Port-a-Band is to cut almost all the way through a piece, but not quite, so that the piece doesn't fall on the floor when done. I can be that precise. One of the things these tools are great for is in situ or ariel cutting where you've gotta cut a piece of rebar that's way up on a crane or somewhere precarious. This will cut through rebar all day, without shattering or shaking. Blade replacement is trivial. It's expensive though, and the batteries themselves are about $100. Still, I like these cordless portable band saws so much I bought the little baby portaband version that Dewalt makes. I recommend the baby version for most folks — the cutting throat is obviously more minimal, but you get that precise shake-free silent cutting.

-- Adam Savage

Reciprocating Blade for Tight Spaces
Multi-Master Tool

$200 Fein FMM 250Q START Bag In Box feinus.com

I'm in the process of restoring an old lapstrake wooden boat. The MultiMaster with a saw blade was the perfect tool for cutting out a section of a board. The boards overlap each other, and the travel of the blade of a jigsaw or reciprocal saw was too great to target the piece of the board that overlaps another board. Even doing it with a handsaw was too difficult to control on this tough wood.

The MulitMaster tool is just a vibrating head. So it vibrates this little sawblade and it cuts right through with great accuracy. The blade itself has very little travel, making it perfect for this application. I shoved a thin piece of sheet metal between the overlap of the planks to keep from sawing into the other board, and I was able to cut exactly where I wanted to. I know of no other tool that I could do that with, though I'd love to hear of any alternatives.

-- Monty Zukowski

I wouldn't have seen it if I hadn't believed it. - Marshall McLuhan

Adaptive woodworking system
EurekaZone Power Bench System
$1250 prebuilt, DIY available EurekaZone

Eight months ago I started searching for a small quality table saw for my personal shop. Spoiled by being raised around an Altendorf sliding table saw, I dreaded having to compromise with an undersized contractors saw. A commenter on Cool Tools led me to the EZ-One Power Bench. After using EZ tools for 8 months I don't know how I ever lived without. They're brilliant.

The EZ-One Power Bench makes repeatable, straight, clean cuts better and more safely than a table saw. For most woodworkers, including myself, it can inexpensively replace a table saw, panel saw, miter saw, joiner, and router table.

This system has so many advantages over the traditional power tools I grew up with: the ability to get clean cuts with cheap blades, excellent dust collection, increased safety from accidents, pinching, and kickback, and all using any circular saw or router. The system requires far less space and can be adapted to work in more ways than I can imagine.

The EurakaZone (EZ) system is remarkably affordable. One can get started with a basic track for around $150 and use any circular saw you have around to make clean straight cuts. One isn't penalized for starting with a smaller system. EZ sells parts individually for everything they make. You can build up as needed - everything works together - and there's plenty of help and DIY ideas on the forums to make your own customizations.

In my own experience with the EurekaZone tools, it's hard to find words. I love these things. I sincerely believe it's an extraordinary leap forward for woodworking. It's like an alien from The Planet of Common Sense came and showed us all what power woodworking tools should be. And the logic truly is alien at first.

It was difficult to get my head around after being raised with traditional tools. (The Core77 video helped immensely, but I am still learning).

In fact, the one downside to the EurekaZone system is the time and attention it takes to learn the new paradigm; wood is always safely clamped in place, expensive blades aren't needed for clean cuts, crosscut before ripping, and more. So far I feel

challenged by the tool and smarter for using it. Whenever I think I found a limitation, I discover a smarter way.

If you relish using a great jig, or programmed a computer to find a better, more efficient way of working, then you'll love the EurekaZone system.

-- Steve Lambert

- Bench Ends Kit
- Frame Kit
- Top Kit
- Bridge
- Tool Track
- Beam Kit
- Leg Kit
- Stop Kit
- Squaring Rod Kit

eurekazone.com

EZ SMART
a system by eurekazone inc.™

Wood dowel joinery system
Dowelmax
$310 Dowelmax

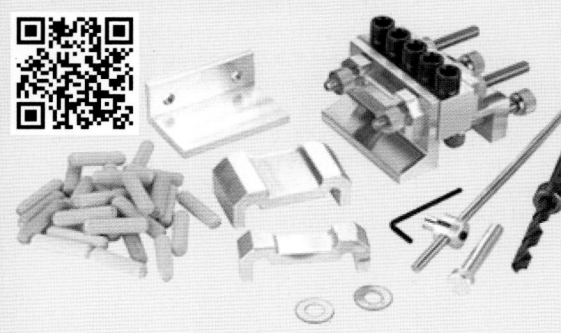

The Dowelmax is a tool that allows you to make incredibly strong wood joints quickly and accurately. I've been using the Dowelmax for about 3 years now and find new ways of using it most times it comes out of the case.

The joy of this tool is its simplicity. It is fabricated with such accuracy that it allows even beginners to create the strongest of joints in furniture making. Doweling is far superior to biscuit joining allowing almost total dry-fitting of a project before gluing, greater accuracy of surface matching, and a joint that is stronger than even a mortise and tenon in a fraction of the time. As the vast majority of connections a woodworker makes are invisible, this tool saves an immense amount of time over traditional joinery techniques and results in a joint as strong or stronger than any of them.

The tool is adjustable to suit any thickness of wood and, using the included spacers and register pins,

one can dowel any length of board with pin point accuracy. The tool can be taken apart and re-assembled in different geometries for various kinds of joints and you can also, as I often do, build your own jigs to use the Dowelmax in ways that probably were not intended.

This is a tool you'll quickly learn to love. I make my living as a woodworker and I don't own another tool that gives me greater satisfaction to use. At about $300 for the kit one might think its only for the professional however I've had friends using it after only a ten minute lesson who were putting together joints as well as they can be made! Check out the website which shows quite clearly what it can do.

-- Colin Farrell

Simple & strong wood joints
Kreg Pocket Hole Jig
$100 Kreg Tool

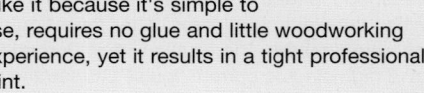

I've used the Kreg pocket hole jig to repair a broken chair, build shelving, and customize framing around a media box. I like it because it's simple to use, requires no glue and little woodworking experience, yet it results in a tight professional joint.

I also bought the right-angle clamp (basically a Vise grip with a pocket hole clamp end, model KHC-RAC), and it works very well. It helps keep boards straight and steady when making a 90-degree joint, and therefore made this unit superior to a more-portable plastic jig I had previously used. The best thing about the Kreg jig is it's simple, doesn't require a lot of space, and all you need is a drill to make it work.

-- Joesph Mayerik

Assembly-line style woodworking
Festool Domino Joiner
$825 Festool USA

Never before has a woodworker been able to make loose tenon joinery simply, quickly, accurately and anywhere. Loose tenon work is a process that has long been done by hand and/or large expensive stationary machines. With the Domino, you can now bring the tool to the wood. Anywhere. No back and forth to the shop, which can take hours. The Domino has locator pins in the face for precise alignment, meaning you can actually build something and test fit it together with no glue; the tolerances are that tight and perfect. The Domino really has the ability to turn a neophyte weekend bookcase maker into a pro -- I am a professional trim carpenter and in my line of work that's scary! Here's why it work's so well: the cutter is an oscillating carbide plunge bit similar to a router bit and it's interchangeable. It takes 5 seconds to set up for plunge and 2 seconds to do the deed. The time savings can be counted in days if not weeks on a big project. I used to scoff at overpriced stuff like this. Silly me. It's well made and, in the short and long run, it really increases productivity, which both saves and makes me money.

It's expensive, but I'd still recommend getting the set, as opposed to just the Domino itself. The set comes with two attachments that are a must for two different applications. One is for end joining, as you do with a face frame (the front of cabinets, which are made out of 1x2 or slightly larger stock). This attachment allows you to fit the narrow piece of wood perfectly on the end and it prevents wobbling (without it, the mortise would not be straight and at 90 degrees). The

attachment also adjusts to take a 2 ¾ inch wide board, mean-

ing you can mortise anything from an inch wide up to 2 ¾ inch. If you are making face frames you have a lot to do, but with this attachment, once you set to your size lumber, there is no more thinking. The other attachment allows you to align dominos that are farther apart than the factory pins. The factory pins allow mortises spaced about a 1 1/2"; apart. With this attachment, you can space them anywhere from 4 1/8"; to 8 3/8"; and the pins hook into the last hole/mortise made, so all your holes are evenly spaced and line up exactly. No marks or measuring.

-- Per Swenson

Saws

Safest saw
Sawstop Table Saw

$1800 sawstop.com

You've probably heard about the Sawstop table saw -- the one that instantly brakes itself to prevent its spinning blade from cutting flesh. I bought one last month, and finally got it all set up. It saws like a charm! I couldn't be happier with its performance. In particular, dust collection is very good, the hand cranks are a dream (smooth and repeatable), and ripping or cross cutting a 2x6 board had no discernable reduction in RPM. The cuts were smoother than what I get from my surface planer, and that was with the stock blade that came with the saw. I've used a number of other table saws, and the Sawstop was relatively easy to make all the adjustments, and is very repeatable.

As for the safety features, I haven't put the brake to the test. Like the air bag in your car, the Sawstop system includes an extensive startup and continuous self test while idle and running. And like your air bag it's very costly to "test." You get only one emergency stop per blade and brake. Besides $70 for a new brake, it's another $50-100 for a new blade. It's pretty high tech. The brake is a special aluminum block and electronic assembly with a fusible (i.e. burnable) wire holding the spring loaded brake block assembly in position. When the electronics "fires" after detecting contact with human flesh, the fusible wire is burned through by a high electric current "pulse". When the wire burns through, the spring loaded aluminum block is shoved into the spinning blade. The blade cuts deeply into the block, and the block absorbs the considerable momentum energy of the blade, arbor, belt and motor. The result is that the blade and block get hot enough near the teeth of the blade to unsolder or weaken the teeth on the blade. In short the blade is ruined 50% of the time according to one web site I found that had tested the unit. Once the emergency brake

has been fired you need to replace the whole brake assembly (like the air bag), which includes the brake, spring, retaining fusible wire, firing electronics including capacitor, and brake frame assembly. Replacement only takes a couple of minutes. Despite the cost, it is still better than paying for a new finger. Two friends have lost 2.5 fingers collectively from table saws. And both were experienced woodworkers.

The Sawstop has other safety features, too. The riving knife and blade guard are both first rate, much better than others I've used (the guard is small, low profile, and narrow, making narrow rips easier with the guard in place). Both are very easy to swap in and out. Lastly, the start/stop switch is a large paddle, perfectly placed for shutting off with a twist of the knee while you hold that thin strip tight against the fence, to prevent the smooth cut from being ruined while you fumble for the off button. So, so far, it is great.

I've never had a close call on a saw yet, but as I age, I know the extra insurance of having the Sawstop system might save a finger or two.

-- Ben Bishop

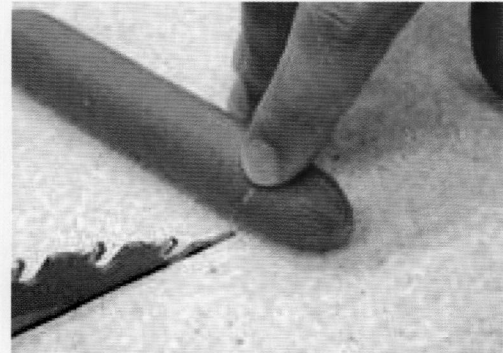
A hot dog proxy for a finger gets only a nick when pushed into a turning saw blade

---

Precision cutting tools
Proxxon Mini Saws

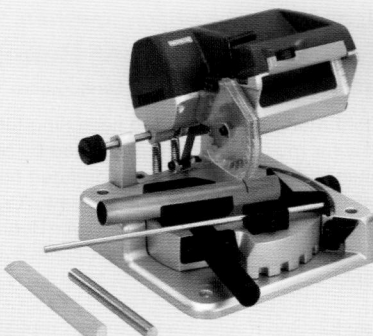

For my work building models and automata, I own two Proxxon miniature power tools, and they are both amazing. Not amazing for their size; just plain amazing.

The Proxxon Miter Saw (table area 9" x 9"; weight 12 lb) has been a valuable addition to my tool collection, and it would also be ideal for anyone who has limited space in his/her work area. The saw has a really clever integrated clamp to hold the material and ensure that each cut stays on the mark. There's also a built-in stop that helps me when I want to cut a bunch of pieces to the same length. Nice.

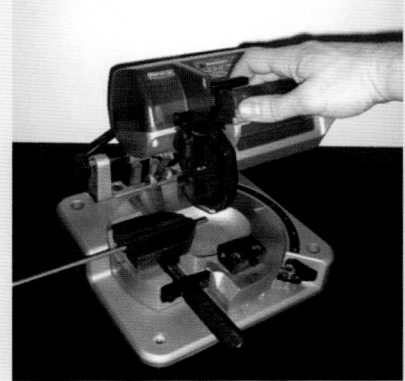

Micro-Mark sells a lesser miter saw that is slightly cheaper ($140), but it only takes cut-off wheels, not blades, so its range of functionality isn't as broad as the Proxxon's. The Micro-Mark allows for angled cuts, but doesn't have the 15-degree latching detents of the Proxxon.

A full-size miter saw is a powerful machine. A small, loose cut-off piece can get swept up by the blade into the blade guard housing. I know; it happened to me. This can be both costly and dangerous. It's not an experience I ever want to repeat. The Proxxon is more appropriately scaled for cutting small pieces, so this is less likely to happen. Compared to free-hand cutting with a cut-off wheel mounted in a

Dremel tool, the Proxxon is safer and produces cleaner, more accurate cuts.

These miniaturized tools are clearly not toys. The Mini Table Saw (overall size 11 13/16" x 10 5/16" x 6 43/64" w/o extension wing; weight 11.5 lb) can make a clean cut in 3/4" hardwood, and it's barely bigger than a toaster. Cutting small very parts on a full-size table saw requires that you spend a good deal of time constructing jigs and zero-clearance inserts in order to make the cuts safely. Unlike another miniature table saw I own, there a ton of useful accessories available for the Proxxon -- some that are simply not available for full-size machines.

The Proxxon's variable-speed control also sets this saw apart from lesser miniature tables saws, allowing me to adjust the speed depending on the blade in use and the material being cut. This can make the difference between clean, smooth cuts and ruined materials.

The truly handy thing about owning the miter saw and the table saw is that they use the same blades, and a surprisingly wide variety at that. I can get blades for slitting, cutting wood and cutting metals, and they're all interchangeable between the two tools. Consider, for example, the diamond-coated blade, which allows me to cut things as hard as tile and stone. I've found the miter saw mounted with an abrasive blade for non-ferrous metals to be a great way to cut brass rod and bars to length.

-- Dug North

$200 37160 KGS 80 MICRO Chop Saw amazon.com

$360 Proxxon 37070 FET Table Saw amazon.com
proxxon.com/us

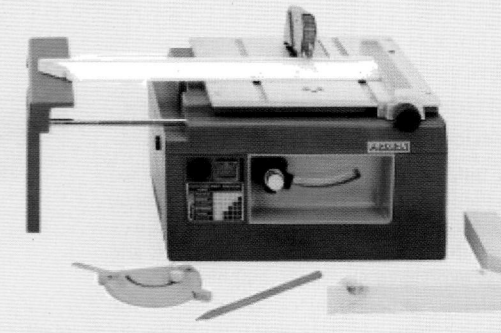

Table saw replacement
Festool Plunge Cut Circular Saw

$550 Festool

I am a fine woodworker and in 2004 I bought a several-thousand-dollar table saw. In 2005, I bought this Festool plunge cut circular saw that runs along a rail instead of being stationary like a table saw. While the Festool doesn't replace my table saw, if I were a home hobbyist or a contractor considering a table saw I think the Festool would be a cheaper and far better substitute.

Though it is on rails, it is fearsomely and effortlessly accurate. I can always get within 1/32" of where I want to be, and the cut is always square. Really square. It fits in a small box and weighs just a few pounds which makes it easy to transport to and from

job sites. It has great electronics, and a riving knife. It is way safer than a table saw, especially for less experienced users. It really shines in cutting down sheet goods. Dead accurate, no tearout. If you want to rip cut lots of lumber it's not the right tool. But every once in a while it can pull that off, too.

This Festool saw is part of a larger system that includes a dust catchment system, expandable rails, and other accessories. As such, it can get expensive, but you only have to buy what you need. I don't always think much of Festool stuff- it is generally way overpriced for what it does. This tool, though, for 5 or 600 bucks can easily replace a table saw of twice the cost. Other circular-saw-on-a-guide-rail setups are not in the same class. The Festool is about the details. If I were contemplating a really low-end contractors table saw, the Festool would still be my choice.

-- Graham Entwistle

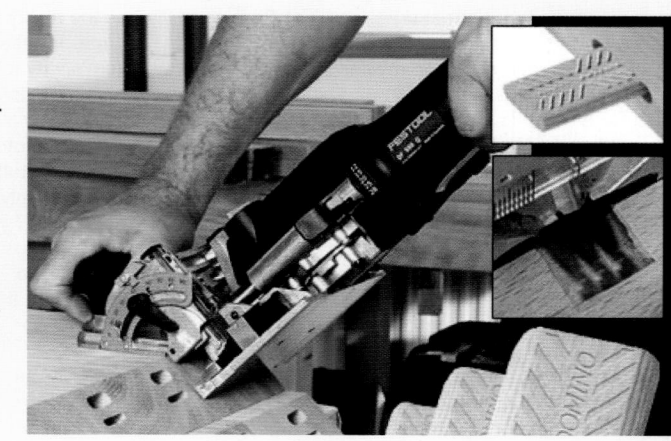

The silly question is the first intimation of some totally new development. - Alfred North Whitehead

Fine Japanese hand tools
The Japan Woodworker

japanwoodworker.com
Or visit the store in Alameda, California

Traditional Japanese tools are not as esoteric as they once were. In part because for 35 years this venerable importer has been publicizing their virtues. Fine cabinet makers in particular have found Japanese-style saws, chisels, and wood shapers to be superior in many ways. But you don't need to be a cabinet maker to appreciate the tools featured in this catalog. I've bought some very reasonably-priced Japanese kitchen knives that we've maintained with razor edges for many years.

-- KK

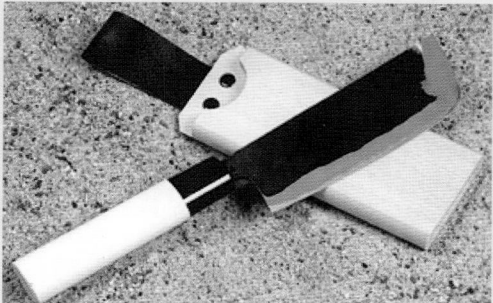

Price: $48.75

Our Harvesting Knife is a hand forged lamination of high carbon steel and wrought iron material, hand tempered to Rc 62-63. It is used by farmers and gardeners for hand harvesting such items as cabbage, lettuce, etc. and comes razor sharp in a wooden scabbard with belt loop. Blade length is 5 1/2" and overall length is 10 1/2".</p>

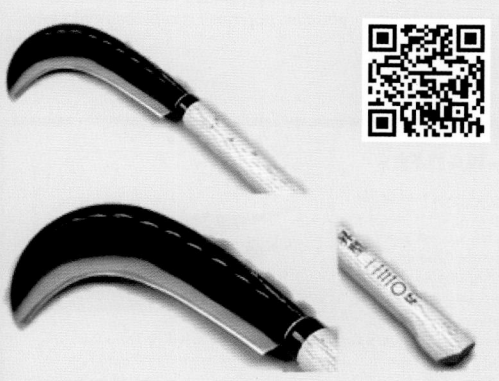

Price: $49.75

Our Brush Hook Nobori Kama is great for removal of brush that is too heavy for a weed cutter and too light for an axe. Swung like an axe, the brush hook's long 14 inch hardwood handle and heavy, hand forged laminated high carbon steel head give it a powerful cut. Cut with a slicing rather than a hacking motion and pull back on the handle at the end of the swing to utilize the 9 inch curved blade. This is a sharp tool and you should always maintain a firm grip on the handle. Comes razor sharp with a sheath for the blade.

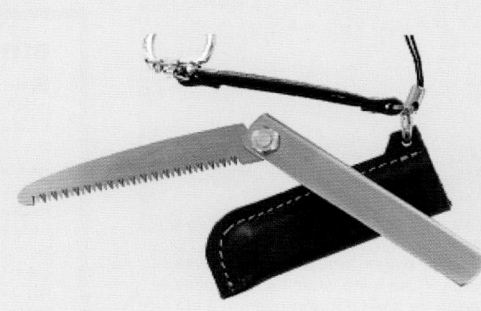

Price: $17.75

Our 2 1/2" folding Trail Saw with its 18 teeth per inch triple facet tooth configuration can quickly and easily cut through branches up to 1 1/2" diameter. It weighs only 0.8 oz and is the perfect addition to your ultra-light gear or pocket survival kit. Wood carvers will enjoy its ability to reach into very small areas. It comes with sturdy leather sheath and detachable key chain. Open length is 5" and folded length is 2 3/4".

Saw different
Japanese Woodworking Saws

$18-$49 leevalley.com amazon.com

I've been hanging out with serious craftsmen/carpenters and virtuoso builders in Canada and ended up buying 4 different Japanese saws they were using. At top is a gem of a keyhole saw. You'll never use an American keyhole saw again. Next down is a springy, elegant razor-toothed saw for flush cuts. Next is the traditional Ryoba, with two different types of teeth. It's the main saw of seasoned Vancouver Island builder Bruce Atkey, what he uses in place of an American saw. It's a joy to use. The last one, the Silky with the black handle, is the gardening saw I should have had 40 years ago. It cuts green (and dead) branches with amazing dispatch. Silky has a great catalog of gardening saws. These tools have got me fiddling around in my shop (and garden) a lot more these days.

-- Lloyd Kahn

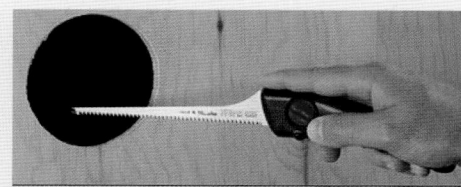

Japanese Keyhole Saw 60T08.01
$32 leevalley.com

Japanese Flush-Cutting Saw 60T19.01
$34 leevalley.com

Traditional Ryoba 60T01.01
$52 leevalley.com

Silky Folding Pruning Multi-Purpose Hand Saw GOMBOY 240 Large Teeth
$49 Amazon

Japanese Hand Saws
Kugihiki Flush-Cutting Saw

$27-$45 woodcraft.com amazon.com

The Japanese Kugihiki flush cutting saw saves me time, makes a cleaner cut, and needs no setup time. Since the teeth have no set, you can slide the saw against a surface without marring it.

These and other Japanese hand saws such as Dozuki and Ryoba have caused me to abandon power tools for many jobs. The cut almost never needs cleaning up and is good for many materials. The Ryoba looks intimidating but can replace a cheap circular saw any day for a lot less money.

-- Alan

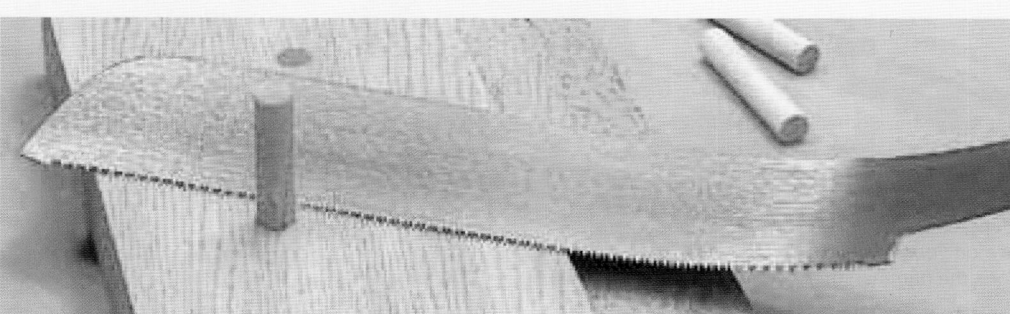

Kugihiki Flush-Cutting Saw
$32 woodcraft.com

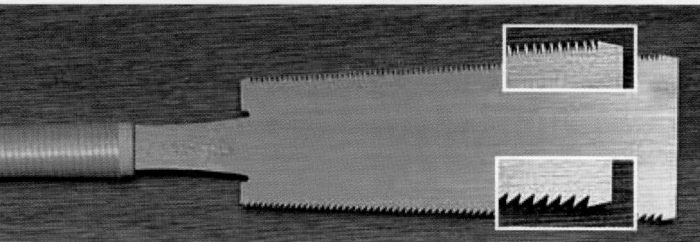

Takumi Ryoba 8-1/4" Super Fine Cut Double Blade Saw
$60 Amazon

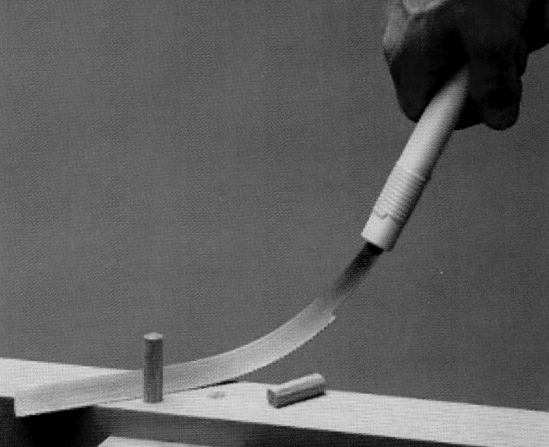

Shark Corp 10-2610 Takumi Dozuki 9" Super Fine Cut Saw
$54 Amazon

Hand tool reviews
Woodworker's Hand Tools

$50 (used) Rick Peters, 2001, 192 p.

This guide by Rick Peters is an exceptionally fantastic review of great hand tools, particularly those for working with wood. Here I discovered cool hand tools I didn't know about (after all these years!), and I learned a lot of useful tricks for tools I did know about. Peters aims his advice at just the right level of intelligence and detail, telling you exactly what is most useful, and nothing more.

This is smartly illustrated book is really a bunch of cool reviews of woodworking hand tools.

-- KK

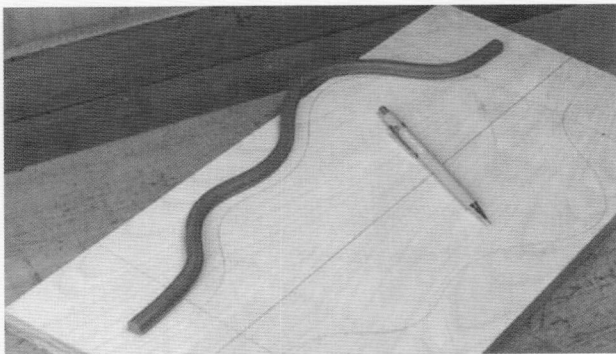

A flexible curve is basically a lead rod that's covered with a vinyl sheath. This clever lay-out tool can be bent into small, graceful curves and is especially useful for reproducing a curve from an existing part, such as pressing it around a cabriole leg that you want to reproduce. Flexible curves can be found in most woodworking catalogs and at most any art store.

For large saws (like a crosscut or rip saw), the easiest way to protect the teeth is to cover them with a short length of garden hose. You can buy this by the foot at most home centers. Make a slit the full length of the hose with a utility knife, and slip it over the teeth. You may need to temporarily attach the hose to the saw blade with duct tape until the hose straightens out.

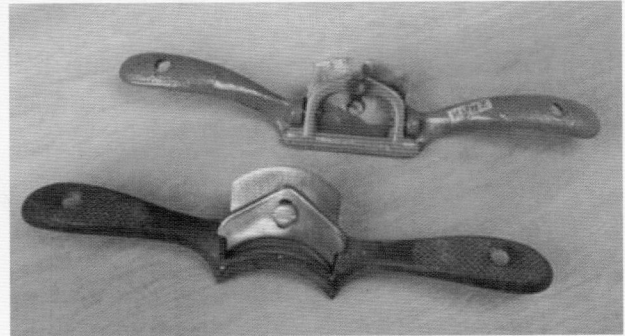

Originally designed to shape spokes for wagon wheels, spokeshaves still find a home in many shops today. I use mine when I shape cabriole legs, add a chamfer to a curved edge, or need a round-over on a curved part. In use, a firm grip is essential, and the tool may be either pushed or pulled. I generally prefer to pull because this gives better control.

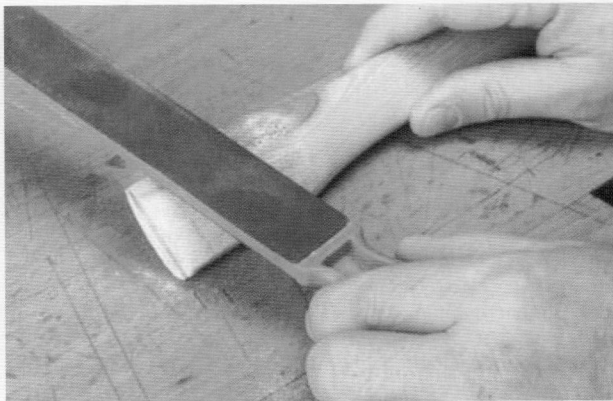

Sandvik files (and other abrasive tools, like their sanding block), are all faced with a special steel plate that has a series of holes punched in the surface to replicate a variety of abrasive grits. What makes this work is that the holes are punched in the metal with great accuracy. And unlike sandpaper, which wears quickly, the sanding plates last considerably longer. When they do wear out, you can purchase a replacement plate.

BLIND-NAILERS

Occasionally, you may need to nail a part in place where the head absolutely cannot show. You could set the brad and apply putty, but this is still visible. To do the job without leaving a trace, consider blind-nailing. With this technique, a tiny sliver of wood is peeled up from the surface to create a hiding place for the nail. The nail is driven in, the sliver is glued back down, and the nail disappears. The sliver can be peeled back with the corner of a chisel, or with a blind-nailer—sort of a tiny plane with a protruding blade (*photo above right*).

Hammerless hammering
Combination Nail Set

$9 springtools.com

I've had the same one for almost ten years. Sometimes called the "two-bit snapper" it's a very simple and clever spring-based hammer that you use instead of the nail set-hammer combo normally used to pound in finishing nails. It's excellent when you need to put up molding in tight spots and corners. Its compact size means that it can always live on your tool belt. You just pull back one end and the spring does the hammering for you.

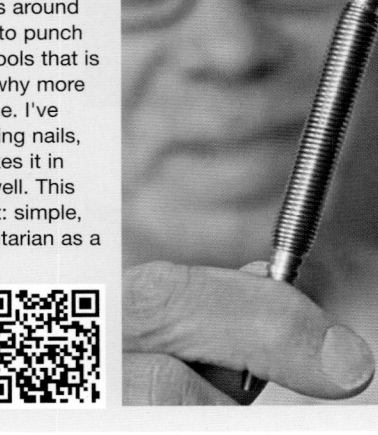

It seems to be a lot more accurate than a center punch-hammer combo, since one hand holds the tool and nail together, while the other pulls back to snap the spring; you get fewer errant holes around the nail you're trying to punch in. It's one of those tools that is so simple, I wonder why more people don't have one. I've only used it for finishing nails, but Spring Tools makes it in other variations, as well. This tool is just so elegant: simple, functional and as utilitarian as a bicycle.

-- Erik Knutzen

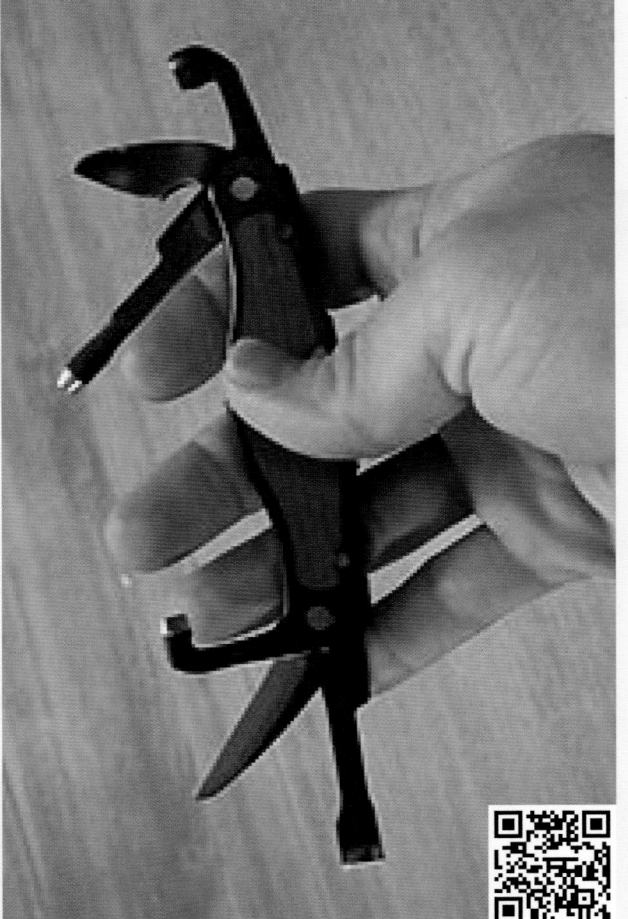

Wood carver's multitool
Flexcut Carvin' Jack

$112 Flexcut

My favorite avocation is carving, and I've built up a modest collection of tools to turn wood blocks into sculpture. The Carvin' Jack adds some new tools to my collection. In total the Carvin' Jack includes six blades. The gouge-scorp and the V-scorp both allow me to gouge or part using a whittling grip and motion. For some work this provides more control. The hook knife can be used to remove a lot of wood quickly or to carve wide shallow hollows.

The other three Carvin' Jack tools are a standard whittling knife, a straight gouge and a chisel. Of these I use the whittling knife most often.

The Carvin' Jack is much more portable than my chisels and Power Grip tools. The Carvin' Jack is also surprisingly light. This was a little disappointing at first but I grew to appreciate this feature.

I'm not aware of another tool like the Carvin' Jack. I have other multitools, but nothing designed specifically for carving.

-- Scott Duke-Sylvester

Precise pilot holes
Gimlet Set

$16

I'm giving gimlet sets to a few lucky in-laws this year. I've found them to be a great time saver whenever I need a hole drilled and precise placement is critical. A few twists and a lovely pilot hole is exactly where you need it.

-- Paul Steger

garrettwade.com

leevalley.com

Superior benefits of wood
Reverence for Wood
$9 Eric Sloane, 1965, 112 pages

Wood was the plastic of the previous era. Better than plastic today it could be found for free, and re-grew itself. This thin beautiful book is a quick orientation to the merits and features of wood. It begins with trees and ends in tools and materials. Should you appreciate the old-timey ways of working with wood, and how these skills shaped early America, as author and artist Eric Sloane does, his sketches will suggest many ways to use and reconsider wood today.

-- *KK*

Charcoal during the 1800's was used for many things other than making iron. People cleaned their teeth with it. Although the first results may look ghastly, there is actually nothing more beneficial for teeth than charcoal powder. Swallow some of it? Also good; there is nothing better for upset stomach. It even sweetens the breath. If you want to purify water or remove an offensive odor from anything, use charcoal. Sailors used to throw burnt muffins into their water supply when it became stale or smelly; meat packers used to pack their meats in charcoal. Ice was stored in charcoal, gunpowder was made with it; printer's ink, black paint, medicines even highways were made form it. In 1865 someone dreamed up this idea, thinking that since charcoal is the longest lasting of materials, a road made of it would be very durable. Timber was piled along the middle of the road and burned right here; then the charred material was raked out and tamped down.

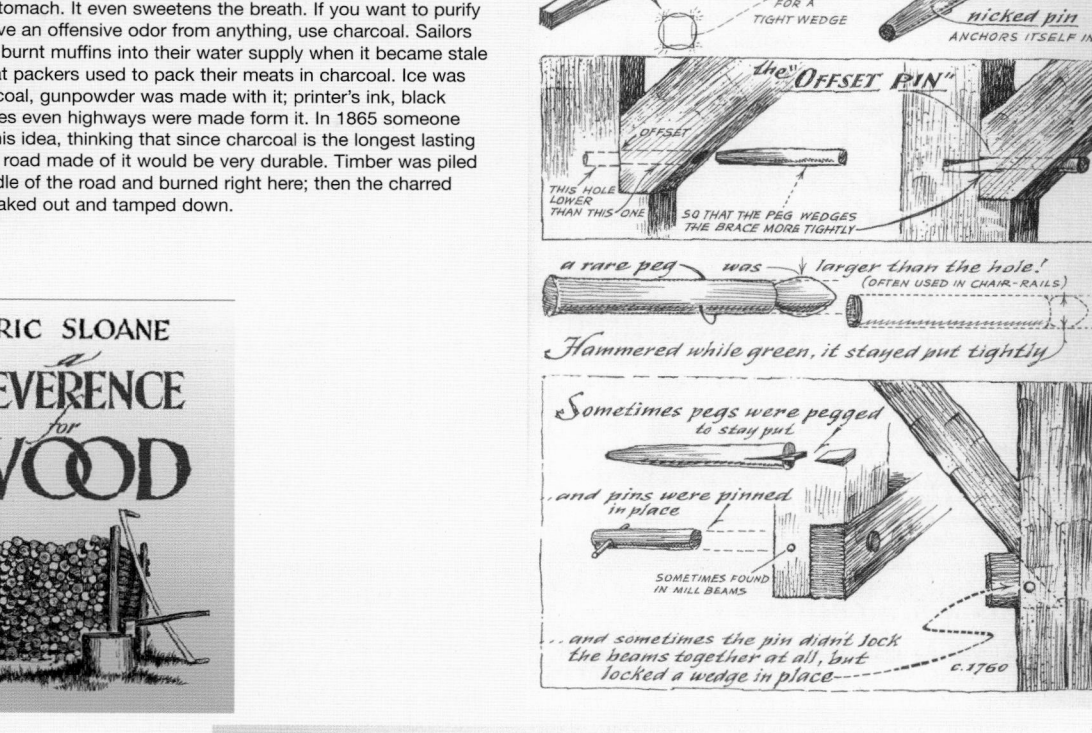

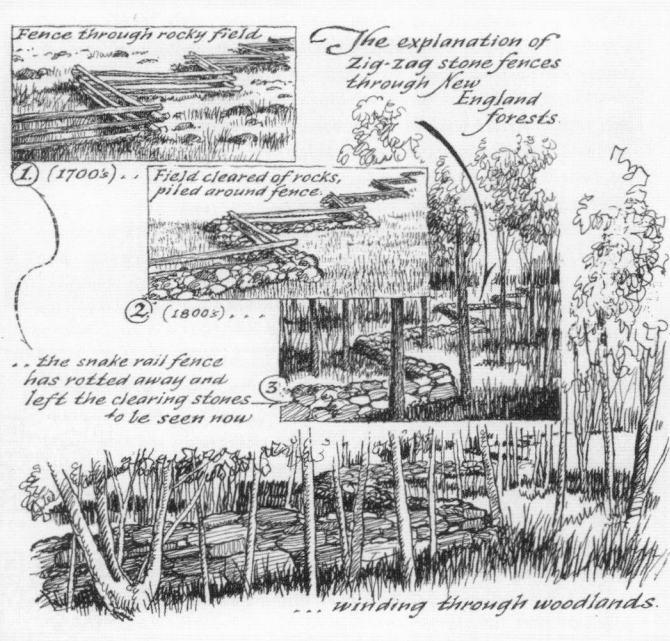

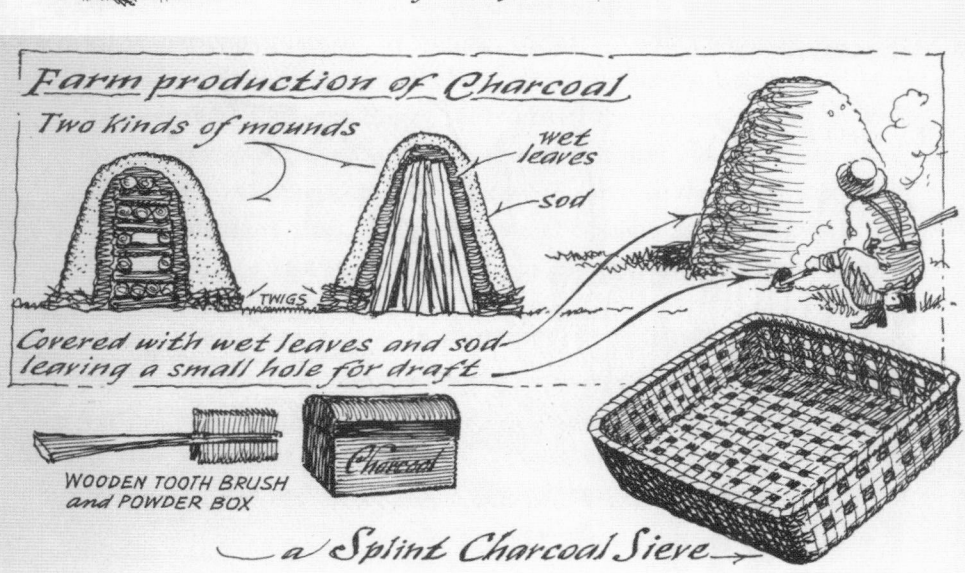

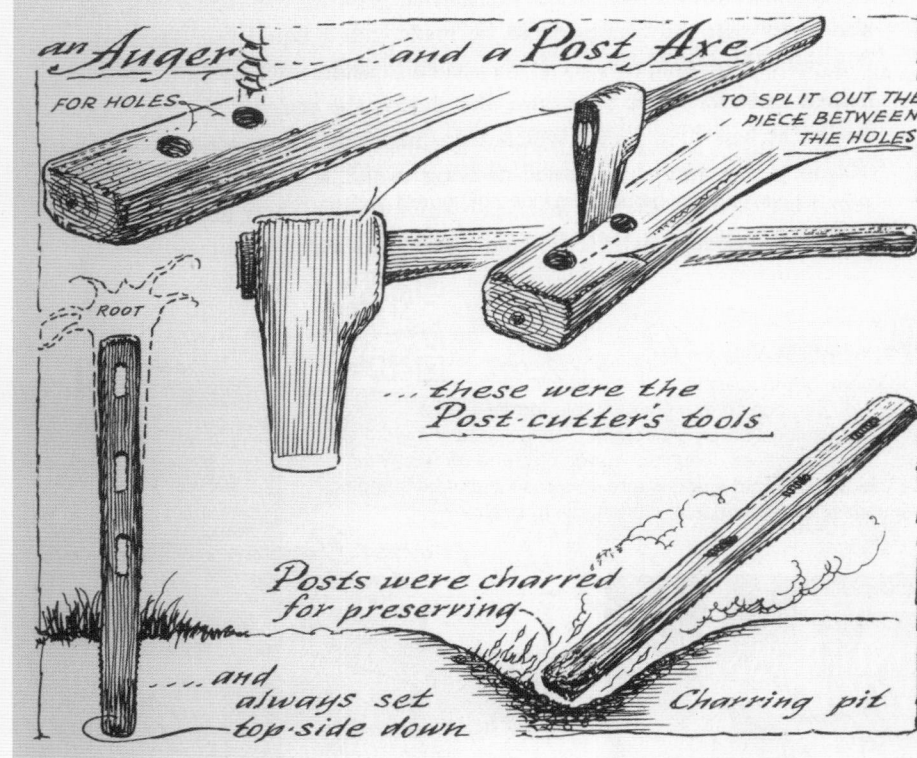

Unusual hand tools
Garrett Wade
garrettwade.com

This is my favorite source for hard to find tools. Garrett Wade has been around since 1975 as a mail order company selling fancy woodworking tools, but in recent years they offer a marvelous selection of hand and speciality tools of all types. They still have the best selection for wood planes and the classic woodworking stuff, but it's their stock of cool and unusual pliers and saws and drill bits and fantastically weird clamps that make it worth a visit. The modern version of the Yankee screwdriver is a Garrett Wade bestseller. In general their prices are on the high side compared to say discounters like Harbor Freight, but quality is usually up a notch as well (and their prices seem better on the web). They produce a paper catalog, which some folks like. Often a great idea begins with the possibilities suggested by the existence of a tool.

-- *KK*

Woodsman's Pal With Leather Handle

Standard US Army issue since 1941. Weighs less than 1-1/2 lbs. If you only work one-handed, this will feel like an extension of your arm.

Very Special Pliers

A modeler's sail rigger tool so unusual, it is really useful for everyone

Imagine having to reach into a very tight space in order to grab something small. Ordinary grippers will be useless, but this unusual tool has its hinge placed way down at the end of a 3" long bent arm. The small mouth opens up 1/4" and will grab whatever you need to retrieve. You'll soon find yourself reaching for it in a variety of situations, and will be mighty glad you have it. Made in India.

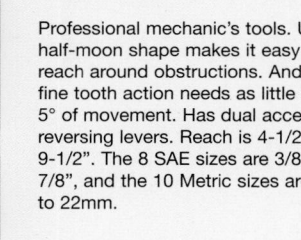

Pro Half-Moon Ratcheting Wrench

Professional mechanic's tools. Unique half-moon shape makes it easy to reach around obstructions. And the fine tooth action needs as little as 5° of movement. Has dual access reversing levers. Reach is 4-1/2 to 9-1/2". The 8 SAE sizes are 3/8" to 7/8", and the 10 Metric sizes are 10 to 22mm.

Heavy Duty Nail Pullers

An old standby - and still great today

This serious tool is a huge time and worksaver, and one you simply don't see around much anymore. When you need it, though, it's absolutely fantastic. It's basically a slide hammer with movable jaws. Position the jaws around the nail head and move the heavy sliding handle down briskly. The jaws dig around the nail head, and you can lever back on the 16" long handle to remove long nails quickly. It's for rough, quick work, so some crushing of the wood around the nail head is inevitable. Weighs 5 lbs.

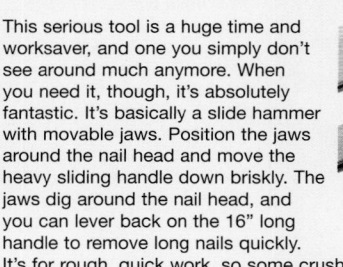

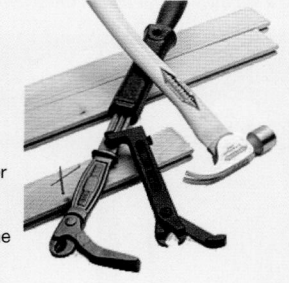

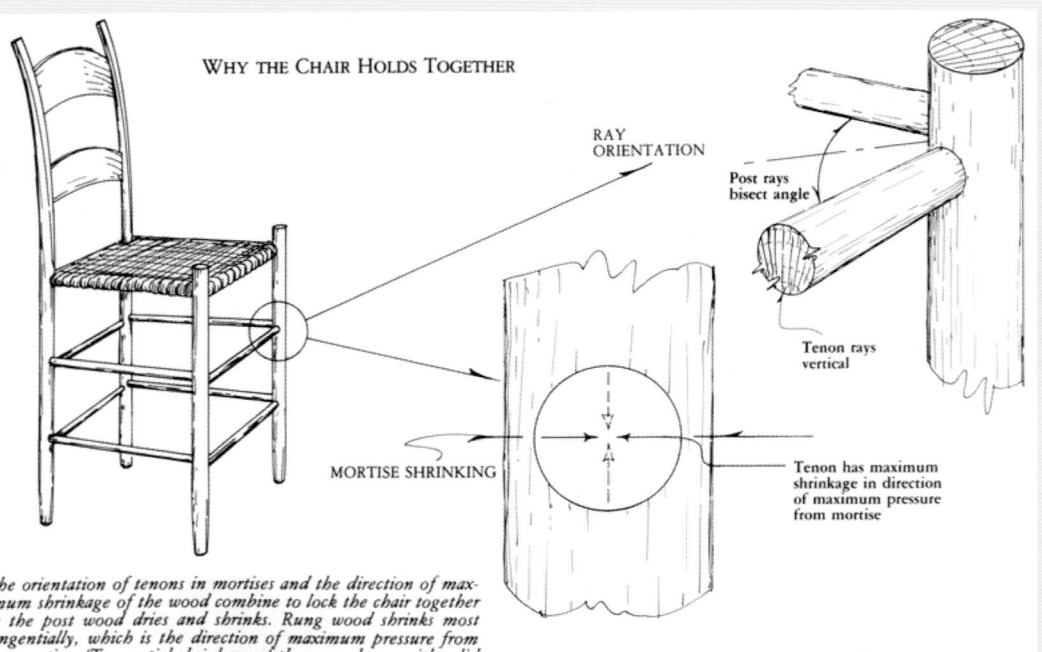

WHY THE CHAIR HOLDS TOGETHER

RAY ORIENTATION

Post rays bisect angle

Tenon rays vertical

MORTISE SHRINKING

Tenon has maximum shrinkage in direction of maximum pressure from mortise

The orientation of tenons in mortises and the direction of maximum shrinkage of the wood combine to lock the chair together as the post wood dries and shrinks. Rung wood shrinks most tangentially, which is the direction of maximum pressure from the mortise. (Tangential shrinkage of the rung shown with solid arrow, radial with dotted.)

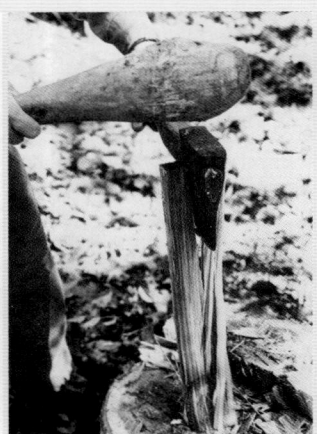

This shaving horse is light enough to be carried into the woods for preliminary shaving right where the tree is felled.

The four stages of shaved rungs: an oversized split; the rung drawknifed square and to size; the corners shaved to an octagon; and the round rung.

Green woodworking
Make a Chair from a Tree

When a tree is felled, its green wood is wet and easy to work with simple hand tools. As the wood dries it becomes hard and difficult. Old timers would shape chair parts from green wood cut from a small tree nearby, assemble them without nails, and as the wood dried it would shrink into a tight, strong, beautiful chair. This lost art was rediscovered by the author of this book, John Alexander. But now the book itself is long out of print, and used copies go for $350.

In the 35 years since the first edition of the book, the author has kept refining his process (while undergoing a gender change; John is now Jennie) and has produced a video of her highly refined process. In many ways the video is even better than the book. Sample excerpts of the video can be seen in the video linked below. Alexander promises a third edition of the book.

If the idea of making a chair from a tree interest you, the Greenwoodworking website is worth checking out.

-- KK

Free video clips and reference
Greenwoodworking

$28 Make a Chair from a Tree DVD
Greenwoodworking

What wood wants
Understanding Wood
$30 Bruce Hoadley, 2000, 280 p.

Wood is one of the most versatile materials known. You can coax it into uncountable forms. However It exhibits extremely complex behavior, as if it were still living. This tome dives deep into woodology, and returns with great insight into what wood wants. It is essential understanding for anyone wishing to master working with wood.

-- KK

Most of the boards in the drying shed at left are restrained by the weight of the others. At right is a similar, simpler setup, where the wood is protected by a sheet of corrugated plastic. In both cases, the boards are stacked in the sequence they came off the saw.

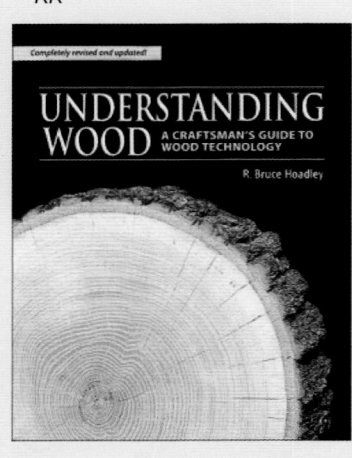

UNDERSTANDING WOOD
A CRAFTSMAN'S GUIDE TO WOOD TECHNOLOGY
R. Bruce Hoadley

A knot is the basal portion of a branch whose structure becomes surrounded by the enlarging stem. Since branches begin with lateral buds, knots can always be traced back to the pith of the main stem.

Stage 1 — Bark
Year of death of branch
Stage 2 — Intergrown knot / Encased knot / Bark
Year branch broke off
Stage 3 — Bark pocket

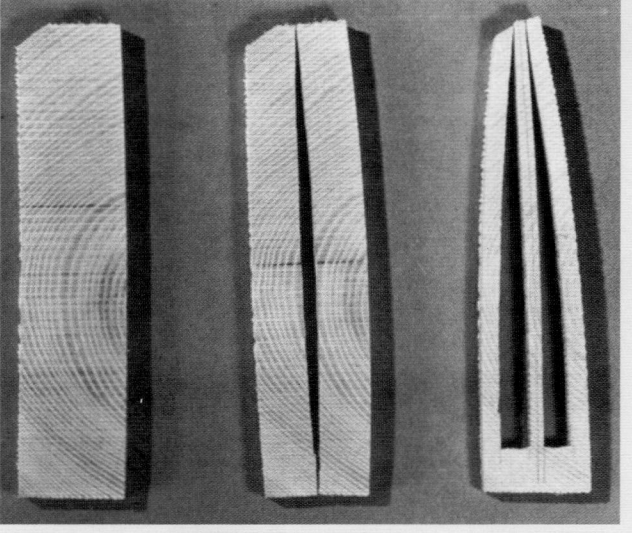

A wafer cut from a kiln-dried plank of white ash shows no symptoms of stress (left). Another section from the same plank, after resawing (center) reveals the casehardened condition (tension in core, compression in shell). Kiln operators cut fork-shaped sections that reveal casehardening when prongs curve inward (right).

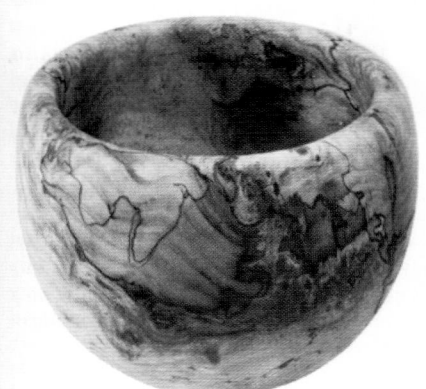

3—As certain white rots develop, dark zone lines form, as on this piece of sugar maple, above. This type of decay is called spalting. Below, turning of spalted maple, by Mark Lindquist.

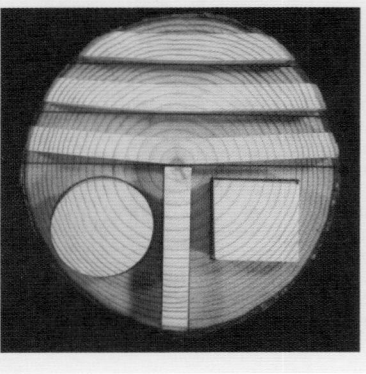

Various shapes of red pine have been dried and superimposed on their original positions on an adjacent log section. The great tangential than radical shrinkage causes squares to become diamond-shaped, cylinders to become oval. Quarter-sawn boards seldom warp, but flat sawn boards cup away from the pith.

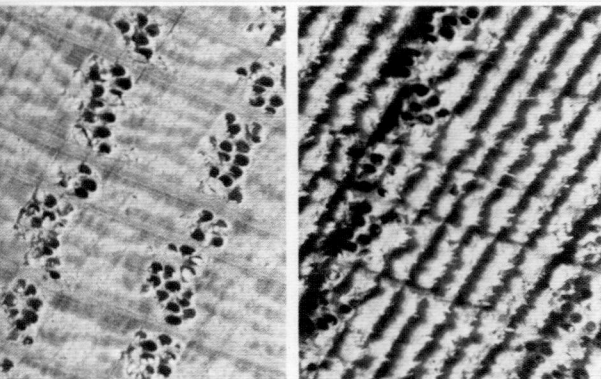

Red oak end grain cut with a ripsaw (right), which mangles the cell structure, and with a crosscut saw (left), which severs the fibers cleanly.

Sandpaper for stone
Diamond Polishing Pads

$45 Amazon

This is sandpaper for stone, ceramic, glass and concrete. The business side of each 4"-diameter pad consists of a polymer honeycomb that looks sort of like the bottom of a sneaker. This "softness" allows it to contour itself to curved surfaces. The elastomer has industrial diamond grit embedded inside. The disc is attached to an electric grinder with an included rubber pad holder covered with black "hook" Velcro on one side and a 5/8-11 threaded brass insert. That's a standard grinder arbor thread. The back of each pad is covered with "loop" Velcro and marked with silver numbers indicating the pad's grit size. The Velcro is also color-coded in case the numerals wear off, which hasn't happened to mine yet. In use, the matrix slowly wears away exposing fresh diamond grit. I used these for jobs that no sandpaper can handle, like polishing a concrete bowl to expose underlying glass aggregate. I could not have done it without these pads.

-- Sean Ragan

Polishing kit
3M Headlight Polishing Kit

$16 3m.com

I originally bought the 3M Headlight Polishing Kit in order to remove the haze on my truck's plastic headlights, but I have since found that it has a plethora of uses. Basically, you use the progressively finer grit sanding surfaces to smooth the plastic and grind away the scratches and finally polish using the 3M rubbing compound. My headlights looked like new and were way more effective after the treatment.

The other day I discovered that the compass for my sailboat was scuffed pretty badly, and I tried using the polishing kit to buff it out (after testing on some safety glasses first). The results blew me away. The compass lens was crystal clear! I've since been polishing anything plastic that I have that's been scratched. Calculators, display screens, etc. You could put this kit together yourself with p500, p800, p3000 grit pads and a foam compounding pad with some 3m rubbing compound but the kit is very convenient and should last a long time as long as you use water with the sanding pads.

-- Jason Tan

Small, multi-functional sanding station
Ridgid Oscillating Belt & Spindle Sander

$200-$330 ridgid.com

The word that best describes the Ridgid oscillating belt sander is "workhorse." It is one of those rare tools which ends up at the heart of your workshop -- fast, precise, durable. The belt rotates like a standard sander, but also simultaneously and automatically oscillates up and down 60 times per minute, giving you better space coverage and a wider stroke (about 1 in.); this is especially helpful with larger pieces, because you don't need to reposition or flip the piece to sand the whole thing.

I use mine almost daily to fabricate parts in wood, metal, and plastic. The metal platen provides plenty of support for serious, precision sanding. I routinely sand to the center of a 1/64 slot on an Incra ruler. Not bad. It's also very quick to swap out the belt and use it as an oscillating spindle sander, meaning you can handle both flat and curved sanding.

It's designed to sit on a bench top, but they also molded slots into the bottom so that it rests stably on a sawhorse. It has an incredibly well made tilt table, with fence, that folds down onto a molded storage bay which holds all the accessories it comes with. And a vacuum port is molded into the back of the unit for clean up.

Two things to know: I find I often have to adjust the belt tension to prevent the belt from rising or falling, but this is easy to do on account of a large, well-placed knob. Also, the belts and spindles it comes with are extremely aggressive and are meant for hogging away wood. If you want to do more delicate work, you need to get higher mesh belts from a specialty store like Rio Grande, Klingspor, or maybe Grainger or McMaster-Carr.

-- Sam Mapadatha

Evolved electric sander
Dewalt Random Orbital Sander

$60 dewalt.com

$15 Mirka 5" 8-hole Assorted Grit Dustless Hook-and-Loop Sanding Disks (50) mirka.com

It's been several decades since I bought a wood sander, but I recently needed a new one for a large finishing job. I was pleasantly surprised by the technological advances now standardly available in inexpen-

sive sanders.

There are three key innovations here: "random" sanding patterns, using sandpaper disks that attach via a velcro-like surface, and a vacuum that works through holes in the paper. Together these three features produce a much superior machine to the simple vibrating sander I had before. Random-orbital sanders spin as circles within circles, leaving little discernible pattern of abrasion on the work. The round hook-and-loop paper is magic. These disks securely attachment and detach in a second, and don't slip. This quickness encourages you to instantly change to the appropriate grit size without hesitation. Lastly, sanding produces massive amounts of dust, and the mini vacuums really decrease the volume of

stuff flying around. The debris is sucked into a small cloth bag that doesn't interfere much with work.

All these features and more are available in higher end machines, but also in cheaper ones as well. I've been using a Dewalt, D26451K which is an entry model at about $55 street price. With a coarse grit paper, its 3-amp motor will eat wood if you need to, but it is light enough to feather touch a fine grit. It takes the standard 8-hole hook-and-loop disk. Many companies make these disks in all possible grades, varieties and types. Although they seem expensive, I found these disks lasted longer than the pieces I used to cut from standard sheets for my old machine. The small dust bag is sufficient for most weekend projects, but

may seem small if you are sanding whole walls; you just have to empty it more often.

None of these features may be new to most woodworkers, but I have not been paying attention; I wish I had got one of these years ago.

-- KK

Super fine sandpaper
Micro-Mesh Abrasives

$19+ micro-surface.com

Micro-Surface makes the finest sandpaper around: Micro-Mesh abrasives. I originally used their sanding pads to get a perfect finish on a plastic model car by sanding each layer of spraypaint I applied to the model. Their finest sandpaper is rated at an incredible 12000 grit. (Although that number isn't using the same ANSI scale as commonly available sandpaper).

I was amazed that I was able to sand a scratched plastic window to perfect clarity, although I shouldn't have been surprised: micro-mesh is used to repair the acrylic windows used on many airplanes. I've since used the same hobby kit for repairing scratches in the clear coat of my REAL car. I've even carefully polished out deep scratches in the bottom of several CDs. You can also polish out scratches on reading glasses.

Micro-Surface makes a wide variety of abrasives, in every size and type I can imagine needing.

-- Mike Gebis

20X Sandpaper 400 grit   *20X Micro-Mesh 1500*

Micro-Mesh is what we like to call a non-abrasive abrasive. It is considered a cushioned abrasive in fact. Conventional sandpaper is designed to be aggressive so that it will dig deeply. In its manufacture the crystals are electrically charged so that they will stand up. They are locked into a hard resin and when you apply the paper to a surface it will literally tear in and remove the substrate of the material you are sanding. The crystals cut in a negative raking motion, leaving inconsistent scratch patterns.

Micro-Mesh does the opposite. The backing is long lasting cloth to which an ultra-flexible cushioning layer is applied. This cushioning layer will determine how far forward you can push crystals before they will penetrate the cushioning layer. On top of this layer, we have a very resilient glue, not a hard resin, but a completely flexible glue that will hold the crystals while allowing it to move and rotate. The crystals can turn in any direction without coming loose. When you start to apply pressure to sand with Micro-Mesh, the crystals will go into the cushioning layer while beginning to cut a bit. When you push harder, they will go further into the cushioning layer, which serves as a safety valve. It determines how much pressure you can exert in a downward direction. Instead of a deep scratch that sandpaper makes, Micro-Mesh produces a refined scratch that is close to a RMS of 1.0. The cushioning layer also allows the crystals to cut with a planing motion that leaves an extremely consistent scratch pattern and allows you to achieve extraordinary levels of gloss.

Everyday Carry

A knife that will get through security
Utili-Key
$9 Amazon

Several nerdy friends of mine who feel naked without their pocket knife have independently discovered that this handy mini-knife disguised as a key will both work in a pinch and — shhhhhh! –pass through airport security checks unnoticed. Here is a way to travel with a knife at the ready. Just bury them with your keys in your bag when you go through the machine!

I've had one, and when I bring my keys I have no trouble getting through security on international and domestic flights. I was surprised to find the other little gizmos incorporated into this miniature thing — particularly the Philips screwdriver — are just as useful. The edge of the knife is only an inch long but it is very sharp. (In theory, this blade is now legal on flights in the US.)

-- KK

Key-ring multi-tool
Swiss Tech Micro-Plus 8-In-1
$7 swisstechtools.com

This 1.6 oz. tool, manufactured by the makers of the Utili-Key, can fit on a key chain or in a coin purse, which is where I keep mine. I most often use it for tightening the tiny screws on my glasses, but the small #1 Phillips and flat, pliers, wire cutter/stripper, sheet shear and rule markings (bonus!) are all unbelievably useful at the frequent odd moments you need the right tool which is anywhere but near (particularly the pliers). I have yet to try to go through airport security with it, but the TSA says pliers/screwdrivers and "tools" less than 7 inches can be carried on.

-- Dale Simpson

Bargain pocket knife
Snap Blade Knife
$2 Amazon

I've gotten more recommendations for various pocket knives as a cool tool than any other tool. Knives are the original tool; everyone has one, and after 100,000 years there's endless variety. They are intensely personal, too. I've seen and tried many of the suggested knives I've received, and I've published a few of the more well-proven ones.

So, after many trials, here is the one I actually carry: it's a dollar plastic box cutter. There is no knife lighter weight, none cheaper, few as sharp, and not very many as quick. I can open it one handed in less than a second from the moment I reach for it. It is as fast as a sheath knife. Keeping its edge a razor is as easy as nicking off the tip. This plastic snap blade is as thin as a pen and so light that I carry in my pants pocket without even knowing it is there; no special holster needed, and it won't wear the pocket out. It's

cheap enough that I hide one in all the clothes I ordinarily wear. I'm not afraid to lose it, and yes, I keep it away from airports.

The cheaper the version of the box cutter the better. You don't want rugged metal ones, like those offered by respectable tool companies; they are bigger, heavier, costlier and no better. What you want is a cheap all-plastic made-in-China throw-away that should cost about a buck. Mine are day-glo orange for easy retrieval if I lay one down.

Other than it being butt-ugly I can't think of why I would want one fancier. I use this one at least 5 times a day, and its quick handiness gives me pleasure each time.

-- KK

Wallet-size multi-tool
Credit Card Survival Tool
$2 Amazon

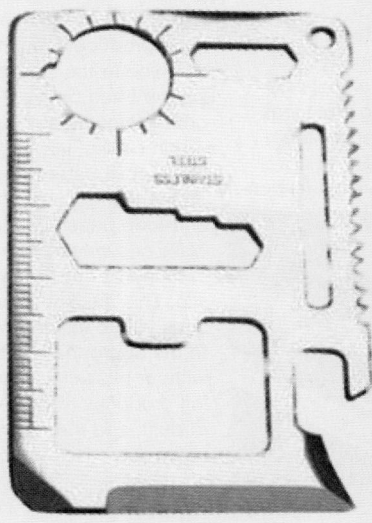

I have two friends who've been carrying these slim, multi-tools for a few years now and swear by them. I've only used the mini-screwdriver and bottle opener, but those functions alone seem worth it. It's stainless steel and will add some weight to your load, but no more than the average metal beverage pop-top. Why junk up your keychain when you can slip another "card" into your wallet? Added bonus: can opener, straight edge, knife edge, et al.

-- Steven Leckart

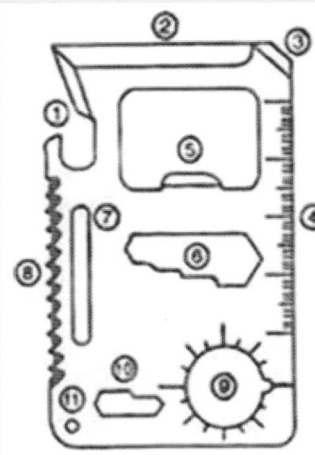

1) Can Opener
2) Knife
3) Screwdriver
4) Ruler
5) Cap Opener
6) 4 Position Wrench
   (For various size nuts & bolt head)
7) Butterfly screw wrench
8) Saw Blade
9) Direction ancillary indication
10) 2 position wrench
11) Lanyard hole (Key chain hole)

Cheap, disposable blades
Derma-Safe Folding Utility Knife
$1.50/each derma-safe.com

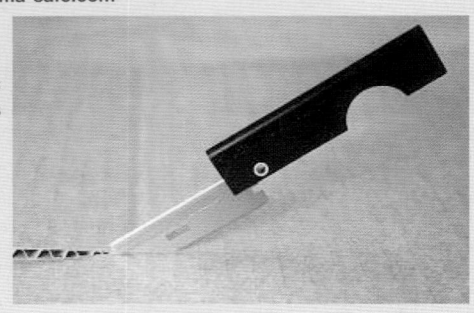

A modern replacement for the classic pen knife, this pocketknife has a thin, 1.5-inch, razor-sharp blade that cuts boxes, cord, tape and tough plastic wrap without effort. Half the charm is its disposability: It costs about as much as a can of soda, so if you get to the airport and have forgotten it's in your pocket, ditching it is trauma-free. I've found the handle grip to be excellent. The slipjoint blade stays in position open or closed. The slim, short design packs a lot of cutting power into a package with about half the volume of a pack of gum. A functional design with aesthetics worthy of MOMA. Derma-Safe also produce a hacksaw version they say will cut through metal as well as wood, which I've not tried.

-- Jonathan Coupe

Keychain cash stash
Cash Can
$30 Sunshine Products

The Cash Can is a small brass tube just big enough for a rolled-up bill. The tube can't be opened unless you remove it from your key ring. It's as easy to remove from the keyring as your keys are. It's also unobtrusive — the whole thing is shorter than most of my keys. Even though I live in a city with an ATM on every block, I'm big on always having a spare $20 bill at hand. I've usually got one stashed in my car and another in my gear bag, and a third tucked into my wallet. The advantages of the Cash Can are its workmanship and stealthiness — unless they read this review, few people are going to know what's inside the brass tube. It just looks like a key fob. Plus, if I lose my wallet, at least I've got the cash attached to my keys.

-- Mike Everett-Lane

Ultra-lightest camp light
BlockLite
$10 (battery included) Amazon

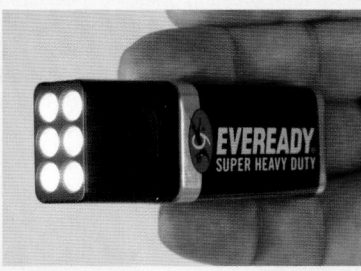

The ultimate lightweight backpacking camp light. A tiny 6 LED chip sits atop a regular alkaline 9-volt battery which acts as handle, stand and power source. Two modes: high (75 hours) and low (600 hours). High mode with 6 LEDs produces about as much light as a small flashlight; low-mode with 2 LEDs on is a candle, only steadier, and whiter. The Pak-Lite is an ideal tent light. You can set down and let it burn hour after hour, night after night. I once ran mine for 48 hours continuously and found no drop off in power. One battery should last the longest thru hike. You can make it last years by substituting a 9-volt lithium battery (200 hours on hi, 1,200 on lo). It's easy enough to grab it and use it as a torch or map reader as well. Since the 9-volt battery has a long shelf life it makes a pretty good hurricane/emergency light too. This one is cheaper than the Pak-Lite, a competitor.

-- KK

An invention needs to make sense in the world in which it is finished, not the world in which it was started. - Ray Kurzweil

Locks-at-any-angle knife
Seber Racheting Knife

$25 seberdesigngroup.com

Available as a utility knife, tanto blade, or traditional straight/serrated blade

I have been using a tanto style, honed edge ratchet locking knife by Seber Design Group, and the only way I would ever recommend a knife is if it was extraordinary. And it is. It's heavy, some people might not like that in a pocket-knife, but I hardly care if it makes my pants sag with its weight, because it is the best blade I have ever used. Thanks to its ratchet it locks at any angle, and is seriously sturdy when it locks. I applied every pound of force in my body to it once, and it did not buckle. It does have a slight play in the lock, but that is normal for this kind of rachet, and does not make it any less effective.

Besides having the brute force necessary to lock the blade in place, it has the ability to lock it anywhere above 45 degrees and be unbreakable to ordinary people with ordinary strength. This means you can adapt the Seber knife to any job. Cutting plastic, cutting any sort of tubing weaker than stainless steel? Cutting rope? Cutting branches, slicing fruit, cutting carpet, canvas, nylon, fabric, paper, cutting woody braches and fibrous stems, cutting anything? You need this knife.

Okay, I admit you don't need the tanto version, the tanto is for stabbing and slashing, adapted from the katana and similar weapons, and I got it for sale on Amazon in the tanto format only, but they make others: a drop point for normal use, in serrated or honed, and both the drop point and the tanto point have 8Cr13MoV steel, similar to 440C stainless steel, hardened up to 58-60 RHC. All that means is they did not cut many corners when it came to sourcing materials. They also make a folding utility knife that features the same ratchet as the other knives, but takes any traditional replaceable utility knife blade, and is (hopefully) as awesome as my knife is.

Seber is, as far as I know, the cheapest, most effective, and most importantly, the only racheting angle locking knife. If I am wrong, and there is something better, I would love to hear about it.

For what you can actually do with the knife, just look around youtube for 'Seber knife' if you are skeptical, and watch it unfold for yourself, or go to Seber's website, and watch them cut everything you can possibly cut with a stainless blade with ease. That's the point I'm trying to make here. Everything you do with a blade, is easier and safer with the Seber knife, and it is as far as I know, one of a kind.

-- David Douglas

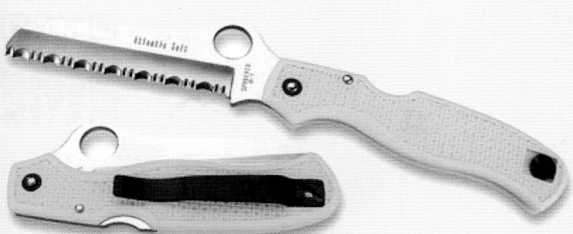

Rustproof aquatic knife
Spyderco Atlantic Salt

$65 Amazon

I work on a tugboat where a sharp knife is important. Rusting is also an issue. I have had my Atlantic Salt model number FRN-C89YL for two years. This knife has not shown any sign of rusting yet. I just bought my second one due to losing the first one.

The H1 stainless steel is amazing. I love this tool.

-- John Brown

H1 stainless steel replaces the carbon in normal steel with non-rusting nitrogen. The outsized hole in this knife blade is useful for gloved hands, and it features a nonslip grip.

--Bruce Sterling

The other half of a knife
Spyderco Sharpmaker

$52 amazon.com

A knife without an edge is worthless, and most knives you find in pockets, sheaths, and kitchens are dull. Every edge you have, including an ax, should be able dry shave hair off your forearm and slice loose-held newsprint without catching.

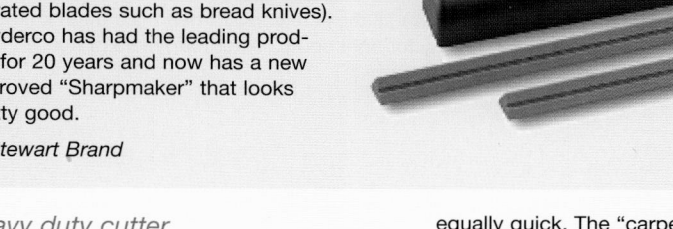

The most effective sharpener I know is also the easiest to use -- just carve straight down on the V of slender stones, a stroke on one side, a stroke on the other. The stones are triangular, so you can use either the flat side or the angle (which permits sharpening serrated blades such as bread knives). Spyderco has had the leading product for 20 years and now has a new improved "Sharpmaker" that looks pretty good.

-- Stewart Brand

Heavy duty cutter
Olfa Carpet Cutter

$10 Model 5011 olfa.com

The single most useful tool I used to carry when blagging it in various builder trades. There are just so many situations where a really sharp blade comes in handy.

This particular model has a simple but sturdy locking wheel that I find much more practical than the usual stepped version. You soon learn to operate it one handed, and for a quick slash of some packing you don't even need to lock it before you retract it and slip it back in your tool pocket. To extend a short steady blade, or the full length is

equally quick. The "carpet tucker", as Olfa calls it, at the rear end is also surprisingly useful when you always have it handy. Opening a can of paint, forcing some casing apart, lifting staples, scratching away some dry glue drippings, or as a screwdriver in a pinch.

I guess there is a reason why I almost never see a painter carry anything else other than this particular model.

-- Gaute Amundsen

A blade for the first responder
Gerber Hinderer Rescue Knife

$67 gerbergear.com

This knife is designed by firefighter Rick Hinderer for the working Firefighter, EMT or Medic. It has a serrated stainless steel blade, a window punch and a foldaway seatbelt cutter. But what tempted me, and what gets used the most, is the built in oxygen tank wrench. It is a deceptively simple slot in the handle, but it has time and again come in handy switching out portable oxygen tanks while on scene. No more sending someone running back to the rig because someone on C-shift forgot to replace the oxygen wrench back in the bag! The oversized thumb studs make it workable even with bunker gloves on and it comes with a 9-piece kit of screw bits.

-- Jesse Hinds

I've used this knife for two years, and found

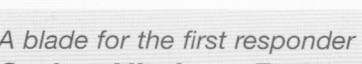

that it has served me well in all my field work. For me the knife is exceptional because of its appropriate sizing and ergonomic hold. It's easy to use with gloves on. The strap cutter on the back side is excellent and I end up using it a lot. The rubber strip with different tools have been useful for hard to access spaces. It does not replace a multi-tool, but is a great compliment to it.

-- Jason DeJong

Multi-purpose machete
Gator Machete Junior

$17 gerbergear.com

This Gerber machete has a normal 16" blade on one side and a serrated saw on the other

side. I go gold prospecting in very overgrown and brushy areas, so the hollow ground machete blade will take care of the smaller stuff and the saw is right there for the occasional limb or larger brush.

This eliminates carrying a saw with me when I already have a lot of other equipment to carry. I had never seen a machete with a saw on the back, and when I noticed it in the catalog I knew I had to have one.

-- Glenn Kangiser

Affordable highly-evolved pocketknife
Myerchin Lightknife

$60 Crew Pro L377P myerchin.com

Bring up the subject of favorite pocketknives with outdoorsmen and you're sure to instigate a pas-

sionate discussion. Knives are potent symbols of power and utility; most men I know have deep paternal (or in my case, grand-paternal) associations with them from their youth. After 35 years of pocketknife buying and using, I have settled on California-based Myerchin as my folding knife maker of choice.

My daily driver is the Lightknife Crew Pro L377P. It uses a featherweight Zytel body (same material that's used in many modern handguns) surrounding a securely locking Japanese 440 stainless blade and a marlinspike (knot untangler). The 3/4 serrated, 1/4 straight edge, 2.25-inch blade is designed to please anyone who works

regularly with line. (On a sailboat, I insist that a serrated blade is a mandatory safety tool.) The body has a unique clip that turns your pocket into a secure sheath. Mine has never fallen in years of regular use. Inside the water-resistant shell is an industrial red LED that's perfect for reading maps and charts without sacrificing your night vision. I've immersed my Lightknife many times without any problems. At 3.8-inches when closed and a mere 2.75 ounces, you won't even notice it's there, and the lack of an obvious sheath eliminates unwanted attention.

A small Sebenza knife, like Reeve's other folders, is a gorgeous piece, but they start at six times the price of a Myerchin. Imagine how you'd feel watching one of those go over overboard! The Boye sailing knives are getting rave reviews but to my eye lack the timeless aesthetics of Myerchins -- particularly the B300. You simply must hold one of these Myerchins in your hand to appreciate the gravitas they generate -- and they cost under US$100 and can be found in any West Marine store.

Need something more substantial? Check out their flagship, the B300 Offshore Folder. If they're good enough for the US Navy and Coast Guard, they're good enough for me.

-- David MacNeill

Multitools

Classic urban survival multi-tool
Leatherman Micra
$22 leatherman.com

Smaller than most pocket knives, and with the ability to unfold into a completely handy pair of snips, the stainless steel Micra contains two functional flat-blade drivers (micro and "regular") and a #2 Phillips-equivalent screwdriver, so I can achieve most anything I need to do inside a server closet or at a customer's desk. You could opt for the Wave, which features more tools. However, the less expensive Micra is lighter (1.75 vs. 8.5 ounces) and smaller (2.5" vs. 4"), and overall it's much more of an urban survival tool. It comes with tweezers, scissors, nail file, and a bottle opener, but the features that make it the most valuable to me are the "Phillips" blade (a flat blade shaped to fit into a Phillips head) and the micro flat driver blade. I'm constantly opening stuff - packages from FedEx (knife,) packages of sunflower kernels (scissors), laptops (micro screwdriver,) data racks (Phillips) and the like. This tool has everything I use on a daily basis in a simple, little package.

-- Steve Sussex

Cheap, small knife care
Gerber Pocket Sharpener
$5 gerbergear.com

Spyderco's previously reviewed Sharpmaker is my edge maintenance tool of choice, but there's no room for it in my grab-and-go bag. I searched around and found a number of pen-sized, high-quality knife sharpeners that wouldn't take up much room, such as those by EZE-LAP. But I wanted something smaller and, well, cheaper, since it was more of an emergency tool than one meant for regular use.

I found this little (2 1/4 x 1 3/4 in.) Gerber sharpener that fits perfectly in my knife sheath's sidecar pocket and cost me just a few bucks. It's easy to use, with one side marked "coarse," the other "fine," and a little thumb-forefinger hold in between. It's actually been effective sharpening the folding knife I keep by my desk, and its light-weight, small profile and low cost make it perfect for leaving in a bag, just in case.

-- Elon Schoenholz

State-of-the-art multi-tool
Leatherman Wave
$55 leatherman.com

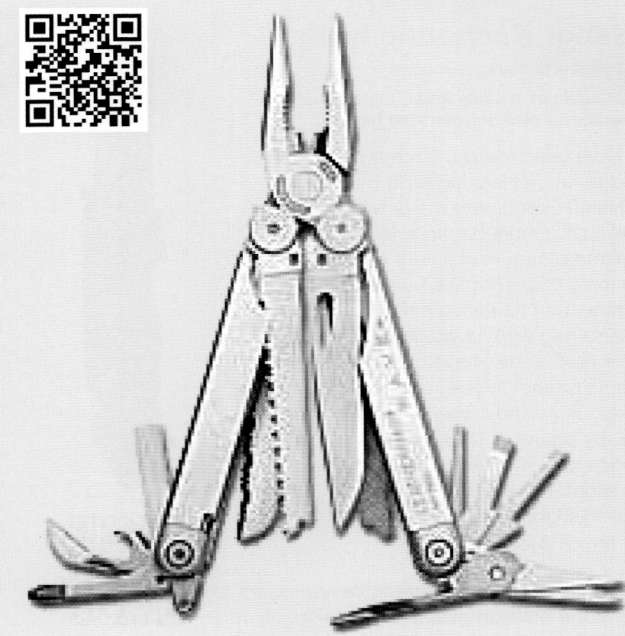

I bought this tool about four years ago in preparation for a backpacking trip around Australia and it has been on my belt ever since. I have used it in every camping situation imaginable. Between the locking straight-edge and serrated blades, I have been able to cut everything from thin sheet metal to steak to wrist thick hemp rope. This tool was a first for me in that the saw blade actually cut wood with ease. Unlike many other models, the blades are on the outside of the tool so you don't have to unfold the whole thing to get to them. This makes it less awkward to use and even allows one-handed use in a pinch. Another nice feature is that the edges of the plier handles are rounded, so they don't dig into your hand when you need to apply a little force. The scissors, can opener and screwdrivers have never let me down. I have found the Wave to be just as useful indoors. I take apart computers on a daily basis, and it is usually all the screwdriver I need, although it is generally too clunky for tight spots. After four years of heavy use it's still going strong.

-- Travis Seay

The classic pocketknife
Victorinox Swiss Army Manager Pocket Knife
$24 Amazon

The Manager Swiss Army Knife has been in my pocket for nearly 2 years. This compact tool has all the useful stuff you expect from the line of Swiss Army knives: blade, scissors, tweezers, file, bottle opener, and separate flat-head & Phillips-head screwdrivers.

What makes it a must-have is the retractable ballpoint pen. It's smooth writing and hasn't dried out on me in the past 2 years. I've taken meeting notes, written checks, and signed receipts. Just extend the combination Philips-head / bottle opener tool for a more comfortable grip during extended composition sessions.

The Manager comes to the rescue time after time for occasional writing needs and tiny DIY tasks because it's always in your pocket. (I just changed the batteries in a Nerf gun with the Phillips-head screwdriver.) It's more comfortable to carry in the pocket than a normal pen and more useful, too.

-- Sean Singh

The Midnite Manager model comes with a built-in LED flashlight in addition to a pen.

-- Mark Frauenfelder]

Pocket-friendly tech tool
Swiss Army Victorinox CyberTool 29
$64 swissarmy.com

I've tried a fair number of pocket knife and combination tools: Gerber, Leatherman, Victorinox, Wenger, and others. The quality and versatility of these tools are quite amazing. I own both versions of the Husky 8-in-1, which are excellent when you have a workspace or are able to carry them in a pack, but not so good to carry in your pocket. I used to work on servers but have been promoted to management, and now don't do as much hands-on work as I once did, but still like to be prepared. For day-to-day use, I want something that fits easily into my pocket, has a small enough profile to work in confined spaces for light-duty computer repairs and other minor jobs. I've found the Swiss Army Victorinox CyberTool 29 to be the best compromise.

It has a nice long 5mm driver that uses four double-ended bits, including my favorite Phillips #2, two smaller Phillips bits, a straight bit, three Torx drivers (#8, #10, #15), and a 4mm hex bit. It also includes the classic straight-blade screwdriver, can opener, awl, two knife blades, corkscrew (yes, I use it fairly regularly!) and a tiny screwdriver ingenuously tucked in the corkscrew. I really like that the straight-blade screwdriver and Phillips driver are at opposite ends. Having the

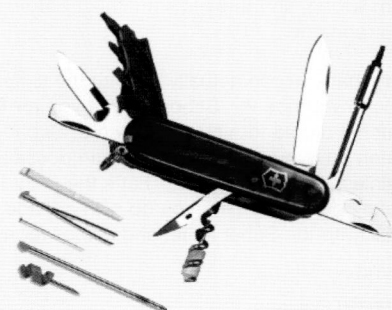

two screwdrivers open at the same time often makes the task go quicker.

-- Rurik Spence

Keychain-size, steel pocket utensils
Atwood Mini Tools
$45+ atwoodknives.com

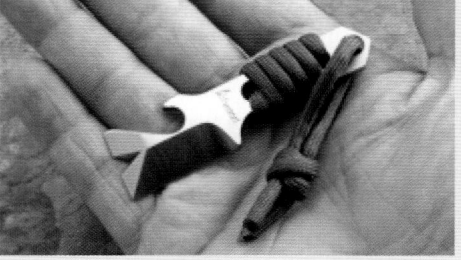

The beauty of these tools is they feel like a fetish item in your hand and, due to their size, you can always have them with you. They're handmade by Peter Atwood and have incredible strength because he uses a specialty stainless steel made via a powder metallurgy process ("The powder is compressed under significant force to a homogenous, solid state and the steel is rolled to required stock size. Molecules are uniform, inclusions of impurities are insignificant").

Both of my EDC knives -- a Swiss Army Cybertool and a SOG Multi Tool -- have slightly bent tips on the main blades because I tried to open or pry something I shouldn't have. That will never happen with the Mini Son of Prything I carry in my pocket or my Prybaby. The trend in tools is to include more and more features. An Atwood piece - and there are a variety of them worth checking out -- is generally designed to do a couple of things really well, and it does: open a package, pull a nail, cut some tape, strip a wire, etc. There are obviously other discovered tasks -- like propping up a new power supply in my computer while I get a couple of screws in -- but it's calling on that intended purpose that is most gratifying.

-- Greg Needham

Pocket-sized driver/Allen set
Doc Allen's VersaTool
$17 docallensversatool.com

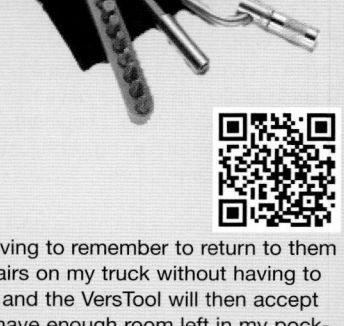

When I am wearing my 5.11 tactical cargo pants, this pocket-sized screwdriver/Allen-wrench with interchangeable bits always goes in the right-hand cargo pocket. I'll often use the screwdriver of my Leatherman several times a day, but the VersaTool does a better job due to the interchangeable bits (better fit to the screws). Also, the handle can be adjusted to provide additional leverage or to fit tight spots. To get greater torque, you just slide the handle into "T" or "L" configurations. Recently, I used it to reinstall a bathroom cabinet door that the kids somehow managed to detach. My kids are good at dismantling things, so having this on hand saves time and allows me to complete repairs immediately without having to remember to return to them later. In one weekend, I also managed to complete several repairs on my truck without having to grab the tool box. Interestingly, the hex adapter will disconnect and the VersTool will then accept any 1/4" socket so that it can be used as a nut driver. I do not have enough room left in my pockets for a set of 1/4" sockets, but I plan on buying a couple more VersaTools, one of which I'll be dropping in my briefcase along with a spare socket set.

-- John Rigby

There are two types of forecasts ... lucky or wrong. - Anon

Non-marring scraper
Lil Chizler
$8 10 scrapers worldwide-usa.com

It looks like only a simple odd shaped piece of plastic -- which it is! -- but it is fantastic used as a pot and pan scraper, pocket or purse sleet scraper, snow ski boot and binding scraper, paint or tar scraper, lawn and garden-digging utensil, putty knife, vinyl remover. Effectively scrapes any surface you don't want to mar or scratch. It is light, small, inexpensive and almost indestructible. It is often given away as a promotional gift; however you can purchase them for as little as twenty five cents or as much as $4.00. They can be found online, and at craft, hardware, office supply, and paint stores.

-- *Larry Zibilich*

More than shears
Fiskars Cuts+More
$10 9" shears www3.fiskars.com

I use shears and scissors constantly while building projects from leather and fabric and other materials. I have tried other types, from kitchen shears to more expensive models, but I have found this model from Fiskars to be the absolute best. In my toolbox, they are indispensable.

The shears are made out of titanium which decreases the need for frequent sharpening. However, the included protective case doubles as a sharpener for when the need arises. They are a true multipurpose tool with a wire cutter, twine cutter, light rope cutter, and even an awl tip for making holes. In terms of use, I have cut leather, fabric, even sheet vinyl with equal ease. They cut cleanly every time, on every material.

They even come apart for cleaning or whatnot. Too cool! Fiskars is a brand I trust, and these shears confirm that fact once again. I believe these handy shears are a great addition to any toolbox.

-- *Stephen Young*

Ceramic safety blade
Slice Safety Cutter
$8 sliceproducts.com

This tiny ceramic blade makes opening plastic packaging and cutting coupons a cinch. It's tiny enough to slip into your travel kit (and it's safe for air travel) and can be used to open all manner of packages. To round it all off it seems difficult/impossible to injure yourself with it and it's magnetic so you can stick on your fridge or PC.

-- *Chris Hecht*

This tool is great for clipping newspaper articles and any other paper related media. With a bit more effort it slices through tough scissor-resistant plastic packaging. Just be sure to cut paper on a surface you don't mind getting scratched as this can easily damage wood and glass.

-- *Oliver Hulland*

Non-scratch scraping
ScrapeRite Plastic Razor Blades
$7 25 blades w/holder scraperite.com

Along with opening blister packages, removing product labels from items is an unavoidable annoyance of contemporary life. After years of scratching with my fingernails and scraping with a sharpened tongue depressor (works well, dulls easily), I've discovered the ultimate solution: ScrapeRite Plastic Razor Blades, double-edged plastic blades designed for light scraping, not cutting. The blades are available in three materials of varying hardness; my experience is with their General Purpose Blades, the softest of the three, which is said to have the consistency of a fingernail and are relatively safe to use on just about any surface, including the paint on your car.

Two years of experience validates

these claims: I've used mine on everything from a stainless steel soup pot and wooden cutting board to countless items from Home Depot or Lowe's. I use mine a few times a month and I'm still on my first blade. The two blades of harder, more rigid compounds are supposed stand up to rougher use, such as paint removal on glass, but may scratch delicate surfaces. Their main advantage over razor blades appears to be safety. (note: I have no experience with these blades).

While the plastic razor blades will fit into most standard blade holders, for around-the-home use, I use the manufacturer's inexpensive and compact plastic holder, which I store under a rubber band stretched around a bottle of Goo Gone. Since I still use my standard metal holder with razor blades for glass, I see

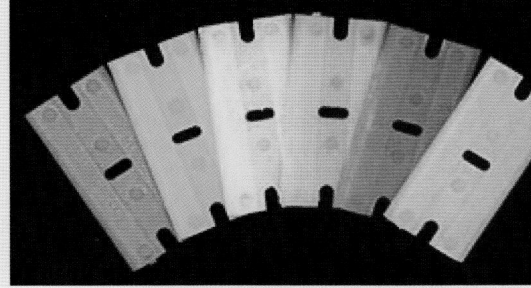

no reason to buy an extra standard holder for these blades.

-- *David King*

Powerful scissors/snips
Titanium Nitride Shop Snip
$16 Fiskars Titanium Nitride 8 inch Shop Snip Amazon

I find myself reaching for this tool a couple of times per week. It is like nice sharp pair of scissors with (almost) the power of tinsnips. It is VERY sharp and will cut through tough materials like vinyl cove base, nylon pallet strapping, or rope quite easily. I recently had to cut some vinyl trim that was too thick for scissors, but got mangled up with tinsnips. This tool cut the material perfectly. Fiskars says this about the Titanium Nitride coating: "EXTREMELY DURABLE Titanium Nitride coating resists wear, nicks and scratches as well as corrosive chemicals and sticky substances while reducing friction for easier cuts." I found the rubber grip is comfortable and the tool is very easy to control. It seems very well made. It has nice little touches such as: the tab that keeps the blades locked closed is powdercoated.

-- *John Nichols*

Inexpensive plastic and sheet metal cutter
Trauma Shears
$3 Amazon

Several years ago I needed about half a dozen tools for a series of workshops I was hosting. I needed a hand tool that could safely and easily shape plastic and thin sheet metal, but not break the bank. I found trauma shears at the local hardware store for a couple dollars each and bought every pair they had. Although I had misgivings about the price they worked great. I still have them and they all get constant use and abuse.

Sometimes called EMT or Paramedic scissors, they were originally designed for emergency responders to cut through seat belts, zippers, denim and leather. The rounded tip and bent handle made to safely cut along skin also make them useful for cutting along other surfaces without snags or jabs.

They're somewhat famous for being shown cutting through a penny, which they'll do without too much trouble. More practically they'll cut sheet metal, wire, cable, plastic, cardboard, staples, rubber, foam, branches, and small bolts, to name a few. They're the scissors I reach for when I don't want to ruin my good scissors, and you'll find them scattered throughout my workshop. They're also great for opening plastic clamshell packages and I've tied them into bows on presents to help get into gifts.

-- *Steve Hoefer*

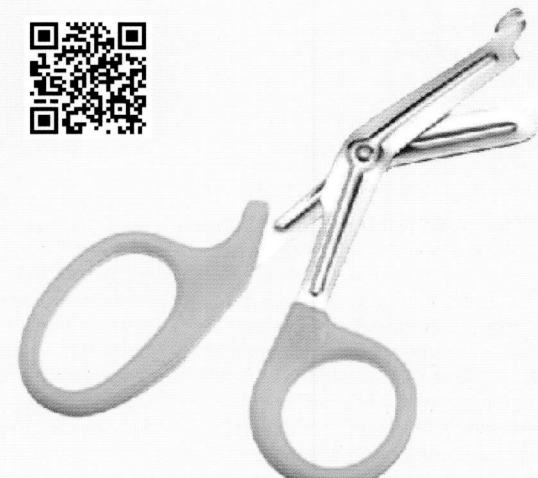

EDC snips
Slip N Snip Folding Scissors
$9 slipnsnip.com

I carry these little, folding scissors with me everywhere. They are very sharp, and fold and unfold very easily. They are also very powerful considering their size. Best of all they have a very slim (flat) profile in my pocket.

I am an avid fisherman, and fish over lunch, on my way to work, etc and I always take these with me. I have found that they cut every type of line I use (according to my dentist, using your teeth is not advisable). They are also safer to hand to my kids to cut something, as opposed to having them fiddle with my Leatherman.

As a daily carry item these are obviously not as versatile as a small

multi-tool, but when cost is a factor (I often fish from a boat and have been known to lose items overboard) or you can't carry a knife, I highly recommend anyone consider these pocketable scissors.

-- *Chris King*

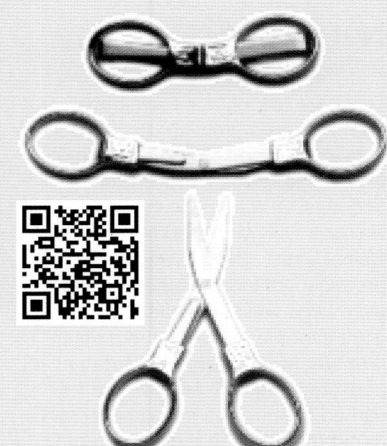

Picker-Uppers

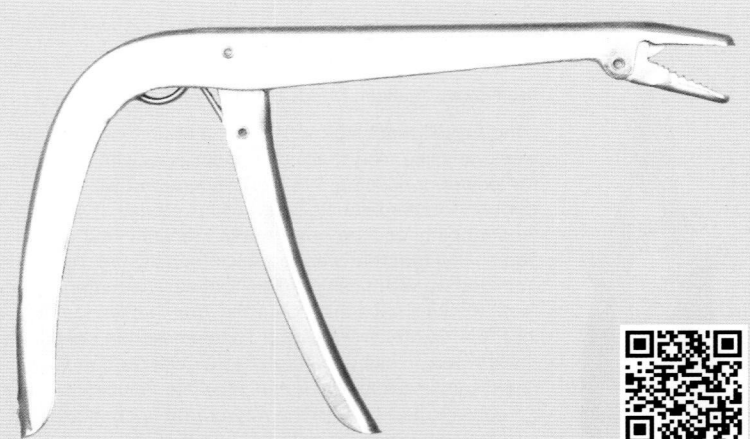

Grip for removing fishhooks & small items
Hookout
$6

The Hookout is specifically designed to get hooks out of fish that have swallowed them, but I have found it's excellent for getting a grip on anything in a tight space. My dad got mine for me in the early '70s. It was part of my fishing tackle box and I used it many times to retrieve fishhooks. I don't fish anymore, but use it all the time around the house.

I keep one in the kitchen drawer since it's especially useful for retrieving items from the garbage disposal (bottle caps, sippy cup valves, etc.). It's also great for automotive work -- retrieving hardware that has fallen into a tight space or, god forbid, down the carburetor throat.

It's perfect because it doesn't require a lot of space to open up, unlike needle nose pliers. The maxi-mum jaw opening is only about 3/8", but the Hookout has a powerful grip. It's useful anywhere you would need some very long skinny needle nose pliers. The jaws are hollow, though, so you're much less likely to drop what you have just grabbed. It does not work like pliers. Instead, when you squeeze the handle, it pulls on a long rod inside the tool and that in turn pulls the little jaw closed. It's spring-loaded, so it opens when you open your hand.

I have the zinc-plated version that's about 9 " long. It looks somewhat cheaply made, but I've tried to bend it by over-squeezing the handle and it won't bend or distort. If I bought another one, I'd be tempted to pop for the more expensive stainless steel version -- just because I have a weakness for things stainless -- but the zinc-plated one has held up very well. I kept it clean and made sure it never saw salt water. After 30 years, it still looks almost new.

-- Jim Barbera

Very long nimble fingers
Flexible Pick Up Gripper
$3 Pick Up Tool mcminone.com

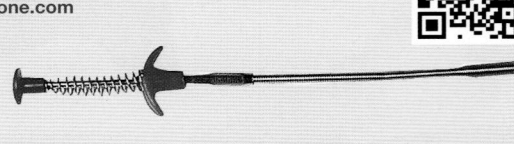

An incredibly handy tool that seems utterly trivial until you have one, but finds its own uses once you do. It's a snaky picker-upper, about two feet long, able to pick up things deep in pipes, behind furniture, in holes, cracks, and gaps. I use it all the time, mostly for rescues that simply couldn't be achieved otherwise. Seems to last forever with occasional lubrication.

-- KK

Crafty stainless steel hook
Steel Spring Hook
$4 8.125" moodytools.com

I was introduced to spring hooks by a repair technician at work around 10 years ago. He was using the tool to get into tight spaces on check processing equipment and gave me one as he thought I'd find it handy around the house.

The tool is quite simple. It's an eleven-inch stainless steel rod with a 90-degree hook at the end. I found it useful for any task in tight places requiring force to be exerted with precision. I used it for a few years before it died of natural causes and I then found a supplier and bought half a dozen; they were only a few dollars each at the time.

I spread the new supply around the house in the kitchen, office, as well as my workshop and I was surprised to find my wife using them more than I. She's used them for sewing projects to thread elastic through a waistband, for craft projects to guide the placement of small parts, and for her own forays into light equipment repair.

I find this tool uniquely capable of getting into tight spaces where no other tool can go making it one of the most versatile tools I own. It is sold in various configurations by numerous suppliers, but the 11" version I was given years ago has proven most useful.

-- Paul Steger

Back-saving picker-upper
E-Z Reacher
$50 arcoa.com

There are various incarnations of these grippers, but I've been using mine all the time for at least three years and it still looks new and works great. It's a rigid aluminum shaft with spring loaded rubber suction cup grabbers on one end and a squeeze handle at the other. Lets me grab things off high shelves and retrieve things dropped in inaccessible places, but it's especially great for repetitive tasks that require bending over, like gathering lots of small things off the ground (fallen walnuts; I hate stepping on them in my yard) or grabbing icky things. I use mine 2-3 times a week, mostly for those quick grabs or a put-back on a high shelf, but also for serial grabbing: I picked up two 5-gallon bucketfuls of squishy rotted peaches off my lawn recently -- no bending, no sticky fingers. When I was done I just used the hose to rinse it off. You can also yank down fruit from on high or pull down a thin branch that needs trimming. It's also gentle enough to pick up an egg if you're so inclined.

Other models made by other companies - even the more expensive reachers -- feel cheaply made, grab less firmly, and often use weaker spring steel. Some use less grabby suction cup ends and others simply have a hook-like grabber which wouldn't be of much use for me. I've seen landscape trash collectors using this model, so I feel that speaks to its strength and longevity. There are shorter E-Z Reachers available, but personally, I find I want as much reach as possible. They also make folding versions (good for those in wheelchairs) and locking versions (for those with less hand strength) and various combinations thereof. Replacement suction cups are available ($4), but I have never needed to replace them.

-- Barbara Dace

Lightweight, long reach
Telescoping Pruner

For the close-to-hand pruning, I have my trusty Felco. For branches further than I can reach with a lopper, I use a big, unwieldy pole pruner with a pull-rope to muscle the clipper. It's overkill for smaller out of reach plants but for decades it was all I knew. Then I discovered the telescoping long arm pruner: easy to extend and collapse, lightweight, and it holds the clipping until you release the trigger, enabling efficient stashing of clippings in a lawn bag. This model, made in Japan, features two pistol grips for two-armed aiming, which most other telescoping pruners don't have. And its telescoping capability unlocks quickly with a lever instead of having to tighten and untighten a collar. This is now one of my favorite tools on a daily basis, considering all the huffing and puffing I used to do to clear ivy or deadhead roses high up on the fence.

-- Howard Rheingold

$95 Nobi Nobi Telescopic Pruning (4'-7') hidatool.com

$75 Fiskars Telescoping Pruning Stik Amazon

Rolling picker upper
Nut Wizard
$60, large nutwizard.com

There are few chores I remember from my years growing up on my family's Missouri farm more thankless, backbreaking, low paying and messier than picking up black walnuts. Our yards had numerous walnut trees, which every autumn produced as many walnuts as there were large whirring cicadas in their giant canopies. Picking them up, however, wasn't just done for the pocket change my brother and I earned as much as it was necessary to get them off the ground and out of the lawnmower's path. As walnuts lay in the grass their soft pulpy shells quickly turn mushy and black, oozing a dark staining juice that makes them unpleasant to handle.

Enter the most effective tool I've come across in a long time, the Nut Wizard. My brother discovered this tool on the Internet and brought one over to our farm during a recent family reunion, amazing everyone with its utility. So simple and elegant, the Nut Wizard is a wire basket reminiscent of an egg whisk, attached to rotating hubs on either end with a long wooden pole handle. You roll the wire basket around on the ground and walnuts or other similarly sized objects just pop right into it. When it's full, you simply lower the wire basket onto a heavy wire spreader (included) that clips onto the top of any five-gallon bucket and, voila, the gathered contents are quickly dumped!

I was impressed that it succeeds in picking up walnuts that have embedded themselves deep in the grass, as well as those that have lost their outer soft shell. Gooey walnuts are picked right up, and sometimes if the outer shells are really rotten, the messy parts get left behind and the rotating basket picks up just the more woody inner shell. By far the most impressive feat of the Nut Wizard is how it can get kids arguing over who gets to push it around the yard.

This tool is available in three sizes, collectively capable of picking up a wide range of items: acorns, pecans, hickory nuts, chestnuts, marbles, apples, baseballs, tennis balls, golf balls. And there's also now an even smaller version, the Ammo Wizard, that will pick up spent bullet casings.

-- James Leftwich

The present is pregnant with the future. -Voltaire

See-thru repair
Transparent Duct Tape

$7 1.88in. x 60ft. Scotch Transparent Duct Tape
3m.com

On application this duct tape is not as invisible as one would wish for, but neither is it the blazing grey badge of desperation you usually get with industrial duct tape. It's a little less noticeable, but still retains duct tape's old magic -- a straight 90 degree tear by hand, durable strength, good sticking power. Another benefit of this transparent version: 3M claims it lasts 6 times longer than the standard variety, having been engineered for extreme temperatures and UV exposure. Since it has only been recently introduced, I can't measure its full longevity but it seems to hold up remarkably well. Dispenses easier too. Good stuff.

-- KK

Quick spot adhesive
Double Stick Tape/Double-Coated Tape

Scotch (3M) sells three varieties of ready-made double-backed tape for sticking together two flat surfaces. Their Double Stick Tape (model #137) does what a self-connecting loop of ordinary tape does, but more tidily and sure. Their Double-Sided Tape (model #667) is similar but you can re-position the tape. For most uses - scrapbooks, posters, etc - I much prefer this kind. Their Photo Mounting Tape (Cat. 002) is double-side, not positionable, but acid-free. This is what you want to use for archival stuff.

-- KK

$6 Double Stick Tape
Amazon

$6 Double-Coated Tape
officedepot.com

$8 Photo and Document Double Stick Tape Amazon

Silicone tape
Rescue Tape

$10 rescuetape.com

Rescue tape is a brand name for silicone tape. I've been using it (and other brands) on and off for a decade now and if there's one thing I had to have and couldn't live without, it's this. I have a roll in my car, in my laptop bag, and virtually every else. I've repaired dozens of pipe leaks with it and have even used it when I badly cut my arm clearing brush miles from a hospital.

Supposedly it can even be used as an emergency fan belt. I've never had to try it, but I

can say it will patch a radiator hose and it even worked (for a little while) on the high pressure side of my car's air conditioner! There are lots of day-to-day uses for it as well. For my electronics work I use it to insulate the underside of the boards I'm soldering so they don't short out, and it has no problem dealing with 750 F high temp soldering either.

The best part is that it's cheap enough that I even use it like shrink wrap, especially helpful if I manage to buy something that has a lot of long unruly pieces that need to be bound together.

-- Jeremy Pavleck

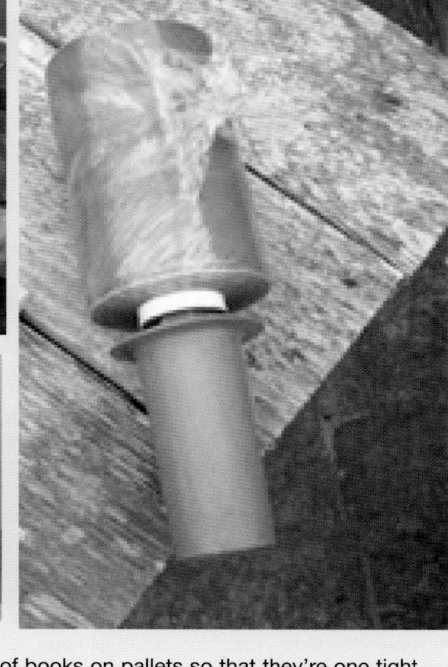

Quick self-binding wrap
Stretch Wrap

$5 5"w x 1000 ft, single roll Amazon

The genius of this product is that it sticks to itself. You just roll it around the boxes or posters or lumber that you want to wrap and it sticks tight. I use it for a bunch of things, as in the garden to stake trees to stakes or to tie say tomato plants to a frame, or as shown in the photo, to keep some nuts together with ball bearings (and have them be visible). It's the same material they use to wrap boxes

of books on pallets so that they're one tight bundle for shipping. Also cool is that it is such a strong yet ultra-thin plastic membrane, not using a ton of resources to produce. They sell them at U-Haul stations. They're cheap!

Above is a pic of stretch wrap I bought at a U-Haul location. I used it to wrap a tube of skateboard ball bearings, with some loose nuts wrapped to the tube. Not only attaches them, but keeps them visible.

-- Lloyd Kahn

Extra sticky duct tape
Gorilla Tape

$12 2" x 35 yards gorillatape.com

Gorilla Tape is duct tape raised to a higher power. It is both stronger and stickier; you can use it on rough surfaces where duct tape won't stick. I have used a variety of similar tapes, from the Army's green 200 mph tape to the fabled Electric Boat tape that Submariners are familiar with. Gorilla Tape sticks better and holds longer than the best quality duct tape in everything I have used it for. It is also waterproof (once applied) and because of the thicker adhesive, less prone to peeling.

-- Stephen Young

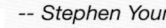

Sticks to a brick.

Duct tape without the residue
Gaffer's Tape

$7 **Camera Tape, P-665**
Small core, 1", 20 yards
permacel.com

If you think duct tape is useful, try Gaffer's tape, known by the brand Permacel (P-665). It's the standard film industry tape. Easy to rip with your hands yet very strong. The adhesive is designed to not rip off paint. My film teacher stuck some on the school wall and left it sit for the whole day under a kilowatt of light a few inches away. The next day it peeled right off leaving the paint on and no adhesive residue.

It comes in many colors and is easy to write on. Uses include sealing film cans and labeling them, marking spots on the floor for measuring, labeling of all kinds. This stuff is really strong. I've heard it referred to as "hundred mile an hour tape" used by NASCAR racers. Also nice is that it comes in a one inch width which I usually have to rip duct tape in half to get. Comes in 2", 3" and 4" widths as well.

Another tape, P-672, is about double the price of P-665 but is weatherproof, twice as thick, and the adhesive is designed for low temperatures. It's the real Gaffer's tape.

-- Monty Zukowski

Velcro double-sided wide ties
Velcro One-Wrap

I carry a roll of the Velcro Plant Ties (see right) in my tool bag, but also keep One-Wrap Velcro strips in the shop. While they're much more expensive, I've found the larger kind to be substantially bulkier and stronger. Here in Toronto, we have alternating weekly garbage, recycling and green waste pickup. We also have rapacious raccoons. I found if I add a simple loop of One-Wrap, screw it into the side of the green bin and loop it over the locking bail of the bin, the raccoons cannot open it. I first tried Plant Ties. They just wouldn't hold. For my purposes, a One-Wrap is good for about a year, after which it is easily replaced. It's available in various colors and sizes. The lower-end of the One-Wrap line is 13 mm wide; however, the One-Wrap also come as large as 22mm. It has deeper loop Velcro (thicker and fuzzier), and as the width of the tape increases, the size of the loops and their grip strength increases. Plant Ties really are great for handling all kinds of tasks, but One-Wrap is strong enough to bundle thicker rope, heavier hoses, and most importantly for me, they keep raccoons out of the recycling.
-- David Keldsen

$4, 50 ties, .5" x 8" Amazon

I much prefer the uncut rolls rather than the precut pieces that are never quite the right size. You can get the rolls in widths ranging from 5/8" to 2" wide, in various colors. Snip off just as much as you need. All my computer cables are shortened by rolling them and wrapping with one-wrap. I use one-wrap anywhere I used to use twist-ties.
-- Charles Platt

$14 - 35, 25-yd roll; sizes vary, velcrosupply.stores.yahoo.net

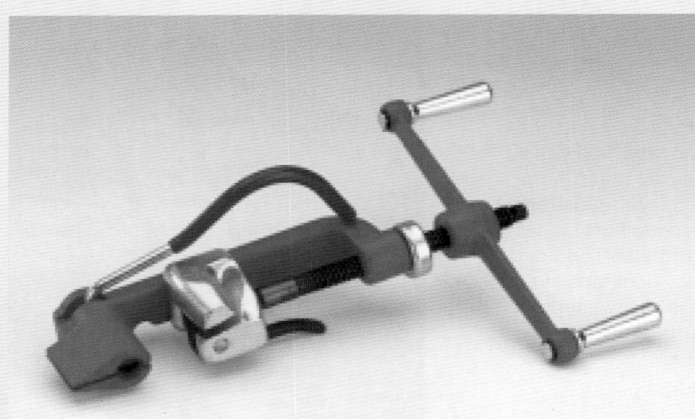

Heavy duty band maker
Straptite

$105 straptiteusa.com

The Straptite appears to be the exact same tool formerly known as the Bandit, a tool I've used forever. This thing works very well indeed; it makes extremely heavy-duty straps. It has long been considered essential emergency equipment by blue water sailors -- for splinting broken spars on long voyages. The device is used to clamp traffic signals to their poles, as well as in more mundane hose clamping duties, for instance to repair the hydraulic hoses on farm machinery. I have used mine as a huge clamp to secure perimeter details of domes, and it has been particularly useful reinforcing wiggly deck railings. Stainless steel strap is ideal and most common (and expensive) but permanent. Of course it can be used with blue-black steel strapping to bundle lumber, pipes, crates etc. (The Poly strapping used in shipping uses a different tool). This tool is not particularly cheap, but it sure does work well; mine is showing little wear after 35 years.

-- J. Bladwin

Heavy duty velcro
Dual Lock Fastener Tape

$18, 3 feet 3M Dual Lock Reclosable Fastener Tape solutions.3m.com

To me, as a commuter, one of the most impressive parts of the EZ Pass toll-paying system is the hard-core industrial "velcro" tape they give you to attach your transponder to your windshield. It's not really velcro, though -- instead of hooks and loops, both surfaces have these tiny hard plastic mushroom-shaped things that grab each other by the hundreds and don't let go. Both sides are the same, so there is only one tape (called self-mating). And unlike the loosy-fabricky velcro connection, the Dual Lock surfaces don't join until you've positioned them exactly, and then pressed them together with a satisfying "chunk." They're primarily used in industrial applications as a replacement for mechanical fasteners, but I use mine to attach my iPod to my dashboard, and tools to the wall in my workshop.

-- S.S. Flanders

Double-side velcro
Velcro Plant Ties

$7 Velcro Plant Ties 2 pk of 1/2 inch by 45 ft. rolls velcro.com

I'm a part-time musician and have to deal with suitcases of coiled cables every time we set ourselves up. I needed a re-useable, quick release kind of strap to keep this kind of gear in order, and wasn't sold on the limits and expense of the plastic zip ties, or beaded ties that I had found.

A roll of Velcro Plant Ties is perfect. Rather than the usual two part Velcro, one side of this stuff is fuzzy, the other side has hooks, so it sticks to itself. I can snip off exactly the length I need, and then with one wrap, the cables are secured. I am finding other uses.... behind the stereo and computer desk, the cables are now neatly routed and secured ... why stop there? Anywhere you need a light-duty, non-marring reusable, quick release wrap. These strips will virtually last forever, and if you lose them, no big deal. Find the roll and snip another length off.

-- Eric Litman

Electrical stores sell black versions of this wrap as Velcro One-Wrap Tape, but in smaller rolls at higher prices. Or in very expensive pre-cut strips. Velcro Plant Ties rolls are a fantastic bargain if you can live with green. They also work great in the garden (bundling hoses, tieing up vines, etc) and you can get it in rolls as long as 70 feet.

-- KK

Heavy duty release mechanism
Seacatch

$283 TR3 (capacity .65 tons)
$595 TR7 (capacity 3.52 tons)

seacatch.com

For heavy-duty release applications, a Seacatch is THE thing to use. I've never found a better way of releasing a heavy line under tension. It's a better solution than a pelican hook (not strong enough, tough to get a smooth release), or a sacrificial line (inelegant, and can foul up launch). Personally I use a Seacatch model TR7LM for homemade trebuchets and ballista releases. Ballista -- as in a giant crossbow, suitable for launching bowling balls, pumpkins, etc. (It's one of the more bizarre hobbies that has arisen in the last 25 years.) But I've also seen Seacatches used by tractor-pull people, construction, you name it. Comes in a wide variety of sizes as well. Beautifully engineered, bombproof, cool.

The action of a Seacatch is smooth, the construction is top-quality. I've never heard of one failing. Their electrically/pneumatically/hydraulically actuated models are commonly used in the Hollywood special effects industry for dropping things at precise moments. They were originally designed for shipboard use (tugboats, fishing boats, etc.) but they've found niches elsewhere.

This is an expensive specialty item for sure, but if you need what it does, it is absolutely worth its price. Before I learned they existed, I spent at least that much on materials and machining yet without being able to create a better release mechanism.

-- Olai Skjaervoy

Versatile fastener
Parachute Cord

$3, 50' 550lb. Type III 7-Strand Paracord Amazon

Parachute cord isn't only light and strong (550lb. rating) for its size (5/32" diameter), it's also more versatile than other types of rope because it can be dissected and parted out, cut and used for its braided nylon sleeve and/or seven separate core strands.

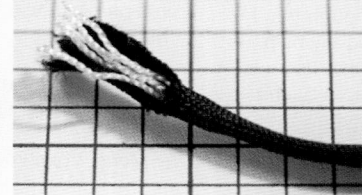

You can get enhanced grip and a little added padding by using paracord to wrap tool handles. It's also used for making lanyards. I recently inserted a length of ball chain into parachute cord sleeve to make a hands-free flashlight for late-night dog walks. The nylon is a lot more comfortable around my neck than ball chain, and the fit is perfect.

-- Spencer Starr

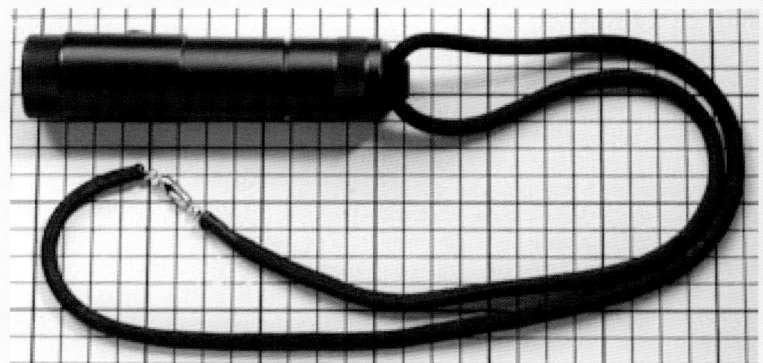

Any theory that can account for all of the facts is wrong, because some of the facts are always wrong. - Francis Crick

Strap supplier
Strapworks.com

You can see all the different strap types

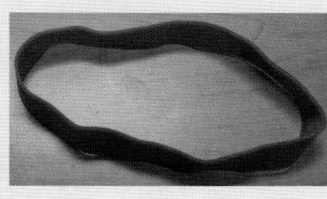

and strap hardware (buckles, tie downs, keepers, clips, etc.) in use on all sorts of stuff swirling around us in daily life. But if you want to get some for your own projects?

Strapworks.com has pretty much all of it. Metal or plastic hardware. All sorts of strap and webbing material.

Inexpensive, easy to work with. Helped me a few times, and I know I will continue to use them when the need arises.

-- Wayne Ruffner

Quick strong tie downs
NRS Heavy Duty Cam Straps
$7+ 1.5" HD Straps nrsweb.com

These straps are incredibly strong. The tensile strength of these 1.5 inchers is 2000 pounds. With their cam locks these NRS straps are easily and infinitely adjustable and can be cinched down very tight. They have almost no flex/stretch and can be used in situations where a bungee would be too weak or stretchy and would not be "bomb-proof" like a cam strap.

If you are a river runner you are already familiar with these straps. They hold your boat, frame and oars on your truck for the drive to the put-in. You then use them to hold the frame to the boat, your bags, spare oar and rocket boxes to the frame. The originals are 1"

wide and come in sizes from 1 foot up to 20 feet. As a commercial boatman I used these for everything from bundling firewood collected for that nights campfire to pulling a truck out of a ditch.

NRS has come out with a 1.5" model that is the perfect width. I have even been using one for several months as a belt. In a pinch it can be used (at the risk of my shorts heading south) to strap/bind/tow just about anything. I keep two of the twenty footers in my truck at all times. These straps are a permanent part of my kit, right next to the duct tape, bailing wire and channel locks.

-- Topher Stephenson

Extra Large Rubber Bands
$4 3/4" x 6", 1lb bag amazon.com

I have been buying one pound packs of rubber bands from LFSMarine for over five years now (along

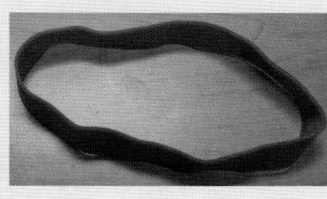

with their cheap and tough nitrile gloves and barge glue). My first buy was an impulse one. I thought, "It's hard to find this size rubber band (3/4" x 6") and, besides, I wanted to make some slingshots so…" I got a one pound bag. When you get them, you realize a pound of these is a lot of banding material. With that abundance, you don't stint their use.

I love them for binding together papers and books (I teach so I always have a few in my desk.) I have used them to hold wood in place for gluing. I use them along with barge glue and duct tape to splice materials together in the garden. And I use them for sling shots., too. In fact they are always in mind and on hand for any kind of kludge. I usually buy a couple of pounds of them at a time for less than ten bucks.

It's fun to give them as gifts just for the odd looks you get now and the thank-yous you continue to get as they too discover that these bands are handier than a pocket on a shirt. Perfect for the maker/tinkerer in you and yours.

-- Terry Elliott

Gigantic twist ties
Griptwist
$8 Nite Ize Gear Ties 18", 2-pack niteize.com

I picked up four of these at my local Container Store, not knowing exactly how I'd use them, but guessing they'd come in handy. Within 48 hours I'd already used them twice-once to secure the barrel of my telescope to its collapsed tripod for easy transport to a remote location, and then to stabilize a table and chairs in the back of my car for a trip across town-both times with great success. These giant, rubberized "twist-ties" were much more efficient and easier to use than a bungee cord in both cases.

Griptwists offer several advantages over bungees in particular. First, they provide "point-to-point" stability, rather than "tie-down" or "net-like" attachment. For example, when moving dining room furniture in the back of my car, I was able to use four Griptwists to connect the legs of chairs to each other, etc., at critical points, so that the entire mass (i.e., of one table and four chairs) was stabilized from within, rather than essentially trying to "net" or "wrap" the mass together from the outside, with bungee cords. Second, with bungee cords, there's always a certain amount of "give," unless you stretch them to their maximum, which isn't always practical; bungeed objects will often move a bit more than you want them to. Third, if you do stretch bungee cords to their maximum, they exert great pressure on the object being contained. I

wouldn't have wanted to use bungees around the barrel of my telescope, for example. The Griptwists remain as tight (but only as tight) as you tie them, with no inherent potential energy to give or take along their own length like elastic bands. Which brings to mind a fourth benefit: no danger of "snapback" when it's time to unload or unpack.

Some things will always have to be netted down, and sometimes the stretchiness of bungees provides a benefit in and of itself (like the ability to squeeze one more last-minute object under the cords, without having to repack). Moreover, from the outside, to the extent they lack handy points where a Griptwist could be employed (e.g., a couch, a canoe, a stack of luggage or boxes). But for temporarily affixing one object to another in point-to-point fashion, with stability, I see more everyday utility in the Griptwist.

-- Adam Zaner

Parcel bands
Four Way Rubberbands
$5, 6 bands flyingbuffalo.com

These hefty four-way rubber bands are so much more useful that a plain old rubber band. Also they can be used decoratively on a simple brown-paper-wrapped gift. Or as a solid tie for bundles of magazines or newspapers.

-- Kaz Brecher

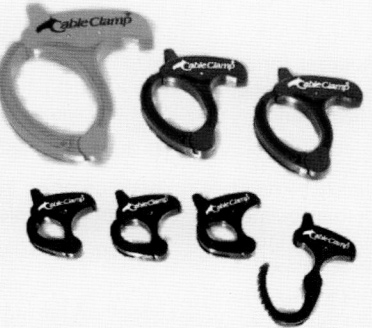

Re-usable cord cuffs
Cable Clamp
$20 - $25 (sets of 4-17 clamps in various sizes) cableclamp.com

The Cable Clamp is a cord/wire/hose organizer I've found helpful, especially in dealing with items that have both long electrical cords and long hoses that can get mixed up with each other. In addition to keeping the long hose and electric cord on my pressure washer coiled separately, I'm using one of these clamps to hang my small electric chainsaw from my belt when climbing a ladder, sort of an improvised tool belt. They come in four sizes, including a Mega-size available from the manufacturer.

They're fun to use -- they close like a handcuff, with ten click-stops. They're more expensive and bulkier than zip ties (i.e. an average tool

chest couldn't carry dozens of these clamps), but they have advantages over tape, cable ties, and other hook & loop products. They're reusable and, unlike tape, leave no gummy residue. They're durable -- won't lose grip after many re-uses. They're less likely to damage delicate electronics cables than a thin cable tie. And they can be opened one-handed (and closed one-handed if there is a backstop handy).

I do find they can be hard to open because the trigger doesn't go back far enough to clear the teeth completely unless it is held down hard. Also, they can get temporarily bent out of shape when under stress -- i.e. the jaw won't go into the catch unless it is guided in by hand. And they are plastic, so they could get broken if something heavy crushed them or fell on them. Nevertheless,

for a relatively inexpensive piece of plastic, they do seem pretty sturdy; I've used mine for about five months and haven't had to replace any.

-- Roger Knights

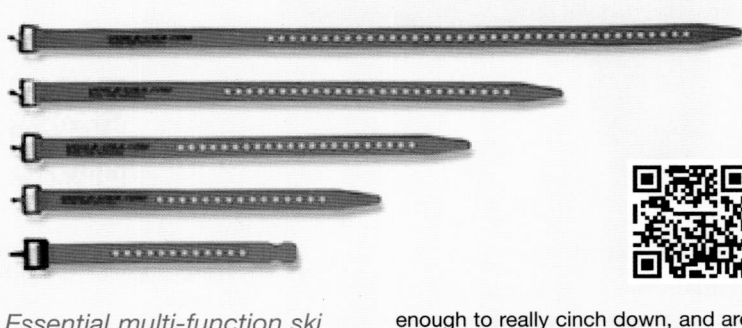

Essential multi-function ski equipment
Voile Ski Strap
$4-$6 voile-usa.com

Every skier ought to own a ski strap. I have used mine to attach skis and poles to my pack, hold the pieces of a broken pole together, attach skis to snowmobiles, affix a tele boot to a ski with a broken cable binding, hold skins to skis, and of course, hold my skis together. I've seen them used to jury-rig backcountry toboggans for patient evacuation, and as an improvised knee strap similar to the previously reviewed Mueller Knee Strap.

Constructed of high-visibility orange polyurethane, they stretch just

enough to really cinch down, and are virtually indestructible. Much more durable and with far greater utility than velcro competitors, this model of ski strap is simply the best. They can be used one-handed with heavy winter gloves on, and come in a variety of lengths. Friends have used theirs for over five years, mine are almost like new after three years.

This strap is an indispensable and indestructible tool for any skier or rider. You could buy one from Backcountry.com or Amazon, but mine was just as cheap from my local ski shop, and is far superior to any other product I have used in a lifetime of skiing.

-- Matt Bresnahan

Ties

Zip tie perfection
Cable Tie Gun

$50 Paladin Cable Tie Gun
paladin-tools.com

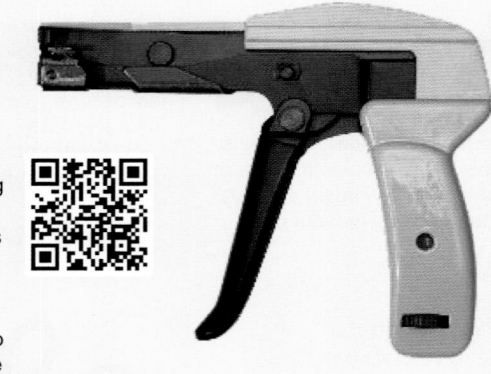

Zip ties are essential tools when it comes to managing cables (among other things), but it can be difficult to get the ties very tight and/or flush. The best tool for the job is a cable tie gun that makes it fast and easy to tighten and cut the cable ties flush. Almost all guns tension and cut in one motion, but the best guns, like this Paladin brand gun, also have a tensioning adjustment. This allows the pull of the gun to be set higher before the blades engage to cut off the tie, but not so high the gun breaks the tie.

-- *Dave Ragains*

The right tool for tightening cable ties is a "tie wrap" or cable tie gun. You gently tighten the wrap, put the gun over the end of the wrap, and pull - it tensions the tie to the RIGHT level for the size of wrap, and clips off the end.

-- *Charles Gallo*

Dirt cheap clamps
Clamptite

$30+ clamptool.com

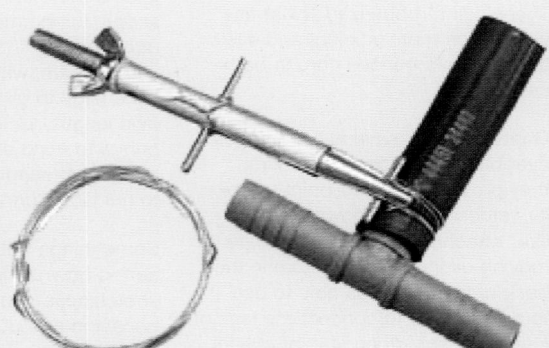

This little-known tool has a cult following. It transforms any old wire into the tightest clamp you can imagine. Unlike a hose clamp there is no limit to the diameter you can tie together. You can bundle bamboo into scaffolding, or twigs into fencing, make brooms from twigs, repair handles, and tie stuff down incredibly secure. Works great as temporary clamping for odd-sided things. Ranchers and farmers rely on cheap baling wire to band anything that doesn't want to move. Fishermen and sailors substitute stainless steel wire to make clamps for pumps and sumps. Also perfect for drip irrigation projects. I've found it takes a bit of skill to tie a clamp neatly, but it ends up far tighter than a hose clamp.

Clamptool.com has the best step-by-step instructions on making the clamps.

-- *KK*

Classic, heavy-duty cable ties
Ty-Rap Zip Ties

$22 (100 ties - TY525MX) tnb.com

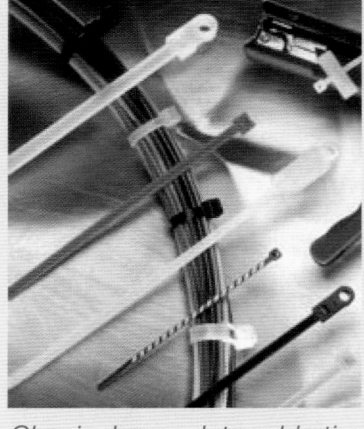

I have had a wide range of work duties and hobbies over the years, and in difficult situations nothing has served me better than the judicious application of zip ties. Neat-ifying cables, creating stand-in hinges, holding car parts on for the trip, fastening bike components, acting as primitive locks on hardsided luggage -- the uses are endless and well-known.

What is less known is that not all cable ties are created equal. The zip tie was invented by Thomas & Betts for aircraft use and the company has continued making higher-quality zip ties while the market of lesser cable ties has proliferated. The brand is called "Ty-Rap" and there are several types of different lengths, colors, and widths. Thomas & Betts makes the only zip ties I use. Despite their additional expense they are worth the effort to find and use.

Wire-tie alternative
Lacing Cord

$14 Waxed Polyester Lacing Twine (165-yard spool) specialized.net

Back before wire ties, cables were bundled with lacing cord -- a flat or round waxed nylon string (flat vs. round require different knots). To this day, lacing cord is used in certain situations where a more flexible bundle is needed, when wire ties are too bulky, or when you need to pull another cable alongside and the lumps of the wire tie would cause problems. Depending on the job, lacing cord comes in a variety

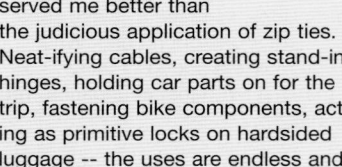

The difference is that the T&B ties use a stainless gripper as the 'ratchet' mechanism, and there are no serrations on the bottom of the tie surface -- it's completely smooth. The stainless locking head actually digs into the underside of the wrap when threaded, leading to infinite adjustability and tight application (the el-cheapo ties always seem to be one "click" too loose.) They are higher-strength material - probably double or triple the strength of standard ties. They resist melting, and seem to be impervious to the worst chemicals I've thrown them into (including lye baths for metal stripping.) They are resistant to abrasions and take a bit of effort to cut through even with a sharp knife. I find that I typically have to wedge a knife blade under the tie, and twist the blade like a tourniquet stick to cut the ties - this also avoids the unpredictable jumping of the blade which is typical of the brute force method of cutting these infernal things once they're on an object.

This preference for a particular zip tie brand may seem like a minor detail, or a slight difference not worthy of attention. However, I have had cheap cable ties stretch, snap, or lose their ratchet grip at the worst possible times, which I'm sure has cost me more than the delta of price that I would have paid for the better T&B ties. In an ugly but unavoidable hack, I needed to hold a set of horizontal computer rack fans on the door of a 19" cabinet. I was not working with my own toolset, and was forced to use "typical" zip ties to hold the heavy fans in place. I came back less than a week later, and the ties had stretched to the

of different coatings, materials, strengths and lengths.

Other advantages of lacing cord are that it's cheap; there isn't a specific size (cut to any length needed); and it's good strong cordage that can be used for other things. The main disadvantage is that it takes a bit of skill with knots. You have to be able to tie a clove hitch for the flat cord, or make a slip knot for the round '12 cord' and then finish with a half-hitch knot.

I've been using lacing cord for over

point where the fans were sagging and rattling horribly against the cabinet door, and would have broken in not too long a time. I replaced them with the T&B Ty-Rap ties and a year later they were as tight as the day I put them on despite the frequent stresses on opening the door.

I have NEVER had a T&B cable tie fail on me under anything less than overwhelming circumstances. They are extremely durable, many of the models are UV-resistant, and the stainless gripper never, ever lets go. A long time ago, after several years and lessons learned using cheaper ties, I have sworn never to use the cheap stuff for anything other than wrapping up cords for storage. The T&B ties are expensive, but worth it. Every year or two I just ignore the price and buy a big bag of them on eBay, and I've never regretted it. I find the TY27M to be a good general purpose model, but take a look at the catalog for ideas.

BONUS TIP: The only way to reliably remove the "tails" of these ties without leaving a razor-sharp edge is to use a pair of flush-cut nippers, such as the Xcelite 170M (available from Amazon). As an add-on tool in any toolbox that has these cable ties, this is mandatory for anyone building a computer rack or doing cable management -- your unbloodied hands will thank you.

-- *John Todd*

20 years. As for brands, one brand is pretty much the same as another.

-- *Charles Gallo*

Indispensable fastening wire
Stainless Steel Locking Wire

$8 .041" diameter, 1 Lb. Coil harborfreight.com

Over the years I have used pipe clamps, zip ties, Velcro straps, and all sorts of other fastening methods, and many have their rightful place for various uses. However, I have discovered a versatile and inexpensive material that, when combined with some other tools for specialized uses, fits the essence of a cool tool: durable, flexible, inexpensive and versatile. Stainless steel wire is sometimes known as safety wire or lock wire; it is used routinely in the aerospace and other industries and conforms to national standards for strength and performance.

Stainless steel wire is available in different sizes measured in nominal diameter for different purposes, and in various quantities depending upon one's capacity needs. For general purpose fastening and use around

the shop and home, I have found that 0.041" nominal diameter wire in 1-lb dispenser canisters (approx. 220 ft) works really well. At about $6 per pound, that works out to less than 3 cents per foot.

This particular size can be bent easily by hand, is durable and strong, and can be manipulated easily with various hand tools. In use it's sturdy yet reusable, and as a fastener it's super inexpensive. It's also corrosion-resistant, non-magnetic and unaffected by UV light.

There are some specialized hand tools that make stainless steel wire even more useful:

Parallel Jaws Pliers put uniform twists in safety wire installations and are generally useful when using wire as a strapping material for multiple twists. The Clamptite hose clamp tool (above) is the best hose clamp solution anywhere, hands-down. And finally Fencing pliers, a great multi-tool when working with wire fences

and general repairs using stainless steel wire.

Here are just a few uses I've found for stainless steel wire:

• Building a bamboo vine trellis

• Keeping posts from splitting when pounding them with a sledge hammer

• Repairing a leaky hose fitting

• Keeping my aging, rusting catalytic converter from rattling

• Repairing my temporary fence until I can get around to building a proper one

With a spool of stainless steel wire, some needle-nose pliers and a pair of wire cutters, there is very little I can't fasten. With a Clamptite tool, some wire twisting pliers and a pair of fencing pliers, the number of possibilities rises exponentially.

Simple, effective and versatile. Inexpensive

and long-lasting. What more could you ask from a tool? Plus, it's a tool that justifies the use of other cool tools. I'd call that a recipe for a Cool Tool, for sure.

-- *Geoff Keochakian*

My interest is in the future because I am going to spend the rest of my life there. - C.F. Kettering

Small precision
Pocket Caliper

$8 General Tools 141ME Pocket Caliper
villagesupplies.com artstuff.net

This yellow plastic caliper is lightweight, reasonably durable (I lose it before it wears out) and pocket-friendly (only 4 inches long). I use it frequently during house or auto repairs to ensure the right size replacement part (such as nuts and bolts, or o-rings and sealing washers) comes home with me from the store or junkyard. I find this easier, quicker, and more accurate in many cases than using a small rule. It is not a precision machinist's instrument. However, in most of the work I need to get done, measurement to the closest 1/32 of an inch or 1 mm will get the right part or a fit which is good enough to work.

-- Ken Johnson

Most reliable micro-measurer
Mitutoyo Digital Calipers

$120 Mitutoyo MyCal Digital Caliper (6in) penntoolco.com

My grandfather, who had been a tool & die maker in San Francisco in the 20's and 30's, instilled in me the habit to always buy the best tools available, period. One of the first tools I was required to buy when I entered trade school was a caliper. At the time you could get either vernier scale or dial calipers. Well the dial calipers were the new thing, so I went out and bought a pair of Starrett Dial Calipers, the best American made tools at the time, at about a week's wages. I was so proud and took extra care of them, but to my dismay, within a year I found that they, and almost all dial calipers, had a fatal flaw. The dial is driven by a very small pinion gear that rides on a very small rack, and the rack had a tendency to pick up fine chips and grit in the teeth that were very hard to clean out. This in turn caused to pinion to skip and would cause the dial to jump its calibration. I had my first introduction to this problem when I was working on a camera part and all of a sudden it seemed all my dimensions were off by .025" (this is a lot in the world of precision). This cost me a day's work plus I had to fess up to my boss, a real tyrant, about my problem, and was he pissed! Well about five years later a colleague of mine showed me the "new new" thing which was a digital caliper. This caliper works on an electro-magnetic field so there are no moving parts to speak of, just the reader head sliding along the scale. This requires a wipe down with a clean rag every couple of days of use. The other features that made the digital version so much better was you could set the zero any place you wanted. So you could zero on a master part, and then

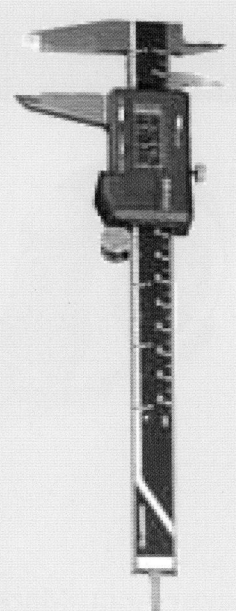

check all succeeding parts and instantly know if they were plus or minus of the master. Also you could switch from inches to metric with push of a button, very handy for working on things made overseas (metric).

Without a doubt my favorite digital calipers are the 6" Digimatic made by Mitutoyo. Mitutoyo is among the first to make digital calipers and seemed to get a jump on everyone else. Remarkably that seems to still be the case 20 years later. The Mitutoyo are the most copied, knocked-off calipers on the market. A friend of mine recently acquired a set of Swiss-made digital calipers and although they work well they are a little clunky and the sliding action is a bit rough.

I never cease to be amazed at the number of things I use my digital calipers for, out side of working in a machine shop. I keep one of my old sets at home and I use them all the time.

-- Chris Rand

Fast angles
Speed Square

Swanson Speed Square
$10 SO101 7 inches

This is the best tool for drawing lines, guiding saws, and basically all carpentry that requires a 90 degree angle. One edge is set perpendicular to the rest of it so you can quickly push it up against a straight side and have a 45 degree angle and a 90 degree angle to mark or saw with, etc. Hard to explain, but once you have one, you won't know how you lived without it.

-- Peter Lawrence

A good metal square is an essential tool for home building, especially framing. It helps you figure out rafter cuts quickly and easily, and it also has a ruler for quick measurements.

There are a number of different models of square out there, but Swanson's Speed Square is the best. Why? Well, sturdy aluminum alloy construction makes it nigh indestructible, and the recessed tick marks and numbers are colored in black so there's good contrast for legibility

The metal construction also makes it super-handy for making square cuts on lumber. Just snug it up and use it as a guide for your circular saw. Plus, all this utility fits in the pocket of work pants without any trouble.

-- Keith Pelczarski

3D vertical
Pole Level

$5

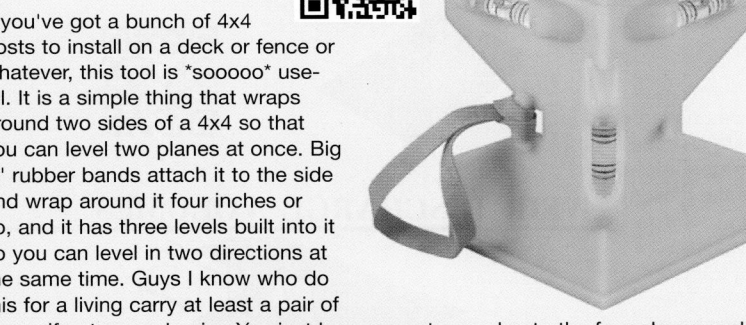

If you've got a bunch of 4x4 posts to install on a deck or fence or whatever, this tool is *sooooo* useful. It is a simple thing that wraps around two sides of a 4x4 so that you can level two planes at once. Big ol' rubber bands attach it to the side and wrap around it four inches or so, and it has three levels built into it so you can level in two directions at the same time. Guys I know who do this for a living carry at least a pair of these, if not several pairs. You just leave one strapped onto the far pole, or each post/corner of a deck, to make sure it remains unchanged while you jiggle the near one. I use one if I'm building shelves in a vertical position, or for anything that requires leveling on two planes at once. It's in that "why didn't I think of that?" category.

-- Paul Hoffman

Square sharpener
Carpenter Pencil and Keson Sharpener

$6 Carpenter Pencil Sharpener Keson

I have been a carpenter for thirty years or so. I started out as a framer on single family homes, where I used the flat carpenter's pencil. Its sturdy lead stood up to marking rough lumber but was a little tricky to sharpen. You want a flat chisel point not a conical point. This is accomplished quickly and easily with an inexpensive Keson pencil sharpener.

My framing days are long gone, thankfully. I have worked in many aspects of the field, from general carpentry to boatbuilding to cabinetmaking and am currently installing interior doors and high-end trim. Through it all I have held on to that flat pencil. It never ceased to amaze me how many employers (and I've been through a few) have told me to lose the flat pencil and get with the program and use a round pencil. To my mind, the only thing a round pencil is good for is taking a lunch order or making out the bill. The point breaks easily when marking wood and is difficult to sharpen unless you have an electric sharpener under your chopbox, which many guys do.

-- Paul Francy

Three-sided ruler
Alvin Architect's Scale

$15+ 2200 Series, 6, 12, 18 and 24 inches
Alvin

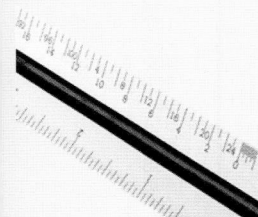

Most of my analog design tools now sit longingly in a cabinet, but one I still use daily is my architect's scale. Aside from a pencil, my scale is the most versatile tool on my desk.

I use a three-sided Alvin brand imperial

unit model with inches and ten different fractional scales. It's a handy basic ruler and straight edge for drawing or cutting, as well as for measuring and creating scale drawings. The aluminum model also makes a fairly intimidating weapon during heated meetings (the corners do tend to bend if it's dropped).

Though so much of my process is digital now, I still use this tool for drafting and measuring drawings almost daily. It's far quicker and less cumbersome to

pull out a scale and create an accurate drawing on the back of a document right in a meeting than going back to a workstation and building a digital model. Sometimes I'll need to explain why something will or will not work because of scale without breaking the flow of a conversation.

Our analog tools were once so precious. Designers built collections over the course of their careers. The most prized ones were cherished and passed

down from mentors and older family members in the field. Who cherishes his copy of AutoCAD -- much less carries an old floppy disk around in a velvet-lined box?

I still cherish my aluminum Alvin ruler. And it rules.

-- Michael Doyle

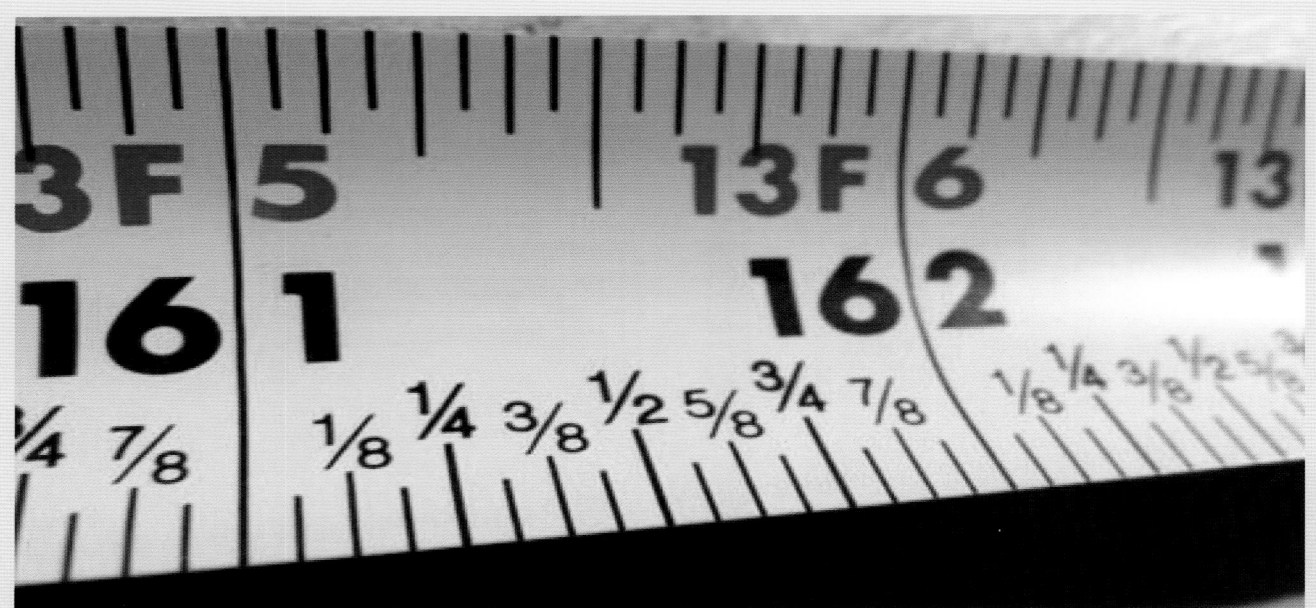

Easy-to-read tape
Komelon Speed Mark Tape

$11 Amazon

Because of improvements in tape-measure technology, even a cheap fat 25-foot tape can extend in the air without support ten feet or more, can deal with 99% of my needs, and will roll up into a pocketable 3-inch case. I don't even bother with tapes less than 25 feet now. I like the Komelon Speed Mark because every inch is labeled with fractional graduations in 1/8 increments (and hashes to 1/16); for instance, the tape will be marked: 13F, 5 and 5/8 inches. In bold easy to read fonts. No figuring needed. A thumbable button will slow its rewind to prevent damage during its return. This one is not expensive and well made.

-- KK

No-math spacing
Rivet Spacer

$35 Amazon

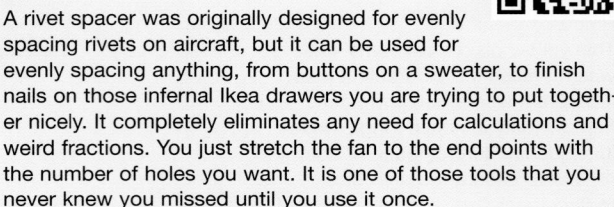

A rivet spacer was originally designed for evenly spacing rivets on aircraft, but it can be used for evenly spacing anything, from buttons on a sweater, to finish nails on those infernal Ikea drawers you are trying to put together nicely. It completely eliminates any need for calculations and weird fractions. You just stretch the fan to the end points with the number of holes you want. It is one of those tools that you never knew you missed until you use it once.

-- Alexander Rose

TABLE 1-1:
NOMINAL AND ACTUAL SIZES OF SOFTWOOD LUMBER

	Thicknesses			Face widths	
	Actual (inches)			Actual (inches)	
Nominal size*	Minimum dry**	Dressed green	Nominal size	Minimum dry**	Dressed green
1	3/4	25/32	2	1 1/2	1 9/16
1 1/4	1	1 1/32	3	2 1/2	2 9/16
1 1/2	1 1/4	1 9/32	4	3 1/2	3 9/16
2	1 1/2	1 9/16	5	4 1/2	4 5/8
2 1/2	2	2 1/16	6	5 1/2	5 5/8
3	2 1/2	2 9/16	7	6 1/2	6 5/8
3 1/2	3	3 1/16	8	7 1/4	7 1/2
4	3 1/2	3 9/16	9	8 1/4	8 1/2
			10	9 1/4	9 1/2
			11	10 1/4	10 1/2
			12	11 1/4	11 1/2

*Thickness sometimes is expressed as 4/4, 5/4, etc.
**Dry lumber has been seasoned to a moisture content of 19 percent or less.

Ultimate guide for hanging
Black & Decker Accu Mark Level

$19 Amazon

I've moved three times in four years, but never quite mastered the art of hanging artwork. Move any frame in our home and you'd be likely to find no less than two sets of holes. Well, not any more. At 36", this level seemed like overkill (especially since most everything I hang is in the 8" x 10" realm), but now that I have one, I don't know how I ever got by without it. On either side of the three bubble levels are two 10-inch rulers with sliding "targets." Each target has a t-shape cut out, allowing you to mark exactly where you want the nail(s) to go. More or less fool-proof. It's also incredibly light and easy to maneuver, even with one hand. These days when we buy art, I don't dread the prospect of putting it up.

-- Steven Leckart

Building with math
Workshop Math

$8 Robert Scharff, 1989, 456 p.

About five years ago I began to build my own house. It's amazing just how much of a house is built on maths! I was never very good at maths at school and I would often have to dredge my deepest memories of that time trying to remember whether it was two Pi x R or Pi x R squared?

My wife was getting pretty fed up with me continually giving her bills of quantities and so on to work out, and bought me this book as a gift. I love it! It's now the most dog eared book on my workshop shelf and even though the house is built and finished I still refer to it whenever I've got one of those "I'm sure there must be an easier way of working this out" problems.

It contains tons of useful stuff from calculating loads on beams over a given distance to calculating the thermal efficiency of a wood burner. It really does cover a lot of ground. Only problem I have found with it is that being from the UK, where we generally work in metric, a lot of the tables in the book are in imperial measurements.

However, Scharff usually gives the formulae as well as the tables so it is usually pretty easy just to do the workings in millimetres or kilogrammes or whatever. If they had used books like this when I was at school I reckon I would have seen the relevance and taken to it much more than I did. Anyway, I think it's a must-have now and wish I had found it years ago.

-- George Graham

Shirtpocket database of tech info
Pocket Ref

$10 Thomas J. Glover, 2010 (4th edition), 864 p.

People who make things keep one of these little books in their truck, one in their tool box, and one in their office. Its tiny pages are crammed with dense tables, charts, lists, codes, conversion formulas–more than 500 pages of numbers, yet it fits into a real pocket. What is the friction rate of water in a one inch pipe? What's cubic feet per second in liters per minute? The country code for Turkey? The voltage drop of number 12 wire over 100 feet? The shear strength of Eastern White Pine? The insulation value of carpeting? You get the idea; it has the numbers for everything, and 95 percent of them found nowhere else (off the web), and no where else in one handy place.

– KK

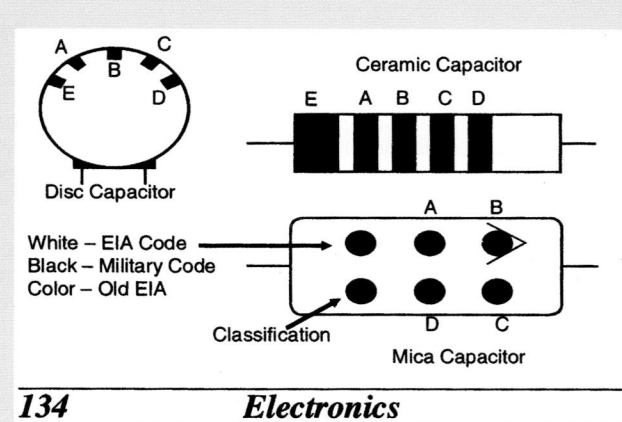

A		C
	B	
E		D

Disc Capacitor

Ceramic Capacitor

| E | A | B | C | D |

White – EIA Code
Black – Military Code
Color – Old EIA

Classification

Mica Capacitor

134 | *Electronics*

WEIR DISCHARGE VOLUMES

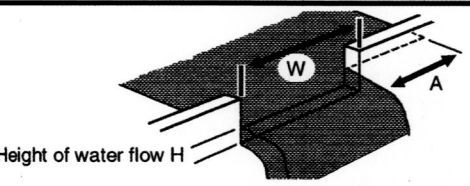

Height of water flow H

Head Inches	GPM for Width of Weir in Feet			gpm/foot over 5 feet wide
	1	3	5	
1	35	107	179	36
1.5	64	197	329	66
2	98	302	506	102
2.5	136	421	705	142
3	178	552	926	187
4	269	845	1420	288
5	369	1174	1978	402
6	476	1534	2592	529
7	...	1922	3255	667
8	...	2335	3963	814
9	...	2769	4713	972
10	...	3225	5501	1138
12	...	4189	7181	1496

Based on the Francis formula:
$$\text{Cu ft/sec water} = 3.33 \, (W - 0.2 H) \, H^{1.5}$$
Where H=height in feet, W=width in feet and distance "A" should be at least 3 H.

Water | **421**

Hand held speed checker
Pocket Radar

$190 pocketradar.com

Hold this thing in your hand, aim it at a fast, moving object and it instantly gives you the speed of that object -- either coming or going. Not only big objects like cars, but little ones like golf balls, too. This little gizmo's accuracy matches that of police scans, so you can check for speeders on your block.

The main use of the Pocket Radar is for sports, which is what we use it for -- measuring ball/running speeds for performance improvement. It's super easy to use. And it will pick up all kinds of things I had no idea radar detected. We were able to get accurate measurements on arrows in flight! Not everyone needs to measure speed, but for most who do, this pocket device is all you need.

-- KK

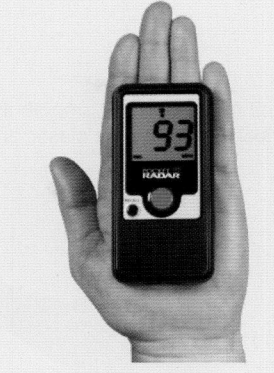

Non-invasive thermometer
Raytek Mini Non-Contact Thermometer

$46 Model MT4 raytek.com

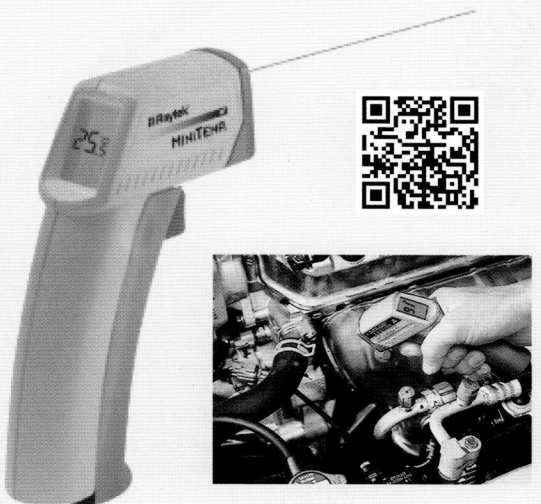

I borrowed one of these non-contact thermometers to test the heat dissipation around a new fireplace I'm finishing. The device worked so well, I found myself running around my house taking the temperature(s) of lots of things I'd often wondered about but had no way of investigating. For instance, I was curious about the results of extra insulation I put in last year. I also found myself using it to follow heat contours around the house. I could follow heat contours in the air by using this device to measure the temperature of the skin of my hand. This method made a rigorous investigation into energy conservation fun as well as informative.

One attribute of IR thermometers I really appreciated is their instantaneous response, even across a distance. Since the device is based on an infrared (IR) light sensor, there is no lag, no hysteresis (like a thermostat), no memory, no need to even be close to the surface being measured, which is a lot different from how I am used to thinking about temperature.

With this tool it was as if I could reach across the room and touch the wall in the back of the fireplace to see how hot the fire was getting. I discovered all kinds of readings that affected my fireplace design. For instance I was able to measure a much sharper gradient across the metal face of the zero-clearance fireplace, where I planned to mount tile with special heat-tolerant silicon adhesive. And so on.

As a homeowner it may be hard to justify buying one, but as a nerd (and especially if I had kids) I want one around. For me it has something to do with an Internet-biased mentality -- I hear an obscure concept, or someone has a question, and I almost reflexively reach for Google. Now it's like that for my home. Is that frying pan at exactly the right temperature for pancakes? Wait, I can get the IR thermometer out of the kitchen drawer...

-- Rick Botman

Laser based measuring tool
Leica Disto 2 Laser Distance Measurer

$160 ptd.leica-geosystems.com

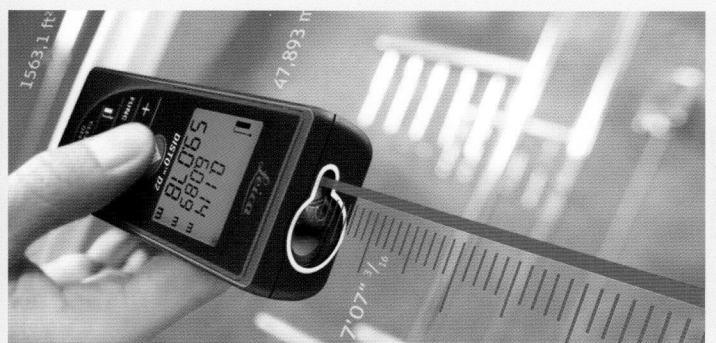

The Leica DISTO 2 allows me to measure accurately from about 1/16 inches to about 197 feet. It can calculate from the measurement, as appropriate, the area or volume. It also has the ability using the Pythagorean theorem to calculate indirect lengths.

The small size, in inches, (4.4L x 0.9D x 2.2W) is conveniently to carry and use. The accuracy requires a steady hand but tool quickly obtains a measurement.

I use the D2 for my construction projects and find it helpful in my photography in setting the aperture to get the depth of field I want.

The combination of small size, accuracy, ease of use and low price is not matched to my knowledge.

-- Walter Smith

Weighs big packages & food
Ultraship Scale

$30 Ultraship Digital Shipping Postal Kitchen Scale Amazon

I have been considering buying a kitchen scale for quite a while, but was often underwhelmed with what was out there. Unlike a garden-variety kitchen scale, which typically weighs up to only four pounds, the Ultraship can handle up to 55 pounds. It reads in ounces, pounds, grams or kilos, so it's perfect for the kitchen, but can also be used for shipping packages and mail. Heck, you could even weigh a small child on it. Also, it features a just plain brilliant design: if you are weighing a really big monster package that blocks the display, you can detach it! The entire face of the unit can be unclipped and pulled away from the scale with a 5-foot-long extension cord.

When I compared the Ultraship to a laboratory-grade scale used at my company, this one went gram for gram with the lab scale. Within the 0-2 pound range, it is actually accurate to essentially 0.035 ounces as opposed to the 0.1 ounces in the specification. If you take baking seriously, this is the only way to go. I fish quite a bit, so it's nice to be able to weight those 30-pound striped bass. From 2-55 pounds, the scale is accurate to within 0.5 ounces. While my initial motivation was for the kitchen, I have also been using it for boxes and packages.

-- Aram Salzman

Weighs 0.01 gram
Super sensitive digital scale

Here are two cheap digital scales that can weigh items to a precision of 0.01 gram. Most kitchen scales are a precision a magnitude lower, at 0.1 gram. You'll need a wind shield for scales this sensitive because air currents will disrupt the reading at this level.

-- KK

Digital 0.01-gram resolution scales are plentiful and very inexpensive.

I used one from eBay identical to one of these and was satisfied with the performance. Note that I was using it for balancing motorcycle pistons, a less demanding task than some others.

Note that you can also obtain scale weight sets for calibration.

-- RCP

$25 American Weigh Scale Scalemate Sm-501 Digital Pocket Scale, 500 X 0.01 G Amazon

$11 American Weigh Scale Ac-100 Digital Pocket Gram Scale, 100 G X 0.01 G

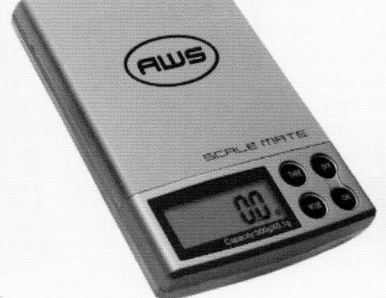

Pliers

Lightweight ratchets
Pittsburgh Pro Composite Ratchets
$10 1/4", 3/8", and 1/2" harborfreight.com

I have multiple Snap On, SK, and Craftsman ratchets so when I first heard how smooth and nice the action is on the Pittsburgh Pro Composite Ratchets from Harbor Freight I scoffed. A metal mechanism inside a plastic and rubber covered ratchet?

So I tried the 1/4" and 3/8" models and all I can say is WOW! I have not tried the 1/2" model yet, but all three sizes are dirt cheap at under $10, feature lifetime warranties, are lightweight, have a non-conductive body, are "warmer" to use in cold weather, and have a butter smooth 72-tooth ultra-fine ratcheting mechanism. This isn't to suggest you ditch your regular ratchets for high torque applications (use a breaker bar) but these are quite nice and have earned a place alongside my other ratchets. These are a real gem.

-- *Warren Flearl*

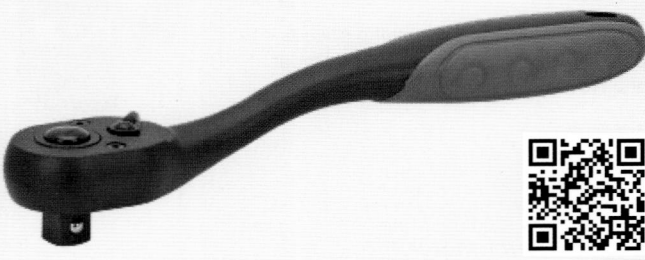

Ergonomic ratcheting wrench
GearWrench X-Beam
$15 (13mm) gearwrench.com

These are not your standard combination wrenches. They literally put a twist in it. The working ends are offset from each other by 90 degrees, which makes for a great handle that reduces stress and increases leverage. Beyond its heft and balance, the design of this crescent wrench/box wrench ratchet is much more comfortable, especially for repetitive tasks. By twisting the axis, that non-working end now makes for a more natural handle that diffuses pressure into the palm and across the fingers. The shaft of the tool is also slightly longer than many combo wrenches (small increases in shaft length greatly increase torque, or conversely decrease force required to achieve required torque).

I've been using this wrench for three months in near daily use. As a solar installer I use my gear heavily in adverse conditions: bolting solar modules to rooftops. When other installers tipped me off to this brand, I did some investigating. They are the only tools I have ever seen endorsed by the Arthritis Foundation. I figured that if they are good for arthritis sufferers, it has to be good for me, too. I was right.

-- *Mark Colacito*

Screwed up pliers
Screw Pliers
$36 Engineer PZ-58 Screw Pliers screw-pliers.com

The first time I used these screw pliers I was amazed that I had lived without a pair for so long. These pliers are designed for screw removal in cases of corroded or stripped heads.

Regular pliers tend to have straight jaws. This works if you grab the screw from the side (horizontally), but if you are in a cramped space and attacking the screw from the end regular pliers fail. I have had many pliers slip off a difficult screw because the jaws are straight where contact is made with the screw, which limits the gripping surface area.

The jaws of these pliers are curved with teeth on the inside of the clamping surfaces. Since the jaws have both horizontal and vertical teeth, these pliers will bite into the circumference of the screw head regardless of the orientation - this makes stubborn screws very, very easy to remove.

It won't handle stripped countersunk screws (those are suited to the extractor bits on the drill) but for other surface screws or bolts it should be fine.

A close-up of the pliers inset teeth allowing for vertical traction.

-- *Ezra Reynolds*

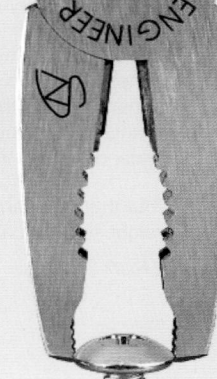

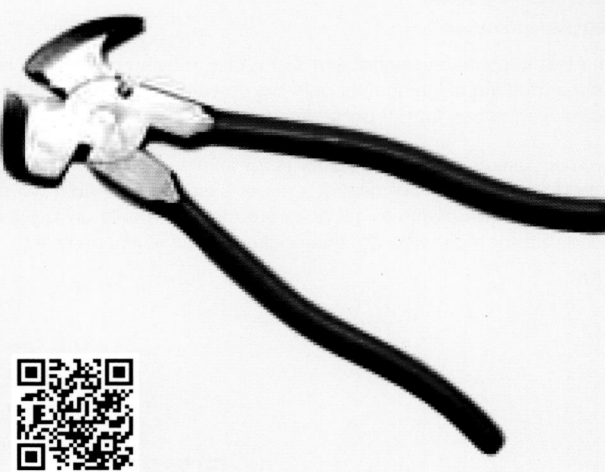

Universal farm tool
Fence Pliers
$7 Amazon

Most useful farm tool No.1 is a pair of Fencing Pliers. These little beauties cost me about $13 and represent the best value for money of any of my tools. In one device it is a wire cutter, a staple puller, a hammer and a great source of leverage on any object unlucky enough to be in its grasp or impaled on its horn.

While most multi-function tools tend to be a jack of all trades and master of none, the fencing pliers hardly compromise at all. They will cut high tensile fencing wire (including our famous New Zealand #8 wire) that would simply blunt most plier-design wire cutters. When it comes to removing staples, they don't only excel at pulling staples that are proud of the post. The flat hammering face can be hit with another hammer to drive the horn into a staple that has been driven too far into the wood. Once you have hooked the staple, levering it out is pretty simple. Try that with a hammer or nipper-design staple puller. The jaws can also be locked over the head of a nail for the same leverage effect. As a hammer, they work pretty well and have a nice weight balance. The only negative is the smaller striking surface, but you can't have everything!

My pair is about 5 years old and despite a few signs of wear and tear, they still function perfectly well. They rate #1 in my farm tool arsenal. When you factor in the relatively low cost, they are an absolute essential in any tool kit.

-- *John Hart*

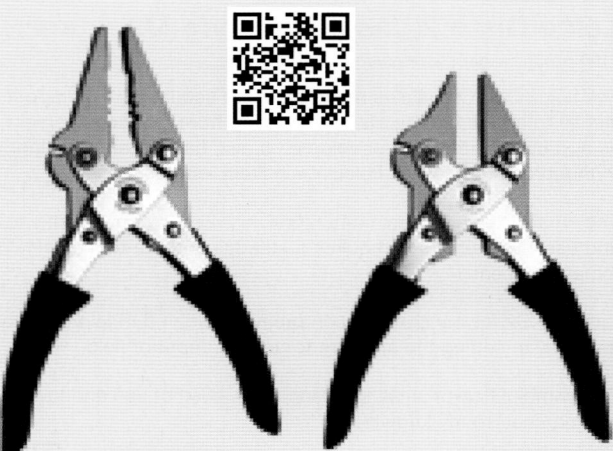

Tight gripper
Parallel Jaws Pliers
$25 Parallel Jaws Pliers tennis-warehouse.com

My favorite general-purpose pliers are parallel-jaw pliers. They excel at crimping and grasping near the tips since they apply uniform pressure across the whole face. Since the jaw faces stay parallel, these pliers may be used in a pinch to hold or turn a small fastener without deforming its face. A small groove running down the center length of one jaw lets you use these pliers to tension cable or wire, and many models come with an effective wire cutter on the side.

I had a pair, passed down from my father, that was stolen -- I despaired of replacing them until I found this robust spring-loaded pair of Shimano pliers made for fishermen. Parallel-jaw pliers are also apparently used by jewellers and tennis-racket stringers among others.

-- *Philip Flip Kromer*

Clippers that cut anything
Knipex High Leverage Cutters
$30 Amazon

This is one of my favorite tools. I own at least two of these nippers. The difference between these and every other cutter is that they are drop-forged and they've got some specific hardening at the tip. They cut through everything. I've snipped through quarter inch bolts with these. I can cut the bane of all cutters — piano wire — all day long and these will never be marred by it. I have ruined so many other tools by cutting the wrong wire or nails. There may be other brands that do this, but this is the one I've been using for 20 years. The Knipex are expensive – they're about $60 a pair — but it is one of those classic examples of how you can ruin a couple of pairs of something else and you've paid for these. I've never had these fail.

-- *Adam Savage*

We can't leave the haphazard to chance. - N.F. Simpson

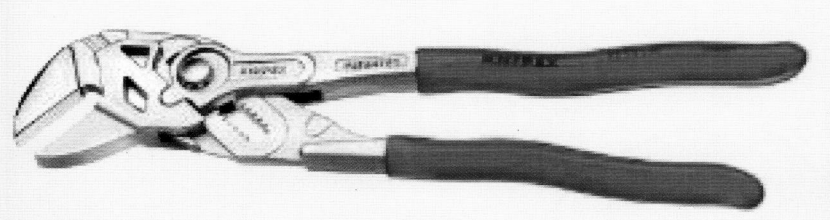

$50 (10in)
knipex.com

Rapidly: an adjustable crescent wrench is not rapid. One must adjust the opening to the nut or bolt head, and between tightening turns, in removing and replacing the wrench, inevitably the wrench loosens a bit and must be retightened. An open-ended or box wrench or socket is the best tool to use, but then one must keep in hand a range of sizes for each size of nut/head. In contrast the Knipex pliers wrench loosens and tightens like a pair of pliers or channel lock wrench.

Safely: an adjustable crescent wrench tends to loosen, rounding off the corners of the nut or bolt head. Pliers or vice-grips are worse, putting teeth-marks on the nut or head. In contrast the Knipex pliers wrench has flat, smooth, and parallel heads ensuring no rounding or gouging of the nut/head.

Strongly: the lever arm of the Knipex ensures a strong grip on the nut/head. I've used them to squeeze small solid aluminum rivets in building an experimental airplane.

Rapid, safe, strong pliers wrench
Knipex Pliers Wrenches

The Knipex Pliers Wrench is best described in the US as a smooth-faced channel lock plier/wrench. Or, as a pliers-handled crescent wrench. I have a set of 3 different sizes and have used them for a year. They allow one to rapidly, safely and strongly grip nuts or bolt heads for tightening or loosening.

To summarize, the Knipex pliers wrench combines the best features of other tools, enabling one to grip and turn nuts and bolts with a single tool, and apply considerable squeezing pressure on objects without gouging or tooth marks.

-- Ralph Fincher

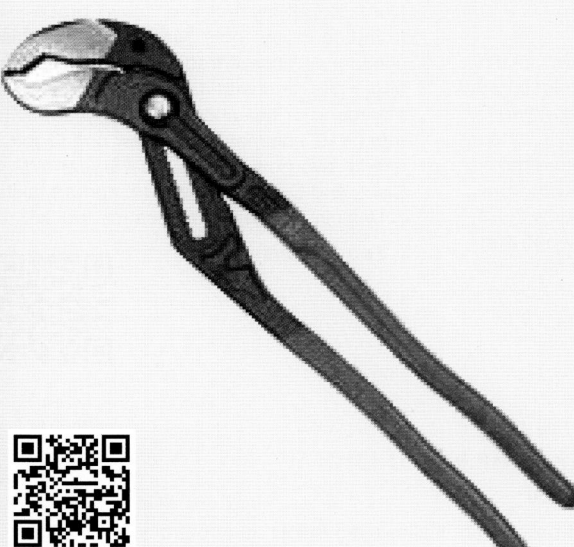

Tenacious wrench
Knipex Cobra Pliers

$30 10in

This unique tool provides instant adjustment, memory retention of jaw opening and single handed, self gripping operation with a grip that won't let go. The Knipex jaws really grip. You can literally hang from the handles and they will not slip. The upper and lower jaws are notched. This allows the user to grip a hex nut on the corner and the flat side so as not to round off the nut. They have a flat nose where the jaws meet that allows you to do some pretty fine work. The jaws are very tough. The Cobra is designed to eliminate "knuckle-busting" and the "burring" of nuts, bolts and fittings. Its thin profile and light weight ensure ease of operation.

On first glance they look like the classic Channel Locks (on the right in the picture below). But the Channel Lock handles actually touch together in the extreme "wide" position. This can and has led to pinched hands and fingers if you slip off the work piece. The Knipex handles do not touch, which leaves you with that little bit of saving grace if you slip off the work piece. Also the Channel Lock has 5 jaw positions that slip/slide into place, while the Knipex has 12 jaw positions and, each position is spring-pin locked into place. For example you are working in a blind, tight space and drop the Knipex: the jaw will still be set to the position you started with and you suffer no aggravation except that due to your own clumsiness. Not so with Channel locks. You will have to fiddle around with them to get them back where you want them, and if you bump or roll them around the work, while trying to get a bite, the jaws will slip back out of position.

I have used this tool almost every day for the past 18 years working with elevator and escalator system installations, repairs, servicing and maintenance. It is always the first tool I grab to take with me to do a job at home or at work.

-- Shaler Derickson

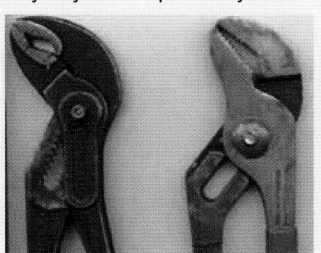

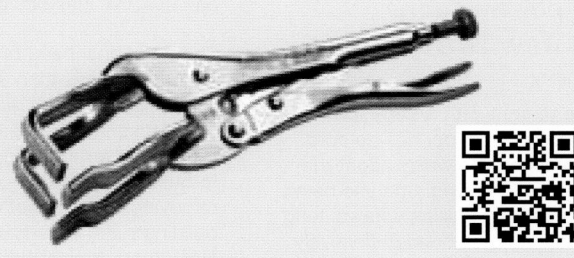

Old reliable
Vise-grips

$10 5WR maxtool.com

If one needs a single tool, Vise-grips are it. On a motor-cycle I have used one as clutch or shift lever or attached to a broken throttle cable. You can turn a screw if you can reach the side of it with this tool . Lock one down to something under the hood; you might not like to bugger up a bolt, but you won't care if you are no where near tools. If required, you can rip sheet metal with one. Wire cutting too. You can clamp it down hard enough to hit it with a hammer. Vise-grips and a crowbar are thieves' favorite tools. Buy the small size; and only the brand name: these are made of high-strength steel.

-- C. Bridger

And they come in a whole tribe of specialty varieties. The standard should be in everyone's tool box, the small one in every emergency pouch, and you should at least know about the others. The same relentless leveraged but sensitive clamping action works with super wide vise-grips, narrow ones, wide necked ones, nut cutters, curved necks and so on. They are extremely handy.

-- KK

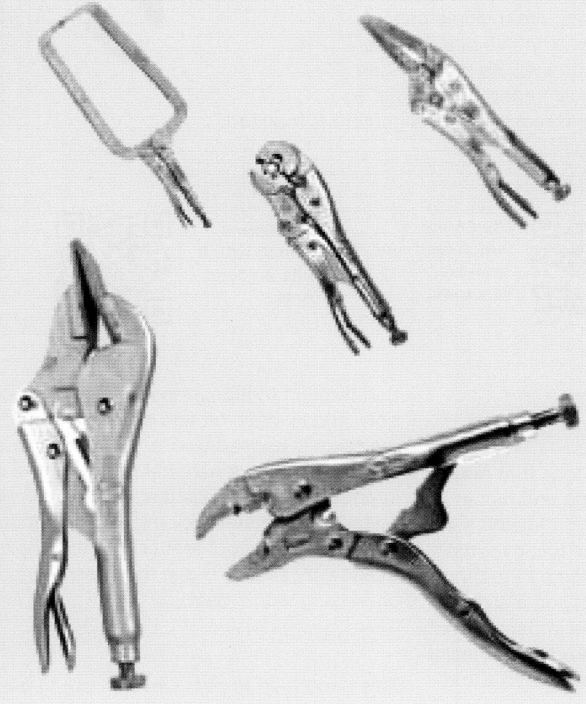

Essential wrench
Vise-Grip Locking Wrench

$13 Model 7LW irwin.com

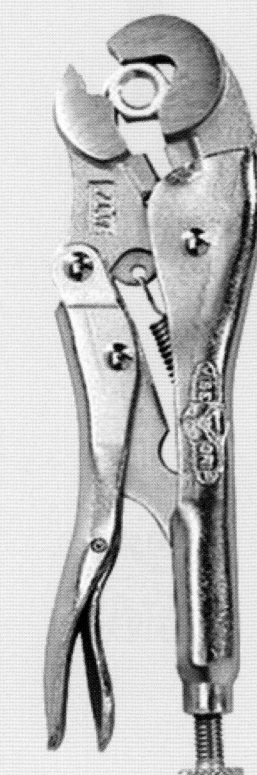

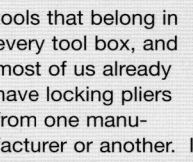

There are some tools that belong in every tool box, and most of us already have locking pliers from one manufacturer or another. Irwin Tools, maker of the original Vise Grips brand product, is the best known. This new version of the tool looks and works nearly the same, but has a vastly improved jaw shape made specifically for grabbing on to damaged hex nuts and bolts.

I used mine just yesterday while working on restoring an old car for my daughter. I had to remove the heat shield from the exhaust manifold, and after 10 years of service those bolts were not in good shape at all. One of them was so bad that my sockets and box wrenches would just spin, getting no bite at all. My usual pair of locking pliers didn't help either. The unique jaw shape on the Irwin Locking Wrench grabbed the head of the bolt from three sides and fastened firmly enough to do the job. In just a few seconds I had that old bolt out without having to resort to cutting it with an angle grinder or torch.

I've seen these online for less than fifteen dollars, and for the amount of headache they save I'd call it well worth adding to any tool box. If you've ever used regular locking pliers to try to get a stripped bolt out, you'll find this new style of locking wrench works wonders.

-- Andrew Pollack

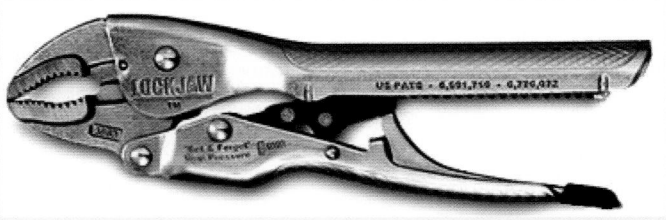

Better ViseGrips
LockJaw Self-Adjusting Pliers

$17 lockjawpliers.com

These tools work similar to ViseGrips except they automatically adjust to the size of the object they're gripping. The tension desired is adjustable via a set-screw, but once the tension is set, different size objects can be clamped without readjustment.

Also, the release lever is opposite that of the ViseGrip in that you pull on the lever with your ring finger while maintaining full grip of the pliers. No more pliers flying across the room and no more pinched fingers between the release and handle!

-- Bob Muir

Classic Hand Tools

Tenon cutter, bit and socket not included.

Professional, shock-absorbing hammer
Stiletto TiBone Titanium Hammer

$200 Stiletto Tools

I drooled over and pondered getting this hammer for a year before I finally took the plunge -- and it was well worth the very high price tag. This hammer really absorbs the vibrations as you pound it. I have been framing for about 14 years and have been swinging an Estwing 25-oz. California-style framing hammer for most of that time. My elbow is almost shot from the vibrations of using those all-steel hammers. Since buying the much lighter titanium T-bone (15 oz.), I have noticed a dramatic difference in my elbow.

All-around it's an absolutely wonderful hammer. The magnetic nail starter isn't a new invention, but it's handy, and I use the side nail puller every chance I get instead of relying on the claw. The hammer also features a removable steel head (or face), which can be replaced with a milled waffle or smooth head (depending on which face you purchase to begin with). Stiletto makes other cheaper hammers with a titanium head and a wooden or fiberglass handle. They absorb a lot of shock, too, but tend to break fairly easily - unlike this model, which has a titanium handle covered in rubber.

If you are serious about building and/or want to lessen the impact on your elbow, arm, etc., this hammer is certainly worth the investment. I don't know offhand what a shot of cortisone costs, but they probably add up. I wouldn't recommend this hammer for the average Joe, but if you use a hammer a lot, this is the one to get. They come with a curved or straight handle. I have one with a curved handle, which just feels right.

-- Greg Morris

Precise start on metal
Auto Center Punch

$7

A simple superior tool about the size of a stubby pencil that punches a tiny depression in metal. It's used to start a hole, or mark a point. But unlike standard punches, which you need to hit with a hammer -- whose impact usually misaligns the spot you intended to punch -- this one gets its punch from a tiny internal spring that flexes as you press the tip down. You simply press the punch where you want a dent and there it is exactly. A classic.

-- KK

We in the rescue trade also use these pretty routinely to safely remove the glass in automobiles. They work particularly well on the glass in the side and rear windows and leave all of the little glass bits intact in the window frame until you gently remove them with gloved hands. The bits then go where you want (generally) and not on your patient. I assume that keeping one in your car would let you punch out your own windows in case of emergency. Just remember that it is key to use the device on the lower corner of a window or the glass can shatter and go everywhere.

-- J. James Bono

Human-powered driver
Three Jaw Brace

$67 Lee Valley

Ever have to fight with a thirty foot cord on a cold day? This tool has no cord. And no batteries. No worry about theft, obsolescence, charging. Imagine being able to remove #4 Phillips screws, long embedded with their heads effectively stripped before they were painted over. By hand. The same tool, with a "no moving parts" adapter, is a speed wrench for 3/8" drive sockets. And you can use 1/4" hex bits as well.

The traditional hand brace does all this, and weighs less than a commercial-duty battery pack. That's why I have two old braces in my on-site tool kit, where I do a vast array of kludge-like repairs to building systems -- everything from removing the third set of windows in a building's life, to re-hanging wood and steel doors (remember those stripped, self-tapping, Phillips screws?), boring holes to run a fish-tape through, and taking mechanical stuff apart.

I just bought my first-ever "new" brace from Lee Valley Tools. Made in France this version will accept traditional square-taper auger bits, and with its three jaw chuck, any round or hex shank tool up to about 15 mm (9/16") diameter. This new one together with two power tools -- a 25-year-old Black and Decker screw gun, and a Makita 7 1/4" circular saw -- makes my tool kit.

-- Lou Parsons

Hole maker
Japanese Screw Punch

This lovely tool can punch through multiple layers of paper, mat board, etc. It is great for making eyelet holes in fabric as well as leather. Used by book makers and mixed media artists. It is amazing in its ease and is very durable! Earns Extra Foofy Points to be able to say you have a "Japanese Screw Punch."
-- Jane Wynn

The advantage of this tool (sometimes called a Paper Drill) is that unlike your usual plier-like paper punch, this one is not constrained by where you want a hole. You can drill a hole anywhere on any size sheet -- not just the edges -- by bearing down on the handle. To compensate for the lack of leverage you do get in a plier-like punch, the shaft of this screw punch rotates as you press, neatly slicing a trim hole. It will go through 15 pages of paper at once; thicker materials will require multiple passes. It comes with five bits, but the largest one will be smaller than the typical paper punch hole, so I've found more careful alignment is required.

-- KK

$38 Screw Punch with one 3mm bit Yasutomo

$82 Screw Punch with 9 bits Volcano Arts

Tough analog drill
Schroeder Hand Drill

$23 Amazon

A hand-powered drill allows a subtlety and control you don't get from a power tool, so very much more direct and satisfying to use. From a sheer utilitarian perspective, my Schroeder 1/4" drill is a wonder to behold and use. The gearing is all-metal, so it's built to last. For the price, you won't find a tougher drill. I've used it for building cabinets and tables, puttering around the house and garden, pre-drilling screw holes, and mounting things to walls, etc. and it works like a champ. I used Fiskars hand drills for years but their inner gears are made of plastic and will strip out if you apply too much torque. They also can't be opened up for repair either, so once that happens it goes straight to the landfill, which is really disheartening. With the Schroeder, the solid, single gear is right there in the open. You have to hold it in your hands to appreciate it. Like the engineering in a 1970's Beemer or a piece of Shaker furniture, it's logical and simple, direct and pure. It makes me happy just to spin it.

-- Charles Henry Frieder

Human powered high torque
Impact Driver Wrench

This hand tool is used to unscrew bolts that may have become rusted into place. One end has a 3/8th inch socket stub over which you fit with the appropriate socket head. You place this over the bolt and then use a hammer/mallet to hit the other end of the cylindrical tool while applying a slight twisting force on the the body of the impact wrench. The perpendicular motion of the hammer is translated (via a system of springs and prawls) into a sudden twisting motion at the head of the troublesome bolt. Since static friction decreases so much when the force is applied over a very short duration ---like the time it takes a hammer to smack the end of the impact wrench -- bolts that would otherwise require so much force that they might snap off can be easily removed. Very cool tool. Other tool makers make things very similar, but in my experience, the Snap-on version works best.

-- Gabriel Pilar

This hand-held Impact Driver is not to be confused with the hundreds of pneumatic and power Impact Drivers which have largely replaced it. For occasional use, this little guy will do -- although it takes some skill to keep it on the bolt when you hammer it. I've used the Craftsman's brand, which is half the cost of the Snap-On.

-- KK

◀ **$55 Impact Driver** Snap-On

▶ **$25 Impact Driver** #00947641000 Craftsman

I shut my eyes in order to see. - Paul Gauguin

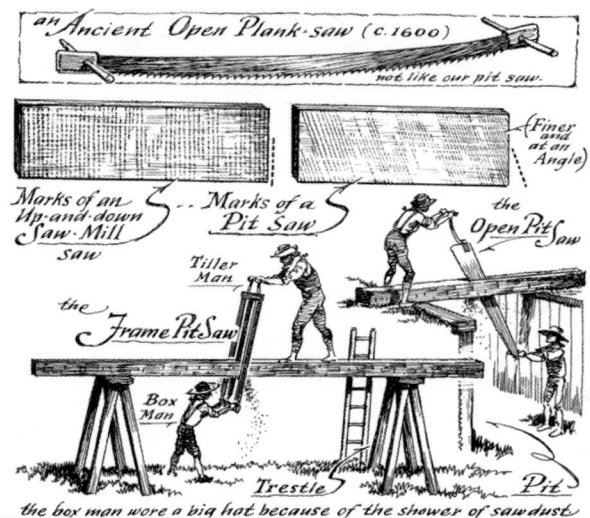

The Biggest Saws

Its teeth raked to cut downward, the long pit saws (both open and framed) did most of the earliest American plank-sawing both from trestles and in pits. The open type was more recent in the New World than the framed model. Factory-made, the open pit saw was used until the late 1800's.

There was an ancient open plank saw (see below) that some collectors regard as an open pit saw, but the curved blade and matching handles indicate otherwise.

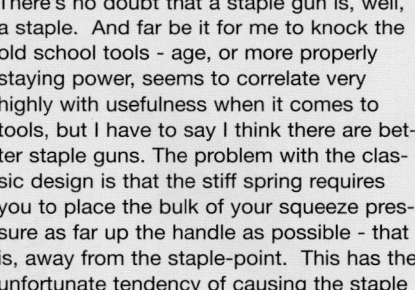

Owner-made tools

Museum of Early American Tools

$9 Eric Sloane, 2002, 128 p.

A story is told by each tool archived in this paper museum. The tool reveals the amazing things that can be done with your own body's power, regulated by your eye and mind. Listening to the tool, you can understand how things are made. Not only do these tools run without electricity, they can be made with other hand tools. There's enough information in these packed drawings by Eric Sloane to enable you to make them yourself, to use to make other things. It's kind of magical.

-- KK

Essential glazing knife

Lamson 3/4-Inch Bent Stiff Putty Knife

$17 GlassWarePro

I have pushed literally thousands of linear feet of putty in the process of window glazing, and have been using this putty knife for the last twenty years (yes, the same one).

If you really want the professional edge when glazing an old wood window then you need this tool. The bent blade allows you to point the putty exactly where it needs to be. With very little practice the tip of the blade becomes an extension of your index finger or thumb for exact setting and cutting of glazing putty.

Simple, cheap, highly effective and very satisfying. Means it's a cool tool in my book!

-- Seamus Holley

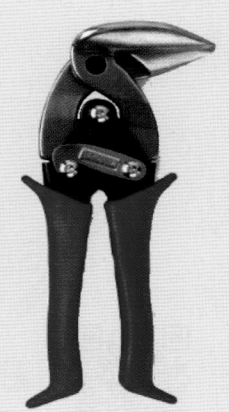

Painless metal cutters

Upright Snips

$26 Midwest Snips

These 90 degree angled snips eliminate the inevitable cuts your hands endure when snipping sheet metal by holding your hands above the work. There's a small price in slightly less finesse, but for most jobs pushing these is superior. You can work under the sheet as well. Comes in left or right handed.

--KK

A better staple gun

Forward Action Stapler

masco.com

One of the joys of producing Cool Tools is the delightful moment a reader turns me on to a better tool than the one I just reviewed. I got a note (below) letting me know that the good old standby Staple Gun which I ran last week has a superior improvement: the forward action stapler. You increase impact by squeezing toward the point of contact (on the left side in the illustration here.) I immediately got one and was hooked. It's ergonomically ingenious, more effective, and no more expensive than the standard type. Takes the usual T-50 staples. It is so much better

that I will retire that early review. This good "new" standby is the one that belongs in the most basic toolbox.

-- KK

There's no doubt that a staple gun is, well, a staple. And far be it for me to knock the old school tools - age, or more properly staying power, seems to correlate very highly with usefulness when it comes to tools, but I have to say I think there are better staple guns. The problem with the classic design is that the stiff spring requires you to place the bulk of your squeeze pressure as far up the handle as possible - that is, away from the staple-point. This has the unfortunate tendency of causing the staple

point to lift in a sort of pre-recoil when the trigger engages, leaving you with staples that are not-quite-in. Experienced users learn to counterbalance and apply extra pressure to the front -- also to anticipate the recoil -- but these adaptations speak to a need for revision.

The newer school of staple guns have very sensibly reversed this arrangement. The handle now inclines towards the front, with the trigger mechanism at the rear. Now the strain of battling the spring causes you to bear down directly on the staple point. You can get both consumer and contractor-grade "forward action" staplers.

-- Johnathan Nightingale

$28 Model 800KB

$24 EasyShot Light Duty

Indestructible multi-use trowel

Marshalltown Margin Trowel

$12 Amazon

I was first introduced to the many uses of the margin trowel fifteen years ago on a heavy construction site. I left the job but have carried the tool on every job and project ever since. When I moved to a desk I threw the tool into my tool bucket and still use it for just about everything.

The trowel is a simple piece of flat, quality steel attached to a wood handle. You can use it to finish concrete, set mortar, sling stucco, lay tile, scrape, pry, chip, hack, or cut anything not tougher than high-carbon steel. It is especially effective for cleaning other tools, such as shovels, concrete trowels, bbq's, and garden implements. With only a modicum of care it will last for years. If you're foolish or careless enough to permanently bend it then shame on you, but you can get another one for about $10.

It is superior to others because it's cheap, reliable and robust. I prefer the feel of a wood handle to rubber, although the wood handle will chip if used as a hammer.

-- Case Farley

Malleable, tight-fitting hexing

Pivot Head Hex Wrenches

$41 (metric or inches) Garrett Wade

The head of these hex wrenches pivots, allowing you to get access into numerous tight places and achieve speedier running in for final tightening (with the same hex or via torque wrench). Unlike a standard hex that only gives you 90-degrees, the flex head can be quickly adjusted. You simply move the handle to the angle that works best in the situation then turn (it's like a tight, square drive U joint adapter; there is no screw to lock it). Often you can simply flip the handle for another turn without disengaging from the socket head. The short end or long end can be used as the driver. I start screws with the long end then simply flip the wrench for snugging down.

I bought mine after I saw a bicycle mechanic using one. I've used mine *hard* for bicycle maintenance for over a year with no appreciable wear (they're chrome-plated vanadium steel). While elegant looking, they have never failed to bust loose stuck bolts, especially stainless ones in aluminum or even steel threads. I gave a set to a Mechanical Engineer whose hobby is designing high-end racing recumbents for setting human powered vehicle records. He was also thrilled with them.

-- Fred Larimer

$27 Amazon

Hole Makers

Perfect guides
Transfer Punches
$26 Transfer Punch Set Central Tools

These simple punches are incredibly useful when laying out things, yet nobody outside of machinists seems to know about them (some woodworkers know about the special ones for dowel holes). You can get them from most industrial tool distributors (like MSC), but they are also one of the early tasks for apprentices to make on a metal lathe.

Essentially, they are just a set of rods, in standard drill diameters, with a center punch tip in one end. When trying to drill pilot holes for things (say a shelf bracket) clamp it in place, and use them to mark the bolt holes. You wind up with marks dead center in the pattern, no more ovaling out holes so you can get the bolts through.

Similarly, there exist punches for transferring threaded holes – screw them in, and tap the sheet you want to transfer to.

-- Jeff Del Papa

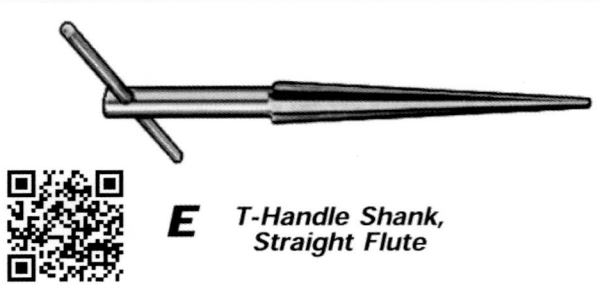

E *T-Handle Shank, Straight Flute*

Hole expander
T-reamer
$6 Grizzly

The handiest simple tool in the world (that most people don't own) - a sheet-metal worker's T-reamer. This utterly simple no-working-parts hand tool will easily, smoothly, safely, and precisely enlarge round holes (and keep them perfectly round) in any rigid, non-brittle material (i.e. not rubber or leather, not glass, but almost anything else). I discovered this tool by accident when I was twelve years old and have owned one, more or less, ever since. When I lose one, I have to buy another. Costs a few bucks, and, with regular household use, never wears out. Try it. You'll like it. Don't get marooned on a desert island without one.

-- William Gibson

Precise drilling device
G8689 Mini Milling Machine
$625 Grizzly

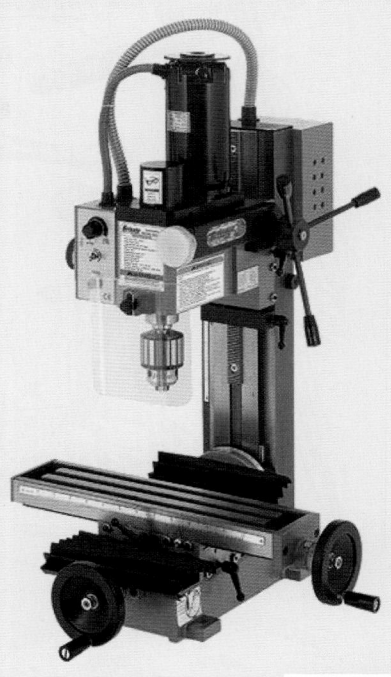

I don't do enough serious fabrication work to spend thousands of dollars on a real milling machine, but for about $500 this provides much more precision and versatility than a drill press. The handle on the right moves the table from side to side. The handle in front moves the table in and out. Both are calibrated in 1/1000 of an inch. Add a couple of small vises (I bought mine from McMaster-Carr) and you can position holes exactly where they should be, or make slots and more intricately shaped cutouts using an appropriate bit while moving the table. The speed control is a simple knob, like a lamp dimmer, enabling me to reduce the speed conveniently when drilling plastics.

The Grizzly catalogue has other similar tools in what I would describe as the intermediate category: Not quite professional level, but more upscale than Home Depot.

-- KK

Drills for sheet material
Unibits
$14 Neiko

I use unibits, or stepped drills, constantly because there's nothing better for drilling sheet material. Let's say you need to make some holes in 1/16th-inch thick acrylic. Your standard two flute drill bit will just tear it to pieces. But the unibit does it without any chaff or shattering or anything. This is because it's not fluted; it doesn't pull itself into the cut. It makes the cut with its leading edge, and it's effectively a scraper. The stepped shape — giving different sized holes in one bit — is simply an added bonus. I use them for all kinds of sheet materials, so I've got a ton of them.

-- Adam Savage

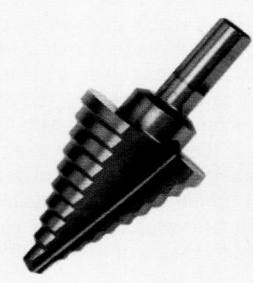

Precision large holes
Rotabroach Hole Cutters
$100 Blair Equipment

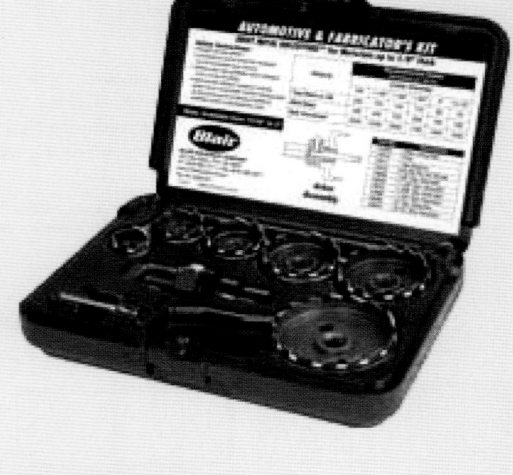

You can use a regular hardware store hole cutter on soft material like wood, but it is difficult to cut really accurate large holes through hard materials like steel or tricky thin materials like sheet metal. For that you'll need a Rotabroach Hole Cutter, which can make precise circular holes in plate steel and other metals. It can do this because it has machined teeth like a skill saw blade, rather than the stamped metal of a normal hole saw. It also only requires a dimple in the center instead of a drilled hole which can make it trickier to get started, but you get the center piece out whole which is sometimes helpful.

-- Alexander Rose

I've been easing into more and more metal work over the last year and half (propane art, collapsible fire fans and fire hula hoops a la Burning Man), so I drill a lot of multi-size holes in aluminum tubing. This is by far the best bit I've found for drilling through such thin materials. To get precise placement and a clean hole, normally I'd drill a small pilot hole, then run a larger drill bit in that hole to get the size and placement right. With this bit, I do not need to create a pilot hole (though, a center punch can help). I simply drill until I get to the right size (1/4" and 1/2" mostly). Because the bit has a single flute (cutting edge), it makes very clean holes. It's also very accurate: the bit is very stiff, so it wanders less when starting a hole. Since I don't need to change drill bits in my drill press to successively drill larger holes or change the jig I'm using to hold the part, it's become a real time saver.

-- Sean Rutledge

Best bits for quick hole-making
Threaded Tip Spade Drill Bits
$15 Bosch

Spade drill bits are normally used only when you only need a hole that's "good enough" and you care about how much time and effort it takes to drill the hole. For example, holes through studs for electrical wiring will be hidden in the wall when you are done, but you need to drill a lot of them. That's when a spade drill bit is useful.

I recently purchased a set of Bosch Daredevil Spade Bits at a big box store because they were a good deal (set of 6 for $10) and my existing bits were dull and not hex shank. I thought the threaded conical tip, like a wood boring bit, was an interesting feature.

I was amazed at how much better these worked than other spade bits I have used. The threaded tip serves several purposes:

Keeps the bit centered when starting.

Literally pulls the bit through the material. I did not have to push the drill at all until it got to the point the tip came through the

other side (and if you were drilling something backed with scrap wood you wouldn't need to, or you could switch to drilling from the other side).

Prevents vibration/chatter and the bit bouncing around the hole.

The resulting holes were where I wanted them, were more round than holes from other spade bits, had fewer blow out" splinters, and were easier to drill.

I also looked at Irwin Speedbor MAX (which have three cutting blades) as they also have threaded tips, and probably work as well or better due to the extra cutting edge. But I like that the Bosch bits lay flat (taking up less room in a tool box) and were cheaper.

-- Matt Taggart

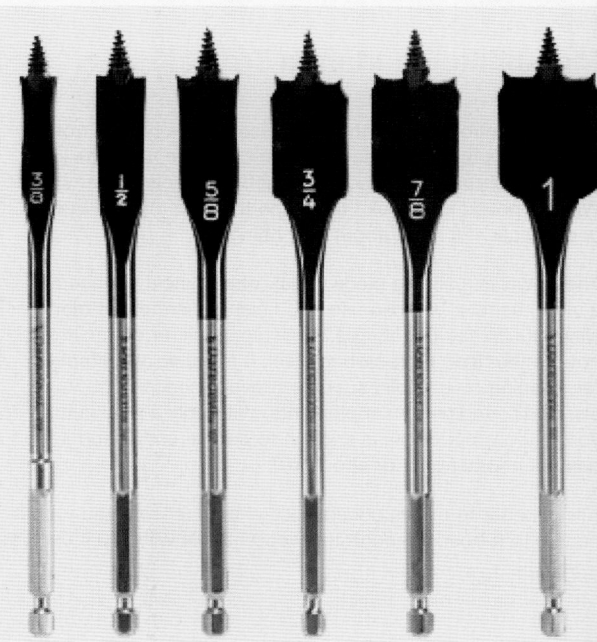

A physicist is an atom's way of knowing about atoms. - George Wald

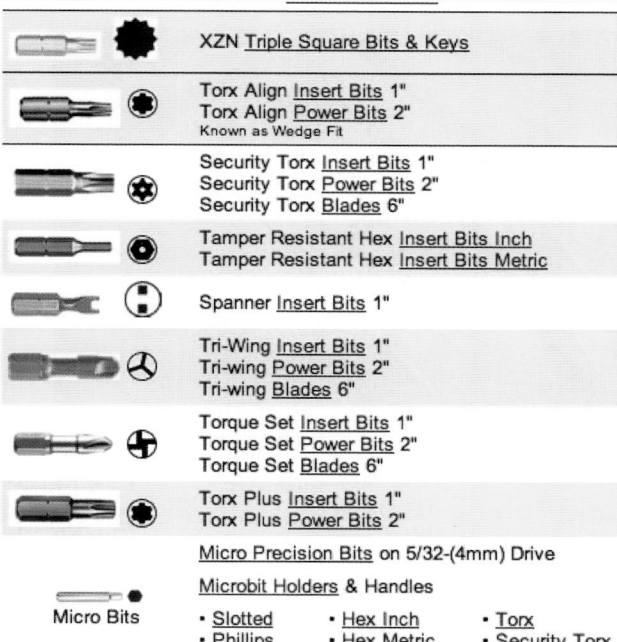

	XZN	Triple Square Bits & Keys
		Torx Align Insert Bits 1" Torx Align Power Bits 2" Known as Wedge Fit
		Security Torx Insert Bits 1" Security Torx Power Bits 2" Security Torx Blades 6"
		Tamper Resistant Hex Insert Bits Inch Tamper Resistant Hex Insert Bits Metric
		Spanner Insert Bits 1"
		Tri-Wing Insert Bits 1" Tri-wing Power Bits 2" Tri-wing Blades 6"
		Torque Set Insert Bits 1" Torque Set Power Bits 2" Torque Set Blades 6"
		Torx Plus Insert Bits 1" Torx Plus Power Bits 2"
		Micro Precision Bits on 5/32-(4mm) Drive
Micro Bits		Microbit Holders & Handles • Slotted • Hex Inch • Torx • Phillips • Hex Metric • Security Torx • Hex Security

Wiha Quality Tools

$45 for a set of 31 bits Wiha Tools

Manufacturers sometimes deliberately make it difficult to open their products. A common method is to use odd-shaped specialty screws. Without the right driver, the unit remains sealed. Wiha makes very high quality hand tools, and likes to offer them in great variety. They are a great source for premium versions of specialty screwdriver and screwdriver tips. This table gives a sense of what you can find. Of course they carry a great variety of premium tools in "ordinary" styles (Phillips, slotted, etc.) as well.

-- KK

Self-contained, tiny drivers
Husky 8-in-1 Precision Screwdriver

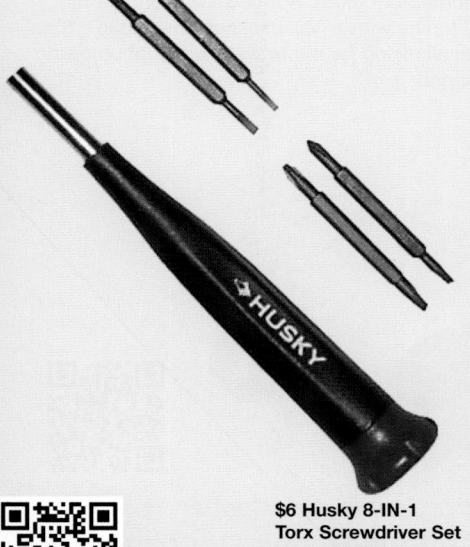

I've encountered many precision screwdriver kits intended to help you get past the tiny screws that keep you out of the most interesting parts of electronic equipment. Most are poorly made. I have long used tools similar to the jeweler screwdrivers previously reviewed on Cool Tools. The metal grooves in the shaft wear on your fingertips after awhile, making longer projects a real pain. You also can't exert quite as much torque, since each tool is so spindly. They don't come close to the usefulness and execution of the Husky 8-in-1.

The Husky 8-in-1 uses removable, double-sided, magnetized bits, and stores them all inside the driver handle. The result is a versatile, compact, easy-to-carry tool. The best part is knowing that everything you need is contained in one small organizer.

The Husky's handle is made from rugged, squared-off plastic and is easy to grip without being clumsy or too large for practical use in narrow spaces. It also has the rotating top you'd expect for this kind of tool, allowing you to apply pressure on one axis while rotating the driver from another. Thoughtfully, the handle tapers to a long, narrow metal shaft for access to out-of-the-way screws. The most satisfying part is how cleanly the bits engage with the screws. They fit perfectly every single time.

Husky makes a Phillips/slotted version and a Torx version. Having both sets gives you 16 screwdrivers that can pry loose just about any tiny screw you might encounter in an electronic device. For the low price and lifetime warranty, they're tough to beat.

-- Danilo Campos

$6 Husky 8-IN-1 Torx Screwdriver Set Home Depot

$6 Husky 8-IN-1 Phillips and Slotted Screwdriver Set Home Depot

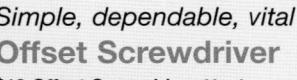

Simple, dependable, vital
Offset Screwdriver

$13 Offset Screwdriver Husky

My neighbor turned me onto this elegant hand tool. It allows you to work in tight places where the usual screwdriver wouldn't fit. It's not a new tool (actually it's a classic), but what's special about this one is that it has four different heads, including two Phillips, so you get four-in-one opportunities to have it fit.

-- KK

Essential screw-aid
Magnetic Drive Guide

$6 Compact Magnetic Guide Dewalt

Long ago a contractor friend of mine turned me onto a simple fixture for a powerdrill. It's an inexpensive gizmo that allows anyone to drive long screws in straight and fast. That's a huge plus now that sheetrock screws have replaced nails for most homestead projects. The guide fits into any chuck. You slip the screw head-first into the extended tube. A magnet at the bottom holds it. You place the loaded guide with the tip of the screw poking out over the place where you want to screw and the tube collapses as the screw goes in. The result: no muss, no-hands, quick, straight-in screw first time. Kids and newbies really love it. I keep one permanently affixed to my drivers. I use it for short as well as long screws. In fact I had forgotten how dependent I had become on the guide until I misplaced one recently and had to work without it. Now I have multiple backups. I don't think the brand matters; I use a $5 one. Make your life easier: keep one on your driver.

-- KK

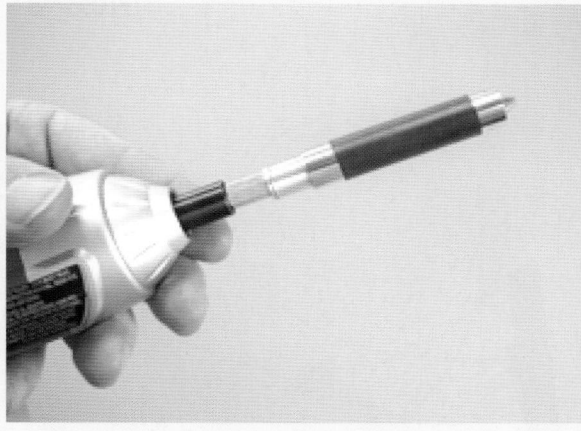

Better bits
Power Bits

$16 10-Piece Power Bit Set Wiha Tools

For too long I relied on traditional insert bits for my power drill/driver. I liked the easy variety of "ends" that were available, but I was also frustrated by the magnetic holders that would drop the bits at the wrong moment.

Then I discovered power bits (bits that fit into Power Bit base, also known as a 1/4" hex shank base). These are usually seen on the magnetic insert bit adapters for power drills, and are designed so that the machine-end of these bits lock in mechanically. Not only do they lock, but they offer 1/4" shaft slimness for their entire length, while also offering varied lengths.

For instance, at work I frequently use a 12" shafted #3 Phillips bit. I also use 2" Torx bits, a variety of 6" bits (tiny Phillips, security or plain Torx, and #2/#3 Square), and a larger set of Ryobi drill bits, all with the Power Bit base. I've also got a full set of nut drivers, 1/4", 3/8" & 1/2" socket adapters (straight & wobble), extensions, and flex shafts. All these fit in drills (with a locking adapter in the chuck), and impact drivers. I still have some insert bits, but I've found that I'm seriously reluctant to use them. The design difference may seem minimal, but the impact is significant when you work with these tools all day.

Power Bits have been a major boon for me, and I thought it worthy of Cool Tools. In terms of brands, I've found Wiha Tools makes 90% of the Power Bits I need and use.

-- Wayne Ruffner

Offset drill adapter
Milwaukee Off-Set Power Screwdriver Head

$36 Milwaukee Tool

I have used my offset screwdriver head for around 15 years and it enables me to get to screws in tight places where you might otherwise only be able to use a stubby screwdriver.

I find that the torque transfer is excellent, although sometimes the extra grip does come off. I have used it in my cordless drill as well as hand held, and it is designed for any combination of bits to be fitted. It does require the use of both hands but this means that one hand is being used to steady or apply downward force to a screw while the other imparts the turning force.

-- Wayne Higgins

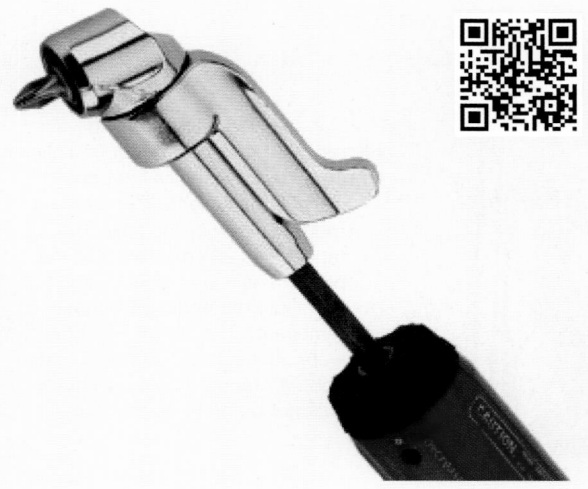

Plumbing

Easiest pipe cutter
Ratcheting Tube and Pipe Cutter
$33 Sears

The Craftsman Ratcheting Tube and Pipe Cutter is, like its cousin the Craftsman Ratcheting Screwdriver (reviewed previously), a well thought out tool. This Ratcheting Cutter works great for cutting pipe in tight spots and is so ergonomically correct I often use it to cut pipe on my workbench. The only reason I hesitate using it on the workbench is I don't want to dull the cutting blade too fast. Oh, did I mention it comes with a spare blade that is nested in the handle so it's sure to be there when you need it? It's also very well built, sturdy, and has the ever so wonderful lifetime replacement policy.

Certain tools are what I refer to as "lifers" — buy it one time, have it for life, need it throughout your whole life, and it makes life so much easier. It would be a mistake for the homeowner and/or professional not to own this one.

-- Eric G. Yukins

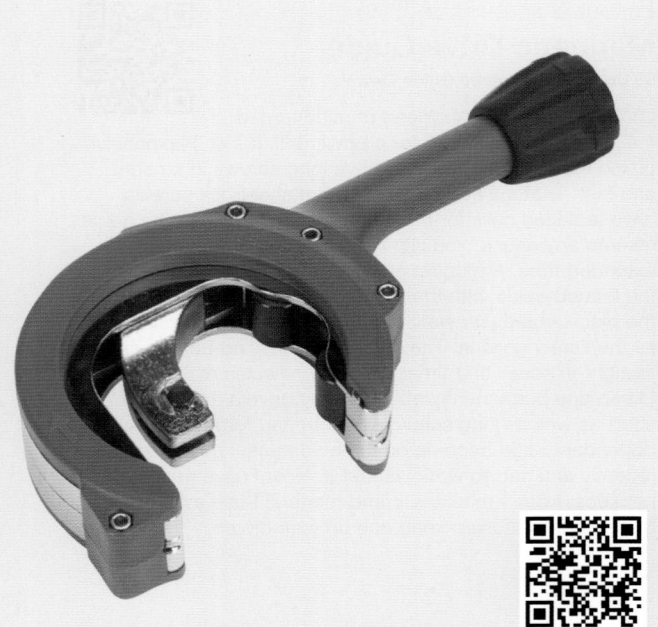

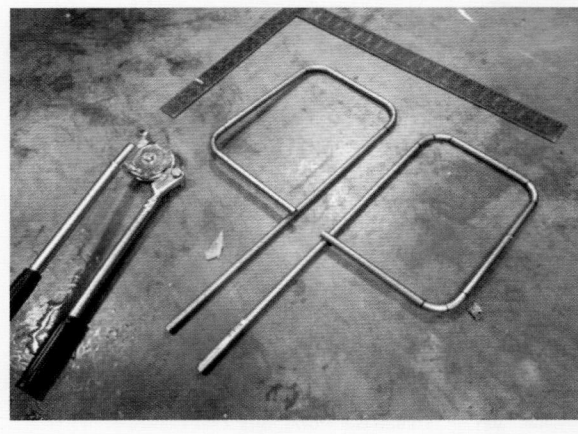

Kink-free metal tube bends
Hand Tubing Bender
$80 Imperial Eastman

I own an inexpensive MIG welder that I use to make the occasional small metal project or repair. Until recently, I've been using bar, or angle stock for my projects, and my work usually ends up with a fairly crude and heavy look.

Recently, I needed to make a set of motorcycle pannier racks, and wanted them be lightweight with a more professional appearance, so I decided to make them out of 1/2" steel tubing.

To bend steel tubing without kinking it, you'll need to use a tubing bender. These benders are basically a pair of matching dies with long handles attached to them, which allow you to gain leverage. Each die has index marks on it, which allow you to make very accurate bends, to specific angles.

You can buy hand bender sets that have interchangeable dies to allow you to bend different sizes of tubing, but the inexpensive ones only do a single tube diameter and bend radius. I found a 1/2" bender on eBay for $36. The one that I bought was marketed as an "Imperial Eastman" brand, but there are many to choose from.

My pannier racks turned out great. But beware, I found it difficult to bend steel tubing with a wall thickness over .035". Steel tubing this thin is challenging for me to weld withought blowing through, but I managed.

-- Steve Lodefink

Cheap & efficient PVC cutter
Klein Tools Cutter
$14 Klein Tools

I was introduced to this tool when I hired a friend who's a professional landscaper to install a sprinkler system on my three-acre property. I was amazed at how quickly and efficiently the Klein tool was able to cut 3/4 inch PVC pipe as well as flexible 3/8-inch sprinkler pipe. The end cuts were clean, burr-free and square, which is helpful when gluing sections of pipe and fitting sprinkler heads. This tool was in constant use, and when it wasn't in his hands it was light and small enough to be placed in his back pocket. The spring that opens the jaws and the ratcheting mechanism allow for easy one-handed operation. My friend also had an older, simpler model that I used that didn't have the spring to open the jaws or the ratcheting mechanism that this Klein Tools model has. That older model wasn't as efficient and required me at times to set down my work and use two hands to open the jaws.

My friend said this tool's only drawback was that his crew often loses them as they are working in trenches with a lot of loose dirt around. At least they're relatively inexpensive to replace. A safety orange-colored model might be an improvement. I liked this tool so much I bought my own and use it to cut just about anything that will fit in its jaws.

-- Charles Dean

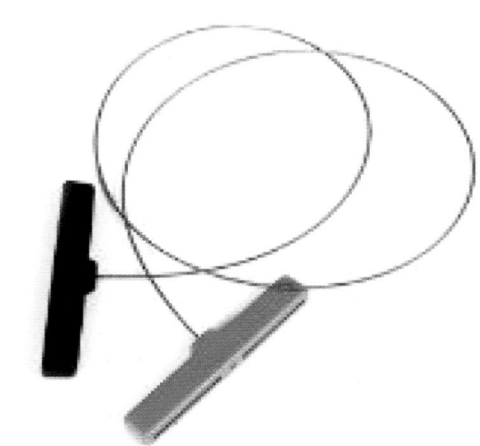

Simple PVC saw
PVC Cable Saw
$8 Black Rhino

I've been using these since high school, and haven't found a better solution for cutting PVC..

Basically, you slip the wire around the PVC pipe and start working it back and forth. It seems to melt through the pipe once you get going, which means less dust and a smoother cut than other saws I've tried.

It also has an advantage over other dedicated saws due to its flexible nature. I actually used one of the longer versions to cut a bit off of a kitty litter box once (it had a spot to hold a scooper, which made it a bit too big for the space). That would have been impossible with other PVC saws that hold onto the pipe. It also would have been tricky with a hack saw due to the size.

At less than $10 for even the most expensive ones, it's a great thing to pick up for an occasional job. And not that painful if you end up losing it.

-- Michael Farnette

Under-the-sink wrench
RIDGID Faucet and Sink Installer
$24 Ridgid

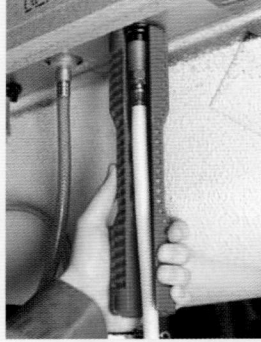

I've installed, removed and replaced quite a number of sinks in my day. Recently, I set out to replace the leaky faucet on my mother-in-law's slop sink. The faucet was 22 years old and the plastic basin was glued to the wall and I just did not want to have to remove it. The supply line bolts were up inside the sink and rusted tight. A standard basin wrench was not going to do the job.

The Ridgid Faucet and Sink Installer is incredibly specific in a clever way. Its two removable and reversible ends have a combination of sizes and shapes to grip all the most common faucet nuts and supply line ends. Looking more like a flashlight than a basin wrench, the orange handle has a slit to fit around the supply lines, and a raised pattern for a good grip.

I'm convinced that this wrench, combined with plenty of WD40, saved me the ordeal of having to remove both the sink and the faucet.

-- Mark Dellamonte

No-Solder Repair Coupling for Copper Pipes
Compression Pipe Repair Coupling
$13 Amazon

Rigid copper water pipe is generally sturdy stuff but it is not indestructible. Errant nails and screws will pierce it and deep freezes in uninsulated spaces can split it. Consequently, when copper pipes do fail, they tend to do so at the most inopportune times and in the most unforgiving places. (I once gutted an 1826 post-and-beam schoolhouse in the frozen depths of a Vermont winter, so I know whereof I speak.)

Rigid copper pipe is typically joined by soldering — using an open-flame torch in tight spaces next to wood framing — so replacing damaged pipe sections can be perilous. Unless, that is, you use a copper compression repair coupling, also called a copper slip-repair coupling.

A repair coupling is a straight length of pipe (typically 12" long) with a compression fitting at each end. Each fitting contains a brass ferrule which, when compressed, creates a watertight seal. (Lavatory risers typically use compression fittings.)

No-solder repair couplings cost roughly $25 at Sears or Home Depot; Amazon offers a ½" repair coupling for about $15.

-- Mike Litchfield

Happiness is the absence of striving for happiness. - Chang-Tzu

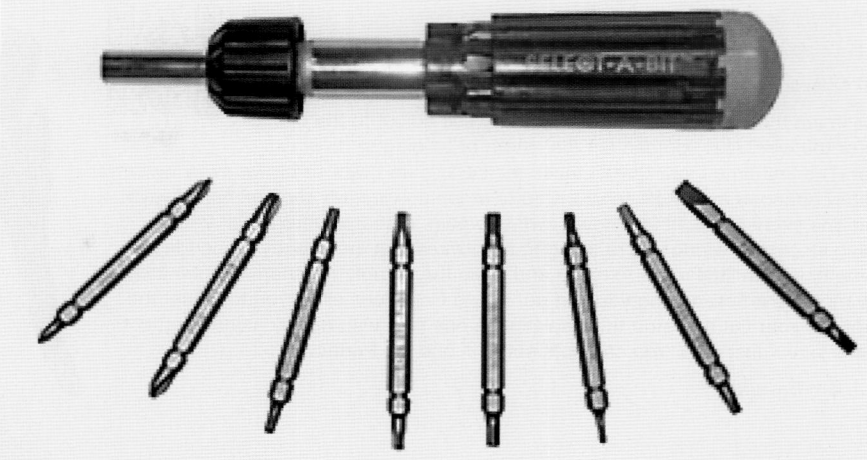

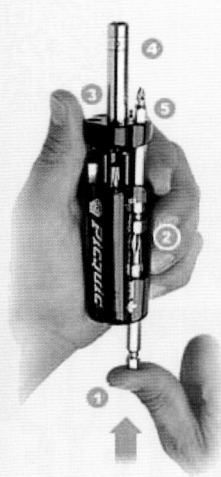

Best multiple-bit screwdriver
Picquic Sixpac
$16 Picquic

The Picquic Sixpac may be the last multi-bit screwdriver I'll ever need to buy, but it wasn't the first. I've gone through a dozen less successful attempts at this kind of tool, always losing at least half the bits in the first month or so of use. When I try to use the few bits I haven't lost, they invariably fall out of the bitholder, which weakens over time.

The Picquic Sixpac fixes both problems. Each bit is stored in a separate compartment in the screwdriver handle. You remove the bit you need by pushing it out of the handle with the bit you are finished with. Since there's no other easy way to get at the bit you need, you always put bits away as you finish with them. I've had mine for three years and it still has all its bits!

Additional features include a solid, spring-lock bitholder that holds as tightly now as it did the day I bought it, and a stainless steel shank that has stood up to everything I've thrown at it. It comes with six bits: two flathead, three Phillips head, and one Torx T15. Other bits are available in Bitpacs from Picquic.

-- *James Home*

4:1 Hyperdriver
Klenk Ratcheting Screwdriver
$25 Select-A-Bit Ratio Multi-Driver DA86450 Klenk

I found this Klenk 4:1 Multi-ratio driver. It is a basic ratcheting screwdriver with two big advantages over the Sears or Snap-on model.

First, it has a black knob on the shaft that when held, allows the bit to turn four times for every one handle turn. It's phenomenally fast and rivals drill drivers on small to medium jobs, where you don't want to drag out the heavy equipment. It's best suited for long screws, where the 4:1 gearing can really speed them in or out. However, since it is essentially high gear, you can't put a lot of torque on it.

The second improvement is the bit storage and retrieval. The Sears version has these clips to stick the single-sided bits in. Getting them in or out isn't smooth. The Klenk has a system with a hole in the top and you sort of lift to disengage the lock and dial the hole to the bit you want, which you can see through the side of the handle. The bits are also double-ended. It holds 8 double-ended bits for a total of 16 heads.

One improvement I'd like to see on this tool is for the ratchet mechanism to be tighter, since in narrow spaces where you can't turn your hand much, the play in the ratchet can result in not getting much of a turn. Also, the 4:1 knob prevents it from reaching in narrow places to begin with. Overall, though, the 4:1 gearing is worth the $20 even if you already have a Snap-on or Sears model.

-- *Mike Numamoto*

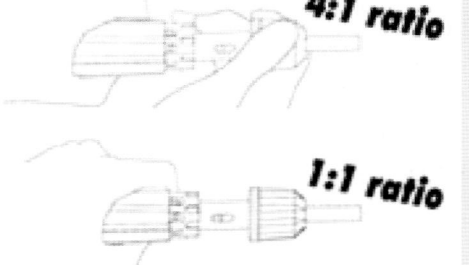

Hold the nosepiece:
4:1 geared ratio nose turns the bit 4 times for each turn of the handle.
4:1 ratio

Use it one-handed:
The nosepiece and handle turn together for standard (1:1) driving action.
1:1 ratio

Easier hex key
Ball End Hex Wrenches
$9 Bondhus Balldriver L-Wrenches Amazon

When you buy a hex key (Allen wrench) set, get them with ball ends. The advantage is that their ball end make it easier to slide the wrench into the receiving slot. You can reach in at an angle and feel your way to the needed drop-in position faster. Good for blind or inaccessible places. It's a small thing, not worth replacing other hex wrenches for, but if you need to buy some hex wrenches, these ball ends are better. Different brands make them in many varieties, format, and handles.

-- *KK*

Compact all-in-one
Switchblade Screwdriver
$20 Tools For Stagecraft

I work as a grip in the motion picture industry, and it's always been difficult to find one place that stocks every specific tool and supply you need for film work. Studio Stores often have everything, but they're too expensive; hardware stores are affordable but not specialized enough. When I found Toolsforstagecraft.com, I knew I'd scored big. They have some wrenches, etc. that I assumed were one offs, made in people's garages. Plus they're interdisciplinary, not just film but stage as well, not just grip, but electric and even carpenter. Check it out, it's a small operation with really good service that deserves more business. My favorite purchase was the switchblade screwdriver. Everybody asks me where I got it, It has a bunch of bits, and it takes up less space on my belt than a 4-in-1 screwdriver.

-- *Eli Golub*

Pocket-size driver
Teeny Turner
$6, or $164 for 36 FireHawk Technology

The small size and stubby shape of this cheap driver allows me to reach tight spaces and still apply considerable torque. I've used it to adjust tension on folding knives and my SOG PowerLock multi-tool, and to open cases on remote controls, my PDA and cell phones. I have a set of jeweler's screwdrivers, Wiha Precision Tech screwdrivers and a Craftsman All-in-One screwdriver (overall length: 8.75 inches) with captive bits that store in the handle. The 2.5-inch Teeny Turner fits easily in a pocket; it's made of aircraft alloy shank, has a magnetic bit holder and the included bits (Phillips 00, Phillips 0, Torx 5,6 & 8, Flat 2mm and 3mm) are generally smaller and much easier to change out than my Craftsman. One small negative is the Teeny Turner has one more bit than storage positions, so you have to choose the least pointy bit to keep in the drive shaft if you carry it in your pocket. That said, the portability really is key. Plus, I do like the name.

-- *Chris Jacobs*

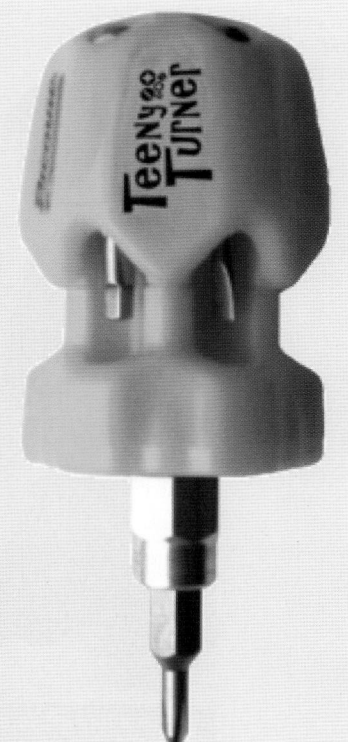

Cadillac of screwdrivers
Ratcheting Screwdriver
$64 Snap-On

Although it will never replace a cordless drill in terms of speed of driving/removing screws, my trusty Snap-On ratcheting screwdriver requires no batteries and is far less cumbersome in both weight and size. And for a 1- or 2-screw job is actually faster.

This unit has a smooth-action, incredibly durable RATCHET action that will send the shaft merrily cranking in whichever direction you desire with a flick of the easily rotated ring. It can also be set in the fixed, non-ratcheting position. I have tried another ratchet screwdriver and found the action laughably rough with plenty of slop. The stainless shaft on the Snap-On is magnetized and bored out in the end to accept the standard hex-shaped bit tips. A durable plastic cap screws into the butt of the hollowed-out handle and has a gasket to keep the interchangeable bit tips that rest inside moisture- (and therefore rust-) free.

-- *Carolyn Branson*

Creativity is allowing yourself to make mistakes. Art is knowing which ones to keep. - Scott Adams

67

Wiring

Ultimate wire stripper
Greenlee Kwik Wire Stripper
$70 Amazon

These are the ultimate wire strippers. They self adjust to the diameter of the wire. And you can set the length of striping to be consistent. The first time I saw one of these tools 20 years I was so blown away it completely changed my whole relationship to stripping wire. My toolbox has always had one ever since. In fact now I own two pairs of them. Often when you're doing electronic wiring you're trying to strip wires that are already embedded in something with little room to move and often the stripping of them is potentially the most destructive thing you can do. These Greenlees allow you to adjust the depth of your cut and strip the insulation in one snip with hardly any movement of the wire. Just snip. You can do it softly in one try. Perfect.

-- Adam Savage

Stripper-crimper
GB Wire Stripper and Crimper
$12 GB SE-94 gardnerbender.com

A tool I love is the GB SE-94 Automatic Wire Stripper and Crimper. The Kronus Wire Stripper, previously reviewed on Cool Tools, used to be the bane of my electrical-work existence. It would only properly set and strip the wire in one quick motion half of the time, and the other half I'd have to spend a few minutes fumbling around getting the clamp to hold on tight or the blade to cut deeply enough to strip the wire. Averaging out the two amounts of time, it really wasn't any more effective than the classic manual strippers. When I got my hands on the SE-94, it was as though someone gave me a hammer after years of driving nails in with rocks. It can grab and strip a wire with just a simple clench of the fist. It's also been extremely handy in those cramped-in-a-sink-cabinet-wiring-up-a-garbage-disposal situations, when I don't have the time to comfortably mess around with an inconsistent tool to get it to do what it was designed to do.

-- Cavan Gahagan

Ergonomic crimpers
Universal Crimping Connector Pliers
$42 Amazon

If you tinker, you find yourself needing to make firm but reversible connections. The standard solution is based on a male-female connectors system, and the only tool you need to make such connection is a set of crimping pliers.

These connector systems are based on the principle of a mechanical connection: the bare wire is literally crushed between small overlapping pieces of metal. The friction between the bare-wire and overlapping metal creates a sound electrical connection as well. Creating a proper "crimp" allows the connection to be made and unmade hundreds of times without failure. Moreover, once you become good at crimping, it will take literally 15 seconds to make a connection—in comparison, a solder gun requires 1 minute just to warm up.

There are a variety of crimp standards, but for POWER connections, I find the JST-style connectors are the best because they are keyed so that the connectors cannot be accidentally joined in the wrong way. To make such connections, I must admit that I love the following set of PA-09 crimping pliers, shown here, from a Japanese company that names itself Engineer, Inc.

I own another set of crimpers, the SN-28B, shown here. Although these were slightly cheaper, and even though they tout the ability to perform both crimps at the same time, I prefer the ergonomics of the PA-09. Moreover, because they are designed to perform two crimps at once, the spacing between the first and second crimp forms is too big to handle the JST-style connectors.

The PA-09 can also crimp the very popular .1" header pins that are used on Arduino boards, etc. Again, the pliers require two crimps. You can see a full list of the types of connectors that the PA-09 can handle. In the US, I purchased mine from the previously reviewed Sparkfun.

In summary: the tool has perfect ergonomics, the material on the grip and the steap is high quality and a pleasure to use, and because it was designed to do one crimp at a time, it is extremely flexible and precise.

-- Abhi Shelat

Here is a JST-style female pin that the PA-09 can be used to crimp. Notice there are two crimps that must occur. The lower, longer flaps of metal are crimped around the insulation of the wiring to hold the wire; the upper, smaller flaps are crimped around the bare, stripped wire. I find the 1.4mm setting in the PA-09 pliers are perfect for both flaps

Best electrical DIY
Wiring Complete
$15 Michael Litchfield, Michael McAlister, 2013, 272 pages

The clearest, most intelligible, most up-to-date, step by step instructions of how to wire most household electrical jobs. Heavily (1,000 photos), smartly illustrated. Besides unraveling the complexities of 3-way switching (I always need help with this), this second-edition deals with other wiring besides electrical power: cable, phone, ethernet. Despite the wireless era, I've got more wires in our home every year, and this book has encouraged me to tackle them myself. The guide is supremely practical, full of great tips for working with real wires in real walls. It helped me figure out how to tap a power outlet inside my house for an outdoor line. I can't think of anything it misses.

-- KK

They then use a plumb laser to transfer marks to the ceiling.

▲ *Each multimedia connector is to the left of the cable It terminates. From left: RG6 F-connector, dual-shielded RG6 coaxial cable; RJ-45 (eight-pin) jack, Cat 6 UTP data cable; RJ-ll (six-pin) jack, Cat 3 phone cable; two RCA audio jacks (sometimes called banana jacks), 14-gauge low-loss audio cable.*

In some old houses, the neutral wires -- rather than the hot wires -- may be attached (incorrectly) to receptacles or switches, in violation of code. So when testing existing receptacles, switches, or fixtures, test /all/ wires for voltage.

A nut-driver bit speeds up splicing, but be careful not to over twist wires.

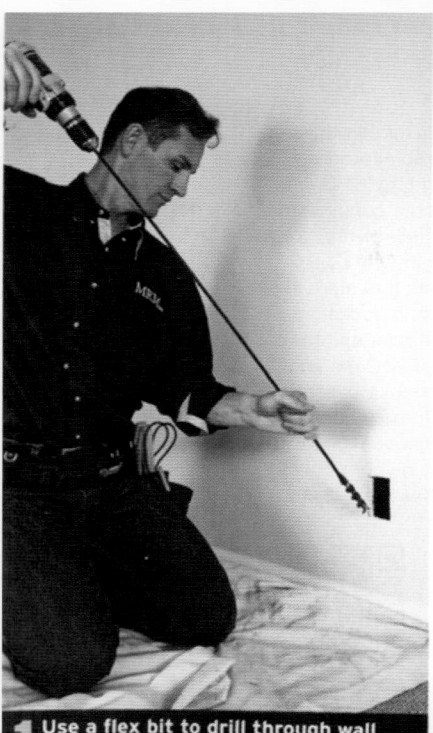

1 Use a flex bit to drill through wall plates.

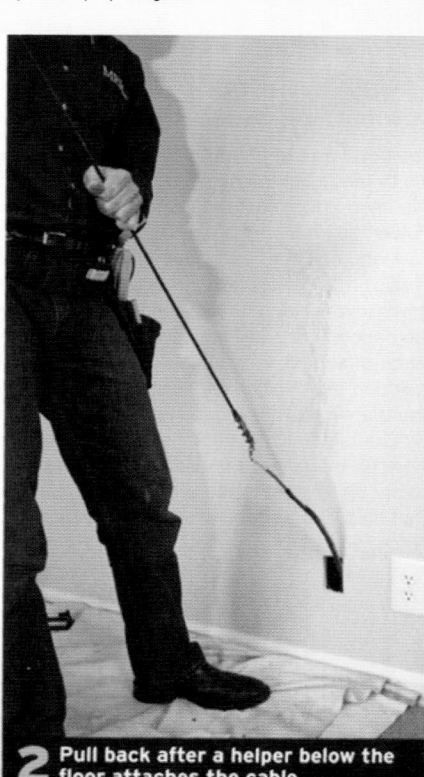

2 Pull back after a helper below the floor attaches the cable.

If you wish to live, you must first attend your own funeral. - Katherine Mansfield

Cordless Soldering
Weller Pyropen
$150 Amazon

The Weller Pyropen is one of the best portable soldering irons out there. I like them because I get almost an hour and half of heat, and I can move around — no cords. So, while I have an electric soldering station, I almost exclusively end up using this Weller, even when I'm near the station. I just find it easier. So, you switch it on, it lights the butane up, and it makes this cool high-pitched scream. And when it glows red its very hot. It heats up faster than an electric; it will reach full heat in about 30 seconds. I love these things.

-- Adam Savage

[Note: According to a spokesman at the manufacturer, the Weller Portasol (review at right) and the Weller Pyropen are nearly identical products. The Portasol is about half the price and has a slightly hotter max temperature and is made in Japan. The Pyropen is currently made in Ireland. Both are considered the same high professional quality. --KK]

Easy waterproof connection
Adhesive Lined Shrink Tubing
$14 Ancor Marine Grade Electrical Adhesive Lined Heat Shrink Tubing Kit Amazon

Double-walled, or adhesive-lined, heat shrink tubing is how you make easy waterproof connections. As you heat the tube and it shrinks, it compresses a heat-sensitive adhesive inside the tube to melt into one waterproof seal. This sample set is a good place to start.

-- Alexander Rose

Cordless, self-igniting soldering iron
Weller Portasol Portable Butane Soldering Kit
$60 Model: P2KC Cooper Handtools

I have used butane-powered soldering irons for about 17 years. This one is compact, well made and lighter than most other butane type irons I have used. It is made of a thermal plastic resistant to high temp and the cap is vented so you can put it back on while the head is still hot. The exterior is textured slightly, which makes it easier to hold. It gives a sharp, well-defined flame front with a very efficient burn.

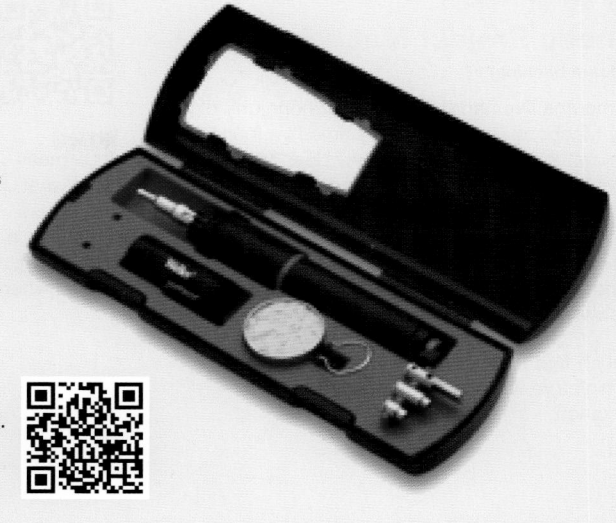

The torch has enough power to tin the ends of large cables and shrink large diameter heat shrink insulation. Unlike the cheaper ones from Weller, it comes with inter-changeable tips, including a hot knife tip, so I can use it occasionally on close pitch SM components. There's a wire rack in the case that allows you to set up the torch with a platform so you can use both hands. The fuel window is a nice feature, too. The run time is advertised at 90 minutes -- of course it depends a lot on how hot you run it. I usually use it at 50% or less. I always refill the butane whenever I store the torch in its case, so I have only run out once in 17 years of using this type of soldering iron (I was 35 feet in the air and that was the last time).

The lab I work in is busy and crowded, so I work outside of the lab a lot. I can tuck this soldering iron in my lab coat pocket and forget about until I need it. I use it two to three times a week. The iron is great for soldering crimped pins on a new cable and the torch is good for heat shrink when I don't want to go get the heat gun. I have yet to use it to cut poly rope, but it is nice to know I can. It is also great for lighting fireworks. I have not used the hot knife yet but I gave one of the kits to our mechanical engineer and he, being a sailor, thought it had real potential. The only draw back I have found is the TSA will not let you carry it on a plane.

Hint: I put the cap on the iron in the case and dropped a Leatherman E4 in the cap holder cut-out to create a more complete kit. You still need some flux cored solder, but one can tuck a small coil in the sponge can or carry a small tube separately.

-- Gary K.

Cheap, classic Romex stripper
Gardner Bender Romex Cable Ripper
$4 Gardner Bender

The recommended Cable Slitter reminded me of this little thingamawhoogy. My father, who made his living as an electrician, always had one on him for stripping cable. You slip it over the wire however far you want to cut it. The electrical cable passes through a hole in the wide end of the CR-100 (note: the holes running along the side are only for checking the gauge of the wire). Then, gripping the tool firmly, you just slide it toward the end of the wire, pulling the wire through and causing the cutting blade on the open end to slit the length of the sheathing, without damaging the wires inside. You can then pull the inner wires out and cut off the sheathing with a knife. Or in my father's case, the cutters on his pliers. This Cable Ripper and a pair of pliers was all he ever used (he could also strip wires with pliers, but that's really an acquired skill).

It's virtually impossible to accidentally cut yourself with this tool, which makes it safer than trying to slit a cable with only a utility knife. I also find it's better than the strippers on a set of pliers, because it's specifically made to slit romex (NM or non-metallic) cable, not strip insulation off the wires themselves. Two drawbacks: it's intended for romex cable and really isn't too useful for anything else. Two, you need another tool to cut the sheathing off. Still, it's inexpensive, works great and you can get them at Lowe's, Home Depot or any electrical supply place and probably your local hardware store.

-- Keith Perkins

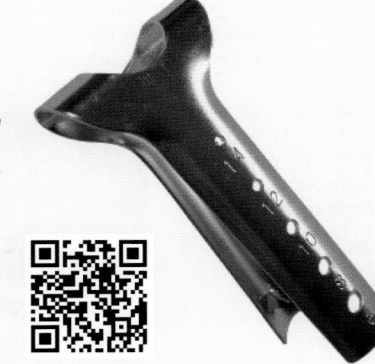

---

the tip are for a thermocouple near the tip for precise and stable temperature regulation.

The pencil itself is very lightweight and is attached to a lightweight, flexible silicone rubber-insulated cable.

The tip heats up very rapidly upon turning the unit on and setting the temperature on the dial. The user is informed when the desired temp has been reached when the LED goes out. During a soldering session, the LED will be observed turning on and off as the selected temperature is being accurately maintained.

There is nothing fancy about it such as a digital temp readout; just a solid, no nonsense, precise and stable soldering tool. Before acquiring this unit, I thought of soldering as something of a chore. With the Hakko I can do precise, quality soldering with minimal effort. The manufacturer has recently discontinued the

---

Dependable soldering iron
Hakko 936 Soldering Station
$83 FX-888 Hakko USA

For someone looking for a high quality soldering station at a reasonable price the Hakko 936 is hard to beat. I've had mine for a few years and use it mostly for electronics and instrument cable work. I think I paid around $80 new for it, and the price included a separate cast metal pencil rest with an integral sponge tip wiping pad.

The power supply is a transformer type, controlled by a rheostat mounted on the front panel graduated in both Celsius and Fahrenheit. The only other control is the on-off switch mounted on the right side. There is a red LED pilot lamp on the front which illuminates only when regulated power is actually being applied to the pencil. The pencil's cable plugs in to a 5-conductor receptacle and locks in via a threaded collar. The extra wires going to

---

Portable flameless soldering iron
Portasol
$17 P50 Cooper Handtools

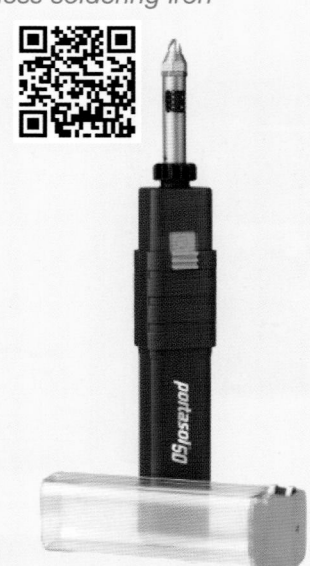

Just the other day I had to solder some wires on our irrigation valves out back in the garden. Completing the job quickly was a breeze with this tiny flameless soldering stick that will get red hot anywhere. In my experience soldering jobs always seem to happen beyond the reach of electrical outlets, so this inexpensive cordless tool is now part of my kit. A tiny catalytic converter burns ordinary lighter butane to a steady orange glow without flame, keeping the tip super hot. It's perfect for small electrical and wiring jobs. I know some hardware hackers who work inside near power yet swear by the Portasol because it heats up so quickly. Comes in a plastic lid which allows you to pack it away while still warm and doubles as the flint sparker to ignite it. This is the low-end cheap one -- $ 15 (includes small bottle of butane) -- which suits my occasional use fine. Weller makes fancier Portasols with piezo self-starters ($35), more wattage and temperature control ($70), and many accessories.

-- KK

Cheap micro flame
Micro Torch
$17 Bernzomatic

For soldering wires in places beyond an extension cord, or for burning stuff with fine details I use this butane-fueled micro torch. It is like a propane torch, only 10 times smaller. The micro torch generates a tiny, precise, very hot blue flame. Uses typical butane refill liquid. It's lightweight and agile. But unlike other self-igniting micro-torch models, including the previously-reviewed Weller Portasol, or the ones used by jewelers, this one is cheap at $12. It is good enough for the occasional heating I do.

-- KK

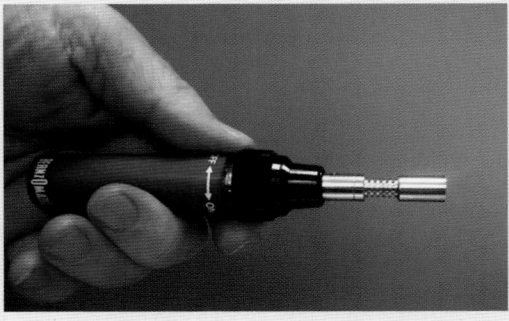

---

936 but they still seem to be widely available on eBay.

-- David Zarn

The Hakko 936 has been replaced by the newer FX-888, but can still be found new and used online.-- OH

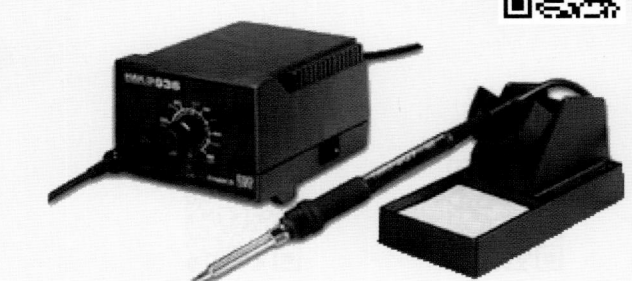

Electronics

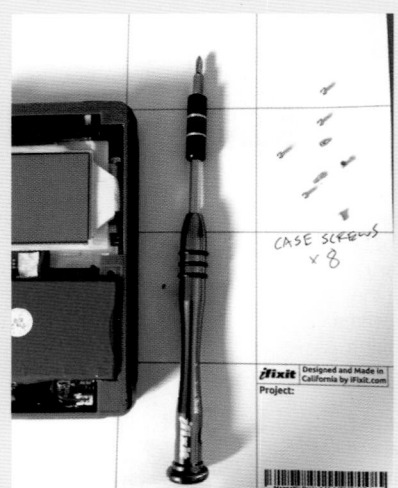

Magnetic DIY repair station
iFixit Magnetic Project Mat
$13 (or $19 with foam backing) iFixit

In the past few months I've had to repair my iPhone, my digital camera, and my Macbook Pro. During this time I've found the iFixit's magnetic mat indispensable. Not only does the magnetic surface mean fewer lost screws, but it's whiteboard surface means I can keep track of what came from where. Intelligently, iFixit includes a very nice fine-tipped dry-erase marker from Staedtler for quickly jotting down repair notes (that also features a bit of wool on the cap for erasing them, too). The pro model mat, which I own, also features a nonslip foam backing much like that of a mousepad which when flipped upside down features cutouts that act like cups.

I like mine so much that it never leaves my desk as it serves as miniature whiteboard, mousepad, and DIY repair station.

-- Oliver Hulland

Non-soldering connections
Wire Wrapper Tool
$7 RadioShack

This is a beautiful and inexpensive tool; a rare mechanical hand tool with precise tolerances. To attach fine wires, such as wiring up LEDs into circuits, wire wrap makes soldering unnecessary. Strip about 3/8 inch on the end of a wire, thread the exposed wire up one of two incredibly tiny slots in the end of the wirewrap tool, put the other tiny slot of the wirewrap tool around the wire it is to be connected to, like the anode or cathode of an LED, then twirl the wirewrap tool in your fingers, leaving a tiny tight spiral of wire wrapped around the connection.

-- Howard Rheingold

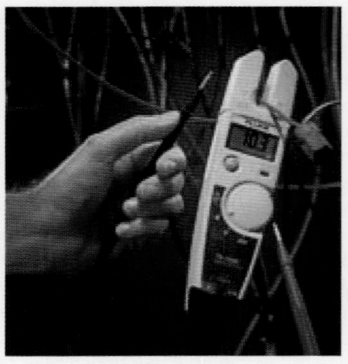

Digital multimeter w/built-in AMP meter
Fluke Voltage, Continuity & Current Tester

The T5 is as reliable as a good, old-fashioned "wiggy" voltage tester, but adds the functionality of a digital multimeter (DMM) and an AMP meter combined. I've found the T5 to be a bit more robust than the average DMM and very reliable for a device in this price range. More importantly, it has a "fork" or "OpenJaw" that can be extended over a current-carrying cable so that it acts like an AMP-clamp, except you don't have to maneuver or close the jaws, making it quicker and easier to use. The fork is also a lot less intrusive and requires less space than the old open-and-clamp design. Perfect for a cramped motor panel or junction box. For most functioning/troubleshooting, it's helpful to know first if there is voltage and then if there is current (the garden hose comparison: do I have water pressure? is water flowing?). And, for service work for instance, it's great to be able to check both voltage and amperage of a motor running with one very lightweight, ergonomic tool.

I have been using a range of Flukes for well over 20 years — everything from a multimeter to a scope meter and other devices. However, this relatively small unit remains my go-to instrument. It is the first one I grab both at home as well as on my job (I oversee the installation of packaging lines nationwide and, at times, do trouble shooting on pieces of automated equipment). There are two version of the T5, the 1000 and 600 models. The main difference between the T5-1000 and the T5-600 is their maximum voltage ratings, 1000 and 600 VAC respectively. To me, the relatively small price difference between the 600 and 1000 was worth it, but for general work around the house, the 600 should be perfect.

-- Ad Verkuylen

$90 T5- 600
model Fluke

$125 T5-1000
model Fluke

A better tape for electronics
Kapton Tape
$13 (2" x 36 yards) Amazon

I do a lot of work with electronics assembly and disassembly, rewiring, and removing and adding components. Kapton tape (generically known as polyimide tape) is a cool tool in these cases and better than regular black electrical tape for a number of reasons:

It is heat resistant. You can put a soldering iron on Kapton tape and it will not melt. In fact, numerous flexible circuits are made with copper on a Kapton substrate where the components are soldered directly to the copper.

It does not stretch. This may be either a pro or con, but it's good when you just want to tape down wires.

It is thin. Actually, it comes in various thicknesses. I usually get the 2 mil (0.002") thick stuff in the 1/2" wide rolls. When you're trying to cram as much as possible into a given space, the low profile and smooth, slick surface help tremendously.

The adhesive leaves no discernible residue. You can pull the tape off after a year and not worry about having to clean anything else up.

As mentioned before, the tape comes in different widths and thicknesses, depending on your need. You can also get it with adhesive on one side or both, though there may be limited width/thickness availability for the two-sided tape.

If you take apart any consumer electronics device nowadays, you'll notice three or four different kinds of adhesives and tapes being used (I'd cover the rest because they're also great, but I really don't use them that much and don't know what they're called nor how to source them).

Mostly, I use this tape as insulation on either a PC board or wires, especially if I think I'm going to have something on top of it that I'll be soldering. It's a bit overkill for just taping down wires, but still, that's better than Scotch tape or electrical tape.

I have no favorite brands of Kapton tape, I just buy a roll from my local electronics supply house when I need more.

-- Mark Huie

Bench-grade digital meter
Fluke DMM
$330 87-5 Digital Multimeter Fluke

My needs are served half the time by a simple sub $100 DMM. Other times, I need a more complex and reliable meter. The Fluke 87V is that meter for me.

The 87V is more a general-purpose tool than Fluke's T5. The T5 is a compact, limited resolution (only four-digit display) tester. It does not appear capable of measuring many of the things that the 87V can handle. The 87V can measure a much wider range of voltages and currents with greater accuracy. It also has an analog-style bar graph to help show trends, stores max./min. readings and will sound warnings if limits are exceeded. It can answer all the same questions as the T5, except in some cases it would need a probe (the open jaw mechanism for measuring current without breaking the circuit is the T5's killer feature).

The 87V can also measure temperature (with a probe), frequency (for control circuits) and handles in-line current measurement to 20A. The peak capture will let you see spikes on a signal/control line as short as 250 us. It also has built-in filters for measuring voltages on noisy lines (as with motors).

If you only need to know how many volts or how many amps in a household setting, the T5 is surely sufficient. If you want a bench-grade tool for the homeowner, automotive and/or electronics hobbyist, the 87V is the real deal. For me, most of the time, the application is automotive or motorcycling (ensuring that things are charging and within spec); or that I can confirm the homemade wiring harness is assembled correctly prior to plugging in the $100-plus parts and accidentally cooking them. For more complex things, like servo controls in remote control applications, the duty-cycle measurements the 87V gives help confirm that the servos are in the right position.

I don't use the frequency feature very much, but temperature measurement is useful in a few applications when debugging cooling problems in equipment, too. When trying to solve a problem with a power supply or load-induced glitch, the max/min hold functionality is great. You can stress and test the circuit and see the min. (or max.) readings after the fact to confirm, or refute, the problem.

The Fluke 87V is the benchmark by which most are measured. Knowing that it can be beat on and abused, yet continues to give me lab-grade results year after year means I just depend on it and stop wondering what is going on. It tells me.

-- Alan Hawrylyshen

Electricity finder
Fluke VoltAlert
$23 Fluke Voltalert 90VAC to 600 VAC Amazon

This is a non-conductive (plastic), non-contact voltage sensor that glows red and/or beeps in the vicinity of an energized conductor. In other words, it lights up near a "live" wire. You don't actually have to make contact to see if the line is hot. It lights up even if there is no load on the line, since it senses the electric field, not the magnetic field. It's much easier to use than a contact indicator light or meter. It works for AC line voltages. Also it only lights up when near the "hot" line, not the ground or neutral, so you can immediately see if an outlet is wired backwards. Works great for finding the dead Christmas light bulb on a series string of lights too (not as easy though when you have two or more strands braided together.) I always rub it against my shirt first to see if it is working. Static discharge sets it off. A number of vendors besides Fluke make this type of device, but Fluke is a high quality name brand.

– Bruce Bowen

The superfluous is a very necessary thing. - Voltaire

Handy electronic source
Mouser Electronics
mouser.com

The venerable Mouser catalog should be on your list of recommendations. Mouser provides electronic components with no minimum purchase required. I don't know why Mouser is seldom a hit in Google searches. But if I want anything from neon indicator bulbs to video cabling, Mouser is my first and usually last stop. Their complete catalog is searchable online and is viewable as PDF pages. They offer a huge range of shipping options (using five different carriers) and charge only the actual shipping cost, no "handling." Until relatively recently, you had to telephone one of their operators to place an order, but they now have online ordering in place.

-- Charles Platt

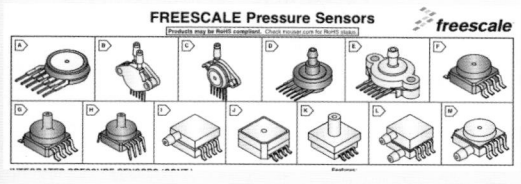

Hardware hacking magazine
Nuts and Volts
$27 12 issues nutsvolts.com

A monthly for the hardware hackers. Lots of electronics, robots, and small mechanical projects. Informative ads, too.

-- KK

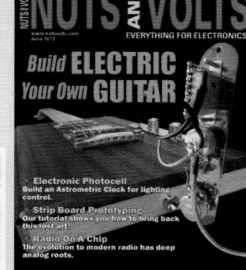

16 bit Experimenter populated with dsPIC

Graphics display with FFT example

Mini-kit

Figure 2 Actual DSP Experimenter Prototype w/o Keyboard

Enthusiast source
SparkFun Electronics
sparkfun.com

SparkFun Electronics sells electronic components aimed at people creating DIY projects. The unique thing about SFE is that they don't just sell a component (such as an accelerometer), they read the data sheets for the component and figure out what other parts would be helpful to add on a board, making it vastly easier for mere mortals to incorporate into a project.

Best course on learning electronics
Make: Electronics
$23 Charles Platt, 2009, 352 p.

When I was a boy I took apart radios and old TVs to mess with their innards. I learned enough to keep the old sets going but not enough to master electronics. Whatever meager electronics understanding I had was lost when computer chips came along. To compensate I am now working my way through Charles Platt's master course on practical electronics -- which includes chips -- taught in this magnificent and rewarding book. His tutorial is project-based; learn by doing a series of demos you wire up yourself. This really is the best way to learn. One cool thing Platt guides the reader to do is lean into failure by pushing circuits and components past their limits. Sort of like learning to skid a car. By deliberately blowing out things I gained a sense where limits lay, and how things work by how they break.

Every step of this structured instruction is expertly illustrated with photos and crisp diagrams. I am looking forward his upcoming volume 2.

--KK

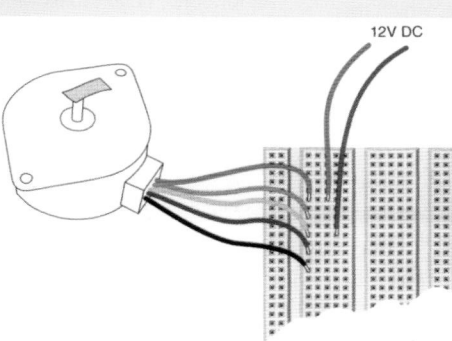

Logic gate basics (continued)

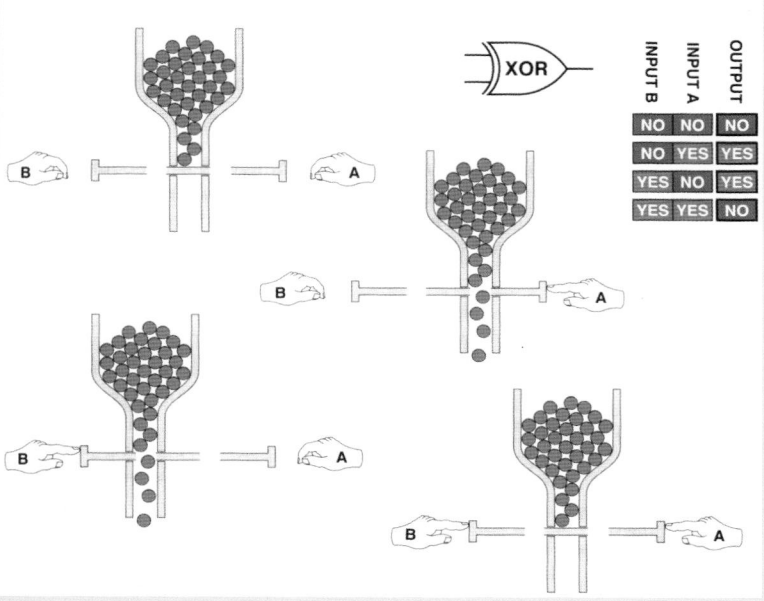

INPUT B	INPUT A	OUTPUT
NO	NO	NO
NO	YES	YES
YES	NO	YES
YES	YES	NO

Heavy-duty wire stripper
Paladin Universal Cable Slitter
$30 altex.com

If you've ever tried to slit electrical cable very far without ruining the inner wires, you know how hard it can be. This amazing little tool does in two seconds what can take a frustrating five minutes with a knife or wire cutters. You adjust the blade to the outer jacket thickness, clamp the thing on the cable, revolve it around the cable for the periphery cut (it rotates 90 degrees), flick the lever with your thumb, slit the cable lengthwise as far you want it, and the outer stripped jacket just falls off. Otherwise, especially on a long strip length, you either have to yank the jacket off the wire by hand or try to slit it with a knife, which is when you start damaging wires. This works great on heavy rubber SJO cord, coax, multiconductor, you name it. No nicks or cuts on the inner wires. You can even remove the jacket from the middle of a length of wire by making two periphery cuts and slitting away what's in between.

Even among electricians who strip cables for a living, this tool is surprisingly lesser-known. I've shown this to guys who wire up large industrial machines for a living and had their jaw drop open. And then I never see my slitter much after that anymore since it's always out on loan. It's a hard tool to find at any store (Berlands house of tools used to carry it). I discovered his tool in 1993 or so. Usage seems to go in spurts, depending on projects and which phase of machine building we are in (I design custom automated machinery for a living). Sometimes these five-foot tall electrical cabinets will have 100 wires running out of it, each having to be stripped & terminated. The electricians I work with especially love this tool.

-- Jon Kroninger

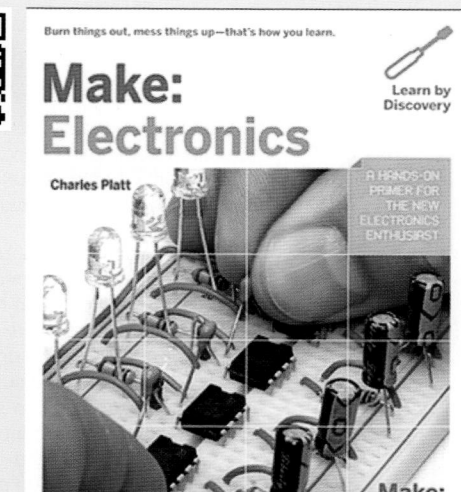

Burn things out, mess things up—that's how you learn.

Make: Electronics

Learn by Discovery

Charles Platt

A HANDS-ON PRIMER FOR THE NEW ELECTRONICS ENTHUSIAST

O'REILLY® Make: makezine.com

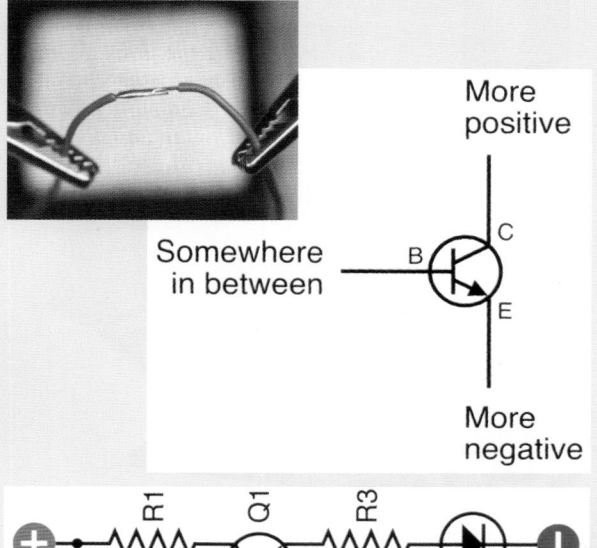

More positive

Somewhere in between

More negative

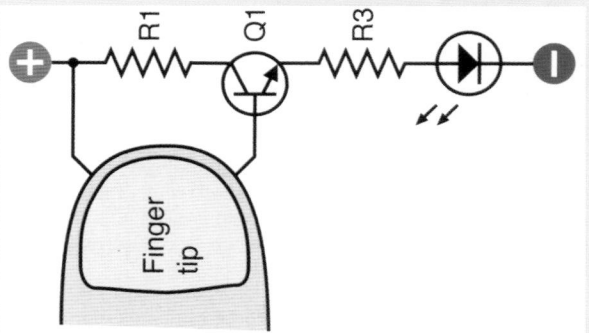

The electronics industry supplies components to manufacturers who build things in huge quantities. Increasingly, however, there are people interested in building things in very small quantities, where a low unit price is not as important as an understanding of how the component works. SFE caters very effectively to this latter audience, not just with their designs, but with tutorials, projects, and their customer forum. I've used SFE as a source for the Arduino, a very inexpensive microcontroller board available in a variety of sizes programmable with open-source tools. They also

sell a variety of add-on components for this system. SFE is an example of an enthusiast source that not only serves a community, but enabled it to exist in the first place. They've done this in at least three ways: 1) connected with tool makers to provide a retail outlet for their work, 2) designed example projects and boards to make the use of raw electronic components more accessible to a larger audience, 3) provided a way for people building stuff to share their experiences.

-- David Zicarelli

sparkfun ELECTRONICS

It's blue! It's skinny! It's the Arduino Pro! SparkFun's minimal design approach to Arduino. This is a 5V Arduino running the 16MHz bootloader in a super-sleek form factor that will fit easily into your next small project.

Adhesives

Not just for construction sites
Construction Adhesive
$6 Amazon

Construction adhesive has a major role in building construction, but I have been using it as a household adhesive. It has a number of unique characteristics that make it possibly more useful than most of the alternatives.

It fills gaps with strength, unlike cyanoacrylates like Superglue or polyurethanes like Gorilla Glue. It is somewhat flexible, which often makes a more durable repair for things like shoes, clothing, tents, etc. It is much stronger than Shoe Goo or urethane sealers, which the clear versions resemble superficially. It has tremendous initial tack. Often you can spread it, stick the two pieces together, and you are done. The glue is sticky enough that often you don't need clamping (which is a virtual necessity for Gorilla Glue and its relatives).

It is easy to apply. Unlike contact cements like Barge Cement, you don't have to apply it to both sides, let them dry, then carefully stick them together (and get an instant that you cannot realign if you didn't bring the pieces together perfectly.) You just spread it on one piece, jam the two pieces together and adjust, and you are done.

It also cleans up with soap and water, unlike epoxy, polyurethane glue, cyanoacrylate glue, contact cement, etc. It is waterproof in non-immersion settings, unlike white or yellow glues. It comes in a variety of formulations with a variety of characteristics, so you can choose high-strength, UV-resistance, clear or a kind of beige, ability to stick to foam insulation, even low VOC, etc. as needed. It is also sold in small tubes, though only in a few varieties.

As for cons, I can't think of any real disadvantages. If you want to bond two rigid things that mate perfectly, use Super Glue. If you want to bond two rigid things that don't mate perfectly, use epoxy. For wood, use carpenter's glue. For pretty much every other material, porous or non-porous, flexible or not, construction cement works great, at least so far.

I guess it isn't completely clear whether the stuff in the little tubes is the same stuff sold in the large tubes that require a caulking gun. But the large tubes are cheap, so some experimentation isn't out of the question.

The clear version from Liquid Nails let me make the only successful shoe repair I have ever made of a peeling sole. I stuffed the shoe full of newspaper, masked off the uppers, applied the glue, then applied blue masking tape on the outside to pull the sole close to the shoe. When it dried, it looked perfect, and for the last few years the glue has held strong while flexing with the shoe. I never had such luck with Shoe Goo, Super Glue, urethane sealants, Barge cement, etc.

I have used construction glues from both Loctite and Liquid Nails, and both brands seem to work well. You have to be careful to get construction cement, and not silicone sealant.

-- Karl Chwe

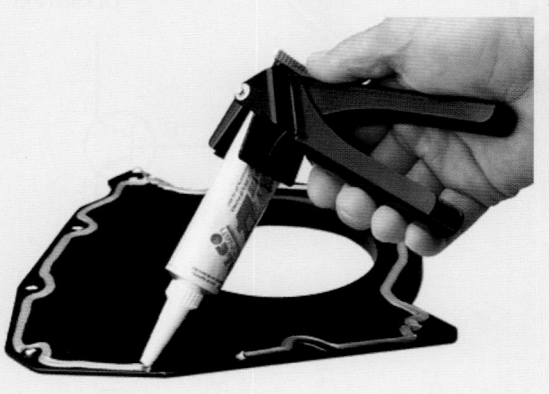

Squeezes tubes dry
Tube-Grip Dispensing Plier
$28 Amazon

This Tube-Grip easily squeeze tubes of adhesive, calk, sealant, etc. with more precision, less waste with better finished results than other methods. Learning curve is short for starting and stopping applications. Tubes are squeezed beginning from the tube's bottom seam, and 96% use of product efficiency is claimed. Very thrifty.

Mechanical advantage is claimed to be ten times more than by hand whether gripping vs. pinching. Less fatigue, more control. Concentration on product flow is enhanced because less physical effort is used during application. Tube squeezers for toothpaste and art paint are a different category. Some calking projects are too small for standard tubes of calk, or are in confined areas where a large gun won't fit.

Tent seam sealing with drippy sealer is controlled better with whole arm movements and a hand grip vs. finger squeezing. I've used this 2" dispensing plier for at least 5-years and would not consider many squeeze tube projects without it. A 2 1/2" model also exists.

-- David McKenzie

Safe hot glue
Low-temperature Glue Gun
$7 Mister Art or Amazon

A favorite tool, the glue gun, now comes in a low-temperature version which works much better with some materials like foam, and is the preferred one to grab at our house because it is slightly less dangerous for kids to use.

-- KK

A strong hold on brake fluid
Seal-All Adhesive & Sealant
$3 Amazon

Like other adhesives, this one can be used on metals, glass, wood and leather, but it is the only household product I have ever used that will withstand constant exposure to gasoline and/or brake fluid. J-B-WELD will work in some cases, but you have to thoroughly clean and dry the surface or it will fail. Seal-All will seal a leak in a master-cylinder-reservoir (non-pressure side) even if you apply it over brake fluid that has already wept out onto the surface. I have also used it to seal an old Coleman fuel tank, and also a weeping fuel fitting on the bottom of a gasoline tank on my bike. This stuff is not what I would consider a toolbox item, but I ride my bike far from home on occasion, and this is one of the items I like to keep in the "just-in-case" bag.

-- Jackie Gregory

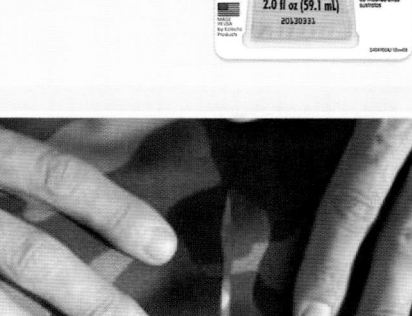

Quickly fixes tears and holes
Tear-Aid
$4-35 Tear-Aid Type A (for fabric), Patch kit, or 3" x 5' roll Amazon
$9-28 Tear-Aid Type B (for vinyl), Patch kit, or 3" x 5' roll Amazon

Tear-Aid is watertight and airtight adhesive repair tape marketed for use in repairing outdoor products. I first found it when I was looking at options for repairing a tear in a self-inflating sleeping pad and read a recommendation of Tear-Aid from a former bouncy-castle operator. That real-world endorsement was enough to get me to try it and it has performed well for me.

I didn't want to experiment with a liquid patch because I couldn't be sure if the solvents would interfere with the composition of the sleeping pad, so this option was attractive. The instructions are clear and application was simple. After preppng the area with alcohol, I peeled the backing off and pressed the tape over the problem area. The tape is tough but flexible, and is transparent. It sticks very well and the sleeping pad now stays at pressure perfectly.

Tear-Aid Type A is for fabrics and Tear-Aid Type B is for Vinyl only. I have tried Type A, but not Type B. My local sporting goods store stocks the small repair kits for around $10, but the product is also available in rolls or by the foot from some vendors online.

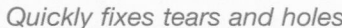

The small repair kit I bought includes a 30 cm length of the 7.5 cm width material, as well as some small patches and a length of monofilament provided to add durability in making edge repairs.

This tape is useful, versatile, and compact, and I plan to keep it on hand for emergencies. You can get it from their website but it is widely available in stores that cater to camping, boating, and other outdoor pursuits.

-- Erik Hoover

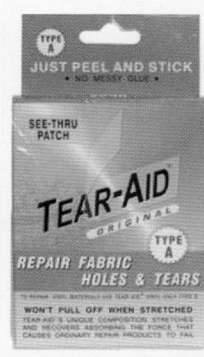
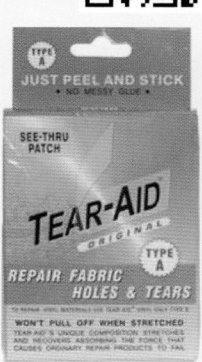

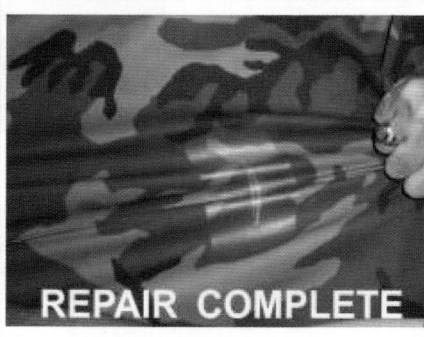

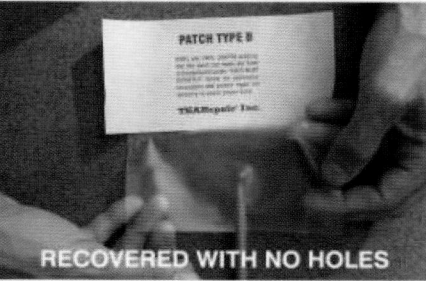

PEEL & STICK

REPAIR COMPLETE

PATCHES ARE ELASTIC

RECOVERED WITH NO HOLES

When I came home I expected a surprise and there was no surprise for me, so, of course, I was surprised. - Wittgenstein

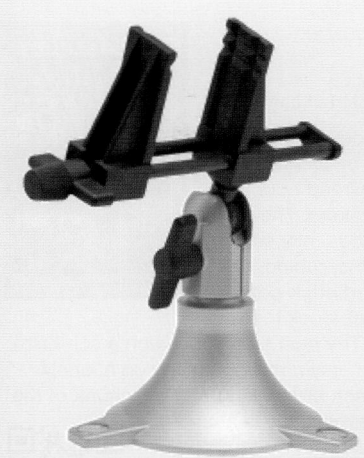

Hold anything mount
Mini-Vise
$24 panavise.com

I have been using this little vise since my interest in electronics was sparked by Make and Hackaday.com. Before I was just using the standard two-arm alligator-clip and magnifying glass holder from Xacto.

The Panavise is much more stable, adjustable and appropriate for breadboard soldering. It has the little grooves on the arms that your board can slip right into and a nice heavy base which means it doesn't need to be attached to a table if you like to move where you work around a bit. I've built several kits and designs of my own using this little vise. I am comfortable knowing *before* I start any project that this is one problem I am not going to have to solve.

-- David Van der Voort

Little lifters
Bench Cookies
$14 rockler.com

I discovered Bench Cookies at the Rockler woodworking store more than a year ago. Billed as "work grippers," they have smooth plastic sides and textured rubber surfaces on top and bottom. You just place them under objects you're sanding, sawing or painting to hold the object in place. There's no clamping or screwing involved. They're amazing. Wood chips and dust have no effect - they do exactly what they're supposed to. So instead of rummaging for scraps of wood or an old book or two to prop up a project, I reach for bench cookies.

I took them to the print shop where I do intaglio printing. Inking and wiping a large copper or zinc plate on a glass table used to be a nightmare - bench cookies make it a breeze. They hold the plate in place and I can pick it up and turn it as I work, and since it's off the table I can wipe the edges, too. I don't think Rockler had any idea how useful they'd be in an art studio.

Their great function and inexpensive price make them a perfect present for anyone that does any kind of project. Turns out Rockler's even made some nice black ones now for uses outside the workshop, like holding up your turntable, keeping it stable and providing vibration reduction.

-- Jeff Woodbury

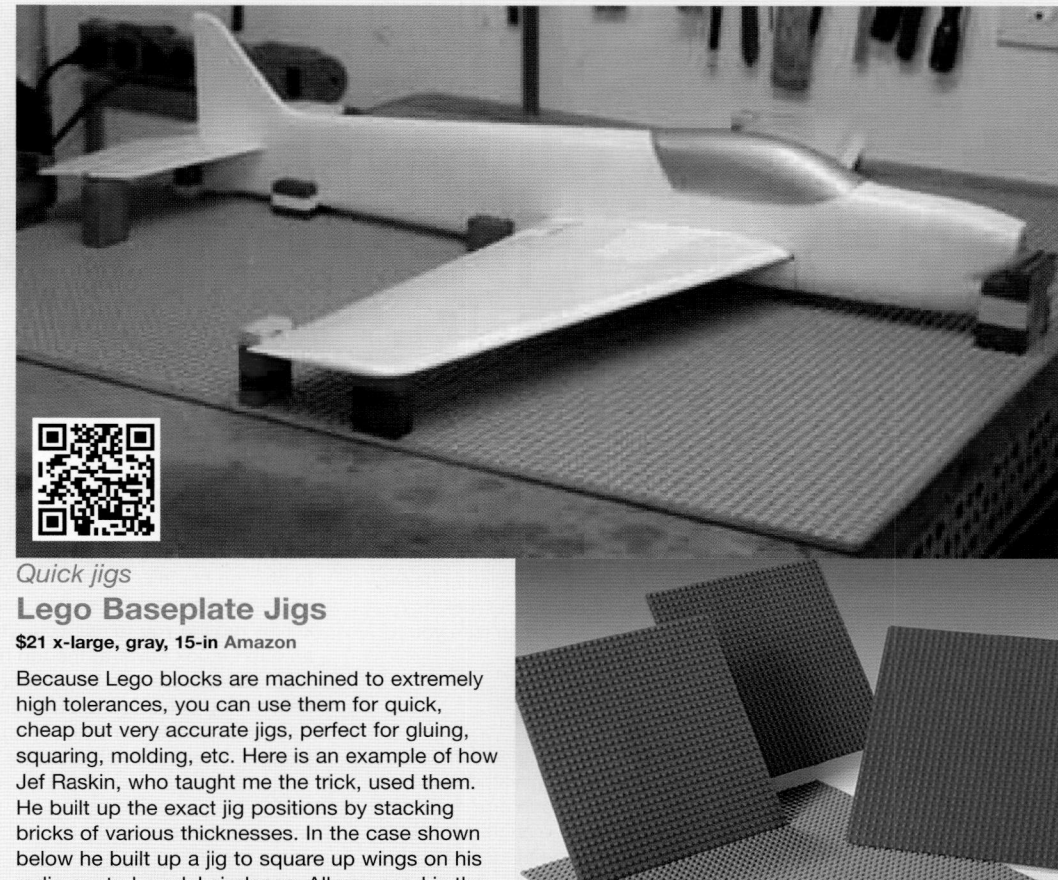

Quick jigs
Lego Baseplate Jigs
$21 x-large, gray, 15-in Amazon

Because Lego blocks are machined to extremely high tolerances, you can use them for quick, cheap but very accurate jigs, perfect for gluing, squaring, molding, etc. Here is an example of how Jef Raskin, who taught me the trick, used them. He built up the exact jig positions by stacking bricks of various thicknesses. In the case shown below he built up a jig to square up wings on his radio control model airplanes. All you need is the large Lego baseplate glued to a heavy duty flat foundation.

-- KK

Adjustable woodworker's clamp
Bessey VarioClippix Spring Clamp
$10 (4-inch) besseytools.com

While I have a wide variety of woodworking clamps in my workshop, over the past year, this adjustable plastic clamp is the one I've found myself reaching for first. It has an adjustable arm that slides easily on a notched shaft and locks into position when pressure is applied, allowing me to quickly resize a 4" clamp for 1", 2", and 3" jobs. It is feather light with comfortable handles and a decent throat depth. The spring pressure is just right and the pivoting faces provide a firm but soft grip (other spring clamps have narrow pads that contact the surface, causing possible indents on softer wood, for instance). If you're a woodworker you already have plenty of clamps. I've been doing woodworking for almost 50 years and currently have four pipe clamps and about ten old traditional all-steel medium to large screw-type C-clamps. Most have either deep throats or an extra-wide opening. I also have a number of simple metal spring clamps in a variety of sizes. I seldom use them anymore. Since the VarioClippix clamps are adjustable, a single clamp replaces all the various-sized ones, which also

reduces the clutter in my workspace. Ever since I spotted them in the Lee Valley catalog, these clamps have single-handedly handled about 70 percent of my clamping requirements.

-- David King

Crafting assistant
Third Hand
$7 Jameco Part#: 26690 jameco.com or **Amazon**

You can also find these at most dollar / discount type stores too for $3 or $4

The "Third Hand" is a low cost helper that has been an indispensable assistant for many of my projects in electronics. It holds circuit boards in place as you put in components, or if you need to solder delicate parts which require a steady hand (sometimes, more than two) it gives you a few more. It's also pretty tough to find someone to help you at 3am when most of the important work seems to happen. Two adjustable metal clips hold in your circuit boards (or whatever else) and a magnifying glass gives you a little zoom in action for the really tricky constructions. Perhaps I anthropomorphize useful things, but on an otherwise cold work bench, the Third Hand looks like a little robot pal with claws raised, always eager to help.

-- Phillip Torrone

Quick-release clamping
Bessey Ratcheting Spring Clamps

A significant improvement to the original screw clamp, these ratcheting spring clamps feature quick releases similar to a vice grip. You can hold your project in place with one hand and attach the clamp with the other -- all with one squeeze of a trigger. Allows you to spend more time on your project and less time screwing around (...and around, and around).

We purchased two of the four-inch clamps at Lowe's about a year ago and use them a lot in our boat repairs. In the last month, they've come in handy on two projects: to hold an awkward-shaped piece of fiberglass in place while we trimmed it; and to clamp some teak to the workbench so that it could be sanded. We have also used them to attach a straightedge to 4x8 pieces of plywood to provide a cutting guide.

$10 (4-inch) besseytools.com

We don't normally take the clamps with us out to sea (or let any of our tools get wet for that matter) so they should hold up fine. The clamps are made out of heavy duty resin, so they should never rust; this also explains why they're so lightweight, especially compared to old-fashioned metal clamps.

-- Nancy Roth

Model Making

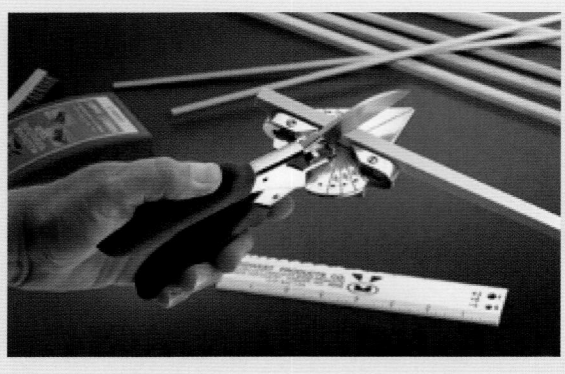

Powerful, portable model part manufacturing

Easy Cutter Ultimate

$24 midwestproducts.com
$24 Amazon

Most people might not know about this lovely tool unless you're a model maker. It is for precisely cutting things on a bias. The Easy Cutter has guides that make sure you get your angles correct and consistent. It can handle styrene, wood, foam core and plastic stuff. For model making, when you're making little parts, this is a terrific way to make sure you're cutting precise little pieces.

-- Adam Savage

This handheld tool allows miter cuts from 45 to 135 degrees of small pieces of wood, plastic, rubber, and even metal. As a miniaturist and model maker, this tool has been invaluable for cutting one or a myriad of small parts at various angles and sizes -- to change the angle you slide a self-indexing metal guide that runs perpendicular to the blade. When I'm in the middle of a project, such as the architectural model I'm working on currently, I use the Easy Cutter fairly constantly -- a few hours at least a couple of days each month. I have been using my cutter about three years now and a friend has been using hers well over 5 years without any trouble. You can buy new blades for this tool, but neither of us has found the need, thus far.

-- April Canady

Fast built models

Styrene

$7 12" x 12" x .06"
Sheet Amazon

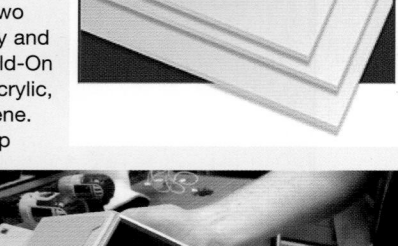

You should know about styrene. It is a really easy material to work with because two pieces melt together really easily and fast with a solvent glue like "Weld-On 3." It's the same Weld-On for acrylic, but it works even faster on styrene. For example, I've made this prop (see below) in about four hours. On movie sets, most of the props are nothing but styrene. You can paint it to look like anything. And styrene is sold in about a bazillion form factors — rods, tubes, sheets, textures.

-- Adam Savage

Turn here

Safe and sane blade holder

Testors Hobby Knife

$7 #50627C

It boasts a small but significant detail. When you need to change blades -- a fairly frequent exercise when cutting cardboard, matts, plastic parts, etc. -- most exacto knives require you to use your finger tips to unscrew an often-stuck collar at the top hugging the exposed razor itself. A slip can be severe. This one moves the unscrewing collar to the other end of the stick -- way way safer. And it has a nice grippy feel, cap, and roll stopper. Thank you, considerate knife.

-- KK

Really instant glue

Zip Kicker

$8 Amazon

When you are working in the special effects industry there's never enough time. You have to make things — and make them work – right now. One of the secrets of every special effects master is the use of cyanoacrylate glue with an accelerator. The accelerator is called "Zip Kicker" and it makes super glue dry and cure instantly. You lay down the cyanoacrylate glue, and you put your piece of material in it, and then you lay down a little bit of the kicker right on top of it. The kicker increases the evaporative effect of the cyanoacrylate glue and it sets almost immediately. When you are making something complex with many parts, instant glue makes a HUGE difference.

-- Adam Savage

The modelmakers' source

Plastruct

$5 print catalog, free pdf plastruct.com

This is the scale plastic stock and model parts catalog used by architects, scratch-build modelers, railroad hobbyists and other miniature makers. They have EVERYTHING at various mini scales: I-beams, T-beams, H-beams, tubing, tiny plumbing fittings, stone and brick-patterned sheets, plastic sheet stock in every size, color and thickness. The next time you watch a sci-fi film and see a far-away shot of, say a mining colony on a lonely asteroid, you're probably actually looking at a big chunk of the Plastruct product line. Their website is abominable; get their paper catalog.

-- Gareth Branwyn

•

To avoid gluing your model to your work surface, especially when working with a fast acting solvent cement like Bondene, we recommend you do all cementing on a sheet of polypropylene. Even better, purchase a few serving trays (cafeteria style) and cut the polypropylene sheet to snugly fit inside. This way, the sides will capture any spilled solvent cement before it spoils furniture, and you can use different trays for different in-progress projects.

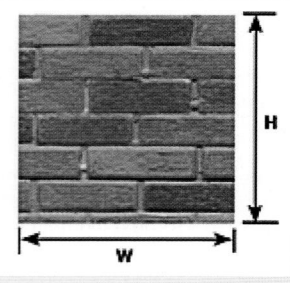

Micro tools

Disposable Suture Set

$20 Amazon

The next time you or a friend are in the ER getting stitched up, ask your provider if you can have the suture set when he or she is done. Most places will hand them over if they are the disposable type. Hospitals use disposable suture sets since they are fairly inexpensive and decontamination of the reusable ones can be costly. The curved hemostat, the toothless needle driver, small surgical scissors and the pickups (tweezers) come in handy around the house.

-- Fritz Araya

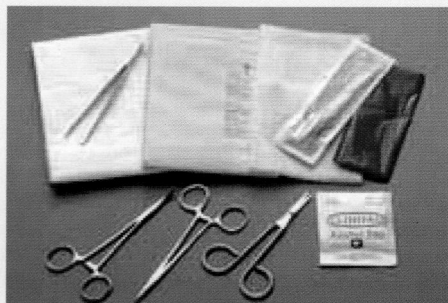

The source for model makers

Micro-Mark

micromark.com

The target audience seems to be HO railroaders and model builders, but there are tons of things in here useful to anyone who fixes stuff, especially small stuff. Every Dremel bit and attachment you could imagine. Tiny vacuums, gram scales, grippers, dental piks, tiny saws and sanders. And every flavor of small organizer container one could imagine. I bought a bunch to organize electronics parts and small screws.

-- Paul Saffo

Ear Polypus, 5-1/2 Inch

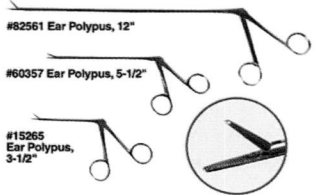

#82561 Ear Polypus, 12"
#60357 Ear Polypus, 5-1/2"
#15265 Ear Polypus, 3-1/2"

Pin Insertion Plier

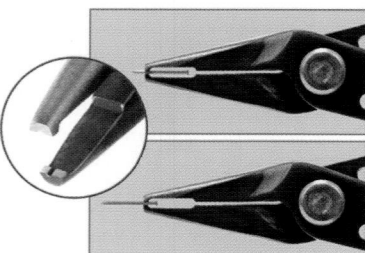

Handle and lock knob vary.

Miniature Clamps

Description

Universal Clamp Holds the Oddest Shapes

Rust n Dust

Best maker skills how-to
The Prop Building Guidebook
$37 Eric Hart, 2013, 383 p.

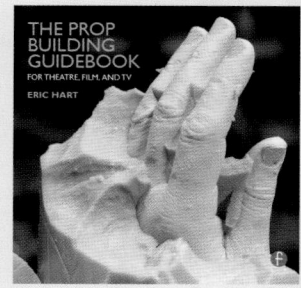

Sold as a guide for theatrical prop makers, this thick dense manual is excellent. But its real audience is the emerging tribe of hobby basement prop makers who create precise replicas of popular Hollywood props. And for this it is brilliant. It's so good in fact, that this guide is the best one-volume manual to general shop skills anywhere. It offers the best information I've seen on using contemporary plastics, foams, resins, adhesives, and composite materials. No where else can you find out how to glue various plastics to other materials. It gives great prototyping tips (since props are one-offs), and has really good guidance on making jigs, mock-ups, finishing, and general shop skills. Props are made from many types of things all at once. So this guide's range of materials and techniques is awesome and refreshing. It is the best "maker" how-to book in print.

-- KK

•

HDPE is used to make milk jugs, plastic bags, and paint buckets, among other things. Because it is a thermoplastic, it can be used for vacuum forming; some prop makers cut apart milk jugs to form small parts.

Polyethylene-based plastics are so chemically resistant that modern science has not invented a solvent glue to bond these plastics. This also means that no paint will bond to them. You may think you have found a glue or paint that sticks, but it is merely sitting on the surface and will eventually peel or flake off. Using polyethylene buckets for mixing and applying paints and adhesives is preferred for their ease of cleaning.

•

All plastic resins, such as polyester and epoxy, are particularly toxic in their uncured form. Keep them off your skin, as they are sensitizers. With enough exposure, you will develop an allergy. This can take a long time, but it can be drastic when it does manifest; you can work with resin every day for ten years, and then suddenly one day when you use it, your skin breaks out into rashes and blisters and your throat begins to close up (this differs among people; some can develop an allergy on the first exposure). It can take weeks to recover from one of these attacks, and afterward, even just a tiny amount of exposure will cause a new reaction.

You need to take appropriate safety precautions to reduce exposure to uncured resin as well as when you are sanding, cutting, or machining cured resin. All cured resin still contains bits of uncured resin that is released into the air when it turns to dust.

When plastic auto body has cured for around five minutes, it ceases to be spreadable, but is not yet rock hard. You can rasp or surform it down easily to save time sanding later on.

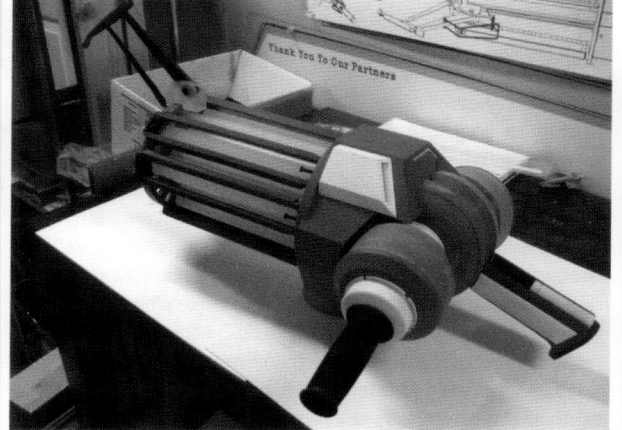

These "before and after" pictures of a gun show how aging and weathering transform a prop from a flat object to an item with a life and a history.

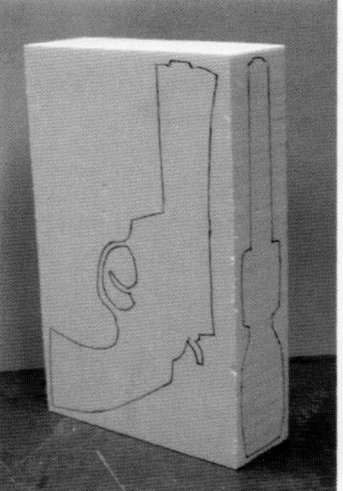 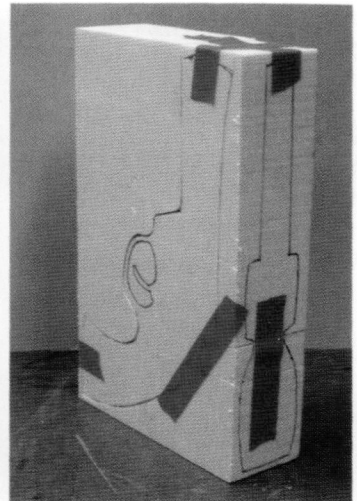

If you are cutting the object out on a band saw (or any stationary saw with a table), a good tip is to save the offcuts and temporarily reattach them so you retain a flat surface from which to cut the other sides out.

A mock-up of a saddle built out of cardboard

From left to right: white/bead foam (EPS), pink foam (XPS), blue foam/Styrofoam (XPS), dry floral foam (also Styrofoam), white craft foam (also Styrofoam).

Perfect tool organizer
Vinyl Zipper Wallet
$7 11" x 6" mmfind.com

A clear vinyl bank bag is a great and inexpensive way to organize tools or materials. I've been using these for years in the field, and I love them. Yes, they stiffen up in the winter, but none of mine have ever been damaged, winter or not.

These are better than the typical canvas bags because it's easy to see what's in them. I use a bunch of these for very different purposes, and the old Klein bags I had were frustrating because I didn't know which was which - unless I wrote on the blank side, and then the bag was kinda locked into that purpose forever more.

These things are just too easy. A perfect Cool Tool.

-- Wayne Ruffner

Score knife
Plastic Cutter
$4 Amazon

This is just a cheap little knife with a sharp draw blade. You use it to score acrylic sheets (up to 1/4 inch or 6 mm) to cut them by snapping them along the score line like glass. This is easier than using a saw. Any make will do; this is a cheap one.

-- KK

Easily applied plastic coating
Plasti Dip
$9 for 14.5 oz plastidip.com

This stuff rocks. Available in spray or dip form, I use it on anything and everything from tool handles to 2.4ghz wardriving antenna. It's available in most home improvement stores (Lowes, Home Depot). I prefer the dip for small things like keys and tools and the spray for things that are bigger.

-- Heath Dieckert

Catchall bowl
Magnet Parts Tray
$3 4" harborfreight.com

These are pretty much required tools if you're going to work on a car. Super handy for keeping track of small metal parts.

Sure, Harbor Freight stuff is primarily shoddily made, but my rule for buying their stuff is if it has no moving parts, it probably won't break.

-- Jason Kavanagh

We argue with our biology, and the result of that argument is civilization. - Charles Siebert

Painting

Extra tough spray paint
Rustoleum Epoxy Appliance Paint
$9 rustoleum.com

I learned about this spray paint a while ago from an old gent that restores appliances. The paint is a super-hard washable epoxy coating for appliances that have scuffed or discolored surfaces. The spray paint goes on very smoothly; I've used 4 cans worth, and have not had any drips or runs. I used it first on an old refrigerator, the front of a gas stove and the vent above.

Heat doesn't seem to bother it, or at least it hasn't bubbled. The paint dries in about 2 hours to a touchable surface, but it is best to let it sit for a few hours, and it really looks good. Price at Home Depot was $6.00 a can, same as any other Rustoleum product. It comes in several colors and can also be purchased, apparently, in gallon cans. For the price it is hard to beat, and for this application I haven't seen any comparable product that works as well. It is a very easy and practical way to refurbish old appliances. My wife even likes it.

Note: For those looking for higher heat applications, Rustoleum makes a high-heat enamel spray for restoring grills and other hot appliances that can withstand a wider temperature range.

-- Stephen Young

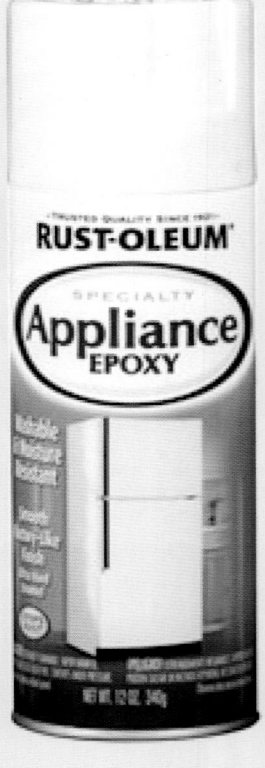

Comfy spray can gun
Can-Gun 1
$7 cangun1.com

Using your index finger to press and steer a can of spray paint gets old very quickly. If your paint job lasts more than a few minutes, you really should use a snap-on pistol grip. It saves your knuckle, keeps paint off your trigger finger, and gives you an easy way to guide the spray. For years I've used an earlier model of this grip (called simply Can-Gun), but that one was only operated with a single finger trigger. This new version uses your whole palm. It's comfortable, quick-on and off, and the only way to spray. I had a 5-can job on a chain-link fence and the Can-Gun made it kind of fun. Even for small spray paint jobs, I slip one of these on.

-- KK

Everlasting foam dispenser
PU Gun
$30 Amazon

If you ever had occasion to use expanding polyurethane foam to mount a window or the like, you may have thought like me "Great stuff, wonder what else I could use this for?"; But standard polyurethane foam cans are only good for a short while. Once used, the valve and application tube glues itself shut within a few hours, regardless of how much product was left in the can. Keeping a can around for those odd jobs and bright ideas is just not worth the waste.

Enter foam guns. The point of foam guns is right up front, so to speak. The exit valve is right up at the very tip of the rigid application tube. When you mount a can to the gun, the whole inside of the gun is pressurized with product just like the can. There is nowhere inside where the foam can expand or harden.

That's the theory, at least. In practice it still won't keep indefinitely. On first try mine hardened right trough in two weeks, and I had a nasty job cleaning it out mechanically. Subsequently, I have taken care to store it with the can upside down, and I tested it every few days for a while, and now it seems to keep fine for at least two weeks. Perhaps it just needed to self-seal.

I don't have a particular brand to recommend. I just got the cheapest all-metal model on eBay at the time, which I've seen since both branded and unbranded, and at wildly different prices. My experience seems to indicate, though, that staying away from the plastic models was a good idea, as I had to use considerable force to disassemble the gun for mechanical cleaning.

With these caveats, I'm still pretty happy about this discovery of mine. Only this week I used it to assemble a life-size doll my girlfriend made, and fix it to its plastic pipe skeleton. It really feels like I've got a whole new material in my kit.

Discovering what else it's good for is going to be fun.

-- Gaute Amundsen

Generic HVLP Sprayer
$55, Wagner Control Spray

HVLP means High Volume Low Pressure. It's a more efficient way of spraying. More media (paint) gets deposited than the old style sprayers. The difference is the air. It's not run with a high pressure compressor (like you use for filling up your tires) but a low-pressure blower making a large volume of air (essentially a reversed vacuum motor). Works fine, it's portable, and inexpensive. You can get a generic HVLP sprayer for $99, but some places are selling them for $79. I wouldn't paint a house with it, but for small furniture projects, it works great.

-- James Crum

Hand-size air-compressed hammer
Palm Nailer
$90 bostitch.com

A palm nailer is a magic hammer. Like a nail gun, you hook it up to an air compressor, but unlike a nail gun, it can be held in the palm of one hand. Its appearance doesn't make its usage obvious, but this air tool pounds in nail after nail without hurting my hand at all. Just place a nail exactly where you want it. Press the opening on the nailer over the nail, and BAP! BAP! BAP! BAP! BAP! -- compressed air drives a little hammer head inside the sleeve to gently pound in the nail. It takes about 10+ taps to get a nail all the way in, but in under a second.

I never knew about palm nailers until my brother-in-law clued me in -- and he learned from a friend who is a carpenter. They're perfect for working with precise positioning, like if you are putting together something with the previously-reviewed Simpson Strong-Tie connectors. I specifically bought mine to do the siding on a backyard shed with a fort for my kids. I just wish I'd known about it when I was doing the framing. I used a lot of Strong-tie connectors that required a whole lot of manual wrist-busting hammering of nails, because -- unlike the palm nailer -- a framing nailer just isn't accurate enough for the Strong-tie holes.

The palm nailer is a total joy to use. I love my air compressor and air tools (and have three nail guns already), but another plus is the palm nailer works with any single nail, not just framing nail-gun feed nails. Also, the size of the palm nailer lets you get into places either a framing nailer or a manual hammer simply can't fit very well. I've only used a Bostitch-branded palm nailer that I picked up at Lowe's. It was like $80, so not what I'd call cheap, but it's made by a solid manufacturer and it's readily available online and if you're walk-

ing into a big box hardware store.

-- Eric Lundquist

Low-odor, low-VOC, fast-drying paint
Benjamin Moore Aura Paint
$55 1 gal. benjaminmoore.com

Unlike a lot of VOC-free paints (VOC = volatile organic compounds), Benjamin Moore's Aura line of low-VOC acrylic paints isn't thin or runny, dries really fast (literally an hour or less) and it's available in a satisfying array of colors in eggshell, matte, satin, and semi-gloss. It's VOC rating is less than 50 grams per liter (a standard paint might have 250 grams; VOC-free paints can still have up to 5 grams per liter). The Aura paint isn't cheap — I think we spent $10-15 more per gallon than we normally do — but I have always been partial to more expensive paints because the colors appear truer and in, many cases, they require just one coat. With Aura, we found even the deepest of wall colors only required two coats to cover, and we didn't use primer. The best part is there was no stinky paint smell residue, only beautifully-painted walls to gaze at with our little one.

-- Amanda Hughes-Watkins

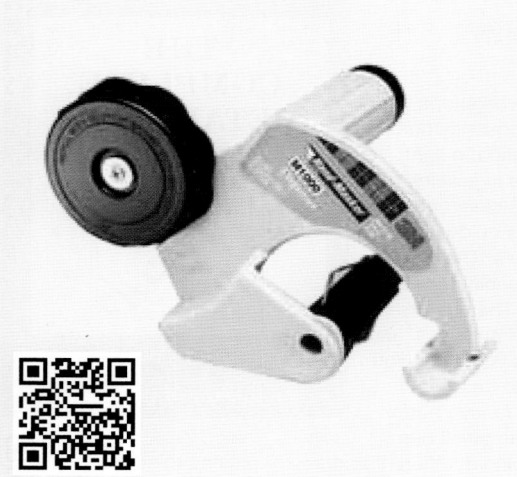

What painters use
3M Masking Tape Dispenser
$20 Model M-1000, 3m.com

The one thing that I hate most about painting is the taping. We all know that if you don't tape, then it will not look as good. So, I'm always looking for an easier way to tape. This little device holds a roll of tape and has rollers to ensure adhesion of the tape to the surface. This is the first device that I've ever used that would work on baseboards, my personal nemesis in painting. I picked mine up at Home Depot and was able to tape an entire room in less than half the time of doing it without a dispenser.

-- Michael McDonald

Paint Roller Cleaner
Wagner Roller Washer
$6 Gleempaint.com

This is the best way I have found to clean paint rollers.

After squeezing and/or scraping as much paint out of the fur of the roller as possible, it only takes the Roller Washer about a minute or two to blast water deep into the roller and rinse away the remaining paint.

I usually then give my rollers a "shampoo" with some liquid soap, and moving the roller up and down inside the Roller Washer until the soap bubbles disappear. This is followed by spinning the roller on the frame with an air compressor blow gun to remove the water and fluff the fibers.

-- Andy McConnell

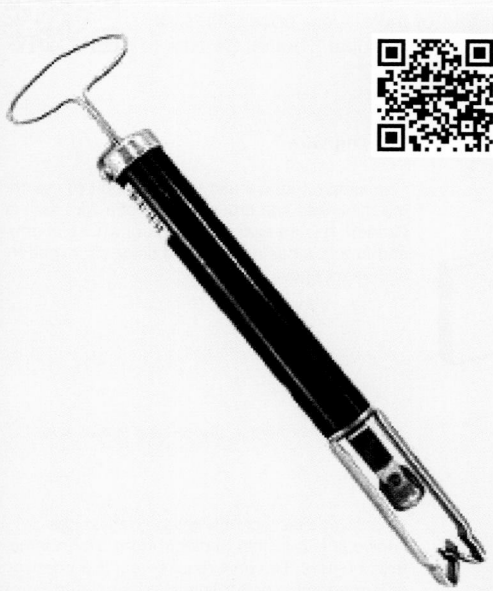

Centripetal brush cleaner
Paint Brush Spinner
$14 Linzer, arroworthy.com

A paint brush spinner is used to clean paint brushes or roller covers. With water-based paints or varnish you simply insert the brush handle into the tongs or grippers, or slide the roller cover over the outside of the tongs. Then while running the brush or roller cover under water from the utility sink (or garden hose and garbage can) you get it spinning.

The brush spinner has a spiral shaft that when pushed into the body rapidly spins the brush or roller cover. The whole process is similar to a child's spinning toy, with the end result being that dirty water and paint is flung off. A similar process can be used with oil-based products.

The only downside is that the spinner spiral shaft eventually gets rusty and needs lubrication. In the past I've used DL Waterless Hand Cleaner to remove any rust that builds up.

-- Peter Klemann

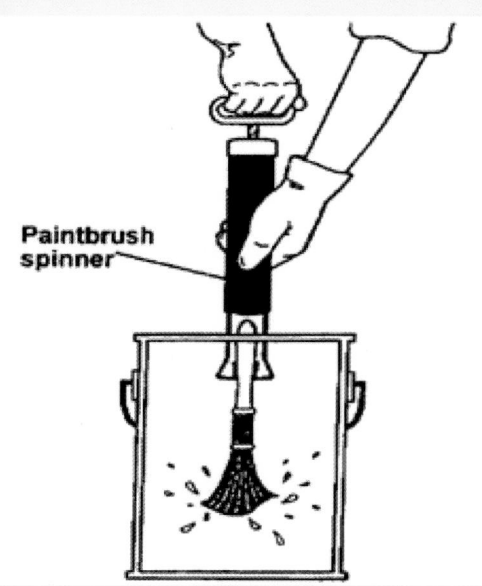

Paintbrush spinner

The best paint removing method
Silent Paint Remover
$395 silentpaintremover.com

I'm currently stripping the exterior of an 1885 vintage Victorian home. There are so many coats of paint to remove it was going to be a nasty job. I spoke to my neighbors who said they had an infrared paint remover (Silent Paint Remover) that worked great. I was hesitant to put out a lot of money for a new, unproven tool so I asked to borrow it for an evening.

I used the tool for 20 minutes and immediately went inside and placed an order! You apply the tool to the clapboard for about 20-30 seconds. Then scrape; the paint really does come off easily. I also purchased the wall attachment so I can slide the tool across the row of clapboards and have one section "cooking" while I'm scraping recently heated area. This allows me to cover twice as much area as I would without it.

Their scrapers are also superior. Unlike most pull type scrapers, their large triangular design provides a lot of open space so the scraper doesn't get clogged when scraping multiple coats of paint. They also have several different shapes of blades. I'm using the clapboard blade which is nice because it gets the underside of the clapboard, above, and the surface of the clapboard below. I also have the profile blade which is making easy work of scraping rounded corners on the house.

Their line isn't cheap, but it's well worth the money in the time you save. It also doesn't release any lead which was a concern when working with a house this old. The tool has apparently been around in Sweden for some time and there is an extensive set of accessories in addition to those I've purchased. When people walk down the sidewalk and see it they're amazed. Now if I could just stop people from wanting to borrow it before I finish the job!

-- Scott Sipiora

Instructions for making your own DIY version from a quartz heater oceanmanorhouse.com/paintremover.html -- KK

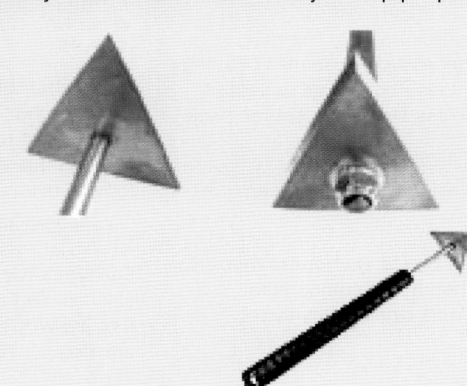

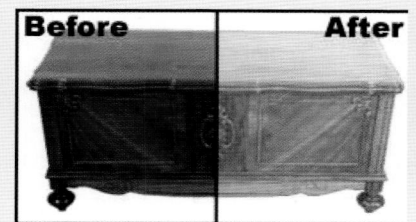

Before   After

$25
Amazon

Biodegradable paint stripping
SoyGel Paint & Urethane Remover

This soy-based, biodegradable stripper is not the cheapest stuff around, but it's easy to use and can be used indoors because it doesn't have the harsh fumes of typical strippers. When I first used it about five years ago, I was shocked. I used two gallons to strip an entire room: it went on like honey and smelled almost as good. Three hours later, almost all the paint came right off in one fell swoop. I've since used it on several pieces of wood furniture and a metal gate.

I've been restoring and renovating old homes and furniture for over 25 years, and always used those harsh chemical strippers that are environmentally unsound. I'll NEVER go back. There are several citrus-based strippers out there that are cheaper, but they're just not very strong. SoyGel really is the most impressive eco-friendly stripper I've run across.

One recommendation: it takes ages for this stuff to dry out. Frequently you can cover whatever piece of furniture you are working on with thick plastic sheeting to keep the stripper moist longer.

-- Justin Anthony

Better paint & roller holder
Bercom Ladder Pail
$22 BER-4500-CC, handypaintpail.com

I've always done my own painting. I've owned a number of boats and have restored an 80-year-old house. Through all that I used dozens of metal and plastic roller pans, the standard variety that are widely available for next to nothing. While they are ubiquitous and cheap, they don't keep the roller out of the paint; they don't have a place to keep a brush out of the way and out of the paint; and they're easily knocked off your ladder's paint shelf. This one by Bercom rules them all and is well worth the money.

It's listed as a ladder pail, but it's really best as a replacement for a standard paint tray. I can fill this bucket with paint, hook my roller on one side, a good brush on the other and proceed to neatly and easily paint both from the ground and from up on an extension- or step ladder.

I've used it for more than a year and have done a number of rooms with high ceilings in two different houses. The ability to suspend both the brush and the roller above the paint and use either without interference, easily, on a ladder make this bucket a joy to use. All the fittings are first rate. The shape is perfect. Even the little details shine, such as the molded-in channels to make pouring the paint from the bucket back into the can smoother.

And the magnet that holds the brush is removable for cleaning, which means I can easily get the bucket back to like-new condition. All in all, I highly recommended it. I won't paint on a ladder without it.

-- Dennis Faust

Metalworking

The machinists bible
Machinery's Handbook

$80 Erik Oberg, 29th Edition 2012, 2800 p.

I have been using the Machinery's Handbook for 30 years. My first was the 14th edition when I started out as a machinist. Throughout my engineering career this handy reference has served in projects large and small.

My 26th edition has accompanied me on three continents and has never disappointed. Machinery's Handbook is the Bible of the mechanical industries. It provides mechanical and manufacturing engineers, designers, draftsmen, toolmakers, and machinists with a broad range of material data, from the very basic to the more advanced.

It has always provided accurate, concise and easy to locate reference material for any mechanical project. The only thing that could improve this fantastic reference is to have a digital copy on my smart phone.

-- Scott Trube

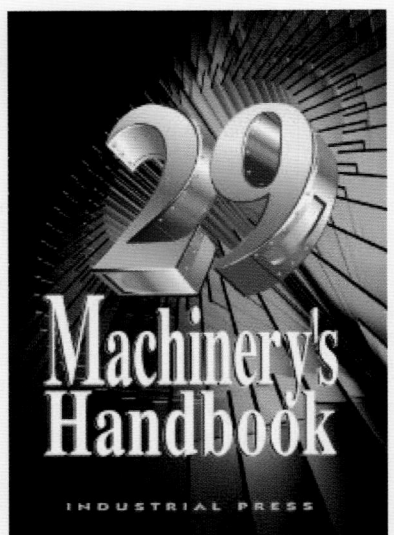

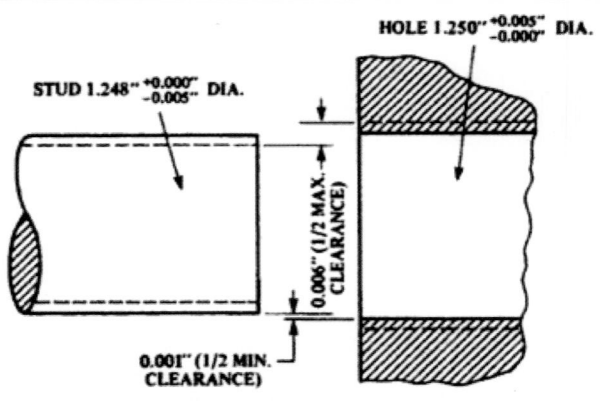

Fig. 3. Graphic Illustration of the Meaning of the Terms Maximum and Minimum Clearance

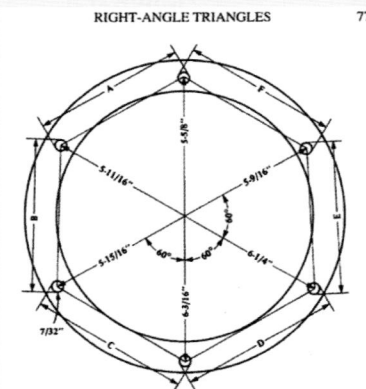

RIGHT-ANGLE TRIANGLES 77

Fig. 16. To Find the Chordal Distances of Irregularly Spaced Holes Drilled in a Taximeter Drive Ring

Essential metalworking tool
Beverly Throatless Shear

$536 Bench Shear B-1 ottofrei.com beverlymfg.com

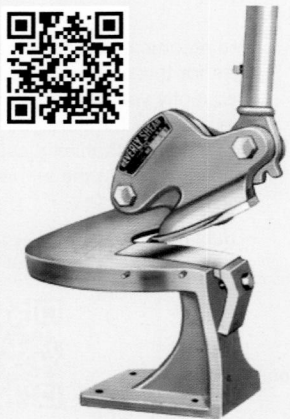

Twenty years ago, when I was first starting out as a metal sculptor, I was advised by my art teacher that if I made only one purchase I should get a Beverly Shear. It remains the best advice I've ever received.

Sounding like a 1940's B movie star, this wonderful tool has been the center of my studio ever since. It lets me cut metal and other materials into complex shapes without misshaping the metal and leaving a clean edge that needs only light finishing. I use it not only for my sculpture work, where I cut parts out of salvaged sheet metal without harming the patina, but also to cut plastic, rubber, old vinyl records, and even cutting corrugated roofing diagonally and along the ridge.

Though I have used the larger models that the company offers, I find that the B1 is the perfect size for almost any task, and does a great job of cutting out small and delicate parts. It is rated to cut 14 gauge steel (18 gauge stainless) and does so with minimal effort with its geared rack and pinion mechanism. There are imitations that go for less money, but I wouldn't trade my Beverly for anything.

-- Scott Randolph

Precise metal saw
Dewalt Multi-Cutter Saw

$450 DW872 dewalt.com

It is difficult to saw stainless steel very precisely without discoloring it as a result of heat. A chop saw using an abrasive blade is not suitable. A band saw using a metal cutting blade (like a hacksaw) is insufficiently precise. What you need is the (relatively) new class of saws which run relatively slowly and use specially designed circular toothed blades. I opted for the DeWalt DW872 after watching the very nice QuickTime video on their web site.

This saw, with a default general-purpose metal cutting blade, costs about $420. I also bought an accessory blade specifically for stainless steel. This set me back an additional $200.

It is, without doubt, the best way to make clean, precise cuts in metal.

One word of warning: Don't try to economize by using the special-purpose toothed metal-cutting blade in a regular chop saw, which runs significantly faster. This generates safety issues.

-- Charles Platt

How to work metal
The Complete Metalsmith

$13 Tim McCreight 1991, 208 p.

I've spied this book in the cluttered workshops of many amateur craftsmen, and it is frequently nominated as the best all-around introduction to light metal work. If you take an entry class in jewelry, this is often the manual. (Complete in this case does not include welding or blacksmithing; this guide is best for metal projects smaller than a bowl.). The reason I like this manual is that it is quick, succinct, clear, and dense -- sort of like metal itself. The author assumes you wield a certain level of handiness, and that you can kind of figure out things yourself if you get a general sketch of what needs to be done. It shows you with simple drawings (no fancy photos here) things you might want to do with small bits of metal -- different methods of shaping it, different textures or patinas to coat it with, ways to cast it in molds, how to set stones in it, what metals to even use. In other words, it's a quick tour of metal work possibilities. It also lays flat on the table with its thoughtful metal spiral binding. Be sure to get the revised edition.

-- KK

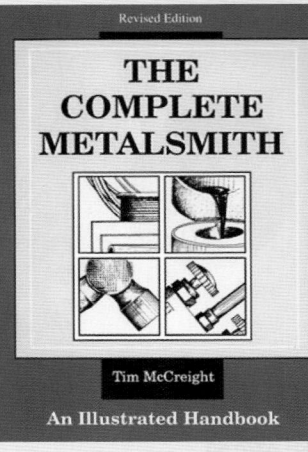

Revised Edition

THE COMPLETE METALSMITH

Tim McCreight

An Illustrated Handbook

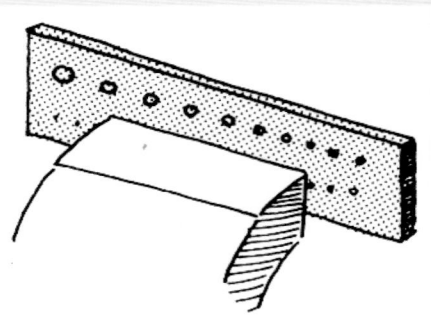

Drawing Wire

This simple tool will allow a craftsman to create the thickness and cross section of a wire as it is needed. It is an example of a tool whose shape and function has no changed since its invention 500 years ago.

◄ The plate is held in a vise so it is well supported.

As anyone blessed with bronze babyshoes knows, it is possible to electroform over nonmetallic objects. The only requirement is a coating of a conductive paint. This can be painted onto a matrix of wood, plastic, paper, stone or about anything else.
◄ If a vise is not available, hold the draw-plate on a board with a hole in it, braced across your door jamb. Native American silversmiths used to anchor their plates against pegs in the ground.

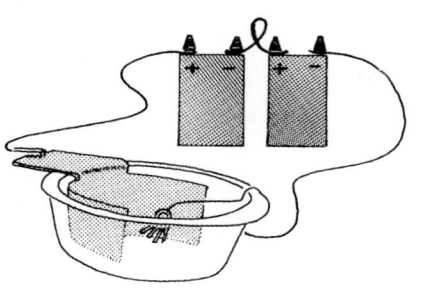
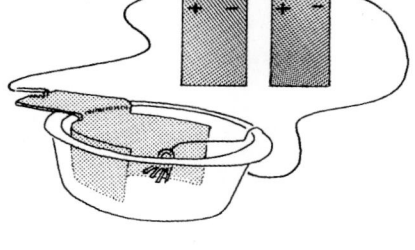

Gold Solder

Gold may be joined with silver solder but to achieve a color match a gold-based alloy is usually used. Gold solders are available in many colors and melting points. When buying solder, specify the metal you are joining. 14 karat yellow solder refers, not to the quality of the alloy, but means it is used on 14K gold. In fact, solder will be a karat or two lower than the metal it will join. Any gold of a lower karat can be used as a solder. 10K will be a solder for 14K; 14K will solder 18K, etc.

Electroforming equipment

Special metal working tools
Eastwood Supplies

eastwood.com

Eastwood is primarily an auto-body parts and tools supplier, but oh what tools. For example, welding equipment. You might not need TiG welding equipment, but you might find use for the gloves (fireplaces) or the jeweler's torch. Or painting equipment. You probably don't need to powdercoat brake calipers, but you *could* powdercoat your grill, lawn furniture, whatever.

Or maybe you need shop tools. Specialty tools like garage wheel alignment on the cheap, or your own garage lift (user-installable!). Wheel dollies for moving cars in your multi-car garage laterally. I first encountered the catalog because I needed tracer dye for a head gasket leak; I ended up buying hard-to-find 3M abrasive pads for removing the old gasket material as well as the dye and the UV lamp. Best thing about it? Buy something once and you get the catalog for well over a year. There's always something in it if you're a handy kinda person....

-- Christopher Wanko

Original Hotcoat Powdercoating Gun
Item No. 10198
$99.99

BUY NOW >>

Eastwood has long been one of my favorites. I have found their stuff to be just what they say it is, and their service all one could ask. I have especially liked their lineup of tools that are very hard to find elsewhere. Many times, just seeing items in the catalog has enabled me to come up with design solutions, and let me make the parts I need. Yummy Yum.

-- J. Baldwin

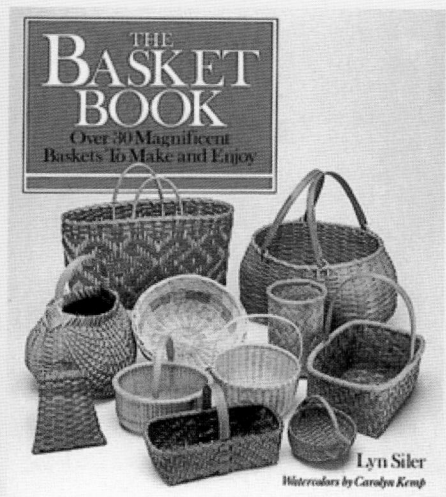

Durable, textured, useful
Building Bamboo Fences

$14 Isao Yoshikawa, 1999, 142 p.

Step-by-step instructions for making scores of stylized ornamental bamboo fences. From Japan where they take this art seriously. Bamboo can grow anywhere most trees grow and is ideally suited to fence making.

-- KK

Elementary basket weaving
The Basket Book

$8 Lyn Siler, 1998, 144 p.

One of several books that can teach you elementary basket weaving. This one's particular virtues are that it has very clear instructions for a large variety of baskets you might actually use (more than other guides), and that it can be had for a few dollars online, used.

Beyond the standard " flat reed" rolls, its hard to find unusual weaving fibers -- unless you make your own.
-- KK

Natural basket fibers
V.I. Reed & Cane

basketweaving.com

Beyond the standard "flat reed" rolls, its hard to find unusual weaving fibers -- unless you make your own. This source has a few natural fibers, and a lot of basketry supplies.

-- KK

We Guarantee:
• No "seconds"
• No "slightly hairy"
• No "slightly darker"
• No "slightly irregular"

Simply the Highest Quality at the Best Price. Superior Quality. Try it and see for yourself!

SPECIAL: Discount priced 25 lb. package ($9.95 lb.). You choose the quantities and sizes that you need

Ash Splits

2 different widths. 2 different lengths.

Preparation: soak for 10 to 20 minutes until splints are pliable.

Basic Techniques

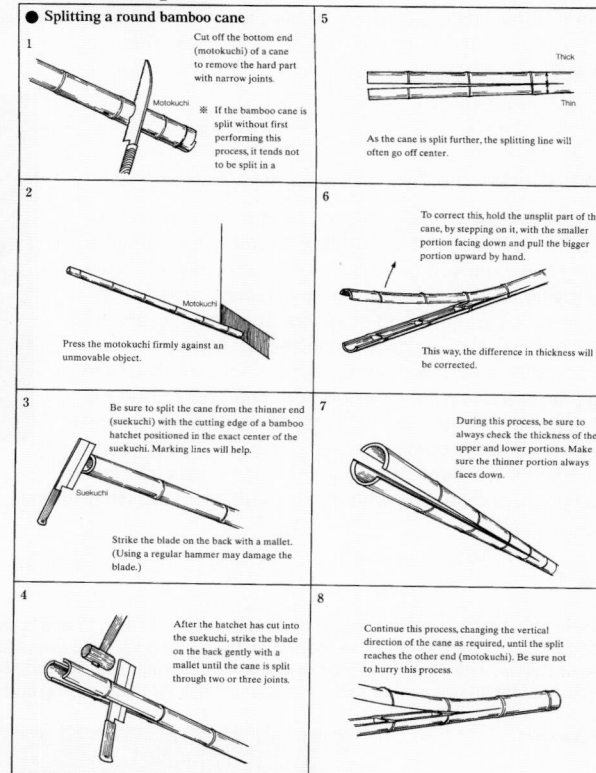

Round Reed Flat Reed

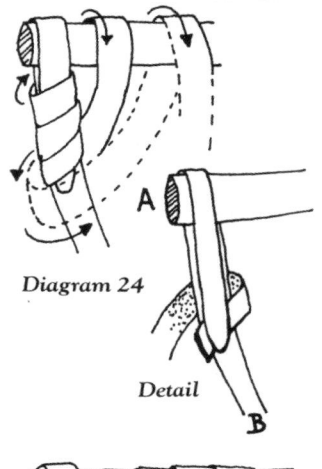

Diagram 24

Detail

Basket possibilities
Art of the Basket

$7 Bryan Sentance, 2007, 216 pages

Baskets can be magnificent. There's a thousand ways to weave strands into objects, for art or for use. This absolutely stunning catalog of traditional basketry from around the world can guide you to what is possible. All materials, all shapes -- 800 amazing basket-y artifacts here! You'll not think of baskets in the same way. What else can be woven in 3D?

-- KK

Baskets, from the Philippines, made using fibre from banana stems.

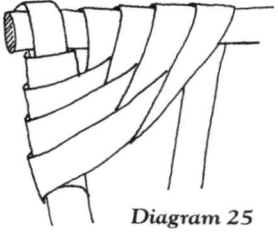

Diagram 25

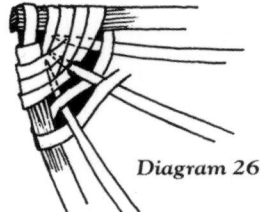

Diagram 26

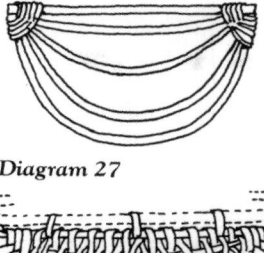

Diagram 27

Diagram 28

Fish creel worn at the hip by fishermen from Lombok, Indonesia.

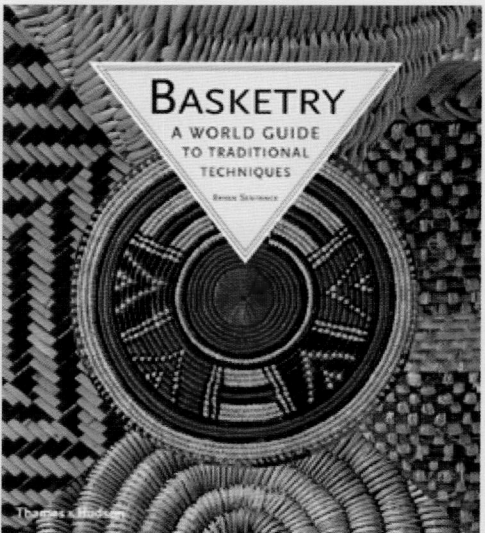

Fabrics

On-demand fabric printing
Spoonflower
$18+ per yard Spoonflower

I am an architect and have been working with programs like Photoshop for years, but Spoonflower really opened up a new world for me: fabric design. It's a service that let's you upload an image to a web site and the company prints the design as a pattern on 100% cotton fabric. Their customer service is great, and I think the fabric is reasonably-priced: it costs $18/yard, not counting shipping, and an individual 8×8-inch swatch is $5. The site is still in beta, so I had to request an invite to use Spoonflower, but a week after contacting them I was experimenting with patterns and ordering fabric.

So far, I've placed three orders with three different designs (3×3 yards worth) at $ 66 per order, shipping included. The trickiest part was preparing the image file so the pattern matches up. I used the "define pattern" command in Photoshop to test my image files before I uploaded them. I defined the image size (150 dpi), set colors to LAB color space and saved the files in TIF format. After I uploaded them to the Spoonflower site, they were automatically tiled to fill the desired fabric size. Then I speci-

fied the shipping address, paid using my credit card and that's it! The turnaround was reasonably quick: my fabric arrived in a month (I live in Switzerland). I made a skirt with the fabric from my first order — a present for my Mom (pic below).

A couple caveats: I have noticed some distortion after washing the fabric and there was a little color shifting from my original designs. Still, the color shifting and fabric distortion really are minor. Overall, I'm happy with the color accuracy and I've been very satisfied with my orders. I have been having a lot of fun with Spoonflower and will likely place my fourth order very soon. I am even considering setting up an Etsy shop to sell some of my fabrics.

-- Isabella Kuntz

Global woven technology
World Textiles
$22 John Gillow and Bryan Sentance, 1999, 240 p.

Anything with a global perspective wins extra points for me. This is the world's best book on the world's textiles. In a single volume you get a taste of all the varieties of weaving, dying and cloth-making on this planet, now and in the past. It's yummy, and stunning. The book is very intelligently designed, logically organized, and magnificently printed (full color). No how-to, but a whole library of inspiring patterns and traditional loomed, tied and knitted methods from all over the world in one portable tome. There's no single volume comparable to this book. Great source material for weavers, of course, but also artists, designers, craftsmen, and anyone who makes stuff. Here are what threads can be!

-- KK

Lace

Lace is a European invention, made by the poorest of women to adorn the clothing of the rich. Probably the most recent traditional textile-making technique to come into existence, it seems to have originated in Italy or Dalmatia (the coastal region of of the Former Yugoslavia) in the 15th century, but the technique and the fashion for its use spread rapidly to countries as far apart as England and Russia.

Stripweave

It is a widespread practice to sew two separately woven pieces together to make one textile which is too large to be woven in one piece on any available loom. This is the method of construction, for example, of rugs made by the Balouch in Afghanistan or of hinggi mantles woven on Sumba in Indonesia. In a very few places textiles are made by sewing together a large number of very narrow strips. Apart from the ghudjeris, or horse blankets, of Uzbekistan virtually all stripweaves are to be found in West Africa. The best known is the kente cloth of Ghana.

Untying wefts for weft-ikat cloth at Sukarara, Lombok, Indonesia. The pattern was resist dyed into the wefts before they were woven. This may involve tying, untying, and retying the yarn several times to dye different parts of the pattern in different colours.

Women, from Uzbekistan, wearing ikat fabric known as abr or "cloud" cloth. On their laps are the tied bundles of threads for abr after dying, which they will unravel.

Rethinking fabric
The Art of Manipulating Fabric
$20 Colette Wolff, 1996, 322 p.

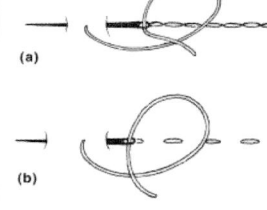
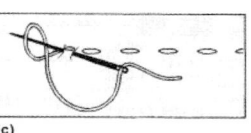

I have used this book for at least 8 years as a source of inspiration for my work as a designer. The author, Colette Wolff, systematically explores the many different ways that fabric can be folded, gathered, tucked and quilted, creating categories for each type. Her explorations start with a simple fold or pleat but become successively more and more complex, and more creative. In the last chapter she includes examples that combine different techniques. She always maintains a clear line of thought as she branches out, providing precise instructions and beautiful black and white photographs of all the "manipulations" executed in plain white muslin.

What I find so remarkable is Wolff's ability to be at once so methodical and exacting, and at the same time to be so imaginative in her approach. She has created an encyclopedia of fabric manipulation, an incredible resource that anyone involved in working with fabric, from clothing and textile designers to quilters and home sewers, would find not just useful, but truly inspiring.

-- Antoinette Indge

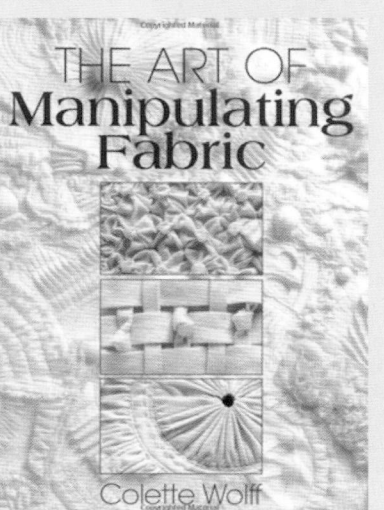

HAND STITCHES

BACKSTITCH
—Strong, versatile hand stitch used where firm sewing is required for structural seams, for mending breaks in machine-stitched seams, and for hand quilting. Backstitches are also used to secure sewing thread at the beginning, replacing a knot in the end of the thread, and at the end of a row of stitching. Work backstitching from right to left (reverse all directions if left-handed). Bring a threaded needle up to the surface; insert the needle back into the fabric ⅛" (3mm) to the right of the emerging thread. For an **even backstitch**, make a stitch ¼" (6mm) underneath and bring the needle out ⅛" (3mm) in front of the emerging thread. For all succeeding stitches, insert the needle into the needle hole ending the previous stitch and bring it out ⅛" (3mm) in front. Even backstitching looks like straight machine stitching ((a) in Fig. A-1). The **half backstitch** looks like running stitches. Making a stitch ½" (1.3cm) long underneath, bring the needle out ¼" (6mm) in front of the emerg-

Fig. A-1. (a) Even backstitch. (b) Half backstitch. (c) Securing with backstitches.

BASTING
—Temporary hand stitching that holds fabric layers together in the desired alignment until permanent stitching is in place. Baste from right to left (reverse all directions if left-handed). For **even basting**, make

Hand stitches, p 295

XIII-4 GATHERED CORDED TUBING—Tight- and loose-fitting casings gathered over cords while turning right side out. For contrast, a stuffed ball ends a length of smooth, corded tubing.

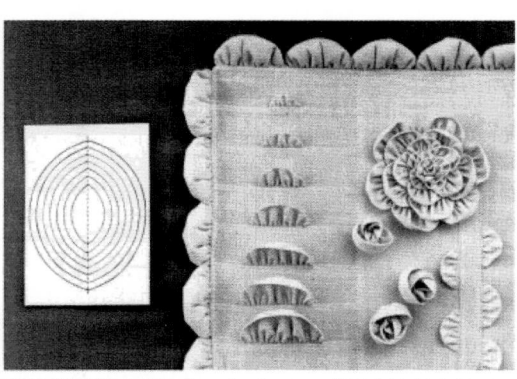

XIII-5 SHELLS—(left) Graduated oval patterns. (right) Folded in half and gathered until straight, graduated shells are inserted in seams, arranged into a large flower-like circle, and rolled into three bud-like shapes. Shells border an appliquéd band and stuffed shells border the sample.

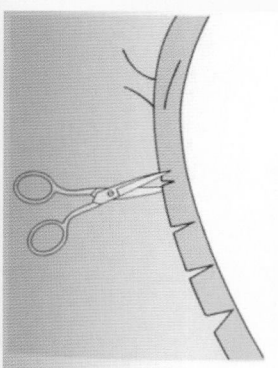
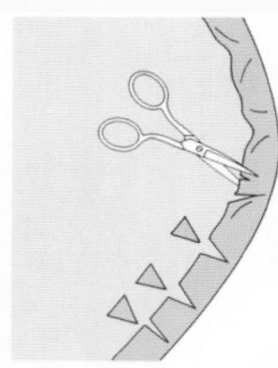
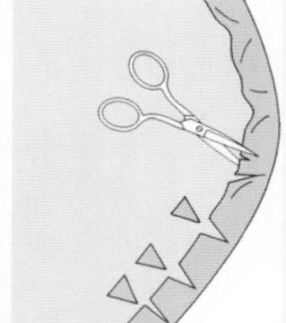

Clipping and **notching** are used on curved seams to allow them to lie smooth. *Clips* are slits cut into the seam allowance of concave, or *inward*, curves that permit the edges to spread. (With either technique, hold scissor points just short of seamline to avoid cutting past

stitching.) *Notches* are wedges cut from seam allowance of convex, or *outward*, curves; space opened by removal of fabric lets edge draw in. When clips and notches face one another, as in a princess seam (see next sketch), they should be staggered to avoid weakening seam.

Hemming stitches, blind

These stitches are taken inside, between the hem and garment. In the finished hem, no stitches are visible. The edge of the hem does not press into the garment.

Blind-hemming stitch is a quick and easy stitch that can be used on any blind hem.

Blind-hemming stitch: Work from right to left with needle pointing left. Fold back the hem edge; fasten thread inside it. Take a very small stitch approximately 1/4 in. (6 mm) to the left in the garment; take the next stitch 1/4 in. (6mm) to the left in the hem. Continue to alternate stitches from garment to hem, spacing them approximately 1/4 in. (6mm) apart. Take care to keep stitches small, especially those taken on garment.

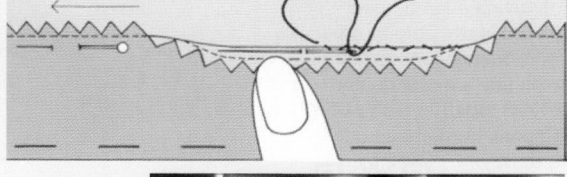

Best sewing skills guide
New Complete Guide to Sewing

$20 Reader's Digest, 2010, 384 pages

When a struggling new fashion-designer needs to hone their sewing skills, Project Runway guru Tim Gunn steers them to this Reader's Digest Guide to Sewing. It's got the best, clearest, and most complete introduction to 95% of the sewing skills you'll ever need. It's practical and methodical in its instructions. Not as good as grandma, but anyone will be able to pick up stitches, cutting and machine use from it.

-- KK

Easy threading needles
Spiral Eye Needles

$25 for three Spiral Eye Needles

These ingenious sewing needles can be threaded blindfolded. You pull the thread into a spiral from the side, and for the most part the thread will remain in the eye as you sew. That is not true for calyx eye needles (invented a hundred years ago) as a solution to the vexing problem of threading the eye. It's as easy for the thread to slip out of the open slot at the end of the calyx needle as it is to slip in, and this wavering can fray the thread. The spiral eye needle doesn't snag, but in my experience it will occasionally let the thread slip out. Expert sewers might find that annoying. It is dead simple to slip back on, and the thread is not frayed, so I can put up with that small inconvenience.

Spiral Eye needles are expensive: $5 each. However they should last a lifetime if you don't lose track of them (they look very similar to regular sewing needles). What I really want is a side-threading sewing-machine needle. Schmetz makes some in limited sizes, but of a less ingenious design.

-- KK

Cheapest portable sewing machine
Brother Sewing Machine

$67 Amazon

I own, use and occasionally drag around my Brother sewing machine. Like the previous version of this machine recommended in Cool Tools, it's light, small, cheap and reliable. I use it for occasional household work and mostly to make repairs to uniforms and sew on patches. It can do ten stitches and that's more than enough for me. Especially handy is the buttonholer. This little box, in combination with a beginner's sewing book, can help you do everything that you can imagine short of embroidery. It has held up most admirably considering how much I use it.

-- Angus mac Lir

Sag-B-Gone Jean Button

$ source-mfc; Paragraph style: Access-Info

Larissa Holland of mmmcrafts came up with a good solution for people who don't like belts or suspenders and also don't like it when their jeans start to stretch and get saggy as the day goes on: a "sag-b-gone" button! The no sew dungaree buttons are available on Amazon.

-- Mark Frauenfelder

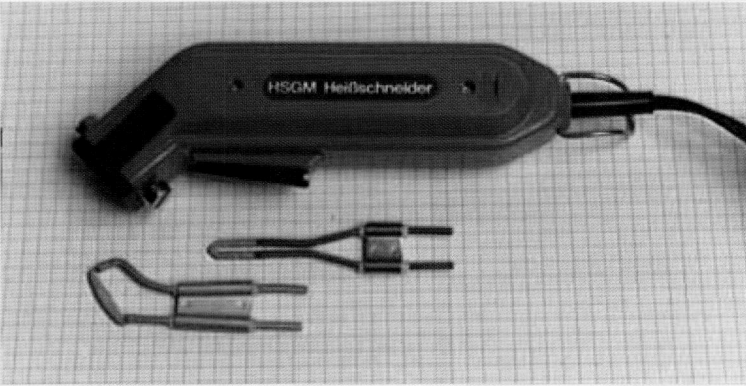

Superior textile cutter
Engel Hot Knife

$168 Rochford Supply

The Engel Hot Knife is fantastic for cutting and sealing synthetic ropes and textiles in one hot cut. Particularly when making kites, bags, tents, or anything with textiles this is faster by a factor of 10 than scissors, more accurate, and also seals the edges against fraying. It has two blade types, one long and arced, great for fast large things, one pointed and small for detail work. The fact it has a work light directed at the blade is a tremendous detail only the German's would have thought of including. I use it for other things as well, like sealing plastic bags and various plastic welding jobs. This is probably a misuse of the tool, but periodically I find that useful. I own two of these, and have owned them for 5+ years, and I love them.

-- Saul GriffithPU

Tough sewing line
Kevlar Thread

$4, 50 yds. dupont.com

I tend to be rough on buttons (or maybe I'm just gaining weight). I started using Kevlar thread to sew fire toys and found it is very strong. I now use Kevlar thread for all my sewing. On buttons, I don't need to use as much thread to secure them and the thread is tougher than the fabric I sew into. By weight, Kevlar is five times stronger than steel wire and is used in bulletproof vests. Do NOT try to break it by hand -- you'll just hurt yourself. The very thin thread works well with beads -- it's very abrasion resistant -- and there are thicker varieties that I use for sewing leather.

-- Sean Rutledge

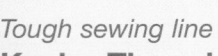

Elemental sewing machine
Sewing Awl

$17 Amazon

One of the world's oldest tools, but one that is often overlooked. This is a heavy-duty needle with its eye at the working end, mounted in a handle. For mending leather, shoes, bags, sewing canvas, or stitching heavy materials, there's no better tool. I don't use mine often, but it has a place in the essential toolbox. Your local Ace Hardware sells a kit with tool, extra needles, and waxed thread.

-- KK

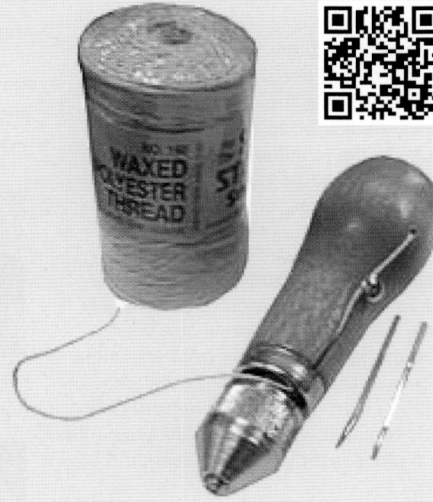

Knitting

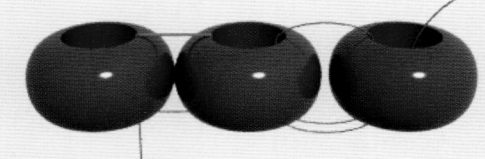

Fire Mountain Gems
Beading, jewelrymaking resource

Prices Vary Fire Mountain Gems

Fire Mountain Gems and Beads is, in a sense, the McMaster Carr of the jewelry world. The company's 400-plus page print catalog, with its to-scale photos of beads, gems, clasps and findings (roughly, the jewelry-making hardware), rivals any catalog in terms of introducing creative possibilities, and enticing you to buy stuff. For me, having the physical catalog makes navigating the extensive website easier.

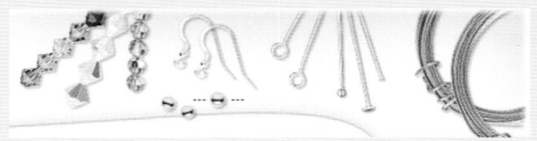

If you're interested in making bead jewelry, I'd recommend taking a beginner's class at a local bead store to get started and gain a basic familiarity with the tools. I took a wire wrap class at a local shop and then had a foundation from which I was able to learn knotting and stringing pearls watching Fire Mountain's instructional videos.

One of my favorite aspects of having even a basic ability to make jewelry is that I'm always able to create a last-minute gift, at least for friends whose taste is similar to mine. I keep a small stash of beads and findings around, and then can put together a pair of earrings in 10 minutes—a personal, homemade gift I didn't have to go to the store to buy.

-- Bryn MacKinnon

Knifty Knitter
Knitting templates

$18 Provo Craft

The problem I have with regular knitting is getting started. With a hat, for example, I have a lot of trouble getting my size just right and having the first row look neat and not sloppy. Knifty Knitters completely eliminate the size problem and allow you to make the first row just as neat as every other row. Each loom is basically a round circle with pegs on it. Since you are wrapping the yarn on preset pegs, the problem of keeping the stitches the same length is eliminated. I have the round set for hats and the long set, which is mainly for scarves and blankets. Each set comes with four looms. The round set labels the looms by size: baby, child, adult and the largest is either for a big-headed adult or for other projects (like ponchos). They come with directions, which are really easy to follow. I made my first hat while watching a movie. As you work, your hat starts to build up and hang down underneath as you go, which is pretty neat to watch. When it is long enough (the directions tell you how long for different sizes), you use this plastic needle to thread a piece of yarn through the loops at the end and drawstring it tight and tie. Then you use this little hook to pop it off. Done.

I totally recommend these for the serious and the totally not serious crafter.

They're pretty cheap. They're easy. And even on your first try, you end up with a really good finished product you can wear or give to someone. I have about a dozen friends who have gotten them since my recommendation and all of them are really into them. Even my husband made a hat for his sister's kid while watching a movie and it came out perfect. The looms are made for thicker yarns, but if you have tons of old thin yarn you can double it up and use two strands as one (or even three) and that makes it so you can do all kinds of color combinations.

I found the long set a tiny bit harder when I got started (i.e. figuring out the corners), but after a few minutes messing with it I was rolling out a scarf. There are other looms I have not tried from Knifty Knitters, like a flower one and a rectangle one, which all make different things. They also have pompom and tassel makers and one that lets you make tube scarves. But there are tons of other things you can do with the same hat loom, too. My friend got a great book from her library; Knifty Knitters' web site has a few ideas; and I recently found a sock pattern on the Internet and made a pair using the smallest loom in the round set. It was way way way easier than it looked and they came out perfect.

-- Krista Wilson Muldoon

Community Quilts
Sewing together

$3 Karol Kavaya and Vicki Skemp, 2001, 136 pages

Modern quilting bees. How (splendid detail in color here) and why (because you make more community than quilt).

-- KK

One advantage of group quiltmaking is that one person doesn't carry the entire load. The desire to create and the willingness to work with others are all that is needed.

●

Some of these quilts took hundreds of hours to complete, many of those hours spent in the convivial company of old and new friends. The subjects that we covered in conversation while quilting allowed us to get to know each other, and sometimes ourselves, better.

Every year we have a party in the spring. We gather the quilts together and hang them up for all to see. It is our time to remember, to reminisce, and to celebrate where we come from and who we are. These quilts are a record of our lives as a community.

●

In general, we think it is a good rule to allow participants no less than two weeks for completing and returning an easy pieced block, and not more than six weeks for a difficult block involving fine embroidery. When you give participants more time than that, blocks seem to get forgotten, lost, or eaten by the dog.

●

We often hang the quilt rather than gift wrap it. This provides for a wonderful shock effect. Furthermore, people are able to enjoy and admire the quilt all through the party.

Ravelry
Knit and crochet community

Free Ravelry

If you knit or crochet, then chances are very good that you've already heard of Ravelry. If you haven't, then you're really missing out.

In the simplest of terms, Ravelry is an online community of 3,000,000+ (yes, that's million) fiber enthusiasts. You'll find users ranging from novice to Master Knitters (and the equivalents in the crochet world). Designers, dyers, and people generally dedicated to the world of making things with yarn are all to be found in the multitudinous forums. There are forums based upon region, favorite local yarn stores (LYS), particular techniques, designers, specific patterns, and just about anything else you can imagine.

But Ravelry is much more than a giant online chat room. In addition to the community that it fosters, Ravelry also provides a number of hugely popular tools for its users. Users may keep track of (and share) their projects, complete with pictures. You can queue projects from anywhere on the Internet, including Ravelry's own voluminous pattern database. You can keep track of what patterns you own, even if they're from printed / offline materials. There's a handy tool that will let you track your stash (and if you're like me, then that alone is a huge time saver) and your needle and / or hook collections.

My favorite tool at Ravelry is the pattern search. If I want to find a knitting pattern for a dress for a toddler, using sport weight yarn, using size 4 needles, that has a picture, is purchasable online, and has at least a 4-star review, Ravelry's got me covered. Need a pattern that doesn't use more yardage than what you have on hand? You can limit your pattern search by yardage. Want to work on lace, cables, or entrelac? The pattern search lets you search by fabric characteristics. The combinations are limitless, and I have lost hours to searching for the perfect pattern.

--Mary Alderdice

The why of knitting
Knitting Without Tears
$12 Elizabeth Zimmerman, 1995, 120 pages

This book is a classic. It is a relatively small instructional book on knitting. It is wonderful because it teaches one how to construct good looking garments without the use of knitting patterns. Her hallmark is a seamless pullover sweater. This book not only delivers quality knitting instruction – it is a great read!

-- Mary Cavanaugh

This is not so much a how-to-knit book, though it excels as that, as much as it is a glorious how-to-enjoy, and how to live while knitting book, penned by a remarkable woman who found happiness at the end of her yarns. This short but famous primer is a good place to start knitting for life. I doubt I personally will suddenly pick up needles — although my teenage kids and all their friends have — but nonetheless I did read every page of her instructions with great pleasure.

-- KK

If you are a habitually tight knitter, try to kick the habit. Loose knitting tends to make your stitches look somewhat uneven, but what of it? Are you trying to reproduce a boughten machine-made sweater? Besides, it is surprising what blocking and a few washings will do to uneven knitting.

I used to think that people in the Olden Days were marvelously even knitters, because all really ancient sweaters are so smooth and regular. Now I realize that they probably knitted just as I do, rather erratically, and that it is Time, the Great Leveller, which has wrought the change – Time and many washings.

The human being is so constructed that it can be completely covered by a series of shaped tubes. Tailors and dressmakers succeed excellently and skillfully in making tubes out of flat woven material; their achievements are nothing short of marvelous. But we, the humble knitters, can fabricate natural-born tubes by the very nature of our craft of circular knitting. With the techniques of increasing and decreasing at our command, we can shape or even bend the tubes as we will, without seams, gussets, or darts. It is then only a matter of uniting the various tubes by knitting them together, or sometimes weaving them together, and we could, if he desired them, make long-johns for an octopus.

For a small baby, take 4 ounces of baby wool, work at any GAUGE you feel like, and see what happens. Babies vary so much in size, and grow so fast, that the jacket will be gratefully worn at some period during the first year.

Caps are quickly made, and invaluable for using up scraps of wool for color patterns and stripes. They are excellent bazaar material, as people will pay more for them than for mittens, and they are quicker and more fun to make. (For me the great drawback to knitting mittens is that, having created one, you have to turn around and copy it exactly, for a pair.)

Knitting can be solace, inspiration, adventure. It is manual and mental therapy. It keeps us warm, as well as those we like and love. It has existed almost as long as the soft sheep, and in giving us wool they deprive themselves of no more than an uncomfortably warm fur coat in the heat of summer.

Knitting Without Tears

Elizabeth Zimmermann

Best sources contest
Sewing and Quilting Sources
Prices vary Clotilde

The best resource for sewing and quilting needs is Clotilde.com. It's been around for ages and offers a complete selection of templates, needles, scissors, rotary cutters, patterns, fabrics and on and on. They have the largest array of seam rippers I've seen anywhere: lobster-clawed, flat-handled, round-handled, two-sided with an awl, lighted, retractable. They sell many unusual and specialized"feet" for sewing machines with adapters to ensure fit on your particular model.

eQuilter

The best online source for quilting fabric is eQuilter.com. It's a very personal, small company out of Boulder, Colorado with the largest online selection of fabrics in all genres: batiks, Asian, novelty prints, solids, tonals, etc. They have great prices and sales, rapid shipping, and excellent customer service. I usually try to patronize my local small quilting shop, but this is my go-to source for things I can't find locally.

Keepsake Quilting

The best resource for quilting kits is Keepsake Quilting.com. Why kits? It's easy to overbuy fabric for quilting projects and the fabric is expensive. Also, Keepsake puts together breathtaking combinations of colors and designs. My most recent purchase was #2990 which I had been lusting over for some time and it would have easily cost more buying the fabrics individually. If you want to use your own quilt pattern, try their medleys of fabrics like Nara Gardens #1646 or the Aquatica Medley #7582 or the Intergalactic Medley #7564.

-- Madame Tut

No trace fabric marker
Hera Marker
$6 Sewing Machines Plus

The Hera marker is an ingenious little plastic marker that makes a shiny line on fabric, perfect for marking hand quilting lines that needs no removal. Technically this is called a "tracing spatula." The shine on the line on the fabric is caused by the friction of the edge of the tool on the fabric fibers, and it makes a small crease in the fabric as well. The shine and crease will be covered by stitches or will be smoothed out when the item is washed, leaving no trace.

-- Lesley Creed

Best sewing scissors
Gingher Sewing Shears
$16 Gingher 8-Inch Knife-Edge Dressmakers Shears Amazon

Ask almost any tailor or sewer which scissors they use and you'll hear universal acclaim for these venerable 8" Gingher Shears. They've been making them in this style forever (although they are now manufactured by Fiskars in Italy). Ginghers are durable enough to pass on to the next generation. These hefty scissors slide through layers of fabric with ease, are comfortable with long use, and stay sharp all the way to the tips. (Pair them with the previously reviewed Gingher snip scissors.) Bless them, they also come in a left-handed version. The key to keeping sewing scissors in top shape is to never use them to cut paper or anything else in the garage. A good idea for those who live in a large household is to tie a bit of fabric or ribbon on the handle as a red flag: "CLOTH ONLY. Do not even think about using this for anything but fabric."

-- KK

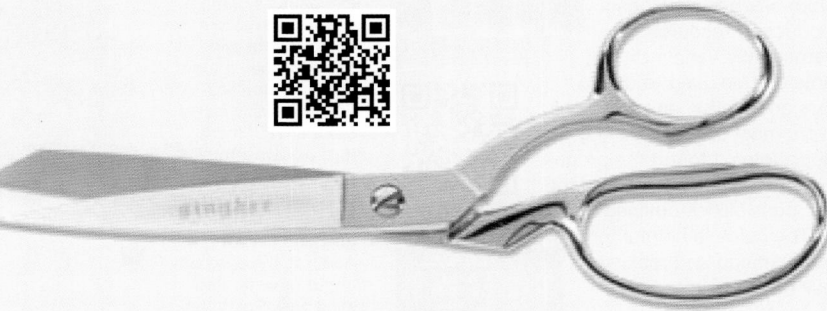

Classic sewing scissors
Gingher G-4C
$20 Amazon

These Gingher scissors are simply stellar. They are strong, durable and well-made. They have extremely sharp points which can make smaller, more precise cuts than any other scissors I have ever owned. As such, I have had numerous Gingher sewing scissors over the years.

I have also discovered that Gingher offers repair and reconditioning for all of their products. Simply ship any Gingher item to them and they will sharpen, repair and recondition it for $7.50. What a deal! I sent in a few pairs of scissors that I have used for years, including one which had mistakenly been used to cut wire (ugh!). A couple of weeks later they came back working as if they were new. Such a service for such a price is something truly rare these days.

-- Elissa Vigil

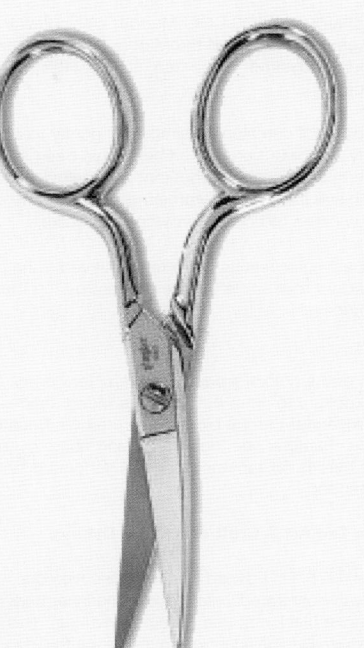

Quick ruler
Sewing Gauge
$2 Sew and Knit Gauge Nasco Online Products

I wouldn't want to run a home without this small sewing and knitting gauge (approx. 6 inches long, metal with a movable plastic marking guide) Helpful for all household projects which require consistent simple measuring and marking. Used for craft projects, or just to help children learn how to measure equal distances when they want to do some kind of art project requiring parallel lines. The small size makes the gauge convenient to cart along for measuring/adjusting/adding lines of sequins, or decorations to costumes. Most families need to hem things (blue jeans, curtains, skirts, costumes) and the gauge is PERFECT for this use. This is as basic a tool in my home as scissors or a ruler. Can be purchased in any sewing store or the sewing department of a discount store.

-- Jane Seitz

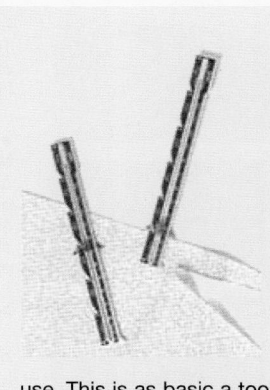

Dharma Trading Co.
Textile Craft Supplies & Clothing Blanks Since 1969

Best fiber supplies
Dharma Trading Company

Prices Vary Dharma Trading Company

Dharma Trading Company has EVERYTHING for the knitter and home fiber craftsperson. Excellent dye supplies, and blanks — white clothes for dyeing — and lots of great (white) fabric for all kinds of projects at very reasonable prices.

– Lesley Creed

I get my batik and tie-dye supplies from Dharma Trading. Great selection and good service.

-- KK

Natural Yarns for Dyeing

Natural Yarns to dye in solid colors or hand paint into variegated yarns. They are natural in color and come in skeins averaging about 8 ounces unless otherwise noted.

The Sample Card (#YARNFS) comes with 8" samples of every yarn, so you can get a better idea of how they look and feel.

Better Tjantings (Batik Tools)

Here's a better Tjanting from Indonesia, the home of batik. Carefully handmade in a small village with all copper parts and Teak wood handles. Copper is easier to heat than the brass ones, and the tips produce a finer line. Some also use the size #1 for drawing very fine lines of wax to make Ukranian Easter Eggs! These tools just look good too!

–KK

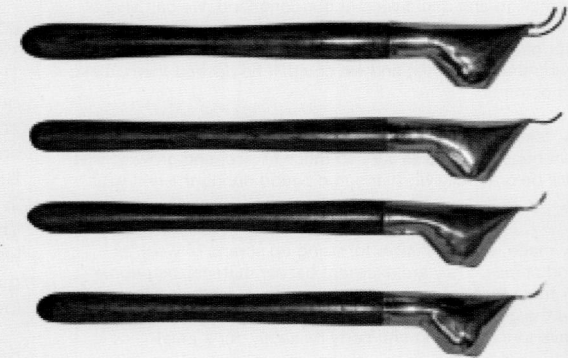

Vanishing Fabric Markers (Purple)

Use these to draw your design on the fabric. The lines disappear "like magic" with water or within 48 hours. On thin silks, it fades away very fast. Test that you have enough time.

Purple for white fabrics.

Procion Dyes

$6 Jacquard Procion MX Fiber Reactive Dye, 2/3 oz. Amazon
$3+ Dharma Trading Company

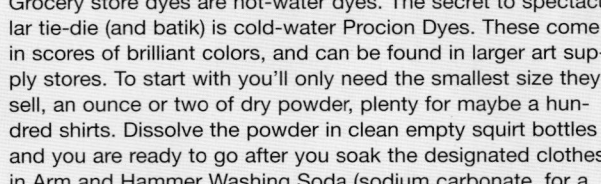

Grocery store dyes are hot-water dyes. The secret to spectacular tie-die (and batik) is cold-water Procion Dyes. These come in scores of brilliant colors, and can be found in larger art supply stores. To start with you'll only need the smallest size they sell, an ounce or two of dry powder, plenty for maybe a hundred shirts. Dissolve the powder in clean empty squirt bottles and you are ready to go after you soak the designated clothes in Arm and Hammer Washing Soda (sodium carbonate, for a fixative). In our experience you'll want to maximize the concentration of the liquid colors to keep the end result brilliant.

-- KK

How to maximize color on clothes
Tie-Dye!

$11 Virginia Gleser, 1999, 95 p.

Hippies got one thing right: Tie dye clothes make people happy. As a group project, for family reunions, or summer camp, a massive tie dye happening is a real blast. The process of dying is simple enough for toddlers to do, yet potentially sophisticated enough that a real adult artist can be challenged. For general instructions and for examples of patterns to tie, I found this guide, though simple, to be useful to most dyers.

-- KK

Natural dyes
Wild Colors * The Art & Craft of Natural Dyeing

$18 Wild Color Jenny Dean, 2010, 144 p.
$20 The Art and Craft of Natural Dyeing J.N. Liles, 2006, 22 p.

In our experiments with using natural dyes, Wild Colors has been the best introductory resource. A remarkable variety of plants can be used to dye fibers and cloths, and this book covers most of them, all in great color photos. I found the preparation instructions clear, and the color possibilities outlined inspiring. The guide is helpful for experimenting and making small batches.

But achieving deep colors consistently requires a lot more attention and knowledge. The finest steadfast colors may require 10 steps or more to process the natural ingredients. You'll need J.N. Liles' heavily researched tome on traditional methods, The Art & Craft of Natural Dyeing. It's not well organized, but it is chock full of historical knowledge. An ease with chemistry will also help get the most from this exhaustive treatment of ancient dyeing skills.

-- KK

From Wild Colors:

Note: Bear in mind that it is not the amount of water used in the dye bath that affects the strength of the dye bath. The amount of water does not "dilute" the dye color: The strength of the dye bath is only affected by the amount of fibers added in relation to the amount of dye color present, as it is the color particles in the solution that have to be shared among the fibers being dyed.

- Iron modifiers improve the fastness of most dyes and tend to make colors darker and more somber in tone. This iron modification process is called "saddening." It can turn yellows into olive-green and, if used with dyes rich in tannin, it can make colors dark gray and almost black. Add it to the dye bath or pot of water and stir it well. Put in the wetted fibers and simmer them for about five minutes. Iron usually take effect very quickly. It can also be applied without heat to many plant dyes. Rinse and wash fibers.

- Washfastness

To test whether colored fabrics will stain or run, make two samples of each color. Sew one between two layers of undyed woolen fabric and another between two layers of undyed cotton fabric. Wash the samples, following the most likely procedure for the finishing item to see the degree of staining in the washing process.

- In Himalayan regions, species of rhubarb are particularly valued for their contribution to the dye pot. In parts of Tibet and Ladakh, and among Tibetan refugees in Nepal, rhubarb root is the most common source of yellow dye, and species of rhubarb have long been sought after locally. The roots are dried, chopped up, and ground into powder before use, and give strong, fast shades of yellow, gold, and orange.

- Madder is one of the most ancient dyes and its existence can be traced as far back as the Indus civilization of around 3,000 BCE. Madder was cultivated throughout Europe and the Middle East, and the finest quality dyestuff came from Turkey, Holland, and France.

Madder root can also be simmered gently to extract the dye color but once the fibers have been added, the temperature should be kept well below a simmer to achieve clear reds. Simmering or boiling the dye bath will turn red colors browner and duller.

The best color results are often achieved if the pieces of madder root are left in the dye pot during the dyeing process.

- Most of the colors produced from elder berries fade on exposure to light, but even the faded shades of pale lavender can be pleasing to the eye. Because of this characteristic, however, using fibers dyed with elder berries for tapestries or wall hanging is not recommended.

From The Art & Craft of Natural Dyeing:

About 1775, Dr. Edward Bancroft discovered a highly concentrated yellow dye in the inner bark of the American black oak tree (Quercus velutina). This was an extremely significant discovery since this dye, which he named "quercitron," was as fast or faster than weld, and it was much cheaper because the dye in weld is present in lower concentration. Thus, quercitron was to become the best natural yellow dye for the next century and was used commercially until about 1920.

- Again, according to Pellew, in about 1908 a German dye chemist, Dr. Friedlander, spent the summer in Naples and collected approximately 12,000 Murex snails for dye extraction. From this quantity of snails he was able to extract about three-fourths of a gram of pure dye. Upon analysis, the dye proved to be 6, 6" dibromoindigo. Part of Friedlander's interest was in determining whether Tyrian purple was identical to thioindigo red B, a synthetic indigo derivative that he had recently produced. The dye was not the same, and Tyrian purple was synthesized and used only for a short while.

- A good black may be obtained by over dyeing a deep indigo blue with strong walnut. In this case sumac leaves or berries or a little tannin, and a little copperas, are added to the walnut. This works well on cotton, wool, or silk.

ROOTS

BERRIES

The main thing is to keep the main thing the main thing. - Stephen Covey

Photochromic safety, sun specs
Mag-Safe Safety Glasses
$45 Amazon

These photochromic safety glasses have an ANSI Z87.1+ rating, which means they're shatter-proof even when struck by a 1/4-inch steel ball at 150 feet/second. The lenses are polycarbonate, so a significant scrape against sand, ground, etc. would probably scratch them. In the six months I've been using them, I've dropped them lightly a couple times and they're still pretty much like-new.

The benefits of these is not only their relatively-low cost and snug fit, but also their versatility. The lenses run almost perfectly clear to a nice, dark tint in the sun, with nearly 100 percent UVA/B protection. When they are dark they keep off glare when I'm driving. They also protect me from wind when I'm biking — day or night — and shield my eyes when I go to the machine shop to work on projects.

Over the summer, I worked in a machine shop lathing, sawing, drilling, tapping metal and wood twice a week for 3-4 hours and a couple weekends straight through until Burning Man. Unlike the cheap, standard shop glasses which I'd constantly put on and remove and occasionally forget to put back on, these are so comfortable I rarely take them off. It's important to note they do not seal all the way around your face the way some safety goggles do — i.e. the ones with flexible rubber sides that press up against the skin. On the one hand, that's why these are much more comfortable, but then again, that makes these potentially unsuitable for tasks where full coverage is recommended. For my usage, though, which is primarily partial-coverage tasks, they're great. Definitely one of the most functional things I own, and considering they're safety glasses, they look pretty good.

-- Eric Nguyen

Magnifying safety glasses
Pyramex Onix Plus Reader
$12 Enviro Safety Products

The outer lens of these safety glasses flips down for welding, and when you're done, you simply flip them up. Nothing special. However, I've been wearing the recommended Mag-Safe safety glasses for years (above), and the Onix Plus is the only flip-up pair I've found that also has a reader's bifocal lens. The inside lens is available in two magnifying strengths (+1.5, +2.5), and outer lens in two different IR shades (3.0, 5.0). Makes it much easier for me to see while welding. Preferable to spending an arm and a leg for prescription safety glasses. Quicker than switching between protective eyewear and reading specs.

-- Byron Hill

Best cheap eyeglasses
Zenni Optical
$7 Zenni Optical

For the past 5 years I had been using Zenni to purchase inexpensive prescription eyeglasses online. Zenni offers decent glasses for super cheap, is quick to deliver, has a better selection than other online services, and their website is much easier to use and order from. Reordering from the same prescription is a no-brainer, too.

Over the past 5 years I've ordered about 10 pairs of glasses from Zenni for different family members and myself, in all different strengths and styles, including sunglasses. The frame quality is okay (great for the price) and the optical quality is A+. My wife has extreme corrections, and I have a very odd combination of factors, while my daughter's prescription is mild. I've ordered single, bifocals and progressives – and the results have all been good. A simple correction and simple frame can cost as little as $10, but our typical glasses will cost about $35. Still a fantastic bargain. Even if you are style conscious, these are great for backup pairs.

One detail you have to pay attention when selecting a frame online is the width of the frame, which varies between models. Pay attention to the size indicator. I once ordered a pair too narrow. Delivery takes only about 2 weeks to my home in California.

-- KK

Break-away eyewear
CliC Readers
$35 Amazon

For anyone requiring reading glasses intermittently, these specs are heaven sent! The frame breaks in the front and clicks together once, resting on your nose by way of two magnets. When not in use, they stay out of the way — the glasses have a hard frame 'loop' that slips around your neck. As soon as you need them, you reach down and pull them up into place. I've tried lanyards — they get caught on your seat belt strap and tangled around your collar. I've tried my pocket — they fall out. Nothing seemed to work, so I ended up buying eight or ten pair of cheap glasses and leaving them all over: habitat, car, at work, etc. CliCs are a wonderful way to avoid all that clutter.

-- Dennis Brittain

Keychain pince-nez
Pocket Eyes Reading Glasses
$16 (with shipping) Pocket Eyes

I've stashed cheap reading glasses everywhere in my house. But inevitably, when traveling around the planet, I have struggles with menus and bank documents and so on. A convenient pair of portable readers is a blessing.

I started with one of those slim fresnel lenses, shaped like a credit card, in my wallet. They're fine for emergencies but useless for comfortable or extended reading. An ideal solution would be a small pince-nez. But the cheapo versions – with a plastic nose-

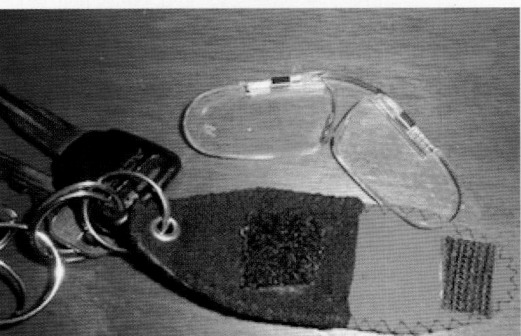

bridge – soon break, or they pinch and hurt.

What you want is for the bridge to be made of flexible metal, squeezing the two lenses against your nose with just the right pressure. They can slip off, if you're sweaty, and there are (ahem) some places you do not want to let them drop-off. But the good ones can squeeze together so the lenses overlap and they fit into a tiny pocket pouch. It's surprising how comfortable they can be, feeling so natural you forget they are there.

Alas, my first trio of pocket pince-nez all broke in the same place; where the metal bridge was riveted into the glass. I searched all over and finally found better ones from Pocketeyes. These have an improved, adjustable metal-to-glass attachment, a corrugated spot on each lens to help grip the nose, and a split pouch that lets you keep the lenses from rubbing against each other in your pocket. The keychain grommet is another plus.

They also have a fun factor. People do double-takes and even strike up conversations asking about them. They won't help with driving or distance. But if all you need is readers to help while traveling around, this may be your answer.

-- David Brin

Safety bifocals
Bifocal Safety Glasses
$12 Amazon

I happened upon these while on vacation in a hardware store (yes, I go to hardware stores while on vacation). These safety glasses provide great eye protection and the bifocal lens allows me to perform closeup tasks without resorting to pulling them off for my reading glasses. Essentially a perfect solution for those who work in a shop with 'older' active eyes.

-- Mark Ramirez

Stick-on magnifiers
Soft Reading Lenses
$28 Amazon

I've been using these soft reading lenses for at least 10 years — so long, I forgot how cool they are. I used to windsurf and would spend time at the beach repairing and maintaining gear while waiting for the afternoon thermal breeze to kick in, detail work that required reading glasses or Optx 20/20s on my sunglasses. I also used the same pair of sunglasses for driving, skiing and general daily wear. The glasses have to be wet slightly to get the 20/20s to stick, so it can be a little fiddly getting both lenses parallel and then squishing out the air bubbles without moving them around (also, if your frames don't have a rim at the bottom, it's more difficult to get them aligned properly). But once that's accomplished, voila! $300 bifo-cal sunglasses for just 20 bucks. Once they're stuck down on the glasses they don't move unless you mess with them when cleaning the glasses or if you get them wet. Peel them off with your fingernail if you change your mind. What could be simpler?

– Evan Marks

I've used this, to great effect. With my prescription sunglasses that I always use when outdoors, I had a problem that I couldn't read maps while driving or hiking. Sticking on just ONE of these bifocal semi-circles was a total solution. The water adhesion has held for two years, and cleaning the bifocal part has not been an issue.

– Stewart Brand

I've used these, but not in the intended fashion. I ride a motorcycle and wear a helmet (though my state doesn't require it). In my 40's I've started wearing corrective glasses, but during the day I also need some sort of eye protection from the sun. The solution was wear regular sunglasses and use these stick-on reading lenses. But I didn't care for them being on my sunglasses all the time, so I stuck them on the face shield of my helmet. This allows me to read the gauges on my motorcycle and the GPS. The field of view is quite small because the lenses are further out than intended, but it works better than not being able to read anything. I've since purchased prescription sunglasses and retired the stick-on lenses, but these work in a pinch and, IMHO, are on par with the $12 specials from the big box stores.

– Ken Jones

Headbands

Multi-use warmer for head

Buff

$19 Amazon

Buff is an all-in-one garment. I am picky and a minimalist when it comes to clothing, but the Buff, in addition to being a shape-shifter, also weighs almost nothing, so I thought I should try it. It's pretty neat, now part of my pack.

-- KK

Y'all probably have known about Buff forever, but in case not, this thing is way cool. Described as "the original multi-functional Seamless Wear", it is a stretchy microfiber tube that can be a neckerchief/neck-scarf, headband, wristband, foulard, bandit-mask, hand-warmer, balaclava and more. I mostly use it as a neck-scarf when biking, and on hikes when it turns cool. Because it is microfiber, it has great thermal and wicking properties — and it is a great glasses-cleaner.

-- Paul Saffo

A better Buff

Merino Wool Buff

$20+ Amazon

The Buff has been been a standard part of my clothing for many years. I live in Germany, usually commute by bicycle and love to hike. It keeps me warm, protects me from insects, is used as a sweatband, or, on hikes, even doubles as a towel. In winter, I also use the warmer Polar Buff. I usually wear the buff as a scarf; when cold, I fold it like a balaclava or wear it as a face cover in combination with a cap. It also can be worn under a protective helmet. And last year, I upgraded to an even better product: the Wool Buff made from merino wool.

The wool version is a bit longer, some 12 g (on my kitchen scale) heavier, and a bit bulkier than the standard Buff. It also feels softer and even more flexible than the microfiber version, easily allowing to fold it into several layers and adjust it to one's neck, face or the whole head. The fine merino wool doesn't itch like some wools. It also has a superior dampness control; wool absorbs a fair bit of moisture and still feels warm and dry, but still dries quickly. This is very apparent when the Buff is used as a face mask in cold weather. However, the Wool Buff does not keep as warm as the Polar Buff, which is a combination of microfiber and fleece fabric.

The biggest benefit for me is the odor resistance of wool. The plastic version becomes stinky after some time, but I have worn the merino Buff daily for many days without smelling the need to wash it. Care is easy, I can machine wash it with the delicates program, preferably with a natural wool detergent. Although very fine, the cloth has been resistant so far, except for a tiny hole caused by snagging it with a zipper – though this has not caused any running.

-- Martin Liebermann

Sweat-busting brow belt

Halo Headband

$5+ Amazon

Getting sweat in your eyes isn't fun. And in some sports, such as cycling, it can even be dangerous. Halo headbands provide a heavenly solution. They're made out of a thin, stretchy fabric with a linguine-sized, soft plastic strip affixed inside that acts as a kind of gutter. This strip (combined with the qualities of the fabric itself) keeps your brow dry. An unexpected side benefit: The headband serves as a gasket to keep your bike helmet snug and comfortable no matter how sweaty the conditions. I've been using them for a couple of years down here in Florida and wouldn't cycle without them.

After my ride, I just rinse the Halo and hang it to dry. Once in a while, it goes in the wash. I have a couple of Halos, so I'll always have one dry when I start out for a ride. Neither shows signs of wear after hundreds of rides and thousands of miles. I've grown so attached to my Halo that I accept the few seconds it takes to don it when racing in triathlons. I'll go without gloves and socks, but my Halo always comes along. Halos come in a tie version, which I prefer, but also in solid pullover bands and in a few other varieties.

-- Steve Leveen

$13 Tied Version

Halo Headband

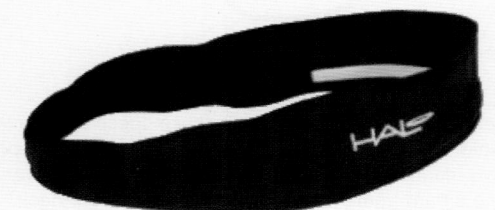

Effective sweat absorbing headband

Halo II Sweatband

$5 Amazon

I live in Ohio and I try to run consistently year round. I've run in sub-zero temperatures on many occasions with no problems. My sweet spot temperature for running is around 55 degrees and when it gets over 70 degrees, I start whining like a baby. My body just does not deal well with warmer temperatures and higher humidity, and I tend to sweat like a pig.

I've tried many products over the years to keep sweat from soaking my sunglasses and stinging my eyes. I have a few Headsweats and SweatVac products, but the king of headbands is definitely Halo. Their headbands are made out of a soft, stretchable fabric they call DRYLINE. It's a polyester/nylon combination that feels similar to a thin neoprene. They also use a thin rubbery strip (dubbed Sweat Block Technology) along the front, inside area of the headband so that excess sweat will be channelled to the sides of your face and not straight down into your eyes. I've got a pretty good-sized melon and I've had no problems at all with fit or comfort.

The amount of sweat that the Halo products absorb is incredible. Naturally, there is a point at which they will become completely saturated. Taking off the headband and giving it a squeeze may amaze and/or disgust you, but you'll definitely know that it's doing its job.

I've personally used the Halo II headband and the Sport Visor (which features a slightly smaller band sewn into the cap) and strongly recommend both.

-- Jason Long

Fleece, drawstring balaclava

Polar Hood

$25 Cartom

This fleece hood features an extra long neck and can be folded up within itself to form a variety of useful configurations, including a face guard, gator, scarf and mombo hat (see diagram). Unlike plain balaclava-style headgear, this has drawstrings which enable it to hug the face exactly as tight as you need in order keep the wind out. I've been using mine for five years to be comfortable outside for long periods of time in the coldest days of a typical Ottawa Winter (-35 Celsius or so). I tend to go for the full-face mode until I want to interact with someone more openly, and then just pull down the face covering (I've become quite conscious of just how much I use my face to communicate). Then if I'm inside for a few minutes I put it in neck-warmer mode.

On its own, the Polar Hood doesn't always provide enough protection from particularly harsh cold and wind, but the crucial service it provides in my winter ensemble is its unmatched facial protection. In the pic below, I'm also wearing my coat's faux-fur hood, along with a Nepalese-style winter hat underneath both hoods. The photo was taken near the beginning of a roughly hour-long walk home in what was apparently -24 Celsius weather, -33 with wind chill. I was happy as a clam the whole walk home.

-- James MacAulay

Hold on to your hard hat

Hat Grabber

$11 Hat Grabber

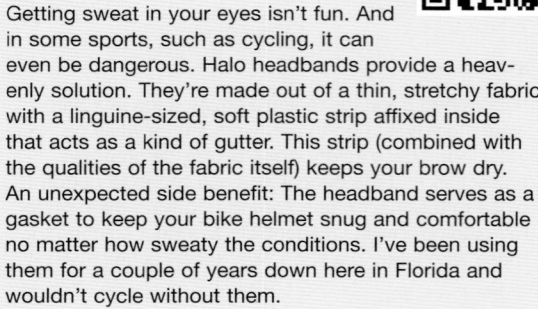

My husband always complained about his uncomfortable hardhat, and how it would fall off throughout the day. About three months ago I ran across the Hat Grabber on another website and thought I would give it a try.

The Hat Grabber is a piece of textured rubber that clips onto the back of the hard hat strap where it provides greater fiction and a larger surface area to resist the leverage that occurs when the wearer leans over, thereby reducing the likelihood that the hat will fall off. It also means you don't have to crank down the tightness of the straps.

He came home after the first day of trying it out and said, "I don't know what you paid for it, but it was well worth it." Now some of his coworkers are wearing them. This is without a doubt a cool tool, and is a must for all the husbands/wives who are in construction.

-- Kerrie Graham

All models are wrong, but some are useful. - George E. P. Box

Most all-around practical
Tilley Hat

$68+ Amazon

Often copied, never quite equaled, the Tilley Hat is the most all-purpose chapeau I know. Its broad brim keeps the sun or light rain off, the bit of foam in the flat crown pads the skull against light whacks and keeps the hat floating in water, and the double strap defeats all wind. (Use just the rear strap behind your head to hold the hat in all but strong winds; the front strap under the chin is effective but dorky looking.) The Canadian behind the Tilley line has generated a humorous but effective fetishism around his durable hats. With one or both side brims snapped up to the crown you get a rakish look which also stiffens the front brim against wind. The Tilley packs well and does last for many years; however, a lot of hot weather use will stain it incurably with sweat. You may not mind.

-- Stewart Brand

Soft helmet
Ribcap Knit Helmet

$128+ Ribcap

My second time snowboarding I got a concussion and lost memory of the day. Since then, I wear a helmet as much as possible when boarding. However helmets are hot and bulky, and if I am traveling, or if it's a nice soft powder day, I have always wanted something that offers protection without the hard shell. D3o Labs has come up with a new foam that is soft in general use, but gets rigid when impacted. This material was used in Olympic slalom ski suits to take the sting out of the oncoming gates and to offer crash protection. A Swiss company, Ribcap, has licensed this material for a set of very nicely made knit caps. These hats have this smart foam sewn in to make them effectively a soft helmet. This is by no means a substitute for a rated hard shell helmet, but I like having the option, especially when traveling where a helmet is bulky. The hat I just got from a retailer in Canada (so far the only place I have found them) is really nicely made, and has a built in balaclava.

-- Alexander Rose

Enduring head warmers
Tilley Winter Hats

$68+ Amazon

I'm bald, and my father was a hat hobbyist, so I come by my hat interest biologically. Furthermore, I grew up in the northern midwest — I know about cold ears.

These two wool-plus hats from Tilley are the best winter head-gear I know for wear-around use.

The "Winter Hat" is a tweed marvel, with short sloping brim all around, fold-down ear flaps, and a fold-down forehead warmer (a great comfort against a chill headwind, but invisible to others, being hidden behind the brim). The ear flaps are slightly cupped around the ear for further wind protection. The wool is teflon-treated, so rain and snow pretty much bounce off. The hat can be folded into a jacket pocket, yet retains its shape perfectly. In two varieties of tweed, plus black, it's a surprisingly handsome hat—"friendly," Brian Eno called it. People call out: "Nice hat!"

The "Winter Cap" looks like your basic New England wool deer hunter's cap, with big baseball-cap brim and ear flaps. But it has the Tilley augmentations—forehead flap, teflon treatment, excellent construction. I love it under a hood in cold precipitation—keeps my glasses dry and clear. Black or red; get the red.

-- Stewart Brand

Durable shade hat
Tilley Airflow Hat

$82 Tilley

The new Tilley Hat is beautifully made of nylon microfiber. It is much lighter (3 oz. total weight) than the original canvas hat and is extremely comfortable to wear, even on the hottest days. The crown is well ventilated and the brim holds its shape well. There is an effective chin strap. It is not suitable for heavy rain wear due to the crown ventilation; use the OR Seattle Sombrero for that. The new hat is guaranteed "forever", even against loss.

-- Carl Bradford

Crushable wide-brimmed hat
The Crusher Hat

$15 Duluth Trading Co.

Crushable hat will return to original shape

Being a man with pale complexion I had received yet another severe sunburn and was on the market for wide-brimmed hats when I discovered the Crusher. It is aptly named. I have squeezed it into a ball and put it into the pocket of my jacket. I have thrusted it in my carry-on luggage. Nevertheless, it still bounces back into shape when I take it out of its cramped storage; the brim remains easily reshaped in the front and back sides to provide the best cover.

This is by far the best head cover I've had in warm climates, and it is made only better seeing as it is affordable.

Finally, a few thoughts: Replace the little piece of leather that Duluth use as a drawcord stopper, it is useless. Create a plastic rain cover for the hat to make it perfect! I have only found those for western style hats, with brims exceeding 4 inches. It's effective but not necessarily comfortable.

-- Per-Erik Ekberg

Lightweight head-and-neck protection
Adventure Hat

$31 Amazon

I spend much of my time outside. Especially backpacking. And this hat always goes with me. It looks a little different, but I've come to like that. Its function is unequaled. Light weight at 2.5 oz and crushable into the pack when not in use. It blocks sun all around with a 4" front brim and a long back tail that can be velcroed up if not needed. It breathes well through side mesh panels and will even scoop water out of a stream to douse your head on a hot day.

-- Carol Corbridge

Helmet rain visor
NRS Visor

$13 NRS

One of the biggest challenges posed by living in Seattle and bike commuting year round has been keeping my glasses clear of rain while riding. I have a small visor that came with my helmet, but it isn't long enough. This visor, which can be attached/detached via velcro, is the best resolution I've come across so far. While my glasses still get wet when it is very windy out (or very misty), the visor drastically increases visibility on most rainy days, keeping my glasses dry.

Although it is designed for kayak helmets (primarily to keep out the sun I assume), it has served me well on my bike helmet and the velcro attachment means I can easily take it off and store it in my pannier on sunny days. Best of all it is cheap at $10 and made by NRS, a company with a strong reputation for quality gear.

-- A. Glosser

Gloves

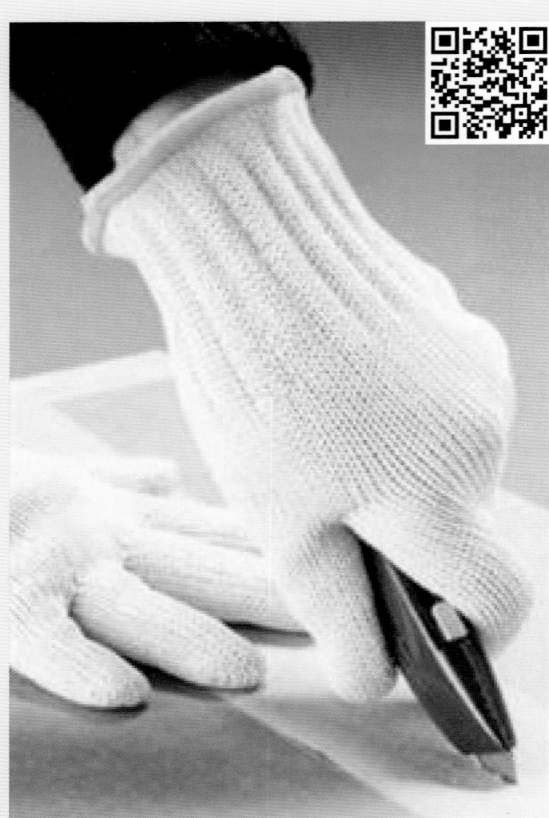

Affordable, cut-resistant hand protection
Whizard Handguard

$20 (per glove) magidglove.com wellslamontindustry.com

These Spectra/Kevlar gloves are used in the restaurant industry to defend against knife and mandolin cuts, as well as handling trash that may have protruding bits of glass and fish bones. I read about them in a cooking magazine, and bought one glove after cutting myself on a mandolin.

I find the glove allows for ample movement and dexterity. It's definitely flexible enough to carve with and feels a lot like wearing a winter Thinsulate glove. These days, when I use the mandolin, I find I can get in closer for a few extra slices. Although the glove hits the blade, my hand's always safe. My gloved hand has even survived an errant cleaver (fortunately I didn't hit myself too hard).

I've used mine about five times a month for the past three years. I've washed it and haven't noticed any deterioration, though it does feel a little stiffer at first. Bonus: The weave is much tighter than with a pricier chain mail glove, so it also seems better for guarding against knife pokes.

-- Steve Golden

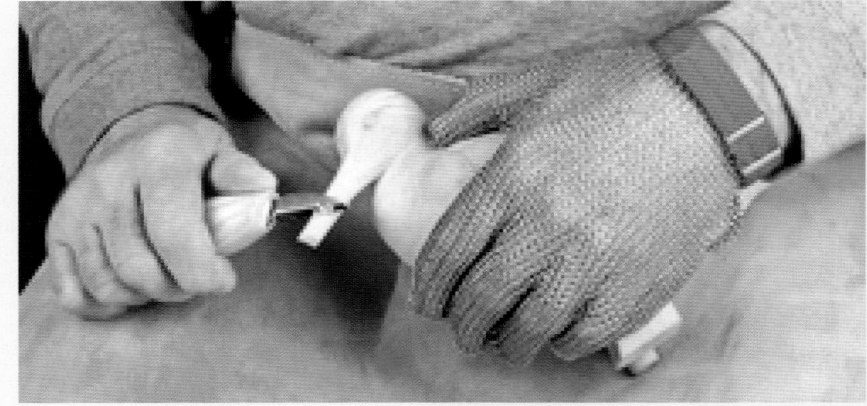

Medieval-style hand protection
Chain Mail Glove

$80 (sizes S - XXL) leevalley.com

If you enjoy carving wood or just working with sharp tools, this glove can save you countless boxes of band-aids as well as a nice chunk of change - and gas money -- from all the trips to the local emergency room for stitches. The chain mail (just like the type medieval knights and shark divers use) is a great safety tool that not only keeps you from slicing your hand open, but also makes you feel pretty tough while wearing it. Much more comfortable and easier to work with than any heavily-padded safety glove. These are similar to the butcher's gloves and also those advertised for shucking oysters, but they're half the price.

-- Josh G.

Tough kevlar work gloves
Tuffcoat Work Gloves

$7 Sperian KV300 TuffCoat Cut Resistant Gloves sperian.com

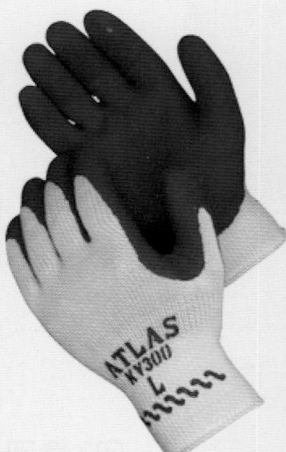

I was left about a dozen pairs of these rubber dipped kevlar gloves by the former owner of my house. Good thing, too! I've removed 4 crabapple trees, buried electrical cable, dug up hundreds of ferns, trimmed pine trees and done yardwork for the whole neighborhood. And these gloves look exactly like they did on day one.

That's not to say they're pretty, because they're surely not, but they can stand up to all kinds of abuse and not seem any worse for the wear. The rubber is flexible enough to grip small objects like nails and screws yet plenty sturdy for sharp thorns and other pokey things. The yellow kevlar mesh on the top makes the gloves feel light and breathable. The gloves pull on and off very easily and they hug the wrists so not much dirt gets inside of them.

The colors may not be pretty but they help make them more visible when you're looking for a pair in your crowded garage or basement. I gave away a few pairs before I realized how valuable they are. Now I just tell other people about them!

-- Matt O'Hara

Note: To those with latex allergies, Sperian makes a nitrile version of this glove.

Fleece-lined neoprene gloves
Glacier Gloves

$45 Glacier Outdoor

The quest for warm hands in a cold demanding environment is a long and frustrating one. The general rule is it takes carrying three pairs of gloves to have one dry pair on your hands. I have not found that to be true with Glacier Gloves, which is hands down the best glove I have ever used. The 824BK is 2mm neoprene lined with a thin fleece nap on the inside; the two layers feel fused together somehow (not sewn or glued), which gives them a comfortable fit, allows easy on and off, and provides excellent dexterity.

I have bought several different waterproof gloves from various makers, including the SealSkinz, other neoprene rubber gloves and a pair of thinsulate-filled gloves with a "waterproof" exterior. Some are OK and allow for moderate dexterity, but I find my hands get cold after working in the water and I then have to switch out to a different glove — and if you have to put some of them on with wet hands, forget it.

With the Glacier Glove, the Velcro strap secures them to your wrist, minimizes heat loss through the cuff, and minimizes water entry through the cuff. I find the cuff, when tucked inside the sleeve of your coat, also prevents rain water from running down your jacket and into the glove from the topside.

My hunting partner bought a pair years ago and was quick to brag about how warm and dry his hands were whenever we complained about how cold and wet ours were. I now wear mine while duck hunting and will generally keep my left glove on all day long, and swap between a thin shooter's glove and my Glacier on the right (that's just my preference; other hunters use them on both hands with no complaints). While I've only used these gloves while hunting, I would recommend them for any cold and wet environment.

-- Max Tullos

Warm hands during wet winters
Youngstown Waterproof Winter Plus Work Gloves

$28 Amazon

I received these gloves about six years ago from my wife, in one of those rare intersections of need and availability. It was Christmastime and I needed to shovel, so I broke these out and went to work. I never gave them a second thought, until I realized I had done a fair amount of ice chopping, opening the garage, and manipulating other things without ever removing the gloves. This is somewhat of a rarity for me since I usually cannot work in gloves. Fast-forward to spring, and I used them to protect my hands when chopping and stacking wood; working on the car; working in the garage. I *far extended* the prescribed use of these, despite the fact that they were winter gloves and waterproof. In a pinch, I've even used them when moving flaming logs in an outdoor fire pit.

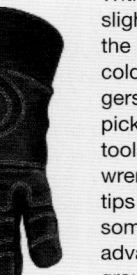

A short word about the waterproofing: I tend to agree with other owners in that these aren't strictly waterproof. If I was a long-line fisherman I may not use them. However, as a north Jersey resident who works on his cars, shovels snow, and builds snowmen for the kids, I can attest to their warmth and utility in the cold and wet.

With respect to function, they fit my slightly larger hand size well, and the back strap does seal in against cold and snow. The palms and fingers are textured and I am able to pick up bolts, thread nuts, small tools and sockets, and work with wrenches rather easily. The fingertips are boxed, not tapered, but in some ways the fingertips work to my advantage in picking up things on the ground.

When they get *really* dirty, you can toss them in the wash. The construction is such that the inner glove liner is not sewn to the shell, but it is a huge pain in the posterior to re-fit the glove components back to original fit. I used a wooden spoon and patience to eventually restore it to normal comfort.

-- Christopher Wanko

Tethered gloves
Glove Guards

$5 Amazon

The problem is keeping my work gloves with me at all times. I've tried putting grommets in the gloves and clipping them with a carabiner, but this isn't as easy as it sounds and is a pain to do all over again when a glove gets lost or worn out.

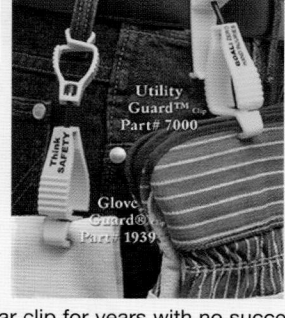

Years ago I saw someone out there with a large battery-terminal clip holding his gloves, and I've been searching for a similar clip for years with no success. This year, though, I found these Glove Guards.

The clips have a "breakaway" feature, so that you won't be trapped if your gloves get caught in machinery or something. This caused me some worry when my gloves got caught in the truck door and seemed to break away too easily but the two pieces of the clip reconnected with ease, and have continued to hold firm ever since.

At less than $5 apiece, I can wholeheartedly recommend getting several if keeping your gloves handy is important to you.

-- Bill Emmack

Wool running gear
Icebreaker GT Wool Running Gear
$49 Amazon

Synthetic exercise clothes have a tendency to get funky after a day or two. They require that you either wash them frequently, or own several pairs. Fed up with the smell and the burden of having to frequently wash my exercise gear several times a week I decided to pick up merino wool running shorts and running vest. After nearly 6-months of use, I doubt I'll ever go back.

I now wear my running clothes for up to a week before I detect any funk, and when it does smell it tends to be a "wet sheep" aroma; a far cry better than the locker room reek I had been accustomed to.

Additionally, wool has antimicrobial properties which can reduce the rate of rashes.

In use, the merino wool isn't itchy, and performs admirably even when drenched in sweat. This is due to wool's ability to absorb significant amounts of moisture before it feels wet which also has the benefit of reducing friction in sensitive areas (for me, it reduces nipple chafing).

At first I was worried that the wool would be too hot for summer running, but I quickly found that it was more comfortable than my synthetic gear due to its breathability, wicking, and absorbant properties. Synthetics are breathable, but I have found that the minute I put them on in hot weather I feel damp (synthetic fibers don't absorb water, but rather wick it away to its surface leaving the fabric feeling wet). Wool, on the other hand, not only wicks but also absorbs, while drying just as fast.

The downside to wool's absorbance is that it has a tendency of feeling heavier during long runs. My second concern was that wool would wear out faster, but after 6-months of near daily use that hasn't been the case. There isn't even the slightest indication of pilling even in places of high wear (between the legs).

Unfortunately, Icebreaker running gear is more expensive than many of the synthetic alternatives, but it's a justified expense given that it feels and performs better. Finally, because a single set of wool running gear can replace several pairs of equivalent synthetics while also cutting down on the number of loads of laundry, you can cut costs elsewhere.

Bicyclists were the first to recognize wool's superiority as an exercise fabric given their historic use of wool biking jerseys. Now that companies like Icebreaker are incorporating soft but durable merino wool into a much wider range of products it's only time before most of my wardrobe is woolen.

-- Oliver Hulland

Quick-refreshing underwear for travel
Exofficio Underpants
$7+ men's Amazon

Travel underwear. These very lightweight, super quick-drying, comfortable briefs are made of a blended material with a new finish that is unusually resistant to the growth of bacteria. You wash them in cold water in your hotel room at night and they are dry before morning. In a pinch, they can be dry in a couple hours if you roll them in a towel and squeeze the water out before you hang them up. I reused one pair of underwear three times on a recent trip.

-- Howard Rheingold

$5+ women's Amazon

Tough, lightweight underwear
Patagonia Silkweight Boxers
$30 REI

Underwear is not a sexy topic. Well, men's underwear isn't. Truthfully most men pay little attention to them other than checking that they're clean. But that's only because many of us think all underwear is equal.

Patagonia's Capilene silkweight boxers are light and well fitting. They keep you dry in the heat and they make a great base under the woolen long johns when it's cold. I live in the Canadian Rockies where temperatures and conditions can swing wildly at any time of the year and these boxers are always the right ones to have on.

I've purchased about ten pair over the last ten years and only one pair has worn out. I've travelled in Africa, Sri Lanka, Indonesia, etc. for a month or two at a time, with just three pairs. Wash them in the sink, hang them up and they're dry in an hour. They're stylish and feel like silk, but are tough as nails. They're built to protect modesty and in a pinch I've worn them into the river and the hot tub.

-- Kevin McIsaac

Stretchy thermal wear
Maxit Workout Clothing
$27 Full Length Motion Tights Amazon
$74 QBZ Long Sleeve Zippered Stretching

Maxit is an amazing material for workouts (and staying warm and dry in general). Maxit is what NFL players wear under their uniforms in winter games. It's a stretchy 92% polyolefin, 8% lycra material that looks like tights you can get in running and biking stores, but it's a different product and not easy to find. My friend Bob Anderson (of Stretching fame) lives in the Rockies near Colorado Springs and goes on 5-7 hour bike rides and all he generally wears is Maxit. I wear one layer when the temp is as low as the '40s. It's a bit cold starting out but as soon as your blood is moving, you're warm (and dry). I think it's better than any of the Patagonia, North Face etc. type hi-tech clothing. I have hats, zip-up shirts, gloves, and tights. My favorite is what's called the QBZ, long-sleeved with neck zipper.

-- Lloyd Kahn

ProMax Fiber

92% polyolefin, 8% lycra

Layering with natural fibers
Icebreaker Merino Wool Jersey
$80+ Icebreaker

This is probably the single most wonderful item of clothing I've ever owned. It's 100% Merino wool. Soft, useful, light, washable, warm, stylish. I've been wearing this whenever it's cold, over a cotton or silk t-shirt. Or if colder, over a lighter weight Merino wool shirt.

I used to wear mostly natural fibers. Then along came Patagonia and other outdoor outfitters with some great artificial (usually polyester)

products: fleece, Synchilla, Capilene, warm lightweight coats, polyester shirts for travel that could be rolled up in a backpack, and look wrinkle-free when worn.

Now I'm back to layering with natural fibers. 100% wool in various combos works wonders. Icebreaker has an elegant line of products (in spite of the very weird cover photo on their home page). They have testimonials from athletes who wear Merino wool clothing in various combos (there are 3 weights): climbing Everest, on kayak trips, wet or dry, hot or cold. How great, natural

fibers outperforming artificial! Also check out Smartwool clothing, another line of beautiful Merino wool products. Go to Backcountry and do a search for "smartwool."

-- Lloyd Kahn

WINTER COAT   SUMMER COAT

Everyday Pants

Durable cargo pants
Tactical 5.11 Pants
$38+ Amazon

Similar to the 5.11 cop shirt, the 5.11 pants are the best tactical (read cargo) pants I own. When you have cool tools you need some way to carry them! Used by the FBI and many other law enforcement agencies, I find that these pants wear well and look great.

-- Charles Kinnear

Slacks w/ cell phone pocket
DutyPro Uniform Trousers
$25 Galls

Until someone sees fit to design a proper pair of dress pants that can accommodate a mobile phone, I found an acceptable solution in the pages of Galls, my favorite law-enforcement catalog. Beat cops wear dress-style slacks as a basic part of their uniforms, and some of those slacks come with a "sap pocket" — a small pocket built into the rear of the leg that's used to hold billy clubs, blackjacks, or flashlights. For civilians, however, a sap pocket is also great for holding cellphones.

Every day I carry a wallet, a chunky set of keys, and a mobile phone. I also spend a lot of time sitting at a desk, so I keep my rear pockets empty to avoid discomfort. That leaves me with two pockets in the front, and three things to carry. The alternatives (belt clips and carpenter's pants) just don't cut it for me. Personally, I think belt clips are conspicuous and a little bit tacky. Carpenter's pants have a slim pocket on the side that's ideal for carrying a phone. Trouble is, it's inappropriate to dress like a contractor when working in a professional office environment.

Galls DutyPro trousers pants aren't as nice as the dress clothes you'll find at Barney's or Saks. On the other hand, they're uniform tough, they're permanent-press for easy care, and they're cheap — less than $25 per pair with free hemming included. The rear leg pocket is perfectly sized for an iPhone, and my mobile slides in without creating a bulge or altering the basic fit. Alternatively, if I ever need to carry a billy club into a business meeting, well, I expect these pants will be good for that too.

-- Todd Lappin

Custom light-weight belt
Tech Web Belt
$29 Patagonia

Better than the smoke jumper cinch belt (I've tried it) is Patagonia's Tech Web Belt. It's lighter and handsomer, comes in colors, and you don't have the noise and debris-collection of Velcro. I've worn mine for six months at all occasions from dressy to sweaty. Trim your new belt to the exact convenient size you want, flame-melt the cut end so it doesn't fray, and you've got the perfect custom belt.

-- Stewart Brand

Convertible activewear
Macabi Skirt
$77 Macabi Skirt LLC

I used to hike wearing trail pants that converted to shorts by unzipping the bottoms. This conversion involved stopping, removing my boots, then unzipping the bottom portion of the pants above the knees, putting the boots back on and stashing the unzipped pant legs in my backpack. I thought, There's got to be a better way.

Then, visiting the website of Sisters on the Fly, I discovered Macabi Skirts. These skirts are a design marvel. It's easy to convert them from a skirt to pants to shorts of various lengths. A pant clip hangs at the end of an adjustable thin strap, which runs down from the waist in the middle of the skirt. It clips quickly to a hook on the inside back of the skirt. Using the strap, it's possible to adjust the length in just seconds! Converting to shorts is just one more step. On the inside of each side of the skirt are snap straps that attach at the bottom of the pockets. Again, it takes seconds to adjust. Unlike the zippered convertible pants I used to wear, there's nothing to store when switching modes in this skirt.

The supplex fabric is lightweight and soft. It resists wrinkles and dries quickly. There's a comfortable elastic waistband with a drawstring, and belt loops. One of my favorite features is the oversize cargo pockets on each side of the skirt. It's possible to stuff them without looking bulky. On the right side there is deep pocket that includes a zippered security pocket that easily fits a passport, thin wallet, and keys. The large left side pocket has an inner pocket that's just right for a phone, iPod or slim camera.

Two of these skirts are the foundation of my travel wardrobe. In the summer the cool fabric and loose fit combine for outstanding comfort. I wear the skirts so often that I bought long underwear bottoms, so that I can continue to wear them during the Colorado winter!

-- Nancy Mulvany

Simple, functional, travel pants
Patagonia Rock Craft Pants
$79 Men's Rock Craft Pants Patagonia
$79 Women's Rock Guide Pants Patagonia

On my recent trip to Bangladesh I wore a single pair of Patagonia Rock Craft Pants for nearly four weeks while in country. Every few days I would wash them in a sink in the evening, hang them up to dry, and in a few hours they would be as dry as anything gets in Bangladesh. After a month of hard traveling and three months of subsequent wear at home I feel confident saying that they are the best travel pants I have ever worn.

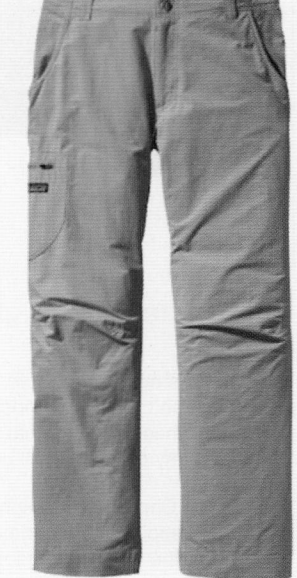

One of the reasons why they work so well is their simplicity. They are not overwhelmed with pockets.

The pants are made out of a lightweight nylon and spandex blend that provides the perfect amount of stretchiness and flexibility. My pair weighs around 11-oz, and unlike every other pair of pants I own they don't take up much space when packed. Despite being light, they also resist scrapes and scratches.

Other nylon pants I've worn used thicker fabric and bulkier designs which contributed to them feeling hot, heavy, and burdensome in the pack. This includes pants I've tried from REI, North Face, EMS, and Columbia. All had some critical flaw. The Rock Guides remain the best pair of pants I've owned. As far as sizing goes, they run a tad large due to their stretchiness. Finally, the most significant criticism I've seen about them is due to the lack of different pant lengths. However, it seems Patagonia has incorporated extra fabric in the pant cuff for those who don't mind re-hemming their pants on their own.

-- Oliver Hulland

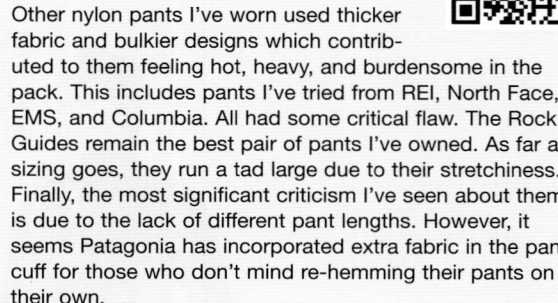

Concealed cargos
Scottevest Hidden Cargo Pants
$70 Scottevest

I often carry far too much stuff in my pockets, and these pants allow me to do so without showing it. They're durable, and I have not been able to find any other pants that do what these do. I wear these and Scottevest's Ultimate cargo pants almost exclusively, because after wearing each type a few times, standard pants with standard pockets feel awkward.

The Hidden Cargo Pants are more formal than the Ultimate Cargos, or 5.11 Tactical Pants (see above). The Hidden Cargos feel more like dress pants. The main difference between the Ultimate and Hidden is that the Ultimate has a rougher fabric, cargo pockets, and zip-off lower legs. The main pocket suspension is the same.

Access to pockets is excellent in the Hidden Cargos. The main pockets on each side of the front consist of three pockets in one. There's a magnetic clasp to access the outer pockets, which are very large (they come down almost to the knee) and are divided into front and back sections.

As long as you're wearing a good belt it doesn't really get too heavy. The design of the pockets means it is far less cumbersome than standard pants, but it can, of course, get cumbersome if you really stuff them full– which would be a feat. Without a good belt, however, the pants can get a bit heavy and slide down if they are loaded with stuff.

-- TJ Wasik

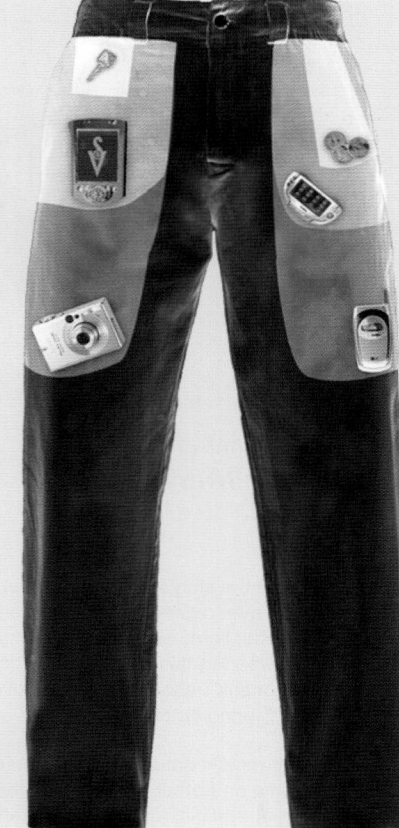

The explorer is the person who is lost. - Tim Cahill

$65 Duluth Firehose Work Pants Duluth Trading Company

$17 Duluth Side Clip Suspenders Duluth Trading Company

Farm-proof work wear
Duluth Firehose Work Pants and Suspenders

Duluth's Firehose Canvas Work Pants are made of strong stuff. I have been using them on my farm for 12-months and have found that they are comfortable and durable. They have a generous cut so I have room to move when I am crawling around the tractor. They have wide and numerous belt-loops, velcro-flapped cargo pockets and hip pockets, and a handy loop for a tape measure, as well as a long pocket for a wrench or screwdriver on the thigh on each side (so they suit lefties and righties equally).

I hang them from Duluth's wide side-clip suspenders so I can load up the pockets without losing the lot around my ankles. These suspenders have two inch wide straps and just two clips; the front and back straps meet at your waist (or where it once was) at the side under your arms. Normal front-and-back suspenders like to catch on stuff when I am crawling around, and often let go. The side-clips have never come unfastened. Great clothes.

-- Russel Day

Multi-function pants
Skillers Super Canvas Work Pants

$38 RepconNW

I've spent about two years in these work pants and believe they offer the most utility for anybody needing to carry a lot of equipment while staying comfortable on the job. They are the perfect pants for anybody in construction. My current pants are six months into their life and are going strong. I'll need to get new ones for aesthetic reasons long before they even start to wear out.

There are pockets on the knees to insert knee-pads into that don't scratch, cut off bloodflow or bind leg motion in any way. I really don't

even think about having kneepads as they're just always there. The pads are sold separately for about $10.00.

The most useful pockets (for construction) are the nail bag pockets. They're located right over your normal hip pockets, and can be tucked in when not in use so they look just like normal pants. You can put nails, screws, tape measure, chalk line, etc. in these pockets and not get poked or feel bulky in any way. The other pockets I use the most are the three pencil pockets (mine are located on the left leg which is perfect for me because I'm left handed). I keep at least two carpenter's pencils at all times (I hate looking for a pencil, or not having a backup when I'm on a ladder and drop the one in my hand). A nail punch goes in one pencil pocket, and in front of the pencil pockets is a buttoned pocket about two inches wide and four inches deep where I keep my Leatherman multi-tool unfolded (in plier mode) and securely buttoned in. Above these pockets is a wide button closed pocket that is about five or six inches deep. I keep a bandana in there, and it'll hold much more if I need it to. The right leg has three long slender pockets that will hold a torpedo level, a pocket T-square, and other similar sized and shaped tools. I keep a speed square in my right back pocket, and a hammer holster and utility knife pouch are attached to my belt.

You may put things in different places, but these will hold pretty much everything a large, bulky, heavy toolbag will hold. These pants keep the weight spread out too, so the perception of the weight is reduced. You can even buy accessories designed to work specifically with the pants if you need extra pockets for anything.

Oh, and you probably want to know how much all this costs. These retail for a whopping $60!!! Probably less than you pay for your Carhartts.

-- Nathan Sharp

Hefty, comfy suspenders for working
Duluth Trading Suspenders

$20 Trading Button Suspenders Duluth

I'm a big fan of the work clothes from Duluth Trading Company. My latest score is a set of $16 suspenders that I can highly recommend. They are uncommonly comfortable, because the straps are two inches wide. They attach to your pants with buttons, not clamps. I hate clamps: they loosen, they break, and they're ugly. The harnesses that hold the straps onto the buttons of your pants are nicely made of leather that is a good balance between handsome and sturdy. My galluses are an attractive red. (They also come in navy.) These braces are best used with a $4 set of brass buttons to attach to your pants. And best of all — best of all — these buttons are actually rivet-like affairs. You don't sew them on. You put them on your pants by taking a little nail that comes as part of the kit, pushing it through the waistband of your pants from the back, then sticking that nail into the brass button that you wear on the front, and whamming it home with a hammer. I can't tell you how entertaining I find it to tailor my clothes with a 16-ounce hammer. I wish all my clothes were this satisfying.

These suspenders are best used, I think, with the Skillers Work Pants with the removable knee pads and the nail pouches that fit inside your front pockets when empty.

-- Joel Garreau

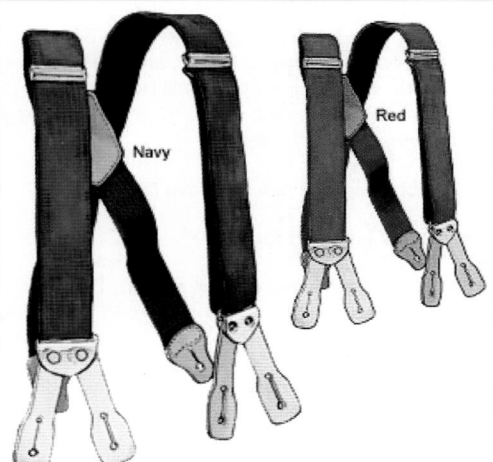
Navy / Red

Duluth

Adventure clothing
Rail Riders

I often split my days between working in the shop, riding a bike, and working in the office. In addition, I do a lot of adventure sports in the evenings, weekends and vacations. I have long been looking for clothes that can stand up to the rigors of hiking, biking, canyoneering, traveling, and still work for the office. I have finally found it in Rail Riders, a small clothing manufacturer that came out of the sailing world. Unlike a lot of the heavy cotton tactical clothes like the 5.11 shirts and pants, Rail Riders' synthetic fabrics are all chosen for their light weight, ruggedness, and water shedding capabilities. The added bonus is they offer several styles that can also work in an office setting, without making you look like you're an off-duty SWAT team member.

Prices reflect the high quality and short-run nature of the garments, but I have yet to be disappointed with anything they sell. Their clothes are used by adventure racing teams, Himalayan expeditions, and world sailors. On a recent all-day canyon trip, everyone but me came back with the seats of their pants shredded. While this stuff is extremely rugged, it's not overweight. Many of Rail Riders' fabrics also have a water repellent treatment that has saved me from some embarrassing accidents while eating or drinking in the car or at my desk.

$59 Men's Yukon Work Pants Rail Riders

These are made of a synthetic fabric that drapes like canvas work pants but feel way better and have great extra stealth pockets for cell phones etc. The lined ones are a fave in the cold weather.

$59 Oasis Shirt Rail Riders

Excellent hot weather button down, that has mesh in the underarms and down the side to keep you exceptionally cool.

$69 Men's Backcountry Khakis Rail Riders

These work in the office and on the mountain (I wore these for a week in Nevada back country). A little stretch makes them extra comfy, and they are treated to repel water.

-- Alexander Rose

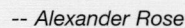

BlueFlower / Honeydew / Pale Yellow / SandFlower

Cop shirts
5.11 Tactical Shirts
$48+ Amazon

I have five now and plan to get more. The 5.11 does everything I want in terms of comfort and pockets and yet looks dignified enough to serve as duty shirts for police, who are its primary market.

The 5.11 Tactical shirt is based on Royal Robbins' excellent Expedition Shirt; the main difference is that it's 100% cotton. The most appealing functional features for me are: 1) large document pockets hidden on each side of the shirt front (my cell phone lives in one, my notepad in the other); 2) a subtle vent on the back, with non-cotton wicking lining for the back and shoulders (which makes it a four-season shirt, good with or without a T-shirt underneath); and 3) the best keepers for rolled shirtsleeves (also a help for four-season use or variable weather).

Appearance features: 1) nifty upper-sleeve pen pocket, an improvement on noising up your chest with metal in a breast pocket; 2) shirt buttons that are colored to blend in with the fabric color, so you're not a row of dots; 3) velcro pocket closures, less conspicuous and handier than buttons; 4) sensible colors. There are optional features of interest to cops but not to me—hidden button-down for collar, sew-on epaulets, sew-on badge holder.

The shirt is available for women as well as men. Also comes in a short-sleeve version. Colors are white, sage, khaki, olive green, charcoal, navy blue, and black; I most like the green and black. (There is a variation of the 5.11 shirt called "A/B" which I suggest avoiding. It's too coppy—sewn-in pleats, epaulets, and badge-holder, and an unpleasant synthetic material emphasizing rayon. Get the cotton.)

-- Stewart Brand

The 5.11 tactical shirt is simply the best field/hiking shirt I have owned. If you are the kind of person who juggles maps and notebooks while outdoors, this is the only shirt to wear. At first glance, it looks like a typical hiking shirt, but the difference is in the details.

For example, the "Napolean" pockets (large horizontal velcro-closed slash pockets behind the visible breast pockets) are huge –7-inches by 8-inches. Large enough to comfortably hold a folded topo map and notepad in the field or a wallet and a PDA in town. The pockets were originally designed to hold pistols for cops, so one can comfortably carry heavy objects in them. Other details include pen slots on the left pocket and the upper left sleeve. The right pocket has a hidden zipper to securely store small items, and the sleeves have the first practical roll-up keepers I have found.

This is a truly versatile shirt, that fits in anywhere from the Sierra to casual business meetings. I was grateful to have all those pockets recently while standing on a wilderness ridge in a driving rain at midnight, juggling a radio and map and scribbling on a rite-in-the-rain pad. But I also wear my navy blue version of the shirt (I own five) as my standard casual business dress. It goes nicely with khaki dockers and lets me carry my wallet and other junk without resorting to the usual pants-pocket bulge.

-- Paul Saffo

Utilitarian daily-wear vest
Filson Mackinaw Wool Vest
$120 Amazon

My Filson Mackinaw Vest is the single most utilitarian piece of clothing I own. And during the fall, winter, and early spring I wear it nearly every day. We've reviewed Filson in the past. They have a legendary reputation among hunters and outdoorsman for wool clothing that stays warm when wet, and holds up over time. This holds true for this vest, but I love it because it's just as functional at home or in an office as it is in the field.

It also features two chest pockets; the right easily fits a notepad, while the left is designed for holding writing instruments, or other tools (I keep a Maratac AAA flashlight, and a few pens and pencils).

Most vests are NOT built for daily wear. Stitching comes undone, fabric begins to tear or pill, and in general they become limp and lifeless after just a few months. The beauty of the Filson is that its heavyweight felted wool and heavy-duty stitching make it near bulletproof. It doesn't shed, pill, or wrinkle, and it looks good day in and day out. And because it's a vest made of thick felted wool it can be worn over three seasons and across a really wide temperature range.

-- Oliver Hulland

Ultralight windbreaker
Montane Featherlite Smock
$60 OutdoorGBr

When folded into its stuff sack, this Pertex windshirt is the size of a small apple and weighs only about 100g. Unlike a "real" coat, the smock can disappear into a jacket pocket or cargo pocket of your combat pants or it can lurk, weightlessly, for weeks in a backpack until needed. Other than being a carry-all-the-time item allowing minimal bulk, it's extremely versatile. It blocks the wind, preventing windchill, while still feeling as breathable as a lightweight cotton t-shirt. Pull up the neck zip and the smock will trap a layer of air around your body. Because the smock keeps this air dry instead of letting it saturate with sweat, it's a superb insulator: the ground out-

side has been white with frost recently, but I've been quite happy walking around with the smock over my sweater (about 0 Centigrade). Shower resistant, but not waterproof, it's much more breathable than anything I've tried that is waterproof — while Goretex may transmit about 25% of water vapor in even ideal circumstances, Pertex scores closer to 100%. As such, the windshirt is a great outer layer for hikers, cyclists and runners to wear in all conditions where real rain wear isn't essential. It's also terrific for commuting and tourism, especially when added to a light umbrella, which allows you to leave heavier-to-carry and sweatier-to-wear just-in-case clothes at home.

-- Jonathan Coupe

Maximum movement with maximum comfort
Schoeller Softshell Fabrics

My latest revelation in gear: all the new outdoor clothes I really like share this common thread, that they are made of hi-tech softshell fabrics produced by the same Swiss company, Schoeller. Softshell outdoor clothes are more than just stretchy. They mark a better way of constructing the clothes that you wear while exerting energy. Essentially the Schoeller fabrics are similar to GoreTex but they are more permeable and they stretch. This allows much more free motion, more breathability, and allows the clothes to fit tighter saving material weight.

Softshells shed moisture/heat/sweat *much* faster than GoreTex and they are super comfy at the end of the day around camp or even in your sleeping bag. However my favorite characteristic of these new fabrics is that they act similar to fleece so that they keep their ability to insulate and feel good against the skin even if they are saturated with water, whereas hardshell fabrics just feel like a wet plastic bag against your body. These Schoeller fabrics are super good for cycling, climbing, and mountaineering… basically sports where you sweat. I still like hardshell garments for sailing and snowboarding where for the most part you are being eaten by the wind and weather.

The best softshell clothing companies I have found:

• Cloudveil: Excellent pants and tops

• Arcteryx: Bad web site, amazing gear all around. They also have hybrid soft/hardshell clothes that I have yet to try but look very promising.

• Beyond Fleece: Allows you to customize the gear you order. Add pockets, hoods, waterproof zippers etc…

Much of this gear is prohibitively expensive, like $300 for a jacket. I usually go to local dealers and figure out the sizing and then shop around on the outlets.

-- Alexander Rose

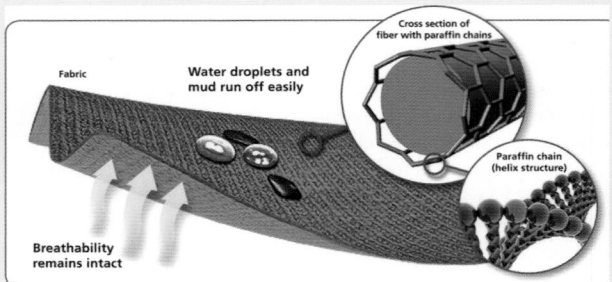

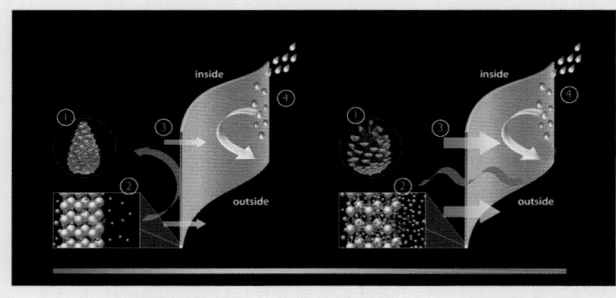

Lightest down jacket
Montbell Ex Light Jacket
$199 Amazon

At first sight it's a nice-looking puffy jacket. Then someone picks up said puffy jacket and throws it at you. You put your hand out ready to catch a pound or so of duck-filled garment and then – nothing. Not what you expected. It's as though a helium balloon just brushed against your hand. It's thick and puffy and warm, but it doesn't weigh anything.

And so began my love affair with the Montbell Ex Light Jacket. Not to be confused with its heavier cousin, the Montbell UL Jacket, the Ex Light weighs in at a scant 5.7 oz for a medium. Don't expect frills such as pockets or hemmed waists, or the insulation and more durable exterior of a thicker down coat.

I wore this jacket whenever I had a chance on the Wonderland Trail. Rest stops, camp, heck I even slept in it on most nights. It's a perfect complement to my lightweight summer bag when things get a little chilly at night.

Granted, I've spent more time in this jacket off the mountain at this point. It's so snug, so cozy that I've been living in it for most of the winter. It replaces my Bozeman Cocoon Vest, and for 0.4 oz more it packs a whole lot more warmth. The downside is that I'm more vulnerable to rain as the Cocoon was synthetic and this is down, but I've found it to be a worthwhile tradeoff.

-- Brett Marl

Traditional wool wear
Filson
$298 Filson

Filson's gear is made in Washington state and is superior to almost all of the winter/outdoor gear I've used. They are a bit spendy but spectacularly well made, and they wear like iron. I imagine my Filson Mackinaw will be handed down to my daughter and then to her children before its usefulness has departed. The woolen gear is quiet in the woods, keeps you warm even if damp or wet, and smells just fine to boot. Thumbs up.

-- John Coates

Best cold, wet outerwear
Paramo Directional Clothing System
£190 The Gorge Outdoors (UK, but ships to the US)

Normal "breathable" shells have three great failings. The worst is that they're just not that breathable, especially in rain, and extra-especially for people who carry on high-energy activities when it rains. This is because they're based on a pored membrane that works by letting water vapor go from drier to wetter air, so when the air outside is wet you're stuck with living with your own sweat. Their two other failings are that repairing rips with a needle is disastrous, because water flows through the holes the needle makes in the membrane, and that getting dry once you're soaked – whether by your own sweat or a fall in a river – takes forever. Softshells try to get around some of these problems, but at the cost of letting in moderate to heavy rain.

A company that has found the answer is Paramo with their "Directional" shell fabrics. Instead of using a membrane they use a "pump liner" that sucks water away from the inside of their shells. So sweat is still expelled in the rain, needle holes don't matter because water trying to enter via them is pumped back, and if you get soaked under your shell when you fall out of your kayak your baselayers will dry out faster with your Paramo on, sucking water away, than if you took it off.

In other good news: Paramo is rustle

free, completely windproof (it's a popular choice of Antarctic exploration teams), is easily washed and re-proofed in a washing machine, and the average hard-used shell seems to last about a decade.

The downside of Paramo shells has been that they combine a shell with a midlayer, making them too warm for many people except in winter, and slightly bulky to carry. However the latest Paramo Velez Light has fixed this problem with lighter insulation and excellent venting. You simply put it on a over a baselayer and work the venting (and roll up the sleeves – something you can't comfortably do with a normal shell) as needed – the shell stays on all day. Because sweat transport and venting are so good this works in all

but summer weather. The Velez Light also has an exceptionally good hood that keeps goggles and spectacles dry in the rain but provides more than adequate side vision even for cycling in traffic.

The bad news is that although discussed excitedly on ultra light-weight hiking lists from time to time, Paramo doesn't seem to be stocked widely – if at all – in the US. However, ordering from the UK is hardly the adventure it was before the invention of the steamship and wireless telegraph.

How good is Paramo? Good enough so that I can crank a cyclocross bike at maximum speed cross country in heavy rain and ice cold wind and my torso is as warm and dry as it would be if I was cycling on a summer day wearing only a wicking tee shirt. In short, ***astoundingly*** good.

-- Jonathan Coupe

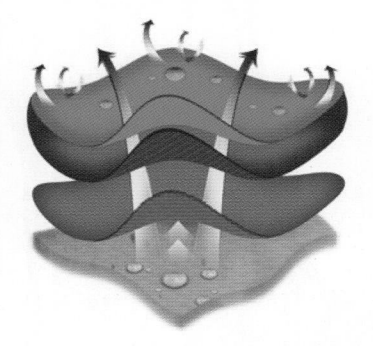

Ultimate cold protection
RefrigiWear
$185 RefrigiWear

Having to work outside in really tough conditions is bad enough, but many times worse if you're cold too.

I found RefrigiWear suits years ago. They're made for workers in blast freezers, so they're tough, not super expensive and come in lots of sizes. My whole crew got these suits and they kept us fully functional while outside overnight for February-in-Wisconsin telecom projects.

I have no idea what Iditarod racers wear, and I'm pretty sure these won't have the right cache for the ski set, but for working people these suits help you get the job done in the cold and won't drain the piggy bank.

-- Wayne Ruffner

Tips

•
A bit of research online shows that 70% isopropyl alcohol in a 2:1 ratio with water seems to be the optimal solution to deice windows (if you have it on hand, methanol is recommended as well), and that it won't hurt your car's paint-job (although it might remove some wax).

--Oliver Hulland

I have a small wet/dry vac that I use as a substitute for renting a rug cleaner to spot clean my rugs and furniture. Use soap and water in a spray bottle or just pour it out of a glass on the spot. Rub it in with a brush or your fingers and then suck it up with the wet/dry vac. Rinse the spot with plain water two or three times the same way. It works great. I've done this to get juice off of my car seats as well.

-- Stephen Foss

•
Two-inch diameter concave mirror from Edmund Scientific magnifies your face when you look into it, and the shorter the focal length, the more magnification you perceive. While this mirror is intended no doubt for high school students conducting optics experiments, I use it to examine my own eyes. Why, you ask? Because when I am traveling, there is a small but tangible chance that I may get a particle of foreign matter in one of my eyes at a time when there is no one around to see it and remove it. (I once paid $200 to an emergency room, merely for removal of a tiny piece of soot adhering to the underside of an eyelid.) I don't use contact lenses, but I imagine this problem is more acute for people who do. The downside of transporting the mirror is that it is fragile, but I have managed to avoid breaking mine for a couple of years now, and recently I was glad that I had it when I was in Florida on my own, everything was shut down because of a hurricane…and I got something in my eye.

-- Charles Platt

•
I had a white board with old writing on it – I tried Windex, alcohol, etc, to little avail, then my girlfriend suggested using a whiteboard marker – they are full of the correct solvent! Just color over what you want to erase and wipe it away. Doh!

-- David Spargur

Winter Boots

Affordable muck boots
Iron Duke Safety Knee Boots
$27 Farm & Fleet

Sometimes you just need to go around in the muck. Since 2006, these American-made boots have kept my feet dry in snow, ice, mud and everything in between. They have excellent, deep cleats for traction, a steel shank for stability and are steel-toed for safety.

A heavy fabric liner is bonded to the inside of the boot, to make it easy to slide your feet in and out. They're not insulated, which is a virtue for me: if water comes in over the top, a change of socks will put you back to work.

What makes this a Cool Tool is that you can get these in farm supply stores for under $30.

-- Robert Paxton

Ultimate shoe horn
Long Handle Shoe Horn
$20 Amazon

You can get a long bamboo shoe horn at any Asian market for $3, or the previously reviewed one from IKEA, but I have one I really like that is sturdy and long-lasting and expensive. But it is SO worth it. Because of the spring at the bottom it is more maneuverable than regular long shoe horns, ending a lot of frustration. Over the lifetime of the shoe horn, the price is justified in my book.

-- Olivia M. Brown

Extra-long shoe horn
IKEA Omsorg
$1 (in-store only) IKEA

I know it's not sexy, but this tool to me is as simple as it is indispensable. I've used it almost every day since I bought it years ago. It's just the perfect shoe horn, especially if you have lower-back problems. And it costs a dollar, which might very well be the best dollar I've ever spent.

-- Sean O'Brien

Quick-zip, heavy-duty footwear
Rocky Side-Zip Paraboots
$135 Galls

I basically own three pairs of shoes. One is a pair of flip-flops that I wear around the house like sandals. Another is a fancy pair of dress shoes that I dust off for weddings, bar-mitzvahs, funerals, and schwanky dress-up events. But for everyday wear in professional office environments, during travel, and for general romping about, I keep a pair of 10" Rocky side-zip leather boots on my feet seven days a week.

The handy side-zip means that getting in and out of these boots is loafer-fast — an essential feature for daily wear or moving quickly through airport security lines. The lacing enables me to customize the fit for my feet, but once that's done, I go months without retying the laces. These boots are designed for use by police officers and other law enforcement and EMS-types, so they're versatile, rugged, and incredibly comfortable (once they're broken in). The black, all-leather uppers have clean and simple lines, so they look good in any casual office environment. The

boot styling provides ample ankle support, which is nice for hiking, long walks, or keeping my feet dry in wet, snowy, sandy, or muddy environments.

During a typical week, I'll wear these boots to work from Monday to Friday, then keep them on my feet during the weekend as I wander through the deep snows of Lake Tahoe, or explore abandoned buildings, or stroll along sandy beaches of the Pacific Coast. Yet even after all that abuse, 20 seconds' worth of buffing is all it takes to clean the boots up in time to walk to work on Monday. When new, there's an initial break-in period that lasts for three or four days (during which I carry band-aids to prevent blisters). But the leather softens up quickly, and thereafter they feel perfectly natural on my feet. An occasional dose of shoe polish is all that's needed to keep them looking great. I'm on my third pair now, and with regular shines to condition the leather, I easily get 3 years of daily wear out of 'em before all the cumulative abuse makes them sub-optimal for office wear. I buy mine from Galls. Check out all the testimonials — kind of hilarious.

-- Todd Lappin

Superior outdoor socks
Smartwool Socks
$17 Amazon

Warm wool socks that don't itch. Using a terrycloth weave of 100% Merino wool, these socks are blister-proof, machine washable, and come in four thicknesses, from a very light liner, to a heavy mountaineering sock. I use the Light or Hiker styles, which give incredible comfort with no feet moisture. They stand up to wear and repeated washing amazingly well. I haven't had a blister yet, even with new boots. And they really don't itch. Well worth the extra dollars.

-- KK

Very warm feet
Steger Mukluks
$180 Mukluks

Ya-shure, winter in Minnesota is cold and dry –and sometimes sunny and lovely. It can be a blast if you know how to get out and tromp around. As a non-native it took me 30 years to learn what to wear up here. Don't wait that long. Here's a key to Minnesota winter survival: Steger Mukluks. I cry when I think about the first time I put on a pair of these. Lightweight, warm, and comfortable — at minus 20F! It's an incredible feeling of winter freedom. Like wearing your favorite bedroom slippers as you hike over the tundra, all day long. I rarely take them off once I hike to the office.

Steger and company, and the original Inuit designers, should be blessed by the Pope for finding a cure for frozen feet. The secret is in the soft (moosehide) sole which allows nerve endings in the feet to be constantly stimulated by movement, so more warm blood goes to that area.

My favorite style is the Arctic Weathermate which has "traveled to both the North Pole and South Pole on the feet of expeditioneers and others." At $180, they're well worth it. I'm thinking of getting a shorter, moccasin style, too. Get the right size by sending a tracing of your foot up to Ely, MN. The crew there is fantastic.

-- Ann Potter

Hand-made, custom-fit shoes
Russell Moccasin Footwear
Varies. $460 for the Cavalier Boot Russell Moccasin

Russell is a hundred-some-odd-year-old shoemaker I've been ordering from for the past 15 years. In addition to the quality of the workmanship and materials, you get the simple, timeless pleasure of a hand-crafted, made-to-order shoe/boot. Options include any number of various soles, hides (including supplying your own!), styles, insulation, toe cap, steel shank, and other custom options. For me, the Vibram sole was perfect. But others might be after oil resistance, traction, silence, longer life, etc. For instance, I'm not a hunter, but for those that are, Russell also has snakeproof boots and options for preventing thorns/cactus. That ability to customize your sole/leather/style per application is great.

There's a downloadable instruction form for sending in your measurements, which they keep on record for a decade. I am very flat-footed and they were able to accommodate the necessary additional space for orthotics. Not that unusual, but I recommended Russell to a friend with extraordinarily narrow feet (especially for how long they are). They were able to create his size no problem; and he's since ordered a half dozen different pairs over the years. One other thing I'd add is they do repair work as well, so you won't need to toss them as they get really old — and you get the added bonus of having someone who knows the shoe doing the work. I have both the Cavalier boot and the Buckle Chukka. They're not cheap, but the Cavalier boots I mainly wear now I've had for at least 10 years, and the pair has only gotten better with age.

-- Wrye Martin

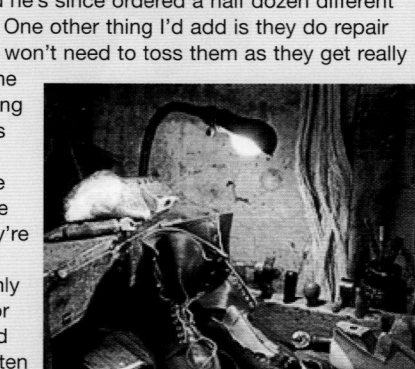

If you don't fail at least 90 percent of the time, you're not aiming high enough. - Alan Kay

Justin
L2561
$148.00
★★★★★

Hatley Kids
Rain Boots
(Infant/Toddler/Youth)
$32.00
★★★★★

Justin
L4332
$198.00
★★★★★

Kamik Kids
Stomp (Infant/Toddler/Youth)
$35.00
★★★★★

Tretorn
Skerry Rubber Rain Boot
$51.99 $65.00
★★★★★

Sperry Top-Sider
Falcon
$52.99 $78.00
★★★★★

Bogs Kids
Glosh Solid Rain Boot
(Toddler/Youth)
$50.00
★★★★★

Kamik
Jennifer
$65.00
★★★★★

UGG
Bailey Bow Tall Boot
$159.99 $230.00
★★★★★

Gabriella Rocha
Soma
$39.99 $49.00
★★★★★

Hunter
Original Short
$130.00
★★★★★

Ariat
Heritage Western R Toe
$107.99 $173.95
★★★★★

All shoes all the time
Zappos

Zappos

Shoes of any sort. Wide, kids, vegetarian, everything. Zappos has flat out the best web shopping/catalog experience on the Web. They have awesome policies — free shipping on most orders AND free shipping on returns up to 365 days! Click on the "sale" link, select your size, sort by price and shop until your heart's content.

-- TDW

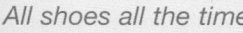

Non-skid shoes
SFC Slip-Resistant Shoes

$35 Shoes For Crews

Architects love to build walking surfaces that are horrible to walk on when wet. I found the elegant and foolproof answer to that — Shoes for Crews. This company has a shoe that I defy you to try to skid in when on slippery wet surfaces. They come in 50 or so styles for men and women, for work, play, casual and formal situations. The work models have steel toes. These darn shoes really work!

-- Don Bierey

Oven-baked, supportive orthotics
SOLE Ultra SOFTEC Insoles

$45 Amazon

Custom fit insoles created by professional podiatrists and orthotics constructors can make running faster and safer, walking more comfortable, reduce back problems, and improve agility and precision of movement. Unfortunately, this sort of work can costs hundreds of dollars per shoe. The SOLE Ultra SOFTEC bring the benefits of a custom fit insole at a mass production price. You simply trim a pair of insoles to fit, briefly heat them, then fit the insoles into your shoes and stand in them in a neutral, well-balanced position for two minutes. At the end of that time you have a pair of custom fit insoles with excellent Poron cushioning and exactly the

fit you need; my friends and I found that SOLEs provided optimum arch support for high, normal, and low arched feet. At $45 they're excellent insurance against running injuries (especially the low arch that eventually afflicts most runners) and a great way of getting extra safety, comfort, and performance for snowboarding, hiking, soccer, or skiing.

Fancy comfortable shoes
Mephisto Shoes

$340 Amazon

French and expensive, Mephistos are what walking sneakers should be: good looking, hard wearing, and very comfortable. I wear the basic black model all the time, so much that I now take advantage of Mephisto's offer to resole their shoes indefinitely. Since the shoes are leather, they adapt to your peculiar foot (such as my bunions), and they're robust enough to carry on for many years with occasionally refreshed soles. I own two pair, so one is working while the other is in the shop.

-- Stewart Brand

I have a high arch, which means I have a greatly increased stress on footfall, with energy being lost from the gait cycle into impact force. The SOLEs corrected this not so much through cushioning, but through restoring correct contact of the load bearing areas of my foot — more energy is now transferred from one step to another instead of into impact.

If you're not impressed with the difference they make, they come with a strong money back guarantee.

-- Jonathan Coupe

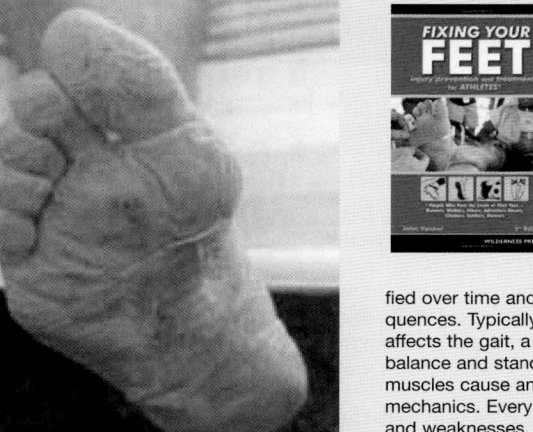

A macerated foot resulting from exposure to moisture.

The foot bible
Fixing Your Feet

$14 John Vonhof, 2011, 392 p., 5th edition

Your feet uphold you. They're easy to abuse, hard to repair. This book is considered the authority on maintaining feet by those who most depend on them: athletes, dancers, soldiers, runners and hikers. Keep 'em happy with the great advice and proven remedies in this portable foot hospital. No other source is as reliable and complete, or more recommended by pros.

-- KK

Many athletes who have participated in extreme sports have learned firsthand how one minor problem can be magnified over time and eventually have major consequences. Typically this happens when a blister affects the gait, a backpack's weight throws off balance and stance, or stressed or weakened muscles cause an imbalance in the body's mechanics. Every athlete has different strengths and weaknesses, different degrees of flexibility, and different muscle skills and body types.

Tips for a Good Fit with New Shoes:

* Do not buy a pair assuming they will fit better later unless they are leather boots. In most cases, today's shoes and boots require no breaking-in period.

* Have your feet sized each time you buy new footwear. Measure both sitting and standing to determine your elongation factor.

* Fit new shoes to your larger foot.

* Try on shoes at the end of the day, preferably after running or walking, because your feet normally swell and become larger after you have been standing and sitting all day.

* Today's running shoes and lightweight hiking shoes are very well made and in most cases will wear as well or better than many of the heavier boots.

* Try a silicone-based lubricant, which helps drive moisture away from your skin and reduces friction between your feet and shoes. Sportslick and Hydropel are both good products.

Empty your socks of rocks and junk. The debris that accumulates as you thrash around in the forest can cause blisters, sores, abrasions, and cuts, all highly contraindicated for happy feet. Best of all, use a light gaiter to keep things out to start with.

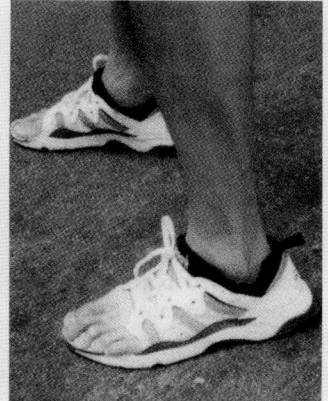

As odd as it may look, cutting the toes off shoes helps prevent common foot problems.

Guide to footwear-lacing
Ian's Shoelace Site

Free Ian's Shoelace Site

Even if you have the least interest in shoes, do yourself a favor and experience this quirky site devoted to shoelaces. Thanks to an active community of contributors, there is an ever-growing abundance of excellent user photos exemplifying almost all of Ian's already-detailed lacing illustrations. The combination of drawings and photos (and ratings!) has really enabled me to find and create any pattern I wish (Ian's was the source for the previously-reviewed Surgeon's Knot). Every article details the pros and cons of each particular pattern, and sometimes an article is supplemented with "work-arounds" which help readers tackle odd situations not covered originally. Quirky, entertaining, and above all, informative.

-- Jacob Musser

Mike Baldwin

Walking naturally
The Barefoot Hiker

$15 (used) Richard Keith Frazine, 1993, 98 pages
Free (online) bhthom.org

Most of the hikers who have ever lived have gone barefoot. Throughout history shoes have been expensive or unknown. Naked feet quickly adapt to stones, twigs, and cold. I've hiked alongside thousands of barefoot hikers, and there's little terrain they can't comfortably negotiate. However the forced-shoeless will immediately adopt a pair of flip-flop sandals for a bit of cushion if given a chance. So why would the well-heeled give up shoes on the trail? *Barefoot Hiker*'s answer: "The soles of our feet function as wonderful sensory organs and the myriad of sensations from earth, grass, moss, pine-needles and other ground textures can both fascinate and delight. Barefoot Hikers appreciate their "vistas" of ground textures as much as others hikers enjoy their vistas of hills, mountains, forests and plains. Walking barefoot adds a rewarding tactile dimension to any outdoor hike."

In short, hiking barefoot is a liberation and a sensual enjoyment — the very reasons why people who can drive will hike in the first place. Once you get over the fact that, like natural childbirth, barefoot hiking is not only possible, but preferable, you're halfway there.

Europe has more barefoot hikers than in the US, but one dedicated women recently hiked the entire rocky 2,000 miles of the Appalachian trail barefoot. Yet if we consider the indigenous tribes of old, she was probably not the first. (Then there's running barefoot, another whole subject.)

There's one book explaining barefoot hiking, a decent short how-to and why-to. It'll go over objections and practical advice on getting your feet toughened up and so on. Tells you how to avoid stares by the disbelieving, which you will get. The book is also available as a free text on the web, courtesy of the author. (I find the printed book form ideal to hand out to others.) Of course there are plenty of websites for enthusiasts.

Because this ability is so primeval, no information is really needed. About all you need to know is that it is easy, natural and fun. Your feet will take it from there.*

-- KK

•
In very stony areas, you will do best to try to walk on the larger stones, selecting one for each footfall and literally gripping it with your toes as you step on and off it. Your heels should not touch the ground at all at such times. When there are not enough of the larger stones to permit you to apply this technique, you will simply have to fall back on your preparation of walking barefoot on gravel and tough it out. Here again, stay on your toes. They are designed to be able to cope with such situations much better than your heels could. Remember that as long as you do not push yourself too far, the experience will ultimately toughen your soles all the more – so think positively and do not let the shod see you wincing. A good pair of strong, healthy, well toughened bare feet should have little difficulty in coping with the equivalent of two or three miles of even the most punishing railway bed gravel in the course of a day's hiking in mild weather; but, as I shall explain more fully in Chapter XI, you must never subject your bare feet to any sort of rough ground in freezing or even near freezing temperatures.

•
Melting snow on a fairly warm winter day is perhaps the most perfect pleasure that nature affords bare feet. Soft and sensuous, cool and cleansing, it is a sensation delicious in the same sense — though not to the same senses — as eating the very best sort of ice cream. Although the opportunity for this singular pleasure may present itself (at least in the climates that I am accustomed to) several times in the course of

a single winter, it is quite ephemeral and rarely lasts more than a day. Thus it may, quite sadly, be a year or so before such a day coincides with one wherein you are so free of the constraints of clock and calendar that you can afford to leave both shoes and watch at home with an heart-felt "good riddance" as you set off for several miles of happy hiking. Nevertheless, even if you cannot afford your bare feet the whole of such a day, you should at least promise them some part of it, even if it be only a lunch hour taken at a park or a very brief visit to a nature centre on your way home from running some errand.

Although melting snow is all the more sensuous on one of those warm-enough-for-shirt-sleeves days that here in Connecticut tend to arrive to relieve the chill at some time in the middle of most winters, you can enjoy this pleasure quite comfortably on any calm sunny day when the temperature is even a few degrees above freezing.

The initial time and effort needed to condition bare feet for hiking is very much less than anyone who has not had experience in the area would tend to suppose. Two or three miles of walking barefoot on good forest trails, two or three times a week, for two or three weeks will prepare almost any hiker to set off quite confidently barefooted on almost any hike that might be included in the programme of any hiking group provided only that the weather be relatively mild.

•
What comes the most to mind at Autumn's mention, are mountains of dry leaves. Take a walk in the woods on one of those delicious days when Autumn deigns to step aside for a late Indian Summer and the leaves are several inches deep on the forest floor and let your bare feet feel them — sometimes crackling with all the crispness of the Autumn air — sometimes whispering sensuously back to your bare soles with what seems a slightly soapy softness.

•
The Brief Rules

1. Always step straight down! Never allow your feet to kick, shuffle or drag along the ground. This is more important than all the other rules together. This may require some conscious effort at first.

2. Always watch the path ahead of you. Learn to keep your eyes on the path a few yards ahead and pick the spot for each footfall a few paces ahead.

3. Try to keep your weight on the balls of your feet and not on your heels.

4. Never forget that you are going barefoot. Always devote a part of your attention to the soles of your feet.

5. Try to walk barefoot on as many different things as possible to sensitize your bare soles. A well developed sense of touch is very important both for safety and enjoyment. You must consciously work on developing this sense.

6. Be especially careful when you cannot clearly see the ground itself because of grass, leaves and snow. Step lightly and carefully under these conditions and be prepared to retract a step if you don't like the feel of what you are stepping on. Never run barefoot unless you can both see the ground surface and have walked over it before.

7. Be especially careful at styles and fences – especially metal ones that have been abandoned. Stubs of former metal fence posts just protruding through the ground are very dangerous. If you see one of these, watch carefully for others which may be in line with it.

8. By all means, try walking barefoot in snow – it is extremely pleasant, but only if it is no more than an inch or so deep and melting.

9. You can walk barefoot on dry ground in freezing weather, but never past the point where your feet become numb and in no case for more than one or two miles, especially on rough ground which is many times as punishing to cold flesh as to warm.

10. Once properly conditioned, your bare feet will give you a great deal of pleasure, but only if you care for them. Bathe them and remove any small thorns after each hike, rub them each day with oil, lotion, or lanolin – especially in winter. Take the time to keep them in the very best condition and take pride in them.

Almost barefoot shoe
Vibram FiveFingers

$60+ Kayak Shed

These shoes allow you to walk with a barefoot gait, without a bare foot, avoiding the injuries that could sideline you. Rocks piercing the foot or breaking a toe on a curb are the end of a barefoot experiment, so I'm looking at this as an urban stepping stone to barefoot hiking when I'm better conditioned and more aware.

The flexible but rugged soles force you to adopt a more natural bio-mechanical stride. Rather than landing on your heel, as we're accustomed to doing with cushioned soles, you land on the mid-foot or ball of the foot. This gait is less stressful on your knees and forces you to place the "strikepoint" of your foot beneath your hips, which also means you initiate forward movement with a lean instead of leg drive. The shoes' toe channels don't cause any discomfort, though I have found the five-channeled Injinji brand socks somewhat uncomfortable to wear beneath them, as the stitching pulls into the webbing between the toes.

The added articulation of the Vibram FiveFingers strengthens your metatarsal ligaments and muscles, which is noticeable in general balance and, oddly enough, upper body pressing strength. Since wearing these shoes every other day (every day can create arch and heel soreness) for two weeks — which took some adjustment in my walking style — I have almost eliminated lower back pain that started several years ago. I attribute this to the lack of elevated heel, which projects your knees forward and affects posture, often encouraging lordosis.

Within minutes of wearing these shoes there is a surprising new awareness of the ground, and a sense of tactile awakening. After all, when is the last time you walked on grass or any surface barefoot for more than a few minutes? I'm rediscovering the most natural means of bipedal movement in the world, which — in a concrete jungle — is a forgotten skill, and a forgotten joy.

-- Tim Ferriss

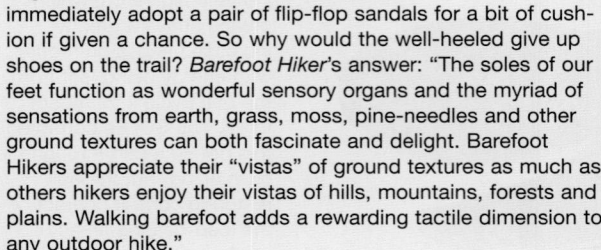

Funky blister-free socks
Injinji Toe Socks

$12 Amazon

I first started wearing Injinji toe socks when I began working out in the previously reviewed Vibram Five Fingers. However, it didn't take me long to realize the benefits of wearing them with normal shoes as well.

When worn with traditional shoes these socks provide a barrier of fabric between your toes that cuts down on moisture and friction thereby preventing the formation of blisters. While hiking you can wear them with another pair of traditional socks layered over them for added warmth and comfort.

For anybody interested in wearing Vibram Five Fingers, these are a must-have as they significantly cut down on the well-known odor problem. The toe socks that I ordered are a wool poly-blend (they make them with a variety of different fabrics) that do a great job of keeping my feet dry while running and minimize any odors. I have only blistered once since wearing them; and that was on the third day of the fantastic Lost Coast hike which included wet sand, mountain climbing, and soaked feet. They make the already comfy VFFs even better, especially in the winter when the minimal protection leads to chilly feet.

The only downsides to these socks are that they wear quicker than traditional pairs, they are more expensive, it takes a little longer to put them on, and it is all too easy to mix up left and right when doing the laundry.

I love my toe-socks, and I highly recommend them to anybody who wears VFFs, easily blisters while hiking or running, or is simply looking for a more comfortable alternative to traditional socks.

-- Oliver Hulland

Amphibious shoes
Keen Sandals

$32+ Amazon

Cooler than shoes, warmer than sandals, and ready for water.

-- KK

Keen sandals have a solid shoe-like toe covering that I've never seen in Tevas-like amphibious sandals. This covering keeps the sand out and eliminates stubbed toes. They're warmer than Tevas and almost not sandals at all. I think of them as very sturdy water shoes. They have arch support and sturdy, gripping soles. They lace with an elastic gizmo that fastens easily and securely. Best of all, water runs right out of them and they dry very quickly. No more dreading the wet footwear as I head off on my daily trek on the beach. I've put about 300 miles on the current pair and they show little sign of wear. My beach has some steep vertical climbs that I traverse without fear of slipping. They seem to carry me easily between the water and the land. It took a little while to adjust to the idea that I could wear socks with them.

-- John Sumser

I've searched for years for give-me-everything sandals and after trekking with my pair of Keens through Europe and a hot New England summer I actually ordered another pair of them, just in case I can't find them again in ten years when my current pair wears out. My Keen sandals are easy to slip on and off, and provide that cooling breeze as I stroll along. If I want to run, bike, hike, or climb a wall, I just use the handy cinch, tighten them up, and go. They are waterproof and quick-drying, which makes them beach-useful as well.

-- Scott Walker

Open-toed hikers
Chaco Sandals

$60+ Amazon.com

When weather permits, I live in sandals. Over the years I've tried all the major brands. A few years ago a friend suggested that I try a brand, Chaco, that I had never heard of. Initially I balked at the price, but when I found a pair that was closeout priced I decided to give them a try. I've never looked back.

While I own a variety of Chaco sandals, I primarily wear the general purpose Z/1. The primary advantage of these sandals is their unique means of attachment to your foot; a single slide buckle. The strap for the front of the sandal is one continuous length that is threaded through slots in the sole. You initially adjust the sandal to your feet by pulling until you've got the fit you want. You then take the sandal off and on by using the slide buckle. To put the sandal on you slip in your foot and pull down on the buckle strap. To loosen the strap to remove the sandal you pull up on the buckle bottom. This is so easy and natural to do that with reasonable balance you can take them on and off while standing on one foot, then the other. This design provides a superbly comfortable fit, primarily through the elimination of the typical stiff Velcro closures.

Another feature of all Chaco sandals is their unique contoured footbed. First, it has an aggressive arch support (that the manufacturer claims counters pronation). Second, it has a deep heel cup that helps your foot stay centered. For my foot, they are more comfortable than any other shoe I have ever worn. This is, of course, a very personal observation, and you should probably try a pair on before buying. Also, the company has recently switched to a newer footbed material that I haven't yet tried.

While they aren't marketed as such, I consider them a hiking sandal. They have a stiff Vibram sole with a very aggressive tread, just like what you'd find on a hiking boot. The slightly oversize footbed protects toes from being stubbed. I wear them for everything: strolling around town, driving, canoeing, biking and hiking. In all these roles they are every bit as comfortable as well-fitting shoes, while also providing the glorious open-air experience. As added bonuses, they float, and can be re-webbed or re-soled.

In competitor Keens, your feet are quite confined. I don't really think of the Keens as sandals; they are really quick-dry athletic shoes with cut-outs. The Keen's soles are similar to those of an athletic shoe, while the Chaco's are more similar to the soles on hiking boots.

Keens definitely offer better toe protection. Still, I've put many hundreds of hiking and biking miles on my Chacos and have never once stubbed my toe. I think that the thick, oversize soles are what provide the protection. If you don't seek the open-air feeling of true sandals such as the Chacos, the Keens would be a fine choice for everyday use. However, for serious hiking and river travel, Chacos are the answer.

As far as cost, the sandals list for $95, but annual design updates result in numerous Internet closeout opportunities in the early spring, and I've never paid more than $65 for a pair.

– Dave King

Shaolin-style barefoot shoes
Feiyue

$15+ Amazon

Why do I prefer Feiyue to the Vibram FiveFingers shoes (see previous page)? Price is half of the benefit. Another 30% of the benefit is that they don't look like Vibrams. You can wear them around and not get stared at. There are other barefoot-style shoes, such as Terra Plana, that look good but they are still expensive as sin. The final 20% of the benefit is in durability. I generally wear a pair of Feiyue from autumn to summer and then go through another pair in the summer when I walk everywhere on concrete in Chicago. The soles aren't exactly thin, but they allow you to feel a lot more without getting jabbed all the time. I have walked on railroad ballast with these and it's not the most pleasant experience but certainly better than barefoot, and nimbler than with heavy boots.

I find that these shoes are good not only for wearing sockless in summer, but also I've been wearing them with double layers of socks in winter and they hold up pretty well (again I live in Chicago). I've also noticed that my feet are feeling much stronger, though the flexor digiti minimi is a bit sore as I start walking in them more.

I also have a pair sized smaller that I use for running and exercising in the gym, which is more along the lines of what the shoes were actually intended for.

Another thing to note when purchasing is that they run about a half size too big. I normally wear a size 41(EU) but in these I'll wear a 40(EU). Also, if you plan to wear them sockless they stretch a bit, especially in summer if you wear them in the water which, I find, is a great way to get them to mold to your feet.

-- Ian Hall

Heavy duty flip-flops
Reef Sandals

$24+ Amazon

I've worn several pairs of Reef sandals for more than 10 years now, and they are simply the most solid "flip-flops" I've owned. I've tried other brands, but they fall apart in stressful conditions or delaminate after a few months of wear. Reef consistently holds up, and I usually wear mine until the rubber is paper thin on the bottom. Right now I'm wearing the "Leather Smoothy" in black – the leather top seems to hold less odor. They have many different styles and colors to choose from for guys, girls, and kids.

-- Camron Assadi

Kevlar-soled moccasins
VIVObarefoot Shoes

$100 Amazon

I'm fascinated by feet, their function and potential, particularly. For the past year and a half, I've been exploring the "barefoot running" scene, and found a wealth of information regarding footcare and advice for those who wished to traipse 'round unshod. Unfortunately, without the proper sensitivity and calluses, it's near impossible to walk/run in urban areas unafraid.

Thus, I went looking for a shoe that would emulate the foot as closely as possible. I tried the famed "ninja" tabi-boots as well as Nike's much hyped "Air Rift" running shoe, without satisfaction. I wondered, what would be the most effective material to construct a sole that would make for a thin, yet durable shoe…and hit upon the jackpot: kevlar. I googled "kevlar sole", and came across a mention of the company "VIVO barefoot" in a podiatry forum by the CEO and creator.

Vivos are without a doubt the most lightest and most comfortable shoes I've ever worn. Their lack of "arch support" and elevated heel is actually a boon, as it allows you to walk/run normally and regain natural posture. They also have a wide toe-box, to accommodate your feet without crunching, even have a zippered sole so that you can just replace them when they wear out, instead of buying a new pair! While the zipper tab does have a tendency to snap off, (a design flaw I hope will be remedied in future runs) I've never felt any discomfort from wearing them, and surprisingly enough, they even kept my feet darn warm in the most recent Maine winter time with their removable "insulated sole insert". They also come in a variety of designs from slip on loafers to casual tennis shoes and look like totally normal shoes. While they generally run on the more expensive side, I managed to find a pair on eBay for forty-five bucks.

-- Josh Samuels

Off-road all-terrain shoe chains
Kahtoola Microspikes
$50+ Amazon

When I met up with my normal winter hiking crew this season, everybody but me had Microspikes. After I fell twice on the icey trail (and I'm an agile hiker!), I came out of it with three gouges on my left hand. So I went ahead and got a pair. The next weekend we did an 8.5 mile hike on trails that were 30 percent ice. I wore my Microspikes, as did all but one of the other ten hikers. We saw only one other person farther up the mountain — a thin, gray-haired trailrunner with headphones on. As he zoomed past with a nod and a smile, I saw he was also wearing Microspikes. The first time I was able to run down a completely ice-covered hiking trail and feel secure, I said, "That alone was worth it right there!"

Prior to purchasing the Microspikes, I vetted them against other products in the same category, including the Yaktrax or STABILicers. At $60 retail (I found mine for $44), Microspikes are expensive, but for anyone out on real trails, they're the best. Yaktrax are the low-end, low-durability cheap version. STABILicers's cleats are OK (and fine for walkways and everyday use, as the reviewer says), but for more rugged terrain, the Microspikes are preferable. Easy to put on, they're much lighter than STABILicers (14.4 oz vs. 28.5 oz for a comparable size — almost a full pound lighter!). They also grip ice much better.

Of course, none of these products are intended to compete with crampons, which excel in exceptionally-high vertical grades and when ice is very hard. They do not have the flexibility in range of use that Microspikes do, however, and are much heavier. Microspikes are not ghetto crampons either; they're the best of a set of products that fill a different, more diverse niche.

While Microspikes are tough, they're not without their flaws: they can gather snow under some conditions, do not provide any additional edging and some people report rubber grommet failures/tears over time. In the case of the latter, Kahtoola will ship a replacement pair to you — and if you've sent in the undamaged one with the damaged one, they will even send the good one back to you so you'll have a spare.

Honestly, I was hoping to find a better-competing product to the Microspikes. It's unusual to find such a monopoly in hiking/backpacking stuff. But I believe they have risen to prominence for a reason.

-- Adam Skinner

Heavy-duty urban shoe chains
STABILicers
$41 Amazon

I have used STABILicers for the past five years for daily outdoor work in the winter. There is no better, more reasonably-priced, long-lasting tool for keeping traction on ice and snow. They feature case-hardened, replaceable cleats screwed into a Vibram Sole with sturdy Hook-and-Loop straps that will fit most boots and shoes (STABILicers come in three sizes). They take just a sec to put on and take off.

I spend my day outside all year delivering residential heating oil, so I am in and out of yards where there is no shoveling or clearing. After my first run-in with ice, I started a hard search for something to keep me from killing myself or, at the least, from getting seriously hurt. First I tried the previously-reviewed Yaktrax. I liked them, but went through my pair in a week ($20 down the drain!). If you want a product for occasional use then go with the Yaktrax. If you want a product that will perform all day, every day then buy the STABILicers.

I put my STABILICERS on in the early AM and do not take them off for eight to ten hours a day. I tend to go from pure ice-covered walkways to snow-covered slopes pulling heavy loads, but I also walk on hard ground between the ice and snow. As such I tend to go through the cleats quickly. I go over my cleats nightly and may go a week without changing a cleat (sometimes it's one or two a day). If you stick to using these on ice, the cleats will last for some time. Easy to change with a screwdriver or electric drill, they sell sell for around $5 for a bag of 50. I recommend buying one or two bags just to keep around. Personally, I buy ten bags at once, which lasts me a couple of seasons easy.

STABILicers are not indestructible. After a few years, I started to wear out one of the straps near the heel, so I bought another pair and now alternate. I find it is easier and less messy to change cleats when they are dry anyway. I also bought a set of the STABILicer Sport model which are rubber and fit over the shoe like a Yaktrax. Since these require a different, more expensive cleat, I use them only for hiking hard-packed snow trails and ice fishing, and never wear them on the pavement.

-- Robert Ferguson

Occasional shoe chains
Yaktrax Walker
$12+ Amazon

Back in December we got some wet sloppy snow which mostly got walked on before people got around to trying to shovel. As a result, there was lots of icy, treacherous, packed snow on sidewalks. Now, I'm not a little old lady (yet) but I don't want to fall on ice on my way to the bus stop, either–especially not while carrying my laptop back and forth to work! These things, which fit over shoes or boots, really work well! I can walk almost normally over packed snow, as long as the surface has a bit of texture–and the added confidence has been great! (Smooth ice is still pretty challenging…)

-- Marie in Toledo

Goose down for your feet
Western Mountaineering Down Booties
$80 Backcountry

I am not prone to getting cold very often, but when I do it is almost invariably my feet that suffer. And there is nothing more uncomfortable than cold feet, or the inordinately long time it takes to warm them up again.

After having mentioned this repeatedly to my fiancee I was recently given a pair of Western Mountaineering Down Booties as a gift. They are, I will be the first to admit, absolutely ridiculous looking when worn, but also the warmest things I have ever had the pleasure of wearing on my feet. Designed for winter camping, they are filled with 800-fill power goose down that provide an impressive amount of insulation (which, when puffed up around your feet, also gives the impression of wearing clown/astronaut shoes).

Unlike other models designed solely for wear around the house, the WM down booties have a tough and water proof bottom (with a thin layer of foam insulation) that can be worn while camping or on quick trips to the mailbox. Another useful feature is an elastic collar that wraps around the ankle that traps in hot air (similar to a down collar in a sleeping bag). This amount of warmth the down provides is impressive and far greater than any other slipper I've tried. The fact that they weigh 6-oz total (while being significantly compressible) means I can easily travel/camp with them.

While the booties are not cheap they are definitely worth the cost to keep my feet warm around the house (while also allowing me to turn down the thermostat a degree or two) or while out camping on a cold night.

-- Oliver Hulland

Waterproof, thick-soled boot covers
NEOS Overshoes
$89+ Amazon

NEOS (New England Overshoes) are basically big insulated, gusseted bags with soles. They fit over my hiking boots, sneakers or, if it's just a quick errand outdoors, my socks. The gusset folds over the top of the foot and ankle with a hook and loop (Velcro) closure. A strap across the instep makes for a snug, secure fit. I discovered NEOS a couple of years ago working as a film extra in rural Pennsylvania. We were outside in cold, wet snowy weather all late fall and early winter. Several members of the crew wore them and the wardrobe folks used them to keep the principal actor's shoes out of the mud and slush. Insulated and uninsulated models are rated for temperatures as low as -20F and 0F respectively. I chose the insulated Explorer version, because I often work and play outside during the winter. As a Scoutmaster, I have worn mine on snowy weekend camping trips when temperatures are down in the teens and kept my feet warm and dry. NEOS also makes light, ankle-high models for commuters with a lining that actually shines dress shoes and heavier expedition weight models suited for intense outdoor activities.

-- Clarke Green

I reappropriated a pair of these boots when my son needed an operation on each leg, requiring recovery in a cast for more than six weeks (one leg at a time). I bought a pair of the NEOS over shoes that fit over my shoes, and it so happened they fit over my son's cast(s) as well. This allowed him to go out during the winter. He could walk to the bus stop, go sledding, etc. It really took some of the suffering out of his recovery, because he could lead a more normal, active life.

-- Alan Brandon

Imagination is more important than knowledge. - Albert Einstein

Casio MQ24 Analog Watch

Simplest analog watch

Casio MQ24 Analog Watch

$11 Amazon

Men's watches are complicated by superfluous amenities, but if you're looking for a simple affordable men's watch this black and white-faced Casio is an excellent analog model similar to the previously reviewed F-91W. This analog Casio keeps the time without frills.

The watch isn't backlit, doesn't have a calendar, or any other function for that matter outside of keeping the time. But I love it, and in all honesty, there are few circumstances where I am forced to check the time under cover of darkness, or while under 100-meters of water. If I need a calculator I can get one, and most days I know the date already.

Overall I am very pleased with this minimalist $10 timepiece. It is simplistic in style (lucky for me black goes with anything), and if I lose it or it becomes scratched it is easily and cheaply replaced.

-- Sean Moriva

Utilitarian digital watch

Casio F91W

$9 Amazon

This $9 watch is the simplest and most utilitarian timepiece I have ever worn. It is easy to read, has an adequate (not blinding) illumination, is small, light and comfortable but also tough, and has a battery that will last up to 8 years (with many other reviewers noting that it lasts even longer).

The F91W is a distillation of a digital watch. It has three features: tells date and time, has an alarm clock, and works as a stop watch (only up to an hour before it turns over). The functions are easy to use, and aren't distracting.

I originally purchased this watch to use while running, but found that I liked it so much that I now wear it all the time. It has replaced my larger, more expensive Citizen Eco-Drive which is now reserved for dressier occasions. After swimming and showering while wearing the watch I trust its "water resistance" and am impressed with its durability. Its also cheap enough that I don't worry about it breaking or getting stolen.

If you are looking for a simple, capable digital watch that will last for years, this is the one to get.

-- Oliver Hulland

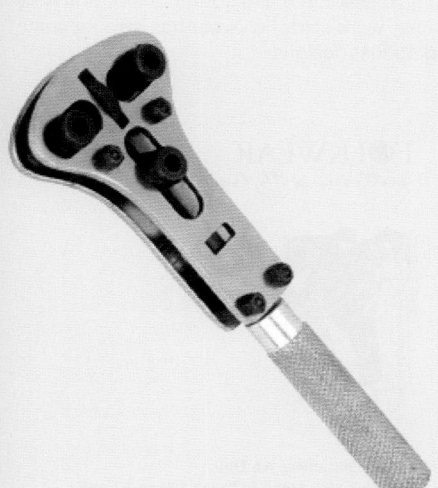

Timepiece caseback opener

Pittsburgh Watch Case Opener

$5 Harbor Freight

This is, in my experience, the only tool one needs to open a threaded watch caseback, which are found mostly on 'waterproof' or water-resistant wristwatches. It's definitely a two-handed operation, but can be done by hand, with no other tools. The wrench comes with several sets of different-shaped pins, which you arrange on the tool to match the precise notch pattern on the caseback. This wrench will work with casebacks that have notches in amounts divisible by 3 and divisible by 2, which makes the tool adjustable to just about any size caseback.

It's not apparent from the appearance, but the tool's large handle rotates to adjust the bottom pin, and the thumbwheel in the middle adjusts the two pins above. Takes a little getting used to, but it's a good, solid feel when the adjustments are correct. Slow, constant force works best; no need to quickly jerk anything.

This type of tool is available from other stores, but Harbor Freight offers the best value. I'd say mine paid for itself about fifteen times over during the first week I had it. Over the last few years I've had several batteries run down on watches I own, including a Fossil titanium watch and a no-name Army field watch. So far, I have only used the tool's round, pin-end pegs. I'm actually not sure what watches require the other types of pegs included, but it's nice to be prepared.

Be aware the possibility of marring the caseback exists, and therefore you should be moderately careful when using this tool. Marring hasn't been an issue with the watches I've fixed, but if the metal is soft (gold alloys, for example), or if you're not careful, this could easily happen. The pins on the wrench appear to be hardened steel and would very likely be much harder than the watch caseback.

-- John Spurlin

Clip-on lens carrier

KABACLIP Contact Lens Case

$5 Amazon

This simple little carrier hugs a bottle of contact lens solution, so the two are always together and easy to find at the bottom of your pack. In the past, I've relied on rubberbands and plastic baggies, but of course they tend to break and they add an extra packing step. This clip pops conveniently on and off. The colors make it easy to distinguish right from left. And it's reduced a bit more clutter from my dopkit. The price is a tad extravagant, but the case is so effective I'm done using the freebies.

-- Steven Leckart

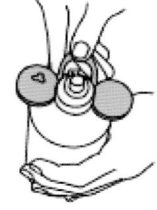
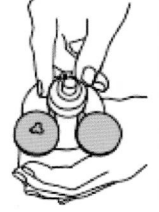

Rubbery ball unscrews watches

Watch Case Ball

$6 Esslinger

If you have a screw-back watch that won't open, get one of these plastic balls. They actually work, and they will not scratch the watch case.

I own the Pittsburgh watch case opener, and it will usually open watches. However, I have one favorite watch that defied the Pittsburgh tool. I read about the Watch Case Ball, and bought one online. Within five minutes of picking up the mail, the watch was open. (I had to inflate the ball; it's shipped flat.)

The ball is made of plastic. It's not actually sticky, but when you press it onto a watch back, it conforms to the surface and won't readily slip on it. Now I go to this tool first, because there's no chance of marring the watch case with it, and it works on all screw-back watches with no set-up at all.

-- Dan Hoyt

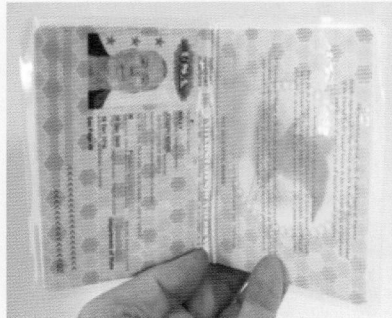

Passport Proxy Tip

A seasoned traveler who ventured further into third world slums than I ever would told me about this nifty trick-of-the-trade. Make a good color copy of your passport, including the covers. Align the inside sheet of your passport data with the outside passport cover sheet. Glue together. Laminate. Score and fold. You now have a fairly official looking travel document.

I have found that for most purposes — changing money at a bank, rentals, hotel front desks, and even police — this passport clone is sufficient. You hide or store your real one and use this one for everything else except crossing borders. I don't know why, but most people seem happy to accept it. It may be because it seems like some new futuristic version 2.0 passport and who are they to question it?

(According to the US Passport Agency, it is perfectly legal for you to make a color copy of your passport — although Kinko's can't — and in fact they recommend you do so.)

-- KK

Folkwear

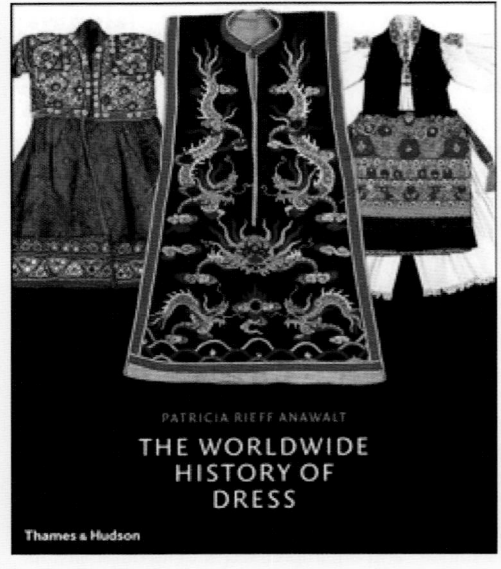

The definitive costume inspiration

The Worldwide History of Dress

$66 Patricia Rieff Anawalt, 2007, 608 p.

I'm guessing that when technology permits us to design and produce our own clothes as easily as we do our websites, we'll go beyond jeans and start making our outfits a little more distinctive. These one-at-at-time items will be supremely personalized, unique. And a return to the way wardrobes of past were once also made one-at-a-time into distinctly personal items. When that moment comes, you might want to lose yourself in this massive 600-page archive, which catalogs the full diversity of costumes from around the world. Over 1,000 glorious illustrations, in astounding ethnographic variety. Tribal, royalty, folk. Outerwear, footwear, headgear, armor. It is the best one-volume summary of Fashion on Earth I've seen. (It's expensive, so check it out at your library.)

-- KK

A circumcision waistcoat possible from the Hebron Hills during the British Mandate period, or earlier. The groundcloth is Atlas satin, a luxury fabric woven with a silk wrap and a cotton weft. The front of the waistcoat is thickly cover with a variety of coins, the better to express the high social value of the boy wearing it. Length 11 7/8 in. (30cm).

The 19th-century tall hats and enveloping cloaks of certain of the Welsh peasantry were markedly behind the times. These garments bear a decided resemblance to the popular image of a witch precisely because they were the characteristic wear of the time of witchcraft persecutions of the 1630s.

Above her richly patterned sleeveless coat, worn over an ornate red silk dress with high shoulder pads, a stand-up collar and blue turned-up cuffs--an outstanding example of the festive dress of the 19th-century Mongolian nobility--this Chalka tribeswoman models the "sheephorn headdress."

Front and back views of a Micronesian warrior suit made of knotted coconut-palm fiber. The accompanying upper-body armor is sturdily constructed of plaited bast fiber. Length 32 1/2 in. (82.5cm), width 15 in. (38cm).

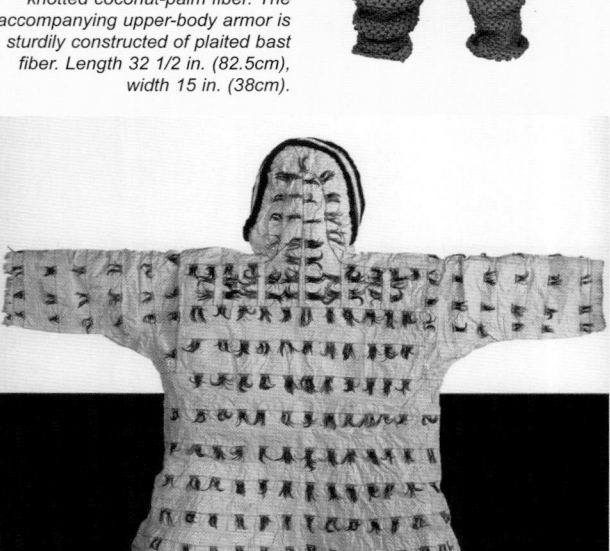

A walrus-gut kamleika made by the Yup'ik people of St. Lawrence Island, Alaska, in the mid- to late 19th century. It is adorned with eats and small feathers of the crested auklet. Length 43 in. (109.2 cm), width 54 in. (137 cm).

This 1950s Conibo man is clad is a cushma, a long, wide, poncho-like cotton tunic that has been worn in the area since per-hispanic times. The brown to black dye used in decorating these garments is obtained by boiling mahogany bark.

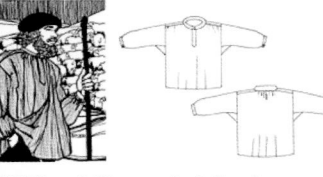
Traditional clothing patterns

Folkwear

Prices Vary Folkwear

Folkwear is a sewing pattern company that was founded in the 1970's by Alexandra Jacopeti. Over the years they have built up a selection of patterns based on traditional folk clothes of the Middle East, Asia and Europe. Their first patterns were based on garments that worked with the full width of the woven fabric, using rectangles and squares. The old adage was to "cut my coat according to my cloth," that is, cut with as little waste as possible. These clothes were frequently used for work and had to have enough ease to move in. One of the Folkwear patterns I've made is the Cheese-Maker's smock. This is a pattern based on a classic French work-shirt. It has several sizes that fit both men and women. The small square gusset set under the arm makes for a complete range of movement and comfort. Wearing it I am covered from neck to wrist — perfect for garden work. I have made several in cotton and linen and could also see it in a fine cotton or silk. It is now my favorite hot weather work shirt. Folkwear has also recently added Victorian and 1930s' designs.

-- Lesley Creed

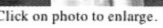

Art is in what you leave out. - Kevin Kelly

Totally inspiring street fashion

Fruits

$20 Shoichi Aoki, 2001, about 200 p.

Anti-fashion snatched off Tokyo's streets. Pages and pages of exuberant color and wild forehead slapping design. Clothes made at home, altered from the store (called "kustom") or piled on without regard to previous styles. You get the ugly and the brilliant. There's little text, just full-page snapshots of real kids with other-wordly outfits unfettered by normalcy. This is one of our favorite books at my house. We open it up every month or so, giggle, and feel inspired to loosen up a bit. Blue, yellow, and pink? Why not, color is free. This is what clothes could be, or ought to be.

-- KK

Atan age 17
Jumper — second-hand
Blouse — at Half Fish
Shirt — handmade
Point of fashion — cheap
Current obsession — meditation

Chee age 23
Shirt — second-hand
Skirt — second-hand
Trousers — handmade
Shoes — Buffalo
Point of fashion — a free lunch
Current obsession — Lamb Chop

Street fashion free-for-all

Fresh Fruits

$20 Shoichi Aoki, 2005, 272 p.

Wouldn't the world be a better place if everyone wore more colorful clothes? You can get a glimpse of that heaven in this never-boring album of Japanese street costumes. Like its predecessor volume *Fruits*, this sequel, *Fresh Fruits*, preaches freedom of color and is meant to be browsed while standing in your closet tossing out the black.

-- KK

Total inspiration

Natural Fashion

$18 Hans Silvester, 2009, 168 p.

Astounding portraits from the Omo Valley in Ethiopia, Africa, where tribal people decorate themselves with natural vegetation and found pigments. This type of natural fashion, which began as sun protection, is art that probably predates cave paintings. There are 160 examples in this stunning book and each one outdoes the creativity of the one before. In sensibility, this is high fashion: total surprise and delight. This book works as inspiration not only for fashion mavens but for all artists.

-- KK

• In this region of East Africa, the savannah landscape presents a picture of large, scattered trees and bushes, and tall dry grasses. In contrast, the vegetation near the water is almost lush - papyrus, flowers, and wild fruit trees. This luxuriance is like an incitement to self-expression, to putting on a show. Within easy reach is a multitude of plants, each one an invitation to indulge in all kinds of imaginative decoration. A tuft of grass serves as a hat, and banana leaves, woven tendrils or flowers are knotted together like a scarf or neckerchief. For Westerners, any such activity might demand great intellectual effort-- which branch, what colour, how and where should they be arranged?--and the whole process could seem laborious, but here the people make their choices spontaneously but firmly, and with a particular instinct for what will work. They do not spend any time thinking about it.

Visual Reference

Visual Reference I go to books when I need to stimulate my imagination. Books never fail. I am a visual thinker, even when I write words, so I especially respond to visual books full of images, graphs, and pictures. Over the years I've accumulated a pretty good library of visual source books. Today, used books are cheap. You can build a good library of inspiration rather easily and inexpensively. These reference books will be the last to be replaced by digital screens, and they will still work perfectly well in the next century — no obsolescence. If you can find space to keep them, a good reference library is a working treasure. I probably have several hundred visual reference books, so I will list only the two dozen or so that I would truly hate to lose. I am mostly omitting single-artist retrospective books, including my favorites, since these are easier to find than the ones I include here, which are not obvious and less well-known. Oh, the possibilities!   – KK

An Album of Fluid Motion

Milton Van Dyke, 1982, 176 p.

Spirals. Vortices. Waves. Cyclones. Turbulence. Ripples. An engineer collected 400 of the classic photographs of hydraulic movement he could find in old scientific volumes and self-published a reference book for engineering students. He's been surprised that mostly artists, animators and poets have been buying it. I'm not surprised.

--KK

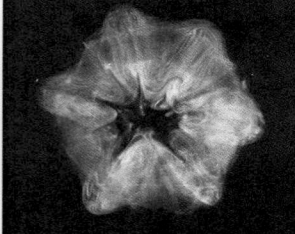

Parallel Encyclopedia

Batia Suter, 2007, 592 p.

A fat encyclopedia of thousands of pictorial gems taken from old books. These old-timey results won't show up on Google image search. Each page is a wonderful orthogonal view of our world-- Items are roughly grouped by category. It's a constant source of amazement, kind of a visual curiosity cabinet.

-- KK

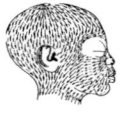
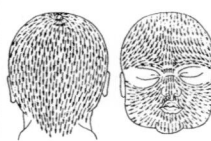
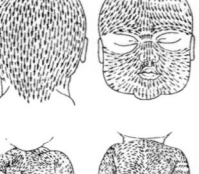
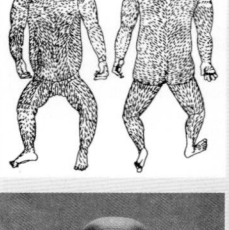

Secret Museum of Mankind

David Stiffler, 1999, 576 p.

This hefty softcover is a facsimile collection of thousands of exotic and sensational photographs dating from around the turn of the century when news of any sort from far away lands was rare. It's sort of a combination of early uncensored National Geographic and Ripley's Believe It or Not. Reproduced without a known author, or copyright, or even authentication of the captions, it was for many years a "secret" underground publication. And for pure gawking pleasures it still can't be beat. Cannibals, executioners, and fakirs, oh my! I use it as a mighty sourcebook of amazing costumes, body modifications and hairdos, architectural novelties, and extinct strange rituals. (I'm convinced science fiction film directors mine this for alien worlds.) I like to think of this book as the best one volume catalog of cultural diversity on Earth. For the most part these societies are long gone, and remain only in rare books like this one.

-- KK

How to Wrap Five Eggs

Hideyuki Oka, 2008, 224 p.

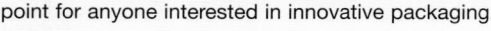

Packing has always been a high art in Japan, even for the most lowly common article. These studio photographs of traditional Japanese packaging from the 1950s and 60s capture Japanese creative packing at its peak before it was sidelined by plastic and printing. With the advent of 3D printing, we may return to this tactile stunning and elegant practice. This book will serve as a starting point for anyone interested in innovative packaging.

-- KK

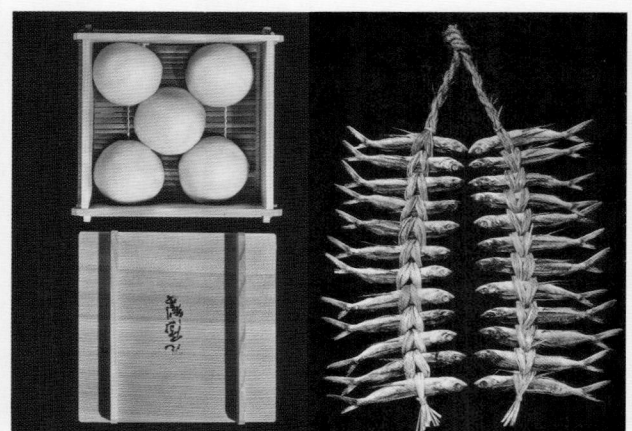

Art Forms in Nature

Ernst Haeckel, 1998, 139 p.

Long a favorite of designers, this 1904 album is a library of possibilities. Its etchings depict lesser-known life forms as drawn by the German naturalist Ernst Haeckel. These organisms appear to be from an alien planet, although they are all found on earth, in soil or water. They contain the future forms of cars, gadgets, architecture, and so this book will serve anyone thinking of the future. Artists, engineers, and natural scientists have used this album for inspiration for the past century. The Dover edition of the book shows all 100 pages in black and white; while the slightly more expensive Prestel edition shows the 25 pages that are in color, and the other 75 in their original black and white.

-- KK

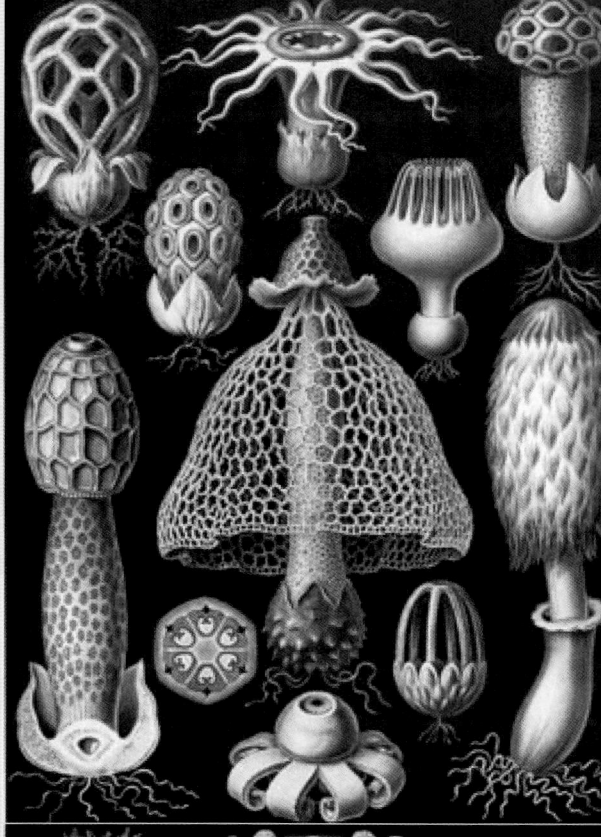
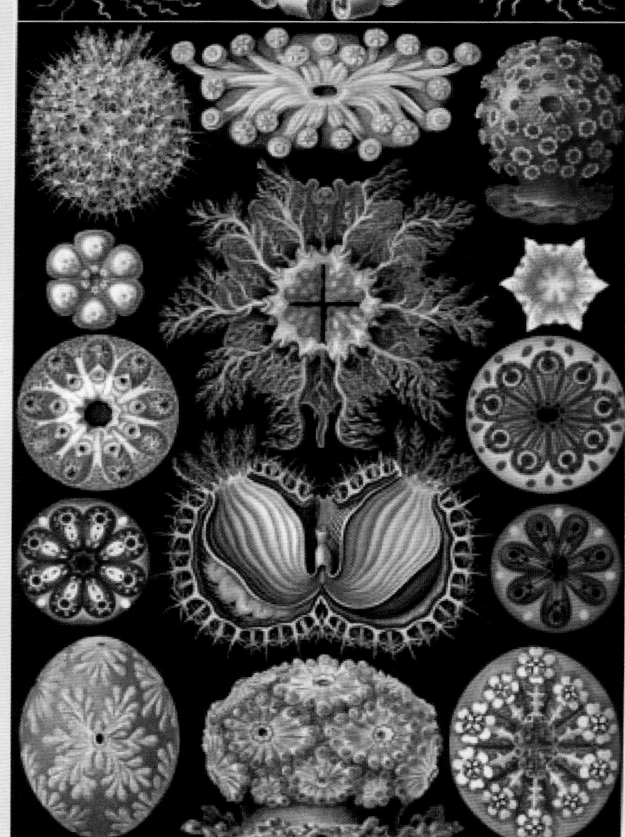

We have to believe in free will. We've got no choice. - Isaac Bashevis Singer

The Deep

Claire Nouvian, 2007, 256 p.

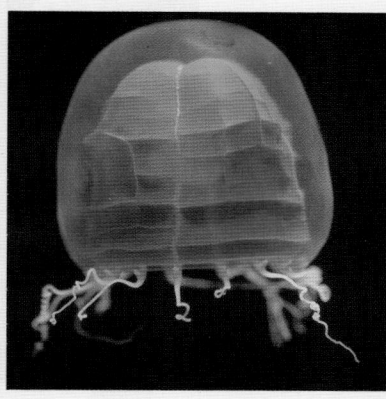

Photographs of fishes and invertebrates from the deepest parts of the Earth's oceans. The forms, colors and appearances of these distant species are so warped by the deep pressure and blackness they they might as well be machines made on another planet, and as such they can ignite alternative ideas in the reader.

-- KK

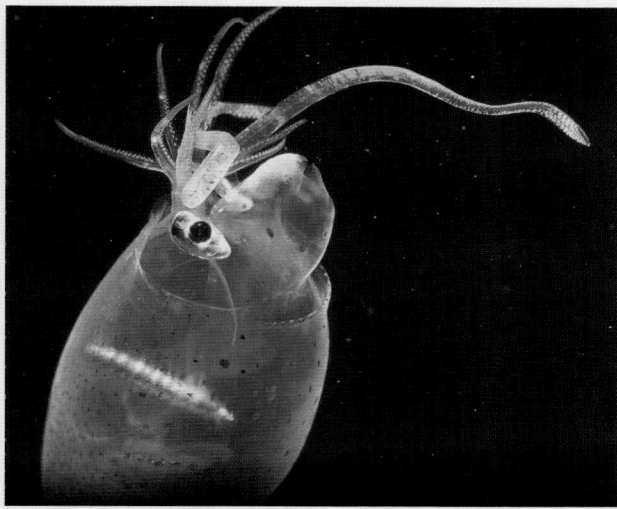

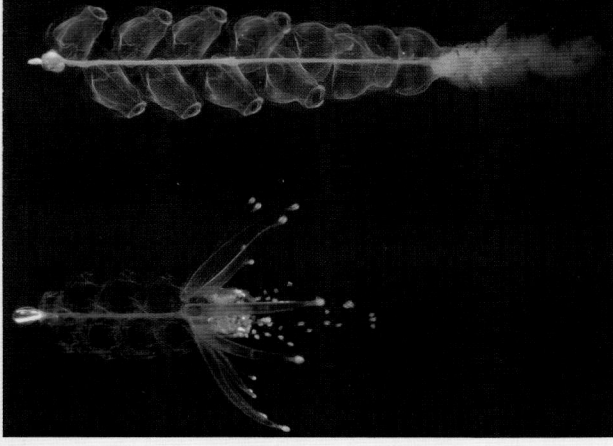

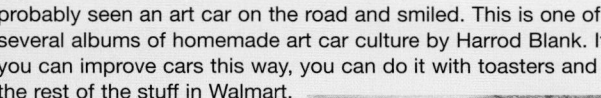

Art Cars

Harrod Blank, 2012, 160 p.

Why are cars so boring, uniform in color, undecorated, unpersonalized when they could be.... covered in pennies, painted in polka dots, or traced in iron? You've probably seen an art car on the road and smiled. This is one of several albums of homemade art car culture by Harrod Blank. If you can improve cars this way, you can do it with toasters and the rest of the stuff in Walmart.

-- KK

Russian Criminal Tattoo Encyclopedia

Danzig Baldaev, 2006-2009, 400 pages each

In three volumes! Tattoos in the Russian prison system were coded messages meant to communicate to other prisoners the wearer's status and gang affiliation, to send insults to the guards, to scare innocents, and as badges of accomplishment for the owner. Russian prison tattoos thus contain multiple layers of subcultural references which give them strange and disturbing powers. Russia's prison system was so vast, indigenous, and generational that prisoners had their own verbal language, culture, and iconography. For instance many of the pornographic tattoos were punishments doled out to losers of card games who could not pay. There are so many levels to these tattoos that they were officially collected and copied by the authorities in order to decipher them. Each one is a small bomb of meaning; as visual source material you can't have more power than these.

-- KK

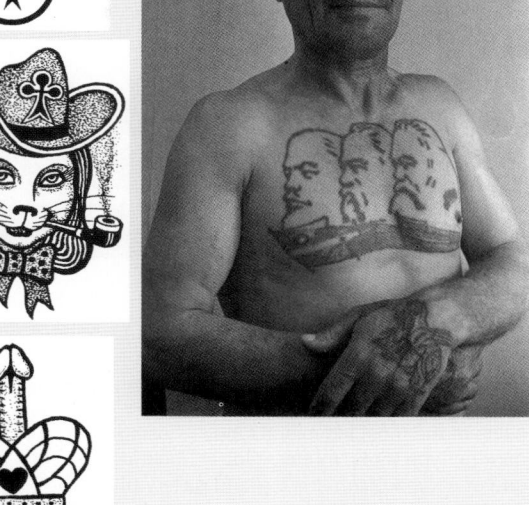

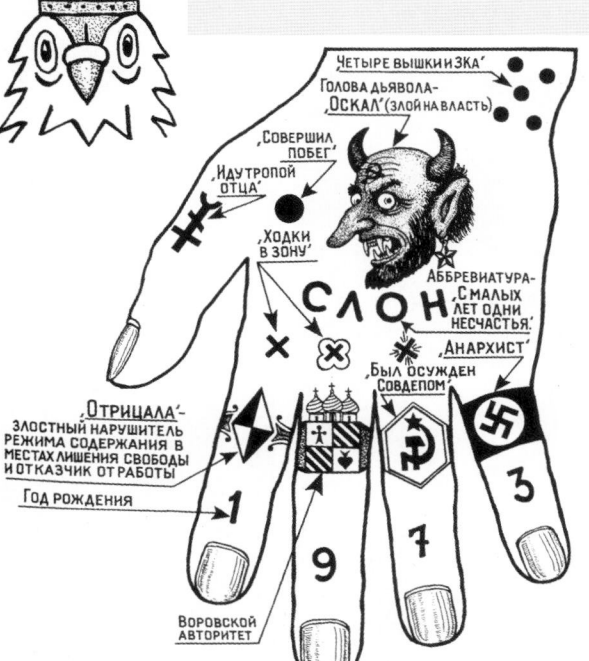

Fantastic Illustrations of Grandville

Jean-Ignace-Isidore Grandville, 1987, 156 p.

Surreal and whimsical did not start with hipsters. These book of 266 pen and ink illustrations by the Parisian Jean Grandville in the early 1800s depicts fantastical chimera, and phantasmagorical visions. It's old-timey hallucinogenic scenes, often switching animals for people. Always guaranteed to wake you up.

-- KK

Auspicious Designs of China

Ye Yingsui, 2004, 239 p.

A small paperback crammed full of vernacular designs of traditional China taken from throwaway paper cutouts, stencils, wood block carvings and front door banners. A great and varied collection, all in black and white. Good for logos and such.

-- KK

Natural Art Forms

Karl Blossfeldt, 1998, 128 p.

Similar to Haeckel's book, but primarily close ups of plants and seeds. There is an other-worldly aspect to these organic forms, in monumental black and white. A great inspiration for sculpture and 3D thinking.

-- KK

Visual Reference

Open Here

Paul Mijksenaar and Piet Westendorp, 1999, 144 p.

I thought I was the only one in the world stealing the safety instruction cards from airline seats because of their terrific graphics. Apparently others see the genius of language-free charts. For radically clear thinking nothing can beat a really good set of wordless diagrams; you know, the kind found as instructions for assembling furniture, or opening a container. They have a rarified beauty. Hundreds of examples from around the world are paraded here.

-- KK

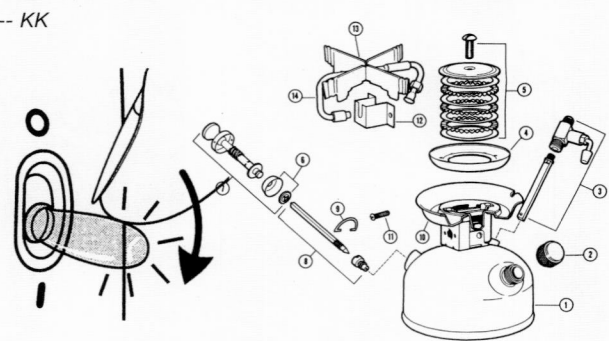
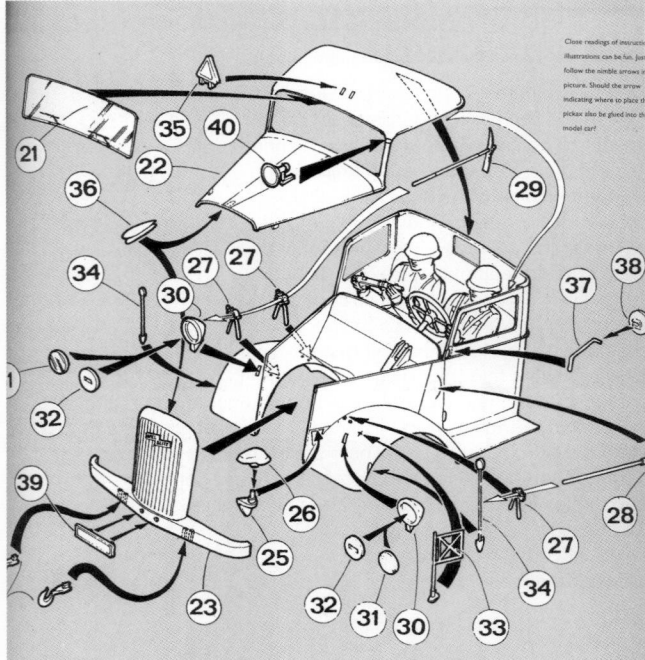
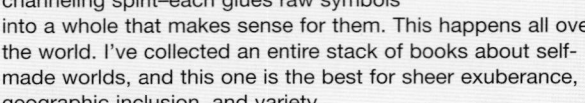

Fantasy Worlds

John Maizels, Deidi Von Schaewen, 1999, 335 p.

Sometimes, despite all pressures toward normalcy, people are compelled to construct their own worlds. The old lady who over the years arranges broken bottles into a house, or the man down the road covering his barn with tiny quotes from a channeling spirit—each glues raw symbols into a whole that makes sense for them. This happens all over the world. I've collected an entire stack of books about self-made worlds, and this one is the best for sheer exuberance, geographic inclusion, and variety.

-- KK

Dover

922 Decorative Vector Ornaments, 2009, 48 p.

For 50 years Dover Publications has been selling cheap editions of copyright-free clip art. Their inexpensive books are still a great bargain for reams of images at low cost, and their catalog is impressive -- calligraphy, old letterpress fonts, folk stencils, celtic knots, bygone engravings, you name it. I have a fair number of Dover clip art books and wish I had more. Recently Dover has issued some of their art books with companion CDs to save you the trouble of scanning the material. Their newest offerings include a CD with vector graphics of the images, which means you can re-size them without losing detail or acquiring distortions. In 5-years CDs will be obsolete, and perhaps then Dover will sell downloads online. In many ways their clip art paperbacks are a sensible investment, since they can always be scanned, and I find thumbing through a book the most efficient way to scan a large collection.

-- KK

Infinite Worlds

Vincent Di Fate, 1997, 320 p.

Past visions of the future. Several thousand science fiction book covers and illustrations (sorted by artist) from past decades. This is the imagination unleashed.

-- KK

Masters of Deception

Al Seckel, 2007, 320 p.

In one tome, a glorious collection of visual trickery, the best I've seen. Optical illusions of the most ingenious types — using mirrors, type fonts, murals, globes, junk, and of course paint. It is a grand gallery of nerd art and visual wit.

-- KK

African Ceremonies

Carol Beckwith, 1999, 744 p.

This two-volume oversized celebration of contemporary ritual in Africa is shocking in its lushness. It seems to explode with possibilities of what ritual and ceremony could be, of how many different ways there are to find meaning in life. It captures the artistic genius found in traditional Africa, now vanishing. There's a one-volume smaller paperback selection called *Passages: Photographs in Africa*, which presents highlights from *Ceremonies*. But this abridgment has only one-tenth the 850 images in *Ceremonies*, and I feel it misses the point of the larger work: glorious, extravagant diversity.

-- KK

Sensacional! Mexican Street Graphics

Juan Carlos Mena, O Reyes, 2002, 339 p.

A thousand amazing wall ads, hand-painted signs, and posters from the streets of Mexico. Tons of energy, color, wit and boldness. Opening this brick of a book is opening a cornucopia of folk art.

-- KK

Street Art San Francisco

Annice Jacoby, Carlos Santana, 2009, 304 p.

A deep and wide collection of the best of San Francisco's murals. A bit of hippy style, plus Mexican, plus punk, plus hipster. Great mix, hundreds of examples.

-- KK

 Nobody is bored when he is trying to make something that is beautiful or to discover something that is true. -William Ralph Inge

1000 Record Covers

Michael Ochs, 2005, 576 p.

This is merely one in a whole series of "1,000 X" visual references that Taschen publishes, but it is my favorite for several reasons: For years the most innovative graphic design in the world was featured on record covers, and now this art has vanished from view. Also, this collection of 1,000 covers is part of a personal collection of 100,000 albums, and these 1K are curated by the owner not for the album's graphic beauty but for their musical and cultural influence, so one gets a whole spectrum view of the art as well. Catalogued roughly by decade, from the 50s, through the 80s.

-- *KK*

Full Vinyl

Ivan Vartanian, 2007, 164 p.

Vinyl figurines and toys are the latest fashionable collectables. Designer toys are being propelled by cheap manufacturing, and will be accelerated even further by 3D printing, which makes it possible for almost anyone to make small objects. There's plenty to study. Among the several vinyl toy books I have this one has the widest range of material, including much from Japan.

-- *KK*

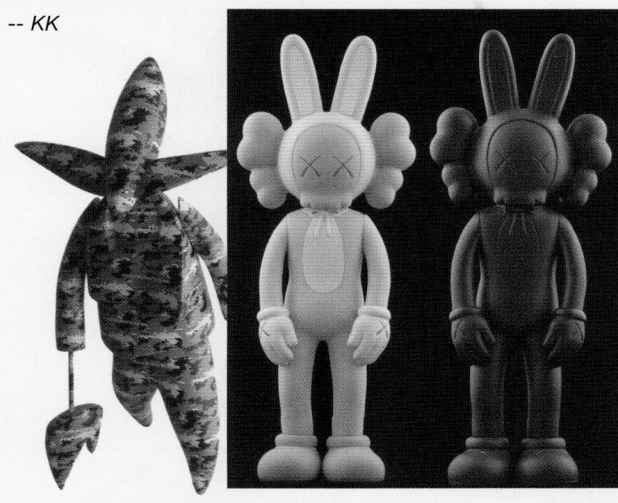

1894-95 Montgomery Ward

Jr. Joseph J. Schroeder, 1977, 600 p.

A page by page reproduction of the mail order catalog from Montgomery Ward in the winter of 1894-95. You get a snapshot of *everything* that was made at that time, plus the description of the item in text. Everything as in: screws, bolts, carpets, curtains, toys, guns, hats, pins, books, tractors, saddles, bullets, bicycles and buggies. It's a time machine and museum in a book.

-- *KK*

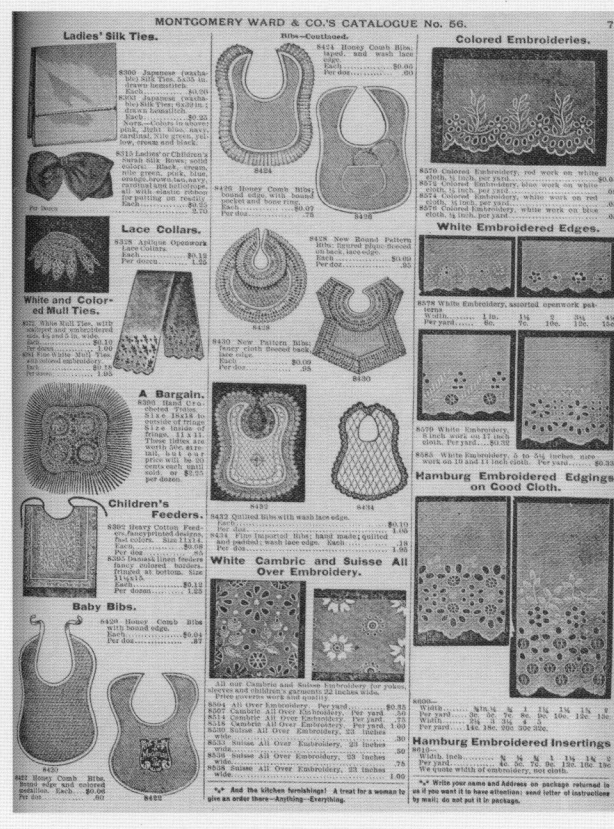

1000 Steampunk Creations

Dr. Grymm, Barbe Saint John, 2011, 320 p.

Steampunk is a contrarian reaction to the sleek minimalism of modernity and the "nothingness" of an iPod. It takes inspiration from the visible workings of brass pipes, rivets, and gears of Victorian technology and transfers that maximalism -- how many doo-dads, filigree, extra decorations can one add? -- to artifacts and clothing today. While this extreme counter-style is dated (by definition), it holds many potential ideas. This one volume compendium contains a thousand vibrant examples of excessive transparency.

-- *KK*

Street Graphics India

Barry Dawson, 2001, 112 p.

This book inspired me to begin recording street graphics as I traveled so now I have my own collection, but this modest book will give anyone a good representation of the graphic landscape in India -- from Bollywood billboards, to painted rickshaw covers, matchbox covers, wall advertisements, signage, and household symbols.

-- *KK*

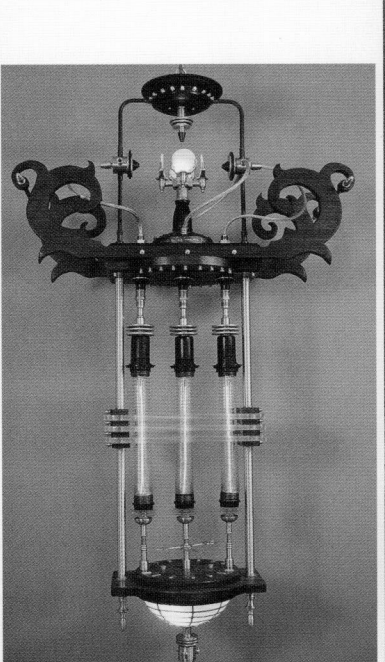

Always side with the truth. It's much bigger than you are. - Teresa Nielsen Hayden

105

Design Constraints

Space-saving possibilities
Collapsible

$15 Per Mollerup, 2001, 240 p.

Witness this marvelous gallery of ingenious objects that unroll, unfold, and unstack in order to save space or become more portable. The examples range from the obvious unfolding umbrellas and strollers, to non-obvious unfolding cameras, bicycles, and ladders. As we become (or return to) more nomadic beings, collapsible products are ever more desirable. Almost anything could be designed to collapse. This collection is an inspiring catalog of what is possible.

-- KK

▼ The Polaroid SX-70 from 1972 includes a number of improvements on the original 1948 model. Among these is the space-saving SLR (single lens reflex) and the power source included in the film pack. Dr. H. Hand was the inventor, with Henry Dreyfuss Associates acting as design consultants.

◄ The GF chair designed by David Rowland in 1964 is the world champion of stack ability. Forty chairs form a tower of just 120 cm (3 ft 11 in). The seat and back of vinyl-covered steel offer a reasonable measure of comfort. Manufactured by GF Office Furniture, USA.

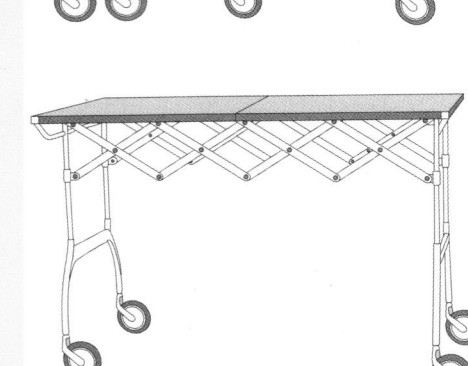

◄ Battista, a length-adjustable, concertina-collapsible table designed by Antonio Citterio and Oliver Low. Manufactured by Kartell, Italy.

► The Columbus foldaway staircase by Trip-Trap, Denmark.

► Stockholm folds out for inspection on this map handed out free by the city's cabdrivers. Produced by CR Grafiska.

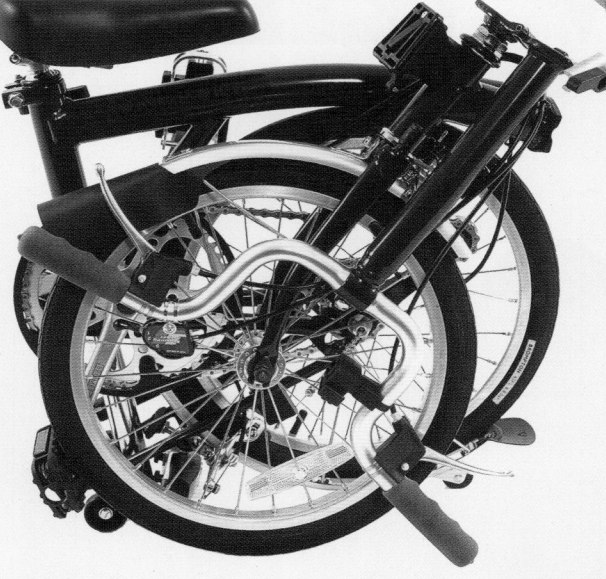

▲ The first Brompton Bicycle was designed in 1975 by landscape gardener Andrew Ritchie, in his bedroom overlooking London's Brompton Oratory.

Collapsible
The Genius of Space-Saving Design

Ergonomic guidance
Human Dimension & Interior Space

$27 Panero and Martin Zelnik, 1979, 320 p.

When designing a space or wearables for humans, you'll need precise measurements of our size. How high to put a door knob, the circumference of our necks, how far we can reach overhead? There's no such thing as an average person, so you'll also need to know what the variances are, too. There's a number of good sources for this data, but the most complete set, with the greatest clarity, and most affordable price is Human Dimensions. This data set was distilled from ergonomic research started by NASA for designing space capsules and broadened over the years to include the ergonomics of wheelchairs and crutches, bathtubs, workplaces and public spaces among many other everyday situations. I prefer its very graphic presentation. Good for architects, costume designers, gadget makers, interface designers, and interior decorators.

-- KK

Figure 1-4. The human body and the Golden Section

Adapted from Human Factors Engineering, U.S. Air Force Systems Command Handbook, DH1-3, P. DN2B11, 19.

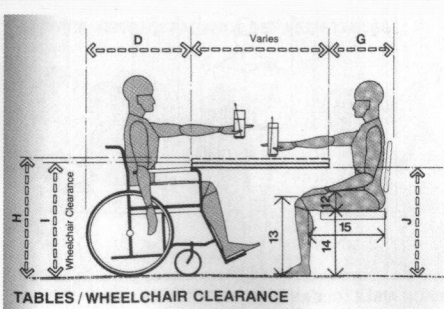

TABLES / WHEELCHAIR CLEARANCE

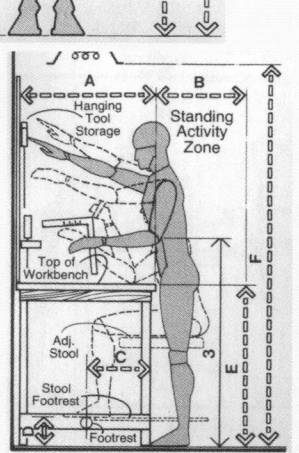

HIGH WORKBENCH

LANDSCAPE PARTITIONS / MALE ANTHROPOMETRIC CONSIDERATIONS

One can resist the invasion of armies; one cannot resist the invasion of ideas. - Victor Hugo

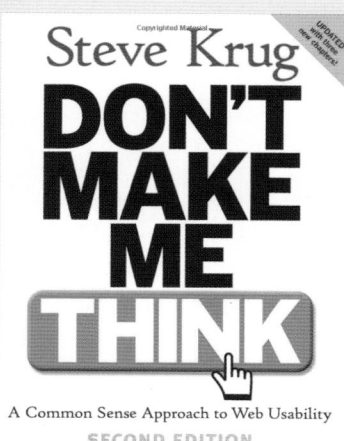

How to make your web site useable
Don't Make Me Think

$22 Steve Krug, 2005 (2nd edition), 216 p.

Here's a cure for badly designed web pages. (This is major news since everything is now on the web.) Follow Krug's key heuristic: "Don't make me think." It works. His manual is a model of what it preaches. It is the best, clearest, most succinct hands-on guide for amateurs and pros engaged in making the web a useable public space. You don't need a consultant; you need this book. I pray everyone reads and obeys.

-- KK

When you're creating a site, your job is to get rid of the question marks.

●

We don't read pages. We scan them.

●

Create a clear visual hierarchy. One of the best ways to make a page easy to grasp in a hurry is to make sure that the appearance of the things on the page — all of the visual cues — clearly and accurately portray the relationships between the things on the page.

●

Jakob Nielsen and Tom Landauer have shown that testing five users will tend to uncover 85 percent of a site's usability problems, and that there is a serious case of diminishing returns for additional users

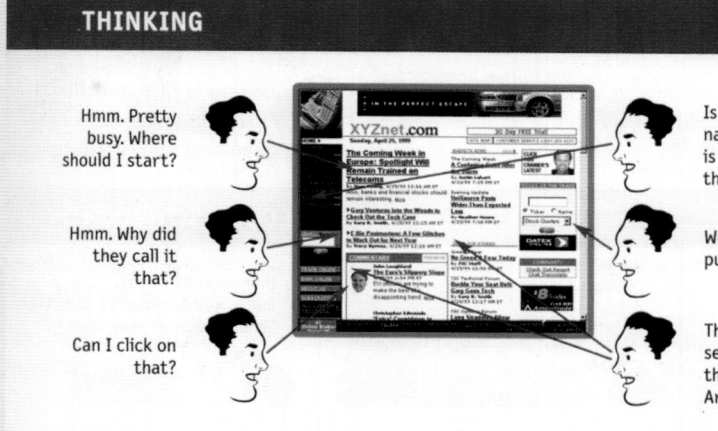

Best UX Guide
100 Things Every Designer Should Know About People

$20 Susan M. Weinschenk, 2011, 256 p.

This is the most helpful guide to user-interface design I've seen. It conveys what science knows about human behavior and how that should influence your design of a website or app. Why fight instincts? Here are 100 useable tips, explained, on taking advantage of the natural tendencies in the way our eyes, brains, and emotions work. Some of the 100 tips are common sense, and some are revelatory. Each is revealed with a principle, some examples, and a takeaway. I use this set as a kind of informal check-list of possibilities. As more of our life migrates to the web, it is ever more important to remember that design is about function, and not just good looks. This overlooked gem of a book encapsulates a lot of wisdom on how to make the functional work for people.

-- KK

●

People believe that things shown close together belong together

●

People process information better in bite-sized chunks

Applying the concept of progressive disclosure:

Progressive disclosure means providing only the information people need at the moment.

Progressive disclosure requires multiple clicks. You may have heard it said that Web sites should minimize the number of times that people have to click to get detailed information. The number of clicks is not important. People are very willing to click multiple times. In fact, they won't even notice they're clicking if they're getting the right amount of information at each click to keep them going down the path. Think progressive disclosure; don't count clicks.

Steven Palmer (1981) traveled around the world and asked people to draw a coffee cup. Figure 5.2 shows examples of what they drew.

What's interesting about these drawings is the angle and perspective. A few of the cups are sketched straight on, but most are drawn from a perspective slightly above the cup looking down, and offset a little to the right or left. This has been dubbed the canonical perspective. Very few people would draw a coffee cup as in Figure 5.3, which is what you'd see if you were looking at a coffee cup from above.

What most people drew when asked to draw a coffee cup.

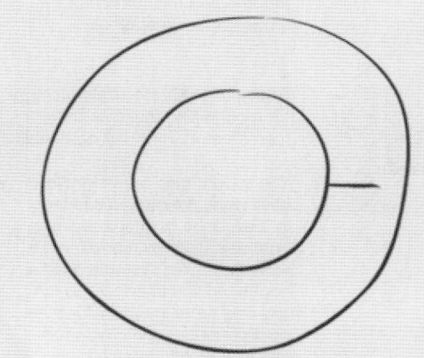

Most people don't draw a coffee cup like this.

●

People read faster with a longer line strength, but they prefer a shorter line length

Have you ever had to decide what column width to use on a screen? Should it be a wide column with 100 characters per line? Or a short column with 50 characters per line? Or something in between? The answer depends on whether you want people to read faster or to like the page.

Mary Dyson (2004) conducted research on line length, and combed other studies to determine what line length people prefer. Her work showed that 100 characters per line is the optimal length for on-screen reading speed; but we prefer a short or medium line length (45 to 72 characters per line).

●

Takeaways

Use concrete terms and icons. They will be easier to remember.

Let people rest (and even sleep) if you want them to remember information.

Try not to interrupt people if they are learning or encoding information.

Information in the middle of a presentation will be the least likely to be remembered.

51 ways to brainstorm
IDEO Method Cards

$49 IDEO Method Cards William Stout Architectural Books
$5 IDEO Method Cards iOS Application iTunes Store

The IDEO method cards are a great resource for people interested in finding new ways of thinking and brainstorming solutions. By picking a random card and following the prompts I have been amazed at the trail of thoughts that it helps to produce. As you work your way through more cards the ideas can become refined, and I have been impressed with the quality of practical ideas one can come up with (just don't forget to capture them somehow). The cards have four different categories including learn, look, ask, and try.

You can use the cards by yourself or in small groups. I have found that even shy people are empowered (and inspired enough) to contribute ideas. You definitely don't have to be an architect or a design expert to use them. This is definitely the best brainstorming tool I have seen. As a freelance Tamil journalist I use it to come with good story ideas. I can imagine small companies who can't afford costly consultants might be able to use the simple prompts to solve some of their problems. They definitely make innovation and brainstorming, whether radical or incremental, into a low hanging fruit. Just jump and give them a try!

-- Sadashiva M

Try

Predict Next Year's Headlines

How: clients project their company into the future, identifying how they develop/sustain customer relationship

Why: helps clients to define which design issues to pursue in product development

Tap twice to flip card:

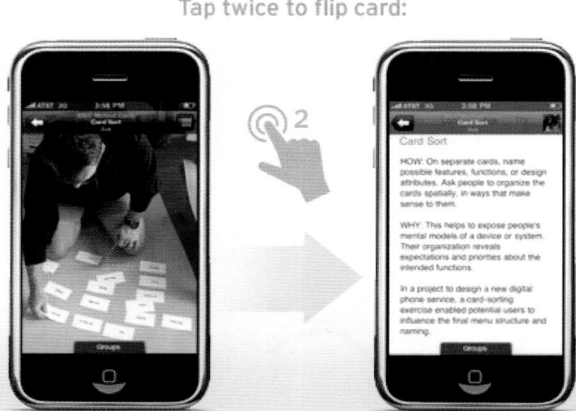

Design Principles

Universal Principles of Design

Practical design solutions

$17 William Lidwell, Kritina Holden, Jill Butler, 2010, 272 p.

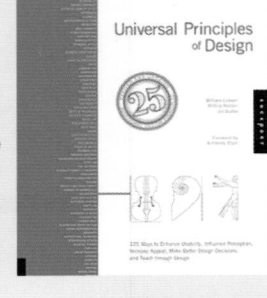

This is a fantastic catalog of design guidelines that apply to almost anything you might want to design. These 125 principles are not infallible rules, but rather recurring patterns that are found in the best designs. This tome is sort of a "pattern language" for industrial, graphic, and system designers. The different patterns can be combined and recombined in many ways. It will be most useful for engineers, architects, product designers, inventors and prototypers. It can be used in tandem with the previously reviewed *40 Principles*, which is a "pattern language" of engineering principles.

-- KK

Contour Bias: A tendency to favor objects with contours over objects with sharp angles or points.

...This seems consistent with the kind of innate response one would expect from potential threats and suggests a tradeoff between angular and contoured features: Angular objects are more effective at attracting and engaging thought; contoured objects are more effective at making a positive emotional and aesthetic impression.

◄ *From the top left to bottom right, the Alessi il Conico, 9093, 9091, and Mami kettles arranged form most angular to most contoured. At the extremes of this continuum, the il Conico will be most effective at grabbing attention, and the Mami will be most liked generally. The 9093 and 9091 incorporate both angular and contoured features, balancing attention-getting with likeability. Historically, the il Conico and 9093 are Alessi's best-selling kettles.*

Interference Effects: A phenomenon in which mental processing is made slower and less accurate by competing mental processes.

In populations that have learned that a traffic arrow always means go, the introduction of a red arrow in new traffic lights creates potentially dangerous interference.

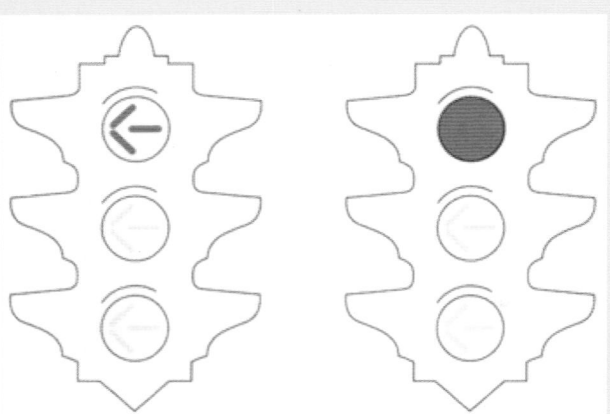

Law of Pragnanz: A tendency to interpret ambiguous images as simple and complete, versus complex and incomplete.

The law of Pragnanz is one of several principles referred to as Gestalt principles of perception. It asserts that when people are presented with a set of ambiguous elements (elements that can be interpreted in different ways), they interpret the elements in the simplest way. Here, "simplest" refers to arrangements having fewer rather than more elements, having symmetrical rather than asymmetrical compositions, and generally observing the other Gestalt principles of perception.

Therefore, minimize the number of elements in a design. Note that symmetrical compositions are perceived as simpler and more stable than asymmetrical compositions, but symmetrical compositions are also perceived to be less interesting. Favor symmetrical compositions when efficiency of use is the priority, and asymmetrical compositions when interestingness is the priority.

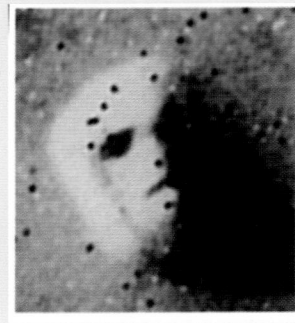
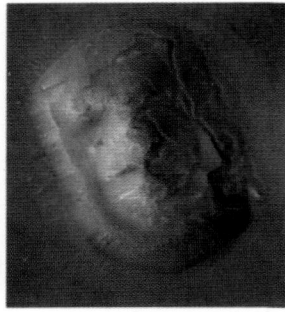

▲ *Low resolution images (let) of a rock formation on Mars led many to conclude that intelligent life once existed there. Higher-resolution images (right) taken some years later suggest a more Earth-based explanation: Humans tend to add order and meaning to patterns and formations that do not exist outside their perception.*

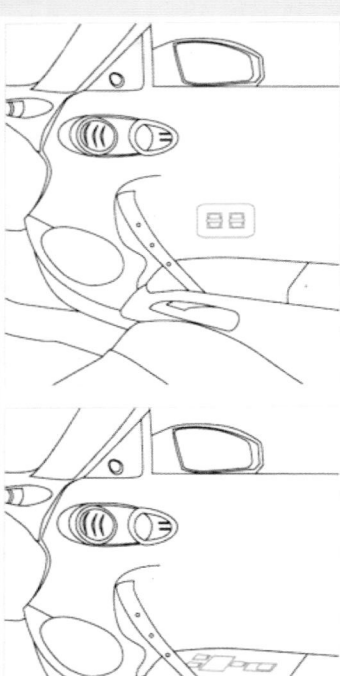

Mapping: A relationship between controls and their movements or effects. Good mapping between controls and their effects results in greater ease of use.

The relationship between the window control and the raising and lowering of the window is obvious when it is mounted on the wall of the door (good mapping), but ambiguous when mounted on the surface of the armrest (poor mapping).

Recognition Over Recall: Memory for recognizing things is better than memory for recalling things.

The advantages of recognition over recall are often exploited in the design of interfaces for complex systems. For example, early computer systems used a command line interface, which required recall memory for hundres of commands. The effort associated with learning the commands made computers difficult to use. The contemporary graphical user interface, which presents commands in menus, allows users to browse the possible options, and select from them accordingly. This eliminates the need to have the commands in recall memory, and greatly simplifies the usability of computers.

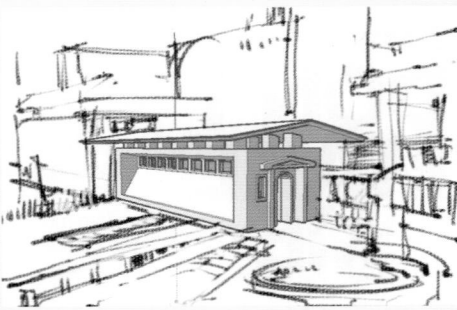

SketchUp

Superb design visualization tool

Free Google SketchUp SketchUp

This software is the opposite of CAD— Computer Aided Design— which is detail-driven. SketchUp gives you total flexibility messing with the FINAL look of something. You work directly with the vision you have, learn what's wrong or right with it, and keep trying variations or starting down new tracks.

You can flick details in and out. How about a corrugated steel roof on the house? No, try standing-seam metal, um, in red. Not bad. Could the pitch of the roof be steeper? That's better. Where should the chimney go? Here on the peak? No, put it over the wall corner for a corner fireplace. Going inside, how would a kiva fireplace look in that corner? It would be better if it was bigger, like that. Plop a couch in there for scale. Better move the doorway over a bit. Yeah that's good enough for now.

I came to this program because I was designing a house I want to build, and I could NOT draw a convincing hip roof. Suddenly with SketchUp I was drawing the whole house, and a basement, trees, and an adjoining building and visualizing the whole site with textured surfaces, in wireframe, in X-ray, with sun shadows, at night with lights on, in walk-through mode. I tried a clerestory my wife fancies and found that it probably wouldn't work with this design. I tried a house based on an existing barn's dimensions and found that wouldn't work either.

This is one powerful program, shockingly intuitive to use. It works for a lot more than buildings— landscapes, worlds. Video game designers use it. Architects use it but don't let their clients touch it for fear of being replaced. There's a whole online community of people creating new downloadable components and textures for it— humans, pets, kitchen sinks, cappuccino machines, beds, wallpapers, stones, masonries, cars, trees, fences, doors…

-- Stewart Brand

Design Thinking for Educators

Best guide to design process

Free IDEO, v.2, 2011, 81p.

designthinkingforeducators.com

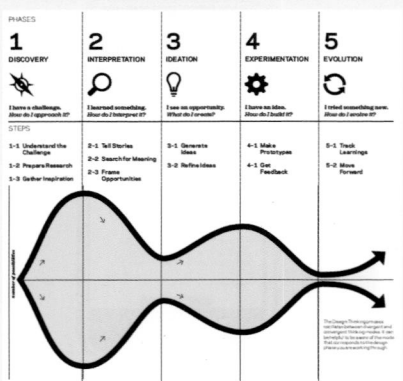

This is the best intro to design thinking, ever. For 30 years IDEO has pioneered a formal process for designing high tech and social products. Recently they crystalized their approach in order to teach it to K-12 students, and released the course as a free 80-page PDF. It is unusually clear, useful, and practical. Remarkably, while this step-by-step guide is aimed at kids, it's the best guide to design process I've seen for anyone. It would work perfectly for any organization or team taking on a design project for the first time.

-- KK

Think of extremes: Consider meeting people who represent "extremes:" people that are either completely familiar with and involved in your topic, or don't have anything to do with it. Extreme participants will help you understand unarticulated behaviors, desires, and needs of the rest of the population that they feel or express more powerfully than others.

Select what surprised you: Look across your buckets and themes and choose the information that you find most surprising, interesting, or worth pursuing. What have you learned that had not occurred to you before? What did you find most inspiring? What sparked the most ideas?

Make Insights Actionable Insights only become valuable when you can act on them as inspiring opportunities.

Ways to Prototype

Prototyping is not about getting it right the first time. The best prototypes change significantly over time.

Challenge yourself to come up with at least three different versions of your idea to test multiple aspects of the possible solutions your team has come up with

List constraints: Make a list of all the challenges and barriers you are facing with your idea. What are you missing? Who would oppose this idea? What will be most difficult to overcome? Put the list up on the wall so it is visible to the team. Remember, constraints are helpful for design.

RULES FOR BRAINSTORMING

Defer judgement. There are no bad ideas at this point. There will be plenty of time to narrow them down later.

Encourage wild ideas. Even if an idea doesn't seem realistic, it may spark a great idea for someone else.

Build on the ideas of others. Think "and" rather than "but."

Stay focused on topic. To get more out of your session, keep your brainstorm question in sight.

One conversation at a time. All ideas need to be heard, so that they may be built upon.

Be visual. Draw your ideas, as opposed to just writing them down. Stick figures and simple sketches can say more than many words.

Go for quantity. Set an outrageous goal— then surpass it. The best way to find one good idea is to come up with lots of ideas.

You can't say civilization isn't advancing, because in every war they kill you in a new way. - Will Rogers

◀ *Make a transition space between the street and the front door. Bring the path which connects street and entrance through this transition space, and mark it with a change of light, a change of sound, a change of direction, a change of surface, a change of level, perhaps by gateways which make a change of enclosure, and above all with a change of view.*

building to the north

outdoors south

▲ *Always place buildings to the north of the outdoor spaces that go with them, and keep the outdoor spaces to the south. Never leave a deep band of shade between the building and the sunny part of the outdoors.*

Each creates the transition with a different combination of elements.

the more obvious,the more it shouts, the sooner it will fade. Gradually it will become part of the building, like the wallpaper; and the intensity of its beautify will no longer be accessible to the people who live there.

Therefore:

If there is a beautiful view, don't spoil it by building huge windows that gape incessantly at it. Instead, put the windows which look onto the view at places of transition–along paths, in hallways, in entry ways, on stairs, between rooms.

If the view window is correctly placed, people will see a glimpse of the distant view as they come up to the window or pass it; but the view is never visible from the places where people stay.

●
Balconies and porches which are less than six feet deep are hardly ever used.

▲ Everybody loves window seats, bay windows, and big windows with low sills and comfortable chairs drawn up to them.

It is easy to think of these kinds of places as luxuries, which can no longer be built, and which we are no longer lucky enough to be able to afford.

In fact, the matter is more urgent. These kinds of windows which create "places" next to them are not simply luxuries; they are necessary. A room which does not have a place like this seldom allows youth feel fully comfortable or perfectly at ease. Indeed, a room without a window place may keep you in a state of perpetual unresolved conflict and tension–slight, perhaps, but definite.

Design heuristics

A Pattern Language

$40 Christopher Alexander, Sara Ishikawa, Murray Silverstein, 1977, 1171 p.

Don't go to architecture school; devour this book instead and use it to design buildings and places that really work. This 1,000-page encyclopedia contains two hundred design patterns found in the buildings and cities that people love. For instance, pattern number 167: "Balconies and porches less than 6 feet deep are hardly ever used." Therefore make balconies wider than 6 feet. Each pattern is what computer programmers call a heuristic: a compressed principle that can be unpacked in many ways. Each pattern is illustrated with exemplary examples and photos, and sociological evidence from studies of real places.

Employ this book to design attractive, timeless buildings (or towns) by combining as many of these patterns as can be consistently contained in one project. Does the house have a hat? An obvious central entrance? A transition zone between public and private? All these are eternal patterns that have worked in the past and will make a place better. First published 45 years ago by Christopher Alexander and team, this book has influenced tens of thousands of architects and urban planners who credit it with giving them tools to make buildings and towns that operate at human scale.

I used this pattern language to design our own house and my studio and both are structures that people love to be in. Among the many fancy homes I have visited, my three favorites are houses designed by the owners using Alexander's pattern wisdom. These spaces are comfortable, humane, inviting, and the structures treat inhabitants intelligently.

In both format (patterns) and content (timeless wisdom) this is a core text for anyone building anything at human scale. The idea of a pattern language is now used in other design fields, including software design.

-- *KK*

●
A building cannot be a human building unless it is a complex of still smaller buildings or smaller parts which manifest its own internal social facts.

●
Ceiling Height Variety

A building in which the ceiling heights are all the same is virtually incapable of making people comfortable.

In some fashion, low ceilings make for intimacy, high ceilings for formality. In older buildings which allowed the ceiling heights to vary, this was almost taken for granted.

●
Pools of Light

Uniform illumination–the sweetheart of the lighting engineers–serves no useful purpose whatsoever. In fact, it destroys the social nature of space, and makes people feel disoriented and unbounded.

●
On no account place buildings in the places which are most beautiful. In fact, do the opposite. Consider the site and its buildings as a single living eco-system. Leave those areas that are the most precious, beautiful, comfortable, and healthy as they are, and build new structures in those parts of the site which are least pleasant now.

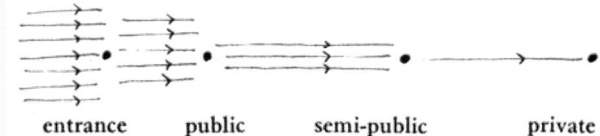

entrance   public   semi-public   private

▲ *Lay out the space of a building so that they create a sequence which begins with the entrance and the most public parts of the building, then leads into the slightly more private areas, and finally to the most private domains.*

●
A Buddhist monk lived high in the mountains, in a small stone house. Far, far in the distance was the ocean, visible and beautiful from the mountains. But it was not visible from the monk's house itself, nor from the approach road to the house. However, in front of the house there stood a courtyard surrounded by a thick stone wall. As one came to the house, one passed through a gate into this court, and then diagonally across the court to the front door of the house. On the far side of the courtyard there was a slit in the wall, narrow and diagonal, cut through the thickness of the wall. As a person walked across the court, at one spot, where his position lined up with the slit in the wall, for an instant, he could see the ocean. And then he was past it once again, and went into the house.

What is it that happens in this courtyard? The view of the distant sea is so restrained that it stays alive forever. Who, that has ever seen that view, can ever forget it? Its power will never fade. Even for the man who lives there, coming past that view day after day for fifty years, it will still be alive.

This is the essence of the problem with any view. It is a beautiful thing. One wants to enjoy it and drink it in every day. But the more open it is,

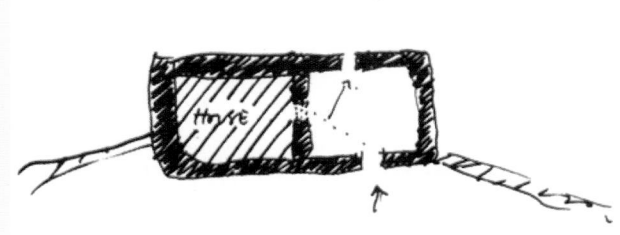

The monk's house.

● *Bed Alcove*

Bedrooms make no sense.

Don't put single beds in empty rooms called bedrooms, but instead put individual bed alcoves off rooms with other non sleeping functions, so the bed itself becomes a tiny private haven.

●
Now, try to imagine how, on your particular site, you can establish this pattern. Stand on the site with your eyes closed. Imagine how things might be, if the pattern, as you have understood it, had suddenly sprung up there overnight. Once you have an image of how it might be, walk about the site, pacing out approximate areas, marking the walls, using string and cardboard, and putting stakes in the ground, or loose stones, to mark the important corners.

While you are imagining how to establish one pattern, consider the other patterns listed with it. Some are larger. Some are smaller. For the larger ones, try to see how they can one day be present in the areas you are working on, and ask yourself how the pattern you are now building can contribute to the repair or formation of these larger patterns.

Oblique Strategies

Useful dilemma prompt cards; a portable oracle
Oblique Strategies
$50 Oblique Strategies: One Hundred Worthwhile Dilemmas, 5th Edition cards Eno Shop

Web version
obliquestrategies.ca

How to get unstuck:

Pick a card at random from this deck of 100 and either 1) do what it says or 2) let it lead you to another idea. It's amazingly effective. This handsomely boxed stack of cards was created by the lateral genius Brian Eno and good friend Pete Schmidt in 1975 to get themselves and other musicians unstuck in the studio. It's been through four updated editions since.

I use this tool in any design situation to think differently. In life I've found it more productive than throwing the I-Ching or staring at the wall.

The cards on this fifth edition are printed on heavy silky stock and will pop your rut. The deck is a significant, weighty artifact. It urges you to linger and make drawing a card a ritual.

Or, you can click on over to several unofficial web sites where a button will reveal a random card on the screen. My favorite site is obliquestrategies.ca and is easy enough to bookmark. It sits right there only a click away. What to do? Let's see, it says "Abandon normal instructions."

But the most convenient form of Oblique Strategies is a phone app. The official iPhone version is no longer available and the substitute one won't randomize. But the Android version is easy and well-done.

I am so enamoured of this portable oracle that I've been collecting my own small set of instructions. I've mixed mine in with the Eno/Schmidt set, to produce this small selection below.

-- KK

Permit the unacceptable	**Remove ambiguities and convert to specifics**	**Ask people to work against their better judgment**
Call your mother and ask her what to do	**Do nothing for as long as possible**	**Use "unqualified" people**
Enlarge the doubt	**Humanize something that is free of error**	**Make a pause valuable by putting it in an exquisite frame**
Faced with a choice, do both	**Imagine the piece as a series of disconnected events**	**Do something boring**
Try faking it	**Fill every beat with something**	**Don't stress one thing more than another**
Do it like a robot would	**Return to the first sketch**	**Use fewer notes**
Remove the mystery	**Take away elements in order of apparent non-importance**	**Discover the recipes you are using and abandon them**

All progress depends on the unreasonable man. - George Bernard Shaw

▲ *British WWI dazzle-painted ship model*

How to hide with wit
False Colors: Art, Design and Modern Camouflage
$20 Roy R. Behrens, 2002, 223 p.

An exhilarating kaleidoscope of artists fooling around, making visual puns, tricking society, and conjuring up novel solutions – all tucked into the margins of this astonishing untold history of military camouflage. I had no idea that both Picasso and Matisse assisted their navies in designing new camouflage patterns. This collection of visual wit is really a how-to book on the best way for serious people to employ artists. "Oh God, as if we didn't have enough trouble! They sent us artists!" – American Army Officer, World War I

-- *KK*

"Salle and her boyfriend, who is a surrealist, staged a weird performance in Hyde Park (in June 1939, at the outset of World War II), reading bits out of Alice in Wonderland and the telephone directory, but the police thought it was some sort of code and took it all down." – Joan Wyndham, Lessons: A Wartime Diary, p. 79.

"There is only one difference between a madman and me. I am not mad." – Salvador Dali

► *WWI American soldier with a papier-mâché head on a stick, used to draw the enemy's fire.*

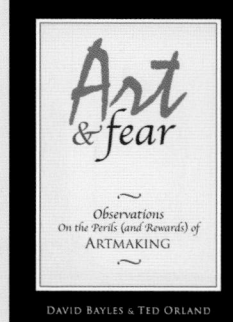

Hand-drawn metamorphosis in which Beethoven becomes a clarinet

Why to do art
River and Tides
$10 Thomas Riedelsheimer, 2001, 90 min.

This is one of the best films about art, by one of our best living artists, Andy Goldsworthy. Any number of great artists could serve as a focus, but I recommend this documentary because it demonstrates more than anything else I've seen that art is process not product. Drift into Goldsworthy's dreams as he summons temporary monuments -- an arc of icicles, a train of flowers, a hive of sticks -- from bits of leaves, twigs, rocks, ice and mud. He makes things you could easily make -- if only you saw the world as he does -- and if only you decided it was worth a day to make them. By the end of this beautifully lyrical film, you DO begin to share Goldsworthy's mystical vision of a world swimming in energy and flows. My favorite moment: when he despairs as his painstakingly constructed pieces fail before they are finished. But a little later, after he tries again, he watches in boyish glee as they naturally fall apart. There's an angelic sweetness about that switch. THAT is what art is about. That IS art.

(Since Goldsworthy sees his photographs of his creations as essential to his art, a gallery of his best work is available in several books. The best one to start with is *Andy Goldsworthy: A Collaboration with Nature*.)

-- *KK*

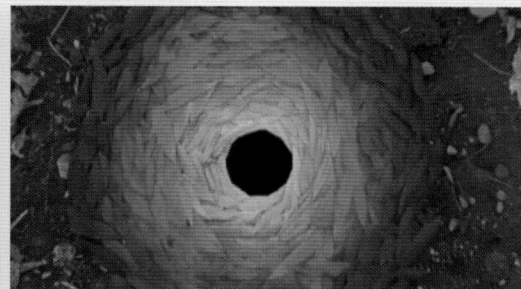

Best advice on how to do art
Art & Fear
$11 David Bayles & Ted Orland, 2001, 122 p.

Astoundingly brilliant (and blessedly short). Easily the keenest insight into making art that I've ever read. One continuous aahhaaa.

-- *KK*

• This book is about making art. Ordinary art. Ordinary art means something like: all art not made by Mozart. After all, art is rarely made by Mozart-like people – essentially (statistically speaking) there aren't any people like that. But while geniuses may get made once-a-century or so, good art gets made all the time. Making art is a common and intimately human activity, filled with all the perils (and rewards) that accompany any worthwhile effort. The difficulties artmakers face are not remote and heroic, but universal and familiar.

• Art is made by ordinary people. Creatures having only virtues can hardly be imagined making art. It's difficult to picture the Virgin Mary painting landscapes. Or Batman throwing pots. The flawless creature wouldn't need to make art.

• Making art and viewing art are different at their core. The sane human being is satisfied that the best he/she can do at any given moment is the best he/she can do at any given moment. That belief, if widely embraced, would make this book unnecessary, false, or both. Such sanity is, unfortunately, rare. Making art provides uncomfortably accurate feedback about the gap that inevitably exists between what you intended to do, and what you did. In fact, if artmaking did not tell you (the maker) so enormously much about yourself, then making art to you would be impossible. To all viewers but yourself, what matters is the product; the finished artwork. To you, and you alone, what matters is the process: the experience of shaping that artwork. The viewers' concerns are not your concerns (although it's dangerously easy to adopt their attitudes.) Their job is whatever it is: to be moved by art, to be entertained by it, to make a killing off it, whatever. Your job is to learn to work on your work.

• The function of the overwhelming majority of your artwork is simply to teach you how to make the small fraction of your artwork that soars. One of the basic and difficult lessons every artist must learn is that even the failed pieces are essential.

• Artmaking has been around longer than the art establishment. Through most of history, the people who made art never thought of themselves as making art. In fact it's quite presumable that art was being made long before the rise of consciousness, long before the pronoun "I" was ever employed. The painters of caves, quite apart from not thinking of themselves as artists, probably never thought of themselves as artists at all! What this suggests, among other things, is that the current view equating art with "self-expression" reveals more a contemporary bias in our thinking than an underlying trait of the medium. Even the separation of art from craft is largely a post-Renaissance concept, and more recent still is the notion that art transcends what you do, and represents what you are.

In the past few centuries Western art has moved from unsigned tableaus of orthodox religious scenes to one-person displays of personal cosmologies. "Artist" has gradually become a form of identity which (as every artist knows) often carries with it as many drawbacks as benefits. Consider that if artist equals self, then when (inevitably) you make flawed art, you are a flawed person, and when (worse yet) you make no art, you are no person at all! It seems far healthier to sidestep that vicious spiral by accepting many paths to successful artmaking – from reclusive to flamboyant, intuitive to intellectual, folk art to fine art. One of those paths is yours.

• Those who would make art might begin by reflecting on the fate of those who preceded them: most who began, quit. To survive as an artist requires confronting these troubles. Basically, those who continue to make art are those who have learned how to continue – or more precisely, have learned how to not quit.

• The truth is that the piece of art which seems so profoundly right in its finished state may earlier have been only inches or seconds away from total collapse. Art is like beginning a sentence before you know its ending. The risks are obvious; you may never get to the end of the sentence at all – or having gotten there, you may not have said anything. This is probably not a good idea in public speaking, but it's an excellent idea in making art.

• Talent, in common parlance, is "what comes easily." So sooner or later, inevitably, you reach a point where the work doesn't come easily, and – Aha!, it's just as you feared! Wrong. By definition, whatever you have is exactly what you need to produce your best work. There is probably no clearer waste of psychic energy than worrying about how much talent you have -and probably no worry more common. This is true even among artists of considerable accomplishment.

• A brief digression in which the authors attempt to answer (or deflect) an objection:

Q: Aren't you ignoring the fact that people differ radically in their abilities?

A: No.

Q: But if people differ, and each of them were to make their best work, would not the more gifted make better work, and the less gifted, less?

A: Yes. And wouldn't that be a nice planet to live on?

• The ceramics teacher announced on opening day that he was dividing the class into two groups. All those on the left side of the studio, he said, would be graded solely on the quantity of work they produced, all those on the right solely on its quality. His procedure was simple: on the final day of class he would bring in his bathroom scales and weigh the work of the "quantity" group: fifty pound of pots rated an "A", forty pounds a "B", and so on. Those being graded on "quality", however, needed to produce only one pot -albeit a perfect one – to get an "A". Well, came grading time and a curious fact emerged: the works of highest quality were all produced by the group being graded for quantity. It seems that while the "quantity" group was busily churning out piles of work – and learning from their mistakes – the "quality" group had sat theorizing about perfection, and in the end had little more to show for their efforts than grandiose theories and a pile of dead clay.

• Art is human; error is human; ergo, art is error. Inevitably, your work (like, uh, the preceding syllogism) will be flawed.

• What you need to know about the next piece is contained in the last piece.

• Filmmaker Lou Stouten tells the painfully unapocryphal story about hand-carrying his first film (produced while he was still a student) to the famed teacher and film theorist Slavko Vorkapitch. The teacher watched the entire film in silence, and as the viewing ended rose and left the room without uttering a word. Stouten, more than a bit shaken, ran out after him and asked, "But what did you think of my film?" Replied Vorkapitch, "What film?"

The lesson here is simply that courting approval, even that of peers, puts a dangerous amount of power in the hands of the audience. Worse yet, the audience is seldom in a position to grant (or withhold) approval on the one issue that really counts – namely, whether or not you're making progress in your work. They're in a good position to comment on how they're moved (or challenged or entertained) by the finished product, but have little knowledge or interest in your process. Audience comes later. The only pure communication is between you and your work.

3D Printing

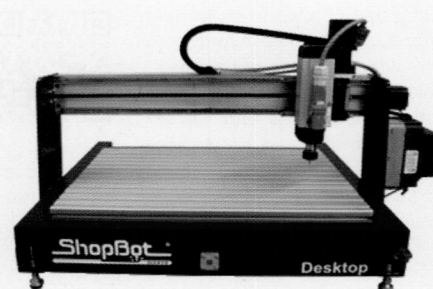

Programmable 3D router
ShopBot
$5,000 ShopBot Tools

The ShopBot is a low-cost CNC, or computer controlled router. Think of it as a large-scale milling machine. It is great for small-scale production runs of machine parts in wood or metal. A friend of mine used his ShopBot to cut the gears and mechanism (other than the chime) for a full-scale replica of a grandfather's Clock. ShopBots (and their kin) can also fabricate extremely detailed 3D contour maps (whole cities!), and other intricate 3D surfaces.

We have one at the design school I teach at. It can cut anything programmable like the hull plates for a full scale sailboat. On a big boat, each plate of the hull is a different shape, but the ShopBot just

follows its orders and spits them out ready to install. It is very accurate. Hey, you can even equip it with a pen or the like, which permits very intricate drawings. The cheapest Shopbot is the small Shop Bot Desktop for $5,000. They are getting cheaper every year, but if you only need one occasionally, you can buy time on one at shared workshops like Techshop.

– J. Baldwin

I work at Stanford's design school — called the d.school. We designed and made much of the furniture we used in our new building space in Google's Sketchup and machined the material using a 4' x 8' ShopBot owned and operated by Rob Bell. The process was very fast, and relatively cheap. ShopBot + Sketchup allowed us to do many cycles of design/build/test, which ultimately yielded some very refined artifacts.

I have also used a Shop Bot while working with a podiatrist who practices as a foot surgeon. The folks in his practice spent a lot of time hand-crafting custom orthotics and insoles, which was very inefficient. Because of my experience at Stanford I realized that the high spindle speed of a wood router could effectively cut the medical grade foam he used in his orthotics. I modeled insoles in CAD (using Solidworks) and we purchased a 4'x8' ShopBot PRS Alpha to cut 20-30 pairs of insoles out of 4'x8' foam sheets. We even-

tually upgraded to a much smaller benchtop ShopBot and installed it in his practice. We reduced machining time to about 15 minutes.

ShopBot has a very strong user community and were always very responsive with tech support. The price of this computer controlled milling machine and modeling software is best of all. It would have been previously inaccessible to a private practice physician even a few years earlier.

-- Dave Baggeroer

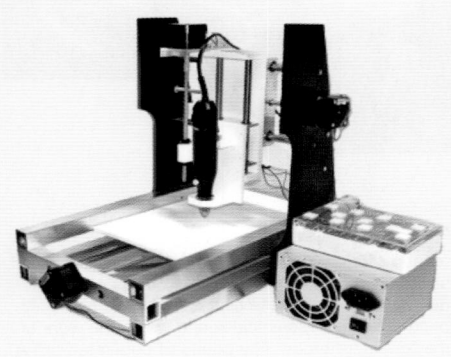

Desktop CNC machine
MyDIYCNC
$590 MyDIYCNC

I'm just getting into desktop CNC. It's the essential element in scaling up from 3D printing to injection molding. The tools are five years (or more) behind 3D printing in ease of use (in part because CNC is an order of magnitude more complex) but it's a field on the brink of a consumer reinvention, just like 3D printing was in 2007.

I use a MyDIYCNC, with MeshCAM software. It's small but a cheap way to start, $590 fully assembled.

The previously reviewed Shopbot CNC has a much bigger build area than the MyDIYCNC. We use our little one for things like making Warhammer battlefields (carved out of foam) based on downloaded videogame maps. Mostly just silly stuff for now, while we're learning how to use it.

I would advise people to wait until the USB interface is standard. Mine is a USB, but it's a beta unit. Works fine, but the version on the website still is based on an archaic parallel port (!!!) cable. I'm telling you, CNC is the land time forgot....

-- Chris Anderson

CAD for kids
Tinkercad
Free trial, or $19/month for personal account Tinkercad

If you want to introduce a kid (or yourself!) to CAD (computer aided design), Tinkercad is by far the easiest and most fun way to begin. Today I mentioned to my 10-year-old that our CNC machine would soon be up and running. He asked what a CNC could do, and I said one example would be to carve a battlefield out of stiff foam for Warhammer figures.

That got his attention. He wanted to know how to tell the CNC what to do. I explained a bit about CAD, and showed him Tinkercad, giving the example of one cube that you could stretch and change.

Then I got busy with something else and left him to figure out Tinkercad himself. I came back an hour later and below is what he'd designed. A ten-year-old. No training. One hour.

The green stuff we're going to CNC out of a sheet of stiff foam. The rest we'll probably 3D print on the Makerbot. It will take a weekend, but this could be our first 100% digital craft project.

This is an example of what I talk about in Makers: manufacturing technologies are getting so easy and cheap (even free) that anyone can use them. Kids today can grow up as fluent in CAD as they are in everything else on computers. Democratizing the tools of publishing brought us the Web. Just imagine what democratizing the tools of manufacturing will do.

We've used the previously reviewed Sketchup and Autodesk 123D, and both are great. But Tinkercad just runs in your Web browser and its simple interface disguises a very sophisticated cloud-based CAD engine.

-- Chris Anderson

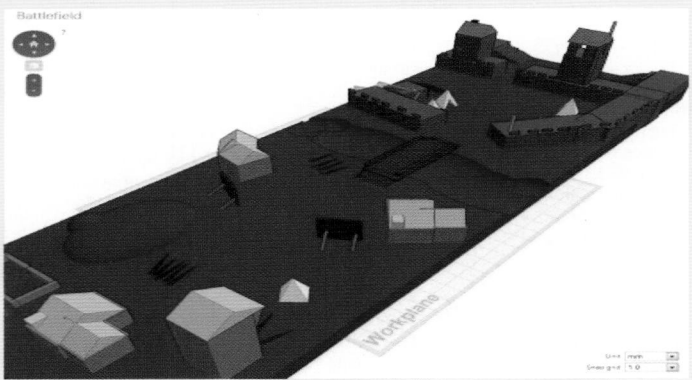

Cheapest 3D scanner
Matterform
$583 Matterform

Part of the 3D printing revolution requires being able to scan an object you want to print. Perhaps you scan it in 3D to merely copy it, or perhaps to use the scan as a basis for modification for your own designs or needs. Until now 3D scanners have been large and expensive. The Matterform is a consumer-level 3D scanner that Make magazine calls the best buy as of 2013. It is relatively inexpensive, and will scan an object as large as a half-gallon of milk, with a decent (but not spectacular) resolution. In the picture above, compare its beta scan of a Dristan bottle with the original. For many purposes this machine will give you good-enough 3D files.

-- KK

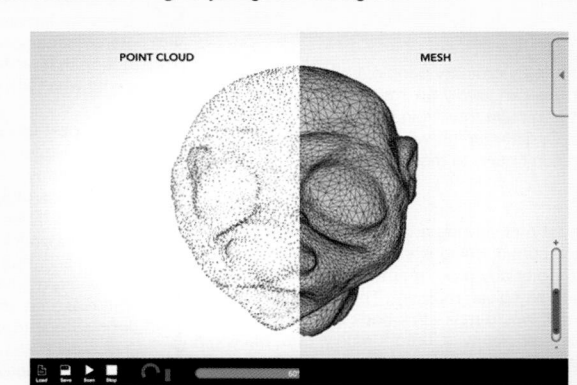

Best 3D printing guide
Ultimate Guide to 3D Printing
$7 Maker Media

3D printing allows you to make a small complex object from a digitally composed file using a 3D printer. However 3D printing technology is changing so fast that Cool Tools can't recommend a specific printer. The best we can do is to point you to people who are seriously tracking this corner of the technium.

By far the best guide to the rapidly emerging world of 3D printing is this special issue of *Make* magazine. This timely guide will spell out the differences in 15 home printers now available, and steer to you the best stock materials to use, the design software options you have, and even how to use 3D print services instead of buying your own (soon to be outdated) machine. Included is a whole chapter on the brand new art of how to scan existing objects so they can be replicated. Their comprehensively researched and test 3D printer buyer's guide is worth thousands of dollars in savings. The 114-page guide is impressively well done, brilliantly illustrated with diagrams and instructive photos, tons of tips and inspiring projects, and will answer 99% of the first questions any beginner will have, while constantly pointing you to the websites and experts generating even more recent information. I hope they keep this excellent tool updated. (Mark Frauenfelder, now editor of Cool Tools, was editor-in-chief of *Make*).

-- KK

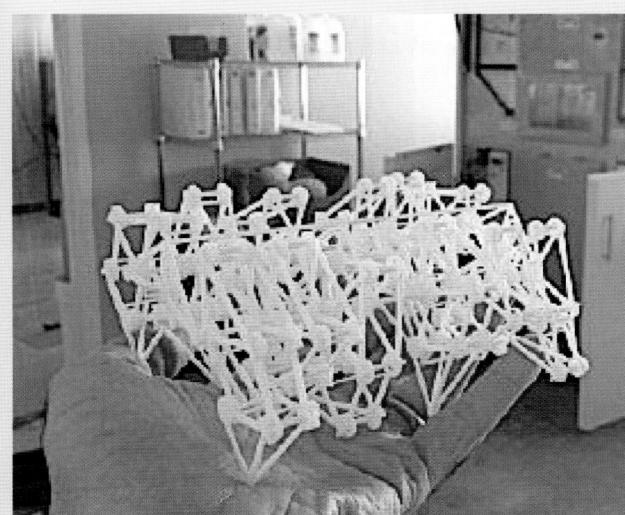

A Strandbeest mechanism by Theo Jansen, printed in nylon on an EOS selective laser sintering (SLS) machine at Shapeways headquarters in New York. Dust it off and it's ready to walk.

A word of warning: when buying a turnkey printer, be wary of "razor vs. blades" business models. 3D printers exist that are seemingly cheap, but which require proprietary filament cartridges, where the consumable filament costs two to three times the going market rates.

Generating STL files – STL files are the lingua franca of the 3D printing world. If an application can export a 3D model as an STL file, then that STL file can be sliced and printed. STL files can be generated using a CAD program. SketchUp is quite popular, as are a number of open source 3D modelers. On Mac OS X, Autodesk has released Inventor Fusion, which combines significant power with a relatively easy-to-use package. Both are free.

Ponoko offers 3D printing in a wide range of materials, from plastics and ceramics to stainless steel, gold plate, and Z Corp plasters. They also offer laser cutting and CNC routing in a huge variety of materials, so you can supplement your 3D-printed project with other custom parts. Prints from Ponoko are generally very good quality and reasonably priced, but their pricing structure and system for uploading models are confusing. They do have a very good support staff who will go above and beyond to help you with any questions. Ponoko operates several regional production facilities, so printing and shipping times vary.

PLA (polylactic acid or polylactide) is a biodegradable plastic typically made from corn or potatoes. PLA filament is extruded at a lower temperature of 160°C–220°C and does not require a heated bed (painter's tape is just fine). When heated, PLA smells a bit like sweet, toasted corn. PLA tends to be stiffer than ABS. While PLA does not require a heated bed, it can warp a bit during cooling, something that a heated bed can greatly improve. Note that there is a "flexible PLA" variant that, while trickier to use, will result in objects that are squishy.

Slicing/CAM Software — Once you have a manifold, error-free 3D model, it must be converted into specific toolpath instructions that tell the printer where to move the hot end, when to move it, and whether or not to extrude plastic along the way. This process is sometimes referred to as skeining or slicing. The standard format for these instructions is a

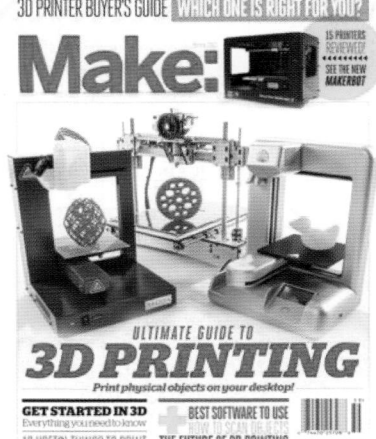

simple programming language called G-code. Historically, most printers have relied on the open source Skeinforge engine for preparing G-code from model files. Recently, however, alternative slicing programs have started appearing, most notably Slic3r, which has been slowly overtaking Skeinforge as the tool of choice.

10 Coolest Objects

McCormick D326 Tractor
Juan Esteban Paz
The detail on this model is amazing.
thingiverse.com/thing:29669

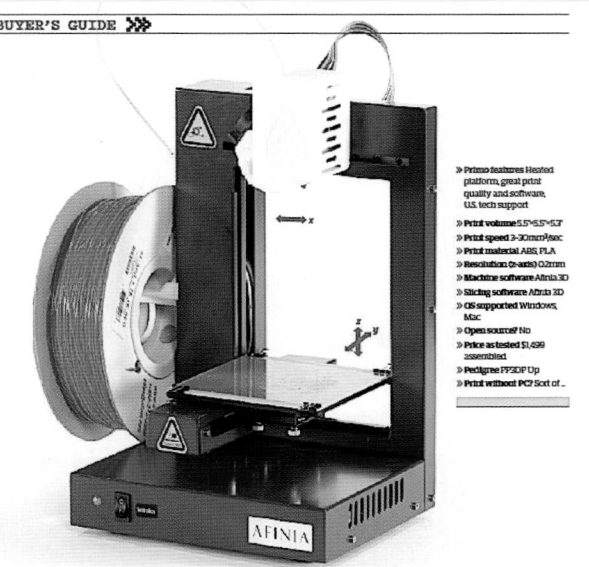

» Primo features Heated platform, great print quality and software, U.S. tech support
» Print volume 5.5"x5.5"x5.3"
» Print speed 3-30mm/sec
» Print material ABS, PLA
» Resolution 0-.xxb0 0.2mm
» Machine software Afinia 3D
» Slicing software Afinia 3D
» OS supported Windows, Mac
» Open source? No
» Price as tested $1,499 assembled
» Pedigree PP3DP Up
» Print without PC? Sort of...

Afinia H-Series
Microboards Technology afinia.com
Easy to use, with feature-rich software and impressive print quality.

Thingiverse
thingiverse.com

Thingiverse is a swap meet for exchanging digital files for 3D printing of tiny objects, like the stuff for doll houses. You download a file and print out the object using the previously reviewed Makerbot or 3D printing service. Eventually, the objects will be larger, and the selection larger, and you'll be able to print out complex things. For now, 3D printing is a thrilling hobby, and this exchange site is a real tool for model makers.

-- KK

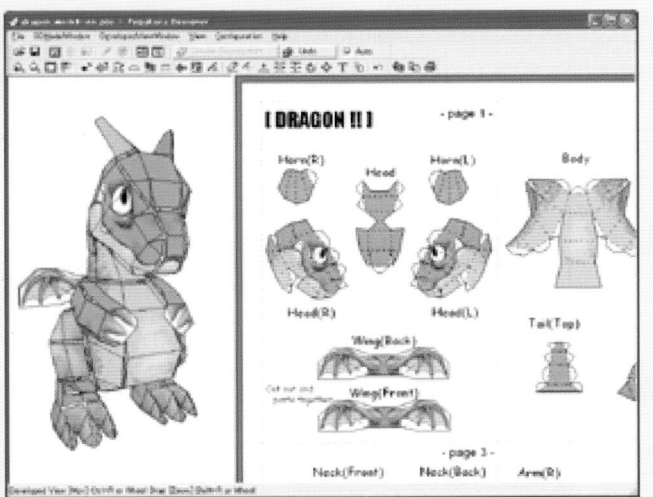

[DRAGON !!]
- page 1 -

Horn(R)   Head   Horn(L)   Body

Head(R)   Head(L)

Wing(Back)   Tail(Top)

Wing(Front)

Neck(Front)   Neck(Back)   Arm(R)

- page 3 -

Paper 3D-printer
Pepakura
$38 Tamasoft

A great complement to "Sketchup" is a handy little product from Japan, "Pepakura". This tool creates a printable, origami-like pattern from which 3D models may be translated into paper "reality".

Here at the University of Texas, I write 3D games that deliver educational content for middle-school children. I use Sketchup as the starting point in my workflow for all the 3D buildings and many of the other objects that the kids move through, as they navigate within their virtual world. For $38, this gadget allows me to push my models through a color printer — I fold the output and paste a few ends together with a gluestick, and I have something to hand to the kids as an incentive when they finish the program. They think it's neat to hold something in their hands that they had just been interacting with in the virtual world.

-- Charlie

Cybernetics

Guide to systems logic
Systemanitcs

$23 John Gall, 2003 (3rd Edition of Systemantics), 316 p.

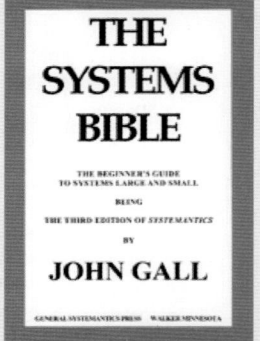

Originally published as *Systemantics*, the pun in the title carries the important message that systems have "antics" — they act up, misbehave, and have their own mind. The author is having fun with a serious subject, deciding rightly that a sense of humor and paradox are the only means to approach complexity. His insights come in the form of marvelously succinct rules of thumb, in the spirit of Murphy's Law and the Peter Principle. This book made me 1) not worry about understanding a colossal system — you can't, 2) realize I can change a system — by starting a new one, and 3) avoid starting new systems — they don't go away.

The lesson is that whatever complexity you are creating or have to work with -- a website, a company, a robot, a tribe, a platform -- is a system that will over time exhibit its own agenda. You need to understand the basic laws of systems, which this perennial book (now in its third edition) will cheerily instruct you.

-- KK

COMPLEX SYSTEMS EXHIBIT UNEXPECTED BEHAVIOR.

- A complex system that works is invariably found to have evolved from a simple system that worked. The parallel proposition also appears to be true: A complex system designed from scratch never works and cannot be made to work. You have to start over, beginning with a working simple system.

- We begin at the beginning, with the Fundamental Theorem: New systems mean new problems.

- The system always kicks back—Systems get in the way—or, in slightly more elegant language: Systems tend to oppose their own proper functions.

- Systems tend to malfunction conspicuously just after their greatest triumph. Toynbee explains this effect by pointing out the strong tendency to apply a previously successful strategy to the new challenge. The army is now fully prepared to fight the previous war.

WHEN BIG SYSTEMS FAIL, THE FAILURE IS OFTEN BIG.

Error avoidance tips
Mistake-Proofing

Mistakes are NOT inevitable, but the logical consequences of remediable design. As such, it's so much easier to avoid them than to correct them, especially if each one becomes a link in a chain of events that go off the rails as a result. If I'd continued in academia, perhaps eventually chairing a department, I'd buy as many copies of this book as there were members of my department — faculty, residents, nurse anesthetists, medical students. It's slim (72 pages) and easy to understand — no formal process(es) to follow. Instead, the book provides several seemingly simplistic but very useful rules of thumb anyone can adopt. As Chase & Stewart write: "You don't need a Ph.D. in statistics to apply it. In reality, mistake-proofing is more like a structured form of common sense." For example: "The key to creating mistake-proofing devices and procedures is not to do too much at once. Instead, concentrate on clever, inexpensive methods to check for only one mistake at a time. If you have two possible mistakes, develop two separate devices or procedures to catch them." Right on!

-- Joseph Stirt

- The best way to ensure the detection of a mistake is to make sure that something in the environment makes it very obvious that one has been made. A good example of an environmental cue is the inevitable "extra" parts that remain after a do-it-yourself repair project. These parts make it very clear that you have not reassembled the item correctly.

- Machine mistakes, being generally mechanical in nature, are better understood than human mistakes. They are, therefore, more predictable and easier to control. If we look closely at the different types of machine mistakes, we see that they fall into two categories: those mistakes we can see coming and those that catch us unaware.

- Employees experience a continuous stream of encounters – one defect is a low failure rate. Customers experience a single defect as a 100% failure rate.

- Toyota, which is very experienced at mistake-proofing, averages about twelve devices for each machine.

- Go/No-Go gauges are not limited to the shop floor. Customers often use such gauges to detect and prevent mistakes.

Some amusement park rides require riders to be above a certain height (so they do not slip through the safety restraints) or below a certain height (to keep larger people off of rides meant only for small children). Parks do not want customers to discover they are too small or large after waiting in a potentially very long line. By placing a gauge at he front of the line, customers can tell if they are tall enough (or short enough) to go on the ride without waiting in line.

- Mistakes are random events and therefore we must continuously watch for them. Sampling is not good enough. It looks at only a small proportion of the outputs in a process.

- Most importantly, mistake-proofing is the only method we know that includes customers' actions in the quality control system. The importance of this is emphasized by one study that estimates that customers of services are responsible for one-third of the problems they complain about.

- Remember that the goal is to develop clever, simple and inexpensive devices. Don't immediately opt for the high-tech solution.

$16 Richard B. Chase & Douglas M. Stewart, 2008, 72 p.

$16 download Lulu

Lateral strategies for innovation
40 Principles

This overpriced book contains a set of 40 design strategies for inventing. It is a summation of engineering design principles devised by a Soviet patent examiner in the 1960s who extracted these principles from a study of 200,000 patents. This guy, Altshuller, says that the 10% most innovative patents would use one of these 40 strategies for their novel solutions. Altshuller then went on to construct a system to help engineers consider these elemental strategies for the problems they were working on. His system is called TRIZ, and it has a cult following among process engineers. I like to think of it as Oblique Strategies for engineers.

To employ the system you apply a principle (from the list) at random to the problem, no matter how unlikely, in the hope that this lateral mode of thinking will hatch a novel solution. The best inventors combine these heuristics intuitively, and many veteran engineers have their own set which they have developed over the years. But if you are just starting out as an architect, tinkerer, engineer, hacker, designer, and do-it-yourselfer, you may find this a good place to start. I did, and have already added to the 40 some additional heuristics that work for me.

You can find the entire text of the 40 Principles posted on the TRIZ website; the only advantage of the book are some crude drawings and handy reference format. However I did find the small additional illustrations and real world examples helpful in grokking the often cryptic rules.

-- KK

$55 Genrich Altshuller, 2005, 144 p.

40 Principles

TRIZ Keys to Technical Innovation
By Genrich Altshuller

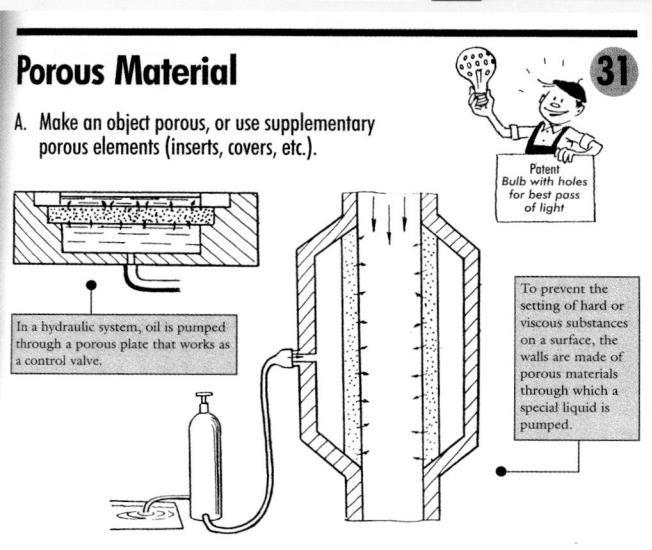

Porous Material
31

A. Make an object porous, or use supplementary porous elements (inserts, covers, etc.).

In a hydraulic system, oil is pumped through a porous plate that works as a control valve.

Patent Bulb with holes for best pass of light

To prevent the setting of hard or viscous substances on a surface, the walls are made of porous materials through which a special liquid is pumped.

B. If an object is already porous, fill pores in advance with some substance.

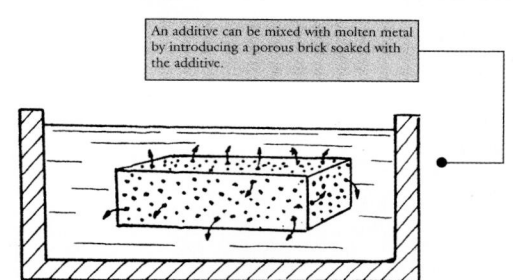

An additive can be mixed with molten metal by introducing a porous brick soaked with the additive.

85

Life must be understood backward. But . . . it must be lived forward. - Soren Kierkegaard

How to add a second unit
In-laws, Outlaws, and Granny Flats
$17 Michael Litchfield 2011, 218 p.

The advantages of having an extra place for guests or relatives to stay are pretty obvious. And more so today as parents live longer, kids remain at home after graduating, and renting a unit helps your paycheck. But actually building an in-law, granny flat, or guest studio on your property is neither easy nor obvious. I know from the experience of building two different in-law apartments in our homes that the design, permitting, and construction hurdles are serious. This book is chock full of very practical tips, great advice, and plenty of real world examples. Because in-laws, converted garages and guest cottages, are by definition small and compact, you'll need the kind of efficient design tips offered here. I can't think of a similar or better source of help that would be useful from the moment you start fantasizing about adding a second unit, till you apply for permits (or not), and finish the last coat of paint. And BTW, if you ever dream about building your own house, even with hired hands, adding an in-law is a great way to practice your contracting skills.

-- *KK*

●
Bump-outs have great appeal because they conserve yard space and, because they adjoin the house, there's one less wall to build. If you want to create a living space for an elderly parent or a caregiver, they'll be right on the other side of the wall.

Carve-outs are even more intimate. Created by carving out a suite of rooms within a house, they are the least expensive and least disruptive type of in-law to build. Close off an interior door or two, add soundproofing, install a kitchenette, and, voila, a second home.

Living in an attic in-law can be a great adventure for the right person. Sloping roofs, skylights, quirky nooks, and long views create an inherently romantic, cozy living space. Because of the stairs involved, though, such units are probably best suited to a younger person, or at least someone with strong legs and a good back.

Most municipalities will allow you to convert an old garage to another use. But often you must first create new parking spots to replace the ones lost by the conversion.

●
When there's a living space above a garage, getting the details right is important for health and safety. Your local building authority has the final say, but the following tips can help make your unit a safer, more pleasant place to be:

Install fire-resistant (Type X) drywall on garage walls and ceilings. The thicker the panel, the higher its fire rating; a thickness of 5/8 in. is often specified. On walls and ceilings between a garage and living space, fire codes may require two layers of Type X drywall.

Egress Well Details

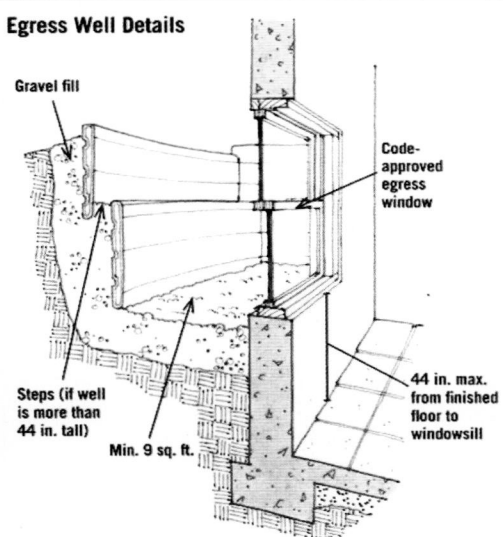

- Gravel fill
- Code-approved egress window
- Steps (if well is more than 44 in. tall)
- 44 in. max. from finished floor to windowsill
- Min. 9 sq. ft.

Spray insulation is a good choice to insulate the floors of in-law units over garages. It seals cracks and effectively deadens the transmission of sound.

Install a motion-sensor exhaust system to clear the garage of noxious fumes. Typically an exhaust fan starts when a car pulls in or out, and runs until a timer switch shuts it off.

●
Older people appreciate the lack of steps going from indoors to outdoors, but completely flat and level surfaces aren't' ideal. Place patios at least 2 to 3 in. below the level of interior floors. Otherwise, water collecting on the patio could run inside the house and cause water damage. In addition, slope patios gently away from the building at a rate of 1/16 in. to 1/8 in. per lineal foot so they'll drain properly.

●
To enable occupants to exit quickly in case of a fire, building codes require a method of escape--egress--for sleeping rooms on every level of the house, including the basement. Because egress windows must also be large enough to allow a fully equipped firefighter to enter, codes specify the

Attic Conversion Design Issues

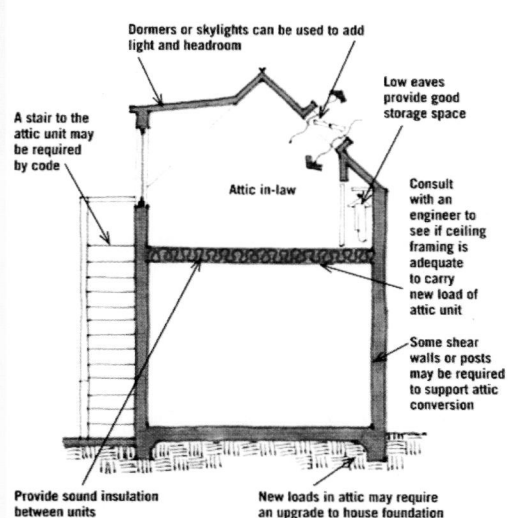

- Dormers or skylights can be used to add light and headroom
- Low eaves provide good storage space
- A stair to the attic unit may be required by code
- Attic in-law
- Consult with an engineer to see if ceiling framing is adequate to carry new load of attic unit
- Some shear walls or posts may be required to support attic conversion
- Provide sound insulation between units
- New loads in attic may require an upgrade to house foundation

size of the egress - typically at least 20 in. wide and at least 24 in. tall, with a combined net-clear opening of at least 5.7 sq. ft.

To make it possible to clim out of an egress window, codes generally specify a maximum sill height of 44 in. above the floor, although a 32-in. sill height seems more reasonable if there are kids or elders present. (Check your local codes; some require two egress points for basement in-laws.) Installing an egress window in a concrete foundation all is a job for a pro and may require the installation of an egress well.

●
Most of the time, wastes flow freely out of a house via downward-sloped drains. All it takes is gravity. If, however, you have a basement unit whose drainpipes are below the city sewer main, you'll need to pump wastes up to the main. This can be achieved by using a sewage ejection pump or a macerating toilet unit.

Sewage ejection pumps can be used with standard toilets. If the floor is concrete, you must first cut a slot in it and then excavate a trench large enough to accommodate drainpipes and a sewage-holding tank. (You can rent a concrete-cutting saw but it's a miserable DIY task; hire a concrete-cutting specialist instead.) In the bottom of the tank is a pump that propels sewage up to the sewer main via a 2-in. or 3-in. discharge pipe rising from the top of the tank.

ATTIC CONVERSION

PROS

- Space-conserving choice, appropriate for a small lot
- If there is adequate headroom, conversion may be economical
- If enough windows and skylights, can feel light-filled and spacious
- Well-suited to adult child living at home, younger renter

CONS

- Can be the most expensive and complicated in-law to build
- Noise can bother people living downstairs
- Codes may require second egress
- Stairs are difficult for older people or those with mobility problems
- It can be difficult to provide adequate heating, cooling, and ventilation

---

Bargain, super easy online real estate
Redfin

This website/service can save you ten thousand dollars or more when you buy a house in certain cities. It is an online real estate broker that rebates 2/3rds of the usual agent sales commission back to you. Since you are probably doing most of the hard work in research, looking, and evaluation while shopping for a house anyway, why pay a real estate agent? On the other hand, there's a lot of paperwork, regulations, and legal issues you really don't want to handle, and a qualified agent should. So this is how Redfin works.

Redfin has a great online real estate website which we quickly found is one of the easier ones to use, with nice virtual walk thrus of each home, and good comparison data for the neighborhood. (The site is a joy to navigate, and we'd use it even if we did not get a rebate. And they have phone apps.) Then you, in the role of buyer and self-agent, do all the footwork of finding, visiting the various homes, checking out the disclosures, etc., and finally choosing which property you want. You are your own real estate agent up to this point. When you are ready to make on offer on a home, you do so online via Redfin, completing the necessary forms on the web. Then a human Redfin employee will take you through the final paperwork and signatures, and eventually visit the house with you. At the close of the deal they will rebate 2/3rds of their buyer agent commission paid by the seller, or 2% of the sale price, which in some areas of the country will mean at least ten thousand dollars.

We used this recently to purchase a home in the Bay Area and saved $15,000 this way. That is, after we closed the deal at the agreed-to price with the seller, Redfin gave us a check for $15K, in effect reducing our cost of the house by 2%. In our book that was enough to make the deal work.

The current drawback? This service is only available in about 35 metro regions in the US. I have no experience in using Redfin in selling a house, although they claim you can save a similar amount.

-- KK

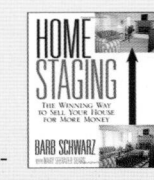

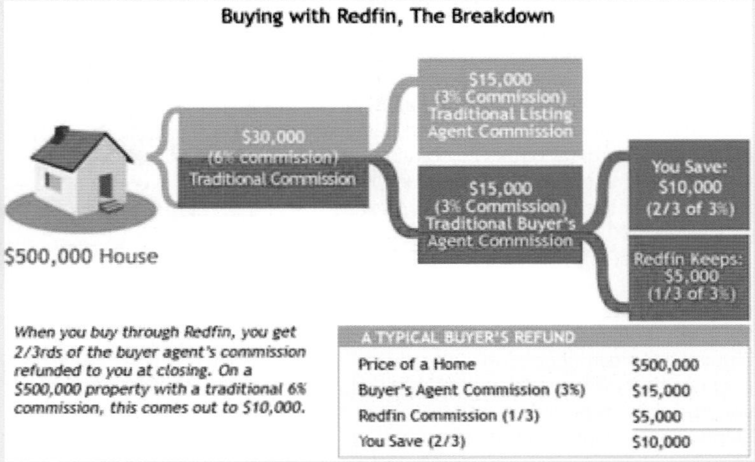

Buying with Redfin, The Breakdown

$500,000 House — $30,000 (6% commission) Traditional Commission → $15,000 (3% Commission) Traditional Listing Agent Commission / $15,000 (3% Commission) Traditional Buyer's Agent Commission → You Save: $10,000 (2/3 of 3%) / Redfin Keeps: $5,000 (1/3 of 3%)

When you buy through Redfin, you get 2/3rds of the buyer agent's commission refunded to you at closing. On a $500,000 property with a traditional 6% commission, this comes out to $10,000.

A TYPICAL BUYER'S REFUND

Price of a Home	$500,000
Buyer's Agent Commission (3%)	$15,000
Redfin Commission (1/3)	$5,000
You Save (2/3)	$10,000

Optimizing the selling price of your home
Home Staging
$14 Barb Schwarz, 2006, 212 p.

A couple of times in your life you may need to sell a house. If you do, try to remember the advice in this book. It could be worth several thousands of dollars for a few hours of your time. The message is simple: when it comes time to sell your home, strip it of all the things that make it a personalized home, and turn it into a bland product that can be personalized by someone else. This book, the best of about half a dozen on the same theme, provides simple ideas on how to reduce your home to a house. The same philosophy also applies to rental property.

-- KK

●
Staging is not decorating. Decorating means personalizing your space; staging is depersonalizing it. Staging is not about the ruffles you love or your favorite color rug. Staging is about getting a property sold. Decorating is optional. Staging is mandatory.

With personalized clutter.

●
The way you live in your home and the way you sell your house are two different things. If you're one of those people who doesn't know what clean really is, ask a persnickety friend to come over and point out things that need attention.

●
My Staging mantra is "Less is more." You're selling your space, not your stuff. All those little tchotchkes? Pitch 'em, pack 'em, but whatever you do, put them away or out of sight.

In marketplace terms, your house is merchandise. In Hollywood terms, your house is the set. You're Staging it to look appealing, just like the set in a movie. Your favorite television show has a set you remember and connect with. Your house is a set too.

Staged, without personalized stuff.

I do not know which makes a man more conservative - to know nothing but the present, or nothing but the past. - John Maynard Keynes

115

Handmade homes

How to build a DIY house
Tiny Homes
$18 Lloyd Kahn, 2012, 228 p.

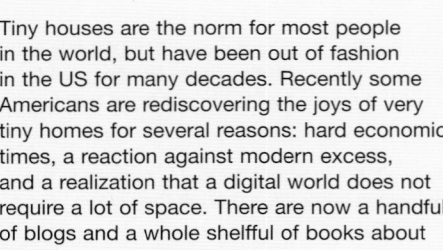

This book will convince you to build your own house. The key is to make it small. A really small house costs less, liberates time, and encourages you to spend that time making the details personal. Because everything is scaled down, the space is much more customized. The result is a home that grows out of your life.

Tiny houses are the norm for most people in the world, but have been out of fashion in the US for many decades. Recently some Americans are rediscovering the joys of very tiny homes for several reasons: hard economic times, a reaction against modern excess, and a realization that a digital world does not require a lot of space. There are now a handful of blogs and a whole shelfful of books about tiny homes. Mostly good stuff.

This new book is the best of those guides and eclipses the previously recommended *The Tiny Book of Tiny Houses*. Lloyd Kahn has built several of his own small homes, and has edited a number of great books celebrating owner-built shelters, including *Home Work*. Here he focuses on tiny homes, which he defines as shelters 500 square feet or less. Some are on wheels, a few float, some are pre-fab, but most are handmade shelters placed in odd corners in cities, suburbs and the country. Their variety is stunning. This large book erupts with a cornucopia of 1,300 photos featuring 150 different tiny homes, showing you how they were built, giving resources and helpful tips of their construction, supplying design solutions and inspiration for others, but also conveying WHY they were built. Tiny though they are, they are much more than mere shelter.

What I love most about this book -- as a tool -- is the way it explodes the possibilities of what a tiny house can be, and how every page conveys the important message that the challenge in building such a tiny structure is not the material, which is almost trivial by definition, but the immaterial. A tiny home is a matter of gumption, resourcefulness and imagination. This book, like all Lloyd Kahn's work, cultivates those virtues.

You leave the book realizing, knowing for sure, that you, yes you, can build a tiny house. And should.

-- KK

•

[This 97 sq. ft. house] was originally a pump house built over a well in 1900. At some point in the '70s it was converted to a chicken coop. A couple of years ago I converted it to a stationary yacht. The design was inspired by living on a small sailboat in Alaska. It's superior to a sailboat in that it needs less maintenance, is unlikely to sink, has lots of windows, and is surrounded by a garden so you don't need to row ashore. It's inferior to a sailboat in that it can't sail anywhere.

The theme of our eco-resort has always been Adirondack Style, which translates to "built with time and no money." Each year we renew our contract with the state to harvest "dead and down trees." It's like building structures in the middle of Mother Nature's lumberyard.

▲ The key to designing my happy home was designing a happy life, and the key to that lay not so much in deciding what I needed but in recognizing all the things I could do without.

▶ The pentagonal floor is made from lumber milled on site. At center is a pentagon. On Mike's birthday, October 29, a beam of light shines through a hole in a 5-pointed star in the door, and falls on the central pentagon!

▼ I did a quick sketch of what I needed.

▲ It is not a building. It's MY building.

Guide to west coast DIY shelters
Builders of the Pacific Coast

I've lived on the California coast all my life, so I'm no stranger to homegrown architecture. I've driven by geodesic domes tucked into canyons and hiked passed shack-like mini-mansions perched on solitary hilltops. These encounters have always been brief and, most notably, from afar. As he did with *Home Work*, Lloyd Kahn takes us inside the structures many of us wouldn't and couldn't even stumble upon. From Northern California all the way up to British Columbia, he brings us the coastal creations of more than a dozen builders. Driftwood saunas and stairwells, wave-like green roofs, bright wide-eyed yurts, hand-carved pillars and more. A wonderful collection of imagination and possibility.

--Steven Leckart

$18 Lloyd Kahn, 2008, 256 p.

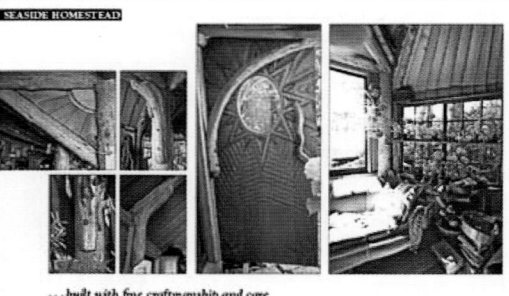

...built with fine craftmanship and care

....a magical homestead built mostly out of driftwood

© 2008 Shelter Publications, from *Builders of the Pacific Coast* by Lloyd Kahn

© 2008 Shelter Publications, from *Builders of the Pacific Coast* by Lloyd Kahn

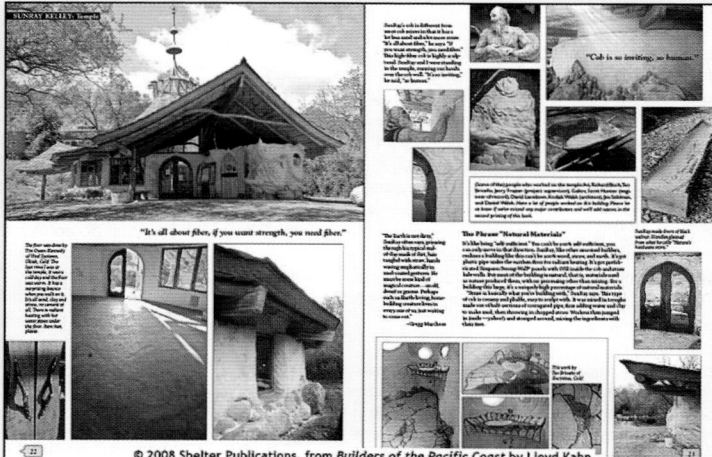

© 2008 Shelter Publications, from *Builders of the Pacific Coast* by Lloyd Kahn

Don't confuse a clear view of the future with a short distance. - Paul Saffo

Why to build your own home
Home Work
$18 Lloyd Khan, 2004, 256 p.

Imagine you were about to build your own home, perhaps with your own hands, and you wanted a few ideas of what others have done, so you set out around the world for 40 years visiting unusual homes, snapping pictures, making notes, and gathering evidence of homes that serve as a personal extension of the people living in them -- the kind of home that is most satisfying both for the owner and for their guests -- the kind of home you want.

You don't have to do that now because Lloyd Kahn has done it for you. For far less in cost, and probably with far more effectiveness, Lloyd has collected homes that work for people. He has crammed a life-time of photos, notes, and insights into this amazing catalog, overflowing with wild, zany, practical ideas, hard-won evidence of successful homes in all cultures, chock-full of amazing glimpses of genius homes, owner-built glories, unique, one-of-a-kind, offbeat, think-different, homes, mindful places, sketches of long-gone shelters, bits of building wisdom, and actual how-to-advice, all offered visually, in vast color plates, at a modest price for such an intense and dense tome. The entire aim of this book is to expand your notion of what your own house could be. It works.

At least once in their life everyone should make their own shelter. This is the book I would hand to them.

Here is how I think *Homework* compares with the other inspirational home books I have recommended here: *Architecuture Without Architects* is timeless, *Built by Hand* is global, *Home Work* is contemporary and personal.

Just build it.

-- KK

▲ The yurt shown here is Bill's home in the Maine woods. It is 54' (eaves) in diameter and was designed so it could be built over a period of several years and still provide shelter during the process. It is a tri-centric, or three-ring yurt with 2700 sq. ft. of floor space. You can first build the 16' inner core as a room to move into. In the second stage, you can build the large sheltering roof over a gravel pad, allowing the major cost, floor construction, to be delayed. In the meantime you have a spacious area under the roof that can be used for a workshop, greenhouse, garage, or for play.

Straw

▲ Reception room of Save the Children Office Building, frescoed lime plaster [over straw bale] walls. Blue color comes from azul anil, a blue pigment commonly found in the Dulcerias or candy stores.

◄ The "honey house" by builders Kaki Hunter and Doni Kiffmeyer in Moab, Utah. This dome/vaulted structure was constructed from earth-filled sandbags and plastered with earth and lime plasters.

Highly-evolved home design
Architecture Without Architects
$25 Bernard Rudofsky, 1964, 128 p.

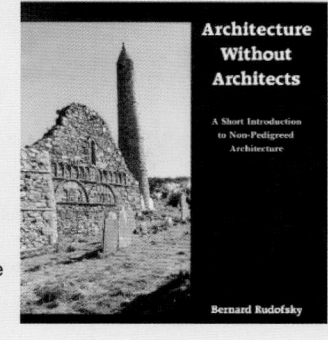
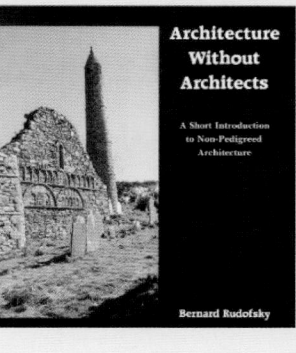

The granddaddy of all books about hand-built homes is the legendary *Architecture Without Architects*. Fifty years in print, it continues to inspire architects, despite its title. Savor it slowly as a black and white poem on what a house might be if you had two thousand years to refine it. These shelters have visible souls. They honor your hands and mind. I consider this small book to hold essential wisdom that no high-schooler should graduate without encountering.

-- KK

One of the most radical solutions in the field of shelter is represented by the underground towns and villages in the Chinese loess belt. Loess is silt, transported and deposited by the wind. Because of its great softness and high porosity (45 percent), it can be easily carved. In places, roads have been cut as much as 40 deep into the original level by the action of wheels. In the provinces of Honnan, Shansi, Shensi, and Kansu about ten million people live in dwellings hollowed out from loess.

Best of vernacular buildings around the world
Built By Hand
$10 (Kindle) Steen, Steen, and Komatsu, 2004, 480 p.

Without qualification, this is the greatest account of vernacular architecture, indigenous shelter, and traditional folk-built home images ever published. And it won't likely be surpassed, since fanatical photographer Yoshio Komatsu spent 25 years traveling the globe to document the full jaw-dropping variety of shelter on earth. He's been EVERYWHERE. I can't think of a remote region of Asia, Africa, South American and Europe that he missed; most of the styles are new and stimulating to me, and I've been around. While *Architecture Without Architects* hints dreamily at this diversity, *Built By Hand* completes the thought by explicitly celebrating this abundance in vivid in-your-face technicolor. It's in a different league from all previous vernacular architecture books. This one is a stupendous 480-page cornucopic tome overflowing with 700 photographs, and thousands of details, hopes, and design ideas. Totally breathtaking, totally awesome! If this doesn't get you to grab a hammer, nothing will.

-- KK

Moula, Cameroon. Arched earthen doorway.

Sumba, Indonesia. Four main posts provide the structural support in this building, and bamboo is used for everything else. Symbolically, the tall section of the roof is for God, the middle space for man, and the ground level for animals.

Renovation

Complete house building know-how
Renovation
$35 Michael Litchfield, 2012, 624 p.

This is a book I wished I'd had when I started building, but it is also one that's extraordinarily useful to more experienced builders. Mike Litchfield was the original editor of *Fine Homebuilding*; in 1982 he published the first version of *Renovation*, and it's been updated periodically, this being the latest and 4th edition. *Popular Science* called it "The most comprehensive single volume on renovation ever" — which is totally true.

What differentiates this book from others of its ilk is that the author has gathered all this information in the field, interviewing carpenters, electricians, plumbers, and contractors, finding out what's important, what works, what's new. These guys love to talk about what they do well, and in this sense, the book is one of collective wisdom. It's at the same time highly useful to professionals, but also one that's invaluable for homeowners and people of the fixer-upper persuasion.

The chapter "Planning Your Renovation" is completely new, reflecting the current interest in smaller projects, spending wisely, and energy efficiency. The chapter on wiring covers code changes, and tells you things like how to fish wire, install wireless switches, or replace old incandescent ceiling lights with energy-efficient LEDs.

There's a section on installing IKEA cabinets, tips and instructions on energy retrofits, working with paperless drywall (in wet areas), soundproofing, cutting into a concrete floor, working with PEX plumbing tubing, and installing engineered flooring. I found myself flipping through the book at random, and learning a lot.

-- *Lloyd Kahn*

Submanifold System

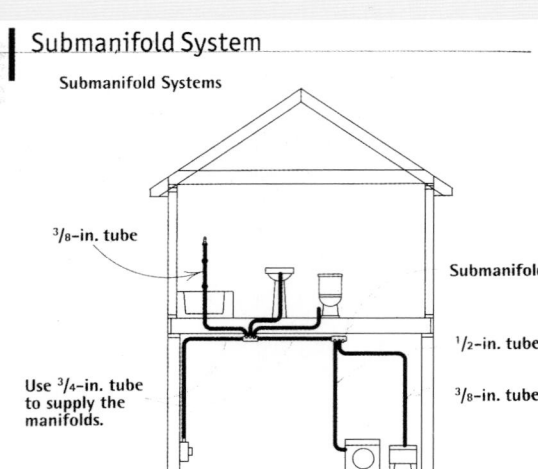

Submanifold Systems

$^3/_8$-in. tube

Submanifold

$^1/_2$-in. tube

$^3/_8$-in. tube

Use $^3/_4$-in. tube to supply the manifolds.

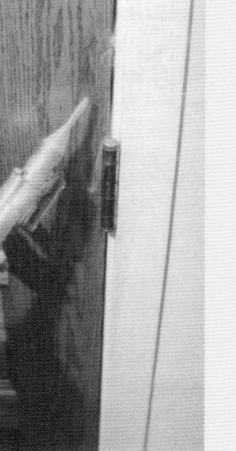

A smoke pencil helps make air leaks visible.

Patching Cracked Plaster

Plaster   Lath

Plaster washer

$^1/_8$-in. recess

Spade bit

Cracked plaster often means that it has pulled free from its lath. Use screws and plaster washers to reattach it, countersinking them so they'll be easier to patch.

Bottom leg of groove removed

To insert a replacement board into an existing tongue-and-groove floor, use a tablesaw to remove the bottom of the groove. Slightly back-cut the ends of the new board so it will slide in easier.

Subfloor

Trim on older buildings is rarely level or parallel. Thus new trim maybe look better if it's installed slightly out of level so that it aligns with what's already there. For example, when stretching a chalkline to indicate the bottom of the water table, start level and then raise or lower the line until it looks right in relation to nearby windowsills and the like. Once the chalkline looks more or less parallel to existing trim, snap it on the building paper, and extend it to corner boards.

Avoiding Direct Sun

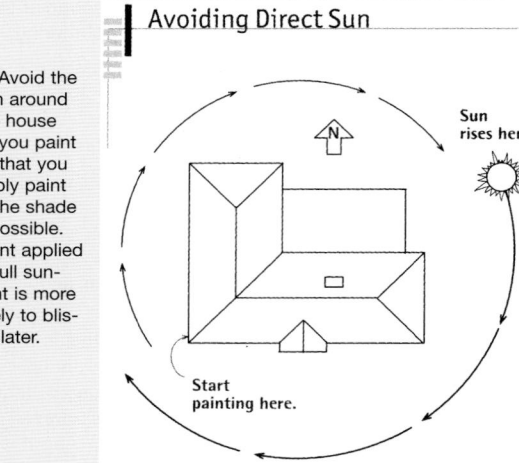

► Avoid the sun around the house as you paint so that you apply paint in the shade if possible. Paint applied in full sunlight is more likely to blister later.

N

Sun rises here.

Start painting here.

Making adaptable shelter
How Buildings Learn
$24 Stewart Brand, 1995, 252 p.

HOW BUILDINGS LEARN
What happens after they're built
STEWART BRAND

Every building that endures will be modified. Yet few structures are built to be easily modified. The more stylized a building is now, the harder it is to change. Stewart Brand (who invented the ancestor of Cool Tools) teases out design principles for making buildings that can adapt -- or "learn" -- to new needs, new uses. While his examples are architectural, showing how the greatest buildings evolve, his advice is aimed at any kind of hard-to-change organization. Software programmers think this book is talking to them since they are often asked to adapt skyscrapers of code built with no concern about adapting it later. This book will be useful to anyone trying to build complicated things that will outlive them.

-- *KK*

▲ **PEX Advantages**

It installs quickly. Because lengths of flexible tubing easily turn corners and snake through walls, PEX systems require far fewer connections and fittings than do rigid materials. For that reason, it's particularly well suited to renovation work.

Fewer leaks. PEX tubing runs to fixtures from hot- and cold-water manifolds with multiple takeoffs. Most of the fitting is simple, consisting of crimping steel or copper rings onto tubing ends. Because most leaks occur at joints, fewer fittings also mean fewer leaks.

It's quiet. The tubing expands slightly, minimizing air hammer– the banging that takes place in rigid piping when taps are turned off suddenly and running water stops abruptly. That ability to expand also means less-pronounced pressure drops (fewer scalding or freezing showers), and PEX tubing is less likely to rupture if water freezes in it.

The beauty of working with PEX is that it required relatively few specialized tools. An inexpensive PEX-cutting tool with a replaceable blade produces a clean, squared-off end.

1900 - The church of San Estaban at Acoma was begun by Fray Juan Ramirez after his arrival as the mission padre in 1629. The construction labor took ten years.

ca. 1915 - An attempt at restoration in 1902 produced blocky bell towers. Earlier known restorations occurred in 1710 (when the bells date from) and 1810. The loggia in the foreground is part of the convent attached to the church.

Share

ca. 1940 - A group of Anglo preservationists called the Society for the Restoration and Preservation of New Mexico Mission Churches raised money to restore the church and put Santa Fe architect John Gaw Meem in charge of the project. The work ran from 1924 to 1930, employing Acoma labor. For structural as well as aesthetic reasons Meem designed a slight batter (slope) in the bell tower walls, which were rebuilt of stone set in adobe mortar.

Modified geodesic dome
Hexayurt

Free

The hexayurt is an update on Buckminster Fuller's geodesic dome and is a sturdy, affordable, easy-to-build temporary shelter. The geometry has been adjusted slightly to make it easier to build domes from materials like plywood, insulation, plastic, cardboard and more. The hexayurts are made from only one kind of triangle: an 8' x 8' isosceles triangle, rather than the strangely-shaped triangles which are standard for Fuller-style geodesic domes. They are not strictly geodesic, either, but it doesn't seem to matter much in practice. The slightly stiff, angular lines look a lot like any other dome.

The most common place to see hexayurts is at Burning Man. The first one was built there in 2003, and was only a little bigger than a tent. There now range in size from 50 to nearly 500 square feet. A typical year at Burning Man will see a hundred or so of the silver huts lined up on the playa.

The design is public domain and build-it-yourself. People using the shelter for Burning Man usually buy the materials (about $300) ahead of time, including mail ordering the hard-to-find extra wide tape which is used to hold the shelter together. It takes about a day's worth of effort to cut out the roof pieces, playa-proof the edges and do a test assembly. Putting the hexayurt together on the playa typically takes a small group of people about two hours and can be a struggle if there is wind or a dust storm which coats all the pieces in a fine layer of tape-defeating dust.

The joy of the thing is a building which stays relatively cool in the desert. The shiny surface of the hexayurt reflects away a lot of the sun's heat, and a mix of pump sprays, swamp coolers and even the occasional air conditioner make the inside quite habitable even in the middle of the day when tents are far too hot for comfort. There are lots of plans and instructional videos on the Hexayurt web site, and handy people seem to have little difficulty putting them up.

A few simpler units, made from plywood, have been tested by local charities in Sri Lanka and Haiti. The jury is still out on whether this shelter will be useful beyond recreational use in the desert, but field trials are underway.

-- Howard Rheingold and Vinay Gupta

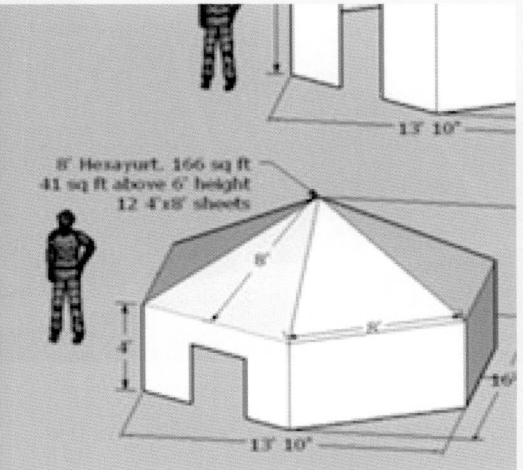

8' Hexayurt. 166 sq ft
41 sq ft above 6' height
12 4'x8' sheets

How to build a seasonal tent-cabin
Mongolian Cloudhouses

$12 Dan Frank Kuehn 2006, 152 p.

Although I have spent time in a yurt I have never made one. But I'd like to. This book tells you how. It assumes you have more time than money.

A yurt is a temporary tent house. It's not really portable. The Mongolian version weighs 200 pounds -- strong wooden frame covered in thick felt. If you really want portable, get a modern dome tent. But if you want a compact summer house, a cabin, a seasonal shelter encased in the mythical round, then a yurt could be perfect since you can make one of these yourself, with the added bonus that you can move it if you have to.

This book is an update of a 1980s classic. It takes the hippie approach. The drawings are all you need. Their instructions are rough, approximate, but satisfyingly visual. The book is motivational simply by being clear and rustic. Precision is not required, craft-smarts are. It assumes you are a do-it-yourself person.

--KK

•
When nomads gather, the topic of tipi vs. ger/ yurt may surface. It's a circular argument. Both are functional and beautiful; the pros and cons balance out. Choose the lodge that best fits your situation and personality.

The straightforwardness of the tipi, its pyramidal shape, the feeling of infinity inside looking up at the apex of the cone, make this Native American design a masterpiece. Because of the slope of the roof, the tipi can shed rain and handle a snow load better than a yurt.

On the other hand, the basket-like frame of the ger culminates at the smokehole, the crown, the tono. A low ceiling makes it easy to heat and the short poles fit on or in most vehicles. The straight wall of the yurt give you as much head space as floor space, unlike the tipi.

As some kind of comparison, this drawing (above) shows outlines of an 18-foot tipi and a 13-foot yurt, both using the same amount of cover material (33 yards, 6 feet wide).

Best dome resource
Domerama

Free

Domes are the most efficient way to build a shelter, covering the most space with the least material. But all domes leak in the rain (ask anyone who has lived in one). Yet, because they can be erected quickly, cheaply, and make wonderful, uninterrupted, open, almost magical, spaces inside, domes are perfect where it does not rain. Or on a temporary basis. Or both. Like Burning Man.

Once popular in the 1970s as alternative housing, then abandoned as impractical a decade later, domes are now in a resurgence because they are nearly ideal structures for arid and temporary shelters at Burning Man. This instant city now sports more domes than anywhere else in the world, and many of these are quite large. Considering how vast they are, it is amazing they can be thrown up in a few days by a small dedicated crew. And then be re-erected the next year.

You can use any set of long uniform pieces for the structs of a dome, from 2x4s, to electrical conduit pipe. The key critical pieces are the hubs which connect the structs, and the struct lengths. These must have a mathematical precision, and their dimensions vary by the size and variation of the dome species.

Therefore if you want to build a geodesic dome structure, you need to be able to construct strong hubs accurately. Domerama is the guide you need. This website shows you how to calculate struct lengths and how to make (or where to buy) dependable hub connectors. Using this site many amateurs have successfully built domes that worked the first time; you'll need help: remember this is a very math-intensive endeavor.

The site has tons of materials on the varieties of domes, erecting domes (not as easy as you think), designing them, what to use as coverings, and introduces global dome culture. It is the best place to keep up on dome innovations: one cool new idea is to shrink wrap domes. Find out how here. Domerama is better than any current book on domes by far.

-- KK

A chill out dome erected at Burning Man

•
Advantages of shrink wrap covering:

· Will hold up under extreme weather conditions

· Translucent to let a large amount of light inside the geodesic dome structure

· Easy to repair, simple to create ventilation in the form of windows

· Strong enough to handle freeway and railway speeds

· Seams bond through heat, creating a seamless containment

· Will last up to 2 years in fully exposed outdoor conditions

•
Tyvek for covering geodesic domes:

Noise factor: when the wind hits the Tyvek® covered dome there may be flapping and so a lot of noise at high winds. Hard structure Tyvek® (the one you normally find at the hardware store) is stiff and noisy when new, but if you put the Tyvek® in a washing machine on the delicate cycle with no detergent for 2-3 cycles, it comes out soft and much more fabric-like. Washing this type of Tyvek® does not seem to affect the water resistance but can cause some shrinkage. 5% should be added to measurements to allow for shrinkage if you are going to wash your Tyvek®.

•

This is the classic way to connect geodesic struts together. A hole is drilled into the flattened ends then bolted together. To accommodate a drilled hole in your struts, the length of the strut needs to be longer. For example a 36 inch pipe/conduit strut will need to be extended at both ends to drill holes. A rule of thumb is to add 2 X 3/4 inch = 1.5 inches (or about 8cm) more to all struts. That means the center of the holes would need to be drilled 3/4" from each strut end.

•

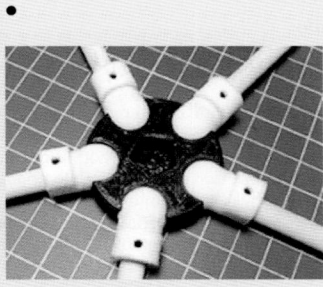

Domekit.cc is a project looking to make dome building simple and fun. They developed a hub connector featuring a robust ball-and-socket joint and an integrated thumbscrew that securely locks the strut to the node. These 3D-printed connectors are made in small batches in workshops and garages across the USA by fabricators with open-source 3D printers like the Makerbot. The principal fabricator for the 3D-printed connectors is Mark Cohen, who operates five 3D printers out of his garage in Brooklyn:

This is the Starplate system offered by Stromberg's. Starplates are steel plates, with channels to hold 2×2's, 2×3's or 2×4's. You simply drill holes in each end of 25 struts of equal length and bolt them into the 11 star plates to build a solid, mini-dome framework in a couple of hours.

A tightly-fitting round notch. Note that there are no saddles, so it is not a saddle notch.

Premium log fitting
The Owner-Built Log House
* Log Construction Manual

Log homes are fashionable. You can order one pre-manufactured from a catalog. Or you can make your own crude log shell for under $5,000 (see *Build This Log Cabin...*).

Or you can use the system featured in these books to make a log home so finely crafted that it is more like living in a gigantic piece of dove-tailed furniture. Called scribed-fit, this method produces handcrafted joints thinner than a piece of paper. You won't save any money this way, but you'll live in a hand-made shelter of utmost craftsmanship. That joy can be worth the trouble.

And trouble it is. Building with logs this way is similar to post-and-beam construction: the scale and details are beyond a single individual. You need a team, and you should try something small first. Your path is made much easier by either of these two books.

The Owner-Built Log House is geared to the dedicated individual willing to do as much of this hard work as they can themselves, from peeling logs, to hoisting them using pulleys, to carving notches and chinking. It presents the task of building a log house as part construction project and part lifestyle -- since it will consume your life. Remember, a shell of a house is only a fraction of the work. This guide is good about detailing the ways to finish it off, and the tricks need to say, get wiring in the logs.

At the highest end of quality is *Log Construction Manual*, the Ferrari of log homes. These aren't houses as much as wooden jewel boxes. Most guides are based on the personal experience of the author building their own house (see above); this one is based on the author's experience teaching thousands of others to build theirs. You get a comprehensive course, laying out the steps, the logic of the steps, and much hard-earned wisdom anticipating your problems as you learn how to scribe-fit logs into a house. But to be honest, the precision and energy needed to build this way demands you hire contractor help. You'll probably end up working alongside the pros, perhaps teaching them some new notching skills.

In many ways, building a fitted-log cabin is like building a wooden boat in your backyard. Many will begin, few will finish on their own. The magnitude of this quest should not be underestimated.

- KK

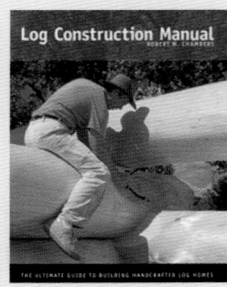

$35 Log Construction Manual Robert Wood Chambers, 2002, 272 p.

From *Log Construction Manual*

On each wall, we alternate the direction that tips and butts point every time we add another log. This helps keep walls from becoming tipped.

Cutting the groove while standing on the wall. You need a steady hand and a good sense of balance.

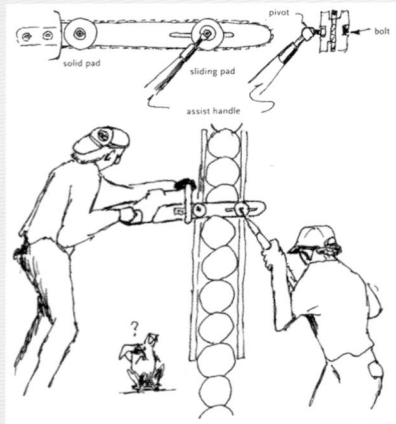

A true and accurate cut may be obtained with a chainsaw equipped with guide pads. These are now available commercially, or they can be made.

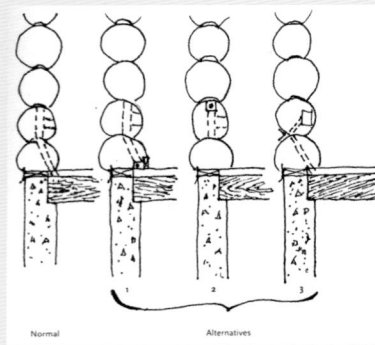

Log Homes Don't Waste Trees

One of the most widespread and damaging myths is that log homes use extravagant amounts of wood. It does appear that "you could build a couple homes out of the logs that go into one log house," as I've heard people say. But, an average log home uses about the same volume of trees as a conventional, stickframed house of the same size.

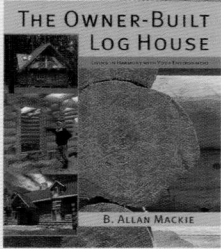

$24 The Owner-Built Log House B. Mackie, 2011, 248 p.

From *The Owner-Built Log House*:

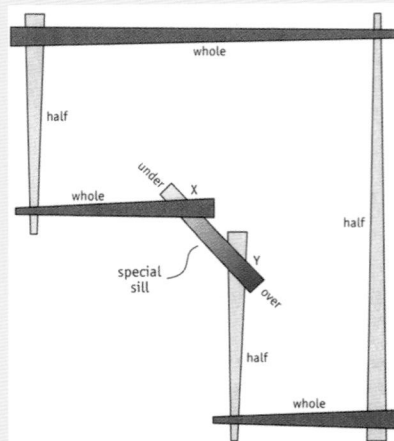

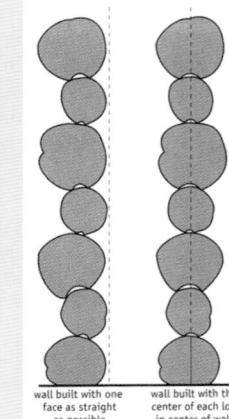

▶ I recommend you build walls so that the centerline of each log is plumb above the center of the wall. Trying to make one side of a wall more or less plumb can be difficult, unattractive, and perhaps unstable.

wall built with one face as straight as possible | *wall built with the center of each log in center of wall*

Top: Husqvarna 362XP with 24" bar.

Middle: Husqvarna 354XP with 18" bar.

Bottom: Jonsered 2016 electric with 16" bar.

I have taught more than 1,000 people to cut notches, and I have seen chainsaws of almost every model, age, and condition. I'll be blunt- an average student with a great saw does a lot better than a great student with an average saw.

Husqvarna and Stihl are the saws that I recommend. Most chainsaws are not suited for log building. And, buy a professional model saw, not one designed for homeowners. Stihl and Husqvarna both have a "pro" line of saws, and you should choose from these. Expect to pay $550 to $725 USD (in 2011).

Every saw has its own feel and character. These differences are not easy for beginners to recognize, but they are real, and important. Stihls are easy to start-when cold or hot. They have a distinctly softer suspension than Huskys-the handles have a more flexible attachment to the motor, and the bar also has a softer connection to the motor. Stihls drive like a Cadillac. My choice for heavy ripping is a Stihl: the big Stihls (bigger than 80cc) have power, are easy to start, and have soft suspension.

Husqvarna saws are more difficult to start than Stihls, especially when they are hot. Huskys also have a harder feel to their suspension. I have more control over the bar and chain-it's like there is a more direct link between what my hands are trying to do, and what happens. Huskys drive like a Ferrari. My choice for notching is definitely a Husky: great power-to-weight ratio, high chain speed, finesse, and superb control.

Cheap primitive shell
How to Build This Log Cabin for $3,000

$23 John McPherson, 1999, 140 p.

A log cabin is one route to cheap housing. You need land with access to lots of tall straight trees. And time. Lots of time. With a chain saw and winches you can erect a modest uninsulated shelter for less than $5,000. People spend up to a million dollars making artfully styled log homes; this is not one of them. It's a quick and dirty home-made shell without wiring or plumbing. This guy shows you how.

-- KK

One specialized logging tool that will be handy is the can't hook (or peavy ... one has a pointy end, the other, as here, don't). This is of special help when rolling uneven logs ... especially when fitting in and out several times while notching.

◀ *Ripping logs into boards may seem daunting at first, but it ain't that bad. There are more efficient ways to cut lumber but not that I am aware of "straight from the saw". The main thing is to have sharp chain ALWAYS! The sharpness will allow the saw to do the work and all you need do is concentrate on following the guide string.*

This was my log raisin' challenge. As the main support purlin, it was 32 feet long with a small end diameter of 12 inches. Lotsa log! I set up two logs as a ramp, hooked up (as described in that chapter) and pulled away. There were so many points of contact of the cable between the winch and the tie off points that the winch never strained.

Tree house wisdom
Tree Houses

Tree houses are impractically romantic. There is no one book on how to make this recurring romance as practical as possible, but these two books by Peter Nelson contain the best suggestions and useful advice for building a real live-in tree house I've seen so far. The *Treehouse Book* has lots of fabulous examples in the US and a few chapters on how-to. His follow-up book, *New Treehouses of the World*, gathers inspirational examples from Thailand, New Zealand and other spots with tree-house culture, and has a short chapter on new tree-house technology. Main thing to remember when building a tree house is that trees move, over minutes and years. It's closer to building a boat in the air. That's why there's plenty ideas in these books for any small house, even those not arboreal.

– KK

• Trees in the northwest grow surprising quickly, so I prefer a GL (Garnier Limb) with a longer stem, the part of the GL that sticks out from the tree. While trees grow taller only at their tips, they grow in girth along their length. As a tree puts on rings it envelops the GL, making the artificial limb even stronger. The tree will eventually push a beam out along the stem of the GL (the reason I prefer a longer stem) in much the same way the tree's roots might lift a heavy concrete sidewalk.

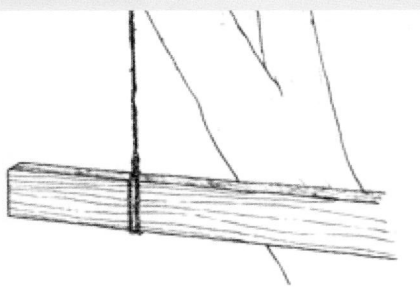

A suspended-point load. The most flexible of treehouse supports.

A fixed-point load with a safety cable. Good for treehouses close to the ground.

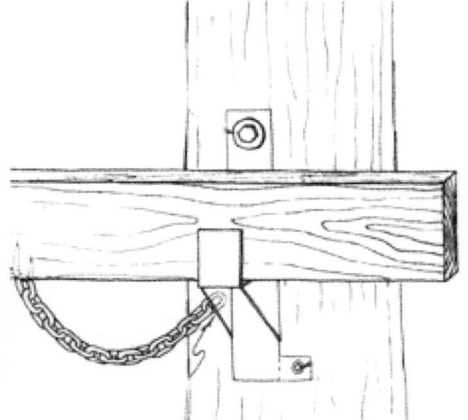

A floating-point load. Good when using more than one tree. The Garnier Limb would be an excellent alternative to this custom made bracket.

▲ *A "heavy limb," also designed by Greewood, holds up a bucket-style bracket attached to a large glue-laminated beam. There are numerous styles of artificial limbs, or tree anchor bolts (TABs).*

The Treehouse Book
$20 Peter and Judy Nelson with David Larkin 2000, 224 p.

New Treehouses of the World
$25 Peter Nelson 2009, 223 p.

An elegant platform takes shape around the old-growth Sitka spruce. Occasionally a tree will resist a building project, but this magnificent specimen remained calm and allowed us to proceed without protest.

Sweet Birch

▲ *Sweet Birch — A strong tree with shiny, waterproof bark that used to be stripped off for wintergreen or birch beer. Use in a group.*
70' high — spread 50'

One machine can do the work of fifty ordinary men. No machine can do the work of one extraordinary man. - Elbert Hubbard

121

How to build a wilderness home

Homesteading Alone

The uber American dream is to build your own comfy place on the edge of wilderness with your own hands. The attraction of this self-reliance is the chance to rewind civilization personally, to start over and do it your way. To own your own progress. Thoreau wrote the prime document of lifestyle self-reliance in his shed at Walden pond, an hour's walk away from his home. *Walden* is still worth reading as a how-to and why-to book (See p. 131). Yet as the world's wilderness shrinks, each generation seeks the wild further afield in order to retell the story of sprouting kernel of humanity in a small homestead.

The evening's haul. I was never short of fish.

There's a lot to be learned from the few diehards who have homesteaded far off the grid in modern times, and who have written honestly about the practicalities of this adventure. I found three recent accounts to be most helpful. Listening to them you get to see how much of a subsidy civilization gives us, and how challenging it is to recreate it in even a small measure.

In *An Island To Oneself*, Tom Neale took over an uninhabited island in the Pacific in the 1950s and constructed a beach shack for his solitary home. He's a sort of Robinson Crusoe, or *Cast Away*, for real. He voluntarily lived alone, separated from the nearest human by hundreds of miles of open sea. He had to be his own contractor, gardener, shipbuilder, fisherman, and doctor. The amount of household stuff he recreated from scratch is amazing. Neale had a lot of leisure as a full-time beach bum, but it's a surprise how constantly he worked, and how thoroughly he had to prepare for everything. His account supplies great details about the reality of living on a deserted island. In a place like his, the littlest mistakes could be fatal. His journal is a page turner with one small upset after another. It was no day at the beach.

In a parallel world up in the cold wilds of Alaska, Dick Proenneke flew to a remote lake and built himself a log cabin to live year-round alone among the snow, bears, and blueberries. This achievement is not uncommon for Alaska. What makes his account in *One Man's Wilderness* special and useful is that Proenneke thoroughly documented his work in 16mm film movies, photos, and diaries. From his meticulously vivid accounts you get a clear and exact recipe for what it takes to chop trees with an axe, peel them by hand, and erect an airtight cabin. And then to heat it all winter in minus 30 degrees. Proenneke complicated his chores by filming and photographing himself the whole time while doing them, no easy feat with bulky, balky film movie cameras of the 1970s. While his "video" clips online are fascinating, I found his journal far more helpful, more impressive, and more inspirational. *One Man's Wilderness* is a great account of how to build a tidy cabin from logs you cut and hew, and keep warm and content in the northern wilderness.

Somewhat related to the Alaska romance is the story of Sylvan Hart, who called himself the last mountain man. In the 1960s and 70s Hart homesteaded in a remote part of Idaho. He lived near a road, and had neighbors and mail delivery, but he spent a lot of time making his own tools, and practicing what are now called primitive survival skills. He mined copper, made metal, forged iron, made his own guns, and hunted bear for food and clothing. In other words he was trying to bootstrap civilization as much as he could. His story, written by a sympathetic journalist in the book *The Last Mountain Man*, gives a somewhat romantic picture of Hart's life, but even this dramatic view will quell most fantasies about how romantic bootstrapping it is.

Yes, you can build a home in the wilderness using only hand tools, but as all each of these stories make clear, self reliance is relative. Thoreau went to town to do his laundry, Neale brought a boatload of supplies with him, and Proenneke in Alaska had the bulk of his food flown in every month. The larger lesson from these books, and the reason they are cool tools, is that every small step we take toward self reliance is rewarded with heaps of wholeness, self-knowledge, and personal clarity. These books will give you confidence and tips on taking your own small steps toward doing things yourself.

-- *KK*

One Man's Wilderness

$12 Sam Keith, Richard Proenneke 1999, 223 p.

•

Learn to use an axe and respect it and you can't help but love it. Abuse one and it will wear your hands raw and open your foot like an overcooked sausage. Each blade was nursed to a perfect edge, and the keenness of its bright arc made my strokes more accurate and more deliberate. No sloppy moves with that deadly beauty! Before I started on a tree I carefully cleared obstructions that might tangle in the backswing. It was fun planning where each should fall, and notching it for direction. Snuck! Snuck! The ax made a solid sound as it bit deeply into the white wood.

•

Anyone living alone has to get things down to a system -- know where things are and what the next move is going to be. Chores are easier if forethought is given to them and they are looked upon as little pleasures to perform instead of inconveniences that steal time and try the patience.

•

I included in the first trip a .30-06 converted Army Springfield, a box of cartridges, a .357 magnum pistol with cartridge belt and holster, the backboard, the camera gear (8mm movie and 35mm reflex), cartons of film, the foodstuffs (oatmeal, powdered milk, flour, salt, pepper, sugar, honey, rice, onions, baking soda, dehydrated potatoes, dried fruit, a few tins of butter, half a slab of bacon), and a jar of Mary Alsworth's ageless sourdough starter.

The second pile consisted of binoculars, spotting scope, tripod, a double-bitted axe, fishing gear, a sleeping bag, packages of seeds, *A Field Guide to Western Birds*, my ten-inch pack, and the clothing. More bulk than weight.

The third pile held the hand tools such as wood augers, files, chisels, drawknife, saws, saw set, honing stone, vise grips, screwdrivers, adze, plumb bob and line, string level, square, chalk, chalk line, and carpenter pencils; a galvanized pail containing such things as masking tape, nails, sheet metal screws, haywire, clothesline, needles and thread, wooden matches, a magnifying glass, and various repair items; a bag of plaster of Paris; and some oakum.

•

It is always interesting to see what a fish has been eating. Several times I have found mice in the stomachs of lake trout and arctic char. Now how does a mouse get himself into a jackpot like that? Does he fall by accident, or does he venture for a swim? Tough to be a mouse in this country.

•

It is important to put the notch on the underside of a log and fit it down over the top of the one beneath. If you notch the topside, rain will run into it instead of dripping past in a shingle effect. Water settling into the notches can cause problems.

•

Had my first building inspector at the job. A gray jay, affectionately known as camp robber, came in his drab uniform of gray and white and black to look things over from his perch on a branch end. The way he kept tilting his head and making those mewing sounds, I'd say he was being downright critical.

•

1) These simple hand tools will challenge anyone's self-reliance. 2) Notice how the notches fit snugly over the tops of the logs below them, as if fused.

•

Wood to saw and split everyday. Got to keep up my payments at the Firewood Trust if I want to stay warm this winter. No real problem at all. Some folks had led me to believe it would be an everlasting job -- cut wood all day to keep warm all night.

1) Dick readies the roof poles for installation. 2) With the poles in place, the slots between the pole ends under the eaves need to be filled in. These fillers should be called "squirrel frustraters."

An Island to Oneself

$25 Tom Neale 1966, 255 p.

•

On August 4, 1953 -- ten months after I had landed -- I welcomed my first visitors.

It was unexpected because I had long since stopped wondering whether one day I would wake up to discover a strange yacht or schooner anchored in the lagoon. I had become so engrossed with my life on Suvarov that I rarely gave a thought to the outside world.

They were very happy days. I was never lonely, though now and again I would walk along the reef wishing somebody could be with me -- not because I wanted company but just because all this beauty seemed too perfect to keep to myself.

•

Of course, I had heard of this great lagoon, with its coral reef stretching nearly fifty miles in circumference, but I had never been there, for it was off the trade routes, and shipping rarely passed that way. Because its reef is submerged at high tide -- leaving only a line of writhing white foam to warn the navigator of its perils -- Suvarov, however, is clearly marked on all maps. Yet Suvarov is not the name of an island, but of an atoll, and the small islets inside the lagoon each have their own names. The islets vary in size from Anchorage, the largest, which is half a mile long, to One Tree Island, the smallest, which is merely a mushroom of coral. The atoll lies in the centre of the Pacific, five hundred and thirteen miles north of Rarotonga, and the nearest inhabited island is Manihiki, two hundred miles distant.

Fishing in the shallows with a single pronged spear.

•

Morning and evening from that moment on I scattered the split uto nuts on the square of ground where the run was to be built, and then banged lustily on the old iron crowbar made from the transmission shaft of a Model T Ford I had acquired in a Raro junkyard. The result was really extraordinary. Up till now I had spent weeks unsuccessfully trying to cajole the fowls into a regular feeding tie. Now, within a week, they were recognizing the familiar sound of the beaten crowbar, and came running as fast as they could, determined not to miss a good feed. They brought all sorts of surprises with them too -- in the shape of at least two clutches of chicks which I had no idea even existed. Although this achievement did not immediately solve my egg-collecting problems, at least I was able to keep track of the island's hen population, and now I started building the chicken run in earnest.

•

I knew the portents only too well (that trite old phrase about the calm before the storm) and strode back to the shack. There was no immediate hurry -- but equally there was no doubt that serious trouble was on the way. Before doing anything else, I checked my survival cache of tools, making sure my extra matches in their sealed tin were dry, and then took the box over to the "burial hole" in the outhouse. Next I lit a good fire on my brick hearth, and while it was burning, went out with my spear for a concentrated hour of fishing. It seemed provident to lay in some emergency rations, for there was no telling with a big storm; it could last a few hours or a few days.

I had plenty of cooked uto, but I foraged around for a couple of dozen more, which I cooked, and then I laid out double rations for the fowls. Next -- as the first puffs of wind ruffled the palms -- I inspected the garden for any ripe fruit which would be mercilessly blown off the plants when the inevitable storm broke.

I had sufficient uto to withstand a siege of several days -- and in a way it was rather like preparing for a siege against an implacable foe. In the outhouse I had a plentiful supply of wood, and in the kai room a good stock of arrowroot, plenty of fresh vegetables, including yams, cucumbers, tomatoes, spinach and onions. A dozen drinking nuts, a couple of ripe breadfruit and a stem of bananas completed my emergency rations.

By mid-afternoon gigantic seas were visible breaking all along the reef to the north, and before sunset, when the storm was beginning to reach its height, seas more huge than I had ever seen before began breaking right across the half-mile width of the entrance to the passage.

The Last of the Mountain Men
$12 Harold Peterson 1969, 160 p.

●
As a young man, dismayed by the destruction of the final frontiers, Sylvan Hart recanted civilization and marched off into this Idaho fastness armed with a few staples, an ax, a rifle, and a master's degree in engineering. There, in the last wilderness, where one winter's snow might fall into another's before a visitor came, he became the last of the Mountain Men. Soon to be known as Buckskin Bill, he fashioned his own clothes of deerskin. He constructed an adobe-covered building with hand-hewn timbers. He mined copper, smelted it, refined it, and made utensils. He even made his own flintlock rifles, boring them on an ingenious handmade machines, to "save the bother of store-bought ammunition." To pay for infrequent trips to Burgdorf (pop. 6, in winter 0), where he purchased only powder, books, and Darjeeling tea, he panned gold.

Sylvan's pole bridge, pinned precariously to the sheer face of a cliff high above the roiling River of No Return, constitutes the only path to the outside world.

Classic guide to low-cost subterranean dwelling

The $50 and Up Underground House Book
$20 Mike Oehler 1981, 116 p.

My wife and I had some property, but not enough money to build a house without going into debt. We enjoyed staying in a cave B&B in France and love the Troglodyte dwellings in Troo, France. After consulting several books, including one by Rob Roy, this book just made the most sense. The methods are so low tech, a bum could make himself a mansion. Other books get into engineering with concrete, steel, rebar, etc., which cost a fortune and don't necessarily function any better and, in some cases, maybe not as well. With this book and the videos, which are a must if you get serious, you really can build a home for the cost of a roll of plastic and a few other items, provided you do the labor by hand and scrounge materials.

Mike explains succinctly what took him years to figure out and you may might never discover otherwise: how to get in light from all four sides, how to protect untreated wood, how to connect the log post and beams together with pins made of low cost rebar, how to evenly compact the earth backfill by hand as to allow nature to finish the job (the backfill also functions as earthquake bracing keeping you tight under the surface rather than hinging at the point where the building meets the ground, a method similar to what Frank Lloyd did to prevent quake damage in Japan). Mike shows how to make a foyer or a gable to keep water flowing around the door opening rather than across it. Skylights are notorious for leaking, even on a conventional house. So Mike invented the "sun scoop," a method I used that allows natural light to shoot right through the full length of the underground complex at different times of the day and year depending on your design and desires. He also shows how to make clerestory windows to let light into the high side of the house through an uphill patio or a wraparound.

I was a bit skeptical at first. How could all of this work and be so cheap? This type of dwelling is not for everyone, but if you do it right it really does provide great shelter. There are engineering tables in the back of the book providing rule of thumb guides and safety information. It won't get you something that will pass a code inspection, but I'm of the opinion codes and building regulations are written in part to provide sales for corporations and taxes for the government. A friend of ours designed a small underground house. She wanted to go with engineers and permits. Last estimate: $1.5 million dollars. And she has yet to get it approved. Sadly, she will never build her dream. This book even has a chapter of strategies for getting around that. Keep in mind, too, this book is not a house plan. You learn how to build nearly any design you want. Just put the safe framing building blocks together in a design that suits you, keeping the important rules and directions in mind. After the basic structural requirements are met, the only limit is your imagination...

We started our house in 2002 and had a very crude shelter within a couple months. I framed in about 2,000 square feet, made about a thousand or so fairly comfortable, and continue to expand into it as we need it. We have a studio apartment area, a master bedroom and two bathrooms, as well as a porch area with a conversation pit, uphill patio, green house and shop. We have added a large garden to raise much of our own food, a carport, wood shed and two-story rammed earth, rock and salvaged boat dock and bridge timber garage. With natural earth temps around 50 at night, only a small fire in the wood stove is required to keep things warm. The roof is a garden. It feeds and shelters us and provides a park-like setting with flowers all around. There is no exterior painting required. Nothing to become an eyesore as the paint chips and deteriorates and the shingles rot off. Sure it takes maintenance and there are issues to deal with but if you build it, you will be intimate enough with it to know what to do.

My home is growing. It's alive. It changes with time and will be here as long as we want it. Or if we leave and no one cares for it, it will someday revert back to the earth from which it came, to be just another one of natures reclaimed gardens.

-- Glenn Kangiser (his underground patio and bedroom) ▼

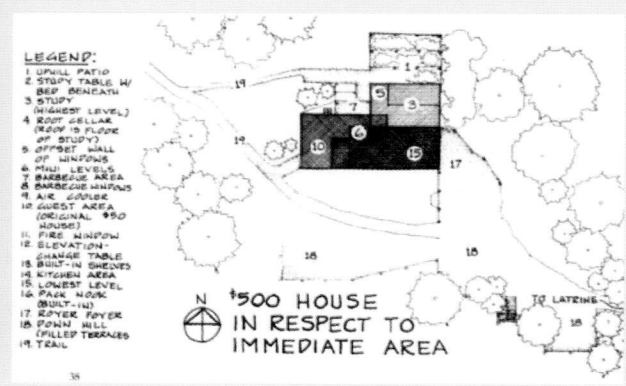

Boat living

The Essentials of Living Aboard a Boat * Living Aboard

Start with the *Essentials* book and proceed to the magazine if you are not dissuaded.-- *KK*

Real advice for boat living
The Essentials of Living Aboard a Boat

$13 Mark Nicholas, 2005, 284 p.

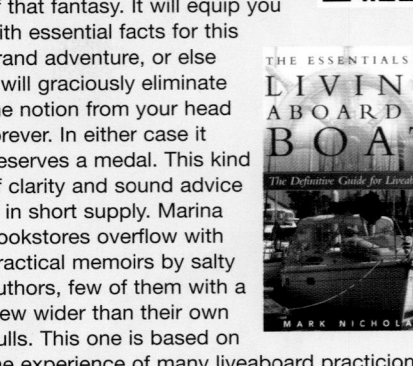

Everybody's dream: to live aboard a boat. This book's job is to wise you up about the reality of that fantasy. It will equip you with essential facts for this grand adventure, or else it will graciously eliminate the notion from your head forever. In either case it deserves a medal. This kind of clarity and sound advice is in short supply. Marina bookstores overflow with practical memoirs by salty authors, few of them with a view wider than their own hulls. This one is based on the experience of many liveaboard practicioners in many styles, and is the most useful way to answer the persistent question: "What is really involved living full time on a boat?" To clarify: *The Essentials of Living Aboard* is concerned with life on a boat that spends the bulk of its time docked, and only cruises occasionally. Your neighborhood will be other boats instead of open water. It is not too much of an exaggeration to say this lifestyle is less about living on a boat and more about living in a marina.

-KK

Speaking of investments, in general, boats are not good ones. Not only do boats depreciate in value, but the difference in value between a boat that is 19 years old and 20 years old may be significant, because many financing companies will not lend money for a boat that is 20 or more years old. You may find that you own a boat you cannot one day sell, which makes your boat virtually worthless.

Even adding electronics and fancy gear to your boat won't help much in maintaining value. Once installed, the electronics will immediately depreciate. This isn't like a house (on real land) in which a $15,000 kitchen renovation might bring about $35,000 in increased market value. On a boat, a $2,000 radar system might bring an increased market value to the boat of $500-$1,000. That's an immediate net loss of 50-75 percent. Then, after just a couple of years, the electronics, valuable if separated from the boat, will bring no market value increase at all to the boat.

●
A better deal will always come along, even if that deal does not exist today. When you think that a great deal is passing you by, don't be nervous, because there is

another one coming. ... So be patient, my liveaboard brothers and sisters. Relax and enjoy the ride. Don't panic. A better boat is right around the corner. If you remember that, and learn to believe it, this process will be less stressful and more fun; you will be a much better negotiator knowing that you can walk away and still have terrific options. And you will be more emotionally willing to take the time necessary to choose for yourself the best possible boat.

●
We already talked about how accessories are not worth their original prices once installed. Good accessories do not make for a good boat. A good boat is a good boat whether or not it has a good radar system. Unfortunately, a bad boat does not become anything other than a bad boat just because it has a $2,000 chartplotter.

●
Power vs. Sail. Most of the time, your preference is in your heart. Sailors want sailboats. Powerboaters or fishermen want powerboats. The decision is often part of the personality.

Sailboats are slow and quiet, with unlimited range under sail, provided there is wind. They require manual labor to operate. A sailboat that is the same weight as a powerboat will typically have a lower center of gravity because of the keel and ballast; the counterbalancing between the keel and the mast will often give the sailboat greater stability under difficult conditions, both at dock and at sea, than a powerboat of similar displacement. While the rigging and sails can be expensive to maintain, a sailboat in good overall condition has much less operating expense than a powerboat.

●
So the question is: Who in his right mind would want to buy a wooden boat?

The advantage to wooden boats is that they are cheap. An old wooden boat can be purchased for far less than a comparably sized fiberglass boat. Consequently, you get more space for the money. Wooden boats also tend to look and smell nice, and even an inoperable boat might be an excellent choice for someone who does not want to leave the dock or perform much maintenance.

If you don't plan on operating the boat, but have enough cash to buy the boat outright and want to avoid insurance payments, an old wooden boat might provide you with the perfect floating house for a fraction of the money.

As another word of caution, many marinas require that their tenants carry insurance, which might be difficult to acquire for a wooden boat.

●
If logic dictated, very few new boats would be produced. But lots of new boats are produced -- lots and lots, despite the fact that there must be a million used boats for sale at any one time.

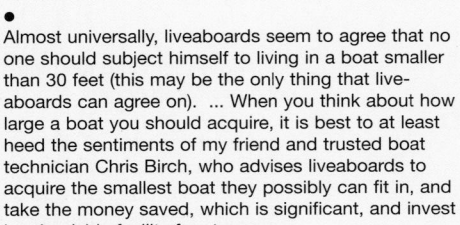

●
Almost universally, liveaboards seem to agree that no one should subject himself to living in a boat smaller than 30 feet (this may be the only thing that liveaboards can agree on). ... When you think about how large a boat you should acquire, it is best to at least heed the sentiments of my friend and trusted boat technician Chris Birch, who advises liveaboards to acquire the smallest boat they possibly can fit in, and take the money saved, which is significant, and invest in a landside facility for storage.

●
There is an upside that I truly enjoyed: it is impossible to buy anything else. Spending sprees are no more. There is no room for furniture or wall space for artwork. And since everything on board must be properly secured/stowed before cruising, there is an incentive to limit unsecured possessions. My relatives and friends were all told that gifts should be limited to beer (in cans) and wine, trips to restaurants, and other things that do not take up any space. For everything that is added, something must be removed.

●
Yet another person at a well-known publication told me that the reluctance to discuss costs was tied to an internal policy of trying to avoid discussion of specific topics that could scare people away from boating, and thus, the purchase of the publication.

●
Boats make noise. Noises aboard your boat will be magnified and will reverberate throughout your boat; noises aboard other boats and upon land will be heard, depending on how far away and how sound-

proof your boat is. Noise travels well over the water (they--I don't know who they are--said that one of the biggest tortures of being a prisoner in Alcatraz Prison in the middle of San Francisco Bay was that one could so clearly hear parties in the city, more than a mile away over the water).

●
Care to guess how much insulation a boat has? None. ... Lack of insulation means that (in addition to added noise) when cold water surrounds the boat, the interior hull and surfaces will chill. We will talk about this in the "Climate" chapter. When there's cool or cold air, the boat's topsides will chill. When it is cold and damp/rainy outside, everything will chill. This is not only uncomfortable, but it also results in condensation.

●
Boats are hard work, and while having a team of people participating in the chores sounds like a blessing for most liveaboards, having less than a team effort is sure to add resentment to the already tight space. Throughout this book, we've talked about how small a boat can be for just one person; add another and the space diminishes substantially. Add a few more and you create a wonderful system of communal living... in a fraction of the space of a commune.

●
Dogs present other challenges. One family in my marina has trained their dog to use the foredeck as his bathroom. I have always found this to be a bit off-putting, but since this family did some extensive cruising, this was the only acceptable location for this activity. The family would clean the waste whenever they noticed it and hose the urine off daily.

Living Aboard

Living Aboard Magazine is devoted to the concerns and needs of liveaboards. It's a pretty cozy subculture, in part because the cost of mistakes on water are very expensive and possibly dangerous. Think of this as an old fashioned newsletter for liveaboard users; all material is generated by readers. It recently stop publication, but its archives are useful and a good place to start.

-KK

●
Living aboard is a dream many share and more and more are achieving. As jobs become more flexible, home offices become more powerful, and people demand more from their lives, the trend is on the rise. Many thousands of people from all walks of life live on all kinds of boats, forming a diverse community with a wide range of personal interests and experience. It is a lifestyle that transcends economic and social boundaries. A sailor in Seattle described the liveaboard community in his marina as comprised of engineers, nurses, mechanics, naval architects, entrepreneurs and salespeople. There are families with young children who live aboard, there are retired couples, single men and women, college students, and nine-to-five professionals. They live wherever there is water on all kinds of boats - of all sizes and makes. They live on lakes and rivers and oceans, north and south, east and west, in all kinds of climates. Some live in marinas, some live on the hook, some cruise, some stay put, leading different lives in different places. What they hold in common is a fierce independence, love of the water and a spirit of adventure. They are a community,

albeit a diverse one, bound by their unique lifestyle.

●
We gradually realized that what had started out to be a vacation or a lark, a mid-life dalliance, had become something more. In our 50s, when most of the daily tasks ashore demanded only that we repeat what we already knew how to do, we learned new skills and rejoiced in knowing we could. At a stage when we had come to rely on a circle of old friends and family, we constantly met new people whose friendship we now prize.

●
Moving aboard a small sailboat meant leaving behind the accumulation of stuff that had clung to us over the years. I disposed of former treasures at a series of yard sales and rented a storage unit for the bits of furniture, ski equipment, winter clothes and memorabilia that we would use to jumpstart our lives when we stopped wandering. I enrolled in classes called "Medicine at Sea" and "The Offshore Cook." We took part in a weekend seminar demonstrating rescue-at-sea techniques. I took scuba diving classes and Ham radio license exams. Finally, we sold our home in the suburbs, quit our jobs, and closed the bank account. It took six years from the time we decided to "live differently" until we were ready to go.

Among all the lessons learned, the most lasting and important was neither how to safely negotiate a lock on the Erie Canal nor how to navigate through a Maine fog. It was an appreciation for time; the realization that what time we squander today will not be available tomorrow.

●
How much does it cost?

Once the dream of living aboard begins to take shape, reality intrudes with the question, "What will it cost?" One answer is, "How much do you have?" It can cost as much to live on a boat as it does to live on land - it

all depends on your lifestyle. Some people cheerfully eat macaroni and cheese, others won't leave the dock without a pasta maker. Some live for a month on what it takes another to pay the cell phone bill. Living Aboard surveys show that most fulltime liveaboards have retirement or investment income; others, however, choose to begin enjoying their boats while still working, keeping their jobs on land and commuting from their boat. A select few move their office or business aboard. And some take their retirement in pieces, cruising until the money runs low and then dropping anchor and obtaining temporary jobs to refill the cruising kitty.

●
The Potti is a stand alone alternative which requires no plumbing, holding tank, macerator, maintenance, etc. The potti is a two part system, flush water sits in the top unit.
At the push of a button the water fills the bowl. After use the waste is dispensed into a lower unit which does have a deodorizer added. I've been utilizing one now in our camper van for several weeks with my two year old, and I can represent that there has been no odor whatsoever. The unit does need to be dumped manually, but I can also say quite honestly that this was a simple no-mess process.

Technology is anything that was invented after you were born. - Alan Kay

Snow shelter construction
How to Build an Igloo
$14 Norbert E. Yankielun, 2007, 208 p.

A wonderfully illustrated guide to making snow shelters. How to build with snow, how to work with snow rather than against it, and what not to do. Amazingly informative, succinct and fun. This book is the kind of expert you dream of.

The Canadian Film Board has an unrelated but excellent 10-minute film by the same name on their website http://beta.nfb. ca/.

-- KK

•
One of the challenges faced by the beginner quinzee builder who excavates the interior of the snow mound is not to weaken the structure by breaking through to the outside of the mound or causing a thin spot in the wall. It is difficult while digging inside the quinzee to maintain a uniform wall thickness. To overcome this challenge, try this trick: After completing the snow mound, and before it begins to sinter, gather a few dozen footlong (30 cm) thin, dead twigs, dried plant stalks, or stiff lengths of straw. Completely push them into the snow mound at various places all over the dome. They will act as depth gauges. During excavation of the interior, if the ends of the twigs or stalks become visible, you will know that enough snow has been removed from that section of the dome. Digging to the point where most of the ends of the twigs become visible inside ensures a uniform 1 foot (30 cm) wall thickness.

Placing twigs of approximately the same length into the snow mound will help to keep the dome of the quinzee a uniform thickness.

A surface entryway should have a header block, or lintel (shaded), bridging the top of the arch opening.

▲ *A snow block wall can be used to protect a mountaineering tent from strong and damaging winds.*

The fragrance of spruce can make for a pleasant night spent in this shelter.

Mounding the snow on several backpacks and then removing them once the mound has sintered saves a lot of shoveling.

Igloo-making tool
Icebox
$180 Grand Shelters

The Icebox tool lets you build an igloo out of any type snow. I made 4 igloos last winter - all with different types of snow: one with heavy, wet, "packing" snow, two with new powder, and one with "sugar snow" - ice crystals that pour like white sugar. No problems. But this is definitely not a kid's toy. You need to shovel snow fairly high -- the 8 foot diameter igloos that I've made stand about 8 feet tall when completed. It took me (and a helper), approximately 4 hours to build each igloo. The whole igloo is free standing. The post device is used during construction to assure a circular igloo and to properly position the blocks. It works fine, although I did need to take my gloves off to extend and shorten the pole. The only difficulty that I've had is properly angling the first course of blocks -- if you don't get the box lined up properly, you have difficulty aligning the second course of blocks.

I'm not into winter camping but the system does fold up and pack. It weighs two kilos. The guy that introduced me to the Icebox has used it for camping in the Adirondack mountains. The igloos are really quiet inside, and noticeably warmer than being outside. If you want to make igloos, this is an awesome cool (no pun intended) tool. Includes video.

-- Tom Connors

Cheapest way to live on water
Handmade Houseboats
$36 Russell Conder, 1992, 240 p.

Oh, it's an ancient yearning. I lived on a houseboat once; you definitely need more than a log raft. But you don't need a million dollars more. The techniques here rely on modern materials (barrels and composting toilets), and cover all aspects of building and maintaining a floating cottage, mindful of the constant threat that constant water presents. In my experience, however, the main hurdle is not construction, but finding a place to dock. If you have a location, you can build it.

-- KK

•
Are You Crazy?

This book is about how to build your own houseboat, and thereby sidestep the twin ogres of twentieth-century survival: mortgages and landlords. If you can hold these pages open, dear reader, then you have the manual dexterity to hold a hammer. If you can do that, then armed with this book and a smidgen of imagination, and at least a little gumption, you can build your

own floating home, and be comfortably ensconced inside it, within a few weeks.

Barrels beneath a raft frame to support a 54-foot houseboat.

•
Steel barrels are the cheapest option; however, they will eventually rust away. Where wind and water meet, there is enough readily replaced oxygen being thrown promiscuously about to equip the intensive-care unit of any hospital. Oxygen is one of the most corrosive elements known, and it will attack steel houseboat barrels with glee. Not only do the drums deteriorate, but flakes of rust fall into the mud and sand, poisoning the benign environment where minuscule creepy-crawlies used to live, before the kamikaze debris started to rain down. If you have acquired a houseboat with steel drums, they'll undoubtedly need replacing soon. If you are building a new house and choose steel for reasons of economy, you are simply putting off the painful necessity of opening your wallet and buying plastic barrels, which will last as long as the houseboat does.

•
Ordinary plastic barrels are readily found, and they are strong and durable. Due to their rounded shape, they will support the weight of a house, on the shore or afloat. The plastic barrel

compresses as load is applied; that is, it transfers the load away along its curve, rather than attempting to support the weight in one place and then breaking, like a flat surface will. All a plastic barrel requires in the way of consideration is that it be placed out of, or protected from, the direct rays of the sun: Ultraviolet light will eventually weaken the material and cause it to become brittle. This should not be a problem with houseboats, for the barrels are placed underneath the raft, in the shade.

•
Houseboats can be designed to float in as little as 6 inches of water, so finding a suitable site should not be a problem.

•
Enclosed is a photo of my little 18'x7' houseboat. Designed by William Atkin in the 1940s, she was built in 1985 by David Scarborough of Rock Hall Boats: cedar-planked, fiberglassed to the waterline, canvas-covered plywood deck, plywood house, powered by a 9.9 outboard. I had her built as a weekend retreat, but before completion, I had a stroke. When I recovered enough to live alone, I moved to the St. Johns River in Florida and have lived aboard since 1987. (Beats living in a nursing home.)

If the human brain were so simple that we could understand it, we would be so simple that we couldn't. - Emerson M. Pugh

125

1 Where will the furniture go?

2 Easily figure it out with our durable furniture shapes

3 You are the interior designer!

Furniture cut-outs for visualizing
Lay-It-Out
$20-100

Last time I moved I threw out my back repositioning Grandma's china cabinet for the 10th time. My latest (and hopefully last) moving experience was a dream because of the Lay-It-Out furniture templates. These unique life-sized paper furniture templates are the shape of your bed, sofa, tables, chairs, rugs, billiard table. After trimming them to the appropriate size (measurements are in inches and centimeters), we placed them on the floor and -- as I was directed to the appropriate location -- continued moving them around with no effort. I had the whole house planned out before the moving truck arrived and it cost less than the physical therapy and pain killers I had to use before. They are a breeze to use. Measure, trim, position, then reposition and reposition and reposition again... You could buy a roll of something like cheap brown crate paper of course, but I liked that Lay-It-Out was ready to go, sizes already measured, and in pretty colors. You can buy a "Total Home Package" or purchase smaller packages specific to the Living Room, Dining Room, Bedroom, Game room, Accessory Tables or Rugs packages. I purchased the whole house package and used most of the pieces, except the billiard table, which I kept pinned to the wall for two weeks as a piece of pop art.

-- Rick Sievering

Keeps your carpet clean
Carpet Film
Carpet Shield $18 24" x 50' Surface Shields
Reverse Wind Carpet Film $53 36" x 200' KleenKover

Ever wanted to have friends over for a party at your house? Ever wanted to have a LOT of friends over for a party? Worried about spilled drinks staining your carpet? One solution is to cover it before the party with carpet film.

What is it? Picture a roll of Saran Wrap. Now imagine it thicker and more durable. Now imagine one side sticky. Voila! Carpet film.

I don't cover every carpet, just the most highly trafficked areas where people will be drinking and spilling: outside the bathroom where there's usually a line, up the stairs, by the entrance, in the coat room, and in the people-watching areas.

When the party's over, it pulls up easily. Best of all, all of the traffic on the carpet film will have pushed the adhesive side down into the carpet's nooks and crannies. When you pull the film, dirt will come out too. Free carpet cleaning!

Several companies make carpet film. You can get it at Home Depot, Lowes and Amazon for $10-20 per 2'x50' roll. Wider widths and longer length rolls are also available. Make sure to buy it reverse wound (with the sticky side on the outside of the roll) to make the application process easier.

-- Joshua Keroes

Recycled moving boxes
U-Haul Box Exchange

I have mixed feelings about U-Haul and their prices, but one thing they have done that is priceless is create and maintain a surprisingly helpful Box Exchange forum. It's a standard web forum divided into geographical areas so people can request free used boxes or make theirs available for free or cheap. We just saved ourselves $250. After responding to two posts, we had something lined up in no time. We drove into the city (Manhattan) the next day from where we live in Jersey City and picked up a bunch of boxes in various sizes that were practically brand new -- all for free. I basically ignored the "buy" forum as the "free" one was successful in under 24 hrs. We first tried Craigslist, but found that most people in our area at the time wanted money for boxes. From our experience, people on the U-Haul forum seemed willing to go a little out of their way to get rid of their boxes. Most of the posts are definitely from individuals, but interestingly, there were a couple of business disposing of boxes (we got ours from an electronics importer in Chinatown). We have not yet completed our big move to Wisconsin, but will be giving away our boxes the same way when we do.

-- Guil Barros

Clearest box labeling
Smart Move Tape
$12 Two Bedroom Kit (2 bedroom rolls, 2 kitchen rolls, 1 living room roll, 1 bathroom roll) each roll is 2" x 30yd U-Haul

Two things smoothed out my family's move a few years ago: designating Open First boxes for each room in our new home, so that on the first night after the move we wouldn't be missing any essentials; and this Smart Move Tape.

The clearly marked and color-coded designations (Office, Bedroom, Bedroom #2, Kitchen, Storage, etc.) made unloading go quickly for our movers, and organizing our many cardboard moving boxes much easier for us later on. No doubt we could have accomplished something similar with a handful of colored Sharpies, but it would have taken a lot of consistently careful writing to even approach the same effect -- at a time when we were looking to make less work, not more -- and the colored tapes really help make sorting a breeze.

-- Elon Schoenholz

Relocation advice
Moving Tips

Since I seem to move house every six months or so, I have ample opportunities to test new strategies. This time around I experimented by putting plastic storage totes through FedEx Ground, and for the items I moved myself I used cardboard boxes with the addition of nonadhesive strapping tape and tubular handles. Much quicker and easier, less effort, no breakages, big success.

-- Charles Platt

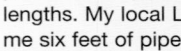

Plastic Totes via FedEx

Wal-Mart sells them for storing items such as bedding and clothes in the home, but their semi-rigid construction makes them ideal for moving fragile possessions such as dishes and stereo components. They are stackable, waterproof, easy to pick up (recessed handle at each end), reusable (can be nested during storage), and will pass unscathed through FedEx ground. Best of all they barely cost more than cardboard boxes! My local FedEx-Kinko's was skeptical about accepting them for fear that the lids would pop off during transport. I allayed their fears by putting 2-inch tape around the perimeter of the lid and folding it under the rim. I had to make little notches in the tape so that it would seal properly either side of plastic strengthening ribs under the rim, but this was still much easier, quicker, and safer than using cardboard. Wal-Mart sells gray Sterilite brand totes (the type I prefer) through its stores, but not online. Models 1830 and 1835 are the ones I have tested through FedEx without any problems. You can pay a little more and get "latch totes" (models 1940 and 1945 with a flip-up latch at each end) but since you'll still need to add tape, I feel the latches are unnecessary. (NOTE: One reader pointed out that plastic totes may buckle if they are stored in a very hot place with heavy objects on top of them. I haven't encountered this problem myself, but I do follow the standard practice of filling each container to minimize empty space inside it)

Strapping Tape

If you still want to use cardboard boxes for items you move yourself, or if you are moving stacks of books secured with cling wrap (as I have suggested previously), consider adding half-inch nonadhesive plastic strapping tape. This is the stuff you sometimes see wrapped around boxes containing big items such as refrigerators being transported as freight. Often it's yellow in color. Shipping departments have a tensioner that they use to pull the tape tight, but you don't need that. You can get 3000 feet of half-inch strapping and a lot of little buckles, with a manual tensioner, for ~$45. You thread the tape through the buckle, pull up on it while bearing down on the box, and you have it as tight as you need it. You trim the tape near the buckle. The advantages are that it greatly strengthens the box while giving you something to grab it by, especially if you augment it with a handle (described below). Also you can link two or three boxes together so that you can carry them easily with one hand, especially up and down stairs. Much more efficient and secure than cradling boxes in your arms, less hazardous (you can see your feet and obstacles in your path), and less risk of back injury, since you don't have to stoop to pick them up. Note that FedEx and UPS don't like string or strapping that can snag their package processing machinery, so strapping is for transporting packages yourself or with assistance from movers.

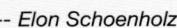

DIY Box Handles

Make handles from half-inch plastic water pipe sawn into 5" lengths. My local Lowe's sold me six feet of pipe for around $3 and you can use any wood saw to cut it. You may feel this is a luxury, but if you want to protect your hands from the edges of the plastic tape, handles are nice to have.

Thread tape through handle.

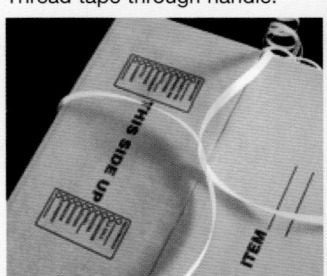

Turn box upside-down and cross the tape ends.

Turn box right-side-up and thread one of the returning tape ends through the handle

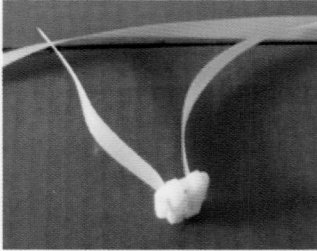

Add the buckle.

After pulling the tape tight, your box is now very easy to carry.

Quiet AC power
Honda EU Series Generators

Honda EU Series Generators
EU 1000iA, $950
EU3000iS, $2,330
Find a dealer through Honda
Honda

These generators are ridiculously quiet. The secret, as I understand it, is that they are low-volt 12v DC generators that take advantage of the new, very efficient inverter technology to produce the needed 120v AC. There are several sizes to choose from in the EU series. All have the ability to be hooked up to another generator to double the rating. The 1,000-watt model weighs less than 30 lbs., fits in a trunk, and can power a few appliances. On the other hand, I have used the 140-lb., 3,000-watt generator to power a camp of twenty people in the desert, including a full sound system, for ten days round the clock, and it hardly was breathing hard at all. With an optional cord you can use the 12v DC current directly to charge batteries. These generators also automatically shut off if they get low on oil. They have electric start with pull-start backup. Best of all they completely decimate the track record for efficiency of most gas gennys. Instead of the usual one gallon per hour they can operate for between seven and twenty-four hours (depending on load) on a single 3.5-gallon tank. In short, they take all the usual horrors and worries out of using generators.

-- Alexander Rose

Efficient home electrical generator
Listeroid Diesel Engine

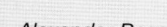
Utterpower, Power Anand, Lister Engine

From 1930 to 1987 the Lister company made diesel motors for pumps, generators, and general-purpose use, using mostly the same design of big, slow-speed, heavy flywheels and simple, easily-repaired parts. The Lister company then sold the designs. Today there are many Indian and Chinese companies that produce Lister copies (aka: "Listeroids") for export. These are fairly faithful to the original design -- with varying quality. The price for these engines *per kilowatt* is cheap, when compared to the more commonly found gasoline-powered generators, though they are not very portable. What is truly amazing is the efficiency of the Lister: one user reports an average of 8000 watts and 0.3 gallons of diesel per hour. They can be made nearly silent with cheap car mufflers or a water muffler. They run fairly cool, and home-built radiators (water tanks, house radiators, car radiators) seem to work well. These slow-rotating workhorse machines are good for nearly 100% duty cycle if properly maintained. (A 100% duty cycle means running 24/7, with no down time due to heat and lubrication needs). The Listers can run all the time, and there are even some people who have figured out how to do oil changes while the motor is still running, thus removing even the lubrication issues. Their efficiency and raw power makes them perfectly suited for electrical generation for long-term use versus "emergency-only" generators which have an extremely short lifespan. They are also works of mechanical art, and will keep a mechanically-minded hacker occupied for weeks, experimenting and tuning. I'm sure that vegetable oil or waste motor oil would work as fuel in these engines as well, but more research is needed.

-- John Todd

One home-built Listeroid-powered 7.5 kilowatt generator with water-tank cooler.

The editor of the Utterpower website, which previously sold the engines, explains that the EPA has made these engines illegal to sell. Most people buy a short block, and build the engine themselves using information on the website.
-- KK

Portable generator
800 Watt Portable Generator

I've owned this generator for two years and it's great for light field work. Turn all your electric tools (weed trimmer, hedge trimmer, leaf blower, even electric chain saws) into gas tools. This generator is OEM'ed to a lot of distributors, who then put their own facade on it. The cheapest version appears to be available at Harbor Freight for ~$99.

It's very robust and endures overload gracefully (it just peters out without any damage.) It's the antithesis of the previously reviewed Honda EU Series. You could wear out and throw away a lot of these generators for the price of one of the Honda inverter generators. And the electronic Honda's don't take even a momentary overload gracefully. A momentary surge from a power tool will trip the Honda's breakers even if the nominal power of the load is within spec.

-- Bruce Bowen

$135 Electric Generator 800 Rated Watts/900 Max Watts Portable Generator
Chicago

$150 SP-GG100 1,000 Watt 1.5 HP 2-Stroke Gas Powered Portable Generator
Steele Products

Heavy-duty backup home power
Generac Guardian Automatic Standby Generator

$2,850 Guardian Automatic Standby Generator (10 kW) Generac

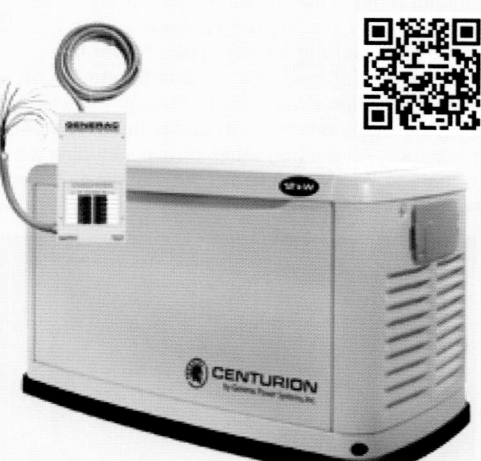

Right now, the electrical power I'm using to submit this entry as I watch television in my warm home is being supplied by my Generac Guardian 12kw generator. It's been running continuously for more than 40 hours now since the latest ice storm left 250,000 people in Maine without power. I've had this unit for nearly ten years now, and it has reliably provided power whenever the grid fails, which can happen a few times a year in this pretty rural part of the country.

The exact model I have is a 04456-0 which is 10kw when used on Natural Gas or 12kw when used with LP (Liquified Petroleum) Gas. Ours sits on a small pad in the backyard hooked up to the same buried LP gas tank I use to heat the house, provide hot water, etc. Since the unit is air cooled, there's no radiator or water pump to worry about. No fan belts. And very little maintenance. Essentially, you have a 5-year battery to replace and an oil change every six months. It "exercises" once a week for 20 minutes and will indicate if there is a problem. The most that's ever gone wrong with it in all these years was a bad spark plug that I fixed in minutes. Mostly, you ignore it until the power goes out. I test mine in the fall or if I hear a big storm is coming; I do that by walking over to the master breaker switch from the power company and shutting it off. Like clockwork, 45 seconds later the house is lit back up as the generator is up and running.

Most importantly, this generator is automatic. As a volunteer firefighter, I wanted a unit that would start up and run automatically, since when we lose power there's a good chance I'll be too busy out on the fire trucks to go dragging a portable out of the garage and wiring it in.

Back about 10 years ago, this kind of permanently-installed generator was less common. The Generac line was really one of the first for consumers. At the time, automatic standby units were for businesses and public safety use. Big commercial units were simply out of the range for home use. My Guardian was purchased and installed professionally -- including the transfer switch and wiring -- for around $5500. I'm told they're available for much less now. There are also other products out there -- mostly higher-end ones like those from CAT

-- that are great, but still too expensive for the average rural homeowner.

Honda makes great portable generators, like the previously-reviewed EU Series, which is enough to keep the fridge or freezer cold, or switch over and run the furnace to keep the house warm, but they're heavy, tricky to set up for many people, and don't hold as much fuel. At 12kw, the Guardian can run my whole house as long as I don't go crazy. The electric dryer and the air conditioner in my server room are not connected to breakers served by the generator, but everything else is. We're careful not to use all the burners on the stove and the microwave and oven all at once, but otherwise, it's just like being on the grid. The generator burns just under a gallon of LP gas per hour on a light to average load. With the tank I have, I can go several days if need be, which is plenty of time to arrange for a delivery of more fuel. During this blackout, my neighbors have even come over to cook and use the shower while their houses are still without power and they're struggling to keep enough heat in to keep the pipes from bursting. I can't think of a better testimonial than that.

My older model doesn't have Generac's new "True Power" feature that provides a cleaner power cycle for sensitive electronics, so I use battery backup units with AVR (automatic voltage regulation) on that gear. Newer Generac models provide this themselves. The one linked to below appears to be the newer version of mine in terms of size/market/capability, but it's only $3k. Given that it includes the transfer switch, that's a hell of a deal. For a cheapo 1 or 2 kw portable generator and transfer switch you'd pay around a thousand bucks.

-- Andrew Pollack

It isn't that secrets are never needed in security. It's that they are never desirable. - Whitfield Duffy

127

Preparedness

Bright, oil/kerosene-powered lighting
Aladdin Lamps

$111 Aladdin US

Aladdin lamps have been around for 100 years. At their brightest, they're about as radiant as a 60W incandescent light bulb, so you can easily read by them. They burn kerosene or lamp oil, and employ a cylindrical wick that heats a Welsbach mantle (it's bright incandescence comes from thorium and cerium oxides). Similar to a lantern, but without the pumping and compressed air hissing. As such, the Aladdins are perfectly silent. They're also more fuel-efficient than a pressure lantern, yet provide almost the same amount of light. Though they're not more fuel-efficient than an average oil lamp, they can make a typical oil lamp look like a nightlight.

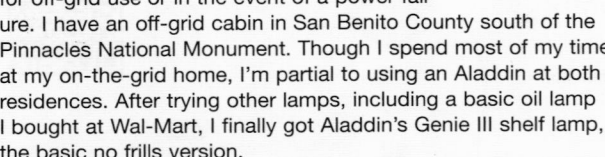

The lamp on the right (above) does not use a mantle, just a wick. They are both using the same fuel; I use Klean-Strip's "Klean-Heat" which is a purified kerosene substitute usable anywhere kerosene is specified. A bowl of fuel can put out a lot more lumen-hours than a battery-operated lamp, making the Aladdins perfect for off-grid use or in the event of a power failure. I have an off-grid cabin in San Benito County south of the Pinnacles National Monument. Though I spend most of my time at my on-the-grid home, I'm partial to using an Aladdin at both residences. After trying other lamps, including a basic oil lamp I bought at Wal-Mart, I finally got Aladdin's Genie III shelf lamp, the basic no frills version.

When properly adjusted they are essentially odourless and smokeless (the only time there is a slight smell is right after extinguishing the flame). By raising and lowering the wick, you can dim the lamp, too. If you raise the wick too high, though the fuel/air mixture becomes too rich and they start to soot/smoke, just like any other oil lamp. Properly adjusted, the wicked fuel creates a blue flame that heats the mantle. An optional chimney extender creates more updraft allowing you to operate the wick higher and get even more light. They recommend this for high-altitude (5000-ft.) operation.

-- Bruce Bowen

Simple lamps
The Book of Non-Electric Lighting

$12 Tim Matson, 2008, 104 p.

For off-the-grid living, you have a lot of options for non-electric lighting. (Solar-battery powered LEDs are not covered here.) This booklet goes through the advantages and disadvantages of different types of petrol-burning lamps.

-- KK

Fuel

Kerosene is the standard fuel for wick lamps. The term kerosene is used loosely to describe a thin flammable oil with a rather high ignition or flash point, roughly 160°F. That high

ignition temperature makes kerosene safer for household use than more volatile alcohol or gasoline--in fact, a lighted match can be dunked in a pot of kerosene without igniting it.

Kerosene and paraffin fuel lamps are distinguished by their wicks and fuel reservoirs. Pictured here left to right are a single wick with transparent glass reservoir, a duplex wick with ceramic reservoir, and a round wick with brass reservoir.

The Chimney

The Aladdin chimney is easy to recognize. At 12.5 inches, it is taller than most lamp chimneys. With only a slight outward curve to accommodate the mantle, it looks more like a glass smokestack than a traditional bell-shaped tapering lamp chimney. This sleek design represents a pinnacle in firelight aerodynamics: the high-velocity draft chimney makes it possible for the Aladdin to burn 94 percent oxygen and 6 percent kerosene, producing 125 candlepower. No other unpressurized liquid fuel lamp delivers such brilliant light.

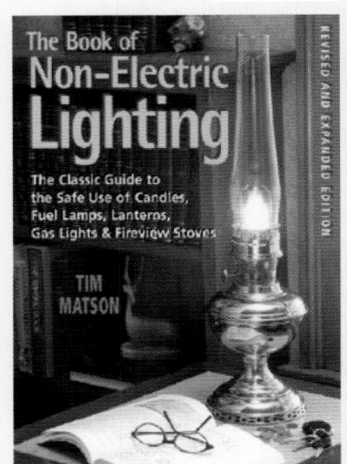

Classic prepper guide
Making the Best of Basics

$8 (used) James Talmage Stevens, 1997, 237 p.

The latest end-of-the-world scenario is past. As usual I did nothing. But now that the apocalyptic hysteria is over, and no one expects Armageddon, I'm convinced this is the time to treat preparedness seriously. This dense workbook has long been considered the bible of the food storage and family preparedness crowd. Preparedness as in: be ready for any long-term disaster or crisis. A newly revised and expanded 12th edition has everything from how to store the basics (and how much), to how to cook 'em, and how to keep water and stay healthy. Up-to-date and exhaustive. Yeah, it's from Utah, so it dispenses well-worn, almost comfortable, anxiety.

-- KK

Water that is bacteria-free when stored in thoroughly clean containers will remain safe for several years. Tests of water quality after long-term storage showed that water stored properly for several years could not be distinguished by appearance, taste, or odor from water recently drawn from the same source. However the principle of rotation is the best guarantee for monitoring stored water's purity and taste.

Treating Contaminated Water: Basic Bleach Method

For emergency treating of water of unknown quality, use any household bleach containing sodium hypochlorite (5.25% solution) without soap additives or phosphates. By using common household bleach as a chemical treatment method, large amounts of safe drinking water can be provided quite inexpensively.

Inventory management for basic in-home food storage is very simple–and hopefully, by now, very familiar:

1) Store what you eat.

2) Eat what you store.

3) Use it or lose it!

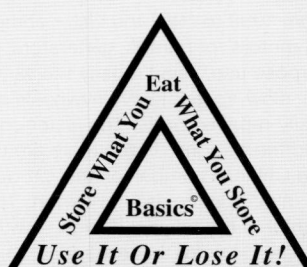

Fumigating Wheat for Storage

Carbon dioxide released from evaporating dry ice will kill all animal life in the container. The freezer will kill all live bugs–but not necessarily the eggs–over an extended period of time. It's always best to refreeze the previously frozen wheat after 30 days to assure that any eggs hatched since the last treatment are killed.

Chart 1
Nutritional Losses by Selected Preservation Processes

Preservation process	Normal loss of nutrition	Processing method
Canning	60%–80%	high temperatures and water-logging
Freezing	40%–60%	rupturing of cells
Commercial Dehydrating	5%–15%	moderate heat and moderate air flow
In-home Drying	3%–5%	low heat and gentle air flow

Free archive of survivalist info
Survival Library

Free Survival Library

Tomorrow, the end of the world won't happen. Even world economic collapse, or the total failure of the US government won't happen without preliminary disruptions. Prepping now for that vague doomsday scenario is plain nuts. But regional natural disasters are almost a certainty. Prepping for survival of a large-scale hurricane, tornado, earthquake with a few days backup at home is a good idea. How do you prep? Most die-hard survivalists take the the "stockpile and defend" strategy, constructing doomsteads, which may or may not work in a natural disaster. Usually going with a "mobile and agile" strategy, with a ready "bug-out bag," is better — but this is mostly a matter of temperament because we don't have a lot of data of what actually worked in actual past disasters. (If you know of real

data examining the value of home preparation please leave a link. Most of the evidence used in the survivalist prep world is Hollywood movies.)

But at the very least you should know what your survivalist options are. There are a zillion "prepper" books each one with more elaborate schemes and crazier than the one before it. Underground bunkers are only the tip. Selling doomsday (vs wilderness) survivalist advice is big cottage industry. I refuse to pay for this nonsense. The Survival Library is an open online archive of self-sufficiency, self-reliance instructions, PDFs, and videos that appear on other sites for free. It is easy to weed through. Some of the information, like welding instruction, or raising rabbits, or how to start a fire with no matches is useful whether or not you believe that the UN is sending black helicopters to take away your machine gun in the basement. The free downloadable PDF of the 500-page LDS (Mormon)

Extras if you've got the pockets or the inclination:

1. **Small radio w/extra batteries.** Why carry a radio? Because your cell phone may become unusable in fairly short order. Or worse, your cell phone may serve as a means for people who are not your friends to locate you. Look for a 22+ mile range GMRS/NOAA weather combo. If you've made arrangements with others to meet up, that type of radio can be invaluable. Be secure about using one, though. Learn its use and its useable range in advance. Practice.

2. **25-50 ft of parachute cord.** Whatever and wherever it fits. Very, very useful. That cord, some branches and your poncho or a couple of 3 mil contractors' bags can construct a decent impromptu shelter. Which could be a life-saver for you or someone else.

Figure 31 - Midland GMRS radio set - about $60

Prep Manual is particularly interesting and for most normal people, all the prep literature you'll ever need.

-- KK

The greatest danger of bombs is the explosion of stupidity they provoke. - Octave Mirbeau

Emergency hot meals
Ready Meals

$70 per 12 A-Pack

Self-heating meal packs give you hot meals without a stove. Developed by the US military for battlefield use, these 1,200 calorie food packages, known as Meals Ready to Eat (MRE), are also widely used by firefighters and emergency workers out in the field. In theory you could live off two per day.

Each meal comes in a complete package of two appetizers, main course, powdered drink, and dessert. The main course is contained in a sealed pouch that you insert into another pouch that chemically reacts to produce an intense heat. The meal inside gets steaming hot, surprisingly hot.

There are 6 standard menus, like spaghetti or beef stew. The taste is okay. If you were hungry enough you might think it good. We've never had trouble finishing a meal. Sometimes just the fact they are steaming hot hits the spot. The other stuff in the meal pack is pretty much generic and always edible. Each of the seven parts in each meal is individually vacuum packed so there is a

pile of litter generated. Also, all the food is ready-to-eat and hydrated; together with massive packaging, these are heavy dudes. Not ideal for backpacking, but one overnight wouldn't hurt.

Self-heating meals are great as easy car camping food. We've used them when we arrive late and are too lazy to set a stove up. Or at events like Burning Man when cooking is the last thing you want to do. I've used them canoeing, too, where weight is not an issue.

These self-heating MREs have an official shelf life of 3 years so that can be stockpiled in your pantry and rotated out as backup emergency rations. I have stuffed two meals for each person in our household into our go-bag.

Until recently all MREs were manufactured solely for military use. You could find wayward MREs on eBay; they may have been past their expiration date, or resold through gray markets, or missing their heater envelopes. Now the makers of MREs are selling directly to the public. The minimum order is a carton of 12, two units of each 6 varieties. They go for about $5 per meal. The brands are pretty indistinguishable. I've been using the A-Pack Ready Meals and am a happy camper.

You can also get consumer varieties. See Chef 5 Minute Meals (below).

-- KK

Self-Cooking Meal-in-a-Box
Chef 5 Minute Meals

$40 for 6 Amazon

I bought six of these two weeks ago just because the technology — a totally self-contained heating element that gives you a hot meal via steam heat in 10 minutes or less no matter where you are —- seemed so amazing.

Guess what?

I'm sitting here eating one of these meals right now, with no power since 14" of snow descended on my podunk town overnight, and it is delicious.

Cheap at twice the price.

And the delight of preparing it: you simply open the included pouch of salt water, pour it on the heating element, place your sealed food container on top, put the whole shebang back into the insulated box, and wait and watch in wonder and delight as:

1. The box starts to puff up

2. Steam starts pouring out

3. Sounds — amazing sounds — emanate from the box

4. The smell of cooking food pervades the immediate vicinity

5. You open the box and peel back the plastic lid and darned if your chicken cacciatore isn't all piping hot and smelling scrumdiddlyumptious — tastes great too!

Fantastic stuff.

-- Joe Stirt

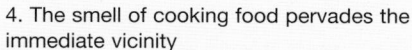

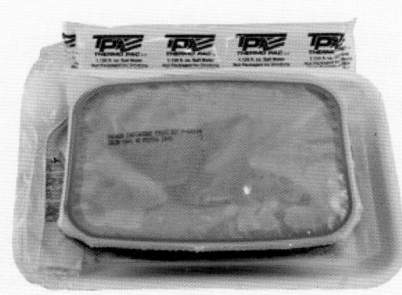

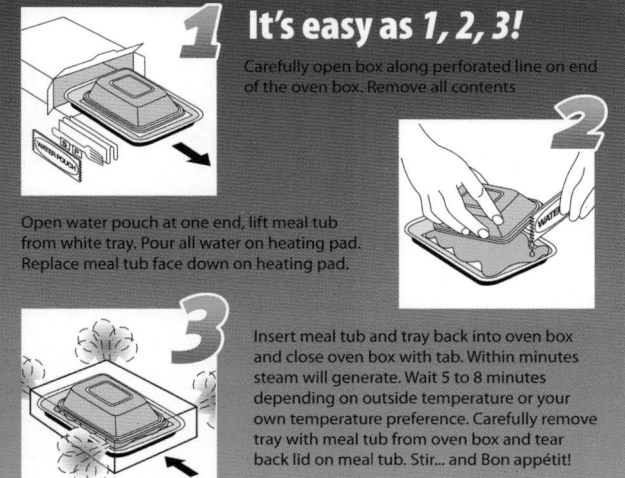

It's easy as 1, 2, 3!

1 Carefully open box along perforated line on end of the oven box. Remove all contents

2 Open water pouch at one end, lift meal tub from white tray. Pour all water on heating pad. Replace meal tub face down on heating pad.

3 Insert meal tub and tray back into oven box and close oven box with tab. Within minutes steam will generate. Wait 5 to 8 minutes depending on outside temperature or your own temperature preference. Carefully remove tray with meal tub from oven box and tear back lid on meal tub. Stir... and Bon appétit!

Disaster Lessons

Right after a major disaster, nobody's in charge. You self-start or nothing happens.

Assume that people can be trapped in any collapsed building. When searching a building call out "Anybody in there? Any body need help? Shout or bang on something if you can hear me." Give trapped people all the information you've got. Enlist their help. Treat them not as helpless victims but as an exceptionally motivated part of the rescue team.

Join a team or start a team. Divide up the tasks.

Encourage leadership to emerge. Most action in a disaster is imitation. Most effective leadership is by example.

Bystanders make the convenient assumption that everything is being taken care of by the people already helping. That's seldom accurate. If you want help, ask. If you want to be helped, ask!

Volunteers are always uncertain whether they're doing the right thing. They need encouragement -- from professionals from other volunteers, from passersby.

-- *Stewart Brand, Essential Whole Earth Catalog*

Tips

- To track whether the dishes in your washer are clean, use a wet erase marker to write "Dirty" or make a fancy "D" on the inside door of your dishwasher when loading dirty dishes. When you run the dishwasher the mark washes away, so you'll know they are clean.

-- *Carl DeCesare*

- When I need to make a hot compress I put dried beans (preferably lentils) in a pillowcase and heat in the microwave for a minute or two. It's cheap, easy, doesn't smell horrible, and retains heat for quite some time. Reusable, too.

– *Courtney Ostaff*

- Wooden, spring loaded clothes pins are one of the handiest gadgets in the kitchen. They are very cheap and long lasting. I have a couple dozen in use at any one time fastening the open tops of almost any kind of food that comes in a bag. This can be a bag of chips, bread in a bag, the cereal package inside the box, bags of half used frozen foods. Clothes pins are way better than twist ties, rubber bands, and the standard bread bag clip. They can also be used to hang up damp dish clothes, towels, and pot scrubbers. I have a wire rack over my sink that holds many sink related tools, as well as items hung by clothes pins to dry.

-- *Michael Kuhn*

I cook a lot and like to use garlic. One downside of properly cleaning and chopping and slicing garlic is the smell permeates your skin. Years ago, I heard on NPR that if you rubbed your hands under cold water with something made of stainless steel, the smell would be eliminated. I didn't believe it, but it works. You can buy "fancy" soap-shaped or garlic-shaped stainless steel objects to do this with, but no need. Go into your drawer and get out a butter knife or spoon instead. This really works!

-- *Michael Raab*

Self-reliance how-to

Mother Earth News

motherearthnews.com

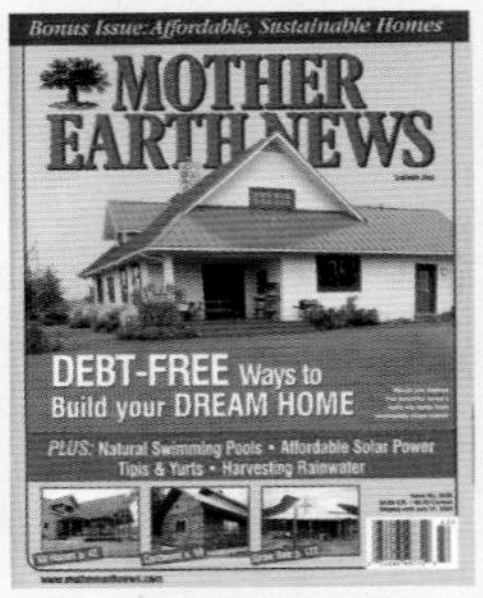
MOTHER EARTH NEWS
DEBT-FREE Ways to Build your DREAM HOME

I've been a reader for 35 years, and I'm finding it pretty useful these days. This old hippie magazine is the only place to keep current with back-to-the-land news. The old dream of thriving on a few acres of land is still serviced with enthusiasm here. Familiar subjects like backyard animals and all-year gardens are reliably addressed, but they also have solid reporting on such technological innovations as the latest in modern cabin toilets, microgenerators, the best chain saws and solar panels, and so on. However, since a lot of homesteading chores haven't changed much, their website offers 35 years of back issues online — some of the best stuff they published was written in the 1970s. (You can also get the archive on CDs).

At ten bucks per year, this magazine is essential reading for anyone attempting to homestead in the country, or to live self-reliantly in a town. But I also find it a great bargain for anyone with a do-it-yourself mentality. Despite the glossy sheen, the pages radiate with reports of reader's hands-on, can-do, think-different attitude.

Why I subscribe: Most magazines are about consuming. This one is about producing.

-- *KK*

•

Tool Sharing Start Up Advice

Are you thinking of starting a tool-sharing program in your community or neighborhood? Here are some helpful tips:

- Hold a meeting to find out people's needs and available resources.
- Determine the scope of the program; it's often best to start with simpler hand tools.
- Determine storage-will tools be stored in homes or in a common space?
- Determine how costs will be covered for tool purchases and ongoing maintenance.
- Develop a clear set of lending, repair and tool-return rules.
- Develop a list of "experts" who can share skills.
- Organize a system to track checkout and return of tools.
- Assign responsibility for maintenance and repair.

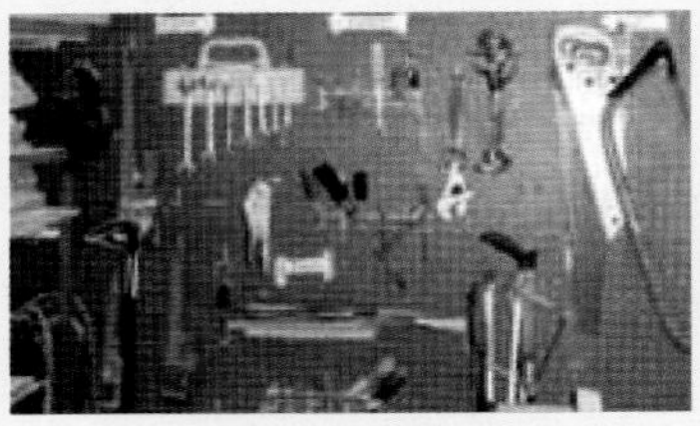

•

You can easily make your own parched (dry-roasted) grain corn at home for a sweet, crunchy snack with "flavors like nothing you've ever tasted before. To get the full flavor from any type of culinary grain corn, Roberts says, it's essential for the corn to ripen and dry on the stalks. Slow drying, low-temperature milling and immediate refrigeration of freshly ground corn keep the flavors alive. Because whole-grain cornmeal retains its natural oils, you often don't need to add butter or other fats when baking with it. "I never add fat to corn bread, since the (corn) meal already has fat in it," says Zoe Caywood, owner of War Eagle Mill in Rogers, Ark.

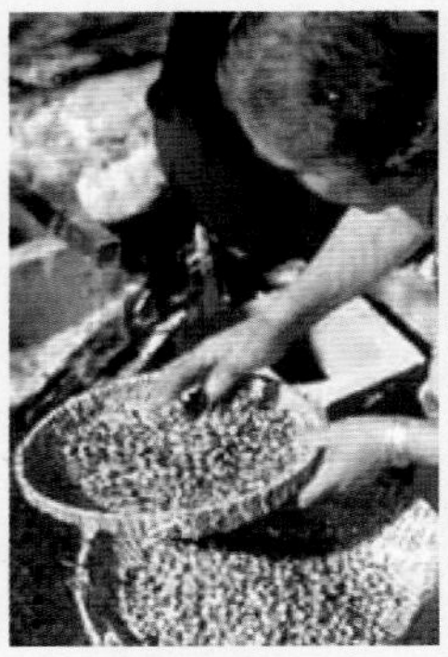

•

It usually does cost a bit more to buy meat from heritage [pork] breeds, but Small says there are good reasons for the higher price tag: Heritage breeds take longer to reach market weight than conventional breeds, and because they also produce a higher percentage of body fat, fewer of those pounds consist of marketable cuts. Small says the high quality and great flavor of the meat nevertheless creates steady demand from customers willing to pay the premium. "Cost per pound of our meat is definitely higher than cheap factory-farm pork," she says. "What we tell our customers is to eat less meat, but eat better-quality meat."

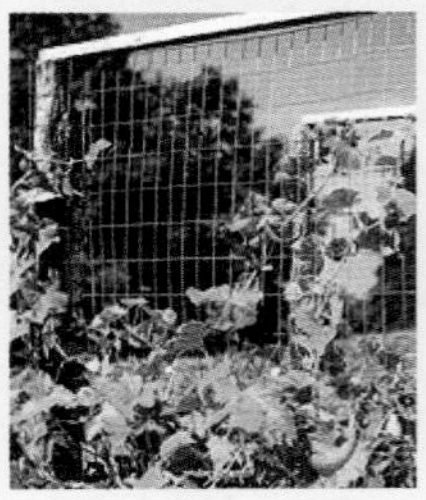

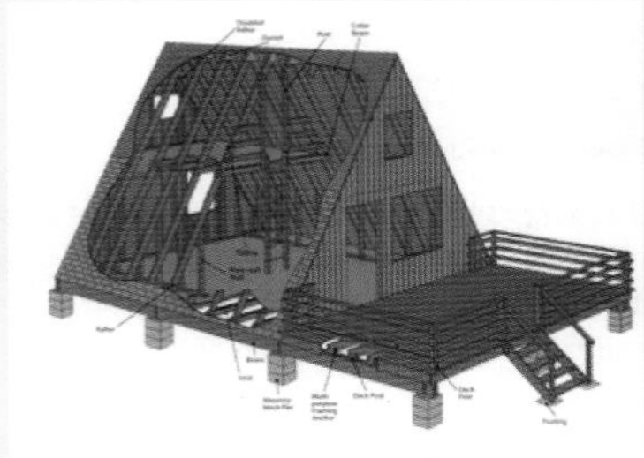

How to Build an A-Frame

•

Unfortunately, in cases of severe flea infestation it may be necessary to "bomb" your house with a commercial insecticide to annihilate the adult fleas before a natural-insecticide program can be implemented effectively. If you find yourself faced with this necessity, take the time to search out a bomb that contains either pyrethrins (natural) or resmethrin (one of the less dangerous synthetics) as the active ingredient. These are the safest of the "bombers," but, nonetheless, follow the directions on the container exactly. After this initial treatment, an ongoing natural flea-control program should preclude the necessity for further chemical "fogging" in your home.

◀I know many a home gardener has used chicken wire for a trellis, but I don't recommend it. Sure, the price is low, but chicken wire is too flimsy for circular freestanding cages, has too small a mesh to fit your hand through and is too effective for trellises. Too effective? Well, yes. I'd far rather untangle a wad of fishing line than have to spend the time and effort needed to remove a fenceful of spent vines from chicken wire.

Backwoods Home Magazine
practical ideas for self-reliant living

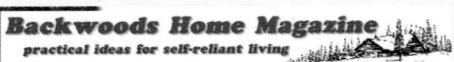

Practical ideas for self-reliant living

Backwoods Home Magazine

$25 (6 issues) **backwoodshome.com**

Imagine Martha Stewart as a gun-toting Libertarian and you'll have good notion of the editorial outlook of *Backwoods Home Magazine*. What makes this magazine useful, regardless of your political persuasion, is the wealth of information written by practitioners in the arts of walden. You'll find articles on everything from growing vegetables to baking bread to, yes, cleaning your Glock. Even if you live in the city there's plenty to learn in the pages of BHM, in particular from Jackie Clay, *Backwoods Home*'s resident advice columnist. Clay can parse out and troubleshoot what have become almost lost arts, things like food preservation, soap making and small-scale poultry keeping. The rambling, unedited reader letters and the thrift-store-painting cover art are endearing bonuses.

Backwood Homes converges with *Mother Earth News* in terms of subject matter lately, but where MEN is liberal/progressive BHM is libertarian. MEN is professional, BHM homespun. MEN is rock and roll. BHM is country.

And what makes *Backwood Homes* magazine different from other DIY publications is that all of the columnists walk the walk in addition to talking the talk. They don't just theorize, they actually do the things they write about. While the Libertarian rants may be off-putting to some, with what I've witnessed of our local government in action, the more I tend to agree. Even if I may never shoot, skin and make raccoon stew, I can appreciate the self-reliant activities profiled in BHM as part of an essential American skill set that needs to be recovered. We urban dwellers have been too busy in recent years with less useful activities such as selling mortgages and collateralizing debt obligations. Time for some tasty squirrel!

-- *Erik Knutzen*

•

Restoring Rusty Cast Iron: Rusty cast iron is easily reclaimable unless the rust has deeply eaten into the iron, causing deep pits or holes. This is not commonly seen, but is always a possibility. Most of the time, all that is needed is a good washing with hot, soapy water and a green nylon scrubby. With lots of elbow grease and a couple of trips through the sink, the pot or pan is often smooth and nearly as good as new. If the rust is more tenacious, you can use a steel wool pad and scour it off with that. In severe cases, I've taken a sanding disc to it, removing the rust first, then using a very fine grit to repolish the surface of the iron.

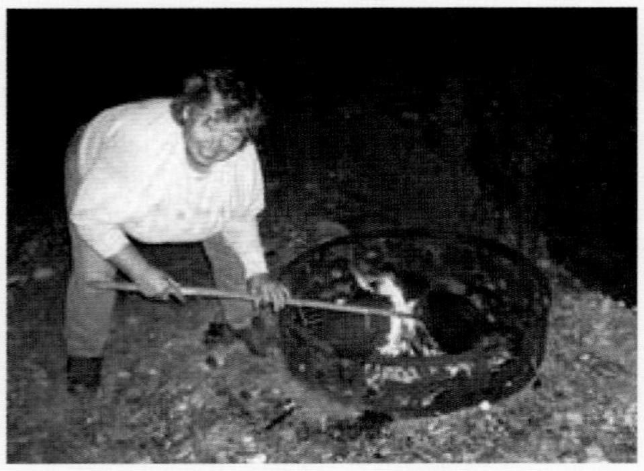

Jackie burns two of her cast iron pans in a fire to remove years' worth of crusted-on food and grease.

Once your pan is clean and smooth, rinse it well with boiling water, then dry it with a kitchen towel. As the iron is now unprotected, even a little moisture can quickly rust your new pan. You will now season the pan, as if it were new.

•

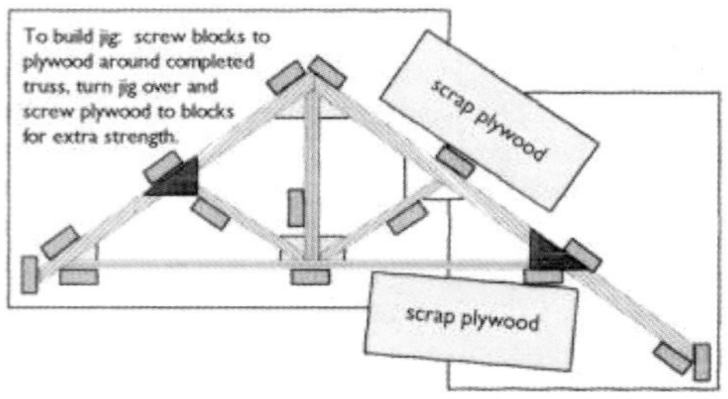
To build jig: screw blocks to plywood around completed truss, turn jig over and screw plywood to blocks for extra strength.
scrap plywood
scrap plywood

Trusses

Wood is not a homogeneous material. It is much stronger in one direction than in others. Wood's greatest strength is in resisting compression along its length. Wood is also quite good at resisting pulling tension, but it is weakest at resisting bending (flexion) and twisting (torsion). One way to make a wooden building as strong and rigid as possible is to arrange the wood so it is being used in its strongest dimensions.

Here's an example. A typical peaked roof frame consists of two rafters with a cross-tie to keep the tops of the walls from spreading. The cross-tie exerts its strength in tension, so it can be made of smaller size lumber, such as a two-by-four. But the rafters must resist bending (flexion), where they are relatively weaker. So the rafters must be made of two-by-sixes, two-by-eights, or even bigger stock. Such lumber is expensive. Long ago, engineers learned they could add greatly to the strength of a roof by inserting compression members within the frames.

Cantilever truss in a jig made from two sheets of plywood and scrap blocks. Some plywood gussets are not shown, to reveal joint details. Cut and set all truss members. Shim tight, then glue and screw gussets from top side. Pull shims and remove truss from jig. Turn truss over on a flat surface, and glue and screw gussets on the other side.

•

Solar Hot Water Systems

Except for batch heaters which have no electronic control devices, any solar system that includes automatic valves or solar loop pumps will require a differential temperature controller. More expensive temperature controllers will include a digital display to indicate system temperatures and alarms, but all are based on a very simple control strategy. One temperature sensor is mounted inside the solar panel on the roof, and one temperature sensor measures the water temperature inside the solar storage tank.

The control concept is simple; when the solar panel sensor is hotter than the water in the tank, a relay inside the controller is activated which turns on the pump. When both sensors read the same, the relay opens and the pump stops. More sophisticated controllers allow the installer to adjust these temperature setpoints to fine tune the system.

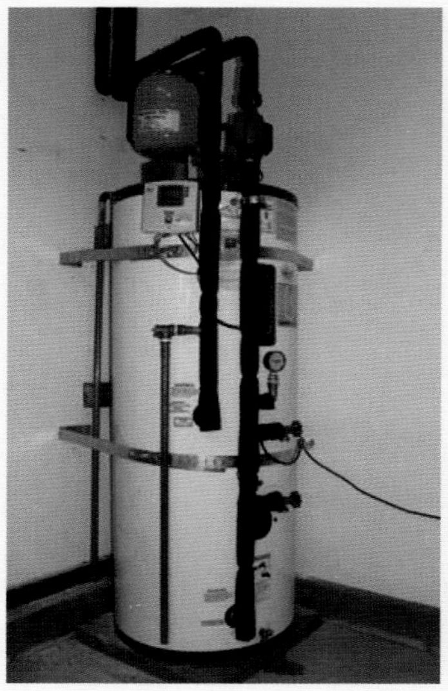

homegrown Evolution:
vegetables, chickens, hooch, bicycles and cultural alchemy

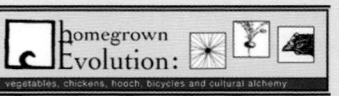

Urban self-sufficiency

Homegrown Evolution

Free rootsimple.com

Mead making, beer brewing, bread baking, urban poultry raising, container planting, pirate gardening, foraging, pickling, bicycle-powered hauling, solar-oven making and anti-car culture ranting are just a fraction of what you'll absorb plumbing the archives of HomegrownEvolution.com. Kelly Coyne and Erik Knutzen, husband and wife urban homesteaders, guide those of us who can't make it back to the land on how best to incorporate aspects of it into our modern city-bound lives.

They're encouraging, but don't preach or pretend to be perfect, and therein lies their appeal.

-- *Elon Schoenholz*

Make a Garden Work Table from a Pallet

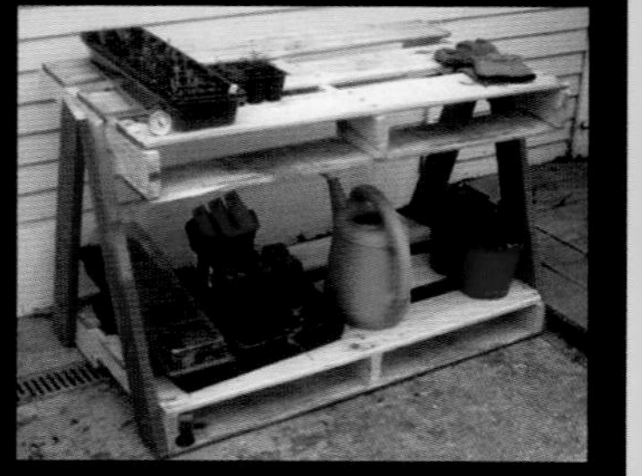

Pallets are a ubiquitous building material, your free lumber yard in tough times. Homegrown Evolution patched together the garden work table above for use with seedlings and storing pots and watering cans. Hopefully the picture is all you need to put one together yourself.

Some tips for working with pallets:

1. We prefer projects that don't involve disassembling the pallet. The nails in pallets aren't meant to be removed. Trying to take one apart with a crowbar will, in most cases, result in a lot of split, useless wood. A Sawzall reciprocating saw would work better if you must take one apart. For the table above we simply cut the pallet in half with a circular saw and handsaw.

2. Use screws not nails and predrill all holes. Pallet wood is very brittle and splits easily.

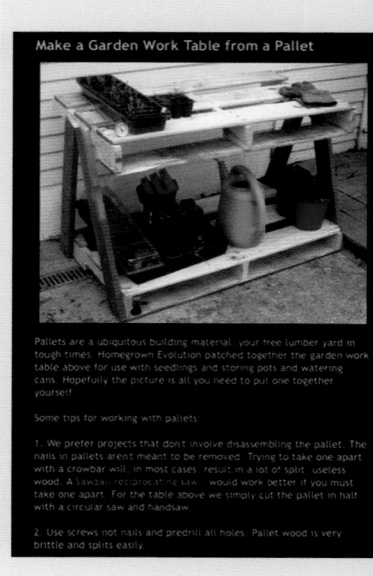

Sometimes interesting opportunities arrive dressed as a huge pain in the ass. - Thomas Edison

Best introduction
The Backyard Homestead

$13 Carleen Madigan, 2009, 368 p.

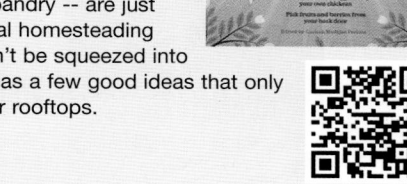

A pretty good introduction to all the homesteading tasks you can do in a small urban space. I found it a bit more helpful than similar tomes like *The Urban Homestead*. Most of the subjects covered -- vegetable gardens, bees, composting, fermenting, animal husbandry -- are just scaled down versions of rural homesteading -- a huge education that can't be squeezed into one volume. But this book has a few good ideas that only work in smaller city patios or rooftops.

-- *KK*

Threshing wheat in a large, clean trash can helps keep the released grains contained.

Tips for Buying Feeder Pigs

The greatest variety and highest quality of pigs is available in the 40- to 60-pound weight range.

Crossbred pigs are generally more vigorous and faster growing than purebreds.

Male pigs should be castrated and healed.

Buy pigs that have been treated for internal and external parasites.

Buy pigs that are well past the stress and strain of weaning.

Bear in mind that while females (gilts) may grow more slowly than barrows (males), they will generally produce leaner carcasses and can be pushed harder with more nutrient-dense rations.

How to Milk

Apply pressure with your thumb and index finger to keep the milk from going back up into the udder.

Use your remaining fingers to move the milk downward into the milk pail.

Holds:
3 hens
1 nest box
1 roost

Ultimate self-reliance
Walden

Free Internet Archive

What revolutions still hide in this evergreen book written in 1854! I owe every ounce of my urgency for living to this journal. Even now I can scarcely read a page without aching to shed everything I own. This account of Thoreau's two-year experiment in self-reliance, a hand-built hut at the edge of a pond, is a dangerous instrument, aimed at youth. It is the Ur-text for do-it-yourselfers. And the trumpeting herald for living with less. Many readers have been sent on a journey to the core of life by these pages. Read, and simplify.

In the true spirit of his message, this free copy (multiple formats) is the one Thoreau would have used.

--*KK*

• When I wrote the following pages, or rather the bulk of them, I lived alone, in the woods, a mile from any neighbor, in a house which I had built myself, on the shore of Walden Pond, in Concord, Massachusetts, and earned my living by the labor of my hands only. I lived there two years and two months. At present I am a sojourner in civilized life again.

• Most of the luxuries, and many of the so-called comforts of life, are not only not indispensable, but positive hindrances to the elevation of mankind.

• Near the end of March, 1845, I borrowed an axe and went down to the woods by Walden Pond, nearest to where I intended to build my house, and began to cut down some tall, arrowy white pines, still in their youth, for timber. It is difficult to begin without borrowing, but perhaps it is the most generous course thus to permit your fellowmen to have an interest in your enterprise. The owner of the axe, as he released his hold on it, said that it was the apple of his eye; but I returned it sharper than I received it.

• I dug my cellar in the side of a hill sloping to the south, where a woodchuck had formerly dug his burrow, down through sumach and blackberry roots, and the lowest stain of vegetation, six feet square by seven deep, to a fine sand where potatoes would not freeze in any winter. The sides were left shelving, and not stoned; but the sun having never shone on them, the sand still keeps its place. It was but two hours' work. I took particular pleasure in this breaking of ground, for in almost all latitudes men dig into the earth for an equable temperature. Under the most splendid house in the city is still to be found the cellar where they store their roots as of old, and long after the superstructure has disappeared posterity remark its dent in the earth.

Realistic expectations
Living on an Acre

$12 U.S. Department. of Agriculture, 2010, 336 pages

Living on a few acres is the classical American dream. But before you leave, best read this realistic advice produced by the US Department of Agriculture for the wave of young back-to-the-landers in the 1970s, updated and rewritten for 2010's young homesteaders. Think of this as a wise uncle who's seen a million folks try this and has a few words of caution -- and encouragement -- for you.

You'll get an informed overview of the thousands of things you need to think about (water, sewage, markets, pests, machines, etc.), and the hundreds of options you have for using the land (flowers, a dude ranch, raising pets, a country B&B, speciality herbs, etc). It won't tell you the right answers or how to do any of them. It serves more like a checklist of all the possibilities and drawbacks to help fit your dream to reality.

Most folks caught in the fever of this dream don't want this kind of overview, they only want to know how many rows of beans to plant and the plans for a chicken coop, in one book. If you do try to live on a few acres, you'll need tons of how-to guides, videos, and forums; I know of no single source that can give sufficient details for the myriad tasks needed.

WALDEN; or, LIFE IN THE WOODS. By HENRY D. THOREAU.

BOSTON: TICKNOR AND FIELDS.

• I thus found that the student who wishes for a shelter can obtain one for a lifetime at an expense not greater than the rent which he now pays annually. If I seem to boast more than is becoming, my excuse is that I brag for humanity rather than for myself; and my shortcomings and inconsistencies do not affect the truth of my statement.

• I got out several cords of stumps in plowing, which supplied me with fuel for a long time, and left small circles of virgin mould, easily distinguishable through the summer by the greater luxuriance of the beans there. The dead and for the most part unmerchantable wood behind my house, and the driftwood from the pond, have supplied the remainder of my fuel. I was obliged to hire a team and a man for the plowing, though I held the plow myself. My farm outgoes for the first season were, for implements, seed, work, etc., $14.72 1/2.

• Bread I at first made of pure Indian meal and salt, genuine hoe-cakes, which I baked before my fire out of doors on a shingle or the end of a stick of timber sawed off in building my house; but it was wont to get smoked and to have a piny flavor. I tried flour also; but have at last found a mixture of rye and Indian meal most convenient and agreeable. In cold weather it was no little amusement to bake several small loaves of this in succession, tending and turning them as carefully as an Egyptian his hatching eggs.

• Wherever I sat, there I might live, and the landscape radiated from me accordingly. What is a house but a sedes, a seat? better if a country seat. I discovered many a site for a house not likely to be soon improved, which some might have thought too far from the village, but to my eyes the village was too far from it. Well, there I might live, I said; and there I did live, for an hour, a summer and a winter life...

• I left the woods for as good a reason as I went there. Perhaps it seemed to me that I had several more lives to live, and could not spare any more time for that one. It is remarkable how easily and insensibly we fall into a particular route, and make a beaten track for ourselves. I had not lived there a week before my feet wore a path from my door to the pond- side; and though it is five or six years since I trod it, it is still quite distinct.

The key to successfully living on a few acres is not doing all the jobs right, but selecting the right jobs to do. This earnest Wikipedia-ish tome is an aid to that meta-job.

-- *KK*

Leasing machinery or hiring custom operators are alternatives to owning farm equipment. In some cases custom operators can complete the work faster and cheaper than you can. This is especially true when you have only a few acres and specialized machines are needed. When considering hiring a custom operator, talk to other people who have used his services. Waiting for a custom operator to arrive can be expensive if the crops are no planted or harvested at the optimum time. Timeliness is important when you compare leasing equipment, owning equipment, or hiring a custom operator.

Bob and Peg Cremin have devoted their retirement years to a small egg farm at the edge of a residential neighborhood in Wallingford Connecticut. Their handmade signs tempt passing cars.

Backyard Chickens

our-coop-adventure | cajunhillbilly's Coop | the-coop | kippenhouse's Coop

c00p3 | KinderKorner's Coop | <3ChickenS<3's Coop | Knittycat's Coop

NCchickenmommy's Coop | chris10sen's Coop | time4chickens's Coop | crossgirl's Coop

ki4gots-small-coop | ks_twin_mom's Coop | The Burg Peeps's Coop | greenpeeps's Coop

Our first egg!

a

Best for backyard beginners
Raising Chickens for Dummies
$11 Kimberly Willis and Rob Ludlow 2009, 408 p.

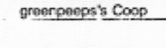

A few years ago we decided to join the growing back-yard chicken movement. We knew zero about chicken raising. We were interested in keeping a handful of hens for eggs, so we didn't want info on raising flocks of them (how many eggs can you eat a day?). I read every book for backyard beginners I could find, and after studying ten of them, the one that was most helpful to us was *Raising Chickens for Dummies*. It did the best job of anticipating our questions for a low-rent minimal approach. For instance, we had no desire to be cleaning chicken-shit every week, and we opted for deep bedding in the coop, a tip suggested by the book.

We've had chickens for four years now, and the book is still answering questions. The author runs a website, Back Yard Chickens, that has very active forums where you can ask other backyarders questions not found in his book. The site's albums of photos of homemade coops proudly posted by members is very helpful and inspirational.

If you decide to graduate to larger flocks I would point you to the recommended book (below) *Storey's Guide to Raising Chickens*, which is extremely comprehensive, but often more than a beginner needs.

BTW, I was initially skeptical I would be able to tell difference with backyard eggs, but it's true. Backyard eggs do taste better; they are more...well...eggy. However, they won't be cheaper, even if you don't count your time. We kept our initial costs down by constructing a coop from scraps from a building site in the neighborhood (after asking permission). We had to buy the screening, which is double layered at the bottom (another book tip) because we have pretty serious predators around. We installed the previously reviewed automatic watering dish from the mail-order hatchery McMurray, which means that overall, the five chickens are very low maintenance. Four years later we have 6 hens producing 6 eggs a day!

-- KK

Keeping our days-old chicks warm under a heat lamp.

Classic how-to
Storey's Guide to Raising Chickens
$13 Gail Demerow 2010, 448 p.

I'm not convinced you need a how-to book to raise chickens; they're pretty resilient and will eat damned near anything and still lay eggs. But the best reference guide we have is the *Storey's Guide to Raising Chickens*. Easy to read, full of information, and covers the whole range from hatching to keeping layers to raising meat birds to dealing with problems.

-- Mike Gunderloy

• The standard catching hook consists of a 30-inch (75cm) length of 8-gauge (4mm) wire bent at one end into a hook and firmly attached at the other end to a wooden rake or broom handle.

• Scratch can be used to trick chickens into stirring up their coop's bedding to keep it loose and dry.

Toss a handful over the litter once a day (traditionally late in the afternoon when birds are thinking of going to roost) and your chickens will scramble for it.

• Depending on the weather and on the bird's size, each chicken drinks between 1 and 2 cups (237-474 ml) of water each day. Layers drink twice as much as nonlayers. In warm weather, a chicken may drink two to four times more than usual.

Chicks by mail
Murray McMurray Hatchery

mcmurrayhatchery.com

We've been buying baby chicks by U.S. mail from Murray McMurray Hatchery for 30-plus years. We'll get a call from the postmaster, sometimes a bit flustered, because there's a box there with peeping chicks awaiting pick-up. We'll go get them and set them up with a light and feed and water, and lo and behold in three months we'll have laying hens.

Minimum order is 25, so the chicks can warm each other in transit. We raise all of them and when they are teenaged, give or sell to neighbors. Raising 25 is no sweat.

Why get chickens by mail and not from your local feed store? McMurray has been in business for 90 years and their birds are of excellent stock. Lots of varieties to choose from. We've had not only Rhode Island Reds, Partridge Rocks and Auracanas for steady egg production, but exotics such as Cochins and Polish, as well as meat birds. They've all been top quality.

Get Murray's hard copy catalog if you want to start a flock. Wonderful to look through. A few tips:

1. A dozen hens will give you plenty of eggs for you and your neighbors.

2. If you want fertile eggs, plan on ending up with one rooster for every dozen hens.

3. In more urban areas, get 4 or 5 hens, no rooster.

Once you have your own fresh eggs, you'll never want store eggs again.

-- Lloyd Kahn

Red Cap

This Old English Breed with reddish brown feathers tipped with black spangles has a large rose comb covered with prominent points. They are white skinned and lay tinted eggs. Chicks (picture above) are a light reddish tan with black speckles and some stripes.

● **Egyptian Fayoumis**

These small, active, lovely chickens have been raised along the Nile River in Egypt for centuries, and even though quite common there, are practically unknown in this country. We got our start of this very rare breed from one of the state universities whose poultry department was using them for special studies in genetics. No other breed matures quite so quickly as these do and the young pullets are apt to start laying their small tinted white eggs at 4 to 4-1/2 months while the cockerels will start to crow at an unbelievable 5 to 6 weeks. They are attractively marked with silvery white hackle and white bars on black background throughout the body plumage. Leg color can be either willow green or slate blue. Baby chicks are highly colored in brown, black, and white markings on the back and a brownish purple head color.

We are spiritual beings having a human experience. - Teilhard de Chardin

How to butcher
Basic Butchering of Livestock and Game
$13 John J. Mettler, 1986, 208 p.

You can probably learn to butcher an animal better from watching a YouTube video than you can from reading text, but this classic book will help you evaluate what you see on YouTube. It gives you the context, reasoning, and background of the moves you see in the videos. It also gives you the instructions in clear text. I find it helps me sort out the cacophony of the different methods seen in amateur videos. Beef, pork, lamb, venison, rabbit and poultry are covered. And of course, if the Internet goes down, this clearly illustrated book is always there.

-- KK

Shoot or stun the lamb as close as possible to the point where two imaginary lines drawn from eye to ear intersect, as shown.

The animal must be killed quickly, with little or no pain, but more important is that death comes without fear. To allow an animal to become frightened at slaughter is not only cruel, but unwise, for it causes the release of adrenaline, which some believe can affect the quality of the meat. Also, fear may cause the animal to struggle, doing damage to its meat or injuring the person slaughtering. Select the method of killing that will upset the animal's routine least, thus avoiding fear, and select a method that is sudden, thus avoiding pain.

A. Hang the animal by one hock on a screwhook, and remove the other rear leg at the hock joint, the front feet, and the tail. B. Start to skin the carcass with a knife, but then peel the entire hide down the body.

Rabbit bible
Storey's Guide to Raising Rabbits
$15 Bob Bennett, 2009, 256 p.

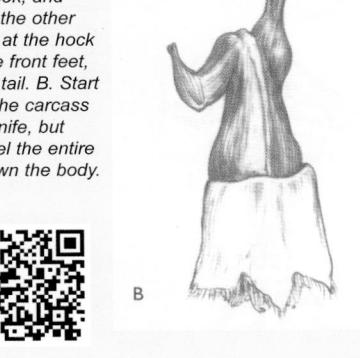

For nearly 40 years this guide has introduced boy scouts, 4H-ers, homesteaders, survivalists, and pet keepers to the practicalities of raising rabbits. Now in a new 4th edition, it's still the best manual for getting started with rabbits for food or show.

-- KK

If you run your hand over each rabbit at feeding time, you will know if you should increase the ration or not.

Watch carefully at feeding time

A good raiser watches stock closely at feeding time. While they are eating, run your hand over each rabbit. A rabbit that's a bit bony should get more feed. If a rabbit hasn't cleaned up its pellets something is wrong.

To determine the cause of appetite loss, first check the water supply. Is the crock or jug empty? Is the valve plugged? Rabbits don't eat when they are thirsty. They must have plenty of water. Most of the time a rabbit that isn't eating isn't drinking.

If the doe starts to carry straw around, she probably will kindle in a day or so.

The doe needs peace and quiet a few days before the litter is born and a few days after. Dogs and children can be particularly disturbing at this time. Upsetting the rabbitry routine can cause the doe to kill her young or abandoned them, so it it is vital that you keep things calm and quiet.

You will, of course, be very curious to see the litter. If you have placed the nest box in the back of the hutch but in full view from the front, you will be able to see into it, and by the 31st day you should see a pile of fluffy fur toward the rear of it, moving slightly up and down.

Ten-day old babies in the nest. Newborns should be handled rarely if at all, so the doe will not be upset by the intrusion in her nest and so you avoid passing your scent to the young.

Guide to goats
Natural Goat Care
$13 paperback Pat Coleby 2001, 372 p.

Angora goats.

On my little homestead near downtown Oakland, CA, I've dabbled in chickens, bees, turkeys, rabbits, and pigs (i.e. eggs, honey, meat, fur pelts, and wonderful manure for the garden). Recently the dabbling got a little more serious: two Nigerian Dwarf goats named Bilbo and Bebe (the one thing missing was milk; And I love milk. And goat cheese). Trouble was, I didn't know anything about goats, what they eat, how they behave. Luckily, a goat herder told me about this guide published in Australia. It put my fears to rest.

With all of the other farm animals (includ-

ing the pigs!), it's mostly a matter of throwing down some food, making sure everyone has water and enough space, and we're all good. Goats turned out to be way more compli-

cated than any other animal on the farm. They have psychological needs. They have a rumen for digesting food. They can get sexually transmitted diseases. They have hooves that need to be trimmed. They are a long-term relationship, which --- from day one -- kept me up late at night worrying. With this guide, I'm far less worried. And now that Bebe is pregnant, in a few weeks we'll have milk!

Bonus tip: I order all manner of goat-related items from Hoegger's.

-- Novella Carpenter

Homeopathic methods...

Cider vinegar maintains correct pH in the body, which is probably one of the reasons it is so useful. Because of its potassium content, it is invaluable for all animals coming up to breeding.

Mistletoe. This parasitic plant is a great tonic for goats, ell or ill. I pull it down from trees and feed it directly to my animals. Be warned, it turns the urine bright red for the next 24 hours--the goats have not developed bleeding kidneys.

Kidding...

The legs appear first and the kid's nose will be level with its knees. If the head is turned back, it is a good idea to scrub up (short nails, clean hands and plastic gloves if the farmer's hands are cut or scratched) and pull the head forward. The kid can be born with the head turned back, but it is not easy. Ease the kid out as the doe contracts and give it to her to wash and suckle or use whatever system of rearing

has been planned. Each kid must have its ration of colostrum, the first thick milk that contains the antibodies for that kid.

Psychological needs...

All goats, particularly the older ones, should have names--ones that do not sound too similar. Goats soon learn to recognize their names when called or reprimanded.

Good rear end and udder

Cow hocks and divided udder

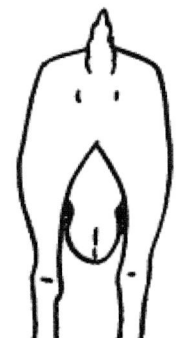

Well attached scrotum

Poorly attached scrotum — pendulous and uneven

Udders and scrota.

It is well to remember that the entire universe, with one trifling exception, is composed of Others. - John Andrew Holmes

133

Catalog for independent living

Country Wisdom & Know-How

$13 Editors of Storey Books, 2004, 488 p.

Originally intended for the wave of back-to-the-landers in the 1960s, this series of pamphlets has been re-issued for DIY city-dwellers. *Country Wisdom* is thick with possibilities for anyone looking to live, do and think more independently. Sure the content and format resembles the *Whole Earth Catalog*, but if anyone can -- and should -- carry that torch, it's the folks at Storey Books. The copy is clear and concise, accompanied by simple line drawings that are fun to ogle, even if you have no intention of mulling wine, weaving baskets, building a smokehouse, raising ducks or rabbits, composting, candle making, creating a bat house, constructing an underground root cellar or butchering livestock. I didn't grow up on a commune, but I recall a tattered copy of the *WEC* lurking around the house. It was only years later I realized what it was. Here's to another life-altering book for the next generation of kids to discover.

-- Steven Leckart

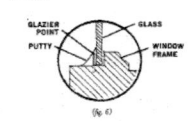

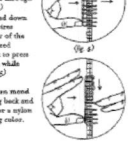
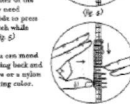

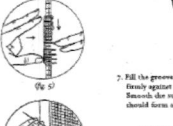
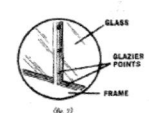
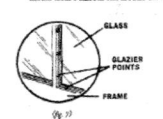
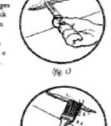
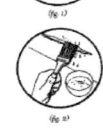

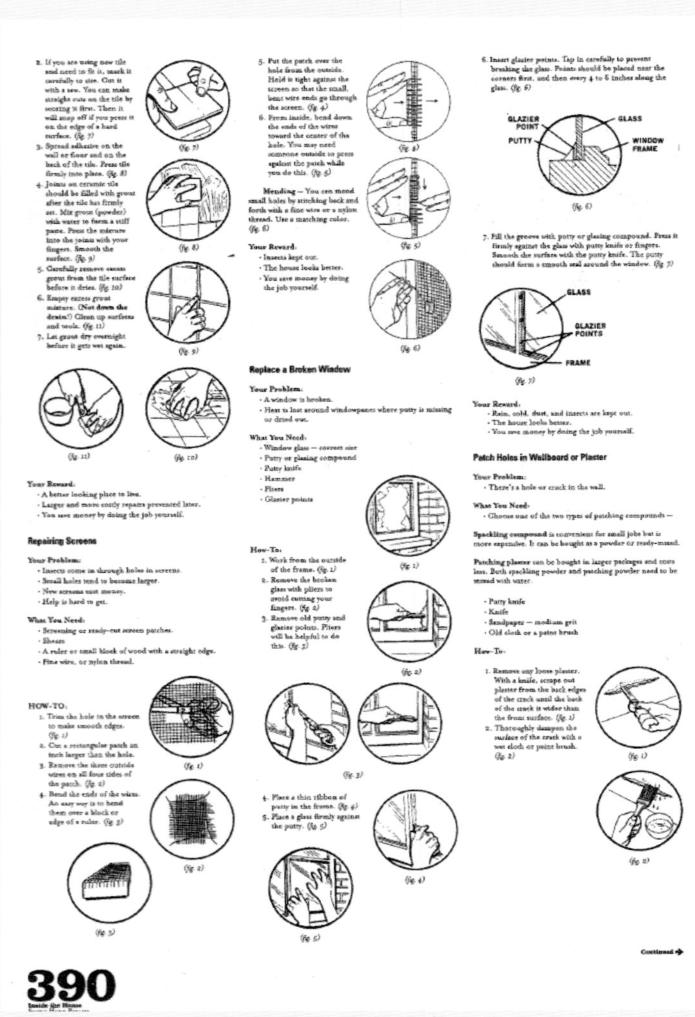

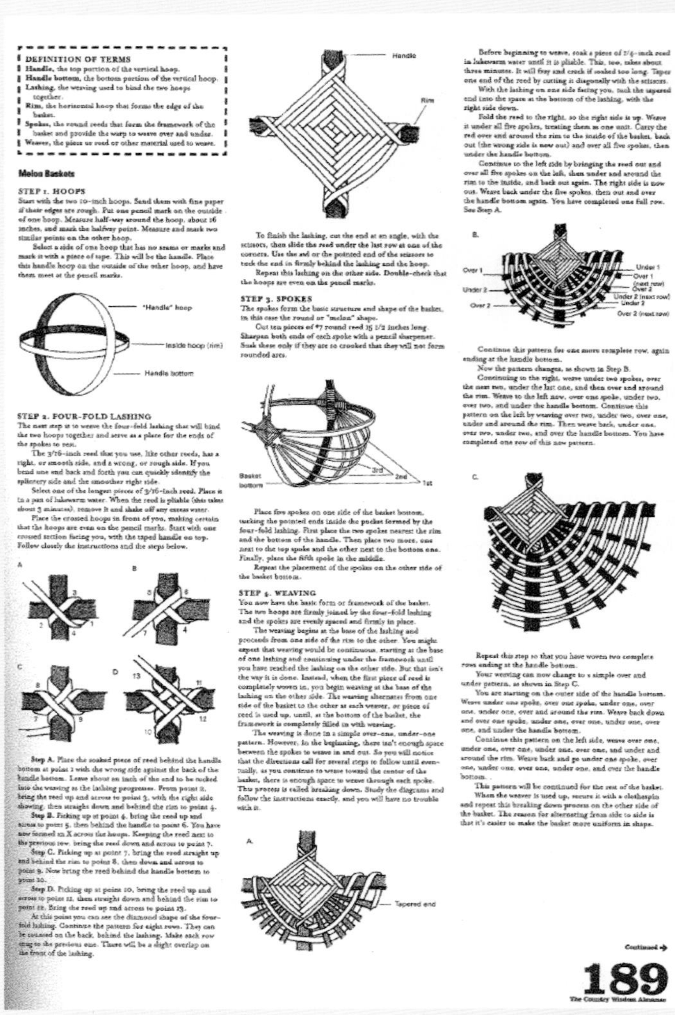

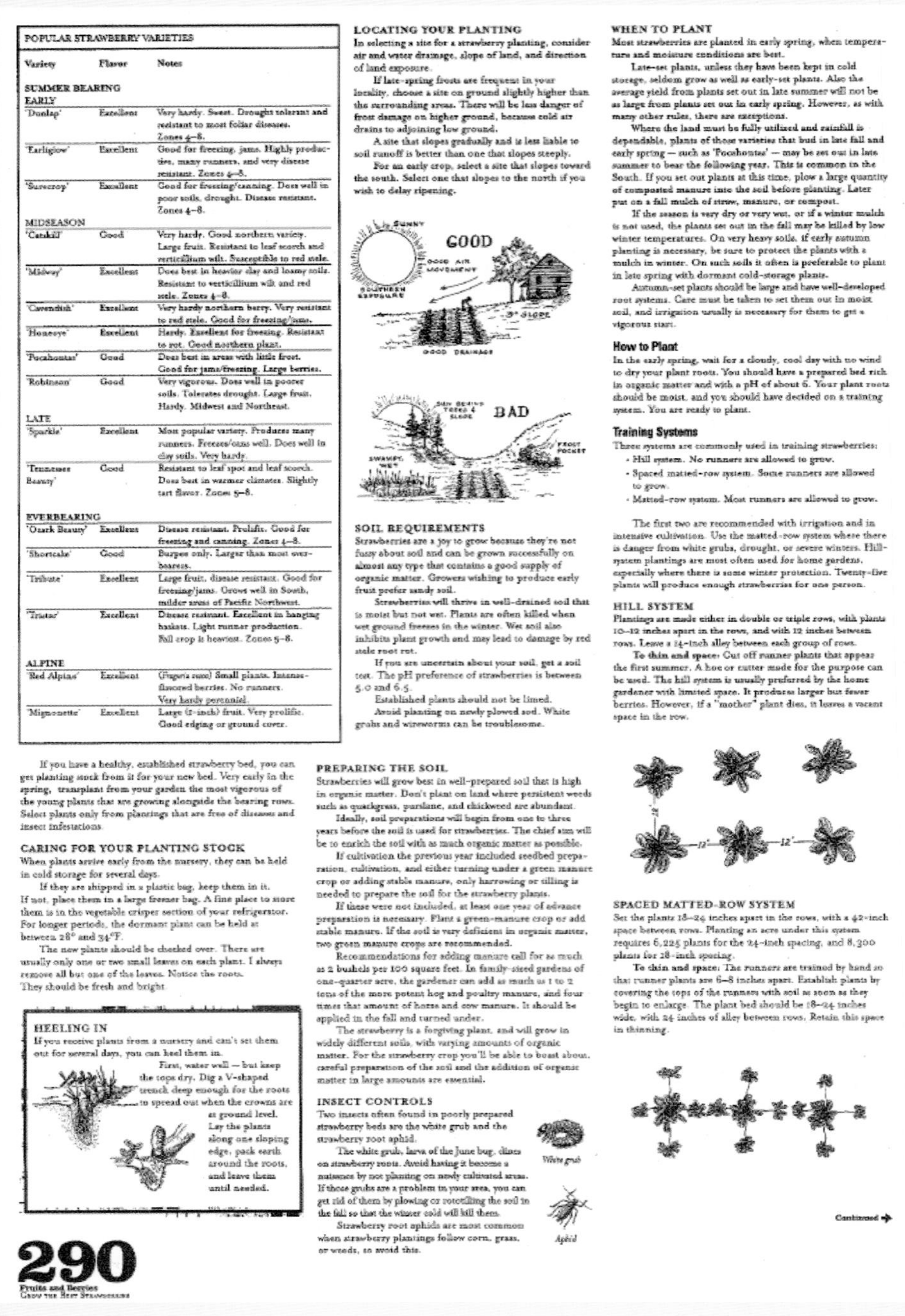

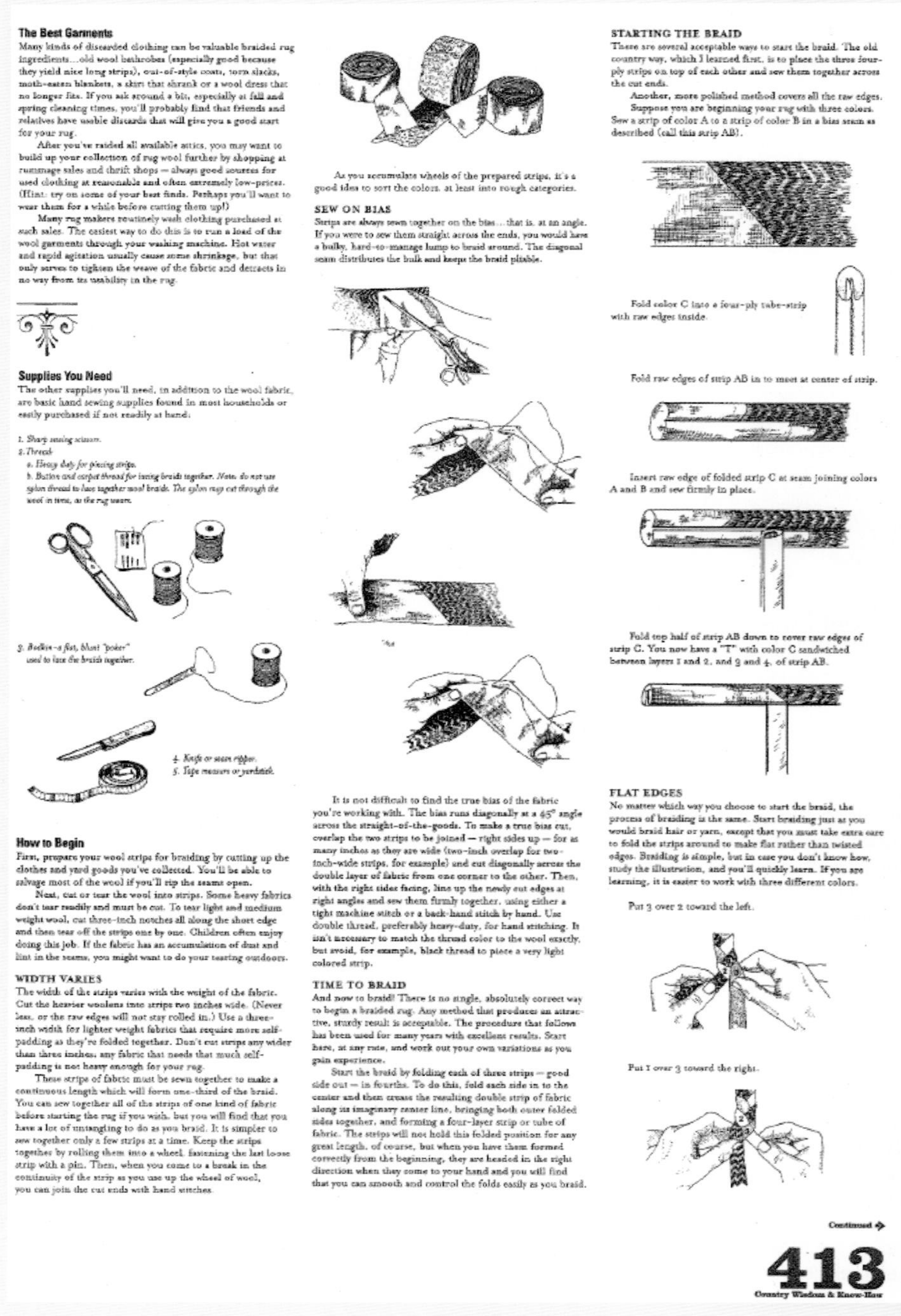

390

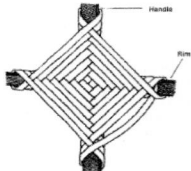
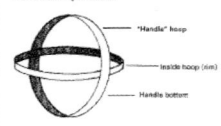
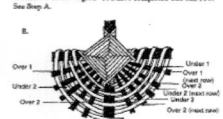
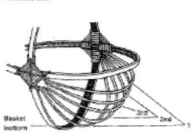
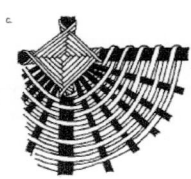
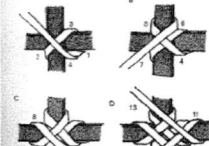
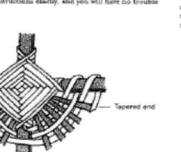

189

POPULAR STRAWBERRY VARIETIES

Variety	Flavor	Notes
SUMMER BEARING EARLY		
'Dunlap'	Very hardy	Very hardy. Sweet. Drought tolerant and resistant to most foliar diseases. Zones 4–8.
'Earliglow'	Excellent	Good for freezing, jams. Highly productive, many runners, and very disease resistant. Zones 4–8.
'Surecrop'	Excellent	Good for freezing/canning. Does well in poor soils, drought. Disease resistant. Zones 4–8.
MIDSEASON		
'Catskill'	Good	Very hardy. Good northern variety. Large fruit. Resistant to leaf scorch and verticillium wilt. Susceptible to red stele. Zones 4–8.
'Midway'	Excellent	Does best in heavier clay and loamy soils. Resistant to verticillium wilt and red stele. Zones 4–8.
'Cavendish'	Excellent	Very hardy northern berry. Very resistant to red stele. Good for freezing/jams.
'Honeoye'	Excellent	Hardy. Excellent for freezing. Resistant to rot. Good northern plant.
'Pocahontas'	Good	Does best in areas with little frost. Good for jams/freezing. Large berries.
'Robinson'	Excellent	Very vigorous. Does well in poorer soils. Vigorous. Drought. Large fruit. Hardy. Midwest and Northeast.
LATE		
'Sparkle'	Excellent	Most popular variety. Produces many runners. Freezes/cans well. Does well in clay soils. Very hardy.
'Trumpeter Beauty'	Good	Resistant to leaf spot and leaf scorch. Does best in warmer climates. Slightly tart flavor. Zones 3–8.
EVERBEARING		
'Ozark Beauty'	Excellent	Disease resistant. Prolific. Good for freezing and canning. Zones 4–8.
'Shortcake'	Good	Burgess only. Larger than most everbearers.
'Tribute'	Excellent	Large fruit, disease resistant. Good for freezing/jams. Grows well in South, milder areas of Pacific Northwest.
'Tristar'	Excellent	Disease resistant. Excellent in hanging baskets. Light runner production. Full crop in harvest. Zones 4–8.
ALPINE		
'Red Alpine'	Excellent	(Fragaria vesca) Small plants. Intense-flavored berries. No runners. Very hardy perennial.
'Mignonette'	Excellent	Large (2-inch) fruit. Very prolific. Good edging or ground cover.

If you have a healthy, established strawberry bed, you can get planting stock from it for your new bed. Very early in the spring, transplant from your garden the most vigorous of the young plants that are growing alongside the bearing rows. Select plants only from plantings that are free of diseases and insect infestations.

CARING FOR YOUR PLANTING STOCK
When plants arrive early from the nursery, they can be held in cold storage for several days.

If they are shipped in a plastic bag, keep them in it. If not, place them in a large freezer bag. A fine place to store them is in the vegetable crisper section of your refrigerator. For longer periods, the dormant plant can be held at between 28° and 34°F.

The new plants should be checked over. There are usually only one or two small leaves on each plant. I always remove all but one of these leaves. Notice the roots. They should be fresh and bright.

HEELING IN
If you receive plants from a nursery and can't set them out for several days, you can heel them in.

First, water well -- but keep the tops dry. Dig a V-shaped trench deep enough for the roots to spread out when the crowns are at ground level. Lay the plants along one sloping edge, pack earth around the roots, and leave them until needed.

LOCATING YOUR PLANTING
In selecting a site for a strawberry planting, consider air and water drainage, slope of land, and direction of land exposure.

Late-spring frosts are frequent in your locality; choose a site on ground slightly higher than the surrounding areas. There will be less danger of frost damage on higher ground, because cold air drains to adjoining low ground.

A site that slopes gradually and is less liable to soil runoff is better than one that slopes steeply.

For an early crop, select a site that slopes toward the south. Select one that slopes to the north if you wish to delay ripening.

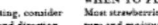

SOIL REQUIREMENTS
Strawberries are a joy to grow because they're not fussy about soil and can be grown successfully on almost any type that contains a good supply of organic matter. Growers wishing to produce early fruit prefer sandy soil.

Strawberries will thrive in well-drained soil that is moist but not wet. Plants are often killed when wet ground freezes in the winter. Wet soil also inhibits plant growth and may lead to damage by red stele root rot.

If you are uncertain about your soil, get a soil test. The pH preference of strawberries is between 5.0 and 6.5.

Established plants should not be limed. Avoid planting on newly plowed sod. White grubs and wireworms can be troublesome.

PREPARING THE SOIL
Strawberries grow best in well-prepared soil that is high in organic matter. Don't plant on land where persistent weeds such as quackgrass, purslane, and chickweed are abundant.

Ideally, soil preparations will begin from one to three years before the soil is used for strawberries. The chief aim will be to enrich the soil with as much organic matter as possible.

If cultivation the previous year included seedbed preparation, cultivation, and either turning under a green-manure crop or adding stable manure, only harrowing or tilling is needed to prepare the soil for the strawberry plants.

If these were not included, at least one year of advance preparation is necessary. Plant a green-manure crop or add stable manure, if the soil is very deficient in organic matter, two green manure crops are recommended.

Recommendations for adding manure call for as much as 2 bushels per 100 square feet. In family-sized gardens of one-quarter acre, the gardener can add as much as 1 to 2 tons of the more potent hog and poultry manure, and four times that amount of horse and cow manure. It should be applied in the fall and turned under.

The strawberry is a forgiving plant, and will grow in widely different soils, with varying amounts of organic matter. For the strawberry crop you'll be able to boast about, careful preparation of the soil and the addition of organic matter in large amounts are essential.

INSECT CONTROLS
Two insects often found in poorly prepared strawberry beds are the white grub and the strawberry root aphid.

The white grub, larva of the June beetle, does damage on strawberry roots. Avoid having it become a nuisance by not planting on recently cultivated areas. If these grubs are a problem in your area, you can get rid of them by plowing or rototilling the soil in the fall so that the winter cold will kill them.

Strawberry root aphids are most common when strawberry plantings follow corn, grass, or weeds, so avoid them.

WHEN TO PLANT
Most strawberries are planted in early spring, when temperature and moisture conditions are best.

Late-set plants, unless they have been kept in cold storage, seldom grow as well as early-set plants. Also the average yield from plants set out in late summer will not be as large from plants set out in early spring. However, as with many other rules, there are exceptions.

Where the land must be fully cultured and rainfall is dependable, plants of those varieties that bud in late fall and early spring -- such as 'Pocahontas' -- may be set out in late summer to bear the following year. This is common in the South. If you set out plants at this time, place a large quantity of composted manure into the soil before planting. Later put on a fall mulch of straw, manure, or compost.

If the season is very dry or very wet, or if a winter mulch is not used, the plants set out in the fall may be killed by low winter temperatures. On very heavy soils, if early autumn planting is necessary, be sure to protect the plants with a mulch in winter. On such soils it is often advisable to plant in late spring with dormant cold-storage plants.

Autumn-set plants should be large and have well-developed root systems. Care must be taken to set them out in moist soil, and irrigation usually is necessary for them to get a vigorous start.

How to Plant
In the early spring, wait for a cloudy, cool day with no wind to dry your plant roots. You should have a prepared bed rich in organic matter and with a pH of about 6. Your plant roots should be moist, and you should have decided on a training system. You are ready to plant.

Training Systems
Three systems are commonly used in training strawberries:
- Hill system. No runners are allowed to grow.
- Spaced matted-row system. Some runners are allowed to grow.
- Matted-row system. Most runners are allowed to grow.

The first two are recommended with irrigation and in intensive cultivation. Use the matted-row system where there is danger from white grubs, drought, or severe winters. Hill-system plantings are most often used for home gardens, especially where there is some winter protection. Twenty-five plants will produce enough strawberries for one person.

HILL SYSTEM
Plantings are made either in double or triple rows, with plants 10–12 inches apart in the rows, and 12 inches between rows. Leave a 14-inch alley between each group of rows.

In the thick spaces: Cut off runner plants that appear the first summer. A hoe or cutter made for the purpose can be used. The hill system is usually preferred by the home gardener with limited space. It produces larger but fewer berries. However, if a 'mother' plant dies, it leaves a vacant space in the row.

SPACED MATTED-ROW SYSTEM
Set the plants 18–24 inches apart in the rows, with a 42-inch space between rows. Planting an acre under this system requires 6,225 plants for the 24-inch spacing, and 8,300 plants for 28-inch spacing.

To thin and space: The runners are trained by hand so that runner plants are 6–8 inches apart. Establish plants by covering the tips of the runners with soil as soon as they begin to enlarge. The plant bed should be 18–24 inches wide, with 24 inches of alley between rows. Retain this space in thinning.

290

The Best Garments
Many kinds of discarded clothing can be valuable braided rug ingredients...old wool bathrobes (especially good because they yield nice long strips), out-of-style coats, torn slacks, moth-eaten blankets, a shirt that shrank or a wool dress that no longer fits. If you ask around a bit, especially at fall and spring cleaning times, you'll probably find that friends and relatives have usable discards that will give you a good start for your rug.

After you've raided all available attics, you may want to build up your collection of rug wool further by shopping at rummage sales and thrift shops -- always good sources for used clothing at reasonable and often extremely low-prices. (Hint: try on some of your best finds. Perhaps you'll want to wear them for a while before cutting them up!)

Many rug makers routinely wash clothing purchased at such sales. The easiest way to do this is to run a load of the wool garments through your washing machine. Hot water and rapid agitation usually cause some shrinkage, but that only serves to tighten the weave of the fabric and detracts in no way from its usability in the rug.

Supplies You Need
The other supplies you'll need, in addition to the wool fabric, are basic hand sewing supplies found in most households or easily purchased if not readily at hand.

1. Sharp sewing scissors.
2. Thread.
   a. Heavy duty for piecing strips.
   b. Button and carpet thread for joining braids together. Note: do not use nylon thread to lace together wool braids. The nylon rug can cut through the wool in time, as the rug wears.
3. Bodkin -- a flat, blunt "poker" used to lace the braids together.
4. Knife or seam ripper.
5. Tape measure or yardstick.

How to Begin
First, prepare your wool strips for braiding by cutting up the clothes and yard goods you've collected. You'll be able to salvage most of the wool if you'll rip the seams open.

Next, cut or tear the wool into strips. Some heavy fabrics don't tear readily and must be cut. To tear light and medium weight wool, cut three-inch notches all along the short edge and then tear off the strips one by one. Children often enjoy doing this job. If the fabric has an accumulation of dust and lint in the seams, you might want to do your tearing outdoors.

WIDTH VARIES
The width of the strips varies with the weight of the fabric. Cut the heavier woolens into strips two inches wide. (Never less, or the raw edges will not stay rolled in.) Use a three-inch width for lighter weight fabrics that require more self-padding as they're folded together. Don't cut strips any wider than three inches; any fabric that needs that much self-padding is not heavy enough for your rug.

These strips of fabric must be sewn together to make a continuous length which will form one-third of the braid. You can sew together all of the strips of one kind of fabric before starting the rug if you wish, but you will find that you have a lot of untangling to do as you braid. It is simpler to sew together only a few strips at a time. Keep the strips together by rolling them into a wheel, fastening the last loose strip with a pin. Then, when you come to a break in the continuity of the strip as you use up the spools of wool, you can join the cut ends with hand stitches.

STARTING THE BRAID
There are several acceptable ways to start the braid. The old country way, which I learned first, is to place the three four-ply strips on top of each other and sew them together across the cut ends.

Another, more polished method covers all the raw edges. Suppose you are beginning your rug with three colors. Sew a strip of color B into a bias seam as described (call this strip AB).

SEW ON BIAS
Strips are always sewn together on the bias...that is, at an angle. If you were to sew them straight across the ends, you would have a bulky, hard-to-manage lump to braid around. The diagonal seam distributes the bulk and keeps the braid pliable.

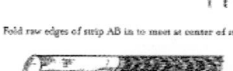

Fold color C into a four-ply tube-strip with raw edges inside.

Fold raw edges of strip AB in to meet at center of strip.

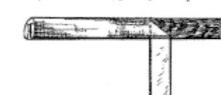

Insert raw edge of folded strip C at seam joining colors A and B and sew firmly in place.

Fold top half of strip AB down to cover raw edges of strip C. You now have a "T" with color C sandwiched between layers 1 and 2, and 3 and 4, of strip AB.

It is not difficult to find the true bias of the fabric you're working with. The bias runs diagonally at a 45° angle across the straight-of-the-goods. To make a true bias cut, overlap the two strips to be joined -- for right sides up -- for as many inches as they are wide (two-inch overlap for two-inch-wide strips, for example) and cut diagonally across the double layer of fabric from one corner to the other. Then, with the right sides facing, line up the newly cut edges at right angles and sew them firmly together, using either a tight machine stitch or a back-hand stitch by hand. Use double thread, preferably heavy-duty, for hand stitching. It isn't necessary to match the thread color to the wool exactly, but avoid, for example, black thread to piece a very light colored strip.

TIME TO BRAID
And now to braid! There is no single, absolutely correct way to begin a braided rug. Any method that produces an attractive, sturdy result is acceptable. The procedure that follows has been used for many years with excellent results. Start here, at any rate, and work your way through any variations as you gain experience.

Start the braid by folding each of three strips -- good side out -- in fourths. To do this, fold each side in to the center and then crease the resulting double strip of fabric along its imaginary center line, bringing both outer folded sides together, and forming a four-layer strip or tube of fabric. The strips will not hold this folded position for any great length, of course, but when you have them formed correctly from the beginning, they are headed in the right direction when they come to your hand and you will find that you can smooth and control the folds easily as you braid.

FLAT EDGES
No matter which way you choose to start the braid, the process of braiding is the same. Start braiding just as you would braid hair or yarn, except that you must take extra care to fold the strips around to make flat rather than twisted edges. Braiding is simple, but in case you don't know how, study the illustration, and you'll quickly learn. If you are learning, it is easier to work with three different colors.

Put 3 over 2 toward the left.

Put 1 over 3 toward the right.

413

Best beginners' guide to bees
Beekeeping for Dummies
$12 Howland Blackiston, 2009, 392 p.

Over the years I've kept a few hives of bees for honey. And I have a whole shelf of bee books. *Beekeeping for Dummies* is my current best choice for a beginner's introduction to bees. As in many subjects, there is nothing like attending a local hands-on workshop as way to learn fast, but you could get a few hives going in your backyard using just the clear step-by-step instructions in this book alone. It'll guide you through basic bee biology, safety concerns, using the gear, and how to get bees. More than any other bee-keeping tutorial it anticipates most questions newbies will have. It also offer guidance on what to do with your bounty of honey and wax. Bees are eternally fascinating and there's a library of other classic bee books to follow up with, but this one is the best place to start.

-- KK

A little smoke under the hive cover calms any of the colony's guard bees that may be upstairs.

Knowing when it's time for more smoke

A few minutes into your inspection, you may notice that the bees all have lined up between the top bars like racehorses at the starting gate. Their little heads are all in a row between the frames. Kind of cute, aren't they? They're watching you. That's your signal to give the girls a few more puffs of smoke to disperse them again so that you can continue with your inspection.

Having Realistic Expectations

In your first year, don't expect too much of a honey harvest. Sorry, but a newly established colony doesn't have the benefit of a full season of foraging. Nor has it had an opportunity to build its maximum population. I know that's disappointing news. But be patient. Next year will be a bonanza!

Beekeeping is like farming. the actual yield depends upon the weather. Many warm, sunny days with ample rain results in more flowers and greater nectar flows. When gardens flourish, so do bees. If Mother Nature works in your favor, a hive can produce 60 to 100 pounds of surplus honey (that's the honey you can take form the bees), or more. If you live in a warm climate (like Florida or Southern California) you can expect multiple harvests each year. But remember that your bees need you to leave some honey for their own use. In cold climates leave them 60 pounds, in climates with no winter, leave 20 to 30 pounds.

A fume board looks like an outer cover with a flannel lining. A liquid bee repellent is applied to the flannel lining and the fume board is placed on top of the honey supers (in place of the inner and outer covers). Within five minutes, the bees are repelled out of the honey supers and down into the brood chamber. Instant success! The honey supers can then be safely removed and taken to your harvesting area.

A safe and fast way to get bees out of honey supers is to use a fume board with Fischer's Bee-Quick.

Carefully lift out the first frame and set it aside. Now you have room to manipulate the other frames.

Cheapest way to start bees
Mann Lake Beekeeping Starter Kit
$187 mannlakeltd.com

This is the least expensive kit for starting beekeeping. It has everything you need to raise some honey, except 3 things. You'll need bees; order them by mail separately, or find a swarm. You'll need to add at least one "upper" story of frames to store your share of the honey, and you'll need access to an extractor -- extracting honey by hand from this upper is possible but extremely messy. With care the equipment included should last many decades. You need only keep adding boxes of frames.

Used bee equipment is not advisable these days because of rampant bee disease. A beginner should start with new gear. There are a few sources with cheaper kits, but their shipping costs -- between costs $60-$90 -- will kill any bargain. Mann Lake offers free shipping, a fantastic deal with such bulky stuff. Also, their boxes and frames come fully assembled, which is also not the norm. That can save you several hours, and for a beginner, it provides assurance everything is right. Get the unpainted option; that's easy enough to do and you can choose your color (they don't have to be white).

If you have Amazon Prime you can get the same deal through Amazon.

--KK

The Basic Starter Kit Includes:

Assembled Hive Bodies or Supers

Assembled Frames with Rite-Cell Foundation

Waxed Standard Plastic Frames

Assembled Telescoping Cover w/ Inner Cover

Assembled Bottom Board w/Reducer

9 1/2" (24.13 cm) Hive Tool

Economy Leather Gloves (Large, color may vary)

Alexander Bee Veil

Dome Top Smoker w/Guard

"The New Starting Right With Bees" Book

Human-powered honey removal
Hand Crank Honey Extractor
$330+ Mann Lake, LTD

This gorgeous, stainless steel spinning extractor, made in Italy for Mann Lake, sits in a privileged part of our living room and sometimes serves as a coffee table. But come extraction time, I not only use this beauty in my yard, I share it with my beekeeping friends. It's about the size of a medium garbage can, so it's easy to load into the car. It fits three frames at a time — the perfect amount for backyard beekeepers who often need to extract only 9 frames at once.

There's no plug, no motor, just human arm power.

Inside is a metal carriage or rack you slide your frames into. Each side of the frame has honeycomb, so you need to flip the frames to get the honey out of both sides. But most backyard beekeepers are curious and want to check out the progress of the extraction process, anyhow. Watching the honey splatter on the inside edges of the extractor is very satisfying.

It's also very satisfying to hold up the frame to the light and see that the honey has been

sucked out of the comb and is now dripping down the inside of the extractor. And therein lies the beauty of this hand-crank model: the spigot. The honey flows down the sides of the extractor and coalesces in a pool. One only has to turn the spigot and out drips your liquid gold. I never filter or heat my honey so we just hold jars under the spigot. Viola!

Clean up is simple — just put the extractor near the beehive. The bees will lick up the remaining honey. And before I put it back in the living room, I like to pour a few buckets of hot soapy water just to make sure.

Mann Lake makes a few extractors, including a cheaper 3-frame model. However, cheaper models have the crank on top instead of on the side, which makes it more difficult to spin (can you say instant tennis elbow?). I've also heard it's harder to get the spinner moving fast enough to splatter the honey. With this extractor (the HH-190), the crank is on the side, which is more ergonomically friendly. The next model up is motorized, which I think you need only if you're a commercial size beekeeper or elderly.

Beekeeping involves buying a lot of equipment (an urban farmer, I have been beekeeping since 1999 and bought this extractor two years ago).

Paradoxically, while we're in it for the long haul and strive to buy quality, long-lasting equipment, we also pride ourselves on being thrifty, and some of us border on the edge of being Luddites. For example, in order to extract the bee's hard-earned honey, a beekeeper must remove the frames of honeycomb, slice off the capped honey and then somehow extract the sticky ambrosia. I'm proud to say I've never used one of those electric, plug-in hot knives for uncapping the comb. I use a pot of boiling water and a good kitchen knife, and simply dunk the knife in the water for a time, wipe it off and then slice. No cord, no expense.

I feel the same way about my extractor: It's a nice synthesis of human and machine. Before I got on I used to try to use a bowl, some pans and gravity. This is impossible in a place like California with all these ants! And it just takes forever to let the honey drip out. This machine allows us to speed up the extraction process, but not too much.

-- Novella Carpenter

Incredible, edible plants

Nature's Garden * The Forager's Harvest

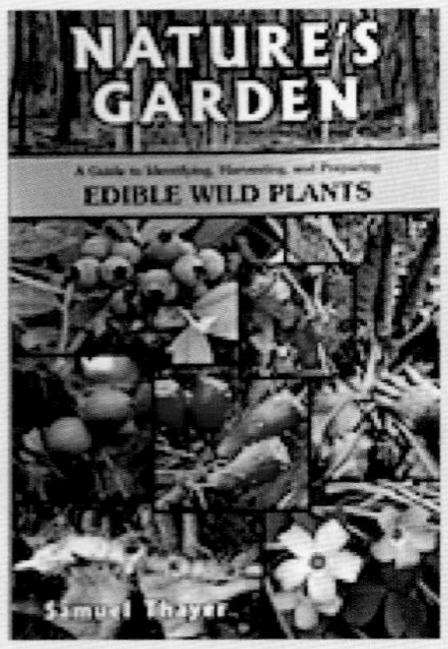

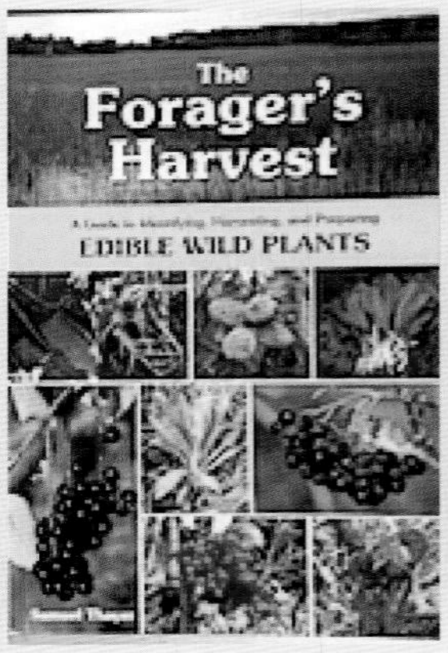

These are the most AMAZING wild food books ever written. Samuel Thayer knows his stuff. And he is a great teacher. He is to wild food plants what David Auroa (see next page) is to mushrooms -- the guru who has mastered encyclopedic details through personal experience. I believe he knows more than Euell Gibbons (see p. 141) did. I've spent many evenings reading his findings till late at night. He has completely re-invigorated my interest in wild greens.

What makes his advice great: Thayer does not include any plants unless he has gathered and eaten it at least 50 times! So he shows the plant in all of its life cycle from seedling, to mature, to seeding, and in great detail of how to find it, and how to harvest it -- not just a few plants but enough for a meal. And he points out the common lookalikes and their stages. And what not to do while harvesting. There's tons and tons of photos of his process. His chapter on acorns is majestic. Acorns are mentioned in passing by all wild food books but not really addressed by any. Thayer's treatment of acorns is born out of years and years of making meal from dozens and dozens of varieties in dozens of different species in dozens of different states. His thoroughness is stunning. Overall he is pretty picky about laying out what tastes good based not on one try but dozens and dozens of tries. His wisdom comes in two volumes. Yet because his expertise is based on his own first-hand knowledge, his books are biased to the midwest where he lives. (If he cites any second hand knowledge beyond his own he humbly gives a full citation of the source.) *Nature's Garden* is a bit broader in geography, but really you want both volumes. They are similar with no overlap of plants, but each contains his general orientation, so can stand alone.

-- *KK*

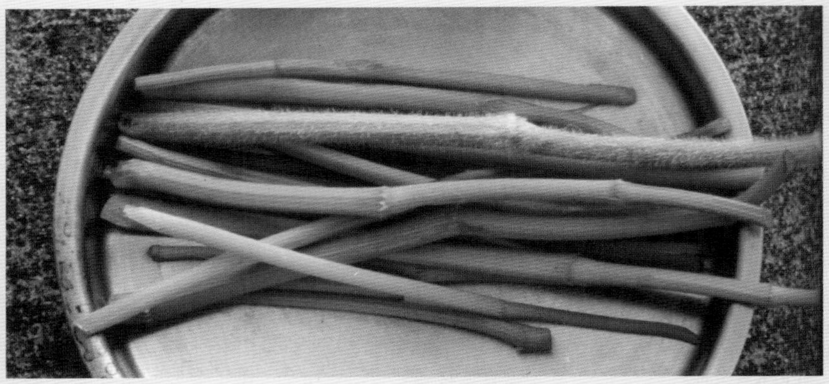

Wild carrot shoots, all but one peeled. These have a pleasantly carroty flavor and are more tender than they look.

$16 Nature's Garden Samuel Thayer, 2010, 512 p.

$15 The Forager's Harvest Samuel Thayer, 2006, 360 p.

From *Forager's Harvest*:

The first time you talk to a certain landowner, ask permission to harvest a specific plant that can be seen from the road; make it something like elderberries or butternuts that the landowner is likely to have heard of before. Offer to share your harvest with him. (Don't worry, he won't want any.) If the landowner was kind and the property seemed like a promising one that you'd like to return to, bring a gift of some foraged product, such as a jar of jam or jelly, as a thank you at a later date. After feeling assured that foraging really is a hobby of yours and that you're not up to anything else, the landowner will trust you more.

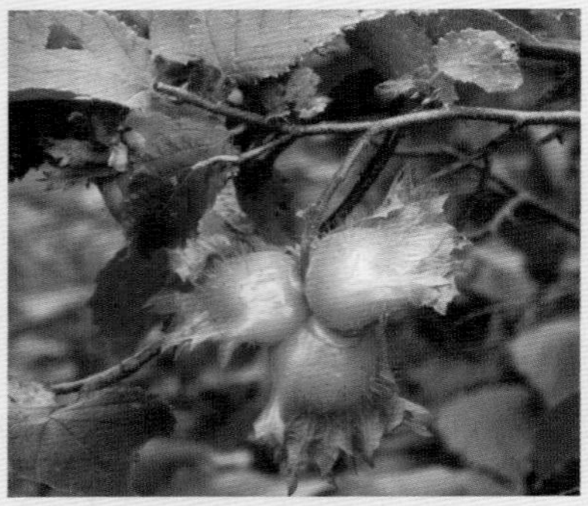

American hazelnuts on the bush. The husks are green, but the nuts are ripe.

•

If you substitute a single wild ingredient in a familiar recipe and the result is disappointing, you may consider the recipe a failure but don't give up on the plant - it may be perfect for another dish. Be patient - it can take a while to figure out how to cook with an unfamiliar vegetable, especially those for which we don't have culinary traditions to guide us.

The Five Steps of Identifying Edible Plants

1. Tentative identification: You have located what you think is a certain plant.
2. Compare your plant to a reliable reference: Do this carefully, thoroughly, critically, and reasonably.
3. Double and triple check: Compare to several more reliable references
4. Find more specimens: Do this until you can effortlessly recognize the plant: it may take minutes, hours, days, or even years.
5. Assess contradictory confidence: Do you really have it? Are you sure? Are you willing to bet your life? Would you proclaim it in front of a group of botanists?

Here's another good rule to follow: if you need to use a book to identify a plant, you are not ready to eat it.

•

The first time that you eat the plant, exercise some restraint. Cook it by itself and taste a small portion carefully. If it is bitter or otherwise distasteful, spit it out. This is an extremely important secondary line of defense. The tongue was designed to tell us which foods are safe and which aren't, and it does a remarkably good job of this. Most toxic plants taste terrible.

•

Most of our common spices and seasonings are toxic enough that consuming a few ounces would make a person very ill; in large enough doses they could be fatal. But who eats a few ounces of rosemary, mustard, or nutmeg? Who slurps down a glass of horseradish? What person, given alternatives, would choose to eat maize gruel as the main course of every meal for months on end? And who in the world gets locked in the chicken truck?

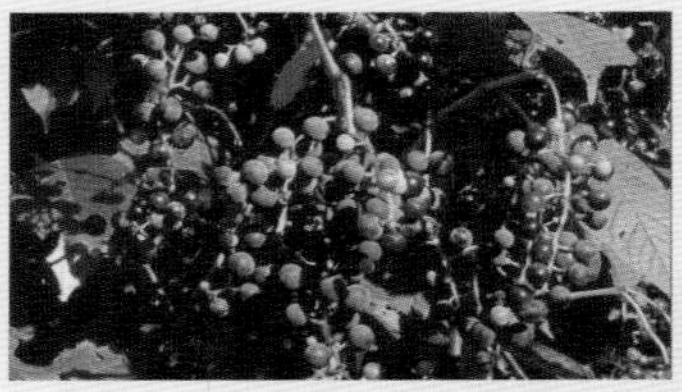

▲ *Tartrate is present in all grapes but is highly concentrated in riverside grape and some of the other small-fruited species. Fortunately, it is easy to get rid of. Just let the juice sit in a container in the refrigerator or some other cool place for a day or two. The tartrate will settle to the bottom; you will recognize it because it forms an ugly grayish sludge. Pour off the good juice and then discard the tartrate sludge, which is usually about one-third of the volume of the grape juice. Never make anything from fresh-pressed small wild grapes without subjecting the juice to this purification process.*

From *Nature's Harvest*:

•

Stinging nettle is a tall and elegant perennial herb that grows in dense colonies connected by a network of narrow rhizomes. The stalks rarely exceed .4 inch (1 cm) in diameter. They are hollow and squarish with four deep grooves running their length, and rarely branch except where the plants have been injured. The stalks are typically 5-8 feet (1.5-2.5 m) tall at maturity. The bark of the stem is composed of strong fibers, which can easily be noted when the plant is broken. The main stem, petioles, and leaf surface bear stinging hairs, although these are generally absent from lower parts of the main stem after the plants reach full size.

•

Fiddlehead Ferns

Almost everyone has heard of "fiddlehead ferns," a gourmet wild vegetable found across much of North America in the springtime. Few wild edibles are so well known, so convenient and tasty, or so widely available. Yet unfortunately, few of them are surrounded by so much confusion. Many people mistakenly believe that all fern fiddleheads are edible. Not surprisingly, stories of people getting sick from fiddleheads are common, and this has caused many to steer clear of these wildlings. All of this confusion is unnecessary, for learning to identify the edible species of fiddleheads is rather easy - and the reward is a lifetime of free and delicious vegetables.

Bracken Fern

Bracken fern is the common, large fern with a single, erect stem, of northern and mountainous regions. By biomass, it is probably the most prolific herbaceous plant in North America and in the world.

There is a great deal of debate about the edibility of bracken fern. On one hand, there is an enormous body of ethnographic evidence that it is edible. It is regularly eaten by hundreds of millions of people today, and in North America was a traditional food for many Native American cultures. Compare this to ostrich fern, which is consumed by far fewer people today and for which there is virtually no evidence that Native Americans traditionally consumed it anywhere. Despite this, a search on the internet will turn up hundreds of sources telling you that this plant is poisonous, even deadly, and should never be eaten. This is due to the presence of a very potent carcinogen called ptaquiloside. However, ptaquiloside is not heat-stable and is apparently destroyed by cooking. Interestingly, Americans don't seem too worried about the equally well-established facts that bread crust and grilled meats contain potent carcinogens. And orientals don't seem to worried about bracken fern.

While it is advisable to eat all fiddleheads cooked, bracken fern fiddleheads should definitely be cooked to destroy the ptaquiloside.

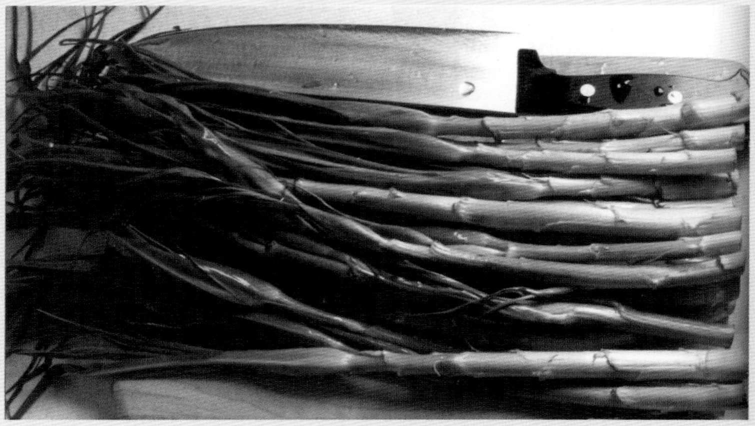

Salsify shoots--a fantastic and little-known vegetable. It only took a few minutes to gather these.

•

Making Your Own Apple Pectin

When making homemade jams and jellies, commercial powdered pectin is usually the most expensive ingredient. A few generations ago, powdered pectin wasn't readily available, and the skill of making pectin at home was common knowledge for the family cook — yet today it is a rare individual who knows how to do this. I learned how to extract pectin from apples a few years ago when I made jams and jellies for a living (as many as 600 jars per day). Not only does this save money, but more importantly, it provides the satisfaction that only comes with doing things from scratch - one of the reasons that I love using wild foods.

To prepare liquid apple pectin, it is best to use under-ripe apples that are still a bit green, hard, and sour. Ripe apples contain less pectin, but the level varies greatly from one tree to the next; some varieties are suitable when ripe, while some have virtually no pectin by that time. Over-ripe apples are the worst. You can use your damaged or misshapen apples for making pectin. Chop them in halves or quarters, fill a large pot, and then add just enough water to almost cover the apple chunks. Cover the pot and place it on low heat for a long time, until the apples are fully cooked and you have something that looks like runny applesauce with skins and seeds in it. Stir the apples every twenty minutes or so while they are cooking.

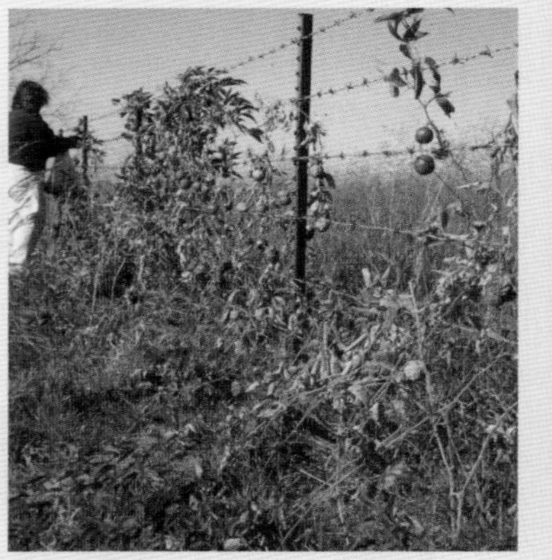

Picking maypops. As usual, on a fence. The wrinkled yellow ones are also good to eat--very good.

I arrange a strainer for this "sauce" by placing a cheese cloth (actually a white T-shirt) over the top of a five-gallon pail, secured by a cord tied around the rim. (A piece of cheese cloth in a colander works fine for smaller amounts.) The hot applesauce is then poured into the strainer; what drips out the bottom should be a clear, thick liquid that's a little bit slimy to the touch. That's your liquid apple pectin. I usually let mine strain overnight, because it drips slowly. You can get more pectin by pressing it, but then it comes out a little cloudy and carries more of the under-ripe apple flavor. I like to make a few gallons of this pectin at a time and then save it by canning or freezing - it's not hard to get a year's supply with one batch.

Dates correspond to an average growing season at 45°N latitude and 1000 ft (300 m) elevation	Early Spring Mar 25 – Apr 25	Mid Spring Apr 25 – May 10	Late Spring May 10 – June 5	Early Summer June 5 – July 1	Mid Summer July 1 – Aug 10	Late Summer Aug 10 – Sep 10	Early Fall Sep 10 – Oct 10	Late Fall Oct 10 – Nov 15
Trout lily bulb								
Trout lily leaf								
Solomon seal shoot								
Solomon seal rhizome								
False solomon seal shoot								
False solomon seal rhizome								
False solomon seal berries								
Lotus tuber								
Lotus nut (soft)								
Lotus nut (dry)								
Lotus leaf								

The empires of the futures are the empires of the mind. - Winston Churchill

These are summer ceps. However all ceps, summer or autumn, show a fine white network on the top of the stem right underneath the tubes.

Introduction to edibles
Mushrooming Without Fear

$10 Alexander Schwab, 2006, 128 p.

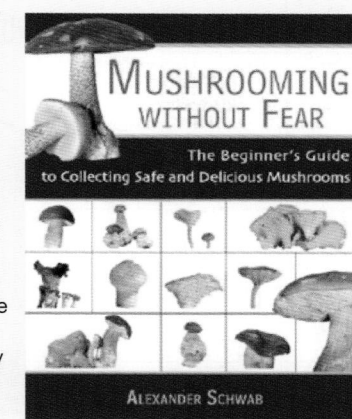

MUSHROOMING WITHOUT FEAR
The Beginner's Guide to Collecting Safe and Delicious Mushrooms

ALEXANDER SCHWAB

Can you tell the difference between a head of cabbage and a head of lettuce? Then you can safely pick and eat some wild mushrooms. The key is to learn to identify a few easily identifiable delicious species, and then stick with these easy ones for a while. This book does a fantastic job of holding your hand every step of the way. It gives you reliable rules for learning 10 or so yummy and safe mushrooms. I wish I had this book when I was first starting out. It is a great substitute for going out with an expert.

-- KK

Hen of the Woods

The hen of the woods is a cluster of fan-shaped overlapping caps.

On the underside of the cap (approx. 2 inches across) the tubes are at this stage visible to the naked eye. At this point the hen of the woods reaches gourmet status. Start picking now.

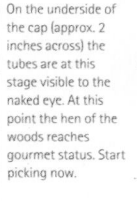

Actual size 2 inches

The fan-shaped caps with radial furrows are typical of the hen of the woods.

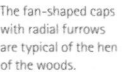

Portable mushroom guru
All That the Rain Promises and More…

$13 David Arora, 1991, 256 p.

The best mushroom hunting book ever. Delivers amazing lore, practical tips, and the most concise (yet reliable) bullet points for identification of fruiting fungus. The seasons and species are biased to the west coast but this back-pocket-sized book is perfectly useable anywhere in the country. It's inspiring and delightful. Puts the fun back in fungi.

-- KK

● **Mining for Mushrooms**

It was a long time ago, in my hippie days. I was living on a commune, and I was sick and tried of all the bickering and brown rice. I really needed some space, so I split for Arizona, where I heard that there was nothing but, to see the spring wildflowers. So get this: we're driving down this crusty, dusty desert road on the way to a scenic overlook — the most unlikely place in the world for mushrooms — and I see this glimmer of white in the ditch by the road. We stop for a look and, sure enough, it's an old Agaricus bitorquis. Jade says it must be the only shroom in the state of Arizona, and I'm about to agree when I start noticing all these cracks everywhere in the hard red clay along the road. It was shroom city. There were hundreds, big clumps of them, veins of them , but all underground! Most were several inches under, some more that a foot. "Dig this!" I said to Jade. "With what?" she wanted to know. We used our hands, making piles of them on the road as we walked along.

Of course we were noticed. An RV stopped, and this older couple from Long Beach got out and wanted to know what we were doing. "We're mining for mushrooms," I said, pausing for effect, "and we've just struck the mother lode." We could tell they really wanted to try their hand at it. They sold life insurance and had been traveling for three months, visiting every national park in the country and this was their final stop, their last scenic

An extraordinary haul of wild Matsutake

The mushroom bible
Mushrooms Demystified

$26 David Arora, 1986, 1020 p.

Veterans of wild mushrooming quickly graduate to author David Arora's masterpiece, *Mushrooms Demystified,* which is the undisputed bible of mushroom knowledge in North America. *Where All That the Rain Promises and More…* is breezy and succinct, *Demystified* is encyclopedic and exhaustive. You take *Rains* out to the mushrooms in the woods; you bring the mysterious ones back to the heavy *Demystifed* tome at your kitchen table.

-- KK

The latest edition of the most comprehensive field guide to wild mushrooms — over 2000 species, over 800 photos

Mushrooms Demystified by David Arora

overlook, and they were so burned out, they really wanted to do something exciting. But duty called, they just had to go on to the overlook.

Five minutes later they were back for some fun. Along with everything else in the world they had brand new shovels with them which they'd been wanting to use for months, and they started pulling giant buttons out of the ground like clams. Boy were they stoked! Mushrooms, edible mushrooms, under the sun-baked desert crust! It was totally incredible to them. It wasn't in their tourist guides or on their itinerary, the auto club hadn't said anything about it, it had never occurred to them to eat wild mushrooms, so they just got more and more excited and started scurrying around yelping and babbling like kids, "Look at this sonofagun over here!"; "Mine's even bigger than yours!"; "Holy Cow, it's hard as a rock!", I can't believe I'm doing this!"

Another RV pulled over to see what all the commotion was about. One of them also sold insurance and of course they had shovels, so they dug right in. Then another RV joined us, a Mormon family from Moab, a bicyclist bound for Lubbock, and two local Navajo. We must have pulled up a couple hundred pounds, and we left lodes behind. Talk about "overlook" — we wouldn't have gotten any if that one old cap hadn't made it above the ground!

A truly gigantic Western Giant Puffball

There was only one campground in the area and we were all staying there, so that night we had this incredible spontaneous mushroom feast with gourmet foods and drinks they'd stashed away in their RV's for that one really special occasion, and what could be more special than this? We ate fabulously and got along famously, and the couple from Long Beach wanted to know if this was what it was like to live communally and I said: "Sure, we do this every night."

I guess you could say we made their day. In fact, they said it was the best thing that happened to them on their whole trip! We had more for breakfast the next morning, and sun-dried the rest, and that one couple just couldn't stop talking about how excited they were. I kept getting letters from them afterwards, and I bet they're still talking about it, twelve years later, telling their grandchildren about the mighty once-in-a-blue-moon shroom bloom beneath the Arizona desert. Me, I'm not much of a talker, but I'm sure tempted to go back — I never did make it to that scenic overlook.

Boletus appendiculatur (Butter Bolete); pores normally stain blue when bruised.

● LBM's: Little Brown Mushrooms

The cap is brown, the stem a shade browner, the gills browner still. This can be said of nearly one half of all the mushrooms you find. On even the most casual jaunt through the woods, you'll find dozens and dozens of Little Brown Mushrooms sprouting at your feet, and very likely under them as well. The fact is, Little Brown Mushrooms ("LBM's") are so overwhelmingly abundant and uncompromisingly undistinguished that it is more than just futile for the beginner to attempt to identify them — it is downright foolish.

ATTACHMENT OF THE GILLS TO THE STALK (as seen in longitudinal section)

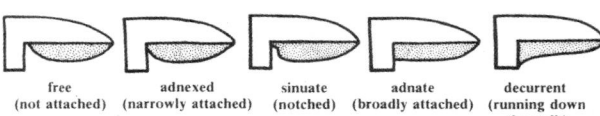

| free (not attached) | adnexed (narrowly attached) | sinuate (notched) | adnate (broadly attached) | decurrent (running down the stalk) |

DIY sweets from trees
Backyard Sugarin'
$10 Rink Mann, Daniel Wolf, 2006, 96 p.

I really like this small guide because Mann emphasizes the cheapest possible way to get up and running. While commercial maple sugaring has gone all high tech with miles of plastic tubing and vacuum pumps, a weekend backyarder can use traditional homemade apparatus to produce a few gallons of golden syrup each season. Don't need much if you have the minimum trees, scrap wood, outdoor workspace and time. (And BTW, you can get syrup form all kinds of maples in the right climate zone.)

From my few clumsy experiments using an earlier edition of this book, I can tell you it's a lot of work for a little syrup -- but because its your syrup, it tastes like ambrosia.

-- KK

• So, let's sum up the things you ought to be thinking about well in advance if you're aiming to make 5 gallons of syrup.

Save up at least 20 plastic milk bottles or other containers to serve as sap buckets.

Pick out your trees for tapping and get permission, if necessary, to tap them. You're going to drill 20 holes.

Collect about a half cord of good dry wood, pile it near your planned evaporator site and cover it over.

Save up 10 2-pound coffee cans with plastic lids, or something comparable for storing your syrup.

There are other preparations that can be made in advance, too, like designing and collecting parts for your homemade evaporator, and perhaps whittling your own sap spouts, but these things can be done over the winter.

▲ Apart from eliminating the high cost of buckets, the Idlenot Dairy Low-Fat Sap Bucket has some very real advantages over conventional buckets. For one thing, except for the 3/4" hole, it is completely enclosed, so you don't get any debris or unwanted predators in the sap. For another thing, it's semi-transparent, so you can see from a distance whether or not it will be worth slogging through the snow to empty it. And, maybe best of all, when the season is over, you don't have to go to all the bother of washing and storing your buckets. You can just drop them off at your local recycling center and start with a fresh set of buckets next season.

• Canning maple syrup presents the same problems as the hot canning of cooked vegetables, with at least one important (and happy) difference. If a jar of canned tomatoes goes bad, you've had it. With syrup, if it gets moldy, you can scoop off the mold, bring the syrup back up to a boil, and you're back in business.

▲ This is what syrup looks like when it's about to boil over. Quick! Someone lift the pot off the burner (or touch the syrup with a bit of butter).

◄ Remember that if you're standing on top of a four-foot snowbank when making your tap holes at the beginning of the season, those taps may be seven feet off the ground near the end of the season when the snowbank has melted. It's hard to collect sap from buckets seven feet off the ground.

Best tutorial on growing mushrooms
Growing Gourmet and Medicinal Mushrooms
$30 Paul Stamets, 2000, 614 p.

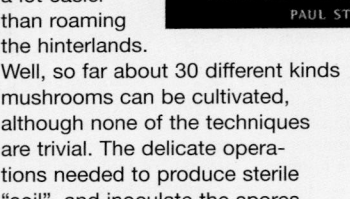

Once you get hooked on foraging for wild mushrooms, you begin to wonder why you can't just farm them. Picking mushrooms from your backyard or basement would sure be a lot easier than roaming the hinterlands. Well, so far about 30 different kinds mushrooms can be cultivated, although none of the techniques are trivial. The delicate operations needed to produce sterile "soil", and inoculate the spores has been streamlined for some species (by using pre-inoculated plugs), but there is still a lot of skill and laboratory expertise needed to grow the rest. Most of what is known about mushroom cultivation has been distilled into the 3rd edition of this irreplaceable book. This is simply the best guide to growing edible, medicinal, and psychoactive mushrooms.

This is a fast-changing field where enthusiastic amateurs lead the way. To keep up with new possibilities, check the author's website at Fungi Perfecti (fungi.com/home.html). Farming mushrooms is also becoming a business, and the Mushroom Growers' Newsletter (mushroomcompany.com) is the hub.

-- KK

In one of my outdoor wood-chip beds, I created a "polyculture" mushroom patch about 50 by 100 feet in size. In the spring I acquired mixed wood chips from the county utility company--mostly alder and Douglas fir--and inoculated three species into it. One year after inoculation, in late April through May, Morels showed. From June to early September, Kind Stropharia erupted with force, providing our family with several hundred pounds. In late September through much of November, as assortment of Clustered Woodlovers (Hypholoma-like) species popped up. With noncoincident fruiting cycles, this Zen-like polyculture approach is limited only by your imagination.

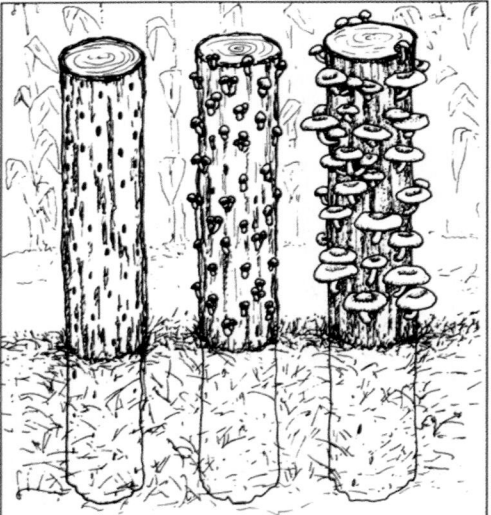
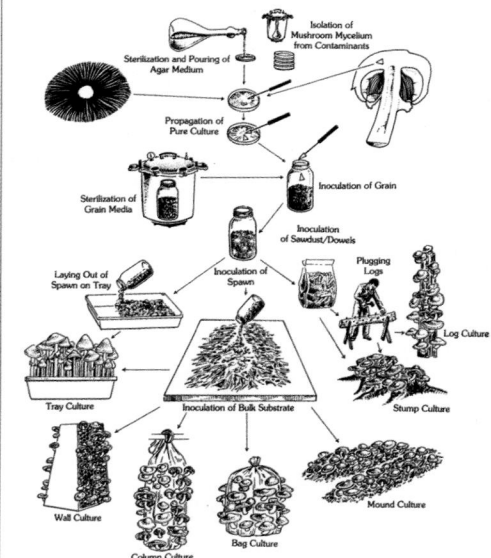

When logs are buried in sand, subsurface moisture is drawn up into the log, encouraging mushroom formation and discouraging competitor fungi.

DIY mycology DVDs
Let's Grow Mushrooms!
$49 Amazon

I have *Mushrooms Demystified* and I just joined a local group so I can find my own mushrooms to start, but this DVD set my wife got me is all about growing mushrooms and is easier to get to grips with. It is two DVDs that start out from very simple (growing oysters/lions mains in a fish tank) to hunting in the forest and isolating your own strain. There's also a great section on how to grow oysters in a laundry basket. Everything in these DVDs is all done step by step, so it's easy to follow and understand — very hands-on with lots of little hints and tips.

The first DVD is great for novices or kids, but the second DVD moves in to agar work, which is more for the professional. I have been growing oyster mushrooms, but the DVD shows how I can move up my production so I'm not just growing a couple of meals at a time. I had no prior experience with mycology, but my wife and I have a small garden and we're trying to see how much we can produce to save on bills. After watching this DVD, I think this could help people start their own small business. I've actually looked into growing for local farmers markets for a bit of extra cash.

-- Jo Fas

Classic fly fishing primer
The Curtis Creek Manifesto
$9 Sheridan Anderson, 1978, 48 p.

Cartoons rule as the densest form of information packing known to humans. This slim 48-page book of cartoons contains just about all you need to know about fly-fishing, and covers more material than most wordy 480-page books on the subject (of which there are many). First published in 1978, this funky manual is still the one that veteran fly-fishers hand out to newbies with the command: "Read this first." It is not the last word, but everyone agrees it is where you start.

-- KK

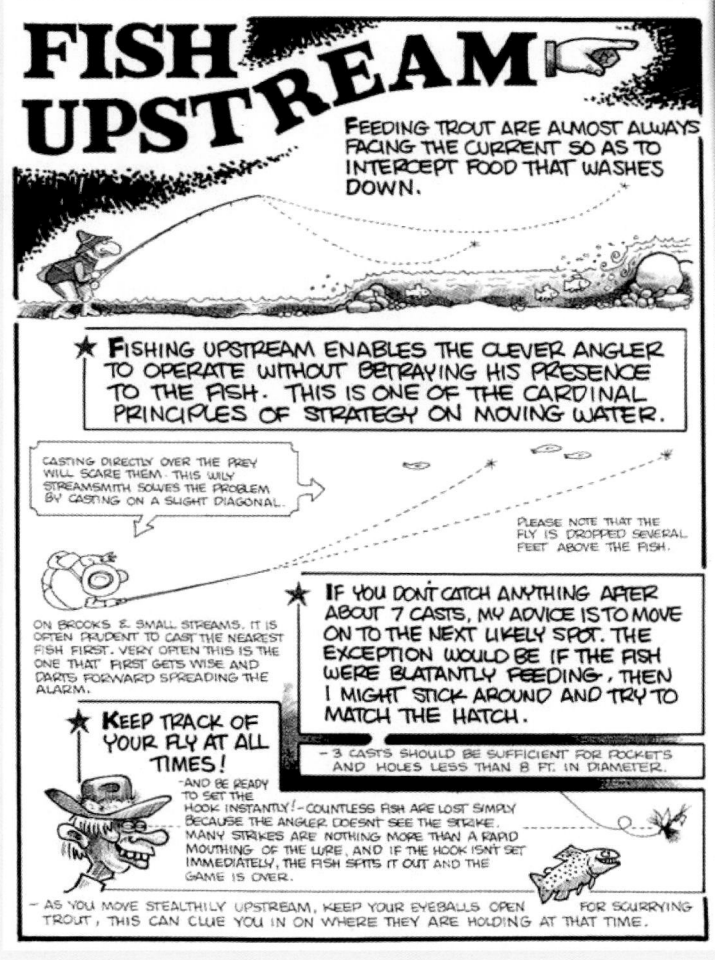

No snag landing net
Brodin Ghost Net

Part of finding my "zen" in fly fishing has been simplifying the stuff I fish with.

One of my best discoveries has been the Brodin Ghost Net. Unlike traditional mesh nets, the Ghost Net is made of clear thermoplastic rubber webbing. It might seem strange to replace lightweight mesh with something slightly heavier, but the advantages become clear the second you walk along a stream.

Fine mesh nets are fragile. They catch on branches and thorns, and they have a tendency to tear. Not only that, but small hooks, especially nymphs, tend to catch and snag in the mesh. The Brodin Ghost Net resolves this with its rubber webbing. The tough clear webbing is robust in the face of snags, doesn't get caught on thorns, and I have never had a fly get snagged or snarled. What this means is that I can spend less time hassling with my net, and more time fishing. I have also read elsewhere that the clear webbing is less visible underwater and less likely to spook the fish (I haven't been able to confirm this personally, but it makes sense).

For those who are less inclined to spend $100 for a new wooden net, Brodin sells the thermoplastic rubber webbing independently, providing instructions on how to affix it to existing wooden nets, or as demonstrated by other DIY-fishermen online, tennis racket frames. This also makes it easy to fix or replace in case something goes wrong.

-- Oliver Hulland

$97 Brodin Ghost Landing Net Amazon

$23-28 Brodin Ghost Netting, various sizes Brodin Landing Nets

Ultimate fishing canoe
River Ridge Canoe
$2,095 River Ridge Sportsman Canoe
River Ridge Custom Canoes

I found these guys a about three years ago while researching small watercraft for fishing lakes/ponds in my area. I was originally looking at flat-bottom boats onto which I would mount a trolling motor, but I read an article about these canoes that described how the owner was trying to build a better fishing canoe that was more stable/comfortable/fishable than a traditional canoe. The result is a pretty tricked-out little watercraft, and at just under 13 feet it's small enough (and light enough) to transport easily on my car-top. They come in various configurations, and are extremely stable; I've even fly-fished standing up in the center of mine.

I went the canoe route as I wanted something that was small (and most importantly thin) so I can get in-and-out of hard-to-navigate places. In the areas where I fish, there are lots of off-shoots and channels through marshes where anything wider than a canoe wouldn't allow you access. And a skiff (in my opinion) is really a lot of wasted space (deeper and wider) that I'd simply being throwing all of my gear into. I also wanted a craft that would take a small trolling motor and be navigable with such under-power (anything larger can be a bear to manage nimbly) and a skiff (or similarly-sized craft) really demands an outboard.

So, while the cost was obviously high for a canoe, this little bugger fit all of my needs — small, nimble, well-laid-out, and most importantly created with fishing as the primary design principle.

Of all the options available, my personal favorites are the integrated drink-holders, the swivel seats with umbrella mounts, and the fact that all of the wiring for the trolling motor is run through the gunwale with hook-ups along the way. My wife loves this thing as well, which is a bonus as it wasn't cheap. I ended up getting the complete package and the only thing I've found a little less than useful is the solar panel battery charger because it doesn't really provide that much juice. Many of the options they use are available through Cabela's or other outfitters, but I like how they incorporated everything into a single package.

-- John Robinson

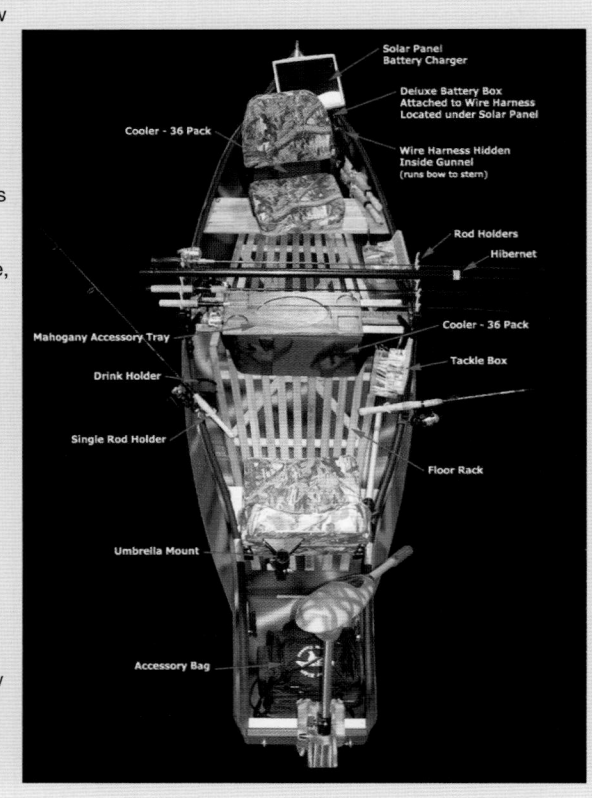

An adventure is only an inconvenience rightly considered. An inconvenience is only an adventure wrongly considered. - Chesterton

139

Primitive Skills

Intro to wild game
Hunt, Gather, Cook
$14 Hank Shaw, 2012, 336 p.

Over the years I've looked at a number of books on hunting, fishing, and foraging, but this turns out to be my favorite. The first sentence: "We live in an edible world."

There is good info on things like aging game birds, gutting and skinning a deer, even how to get started hunting. Or how to net herring -- an annual ritual in NorCal. For the boatless, this can be practiced from shore with a cast net, 5-gallon bucket, and hip boots. Onto harvesting clams, rock crabs, rock fish. How to kill eels with salt (almost impossible otherwise), manzanita cider, madrone bark tea. Making sausage from wild boar, eating squirrels, (there's a bluegrass song, "Why Would Anyone Eat Beef When They Can Have Squirrel?"), and recipes for everything.

-- Lloyd Kahn

● Catching crabs is pretty easy. You need bait, a cooler, some string, and patience. A trap of some sort helps a lot, but I've caught crabs hand-lining a chicken leg off a rowboat in a back bay or off a dock. You lower the chicken to the bottom and wait until you feel little tugs. Slowly bring the line up, and if you see a crab munching on the chicken, you carefully slip a net underneath him-he'll let go of the chicken as soon as he sees you or the boat.

Trap crabbing is basically a combination line and net. You toss the trap in and wait, then haul it in from time to time. Remove crabs from the trap and toss them in a cooler. Repeat as necessary.

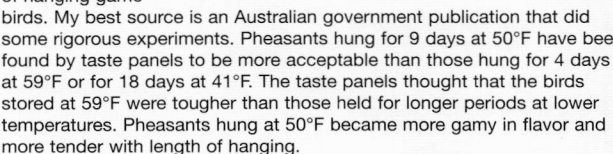

Where to go? Piers are good places, as are jetties or breakwaters. You want to put the trap near places where crabs hide. They will run out and start eating your bait, and you can collect them. If you have a boat, look for underwater grass beds near rocks.

● Always be ready. Rabbit hunting is an exercise in active relaxation. You never know when a rabbit or hare will show itself, and then you might only have a second to make the shot. Peering intently at everything will wear you out in an hour, so you need to let yourself go and absorb everything as you slowly move through an area. Listen. You can often hear rabbits before you can see them. I've heard rabbits chewing before I could spot them.

…Above all, watch. Don't look for the body of the rabbit or the hare, look for its eye or an ear. I've spotted hares staring at me that were standing stock-still. I never saw the hare; his coat melted into the surrounding scrub, but his eyes looked like polished pebbles. Aim for the head, especially with a shotgun. A full blast with a shotgun in the body can destroy the meat on a rabbit or squirrel. A head shot is both more humane and wastes less meat. Remember, the most and best meat in any of these animals is in their back legs.

● **Aging Game Birds**

I used to recoil at the idea of hanging shot pheasants or partridges ungutted and in their feathers for days. It did not seem terribly hygienic or sane to me. Old texts wax rhapsodic about the sublime flavor of "high" game, which usually means pheasants that have hung for more than a week. This, I'd decided, was madness. I was wrong.

● Fortunately, science exists on the topic of hanging game birds. My best source is an Australian government publication that did some rigorous experiments. Pheasants hung for 9 days at 50°F have been found by taste panels to be more acceptable than those hung for 4 days at 59°F or for 18 days at 41°F. The taste panels thought that the birds stored at 59°F were tougher than those held for longer periods at lower temperatures. Pheasants hung at 50°F became more gamy in flavor and more tender with length of hanging.

A few things you should know. First, aging works with any game bird. The general rule is the larger the bird, the longer you can hang it. Doves and quail need just a day or so, while grouse, partridges, woodcock, and pigeons can go as long as 5 days. Don't try to wet-pluck an aged game bird. You must dry-pluck these birds because the skin gets looser, and scalding (more on this ahead) does not seem to help with the feathers. It was a major bummer to scald one bird and rip some of the skin. Dry-plucking, you should be warned, takes forever, but the results are worth it.

Bootstrapping tools
Primitive Technology

You can't learn how to make friction fire by reading a book. Nor can you learn how to knap a stone edge from diagrams on a page. But you can learn what there is to learn. These two remarkable books collect what is known about primitive tool making skills. Both are compendiums of a research-intensive newsletter published by the Society of Primitive Technology. The depth of their investigations and re-discoveries are extraordinary. Using a recursive chain of simpler tools making the more complex, modern enthusiasts can create artifacts of astounding complexity and beauty entirely by hand. These hefty tomes collect recipes for stone-tool-made compound bows, razor sharp knives, bark canteens, pump drills and reed boats. I get more than survival skills from them; they are the first lessons in material hacking.

– KK

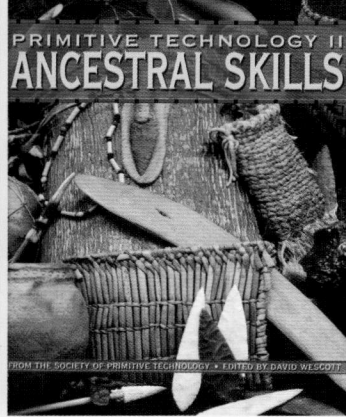

$17 Primitive Technology: A book of Earth Skills, Edited by David Wescott, 1999, 248 p.

$20 Primitive Technology II: Ancestral Skills, Edited by David Westcott, 2001, 248 p.

Fire By Friction Anywhere

Making fire by friction is a deceptively easy process once the principles are understood and the technique well practiced. It's a trip to watch a master walk over to a bush, snap off a twig and begin rubbing it on a log until smoke begins to rise from the resulting trough. Or a straight twig is cut, roughly straightened, and spun between the palms, while resting on a softwood hearth to create that magic spark.

Or better yet, splitting a section of bamboo, scraping off the lacquered layer to be used as tinder, creating a notch with a slice of rock, and then rubbing the notch along the edge of the bamboo until the tinder ignites.

Tools of the trade – hearth, spindle, and blisters

▶ The primary construction crew on the finished frame. Built with homemade hand tools.

The house was commissioned by the Texas Department of Parks and Wildlife for the Caddoan Mounds State Historic Site, 6 miles south of Alta, Texas. It has withstood a tornado and 10 years of exposure to the elements and vandals, however, it [was] scheduled to be burned this spring (1994).

The Caddoan house reconstruction conducted in Texas by Scooter Cheatham followed closely the methods of the past. The structure was duplicated from the post molds of Domicile #10 at the Davis Site. 3 mounds of a large Confederated Caddoan Center dating back to the 8-12th century were excavated here. The house was 25' in diameter, 30' high and contained 4 interior living levels. Tools for the reconstruction were prepared beginning in September, harvesting of the thatch took over two weeks in October, the poles cut, peeled and placed in position by the 1st of November, and the final touches were being added shortly before Christmas day.

▶ Pitch [glue] sticks ready for just about any job.

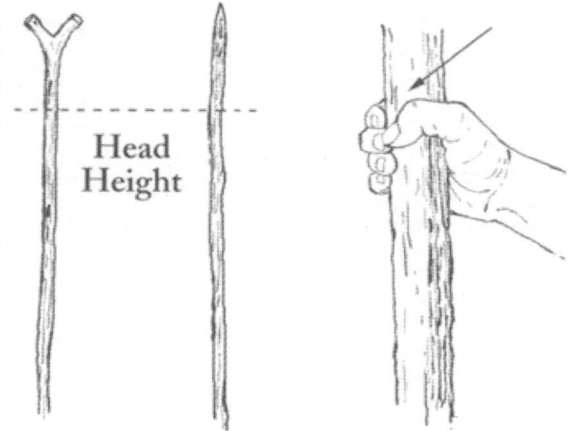

The survival stick

Best wildnerness survival guide

Hawke's Special Forces Survival Handbook

$11 Mykel Hawke, 2011, 256 p.

Let's get this straight: you will not have your wilderness survival guidebook on you during a survival emergency. That's not how emergencies work. A great survival guide book will a) assume you won't have it with you, and b) will prepare you to survive bookless by preparing you with real details beforehand. Out of the many dozens of survival guidebooks in print today, this is the only one that accomplishes this, and this is the only one that I would recommend. (This is not a Prepper's guide, but focuses on wildnerness survival.) It can get you thinking about real solutions to real problems. Survival is all about priorities, and I think this book lines them up in the right order. It will still be up to you to rehearse them beforehand — you won't have this book with you.

-- KK

Last Resorts

You can drink urine! The rules for urine drinking are straightforward: drink it as soon after you urinate as possible; the first time you urinate is usually fine to drink; and you can drink the second pass in dire circumstances. After a second pass, chances are that you won't be urinating again anyway if there is no more fluid going in. There simply won't be any fluid left to be passed.

Myth: You will not die or get sick if you drink urine. It is not poisonous. It is actually sterile the moment it leaves your body, and only contact with the air allows for bacteria to grow. This is why you shouldn't urinate and then store it for later.

●

Choose a stick slightly taller than you; if the stick is too short, it may jam into your neck if you fall. It can serve as a measuring device–how deep a river is or could you jump over a chasm? If the stick is strong enough, it might even be used as a small bridge. It can be used as a rafting pole, a crutch, a spear, a reaching tool and a digging tool, etc.

●

Levels of Pain

Alert — If you can hear a person yelling and screaming, he's okay for the moment. The noise means he's conscious, breathing, awake and talking. It's a good sign that his body is stable enough that all systems are still functioning.

●

A good rule of thumb is that green pus is bacterial, yellow is viral. This is useful for determining if you actually need that antibiotic or not when there is a cough, runny nose or phlegm.

●

Otherwise, the best source of water when surviving at sea will come from the atmosphere. If it rains, drink all you can, catch all you can, store all you can. If you have fog, then use all the cloth you can to capture that and squeeze its moisture into a container or your mouth. Try to make a solar still.

●

Try to concentrate your power-based communications in the first 24 hours, as this is when most search parties will be initiated. Broadcast your signal continuously during this window if you're able.

Consider delaying your 24-hour broadcast period for a day or two if you have reason to believe it will take folks that long to begin looking for you.

After the initial broadcast period, you'll need to go into power-conservation mode. This means spacing out the broadcasts and standardizing their length.

Transmit at dawn, dusk, noon, and midnight. Dawn and dusk are when atmospheric changes can help broadcasts travel enormous distances.

Hawke's Laws of Survival (for starters. . . .)
Never quit
Everything you plan and pack, will be lost in the event that causes the survival scenario
Survival situations happen to those who haven't studied, or have but aren't ready
The best-trained, most-equipped survivalist will be the first one killed in the crash
The person least likely to survive will be the one left to face surviving
When you lack everything but misery, you are surviving
When you think you got it all handled, you're in the biggest trouble

●

The Rule of Threes: There are 3 dots and 3 dashes in the 3-letter Morse code for SOS. That's no accident. The universal distress signal is anything in threes.

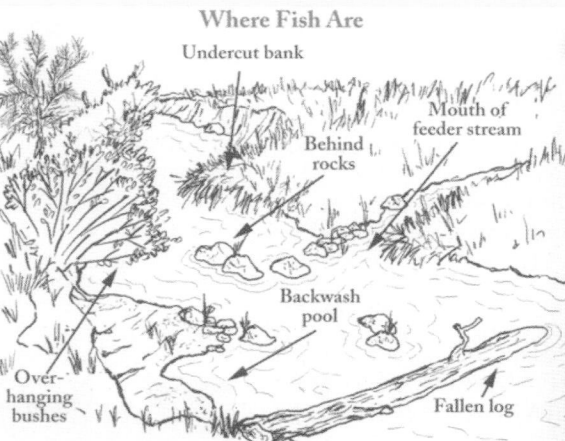

Where Fish Are

Berry rules:
90% of purple, black & blue are good for you.
90% of yellow and white just aren't right.
50/50 on the reds—could be good, or could be dead.
If singletons or cluster berries, eating them could be merry.
But if they grow in a one-stem batch, best not put them down the hatch.

Classic guide to wild foods

Stalking the Wild Asparagus

$12 Euell Gibbons, 2005, 303 p.

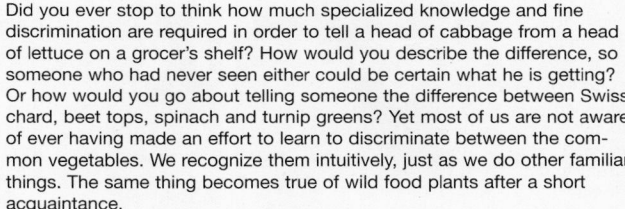

There's a bunch of watercress growing wild at the low end of our creek. And wild plums thick at the upper end. And stinging nettles in between, and all three of them delicious. I know this because I first read Euell Gibbon's charming book on foraging for wild food 50 years ago. All these years later it's still one of the best books on finding wild foods in North America. It won't help you identify the edible plants and critters (use Thayer for that, p. 136); there are no photos, only a few minimal line drawings, and very little in terms of identification help. Gibbons assumes you'll use other sources, including friends, to help you learn to distinguish them.

What Gibbons offers in his books (including his sequels on herbs and beachcombing), is what to do with what you find, and why bother. He is a delightful writer who tells memorable stories about his life-long adventures in discovering wild foods and uncovering (through historical research) how they can be prepared. Gibbons is not concerned about the survival aspects of wild food. For him the adventure is culinary, and an antidote to white bread and office work. It is hard to convey the paucity of cuisine in suburban America at the time he was writing. His passions helped open up American palates. And despite the fact that you can buy dandelion greens, fern fiddles and wild mushrooms at some farmers' markets today, his books can still open your eyes to the edibles and adventures that lie unseen in your own neighborhoods. I enjoy re-reading him every now and then to be reminded of wild foods I overlook. I've used his advice many times. I get an immense and distinct satisfaction from adding even a small bit of wild food to a meal.

-- KK

Did you ever stop to think how much specialized knowledge and fine discrimination are required in order to tell a head of cabbage from a head of lettuce on a grocer's shelf? How would you describe the difference, so someone who had never seen either could be certain what he is getting? Or how would you go about telling someone the difference between Swiss chard, beet tops, spinach and turnip greens? Yet most of us are not aware of ever having made an effort to learn to discriminate between the common vegetables. We recognize them intuitively, just as we do other familiar things. The same thing becomes true of wild food plants after a short acquaintance.

Since then, each spring I go out along the field borders and byways and gather wild asparagus, not only enough for current use, but some to store in the freezer, so I can bring back the joyous spring days any time of the year merely by cooking a dish of wild asparagus. That five minutes I spent so long ago, concentrating on one dead asparagus plant, has led me to many pounds of this most delicious of early vegetables. The eyetraining it gave me has lasted until now. Whenever I drive, in the late winter or early spring, my eye automatically picks up the dead asparagus stalks by the roadside, and I make an almost unconscious mental note of the places where the green spears will be plentiful when warm weather returns.

Black Birch

To make a wintergreen-flavored tea, cut some sweet birch twigs in small pieces and cover them with boiling birch sap. Let it steep for a minute or two, then strain out the twigs and sweeten the tea to taste. Some like to add cream or hot milk. Children are usually very fond of this beverage and it's perfectly harmless and wholesome.

●

For the number of different kinds of food it produces there is no plant, wild or domesticated, which tops the common Cattail. In May and June the green bloom spikes make a superior cooked vegetable. Immediately following this comes the bright yellow pollen, fine as sifted flour, which is produced in great abundance. This makes an unusual and nourishing ingredient for some flavorful and beautifully colored pancakes and muffins. From fall until spring a fine, nutritious white flour can be prepared from the central core of the rootstocks for use as a breadstuff or as a food starch. On the leading ends of these rootstocks are found the dormant sprouts which will be next year's cattails. These can be eaten either as a salad or as a cooked vegetable. At the junction of these sprouts and the rootstock there is an enlarged starchy core the size of a finger joint. These can be roasted, boiled or cooked with meat. In the spring, the young shoots can be yanked from the ground and peeled, leaving a tender white part from six to twelve inches long which can be eaten raw or cooked.

●

Don't feel like a vandal while digging day lily tubers. A spading fork full of plants removed here and there from the clump will only give it a much-needed thinning and cultivation. If you would like to see more of these interesting and useful plants growing, then set out some of the plants in new places after you have remove the tubers. They will live and each one will soon form a new colony about itself.

●

Once I stopped my car by a roadside stream, and in ten minutes speared eight large frogs. A good way to get right up into the stream, wearing old clothes or fishing waders, and walk up the middle of it, spearing or shooting frogs on either bank.

A head for a frog spear can be bought at most any sporting goods store. It is a small three- or five-tined fork looking something like the trident carried by Poseidon. Many frog-hunters will disagree with me but I think the best handle for a frog spear is made of a good stout piece of bamboo ten to twelve feet long. Such a rig looks as if it were all handle and no spear, but I have walked along narrow streams spearing frogs on the opposite bank with such a long-handled spear very successfully.

●

Another point in favor of foraging as a family is the handiness with which it can be practiced. One doesn't need to go to the mountains or virgin forests to find wild food plants. In fact, mountains and dense forests are among the poorer places to look. Abandoned farmsteads, old fields, fence rows, burned-off areas, road-sides, along streams, woodlots, around farm ponds, swampy areas and even vacant lots are the finest foraging sites.

Stone building essentials

The Art of the Stonemason

$16 Ian Cramb, 1992 (updated 2006), 174 pages

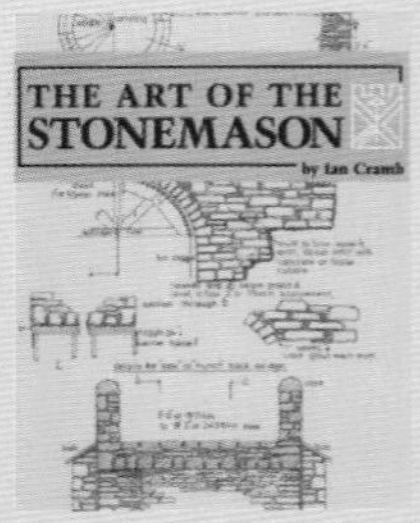
THE ART OF THE
STONEMASON
by Ian Cramb

This book by Ian Cramb is a classic. Straightforward and elegant, everything you need to know about putting one stone on top of another. I've been through many tons of stone with only Ian's stern Scottish advice to guide me. Never looked back.

I don't remember where I heard it (this book doesn't cover drywall), but the best short course I've seen on dry-stack stonework is this:

1. Gravity always works.

2. If a stone can move, it will.

That sums up pretty much everything you need to know to ensure a wall will still be there for people born after you die.

-- Matt Thornton

•

The most reliable test for stone is to examine an old building nearby that has been built of the same stone. The arrisses (edges where the surfaces meet at an angle) should be firm, fine, and the members of moulds sharp and clean. The lines of stratification should not be prominent. The faces must be hard and solid when struck with a chisel. A loose or spongy appearance would denote decomposition of the chemical constituents.

The following are some specific tests for stone.

Water test — A few stone chippings are placed in clean water and stirred about. If the water becomes muddy, the stone should be rejected.

Chemical test — Immerse a stone in a solution of 1 cup sulfuric acid, 1 cup hydrochloric acid, and 1 gallon of water for a few days. When taken out and dried, the grains should be sharp and firm. Loose sand would mean the stone could dissolve in a polluted city atmosphere. NOTE: These acids are very dangerous. Every precaution must be used in handling and disposal.

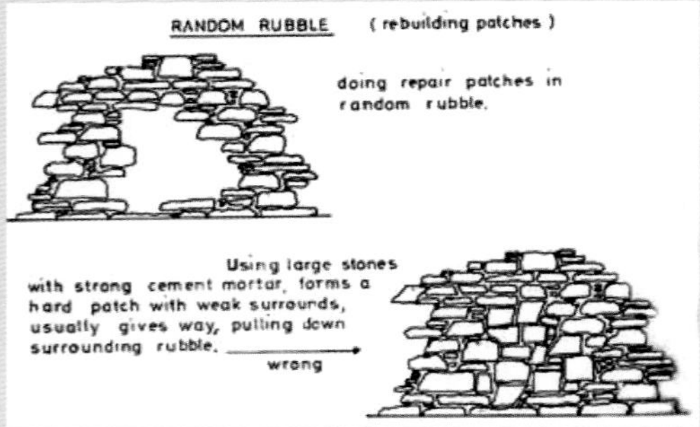
RANDOM RUBBLE (rebuilding patches)
doing repair patches in random rubble.
Using large stones with strong cement mortar, forms a hard patch with weak surrounds, usually gives way, pulling down surrounding rubble.
wrong

To detect the presense of lime — If a few drops of acid are placed on a stone and the drops cause effervescence, carbonate or lime is indicated. Such a stone would not weather well.

Absorption — A sandstone shell should not absorb more than 10 percent of its weight in water; a limestone not more than 17 percent.

•

Points to remember

All random rubble is built in courses. This is the traditional method; there is no such thing as uncoursed random rubble.

A hole for every stone, and a stone for every hold. What you lift, you build.

•

To fit your center key stone, spread mortar on each joint surface of the stone already in position ("h"). Lower the stone into the opening — do not use a hammer — until it rests on your sand-lime mix. If joints are too slack, adjust each joint a little to make them all look equal, then flush point the face joints, pressing the mortar in gently. The stones of the arch are now in position, with the face joints pointed. Add a touch of

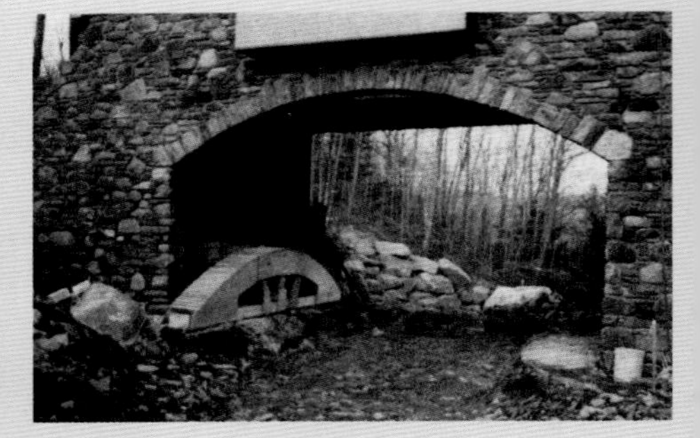

water to your mix, making it into a grout or slurry. Pour this into the back of your arch stones and into any voids in the joints, making sure it does not push out your stones. The lime mix the stones are resting on will prevent the grout from running through. Once your joints are filled up, insert small slivers of stone into each joint, pushing them down gently into the grout, until they are tight. These small stones act as a wedge in each joint.

In grouting stonework, I use a lime-based grout, not a strong cement grout as some recommend. Open up a wall that has been cement-grouted, and you will find little adhesion to the surrounding material. Examine any cement pointing on stone, and you will see hairline cracks between the pointing and the stone, allowing for penetration of water.

Work horse bible

The New Horse-Powered Farm

$27 Stephen Leslie, 2013, 368 p.

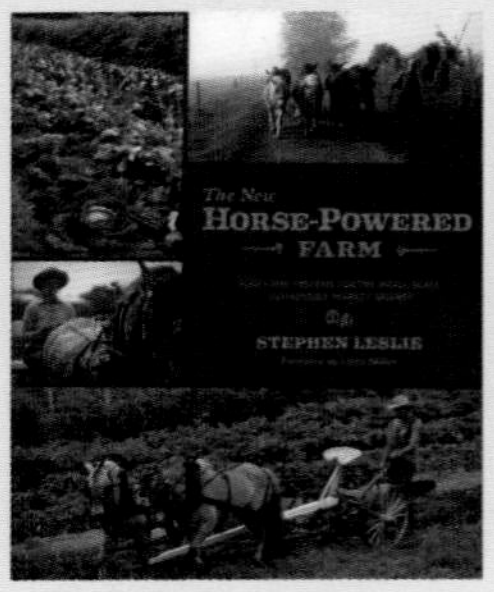
The New
HORSE-POWERED
FARM
STEPHEN LESLIE

Using draft horses instead of tractors is not as crazy as it sounds. Horses self-reproduce, are fueled by what can be grown on a farm, and can be amazingly agile. The only farms in America increasing in numbers are very small farms of the size that can be powered by horses. An emerging renaissance is bringing back work horses coupled with high-tech implements and gear. My horse-powered Amish friends say this book is the bible for small-scale growers converting to horses, and is by far the best book on using horses on a farm. It's very forward looking, packed with practical know-how, and aimed at using horses to increase soil fertility and productivity.

-- KK

•

Horses only need to sleep about 6 hours a day. A lot of this sleep is caught in the form of short naps, sometimes while standing, but 1-2 hours of this sleep is of the lie-down dead-to-the-world variety. The very shy or nervous subordinate horse housed in a group might never feel comfortable enough to take this kind of rest and actually suffer from sleep deprivation. In such a case, alternative housing will have to be created.

•

A draft horse needs to consume about 2 percent of its body weight in hay every day. For a full-size draft weighing 2,000 pounds this will mean a 40-pound bale of hay. It is almost universally agreed among horse people that timothy grass makes the best hay for horses. The problem with timothy is that it will only persist in a hay field for

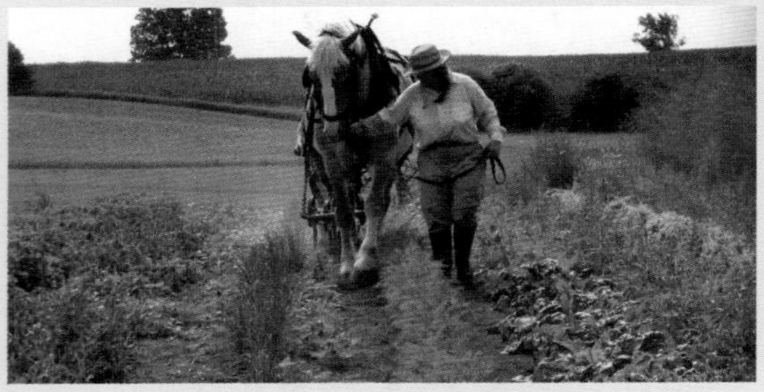

Cultivating with a single horse at Meeting Place Organic Farm

about 3-4 years and then needs to be reseeded.

THE PROS AND CONS OF HORSE POWER

By David Fisher, Natural Roots Farm, Conway, Massachusetts

Pros

Horses are extremely versatile power units. They can be used for heavy tillage, light cultivation, hauling, haying, harvesting, logging, even digging—nearly anything when used with the appropriate tools. Multiple horses can be used singly for lighter work in tight spaces, or hitched together in any number for heavier work.

- With an adequate land base, all the horse's fuel needs can be raised on the farm in the form of pasture, hay, and grain crops.
- Waste products from horses are nontoxic, life-giving fertilizer that can be recycled into their own feed crops or other crops on the farm.
- Horses always start, almost never get stuck, and generally remain in good working order, provided appropriate care and maintenance are applied.
- Unlike some machinery, horses perform better and appreciate in value with increased use until late in their working lives (usually age 3–25).
- Horses have the capacity to be self-replacing. With the right breeding program, you may only have to purchase stock once in a lifetime, or for generations!
- Horses are extremely light on the land. They don't make ruts and they cause a minimum amount of compaction.
- Working with horses will stimulate personal growth and communication skills.
- Horses are very pleasing to the senses and can be kid-friendly. They are a great draw to involving the whole family in farmwork.
- Horses are also very appealing to the community and to customers and enhance the image of the farm.
- By helping to create a sustainable agricultural system independent from petroleum dependence, the use of horse power can help to address many pressing environmental and political issues.

Cons

- Horses can require a lot of maintenance in the form of feeding, watering, stall mucking, and grooming. Hoof care and harness maintenance also take time.
- Like other livestock, working horses require daily care even when they're not working.
- Working with horses requires a skill set and a mind-set that take time to cultivate. Inexperience can result in frustration and hazardous situations.
- The less feed and care the farmer can provide (from on-farm sources), the more expensive keeping horses will be.
- Horses work most smoothly and are most cost-effective when there is work for them on a regular basis. Relying on them will probably not make sense if you need a lot of horse power for only a few brief periods over the course of the year.
- Good working stock and horse-drawn farm equipment in working order are not as readily available in the Northeast as they are in the Midwest, not to mention the necessary skills and the parts and expertise in maintenance and repair.

•

Spring Training

Unlike a tractor, you can't let your horses sit idle for months in the winter and then expect them to jump right into spring plowing. You will either need to invent ways to keep them useful and active in the winter--clearing snow, sleigh rides, skidding firewood, feeding out hay to livestock, collecting maple sap--or build them back up gradually to a physical condition capable of taking on the plow. One of the most common training devices is the stone boat. If you happen to live in a region of the country that has stony soil, then spring training with the stone boat can take on the very practical task of picking rock from the fields. The strategy is to start out loading the sled lightly. Over the course of several days and several work sessions the load the horses are asked to haul is gradually increased until it approaches the pull of the plow.

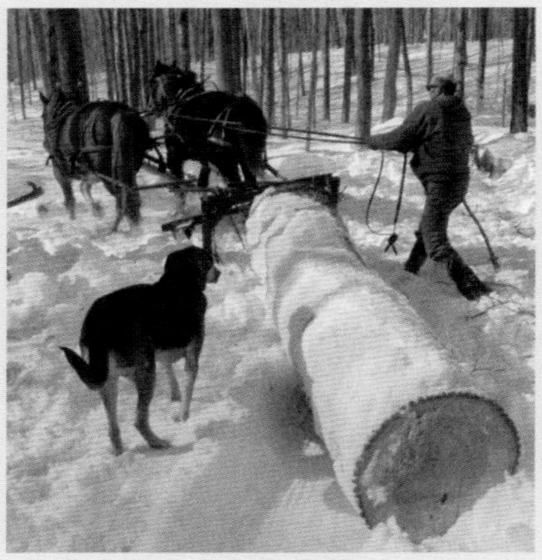

Skidding out a saw log at Northland Sheep Dairy

•

We could state in very general terms that if a team of horses is used to manage a small farm with 20 tillable acres and a diversified cropping system, not quite a third of that land would be required to feed the horses.

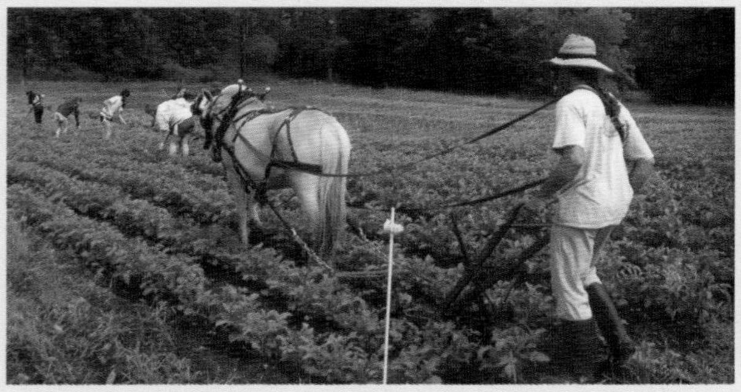

High school students, horse, and farmer cultivating potatoes at Cedar Mountain Farm

Natural food storage

Root Cellaring

$12 Mike and Nancy Bubel, 1991, 320 pages

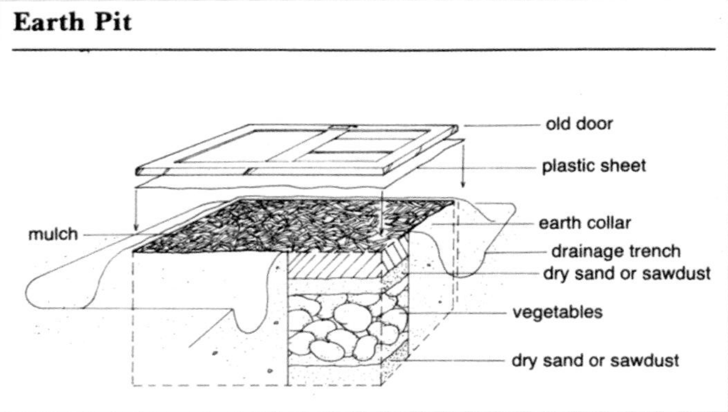
Earth Pit
old door
plastic sheet
earth collar
mulch
drainage trench
dry sand or sawdust
vegetables
dry sand or sawdust

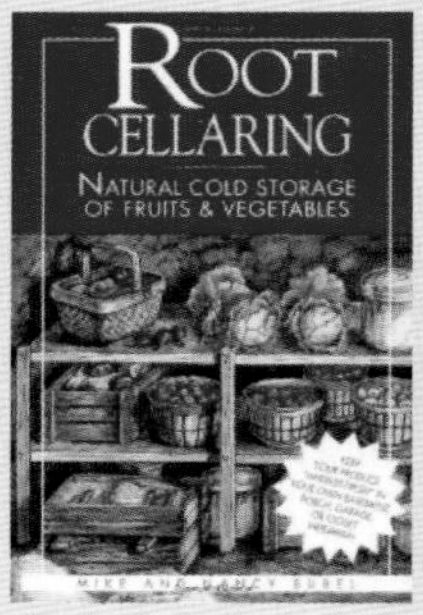
ROOT
CELLARING
NATURAL COLD STORAGE
OF FRUITS & VEGETABLES

It's natural cold storage. A place to store excess produce from your garden at no-energy, low-cost for up to half a year. It works on the idea that when you dig down anywhere, the subsoil maintains a uniform cool temperature no matter the high or low temperature outside. Over 100 different kinds of crops can be kept in this easily made traditional storage. Included are plans for many types, from elementary earth pits to full-fledged basements. And instructions on how to prepare the harvest. These principles can also be used on urban homesteads. This is the definitive book on the subject.

-- KK

•

I dug my cellar in the side of a hill sloping to the south, where a woodchuck had formerly dug his burrow, down through sumac and blackberry roots and the lowest stain of vegetation, six feet square by seven feet deep, to a fine sand where potatoes would not freeze in any weather....I took particular pleasure in this breaking of ground, for in almost all latitudes men dig into the earth for an equable temperature. Under the most splendid house in the city is still to be found the cellar where they store their roots as of old, and long after the superstructure had disappeared posterity remark its dent in the earth. The house is still but a sort of porch at the entrance of a burrow.

-- Henry David Thoreau in Walden

•

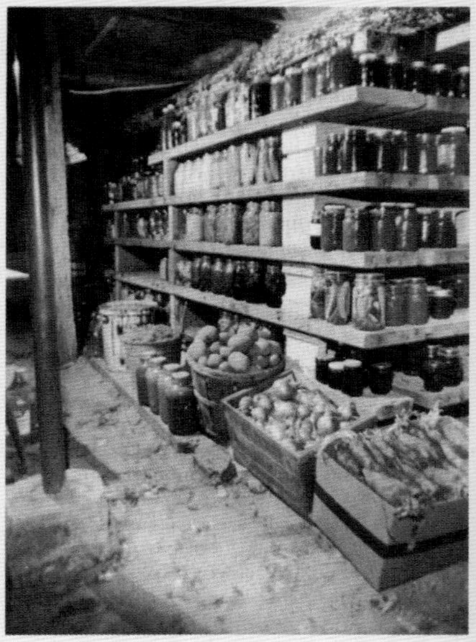

The dirt-floored root cellar in our old house.

142

God is alive and well, but has moved onto a more ambitious project. - Kevin Kelly

Portable, precise lumber cutter
Alaskan Chainsaw Mill

To cut your own boards from a felled tree, you need either an expensive bandsaw mill, circular saw or a bad-ass chainsaw and a bracket to hold the chainsaw parallel to some reference surface. The Alaskan mill attaches to the saw's chain bar and keeps the chainsaw in line with a flat surface, allowing you to cut slabs as thin as 1/2 inch thick. The Alaskan is easy to set up. There is really only one way the saw can fit into the mill. Then, you adjust the two posts on either end to the desired clearance (make sure both posts read the same distance). To make sure your first cut is straight, you use a slabbing bracket; I used the aluminum slabbing rails made by Granberg. Then, you just adjust the clearance to the width of your slab and use

the surface of the previous cut to guide the next cut, and the next, and so forth.

After moving into a new house in a wooded area, I realized a dead, 100-foot Red Oak was just 50 feet from the house. Following a few spells of high winds, I knew it was just a matter of time before it might give out, so I hired a local arborist who methodically cut off the upper part of the tree (a 20-ft. section), then worked his way down, cutting more of the tree into 8-ft sections. We had a nice surprise when we finished: the wood looked to be in great shape and seemed like it might make nice flooring. But I soon discovered the professional sawmills near us won't touch a log less than 9 feet long. Instead of hiring someone with a sawmill to come to my property, I decided to get my own rig.

There are three different kinds of sawmills: circular saw, bandsaw, and chainsaw. I looked at the Lucas Swing blade, several different bandsaw mills and other chainsaw mills. If you have plenty of space and lots of money, Timberking makes some good mills. Most bandsaw mills and circular saws are portable in the sense you can hook them up to your pickup truck and tow them to the site, but they are not portable in the sense you can pick them up and haul them down the hill and through the woods. My number one consideration for the mill was that I should be able to take the saw to the log since I didn't think I could take the log to the saw. One thing to consider about a chainsaw mill is that it wastes a lot of wood. If you're going to build a fixed installation, a bandsaw or circular saw is the way to go. As I've learned, though, Red Oak is *heavy*, espe-

cially when it is wet. Getting the log to the rig wasn't an option, so I went with a chainsaw mill. I chose the Husqvarna 385XP saw with a 28-inch bar, along with a 30-inch Alaskan mill. That means the mill can be adjusted to fit any bar up to its maximum size, in this case 30 inches. You can install basically any size bar into a chainsaw. I chose 28 inches since it would be big enough to work with any of my logs (my largest log was about 20 inches in diameter).

What's impressed me about the Alaskan mill is its simplicity, sturdiness and the geometry of the bracket. The bracket on the mill allows the user to keep the mill flat against the log. With other mills, like the more expensive Logosol system for instance, you attach a bracket to either end of the log and use it to index down through the log. This is probably a better system for indexing, but seems like a lot more work; plus the Logosol also supports the chainsaw only from one end. The Alaskan bracket provides support at both ends of the bar, and it comes in a size as short as 24 inches and as big as 56 inches. Granberg also makes a kit with a bar to allow you to attach *two* 385 power heads to the saw. They also offer an oiler kit to increase the amount of oil on the chain, and they manufacture special ripping chains that make cleaner cuts (I used one). I read one guy's review where he said you needed three sharp chains before starting a days worth of cutting. Maybe that's about right; I could never last more that one sharp chain worth of work before petering out. Some reviewers have mentioned the effort that goes into sharpening the chains makes a chainsaw mill unacceptable. I didn't really find it to be onerous. Since the Alaskan mill is basically the same size as the saw, storage isn't an issue. I just leave the saw mounted in the mill. (NOTE: I learned the hard way, that it is important to store the saw upright. When I stored the saw on its side one time, the next time I used the saw, it took me about 5 hours to get the saw started.)

A few things to remember about chainsaw mills: This is hard work and the going is slow. On my best day, I only managed to finish two logs. Had I been cutting 1- inch boards (instead of 2-inch ones), this would have been much slower. Admittedly, though, my wood was Oak; maybe, just maybe, pine is easier. Also, the saw vibrates a lot. I exchanged my saw's plastic handle for a foam grip, which helped some. Lastly, while the Alaskan rig makes the saw safer, you can never forget there is a lethal weapon in your hands. Although I've given up on the flooring idea, I still have all this good lumber which I'll certainly use for a woodworking project.

-- Jack Tomlinson

$180 (24-inch)
granberg.com

Sizes 20"-48"
leevalley.com

Locate metal before woodcutting
Lumber Wizard
$130/$30 wizind.com

With the price of lumber going up all the time, I'm recycling wood more than ever. But I ruined a blade on my circular saw after hitting an old nail I'd missed when cleaning the wood (my eyes ain't what they used to be). The Lumber Wizard is a lot less expensive than those security metal detectors, and it's saved my new blade a couple times. It takes less than a minute to check a big sheet of ply. If it finds something and I still can't see it, I use the Little Wizard (when I purchased my Lumber Wizard, this came bundled with it).

I guess you could just use the Little Wizard to scan lumber, but it would take longer since it only covers a few square inches at a time. The bigger Lumber Wizard covers about a 6" x 6" area, so sweeping it over a big ply or 2 x 4 goes pretty darn quick (for thicker wood, I usually flip over the lumber and scan both sides just to be sure). The battery life is pretty good, too. I went three months on a single nine-volt battery, using it several times a day, three to four days a week. The Lumber Wizard also has a vibrate setting, which is helpful if other machines are going in the shop, since my hearing ain't what it used to be.

-- Robert Palembas

Chainsaw protection
Husqvarna Helmet
$42 ProForest Helmet System husqvarna.com

I've been using chainsaws for many years. Over the decades I have probably owned 5 or 6 different ones. In the 1960s and '70sI used chainsaws extensively, cutting up redwood (from the beaches or windfallen trees in the woods) into bolts, and which I then split into shakes for roofs and siding. These days I use a Stihl Woodboss MS270, 24" bar for firewood. Every year I find wind-felled oak on country roads, haul it home, cut it into stove-size lengths, then rent a splitter for a day and stockpile a year's or more worth of firewood. Point is, I've had a lot of chainsaw experience.

The other day I was sawing through a piece of wood on the woodpile and as I finished the cut, the blade hit a log below it and snapped back towards my face. It sent a chill of adrenaline that I somehow felt in my ears. Very scary.

BUT I was wearing my Husqvarna helmet, which combines skull protection, ear guards, and a metal mesh facemask. I've only been using the helmet the last few years, prompted by a log rolling down the hill and knocking me down. I felt then I should have had one of these helmets all along. Good thing. This time the blade didn't reach my face, but if it had, the mask would have blocked it from carving up my flesh.

I urge you chainsaw users: get one of these. $40 or so. Play it safe, please. The more hours you've operated chainsaws, the more the chance of a freak accident. Experience doesn't make you invulnerable.

-- Lloyd Kahn

Chain Saws

Best chainsaw
Stihl Chainsaw 280

$500+ (varies with dealer) Stihl

Long ago, I saw a tree guy toss a small Stihl chainsaw 25 feet to the ground. His partner picked it up, refueled it, and started it on the first pull. While I certainly don't plan to abuse any of my tools to that degree, the incident stuck in my memory.

I've used three or four other brands of chainsaws but when a 50-foot-tall, 34-inch-diameter walnut tree fell on my barn, I decided I needed a better chainsaw than I could get at Sears. A brand new Stihl model 280 with a 20-inch bar cost $420 USD at my local store and I don't regret one penny. I've run my 280 continuously (well, with stops for refueling and lemonade) for eight or nine hours without problem. I pinched the blade at one point (user error) hard enough that I had to use a come-along and bow-saw to get it free, but afterwards it still worked fine! The balance is excellent, the weight is manageable (the less expensive model 290 "Farm Boss" is heavier) and there is noticeably less kickback than any other chainsaw I've ever used. All Stihl saws have a "recommended" or "stock" bar length but are capable of running shorter or longer. I wanted the lightest saw that could actually cut through a 36" diameter tree… so I got the lighter 280 with an extra-long 20" bar which fits perfectly and runs fine; it's chewed through 34" of black walnut, 24" of maple, and 10" of oak so far without complaint.

I'm less than happy about owning anything with a 2-stroke motor — after all, I've been using an electric lawnmower for decades and driving a Prius since 2001 — but Stihl has even addressed that concern. Their motors use a 50:1 gas/oil mix rather than the 40:1 ratio of cheaper saws, and they sell a (relatively) environmentally friendly bar oil. They also claim to use 50% less bar oil than other brands, and unlike every other saw I've ever used my Stihl 280 never leaks oil on the ground or into the carrying case.

Real pros — men who use chainsaws eight to ten hours a day for a living — will want to spend around $900 USD for the model 361, with weight somewhere between the 280 and 290 and *significantly* more horsepower. For the rest of us, a model 280 or 290 is a big, burly tool that will be more than sufficient.

When asked why the word's best selling chainsaw (it's pronounced STEEL, like the metal) is not carried by Walmart or Home Depot, Stihl representatives will proudly state "because we don't have to!" To find the Stihl distributor nearest you, use their web site's store locator.

-- Charlie Brooks

Keeps chains sharp
PFERD Chain Sharp

$22 Bailey's

We heat our home with wood, and this has made my favorite fall/winter tool a Stihl MS260 chain saw. But if the chain isn't sharp, the saw is tiring and dangerous. The best tool for keeping a sharp chain is the Pferd Chain Sharp: a device that files both the saw teeth and the depth gauges in one operation.

It's not only time-saving, but it also makes sure the depth gauges are at the right height. This is something that's easy to ignore since most chain saw sharpening tools are designed to hold only the saw tooth file. But if the depth gauges are too high, they'll prevent sharp saw teeth from engaging the wood correctly.

I've been using the Pferd Chain Sharp for 5-years, sharpening my saw chains every second tank of gas. Since I've started using the Pferd, I have never had to take a chain to be sharpened "professionally."

-- Terry Beck

Electric Lopper
Black & Decker Alligator Lopper Chainsaw

$80 Amazon

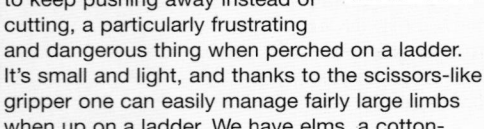

This unique chainsaw is especially good for sawing slender limbs that a traditional chainsaw tends to keep pushing away instead of cutting, a particularly frustrating and dangerous thing when perched on a ladder. It's small and light, and thanks to the scissors-like gripper one can easily manage fairly large limbs when up on a ladder. We have elms, a cottonwood, a pear tree, a crab apple, and a box elder, and I use mine generally one to two times a year unless wind damage or heavy snowfall breaks some limbs. Manual loppers are longer than the Alligator, so they have better reach. However, they require greater arm spread, too. The advantage of the Alligator is cutting speed, gripping-power, and its light weight and maneuverability.

-- Dirk Murcray

This lopper-on-steroids is also great for those of us with a touch of chainsaw-phobia, since the cutting chain is covered by the guards and you don't have to worry as much about kick-back and such.

I had procrastinated for months about cutting a stand of saplings because I dislike chainsaws, but I breezed through them in a few hours with my trusty Alligator — it was even kinda fun! If you dread using a chainsaw, but have to cut branches too big for your lopper, get one of these puppies. Cuts anything up to 4 inches in diameter. I've had mine for about 8 months and have since gotten a lot of yard clean-up done that I was putting off (anything too big for a standard lopper). One unforeseen problem: all my friends keep wanting to borrow it…and keep it. Get your own, guys!

-- Barbara Dace

Mess free fueling
No-Spill Gas Can

$22 2.5-gallons (other sizes available) nospill.com

This No-Spill Gas Can has a push button spout that almost completely eliminates spilling gas when you fill a small fuel tank on a lawn mower or weed whacker. The first time I tried it, I filled a chain saw to exactly the spot I wanted. Since most chain saws have small and oddly-shaped tanks, I was really impressed.

Most gas cans have an unreliable separate vent cap that you have to remember to open and close, and even worse, a leaky main cap that lets the gas vapor escape when you leave it in the sun and the tank can't hold the pressure. The No-Spill can has a single push button that controls both pouring and venting, and the only thing to remember is to push the button with the can level to relieve the pressure. (And don't make the mistake I did, and look into the nozzle, because you get a puff of gas fumes in your eyes. I'm lucky I wear glasses.)

No-Spill also has a line of fuel cans that meet CARB (California Air Resources Board) requirements, and that are required in many states. I live in Ohio, and had never even heard of this requirement, though I'm aware that gas cans pressurize in the sun, and I make sure to keep them in the shade.

-- Matthew Robbins

Gas-powered mule
Powerwagon

$2,300+ DR Powerwagon Pro drpower.com

My wife and I are both Master Gardeners who live on mountain land where there is not a single level square foot. We have less than 1000 square feet of grass stuff (not really turf) so I have no use for a lawn tractor. Instead we use a Powerwagon. Think of it as an ATV wheelbarrow. It can haul hundreds of pounds of rock, logs, soil, or what have you up steep grades. My wife enjoys building stacked stone walls in almost inaccessible places, and this is the only way that I can get the material to her. I doubt that I could work our property without it. Warning: it is not cheap, but for me it is worth it.

-- Mike Saunders

Outdoor tool supermarket
Gempler's

Free catalog with order Gempler's

The most he-man cool tool catalog I've come across yet. Gempler's began by supplying the hardware needs of commercial farmers. It now also serves gentleman farmers and dude ranchers, and anyone else working outside — like contractors, surveyors, landscapers and groundskeepers. The catalog is huge: 563 pages of outdoor gear and heavy-duty tools that real men covet. Many of these are specialized or little known. Not just another industrial supply catalog, it's the ultimate backyard wishbook. Their service is good.

-- KK

If you're not prepared to be wrong, you will never come up with anything original. - Sir Ken Robinson

Classic ax-wielder's guide
An Ax To Grind

I've never felled a tree and can count with my hands how many times I've chopped wood. Enough swings to have stumbled on the sweetspot, but also uncomfortably close to injury. This free guide published by the USDA Forest Service is an incredible resource for everything ax-related, from beginner to advanced (and it's free!). Filled with succinct and wise passages, clear photos and helpful diagrams, the book explains the in's and out's of felling, limbing, splitting, chopping, bucking, and hewing. Plus, no-nonsense tips on how to swing, grip, sharpen, maintain, select and purchase the right ax for the right job. The subtitle is right: practical.

-- Steven Leckart

On a knotty, gnarly block of wood you'll need to start your split from the outside edges and slab off the sides. Inevitably, your ax will become stuck in

the block you are trying to split. The best way to remove it without damaging the ax is to rap the end of the handle sharply downward with the palm of your hand without holding the handle.

Accuracy is the only thing that counts; the force of the swing is not nearly as important as its placement. Chop with a series of strokes: the top, the bottom, and then the middle (Figure 80). If you chop in that order (top, bottom, middle) with both the forehand swing and the backhand swing, the

chip will fly out after your last cut. On your last cut in the middle on the backhand swing, you should give a slight twist to the ax as you sink it into the wood to pop the chip out. Swing with a natural rhythmic and unforced motion. Always watch your aim. Leaving one edge of your ax blade exposed will help ensure it doesn't get stuck in the log.

Clamp the ax to the bench at a comfortable height (Figure 65). Put on gloves to protect your hands. Hold the file as shown. Because you file into the edge of the ax, not away from it, you need gloves in case of a minor slip. Always file into the edge, toward the center of the ax handle, because this creates the least amount of burr to remove on the other side. The single-cut file sharpens only on the push stroke. Lift it away from the ax head on the return stroke. If you "saw" with your file, it will fill with metal particles. It will not cut well and it can also be ruined as the file edges are peened over.

Free PDF USDA Forest Service

Free PDF Scoutmaster

Kindling splitter
Froe

$43 Lehman's

When I think of tools that I love, this one is near the top of the list.

Most folks will tell you that the way to make little sticks (kindling) out of big sticks (chunks of firewood) is to hold the firewood chunk upright on a chopping block in one hand and take a good swing at it with a hatchet. It's pretty obvious what's wrong with this picture: you have a sharp bladed instrument moving at high speed in the direction of your bare hand. After some practice, you'll get the hang of it; the problem is reaching that level of skill without a few trips to your local suturist or finger-reattachment specialist.

There's a better way: the Froe. Traditionally used for splitting shingles, it serves equally well for bloodless, fear-free kindling. The iron blade is driven into the log (another piece of firewood makes a perfect "mallet" for this), and then torque is applied using the wooden handle to complete the split.

Your fingers will thank you.

-- Karl Bunker

Easy splitting
Fiskars Splitting Axe

$47 for 17", 23 1/2", 28", and 36" models Amazon

The Fiskars 36" Splitting Axe is like night and day when compared to other splitting tools I've used in the past. While I'm envious of those who have a hydraulic wood splitter,

I can't emphasize enough how painless this splitting axe makes the process. Whereas my previous axe would get stuck, and require swing after swing, the Fiskars cuts like butter. The head, unlike a traditional axe blade, is closer in design to a splitting wedge which helps cleave through wood with ease.

-- Oliver Hulland

Sharp, tough hatchet
Fiskars Pro Chopping Axe

$32 Amazon

Fiskars makes the best axes for the money—light, sharp and virtually unbreakable. The handle

is a fiberglass reinforced composite that is amazingly strong. A couple years ago I was carving a dugout canoe with my 28" Pro Chopping axe. The handle held up through a 30" diameter tree before breaking while I was working on the canoe (a quaking aspen log — not the best for a canoe, but all I could get at the time). Still, the axe was returned to Lowe's and replaced for free. I have used similar-priced axes in the $30 range and the wooden handles either break in no time or the blade is dull or both. I have used my axe for around three years now and went quite a while without sharpening it. Eventually, I bought the Fiskars companion sharpener for $10 and with a few passes through it, the axe is ready to go.

-- Benjamin Thompson

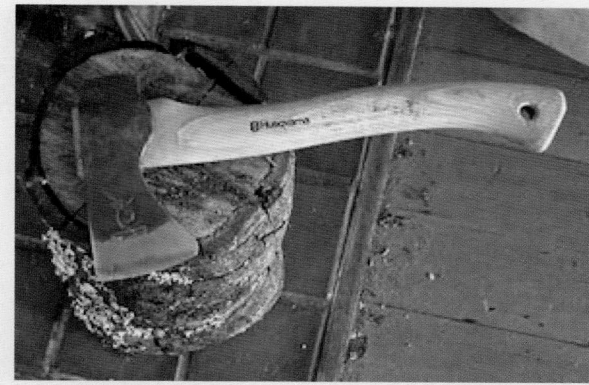

Hand forged hatchet
Husqvarna Hatchet

$45 Amazon

I've had this little hatchet for a few weeks now. Seldom have I had a tool give me so much pleasure. I love to look at it as it sits by the fireplace. It makes me happy. And using it is a whole other hatchet experience – it's razor sharp and cuts beautifully. It makes me want to split wood or sharpen stakes. Hey, I think I need to trim the branches on that dead oak I'm about to cut up for firewood.

Once in a while, a tool has just got it.

It's hand forged of Swedish steel (not made in China, by golly) by Husqvarna, the chain saw guys. This is on the smaller side of a hatchet, but they also make a larger version. The Husqvarna holds its edge well, and I don't think I'll need to sharpen it for awhile.

All my hatchets up to now have been clunkers compared to this (other than my shingling hatchet, which is specially designed for shaking and shingling).

-- Lloyd Kahn

Log splitter
E-Z Split

$1305 Amazon

We heat our home with wood — four full cords per year — and began to feel guilty about borrowing our neighbor's wood splitter for our annual restocking project. We don't have room to store a full-size splitter, so I researched and found the Brave EZ split log splitter. At about 1/3 the size and 1/4 the weight (140 lbs) of a standard splitter, it doesn't take up much more space than a lawn mower and can handle all but the most gnarled logs. The splitting wedge is quite narrow, so sometimes it actually cuts through the log rather than splitting it apart. A full cycle is about 18 seconds, so it's not as fast as a full-size splitter (closer to 12 seconds). Since the wedge isn't as tall as on a full size splitter, I occasionally have to turn the log over to get a complete split. Also, the splitter only takes logs up to 18 inches long, but these are small trade offs for the ease of storage and transport. If someone wants to borrow it or if there is a downed tree that someone is willing to let us have, we can put it in the back of our van and not worry about a tow-behind-splitter bouncing all over the road. The engine, which runs on regular gas, always starts after one or two pulls.

-- John Savereide

Wood Burning

Best advice for wood heat
Woodburner's Companion

$13 Dirk Thomas, 2006, 176 p.

If you burn wood for heat, read this book. I was amazed at how much I learned, and I've relied on wood heat for a number of long winters. Read it twice if you are just thinking about burning wood. It'll help you sort out whether you want a furnace, or stove; pellet or logs; masonry or metal, buy wood or cut it yourself, and so on. This is first-rate advice, pithy and to the point, up-to-date, well-written and insightful. The author is a professional chimney sweep and his instructions on how (and why) to clean your chimney are worth the price of the book alone.

-- KK

The Woodburner's Companion
Practical Ways of Heating with Wood
THIRD EDITION
From the Lore of an Ancient Art to the Science of 21st Century Woodburning Technology
by Dirk Thomas
Foreword by Castle Freeman, Jr.

Does it make economic sense, then, to heat your home with wood? Yes, if you have more time than money, and yes, if you enjoy the work and ritual unique to this form of heat. Burning wood fits some ways of life in the same way that vegetable gardening and livestock raising do: it also saves money, but the savings are almost incidental to the satisfaction it can provide.

Is heating with wood ethical? It may not be if you live in an area plagued by air pollution. It probably isn't if you live in an area with little forested land. It isn't if you harvest and burn your wood irresponsibly. If, on the other hand, your circumstances permit and you decide to become a responsible user of the resource, wood burning can be an integral part of a contained and conserving way of live with positive ecological impacts balancing the negative.

Wood as the Primary Source of Heat

This strategy will fit a few more households than the first: you've got a back-up heating system, so you have more flexibility. Your stove won't completely run your life six months a year, but you'll probably burn nearly as much wood as will those in the first category, so your house, location and lifestyle need to be nearly as accommodating.

Wood as Supplementary Heat

Even if your circumstance make major reliance on wood heat impractical, you might find that a stove or fireplace stove which heats part of your house some of the time will give you substantial savings on your fuel bills and a good deal of pleasure and comfort in the bargain.

Wood as an Emergency Back-up Heat Source

I mentioned the catastrophic ice storm of 1998 earlier, but even the lesser power outages to which rural areas are prone can be uncomfortable or even dangerous in severe weather. A just-in-case wood stove and a small supply of wood can turn a wretched situation into a merely inconvenient one.

Masonry Heaters

Instead of a round-the-clock fire maintained by periodic stoking and control of the air supply--the modus operandi applied to other serious wood heating equipment--masonry heaters rely on very hot fires--at times in excess of 2,000 degrees Fahrenheit--of short duration. Fires lasting only an hour or two heat a masonry mass weighing a ton or much more. The mass then radiates the stored heat for 12 to 24 hours, depending upon the weather. The extremely hot fires result in very clean burns.

A well-designed masonry heater, on the other hand, stores and radiates something on the order of 80% of the heat it produces. It does this by directing the intensely hot gases through a series of channels in the masonry mass. By the time the exhaust reaches the top of the chimney, it is almost cool, having left its heat in the masonry. The smoke does not deposit creosote if the heater is properly operated, because the fire is so hot that the tars and organic compounds are consumed in the firebox.

Disadvantages

Price. Pellet stoves usually cost more than wood stoves, and the fuel isn't cheap. As a national average, pellets currently cost about $3.50 per 40 pounds, or $165-$175 per ton. With 1 ton of pellets having the heat value

Round wire | Rectangular polypropylene | Flat wire

of 1 1/2 cord of hardwood, fuelwood must cost $100 per cord in your area for pellets to be an economical fuel.

Keep the chimney inside. Chimneys that are in the house for most of their length stay cleaner, work better, last longer and return more heat to the house than do chimneys outside the exterior walls.

If you see 1/4-inch of creosote, you'll know that the chimney needs cleaning, but the absence of creosote where you can see doesn't mean that there's none elsewhere.

Detection of a chimney fire is not usually a problem. It will likely announce itself with a prolonged roaring noise, smoke and odor in the house and thick, dark smoke and/or sparks and flames coming out of the top of the chimney. Some chimney fires are not so dramatic, probably because they haven't enough fuel or oxygen to really take off, but all chimney fires are potentially destructive and should be taken seriously. To people who regard them as a harmless way to clean a chimney, I can only say that physicians used to bleed people who were ill, too; all of the available objective evidence indicates that both practices are foolhardy.

Fire bellows poker
FireDragon Bellows

$35 mangoenergy.com

I've been using the FireDragon for the past five years to quickly and efficiently get my woodstove burning. It allows me to get a fire started using a minimal amount of tinder and kindling, and without any other firestarters. This is one of those simple, good ideas. You blow into the FireDragon to shoot a directed, bellows-like blast of air into your fire, creating a supercharging effect. This helps get larger chunks of wood to ignite and burn steadily when lighting a fire or adding a new log to a fire that isn't burning well, and it can return a smoldering fire to blazes with a few puffs.

It's basically a 3-foot long steel tube with a brass mouthpiece (that makes me think of a flattened trombone mouthpiece) and a forked end that can serve as a fire poker, log re-arranger, and coal raker. The manufacturer says they got the idea from Civil War soldiers that would take the barrels off their rifles and blow through them to fan their campfires.

Now I find I want the FireDragon any time I'm around a fire, so it goes along camping. It is plenty sturdy. No moving parts, and easy to use.

-- Brent Inghram

Automatic wood heating
Wood Pellet Stoves

Pellet stove manufacturers earthsenseenergysystems.com
$1,400 England Stove Pellet Stove 55-Shp10 Amazon

Wood pellet stoves are an alternative way to heat a home. The stoves use wood pellets, which look exactly like rabbit food, and are made out of dried recycled compressed sawdust from lumber mills that otherwise ends up in landfills. They were invented in the 1980s and were popular for a while then declined some in the late 90s but have recently made a big comeback. The industry for stove manufactures, pellet distribution and stove technology has greatly matured and is nationwide.

Wood pellet stoves have a number of advantages over normal wood stoves. Because the stoves are so efficient, there is almost no smoke or creosote produced, in fact the exhaust is barely even hot so the stove doesn't need a masonry chimney and can be installed anywhere a tin metal liner can be put in, either directly into the roof, or sideways out a wall. They can be stand-alone stoves on legs in the corner of a room, or chimney inserts using an existing chimney. Unlike wood stoves, pellet stoves work well in urban environments because of little exhaust and no need for a chimney and can be installed in any room.

The pellets come in 40 pound plastic bags, about the size of a mulch bag, which makes transport and storage a snap compared to dealing with cord wood. A fully automated stove requires filling up with the pellets and turning on; the stove does the rest: it automatically lights, automatically feeds the pellets into the flame with an auger, automatically adjusts the rate to keep the room at a pre-set temperature with an electric thermostat. At the low setting I can go 76 hours on one load in my Harman stove, which is a fireplace inset so it is limited in hopper size. There are other stoves that have bigger hoppers. Indeed there are pellet furnaces that can hold weeks worths of pellets and heat an entire central heating system.

A 40 pound bag of pellet wood produces less than a

cup of ash so it rarely needs to be emptied. I need to vacuum the ash pan in my Harman stove after burning fifty 40lb bags --about every two months during heavy use.

Typically pellets are sold by the pallet, which is 50 bags or 1-ton, for $120 to $200. Wood pellets can be found at most hardware stores around the country including Home Depot, Ace, etc. Pellets come in 3 grades, depending on ash content (less ash the better), the higher grade pellets are hardwood while the lower grade is pine, most of the major hardware chains sell the middle grades.

The stoves require electricity to run so if you lose power it won't work, which is a notable drawback, although there are solutions such as a generator or battery back up. I personally have a long extension cord to an inverter in my car in the driveway in case of a heating emergency.

Pellet stoves range in price from $1200 to $3000. Harman is way ahead of the game with computerized sensors and controls and is the brand I recommend. The stove I own is Harman's Accentra Insert, and it was $2800 installed complete.

Are wood pellets cheaper than gas or oil? Probably not, although they may be in some areas, but there are environmental "costs" to consider as well.

-- Stephen Balbach

Intelligence is the capacity to acquire capacity. - H. Woodrow Wilson

Cubic-foot heat
Extremely Tiny Woodstoves

The need: a very tiny woodstove suitable for a small space in a home.

The original Very Small Woodstove is the Jotul 602, from Norway. This model is a mere 12 inches wide, 19 inches deep. They are found most often in cottages and cabins in the woods, where the 602's good looks are a highlight. It's been around almost forever. Jotul claims over 1 million of these have been manufactured. Waterford and Garden Way produced a near identical stove called the Reginald 101, but it is no longer in production, but available used, as is the Jotul 602. Although very small it can heat amazingly well.

$700 Jotul 602 12 x 19

jotul.com

But the tiniest very small woodstoves are those built for boats. These are designed for very tight quarters, and often have a railing on the top to keep pots from rolling off. Here is a typical one from the Canadian coast measuring all of 12 inches by 12 inches. They are made of cast iron and porcelain and are so cute and enchanting, folks have thought of getting a sailboat just so they need one.

$763 Sardine 12 x12

marinestove.com

The third option for extremely small woodstoves are those manufactured for camping. Sometimes known as wall tent stoves, or pack trail stoves, or ice shack, or even shepherding stoves, these are meant for nomadic or seasonal camps. Like the marine varieties they double as cookstoves. More expensive varieties are produced in titanium, the cleverest are even collapsible, but the cheapest are steel, and they are as plain and basic as camp coffee.

$185 Two Dog Stove 10 x 12

walltentshop.com

THE source for pack trail stoves is Pack Saddle Shop.

$140 Wilderness Shanty Wood Stove 8 x 15

goodoutdoors.
theshoppe.com

Slightly larger-- that is small, but not extremely small -- home woodstoves can also be found at Lehman's.

Tiny convection stove
Morsoe Wood Stove
$1200 1440 morsona.com

This low-clearance stove sits in a corner of our family room, which is not huge, so I wanted to nestle it in as close to the corner as I could. The big difference between this Morsoe and the previously-reviewed Jotul isn't the physical dimensions so much as just how close to the walls each stove can be. The Jotul needs to be situated 13 inches off the walls. The clearance for the Morsoe: 7 inches. A significantly smaller space clearance-wise than any other stove I've found. When I plotted just how far the Jotul would protrude into my room versus the Morsoe, the difference was dramatic.

In lieu of legs, the stove has panels bolted on either side which run from the floor to the top. Since they are not the same casting as the main body of the stove, the panels do not get incredibly hot. I can have the stovetop at 700 degrees F, and still touch the panels with my hand without getting burned. Air is drawn from beneath the stove up between the panels, and flows up into the room providing most of the heat output.

Aside from the clearance, this is a really nice little stove -- easy to start and burns great. I've used mine for two seasons now, two to three times a week during the winter months. While the rest of the house is kept around 65 degrees, the family room is 75. The downsides: requires small (10") wood, and the firebox is somewhat small, so it needs reloading pretty frequently. However, I shouldn't forget to mention the stove has cool squirrel symbols on the side panels.

-- Paul Mitchell

Propane heater
Dickinson Marine Fireplace
$990 P-9000 dickinsonmarine.com

We live in a tiny house and love our Dickinson Marine fireplace -- it does an excellent job of heating our 105-square-foot space. Watching the flames makes things very cozy on a cold day.

We generally use our fireplace beginning sometime in November through about April, depending on the weather. It uses very little propane; I think it cost us about $40 for heating this past winter. We use the 12v built-in blower when it is particularly cold or when we are trying to heat things up quickly. But forced-air heat blows around dust, which makes me sneeze, and it is a little noisy, too, so I prefer to leave the fan off when it's not necessary. Without the fan on the heater is very quiet. For our small space and compared with electric space heaters or even central forced-air systems, this little guy takes the cake.

One nice side bonus: When the heater is on, I can place my coffee cup on top next to the flue to keep my coffee warm!

-- Derek Raedeker

Resin-rich fire starter
Fatwood
$15 for 10 lbs. amazon.com
$30 for 25 lbs. llbean.com

fatwood.com

There's not much new in the art of firemaking, and most methods are a few hundred thousand years old. But in the 21st century, getting a fire started in the fireplace can still be more difficult than it needs to be. Crumpling up inky newspaper as tinder under a full size split log is hit or miss at best, and gathering up sticks as kindling is a pain, especially for city dwellers.

This winter, I've solved the problem with the discovery of "fatwood" firestarters: small sections of resin-rich pine (most commonly from the longleaf pine Pinus palustris) produced from stumps. They just work: criss-cross two of them, light them and they will quickly catch and burn long enough to get the big logs going. They work every time. They smell good, they're inexpensive and they're sustainable. They come from existing stumps and the Fatwood company plants three trees for every one they use. Start a cozy fire faster with a clear conscience this winter.

-- Matthew Perks

Portable wood heat
Wall Tent Stoves

Wall Tent Shop
walltentshop.com

Kifaru Foldable Tipi Stove
$249+ 4.5 lbs. 8" x 9" x 12"
kifaru.net

KniCo Stove
$120+ 12.5 lbs. 10" x 10" x 23"
packsaddleshop.com

Portable wood stoves are for tents, tipis, huts or other temporary shelters. More efficient than a campfire, and more powerful than a backpacking stove, they are often used by ranchers, hunters, fisherman, and other trail groups who need to set

up a moveable camp. These little guys will heat a large tent/small room, and cook meals. It's overkill for overnight use, but quickly becomes beloved in cold weather, large groups, or extended summer camps. Once upon a time you needed a pack horse or off-road vehicle to carry one -- and the stove pipe it requires. Now there are lightweight versions. The Kifaru, for instance, will fold into a backpack. However the heavier ones will last longer and warp less due to high heat and burn-out of the stove bottom.

The best single source for information, comparison evaluations and ordering various brands and models of these stoves is the Wall Tent Shop. (And yes, they also sell traditional wall tents.)

-- KK

Wood powered hot tub
Snorkel Hot Tub

$4,000 6 x 4 ft Cedar snorkel.com

Our neighbor has one of these which we've used with great appreciation and delight. It's your basic wood-fired, fresh water, aromatic wooden hot tub. Takes two or three hours to heat up, but it's pretty thrifty with the fuel. The gut is a marine-grade aluminum stovebox, which you can purchase alone (choice of large or small) or in a cedar/redwood tub and stove combo that costs about half of a modern fiberglass version. Even the small one is roomy enough for three. Bathers are safely protected from the submerged stove by a metal and wood shield. A drip of Clorox between soaks keeps the water tame. Discounting your labor in making firewood and keeping the firebox stoked, the upkeep is free. This tub is ideal for a remote cabin, cottage or hideout anywhere off the grid -- precisely the kind of place where a steaming hot bath with an open view is most welcomed.

-- KK

Efficient, compact hot water
AquaStar Tankless Water Heater

$403 bosch-climate.us

I have lived on a boat since I was 13. We have tried just about every way of heating water (including one kettle at a time on a wood stove). Since boats usually don't have room for a big water heater, nor the natural gas hookup, we usually had a hardly-functioning on-demand propane water heater. They were infernally breaking down. However these "instantaneous" water heaters have finally come of age due to market pressures, so now you can buy a highly efficient mainstream tankless heater for home use.

I now have a Bosch AquaStar 125HX. Not only is it smaller and more efficient than any water heater that uses a tank, it gives endless hot water at good pressures, and has worked flawlessly in a marine environment for the last three years on my houseboat. This water heater instantly lights up a propane heating system automatically the moment I turn on the hot water, yet it does not need a power cord (important if your power goes off, or if you aren't on the grid). It does this by cleverly generating electricity from the water pressure in the pipes to spark a piezo igniter.

There is a whole AquaStar line from large ones for multi shower households, to the smaller ones like mine. Some are made to work in line with solar radiant heating, some with propane, some with natural gas. I really like the HX model because it works with no outside power source

Guide to sun-heated H20
Solar Hot Water Systems

$90, or $40 for the black and white (shipping included)

Tom Lane 2004, 194 p., ecs-solar.com

Way back in the 70s and decades before, too, hundreds of us tried lots of ways of heating water with sunlight. Some schemes worked fine at first, but later succumbed to failures of materials and technique. Some defiantly produced only lukewarm water available only at awkward hours. Some defied the laws of physics and didn't work at all. A few exploded. It wasn't long before it was common to see deteriorating solar water heaters perched disconsolately on rooftops, abandoned by humiliated, exasperated owners.

Time to try again! This inspiringly-comprehensive book presents what has been learned the hard way over the past 30 years or so. Clear illustrations (many in color) show the layouts that have proved to be the best in every way. Recommended hardware is here complete with brand name and even the part numbers. Here are the most effective pipe sizes and materials and why they are chosen. Classic mistakes are attended along with their corrections. Cautions are noted; success is celebrated.

My experience in the field and 25 years at the *Whole Earth Catalog* tells me that every aspect has been well covered and detailed. If you follow the recommendations, your solar hot water system will be sure to work and last a long time. I consider this book as a model for collected experience on other subjects as well.

-- J. Baldwin

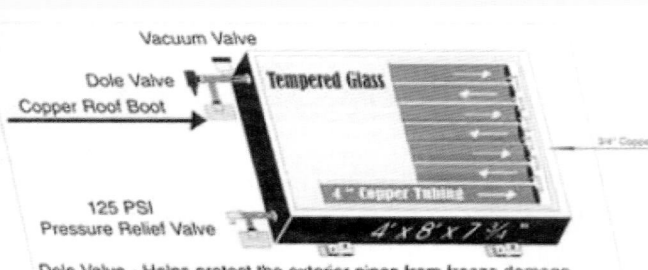

Dole Valve - Helps protect the exterior pipes from freeze damage.
Vacuum Valve - Allows air in for draining the system.

Small, battery/propane-operated shower
EccoTemp L5 Portable Tankless Water Heater

$120 eccotemp.com

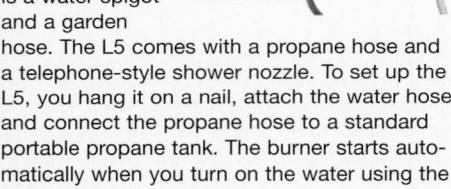

While most tankless water heaters require expensive permanent installation, the Ecotemp L5 water heater provides hot water anywhere there is a water spigot and a garden hose. The L5 comes with a propane hose and a telephone-style shower nozzle. To set up the L5, you hang it on a nail, attach the water hose, and connect the propane hose to a standard portable propane tank. The burner starts automatically when you turn on the water using the control on the shower nozzle.

My wife and I have a tiny cabin on a piece of mountain land that has a water supply, in the form of a frost-free water spigot, but no other utilities. We bought the L5 two years ago when we got tired of heating water for washing and showers in a pan on our Coleman stove. The L5 makes this glorified camping spot feel luxurious. The heater weighs about 12 pounds, making it easy to move back and forth between the spot where we wash dishes and a small enclosure I built for taking showers. When we leave, we disconnect it, drain it, and store it in the cabin.

The heater uses two D-cell batteries to run its automatic igniter. In two years of summer-weekend use, we've not yet had to replace the batteries. The heater has two controls: a water-flow dial and a gas-flow dial. In practice, you just turn the gas dial to "max" and adjust the temperature by varying the water flow. When adjusted to a decent temperature for a hot shower, the flow is perfectly adequate.

The heater must be used outdoors. Conceivably, you could mount it to the outside of a cabin and pipe the hot water inside. The water outlet accepts the same kind of flexible water supply hose you use to connect a sink's faucet to your household water supply.

The L5 is not the only on-demand portable water heater. Coleman's table-top unit uses small, disposable propane canisters, and has a built in pump, allowing it to be used without a pressurized water supply. The pump's battery must be recharged every 40 gallons. Available accessories for the Coleman include a shower handset and adapters for bulk propane containers and pressurized water supplies. The Coleman unit's built-in spigot makes washing hands and dishes more convenient than the L5's shower handset, and it has a special mode for producing 160 (F) degree water for hot drinks. However, it has 20% less heating capacity than the L5 (which is rated at 37,500 BTUs) and costs substantially more, especially with accessories. Another option, the Zodi travel shower, also uses a battery-powered pump, but provides only 10,000 BTUs and lacks the instant-on feature of the L5 and Coleman heaters. Both the Coleman and the Zodi are free-standing, and do not require a place to hang them. The Coleman costs about $185 (plus $30 for the bulk propane adapter, $25 for the water supply adapter, and $15 for the shower handset), the Zodi $130, and the L5 $120.

In the two years we've had the L5, we've had a couple small problems. We had to replace the short hose that connects the heater to the shower handset. More recently, the handset itself broke when we left it outside on a very cold night and the water in it froze. Occasionally, the burner will go out in a high wind. On the whole, however, the L5 has been very reliable and convenient. Besides luxury camping, I could see the L5 being useful in a potting shed or an outdoor kitchen.

-- Tom Sackett

Changing sunlight into electricity (PV or photovoltaic systems) captures everyone's imagination and the publicity causes them to contact solar contractors. Once they focus on KWH's [kilowatt hours] saved, it becomes clear that for every $20 to $30 spent on a PV system you can save the same amount [of KWH] for $1 spent on a solar hot water system.

• NEVER RUN THE INSULATION THROUGH THE FLASHING THROUGH THE ROOF DECK WITH THE PIPING. This can cause rain to run between the insulation and the piping into the home. Seal under the stand pipe before soldering around the "coolie hat." DO NOT USE SILICONE SEALANTS.

or pilot for ignition, making it very efficient, safe and reliable. They cost more than standard water heaters (mine was $550) but they pay for themselves fast in power bills since you don't have to keep a large tank of water heated all the time; you only make hot water exactly when you need it.

I would absolutely use one of these even if I lived on land with access to a gas line. The hot water never runs out (which would be great in a household with a lot of people, or if you just like long showers) and it's more efficient because it's not heating a whole tank of water all the time.

-- Alexander Rose

A drug is something that, injected into an animal, produces a paper. - Albert Sangiorgi

Vent-free, clean-burning heater
ProCom Unvented Propane Heater

$200 MD300TBA* Norther Tool

If you have an unheated outbuilding or basement and you want to warm it cheaply with minimal installation hassles, the ProCom "Blue-Flame" ML300TBA is an interesting option. A combination radiant/passive-convection heater powered by propane, the ProCom burns cleanly and needs no vent or chimney. A bit more civilized than the brute-force, rocket-engine-style of the, portable Dyna-Glo workshop heater (this page). Granted the Dyna-Glo has the raw power to bring a very large, cold space up to a comfortable temperature within minimum amount of time, but it is relatively expensive to run and does make a distracting amount of noise. The Procom, on the other hand, just simmers almost silently in the background.

During use, the heater creates virtually no odor detectable by my nose, and because no heat is lost through an outside exhaust, it's super-efficient. Just to be on the safe side I bought a carbon monoxide detector from Home Depot for around $20, but it has not registered any hazard. Of course any flame will consume oxygen, and for this reason alone you should crack a window a little if you keep the heater burning for prolonged periods. The heater is not recommended for very small spaces, bedrooms, or bathrooms. Be sure to follow all the instructions in the manual.

Since the combustion of propane unites hydrogen in the gas with oxygen in the air, the heater liberates more than one-and-one-half pints of water per hour at its maximum setting, in addition to some carbon dioxide. The water is a bonus for me, as my sinuses prefer some humidity. The heater is silent unless you buy the optional (overpriced) circulation fan. Personally, I prefer to use a ceiling fan to spread heat around more actively.

Is it really safe?

Well, consider the alternatives. A wood-burning stove is generally regarded as benign, yet can emit significant carbon monoxide through incomplete combustion if you use it in "slow burning" mode. Fragrant wood smoke is rich in tars that may be carcinogenic, some escaping into your living room while the rest circulate through your neighborhood via that convenient device, the chimney -- which is not only horribly inefficient but becomes a notorious fire hazard as residues accumulate inside it.

For those who don't want to install a chimney, or don't have a municipal gas supply, or don't want to pay a plumber to extend an existing gas line to an additional location, an unvented heater is a convenient option. Propane is not an irritant, does not cause sensitization, and has no known teratogenic or mutagenic effects. Also, unlike a wood stove, the ProCom heater contains an oxygen depletion sensor that will shut it down if necessary. Of course if you allow it to become very dirty, it may burn less efficiently, creating some carbon monoxide, like a kerosene stove, which is why you may find a carbon dioxide detector reassuring.

Northern Tool also sells a natural-gas version of the ventless gas heater, which I have not tried

-- Charles Platt

Portable, forced-air, fuel-flexi heater
Dyna-Glo Pro Heater

$200 KFA75H Home Depot

For heating a cold garage, this crazy-macho heater really does the job. It's very powerful (75,000 BTU) and, amazingly, creates no detectable odor while burning kerosene. Sold only in Home Depot stores (not available anywhere online) it retails for around $200, which is slightly less than similar models by other manufacturers. While many forced-air heaters of this type are propane-powered, this one allows you a choice of kerosene or diesel, eliminating the hassle, weight, and expense of a propane cylinder.

Inside the heater a pump vaporizes the fuel, which is ignited in a tube containing a powerful fan. The blast of hot air feels good and is much more effective than a passive convection heater. The device looks and functions like a small rocket motor, which adds to the fun of it for me, since I feel nostalgic for the days when consumer products were unencumbered by tiresome safety features. Some people however may be disconcerted by the yellow flames that emerge about 1 to 2 inches from the business end during normal use. If you live in Massachusetts, you're supposed to get a local fire department permit before you plug it in and induce ignition.

You must have a fresh air supply through a partially opened door or window, and you don't want pets or children around. Probably a concrete floor is advisable, and (even though the instructions somehow fail to mention this) you should not stand directly in front of the heater while switching it on! In 35-degree weather, in a workshop of 20 x 25 feet with a very

high 16-foot ceiling, the heater created a 70-degree environment within about 15 minutes. The burning vapor makes a muted roaring noise, but you probably won't need to run it for more than a few minutes at a time.

Although the heater has a thermostatic control, I prefer to use mine manually, since a gadget resembling a small rocket motor which ignites itself at unpredictable moments is enough to make me a little jumpy. Dyna-Glo also manufactures a smaller, propane-powered version, which I tried but didn't like as much. They offer two larger liquid-fueled models which I haven't tested, because I don't have that much space to heat.

-- Charles Platt

Wood stove thermometer
Magnetic Stove Pipe Thermometer

$13 SBI International

I have a wood stove in the basement that is connected to the chimney flue with stovepipes. It has adjustable air inflow like most wood stoves, but it has always been a guessing game where I should set the intake ports. Too hot and you risk a chimney fire, too cold and you get creosote buildup in the flue.

I purchased the Magnetic Stovepipe Thermometer on a whim a few months ago. I thought it might be interesting to know how hot the stovepipe got. As it turns out it's a great guide for how to set the air inputs on your stove. Now, every time I walk downstairs to check the fire, the first thing I look at is the stovepipe thermometer. If it's pointing near to straight up I know the temperature is about right. If it's pointing left I know it's too cold, so I open up the air ports and/or add more wood. If it's pointing right I know it's too hot, so I close down the air intake ports.

I don't believe the model I purchased is any better than the half a dozen or so I found on Amazon. Others could very well be superior. The fact that it is magnetic, however, is very convenient, as you can move it around on the stovepipe till you find the hottest spot or the right angle.

-- Gary Klaus

Versatile material reflects heat
Reflectix Foil Insulation

$24 24"x25' Reflectix Inc.

Reflectix is a reflective insulation that looks like silver bubble wrap. It's commonly used in attics as insulation. It reflects heat, and works best if there's a small dead air space between it and whatever you're insulating (you can use a small strip of reflectix to create that space). It's lightweight, you can buy a 4'x25" roll of it for less than 50 bucks, and it's easy to work with.

I use it in a lot of ways beyond its traditional use as a radiant heat barrier in attics. It's great for small-scale insulation projects, covering frost-sensitive plants at night, covering a window when the sun's blasting in.

Last winter, I threw some over the chicken coop when it got really cold at night, and I'm planning to use it to shade their coop when it gets hot this summer. While I've never used it this way, it might make a great parabolic reflector for solar uses, as long as it didn't get too hot. I can see lots of backpacking uses for a length of this lightweight stuff (as a thermal barrier under a sleeping pad), as a reflector behind you when you're sitting by a fire to reflect the heat back (though you should take care to anchor it well so it doesn't get into the fire), or as a sunshade on a hot day.

-- Amy Thomson

Composting Toilets

cover material

Make your own emergency toilet
Humanure Handbook Sawdust Composting Toilet

Everything you could possibly want to know about recycling human waste is found in the third edition of the *Humanure Handbook* (see right).

In addition this heroic book tells you how to make your own small homemade composting toilet using 5-gallon buckets and a regular toilet seat, and how to compost the deposits usefully. This can be used for an emergency toilet, for a cabin, or in a motor home, or for everyday use if you have a garden. One of the videos on the book's website details the clever idea of how a music festival used sawdust toilets instead of porta-potties to much relief.

The book is also available as free PDFs; the chapter on building your own sawdust toilet is Chapter 8.

-- KK

After using composting toilets on a few sailboats and one in a relative's cabin, I would say they are all prone to smells, breakage and disappointment. EXCEPT for the DIY five-gallon sawdust bucket described in *The Humanure Handbook*. Nothing to go wrong. I've never had a smell issue either in the toilet or the compost pile. It requires a little bit of ongoing effort, but in my opinion this is 'positive' maintenance as opposed to negative maintenance when any other toilet breaks down. As an added bonus the bucket can be built into an attractive box to match the style and material of your space and looks far better than almost any toilet on the market including water closets.

-- Mackey McLelland

I have used this sawdust composting toilet for 10 years now without problems. There really is nothing to have a problem with. I originally envied a neighbor who had shelled out for one of the big production composting toilets. It broke in less than two years (an important mechanical part of the 'tumbler' was poorly designed and failed). He was left with a

couple hundred pounds of incompletely composted humanure in his house. To say that he was unhappy is an understatement. He has used a sawdust toilet since then. In short, unless local regulations require a production toilet (increasingly they do not) a sawdust toilet is the way to go.

A couple of suggestions: use wood pellets if you find sawdust hard to come across; they quickly turn to sawdust. Don't turn your humanure compost piles, just leave them...for years. They will take care of themselves. You can find instructions for a sawdust toilet online easily. It is embarrassingly simple and much more hygienic (even though most people's first reaction, including mine, is, "Ewwww.").

The sawdust toilet also provides a perfect emergency toilet (for hurricanes, power outages, etc) Just keep a 5 gallon bucket, 2 lids, and a bag of wood pellets in a closet. Cut a salad plate sized hole in

one of the lids for use as a 'seat' and put the other over it to 'close the lid'. Just make sure to dispose of the humanure responsibly after the emergency.

-- Rob Groesbeck

Free, Humanure Handbook PDF
Humanurehandbook.com

Free Humanure Youtube Channel

Composting crapper guide
The Humanure Handbook
$19 Joseph C. Jenkins, 2005, 256 p.

This is the definitive source on composting crappers, from why to how, and yes, the scatological humor abounds. Yet this is a serious issue. Biosolids are recycled and used in the U.S. and around the world by governments and municipalities, and not always in the most responsible ways. Jenkins gives you the knowledge to do it yourself, and do it responsibly. The entire contents of this comprehensive guide are available as a free PDF download, and the Jenkins Publishing site offers up instructional videos, too. Very helpful when I constructed my own bucket toilet.

-- Erik Knutzen

• "We don't want to eat shit!" they informed me, rather distressed (that's an exact quote), as if in preparing dinner I had simply set a steaming turd on a plate in front of them with a knife, fork and napkin. Fecophobia is alive and well and running rampant. One common misconception is that fecal material, when composted, remains fecal material. It does not. Humanure comes from the earth, and through the miraculous process of composting, is converted back into earth.

• That's also why humanure and urine alone will not compost. They contain too much nitrogen and not enough carbon, and microorganisms, like humans, gag at the thought of eating it. Since there's nothing worse than the thought of several billion gagging microorganisms, a carbon-based material must be added to the humanure in order to make it into an appealing dinner. Plant cellulose is a carbon-based material, and therefore plant by-products such as hay, straw, weeds or even paper products if ground to the proper consistency, will provide the needed carbon. Kitchen food scraps are generally C/N balanced, and they can be readily added to humanure compost. Sawdust (preferably not kiln-dried) is a good carbon material for balancing the nitrogen of humanure.

• A wide array of microorganisms live in a compost pile. Bacteria are especially abundant and are usually divided into several classes based upon the temperatures at which they best thrive. The low temperature bacteria are thepsychrophiles, which can grow at temperatures down to -10°C, but whose optimum temperature is 15°C (59°F) or lower. The mesophiles live at medium temperatures, 20-45°C (68-113°F), and include human pathogens. Thermophiles thrive above 45°C (113°F), and some live at, or even above, the boiling point of water.

• If a backyard composter has any doubt or concern about the existence of pathogenic organisms in his or her humanure compost, s/he can use the compost for horticultural purposes rather than for food purposes. Humanure compost can grow an amazing batch of berries, flowers, bushes, or trees. Furthermore, lingering patho-

gens continue to die after the compost has been applied to the soil, which is not surprising since human pathogens prefer the warm and moist environment of the human body. As the World Bank researchers put it, "even pathogens remaining in compost seem to disappear rapidly in the soil." [*Night Soil Composting*, 1981] Finally, compost can be tested for pathogens by compost testing labs.

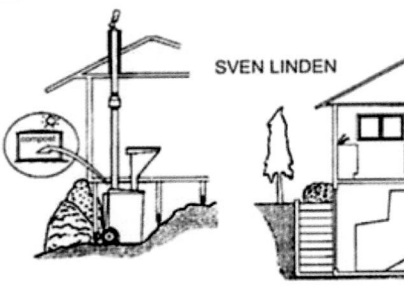

SVEN LINDEN

AQUATRON

SUN-MAR

BIO-SUN

TECHNISCH BUREAU HAMAR

ALASCAN

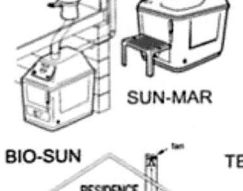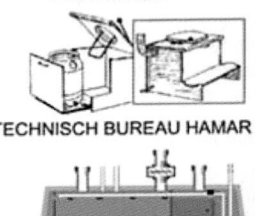

Clockwise from top left: Sven Linden, Sven Linden, Aquatron, Dutch Hamar, Alascan, Bio-Sun, Sun-Mar.

120 *The Humanure Handbook — Chapter 6: Composting Toilets and Systems*

• Allow me to make a radical suggestion: humanure is not dangerous. More specifically, it is not any more dangerous than the body from which it is excreted. The danger lies in what we do with humanure, not in the material itself. To use an analogy, a glass jar is not dangerous either. However, if we smash it on the kitchen floor and walk on it with bare feet, we will be harmed. If we use a glass jar improperly and dangerously, we will suffer for it, but that's no reason to condemn glass jars. When we discard humanure as a waste material and pollute our soil and water supplies with it, we are using it improperly, and that is where the danger lies. When we constructively recycle humanure by composting, it enriches our soil, and, like a glass jar, actually makes life easier for us.

Commercial options
Carousel Composting Toilet
$2,700 Medium Carousel Ecological Engineering
$1,800 Sun-Mar Excel Sun-Mar

I grew up with a Carousel composting toilet in our house. It works well. Draining the urine, using a scoop of sawdust every time, and the occasional insertion of beneficial bacteria, all help prevent odors. We had a 12V fan, as well. Two years is the recommended time between deposition and cleaning. We used it as our primary family toilet for over 15 years, before my father no longer wanted to clean it. It never broke down, and never had any issues. It can handle a whole family year round.

For individuals or occasional vacation use, I'd recommend the Sun-Mar standard Excel.

-- Courtney Ostaff

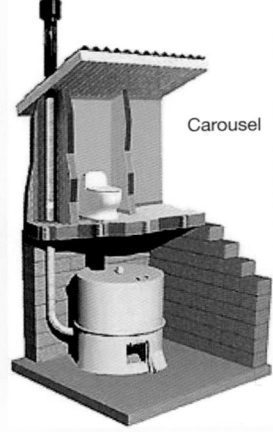
Carousel

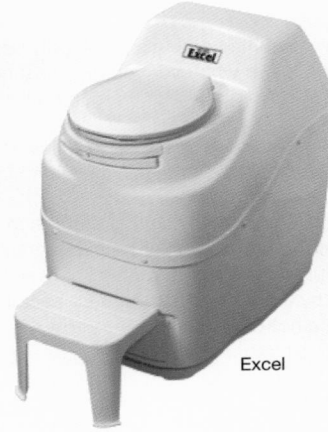
Excel

Tips

• A useful source of strong wire that is universally available in every closet is a coat hanger. Keep one in the car and one in the toolbox. Uses include tieing things, creating temporary supports, unblocking drains, opening cars, fishing for lost items that are out of reach, replacement aerials, weird 12v lighting tracks, and fabricating special tools and jigs. I've even seen them used to make Christmas decorations. Probably as useful and universal as duct tape, only cheaper.

-- Steve Burrows

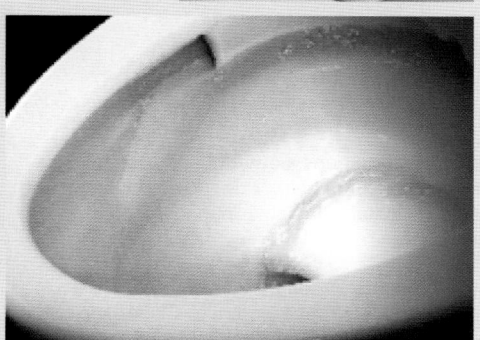

Never fail flush
Toto Ultra Low Flush Toilet
$445 Toto UltraMax,
$226 2 Toto Drake 2 totousa.com

Where I live, new toilets must be ultra-low flow using only 1.28 gallons per flush. We had trouble with our previous 1.6 gallon low flow toilets of various makes not dealing with large turds. But a few years ago I discovered Toto's UltraMax toilets. Hurray! They never ever clogged. I replaced three of our low-flows with Totos and put away the plunger for good. I was a little skeptical about the new super low-flow 1.28 gallon UltraMax 2 but they flush as reliably and forcefully as ever. In the year that we've had two of them, not a single incident. The UltraMax 2 is a one piece unit; you can save $200 with the two piece Toto Drake 2 using the exact same "double cyclone" flushing design. Either one, this is the cheapest first-time, every-time, never-fail ultra low flush.

-- KK

Deluxe mid-priced bidet
GoBidet
$128 gobidet.com

Instead of the Toto Washlet Toilet, there's another bidet attachment option that is easier to install and use while being cheaper. The GoBidet is an adjustable arm that affixes to your existing toilet and swings into position when needed. I've been using mine for at least six years. We had one in a hotel down in Costa Rica and I liked it so much I found a stateside supplier. I find it much more flexible than the fixed bidet seat variety. Although it costs more than the BioBidet, the remote control handle makes a world of difference compared to a fixed tip. With the GoBidet, you're actually able to aim the nozzle. It's kind of like playing a twisted version of Space Invaders.

The bidet can be set to spray both hot and cold water, and the water hookups and mixing control are just like those in a single lever sink faucet. You move the water control lever up to increase water volume and to the left or right to make it colder or warmer. I have it hooked up to just the cold (attached to a 'T' from the toilet supply spigot). While it initially required some getting used to, I found it was easier than running a longer hose from the hot water hookup under the sink. Of course, in a new bathroom install you could run another hot water spigot next to the toilet supply. I've used warm water bidets before and would definitely recommend setting it up with the hot water, if at all possible. It's $130, but they can be frequently found for less on eBay (new, of course).

-- Ed Tapanes

Luxurious, squirting WC seat
Toto Washlet Toilet
$800 washlet.com

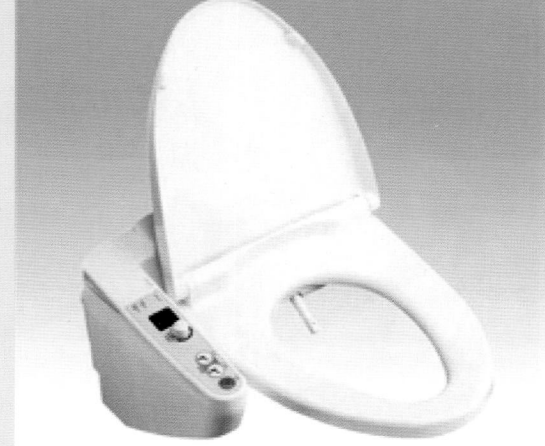

Compared with my previous visit to Japan 12 years ago, the most noticeable change I find today is in the bathroom. The "Incredible Squirting Toilet" has achieved almost total market penetration, and not just in middle-income homes. It even appears in fast-food restaurants and in public facilities in railroad stations.

As you lower yourself to the thermostatically warmed seat, a concealed motor whirs briefly, providing your first clue that you are about to encounter a piece of highly sophisticated technology. The toilet then remains silent and passive until you reach the point where you would normally apply paper. Instead, you hit the spray button. A hidden tube extends itself beneath you, and with the precision of a heat-seeking missile, it directs a spray of warm water that simultaneously tickles, stimulates, and cleans the place that needs it most. While its aim is meticulous, you can adjust its penetration by gently flexing your sphincter muscle. The experience is so unexpectedly and uniquely pleasurable, I found myself tempted to visit the toilet repeatedly just for recreational purposes.

Paper is needed only to mop up the water when the spray jet has done its work, but such is the effectiveness of the washing action, you will find no visible trace of fecal matter on the sheets of tissue, and can don your underwear in the happy knowledge that you have been cleaned by the same impeccable Japanese engineering that brought the world Honda motorcycles, 170-mile-an-hour trains, and robotic talking dogs.

Higher-end versions of the squirting toilet eliminate the need for paper entirely, by allowing the option of warm-air drying. They also provide adjustment of the water-cleaning jet, including a pulsatile flow which I found especially pleasurable. And for those in Western countries who are sufficiently uninhibited to allow themselves the pleasures of using this rectal equivalent of a water-pic, I have good news: The squirting toilet is available as an imported item and can be retrofitted to older bathroom equipment (you simply swap out the seat). Toto, the primary Japanese manufacturer, offers the most basic model under the name Washlet C100, and if you browse online you can find it for around US$500. This has only the most basic features; you can pay more for more advanced models, including one that welcomes you by raising its lid when it sees you approaching.

A note for female readers: The squirting toilet has a second tube which can be deployed by women who wish to cleanse their labial areas. For anatomical reasons, I was unable to test this personally.

-- Charles Platt

Dual TP dispenser
Double Paper Holder
$14 lwws.com

Modern public toilets employ versions of these dual TP holders, and even though a private household has no similar absolute need for one, it's very nice to permanently eliminate one of life's little nagging gotchas. I've been using this model for 15 years, and it's served its purpose admirably: having an at-hand spare roll when the primary roll unexpectedly runs out. It's bound to happen someday to someone (maybe to a visitor), so why not attack the problem proactively? Rather than being haphazardly located under the sink, next to the john, etc., the spare roll is rather tidily found; neither in the way nor out of the way.

Also, there is no spool to thread through the roll(s), meaning there's no detachable part to drop while re-threading or misplace while moving or painting. Instead, there are a couple of 3/8" circular projections on each side that fit snugly into each roll's cardboard center. Press a little black button and an arm on the side pivots out an inch. Insert one side of the roll onto the center (fixed) post and swing/click the arm back into place -- fast and foolproof. This design also fits the roll more tightly than a spool, so the TP doesn't rattle on its axis while being turned and thoughtfully stops turning when the pulling stops. There are slightly cheaper versions of this style of holder, but they have spools. Besides, in 15 years mine hasn't failed, tarnished or scratched. I think building codes should encourage such dual TP holders.

-- Roger Knights

A sink in the top of your toilet
Toilet Lid Sink
$140 eco-buildingproducts.com

After you flush the toilet, incoming water cycles up through the sink before going down to refill the toilet tank. Water is used twice: Once for hand washing, and a second time for the next flush.

-- Charles Platt

▼

Cheapest bidet
BB-50 Natural Water Bio-Bidet
$34 biobidet.com

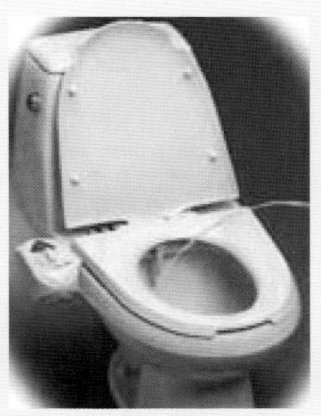

I've never felt completely clean after taking care of the paperwork end of visiting the restroom. This bidet attachment is cool because it fits on most toilets, is really cheap compared to a standard bidet, is easy to install and doesn't require you to modify the plumbing.

Just remove the toilet seat, place the bidet on the bowl, put the toilet seat back on top of the brackets that hold the bidet, and use the longer bolts (supplied) to tighten the seat and bidet to the bowl. As far as the water connection, simply introduce a valve into the tubing in between the pipe coming out of the wall and where it enters the bottom of the toilet tank. There is a pressure dial off to the right of the seat (it allows you to go to the full pressure of the water coming out of the wall, so be careful!). The higher priced models have heaters, but that requires either patching into a hot water line or snaking an electrical cord around your bathroom for the models that come with mini hot water heaters. For me the basic, inexpensive one works just great, and the ease of installation was important (I am not the slickest with tools). The only maintenance I do is spray the bidet nozzle with a bleach/water mixture whenever we clean the toilet. I have used mine in three different houses in the last two years, and it's truly enhanced my life. Why take two showers a day unless you really have to?

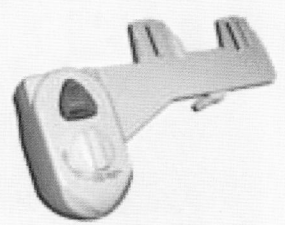

-- Ryan Combs

Solar

Zero down solar panels
Solar Lease

SunRun sunrunhome.com
SolarCity solarcity.com

The cool tool here is creative solar financing. Solar-electric panels are pretty much a commodity, but still high priced. What's new is an innovative way for a homeowner to afford an expensive solar set up. Five years ago I covered my studio roof with 5 kilowatts of solar panels financed by a solar company (our roof shown above). We are generating about 85% of the electricity we use now. Here's how it works.

You sign up with a company that installs high-quality panels on your property for no money down. Zero dollars! On sunny days the panels make electrons which run your meter backwards. The quantity of panels are sized to cover about 80-90% of your current electric bill, so that you should be expected to pay the utility only 10-20% of what you pay now. In addition to the much smaller payment to your electric grid company you will also now pay the solar company a fee based on the number of watts you send into the grid. This is how they make money to cover the costs of installing the panels and their profit. The rates they will charge you per kilowatt will be less than the utility rates, so your total bill for electricity will be less each month. (Not zero, not half, but less.) Because the solar company makes money by how much electricity your panels produce they have a clear incentive to maintain the panels' performance and keep them clean and the inverters going. After 15-18 years, you can buy-back the panels for a fraction of their costs, but I suspect they will give them to you free since it will be cheaper than removing them from your roof.

You could think of this as a lease-to-own option for solar panels, where the solar company's rents for electricity are cheaper than the utility grid's. Those cheaper rents are made possible in part by government solar subsidizes, which the solar company will claim on your behalf. But this is a busi-

ness. While you may be generating 90% of your usage, because you are leasing the panels, your total combined bill will not be 90% less. It may only be 10% less per month. But since it costs you nothing or little up front, over 18 years that 10% adds up. In California, one company providing this zero down financing is SolarCity.

While I got a bid from SolarCity, we went with a slightly different deal from SunRun. Rather than zero down, we paid for half of the installation. That investment bought us a better rate for the electricity that we generate. In fact for the next 18 years we pay a fixed rate for electricity. The average California rate is expected to at least double, and we are projected to save $80,000 over 18 years. We could have gone all the way and bought the panels outright and then paid no lease. But we went with SunRun because this path requires either half, or no, down payment, and because SunRun specs out, installs, insures, owns and maintains the solar panels on our roofs. Also, they guarantee a certain level of output performance.

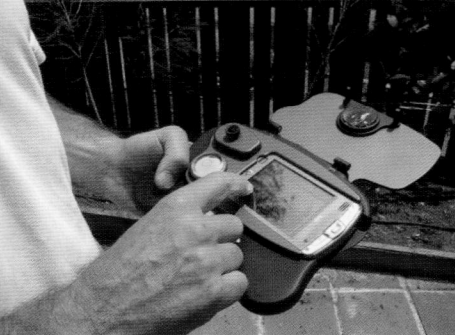

Calculating the proper orientation of the pannels with a speciali solar meter.

The actual rates that SunRun or SolarCity charge you depends on the particulars of your place -- the solar climate in your town, the pitch and orientation of your roof, potential shade, and local electric rates. Solar engineers use a really cool computerized tool (above) which takes an annualized panoramic to determine your solar potential. From this they can accurately predict your site's solar potential and lay out a design to maximize it by the hour. The image below was taken on the roof of my studio where our panels now lay.

Solar panels these days are low profile (you can't see ours from the street), modular, and require a minimum penetration into the roof. (The picture at the beginning of this review shows the panels being installed on our roof.) Our 28 panels made it through the rainy season with no problems. If there is a problem, the owner -- SunRun -- takes care of it. (There are escrow mechanisms should SunRun go out of business.)

The technical term for this kind of financing is a "solar power purchasing agreement" or a Solar PPA. Solar PPAs were first used for commercial properties -- huge flat roofs converted for collecting electricity. SunRun, SolarCity and a few others have adapted solar PPAs for home residential use in some states. Coverage is being expanded rapidly so it's worth rechecking.

Like a lot of folks, we've wanted solar electricity for a long while but the significant up-front costs of installing it didn't seem to make sense. Zero dollars down makes sense. Half down and a fixed 18-year rate makes sense.

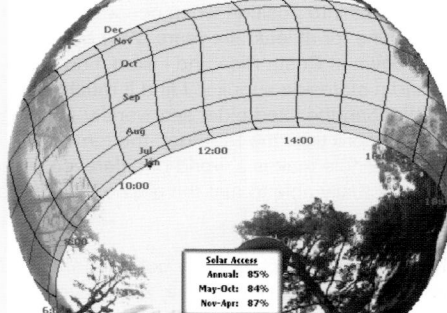

Data by Solmetric SunEye™ -- www.solmetric.com

And watching my daily stats on the SunRun website, seeing the meter run backwards, really makes sense.

-- KK

Alternative energy
Home Power

$15 print $10 digital 1 yr. subscription (6 issues)

homepower.com

A great resource on renewables and other off-grid techniques written by people who've done the work for people who are ready to do the work themselves. Last I heard (probably more than a decade ago now), there were at least 100,000 homes and buildings off the grid in the USA. *Home Power* is the magazine that shows them how to do it, what works and what doesn't. For those who aren't afraid to pick up a wrench and get dirty, good stuff.

-- George Mokray

Off-the-grid store
Real Goods

Prices Vary Real Goods

A good source for reliable off-the-grid appliances is Real Goods. Located in the hippy heartland of northern California where many folks live year-round off-the-grid, this store has been selling highly selected solar and eco-friendly gear since 1978. It's a good place to get 12-volt freezers, refrigerators and solar well pumps.

-- KK

Solar Well Pump Kit - 100' Depth

Price: $2,199

Our basic solar well pump system can be submerged up to 100 feet underwater with a total of 230 feet of lift, giving an additional 130 feet of lift out of the well, ideal for pumping to elevated watertanks without the use of booster pumps. This system contains everything you need to ditch the noise and costs of the generator.

The Shurflo pump is 100% field serviceable, and we offer a full line or replacement parts from gaskets to motors.

The following items are included with this kit:

1 Linear Current Booster 12/24 Volt DC, 7A, PPT 12/24-7

240 Submersible Pump Cable 10/2 Per Foot

1 SJE PumpMaster SPDT Float Switch

1 SHURflo 9300 24VDC Submersible Pump

1 MC4 PV Output Cable 15'

1 DP Custom Top Pole Mount

2 ET Solar 95w Polycrystalline Solar Panel ET-P63695

1 MidNite Solar 10A 150VDC Din Rail Mount Breaker MNEPV10

1 MidNite Solar Combiner Box MNPV3

2 PV Grounding Lug 980010

Never confuse a clear view ahead with a short distance. - Paul Saffo

Off-the-grid source
Backwoods Solar

backwoodssolar.com

One version of solar electric is off-the-grid power. This technology is most useful for homes located beyond the power lines, in a cabin, or a boat, or Amish-like, opting out of the system. The size and costs of photovoltaic panels makes it difficult to generate a lot of off-the-grid power so in addition to the solar gear, you need to modify or replace appliances and lifestyles within your home. Wiring up even a small cabin to the sun is not a simple task. The best source for current information for family residences off-the-grid, including a store that sells select gear, is Backwoods Solar. They have a large website, a paper catalog of gear and advice, and they keep up with the latest. They also run a consultancy for projects, but based on customer feedback, they will cheerfully use email and phone to help you get what you need if you ask.

-- KK

●

Refrigerator / Freezer

Many standard refrigerators and freezers use so much power that battery charge is depleted very quickly. It is not practical to use most standard electric refrigerators or freezers with independent power unless you have a powerful water turbine generator. Super efficient refrigerators designed and tested for solar power, listed in this website, operate on less than half the usual power. Some carefully selected Energy Star rated conventional refrigerators using under 400 - 450 kilowatt hours a year may be acceptable.

●

Surrette Heavy Duty Industrial Batteries, $378

This new generation, deep cycle, flooded lead acid battery offers high capacity and heavy duty plate grids which resist positive plate breakdown. The plates are double insulated with glass mat and polyethelyne envelope, eliminating the possibility of separator misalignment, cracked separators, and shorting.

Each 2 volt cell is built into its own lightweight container made of durable polypropylene. The cells are then assembled into a tough outer container with a removable lid. Even if this outer container cracked, acid spills are prevented and the battery still operates. The individual cells are bolted together allowing the battery to be disassembled and the cells individually removed for easy on-site installation. Free battery book and Hydrometer included with each purchase.

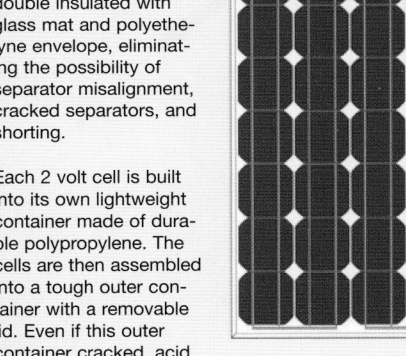

●

ET 135W Poly, 12V, $319

ET Solar ET-P636135 Polycrystalline PV modules generate very reliable solar power for on-grid and off-grid applications, as well as residential and utility-scale solar power systems. These polycrystalline photovoltaic modules are designed and manufactured to comply with very strict international quality standards. Strong design, procurement and production efforts ensure that these products generate high solar power and take up small spaces. Backed by a 25-year warranty on power output, ET Solar modules bring lasting values. Made in China, UL listed for the US and Canada.

DIY solar
Build It Solar

Prices Vary Build It Solar

I think it's best to leave household solar electricity up to the pros right now. The panels are still expensive, improving every month, and the layout and installation, hookup, etc. are very tricky. (Check out Solar City or SunRun, previous page, for your home.) But this is also a fine time for DIY-ers to leap ahead. A lot is happening among the maker crowd and the place to keep up with it all is Build It Solar, a free site with a sprawling collection of tutorials, recent projects, experimental results and handy resources. Not just solar, they cover alternative energy sources and conservation was well. The site is pretty well managed, and will follow up with updates on earlier experiments as much as possible.

-- KK

$2K Solar Space + Water Heating -- One Simple DIY System

These pages describe a very simple solar system that provides both solar space heating and solar water heating in one simple design that you can build.

Using all new, high quality materials, this system can be built for as little as $2000 -- about one 1/8th the price of an equivalent commercial system. Nearly all of the materials will be available at your local hardware or lumber yard. The system can be built with simple tools, and with ordinary DIY skills....

The PEX tubes efficiency of the heat

DIY wind power generation
Wind Scorpion Wind Turbine

$480 Wind Scorpion 500 Watt Wind Turbine Thermodyne Systems

I bought a Wind Scorpion wind turbine to augment the solar panels in the off-grid power system I use for my cottage. At the northern latitudes where I live the solar panels get covered with snow for most of the winter. This meant that there was always the danger that the batteries would get run down and freeze, which would ruin them. A wind turbine looked like a good option and Thermodyne Systems had what looked like the best bang for the buck.

I installed it last year, and so far it has run without any problems. I was concerned that it would be noisy, but the noise at full speed is equivalent to an electric induction motor running, which is okay. It's cool to look up and see it spinning away generating electricity.

The turbine itself costs around $500 shipped, but you also need a tower and wiring. I used an old TV antenna tower and a length of pipe. The tower was free and the material and shipping brought the total cost to

transfer from the PEX to the floor is greatly improved by using these heat spreader plates. This means that lower temperature water can be used to transfer the same amount of heat to the floor, and this will make the whole solar system more efficient. The heat spreader plates are homemade and are exactly the same ones I have used in some of my solar collectors...

...So, for the conditions and energy prices assumed the payback period ranges from 2.5 years for propane up to up to 3.4 years for NG. Also bear in mind that you may qualify for some rebates or tax credits, and that as the price of fuel goes up the payback period, return on your investment, and peace of mind all improve.

●
Bubble Wrap Window Insulation

I've used bubble wrap on windows for two three+ years now, and I'm amazed how quick and easy it is. This year, we are even covering the windows in the guest room -- we just take the bubble wrap down when guests come, and put it back up when they leave -- 15 seconds a window.

This is a simple technique for insulating windows with bubble wrap packing material. Bubble wrap is often used to insulate greenhouse windows in the winter, but it also seems to work fine for windows in the house. You can use it with or without regular or insulating window shades. It also works for windows of irregular shape, which can be difficult to find insulating shades for.

It's been five years since, and I've heard from MANY people who are quite happy with using bubble wrap for window insulation.

The view through the bubble wrapped window is fuzzy, so don't use it on windows where you need a clear view. But, it does let plenty of light through.

Installation:

Cut the bubble wrap to the size of the window pane with scissors. Spray a film of water on the window using a spray bottle. Apply the bubble wrap while the window is still wet and press it into place. The bubble side goes toward the glass. To remove the bubble wrap, just pull it off starting from a corner. You can save it and use it for several years. It does not leave a mess or stains on the window glass. A few small pieces of double back tape can be helpful on really stubborn windows. The bubblewrap can be installed in the fall, and removed in the spring. Judging by how mine looks after a year, it may last quite a while. When you take the bubble wrap down, put a small number on the upper right corner of each piece of bubble wrap, and write down which window that number goes with on a piece of paper. Save the paper for the installation next fall. This tells you instantly where each sheet goes, and which way it's oriented.

about $750. This is for the add-on to an existing solar system. If you are starting from scratch, the solar panels, charge controller, batteries and inverter for a small system will set you back a minimum of $1,800. That and your free labor is the cost of not having an electric bill in your mailbox every month.

The result looks a bit jury rigged, which I take a perverse pride in. You need to a have knowledge of electrical and construction technology together with tools and skills to do it yourself. Raising a 40' tower requires planning and a bit of overarching self-confidence. A similar system I looked at that was put together by a professional contractor reportedly cost over $15,000. I am on the lookout for more tower sections so I can raise the turbine up another 20 feet to catch more wind. The challenges never stop.

Thermodyne operates through their website and pride themselves on being paperless. Email inquiries were promptly answered and the order was shipped the next day.

There are competing wind turbines, but I haven't had any experience with them. They look more finished, but the advertised prices are about double for a machine with equivalent output.

-- Brian Hughes

Brian's wind turbine at home. ▶

Power Gear

Simultaneously power up multiple tools
Craftsman Auto Switch
$20 craftsman.com

Like most people I don't have a dedicated workshop, meaning my power tools share the garage with lots of things that aren't happy about sawdust wafting over them like the morning dew. The solution is a Shopvac, but it can be a real hassle remembering to turn it on/off as I turn on/off my table saw, hand sander, Ridgid Oscillating Belt & Spindle Sander, etc. I've been woodworking at home for perhaps 18 years, and the best solution I've found is one of these little outlet boxes, which powers up multiple tools automatically.

You simply plug your main tool into the top outlets, then plug your vacuum or work light into one of the other two accessory outlets. Whenever you turn your tool on, it will automatically turn the other outlets on. When you turn your tool off, it waits a few seconds before turning the accessory outlets off, which is useful for clearing the line of dust, etc. I have two in my shop -- one for each Shop-Vac so I never have to reconnect power cords or vacuum hoses!

I've been using these switches for four years. They definitely save time. On a given woodworking project, I generally turn machines on and off every few minutes and move from machine to machine. Without this switch, you would spend an extra 3 seconds and 2 steps turning it on and another 3 seconds and 2 steps

turning it off. Doesn't sound like much, but in reality those seconds and steps really start to add up, so you'd just end up leaving the vacuum on or using some other less effective dust collection (for example, an on-tool dust collection bag).

I had a discussion with someone about 9 or 10 years ago about how you could build one - and I actually found schematics for a load sensing relay that you could make one with. But for $20, this switch certainly beats trying to round up the components and DIY.

-- Yitah Wu

Electrical usage meter
Kill-A-Watt
$19 p3international.com

My electric bills are killing me, and now I can finally figure out exactly why.

The Kill-A-Watt plugs into a wall outlet and will measure the actual electricity usage of any appliance. I've been wanting one of these things for years, to the point of seriously considering manufacturing one myself. I'm glad someone has finally done it for me. It looks like my computer costs me something like $216 a year to run. Trouble is, I have five of them. Something's gotta go.

Street price for this device is about $30. I should save that much in the first month.

-- Curt Nelson

Outlet w/individually-powered switches
Ultra Surge Protector
$25 Tripp Lite TLP76MSG tripplite.com

In the old days, I plugged all my computer equipment into a power commander, a large pizza-box device that sat underneath my monitor. It had many outlets with individual power switches and a master switch on the front, allowing me to regulate which devices were draining power. I haven't been able to find those power commanders anymore, but after more searching than I expected, I finally found this surge protector that has per-outlet power switches. For the last year, I've used two of them as cheap insurance for power regulation in my RV.

Power in an RV can be at a premium, especially if it's coming from a generator or inverter (batteries/solar). A lot of the equipment in my RV is rarely used nowadays, but drains power if plugged in (vampire appliances!). Disconnecting specific devices is an easy solution -- flipping a switch for each outlet is even easier.

I use one for the TV, DVD player, satellite, etc., and one for my computer, monitor, phone charger, external hard drive, etc. I'm now able to turn my computer on and off with the

master switch, and turn rarely-used devices on and off only if needed (TV/DVD especially).

I've yet to analyze the electric bill -- I'd need the previously-reviewed Kill-A-Watt (coincidentally on order) to know exactly how much power I'm saving. But this definitely helps me prevent using more than I expect. A great device for a cabin, RV or anywhere power use might be at a premium.

-- Mike Polo

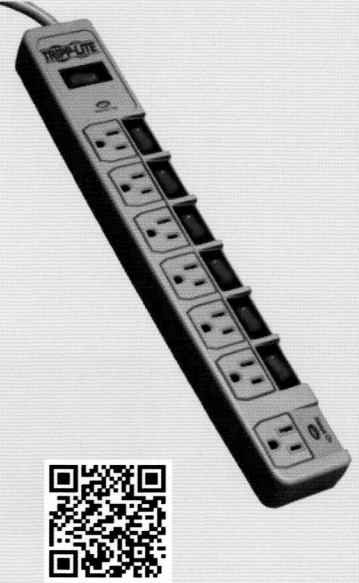

Wall wart solution
Yellow-Jacket 5 Outlet Adapter
$12 woods.com

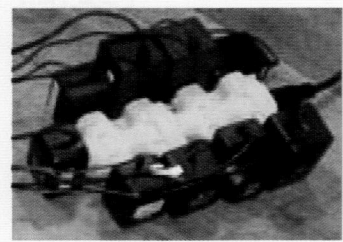

This in-door, out-door adapter is the best I've found for dealing with multiple wall-warts. The outlets are spaced just far enough apart to allow virtually any size wall wart to fit, and you can chain together the adapters (each outlet has five outlets, so every additional one in the chain gives you four more outlets). It's cheaper than specialty adapters like the PowerSquid, and it's inherently more organized. If you chain a couple PowerSquids together, you've

got a mess of extra cords on account of that model's 'tentacle' design. If you daisy chain two Yellow-Jackets together, you've got a tidier package.

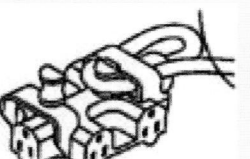

The Yellow-Jackets also feature cable restraints or 'cord locks' you can run the cables through. Personally, I cut them off to make the outlets more compact, but if you had five people working outside -- each using a power tool and each pulling the adapter in a different direction -- these restraints make it so that you'd have to pull a lot harder to cause an accidental unplugging.

-- Stephen Malinowski

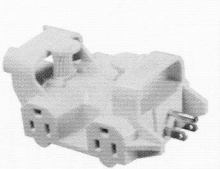

Better than a power strip
PowerSquid
$13 powersquid.com

Lets you connect multiple devices, even with big power converters, to a single outlet.

-- Zimran Ahmed

Easy 120 to 220 volt converter
Quick 220
$200 quick220.com

When I moved into my apartment I found it had a through-the-wall air conditioner sleeve. I ignored it and installed my window air conditioner. When that old AC died about 3 years ago, I was told by the co-op board that the rules had changed and I had to use the sleeve. I guess I should pay more attention to coop board announcements. My problem was that next to the sleeve was a 110V outlet but every AC that fit the sleeve required 220V.

After being quoted over $1000 to run 220V to the sleeve I was desperate to find another solution. Luckily, I found the Quick 220 Power Converter. All it took was the 110V outlet near the sleeve and an extension cord from another 110V outlet on a different circuit. Instantly, I had two 220V outlets. And at $160.00 I was very happy with the price. They also throw in an outlet tester because both 110V outlets must be wired correctly (not something you can assume in an old apartment) for the Quick 220 to work.

-- Donnie B

This is a good well done hack but probably best for technology uses - when you really need 220 volts, but don't intend to have it permanently.

-- KK

The multiverse is the smallest possible place which can contain all possibilities. - Kevin Kelly

Long-lasting, efficient invisible lights

Flexible LED Strip Lights

Sun Bright LEDs

We installed flexible LED light strips in our kitchen for under cabinet and within cabinet lighting. These are very low energy consumption, cool to the touch, and rated to last for 50,000 hours.

The strips are about 1 cm wide and 2 mm thick. The strips come on a spool with a sticky tape side. You press the sticky side to the bottom of the cabinet (or the sides inside) and the strip gives a very diffuse effective and efficient light. They are so thin, you can't really see the light strip itself, only the glow. The strip is a circuit of LEDs in a row. They have marked segments about every 2-3 inches where you can cut them to fit. They typically run off of 12 volts; the transformer can sit in a cabinet, attic, or basement. You can also specify different color temperatures (very warm to very cool). The lights are dimmable.

We used them under our cabinets and inside of one cabinet (picture above).

There are tons of manufacturers peddling flexible LED strips now. You can purchase them in meter strips or on 5 meter reels. Here is one supplier with many products and variations: Superbrightleds.com. I have no experience in using this outfit. It is a new market so quality varies.

We used a local California-based manufacturer, Aion. Their prices are higher than many of the imports (usually from China), but they had a deliverable guarantee of 5 years. Unfortunately they don't deal retail, wholesale only through electricians, who can reliably install it.

If anyone has experience with installing DIY LED strips, please let us know.

And these nifty strips can be used for all kinds of other illumination where flexibility and thinness is desired.

-- KK

Cheapest 60-watt LED bulb

Cree 9.5 watt LED light bulb

$13 cree.com

I have used the Cree LED warm bulbs for a month and they are an excellent replacement for a 60 Watt incandescent bulb. The light is better than CFLs I have used. This new 800 lumen light has a color temperature of 2700K, on 9.5 watts. It has the shape and general look of a incandescent bulb and is a screw-in replacement. Its rated life is 25,000 hours and comes with a 10 year warranty At $13 from Home Depot, I see this as a game changer and a CFL killer. They work with dimmer switches.

-- Louis Nettels

Best 60-watt LED bulb

Philips L-Prize Bulb

This is the best household LED bulb at the moment. It's not the cheapest (see left) but it throws a bit more light, runs cooler and is guarenteed to run twice as long as the Cree. It runs on only 10-watts, gives off the light of a 60-watt tungsten, delivers a soft white light, with the even distribution of the old bulbs. It's dimmable. And it is promised to last 22-years. Since we've installed a bunch in our kitchen and dinning room and den, I can confirm all these claims except the last (too early to tell). It is exactly the same shape and size of a 60-watt tungsten bulb, which many other LEDs are not. This makes it easy to swap out. Also, this one is brighter than most other LED replacements that I've used, including the previously reviewed Lemnis 40-watt LED bulb. It is more energy efficient than other 60-watt LED equivalents. Believe it or not, at $25 it is among the cheaper hi-powered LED bulbs — although the price is still too high for me to swap all my household bulbs (most of which are compact fluorescents).

Besides the price, two minor caveats. The bulb is heavy. It seems to be made of solid ceramic. It may not work in a counter-balanced fixture like an extended arm lamp. And if the bulb is exposed it shows bright yellow-orange markings when off, which may (or may not) be distracting design-wise.

Compared to tungsten bulbs, this is crazily expensive at $25. But it's a steal if it lasts 22 years. (By Philips' calculation you'll save $137 in the end.) Compared to other LED lightbulb replacements, this one is brighter, more efficient, better color light, smaller, easier to swap, and more affordable.

-- KK

Check with your local utility company as they often feature rebates on LED bulbs. Home Depot is known for selling this bulb cheaper in-store than they do online for this reason.--Oliver Hulland

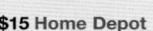

$15 Home Depot   **$25** Amazon

Rechargeable Batteries

Still the best batteries
Eneloop Rechargeable Batteries
$9 750 mAh, AAA 4-pack or $44 2000 mAh, AA 16-pack eneloop.info

No No doubt, the best batteries I've used are Sanyo's Eneloop cells. They're NiMH but the self-discharge problem is pretty well licked, and Sanyo are the ones who solved the problem.

Eneloops are still the best, but there are more makers now of LSD (Low Self-Discharge) NiMH cells. Usually marketed as "ready to use", their initial charge should still be available at time of purchase.

Sanyo has a fairly broad range of chargers available to go with these things, of which I have a couple. But to really get the most from my cells, I use the LaCrosse Technology BC700 Alpha Power charger. A very good combination for me.

-- Wayne Ruffner

12-volt battery juicer
Xtreme Charge
$80 xtremecharge.com

I have a collector car I won't drive in the snow, so I'm forced to use a battery tender to keep the battery alive while it collects dust during the winter. In years past, I've used a variety of chargers/tenders (I also had a Harley I stored in the winter), but none has worked as well as the Xtreme Charge I've been relying on this last year. Though my battery used to die all the time within hours of being removed from previous chargers, it now holds a charge for days on end. I am certainly no expert. What I know about how the system works is from what I've read online. It's my understanding that once the battery's gotten a full charge from the unit, it switches to a "pulsating DC current" mode. Apparently this pulse technology does something to reduce and keep sulfate deposits from building up again.

What I know about whether the charger works comes from the old, off-brand battery that, by all rights, might have been relegated to the recycle bin last year but is still holding a charge like a champ. At about the same time I bought the charger, I had already bought a new battery for the '88 Rolls Royce Silver Spur. But rather than use the old battery to recover a "core" charge on the new battery, I kept it and used the Xtreme Charge on it, just to see what would happen. It brought the old battery back to life so well that today I use the charger to keep the old battery alive as a backup power source for my sump pump!

I really appreciate the charger's LED display, too, which provides a constant readout of the state of the charge. Makes it easy to monitor its progress at a glance. After it first reads the current charge, a series of small lights begin pulsing. As the battery charges, the display expresses the status as a percentage of full: 25%, 50%, 75% and 100%. Another great feature: if a battery is dead and cannot be charged, the display tells you bluntly "battery dead". In years past, I would waste time and effort hooking up more than one battery to a charger when it was simply impossible for the battery to take a charge. I went with Xtreme Charge's "marine" charger because it's water-proof and comes in a rubber casing. These days my battery is fresher in the spring than it is at the end of the driving season.

-- Ken Herrera

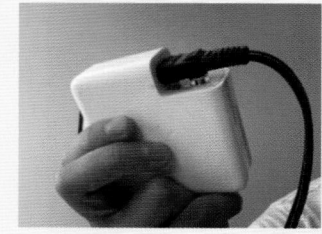

Customizable charge times
La Crosse Battery Charger
$60 BC-1000 lacrossetechnology.com

Rechargeable technology has gotten to the point where you can get almost as much power out of reusable batteries as disposables. Most battery chargers, however, are dumb circuits that simply jam a current through the battery no matter its current state of charge, which can ruin a perfectly good battery. With La Crosse's BC-900, you can not only monitor the charge on the battery at any given time, you can do a discharge + recharge cycle, or even a full refresh where the battery is discharged and recharged several times in a row. I've found the BC-900 can actually revive a battery that was rendered unusable via a less effective charger.

Previously, I owned a Panasonic that worked OK. Though I haven't done a completely exhaustive search of this space, after reading a lot of reviews and then using it, I really would rate the BC-900 as being one of, if not the best little charger for the money. With mine, I find I can get anywhere between 50 to 100 percent more cycles.

Plus, this unit has selectable charge rates, which allows you to charge batteries quicker if you need them ASAP, like within

15-30 minutes. Doing this does require a lot of current to be jammed through the batteries in a shorter period of time, which stresses them and shortens their lifespan. But it's helpful to at least have the option of optimizing for speed over longevity. The charger comes with eight batteries (4 AA and 4 AAA) and 4 C and D cell adapters, too, so you get a nice start all in one package.

-- Dave Cortright

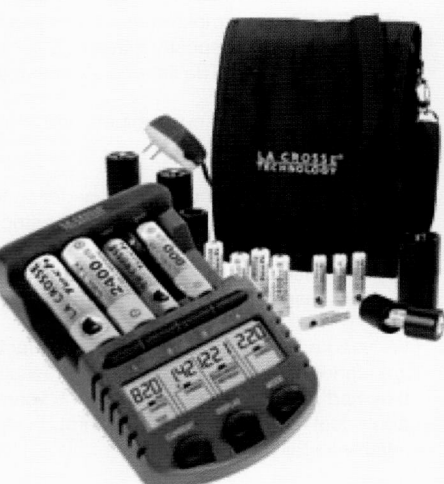

Multi-cell battery holder
Storacell Battery Caddy
$6 Storacell A9 Pack Battery Caddy Amazon

These battery holders are a clear winner over other cell containers. Mine's loaded with Eneloop AA & AAA cells (and a Duracell 9V), in my tool kit, ready to keep me moving. Regular Alkaline cells fit in there too, of course.

I've got a lot of small equipment that uses these small batteries. Being prepared to change them when they're low is easier than Periodic Preventative Maintenance like charging everything monthly or something. And less time consuming than zooming off to get replacements when something quits. Better for the cells, too, than charging them when they don't really need it.

I don't know yet if these will survive a winter, but the plastic seems of a type that should fare well. Certainly better than the other types of plastic battery boxes that seem to explode when the temps drop. A pretty good variety of shape/combos and colors are available.

While these do a good job of protecting the cells from shorts, they're not absolute, so be careful about jamming them into spaces with other things that could lead to short circuits. Like my tool bag. And in a camera bag, no problems.

-- Wayne Ruffner

Rechargeable battery tip
Eneloop Batteries in bulk
$44 Eneloop NiMH Rechargeable Batteries, 16 AAs Amazon

The key to using rechargeable batteries in a heavily electronic household is to a) hide the non-rechargeables, and b) have lots of rechargeables already charged and handy. The problem we had in the past was not having enough rechargables in stock and charged, which meant we had to have a cache of regular batteries, which meant we tended to reach for those first, defeating our efficiency intentions. Now we have a decent stockpile of charged rechargeables and no reason to dip into the outmoded stuff. You want to have an inventory of about 1.5x the number of batteries in active use, so you always have a stockpile of ones already charged. You are probably using more than you think.

Eneloop rechargeable batteries, which we have reviewed twice before, come somewhat charged in the box, recharge fast, and can be acquired in bulk packages of 20.

-- KK

Mac Laptop Power Cord Tip
$4 Sony PlayStation Power Cord Amazon

Every Mac comes with a long, bulky power cord and a small 2-prong nub. You can interchange them, but both are far from optimal for travel. Here's my fix: use a power cord from a Sony PlayStation. There are other cords that will also fit, but the PlayStation cord is easy to find. It fits into the power brick, coils up nice and small and has two prongs. Plus, you can leave your giant Mac cord at your desk back home. I always keep one PlayStation cable stashed in my bag, so I only have to transfer the brick to the bag. This trick's good for any Mac laptop from the last 4-5 years.

-- Brian Lam

The universe is full of magical things, patiently waiting for our wits to grow sharper. - Eden Philpotts

Home automation superstore
Smarthome

smarthome.com

Here it comes, ready or not: the Smart House. A whole avalanche of products in mind-numbing diversity is available via this mail-order catalog and Web site. A lot of the equipment I find creepy (networks of concealed in-house mini-video cameras for "security" purposes), but some I covet right now (I want to be able to beep my front door open like I beep my car door open; $69 uninstalled). The rest can wait (the caller ID of your incoming phone call shows up on your TV). The avalanche is only picking up speed and this store, which has the widest collection I've seen, is the best way to keep up.

-- KK

Luxe Bidet BidetNeo320S Fresh Water Bidet with Hot and Cold Water, Dual Nozzle
Price: $75.92

Touchless, Stationary Vacuum Removes Swept Debris Automatically $99

Increase Security with a Door Lock that Opens Only when a Registered Fingerprint is Recognized

Overview
500 DPI fingerprint sensor
Reversible handle
Simple user interface with LED programming
Disable fingerprint to operate like a regular handle
Emergency unlock with a standard battery or backup key
Fingerprint can not be duplicated
Zinc alloy die-casting body
Up to 99 users

Closer to the Jetsons
Smart Home Hacks

$18 Gordon Meyer, 2004, 328 p.

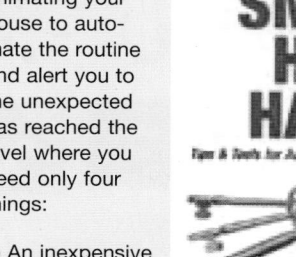

The dream of animating your house to automate the routine and alert you to the unexpected has reached the level where you need only four things:

1) An inexpensive software controller program for your PC or Mac.

2) Off-the-shelf X-10 components, which send signals along your 110 volt room wiring.

3) The Smarthome catalog of devices, hardware and parts.

4) This book, which tells you in satisfying detail how to use 1, 2, and 3 to accomplish (and extend) your fantasies.

No-fuss home automation
Belkin WeMo Switch

$45 Amazon

Home automation is finally plug-and-play. Setting up this wifi-connected box takes minutes:

1) Plug the WeMo into a three-prong outlet

2) Download an iPhone app (Android is rumored to be on the way)

3) Type your wireless password into the app to connect the switch to your home network

4) Plug a device into the WeMo (lamp, TV, fan, etc.)

That's it.

You can toggle the switch on/off by pressing a button in the app. You can also quickly set an automated timer that automatically turns

Hot and cool energy tool
Nest Learning Thermostat

$179 First Generation model Amazon

Last year I replaced my old-looking but perfectly functional programmable thermostat with a better looking, WiFi-equipped model. The remote aspect of it was good. We could set "away" temps, and restore normal temps on our way back home. And the programmable part was always good – cool at night, not working so hard when we're at work, etc.

But even though the thing was from a "major name", it was a true PITA. While it worked most of the time, any time we wanted to tweak things, ugh. It was miserable. Then Nest came out with their Learning Thermostat.

I recently put one in and it's well beyond what I was hoping the other might be. Superbly easy installation and activation, beautiful to look at, and as user-friendly as anything can be. It's still in learning mode which basically means it is figuring out our daily schedules. But so far they've thought of everything, and this has given me complete confidence in its long term purpose.

Nest also provides apps that allow you to control your thermostat from your iOS or Android phone or tablet. You can also track energy usage history, etc. At $249 it's a lot more than other thermostats, and so maybe not suited for everyone's budget. But I'll say it's more than suitable for any home. It's a beautifully designed and exceptionally functional thermostat that continues to do its job very well.

-- Wayne Ruffner

For an avalanche of smart products in mind-numbing diversity, see the previously reviewed Smarthome catalog.

-- KK

• Not everyone in your household will be as enthusiastic about home automation as you are. That's to be expected -- everyone has different interests -- but unlike some hobbies, automating your home has a profound impact on others. If it's not done in a careful and considerate fashion, it can disrupt and bring frustration to a family's ultimate retreat: their home. For this reason, and just for common courtesy, it's a good idea to discuss your plans before you implement them. The results of some automation projects can be surprising, such as a talking house [Hack #28], so it's best to make sure you aren't the only one who will enjoy them.

• **Hack #55. Know if the Garage Door is Open.**

Use a magnetic switch and Powerflash module to keep track of the status of your garage door.

• A keystone in my home automation system is that it knows when the house is unoccupied [Hack #70]. When the house is empty, the alarm system is activated, visitors coming to the front door are logged [Hack #74], and the network camera that I use to check in on my dog [Hack #82] is turned on. Furthermore, the first person who comes home to the previously unoccupied house is greeted with appro

the switch on/off at different times on different days.

My WeMo Switch controls a huge floor lamp in the corner of our living room. It's programmed to shut off every night at 9pm. No more playing footsie with the floor dimmer! Also, a nice reminder to stop watching TV and go read in bed. Typically, we turn on the lamp via an iPad in our kitchen. Dinner guests love it.

$50 isn't cheap. The company sent me a complimentary switch to test, because I write about technology. That said, I'm buying another switch at the full price for my office. I don't mind paying for the convenience.

If you're handy with a soldering iron, go ahead and hack your own Arduino-powered switch. Or, assuming you don't mind playing with wires, you might find a cheaper alternative in the

The PowerLinc USB power-line interface

priate lighting and thermostat setting, and important reminders and announcements [Hack #28].

Hack #48. Put the House to Sleep for the Night.

When it's time to go to bed, have your house turn off all the lights, check to make sure things are secure, and ready your motion detectors to light the way should someone get up for a drink of water.

Smarthome catalog. Up until now, most of the previously-available gear I've seen has been a combination of too complicated, cost-prohibitive, and/or aesthetically blah.

This thing works. It looks cool. And whenever my lamp automatically turns on, it feels magical.

-- Steven Leckart

Energy conscious switch
Smart Light Switch

$36 Amazon

We just had a new light switch installed in our bathroom, the Lutron Maestro Occupancy Sensor. It is smart and cool but it needs a user manual! Yes, a manual for a light switch!

Because of new building codes, bathroom gear needs to conserve energy by keeping electricity use to a minimum. One way of low use is via LED lights; the other is via a smart switch that has a motion detector built in, which will fade the lights after X minutes if no one's moving inside. And it will turn them on when you enter. It also remembers what level the light was last when you turn it on. The downside is that you have to PROGRAM the light switch — what levels, when, and how long it takes to go off. It comes with a dense how-to-manual. But the default settings seem fine and the device is pretty cool. Here is a shot of the instructions, which also cover the other side of the paper.

-- KK

Ladders

Sturdy with tool compartment
Deep-Step Safety Ladder
$200 (8-step) frontgate.com

Unlike conventional step-ladders, the top step of this nifty aluminum step-ladder is the most stable because of its extra size (100 square inches, the biggest of all the steps). It also makes tasks lickity-split efficient, especially with its thoughtful storage bin 11.5"W x 4.25"L x 1.25", meaning no more lost nuts, etc. And if you're changing light bulbs, for instance, you can leave the top open and place tons of stuff inside.

There are three, four, five and eight-step models. I bought the four-step version ($99) which weighs 9lbs, so it's easy to lift with one hand and much lighter than my rickety old wooden ladder. It folds to 4.5" wide, so storing it is easy.

-- Joseph Stirt

Two-person stepladder
Green Bull Double Front Ladder
$90 westerntool.com

These ladders have steps on both sides, which really helps if you're doing something where some-one has to climb up and help you, like hanging fans or light fixtures. It has a higher rating (375 lbs) than most other heavy-duty commercial grade ladders. Its exceptional build quality and strength make it pretty much bullet proof. A friend introduced me to these after his painter had left one for him to repair some fallen gutters at his home three years ago. He loved it and bought one. I saw it, loved it and bought one and have been using it ever since.

-- Velemir Cicin

Compact multi-purpose ladder
Little Gorilla Ladder
$99 Walmart

The Little Gorilla is like the Little Giant Ladder sold on TV. Both are pretty nifty 4-in-1 ladders. You get: 1) Standard extendable A-frame ladder, 2) Adjustable for uneven terrain such as having one side on a stairway, 3) Flat extension ladder to lean against a wall, 4) Divided into two smaller A-frames which can support a scaffold or 2x12 plank between them.

The Little Giant is very expensive ($300 plus), while the Little Gorilla (different company) is much cheaper -- $99. The Little Gorilla Ladder does all the Little Giant does but better. It is light weight -- 29 pounds; anyone in normal physical condition can lift it. It is strong -- 300 pound rated steps, stronger than most ladders. And it is small -- when folded for storage, only 43 inches long. It fits easily in a car or in a closet. I can carry it around the house without bumping into walls or precious deco-rative objects.

Although it is advertised as a 13-foot multi-position ladder, the maxi-mum length of the Little Gorilla is actually 11 feet. There are larger sizes of the Gorilla but they are bigger than I need, heavier and cost more. The Little Gorilla is best.

-- Jim Teter

Heavy-duty, multi-purpose double stepladder
Werner Combination Step/Extension Ladder
$350 (7ft.) wernerladder.com

This is the only big ladder I own. It works great as an exten-sion ladder for painting, cleaning the gutters or reaching any of those high places. Like the Little Gorilla, it can be re-configured as a step ladder, so you can use it anywhere there is no wall to lean against. But like the previously-reviewed Green Bull Double Front Ladder, this ladder also has steps on both sides, allowing two painters to work at the same time (the max capacity is 375 lbs). The Werner definitely offers the best of both worlds. More expensive, yes. But surprisingly lightweight for a ladder this strong. I've had mine for more than 10 years with no sign of wear or tear. My dad is still using the one he bought in the '70s.

-- Dan McCulley

Folding, mini step-up
E-Z Foldz Turtle Stool
$11-21 Amazon

I have other step stools, but none so handy, sturdy, easy to use, and simple to store away as this small, plastic fold-ing step stool. One lives in the narrow crack between my refrigerator and wall—it breaks down to less than two inches flat, but pops out easily to give me the extra nine inches I need to root around in the back of the top cupboards. Very sturdy: rated for 300 pounds. Reasonably light-weight: less than 2.5 pounds. And it has a nice handle when folded, so it's great for use wherever, whenever.

-- Barbara Dace

We have a Turtle Stool in our kitchen which we use all the time. It's quick to unfold, easy to store, lightweight, and

incredibly strong and stable. The inventor of the stool also makes wooden versions, in difference sizes. No prices, but lots of choices and inspiration at his Tower Stool website.

I've used mine for nine years, inside and outdoors, and it's not showing any signs of age; I just hose it off on occasion. Really good to have on hand anywhere space is at a premium -- apartments, boats, RV's, etc. They're also available in 6- and 12-inch heights, plus a two-step model (17 inches high), that folds to 4.5 inches (haven't tried those models myself, though). The stools also come in a variety of colors.

-- KK

This knock-off of the folding Little Giant Ladder is no longer pro-duced. But the an identical knock-off (knock-off of a knock-off), at the same $99 price is now sold as the Cosco World's Greatest Ladder at Walmart.

-- KK

Maximizing safe levelness
Ladder Levelers
$81/pair mcmaster.com

What makes a ladder really useful is individually adjustable legs. I've had adjustable legs on my ladders for 30 years. You can bolt them to almost any ladder. (Ours is a 12-footer straight convertible into a 6 ft stepladder.) They let you level the bottom end of the ladder on uneven ground. Mine will handle 18 inches of difference.

There are several brands, many of which will only fit certain ladders. Most of those only accommodate three inches of difference, which is not enough. Also, the levelers you want are like this kind from McMasters, which are infinitely adjustable; most accessory levelers I've seen have a selection of set incremental positions that are, of course, not quite right most of the time.

Mine make their variable adjustment by means of a stack of tightly-fitting washers on the extension tubes. A spring holds them free when you squeeze the stack. Let go and the washers jam tight permit-ting no slack at all. They are very easy to adjust without tools. I think that there must have been a problem with liability lawsuits, otherwise the things would be in every hardware store. But even a ninny couldn't mess them up. A guard protects the wash-ers stack. They've never slipped or failed me in any way for 36 years.

The kind here costs less in real money than mine did in 1970 when I paid $20. I literally use mine every time we use the ladder here, at the chicken farm. They can also give you another 15" or any-thing in between when leaning the ladder on some-thing. You'll love 'em.

-- J. Baldwin

I prefer most of all to remember the future. - Salvador Dali

Fire-proofing your suburban home
Will Your Home Survive?

$8 R.D. Harrell, William C. Tie, 2001, 56 p.

It's in the headlines every summer: The number of homes built -- and burned -- at the wildland-urban interface is mushrooming. If you live on the interface, don't count on the fire department showing up. Safety-conscious fire departments across the country are changing their policies, and will no longer risk firefighters' lives to protect mere property in these conflagrations. The survival of your house is utterly dependent on the steps you take to protect it.

This is a short (56-pg.) booklet that provides a complete overview of how to make your home more survivable in a wildfire. It covers the same material as many brochures published by fire departments on the same subject, but covers the subject in just enough additional detail to make it worth the $8 price tag. Important details not covered elsewhere from the theoretical (e.g., a detailed but not overly technical assessment of different terrain types and their effect on firs burn rates) to the practical (e.g., be sure to leave a ladder leaning against your roof when you evacuate - it might encourage firefighters to stop and save your house.)

Above all, the book has a refreshing and welcome bluntness that begins right on the cover -- two house photos, one labeled 'winner' and the second labeled 'loser' In an actual wildfire situation, fire crews will be making exactly the same snap decisions as they drive down a row of houses and decide which to save and which to sacrifice, so this is a good mindset for any homeowner to adopt.

The book thoroughly covers the basics of all aspects of passive fire protection, from vegetation clearances, to construction details and even evacuation practicalities. It doesn't cover active measures such as pool fire pumps and stand-and-defend tactics. But this is just as well: such steps are at best risky and should not be undertaken without a level of planning and commitment (and perhaps sheer crazedness) that is beyond the scope of a short book.

-- Paul Saffo

●

Prepare the house to withstand the wildfire by closing all doors and windows, closing mini-blinds and heavy drapes, and removing lightweight curtains. Turn on the lawn sprinklers and the roof sprinklers, if you have them. Fill the bathtub and sink with water you can use to try to extinguish spot fires on/in the house if the water system fails. Shut off the heater/air conditioner to avoid drawing more smoke into the house. Turn on the porch light so that firefighters can see your house through the smoke.

●

However spectacular the view, don't build your home at the top of a steep, fuel covered slope. Setting the structure back from the slope will allow most of the heat, flames and firebrands to go over the house rather than contact it.

Instant lock re-keying
Kwikset Smartkey

$50 Kwikset featuring Smartkey 991J 15 SMT CP Juno Entry Knob and Single Cylinder Deadbolt Amazon

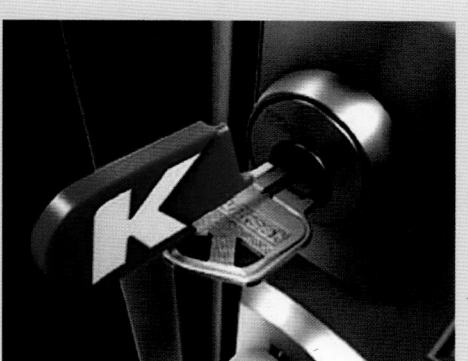

I installed this lockset system on my last property, and love it so much, I'll never use another. You can re-key an entire house literally as fast as you can walk from door to door! For landlords, this is dream: a tenant moves out, you "change the locks" and the next folks feel secure because they have a new key. The system works with both knobs and deadbolts, so there's only a single key to the entire house. You pay a bit more up front, but you never have to change the hardware or call a locksmith for an expensive house call!

To re-key, you put in the existing key and give it a quarter-turn. Then, stick the special Kwikset Smart Key tool into the little hole next to the lock's keyhole. Remove the first key and stick in the new key, remove the tool, and you're golden! You have to have the working key to re-key, so security is maintained.

Here's a hint: When you buy a quantity of these locksets, be sure that the lock serial numbers on top of the box DO NOT match. You pick a key from one of the sets, and have dupes made from that. Match the rest of the sets to this key. File the rest away — that way, you have your next master key ready when you want to change the locks.

-- Doug Barnard

Keyless deadbolt
Combi-Bolt Sliding Bolt Lock

$22 combi-bolt.com

The Combi-Bolt is a traditional sliding bolt, but it has a 4-dial, 10,000 number possible combination lock for keyless security. I used to have a Hasp and padlock on my backyard shed and had to cut the padlock off more than once because one of my kids lost the key. I've now had this lock on my shed for over a year and I love it. I keep my garden tools, the dog toys, basketballs and even a spare house key in my shed, and I no longer have to worry about my kids losing yet another key or myself having to destroy another padlock! Everyone has access when they need it and if for some reason I want to change the combination, it's easy to do. It's constructed of solid metal and has held up well over our snowy, rainy, windy winter and works just as well as it did the day I installed it. It also came with "one way" screws so that once it's installed, you'd have a tough time getting them out (luckily I positioned it correctly the first time). You can even use this lock as a child safety device to keep the kids out of the cupboards in your home or workshop.

-- Mary Freeorn

Rehearsing the worst
The Worst Case Scenario Survival Handbooks

The Worst Case Scenario Survival Handbook: Travel
$13 Joshua Piven and David Borgenicht 2001, 190 p.
The Worst Case Scenario Survival Handbook
$12 Joshua Piven and David Borgenicht 1991, 176 p.

I know these are supposed to be joke books, but they contain sensible answers to sensible questions. Why not rehearse the solution to a worst case scenario if it ups your chances of survival even a few percent?

-- KK

How to Jump from a Moving Train

Stuff blankets, clothing, or seat cushions underneath your clothes. Wear a thick or rugged jacket if possible. Use a belt to secure some padding around your head, but make certain you can see clearly. Pad your knees, elbows, and hips.

Cover and protect your head with your hands and arms, and roll like a log when you land. Do not try to land on your feet. Keep your body straight and try to land so that all parts of your body hit the ground at the same time. You will absorb the impact over a wider area. If you land on your feet, you will most likely break your ankles or legs. Do NOT roll head over heels as if doing a forward somersault.

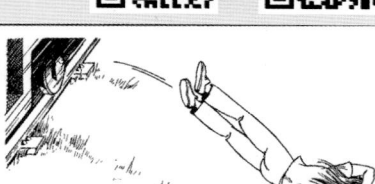
Pick your landing spot, and jump as far away from the train as you can. Protect your head.

Try to land so that all parts of your body hit the ground at the same time.

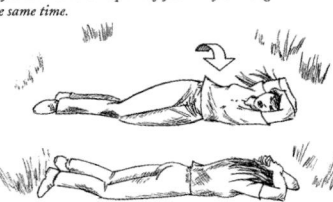
Roll like a log, keeping your head protected.

How to Fend off a Shark

Hit back. If a shark is coming toward you or attacks you, use anything you have in your possession - a camera, probe, harpoon gun, your fist - to hit the shark's eyes or gills, which are the areas most sensitive to pain. Make quick, sharp, repeated jabs in these areas. Sharks are predators and will usually only follow through on an attack if they have the advantage, so making the shark unsure of its advantage in any way possible will increase your chances of survival. Contrary to popular opinion, the shark's nose is not the area to attack, unless you cannot reach the eyes or gills. Hitting the shark simply tells it that you are not defenseless.

How to Perform a Tracheotomy

This procedure, technically called a cricothyroidotomy, should be undertaken only when a person with a throat obstruction is not able to breathe at all - no gasping sounds, no coughing - and only after you have attempted to perform the Heimlich maneuver three times without dislodging the obstruction. If possible, someone should call for paramedics while you proceed.

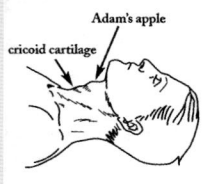
Find the indentation between the Adam's apple and the cricoid cartilage.

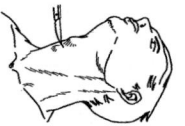
Make a half-inch horizontal incision about one half inch deep.

Pinch the incision or insert your finger inside the slit to open it.

Insert your tube into the incision, roughly one-half to one inch deep.

Password lock
Wordlock

$15

Why didn't we think of this earlier? A lock with a password. Much easier to remember. Because there are only 10 letters per ring, you are limited to a mere 1,000 dictionary words and names. I could not program my usual password, or my favorite names, but I did code in a memorable nonsense word, of which many abound. The mechanism has the heft of your standard gym locker lock.

-- KK

Icebreaker extraordinaire
Razor-Back 4-Inch Ice Scraper
$20 Amazon

When you should have shoveled but didn't get around to it you're probably going to need an ice chopper/scraper. If you don't catch a snow before the first melt-freeze cycle, or the first few hundred people walked by, what you end up with is a two inch thick layer of ice that laughs at your snow shovel.

After breaking numerous shovels, garden hoes, and edgers I finally bought a good, heavy scraper. The sharp edge slips under the layer of ice, and the wooden handle mutes some of the eventual wrist pain from slamming the end into the concrete/ice inter-

face a few thousand times. The Razor-Back scraper I use has a heavy, narrow forged head for maximum energy transfer. Save your shovels for pushing snow and get a heavy-duty ice scraper.

-- Ry4an Brase

Bionic snow shovel
Sno Wovel
$130 wovel.com

As a Montrealer who has shoveled more snow than you can shake a very big stick at, I was intrigued when I first came across a video of this wheeled shovel in action. I live in the suburbs south of Montreal, on a street where there's a popular bus route; the snow plow can pass my house several times a day during heavy snow falls, repeatedly depositing a compacted mound of snow in my driveway entrance.

I bought a Wovel, and what was once a dreaded exercise in futility has now become a looked forward to workout! Thanks to the Wovel's design, all the snow's weight gets transferred to my arms and legs. The fulcrum at the center of the big wheel effectively allows the Wovel to do the heavy lifting for me. After becoming proficient in its use, I was able to master the natural seesaw action and launch the snow surprisingly high. Now, after a season and a half of use, I can consistently build snow banks up to five feet high. It's like having my own little nonnmotorized bulldozer.

I've been using mine to shovel my walk/driveway as well as my neighbor's for more than a year, and I've been beating the crap out of the thing. It won't quit. It's made from a thick-gauge steel and is covered by a lifetime warranty. What was once about an hour of back-breaking work has been cut down to about 20 minutes, which makes this purchase one of the best expenditures I have ever made.

-- Billy Zavos

Ergonomic snow remover
SnoBoss Pusher 4-Way Shovel
$36 24-Inch ames.com

This new fangled snow shovel is sometimes referred to as a four-way shovel. It is a true innovation in the area of manual snow removal.

The curved shaft offers the advantages of a regular "back saver" shovel. The broad top handle allows for easy 2-handed use when using it as a snow pusher. When using your foot to cut through packed snow you can place your foot in the center of the shovel. This pre-

vents the flexing and possible breakage of normal snow shovels.

But perhaps the best feature is the addition of 2 forward grips. These grips, being parallel to the top handle, are more comfortable to use than twisting your hand 90 degrees to grasp the shovel shaft.

The large scoop will move a LOT of snow. If the snow is heavy, just scoop less at a time.

-- Andy Bajorinas

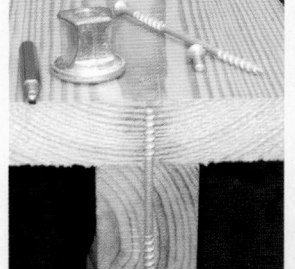

Fixes squeaky floors
Squeak No More
$20 Amazon

This tool is a system for eliminating squeaky floors. First, you locate the joist by chucking the joist finder, which is a long screw threaded only on the end and has a hex end for the drill/driver. Pick a place and go for it. If you are over a joist, once the screw is down a couple inches, when you back it out it will push itself out. If you're not over a joist, it spins freely. It's pretty easy to tell even when the screw goes in if you are on a joist.

Then you set the tripod stand over the joist and drive a screw through the center into the floor. The screw goes through the carpet, through the sub-floor, and into the joist. Once a few screws are in place, you can use the side of the tripod to rock the screws back and forth to break it off where grooved. The screws' depth is set by the tripod so that they break off slightly below the surface of the sub-floor. After a little brushing with your hand, the carpet reveals no evidence of the screws.

We had a large area about 1' x 3' in our bedroom that squeaked a lot. You could feel the give in the floor. I put about 15 screws into the area, about every 4" in three different joists. Now it is almost completely silent. -- Jason Melvin

Life consists of propositions about life. - Wallace Stevens

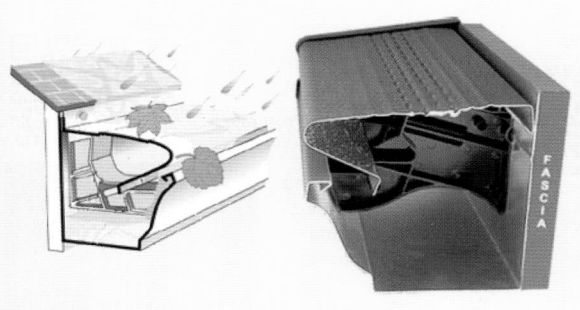

Premium clog-free gutters
GutterShutter
guttershutter.com

This is the Bradley Tank of gutters. It is insanely engineered and overbuilt to last a lifetime without clogging with leaves, pollen, pine needles, twigs, etc. Like several other brands of gutters it ingeniously uses water's natural surface adhesion to bend rainwater around its blunt edge and into the drain. The water drips in upside down, but the leaves and gunk do not. This idea really works, even in very hard rains. I've spent some soaking wet time closely inspecting how well this clever system works in the worst downpours of the winter, and the physics caught about 98% of the rain (and zero debris).

GutterShutter distinguishes itself because of the quality of their build. They use 0.032 inch aluminum which means that you can hang from the gutters, or throw a heavy ladder on it without fear of denting it. I was very impressed with the solid construction details because of previous experience with wimpy metal gutters that bent or rusted. There's no doubt in my mind these will outlive me. Finally, the company guarantees there will be no debris in the gutter ever -- and will come clean it out themselves if you do find any. That's a promise hard to beat.

So far I've found none. Which is amazing. We live directly under several 100-foot Pine and Redwood trees that drop leaves and pollen cones year round. I would spend a weekend twice a year cleaning out several inches of crap, and the rest of the year knowing I should do it more often. I tried all kinds of gutter guards but without success.

The downside of GutterShutters is their very high cost. They are expensive, no way around it (and they have heavy duty sales pitches). Probably $30-40 per foot installed (in San Francisco area). Because of that cost we limited where we put them -- wherever I was tired of hanging off a 30-foot ladder several times a year.

So far, I've had zero work to do on the gutters, so their cost has been worth it. I'd recommend these for homes with a heavy load of leaf debris and/or high or hazardous roofs. Or if you simply want gutters you don't ever have to worry about again.

Other systems that work on this same principle, such as Gutter Helmet, and Leaf Guard, are a whole lot cheaper and probably just as effective, although I found them to be less substantial, and presume them less long-term. Some pop on top of existing metal gutters. They just were not built like tanks.

-- KK

Old-fashioned window/door insulation
Metal Weather-Stripping
Accurateweatherstrip.com

Unlike the plastic, foam or rubber weather-stripping one mostly finds at the big box stores, metal weather-stripping lasts for decades and truly keeps out the wind and weather. I live in NJ about 5 miles from the ocean and we encounter typical northeastern freezing-to-steamy yearly variations. Very nearly every old (80-100 years) house I know of in my town has some of this installed on the doors or windows (that haven't been ripped out since in a hasty renovation). I recommend this specifically for retrofitting and sealing old homes' doors & windows to keep out drafts & winds. Even an old drafty window can keep the rain & snow out, but the air infiltration is tougher to seal against. These weather strips do this every bit as well as newer plastic strips, but last longer and add the advantage of smoothing out the travel of the sash as compared to the wood-wood sliding surfaces of old sash windows. I've seen metal weather-stripping described as "carpenter's weather strip" because it does require someone with some

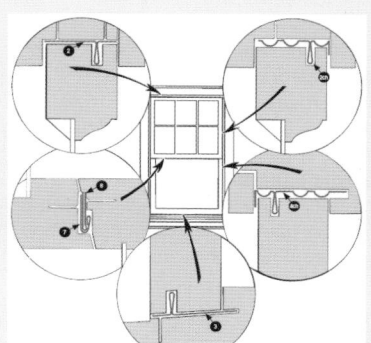

skills & tools to install, but an investment in a day's effort and a few dollars' worth of materials has allowed me to refit & tune up 100 year-old sash windows, inswinging casement attic windows, and doors that have clearly already outlasted those with new, more expensive vinyl stuff. I obtain mine straight from a manufacturer in Mt. Vernon, NY (est. in 1898!). They offer a vast selection in zinc, bronze and brass for all types of doors and windows. I usually choose zinc because it's less expensive and the old stuff I see around town is zinc also, so I figure it must have lasted some time already.

-- Michael Barrett

Simple removable draft barrier
Twin Draft Stopper
$11 Amazon

Lots of people visiting my house comment on all the different gadgets I have, but the only one they ask me about -- where can they get their own? -- is my double draft stopper. Sometimes the simple and cheap is more impressive than the complex and expensive. It's just two long cylinders of styrofoam that slide into a cloth cover which is then slid under the door and holds the foam in placed to stop drafts. The foam can be trimmed to fit your door and the extra fabric folds back and fastens with velcro. The whole thing moves with the door, is easily removed, and the cover is machine washable. They're available all over the web for less than $10.

-- Jimmie Whipple

Bird-strike window decals
Window Alert
$7 windowalert.com

I have tried many different methods to stop birds from striking my windows including sticking white label dots all over the window. I found these UV decals that go on the exterior of your window to be the easiest and most successful of any solution.

Birds read the reflection of nature in your windows as real and think they are traveling towards trees or sky--whatever is reflected. The WindowAlert decals are nearly invisible (so you don't have to look at decals) but the birds see UV light reflected back at them from the decal. Before applying the decals I washed the window and used rubbing alcohol to remove any residue.

It also helps if you place feeders and bird baths either very close to the window or away at an angle.

--Terry Powell

For a number of months, my large glass windows were a killing field for birds. Three or four a day were ending their lives smashing into glass they could not see. I tried a number of things--gel stickers, vinyl stickers, etc. But the best thing I've found are these Window Alert decals. These static-cling decals reflect UV rays,invisible to people, but startling and bright for birds. I haven't had a bird hit a window that has these decals on it. Great product!

-- Joni Jordan

Quick and dirty crack sealer
3M Weather Sealing Tape
$6 1.5" x 30' roll 3M.com

This weather sealing tape seals cracks in and around doors and windows. My solid wood front door for many years has had two vertical cracks each about two feet long. I've tried many times to seal them with all manner of materials — putty, silicone sealant, caulk, you name it — but within months the cracks reopen. I happened on this tape somewhere and bought a roll. Problem solved.

Goes on just like Scotch tape and is pretty much invisible on the door. A heckuva lot easier than the old seal-and-repaint routine. Cheaper and faster, too. What's not to like?

-- Joe Stirt

What We See... *What Birds See...*
Ultraviolet Technology visible only to birds

Drain Hygiene

Far reaching drain cleaner
25' Cable Auger
$26 Cobra

Recently our kitchen sink became completely blocked. Neither the previously reviewed Zip-it Drain Cleaner (too short) nor the Drain King (explained later) would have been able to fix the blockage, and we ended up buying an affordable 25-foot cable auger after two doses of chemicals failed to clear the blockage.

Our kitchen sink connects to a pipe in a wall at a right angle bend, and another pipe under the house after which it runs about 15 feet before connecting to a second drain. In order to insert the auger I disconnected the U-bend under the sink (use a bucket to catch the contents) and ran the auger slowly down the pipe into the wall.

When it hit the first 90 degree bend, I tightened the thumbscrew on the canister, and with a little pressure and turning the handle the cable turned the bend (practice makes this easier). When I hit the first real blockage I repeated the procedure and after a few turns and a little more cable I pulled the auger back up. Recognizing a blockage compared to a bend is fairly easy; with a bend a few turns should send the auger end past the bend and it will "jump" around the bend. With a blockage it will remain harder to push more auger down.

In my situation we had multiple partial blockages all the way down to the joint with the second drain, so in all it took about six hours of auguring to clear the drain (the good news is that the drain is now clear the whole length). With practice I can now run about 23 feet of cable down the drain in about five minutes. Any pressure tool would be likely to just push the partial blockages together creating one super blockage. I've also seen warnings about using those with older pipes (Our house was built in the 1930's) as they can blow out some joints under the wrong circumstances.

While much more expensive versions are available (30' electric augers start at around $140, 100' ones seem to be more like $2,500) I prefer the simple manual canister auger. You can also get versions that attach to your electric drill, but I find that screwing the end into the blockage and pulling a chunk of it back up (most of it is hair based) seems to work very well. In our house no plug hole is more than about 23 feet from another access point to the drains so this length is both cheap and sufficient for my needs.

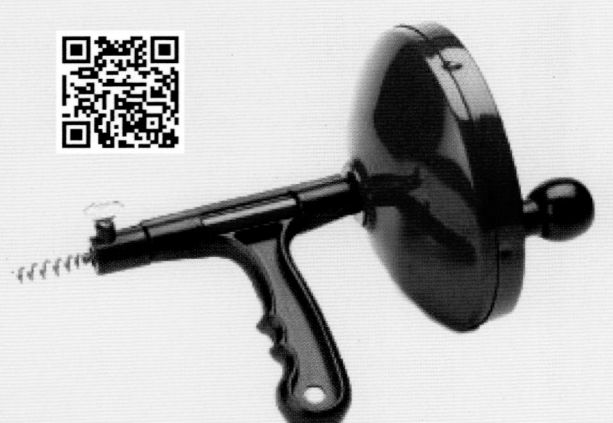

It is important to wear gloves as your hands will get dirty when you pull the auger back up. Also, too much pressure on the cable (including too many turns) and you risk kinking it. A kinked cable should be replaced as it is almost impossible to use. All in all, the investment in a cable auger saved an expensive call to the plumber.

-- Adam Morris

Exhilarating, manual drain blasting
Pressure Pump
$22 Cobra

This cheap, no-name, pump-action drain unblocker is a great alternative to professional models that can cost more than $50. This pump is also really fun to use. Rather than poking a hole in blockages, it really dislodges them: I put one end of the unblocker on the edge of a chair, pump down up to 35 times, place one of the item's four gaskets over the business end, position that end in the drain, put most of my weight behind the handle and pull the trigger -- Ka-POW! Very satisfying.

It takes less than five minutes, not counting the prep: open a tap until a couple of inches of water are in the basin and pound rubber stoppers into the two circular overflow-drain outlets. Important: in bathroom sinks and tubs, the overflow drains have to be plugged first to ensure the blast doesn't spray backed-up water all over the bathroom. An extra pair of hands and/or lots of Gorilla Tape over the wadding are needed for non-circular overflow drains.

Unlike an auger, which I've had trouble getting to follow a 90-degree pipe-turn, there's no yucky clean-up of the tool afterwards or any need to get your hands into the backed-up water. The Zip-It drain cleaner is no doubt a cool tool in some situations, such as a clogged trap beneath a low-height sink, or perhaps a clogged bathtub or toilet trap. But it doesn't do as thorough a job in cleaning the trap, and it wouldn't clear a pipe that's up behind the wall. It's too short (less than 18 inches below the handle) to reach to the bottom of my unusually tall bathroom sink's trap. It's also too wide -- it barely fits through the four slots in the drain-guard of my kitchen sink. When I withdraw it, every barb catches on the slots' edges, which means that much of the gunk it snags falls back down the drain. I'm glad to have the Zip-It, and it does cost very little, but it's only a partial solution. When you have a stopped-up drain that seemingly only a pro could unclog, you need a Pressure Pump (or Air Pressure Drain Opener, more info below) - and again, its cost is modest in comparison to a pro model.

I have also tested the Drain King, a pulsing expanding-rubber-gasket drain unblocker. Its main defect is that the guard-fence beneath the drain inlet must be removed to thread it through, which is usually impossible, or a plug in the basement must be unscrewed, which dumps a pail full of nasty water into the pail you've thoughtfully placed beneath it (or not). You can get around this if the trap, etc. beneath the sink is removed -- but that's still a messy hassle -- and it doesn't always work. Further, if you have a larger pipe, an additional, wider-diameter Drain King must be bought to cope with it. Another drawback to the Drain King is that few apartment dwellers will have the garden hose and faucet fittings that are necessary to drive it. And even for those persons who live in a house, it's a pain running a hose in through a propped-open door--and it can be a bit messy

That's why the blaster is so cool -- even though it's not a do-all product, it fills a crucial niche where other products work poorly or with difficulty.

The Kleer Drain is a better-publicized, award-winning home-style drain blaster sold at Home Depot, but it costs $30 (more than twice the Pressure Pump and a few bucks more than the Air Pressure Drain Opener). The Kleer Drain also requires carbon dioxide cartridges to power it, which might be impossible to obtain in a dire emergency situation (i.e. social collapse) and obviously it costs money to buy refills. The Kleer Drain does come with a "splash guard" -- a piece of plastic wrap with a hole in it - but with the Pressure Pump or Air Pressure Drain Opener one could easily make one, or just wrap a towel around the barrel. More important in reducing blowback is to put a lot of straight-down weight on the barrel before pulling the trigger.

Hooks out gunk
Zip-It Drain Cleaner
$4 Amazon

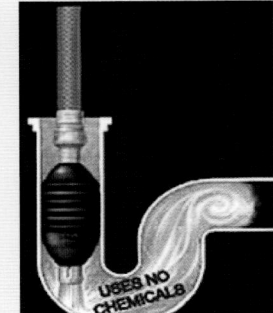

I bet this cheap tool is the best bargain in this book. For 2 dollars you get a flexible 24" plastic probe that will remove an alarming amount of hair and gunk clogging your sink or shower drain. It descends easy. You can snake it down without taking off the usual drain plug. The many little reverse (and very sharp!) spines hook hair balls and other unmentionable crap as you carefully back it out. It removes grunge that liquidators won't budge. Sold as disposable, a cautious wipe will keep it going forever. We have a very hairy household; I can't keep the plumbing going without it. I got mine years ago for 99 cents at our local Ace Hardware.

-- KK

Simple emergency sump pump
Pumps-a-lot Water Pump
$16 WP10

This is a cool tool. It is a powerful water pump you can use without electrical power; instead it uses the Bernoulli effect from water pressure in a hose. This pump saved us a few weeks ago. It rained all day and then at about 5:15 the power went out. Our sump pump in the basement had been going every two or three minutes but there were still two or three inches of water covering the cellar floor when I got home from work. I was desperate to keep the level from getting up to the furnace. Our neighbor Jan had a generator to run their sump pump, so she could offer me her PUMPS-A-LOT which they'd use before they got the generator.

You connect the pump to a faucet with a garden hose. Inside the unit there's a nozzle pointed at the output hose. It sucks water from below, spitting out that water together with the propelling water via the output hose. In truth, I didn't believe

it would work. The makers claim you can pump 800 gallons per hour, or 6 gallons for every one gallon of water you use. But if it didn't work, I'd be filling my cellar with more water. So I tested it in a bucket of water first. It worked! Like magic. It emptied the cellar in a few minutes! Since it has no moving parts, takes up little space, it is an ideal emergency tool.

-- Michael Shook

Unplugs pipes without chemicals
Drain King
$14 GT Water Products

Brilliant invention for clearing clogged drains without caustic chemicals. Comes in different sizes for different drain diameters. You attach it to a hose, and say for the kitchen sink, take off the p-trap, and slide the hose down the drain pipe as far as it will go. You then turn on the hose and it builds up pressure inside the wedged bellows to the point where it releases in a burst, expanding and contracting, ka-chunk, ka-chunk . . . You can clear one obstruction and then push the hose further to get to others. It really unclogs crap. Marveloso!

-- Llyod Kahn

There is no lettering on the Pressure Pump itself. There is an 8.5 x 11 sheet folded into a booklet format with humorously inept-English instructions. It says the manufacturer is "Yidatong Pumps." The title or brand name is "Dongsheng Drain Unblocker." No address or other info is provided. The only lettering on the plain white box is "Country of origin: China."

I recently learned that the stock is limited for the Pressure Pump, but I found a similar manual pump being sold as the Air Pressure Drain Opener that also comes with four gaskets.

-- Roger Knights

Every word was once a poem. - Ralph Waldo Emerson

Automatic water main shutoff
WaterCop
$405 3/4-inch Valve and Three RF Sensors watercop.com

This tool literally saved me thousands of dollars and incalculable emotional stress. Watercop attaches to the water main on your house and is triggered by remote RF water sensors that can be placed anywhere. When triggered, it shuts off the main and stops all water flowing into the house.

I installed the Watercop 5 years ago with remote sensors in 4 locations and it sat silently, doing absolutely nothing for all that time. A few weeks ago we got back from a week long vacation and immediately discovered that there was no water coming through our faucets. My first thought was that the Watercop had experienced a power fault and failed closed.

I went down to the basement and, in fact, the Watercop was closed. I turned it back on and heard a gusher from our furnace room. You can imagine my shock when I ran into the furnace room and discovered that the floor of our 15-year-old hot water heater had burst and the Watercop sensor in the room was submerged.

I don't even want to contemplate what would have happened during that week if there had been no automatic shutoff on the main. The damage to our house and personal possessions, along with the inevitable mold, would have been a disaster.

Not only did it work flawlessly, but you can qualify for an insurance discount if you you have it installed by a licensed plumber (you can install it yourself, but it does require decent plumbing skills). As far as setup, you can place the sensors anywhere. The only downsides I have found is that it is not cheap, you have to replace the batteries annually, and it runs on A/C power meaning that when the power fails so does the device.

Despite these few drawbacks, I can not recommend the WaterCop highly enough. This is, without a doubt, the most valuable tool I have ever purchased.

-- Peter Bee

Bucketless bailing
West Marine Manual Bilge Pump
$40 (24-in. pump with 72-in. hose) westmarine.com

This is a hand pump for pumping out the bilge of a small boat. I'm sure it is good for that purpose. However, what it does better than anything else I have ever tried is to pump off a sports field after a downpour. Many fields have no power access for electric pumps. With this hand pump you can dig a small hole, let the water drain into it and then pump it off quickly, into a bucket or just off the field, to help it dry.

I travel around with this bilge pump during baseball season in eastern Massachusetts, and it has probably given my teams three or four games extra each year, by making inundated fields usable.

It's not hard to work the pump -- in fact, I had my nine-year-olds pump it this year -- and the design is simple and industrial. It has a small crosshatch filter to keep material out of the mechanism and the outflow rate is pretty good if you pump it steadily.

-- Benjamin Grassly

Low-maintenance, liquid-resistant floor covering
Chilewich Woven Vinyl Rugs
$125+ unicahome.com

These woven vinyl floor coverings are synonymous with high-priced "design" boutiques and museum gift shops. Translation: $$$$. But boy are they resilient. After three years of countless beverage spills, dirt, dust, mud, food, foot traffic, and housebreaking a dog, the 5'10" x 9' rug we keep in our living room looks as pristine as the day we first laid it out. I thought a rubbery rug might feel a bit too industrial. It's functionality won me over. The entire backing is vinyl so it never slides around on our hardwood floors. Best of all, in the event of a spill or restless canine bladder, you wipe it down with a damp cloth. No trips to the cleaners, and less likelihood of stains, depending on the color (our tan/dark brown one has yet to harbor a permanent spot *knock wood*). You vacuum it as you would carpet or a hardwood floor. The only other maintenance is to scissor the edges if part of the weave frays (we've done that maybe three times in three years). Though we scored a substantial discount, I'd pay full price if another room in our home ever calls out for a rug. Chilewich also makes a variety of indoor/outdoor mats, coasters and place settings. The small kitchen mat we've had for two years has been sprayed with dishwater, food droppings, you name it, and it still looks great. It's also much kinder to bare feet than our home's frigid, wintertime tiles.

-- Steven Leckart

Custom wallpaper and flooring
Printed Space
$76 for 24"x16" unframed canvases
$6+/ft2 for wallpaper
£108 for 60cm2 blinds (prices not given in USD for blinds)

printedspace.com

My initial experience with Printed Space came about when family in England bought my wife and I a couple of canvases that used photos from our wedding. An artist at Printed Space worked with my brother to edit a batch of 300 photos down to 60, then cropped and arranged them and gave my brother various digital proofs, from which he selected the one he thought we'd like the best. The canvas was shipped from England to our home in San Francisco in a custom-made picture-frame box, in perfect condition.

When we found out that Printed Space also puts your images (or stock images) on blinds and wallpaper, we got a bedroom decorated for a friend's 4-year-old son. (Pictured here).

The company now does flooring too, so I'm planning to get the lobby and other areas of my office covered with custom flooring.

What we liked: Limitless choice in images -- use your own, or images you can buy from any online source. Printed Space has partnerships with a number of stock image sources, photographers and artists, so you're not going to end up with the same all-too-obvious images you see elsewhere.

Fully customized to your space. These are not posters. I've had other canvases made by online poster vendors, but they've been just that -- posters printed on canvas. These are images that can be enlarged, cropped, rotated, whatever, to suit the space you're trying to decorate. Printed Space gave us advice about planning around windows, doors, light switches and power outlets. You pay no extra for this design service.

I couldn't be happier with the quality of their work.

-- Philip Leonard

Art you can sit on
Oriental Rugs Today
$4+, used Emmett Eiland, 2000, 199 p.

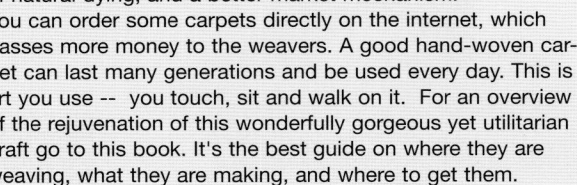

You would think that natural dyed, hand spun, hand-woven carpets from villages in the Mid-East and Asia have disappeared with the caravans, but you'd be wrong. Like the revival of other gourmet goods around the world, traditionally made carpets are in a renaissance. Some experts feel that these contemporary wool carpets exceed the quality of the classic old ones, which command classic antique prices (hundreds of thousands of dollars). At the moment, the new, better ones are far more affordable (and yes, this book deals with the issue of child labor). Fueling the revival of these traditional ways are improved methods of natural dying, and a better market mechanism. You can order some carpets directly on the internet, which passes more money to the weavers. A good hand-woven carpet can last many generations and be used every day. This is art you use -- you touch, sit and walk on it. For an overview of the rejuvenation of this wonderfully gorgeous yet utilitarian craft go to this book. It's the best guide on where they are weaving, what they are making, and where to get them.

-- KK

Sweeping/Vacuuming

Quicker than a vacuum
Hoky Carpet Sweeper
$47 PR-2400 hoky.com

I've been using one of these carpet sweepers so long I forgot to think of it as a Cool Tool. You've probably seen them used in restaurants and hotels. They just plain work. No electric, no plugs, no noise & lightweight. So convenient to grab for a few second cleanup. Just push and they clean, even small crumbs. They go forever. Around $50. And when you flip them over to empty, you're always amazed how much stuff they picked up.

-- Vincent Crisci

Fastest carpet cleaner
Bissell Natural Sweep
$23 Bissell Natural Sweep Dual Sweep, 92N0A Amazon

Like the classic Hoky, this quick and quiet carpet sweeper is what I grab for when touch-up "vacuuming." Lightweight, never needs recharging, no noise, very little to break, it's much superior to a dustbuster. Cleans low carpets fast, empties fast. All the same satisfying benefits of the Hoky -- but half the price! *-- KK*

Affordable robotic mopping
Scooba Floor Scrubber
$279 amazon.com

The Scooba 230 floor scrubber doesn't do as good a job as a professional house cleaner, but my wife and I are lazy, and we figured an automatic floor scrubber that washes the floor and does an ok job would still be better than the job I do. I used the same logic on vacuuming and bought a couple Roombas. We've come to find out these robots don't do just an ok job, they actually do a very good job each and every time they run. I'm always amazed at how dirty the water is when I clean out my Scooba and I cannot believe how clean our floors are. My floors are now automatically swept, then mopped every week. I only spend 10 minutes preparing the Scooba robot: adding hot water and a cup of the Scooba Clorox solution, then emptying the dirty water, cleaning a few parts and putting it on the charger for the day after tomorrow (we now sweep and mop up to three times a week). The robotic brothers and sisters all like to entertain. I clearly have the cleanest floors; and the best thing is I'm not the one doing the scrubbing anymore.

-- Don Tharpe

A household robot that works
Roomba Vacuum
$350 on up Model 630 amazon.com

It finally happened, an off-the-shelf household robot that works and pays back even the early-adopter price.

What makes it work is the combination of clever robot design AND clever vacuum cleaner design. Its job as a robot is to cover an entire room and not get trapped somewhere or wander off where it's not wanted. The first time you use it, you watch with fascination as the Roomba goes through its repetoire of exploration (spiral till a wall is encountered, then scrub along keeping the wall on the right, etc.) and avoidance of trouble (detect drop-offs and deflect; when blocked, keep rotating and trying again; etc.) It will happily go places that most vacuums don't, like under beds. For keeping it from openings into other rooms or from entangling wires or such, the Roomba comes with a separate device which puts out a keep-away beam up to 13 feet.

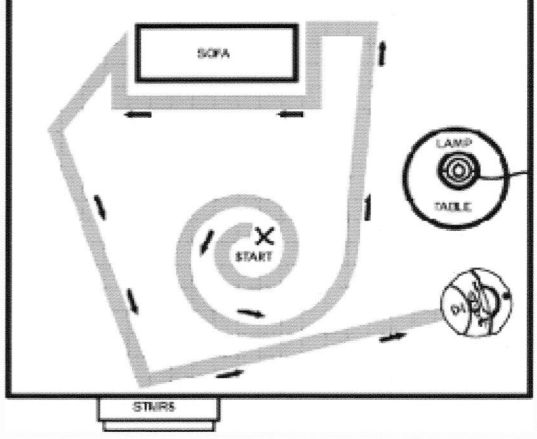

Plugged into a wall socket for battery charge, the Roomba is always ready to grind away diligently in a room. Weekly, daily, who cares? After the first time, you'll leave it to work alone, or you'll find yourself giving it advice, which it does not need.

-- Stewart Brand

Micro suction cleaner
Vacuum Micro Attachment Kit
$9 Item #114 0210

I find that compressed gases just don't work for me on computer accessories (e.g., keyboards and cases) or cameras -- the junk just gets blown deeper inside or I am afraid that the "condensate" will gum things up. A vacuum seems a better solution, but the teeny-tiny ones sold for these purposes don't suck enough(!). The answer -- an $8 Vacuum Micro Attachment Kit. This is an ingenious set of attachments and connectors that turns any upright or canister vacuum into a powerful "micro vacuum" that really does the trick on keyboards, PC cases, cameras (bodies and lenses) in a safe and effective manner.

-- Bryan Quattlebaum

Whizzbang pet cleaner
Bissell SpotBot
$150 Model 338N bissell.com

The SpotBot uses a water and fluid combination to clean a spot about 10-inches in diameter. To clean up a spot, you pick up what you can off the surface of the carpet and then place the SpotBot's circular brush over the spot. You press a button on the SpotBot and 5-minutes or so later it will have shampooed and brushed the spot away, and you're done! I've been using the SpotBot for a year now and when this one breaks I'll be getting another one. It has already paid for itself many times over.

-- Stan Smith

14 gal. quiet wet/dry vac
Ridgid Wet/Dry Vacuum
$155 WD1450 ridgid.com

I purchased this shop vac after multiple online reviews recommended this model. The feature that stands out the most for me is its Scroll Noise Reduction, which I find is actually effective. Most vacuums are extremely loud, but with this one it's possible to have a conversation while it's running.

I initially sought out this shop vac after renovations left our house coated with a layer of dust. We used the Rigid vac to clean up drywall dust, sheetrock dust, sawdust and other debris. Later we confirmed its wet application utility when a pipe burst in the bathroom. When not being used elsewhere our vac sits attached to saws in the garage, keeping the space clean. The whole unit is light enough (22 lb.) and easy to carry around. It uses a three-layer replaceable air filter, and though it's not included, there is an option of a HEPA replacement filter.

While the 2-gallon Singer wet/dry vac previously reviewed on Cool Tools seems useful for smaller clean-ups, this 14-gallon Rigid has been well worth its purchase price.

-- Wes Sisk

Self-education is, I firmly believe, the only kind of education there is. - Isaac Asimov

Superior mop
Mary Moppins
$29 goclean.com

I previously used a basic cotton deck mop, which is the best of the conventional choices, as far as I'm concerned. Most of the grocery store alternatives to the cotton deck mop are flimsy and don't work very well. This mop is superior to others in several respects. First is that it is solid and sturdy. It is a real tool rather than a flimsy piece of junk. Second is that it works so much better. It takes less water and cleaner and less effort but picks up dirt better and faster. I use mine with vinegar and water or other environmentally preferable cleaning solutions. Third is that you don't have the problem of storing a wet, dirty mop.

This mop is basically a cylinder at its base, with Velcro-like hook fasteners that hold onto a typical terry cloth towel. The towel or rag you use comes off the mop head when you are done and goes into the wash. Nothing hangs around wet in your cleaning closet getting funky. It's similar in design to the Cuban Mop previously reviewed on Cool Tools, but with a better means of keeping the towel on the mop head.

-- Katie Bretsch

Affordable, everyday cleaning cloths
Microfiber Cleaning Towels in Bulk
$15 12 towels, 16"x16" clean-rite.com

Microfiber towels are listed in Cool Tools as great for drying and travel and camping, but have you used them for everyday cleaning, dusting and wiping? I buy my 16x16-inch towels in bulk. I've used the previously-reviewed MysticMaid cleaning towels and, personally, have seen no difference in cleaning power. Of course, mine may not last as long in the end, but they are are a heck of lot cheaper, so I'm more inclined to use them for everything and anything. And they really are holding their own so far. I've washed my current kitchen cleaner over 50 times with no loss in cleaning power (the packaging says good for over 100 washes). Dampen with water and you can clean the kitchen top to bottom without leaving a streak. It removes grease, grime, and the odd stuff on the stove top. Around the house it cleans glass without leaving a streak, removes the haze from inside of your auto windshield, cleans the car interior and removes all the muck the kids have built up on the plastic, doors and even car seats. Around the desk it cleans up coffee spills and rings. I've also used mine for cleaning monitor screens, brass, cameras (I collect Minolta 16 mm and Minox cameras), jewels, coins, glass objet d'art, lexan screens, fine wood carvings, some photos, and find no scratches or wearing away of labels, paint, or important stuff -- and I've looked hard with my loupes. Cleaning wood work is easy and quick, as well. And in the wood shop it does wonders in getting dust off surfaces before staining or painting. A bonus for ribs lovers -- it's better than any napkin or moist towelette.

-- Patrick J. Meyer

Best stain remover
OxiClean
$10 5 lbs. Amazon

This powder is a non-toxic, non-chlorine bleach. Chemically it works like hydrogen peroxide, which is a water molecule with an added unstable oxygen. OxiClean is chiefly sodium percarbonate, which is washing soda with additional unstable oxygen. As in hydrogen peroxide, the excitable oxygen bubbles off when it reacts, chemically oxidizing smells, films, germs and stains of all kinds. But because OxiClean is a dry powder it is far more durable and stable than hydrogen peroxide, easier to concentrate, and cheaper in bulk. (Drugstore hydrogen peroxide is 2% solution; OxiClean is equivalent to 27% peroxide.) Best of all, percarbonate degrades to simple oxygen and washing soda (sodium carbonate). Greenies love it, and it is sold in many environmental friendly stores. I feel comfortable using it in the kitchen, and will freely work it in my hands; it has an alkaline soapy feel and fizzes satisfyingly.

Dissolved in water, it works wonders on carpet stains, soiled clothing, weird gunk on counters, mildew, trash cans, refrigerator smell and so forth. American Test Kitchens tested all available cleaners and found that sodium percarbonate was the all-around champ on getting severe grease, food, coffee and wine stains from clothes. Generally, oxygen bleaches won't fade or affect colors like chlorine bleaches will.

Sodium percarbonate is an old chemical, but manufacturers only recently learned how to make this stuff in the vast quantities needed to be tossed by the cupfull into laundry machines. For around-the-house chores, I've found that a very little of this stuff will go a long way. You can mix it to your own preferred concentration. There are a number of powdered cleaners based on sodium percarbonate and they all have "oxy" in their names. (Liquid cleaners with "oxy" in the name are usually hydrogen peroxide.) But of these, OxiClean, versatile stain remover is a best buy for laundry use. Most general stores, like Walmart and Target, carry it.

-- KK

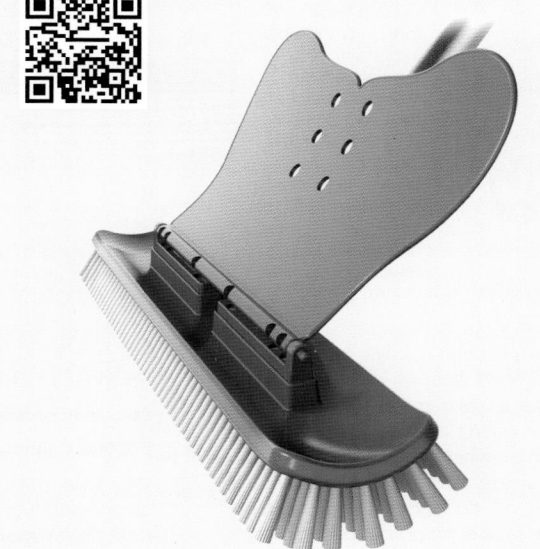

Tenacious pool brush
Wall Whale
$20 wallwhale.com

I used a normal pool brush before, and always had the problem with the brush not sticking to the wall. I would normally have to use a lot of force to successfully brush a vertical section of pool wall. Then the brush finally broke. So I went to a local pool supply to get another brush and came across the Wall Whale brush. It's unique because in addition to the brush, it has a fin, which creates a powerful force, that basically sticks the brush to the pool wall. It's pretty effortless to use, and successfully cleans the area that I brush.

I have had it for a few months and love it.

-- Mike Hedge

Old school stain remover
Fels-Naptha
$4 felsnaptha.com

Fels-Naptha is old school soap that works great when it comes to stains. I had a pair of khakis that I got old chain grease on, washed them regularly about 3-4 times. Regular wash didn't get the stain out, so I called it a bust. Then 3-months later I used a little elbow grease and Fels-Naptha, just rubbing the fabric against itself for 5 minutes, and sure enough, the grease came right out. The soap is good for plenty more as well.

-- Tanner

Household

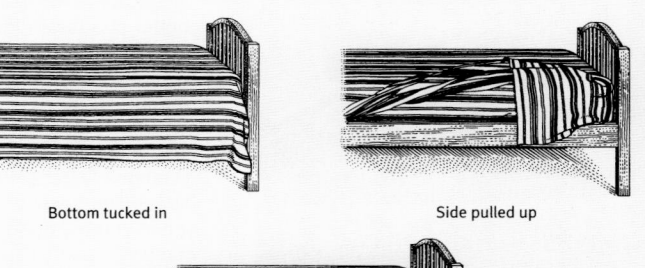

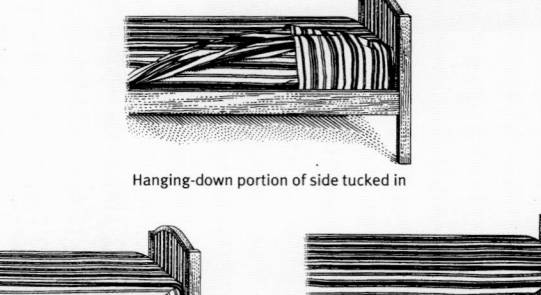

Minding the small stuff
Home Comforts: The Art & Science of Keeping House

$14 Cheryl Mendelson 2005, 896 p.

This appears to be a book of tips for housekeeping, but it is as much about housekeeping as Moby Dick is about fishing. It's about doing mindless chores mindfully. If you cook, clean, and dress, why not do it with full knowledge of what the most scientific method is? There is something attractively nerdy about Mendelson's obsession with getting to a deep technical understanding of whatever needs to be done. So much good-spirited lore swims in this book, that you can pick it up anywhere and find yourself reading hours later about the absolute best way to iron. Ordinary chores are given a new life. I haven't seen such behavior-changing information in ages. I'm thinking I'll give each of my kids a copy when they depart for their own places.

-- KK

avoid crushing the cloth, giving it a shine, or stretching or scorching or otherwise harming it with the heat of the iron. This is done partly by not sliding the iron and partly (and usually) by using a "pressing cloth." This is simply a cloth that you lay over the fabric, pressing through it rather than touching the iron directly to the garment.

- Washing the Dishes. Begin with perfectly clean, hot, sudsy water. Wash the dishes that are least soiled first and progress to those that are most soiled, as this entails the fewest changes of water. As noted above, you usually begin with glass and silver or flatware, which need very hot water so that they dry quickly without streaks or spots.

- As an experiment, I once sorted my laundry according to the exact instructions on the care labels. Although in quantity I had enough to make up three or four good-sized loads, if I had obeyed the labels I would have had to wash at least three times that many loads, as practically no two garments were labeled identically. No experienced home launderer actually washes twelve or more loads instead of four. Thus we all become care label skeptics, defying the labels without hesitation.

- Inaccurate labeling and "low labeling" (labels that prescribe more conservative care than the garment really needs) are both quite common. Nonetheless, some of our skepticism about labels is in fact mistaken. We may fail to recognize that a label is accurate if (for example) a garment labeled "Dry-clean only" seems perfectly all right after being laundered. The effects of laundering may become apparent only after the third or fourth wash, and those effects may include shrinkage, fading, weakening, or the loss of beneficial treatments and finishes. By the time you discover that the label was right all along, it is too late to save the garment.

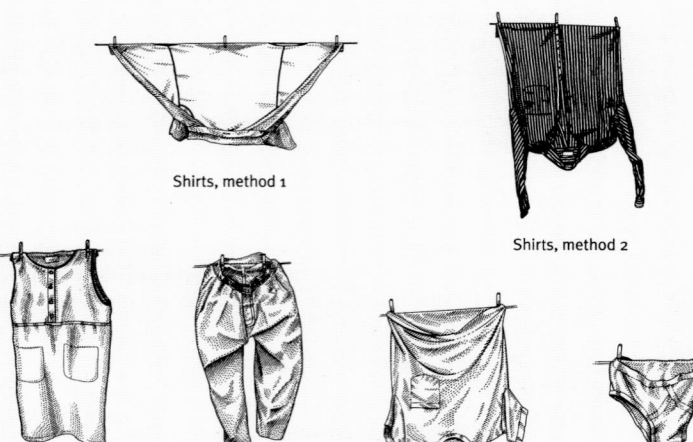

Shirts, method 1

Shirts, method 2

Hanging clothes and linens for line drying

- The terms "ironing" and "pressing" are often used interchangeably, but they are in fact different things. In ironing, you slide the iron back and forth over the cloth; in pressing, you simply press the iron in one spot and then lift it. Pressing is used on tailored and lined suits, especially on men's, on wool, on silk and some rayon, on net, and on pile fabrics. Pressing is used to

Bottom tucked in

Side pulled up

Hanging-down portion of side tucked in

Side hanging down

Tuck-in of entire side of sheet (optional on top sheet)

How to make "mitered" or "hospital" corners

Collapsible, horizontal laundry cage
IKEA Frost Drying Rack

$20 ikea.com

Drying clothing on a rack is cheaper and better for the environment than using a dryer, but the design of a lot of drying racks is far from ideal. IKEA's Frost rack is a long series of bars that are horizontally parallel to one another, which maximizes the use for each bar. The closely-spaced bars allow me either to pack in small laundry or put sweaters and thicker laundry across two or more bars to let more air pass around it. On the other hand, many racks are situated with each bar immediately above or below another bar, so if you hang pants from the top bar, they hang down making all of the bars below them useless (i.e. wet). A few companies make potentially-good racks you hang from the ceiling, but they're usually permanent, more expensive and not so nice to look at. The cheap Frost rack can easily fit an entire load of laundry, whether it's socks or jeans, and it folds into a large, flat rectangle when not in use. A few racks can easily fit into the back of the closet.

I bought my first Frost rack when I lived in an apartment. But even when my wife and I moved into a house two years ago, we decided to get by without a dryer for a while, mainly to save money. To our surprise, it wasn't difficult. It's no problem at all in the summer, when we can supplement our drying with an outside clothesline on sunny days. During the winter, our two racks are in constant use (hint: put the rack beside or above heating vents or radiators to speed drying). We might eventually buy a dryer, but only to make it easier to catch up when we fall behind. I've been using one rack for about four years and bought the second about two years ago. I cannot tell which is the old one. They've held up quite well. Granted the rack is not perfect: it could be both wider and higher -- tall people will have to stoop a little bit to use it. Still, it's far better than any of the alternatives I've found.

One unexpected benefit: our clothing seems to last a lot longer. We'd never realized how rough the dryer can be on clothing. I have shirts that are a few years old I wear regularly and they still look new. I suppose all of the lint in the dryer trap has to come from somewhere.

-- Willie Beegle

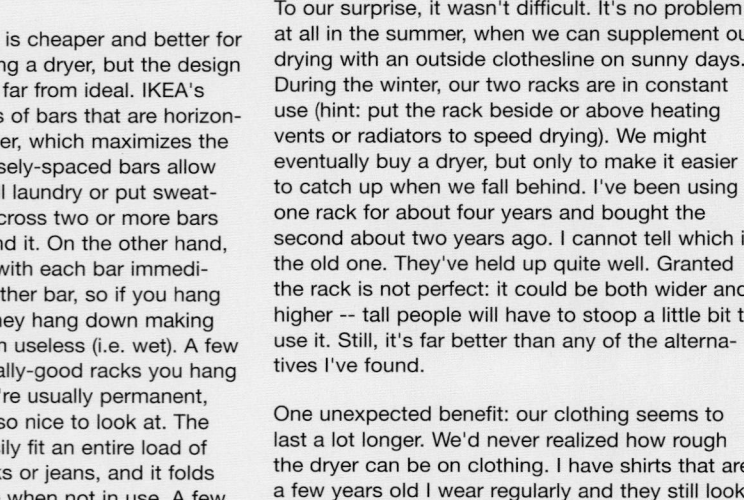

Centripetal-only laundry
Spin Dryers

$145 laundry-alternative.com

$70 Mini Countertop laundry-alternative.com

When we moved out to a farm, we decided to line dry whatever we could, but handwringing all our clothing, linens and towels is time and energy consuming. And the hand wringing was hard on my more delicate clothing. These electric-powered spin dryers do a fantastic job; the clothes come out just slightly damp and dry quickly. The dryers are also much gentler on stuff like sweaters, delicates and lingerie. Two years ago we bought a small counter-top dryer for the apartment we keep in the city (to avoid schlepping linens and towels). It worked so well and we were so impressed with it I then bought a larger one for the farm. The smaller one spins at 1600 RPM and the larger one at 3600 RPM, so they greatly reduce the time needed for line drying (probably only 1-2 minutes on average). They also help get much more water and detergent out of our laundry than a conventional washer does. There's much less detergent smell. We are most definitely not into the fragrances put in many detergents. It usually smells like nasty chemicals to us, so the more we can get out of our clothes and linens, the better. And avoiding the dryer frees us from that "cooked" smell.

Both systems are completely contained and the water drains into a sink or bath tub. We put the mini one on the kitchen counter (on the dish drainer tray) so we can load wet stuff right from the sink into it. It has a flexible hose that comes out of the bottom in the back, and you just snake that over to the sink and the water goes right back in — makes it easy to use the same wash water and detergent several times, saving on water and detergent. The large one has a spout in the front at the bottom, which we position over the bath tub. My husband actually built a plywood triangle fitted with some rubber matting on the underside (so it wouldn't mar the tub). The larger one is especially great for cleaning and freshening up bed pillows. They're almost completely dry after only spinning a couple minutes! A couple caveats: you can't turn them on and go off and leave them unattended. And you do have to ensure they're balanced — if the big one ever got away on you, I'm sure it could do some damage. But after using it a couple times, you get onto how to load for balance.

-- Christine Mank

Faith is, at one and the same time, absolutely necessary and altogether impossible. - Stanislaw Lem

Build yourself extra space
OP Loftbed
$10 OP Lofts

My girlfriend and I were sharing a single room in a shared apartment, so we didn't have much space. I suggested getting a loft bed, and she surprised me by liking the idea. Searching online to purchase a loft, I couldn't find any great designs, and shipping all that wood wouldn't be cheap. But I didn't really want to put the time into designing one I'd like.

When I found plans for an OP Loftbed, I instantly recognized a quality design. OP stands for "Orgy-Proof" and though we haven't tested it that way, it's a good bet the bed would have NO problems.

I took my time and built it over several weeks, but it could be done pretty quickly (a long weekend). That's with basic, though not complete beginner, tools and skills. The website estimates that for a twin-sized bed, it'll be around $100 for lumber, and $25 for fasteners if you buy it from their online partner. The queen-sized, which is what I built, cost me more like $300 to $400. The difference is that:

1) The queen-size needs 2 sheets of plywood (and I used nice $30/sheet ply).

2) The fastener deal wasn't around, so I probably spent around $60.

3) I made a desk, which needed more wood and another sheet of good ply.

4) It's all painted and the shelves/desk are all poly'd.

Joel's queen-sized loft ▲

It's like buying a car — the basic model is probably around $150 or so, and you can spend a lot more for the accessories. There are free plans for bookshelves, a desk, and a telephone table, all of which I've modified slightly for my queen-sized loft, and all of which are fairly ingenious in their use of space.

Overall, the loft makes the room feel much bigger. I built mine to last, either for my own use, or for resale value. It was a good investment.

-- Joel M Rosenberg

[Plans for bed mods, bookshelves and desks are free from here:]

Next generation of hideaway beds
Murphy Bed
$2,000 Jefferson Library Bed More Space Place

We moved to a much smaller house recently in an effort to downsize. We found, however, that no matter how carefully we shopped we were not going to find a house in our price range with all the rooms we needed. Then an idea struck me. What about a Murphy Bed? My memories of them consist of people being trapped in them in TV comedies. You know, the ditzy one, sits on the end of the bed and up it goes into the wall taking him or her with it.

But, oh my, how they have changed. Murphy Beds are still in use, more than ever, and they have some beautiful and ingenious models. What was more important to us, however, was that by using a Murphy bed we got another room. The room that will be my library will, now, also be the guest room. By having a bed that folds inconspicuously into the wall and is then fronted with bookcases our guest room serves as 2 rooms. What a bonus.

The fronts of these beds come in any configuration and serve as many purposes as you can imagine. They start at about $2000 and can go quite high from there depending on what you want. But when you consider you are adding a room to your house for that price it is a true bargain.

We purchased our Murphy Bed, called the Library, from more SPACE place in Salem, NH and I cannot say enough about the quality of the product and the service this company provided. The cost of the bed includes delivery and installation and they did this quickly and professionally. I would suggest you start your search here to get an idea of what a good bed costs and branch out from there. My bet is you'll be back here. We found that they were superior to their competitors in price, variety, durability and service. What else is there?

The best thing of all is that the bed is really comfortable.

-- George Christin

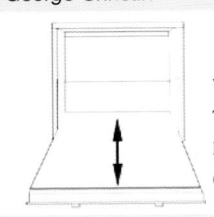

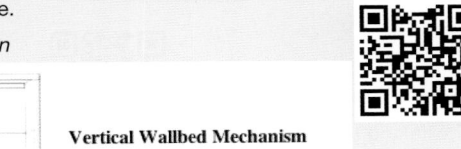

Vertical Wallbed Mechanism	
Twin	$299.00 each
Full	$299.00 each
Queen	$299.00 each

Sheets with pockets
Neat Sheets
$60-105 Twin to California King store.
neatsheets.com

I have a small amount of stuff that I want within easy reach at night, including my cellphone, lip balm, and a small bottle of water. I was considering housing it in a bedside caddy or organizer, but wasn't thrilled by the idea of buying a uni-tasking extra product just for that one purpose. Searching for a better solution, I stumbled across Neat Sheets sheet sets from a company called Everest Luxury Linens. These sheets come with sewn-on side pockets on the fitted sheets which serve as convenient repositories for whatever you want within reach while you're in bed.

Neat Sheets also have sewn-on tags at the foot of the sheet, to (as the company says on its site) help you get the right corner of the sheet on the right corner of the mattress, every time. I hesitated to buy Neat Sheets, because the site had a slightly gimmicky infomercial-style vibe. But a few months ago I did buy them, and they are terrific. They are exactly what's described on the site, and I find they make my life just a tiny bit easier every single day. As a minimalist and a fan of good design, I'm really pleased.

-- Sue Gardner

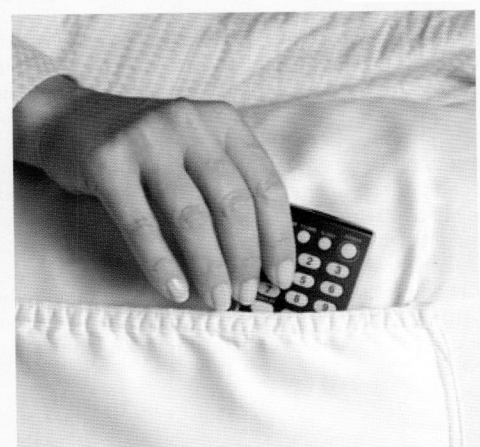

Body-shaping foam sheets
Visco-Elastic Memory Foam
$72 2" Twin Foam Topper memoryfoamsource.com

Visco-elastic foam (aka memory foam, or Swedish foam) is rather odd stuff. When you poke it, it takes a while to gloop back into its original shape. This isn't the neat bit though. The neat bit is that it becomes softer at higher temperatures, so it can react to human body heat. The result is to spread pressure very evenly over the bits of you that touch it.

It's currently used mainly as pillows and mattresses, but could probably be used for anything that exerts pressure on the human body. I recently bought a pillow and mattress topping made of the stuff... very nice :-) I'm planning on using it for a seat cover and to pad my backpack straps as well now.

In terms of working with it, it seems to be just like ordinary foam except slightly heavier. I cut a slice off my mattress overlay with scissors: no problems, nice clean cut. At a place like Target or equivalent a memory foam pillow goes

Ultimate air mattress
Insta Raised Bed
$130 Insta Raised Queen Bed Amazon

You never seem to have an inflatable bed when you need one. Then you buy one and the piece of crap leaks or is really uncomfortable. This one works well. A typical two-prong power outlet nearby lets you fill the Insta Bed quickly with the mattress's built-in air pump — and this is key — it quietly keeps it inflated to your desired pressure all night. You also deflate it via that pump. Folds into a small twin pillow-sized bundle for storage. It is firm enough to fool me, doesn't lose air very fast either. Guests have commented on its comfort. Returning guests pick the room with that mattress over a guest room with a real queen-sized bed for some reason.

-- Jason Weisberger

for $35, a (fairly thin) mattress overlay for $90. A company called "Tempur" has been marketing the stuff fairly heavily.

-- Paul Harrison

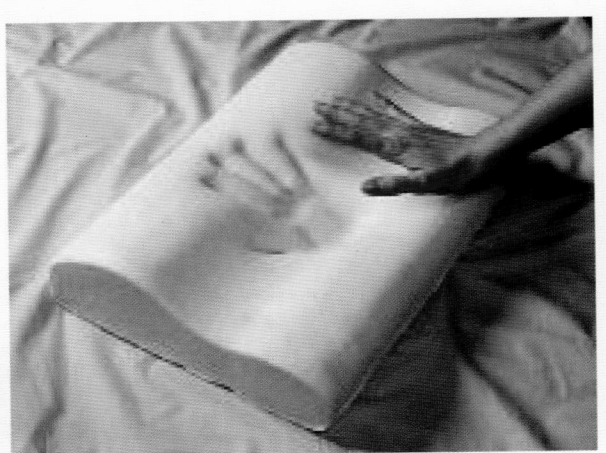

Salvage

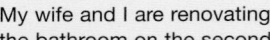

Unbreakable trash bags
Demo Bag
$22 for 10 demobags.com

My wife and I are renovating the bathroom on the second floor. We needed a way to get debris out of the house and into the dumpster parked on the street. Since we preferred to not carry buckets of plaster through our house, we needed an alternative. I found a link online and thought I would give Demo Bags a try. We sealed ourselves into the bathroom, filled the bags, and duct taped them shut. Then we threw them out the second floor window and dragged them to the dumpster. Not one of the 40 that we filled broke open. For a small remodel these are ideal! Our only mistake was to make them too heavy. Do yourself a favor: buy a lot of 'em, and make them light!

-- Matthew L. Cartwright

Salvaged building materials
Habitat for Humanity ReStores
habitat.org/env/restores.aspx

As a builder, woodworker and general do-it-yourselfer, I've been in my local ReStore every week since they opened. The concept behind

Habitat for Humanity's ReStores is a building supply thrift outlet whose proceeds go to funding more Habitat projects. Everybody wins. Everything in the stores is salvaged, used, donated or surplus, so the prices are incredibly reasonable. I just refinished a garage for well under half of what I would have paid retail by buying most of the supplies from a ReStore

-- everything from the lighting to OSB board and 2x4's we used to make the temp walls. We even found some sound-deading insulation which helped sound-proof the place. So you never know what you might find.

The store in Dover has a volunteer demo crew that goes a few times a month on various demo projects and they usually produce a lot of usable material. The stock and materials do vary from week to week, but they have everything from engineered hardwood floors to tools to kitchen sinks. The quality also varies, but really only when dealing with items such as sheetrock and lumber. All the appliances are in working order and, at least at the one in Dover, there's a large selection of very nice kitchen cabinets. As a carpenter, I also go in during the day just to buy extra nails, joist hangers, and other little odds and ends that add up at the end of the year.

Currently, there are ReStores in 47 U.S. states and 9 Canadian provinces.

-- Dave Marcoux

Non-explosive demolition agent
Dexpan
$100 dexpan.com

Problem: 50 feet of reinforced concrete curb where we wanted to build our community workshop. Plan A: Rented two pneumatic jack hammers. After a long afternoon, we had made progress, but only broken up about 10 feet. Plan B: My co-housing neighbor came across the previously-untried Dexpan. A non-explosive demolition agent, Dexpan is a mortar-like powder you mix with water and apply to rock, concrete and even reinforced concrete in order to break the material apart. As it dries, the powder expands a slight bit, but with a tremendous force. It's easy to use. We followed the guidelines for the most part. With a 1.5" carbide bit in a hammer drill, we made a series of strategically-placed holes on 12-16" centers, mixed up the mortar, and poured. It takes 24 hours or longer for maximum effect. As I recall, some holes didn't crack at first, but did after I added additional water and gave it more time. We did end up using a 20-pound sledge hammer and a 5-foot long solid steel pry bar when necessary to open up cracks so we could use an angle grinder to cut the rebar. The pry bar also was crucial in moving the chunks, which tended to be very heavy. Nevertheless, the Dexpan was responsible for breaking up the concrete into reasonably-sized pieces. The rebar had to be cut and required a lot of prying, but there's no way we could have broken all this up using a sledge hammer in any reasonable amount of time. There are other non-explosive demolition agents out there, but my recollection is that Dexpan was by far the easiest to buy in small quantities. They say their 44-pound box will cover 34-36 linear feet. You must order one of three mixes depending on the temperature you will use it at.

As I recall, it was probably the low 60's on average when we used it so we got the middle mixture. If we had to do it over again, we'd probably price out having a professional remove the curb -- it really was a lot more work than we thought. But if you're going to do it yourself, this makes it a lot easier than just relying on a jackhammer.

-- Dale Grover

Best new old-house fixtures
Rejuvenation
rejuvenation.com

Our family has owned three houses in the past 12 years. All have been older homes. Our current home was built in 1911. As you'd expect, old homes take some work. We're fortunate enough to live near the Portland, OR, Rejuvenation storefront (there's one in Seattle, too), which stocks everything that's in the catalog, and then some. They've even got a decent selection of architectural salvage like old doors, mantelpieces, and other old house ephemera.

If you're a little farther away, you'll want to get your hands on a copy of the Rejuvenation catalog. The catalog is primarily focused on period lighting products, but also has a solid selection of period hard-

ware, bath items, and other fixtures for old houses. The company takes great pains to recreate authentic pieces and assembles most of their lighting pieces in their Portland factory. Their range of recreation runs from the Victorian era right up through the funky 1970s. I've long loved their Sunset fixture (pictured), but have never quite been able to convince my wife that it fits our house.

The fixtures and other parts manufactured by Rejuvenation aren't cheap, either in quality or cost. These are the real deal, made with painstaking detail. In addition to awesome old house lighting, the catalogs contain a wide range of hard-to-source doorknobs.

In addition to being an excellent supplier of new old house parts, Rejuvenation is an outstanding corporate citizen. The company started back in the '70s as an architectural salvage store, with just a couple of guys tearing apart old houses and selling what they could to folks fixing up other old houses. Today the company employs over 200 people from 21 countries, and they donate 10% of their after-tax

profits to help support the communities where their employees live.

Rejuvenation supplies what I need to fix up our old house, but it's also a company that I can feel really good about patronizing. Be sure to check out their blog for some good project inspiration.

-- Brendon Connelly

The future is here. It's just not evenly distributed yet. - William Gibson.

Maximize contents held in tube containers
Tube Wringer

$25 heavy duty tubewringer.com

My new favorite tool is the Tube Wringer, from Gill Mechanical.

From their website: "The Tube-Wringer efficiently squeezes the contents from tubes of caulk, glue, medical compounds, adhesives, and toothpaste. Nearly indestructible, the Tube-Wringer will last a lifetime under normal use and pay for itself in short order."

In addition to sqeezing every little bit out of just about any tube, the squeezed part is left with a zig-zag texture so future usage doesn't undo the squeezing. Tubes are left efficiently squeezed, and cool looking. My only problem is that I wish I had more partially-used tubes available because it's so satisfying to squeeze every last bit out of them.

They come in light, medium, and heavy duty versions.

-- Sally Rosenthal

Stabilizing plastic shim
Wobble Wedge

$7 (6-pack) wobblewedge.com

As a grad student, I spend a lot of time working on a laptop in coffee shops and living in old houses. What that means: sitting at notoriously-wobbly cafe tables and shimming furniture on uneven old wood floors. Wobble Wedges are small, clear plastic shims with a ridged surface that are invaluable in both instances. Since they weigh just an ounce or two, I always keep a couple in my computer bag (better than jamming newspaper under a coffee shop table). I usually go to a coffee shop twice a week, sometimes more, and find myself having to use them about 30 percent of the time. Sometimes I forget and leave them behind, but they're cheap enough it's no big deal. At home, these also work great because they are clear enough to be almost invisible. They are plenty strong enough for a fully-loaded bookshelf and, in the five years I've been using them, I've never had one break down or crack. Losing them is another story: I once used some to shim a pedestal sink and never saw them again. But the sink never wobbled either!

-- Donovan Finn

Better door closer
Touch n' Hold

$15 touchnhold.com

If you have a storm door or screen door, you probably have a pneumatic device that closes it. And the device has a little washer thing that will hold the door open if you put down your bags, and the baby, and let the dog go free while you fiddle it down the bar, so it can jam against the piston. It's a hassle.

The Touch n' Hold is a device that makes this a happier moment. The Touch n' Hold door closer lets you set the door open with a simple tap of your toe or elbow. Then once you've got all your stuff inside, just nudge the door (not the thing) open a little more and it will go back into closing mode.

I use it every day, and it always makes me think of Cool Tools.

-- Thomas T. Ballantine

Stick-ons, boosts visibility
SOLAS Marine Reflective Tape

$40 (1" wide)
$55 (2" wide)
(both, 30' long)

shop.reflectivestore.com 3m.com

We've been using 3M's SOLAS reflective tape for several years. It was designed for the Coast Guard to use on life jackets, so you know it has to be tough and withstand time, bad weather and wet conditions (SOLAS = safety of life at sea). It is a bit expensive, but it is the brightest and most durable stuff I've ever found. We use it everywhere and have put in on just about everything: garbage cans, walking sticks, jackets, kayaks, a bicycle, a stroller, a trailer, traffic cones, automobile door jams (so oncoming traffic sees me right away), the trunk of my car (an instant safety device if I get stuck on the side of the road) and the car's mudguards. The strips on our mudguards -- which take a lot of abuse! -- are still sticking after more than seven years. Now that I've seen how effective it is, I really think it should be a law that all cars come stocked with reflective stripping on door jams.

-- Jeff Ellis

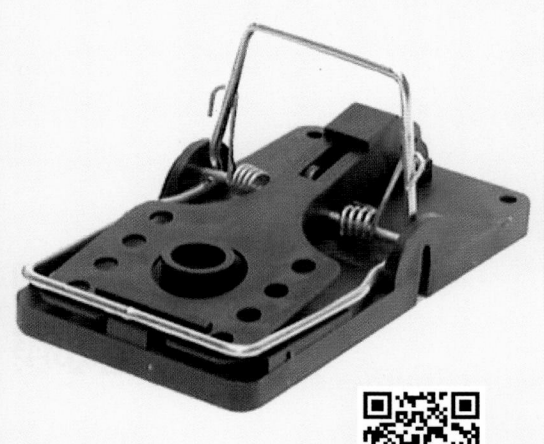

The Best Rat Trap
Snap-E Rat Trap

$7 Amazon

There are certain less-than-glamorous homesteading chores that I am really good at. Shoveling, doing dishes, and trapping rats. Sigh.

Rats around here are not the loathsome Norwegian variety, but rather wood rats, or pack rats, which look like a big mouse — kinda cute. In the woods, rats build pyramids of twigs 3 feet or so high — rat architecture — always in secluded spots, so you have to be bushwacking to come upon them. In semi-rural areas like mine they cruise human habitations for easy pickins. One year I trapped over 40.

For years I used the standard wooden Victor traps and would put peanut butter in a little piece of plastic (with punched holes), tied to the trigger with baggie ties. Then I started sheet-metal-screwing a 1/2" copper pipe cap to the trigger, which I filled with peanut butter.

I went through maybe 4 types of other traps until I discovered these. They have a bait cup so the rat has to tug at it, thereby releasing spring—plenty strong enough to ensure fatality.

I'm writing this after getting one last night that had been eluding me for a week. Outwitted by a rat night after night.

Method: I washed 3 traps (getting rid of scent), smooshed some bacon in the cups, surrounded by smears of Skippy peanut butter — mwah!

And whack! Mighty hunter.

-- Lloyd Kahn

World's best mousetrap
Ketch-All Multiple Catch Mousetrap

$17 Cooperseeds

I once had to get rid of a lot of mice. Standard mouse traps were too messy to reuse, but too expensive just throw out. Have-a-heart traps were too finicky, and traps were too cruel. Finally, I found the proverbial better mouse trap: a wind-up repeating trap. No bait required. Just put it two inches from the wall and for some reason the mice climb right in. A spring loaded trap door flips them into a little chamber, and they call their friends to join them. One trap catches ten a night, and the mice don't seem to mind at all. The one I used is the Trap Man, sold as the Ketch-All in the US.

(Of course, it does leave you with the problem of what to do with a daily box of live mice.)

-- Danny Hillis

No more slamming doors
Magnetic Doorstop

$9 stanleyhardware.com

I frequently have windows open in the house and have for years put up with doors slamming closed when the wind catches them. I have finally found a solution in the form of these magnetic door catches.

They work excellently and I have installed them on most doors throughout the house. I have used them for several years and always show them off to the house guests. I can now leave windows open without a door slamming shut. One minor drawback is that they are a little loud when the magnet makes contact with the catch. Finally, care should be taken when installing to make sure the two parts align well otherwise the magnetic hold will be weaker.

-- Don Allen

Sharpening

Idiot-proof wake-up alarm
Screaming Meanie
$25 Amazon

When I travel I often use earplugs at night (E.A.R foam are my preferred brand, p. 330) to mute the sounds of strange places and get a good night's sleep. Only problem is, the pathetic "eep eep" sound of a typical travel alarm cannot penetrate the earplugs. For years I have searched for a truly heavy-duty portable alarm, and finally found a good candidate at the Petro Truck Stop in Kingman, Arizona: The Screaming Meanie.

Also available from online sources, the Screaming Meanie is not a clock. It is a countdown timer. You set the number of hours and minutes between now and the time you want to wake up. You can also set the volume, either to "loud"

or "frighteningly loud." In case 110 decibels is not enough ("loud enough to wake the dead!"), they have a 220 decibel version too!

When you start the Screaming Meanie the alarm is ON by default. This eliminates my habit of waking up five or six times just to check whether I set my travel alarm correctly. You just know this thing is going to work. You can't possibly sleep through it because while the 10 and 5-minute warnings can be turned off with one button, it takes 3 buttons pushed simultaneously to silence the final alarm. My only quibble is that it should be smaller (it is a rounded plastic block, 1" by 2.25" by 5.25") but hey, it was designed for truckers.

-- Charles Plattt

Constant automatic accuracy
Analog Atomic Wall Clock
$25 14" Radio Controlled Clock amazon.com

Like many households we have clocks and watches, but none of them are set to the precise time (I think). With constant advancing or retreating because of daylight savings, no timepiece is safe from being infected with inaccuracy. (Who has time to set the time?) Most clocks and watches linked to the exact time from Boulder, Colorado, are digital, but I'm an analog man. The 14" Atomic Wall Clock is large, analog, and self-correcting. (It's like having an atomic clock in your basement.) It's spooky to watch the hands whirl around until they find their spot as it adjusts itself in and out of daylight savings time, a chore worth at least its price. Someday all clocks (and appliances!) will be this smart.

-- KK

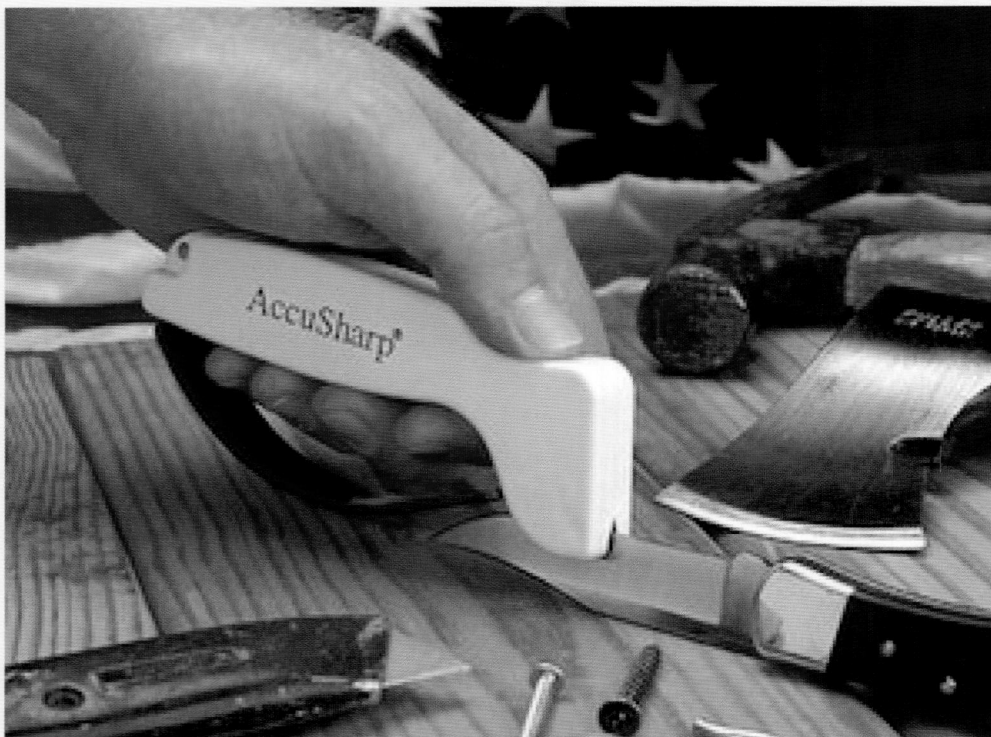

Budget edge sharpener
Accusharp Knife Sharpener
$9 accusharp.com

One Amazon reviewer called it the "sharpening tool of the century." I won't argue. My knives have been getting progressively duller over the years but I'm not about to try to sharpen them myself with a stone, nor am I taking them in anytime soon for expensive professional sharpening. I've been content to use them as they are. Then I came upon the Accu-Sharp somewhere and read the Amazon Reviews and decided to pony up $9.10 for one.

Amazing would be an understatement for the ease of use once I figured out I was doing it backwards. I cannot recommend this tool highly enough after seeing the results obtained from a few swipes of the device along the blade. There are probably many who would tell me how I'm wrecking my knives (Henckels 5-Star) by using a $10 sharpener, but you know what? There's an Arab proverb for that: "The dogs bark, but the caravans move on."

-- Joe Stirt

Some of my knives had so little edge that they would turn tomatoes into a mushy watery mess on a cutting board.

After a few swipes with the Accusharp I could cut tomatoes into perfect slices, and it took a measly 15-minutes to clean up the edge on almost every knife I own (it even worked on my breadknife!).

The sharpener is a simple device built around two pieces of carbide that form a "V" in a plastic handle that when run along a blade shaves the edge to a sharpened point. Unlike a whetstone, the carbide pieces will eventually wear away and lose their ability to produce an edge, but the Accusharp is designed so that the carbide can be flipped or replaced. I've had mine for three-months and see no sign of wear, and Amazon reviewers say that they get a few years of sharpening before they need to replace the carbide.

For $10, this sharpener was able to rejuvenate most knives in my kitchen. The few it couldn't sharpen were blades that had been bent or misshapen beyond simple repair.

-- Oliver Hulland

Cheap, disposable scissors sharpener
Fiskars SewSharp Scissors Sharpener
$3 fiskarscrafts.com

Shaped like a worry stone, this low-tech scissors sharpener features a ceramic whetstone piece set in plastic. The tiny tool (about the size of a poker chip) is designed specifically for the user to sharpen the two blades simultaneously, a process that's safe and controlled due to its design. The textured tab is to be held between thumb and forefinger. Mounted inside is a small ceramic rod that serves as the whetstone. One blade is inserted below the rod and the other above. As you draw both blades through, the open scissors close themselves. The Jiff V Sharpener (below) might be the best all-around inexpensive sharpener for the home -- it can handle knives and the blade is replaceable -- but it's still too big to keep in crowded or small spaces. The SewSharp is perfect for an office desk or sewing kit. It also costs half as much as the Jiff V, so you can buy multiples to stash in crafts kits, tool drawers, and scrapbooking boxes. The life of the ceramic rod is not indefinite, so I'd recommend buying more than one anyway.

-- Anne Morris

Least expensive scissor sharpener
Smiths Jiff V Sharpener
$8 amazon.com

This $6 plastic sharpening tool has the cheap feel of a "as advertised on TV" item. But it does work and is super quick and easy to use. It holds a carbide V that sharpens knives and scissors when you run the blade through it. The groove keeps the blade pretty steadily angled. There are similar products for serious knife sharpening but they are more expensive. When compared to the Tormek, I have to qualify my definition of sharp -- however the V does significantly improve the edge in seconds. Often that small honing is sufficient for most household chores. This gizmo is especially great for scissors, which in my experience are hardly ever sharpened after they are bought. I keep mine in my desk drawer.

-- KK

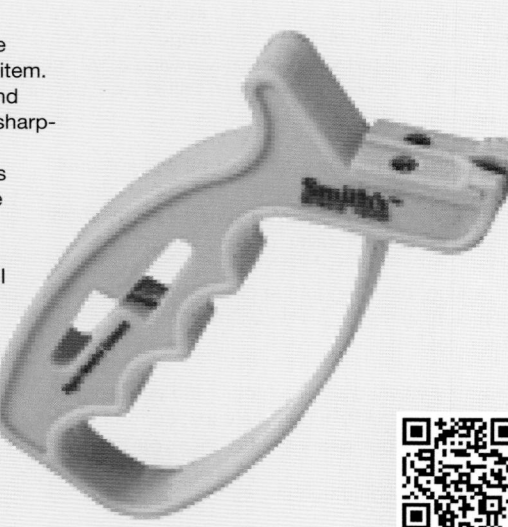

The future of cat flaps
SureFlap Microchip Cat Flap
$133

This is a battery operated cat door that unlocks (going inside) by reading the cat's microchip. Our cat was chipped at our shelter for around $10, but commercial vets are also able to do it for a bit more. No need to worry about lost collar keys, or magnets. Keeps out unprogrammed animals. The door also has the standard four-setting mechanical override locking feature of: in-out, in only, out only, locked. If your cat is not chipped, you can also use an RFID collar key (not included).

We previously had a magnetically keyed cat door, but you then have the choice of using a safety collar and losing the (not cheap) key every now and then, or using a non-safety collar and risking the cat strangling itself.

Raccoons eventually defeated our magnetically keyed door. They haven't defeated this one (yet), although the mechanical parts of the latching action are similar.

-- Bruce Bowen

Cheapest little robot
Omega Paw Self-Cleaning Litter Box
$35 omegapaw.com

Ever since I've had my cat, I have found the litter task quite unbearable. I've read a lot of reviews for various automatic litter box cleaners and most of them are too expensive, too error prone, and usually a combination of both.

Eventually I found the Omega litter box and I've never been happier. It is similar to the previously reviewed The Litter Robot, but it is cheaper and is NOT automatic which means a reduced likelihood of it breaking.

I've been using this litter box for almost 2 years now and the process is simple as ever: roll the litter box to the right, then roll it back.

Get the shelf with the litter out and throw it in the garbage. DONE. No mechanical issues, no special sand, no electricity usage and NO SCOOPING. I love it.

-- Vitaly Belman

Feline meds delivery
Pill Pockets
$6 Greenies Pill Pockets for Cats, 1.6-Ounce Amazon

If you've ever tried to give a pill to a cat, you know it's not only not fun, it can be downright dangerous. Dogs will eat anything. Cats, not so much.

I had a cat that was on medication for years, and every day it was the same struggle to get a pill down her throat. Now, I have a semi-feral, and very strong, older cat who needs thyroid medication every day. I would probably have lost a finger or two if I hadn't found these things. You just fold the pill up into the little pocket, drop it in front of the cat, and it's gone, like magic. Everyone's happy, especially the cat. And you don't need the asbestos gloves anymore.

-- Charles Richardson

Intense feline grooming
FURminator De-Shedding Tool
$17 furminator.com

The FURminator is the only really functional cat-grooming tool I've ever found. The stiff steel rake grabs the undercoat while leaving the topcoat intact. It does a tremendous job of removing loose fur. Be prepared, especially the first time you brush your cat. For my cats, the big difference between the FURminator and regular brushes is that the softer bristles of standard brushes just get hair from the surface -- the topcoat, and a bit of undercoat -- whereas the stiffer teeth of the FURminator primarily snag the undercoat (and lots of it!) as well as loose hairs of the topcoat. The best part is that all that fur goes in the trash, and not on your sofa, bed, or carpet. The environment of my apartment has been improved dramatically, and I no longer need to spend a lot of time vacuuming up cat hair. While the FURminator is expensive for a grooming tool, it's solidly constructed and ergonomically designed, and best of all, it really works. My vet used it on my cats while they were in for a visit. I was shocked at how much hair came off in just a few strokes, so I bought one to take home and have been using it for several months. I then threw out the other standard, cat/slicker brushes I had acquired over the years, and bought two more FURminators to give to cat-owning friends. The one I use is 1.75" and is intended for cats, so although the FURinator comes in larger sizes for dogs, I can really only speak to its utility when it comes to cats.

-- Debbie Chachra

Guide to vet care
The Merck/Merial Manual for Pet Health
$17 Merck Publishing and Merial, 2007, 1300 pages

The Merck Veterinary Manual has long been the standard guide found in most veterinarian's back offices. Vets are required to serve the needs of many animals, not just one, and so this venerable book is their operating manual for lesser known species. It also serves as a reminder for uncommon ailments in the common species of pets. Recently Merck/Merial has published a one-volume paper-bound home edition of the Vet Manual. It is less technical, but still remarkably deep, and by far the best pan-species health guide for pets. It is often even better than many single pet health guides.

Besides the expected dogs, cats, and horses, it covers the health needs of rabbits, rodents, ferrets, birds, reptiles, and exotics such as pot-bellied pigs and sugar gliders. At 1,300 pages, it's an old-fashioned book, but intelligently designed, and easy to browse and study.

This book won't eliminate visits to the vet, but it will reduce their number, and make you smarter when you do visit. The real value of a pan-animal tome like this is when you take charge of an unfamiliar animal. It also gave us confidence to adopt pets we hitherto knew little about.

-- KK

Ssscaredy cat trainer
SSSCat Cat Training Aid
$22 innotek.net

This terrific product is perfect for dealing with minor stubborn behavior in your cat. I didn't like our cat going up on the counter behind our kitchen sink to look out the window, but every time I went outside, there she was laughing at me. I tried many different deterrents, but she was like the Borg from Star Trek. She would just adapt. SSSCat solved the problem.

SSSCat is a can of compressed air (like for cleaning the dust out of your keyboard), but with a motion sensor that sprays when the cat gets near. It doesn't harm or hurt the cat in any way, but it does condition them to avoid the area where the SSSCat has been.

We've also used it outside of our bedroom door to prevent the cat from persistently meowing and jumping up at the door in the wee hours of the morning.

The can of compressed air the unit comes with is about half the capacity of the cans you get for dusting keyboards. After it ran out, I found that I could use the keyboard duster cans. Just popped the trigger off the keyboard duster and attached the SSSCat nozzle.

-- Bill Dorfmann

Cat hair remover
Love Glove
$6 fourpaws.com

With three cats in the house, fur gets all over our furniture and clothes. I bought a Love Glove to attack the problem at its source – on the cats.

The Love Glove looks like an oven mitt. The palm side is covered with rubber nubs. To use it, you simply pet your cat. The loose fur comes off and sticks to the glove. It's easy to peel off. My cats go into throes of ecstasy when I use the Love Glove on them. They even get excited just seeing me approach them with the glove on my hand.

-- Mark Frauenfelder

Dog Care

No more taut leads
Premier Gentle Leader

$12 Amazon

I have had the Premier Gentle Leader Headcollar for about a year now. We have a somewhat rambunctious Bearded Collie (which is to say, a typical Bearded Collie). And whenever we walked him he would go somewhat bananas pulling at the leash or jumping off in random directions no matter

what we tried: treats, collars, harnesses, even that "CHHHHT!" noise that Cesar Millan recommends. Nothing kept him consistently manageable.

The Gentle Leader, on the other hand, just works. It is some sort of black magic from the Animal Gods.

I went from a leash that was as tight as piano wire on most walks, requiring a lot of upper body strength to keep our 45lb Beardie in check, to a pretty much completely slack leash — allowing a much more leisurely, less tiring, and more enjoyable walk.

-- Steve Coallier

The headcollar uses a nose loop and a neck strap. The nose loop encircles the dog's muzzle in the same way a "pack leader" gently but firmly grasps a subordinate's muzzle in his mouth, giving the dog a clear signal that you are the leader. The neck strap puts pressure on the back of the neck, working with the dog's "opposition reflex," the natural instinct of dogs to push against pressure rather than move away. Thus the dog instinctively leans

back against the pressure, putting an end to leash pulling. The literature that comes with the collar claims that most dogs respond with a dramatic change in behavior in less than 10 minutes. I can attest to this. Our dog Maroon gave a few good tugs, bucked a few times and then began walking calmly beside me, not once pulling.

-- Michele McGinnis

Remote control stimulation for canines
Innotek Dog Training Collar

$120 Innotek

I no longer apologize for using this "shock collar." Not only has it potentially saved our dog Jolie's life on at least two occasions, but it has given us a measure of security and Jolie a degree of freedom that wouldn't be possible otherwise.

We adopted Jolie as a young adult and while she quickly learned "sit", "stay", "down", etc., she would not respond to "Come!" in the park amid the distraction of scents and dogs. We tried everything: two series of training classes, a personal trainer, and an armload of dog training books. To no avail Jolie would NOT come. Her rescue group suggested an electric collar and loaned us the Innotek collar (one of its volunteers met with us for a training session). Within one afternoon, Jolie was coming when called - and it took only a couple of weeks until we no longer had to activate the stimulation on the collar to reinforce the command.

The system works like this: the collar has a receiver on it with two stimulation-delivering prongs that fit snugly against the dog's neck or throat, depending on how the collar is positioned. The human carries a transmitter (about the size/weight of a deck of cards), which will deliver stimulation at a range of up to 300 yards.

The dog must first know the command you want. It won't work if the dog does not know what you are asking of her. Once you are sure the dog knows what you want (we found that Jolie would "come" indoors but not outside), give the "Come!" command. When the dog doesn't come, immediately say (shout!) "No!" while simultaneously pressing the "tone warning" on the transmitter. This will cause the collar to make a quiet beep the dog can hear. Again, try the "Come!" command. If the dog doesn't come, immediately say "No!" while simultaneously pressing one of the stimulation buttons on the transmitter to deliver the shock. You can choose "momentary" to deliver a brief, pre-measured tap or "continuous" which delivers stimulation for up to 10 seconds. Call "Come!" one last time -- either after the tap or during the continuous stimulation -- and this should get the dog on her way. As soon as the dog starts to come, stop the stimulation and immediately begin to praise her. If she gets distracted on her way, she gets another "No!" accompanied with more stimulation. As soon as she complies, the stimulation stops and she gets lavish praise.

This sequence of commands and activations is fast. At the start, you will have more difficulty fumbling with the buttons and timing than your dog will have responding to the collar. The stimulation level (controlled by the transmitter) ranges from 1 - 7. It usually takes a 3 to reinforce the "Come!" command with Jolie. Only on two occasions did I have to go higher and that was when she was in hot pursuit of a cat. Imagine the relief I felt as she was heading full speed, headlong toward the street and was stopped in mid-flight by a jolt from her collar.

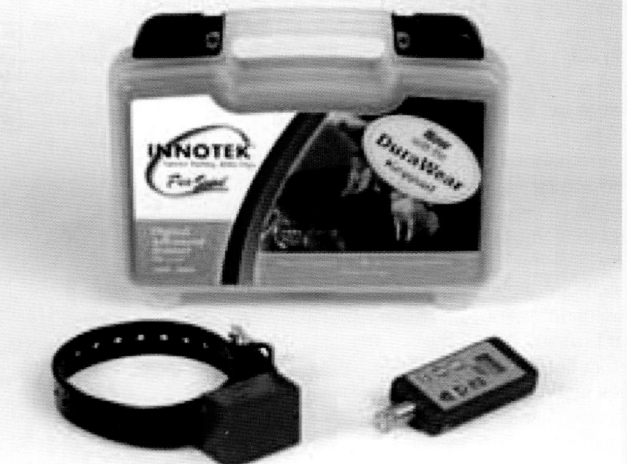

We've now been using the collar for 8 months. Only very rarely do we need to deliver stimulation as reinforcement. Almost every time, she comes on command. For those rare times she doesn't come right away, usually a tone or "No!" will get her moving in the right direction. I'm not exactly sure how the dog knows to come when she receives stimulation, but I'm guessing it's the quick, consistent, and proximal combination of negative stimulation and positive praise.

I have tested the collar on my wrist (not neck) on all levels (I also taste new dog food and treats). The collar goes up to Level 7. It's hard to describe the differences in the shock experienced as I have no experiential gauge. I touched an electric fence once at the zoo when I was 10, but that's about it. Level 3-5 give me an involuntary jump reaction. They are uncomfortable. But the discomfort or pain of an electrical shock is different from other types of pain. As soon as the shock stops, so does the pain. Level's 6&7 are very uncomfortable, in a startling, well, shocking way. As I said, we've only gone to that level couple of times. It made her leap into the air. I'm sure it was painful, shocking. But when I compare it to the pain and trauma of getting run over (remember, she was in hot pursuit of a cat), or getting away from us and fighting with another dog (she's a pit bull, she'd win) I'd do it again.

The loaner collar from the rescue agency was not working properly (it had been submerged in the ocean and would not consistently deliver stimulation - even though the collars are supposed to be waterproof). We decided to purchase the same brand and model due to its good reputation in the dog training industry and its low price compared to its main competitors (we bought ours on eBay for $100). Our collar has gotten fully wet and continues to work perfectly.

-- Michele McGinnis

Although the Innotek Training Collar is no longer available, the Petsafe PDT00-12470 is comparable. It has positive and negative tones, and a 400 yard range. It's also the highest rated dog training collar on Amazon. *-- KK*

No tangle two dog leash
Double Dog Leash

$7+ Add A Dog Couplers Super Leash

This leash lets us walk the two dogs simultaneously with no tangles. Thanks to the riveted connectors, they can cross back and forth to their hearts' content, with no adjustment necessary on our part.

It looks like several companies make these, but I couldn't find a link for the exact kind we use. This one promises its version can accommodate three or more dogs.

-- John Endicott

Highly natural pet foods
Wysong

$41 32-Pound Case Amazon

The Wysong line of pet foods was started by veterinarian Randy Wysong, a long-time critic of the pet food industry. Wysong foods are specifically designed to optimize health, not simply meet regulatory standards. Their ingredients are made from fresh meats and non-processed living foods. They are additive free and use only natural preservation. A diet of Wysong pet food is only part of the philosophy of Wysong's Optimal Health Program. According to the program, a diet of hunted, raw prey is the healthy ideal for carnivores. At the unhealthy end of the diet spectrum would be generic foods alone. And in between these extremes are various combinations of Wysong foods, supplements, nutritional supports, and raw and cooked foods.

I've tried many brands of generic, premium, and high end "healthy" pet foods over the years. Wysong is simply the best. Whether or not you subscribe to Wysong's philosophy or follow its optimal health pyramid, its maintenance diets (just the dry food alone without the supplements, supports, raw & cooked foods) have made a discernible difference in our dogs' health. There is a noticeable improvement in coat health – their coats are much smoother and shinier whereas before Wysong they were more coarse and dull. However, the most significant difference has been with our dog, Maroon. For six years, he suffered from an undiagnosed gastric upset that caused him to vomit several times per week. Since switching to Wysong Senior almost 1 year ago, his vomiting has stopped completely.

Wysong can be purchased at most stores selling pet food products and online from Wysong. A 40 lb box of food costs $40 at my local pet store.

-- Michele McGinnis

Basic canine care
Dog First Aid
$17 American Red Cross, 2008, 116 p.

If you're caring for a multitude of critters, the previously-reviewed *Merck/Merial Manual For Pet Health* is essential. If you've never had a dog or, for whatever reason, never took the time to do your due diligence, the Red Cross' *Dog First Aid* is an excellent primer and quick emergency guide worth reviewing and keeping handy. Beyond the basics of general care, the guide provides short, clear instructions and photos (plus a DVD) on how to diagnose and tackle everything from choking, pad wounds, anal sac swelling (it happens), constipation, bite wounds, burns and ear infections to frostbite, electric shock (cord bites), parasites and the more esoteric afflictions you hope never to see, like "rectal prolapse." There's also a checklist and instructions on how to assemble the ultimate first aid kit (the list is much longer than I would have imagined).

Our best buddy's been with us for five years and — *knock wood* — we've had only one serious emergency, which luckily happened outside the vet's office: anaphylactic shock due to an allergy. As time passes, of course, the chances of potential emergencies and health issues will inevitably increase. I know the little dude appreciates our preparedness.

-- *Steven Leckart*

Nails (Broken or Torn Toenails)

What You Can Do.

If the nail is bleeding, apply styptic powder to the area… You can also try applying direct pressure to the nail with a piece of gauze or clean cloth for 5 minutes. If you do not have these items available, try the following:

1. Take a bar of soap and push it into the bleeding nail, or apply flour or cornstarch to the area with firm pressure for 5 minutes.

2. If you are not successful, wrap the paw (See Pad Wounds, page 89.) After bandaging the paw, transport your dog to a veterinary hospital.

If you are able to stop the bleeding at home, wait 1 day (to make sure you do not disturb the clot that has formed) then soak the paw in warm water and a saline solution to help it heal. Monitor the site for infection, as evidenced by swelling, pain, redness and reluctance to put weight on the paw. If any of these signs appear, take your dog to a veterinarian.

●

Tourniquet Technique

Use only on limbs — never place a tourniquet on the neck!

1. Wrap a strip of cloth or gauze (about 2 inches wide) twice around the limb above the bleeding area. DO NOT MAKE A KNOT.

2. Tighten the gauze or cloth by wrapping each end around a rigid object, such as a stick.

3. Turn the stick slowly and just enough to stop blood flow. Write the time on a piece of tape on the tourniquet.

4. Loosen the tie for several seconds at least every 10 minutes to help avoid permanent tissue damage.

5. Be aware that the interrupted blood supply may cause your dog to lose the limb.

6. Take your dog to a veterinarian immediately.

Good behavior training leash
Gentle Leader Headcollar
$13 gentleleader.com

As a dog owner of many years, I've trained my own dogs to walk nicely at heel. I've escaped receiving that "are you walking that dog or is he walking you" look from passerbys. Enter Maroon, my housemate's dog. He is 85 lbs of pure force pulling on the leash. On weekends, when I have the choice of whether or not to take him on an outing, I find myself declining to have him along because I just didn't want to fight him the whole time. Out of desperation, I finally decided to try the Gentle Leader Headcollar. I'd seen them frequently on other dogs, but they looked so wimpy. I was wrong ...this leash is unbelievable. It has changed our lives.

The headcollar uses a nose loop and a neck strap. The nose loop encircles the dog's muzzle in the same way a "pack leader" gently but firmly grasps a subordinate's muzzle in his mouth, giving the dog a clear signal that you are the leader. The neck strap puts pressure on the back of the neck, working with the dog's "opposition reflex," the natural instinct of dogs to push against pressure rather

Dogs as transportation
Black Ice Dog Sledding Equipment
$45 #HS62 blackicedogsledding.com

Dogs for locomotion. Esoteric, but durable dog sledding gear, and apparatus for dog carts.

-- *KK*

Weight Pull Harnesses

These are the harnesses you need for hauling heavy loads or for weight pulling competitions. Sewn with competitive weight pulling in mind, they are strong and durable harnesses designed for a dog's safety and comfort while working. Each harness is made of wide, heavy-duty nylon webbing to better distribute the work load and thick padding for extra comfort. The hardwood spreader bar prevents side straps from pressing against the dog's hind legs. The sturdy 1-1/2 inch stainless steel attachment ring allows for easy

Best haircutting tool for dogs
Master Grooming Tools
$31 petedge.com

I've used this tool, for about 6-months on a long-haired Chow/Labrador mix and on a Corgi. They both shed like crazy and the undercoat is a serious challenge with the Chow. This grooming tool takes care of the undercoat like nothing I've ever used. It's also apparently less painful for the dogs, as it doesn't have the tendency to dig straight in like the previously reviewed Furminator, which I liked well enough before trying this one.

I have the 16-blade version. It gets down deep and pulls the undercoat and dander OUT. The blades are much more robust than the Furminator, and there's no chance of bending. It's a VERY well-built device, and the rubber handle looks weird but feels good in the hand. I can't think of a single improvement I'd make.

I will say that the first time you use this tool, try not to be too ambitious. It took three or four sessions with my chow (an outside dog, and it had been awhile) before I got all the lumps of undercoat off him. Not because the tool was rough with him, but just that he had so much to remove. The Corgi was done in one session, and despite her shorter hair, this tool removed huge volume of fur. Her haunches are very thick, but this tool goes right through it without the tearing I'd been so careful to avoid with the Furminator.

Now, both my dogs love this thing. When I'm working on one, the other dog comes up to pester me so he gets a turn. Once the major de-undercoating is done, it's a simple matter to use this weekly or as-needed to keep things fluffy. Both dogs really look forward to their grooming.

-- *Bill Womack*

than move away. Thus the dog instinctively leans back against the pressure, putting an end to leash pulling. The literature that comes with the collar claims that most dogs respond with a dramatic change in behavior in less than 10 minutes. I can attest to this. Our dog Maroon gave a few good tugs, bucked a few times and then began walking calmly beside me, not once pulling.

I'ts been a couple of months since we started using the Gentle Leader. Maroon is pulling a bit more than he did at first, but I'm convinced that is due to inconsistent and sometimes incorrect handling techniques that arise when more than one person in the household share in dog walking duties. And even with a slight amount of pulling he is easily managed and controlled and no longer a source of unhappy person or dog. The main thing is I no longer dread the nightly walk, and Maroon is now welcome on special outings. The pet store owner who raved about it and sold it to me said, "A happy person makes a happy dog."

-- *Michele McGinnis*

drawing not to scale

hookups. These harnesses meet IWPA, ISDRA and AMCA requirements for weight pull competition. Although built to tough competition standards, these harnesses are also one of the most comfortable and durable harnesses available for recreational use. They are excellent harnesses for all forms of pulling, although the lower point of attachment does not lend itself readily to skijoring.

Always handy tick remover
Tick Key
$6 Amazon

Though I wish my dog's tick prevention worked 100% of the time, it just doesn't. The Tick Key makes the unpleasant task of removing ticks much easier. I purchased the key shaped tool a year ago after noticing it by the cash register at my local outdoor store. All I do is align the larger end of the key's opening over the tick, draw the tool toward the narrow part of the opening, and the little sucker just pops right out. My favorite canine, who always dreaded our approach with tweezers and made tick extraction an exercise in fortitude and contortionism, is not bothered by this method at all.

-- *Amy Reavey*

Dogproof chew toy
Hol-ee Roller
$8 Amazon

A friend gave my dog this ball in January, and my dog and I like it so much that I have since started to phase-out other dog toys. It is durable. My dog is a strong chewer, and has destroyed many a lesser toy. It is attractive. Who doesn't love a geodesic dome? It is light and squishy, bouncing off objects denser balls would damage. It is large. This might not seem important, but my dog has been known to attempt furniture disassembly while attempting to retrieve a ball that has rolled under the sofa. Despite its size, it is easy to pick up. Dogs can chomp on a vertex, and I can hook it with a finger. Touching it is not disgusting. Despite its size, it has little surface area to get slimy. And no tennis ball fuzz.

-- *Jonathan Harford*

It's a goofy cliche to say outdoor cooking stirs in men some sort of cellular caveman memory about fire and roasting Mastodon shanks or whatever. But given how firmly the obsession has taken hold of me, there may be something there. I grill at least three times a week, from as early in the spring as possible until I have to start scraping ice just to get cooking. People kept telling me I had to get Steven Raichlen's *How To Grill*, so to kick off this year's grilling season, I bought it. Now I know why people rave. It's not only the best grilling book I've seen, but it's probably one of the best cookbooks in print. Beautifully designed with great recipes, step-by-step photos and useful marginalia. Warning: Raichlen puts butter or oil on everything, even steak. Beyond meat, there are lots of recipes for grilled veggies and even grilled deserts.

-- Gareth Branwyn

The pros use the poke test to gauge the desired degree of doness: A quick poke of the meat with your finger will tell you whether it's rare, medium, or

(heaven forbid) well-done. Use the following guide to help you, but remember: A steak will continue cooking even after it comes off the grill.

● "Bizarre" and "outrageous" aren't necessarily words you expect to find in a cookbook. But how else would you describe roasting a chicken in a vertical position over an open beer can? I first encountered the method at the Memphis in May Barbecue Festival and described it in *The Barbecue! Bible*. Since then, I've prepared beer-can chicken hundreds of times, and each time this astounding technique produces an exquisite bird. The fact is, the upright position helps drain off the fat, and crisp the skin, while the beer in the can steams and flavors the bird from the inside. Needless to say, the sight of a roasted chicken standing erect on an upright can of beer will astound your guests.

 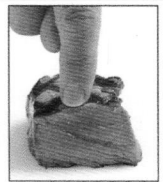  

VERY RARE STEAK (a.k.a. still mooing): The meat is bloodred in the center and barely warm. The steak will feel soft and squishy to the touch.

RARE STEAK: The meat is red in the center and warmish hot. The steak will feel soft to the touch.

MEDIUM-RARE STEAK: The meat is pinkish red in the center and hot. The steak will be gently yielding to the touch.

MEDIUM STEAK: The meat will be pink in the center and quite hot. The steak will yield only slightly to the touch.

MEDIUM-WELL STEAK: The meat will be mostly graybrown in the center, with only a trace of pink. The steak will feel firm to the touch.

WELL-DONE STEAK: The meat will be uniformly graybrown and will feel almost hard to the touch.

From BBQ to chef
How to Grill
$14 Amazon

The best way to start a charcoal barbecue
Weber Rapidfire Chimney Charcoal Starter
$15 Model 7416 weber.com

No need to buy charcoal lighter fluid (or "boy scout water" as they call it in my home state of Colorado) or self-starting charcoal briquets. Just put two crumpled sheets of newspaper in the bottom chamber of this metal chimney and add briquets (I buy the large bags at Trader Joe's for $7 each) to the top. Light the newspaper with a match and go back into the kitchen to prepare food for grilling. In 20 minutes the briquets will be cherry red and ready to use. Once you use this you'll wonder how you grilled without it. Take a look at the insanely happy Amazon reviews (4.9 star average with over 800 reviews.)

-- Mark Frauenfelder

High-powered nautical BBQ
Solaire Anywhere Portable Infrared Grill
$345 Amazon

The Solaire Anywhere Portable Infrared Grill is a full-sized, no-compromises top-quality grill wrapped up in a super-portable package. This grill is small in size, but not cooking power; it puts out 14,000 BTUs, nearly twice what is typical for portable grills. The secret is that instead of conventional burners, it uses a ceramic infrared grid that heats in seconds (full-blast in less than three minutes), cooks in a flash, and cools down in about 15 minutes with no coals to dispose of. It uses 1-lb. propane bottles or a 20-lb. tank with optional adaptor. It can also be converted for use with natural gas.

The grill's surface area may seem small (155-sq. inches), but food cooks so fast, it will handle a meal for four without any trouble. The unit is super easy to clean: The burner self-cleans if you let it run on high for a few minutes after everything is off the grill — anything on the burner simply vaporizes. Both the grilling grate and burner easily lift out, allowing for easy wipe-down of the steel housing. Best of all, the Solaire is elegantly designed and ruggedly built for a lifetime of use. The basic unit is made from commercial-grade 304 stainless steel; there's also a marine-grade version in 316 stainless.

Mine is 21"x12"x 3", including the carrying handles, and weighs 20 lbs. with the carry bag. The Solaire is designed for RV-ers, car-campers, tailgaters and boaters. It also has some nice accessories: Car-campers will like the collapsible tripod base, while boaters should check out the gimbaled deck rail clamp.

The only hitch is cost: At $285-$400 the Solaire is more expensive than other portable grills. But as our parents told us, sometimes spending a bit extra on quality saves money (and grief) in the long term.

-- Paul Saffo

Classic, cast iron cooking
Lodge Hibachi Grill
$70 Amazon

The first time I saw one of these finely crafted grills was on a ranch I visited back in the late '70s. They've changed very little over time: the one I have now that is a few years old is essentially the same as the first one I saw almost 30 years ago. Being cast iron, it absorbs and retains heat, radiating it evenly, so the whole stove is part of the heat source — not just the coals.

It's cast iron instead of stamped tin or steel, so it's heavy, but substantially built. And it's a hibachi, not a lidded grill, so it's not a smoker. It is small enough to put in the trunk or chuck box and take camping, or to use on the patio (about 20" x 10" x 9" and the legs lift the bottom about 4 inches off the ground). But what I like best is it fits in the fireplace, so you

can grill in wet or cold weather indoors.

It is lower in profile than most charcoal grills, but about twice as big as most hibachis. If you are cooking for 8 or more people, obviously it will stretch its capabilities, but for the two of us or when we have a couple of friends over for kabobs, it can't be beat. It is just about perfect for a couple or small family.

The grate you place the food on is not welded wire — it is cast iron like the rest, so the cross pieces are as wide as the slots in between. They hold food well, hold heat well, and when you sear your food, you can see the wide dark sears on the food. The grate is also strong enough to hold pots, pans, coffee pots, etc., — thus, it can function as a small stove.

There is a door that opens down on the front to add coals or help the dampers to adjust the heat. The damper doors adjust by sliding side to side so you can adjust the draft perfectly. The grill disassembles for cleaning. It's only four parts: the base with the front door, pin-hinged at the bottom, the top grate, the bottom grate, and the sliding damper.

Again, the lower grate the coals rest on is cast iron, so it won't burn out or warp over time. The whole grill is really well made. I burned out several imported hibachis before getting this grill. It should last a lifetime.

-- Rick Shannon

Compact travel BBQ
Tool Box Grill
$72 Amazon

The Tool Box Grill is the best portable, tabletop barbecue grill we've ever owned. This gas-powered grill is a good size and is easy to use anywhere (we are full-time RVer's). The handle on top makes it easy to carry, the grill is very stable, and there are no vents in the bottom, meaning no greasy mess (there's a built-in grease tray, too) and the grill doesn't dirty up the compartment where we store it. The grill heats up quickly (I mostly cook with medium heat, sometimes low), but is completely cool and ready to store by the time the meal is finished, and it closes up quick just like a tool box. We used the less expensive charcoal model several years ago and switched to gas when it became available (no ash to empty out after).

-- Gwen H.

cooking ranges. The elite brands like Viking or Wolf were in the $7,000 range for a 6-burner. Worse, their recent reputations for quality, service and dependability were in decline. (No appliance is without horror stories; missing were sufficient new testimonials about great satisfaction to counterbalance accounts of the awful; the higher the premium, the higher the ratio should be.) In the hunt for an alternative pro quality stove, we settled on a Blue Star stove, which was significantly cheaper yet had great user reviews and a big enthusiastic following online. Blue Star is a newcomer with several advantages for us.

First its large open burners produce really high BTUs. I had hacked our previous stove to increase the heat by drilling larger orifices in the brass gas jets, but Blue Star's high-heat burners came already engineered for a maximum flame of 22,000 BTUs. (Typical high burners are only 15K.) It could also simmer great. Second, the circular burner design features a ring which can easily lift out so that a

High performance stove
Blue Star Range
BlueStar

When we remodeled our kitchen we were shocked at the prices for professional quality

wok (which needs super high heat) can seat perfectly near the jets. Thirdly, the dials are analog, no fancy electronics to fail. Fourthly, the cast iron grate above the burners forms a single uninterrupted plane so pots can be slid around easily, like a second work surface. Lastly, you have a choice of 200 custom colors for the stove. We went with a yellow to brighten up the kitchen. We've been using the Blue Star for a year and a half and really love the craftsmanship and intelligent placement of knobs, trays, switches. It's super easy to keep clean as well.

There are plenty of far less expensive stoves that cook food. We'd been using one of those for years. In aiming for a life-time purchase of a high performing stove, with great user design, we found Blue Star offered the most for less compared to other high-end stove brands.

-- KK

Classic ceramic smoker
Big Green Egg

$630 (medium) Big Green Egg

The Big Green Egg is an awesome-looking ceramic smoker with amazing heat retention. Modeled after the ceramic kamado pots used in Japan, the "BGE" has been around since the 70's, but has developed a rabid fan base in recent years (They call themselves "eggheads"). It's easy to see why people love them. The BGE gets to temperature in 10 minutes, allows a bag of charcoal to last for 6 months, and can cook from 150-700F. Thus, it enables proper smoking and grilling, where the flavor gets right into the meat.

The top and bottom halves feature a felt seal that's virtually airtight; the only holes are a variable intake vent at the bottom front and a variable exhaust. With the combination of these vents you can vary and maintain the temperature to around 25 degrees of accuracy within that 150-700F range. This keeps all the smoke and heat inside, while also limiting the amount of fuel burned. Like an oven, the ceramic doesn't develop hot spots, so the cooking is completely even and food stays moist and juicy (We've had awesome pulled pork, ribs and steaks).

With the right accessory, you can also use the BGE as a clay oven for cooking pizza, tandoori and even pies. We have the XL BGE, which is massive enough for smoking 15 chickens at once! The smaller BGEs are cheaper, of course, though not cheap. Still, you can basically do everything on a BGE that you can on a regular grill. Our old bbq and BGE sit side-by-side on our back patio; these days, we only use the BGE.

-- Matt Field

Dirt cheap art oven
Build Your Own Earth Oven
$14 Kido Denzer, 2007 (3rd edition), 132 pages

My friend has built several of these. It's art you use. Take clay dirt, water, and imagination. If you make a mistake, you just smash it and start over. Many in the world still bake their bread in these.

-- KK

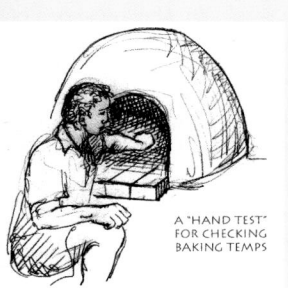

A "HAND TEST" FOR CHECKING BAKING TEMPS

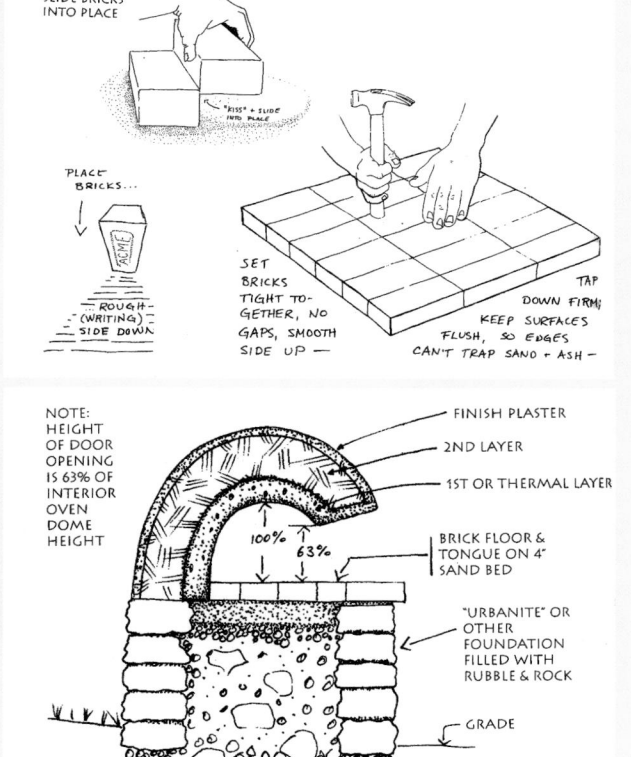

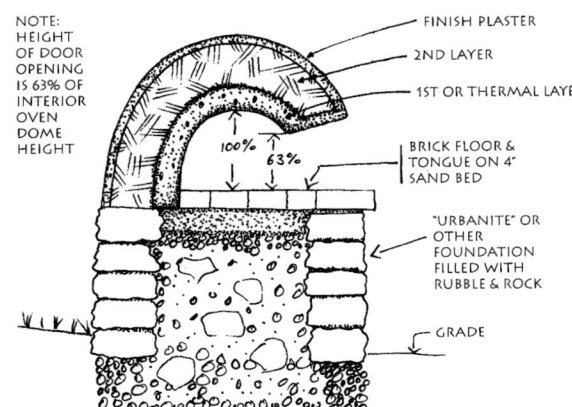

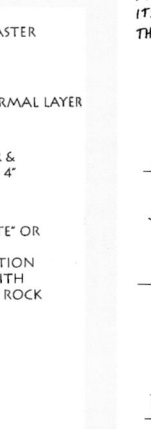

Onion Bag Scrubbing Hack

Everyone knows the worst part about baking bread: Having to clean up the sticky, floury mess from counter tops, bowls, and utensils. The gluey mass refuses to come out of sponges, and gums up anything it touches.

I recently discovered a solution: The netting that onions and other vegetables come packaged in. By cutting up the stiff netting into about 6-inch squares you can make reusable super scrubbing tools. A few bags will produce more than you'll need. When you're finished scrubbing, just rinse off the gunk, recycle the netting, and marvel at your flour- and cheese-free sponges.

-- Pen Duby

Compact portable hot plate
Butane Burner
$25 Amazon

These stoves are great for backyard cooking, partying, tailgating, car camping, and/or power outages. They're too big for most backpacking, but for most other uses they're much more convenient than larger propane and or liquid fuel stoves. They come in their own lunch box sized plastic or nylon carrying case. The hairspray-sized butane canister is contained within the stove instead of sticking out on the side like most propane stoves, and it just drops in. They all have piezoelectric ignition. Most models are dirt cheap. I bought mine at Target a few years ago for $30, but Big 5 had them on sale for $16 a few weeks ago.

-- Bruce Bowen

These handy stoves, good for one-room studios, huts, and emergency use can be found at Asian grocery stores, which also sell the butane fuel cans. Quality varies tremendously among "brands", but this $25 version gets good reviews on Amazon.

-- KK

Quality entry level smoker
Brinkmann Electric Water Smoker
$105 Amazon

I have used at least a half-dozen of these watersmokers for the past forty years. They hold up well, and the flavor options they provide are unique. I recommend this electric model from Brinkmann. Cooking times are often six or more hours, and can vary significantly when using charcoal, especially if the smoker is full or if it rains.

Once you have started it, it should not be opened except through the side to add hickory or fruitwood sticks. Opening the lid loses you a half hour of cooking time. A second standard charcoal BBQ grill is a great accent – water smoke until almost done then just finish off to taste on the BBQ.

Rust can be an issue because you are cooking with water, heat and smoke. Luckily, the most important parts are stainless steel, and for everything else Brinkmann makes replacements.

If you've got a few ugly pots laying around you can use them to cook a pot roast in the smoker, too. For that matter, Brinkmann includes a cookbook with all the recipes you'll ever need.

-- David C. Clark

Baking Bread

Best guide to artisan bread making
The Bread Baker's Apprentice
$20 Peter Reinhart 2001, 304 p.

New to bread-making, I've been looking for a great guide. I found and fell in love with Peter Reinhart's book. It has beautiful photographs, and has motivated me to experiment. I'm now one-third of the way through baking every formula in the book. His explanations are very clear. He includes enough theory, which allows me to make my own informed decisions about baking different styles of bread. It is not rocket science, but there are a lot of non-intuitive details he covers well. Needless to say, all this teaching has elevated the quality of my own breads. He also provides detailed recipes for each type of bread he describes, so those who are uninterested in the fundamentals can still bake quite easily. When I got the book, about the only thing my breads had going for them was that they were "homemade." Now I like my breads just as much or more than the expensive artisan-style breads I buy at my local bakeries.

-- Christopher R. Carlson

Some masters are great at craft, and some at teaching, and every once in a while a person like Peter Reinhart comes along who is grand master of both. This book is considered the best all around guide to making fancy and rustic artisan breads; some would say for making any bread, period. Grounded in theory and practice, it is superb teaching.

-- KK

• It is easy to see the subtle difference in color and texture of various flours when they are placed side by side. These are, from left to right, cornmeal, semolina flour (coarse durum), fancy durum, dark rye, white rye, bleached cake flour, unbleached pastry flour, unbleached bread flour, clear flour, and whole-wheat flour.

• For perspective, here are the twelve stages in order:

1. Mise En Place ("everything in its place" is the organizing principle)

2. Mixing (in which three important requirements must be met)

3. Primary Fermentation (also called bulk fermentation, in which most of the flavor is determined)

4. Punching Down (also called de-gassing, in which the dough begins to enter its secondary fermentation and individuation)

5. Dividing (in which pieces are weighed or scaled, while continuing to ferment)

6. Rounding (in which the pieces are given an interim shaping prior to their final shape)

7. Benching (also called resting, or intermediate proofing, during which time the gluten relaxes)

8. Shaping and Panning (in which the dough is given its final shape prior to baking)

9. Proofing (also called secondary or final fermentation, in which the dough is leavened to its appropriate baking size)

10. Baking (which may also include scoring the dough and steaming, but in which three vital oven actions must occur)

11. Cooling (which is really an extension of baking but must occur before cutting into the bread)

12. Storing and Eating (in production baking it's primarily storing, but home baking usually emphasizes, ahem, eating)

No-Knead Bread
$30 Dutch Oven Amazon
Free Bread Resource Breadtopia.com
Free No-Knead Bread Recipe New York Times

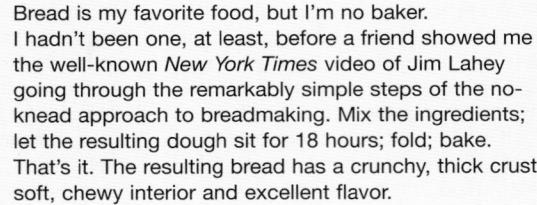

Bread is my favorite food, but I'm no baker. I hadn't been one, at least, before a friend showed me the well-known *New York Times* video of Jim Lahey going through the remarkably simple steps of the no-knead approach to breadmaking. Mix the ingredients; let the resulting dough sit for 18 hours; fold; bake. That's it. The resulting bread has a crunchy, thick crust, soft, chewy interior and excellent flavor.

No-knead bread is baking for nonbakers, perhaps also for skilled bakers too busy to bother with more labor-intensive approaches. This process requires so little effort but yields a beautiful, satisfying, delicious creation. It's really not much harder than making toast.

Since learning this technique, I've begun baking bread at least twice a week, finding the process as fun as it is a pleasure not having to buy inferior bread from the market. I've also used resources such as Breadtopia.com to refine my recipe and experiment with different ingredients. It's given me the confidence to try more complex recipes.

Most, if not all, of the fundamental baking tools necessary for making no-knead bread will likely already be around your kitchen. If not, Breadtopia is one of many sources for the tools you'll need to give it a try. I use a

Lodge cast iron Dutch oven that's been in the family for ages, a very cool tool. The web offers many resources regarding no-knead breadmaking, but the *NYT* video is the best I've seen, especially as a starting point for novices, thanks to its utter simplicity.

-- Elon Schoenholz

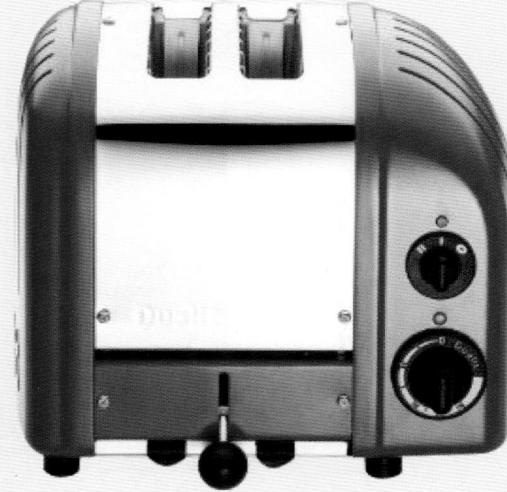

Ultimate analog toaster
Dualit Toaster

We have had a Dualit toaster for the past 5 or 6 years, and to this day, it works perfectly. My parents have had their Dualit toaster for at least 15 years, and it still works perfectly, too. These machines are manually-operated with levers (to move the bread up or into the toaster slots as it doesn't pop up with a spring), switches (to choose whether you have one or more of the slots heating) and dials (the clockwork timer to decide how long you want the elements to remain on), so there is nothing to go wrong, digitally. And if the heating element fails (something I've never heard

of it doing), they are easily replaceable. The toaster we own is a 2-slice unit. You can also get them in 4-slice units, and you can purchase a basket for sandwich making that fits into the nice, wide slots for the toast slices. We have this sandwich basket, and use it often.

The Dualit isn't a cheap toaster, but it's well worth the investment. When our last "normal" toaster quit several years ago, my wife refused to purchase another until we could afford the Dualit. While they normally ran about $200 for the 2-slot unit, she found one on clearance in Kitchenkaboodle, and snatched up the last one they had. We've never looked back, and we've never regretted our purchase. The only thing my wife says she'd change is that, if it had been available on clearance, she would have purchased a red one. As it is, ours is dark blue. It still looks great!

Beware of look-alike imitations! If it's got spring-loaded slots, it ain't a Dualit!

-- Adam Morris

$210 (2 slice) Amazon $340 (4 slice) Amazon

No-knead bread on your schedule
Artisan Bread in Five
$17 Jeff Hertzberg, Zoe Francois, 2007, 242 p.

As a practical guide to incorporating No-Knead Bread baking into daily life, regardless of your schedule, I highly recommend *Artisan Bread in Five Minutes a Day* and the follow-up *Healthy Bread in Five Minutes a Day*. I've been baking from the instructions in this book for some time now, and now I hardly ever buy commercial bread. My young ones love the bread, especially warm from the oven, and there's something special about bringing your own fresh baked bread to a get-together.

This is literally five minutes of effort. Throw the ingredients together, mix, pop the dough into a bucket and then into the fridge. After a couple hours of rising, I have enough for three big loaves. The dough keeps very well in the refrigerator for a couple weeks (and tastes noticeably better the longer it's been sitting,

though mine rarely makes it that long). When I want fresh bread I pull out a bit of dough, get the oven heated up and bake away. There are plenty of no-knead recipes about, but Jeff Hertzberg and Zoe Francois perfected a process that works for me. The main advantage I've gotten out of *Healthy Bread in Five Minutes a Day* is feeding the kids a bit more whole grain and some protein as well. I find the flavor richer, too (beer helps that a bunch, but also subtracts a few healthy points). I do prefer the texture of the white loaf, and for guests or as a host gift, I'd likely choose the original recipe. Of late, our everyday breadbox loaf comes from the *Healthy* book. Slices, toasted a bit, make a heavenly sandwich.

-- Angus Long

• **Yeast Love to Keep Cool**

Jefferson University yeast biochemist Hannah Silver, Ph.D., loves great bread, and bakes her own with our method. We asked her where the great flavor comes from, especially with dough that has aged a few days: "Yeast extracts are sometimes used as a flavor enhancer in commercial food, and they introduce a savory, complex flavor, sometimes called umami, the so-called fifth basic taste recognized by the human tongue (in addition to sweet, salty, bitter, and sour). The flavor you get with stored dough comes from chemicals produced by yeast as they use sugars and starches to make carbon dioxide gas (which forms bubbles to leaven the bread) and alcohol (which boils off in baking).

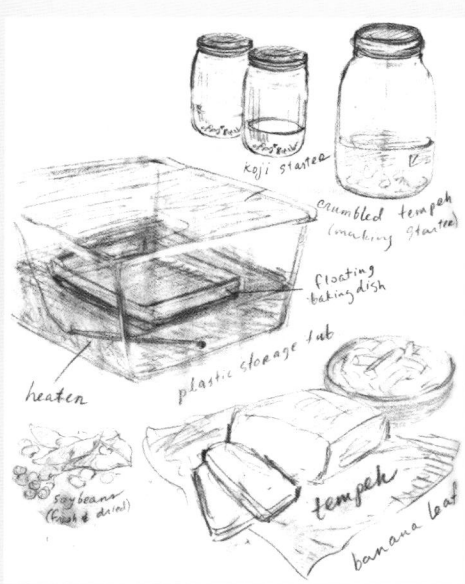

Fermented food cookbook
Art of Fermentation
$26 Sandor Katz, 2012, 528p.

Yogurt, bread, beer, kimchi, wine, cheese, miso, kraut, and vinegar are among the many foods produced with the aid of microorganisms. Those are living beasties of a type that we ordinarily try to remove from what we eat. This cookbook is full of fermentation recipes. It presents a unified theory of "live-culture foods," a way of connecting their different methods in order to understand why fermentation is a Good Thing, and why there should be more of it.

Fermentation is fairly easy to do. It can self-correct many beginner's errors. It is definitely a slow-food process, but at the same time, a low-effort process since the bugs do most of the work. The recipes here are starter ones, broad in scope, easy to do, just to get you going. The appendix contains a good roundup of sources for a large variety of live cultures. You can find deeper more complex recipes in specific books, but here in one slim volume is a great introduction to how to ferment. At least once, you should make your own yogurt, bread, beer, kimchi, wine, cheese, miso, kraut, and vinegar. Find what you do well and make more of it.

-- KK

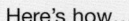

● Kefir is notable among milk cultures in that rather than using a bit of fermented milk to start the next batch, it relies upon a SCOBY, a rubbery mass of bacterial and fungal cells that has evolved an elaborate symbiotic arrangement, sharing nutrients, coordinating reproduction, and co-creating a shared form, which is not microscopic.

● I've made a couple of batches of *Keckek el Fouqara*, and they've been very popular. To start, mix bulgur with just a little more than its volume of water. Stir daily. After about a week, it develops a sharp flavor, which keeps getting better as the days pass. After two to three weeks, add spices. My best batch included garlic, caraway, cumin, and sage, crushed together with salt with a mortar and pestle. Mix spices into the bulgur mix, adjust as necessary, and form into balls about 1/2" (4 cm) in diameter. Pack spiced fermented bulgur balls into jars, cover with olive oil, and age at least a few weeks, or up to about six months. Serve with crackers as a cheese alternative.

● Sourdough smells awful

A sourdough is a complex community of microorganisms. When it receives a fresh high-proportion feeding, yeast activity is most vigorous and the sourdough develops a yeasty smell. Then, as lactic acid bacteria follow yeasts into dominance in the sourdough environment, it becomes increasingly acidic. But if you neglect feeding your sourdough and the lactic acid bacteria exhaust their nutrients, the putrefying bacteria, also part of the community, can rise to dominance. This is what it means when your starter smells awful. Rather than discarding it all, retain a small amount from the very bottom of the jar. Give it a high-proportion feeding to reawaken the dormant yeasts and lactic acid bacteria. Pamper it: Stir daily, keep it warm, and feed it every day or two, even if it doesn't bubble right away. Sourdoughs are very resilient and can come back from even extreme neglect.

● The first mold I learned to make was tempeh (sometimes spelled tempe), from the Indonesian island of Java. Tempeh is made by growing molds, predominantly *Rhizopus oligosporus*, usually on soybeans; the mold pre-digests them, binds them together, and greatly reduces required cooking time. Fresh tempeh is truly delicious, vastly superior to what is typically available commercially. Although tempeh IS best known as a soybean ferment, it can be made from any combination of legumes and/or grains (and other substrates as well). For years I thought that some legumes were necessary, but my friend and helper Spiky, an irrepressible experimentalist, insisted on trying a batch of all-grain millet oat tempeh, with no legume whatsoever, and it not only worked but was quite delicious, lighter than soy tempeh and almost nutty. I typically make tempeh that is half legumes and half grains.

Countertop yogurt maker
Waring Pro YM350
$60 Amazon

I've been making my own yogurt for the past couple of years. Not only is it much tastier than store-bought yogurt, but it's also much cheaper. At my local supermarket, an 8-ounce container of yogurt costs $1. That adds up to $16 per gallon. At the same supermarket, one gallon of low-fat organic milk costs $4.

Since I'm a believer in the power of probiotics (i.e. bacteria is good for your immune system), I usually eat three cups of home-made yogurt a day. That translates to a savings of $2.25 per day, or $67.50 per month — which means my $89 Waring Pro YM350 yogurt maker paid for itself in just a few months. Even if you don't eat as much yogurt as I do, I recommend you try making it yourself. It's so easy, and even fun.

Here's how…

1. Pour 4-6 cups of low fat milk into a microwave-proof glass bowl, and heat it until the milk begins to boil. (Boiling changes the milk's composition so it will solidify when mixed with the starter culture.) If a skin forms on top of the milk, that's a good sign you boiled it long enough.

2. Let the milk cool to the point where you can tolerate holding your hand against the bowl. Remove and discard the milk skin. Add one tablespoon of your previous batch of yogurt (or plain store-bought yogurt if you're just starting out), and mix together with a whisk. Do NOT add more starter yogurt to the mix in an attempt to speed up the process. Paradoxically, it will only slow down the fermentation (I've read that too much starter crowds out the bacteria from doing its job).

3. Pour the yogurt into 8- or 16-ounce containers. Do NOT put on the lids yet. If you have an older-style oven with a pilot light, you can stick the glass jars in there and allow the warm oven to act as an incubator. Otherwise, use the yogurt maker or a seed-starter warming pad to ferment the milk into yogurt.

4. Wait 8-10 hours, then screw the lids onto the jars and place them in the refrigerator.

Tip: I like to mix my yogurt with nuts, blueberries, and honey from my beehive. My kids love yogurt, banana, and berry smoothies.

-- Mark Frauenfelder

Sauerkraut stoneware
Fermentation Pot
$90 Amazon

After reading the previously reviewed Wild Fermentation, I ended up getting this Polish-made crock pot. It has a lip you fill with water to keep unfriendly bacteria out. Note: If you want weight (recommended), get the 20-liter stone weights, not the smaller ones. Anyway, sauerkraut (great for digestion) is composed of: cabbage and salt, nada mas. Simple! First batch worked great. Centuries-old low tech.

-- Lloyd Kahn

Easy homemade soy milk
Joyoung Soy Milk Maker
$99 Amazon

I used to buy soy milk from the store in cartons. Aside from the fact it's heavy (I transport groceries without a car), it comes in a tetra-pack, which is difficult to recycle. More importantly, commercial soy milk tends to include a number of ingredients I can do without, like chalk (calcium carbonate) and guar gum.

Unless you really like mucking with cheesecloth and lots of pots covered in soy scum, you owe it to yourself to buy a soy milk maker. After some research, I settled on the Joyoung CTS1048. This "filterless" model is a major improvement compared to earlier soy milk makers. Other devices require filter cups, which tend to get clogged with gummy okara (soy pulp) and are a terrible headache to clean. Instead, the CTS1048's immersion blender head is contained inside a small steel cage. From there, the milk strains through a second, basket-style strainer. Clean-up is no harder than what's required by a food processor.

Since the Joyoung makes 1.6 Liters per run, there's plenty to serve up hot and/or store in the fridge. It doesn't take long either, so you can always run it twice. Plus, it only costs around 15 cents a batch. I drink four times as much soy milk now, so the machine paid for itself in two months.

If you've never had fresh, hot soy milk, the way the Chinese like it, you're missing out; it's rich, foamy and all-around delicious. I always enjoy a warm glass as soon as a batch is done. Bonus: Aside from soy beans, you can add other ingredients. The Joyoung makes excellent coconut milk, for example, which eliminates an often preservative-laden canned good from the kitchen.

During my research, I discovered that most of the more-expensive soy milk makers are just rebranded Joyoung appliances, making the Joyoung the smart and economical pick. This is that rare product I can recommend with no reservations.

-- Sam Putman

Tip: Before starting, soak the beans until they're plump. Although the Joyoung features a dry-bean mode, reviewers says the end product is inferior and your patience will be well-rewarded.

Moonshine and Mead

Starter home distillery
EasyStill
$199 Brew Haus

I've been brewing beer on occasion for over 20 years, starting when I was in college. Always lurking out beyond the homebrew scene was the idea of making spirits. More complicated than making beer or wine and requiring the use of a still, it seemed out of reach. Being officially illegal didn't help either. But the idea lingered on in the back of my mind.

Then I stumbled upon a device called an Easystill. Basically, it is a water distillation unit that can also be used to distill alcohol as well. The idea of spirit distillation is simple. Alcohol boils at a temperature less than water, so if you get temperature above 78 °C but below 100 °C, the alcohol becomes vapor, leaving the water behind. A still captures the vapor, cools it enough to turn it back to liquid, allowing you to capture it.

The EasyStill does all that in a 110-volt tabletop device that you can store in the closet or garage when you are finished. The still handles about a gallon of mash at a time, so if you make a small 5 gallon batch of fermented mash, you are running the thing at least 5 times to produce a liter of alcohol. The process is slow to start but does work. I've made drinkable moonshine. It's not for any serious distilling, but for cooking up a batch on occasion.

I'd recommend EasyStill for someone that wants to see if distilling is for them. If they like it, they'll want to buy a real still with bigger capacity and full features. If it's not for them, they haven't spent a lot. Most people getting into 'firewater' have already tried homebrewing beer and likely already had all the stuff for the initial fermentation. I did.

-- Michael Pusateri

Making beer and wine at home in the US is perfectly legal. Owning a still (for water or making fuel) is legal. But making distilled spirits at home is currently illegal in all countries of the world except New Zealand. However, technological advances, local craft breweries and artisian spirit-making is rapidly shifting the legal landscape in in the US in favor of home production. In the meantime, if you don't sell it and don't kill anyone, no one will likely mess with you. The best source for home distillery information, including legal updates, advice about all types of stills, recipes, what gear works, aging caskets, flavorings, and so on, is a really great website (based in New Zealand) called Home Distiller. It will probably answer any questions you may have about making your own liquor.

--KK

Home Distiller

How to make honey ale
Compleat Mead Maker
$14 Ken Schramm, 2003, 316 p.

Of all homemade alcoholic beverages, my favorite is mead -- that is, fermented honey. I find mead easier to brew than beer but not as finicky as wine. Also, since it's not commonly sold, mead is a sensible thing to make it yourself. This book delves into the varieties of mead one can make, and how to do it. Different honeys and different yeasts yield different flavors. My best batch of mead ever was a golden 5-gallon carboy of it I made to serve at our wedding -- bringing the term "honey moon" to life. This book is the all-around best guide in print for making your own mead and covers everything for both beginners and more advance mead-making.

-- KK

Raspberry. The very high ash content may seem to make this honey somewhat suspect, but it expresses a dynamic nose and flavor out of the jar, and this character carries over impeccably to finished mead. The interesting sugar blend may be responsible for this honey's complexity, and the higher nitrogen is of benefit during fermentation. Dan McConnell and I took 5 gallons of this mead to the 1994 American Homebrewers Association conference, and it was the most popular of the thirteen meads we brought. The meads we have made and tasted from this honey have all been of very high quality.

As a general rule, honey from the earlier flows tends to be lighter in color, milder in aroma, and lower in wild yeast count than that of later flows. Most apiarists attribute this to the fact that wild yeasts tend to peak in airborne concentration later in the summer.

Most people think of honey in much the same way they think of sugar or flour: it's something you can keep around at room temperature until you use it without much thought of spoilage. For really fine meadmaking, however, we advise a different approach. Honey should be thought of in the same way you would think of any other agricultural product you use -- the fresher the better. We already know that the volatility of the aroma constituents make pasteuriation an unappealing option, but a number of other problems can also result for age and improper storage.

When you add the yeast to your fermentor, wonderful things begin to happen inside. The yeast gobble up all the oxygen you stirred in, grab a bunch of the nutrients you added to the must and then reproduce until their numbers are approximately five times what you originally put in the fermenter. Then, assuming all goes well, they begin a robust fermentation of all that sugar that the honey provides.

During fermentation, yeast convert sugar into carbon dioxide and alcohol. When this is happening, you'll see bubbles of carbon dioxide escaping through the fermentation lock. In most cases, you should see this starting to occur about 24 hours after you add the yeast. If it doesn't happen that quickly, don't worry. It will most likely kick in after a few days, and everything will be fine.

Cotes des Blancs (Red Star, Wyeast 3267, White Labs WLP745)

Has a reputation for being a slow fermenter, with higher nutrient requirements in low nitrogen mead or wine musts. Accents fruit aromas; a good choice with varietal honeys. Red Star says this yeast is the same as Epernay but with less foaming. This was a favorite yeast of Bill Pfeiffer, winner of many mead competitions.

Citric, Tartric, Malic Acid, Acid Blend

Acids are used to impart the tart twang on the tongue that balances the residual sugar in your mead. The primary acid in honey is gluconic acid, but you won't find that at your local winemaking supply store. The three most common prepared acids available in dried form are citric, tartaric, and malic. Citric acid is, of course, the acid produced in citrus fruits.

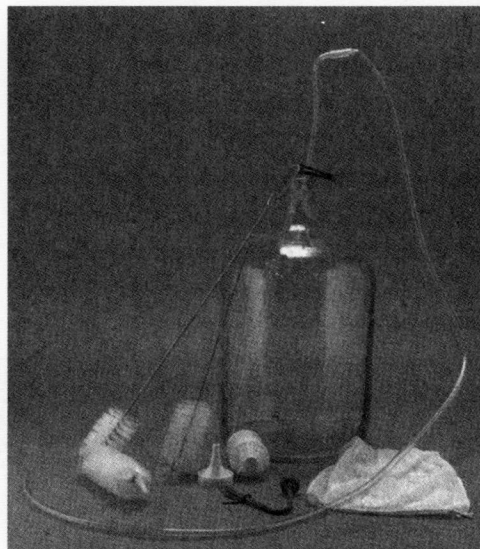

Basic equipment from left: carboy brush, large bottle brush, plastic siphon starter, jet bottle washer, 5 gallon glass carboy with racking cane, hose and cane/hose clip, and nylon hop straining bag.

Home-brewing software
ProMash
$25 (for Windows) ProMash

For the closet beer geek in all of us, ProMash allows a brewer to virtually brew a recipe before ever setting foot in the home or professional brewery. It frees the user from the tedious "carry the 1" calculations that abound in the brewing process

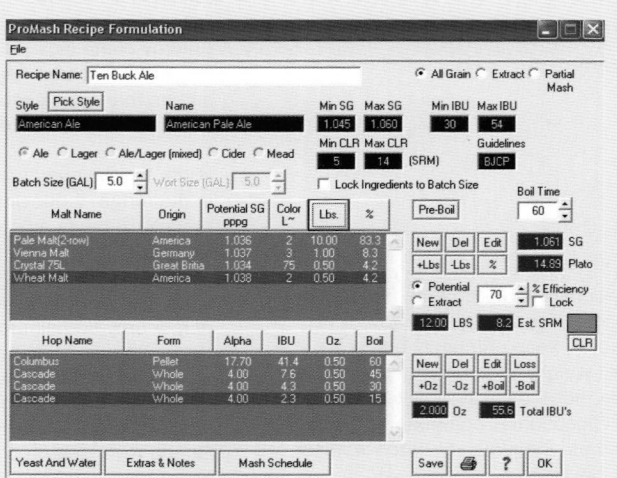

and helps you keep track of the history of a beer as it develops over time. Updates are provided yearly, free of charge to registered owners.

-- Drew Beechum

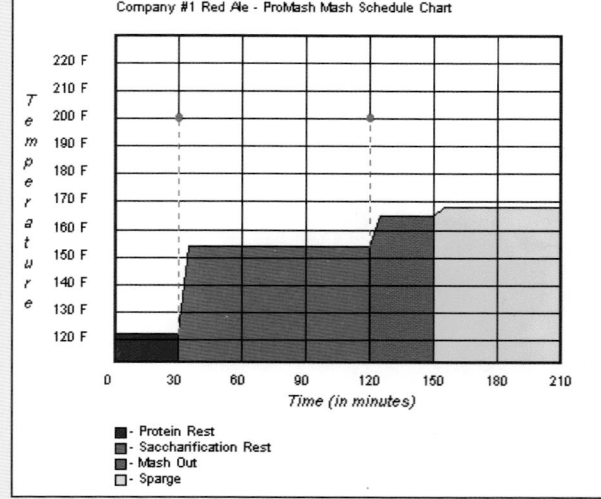

Making your own brewery
Brew Ware
$13 Karl F. Lutzen, Mark Stevens, 1996, 272 p.

These two guys are deep into making DIY gear for home beer brewing. Serious nano-scale brew pub.

- KK

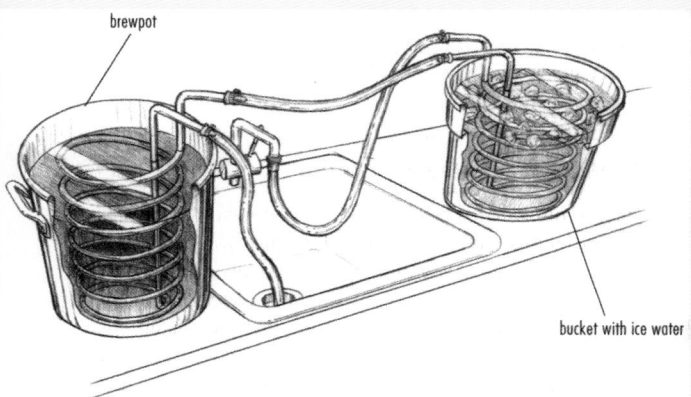

Double-coil chiller. This one calls for two coils, the first to lower the temperature of the cold water, the second to chill the wort.

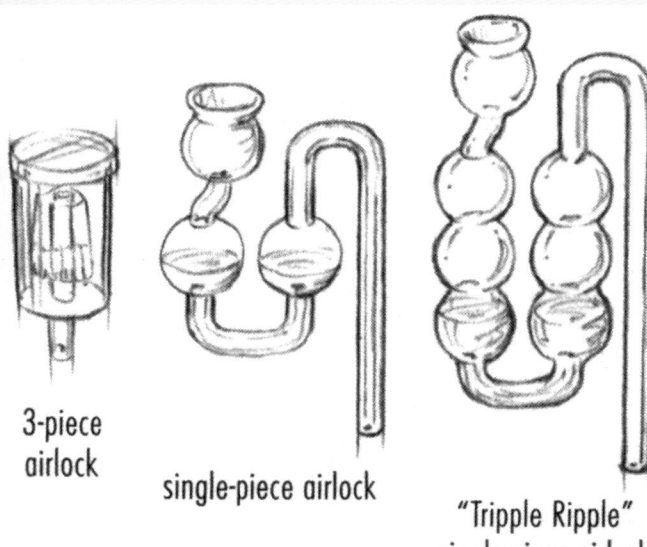

3-piece airlock

single-piece airlock

"Tripple Ripple" single-piece airlock

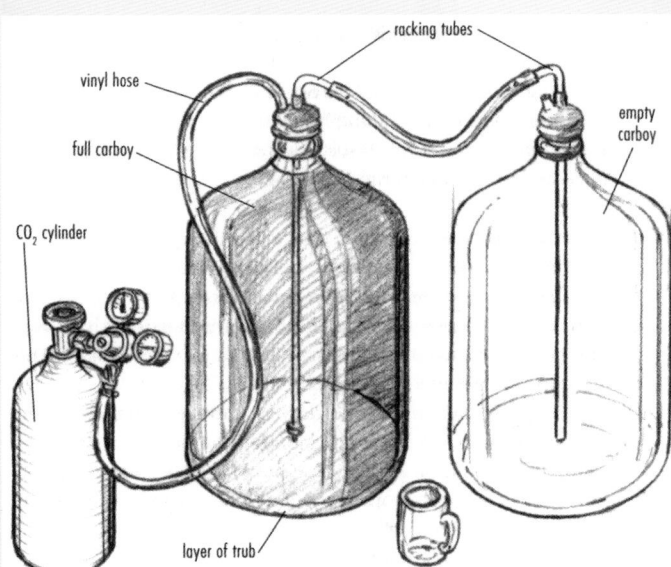

If you have a kegging setup, there is no need to siphon beer from your carboy. Use your CO_2 cylinder and a racking configuration like this.

Best one-volume homebrewing guide
The Complete Joy of Homebrewing
$11 Charles Papazian, 2003, 432 p.

There is not a better introduction to the universe of homebrewing than *The Complete Joy of Homebrewing* by Charles Papazian. It covers history, equipment, ingredients, chemistry, beer styles, and methods, while appendices cover various topics from recipe formulation to meadmaking. I've used this guide quite extensively in my first batches of home brew beer and I still consult it on occasion, especially as inspiration for experimentation. It also contains enough on advanced topics to lead in the right directions when I want to learn more.

Of many introductory books to brewing this one has the ideal integration of simplicity and thoroughness. Experienced brewers may find the book rather "incomplete" on advanced issues, but online resources and brewclubs are better sources of advance information than most books.

Papazian's passion for beer brewing will pique the interest of any brewer, regardless of expertise and experience. His enthusiasm has even pushed commercial brewers to experiment with new procedures and ingredients. For instance in a passing comment in the 2nd edition Papazian mentioned maple beers, and now maple beers are brewed at several brewpubs.

What is perhaps most important about the book is the philosophy behind it. Papazian's recurrent admonition is to "Relax, Don't Worry, Have a Homebrew." We can't control everything in home brewing. It represents a whole perspective on beer, the universe, and everything.

-- *Alexandre Enkerli*

Swollen glands! Tiny lupulin oil glands coat the base of the hop's flower petals. The lupulin contributes to the bitterness and aromatics of the hop.

The Cornelius "Keg"

The Cornelius draft system is one of the most versatile systems for the home-brewer. Cornelius "kegs" are actually stainless steel canisters that serve as containers for the soft drink industry. They come in 2.5-, 3-, 4- and 5-gallon sizes--perfect for your 5-gallon batch of beer and small enough to fit in a refrigerator. They are very easy to clean and sanitize. Beer can be dispensed as needed with a CO_2 tapper system.

Having a crush! It may not be love at first sight, but with proper adjustments, the grinding plates on this type of flour mill can serve your malt-grinding needs.

Don't roll out this barrel! Brewery kegs can be used to hold draft homebrew. The sediment will be drawn off with the first pint of brew. A hand pump or tapper system can be attached.

Opens and closes
Hermetus Bottle Opener and Sealer
$9 Kafmann Mercantile

I often make my own beer at a local brew-it-yourself taproom. The bottles we use are 22-ounces, so drinking one is almost like drinking two. Often times I'll end up drinking more than I wanted or drinking none at all (oh, the horror).

Stumbled across the Hermetus Bottle Opener and Sealer while looking for a Father's Day gift for my dad. Bought one for him, a couple guys in the brew group, and myself. To create an airtight seal simply slip it over the top of the bottle. It works perfectly.

Drank half a bottle one night then sealed it and put it in the fridge. Drank remaining half the second night, and it tasted the same and still had a nice head on it. I love the simplicity of the design!

-- *Mark Prasek*

Best wine-making guide
The Way to Make Wine
$22 Sheridan Warrick, 2010, 272 p.

It's not difficult to make your own drinkable wine. Almost any wine-making book or the internet will tell you how. Making a good or great wine is more challenging, and the aim of this book. Sheridan Warrick, who has been making great homemade wines for 30 years, gives guidance that is level headed, exact, and well-written. I find his advice neither too general nor too detailed, but just right, which is important in a field like winemaking where jargon and mystery are rife. I'm still a beginner, but his guide treats me intelligently, not wasting my time. This is best introductory book out of the dozens available; follow it and you'll make some great wilne.

-- KK

Won't I have to wait years to drink my wine? Not necessarily. When it comes Zinfandel, Syrah, and today's other fruit-forward wine, drink up and don't look back. It's true that vintners need a bit of patience that beer brewers do without. But if you've ever planned ahead for a vacation, you'll have all the patience you need. Suppose you follow the classic schedule: fermentation in fall, cellar work in winter and spring, bottling in summer -- say, June. When can you start pulling corks? RIght away!

- Frozen grapes. Many brew shops now sell high-quality crushed red grapes and white grape juices (in making white wines, the skins are always excluded). They come frozen solid in small tubs and large drums. More than a dozen different wine grape varieties are offered.

- Stinky! The must during active fermentation should smell clearly! grapey and pleasantly yeasty, and in fact it's wise to give the fermenter a pointed sniffing each time you punch down. If you begin to notice a strong dirty socks or rotten-egg odor, think about taking action.

- Is your wine truly clear? Before declaring your wine ready to bottle -- either before or after finning -- pour a generous amount into your tasting glass, set it in a shady place, and shine a strong light through it from the side, perpendicular to your line of sight. If you can see the light beam in the wine, you may want to help the wine clarify further.

Racking -- that is, siphoning -- th enewlyl made wine away from the gross lees (spent yeasts and pulp) that have settled in a thick layer at the bottom of the carboy.

World's easiest wine bottle opener
Screwpull Lever
$86 Amazon

The Lever model makes pulling corks a literally four second operation: clamp it around the neck of the bottle, pull the lever down, pushing the screw into the bottle, pull the lever back up, pulling the cork out of the bottle, open the clamp slightly to remove the bottle, then close the clamp again push the lever back again, removing the cork from the screw. There are cheaper models than this one — Rabbit comes to mind — which may be good, and even really cheap models which are distinctly inferior, but this one is still a bargain for how simple it makes getting between your intention to have a glass a wine and actually sipping it.

-- Louis Rossetto

Reliable wine opener
Pulltap's Double-Hinged Waiter's Corkscrew
$7 Amazon

We use these wine openers in the tasting room at our winery, as well as at home. They work. Better than everything else we have tried. We've been through most all the types out there. Some of our baby-boomer staff have arthritis and find that the "rabbit" openers are unusable, not to mention clumsy even for the most deft of hands. They also take up too much room and require an inordinate amount of force. The two step feature of the double-hinged model saves broken corks and sore wrists (we open 30-40 bottles of wine in a shift!). We use the bottom of the line version, but it is still very well made. It has a Teflon coated worm that far outlives the "rabbit" worms; sharp, easy to open, easy to use foil cutter, and tight hinges throughout.

They even work well with the accursed synthetic "corks". After engaging the worm, use the shorter of the two fulcrums to start the cork out. If the closure is stubborn, move your grip on the handle to the very end, increasing your mechanical advantage. After you start the cork moving, switch to the longer fulcrum. The Spanish manufacturer Pulltex makes some pricy elegant wood/chrome/brass models that I have not tried. And per the manufacturer's web site there are forgeries on the market. Caveat emptor.

-- David Ott

Cutaway view of boxed wine.

Unoxidated wine as medicine
Box Wine

Wine never tickled me either. Hard stuff had no appeal at all. But recently the medical benefits of wine have become so established that it's hard to ignore, my doctor prescribed it. One respected study published in *JAMA* in December 2002 claims that not drinking at all was as bad for the heart as morbid obesity, and that moderate alcohol has health benefits equal to one hour of physical exercise a day. Take that you gym rats!

I decided that I would take one glass of wine a day, as medicine.

Unfortunately, the pharmacologically active ingredients in wine easily oxidized, disappearing within hours of opening the bottle. Since my consumption was so low, the medical effects I wanted from the wine would evaporate quickly, to say nothing of the wine's taste. I discovered however, that boxed wine retained the freshness of wine almost indefinitely. By means of a tap on the bottom, and a collapsible bag, the wine is never exposed to air at all before it is dispensed. I can drink at a nibble and retain the goodies. Even better, the economics are impressive: about 35 cents per glass. No one should depend on my evaluation of taste, but several wine connoisseurs, including ones in *The New York Times*, have declared their surprise at how good the box wines are. A few upscale wines are now being package this way, too. I find the tap extremely handy to use (no drip) so the box sits on a shelf in the pantry awaiting my daily draft. Here's to taste, longevity and the good life!

Box Wines can be found in supermarkets. The elixir of youth I am drinking:

$17 Almaden Mountain Burgundy 5 L
Amazon

$13 Franzia Cabernet 5L BevMo

Private Preserve Wine Preserver

For those wine snobs who must drink wine from a bottle, there is one tool that can prevent oxidation in bottles fairly well. Devices that try to make a vacuum often don't succeed for long, but an inert gas called Private Preserve can make a usable seal. A few zips of this mixture of heavy inert gases (nitrogen, carbon dioxide, argon) down the neck of the wine bottle creates a barrier to oxygen which preserves the wine's freshness for up to a year. Each seemingly weightless can holds enough for more than 100 applications. Easy enough to use when boxed wine might embarrass the guests.

-- Stewart Brand

Private Preserve is also useful for preserving anything in bottles. I keep gallon jugs of genuine maple syrup going indefinitely with Private Preserve (or some lookalike).

-- KK

$9 Private Preserve Wine Preserver
Oenophilia

Quiet, versatile juice extractor
Omega 8003/ 8004 Juicer

$216 Amazon

I eat fruits and veggies, but based on everything I've read, the potential health benefits of juicing are too great to pass up. Unless you're an impatient person, the Omega 8003 is great for a beginning juicer. It not only handles apples, oranges and carrots, but won't get bogged down with wheatgrass, spinach and other leafy greens. Unlike a centrifugal juicer (vita mix), which violently shreds what you put in it, the Omega 8003 uses what is known as a dual-screen, single auger. That means it doesn't cut or chew as much as it mashes pulp forward into the end of a cone using the pressure of a spinning auger. The juice yield definitely trumps my old Braun centrifugal juicer, which can't handle wheatgrass. The pulp I get from the Omega is drier and if need be, I can easily put it back through for a tiny bit more juice.

Of all the machines I've researched, tested and used, the Omega 8003 just crushes every piece of machinery, especially at this price. After eight months, I still use the juicer almost every other day and nothing has broken or malfunctioned. Juice extractors tend to be jet-engine loud. While the Omega's motor is strong and hums with authority, it's killer quiet. I can easily juice in the early morning or night without waking my wife or the neighbors. It's also not too large in size and the folding handle on top makes moving the machine around much easier than other machines. The construction is solid. Omega backs it up with 10-year warranty.

-- Jim Rubel

$256 Amazon

Before purchasing a juicer I extensively researched what was available and ultimately purchased the Omega Juicer 8004.

I have been using the Omega juicer twice daily for the past few months. There are two major types of juicers, centrifugal and masticating. The Omega 8004 is the latter. Centrifugal juicers have higher juice yields for some kinds of fruits and vegetables and are a bit faster than masticating juicers, but masticating juicers are better for a litany of reasons.

First, they're quiet. The Omega juicer operates at about 80 RPM at a tolerable decibel level. Centrifugal juicer are LOUD. They also work better with leafy greens like kale, swiss chard, spinach, etc. They also can be used for a variety of tasks. Masticating juicers are multifunctional in that they can be put to use making pasta, nut butters and milks, and baby food.

One of the biggest reasons the Omega 8004 is superior is because it is easy to clean. It disassembles quickly and the parts can be cleaned in just a minute or two. The construction is also quite solid. The Omega 8004 and its slightly more expensive counterpart the Omega 8006 are the only juicers on the market that have a 15 year warranty. And the only difference between the 8004 and the 8006 is the finish: the 8004 is white plastic and the 8006 has a black and chrome finish.

On the downside it is ugly, but in my opinion all juicers are ugly and in this case it is a question of function over form. It also has a large footprint compared to other juicers, and this is an issue for people who have small kitchens. I live in New York, but am fortunate enough to have a decent sized kitchen.

One other small issue is the size of the feed tube, which is rather narrow (about an inch and a half in diameter), which makes it necessary to cut up fruits and vegetables a bit more than some other juicers on the market.

Omega has another line of masticating juicer which are "vertical" taking up less counter space, have larger feed tubes, and are highly recommended by people who seem to know what they are talking about on the Internet. However, they are a lot more expensive.

I chose the 8004 over the Omega vertical models, because the 8004/8006 seemed mechanically simpler and has a 15 year vs. 10 year warranty. Overall, I have found the Omega 8004 easy to use and actually fun. The variety of juice you can make is amazing. I will let others discuss the health benefits of juicing, but unscientifically after using it I have lost some weight and feel really great.

-- Max Abramowitz

The ultimate blender
VitaMix 5200 Countertop Blender

$499 Amazon

$350 for a blender!? But man, this thing is an incredible MACHINE.

I once believed that a blender only needed two speeds: Off and High. I was wrong. With ten variable speeds, it makes short work of anything and everything we've ever put in it. We use it every single day, often multiple times. The 1380-watt motor surprisingly quiet on low, and a barracuda at high speeds. Clean-up is incredibly quick: Add water, a bit of soap, turn on high for ten seconds, and then rinse and dry.

The 64-ounce Lexan pitcher is amazingly tough. I always figured plastic was plastic, but this stuff is really tough. If you do happen to somehow break it, the company will replace it free of charge through its seven-year warranty. After that, you can simply purchase parts/replacements.

After using it EVERY day, usually multiple times a day — I realized it's worth $350. Anyone who uses a blender regularly will find this to be the best blender they ever own. My previous $45 blender, which I once thought was pretty good, now sits gathering dust. I've been spoiled.

-- Jeff Jewell

Hand-powered juicer
Ra Chand Citrus Press

$162 Amazon

Living in Southern California, we have an abundance of citrus nearly year round — lemons, limes, kumquats, grapefruits, and more. I also have a household of beverage enthusiasts, from my kids who love to make lemon-, lime-, etc. -ades, or "kid drinks" as they call them, to my wife and I who are crazy about cocktails, flips, fizzes, and sours. This is why I graduated from my fine, but slow, hand juicer, to the monstrous, restaurant-calibre Ra Chand J210 Bar Juicer. It makes quick, efficient work of juicing tons of citrus. Rather than dread all the labor, I'm now happy to juice enough fruit to make a full pitcher of Ginger Limeonade with my kids to sell in their DIY juice stand.

The Ra Chand is dead simple. No motors or fragile plastic parts to break — in fact it only has six parts, made of cast aluminum, plus a wire return spring and a few bolts. The mechanical advantage it provides is tremendous. With its long lever and offset pivots, even my six-year-old daughter can use it to easily squeeze a half-lemon dry. The Ra Chand is big enough for me to juice a medium grapefruit — when I have a larger-sized one to contend with I quarter it (and secretly wish I had the even-larger model, the J500).

The straining cone (which looks like a half beehive) allows juice and the occasional small seed through, but very little pulp. This is also due to the fact that pressing (rather than twisting like a motorized juicer) bursts the cells of the fruit, but doesn't shred the membranes.

If I have one complaint it is that the juicer can be tipped forward easily until you get the hang of pulling the lever down, not down-and-toward-yourself. I've gotten used to this, but I do hold onto the base when my kids use it to avoid a mess.

In all, the Ra Chand is hands-down the best citrus juicer I've used. I appreciate its size, speed, power, ruggedness, and simplicity. I imagine it'll be in our family for many years, hopefully providing juice for generations.

-- John Edgar Park

We have this rugged, indestructable juicer. Note: It's very tall, and at rest won't fit under most counter cabinets.

-- KK

Coffee Resources

Coffee technical reviews
CoffeeGeek
coffeegeek.com

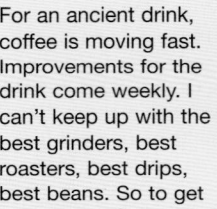

For an ancient drink, coffee is moving fast. Improvements for the drink come weekly. I can't keep up with the best grinders, best roasters, best drips, best beans. So to get the latest coffee techniques and tools, by the most serious fans, I head to CoffeeGeek. Great equipment reviews, buyer guides, and tutorials for enthusiasts. They are fanatical about good coffee, but also eager to speak to beginners as well.
-- KK

Where to Buy
→ Seattle Coffee Gear
→ 1st in Coffee
→ 1st-line Equipment

List your business site here.
About "Where to Buy"

Product Details
Overall Rating 8.5, Based on 18 Reviews

La Pavoni Professional Lever Machine
This direct lever machine uses your hand as the pump. Note it has the froth aiding device attached - fortunately, La Pavonis can easily swap this out for the traditional steam wand (both are included with the machine).

Luxurious, simple everyday brewer
Mono Filio Teapot
$145 In Pursuit of Tea

I've used numerous tea pots, ranging from traditional to modern, built with materials from clay to plastic. The stainless steel and glass Mono Filio is the best one for regular tea drinking. I've been using this teapot daily for about a year and a half, drinking mainly green, oolong and white tea. I'm not sure the suspended design has any benefit besides looks, but it will prevent condensation and heat from reaching wood counters or tables. The real design innovation is the very large strainer basket. Aside from having a metal handle that makes removal easy, the basket is almost the full size of the pot itself, allowing a lot of space for the leaves to float freely. When tea leaves can float freely they release flavors more evenly, making for better-tasting tea. The tea bag is a modern convenience. What you typically get inside is crushed dust rather than intact leaves (this is why it often tastes bitter, especially in the case of black tea). When you put a tablespoon of oolong leaves in this pot, after two infusions the leaves expand to fill perhaps a cup in size. Like the smaller plastic IngenuiTEA, the transparency of the glass provides something interesting to watch while the tea brews. While the IngenuiTEA looks to be more of a travel device or something you use at work, the Mono is something you want to use in your house on a daily basis. The 20 oz. size creates the perfect amount of tea for two people and cleans up nicely. $100-plus is incredibly expensive. The matching cups I bought are $70 — ridiculous. With this one, you have to already know you really like tea. But unlike a lot of modern revisions of traditional objects where radical originality in looks creates some level of annoyance in use, Mono Tabletop's teapot is exactly the opposite. It's much different from the traditional clay pot, yet, for me, easier to use and a better experience. After some 4,000 years of tea culture, that achievement is worth $110.

-- Wayne Bremser

Durable, insulated coffeemaker
Frieling French Press
$80 Amazon

After breaking two glass carafes while living in the middle of nowhere, I knew there had to be a better answer to the standard French press. The Frieling is; made of all stainless steel parts, it's insulated and has no plastic anywhere. It is awesome.

Some people think that allowing the grounds to sit in the bottom of the Freieling for an extended period of time (because the water stays hot) will make the coffee bitter. My experience is that it doesn't. Even if you choose not to let coffee sit in the press for the two hours that it'll remain hot, the insulation still makes a difference in the initial four-minute brewing period. Though the temperature of the water in a typical glass French press will decrease immediately, the water in the Frieling retains its heat while my coffee is brewing.

Cadillac of coffee carriers
Thermos Nissan 61 oz Insulated Bottle
$40 Amazon

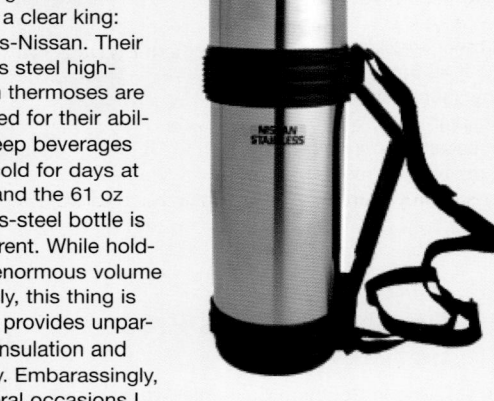

In the modern world of insulating containers there is a clear king: Thermos-Nissan. Their stainless steel high-vacuum thermoses are renowned for their ability to keep beverages hot or cold for days at a time and the 61 oz stainless-steel bottle is no different. While holding an enormous volume (seriously, this thing is huge) it provides unparalleled insulation and usability. Embarassingly, on several occasions I have made coffee and forgotten it on the counter only to find it piping hot a full 24-hours later.

In terms of use, pouring a thermos can be a drippy affair (especially those with larger volumes), but the foldable handle built in to the 61-oz model coupled with the flow controlling lid makes it easy. And while I was initially wary of any coffee container that needed a shoulder strap, after putting it through months of use I have found it incredibly handy for when I'm carrying anything else. Be warned, though, as people will struggle to understand why you're carrying something that looks like a cross between a battering ram and a missile launcher (someone else mentioned that it looked like it should carry radioactive material).

Admittedly a thermos is a weird thing to geek out about, but in this case the praise is well deserved. Between the heating and cooling curves provided in the literature that are proven on a daily basis, to the lifetime warranty and solid stainless steel build, this is one hell of an insulating bottle.

-- Oliver Hulland

The only downside of this outstanding pot is that I don't get to watch the brewing process. I've found it well worth the trade-off. It's beautifully designed and not easily broken – dishwasher safe, too. I've had my Frieling French press for almost two years now, and the mirror finish still looks great except for a dent or two. It doesn't scratch easily, and it still looks and performs just like it did out of the box. It's the best investment for my kitchen I've made in years.

-- Brechelle Ware

Coffee roasting supplier
Sweet Maria's
Sweet Maria's Coffee Roasting Supplies

My particular enthusiasm is home-roasted coffee and Sweet Maria's is my go-to supplier. Not only do they offer everything you need to roast your own coffee at home, but they also carry a great range of products from inexpensive entry-level roasters to top-of-the-line home roasters. (I've been using the Hottop roaster for many years now and am very satisfied).

The best thing about Sweet Maria's is that it is also a great source of information about coffee, roasting, brewing, and drinking. I've been a coffee nut for quite a few years now and have learned a fair bit about the subject. As far as I can tell, everything on the Sweet Maria's site is either correct or clearly marked as opinion. What more could you want?

-- Dudley Irish

For Canadians, a good analogue to Sweet Maria's is Green Beanery in Toronto. They sell roasting, grinding, and coffee-making equipment, as well as beans from small-scale farmers in Africa, Asia, and South America. Everything's available online. I've bought a few things from them and visited their shop once during a trip to Toronto. They do good work.

-- Brad

Improved instant coffee
Starbucks VIA Instant Coffee

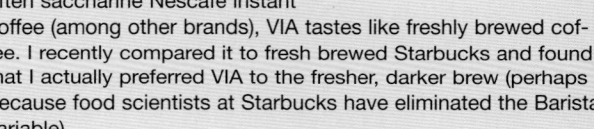

Since learning how to roast my own beans I have come to appreciate the broader art of coffee making. However, I don't always have time to roast coffee weekly or bring along my burr-grinder and kettle to brew a fresh cup. This is especially the case while camping and travelling.

The best solution I have found for caffeinating while abroad or on the go is Starbucks VIA instant coffee. Unlike the distasteful and often saccharine Nescafe instant coffee (among other brands), VIA tastes like freshly brewed coffee. I recently compared it to fresh brewed Starbucks and found that I actually preferred VIA to the fresher, darker brew (perhaps because food scientists at Starbucks have eliminated the Barista variable).

Not only does the VIA taste better than other instant brands, but it also dissolves better. The fine powder (described in the marketing as soluble micro-grounds) dissolves equally well in cold water as hot, allowing for instant iced coffee in the summer (or when I need to run out the door and don't have time to wait for the kettle to boil). Each packet is supposed to make a strong 8-oz cup, but I find that it tastes best when diluted in about 12-oz of water.

The form factor is incredibly small (4 grams per packet) and as such the folks at Backpacking Light swear by it as a replacement for camp coffee.

The only downside to VIA is its expense with each packet costing around 60 cents which when compared to Nescafe's 12 cents a cup seems a bit costly. However, it's still cheaper than buying a cup at the coffee shop, and probably on par with how much my beans cost from the store. Finally, I'd recommend that people stay away from the sweetened variety of VIA as they are more expensive, less compact, and not as good as the simpler stuff.

VIA represents a quantum leap in the quality of instant coffee I've tried, and I remain blown away that I find myself choosing instant coffee over fresh-brewed stuff. I highly recommend that people set aside any lingering instant coffee prejudice and try a cup for themselves.

-- Oliver Hulland

$11 twelve pack Amazon $30 fifty pack Amazon

Predicting the future is easy. It's trying to figure out what's going on now that's hard. - Fritz R. S. Dressler

DIY beverage bubbles
Home Carbonation System
Free Information Richard J. Kinch

I drink a lot of seltzer. So much that my fiancee says I couldn't survive without bubbles in my water. After trying a SodaClub home soda maker (above right, in the picture) and realizing it would cost $70 to buy a special part for it, I found a really detailed resource for building my own, simple home carbonation system for under a $100 using a CO2

tank, regulator, hose and a carbonator cap (details below). It took ten minutes to build. I love having very good homemade soda on the cheap and not having to lug around seltzer bottles or worry about it going flat. With a scuba-like tank in the kitchen, guests always ask "What is that?!" and I really love demonstrating. When one friend of mine said he didn't like soda, I whipped him up a mango soda from this special puree of mango I had. He absolutely loved it! And a by-product of the cost of producing low cost seltzer water is that I can experiment with different flavored sodas. I mean some really wacky stuff, like lychee-tangerine or coconut-lucima. If I don't like it, or it tastes weird, I don't feel guilty about draining the entire liter or two-liter bottle.

My 20lb system makes over 1133 liters of carbonated water. In practice, efficiency is not perfect, with unavoidable losses in the hose and headspace. But at current prices of $20 per 20lb tank-fill, the cost to convert tap water to seltzer is under $0.02 cents per liter. A single fill of a 20lb tank charges over 500 bottles, which will keep you supplied for 1.5 years if you consume an average of one bottle daily. In terms of break even, assuming that you can find liter bottles of seltzer water for $0.99 per bottle, then it'll take roughly 100 bottles for the system to break even. I definitely drink a liter a day, so it only took about 3 months for me to break even — not to mention all of the labor and space that it saves to lug in and store 8.3 dozen liter bottles of seltzer water.

I found a CO2 tank on eBay for about $30 bucks, including shipping. I use a dual gauge CO2 regulator; a single gauge one for CO2 output would work also, but I prefer the dual as it also tells you the amount of gas in the CO2 canister ($20 on eBay). You also need a hose (or "gas fitting tube"). To avoid the site's detailed instructions on how to fit the CO2 hose onto a 1-liter bottle of soda, I bought a special carbonator cap that lets you easily insert the hose ($11 from Northern Brewer). You can't refill a CO2 tank in NYC, as it violates several ordinances. However, you can exchange your empty tank for a full one for $20 at a local welding supply place; other spots include keg brewers and anywhere that refills fire extinguishers.

The operating instructions are fairly straightforward. On a dual gauge tank there are two gauges and two valves, one for the main tank and one for the output. The valve between the CO2 tank and the regulator, I'll call the CO2 valve and the valve between the regulator and the carbonator cap, I'll call the output valve:

1) Fill up a one- or two-liter bottle.

2) Screw on the carbonator cap fairly tight (it's a ball release cap, so you simply push the entire cap to release it from the hose afterwards).

3) Make sure the Output valve is completely shut off.

4) Turn on the CO2 valve and watch the CO2 tank gauge shoot up (this will be the remaining pressure in your tank).

5) Slowly turn the Output valve open until the pressure reaches about 50 PSI. (I've been experimenting with various PSI's — 50 PSI works best for me.)

6) As you feel the bottle get full (don't worry, I read recently that two-liter soda bottles are rated to handle 200 PSI), pick it up and start shaking vigorously as you would a bar drink (this helps carbonate the water).

7) Turn off the CO2 valve and then the Output valve.

8) Remove the carbonator cap.

Incidentally, it was a SodaClub home soda maker I bought on eBay that inspired me ultimately to build my own home carbonation unit. The SodaClub unit has a proprietary design whereby it is nearly impossible to refill without a special adapter and the adapters I found online cost $70 bucks (more than I paid for the SodaClub). So rather than spend $70 to fix an inherent problem with the SodaClub (and I would still need a 20lb canister sitting somewhere in my house), I did some research and found this site. For about $95 bucks — less than the cost of a new SodaClub (they retail new for about $100) — I have more than 10 times the soda making capacity (SodaClub claims you can get 110 liters of soda). I should add that I've seen plans on eBay for $5 or $10 bucks for how to construct your own soda fountain gun that spurts out bubbly water on demand. With mine, the end result is the same, but the carbonator unit I built is so much simpler and cheaper and it doesn't require a heat sink or a refrigeration unit.

-- Alastair Ong

$8+ Soda Supplies & Parts Northern Brewer

Easy carbonated water maker
Sodastream Home Soda Maker
$115 Amazon

Concerned with our household's waste-stream of plastic bottles and cans, we started using this counter-top soda maker to concoct our own soft drinks with tap water processed through a Britta. It's easy to use. The durable bottles are said to be good for three years. Best of all, Sodastream's proprietary CO2 cartridges can be conveniently exchanged either by mail or at accessible chain stores like Williams-Sonoma.

If you're looking to save a little money, see above. However, the Sodatream has the benefit of being plug-and-play; it's smaller and less clunky; and it's only about $30 more than the DIY set-up. Plus, the DIY set-up requires you to lug around a big scuba tank every time you refill the CO2. But hey, to each his own, no?

After the initial investment, the only things I ever need purchase are carbonator refills and new bottles of flavoring. So far, we've enjoyed Sodastream's cola, faux Dr. Pepper, tonic, and pink grapefruit — all diet with Splenda instead of aspartame (They also sell sweetened syrups without hi-fructose corn syrup). I find the taste is excellent. The pink grapefruit is one of the best soft drinks I've had anywhere.

Aside from reducing our waste, we no longer have to lug bottles back from the store. I also like to think about all the energy we will save annually by not buying water that's been shipped from one part of the country to another.

-- Brad Zebal

From tutorial
Cloning Your Own Mineral Water
Free Tutorial How to Clone Mineral Water Edible Geography

You can start with a carbonation water machine, like a SodaStream, Soda-Club, or the previously reviewed home system, and then you can add minerals to make your own artisan mineral waters. There are several ways to calculate how much mineral you need to add. In general you start with an analysis of your tap water (often provided by your water company), then you get a list of branded mineral waters to imitate, and then use a spreadsheet to figure out how much mineral to add. Of course you can also refine your own personal mix that suits your taste, too. Finding a source for the minerals is a little bit trickier, but I suspect selling such salts will soon become a small cottage business for someone. Right now check out this tutorial which tells you how:

How to Clone Mineral Water, Edible Geography

A spoon full of mineral salts is required for the preparation of 1 liter of San Pellegrino mineral water. Image from Khymos, Mineral waters a la carte

One of the commenters on the Khymos blog noticed that Burton salts, used in beer brewing, and available from supplier like AHS, is very close to the mix of the salts in San Pelligrino mineral water. A quick experiment awaits…

– KK

Mugs

Hot/cold double-wall mug
Bodum Insulated Glassware
$18 Bodum

I've tried those insulated stainless steel mugs for keeping coffee hot, but the coffee never tasted right — even though stainless is supposedly impervious. Recently, we discovered these wonderful insulated glasses made by Bodum, best known for its plunger coffee pots. They keep drinks hot, are cool to the touch, and are elegant looking. A latte made in one is rather spectacular, with layers of espresso and milk. There are a few sizes in the "Pilatus" collection, including glasses 6- and 4.75-inches high. Pricey, but high quality. Bodum's description:

"…a strong heat-resistant glass that

weighs less than traditional glassware. Used to make scientific lab glass, borosilicate glass (medical grade glass) is stronger than traditional "soda-lime" glass….

Borosilicate glass substitutes boron oxide in place of the soda and lime used in traditional glassware. The boron oxide acts as a glue holding the silicate together and due to the small size of boron particles, the glass is held together tighter, resulting in a stronger glass."

I use the taller one every morning for fresh ginger tea.

(Bodum also offers a range of other double-walled glassware, including a 20-oz. beer glass.)

-- Lloyd Kahn

Stackable tempered glassware
Duralex Gigogne
$25 (set of 6, 5.75- or 7.5oz.) Duralex

We have two active kids who are experts at breaking all manner of things. We also have been a bit concerned about plastics and, in particular, microwaving food in plastics. These lovely glasses solve both problems elegantly. We've had the Gigone (nested or stackable in French) glasses for about 6 months and I absolutely love them. Although they are "for the kids," I find that I use them the most. Beautifully shaped and feeling great in the hand, these are my go-to glasses for wine now. Something about the shape, size and heft makes them special. The impres-

sive durability of the tempered glass is a wonderful bonus. They're good for hot and cold drinks.

We've dropped them several times on our hardwood floor without breaking them. I can say that other glasses have broken on our floors, precisely the reason we sought these out in the first place. After 6-plus months of dishwashing, they look brand new. I haven't tried their other glassware, but I have it on my list to try for sure.

-- Peter Lio

Easily cleaned bottle
Clean Bottle
$10 Clean Bottle

The Clean Bottle is a 22-oz sports water bottle with removable bottom. It is one of those products that seems like a no-brainer the instant you hear about it.

Many athletes put electrolyte/endurance/recovery drinks into their bottles. Some of those bottles inevitably get forgotten in the bottom of a bag, under a car seat, or in a closet where they develop lush colonies of mold and bacteria which are impossible to clean out completely, so the bottle gets tossed. With the Clean Bottle you just unscrew the bottom, scrub the pieces and you're back in business; no moldy residue left to taint your drink.

I train 6-7 times a week, and while I haven't forgotten a dirty bottle in my car, I did leave one there on purpose for a week. It molded up as expected but was a cinch to clean out. I've been using the bottles for about 3 weeks and so far I'm very happy with them, as are the friends I've recommended them too.

At $10.00 each they aren't cheap, but the savings from not having to replace dirty bottles (as well as keeping that plastic out of landfills) offsets the price.

The bottles are BPA-free.

-- Galen Pewtherer

Non-plastic beverage containers
Sigg Aluminum Water Bottles
$15 Sigg

These bottles are a great solution for anyone looking to get away from plastic. In the last few years, studies have suggested that using plastic bottles may be harmful to your health. For instance, plastic bottles made of polycarbonate (#7 recycle code) contain a substance called bisphenol-A (BPA), which acts as an endocrine disrupter that mimics estrogen and has been linked to aneuploidy, adipogenesis, and other scary problems with funny names. Found in plastics with recycle codes 1-5, phthalates (the chemical that softens plastic) can be carcinogenic and act as endocrine disrupters, too. Even water standing at room temperature in a plastic bottle can leach phthalates from a bottle, not to mention a bottle that goes through temperature changes throughout a day.

Granted there's been great debate over all these studies and whether the levels of leached phthalates in the average plastic bottle are really high enough to merit health concerns. Either way, just think about the toxic byproducts of plastic production: dioxin (a carcinogen) and plastic waste. Enormous amounts of plastic waste from all those bottles that aren't recycled create equally enormous vortexes of plastic garbage in various oceans, where they wreak havoc on marine life. Moving away from plastic is healthier for the planet.

The Sigg bottles are just a tad heavier than their plastic counterparts. The water-based, polymer coating is taste-neutral and acid-resistant (think fruit juices), and guaranteed for the life of the bottle (5 years according to the manufacturer). They come in a variety of eye-catching designs and sizes. You can also purchase a variety of caps (i.e. the sport top) that increase the utility of the bottle for your specific needs.

-- Ari Cohn

Simple tea filter
Finum Goldton Tea Filters
$20 Finum

I make at least five cups of tea daily. Some at home and some at work. Over the years I've learned to appreciate nice loose-leaf teas that brew best in a basket that gives them room to "breathe." While I'd love to use a beautiful teapot, it's not always practical. The usual solution is these tiny mesh tea balls, but they don't allow the leaves to really expand. There are also tea tumblers with baskets, but I found most of their baskets tiny and hard to clean.

Luckily, I stumbled upon these Finum Goldton Filters. They are perfect for making a single cup of wonderfully brewed tea in whatever mug or cup is around. They have ample room and the tea infuses really well through the fine gold chamber. It's really easy to just spoon the tea in, no wrangling with stray leaves like with a tea ball.

Unlike traditional mesh, the gold walls are very easy to clean and I hardly ever have to pick stray leaves out. They also come with a cap that can allow a stronger brew as it keeps the temperature more constant. I recommend this simple Adobe Air app Tea-Timer to prevent over-steeping. After brewing the cap doubles as a stand for the filter, which keeps it from dripping all over the place. Another advantage of brewing a single cup at once is that I can serve guests any type of tea they want instead of sharing one single pot of tea. I originally got these for work, but I bought some for home and use mainly these instead of a tea pot.

-- Melissa McEwen

Leak-free, insulated mug
Contigo Autoseal Mug
$18 Contigo

Far and away the best travel mug I've used is the Contigo Autoseal Stainless Steel Mug. The Autoseal mechanism is the most leak-proof design I've found; it seals automatically when you're not actively drinking from it, so there's no worry about knocking it over with the top open. This is the only mug I'll use around my computers now.

I had a terrible experience with the Oxo mug. It was impossible to clean due to the enclosed design of the lid, and eventually accumulated way too much gunk inside for me to be comfortable using it. The lid on Contigo's mug is fairly open and easy to clean, and the entire thing is dishwasher safe, though they also sell a model with a colored body that isn't. They sell replacement lids for $7 if you have a problem, but I've been using four of them for over a year in heavy rotation with no issues.

Contigo also makes plastic smaller containers for kids and larger water bottles (both of which are BPA-free) with the same Autoseal design.

-- Adam Fields

Our task is not to foresee the future, but to enable it. - Antoine de Saint-Exupery

How to cook in small spaces
The Itty Bitty Kitchen Handbook
$12 (used) Justin Spring, 2006, 240 p.

I happened across this Cool Tool at the local library, and the subtitle ("Everything you need to know about setting up and cooking in the most ridiculously small kitchen in the world: Your own") caught me instantly. The cute cover suggests charm over content, but the book itself doesn't waste a paragraph. It's pithy, insightful, inspiring, and entertaining.

Justin Spring grew up on a boat, with a kitchen even smaller than mine — essentially a camp stove, an ice chest, and a bucket. He has huge insight into the problems of small kitchens, including the 'shut-off point' where clutter stops most food preparation and the local takeout place gets a lot of business.

He is not hesitant to make solid, practical suggestions, and includes websites for sourcing. He weighs in on everything from the best tool cabinet to repurpose for a kitchen, to the best sources for cheap, lead-free, by-the-stem crystal.

This is a truly holistic guide to getting the most possible use and enjoyment from a tiny kitchen. It includes 100 recipes tailored for the small kitchen ("one-pot, toaster oven brownies").

I have only had this book for a week, but it has inspired one full day of kitchen cleaning (!) and doubled the number of meals I eat at home. It is not comparable to anything else I've seen, either on the web or in print: no glossy photos of gleaming granite countertops, no vague, sentimental, market-friendly prose. The closest thing I've seen was Mark Bittman's guide to stocking a minimalist kitchen, but that was four pages and this is over two hundred.

If you are struggling with a tiny kitchen and have almost given up on eating at home, this book is a lifesaver. If you want to eat well, eat healthily, entertain occasionally, and generally live like a normal person despite your itty bitty kitchen, I can't recommend it enough.

-- Tricia Postle

And Also A Quick Word about Blenders

The best new blenders will now do the work of mixers and food processors– and in itty bitty kitchens, where limited counter space cuts down on the possibilities for countertop appliances, multitasks of this sort are particularly valuable. Nearly any blender will do for basic blending tasks (for ten years I managed very well with a used bar blender purchased for $5 at an Episcopal Church tag sale; I have no doubt it blended up many a daiquiri before it came into my life.)

●
The Refrigerator

Consider washing out your refrigerator interior with a deodorizing solution of baking soda and water and (after unplugging the appliance) cleaning the coils on the back– they attract dust, which interferes with the refrigerator's ability to cool and thus drives up your energy costs. If the refrigerator has wire shelving inside, install sheets of plexiglas over them– they will clean up easier, and your food items won't topple over so much. Just take the measurements to a hardware store and have the inexpensive Plexiglas cut to order.

●
Arrange it in a cook-friendly way. Try consolidating all your food into one cupboard or area so that you know what you have at a glance, and keep that list of your staple items handy—preferably in a clear plastic sleeve on the cupboard's inside shelf. In elevated cabinets holding many small items, consider buying stepped shelving for visibility all the way to the back. (Incidentally, you can make your own stepped shelving by cutting 2 x 4 lumber to fit, stacking as needed.) If you are a short person (or your cabinets are up high), consider buying yourself a foldaway step stool so that you have access to every last inch of IBK space.

Better than a blender
Cuisinart Smart Stick Hand Blender
$30 Amazon

I hate most kitchen gadgets with a passion. Seeing things like an avocado slicer, mango corer, or left-handed inverted egg whatsizinger give me the hives. For the longest time, I prided myself on being able to do the most with the least in the kitchen.

I'm saying all this because I wanted to convey just how hard it was to buy the Smart Stick a year ago on the recommendation of my wife. Normally blenders are hard to clean, bulky, loud, and can only be used for low-viscosity liquids; if the mixture is too thick, the blade just whirs uselessly.

The Smart Stick solves all that. It takes up virtually no space. It is easy to clean. Instead of scrubbing out a blender, you just pop off the Smart Stick's head, so it can be cleaned in eight seconds under running water. It's impressively powerful and can be jammed full force down into a glass of ice to chop it up quickly. Yet, it's still much quieter than a blender. The measuring cup it comes with is also well designed to break up the vortex the blender creates.

The Smart Stick is the cheapest and most basic hand blender I could find. Others come with whisks and choppers and brushed metal finishes, but I think the regular head works just fine. I found that the Smart Stick did 150% of what I've used a blender for and 75% of what I used a food processor for.

It's very versatile. No more "pour boiling hot broccoli soup into blender to cream it, then pour back into pot." You can use the Smart Stick right inside a stockpot on the stove. You can use it on thicker foods because you can stir and mash while blending, continuously bringing new material into the blade as opposed to a stand blender's reliance on gravity to find unblended parts.

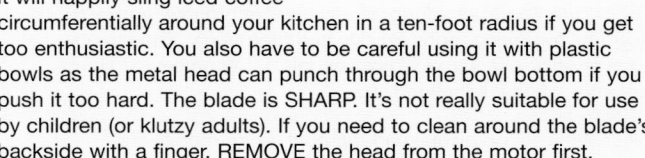

Making hummus, salsa, applesauce, and pesto went from "giant mess" to "easy." Making smoothies went from "big production" to "two minutes." Guacamole and whipped cream turn out wonderfully smooth. Margaritas can be made right in the pitcher. Almond butter can be made without too much trouble. I imagine this would also be a lifesaver for making baby food.

There are some downsides: It only has one speed (high!), so you have to be careful and use it in bursts if chopping ice, as it will happily sling iced coffee circumferentially around your kitchen in a ten-foot radius if you get too enthusiastic. You also have to be careful using it with plastic bowls as the metal head can punch through the bowl bottom if you push it too hard. The blade is SHARP. It's not really suitable for use by children (or klutzy adults). If you need to clean around the blade's backside with a finger, REMOVE the head from the motor first.

Again, I really really wanted to hate this thing and didn't buy one for the longest time because I considered it useless. Now it's the only electric kitchen tool that remains permanently plugged in on my counter other than a Kitchen-Aid six-quart mixer.

-- Jon Braun

Space saving funnel
Collapsible Silicone Funnel
$8 Amazon

My kitchen is on the small side, which means every inch of space must be efficient and tidy. While most funnels are bulky and take up valuable room, this one is compact enough to fit in a studio-size kitchen or be a welcomed addition to any camping pack.

The accordion-style pleats not only allow you to collapse the silicone funnel so it fits neatly even in a shallow drawer. The pleats also allow you to adjust the height and width of the funnel for pouring into various-sized containers.

Since the funnel is made of high-quality silicone, it is dishwasher safe and heat and cold resistant, making it more durable and longer-lasting than plastic funnels. Other potential uses: changing your car's oil or adding washer fluid. If you plan to use it in the garage, of course, I'd recommend getting a second one.

-- Kelly Spitzer

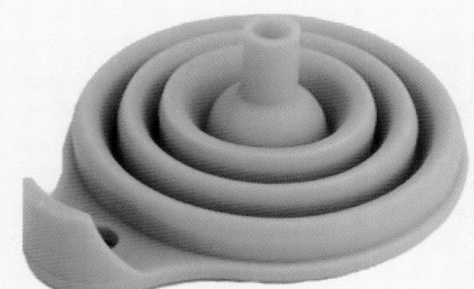

Easy, no-soap wok and pan cleaning tool
Bamboo Wok Brush
$7 Amazon

I use well-seasoned cast iron and carbon steel pans for the better part of my cooking. To clean them, I've used the same bamboo wok brush than I bought at a corner market in Sacramento in 1990. I've been thinking of buying a new one, just so I can phase it in over a few years while I slowly retire the original. It only takes a few swishes around the inside of the pan with hot water

(no soap!) and a rinse to clean a pan. In the time I've been using it on my iron and steel pans, including the wok I use occasionally, I've gone through countless sponges, scotch-brite pads, and those looped-plastic scrubbies that I use on stock pots etc., all of which get pretty hinky once put into use and have to be run through the dishwasher to get free of food particles. It also looks dignified and fine sitting on the countertop by the sink, has just gotten more seasoned, and never needs more than a rinse to get clean. The edges of the cane bristles are pretty blunted by now and a new one might work better for attacking the occasional nuclear cooking mess. On the other hand, it's gentle enough on the built-up seasoning in my pans that they keep getting non-stickier and shed scorched cheese like schmutz on teflon.

The brush I bought way back when has flat bristles, about 11 inches long by 3/16 wide, and stouter than most of the wok brushes I've seen recently in Asian groceries. I can't imagine that there's been much innovation in wok brush technology in the last 3000 years, but quality is probably inconsistent on an item like this, even from the same seller. Unless you have access to Asian markets and can shop around while you're out making your weekly durian run, Amazon has a variety to choose from, all about $7.50 with shipping. The Wok Shop seems to be reputable, but it might be prudent to order a few just in case yours only lasts as long as a good hamster.

-- Brian Garber-Yonts

No more burned fingers
Bamboo Toast Tongs
12" $4 Amazon

My wife brought home a pair of bamboo toast tongs from a "Pampered Chef" housewares party, and I've been surprised at how useful they are. We have a standard toaster, and also make homemade bread in small pans. I hadn't realized how many times I'd been burning myself on the toaster or what a hassle removing smaller slices had been until I started using these.

I guess I find the concept more useful than any particular implementation as I imagine that the adept use of chopsticks would serve the same function.

-- Mark Crane

Dehydrators

Affordable dehydrator
Nesco Food Dehydrator

$60 Amazon

The Nesco Food Dehydrator is a simple, affordable, and well-built tool for drying foods quickly and thoroughly. Though not an every-day-use item for most people, it becomes absolutely essential when it is needed.

I recently went on a weekend trip hunting for morels and returned with far more than I could eat. Luckily, this dehydrator made short work of the excess. The stackable trays easily fit 60 whole small morels and many of the larger ones which I'd cut in half. Altogether, I fit about three pounds of mushrooms in five trays.

Like the previously reviewed Excalibur Food Dehydrator, the Nesco model has a temperature control, fan, and heating unit.

The Nesco's heating unit is built into the top (cheaper models heat bottom-up) that sits atop the stack of trays and blows air through a central column allowing for better distribution and airflow throughout.

I used a temperature of 110F when drying morels, and left them to dry over night for about 8 hours. Since any moisture can lead to a ruined batch, I made sure to let them dry out for a little longer than necessary. They were perfectly dried the next morning, and ready for storage in an airtight container.

While I have mainly used this model for mushrooms, the large trays and variable temperature dial (95-160F) allow for a wide range of dried foods to be made. This particular model is also expandable to 12 trays if you need to dry a truly astonishing amount of food.

The Nesco, when compared with the Excalibur, has the benefit of being nearly $125 cheaper combined with a smaller (though expandable) footprint, a relatively-quiet fan, and similarly adjustable temperature.

-- JC

I have experience with both the Excalibur and the more recently-reviewed Nesco, a smaller and less expensive dehydrator. The Excalibur is a superior product if you are a heavy user and tend to be drying large batches of produce at

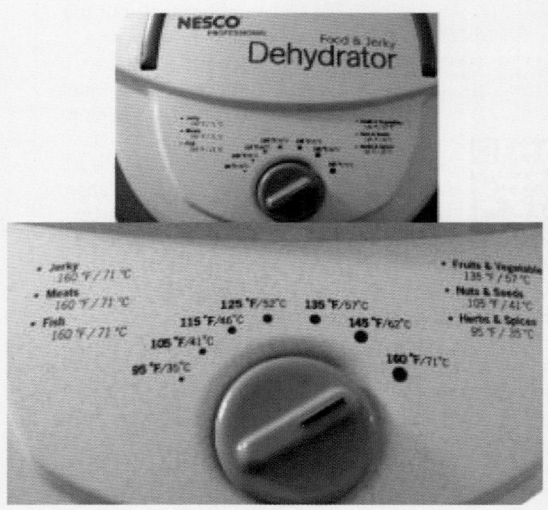

once. It has quite a bit more capacity due to the design (no center hole and square racks make a big difference). The horizontal airflow system does dry large batches more uniformly. Although you can add racks to the Nesco, it dries less efficiently, and once you add in the cost of extra racks you are approaching the same price as the Excalibur.

Having said that, the price on the Nesco has really dropped and the top-down heater/blower is a nice upgrade over the older bottom-fan models. Heck, you could almost get three of them for the same price as an Excalibur, although that would take up a lot of storage space and use more energy to power 3 units.

-- Oliver Hulland

DIY dried goods
Excalibur Food Dehydrator

I've been using this 9-tray dehydrator once or twice a week for the last three years to make dried fruit, veggies, jerky, dog treats, and dried bread crumbs. Other uses include re-crisping crackers, cookies, and chips, and thoroughly drying wet photographs and flowers.

Overall, this is truly the most flexible dehydrator I've found. The thermostat is adjustable (85-145F), so you can customize your dehydrating. The removable trays allow you to experiment with sizes, quantities and varieties of foods sorted by temperature range. If you group shorter-term items by tray, you just remove those trays first, then keep the remaining items/trays inside a bit longer.

Other units heat unevenly from the bottom, require you to manually rotate trays, and — in the case of cheaper units — don't let you control the temperature. Along with a thermostat, the Excalibur has a fan that distributes heat more evenly; it also features a timer, so it will automatically turn off at a desired time whether you're around or not.

All of the dehydrators I've used generate noise (I now use my Ronco and Home Essentials models exclusively for making dog treats). Since the Excalibur isn't quiet, I keep it in our craft room. It's very easy to clean. I enjoy not throwing out spoiled food. We always have

healthy snack alternatives for us and our grandkids — and they enjoy contributing to the process as much as they eating the rewards. Ever since we moved to a property with grapevines, they've helped us make copious amounts of raisins.

Tips:

1) To make fruit yogurt leathers or work with items high in moisture content, you'll need ParaFlexx non-stick drying sheets. Excalibur provides a pretty good guide on how to work with different foods.

2) If you buy direct from the manufacturer, it may be slightly more expensive, but I understand they'll guarantee the unit for 10 years; otherwise, you can purchase a 10-year extended warranty.

-- Chris Lewis

I have experience with both the Excalibur and the more recently-reviewed Nesco, a smaller and less expensive dehydrator. The Excalibur is a superior product if you are a heavy user and tend to be drying large batches of produce at once. It has quite a bit more capacity due to the design (no center hole and square racks make a big difference). The horizontal airflow system does dry large batches more uniformly. Although you can add racks to the Nesco, it dries less efficiently, and once you add in the cost of extra racks you are approaching the same price as the Excalibur.

Having said that, the price on the Nesco has really dropped and the top-down heater/blower is a nice upgrade over the older bottom-fan models. Heck, you could almost get three of them for the same price as an Excalibur, although that would take up a lot of storage space and use more energy to power 3 units.

-- JC

$212 Excalibur Food Dehydrator Amazon

$16 ParaFlexx Sheets Amazon

Affordable, freeze-dried goods
Dehydrated Food In Bulk

Backpackers, canoeists, campers and scouts have two basic ways to stock their food supply: classic prepackaged freeze-dried meals or building your own menu. Commercial freeze-dried camping food is expensive, limits menu choices and is hit or miss in the flavor department. Most of us have learned to shop carefully at the grocery store and put together a fairly lightweight, nutritious menu for weekend trips. But add a couple of people and extend the trip for two or three days and grocery store options get a bit heavy. Supplementing with bulk freeze-dried or dehydrated food expands the choices and cuts down the packed weight while developing a tasty, nutritious menu without blowing the budget. If you are planning an extended trip, I highly recommend assembling your menu with these two suppliers in mind.

-- Clarke Green

Honeyville Food Products

I've organized six days of food for 18 people in two crews for a canoe trip (18 meals, 324 servings), which would have been impossible — or just plain expensive — had I not ordered Honeyville's goods. They offer a wide variety of vegetables, fruits and other foodstuffs in bulk (#10 tin cans, and cases even). While a single-serving package of freeze-dried strawberries (.06 oz.) from Mountain House is $3.00 ($50.00 an ounce!), Honeyville's #10 can of freeze-dried strawberries (6 oz.) costs just $17.00 ($2.83 an ounce). They will ship an order of any size anywhere in the continental U.S. for under five dollars — just a little more than a gallon of gas!

Prices Vary Honeyville Food Products

Harmony House Foods

Soups, vegetables, fruits and textured vegetable protein (i.e. soy-based meat substitute) in large AND smaller quantities so you customize freeze-dried meals for long, big, short and small trips. They also offer a Backpacking Kit, a pre-selected assortment of dried foods that will make a variety of dishes. Don't miss these two very helpful PDF files: Using Dehydrated Products and a Serving Size Chart.

$65 Deluxe Sampler Harmony House Foods

When you ask for an adventure, there will be detours. - Kevin Kelly

Versatile one pot meals
Fagor 3-in-1 Multicooker
$90 Amazon

Last summer I tried some carrot soup that tasted like buttered toffee. It had been made in a pressure cooker, which heats water vapor above boiling temperature, greatly reducing normal cooking times. I told my parents I was going to get a pressure cooker, and they recommended the Fagor multi cooker, because unlike most pressure cookers it has an electric browning feature, which lets you brown beef, fish, or chicken right in the pot before you pressure cook it, greatly improving the flavor.

The Fagor is also a slow cooker and a rice cooker. Because it is so versatile, I use it almost every day. The throw-everything-in-the-pot-and-push-a-button approach has broadened my cooking horizons. I've made rib roast in the slow cooker that had my in-laws coming back for thirds. I've made mouth-watering chicken stuffed with sun-dried tomato pesto, basil and goat cheese in a matter of minutes. I've made salmon with spinach and lemon sauce, fennel and Italian sausage, creamy risotto, and spicy Bolognese sauce. Thanks to an online army of pressure-cooker devotees, I'll never run out of recipes.

The only negative thing about the Fagor is that the user interface doesn't make it clear when it is cooking. A couple of times I've set the timer and forgotten to press the start button, only to find out twenty minutes later that it never started. I've learned not to do that.

-- Mark Frauenfelder

Smart grain cooker
Zojirushi Rice Cooker
$167 Amazon

This is the best thing with a plug. Pop water and rice in the bowl, set the timer, and you'll have a perfect bowl of rice waiting for you when you get home. Don't worry if you get hung up in traffic, the Zojirushi will keep your rice perfectly moist, and warm.

-- Chris S.

Commonly used in Japan, this type of fuzzy-logic rice cooker can be set ahead of time. I've purchased several for friends and family and have settled on the Zojirushi brand. I've used a Zojirushi for several years, and it has held up well and completely changed my cooking habits.

In the evenings I load up the pot with oatmeal and/or grain mixture for hot breakfast the following morning. And the mornings, I load up the pot for dinner – rice, whole grains, barley, lentils, beans, and/or spices. When I walk into the house after work, the air is fragrant with cooking. The cooker can keep its contents warm and fairly fresh for a few hours after the timer goes off.

My favorite model is the Zojirushi NS-ZAC10 (5 cup capacity) though I'd get the larger model if I had a bigger family.

-- Douglas O'Heir

Instant hot water source
Zojirushi Electric Dispensing Pot
$127 Amazon

Like the rice cooker, the electric dispensing pot is an appliance that EVERY Japanese household has. Its function is simple: It heats and dispenses hot water at just-below-boiling, as much or as little as you want. Perfect for a cup of tea or a cup of noodles. There's even a "Keep Warm" feature for maintaining the water temp at 208F, 195F, or 175F for a set amount of time.

We picked up Zojirushi's 3.0-liter US version when we moved back from Japan. It's performed flawlessly for well over a decade. Lots of nice little touches: The "MagSafe" magnetic power cord featured in Apple's laptop computers? Zojirushi did it first; makes it easy to move the pot to the tap to fill it up.

-- Robert Woodhead

Non-Electric Slow-Cook
Nissan Thermal Cooker
$166 Get Prepared Stuff

Ever wish you could whip up a pot of chicken and dumplings, go on your bike ride or canoe paddle or even just hike, and have it piping hot and ready for you when you get back to the car? Ok, more likely it rained or snowed on your ride/paddle/hike and you're shivering and wish you had any hot food back at the car. This is experience speaking.

Nissan, the makers of vacuum mugs to keep your coffee warmer longer, also makes a 4-quart powerless crockpot. No plugs. No heater. It's wonderful.

Here's how it works: pull the inner pot out of the device and put it on the range at home (or the stove at camp). Insert ingredients. Heat 'em up to a boil. Put the inner-lid on, then insert the inner pot into the outer pot. Seal the outer-lid. Put the whole device in your car (or your boat, or your dogsled). Have some fun for 3-6 hours. Open the pots and dish out the steaming food..

The crock-pot has recently come back on the market, and is again being hyped as a tailgater essential. Bah. Tailgaters

Best cheap nuke-it popcorn maker
Nordic Ware Microwave Corn Popper
$9 Amazon

This microwave popper is simplicity itself: 1/2 cup of corn, a little oil (or not), and a little time in the microwave yields a low-cost, low-cal snack you can eat right out of the popper. Unlike other poppers or Tupperware containers, the Nordic Ware's top cover has nifty ridges that facilitate comfortable removal — i.e. when everything is very, very hot (If you don't remove the cover immediately, the popcorn gets too moist).

I've tried a variety of devices on my long march to the perfect popper… table-top poppers often made a mess (and big noise) and they're not machine-washable. Some microwave poppers require pads that deteriorate with use and need to be replaced, but are difficult to find. The stove top method, I just could never fully master: burned pans, burned corn, mess to clean. Lastly, microwavable bags of popcorn: If you eat a lot popcorn, you'll be spending exorbitant sums and — depending on which brand — consuming chemical additives. The Nordic popper does not require oil, so the end-product is essentially the same as an air popper. The Nordic can go in the dishwasher, or just be wiped clean. Plus, the Nordic is perhaps the least expensive one out there. As of late, we've been producing popcorn five nights a week.

-- Daniel Wilson

and church-potluckers aren't going to shell out $149 for a crockpot. People who do endurance races in the northern climates: now there's your target audience. And don't forget that this crockpot is more electricity-efficient than the normal kitchen plug-in models; it takes none once it's hot so it makes a great kitchen addition for the average treehugger.

-- Rita Nygren

Simple recipes:

1 lb hamburger, browned

2 cans diced tomato

1 lb of elbow mac

Combine ingredients, bring to boil, seal, wait 3 hours. Serves 2-4 people.

Rice-a-roni (any flavor)

Butter

Canned chicken

Fresh veggies, diced

Prepare rice as directed on box. When you get to the cover and simmer stage, dump in the chicken and veggies, then seal in pot. Cook a little longer then directions call for. Servers 2.

2 cans chicken broth

1 can chicken

2 cups wild rice blend

2 cups Simply Veggies (freeze dried vegetables)

Bay leaf

Salt & pepper

Combine ingredients and boil, leave over heat for 5-10 minutes. Seal in pot. Wait 2-4 hours. Serves 4-8 people.

Cooking Hacks

Best popcorn & coffee roaster
Whirley-Pop Popcorn Popper
$30 Amazon

My Aunt Lee bought several of these popcorn poppers and gave them away as Christmas presents over 20 years ago and I am so happy with the one I received that I still use it today.

It makes the best tasting popcorn with very few "old maids" in minutes. Put just a splash of oil in it, add a couple of kernels of corn, turn the stove to Med-High, wait for the few kernels to pop, add a half cup of popping corn and turn the handle. They seem really cheap because they are made from very thin walled aluminum but that's why they work so well as they transfer the heat instantly.

You get light, fluffy, wonderful popcorn every time and virtually all of it pops. I can make a batch of popcorn during a commercial break and never miss a beat. You use very little oil so it's better for you than that microwave stuff and tastes much better than an air popped batch.

If you enjoy fresh popcorn, the Whirley-Pop Theater Stovetop Popcorn Popper is the best way to make it.

-- Mark Wialbut

Roasting coffee at home is one of the best kept secrets. You get far superior coffee at a much lower cost – and I live in Seattle so I'm comparing this with the best roasters around. It's easy to do, takes about 20 minutes (basic instructions and links below) and produces about a pound at a time. I've been roasting 1-2 times a week for over 2 years.

Many home roasters use old air poppers as roasters. These can work fine but you need to get the correct air popper (new ones usually don't work). They are much harder to control and they make a serious mess (when fresh beans are roasted the outer skin cooks off as a light chaff which air poppers blow all over the place). Home roasters (previously reviewed here) give you far less control and typically involve somewhat laborious cleaning of parts. Also the inexpensive ones don't handle the chaff problem. Air poppers and home roasters also provide almost no way to control the considerable smokiness of the process which is why most people use them outdoors.

I use a popcorn popper very much like the Whirley-Pop Theater Stovetop Popcorn Popper but it is significantly more durable in material (stainless steel vs aluminum), gauge (much thicker) and gears (metal vs plastic). This is important when roasting coffee (vs. popcorn) because it is much heavier and puts significantly more strain on the parts. Also, heavier pots distribute heat better.

I've been using this popper for almost 2 years and it's never been cleaned and it works like a charm – well worth it. Replacement gears are available for a few bucks online and they will eventually wear out (especially if you use a drill for stirring instead of your hands).

Jump In!: Reading about coffee roasting is worthwhile and Sweet Marias (see p. 182) has everything you need to know. The only problem is that it will make you think it is far more complicated than it really is. The bottom line is that it takes a little practice and once you have done it you realize you just have to get the temperature right and watch/listen/smell for the obvious signs of it being ready. Don't be put off, just jump in and try it. I've tried many DIY things from the Arduino to making jam and I can assure you that this is the easiest and most rewarding of all them.

-- Charles Borwick

Low temperature cooking
Beginning Sous Vide
$23 Jason Logsdon, 2010, 201 p.

There's a new way of cooking. When food is simmered in a sealed pouch at low temperatures for long periods of time the food flavors are surprisingly enhanced. Meats in particular benefit from this type of preparation, called sous vide in French. I found fish and veggies made by this method to be amazingly tasty, with a unique texture and bursting with savories. Meats are stunningly moist without being overdone or underdone. This method is neither roasting, stewing, or searing. It's a whole new method of cooking that brings a new set of flavors, textures, and treats.

But lower cooking temperatures require more exactitude, and the food pouches need to have their air removed to ensure even cooking, so the equipment to cook this way has been expensive and confined to fancy restaurants. Naturally, amateurs quickly figured out home versions, while appliance makers started selling cheaper residential gadgets.

But know-how was still in short supply. I found this cookbook the best one to start out with. Low temperature or sous vide cooking requires a whole new set of recipes. Cooking times are so different you need charts to determine duration and temperature, which this book provides. This guide explains the principles extremely well and they assume you'll be using homemade or home grade equipment. Basically what you need is a water bath that can maintain its temperature to within a few degrees over several hours or more. Dedicated units have bubblers and thermostats to keep very even water temperatures. And an ordinary FoodSaver freezer vacuum unit will produce airless watertight pouches of food.

However there is an extremely easy and cheap way to try out sous vide cooking for the first time without buying any equipment at all. You are limited in what you can do, but you'll get an idea of what the process can do. All you need is a cooler, a kitchen thermometer, and a vacuum packed hunk of food from the grocery store.

As as example, we took some frozen vacuum packed fish from Trader Joe's. First you defrost it.

Then you fill up the cooler halfway or so with water heated on the stove to the appropriate low temperature (found in the book or online). In the case of fish it's probably not much above the maximum temperature coming out of your water heater. Let the food

steep in the water for the required time. (It can be up to hours for meat.) You may need to add some hot water if your thermometer shows the water cooling. Unwrap the finished fish and add sauce.

If you like the results you can build your own bath, or purchase a home unit, and use this book to guide your exploration.

-- KK

- The basic concept of sous vide cooking is that food should be cooked at the temperature it will be served at. For instance, if you are cooking a steak to medium rare, you want to serve it at 131°F.

With traditional cooking methods you would normally cook it on a hot grill or oven at around 400°F-500°F and pull it off at the right moment when the middle has reached 131°F. This results in a bulls-eye effect of burnt meat on the outside turning to medium rare in the middle. This steak cooked sous vide would be cooked at 131°F for several hours. This will result in the entire piece of meat being a perfectly cooked medium rare. The steak would then usually be quickly seared at a high heat to add the flavorful, browned crust to it.

- A great low-cost method of sealing your food is food-grade ziploc bags. They have a few drawbacks but work great for short cooked foods, especially if you are just getting started with sous vide cooking and do not want to spend any up-front money. In most cases sealing your foods with ziploc bags is also a lot easier than using a vacuum sealer.

- Many home cooks prefer a standard home vacuum sealer like a FoodSaver. These vacuum sealers work by inserting the opening of the sous vide food pouch into a small depression in the machine. The sealer then sucks the air out of the pouch and seals it using a heating element. They are the most cost effective method of vacuum sealing your food.

- The main advantage is price. If you already have a cooler and ziploc bags then it is basically free to try.

Another advantage is that the water coming out of many home faucets is around 131°F-139°F, meaning it is the perfect temperature to cook steak in. If your faucet is in that range it just means you open up the tap water, fill the cooler, and throw in the steak. It can be very simple.

- Some of the most impressive results of sous vide are created with tough cuts of beef. Sous vide allows you to do things that traditional methods are unable to accomplish, such as cooking short ribs medium-rare but still tenderizing them, or creating fall-apart medium-rare roasts.

This is accomplished because cooking tough cuts of beef with sous vide allows you to break down and tenderize the meat without cooking it above medium-rare and drying it out. Once temperatures in beef go above 140°F the meat begins to dry out and become more bland. However, they also start to tenderize more quickly above this temperature which is why tough roasts and braises are done for hours at high temperatures. Using sous vide, you can hold the meat below 140°F for a long enough time for the tenderizing process to run its course.

- Most tough cuts of beef are cooked sous vide for between 1 and 2 days. However, for some more tender beef roasts shorter cooking times of 4 to 8 hours will be enough time to tenderize the meat fully.

- If adding a sauce or marinade make sure your vacuum sealer does not suck it out, you can normally seal it before all the air is out to prevent this just fine. Also, we do not recommend using fresh garlic, onions, or ginger, as they can begin to take on a bad flavor over the long cooking times.

Whatever has not happened yet will happen. - J. B. S. Haldane

Cooking with hot water
Sous Vide Supreme
$429 Amazon

My wife and I both work long hours, and getting dinner on the table can be a challenge. Often our window for doing so may be as little as 15-20 minutes from the time we walk in the door, otherwise the kids will start to get hungry and have a hard time settling down to eat. In the past year we've missed that window more often than I'd like, and if we have a half an hour or more of cooking ahead of us, we'll usually end up ordering instead. In addition to being less healthy overall, this can cost us around $30-$40 per meal over the cost of what we would have paid for ingredients for dinner, even buying top quality ingredients at the farmer's market.

At $400 the Sous Vide Supreme is pricey, but if it can prevent us from ordering out even once a week, it will literally pay for itself in four months. We used it five times in the first week. Time will tell if this is a novelty effect, but so far I've been overwhelmingly thrilled with the results. There's been a lot of focus on 30-minute meals, but for a busy working parent or two, that can be an eternity. Pair the Sous Vide Supreme with a rice cooker with a timer and a microwave vegetable steamer and it becomes possible to get a completely freshly cooked dinner on the table with minimal work in less than ten minutes. Even without going to that extreme, it significantly cuts the amount of stove time required for a "regular" meal. It's completely changed the way I look at preparing large portions of food in advance.

Sous vide cooking is actually pretty simple. You seal the food in a vacuum bag (like a Foodsaver bag) and then cook it in a precise temperature water bath at very close to the temperature you want the final product to be. When the food is done (at minimum, enough time for the middle to reach the equilibrium temperature), you take it out of the bag, sear it in a hot pan if needed (most proteins will benefit from a little browning to develop more flavor, but they really only need about 30-seconds per side in a very hot pan on the stove), and serve it right away. If you leave it in the water bath for a few extra hours, it's no problem; the texture of some food will break down after an extended period of time, but for the most part, it's hard to overcook things (fish and eggs are two exceptions – they're more finicky about timing, but that still buys you a margin of an hour or two over). Because you can set the Sous Vide Supreme at 1-degree increments and it will stay at pretty much exactly that temperature, you can get exquisite results with very little effort, and if you get distracted, it's no problem.

Sous vide cooking certainly requires some planning ahead – it's not for quick dinners unless you start early, but you don't have to really figure out how early to start – putting the bag in before you leave in the morning is just fine. It's also a huge psychological boost, because when you get home, dinner's already on the way to being cooked. When all you want to do is sit down after a long day and the kids are hungry, it really helps to have things already started.

We've done chicken breasts, steak, 30-hour country style pork ribs, carrots in butter – all pretty perfect. Soft boiled eggs and pork chops deserve special mention. Eggs do completely different things in sous vide, because the yolk actually cooks at a lower temperature than the white, and so it cooks first. A soft boiled egg in sous vide gets you a creamy but cooked yolk and a runny white. It's strange, but entirely delicious. Hard boiled eggs were a little off, because cooking at a high enough temperature to set the white actually overcooks the yolk a little bit. I prefer 8 minutes in water just off the boil. Big fat scallops came out intensely creamy and tender.

The oven comes with a few recipes with common timings, but there's little news there if you know what your target temperatures are for regular cooking; steak at 130F, pork chops at 135F, chicken at 142F, fish at 140F, etc. There is no shortage of recipes on various food blogs though some are meant for a more industrial setting. There are some extra safety considerations, but it's mostly just common sense, and much of it doesn't come into play in a home setting where you're not storing the bags for long periods of time. You just have to be careful that you're dealing with a somewhat anaerobic environment that can breed microbes that usually aren't a problem in home kitchens. As long as you're buying quality food, treating it with respect (understanding the rules of heating, chilling, and storage), and eating it promptly, you shouldn't have any problems.

In short, this device is amazing, and it's the future. For me, it fulfills every convenience promise of the microwave and the crock pot, neither of which I've ever been happy with from a culinary perspective. There is a small consideration of the extra waste in plastic bags, but I balance that against the amount of waste generated from takeout, which is far greater.

I can't recommend it enough.

-- Adam Fields

Best early economical sous-vide
SideKIC Immersion Circulator
$170 icakitchen.com

At present time, this food-grade heated water pump controlled by a thermostat is the cheapest commercial way to do slow cooking at the critical precision of sous vide. It can maintain a large pot of water at plus/minus 0.5 degree, which is what you want to cook a hunk of meat to perfection. How it works: the small submerged pump in the device keeps the heated water circulating past the heater to maintain a constant temperature. It's a poor-person's sous vide machine, although it has many limitations, including how long it takes to get hot. According to the Wirecutter, it's the best of the current inexpensive options. There will be better and more complete slow-cook appliances coming. This one is for early adopters.

-- KK

Easy home vacuum preservation
Vacuum Food Sealer V2244
$80 FoodSaver

I first saw the FoodSaver on an infomercial years ago and bought it on a late-night whim but it has turned out to be the coolest thing I ever bought for the kitchen. It has changed my approach to food entirely. There are lots of attachments available but  all you need are roll bags, and a box of mason jars from the local hardware store (cheap). You then vacuum seal everything in the cabinet and fridge (jars) and freezer (jars or bags) — including veggies, milk, rice, etc. Everything lasts 4 to 5 times as long plus tastes better and retains the nutrition better. Food savings alone make up for any costs, but that nice "swoosh" sound of prying off the lid from a mason jar is very satisfying and reassuring.

I did an experiment leaving fresh parsley in the veggie drawer of the refrigerator, and putting some in a vacuum sealed mason jar. After 2 weeks the drawer stored parsley was still usable but smelled and tasted "off" like mold. Opening the mason jar the smell of fresh parsley came out and it tasted like it was just bought. I can only imagine the vitamin and mineral content was retained better too. One side effect is my refrigerator has more room and is easy to manage as mason jars are uniform to stack and pack.

I store all my pantry dry goods in vacuumed mason jars. Beans, rice, coffee, hot chocolate, sugar, etc., and label everything with the date. Most dried goods pick up bacteria and molds that are not visible which is why you should not buy from bulk food bins that have no expiration date. The typical life is around 6 months to a year for most dry goods but with vacuum sealing it can last much longer and retain more nutritional value.

If I come into a large quantity of food and want to save it longer than a week I freeze. The best way is to first freeze it so it gets hard, then vacuum seal, this way the strong vacuum does not mush it. For liquids like soup, freeze it in the serving bowls, run under hot water to remove from the bowl and you have a chunk of soup in the shape of a bowl, vacuum seal and it is an instant meal that can be re-heated in the original bowl. For example, turkey and ham from the holidays: Cut the meat off the carcass into small chunks, freeze it, vacuum seal it in small portions (I have 5 or 6 bags of turkey from Thanksgiving) and you have cooked meat packets for recipes without having to dethaw the entire amount.

I was at first worried about recurring bag costs. But a case of 12 11"x18" rolls can be bought from the manufacture's website for $130 and so far it has lasted many years. That is a lot of bags at 18 feet per roll and it is possible to re-use bags. The pre-cut bags are nice but costly, the roll bags give you more control over bag size and thus usage. Do not get the Tilia canister or bulk storage items because they lose their seal and are flimsy materials; mason jars work better and are cheaper.

I recommend the lowest-cost Food Saver as it does everything you need and is entirely manual operation. The more expensive models will automate some tasks like cutting the roll and have more capacity, but they take up more counter space. Mine has lasted over 7 years of regular use and still going strong. The 550 comes with the wide-mouth jar sealer attachment which fits wide-mouth pint, 1Q and 1/2 gallon mason jars. It uses normal mason lids sold in hardware stores so you don't need to buy anything other than the attachment.

What and how you vacuum seal is up to you and creativity is the name of the game. If you're looking to buy on the cheap they often show up on the police auction site and eBay.

-- Stephen Balbach

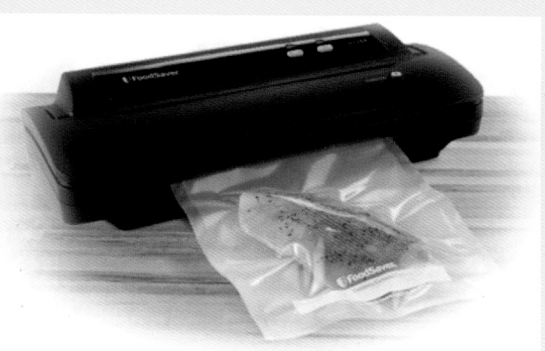

The original model this review was based on is no longer produced. The current low-end FoodSaver model V2244 ($80) does not include the jar attachment.. It needs to be ordered separately..

-- KK

Kitchen Safety

Kitchen fire-killer
Food-Safe Fire Extinguisher
$25 Amazon

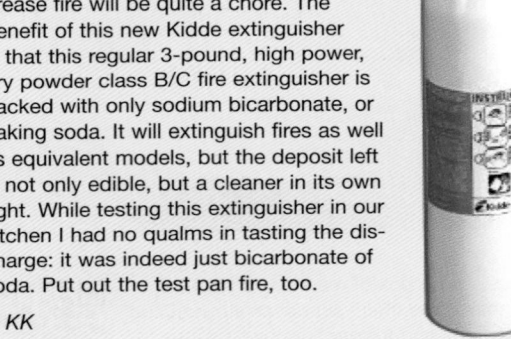

You need a fire extinguisher in your kitchen. One that really works well rather than one that looks really good. Most fire extinguishers that easily put out a kitchen-type fire use a mix of chemicals that are not food safe. Cleaning up the sticky powder left after a short blast for even a small grease fire will be quite a chore. The benefit of this new Kidde extinguisher is that this regular 3-pound, high power, dry powder class B/C fire extinguisher is packed with only sodium bicarbonate, or baking soda. It will extinguish fires as well as equivalent models, but the deposit left is not only edible, but a cleaner in its own right. While testing this extinguisher in our kitchen I had no qualms in tasting the discharge: it was indeed just bicarbonate of soda. Put out the test pan fire, too.

-- KK

Hot science mitts
Bel-Art Autoclave Gloves
$34 Amazon

I've always thought that autoclave gloves would be tremendously useful tools in the kitchen despite only ever using them in the lab.

For one thing, almost all oven mitts are just that; mitts. They're unwieldy and often so thin you can't pick things up for more than a couple seconds before the heat passes through the material.

Autoclave gloves also allow for a vastly greater degree of articulation. They come in pairs and have individual fingers. And they stand up to heat (up to 450 F, or 100F more than the Ove Glove) really well, too. I've picked things up that were fresh out of the autoclave, so just a step below boiling, and even though I was holding a one liter glass flask full of completely scalding water, it was a good ten to fifteen seconds before the heat coming through the gloves started to get anywhere near uncomfortable. And unlike the previously reviewed Ove Glove these autoclave gloves protect your forearm as well.

My point is that these gloves are perfectly made for grabbing things out of the oven without having to worry about fumbling the pan because you didn't get a good grip with the mittens or because it got so hot you had to set it down immediately.

-- Chevan C.

For those looking for the ultimate in heat protection you can get a pair of Kevlar glassblowing gloves that are rated to up to 1,000 degrees Fahrenheit from Artco for $34. They are, however, significantly less dextrous than other gloves. --OH

$34 Kevlar High Temperature Gloves Artco

Apron with pot holders
Royal VKB Oven Mitt Apron
$25 Amazon

We avoid clutter in our kitchen, so all towels, pot holders and oven mitts live in a drawer next to the stove. Accessible, but nowhere near as handy as this apron that literally puts two padded mitts at your side, right where you need 'em, whenever you need 'em. So simple, so elegant. The slits lessen your below-the-belt coverage, of course, but the convenience is a worthy trade.

-- Steven Leckart

How to cut correctly
Knife Skills Illustrated: A User's Manual
$20 Peter Hertzmann, 2007, 256 p.

I have used this fantastic reference book for about three months and it has greatly improved my time in the kitchen. Cooking consists mainly of three basic skills: heating things, putting things together (mixing) and taking things apart (cutting). This book is focused exclusively on the last set of skills.

Why are good knife skills so important? They allow you to cut food without hurting yourself. Also, as the author explains, "you are able to cut it into evenly sized pieces that will all cook at the same rate." In many cases, you can reduce waste by using a well-thought out cutting technique. In practice, the book has also improved my efficiency in the kitchen, since I can now dice an onion in about a dozen or so deliberate strokes of the knife, rather than chopping haphazardly until I get it into roughly the shape I want it in. There are also aesthetic advantages–good presentation is easier to achieve with consistently cut pieces of food. Finally, as the author notes: "With good knife skills, cooking becomes fun." I couldn't agree more.

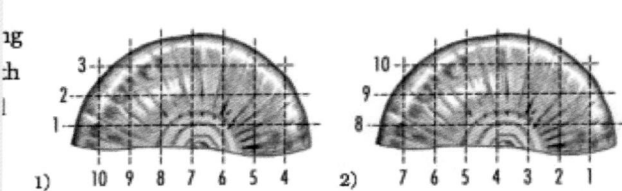

horizontal cuts, as indicated in (2). The numbers represent

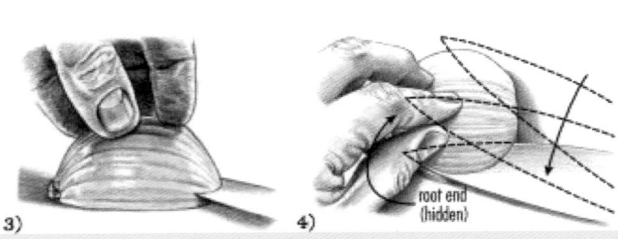

Dicing an onion, the traditional method.

The book walks readers through the process of selecting the proper tool for the job and illustrates the pros and cons of various shapes and blade materials for various tasks. After getting familiar with the two basic grips (yes, you have probably been doing it wrong all your life), knife care and cutting boards are covered briefly and then the real fun begins.

Heatproof Glove for Outback Cooking
JML Incredible Oven Glove
$16 JML Direct

I could see the utility of a fireproof glove on a camping trip; I didn't want to take a "spondonicle." Nomex flight gloves looked to fit the bill. But before I could buy a pair, I came across the significantly cheaper 'Incredible Oven Glove' at the supermarket. It's a five-fingered Kevlar and cotton glove that's quite thick.

I used it for adjusting the fire and for handling my billy, utensils and metal cup. The glove worked admirably, giving plenty of mobility. I could hold on to very hot things for long enough for them to cool down without feeling any of the heat. It fits both hands (the one-size-fits-all was just adequate for my large hands). Mine was blackened from soot, but a run through the washing machine when I got back had it good as new.

Be careful, as the glove doesn't protect from hot water and steam penetrates a little. But if I intend to cook again while in the bush, the oven glove will come with me. I haven't used it in the kitchen yet but I see no reason why it would fail to work there.

-- Adam Farrow-Palmer

The subsequent chapters explain the best way to cut a wide variety of common vegetables, fruits, meats, fish and poultry. Explanations are clear and concise and are accompanied by beautiful hand-drawn illustrations in both right and left-handed versions. In many cases, multiple techniques are covered.

CUTTING ONIONS (right-hand version)

Trimming the Root

Hold the onion firmly in your left hand and a sharp paring knife in your right hand, with your forefinger wrapped around the blade. Support your knife hand by resting your right thumb firmly against the side of the onion (1). Cut the tendril-like portion of the root from the onion: using a slight sawing motion, make the cut at the juncture of the skin and the root so that the skin remains intact and the root is cut flush with the surface of the onion (2). The reason for trimming the root is more aesthetic

Much of this information can be accessed in Youtube videos or other online resources. However, I find this book to be far superior for several reasons. First, the book clearly spells out each step in the process, together with an illustration from an ideal angle. With online videos, the steps often run together, forcing you to start/stop and rewind the video in order to completely understand the process. Also, videos are often shot facing the chef, who narrates the process along the way, making it difficult to see what is happening. The written explanations also often contain much more detailed explanations than would be possible in a video voice-over. Critically, I can spread the book out in front of me in the kitchen while I attempt the technique that I am learning. It is easy to look forward or back a step and then pick up where I left off. This is potentially workable using videos on an iPad, but in practice the book is much more convenient. All of the information in the book is consistent in terms of presentation and quality. With online resources, you never know what you are going to get.

Last but not least, it's very satisfying to pull the book down from the shelf and thumb through it during a spare moment, enjoying the artwork and layout. It sometimes inspires me to attempt a new dish that I would not otherwise have thought of. This book is a cool tool that is also a beautiful object in its own right.

-- Adam Clark

[For those interested, Peter Hertzmann has made a sample chapter covering how to properly chop onions available in PDF-form here.]

Inexpensive great chef knife
Forschner Victorinox Chef's Knife
$28 Amazon

A really great chef's knife is insanely sharp, yet retains its edge easily and feels well-balanced and welcoming in your hand. These days, a decent high-grade chef's knife can cost $100-$200. Several cooking publications, including *Cook's Illustrated*, recently tested a bargain $30 chef's knife that rated just about as good as the $100-plus knives. It's the Victorinox Chef's Knife; the one we use.

The Victorinox is a hybrid of a thin Japanese blade with a 15-degree edge (western knives have a 20-degree edge), but with the longer, broader blade of European knives. It is lightweight, nicely-balanced, and lethally-sharp. It has a comfortable, grippy handle that won't slip even when wet. There are five cooks in our household. This is the knife they all grab first. It may not be quite as super great as some of the other previously-reviewed chef's knives, but considering the price, it can't be beat.

It comes in two sizes. We have both but use the 10 inch version more oftem.

-- KK

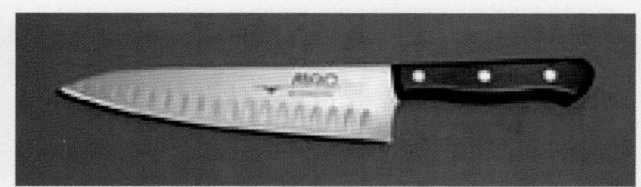

Insanely sharp chef knives
MAC Hollow Ground Chef Knife
$95 MAC Hollow Ground Chef Knife 8" JB Prince

This knife is extremely sharp. I use it mostly for vegetables which need a clean cut (carrots, parsnips, etc.) but which are soft enough that they won't damage the blade (I'll cut through chicken bones with others, but not this). The kullens and thin blade also make it uniquely suited for very thin slices.

-- Adam Fields

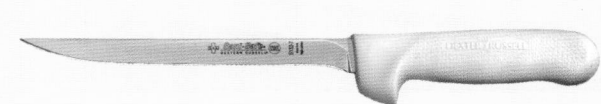

Reliable fish cutters
Dexter-Russell Fillet Knives
$18 Dexter-Russell 9" Fillet Knife Sportco

This filleting knife does not rust, does not dull easily, is easy to sharpen, and the handle is sanitary, comfortable, and good in cold conditions. Most importantly, the blade is flexible, thin and the shape is just right for filleting.

I've used mine for about eight years. It came razor-sharp from the factory and stays sharp for a good deal of time. These days, I usually sharpen it a little bit before every use. A couple laps on a 220-grit Japanese waterstone does the trick.

There are plenty of fancy fillet knives you can get. This one is not particularly expensive, and it's the brand I see most commercial fishermen using. There's also a plastic scabbard you can buy. Dexter's filleting knives come in a few varieties of size/length, etc. There's the 9-inch narrow one, for instance. Personally, I find that one a bit bulky, so I use an 8-inch narrow.

$22 Dexter-Russell 8" Fillet Knife w/Sheath Sportco
-- Michael Krakovskiy

Bargain Japanese chef's knife
Tosagata Hocho 6-inch Santoku Knife
$47 JustKnives

I decided about six years ago that what I really needed was a Japanese Chef's Knife – not because I'm an expert in the kitchen, but because I didn't have a decent chef's knife and the Japanese ones looked exceedingly cool. (My wife and I were at the time in the grips of a modest Iron Chef addiction). When I looked online, most of the ones I found were over $100.

Then I found this Tosagata Hocho 6" Santoku, in blue steel and wrought iron, for ~$35. I ordered it, thinking that even if it turned out to be a lesser knife, it was a good way to try out the idea of a Japanese knife.

Six years of hard use later, this knife is still frighteningly sharp. It's my utility knife – I reach for it for about 80% of my cutting jobs in the kitchen. The blade has maybe six almost undetectable nicks on it, and I have never sharpened it or done any maintenance beyond occasionally wiping it with a little oil before putting it away.

An importer's website says: "Tosagata Hocho Cutlery are finely crafted kitchen knives that come from Tosa on Shikoku Island. This region is much more rural and forested than other parts of Japan, and the blacksmiths still adhere to the old ways. The master blade-maker sandwiches a layer of Aogami Hagane (blue steel) between two pieces of soft wrought iron, and by hand very slowly hammers the blade into shape."

And it looks it – a black/grey surface, complete with hammer marks, makes this look like the serious implement it is. It gives me the thrill of using a well-made tool every time I pick it up. I've even come to love the fact that it's not stainless – having to spend just a moment cleaning it soon after use reminds me that I'm using something a little special, and gives even mundane kitchen tasks a little sense of occasion.

An unbelievable bargain for a terrifically cool tool.

-- RJT

Based on this review, we got one of these for our kitchen 5 years ago and it has become one of our top two kitchen knives. Sharp, well-balanced, rugged.

-- KK

Cheapest high-quality cutlery
Kiwi Knives
$3 - $15 The Wok Shop

As I got more serious about cooking, I splurged and bought myself a very nice Kai Shun santoku like the Tosagata Hocho. I used its preternaturally sharp edge with joyous dispatch for about 6 months, until I woefully cut some citrus with it and left it dirty overnight, eroding that wonderful edge. I've never been able to get that magic edge back, even with pro sharpening.

On a visit to a local Asian market, I found a series of Thai-made Kiwi brand knives. In the store, they were nearly free: The large tapered chef's knife (model #21) that soon stole my heart cost around $4; the paring knife was $1.50.

These knives are very sharp and schuss through veggies and meats like it's nothing. Don't go hacking at bones with the thinner models, but Kiwi also makes quite usable cleavers for around $8. The miraculous part is, the knives hold an incredible edge for months with proper use of your steel, and they take a new edge with aplomb after a few strokes on a stone.

I have owned knives by Wusthof, Kyocera, Calphalon, and Ikea (::shudder::) and the Kiwis are the most consistently sharp, most durable, and have the most effective shapes. I've bought or suggested them for all of my foodie friends, and people can't get over how wonderful they are. They don't look like much, but they're well-balanced, very sharp. It doesn't hurt that I could have picked up a full set for less than my crappy block-o-food-manglers cost 10 years ago.

As far as longevity goes, I've had my main chef's knife for about four years, have steeled it every time I used it and given it a few good hones on my Spyderco Sharpmaker. It's still wicked sharp, and while I haven't babied it, it looks none the worse for wear. I used my paring knife to whack the lid off a persnickety glued-shut can of Lyle's Golden Syrup, and in my zeal, the tip bent over almost double. I thought, Oh no! But then I bent it back in place with a pair of pliers, and it's basically good as new.

They're definitely the Jeep Wranglers of the kitchen. I suggest buying them locally if you live in an area with Asian markets; if not, they can be picked up online at generally higher prices.

-- George Cochrane

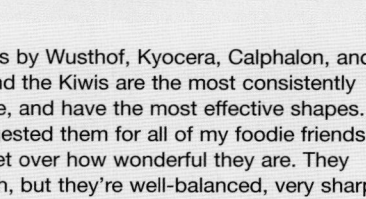

Where to buy kitchen knives on the web
Chef Knives to Go
Prices Vary Chefknivestogo.com

Chef Knives to Go is a small Madison, WI, company that specializes in high-quality Japanese kitchen knives. They have helped me out professionally (as an editor testing samples) and personally (I own and have made gifts of several different models). The owners, Mark Richmond and Susan Brown, really know their products and have always given me honest, dependable, and prompt service. If you are a professional chef needing a special knife or just a kitchen hobbyist wanting to upgrade, I'm happy to recommend CKTG. Good folks and great products.

-- Tim Heffernan

I don't paint things. I only paint the difference between things. - Henri Matisse

191

Kitchen Measurers

Still the best thermometer
Thermapen

$89 Amazon

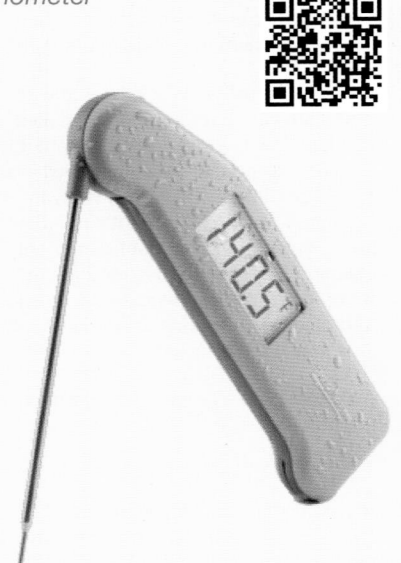

Over the past few years I've experienced everything from burnt caramel to undercooked turkeys and overdone steaks because of crappy thermometers. Most were either slow, inaccurate, or both, and it made for imprecise cooking.

I left that all behind a few months ago when I started using a Thermapen digital thermometer. It's fast, accurate (within +/-0.7 F), and tough (the newer models are splash proof, just don't fully submerge it). It turns on the instant the stainless steel probe is flipped out, and is ready to read in three seconds. It's got a professional thermocouple, and if you ever find it's become inaccurate (you can test with a glass of ice water, or a geographically determined boiling point) they'll calibrate it for free.

The quick reading time means that there is no need to leave it in the oven (or leave the roast out of the oven for that matter). My old $10 thermometer took 30 seconds to stabilize, which, when cooking a nice piece of steak, is the difference between perfectly cooked and over-done. Not only that, but the narrow probe is far better at determining the temperature of thinner cuts of meat without leaving gaping holes.

While it may seem like an extravagance to most, I've found this thermometer to be an essential cook's tool.

-- Oliver Hulland

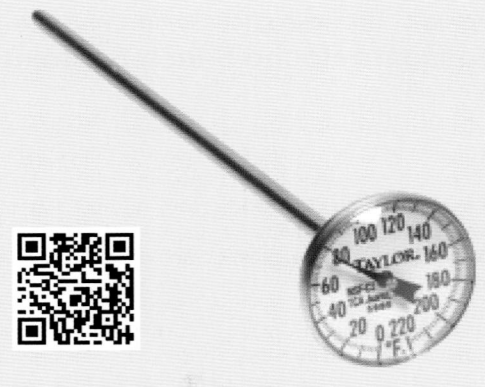

Classic, simple, reliable cooking gauge
Taylor Analog Instant-Read Dial Thermometer

$5 Amazon

Whenever I need a temperature read from an item in the oven, I use this inexpensive, stainless steel thermometer. It's well-designed: I can read the numbers without my glasses or contacts, and a plastic sleeve protects it when not in use. Using my thermometer and the internal temperature specified (for rare, medium, etc.) in whatever recipe I'm working from, I always achieve the required degree of cooking. During the holiday season, I cook a goose, prime ribs, hams and other meats — special meals for my family that have to be just right. I've been using this thermometer for at least 9 years and it's always accurate. When I needed a new one (the first one was dropped accidentally on a cement patio a couple years ago), I knew I wanted another Taylor since I had been so satisfied with the first one and the company has a great reputation. There are digital thermometers with timers and alarms available from Taylor, and other $20 – $90 digital incarnations like the Thermapen. I'm not anti-tech by any means, but simplicity and efficiency are a very nice duo. This thermometer serves one purpose. It's easy to read, easy to use, requires no batteries and can last a long time if take care of.

-- Cheryl Hassell

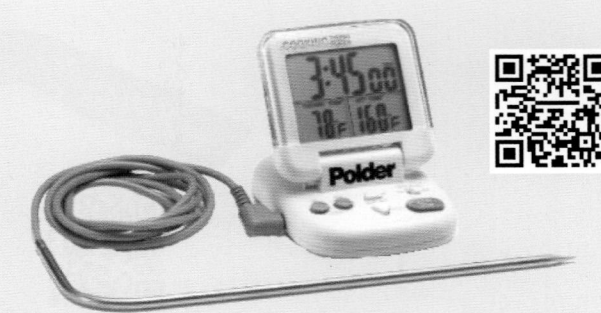

Versatile kitchen timer/thermometer
Polder Thermometer/Timer

$24 Amazon

The Polder timer/thermometer features a 43-inch cord running from the thermometer to the probe, which allows you to take active readings without opening the oven. I really like being able to adjust the cook time or reset the finish temperature on the fly. Plus, there's a magnet on the back, so you can attach the thermometer to the side of the oven.

The Polder also allows you to preset a desired high/low temperature simultaneously. When either temperature is reached, the unit's beeping alarm sounds. It's helpful for remembering to check on liquids and meats. My 8-year-old son has even used ours to check the temperature outside: You can insert the metal probe underneath your window, and it's quite accurate.

The timer, which counts up or down, is very handy for a range of other household uses, such as, "You have three minutes to pick up your room before I come in with a trash bag that's headed for Goodwill!" Best of all, the thermometer is amazingly durable. We've had ours for at least four years and have dropped it many times.

Lastly, it can be set to display in Celsius or Fahrenheit, which proved to be a huge help when we spent some time living in Ireland. I had my American recipe books and was able to use the Polder thermometer to convert temperatures for a Celsius-based oven.

-- Ginger Cooper

Easy-to-read measuring cups
OXO Angled Measuring Cups

$20 (set of three) Amazon

I have used these cups for about two years and they are far better than other measuring cups because you can measure the amount from the top while filling. You don't need to stop and look from the side. This is achieved via a patented angled surface with clearly marked volume indicators. It is a simple, unique, improvement to something I use all the time!

-- Paul Hanna

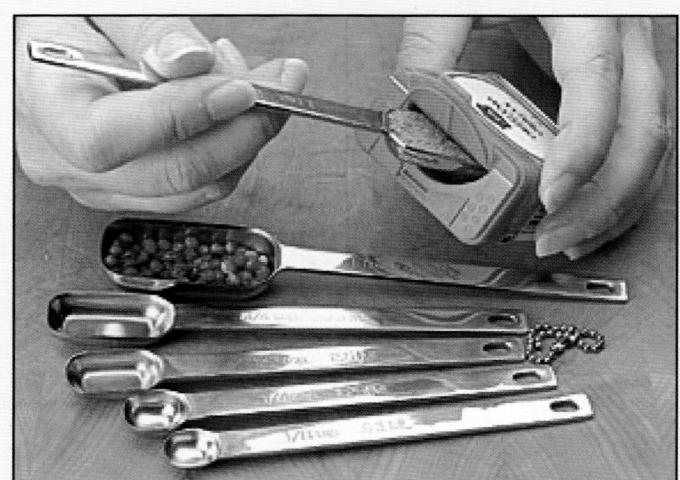

Slim, mess-free portioning
Spice Jar Measuring Spoons

$14 Amazon

Unlike traditional measuring spoons resembling those intended for stirring and eating, these stainless steel Spice Jar Measuring Spoons are rectangular in shape with a narrower profile. Translation: They fit easily through the small opening of a spice container. Bonus: If the container's opening has a straight edge, you can level the scoop as you withdraw the spoon.

In addition, the set contains two sizes that aren't normally included with the average measuring spoon set: 1/8 and 3/4 teaspoons. I find the 3/4 spoon particularly handy in that two 3/4 teaspoons equals 1/2 tablespoon, a measurement I frequently encounter after scaling down a recipe.

After three years of daily use, I've found no down-side to using these sturdy spoons for all my measuring needs — liquid or dry. Given their advantage with small containers, I see little reason to use traditional measuring spoons other than a slightly lower cost.

-- David King

Measuring miniaturized
Mini Measure Shot Glass

$6 Amazon

I've always had at least one of these on hand over the last four years. For small amounts of liquid ingredients in recipes, like vanilla extract and soy sauce, it's much easier than trying to fill a measuring spoon to the rim. For mixed drinks, it's more precise than a jigger, albeit a bit slower. If nothing else, it makes a perfectly serviceable (and somewhat geeky) shot glass.

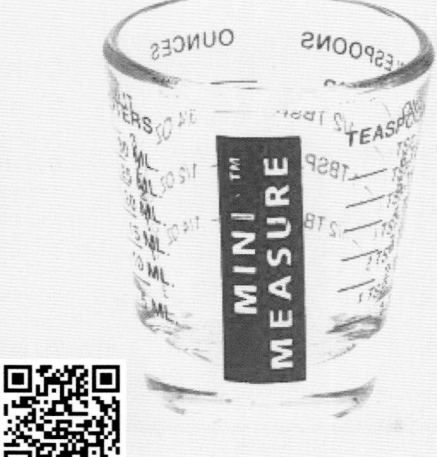

The measurement markings are in fluid ounces, milliliters, teaspoons, and tablespoons. A few different companies make them, and while they're available online for $3-$5 a pop, I've seen them cheaper in brick-and-mortar stores like Bed Bath & Beyond and Target.

-- Jason McCay

Without expectations, there's no future, only an endless present. - Francois Jacob

aging cheese), helps me remember what food was like when I was a kid and my mom and dad did these things, and what it might have been like when they were kids.

Low-sugar jams and preserves

The jams and fruit preserves in this book are all quite low in sugar, simply because I think looser, less-sweet spreads taste better than sticky, cloying ones. Most contain fresh lemon juice, which is added primarily for flavor but also to up the acid content a bit. The jams and preserves have a remarkably intense fruit flavor because excess water is cooked out rather than gelled with store-bought pectin.

Real pickles

Here you'll find everything from refrigerator pickles in vinegar brines that will last a few weeks or months in the fridge and don't need any processing, to canned quickly brined pickles that will last a year in the pantry, to long-fermented pickles made sour by fermentation, to Indian and Middle Eastern-style "pickles" such as citrus preserved in salt. Most pickles are low in sugar, but not low in salt (which I fervently adore), whether it's that sharp bite of the acetic acid in vinegar or the mellow tang of fermentation-produced lactic acid.

So there you go. Heating to kill off existing microorganisms, processing to create a vacuum and prevent introduction and growth of microorganisms, and using high-acid foods or acidulating those that are not in order to create an acidic environment that's inhospitable to microorganisms.

●
Quick, High-Yield Strawberry Jam: Makes about 7 half-pint jars

Here's a basic jam recipe that uses Pomona's Universal, a commercial sugar-free low-methoxyl natural pectin derived from citrus rinds. It can be used in low- or even no-sugar recipes because it's activated by calcium rather than sugar. You can adapt it to just about any fruit. If what you want is a lot of jam from not a lot of fruit (say, if you're making a big batch

to give as gifts), and if you want to cut back dramatically on the sugar content, this is the way to go. This jam, while not as intensely fruit-flavored as the no-commercial-pectin preserves in this book (here you're essentially gelling the water that in other recipes is cooked off), will be thick, semi-firm, and light–a refreshing jam, if you will allow that such things exist. Pomona's Universal can be found at health-food stores or online (see Sources, page 291).

●
Strawberry Jam with Thai Herbs: Makes about 4 half-pint jars

This is a sweet-tart preserve, but the mineral cilantro, fragrant thai basil, and fresh mint give it a complexity reminiscent of a good, well-balanced yum, or thai salad. Strawberries pair so well with herbs, and indeed all sorts of crazy savor things–balsamic vinegar with strawberries being one surprisingly long-lived trend–that it didn't take much to come up with this extraordinary jam. Try this: Go out into the herb garden with a plate piled with halved berries and a little mound of sugar. (Or gather a bunch of leftover herbs from the refrigerator, or befriend a generous herb grower.) Dip a berry in the sugar, and pop it in your mouth with a few leaves of different herbs, tasting and tasting until you come up with a combination you like. It'll be a little different from the actual jam, of course, but you'll be able to tell if you'll like the finished result.

Best modern canning guide
Canning for a New Generation
$15 Liana Krissoff, 2010, 304 p.

New fashions in canning. Preserving is not really cheaper, nor is it a survival and disaster remedy. Canning these days makes sense as a culinary endeavor — because you can make preserves that taste better, or are far more varied than anything you can buy. This book is the best of a bunch of new guides on modern canning techniques and recipes (like *Put 'Em Up*, which is decent but not as good). I prefer the recepies in Canning for standard items like jams and jellies because it calls for far less sugar than other books, and it has a wide range of culinary influences. The book is also intelligently and simply designed with beautiful illustrations of the preserved treasures.

-- *KK*

●

When I was growing up, canning was for old folks and cranks and separatists –oh, and for my parents, who spent every summer of my Virginia childhood scrambling to convert overflowing bushel baskets of fruits and vegetables from their garden into a pantry lined with shelf upon shelf of colorful canning jars, not to mention a stuffed-to-the-rim chest freezer or two. Not for me. I had better, far more important things to do. I can't remember what they were.

For me, putting up the very best produce I can find in season–especially if it's homegrown or from a nearby farm–is quite simply a way to spend some marginally productive time in the kitchen, preferably with my family and friends. Opening the jars and enjoying them later, I'm reminded of those fun times of tasting and talking, usually about food but also about music and politics and everything else that matters. In addition, taking on a kitchen project of a certain complexity, like canning or pickling or fermenting (or smoking meat or stuffing sausage or

The best pot under pressure
Kuhn Rikon Pressure Cooker
$199 Amazon

This is not your grandmother's pressure cooker. Modern day versions are safe, easy to lock tight and are far quieter than units of yore. I can't imagine my kitchen without one. The convenience plus time and energy savings associated with making things ranging from roasts to perfect risotto and even desserts is incredible. On top of that, everything inevitably turns out tastier and more nutritious than it would otherwise.

For the uninitiated, pressure cooking is a method of cooking in a sealed vessel that does not permit air or liquids to escape below a certain pressure. Pressure is created by boiling a liquid, such as water or broth, inside the closed pressure cooker causing the trapped steam to increase the internal pressure and temperature. This causes wet steam (or "saturated steam") to be forced through the food and results in faster cooking times compared to conventional cooking methods. Once pressure is reached, the heat source can be dialed down significantly to maintain proper pressure for cooking. Pressure is slowly released through an external venting mechanism so that the vessel can be safely opened. A pot roast can be ready in 45 minutes, potatoes are cooked through in 10, broccoli and other vegetables barely take 5 minutes (at pressure) to become tender.

I've owned several brands and sizes over the years, but my favorite by far is the 6 qt. stockpot model made by Kuhn Rikon of Switzerland. This unit, while not cheap, is extremely well-built, whisper silent and has multiple safely mechanisms built-in. Unlike the classic stream-release versions with the loud jiggly knob on top, this design retains most of the moisture, thus minimizing the amount of liquid required to get up and stay pressurized.

There are many less expensive, good quality pressure cooker alternatives out there that will serve you well, but I believe my Kuhn Rikon cooker will last for years of frequent use and look good doing it.

-- *R. S. Parikh*

Countertop flour mill
The Wondermill
$260 Amazon

For 30 years we had an electric stone-ground flour mill. It finally gave out and I got a steel-ground mill, and is it great. I realize that stoneground is the better way to go, but the new mill is so fast (20 times faster), and a joy to use.

We're grinding most of our own flour for bread, etc. We grind organic California short-grain brown rice for cream-of-rice cereal. Easy to cook, delicious (a little butter, dark sugar, milk), and it's a meal of freshly ground whole grains. I also use it to grind whole oats (called groats) into flour to make sourdough pancakes. No wheat. They're delicious, and thanks to the sourdough, chewy. Fresh ground whole grains. Easy to do.

-- *Lloyd Kahn*

Grind your own oats
Roller Mill
$120 Lehman's

This elegant little Italian grain grinder has three hardened steel rollers that flatten grain for making flakes or crack it for making hot cereal or granola. I'd never had fresh oats before until my friend showed me this device, just after he gave me a breakfast bowl of fresh oatmeal along with flax seeds, shredded coconut, a little hemp oil for flavor, and brown sugar. As you grind oats you're taking the whole oat grain (groat), and crushing and flaking it just before you cook it. You get nutty, delicious oatmeal, the flavor of the whole grain just released. Clamps to any surface up to 2" thick.

-- *Lloyd Kahn*

Durables

Glass-based airtight containers
SnapWare Glasslock
$33 Amazon

Storing food in plastic containers is an imperfect solution. Not only is there the likelihood of the plastic deteriorating and contaminating the food, but it also tends to stain and retain the taste and smell of whatever was last stored in it.

After years of frustration with plastic containers I recently picked up an 18-piece kit of SnapWare Glasslock, a glass-based alternative to plastic food storage containers. As their name implies, the glass containers come with a rigid plastic top that snaps shut with four hinges. This coupled with a durable silicone seal renders the containers leak-proof (something I definitely couldn't do with my old plastic ones). I have biked with one filled with soup and arrived at my destination without a drop missing, and I didn't have to waste another bowl in order to microwave it.

The biggest downsides to this container solution is the expense and added weight. Plastic containers are cheap, near-disposable, and almost weightless. But I'll happily tote the extra ounce or two of glass if it means I don't have to worry about plastics leaching into my now unspilled soup.

The containers themselves are freezer, microwave, and dishwasher safe, but are not recommended for the oven. I have read many accounts of people successfully using them in the oven, but I do not believe they are made with the same borosilicate they use in Pyrex, so it is at your own risk.

The 18-piece set is enough for my partner and me, but may not be enough for a family of more than two or three (given how fast some people go through containers). I bought my set at a Costco warehouse where they are sold for quite a bit cheaper than elsewhere. I believe the Container Store has a near identical solution for comparable prices. Finally, for those not concerned about using plastics, SnapWare recently released a near identical product with BPA-free plastic.

-- Oliver Hulland

Best container system. I love this stuff. We use it nightly. Closes with a satisfying and very secure snap. Stackable in the frig. Near indestructible. We bought another set.

-- KK

Heavy-duty sheet pans
Restaurant Grade Sheet Pans
$12 Amazon

After screwing around with grocery-store sheet pans for years, I went to a restaurant supply store and bought three plain metal sheet pans (technically "half-sheet" at 13×18, but true "full-sheets" are only used in commercial ovens). I've used them for over three years now, and am totally convinced that they are awesome.

Here's why people buy grocery store sheet pans: they're cheap, non-stick coated, and easily found at the grocery store. And here's what's wrong with them. They're flimsy metal, so they warp in the oven if you use them at high temperatures (over, say, 425F). They come in non-standard size, so you can never be sure that a cooling rack will fit into them. And their fancy-schmancy non-stick coating means that you baby them.

Here's why plain old restaurant-grade sheet pans are awesome:

They're not much more expensive than the cheap stuff you buy in the grocery store. Going from a $7 grocery-store pan to a $12 restaurant-grade pan is a significant percentage markup, but it's only $5. If you have a restaurant supply store near you, you may be able to get the restaurant-grade pans for basically the same price as the grocery-store pans.

They are heavy metal, which means that you can toss them into a 500 degree (F) oven to bake bread on them and not worry about warping. And they don't have any non-stick coating to worry about. I have used my sheet pans for everything from crafting trays to putting them under gardening flats when starting seedlings. No matter how nasty and dirty they get, I know that I can just take a steel wool pad to them and they'll come back to like-new.

You might think the lack of a non-stick coating is a minus, but seriously, you just spray the pan with non-stick or use baking parchment or silicon mats. It's not that hard. Every baker I know backs up "nonstick" pans with non-stick spray or parchment anyway, so it's not like there's any change in your cooking process.

-- Joshua Bardwell

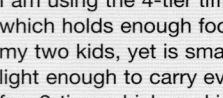

Even-cooking pans
All-Clad Roaster
$250+ All-Clad Stainless Steel Flared Roaster Williams Sonoma

In 2008, Williams-Sonoma released a line of exclusive All-Clad flared roasters. They are expensive, but well worth it if you use your oven a lot. The unique design makes for very even cooking, especially if you don't have a convection oven. The lower sides give good heat exposure, so you get excellent browning on the underside of roasts. The aluminum core provides outstanding heat distribution.

Last year, I cooked a 27-pound Thanksgiving turkey in the extra large roaster, and I've since used this pan for all kinds of dishes. Since it's basically a very large saute pan, it works great on the stove as well. I've used it to cook a huge portion of mac & cheese (mixing the roux/bechamel right into the pan on the stove). I also use it regularly for large batches of braised lamb shanks and short ribs. The roaster's low and wide design encourages a lot of reduction of the braising liquid, which yields a more flavorful sauce.

Warning: The extra large size is unwieldy. Before buying, make sure it can fit in your oven and sink. Although the curved design makes it very easy to clean with a brush, this size barely squeezes into my sink. Though it's a bit of a beast to handle, it's nevertheless indispensable if you need the capacity.

If the large version also seems a bit much, there's now an even smaller and cheaper version for roasting chickens. This has quickly become my standard everyday pan for most things. It also comes with a suspension arm for cooking a chicken elevated.

Regardless of which size is right for you, these are great roasting pans. The images are pretty deceptive with respect to the size differences and just how big they actually are. It's worth a trip to the store to see which size is best for you.

-- Adam Fields

Stainless steel tier lunch box
Tiffin Carrier
$20 4-tier Om Goods
$15 3-tier Om Goods
$12 2-tier Om Goods

As the name suggests, the tiered tiffin carrier is comprised of stackable tiers of storage which can be laid out for all to enjoy. When you are done, you just stack 'em back up, lock the clasps, grab the handle and go. They are made out of a high quality stainless steel which makes them very sturdy yet quite light, and so easy to clean.

I am using the 4-tier tiffin, which holds enough food for my two kids, yet is small and light enough to carry everywhere. I also have a few 2-tiers which my kids take to school. Recently, I began taking my tiffins to pick up my take-out orders. This beats using disposable items provided by the restaurant. My favorite take-out places are quite happy to oblige and love the concept.

Not all tiffins are the same. In my quest to find a stainless steel lunchbox, I tried a no-name brand tiffin sold through Amazon. It is poorly-designed, made from a poor quality stainless steel and it's massive. This new one I have is a perfect size (6.75 x 4.25 inches) and you can see the quality in the steel and workmanship. It's also less than half the price of fancier tiffins like the pyramid, which I'll admit looks pretty neat.

-- Meeta Dhillon

Multipurpose bamboo vessel
Bamboo Steamer
$25 Amazon

Nothing in my entire house so perfectly combines utility, simplicity, sustainability, beautiful design and tradition as my set of inexpensive, generic bamboo steamers.

I use the two-tiered, six-inch set daily for steaming small servings of fresh vegetables (over boiling water in a cheap wok–another cool tool). Potatoes steam to mashable softness in about 12 minutes.

The big twelve-inch set accommodates a whole batch of steamed buns, masses of vegetables, or even a plate of leftovers to be gently reheated– and it's fantastic for carrying pies and cookies to parties, and so much more attractive than plastic ware.

These common everyday items of Asian cookery are craft works of real beauty, with their woven-bamboo lids, their curved and stitched side walls, and their beautifully slatted and fitted bottoms. They darken as cooking heat caramelizes the sugars in the bamboo, but they last a long, long time (I've been using mine daily for four years with no sign of failure), and when they do finally give up the ghost, I can burn or compost them, and easily afford a replacement.

-- Elissa Vigil

Reusable non-grease baking sheet
Silicone Baking Mat

$12 Amazon

For years professionals have baked their goods on inert silicone-impregnated mats. These simple, inexpensive, oven-proof, non-stick sheets slide into baking trays and are now quite common in households like ours. Instead of consuming rolls of aluminum foil or parchment paper, you just lay everything out on these reusable durable mats, and bake. The nicely-browned goods slide off with no effort and no added grease. There's less burn on the bottom, too. Multiple mats can feed one expensive baking tray for serious cookie production. Clean-up is a simple rinse. As an added bonus, they make great kneading boards. The mats also roll up for easy storage. We've used several of the five brands available. So far, they all seem similar. Silpat was the original, but SiliconeZone is the least expensive I've seen.

-- KK

Life can only be understood backwards, but it must be lived forwards. - Soren Kierkegaard

Precise sharp slicer for kitchen
Microplane Grater
$13 Amazon

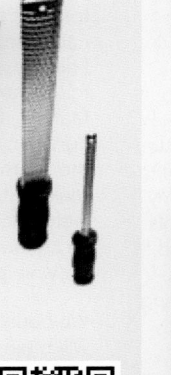

Microplane began making micro-blades for woodworking use, but they've diverged into making fantastic kitchen tools. Their kitchen graters will turn a little block of Parmigiano-Reggiano into a huge cloud of billowy cheese wisps. Vegetables grate into little strips that almost melt in your mouth. My favorite use is with citrus zest. My lemon bars, lemon tarts and key lime pie have a much greater depth of flavor than ever before.

With most zesters, you end up with too much of the pithy white rind of the citrus fruit, but the Microplane takes off only the very thinnest layer of the outside of the fruit, the part which contains the intense and volatile citrus oils. Hands down, these are the best tools I've tried for fine-grating and zesting.

-- Jeff Zimmerman

Quick apple peeler and corer
Progressive Apple Peeler
$20 Amazon

My wife's grandmother seems to effortlessly make dozens of wonderful apple pies. And yet, she has poor hand strength due to advanced rheumatoid arthritis. Finally, we convinced her to pass along the secret behind her pie-making success: She uses one machine to peel/slice/core her apples.

Simply poke the three prongs into the base of an apple and turn the crank. Before you know it, a lovely spiral of apple skin will unfurl before you, leaving a perfectly cored and peeled apple that can be quickly cut into quarters and thrown into a pie.

As soon as you see the device in action, it's obvious just how elegant the mechanism is. It's safe for children to use, once the apple is situated on the prongs. Best of all, it makes prepping apples so simple you'll wish you had one years ago. There's a version that clamps to a kitchen bench, but I find the models with a vacuum base are the same price and are far easier to set up and use.

-- Steve Allen

Best garlic and ginger press
Kuhn Rikon Epicurean Garlic Press
$38 ch.kuhnrikon.com

I've used this tool for about 10 years and it's still going strong. It's probably the best garlic press in the world. It's constructed very robustly from stainless steel; it has an unusual lever-action which is far superior to the one-to-one action of most garlic presses; it opens up easily and is trivial to clean.

To see a demo, have a look at America's Test Kitchen Equipment Review (below) where they come to the same conclusion.

But note that Kuhn Rikon have another garlic press called the Easy Squeeze, which is a lot cheaper. It has a slightly different action and plastic handles. It's not nearly as good.

-- Stuart Wray

Tears through tomatoes
Tomato Shark
$6 Amazon

I have dozens of tools and gadgets in my kitchen. Years working in the restaurant and catering world left me with an inventory of items that I bought for this job or that party. Some were quite expensive and most were probably only used once or twice (I'm looking at you, Mother of Pearl Caviar Spoon!).

But there's one tool that cost me less than $2.00 at a restaurant supply store over 10 years ago that I still use on a fairly regular basis, at least during the summer. Anytime I need to core a tomato or hull a strawberry I reach for my Tomato Shark.

Healthy snacking in 30 seconds
OXO Apple Divider
$10 Amazon

I like apples but I've never been a fan of the form factor, which tends to be tough on the teeth and jaws. The OXO Apple Divider cores and chops in one fell swoop. Total prep time, including rinsing the apple

Superior vegetable peeler
OXO Peeler
$9 Amazon

It is hard to image how the traditional kitchen peeler could be substantially improved. Remarkably, the OXO Peeler accomplishes this. Easier to use, vastly more comfortable for long stretches, sharper, and more productive. The OXO Peeler continues to win awards in test kitchens. A superior tool; worth the few extra dollars.

-- KK

(Tomato Shark, continued)

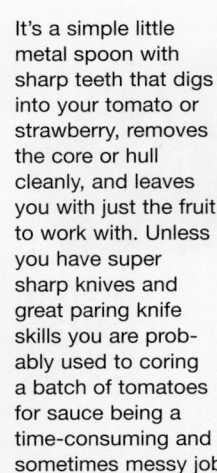

It's a simple little metal spoon with sharp teeth that digs into your tomato or strawberry, removes the core or hull cleanly, and leaves you with just the fruit to work with. Unless you have super sharp knives and great paring knife skills you are probably used to coring a batch of tomatoes for sauce being a time-consuming and sometimes messy job; the Tomato Shark makes this job easy, tidy and quick.

This is one of those items where you should buy the actual Tomato Shark brand. I've found similar items just don't hold up over time: the teeth get dull quicker, and you just don't need to spend the extra money on a fancier version (unless you have problems with your hands and need a plastic handle for ergonomic reasons).

-- Caryl Shaw

[The original Tomato Shark is remarkably difficult to find online, and your best bet might be hitting up a restaurant supply store. With that being said, Amazon reviewers have good things to say about these off-brand stainless steel tomato corers being sold for $10 a dozen.--OH]

beforehand: 30 seconds max, 20 if I'm in a hurry. Like other OXO products I've tried, the OXO Apple Divider is a well-designed, well-built version of a classic tool. The company's included its trademark "good grips" and sharp blades.

I appreciate it every time I use, it because I'm a chocoholic with easy access during the day to cookies and hot chocolate. Bringing a plastic container filled with wholesome, fresh, organic apple chunks makes it easier for me to resist the lure of chocolate. Even if you don't consume apples as frequently as I do, the OXO Apple Divider is one single-use tool that's worth keeping around.

-- Jonathan Steigman

We we bought this and use it regularly on potatoes to make oven fries. Slice the potato, toss the pieces in olive oil and spices of your choice, and bake on a non-stick sheet for 20-30 minutes at 450F, turning once. I didn't even know this device was actually for apples until I saw it in Cool Tools!

-- Julee Bode

Bulk pineapple slicer
Pineapple Slicer/Corer
$10 Amazon

I'm not usually a big fan of single-use tools, but this is by far the only tool for this job. We had a party where I needed to core and slice three cases of pineapples, and what could have taken all day took but a few hours. No skill is needed. You just cut off the top of the pineapple and screw down the corer. Once you are at the bottom, pull out the meat and you're done. The pineapple is evenly-sliced and you are left with a usable hull (for serving fruity drinks in, of course). I have seen these on sale for as little as $7.

-- Walter Susong III

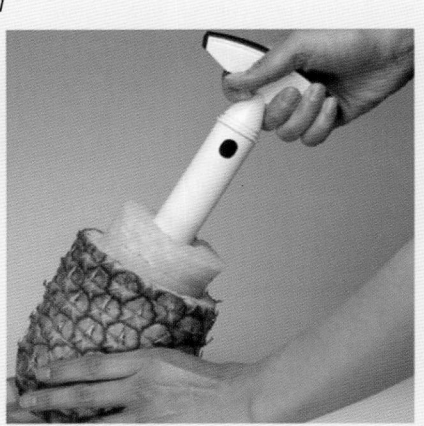

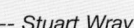

Utencils

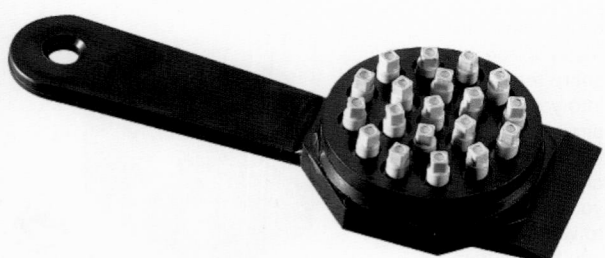

Quick fish cleaner
Magic Fish Scaler

$13 Cabela's

Sure, you can scale a fish with the back of your knife blade. I did for years — until I drove my thumb into the dorsal spike of a striped bass. After having surgery, I picked up this little device at the tackle shop. It offers more than self-defense. It's just absolutely good at what it does, and costs less than 15 bucks. Show it to your friends and make them guess what it's for; they'll be stumped. What would make you design a fish scaler with what looks like plastic hex-head bits loosely attached to the underside of a circular disc? It doesn't make sense. But it works! It defends your thumb (thank you) and prevents scales from scattering all over and flying up into your face. Only a little pressure is needed, and the fish is completely clean in seconds.

-- Jay Allison

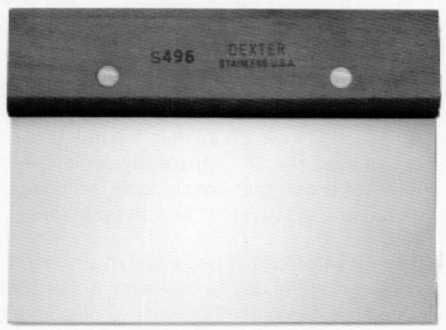

Dough Scraper
Dexter-Russell Dough Scraper

$15 Dexter-Russell

Although it was designed specifically for bakers, this low-tech tool is absolutely indispensable in the kitchen. Beyond scraping bread dough off the counter, we use ours to transport all types of chopped foods from counter to bowl, counter to skillet, etc.

There are other dough scrapers out there, but Dexter-Russell's S496 features a wide wooden handle that helps make it the best. Don't want take my word for it? I was in a local Sur la Table recently. They had various bins filled with dough scrapers; the Dexter bin was empty!

-- Mark Esswein

Heavy duty kitchen scissors
Fiskars Kitchen Shears

$17, #9474 Fiskars

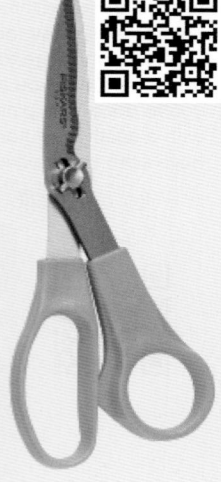

I don't consider myself a great cook, but I've found that for a multitude of kitchen activities, scissors are important. Whether for cutting cooking twine, small bones or a chicken breastbone, they can be very useful. Normal office scissors don't have the right length of blade and the joint can harbor germs and food residue.

The Fiskars shears are one of a number of scissors specially made for the kitchen. They feature shorter, stainless steel blades and a take-apart joint for cleaning. However, these shears are one of the least expensive, yet still reliable pairs.

-- AK

Essential pot and pan scraper
Norpro Comfort Grip Deluxe Scraper

I am the kitchen staff in our household: cook, dish- and pot-washer. We are suspicious of non-stick cooking surfaces, so all of our pots and pans are steel, enameled iron or cast iron. No matter how much care I take in seasoning pans or paying attention to my cooking, I invariably end up with something stuck to the bottom of something at least once a week. Witnessing my frustration at having to soak, wipe, and then scrape with tools designed to do other things besides remove cooked-on food, my wife said, "Why don't you get one of those plastic scrapers like my mom used to have?" I scoffed at first, never having heard of this kind of thing (growing up as I did surrounded by Teflon).

We found a scraper at an upscale kitchen store and gave it a try. This first scraper (Norpro 239) was cheap and flimsy and visibly wore down over a month of vigorous scraping, but it was still a revelation. Then I found this thicker scraper and I am quite impressed by its simple, sturdy functionality. After almost a year, it's just starting to wear, and it kicks potwashing butt on almost a daily basis. It also comes in fun colors!

Unlike other, similar products, this scraper is significantly thicker in the middle than at the edges, making it rigid in use with a little bit of flexibility where the edge meets the pot or pan; it also has a rounded handle along the top edge (mimicking the handle of a European dough scraper) that fits securely along the inside

Evenly floured surfaces
Best Flour Duster

$10 Amazon

This flour duster allows for remarkably light and even dusting of dough or a work surface. You simply squeeze the wire handle, which expands the spring bulb so that the wires have space between them. Stick it in a bag of flour, stop squeezing and the spring bulb closes around a golf-ball-sized wad of flour. Then, shake it over a work surface squeezing gently — I tap it over my free hand ala David Byrne's "Once in a Lifetime" — and voilà: A very even dusting is achieved. I've used this flour duster for five years, and have found nothing else that can compete.

-- Robert Narracci

Better banana protection
Banana Guard

Most parents would agree that the venerable banana is a staple of the toddler diet. Unfortunately, they tend to not to fare very well when tossed into a diaper bag filled with wipes, water bottles, and the other dizzying array of items that have to be hauled around everywhere with your little ones. The Banana Guard makes this problem go away completely.

We were given one of these shortly after our daughter was born, and two years later, it goes everywhere with us. The sturdy, BPA-free container protects bananas in even the most over-stuffed of diaper bags, and there's something particularly ingenious about the size and shape: I've yet to encounter a banana that didn't fit.

The ventilation holes help keep the banana fresh, and while the locks can be opened fairly easily, they won't accidentally pop open if the bag is tossed about, or if the guard is discovered by

Roasting rubber bands
Architec Stretch Cooking Band

$8, pack of 20 Amazon

I picked up a pack of these medical-grade silicone rubber bands for cooking at my local commissary. They work well for my original intended purpose of trussing chickens. Since they are made out of silicone they are safe up to 600°F and elastic enough to easily stretch around a 5-lb chicken and still hold the wings tight. And they clean up easy for reuse.

What makes them a really cool tool to me is the fact that while they have the elasticity of a similar sized rubber band they don't degrade like rubber bands. I have had my initial pack for over a

of your index finger. These two features give it a really nice hand-feel, which is something I appreciate in any tool, even a mundane pot scraper. Its best feature, though, is the gradual curve on one scraper edge and the sharp curve on the other, making it useful for saucepans with rounded bottoms as well as square-bottomed pots or brownie pans.

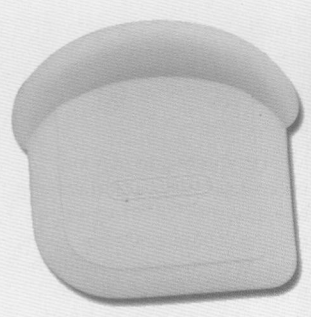

We bought a bunch of these (they are pretty inexpensive) and will often give one to friends, house guests, and family members who express even the slightest curiosity. The gift is invariably met with a quizzical look, but almost everyone we give one to contacts us later to tell us how amazed they are that they lived this long without it.

-- Jeff Morrison

$5 (set of two) Norpro

$4 (similar set) Progressive

Portable pepper mill
Vic Firth Pump and Grind Pepper Mill

$18 Vic Firth

I never go anywhere without my portable pepper mill. I have one stashed in my desk and another in the glove box, and still another couple in the kitchen. Trader Joe's sells an outstanding disposable model for a couple bucks, but by far my favorite is the thumb-operated pump mill made by Vic Firth.

The sleek designed cylindrical metal and glass device stands 5-1/2-inches tall, and you can tell from its weight that it's a serious tool. Fill the tube with peppercorns, push the plunger, and presto! Delicious, calorie-free pepper.

-- Andee Beck Althoff

a curious toddler.

Of course, this isn't just for kids. When I eat bananas on the go the Banana Guard is the answer. The $15 price tag is perhaps a little steep, but the guard is definitely built to last and in the long run probably costs less than all the bananas you might lose otherwise.

-- Darin Wilson

$7 Aerostich

$6 (generic version) Amazon

year and have found no degradation, the only broken ones were cut. I have used them for many things, lashing together a broken drying rack, bundling together bags, holding mesh filter on a racking cane.

-- Marvin S.

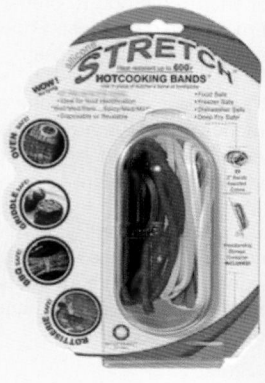

We have art in order not to die of the truth. - Friedrich Nietzsche

Best spatula
Dual-Ended Silicone Spatula
$11 Chef'n

This is the silicone spatula that will replace all your silicone spatulas.

If you've already made the switch to silicone spatulas, you know that the silicone variety do a really wonderful job scraping bowls of cookie batter, getting the last bits of sauce out of a pan, and generally making the process of cooking cleaner and more efficient. In addition, silicone has a much higher melting temperature than the thermoplastic typically used–650?F v 230?F–so you can use these spatulas in the fry pan (usually ~375?F). The soft silicone is safe for coated pans, which is a definite plus.

This particular silicone spatula is made with the silicone cast around a steel core. This gives the handle the rigidity of other spatulas, without the awkward and ingredient-trapping transition from spatula to handle. The silicone over steel makes a very comfortable grip, and the whole thing can be cleaned in the dishwasher. This design also allows them to make the spatula dual-ended, with a useful narrower scraper that is great for getting the last peanut butter out of jars.

I've been using mine for over a year, and it shows no wear. It is easily my most used utensil in the kitchen, and has relegated many other tools to the Goodwill bin.

-- Wendy Ju

Easy-To-Clean Multipurpose Kitchen Tool
Silicone Spoon Spatula
$8 iSi

I've had this spoon spatula about four years and it's the single kitchen utensil I use the most.

It's perfect for mixing brownie batter, stir-frying vegetables, scraping jars, serving food from the pan into bowls, and pretty much anything and everything you can think of. I spread butter, jelly, and peanut butter with this thing. I use it to cut brownies, break apart cooking cauliflower, scoop cookie dough onto pans, scrape cut veggies off the cutting board, and I've even flipped pancakes with it (though I recommend the turner for that).

The seamless design is super quick to clean, doesn't hold food flavors, and it's never melted or deformed despite years of constant use and abuse (like being left on a cast iron pan of smoking olive oil). It can be cut though, as I found after carelessly stuffing it into my Vitamix!

Avoid using this with sharp blades and it'll last a lifetime.

I also highly recommend the Silicone Slim Spatula and Silicone 13 Inch Turner as a complement to the spoon spatula, but the spoon spatula is really my go-to tool and rarely leaves the countertop.

-- Ian Hall

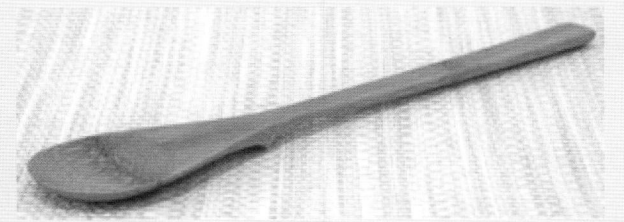

Self-elevating cooking tools
Give It A Rest Bamboo Utensils
12" spoon $8 Give It A Rest

Bamboo utensils are great for cooking with nonstick pots and skillets. Recently, I found an even better version: Bamboo utensils with rests carved right into the handles. Lay down the utensil, and the business end won't touch the surface. You don't need a spoon rest, and you don't need to clean a spoon rest either. Thus far, I have purchased a spatula and two spoons; I intend to buy more. I converted overnight. The other wooden utensils I'd been using for years? They're all gone.

-- Bob Callaway

Durable steel hands
Stainless-Steel Locking Tongs
$13 OXO

As a former cook in four restaurants, I've found these simple tongs to be an indispensable utensil day in and day out. Stirring, cooking and tossing pasta, flipping steaks, and grabbing anything hot including pans. They become an extension of your hands. I continue to use them in my own kitchen. I often see a lot of inferior, cheap and just plain useless tongs included with BBQ sets. They are usually too long or poorly designed to be effective. Get these: Williams-Sonoma Stainless-Steel Locking Tongs, or a pair of OXO Stainless-Steel Locking Tongs.

-- Alan Hachey

I learned how indispensable a decent pair of tongs can be around the campfire while working as a river and ocean kayak guide. We cooked as much of the meals as possible on a grill over the fire to conserve fuel on multi-day trips. I still cook this way whenever possible and use these OXO

Mini squishy bowls
Silicone Pinch Bowls
$7 Norpro

I've been using these little Norpro silicone pinch bowls for about a year now. I picked them up on a whim at the grocery store and they are now easily one of the most useful and well loved items in my kitchen. Tiny, colorful and versatile with a seemingly never ending number of uses.

My family uses them for prep work in cooking (their intended lot), but also as dipping cups for any variety of condiments. I also use them to hold small servings of dried fruits or nuts to snack on, to hold screws in while doing simple housework, to mix spice blends in or when I need to ingest small amounts of liquids for taking medicine. Their flexibility of form allows them to fit into tight spaces and their durability allows them to be used without fear of breakage or wear. They are simply more attractive, versatile and easier to use than other small bowls of their small size.

-- Shad Miles

Best cooking spoon
Spout Ladle
$6 Winco

A spout ladle is the optimal tool for basting. I've tried spoons, suction basters, basting mops, and even those new silicone basting brushes. All but the first are less efficient at getting enough liquid out of the bottom of a pan.

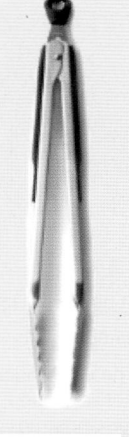

Stainless Steel Locking Tongs to not only move food around on the grill, but also to move hot coals or briquettes! These tongs lock closed for easy storage and have a 'hook hole' for hanging up. The non-slip rubber grip has held up for years in the dishwasher. Available in 9-inch, 12-inch, and 16-inch models. For obvious reasons, I would suggest the 16-inch ones for outdoor cooking. Buy one of these for that unfortunate soul still using — gasp! — a fork at the barbecue.

-- Lewis Duffy

The OXO Stainless-Steel Locking Tongs sport handy rubber grips, lock closed for storage, and are the ideal surrogate hands in the kitchen. It's the pair we have.

-- KK

Last bit o' jam scoop
Bottle Scraper
$3 Fante's

I first used this bottle scraper twenty years ago while boarding with a family in the Netherlands. At the time, Dutch pudding came in glass jars similar to traditional milk bottles. This spatula was the only way to get out the last drop. Since then, I've thought wistfully about the bottle scraper every time I've tried to get gooey foods, sauces or peanut butter out of a bottle or jar.

Unlike most spatulas, the long handle reaches the bottom of tall bottles. The small silicone head bends to enter small openings, then re-opens inside. The curved head fits snug against interior bottle walls, making it easy to scrape the contents out.

On a recent trip to The Netherlands, I made sure to purchase one for my home kitchen. Of course, travel isn't required. They're sold online at Fante's Kitchen Wares Shop.

-- Debora Dekok

Regular spoons, even so-called "basting spoons," aren't the right shape for getting down deep into the pan while simultaneously letting you scoop up enough liquid without having to tilt the pan too much. Enter the spout ladle, which is the perfect shape for this. The angles line up; the tilt is right; and it's long enough you don't run the risk of burning yourself on the pan or the rack while doing it.

I got mine in Chinatown, which is the only place I've ever seen this exact shape. You want a slight angle, not a 90-degree between spoon and handle as in most serving ladles. You can get one close to, but not exactly, that design online.

-- Adam Fields

Simple Kitchen Aids

Easiest jar opener
JarPop
$5 Spring Mill

The JarPop jar opener is the best five-dollar gizmo I've ever bought. It's what I gave my mother for Christmas last year. It's a beautifully simple bottle-cap-opener for lidded jars. It breaks the seal on a jar of applesauce (or anything else), and then the lid twists right off. I'm a little embarrassed how strongly I feel about it.

-- David McIntosh

Really big ice cubes
Tovolo King Cube Ice Tray
$8 Amazon

I don't own a fridge with an ice maker, and so for the past few years have been relying on the cheap white ice trays that seem to inhabit everybody's freezer. They've done their job, but never very well. Recently, however, I picked up the Tovolo King Cube Ice Tray, and have been blown away with the oversized ice cubes it produces.

The silicone ice tray produces the largest cubes of ice (they're 2" x 2") of any tray I've seen. Outside of being a gigantic novelty, the increased size is a boon as it reduces the surface area to volume ratio. This means the ice melts slower in your drink keeping it cold longer while minimizing how much it waters down your drink. I hadn't expected it to make that much of a difference, but it's really astonishing how much longer the ice remains in the drink. I've found these large cubes are downright perfect for cocktails like a gin and tonic, and while I'm no whiskey connoisseur I imagine they'd be even more at home in a scotch on the rocks. Simply put there's something special about having an oversized piece of ice clinking in your glass.

Another design plus is that the silicone tray holds a greater volume of water than other ice cube trays I've tried (which all seem to hold a pitiful amount of water), while taking up less valuable freezer real estate (the tray is significantly taller, and not as long as my old trays). Popping the ice cubes out takes a bit of wrangling, but no more so than cracking traditional ice trays, and because silicone is a good insulator you're not left with ice cold hands in the process.

The only downsides I've found so far are that the flexible silicone tray can twist and bend and slosh while finagling it into the freezer, and the fact that it only makes six cubes at a time. This hasn't been a problem for me as it takes fewer cubes (read: one) to cool down most drinks.

Overall, these big ice cubes are just plain cool, and for $8 it's a cheap and functional upgrade to any freezer.

-- Oliver Hulland

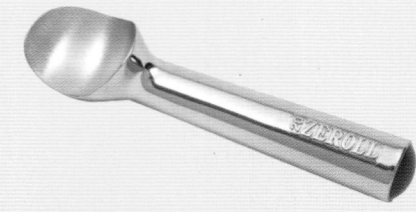

Heat-activated frozen treat scoop
Zeroll Ice Cream Scoops
$16 Zeroll

Unfortunately for my waist, I love ice cream. For a long time, I accepted the fact I either had to strengthen my wrist muscles, leave out the ice cream to soften up, or run the frozen tub or spoon under hot water before digging in (which dilutes the ice cream if you forget to dry it off beforehand). Not anymore.

The trick to this scoop is a heat-conductive fluid sealed inside the handle and business end. The heat from your hand warms the fluid, which lets you scoop easier and quicker. I find it can scoop ice cream from ice cream tubs that are hard as a rock, like a spoon through a tub of margarine.

This Zeroll scoop is not dishwasher safe, and must be hand-washed in warm or lukewarm water (the fluid in the handle can't take any hotter). It comes in different sizes from two to four ounces, in either a silver aluminum or Anodized Teflon finish. I opted for the two-ounce aluminum scooper because I've heard the Teflon finish wears off over time.

It's worth mentioning that I learned of the Zeroll from a cooking magazine. They tested various scoopers to settle on one that makes the "perfect, round scoop." The Zeroll won.

-- Ethan Stettner

Personal ice cream security
Ice Cream Pint Lock
$6 Ben & Jerry's

Due to roommates that didn't quite understand my displeasure at my constantly disappearing ice cream, I had to resort to this. Not a gag, it is actually is designed with the intention to work. Though I suppose that since the container it is "locking" is made of waxed cardboard (which can be deformed a bit) it won't keep out a serious professional penetration attempt.

I found that it sends a warning message, sort of like one of those little LED's you put in a car to give the appearance of having an alarm.

-- Morgan Davis

Safe can opener
Kuhn Rikon Safety Lid Lifter
$20 Kuhn Rikon

It may be a terribly long and unwieldy name, but it is far and away the coolest can opener I have ever used.

Why? The blade cuts into the can *below* the rim so the lid never falls into the food, and the blade doesn't touch the food either. You can use it to open "pop top" lids as well. A can opened with this tool will have no sharp edges. Apparently it works for both righties and lefties (not tried). Best of all you can challenge your friends by handing them the opener and a can and watch them figure out how to use it.

-- Marsh Gardiner

One-handed towel dispenser
Kamenstein Paper Towel Holder
$29 Kamenstein

Most free-rolling paper towel dispensers just don't work for me. Since I do a lot of food prep from my wheelchair, I can only grip with one hand. The genius of this "Perfect Tear" dispenser is how it allows enough freedom for the roll to unwind with a steady pull; yet, there's still enough friction to prevent further unwinding when you pull to detach the sheet.

The secret? 1) The center post is a series of bowed wires that contract and hold the paper roll snugly in place; and 2) The base weighs about four pounds, which adds stability.

No more chasing unwinding rolls of paper across the kitchen floor. Or getting five sheets when I only need one. Better still, it works just as well at the end of the roll as it does at the start. When a roll is out of sheets, just unscrew the top cap, slide off the cardboard tube, push on another roll and replace the cap. All of this can be easily performed one-handed.

After a couple of years, it's still well worth the precious space it's claimed on my very limited counter.

-- Eric Eales

Fridge-free butter
Butter Bell
$20 Tremain

Some folks are comfortable leaving out the butter, as-is on the counter for days on end. For those who aren't, but still want the convenience and pleasure of a steady, safe supply of spreadable-yet-fresh butter: You'll love the Butter Bell.

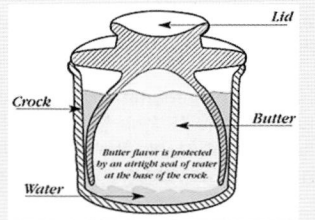

Begin by leaving a stick of butter on the counter for an hour, or just long enough to soften it up. Place the butter in the Bell, then add a little water to the base. This creates an airtight seal around the butter, discouraging bacteria. Voilà! You'll never again be stuck trying to spread rock-hard butter on a piece of toast.

It's a design that's been around in various forms for centuries.

-- Bryn-Ane MacKinnon

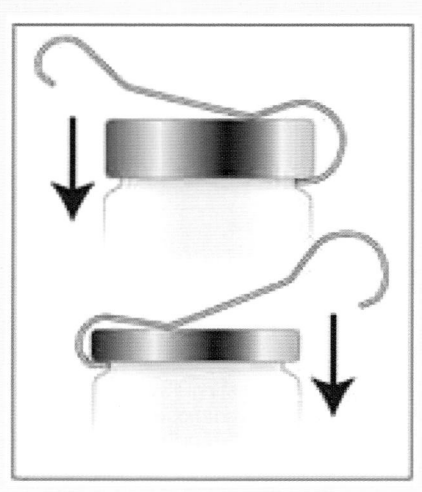

Metal seal popper
Lee Valley Jar Opener
$10 Lee Valley

I always used a spoon, until I was given one of these lid poppers. I was skeptical, but I now find myself reaching for it without even thinking. An 8.5 x 5-cm piece of metal, it's bent in the middle and curved at each end to accommodate just about any size jar lid. It's very simple and straightforward: Simply place it on the jar top with either of the rolled sides caught under the lid's lip (which side of the opener depends on the lid size); then, hold the opener in place and use it as a lever. The bend in the metal serves as the fulcrum. The downward pressure of your hand provides enough force to release the vacuum seal without distorting the lid. I can happily report no more bent spoon handles, no more splatters, and no more spills. Just a nice "pop" when the vacuum breaks, and I'm home free. I have not tried the previously-reviewed plastic JarPop, but I've had this steel one for at least 3 years. It has never bent, nor has it rusted.

-- Ellen Rocco

We drive into the future using only our rearview mirror. - Marshall McLuhan

Best vegan cookbooks
Veganomicon • Simply Vegan

$17 Isa Chandra Moskowitz, Terry Hope Romero, 2007, 336 p.

Veganomicon is the best vegan (no meat or dairy) cookbook out there. Its reputation is based on the quantity and variety of its recipes, and the complexity and deliciousness of the resulting dishes. There are more than 250 recipes, presented with wit and lighthearted punk-rock irreverence, as well unpretentious and helpful instructions. These vegan dishes don't only try to mimic meat-based meals; they are just good food. Our household doesn't adhere to a vegan diet, yet we've found some of these recipes great eye-openers as to how tasty and accessible homemade vegan food can be.

-- Elon Schoenholz

$11 Debra Wasserman, Reed Mangels, 2006 (4th edition), 224 p.

SIMPLY VEGAN
QUICK VEGETARIAN MEALS
By Debra Wasserman
Nutrition Section
By Reed Mangels,
Ph.D., R.D.

Updated 4th Edition

When I went vegan, I was 14 years-old (14 years later, I still am). At the time, my parents made me sell them on the idea of maintaining my health sans animal products. At first the task seemed incredibly daunting. Once I found *Simply Vegan*, I had all the answers.

This book is perfect for beginning vegans because it has specific sections on how to be a healthy vegan, as opposed to a "Fritos and Sprite" vegan. The text goes into various sources of proteins and minerals, and includes ready-to-go weekly shopping lists and daily meal lists. If you're getting into veganism, you can do it safely and intelligently with a minimal amount of work; just buy the stuff on the shopping list and cook it.

I won't say the recipes in this book are the best ever. They certainly can't hold a candle to much of *Veganomicon*. But if you know your way around a spice rack, they're pretty good. Either way, there's no better book I've found which covers the nutritive bases and really can set a new vegan on the right path to whole health. 14 years later, I'm still vegan and my folks are mostly vegan as well.

-- Ian Hall

●
from *Veganomicon*:

Chickpea Cutlets

We try not to play favorites, but this is one of our babies and a recipe that we are sure will take over food blogs worldwide. A combination of chickpeas and vital wheat gluten formed into savory cutlets, it's perfect for when you want something "meaty" buy don't want to go to the trouble of making seitan. We serve these cutlets in myriad ways, packed into sandwiches or smothered in mustard sauce, with a side of mashed potatoes and roasted asparagus. It's vegan food that you can eat with a steak knife and, best of all, it is fast and easy. You'll probably want to double the recipe if you're serving it to guests.

●
Beanball Sub

This is a conglomeration of a few recipes from the cookbook that also would make great use of leftover Beanballs (page 189). We throw in a handful of spinach just for posterity; you need not be so healthy if you don't feel like it. Also, if you don't want to make the Pine Nut Cream (page 164) and just want to use some soy cheese, we won't judge you. These would be perfect for a Super Bowl party, or since you are a vegan and hate football, a Nobel Prize party. Ooh, we can't wait to see who wins for physics this year!

1 recipe Beanballs (page 189)

1 recipe (4 cups) Marinara Sauce, or any of the variations (page 205)

1 recipe Pine Nut cream (page 164)

4 hoagie rolls, split open

2 cups fresh spinach leaves, well washed

●
Tip

To toast sesame seeds: Preheat a small pan over medium-low heat. Pour in the sesame seeds and toast them, stirring often, for about 3 minutes. Once they are browned, immediately remove them from the pan to prevent burning.

●
Tip

This is our favorite way to prep collards: To get rid of the tough stem without having to sit there cutting it, you can actually easily tear the leaves from the stem with your hands. Fill the sink with water, pull off the leaves, rip them into large pieces (collards are tough, they can take it) and put the leaves into the water to rinse them. No need to drain, just give them a shake before adding to the pan.

●
from *Simply Vegan*:

Summary: It is very easy for a vegan diet to meet the recommendations for protein, as long as calorie intake is adequate. Strict protein combining is not necessary; it is more important to eat a varied diet throughout the day…. This concern about protein is misplaced. Although protein is certainly an essential nutrient which plays many key roles in the way our bodies function, we do not need huge quantities of it. In reality, we need small amounts of protein. Only one calorie out of every ten we take in needs to come from protein (1).

(1) Food and Nutrition Board, institute of Medicine. Dietary Reference Intakes for Energy, Carbohydrate, Fiber, Fat, Fatty Acids, Cholesterol, Protein, and Amino Acids. Washington, DC: National Academy Press, 2002.

●
Generally, vegan diets can be low in fat if they emphasize grains, legumes, fruits, and vegetables. Some foods vegans eat such as oils, margarine, nuts, nut butters, tofu, tahini, avocado, and coconut are high in fat. These foods should not be the center of one's diet but should be used sparingly. For example, tofu is high in fat. If you ate a pound of tofu, you would eat about 22 grams of fat. Eating a smaller amount of tofu (4 ounces) and serving it over rice with vegetables could provide the same number of calories and less fat.

●
Calcium, needed for strong bones, is found in dark green leafy vegetables, tofu made with calcium sulfate, calcium-fortified soy milk and orange juice, and many other foods commonly eaten by vegans. Although lower animal protein intake may reduce calcium losses, there is currently no real evidence to suggest that vegans have lower calcium needs. Vegans should eat foods that are high in calcium and/or use a calcium supplement.

Handy reminder for responsible fish eating
Seafood Watch

Free download Monterey Bay Aquarium

It's no secret that fish stocks of many species have been over-harvested to the point of extinction, but whenever I'm ordering fish at a restaurant I can't remember what's good fish and what's bad fish. I now rely on this very app. Tells me which fish species to avoid (severely overfished), which are okay, and which are borderline narrowed to my location.

-- KK

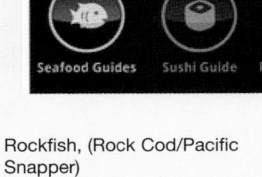

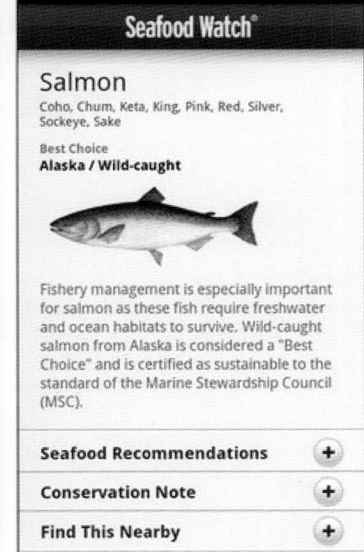

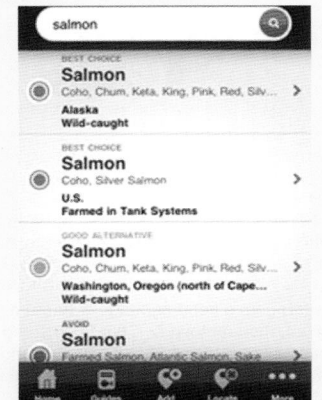

AVOID	
Caviar, Beluga/Osetra/Sevruga	Rockfish, (Rock Cod/Pacific Snapper)
Chilean Seabass	Salmon, (farmed/Atlantic)
Cod, Atlantic/Icelandic	Sharks, except U.S. West Coast Thresher
Crab, King (imported)	Shrimp (imported)
Lingcod	Sturgeon, wild-caught
Monkfish	Swordfish, Atlantic
Orange Roughy	Tuna, Bluefin

Food with few dishes
Glorious One-Pot Meals
$13 Elizabeth Yarnell, 2009, 240 p.

Elizabeth Yarnell has developed an easy, tasty, and fast method of one-pot cooking she calls "infusion cooking." More or less, it's the opposite of slow-cooker cooking. The ingredients are layered in a two-quart cast-iron Dutch oven, which is covered and placed in a 450F oven for 45 minutes. I've found that I can assemble one of Yarnell's meals in the time it takes the oven to heat. That makes two servings: one for a couple or, in my case, one for lunch and dinner. Although the recipes in *Glorious One-Pot Meals* need a bit of spicing up, after making a couple, you get the idea and improvisation is easy.

Yarnell recommends an enameled cast-iron Dutch oven. Although it's not enameled, I've found the Texsport two-quart Dutch oven ($25 at Amazon) to be my favorite. It's pre-seasoned and easy to clean and use. Most of the two-quart Dutch ovens are squat and short. The Texsport is narrower and taller, which seems to work best for this method of cooking (I've tried several different ovens). Plus, when it's filled to the brim, the Texsport is actually 2.5 quarts. The extra room is useful if you're including leafy greens. If you have your heart set on using an enameled pot, I recommend the Staub 2.25-quart round cocotte ($100 at Amazon) instead of the Le Creuset dutch oven ($185), because the Staub is higher quality and better made.

-- Michael Ham

Cookbooks

Ingredient substitutions
The Cook's Thesaurus

Free The Cook's Thesaurus

Although it has been online for years, I only recently discovered this incredibly handy resource. Use this simple website to find substitutes for cooking ingredients. Say a recipe calls for buckwheat flour, which you most likely don't have on hand. What do you use? Type in the term and presto: The links take you to an entry which will suggest alternatives. I also find the site helpful in quickly introducing myself to new ingredients. While not exhaustive, it lists about 90% of the ingredients you'll probably encounter, including many exotics, usually with a helpful photo and a short summary of its origin. This thesaurus of ingredients is fast, simple, and just right.

-- KK

▲ Pigeon Pea = goongoo pea = gunga pea = gungo pea = congo pea = congo bean = no-eyed peas = gandules Shopping hints: These are usually sold dried, but fresh, frozen, and canned peas also are available. They have a strong flavor, and they're popular in the South and in the Caribbean. Substitutes: yellow-eyed peas OR black-eyed peas

► Jocoque = labin Notes: This is a Mexican product that's halfway between buttermilk and sour cream. Substitutes: salted buttermilk OR sour cream OR yogurt OR crema

Best basic cookbook
How to Cook Everything

$21 Mark Bittman, 2008, 1056 p.

In our household, this is the book that has replaced *Joy of Cooking* as the first cookbook we reach for. It educates the ignorant, rewards the expert, and gratifies the harried with steady and sure knowledge about how to cook everything. By everything it means: wholesome everyday food. Its 2,000 recipes are unpretentious, yet diverse.

-- KK

●
Each year, I experiment less and less with complex dishes, and try to master the simple staples both of our widely divergent culture, and of other cultures from around the world. I look for good ingredients, and handle them minimally. I am usually satisfied with the food I prepare, but I am the first to admit that it is very rarely on the same level as that served in the world's best restaurants. (It's better, however, than that served in the vast majority of restaurants.)

Striving for brilliance in everyday cooking is a recipe for frustration. Rather, everyday cooking is about preparing good, wholesome, tasty, varied meals for the ones you love. This is a simple, satisfying pleasure. Your results need not be perfect to give you this gift, to which all humans are entitled.

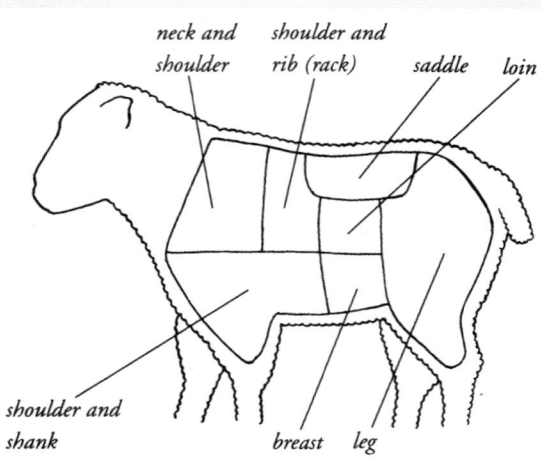

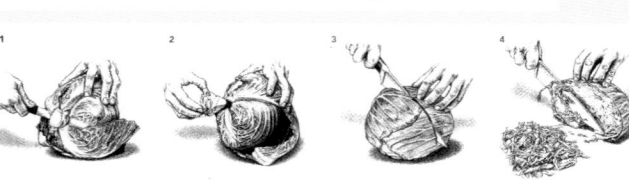

●
Spiced Melon Balls

Makes 10-15 servings

Time: 20 minutes

Melon balls are melon balls, until you do something to them. This converts them to an exotic Asian-style dish, easily eaten with toothpicks.

1 ripe cantaloupe or other orange-fleshed melon

1 ripe honeydew or other green-fleshed melon

1/2 teaspoon salt

1 teaspoon ground coriander

1/4 teaspoon cayenne, or to taste

1 tablespoon very finely minced cilantro leaves

2 tablespoons freshly squeezed lime juice

Sugar to taste (optional)

1. Use a melon baller to remove all the flesh from the melons. Combine the balls in a bowl with the salt, coriander, cayenne, cilantro, and lime juice.

2. Taste and adjust seasoning; you may add more of anything. If the melon is not sufficiently sweet, add a bit of sugar. Cover and refrigerate until ready to serve, up to 2 hours.

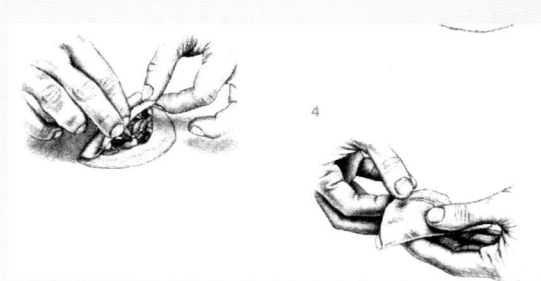

First, remove the leg-thigh section by cutting straight down between the leg and carcass, and through the joint holding the thigh to the carcass. Set aside for the moment.

Cut the wing from the carcass.

▲ **Making potstickers**

(Step 1) Place a teaspoon of filling on one half of the dough. (Step 2) Brush circumference of the circle with a little water or beaten egg. (Steps 3-4) Fold over and pinch tightly to seal.

◄ (Steps 1-2) The easiest way to core a head cabbage is to cut a small cone-shaped section from the bottom, then remove it. (Step 3) To shred head cabbage, first cut it into manageable pieces. (Step 4) Cut thin sections across the head; they'll naturally fall into shreds. (You can also use a mdoline for this.) If the shreds are too long, just cut across them.

Essential iPhone cook book
How To Cook Everything

$5 iTunes Store

This $5 iPhone app contains all the content of Mark Bittman's original book. Since the information is stored offline, unlike many other recipe apps, you can access it whenever. In addition, there are useful features including a recipe timer, fast searchable index (by main ingredient, cook time, vegetarian, etc.), an emailable grocery list from recipes, and reader-recommended recipes. I have used it almost every day since it was released. It's what a cookbook for the iPhone should be.

-- Oliver Hulland

Chopping Illustrated

Cutting vegetables—or any food—into small pieces is best done in a series of steps.

First, cut the food into manageable and

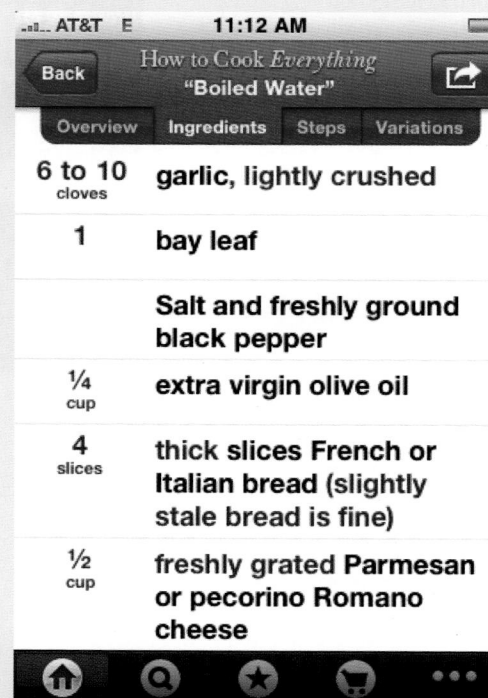

"Boiled Water"

Overview	Ingredients	Steps	Variations

6 to 10 cloves	garlic, lightly crushed
1	bay leaf
	Salt and freshly ground black pepper
1/4 cup	extra virgin olive oil
4 slices	thick slices French or Italian bread (slightly stale bread is fine)
1/2 cup	freshly grated Parmesan or pecorino Romano cheese

I paint objects as I think them, not as I see them. - Pablo Picasso

SCIENCE
The Benefits of Boiling Brown Rice

When rice is cooked on the stovetop via the absorption method, the grains absorb almost all of the small amount of liquid that's in the pot early on in the cooking process. This can lead to uneven results, since only the grains that fully hydrate at the start will completely soften, while the grains that didn't initially absorb enough liquid will remain firm.

We found that boiling brown rice in an abundance of water not only cooked it more evenly but also shaved a good 25 minutes off the usual 50 minutes needed for the absorption method (i.e., simmering the rice in a set amount of liquid). With a large volume of boiling water in the pot (which is drained off when the rice is done), the liquid can penetrate the grains evenly from all sides, so their starches gelatinize more uniformly as well as more quickly. Boiling the rice (versus simmering it) also speeds up cooking because boiling water contains more energy than simmering water. All in all, boiling is an excellent way to cook brown rice. –A.R.

ABSORPTION APPROACH
Simmer rice, covered, in small amount of water.
Cook Time: 50 minutes
Results: Uneven. A small amount of water can't penetrate all of the grains at the same rate.

BOILING METHOD
Cook rice in lots of boiling water; drain.
Cook Time: 25 minutes
Results: Every grain absorbs the same amount of water, so the whole pot cooks evenly.

The magazine for cooking nerds
Cook's Illustrated

$25 (1-year subscription, 6 issues) Cook's Illustrated

The technical aspects of cooking are usually overlooked. Kitchen gear is addressed by most publications, if at all, when it is fancy and untried. This paper magazine, however, tests equipment, gadgets, and recipes — new and old — in a relentless quest for the best kitchen stuff. *Cook's Illustrated* is at liberty to be honest in their recommendations because they have no ads — no one to please but avid readers. The tests are amazingly thorough, and astoundingly informative. They examine everything from basic ingredients (sea salt, bread flour, olive oil) to high-end equipment (what is the best mixer?), as well as state-of-the-art

BREADWINNER
UDI'S Gluten Free White Sandwich Bread
Price: $5 for 12-oz loaf
Comments: Thanks to its high protein and salt levels, our favorite gluten-free bread "looked good," "smelled nice," and boasted an "airy texture." Toasted, it was "crunchy yet yielding"—"close to 'real' bread," according to some tasters.

THINGS FALL APART
FOOD FOR LIFE Gluten Free White Rice Bread
Price: $6.79 for 24-oz loaf
Comments: A measly amount of protein left this second-to-last-place bread with "no structure at all." Its flavor also seemed "super-stale" and was marred by a "horrible aftertaste."

ON THE BORDER
CANYON BAKEHOUSE Mountain White Gluten Free Bread
Price: $5 for 18-oz loaf
Comments: This second-place bread tasted "boring but not actually bad." But its texture was "rubbery"—like "chewing gum."

DON'T BOTHER
ENER-G Gluten Free Tapioca Loaf, Regular Sliced
Price: $5.79 for 16-oz loaf
Comments: Tasters forced down bites of this losing loaf, which was "flat" and "dense," like a "coaster," and regretted its "scratchy" texture.

in standard instruments like garlic presses, frying pans, oven thermometers, etc. I find their comparison methods to be more realistic and far more useful than *Consumer Reports*; and, of course, they evaluate far more items than *CR* ever would. They also obsessively taste-test popular recipes in hundreds of variations, and research the mysteries behind each ingredient. I learn tons each issue — about foodstuffs, about cooking, and about eating.

EXPLANATION
It turns out that salad leaves have a protective waxy cuticle layer that prevents water-based liquids (vinegar) from having much effect on them, but oil easily penetrates this film. Tossing the greens with vinegar first provides a barrier that blocks the oil, keeping it from penetrating the cuticle. The emulsified vinaigrette works the best at keeping the salad crisp because in this state the vinegar surrounds droplets of oil, keeping them trapped and preventing contact with the greens.

SOGGY   SLIGHTLY WILTED   CRISP
Tossing a salad with a fully emulsified vinaigrette (right) is the only way to ensure that greens keep their crisp texture. But if you prefer to add oil and vinegar separately, introduce the vinegar first, followed by the oil (middle).

Best of all, these folks make it very clear when a new tool or technique is not worth the trouble, and how you could manage with an old version. Unlike most magazines, back issues don't age. You can also get online versions. And recently they've launched video and TV episodes. Their "Best of" compilations are well-used in our kitchens.

-- *KK*

TECHNIQUE | THE NEW BASICS OF COOKING LOBSTERS

1. FREEZE FOR 30 MINUTES
Chilling lobsters in the freezer for 30 minutes induces a comalike state that makes it easier and safer to maneuver them into the pot.

2. COOK TAIL TO 175 DEGREES
A tail temperature of 175 ensures perfectly cooked meat. (We cook fish to between 130 and 140 degrees, but lobster requires a higher temperature since its muscle fibers are longer and require more heat to shrink.)

What other people eat
Strange Foods

$17 Jerry Hopkins, 1999, 232 p.

People (collectively) will eat anything. But one man's meat is another man's ugh. This color-rich volume features the strangest (to us) foods served in the world. It highlights two global trends: a hunger for increasingly exotic foods, and the worrisome increase in hunting bush meat from endangered and rare animals – at crisis levels in parts of Africa and Asia. Nonetheless, the full variety of things-humans-eat, in all their strangeness, are captured in fine photography and readable history here. The author also provides sources and recipes for farm-raised exotic foods and meats. This guy, at least, has tried everything.

-- *KK*

When I tell people that I took the placenta home following the birth of my son and the next day served it as a pate, they generally (1) don't believe me or (2) recoil in horror, calling me a cannibal. My wife was to return home the day following and my plan was to cook the placenta and make it into a pate to serve visitors who had been invited to meet the baby. When I asked, the doctor agreed in wonderment, but then didn't know what to put it in for transport to the flat. Unlike restaurants, medical clinics don't have Styrofoam "take-away" containers for leftover food.

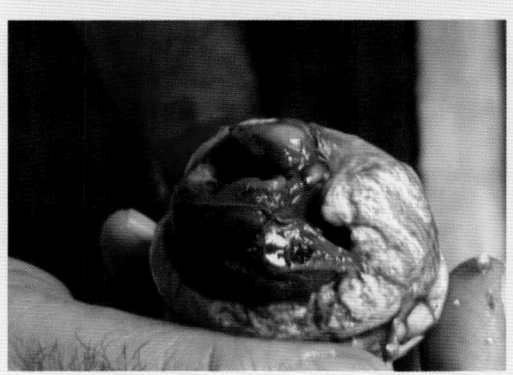

Bird's nest soup is one of the true culinary enigmas, a high-priced delicacy that is made from the nests of swifts, found in bat-filled caves in Southeast Asia. The nests are made of seaweed, twigs, moss, hair, and feathers glued together by the birds' saliva and the spawn of small fish. Is this something you would pay up to US $300 a bowl for?

Why so expensive? Well, first of all, it's considered by many to be an aphrodisiac, a word – some say myth – that is driving many animal species to the edge of extinction. For centuries, Chinese have given their children the soup, believing it will help them grow. Others consume it to improve their complexion and defeat lung problems, or as an all-purpose tonic.

Two handfuls of rats that will either be eaten, or sold for one-and-a-half rupees each under a program set up by the Oxfam Trust and India's Department of Science and Technology.

Outer limits of food
Bizarre Foods

$10 Andrew Zimmern, 2007, 338 min.

I think we owe it to ourselves to explore the world's cuisine and outer boundaries of food. You don't have to like everything you try, but you should try everything. Humans somewhere will consume just about anything that moves, or is grown, so there is plenty of material. The balding fat chef, Andrew Zimmern, who is the host of this TV show goes on a quest to eat the weirdest, strangest, most bizarre foods in world. He'll try anything twice, and then give his "review" of it. Strict vegetarians may want to avoid watching. Not only is any animal, insect, fish, invertebrate eaten, any part of it is gobbled down as well. Better than several books on the subject, this series will make you rethink your food limits. It's comparative foodology 101. All weird foods have a good story behind them, as revealed in these fun documentaries, which now comprise at least 75 episodes. If you can't find endless repeats on his show on cable TV, there are collections on DVD.

-- *KK*

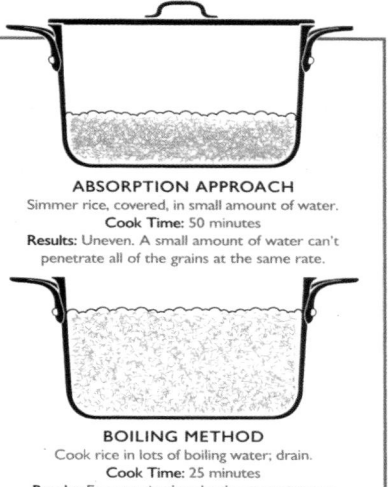

Basic principles

The Science of Good Cooking

$26 Editors of America's Test Kitchen and Guy Crosby, 2012, 504 p.

I've learned more about cooking from this hefty volume than from reading or watching anything else.

There are other fine books about the science of cooking, including Harold McGee's classic *On Food and Cooking,* but this big book is by far the most practical and helpful. While McGee's is authoritative and complete, this one is better organized for your average cook. The science is condensed into 50 principles, and each easy-to-remember principle is illustrated by half a dozen tested recipes. If you can master these 50 you'll have the equivalent of a culinary degree.

An example of a principle would be: Salting vegetables removes liquid. You'll hear the evidence why this is true, what difference it makes in dishes, and how to apply it to any recipe in the future. Every claim is tested by experiments run by the nerd chefs at *Cook's Illustrated*, so that you have full command of the idea and its exceptions. Although this book is jam packed with "best recipes" this is not a traditional cookbook: it is more of a cooking course. The teaching is a model of clarity and insight.

-- *KK*

BAKING SODA VS. BAKING POWDER

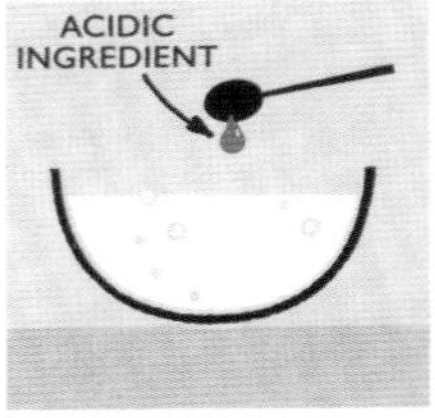

BAKING SODA *When baking soda and an acidic ingredient interact, they immediately begin to produce carbon dioxide, creating bubbles that help batters and doughs to rise.*

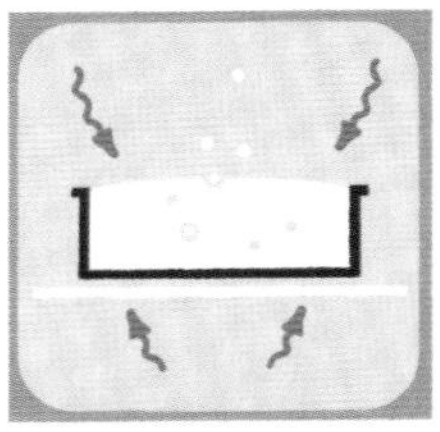

BAKING POWDER *Most baking powder produces bubbles of carbon dioxide a second time—when it is heated in the oven.*

•

The way you cut an onion affects its flavor. To prove the point, we took eight onions and cut each two different ways: pole to pole (with the grain) and parallel to the equator (against the grain). We then smelled and tasted pieces from each onion cut each way. The onions sliced pole to pole were clearly less pungent in taste and odor than those cut along the equator.

PRACTICAL SCIENCE AVOIDING UNEVEN BAKING

Bake one sheet at a time, and be sure to rotate.

Baking two trays of cookies at a time may be convenient, but it leads to uneven cooking. The cookies on the top tray are often browner around the edges than those on the bottom. If you have two sheets in the oven, switching their position halfway through cooking helps. But for cookies with an especially finicky texture, we find it best to bake the cookies one sheet at a time to ensure the best results. And just because there's just one baking sheet in the oven, don't assume you can walk away. Even the best ovens have hot and cold spots and you must rotate the baking sheet at the halfway mark to ensure even baking. Simply grab the front of the baking sheet and rotate the pan until the cookies that were in the front are now in the back of the oven.

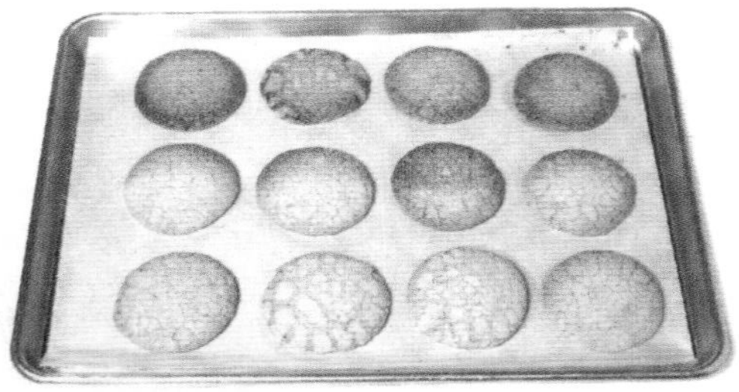

NO ROTATING = UNEVEN BAKING

•

Perhaps just as important as cookware material is the pan shape and size. Crowd four chicken breasts into a 10-inch pan and they will steam; space them out in a 12-inch pan and they will brown.

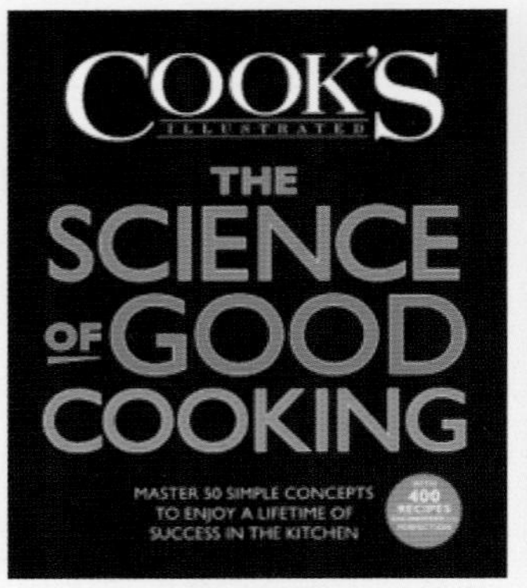

•

Salty Marinades Work Best

Marinating is often regarded as a cure-all for bland, chewy meat. Years of testing have taught us that while many marinades can bump up flavor, most will never turn a rough cut tender. Well, not without the right ingredient. What's the secret to a marinade that can add complexity to steak, chicken and pork and enhance juiciness? You guessed it: salt.

•

Gentle Folding Stops Tough Quick Breads

As we learned in concept 39, yeast breads depend on a well-developed gluten structure to rise properly. Gluten also gives bread its resilient, chewy texture. In contrast, quick breads (such as banana bread), as well as muffins and pancakes, can be ruined by excess development of gluten. That's because tenderness–not chewiness–is the goal.

•

Two Leaveners Are Often Better than One

The advent of chemical leaveners, such as baking soda and baking powder, in the 19th century made it easier for cooks to bake at home. No need to rely on fickle yeast in order to make a cake. Chemical leaveners are quick and reliable. But they are also confusing. Some recipes rely on baking powder, some on baking soda, and many on both. Why do you need two leaveners in something as simple as a cookie that doesn't even rise all that much?

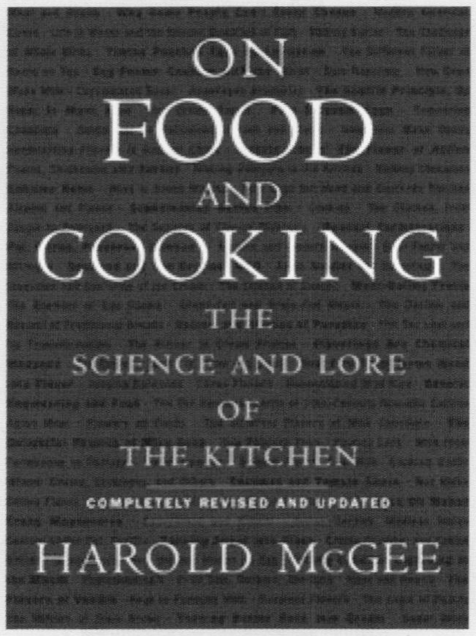

Food answers

On Food and Cooking

$27 Harold McGee, 2004, 884 p.

This is the smartest book in my kitchen. It's where I go whenever I have a question about what I am eating, or the science behind its preparation. Simply the best source for understanding food and how it works. Now in its updated second edition. Covers ingredients from all over the world and time. Awesome, encyclopedic.

-- *KK*

•

Aromas from Altered Carotenoid Pigments.

Both drying and cooking break some of the pigment molecules in carotenoid-rich fruits and vegetables into small, volatile fragments that contribute to their characteristic aromas. These fragments provide notes reminiscent of black tea, hay, honey, and violets.

•

Green Chlorophyll.

One change in the color of green vegetables as they are cooked has nothing to do with the pigment itself. That wonderfully intense, bright green that develops within a few seconds of throwing vegetables into boiling water is a result of the sudden expansion and escape of gases trapped in the spaces between cells. Ordinarily, these microscopic air pockets cloud the color of the chloroplasts. When they collapse, we can see the pigments much more directly.

•

Soba: Japanese Buckwheat Noodles.

Buckwheat noodles were made in northern China in the 14th century, and had become a popular food in Japan by around 1600. It's difficult to make noodles exclusively with buckwheat flour because the buckwheat proteins do not form a cohesive gluten. Japanese soba noodles may be from 10%-90% buckwheat, the remainder wheat. They're traditionally made from freshly milled flour, which is mixed very quickly with the water and worked until the water is evenly absorbed and the dough firm and smooth. Salt is omitted because it interferes with the proteins and mucilage that help bind the dough (p. 483). The dough is rested, then rolled out to about 3 mm thick and rested again, then cut into fine noodles. The noodles are cooked fresh, and when done, are washed and firmed in a container of ice water, drained, and served either in a hot broth or cold, accompanied by a dipping sauce.

•

Maple Sugaring Without Metal or Fire.

In 1755, a young colonist was captured and "adopted" by a small group of natives in the region that is now Ohio. In 1799 he published his story in *An Account of the Remarkable Occurrences in the Life and Travels of Col. James Smith*, which includes several descriptions of how the Indians made maple sugar. Here's the most ingenious method.

"We had no large kettles with us this year, and the squaws made the frost, in some measure, supply the place of fire, in making sugar. Their large bark vessels, for holding the stock-water, they made broad and shallow; and as the weather is very cold here, it frequently freezes at night in sugar time; and the ice they break and cast out of the vessels. I asked them if they were not throwing away the sugar? they said no; it was water they were casting away, sugar did not freeze and there was scarcely any in that ice…I observed that after several times freezing, the water that remained in the vessel, changed its color and became brown and very sweet."

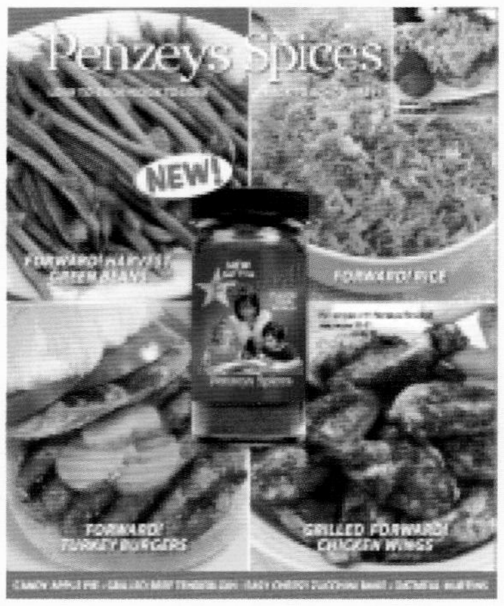

Global spice source

Penzeys Spices

Prices vary Penzeys Spices

The spices of life. All of them, in subtle variations, from around the world. By mailorder.

-- *KK*

Saffron

Saffron is the stigma of the fall flowering crocus. Peek inside most any flower and you will see three thread-like filaments. These are stigma–but only in the saffron crocus are these stigma worth thousands of dollars per pound. Saffron is so valuable because it is a very labor intensive crop; only 5-7 pounds of saffron can be produced from each acre of land. This makes saffron the most expensive spice by weight–it has always been–but by use saffron isn't that expensive, because a little goes a long way. A single gram of saffron easily translates into golden color and fragrant flavor.

Saffron contains 450-500 saffron stigmas to the gram. The stigma are also called threads, strings, pieces or strands. 1 gram equals 2 tsp. whole, 1 teaspoon crumbled or 1/2 teaspoon powdered. Don't buy pre-powdered saffron because it loses flavor quickly and is usually cut with turmeric or something else.

Mace

Mace, the lace-like, dried covering of the nutmeg, is a sweet and flavorful spice well worth using. Mace has a softer flavor than nutmeg, and for a nice change of pace it can be used in place of nutmeg in any recipe. Blade Mace can also be added to clear soups and sauces where nutmeg powder might spoil the appearance. Mace is a traditional flavoring for doughnuts and hotdogs.

Ajwain Seed

Ajwain (or Ajowan) is a traditional addition to many Indian and Pakistani dishes. It's especially useful in vegetarian lentil and bean dishes, as a flavoring, and to temper the effects of a legume-based diet. From Pakistan.

50113 1 lb bag 13.90

50184 8 oz bag 7.49

50142 4 oz bag 4.29

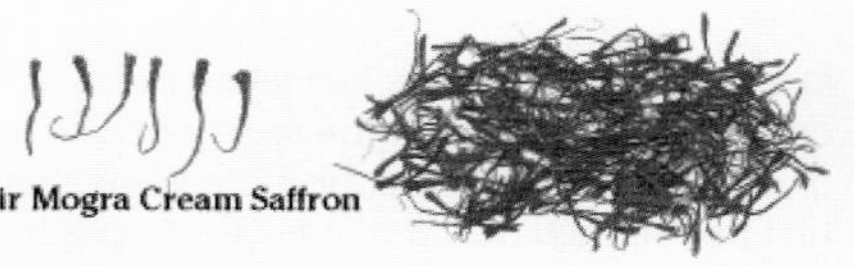

Kashmir Mogra Cream Saffron

Kashmir "Mogra Cream" Indian Saffron is the world's finest saffron. The dark red color and long perfect strands are as beautiful as they are colorful and flavorful. Kashmir saffron is awfully tough to obtain, which makes it higher in price, but Kashmir Mogra Cream Saffron is truly wonderful.

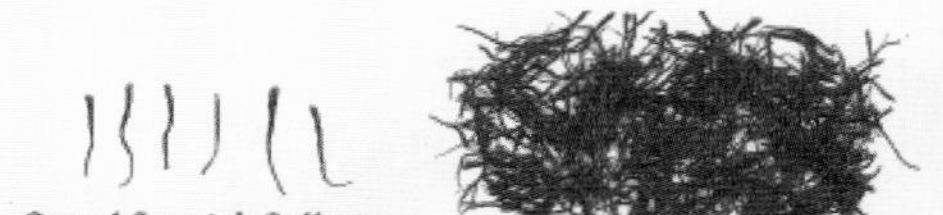

Coupé Spanish Saffron

Spanish Coupe Saffron is the top grade of the Spanish Saffron crop. Extra hand labor is used to remove every bit of the yellow saffron style material, leaving 100% beautiful pure red saffron threads–hence the name: coupe means "to cut", as in cutting off all the yellow bits. Spanish Coupe Saffron is a truly excellent crop, especially nice for the traditional Spanish dishes.

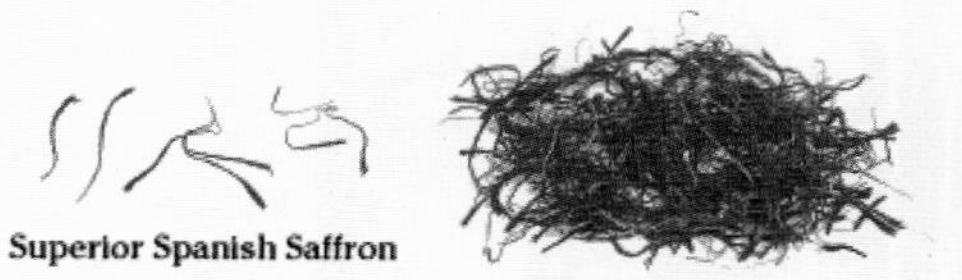

Superior Spanish Saffron

Spanish Superior Saffron is the most widely available saffron and is a very good crop. Spanish Superior Saffron has a bit of the yellow style material left attached to some of the saffron stigmas (see photo), so it is not quite as strong as Spanish Coupe or Kashmir Indian Saffron.

Your theory is crazy, but it's not crazy enough to be true. - Niels Bohr

All foods
Cooking Ingredients
$19 Christine Ingram, 2010, 512 p.

For the straight dope on cooking ingredients, this is your one-stop compendium. Aimed at global foodies, it explains the differences between similar ingredients, and how they are used in cooking. Unravel your various pastas, cheese types, strange fruits and confusing meat parts. Over 1,500 ingredients are covered, so you get only a brief paragraph or two on each, plus a picture. The only source that comes close to the comprehensive range of this fat, affordable book is Wikipedia, but it lacks this tome's wonderfully informative photographs. Food likes to be seen. I use this book for both browsing and searching. (It's out of print, but you can get remaindered copies pretty cheap. The same information is sold in a larger format and much more expensive edition entitled *The World Encyclopedia of Cooking Ingredients*, but it is not worth it.)

-- KK

•
Also known as blachan, terasi, kapi and ngapi, according to its country of origin, shrimp paste is an essential ingredient in scores of savoury dishes from South-east Asia. It is made from tiny shrimp that have been salted, dried, pounded and then left to ferment in the hot, humid equatorial conditions until the aroma is very pungent. The color of the paste can be anything from pale oyster pink to purplish brown,

depending upon the type of shrimp and the precise process used to produce it.

There's no disguising the main constituent of this paste. The moment you unwrap it or lift the lid, the smell of rotten fish is quite overwhelming. Do not let this put you off, however. The odour vanishes when the paste is cooked, and this is one of those ingredients that really does made a difference to the food, adding depth, pungency and a recognizable Southeast Asian signature. it should be used sparingly – a piece about 1-2 cm/1/2-3/4 in long is sufficient for most dishes.

Shrimp paste is compressed and sold in blocks or packed into tiny tubs.

Calf's and lamb's sweetbreads

•
Sweetbreads are the thymus glands taken from the neck and heart of young animals such as calves and lambs. They are pale and delicate with a tender meaty texture when braised or boiled. They are often pressed and fried or sauteed after blanching.

Spelt flour is ground from the small brown grains of an ancient variety of wheat, which is quite different from modern types of wheat.

•
Spelt is one of the oldest cultivated species of wheat. It is grown in only a few areas of Europe today, but some of the smaller flour mills produce a spelt flour that is available in some health food stores. It is popular in northern Europe, especially Germany, Switzerland and France, and is beginning to enjoy a revival in some other countries. This may be because the gluten it contains is fragile, so people with a gluten intolerance may be able to use it. It contains more B vitamins than other wheat grains.

Handy substitutions
Food Substitution Bible
$24 David Joachim, (Second Edition) 2010, 695 p.

This is pretty handy. An alphabetical listing of 6,500 types of food (and a few tools) with their possible substitutions. It's particularly powerful with exotic foods you are unlikely to have, know where to get, or to even recognize. This big fat tome will give you alternatives in descending similarity. Two reasons to use it: 1) to find a simple substitution to achieve the same results; or 2) find an alternative that will take the dish in a slightly different direction. This book should also be an app.

--KK

Cashew Butter

A paste of ground roasted cashew nuts, oil, and salt.

If You Don't Have It

Substitute 1 cup (250 mL) cashew butter with:
- 1 cup (250 mL) Homemade Cashew Butter: Put 2 cups (500 mL) roasted cashews and ¼ tsp (1 mL) salt in a blender or food processor fitted with metal blade. Process, gradually adding 4 to 6 tbsp (60 to 90 mL) vegetable oil, until the mixture forms a paste. Add sugar to taste. Makes 1½ cups (375 mL).
- 1 cup (250 mL) peanut butter or almond butter
- 1 cup (250 mL) tahini (strong sesame flavor)

Cassava

Also known as mandioca, manioc, and yuca. A starchy root that is popular in Latin America and a staple in many parts of Africa. Tapioca is one by-product.

If You Don't Have It

Substitute 1 lb (500 g) cassava with:
- 1 lb (500 g) mandiba
- 1 lb (500 g) yautía or malanga
- 1 lb (500 g) taro
- 1 lb (500 g) potatoes

See also GARI; TAPIOCA.

Pheasant

The flesh of female pheasants is plumper, juicier, and more tender than that of the males. Very young hens are delicious roasted.

1 average = 3 lbs (1.5 kg)

If You Don't Have It

Substitute 1 lb (500 g) pheasant with:
- 1 lb (500 g) guinea fowl
- 1 lb (500 g) grouse
- 1 lb (500 g) quail
- 1 lb (500 g) partridge
- 1 lb (500 g) squab
- 1 lb (500 g) Cornish hen (fattier)

Efficient recipe search
Recipe Aggregators

As much as I like cooking from any of the several cookbooks in my library, I often look for new recipes online. It's not an easy task. I'm amazed at the number of ad-riddled pages I find by Googling the name of a dish. I do have an online subscription to *Cook's Illustrated*, and there are a handful of other individual free sites I turn to for recipes and technique info. However, as a research librarian, I'm always keen to execute a search in a manner that maximizes the number of relevant results. When I put my home-cook hat on, I approach recipe-finding with a similar set of expectations. Though there's no shortage of recipe information online, there's not really an equivalent set of databases for cookery. Here's a round-up of the best recipe aggregation resources I've found.

Epicurious is my go-to recipe site; I've used it for four years. One of the aspects I like most about it is the user comments. Because the site is older, most recipes have at least a handful of comments, and I've found that most users leave really helpful feedback (usually suggestions for how to scale or tweak recipes). However, it's also very easy to ignore user comments if you just want to stick to the original recipe. I usually cook from printed versions of the recipes (rather than bringing my laptop in the kitchen), and Epicurious offers several options for the size of the printed page, whether or not images are included, and even the option to print a separate shopping list.

Most recipes come from *Gourmet* and *Bon Appetit* magazines (the site is owned by Conde Nast). Some come from cookbooks published by Random House, with whom Epicurious has some kind of republication agreement, it seems. Some have also been reprinted from other cookbooks, with permission. In addition to the 25,000 recipes from these professional resources, they also boast 50,000 member-submitted recipes. Epicurious is the online food site to beat.

Cookstr publishes recipes by professional chefs, including Mario Batali, Jamie Oliver, Alice Waters, Jacques Pepin, Michael Recchiuti, Mark Bittman, and on and on. In addition to recipes, the site also provides informative profiles for each chef. Features are fairly minimal, with a video section, but I do like the simplicity of the site. Site registration allows you to save and comment on recipes. Although Cookstr only has a few recipes from each chef, it's the closest thing to a massively cross-cook[book] database I've found. I hope it grows.

I learned about Food52 when the New York Times ran a round-up of new, crowd-sourced food sites. The hook of this site, founded by two food writers, is that every week there's a theme-based competition; after a year of these contests, the winning recipes will be collected in a book. Any registered user can compete in the competitions, the founders select finalists and post slideshows of them testing the recipes, and then users vote for a winner. The focus of the site is the contests, and all recipes submitted for the contests are accessible, but registered users can upload any type of recipe. Although there is a pretty sizable diversity of recipes on the site, I most often use it when I'm looking for inspiration to try something new, not when I have a few keystone ingredients I'm trying to hang together.

Serious Eats is another curated food community with some social features, including a set of forums, and original video content in addition to a large collection of recipes. Recipes come largely from featured cookbook writers and chefs, but also the wider community base (in the forums). It's more inclusive than Food52, because of its forums, and it's more polyphonous because its cast of contributors is quite long and revolving. However, it's less inclusive in the sense that the Recipes section of the site is limited to those curated by contributors (mostly recipes from featured books and chefs).

Foodbuzz is a network of foodbloggers (more than 10,000). They offer a set of services for "featured publishers," including ad management and other perks, as well as several social networking-type features for individual users. Foodbuzz is one of the few sites I've found that actually aggregates recipes from across the web. You can submit links to recipes to be indexed, and you can also submit recipes for direct publication at the site. It displays some characteristics of a curated site in as much as it highlights recipes from members of its featured publishers network, but overall it's quite open since anyone can submit a recipe or recipe link.

Epicurious, Cookstr, Food52, SeriousEats, and Foodbuzz are my favorite recipe aggregators. To reduce my search load even further, I've created a custom Google search engine that queries these sites in addition to a few of my favorite individual sources.

-- Camille Cloutier Hartsell

BCS – Harvester 722 Tiller

Seedling Tray 128 Cells (1-1/2" sq x 2-1/2" deep)

Best source for gardening tech
Peaceful Valley

GrowOrganic.com

Organic gardeners, both backyard and commercial, know this mail-order outfit as the premier source for organic farming supplies. They've got everything: Natural pest controls, insect traps, cover crop seeds in bulk, sticky tape in all varieties. I mean where else can you buy a gallon of milky spore disease (for Japanese beetles), or white fly parasites in quantities of a thousand, or red worm *eggs*, with a side order of bat guano? Not only do they carry mulching film in standard black, but they also have it in innovative silver, green or red colors as well — each spectrum producing different effects for different plants.

But this catalog is also useful in other ways. Non-gardeners and green householders will find hard-to-find products such as poison-free cockroach traps which use cockroach pheromones.

Best of all, Peaceful Valley collects the best gear for growers of any type. Here is your source for plastic deer fencing, the world's best walk-behind Italian tillers, superlative hand tools, the best selection of drip irrigation supplies, and — my favorite — reusable foam seedling trays. You'll find this source absolutely essential if you grow anything.

This catalog is a throwback to the mail order catalogs of old. 1) They tend to only sell the best stuff, not just the best-selling or most profitable, and 2) they still print it on paper. You can spend several evenings reading it with great profit. You get a short course in state of the art practices for small time farmer and serious gardening.

They have a pretty good website, too (but not as informative as the paper catalog). And they are easy to work with.

-- KK

Optimistic dreambooks
Garden and Seed Catalogs

Seedsavers Exchange, Johnny's Selected Seeds, Gardens Alive

Gardening catalogs are the very epitome of dreambooks. Some are quite beautiful, all ripe with the promise of fulfillment in a slightly other universe, but here are the three that make late winter in the heartland a little less bitter:

Seedsavers Exchange puts out a gorgeous catalog and promotes Earth-respecting attitudes with no preaching or guilt-laying. Their online version is, to my mind, among the best designs of its kind. Their descriptions usually include a few words about the histories and sources of their heirloom varieties — makes it hard not to feel involved with the ancient epic of how "weeds" got turned into the exquisite diversity of crop plants we take for granted these days.

Johnny's Selected Seeds is a commercial version of a labor of love. It's a real working catalog with limited color photos but a large and well-selected inventory of standard, heirloom, and organic veggie, herb, flower, grain, and covercrop seeds. What makes the catalog special is its generosity with information. If you need a tomato that resists some particular kind of rot, you'll probably find it here. You'll probably find it in other catalogs, too, but won't necessarily know it. There's extensive cultural, climate, and harvesting info that makes me resent almost all other catalogs for their lack of same. Johnny's really wants their seeds to grow strong and prosper.

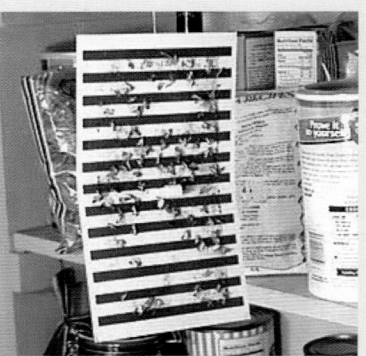

Cupboard Moth Trap. Signature Product. Our easy-to-use traps stop Indian meal moths from ruining food in your pantry. As low as $6.95 each (Gardens Alive)

Gardens Alive is a southern Indiana seller of products for organic/"environmentally responsible" gardening and growing. Natural fertilizers, biocontrols (they grow critters like parasitic wasps and nematodes themselves), natural lawn magic, redworms, composting accessories — a fairly thick little catalog with basic graphics and all kinds of dreams for the garden geek. Dozen-page guides to plant diseases, nutritional lacks, bugs. I get the same kind of thrill pawing through this jammed volume that I used to get with *Edmunds* or *American Science and Surplus* or the fireworks spreads, or, well, *Whole Earth Catalog* — It just makes my hands itch to get out there and tinker.

-- David Walker

Black Prince Heirloom Tomatoes. New last year! Mahogany brown with flavor. Unusual mahogany brown shoulders become orange-red at the blossom end. Color will be deeper and more pronounced in sunnier locations. Distinctively rich, fruity, tomato flavor. Relatively smooth, 3-5 oz., 3" globes show less cracking than typically seen in most heirlooms. This is an heirloom from Irkutsk, Siberia. Indeterminate. Organically grown. Mini: 40 seeds. $2.70. (Johnny's Selected Seeds)

Specialty root source
Potato Garden

Free Catalog Potato Garden

Ever since I encountered fingerling potatoes in European restaurants I wanted to grow some of my own. I find these small fat-finger-shaped tubers have a nuttier, richer taste than regular potatoes. Potato Garden in Colorado is a mail order source that sells a dozen varieties of fingerlings and it's been fun trying various breeds. Potato Garden also introduced me to scores of strains in "main" potatoes. And they offer an exotic variety of live starters for other root crops, such as garlic, onions, and sun chokes. Their catalog provides enough basic info about growing and storing roots that it serves as a one-stop short course. For spring delivery you need to order early.

-- KK

French Fingerling - Certified Seed Potato

Added to Basket: *No*
In Stock

1 lb. -	$7.50
2 lbs. -	$12.00
3 lbs. -	$18.00
5 lbs. -	$18.75
10 lbs. -	$30.00
25 lbs. -	$69.38
50 lbs. -	$120.00
100 lbs. -	$225.00
200 lbs. -	$420.00

Quantity: [1]

[Add To Basket]

A gourmet quality fingerling with satin red skin and yellow flesh with an interior ring of red when cut across. Produces good-quality, medium sized tubers which are a great addition to any plate. It is said that this fingerling arrived in this country during the 1800's in a horse's feedbag. Mid-Season

- Sunchokes: Native of North America, a type of sunflower whose tuberous roots have been eaten for millennia by Native Americans. The first recorded discovery of sunchokes in America apparently occurred in Native American gardens along the eastern coastline in the early 1600's. The Indians called them "sun roots". Sunchokes are delicious eaten raw as they have a crisp, juicy texture like water chestnuts. We like to slice or grate them for a zesty addition to any fruit or vegetable salad. We have found that steaming or boiling is the best way to cook them, with a little butter and Real Salt.

OZETTE (NC, N)
Originally, potatoes were taken from South America to Europe before they made their way to the Americas. However, it is believed that the Ozette was brought directly from South America to Neah Bay Washington by Spanish Explorers in 1791. They planted them in a garden that was later abandoned when the Spanish left. Discovered by the Makah people, they began to grow them in their own gardens and named them after one of their villages. Introduced to the market by David Ronniger in the late 1980's, the Ozette is one of the tastiest of all fingerlings. Classic in appearance with pale gold skin and creamy yellow flesh. The slightly earthy, nutty flavor comes through beautifully when lightly steamed or sautéed. A Slow Food USA, Arch of Taste selection. Late variety.

RED THUMB (CS, O)
The Red Thumb is a relatively new fingerling and with its one of a kind brilliant red skin and unusual red flesh, it cries out for a place in a gourmet setting. The uniformity of this particular potato makes it a favorite among chefs. Early variety.

ROSE FINN APPLE (CS, O)
A rosy colored skin with deep yellow flesh and a waxy, firm texture. A great roasting potato, very popular and fun to grow. Delectable flavor and a fine keeper with vigorous vines. Many chefs are finding that these potatoes cooked and pureed lend themselves well as a soup thickener for sauces and gravies. A fine keeper with vigorous upright vines. Mid-Season.

Marbled Purple Stripe Garlic

- Bulbs are striped, marbled or dappled with purple
- Typically has fewer cloves per bulb
- Extremely strong bolting cultivars
- If the scape is left uncut, it can grow as tall as 6ft
- Larger cloves make it easy to peel
- Large squatted, fat tan cloves with a hint of purple coloration
- Removal of scape is recommended for large bulbs
- Stores well
- Can be quite hot raw; more garlicky when sautéed

57SIBE15 Siberian - Marbled Purple Stripe - Large

Sold Out

Best intro to backyard vegetables
All New Square Foot Gardening

$17 Mel Bartholomew, 2013, 272 p.

Outlined in this classic book is the best foolproof way to begin vegetable gardening. It's a simple system that works on the small scale of an introductory backyard garden for someone who has never gardened before. In brief, you do this:

* Make raised beds with a square frame of boards. Staple chicken wire on the bottom.

* Size it so you can reach every part of the inside without ever stepping in it.

* Fill it with potting soil, or as much compost mix as you have.

* Place it near your kitchen or somewhere that is easy to see and use.

* Plant your seeds/seedlings very close together but only a few of each type.

* On the north side you can erect a vertical net to gain extra "space."

This works. Essentially, these beds are flat growing containers that use whatever soil is under them for bonus nutrients, and the crowded foliage keeps out weeds. There are disadvantages to this system of course, but this is a good way to start. Our garden today is a larger version of this. Our frames are 6 feet square and 12 inches high, and we have lots of them.

The information above is really all you need to do this but if you'd like more details about this approach read *All New Square Foot Gardening*, a book that's been around for 30 years and is still helpful. The author is a relentless self-promoter (his picture is on every other page), and "his method" is actually an ancient one with many other modern interpretations (such as biointensive gardening). But Mel Bartholomew makes the process and logic of this food garden coloring-book simple. With grammar-school repetition he'll get you going, and soon it will all seem obvious and trivial.

-- KK

●
Your garden doesn't have to be all in one place. You no longer have to rototill or water one big garden area all at once. You can split up your SFG so that a box or two are located next to the kitchen door, while more boxes can be located elsewhere in the yard. Small, individual garden boxes allow you much more flexibility in determining location. Now your garden can be located near where you walk and sit, or where you can view it from the house. It can even be located in a patio or pool setting, where you relax. Your SFG becomes a companion rather than a burden.

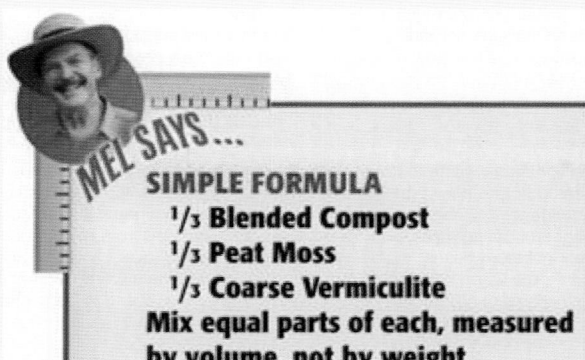

MEL SAYS...

SIMPLE FORMULA
$1/3$ **Blended Compost**
$1/3$ **Peat Moss**
$1/3$ **Coarse Vermiculite**
Mix equal parts of each, measured by volume, not by weight.

Malabar spinach is a climbing leaf crop that makes a beautiful ornamental.

Lazy veggies
Perennial Vegetables

$24 Eric Toensmeier, 2007, 224 p.

In the gardens of paradise, all the vegetables would be perennial. No endless replanting. Just keep picking year after year. Like fruits and nuts. On earth there are more of these heavenly plants than you might think. This book rounds 'em up, with terrifically informative summaries, clear photos, and useful hints. A few of these recurring veggies are familiar — asparagus, rhubarb, artichokes — but most are exotics, so eating/cooking suggestions are given as well. I am a lazy gardener who favors perennials in our landscape garden, so I am inclined to be lazy in the food garden as well. But besides laziness, this is a great culinary adventure — all kinds of Andean root crops I've never heard of, and bean trees, and bush spinach — oh my! One hundred new friends. As a bonus the author takes the long-view and makes suggestions about promising varieties that amateurs could breed into better perennials. This is a fabulous book.

-- KK

One of the moments that really changed my life in terms of understanding the potential of perennial vegetables was the day I grazed on the leaves of this beautiful shrub at Plants for a Future (PFAF) in Cornwall, England. To see a hedge of this beautiful silvery gray shrub producing copious quantities of edible greens virtually year-round, and to just stand there and stuff the tasty, salty leaves into my mouth, was a remarkable experience.

Every spring on the East Coast, from New England to New Brunswick, foragers go hunting along riverbanks and in floodplain forests for the shoots of this native fern, known as fiddleheads because their spiral shape looks like the head of a violin. These foragers harvest large quantities to sell to restaurants and supermarkets, where they bring a good price. Strangely, while many people grow this fern as an ornamental few home gardeners seem to grown it for fiddleheads.

In the wild, ostrich fern is found primarily in floodplain forests and riverbanks, but under cultivation it succeeds in a variety of moist, shady conditions.

This crop, virtually unknown in the United States and Canada, is second in importance only to potatoes across vast areas of the South American high-lands. It has become a commercial crop in New Zealand and has the potential to become a much more important crop worldwide. In gardens oca can provide high yields in tiny spaces.

Oca's beautiful tubers are shaped like fingerling potatoes and come in bright colors like yellow, orange, red, and purple. They have a crisp, moist, waxy texture, and unlike many root crops make a sweet and tart, almost candy-like snack raw. Flavor varies dramatically among varieties. The varieties I have tested were mild, sweet, and tart when eaten raw, like a good star fruit. When baked they lived up to their reputation of tasting like potatoes with sour cream already added.

vegetables have rather strong favors, especially those adapted to cold climates.

* Many perennial vegetables are so low-maintenance that they can become weeds in your garden, or escape and naturalize in your neighborhood.

Fiddleheads emerging in spring.

Drawbacks of Perennial Vegetables

* Some perennial vegetables are slow to establish and may require several years of growth to begin yielding well. Asparagus is a classic example.

* Like annual crops, some perennial greens become bitter once they flower. Thus their greens are available only early in the season. Perennial vegetables are not meant to replace annuals, but to complement them. In this case, perennial greens are available early in the season, providing greens until the annuals are up and running.

* Many of the minor perennial

The author grazing on saltbrush as PFAF in England in 1997. It was hard to tear me away from that salty spinach: like pretzels in a shrub!

Oca tubers come in many beautiful colors and have a delicious sweet, tart flavor.

Composting

Minimal worm compost
Worms Eat My Garbage
$10 Mary Appelhof, 1997, 162 p.

Worms convert kitchen scraps into high-potency garden fertilizer. In the process they multiply, and can be used for fish bait or for chicken snacks. The worms reduce your trash load. The fancy name for this is "vermicomposting." It requires little beyond a modified wooden box or plastic tub in the kitchen, basement or backyard. This perennially best-selling, and now up-dated, book will tell you all.

Wormpoop.com is an all-worms site that sells worms (by the pound) and worm poop fertilizer (by the gallon), and worm raising information and supplies.

-- KK

● Whichever you start with, breeders or bedrun, when they produce more worms than the garbage you are feeding them will support, many will get smaller, some will slow reproduction, and others will die. Eventually, no matter how many worms you start with, the population will stabilize at about the biomass that can be supported by the amount of food they receive.

● Any vegetable waste that you generate during food preparation can be used, such as potato peels, grapefruit and orange rinds, outer leaves of lettuce and cabbage, celery ends, and so forth. Plate scrapings might include macaroni, spaghetti, gravy, vegetables, or potatoes. Spoiled food from the refrigerator, such as baked beans, moldy cottage cheese, and leftover casserole also can go into the worm bin. Coffee grounds are very good in a worm bin, enhancing the texture of the final vermicompost. Tea leaves, even tea bags and coffee filters, are suitable.

● Still another method for harvesting worms is the divide and dump technique. You simply remove about two-thirds of your vermicompost and dump it directly onto your garden's surface. No digging nor turning; no muss, no fuss. Add fresh bedding to the vermicompost still left in the box. Enough worms and cocoons usually remain there to populate the system for another cycle.

From From Wormpoop.com

The worm bed is 36" high (about waist level), reducing stress on the back and legs from bending. This worm bed has four removable partitions for easy access for feeding and harvesting the worms and wormpoop castings (also called Vermicompost). It allows the person working with the worms to do so with less effort. It also helps reduce the workload when harvesting the worms.

Adding Vermicompost to soils aids in erosion control, promotes soil fertility, stimulates healthy root development in plants. This life cycle is the process of things being born, living, dying, and being reborn again. This is nature's way of recycling and keeping the earth in balance.

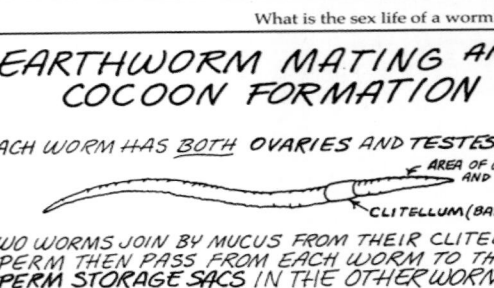

EARTHWORM MATING AND COCOON FORMATION

EACH WORM HAS BOTH OVARIES AND TESTES.

TWO WORMS JOIN BY MUCUS FROM THEIR CLITELLA. SPERM THEN PASS FROM EACH WORM TO THE SPERM STORAGE SACS IN THE OTHER WORM.

LATER, A COCOON FORMS ON THE CLITELLUM OF EACH WORM. THE WORM BACKS OUT OF THE HARDENING COCOON.

EGGS AND SPERM ARE DEPOSITED IN THE COCOON AS IT PASSES OVER OPENINGS FROM OVARIES AND SPERM STORAGE SACS.

AFTER BEING RELEASED FROM THE WORM, THE COCOON CLOSES AT BOTH ENDS. EGG FERTILIZATION TAKES PLACE IN THE COCOON.

TWO OR MORE BABY WORMS HATCH FROM ONE END OF THE COCOON.

Figure 17. Worms are **hermaphroditic**.

HARVESTING TECHNIQUE: DIVIDE AND DUMP.

1. TAKE OUT ALL BUT 1/3 OF WORMS AND VERMICOMPOST. ADD NEW BEDDING.

2. ADD VERMICOMPOST TAKEN FROM BOX TO THE GARDEN...WORMS AND ALL.

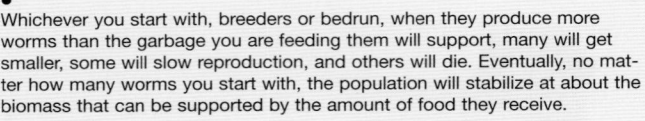
WORM TO GARBAGE RATIO 2:1

½ LB GARBAGE PER DAY (AVERAGE)

1 LB REDWORMS

Varmint-free compost maker
Urban Compost Tumbler
$290 Amazon

This is a great composter, made out of a recycled pickle drum. It comes via UPS and you assemble it. It has end-over-end tumbling action (unlike the larger, more expensive drums that roll horizontally) and it has solved the problem I've had for years of composting kitchen scraps and fending off coons, skunks, foxes, and possums. Here it's locked up and impenetrable. It takes a while to get it working right, with the proper amounts of green stuff, dry stuff, and soil organisms. I've transferred some worms from my old compost bin into it, to get them processing the organic matter.

-- Lloyd Kahn

Omnivorous composting
Green Cone
$185 SolarCone

I was more burdened by wet garbage than I thought, and more relieved than I expected by a fiendishly simple device called the Green Cone.

Regular composters are notoriously picky: no bones, no meat, no oil, no avocado pits or shells, no citrus peels, no dairy products. The Green Cone happily devours all that stuff, which means that pretty much all your kitchen waste can go in it, right now. File and forget.

All you need is some yard and a spot that gets sunshine. The Cone's perforated plastic basket is sunk two feet into the ground. The Cone stands 28 inches above the ground, collecting sun warmth to encourage the bacteria down below who are chowing on the garbage and seeping the resultant nutrients into the soil. Thanks to the ground seal around the basket, there's no smell at all, except when you open the top of the Cone to add more yummy garbage for the microbes.

Garden wastes should not go in the Cone, because they would overwhelm it with volume. Nor should paper or plastic products, which is about all you'll have left in your now light and odorless kitchen trash bin.

-- Stewart Brand

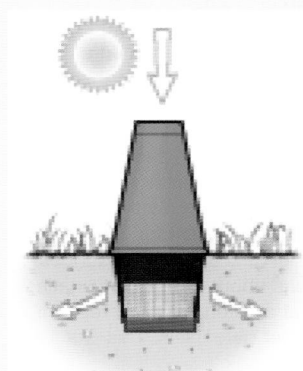

How to utilize urine

Liquid Gold

$11 Carol Steinfeld, 2007, 95 p.

Logically, we should recycle our urine to capture its many nutrients for growing new food. Here's a fuller case for that argument, and if you buy it, how to practically accomplish this export on the small scale of a homestead. Most likely you'll be the only person in your neighborhood mining "liquid gold," but you may also be an outlaw, two issues this book anticipates. The small book is also chock full of urine lore, including the historical medical, cooking (!), chemical, and agricultural roles urine has had. This small booklet changed my mind.

-- KK

•

According to sanitation researcher Caroline Schonning of the Swedish Institute of Infectious Disease Control, humans rarely excrete disease-causing organisms, orpathogens, in urine. Also, most pathogens die when they leave their hosts, either immediately or shortly thereafter. The only significant urine-transmitted diseases are leptospirosis (usually transmitted by infected animals), schistosoma, and salmonella. The first two are rare–usually found only in tropical aquatic environments–and the last is typically inactivated shortly after excretion. The more likely health risk is urine contaminated by feces that were misplaced in a urine-diverting toilet.

•

There are other ways to use liquid gold. For small amounts of urine, you can make a urine planter. Layer shredded cardboard or paper with chunky sand or peastone. Add more material when the contents shrink as the paper decomposes. Plant hearty nutrient-loving plants, shrubs, or small trees. Urine also works well in hydroponic planter systems.

Hakan Jonsson fertilizes his lawn with a device he made that distributes urine evenly through perforated pipe while he dilutes it with a garden hose.

Applying urine to leaves, not roots, is its most effective use, according to Paul William. "Foliar feeding is much more efficient at stimulating plant growth than fertilizing via the root system only," he says. "The leaves respond within hours of the application."

To determine the best dilution to prevent the mis from getting too salty, he uses a TDS (total dissolved solids) meter available from hydroponic garden supply stores. "My tap water has 600 ppm (pars per million) as a result of the chlorine salts before I add any urine. I add urine until I get around 1,700 ppm." He also adds a bit of soap so the spray better penetrates the leaves.

"Urine foliar feeding is amazing," he says. "My friends are having huge success growing all kinds of tropical plants doing it, and my temperate plants are so lush and green, it boggles the mind!"

Urinals for women are not new, but the demand for these has been limited.

The largest ears of corn on the left were fed a 3:1 water-urine mixture three times a week. The others were fed far less.

Layer sand and peastone with shredded cardboard in a planter to create a urine planter. Over time, the mix will decompose into a soil.

Paul William applies diluted urine to fruit trees.

◀ *Lately, women's urinals have popped up at music festivals where disposable cardboard personal urine diverters, such as the P-Mate, are provided with which to use them.* ▶

The advantage: More service in a smaller space and shorter waits for portable toilets.

Amplified easy slicing

Fiskars PowerGear Bypass Pruner

$20 Amazon

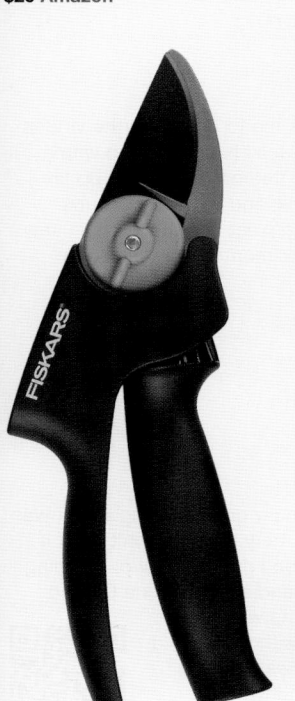

This hand clipper is a really cool ergonomic innovation. It uses an ingenious gear design to easily slice off sticks that are 3/4 inch in diameter. As you squeeze, the bottom handle rolls slightly and this motion leverages the power in the scissor cut. I find I can now tackle stuff that ordinarily I would have had to run back to get the larger pruners for. Your Felco pruning clippers will last you a lifetime, but as my grip wanes, I find I this lightweight Fiskars pruner is the clipper I grab first.

-- KK

Precise garden snip

Fiskars Softouch Micro-Tip Pruning Snip

$12 Amazon

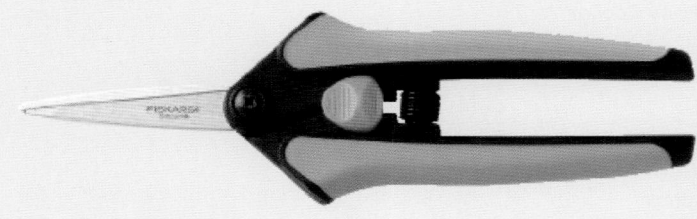

Fiskars' PowerGear Bypass Pruner, previously reviewed, is the handiest, most used tool in my vegetable garden, but it's too big and clunky for precision cutting of young salad greens and herbs. For that task, the company's Pruning Snip is an outstanding and inexpensive tool.

Snipping action requires little effort because the short blades are quite sharp and a spring in the center of the handle returns the shear to its open position after each cut. A small garden scissors could work almost as well as this tool, but the spring-activated light-action cutting makes a big difference for ease of use. Like the larger pruner mentioned above, this model gives a lot of cutting output with disproportionately little input. This shear is also useful for carefully thinning densely grouped seedlings by cutting the excess plants at their bases.

-- Elon Schoenholz

Superb garden clippers

Felco Pruners

$55 Amazon

My garden includes roses, blackberry and ivy vines, five kinds of fruit trees — all plants that need constant pruning. So I carry my pruner on my belt. I probably use them a few dozen times every day. I have no idea why it took me so long to buy a pair of the best available — Felco. It's got leverage! A handle shaped to the hand. If you prune a lot, you'll know immediately by the feel that these are the best. You can buy models for small hands, ergonomic models for gardeners with arthritis, left-handed ones. Forty dollars seemed like a lot for clippers when I bought them, but after decades of using inferior pruners I get pleasure every time I snip the Felcos.

-- Howard Rheingold

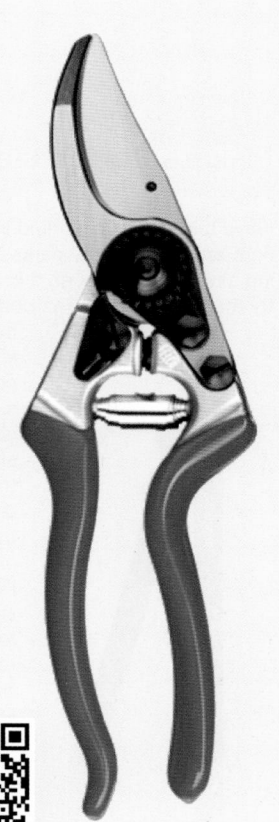

Pruning

Lightweight tree pruner
Fiskars Telescoping Tree Pruner

$80 Amraroozn

I like this new telescoping tree pruner from Fiskars. It is much better than the old tree pruner I used to have that was just a long wood stick with a pulling string attached to the blade. Not only was it heavy, but the string easily tangled. The new one from Fiskars is made with aluminum and is much lighter. The best feature is the pulling mechanism built into the handle. It is convenient, easy to use, and doesn't tangle. It also comes with an attachable saw for branches that are too large for the pruner, but I have yet to try that out.

I use the tree pruner every summer to keep the branches from growing too close to the power lines in my garden in order to prevent fires.

-- Horace Chan

Telescoping pruning tool
Fiskars 12' Pruning Stik

$73 Amazon

We've got a line of trees standing over an old fence line covered in grape vines. For pretty much the last 10 years, I've been keeping the trees healthy and vine free with the help of my Fiskars Pruning Stik.

I've had some of the traditional long handled pruners, and they all broke or something, I don't have them anymore – no reason to remember anything other than disappointment. When I found the Stik, I knew I had the right thing.

The telescoping version gets well into underbrush, up into trees, all over. The angle-adjustable head helps too. It's easy to use, reliable and easy to maintain (a little WD40 on the cutter, occasionally). The only hair to split is that the locking lever on the head catches on stuff now and then and unlocks, but no big deal.

The "tape" line (not a rope) that transfers your effort to the head lays flat, and is very hard to tangle. The head separates from the pole (but stays attached by the line) when you ask it

to bite more than it can chew and it locks up on something or gets tangled in brush. The "tape drive" and the telescoping stick work perfectly without any adjustment other than your extending the stick. All very slick.

Our trees have grown very nicely with the vines taken out of them, over and over. Maybe some day we'll get more to the root of the vines, but so far this thing truly helps our trees

-- Wayne Ruffner

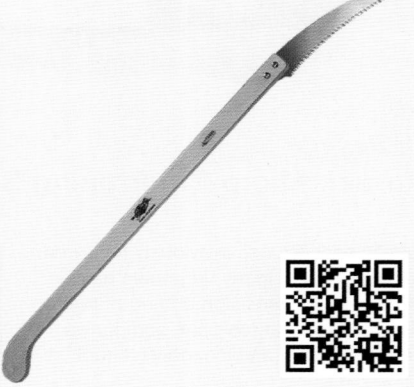

Mechanically advantaged pruners
Florian Ratchet-Cut Pruning Tools

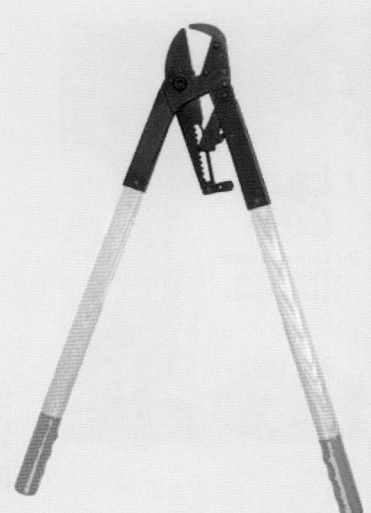

My wife and I have used Florian tools for 12-to-15 years including their hand pruners, brush loppers and pole-pruner. What makes Florian tools so excellent is the ratcheting mechanism. It lets you bite down with the jaws, then as you release the handle (or rope, in case of the pole-pruner) the jaws stay set. The ratchet then moves up a notch for a better mechanical advantage on the next stroke. Very powerful and very fast. And you don't wear yourself out cutting super-size stuff.

Here's what my wife has to say: "I can cut fat stuff that I can't cut with any other loppers, and I don't get tired doing it." That's it in a nutshell.

-- Chuk Gleason

$34 Florian Pruner Amazon	**$189** Florian Maxi Lopper Florian Tools

Light, strong retractable saw
Fiskars Pruning Saw

I'm a backpacker who takes only the essentials; my three-season multiday pack weight without food and water is around 11 pounds. This saw still finds its way into the pack. It weighs about 8 ounces, and cuts great. The blade is of a comparable quality to my Japanese carpenter saws. The handle is made of Zytel, superstrong and superlight. The teeth are very sharp and made of good stainless. I took it on a two-week BC kayaking trip, and it shows no staining despite the salt that everything is exposed to on such a trip.

With a simple twist of the locking nut, the blade is securely locked open or safely closed inside the handle. It also has a belt clip that allows easy and secure access, though I haven't used this feature.

This saw can do it all from opening the chest of an elk, securing firewood or building an emergency shelter. It sure beats the tiny saws of a Leatherman tool or a Swiss army knife, and with a comparable weight. I looked a long time for a saw of this quality that weighs so little.

-- Harry Cooney

$14 (6" saw) Amazon	**$17** (10" saw) Amazon

High-powered cutter
Fiskars PowerGear Bypass Lopper

$32 Amazon

I love this tool. I've worked in landscaping, and for one very long winter I cut brush in our city parks. I wish I had these then. If you think a pruning saw can go through a branch like a hot knife through butter, just try these Fiskars! Not as portable as my little folding pruning saws, but oooh the leverage action is sweet and effortless! One landscaping company I worked for used Sandvik loppers, and they were impressive, but I still think the Fiskars are the best so far. They have more leverage than similar sized loppers I've used. And they're easy on the elbows and shoulders, too. When the jaws close, they don't hammer together like those usual cheesy excuses for a tool.

I've tried the 18" (or thereabouts) short version of these Fiskars PowerGear loppers, and for their size, they're very nice too. Friends of mine used that model to clear honeysuckle bushes from their back lot. So far, every Fiskars product I've used has been top notch.

-- Margaret Halpin

All-Purpose Yard Maintenance Saw
Fanno Pole Saw

$35 Amazon

I have had this saw for at least six years and use it quite often clearing and maintaining trails for cross-country skiing and walking. The handle is plywood, nicely edge-rounded and fits my hands well. The hook on the top end of the blade near the handle is great for dragging cut vines and brambles out without losing blood.

-- David Wing

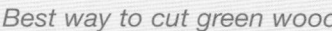

Best way to cut green wood
Pruning Saw

$25 Amazon

I am shocked at how long it took me to figure out the virtues of a pruning saw. For three decades I have sweated with a regular hand saw to lop off hefty tree branches, tidy up firewood, trim Christmas tree stumps, and cut down shrubs. (Trimming branches is really not a place for a mini-chain saw even if I had one). Yet month after month my regular saw would bind up in green, wet or frozen wood. On principle I avoid one-job tools, which is what a pruning saw sounded like. However when I finally got a pruning saw it was like a hot knife slicing through buttery wood. I don't think it matters much what brand you get. I now have two: a folding 7" Coleman I take car camping, and a 13" Corona Curved I use for landscaping at home. The wolfishly large teeth bite off visible chips without binding, and in no time the wettest, greenest wood is cut. But you already knew this, right?

-- KK

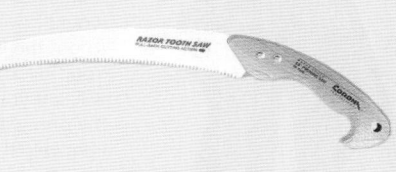

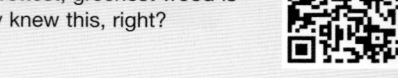

It's not that I'm so smart, it's just that I stay with problems longer. - Albert Einstein

Wheelbarrow handles
Simply Dump It

$22 Amazon

These pivoting plastic wheelbarrow handles let you go from a walking position to lifting and dumping without repositioning your hands. They're also amazing for me, because I am tall: When walking with a wheelbarrow the nose can sometimes catch the ground causing several problems. The handles lower the wheelbarrow's handles several inches, allowing me to walk upright instead of hunched.

Although I've only started using them, they've already had quite a workout. I am replacing the gravel pushed off of my 350' driveway by the snow plow. I load the wheelbarrow quite heavily. These handles have eliminated my

hunching AND they let me dump the gravel easily.

Installation took me about ten minutes, being very careful, as they require you to drill permanent holes. They come with clear directions, a long screw, and nylon lock nut for each handle (also included are tubular shims to adjust the fit, if necessary). The steps are: 1) Slip it over the handle; too tight? Sand the handle. Too loose? Add shims. 2) Position as desired. 3) Drill hole in marked location through entire handle. 4) Put screw through the hole, apply nylon lock nut on the other side. Done.

I've found them to be stable. UV degradation is my primary concern, since

I leave my wheelbarrow outdoor all year. Still, they are cheap enough that a second pair in 4-5 years would be acceptable to me, considering the convenience and back saving.

-- Andrew Bajorinas

Foldable cart
Tipke Fold-it Utility Cart

$226 Amazon

This nifty, lightweight (33 lbs.) garden cart will fit into any spare cranny in the garden shed or garage. It folds into a long, slender package about six inches wide at the wheel hubs, and three or four feet long. While I wouldn't go dropping jagged boulders into it, it's proven a tough, sturdy and useful hauling tool for gardening or otherwise over the couple years I've had it. I've mounded it high with bark, manure, compost and brush (the load limit is 330 lbs.), and it's performed like a champ.

Because of its smooth aluminum surface, it hoses clean for transporting non-dirty items. The gate on the front of the cart is basically a reinforced flat sheet

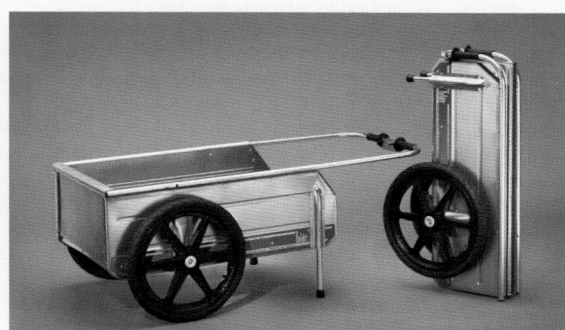

of metal with a folded U-shaped channel that interlocks with a similar folded U-shaped channel on the cart. I feel obliged to mention that one time I was hauling a composted sawdust/manure mixture and some of it got caught in the channels of the lift gate. Since then I haven't been able to get the gate all the way down, but it's really a minor issue. The gap is only about an inch and stuff doesn't seem to leak out the front.

Overall, this cart is just a marvelous, very maneuverable device for the storage challenged person. There is a slightly cheaper folding cart by Bully that can haul up to 400 lbs.

-- Amy Thomson

Versatile walk-behind tractor
BCS Two-Wheeled Tractor

$4,049 (Model 853) BCS

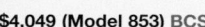

Like traditional tractors, two-wheeled tractors (aka 'walk-behinds') use an independent power take off (PTO) for attaching and powering various farming and landscaping implements. Rather than purchasing specialized power equipment (i.e. mowers, branch chippers, snowblowers, soil tillers etc.) that each have their own engines that perform only one or two functions, the walk-behind owner has to maintain only one engine and attach whatever tool is required for the job at-hand.

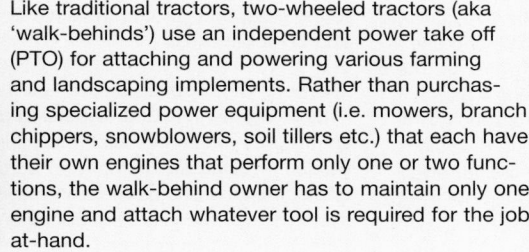

The beauty of a walk-behind tractor's design is that it is quite nimble, and can work in spaces where traditional tractors can't. Ours is equally comfortable in the forest – shredding branches and hauling out firewood – as it is in open areas tilling soil, removing snow and baling hay. It can also serve as a material transport machine by attaching a cargo trailer (with the added bonus of giving the operator somewhere to sit!). A cool and unique feature is that the handlebar steering mechanism can be rotated 180° so the business-end of the PTO can be positioned in push mode (mowing, tilling etc.) or pull mode (dozing, transport, etc.).

Two-wheeled tractors have a long history of agricultural use in Europe. The two major manufacturers, BCS and Grillo, are both based in Italy and make commercial-grade lines of machines that are built to last. Unlike two-wheeled units one finds at the big box stores, these machines have all-gear transmissions, and wheel differentials on the higher-end models which allow for quick and easy turns. There are multiple attachments and implements available from the manufacturers and third-party providers, and a reasonably-wide US dealer network.

The upfront costs are higher, but the long-term benefits of owning equipment that will last for decades, plus the convenience of only maintaining one 12HP Honda gas engine for all our needs, made for an elegant and practical solution for our property (diesel versions also available). While these machines may not be the best tool if you are working 40 acres, they can serve as a practical alternative to a full or medium-sized tractor if you have the right mix of homestead, farming or gardening needs.

-- RS Parikh

Handled garden tarp
Burden Cloth

$35-40 (4×4', recycled) Timeless & Daughters

I never seem to live anywhere a cart is usable, and I hate wheelbarrows. Working in my garden, I've hauled everything from straw bales to gravel with the help of Burden Cloths. I've been using them for about 20 years, and have the patio (3×3') and farm (5×5') sizes right now.

As opposed to a tarp or burlap, the Burden Cloth has one-inch-wide stout cotton webbing double-sewn around the entire edge of the cloth, adding strength and durability. Burlap just isn't as sturdy as the material used in Burden Cloth. At the corners, the webbing comes out and forms a loop before continuing onto the next side. The loops are probably 6 to 8 inches in radius; you can custom order them larger. I get the recycled cloth option (canvas is available for a little more), and they always come in interesting colors or patterns.

You could certainly make your own: get sturdy cloth, stout webbing, and sew away. You probably wouldn't have to have a commercial sewing machine to do it, but I'm not sure. I could knit socks too, but I don't do that either.

-- Gani Ruthellen

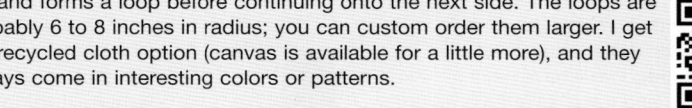

Best post hole digger
Fiskars Post Hole Digger

$50 Amazon

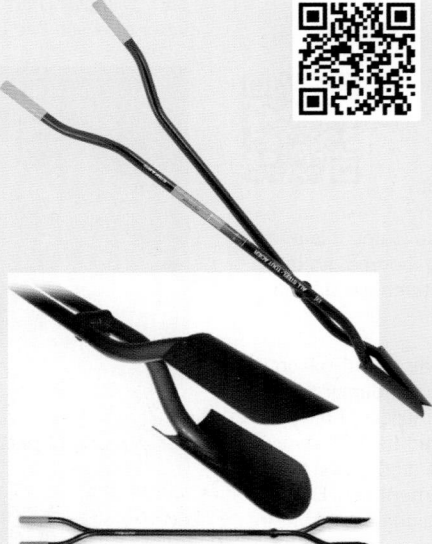

To bury posts you want straight narrow holes in the ground. Traditional post hole diggers tend to flare the hole at the top as the hole deepens because the handles must swing out further. This clever improved design from Fiskars crosses the handles so they don't swing out as far in the hole, yet they still bite as the hole gets deeper. The narrower the hole, the less dirt to remove, the less work. I found I could get a tight cylindrical hole almost one foot deeper with this tool. Also, this design prevents that dreaded knuckle-banger when the handles crash into each other on the closing stroke, which alone makes it worth using.

-- KK

Watering

Fine-tuned watering
Haws Watering Can
$33 Amazon

When I began gardening I used a generic plastic watering can from a hardware store, but it didn't give a gentle enough flow for newly planted seeds, nor a fast enough stream for larger plants that drink a lot. The polyethylene Haws can's separate spout attachments (right angle downspout and oval brass rose) are outstanding features that make it a versatile performer. The right angle is useful for pinpointing the spot I'm aiming to water and also for avoiding watering a plant's leaves. The brass rose angled upward lets forth a gentle rain for delicate seedlings; angled downward it gives a still-gentle but stronger dispersed stream. With both spouts removed, a solid stream shoots straight out of the can for deeper watering and hitting the tough-to-reach corners of my raised beds. Two "parking spots" on the body of the can hold the spout attachments not in use, so they're never misplaced. Changing modes — and changing back — couldn't be easier. The only drawback I've encountered is that the fine holes in the brass rose clog easily and need to be cleaned regularly to work well. But until I graduate to drip irrigation, this is the perfect tool.

-- Elon Schoenholz

Self-regulating plant watering & feeding
Volkmann Reservoir Wick Pot
$4 Volkmann Brothers Greenhouses

I've over-watered my share of temperamental plants into oblivion. This pot uses a simple method of providing the right amount of water and nutrients to a plant so you don't forget and let it go dry or over-water the plant. There is a water reservoir below the plant pot that supplies water to the pot through a wick that is in the bottom of the pot and extends into the reservoir. Just add nutrient to the water (about a teaspoon of something like Miracle Grow in a gallon of water) and the plant takes care of the rest. Now I just have to remember to refill the reservoir every month or so, and our African violets grow and bloom with only rare attention from us.

We tried raising African violets with limited success, until one of our friends gave us this Wick Pot. The violets come with a long list of care and feeding instructions regarding watering schedules, humidity, temperature, and the like. This planter is a godsend to those of us with brown thumbs looking to grow non-native plants (we live in Houston). The pot obviously will not change ambient light or humidity levels, but using one means the plant requires almost no care and feeding whatsoever. The Wick Pot also lets you be much less precise about the amount of water you refill because you're filling the reservoir as opposed to putting it directly into the pot.

There are other self-watering planters out there, but Volkmann's provides a cheap option and they also have full kits available (includes feed fertilizer, wick pot and soil) that are very reasonably priced. Of course this method is so simple, if you wanted to you could also fabricate a pot for yourself by using a recycled plastic container, a potted plant and a short piece of wick placed between the pot and reservoir.

-- Durwin Sharp

Plant and soil data tracking tool
EasyBloom Plant Sensor Plus
$60 Amazon

I love to garden, but I have a hard time figuring out whether a particular spot is ideal for a particular plant. I recently discovered the EasyBloom, a tool that when staked into the ground tracks data for sunlight, humidity, soil drainage, temperature, and, for an added monthly fee, soil fertility.

By tracking these variables the tool is capable of identifying whether an environment is suitable for a particular species of plant. It can be used to analyze why a plant is not doing well, and even alert you when the plant needs water. It functions indoors and outdoors. I have used it multiple times and it has saved me time and money, since I now know what to plant where.

The EasyBloom connects to the computer via USB and includes software to analyze the data that it produces.

-- Erin Boyle

Tree watering device
Treegator
$23 Amazon

We've recently planted trees in the midst of a dry-spell and have struggled to keep them watered. We have since discovered the Tree Gator. It is a bladder filled with water that wraps around the tree. As the water slowly leaks out it keeps the tree watered for as long as a week.

We use the 15-gallon Treegator Junior for the smallest of newly planted trees. They also make a 20-gallon version for larger trees. Beats dragging hoses from tree to tree.

-- Margaux D

Harnessing greywater
Create an Oasis with Greywater
$15 Art Ludwig, 2009, 144 p.

Greywater is the term for all household wastewater except for the toilet and kitchen sink. This is the only comprehensive book I know of on the subject, and in this fifth and expanded edition, Art Ludwig explains how to choose, build, and use a variety of simple greywater systems. There are clear drawings for sending washing machine water into the garden (with or without a drum), for putting diversion valves on bathtubs or showers, for creating "mulch basins," for ultra-simple setups like "Garden Hose Through the Bathroom," and "Dishpan Dump (Bucketing)" — the latter of which I've been practicing lately

to the great benefit of both septic system and compost piles.

There's a large section on branched drains — splitting the flow and dispersing greywater to a number of mulch basins in the garden — using gravity flow, no pumps or electricity. Mistakes made in greywater systems over the years are documented here, along with suggested improvements, and there's a two-page System Selection Chart with a comparison of 18 different systems.

-- Lloyd Kahn

Simple Laundry Drum with Rainwater Harvesting

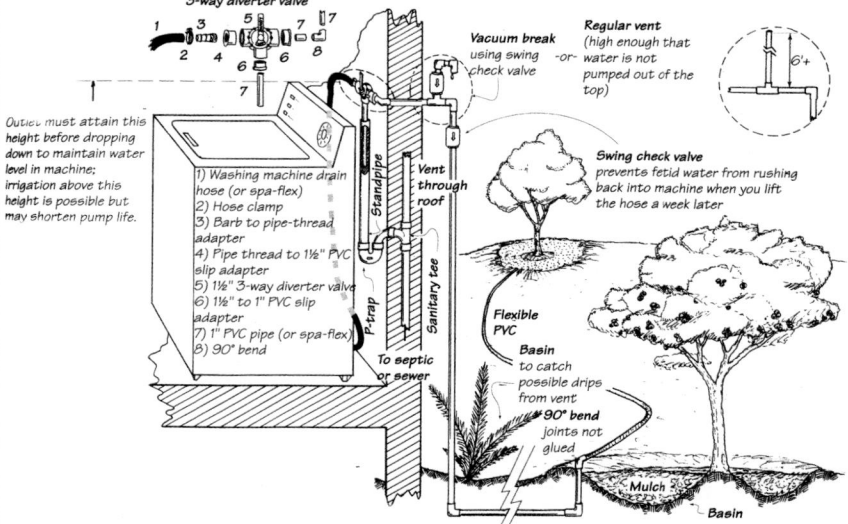

Figure 7.6: Laundry Drumless Laundry

Complete plans for one of the book's most broadly appealing projects -- a Laundry to Landscape Grey Water System -- are available, free, on the Oasis Design site.

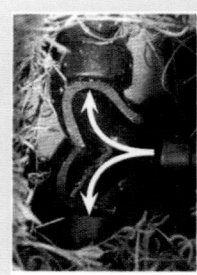

Cutaway view of a double ell, a flow-splitting fitting that is largely self-cleaning with no filtration. This one is part of the first known Branched Drain network. I valiantly tried to clog it with pure kitchen sink water—took the sink strainer out and pushed bowls of soggy granola and pot scrapings down the pipe for half a year. The p-trap clogged every other day, but the Branched Drain network never did.

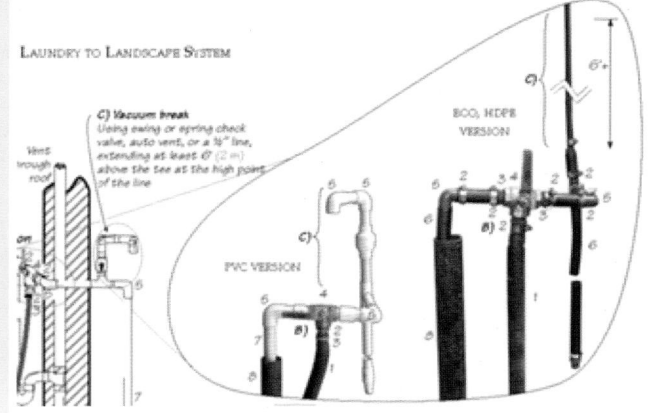

Everyone can read. The illiterate of the 21st century will be those who cannot learn, unlearn, and relearn. - Alvin Toffler

Push & click hose adaptors
Melnor Quick Connects
$13 Amazon

These plastic quick connects from Melnor are the go-betweens for the hose and whatever nozzle, sprinklers or other hose-end attachments you may have. They're especially good for quickly moving and attaching hoses from one faucet to another. I installed them on ALL my faucets (5) and hoses (perhaps 7) and external attachments (probably 10). I have used them for about a year and wonder how I ever got along without them. It takes less than a second (maybe 1/2 second) to attach or detach any hose or attachment. They are installed in pairs, a male and corresponding female connector, with the appropriate threaded fitting to attach to the faucet, hose or nozzle attachment, one on each side of the connection. You just firmly push the connector into its counterpart, and it easily pops into place — firmly means it does need a little pressure, but even a small child could do it. To disconnect, you push the green collar about an eighth of an inch in the one direction it's capable of moving, and it pops off. (Similar devices have been in use in industry for a long time — on compressed air lines, for example). No more screwing and unscrewing (no more scraped knuckles); no more leaks from incompletely tightened hoses; no more stuck connections because some gorilla (i.e. me) tried to stop a leak by tightening too hard.

One type is designed so that when you disconnect from it, an internal plug pops into place and stops water from coming out. The other type, for between a faucet and hose, does not have the shutoff. When you disconnect the hose from the faucet, water will still flow and the faucet can still be used. There are other brands and styles; some are even made of pricier brass, but I recommend you stick with one manufacturer because connectors are generally not interchangeable between brands. And these inexpensive plastic ones from Melnor are well made: I have (intentionally) very high water pressure (> 100 psi, sufficient to burst hoses) on my garden faucets, and I have had no leaks from these connectors.

-- Robert Ando

Brass connectors
Nelson Quick Hose Connectors
$7 Amazon

These brass connectors are MUCH better than the plastic Melnor Quick Connects.

These little brass hose connectors make the job of attaching and detaching hoses quick and simple. You pull the collar back on the female connector, and insert the male connector, and you're ready to roll. Really, it just takes a second or two to provide a secure, leak-proof connection. There are several brands of cheap plastic connectors out there, but these brass ones will last a lifetime. I have a number of them that are 10+ years old, and they work amazingly well. I attach these to everything hose-related: faucets, both ends of the hoses, and all the attachments, and they save me a lot of time and annoyance.

There are two drawbacks to these connectors: people unfamiliar with them will unscrew the whole set up, so if you have handymen, contractors, or yard men who are going to deal with your hoses, you'll need to explain how they work. The second is that they're easily lost and misplaced. Even though these connectors are easily lost, they're so long-lasting and sturdy that when they turn up again, they'll work perfectly!

-- Amy Thomson

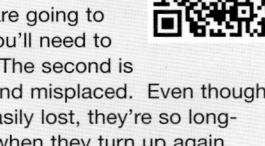

Reaching the high spots
Trombone Tree Sprayer
$51 Hudson

We are lucky to have a few apple & peach trees, but they have to be sprayed to insure tasty fruit. Trouble is some are about 20 feet high. I tried a bunch of sprayers, all poor performers, until I discovered the Hudson Trombone Tree Sprayer. It works like using a trombone and throws a great spray — they claim to around 25 feet high and that looks about right. A connecting hose maybe 7-8 feet long rests with a sort of small shower-head-like filter in the bottom of a bucket (not provided).

It uses plain old arm power. You feel like Elliot Ness in the "Untouchables" wielding a Tommy gun, but it works great, is only about $50 (get the one with the two gun grips) and even builds up your forearms and shoulder muscles. It's also got an adjustable nozzle to adjust spray. It really throws a good heavy directed or dispersed spray; I'm surprised at how much more quickly it gets the job done. Way outperforms pump-up pressure tank ones.

-- Vince Crisci

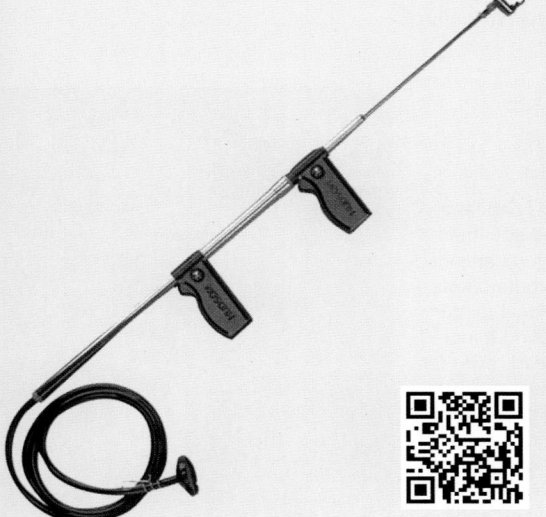

Fine misting nozzles
Dramm Fogg-It
$13 Amazon

I have used Dramm Fogg-it hose nozzles for a variety of watering and irrigation purposes for more than ten years. They deliver a fine mist of water and are available in different strengths, measured as gallons per minute: ½ GPM, 1 GPM, 2 GPM and 4 GPM. I've used all but the 4 GPM model. The ½ GPM nozzle, attached to a wand, is perfect for laying down a fine mist of water on a hot deck to cool things down using a minimal amount of water. You can also water very fragile seedlings, or mist cuttings with it. I use the 1 GPM nozzle for watering seedlings and seed beds. The 2 GPM nozzle is great for general watering of established plants. The fine mist will not break down soil structure, and delivers slowly enough for the soil to take in the moisture without run-off.

I like the fact that I can tweak the flow rate by switching nozzles. If one takes too long, I use a nozzle with a higher flow rate. Or if the spray is damaging tender seedlings, then I use a more gentle nozzle. The fine spray is also a great way to revive a heat-wilted plant.

These nozzles are solid brass, tough and well made. I toss them around mercilessly. Also, mine have never clogged. They fit onto a standard ¾-inch fitting, so you can screw them onto your hose, or any water wand with a hose fitting. Their only drawback is that they're small enough to get lost easily.

-- Amy Thomson

Superior garden hose reel
Rapid Reel
$140 Amazon

This is a heavy-duty cast aluminum garden hose reel. It costs about twice as much as the plastic reel I replaced and is at least four times the quality and longevity. The materials used are thick cast aluminum, powder-coated, with real stainless steel fasteners and brass fittings. The fittings and bearings are replaceable and heavy duty. The term bullet-proof comes to mind.

The reel is configurable as a parallel or perpendicular mount with either a right or left hand hose mount. The design is modular and well thought out. Even the included hex wrenches are well thought out and long enough to reach easily and are of high quality. As a mechanical designer myself, I am able to appreciate a nice robust design and execution.

-- Jack Kellythorne

Best garden hose
Craftsman Premium Rubber Hose
$44 Craftsman

I spent 20 hours researching garden hoses and discovered that the 50-foot Craftsman Premium Rubber Hose for $40 is the best choice for a garden hose. It is built like a tank -- heavy rubber construction and nickel plated brass connectors. It should last years if cared for properly. Not only is it affordable, but it comes with a lifetime warranty that covers you when, not if, the hose eventually breaks.

-- Oliver Hulland

Seeds

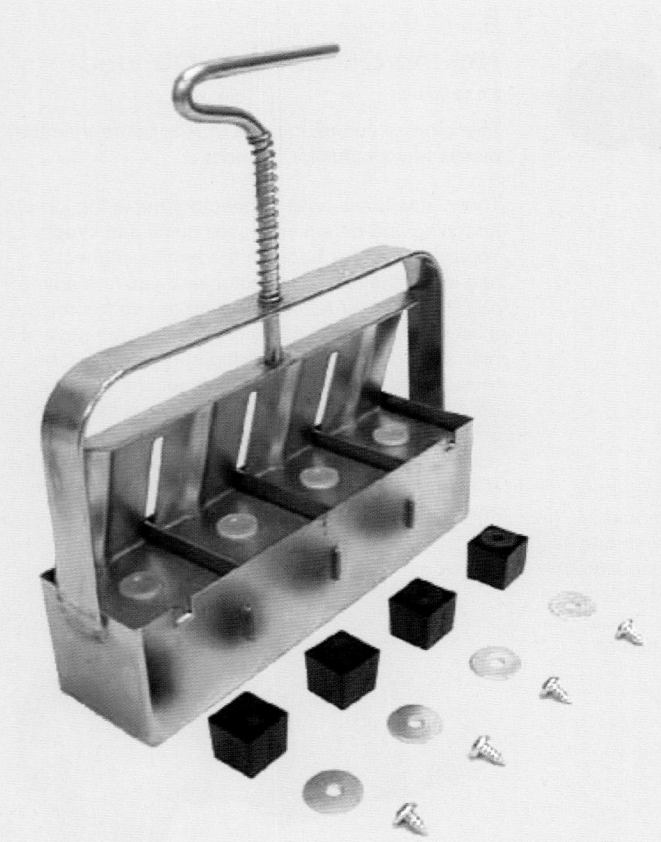

Cheap, efficient seed starting
Soil Block Makers

I've been using these for a dozen years to start seeds for annual flowers and a vegetable garden. They are superior to most methods when it comes to reducing transplant shock and simply make transplanting easier. Additionally, they allow me to save money on supplies at the expense of a little extra labor.

Soil block makers are hand-operated presses that make a compacted soil cube. You start seeds directly in the cube of compressed soil; no container is necessary. Since the cubes' sides are in contact with air, roots will stop growing when they reach the side of the block. Contrast that with seedlings grown in the typical retail greenhouse's flimsy plastic tray, in which the roots wrap around the space between the soil and plastic, becoming pot-bound.

When it comes time to transplant the cubes formed with soil block makers into the garden, just drop the block into the prepared hole. There's no prying a pot-bound seedling from a container; no accidentally damaging the root system. I've tried various biodegradable containers designed to go right into the garden soil, including peat pots, peat and coconut blocks, even small paper bags designed to hold potting soil and seedlings. None of them decompose as quickly as advertised; this results in slower root growth after transplanting. Plus, buying new containers each year is an added expense. I also tried a tray system that's sturdy, designed to be easy to water, has a better shape than greenhouse trays, and an integrated greenhouse cover. While it's the best tray system I've ever used, buying enough of these trays to start all my seeds would be several hundred dollars in up-front expenses, and they're a pain to store when not in use. My block maker is less expensive and only takes up about the space of a hardback novel.

Block makers come in several sizes, designed to handle different sized seedlings, or to allow potting-on from one size to the next. I've found the two-inch size covers most of my home-gardener needs.

The only downside I've found is you must water the blocks frequently or they dry out. I put my blocks on disposable foil cookie baking sheets, placed on shelves. Some people put the blocks on capillary mats, which stay wet and wick water into the block bottoms, so you don't need to water as often. I've found that you still need to mist the blocks, and worse, plant roots can grow into the mat, causing the very root trauma you are trying to avoid. When it's time to transplant, I slide the foil sheet onto a piece of plywood and carry it out to the garden.

The block maker I have is the Mini 4, by Ladbrooke. You can also purchase them, as well as soil block mix, or find more soil recipes and instructions for making your own soil blockers at Pottingblocks.com. Great advice and instructions for homemade blockers are here.

-- Brian Costlow

$30 Ladbrooke Soil Blocker (2" blocker, 4 blocks) **Peaceful Valley**

$30 Hand-held Soil Blocker (2" blocker, 4 blocks) **Johnny's Selected Seeds**

Cheapest way to grow
A Garden from a Hundred Packets of Seed

$6 James Fenton, 2005, 125 pages, 2nd Edition

With patience and discretion, one could grow the most magnificent flower garden with only $100 worth of seeds. Author and poet James Fenton brings the wisdom (and a highly evolved list of plants); you'll need to bring the patience.

-- KK

As for the design of this flower garden, I insist on keeping it vague. A hundred varieties of flower might look cramped on a balcony, spectacular in a situation only one size up from there. For it is amazing what can be crammed into a small space. Conversely, it is amazing the number of plants that could, in theory, be raised from so large a number as a hundred packets of seed.

Electric blanket for seedlings
Seedling Heat Mat

I've owned one of these for a couple of years now. I keep meaning to use it for plants, but It keeps getting hijacked for other uses. Last spring, I put it under my chick brooder to keep my baby chicks warm. Right now, it's warming the mealworms that I feed to those same very spoiled chickens. I expect it would be a total cat magnet if I threw a towel over it and left it out for them to lie on. And it's great for encouraging the seedlings of heat-loving plants to sprout more quickly.

Basically, this is a rectangular black plastic flexible mat that plugs into a standard electrical outlet. It feels like a pleasant sun-warmed surface if you put your hand on it, maybe 80 or 90 degrees Fahrenheit. If you put it on an insulated surface it's warmer than on an uninsulated one. Because they're designed for greenhouse use, they're waterproof, though I'd still use care, especially with the electrical cord.

If I were putting it under animals (especially baby animals) I'd keep the cord and the mat where it couldn't be chewed on. I'd also monitor the animals for overheating and make sure there was a part of their cage that wasn't on the heat mat so that they could self-regulate their temperature.

If you need a precise temperature, you can buy a thermostat control. I haven't used the thermostat, so I can't report on its reliability. These heat mats come in a variety of sizes, from 9" x 9" inches up to 20" x 48" inches, with the price increasing according to size.

-- Amy Thomson

$23-54 Seedling Heat Mat (9"x9", 20"x20", 20"x48") **Amazon**

$35 Heat Mat Thermostat Amazon

How to grow your own seed
Seed to Seed

$18 Suzanne Ashworth, 2002, 228 p.

You don't have to buy seed. You can take seeds from your own plants and sow them later. By going "seed to seed" you can selectively breed new varieties of favorite plants, or custom tailor plants to your local microclimate. At the very least I've found it incredibly satisfying to use my own seed, even for a few plants. You realize, oh, these are self-replicating goods! And you can share rare or exotic heritage varieties not for sale kept by other seed savers. Since garden plants are optimized to produce edibles or flowers, rather than seed, getting good seed can be tricky. This book is the bible for a network of folks around the world — the Seed Savers Exchange — providing tips and methods on how to raise, save, and germinate seed, plant by plant.

-- KK

●

The basic general rule is that seed should be saved from 20 inbreeding plants or 100 outbreeding plants.

Always attempt to grow as many plants as possible in the space available in your garden, and that will usually yield an adequate range of genetic diversity for your particular gardening situation. This technique has worked well for gardeners throughout the last 12,000 years, creating the amazingly diverse richness of the world's food crops.

●

Small-scale seed savers should also rogue their plants, being sure to plant large enough populations so that roguing is meaningful and doesn't lead to inbreeding. Garden plants undergo almost daily inspection during watering, weeding and picking. Off-type plants are easy to spot within a population, and their removal helps eliminate the effects of any slight crossing that may have occurred during a previous generation or any accidental mixing of home-saved seeds.

Pollen-covered anthers of the petal-less male flower are used as a brush to transfer pollen onto the stigma of the female flower.

For many gardeners, who often are concerned with food production and seed saving simultaneously, roguing is a hard thing to do. Letting an off-type plant remain in the garden is fine, if the plant is harvested for food before it flowers.

●

Vegetable seeds are at their peak when they reach maximum dry weight on the mother plant. Vigor is the seed's ability to germinate rapidly with good disease resistance. Home-saved seeds will retain maximum vigor when thoroughly dried and stored in a moisture-proof container. The most vigorous seeds at harvest time will keep the longest in storage. The two greatest enemies of stored seeds are high temperature and high moisture. Seeds that are stored at fluctuating temperature and moisture levels will quickly lose their ability to germinate. As a rule of thumb, the sum of the temperature (degrees F.) and relative humidity should not exceed 100. In actuality, humidity is probably more important than temperature, because it allows for the growth of microorganisms that degrade seed quality.

Begin with the assumption that any commonly held belief is wrong. - Ken Olsen

Easy, rapid plant cloning
Rooter Pot
$15 (set of 5) Lee Valley

This is a new plant propagation method/tool that allows you to produce large, rooted plantlets from woody plants (with stems up to 25 mm diameter) within one growing season (~ 2-3 months). Since I got them 2 months ago, I very easily rooted a large, marketable Schefflera in about 45 days and a 12" – 14" tall Ficus in ~60 days. I talked to an associate in Australia who has rooted almond. The concept is exciting because you should be able to produce a usable plant in 1/3 the time (one growing season vs three). I do expect that, with grower experience, almost any woody species that can be grafted can be propagated faster / less expensively using the Rooter Pot.

I bought them specifically to (try to) clone American chestnut selections for preservation without grafting. I expect to successfully clone mature conifers which are usually grafted for seed production. Rooter Pots are reusable. A larger-sized pot is now available for stems up to 1 inch in diameter.

-- Carl L. Haag

Mail order xeric seedlings
High Country Gardens
High Country Gardens

An online supplier of dazzlingly hardy plants (mostly perennials) adapted to west of the Rockies. They specialize in drought resistant (xeric) varieties, which of course can be established in non-desert areas. Unlike many mail order outfits, they don't deal in seed, but in young seedlings. Although more expensive per plant, I've come to seek out seedlings as the way to plant flowers and shrubs. They seem to take off faster than both seeds or potted plants. Specimens arrive live in minimal (lightweight) but remarkably adequate packaging. I've experienced very low failure rates, and good growth rates.

-- KK

Silene laciniata (Mexican Catchfly)

15" x 15" wide (seed propagated) This brightly colored wildflower species blooms most of the summer and is a favorite nectar source for hummingbirds. Plant Mexican Catchfly in a lean, infertile soil and avoid too much water after it's established; this causes the plant to get floppy. It makes a nice companion plant for another long-blooming wildflower, Berlandiera lyrata. Silene will reseed readily, especially if mulched with crushed gravel. Zones 5-9.

#9170, $5 each, cheaper for 3 or more (currently unavailable).

Calamagrostis arundinacea "Karl Forester" (Karl Forester Feather Reed Grass)

4-5" x 24" wide (division propagated) This is one of the best ornamental grasses for the western U.S. being rather drought tolerant (but not quite xeric) and tolerating a wide range of garden soils. Feather Reed Grass has a wonderful upright growth habit, making it very useful to place behind perennials with a spreading or rounded shape. The feathery plumes emerge in early summer and ripen to handsome wheat-colored seed heads by fall. Combine with Artemisia "Powis Castle" or Blue Mist Spiracea. Plant in groups of three or five for best effect. Zones 5-9.

#27550, each $9, cheaper for 3 or more

HIGH COUNTRY GARDENS®
Beautiful Plants for the Waterwise Garden

Mail-order analysis
UMASS Soil Testing
$10 (standard), $15 (with organic matter) UMASS

If you take gardening seriously, then you know it all starts with soil health. But you can't just look down and analyze it. The University of Massachusetts at Amherst offers cheap soil tests that will provide you with a comprehensive rundown of what your soil contains and what it needs.

I first had the soil test done years ago, and it showed low phosphorous, and very low levels of heavy metals. It gave specific instructions for adding nitrogen, phosphorous and limestone. For $9 they perform a standard soil test resulting in the following information: pH level, buffer pH, extractable nutrients (P, K, Ca, Mg, Fe, Mn, Zn, Cu, B), extractable heavy metals (Pb, Cd, Ni, Cr), and extractable aluminum, cation exchange capacity, percent base saturation. For $13 you get everything in the standard soil test and the amount of organic matter in your soil.

One of the most vital tests is the extractable heavy metals. Anyone planning to grow food near an old house that may have been painted with lead-based paints should perform this test to make sure you're not growing your organic veggies in poisoned soil, which pretty much defeats the purpose.

The soil test also provides specific fertilization recommendations, based on what you're growing. This helps you customize your fertilizing practices, by letting you know what you need to add to make your soils more fertile. More importantly, you can use that soil test to cut back on the stuff your soil doesn't need.

These are some of the cheapest soil tests available anywhere, and they provide immensely useful information. I first heard about them during my Master Gardener training a couple of decades ago. My only caveat is that the test is only as good as the sample provided. Make sure you follow their directions carefully.

I'm planning to redo the soil test, since I had raised beds added recently. The raised beds were filled with topsoil from a local company that composts yard and food waste. Now that I have good raised beds and drip irrigation, I'm gardening on a much larger scale and need better information. I took half a dozen large plastic sacks full of lettuce and spinach to the local food bank last year, and am hoping I'll be able to do that again next year.

-- Amy Thompson

Landscaping tools
A. M. Leonard
Varies A.M. Leonard

The source for all your nursery, grounds-keeping, and landscaping needs. Pages and pages of every variety of rakes, rows of shovels, more carts than you knew, sprinklers, clippers, pruners, and so on. These tools are aimed at pros, but creative and diligent amateurs will find plenty of interest here.

-- KK

Super dexterity
Atlas Nitrile Garden Gloves
$8 Amazon

My wife used to come in after a day of gardening with her hands roughened and scratched. Sure, she had gardening gloves, but they'd always get pulled off and forgotten the first time she had to do anything delicate. Leather, canvas, cotton — nothing would stay on her hands.

Last year she picked up a pair of Atlas 370 gloves at the local garden store. They're extremely thin, lightweight, and flexible, so there's no need to take them off. The palm is tough nitrile — made it through a season with no punctures or tears — while the back is a cool, breathable knit. You could tie your shoes without taking these off.

These gloves were actually designed for precision assemblers. Gardeners discovered them and adopted them in a heartbeat. They're pretty easy to find at local garden centers (many of which also carry a heavier cold-weather version), but several on-line retailers stock them.

-- Jonathan Rice

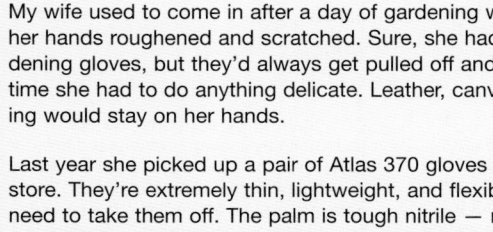

Non-toxic skeeter eliminator

OakStump Farms Mosquito Trap

$13 Amazon

When I saw this cheap trap at Logan's Trading Post three years ago, I figured what-the-heck, but we've been amazed at how effective they are. About three fourths of the way up from the bottom of the jug a tube runs through a hole in each side. Fill the jug with water up to the bottom of the transverse tube, add a pheromone pack, let it sit for a week with the top off (to make sure it gets the right attention), then close it after topping the water off. The mosquitoes fly into the tube and lay their eggs. When they hatch, the little mosquitoes can't figure out how to get out. With luck, in about three weeks the trap will literally be swarming with skeeters.

We empty ours once a year and add new water once a month or so; as long as you break the breeding cycle early enough in the spring it's not a big deal if you forget to water them later in the season. On our quarter-acre lot, I've found that three traps is plenty. So far this season, I haven't seen a single mosquito (except for the two or three I let out when I opened up one of the traps to top it off w/water). Only one of the three traps has looked really busy this year (last year, it was two of three).

We don't get many bugs inside. We live in an 1872 farmhouse, so we do get the occasional palmetto bug, but never up so high as to need the Bugzooka. However, living as we do, in the North Carolina piedmont, we're plagued by mosquitoes; particularly the new "Asian Tiger" mosquitoes, which leave me and my sweetheart itching and inflamed for days after working in the garden or yard. We tried the "propane to human breath" machine (the Mosquito Magnet) for a year or so, and it simply didn't catch any mosquitoes. The fan was not powerful enough to suck in the little buggers, so the mesh bag they said would be full of bugs was full of dust and pollen. We tried the doughnuts you're supposed to dunk in places (like gutters) where water stands from time to time, and they didn't help. We drilled holes in all of our trashcans and recycling bins, but they still bred mosquitoes. We heard about services that will spray some sort of natural insecticide all summer long, but they were too expensive.

With these traps, we can now work in the yard or garden or sit on our porch — one of the small joys that defines Southern living — without fear.

-- *Steven Champeon*

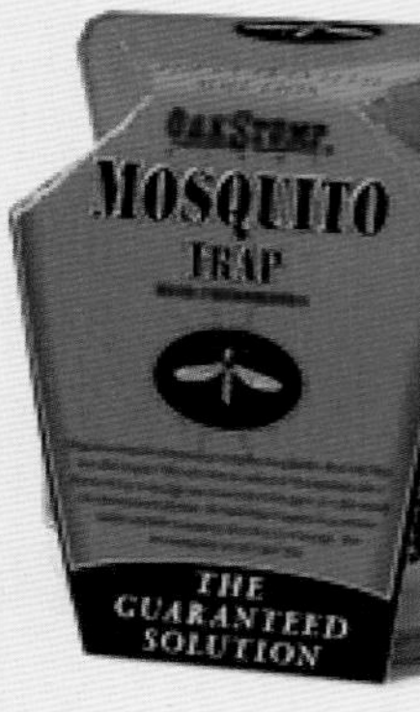

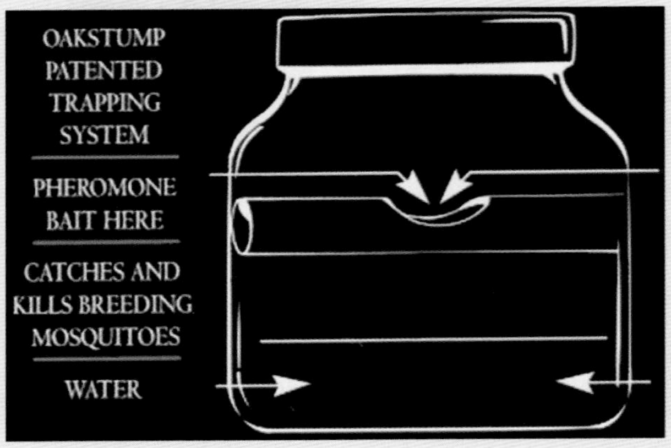

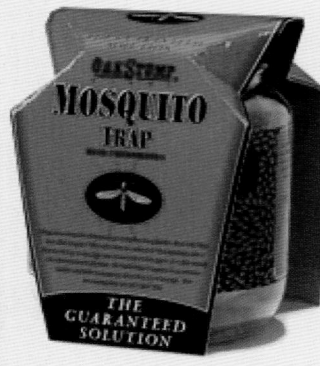

Hurts bugs, not plants

Bug Blaster

$29 with Water Wand Lee Valley

The Bug Blaster is a great insect control tool for the garden. It is completely organic–it only uses the force of water. I have used the tool for three years and love it. You just attach it to your hose and turn it on. The water is forced out a tiny hole and guided in such a way that it comes out in a fine spray that is a flat circle. Stick the nozzle in your plants and it knocks all the insects and eggs off, those below the leaves and those above.

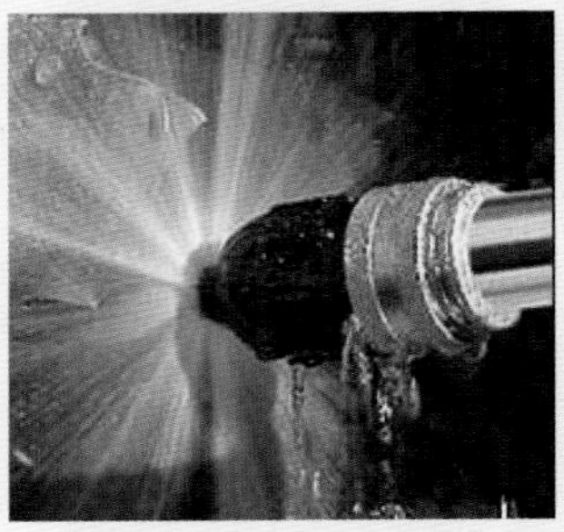

Every gardener knows you can remove aphids by hosing the plant, but it is difficult to get the ones under the leaves. On delicate new growth, the hosing can injure the plants. But the Bug Blaster has such a fine, controllable spray that it cleans the plants of all the pests and doesn't harm the plants. The good insects are usually hard shelled and aren't injured. Since I bought this tool I haven't used any other pest control method.

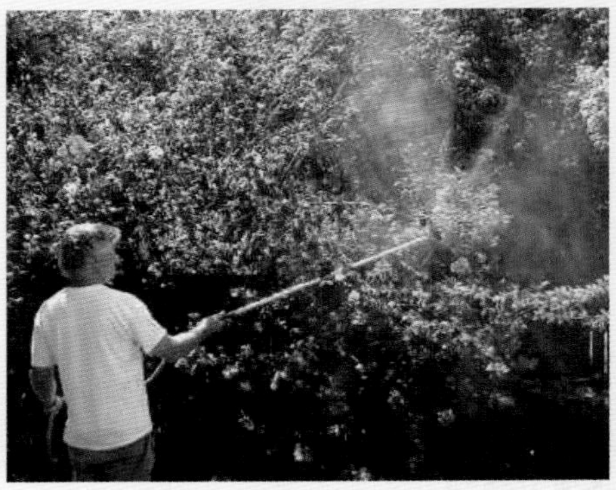

-- *Terry Powell*

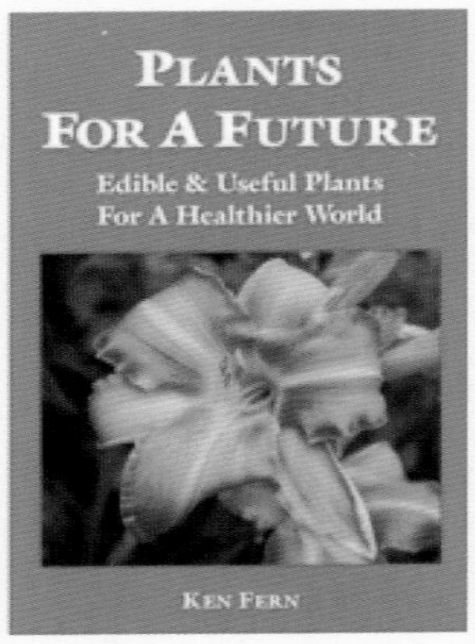

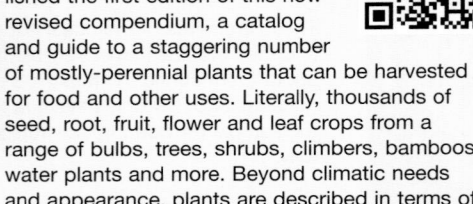

Guide to edible & useful foliage

Plants for a Future

$21 Ken Pern, 2000 (2nd edition), 300 p.

In the 1970s British bus driver Ken Fern went back to the land. Twenty-five years later he published the first edition of this now-revised compendium, a catalog and guide to a staggering number of mostly-perennial plants that can be harvested for food and other uses. Literally, thousands of seed, root, fruit, flower and leaf crops from a range of bulbs, trees, shrubs, climbers, bamboos, water plants and more. Beyond climatic needs and appearance, plants are described in terms of their taste and, often, highly-specific use (e.g. Asarum canadense. SNAKE ROOT: "a ginger substitute in flavouring cooked foods."). The index is conveniently broken up into edible uses, like condiments and egg and salt substitutes, and non-edible uses, like basketry, disinfectant, and tooth care; for more, check out 100 Other Uses. And actually, the Plants for a Future web site offers a searchable database of 7,000 plants. While much of the info from the book is available online, the printed format can be easier to parse and digest. There are sections on "green manures" and how to mulch with cardboard boxes or newspaper and straw, as well as how to make a pond. Despite all the ideas and potential outlined in the book, the final chapter, "Future Possibilities," truly emphasizes the magical allure of cultivation and experimentation.

-- *Steven Leckart*

•

Most organic gardeners, when confronted by a heavily weed-infested site, will reach immediately for the fork or spade and spend many hours laboriously digging out as many weeds as they can. Not only is this exceedingly hard work, but it is often far less than successful. Many of the weeds, such as couch grass or thistles, will soon regrow with renewed vigour if even small parts of the roots are left in the ground. There will also usually be an explosion of germination from literally millions of seeds that have been given ideal germination conditions. The newly-dug ground will very soon be covered in weeds again.

The alternative, once more, is to mulch. But this time there must be some organic barrier placed below the mulch to prevent all the weeds from growing through. We have found that cardboard boxes are an ideal barrier to use. They are usually freely available in quantity from local shops, etc., will form an excellent barrier for a year or so, in which time most of the persistent weeds will have died, and then will rot down nicely to add their own organic matter to the fertility of the soil. Other materials that can also be used include newspapers (but try to avoid too many with colour printing and do not use colour supplements on land where you intend to grow food) and carpets (but only those made of natural materials such as hessian — avoid foam-backed carpets).

It is very important to ensure that you apply a sufficient thickness of barrier mulch, otherwise the more vigorous weeds such as thistles and docks will push their way through it. A carpet that is not too worn is usually sufficient, carboard boxes folded flat but not opened out are generally enough, and newspapers about 15 sheets thick are also adequate. Make sure that the edges of the boxes or whatever overlap by at least 8 cm, otherwise the weeds will soon find their way to the surface. Autumn and early winter is the ideal time to mulch weed-infested beds, though it can be done at any time of the year so long as as the soil is not dry.

Best gardening innovations

HortIdeas

$15/year via email, HortIdeas

Do plants have ideas? Yes.

I use this monthly to troll for the best in the art and science of gardening. Each month editors Greg and Pat Williams extract the meatiest, handiest, most practical innovations in vegetable, fruit and flower horticulture. They tirelessly glean material from obscure ag-extension bulletins, garden club newsletters, seed catalogs and dusty journals, reading it all so you don't have to, and translating it into clear English so you can use it. They run no pictures, no ads; only concepts, tools, and techniques. It's sort of like a *Cook's Illustrated* for your garden — the advice is based on scientific testing, and the tools born out of genuine need.

The newsletter is emailed as a PDF file. Because *HortIdeas* reports "news that stays new", I recommend the nifty CD of all their back issues. This humble yet intelligent newsletter is an amazing service which should appeal to anyone with a love of perfecting what is possible.

-- *KK*

•

Ohio State University horticulturists have been evaluating underutilized low-growing willows (Salix species) for their ornamental potential and hardiness. They gathered around 200 willows from a variety of international sources.... Several of the low-growing willows have interesting ornamental features and appear to be excellent candidates for use in small-scale gardens in the Midwest. Some are well-suited to container-growing. We hope that commercial nurseries become interested in propagating and marketing some of these trees! According to the OSU horticulturists, because of extreme variability among seed-propagated willows, it is imperative that individuals with unique qualities be propagated vegetatively.

•

Several years ago, there was considerable interest in adding hydrogen peroxide to irrigation water to enhance oxygen in the root zones of plants. At the time, some investigators reported increased crop yields with hydrogen peroxide, but, as far as we know, no commercial apparatus was developed. Perhaps the results of recent experiments conducted in Australia will rekindle interest in oxygenated irrigation systems. The Australian researchers injected 0.6 pints per 1,000 square feet of 50% hydrogen peroxide solution via subsurface drip irrigation tape into heavy clay plots following flooding of the soil. Zucchini plants grown in the plots produced 29% more fruits weighing 25% more than the fruits produced without hydrogen peroxide treatment. The researchers also tried injecting hydrogen peroxide at a rate of 0.1% by volume with the irrigation water provided to container-grown vegetable soybean plants in "heavy cracking" clay soil that was kept water-saturated. Yields of soybean pods (fresh weight) went up by 82-96% relative to the yields with no hydrogen peroxide.

Clearly, oxygenated irrigation is a highly promising way to boost production of crops growing in waterlogged heavy clay. We believe there could be a substantial market for a mechanismthat automatically injects hydrogen peroxide into drip irrigation systems.

•

Moss loves buttermilk and beer. Where did this "old school" formula of mixing moss fragments with buttermilk and/or beer in the family blender come from, and does it work? Moss craves acidic conditions which buttermilk and stale beer provide. While the "moss think tank" at Moss Acres prefers some less odorous methods of preparing a moss shake/slurry, this oft-prescribed method has about a 60% success rate when the moss fragments are kept consistently wet. Al Benner, president of Moss Acres, says: "Our customers tell us the applications for moss are expanding. Moss has always been ... popular ... in Asian gardens, rock gardens, water gardens, and shade gardens. But every day we are helping clients use moss for creative projects such as interior landscaping, stone walls, and moss roofs."

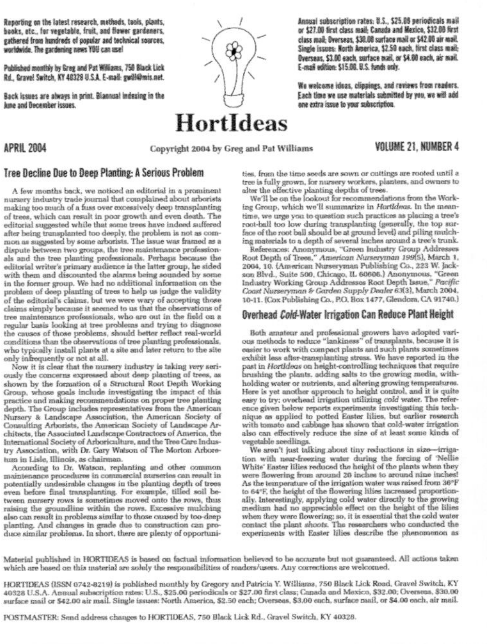

Reporting on the latest research, methods, tools, plants, books, etc., for vegetable, fruit, and flower gardeners, gathered from hundreds of popular and technical sources, worldwide. The gardening news YOU can use!

Published monthly by Greg and Pat Williams, 750 Black Lick Rd., Gravel Switch, KY 40328 U.S.A. E-mail: gwill@mis.net.

Back issues are always in print. Biannual indexing in the June and December issues.

Annual subscription rates: U.S., $25.00 periodicals mail or $27.00 first class mail; Canada and Mexico, $32.00 first class mail; Overseas, $30.00 surface mail or $42.00 air mail. Single issues: North America, $2.50 each, first class mail; Overseas, $3.00 each, surface mail, or $4.00 each, air mail. E-mail edition: $15.00. U.S. funds only.

We welcome ideas, clippings, and reviews from readers. Each time we use materials submitted by you, we will add one extra issue to your subscription.

HortIdeas

APRIL 2004 — Copyright 2004 by Greg and Pat Williams — VOLUME 21, NUMBER 4

Tree Decline Due to Deep Planting: A Serious Problem

A few months back, we noticed an editorial in a prominent nursery industry trade journal that complained about arborists making too much of a fuss over excessively deep transplanting of trees, which can result in poor growth and even death. The editorial suggested while that some trees have indeed suffered after being transplanted too deeply, the problem is not as common as suggested by some arborists. The issue was framed as a dispute between two groups, the tree maintenance professionals and the tree planting professionals. Perhaps because the editorial writer's primary audience is the latter group, he sided with them and discounted the alarms being sounded by some in the former group. We had no additional information on the problem of deep planting of trees to help us judge the validity of the editorial's claims, but we were wary of accepting those claims simply because it seemed to us that the observations of tree maintenance professionals, who are out in the field on a regular basis looking at tree problems and trying to diagnose the causes of those problems, should better reflect real-world conditions than the observations of tree planting professionals, who typically install plants at a site and later return to the site only infrequently or not at all.

Now it is clear that the nursery industry is taking *very* seriously the concerns expressed about deep planting of trees, as shown by the formation of a Structural Root Depth Working Group, whose goals include investigating the impact of this practice and making recommendations on proper tree planting depth. The Group includes representatives from the American Nursery & Landscape Association, the American Society of Consulting Arborists, the American Society of Landscape Architects, the Associated Landscape Contractors of America, the International Society of Arboriculture, and the Tree Care Industry Association, with Dr. Gary Watson of The Morton Arboretum in Lisle, Illinois, as chairman.

According to Dr. Watson, replanting and other common maintenance procedures in commercial nurseries can result in potentially undesirable changes in the planting depth of trees even before final transplanting. For example, tilled soil between nursery rows is sometimes moved onto the rows, thus raising the groundline within the rows. Excessive mulching also can result in problems similar to those caused by too-deep planting. And changes in grade due to construction can produce similar problems. In short, there are plenty of opportunities, from the time seeds are sown or cuttings are rooted until a tree is fully grown, for nursery workers, planters, and owners to alter the effective planting depths of trees.

We'll be on the lookout for recommendations from the Working Group, which we'll summarize in *HortIdeas*. In the meantime, we urge you to question such practices as placing a tree's root-ball too low during transplanting (generally, the top surface of the root ball should be at ground level) and piling mulching materials to a depth of several inches around a tree's trunk.

References: Anonymous, "Green Industry Group Addresses Root Depth of Trees," *American Nurseryman 199*(5), March 1, 2004, 10. (American Nurseryman Publishing Co., 223 W. Jackson Blvd., Suite 500, Chicago, IL 60606.) Anonymous, "Green Industry Working Group Addresses Root Depth Issue," *Pacific Coast Nurseryman & Garden Supply Dealer 63*(3), March 2004, 10-11. (Cox Publishing Co., P.O. Box 1477, Glendora, CA 91740.)

Overhead *Cold*-Water Irrigation Can Reduce Plant Height

Both amateur and professional growers have adopted various methods to reduce "lankiness" of transplants, because it is easier to work with compact plants and such plants sometimes exhibit less after-transplanting stress. We have reported in the past in *HortIdeas* on height-controlling techniques that require brushing the plants, adding salts to the growing media, withholding water or nutrients, and altering growing temperatures. Here is yet another approach to height control, and it is quite easy to try: overhead irrigation utilizing *cold* water. The reference given below reports experiments investigating this technique as applied to potted Easter lilies, but earlier research with tomato and cabbage has shown that cold-water irrigation also can effectively reduce the size of at least some kinds of vegetable seedlings.

We aren't just talking about tiny reductions in size—irrigation with near-freezing water during the forcing of 'Nellie White' Easter lilies reduced the height of the plants when they were flowering from around 20 inches to around nine inches! As the temperature of the irrigation water was raised from 36°F to 64°F, the height of the flowering lilies increased proportionally. Interestingly, applying cold water directly to the growing medium had no appreciable effect on the height of the lilies when they were flowering; so, it is essential that the cold water contact the plant *shoots*. The researchers who conducted the experiments with Easter lilies describe the phenomenon as

Material published in HORTIDEAS is based on factual information believed to be accurate but not guaranteed. All actions taken which are based on this material are solely the responsibilities of readers/users. Any corrections are welcomed.

HORTIDEAS (ISSN 0742-8219) is published monthly by Gregory and Patricia Y. Williams, 750 Black Lick Road, Gravel Switch, KY 40328 U.S.A. Annual subscription rates: U.S., $25.00 periodicals or $27.00 first class; Canada and Mexico, $32.00; Overseas, $30.00 surface mail or $42.00 air mail. Single issues: North America, $2.50 each; Overseas, $3.00 each, surface mail, or $4.00 each, air mail.

POSTMASTER: Send address changes to HORTIDEAS, 750 Black Lick Rd., Gravel Switch, KY 40328.

•

The researchers conclude that the results of the storage trial show that high storage temperatures—apparently achievable simply by having a fairly large pile, without periodic turning— can speed destruction of pathogenic bacteria in solid manures.They also warn of the potential dangers of consuming produce-harvested soon after applying fresh manure.

Intelligently designed bird feeder
Effort-Less Bird Feeder
$87 Amazon

The Effort-Less birdfeeder is a gravity-fed dispenser that is easy to fill and clean, holds a lot of seed, provides a second lower tray for spillage for birds that typically feed on the ground. It is elegant, durable, and allows large numbers of birds to feed peacefully for long periods of time. It has an effective squirrel guard and is free-standing on a hefty base.

The quality and design of this simple bird-feeder stand out. The design is a total rethink of many traditional styles that obviates all of the problems with other feeders. The quality is in the myriad thoughtful details of materials, construction and presentation that make it perform perfectly.

All of the parts fit together exquisitely when one follows the extremely clear instructions. Assembly was actually fun and without stress.

We have numerous feeders and fountains for the birds. After introducing the Effort-Less, we have seen a sudden influx of numerous kinds of rare birds, sometimes in large flocks. Not sure if this is coincidence or an overlapping of factors. Nonetheless, the birds are surely making good use of the feeder. We have owned this from spring to the beginning of autumn and it has made birdwatching a great pleasure in our lives.

-- Erica Heftmann

Automatic bird bath filler
KozyFill
$54 Amazon

I sent one of these to a friend who lives in Tasmania. She has a wonderful assortment of southern hemispherical birds that she likes to feed and provide water for, but she travels on a regular basis, and the birds empty the bath in a day. She tried various home-brew ideas for automatically filling the bird bath, but none really did the trick for her. Also, this one's the most aesthetically pleasing I could find, as the reservoir sits separate from the bird bath.

I sent her the KozyFill, she set it all up, fine-tuned the height of the various tubes, and voila! She's got a yard full of happy Eastern rosellas, wattle birds, the occasional cockatoo, and other sundry birds of the Antipodes. Watching the birds beats TV any morning: you've got drama, conflict and humor in dazzling color right outside the bedroom window.

-- Rick Turner

Plans for a homemade automatic bird bath purger-filler by James M. Clark here.

--Elon Schoenholz

Perfect hummingbird feeder
HummZinger Hummingbird Feeder
$16 Amazon

There exist a seemingly endless variety of hummingbird feeder designs, and over the years we've tried many only to encounter a variety of annoying shortcomings. However, we have finally discovered the perfect feeder: the Aspects HummZinger Hummingbird Feeder. We have been using 4 of these feeders for about 5 years, and are completely satisfied with their design.

Where we live, mold growing inside a hummingbird feeder is a constant problem. Most feeders are extremely difficult to clean due to their vacuum feeding system that requires a narrow-necked food reservoir. The HummZinger feeder solves this problem by using a simple bowl reservoir, not a gravity feed. Thus, when you pop off the top you have a completely open container that couldn't be easier to clean. Another problem is that ants would occasionally find one of our feeders. Once this happens the only solution is to move the feeder and hope they don't find it in the new location, or add an ant trap, which are hard to find. The HummZinger feeder solves this problem by having an integrated ant trap. Just fill it with water, or let rain do it, and

you'll be ant free. A final problem we've experienced with some feeders is that rain water can easily run into the feeding holes, diluting the solution to the point where it no longer attracts the hummingbirds. The HummZinger feeders address this problem by having a raised flower design around each feeding port that diverts much of the rain water. While this isn't a complete solution, this feature definitely reduces the problem.

The feeders come in 8, 12, and 16 oz sizes, with 3, 4, and 6 feeding ports respectively. The feeders are constructed of an "unbreakable" polycarbonate and come with a lifetime guarantee. We use multiple feeders in the "Mini" 8 oz. size because we find that the eastern Ruby Throated hummingbirds don't "play well with others", and too many ports on a single feeder lead to excessive squabbling. However, in the western US, where I have seen swarms of hummers happily sharing a feeder, the 16 oz model may be a better choice.

The only potential fault I can see with these feeders is that even the 16 oz model has much

less capacity than many gravity-feed brands, which means that they must be refilled more often. We don't find this a problem because by the time one of our feeders is empty it is also in need of a cleaning to avoid mold.

-- Dave King

Best bird attractions
The Backyard Birdfeeder's Bible
$15 Sally Roth, 2003, 384 p.

Of the many backyard birdfeeding books on my shelf, this one is my favorite. Serious birders treat it as the best too. It introduced me to some neat tricks -- using dried dog food as substitute feed, making suet holders from slab wood, planting small patches of grain as attractors.

-- KK

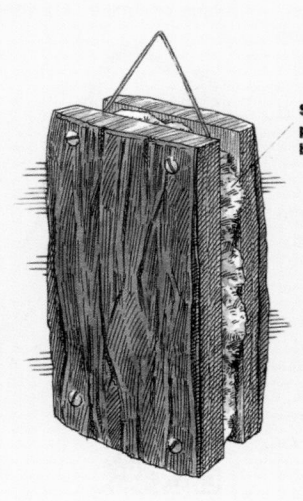

Suet or peanut butter

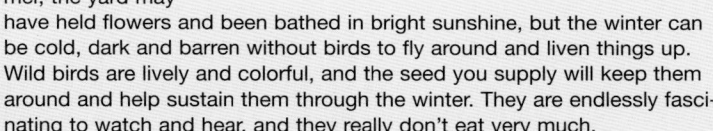

Open

Closing

Feeds birds, not squirrels
Brome Squirrel Buster Bird Feeder
$87 Amazon

During the summer, the yard may have held flowers and been bathed in bright sunshine, but the winter can be cold, dark and barren without birds to fly around and liven things up. Wild birds are lively and colorful, and the seed you supply will keep them around and help sustain them through the winter. They are endlessly fascinating to watch and hear, and they really don't eat very much.

Squirrels, on the other hand eat quite a bit. You don't need to feed them, but if they can get to your bird feeder, they'll empty it in no time at all.

Here's where the Brome Squirrel Buster Plus comes in. The endless battle of wits between Bird Feeding Man and Squirrel is won most of the time by Squirrel. You will start off grossly underestimating the squirrel's athleticism and sheer persistence. They can jump, and hang, and climb better than you can ever imagine. Happily, the human's superior intelligence is manifested by many models of "squirrel-proof" bird feeders.

The best of which, especially for the price, is the Brome, made by a company in Canada. Birds, having evolved to be light for ease of flying, perch on the bottom and eat at will. Squirrels, being larger and heavier, weigh the bottom down and close off the openings (thus keeping them from just trying to shake the food out). The quality is high, the pressure is adjustable (to keep out starlings, grackles and other possibly large, unwanted birds) and all the parts are replaceable. It also has a lifetime warranty against squirrel damage. Your bird seed supply will take a long time to run out – the feeder has a large, 3 quart capacity and there will be no thievery.

-- Matthew Perks

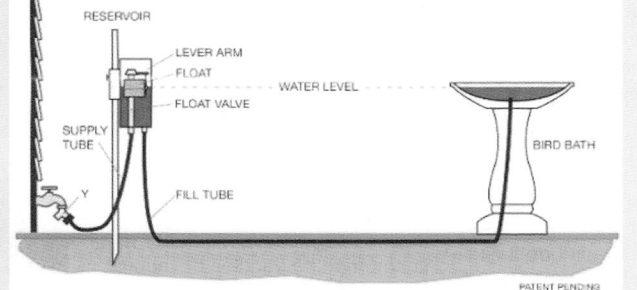

RESERVOIR
LEVER ARM
FLOAT
FLOAT VALVE
WATER LEVEL
SUPPLY TUBE
FILL TUBE
BIRD BATH
PATENT PENDING

Landscape Tools

Best compost turner
Garden Fork
$23 Amazon

Shovels get stuck turning thick compost piles. A garden fork, known also as a compost or spading fork, moves more freely through the debris, and is my favorite means of turning compost, a task that, with this tool, I enjoy. I've seen devices such as the Compost Crank, designed solely for aerating a pile of decomposing organic matter, but they're apparently not up for much else.

I value my garden fork because it's also the best tool I have for aerating soil without tilling it. It's good for lifting and moving stuff around the garden, some digging and uprooting, too. I bought mine from Seeds of Change a few years ago, recommended by a friend who's had one for many years. It has a hearty ash handle and a head of four pointy sharp carbon steel tines. There surely are other worthy versions of this essential garden tool. I'm more than happy with this one.

-- Elon Schoenholz

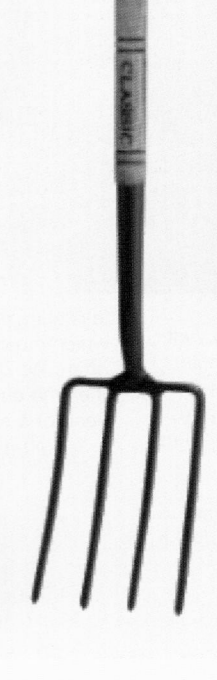

Ergonomic pitchfork
Broadfork
$189 Johnny's Seeds

This broadfork is what I use anytime I have a garden bed to prepare and want to loosen up the soil and add amendments before planting. Tillers are unwieldy, destroy soil structure and vital organisms and are generally unsuitable for raised beds. A standard pitchfork is fine but an ergonomic nightmare if you have a large area to work. The best solution I have found is the broadfork. It uses your body weight and two long handles for leverage and loosens a large swath.

I bought the Johnny's 520 Broadfork from Johnny's Seeds as it was large enough for my needs, although there are various sizes available. I use it regularly and the amount of soil it can turn with a modicum of effort is remarkable. I started using it this year and think that any serious vegetable gardener looking to avoid the roto-tiller would welcome this in the shed.

-- J. Sciarra

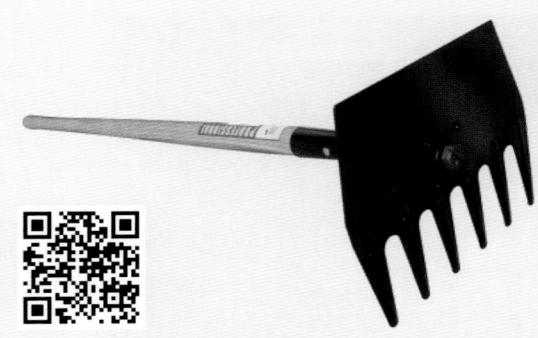

All-in-one landscape tool
McLeod Fire Tool
$59 Ben Meadows

An ordinary tool with extraordinary utility and ruggedness is something called a McLeod. It's a heavy duty combination rake and hoe with a 12" steel blade, introduced to me by friends in the US Forest Service who use McLeods for a variety of firefighting tasks; I use mine for gardening and landscaping (and fire protection, too). It does almost everything I need outside, from chopping weeds to smoothing planting beds, cutting trails, and raking up leaves and brush. A McLeod eliminates the need for dragging around a shovel, and a hoe, and a rake and a pick. There are multiple vendors online. Recently we bought one to be used at a remote cabin for $60 from Baileys, suppliers of a wide range of professional fire fighting tools.

--Mike Liebhold

No pesticide weed killing
Red Dragon Torch Kit
$55 Amazon

Are you kidding? A 500,000 BTU heat source to kill weeds? The Red Dragon is not really intended for garden weeding. Because we have a no-pesticide agreement, I use the torch to control weeds on our 600 ft long gravel driveway in the North Georgia mountains. In addition, it would be useful if you just wanted to light something on fire: burning off fields, starting piles of damp wood, etc.

There are cheaper smaller ones (only 100,00 BTUs) also made by Flame Engineering, but I sure like the one I have. Do you really need those extra 400,000 BTUs? A friend of mine has a smaller one that takes *forever* to show an effect. With mine, you can just wave it across a weed and it discolors almost instantly (usually enough to kill it). However, that's not much fun. A few more seconds of flame will incinerate the weed completely. Yeah, the extra heat makes a huge difference. When lit, the torch produces a 2 foot long, 5 inch wide column of blue flame that sounds like a (quiet) jet engine. That said, the flame doesn't spread much, so it's fairly easy to control. Every pyro needs one.

-- Greg Baumann

Swift, fun-filled brush maintenance
Bahco Swedish Clearing Axe
$66 Amazon

This tool came into my life years ago when preparing a campsite. While the rest of us were clearing the area with loppers and bow saws, one fellow was blazing past all of us with one of these — and actually enjoying it! I borrowed his funny-looking axe and was impressed enough to get my own from Gemplers. It's sturdy (a hickory handle) and has a good feel when you swing it.

With loppers, you have to grab the branch and squeeze two handles. Using a saw takes even longer. Swinging an axe handle is much quicker, but a small axe doesn't extend your reach like the brush axe does. The handle is 20" long and the head is lightweight (it really feels as if you're swinging just an axe handle), so it's easier to swing and less awkward than a typical axe.

I also feel safer wielding the brush axe instead of a machete, because the area of the exposed blade is smaller. I haven't had to sharpen my blade yet, but I have removed it from the head to see how much trouble it would be. Once I figured to clamp the head in a vise and lever the handle to "pinch" the ends of the head closer to each other, the blade came right out. Assembly is just as easy, and I imagine the blade will be much easier to sharpen when it's free from the axe!

Whenever an ice storm fills my backyard full of tree limbs, I now reach for the clearing axe. Chainsawing through the big stuff isn't a problem, but getting to it can be tedious — usually you have to chainsaw away the smaller stuff so you'll have enough room to work on the big stuff safely and easily. With this axe, that clearing work is now safer, often quicker, and certainly more enjoyable than maneuvering a chainsaw the whole time.

-- John Bodoni

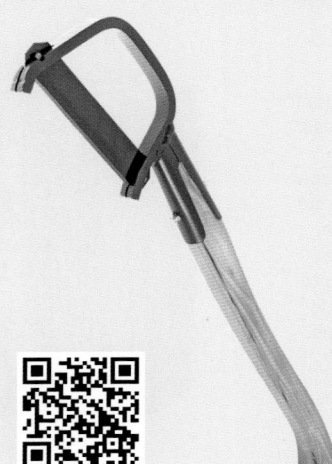

Backache-reducing rake/shovel handle
BackSaver Grip
$12 Lee Valley

We live in Cleveland and shovel lots of snow (two feet last Easter Sunday!). I didn't have a lot of pain, mostly "tired" back, but this handle definitely worked. If you're older or have a bad back or do not want the expense of a snow blower, this thing is probably indispensable and I recommend it enthusiastically. I found the handle itself loosened up after a few snowfalls, maybe three, but it's easy to retighten. That can be kind of annoying, since we shovel on average weekly during the two peak snow months, but considering the price point, this is absolutely worth the money. And aside from being a lot better for the wallet, it's also better for the environment (air and noise) than a snowblower.

-- Glenn Mercer

I bought a BackSaver grip when I was in the midst of the arduous removal of about 2000 sq. feet of rocks from my backyard. I didn't do it all personally, but I did a lot of shoveling and after a few hours per day, I always developed some degree of back strain, which tended to get worse the next day (eventually I had to get the build-up of muscle torque massaged out of my back). In the middle of the project I found the BackSaver at Ace Hardware. If it were cheaper, I'd get one for every long-handled tool I own because it made a huge difference finishing the rock-shoveling. I was grateful again when I went on to move 15 cubic yards of compost from my front driveway to backyard. It allows you to lift the shovel without reaching down as far, and although it looks like a short difference in distance, you can really feel the difference. I recommend this to anyone who has a big job ahead of them or just fears the freak movement that causes their back to give out. I've only had to retighten the grip once, although, to be fair, I have moved it from one tool to another a few times since I've had it. One thing to know: in order to accommodate handles of various diameters, the bolts that it installs with are long enough that they stick out a bit when installed on a narrow handle. However, the manufacturer provides little rubber caps so the sticking out bolts don't catch on stuff.

-- Amanda Redmond-Neal

Without the Grip.   With the Grip.

Workhorse lumber breaker-upper
MacKissic Mighty Mac Chipper Shredder
$1,400+ The Lawnmower Shop

I bought a Mighty Mac shredder/chipper about 25 years ago, have used it — heavily at times — all these years and, with a few engine repairs and turning the shredder blades around once (they are 2-sided), it's worked flawlessly on our 1/2-acre homestead. This is a "hammermill" chipper with free-swinging hammer blades for the top-feed hopper, as well as a chipper, a side feed where you put in larger branches (it will grind up a 2×4) at a 90-degree angle to the balanced flywheel blade that runs on the same axle as the shredder blades. If you get one of the bigger professional type units you don't need a separate grinder, but for home-style operation, I wouldn't fool with any of the lower-cost feed-it-in-the-top units. You don't really need to shred stuff like oak leaves (they compost nicely as is), and the smaller shredders tend to choke on stuff such as 1-inch diameter branches. This unit has changeable screens so you can adjust from fine to coarse output.

Be aware: these are dangerous tools. If you get careless and push down on brush in the hopper and get a sleeve caught in the blades, you'll end up with a mangled (or no) hand. See the simple 2×4 pusher tool below for pushing stuck vegetation into the blades. I also use a Collins machete for chopping up branches for easy feeding and of course — Grandma speaking here — goggles (chips fly), earphones, and gloves.

Mine (depicted above) has a 7HP Briggs and Stratton motor. The current models have a 10 HP. I wouldn't bother with the electric starter; the rope pull works fine.

-- Lloyd Kahn

Pusher safety tool made from 2X4: cross piece an inch or so narrower than hopper's bottom opening (9-1/2"), screwed on to a 21" handle

Weeder-cultivator
Stirrup Hoe
$17 Sears

The most recent addition to my quiver of essential landscaping tools is the stirrup hoe. The stirrup hoe is a deceptively simple device which, as the name implies, is a stirrup-shaped blade attached to the end of a stout wooden handle.

The stirrup hoe has two primary functions: First, it is useful for loosening the top layer of soil in a garden or flowerbed. The horizontal blade tends to glide about an inch beneath the surface of the soil without noticeably disturbing the soil. Weeds can deposit seeds that remain dormant in the soil until exposed to sunlight. While turning the soil with a spade brings these unwanted seeds to light the stirrup hoe leaves them in the dark. I prefer using a long pulling motion with this hoe while others recommend working it back and forth.

The second use for this tool is weeding. As the stirrup hoe glides through the soil, it snags weeds at their roots. The entire plant usually comes out of the dirt with less mess than if you pulled it by hand. Using my stirrup hoe, I recently weeded 30 feet of an abandoned flowerbed in about 10 minutes. Normally, this job would have taken at least an hour.

Prices range from about $17 for the Sears Craftsman model (with lifetime warranty) I use to $33 for the high-end Swiss-made Glaser (handle sold separately).

-- Sherard Edington

Portable tiller
Mantis Tillers
$326 (7225 2-cycle) Amazon
$430 (7262 4-cycle) Amazon
$350 (electric version) Amazon

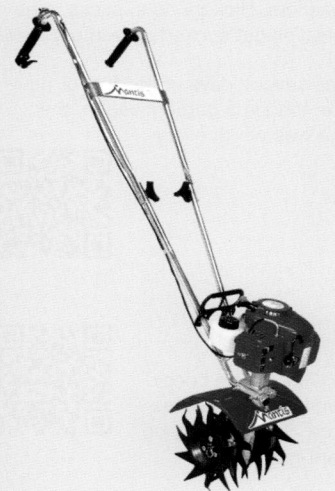

The Mantis tiller is a lightweight tiller (about 25 lbs), which allows for better portability than heavier tillers. It is easily moved from location to location (try that with a big Troy-bilt), and will handle a variety of jobs with various blades on the tiller shafts: tilling, digging shrub or tree holes, aerating lawns, de-thatching lawns, edging sidewalks or planting beds, making the vertical cuts in sod to be (re-)moved, mixing compost, or even a new metal steel spring wheel designed to clean cracks or debris and weeds in sidewalks or patios. I have three large bins (4x4x6-feet each) that I use for composting leaves and grass clippings. I simply take down the front boards and use the Mantis to mix the compost inside and in front of the bins. Then I put the boards back and reload the bins with the mixture. Short work with the Mantis. After viewing my Mantis in action, a landscape company supervisor in Peachtree City bought ten (10) of them for his company use, one for each of their work trucks.

A Mantis is better than competing small tillers like the Honda or Sears, because of the unique design of the tiller blades. They can be swapped side to side to till deeply or lightly, are very sharp and have a squiggly (my word) design that thoroughly mixes the soil. The tiller blades are warranted against breakage. The worm-gear design of the shaft that drives the tiller axles may be unique, as well, since it is very hard to stall this tiller, no matter how many vines you wrap around the axles. The variety of blades, plus the ability to use them for light or heavy penetration (e.g., tilling, aerating and edging) makes the Mantis somewhat unique.

It is not a "heavy-duty" tiller that you would usually use to till an acre of ground. If I needed that job done, I'd rent a Troy-bilt or other massive tiller for dedicated tilling of large areas, even though they are not very easy to transport or use. However my brother used his Mantis to till a large lawn (1/3 acre) which need to be re-sodded.

-- Jim Stagg

The Mantis is a little jewel. They are exceptionally easy to work with, being easy to start and incredibly lightweight. I have two caveats though: 1) To use it most effectively, you have to put it in front of you and then walk backwards, dragging the machine with you while simultaneously trying to keep on eye on the machine and where you're about to step. 2) Tough plants have a tendency to get tangled up in the tines. Fortunately, the tines can be removed, cleaned of offending material, and replaced very quickly.

By the way, Mantis offers a lifetime guarantee on the tiller's tines. If a tine ever breaks, they'll replace it. Hmm.. I guess that would be a "lifetime" guarantee! Every home with a garden should have one of these. They're that good.

-- John Bodoni

Removing big weeds
Weed Wrench
$155 Weed Wrench Company

THE tool for the job if you're uprooting alien and invasive plants such as French broom and Scotch broom. Those plants, like other invasives, tend to form aggressive monoculture areas that drive out local biodiversity, and they often make dense undergrowth fire hazards. Ripping them out is a kind of joy — a fine workout, more productive in every way than a couple hours at the gym.

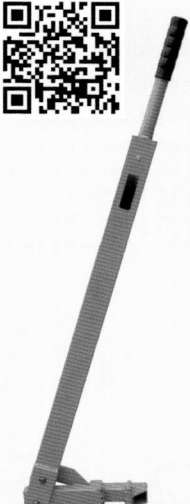

Built like a cast-iron frying pan, the Weed Wrench is a seriously macho tool. Its fierce jaws grip the miscreant plant or small tree by the throat (base of stem), and big leverage yanks it bodily out of the ground. If you get the smallest (mini) and the largest Weed Wrenches, you've got everything covered up to 2 inch diameter (beyond that, use a saw).

-- Stewart Brand

Many of us who own land in coastal northern California have a constant problem eradicating (or even keeping under control) Scotch broom, that ubiquitous plant with the yellow flowers that covers more of the hills every year. After a rain it isn't too hard to pull out if you have a strong back and the right warrior spirit. But sometimes they are just too big or the ground is too dry. That's when you need the Weed Wrench. It's basically a big lever with a set of jaws at ground level to grip the trunk of the plant. You pull slowly until the jaws engage then yank it out of the ground, roots and all. If broom or other woody weeds are a problem for you, get one of these things. There's nothing else that even comes close for effective broom removal. It amazes me that they aren't in every hardware store in northern California, but so it is. Order it from the web site. They come in four sizes. The medium is probably best for most jobs.

-- John Coate

Affordable quality tillers
Rogue Hoes
$30 Rogue Hoe

After trying several types of gardening on my homestead in the rainy Pacific Northwest (where my favored "no-till" sheetmulching seems to fail miserably), I've settled on the lightly-cultivated approach of Steve Solomon (soilandhealth.org). The old-fashioned and well-sharpened garden hoe is the workhorse of this technique.

After going to every garden center and hardware store around, and going through a few cheaper units with bad handles and unsharpenable blades, I decided to spend what it takes to get a good one. Imagine my pleasant surprise when the finest hoes I could find online were the same price OR CHEAPER than the flimsy, cheaply made Mexican and Chinese imported units.

Rogue Hoes are all about $30 and come in a myriad of sizes and blade shapes. I use the 65g for general soil-mixing-and-moving and weed slicing and the 60S "stealth bomber" to remove weeds from tight spots. The blade takes a very keen edge with a little filing and the handles should last a very long time with occasional oiling and the most basic of care: keep them out of the rain and hang them with the blade and handle off the ground.

-- Rob Campbell

Mowers

Lawn mower, weed whacker hybrid
DR Trimmer Mower

Twenty years ago when I moved from the city to the rural acreage I now inhabit, I started researching all kinds of tools. I came across a small ad for a strange-looking contraption called a DR Trimmer/Mower. Picture a rotary lawn mower with an oversize weed whacker instead of a blade, and you'll have it. I ordered one and was VERY glad I did. Nothing else comes close in keeping vegetation under control, even in tight spots like under fences. If I could only have one yard-maintenance tool, this would be it, hands down. In a pinch, it can even serve as a conventional lawn mower.

My original DR served me faithfully, and in fact still works well though it's showing its age. But recently the manufacturer made an offer I couldn't refuse

$800 DR Trimmer/ Mower Pro 6.75
DR Power Equipment

$15 Trimmer Line
Amazon

to us early adopters of the original, so I updated to this new model. It has a few nice refinements but isn't fundamentally different from my 1992 model. Highly recommended for people with lots of weeds, grass, and even brambles to keep under control.

Tips: the optional bigger engine in the 8.75 model is nice but not essential. Electric start is an optional luxury; my engine starts easily with a pull cord. I don't think the self-propelled option is worth the money and added weight and complexity (YMMV). Don't be afraid to experiment with different cutting line sizes and types: the stock line lasts a long time but I don't think cuts as well as Oregon's Nylium Starline.

-- Rob Lewis

Leaf solution
Cyclone Rake

$1,035 Cyclone Rake

I have about an acre of land with a lot of mature oak and hickory trees. They drop a lot of leaves each fall. I got the cyclone rake about 11 years ago, and it is just amazing. In one full day I can clean the entire property of leaves and be ready for winter. I'll fill it 40 or

so times throughout the day and emptying is reasonable. I make a leaf pile in a back area of the property for compost.

The 5-HP engine pulls the leaves from the mower discharge and grinds them further into small bits. One time using the attachment hose I sucked up a small block of wood with no damage to the impeller. However, there was a minor crack in the housing which I was able to patch with a short bolt and a couple

The best electric trimmer
Stihl FSE 60 Trimmer

$110 Stihl

I have used several borrowed models of both electric and gas powered trimmers. The electric plug-in Stihl FSE 60 is my favorite by far. It is quiet and strong. The only concern is that when used continuously for half an hour or more, it gets very hot. I find that it is better to use it in shorter intervals.

It works better than other models and is easier to clean. While I have to wear earplugs when using it, it is far from the teeth-shaking monstrosities that disturb the neighborhood. I couldn't see going to a gas powered trimmer unless I were very far away from an electric outlet. It is a bit more expensive than big box electric trimmers, but way better. The only reason to buy something like a Black & Decker or McCullough electric model is if you were only going to do a few light jobs one season and never use the thing again.

I was surprised that this dealer distributed model was so much better than the big-box online-marketed alternatives. In value, it's one of my best tool purchases ever.

-- Bill Owens

I initially bought my Stihl FSE-60 after reading a review at Consumer Search. The Stihl FSE-60 is not available at big boxes. They are only available at stores who function as local Stihl dealers. Presumably, this makes customer service a more personal experience and does a positive service to

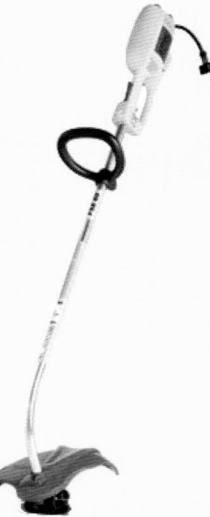

those smaller hardware stores trying to survive the big box onslaught. In any case, I bought mine a year ago in Kearny, NJ.

The balance is a bit weird. In your hands it has a bias to the rear, which is helpful, but necessary because it is powerful. VERY powerful. It uses a two-string configuration, and it's a bump-feed. I found it to be efficient and effective. I may have only bumped it twice during a day's use, whereas the Black and Decker it replaced was more bump than trim. It's heavy, but not so heavy as to make it a terrible chore. It's solid and quiet for a trimmer. Cleaning is easy after use as well. I suppose in comparison to the old B&D I had it's superior, but I don't do enough yard work to say definitively that it's the best. I like it a lot, and I'm glad I bought it from a local dealer.

-- Christopher Wanko

Easiest hand mower
Brill Push Mower

$212 Amazon

When I first realized that my housemates were serious about me using a push mower to cut our yard, I was a little skeptical. Eventually I was won over by the environmental benefits and the sense of accomplishment that I received from using a "reel mower". The first mower we purchased is literally called the "Prison reel mower" and I wouldn't recommend it. The Brill Luxus 38 Reel Mower on the other hand is a sweet piece of engineering. It is very light at 17 pounds, weather resistant, and has variable height ranges. It feels good in your hands and seems very well designed. Now that I use it, I wouldn't even consider buying a gas or electric powered mower for an average size yard. But let me warn you, using a manual mower is physically much harder, takes more time, and is very difficult if not impossible with tall grass (which means regular mowing). Whether you choose to look at that as an environmentally friendly and money-saving workout or a punishment is up to you.

-- Patrick Chen

For the past 20 years I've cut my lawn with a hand reel mower. Reel mowers are wonderful — when they are new. The major drawback is not the mild workout, but keeping the blades sharp over time. You can't sharpen the helical blades of a reel mower

without a special jig (at least I can't). Yet getting it sharpened at the shop will set you back $50 each time. That adds up real fast. And if a reel mower isn't razor sharp (unlike a power one) cutting the grass does turn into punishment. That's why the Brill is so interesting. Because its blades do not touch the cutter bar, it claims the average interval for resharpening is 8 years. I don't know anyone who has had one that long (German-made Brill is big in Europe but new in the US), but in theory this could prolong the duration between sharpenings and change the equation for keeping a manual reel mower going. That is good news because I've found that I can cut our small irregular lawn just as fast, and with no more sweat, using a sharp push mower.

-- KK

of fender washers. Hickory nuts, sticks, pine cones and leaves get sucked up without issue.

Before it was several days of hard labor hauling load after load in a garden wagon, the cyclone rake was worth every penny.

-- John Dyer

Most efficient mower
European Scythe

$190 (full kit w/sharpening tools) Scythe Supply
$62+ (blades) The Marugg Company

Light, sharp, ergonomic and quiet, this European scythe is not what you'll find in your local hardware store. The handle (snath) is custom-fit, so you stand comfortably upright while 'sweeping' weeds and grass down with ease. Potential uses range from small-acreage hay cutting to weed and brush clearing in variable terrain. I use it as a weed-whacker replacement on my long driveway. You can talk to people and hear birds while 'weed-whacking'. Pretty sweet. The price for a new one puts it up there with gas-powered weed-whackers, but I find the experience much more enjoyable. Honestly, I believe you can clear more area with less sweat using a European scythe than a powered string-trimmer. The key is the light weight of the tool and the sharpness of the blade.

Most people are stunned when they see me take down grass or weed stalks with little more than a gentle nick from the blade.

Furthermore, getting it custom fit will make it probably the most pleasant-to-use garden tool you'll ever have. (I'm unusually tall, so maybe this impresses me more than it would a 5'9" man, for example.) Here's how a European scythe and string-trimmer weed whacker tally up to each other:

Scythe Pros

Scythe is lighter. Likely to be considerably more ergonomic. Quiet. Free from power source. Stalks intact, no pulverizing of plant-matter.

Scythe Cons

Must keep the blade *sharp* (The $170 kit comes with peening jig and whetstone). Sometimes the direction of approach makes a particular weed hard to cut. You won't be able to pulverize a weed in between rocks or hard things. You must not let the blade hit hard things like rocks or metal.

For those considering a scythe, be sure to get the European style and help end this sad era that has had Americans breaking their backs with horribly un-ergonomic, heavy scythes. For instance, European blades weigh 15 oz, while American style ones weigh twice as much, at 30 oz! Besides the weight difference, the tang on the American style is not angled to help you cut the stalks. The blades are thicker and not as sharp, etc. You'll find a lot more info on why and how to use this tool at Scythe Supply.

-- James Zimmerman

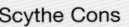

If you are not confused you aren't keeping up. - Kevin Kelly

A selection of bamboo culms showing variation in shape and form.

Best growing instructions
Practical Bamboos
$16 Paul Whittaker, 2010, 176 p.

You can grow bamboo where you live. In our yard we've been nursing along some small clumps of bamboo, and since then I've been investigating other hardy bamboos. I own a lot of bamboo books, but *Practical Bamboos* is by far the most useful of all. Other bamboo books are more encyclopedic; this one focuses on "only" the 50 most useful bamboo species, spelling out what types are good for fence rows, which are drought resistant, which work well in containers, and how to identify those variants from lookalikes. There's very specific growing tips for each variety and solid advice about the principles of growing bamboo plants in general. This is the manual to get.

-- KK

Simple division using a saw.

Using bamboo
The Book of Bamboo
$38 David Farrelly, 1984, 352 p.

Bamboo works. Bamboo does more things than any other material. Many of its traditional uses are inventoried here. A shape-shifter, bamboo's super-human abilities are amazing. Its grass fiber is all that plastic would like to be, plus more. This is an encyclopedia of bamboo ideas.

-- KK

• Arundinaria gigantic: 30 feet by 1 1/4 inch, - 10°F

(Arundinaria macrosperma).

One of two bamboos native to the continental United States, its "canebrakes" once covered large areas from Virginia to Texas and provided an effective exit from the South for runaway slaves headed north for freedom before the Civil War.

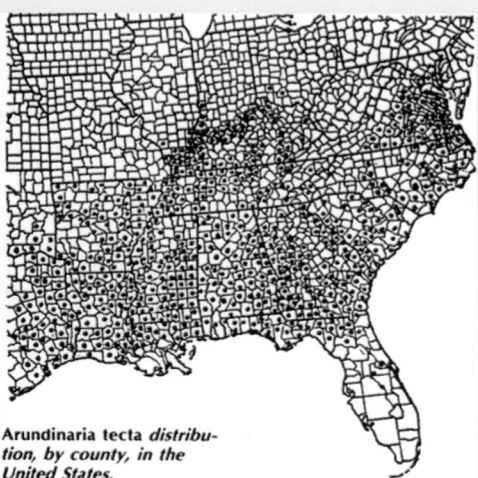

Arundinaria tecta *distribution, by county, in the United States.*

We live surrounded by such an abundance of tools that the advantage of a material that requires few tools, and those hand powered and even handmade in many cases, is not so apparent in industrial centers as in the hinterlands where bamboo is most abundant.

Bamboo's high silica content is famous for dulling tools. Tool effectiveness will be increased, time spent sharpening reduced, and work in general cheered by using molybdenum steel or an equally hard alloy. Many a bamboo house has been machete built, but more tools are demanded for more refined work, some peculiar to processing bamboo and therefore unavailable at standard tool sources. The Chinese bamboo tub and bucket maker requires some thirty different

tools and gadgets to measure, cut, fit, and assemble his wares.

• For kites or other miniworks, soak the pieces to be bent overnight in water with a dash of ammonia, then tie in desired shape around a mold to dry. You can heat small pieces in a candle flame. The mortar holding the fibers in place becomes flexible with heat and permits bending to chosen shape, which is retained after cooling. Take care not to scorch or burn bamboo by leaving candle too long in one position. Try using a bucket of hot sand to shape small pieces, as eyeglass doctors do to shape plastic frames. Don't force the bamboo's pace, nor try to bend it too far, or you'll crack it.

Bending strips or small culms.

• Bamboo animal cages and feeding troughs reduce expensive importation of metal cages, are more amiable to the cages, and can be repaired from locally available material.

Bamboo

Sustainable wood harvests
Coppicing & Coppice Crafts
$27 Rebecca Oaks and Edward Mills, 2012, 192 p.

Coppicing is an old art of the repeated harvesting of small-diameter wood from the same bush or tree. Once cut, the branches grow back, often pretty fast. Coppicing is common tradition around the world, particularly where big lumber is scarce. This book teaches the traditions and skills of coppicing as practiced in England. Coppicing is a useful art for homesteaders because you can sustainably extract wood products from a small lot or even fence row. Coppiced wood can be woven, used for carving, making chairs, charcoal, and for firewood. This English book is the best guide to the craft, instructing you in how to grow, manage, and use coppice bounty. One note, emphasized by the book: the biggest challenge in coppicing today is controlling deer, which were not a problem in old days (everyone ate them), but their huge populations now devour coppice shoots indiscriminately.

-- KK

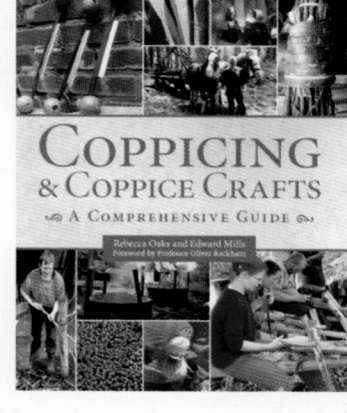

Seven-year-old hazel ready to be cut again.

New growth on hazel — only a few days old.

Finished hurdle with arch and gate.

Splitting post and chopping block all to hand.

Coppicing makes use of a mysterious property that most trees have: when cut down they do not die but grow again from the stump or roots. People have used this behavior for at least 6,000 years to generate renewable supply of wood for fuel or to use for many crafts, simple or specialized.

Tips on dealing with brash

If there is a lot of waste, burn brash on fires raised off the ground, or on areas of little value such as rhododendron stumps.

If there is not much waste, scatter it around and it will rot away very quickly.

Make brash piles but keep them small and dense.

Consider chipping but remove the chips and compost elsewhere.

Making dead-hedging keeps brash relatively tidy and in one place, and helps to deter deer if tall enough (a dead hedge is really just a tidy wind-row).

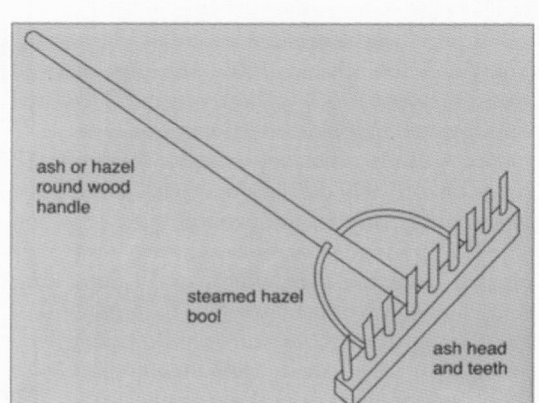

ash or hazel round wood handle

steamed hazel bool

ash head and teeth

A Northern style hay rake with a bent hazel bool.

Science gives man knowledge which is power; religion gives man wisdom which is control. - Martin Luther King, Jr.

Pond-making how-to
Earth Ponds
$17 Tim Matson, 2012 (Third Edition), 152 p.

Ponds can be used for swimming, wildlife magnets, irrigation, iceskating, fire protection, water gardening, landscaping, and fishing. You can build your own pond in your backyard, farm, or wherever.

Tim Matson is the established guru of building ponds with an earth-seal, rather than with a plastic or concrete lining. For 30 years he's been creating, advising, and collecting knowledge about pond-making. His classic *Earth Ponds* (2nd ed.) is the basic how-to, and comes with a DVD. It supplies the needed lessons in siting a pond, building it, maintaining it, enjoying it, and also restoring old ponds. This is not your average how-to; it's beautifully written and a joy to read. If you find the basics to your liking and need more, Matson has an updated *Sourcebook* with plenty of

resources, and an illustrated encyclopedia of pond variations and building techniques. Finally, Matson has a helpful website with more videos and sources.

-- KK

● The sand drop is another well-esteemed pond keeper's trick that takes advantage of the ice deck. It's an upkeep technique well suited to older ponds in need of restoration, particularly where aquatic vegetation or mud get unruly. To set up a sand drop, the pond keeper spreads a two-to-four inch layer of sand–not salted road sand–over the ice. In spring when the ice thaws, poof! The sand falls in a uniform layer over the basin floor. Sand works like an inorganic mulch, shading out weeds and, like the finings in a beer crock, holding down sediment. In muddy ponds, it's a good carpet material for the basin floor. One of my neighbors was able to use a sand drop to eliminate the slimy bottom in her family's pond, along with snakes and leeches. True, the sand drop does fill in the pond to a minute degree, but it's not often done, and it sure beats herbicides.

● Trout have a reputation as fussy feeders, picky as spoiled Siamese cats; yet for three years I've watched my brook trout gain weight without an ounce of supplemental feed. I see them feast on the bottom as much as in the air: the water is as transparent as an aquarium. I recall my neighbor's drawdown and follow-up trout stocking: clearly, the fish were pitching in to keep it clean. And I recalled an old Vermont tradition: to keep the farmhouse water clean, a trout was dropped in the well.

● Fixing low-tide ponds begins with a search for leakage. Ponds with piping often leak around the outside of the pipe or through seams, gaskets, and valves. In most cases, unless a fitting can be easily replaced, pipe repair involves digging up the line to repair joints or to implant anti-seep collars.

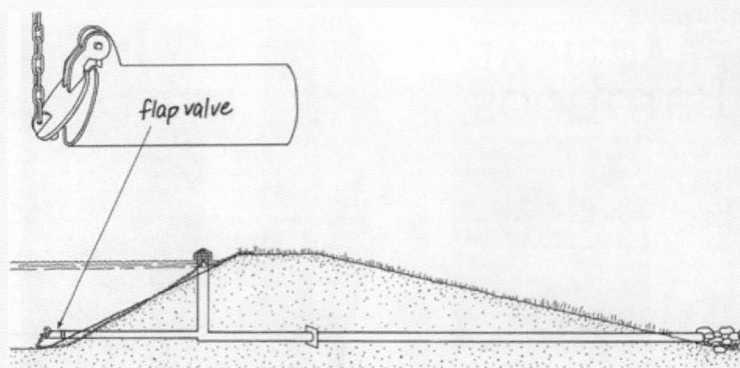

Scraping bottom in the pond basin Ray searches for flaws in the earth seal–clusters of pervious stone or gravel that would be the source of potential leaks. He carves out these patches and substitutes watertight soil. A good seal is the best defense against seepage. Pond makers who claim they can waterproof impossible sites with chemical additives and underwater dynamite blasts should run out of town. Like a potter's bowl, the earth pond is molded with a blend of materials. In addition to drawing a sufficient supply of water, this site consists of good watertight soil: about 10 to 20 percent clay and an even mix of silt, sand, and gravel. Preliminary test holes in the pond basin are crucial in evaluating the worthiness of a site.

Sensible woodlot management
Common Sense Forestry
$28 Hans W. Morsbach, 2002, 240 p.

A woods can be managed to maximize recreation potential, or increase wildlife for hunting, or maximize timber. This guidebook assumes you'd like to optimize your woodlot's timber potential in a sustainable fashion. Small-time woodlots with selective harvesting are a lot of work yielding little money, but with applied intelligence they can produce wonderfully rich and productive forests. This detailed manual will teach you intelligent woodlot management. What the author learned over 35 years is that you the forester should do as little as possible -- just enough to encourage the woods to do as much as possible.

-- KK

● Some time ago, I surmised that I could establish an exciting mixed-species forest simply by planting as many seedlings of different varieties as I could fit in a given plot of land. As the stand matured, I could decide which trees to keep and which to cull, creating the mixture of trees I wanted. The stand would form an early canopy and the trees would side shade each other, meaning I'd never have to prune. Natural selection would favor the best trees to survive. They would become perfectly shaped veneer logs with little lateral

A typical oak seedling before trimming. Its roots are too long for spud planting.

branching. ...By any reasonable standard of investment analysis, planting in this fashion is fiscal insanity. Yet this experimental plot promises to develop into a wonderful forest better than any other scheme I've witnessed for planting seedlings. It will require virtually no maintenance beyond thinning, which means it will flourish even if I do nothing.

● A site I had prepared for walnuts suddenly was inundated by giant ragweed, which grew to twelve feet in a couple of weeks, totally smothering all my seeded walnuts and oaks. Elsewhere I disced ash seeds between the rows of a walnut plantation. The ashes never appeared, but an influx of Queen Anne's lace dominated the ground. Along a hedgerow of cedars I planted years ago, little cedars germinate in one particular spot and nowhere else. There must be something special about this spot (a "site-specific" condition, as ecologists and foresters say when they can't explain such a peculiarity). Similarly, on property I own miles away from my main farm, I see new white spruces popping up next to their parents, while I seem to be incapable of making them germinate on my farm. The pH is not low enough at my farm, and conifers prefer acid soil.

● I have never seen or heard of a seedling that resulted in too many trees. Experts suggest that about fifteen thousand seedlings an acre is a good number, which means about three seedlings per square foot. I suggest that you plant whatever seeds you have.

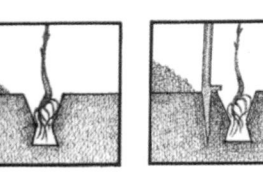
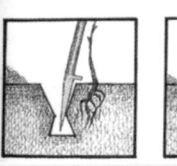
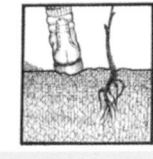

Here are eight steps for planting a seedling with a spud.

● After having planted two fields next to a forest where squirrels stole every single nut in two successive years, I decided that I can live without walnut trees.

● You should also remember a suggestion I made earlier: Always cut the most inferior tree before cutting your best. You should upgrade your forest so as to maintain large, well-formed trees for future harvests. I urge you to be personally involved in deciding which trees are to be cut.

● Mark your harvest trees carefully. Most commonly trees to be harvested are marked with a paint gun by you or a forester. It is best to mark two spots on the tree: one at eye level to be seen by the logger and a second spot at the base to assure that only designated trees are harvested.

● An environmentally friendly method of getting logs to the logging roads is a system of winches and cables. Extracting logs by suspending them from cables does less damage to the forest than the use of heavy equipment. German foresters don't allow skitters to move about in the woods, so all logs are dragged by cable to a logging road.

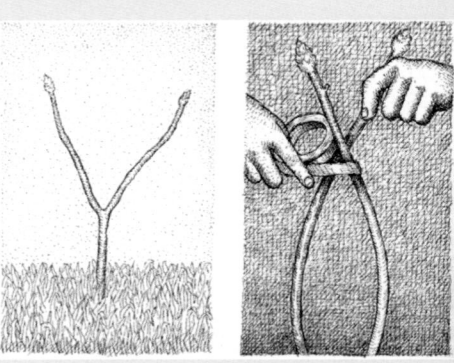

Taping a fork as shown will strengthen the branches. Later, you can remove one branch and the other will become the new leader.

Science has made us gods even before we are worthy of being men. - Jean Rostand

Trail building best practices
Lightly On The Land

$17 Robert C. Birkby, 2006, 341 p.

Say you need to lay a new bike trail in the hills, or you have a piece of property that could use a footpath down to the creek, or you volunteer one weekend to repair some trails for a local wildlife organization but none of the other volunteers know what to do. You need this fabulous manual. It will instruct you in the better ways to build and maintain footpaths with sensitivity, and how to deal with the three primary enemies of all roads: water, water, and water. I've made some trails and I sure wish I had this book long ago. It's the best of a few alternatives. The insights are hard-earned and not commonplace, and will make a huge difference in how often you'll have to come back to fix what you thought you already fixed. I've spent enough of my life living on trails to really appreciate a well-made one. Here's how to make great trails.

-- KK

• Measuring Distances by Pacing

In ancient times, distances were often determined by the length of a person's stride. Knowing how to pace is a valuable skill in our day, too, since it allows a trail worker to estimate distances simply by walking.

Developing an accurate measuring pace is a learned skill. Use a tape measure or measuring wheel to mark off a 100-foot distance on flat ground. Beginning at one end, walk to the other with a normal stride, counting your steps as you go, then divide 100 by the number of steps.

Early forestry manuals make the distinction between a step (count every time either foot strikes ground) and a /pace/ (two steps--count only when the left foot strikes ground). Some strides are easier to calculate in paces, others in steps.

• Stump Removal

The tribulations of stump removal will try your patience as do few other tasks in trail work. When you match your intelligence to that of a stump, though, chances are better than even that you will be at a slight advan-

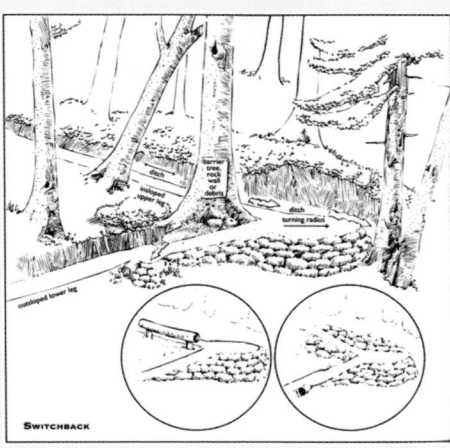

SWITCHBACK

tage. Granted, the stump has nothing to think about except how to stay firmly situated in the center of your trail, but a bit of cleverness on your part may persuade even the most tenacious root ball to ease its grip and go away.

• Advantages of Building Downhill

Because of the nature of switchback design, the likelihood of accurate treat placement is much greater

An ever-widening braid of beaten-down trails is a common problem in meadows and alpine tundra.

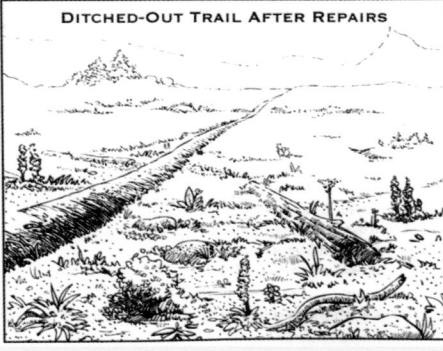

Close off unwanted trails and make the remaining tread the most inviting route for travelers.

when you build down through the turn than if you try to go the other way. If the general direction of trail construction has been uphill, stop the upward excavation about 100 feet from a proposed switchback. Move up the stake line 50 feet beyond the turn and build the track back down to the switchback location. Construct the switchback itself, and then continue downhill construction, fine-turning the location until you link up with the tread that has already been completed.

All-thread rods can be tightened during maintenance to keep railing posts secure.

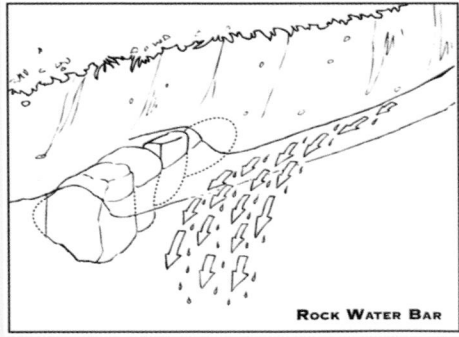

ROCK WATER BAR

The rocks embedded in a rock water bar are the last-resort barrier; the slope of the trail itself should shed most of the water.

Professional, scientific outdoor supplies
Ben Meadows Catalog

Free Ben Meadows

If you measure value in decades and don't care about appearances then industrial supplies are always the way to go. The McMaster-Carr Online Catalog (see p 15) is the granddaddy of all industrially-minded geeks, but their focus is on tooling and indoor industrial items. If I'm considering anything for the outdoors, Ben Meadows is the first catalog I pick up and the only other paper catalog on my shelf I use regularly.

Its categories span the spectrum of possible industries: loggers, farmers, ecosystem scientists, surveyors, animal control & management, spelunkers, cable locators, miners, hydrologists, oilfield workers — and dozens of other areas. It's a weird and wonderful combination of both rugged equipment for burly log-throwing types as well as instruments, equipment, and books that the more scientific-minded person would be interested in. This is the place where pros (or their purchasing departments) come to find the best gear, and I suspect much of it is worth the cost and slight delay even for an amateur.

The inventory of the Ben Meadows catalog is impressive: Six pages of pH meters! Seven pages of measuring tapes! Five pages of arborist ropes! Portable lightning detectors, safety equipment of all types, windsocks, night vision gear, throw nets, waders, fire jumper supplies, forestry cruising equipment — there is no way I could do justice to the huge variety. I've been getting

the catalog for 10 years, and every year find a new person who has never seen it and been just as excited with all the stuff they have never known where to get ("So THIS is where I can get bright green non-toxic water dyes!"). Keeping this catalog handy is a dangerous thing. You'll almost certainly find that tool that makes you think: "If only I knew this existed last summer when I needed it!" And then you'll go order whatever it is so next summer's job is much easier.

The descriptions of certain tools give quick insight into how things are done by the professionals. It's like seeing a shadowy, partial image of an instruction set of how to perform certain tasks. For instance, there is a "Plant Tissues Color Chart" book which allows comparative color examinations of certain plant leaves to determine soil nutrient or toxicity makeup. Well, there's something I didn't know you could do, and now I know how to get more information.

Looking through the field test kits, I was surprised to see how many possible test elements there are for groundwater; maybe now I'll test the spring in my backyard to see what kinds of mineral content it has. I would be very surprised if you couldn't find a significant portion of previously-reviewed Cool Tools in this catalog.

-- John Todd

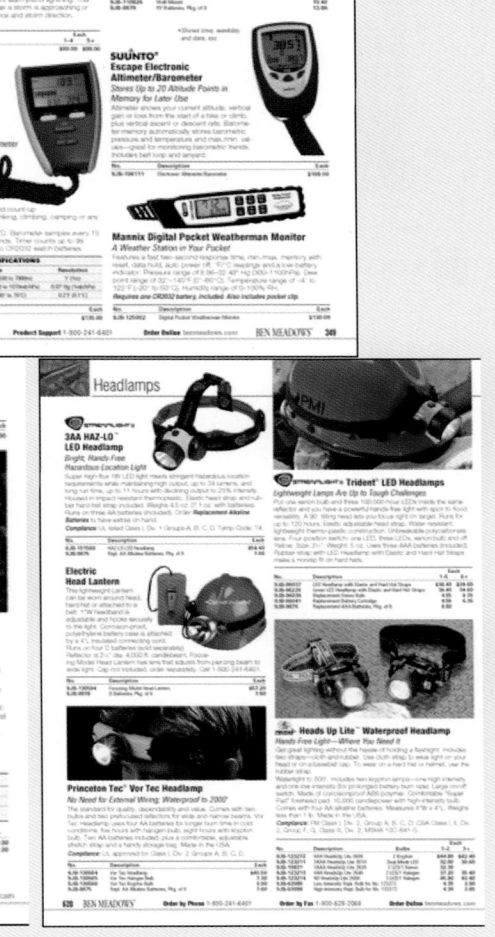

How to set one up

The New Farmers' Market

$18 Vance Corum, Marcie Rosenzweig & Eric Gibson, 2001, 257 p.

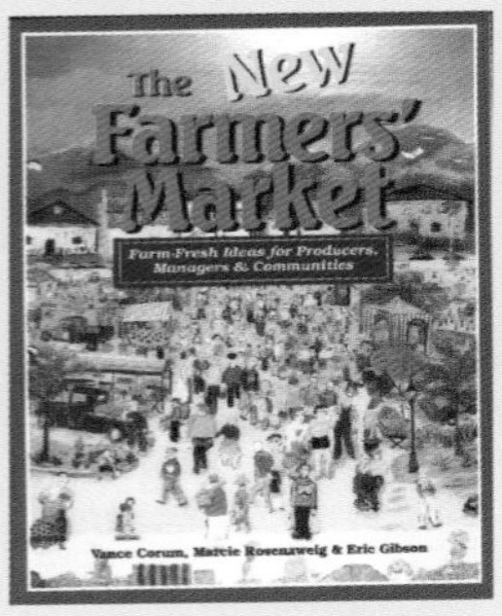

How to make a Farmers' Market in your town succeed for everyone. Selling on your own is scary; and buying at a stall is different. This fun book is chock full of great advice about market smarts, guerilla marketing, niche marketing and having fun peddling good food to eager customers. Tons of "what's worked" for many others. And if you haven't been to a local one lately, check one out.

-- *KK*

•

"Making Lemonade from lemons." For example, when drought in '91 left the couple swamped with golfball-sized potatoes, they promoted them as gourmet "PeeWee Potatoes" in $2 pint boxes. The lemonade theory worked in other ways, too. They put 8-10 peppers of various colors that were too small to sell individually into $1 "Bag O'Peppers." They almost always sold out, Peterson notes.

•

Farmers' markets offer:

minimal marketing start-up costs – requires only truck and selling area;

exemption from standard size and pack regulations (at most markets);

little or no packaging, advertising and promotion costs – farmers' markets are usually well established and centrally located;

better prices – substantially higher than wholesale; and

immediate, direct feedback. Customers are the best ones to tell you about price, quality, variety preferences, and ideas for other crops to plant.

•

One Southern California farmer was considering pulling out his exotic chocolate fuyu persimmon trees, but when he tried selling them at the Santa Monica Farmer's Market, at least 80% of those who tried his samples bought a bag! Instead of ten flats a week on the wholesale market, he was moving a full truckload because of direct consumer contacts and aggressive sampling.

An intriguing press release may focus on a unique, humorous event which has human interest. Be sure to set the scene with a specific reference to the visuals that a photographer or news team can capture as at this individually oriented, all-you-can-carry pumpkin contest (Santa Monica FM) for $5.

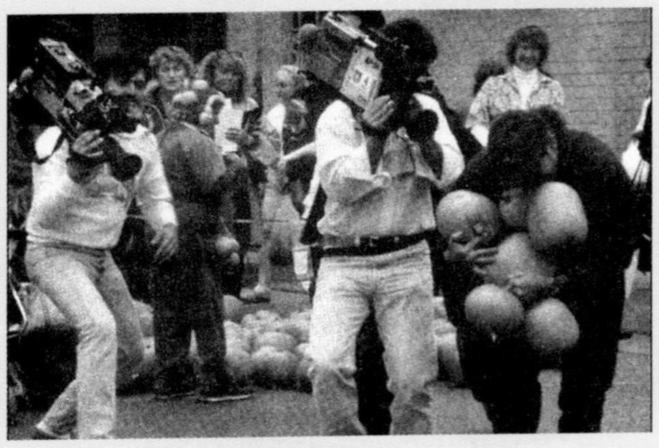

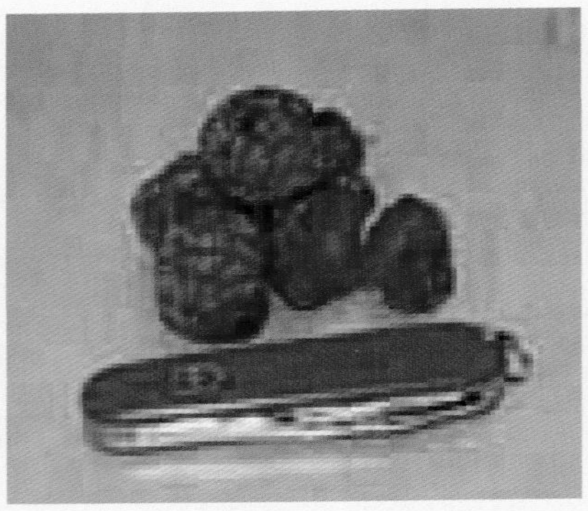

Growing your own exotic fruits

Uncommon Fruits for Every Garden

$15 (paperback) Lee Reich, 2004, 308 p.

These days specialty markets even in small towns sell once-exotic fruits. Asian pears, Japanese Persimmons, Kiwi fruits, and so on. This book is an inspiration and guide to planting these and other exotic fruits in your own backyard. Many uncommon fruits are hardier and easier to grow in the US than the traditional backyard fruits. Much uncommon fruit featured here you can't buy anywhere: Nanking Cherries, Medlars, Pawpaws. We have a few in our yard and cheered by this collection of fruits I've never heard of, and encouraged by the mail order sources and horticultural instructions, I'm ready for more.

-- *KK*

•

Millions upon millions of people have enjoyed eating persimmons, so why include this fruit in a book about uncommon fruits? Because most of those people are in Asia. The kaki, or Oriental persimmon, was the most widely grown fruit in the Far East until the twentieth century, when apples became popular. Few people outside of Asia are familiar with — let alone grow — the kaki. Few people anywhere in the world know or grow the American persimmon.

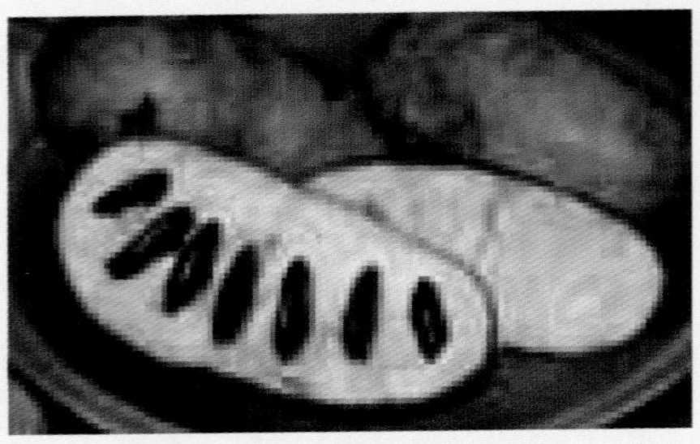

A row of dark brown, inedible seeds lined up within the custardy, rich flesh of a pawpaw fruit.

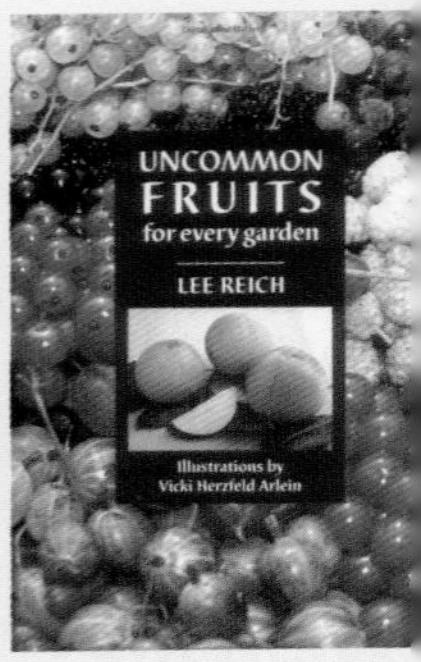

•

Medlars are rock-hard and puckery when ready for harvest and must be allowed to soften before becoming edible. This softening is called "bletting," a word coined in 1839 from the French world blessi, which denotes a particular type of bruised appearance found in fruits such as the medlar and the persimmon. Chemically speaking, bletting brings about an increase in sugars and a decrease in acids and tannins (tannins cause the unripe fruit to be puckery).

•

Combine the appearance, flavor, and texture c mulberry and fig fruits and you get something that looks, feels, and tastes like these che fruits.

Online agriculture marketplace

AgriSeek

Free AgriSeek

Buy from the producer, sell your own. Just about anything 'agricultural'; llamas, cotton, flower seeds, bean seeds, farms, farm trucks (or trucks in general), bulk wine, employment ops, whew. I found this site while looking for a cacao plant to buy. Some fellow is selling his here. There's sort of an online list that's updated when anyone puts something on the list.

-- *Melissa Keyes*

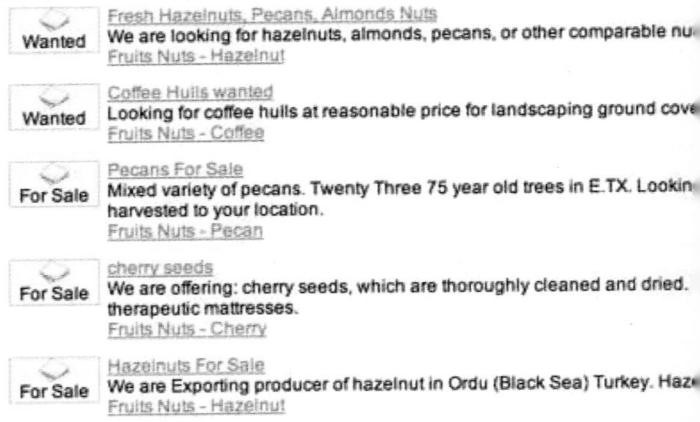
Wanted
Fresh Hazelnuts, Pecans, Almonds Nuts
We are looking for hazelnuts, almonds, pecans, or other comparable nu
Fruits Nuts - Hazelnut
Wanted
Coffee Hulls wanted
Looking for coffee hulls at reasonable price for landscaping ground cove
Fruits Nuts - Coffee
For Sale
Pecans For Sale
Mixed variety of pecans. Twenty Three 75 year old trees in E.TX. Lookin
harvested to your location.
Fruits Nuts - Pecan
For Sale
cherry seeds
We are offering: cherry seeds, which are thoroughly cleaned and dried.
therapeutic mattresses.
Fruits Nuts - Cherry
For Sale
Hazelnuts For Sale
We are Exporting producer of hazelnut in Ordu (Black Sea) Turkey. Haz
Fruits Nuts - Hazelnut

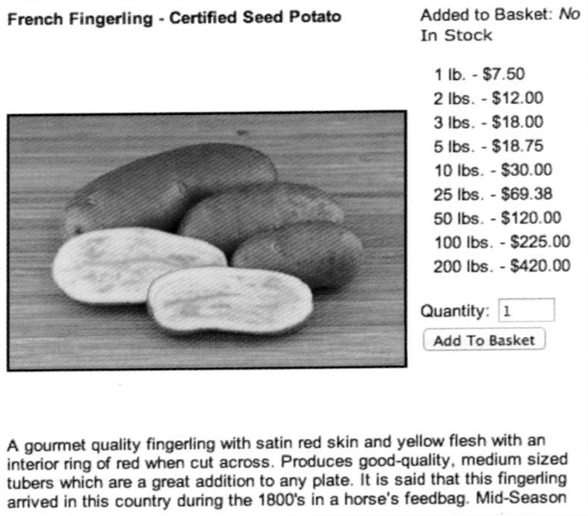
French Fingerling - Certified Seed Potato
Added to Basket: No
In Stock
1 lb. - $7.50
2 lbs. - $12.00
3 lbs. - $18.00
5 lbs. - $18.75
10 lbs. - $30.00
25 lbs. - $69.38
50 lbs. - $120.00
100 lbs. - $225.00
200 lbs. - $420.00
Quantity: 1
Add To Basket
A gourmet quality fingerling with satin red skin and yellow flesh with an interior ring of red when cut across. Produces good-quality, medium sized tubers which are a great addition to any plate. It is said that this fingerling arrived in this country during the 1800's in a horse's feedbag. Mid-Season

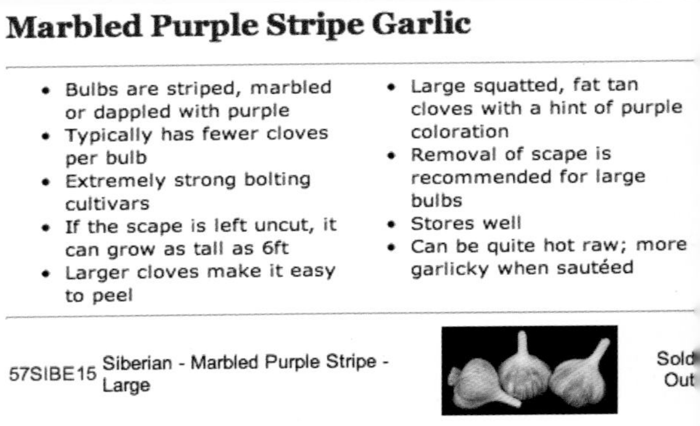
Marbled Purple Stripe Garlic
Bulbs are striped, marbled or dappled with purple
Typically has fewer cloves per bulb
Extremely strong bolting cultivars
If the scape is left uncut, it can grow as tall as 6ft
Larger cloves make it easy to peel
Large squatted, fat tan cloves with a hint of purple coloration
Removal of scape is recommended for large bulbs
Stores well
Can be quite hot raw; more garlicky when sautéed
57SIBE15
Siberian - Marbled Purple Stripe - Large
Sold Out

CSA finder

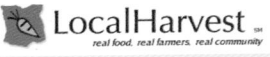

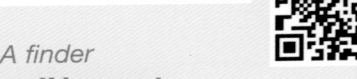

LocalHarvest

Free LocalHarvest

LocalHarvest is a comprehensive one-stop resource for finding locally-grown food in the continental U.S. The site provides a customizable search feature on its homepage, and a simple zip code input provides you with a description and link to your closest Community Supported Agriculture option. Other search options include farmer's markets, grocery co-ops, and restaurants that serve food made with organic ingredients.

-- *Elon Schoenholz*

•

Shared Risk

There is an important concept woven into the CSA model that takes the arrangement beyond the usual commercial transaction. That is the notion of shared risk. When originally conceived, the CSA was set up differently than it is now. A group of people pooled their money, bought a farm, hired a farmer, and each took a share of whatever the farm produced for the year. If the farm had a tomato bonanza, everyone put some up for winter. If a plague of locusts ate all the greens, people ate cheese sandwiches. Very few such CSAs exist today, and for most farmers, the CSA is just one of the ways their produce is marketed. They may also go to the farmers market, do some wholesale, sell to restaurants, etc. Still, the idea that "we're in this together" remains. On some farms it is stronger than others, and CSA members may be asked to sign a policy form indicating that they agree to accept without complaint whatever the farm can produce.

•

Advantages for consumers

Eat ultra-fresh food, with all the flavor and vitamin benefits

Get exposed to new vegetables and new ways of cooking

Usually get to visit the farm at least once a season

Find that kids typically favor food from "their" farm – even veggies they've never been known to eat

Develop a relationship with the farmer who grows their food and learn more about how food is grown

It's a simple enough idea, but its impact has been profound. Tens of thousands of families have joined CSAs, and in some areas of the country there is more demand than there are CSA farms to fill it. The government does not track CSAs, so there is no official count of how many CSAs there are in the U.S.. LocalHarvest has the most comprehensive directory of CSA farms, with over 2,500 listed in our grassroots database. In 2008, 557 CSAs signed up with LocalHarvest, and in the first two months of 2009, an additional 300 CSAs joined the site.

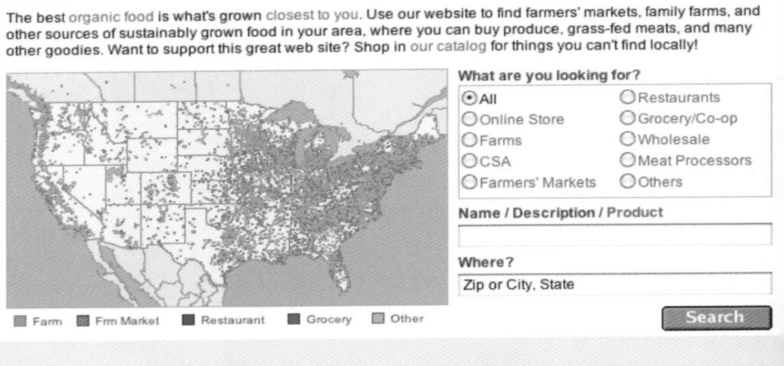
The best organic food is what's grown closest to you. Use our website to find farmers' markets, family farms, and other sources of sustainably grown food in your area, where you can buy produce, grass-fed meats, and many other goodies. Want to support this great web site? Shop in our catalog for things you can't find locally!
What are you looking for?
All
Online Store
Farms
CSA
Farmers' Markets
Restaurants
Grocery/Co-op
Wholesale
Meat Processors
Others
Name / Description / Product
Where?
Zip or City, State
Search
Farm
Frm Market
Restaurant
Grocery
Other

•

Variations

As you might expect with such a successful model, farmers have begun to introduce variations. One increasingly common one is the "mix and match," or "market-style" CSA. Here, rather than making up a standard box of vegetables for every member each week, the members load their own boxes with some degree of personal choice. The farmer lays out baskets of the week's vegetables. Some farmers encourage members to take a prescribed amount of what's available, leaving behind just what their families do not care for. Some CSA farmers then donate this extr produce to a food bank. In other CSAs, the members have wider choice to fill their box with whatever appeals to them, within certain limitations. (e.g. "Just one basket of strawberries per family, please.")

222

All good work remembers its past. - Wendell Berry

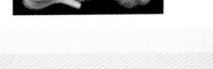

Best tree guide
The Sibley Guide to Trees

$28 David Allen Sibley, 2009, 426 p.

Naturalist David Sibley, like Tory Peterson before him, made his reputation painting and annotating birds before expanding to other biological realms. Sibley's guides to birds and bird behavior (recommended this page) are the best all-around guides to the birds of North America. Sibley's beats out Peterson's, and the dozens of others published today. Sibley's newest book, also written and illustrated by him, is the best all-around guide to the trees of North America, again displacing the many other field guides to trees in print.

Sibley's illustrations are clear, crisp, and accurate. He manages to maintain distinctions in tree types where species get fuzzy, like in the oaks, or firs. His maps are specific. He includes more parts of the tree than most guides — buds, bark, branches, seeds, silhouettes, flowers, cones, etc. — which really help in identification. And he includes not only native trees but many feral varieties, and even widely planted ornamentals. One detail I appreciate: he lists alternative common names to trees, since trees seem to have local names.

With Sibley's guide I've been able to identify more trees than with other guides. However the book is big, not at all pocketable, or the kind of thing you are likely to take with you into the field on a hike. Perhaps future editions might remedy this. I use this quality softcover edition (a delight to browse) by taking samples and photos outside and returning home to identify.

-- KK

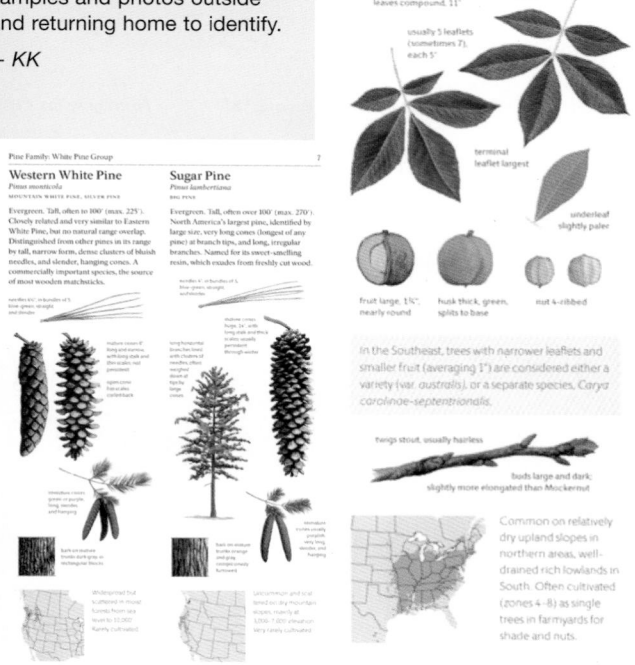

How to see birds
Sibley's Birding Basics

$13 David Allen Sibley, 2002, 168 p.

Our contemporary Audubon, David Sibley, will mentor you in seeing birds. This is not one of his legendary field guides; instead it's a masterful course on how birds work, distilled into a small compact book, and illustrated with his impeccable drawings. Even if you've been birding all your life, every page will illuminate the art of seeing them. How can you tell just from a flitting glance in the dark that was a white-throated sparrow? Sibley the grand master tells how he does it. It will be a very long time before anyone else understands and communicates this hard-won knowledge better.

–KK

▲ Western Sandpiper in fresh (left) and worn (right) alternate plumage, with representative scapular feathers from each, showing the striking changes that take place gradually, over a period of about four months, with no molt. Most field guides can show only one example of each plumage, so they illustrate an "average" bird, somewhere between these extremes.

The making of hissing, shushing, and squeaking noises (known among birders as "pishing") is done in imitation of the scolding calls of certain small songbirds. It is often combined with imitations of the calls of a small owl in order to simulate the sound of an owl that has been discovered by songbirds. Birds approach to see what's going on and to join in scolding the predator. Pishing is most effective when you are somewhat concealed within vegetation. The birds need to be able to get close to you without leaving their cover, and ideally there should be an open spot for them to sit when they do reach you. Curiosity will bring the birds in and then draw them to a perch where they can take a clear look at you.

A Purple Finch with representative feathers from different parts of the body.

► The visible outline of a bird changes with feather movements: bird with puffed out (left) and sleeked down (right)..

Identifying bird technology
Western Birds' Nests + Eastern Birds' Nests

The baskets and fabrics made by birds are as admirable as their feathers. For years I've collected bird nests (a few in the image below right) without knowing much about them. It took one obsessive Hal Harrison to find and photograph all of the nests and eggs of the birds in North America before I could begin to identify them.

Unfortunately, there is no real taxonomy for nest types, so identification is still a somewhat trial and error visual match. Environmental context — where a nest is found — is a bigger ID factor. But with some sleuthing in this book (two volumes, east and west) I've begun to identify species of nests. That has enlarged my appreciation of birds.

Oh, and these catalogs of many hundreds of nests also serve as splendid inspiration for human weavers.

-- KK

The site at which the nest is located is often diagnostic. While some species will choose a variety of sites, many are highly specialized, and this is important in identification. Water Pipits nest on the ground in tundras; Chimney Swifts nest in chimneys, and White-throated Swifts nest in steep cliffs; all wood-peckers nest in tree cavities and so do Prothonotary Warblers; storm-petrels, kingfishers, and Bank Swallows nest in burrows; MacGillivray's Warblers nest in low bushes while Olive, Hermit, and Townsend's Warblers nest high in conifers; orioles build beautiful hanging baskets but Poor-wills build no nest at all.

The nest itself is described in detail. Material used will vary with availability. For some species this has been noted, but readers should bear in mind that Spanish Moss would be no more available to a bird in Montana than spruce needles would be to a bird in the Rio Grande Valley of Texas. The basic structure of the nest of most species is so uniformly true to type that even though the materials used may vary, the format generally does not. An American Robin's nest in Washington or Oregon with mosses built into it still looks very much like a Robin's nest in Arkansas with mud and grasses predominating.

PYRRHULOXIA

BLUE GROSBEAK

DICKCISSEL

BLACK-HEADED GROSBEAK

LAZULI BUNTING

ROSE-BREASTED GROSBEAK

HOUSE FINCH

AMERICAN GOLDFINCH

Western Birds' Nests

$14 Western Birds' Nests, Hal H. Harrison, 1979, 279 p.

$14 Eastern Birds' Nests, Hal H. Harrison, 1998, 288 p.

Eastern Birds' Nests

The brain is wider than the sky, For, put them side by side, The one the other will contain, With ease, and you, beside. - Emily Dickinson

223

Tracking

How to see the unseen
Mammal Tracks & Bird Tracks

Mark Elbroch is a young tracker quickly gaining a reputation for his obsessive devotion to craft and comprehensive style of seeing. He once spent a whole New England winter tracking a single red fox — which wound up tracking him! More than stories, Elbroch offers an astounding encyclopedia of observed animal signs and visualizations that are the most helpful I've ever seen. Pages and pages of life size paw prints, a whole long chapter of diverse specialized burrows, dens, nests, and cavities — many in life size — and all photographed. Elbroch is not only an ace naturalist, but a fabulous communicator. He must sleep with his camera because he captures every nuanced disturbance on film. There's distinguishing scat, urine and other secretions, by species. And most wonderful of all, several hundred pages on feeding patterns left by each mammal on vegetation and prey. This immense guide (almost 800 pages of full color illustrations and images) is by far the most ecological of any tracking guide ever written. It shows you how to see animals through their effects upon the other living organisms around them. The amount of knowledge, respect, and insight packed into this brick of a book is stunning. I'm sure it will become a classic.

Equally astounding is a companion book on bird signs. Imagine going birdwatching without looking at birds. All you inspect are the ripples each bird makes as it disturbs the environment in its daily routine. At first the ripples are faint, but soon with practice they swell in size and plenty until they seem a wave that all but shouts out the bird's identification. That's the Elbroch way of seeing.

These fat books, lovingly published by Stackpole Books, will change the way you walk in the woods.

– KK

● Finding a hair. This is an exercise I have practiced over the years to help myself look deeper. Whenever I sit down in the woods, I won't allow myself to stand until I've found a hair within approximately an 8-inch-square patch of earth. When I'm relaxed, it's a short exercise, but when I'm tense, it may last 30 minutes. When I'm struggling, it's usually just after I've proclaimed that I've finally found the first piece of earth devoid of animal hair that I find the first one. The second one is easy.

A great horned owl has swooped and picked up a mouse.

Negative space. The spaces between the toes, between the toes and palm pads, and between the individual interdigital pads form shapes that are incredibly useful to track detectives. I often look for an X, H, or C shape to help distinguish feline and canine tracks. The front tracks of gray foxes and domestic dogs tend to show an H, while those of red foxes and coyotes show an X. Look for a C in the front tracks of cats.

Front bobcat: "C"   Front eastern coyote: "X"   Front gray fox: "H"

$32 Mammal Tracks & Sign, by Mark Elbroch, 2003, 792 p.

$27 Bird Tracks & Sign, by Mark Elbroch and Elearnor Marks, 2002, 464 p.

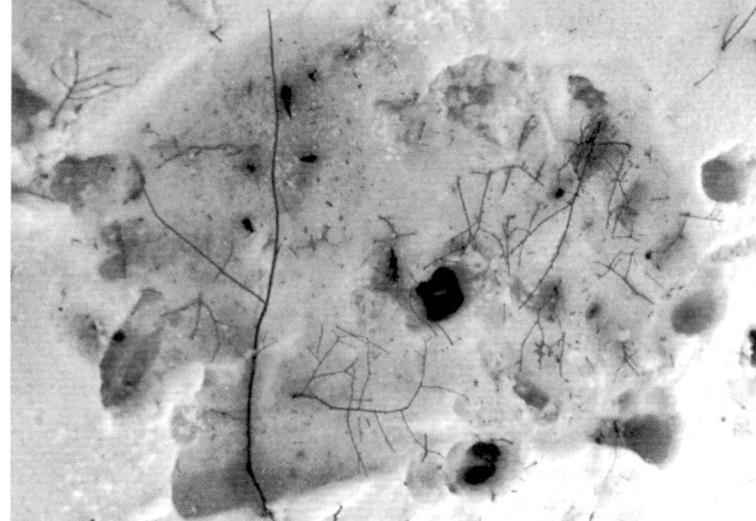

White-tailed deer beds may show a lot of detail. In this one, the impression of the deer's rump is to the lower left, the hind leg is to the lower right, and the two folded front legs are to the upper right. You can determine the size of the deer by measuring the bed from the center of the lower folded front leg diagonally across to the rump. A large deer's bed measures 41", a small deer's 25".

Since white-tailed deer have only bottom incisors, they leave rough, torn, or squared-off cuts when browsing.

Red squirrels opened these hickory nuts, leaving large, jagged holes. When gray squirrels open hickory nuts, they chip away at them, creating a ragged appearance, and often break them into small fragments. Red squirrels and flying squirrels leave the shells more intact.

How to see
Tracking & the Art of Seeing
$17 Paul Rezendes, 1999, 336 pages

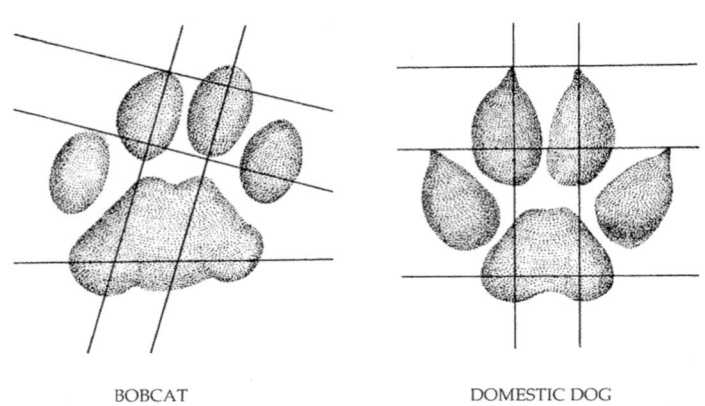

BOBCAT   DOMESTIC DOG

A comparison of cat and dog tracks highlights the asymmetrical shape of the cat's track. The toes point in a different direction from the heel pad, and the two inner (front) toes have one slightly ahead of the other, as with the two outer toes. In contrast, the dog track is more symmetrical.

The scat of snowshoe hares (left) and cottontails (right) is not always this dissimilar. Notice that one of the cottontail pellets looks exactly like those of the snowshoe hare. You cannot rely on scat to differentiate between most of the rabbit family members.

I've had meager success in tracking animals using other guide books. This one employs color photography which matches what I see on the trail much closer that black and white sketches. Also it emphasizes animal scat and browsing patterns. It includes primarily North American mammals.

-- KK

Handiest guide to bugs
Kaufman Field Guide to Insects

$14 Eric R. Eaton, Kenn Kaufman, 2007, 392 p.

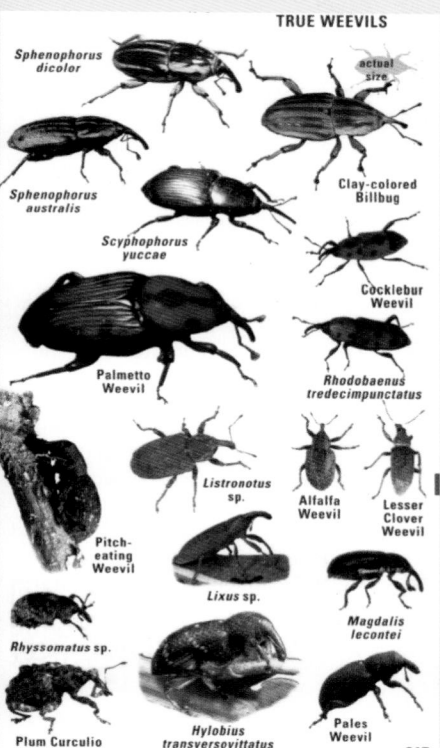

TRUE WEEVILS

This is the all-around best one volume field guide to insects in North America. It employs retouched photographs for the images and includes representative profiles at actual sizes, which are very handy. The most difficult task for a guide like this is helping you find your way through 2,350 pictures of bugs. Its solution is a rough categorization of 13 body types, which are fairly easy to browse visually, so generally we've been able to identify most of what we find to the genus level. (Species level identification of an insect often requires more information and a microscope. This book assumes you are doing "naked eye" identification.) It is more up-to-date and comprehensive than other equivalent guides. It is also backpackable and ruggedly made. All-in-all a solid dependable guide to this vast kingdom of life.

-- KK

MOTHS: WASP MIMICS, ETC.

215

263

Bug stuff
BioQuip

$14 Pocket Net Bioquip

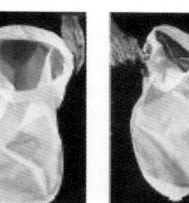

Bioquip.com is the best supplier of professional grade entomology tools there is. Everything you could want to collect/examine insects and other small creatures.

As a teacher with a strong interest in science, I've owned two of their collapsible pocket butterfly nets for many years. The hoop rims are made of a narrow band of spring steel. When twisted, they result in three smaller loops which are secured with the net bag. A full 12 inch folding net thus fits nicely in my pants pocket while birding in the forest. I just cut a piece of bamboo to make a temporary handle.

– Mike Brady

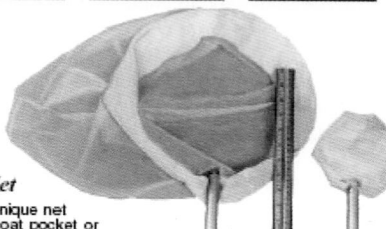

Pocket Net
BioQuip's unique net fits into a coat pocket or briefcase and is ideal for inconspicuous use. Spring steel net ring folds to a 4" (10.2cm) diameter, and flicks out quickly to a 12" (30.5cm) diameter polyester aerial net.

This collapsible net is refolded simply by twisting the top of the net ring and the handle each 180° in opposite directions so that sections of the ring fold into each other. It may be locked in closed position by slipping one of the three loops of the net ring over the "T" knob with the thumb. The 5-inch (12.7cm) anodized aluminum handle may be extended by adding 7312 aluminum extensions described below, or by inserting a 5/8" (1.6cm) wood dowel of desired length.

	Price each	1 - 11	12+
7112CP	Pocket net, 5-inch handle, 12" ring dia.	13.95	13.25
7112CPA	Replacement net bag	5.60	5.35

Best tarantula how-to
The Tarantula Keeper's Guide

$14 Stanley A. Schultz, Marguerite J. Schultz, 2009 (3rd edition), 384 p.

I'm into very low maintenance "pets." I've got my autonomous brine shrimp and have been looking for other critters I can keep and then abandon on a two-week vacation without external care or worry. I was given two tarantulas that fit the bill.

Tarantulas are big, beautiful, active and fascinating. I feed mine crickets. Since they sit on my desk basking in the warmth of the computers and electronic adapters, they've grown quite large. They burrow, cling, and pounce. Every once in a while they crawl out of their skins and molt. They are far more entertaining than I imagined. That's not too hard because I knew nothing about such creatures.

This wonderful book cured my ignorance. It is the best and most complete of the few volumes on the subject, and far more organized than any of the many web sites. It got me going by answering most of my newbie questions, and hasn't exhausted my spider curiosity since. Like many insects, tarantulas have lives that need books to explain and that can mesmerize readers for hours. This guide serves up natural history and practical how-to instructions for keeping these wonderful arachnids in your home.

– KK

•

How can the right kind be selected? Remember, these creatures don't live for only a few months like hamsters. They will live for years, perhaps for decades. Once purchased, it could be yours for a major portion of your life.

Not So Deadly Tarantulas

Virtually every reference is anecdotal with no firm medical evidence or authoritative species identification. There are also allegations that some South American species are dangerously venomous (e.g., one or more Phrixotrichus species); but again, there is little factual evidence, merely unverified anecdotal attempts to impress the gullible tourist with giant

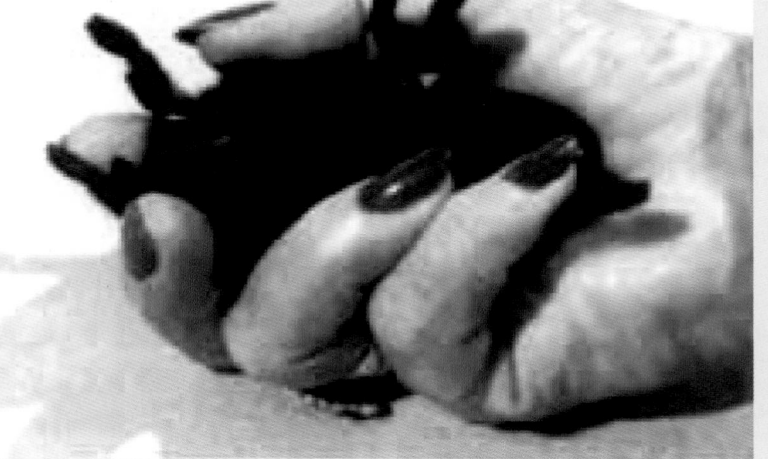

Picking up the tarantula

spider stories.

Too many people have cried wolf too many times. To say that these authors are skeptical is a vast understatement. With the exception of those listed above, none of the species commonly sold in pet shops are dangerous, and most make safe, reliable pets for the novice. The experienced aficionado may wish to acquire some of the rarer varieties, but is urged to take precautions when handling them until their identity is confirmed and verifiable evidence of the

The fresh exuvium [shed skin] of Brachypelma emilia. How much of the anatomy can you identify?

effects of their venom is obtainable. Other than that, neither the enthusiast, roommates, the spouse, nor the mother need worry.

•
Alternate Foods

It may be very tempting to feed ants to a tarantula. After all, ants are among the most plentiful of insects. However, there is something about ants that nearly all tarantulas abhor, formic acid or some other chemical perhaps, or their proclivity to crawl over or attack the tarantula in vast hordes. Many ants are capable of delivering a potent sting. In nature, if ants invade a tarantula's burrow, it evacuates if it has time.

•
Cagemates

With one possible exception, which we will discuss shortly, it is best not to try to keep other pets with the tarantula. American chameleons (actually Anolis caroliniana), European wall lizards (Lacerta species) and other small lizards will only make good, though expensive, food for the tarantula.

•
Rats or mice, however, have good reason for avoiding tarantulas. Rodents, it would seem, are abnormally sensitive to tarantula venom, and therefore are notoriously unreliable as predictors of toxicity in humans. Or, stated the other way, the venom of many tarantulas seems to be intended specifically for killing rodents.

•
Acquiring and

maintaining a breeding population of tarantulas can be a very expensive proposition. Because of the number of tarantulas that must be individually housed and cared for, and because of the long period of time required by these creatures to mature, it is virtually impossible to turn a profit. The enthusiast must be resigned to doing it only for the love of it.

With this in mind, the enthusiast who resolves to breed tarantulas could make an inestimable contribution to their preservation. Even if unsuccessful, at the very least a greater insight into the lives of these remarkable creatures will be gained. Whatever losses incurred are well worth the risk.

The Tarantula Keeper's Guide

Digging out a tarantula.

Coral

Coral Reef Guides
Key to alien life underwater

$27 Reef Fish Identification, 2002 (3rd Edition), 512 p.
$28 Reef Creature Identification, 2002 (2nd Edition), 448 p.
$25 Reef Coral Identification (2nd Edition), 2002, 288 p.
All by Paul Humann and Ned Deloach
$35 Coral Reefs, Kaplan 1982, 289 p.

A few summers ago I spent a week snorkeling in the Bahamas. Descending underwater, I had an out-of-the-planet experience. Minute by minute I realized that I was encountering creatures whose general business in life I couldn't identify. How did they make their living? Animal, plant, or alien? I couldn't tell. Life is simply far stranger than we can imagine, and nowhere is that more evident than in the compressed diversity of a coral reef. I needed a Who's Who to introduce me to the characters of this underworld. The best beginner's orientation I found was in *Peterson's Guide to Coral Reefs*. It's fine for a start.

Then a diver tipped me off to Paul Humann's work. Working with 50 professional biologists, Humann has collected pictures and descriptions of Caribbean marine life into three color bursting field guides: *Reef Fishes*, *Reef Creatures*, and *Reef Coral*. These are working identification books used by divers, biologists and taxonomists themselves. (Comes in durable plastic protection cover; includes species life-check list.) Many of the species ID'd are little known. Most are weird. All are beautiful and wonderful. The guides contain a sufficient critical mass of species that you can be confident you actually saw what you think you saw.

The other way I use these: I sit late at night and page through them. My favorite is *Reef Creatures*, with backup by *Reef Coral*. I boggle at WHAT'S DOWN THERE. I read the bios. I swoon over the shocking images in full color. I stare. I re-read the bios. I feel holy, blessed.

Humann (and Peterson for that matter) covers the west Atlantic. There is no equivalent portable guide for waters in the rest of our ocean globe that I am aware of. Like Audubon's masterpiece of birds in North America it can be used and appreciated in other locales.

-- KK

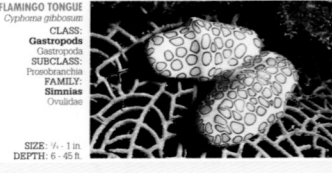

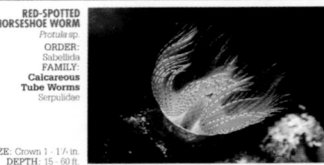

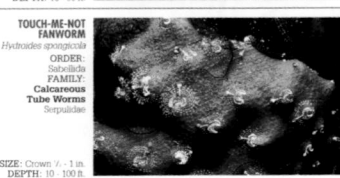

◄

1. Iridescent Tube Sponge, *Spinosella plicifera*. Dull purple with iridescent light blue overtones.

2. Knobby Candelabra, *Eunicea* species. Thick, bushy, knobby, yellow-brown branches.

3. Stoplight Parrotfish, *Sparisoma viride*. Gray with red belly; large scales outlined in black.

4. Crenelated Fire Coral, *Millepora alcicornis*. Tan, smooth; no visible cups; pointed white branch tips.

5. Large-Cupped Boulder Coral, *Montastrea cavernosa*. Cups distinct, blisterlike, greenish with bright green centers.

6. Tan Lettuce-Leaf Coral, *Agaricia agaricites*. Flat leaflike plates with concentric rings of cups in connected valleys.

7. Flower Coral, *Eusimilia fastigiata*. Yellow or tan; cups large, oval, at ends of short branches.

8. Black Wire Coral, *Stichopathes lutkeni*. Brown or cream; wirelike. Black corals (antipatharians) are found only in deep water.

9. Pillow Stinking Sponge. *Ircinia strobilina*. Gray; large pointed warts.

Natural Reef Aquariums
Intense underwater gardening

$35 John H. Tullock, 2001, 336 p.

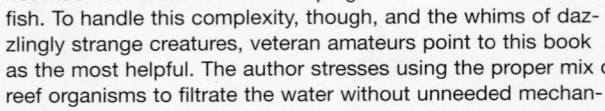

The folks who know the most about reef ecology are the amateur reefers. These passionate hobbyists explore the essentials of marine life by creating artificial salt-water reefs at home. They can cram an amazing diversity of species – sponges, coral, mollusks, fishes — in a few square meters. The coolest residents are the invertebrates. So much of this craft is like high-performance gardening. You've got grow-lights, pumps, salts, and lots of technical gear. Technology makes the chores not much more difficult than keeping fish. To handle this complexity, though, and the whims of dazzlingly strange creatures, veteran amateurs point to this book as the most helpful. The author stresses using the proper mix of reef organisms to filtrate the water without unneeded mechanics. He guides novices easily through sophisticated methods, keeping it as "natural" as possible. Because home reefer enthusiasts are so attuned to the life cycles of their captives, I learned more about marine life from here than any other source.

– KK

● Your grandfather, perhaps 100 years ago or so, could only imagine what wonders the world beneath the sea might contain. Your father could follow the exploits of the first explorers of the undersea realm and could just begin to see and experience the explosion of life on a coral reef. But you and I, we can not only visit this world whenever we wish, but we can also capture a small part of it in an oceanic microcosm of our own making in our own homes.

Open (top) or closed polyps, as in this Palythoa colony, can be an indicator of water conditions. Constantly closed polyps are a sign of trouble.

● Even in the most northerly regions, an aquarium placed in direct sunlight can overheat. Aquarists should avoid placing the aquarium in a sunny window, as seasonal fluctuations in temperature in such a location will make maintaining the correct water temperature a challenge. Artificial lighting, for most home situations, is the better choice, being more controllable, predictable, and programmable for the most convenient viewing period.

Alternatively, organisms from deeper waters, or specimens that have languished for too long in dim light, may have ceased production of protective pigments. When these specimens are then placed under bright lights, the effect is similar to that experienced by someone who, having spent a long winter indoors, rushes out on the first sunny day and spends an afternoon sunbathing. I believe that the alleged burning of corals by metal halide lights can be attributed to a lack of understanding of how these organisms respond to light and not to any inherent detrimental effect of the lights themselves.

● One of the more vexatious challenges, even for experienced reef keepers, is the appropriate placement of corals within the aquarium. Finding just the right level of light intensity and water motion can mean the difference between a specimen that thrives and grows, showing full polyp extension and brilliant coloration, and one that leads a lackluster existence, with polyps retracted or shrunken, dull coloration, and no growth.

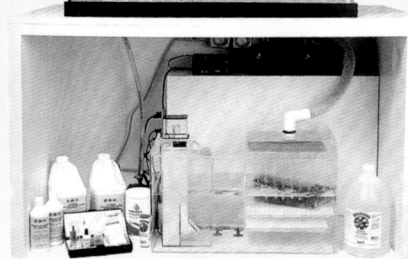

Metal halide pendants provide intense illumination while permitting easy top-down viewing of the clam reef. A convenient acrylic sump houses the skimmer, heaters, pouches of activated carbon, and phosphate remover.

The Shape of Life
Presents life's full diversity

$27 4 DVD set Amazon

This 8-part (4 DVD set) series is a National Science Foundation/PBS production that is the most taxonomic of any presentation I've seen. *The Shape of Life* addresses the 8 major categories of animal life — phylum by phylum. Starts with sponges, heads toward round worms, and so on. You get the full diverse view of life — all intelligently organized around a taxonomic framework (without the vocabulary), and expertly illustrated with great (mostly undersea) BBC-type footage. Despite the wonderful nature photography, the creators work really hard to convey the innovations offered by each phylum, and it works. This series cured me of a rather vague notion of animal diversity, despite my work at All Species. I'd love to ingest the same mind-opening treatment for the plant world, as well as the other 3 kingdoms.

-- KK

Failure is probably what you fear most, but failure is where you get your best material. - Bono

How to hear the natural world
Wild Soundcapes

$25 (used) Bernie Krause, 2002, 168 pages, with CD

What a rare gem: a how-to book that changed my mind. Or at least my hearing. Audio recordist Bernie Krause has captured the sounds of ants eating, of sand dunes shifting, of frogs croaking in duets with airplanes, and the winds sweeping over prairie grass. This subtle yet omnipresent universe of natural sound was something I had mostly ignored. Krause's practical guide is a fantastic re-education. Using a tiny digital recorder as my new ears, under his guidance nature is reborn into ever-changing radio-stations of novel sounds. His how-to advice is among the best how-to I've read; smart, specific, just the right level of detail and backed by 30 years of doing it. Since sounds often trigger more memories than snapshots, recording soundscapes should be as easy and satisfying as photography, and with Krause's advice it is. His book is dense with sonic adventures in the wild, and a 55-minute trophy CD. It's the ultimate guide: every page compels you to get up and do it. See with your ears!

-- *KK*

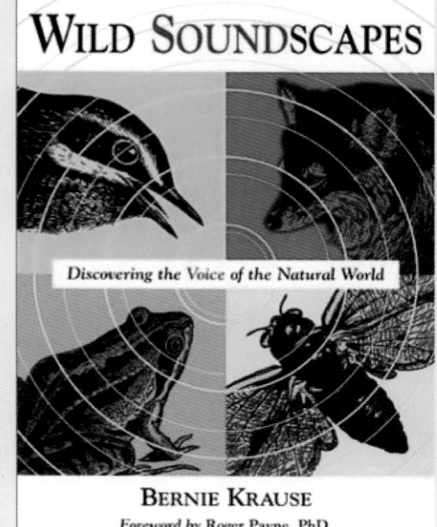

•

Every living creature has a sound signature—from the smallest microorganism to the largest megafauna. Even vegetation! Once, I was sent to record corn growing in Iowa. I sat in a remote field for two hot August nights with my recorder and mics, swarmed by mosquitoes and fighting off flies. Around midnight, I heard slight popping sounds which grew into lots of popping sounds as the stalks of corn telescoped and grew in length almost imperceptibly in the moonlight. The friction caused them to squeak and pop, hence the sound signature of corn growing. Every sound connected in a vibrant interrelationship magnified by the use of my recording gear. I'm still trying to find words to describe the voice of growing corn.

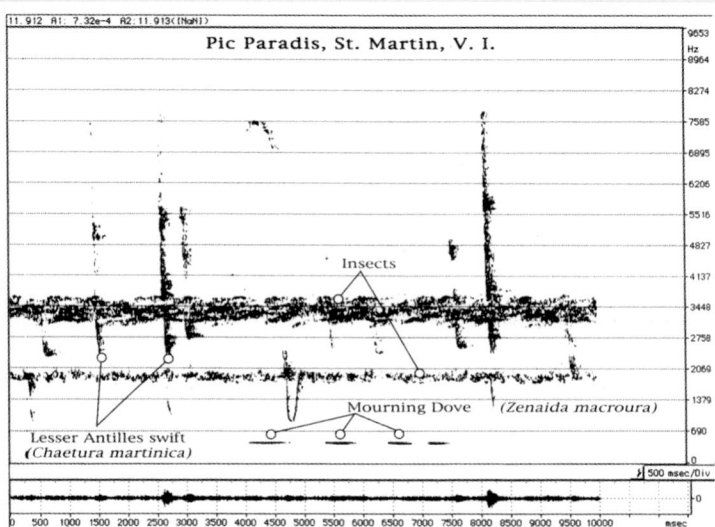

Fig. 3.1 Pic Paradis, St. Martin, V. I., secondary growth biophony spectrogram

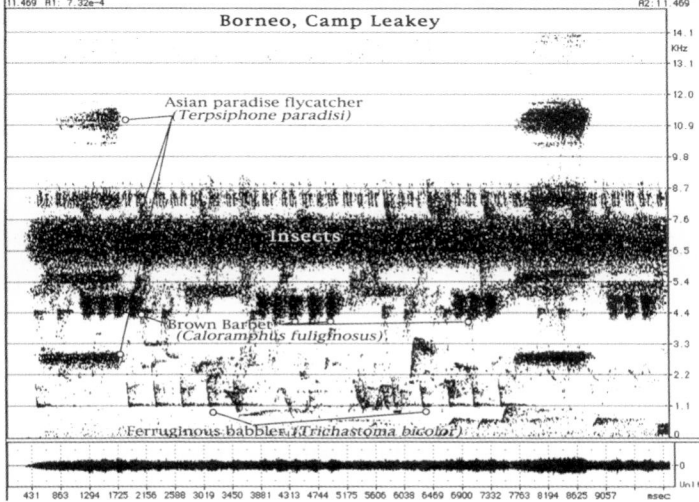

Fig. 3.2 Camp Leakey, Borneo, primary old-growth biophony spectrogram

---

Bargain superior binoculars
Nikon 7540 Monarch Binoculars

$230 Amazon

Do high-priced optics really make much difference in a pair of binoculars? Yes. Great optics create a very bright image within a large viewing area, so that it feels as if you are looking through a magic window rather than squinting through a tiny peephole. Your eyes scan the scope easily, as if there were no glass in front of them — except everything is closer. You can watch longer, in dimmer light, without fatigue, which is what you want for birding, sporting, or boating. If great optics are squeezed into a lightweight waterproof small object you can hold this magic window longer without the shakes. In short, superior optics make distance viewing clearer, easier, weather tolerant and all around better. According to the Cornell Ornithology Lab and Birder's World, the best buy for high-quality optics birding binoculars are the Nikon Monarchs. The go for about $230 on the street.

These are startlingly bright, wide-eyed, and lightweight (21.5 oz), which has made the Monarchs a best seller. Because they are waterproof and shockproof — with an amazing 25-year warranty — they are also very popular with hunters. They can also focus as close as 8 feet — ideal for dragonfly and butterfly viewing (thus the name Monarch).

If you have not examined binoculars recently they are undergoing a performance curve similar to cameras, getting better and cheaper each year. These $340 binocs would have cost $1,000 only 5 years ago. When friends view these Nikon Monarchs, they go "Wow! It's like a movie screen!" I've found the ease of viewing — sort of like watching a flat screen rather than peering through a tube — encourages me to use them more. I also like the fact they are waterproof so I can use them in the rain and mist without worry. I wear prescription sunglasses and these work perfectly fine with them. They also feel well-balanced in my medium hands. I find I can hold them fairly steady for long periods of time with one hand. None of this was true with my inexpensive binoculars in the past.

The very best binoculars today go for $2,000. But for only $230 (what I paid), or one tenth the price, you can get a pair of these Nikon Monarch binoculars and get 95% of the same performance. Sure, in a one-to-one comparison, a pair of $2,000 binoculars may be a little better, but they are not 10 times better.

Other new models share many of the same features of these 8×42 Monarchs, including sealed optics, waterproofing, coated glass, and bright viewing, but these others cost a minimum of $500-600. There are certainly cheaper binocs (you can get decent ones for $50) but they suffer from dim views, narrow fields, short lives. The Nikon Monarchs make a fantastic tool: You get most of a thousand-dollar view for a bargain price.

-- *KK*

$24 Nick Baker, 2005, 256 p.

Best nature how-to
The Amateur Naturalist

The best hands-on-guide to nature experiments in print. Chock full of projects doable in a few hours to a day, whether you are an adult or kid. Just outside your door, no matter where you live, is the largest laboratory available anywhere. Hello, living neighborhood!

– *KK*

Mounting and displaying bones.

Forget plastic model-making – this is the ultimate model kit!

•

Resist the temptation to collect lots of spawn or tadpoles. Though you often come across huge quantities in the wild, only a few percent of it will survive. So collect a small quantity of newly laid spawn – it should be quite firm and easy to separate with your finger. Half a cupful is an ideal quantity to achieve a ratio of three to five tadpoles for every liter of water (14-22 per gallon).

Take spawn from garden ponds wherever possible – it keeps your impact and disturbance of wild populations to a minimum. It is also good practice not to risk contaminating a habitat by introducing spawn, pond weed, or any other form of life that you have collected elsewhere. This is commonsense herpetological hygiene. Frogs in particular suffer from contagious diseases that may be spread unnecessarily in this way.

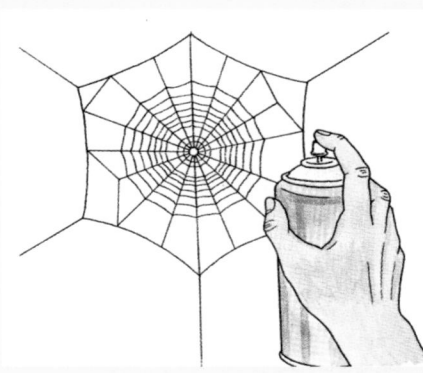

Although the very fragility of a spider's web is part of its attraction, it is a shame to think that these phenomenal feats of design and construction rarely last longer than a day. However, if you find a web without a spider in residence, it is possible to collect and preserve one of these fabulous structures. Choose a still day and make sure the web is dry, with no droplets of dew.

You will need:

the most gorgeous orb web you can find

a sheet of newspaper

a can of white or black spray paint

a can of artist's fixative (available at art shops) or hair spray

a sheet of cardboard large enough to fit the web on and in a color that contrasts well with the paint

scissors

1. Position the newspaper behind the web so that you don't get paint all over whatever is behind it, then spray the web evenly and lightly on both sides from a distance of about 40 cm (16 in) – much closer and the pressure of the paint will damage the web. Leave it to dry for a while and repeat.

This book was produced right about here, at 37.61407, -122.47339

Are You Really Here Now?
The Big Here Quiz

You live in the big here. Wherever you live, your tiny spot is deeply intertwined within a larger place, imbedded fractal-like into a whole system called a watershed, which is itself integrated with other watersheds into a tightly interdependent biome. (See the world eco-region map above). At the ultimate level, your home is a cell in an organism called a planet. All these levels interconnect. What do you know about the dynamics of this larger system around you? Most of us are ignorant of this matrix. But it is the biggest interactive game there is. Hacking it is both fun and vital.

The following exercise in watershed awareness was hatched 30 years ago by Peter Warshall, naturalist extraordinaire. Variations of this list have appeared over the years with additions by Jim Dodge, Peter Berg, and Stephanie Mills among others. I have added new questions, and I have edited or altered most of the rest. It's still a work in progress. If you have a universal question you think fits, submit it to me.

The intent of this quiz is to inspire you to answer the questions you can't initially.

-- KK

30 questions to elevate your awareness (and literacy) of the greater place in which you live:

1. Point north.
2. What time is sunset today?
3. Trace the water you drink from rainfall to your tap.
4. When you flush, where do the solids go? What happens to the waste water?
5. How many feet above sea level are you?
6. What spring wildflower is consistently among the first to bloom here?
7. How far do you have to travel before you reach a different watershed? Can you draw the boundaries of yours?
8. Is the soil under your feet, more clay, sand, rock or silt?
9. Before your tribe lived here, what did the previous inhabitants eat and how did they sustain themselves?
10. Name five native edible plants in your neighborhood and the season(s) they are available.
11. From what direction do storms generally come?
12. Where does your garbage go?
13. How many people live in your watershed?
14. Who uses the paper/plastic you recycle from your neighborhood?
15. Point to where the sun sets on the equinox. How about sunrise on the summer solstice?
16. Where is the nearest earthquake fault? When did it last move?
17. Right here, how deep do you have to drill before you reach water?
18. Which (if any) geological features in your watershed are, or were, especially respected by your community, or considered sacred, now or in the past?
19. How many days is the growing season here (from frost to frost)?
20. Name five birds that live here. Which are migratory and which stay put?
21. What was the total rainfall here last year?
22. Where does the pollution in your air come from?
23. If you live near the ocean, when is high tide today?
24. What primary geological processes or events shaped the land here?
25. Name three wild species that were not found here 500 years ago. Name one exotic species that has appeared in the last 5 years.
26. What minerals are found in the ground here that are (or were) economically valuable?
27. Where does your electric power come from and how is it generated?
28. After the rain runs off your roof, where does it go?
29. Where is the nearest wilderness? When was the last time a fire burned through it?
30. How many days till the moon is full?

The Bigger Here Bonus Questions:

31. What species once found here are known to have gone extinct?
32. What other cities or landscape features on the planet share your latitude?
33. What was the dominant land cover plant here 10,000 years ago?
34. Name two places on different continents that have similar sunshine/rainfall/wind and temperature patterns to here.

My 8-inch home-made ecosphere adjacent to a commercial 4-inch Ecocosm. Mine has been going 10 years.

No maintenance micro-world
EcoCosm/EcoSphere

As I write, a dozen brine shrimp dart about in the bowls on my desk. They nibble on green algae coating the rocks inside. I have never fed them, nor cleaned the bowl, nor aerated their water. In fact their home is sealed airtight in a glass globe; nothing goes in or out. They are completely carefree pets, living in a completely self-sustaining world. The algae produce food and oxygen from room light, the shrimp and snails make carbon dioxide for the plants. Together all three organisms support each other with no input from me, other than admiration. Their globes are little sustainable planets of sorts, a balanced ecosystem that could in theory continue indefinitely. One of my spheres thrived for many years before accidently being smashed.

I keep these micro-worlds for three reasons: 1) as a lazy-man's aquarium (vacation? You could leave for ten years and they wouldn't care), 2) for the constant reminder of how we humans are kept alive by other species, and 3) for the inspiration of a self-sustaining whole system.

You can purchase a ready-made small 4-inch Ecosphere filled with about three shrimp, one snail and a bit of algae,

sealed airtight in a perfect glass sphere for $65. The same producer has other larger models, but this one is about the size of a softball. A system this small is very sensitive to room conditions, and it is easy to kill off the inhabitants before you find the optimal place in a room — which is warm but (surprisingly) not brightly lit. With this off-the-shelf option you get an instant world (works as a gift), but one with few individuals and a somewhat delicate balance. My shrimp and snails are still going strong 10 years later.

For the same price you can assemble a much larger — and better– eco-habitat at home by purchasing a small kit from EcoCosm in Hawaii and upgrading the bowl. Order the smallest size micro-habitat ($40), which will give you about a dozen or more Hawaiin brine shrimp, a few snails, and a beautiful bit of porous rock and gravel seeded with algae, all afloat in sea water and packed with a small plastic hexagonal container. Discard the container and substitute a glass fish bowl. I found the best and cheapest spherical bowls are not sold in pet stores but in art stores for use in decorating, holding glass marbles and the like. I got an 8-inch globe for $4. I put in the creatures, the rocks, and then added brine water (1 part sea water to 2 parts fresh water) to top it off. I cut a small circle of plastic to seal the top. The shrimp (about 1/2 inch long when mature) are amazingly visible and active during the day. They constantly distract in a good way.

The question many owners of these brine shrimp/algae worlds want to know is, how long will they live and can the shrimp reproduce? My world has been thriving for 10 years so far, with no deaths. While an individual shrimp can live for up to 10 years, unlike most marine invertebrates, the endemic Hawaiian red brine shrimp (Halocaridian rubra) reproduce very sparingly. This is why they are expensive to culture (and why it is illegal to use wild brine shrimp from the rare anchialine ponds). There are reports of Ecospheres hatching shrimp fry, but they are rare enough to offer little hope yours will. However, even if the shrimp die, the algae will continue to live for decades or longer — an additional ecological lesson.

From my observations of the micro-habitats that friends and I have owned it is clear that the usual cause of decline is too much light. Room light, even dull overhead fluorescent in a Dilbert cubicle, is all the light these worlds need. The tiny orbs of self-sustaining life are great instructional aids. If you like living things nearby but don't like the slavery of upkeep, these are perfect pet/gardens, and ideal office mates.

May you be a fine god!

-- KK

$50 EcoCosm Shrimp Microhabitat
ecosaqua

**$60 4"
EcoSphere**
Amazon

Landscape Visualization

$9
Underground
David
Macaulay,
1983, 112 p.

$17 Built to
Last David
Macaulay,
2010, 272 p.

Understanding big buildings
David Macaulay's Visualizations

Few have mastered the big picture better than artist David Macaulay. When a kid wants to know about pyramids or castles introduce him/her to Macaulay's books. Macaulay dissects the parts in kid-obsessive detail while keeping his eye on the whole. And he shows how it all grows in time. His uncanny ability to x-ray complex places makes him the master guide to the built world. Of all his books, *Underground* is his most revelatory. Even adults will find themselves studying each page of "the city underneath the city" in aha enlightenment. Oh, so THAT'S how it works! Macaulay revisited three of his early books -- *Castle*, *Cathedral*, and *Mosque*-- creating new even more amazing visualizations, and combined the books into one new book called *Built to Last*. It's a short course on civilization for kids.

-- *KK*

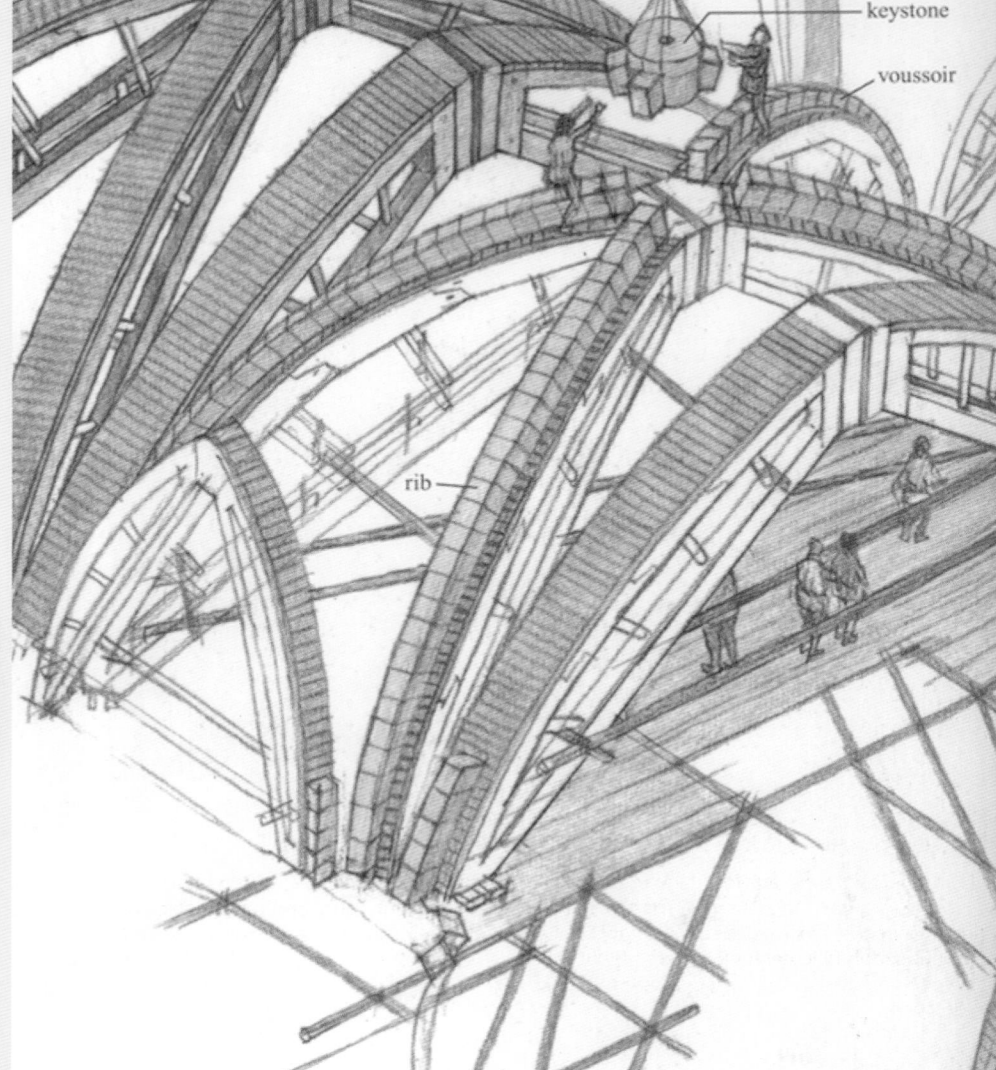

From
Underground

Never waste a crisis. - Anon

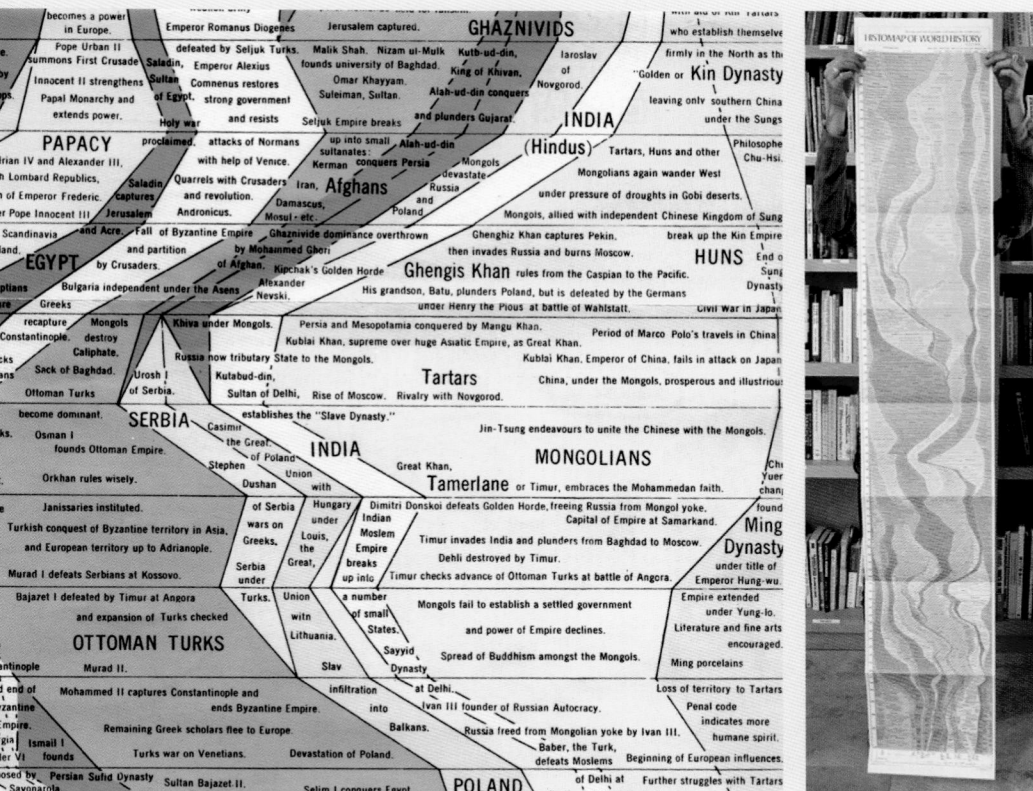

Understanding geological and biological time
Correlated History of Earth

$25, 27" x 37" Correlated History of Earth

The long view. Or rather, views. Geological time and biological time run at such different paces that the two perspectives are not easily brought together. This crisp chart joins them with extraordinary clarity. It lays out the chronologies of continents skittering around the globe, of comet and asteroid impacts, and of life's increasingly diverse groups of living creatures and how they fit into geological time. And more. Ordinarily, combining such staggering amounts of information would yield mush and muddle. But this large, exquisitely printed, laminated poster manages to present 4.5 billion years of geology and biology as the unified whole that it is. Like a good map it teaches something at two feet away, or you can get out a magnifying glass and read down for details.

-- KK

From the chart's Web site:

"Included are plate tectonic maps, mountain building events (orogenies), major volcanic episodes, glacial epochs, all known craters from asteroid and comet impacts, over 100 classic fossil localities from around the world, fossil ranges of plants, invertebrates and vertebrate life forms, and major extinction events as revealed by the fossil record. Also evident on this chart are the "Cambrian explosion" of animal phyla and the juxtaposition of reptiles and mammals across the Cretaceous/Tertiary (K/T) boundary. Hundreds of illustrations add a striking visual dimension to the data."

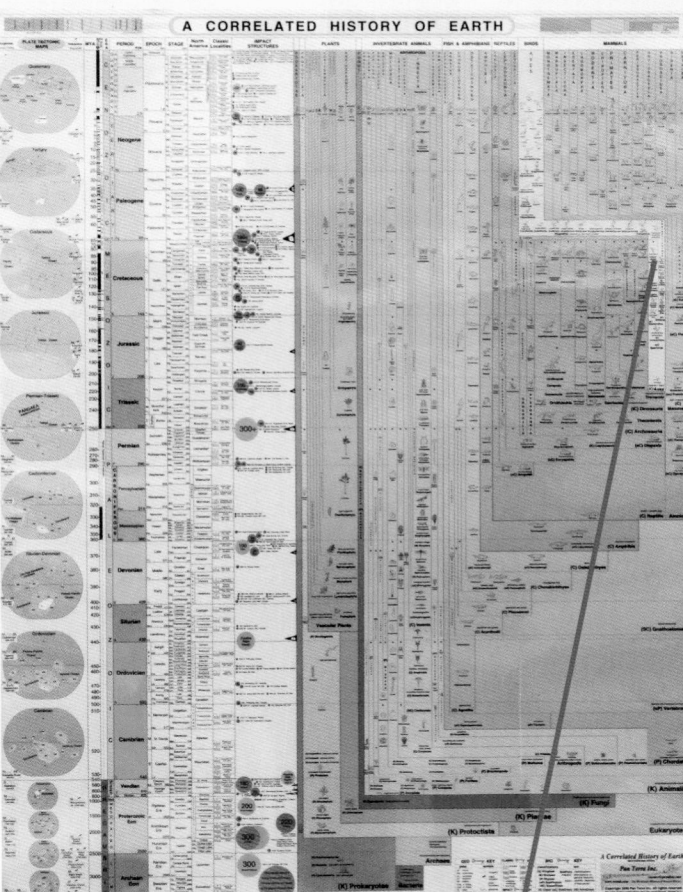

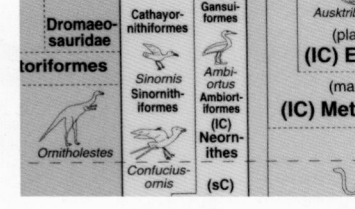

Compact timeline of global history
Histomap of World History

$20 (with $12 shipping), 12" x 78" jacquieglanz@yahoo.com

Not a map really, but a 5-foot-high chart showing in one glance 4,000 years of human history on a global scale. Thirty years ago I saw this on the wall of someone's dorm room and it flipped me out then, and every time I've seen it since. Its beauty is how Mr. Sparks divies up world power (somewhat crudely) into its main factions graphed in each increment of fifty years since 2000 B.C.E. Different civilizations are color-coded so one can easily trace the flow and ebb of culture over the centuries.

It has three uses for me: whenever I am reading about some historical event I can instantly see what else was going on in the world at that time (for instance, what was happening in France during the Ming Dynasty). I also get a very intuitive sense of the rises and falls of civilizations, a pattern that no other chart or book has been able to give me. And hanging on the wall, it never fails to elicit gaps of shock when visitors recognize our modern place in the chart. At twenty bucks, it's a bargain education.

The only way to buy a paper version is to send $32 via PayPal to Jacquie Glanz: jacquieglanz@yahoo.com. Or you can find a free very high resolution interactive scan at davidrumsey.com.

-- KK

5,000 years of history in one square meter
Diagrammatic Chart of World History

€20, 32" x 45" Editions.Sides

Simply the best overview of the *long now* I am aware of. Displays with utmost intelligence 50 centuries of civilization, as revealed in the complex rise and fall of ancient powers. Because it is not as linear as the famous Histomap, it is not as handy for quickly locating a fact in time, but its extra dimensions make this diagram the one I keep returning to to grok the past 5,000 years.

-- KK

Flippant, but painless, world history

Cartoon History of the Universe (Volumes 1, 2, 3)
$16 Larry Gonick, 2002, 307 p.

Larry Gonick, the over-educated cartoonist, doodled an awesome series of book-length comic-strips that illustrate ancient history. The first began at the Big Bang, zipped through pre-history and explored the Greeks. His second tackled everything up to the fall of Rome. His last 300-page installment covers the rise of Arabia and the role of "Orientals" in crafting the culture we have today. In Gonick's hands history is a hoot, and very much about ideas. I particularly savor his last volume because by moving the center of the universe somewhere east of Europe — delving into Islam, Africa and East Asia — Gonick's cartoons can remedy the ignorance and arrogance of the west. Laugh your way to enlightenment!   -- KK

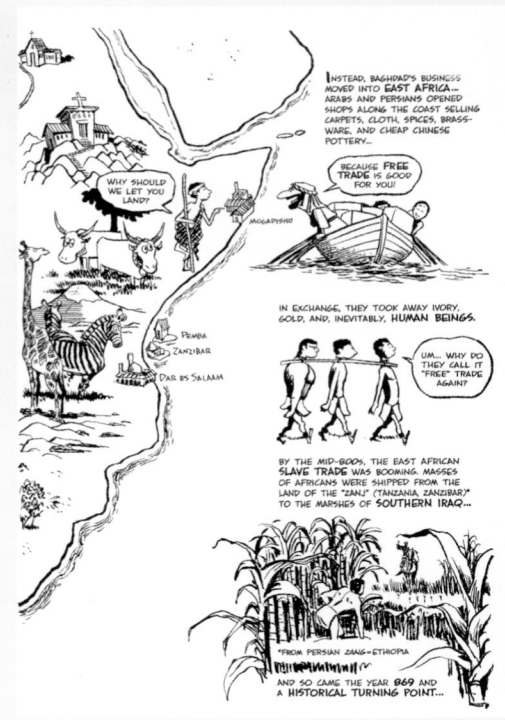

The difference between theory and practice is always greater in practice than it is in theory. - Anon

*Memorable immersive
history series*

1900 House
Frontier House
Colonial House

$90 1900 House DVD Amazon (also on Netflix)
$25 Frontier House * Colonial House DVD Amazon

The premise of these three reality-TV programs is brilliant. For the first, take an ordinary middle class family of the year 2000 and make them live for 6 months like an ordinary middle class family of the year 1900. The London-based producers succeed in this transformation by getting every detail of Victorian domestic life exactly right and complete. The volunteer family is plunked down in a different era as if by time machine, and there is no escape. No shampoo, either. The edited 6-hour result is deep, instructive, and totally riveting. Kids who hate history are mesmerized by it. Because it is so visual and visceral, it changed the discussion of chores and gender roles in our household. Better than 100 essays, this video series reveals the notion of progress. It is now my favorite history "book."

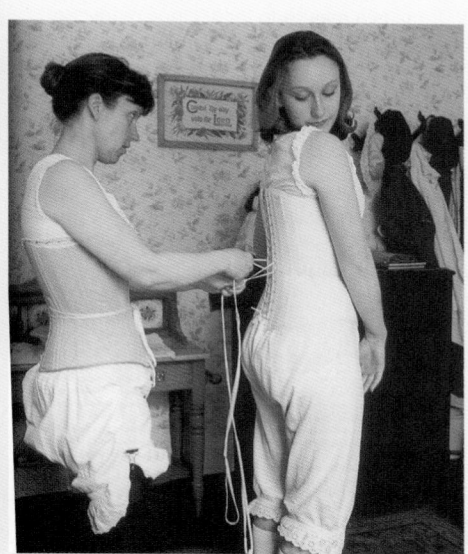

▲ *Two sisters help each other tighten their corsets, a binding which makes housework difficult. Putting one on was a major chore itself.* ▼ *Every morning the family members need to empty the pee pot from the night before.*

The success of *1900 House* spawned *Frontier House*, a parallel experiment that transfers the conceit to the edge of Montana in 1893 during homesteading days. It ups the challenge by requiring the participants to build their homesteads and raise all their own food while sticking to period tools and the lifestyle of pioneers. The three families who settle in a beautiful valley need to stockpile enough food, shelter and firewood to last a Montanan winter. Instead of cooperating, they compete against each other, making this remarkable 6 hours series into what *Survivor* should have been – an authentic test of surviving. There is probably no greater persuader of women's inequality than this pair of films. The guys loved being pioneers, while the women and girls were imprisoned by it.

In the last to be made, *Colonial House*, the premise is now familiar -- only with fewer tools. Make a modern family live with only the tools

▲ *After camping in a tent and cooking outside, one mother rejoices as their log cabin takes shape. Later her husband (above) needs to finish their house before winter sets in.* ▼ *Water is hauled in by the "servants."*

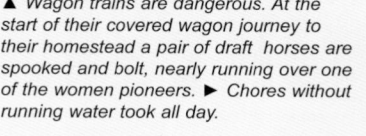

▲ *Wagon trains are dangerous. At the start of their covered wagon journey to their homestead a pair of draft horses are spooked and bolt, nearly running over one of the women pioneers.* ▶ *Chores without running water took all day.*

and resources available four centuries ago. The suburban families are sent to live in the summer of 1628, on a forested island off of Maine. Their task: build a New World colony (20 people strong) that can both survive and pay back its investors in England. Life is pretty grungy. Two families to a room; no outhouses.

Of the three programs *Colonial House* is the best, in part because of the reality show-like drama and bickering between the colonists. They fight over religion, status, and food. Cameras record every detail as the pudgy newcomers scrounge for scraps, learn how to farm Indian corn, all the while slowly starving, and assuming appropriate roles such as indentured servants with astounding ease. Who knew how easy devolution was? Like the hit TV series *Survivor*, it's about how primeval people get when survival is at stake. But unlike *Survivor*, there's genuine historical logic, authentic rituals, and significant meaning in their test. If I had to choose one of these three historical re-enactments, I'd start with this one, the 8-hour *Colonial House*. But if I could, I would require every child in 21st century America to view all three series. These are the nearest things yet to a time machine.

-- *KK*

▲ *Laundry is laid out to dry on the grass beside the huts.* ▼ *Exhaustion adds to the grief when a boyfriend is hurt in an accident.*

First person accounts

Eyewitness To History

Most of what you read about what happened in the past is written by someone who read what someone else read about it. Here is a diverse collection of short first-hand, eyewitness accounts of what proved later to be important events. Vivid, uncensored, naked testimony from someone there at the time. Make up your own mind.

-- *KK*

● Landing in New England, November 1620
William Bradford.

New England had been named by captain John Smith, who explored its shores in 1614. The first permanent settlement was made at Plymouth, Massachusetts, in

1620 by the Pilgrim Fathers aboard the Mayflower, whose arrival is described here.

About ten a clocke we came into a deepe Valley, full of brush, wood-gaile, and long grasse, through which wee found little paths or tracts, and there we saw a Deere, and found springs of fresh Water, of which we were hartily glad, and sat us downe and drunke our first New England water, with as much delight as ever we drunk drink in all our lives.

When we had refreshed ourselves, we directed our course full south, that wee might come to the shore, which within a short while after we did, and there made a fire, that they in the ship might see where we were (as wee had direction) and so marched on towards this supposed River: and as we went in another Valley, we found a fine cleere Pond of fresh water, being about a Musket shot broad, and twice as long: there grew also many small Vines, and Fowle and Deere haunted there: there grew much Sasafras: from thence we went on and found much plain ground about fif-

tie Acres fit for the Plow, and some signes where the Indians had formerly planted their Corne: after this, some thought it best for nearnesse of the River to goe downe and travaile on the Sea sands, by which meanes some of our men were tired, and lagged behinde, so we stayed and gathered them up, and strucke into the Land againe; where we found a little path to certaine heapes of Sand, one whereof was covered with old Mats and had a wooden thing like a Morter whelmed on the top of it, and an earthen pot laid in a little hole at the tend thereof; we musing what it might be digged and found a Bowe, and as we though, Arrowes, but they were rotten; W supposed there were many other things, but because we deemed them graves, we put in the Bow againe and made it up as it was, and left the rest untouched, because we thought it would be odious unto them to ransacke their Sepulchers. We went on further and found new stubble of which they had gotten Corne this yeare, and many Walnut trees full of Nuts, and great store of strawberries, and some vines: passing thus a field or two, which were

not great, we came to another, which had also bin new gotten, and there wee found where an house had beene, and foure or five old Plankes laied together, also we found a great kettle, which had been some Ships kettle and brought out of Europe; there was also an heape of sand, made like the former, but it was newly done, wee might see how they had padled it with their hands, which we digged up, and in it wee found a little old Basket full of faire Indian Corne of this yeare, with some sixe and thirty goodly eares of Corne, some yellow, and some red, and others mixt with blew, which was a very goodly sight: the Basket was round, and narrow at the top, it held about three or foure bushels, which was as

much as two of us could lift up from the ground, and was very handsomely and cunningly made.

$16 John Carey, ed., 1997 (Reprint edition), 752 p.

Free Website
Eyewitness To History

Cosmos

Picture of everything
The Universe Map

$14 20" x 31" map
Amazon

The first modern map of the known universe. Spacey. Trippy. An ingenious design locates our habitat in the very grand order of things.

-- KK

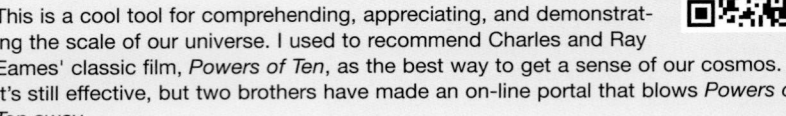

Understanding scale
The Scale of the Universe 2
Free Scale of the Universe

This is a cool tool for comprehending, appreciating, and demonstrating the scale of our universe. I used to recommend Charles and Ray Eames' classic film, *Powers of Ten*, as the best way to get a sense of our cosmos. It's still effective, but two brothers have made an on-line portal that blows *Powers of Ten* away.

Check out *The Scale of the Universe 2*. It takes a minute to load. Once ready, be prepared to have your horizons stretched. I like the way they pile in the expected and unexpected size examples, which anchor the scale in a refreshing way. The continuous zoom is what makes this device work, rather than the quantum powers of ten of the film. (In fact you can read off the powers of ten in this model as well.) And the fact that you drive the slider. And like anytime you drive, you get a better sense of the place than you do as a mere passenger.

For the first time, I really got a visceral sense of our place in the universe. As many have noted before (but none have explained) we — our visible bodies — are located approximately in the middle of the universe's size range. The largest things we know and the smallest things we know are roughly the same magnitude away from us.

And BTW, this app is what electronic "publishing" is really about.

-- KK

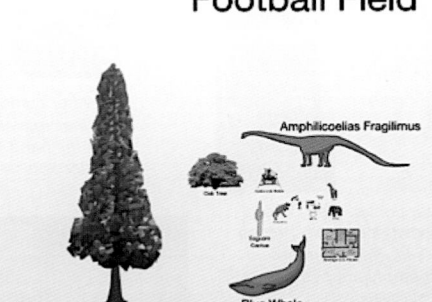

Timeline of the universe and everything
Universal Heritage

Free (must have Scribd account) Scribd

This chart rewards careful study. Inspect one timeline of the universe from the Big Bang to yesterday. It skips through this vast scale in 16 jumps, each period nested inside the preceding epic. Combined here is cosmic history, geological history, biological history and cultural history into one unified, universal snapshot of the Great Story.

-- KK

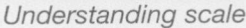

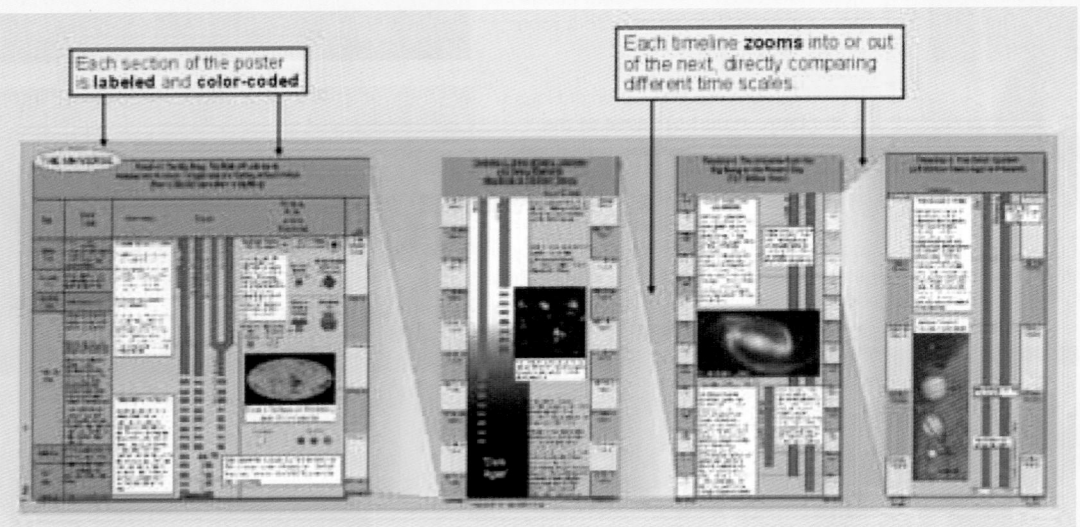

Here we are
Universe

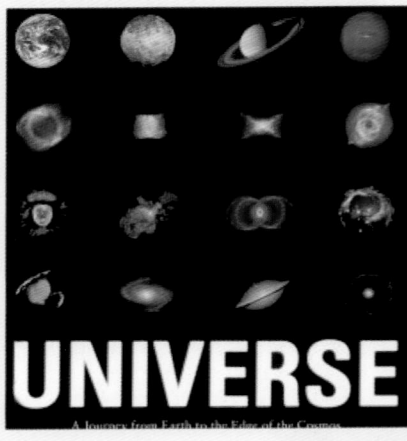

$30 Nicholas Cheetham, 2009, 224 pages

So far this is my favorite one-volume gallery of the other inhabitants in our universe. Organized by ascending distance from us, it includes portraits of known planets, remarkable stars, flamboyant nebulae, and outstanding galaxies. Better than any other atlas, or map, or online source, this book gives you a really good picture of this place called the universe.

-- KK

• Uranus
Planet
163 light minutes

Uranus' northern hemisphere is emerging from the grip of a long, dark, winter. Winters on Uranus are compounded by the fact that at the poles the Sun does not rise for 21 years as a consequence of the planet's extreme axial tilt. As sunlight returns, the frigid atmosphere warms stirring spring storms that blow bright clouds of crystallized methane before them at up to 420 kph (260 mph).

• Ant Nebula Mz3
Planetary nebula
3 thousand light years

Another addition to our menagerie of dying stars is this light-year-sized stellar insect. No common-or-garden variety of nebula, this creature surpasses all its cousins by producing a record breaking 3.6 million kph (2.1 million mph) outflow of charged particles. Such is the spectacular diversity of planetary nebulae, one might be forgiven for eagerly anticipating our own Sun's demise.

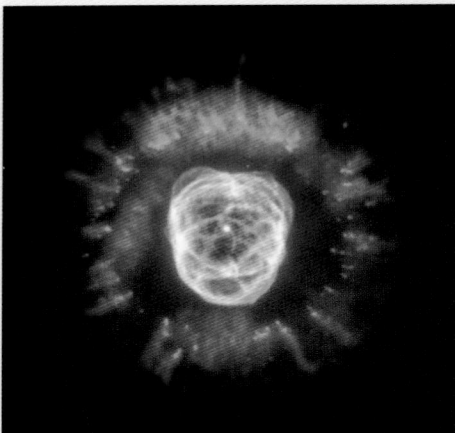

• Eskimo Nebula NGC2392
Planetary nebula
5 thousand light years

This Eskimo's parka disguises another bipolar planetary nebula. Its second lobe is concealed directly behind this one – we are viewing the nebula edge on. The parka's orange fur trim is though to be formed by slow-moving globules of gas streaming in an eroding flow of faster-moving material. And it is moving quickly: this Eskimo's hood is growing at 1.5 million kph (900,000 mph).

The best way to predict the future is to invent it. - Alan Kay

Best beginner telescope
Celestron FirstScope
$42 celestron.com

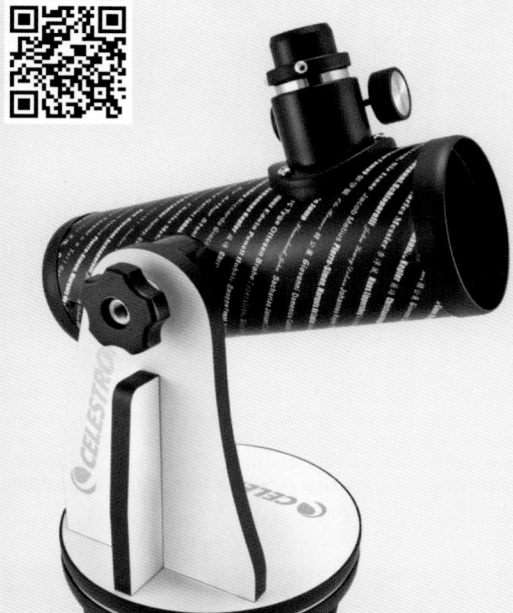

The Celestron FirstScope is the best pick for an absolute beginner level telescope. Most entry-level scopes are crap, and most useable scopes start at $300. Since the FirstScope costs only $42, you might be tempted to dismiss it as more useless junk. But I've been using the FirstScope, and it is sweet. It needs a sturdy chair or table to perch on, but otherwise is easy to handle. It is compact for storage; it can fit onto a shelf -- and it is the perfect size for a small kid. Pretty durable, too. With its 3-inch mirror you can see moons of Jupiter, rings of Saturn, and lunar craters. (I missed that recent comet.) Many other buyers mention that if you substitute decent eyepieces (from another scope) it improves the view tremendously. With one of those you can view a few bright galaxies. It will also focus as close as 30 feet away; we've used it as a terrestrial telephoto lens to scan the wildlife on the mountain behind our house.

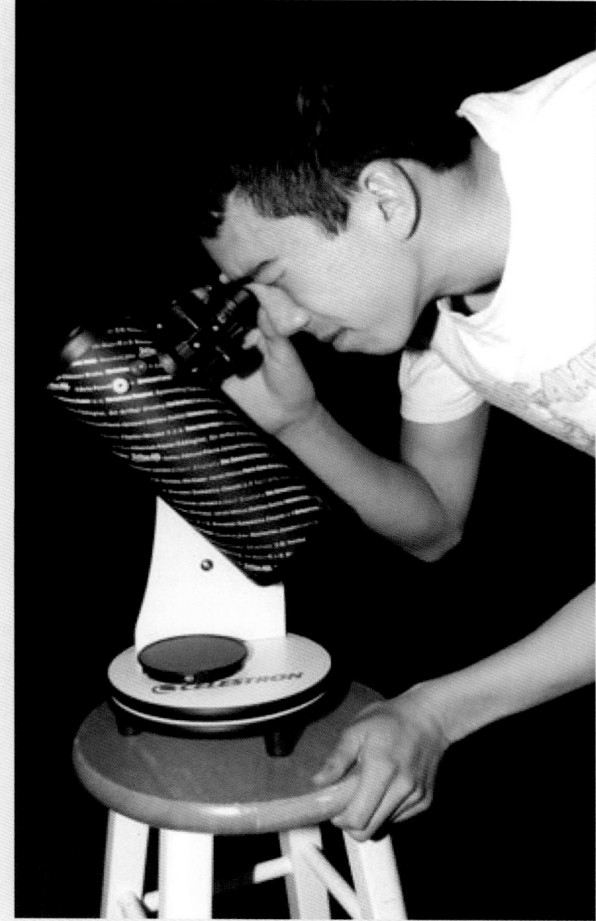

This is an adequate first telescope to try out sky watching for a small investment. If you want to invest into a higher quality telescope, I recommend Ed Ting's reviews at ScopeReview. It was Ed Ting's raves about this little gem that turned me onto the FirstScope in the first place.

-- KK

Map of the greater neighborhood
Sky Atlas 2000.0
$330 (used) Wil Tirion and Roger W. Sinnott, 1999 (2nd edition), 30 pages (26 charts)

This is the definitive atlas of stars for backyard star gazers. Large charts accurately map any star you can see from Earth with amateur optics. There are a lot of them; about 80,000 (visible to magnitude 8.5). Professional atlases list fainter objects, and field guidebooks like Peterson's may be more portable, but the Star Atlas 2000 is now the standard reference star catalog for serious buffs navigating into deep space.

-- KK

[Sky Atlas 2000.0, 2nd edition, is available in a confusing array of versions: Deluxe (black stars, white sky, color deep-sky objects), spiralbound, or hardcover, or in two black-and-white versions: Field (white stars in black sky), or the inverse Desk (black stars in whites sky). Both black-and-white versions are available either as loose charts, boxed, or as laminated pages, spiralbound. The consensus among amateur astronomers is that the spiralbound deluxe version of black stars on white sky with color objects is the most useful.]

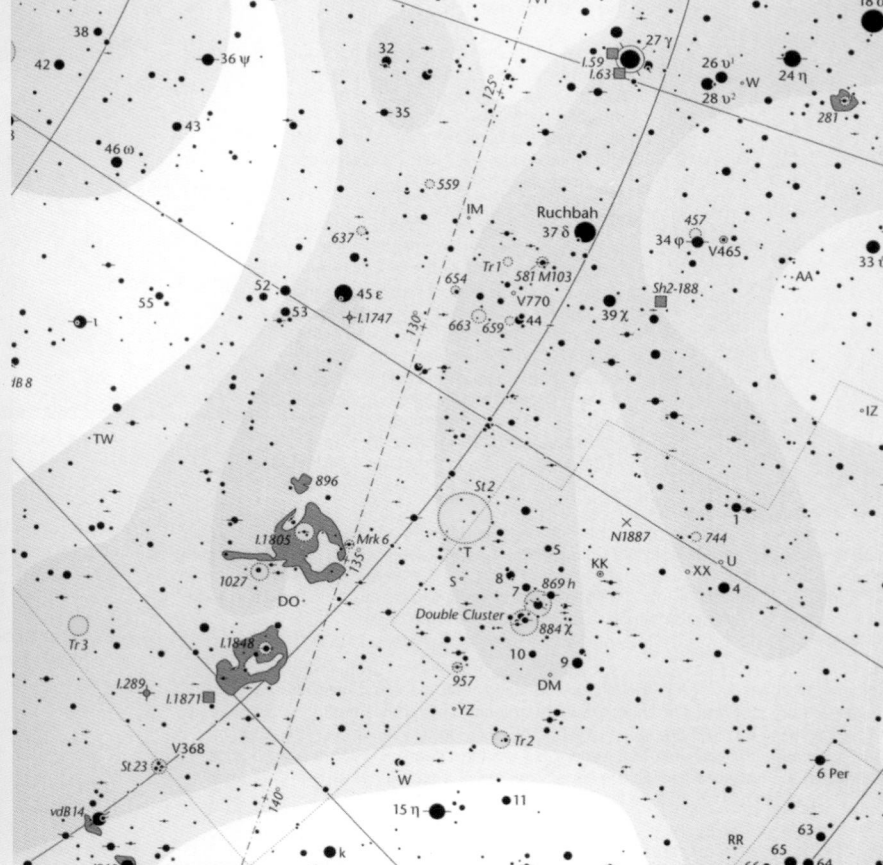

Augmented astronomy iOS app
Sky View
$2 iTunes Store

Judging from the reviews in the App Store I am not the first to be enchanted by Sky View, the augmented reality astronomy app. When I point my phone camera at the night sky this app displays the heavens, as if through a window, overlaid with the specks of stars, at appropriately varying brightness. (The phone's sensors tell the program which way it is pointed, and computes the simulation on screen.)

It also shows planets and satellites in the proper place in the sky. Tap a celestial object, and its name appears, just where the object is in the sky covered by your screen. The effect gives the impression the annotation is happening on the sky itself. It's quite magical and couldn't be easier to use. The paths of the planets are traceable as a thick yellow line, and as your finger slides along the line, you can see the times when the planet will arrive at this point in the sky. Constellations appear as ghostly outlines, good for learning. Recently Sky View has been especially fun, with Mercury, Jupiter, and Venus all visible on the western horizon around sunset, and Mars rising overhead at night.

-- Gary Wolf

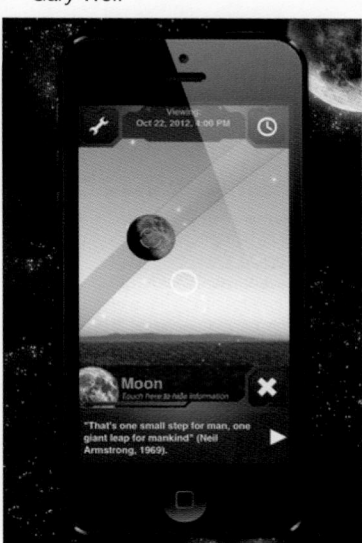

Best backyard astronomy aid
Green Laser Pointer
$58 BTG-3 Class II Green Laser Pointer
Amazon

$80 Starpointer Full-powered 5mW
SkyPointer

$100 Wicked Lasers Classic
WickedLasers.com/Nano

After a telescope, this is the best astronomy educational tool I've seen. At night this AAA battery powered green laser pointer can seemingly touch the stars millions of miles away. Compared to a red laser pointer, the green beam remains visible and penetrates the air much farther. Because of its particular spectrum you see the beam and not just the end dot. Also, it's about 50 times brighter than an ordinary red laser pointer — using the same safe low power. On a clear night it can easily shine a dot a mile away. With its sharp laser beam you can pinpoint the exact star you want, which greatly accelerates mapping and learning the constellations. I've been amazed at how much faster I've learned the heavens with one of these in hand.

The problem with green laser pointers has been their stiff price. Only recently have they dropped below $50, which is still a lot for an educational tool. Manufacturing green laser engines is more art than science so their actual power output varies by final pointer. The lasers are sorted after they are made. The select ones near to the legal "pointer" limit of 5 milliWatts are labeled as such and are priced around $100 these days. The others are labeled as "less than 5mW" or "guaranteed to be up to 5 mW" and are priced as cheap as $40, but their actual power is not stated. For a star pointer all you need is one of these cheap ones. I've been using an inexpensive "up to 5mW" version that works wonderfully.

Incidentally, you can purchase higher powered green lasers from Wicked Lasers that exceed the mandated 5 mW. Their 75 mW green laser goes for $100 and their scary/astounding 1 W for $300. These are incredibly bright at night, but overkill for an astronomy aid.

-- KK

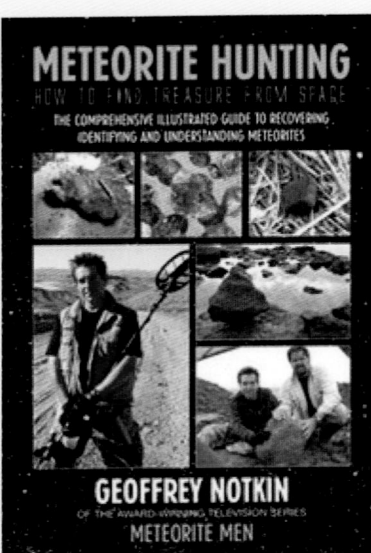

How to find space rocks
Meteorite Hunting
$25 Geoffrey Notkin, 2011, 84 p.

Who can resist the search for alien specimens from space? Most meteorites are small pebbles; they drop all over the planet but are most easily detected in deserts, or in fallen clusters. Finding them requires metal detectors, maps, jeeps, software simulations, chemical analysis, airplane tickets, patience and a lot of luck. The practical lore in this slim how-to manual was previously known only by the close-knit club of professional meteor hunters. As far as I can tell, this is the only book on how to find meteorites; even the web doesn't contain the useful details this guide does. Its 84 color pages discuss the gear, the techniques, and the logical tricks needed to find and excavate a metallic needle in a geographic haystack.

The author is one of the stars of *Meteorite Men*, a TV series which documents the adventures of him and his buddy as they hunt for meteorites in exotic photogenic locations around the world. While meteorite hunting is rarefied hobby right now, it is becoming increasingly regulated as it gains in popularity. Meteorites fall to the ground everyday, but statistically the ones you find will be ancient – a fossil in fact, like gems. You need to obey the local laws even though space rocks are just sitting on (or below) the ground waiting to be picked up. The hard part is still finding them, which this guide will help.

-- KK

The common terrestrial iron oxide hematite is often mistaken for meteorites by novices. Hematite typically does not show any attraction to a magnet and will usually leave a red streak on a white ceramic tile, while an iron meteorite will leave little or no streak. The surface features on some hematite specimens also have a visual resemblance to regmaglypts.

• If you are going to start hunting for meteorites, the one thing I can guarantee is you are going to find meteorwrongs. Your metal detector can only tell you so much; you need to do the rest.

Metal detectors that are used for hunting meteorites are calibrated to return a signal when they find iron. Sophisticated modern hand-held detectors such as the Fisher F75, a personal favorite of mind, have the capability to distinguish between different types of metal.

Picking a meteorwrong from the surface is one thing; digging one up from several feet underground is another. It can be tiring and discouraging to spend half an hour toiling through hard ground with a muddy shovel only to reveal a foot of rusty pipe. That is why, when people ask me what you need in order to be a successful meteorite hunter, I say: "Determination." Be prepared to dig up a lot of trash on your way to finding meteorites, especially in areas that have been farmed, mined, or were once settled.

Excavating a complete 870-gram stone meteorite in the Gold Basin strewnfield. While the exposed surfaces had weathered considerably, fusion crust and regmaglypts were present on the buried sections. It turned out to be the best-preserved fusion crust we had ever seen on a Gold Basin specimen.

A new Nevada stone meteorite lying exactly where it was found. Note the relatively fresh, black fusion crust, indicating a fairly recent fall.

• A "hot rock" is a terrestrial stone that sets off a metal detector. It is an old gold prospector's phrase that has been adopted by meteorite hunters. Is is very important to remember that there are many different types of earth rocks that contain iron, so if your target turns out to be stone, rather than man-made iron trash, do not automatically assume that it is a meteorite.

• The glowing fireballs we see in the sky are caused by atmospheric pressure and friction, but meteors stop ablating while they are at least seven miles high. If you are lucky enough to witness a bright fireball, and it begins dark flight while approaching you or directly overhead, it is possible that meteorites will land nearby. When a fireball apparently lands in the vicinity what we are usually seeing is it arcing away over the horizon, still high up in the atmosphere. Due to the curvature of the earth, the fireball may seem to hit the ground, but has in fact just moved out of our field of view and gone beyond the horizon. Because of their extreme brightness, fireballs can appear — to our human eyes — to be much closer than they really are. It is something I, myself, have been fortunate enough to witness a couple of times, which can be frustrating because it does look as if meteorites landed "just over there." If anything made it to the ground, however, it probably landed hundreds of miles away.

Affordable radiation detector
Pocket Geiger Counter
$300 DX-1 Professional Equipment

The unit is made to check for radioactivity in industrial or geological uses, like testing scrap metal from unknown sources, old uranium glazes on pottery, or possibly contaminated waste sites. The device clicks satisfyingly clearly when it detects three types of radiation. It's bigger than a pocket, but much smaller than the old fashioned vacuum tube variety. It runs off an 9-volt battery.

This device is not sensitive enough to detect natural background radiation, or radiation drift in the atmosphere, or mild exposure on clothing, say. The device has to be very close to the radioactive source. It would have had trouble detecting the radiation during the accident at Chernobyl 500 meters outside of the plant itself. To measure the radiation in uranium ore, for instance, the device has to be just about touching the rock. Stuff has to be significantly "hot" to register, but this is the stuff worth worrying about.

They were hard to find immediately after the Fukushima incidents, but they're back in stock now.

UPDATE: This device is a little bit more sensitive than your classic hand-held geiger counter, and cheaper, and also smaller. It's a good bargain. But geiger counters in general are not extremely sensitive. They can be made more sensitive by wiring them up to count "hits" over hours, days, and weeks instead of per second. See, for example, the Sparkfun geiger kit.

-- KK

• Specs
Operating Range:
0 to 10 mR/hr range on analog meter.
Beeping at 20 mR/hr Continuous Tone at 200 mR/hr.

Sensitivity:
Detects Beta at 35 keV with 90% efficiency or at 1,000 keV with 100% efficiency
Detects Gamma down to 6 keV at 25% efficiency or to 35 keV at 90% efficiency or to 100 keV at 100% efficiency

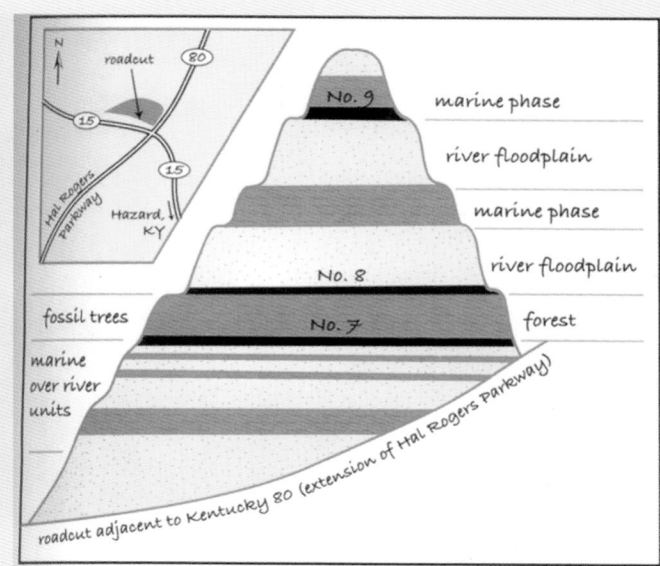

Cross-section (not drawn to scale) of the Four Corners roadcut. The coal seams (black lines) formed in a swamp environment.

101 American Geo-Sites You've Gotta See

$18 Albert B. Dickas, 2012, 264 p.

This will change your vacation plans. Visit your home planet! Geology is a force so huge we don't see it. Yet evenly spread across the US (at least one in each state) are spots where our planetary behavior is made visible, erupting in either grand spectacle or in tiny gems on the ground. I was briefly a geology major in school, so call me geeky: but what bigger vacation can one imagine than inspecting 101 sites where you can see inside the Earth? A surprising number of US national, state, and county parks are dedicated to geologic power points. Other spots may be roadcuts or river beds. Use this guide to find them and interpret their incredible hidden significance.

-- KK

At Dinosaur State Park, intersecting sets of pockmarking footprints give evidence of a well-traveled freeway.

The main attractions at Kelleys Island are the first-order, big-boy grooves deeply scoured into the limestone bedrock at Glacial Grooves State Memorial.

● Gilboa Forest, New York
42° 23' 52" North, 74° 26' 50" West
Devonian Period Fossilization
Only Sandstone casts of stumps and roots remain of this first forest to shade the American landscape.

This Sandstone cast of a Gilboa Forest stump is believed to be the fossilized root remains of a primitive palmlike tree. The basal diameter is 3.5 feet.

● **Meteor Crater, Arizona**

Of the more than 180 impact sites recognized around the world, approximately 25 are in the United States. The recognized godfather of them all, meteor crater is a perfect example of a simple crater — one without a central uplift. It is the most thoroughly investigated and by far the best preserved of the many astroblemes that scar the face of planet Earth.

Fossil Collecting in the Mid-Atlantic States

$25 Jasper Burns, 1991, 216 p.

The only thing wrong with this field guide is that it is restricted to the Mid-Atlantic States. It gives very specific driving directions (alas, no GPS coordinates) to easily accessible sites where one can collect small fossils. And each site and its ancient bounty is depicted in lovely sketches. I wish all guidebooks were like this.

- KK

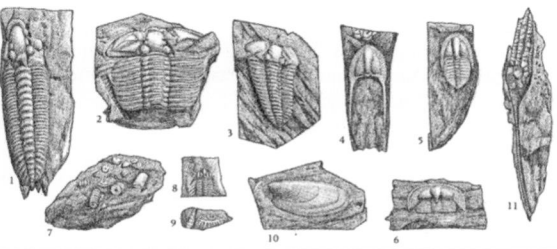

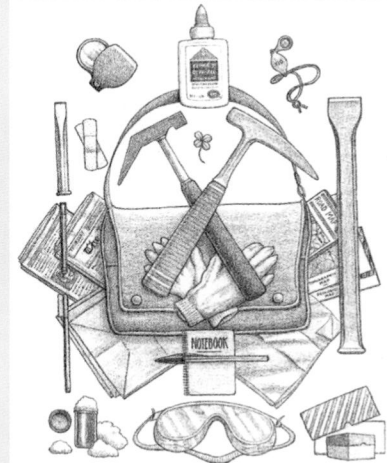

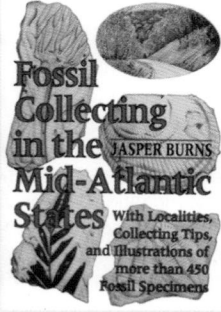

Field gear for the well-equipped fossil collector. Hand lenses (top), Elmer's Glue-All, various sizes of masonry chisels (or cold chisels), bandaids (and other first-aid supplies), a chisel-end and pick-end rock hammer, a rock bag, an assortment of maps, newspapers for wrapping specimens, paper bags, plastic bags, an old toothbrush, a notebook and pen, some cotton, small containers, gloves, safety goggles, and a little bit of luck.

Clouds

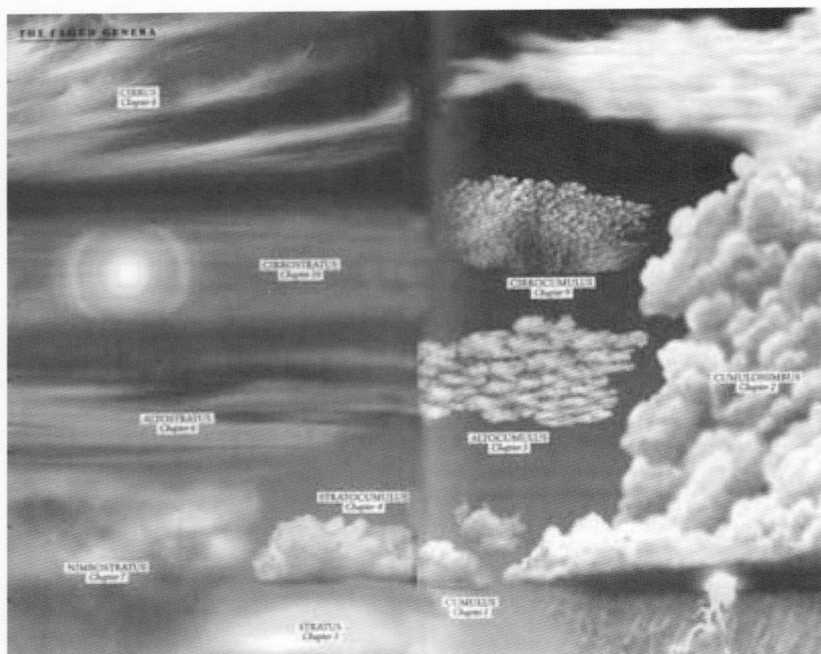

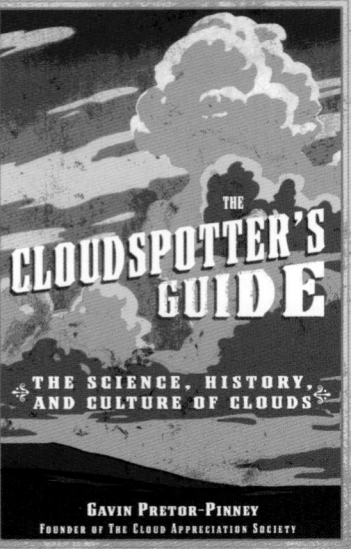

► This rare Cirrus formation is known as a Kelvin-Helmholtz wave cloud and can form in the region between shearing winds, moving in different directions.

► With a population of just 178, Burketown sits in one of Australia's most remote shires. But every September and October, a small group of individuals journey from all corners of the country for the appearance of a remarkable and dramatic cloud called the Morning Glory. Clouds don't usually have names, nor are they normally linked to a particular location, but then the Morning Glory is no normal cloud. Looking like a huge white roll of meringue, it stretches up to 600 miles (about the length of Britain) and sweeps over Burketown at speeds of up to 35mph. The visitors who come to

marvel at this beautiful and awe-inspiring meteorological phenomenon are an intrepid group of glider pilots, for whom the cloud promises the most unique and thrilling flying conditions of anywhere in the world. Each year they come to this sleepy town in the hope of 'soaring' the Morning Glory, an exhilarating gliding adventure that can only be described as cloud-surfing.

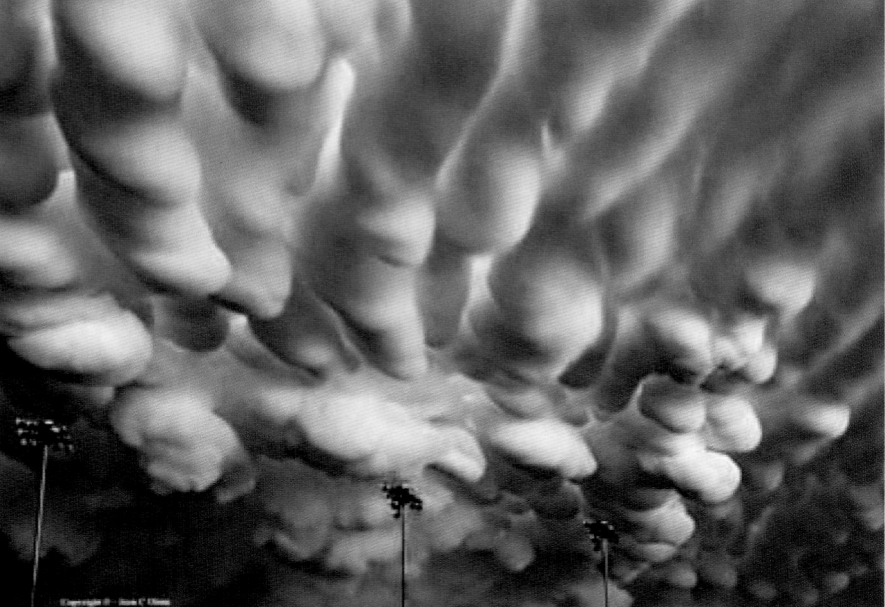

▲ The mamma cloud formations, sometimes known as 'mammatus', are named after the Latin for 'breasts'. As described earlier, these can appear on the underside of a number of different cloud types – Cirrus, Cirrocumulus, Altocumulus, Altostratus, Stratocumulus, and Cumulonimbus – and at their most dramatic look like a field of smooth, globular udders.

They are at their most impressive when wed to a mighty Cumulonimbus. Forming on the underside of its incus, mamma appear when the top of the anvil cools, by radiating heat up into the atmosphere, and parts of it sink into the air below. When this air is relatively warm and humid, some of its water vapour condenses into cloud droplets as it mixes with the cold air. The process is like the reverse of convection currents forming into Cumulus clouds: rather than air warming at the ground level and rising to form clouds, here air is cooling at the top of the troposphere and sinking to form them.

Mamma tend to be far less dramatic on the other cloud types. On the whole they are only plump, full and abundant when there is a mighty thunderstorm in the vicinity. The more powerful the Cumulonimbus, the more buxom the mamma.

Wireless Thermometer With Comfort Level Reading

Indoor/Outdoor Humidex Thermometer
$34 Amazon

We plan activities around weather forecasts. However, the information is often from sensors far from our location. I want data from my backyard with the convenience of not having to go outside to read it. I have been using the wireless Indoor/Outdoor Humidex Thermometer for over two years. It is perfect for my needs. I have placed it in a central location in the house and I take a glance at the readings every time I pass it (at least ten times a day).

Setting it up is a snap. First insert two AA batteries into the back of the monitor and two more into the remote outside sensor. Press the reset button on both and you

should begin receiving data which is displayed on the monitor. Look for a suitable place to locate the sensor. A shady area is recommended for accurate readings. The maximum transmission range is 45 meters but that is in open spaces. Walls will cut down on the separation distance. A signal detector icon indicates how strong the connection is between the two devices. Using this will help you find the best place to put each of the two gadgets. The remote sensor is splash proof but it should not be exposed to heavy rain. I have put mine under the eaves of my garage. The monitor can be mounted on a wall or placed on any flat surface.

This particular model is perfectly suited for cold Canadian weather. The remote temperature sensor is good for -50°C to 70°C (-58°F to 158°F). The main difference between this monitor and the competition is that this model provides decimal temperature

readings, which is a rarity. A temperature of 16.6°C to 17.4°C would register as 17°C on most monitors. I appreciate this precision because I am sure I can tell the difference between these two readings. On the monitor there is a battery indicator icon, letting you know when the power is starting to go. The batteries should last about 12 months.

Besides the indoor/outdoor temperatures, the monitor also displays the outside humidity and a "Humidex" index to indicate how comfortable/uncomfortable the temperature really is outside.

-- Marcel Dufresne

Understanding weather
Eric Sloane's Weather Book
$10 Eric Sloane, 2005, 96 p.

By means of insightful hand-drawn diagrams, Eric Sloane gives the best explanation I've ever seen of how weather works. Originally created to help sailors 50 years ago, it works for pilots, outdoor explorers, and anyone else dependent on a change of weather.

-- KK

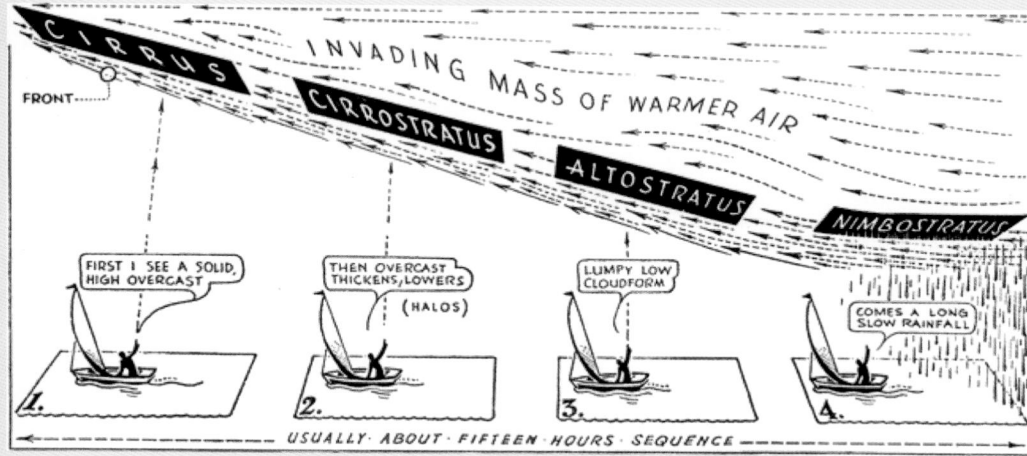

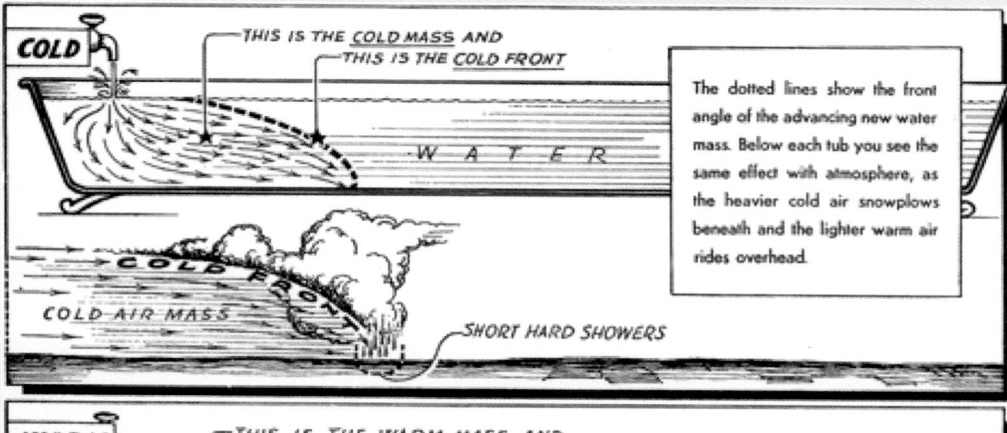

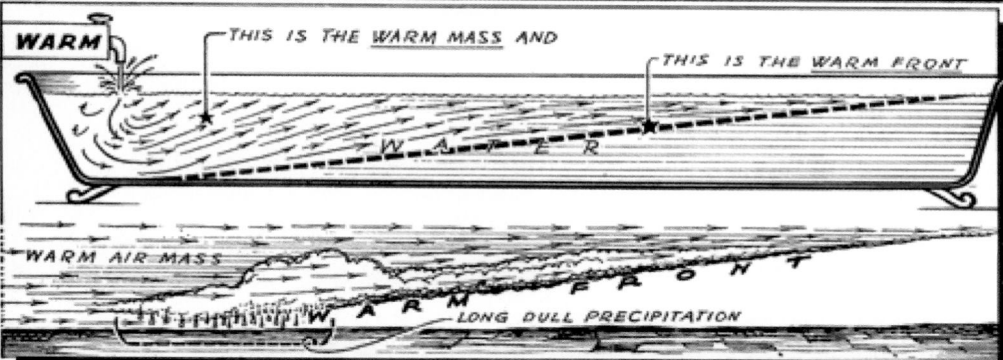

Home weather station
Ambient Weather WS-2080
$110 Amazon

The Ambient Weather WS-2080 is a very full-featured weather station for the price. It uses a radio signal to communicate between the weather station and the display console, and updates the display every 48 seconds. The display shows a lot of information, and has a USB interface that allows a computer to capture the readings and create graphs from them. I haven't used the USB interface yet, but it was one of the features that attracted me to this particular model.

It's possible to adjust the calibration of the various sensors from the console, but for temperature it was close enough out of the box that I didn't bother. We've had some rain a few times in the last month and it seems that the readings produced by the WS-2080 are on the low side, so I might end up calibrating the rain gauge. I did find the configuration procedure to be fairly confusing, with a lot of button-pushing to get to the various settings. You definitely want to have the manual in hand when you do it.

There is software that comes with the WS-2080 to configure it but it's Windows-only and I have a Mac and Linux household so I haven't used it. There is open source software for Linux that is supposed to be able to talk to the WS-2080 to capture the sensor readings, but I haven't had a chance to try it yet.

I mounted the sensor pod on my TV antenna mast above the antenna, which puts it only about four feet above the roof; probably not the best place for the temperature sensor. I did buy the accessory solar radiation shield for the temperature sensor, but a better solution might have been to mount the temperature sensor in the shade on the north side of the house. The various parts of the weather station connect together with phone-cord-like wiring with RJ-11 connectors.

-- David H.

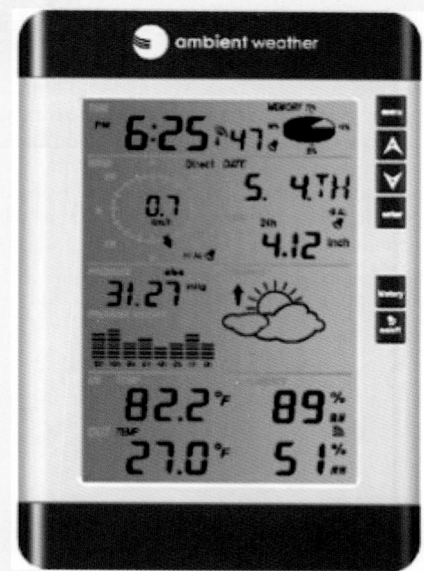

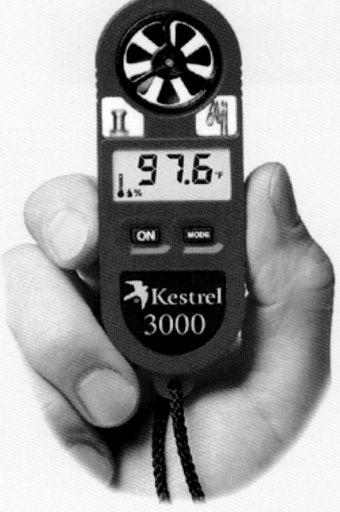

Pocket weather station
Kestrel 3000 Pocket Weather Meter
$152 Amazon

A marvel of compact engineering, this brilliant little device now accompanies me wherever I travel, not just in the wild any more. Two buttons. One is on/off. The other cycles the readout through current wind speed, maximum wind speed, average wind speed, temperature, wind chill, relative humidity, heat index, and dew point. It is shockingly sensitive. Once when I was hiking up into a fog layer, I tracked–while I was walking–the decrease in temperature and rise in humidity, with indicated dew point ever closer to the ambient temperature. As I entered the fog, humidity reached 100 percent and the ambient temperature and dew point temperatures were identical. Precisely! Pocket-small, the Kestrel's slide-on case can't be lost because it's on the lanyard.

-- Stewart Brand

Cycles

Know your snow

Ken Libbrecht's Field Guide to Snowflakes

$10 Ken Libbrecht, 2006, 112 p.

A gorgeous key to the surprising variety of snowflakes. There's more diversity than you think. The taxonomy of snow is categorized succinctly here. You can also find the same information on the author's densely packed website. He offers a companion book of a gallery snowflake photos, and prints, "wallpaper," and US postage stamps! However this small book is the handiest form for all this goodness.

– KK

Stellar plates often show distinctive ridges that point to the corners between adjacent prism facets. When these ridges are especially prominent, the crystals are called sectored plates. The simplest sectored plates are hexagonal crystals that are divided into six equal pieces, like the slices of a hexagonal pie. More complex specimens show prominent ridges on broad, flat branches.

- Surprisingly, no one knows why snow crystals grow into these three-fold symmetrical shapes. (Note however that the molecular structure of triangular crystals is no different from ordinary six-sided crystals. The facet angles are all the same.)

- By growing snow crystals in the laboratory under con-

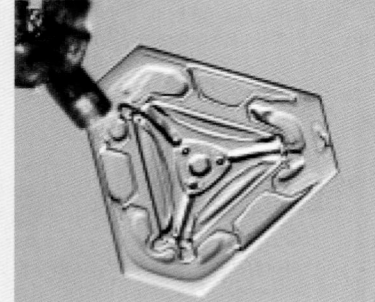

trolled conditions, one finds that their shapes depend on the temperature and humidity. This behavior is summarized in the "morphology diagram," which gives the crystal shape under different conditions.

The morphology diagram tells us a great deal about what kinds of snow crystals form under what conditions. For example, we see that thin plates and stars grow around -2 C (28 F), while columns and slender needles appear near -5 C (23 F). Plates and stars again form near -15 C (5 F), and a combination of plates and columns are made around -30 C (-22 F).

Furthermore, we see from the diagram that snow crystals tend to form simpler shapes when the humidity (supersaturation) is low, while more complex shapes at higher humidities. The most extreme shapes — long needles around -5C and large, thin plates around -15C — form when the humidity is especially high.

Why snow crystal shapes change so much with temperature remains something of a scientific mystery. The growth depends on exactly how water vapor molecules are incorporated into the growing ice crystal, and the physics behind this is complex and not well understood. It is the subject of current research in my lab and elsewhere.

Snow Crystals website

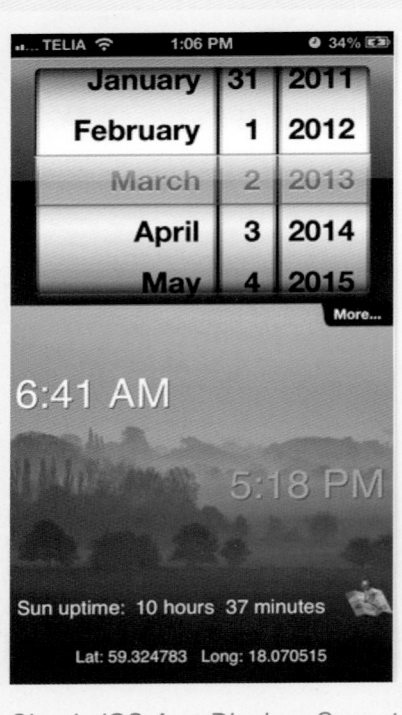

6:41 AM
5:18 PM
Sun uptime: 10 hours 37 minutes
Lat: 59.324783 Long: 18.070515

6:39 AM
5:21 PM
Sun uptime: 10 hours 42 minutes
Lat: 59.324783 Long: 18.070515

Simple iOS App Displays Sunset and Sunrise Times

The Sun: Rise and Fall

Free iTunes Store

This is a dead-simple iOS pp, whose sole function is to tell you what time the sun rises and sets. It has a scroll wheel in the upper right hand corner you can use to scroll backward and forward to see the sunrise and set times on a given day. It also shows the time until sunset during the day, and the time until sunrise at night, as well as the total hours of sun uptime. You can set it to show moonrise and fall, as well as the phase of the moon. There's an icon for the current weather, and the highs and lows for your area are displayed as well. It's not as useful as a full-fledged weather app though, but it does give you a nice idea of what it's like out there.

I find it useful for knowing when to let my very spoiled pet chickens out of their coop, and getting some idea of when they'll stop laying for the winter, and start up again in the spring. You can localize it fairly easily. If you are traveling and need to know the various rise and fall times for, say, scenic Ulan Bataar, you touch the map icon and move the pin there. Sure, I can look out the window and find out what's happening now, but for precise information for other times and places, this app is marvelous. And I can do things like discover when the actual equinox is at my house. Turns out that we get 12 hours of daylight and 12 hours of night on March 17th.

-- Amy Thompson

Tidal updates

TideTrac

$3 TideTrac

Tide data, like time and gps coordinates, now flows freely almost anywhere you desire, so there is no reason not to tap into this stream. Plugged into the data I feel more in tune with the outside, and better prepared when I head to the shores. Most people in the US (and the world) live near a coastline. This will come in handy.

There are many free tide apps out there. For instance, TideApp is free and works on iPhone, Android, the web and as a widget for Mac and Windows. It gives you basic tide tables but has not been updated in a while. I prefer TideTrac which costs $3 (iPhone app) for several reasons. 1) It will give me the tides for the location where I am when I ask, 2) It works even when I am out of cell range (by storing a cache), 3) I can look up tides a year in advance, 4) it gives sunrise/set, moonrise/set data, and 5) I can get a lovely and revealing monthly view of the tides as well.

The interface is smart and fast.   -- KK

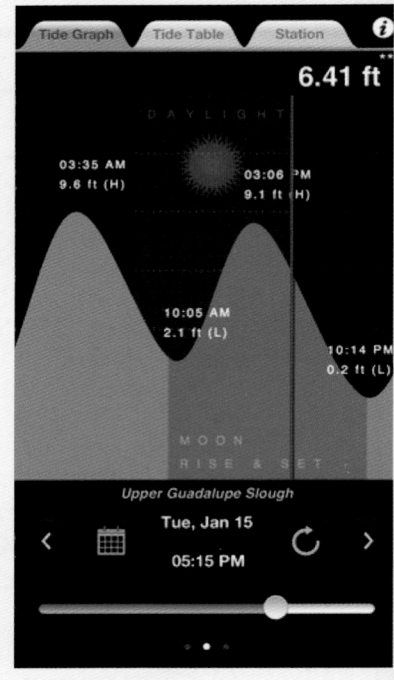

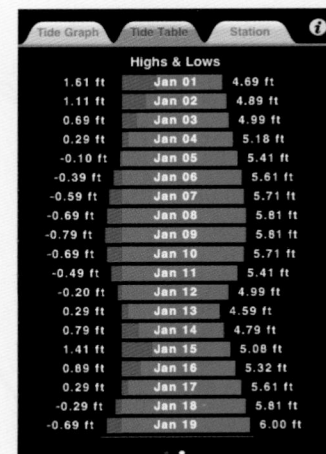

The largest map of the world
World Map Wallpaper

$150 Hammacher Schlemmer

The world's most educational wallpaper. Also the largest map of the world commercially available — 9 feet by 13 feet. It is impressive. Standing in front of it, your gut senses a large blue ocean world. It is pretty crude cartography, however; large cities only are depicted and some countries are out of date. Be forewarned you need a quite large blank wall to contain it (you need to trim 8 inches off the top just to squeeze it onto the standard residential wall), although I've seen folks wrap it around corners, dormers and windows. Think of it as beautiful wallpaper, which it is. Works well in an office — particularly since you can write on the plasticized map with dry erase markers. Doodle in your travels. It could also be used on a floor. It comes in 8 pieces, each 3×4 feet, applied with wallpaper paste (included). That modularity gives you another bonus. You can arrange the pieces so that they center the world on your choice: the Americas, Europe and Africa, or Asia. I like it because it gives me an overwhelming sense of the scale of our planet.

-- KK

Very large up-to-date political map
2nd Largest World Map

$30 National Geographic

Most homes have limited uninterrupted wall space, so I've found this wall map from National Geographic to be the largest practical map of the world. Sized: 70 by 49 inches. Contains adequate political detail, crisp geographic printing, and is current as of 2010.

-- KK

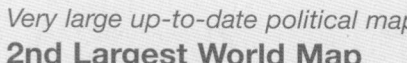

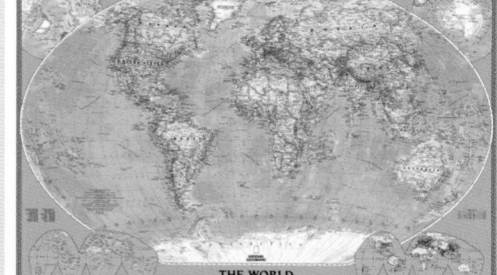

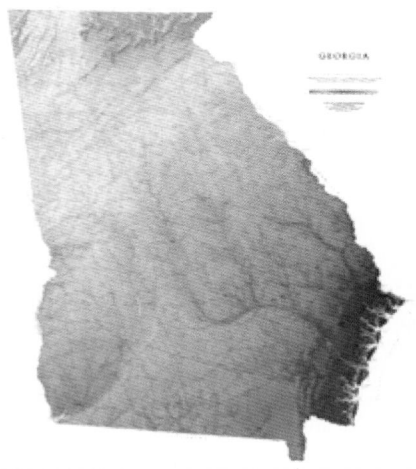

World's best world atlas
The Times Atlas of the World

$132 2011 (13th Comprehensive Edition), 544 p.

This is the best atlas of the world. Period. It is the most accurate, clearest, most-up-to-date, and most comprehensive atlas ever published. Unlike previous atlases, it locates and names those hundreds of thousands of towns where most of the people of the world live. However, even the best atlas is inferior to Google Earth in terms of detail, currency, and searchability. In a world of Google Earth, a great atlas is still superior for browsing and larger overview. Use this *with* online maps.

-- KK

This is the part of the world that is normally left blank. Known as the Empty Quarter, it isn't empty here.

Best US state wall maps
Raven Maps

$50 (Laminated) Raven Maps
$30 (Unlaminated) Raven Maps

Raven maps are artwork. They are the most detailed US state maps you can find on one sheet. Printed in exquisite detail on heavy paper, they radiate clarity. Their colored shaded relief highlights the topology of their place with intelligence and precision. Unlike most maps, Raven maps deliver two perspectives at once — an expansive overview and tiny close-up details — a very rare combination you won't find in an atlas or road maps.

These single sheet maps are also huge — the California map, for instance, is more than 5 feet high. If you have a blank wall, the blend of art and science in these wall maps can't be beat. They act like a doorway or window. I've found that most folks can spend hours studying their home state, reveling in the vast overview and minute discoveries — "hey, I didn't know about that!" — of their own turf.

They also make fine gifts. If you get the laminate version you don't need a frame.

-- KK

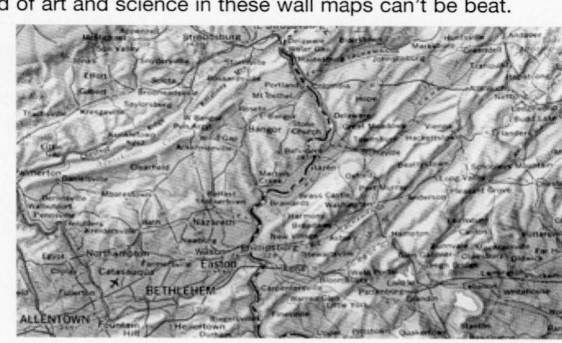

The big perspective
Earth From Above

$39 Yann Arthus-Bertrand, 2002, 464 pages

To change your perspective on things, go up and look down. This volume has a portfolio of aerial views similar to the Georg Gerster classics, *Grand Design* and *Below from Above*, but without those books' lyrical elegance. There's wider variety here, blunter politics (clear-cutting, ugh!), and more of the Earth's bioregions covered.

-- KK

Village of Koh Pannyyi, in Phangnga Bay near Phuket, Thailand. Koh Pannyyi is a fishing village floating on bamboo shoots.

We are not human beings trying to be spiritual. We are spiritual beings trying to be human. -Jacquelyn Small

241

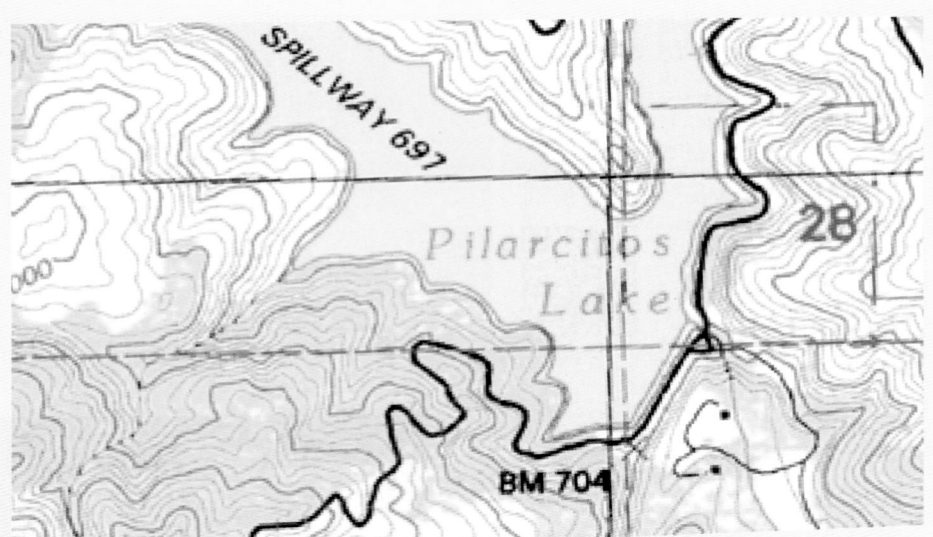

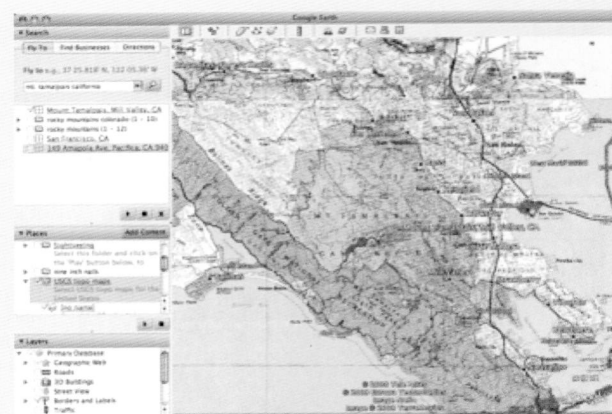

Topographical Overlay layer in Google Earth.

Topographical overlay + Adventure Paper

Free Topo Maps

Free USGS Topographical Overlay
Free USGS Map Locator
$25 Adventure Paper National Geographic

Topo maps have long been friends of all explorers and wanderers. Contours of the land make or break your journey, but this critical relief is not captured by the satellite images or street maps usually found on Google Earth. Togographical maps however do show relief. Topo maps typically display the gradient of the land as concentric contour lines which can be easily followed. Topo maps also label structures, buildings, railways, and other features of interest to someone trying to navigate on their own power. All continental areas of the US have been mapped in topographic detail and these crisply printed topo maps are available inexpensively from the United States Geological Survey.

But this is the age of freeconomics, so there are two ways to acquire topo maps for free.

The easiest way is to download a free nifty app for Google Earth, called the Topographical Overlay, that will add a KMZ "layer" of official US topo maps on Google Earth. Once installed you can toggle it on or off. When on, the Topo Overlay displays the standard 7.5 minute topos as one seamless map of the country. This makes it very easy to center your interest in the

middle of your custom map. (You can buy a similar service on a not-cheap set of CDs from National Geographic, but you get the same thing here for free.) For browsing, this arrangement is hard to beat. You can zoom in, or out, and scroll forever. Its major drawback is printing. I have not been able to get the displayed map to print larger than one half of a standard letter page.

However there is another way to print free topos. You can download, for free, a high resolution PDF file of any US topo map made. These are the same maps that the Google Earth app is using, but here they are dished out one by one in PDF format. Go to the USGS Map Locator page, and search for the quad you want. You can type in an "street" address just like in Google. Click on the appropriate miniature map and then choose which scale map of the area you want to download. The PDF files of the standard 7.5 minute topo map will be between 6 and 16 megs. You'll need Photoshop or equivalent to crop and size them. Be prepared to use some heavy duty processing power. These are big, very detailed maps.

Once prepared, you can then print the topo map out yourself if you have a wide color printer. But since you can order the topo map itself for only $6 (plus postage) from the same government website, why not buy if you have the time?

There are four good reasons you might want to

download and print your own topo maps.

1) It is instant. When you need a topo today, it's worth the hassle of messing with files.

2) It is selective. Way too often the spot you are looking for is in the corner of 4 maps, which means you have to order all four just to center the chosen area. You can eliminate 3 extra maps by combining the parts you want into one map.

3) You can print it on Teslin map paper (see below) which holds up in field use.

4) It can be lots cheaper.

However most of us don't have extra wide printers. You can print a series of cropped portions of a topo on regular 8.5 x 11 sheets at the official scale, but I wouldn't want to do many by hand like that — say a long trail. (Someone should write a utility for that job; write me if you know of one.) Even a slightly wider printer which can handle an 11 x 17 size sheet (Ledger) will give you very usable results. I recently printed a river run by cutting out the relevant sections of 6 topos, then printing each sheet at standard scale on an 11 x 17 page. We got served wonderfully.

Whatever size you print, you can drastically increase the usability of your home-printed map by upgrading to Teslin paper. National Geographic sells cut sheets of Teslin as Adventure Paper. Think tyvek, but smoother and printable. It's available in boxes of 25, 15 or 10 sheets depending on size. You send this this untearable, nearly indestructible paper through your ordinary ink jet printer. The resulting map (see picture above) can then be dunked in the ocean, folded again and again, and it won't break. When applied as if the paper were Glossy Photo Paper, your typical ink jet ink seems to adhere well and hold up pretty good to abuse. It can be printed on both sides, too, to further compact your maps.

-- KK

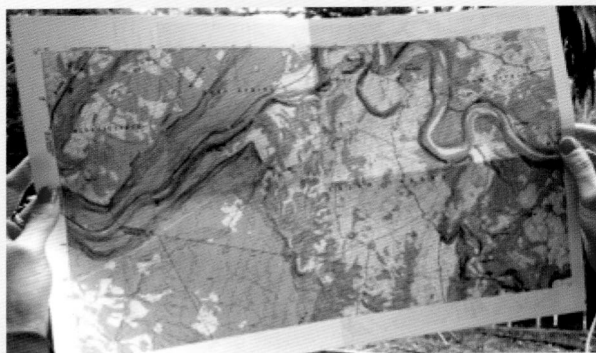

Teslin + ink-jet map, printed on both sides. No-see-through when used horizontally.

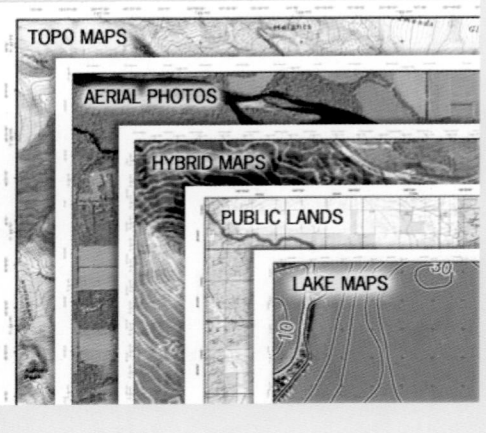

One stop source for global maps

Omni Maps

Omni Maps

Let's say you wanted a maximally detailed topographical map for the area surrounding Louangphrabang, Laos. Where do you go? Omni Maps. They have topographic and road maps for most of the world. There are many reasons to use paper maps over online maps when traveling.

-- KK

Omnimap.com

No-frills custom maps online

Mytopo.com

$10 18" x 24" Topo Map
Mytopo

Mytopo.com makes custom printed topo maps. You can choose where to center a map, on large sheets. You can order folded maps which are cheaper to ship.

-- KK

Best traveler's maps

Nelles Maps

$9 Nelles Maps

Nelles Maps are the best foldable maps for travelers I've seen. I favor them for six reasons: 1) They come at a good practical scale for traveling, fine enough to show most small rural towns. 2) Each map displays shaded physical relief of mountains, highway numbers and even "places of interest" – which are

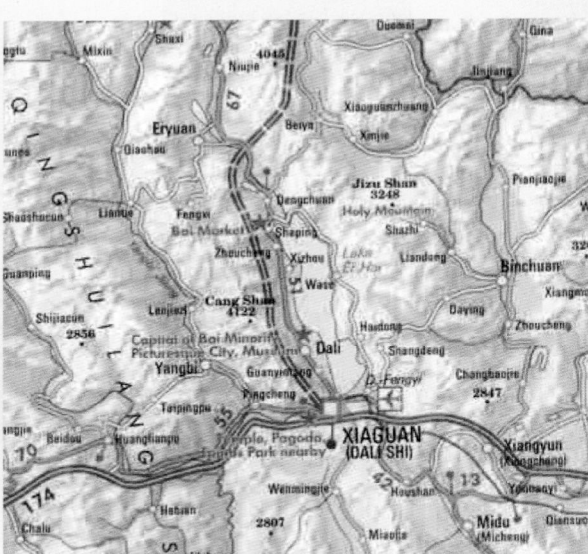

often not listed in guide books. 3) The maps are printed on both sides to maximize coverage. 4) They are printed in a form that folds neatly into a shoulder bag, with cover. 5) They are reasonably priced. 6) Best of all, Nelles seem to keep them very up to date. I haven't found any Nelles maps in print that are more than a few years old.

These qualities may seem expected, but most maps of third world countries are uselessly vague. Nelles maps shine in particular for Asia and Africa, and remote places where good maps are hard to find. I know from personal experience they have the best ones (in English) for China (in 3 maps, a North, Central and South), for India, and for the Himalayas as a whole. And they have the only useable map for Papua Maluku (Papua New Guinea) that I've been able to find. You may be able to find maps that are better for specific countries, but try Nelles (based in Germany) as your first stop.

-- KK

Long-term global travel

The Practical Nomad

$16 Edward Hasbrouck, 2011, 720 p.

Round-the-world travel was my occupation for many years. It's an admirable vocation ignored by the travel industry and travel media. They think in terms of two weeks not two months or two years. Ignore the country-specific info in this thick tome as out of date, but do pay attention to his airline ticketing advice, and his general wisdom about long-term travel. To anyone planning to take some serious time off to explore the far world at a cut above Stompers, start with this book. And then leave it at home.

-- KK

Some people are afraid to have a gap in their resumé. Don't worry about it. Don't leave a gap in your resumé, either. More and more, I hear from returned travelers who are putting their travel experience at the top of their resumé: "A year spent traveling the world, familiarizing myself with the diversity of world cultures, and learning how to understand and deal with people from backgrounds different from my own." Prospective employers may smile, they may laugh, they may be jealous – but they will offer you the job.

•

Every guidebook I've read describes Tashkent, Uzbekistan, as completely without touristic interest – a big, industrialized city. Too civilized. Too modern. Not quaint. Too fast-moving. Too aware of the rest of the world. Too much of an ethnic mix to give one a proper sense of "pure" Uzbek culture. All accurate descriptions. Most tourists don't like Tashkent, for just these reasons.

Reading the guidebooks' denunciations, I knew immediately that Tashkent was the place for me. I found it was everything I had hoped for. I didn't find a mythic past in Tashkent, but I wasn't looking for the past. Tashkent is the future of Central Asia, all brought together in one bustling, cosmopolitan, accessible m lange: an intellectual and ideological center; the largest and richest city north of the Himalayas between Beijing and Moscow; a magnet for the best, brightest, and most ambitious people of a dozen nationalities from a thousand miles around. And, as of early 2000, US citizens no longer need a sponsor in order to obtain a visa for Uzbekistan.

•

My rule of thumb for guidebook prices is to add 20 percent to prices in a newly revised guidebook plus 10 percent for each year since the copyright. It adds up fast: if in 2003 you're using a 2000 guidebook, expect prices to be 50 percent higher than in the book.

•

Where there is a train, take it. Don't think twice about the choice. In comparison with rail travel, road travel is dangerous, polluting, and expensive.

"Comfort, Safety, Speed" was the slogan of the Pacific Electric Railway, the Los Angeles and Southern California streetcar and interurban system that was once, believe it or not, the world's largest. Comfort safety, and speed are the advantages of trains over road vehicles. Even where cars or buses are faster, comfort and safety – especially safety – are the reasons I still travel by rail where I can.

•

Hiring a driver greatly reduces your legal and financial liability. It is thus, in a certain sense, the most effective and often the cheapest form of insurance. If you are driving a car, you are responsible for complying with all the local ownership, licensing, tax, and insurance requirements, and for having all the related paperwork in order.

•

Myth 5: "Tickets will be cheaper locally"

Many people have heard that tickets in some places are cheap and mistakenly conclude that it will be cheaper to buy parts of their tickets en route than to buy them before they leave. Those same tickets can probably also be obtained cheaply in advance, sometimes much more cheaply than if bought en route.

•

Big Business and the People's Airline.

Travelers often wonder why all major international airlines seem to be set up to cosset the rich luxuriously and expensively. How come a major international airline isn't committed to affordable, no-frills transportation for the masses? But there was, and to some degree still is, just such an airline: Aeroflot, the national airline of Russia. Why is Aeroflot different? Because it does things differently,

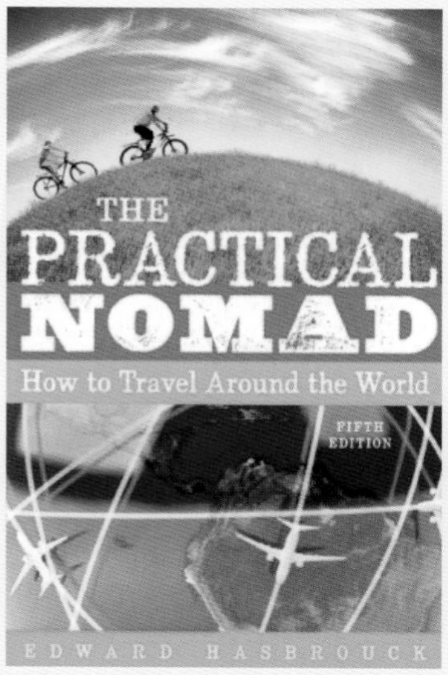

Aeroflot often seems a strange airline, and in some respects it is. It doesn't know much about marketing, and it is often hard to deal with. But travelers who want to keep no-frills long-haul air transportation available as an alternative to expensive luxury owe it to themselves to at least consider Aeroflot (http:/www.aeroflot.org) and Russian aircraft where they are an option.

•

But if you want the cheapest possible roundtrip from the US to India, Ireland, Nigeria, or any other place from which there are large numbers of immigrants, no general-purpose agency, even a general discount agency, is likely to be able to beat the lowest prices of a no-service, bare-bones, specialist agency within that particular ethnic community that sells nothing else but a massive volume of roundtrip tickets to a single destination.

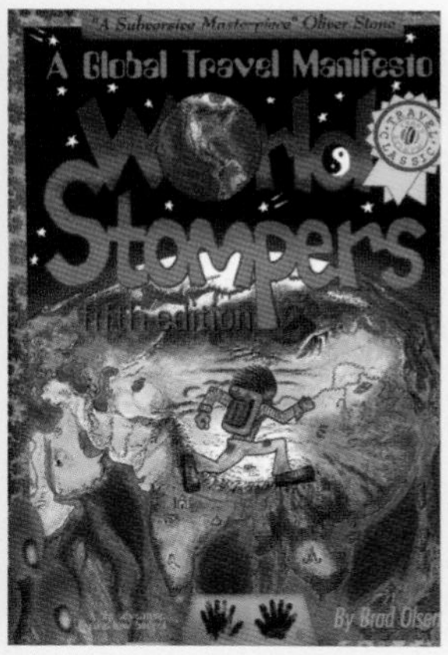

Not a vacation

World Stompers

$18 Brad Olsen, 2001, 288 p.

We used to call ourselves drifters, or freaks, but "stompers" works just as well. Stompers are young, nomadic travelers having a great deal of fun meandering around the world, hanging out, partying in run-down grass shacks in exotic places, hooking up with each other, paying attention to the local scene, while ignoring boundaries. It is more a lifestyle than a vacation. Once centered mostly in Europe during the summer, the entire world from Ghana to Laos is now stomping grounds. This book is subversive, irreverent, bombastic, self-published, and full of the best advice I've seen in print for global vagabonds. It assumes you have very little money, but a whole lot of time and are open to new experiences. Average trip of a stomper: one year. What I like about the author, Brad Olsen, is that he seems to have made every possible mistake, but learns quickly from them.

Here's the acid test: If you need to sleep in a bed on your world tour, *The Practical Nomad* is more your speed (and mine, too, these days). If you don't care where you lay your sleeping bag down for the night, and you intend to be on the road for more than a month, this is the owner's manual for you.

-- KK

•

One Summer when Tommy P. and I lived in Lake Tahoe, we made a bet. We bet five bucks on whether he could last a whole month without spending a single cent on food. He worked as an usher for Caesar's Showroom and was allowed free meals. Security was laid back and lax, so he would munch hard before and after his shifts and smuggle out pocketfuls of fruit, yogurts, puddings, cereal, milk and fruit drinks. I would barter meals with him on his days off to give him a variety, but never any freebies. The bet was only to pay for food.

Well he lost the bet a few days short of a month because he was fired from his job. He got the ax because he got up on stage and danced with Diana Ross during the encore. His boss did not believe she pointed at him for a dance.

•

The World's Top 10 Best Stoner Meccas:

10. The whole country of Laos
9. Dahab, Egypt (page 220)
8. Nimben, Australia (page 179)
7. The ski mountains of Lake Tahoe, CA USA (page 151)
6. Tuk Tuk Peninsula, Lake Toba, Indonesia (page 189)
5. Pokhara, Nepal (page 241)
4. San Pedro, Guatemala (page 158)
3.The Whole Country of India (excluding the cities) (page 244)
2. The state of Alaska, USA (page 153)
1.The whole country of The Netherlands (page 206)

•

Rip-offs are rampant for people commando-crashing outdoors, particularly in Europe. Backpacks are taken, money belts being used as pillows are unzipped and cleared of contents, and even shoes are swiped. If you are going to Europe on a low-budget and plan to sleep outdoors part of the time, consider a few tips. First, it is always best to sleep in a group. There is definitely safety in numbers. Second, sleep with your money belt inside your sleeping bag, but not all the way at the bottom. There have been incidents of thieves feeling the bottom of a sleeping person's sleeping bag for a money belt, then cutting the bag open with a knife and removing it. Third, chain your backpack to something, lock all the zippers, and try to use part of it as a pillow. Lastly, wherever sleeping with a group, lock all the packs together in the middle and position yourselves like spokes around a wheel hub. Detour thieves by making it hard for them to steal anything.

Another Stomper's Budget

To further illustrate expenses, here is Canadian Trevor Zimmer's budget(s) for one day in:

Kas Turkey (on the Mediterranean Sea)	
* Sleep on a rooftop	$2.00
* One bottle of water	.70
* Repair broken sandal	.50
* Two toasted cheese sandwiches	2.00
* Three tomatoes	.40
* Brick of cheese	1.50
* Loaf of bread	.20
Total	$7.30
Pushkar India	
* Bootleg Hudu Guru tape	$1.20
* All-you-can-eat breakfast	.80
* Four hour bike rental	.40
* Made to order vest	1.20
* Three lime sodas	.60
* Photo of a holy man donation	.15
* Fresh pineapple juice	.20
* Train ticket to Agra (300 km)	3.30
Total	$9.60

Trevor also kept records of his ultra-budget days when he was trying to spend the bare minimum (and still have a great time). An example of one such day in India: Orange juice – $.20; vegetable, rice, and sauce lunch – .33; bike parking fee – .03; all-you-can-eat supper – .80; chocolate bar – .20; bungalow on the beach – 50 cents. Total expenses for the day – $2.06.

How to travel cheaply

The World's Cheapest Destinations

$16 Tim Leffel, 2013 (4th edition), 228 p.

So much to see, so little time. You won't ever see it all, so why not select your destination by how inexpensive it is, thus maximizing your journey?

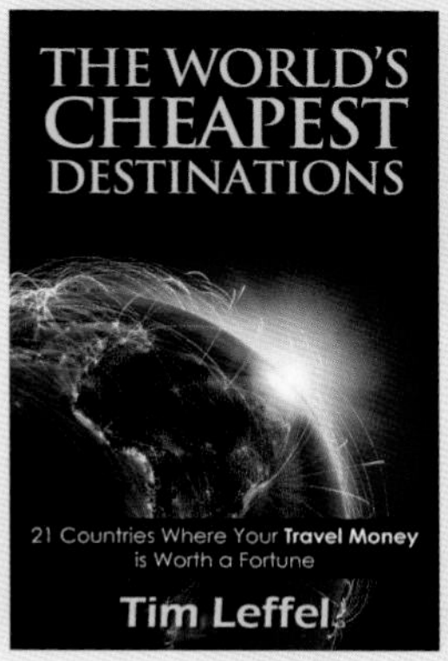

You can spend two weeks in Europe, or 6 months elsewhere. Your choice. Travellers who choose the latter have far more fun, learn more, and bring dollars where it can do the most good. Rock-bottom prices also transform budget travel in these areas into luxury travel. This thin guide is a good investment for this approach. It lists 21 of the world's cheapest countries for travelers with more time than money, with a brief idea of what to expect. Stick to these few and you'll still have a lifetime of adventures.

-- KK

[The author's website has some interesting and helpful links for bottom-fed travel: http://worldscheapestdestinations.com/]

•

Indonesia

Prices plunged to a ridiculous level in the midst of the Asian currency crisis — when my wife and I needed five weeks of travel to spend $350, despite living it up.

•

India

We paid a dollar a night for a great room with bath in Jaisalmer, then found out the guys next to us had bargained the owner down to 65 cents!

•

Morocco

A cheapie room in a basic cold-water hotel starts at around $4 in the villages and averages $7-$10 in the cities. The worst hotel we stayed in was $8 and the best one we stayed in was $8. It just depends on where you are.

Tips for globe-trotting surfing

The Surfer's Journal

$63 The Surfer's Journal

The Surfer's Journal is pure surfing, globablly. For about 22 years now, Steve and Debbee Pezman have been sharing their love of the ocean and waves with other like-minded water people around the world. A unique feature is the absence of advertising except for 2-3 pages from companies that surfers respect. The photography is stunning, the articles are in-depth, and the locations world-wide. There's also a lot of wonderful stuff from the past; it's amazing that after all this time they still come up with unique shots from the 50s and 60s and sometimes earlier, when life was simpler and waves were uncrowded. The soul of surfing, 5 times a year. It's the only magazine where I've saved every copy.

-- Lloyd Kahn

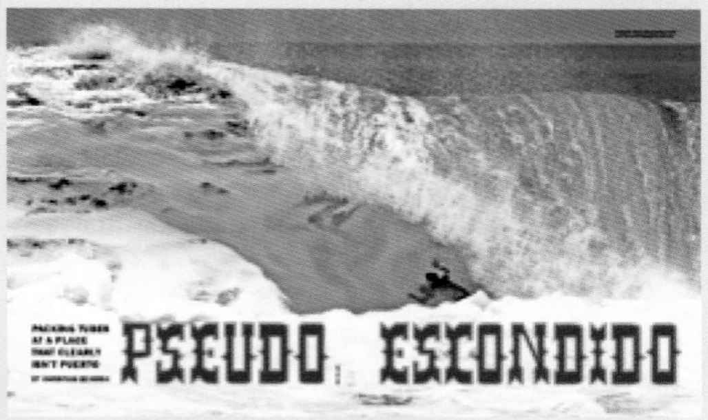

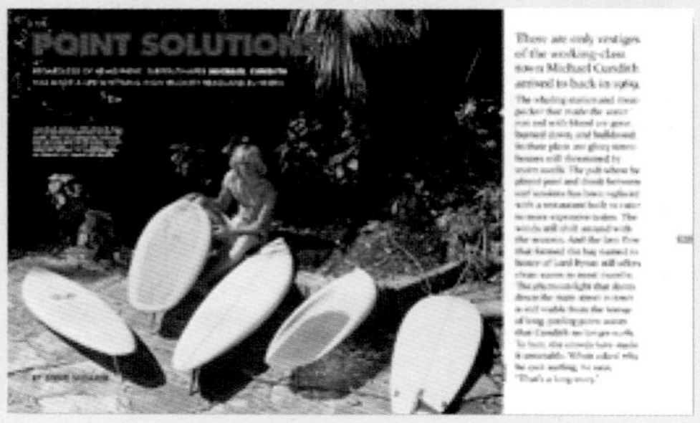

How it feels to vagabond
A Map for Saturday
$25 Brook Silva-Braga, 2006, 90 min.

Don't watch this documentary unless you are ready to quit your job. It's about the joys and woes of long-term traveling. It's impossible to watch this fun film and not confront the fact that you are here instead of there, out on the road, soaking up the mysteries of the world, with all-you-can-eat $3 dinners and $5 rooms, backpacking around the world for a year, as the filmmaker himself did. This kind of vagabonding is more a state of mind than a state of motion. Something weird happens when you travel longer than 10 days, and that wonderful transformation (which no one can explain to their family when they return) is what this superbly written, fabulously edited, deeply personal and wonderfully likeable documentary is all about.

This film explores the mellow subculture of (mostly) young people who trek along an invisible international traveler's circuit. There's a kind of endless distributed global party going on every day of the year (plainly visible here), and to join it all you need is a ticket to any country and the address of the local hostel. I was part of this mind-set for many years and boy, does this film nail the peculiar delights of perpetual cheap travel. Not just the highs (every-day is Saturday, each new person an instant best friend), but also the lows (always saying goodbye, and loss of connection).

This DVD won't give you the how-to specifics of vagabonding. For that I recommend *First-Time Around the World* (to the right). *A Map for Saturday* works best as an orientation course, offering inspiration on why to tackle this once-in-a-lifetime adventure. It's the next best thing to having a good friend come back and tell you what really happens when you find yourself at the other end of the road.

-- KK

You have to get used to the squatty potties in Asia. The bucket of water on the side is used to flush the toilet.

Filmmaker Brook keeps track of his expenses for one day in Laos. He starts out with his $5 room shared with fellow traveler Kym.

A game of beach volleyball on the sands in Thailand. Hanging around for weeks sipping cold beers at sunset is part of the plan.

4-wheel adventurers
Overland Journal
$45, one-year subscription (5 issues) Overland Journal

Last month I helped out a guy stuck on Tioga pass get his vegetable oil powered Gelaendewagen back on the road. He showed me a copy Overland Journal and I was so impressed I subscribed and ordered all the back issues once I got home. To give you an idea of the flavor of the magazine, one of the contributing editors is the author of the excellent *Vehicle Dependent Expeditions* book (see p. 249).

For anyone who does car camping, 4×4 exploring, vehicle trips abroad, or just enjoys armchair exploration, I cannot recommend this publication enough. It has amazing comprehensive comparison reviews of the type of gear no other publication would cover, ranging from vehicle rooftop tents to converting a LandCruiser to bio-diesel. On top of the fantastic information and writing in the magazine, it is gorgeously designed and features beautiful expedition shots from around the world. It is the first publication I have come across in years that has me reading every word, review and even advertisement. They publish four issues per year, plus a gear guide and back-issues are available to '97.

-- Alexander Rose

First-Time Around the World
$18 Rough Guides, 2010, 312 p.

The ultimate trip is a slow transverse of the globe on very little money with lots of time. I've recommended two guides for this way of traveling in the past: *The Practical Nomad* (for budget travelers) and *World Stompers* (for those with almost no money). While both of these books still have some good tips in them, they are both showing their age.

First-Time Around the World is the book I would write if I had to give my advice on how to travel cheaply and globally. It's smart, current, wise, and true. And worth reading even if you are only traveling for a few weeks.

-- KK

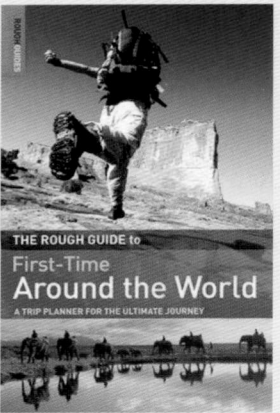

Q: I've got $4000 saved up. Will that get me around the world?

A: No problem. You can find round-the-world tickets for half that price, or hitchhike on yachts for even less. The more important question is what kind of trip do you want to take and how long do you want it to last? To figure out a daily budget that fits your comfort level, and to learn which countries offer the best value, turn to the "Cost and savings" chapter, where you'll find some budgeting tips as well.

• Fake police scam

A kid comes up and asks for change for a small banknote. Not long after (most likely in a city park or on a quiet road), a man approaches, flashes a badge quickly and tells you he's a police officer. He explains that the note you just received from the boy was counterfeit and that he needs to take it back to headquarters and you will be fined for your involvement. At this point, just as you are starting to wonder if it's real, a large muscular "colleague" arrives and pressures you to pay up.

How you beat it: take a good long look at the badge and tell him that, although he is certainly a genuine officer, there are many impersonators and that, according to their own tourist ministry, you're supposed to make all such spot payments at police headquarters, and you'll be happy to follow him there on foot. Under no circumstances should you get into their "unmarked police car".

• Free transport scam

You're met at the train or bus station by a tout who is offering free transport back to his hostel. You follow him onto a city tram and notice that it's not free – he just didn't pay the fare.

How you beat it: ask how you'll be getting to the hotel. If it's by public transport, make sure the tout is willing to cover your fare.

• Time and space

One thing travellers often forget to mentally prepare for is the different conception of time and space on the road. With buses that don't leave until they're full, boats that wait at the harbour for the captain to return from his family holiday, and mechanical problems that require spare parts sent by cargo ship from Australia, the hardcore traveller's mantra of "no watches, no calendars, no worries" begins to seem like a healthy response. Your personal space, on the other hand, is likely to shrink, whether you're speaking with someone who insists on standing almost nose-to-nose during the conversation or you're packed into a six-person minivan with seventeen other passengers. Plan for twice as much transport time as you think you need, try to grab a seat near a window so you can control the fresh-air supply – and make sure you've got something to read.

• Round-the-world tickets

Because of their complexity, round-the-world (RTW) tickets are best booked with a knowledgeable travel agent. London is probably the cheapest place to start such a trip, but that can vary slightly based on route and currency exchange, and it's unlikely that getting a round-trip ticket there to start your trip will provide any (or significant) savings.

• By yacht

Private yachts of all types often need an extra pair of hands during a sea passage. Some are crewed by professional captains delivering a boat to a new owner and some by "old salt" couples who live aboard their vessels full time. They usually follow common routes across seas where anchorages are safe, the scenery is agreeable and (since many are retired) the prices are low – and simply want a little help or a little company on board. In other words, it doesn't necessarily mean seeing the world with a bunch of nouveau riche assholes. It's possible to get a working passage or catch a free lift (though people may request $5-25 / £3-14 per day to cover your food and drinks).

Useful yachting websites

Matching skippers and crew
http://www.sailingnow.com
https://www.crewseekers.net
http://www.globalcrewnetwork.com
http://www.crewfile.com
http://www.partnersandcrews.com

• Meeting locals

It's hard to pick up a travel magazine, brochure or guidebook without seeing an exotic cast of faces. The unspoken message seems to be that this is who you'll meet in these countries. The people you're far more likely to encounter, however, are other travellers. And the local people you'll mostly come in contact with are vendors, taxi drivers, guides and hotel clerks – people serving you. To make more genuine contacts takes some effort. Volunteering or working in a place is one of the best ways. But even if you're just looking to take a picture of someone, a thoughtful approach might lead to a more meaningful connection.

• Free accommodation

Travel exchanges are growing in popularity as a Web-based method of finding a bed for free. Once you've registered on one of the websites below, you gain access to a list of accommodation offered by other travellers. You email those that sound appealing and, if they say yes, you get to use their sofa, bed, hammock or whatever's available. It takes a little advance planning and a good deal of Internet surfing and mailing, but the results can be hugely rewarding. The minimal (and fair) hidden cost is that you have to offer your home to travellers heading your way, although you are under no obligation to let them stay. Check out:

http://www.globalfreeloaders.com
http://www.hospitalityclub.org

Guide to world's best festivals

World Party

$30 Rough Guides, 2006, 400 p.

All the world is a party; you just have to know where to look. My favorite "big happys" are traditional religious festivals, which can't be beat for color, intensity and otherness. This Rough Guide serves as a good guide to some of the world's most interesting celebrations. Besides the famous (Mardi Gras, Kuhm Mela), and the infamous (full moon in Hat Rin, Thailand, Love Parade in Berlin), it also lists a hundred smaller lesser known, but still incredible festivals. It's crammed with color photos, history, reviews, and tips. You could map out a pretty good journey trying to keep up with the possibilities here.

-- KK

•
Maherero Day
Where: Okahandja, Namibia
When: August
How long: 1 day

This very local festival is unique to the Herero people of Okahandja, a quaint little provincial town that's around an hour's drive north of the Namibian capital, Windhoek. The Herero are cattle farmers whose history is littered with bloody conflicts, both with their tribal rivals, the Nama, and with German colonialists

who almost wiped them out in the twentieth century. On Maherero Day, the clans don traditional dress and parade through town in military style to honour their war dead, starting from the cemetery at the graves of two great chiefs, Kahimunua and Nikodemus, both felled by German bullets. It's the women's costumes that make the day a remarkable occasion – they wear elaborate dresses based on a style introduced by German missionaries in the 1800s, with long-sleeved jackets and bodices over voluminous, crinoline-like skirts. Topping off each ensemble is a huge cloth headdress shaped like cow horns, a symbol of wealth in traditional Herero society.

•
Participating in Holi is not always your choice to make, especially in the north, where it's hard to avoid being dragged into the festivities at every street corner. If you'd rather stay clean, then remaining indoors and watching the powder-slinging from the window might be a better option – Holi also involves a number of performances, parades and other pageantry that you can watch from a distance, wherever you are in the country.

Insider info: Coloured powder is available at all marketplaces, but be careful what you buy – many colours contain toxic chemicals and dyes, which are harmful to both the people using them and to the environment, seeping into the soil and the underground water table. In Delhi, the Central Cottage Industries Emporium, on Janpath, and the stalls at Dilli Haat sell natural coloured powders made from flower petals and sandalwood. The Bombay Store and Spencers Hyper Mart, in Mumbai and Pune (Maharashtra) respectively, also cater to a safe and natural Holi.

Everyone gets involved, showering passers by with multi-coloured powders.

Travel different

Eccentric America

$8 Jan Friedman, 2004, 336 p.

Think different. More than just a list of weird kitschy roadside attractions, this enjoyable guidebook points  you to odd festivals, off-beat environments, outsider art, bizarre endeavors and eccentric people in all 50 states. You can have a real adventure in the US by seeking out any of the 900 wacky national treasures covered in this fantastic guide. I found a whole bunch of incredible "never forget" destinations this way. May your travels be as creative as you are. (Someone please make an Eccentric Europe, or Mexico, Japan, etc.)

Alternatively, you can go to the website Roadside America. It's not as complete, not as easy to browse, and not as eccentric (more of what you expect in roadside attractions), but it is free. Furthermore, it relies on tips from readers, so it is improving fast.

-- KK

•
Led by a group alarmed by the increasing presence of surveillance cameras, the Surveillance Camera Outdoor Walking Tours cover most Manhattan neighborhoods, meeting Sundays, rain or shine, for the one-and-a-half-hour tours. The leaders, known as the Surveillance Camera Players, share a great deal of history on the subject as well as pointing out the technological capacities of the various types of cameras.

Surveillance Camera Outdoor Walking Tours (SCOWT) meet on Sundays at 2.00pm sharp in various neighborhoods. Check the website for details. Free.

Sofas, chairs and bathtubs take to the slopes at Big Mountain Resort's annual Furniture Races in Whitefish [MT]. All manner of furniture (very loosely defined) is firmly attached to skis, towed to the top of the slope, and then raced full-throttle down to the bottom. Competitors are judged by speed, ability to stop reasonably close to the finish line and on style. Winner gets a new piece of furniture.

Furniture Races, held annually in April in Whitefish, MT. Contact Big Mountain Ski and Summer Resort, PO Box 1400, Whitefish, MT 59937; 800 8582900.

•
Talk about off the wall – you'll be literally bouncing off padded ones at Flyaway Indoor Skydiving. Flapping around like a bird stuck in a silo, you'll 'fly' in a vertical wind tunnel with updraft speeds up to 115mph. But first you need to attend flight school. Here you learn how to position your body for maximum uplift; practice the 'tuck and roll', which is how you exit the updraft safely; and learn the communication hand-signals. Then you'll watch a lawyerly video explaining all the ways you could get hurt or killed (no-one ever has been); and sign your life away on the liability release form.

After that, it's into your flight suit, knee and elbow pads, helmet, ear plugs and goggles. Then it's into the wind tunnel with up to four of your soon-to-be best friends. Since your body isn't likely to agree with your decision to leap into a void, your flight suit has handles so your trainer can pull you into and out of the maelstrom. The tunnel itself is a giant, padded, cylindrical tube with a turbine engine mounted into the floor.

Flyaway Indoor Skydiving, 200 Convention Center Dr, Las Vegas, NV 89109; 702 731 4768 or 877 545 8093. Open seven days a week. Hours are seasonal; phone for current times.

•
The Indiana Shoe Tree has been featured in newspapers, and on television and radio, for most of the 35 years in which it has been collecting thousands of pairs of shoes and other footwear. Originally local folks shoed it just for fun, but now that it's famous, people come from all over to tie their old laces together, then hurl their old shoes up into the white oak tree. Some people put their name and date on the soles before tossing them skyward. In winter you can truly see just how many shoes reside in the tree since there is no foliage to hide its contents.

Indiana Shoe Tree, located along County-1, 6 miles south of Milltown, IN. Contact Maxine Archibald, Maxine's Market, 402 W Main St, Milltown, IN 47145; 812 633 4251

•
Thirty thousand people show up to hunt rattlesnakes and then eat them at the annual Sweetwater Jaycees Rattlesnake Round-up and Cook-off. In the 40 years since the event was organized as a way to control the deadly snake population, more than 220,000 tons of rattlesnakes have ended up deep fried, barbecued, or otherwise recycled into less-threatening form. There are demonstrations of snake-handling, snake-milking and a Miss Snake Charmer Queen contest. The squeamish might want to sit this one out.

Rattlesnake Round-up and Cook-off, held annually in March in Sweetwater, TX. Contact: Rattlesnake Roundup, PO Box 416, Sweetwater, TX 79556; 915 235 5488 or 915 235 8938.

•
The Kaatskill Kaleidoscope is the world's largest, built inside a converted grain silo by members of the Brewster Society, a group of kaleidoscope craftsmen. To see the show, you lean back against padded boards equipped with new supports, then enjoy 15 minutes of inventive sound and imagery.

Kaatskill Kaleidoscope, Catskill Corners, Mt Tremper, Ulster County, NY; 914 688 5300. Open Sun-Thu 10.00am-5.00pm, Fri-Sat 10.00am-7.00pm.

North Carolina is home to the world's largest chest of drawers

The Mega-sore-ass dinosaur machine crossing the Eel River and traveling to Ferndale in the Annual World Championship, Great Arcata to Ferndale Cross-Country Kinetic Sculpture Race.

digihitch

Hitchhiking encouragement
Digihitch

Free Digihitch

This a website promoting hitchhiking. You didn't used to need a website to hitchhike, only a thumb and pulse. I've spent a lot of time standing by the side of the road with my thumb out, and it led to some of the best days of my life. Times are different now.

What this site offers is mostly encouragement. Stories of other hitchhikers having a blast, reassurances that hitching is safe and legal, and suggestions about where in the world the natives are friendly to hitchers.

If you'll hitch, I'll pick you up.

-- KK

● Isn't hitchhiking illegal in many areas? The short answer is: no.

● Hitchhiking is not as popular in North America as it was 30 years ago, but it is still legal if one follows the laws of each state. Also, hitchhiking is still a viable mode of transportation in many other areas around the world, including Europe, parts of Asia, Africa, Australia, etc.

The most common law related to hitchhiking in the United States has been established in the Uniform Vehicle Code (UVC). It states:

No person shall stand in a roadway for the purpose of soliciting a ride.

What many people fail to realize is that a roadway is defined (in the same UVC) as:

That portion of a highway improved, designed or ordinarily used for vehicular travel, exclusive of the sidewalk, berm or shoulder even though such sidewalk, berm or shoulder is used by persons riding bicycles or other human powered vehicles.

As you can see, the law only states that hitchhikers cannot stand in a driving lane (good idea, huh?), but they can stand on the shoulder or sidewalk of a road. A further code mentions that US States have the right to restrict pedestrians (i.e. hitchhikers) from entering certain highways (interstate routes, for example), but must post a sign if this is the case.

What it all boils down to is this. Hitchhiking is not only possible in the US, but also legal. Many US States have adapted the above code to their own liking, though keeping a similar wording. You can research more about current hitchhiking-related laws in the digihitch USA section.

● I held up a sign in Japanese: "Kaze o fuku mama, ki no mukoo mama," loosely translated to mean: "Wherever the wind blows,

so too will my feelings take me." A folk singer I met thought it would be funny if I tried hitchhiking displaying this old song lyric.

It was funny. So funny, in fact, people stopped their cars to take pictures of me, and then drove away.

● I had been stuck at an entrance ramp for hours [in Belgium]. I was joined by a six foot five fellow hitchhiker carrying what looked like a body bag.

A car stopped for us, and the woman

inside hit the button to lower the passenger side window. She peered out of the opening at us. "Are you dangerous?" I shrugged my shoulders and said "Not me," turning to my fellow hitchhiker, "Are you?" "No."

She let us into the car. She was a child psychologist, specializing in abnormal psychol-

ogy, claiming she could tell by our body language during the response that we were, indeed safe.

● During the past fifteen years I've hitch-hiked through over a dozen countries, spending months at a time begging rides. Everyone from grandmothers to soccer hooligans have stopped for me. Rebels pick me up to bond with a fellow outlier of the system, while law and order types give rides to keep me from harm, or to make sure I cause none. I've been treated to steak dinners, been given free lodging, plenty of free advice and even some cash. I've slept in driver's mansions, in rest stops, and in road side culverts. I've traveled at 150mph with an executive in a new Mercedes across the German autobahn, and I've limped through the hills of central Japan in a sputtering Toyota van with a Japanese rhythm and blues band.

Double your chances of getting picked up by using a cardboard destination sign, like these from a European trip.

Dorm in Glebe Point Hostel, Sydney, Australia

Best gateway to hostels
Hostelz

Hostels range in price but they are usually the cheapest lodging option in most cities. You can often find a bed in mega-cities for less than $20. A hostel has very little to do with youth, although there is still a network of official youth hostels, which anyone of any age can use. A hostel is simply a hotel where you sleep in a shared bedroom, or a dorm, instead of a private room. Shared facilities mean cheap digs. (The exception is South and Southeast Asia where private rooms are as cheap as hostels). Hostels also often have a shared kitchen which residents can use. This means hostels are very social places with lots of interaction between travelers.

I previously used the hostel booking site Hostels.com, but that site has fallen a bit behind the times after a change in ownership. Much better these days, with thousands of more hostels in their database, and a lot more friendly mojo, is Hostelz. It is the most complete and useable portal for global hostelling.

Started by a backpacker, the web site Hostelz list some 22,000 hostels and guest houses around the world. They encourage independent reviews by users and don't censor negative reviews. In addition, they pay back-

packers $7 to officially review hostels for the site. Hostelz graciously provides you with the complete contact and location information of each hostel so you can book a room yourself. But Hostelz also provides the option to book a room through them at the same price. Since they do not charge hostels to be listed, this booking option provides their only income, which so far is enough to keep the site going.

Hostels are a great, often overlooked resource, and Hostelz is your best bet for finding one. -- KK

Kabul Hostel, Barcelona.
17-25 Euros per bed.
Five stars.

This hostel lived up to its name the party hostel. I stayed in a twenty-person dorm for three nights and there was always at least one group that stayed up well past 6 a.m. One night we had twenty-three people (three people on the floor). If you want to sleep, do not stay in a twenty-person dorm. It did not help that I got the biggest party room in the entire hostel. (I'm not really complaining — I had a great time.) Earplugs help. The good — spacious lockers and toilet facilities, hot water. Excellent location if you want to stay where the action is. Lots of French girls. The not so good — never-ending noise when you want to sleep. Staff were generally rude at the front desk. (No big deal but other hostels had friendlier service.) Five internet computers for two hundred-plus guests meant there was always a line. I would stay here again.

Dorm in Itaca Hostel in Barcelona, Spain

Cheapest homestays
Couchsurfing * Airbnb

I travel a lot. I hope to never book a hotel room again. I stay in people's homes, arranged either by couchsurfing or Airbnb.

While I was traveling through Europe as a student I got tired of staying with other American travelers in hostels. I was looking for a more authentic and local experience so I began to stay in homes through Couchsurf.com. Over the years I've stayed in about 25 homes. Once you sign up you can search for locations and hosts with similar philosophy, interests, and traveling tendencies. There is no payment for sleeping on whatever couch/bed/futon is provided. To show my gratitude I make it a rule to cook a meal for my hosts. I've also reciprocated the generosity by hosting couchsurfers in my homes. CS runs on trust,

Kreuzberg. Old Building. Charming. By Joohn - $114

Room-artist loft Berlin Kreuzberg By Judith - $61

interests and positive reviews. Since there is no payment, the main reason to join is to meet like-minded people who have stories and camaraderie to share. As long as you have a detailed profile, you will attract and find people with similar interests. Being a female traveler has never been an issue since I normally travel with a friend, or I choose to stay with primarily female hosts. I have met some of my best travel companions and friends through CS. You can find couchsurfing all over the world now.

Now that I am working I can also use Airbnb. Airbnb offers an elegant interface and large database of ordinary to extraordinary places to stay all around the world, at a reasonable price. The service they offer is the curation of unique places, as well as increased security. Part of why some people will stay in an Airbnb and not a couch on CS is because Airbnb treats security as its primary financial and legal liability. Airbnb offers a 24-hour hotline, secure payment platform, identity verification, verified photographers and profile reviews. They also show whether you have mutual friends with the host, which makes me more inclined to stay with them. I've discovered some unbelievably beautiful and unique places that I otherwise would never have had access to at a price lower than a conventional hotel, almost by two or

Couchsurfing in New York City

three fold ($50 vs. $100-150).

Both CouchSurfing and Airbnb offer "local experiences" and a more affordable way to travel. However, CS requires more of a commitment to engage with your host (share stories, eat a meal together) in exchange for free board vs. Airbnb which requires payment yet is more luxurious and less personal. Think of it as the difference between getting a ride in a taxi (Airbnb), vs. from a rideshare (Couchsurf). In the cab you sit in the back and you don't need to talk to the driver if you don't want to, while the rideshare is more intimate so you sit up front and chat.

When deciding which service I want to use, I always ask myself: Do I want surprise or security? CS always surprises me with interesting people and stories, while Airbnb offers local luxury at an affordable price. -- Ting Kelly

Couchsurfing   Airbnb

Any work of art which is not a mere beginning is of little worth. - Ezra Pound

Cyprus

- (PARALIMNI - Our home is 3 km South-East)

Resources for home swapping
Home Exchanges

$95-$120+ (per annual listing) Intervac International Home Exchange, HomeLink International

In the past seven years I've had 10 occasions to exchange my home with others. Home exchanges, in my opinion, are the logical extension of the "sharing is better than owning" philosophy. I've gotten to use 10 neat homes around the world and pay not a penny for the privilege of living there. And 10 counterparts have gotten the same deal in my home. Exchanging houses is indeed "better than owning."

My experiences have been uniformly good.

The way I analyze it, house exchanges typically save money four ways:

1. House exchange = no hotel or rental cost;

2. Car exchange (common) = no rental car fees;

3. Access to a full kitchen = less need to rely on restaurants;

4. Cellphone exchange = no hassles with establishing a new phone or expensive overseas roaming charges.

House exchanges reduce the cost of vacations to essentially the transportation cost to get to the destination and admissions fees to museums, parks, etc.

The various services have different strengths. Each claims, one way or another, to be the biggest and the best, but it's hard to find numbers to corroborate the claims. Arthur Frommer says HomeLink is the largest, followed by Intervac. Homeexchange.com claims 26,000 listings, but it seems thinner to me than either HomeLink or Intervac. Homeforhome has 500 listings in Spain, about 500 in other countries.

Intervac and HomeLink work similarly (they began as one in 1953): you pay roughly $95-$120 annually to list your home and its attributes in the database (print catalogs are avail-

able, but cost extra). In turn you get to see and search others' listings. Non-members can typically preview the database or a subset of it, but don't get exchangers' contact information.

After joining, members contact others directly via phone, mail or email. I'm an aggressive marketer: I'll contact 15-20 members at a time, sometimes more if time is short. The services aren't brokers, merely information providers. There is no additional fee paid to the service and most typically no money changes hands between exchangers.

Exchange arrangements can be whatever both parties agree to: a simultaneous exchange, or non-simultaneous, even a three-way exchange. I'm doing a non-simultaneous exchange in June, using a North Shore Chicago townhouse while the owners are at their vacation home. They'll use my home in October when I'll be on a road trip.

Exchangers typically prepare a book or document that lists important phone numbers, who to contact, what food and wine to eat, what not to use and so on. It's important to have a local person who can check in your exchangers and act in your stead should a problem come up. All the services have suggestions and guidelines for first-time exchangers. The one at homeexchange.com is both typical and pretty good.

Obviously, it's easiest to exchange if you live in a popular spot and have a beautiful well-furnished home or apartment. But there are all kinds of listings. The important thing, in my opinion, is to pay close attention to the photos and text and try to exchange like-for-like. I don't try to exchange my home for a French chateau (though I did get a 16th-century farmhouse); and I am no longer enchanted by tiny run-down apartments in out-of-the-way locales.

-- Roger Karraker

3 bedroom apartment in the center of tourist area of Limassol
418185

Accomm.:	4	People:	3
Bedrooms:	2	Exchanges:	0
Bathrooms:	2	Children OK:	Yes
Smoking OK:	No	Pets OK:	Yes

House-sitting classifieds
Caretaker Gazette

$30/year Caretaker Gazette

I've used the Caretaker Gazette to live rent-free for the past three years. A friend told me about this publication, which has been around since 1983, and I've used it to find positions living as a caretaker in California and Idaho. In exchange for my accommodations, my duties have included keeping trespassers off the property, taking messages, mowing the lawn, cleaning the pool and generally watching over the home when the owners are away.

My subscription includes PDF listings online, weekday e-mail updates and a print version (same as the online PDF) mailed out once every two months.

-- Jane Smith

● ALASKA

CARETAKER NEEDED late September to May on a self-sufficient comfortable Aleutian homestead. Free housing and stipend. Orcas, eiders, sea otters, caribou, hydroelectric power, Internet, loom, hot tub. Writers and naturalists have prospered here. Please call (907) XXX-XXXX.

● HAWAII

CARETAKER(S) NEEDED. Responsible, competent single man or couple, with one child OK, with strong body and alternative minded. Must be enthusiastic about rustic jungle life, experience with off-grid living and solar equipment. No tobacco or alcohol users please. Maintenance of 2-acre homestead in a beautiful coastal jungle area in an eclectic, but rootsy, neighborhood on the Big Island. Care for orchards, garden, and cats. Small but comfortable cabin provided. Please send a letter explaining why you are interested in this opportunity, to: XXX XXXXXX, XX-XXXX Napoopoo Rd, Captain Cook, HI 96704.

● BELIZE, CENTRAL AMERICA

HOUSESITTER WANTED during owner's absence. You can explore the jungle, fish, snorkel in the coral reef, or take some canoe trips. I need a housesitter for the month of June. Have your own bedroom, living room and bath on 3rd floor overlooking the Caribbean. Pay for telephone, electricity, and your own food. Please write to X. XXXXX, XXXX SW 138th Avenue, Miami, FL 33186 or call (305) XXX-XXXX.

● CALIFORNIA

HOUSE GUEST(S) wanted to occupy a mountain cottage(s). Full time. Located in the foothills, one hour from Sacramento. Bottom of canyon. Four miles from freeway. You can fish off the porch. Keep all gold found in the river. Must love outdoors, remoteness. Pets permitted. References required. No job. No addictions. Please leave a message, including your name and phone number at (916) XXX-XXXX.

Skip the hotel, rent a home
Vacation Rentals By Owner

Varies VRBO.com

Traveling with my family, I prefer staying in houses to sterile hotel rooms. Eating out gets tired after a few nights, and I like to have a full kitchen to make a home-cooked meal. If we're visiting a city where friends live, we'll cook a meal and have them over. It's more comfortable and feels homier.

VRBO.com is an excellent means of finding reasonably priced accommodations, in the U.S. and abroad, that are often larger and more comfortable than hotel rooms, at a lower price. I've used it to find great short-term vacation rentals in California, Michigan and Florida. Making arrangements with the homeowners or property managers is easily handled through e-mail, and a deposit is usually required. You do have to clean up after yourself a little more than you would in a hotel room, but the savings and access to a city's residential neighborhoods rather than its commercial districts make it a worthwhile exchange.

-- J. V.

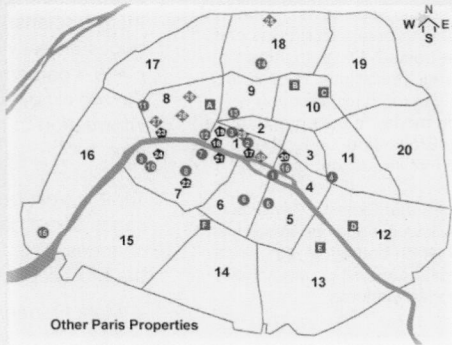

Other Paris Properties

Search over 265,000 vacation rentals worldwide

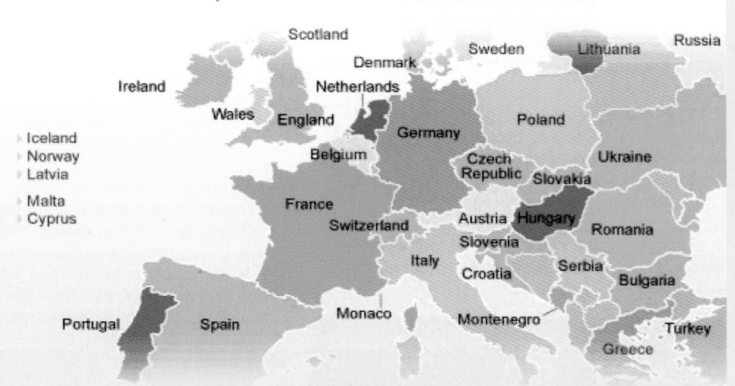

No more cramped seats

SeatGuru

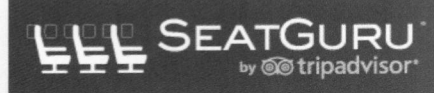

Free SeatGuru

If you've ever picked a seat on an airplane only to find yourself with half the leg room as the rest of the row, you'll appreciate this website. I found this site about 2 years ago after sitting in a cramped seat for 7 hours.

Since I have long legs, this site has been a lifesaver. It gives you a visual breakdown of most major airlines' seat configurations by model of airplane, color coding the iffy seats yellow and the really bad ones in red. If you're really lucky, you might find one of the green seats available on your flight, giving you the best seat in the house.

-- Michael Moscheck

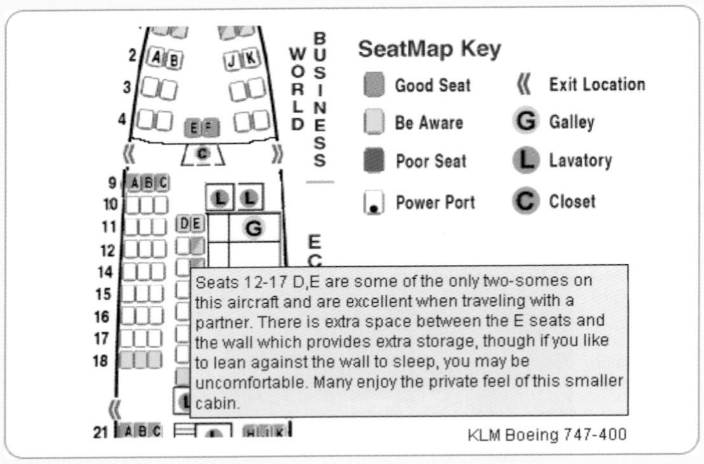
SeatMap Key
Good Seat
Be Aware
Poor Seat
Power Port
Exit Location
Galley
Lavatory
Closet
BUSINESS
WORLD
Seats 12-17 D,E are some of the only two-somes on this aircraft and are excellent when traveling with a partner. There is extra space between the E seats and the wall which provides extra storage, though if you like to lean against the wall to sleep, you may be uncomfortable. Many enjoy the private feel of this smaller cabin.
KLM Boeing 747-400

Cheap European flights

Ryan Air & Cheap European Airlines

There are half a dozen or so low-cost inter-European-city airlines. RyanAir is the largest. I recently got a round trip on them from Frankfurt to Pescara, Italy for about $90 — and this is one of their more expensive destinations. Other flights are ridiculously cheap. If I'd wanted to go to say Pisa or Stockholm from Frankfurt, the one way ticket would be 10-12 euros. London (Stansted) to Rome is 10 euros. These are ultra non-frill flights, and they all offer one-way trips without jacking up prices. One major disadvantage is that the airports can be out of the way. For instance, the Frankfurt one is actually 62 miles from the city, but for these rates I'll take a train or bus to the airport.

An ad from the RyanAir website advertizes limited come-on flights for 99 pence ($1.80) one way, starting next year. On many flights the taxes will cost more than the fare.

In addition to Ryanair, there are others with the same idea, with less extensive routes: Easy Jet, EuropeByAir, Air Berlin, Transavia.

-- Lloyd Kahn

Cheapo airlines in Europe don't all go to secondary airports, although they often do. However they often service secondary destinations. For example, we flew Basiqair to Bordeaux last year from Amsterdam. Not exactly Nice. To get to Milano, some of the low costs fly to Bergamo instead, which

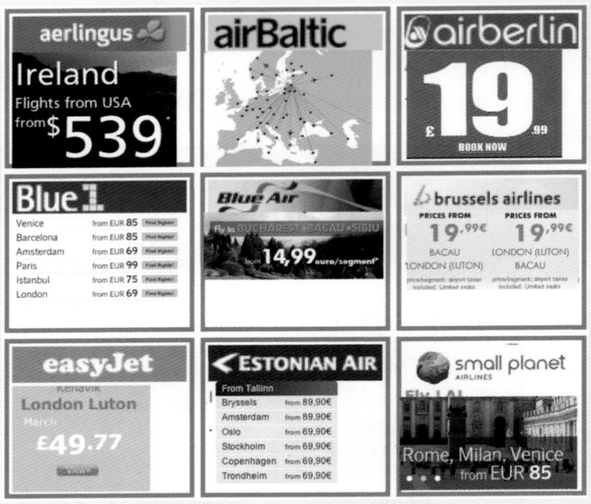
aerlingus
Ireland
Flights from USA
from $539
airBaltic
airberlin
19
BOOK NOW
Blue1
Blue Air
14,99
brussels airlines
19,99€
19,99€
easyJet
London Luton
£49.77
ESTONIAN AIR
From Tallinn
small planet
Rome, Milan, Venice
from EUR 85

is on the Venice side of Milan. Their fares were a fraction of the majors — Air France and KLM. In addition to the airlines you mentioned last time, here are some more choices.

-- Louis Rossetto

Ryan Air, Easy Jet, EuropeByAir

Transavia, Air Berlin, Germania Express

Ground-truthing exotic travel destinations

Thorn Tree Forums

Free Thorn Tree

The most savvy travellers I know log onto Thorn Tree as they vagabond. Thorn Tree Travel Forum is where you get the latest, greatest, most dependable travel advice for exotic destinations. Originally set up by Lonely Planet as an online way for readers to update their guidebooks, this bulletin board now bypasses and surpasses the guidebooks altogether. Reliable travel info has been completely revolutionized by the ubiquity of internet cafes around the globe.

Thorn Tree Forum

Let's say you want to know whether the border between China and Kazakhstan is open this October, or whether it's safe to visit Katmandu, Nepal, or where the newest climbing spots in the Peru Andes are. You log on to the appropriate Thorn Tree "branch" where a traveler who is in Katmandu, or who has just arrived in Almaty yesterday after a harrowing 11 hour border crossing from China can tell you all the specific details of what is true and what is not. Someone else might post that the popular beach shack on Lombok island, Indonesia you were headed for is now closed. And, to complete the circuit, you may be on the road yourself, at a dusty internet cafe in Morocco, when you read this. It's true real-time advice, from real folks who've done it. Thorn Tree is a remarkably efficient way to score hard-to-get facts from and to the field. And for armchair planners at home, the sheer detail available at a distance is heavenly.

I've found that the third world locations, rather than Europe and the US, are best served by the forums; but these after all are the very places instant ground-truthing is so badly needed. Thorn Tree is also a great place to connect up with others bent on long-term Around the World tours, and up-to-the-latest tips on long haul travel. *-- KK*

Jun 11, 2013 11:03 PM
HeatherMay

last reply
Jun 20, 2013 4:20 AM
MattB68

2 replies
327 views

How to Access Facebook In China

I am going back to China in a few days. Last time I traveled I had to find a way of how to access Facebook in China. This time I found this blog post on how to unblock and access Facebook, as well as my other social media and YouTube. Is there anyone in China now who is using Securitales? Can you please let me know how it works? The free trial worked very well. Thanks.

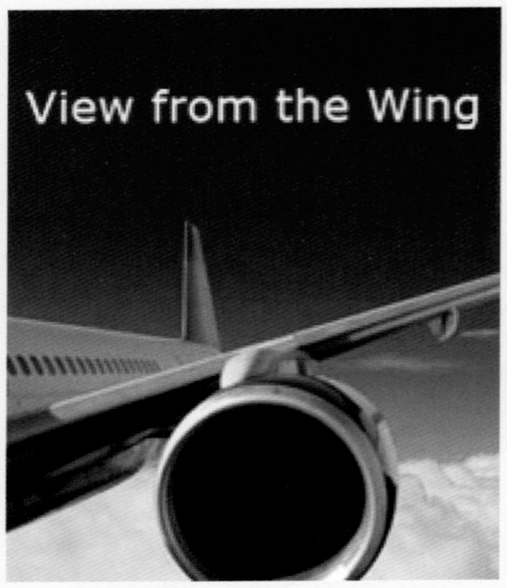
View from the Wing

- TSA's PreCheck is like going through airport security before airport security was federalized. It's a humane process. Not quite as civilized as going through security screening in Lufthansa's first class terminal, perhaps (the screeners there assist me with my jacket). But it's still... civilized, almost.

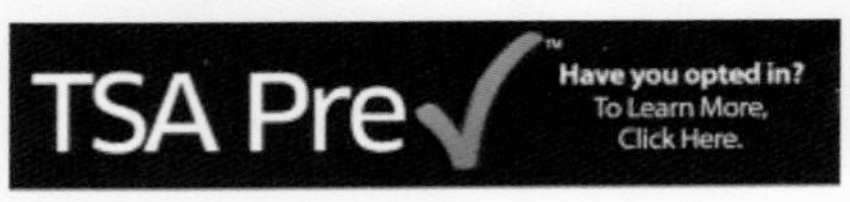
TSA Pre
Have you opted in?
To Learn More,
Click Here.

Maximum free miles

Boarding Area

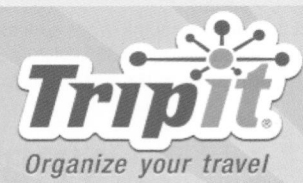

Boarding Area.com - View From the Wing

There's a small cottage industry of avid travelers exploiting loyalty and frequent flier programs to earn maximum free "miles." The best moderated forum I've found for their tricks, tips, and hacks on how best to fly free, or almost free, is a group of bloggers called Boarding Area. They all share great stuff but I am particularly fond of Gary Leff's blog, *View from the Wing*. He specializes in maximizing miles for free trips.

-- KK

- Here's what I believe to be the current 10 best credit card signup bonuses on offer: 1 Chase Sapphire Preferred offers no fee the first year, 40,000 points after $3000 in spending within 3 months, no foreign currency conversion fees, double points on travel and dining, points transfers to United, Hyatt, Southwest, Amtrak, British Airways, Korean Airlines, Marriott Priority Club, and Ritz-Carlton. Probably the best all-around credit card, and with a great signup bonus. There was for a few days a similar offer with just $2000 rather than $3000 as the required spending, but that was pulled rather quickly.

- Six tips for folks just getting started with miles and points. The basics are:

  Start with a goal that motivates you and also helps your choice of program. Nothing worse than finding out you want to go to French Polynesia, but United miles only let you get there flying to New Zealand first.

  Never pass up miles, always sign up for frequent flyer programs even when it's not your primary program. The miles add up eventually. Lots of programs become easily manageable at a site like AwardWallet.com.

- This is the second set of major devaluations for a program that is only two and a half years old. And both times the changes were implemented with no notice whatsoever. Programs that simply make your points worth less one day are not to be trusted. Programs that let you earn with a redemption goal in mind and then change the earning rules after you've invested time and money in their program are like Lucy, Charlie Brown and the football... keeping the goal forever just out of reach.

  I've now concluded that Expedia Rewards is a program that I believe is not to be trusted, and also is no longer worth bothering with, since the cuts to the value proposition are actually worse than I reported yesterday.

Travel plans automatically generated

Tripit

Free Tripit
$49 Tipit Pro Tripit

Keeping track of travel arrangements — hotels, flight schedules, rental car reservations — is a problem for me. I make mistakes writing down the information, I lose printouts, I resent the time it takes to stay on top of everything. That all changed a few years ago when I started using TripIt, an online travel organizer that keeps all my trip plans in one place.

Here's how I typically use it: I purchase a flight on Southwest's website. I reserve a rental car on Hertz's website. I book a hotel through hotels.com. When I get the confirmation emails I forward them to plans@tripit.com. TripIt parses the information and produces an easy-to-read itinerary. It's easy to add meeting and other plans. I can email the itinerary to other people and refer to it while I'm traveling, via the TripIt's free mobile app. TripIt also adds the information to my calendar (I use iCal but it works with everything else, too).

TripIt is free, but I pay for TripIt Pro because I like getting text messages about canceled or delayed flights and gate changes. This feature makes it worth $49 a year for the pro account.

-- Mark Frauenfelder

We are prisoners of our own metaphors, metaphorically speaking. - R. Buckminster Fuller

DIY tours
Hacking Adventure Tours

Packaged adventure tours can be fun and useful. A good adventure tour agency knows how to smoothly sequence events, and on higher-price tours you may get a guide as well.

But I prefer to create my own adventure tours, because I can save many thousands of dollars that way. I use the commercial adventure tour itineraries as a basis for my own travels, and then modify them as needed. The way I figure it, if they can move a dozen people along the route, I should be able to do it with one or two. The most reputable agencies publish their itineraries online in great detail as a sales incentive. But to complete many of the routes they are selling requires private transportation or special accommodations. You might need a pick-up or delivery at a trail-head, or a jeep to reach a village, or even a plane flight, etc. This is where many budget travelers stop. It took me many years to realize that in most places in the world today -- even developing nations -- it is not hard, or very expensive, to arrange private transportation or expert help. And with the internet, these arrangements can be made beforehand. I've pre-arranged jeeps, vans, buses, and boats. The simple rule of thumb is: if a US-based tour agency can pre-arrange it, you can too, and at a great savings.

It will take some time and googling to arrange all the parts of an adventure tour, but the payoff is that you can replicate the same tour for about 1/5 the cost of the glossy professional version. So now I page through the adventure travel sites discovering all kinds of nifty tours I would have never thought about doing. Unlike the unconnected places in a guide book, there's a logical flow to an itinerary, and because of their high prices, these agencies will hone and optimize a trip for peak experiences. A key thing: pay attention to the time of year they run a tour, which is again highly optimized. Still I wind up modifying them in some way for my own use. I usually chop off the leisurely entry in a big city and head directly to the adventure (I call that laser-forward-slow-back travel).

Adventure Tour Agencies

National Geographic Expeditions
Wilderness Travel
Geoex
AsiaTranspacific
Africa Adventure
Zegrahm
Journeys International

Some famous adventure travel companies specialize in highly-refined premium tours around the world, but they may be low on actual adventures. For instance I find National Geographic Expeditions trips (better than their Adventure trips) still involve more car and plane travel than suits me, but occasionally they'll have a nice gem worth replicating. Wilderness Travel gets you walking or kayaking a bit more, but still cover more miles in vehicles than I want, but I have used their itineraries a few times with great success.

Geoex offers pretty cool offbeat trips I've not seen elsewhere, but they also have plenty that are too mileage-hungry to count as an adventure. AsiaTranspacific specializes in Asian trips, a few of which stay close to the bone. For Africa and animals I look to Africa Adventure; they have a really good season chart for best times of year and parks for wildlife viewing. I like Zegrahm for inspiration. They do real off-the road adventures, including trips one might describe as "expeditions" which is more my kind of adventure travel.

But of all the tour sites, the one that has provided me with the most appealing itineraries is Journeys International. They emphasize getting you to walk, hike, bike and kayak and this is really the way to go anywhere. Almost any one of their itineraries would yield a fantastic adventure.

Remember, I have no personal experience with the tours given by any of these outfits. I only use their freely published routes. All these tours are super expensive if you buy them but I would bet they would be really fun and generally well done. I recommend them here only as models to assemble your own.

-- KK

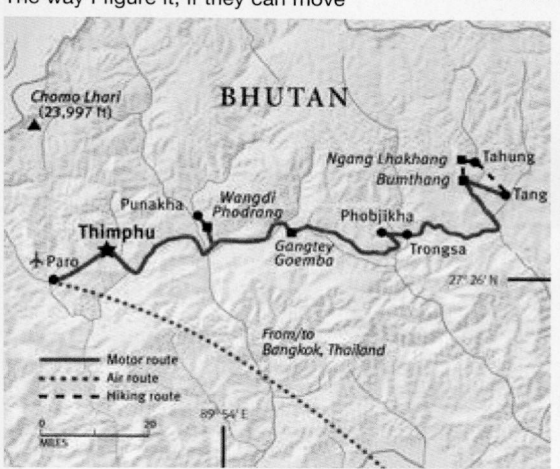

BHUTAN
Chomo Lhari (23,997 ft)
Thimphu — Paro — Punakha — Wangdi Phodrang — Gangtey Goemba — Phobjikha — Ngang Lhakhang — Bumthang — Trongsa — Tahung — Tang
From/to Bangkok, Thailand
— Motor route
····· Air route
---- Hiking route
From Journeys International

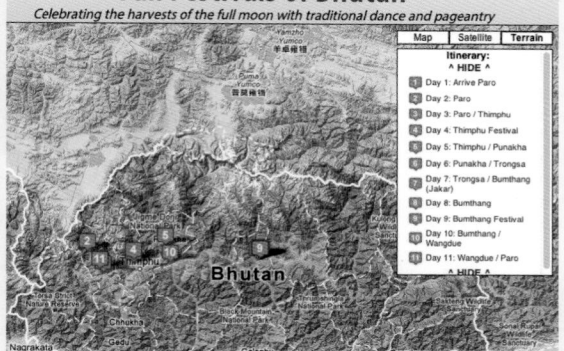

Fall Festivals of Bhutan
Celebrating the harvests of the full moon with traditional dance and pageantry

Itinerary:
Day 1: Arrive Paro
Day 2: Paro
Day 3: Paro / Thimphu
Day 4: Thimphu Festival
Day 5: Thimphu / Punakha
Day 6: Punakha / Trongsa
Day 7: Trongsa / Bumthang (Jakar)
Day 8: Bumthang
Day 9: Bumthang Festival
Day 10: Bumthang / Wangdue
Day 11: Wangdue / Paro

Serious off-road survival
Vehicle-Dependent Expedition Guide
$200 Amazon

This great book is unfortunately expensive and difficult to find. However it is the most stunning collection of vehicle expedition lore anyone is likely to encounter. It lists everything from how many Land Rover Defender 90's you can fit in a cargo container, to what socks to wear while driving in the desert. It is extremely detailed, does not shy away from product names, and is rife with real-world life-saving data. It includes tons of information on planning, visas, customs, shipping, survival, vehicle set up, driving tips, GPS and traditional navigation etc. On top of all that the writing style is matter of fact, the book is very well organized, and the photos and examples are inspiring. The most surprising fact that I learned from this book was how much weight matters, just like backpacking and mountaineering, it is the single most important thing to minimize in vehicle expeditions. Weight adversely affects handling, fuel efficiency, acceleration, braking, and your ability to traverse sand, mud, or steep grades. The $150 spent on this book will save anyone thousands on any offroad trip or expedition they are undertaking.

-- Alexander Rose

Fuel planning reserves – basic formula
Fuel for the actual distance .. | ... plus 25% ... | - plus 100 miles

Best of the world
World Heritage Sites
Free UNESCO

I've slowly clued into the fact that there is a network of "World Heritage" monuments, sites, and natural parks throughout the world -- places that are deemed unique enough, or endangered enough, to deserve funding by UNESCO. A cultural site can be a monument, a group of buildings, or an entire city. But to be granted a World Heritage designation, it must "represent a masterpiece of human creative genius; or bear a unique or at least exceptional testimony to a cultural tradition or to a civilization which is living or which has disappeared."

I like to think of these creations as the Best of Civilization.

Almost every country has at least one site, and sometimes many. Some places are justifiably famous, but many are mysteriously overlooked. Heritage sites are always among the most interesting destinations to visit in any country, well worth going out of your way to see. The sites range from ruins like the famous Inca Machu Picchu, to the less known ancient city of Fatehpur Sikri, India, to preserved towns like Visby, Sweden, to unspoiled wilderness areas like the Galapagos Islands. In total UNESCO lists 788 sites in 100 countries, which also include about 150 natural sites, deemed "areas of exceptional natural beauty and aesthetic importance" or outstanding bio-diversity.

In my travels I've learned to seek them out.

For a full list, and criteria, see World Heritage List.

-- KK

The walled city of Pingyao, China

• BULGARIA (Year added to list)

1979 Boyana Church
1979 Madara Rider
1979 Rock-hewn Churches of Ivanovo
1979 Thracian Tomb of Kazanlak
1983 Ancient City of Nessebar
1983 Srebarna Nature Reserve
1983 Pirin National Park
1983 Rila Monastery
1985 Thracian Tomb of Sveshtari

Exploring with a vehicle
Overlanders' Handbook
$29 Chris Scott, 2011, 750 p.

This is a more affordable version of *Vehicle Dependent Expeditions*. For $30 you'll get most of what is in that $100 plus book. In fact, this *Handbook* is more practical, with the kind of information you would want to take with you on a rough vehicle expedition, while *Expeditions* is more for pre-planning your trip. Think of it as the Lonely Planet guide to overlanding.

-- Alexander Rose

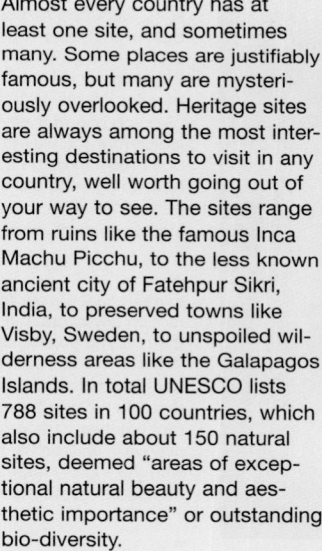

• The single biggest mistake first-timers make is over-equipping and overloading their vehicle.

• Do You Need a Powered Winch?

A powered winch may be crucial to the 'expedition look', but the received opinion is that most 4x4 overlanders who've been there and got stuck is that, unless you're looking to push your 4x4 to the limit, there are many other more useful items.

However they're powered, the typical permanent front mounting will be at the wrong end more than half the time and on many occasions there'll be nothing close enough to winch off unless other vehicles are present. And if they are, chances are they can simply pull you out.

• Shipping involves so many entities that it's very difficult to discern where a service charge ends and a bribe begins.

• You must also be very conscious of your situation and the local culture. In many developed countries, an attempted bribe could land you in a lot of trouble. On the other hand, in some countries, without a small bribe your vehicle could turn to rust before you get the single stamp you need on your temporary import document.

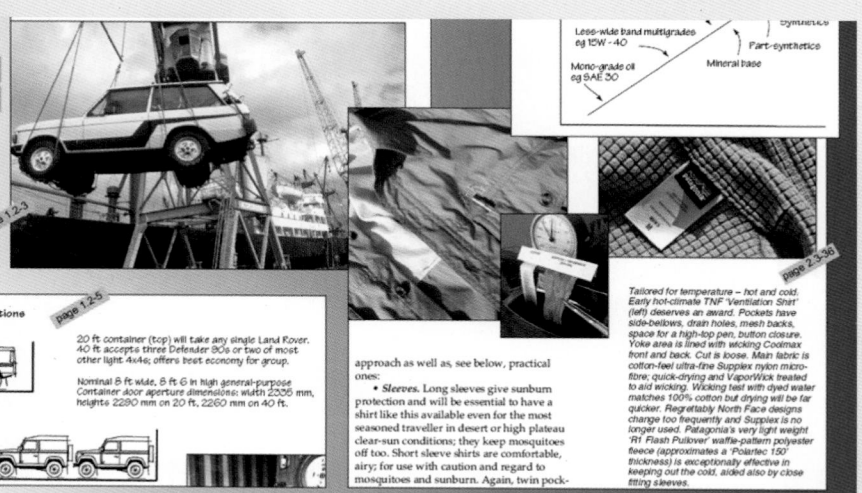

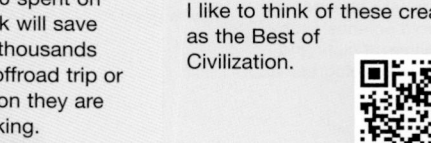

Overlanders' HANDBOOK
CHRIS SCOTT

Exploration

Urban exploration tips
Access All Areas
$15 Ninjalicious, 2005, 242 p.

Echoes of Forgotten Places
$9 (used) Scribble Media, 2005, 63 min.

They call it "urban exploration." Cruising through abandoned factories, tunnels, sewage systems, bridges, and even "live" structures still in use. Why? Because they are beautiful, mysterious, exciting, and not open to everyone. Others simply enjoy "abandonments, decay and industrial mayhem."

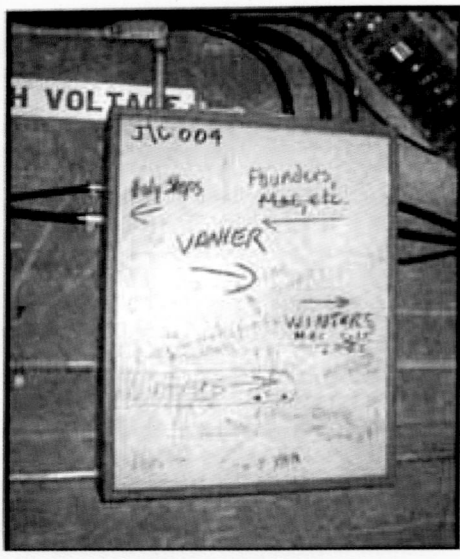

Directions left by past tunnelers can be quite useful, though they should be taken with a grain of salt. People make mistakes.

This book is packed solid with great practical advice on how to explore this unexplored realm. Every page has something I didn't know about gaining access, staying safe, and discovering new paths in the urban wilds. While this activity is generally considered illegal, the respect for the buildings, and the owners, nurtured in this guide is impressive.

There's a related DVD (*Echoes of Forgotten Places*) in the same spirit which contains no advice at all. Rather it's an ode to urban archeology and the love of forgotten buildings.

-- KK

• Sometimes you'll want to head through a room, hallway or stairwell that's off-limits and monitored by a camera. In many cases the best way past such a camera is to calmly walk past the camera. Certainly, this will work more often than snipping the wires, cycling the video feed or any other elaborate spy stunts.

• While I'm a big advocate of properly researching a place to get the inside scoop on how to act like you're supposed to be there, sometimes it's also necessary, or at least fun, to fly by the seat of your pants. In such cases, you may suddenly find yourself questioned by someone, or needing to speak with someone in order to get through a particular barrier, without having any real idea what might be a plausible reason for you to be there.

In such a case, I recommend just stalling for a time and letting the person you're talking to supply your excuse for you. People hate uncomfortable silences and confusing situations and will often rush to supply the information they're looking for themselves. Good stalling phrases include: "I hope you can help me"; "I'm not sure exactly what the procedure is here"; "Do I need to show you some ID?"; "I didn't even know I was going to have to speak to anyone about this" or something of that sort. After you say one of these lines, wait for a response. People generally want to believe that the people around them are rational, so they'll more or less tell you the most rational reason they can conceive of for your presence — "Are you here for the class?"; "You must be looking for Mark"; "Are you one of today's volunteers?"; "I guess you're looking for the way to the observation level"; etc. You don't have to come up with a good reason — you just have to agree to the one they devise for you. Once you perfect the skill of stalling without seeming like you're stalling, this will work for you quite often.

• In most cases, your focus shouldn't be on defeating motion detectors, but on spotting them and avoiding them. If you constantly keep an eye out for motion detectors at all times and in all locations, you'll gradually get a sense of where they're installed, and learn that you have to be especially careful near doorways, roof hatches, outside exits, the tops and bottoms of stairwells and similar locations. And you'll get familiar with the slightly more out-of-the-way routes that can be used to avoid them.

• Many explorers go out of their way to visit abandoned buildings during the day, both to avoid potential problems with flashlights and camera flashes at night and also because buildings tend to look and photograph a lot better in natural light. As an additional bonus, exploring during daylight hours makes you less likely to step into a hole you didn't notice. The main advantage of exploring at night is that darkness, when properly used, can provide a good deal of concealment while you're trying to get into a building, or while you're climbing about on its roof. Exploring an abandoned building at night can also be very pleasantly creepy.

• When we visit abandoned buildings, our senses are so heightened by the idea of having earned a glimpse of something unique and forbidden that we intensely savour the splendour and wonder of the place. But cities are full of beautiful, neglected, charming and authentic places and these aren't all inside abandoned buildings — not by a long shot. Some of the city's most surprising and impressive places are courthouses, theatres, libraries, museums, stadia, office buildings, hospitals, transit stations and similar buildings that are still more or less open for business. Just about any interesting old building is worth a look and so are a lot of newer ones. Go in and find their secrets. Climb every ladder. Open every door. Summit every rooftop, etc.

• In my experience, the absolute optimal time for infiltrating an office tower or similar place of business is between 4pm and 6pm on a Friday night. Between 4pm and 6pm, all the employees are taking off, but the cleaning crews and evening security patrol haven't yet been around. And Friday afternoon is by far the most laid back time at virtually any business.

• Crossover floors, whatever their signs may warn, should be unlocked in compliance with fire codes. They're good routes out of stairwells.

Still from Echoes of Forgotten Places

Ventilation shafts really can be used to move from room to room, and in large ones crawling on your knees and elbows is not normally a necessity.

• Looking unsuspicious is a big part of using elevators for exploration. If you're on the ground floor and you want to go down, or it you're near the top of the building and you want to go up, it may be in your best interest to push the wrong button, just in case a guard or employee joins you. You can change your mind and your direction once the elevator arrives, providing it's empty. If you're sharing an elevator with others, if you worry that others might get on part way through your ride or if you simply worry that you're looking suspicious, you may want to send out similar miscues about what floors you're visiting when you hop onto the elevator. If you seek the roof of a 50-story building, hit 36. If you have the elevator to yourself and you arrive at 36, hit 47, and walk up from there. (If you look and feel confident, you needn't take these sort of precautions — these tips apply only when you feel out of place or out of your league.)

Travel guide to place art
Destination Art
$29 Amy Dempsey, 2010, 272 p.

Some of the best art is a destination; you must travel to it. This lavish guide book is chock full of art that can only be experienced in place, beyond four walls. Some of this destination art is monumental, some architectural, some is art rooted in the physical landscape, some is found in open air art parks. There is a refreshing mix of choices from around the world, each of which is worth making a trip to see. Like the previously reviewed *Geek Atlas*, having a specific unusual destination can enhance ordinary travel.

-- KK

Spiral Jetty in Great Salt Lake in Utah has been covered with water for most of its existence. It recently re-emerged to reveal its new brilliant, salt-encrusted state, as seen in this photograph, taken in 2004.

As you approach Le Palai Ideal, near the rural village of Hauterives in France, the stunning moss-covered, highly ornamented and intricately carved palace emerges from the ferns and trees surrounding it.

Never assume malice when incompetence will suffice. - Robert Heinlein

Your European Guru
Rick Steves' Europe Through the Back Door
$15 Rick Steves, 2013, 828 p.

An award in heaven should be given to those authors who update their good books every year until they are great books. Rick Steves' guidebook on intelligent travel in Europe has been around decades, but it gets better with each yearly edition. That's because for the past twenty five years Steves has spent 130 days each year exploring new and re-exploring odd corners of the continent. From this wealth of experience he delivers not only the best guide to Europe, but the best general guide to smart traveling anywhere. I spent a decade full-time traveling myself, and these days I go to Europe every couple of months; this book has directed me to many specific towns or regions that retain distinctive cultures, places which would otherwise have taken me years of visits to find. Among the techniques Steves offers is a sort of laser traveling (head directly from the airport to the quintessential regions, skip the rest) which only works because he knows where to send you. There are a thousand hard-earned tips on cheap travel, on getting comfortable with a different way of doing things, and, bless his soul, he updates the darn thing every year with the latest prices. I consume travel books by the barrelful, including Lonely Planets, Rough Guides, and so on; this is the one to study, the one you want to re-read. It's not about London and Paris; it is not a guidebook. It's about how to make jokes in beginners' Italian, or attend a wedding on a Greek island. With Steves' guidance you can finally do that inexpensive grand tour of Europe you've always meant to do, or, better, bestow a roundtrip ticket and this book to a recent graduate and it'll be as good an education as they've had.

-- KK

•

In many ways, spending more money only builds a thicker wall between you and what you came to see. Europe is a cultural carnival, and time after time, you'll find that its best acts are free and the best seats are the cheap ones.

•

Travel is addicting. It can make you a happier American, as well as a citizen of the world. Our Earth is home to nearly 6 billion equally important people. It's humbling to travel and find that people don't envy

Extroverts have more fun. If you see four cute men on a bench, ask them to scoot over.

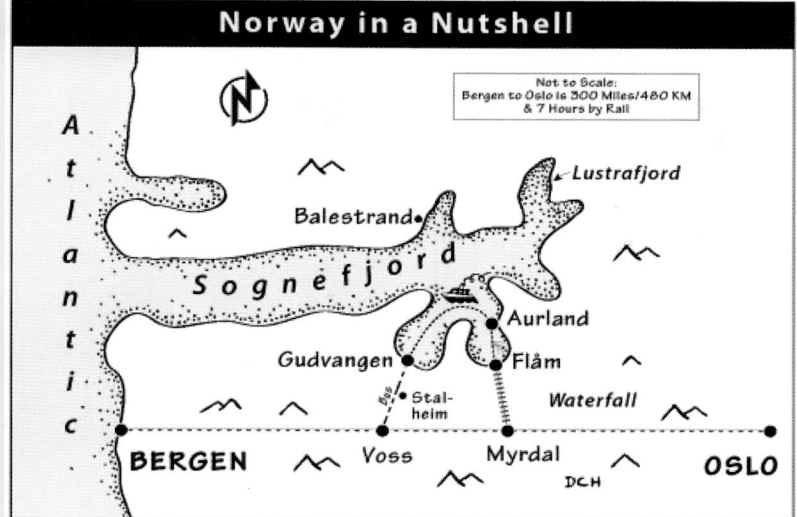

Norway in a Nutshell

Not to Scale: Bergen to Oslo is 300 Miles/480 KM & 7 Hours by Rail

Americans. Europeans like us, but with all due respect, they wouldn't trade passports.

•

The Big Sleep: Arrive 30 minutes before your train leaves. Walk most of the length of the train but not to the last car. Choose a car that is going where you want to go, and find an empty compartment. Pull two seats out to make a bed, close the curtains, turn out the lights, and pretend you are sound asleep. It's amazing. At 21:00, everyone on that train is snoring away! The first 30 people to get on that car have room to sleep. Number 31 will go into any car with the lights on and people sitting up. The most convincing "sleepers" will be the last to be "woken up." (The real champs put a hand down their pants and smile peacefully.)

Museum Strategies

Eavesdrop. If you are especially interested in one piece of art, spend half an hour studying it and listening to each passing tour guide tell his or her story about David or the Mona Lisa or whatever. They each do their own research and come up with different information to share. Much of it is true. There's nothing wrong with this sort of tour freeloading. Just don't stand in the front and ask a lot of questions.

•

For $20, you can rent a couchette (bunk bed) on your overnight train. Top bunks give you a bit more room and safety – but BYOB.

Tips on Creative Communication

Be melodramatic. Exaggerate the local accent. In France, communicate more effectively (and have more fun) by sounding like Maurice Chevalier or Inspector Clouseau. The locals won't be insulted; they'll be impressed. Use whatever French you know. But even English, spoken with a sexy French accent makes more sense to the French ear. In Italy, be melodramatic, exuberant, and wave those hands. Go ahead, try it: Mama mia! No. Do it again. MAMA MIA! You've got to be uninhibited. Self-consciousness kills communication.

Desperate Telephone Communication

Let me illustrate with a hypothetical telephone conversation. I'm calling a hotel in Barcelona from a phone booth in the train station. I just arrived, read my guidebook's list of budget accommodations, and I like Pedro's Hotel. Here's what happens:

Pedro answers, "Hotel Pedro, grabdaboodogalaysk."

I ask, "Hotel Pedro?" (Question marks are created melodically.)

He affirms, already a bit impatient, "Si, Hotel Pedro."

I ask, "Habla Eng-leesh?"

He says, "No, dees ess Ehspain." (Actually, he probably would speak a little English or would say "moment" and get someone who did. But we'll make this particularly challenging. Not only does he not speak English — he doesn't want to… for patriotic reasons.)

Remembering not to overcommunicate, you don't need to tell him you're a tourist looking for a bed. Who else calls a hotel speaking in a foreign language? Also, you can assume he's got a room available. If he's full, he's very busy and he'd say "complete" or "no hotel" and hang up. If he's still talking to you, he wants your business. Now you must communicate just a few things, like how many beds you need and who you are.

I say, "OK." (OK is international for, "Roger, prepare for the next transmission.") "Two people" –he doesn't understand. I get fancy, "Dos people" — he still doesn't get it. Internationalize, "Dos pehr-son" — no comprende. "Dos hombre" — nope. Digging deep into my bag of international linguistic tricks, I say, "Dos Yankees."

"OK!" He understands, you want beds for two Americans. He says, "Si," and I say, "Very good" or "Muy bueno."

Now I need to tell him who I am. I say, "My name Ricardo (Ree-KAR-do)." In Italy I say, "My name Luigi." Your name really doesn't matter; you're communicating just a password so you can identify yourself when you walk through the door. Say anything to be understood.

He says, "OK."

You repeat slowly, "Hotel, dos Yankees, Ricardo, coming pronto, OK?"

He says, "OK."

You say, "Gracias, ciao!"

Twenty minutes later you walk up to the reception desk, and Pedro greets you with a robust, "Eh, Ricardo!"

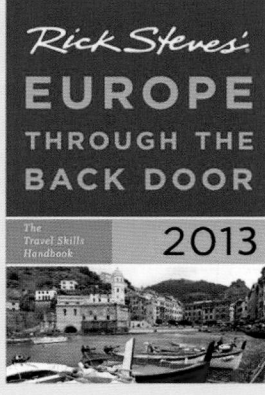

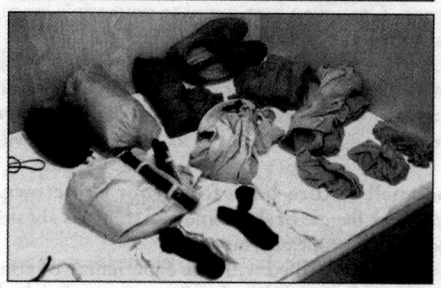

One carry-on-size bag?? Here's exactly what I traveled with for two months (photo taken in a Copenhagen hotel room).

Crash course on budget European travel
Rick Steves' Travel Skills
$16 Amazon

I rely on Rick Steves' masterly command of travel minutia to guide me in Europe. The guy spends 3 months traveling there every year updating his advice in his expanding line of eponymous books. Rick has the drill down perfectly, and possesses a real gift for teaching what he knows. Yet as great as his books are, the very best way to get educated in how to travel Europe with ease and grace is to watch his short course in Travel Skills on DVD or tape. He does great video: quick, dense, informative, easy. I am a hardened veteran traveller and I picked up some handy tips I didn't know. If you are just starting out to Europe, I can't recommend this enough.

-- KK

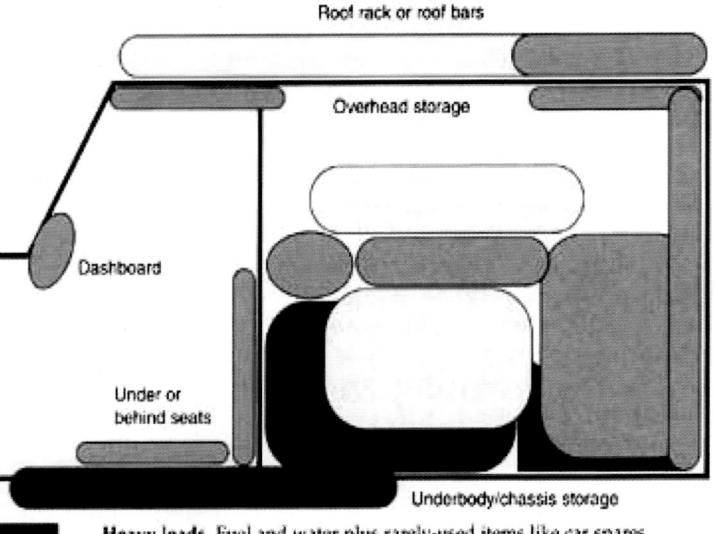

Roof rack or roof bars

Overhead storage

Dashboard

Under or
behind seats

Underbody/chassis storage

Heavy loads Fuel and water plus rarely-used items like car spares.

Daily items Food, cooking and camping gear. In front pockets and behind/under seats: maps, books, documents, water bottle, camera.

Light or less frequently needed items Clothes, tents, sixth tyre, empty containers, extra food.

The bilble of Sahara
Sahara Overland
$32 Chris Scott, 2005, 688 p.

The Sahara is a desert as large as the United States filled with emptiness, ancient cultures, and natural wonders. America has its own recreational deserts in the west, but for Africa and Europe, the Sahara is where you go to test yourself. This book, now in its second edition, has emerged as THE source for getting into the deep Sahara and back, alive and in good spirits. It is uncommonly thorough and immensely practical. It covers the kinds of vehicles and supplies you need, runs along possible itineraries and dangers, and anticipates most of the questions you might have. No stone is left unanswered. The book is a brick — a great big fat bible stuffed with precious overland Sahara lore, hard won by hundreds of trips and mistakes of others. There are not many travel books (or destinations) quite like this one.*

- KK

• Another problem with guides arises when you want to take them away from their prescribed routes. Nervousness about the condition of their own vehicles can play a part, but guides also feel secure following their time-worn 'tram lines.' They can get distinctly edgy when asked to go into areas they don't know or which will push their vehicles hard. The fact that you have a guidebook full of proven GPS points may not necessarily make them feel any better. I've seen one driver (admittedly not the guide) literally freak out at the thought of heading into the dunes, grabbing a wheel brace and all the cars' keys, yelling 'we're all going to die!'

• Tyre pressures

The first-time desert driver quickly learns the huge difference very low tyre pressures make to driving in soft sand. As Ralph Bagnold discovered nearly eighty years ago while drivng a truck into the Great Sand Sea: "Prendergast let more air out of his lorry wheels so that the pressure was only 15 psi instead of 90. The result was marvellous. The lorry sailed along."

• It's possible to arc weld off two (or better still three) 12-volt batteries attached in series making 24/36 volts and plenty enough amps (home arc-welding machines produce about 30-40 volts). A jump lead attached to a pair of Mole grips can hold a welding rod and bits of thick cable or wire can join the batteries if necessary. Take the batteries right out of the car and if unsealed protect them from sparks (batteries produce explosive gas) and prepare the welding area well. It's not going to do your batteries much good in the long term so is best for emergencies only, but I've seen a broken chassis repaired with battery welding.

• At this point, you may want to try asking someone… A lot depends on how you ask. Don't pre-suggest by pointing and asking 'Is this the way to Madame Tussaud's?'. Instead ask 'Which way to Madame Tussaud's?' but don't point. It won't guarantee a correct answer but will avoid the tendency to nod affirmatively to please or to get rid of someone. Although you may be steaming from the ears by this stage, remember to be polite and, as with all exchanges in Africa, start with greetings and handshakes. Avoid showing maps – depending on where you are, only tourists use and understand these – but drawing a mud map in the dirt or in the dust on your bonnet can be useful.

• A final word about guides: you need them, but do not rely on them. They will tell you that lots of things are impossible.

That generally means that they cannot be bothered to do them. They tend to be highly conservative people, who resent being diverted from their usual routes and routines. Do not trust their navigation. If you leave your compass and GPS at home because you are in the hands of a local, you are being very foolish. Try to use guides who have been recommended to you by previous expeditions. And (of course) on no account pay them everything up front.

• An old adage advises that you should never camp in a oued because flash floods from distant rains could rip through your camp causing havoc. Some sources have even claimed that 'more people have drowned in the Sahara than died of thirst' – about as likely as more people dying of thirst than drowning at sea, or freezing to death in the Antarctic. In Morocco, where run-off from the Atlas can be frequent, steep and fast, this warning is valid in certain seasons but in the deep Sahara, oueds often offer some welcome tree shade or vegetated wind breaks, as well as soft sand rather than gravel. Obviously if there are dark clouds in the sky keep to the high ground wherever you are, but dangerous flash floods are only a real danger in mountain areas, and by the time they get to the plain they're all but spent.

• People get nervous about carrying a wad of money abroad but good old-fashioned cash is readily changeable and local currency is what talks loudest in the Sahara. Unless you expect to be visiting large cities or capitals, travellers' cheques are of little use. Despite what you're told, the promise of speedy replacement of stolen cheques requires a phone call – itself a rather tall order in most of the Sahara. Don't rely on cashing travellers' cheques in the Sahara.

It may look drastic, but the only way is to drag this car down to more level ground where it can be pulled back onto its wheels. Within an hour it was running just as before.

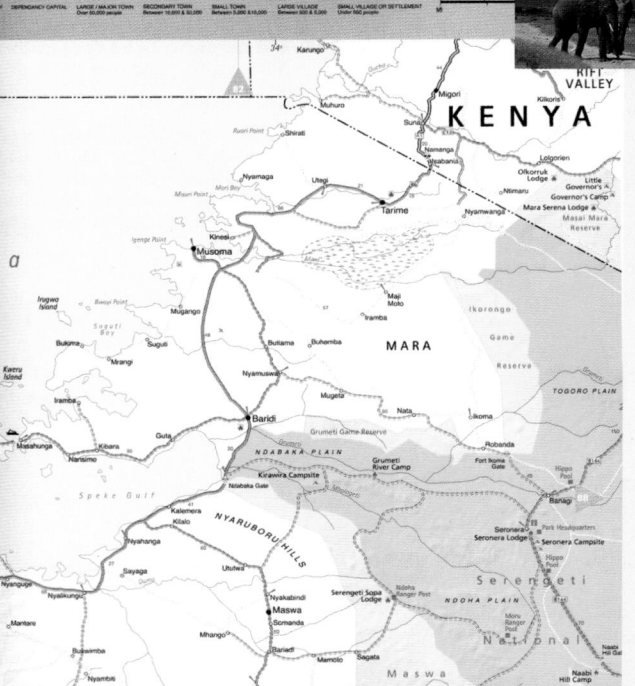

Essential road maps
African Adventure Atlas
$6 (used) Amazon

The vastness of Africa is vastly rural. Driving a car or van is the best way to get around. But African road maps are as scarce and inadequate as the mostly unpaved roads themselves. This heavy, oversized, and humungous 336-page atlas (definitely not backpackable) contains the best — and sometimes only — road maps for the entire continent.

Crafted by the cartographic gnomes at National Geographic, this set of maps is meant to be more of an adventure guide. It succeeds as both. These maps indicate the exact information you need while on the road: known ferry crossings, known border posts, known park entrances, local airfields, ruins, mileage markers, as well as the major African towns and national parks interiors. I can't think of any other maps anywhere else in the developing world that provide this kind of vital information ahead of time. And to top it off, this full-color atlas concludes with 80 good itineraries (with maps!) for creative explorations on the continent. It's a remarkable achievement; I wish there was one for Asia and South America as well.

-- KK

Best guide to Mexico
The People's Guide to Mexico
$18 Carl Franz, Lorena Havens, 2012, 768 p.

I love works that are renewed and improved. Carl Franz and Lorena Havens have been exploring the hinterlands of Mexico and reporting back their travel suggestions in amusing detail since their first edition of this book in 1972. For four decades this venerable guidebook has been the best manual for visiting Mexico, getting better with each edition. It has just been released in its 14th. Franz and Havens are not going to be much help in keeping you up to date with the best hotel in the usual tourist destinations (your standard Lonely Planet-ish guide will handle that). Where *The People's Guide* transcends the usual guidebook is in its devotion to the blue highways and backlands, the off beat places and indigenous living.

This guide is best for those driving around Mexico in a vehicle, camping in its many parks, exploring its meandering dirt roads, hanging out on undeveloped beaches, sampling native foods and immersing yourself into the culture

Building a palapa

Knife blade inscriptions: He Who Acts Bad Ends Bad; Life Is The Road to the Tomb; Beans Are Worth More than Happiness

of our neighbor as much as possible. It's chock full of all the advice you'd expect from a couple who have been noodling around Mexico every year for thirty five years: how to live off the land, keep on the right side of the law, shop for strange and exotic foods, survive, educate yourself in local customs, and remain healthy and sane. It's a fat 700-page book with lots of great stories, and endless good counsel. (They run a supplementary website for updated tips.)

A lot of this lore is universal travel wisdom (the less money you spend the more fun you have). In fact *The People's Guide to Mexico* is one of the best travel guides I've ever seen to anywhere in the world. You could easily transfer many of their tips to traveling in Asia or Africa, and the rest of Latin America. But the bulk of it is very particular to Mexico. Every page yields golden nuggets of fine advice for every part of a very large Mexico. I find myself reading whole chapters for the pure enjoyment of being in the presence of great, gifted guides teaching me useful stuff I didn't know.

The Mexico/US border is one the most abrupt borders in the world. There's almost nowhere else on earth where you can travel so far in so few miles as crossing this imaginary line. This trip has the additional benefit of being guided by this amazing encyclopedia of practical tips and insights. You'd be a fool not to take it with you.

It's the operating manual for people in Mexico.

-- KK

•

I climbed over other passengers and cargo to the cab of the truck, determined to check our speed.

"Hey," I yelled back to Lorena, "It's really not so bad after all. We're only doing 90 to 100 kilometers an hour. That's fast but not so dangerous." I took another peek through the rear window; a curve was coming up and we were slowing to 70. i was just about to turn and work my way back when I noticed a small "MPH" beneath the speedometer needle.

MPH! I felt the blood drain from my face and go roaring through my ears and down to my feet. Seventy into a curve! One hundred on the straightaway!

"Let me off! Let me off!" I screamed, pounding the roof of the cab with my fists. I got a glimpse of the driver's startled face turned toward the rear of the truck.

Many common driving hazards and annoyances found in the U.S. are also in Mexico, though usually in a slightly altered form.

In the U.S., the omnipresent teenager hunched bird-like behind the wheel of his 400-hp candy-colored, air-foiled Supercar, passes you dangerously close at 140 mph as he calmly munches a DoubleBurger and squeezes an annoying pimple.

In Mexico, he's still the same basic teenager, apparently oblivious to other traffic and mesmerized by the blaring radio and the dangling ornaments that festoon mirrors and knobs. But there is one difference: He's behind the wheel of a hurtling semi-truckload of sugarcane. And he's passing you on a blind mountain curve. You glance over, afraid to imagine what is about to happen. He grins, flashes a peace sign and cuts you off as he swerves to miss an oncoming bus.

Low-flying buzzards are a very real hazard, as are piles of drying corn, beans and chili peppers placed on the hot pavement by enterprising farmers who prefer the smooth road surface to the dusty shoulder.

As you fly around a curve and find yourself unexpectedly in the middle of small village, it seems that everyone suddenly leaps up and crosses the street, forcing you to brake madly. Pigs that haven't moved from gooey wallows for a week lurch frantically to their feet and stumble in front of the car, followed by reckless children beating them with twigs.

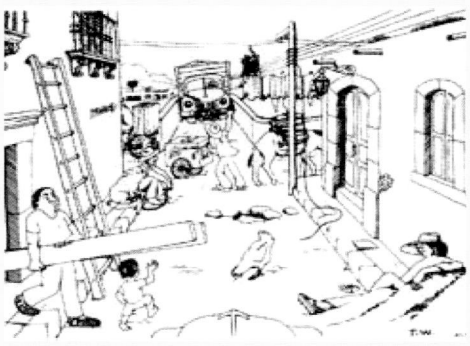

These are relatively minor hazards that you'll soon become used to. For really serious trouble, nothing compares to other drivers.

"They may be wild, but they're damn good!" is a comment you might hear, especially about Mexican truck drivers. If good driving involves good sense, however, they must surely be among the worst. Many truckers would be disqualified from a destruction derby on ground of excessive zeal and disregard for human life.

The good news is that the average Mexican chofer (driver) is definitely getting better. Drivers are more courteous and less likely to indulge in macho grandstanding while behind the wheel of the family car. Bus drivers have also gotten the message about safety and many of them could give lessons to American drivers.

Still, it is dangerously easy for tourists to fall into the same driving habits they see demonstrated by others. When you're breathing fumes behind a slow diesel truck in a steep mountain pass, the temptation to pass on a blind curve can be very strong. At this point, you should seriously consider what the consequences are if you don't make it.

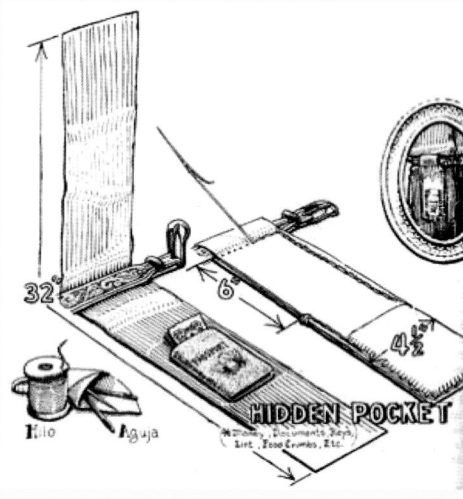

Diarrhea and Dysentery

Powdered scorpions, chia and 7Up, camomile and "dog tea," food enzymes, acidophilus, papaya seeds, dried apricot pits: When it comes to upset stomachs, nausea, diarrhea, and disenteria, I've tried almost everything. As a firm believer in the value of medical plants and folk remedies, I'm sorry to announce that a dose of bismuth solution (such as Pepto-Bismol) seems to beat them all. In fact, our experience clearly shows that taking the pink stuff in moderate doses before, during, and even after traveling can dramatically reduce stomach problems.

Though it is effective, I'm no fan of bismuth's cloying pink taste and I don't like to pour it repeatedly into my stomach. I now take about half of an adults dosage (one tablespoon 3-4 times a day). I start my bismuth program a few days before leaving home and continue taking it once or twice a day for about a week. If my stomach shows no sign of rebellion in that time, I go to "standby" and keep the bismuth close at hand in the event of sudden turmoil.

•

In Mexico, "look before you leap" isn't just an expression, it's a survival tip. Forget about bandits; the greatest threat to your safety comes from slippery cobblestones, uneven sidewalks, knee-high curbs, head-knocking signs, eye-poking awnings, toe-stubbing thresholds, open trenches, unexpected drop-offs and discarded construction debris.

•

Keep track of your personal belongings. When Lorena and I lead tours or travel with friends, we continually pick up our companions' stray cameras, passports, purses and room keys. Tourists routinely walk away from their suitcases, leave their credit cards at souvenir shops and their only shoes at the beach, and can't recall which lavanderia (laundry) they left their clothes in.

A fellow we traveled with in eastern Mexico left his binoculars hanging on a chair in the restaurant of a small hotel. By the time he realized his mistake, we were hundreds of miles away and couldn't go back. When I returned to the hotel two years later, the owner's first words were, "I have the binoculars your friend forgot. … As a postscript, the fellow who lost and regained the binoculars returned to travel with us again. This time he left a very expensive Nikon camera in the washroom of a museum. In this case, however, the camera had vanished by the time we returned for it.

Snow poles mark the road edge for snow plows in scenic Thompson Pass

Alaskan highway guide
The Milepost
$19 Kristine Valencia, 2013, 784 p.

If you're thinking of doing a road trip to Alaska, *The Milepost* is a must-have. This thick publication, revised annually, has mile-by-mile conditions of all the major highways in Alaska and other northern points, including Alberta, British Columbia, Northwest Territories and the Yukon.

It's available in some brick and mortar bookstores, and online from their website.

-- Regis

•

"What is the best time of year to go?" is one of the most frequently asked questions about traveling to Alaska. During the

summer, the weather in the North is as variable and unpredictable as anywhere else. Go prepared for both hot, sunny days and cold, rainy days. Regardless of weather, the Alaska Highway is open all year.

May: fewer people on the road, can be fine weather.

June: long days averaging 20 hours of daylight.

July: busiest month on the highway, can also be the wettest.

August: trees start to turn colors, nights get chilly.

September: fall colors, first frost and snow possible in some areas, uncrowded ferries.

•

Is the Alaska Highway paved?

All of the Alaska Highway is paved, although highway improvement projects- such as

the Shakwak Project between Haines Junction and the AK-YT border-often mean motorists have to drive miles of gravel road through construction areas, bringing into question whether that statement is altogether accurate.

But the Alaska Highway is much improved from what is was even 20 years ago. It was during the 1980s that many of the rerouting and paving projects were completed. By 1992, the 50th anniversary of the Alaska Highway, the last section of original gravel road had been rerouted and paved.

Hotsprings

Where to soak outdoors
Wild Hot Springs

A natural hot spring is not interesting until collected into a hot pool. Hot pools on private land inevitably evolve into hot spas. These can be great in themselves: The Japanese built a robust empire around hot spas, and even in the US, natural spas can be wonderful. But there is nothing like soaking your butt in a natural hot spring bubbling out of the ground in the midst of absolutely-nowhere, surrounded by tufts of green, rock, and drop-dead beauty, and — most of the time — no one else.

By some cosmic gift, most of the hot springs in the US pop up within the publicly owned vastness of the West, thereby guaranteeing the continuation of several hundred recreational hot springs and hot pools that retain their undeveloped wildness. This is me, right, at Spencer's Hot Springs, Nevada. Water temp, about 104. Or below, me, my wife and some friends in Crowley Hot Springs (also known as Wild Willie's), California. Yes, it was a lovely as it looks.

How do you get there? These books will tell you.

The two US-oriented ones here are the best of a very small bunch. They are great updated editions based on the early guides of the late Jayson Loam, who is credited with popularizing rustic hot springs. The Southwest book somewhat counterintuitively includes California, Nevada down to Texas, while the Northwest volume includes Oregon, Wyoming up to Alaska. *Hot Springs of Western Canada (2nd Edition)* covers about a hundred springs in Canada, but the better ones are included in the aforementioned *Hot Springs & Hot Pools of the Northwest*; good enough for most folks.

Each guide lists over a hundred hot springs, including the many developed ones (some extremely built up). You'll have to sort through to find the more primitive and rustic ones. For each

spring there's at least one photo, a description, and street directions if they are developed. In the past the great challenge posed by wild springs was finding them; many quests to reach a fabled hot spot were abandoned by the mapless. Happily that test is now easy to pass if you have a GPS unit. These guides provide GPS coordinates (yeah!) for most of the rustic sites.

There used to be an occasional periodical called the *Hot Spring Gazette*, which kept up on which springs dried up, or were closed down, and what ones newly opened, etc. While they have a website, as far as I can determine they haven't had an issue in 5 years. Your best guide to the latest news in primitive hot baths (other than spring-wise friends) is these websites.

Free soak.net

Free hotspringsenthusiast.com

Lastly, the truly hot-spring obsessed will quote from the legendary Thermal Springs List of the United States. It is nothing more, nor less, than a comprehensive database of ALL known hot springs in the US. Decades ago, a yellowing print-out of this government publication was a badge of true hot-spring aficionado. These days this database is maintained by the National Oceanic and Atmospheric Administration and is available online. Diehard hot-water freaks use the list to hunt for little-visited hot springs, but be forewarned. Most of these springs are but trickles of warm water and not bathable. Furthermore, this database contains only the temperature, flow, and latitude/longitude coordinates of the springs, which won't help the casual user in either finding it, or deciding whether it will be worth the trip. For most mortals, the guide books above offer more enjoyable springs than you'll ever get to.

Happy soaking!

-- KK

$19 Hot Springs and Hot Pools of the Southwest Marjorie Gersh-Young, 2011, 264 p.

Free Thermal Springs List of the United States (database search)

Free Thermal Springs List of the United States (map interface)

$18 Hot Springs and Hot Pools of the Northwest: Jason Loam's Original Guide Marjorie Gersh-Young, 2008, 235 p.

Common Sense and Safety Tips

It's Hot: Always, always check the temperature of the water before entering. Even if you have been to a spring several times, conditions affecting water flow and temperature change constantly.

It's Smelly or Not: Structures built over hot springs often prevent natural gasses from escaping. These can often build up and cause you to become dizzy and pass out. Be extremely cautious about staying within structures for any length of time.

Heads Up: Because many forms of bacteria and other organisms live in hot water, it is recommended by many that you do not put your head in the water.

The Gang's All Here: This is where consideration for other soakers comes in. If you arrive at a full pool, ask how long they plan on staying; or ask if you may join them. If you're the first person there, invite others to join you. You'd be amazed at the interesting people you meet. If people are waiting for you to get out before they get in, determine a reasonable length of time, and leave when agreed upon. Take a walk, watch the sky, read a book, and return later.

●
Kennedy Hot Spring / Undeveloped / 35 C (?) (95 F)

The unusual soaking box at Kennedy is about 2 m (6 ft.) deep and is fed from the bottom. – Hot Springs of Western Canada

A 9 km (5.5 mi.) hike on an excellent trail leads to a very nice pool deep in the Glacier Peak Wilderness. This is one of the more popular hikes in the North Cascades and is well worth the effort. May through October are the best months for this trip.

$18 Hot Springs of Western Canada: A Complete Guide Glenn Woodsworth,1999, 288 p.

Desert swimming holes
Day Trips with a Splash

$19 Pancho Doll, 2000, 216 p.

A swimming hole
in the desert
is heaven.
Splash! Splash!

Here are 100 heavens.

And how to get there, without prayers

With GPS coordinates, topo maps, summaries.

No excuses.

-- KK

●
The Jug

Smoothest water east of the Sierra Nevada. Water pouring out of the Salome Wilderness cuts through an exposed portion of the batholith, a large intrusion of granite that underlies many of the ranges here. It creates a sinuous channel of intriguing shapes. Directly at the bottom of the first access to the creek is a rock that so resembles the torso of a reclining woman that a crack runs directly across her back and shoulders where the bra strap would be. The rest of this miniature canyon has so many sinusoidal curves worn into the rock that you might think yourself in Yosemite except for the saguaro on the canyon walls.

Above the "sleeping lady" is one of the best late season spots I know of. I say late season because the water is awfully cool in the spring. Also because low levels let you appreciate the beautiful lines of this tub. It's a near-perfect rectangle, twelve feet long, seven feet wide and just as deep. Water exits via a narrow spout etched exquisitely in the rock lip at the bottom of the tub. There is a two-person slab adjoining the pool to the right. An overhanging rock is there if you need some shade.

Warm days in spring can attract as many as one-half dozen cars to the trailhead. Consequently, the canyon can seem busy..

●
Cave Creek

The sweetest place to sit in the whole state of Arizona. There's a perfectly flat stone the size of a park bench right next to a tiny waterfall. A juniper provides a low, dense canopy of shade that'll keep you cool when the surrounding vegetation is at the flash point. The adjoining pool occurs where a handful of large boulders have tumbled across the stream. As it rushes over the boulders, the water accelerates just enough to scrape a modest pool out of the sand and gravel streambed. The pool is circular, about 30 feet in diameter, but none too deep, maybe six feet in the center although this will vary with water level and the amount of cobble in the creek bed.

Lots of people with side arms, it seemed. Rationally I know that the reason people carry combat automatics into the mountains is because they are more afraid of you than you should be of them — this or they believe

that rattlesnakes attack in packs. Still, I got a kind of weird vibe and I'm a gun owner myself.

Aside from the firearm notice, be advised to bring something to sit on because the rocks are dark and will get very hot during midday. Also, it's a short steep descent with loose rock. A walking stick is recommended.

Essential guidebook to Old Japan
Japan's Hidden Hot Springs
$25 Robert Neff, 1995, 180 p.

I enjoy Japan because it is so richly Other. Central to Japanese "otherness" is the bath. Like the famous tea ceremony, it's larger than it seems. The shortest route into traditional Japanese culture is a soak in a very hot bath, preferably in a communal bathhouse, more preferably in an intimate, well-crafted hot spring located in a mossy thatched inn with paper doors and tatami floors at the end of a trail. Problem is this romantic ideal is very hard to locate, especially for foreigners. But they do exist. This wonderfully small, intimate and well-crafted book will guide to you the few remaining really traditional hot springs (onsen) in Japan. Despite this guidebook, you'll only find Japanese staying there. The author has visited several hundred Japanese onsen (I've been to maybe a dozen) and will save you the incredibly depressing experience of winding up in a hideous concrete over-commercialized urban disaster – which is what most of the springs have become. Any one of the chosen here are little-known national treasures worth going way out of your way to soak in overnight and soak up.

-- KK

There are better times than others for visiting onsen. Winter is best, since the hot water feels finest against the cold air and the snowscapes are so ethereal. What could be more sublime than sitting in a mountain hot tub at night, sipping sake and conversing with your close ones while gazing at the stars through snow-clad branches? Ideally, a bubbling brook is coursing through the snow just next to the bath. Great for a Scandinavian-style plunge if your heart can take it. The next-best season is autumn, followed by spring and summer. Avoid weekends if possible, although that's when I usually go for lack of other opportunities. And try to take friends. You'll get a better room and price as a party of four (or more) and have more fun as well.

No two outdoor baths are the same, of course, but Myogaya's is uniquely fetching. To get there means negotiating several very steep, covered staircases plunging from the inn to the depths of the Kanomata River gorge. Near the bottom you'll first encounter the separate men's and women's changing rooms. Off to the left, and on about the same level, are several goemonburo, cramped, vat-like tubs that barely accommodate a single bather. They're named for a legendary figure who was boiled alive in a similar pot.

Descend one more short stairway and you're at the sexually integrated bath-site. Here you'll find four sheltered tubs: two smallish but comfortable wooden ones implanted in cement, a larger one of concrete to the back, and a tiny cave-like pool off to the side. All face onto the narrow river, a gurgling mountain stream that's just a hop away. Its other side soars almost vertically, clad in thick vegetation. This ranks among the best outdoor bathing we've enjoyed anywhere.

Somehow, Myogaya's rotenburo manages to combine a sense of both coziness and spaciousness, solitude and fraternity. Rarely crowded in our experience, the baths can be more or less your own private playground if you time things right. That means when everyone else is having dinner or after 10:00 a.m.

Extremely remote getaways
Firetowers, Lookouts & Rustic Cabins for Rent
$25 Carolyne Ilona Gatesy, 1997, 226 p.
$16 Tom Foley, Tish McFadden, 2005, 240 p.

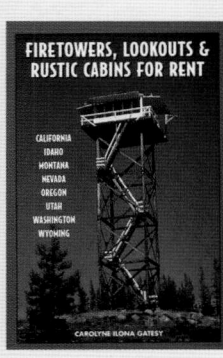

The last wilderness romance: a funky old-fashion shelter with minimal comfort and maximum views. You can rent these remote cabins for about $25 per day, and sleep 4 or 5 people. The 145 described here are all located in the west. The best are difficult to reach. Most are approachable by 4-wheel drive. All need advance reservations. The little-known details and full getting-there instructions, are here.

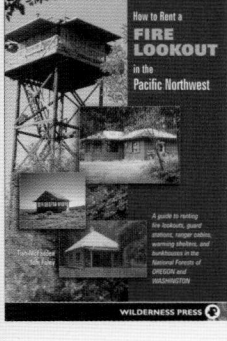

The above original book is showing its age in terms of prices and numbers. While the structures are the same, an even better book, with current fees, web pages and phone numbers is *How to Rent a Fire Lookout in the Pacific Northwest*.

-- KK

All of the firetowers, lookouts and cabins described in this book are rustic in every sense of the word. They are remotely located, and most lack the conveniences of civilization such as running water, electricity or telephones. The interiors look like they were from the 1950s and the furniture included is generally limited. They contain sparse, serviceable, shabby or rough-hewn furniture of the sort you might throw out, after the Salvation Army had rejected it. However, if you hike or ski in, you will appreciate just sitting down with a roof over your head. The beds are usually plywood, built with a plank on top, and occasionally lacking a mattress. (I recommend bringing an inflatable mattress if none are listed by the district as included with the rental.) Upon making your reservation, be sure to ask for a detailed list of what is available with the rental and what to bring.

Squaw Peak Lookout

As long as you have four-wheel drive and patience, you can enjoy this scenic cabin in the summer. There is initially a horrendous road of 2.5 miles of ditches and holes, and then an additional 2.5 mile hike into the Lookout, or you can park your vehicle and hike the five miles. Squaw Peak is a one room painted white cabin with a stone base located on a bare peak in

Acker Rock Lookout

the Cabinet Mountains. There is a stone outbuilding next door in the process of being rehabbed. The cabin does have available a propane refrigerator and stove and if you send for information, included are instructions in the operation of both items. There is also a wood stove, and wood is kept in the basement.

Category: Very rustic lookout
Elevation: 6,167
Road condition: Trail access three miles from Highway 200
Availability: All year except July and August; exact dates depend on fire season
Daily use fee: $25 for up to five people
For further information, contact:
Kootenai National Forest
Cabinet Ranger District
HCR2, Box 210
2693 Highway 200
Trout Creek, MT 59874
(406) 847-2462

Berry Creek Guard Station, built in 1934, sits with gorgeous scenic views in the Shell Creek Mountains. The view includes aspen, many tall trees, and lots of mountains. Deer, elk, and sometimes bobcat and coyote may be seen or heard from the cabin boundary. The old cabin has a living room, one bedroom, and propane cook stove and refrigerator, and a propane wall heater. There is indoor plumbing during the warm season, including a shower and toilet.

Lightning Stool at Pickette Butte Lookout

Ultimate walking
North Cornwall: Exploring the Coastal Footpath
$4 Mark Richards, 1976, 132 p.

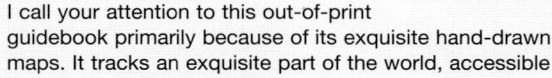

I call your attention to this out-of-print guidebook primarily because of its exquisite hand-drawn maps. It tracks an exquisite part of the world, accessible by foot. A 300-mile footpath winds along the west coast of England, and like most trails in England, it is signed and no-cars the whole way. It cuts along spectacular cliffs, tiny coves, and secluded villages. The path's landmarks are captured beautifully in this one-of-a-kind field guide. I wish there was a guide like this for every trail in the world. I found its sketches indispensable while I walked the path, but now it serves me as a reminder that for hikers, trekkers, and ramblers, there is no place better for short or long walks than England. I have hiked all over the globe and England's network of marked and uninterrupted footpaths is the best there is, as suggested by the details in this artful book. Used copies can be found on Amazon UK. -- KK

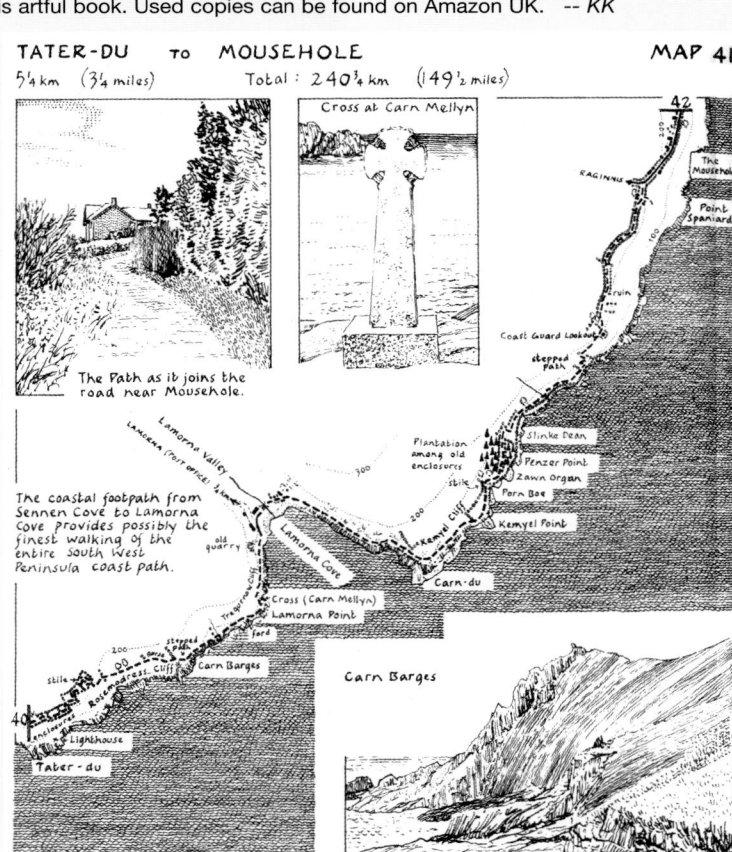

Best guide for nomadic RV life
Boondock RVing

Escapees RV Club and Mail Forwarding escapees.com

Workamper workamper.com

The Complete Book of Boondock RVing
$12 Bill Moeller, 2007, 176 pages

With a little bit of gumption you can liberate your RV from the leash of the RV parks. Run it untethered, off the grid. Camp in a wild place, or in a parking lot. Takes some advance planning, maybe some more gear, certainly a change of spirit. This book will help. While its technical specs are out of date by a few years, the general drift of the book's advice is right on. Like in anything else off the grid, there's much talk about batteries, inverters and cables. There is not much here about mail forwarding, etc., which is best covered by hanging out on the forums at Escapees, the watering hole website for full-time RVers.

You can use flexible water tanks to transport water to the RV.

Escapees is a membership club for full time RVers which offers a popular mail forwarding service. You can get your postal mail and packages forwarded in a hundred different ways and schedules. Since it is based in Texas, your official residence can then be located in a state without income tax. Its 35,000 members are eager to share their knowledge of the RV life with newbies.

Also, Workamper is a good online bookstore full of RV-related titles. Guides to: Finding work on the road, cooking, repairs, shopping guides for new rigs, directories of camp grounds, RVing in Mexico and Alaska, dealing with insurance, etc. Also a book that lists what stores lie at each exit of the interstates! Most of the published lore focuses on snowbirding, and RV parking, rather than boondocking.

Overall, *Boondocking RVing* is the best book about the logistics of long-term nomadic RVing.

--KK

•

Additionally, the cost of staying in private campgrounds is increasing, going up by a dollar or more per night each year. We recently read an article in RVBusiness magazine, written by a campground spokesman, that stated the industry envisions campground prices will eventually reach a level of 50% the cost of a midlevel hotel or more. Consequently, if you would normally pay $100 a night for a hotel room, you would pay $50 a night in an RV park.

•

Retail Stores and Restaurants

Retail and chain stores often have large, well-lit parking lots. We have camped at Fred Meyer, Kmart, and Wal-Mart stores (or Camp Wally as they are more commonly called). In fact, Wal-Mart carries an edition of the Rand McNally road atlas with an insert that lists all of the U.S. and Canadian Wal-Marts. Other options might include discount warehouses, such as Sam's Club, or restaurants, such as Cracker Barrel and McDonald's.

•

Casinos are excellent places for convenience camping. We don't know of any casinos that prohibit overnight camping, unless they have a commercial campground. Of course, they expect you to patronize the facilities, so at least eat in their restaurants, which often have

excellent buffets at reasonable prices. ... With the profusion of casinos being built all over the country, they can make great overnight stops with good food and entertainment. Some casinos have regular RV parks, but still allow boondocking in certain areas of the parking lot.

•

We have two catalytic heaters -- a small one (1,600 to 2,800 Btu), which is mounted on the wall, and a medium-sized one (3,200 to 6,000 Btu) we can move around as needed. We've kept warm in some below-freezing temperatures with the catalytic heaters as our only heat source.

Our catalytic propane heater with the folding doors that we made to protect the cabinetry near it.

•

There is a bit of controversy over whether 6-volt or 12-volt batteries are better in a battery bank. Two of the arguments for using 6-volt batteries are (1) there are fewer cables involved in series wiring, so there are fewer connection to corrode; and (2) in 12-volt parallel wiring, one of the batteries in a two-battery bank will receive most of the load and most of the charge, and therefore will fail faster than the other.

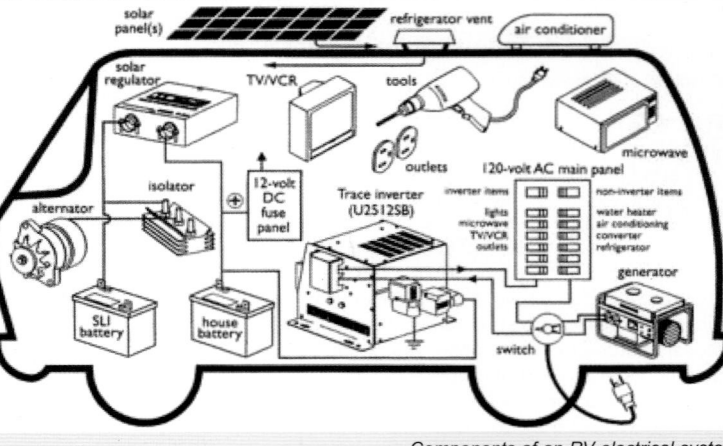

Components of an RV electrical system.

The first argument has some validity as there are fewer cables in series wiring, so there is less corrosion. The second argument is not necessarily true, if you wire the bank as shown above. if a battery goes bad in a 12-volt bank, you can just disconnect it and use the remaining one. You'll still be getting 12 volts. With a 6-volt bank, however, one bad battery means the loss of the whole two-battery bank.

•

Should you tilt your panels and follow the sun? ... We have seen rigs with their panels mounted on racks that allow them to swing around to track the sun. Frankly, this just seems like too much work to us, plus we don't really think it's necessary. Also, when panels are tilted up, they can be more easily damaged by the high winds that occur during the winter months, particularly in desert areas.

Three 100-watt solar panels installed lengthwise on the roof of a friend's motorhome.

Low rent nomads
Cheap RV Living

cheaprvliving.com

Roomier than a car, but cheaper than an RV, a retrofitted van makes a cool inexpensive house. Once popular during hippie days, the ancient American tradition of modifying a van is undergoing a resurgence as rents continue to rise. More folks each year commute from work and then park their home, instead of parking in front of it. On this lovely free website, you can find inspiring examples of cheap nomads, detailed instructions for conversions, gear recommendations, and lots of advice for living in a low rent or homemade RV from "them that's doin' it."

-- KK

•

And what about gas mileage? With a car you may get 50 mpg and with an RV you may get 5 mpg. Since we are living cheaply, this is a very important consideration. It's hard to be too specific with mpg numbers. If you buy a 1975 1 ton pickup with a 454, you might get 6 mpg with a camper, but if you buy a 2005 diesel, you may get 20 mpg with the same camper. If you get a 1985 Ford van with a 460, you may get 6 mpg but if you get a 302 V8 you may get 22 mpg. Or, even better, get an Astro mini-van, you could get 25 mpg.

•

STEALTH PARKING: After I bought the van, I didn't know where to go with it. I couldn't afford to pay for an RV park (and they probably would not have accepted me anyway since my van was pretty beat-up looking) so I slept in the parking lot of the store where I worked. No one even noticed me! The great thing about the box van was that when I parked in front of any large store, it looked like it belonged there. I lived in that van for 6 years and never once paid for parking anywhere and was never bothered for where I did park.

•

I have a cell phone, a loan payment, van insurance, and credit cards. One of the first things I did to handle this was go "paperless" - I now get all my statements by email and pay my bills online. I get wifi on my laptop, and many public libraries have computers & internet available.

•

Kitchen:

This changed several times as I was building it. I needed pantry space, drawers, and fresh/gray water for the faucet/sink. The kitchen is positioned along the passenger side so I can open the doors when cooking on my camp stove. The counter is actual Formica with a drop down leaf to give me more room when cooking. I have 2 six gallon containers, one is for gray water and one for fresh. I use a hand pump for water, or use gallons of water from the store for cooking and cleaning more often now. I may add a small pump in the future. The microwave sits underneath with enough space in the pantry for about a week's worth of food. The spice rack is a must have for me, because while the portions are smaller and more challenging to make, I still don't sacrifice on good food! Under the pantry I store my pans, lids, and plates in a magazine rack from Ikea. The fridge is a standard dorm minifridge I found on craigslist for $20 but I only turn it on when driving or when plugged into shore power, as it can drain my batteries in two days.

Most of the time I use it as a glorified icebox, as I tend to buy fresh foods the day I use them.

•

The Pee Bottle:

First and foremost, the pee bottle must be leakproof and unbreakable for obvious reasons! For all my adventures, I've used a 1 liter, wide-mouth Lexan bottle made by Nalgene. They come in a variety of colors - I've settled on the dark yellow one for my pee bottle so I don't mistake it for my drinking water bottle. Similar, less expensive brands can be found in the sporting goods department at WalMart or Target,

or experiment with plastic food product containers with tight fitting lids and enough volume.

Spill Proof - One fear I have in van or tent is fumbling and spilling the pee bottle before I have the lid screwed on all the way. To safeguard this, I made a wrist loop out of a piece of 1inch wide nylon webbing which I duct taped to the bottle (see photo). The wrist loop is loose enough to slip easily on and off and to hold the bottle with that hand, but tight enough that the bottle won't fall if I loose my grip. Slip the loop over one hand, unscrew the lid, and away you go; just be sure to screw the lid on tightly before slipping out of the wrist loop. A piece of cord would work just as well as the nylon webbing - just get the loop the right size.

I keep two pee bottles in the van just in case I forget to empty one during the day - and on long, cold nights sometimes one liter just isn't enough!

•

What vehicle to buy?

If gas mileage and stealth are most important: Chevrolet Astro minivan--great mpg and super stealth.

If room and stealth are most important: Full-size American van, especially the Dodge with a 318 V8.

If headroom is most important: High-top American conversion van.

For a couple, or if you need lots of room: Box van or Step-van, both with a diesel engine.

If you want to go further into the backcountry: Pickup with a camper with 4X4.

used with discretion). The spotlight is incredibly versatile — you can point/rotate it while sitting in the driver's seat — and it's come in handy countless times for roadside emergencies, setting up campsites, or finding house numbers on dark streets.

This urban camouflage guise is very useful for parking in yellow zones, urban/industrial exploration, and crime deterrence. And the thing is… it really works!

The spotlight, bumper, and rear flashers came from my *all-time favorite* mail order catalog: Galls, "The Authority in Public Safety Equipment and Apparel."

It's a gold mine, full of handy things that you didn't think you were allowed to buy.

-- Todd Lapin

Public safety gear catalog
Urban camouflage

Galls Catalog

My Jeep is camouflaged to look like a commercial fleet vehicle. I made up a fake company name, appropriated a 1950s-era logo that once belonged to a nuclear energy mutual fund, painted safety stripes on the back, and plastered a fake vehicle number all over the place. I also added flashing yellow lights in the rear window, and a police-style spotlight and rubberized push bumper to the front. VERY FUN accessories … and useful too (when

Vagabonding tips
VW Vagabond

Free VWvagabonds.com

This couple penny-pinched their salaries for several years, bought a VW Van, and drove it around the world (US, South America and Africa). They share what they have learned on one of the most helpful websites I've seen for this sort of thing. I really like their sensibility and advice. Very reasonable and very wise. They also "review" the tools and stuff they found vital in their small traveling home on this page. Click on a tool to see more.

They give good advice about shipping vehicles (very complex) and even saving up enough to make the journey. They have a book, too.

While living in a VW Van for three years, they got the idea that even this lifestyle was too complex so they get simpler for the next stage. They are now bicycling across Asia, another adventure and great idea.

Part of the reason their advice and website is so useful is that they have no sponsors — a rarity for ambitious trips like this these days. It keeps them honest and useful. Check 'em out.

-- KK

SUCCESS Merrill Lynch Cash Management Account: We opened an account with Merrill Lynch before leaving home and were happy we did for three reasons. 1) Their Signature Rewards Visa card includes free medical evacuation coverage that costs big bucks to purchase.; 2) We were never charged a transaction fee for the more than 150 ATM withdraws we did while traveling and we got the highest bank rate of exchange; 3) Our card number was stolen and used in Brazil. When we realized something was wrong we called our Merrill Lynch rep. collect and he took care of all the hassles

---

Tips for American nomads
Dwelling Portably

$1 per issue, Back issues available
Dwelling Portably, DP c/o Lisa Ahne, POB 181, Alsea, OR 97324

Practical advice about being homeless or low-budget in-motion by choice — camping on the edges, living simply, getting by on the road and loving it. This old-fashioned zine crams tons of tips onto a few sheets of paper printed in minuscule 6-point type. Holly and Bert Davis have been publishing this resource for several decades (formerly called Message Post) so they have a no-nonsense perspective. It's for modern nomads in the US choosing alternative lifestyles to working 9-5 in the same place. You get hard-won need-to-know wisdom like: How to live in cars. How to buy staples for 25 cents per pound. Can you camp in U-Hauls? Where can you find a cheap dentist? The dangers of social services taking kids without a house. Fixing a free bike for long-haul travel, etc.

Everyone should live in near-poverty at least once in their life, and this humble newsletter provides guidance and inspiration of how to learn the max from it.

-- KK

•
Legality of salvaging from dumpsters. Amy Dacyzyn, who phoned several police officials, said (in The Tightwad Gazettte, July 1993), "Dumpster diving is generally considered to be legal with the following exceptions: — If the container is on CLEARLY MARKED private land, behind a fence or locked up. However, most dumpsters in 'semi-public' areas such as parking lots are fair game. — If the discarded items are outside the dumpster they should not be taken." A deputy district attorney in Santa Clara, CA, where many people rummage for high-tech discards, told Amy: "By putting items in a dumpster, the companies have abandoned ownership…. The idea that people are stealing is not a prosecutable case."

•
For quick earning with little expense, consider cab driving. I can almost always get a job immediately, anywhere in the country. Drivers often quit, and cab owners are anxious to keep their equipment rolling. After 6 months, a driver will usually start to 'burn out' and not put in as many hours.

That's okay: if you've worked hard and not spent much, you'll have enough money to move on. I just quit the best deal I ever had: 38% of meter plus owner paid gas. I did so much business I couldn't handle the stress. But I now have enough to live modestly for two years.

I usually lease a 24-hour (single shift) cab and sleep in it, bathing at public facilities. Generally, if one is working hard, the owner gives you a lot of leeway. You will need a valid drivers license with good record, and a sense of direction and ability to rapidly learn your way around. Cab driving is a good way to scout a new area, and gain information and interesting experiences.

Alas, driving is becoming increasingly competitive and, in big cities, regulated. Also, some cities are dangerous, even if one knows the streets well. I advise: small towns, or working-class suburbs adjacent to big cities. Depressed areas are actually good places to make money as many people there can't afford cars. You'd be surprised how many people I take to welfare offices. Waitresses and bartenders often tip well, because THEY depend on tips. Las Vegas is, by universal acclaim, the best place to earn big bucks. As with anything, ask the old timers — which will be easier after one has 'hacked' a few times.

Vehicle freezer
Coleman Stirling Power Electric Cooler

$460 Amazon

This is a fantastic electric cooler based on the free piston Stirling cycle that will maintain freezing temps even in a hot car. The power consumption is amazing, 24 watts. It's quiet, light weight, works great. Much more practical than the portable compressor or propane based freezers. I've had two in continuous use for two years now and they are wonderful. I think this product has not taken off like it should because of confusion with the cheaper, power hogging thermo-electric Peltier-type coolers.

-- Todd Troutman

Cold tool
Portable Freezer

$510+ CF Series Portable Refrigerators/Freezers Waeco/Dometic
$810 ARB 37 Qt. Fridge/Freezer ARB
$910 MT45F-U1 - Engel 43 Qt. Portable Fridge/Freezer Engel

I have been doing a fair amount of research into a portable fridge for an vehicle expedition I am planning on doing from Baja to Alaska. The problem lies in the Peltier thermoelectric technology used in the new cheap coolers; they just don't make really cold temperatures.

To my knowledge there is nothing great in the sub $100 range, but there are excellent efficient cold fridges made for expeditions. These will actually freeze stuff. Unfortunately the cheapest is about $550. They are the ones with the sealed Danfoss compressors. These portable fridges/freezers are marketed by Waeco, ARB, and Engel and are all basically exactly the same products. You can pick which one you think has the better customer support; I can't say which that is yet. I would probably go with ARB, as they have a very high rep in the 4×4 community. But the Waeco USA site also has a 'factory reconditioned' section that is worth keeping an eye on for the right model.

-- Alexander Rose

Campside

Handiest place to pitch your tent
Car-top Tent

About 10 years ago I came across a Toyota jeep with European license plates parked by Bowman Lake in the Sierras. It was obviously a world-traveling vehicle. On top of the jeep's roof was a tent. I could see the owner down swimming in the lake. Fascinated by this approach to sleeping while on the road, I wrote down the name of the manufacturer: Air Camping in Milano, Italy. Some months later I tracked down the company and ordered one. It was expensive, about $2000 including airfreight, but the expense turned out to be worthwhile.

The unit folds up and can be mounted on a truck or car top. Closed it measures about 4 x 4 feet, and about 14" deep. When you stop for the night, you remove the waterproof cover and unfold it — whereupon the tent pops up. The cantilevered section is supported by a telescoping ladder. There's a mattress inside, as well as blankets and pillow, so your bed is ready as soon as it's set up. I've spent 100s of nights in it, usually in the desert or on Baja beaches with the opening facing the ocean. Its got mosquito netting, is well made and it's great

to be up there for the view and breeze. It's comfortable, and the tent does not take up storage space in the bed of the vehicle. I don't believe Air Camping is still in business, but a German company, Autocamp, makes what appears to be a similar product.

-- Lloyd Kahn

$600-900 Car-top Tent Autocamp

$995 Skydome cartop roof rack mounted tent Outdoor Equipment

Camp coffee grinder
JavaGrind Hand Crank Coffee Mill

$20 GSI Outdoors JavaGrind Hand-Crank Coffee Grinder Amazon

The JavaGrind hand-crank coffee mill is a burr grinder which does a better job of grinding coffee to a uniform size than an electric blade grinder, an important feature when using a press to brew. It is hand-cranked so it works in camp as well as in the kitchen, and it's quiet. It doesn't wake the rest of the camp (or house) when I brew up at 5:30 am. At 11 ounces it doesn't add very much to the camping load. And at 20 bucks it's less than half the price of powered burr grinders. What's not to like?

-- Dave Shaw

Burly folding backwoods saw
Sven-Saw

$35 REI

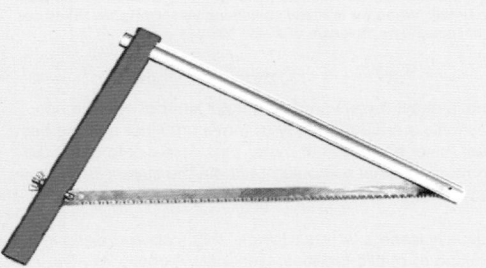

The Sven-Saw is an ideal camping saw. I grew up watching my Dad use one to make short work of the tree limbs I dragged through the woods to the campsite. Now I take mine on every backpacking trip. It makes gathering firewood easier, because you don't have to search for logs you can break or hack through. Larger logs left by others or downed trees that you'd never be able to hack down or break are fair game. I leave my hatchet at home, because this saw is so efficient and well-designed. I've used mine extensively for almost ten years without replacing the

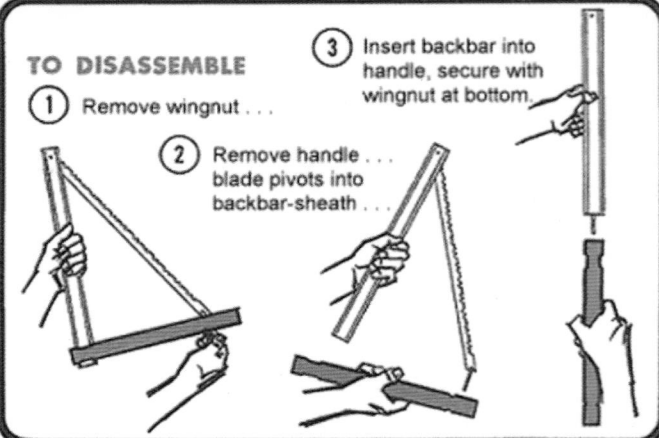

TO DISASSEMBLE
1. Remove wingnut . . .
2. Remove handle . . . blade pivots into backbar-sheath . . .
3. Insert backbar into handle, secure with wingnut at bottom.

blade. It's also great for pruning tree limbs and taking care of downed wood at home.

The original 21" saw weighs less than a pound and folds down to 24" x 1 3/4" x 5/8", which slips easily (and safely) along the inside of an internal frame backpack. A 15" version is now available, which saves even more weight on long treks.

-- Greg Schneider

Instant outdoor room
Flea Market Canopy

King Canopy
$100+ Northern Tool

Cheap portable shade from the sun in hot climates, flea market canopies are used by surfers and fishermen in Baja California. I used this 10' x 12' "peak unit" from Jenkins for several years on Baja beaches. Framework is 1 1/8" electrical conduit put together with special fittings and wingnuts. Tarp is attached with ball bungees, fantastic fastening devices. Mine was held down by 4 canvas sacks filled with sand, hanging from the corner posts (rather than stakes). It all folded up and fit in the Yakima Rocket Box on top of my truck. The guys at Jenkins Crafted Canopies were great to deal with; good products, good service.

–Lloyd Kahn

Hand-powered chain saw
Pocket Chain Saw

$23 Amazon

This little saw is excellent, fast cutting, light weight (at 3 oz without the case), and folds up small making it highly portable. It

can quickly saw branches and trees up to about 4-6 inches in diameter with its 28 inch long chain.

To use it, wrap the chain around whatever you want to cut and then grab the handles and pull back and forth. This flexibility means that it can take on logs and branches too thick for smaller camp saws. I've used it in the back country as well as around the yard.

When one of the metal loops that attaches the saw to the handles came apart at the weld point the company very quickly responded by sending me a new set of loops. It's an excellent product supported by a conscientious and responsive company.

-- Jaime Cobb

An even lighter weight military model can be purchased here ▶

Do-it-all tool around camp
Coghlan's 12-in-1 Scissors

$7 Amazon

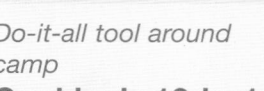

I am a long time tent camper who camps on the cheap at primitve camp sites where I haul in my own water and haul out my own waste. I camp with either a 4X4 truck or Subaru

Outback. My approach is minimalist, and I look for tools that have multiuse and are hopefully inexpensive. I've used the Coghlan's scissors for many years, and found them to be well worth having.

The Coghlan's 12 in 1 scissors is a silly looking and cheap ($7) tool that is surprisingly useful. It will cut fairly heavy material, has a bottle opener, screw-

driver, and will come apart so you can use it as an awl or hole punch in an emergency. Granted, it is not elegant but it is surprisingly useful. I have two pairs of these in my camp gear, and end up using them for stuff like gripping needles to pull through heavy fabric, and other unexpected uses. They are cheap to buy and a useful addition to any kit.

-- Stephen Young

The job of the artist is always to deepen the mystery. - Francis Bacon

Pocket dryer
Travel clothesline
$10 Rick Steves' Travel Store

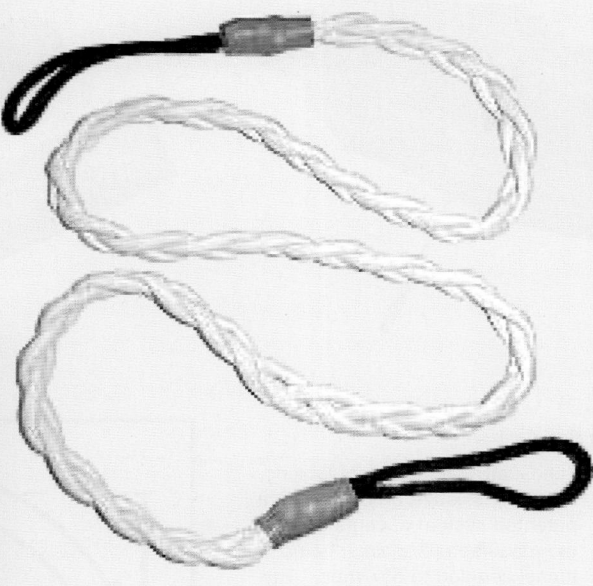

On long vacation trips when we wash our own undies, socks, and whatnots in our hotel room sink, this nifty braided rubber clothes line is the thing we use to dry them. It weighs a mere few ounces. You stretch it between two secure knobs or hooks, which you can usually find somewhere in a room. (Adding string extenders helps.) The ingenious design allows you to slip a corner of wet clothes between braids, which clinches it without clips or stains. Thus secured, we have no fear about stringing the laundry up outside in a breeze, or under a fan, where they dry fast without blowing away.

-- KK

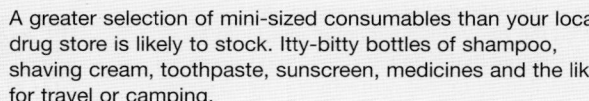

Mini portions of stuff
Minimus
Minimus

A greater selection of mini-sized consumables than your local drug store is likely to stock. Itty-bitty bottles of shampoo, shaving cream, toothpaste, sunscreen, medicines and the like, for travel or camping.

-- KK

Superior travel towels
Aquis Microfiber Travel Towels
$34 Adventure Towel Aquis

A compact quick-drying microfiber towel folds up neatly into a tiny square and is the perfect tool to stuff into your backpack anywhere you won't be provided with clean towels — say traveling in low-budget parts of the world, or an overnight train. This towel comes in a small tidy pouch to keep it clean. It weighs only 3.5 ounces (when dry).

-- KK

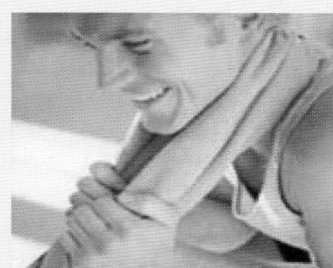

Urban sleeping bag
Cocoon Silk Bag/Travel Sheet
$50+ Cocoon

The Cocoon Silk Bag Liner/Travel Sheet works like a sleeping bag in hot weather. I've used it when staying at hostels as well as when couch surfing so people don't have to hassle with sheets for me. It can be a sleeping bag liner, too. It's light (6.3 ounces), packs down very small (5.5 x 7 inches – it comes in its own satchel) and is really quite comfortable.

– Hulda Emilsdottir

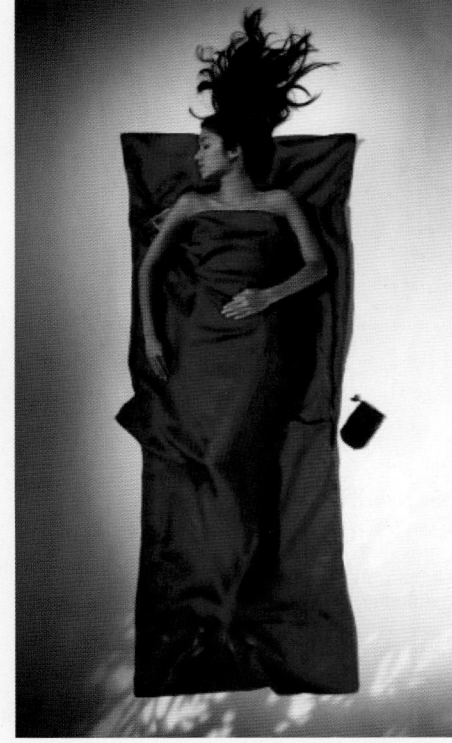

Header-Subtitles
Eagle Creek Comfort Travel Pillow
$20 Eagle Creek

I find a comfortable travel pillow essential for long train commutes. Unlike regular neck-pillows, the Eagle Creek travel pillow is easy and unobtrusive to carry with you. It's inflatable and folds flat to slips into a jacket or hip pocket, though I keep mine in the briefcase. To inflate, pop open the wide cap, and breathe into the valve; a clever rubber flap allows you to empty your lungs comfortably into a wide circular opening without straining.

Three breaths is all it takes, and the flap and cap keep it solidly sealed the whole trip – deflation is nearly instantaneous once arrived. It has a soft microfiber cover, removable and washable, that offers a surprising amount of comfort. It masks the inflatable nature of the pillow admirably, though not completely. It's still going to be a little warmer than a regular "u" pillow, and the cushion won't be as nestle-in soft, but it beats the heck out of "microbead" pillows and the like, and definitely beats a sore neck and shoulders.

After a year of daily service, it developed a small leak, which was easily fixed with a little dab of the previously reviewed shoe-goo cement, and has been going strong for another year.

-- Matt Gabriel

Wide-beamed light source
FoxFury Multi-LED Headlamp
$86 FoxFury

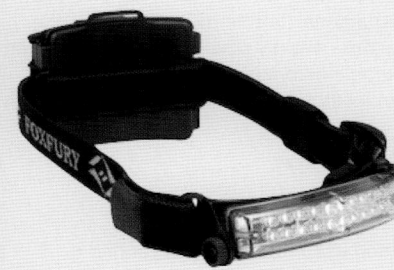

I've used lots of headlamps, and there's a common problem when the light comes from a point source: brightly lit areas with inky black shadows behind the lit objects coupled with a narrow field of view. This FoxFury headlamp uses a bunch of LEDs spread out horizontally so the light washes in and around irregularities while lighting a wide field of view.

I've used this headlamp on a hard-hat for at least 3 years when I'm lowered down into holes drilled through landslides. It's amazingly dark below around 25 feet, and these lights just flood the walls of the boring so we can find the bottoms of landslides and map them.

They are great for changing tires, snowshoeing, and even yard work at night. My neighbors think I'm weird. They sell different models for fire fighting, forensic work, SCUBA diving, you name it. Plus they tune the spectrum to the need: natural light, infrared, etc. In addition, most of the models come with a red LED on the back for safety purposes.

-- Reid Fisher

DIY headlamp
Fenix Flashlight Headband
$19 Fenix

I've been using the Fenix Headband for about 6 months now and I've found it superior to just about any other headlamp system out there.

It's much more versatile since it allows me to rotate the light 360-degrees, instead of just forward and down. And because it is on the side of my head instead of on my forehead, light doesn't hit my eyes. It's designed to fit Fenix lights (most AA and CR123 models), and works with countless others including the outstanding 4Sevens Quark line.

Having a "real" light means actually getting "throw" with a headlamp which is something sadly missing from the older LED technology commonly used on caving/jogging lights on the market. Along the same lines, newer LEDs are more efficient, having a much higher lumen to power consumption ratio, in effect giving me a brighter light for much longer. The plastic light mount is super durable and has a metal hinge, screw and threads so there's no chance of plastic wear on moving parts.

Its unique design means I can have all of the benefits of the latest light technology and the versatility to choose which flashlight features I want, for every type of use I can throw at it. I can choose the batteries, bulbs, and modes I want or need in a light and secure one or TWO to my head leaving my hands free to start a camp fire, steer a bicycle, work on electronics, hold a map, or write a note while standing. I can investigate a noise over 100 feet away while unscrewing my water bottle (a simple task but impossible with an average headlamp) and can point it upward then set my light to SOS mode and signal a rescue team while administering first aid.

-- Joel Mellon

Portable Comforts

Disposable urinal
Travel John
$10 (6packs) Travel John

I've used these for several years, and they're great when the need to urinate calls but no facilities are accessible. I've found them useful while flying in small planes that don't have a toilet, and also when I didn't want to leave my tent in the middle of a rainy night to relieve myself. Long lines for the Port-A-Potties at the airshow with your kids? Problem solved.

I learned of the piddle pack concept while serving in the USAF. Back in the day it was a plastic bag with a sponge that wasn't always successful absorbing all the urine. The technology these days, similar to what you'd find in a disposable diaper, is much better. A biodegradable polymer within the bag turns your liquid input into an odorless gel that won't spill, and a unisex collar makes it ideal for the whole family. Keep some in your glove compartment. You won't be sorry.

-- Sean Lally

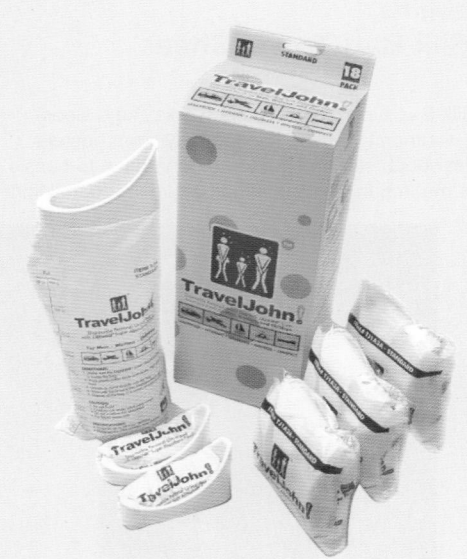

Unflippable umbrella
GustBuster Umbrella
$45 GustBuster Golf Amazon

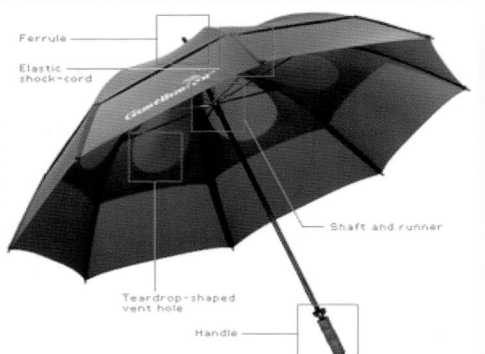

The GustBuster is a cool-looking, lightning resistant umbrella with a patented system of vents that is, the manufacturer claims, "wind tunnel certified to 55+ mph." The other night it started blowing up a storm — winds to 20 miles per hour. Just for giggles I tried turning the GustBuster sideways and it just would not pick up any air — it really does work amazingly well. The holes in the inner surface seem to neutralize all of the typical suction.

The version I decided on for my all-weather walking is labeled a "golf umbrella" and is big enough for a small wedding reception. (I exaggerate but 62 inches is certainly big enough for me and the dog.) The price is right, $45 — a bargain for a good umbrella. If you're concerned about weight (this super-sized version weighs close to two pounds) there are smaller, lighter versions. On their website they say the GustBuster is very popular with professional golfers — seemingly, a good indication of long-term quality and performance. Also comes with a limited lifetime warranty. I'm impressed — very cool tool.

-- Chuck Green

$33+ GustBuster Metro Amazon

Budget trekking umbrella
Euroschirm Trek
$40+ Campmor

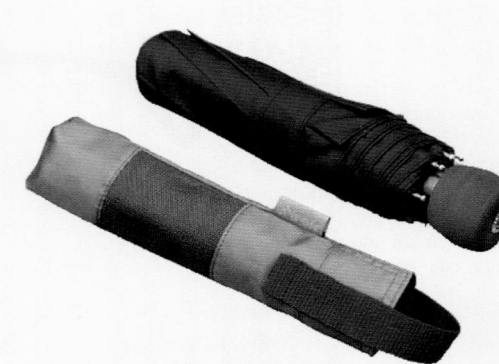

I did research on a travel umbrella for a lengthy South American trip, found this and love it. It's made of tough, lightweight materials, fits in its own sleeve, can be put away wet, and has a tiny compass in the handle. I got mine with a silver reflective top, so that it's also useful in sunny conditions.

At 10 ½ inches long closed and 8 ½ ounces, the Trek's bigger and heftier than the previously reviewed Knirps umbrella, but also less expensive. It also costs less than the previously reviewed Go-Lite umbrella. Forget about parkas and pants, umbrellas are the way.

-- Geoff Wilke

114 cm
100 cm
64 cm
207 g

Pocket chair
Slouch!Buster
Amazon

The Nadachair and Slouch!Buster are based on the ropes that Tibetan monks use to sit upright for hours on end when meditating. The monks use these ropes between their knees and back to help them stay upright. The Slouchbuster is a small, much more elegant version than ropes. The Nadachair is a larger version.

I'm a yank who lives in Perth Australia (West Coast). I fly often to the US and Europe, in coach. I've found this little thing is what allows me to sleep and survive 19-22 hours of crowded coach seats. I use the Slouchbuster when I travel because:

(1) It is very small. It is the size of a paperback book when folded up.

(2) It folds up and then zips up inside itself. It is totally self contained. No bags or anything needed.

I also own a Nadachair, too, which I keep at work. I use that a couple times a day to keep my back straight. I write software for a living, so I'm sitting for hours on end. It really makes a difference, especially if you have any sort of lower back problems (like me). I owned them for a couple of years now and I found that I no longer need a monthly chiropractor visit. So it has paid

for itself within a month.

-- Ron Larson

Feminine urinary director
Freshette
$27 Amazon

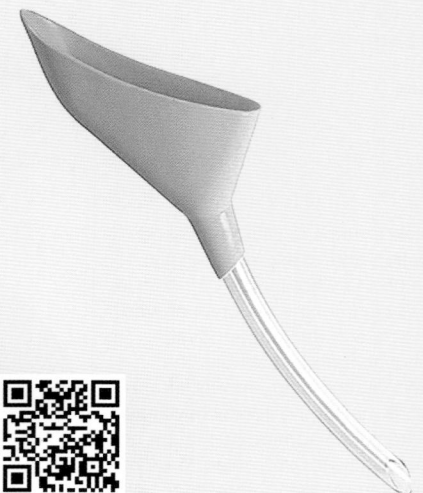

A superior Femine Urinary Director is the Sport and Travel Freshette. It's slightly larger than the TravelMate—just longer than the palm of my hand when collapsed and about half as wide—but still can fit in the hip pocket of a camping backpack quite easily (and you can still use it through your pants' fly). The Freshette's larger cup, similar to the unisex collar on the previously reviewed Travel John (upper right), fits more easily than the TravelMate—and solves the positioning and overflow problems to which the TravelMate is prone. It really is easy to pee all over yourself with the Travelmate due to its small size and smaller throughput (the main reason I can't recommend it).

The flexible outlet tube on the Freshette makes for easier aiming. With practice, it's possible to collapse it after use, store it back in the bag, then get it back out and reuse it without touching any of the wet bits, if you're squeamish about that sort of thing. And if you need the extra feature, there's a "complete portable" kit that comes with sealable bags you can attach, in case there's a need to pack out your waste or you're going to drive like Lisa Nowak.

While it's the best product of its kind that I found, the Freshette is more expensive than the TravelMate, and its weird shape and larger size make it harder to pack. Also, the plastic bag it comes with is not the most durable. Mine lasted through about three weeks of camping before getting a hole. Both models tie for ease of being able to clean yourself off without toilet paper.

There are many other variations on the Freshette, which I imagine would work about as well: The Whiz Freedom—quickdry anti-bacterial flexible medical plastic; the SheWee—slightly smaller and available with a durable hard case; the PStyle—more a channel than a funnel and no tube; the Lady J—wider funnel.

-- Sarah Mercer

Pliable camping containers
Guyot Designs Squishy Bowls
$16 Amazon

For weight- and space-conscious backpackers or car campers, the squishy bowls offer an alternative to old-school non-collapsible aluminum/stainless steel/titanium bowls. And while these food-grade silicone bowls won't stand up to direct fire, they are oven safe up to 500° F. They can be baked, boiled and frozen without ill effect, making them more versatile than the previously reviewed Orikaso campware and the newer Fozzils' take on that design.

Guyot's bowls are entirely pliable, and eating out of a bowl without structural rigidity can be a strange experience the first time. Their flexing and bulging when holding liquids does take some getting used to. But I've never had a problem eating out of them. This amorphousness comes in handy when you want to slurp back the rest of your milk or finish off the end of your camp stew, as you can squish the side of the bowl into a convenient spout. It also means they sit solidly. They hold hot liquids well, and are insulated enough to prevent you from burning your hands when you hold them as commonly happens with a traditional metal bowl.

-- Oliver Hulland

Barring from my mind all remembrance of what I've seen, looking for what has never been. - Rene Magritte

Ashley Bend

Cow Hitch Using End

Cow Hitch using loops

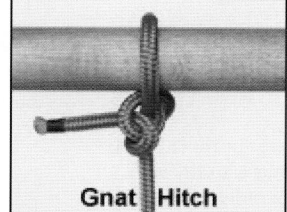

Gnat Hitch

Highwayman's Hitch

Hunter's Bend

Mooring Hitch

Tumble Hitch

All knots are knotty and hard to visualize the first time. This free website is the best knot teacher yet. It beats any of the beginner books I've seen, as well as all the other knot web-sites. The key here is the stepped animations synchronized with instructions, which you can run at any speed. Replay them till you get them right. Animated Knots is the next best thing to having old Pete next to ya. Once you get the basic ones down, try some of the harder ones. There are 75 cool knots animated in total.

-- KK

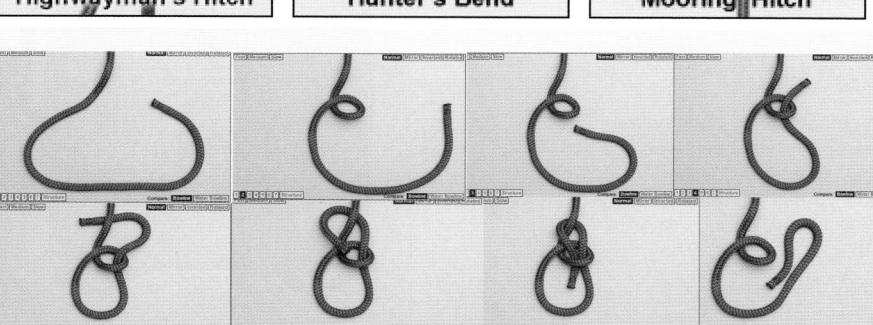

Bowline with Yosemite Tie-Off

Next step beyond the basic knots
Morrow Guide to Knots
$11 Mario Bigon, Guido Regazzoni 1982, 255 pages

Knots are such fundamental tools, and matching the right job with the right knot is so often essential, the important next step from the Klutz Book is the equally lucid and fairly comprehensive *Morrow Guide to Knots*. Last week my wife Ryan gave a glad cry at the clarity in the book when she wanted to see a couple ways to tie a clove hitch, and learned that it's easy to put a slip in a clove hitch for quick release.

-- Steward Brand

Alternative shoelace tie
Surgeon's knot

I was shown this knot earlier this summer as a way to secure my boot laces, which were constantly coming untied. My boss, who taught me it, called it the "super knot." How to make it: (if you tie your shoes with one loop then wrap another loop around it) - pass the loop through a second time. (bunny ears method) - pass one ear though a second time.

I've tested this knot for 8 weeks of hiking around in the forests of New Hampshire and it has never come untied. I noticed that Ian's Shoelace Site has some other recommendations for knots, but I cannot vouch for their security. I know that the Surgeon's Shoelace Knot works for me. See Ian's Shoelace Site for pictures and a clear explanation.

-- Sam Johnson

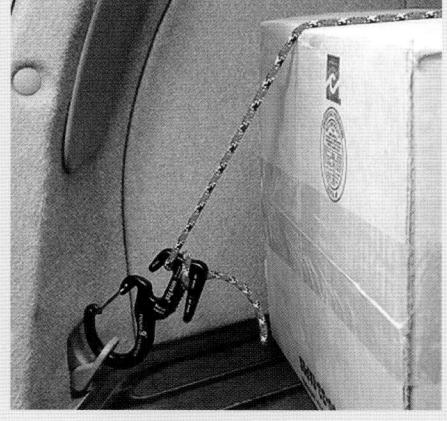

Knot substitute
Nite Ize Figure 9 Carabiner
$7 niteize.com

The Figure 9 carabiner lets you quickly fasten -- and quickly loosen or adjust -- a small-diameter rope to a fixed point without a knot deploying a clever combination of friction and angles. To those of us with knot-dyslexia, this is a real boon. The only requirement: your fixed attachment point must feature either a place to clip the carabiner (i.e. a metal loop in a pick-up truck bed or a thin, sturdy tree branch), or something around which your line can be looped. That could mean securing a Tarptent to a tree, improvising a handle around a bundle of cables, or securing a travel clothesline between window-grate and curtain-rod.

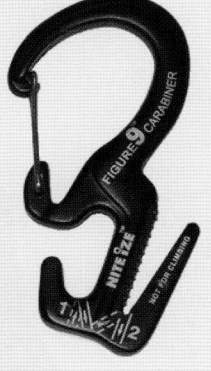

All you need to do is pull the rope through in the right sequence and finish with the rope's loose end tugged into the notched "V" section to keep the rope attached and taut. There are actually multiple sequences and ways to work the geometry. Three methods are diagrammed in the instructions that come with the carabiner (see right).

Thus far, I have used the devices only with standard-issue parachute cord, but they're sized to work with a range of small-diameter ropes. Though the tying system looks suspiciously wimpy, I've found it is as robust as promised. I ordered the Figure 9s to replace the mesh netting that came with the roof-rack basket on my car. Not only do these make a decent replacement (i.e. riding around with a kayak strapped to my car this sum-

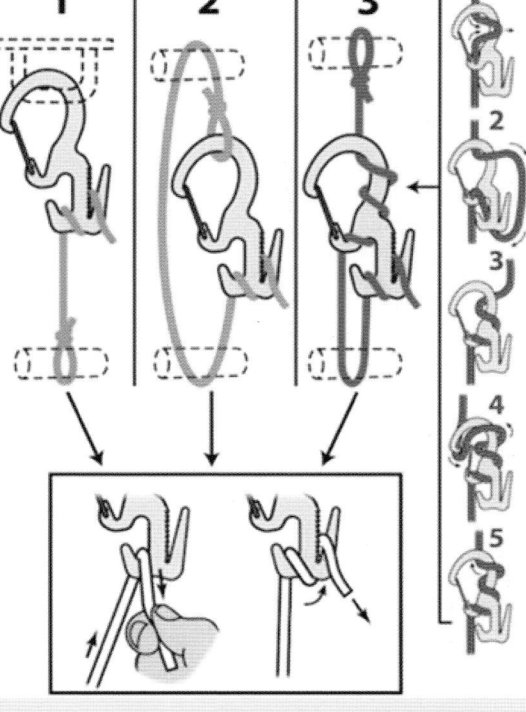

mer), but tying one more knot under the car is something I'm glad to skip. Note: the device is anodized aluminum and weighs a bit more than I expected (slight downside to ultra-light hikers); still, "Not for climbing" is printed on the packaging, repeated in the instructions, and emblazoned on each carabiner. I think they mean it.

-- Timothy Lord

Quick, easy tie-down
Rope Ratchet
$9 - $12 (1/4-inch, w/rope)
roperatchet.com

I wanted to rig a single line of rope across the ceiling of my garage for a storage solution, but was concerned about getting the line tight enough to keep from sagging. Rather than tie up a come-along winch -- which

requires a lot more hook up room and has a tendency to release quite hard -- I saw the Rope Ratchet and decided to give it a try; I'm glad I did. The contraption is basically a rope that's fed into and around a ratcheting wheel and bracket that holds the line and prevents backspin; you can release the line with a lever. It's quite simple, but I haven't seen anything quite like it. I'm using one to hold up a 70-lbs. tackle bag 6 feet off the floor of my garage and another holding about 80 lbs. of plastic lures on a rope stretched across hooks against the ceiling of my garage. I'm using the 1/4-inch

Rope Ratchet that's rated for a working load of 150 lbs., but there are different sizes for different needs: the 1/8-inch will hold 75 lbs. up, while the 1/2-inch will hold 500 lbs. After a number of months, mine are holding strong with no sign of failure.

-- Doug Mainor

Travel Packs

Adaptable luggage
Rick Steves' Convertible Carry-On
$100 Amazon

I lived out of a bag for most of the past year, traveling with my wife. We visited 11 countries and used all manner of transportation. I used Rick Steves' Convertible Carry-On Bag, and my wife used the less expensive Back Door Bag.

These bags were great. They were tough enough to withstand our daily abuse; and quite light. The Convertible Carry-On had just the right number of pockets: enough to keep some organization going, but not so many that the bag is all zippers. None of the zippers on either of our bags has given us any problems.

Wheeled bags like the Travelpro Rollaboard are great if you're going to be places where you can use the wheels all the time. While traveling through poorer countries there often isn't a good surface for rolling lug-

gage, and the instant you have to carry the bag the extra weight really hurts. The harder shell on those types of bags obviously protects your stuff better, but also makes it harder to stuff under seats.

I only expanded my bag (using the perimeter zipper) a few times, and barely used the waist belt, but it sure was useful when I did turn to these features. The small size (9 x 21 x 14 in.) was great when stuffing the bags under bus seats. Despite the fact that the bags conform to maximum carry-on size, we often checked them because we exceeded carry-on weight limits: Our filled bags are about 28 lb., while we encountered weight limits that were typically around 22 lb.

Of the many things I purchased before our trip, this bag was one that I've never second-guessed. I wouldn't hesitate to buy another one if this one ever shows enough wear to warrant it.

-- Tim Newsome

I travel overseas for business and pleasure on the same trips, usually for weeks at a time, where I am both "backpacking" and hoteling in cities. For years I've carried a Rick Steves' bag. It is just the right size. Since it is soft I can stuff it anywhere, yet hoist it on my back when needed. I love it.

--KK

Superior luggage system
Eagle Creek
Conor Flashpoint Daypack, $160 Amazon

There may be a better product here and there in a particular piece of luggage, but it's just not worth my time messing around to find out. I've replaced all of my duffels, carry-ons and backpacks with Eagle Creek products, and have been using them for the past two years. I've standardized on Eagle Creek luggage because I've found their stuff to be uniformly excellent, and it just saves me the frustration of trying stuff out and finding it has deficiencies.

Eagle Creek makes a handful of practical accessories for space-saving and orderly packing. Their Pack-It Folders compress lots of shirts, pants or skirts into a compact, wrinkle-free stack. And their Cubes are ideal for organizing underwear and socks while compressing them and maximizing space. They also offer Compression Sacs, giant Ziploc-like bags with one-way air valves that can compress your dirties into a fraction of their

uncompressed size. All of these accessories work quite well with other brands of luggage; they are by no means specific to Eagle Creek.

Travel Gear Pack-It Folder 20 Organizer, $34 Amazon

Another reason I've chosen Eagle Creek: the company's products are extremely rugged and have a lifetime warranty. I took them up on their warranty on a bag that got slashed. I live in San Diego and found that I could just take it by their headquarters rather than mail it in. They gave me a new bag, no questions asked.

Just to qualify as an experienced traveler, I've accumulated more than 6 million lifetime miles in the American Airlines AAdvantage program, more than two million on United, and a million on two or three others.

-- Don Lyle

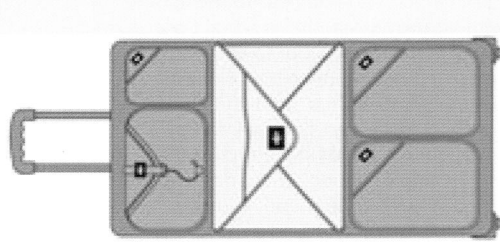

Professional luggage
Travelpro Rollaboards
Crew 9 20-Inch Rollaboard, $170 Amazon

The original rollaboard luggage is still the best, not least because the extendable handle unlocks with one hand on the handle. No bending over to release a lock with your other hand while your shoulder pack falls off your shoulder, adding further unwelcome drama to your episode with the airport security check. Since there are now so many rollaboards out there, most of them black, I add bright yellow bookbinders tape wrapped around the lifting handle of my bags. A huge duffel bag with wheels is sometimes necessary for the long or multipurpose trip, and in this I prefer Travelpro's offerings as well.

-- Stewart Brand

Crew 9 22-Inch Rollaboard, $187 Amazon

Versatile overnight carry-on
Tom Bihn Western Flyer
Western Flyer, $210 Tom Bihn

Why is the Tom Bihn Western Flyer better than my favorite suitcase, messenger bag, or backpack? This bag combines the elements of all of these into one super tidy, easy to use package. Like a suitcase, I can pack everything I need for travel. The main compartment is big enough to store days worth of clothes and a change of shoes. I packed for a ten day trip in Nepal in just this bag! The front compartment has a divider to split the compartment in two and generally

keeps my toiletries, electronics (chargers, etc) and books organized and easy to reach wthout digging through my unmentionables. The front pockets are weather sealed and hold my travel pillow, headphones, keys (and all the other bits and pieces I pick up along the way). The bag has an optional handle, shoulder strap and hide-away backpack straps. Because I like the balance and comfort of a backpack, these padded straps are out all the time and keep my hands free for a coffee and/or a roller bag.

And the Tom Bihn is better than my other options because it is super durable. I don't treat my luggage

lightly, and after several beatings, pushings and pullings, and weeks of over-stuffing, the bag looks as good as new.

-- Kristyna Solawetz

We are nothing else than evolution become conscious of itself. - Teilhard de Chardin

Best external USB battery
New Trent External USB Batteries
$70 Amazon

I have used a New Trent IMP500 external USB battery for the last two years, mostly in the backcountry, to keep multiple devices charged (you need to make sure you have adapter tips or a short cable for each type of device) and am impressed with its capacity and durability. These batteries work when you need them to work.

New Trent has consistently made the most powerful and reliable external USB batteries for USB-devices like the iPhone. Look at the New Trent website to decide which product is right for you, then look at the reviews on Amazon for confirmation of my first sentence.

The newest battery, IMP1000, has 11,000 mAH capacity, about 5-6 recharges for an iPhone 4. Before I bought my IMP500 I researched extensively before buying. Since then I have used this battery under extreme conditions for the last two years, and am more than satisfied.

-- Kim

Portable AC power
Alien Bees Vagabond Mini
$240 Paul C. Buff

The Alien Bees Vagabond Mini is a lithium battery pack which gives USB and AC power, and includes battery, inverter, and charger. I originally bought it to run photo flashes (which it does quite nicely), but I also use it to run my laptop, and it will also run any AC device less than 300 watts.

After seeing the low quality available for other lead acid battery packs, I decided to build my own. Then this came out. The whole package is about $40 more than the price of an equivalent battery pack, and it is a complete package. Other people have verified that it has a "PureSine" inverter.

There are some reports of them not working in 120 degree ambient temperatures of the desert outside of Dubai. They can also apparently be burnt if you run them at 500 watts, and keep pulsing them at 2kw for several hours. I suspect that it is the continuous load and high temperatures internally when pulses are demanded which causes the failures.

-- Michael McMillan

Extra-short iPhone/iPod cable
iStubz

The iStubz is a miniature USB cable for iPhones/iPods. It comes in either 7cm or 22cm lengths, and is probably the best nine dollar purchase I've made in the past year. The reason I'm so in love with this little tool is that it can live permanently in my bag without taking up any space or tangling up on anything. This is great since I regularly forget to charge my iPhone at night and often have to charge it on the go. It's also ideal for charging/syncing from my laptop, keeping cables from getting tangled in my mouse and still allowing my phone to be within arm's reach. It's doubly useful when coupled with the socket-to-USB converter packaged with the iPhone. I keep them mated in my bag, so if I happen to be somewhere without my laptop or a convenient USB port, I can still stay charged.

-- Ian Hall

$6 iStubz 7cm Amazon   **$9 iStubz 22cm** Amazon

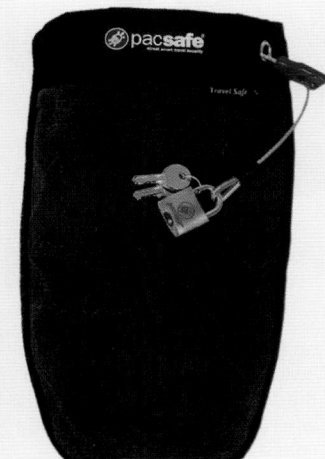

Theft-deterring tourist sack
Pacsafe Travelsafe
$60 Amazon

The Travelsafe 100 is a heavily reinforced, lockable nylon bag with steel cable woven through the fabric and an external steel cable which makes it possible to lock the bag to a stationary item (such as the frame of a bed in a hotel). The bag is 8+" x 13" and quite light. It's more of a deterrent to casual thieves, as a well-equipped, professional thief armed with a hacksaw or 5" bolt cutters could probably penetrate it (a knife would not be sufficient to cut the steel mesh). On a recent surf trip to Costa Rica, the hotel safe at the main office was only open 8am-6pm, and was basically unavailable given our daily schedule. I used the bag to store my digital camera, iPod, passport, wallet, traveler's checks and money by locking the bag to the hotel bed frame (my travel buddy also put some of his things in it, too). If you don't want to be burdened with a key, you can buy your own combination lock, though the spindle needs to be thin enough to fit. Pacsafe also sells lockable knapsacks, shoulder bags, computer bags, and even steel mesh covers to extend over large backpacks or suitcases. I chose the model I did because I wanted something relatively inexpensive and small enough to just hold valuables and electronics.

– Carl Hamann

Lightweight power sharer
Power Cord Splitter
$3 Monoprice

What's so cool about a power cord splitter? Sure, it turns one plug into two, but so what? The genius of this short adaptor is that you can pack it in your travel bag. So when you come upon the lone outlet in an airport, cafe, or hotel lobby that is already occupied, all you need to do is to politely ask to insert this spitter. Now you can add your line without disrupting theirs. And of course, at times you may use its doubling yourself. These little ambassadors should cost less than $3.

-- KK

Solar panel quickly charges cell phone batteries
SunVolt Portable Solar Power Station
$100 Power Station $40 Battery Pack gomadic. com

I've been trying to live off the grid for a while now. I bought land in Cabo San Lucas that I plan to entirely run by solar and wind turbines.

I also use my cellphone a lot. I burn through batteries so quickly, that I only buy phones that use replaceable batteries. My current cellphone is a Samsung Galaxy S3 and I have a 7500 mAh battery (no, that is not a typo) and a fully charged backup 3500 mAh battery that I keep in my pocket.

With my commitment to living off the grid, I have tried those little solar cell phone chargers that you can get in China; I have tried the Solio and I have even tried to fabricate my own solar charger. The problem with all of these devices is that the solar panels are so small that to give your phone even a small bump in energy, you have to keep your charger in the sun for a minimum of 6-8 hours.

Enter the Gomadic Sunvolt Solar Power Station and Solar Cache High Capacity Battery Pack. It is an all-in-one solar charger and high capacity battery in its own sturdy carry case. At first, I thought, wow, it is as big as my laptop, and I would never lug that around. True, it's big, but this is because it contains a large 10 1/2" x 10" solar panel. The case acts as a stand so you simply unzip and position the panel to receive optimal sunlight and you're good to go. The design of this system is really well

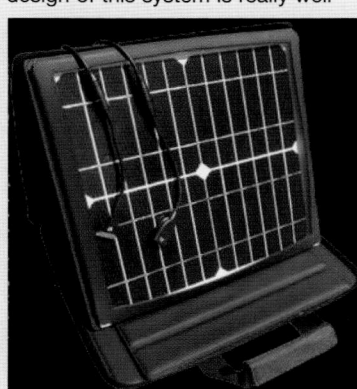

thought out — the outer pockets of the case hold the battery and every conceivable connection to every conceivable electronic device. Even if your device connection is not included, all you'll need is a USB cable to your device as the out port on the battery is a standard USB port. Best of all, the power output blasts all of the other solar chargers in the market. It outputs between 8.0 – 14.4 watts (and I understand that they are coming out with a more powerful one).

The solar panels charge a 3400 mAh battery which is good enough to charge my cellphone for a day's use, although you can hook up your device to be charged directly from the sun.

I recently brought this to Thailand, where it is 100 degrees in the shade, and I found the system to be extremely helpful, especially in the south where modern electronics were sparse. The case is extremely durable and well made. The near-empty battery was fully charged after two hours in the full sun, which is extremely quick. I found that during the day, I would charge the included battery and then at night would use it to replenish my dying cell phone.

The only thing I would wish for is a charging indicator that would confirm that the panels were getting enough sun and that I have a proper connection to be providing a charge.

-- Alastair Ong

Mini Lights

Ultra-bright mini-torch
Fenix L1D-CE Flashlight
$52 Fenix-Store.com

As a flashlight enthusiast, I'm often asked which flashlight I reach for the most. My answer: the Fenix L1D-CE, a pocket-sizeLED light that uses only a single AA battery. That's brighter than the typical 3D cell flashlight -- amazing for a single AA battery!

I always return to the L1D-CE configuration because it's just the right handy size, has brightness levels appropriate for most of my indoor uses, and I can use one rechargeable AA battery for almost no cost and environmentally-friendly illumination.

-- Vincent Tseng

Powerful, pocketable penlight
4Sevens Preon 2 Penlight
$40 4sevens.com

I recently discovered that as one ages you need more photons to see clearly. In particular, when skimming the bookshelves at home it's extremely hard for me to make out titles because my eyes require (a lot) more light than they formerly did.

My wife gave me a 4Sevens Preon 2 penlight last December, and I love it. It weighs 1.6 oz and uses two AAA batteries. No special batteries needed. In addition to the 3 main selections (low - 2.2 lumens; medium - 22 lumens; high - 120 ANSI lumens), it has a strobe and SOS options, not of use to me. When you turn it on, it comes on "low". Pressing on/off switch slightly then switches to "medium," pressing slightly again switches to "high." A full press on the switch turns it off. Actual operation is easier than the explanation suggests.

It gets this much light from the new CREE XP-G S2 LED, a modern LED capable of incredible light output. Low, at 2.2 lumens, is fairly dim, but ideal for reading a restaurant menu in a dimly lighted place. And it's good that the dim comes on first: the "high" setting seems like flashbulb brightness, which would be annoying in (for example) a good restaurant or if you want to read from the program during a play.

It's easily carried, and 120 ANSI lumens is a LOT of light and provides excellent illumination. So far as I can tell, this is the current leader in the penlight format. And my life is easier now that I can readily carry sufficient light for my elderly eyes.

-- Michael Ham

Bright pocketable light
Streamlight Stylus
$14 Amazon

My super-favorite pen light is the Streamlight Stylus. Don't bother with the Pro with fancy housing — go for the simple penlight version. Since the stylus lights are only slightly larger than a ballpoint pen, they go everywhere; in my backpack, my pencil cup on my desk, next to the bed, in my car. Amazingly useful at moments when one needs to look under your seat on an airplane, etc. It's a great EMT light for looking in eyes and ears, etc. And believe it or not, I find them very useful on official search-and-rescue missions. I always have one within arm's reach and keep giving them away to friends (they cost less then $12), so I probably buy 10+ year. They run on hard-to-find AAAA batteries, but I generally lose my stylus lights before I need to change the batteries. However, inside a 9-volt battery are 6 4A batteries if you really need some.

-- Paul Saffo

For light in tight places
StylusReach Flexible Flashlight
$17 streamlight.com

My brother-in-law, who's a tool salesman, gave me one of these lights for Christmas. It's a natural white super bright LED light on a flexible, shielded cable. The LED has a rated life of 100,000 hours. The light is extremely tough. My bro-in-law likes to whack the crap out of 'em to demonstrate how durable they are. Waterproof too. Two settings on the light: blinking and steady. There's also a blue LED version, which is easier on the eyes.

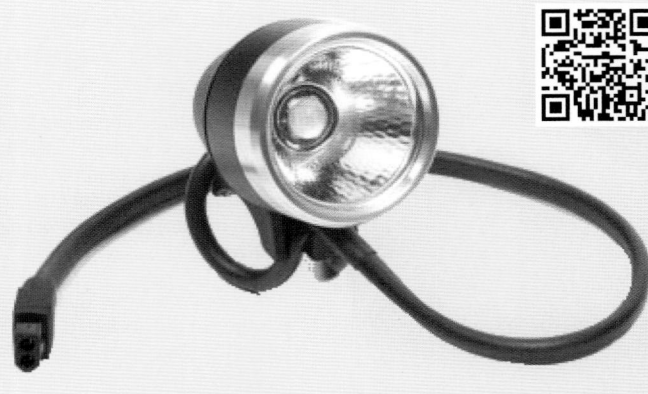

High-output technical LEDs
Lupine Bike & Adventure Lights
$475 Tesla 700 (includes charger/ battery) gretnabikes.com

In the winter I mountain bike one to two nights a week after dark on fast technical single track trails. I have built my own lights and purchased commercially-available lighting systems upwards of $400. I have tried halogen, HID, and LED lighting systems. Until now they were all a compromise. I am now using the Lupine Tesla 700 LED light, and I have to say it makes everything I have used up to this point seem like a silly toy. Weighing a mere 102g, this light outshines my brightest HID system, is more efficient than my smallest halogen, and has the best construction, controls, and mounting system I have seen in a light.

Lupine Lighting Systems is a German company that has been around for a while, and I have always heard they make the best lights in the industry. The one I bought, the Tesla 700, is their new "entry level" light which costs $300 just for the head unit or $488 for a complete package with battery, charger, etc. It is worth every cent. This unit puts out an amazing 700 Lumens in a pattern and color temperature that is perfect for outdoor sports or caving. This is in stark contrast to most LED-based products I have tried which have a weirdly tinged light that even when bright enough, do not give good definition. Lupine makes larger and brighter lights, but I could not imagine what you would need more light for, short of landing a helicopter.

-- Alexander Rose

Stick anywhere solar-powered LED
SolLight LightShip
$25 sollight.com

This solar-powered LED light comes with suction cups and is incredibly handy. I keep one in the car on the back window, so it's always charged in case of a breakdown. It also features a red LED to preserve night vision is, as well as the auto-shut-off with the light sensor. It is weather sealed and it stood up brilliantly to the elements while living in Fiji- sun, salt and sea.

I used this device, along with the brilliant LightCap. This latest version of the SolLight classic LightShip is fantastic as ever. Great for hands free light, camping, and emergencies.

-- Kaz Brecher

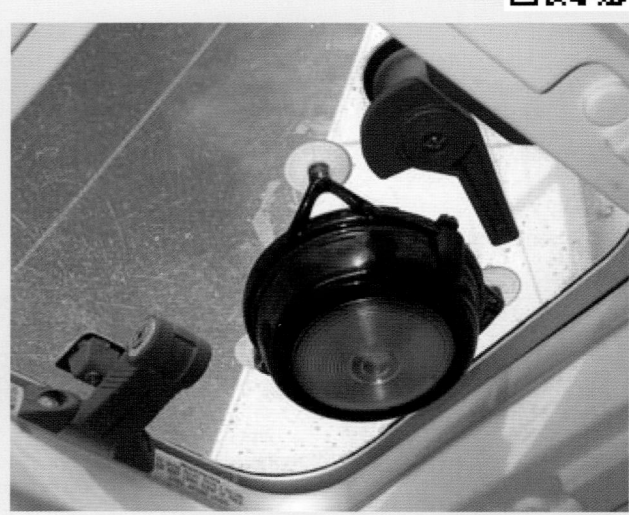

Ultralight and bright
Photon Microlight II
$8 photonlight.com

This is a very handy little light that is small enough to carry around in your pocket on a keychain. It weighs only 4.8-grams and the LED "bulb" is very bright for its size, more than adequate for finding your way around in a dark spot, reading a map, finding key holes, etc, with a simple thumb press on the button. It has a small switch that will lock the light in the "on" position for those times when you need some extended light.

-- Paul Dubuc

The Photon is the original and still superior Microlight -- but expsnsive. I've found I get can similar generic lights for $1 each on Amazon mailed free from China. They don't last as long, but I have 8X as many. -- KK

The StylusReach is pen-sized (when the shaft is folded over and clipped to the battery tube) and 14 inches long when extended. It has a pocket clip (and you thought that Fisher Space Pen made you look like a geek!). I use mine for all sorts of hardware hacking and around the house stuff (like looking under the burner on our stove to try and find out why the stovetop heated up to the point where it shattered the tempered glass stovetop inset!) Inside computers, you can actually clip it to the side of the case to direct the light where you want it. It's also really useful for seeing behind furniture, etc. The light lets me clearly see what I'm going to grab before I reach and grab.

-- Gareth Branwyn

Find something you love to do and you'll never have to work a day in your life. - Harvey Mackay

Warranted fixed-price used cars
CarMax
CarMax

CarMax is a great source for when you are in the market for a certified, warranted, used vehicle. I don't know of any other dealership where you can test drive a used car, in excellent condition, and not have to go through a hard sell sales pitch, or a torturous bargaining phase when you decide to purchase it. The no-bargain price is right on the vehicles, and is often quite a bargain (with notable exceptions, so you have to do your independent price-point research ahead of time). Additionally, if you decide within five days of your purchase that it was not the right car for you, you can return it for a full refund, regardless of how much you drove it (and yes, I have actually tested this out) with no reason needed beyond simply that you didn't like the car. They also make a similar no-bargaining, no-low-balling offer for your trade-in, and let you know

with 30-45 minutes exactly what they are willing to pay you for your car. And, as it should be, the two transactions don't have to be tied to each other. They also have a decent website that lets you find the car you want nearby, or sign up to be notified via e-mail if a car matching your criteria shows up in their lots. Their Service Centers also seem to be squeaky clean and very impressive. They seem to be the elusive Car Dealership with a Conscience. My advice to anyone looking to buy or sell a used car, it behooves you to at least see what CarMax has to offer before making your final decision.

-- Surkhab Niazi

The Autoline "Intelligent Car Buying"

Convenient Car Buying Service
The Autoline
$200 per vehicle purchased or leased, 800-697-9776 The Autoline

To find the best deal when buying a new car I use The Autoline. I can't recommend them highly enough. For $200 they will find the car you want (or recommend the car you

should buy based on your budget and requirements) and call you back with the best no-haggle price they can find. (They also do leases.) I've used them four times now and am very happy with the results. Each time they've arranged for dealer to deliver the car to my house, so I never have to set foot in the dealership or hassle with the guy who pressures you to buy

useless "clear coat" and other pure profit add-ons.

Don't be put off by their 1993-style website — all business is conducted by phone and email.

-- Mark Frauenfelder

GETUSEDPARTS
FIND PARTS FAST.

Used auto parts online network
Get Used Parts
Getusedparts.com

After recently being involved in a minor fender-bender that resulted in a cracked tail light on my Subaru, I found that replacement parts would cost about $300 brand-new. A thorough web search confirmed that no lower prices could be found for new parts. Then I thought of trying to find the parts from a junkyard, but soon realized that would involve calling all of the junkyards in my area and then

traveling to get the part, if one could be found. So I did what any person would do in this day and age and searched Google for used or salvaged auto parts and found this website. Once I entered in the year, make, model of my car and the exact part I needed, I received a phone call a half hour later from a junkyard in Alabama that had exactly what I needed. They sent me the part for $95, including shipping.

There are several other sites that do essentially the same thing, i.e. use a standard-

ized format to send a parts request to multiple junkyards and salvage lots around the country. I use this one because it has the nicest interface and I received the best and fastest quote on the parts I needed. One thing I noticed in using these sites is that they all used the same software for selecting the year, make, model of the car and parts needed. Some entrepreneurial software company must have identified this niche and they now monopolize the market for this specialized type of software.

-- Jason Spitzer

Better car part network
Car-Part.com
Car-Part.com

Getting quotes from Get Used Parts is nice and all but for the more hands-on "just give me the info" approach, Car-Part.com is a better fit. It actually gives you a list of all the places

that have your part, their prices, condition etc. with contact information for the seller and you can filter the results by area or state. A lot of parts are too big/heavy to ship or cost prohibitive so it helps to find nearby sellers. They even have a handy tool to help you figure out what a part is called if you don't know.

The prices quoted online have been accurate and the parts are almost always available when you contact the seller. Most places have 800 numbers so its no big deal to call a few if need be or to find the best shipping prices. My dad has found several items to repair our family's cars and has been happy with them. Of course the shipping costs, accuracy of item descriptions, etc. will vary depending on the seller, but we haven't had any issues to date.

-- Isaac Good

The ultimate dry
The Absorber
$11 Amazon

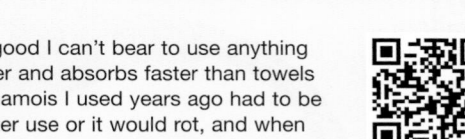

For the last five years I've used a synthetic chamois called The Absorber to dry my boat and cars. It is so good I can't bear to use anything else. It holds more water and absorbs faster than towels or real chamois. The chamois I used years ago had to be thoroughly dried out after use or it would rot, and when dry, was hard to store. Then you had to get it wet before use and wring it out frequently since it didn't hold much water. A towel, once wet, doesn't leave a dry surface (all those spots). The Absorber when moderately wet leaves your surface utterly dry. It's kind of amazing, really.

After you're done using it, just fold it in half, roll it up wet and tuck it in its hard plastic storage tube. It says you can machine wash it but I haven't tried that myself.

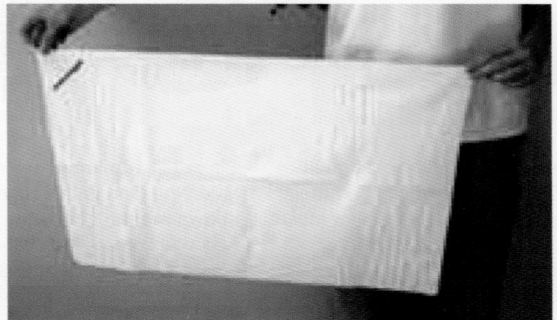

On the company website, you can read details on its PVA open-cell material. The company claims that the product is "the best drying tool you'll ever discover" and I have to agree it is — it is superior drying technology. I now own four of them in different colors. The site says you can use it to dry pets but I have never tried it on my dog (she's a short hair model and doesn't really need it), but I will try it on myself.

-- Steve Leveen

Free car buff magazine
Winding Road
Free Winding Road

Winding Road is a free digital car magazine that arrives once per month — you can either view it online in flash or download it in PDF. Apparently the magazine hired away some of the good writers from the other well-known car magazines. They are doing a pretty decent job. The magazine has cool videos and audio interviews throughout, and the photos are very good. They also have a daily news site. With Winding Road I can get all the car magazine stuff I need, without having to pay, and they

WINDING ROAD
FOR DRIVERS

never asked me for a credit card number or any of that. I've cancelled my Car and Driver subscription because I don't need it anymore.

-- Roy Nesseth

▲ We had the Smart EV for several parade loops around Brooklyn and Manhattan, and certainly the cars were 100 percent in their element here. We do completely adore the in-cabin sitting-at-the-wheel relationship; it's still near perfect and tremendously comfortable. The spatial attitude of the driver and our view out of the car are both near perfect in urban situations as well.

Acceleration to 37 miles per hour is quoted at 6.5 seconds, and top speed is capped at just 62 mph. That speed cap will keep drivers from routinely sucking the 16.5-Kwh, Tesla-Daimler lithium-ion battery pack dry, and thus falling way short of the quoted 82-mile range. The transmission is just an

on/off switch really, with a single-speed system overseeing things. This automatically makes the ForTwo ED better than the gas-powered sibling, as the five-speed simplistic SofTouch automatic is, frankly, quite an awful experience.

Another mixed message: until the 2013 model year, these initial Smart ForTwo ED cars are available only on exorbitant 48-month leases at $599 per month. That's $28,752 total, but the federal income tax credit is bound to be for the full $7500 possible, thus bringing the take down to $21,252 or, in the end, about $4,000 less than the base Nissan Leaf.

▼ Evo has gotten an early drive of the BMW i8 prototype in northern Sweden. When driving, there is a whine from the three-cylinder motor, but it isn't what one would consider bad. They describe it as sounding a bit like an early Porsche 911.

▼ Volvo has introduced a new engine family called Drive-E with two offerings, one of which is both turbocharged and supercharged.

Dashboard

◄ After trying many dash mounts I settled on Garmin's "friction mount" -- a big heavy pliable base that sits horizontal -- as the only one that would keep the screen stable in view, in the sun for years. -- KK

Bargain spoken maps
Garmin Nuvi
$118 Garmin 50LM

The Nuvi is a superbly designed car navigation device that mounts on your dash.

Nav systems are so superior to driving with maps, that I find it hard to drive somewhere new without one. Spoken turn-by-turn directions are one of the great inventions of all time.

The only question today is whether to use a dedicated device, or your phone. While map updates, and added info such as traffic are better on the phone, the Nuvi has a better interface for driving. It shows lane changes in multi-lane roads better for instance. For the moment.

Of the GPS makers (Tom Tom, Magellan) Garmin makes the best models. Their high-end Nuvi50LM has lots of competitive features, while maintaining its highly-evolved interface.

-- KK

Stabilizes items in cars
Sticky Pad
$6 Amazon

By some material genius, this pad holds stuff on your dashboard so it doesn't fly off as you drive. Non-adheasive, non-magnetic, it grips cell phones, PDAs, sunglasses, GPS, binoculars, CDs, anything that you want to grab quickly and easily. I have no idea why it holds things so firmly, but it does without adhering to the object or your dash, keeping all in place on curves, hills, and sudden stops. After a year or two in the sun it will accumulate dust and grime, diminishing its effectiveness. The pad can be restored to most of its grippiness by washing it off with detergent and water. If you can keep out of direct sunlight, it will last longer.

-- KK

Rock-steady arms
RAM Mounts
$10+ Mounts, modular parts RAM

Heavy-duty devices to mount anything in or on any vehicle — car, truck, tank, motorcycle, airplane or boat. What you get while in motion: computers in cars, GPS units on motorcycles, fishing rods on boats, TVs in trucks. You name it, they got a ball and socket expanding-arm rack to mount it. Assemble your own from a modular part system. Says reader Les Hall, who recommends these especially for motorbike or cycle handlebars, "They are easy to adjust and when tightened are rock solid."

-- KK

A movable light for tasks in the car
Hella Car Reading Lamp
$45 Buy Auto Truck Accessories

This is one of my all-time favorite and most-used vehicular tools: a hard-mounted interior reading light on a flexible stalk. This one is manufactured by Hella. I installed one in my first car, and used it for 12 incident-free years. The one in the Jeep is now 13 years old, and is still going strong. Both were/are mounted on the center of my dashboard, right above the radio.

Very handy in an infinite number of situations. Reading, obviously, but the directional nature of the light means a passenger can read in such a way that a driver's eyes are not blinded by glare. There's even a version available with red and white lighting, for night-vision preservation. The new versions are LED. Havent used the new one, but Hella makes amazing stuff, so I'm very confident about a recommendation.

-- Todd Lappin

Gadget car mount
Mountek MK 5000 CD Slot Mount
$25 Amazon

After I bought my smart phone, I wanted to find the best way to play mp3 and navigate with the built-in GPS when I am driving. Since then I have been searching for the best car mount. There are two common types of phone mount on the market, suction cup that sticks to the wind shield or flimsy clips that clip on to the air ventilation. I have tried both and found them to be inadequate and imperfect solutions.

I did some research and came across a mount that uses the CD slot. This is especially useful as I no longer use the CD player, but it is possible to play CDs at the same time. I have found that it is the perfect place to mount my smart phone. The MK5000 phone mount is very sturdy, and it has an adjustable blade than I can slide inside the CD slot and lock it tight. The mount supports vertical and horizontal rotation for easy screen rotation. It is adjustable and fits devices of different size.

I have been using the mount for a couple of months and it works very well. Every day when I hop into my car, I place my smart phone onto the mount and it holds really well. The only downside I have found is that it is more expensive than some of the other mounts, but it is definitely worth it.

-- Horace Chan

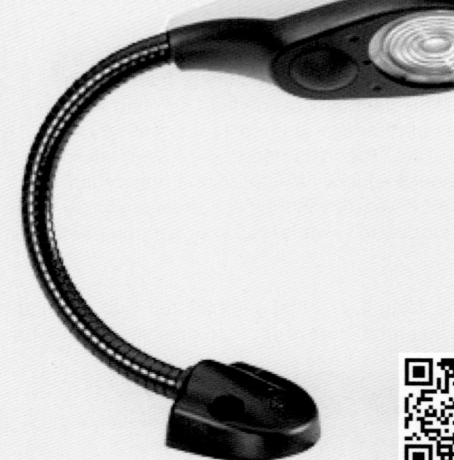

Premium radar detector
Valentine One Radar Detector
$495 Amazon

I carry a Valentine One radar detector in my day bag. I drive multiple cars, so I can I transfer it from one car to the other, and I use it for rental cars as well. A radar detector may seem a wholly unnecessary item for a law-abiding citizen, but as police departments see their budgets threatened, they have become more active in pulling people over for small infractions such as failure to come to a complete stop at a stop sign, or even driving just a few miles in excess of the limit. Modern police radar is designed to be kept in standby mode, activated only when the officer points-and-shoots, but in my experience, many police are lazy and leave their radar guns active all the time.

Since I like to know where they are, the Valentine One is the only detector that shows me the direction of a radar source (whether ahead, behind, or either side). It's very expensive at $495, but can easily pay for itself, depending on your driving habits. The after-sale service is remarkable; when my detector's frequency setting drifted after about 8 years, I sent it in and they fixed it and sent it back without charge. They will also upgrade older models for a small fee.

-- Charles Platt

Cheap brass ice scraper
Fantastic Ice Scraper
$6 Amazon

I bought the one I have now in 1982 at a gas station in Wisconsin. It's such a superior scraper that I've been careful to make sure it transferred from disposed-of vehicle to replacement vehicle four times since then. The thin, stiff, but mildly conforming brass blade slides easily between ice and glass and does so without scratching because brass is softer than glass. Important: don't use it to hack at the ice because you may deform the brass blade, after which it won't slide between ice and glass well at all.

-- Jeff Morrow

Brass blade is the real deal. I've given these to friends and family because they are so much better than the crappy plastic ones. Brass is soft enough to not damage the glass. The blade is thin and not really sharp to the touch, but is great on ice. The plastic scrapers get dull pretty quickly and then just skip over really tough ice.

-- Scott Christensen

Had one of these for years and it was the best I have ever used. You just have to be careful about hitting the rubber gasket with it – it will cut. That is the reason the blade is not as wide as the blade holder.

-- Jim Sheafer

Windshield clearing film
Rain-X
$3 (3.5 oz.) Amazon

If you ever drive your car during rain and you haven't discovered Rain-X, you are probably driving far less safely than you could. Rain-X is an exterior window (windshield, mirror, rear-window) treatment that causes water to shed from the surface rather than sheet. I don't know the composition of the product, but it behaves like a silicone wax for glass. Water beads up and drips off.

Sheeting water on a glass surface, like a windshield, causes significant distortion in the light/images passing through the glass because it isn't perfectly smooth. Rain-X causes the water to bead up so that spaces between the beads give you clear vision of what's ahead. While this is clearly evident during rainstorms, it is UNBELIEVEABLY DIFFERENT during rainstorms at night. You can actually SEE!

During most rain, you can leave your wipers on intermittent when others are swiping furiously – and you will be able to see far better than they can even with the frenetic wiper activity. Better sight is better safety!

If you want a clear demonstration, put a bit of Rain-X on a 10" square patch on your windshield just below the rear-view mirror (on the outside of the glass). The next time it rains, you won't believe how well you can see out of this patch and how poorly your wipers are clearing the rest of the windshield.

I am very skeptical of "patent medicines" so when I try something that actually works I am very pleasantly surprised. This product has astonished me. I have been using it for many years and wouldn't think of sending my kids out in a car without Rain-X.

(I think they are missing a bet by not offering their Rain-X "towelettes" as free samples over the Internet. They don't even accept email on their site. Ah well, at least the product is great.)

-- Durwin Sharp

Applying Rain-X by hand is for people with entirely too much free time :) Take a gander at the windshield wiper fluid with it already added. I have been using this for at least three years now and I give gallons of it for xmas. it is a wonderful invention.

Available from automotive stores.

-- Douglas F. Calvert

Removable windshield appliqué
Sticker Shield

Sticker Shield is a static adhesion sheet that surrounds a decal or sticker, making it easily removable and transferable from one surface to another. I've always had a problem with parking stickers. External stickers are easily scraped off during Chicago winters. Internal stickers are weatherproof, but can only be removed destructively from your windshield. Unlike Un-Du and Grip Solvent, which can ostensibly remove decals easily, Sticker Shield allows you to avoid the hassle altogether and preserves the sticker for re-use. The sheets are 4×6-inches, so if you're using smaller decals, you just cut down the sheet and save the other half for another sticker. Often my partner and I switch cars, so now it's much easier to swap stickers with each other before going to work. Or say a child has an awesome sticker he or she wants to put somewhere, but on a "permanent" basis. Whenever the time comes to remove it, there'll be no need to resort to solvents or scraping.

-- Joel Grossman

These are SENSATIONAL. The plastic holds up perfectly for years and it is impossible to see you've made your "permanent" sticker a temporary and easily movable item. I've been using Sticker Shields (it used to be named something else) for at least ten years: one for my auto registration sticker and one for my state inspection sticker, both on my front windshield. My daughter also uses one for her apartment parking sticker, and gives it to friends when she's not around town. She did that in college, too, so her pals could park on campus when she was off. It's really fun to use, sort of like magic.

-- Joseph Stirt

$5 (two 4×6-inch sheets)
Lemeer Design

$250 (50 sets)
Amazon

Quick retractable auto shade
The Shade
$34+ (varies with car model) Dash Designs

Conventional car shades are unwieldy, prone to slipping off, and awkward to store.

The Shade requires careful installation, but thereafter takes only a second to put up or roll away. This makes one much more likely to use it regularly, resulting in fewer surprises when those clouds vanish midday. It is well built, sturdy, and reliable. The retraction mechanism on my original unit is as strong and smooth as on a new one; I know, because I've bought eight more of these shades over the years for friends and family. The glue for the mounting brackets is strong stuff, my right-hand brackets fell off this summer, but that was after six years of New Mexico sun. Replacement brackets were $5, and my Shade is now remounted and ready for another six years.

They are sized to fit different car models.

-- Ed Santiago

Super wide angle windshield view
LightInSight
$18 LightInSight

I bought a souped-up Mini Cooper from a car-enthusiast friend. As I sat for the first time in the driver's seat, I noticed what looked like an irregularity in the top of the windshield. Peering more closely, I saw it was a little Fresnel lens. "What's that for?" I asked.

"It's the coolest thing," he said. "I found it on one of the Mini sites. It lets you see when the light turns green without having to crane your neck."

Sure enough, it does. Another friend who was riding with me a few weeks later became so enamored with the device, I peeled it off and gave it to him. While waiting for a replacement I had to bend my neck sideways and lean forward to see the light when I'm first in line. What a pain compared to just sitting back comfortably and waiting for that little red dot in the lens to go green.

The manufacturer says LightInSight works for all kinds of vehicles and is "especially helpful for taller drivers, drivers in smaller cars, delivery vans and trucks, and drivers with a mobility problem, such as a neck or back problem."

LightInSight is self-adhering (assisted with a wet paper towel), easily removable and reusable. It measures 7" by 1-1/2".

-- Steve Leveen

Auto Security

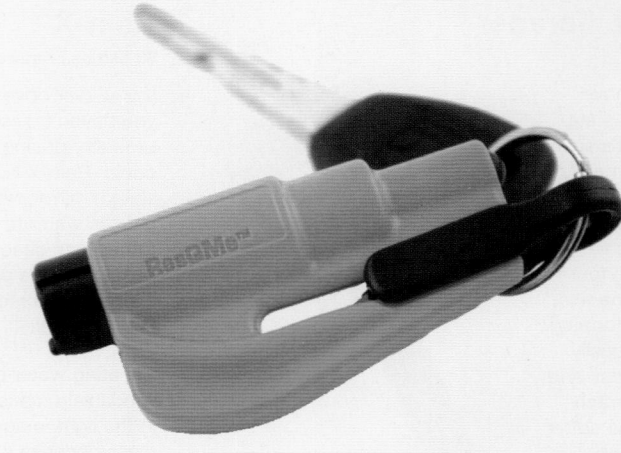

Most secure auto theft prevention
Ravelco Auto Anti-Theft Device
$470 Ravelco

Two years ago I caught someone trying to steal my car. They were doing it in a way that would not set off my alarm. That prompted me to do a bunch of research about the current state of the art of auto security. Much to my chagrin, most of the items on the market right now are easily defeated by car thieves. There was only one product that everyone said worked. Called a Ravelco device, it consists of a multi-pronged plug and socket that disables multiple electrical systems in your car. They claim that in 29 years and in an installed base of 3 million cars, not one of those cars has ever been stolen.

So I got it. They sent a technician to my house to do the install and he did an excellent job. The solution is simple and elegant. It is not an alarm but a device that makes your car undriveable. It uses a coded dongle and the installer will pick multiple systems (electrical, fuel) that are disabled when the dongle is removed so even if the starter is hotwired, the car cannot run without the dongle. The installer will also go to great pains to disguise where wiring has been spliced. My experience with other mass-installed alarm systems is that they use bright red wire for power and always put the controller and the siren in the same spot.

I have used the Ravelco for several years now. It is completely foolproof and couldn't be simpler to operate. When you pull the dongle, the car stops and cannot be restarted, period. No false alarms, no waking the neighbors. I feel confident parking my car almost anywhere. They give you two dongles up front and you get a code to order new ones from the company if you should lose one. That being said, we have had some exciting moments when my wife temporarily misplaced her dongle once.

Then two weeks ago I accidentally left my car door open overnight. When I opened the car door to go to work I realized my mistake. Someone had been in my car and had opened my fuse box to look for the alarm shutoff. They had also opened my hood to start the car. The Ravelco had completely foiled them. I love it!

-- Kurt Wendelken

Window smashing lifesaver
ResQMe
$10 Amazon

The ResQMe tool is something that I believe everyone should own, but I pray that no one will ever need to use.

I have been fortunate enough to have never needed to use this tool myself, but through my work as an EMT I have come across more than one situation where my patients may have benifited from this tool, and one situation where I honestly believe that this tool could have been lifesaving.

When you have been involved in a serious motor vehicle collision your adrenaline starts flowing and, if you are like the large majority of people, your fight or flight instincts kick in and thinking rationally can become a challenge.

If it is safe to remain in your vehicle, that is certainly your best course of action. But in some situations this is simply not an option. If for example the vehicle has entered water, if chemicals or fire are involved, or if you are in an isolated area and assistance is simply not going to find you in your current location it may be necessary to vacate your vehicle. Seatbelt mechanisms may become jammed and pushing the release button may no longer work. Electric windows may no longer work if the electronics were damaged by the collision.

In order to get out of the vehicle you need to find not only an alternate way to undo your seatbelt, but a means of breaking a window specifically designed not to be easily broken, and you must do both these things while in a near panicked state. With other tool combinations that I've used the seatbelt cutter and the window punch have been separate and have had no means of attaching to a keychain.

As a rescuer, these independent devices work well. However, if you are the person trapped inside the vehicle you don't have time to be reaching around looking for one tool, let alone two. Having the ResQMe attached to your key chain means that you will almost always be able to escape from your vehicle.

-- Caity

Velcro hide-a-key
Velcro Key Hider Pouch
$8 Amazon

Locking yourself out of your vehicle is nigh inevitable. Whether your keys are lost, misplaced or dangling tauntingly from the ignition of your locked rig, you've got yourself in a pickle. A recent review of a trailer-hitch key vault proposed a nifty, albeit pricey method to ensure you're not stranded.

But for those too frugal to spend $65 on a solution, there's a cheap and effective solution that has saved my bacon on a number of occasions, including out in the middle of nowhere after losing my keys in a trout stream.

The Velcro key hider is a pouch which can be affixed to your vehicle discreetly. Unlike the magnetic key hiders, it won't jiggle off on rough roads. I still have the original key pouch I purchased a dozen years ago, tucked safely away but readily accessible. I use it often by design, not wanting to carry my keys with me if I'm engaged in sporting events or hikes or such.

They can be purchased for a tiny fraction of the aforementioned trailer hitch (and don't have to be removed if you intend to be pulling a trailer, either.) This one on Amazon's site retails for around $8, but I found mine at my local key shop for a similar price.

-- John Bulger

Secret truck stash
HitchSafe Key Vault
$47 Amazon

I do a lot of outdoor stuff like fishing, hunting, diving, etc. and when I leave my car I am always trying to figure out what to do with my keys. In the past I had three places I hid the keys but I never felt really comfortable about it. I never liked taking keys with me because I worried too much that I might lose them. I used to be able to take them diving, but now that most keys have electronics attached, it has made it impossible.

I recently discovered the HitchSafe, an attachment that slides into my tow hitch that has a compartment that can hold credit cards, drivers licenses, keys, etc. The hitch has four dials on the drawer allowing you to create a custom unlock combination. And it comes with a cover that conceals the HitchSafe.

I recently bought a second for my wife as she is always getting locked out of her car and so she now keeps her spare key in there. In the past she has tried those magnetic boxes that stick to the underside of the car, but they kept falling off and it was hard for her to find it, let alone reach underneath and grab it.

This is exactly the kind of tool I wish I had thought of.

-- John Davis

Nothing is funnier than unhappiness. - Samuel Beckett

TORQUE
Engine Management Diagnostics and Tools
Profile: Mustang

Engine diagnostic tool
Torque Engine Diagnostic App and OBDII Reader

For years, every time I had a "check engine" light pop up I thought about plopping down $100 or more for an OBDII code scanner. I could never rationalize the cost of the device and the limited benefits that it could give me (being limited to simply reading and perhaps resetting codes).

However, that's all changed. Now if you have an Android phone or tablet there is a much less expensive and much more useful alternative. An app called Torque Pro available in the Android Marketplace provides an amazingly customizable dashboard of information. Among others, and depending on the vehicle you own, it can display transmission temperatures, 0-60 speed timings, and track CO2 emissions. The application is capable of graphing all the analytics, or out-

putting to a PC. Recently, the things that I have been using the most are instant and average fuel economy statistics.

The OBDII interface that connects your car to the Torque app can be used by any bluetooth enabled code reader (Torque has provided a list of all compatible devices). The one I use and recommend is the ELM 327 bluetooth OBDII scanner that I picked up on Amazon for around $25, but most compatible units will work just as well.

-- Karl Hafer Jr

$5 Torque Pro App Android Marketplace

$25 ELM 327 Bluetooth Scanner OBDII Car Diagnostic Tool Amazon

Blackbox for your car
CarChip E/X
$76 Amazon

Ever had that darn annoying little "check engine" light come on your dashboard? It costs a ridiculous 75 bucks just to "hook up your car and see what the computer says." And that doesn't include the cost to fix it, if anything really is wrong.

There's a very cool little thing-a-ma-jiggy called the CarChip E/X that lets you do this yourself. Since 1996, thanks to emission control regulations, just about every car sold in the USA adheres to a protocol called an OBDII. This includes an interior plug which allows anyone with a computer hookup or data scanner (like the CarChip) to plug into the car's computer and download information.

With the CarChip E/X plugged into your car, it records up to 300 hours of your driving data. In other words the CarChip acts like a car blackbox. Every trip you make is recorded. The information it records includes: time and date for each trip, distance, speed, hard accelerations and braking, and engine diagnostic trouble codes. In addition, you can pick four other

parameters to record ranging from RPM, engine coolant temperature, throttle position, fuel pressure, battery voltage, etc. Using the included software, you can then graph out the data to show you how your vehicle is performing. And like an airplane blackbox, if you happen to have the misfortune of getting into an accident, the CarChip E/X will automatically generate an accident log showing the last critical 20 seconds of speed.

The OBDII port to plug the CarChip in is pretty easily found, at least on both my and my friends' cars. It is typically located inside the car somewhere under the dash/steering wheel. Here's a great site that helps you determine where to look by car model.

The CarChip software (Windows only) is relatively easy to figure out once you get the hang of it. It makes it pretty simple to get all the information from your CarChip and plot it out in charts and graphs. All you do is connect the CarChip E/X to your USB port, start the program, click on download, tell it which car you are downloading from (i.e. name the log file; separate downloaded info so you can track different cars), then wait for it to finish. Then you have several different views to look at the downloaded info.

If there are any error codes stored in your car, they will show up in the log file. Error codes can be googled. There are tons of sites where they explain what the code

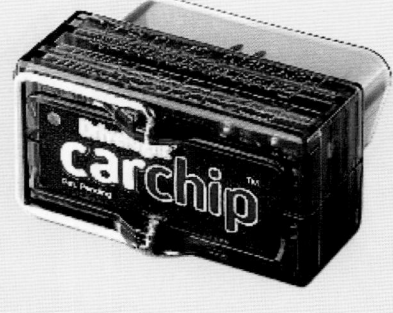

means. The current version of the software doesn't appear to have an export to Excel function, but you can do a cut and paste of the data tables and paste it into Excel if you want to manipulate the data further.

You can monitor trends in your engine and hopefully be able to anticipate system failures before they occur. I can't tell you how much I enjoy looking over the data dumps (charts, graphs) from this thing and chide my wife about how many hard stops or accelerations she's made. Of course you can use this to monitor your kids' driving habits. Because it records when it was installed and removed, they can't remove the device to hide their driving.

This is really one cool tool that I will always have in my arsenal. It's saved me and many friends several unnecessary trips to the dealer. And when I do have to go to the dealer for service, I'm more informed about what the problem is, and what work is probably going to be needed. Harder to get fleeced.

-- Paul Lin

Portable household current
Bestek Power Inverter
$17 Bestek

You plug this solid-state inverter into your car's lighter socket and power whatever 110 volt AC appliance you want, 75 watts max. No need for special DC gadgets. It's made for recharging cell phones and other batteries (it has two USB plugs), but I've used it for my scanner and my printer while on the road. Also, I've run a small B&W TV set (5'5), and more important, my baby's bottle heater (I admit is a small one). You can power almost anything that doesn't use large resistance like hair dryers, waffle makers, bread toasters, small ovens. I haven't tried a coffee maker yet.

The same company offers an assorted line of automobile inverters with more output power (200 watts on up). This is the smallest one.

-- Juan J Gil

Thicker cables, less resistance
2-Gauge Jumper Cables
$55 25' 600 Amp Booster Cable Amazon

I've had these jumper cables for over a year. At least four times I can recall, (and probably more) when someone was already being jumped and all they could get was a click or it barely turned over but wouldn't go far enough to start, I've just put these on instead of the wimpy cables they were using and the engine fired up instantly. Even from a smaller car to a larger one.

If you need to get hundreds of cold-cranking amps over several feet of cable, the voltage drops by the resistance times the current. So even a tiny fraction of an ohm matters when you need that many amps, since you can halve the voltage at the starter. You might barely get enough

to the point of connection of the other car, then there are thinner wires to the alternator and a thirsty battery. Your battery and alternator probably provides more than enough but it doesn't help if it doesn't get there and instead just warms the jumper cables. Once when I didn't have these I managed to get a car to barely start by putting a second pair of the thinner cables in parallel.

Forget anything under 6-gauge. 4-gauge can work most of the time. These 2-gauge cables work every time even though they are 20 feet long.

-- Thomas Z.

Portable jump kit
Jump-N-Carry
$105 National Tool Warehouse

Mechanics here in Boston call this a "jump kit." It's a briefcase-sized, 20lb, 12V battery with built-in 12v/120v charger, and with built-in jumper cables attached. The Jump-N-Carry is a much easier way to jump a car; no jockeying the live car to kiss bumpers, no stretching jumper cables between cars. I tend to keep mine in my car, so it's quick & easy to help anyone who needs a jump. A cute trick for a dead alternator is to hook up the jump kit, lay it inside the engine well, close the hood as well as you can, and drive to the shop. One of my mechanics has a J&C with a case that melted from doing this trick, but it still works fine.

This model can be charged from your car's cigarette lighter, but I just plug mine into a wall outlet with any extension cord that's handy. It holds its charge for months without recharging. I've had one, trouble-free, for a year and a half.

-- Don Davis

Tire Care

Re-inflates tires on the go
Campbell Hausfeld 12-Volt Tire Inflator
$28 Amazon

I have a Campbell Hausfeld 12-volt tire inflator that has kicked around in the back of my car for years. I've lost count of the number of times I've re-inflated a tire with a slow leak, and then gone on my way. The brand isn't nearly as important as the fact that it runs off your car battery; it has a tire pressure gauge built in, and it has a work light.

Small 12-volt compressors like this run from between 15 to 30 bucks new, and will do a fine job of re-inflating tires or rubber rafts or volley-balls. Most compressors come with attachments that will do all of these things. In my case, we often travel on industrial roads that lead to the local dump, so we tend to pick up more than our share of nails and screws. My little compressor has lasted through several cars and many tires.

-- Amy Thomson

Flat prevention and repair
Fix-A-Flat
$8 (16 oz.) Amazon

Yes, this little thing really will fix your flat. Even huge pick-up and SUV tires. No need to jack up. Just press the nozzle — whizzzz — and it repairs and re-inflates your tire. You definitely should carry one in your car or truck. At $8 it is cheaper than getting your tire repaired at a shop.

But that's not the best thing it offers. This amazing can of stuff will also PREVENT flats and slow leaks. Fix-A-Flat inserts a complex liquid into your tire. Leaking air instantly polymerizes it to plug up any hole. This magic material is similar to the stuff which keeps bicycle tires intact — see the amazing video in this review. Although I have not used the industrial version of this invention, farmers and the army use a similar compound to keep their gigantic tires going.

This consumer version works great as a flat cure. I need to pump up my treated tires far less often, even the tires with chronic leaks in them, and have had no flats on well-worn tires.

For non-emergency prevention you can buy the sealant in a non-aerosol squeeze bottle, but I found this hard to find in stores. They make a bicycle version which I have not tried yet…*

-- KK

Shown right is bullet proofing for jeeps; the liquid rubber inside a tire will instantly heal a bullet hole. It hardly notices nail and screw pokes. ▶

$70 Ultraseal Tire Sealant (1 gal.) Gempler's

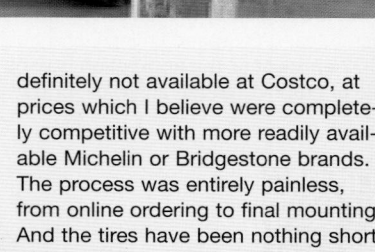

Optimal source for tires
Tire Rack
Prices Vary Tirerack.com

Maybe Costco has cheaper tires (I'd have to be convinced) but I suggest you check out Tire Rack online for real bargains on tires. What Costco can't deliver is the peace of mind that you have actually bought the optimal tires for your car, ones where you have made the correct trade offs regarding handling, ride, quietness, and tread life. And when it comes to your car, these can literally be life and death decisions.

You can't get this information by looking at a tire. You have to find reviews. So who is actually testing tires for your car? Well, it seems like Tire Rack is; their reviews are both quantitative and qualitative, based on user response. Plus they also do their own direct comparison tests, with different tires put on the same car driven over similar conditions to try to achieve objective, repeatable results. And their inventory isn't just the mainstream, largest selling tires, but many more specialized, performance-oriented, or just plain excellent but less popular tires.

How, you may ask, do you buy tires online — like who mounts them? They have local tire retailers they work with who will mount your tires for a fixed fee you know ahead of time. Tire Rack ships direct to the retailer; you bring your car and they mount the tires as if you bought them there. Even with shipping and mounting, the cost of Tire Rack tires is competitive with local prices, even discounters.

I've bought tires for both our cars now through them. Using their surveys and tests, I ended up deciding on Pirelli PZero Neros, which are definitely not available at Costco, at prices which I believe were completely competitive with more readily available Michelin or Bridgestone brands. The process was entirely painless, from online ordering to final mounting. And the tires have been nothing short of a revelation, changing the handling, ride, and quietness of our cars significantly for the better.

-- Louis Rossetto

Accurate tire inflator
Tire-Pressure Nozzle and Gauge
$9 Harbor Freight Tools

I have always hated inflating my tires. It's always a struggle to keep the inflator nozzle pressed against the tire valve stem while alternating between inflating and checking the tire pressure.

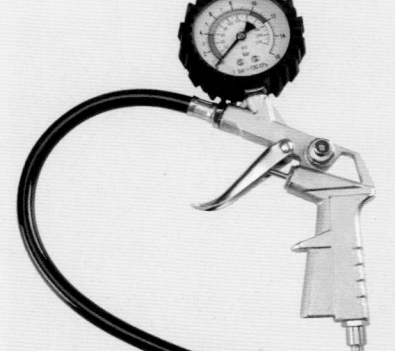

I recently got one of these clip-on tire inflators. It lets me quickly and easily inflate my tires without needing to remove the nozzle to check the pressure. You clip it on, and your tire pressure appears on the gauge. Then you just pull the trigger to inflate. If you over-inflate, you can easily bleed off pressure.

It's an inexpensive addition to your air compressor and well worth the $9.

-- Mike Polo

Emergency puncture fix
Tire Plugs
$10 Buy Hardware Supplies

What happens if you're on a trip in middle of nowhere and you get a flat? You swap to your spare, right? OK, now you are in the middle of nowhere, with no back up. Your only option now is to head to civilization to get your tire repaired, which can wreck a camping trip fast. This weekend I was reminded how few people know about these tire plug kits or how to use them. For under $10 and a few ounces, you can use the same tools that the tire repair shops do. They are available at almost every gas station. You just find the leak (a little soapy water works best) remove the obstruction, rough up the hole with the rasp tool, and push in the sticky rope plug with the other, then re-inflate (which requires a pump of some kind, but even a bike pump will work). This is the same thing they do in the repair shops, but is no harder than changing a tire and sometimes easier as you don't always have to take the tire off the car (but you will have to jack it up or somehow take the weight off of it). This won't work for really large blow outs or slashes, but will fix 90% of all tire punctures you encounter and keep your weekend from getting ruined. -- Alexander Rose

There is moderation even in excess. - Benjamin Disraeli

Easier way to change oil
Topside Oil Changer
$61 Amazon

I have had my oil changed by the dealer, a local mechanic and even those jiffy people. They've all done a good job, but I like changing my own oil. It's a bit of a meditative exercise and gives me a chance to see what's going on with my car. While I enjoy doing the oil change, my least favorite part of changing my oil is getting underneath the car, removing the drain plug and draining the oil. Dealing with the jack, stripping the drain plug every now and again, and spilling the used oil were nearly enough to stop me from changing my oil.

A friend of mine recently had his car serviced at a local dealership and he told me about a new machine that they used to drain the oil without jacking the car or removing the drain plug. The oil change technician inserted a probe into the dipstick tube and used a vacuum to drain the oil. This sounded very interesting and encouraged me to research more about this system and see if it was small enough to be used at home.

My research revealed that there were a number of these systems available for the do-it-yourselfer. After I compared features of the different brands, I settled on the Topsider. Originally designed for the boating market, the Topsider is all-metal. This feature was the one that seemed most important to me. The majority of other vacuum oil changers were made of plastic and I was concerned that the plastic would become brittle over time.

Changing the oil is really simple:

1. Make sure the engine is warm to make the oil flow easily

2. Place tube in dipstick tube

3. Close pinch valve on hose

4. Pump the canister 50 times to build vacuum

5. Release the pinch valve

It takes about 8 minutes for the oil to leave your engine. I usually use this time to remove the oil filter, open oil bottles, etc. Most dipsticks reach all the way to the bottom of the oil pan. I push the hose til I feel the bottom of the pan. When I first got it, I would open my drain plug after vacuuming and very little came out (a few drops) so I suspect the vacuum gets most of the oil out. It will pull sludge out as well up through the tube. The can holds 2 gallons of oil. Once the oil is out of your car you can remove the vacuum pump and suction tube and seal the container for transport to your recycling center.

I think the clincher for me was discovering that this was the technique that Mercedes was using in its dealerships (albeit using a commercial machine).

-- Kurt Wendelken

One-size-fits-all oil filter wrench
Nylon Oil Filter Wrench
$8 Amazon

This is the only oil filter wrench anybody will ever need. I've used one similar to the one available at Amazon since a mechanic friend suggested it to me over 20 years ago. There's no adjustment necessary. It doesn't slip. The tighter you turn it with a ratchet, the tighter it grips. And you don't need to keep several sizes of socket around, unlike the previously reviewed Oil Filter Sockets. Best of all, it's cheap and it will last practically forever.

-- Michael Farris

Spill-free gas can
Smart Fill Fuel Can
$20 (6 gallon) Home Depot

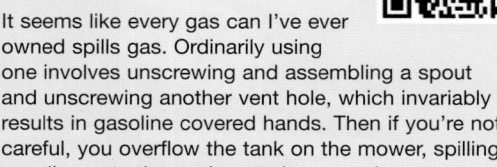

It seems like every gas can I've ever owned spills gas. Ordinarily using one involves unscrewing and assembling a spout and unscrewing another vent hole, which invariably results in gasoline covered hands. Then if you're not careful, you overflow the tank on the mower, spilling gasoline onto the engine, or the ground.

The Smart Fill fuel can is exactly what I always thought should exist. It's self-venting. It has an automatic shutoff. And it even has a hand-hold on the opposite side from the spout.

I've been using it for a few months now, and other than the initial transfer of gas from my old can to the new one, I haven't spilled a drop on myself, the mower, or the ground. (It won't work for your car though...)

-- Edson Freeman

Collapsible emergency gasoline can
Itzagascan
$12 DSK Sales

This disposable fiberboard container folds flat and has a bladder that can hold a gallon of gas (about 14" by 6" by 2"). I've yet to have a car emergency, but I've used it for a prosaic fill up on a lawn mower. No leaks, easy to carry and cheap to replace. Keeping one around is handy and comforting, and it's way better than the bulky plastic ones that have bounced around in the back of my car for years.

-- Vincent

Easy oil filter removal
Oil Filter Socket Set
$6 Harbor Freight

Sometimes, a tool comes along that makes you wonder how you ever got along without it, even if it's a sole-purpose tool. This Oil Filter Socket Set is one of those tools.

Instead of trying to remove filters with oil-covered hands or those silly floppy metal band wrenches in terrible positions, these cup wrench sockets make changing oil filters a snap. If there's enough space around it for your hand to reach it, you can reach it with one of these, and they allow you to apply

leverage with a 3/8" socket wrench, a regular crescent wrench, or even a thumbwheel ratchet so even the most stubborn filter will come off easily. They have little grippy bits inside somewhat like a nut remover socket so they grip really well.

This $6 set of wrenches has fit every round filter I've tried them with. Sure, they're cheap, but oil filters aren't an application where strength and precision are required – all that's needed is "good enough" and that's what these are.

-- Jon Braun

Tidy oil drainer
Fumoto Oil Drain Valve
$24 (F-series) Fumoto Valve

Changing the oil in your car is a bit of a pain, and usually involves fishing around in an oily mess for the drain plug you dropped. The Fumoto Valve makes the process a lot tidier and easier. It's simply a ball valve with a locking quarter-turn action. You install it in place of your oil drain plug, and after that, draining the oil is a matter of a quarter turn on a lever. The lever locks in place in the closed position, making it difficult for vibration to open it. It does project slightly below where the old drain plug would be, but this is not a problem unless you're rock crawling in the Camry.

-- Michael O'Connor

Reliable Vehicles

The people's truck
Toyota 4×4
$20,000+ (new), $5,000+ (used) Ebay

Because I've worked for years at the edges of computer research, and have grown accustomed to flakey and fragile gadgets that only work intermittently, then crash, I have for my private life adopted a farmer's frugal aesthetic when selecting durable tools. I favor poet Gary Synder's measure of dependability*:

I lie in the dusty and broken brush

Under the pickup

Already thought to be old -

Admiring its solidness, square lines

Thinking a truck like this

Would please Chairman Mao

My own people's pickup is a 1996 4-cylinder Toyota Tacoma 4×4 with 110,00 miles. Toyota pickups are widely visible during CNN coverage of the Middle East as the vehicle of choice in the rugged mountains of Afghanistan, and Pakistan. Indeed you find these almost anywhere in the world where reliability is difficult but critical. My mechanic for years, an expatriate Iranian, says that every mechanic he knows admires, and many own, the Toyota 4 cylinder trucks for their durability and reliability.

I use mine to haul feed for the animals, to clear brush from the pastures, to haul firewood, to traverse the high country through deep snow, and for regular commuting over mountain roads and congested freeways. Despite only 4 cylinders, power is ample for any use on or off-road. A used Toyota like mine would sell for $6,000. But I'm pleased to see that prices for a new one are about the same as I paid in '96: dealers sticker is under $18,000, retail around $19,000. The basic four cylinder engine is unchanged throughout the years. It's a classic, like the old GMC/Chevy straight six, and the Dodge slant six; only the running gear and comforts are improved.

It is a truck, I bet, that would have pleased Chairman Mao.

-- Mike Liebhold

Toyota is well known around the world for its durability. In fact the United Nations uses a Toyota fleet for its peace keepers and observers around the world. Most don't realize they are using Toyotas that are not available in the USA due to lower emissions standards. The Toyotas you see NGOs using are made by a special unit of Toyota called Girbraltar. They have SUVs, Pickups, etc.. same lines as you'd find at dealers but different models and configurations. My favorite option is the ballistic mat. It's an explosion-proof padding that goes underneath the carpet in case of landmines.

I just spent the past 8 weeks on a "vehicle dependent expedition" in the deserts of Nevada in a Toyota 4Runner with no mechanical breakdowns (other than flats). It really is wonderful engineering. However, it is not always the best tool for the job. Toyotas are rock solid but they do wear out and when on an extended trip you want a vehicle that is easy to maintain in the field. Toyotas are good for short and medium term trips where breakdown is hopefully not going to happen, for long-term expeditions where breakdown is inevitable, you want something that is fully self-sufficient.

For example, on an extended African trip you won't find a certified Toyota mechanic and parts everywhere. Older Land Rovers are often a better choice because they are essentially fully repairable in the field. Everything is bolted on and can easily be swapped out. Like the windshields come off with a few bolts. Fixing a windshield in a Toyota is more involved and complicated . With a Land Rover it's possible to bring all spare parts and keep the vehicle going indefinitely with no outside help short of catastrophic damage.

To sum up: Toyotas are more modern design using newer technology; the older Land Rovers are basic nuts and bolts. The Land Rover will probably break down more often, but be easier to fix. Land Rovers are kind of like the hackers' vehicle, an old PC running Linux, while the Toyota is more like a Macintosh, well designed and reliable.

-- Stephen Balbach

I have owned three Toyota 4-cyl. 4×4's over the years, but the basic unit is the same.

I had an '88 that I put about 170 K miles on. In 14 years it never failed to start up (except once when the starter motor went out). I went through arroyos, all over the desert, on beaches with soft sand. I pulled people out of ditches. It was also my city vehicle. I sold it last year to a surfer dude for about $1500. The only thing wrong was that the body was pretty completely rusted out, since I live on the ocean (and also I figured in retrospect because I would never rinse it off after hauling surfboards dripping with salt water).

Then I bought a 2003 and it's a dream. Toyota has re-thought every part of it, and redesigned where necessary. The radio, the wipers, the seats, the exterior and interior design.

There's an old Yakima rocket box on the top, and the cylindrical thing is a pull-out tarp for quick shade that I got used . Note the metal camper window on the drivers side (where you don't need visibility).

-- Lloyd Kahn

Superior compact
Honda Fit
$18,000 Honda Fit, 2013 Model

I've been driving 4×4 trucks for over 30 years. The trade-off was the weight and truckiness being that I could pick up firewood, haul lumber and sacks of concrete, and go anywhere, any time. I spent 12 years 4-wheeling in Baja. Three long trips to British Columbia. 4-wheeling it across the river to my friend Louie's house in Mendocino county. I've been a truck guy forever.

But there came the time, several months ago, when I realized I was through with the long truck hauls, the 3,000-mile trips, and hauling the truck over the windy roads homewards from my weekly trips into San Francisco was a chore.

I embarked on a study of cars, and ended up settling on a Honda Fit. Other contenders (in this field of scaled-down, aerodynamic SUVs) were the Toyota Yaris Liftback, Mazda 2, Scion XD, Prius C model, VW Golf diesel. The Cube too cartoony, the Scion xB too boxy. In the end I settled on the Fit largely because of its ingenious cargo space in the rear: 4 x 5 feet with rear seats folded down. 20 cubic feet of space vs. 15 for the other cars. 4 doors and a hatchback so you can get into the rear from all sides. Like a small truck bed. (I could get into my truck bed camper shell on all 3 sides.)

I guess things have come a long way, because this very efficient little car reminds me of going from a truck to this car is like going from logging boots to running shoes. Like a 250 pound guy losing 60 pounds.

360-degree visibility, automatic windows, a

USB connector. There are a dozen things that delight me about this car. I could drive all day and arrive rested. I'm in auto heaven.

-- Lloyd Kahn

Cheapest reliable used car
Volvo 240
$1,000 (1985, 150,000 miles) Cars For Sale

The Volvo 240 series of cars is quite possibly one of the best used car deals for the cooltools crowd. They were made from 1975 until 1993 — so there are plenty of them to go around. In fact, Volvo wanted to stop making the cars three years before they actually stop producing them — the community demand was so great they just didn't stop!

240s are roomy (especially in wagon form), reasonably fuel efficient (20 – 30 mpg), durable (engines with 200,000+ miles are not blinked at), solid (steel construction), safe (one of the many cars that built the Volvo=Safe reputation), comfy (lumbar support, heated seats, et cetera), simple to work on (thanks to a roomy engine bay),

excellent community support (comprehensive FAQ & online forums), excellent parts support (online junkyard parts galore, and you can still get parts at dealerships), good in the winter (with proper snow tires) and best of all, cheap! A 240 in good condition can be had for anywhere from free (it needs a little work and it's so old and has so many miles… who'd want it?) to $2,000+ for a well looked after example. (The 240's latter siblings, the 740 and 940, are both fine cars as well – based on the same mechanicals as the 240)

I've had two previous Vovlo 240s and love my current 1990 240 wagon. I purchased it with 225,000 miles already on the odometer for a trip to Alaska. It may be a 16 year old car, but it brings a smile to my face.

-- Zach Zaletel

When I grow up I want to be a little boy. - Joseph Heller

Ultimate adventure touring bike
BMW R1150GS Motorcycle

$5,000+ (used)

For those with a true yearning for adventure travel, nothing beats a touring motorcycle. Unlike the cocooned isolation experienced by those in a 4-wheeled vehicle, motorcycles immerse you in the environment – smells, sounds, climatic conditions and noise are all immediate and accessible. In addition, motorbikes are a fuel and space-efficient means of commuting or travel. They add a huge fun factor to getting from point A to B.

I've owned about 30 motorcycles. Of all the models available today (new or used) , none beats the BMW R1150GS or its "butch" sibling, the R1150GS Adventure, for sheer versatility, capability and reliability on and off the road. The GS handles well enough in the city to be a commuter bike, yet it is capable of surviving off-road on unpaved tracks when the goal is to do some exploring. It handles as well as many sport bikes when canyon carving or dialing it up in the twisties. And, it has a shaft drive (no chain), which means it's essentially a "zero maintenance" bike. I suppose the only category it doesn't fill is the Harley/cruiser one. I've never understood that crowd anyway….

At over 86 inches in length, with an operational weight of 590 pounds plus, this BMW bike seems heavy and unwieldy to the uninitiated. But, the length and unique suspension make for a controlled and supple ride, whether you're super-slabbing it, or pounding along a dry river bed. The weight powers you through the rough stuff, and a torquey engine with plenty of grunt through the entire power-band makes the bike feel lighter and more nimble than specs alone would indicate. Superb ergonomics make snaking though city traffic a breeze, while keeping you comfortable and upright in the saddle.

In the last two years alone, I've toured over 50,000 miles in over 22 countries, countries as diverse as mainland Mexico, Turkey, the Balkans, China, and Namibia. Properly outfitted, the big GS ("Gelande" and "Strasse", loosely translated German for "off-road" and "street") has carried me, all my gear, and at times, my riding partner, over everything from dry autobahns to rain covered loose-traction surfaces of frightening disrepair. The bikes are reliable, rugged, and designed to sustain minimal damage.

Parts availability world-wise is surprisingly good. BMW has en extensive dealer network, and, their car and motorcycle parts systems/warehouses intersect. If you have a part number, you can order through any BMW car dealership. Outside of the US, many BMW care dealers also sell and service the bikes. But, mostly, you don't need to worry – rarely does anything break!

In the particular category of a multi-continent capable world-class adventure/touring machine, this motorcycle is in a class of its own. Harley makes nothing like it. Neither do Honda, Yamaha or Kawasaki. Nothing out of Italy. BMW has owned this category for over a quarter century.

The next time you see a motorcycle driving along the Haul Road in Alaska, or through the otherworldly red dunes of the Namib desert, take a close look, chances are, it'll be a BMW GS motorcycle. No one does the swiss army knife of two wheels better!

-- Mike M. Paull

Best value all-around motorcycle
Kawasaki KLR 650

$7,000+ (new), $1,000+ (used)

In these days of fancy $20,000 high-tech motorcycles, there is a refreshing alternative for those seeking simplicity and time-tested reliability: the Kawasaki KLR 650. Kawasaki started making this dual sport bike in 1984 and in thirty years has made only minor modifications, other than changing color schemes every four years or so.

There are no computer chips to melt down. Just one carburetor and one piston to maintain. The components are as accessible as on a old tractor. The US military recently converted the KLR to diesel, fulfilling their goal of having all their vehicles consume one fuel.

What sold me on this bike is the community support. Over 3,000 feisty members on the Yahoo group can provide you with anything you want to know (and sometimes more than you want to know). Local groups around the planet get together for rides and maintenance sessions. A long list of web sites show you in full detail any repair or modification you can think of. A former Midwestern corn farmer will overnight parts from his shed in Moab, Utah to anywhere you might be waiting.

Many call this one of the best 'value bikes' you can find. It is certainly one of the top adventure motorcycles, with a huge variety of aftermarket options catering to the countless people who have traveled to every corner of the planet on the KLR.

One advantage for a vehicle that's been around for thirty years is that you can find old ones dirt cheap and easily resuscitate them. New ones are a bit over $7,000.

Maybe you can find a cheaper bike out there, but with the KLR you've got a bullet proof bike you can fix yourself with a network of support. You can comfortably take it back country in rough terrain, use it around town as reliable transportation or head out on a global adventure.

-- Jonathan Foust

Protective gear for welding/motorcycling
Black Stallion Cowhide Welding Jacket

$77 Working Person's Store

I bought this jacket three years ago while shopping for welding supplies, but it now doubles as a motorcycle jacket. Convection is the enemy of anyone on a motorcycle. Leather is naturally wind proof, so its brown cowhide suede finish has kept me warm while riding around on my Harley. The jacket's really well made and an amazing value for about $55. I'm just learning how to weld (my particular interest is to build furniture), so my experience is rather limited. However, it's my understanding the sparks created from arc welding have a tendency to melt through most synthetics, and that heavy cotton and leather seem to work best at shielding sparks. The cheaper welding jackets made by Black Stallion are made of cotton and may work fine, but because they can allow air to pass through, they wouldn't work well as a motorcycle jacket. With this one, I get two jackets for the price of one.

--Velemir Cicin

Jack-based motorbike trailer hitch
Ultimate MX Hauler Motorcycle Carrier

$420 Ultimate MX Hauler

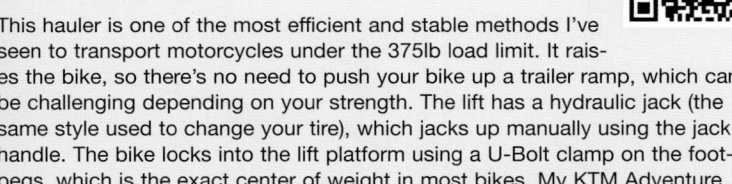

This hauler is one of the most efficient and stable methods I've seen to transport motorcycles under the 375lb load limit. It raises the bike, so there's no need to push your bike up a trailer ramp, which can be challenging depending on your strength. The lift has a hydraulic jack (the same style used to change your tire), which jacks up manually using the jack handle. The bike locks into the lift platform using a U-Bolt clamp on the footpegs, which is the exact center of weight in most bikes. My KTM Adventure weighs around 325lbs (depending on the level of the 7.4 gallon fuel tank) and even when cinched down on a ramp hauler, it tended to bounce around; this rig doesn't have that problem. I love it. It's especially handy when dropping off the bike for repairs — just strap it onto the back of my 4X4 van and I'm off. Fast, safe, solid and simple. The hitch attaches quite easily to your trailer hitch. You will need to purchase an adapter if the vehicle has a lift kit, but Ultimate makes adapters up to 8".

-- Velemir Cicin

Integrated motorcycle helmet lock
HelmetSecure

$60 Amazon

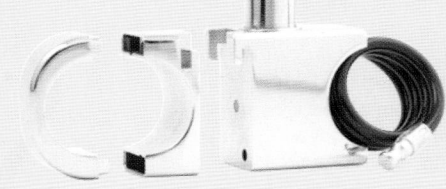

For the longest time I was one of those motorcyclists you see walking along the street carrying his helmet everywhere he goes. I didn't trust the flimsy D-ring lock that came with my motorcycle: it wasn't strong enough, and it left my helmet strap vulnerable to being cut. I wasn't interested in carrying a cable lock in my pocket, in case I crashed and landed right on it.

The solution I found, and have been using for seven months now, is the HelmetSecure. It attaches to my handlebars, and stays there, using hidden bolts that are only accessible if you have the key. I arrive at my destination, loop the 15in.-long integral steel cable through the face of my helmet (and the D-ring of a second helmet too, if I have a passenger) and leave it behind.

And the lock looks great. It's show-quality chrome, and I get plenty of questions about it. It fits the round handlebars on my Ducati, but it also comes with rubber spacers to fit Harleys and a range of different handlebars.

-- Michael Schatzl

Small Boats

How to make classic sails
The Sailmaker's Apprentice

$16 Emiliano Marino, Christine Erikson, 2001, 494 p.

The author covers both traditional and modern sail materials and sailmaking skills. He's not so much about design as technique. I particularly liked the associations with the history and self-sufficiency aspects of learning a skill like sailmaking. The book talks you through a simple version of making a ditty bag while giving you the skills to do it up to your liking. I've made two. One's served me well everywhere including at the top of my boat's mast. Get the book and then buy the materials and tools from SailRite.com and make your own.

-- Dale L.

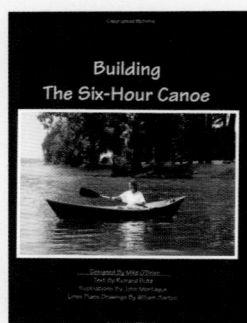

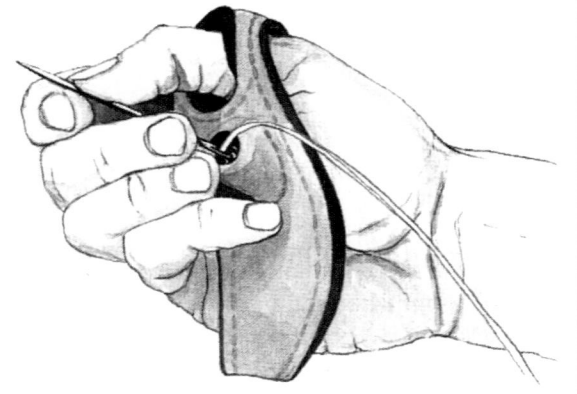

Holding the needle.

In a crosscut sail the first panel, or cloth, is laid along the tack seam, which is the perpendicular from tack to leech.

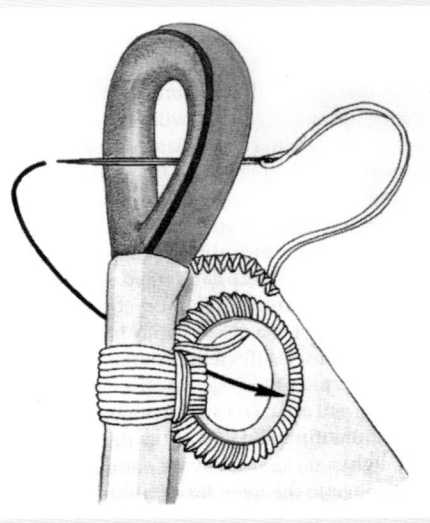

Pass the twine repeatedly back and forth through thimble and ring.

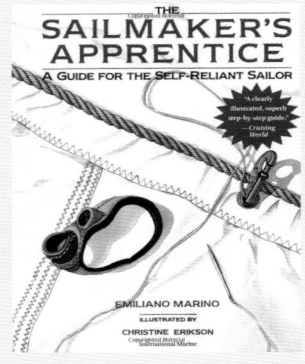

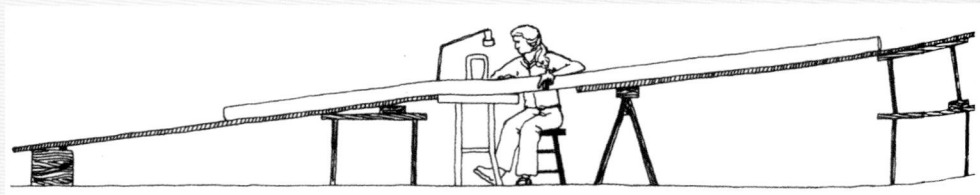

Let gravity help feed a large sticky-taped sail through the sewing machine. Building a temporary chute can be a fun challenge. Tables, boards, cloth—in the door, out the window, up the stairs, whatever it takes to get a big enough run on both sides of the machine. The less friction there is, and the fewer bumps, the more smoothly the cloth will slide.

Cheap way onto water
Building the Six-Hour Canoe

$11 Mike O'Brien and Richard Butz, 2000, 65 p.

Probably the cheapest way to get onto water. Built from a single piece of 4 by 16-foot marine plywood, plus some epoxy, this canoe will set you back $150. It might take a pro six hours, but most builders are happy to complete it in a 3-day weekend. This is the design that community boat building programs use; thousands have successfully launched theirs.

-- KK

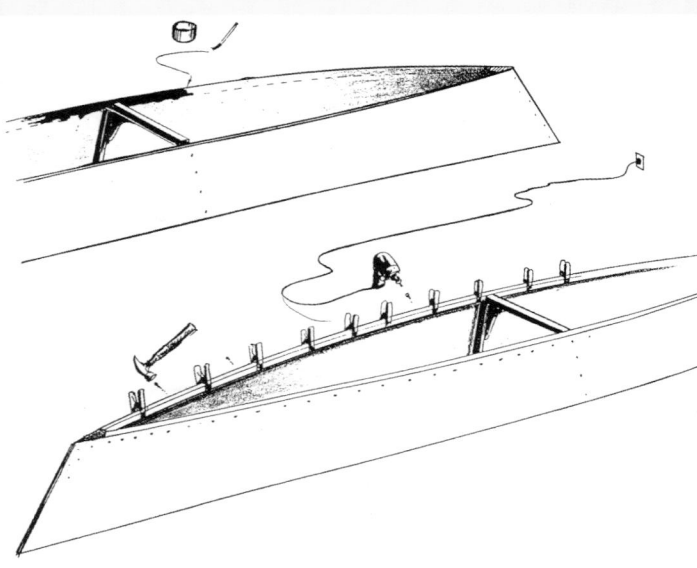

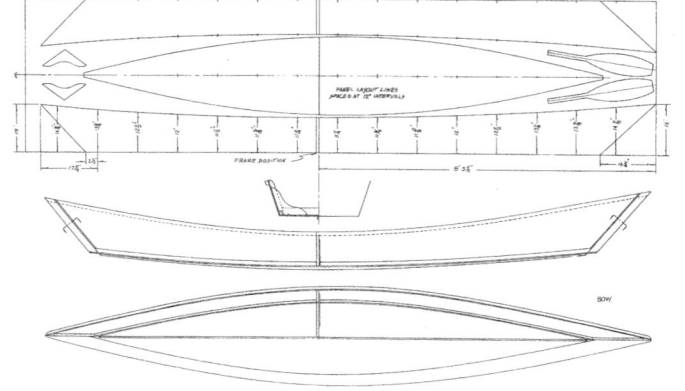

Simple boats a group can make
Community Boatbuilding Manual

$4 Digital book Wooden Boat Books

Building a boat together has proven to be a community and family builder because it allows a bunch of novices to jointly create something they didn't think they could — and to make something immediately and wonderfully useful. WoodenBoat magazine publishes this handy booklet presenting the experience of about a dozen communities and schools who have tried this. It includes suggestions of boat plans that are doable. Each year the magazine itself has hosted a family boatbuilding weekend. It's a sight to see 20 families end the weekend by launching, in unison, a simple boat they've made themselves.

-- KK

- Problems can crop up when you have too many kids for the boat you've chosen. Younger students are not as well equipped as older ones to handle the idle time that comes with too many people working on a boat. An ideal class size might be 10-12 if you had three boats under construction, but putting that number on a single boat is a strain.

- Participants in the program are generally lured by a photo advertisement in the local newspaper. Some children and teens come to build with a parent, but most participants are adults — either individuals or couples. Over the years they've built an estimated 60-70 small craft, most of them skimming the coastal waters from Boston to Portland, Maine.

Sailing tool
Davis Deluxe Rigging Knife

$18 Amazon

This knife/marlinspike/ shackle-wrench/ screwdriver is one of the simplest and most reliable tools I own. It contains a decent sheepsfoot blade, a locking curved marlinspike, a very simple lever wrench, and a nice large flat screwdriver all in one shiny stainless steel package.

Before owning a sailboat I never realized the need for such a thing, and in fact had never even noticed them as real tools. I thought they were some sort of romantic holdover from another era. Not until I started working with ropes, lines and shackles on the boat did I fully realize the critical necessity for such a tool. I can't imagine life without one now. I own two of them, two different brands, but the one I keep abusing is the Davis, the "other" one is pretty but not quite as effective.

It works very well, is relatively inexpensive and even looks cool! Cheap, virtually indestructible, invaluable to anyone who works with rope/line. I've put this tool to the test daily since I bought it a year ago and swear my greatest confidence that this is, hands down, one of the coolest tools ever!

-- Seamus Holley

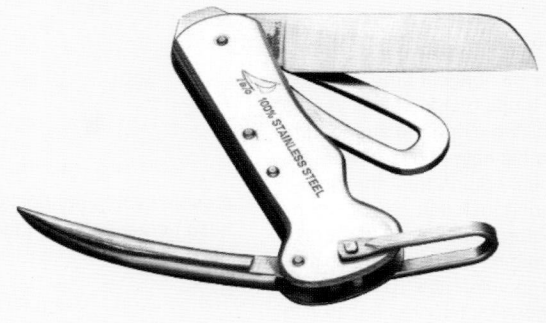

Man can believe the impossible, but never believe the improbable. - Oscar Wilde

Inflatable Collar PFD inflates in seconds

Comfortable water safety
Inflatable Life Jacket

$175 Landfall Navigation

If you mess around in boats (and you should), a life jacket is a very good thing to have, or even better, to WEAR. Over the last few years there has been a revolution in life jacket comfort as a variety of automatically inflatable life jackets have come on the scene. Inflatable PFDs (Personal Flotation Devices) overcome the two primary reasons people don't wear a life jacket: the bulk and heat a life jacket captures. I recommend a full collar auto-inflatable type since it will bring you to the surface if you go into the water unconscious (for example if you knock your head).

I hardly notice mine (a Mustang Survival Classic) when I have it on. Whether you kayak, jet ski, or boat, there really isn't an excuse not to wear one. In addition to the Mustang Survival line, another source for inflatable life jackets is Sterns, which produces the Sospenders line. Both manufacturers are approved by the US Coast Guard.

One important note: Wear your inflatable life jacket OVER your outwear. You don't want to be sharing the inside of your zipped up jacket with one of these when you go in the water. Something will break and it is likely to be you.

– Daren Lewis

Ultra-loud, all-weather noisemaker
Storm Whistle

$6 Amazon

I found this incredibly loud whistle while putting together a disaster preparedness kit for my car. I did some non-scientific testing against my Fox 40 (rated 115 decibels) by having my son blow into each of them across a soccer field. The Storm (rated 118-120db) definitely sounded louder (decibels are based on a logarithmic scale with a base of 10, so the Storm's decibel intensity is almost 3 times the Fox 40). It is also advertised as working underwater (the chambers clear as you blow). I haven't tried it underwater yet, but regardless, this is the loudest whistle I have ever heard.

– Mark Chow-Young

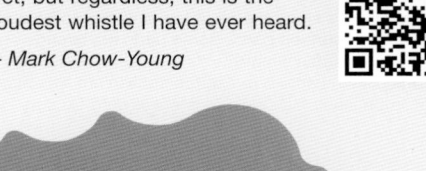

Keeping your boat in ship shape
Don Casey's Complete Illustrated Sailboat Maintenance Manual

$33 Don Casey, 2005, 896 p.

When I need to repair anything on my sailboat this is the first book I turn to. The illustrations are excellent. The book is actually six books compiled into one, which makes navigation of it a bit difficult but not impossible. The explanations are very clear with detailed information on things such as fiberglassing with resin versus epoxy, electrical wiring, and inboard diesel engines.

As a companion to this I find my subscription to Practical Sailor magazine to have up to date first hand reports on sailing equipment and products from porta potty deodorizers to bottom paints to navigation systems.

-- Monty Zukowski

● **Symmetry**

From directly forward and astern, the hull should appear symmetrical and the keel perpendicular to the deck. Sighting the hull through the gridwork of a plastic plotter simplifies this determination. Any detectable difference from one side to the other suggests major trouble. (p 11)

● **Galvanic Corrosion**

A more insidious problem is galvanic corrosion. Connecting the green wire to an underwater fitting completes the circuit between your boat and all other nearby boats with their own green wires grounded. With seawater as the electrolyte, every grounded fitting essentially becomes part of a big battery. (p. 557)

LINES

Walk (or row) away from the hull, then circle it slowly, looking at the shape of the hull.

Symmetry. From directly forward and astern, the hull should appear symmetrical and the keel perpendicular to the deck. Sighting the hull through the gridwork of a plastic plotter simplifies this determination. Any detectable difference from one side to the other suggests major trouble.

Distortion. From either side, look for any change in the flow of the sheer. Overtight stays can permanently distort the hull, revealed by a break in the sheerline, usually at the mast station. Improper support during storage can also cause permanent hull distortion.

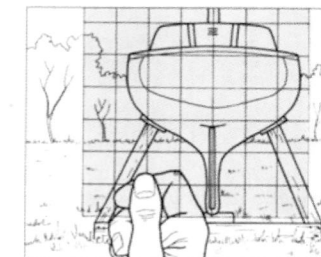

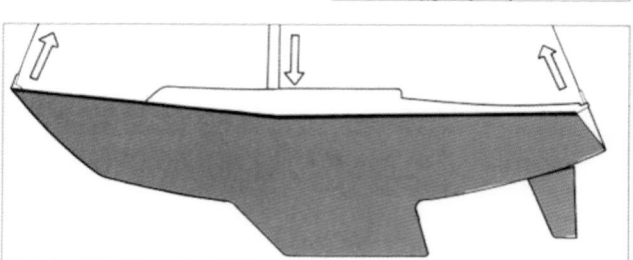

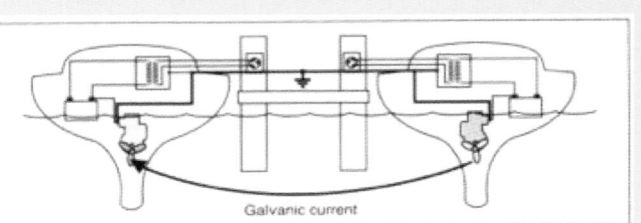

Galvanic current

If your fittings are less noble on the galvanic scale than your neighbor's, they are anodes and begin to erode. This can be bad news if you have an aluminum outdrive in the water and your neighbor's underwater fittings are bronze and stainless steel.

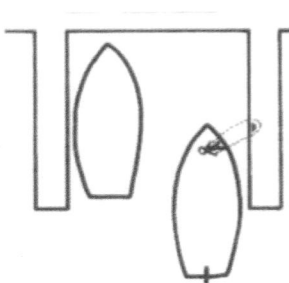

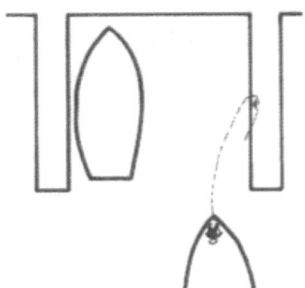

How to dock
Single Handed Docking and Sail Trim with Captain Jack Klang

$10 (Download) Sailing Channel

I have been on the water in one fashion or another for over 40 years and this is the first comprehensive presentation I have seen on how to dock in all types of conditions and situations. Captain Jack, in a mere 53 minutes, covers the main topics that drive sailors nuts: docking and sail trim, especially spinnakers. First he uses models to describe the maneuvers and then we see him on his own boat demonstrating in real time. He shows how to maintain control of your boat with the wind on the bow, on the beam or aft. He covers situations with adverse currents. What I found most intriguing is how he backs his boat into a slip to keep the bow into the wind. He demonstrates a few basic concepts, like prop-walk and spring-lines, and shows how to use a single spring line (a line attached slightly midship) to control the boat's movements. He does this not only single handedly, but without jumping off the boat. Much safer.

I wish I would have had this video when I was a beginner. It would have saved a lot of hard knocks while docking and would have saved my having to unlearn many of the bad habits I picked up trimming sails.The interface between the land and sea is often the most challenging aspect of boating. This is especially true as marinas get tighter and tighter as they pack more and more boats into them. I still sail, but four years ago sold my sailboat and bought a Nordic Tug. Docking has always been a challenge and is even more so with the tug. The tug idles much faster, so everything happens faster. It is also much less maneuverable. Even if you are a power boater, the first half of the DVD concerning docking is still well worth the price. Just fast forward through the sail-handling parts or watch it and be inspired to go sailing.

-- Dean Raffaelli

Hard waterproofing
Otterbox

$19 Amazon

Electronics and water don't mix well. Keeping digital gear dry around water is a tricky job made perfect by an Otterbox. Tough as concrete, lightweight, watertight as a submarine, and padded inside, an Otterbox will keep cameras, cell phones, navigation equipment, or wallets safe and dry through rapids, splashes, or 100 feet of water. They are indestructible.

-- KK

Boats that fit in a closet or trunk

Folding Kayaks

Kayaks are cool tools all by themselves… small, simple boats that give you access to virtually any waterway, big or small. Simple enough for a novice to enjoy, but with skill and experience, kayaks can also used for thousand-mile expeditions far from support.

Folding kayaks are a special breed among kayaks in general. They typically consist of a wood or aluminum frame inserted into a fabric skin, and assembled boats are reminiscent of the bone-and-hide baidarkas used by Inuit hunters. The obvious advantage to a folding kayak over the far more common plastic or fiberglass boats available is storage. When not in use, a folding kayak can be stored in an apartment or car trunk. But the boats are also serious performers–they are truly in their element when the seas get rough–and they tend to last much longer than rigid boats. Cracks in plastic and fiberglass can retire a rigid boat in 6 to 10 years. Folding kayaks can last for decades, not only due to the materials, but also due to the fact the individual pieces can be replaced.

Klepper of Germany has been in the business the longest, since 1909, and their boats have been around the world, including across the Atlantic, twice. They are also used by Special Forces. They are also expensive, but not quite as expensive as Feathercraft of Canada, a relative newcomer. Feathercraft makes boats using a high-tech approach in materials and design. Their boats pack down smaller, but they also cost more. Folbot is an American-made fold-

ing kayak that enjoys good reputation, in part due to their absolute commitment to standing behind their products, pretty much for life. Their boats are highly regarded, and they are significantly cheaper than the competition. They are Ford to Klepper's BMW.

I just took delivery of a newcomer in the folding kayak world, a Longhaul Mark II made by Mark Eckhardt of Colorado. Eckhardt started his business repairing Kleppers and making accessories. He was an official Klepper dealer and service center for time, but has now struck out on his own making his own boats, that are in many respects are identical to Kleppers–a Longhaul frame will actually fit a Klepper skin and vice versa. But Eckhardt has addressed a number of what he sees as design flaws of the Klepper in his new boat.

Folbot Cooper

For an inexpensive folding kayak suitable for a novice, I recommend a new boat just announced by Folbot called the Cooper. Small and light, the Cooper fits into one bag, and has nice profile. And it comes in at a price that is 2/3 the price (or better) of other reputable folding singles, at $1400. As I mentioned, Folbot has been around for decades. A brand new model from them is a boat that has a lot experience behind its design and manufacture. Additionally, Folbot has an unbeatable guarantee… they guarantee that it will be free of manufacturing defects for life, and they'll give you 100% of your money back within 60 days if you don't like the boat and return in "like new" condition. That's a tough deal to beat.

A fine enthusiasts website for tracking the latest in folding kayaks is foldingkayaks.org. For reading I recommend:

$25+ (used) The Complete Folding Kayaker Ralph Diaz, 2003, 256 p.

-- Alex Gray

●
Folbot Aleut I

The Aleut is the least expensive foldable kayak on the market today. Like the double in the Folbot family, the Aleut is designed for the mass market, for people who aren't performance-minded but simply want to enjoy paddling without much fuss. For that market, the Aleut I delivers the essentials of any folding kayak--foldable convenience and stability.

The Aleut's frame consists of aluminum long pieces and polycarbonate ribs. Its hull is Hypalon, and its deck is coated polyester.

Assembly and Portability

Assembly is a snap; the Aleut has only three ribs and only about fourteen parts. Some parts are already held together in subassemblies. You can get the Aleut either in one or two bags, but take the convenient two-bag option because the single bag is awkward to carry.

Stability and Seaworthiness

The Aleut's stability cannot be overstated. No kayak can be termed untippable, but the Aleut goes a long way in that direction. It handles well in open water, and its nose refuses to dive in all but the highest waves and wake.

●
Bailers and Pumps

Bailers and pumps are necessary safety items for any kayaker. They're doubly important in a foldable because, in the event of a capsize, the relatively large interior space could fill with a huge amount of water.

A bailer is a handy way to extract water quickly, but you won't find a single one on the market. Make your own from a pail, plastic bleach bottle, or almost any large, unbreakable beverage container made for refrigerator storage.

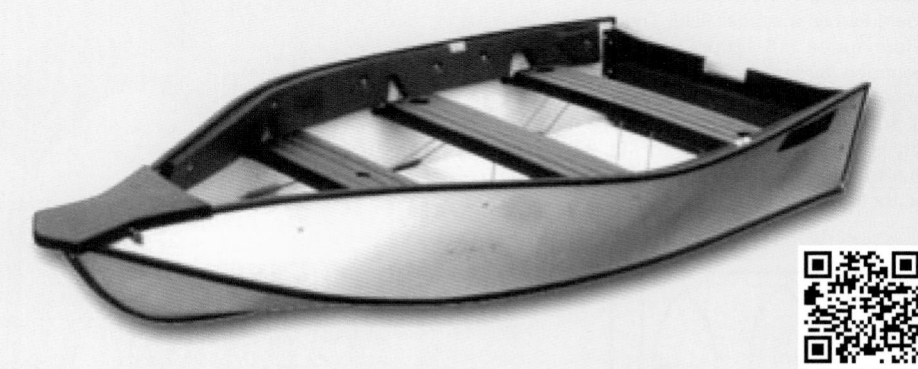

Foldable skiff

Porta Bote

$1,250+ Porta Bote

This is a very cool tool. Its a boat that folds up. It really works great. I wanted a little boat I could keep on my larger 24-foot boat so I could take me and my dogs ashore. This boat is perfect. Very stable and folds up when not in use. I tie it down on the bow when not in use. I have seen a lot of people use these with RVs, mounted to the side. You can use paddles or a small electric or gas engine to get around. It handles great and is easy to plane with a small engine like mine — a 4-horsepower gas engine. The other great thing is that I know the hull is not going to be punctured by my dogs or anything else. Its very stable with 2 people and two small dogs.

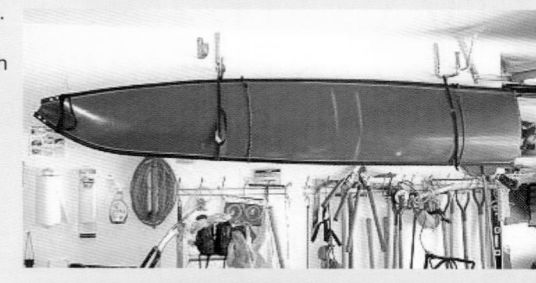

It's very easy to fold up, takes less than 5 minutes. The seats act as braces to hold the boat open, so when you take them out the boat folds up. The boat is made of Polypropylene and has a 10 year warranty. I have the 8 foot model (smallest), which I got for $900 years ago but now goes for $1,250.

-- Bart Snyder

Best kit for building a Coho kayak

Pygmy Coho Kayaks

$975 Pygmy Boats

Using the *Kayaks You Can Build* book, I built my first Coho, a stich-and-glue plywood sea kayak. Before deciding on the Pygmy kit,

I also considered ones offered by Mill Creek, Red Wing, Cheasapeake Light Craft, Dancing Waters, and One Ocean Design. In the end, I settled on Pygmy based on the feedback I got from other builders who touted just how very, very accurate the computer controlled router cut parts are. From the start, I realized I've seen a lot of Cohos out there over the years, which seemed to imply the design

would be pretty well nailed down and refined by now. I was right.

The eight panels in the hull of the Coho make it a multi-chine boat, sort of half way between a strip construction and a four-panel hull. The way the deck fits elegantly onto the hull was also a big factor in my decision. I really like the fact that it is such a simple, but effective attachment.

I was at Eagle Lake, CA and someone had a Pygmy Arctic Tern. The boat paddled like a dream — remind-

Some designs mandate you place screws or nails through the deck to the shear — to me that just seemed wrong. I also liked the more modern vertical stern, though the bow still very much keeps with a classic Greenland kayak shape. The hull is not too wide, but very stable and the deck's extra two panels create a shape that reduces the knocking of your knuckles when you're paddling. Also, the thinner panels of the hull really allow them to twist and create intriguing transitions that are simply not possible with a four-panel hull.

ed me of the first time I rode a high quality road racing bicycle. I was finally sold. Not long after, I bought my Coho kit from Pygmy.

I took a pretty leisurely approach and probably spent about 300 hours, until it was done. After that, there is always something to consider adding — a carrying cart, some kind of a sail rig, etc. So I guess it is never really all finished! There really are only two problems with the Coho: 1) though they are very durable, you have so much time in them, you still really want to take care of them, 2) just about every trip I go on I get about six people a day stopping and asking me questions. It can actually delay your leaving the beach!

-- Mark Forwalter

Inflatable heavy-duty kayak

Advanced Elements Inflatable Kayak

$576 Amazon

The Advanced Expedition inflatable kayak has allowed me to get out on the water more often than I ever would with one of its hardshell cousins.

Because the boat fits in the trunk of my car and can be carried solo in a duffle bag, I find myself using it when the hassle of loading a more traditional kayak onto a roof rack and muscling it around would dissuade me. Using a double action pump it can be set up and ready to go in under 10 minutes, and the break down is even faster. It just deflates and folds back into its bag.

While it doesn't track as well as a hard bottomed boat, it more than makes up for this with its incredible stability. Buoyed by two high-pressure inflatable tubes that form the 13.5 foot frame, the boat withstands moderate waves and can carry up to 400 pounds. Standard spray skirts fit and keep the inside snug and dry.

I have used it to surf waves, paddle with sea lions, and as a kayak escort for swim races. In all cases I have been able to keep up with fellow kayakers.

I highly recommend this for kayakers who want a full size boat but don't have a garage or the space to keep one!

-- Ben Hanna

For those looking to stay dry, the Advanced Element comes with a standard spray skirt.

Guide to constructing Coho boats

Kayaks You Can Build

$25 Ted Moores and Greg Rossel, 2004, 256 p.
$1,039+ Pygmy Coho Kits (17'+) Pygmy Boats

I have built several simple fiberglass canoes and repaired my sailboats, but using this book I was able to build my first "real," high-performance boat, a Pygmy Coho, a stitch and glue plywood construction sea kayak. I read a lot of books on kayak construction, stitch and glue type in particular. I also used the Coho building manual from Pygmy some. But I absolutely would not have been as successful with my boat had I not read this book before building and referenced it during building. The detail, sharing of practical experience, the tons of photos, clarity in explanation and the examples of the exact same boat — the Coho — made this the only choice. The book lays out everything in terms of what you can expect to accomplish on Day 1, Day 2 and so forth. Even if you don't follow it step by step, the book provides the fundamentals to make good alternative building decisions.

I was able to do all of the following alternatives: Rigged up my own plumbing for a built in bilge pump. Added 4-oz glass to the deck for strength. Added the bulkheads to also gain rear deck strength. Doubled the coaming lip for strength and aesthetics. Added in hardwood keys at the coaming spacer joints for strength. Fiberglassed the entire coaming (probably really not necessary). Made my own jigs with hot glue and pop sickle sticks as prealignment tools for bulkheads, seat braces, deck joint, etc.

Above all else, the book explains how to build a very flat, level, elevated worktable with internal/external stations to hold the boat in position. That aspect alone is reason enough to go with this book. I am currently building a skin-on-frame, Greenland style kayak for my wife, but I would re-read this book before building any other stitch and glue boat. I also recommend the Greenland kayak website, Qajaq USA and Guillemont Kayak's boat-building forum, where there is a wealth of information for the construction and use of stitch and glue, strip building and traditional skin-on-frame (SOF) kayaks.

-- Mark Fowalter

•
In order to achieve professional results, each stage of your work should be completed with the least number of steps as well as prepare you for the next stage. For example, if you apply the filler casually with a stick, before the next step can happen the excess will have to be sanded off. Professionals eliminate the cleanup step by placing just enough filler in

the right place to do the job. When the masking tape is peeled off, the step is complete and ready for the next one. Keeping the filler under control saves time and minimizes exposure to the bad stuff. That's a pretty fair payoff, but there's also a bonus that comes with thinking lazy. That bonus is professional results. You cannot build a professional-quality boat when you are doing damage control between each step… We are all good at something; by combining an understanding of what needs to be done with what is already familiar, we find that practical solutions present themselves.

•
The less epoxy you put on, the less you have to sand off. If the epoxy is kept under control when wet, expect about one day of sanding, preferably outside. Tidy glue application brings the additional benefits of less unhealthy dust produced and more efficient — and less costly — use of the epoxy.

5-84
5-85
5-86

How to Begin

So, how to begin? One option, of course, is the free-form approach, in which the kayak is built right on the floor or, as one manufacturer suggests, on something flat like three cardboard boxes. Although this lets you get right to work, there are a number of drawbacks. One is the possibility of introduction funky eccentricities and variables to a process that requires precise control. The other is the questionable practicality of spending hours bent over, toiling on the floor. This is a pretty good sized "some assembly required" project, and at some point in the process either your knees or your back will start protesting.

Another way to go is to build a worktable that will raise your assembly surface to a more civilized altitude. With some forethought the worktable also becomes a modification of the traditional boatbuilder's strongback. A big advantage to the worktable is that you are, in effect, working from the same baseline that the designer used to draw the boat. With the addition of a centerline and station liners, the table becomes an accurate reference and a jig for many of the building steps… Being able to reach in and clamp along the edge of the worktable is convenient, and a step towards making tidy joints that require very little cleanup. This not only saves time but also reduces your exposure to the epoxy.

Building the box beam and fitting and leveling the top of the worktable took the best part of one day and consumed two sheets of plywood. If building this beam sounds like too much work, there are other possibilities for getting a stable base under the top. Consider a straight ladder set up on a sawhorses, laminated floor joints or anything else that will support the length of the table to accommodate your height and the kayak you are building.

Making the long straight cuts necessary for building a straight table could be a challenge for the casual builder. The easiest solution, and one that also simplifies transportation, is to have the plywood sheet ripped into desired widths when you purchase the board. Some big-box home improvement stores offer this service at little or no extra cost, using extremely accurate dedicated panel saws. If you decide to do it yourself and are using a table saw, keep in mind that the panel must be supported at both the in-feed and out-feed ends for safety reasons and to ensure that the cuts are straight. If you are using a portable circular saw, consider clamping a straightedge to the board to guide the saw.

The simple-to-build box beam consists of two 8-foot open-ended boxes held together with a 4-foot section that fits in the open ends of the boxes to tie them together. The important point to keep in mind is that once joined, the top side of the box must be straight.

Cradle forms are the secret to controlling the shape of a plywood kayak. They can make the difference between a twisted hull with a hogged bottom and

the beautiful kayak in your mind. Besides, now that you have a worktable, you might as well add several cradle forms and enjoy the peaceful rhythm of building when the pieces fall into place and stay where you put them. With cradles attached to the predictable base formed by the worktable, the hull will come together at a controlled distance above the baseline and will be centered over the table centerline (3-6 [image]); our horizontal reference will be the level, anytime we need it. As flimsy plank is added to the flimsy plank, the crade forms will hold all the pieces where they should be. The pieces will come together without being stressed or having to be bullied into position.

Cover the path of the cut with masking tape to provide something to mark on and to protect the desk and the edge of the cut. Drill a hole inside the line big enough for the jigsaw blade (5-84). Take your time making the cut. Trust the line and follow it; it is easier to make the first cut to the line than to try to clean it up later. As the cut progresses, bridge the joint with tape to keep the cutout from falling into the hull (5-85). Peel off the tape when you have finished making the cut and clean up the shape with a rasp or a hard sanding block if needed. This opening will be the pattern for trimming the parts to come, so getting a smooth shape now will save correcting the same problem on the spacer and rim later.

Paddling

Ultimate lightweight paddles
Epic Kayak Paddles
$449 Epic Kayaks

"Amazing!" That's the first word my friends say when I hand them my carbon fiber kayak paddle made by Epic Paddles, a company founded by Olympic gold medalist Greg Barton. (Of course, I first make my friends hold a progression of older paddles starting with a wooden one, then moving to a standard aluminum and plastic rental type, then a nice fiberglass one by Werner, and finally to the carbon fiber by Epic Paddles so they really appreciate the dramatic reduction in weight.)

I am only a recreational paddler myself, but even I can appreciate the vast difference between the kind of standard paddle you'll usually get when you rent a kayak, and the carbon fiber paddle I've grown to love. Besides being laughably light weight, the blade itself has a lot of flotation so it pops out of the water by itself. With a feature called length-lock, you can dial your feathering angle (for example, 45 or 60 degrees) and adjust overall paddle length to your liking. A kayak instructor I know calls this the "magic wand" of paddling. I'm such a fan that I insist on taking my paddles with me when I travel to the Caribbean (in a Harmony double paddle travel bag). I'll rent kayaks, but can't downgrade to rental paddles. Like a tennis racket or golf clubs, you want your own good equipment once you get used to it.

Epic has a lot of options for paddle construction. The one I have owned for three years is the Signature Series Full Carbon and I just ordered this same construction but in a wing shape–the Mid Wing. The Full Carbon is about $100 more expensive than the hybrid but gives you the full benefit of carbon fiber technology and the best blade design. The hybrid is a compromise for a lower price. The reinforced version adds some material to the end to protect the blade from damage if you're going to be hitting rocks with it. The ultra apparently is an even more refined full carbon, probably for the competitive racer.

Bottom line: Go for Signature Series Full Carbon and you'll be a very happy paddler!

-- Steve Leveen

Longboard water cruising
Paddleboards
$1,380 12' Surftech Bark Board
The Frog House

Paddleboarding is a great way to stay in shape for surfing, to explore the coast, to watch birds, and to cruise around in almost any body of water. Paddleboards, like surfboards, snowboards, skateboards and other devices used for moving through space, have evolved greatly in recent years. For years, Eaton paddleboards were the primary manufacturers of quality racing boards. Lately, Joe Bark has been turning out beautiful stock and custom boards. This summer I bought a slightly used Joe Bark 12' "Surftek" paddleboard in L.A. for $1,000 ("Surftek" is the nickname for lightweight surfboards/paddleboards built with Styrofoam and epoxy resin, rather than the more standard polyurethane foam and polyester resin). The board is feather light (22 lbs.) and lets me skim through the water like a water skeeter. Boards run from 12-19' or so. The 12-footers are the most popular partly because they are the easiest to transport and store. The longer boards are slightly faster in races (there are over 70 races a year in Southern California), but more cumbersome to deal with on land.

NOTE: There is also stand up paddleboarding (SUP), where you use a physical paddle to propel and steer your way through surf and to catch waves. Giant, heavy surfboards, those have a completely different design. The ones I review above are lie-down (or kneeling) boards, which you *cannot* stand on and are not intended for wave riding (though you can catch small waves).

A full range of boards, including standup* boards, available from http://www.joebarkpaddleboards.com/.

This is the board I'd get if I were to buy a new one:

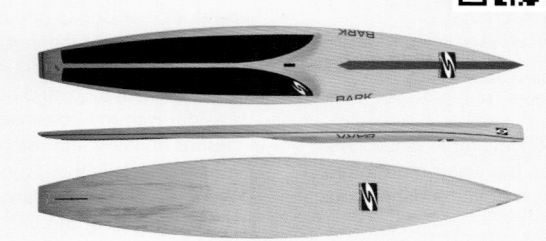

$2,359 Stand Up Dominator Model Joe Bark Paddleboards

-- Lloyd Kahn

Surfing in whitewater
Squirt Boating and Beyond
$20 James E. Snyder, 2001, 235 p.

Think skateboarding on white water. A squirt is a very small kayak, almost a hollowed out surfboard, that skips, spins, jumps, and yes, squirts out of rivers. It is dangerous fun, with a similar underground culture as other x-treme board sports. The funky illustrations tell all.

-- KK

"Attaining" is the term I coined in the late 1970s for paddling upstream. This is quite a fine form of fun. There are even attaining races, which are great entertainment. If you want to perfect your attaining skills, for whatever reason, remember a few basic tips. Timing and accuracy are much more important here than in downstream negotiations: plan your lines well in advance and let the river dictate the timing; and pace your energy expenditure so you will have the fierce energy necessary for the tough attainments. Learn to feel the force around you, and you will be able to attain up paper-thin eddies that are hundreds of feet long.

Guide to oar-making
Canoe Paddles
$17 Graham Warren and David Gidmark, 2001, 144 p.

After a week plying a rented aluminum and plastic paddle on a scouting canoe trip, I wondered just how difficult it would be to make my own out of wood. The answer: not too difficult. As this book explains, making a canoe paddle is part woodworking, part sculpture, part whittling and well within the grasp of anyone willing to work patiently. It requires a minimal number of basic tools (consider that Native Americans used very primitive tools to make theirs). Naturally, power tools will speed things up a bit but they aren't required. Ten or fifteen hours of pleasant work will yield a paddle every bit as good as one you can buy.

Canoe Paddles guides the reader through selecting the right material, laying out the pattern and shaping the complex profile of a paddle step by step. Gidmark and Warren explain and illustrate each operation clearly and offer options for using power or hand tools. They include a thorough treatment of the history and function of this deceptively-simple ancient tool to convey to the reader the huge importance of proper paddle geometry. The book also includes twenty pages of patterns and specifications along with advice on selecting the right paddle for different types of paddling.

I bought this book right after using that rented paddle and returned for our annual canoe trip the next year with my own homemade paddle, which is now a veteran of four or five trips. I couldn't be happier with the way it performs. The paddle is a glue-up of ash, cherry and mahogany, but as the book shows, paddles can be made from commonly-available woods found just about anywhere in the world.

-- Clarke Greene

• Choice of grip is subjective. To be comfortable, it must conform to the shape of your hand; if you paddle both sides, you should verify that it is comfortable in both hands. If it is too thick or too thin, you will probably have to grip it too tightly, which will result in premature muscle fatigue. It should be significantly scooped away at the sides to relieve pressure on the inside of the thumb, which is the classic site of blisters.

• Woods that aren't recommended are oaks, because they are hard to carve; elm and beech, because they warp severely; hemlock and tamarack, because they are knotty and splinter easily; balsam, because it breaks; and walnut and mahogany, because they are not necessary — they are for show-offs.

If people never did silly things, nothing intelligent would ever get done. - Ludwig Wittgenstein

Ebike clearinghouse
ElectricBike
electricbike.com

One of the least-noticed but fastest-moving sectors of technology is electric bikes. Every week a new innovation is released, altering the field, making it difficult to keep up. By far the keenest intelligence on new ebike stuff is Eric Hicks. Eric attends the bike shows, visits the workshops of the leading inventors, and most impressively, he personally rides and reviews in great depth just about every ebike made. He publishes his very fair and impartial findings and reviews on his blog, ElectricBike.com. He really knows his stuff and is eager to help others decide which ebikes to get. ElectricBike is where I go to find out what's worth considering at the moment. His archive covers just about any electric bicycle built, including a lot of small-time builders and prototypes.

I used Erick's suggestions in finding a touring electric bike that would take me 50 miles a day. (I got a Gruber pedal assist, which was perfect for what I wanted.) A year later even better choices were available.

As of 2013, ebikes are huge in China, big in Europe but still only the bleeding edge in the US. An electric bicycle is a great choice for urban commuters, and okay for fanatic mountain trail riders, but not quite prime time for long road touring. What's the difference between an ebike and an electric motorcycle? Good question. ElectricBIke is the place to drill down into this emerging world of cheap electric powered transportation.

-- KK

• The Stromer ST1 is one of the most exciting electric bikes to be released and one of the best production ebikes I have gotten to test so far.

I am not sure if the Stromer Platinum can fairly be considered a 30-MPH bike. I am not even sure if the Platinum would be deemed *illegal* if put to a speed test. It is serious work to get this bike up to 30-MPH, and without pedaling… *forget about it*. The federal law says theres a 20-MPH limit *without pedaling*. It feels like the Stromer Platinum would just barely break 20-MPH without any pedaling.

On the other hand, the Stromer ST1 Elite hits its claimed 20-MPH top speed with little pedaling effort. These two bikes are a lot closer together

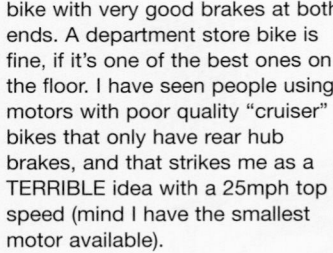
ElectricBike.com

performance wise than you would assume from reading claimed speed numbers. My guess is that under "real world" conditions, the Elite is a 25-MPH bike, and the Platinum a 28-MPH bike. Where as Stromer calls the Elite a 20-MPH bike (low balling estimate) and the Platinum a 30-MPH bike (high balling estimate).

• The Stealth Bomber comes from the factory with a jumper-wire on the controller that limits it's top-speed to 20-MPH. Remove that jumper, and it puts you in "off road mode" and transforms your bomber into a 50-MPH 5,000-watt beast.

Few electric bike manufacturers have decided to ignore the federal definition of E-bike and make a bike that is fast. The Stealth Bomber is a 50-MPH 120-pound monster capable of going up to 40 miles on single charge (flat ground and moderate riding). It has ample acceleration and performance for most users…meaning this bike will scare the hell out of you. The Stealth Bomber and Fighter are at the forefront of electric bike technology, building a bike that is well respected in the e-bike community for quality construction and great performance. They are top of our list of purpose built e-bikes, meaning they are rare examples of bikes built from the ground up to be an electric bike. If you want a reliable and super fast electric bike, turn key and ready to ride and you have the dough to spend, the Stealth Bomber is among your best options.

Electric scooter
eGO Cycle
$1550+ Varsity Cycle

For the last year, I've loved commuting to work on this electric scooter because it's powerful enough to ride in traffic, but doesn't feel like a motorcycle. Before settling on the eGO Cycle 2 SE, I test drove a bigger bike and smaller one from a different manufacturer, but I liked the eGO best, which has turn signals in front and back, a headlight, and a horn. There are two settings: "Go Far" and "Go Fast." I find I can get up to 23 mph or so with Go Fast, though I usually use Go Far, which has a max speed of about 18 mph. The guy who sold it to us said it has a range of about 20 miles and takes about an hour to recharge. I keep it plugged in regularly and have not let it run down much since I got it. I am fortunate to have locked, indoor parking with an outlet at my work, so this is easy. My commute to work is 1.6 miles, but I have ridden the bike up to 10 miles with plenty of charge left. In Oregon, this qualifies as a bike, even though it's motorized, so it does not require a motorcycle license.

-- Mary Gear

250 mpg bicycle assist motor
Golden Eagle Bike Engine
$659 Golden Eagle Bike Engine

I live in Phoenix, Arizona which has a vast network of grossly under-utilized bicycle trails and paths. My daily work commute is 50 miles, which, by car, is environmentally obscene (and not at all uncommon) and further costs about $7/day just in fuel alone.

I tried bicycling the old fashioned way for a couple weeks, but 25 miles urban each way in a Phoenix summer is suicide no matter how good your physical condition. I began looking for an assist-motor for my bike. Most "whizzer" type bicycle engines are a hassle. Electrics don't have the range for a 50 mile daily commute. Two-stroke motors are a pain and become expensive due to the necessity of pre-mixing oil and fuel. Friction-drive bicycle motors wear out tires rapidly and behave badly on rough surfaces & water.

I eventually found a 4-stroke motor and belt drive kit from Golden Eagle Bike Engines that weighs very little, operates quietly, and gets me to work and back for about 45 cents a day in fuel. It took me just under 1/2 hour to install on my $200 department store mountain bike.

This 35cc Honda requires me to pedal a little when accelerating from a stop or climbing steep hills. Doing this is very natural and it feels just like riding a bike the old fashioned way. Top speed with 26×1.95 dirt

tires is about 25mph on flat pavement, or 23mph on flat dirt. Wind, inclines, sand, and other factors significantly impact the top speed, but it will even typically maintain 18mph under most typical adverse conditions. I know from prior experience with the same bicycle that I can sprint it up to 24mph without the engine, so having the engine on is equivalent to being able to sprint all the time. Up very steep inclines I pedal with the engine at partial throttle and maintain 12mph where previously I would go 3 or 4mph without the engine. I have ridden in moderate rain with no ill effect other than getting myself very wet. The drive is unaffected.

Getting to work across Phoenix now takes me about 10 minutes longer than it typically took me by car (yes, traffic is THAT bad) but the ride is far less frustrating or stressful because I'm not stuck behind someone, I'm hauling ass. There are some fun shortcuts and interesting parts of the city to see, as well. One tank of ordinary pump gas gets me 22 to 25 miles, urban riding. The tank on this model is just about 11 ounces, so that equates to somewhere approaching 250 miles per gallon!

I highly recommend a good quality

bike with very good brakes at both ends. A department store bike is fine, if it's one of the best ones on the floor. I have seen people using motors with poor quality "cruiser" bikes that only have rear hub brakes, and that strikes me as a TERRIBLE idea with a 25mph top speed (mind I have the smallest motor available).

Finally, $659 is a steep price, but the ease of filling up your tank for $0.25 cents on regular pump gas and not having to mix expensive smelly 2-stroke oil, and the quiet and easy ride make it worthwhile. If my daily commute were less than 10 miles each direction I would not even consider owning this and would just pedal the old fashioned way. Since I have to go more than double that, it becomes practical due to increased fuel saving and the increased difficulty in riding that distance routinely. For me, it pays for itself financially in 84 trips to work and back.

-- Apanthropy

Cheapest electric bike
Currie Ezip Trailz Electric Bike
$480 currietech.com

This is the electric bike I recommend for anyone on a *tight budget*. The Ezip Trailz is a bargain in terms of how much it can effect your life on little dollars. It is by far the best selling electric bike in the United States, for good reason: For less than $500 it is a decent electric bike with reasonable performance. It uses a sealed-lead-acid battery (SLA), which is heavy and has a short life expectancy, but… is extremely *inexpensive* compared to lithium (and more fire safe). The Trailz weighs in at a hefty 72 pounds because of this SLA battery. It comes with step-through model, which I favor because it is much easier to get on and off the bike, which is a big factor on a 70-pound bike. The Trailz is perfect for anyone who either wants, or needs, a way to get to work without a car or public transport, or for anyone who can't drive

a car for some reason (for instance it makes great transportation for anyone who has lost their license due to a DUI or traffic tickets). At this price point if you just ride the bike regularly it will pay for itself quickly. The Currie Trailz is a simple electric bike that rarely fails and is easy to work on. Any bicycle shop should be able to fix 80% of the problems you will encounter. Probably the biggest electrical issue you will ever face is the battery gradually dying if you don't care for it properly. However its easy enough to buy a new battery from Currie and switch it out -- or better yet upgrade to the Currie lithium battery. The lithium battery will offer slightly more range than the lead acid version, it will be better for climbing hills, and it will lower the weight of the bike by nearly 20 pounds. The lithium battery is pricey, in fact it's as almost as much as the price of this bike ($359 shipped). It is possible to install 2 of these batteries on the rear rack if you want to double your range.

The Currie Trailz is not the fastest, lightest, or sexiest electric bike on the market, but it is the cheapest, and is therefore a great entry electric bike for those who need a little electrical push to get back on the saddle and out riding.

-- Eric Hicks

Folding Bikes

Quick folding bike
Brompton
$1,540 (M6R-NYC model) Nyce Wheels

My new best friend is the Brompton T6, a foldable 6-speed bicycle made by the Brompton company in England. Living in an urban area and having a bike that folds is basically like having wheels for feet; and in the world of folding bikes, Bromptons simply cannot be matched in their compactness and riding quality. They ride beautifully and smoothly thanks to a conical rear shock absorbing block. They take about 10 seconds to go from fully unfolded to fully folded and are compact enough to take inside anywhere — metro, hotels, restaurants. I, at least, have never had a problem storing it. There are other makes of folding bikes (like Dahon) but time and time again I see people that own Dahons who simply won't bother folding them and chain them up outside because they're so cumbersome. What's the point of owning a folding one? Brompton spare parts are amazingly easy to install yourself (the manual is very comprehensive and detailed in how to upkeep the bike). I bought mine six months ago and it has completely trans-formed my day to day existence. It's a true lifestyle changer. Check out the front car-rier accessories too. Fill that with other cool tools and that's basi-cally all you need.

[*Today, the clos-est available model to the T6 is the M6R.]

-- John Root

Premium folding, touring bicycles
Bike Friday
$1,198 Bike Friday

A folding bike is a compromise between ride quality and foldabil-ity. Moulton makes great artisan folding bikes with very unique design. Brompton also makes lovely folding bikes (previously-reviewed), but kind of artisan and pricey. I like the previously-reviewed Strida if all you have to do is ride 1-2 miles to the transit station. It's not much good if you have to ride for more than 15 min-utes. Citizen Bikes are awful, but some people who have never rid-den a nice bike seem to be able to tolerate it. Dahon is starting to make some pretty damn good folding bikes at reasonable prices.

But my favorite is Bike Friday. It can fold into a suitcase that won't incur over-charges on airplanes. Super light. Rides like a real bike, in some ways better. They have a few different models (even tan-dems!); I've ridden most of them — they are all good. I optimized my choice for quality of ride, but you can build them with ease of folding in mind by specifying what you want in terms of tools/no tools. For instance, some models require tools to fold for airline travel, but not for folding to stash on cars/buses. The Tikit models, on the other hand, explic-itly requires no tools for folding at all.

These bikes are not cheap. I am a self-admitting bike snob. I value ride quality. Most low-cost folding bikes just feel cheap. The difference is in the custom-fitted frame, and better design details, higher-quality components and etc. (Bike Friday has been doing it for years). But you can get on a good Bike Friday for $1200. If you want, you can spend up to $3000 or even more for extras, but the frame is the same. These guys have great customer service, too.

I love mine. When it was recently stolen, I was heartbroken. Bike theft is like pet death. If you see my yellow Bike Friday (it has my wife's name "Arwen Griffith" on the top tube), throw rotten fruit and stones at the asshole who stole it.

-- Saul Griffith

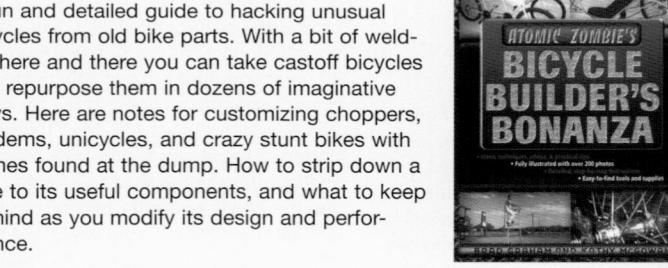

Portable transit for urbanites
Strida Folding Bike
$650 Amazon

This folding bike has won both design and race awards. I've used it for seven years to traverse New York City, com-muting two miles one way: in and out of Grand Central, the subways, buses, etc. A lot of folding bikes break down so that they're bulky and awkward. The Strida is long and narrow, and carries like a photographer's tripod — I can fold it while running down the platform at Grand Central. An easy way to visualize it is to picture three tubes in a triangle. Two points are hinged, and the third is a latch. When unlatched, the tubes fall together to look like a group of parallel tubes with a seat and wheels. Assembly is just forming the triangle, then click and go. This design is very clever, yet simple and robust.

The bike is unusual because there isn't much maintenance (tire pressure and brake adjustments only). Unlike the Brompton, the Strida is a single gear with (dry) belt drive, which means no shifter or greasy chain, no tension adjustments and no caught pant legs. Even though there is only one speed, I can still climb reason-able hills. The tires are mini fat tubes, so you can jump curbs and hit potholes without any problems. The bike has a very, very tight turning radius, and while riding, your posture is quite upright – like a boulevard bike, not humped over like a road bike – so you can see traffic while riding in a suit and tie. The construction is solid, not flimsy in the least. I stripped mine down for size: removing the luggage rack and fenders so that it would easily fit in the overhead rack on the train. No one has ever bothered me for a bike pass on the trains or buses. If you buy one, be prepared: people will stop you often to ask what it is. I once had two teenage girls run out of a restaurant (and hang up their cell phones) to stop me and ask what it is. For a brief moment, I actually felt trendy!

-- Bruce Hartleben

Bike hacking
Atomic Zombie's Bicycle Builder's Bonanza
$17 Brad Graham, Kathy McGowan, 2004, 388 p.

A fun and detailed guide to hacking unusual bicycles from old bike parts. With a bit of weld-ing here and there you can take castoff bicycles and repurpose them in dozens of imaginative ways. Here are notes for customizing choppers, tandems, unicycles, and crazy stunt bikes with frames found at the dump. How to strip down a bike to its useful components, and what to keep in mind as you modify its design and perfor-mance.

-- KK

All parts of a frame after cutting

Make final adjustments before priming and painting.

The completed Skycycle is an awe-some sight. Are you bold enough to ride it?

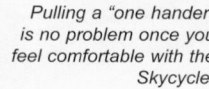

Pulling a "one hander" is no problem once you feel comfortable with the Skycycle.

An ounce of action is worth a ton of theory. - Friedrich Engels

Bicycling sanity
Just Ride
$12 Grant Petersen, 2012, 256 p.

This book returns the fun to recreational bicycling. Biking has been taken over by racing style; weekend riders and bike commuters imitate racers in their gear and approach. The author is a long-time bicycle maker, racer, and advocate, and in this manifesto he deflates common bicycling myths one by one. He argues you can wear ordinary street clothes, and that you will be less tired if you don't use clip in cleats on your pedals, that the weight of the bike does not really matter, baskets are cool to have, plastic saddles are good enough, and so on. I've ridden bikes for 40 years, including long-distance touring and everyday commuting, and the common sense Grant Peterson preaches here is both absolutely true and refreshing. If biking seems less fun than it once did, read this. You'll save a lot of money, and will enjoy riding more.

-- KK

I say, wear underwear–even if it's cotton. That goes against a powerful rumor mill that considers cotton underwear a no-no for any kind of ride beyond a ten-minute commute. The naysayers say it gets wet with sweat; the sweat makes your skin more vulnerable to chafing; the seams are uncomfortable at best and will cause saddle sores at worst.

The only riders who benefit from clipless pedals are racers, and only because their pedals are so small and slippery. If you don't ride tiny, slippery pedals, you don't need stiff, cleated shoes.

The benefits of pedaling free far outweigh any real or imagined benefits of being locked in. They are as follows:

Your muscles last longer. Moving your foot about the pedal shifts the load, even if slightly, to different muscles, and spreads the load around. Sprint up the hills on the balls of your feet and, on long-seated climbs, push with the pedal centered almost under your arch. It's not a turbocharged, magic sweet spot, but it feels better and more natural, and you can't do it if you're locked in.

You reduce the chance of a repetitive stress injury, because your feet naturally move around more, changing your biomechanics.

You get off and on easier at stoplights; there's no twisting to get out of your pedals, no fussing to get back in.

You can walk in stores without walking on your heels. You can run! You aren't handicapped by expensive and weird-looking shoes.

Whenever a rider gets hit and is being loaded, unconscious, into the ambulance, the driver who hit him will testify to the cops, "I swear, I didn't see the dude." If you're looking brilliant and geeky, you're more likely to be seen and less likely to get hit, and he won't have that excuse.

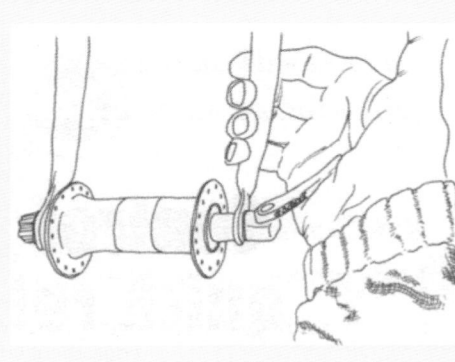

Grab the fork with your fingers, and use the heel of your hand to close the quick release. The convex side of the lever is labeled CLOSE, and should face outward when you're finished.

Closing the lever properly requires enough force to leave an impression on your hand.

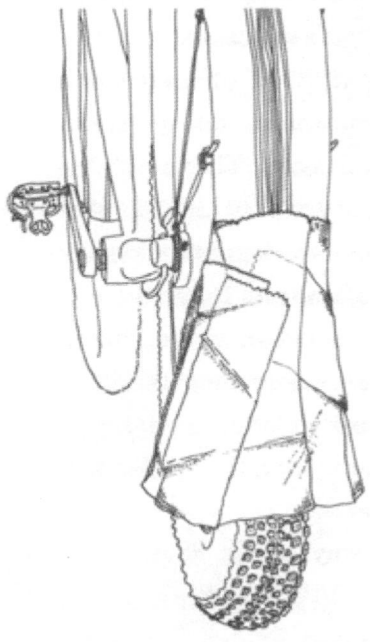

Shock your friends by putting an ugly duct tape mudflap on a nice bike.

On a stop-and-go commute, a red light at the wrong time instantly wipes out even a hundred-pound weight difference.

On a descent, the heavier bike rider is faster.

Light wheels accelerate faster than heavy ones, which helps when you're taking off from a stop, but heavy wheels maintain more of their momentum than light wheels, which helps you keep your speed on rolling roads and trails.

On twenty-five-mile club rides, when you and your club mates are close to the same fitness level, the pack sets the pace, and since you're riding in a partial vacuum (not fighting the wind), it's easy to keep up, even with heavier bike and body.

It's easy to buy tires with an extra layer of rubber, nylon, kevlar, or something else between the casing and tread to stop thorns. Every extra bit of protection adds weight that will always scare off racers and others under the spell, but for all-purpose Unracing rides, I like extra flat protection. Why not? I've fixed at least five hundred flats in my life, I'm really good at it, and I still hate it. Beef up my tires, thank you.

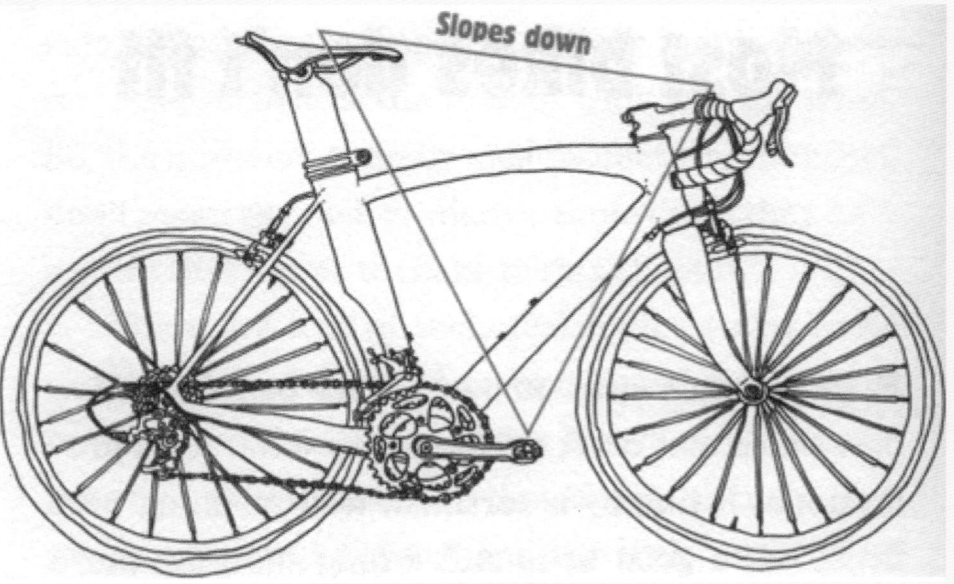

A typical racy road bike gives you a CPT like this:

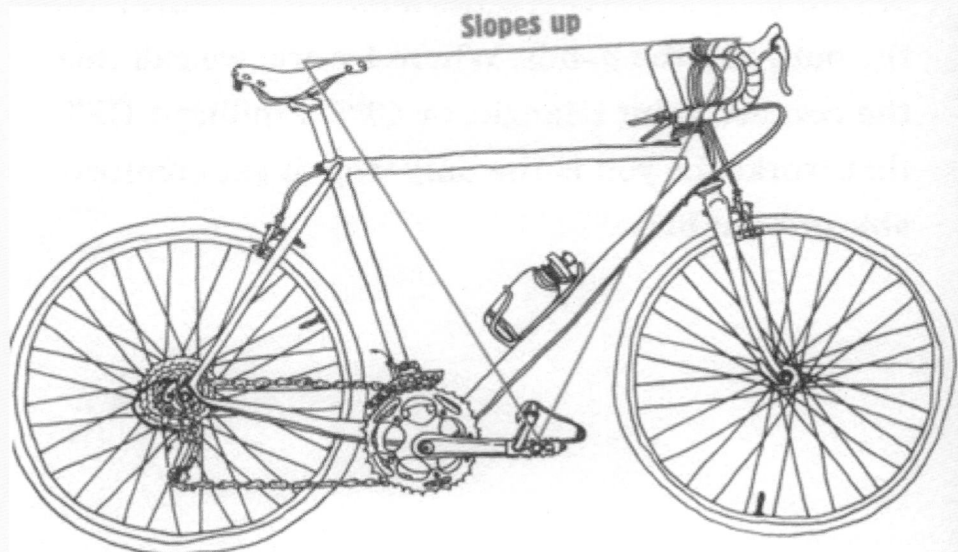

A more comfortable, better all-aournd Unracer's CPT looks like this:

DIY guide to bikes & biking
Sheldon Brown's Online Cycling Encyclopedia
Free Sheldon Brown

Whether you're looking to convert your road bike into a fixed gear or want to learn how a derailer functions, this site has all the info you could ever want — a giant glossary, bits of cycling history and plenty of specific instructions and photos.

His site has helped me purchase, repair and build two road bikes (my Gios Torino and a Tom Ritchey built Palo Alto).

I've seen, in the process, just how precise Sheldon's attention to detail is. I had no idea that there was English and Italian threading. Sheldon has a chart that gives you the measurements for every BB out there, anything from French to Swiss. And I totally didn't listen to his tip on Italian threaded bottom brackets and paid the price.

Even if you have no interest in working on your bike or going deeper than the basics of maintenance, this site can really boost your understanding of how a bike works (it has in my case) and even how to ride. There are great tips for beginners, including articles like "Everything You Wanted To Know About Shifting Your Bicycle's Gears, But Were Afraid To Ask."

-- Benjamin Gaffney

The imagination of nature is far, far greater than the imagination of man. - Richard Feynman

Urban Biking

Bicycle survival skills
Urban Bikers' Tricks & Tips

$11 Dave Glowacz, 2010, 256 p.

I started riding a bike for the first time as an adult, at age 37. After an onslaught of expensive auto repairs and with the encouragement of my partner who is a bike commuter, I sold my automobile. Overnight, literally, I became a bike commuter. Living in San Francisco and facing a 16 mile daily commute to work was daunting, to say the least. *Urban Bikers'* has given me the know how and skills to get around the city and and out of town. This book covers everything – maintenance basics, avoiding theft, getting around in traffic, inclement weather – it's there. What's more, the illustrations make me laugh out loud. It is a savvy and wry vote of confidence for the urban cyclist – novice or otherwise.

-- Michele McGinnis

• Remember that on a street, you either share the lane (cars pass next to you) or take the lane (you ride in the middle, and cars stay behind you or pass in another lane).

• In the door zone (the 3 or 4 feet next to parked cars in which you could get hit by an opening door), keep track of what's behind you: If you have to swerve suddenly, you could get hit by traffic. Also, look for stretches where you can ride out of the door zone.

• Cross locking. When you cross lock your bike, you use two different lock systems at once – such as a U lock and a cable. Cross locking forces thieves to spend more time and use more than one kind of tool. If a thief sees that your bike is cross locked, he might move on to another bike that isn't.

Mounting a standard-frame bike in a skirt

1 Lay the bike on the ground.

2 Put one foot inside the middle of the frame.

3 Pull the bike up halfway.

4 Pull your foot out of the frame.

5 Stand the bike all the way up.

6 To get off the bike, reverse the steps.

What to look for

Square cut in the pavement

Round cut in the pavement

The detectors work by sensing the metal in your bike. If you stop over the symbol and it doesn't affect the traffic light, get off of your bike an lay it down on top of the symbol. This gives the detector more metal to detect.

Detachable cycling hitch for kids
Trail-Gator Bike Tow Bar

$84 **Amazon**

What sold me on the Trail-Gator was that I can attach my son's current bicycle to the back of my bike. We can ride together along the main roads; however, when we get to our destination, I can easily unhook his bicycle and let him ride around and have fun. The towbar tucks away nicely next to the rear wheel when not in use.

I've used conventional bike trailers before, and I can tell no difference in the ride. I had no trouble installing the kit, and it feels very stable when we ride together. My five-year-old son loves riding his bike, and now we can go exploring together. I also really like the fact I can use the Trail-Gator with multiple bikes. When my three-year-old daughter is ready for her first bike, we can easily move the receiver hitch over.

-- Jeff Curry

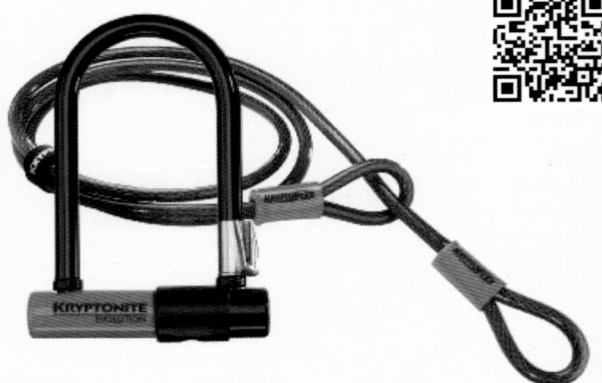

Best urban bike lock
Kryptonite Evolution U-Lock

$49 **Amazon**

I live in Baltimore, a city that still struggles with crime. As such, I take the security of my belongings seriously, and no place is this more evident than with the thing I most often leave in public: my bike.

In the past, and in safer cities, I have used steel cable locks without any problems. However, while locking my bike up around Baltimore I would frequently see the cut remains of thick steel cable locks. My dismay was reinforced when I saw a video of the time (mere seconds) it took to cut through even a thick steel cable lock with a pair of bolt cutters. Disconcerted, I asked my bike-savvy friends for a better solution. The universal answer was a Kryptonite U-lock cou-

pled with a steel cable used to lock both your front and rear wheel to the bike frame and an immovable object.

I have a mixed history with Kryptonite. Eight years ago I owned and used an early version of their U-lock. Its size, weight, and ungainliness left much to be desired. In addition the model I owned had an embarrassing reputation for being picked by nothing more than a simple Bic pen. So I was wary when everybody and anybody with any knowledge about urban bike riding told me to use a Kryptonite lock.

After a few months with the new U-lock it is clear that eight years of substantial design changes have made a difference. Not only have they fixed almost every issue I had with my old U-lock, but they have made it smaller, lighter, and more secure.

Favored by bike couriers, the U-Lock is designed to couple the front wheel to the frame of the bike while locking to an external post, stop sign, or other immovable object. What Kryptonite has done to make this more usable is by shrinking the width and length of the U-lock so that it fits snugly into most back pockets (while the shorter length means it doesn't fall out while riding). This subtle change makes it far easier to carry the lock thereby avoiding the need for a bag, or even for attaching it to the frame of the bike through a plastic connector (which are, at best, unreliable and prone to breaking).

In shrinking the lock for portability Kryptonite has also made it more difficult for bike thieves to steal the bike by preventing them from fitting a car jack between the lock and the steel bar (the main technique used to bust larger U-locks).

The one downside to Kryptonite's U-lock will always be its significant heft. The lock is predominantly made up of a solid chunk of hardened steel, and as such it weighs a considerable amount. But the knowledge that my bike is safer is much less of a burden than the few ounces of steel.

-- Oliver Hulland

Hanging bike storage
Dero Track Rack

$259+ **Dero**

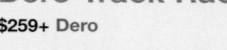

I bought this hanging bike storage system on a recommendation from a bike junkie friend who owned 8 or more bicycles. Tandems, single speed, mountain bikes, road bikes: you name it, he had one, and he stored it on his track rack.

My friend did the heavy work with the research and ultimately recommended the Dero Track Rack when I asked him how to solve my bicycle storage problem. The track went into the basement ceiling with no problem at all: lag bolts into the overhead joists. The track is super strong. The rollers that install in the track look like they are machined to aircraft standards. In short the whole getup is first rate.

The track has rollers that glide along the track and suspended beneath are a number of

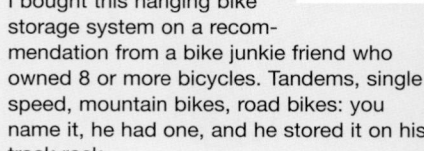

Hooks slide along track for easy access to bikes while providing maximum space efficiency

"S-hooks" from which you hang the wheel of a bike. What is amazing is how you can move the bikes along the track much the same way you slide shirts in your closet…only easier. The Track Rack has been a lifesaver for me, and now all my bikes are neatly organized and hang from the ceiling.

They are secured so there is absolutely no chance they will be knocked over by anybody. The Track Rack has moved from the basement to the garage, and when I sold the house I made sure to take the Dero Track Rack with me. I can't see ever parting ways with my Dero Track Rack. It is THAT cool.

-- Bruce Tunno

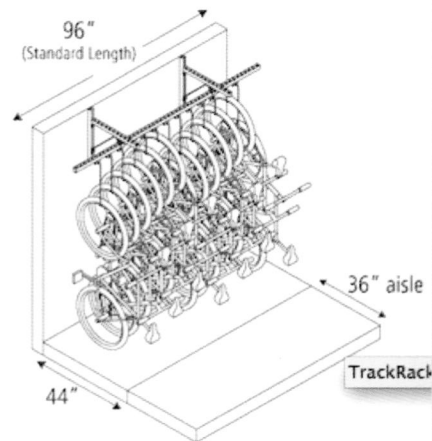

Wisdom begins in wonder. - Socrates

Hybrid handlebar and basket
Origin8 CargoUnit
$106 Amazon

The Origin8 CargoUnit is a great piece of "why did this take so long" common sense technology. These are handle bars that have an integrated basket which is large enough to hold a bike lock, a grocery bag, and anything else that will fit. The construction is rugged, true to Origin8's line of strong/light components.

These are superior to any number of bolt-on accessories because the basket is part of the handlebars. Aftermarket baskets bounce, come loose, and scratch up the finish of whatever they're attached to. Because the basket is one with the handlebars, there is none of that. Plus, there's no way to steal the basket as they are welded together.

Speaking of the weld, these are not toys. The gauge of the tubing and the strength of the joints are on par with pro equipment. This product is serious, and comes at a rise & width to replace bars on fixies, hybrids, or even BMX geometries.

--James Roche

Durable frontside bike cargo platform
CETMAracks
$120 (5-rail, uncoated) CETMA Cargo

I don't own a car, so when I go to the store for large quantities of beer or buckets of cat litter I use the CETMA, a lightweight steel rack that's tough as nails. I know a couple messengers that have crashed and the rack took the brunt of the force dishing it out to car doors or whatever obstacle happened to be there, and the rack only absorbed a slight crinkle or bend without compromising anything at all in it's performance. I've been using a CETMArack for a couple years and currently have a 5-rail on my '81 single speed, all-weather

utility grocery coffee shop beer bike (a 3-rail is plenty big enough if you only plan an occasional twelve pack or a couple library books; they also offer a 7-rail version!). Keeping the load up front over the front wheel lets you control the weight a bit more and doesn't bog down like a rear rack. You cannot ride like you normally would, hopping curbs or diving into corners when you have 27 pounds of cat litter on the front. But it's good to get a change of pace once in a while; a gravity reminder keeps you humble. I also like CETMAracks because of the guy who makes them. Made by hand in Eugene, OR. No outsourcing. No overseas production. And now they even include home-baked cookies with your order.

-- Mark Pilder

Urban bike hauling
Grocery Bag Panniers
$59 Jandd Grocery Bag Panniers Jandd
$45 Novara 'Round Town Panniers REI
$25 Nashbar Townie Basket Nashbar

Most bicycle panniers work well for touring, but don't meet the needs of people who use their bikes for commuting or shopping everyday. The typical pannier has a main compartment sealed with a zipper or flap, plus a few smaller pockets. The tourist packs it like a hiker would pack a backpack. However, these bags don't easily hold the urban cyclists' cargo of shopping bags, daypacks, and laptop computers. An open-topped pannier that works more like a basket than a

backpack provides a better way of carrying this kind of gear. These large bags, usually called grocery bag panniers, or shopping panniers, allow you to carry all kinds of oddly-shaped loads and fold flat when not in use. The key to using shopping bag panniers is to keep your gear in a separate bag that you can drop into the pannier. Day packs or book bags work well. I've used dry bags when it rains, but have found that plastic garbage bags are easier and cheaper. Having an open-topped bag also gives you a quick place to toss your bike lock, and the convenient access makes it easier to shed clothing layers as you warm up.

Several companies make them. The Jandd grocery bag pannier seems to be the sturdiest, but is also the most expensive, at around US$45 for a single pannier. REI sells a similar, but less refined, bag for US$80 per pair. My favorites, which I use everyday, are the Nashbar Townie baskets, which cost US$17 each. Unlike the other grocery bag panniers, they don't use a rectangular metal frame to reinforce the top of the bag. This means that they don't hold their shape quite as well as the others, but it lets the opening at the top adjust to different shaped cargo, like a bulky laptop bag. They're cheap enough that I leave them on the bike all the time, but they remove quickly enough that I can conveniently take one with me to carry stuff while the bike is parked.

-- Tom Sackett

Bicycle truck
Xtracycle
$190+ Xtracycle

This kit transforms a regular bike into an SUB (sports utility bike) by extending back the rear wheel and adding a seat and baggage platform. I've

had my SUB for two years now. I find it makes owning a car completely unnecessary! I've transported my folding kayak on it. I've taken my girlfriend and her Australian Blue Heeler on it. I've moved furniture. It's crazy how stable it is. In many ways I prefer how it handles to my regular

bike! And for giving people tours around NYC people just LOVE it.

You can modify your bike yourself, but I ended up taking it to a bike shop to have it installed.

-- Jens Rasmussen

Front child bike seat
WeeRide Kangaroo Carrier
$60 Amazon

Traveling through other countries, we've often noticed child cycling carriers where the child sits forward of the rider — this allows them better visibility and puts them in reach/view of the rider, unlike seats that mount to a rear rack. My sister even went as far as to bring one back from the UK to use with her kids. We hunted, but couldn't find the same thing in the US until two years ago. Now we use it once or twice a week when weather permits. Aside from being a much safer and secure version of the one my sister has, the WeeRide Kangaroo has some other very clear advantages.

The injection-molded seat mounts to an extremely sturdy bar that clamps to the seat post and steerer tube. This allows the seat to be removed quickly and easily when not in use. This is done by unscrewing a single large bolt. Also, the carrier features a padded "face pad" which 1) keeps your passenger from messing with your handlebars and controls; 2) protects your passenger from smacking his/her face on the handlebars (assuming you left the four-point harness too loose); and 3) gives your passenger a natural place to rest his/her head when sleeping. In addition, the Kangaroo's foot cups are adjustable and flexible, but I've never seen a child get his/her toes anywhere near the front wheel.

A few caveats: The harness probably has six feet more webbing than it really needed, but I was able to clean up ours with a handful of safety pins. The seat is wide enough you have to ride somewhat bow-legged, but you get used to it pretty quickly. The footrests don't go down far enough for larger children. Don't expect to fit a three-year-old kid into it.

Our youngest just turned one, so we have at least another season with it, which we'll relish: We love being able to interact more with our passenger, and I'm sure the kid likes the view a whole lot better.

-- Yitah Wu

Pedals & Saddles

Simple cheap toe clips
PowerGrips
$18 Amazon

PowerGrips give most of the benefits of toeclips or clipless/cleat systems on bicycle pedals, without most of the downsides. The concept is simple: an asymmetrical strap of cloth that attaches securely to most bicycle platform pedals. The strap is attached in such a way that it loosens when you rotate your heel away from the bike, and tightens when you "heel-in". This gives you similar benefits of a clipless/cleat system; greater efficiency in pedalling, because you can pull on the pedals' upstrokes, rather than just being able to push down. They are just as easy (if not easier) to disengage from. The PowerGrips also have a couple of other benefits which fit well with all but the higher-end performance cyclists:

* Can be used with regular shoes or sandals. Almost no lock-in to a particular type of clip/cleat system.

* (Relatively) cheap, at only $20-$25.

* You can get off the bike and walk around without looking like you're doing some sort of odd balancing act, or scratching up whatever floor you're walking on.

Because the PowerGrip strap is directly above the pedal, gravity does tend to flip it upside-down when not in use. Just as with toe-clips I can pedal on the upside-down pedal to get started, then flip it over with my foot when I'm moving and insert my foot into the strap. Since my riding is commuting to/from work, I have a fair amount of stop-go traffic at intersections, and feel less likely to get a foot stuck and fall over sideways when I have to stop. The PowerGrip strap is totally loose enough for me to quickly get my foot out at a stop, and it has the unusual benefit of being as tight as I want it to be (without using my hands), depending on how I adjust the strap, and how far I heel-in to the pedal. So the "float" can be adjusted on the fly, according to my current riding conditions. This takes a little getting used to, but in my opinion, involves a lower learning curve than clipless pedals.

-- Brian

Ergonomic bike pedals
Ergon PC2 Bike Pedals
$80 REI

I've been using these larger-than-usual ergonomic bike pedals this bike riding season. I've always had foot problems from cycling. Almost all bike shoes are too narrow for me and clip-in pedals are small and create pressure points. The Ergon pedals are slightly concave which allows the foot to easily find a position of comfort.

These pedals are extremely comfortable all day long, and I have found that they increase pedaling power. Sure they look geeky, but they are one pragmatic tool.

-- Curtis Wenzel

Supremely elegant and efficient bike pedals
Egg Beater Pedals
$90 Amazon

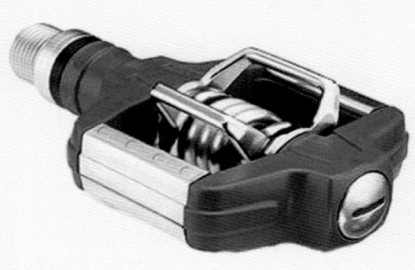

Egg Beater S classic

Egg Beater Candy

Bike pedals have been around forever, and one would assume they would have reached their climax state in sophistication and function. Wrong — Egg Beaters beat every other cleated bike pedal out there. They lock your feet in securely, but also afford effortless release. My road bike friends like them too, but they excel on mountain bikes, as the design self-clears mud and dirt, and the mechanical advantage of the design guarantees that a stray bit of dust isn't going to lock your feet into the pedal.

And they just keep getting better. I bought my first pair — the classic egg beaters — just over two years ago. Then when I purchased my new mountain bike earlier this year, I bought the new Egg Beater Candys — just like the classic, but with tiny platforms wrapped around the egg beater mechanism. This makes it much easier to ride unclipped for short periods than was possible with the old pedals. I haven't tried the Egg Beater Mallets (street shoe ready) yet.

In short, Egg Beaters transformed my ride, and I can't imagine riding a bike that didn't have them.

-- Paul Saffo

Ergonomic handle bar grips
Ergon Cycling Grips
$20 Amazon

I ride single-track trails on a mountain bike in the heart of Colorado's Rocky Mountains and during 20 years of riding I was unable to find a handlebar grip that alleviated numbness and pain in my palms — until I tried the Ergon GP1 grip. Ergon grips differ from normal grips in that they have a contoured, rubber-coated platform under the outside portion of your palm. This platform provides support in such a way that pressure on the ulnar nerve is reduced or eliminated entirely. (I learned my hand numbness arose from pressure on the ulnar nerve in my palm while holding the handlebars.)

Installation is simple, requiring the use of a 4mm allen wrench. Fine-tuning the fit involves riding your bike for a few miles and then evaluating any pain or numbness. If necessary, loosen the bolts, slightly rotate the grips up or down, and retighten the bolts — repeat until your pain or numbness disappears. In my case, rotating the rearmost portion of the grip down from horizontal did the trick. I understand people with carpal-tunnel issues typically rotate the grips upwards from horizontal to reduce the flex angle of their wrists.

Ergon grips are mounted on straight handlebars, such as those found on mountain bikes and some touring bikes, but NOT drop bars. They are available in models with or without bar ends and special short models that work with twist shifters, plus slightly smaller and lighter competition models.

Compared with standard rubber slide-on or "lock-on" grips the Ergon grips are more expensive and heavier. However, the price and weight difference for mine (70-100 grams more) pale next to the increased comfort and pleasure while riding. Since installing the grips, I've ridden 244 miles of expert mountain trails with a total 26,500' vertical gain, and experienced no pain and a huge reduction in my chronic numbness — absolutely no numbness in my right hand and only very minor, infrequent numbness in my left. Everyone I have recommended these to has been pleased, including my chiropractor wife.

-- Graham Ullrich

Comfy classic bike seats
Brooks Saddles
$122 Amazon

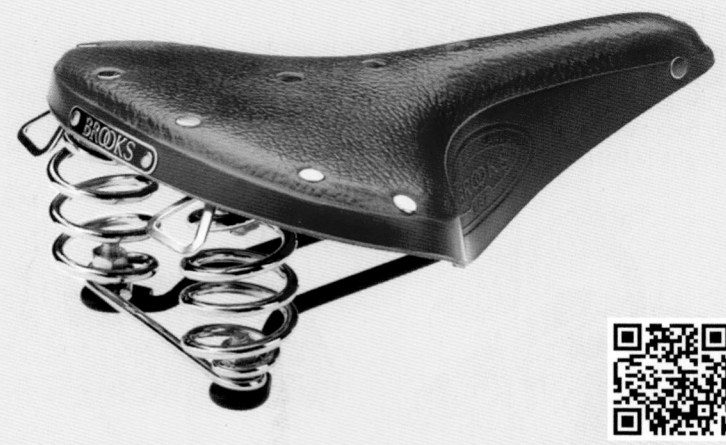

We have three points of contact while riding a bicycle: pedals, handlebar grips, saddle. As anyone who's been uncomfortable on a ride knows well, the latter's by far the most significant in terms of comfort. Saddle choice is as personal as musical preferences; the only way to know if a saddle works for you is to plant your butt on it and take a spin. One general design, however, made by an English company since the late nineteenth century, has proven itself a tried and true favorite.

Brooks leather saddles come in configurations for nearly every type of rider and every mode of riding. Among the choices for leisurely upright cafe bikes is the B67 model, which I use on my utility/errand bike. It's the most comfortable saddle I've ever owned. I'm obsessive about bike fit (bike fit is more important than bike quality), and there isn't a component I've used that makes my bike fit me better than my Brooks saddle. Brooks' B15 model has been around since 1937, and is best suited to a racer hunched over in the drops. Other options include women's models, and wider models with bigger springs.

Like baseball gloves, Brooks saddles require a break-in period, though under you instead of your mattress. After a couple of months mine became noticeably more contoured to my contours. It's felt custom-made ever since. Also like baseball gloves, bike saddles should be chosen for your size and position (on the bike). A wider platform is better suited to an upright riding position/wider body; narrower is better for racing-oriented cyclists/narrower bodies.

Leather saddles don't tolerate wet weather as well as modern synthetic models. They're also heavier and more expensive, too expensive for me to have a Brooks on all of my bikes, though I would.

-- Elon Schoenholz

Uncertainty is an uncomfortable position, but certainty is an absurd position. - Voltaire

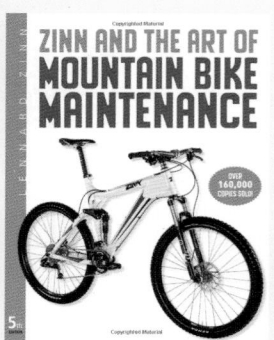

An accessible bike manual
Zinn and the Art of Mountain Bike Maintenance
$17 Lennard Zinn and Todd Telander, 2010, 464 p.

I've been using this book for over a year and so far haven't found anything it doesn't cover when it comes to maintaining my bike. Zinn includes lots of step-by-step instructions with clear illustrations. I was a complete novice prior to reading this, and now it's nice not having to run to the bike shop for every little thing I need fixed. It gives me confidence to tackle things I normally wouldn't attempt.

-- Rob Lewis

● **Chains**

A bike chain is a simple series of links connected by rivets. Rollers surround each rivet between the link plates and engage the teeth of the cogs and chainrings. It is an extremely efficient method of transmitting mechanical energy from the pedals to the rear wheel. In terms of weight, cost, and efficiency, the bicycle chain has no equal, and— believe me— people have tried without success to improve on it for years.

To keep your bike running smoothly, you have to take care of the chain. It needs to be kept clean and well lubricated in order to transmit your energy efficiently and shift smoothly. Chains need to be replaced frequently to prolong the working life of other, more expensive, drivetrain components because a chain gets longer as its internal parts wear, thus contacting the gear teeth differently than intended.

8.5 Removing and installing a Shimano 2007-2010 XTR FC-M970 crankset

4.5 Checking chain wear with the Rohloff gauge. If the curved tooth with the S (steel cogs) falls completely into the chain, replace the chain (A is for aluminum cogs).

Essential bike maintenance tool
Park Team Race Stand
$210 (PRS-20) Amazon

Bicycles need routine maintenance to perform safely and efficiently. But without a bike stand you end up kneeling in a contorted position on the cement floor of your dimly lit garage. And this torture, on your knees and your back and your elbows, which no knight of the Inquisition had the genius to invent, is what causes many of us to abandon bicycle maintenance, and eventually our riding.

Serious riders get the idea. But for the rest of us more casual riders, a bike stand, let alone a Park, seems like a ridiculous expense. After all, a bike stand does nothing more than hold your bike firmly at a height and angle that is convenient for you while you work on it.

Until you've used a bike stand, it's hard to communicate what a difference this makes. Your bike now moves, easily, to a position that is convenient for *you*, rather than the other way around. I think I'm an average primate, and the fact is, I'm not going to do jack squat unless it's easy. And that's what a bike stand does for bicycle maintenance. Once you remove the physical agony from the picture, working on your bike becomes something you actually look forward to. Would you believe that I actually enjoy cleaning my bike now? Well, you shouldn't, because that's crap. But I do keep my bike clean. I do regular maintenance and make significant upgrades to my bikes; all because I know that the bike I am working on is firmly held and at an angle and height that lets me work in comfort. It's such a small thing, but it makes such a huge difference.

The Park Race Stand was designed to be portable, but without sacrificing strength or stability. It's equally at home in your garage or in the field. It's moderately heavy, and a bit ungainly. Getting it in and out of your car is not difficult, but it ain't enjoyable either. To give the unit its strength and stability, it doesn't really fold. Instead, you just lift it up and the legs sort of drop downward by themselves. There are heavy plastic clips to secure the legs, but a Velcro strap does a better job.

A bike stand is a *transformative* tool. It really changes the experience of working on your bike, and the Park Race stand is the best.

-- Verner

Handiest bike tool
Park Tool AWS-1
$9 Amazon

Peer behind the service counter at most bike shops and you'll see a Park Tool workstand. There'll be a waist-level tool tray on the stand, and unless it's already in the hands of a mechanic, the triangle-shaped AWS-1, which features a 4-, 5- and 6mm hex wrench, will likely be one of a handful of tools resting in the tray.

While many general tools are too general, this one is specific and functional enough for excellence. It's useful enough to be taken for granted, one of my hallmarks for a real Cool Tool. So many maintenance and repair jobs on bicycles involve these three hex wrench sizes that it's easily the most used tool in the shop.

Details that make this tool great include a grip-friendly ball in the center (I own an older version without the ball, and it's not as comfortable to hold and also provides less leverage) and color-coded rings at the base of each wrench, so the user can quickly choose the correct size.

I still use my Craftsman T-wrenches when I need a hex with more leverage, and particularly on an 8mm crank bolt, which the AWS-1 doesn't cover. I also use a great set of Pedro's L-wrenches with a ball end on one side for offset access. But the convenient Park Tool AWS-1 is so much my mainstay that it doesn't ever get put away. The company's website also hosts an array of helpful repair how-to's.

-- Elon Schoenholz

Solid state bike tool
Park Tool MT-1
$10 Amazon

I'm sure most roadside bicycle repair multi-tools do their job, but for me the MT-1 is the coolest. Not only does it do the job better than most, its design is so simple, it's so small and lightweight, so ingenious that it has to qualify as a cool tool.

Park's MT-1 is made out of nickel-plated investment-cast steel, weighs next to nothing, has no moving parts, and yet has all the functions one needs for most emergency bicycle repairs, from adjusting derailleurs to tightening crank bolts. Because the shafts are so short and the lever longer, the MT-1 provides superior torque to tools such as the previously reviewed Crank Brothers Multi-19, or a standard folding hex, such as Park's AWS-9. Unlike folding tools such as the Multi-19 or AWS-9, the MT-1 has no retaining bolt that can come loose over time. And because the thin MT-1 has such a low profile, it can fit in tight places, including small saddlebags.

It also offers 8-, 9- and 10mm socket wrenches, which are commonly used on rack and fender hardware, as well as older brake bolts. Overall, the MT-1 is simpler and more usable than the Crank Brothers tool. Though it does have fewer functions, I find the ones the MT-1 does have are all I need for road riding that doesn't involve a long-distance expedition — and they work better. Perhaps the only thing wrong with it is that it isn't blaze orange; I forgot mine in the grass the other day after a quick tune-up, which I might not have done if it had been painted an obnoxiously bright hue.

-- Andrew Wilson

Cable adjuster
Fourth Hand Tool
$38 Amazon

I always knew there had to be an easier, smoother way to change cables on my bicycle or Lambretta. Previously, tightening a brake or clutch cable on my old scooter involved fumbling with a vice grip or begging someone to hold the cable taught while I clamped down the adjustment screw. Enter the 4th hand tool. This little beauty grabs one side of any cable you are adjusting.

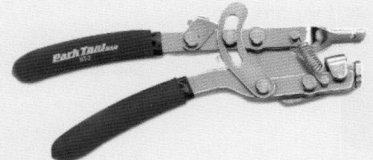

Squeeze the grips and it clicks locked at the distance you are aiming to adjust!.

-- David

Walnut-sized hex set
Topeak Mini 6
$10 Amazon

This incredibly compact, bike-oriented multi-tool has five different sizes of Allen wrench plus a Phillips screwdriver head, all of which folds up into a little pod about the size of a walnut. Sometimes I'll carry it in my pocket or toss it in shoulder bag; mostly I keep it in the under-seat pouch of my bike. It really comes in handy for quick adjustments: raising the seat height, tightening the rear view mirror, adding and removing accessories, etc. Because it's so small it doesn't give enough leverage for really tight nuts (you can't remove a handlebar stem with it), but by extending the tools on the opposite side of the one you're using you can get a handle that's effectively 2.5 inches long, which is enough for small jobs. It also works well as a keychain fob, though at 58g it's slightly on the heavy side.

-- Dylan Tweney

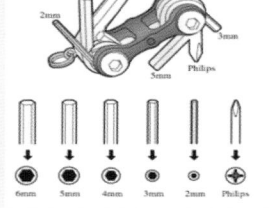

Bike Tires

Dependable bike pump
Topeak Joe Blow Floor Pump
$36 Amazon

After breaking four or five "rugged" bike pumps in four or five years, I made the hefty investment in a Topeak Floor Pump four years ago, which cost about half what I had paid for the "cheap" ones before. It's still going strong and doesn't show any sign of wear.

As to which model to choose, it depends on the bike. For a racing bike you'll want a pump with a small-diameter cylinder, e.g. "Topeak Joe Blow Sport II" while for a commuter bike or a mountain bike you'll want one with more volume, e.g. "Topeak Joe Blow Max II".

These pumps are well-built, large enough (that includes handles, too) and have a good pressure gauge. The tube is long enough. But probably the best thing is the "TwinHead". Depending on the valve type, either side fits. One side for Schrader valves, the other one for narrow valves. No adapter, no hassle, just push on and turn the lever.

-- Bernhard

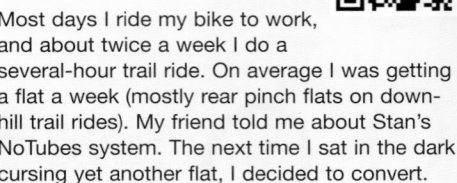

Puncture-proof bike tires
NoTubes
$64 Stan's NoTubes System

Most days I ride my bike to work, and about twice a week I do a several-hour trail ride. On average I was getting a flat a week (mostly rear pinch flats on downhill trail rides). My friend told me about Stan's NoTubes system. The next time I sat in the dark cursing yet another flat, I decided to convert.

In the NoTubes system you remove your inner tube from your tire. No tubes! You add a rim strip that seals your spoke holes. Since there is no tube you need a filling stem to put air into the tire.....this is built into the NoTubes rim strip. Then you add some white liquid inside the tire that seals it airtight. It's one of those things that seems like it would never work, but it works amazingly well. The white liquid sloshes around inside the tire and immediately reseals any punctures as they occur without any air loss. If you still need convincing, watch this amazing video.

I have not had a flat since switching, and I can run at much lower pressures when needed for technical downhill without the danger of pinch flats. The system even saves some weight (and un-sprung rotational weight at that). Installing the system is pretty easy, especially if you use lots of soapy water while installing the rim strip and tire. The only maintenance is that you have to keep adding a bit of the liquid every few months or so. The site also has preferred tires that work the best, and other good installation tips worth looking at before committing. I will never go back to tubes.

-- Alexander Rose

Travel-size floor pump
Topeak Turbo Morph Bike Pump
$33 Amazon

The Topeak Turbo Morph is a lightweight frame pump that functions like a floor pump. It has a fold-out anchor for your foot, and the handle also flips sideways into a T-shape. It's also got a hose, so you can easily inflate the tire while it's mounted on the bike. Before getting the Turbo Morph about two years ago, I had a tiny frame pump that was just this side of useless. Most portable bicycle pumps are designed to be used exclusively with your arms/hands. Since they attach directly to the tire, they're cumbersome to use and difficult to get to the full tire pressure. Compare this to the floor pump in your garage. You anchor it with your feet and use your body weight to power it. Unfortunately, they are also too large to easily carry with you. I tried another "mini foot pump" before the Topeak, but it wouldn't quite work with a Presta adapter. With my other frame pumps, I'd spend more time inflating the tire than I would fixing it, and it would be hard getting the thing past 60 PSI. With this pump, I can get the tire to its full 120 PSI in just a couple of minutes. I have the G model, which has a built-in gauge. More convenient to have a gauge on the pump than to have to carry a separate one. But if you've already got a gauge, then you probably won't want the gauge version. I have puncture-resistant tires, but the key word is "resistant." I still wind up getting a flat a couple times a year. This is well worth carrying.

-- Joe D.

Puncture-resistant cycling tires
Schwalbe Marathon Plus Bike Tires
$36 Amazon

I had two punctured tires in three weeks right before I bought these. Since I switched to the Marathon Plus tires a few months ago, I haven't had a single puncture. The Marathon tires come in two grades: normal and Plus, which is the more flat resistant of the two (Schwalbe also makes a model called the Supreme, which I haven't tried). They are truly for everyday commuting, with tread and real heft. Most importantly, they have Schwalbe's SmartGuard, a layer of "highly elastic, special india rubber" to help better protect your tubes from sharp objects.

The Marathon tires aren't cheap — and it's hard to tell whether it's just been good luck or good engineering — but I feel confident it's the latter. I ride a lot (28 km, two or three times a week, 10 months or so a year) and I used to get tons of flat tires, sometimes once a week. This month in particular is very bad for debris; it's the thaw here in Toronto, so all sorts of junk gets left behind as the snow banks melt.

I'm sure part of why I was getting so many flats is due to the fact I usually ride an EZ-1 Recumbent. With a 'bent, the front wheel is very lightly loaded and the back wheel is heavily loaded. I sit right on top of it (I'm 6'2" and 240 lbs), so it probably carries 90% of my weight. I think this makes the tire more susceptible to punctures because I'm guaranteeing that anything sharp that doesn't bend or move goes right in. I've ridden on a few other kinds of tires: Continental slicks (nice), cheapo knobbies (garbage), some satisfactory tires that came stock, and Primo Comets (dartboards).

I am riding under the same conditions, circumstances and in the same areas as when I used to get the flats, and haven't had any trouble. Just last week I rode through quite a lot of glass with no problems.

-- Adam Norman

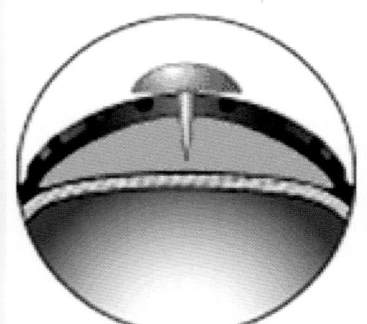

Twice the stability for bikes
Pletscher Two-Legged Kickstand
$45 Amazon

While the need for a two-legged kickstand on a large tandem is fairly obvious, it's not as clear why you'd need one for smaller bikes — until you start riding with children aboard. Whether you're using a front-mounted Kangaroo WeeRide or a traditional rear-mounted child seat, preventing the bike from falling over when a child is strapped into the seat is a serious safety concern.

I first saw this Pletscher kickstand about seven years ago, when it came on our Bike Friday Family Triple. It's an aluminum kickstand with two legs; the second pivots via a cam mechanism, so that it stows alongside the first leg. Made in Switzerland, it's a cool piece of hardware for the folding design alone. Stowed, it looks like a standard Greenfield kickstand, with an extra leg.

The double-legged stand makes a big or heavily loaded bike far more stable when you dismount, and it can also double as a makeshift workstand for back-end fixes, as it lifts the rear wheel off the ground. We now have two bikes outfitted with this kickstand.

-- Yitah Wu

Anti-thorn sealant for cyclists

Tire Slime

$16 Amazon

I have found that anti-puncture strips are often not wide enough to stop thorns from piercing bike tubes, as the strips are only useful in the middle of the tire. I started using Slime, a green liquid sealant, after talking to a bike-borne cop who had very good results. I now use the stuff in my mountain bike and wheelbarrow tires. Actually, I bought pre-Slimed bike tubes when I got new tires recently. No flats at all for six years, despite rough use. I will confess to having to pump up a few times, though. If the bike is left parked in one position in, say, the winter season, the Slime may run down to the bottom of the tire, thus unsealing some of the sealed holes. As such, you will have to pump the tires and ride a while to reseal everything after a month of non-use. In cold weather, Slime puddled at the bottom of a tire while parked will cause a markedly unbalanced tire for the first few miles. This is most noticeable on dual suspension mountain bikes like mine, but it doesn't seem to affect the operation of the bike.

The last time I changed bike tubes, I found 29 thorn holes Slime had sealed! Slime works in both tubed and tubeless tires, but with a few more caveats: it adds weight to the wheels, which is a disadvantage in racing. For normal road or trail use, you won't notice. Also, Schrader valves are what to use with Slime, as the skinny Presta ones clog too easily. Tubeless tires, which are already heavier, also require special rims or rim treatments to prevent leaks through the spoke holes. I'd appreciate lighter wheels and tires, but my present tubed setup is fine for my use. Tubeless tires are much better than tubed tires at resisting "snakebite" (tire damage from striking a sharp-edged bump or hole at high speeds). However, tubeless tires obviously can be punctured by thorns, etc. — Slime will dutifully seal such. I have heard Slime itself will not patch "snake-bite" damage, as it is too far up the sidewalls for Slime to be thick enough to work. As I do not race (especially downhill) at 74 years old, tubeless tires do not tempt me. Slime does not last forever either. After a few years, it isn't as runny, and may not seal a thorn hole in time to prevent needing to pump.

Some people say a Slimed tire cannot be patched by the usual means. Don't believe 'em. You just have to wipe off the Slime from the area before patching it in the usual way. They offer incarnations of Slime for cars and motorcycles, too. Personally, I would not use Slime in automobile tires, as the high temperatures and odd balance changes might prove obnoxious. It'd be expensive to find out I was wrong. Bottom line: if you cycle where there are thorns (we call them "goat-heads" or "concho burrs"), Slime will greatly reduce flats. I have had only one flat in the last 10,000 miles — from running over a broken bottle. Slime couldn't seal the 1.5-inch slit. Neither could my patch kit.

-- J. Baldwin

Combo bike tire levers and flat repair kit

Planet Bike Lunar Levers

$5 Amazon

Every cyclist should have a flat kit to enable them to deal with a flat tire. Most kits include simple levers to get the tire off the rim and a set of patches for repairing holes. The Lunar Levers combine these two needs into one. The levers themselves are better designed to help you remove and remount a tire than standard levers. Ingeniously, the levers store the patch kit inside inside the levers themselves, snapping together, forming a single unit, saving space.

-- Michael Pusateri

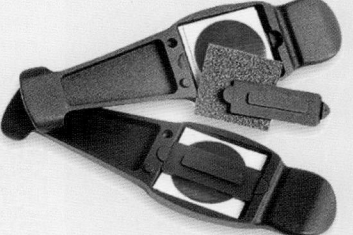

Best bicycle tire iron

Crank Brothers Speed Lever

$4 Amazon

This tool makes removing and replacing a bicycle tire quick, easy and safe — and it does it much better than conventional bike tire irons.

Ever watch an auto tire shop mechanic mount a tire onto a rim? He's got this big power tool that runs around the bead of the tire and pops it onto the wheel. Shrink that to pocket size, a little over an ounce, and you've got the Crank Brothers Speed Lever for bike tires. It reduces the major hassle of a flat tire to a few seconds' effort. You work the speed lever under the bead of the tire, extend it and clip it to the axle. Pull on the end near the tire and zip the tire off the rim. It can take a bit of pull to get started, but this tool is worlds above conventional tire irons. And I've never pinched a tube using the Speed Lever.

One side of the head looks like a conventional tire iron and is used to remove the tire. The other hooks over the rim to lever the tire back on after you patch it. The long handle portion is actually three telescoping sections that extend to allow snapping one end onto the axle to hold it in place while you rip the other end along the rim.

Grab the end of the Speed Lever nearest the rim and pull it along the rim. The other end is hooked to the axle, so pulling the rim end

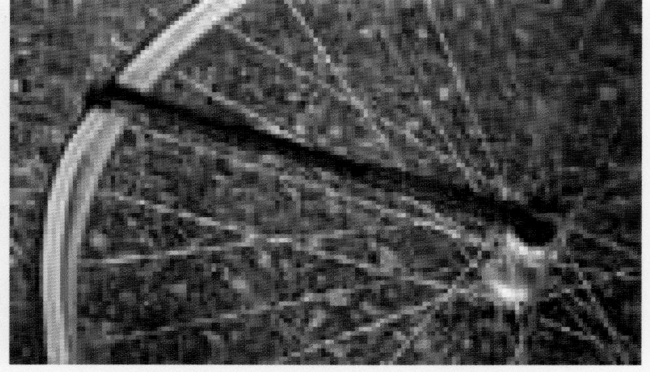

How to ride in the snow

Nokian Ice Bike Tires

Scandinavian bicycle tire manufacturer Nokian makes carbide-studded "ice" tires for winter riding. Their "lightly-studded" 700c model, the Hakkapeliitta, has made my bicycle commuting season here in Boston last year-round. The carbide studs will give you traction through snow and across frozen trails, iced-over gutters, and unanticipated (and very dangerous) black road ice. I've been able to bike on surfaces that I couldn't even stand on. In the worst of winter weather, it gives me great pleasure to smoothly cruise past entire fleets of cars stuck on the ice. For ultimate winter traction control, mount them on a "fixed-gear" bike with wide tire clearances, such as the Surly Steamroller.

I dream of a day, after weeks and weeks of frigid weather, when I can commute from Cambridge to Waltham on top of a frozen-over Charles River.

-- John Rieffel

$78 Nokian Hakkapeliitta 700c tires Peter White Cycles
$92 Nokian Extreme 294 Peter White Cycles

moves it along the rim, levering the bead over the rim. Less force required, and it keeps your hands out of the tire.

The key is that one end of the Speed Lever is on the rim, the other is hooked to the AXLE. This allows the user to pull it along the rim to mount or dismount the bead. Remounting goes in reverse, and is just as easy. You insert the back side of the head of the Speed Lever over a portion of the rim where the tire is already in the rim, extend the sliding sections and hook onto the axle. Then grab the end of the Speed Lever nearest the rim and pull it along the rim. The tire is levered back over the rim and seated.

-- Dave Shaw

Bike Brake Tip

The problem: Nice road bikes that don't have kickstands. You have to lean them against something but sometimes they roll and fall over. Ouch!

Solution: Before your ride, take a wine cork and cut one end into a wedge with two simple cuts that make a nice tapered end. Then squeeze one of your break handles and insert the wedge end into the gap that appears between the handle and the hood. This keeps the brake deployed and your bike won't roll. Viola!

It's free, fast, and the cork stows away unnoticed in your jersey pocket or tool bag.

I learned the trick 25 years ago from a bike shop owner in Virginia, yet I have yet to find a cyclist who knows about it. My biking friends are converts.

-- Steve Leveen

Bike Touring

Excellent long-distance bike routes
Adventure Cycling

$40 (membership and 9 magazine issues)
Adventure Cycling Association

(maps, books, and gear)
Cyclosource

Invisible to most drivers, there is a 26,000-mile network of long-distance bicycle trails criss-crossing the US. These mapped and designated routes offer travelers researched paths with plenty of information on the nearest bike shops, profiles of difficulty, and indicated sleeping possibilities. It all started with Bikecentennial's 1976 TransAm route, the first to cross the continental US, connecting Oregon and Virginia. Thousands still use this route, now overseen by the non-profit Adventure Cycling.

I once rode a bike across America using my own route (more adventure) but I have followed long sections of other Adventure Cycling routes. Their materials are well-worth the price; you will however have lots of companions — which many enjoy.

Adventure Cycling puts out a pretty good magazine for bicycle long-distance touring (a place to solicit travel companions), runs bike tours, has a decent catalog of touring paraphernalia, and continually pioneers new routes. The newest: the world's longest mountain bike trail, running 2,500 miles along the Continental Divide from Canada to Mexico. For that kind of amazingly rugged off-the-road trip (which only a few have completed in full), their maps (waterproof) and guides are essential.

-- KK

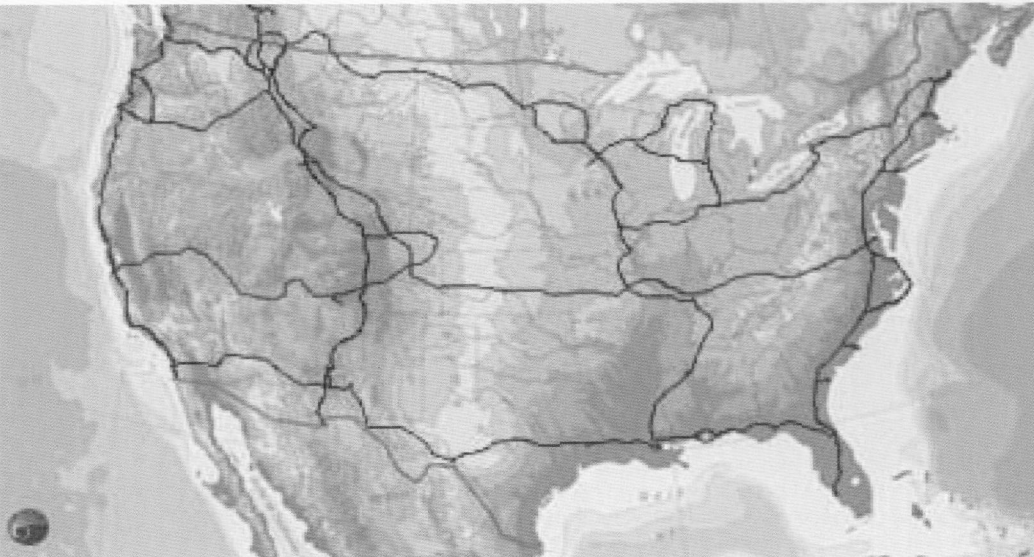

Bicycle-centric maps
Adventure Cycle Maps

adventurecycling.org

For over two months my teenage son and I rode our bikes down the Pacific coast from Canada to Mexico. We followed a route mapped out by Adventure Cycling. The 2,000-mile route is broken into about 80 sections, each annotated with the kind of info you'd like to know on a bike: where the next camp sites are, grocery options, bike shop locations, mileage counts, and most important -- elevation contours for the upcoming hills! These maps are printed with full clarity on waterproof paper. The set is extremely well designed, sized at the right scale, and kept current with frequent updates. It was the best bargain of our trip.

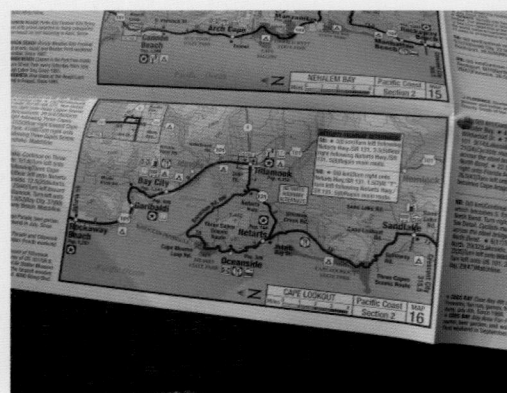

While this Pacific route is very popular, Adventure Cycling offers about 20 other long-distance bicycle routes in the US as well. If you are making a long-distance bike ride in America, chances are Adventure Cycling will have a set of maps for you. These maps are miles better than any automobile road map, and in most ways better than Google maps. Ordinarily, I'd shy away from a well-travelled trail, but in this case, the availability of a set of Adventure Cycling maps would entice me to follow it.

Their web-based video gives a great overview of the maps' benefits, and also serve as a manual for using them.

-- KK

No-car roads
Rails-to-Trails

$4 Ron Quinn, 2000, 256 p.

Rails-to-Trails (or rail trails) are roads without cars. They are where railways go when they die. Bicycles love them.

Every year 2,000 miles of railways in the US are abandoned. So far, about half of the 300,000 miles railways built by 1916 (the railroad peak) have been taken out of service. Some 13,000 of those miles have been repurposed into bike/hike trails.

Why they're great: 1) You get paths with flat to gentle slopes, 2) no cars, 3) no strip development, and 4) they often pass through small towns. These wide, sculpted, relaxing paths are perfect for hiking, horseback, cross-country skiing, skates and particularly bicycles. While most of the rails-to-trails are less than 5 miles long, there are 10 in the country stretching over 100 miles and at least one that is 225 continuous miles. These longer trails are a big hit — easy, civilized bicycle tours: gentle rides without having to compete with cars. As far as I am concerned, riding bicycles on rail trails is the way to go.

The rails to trails movement began in the mid-west, where most of the abandoned railways were. It has now spread to every state. There are about 1,300 rails-to-trails in the US, with another 1,000 in progress. Backpackers have a network of fabulously signed and maintained long-distance footpath trails; we now have the beginnings of a network of long-distance dedicated bikepaths.

Behind most of this work is the very effective non-profit Rails-to-Trails Conservancy. They publish a magazine, newsletter, and a directory of known rail trails in the US, entitled 1000 Great Rail Trails. It's a bare bones listing with no traveling information; but it is where you go to browse where rail trails exist in particular states. The same info, in slightly less useful search-mode is available on their supplemental website, TrailLink, which includes a list of the 10 longest rail trails, and introductory orientations to most rail trails.

For utilitarian logistical details, the Conservancy publishes 8 region-specific books. I've been using the California one, *Rails-to-Trails: California*. It covers about 60 rail trails in the state, including several in my own area that I was not aware of.

-- KK

On-the-road spoke replacement tool
Next Best Thing 2 Cassette Tool

$30 M-Gineering

If you're on a long distance cycling trip and you break a spoke (a common occurrence) on the right hand side of your rear wheel then you're in trouble.

To replace these spokes you need to remove the cassette to get access to the hub. Normally this requires a specialized tool, a very large spanner (about 12") and a large chain whip – all of which are heavy and unwieldy to carry. However, the Next Best Thing 2 is a small and light tool that enables you to remove the cassette using just the leverage of the bike's chain.

Assuming you have the correct spokes with you (as any serious long distance cyclist would) then you should be good to go again without having to limp in to the next town/bike shop – something I've had to do several times over the years.

This is probably in the category of "tool you very rarely use but are extremely grateful when you do."

-- Jamie McMahon

The idea is all there is. Trust me. - Ornette Coleman

Roads without cars

Seven Great Long-Distance Bike Trails Without Cars

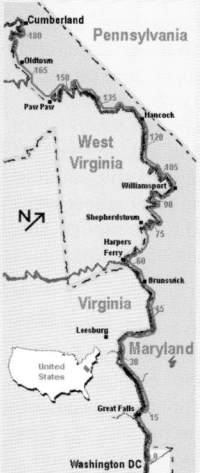

Many years ago I took a meandering 5,000 mile bike ride across the US, from San Francisco to New York via Idaho and Texas. I rode back roads all the way and it was a highlight of my life. But this long bike ride would have been 100 times better if I did not have to share the road with careless drivers, overloaded pickups, and logging trucks, not to mention suicidal teens in hot rods. Wouldn't it be great if there were long-distance trails specifically for bicycles? Basically — roads without cars?

Well, there are! A quickly emerging network of abandoned railway lines are being converted by regional governments into superb bike paths. In addition to offering very gentle grades that are ideal for bikes, many of these new trails are satisfyingly long. The longest rail trail is over 300 miles long, and the longest off-pavement bike trail in the country stretches 2,500 miles. On these bike roads you can cruise along for weeks without ever encountering a car, or worrying about being bumped off the white line by an oblivious motorist. These are not paved roads, but packed gravel or dirt. Many sport spectacular tunnels and bridges courtesy of the former railways. At the same time these trails pass through small towns affording local eateries and rural lodging, as well as the usual camping spots along the way. I tell you, there's nothing like arriving at the soft pillows of a B&B after a long day of pedaling.

Many of these trails did not exist as bike paths even a few years ago. More are being opened every day. There's great effort to sew short sections together into long haul bike-primary paths. Eventually you will be able to cross the country via a series of interconnected car-free roads. In the meantime, the clearinghouse for the latest additions to the bike-road network is the Rail to Trails Conservancy. But you don't have to wait to enjoy some fantastic overnight tours on roads without cars. Here are six of the longest continuous bike trails in operation right now, in ascending order of length.

-- KK

Katy Trail — 264 miles

This bike trail which mostly parallels the Missouri River is a Missouri state park unto itself. It's generally flat and very civilized. There are loads of B&Bs, wineries, and historical sites, and bike support. The path is part of Lewis and Clarke's trail. This well-love week-long trail has its own website, BikeKatyTrail, for the best info.

John Wayne Pioneer Trail — 113 miles

While this trail officially transects Washington state, only 113 miles of the final 200 mile trail have been developed (by 2007) and are presently open. You can get several overnights out of it. Great diversity of terrain: unshaded, dry sagebrush in east, glacial valleys and ranchlands in the west. Hard gravel. Biker/hiker camps. Best source for update info for bikers is from Jennifer's List of Bike Trails. For mile by mile descriptions of the trail try Spokane Outdoors.

Central Lake/Lake Wobegone Trail — 130 miles

A paved hike- and bike-only path in central Minnesota that skirts a dozen lakes. Built on built on an abandoned Burlington Northern Railroad corridor, it has a level grade the whole way and passes through plenty of small towns and lodging. See centrallakestrail.com/trail-map.html

Cowboy Trail — 195 miles

A nice leisurely 5-day trip passing through the small towns every 15 miles on the Nebraska prairie. (The trail is currently being extended to over 300 miles.) Crushed limestone, 200 wooden bridges. Food, lodging, lush grass and flat terrain in abundance. Check the official Nebraska Parks site for current info.

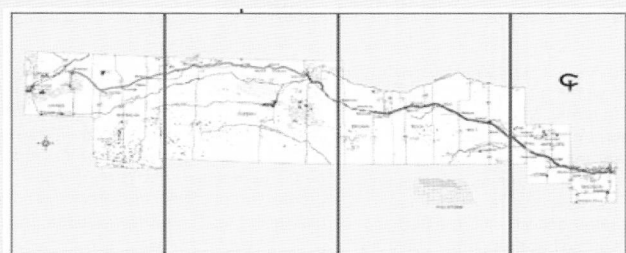

Kettle Valley Rail Trail — 280 miles

Located in lower British Columbia, the big attraction here are the stunning trestle bridges, long tunnels, and mountain scenery glimpsed from an easy grade that never exceeds 2.2%. (Many of the trestles were destroyed in a forest fire in 2003 but are being rebuilt. The photo shows a rebuilt trestle.) Ten days is an easy, decent trip. Most current cycling info can be found at Cycling the KVR. Mile by mile log of the trail is at Trailness.

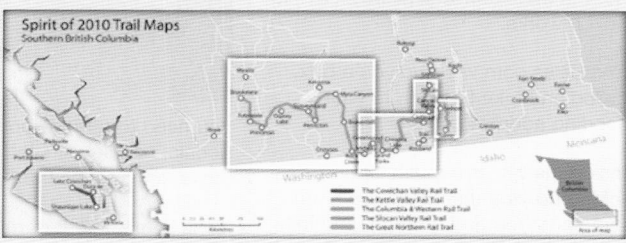

GAP/C&O — 335 miles

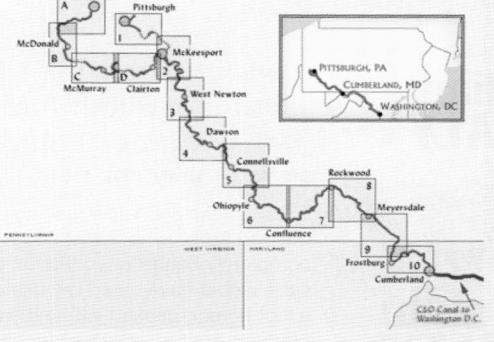

Running along the former towpath of the C&O canal, this well-traveled path crosses the hills of Appalachia. The Greater Allegheny Passage/ C&O trail is unique among bike paths because it begins and ends in a big city. Imagine it: You can ride from downtown Washington, DC to downtown Pittsburg, PA without encountering automobiles along the way! The big city endpoints make logistics a little easier, too. And of course the multi-week trip runs through tons of historical places. The official GAP site and corresponding official C&O sites are best for updates. Best biker info can be had at Bike Washington.

Great Divide Mountain Bike Route — 2,500 miles

Unlike the other five trails, this one is not flat. Anything but. The Great Divide Route is 2,500 miles of rough fire roads that cross summits of the Continental Divide 27 times, earning you over 200,000 feet in changed elevation. The entire trail stretches from Canada to Mexico. It will take an ordinary human 3 months to complete. But unlike any other transnational trail in North America, you won't be squeezed by cars as you ride from border to border. It's a remote trail, in wilderness, with few amenities. Think of it as the Appalachian Trail for bicycles. Adventure Cycling has the best info on this dream.

Off-Road Bicycling

Cheapest bike shipping
EBike Shipper
$41+ ShipBikes.com

This is the cheapest way to ship a bike in the US. Most airlines have hefty charges for your bicycle as accompanied luggage, so this compact box and subsidized FedEx ground rates are the best deal I've found. It will cost about $100 when you are done if you use their full service. While it is the cheapest way, it is not the most convenient way. Here is how it works.

ShipBikes.com will ship you a box, called an Ebike Shipper, to your sending address.

Inside the box is a much larger box folded up. You unfold that box into two parts (top and bottom), and then you disassemble your bike and tie it in.

You need to remove both wheels, pedals, handlebar, seat, fenders, racks, and maybe the front fork.

It will take an hour or more, and can be done with two common tools. (And of course you need to rebuild it at the other end.) Then you tape up the box, print out a label from an email they send you, and then call FedEx who will come to your address to pick it up, and then deliver to the address you designate. This delivery and pick up is really fantastic at the end of a bike trip when you are shipping a bike back home from a far destination.

The shipping box is very cleverly designed to arrive in the mail folded up and to just squeak under a pricing threshold when unfolded. Thus the tight fit and the need to strip the bike down. By coming under the FedEx price threshold the box will ship in the US for about $53. The cost of the box and shipping it to you is $48. You can stuff some gear like a sleeping bag and pad into the box for padding but it won't hold much beside the bike.

The alternative is to use an AirCaddy from the same company, which is a triangular shaped box that takes the bike with almost no disassembly. (The AirCaddy box is also reusable.) You can load it in 10 minutes. But it costs $99 to reach you, and about $96 to ship because of its larger size. That extra simplicity will cost about double the ebike box option. But this is by far the most convenient way to ship a bike: Box comes, you unfold it, pop bike in, they come to get it, then deliver it its destination. Done for $200.

Of course if you have use of a car you can find a free used box from a bike shop, drag it home, and ship it yourself, but you'll pay higher rates, close to $100. ShipBIkes has some kind of deal with FedEx that gives you a discount on the freight. Or you can get a free bike box at a shop and then haul the packed bike-in-box to the airport (and then out of the arriving airport), but for most airlines this will still cost you about $90-$100+, and it requires a car, which you may not have at the end of a long tour.

There are still a few airlines that will ship a boxed bike for $50 as accompanied luggage, but they are rare, and you still have the problem of getting the box and then getting the bike to the airport and back. Lastly, the ebike box is so well designed that there are four layers of cardboard around the perimeter, everything is tied in with straps, the wheel axels protected with rubber bumpers, and the whole thing much more protected and secure than a free bike-shop box, which has been used and is not meant to be shipped in luggage. I recently received a bike shipped this casual way and the front wheel was so damaged it had to be rebuilt. The bike we shipped via ebike was intact.

Any way you do it, it will cost you about $100 to ship a bike in the US. (ShipBikes will ship overseas but the costs vary so much I can't summarize.) But if you count the hassles of the alternatives, the hassles of disassembling your bike into a provided box and having them pick it up to deliver works out to be the cheapest way to do it.

-- KK

Ultimate mountain bike tutorial
Mountain Bike!: A Manual of Beginning and Advance Technique
$12 William Nealy, 1992, 176 p.

A few weeks ago while rushing down a trail on my bike I wiped-out and broke a rib. I wished I had read this book earlier. Its completely hand-drawn tutorial of mountain bike techniques and skills would have cured my mistake. Each page is hand drawn, full of humor, packed with experience, and conveys memorable lessons. Author Nealy's hilarious one page cartoons are more effective in teaching crucial things than either text or video. Although it was written — I mean drawn — in 1992, it's still amazingly valid. The bikes have changed but the skills and challenges are the same. It's a really great how-to.

-- KK

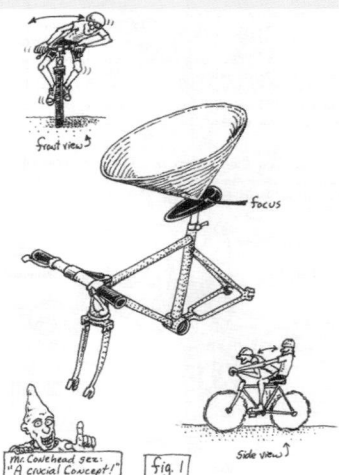

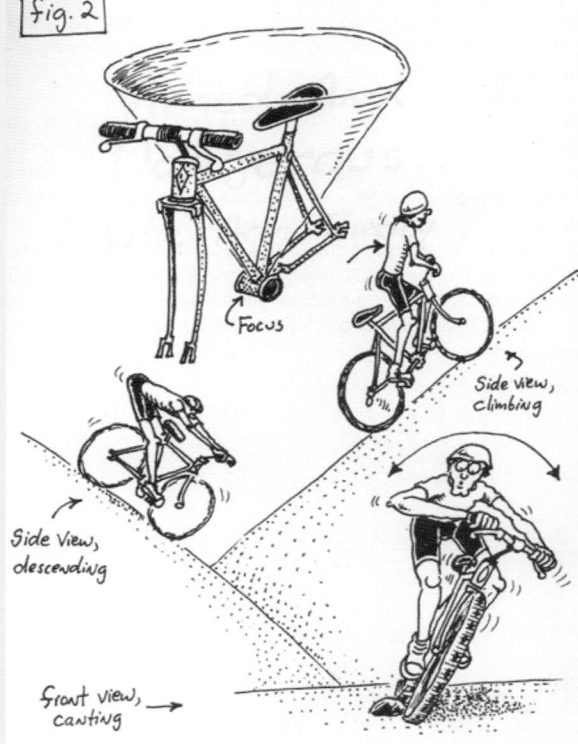

Cone of Movement — The amount of lean a rider can exert on his/her bike is determined by the focus of his/her stance: in a seated position, the cone of movement is focused on the seat [fig. 1] and is relatively small. The greater the obstacle, the larger the cone of movement must be to surmount it. [fig 2.]

From a standing position the cone of movement is huge compared to sitting. This gives the rider an exponentially greater number of options in terms of leans, weight shifts and control.

• Before you begin a self-training session RELAX, this ain't Wall Street. You can't lose riding a mountain bike. If you are working on a technique and you fail two or three times in a row, STOP!! Do something else and try again later. This is called "Training To Failure" (positive progressive training; pushing the envelope). If you push a training session beyond three successive failures you are "Training To Fail" (negative regressive training; more pain than fun). As you become more adept at self-teaching and pushing yourself appropriately you'll be able to discern where good (beneficial) training ends and bad (regressive) training begins. [Hint: lack of fun marks the spot.]

On level or down-sloping trails you can keep your pedals and cranks clear of ground clutter by keeping your cranks more or less level and pumping the pedals up and down.

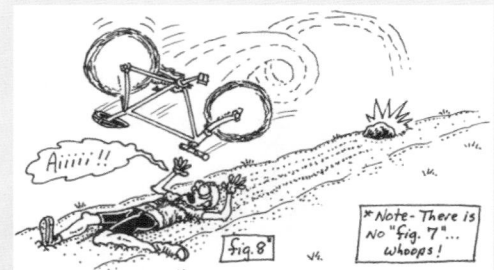

Another excellent reason to hang onto your bike in any fall is a loose bike's proclivity to become a very gnarly projectile during a wipe-out!

USB-rechargeable bike light
Knog Boomer Tail Light
$30 Amazon

I have had countless bike lights stolen over the years. Part of this is due to forgetfulness, but also to the difficulty of quickly removing the light from the bike when I'm finished with my ride.

Knog lights have fixed this problem through the use of silicone cases. The stretchy silicone easily wraps around any bar on the bike, providing a secure, but flexible, attachment on even the bumpiest of roads. In the past, Knog has been criticized for producing lights that were were more ornamental than functional given their under-powered LEDs. However, the Knog Boomer changes that.

Unlike previous Knog lights I've seen, the Boomer tail light is super bright. The three LEDs produce 15-lumens on their highest setting, which, while not significant compared to many high-end flashlights, is plenty for its intended use as a rear tail light.

The unit's battery life is respectable (12-hours flashing on full brightness) and is made even more palatable through the design's inclusion of a USB-port that allows for easy charging on any powered USB hub. It might

seem strange to rely on a USB-port for charging, but the ubiquity of the interface has made it almost more commonplace than outlets (and even without an outlet you can substitute any iOS charger). Not only does my laptop have two, but my desktop monitor has six, while my external keyboard has another.

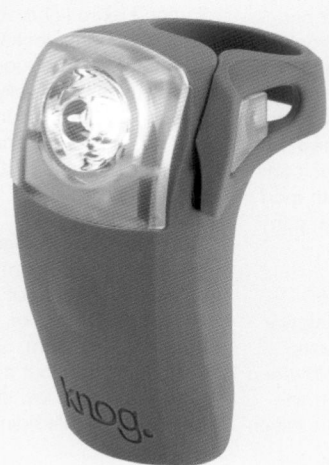

While many may complain about the lack of versatility that is associated with using AAs or AAAs, the convenience of a built in charging unit has, for me, far outweighed the benefits of quickly being able to switch out batteries. For those less inclined to charge via USB, Knog makes a non-USB version.

-- Oliver Hulland

USB Rechargeable Bike Blinky Lights
Knog USB Light
$21+ Knog USB Lights

When riding after dark you really want some good marker lights for your bike to *help* drivers see you. I find though that most of these lights are either too big, or they use short lasting and hard-to-find watch type batteries. Recently though there are more and more companies making USB rechargeable lights. Knog in particular makes a great series of surprisingly bright LED lights for your bike in soft silicone that recharge in any USB plug. This also means that you dont have yet another wall wort to lose, and you can always do a last minute charge at work or even in the car. These lights are also low profile and light enough to just leave on your bike so they are always there when you need them.

-- Alexander Rose

Most visible night alert
Reflective Yield Symbol
$15 Safety Central

I wear a reflective yield symbol pinned to my bike pack. It's arrestingly bright, alarmingly visible. I've been stopped by motorists, pedestrians, and cyclists alike inquiring about or thanking me for wearing it. It can be seen from 3000 feet.

-- Michele McGinnis

Orbiting cycling light
Cat Eye Orbit Bike Light

$18 Amazon

For the past 6 months I have been using the cat eye orbit wheel light. It clips onto my bicycle wheel spokes. By squeezing the housing the light turns on. It makes a soft, but bright, illuminated glow which spins with my bike wheel while riding down the road. I have seen car drivers noticing the lights.

There are two remarkable things about the orbit. First, in 6 months of parking my bike on the street I have not had to change the battery once. Second, ask any cyclist

in San Francisco how long they expect their bike to last before it's stolen by some thieving hipster. The answer is "not long." I don't have to worry about the orbits being stolen because they look like old fashioned reflectors.

I love 'em.

There is a similar product from Nite Ize called the Spoke Lit, but I haven't tried it.

-- Andy Bot

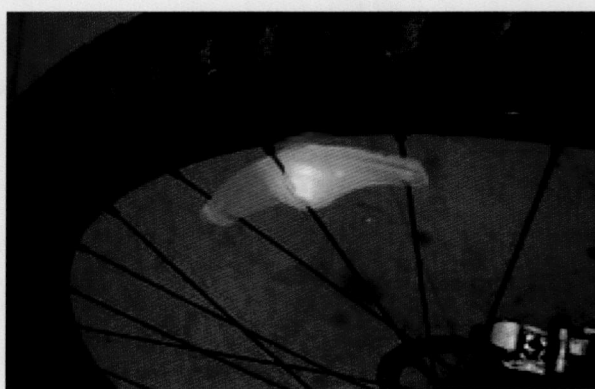

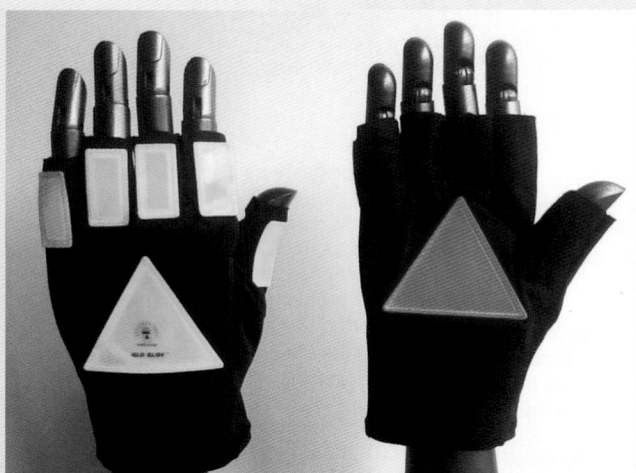

Reflective cycling handwear
Glo Gloves
$26 Amazon

As a year-round bike commuter, I rely on the previously-untried Glo Gloves, which work as advertised — great! — for adding reflective spots. They are a one-size-fits-all, fingerless stretchy nylon glove with reflective patches sewn on. During a winter of bike commuting, with my schedule, that means two hours of riding in the dark each day. When I stick out my arm to signal a turn, the gloves give a strong visual cue to drivers about my intent. I can even twist my hand from vertical to horizontal to make the reflective patches blink in a turn signal pattern. They're intended to be worn over your regular gloves. I've worn them over leather work gloves, fingerless cycling gloves, full finger cycling gloves, Smartwool lightweight wool "lin-

ers", and just my bare hands. They're very thin and don't interfere with touch sensation. I have both the original and sport gloves. All models are designed to stretch and fit over your gloves of choice. I consider them as essential as lights and reflective ankle bands for riding at night.

-- Michael Rasmussen

As a bike commuter, I use these gloves to signal to indicate my intentions at intersections, even to wave traffic through. I have the sports version, which I stretch over regular bike gloves. I've found they can even stretch over ski gloves up to about size M or L, depending on the ski glove. After three years of use on hundreds of rides, the stitching on one of the reflective patches has come a little loose, but otherwise they've worn well. The main difference between the regular and sports versions is a patch of abrasion resistant fabric on the palm.

-- Jun Nogami

Best bike bags
Ortlieb Panniers
$128 Back-Roller City Rear Pannier ortliebusa.com

These Ortlieb bike panniers are not the cheapest, but they are the best. They are 100% waterproof. Sensitive electronic gear inside will stay perfectly dry after riding all day in storms. You roll up the top opening to close (no zipper to break). Extremely rugged, super easy to lift on and off the rack, and will fit inside a tent. They hold a lot in a single bag (no internal pockets), more than I like to carry. I know folks who use them for hauling groceries in the city. I live out of them on the road. They come for either rear or front wheel placement, with very visible reflectors on the ends.

-- KK

Recumbent Bikes

Supremely comfortable pedal-wheels
Sun USX Recumbent Tricycle

$1,300+ Sun Bicycles

The Sun EZ-3 USX is a human-powered, recumbent, three wheeled vehicle. It engages me in a way that the Segway did not. I am amazed this product, what some call a "bent trike," is not better known.

The USX is the most comfortable human powered vehicle ever, more comfortable than many cars. It's safe, practical, and affordable. I hate exercise but I find myself impatient to get my next chance to ride this thing.

Riding the USX is eerie, because it feels like relaxing on a perfect easy chair and performing aerobic exercise at once. You can go fast or slow, and both are wonderful. You can load the thing with 450 total pounds. You can pull carts. Some riders have decked out USX's with ipod sound systems and other amenities. You can get rain roofs and car hitches.

There are some downsides. It's heavy: 65 pounds. Going up hills is pleasant, but slower than on a bicycle. Some of the parts (bolts, screws, and bearings, in particular) are low-end and might need to be replaced sooner than you'd expect. It doesn't come with some essential features, like rear view mirrors. (Mirrycle handlebar mirrors are the best after-market choice.) It's hard to mount a front headlight.

Some other upsides: Unlike a lot of bent trikes, the USX folds for easy transportation. I put it inside the back of our SUV instead of on a rack.

Another big plus: you sit high enough to be noticed by car drivers, though I also added a flag and extra lights to err on the side of caution. Although it looks wide, and encourages cars to give more room than is commanded by bicyclists, it is actually narrow enough to roll through a standard door. You can stand it up on end so it takes minimal room when parked. You can just stop and rest while going uphill - it has a parking brake.

There are lots of other bent trikes — dozens — but most are "performance-oriented" — made for athletes. Some of the athletic brands are Greenspeed, Catrike, and Windcheetah. I have tried some of them, and I think they are fun and interesting, but not what I want. They are expensive, very low slung (you're practically on the ground while riding), and not so practical for non-athletes. What I want is something that's super easy to get in and out of, that's fun to sit on while standing still, that's high up enough to be safe around cars, and that is fun to ride slow, while on the phone or catching up on treo email. I want something for life, not for sport, and there's not much competition in this niche. There is another interesting comfort-oriented bent trike, the Hase Leupus, from Germany. The Leupus is lighter and made of higher-end parts, but is disproportionately more expensive. The seat isn't as comfortable as the USX — though it does have better suspension. Hase also makes super light versions, including titanium models.

The USX is available online. If you buy online, know that Sun ships the USX without the parts well-tightened. If you can afford it, it makes more sense to buy retail from a good local bike shop for about $1,300. The service will be very much worth it!

-- Jaron Lanier

Front wheel drive recumbent bicycle
Cruzbike Freerider

$1,195 Cruzbike

Although it takes time to master the ride, the Cruzbike's a blast once you do get the hang of it. It's a front-wheel drive bike, so it gives you the comfort and speed of a recumbent without the long, long chain. The lack of chain in the rear makes it a perfect complement to the Xtracycle free radical sport utility bike, which is specifically why I bought the Cruzbike. I have the stock 65 psi tires on my Freerider now, but I'm thinking of upgrading to disc brakes and 100 psi tires to make it even more of a cargo-hauling truck. (As much as possible, I try to avoid driving a car entirely.)

I first bought a recumbent in 2000, after testing several, and never looked back. I've ridden bikes like the EZ-1 and have four recumbents currently: a Rans Rocket (my first), a Rans tandem, a BikeE (for my wife) and the Cruzbike, which I bought last fall. The Cruzbike's grip-shift handles the same as any other bike, and it takes hills pretty well for a 'bent, albeit with the proviso that no 'bent climbs as well as an upright because you can't stand up on the pedals (a small price to pay for being able to ride for hours without feeling any pain and for having a pleasurable touring ride experience).

It feels great to glide through the world with your head in a normal, comfortable position, at a comfortable height, instead of craning to see traffic. I find I'm faster because you are more aerodynamic than on an upright. Thus, it also takes less work to maintain the same speed. Even with the Xtracycle, the Cruzbike feels amazingly light.

-- John Gear

Lightweight tri-wheel bent
Greenspeed Trike

$2,390+ Greenspeed

Although I've known about recumbents for years, until recently I had a prejudice against them. Whenever I observed middle-aged riders of two-wheeled recumbents obviously just getting started on regular daily exercise, they seemed unstable when starting to pedal from a dead stop. That led me to trying out a three-wheel tadpole trike, which allows you to remain in a stable, ready-to-ride position. Tadpoles have the two wheels in the front, one in back. Deltas have the two wheels in the back. After just two minutes riding a trike, I was addicted.

The Greenspeed sits closer to the ground and is much lighter than most delta trikes — my GT3 weighs 37.5 lbs compared to the 65 lbs. of the previously-reviewed Sun USX. Unlike deltas, the tadpole provides a greater sense of the same freedom, speed and agility that people are used to on good upright bikes. My GT3 is much faster and infinitely more sporty and maneuverable than a delta. If deltas are sedans; tadpoles are the sport coupes. Sitting with one's head upright enables you to enjoy your surroundings much more than on regular cycles. This is true of all recumbents, but for me, there's something especially thrilling about a tadpole. Though all tadpoles whip around like human-powered go-carts, the Greenspeed has 16-inch wheels rather than 20-inch ones on most tadpoles. Thus, it has a much tighter turning radius and even more responsive steering. It's also really fun to move along at a good clip that close to the ground.

It's worth noting that if you're older and/or fairly overweight, the Greenspeed can be harder to get in and out of than other tadpoles (again, it's lower to the ground).

Greenspeeds aren't the cheapest tadpoles. Sun now makes fairly inexpensive tadpoles and that entry-level Catrike is a real deal. The new Greenspeed GT1 is more affordable than the GT3, but obviously the higher price brings with it better components and a noticeable difference in performance that I value.

Throughout my 20's and early 30's I was an

avid distance cyclist; indeed, one of the most life-affirming events in my life was touring cross country in 1978. That said, I always had discomfort in my neck, crotch and butt and developed some knee problems. Finally, in my late 30's I started to have back problems that became stenosis and sciatica. I had to quit cycling.

Until I discovered bent rides and the GT3, I thought I'd never ride again. Like many people my age (I'm 54), I have battled my weight. Having a significant gut makes riding traditional bikes that are meant to be quick, not feasible. Since starting to ride my GT3, I've lost 30 lbs and have been able to make good progress on a new routine of sensible eating that suits my body and age better. The machine motivates me greatly. During the summer, I rode nearly every day, ten to thirty miles. I've joined a gym to continue conditioning through the Minnesota winter before I begin bike touring again next year.

-- Curtis Wenzel

Inexpensive recumbent bicycle
EZ-1 SX Recumbent

$899 Sun Bicycles

I recommend the cheap recumbent, EZ-1, designed by the makers of the classy Tour Easy touring recumbent. I ride a BikeE recumbent myself, but they went out of business. My bro has an EZ-1. They're not the lightest, fastest, or coolest recumbent, but they have the ergonomics of a $1500 bike and are a blast to ride. They start at $900. The EZ-1 is a comfortable workhorse that lets you stay in the saddle for a *long* time.

-- Mark Crane

The opposite of intimacy isn't conflict. It's indifference. - Joshua Shenk

Wide, fold-up scooter
Xootr
$250 Amazon

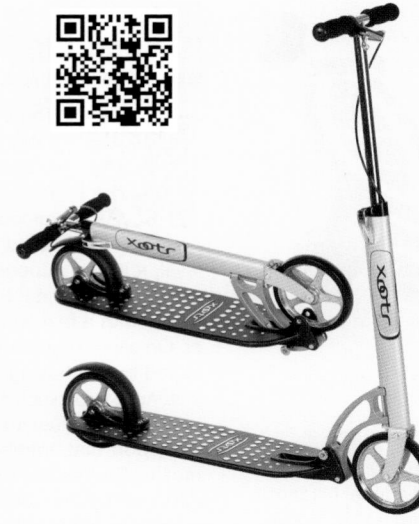

My commute is the typical metro mix: walk to train, take train, walk to work (25 min. of walking; 20 min. of train). There had to be a better way and I found it: the Xootr MG scooter. This is no kids scooter. Made from lightweight magnesium, the scooter weighs a mere 9.9 pounds and folds up small enough to take on public transportation and easily store at home/work. Unlike the Razor, the Xootr sports a big front wheel, which makes it less likely to get stuck on a sidewalk lip and pitch you forward — though you still have to be careful! The wheel is also a hard, smooth, thin black rubber, which tracks in very little dirt (unlike inflatable grooved tires) and loses less energy than skateboards or lesser scooters. I chose the MG model, since its deck is lower and 7.5 inches wide (my feet are size 13). Unlike the previously-reviewed K-2, the Xootr's handlebars are full, two-hand handlebars with agile steering that is the same as a bike. I actually replaced the grips with thicker more absorbent ones from Ergon (I'm a software developer and don't want to screw up my wrists). The Xootr also has a familiar bike-style front brake for when you need to stop in a hurry. You can also push down on the rear fender, but I'm not in the habit of using that method and have read it may wear down the tire more rapidly. The brakes basically don't work in the rain; there's a real loss of friction/stopping power, so I don't recommend riding in those conditions. When it's not raining, though, this scooter makes getting around sans car not a drudgery, but efficient and fun. I've found I can go about 8mph with the Xootr. It's a workout.

-- Jeff Winkler

Superior urban transportation
Kickboard Scooter
$200 Kickboard USA

Since discovering scooters a few years ago, I seldom walk on my weekly trips into San Francisco. I park my truck and grab the scooter out of the back. It's about 3 times as fast as walking, it's good exercise and IT'S FUN! When I go to a popular neighborhood where it's hard to park, I'll park about 8 blocks away and scooter in. No sweat! When I arrive at my destination I fold it up.

These days I ride this beautifully designed high-tech-wheel scooter. The two wheels in front give you a lot more stability. It rides over cracks in the pavement where a one-wheeler would dump you. Like other scooters, you depress the rear wheel guard to brake; unlike other scooters, the deck tilts when you turn. The scooter is hinged ingeniously on the front wheel assembly, where the wheels cant in the direction of the turn. Springs on the front axle pull the scooter back to straight-forward direction after a turn. There's only one wheel in the back because that's all you need. The joy stick (as opposed to handle bars) takes a bit of getting used to; right hand on knob when right foot is forward on the deck, left hand-likewise.

Riding a scooter is a great way to move around in a city, but you have to be careful! People (and cars!) don't expect a human body to be coming along that fast, so you have to be constantly monitoring and alert. Any scooterer's (or cyclist's) nightmare is a parked car's door being opened just as you get there. Oh yes, when you ride long distances you will find that the leg on the deck gets tired (it's holding all your weight), so it pays to get proficient at switching the forward foot every block or so.

-- Lloyd Kahn

Bike + Scooter Hybrid
Footbike
$434 (with shipping) FootbikeUSA

I have used this scooter for three years. I use it to commute to work, about eight miles each way, and it takes about 35 to 45 minutes. It gives an all-around workout much like cross-country skiing. It works the core, glutes, quads, hamstrings, calves, shoulders, and arms. It's different than the Xootr in that it handles and reacts more like a bicycle – and it brakes more safely than a smaller-wheeled scooter, too.

I own the more expensive and higher-end Track model. It is made with aluminum and is lightweight at 14 pounds. I chose it originally because of it's efficiency and performance. They do make a more affordable Express model which is almost a third of the cost but comes with lower-end components.

As far as sizing, it's pretty much a one-size-fits-all type of design. If you're shorter than about 4'8" or taller than 6'2" or 6'3" you can adjust the size somewhat by using a different stem for the handlebars. So they accommodate a pretty wide range.

I carry it in my car just by taking off the front wheel with the quick release. It's a lot lighter than a bike and doesn't have any of the associated grease from a chain, gears, or pedals. Because of this it easily allows for multi-modal transportation: on the days I do drive to work in my car, I park over a mile from my office and take the scooter in from there.

we do it because it's something that's fun and healthy. While racing the marathon distance (26.2 miles), I've averaged 16.3mph, and in a sprint, I've reached 22.6mph.

-- Gary Schmitt

When I go out on the recreational trails, people often want to know what it is and how it works. I have found that it's a great way to meet people! People often call it a "scooterbike" when they first see it.

I recently joined the FootbikeUSA racing team. We are amateur racers and

[For those looking for a more utilitarian version you can find one at Amish Scooters. They are made in the USA by an Amish family and come in three different sizes with a variety of different colors. Prices range between $170-$250.-- OH]

Speedy, local electro-commuting
Go-Ped
$1,195 Amazon

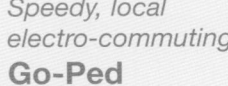

This electric scooter is a fun and practical means of transport for anyone looking for eco-friendly, short-range transport. My 40-minute, 2.5 mile walk to work is now a 15 minute ride. I now get to work without showing up soaked in sweat, like I did riding my bike. And I love avoiding the Seattle public transit system.

The ESR 750 EX has a purported range of 8 miles (12 miles in "econo mode"). With all the hills I have to climb in Seattle, I mostly use it in "turbo mode," which truncates the range, but it's actually a more fun ride that way. Set aside the fact it's taken me up every long, steep hill I've attempted. This thing is a blast to drive. It gives one the sensation of flying.

I looked at plenty of scooters out there. You can get an electric scooter for less, $300-$600 maybe, but not one that will take on Seattle-size hills. For longer range, an electric bike or gas powered scooter may be the way to go. But as I only have to go 2.5 miles to work, I was more interested in something that could also be safely brought into my building, where I don't have to worry about parking and a 'free,' full recharge takes three to four hours. The Go-Ped also breaks down and stows away easily.

You can also buy all sorts of add-ons, including a seat, which I did not get. I prefer to stand and, to me, the seat looks a little goofy. Sure you can spend thousands on fancier models, if that seems worth it to you, but at around $800, this Go-Ped is a good middle ground. Another scooter in this range, the Rad2Go Great White, was a close second in my mind, but it's nearly 100lbs. The Go-Ped is about 60lbs., which seems more practical if I ever have to carry it.

I was concerned that car drivers and pedestrians would view me as an annoyance (I mostly ride on the street, following the same rules as a bike), but that doesn't seem to be the case. I'm trying not to be an obnoxious driver myself and most people seem to regard it with curiosity and amusement, sometimes outright envy.

I should add one thing: these are not 'all-weather vehicles'. The electrical throttle on the handlebar for regulating your speed, is particularly vulnerable to damage from water were you to ride in the rain (I'm considering wrapping it in plastic and trying it anyway). Still, it may be more of a spring-summer option if you live in a wet climate. Regardless, the manual advises against riding in inclement weather, citing concerns of visibility and skidding.

-- Bez Palmer

Superior way to shift bike gears
Rohloff Speedhub
$1,217 Amazon

A German-made 14 speed all-internal gear hub for bikes. Most bike hubs use cogs. In theory you take a bit of an efficiency hit by using gears instead of cogs, but it turns out that most bike's chains are not properly maintained nor in perfect alignment – which lowers their efficiency in practice. Thus the all-internal hub which always has perfect chain alignment and only requires a 1 oz. oil change per year in maintenance ends up being more efficient. You can also shift the full rage of gears while standing still or with pressure on the pedals. You also avoid the usual derailment, fragility, and chainsuck issues of a normal transmission (this is why many professional downhill riders are switching to them). It weighs a bit more than all the components in a traditional bike tranny but gives the bike an overall cleaner look. Also, since normal bike gears overlap their range this hub's 14 speeds is equivalent to 27 or more speeds of the traditional derailleur tranny. I have been riding mine now for a while and would never go back.

-- Alexander Rose

Skateboards

Surfing on hills
Downhill Skateboarding

Downhill skating is like surfing; carving back and forth on long downhills. A note to you guys who skated as kids and have quit: the technology is way advanced these days. Decks, trucks, wheels, designs. It's a different skating world. If you've ever skated, you've got the motor skills (due to "muscle memory"), and

you'll be surprised at how much fun you can have skating downhill with today's boards. Here are three unique skateboards meant for downhill, as opposed to acrobatic street and ramp skating.

-- Lloyd Kahn

Loaded Carving Systems

This is my board of choice, after maybe 20 boards. The decks are made of 1/2 cm strips of vertically laminated bamboo (with the grain running truck to truck), sandwiched between layers of fiberglass. The decks are convex (from end to end) and you can pump to accelerate, gaining speed from the flex of the deck and rebound from the truck bushings and wheels. They produce a graceful and flowing ride. I've got a Dervish model with Orangatang wheels. Check out the film clips on their website.

$328 Dervish complete board w/ wheels Loaded Boards

Carveboard

This is a whole other animal. Surfers love them. They're heavy, have adjustable air pneumatic tires, and the deck tilts off springs so you can carve insanely tight angles. I use one with tires deflated to about 10 lbs. pressure to be able to skate a steep local hill that I can't handle on any other board.

$359 43" Carveboard Carve USA

Landyachtz Evo 2008

From British Columbia, land of heavy-duty mountain bike riders and downhill skaters, come these downhill racing boards. The drop-down decks give you a lower center of gravity and great stability at high speeds. Being closer to the ground makes it easier for skaters to get a padded glove on the ground for sliding (to slow down).

$252 Evo 2008 w/ Gumball wheels Landyyachtz

Skater's pavement paddle
Kahuna Big Stick

$99+ (5' – 6') Kahuna Creations

The Kahuna Big Stick is a lightweight wooden shaft with fixed rubber wheels that allows a skater to push and pull while keeping balanced with both feet as opposed to pumping with one foot. On the level, it is way superior to foot-pumping. Even on uphills, I've found if I do a few foot pumps, then follow with a few paddles, it's faster and smoother. On slight downslopes, I can now get a lot more speed by not having to foot pump. It's got me skating a two-block section in town that used to be too slow. Plus, it adds an upper body workout to a sport that, traditionally, challenges your legs mostly. Surfers see me with it and invariably break into a grin; they instantly get it and are charmed. It really is incredible. The day I got my 5' 6" Big Stick, I tried it out in a parking lot while getting gas. Boy! After about five tentative strokes, I started reaching out as far as I could, zooming around. Later that night I decided to skate in the streets (no cars). I got in a bunch of half-mile downhills in an hour. It is insane fun. One disadvantage: You're carrying this stick rather than free skating down hills.

-- Lloyd Kahn

Skateboard multi-tool
SilverTool

$16 Amazon

Here's a tool I wish existed about 25 years ago. Silver Trucks makes this updated version of the classic skate key, with added functionality, so it works in a complete skateboard build-up and isn't limited (as its predecessor was) to maintenance and adjustments. The SilverTool is a solid, straight, T-shaped tube that feels much better in my hand than other tools I've used and has more features than anything else out there on the market.

Like the old skate key tool that was the standard for years, the SilverTool has openings to adjust the nuts for the wheels, as well as adjusting the nut tensioning on the truck kingpin. What is revolutionary about this tool is that it has a reversible ratchet at one end and a removable Phillips/hex driver. These features allow me to install and adjust the hardware holding the trucks to my deck. (Rush makes a ratcheting skate tool that has a hinged ratchet socket, and a hinged pullout Phillips/hex driver. Rush's tool is smaller than Silver's, but I believe some stability/torque is sacrificed in exchange.)

The SilverTool is also equipped with a medium-grade file for smoothing out the grip-tape edges around the skateboard deck. This is a nice bonus, though it's not quite enough for me to perform a complete setup. I still need to use a separate razor blade or Stanley knife to trim away excess tape.

I hope to purchase, or make, adapters for the ratchet that will allow me to use this tool for basic bicycle maintenance as well. If Silver were to think a little beyond just skateboarding, they could easily manufacture the tool of choice for those who are into both skateboarding and riding bikes.

-- Scott Singer

Customizable, easy-to-ride skateboard
ONDA Core Motion Skateboard

$156 Amazon

I've ridden skateboards for the last 20 years and the ONDA Core has something I've never seen before: two interchangeable bushings on either side of the kingpin. ONDA calls

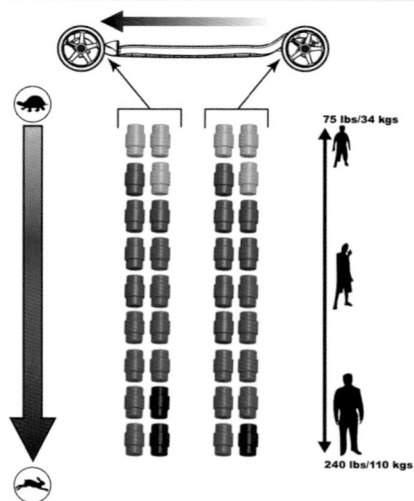

them torsion shocks. Basically, they've rethought how trucks should work and I really like it. They've created a simple way (without any tools necessary) to swap out the "shocks" to 9 different levels of resistance. It's pretty brilliant, as you

can adjust it based on your weight or average speed to be the perfect fit.

The deck is made of plastic, which was what originally kept me from trying it. I'm used to wood decks, but the plastic is more flexible and lasts much longer. It took a few days to get used to it, but now I'm a huge fan.

The wheels are extra large, which definitely gives it a unique look. But they're coming out with a newer model in August which has smaller wheels and a shorter deck. It looks more conventional, but the wheels are still wider and larger than most skateboards.

This board may not be for hardcore skateboard enthusiasts, but it's super easy to ride and a great fit for beginner and intermediate riders. I've owned mine for only 2 months and I'm hooked.

-- Nate H.

Lightest pole
LT4 Trekking Pole

Insanely light trekking pole. The lightness (less than 4 oz) means you can twitch it really fast to catch yourself because the pole doesn't have a lot of inertia to overcome. It means your arm and hand tire far less in a day of swing-and-place. It means when you lash it to your pack, it adds little to your burden.

This pole has proved its durability for me on a range of hikes from casual to intense, on a variety of terrains. Adjusting the length with an untwist and retwist to lock is easy and reliable. Since they're usually sold by the pair, you have a spare in reserve. (Trekking with two poles feels like skiing without snow for me; awkward and hand-encumbering. I like to be a three-legged creature in the bush, always able to brace for stability, striding like a pilgrim with staff.)

-- *Stewart Brand*

$80/pole LT4
Gossamergear.com

$88/pole LT4S (w/ strap)
Gossamergear.com

Comprehensive bank of hiking routes
Traildino

Free The Trail Database / Traildino

Excellent website with useful information on hiking trails all over the world. From it I get an awareness of obscure and out-of-the-way trails globally. It has trails on my secret Greek Island of Karpathos, and in the central Asian neo-countries of Kyrgytzstan and Tadjikistan, where there are presently no trail guidebooks. Even in places with lots of guidebooks (such as the Coltswolds, England) this site has useful first-person notes and suggested routes.

– *KK*

France

France has been quick in developing the modern pilgrim routes to Santiago de Compostela. Four main Ways have been laid out, based on historical relevance. These Ways pass numerous churches and other religious monuments dedicated to the medieval pilgrimage to Santiago, and this alone makes France a splendid pilgrimage destination. Moreover, pilgrims from Europe had to cross the Pyrenees and to have lengthy wanderings through France if they wanted to visit the holy grave of St. Jacob.

Via Turonensis

Let's start with these four main Ways. The westernmost is the Via Turonensis, leaving from Paris, passing Tours ending in Ostabat in the Pyrenees. In modern France this is the GR655. In Spain, this Way continues as Camino Francés. Below are the main and side itineraries:

•GR655, Saint-Quentin - Paris (- Ostabat), 234 to Paris, 9 days

•GR22, Sentier du Mont Saint-Micheal, Paris - Mont Saint-Michel, 250 km, 10 days

•Via Turonensis, Paris tour Saint-Jacques-de-la-Boucherie - Tours - Ostabat, 593 km, 24 days

•GR12, Amsterdam - Paris, 977 km, 40 day

•Via Gallia Belgica, Hélécine - Nivelles - Saint-Quentin, 223 km, 9 days

•Voie des Plantagenêts, Mont-Saint-Michel - Aulnay, 203 km, 8 days

Four legs
Hiking Poles

$10 Poles for Hiking, Trekking & Walking, 2006, DVD, 73 minutes Amazon

Leki Nordic Walking Traveller Poles Amazon

Leki Trail Enzian Poles Amazon

Serious long-distance thru hikers along the Appalachian and Pacific Coast trails use them. Hip continental trekkers use them. Fanatic "nordic walkers" use them. I use them. Hiking poles give you two more legs. They allow you to use your arms to significantly push yourself uphill, and to relieve your legs on killer descents downhill. Two poles add much needed stability on inclined terrain. Instead of being a precarious biped, ready to tumble or slip, you turn into a graceful four-legged gazelle able to hop over the roughest sections. Using poles has eliminated twisted ankles and rubber knees for me. I've reclaimed trails that I had given up as too gravelly, steep, slippery, and treacherous. Now I scuttle along, poles extended, adding arm power to my legs. With added confidence I can scramble up and down much faster, and much safer. All these benefits are multiplied when you add the weight and higher center of gravity of a backpack.

A good set of poles weigh about one pound, cost about $100, and will telescope closed to fit in a backpack or trunk. Leki makes ones popular with hikers. I found that a tiny bit of instruction in how to use them helped me get going. This instructional DVD did the trick.

– *KK*

Plant Push

Setting the poles behind your feet you push, not pull, to ease ascents uphill.

15 Degree Positive Angle Grip

An angled grip is more comfortable.

Motherlode for all outdoor gear
Cabela's

Free Catalog Cabela's

Cabela's started out as a premier mail-order source for hunting gear. It is still known for that, but its coverage has expanded far beyond hunting, far beyond camping, to include anything remotely connected to the outdoors. Its pages overflow with boating tools, trailer hitches, smokers, meat processing equipment, kayaking stuff, binoculars, remote cameras, tent gadgets, pet gear, RV supplies, and so on. The range of tools sold is staggering. It is a catalog of outdoor aspirations. In general the stuff they sell works as advertised, so one can use them as a pretty good guide to what's useful.

Candid customer reviews of purchased items makes shopping at the Cabela's website almost as good as Amazon's. But you really should get your hands on their 500-page master paper catalog. No one is as keen on web shopping as I am, but the Cabela's master catalog is prime evidence that sometimes a big fat paper book is better. You cannot grasp the totality of what Cabela's has to offer on its website, nor can you zip through it in browse mode as you can while flipping through its 500 crammed pages. It would take days to do the same on the web, and you'd still miss stuff.

A big fat paper catalog can be a big environmental waste mailed out each season. Cabela's has engineered an interesting experiment wherein they display scans of the catalog pages with embedded links to the online item. You get the browsability of the paper catalog and the convenience of web ordering. What you don't get is speed. This method is currently too slow to be enjoyable, but it is a handy option. I still take the paper version.

-- *KK*

Best Intro to Ultralight
Ultralight Backpackin' Tips
$10 Mike Clelland, 2011, 144 p.

This is the best introduction to ultralight backpacking there is. Ultralight means you carry less than 25 pounds of gear, food and water for a 10 day trip, and maybe less than 5 pounds for a weekend trip! That's liberating. If you obsessively reduce the mass of things (or leave them behind) by onefold then you can raise your enjoyment of hiking tenfold.

But most of the stuff in a backpack is carried to overcome a lack of knowledge. So whenever you take away weight you have to replace it with knowledge — knowledge that this book supplies.

This book assumes you are persuaded of this zen-like way. If you need to be persuaded that carry-weight is worth obsessing over, or you want the full course of every option available, and the evidence and reasons for each method, and how to make all the stuff yourself, then you'll need Ray Jardines' bible on the subject, *Trail Life*, on page 298.

But instead of a bible, this fantastic book by Mike Clelland will give you cartoons. Lot's of them.

It's jammed packed with dense, informative, easy to digest, and remarkably helpful advice, hints and instructions on how to accomplish and enjoy walking with very little stuff — and this knowledge is mostly compressed into witty cartoons. I am a big fan of Clelland's other cartoon guides to basic backpacking (below) and to snow travel (recommended on p. 303) and I really like how amazingly effective his drawings are. Each one is worth thousands of words. It's fun but not silly. Clelland grapples with the real-world details of, say, not taking a water filter or toilet paper (!!!) and his solutions are born of many seasons of experience. The whole book is authentic and reliable. It will very quickly have you out on the trail carrying a lot less than you once did. Even if you don't get as extreme as he does, you can move in the right direction by substituting knowledge for stuff. I've been going super light for a long time and I learned tons of new tricks on almost every page.

-- KK

Backpacking bootcamp
Allen & Mike's Really Cool Backpackin' Book
$11 Allen O'Bannon & Mike Clelland, 2001, 161 p.

Spot-on cartoons make this crash course in backpacking incredibly effective. No matter how much you think you know about trail living, you probably can't teach it as well as these guys do. The humor is geeky, the advice is excellent, the presentation unforgettable. It is simply the best introduction to the art of living off your back. This is the book you want to hand to the friend, sibling, significant other who has never been backpacking, but is ready to try. If it doesn't click with them, they probably shouldn't be on the trail with you.

-- KK

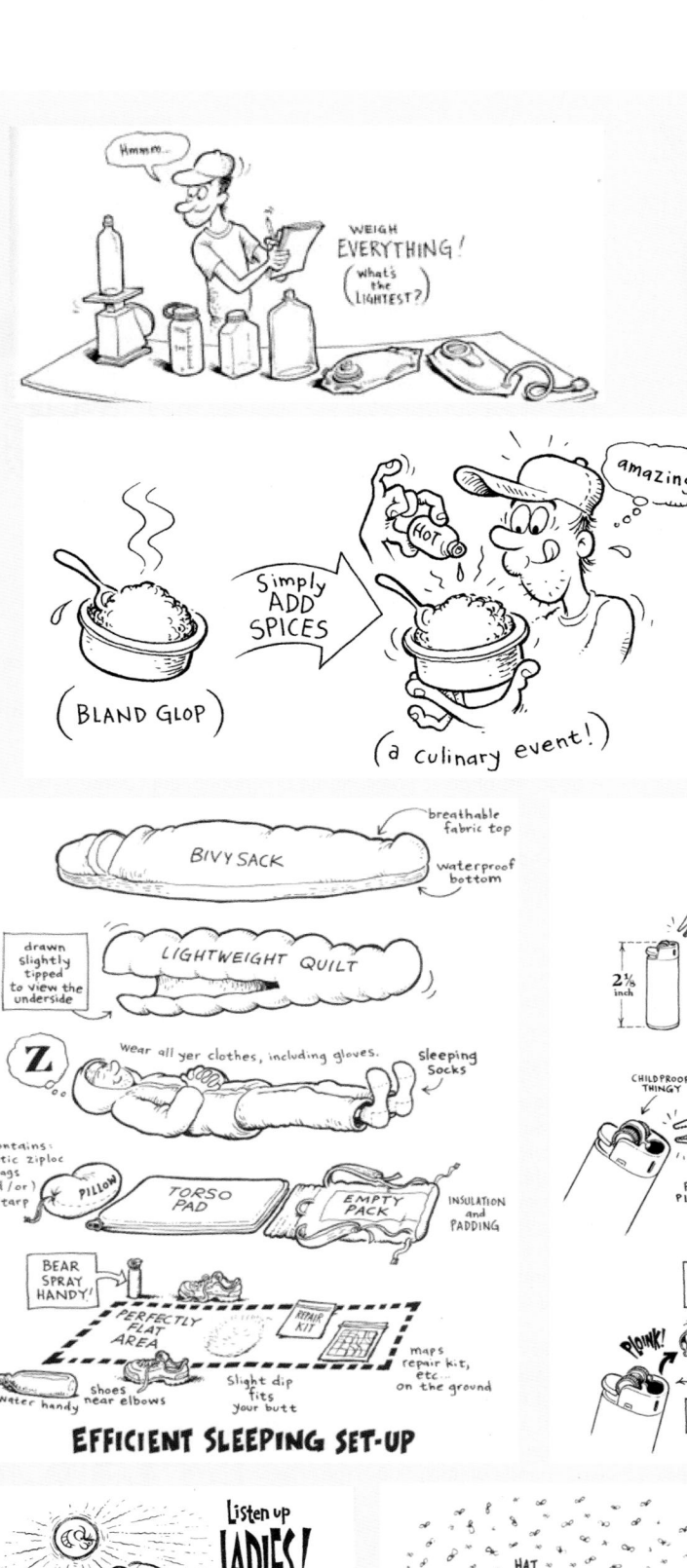

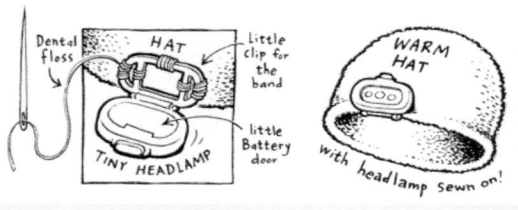

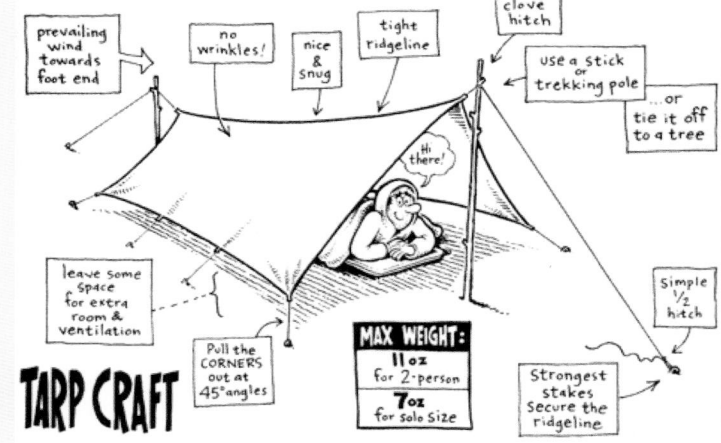

The ultimate ultralight backpack -- only 16 oz.
G4 Pack
$125 Gossamer Gear

My girlfriend Gwen got one of the super-ultra-light G4 packs by GVP (as used by 'Flyin' Brian' in his triple crown hike).

It is truly an ingenious pack. It takes all the lessons of the Go-Lite Breeze and goes a step further. It is a 4000+ cu pack that looks like 3000cu pack and has a waist belt (which many of the ultralights don't have) and still comes in at 16oz.

The most ingenious part of it is that it uses a Z-Rest sleeping pad as the "frame". This feature is shared with the Go-Lite Breeze but the G4 allows you to load it from the outside of the bag so you don't have to unload everything out of the way.

The other key advantage is its configurability. The straps are set up to allow you to add only the bare minimum of foam (or unused clothing) needed for your body type. And you have the option of ordering it made to your specs with various loops, dividers and pockets according to your preference.

The real proof of it being a great pack however is that even with the pack loaded down with camping and climbing gear Gwen, weighing in at 120lb, said it was the most comfortable she had ever worn. (She was a bit skeptical of the whole thing at first and thought it was too light to work at all.)

-- Alexander Rose

No sweat, nice comfort
Air-Cooled Day Packs
$79 Amazon

I have become enamored of new European packs which allow for complete back ventilation. I picked up one by Deuter in Amsterdam last fall and it has become my favorite day and cycling pack. Since I sweat a lot, I generally try and avoid wearing packs while exercising, but this pack has eliminated this problem. The new packs are suspended off your back with a nylon mesh fabric. This web also makes the pack the most comfortable I have ever worn, as weight distributes itself across your back, and the trampoline effect of the mesh absorbs the shock loads you usually get from packs while exercising.

I have found three companies that make them (interestingly all German). I am using one by Deuter called the AC Lite 15. A professional cyclist friend uses one of the small Vaude packs like this and swears by it as well. They all seem to have good allowances for hydration systems, and some have integrated rain covers and helmet holders. The down side is that because of the frame it is not the lightest pack you can get for its size, but even for an ultra-light weenie like me the trade off has been worth it. They are somewhat difficult to find in the US, but I have seen them for sale in some mountaineering and cycling shops. You can get catalogs from the websites and do mail order as well. Each company that makes them also makes traditional suspension pack systems, so inspect the catalogs carefully for the buzzwords like Air Comfort and AeroFlex suspension.

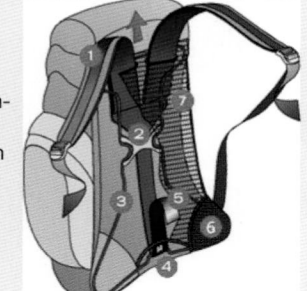

-- Alexander Rose

Heavy-duty waterproof bags
Ortlieb Dry Bags

The German company Ortlieb produce a range of waterproof items. These are excellent for use while trekking, motorcycling, bicycling, caving, canoeing, etc. I usually put clothing and sleeping bags in Ortlieb dry bags inside my rucksack. I am guaranteed that stuff will keep dry, and it makes it easier to organize the backpack.

I also have a larger Ortlieb bag which I use when I go on motorcycling trips. Useful stuff, and excellent quality/durability. They produce a range of items.

-- Helge A. Gudmundsen

$18+ (PD-350 Dry Bags) Ortlieb

$150 (Packman Pro 2) Ortlieb

Portable shade
Chrome Dome Trekking Umbrella
$20 golite.com

While this umbrella will keep you dry, the main thing it dispenses is portable shade. Unless you are deep in the woods, on most trails you blast along day after day under the sun, particularly high and desert places. You end up marching from shady patch to shady patch. What you really want, the serious trekkers realized, is to carry your own shade. This umbrella does that better than any other for a couple of reasons. It is very opaque; many lightweight and light-colored parasols actually let a lot of light through. Black umbrellas block more light, but turn it into heat which radiates downward. Either way your brain basically cooks. The Chrome Dome, on the other hand, is silvery light reflective on top, thus opaque, and non-reflective black underneath, so no light passes and you get to enjoy a deep cool shade. On some trails in the summer you'll be an object of envy from other hikers as you carry around what they are looking for. It's light, only 8.5 ounces, which is important since you hold it up a lot. It has a short shaft, which is easy to brace on your backpack, handsfree. High wind is an issue. But the great luxury of the Chrome Dome is that you can hike without a hat. Your hatless head is more free to sweat, catch the breeze, and without a hat I feel my head is more out in the world.

-- Stewart Brand

Best pannier-backpack
Arkel Bug
$170 Arkel

I have a car but prefer to get around the city by bike as much as possible. I own a pair of Arkel's grocery bag-style panniers — higher-end versions of the previously reviewed Grocery Bag Panniers — which are great for shopping and commuting by bike, but I found myself wanting the carrying convenience of a backpack, so my hands would be free when I was off my bike. Arkel's Bug was the best I found in this category.

I love this bag primarily because converting it to a very comfortable, functional backpack is as simple as pulling the shoulder straps from underneath a pair of Velcro flaps once I've removed the bag from my bike's rear rack. The padding in the straps is good, and I have to remember to move a metal hook, so it doesn't stick me in the back, but that's easy. Carrying capacity is a little smaller than that of the grocery bag panniers, though still sufficient for my needs. Two small mesh pockets along with an easy-access zippered pocket on the Bug's exterior make stowing and retrieving my water bottle and other frequent-use items a breeze.

-- Colin Bogart

Ultralight, waterproof, compression sacks
Sea to Summit eVent Compression Sacks
$19-$45 XS (6 L), S (10 L), M (15 L), L (20 L) XL (30 L) Amazon

I've used these Sea to Summit eVent compression sacks the last few times I've travelled abroad or while backpacking, and found them to be an essential travelling companion. Their main function is to keep stuff dry while also compressing and organizing the contents of my pack. The Sea to Summit sacks are unique in their use of eVent fabric (a semi-permeable membrane) which allows for greater compression and the formation of a vacuum like seal.

Before compressing the sack with the supplied compression straps, the Sea to Summit bag's roll-top is sealed. Then, by pulling the straps taut, air is driven out of the one-way breathable eVent membrane that lines the bottom of the bag. As air is pushed out something akin to a weak vacuum is formed (eVent is impermeable to water and semi-permeable to air). I found that even after loosening the straps the contents remain compressed (it will eventually equalize as air seeps back in, but very slowly). This dramatically reduces the amount of space soft compressible items like socks, clothes, sleeping bags, etc. take up.

I currently own two, in small (10 L) and large (20 L), and have been blown away at how much I've been able to compress into my pack. They are super light (4.5 oz and 5.9 oz, respectively), and as tough as any other compression sack I've tried. While travelling in Bangladesh they kept my moisture sensitive camera gear dry even during downpours, and all my tests at home found them to be 100% waterproof (just be sure to not compress anything with sharp edges). While they are more expensive than traditional dry sacks, the superior compression and vacuum-like seal really make it worthwhile when trying to minimize pack space while maximizing protection.

-- Oliver Hulland

Ultralight Hiking

Super ultra-lightweight camping
Trail Life
$26 Ray Jardine, 2009, 399 p.

The joy of hiking is inversely proportional to the weight of your pack. Carry nothing and your pleasure is unbounded. No one has articulated the benefits and the know-how of carrying little as Ray Jardine. He can show you how to liberate yourself from your tent, water-filter, stove, and most of the rest of your gear. He also has the best tricks for completing long through-hikes. The best times I've ever had in my decades of trekking have been when I was carrying little more than what I was wearing, and hiking the way Jardine preaches.

-- KK

●

Compare one of my packs – weighing 13 ounces and costing $10.40 to make – to a store-bought backpack weighing 7 pounds and costing $275.00. My pack is 12% of the weight and 4% of the cost.

I should point out, too, that the majority of nights we hikers spend in the backcountry are mild. We are not automatically going to encounter the ultimate storm the minute we step out the back door with lighter-weight gear. But should it happen, a properly pitched tarp will handle it. Pitching a tarp is not difficult, but the method differs from that of pitching a tent. The best way to make the transition from tent to tarp is to carry both on a few short outings. Pitch the tarp and sleep under it, and keep the tent packed in its stowbag and close at hand, just in case.

The reaction of these backpackers was typical of the many we met that summer. On paper, our lighter-weight methods may seem "radical" and idealistic. But when these people saw how easily we were doubling and sometimes even tripling their daily mileages, they tended to become less skeptical. The irony was that we were exerting ourselves no more than the backpackers. We were using our energy mainly for forward progress, rather than for load hauling. I see mileage as an effect rather than a cause. Not something to be struggled for, but merely a by-product of a more efficient style. My main focus is on the natural world, my place in it, and how that relates to the joys and the lessons learned along the way. I also find that when we reduce our barriers — our detachment — from the natural world, we stand to better our wilderness connection.

According to conventional backpacking wisdom, giardia contaminates all wilderness water, and we hikers and campers need to purify every drop that we drink; as well as what we use for cooking and brushing teeth. You can read this in hundreds of magazine articles and books. Jenny and I followed this rule faithfully during our first four mega-hikes. And I was sick with giardia-type symptoms many times.

Obviously, something was wrong. If we were being meticulous about filtering our water, then why was I not staying healthy? Jenny remained healthy, and she was drinking the same treated waster as I. Apparently my immunities were lower than hers. But the fact remains that somehow I seemed to be contracting parasites despite the assiduous use of the water filter. The filter cartridges we were using were common, brand-name varieties, and we had no reason to suspect they were not working properly.

Clearly, the conventional wisdom was not working. So we abandoned it and tried a different approach. While training for our fifth thru-hike we drank directly from clean, natural sources, a few sips at first, then gradually increasing in quantity over the weeks and months. In this way we helped condition our bodies to the water's natural flora. Then during the actual journey we drank all our water straight from the springs, creeks and sometimes the lakes - after carefully appraising each source. And for the first time in years I remained symptom-free; and Jenny stayed healthy also -- I doubt whether my illness had anything to do with the filtration or lack thereof. Rather, it had to do with the nature of the water sources we were using. During the initial journeys we were collecting from all but the worst sources, and treating it. In several cases that I can think of, I feel that this treatment -- or any other available treatment -- was incapable of making that water safe to drink. This is why, on that fifth trek, we collected water only from clean sources. Based on these experiments and their successful outcome, the following are my recommendations: Learn to recognize pristine water, and treat it if you prefer. Learn to recognize water that could be microbially contaminated, if only mildly, and treat it thoroughly. And most importantly, learn to recognize water that is beyond treatment, despite any reasonable degree of clarity. Such water can be extremely virulent, and no water treatment system available to hikers is capable of making that water safe to drink. Do not filter, boil or add purification chemicals to this polluted water. Do not use it for cooking or bathing. In the next section we will learn how to recognize such highly contaminated water.

●

Stealth camping. If you can manage to camp away from the water sources, and from the established campsites, then the many wonderful advantages of stealth camping will be yours. Stealth camping is a cleaner, warmer and quieter way to camp, and it offers a much better connection with nature. In all likelihood no one has camped at your impromptu stealth-site before, and the ground will be pristine. Its thick, natural cushioning of the forest materials will still be in place,

making for comfortable bedding without the use of a heavy inflatable mattress. There will be no desiccated stock manure to rise as dust and infiltrate your lungs, nor any scatter of unsightly litter and stench of human waste. The stealth-site will not be trampled and dished; any rainwater will soak into the ground or run off it, rather than collect and flood your shelter. Bears scrounging for human food will be busy at the water-side campsites, and will almost invariably ignore the far-removed and unproductive woods. Far from the water sources you will encounter fewer flying insects, particularly upon the more breezy slopes and ridges. Above the katabatic zones the night air will be markedly warmer. And you can rest assured that your chances of being bothered by other people will be slim.

◀ We pitch the tarp sideways to any wind, and if the wind is stong we pitch the tarp lower and secure the windward edge flush to the ground. A properly pitched tarp is stronger than most tents.

The drift box. On our longer hikes, Jenny and I often use what we refer to as a "drift box", or "running resupply box". This is a small parcel that we send ahead rather than home. It contains items that will probably be needed later, but not presently. These might include spare shoes and fresh insoles, extra socks, a spare water filter cartridge, an extra camera battery, a small whetstone, a utility knife with disposable blades, a tube of seam-sealing compound, a spare spoon, an extra sweater, and a roll of boxing tape. The drift box gives us occasional access to these items without having to carry them. We send it First Class to a station approximately two weeks ahead.

Our 8.5 lb. backpacks at the end of a 2,700-mile hike, 1994.

The 8 1/2 pound packs at the completion of a 2,700 mile journey, 1994.

●

Most large backpacks on the market weigh from five to seven pounds, and more. Yet the pack adds nothing to the journey, other than acting as the container for the equipment, clothing and food. To me, it makes no sense that the container should be the heaviest article of gear.

●

This is because the gear needed for camping one night in the wilds is about what is needed for camping a hundred nights. The same holds true for the clothing, rainwear, and so forth. The only real variation is the supply of food.

●

Where to ford

As a general rule, if the river is swift and knee deep or deeper, we do not attempt a wade. Rather, we scout the bank for a natural bridge. We have hiked as much as five miles along a creek in search of a safe crossing.

●

If we find a place that appears safe to wade, but where whitewater lurks immediately downstream, we do not risk it. One slip, and the current could sweep a person quickly into the rapids.

●

Also, if the creek is swift and its bed is solid rock, as with many places in the High Sierra, we look elsewhere. In all likelihood that riverbed has been polished by grit and coated with a translucent layer of algae that can be unimaginably slippery.

●

Another technique that can help extend the miles is to use waypoints as springboards. Shelters, creek crossings, lakes, and trail junctions can serve to urge us several more miles. But the temptation might be to say to ourselves, "four more miles to Green Lake Shelter; I think we will stop there for the night." This is letting the waypoint dictate progress. Instead, we could say to ourselves: "once we reach the Green Lake Shelter, we will continue for one more hour before making camp." The idea is to use the waypoints as incentives, rather than as destinations.

Nancy Feagin and Mark Twight preparing for a bad night on a bad (small) ledge. Mont Blanc Massif, France.

Going light by going fast
Extreme Alpinism
$19 Mark F. Twight, 2001, 238 p.

I'm struck by any book on a dangerous subject that looks as though it escaped the inspection of lawyers. Extreme Alpinism (with the exception of the title) is the best book I have read on any outdoor subject. It's devoted largely to author Twight's theory and practice of alpinism — his drastic gear weight reduction methods go far beyond simple ultralight camping. Twight has combined new ways of using clothing, equipment, nutrition, and training to survive impossible situations and achieve incredible feats. The sections on Twight's own failures are a rarity and probably the best part. While I'm not an alpinist myself, this book has been inspirational in all my outdoor activities.

-- Alexander Rose

●

Extreme alpinism can mean different things to different climbers. In this book, we define it simply as alpine climbing near one's limits. We use "extreme" to denote severe, intense, and having serious consequences. To survive in the dangerous environment where ability and difficulty intersect, the climber must visualize the goal and the means to realize it. After training and preparation, the climber tackles the route, moving as swiftly as possible with the least equipment required. For a fully trained and prepared athlete at the top of his or her game, only the hardest routes in the world offer sufficient challenges to qualify as extreme.

●

We look upon both the preparation for climbing and climbing itself as a process of self-transformation, of character building. Character means more than strength or skill. We will belabor this notion because it is the core truth at the heart of hard climbing. Extreme alpinism is a matter of will. We all know this to be true. In every endeavor, people who concentrate and refuse to quit become the elite.

An alpinist needs to acquire facility in rock climbing, ice climbing, weather forecasting, snow safety, approach methods, retreat techniques, bivouacking, energy efficiency, nutrition, strategy and tactics, equipment use, winter survival, navigation, and so forth. The more you know, the safer and more efficient you will be in the mountains.

In a dangerous environment, speed is safety. Climbing routes at the edge of the possible is akin to playing Russian roulette. Each time the cylinder spins, the chance of firing a live cartridge increases. Therefore, "Keep moving" is the mantra of the extreme climber. The idea of speed permeates this book.

●

It's impossible to stay fully hydrated while actually climbing, so rehydrating at the end of the day or during breaks between hard effort is essential. Because of the climbing, your body will be dehydrated, your stomach and your entire system will be highly acidic, your muscles will be holding onto metabolic waste, and your glycogen reserves will be gone. First and foremost, you must drink. Plain water is fine. Once you are a quart ahead, start adding your recovery foods and supplements. Avoid acidic food and drink. Your body already is in an acid state, so look for foods that buffer it. Acidic foods also are more difficult to absorb. Citrus juices, for example, are acidic and the high sugar content will impede gastric emptying.

●

Light and fast as a style results in the ultimate autonomy and self-determination — but any time you decide to pare food, fuel, and gear down to a marginal level, you accept great risk and must therefore accept great responsibility. If your style is too light, or you drop a crucial piece of gear, or the weather turns bad, you must retreat. Or if you are too high on the mountain, then you have to fail upward as quickly as possible. You must keep moving at all costs. Movement is your only safe haven.

●

On the other hand, there may be no way in hell to do the route without sleeping on it. If that's the case, live with the minimum. Do not pursue comfort. Aim for success only. On a one-bivy route, don't plan on a good night's sleep. Never take a cup and a bowl. The water bottle and the pan for the stove will do. Each climber may carry a spoon — that's it. Forget your manners. Forget the Ten Essentials. No matter how long the intended route, carry only the genuinely essential.

To be interesting, be interested. - Kevin Kelly

How to live well on foot
Complete Walker IV
$17 Colin Fletcher & Chip Rawlins, 2002, 864 p.

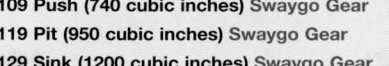
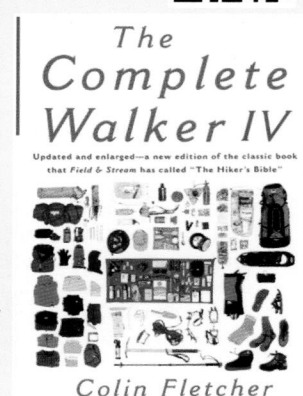

Colin Fletcher is back (at 80 years old!) with a brand new fourth edition of his landmark 1968 book. It was last updated in 1984 — the Iron Age in terms of technological gear. A lot has changed, but the pleasures of walking haven't. While Ray Jardine (previous page) stresses efficiency and accomplishment, Fletcher and co-author Rawlins toast comfort and enjoyment. Like all past editions, *The Complete Walker IV* is astoundingly informative and insanely complete (843 pages, including 62 marvelous ones on the varieties of backpacks). These grey beards not only tell you about gear, they give you its history, and the history of its makers, and the current skinny on their prospects. You feel educated. They consider everything and anything remotely portable, and tell you what else a tool might be used for, where it comes from, and whether it could be improved or left behind. They get you to think about everything too. It's wonderful to read, sly and humorous as the first edition. We don't often associate civilization with backpacking, but that's what Fletcher is trying to do. He's offering wisdom on how to live on the trail, with the emphasis on live.

-- KK

• Yes, Unbearable Lightness offers huge advantages, but it's easy to gloss over uncomfortable facts. Although the lighter load helps--helps a ton--that's not the whole truth, so help me God. Backpacking isn't all traveling. It's also sleeping and loitering and eating, for

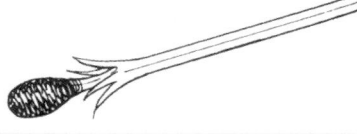

example. So backpacking pleasure is also comfortable sleep, cozy warmth at all times, and perhaps a few heavy luxuries--short of the complete works of Sir Arthur Conan Doyle -- not to mention a full belly. I note that many light-gear enthusiasts seem to skimp on the food. Yet there's general, though not total, agreement that to stay healthy and fully active the average person needs a daily ration of around 2 lbs. of dehydrated food, and some stories of ultra-Spartan rations frankly sound harder to swallow than the food.

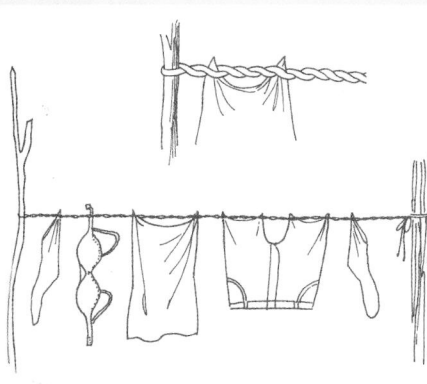

In civilized temperatures I generally try to wash most of my clothes at least once a week…This works out well because I find and I think most people find that about once a week you need a day's more or less complete rest from walking. (In really cold weather you simply don t do any washing of clothes or of yourself, which means that when you get back to civilization that first hot shower is not only sheer heaven but highly necessary).

Rugged waterproof caving pack
Swaygo Caving Pack
$109 Push (740 cubic inches) Swaygo Gear
$119 Pit (950 cubic inches) Swaygo Gear
$129 Sink (1200 cubic inches) Swaygo Gear

Caving introduced me to a fascinating array of tools including one of my favorite possessions; the incredibly durable waterproof roll-top caving pack from Swaygo.

On any trip underground you're almost guaranteed to ruin one piece of gear or clothing. It's a tough environment, and as such it requires unusually tough gear. The Swaygo is one of the toughest tools I own. The minimalist roll-top bag is made entirely out of polyurethane impregnated and coated nylon, that is tough as nails (and closer to a car tire than anything else I can think of). It has RF welded seams, and the roll-top is locked by a carabiner (unlike a previous bag I used that had plastic clips that failed mid-trip). The roll-top combined with the impregnated nylon makes the bag waterproof, and the toughness of the skin means that even in scrapes and falls the gear inside is kept safe and sound.

Unlike other roll-top bags, the Swaygo is designed with durability, flexibility and tight squeezes in mind. The shoulder straps are made out of webbing, and connect to the bag via three carabiners. The carabiners provide additional utility in that when you are crawling or climbing and need to drag the bag behind you, the top carabiner can be looped and clipped to your leg; when pulled this shortens the shoulder straps, drawing the webbing through a grommet creating a single long leash that minimizes snags during tight crawls.

While not designed for comfort, the bag itself feels great while caving. It's designed to be worn with the rolltop on the bottom, minimizing the bulk at the top of the pack when crawling or duck-walking thereby further reducing snagging while also keeping most of the weight at the bottom of the pack.

Swaygo packs come in three sizes. I own the Push (740 cubic inches) which was perfect for my needs (it swallowed my pocket camera, three extra sources of light, a Nalgene water bottle, granola bars, and extra wool underwear). But for those who need something larger on longer trips, they also make the Pit (950 cubic inches) and the massive Sink (1,200 cubic inches) for $10 and $20 more, respectively.

After a recent caving trip I learned of a cave rescue in Tennessee that was made possible, in part, by four Swaygo packs. By inflating the packs with air and lashing them to the injured caver, the cave-rescue team was able to float the patient out of the cave using their packs as pontoons. I mention this only because in a tough situation I know I can depend on a bag as well-designed and built as the Swaygo. It's built by a caver, for cavers, and as such it has the refined utility that, for me at least, is the definition of a cool tool.

-- Oliver Hulland

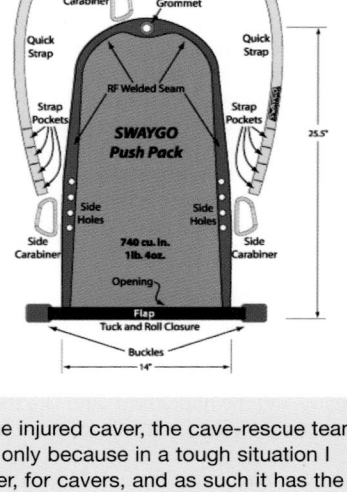

Packable camp shoes
Sanuk Vagabond
$43+ Amazon

These are the perfect camp shoes while backpacking. They are awesomely light and they flatten into almost nothing; you stick them in the side pockets of your bag. They are a total luxury comfort but also a breakthrough product for me because I'm really glad to stop and take my boots off to dry my socks and prevent blisters. With these on the trail I don't have to cripple around barefoot.

-- Stewart Brand

The greatest Army invention
P-38 Can Opener
$2 Amazon

I have carried a P-38 since I first encountered one about 40 years ago in my introduction to US Army combat rations during Basic Training at Fort Jackson in South Carolina. Each case of combat rations had a dozen or so P-38s or more officially "OPENER, CAN, HAND, FOLDING, TYPE I". The older P-38s were made of steel and the later ones of aluminum. In either case the P-38 folds flat and attaches easily to a key ring. In addition to opening a can, I personally have used it many times over the years as a screwdriver, lever, and knife.
-- Steven Cochran

The classic GI Can Opener is an excellent tool. Small enough for a key ring, or worn on a lanyard around the neck, it has been of assistance in repairing a fuel pump, tightening screws, and yes, opening cans. All for ~99 cents. It is sold at many locations online, as well as most Army/Navy stores. In years past I have given them as gifts. Invariably I have heard similar stories from friends, of truing pins on cell phones, adjusting fishing gear, stripping wire, etc.

-- Christian Chambers

Keeps your mitts warm
Dachstein Boiled Wool Mittens
$40 bradleyalpinist.com

I bought these mittens years ago, and have returned to them again and again. The boiled wool is so dense and thick that they are waterproof in practice. They are extremely warm and do not become damp inside. And they are bombproof, much more durable than typical nylon/gore-tex mittens. They are also cheap.

The only downside is the bare wool can be slippery. I have seen people spread a little silicone caulk over the palm to improve the grip. Maybe spray Plasti Dip would work, too.

-- Karl C.

Lightweight Tents

Ultra-lightweight tent
Nemo Obi Elite 1P
$314 Amazon

This is a fantastic featherweight self-supporting one-person tent. It is among the lightest tents you can buy. Together with its fly and tent stakes (but minus its compression stuff sack), the Obi Elite 1P weighs only 2 pounds (0.91kg)! Having an ultra-lightweight tent makes a huge difference when you're on a long hike or bike trip. There are lighter tents that re-use hiking poles for support, or don't have an outer fly cover, but none that are self-supporting and double-walled like this one. (A double wall really minimizes moisture buildup.) The Obi gives me enough room to sit up inside, so I can change clothes and store some gear and be covered by a fly and withstand a good rain and wind.

I used this everyday for a month on a recent trip. I would giggle each time I set it up because it practically assembled itself. I could set up the tent and fly in less than 3 minutes, and pack it up even faster. The technology of all the best lightweight tents is primarily made by one Korean company which manufactures the precision poles, elastic, hubs, and very clever fasteners called Jake's Feet which make it so easy to erect and strike. A great tent these days is a precision collapsable machine. Nemo has arranged these parts into a super design. Every detail is well-thought out, from the placement of zippers, interior pockets, color coding of poles. I can not think of much to improve. For instance it has a large side entrance making entry and exit a breeze, whereas many other lightweight solo tents have a narrow end entrance.

The Nemo Obi Elite 1P is expensive; you can get great one-person tents only a few pounds heavier for hundreds of dollars cheaper, such as the previously reviewed Sierra Designs tent. But over decades of hiking I have discovered a direct inverse correlation between the amount weight I carry and my happiness. And like the best tools, it gives me pleasure each time I use it, and with care will last a long time.

Nemo makes a regular, non-Elite 1P version with slightly heavier hi-tech fabric (total weight 2.7 pounds) and a slightly better pole arrangement that is $50 cheaper. I have used this one with satisfaction. In fact, if you can spare the few extra ounces, the Obi 1P is for sale at substantial discount from Amazon, and is the one I would recommend.

-- KK

Featherweight solo shelter
Sierra Designs 1-Person Tent
$130 Amazon

Two ultra-light poles + rain-fly + nylon case + tent = Less than 4 pounds and slightly larger than a shoebox when packed up. Unpacked, it isn't spacious (about 20 sq. ft.), but there's more than enough room to stash a pack in the event of a downpour or to use as a headboard while reading (try that in a bivy sack!).

Backpackers will appreciate the quick, intuitive set up: Clip the poles to eight hooks, insert the four pole ends into grommets at the base, and drive five stakes (the fifth creates the door). If you need the rain guard, the tent shape — unlike a dome — makes it obvious to surmise what goes where. Throw it on, fasten a couple Velcro straps to marry the fly to the poles, and be sure the stakes go through the holes at the base of the fly. Drive a sixth stake for the "entryway". All of this takes maybe three minutes. The learning curve is rapid.

I spent two months in the tropics crashing in this tent. Even on a sandy beach, a heavy rock or two maintained the tension needed to retain the door's shape. The tent also held its own in a number of windy rainstorms, and I've since used it for wintertime jaunts into the coastal hills of Northern California. Not exactly the High Sierras, but there can be morning frost. To this day: no tears, no leaks, no busted seams. Since I purchased mine in 2000, Sierra Designs has added a more resistant silicone coat to the rain-fly and knocked off a few ounces by switching to even lighter poles.

-- Steven Leckart

Light, quick cool shelter
Hennessy Tent Hammock
$100 Hennessy Hammock

An ultralight gear item which I've been trying out is the Hennessey Tent Hammock. Part tent, part mosquito mesh, part hammock, the thing is pure genius and a pleasure to use — very light, ingeniously designed, and actually provides a comfortable backcountry sleep. Perfect for wet areas. You do have to worry a bit more about insulation under yourself, but not a big minus especially given the comfort of the shelter.

-- Rex Ishibashi

Hennessy Hammock is a brilliant fine-tuning of the hammock concept into a tent substitute. It means I never have to sleep on the ground again! Being asymmetrical it allows me to lie relatively flat for a very comfortable night's sleep. There is a large rain-fly that cocoons around the hammock in cooler weather, a fine insect/dust mesh enclosure, and an entrance that my weight closes behind me. You can even set it up on the ground like a bivvy-bag if there are no trees (or lamp posts, or bumper bars). Great for tropical camping.

-- Toby Gibson

Heavy-duty makeshift shelter
Tundra Tarps
$85 Cooke Custom Sewing

Camping beside a windblown lake or a tundra riverbank, where the wind never really stops, is hard on tarps: grommets blow out, seams pop, and there never seems to be enough spots on the tarp to attach a line. Tundra Tarps are terrifically versatile, stout tarps. Instead of grommets the tarp is ringed with 3/4" nylon ribbon with loops sewn in every two feet on the outer edge and interior seams. The sil-nylon material is stitched together using a single needle lockstitch with double stitched lapped ends — in other words, the cloth will fail long before the seams. The most delightfully ingenious innovation is a central "quad loop" that captures the end of a pole, staff, stick or paddle and hold it firmly in place so that when the wind lifts, the center support does not fall out.

After three years of canoeing, camping and backpacking with the Tundra, the tarp is still one of my favorite pieces of gear. I originally purchased one 10' x 16' tarp for a canoe trip to Canada with a crew of nine Boy Scouts. The tarp has sheltered a crew of nine in violent thunderstorms and been a palatial home for one on backpacking trips. There are cheaper options out there, but from my experience, none matches the true versatility and quality of the Tundra Tarp. Weighing a mere 2 pounds 10 ounces, it does not add substantially to the load; there is also a 1 pound 10 ounce version available for an additional $80.00. Each tarp ships with 80 feet of polyester cord, a tube of SilNet sealant and a stuff sack. They are sized from 8' x 10' to 15' x 15'.

The company will also sew your choice of colors, either a single color for the whole tarp or multicolored panels. My tarps are multicolored — orange, red, blue, and yellow — which makes them very easy to spot when canoing back to camp. I purchased a second tarp this summer when we added a second crew to our annual canoe trip. We're going to get three more to outfit our entire Scout Troop this fall.

-- Clarke Green

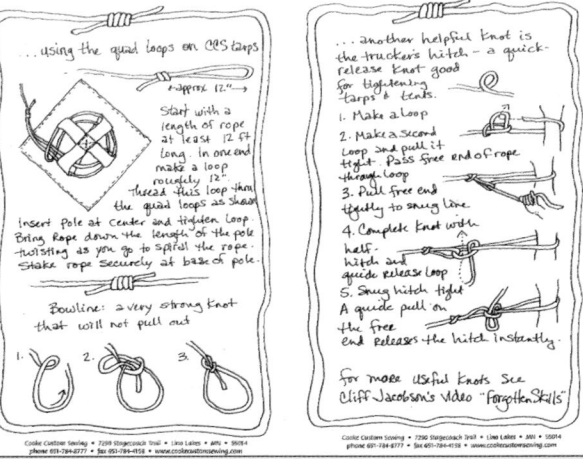

Quad Loop

Ultralight backpacking shelter
Tarptents
$199+ Tarptent

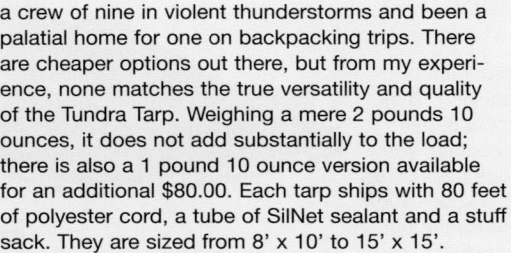

Lots of people on the PCT (Pacific Crest Trail) are using these kind of tents – including myself (I recently completed 560 miles). Many ultralight backpackers use a tarp instead of a tent and swear by it. That can be tricky to set up and doesn't keep all of the bugs off. The tarptent concept is based on the simplicity and lightness of a tarp, but made into a more traditional tent look. While Sierra Designs' one-person tent looks good, it weighs 2lbs 11oz. My Contrail tarptent is 24 oz. It's a single layer silnylon tent with a ground sheet and mesh all around the inside between the groundsheet and the tarp, top. (Models are available with sewn-in floors or floorless; the latter is $30 cheaper and lighter.)

I use my trekking pole as the main upright. Set up took a while to figure out, but now I put it up and down in much less than 5 minutes. I can rig it for strong wind, too (it's designed to be storm rigged in need). It's great for the Sierras, but wouldn't be so suitable for wet climates. If you camp somewhere moist, like near a river, it can suffer from condensation. As such, I have learned to camp differently and now leave the door wide open all the time apart from the mosquito net. It hasn't rained much in the 2 months I have been hiking the PCT, but when it did, the tent was waterproof. You have to seal the seams yourself, but it is very easy to do so. The only modification I have done is to swap the standard 2 rear pegs for 9 in. ones, which work better especially in sand.

-- Carl Myhill

Formal education will make you a living; self-education will make you a fortune. - Jim Rohn

Free homemade super lightweight
Pepsi Can Stove
Varies (DIY Instructions) AntiGravityGear

This little stove is amazing; you make it yourself from Pepsi and Guinness cans, using things that can be found around most households. It takes about an afternoon to make (plus some time waiting for the epoxy to set), weighs only a few grams, and is sufficient for most backpacking trips. I made my first one a few years ago, and I've been handing them out as gifts ever since. The stove is powerful enough to boil a quart of water in a reasonable amount of time, it's MUCH quieter than other camping stoves, if you lose it you're not out $80.00, and you can get the fuel for it (denatured alcohol) at most hardware or paint stores. Mine fits nicely inside of the mug I use for cooking and eating, with room to spare. I usually stuff a spare pair of socks in with it to keep it from rattling around.

The site provides detailed instructions.

-- Galen Pewtherer

Light-weight stove burns fuel found along trail
Sierra Stove
$57 ZZ Manufacturing

There I was, in driving rain, cooking breakfast under a tree over an intense, portable fire. Fresh coffee and scrambled eggs.

It was a Sierra Stove I got for $52. It's a mini-forge, forcing air into a small insulated chamber where a double handful of twigs (or dung or whatever) can heat water in a couple minutes—just a little longer than a butane stove, but with NO fuel or fuel containers to carry. One enthusiast hiked from Mexico to Canada cooking with one, claims Chip in *The Compleat Walker IV.* Chip himself now claims to camp largely solar–with backback solar charged batteries running his flashlights and his Sierra Stove.

The basic unit I got weighs 18 ounces and is clever and well-evolved. Accessory goodies can be found at the manufacturer's site. The newest item is a titanium version that weighs only 10 ounces, for $129.

I was impressed at how little fuel was needed, and how funky it could be. A switch offers high or low speed on the fan, driven by one AA battery. No igniter–my Bic failed me in the rain, but a Lifeboat match and lil' firestarter saved the day. Unlike butane, the Sierra Stove does blacken your pots and pans, which is the main nuisance–they go in ziploc bags anyway though. All in all an impressive little rig.

We'll all want one when the economy collapses completely and we have to live homeless.

-- Stewart Brand

Ultra efficient stove system
JetBoil
$99 Amazon

It's the quickest, handiest, most efficient hot water maker yet. It takes the piezo-ignited butane trail stove to maybe a 50% overall improvement—worth converting for many.

The main tricks are: fin-like heat exchanger ("FluxRing") where the flame meets the pot; pot attaches to stove (vastly less fiddly); pot has a cozy on it to hold heat and make gripping the pot easy; the plastic lid of the pot doubles as a cup lid for sipping direct from the pot; and the stove stows inside the pot. The weight is 12 ounces, the same or less than other light butane stove systems, but you save on weight of fuel, small pack volume, and overall convenience.

The heat exchanger means you can heat 2 cups of water in about 2 minutes, with significantly little fuel expended. So little heat escapes that you can hold the whole thing in your hand while it cooks, and the cozy never burns. The pot works better for eating from than for drinking from—I still prefer an insulated Alladdin cup (with the meaningless handle sawed off), but it's manageable for drinking if you want one less implement.

It's fine for dinner for two, or an instant cup of coffee or tea under way. You could use it riding in a car (open a window).

-- Stewart Brand

Best ultralight cook kit
Snow Peak Stove and Cookset
$50 Stove Amazon

This is a super-light high-performance cook set. I've been hiking since the late '60s and this is far and away my favorite combo. The stove is tiny and it and the gas canister fit inside the nested pots of the cookset. Add a titanium spork and you have a complete cookset weighing under 8 oz and fitting in a space smaller than a jacket stuffsack. It is so light that I use it for more than overnights: I often take it on day hikes instead of a thermos — I pack some powdered green tea, a bamboo whisk and a second cup. In a few minutes, I can whip up tea ceremony style green tea for myself and my hiking companion.

-- Paul Saffo

$50 Cookset Amazon
$50 Titanium Spork Amazon

Rugged multi-fuel stove
MSR XGK Multi-Fuel Stove
$160 Amazon

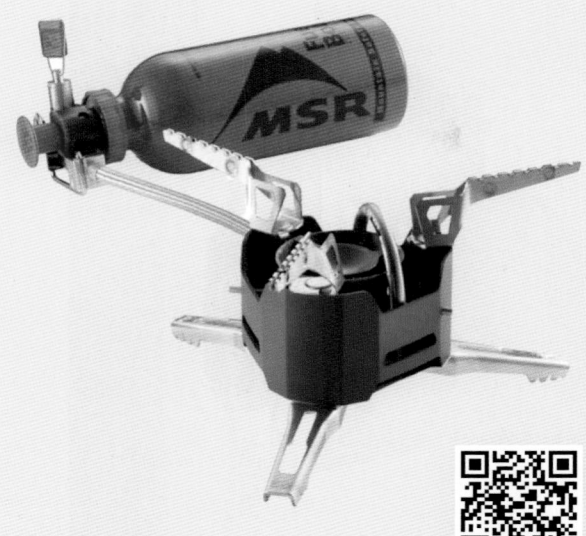

I've been using my XGK stove for over 22 years and it's battered and sorry-looking but still performs wonderfully.

What really sold me on it was that I had a career and life-change about 5 years ago and put all my camping stuff in storage. Last summer I retrieved and unpacked it all for a trip to Nova Scotia and New Brunswick. The stove fired up first time and performed flawlessly. It still sounds like a jet engine and boils water in a very short time. A triumph of simple, solid engineering.

It enables me to cook food and make warm drinks in order to stay alive in challenging locations. I can source multiple kinds of fuel without having to be overly reliant on one type of fuel or (even worse) proprietary canisters. The rocketship sound makes me happy and reminds me of all the times that noise signaled I would soon be fed and warm. Throw the stove in a backpack, duffel, truck bed, helicopter, and don't worry about damaging it. Even if it gets damaged or clogged (on Russian diesel, for instance), you can strip it down with a Leatherman. MSR provides all the spares you need with the stove.

-- Raoul Miller

Super reliable at high altitudes
Optimus Svea Stove
$97 Amazon

Since the 1980's I have used many small camp stoves, but none compares to the Svea 123. This stove is famous for working well at high altitudes. It is light, reliable, simple, and will boil water fast. It does lack a simmer setting, even on its lowest setting. And it can be a bit much for some things, but when camping or backpacking a long simmer is rarely desired.

This uses standard white gas (Coleman Fuel) and can be refilled from partially full, giving it a great advantage over disposable cartridge pressurized gas models. It is fully self-contained which is a nice advantage over other stoves such as the Whisperlite, but at the expense of fuel capacity.

It has been made, nearly unchanged, since 1955. This is a testament to its reliability and usefulness. If I had to choose only one outdoor stove to use ever, this would be the one.

-- Grant Johnson

Water Cleaners

Heavy-duty water filter
Katadyn Pocket Microfilter
$277 Amazon

While bottled water is available in most large towns throughout the world, in many remote locations the water quality is questionable. Even where bottled water is available it seems extremely wasteful to throw away a dozen plastic bottles every day. We used the Katadyn Pocket Microfilter to fill up our own canteens. On a bike trip through SouthEast Asia we were able to avoid purchasing about 20 of those one liter bottles of water every day by having the pump. And of course in places without bottled water, this was a life-saver.

The Katadyn Pocket is different from everything else on the market. The first difference is the price. It costs is two-to-three times the price of it's competition! Also, it is not lightweight. And really it's not all that easy to use.

So what's so great about it? Katadyn has been making this filter for decades. It has been used by the Navy Seals and other special forces for years. The aluminum construction makes it very durable.The filter is fully field-cleanable. That means there is no expensive filter cartridge to replace after a month of use. The ceramic cartridge in the Katadyn Pocket has a life of 13,000 gallons or 50,000 liters. So this filter will last for a lifetime of any adventure.

There are a few things that need to be done regularly to keep the filter in good working condition. The pores of the ceramic filter element absorb the contamination and must be scrubbed clean periodically. Generally I give it a light scrubbing after pumping about ten liters of sink water. If the water source is slightly salty or dirty then the element must be

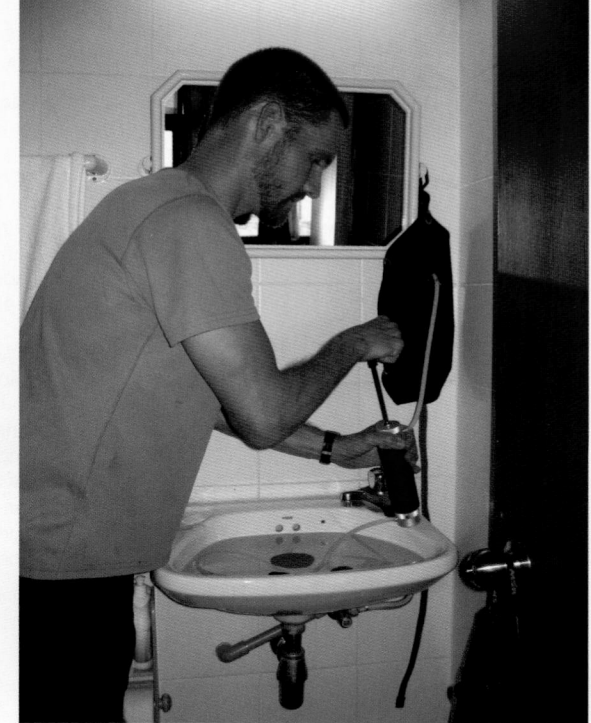

Filling the water bag in a hotel bathroom in Thailand

scrubbed more frequently. I can tell it needs a cleaning when the filter becomes difficult to pump. When I first began using the filter I would scrub it too often and too hard, removing more of the ceramic coating than necessary. The first filter wore our faster than the 50,000 liter limit and I learned my lesson. Now I am careful to scrub it lightly and evenly so the wear occurs at the outer edges of the filter at the same rate as the center. Katadyn provides.an organic lubricant that is applied to the pump handle at the bottom and the point where the rod enters the pump. While the lubricant is a tiny little tube it seems to last a long time.

-- Richard Ligato

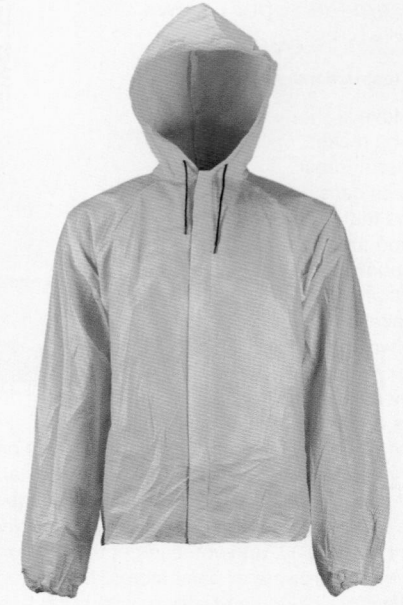

Lightest rain gear
O2
Hooded Rain Jacket
$22+ Amazon

There are more durable and more comfortable rain wear, but none as light. The O2 jacket with hood weighs only 6 oz (175 g)! Pants are about the same. Its featherweight can slip in anywhere without notice. This makes it perfect for backpacking or bicycling when ounces and bulk count. Rather than using the usual Goretex-like breathable fabrics, this uses a 3M Microporous Film fabric which is thinner, lighter and cheaper. The fabric does not feel plasticy, like most lightweight ponchos; instead it feels almost like a soft paper towel. It is perfectly waterproof, even in severe downpours (I even tested it in the shower once; my clothes dry underneath). And fairly breathable. I will wear it as a windbreaker on hikes even in sunny weather, and not sweat.

The garment is minimal and packs small; simple zipper, no pockets (on the basic model). Being so lightweight it is not as robust as more expensive gear — but perfectly adequate for unexpected rains. If you plan to wear it over heavy outer wear, order a size larger.

-- KK

Portable emergency water
MIOX Water Purifier
$130 rei.com

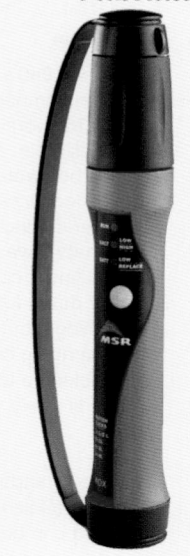

I was skeptical at first but after some practice I've become very attached to my little MIOX purifier. Its about the size and weight of a mini-Mag Light. I've tried iodine and chlorine tablets in the past, but I've always ended up filtering my water a second time to a Nalgene bottle to get the taste out. I was initially turned off by the smell of the MIOX too. It's very strong for about 10 minutes as it off gases, but after the required 30 minutes of "dwell time" it's virtually undetectable in a 100 oz. reservoir.

I've been using the MIOX pen mostly as a backup. It runs on CR123 Lithium batteries and salt. It took some practice to get the water in the salt chamber filled and the solution to travel back through the screen to the diode. There are a couple screw caps and several ways the task can be done. But I can fill my reservoir, treat my water, and get my reservoir back in my pack in about a minute now. I pre-filter my water if it's really cloudy or stagnant.

The pen has multiple settings for different volumes of water. I use a 3L Nalgene bladder with the fist sized screw cap. Spare salt, test strips and a stuff sack come with it, but I carry none of them. A full salt chamber is good for about 12 doses. The rest is extra weight to me. The MIOX was developed for military applications with assistance from Darpa. Cascade Designs (parent company of MSR, Thermarest and others) partnered with the MIOX corporation to develop an entirely new type of portable water purification. I've been using one for 2 years now and have never encountered any problems. Thousands are in use by US and allied troops around the world. I'm convinced it's sound technology and a useful survival tool. When I'm not hiking it stays in my glovebox with a 2L reservoir.

– D.S.

Flexible water carrier
Soft Water Carry Bladders
$15 1 liter cascadedesigns.com

The Evernew Water Carry bladder is the equivalent of a Camelbak that you don't have to drink out of with a hose, and it's the best solution for carrying water on a day-to-day basis that I've found. A few months back I got sick and tired of trying to find a place for my bulky stainless steel water bottle in my day bag, and decided to try out the Evernew bladder after a friend recommended them. They are especially popular amongst the ultra-light crowd given their light weight (mine weighs around an ounce when not filled) and superior packability (they can be rolled up to the size of a hi-lighter). Another bonus is that TSA won't take it away from you when it's empty allowing you to refill it once you get through security.

The beauty of the Evernew bladder is that when it's empty it takes up absolutely no space, and when it's full the flexible nature of the polyethylene means that it conforms to whatever space you put it in. At first I was worried that I would quickly tear a hole or somehow spring a leak in what I assumed to be a less-than-robust plastic, but after 6-months of hard use both of mine are still going strong. I've dropped them on sharp granite, shoved them to the bottom of my pack filled with rigid objects, stored them rolled up and have yet to find any signs of impending failure. The cap has never come loose, and I have never had one leak. Another benefit is that they can be retrofitted to work just like a Camelbak, all you have to do is buy the hose accessory that screws on.

The bottle I use on a daily basis holds .9 liters which is my sweet spot, but you can also find them in 0.6 and 2L varieties. They are designed so that when full they can stand on a flat surface unlike the bags that come in Camelbaks. Given that Evernew is a finicky Japanese supplier, these bottles can be hard to come by, but are well worth it if you can find them in stock. I do know that Platypus has a similar system out that is equally well-reviewed, but I can't personally comment on their quality.

Many will rightfully point out that this bladder is made out of plastic. Like many of you I try to avoid plastic products, but in this case the Evernew is hands down better than anything else I've tried. Unlike other containers I've used it contributes absolutely no plasticky odor or taste to my water. While this may not be an indication of the relative likelihood of contamination I do what I can to minimize any risk (notably, I never fill it with boiling water, or leave it in the sun for too long).

Platypus Softbottles are good alternatives available on Amazon.

-- Oliver Hulland

You can never know what is enough unless you know what is more than enough. - William Blake

How to hike and camp in the snow
Allen & Mike's Really Cool Backcountry Ski Book
$5 Allen O'Bannon & Mike Clelland, 1996, 114 p.

Allen and Mike, two wise hikers, have penned an admirable series of primers that feature cartoons and pithy advice for backpackers. This, the third, is the best of the series so far (see also *Lighten Up* and *Allen & Mike's Really Cool Backpackin' Book*). Its subject is winter backpacking, which often intimidates fair-weather hikers. Their great advice will not only keep you safe, but also warm and happy. There's a fantastic chapter on making snow shelters, presented in such accessible detail that I'm astounded that it was all new to me. Allen and Mike become your best friends as they giggle and chuckle while they give you the straight dope on what you need to live and prosper in the snow. Trust them.

-- *KK*

●

Sidecut is the difference between the width of the ski at its fattest points (the tip and tail) and its narrowest point at the waist (middle of the ski). The more side cut a ski has, the faster it will turn. On the other side of the coin, skis with less side cut are better for touring since they will hold a straighter line.

●

Careful! Liquids that don't freeze at low temperatures, such as alcohol and white gas, can cause frostbite damage because they will be the same temperature as the air.

●

People in the earliest stages of Hypothermia will feel cold and clumsy. They will exhibit improper behavior, such as not putting on a hat. Their personality will show changes, and they will become apathetic, listless or emotional. They may show signs of shivering, although there are many cases where people have passed through this stage without shivering. This is especially true when people have been exercising beyond their normal point of endurance. As hypothermia progresses, a person will start to lose his or her coordination and start to stumble. The person will be unable to do simple tasks, such as zip a zipper. He or she will show more marked personality changes and may become belligerent and irrational.

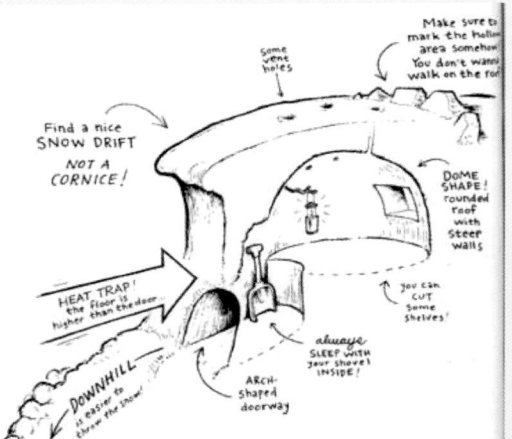

Avalanche wisdom
Staying Alive in Avalanche Terrain
$14 Bruce Tremper, 2008, 304 p.

My mountain rescue friends say this is the bible of avalanche survival knowledge. Now in its second updated edition, it is a readable, immensely informative dissection of how avalanches happen, and how to avoid them — and what should be done when they aren't avoided. Neither overly technical, nor dumbed down, the book is near perfect in pitch, telling you important stuff in vivid and interesting ways. It's generally recognized as the best source on the subject of moving snow. I read almost the entire book even though I am not often in avalanche terrain, just because the information is so clear, insightful, and brilliant in the details. More outdoors fans are winding up in avalanche territory; these insights could save your life.

-- *KK*

●

People are getting slaughtered by avalanches. I don't think slaughter is too strong a word considering that between 1990 and 2007, 423 people have died in avalanches in the United States, averaging 25 per year and 15 per season in Canada, and the trend is on a steep upward slope that shows no signs of abating.

●

Almost all avalanche fatalities involve recreationists, most notably snowmobilers, backcountry skiers, snowboarders, and climbers, in that order. Almost all are very skilled in their sport, male, fit, educated, intelligent, middle class, and between the ages of 18 and 40. Does this sound anything like you?

There is hope. In 93 percent of avalanche accidents, the avalanche is triggered by the victim or someone in the victim's party. Which is good, because as the Pogo cartoon says, "We have met the enemy and he is us."

The good news is that we have two important things going for us: first, we have a choice, and second, we already know the enemy. The bad news is that the enemy is us, and that is the hardest enemy of all to conquer.

●

◄*Cracking snow is an obvious buzz from the avalanche rattlesnake. Don't take another step! Here, a 40-foot crack shoots out from my wife's skis. She was able to crack the fresh wind slab by safely standing on the flat of a ridge and watch the crack propagate below her. Luckily, the slope below is barely 30 degrees and is a good, small, test slope. (Wasatch Range, Utah)*

Snow Is Like Silly Putty

Go to nearly any lecture on avalanches and chances are good that you will see the instructor pull out their trusty Silly Putty. (I've also seen people use a mixture of cornstarch and water.) This is the only way I know how to demonstrate the visco-elastic nature of snow.

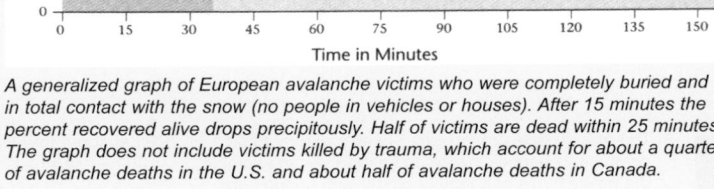

Avalanche Survival vs. Burial Time
422 Total Avalanche Victims Buried

93%

Victims probably did not have an air pocket.

Victims probably did have an air pocket.

Percent Recovered Alive

Time in Minutes

A generalized graph of European avalanche victims who were completely buried and in total contact with the snow (no people in vehicles or houses). After 15 minutes the percent recovered alive drops precipitously. Half of victims are dead within 25 minutes. The graph does not include victims killed by trauma, which account for about a quarter of avalanche deaths in the U.S. and about half of avalanche deaths in Canada.

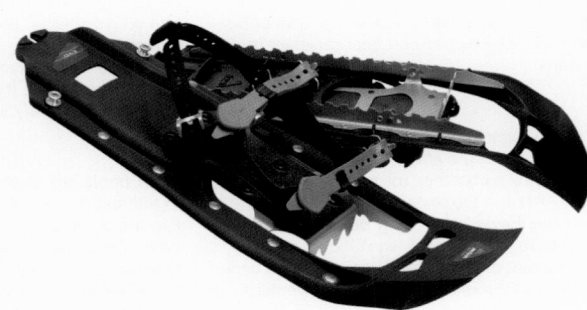

Snow behaves viscously when it moves slowly as demonstrated by this roof glide. When strained to its breaking point, it behaves elastically and fractures.

Silly Putty, like snow, exhibits both a viscous and elastic nature. If you roll it in a ball, you can bounce it (elastic energy). But snow (and Silly Putty) also flow viscously; like the proverbial molasses in January.

The most interesting part of the snow-Silly Putty metaphor is that when deformed slowly, it flows like taffy, but when deformed rapidly, it fractures like glass. The take-home point is: Snow is very sensitive to the rate at which it is deformed. This is probably the most important property to remember about snow, and it's the cause of most avalanche fatalities. In other words, snow, just like people, does not like rapid change.

●

Unless you practice regularly with your beacon, you probably won't be able to find your partners in time to save their lives.

Inexpensive great snowshoes
MSR EVO Snowshoes
$100 amazon.com

Float over snow. Go slow, steady. Be thrifty. One of the least expensive pair of snowshoes you can get is the best. Unfashionably molded of single piece of unbreakable bomb-proof plastic these EVOS are idiot-proof easy to get on and off, very lightweight, and small enough to fit into your carry-on luggage! Try that with fancy ones. A classic model by now, any bugs in the near-solid-state EVOS have long been worked out, so these economical shoes have a huge following. I find them far more comfortable than other snowshoes I've used for casual excursions. They have optional extenders for heavier weight or snow conditions.

-- *KK*

Trail Food

Homemade trail food cookbooks

Trail Food * Backpack Gourmet * Lipsmackin Backpackin

Make your own lightweight backpacking food. To do: At home cook a dish you like, dehydrate it to reduce weight, and then rehydrate it on the trail. This is how commercial trail meals work. The difference is you make stuff you really like, tailored to your preferences (vegan, gluten-free, whatever). And it's cheaper.

There are two camps, so to speak, about homemade dehydrated trail food. One camp dries ingredients separately to be recombined any way you want on the trail; the other makes one-pot meals and dries the entire dish at once and sealed in one bag. Then that one bag is hydrated and heated. This latter way tends to yield better results.

The thin guide *Trail Food* provides good instructions on how to prepare and store dehydrated trail food including drying ingredients separately, but is short on recipes. All the many recipes in *Backpack Gourmet* are single-dish meals, devised by a single author. The 150 recipes in *Lipsmackin' Backpackin'* are a compilation from many hikers and some of the recipes entail separate dehydrated bags, but the book has more variety of foods and snacks than the others.

-- KK

From *Trail Food*:

The Price Is Right

Entire dehydrated meals often cost less than a single component of a commercially packaged entrée. I've been able to eat well and heartily for as little as three dollars a day.

Reduced Weight And Bulk

Anywhere from 50 to 90% of most food consists of water. As a result, dried meals can be reduced to a few ounces that fit in the palm of your hand. Using dehydrated food, I have canoed as long as 60 days without needing a resupply, and my boat has plenty of freeboard left. Dehydrated

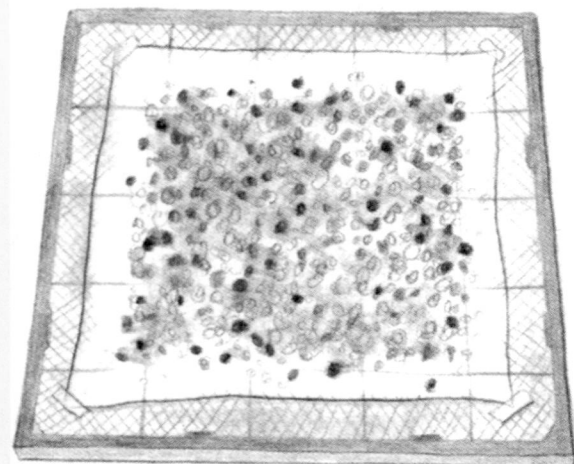

Cover mesh dehydrator trays.

supplies fit easily in bicycle panniers, day packs, kayak hatches, or the cramped cupboards of a sailboat.

When peaches are cheap, lug home a 30-pound box instead of three or four for your fruit bowl. When green peppers are eight for a dollar, get 50! In a matter of a day or two, depending on your drying capacity, they'll be safely preserved.

Farmer's markets and fruit stands are terrific sources of fresh, unpackaged produce. Orchards often have seasonal specials or pick-your-own deals.

Not Worth The Effort

After years at this game, I've come to the conclusion that there are a few foods that simply aren't worth the effort to dry. Take onions, for instance. The first time we took on those little devils we brought home a 50-pound sack, chuckling all the way over our great savings. A week later we finally finished the last one off, having endured the indignities of various home cures for tearing eyes, and vowing never to dry another bloody onion as long as we lived. At one point that week, near midnight, we looked at each other over the pile of onion skins and collapsed in hysterics. Each of us wore a pair of ski goggles and a bandanna, bandit style, and had a piece of white bread stuffed in our mouth. None of it worked, so don't bother. Ever since then, we've found diced onion bits at very reasonable prices through our local health-food store.

Dried potatoes are also cheap and readily available, and save you the chopping, blanching chore. Powdered milk is expensive, but worth the price. You may find other dried products in your area stores that will be worth the laborsaving convenience.

From *Backpack Gourmet*:

Drying One-Pot Meals in a Dehydrator

Time-saving Tip: Prepare extra food, enjoy some for dinner tonight, and dehydrate the rest.

Choose a one pot complete meal recipe from this book. Cook your meal at home, just as through you are preparing tonight's dinner. If you choose a meal such as spaghetti, simply prepare a spaghetti sauce--your choice of beef, seafood, or vegetarian. Then boil the pasta al dente (cooked but still firm.) Toss together the sauce and drained pasta, and put the whole dish, freshly cooked and still warm, into the dehydrator. While preparing the food, chop, grate, dice, or clive the ingredients into small pieces. These will dehydrate

Cover pasta, quiches, or casseroles with water just above the level of food in pot.

much faster and more successfully than large pieces of food.

Virtually all cooked foods are safe and easy to dry at home.

Spread the warm, cooked meal evenly in a thin layer on the dehydrator trays and put them in the dehydrator. Overloaded trays dry slowly. All of the one-pot recipes in this book – which make four servings each – fit comfortably into a typical home dehydrator. For highest quality and food safety, speedy drying is best.

It is nearly impossible to overdry or otherwise ruin your home-dried meals using an electric dehydrator with a heat source and fan. If necessary, you can put the food in the dehydrator, leave the house, go to work for eight hours, and then turn off the dehydrator when you get home.

The one-pot home-dried meal method requires little field equipment. Leave your frying pan, knives, forks, cutting board, plates, an extra pots at home.

Sample excerpt from *Lipsmackin' Backpackin'* ▼

Italian Trail Couscous

Total weight: 9 ounces
Total servings: 1

At home:

Dry the tomato paste on plastic wrap in a food dehydrator. Once dried, break tomato leather into small pieces and package along with couscous, Parmesan cheese, and Italian seasoning in a sandwich-size resealable plastic bag. Package oil separately.

On the trail:

Add all ingredients, as well as oil, to water. Let sit for 20 minutes. Bring to a boil, then reduce heat slightly and stir frequently. The cooking time depends on the altitude but normally takes about 3 minutes. When ready, the couscous should have the consistency of a moist paste.

This is a good and fast recipe. It's one of my classics. I eat it in the evening; and on some trips I have eaten it almost every day.

LUCA DE ALFARO
PALO ALTO, CALIFORNIA

$7 Trail Food Alan S. Kesselheim, 1998, 112 p.

$10 Backpack Gourmet Linda Frederick Yaffe, 1998, 112 p.

$11 Christine Conners, 2013 (2nd Edition), 296 p.

Nice bears

Backcountry Bear Basics

$8 David Smith, 1997, 109 p.
$10 Kindle Amazon

Bears are back in the woods. There's lots of folklore about what to do around them. Most of it wrong. Here, in a small book, is the latest straight dope about what you should do if you meet one — and how not to meet one.

-- KK

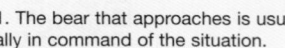

There are three key behaviors you need to be aware of:

1. The bear that approaches is usually in command of the situation.

2. The subordinate bear does not end an engagement with a dominant bear; the dominant bear is the first to leave.

3. Merely standing still has signal value; standing still will often alter the ongoing behavior of an approaching bear.

The magic circle around every bear is different and constantly changes in size and shape. As an example, the magic circle of a female grizzly with spring cubs will probably be larger than the magic circle of the same bear when she doesn't have cubs. … Don't forget that you have a magic circle, too. A seasoned black bear biologist might be comfortable with a bear that's only 10 yards away, but you or I might be nervous about a black bear that's 40 yards away.

Years of experience in Denali and other national parks have proven that properly secured bear resistant food containers work.

For some reason, bears are interested in petroleum products. When they come across a spot of oil or gas on the ground, they sometimes roll in it like a dog rolls on a carcass. After the Exxon Valdez oil spill, some bears looked like they'd been using Brylcream. My friend Hod Coburn, a bush pilot who's flown all over Alaska, told me that a black bear once got into a case of oil he stashed at a remote runway in the western

part of the state. It didn't bite one can and assume there was more of the same in the others – it bit into every can.

What about tree-climbing? You startle a bear that's 100 feet away and decide to run and climb a tree that's only 10 feet away. The bear will arrive in about 3 seconds. You wouldn't have time to climb a stepladder, let alone a tree. Even full-grown black bears can scoot up any tree with astonishing speed. An adult grizzly can "ladder" its way up a tree if the limbs are right, with a known record of 33 feet high.

Bears key on movement and quickly notice a silhouette on a ridgeline. Steve French, an M.D. and bear researcher who's co-director of the Yellowstone Grizzly Foundation, has an excellent rule of thumb regarding the vision of bears; If you can see a bear, you should assume it can see you.

Black bears are creatures of the forest, so in response to a threat they've always had the option of slipping into the underbrush and hiding or climbing a tree. When threatened, black bears flee. Even when black bear biologists hold squalling cubs while mama bear is just yards away, the females almost always retreat.

They may make a blowing sound and clack teeth and make a rush or two toward the biologists, but ultimately, they retreat.

Not so with grizzlies. Grizzlies evolved in more open terrain. At times, there wasn't enough cover for a female and her cubs to hide from other bears or mammals. There were no trees to climb. When threatened, a female had to defend her cubs.

You can't steer unless you are moving. - Fred Brooks

Cheap worry-free sleeping
Mosquito Netting
$13 Amazon

I hate mosquitoes. Serious gut-tightening allergic aversion. One bite at night and I am awake for hours, and I'll itch for days. They'll always find me, too. I've learned to ignore what natives say; there ARE mosquitoes around, and they do bite. When I travel in any remotely warm place, I pack my own mosquito netting. It weighs only a few ounces and can scrunch up small. It's cheap, and lasts forever. I'm still using one I bought 30 years ago for $2. I like the boxy four-cornered variety to fit over a bed or sleeping bag. I tie a 6-foot long string to each corner; that usually enables me to attach the string somewhere to keep the net elevated at night. I tie it to trees if I am camping without a tent.

I haven't figured out why more people don't pack their own. Mine has saved my life more than once. Mostly by allowing me to sleep soundly, but also because with it I avoid mosquito-borne diseases in areas they are common. Studies have shown that sleeping in a net is more effective at preventing malaria than taking prophylactic drugs. I insist my family use netting while we travel in the heat overseas. A quick search led me to Coleman as the least expensive source for a one-person camp-style box net.

There are new self-supporting varieties of mosquito netting, which would be useful where there is little outside support but lots of mosquitoes (tundra, everglades). They are more expensive, but still lightweight. I haven't tried these. Let me know if you do.

-- KK

Premium freestanding net
TropicScreen Mosquito Tent
$75 Mosquito Nets USA

Do you know someone going on a government-paid excursion to the Middle East dressed in Army fatigues? Mosquito netting is a must. There's a misunderstanding that the Army supplies you all you need in the field. Nope. I may have been able to get my hands on an Army issued net a few months AFTER mosquito season… but instead we used the Epco TropicScreen II, the Cadillac of mosquito nets. The Tropicscreen is the only freestanding mosquito net we found that would work with an army cot. It has a floor too! It also turned out to be far easier to pack than the standard "mosquito bar" such as the backpacking nets reviewed in CoolTools. Weight wasn't a huge issue (since we were never too far from vehicles), but speed of assembly/disassembly was crucial.

-- Frank Black

How to survive jungle expeditions
Jungle Travel and Survival
$18 Don Ladigin, 2001, 197 pages

The tropical medical advice here can be found elsewhere, but I've found no other source to deal with the psychological and logistical preparations needed to run a small expedition into the jungle (with a bias toward the Amazon).

-- KK

•

Anecdotally, there is a lot of support for the notion that the tropics somehow engender sexual activity. The experience of those of us who spend essentially all our wilderness time in the hot ones, as opposed to those whose preferences are for high altitude and freezing environments, leads inescapably to the conclusion that group tensions brought on by sex or the pursuit of sex are much more an issue in the tropics than in colder climates.

•

All sorts of problems, especially injuries, seem to increase logarithmically when you get beyond 7 to 10 members in a wilderness group.

•

Indigenous peoples move along the trail at a rapid, sustained pace, somewhere at the upper end of fast walking and just before breaking into a run. They seldom slow down for any reason, but they will speed up when fleeing enemies, pursuing game, or hurrying home to sleep in their own hammock or bed at night. Not only do they move along at this clip on level ground and downhill, but they also keep the same pace going uphill! Chances are, you do not maintain your regular pace when ascending an incline, and initially you will find this trait among natives perplexing and tiring. Tribesmen know what they are doing here…their idea is to maintain a constant rate as they move from point A to point B, and it doesn't occur to them that going up a hill is any more reason to go at a lower pace than when walking on level ground.

Effective tick repellent
Permethrin
Insect Shield Clothing (various) Amazon
ExOfficio Men's Bugsaway Chas'R Tee Shirt $18 Amazon
Permethrin Clothing Repellent 24-ounce spray bottle $11 Amazon
Perky Pet Ant Guard for Bird Feeders $7 Amazon

Permethrin is a man-made version of an insect repellent found in chrysanthemum plants. The molecule repels a variety of biting insects including flies, ants, chiggers, mosquitoes, ticks, etc. The company Insect Shield partners with manufacturers of work and recreational outdoor clothing to produce bug repellant gear: LL Bean, Buff, Carolina Manufacturing (bandanas), Eagle's Nest Outfitters, ExOfficio, Outdoor Research, and REI.

Since deer populations have been exploding in many parts of the country, we have seen a corresponding explosion in the tick population. Some diseases carried by ticks can send you to bed for at least a week and may even have permanent effects (Lyme disease for example). Permethrin seems to be the best alternative for dealing with these pests and is a vastly superior alternative to DEET.

We were clued into this permethrin clothing treatment last year by Rob, a local farmer. He was finding about a dozen ticks a day after working in the fields. Rob started wearing permethrin treated socks, long pants secured at the ankle, long-sleeved shirts and a bandana; he stopped picking up ticks. I have shorts, an ExOfficio Bugsaway t-shirt, and several pairs of treated socks, and that seems to do the trick for me. There are also sprays for applying permethrin to your own clothing and camping gear (please read the warning labels carefully before using them) though I personally prefer pretreated clothing.

One thing to consider before using permethrin is that, as the Wikipedia article notes, permethrin is toxic to fish and aquatic life in general. This is why I dislike the use of permethrin backyard sprays as they seem like overkill, while any runoff can inadvertently damage local water life.

-- Phil Earnhardt

Remember, they are supremely fit, so going uphill really isn't all that much more taxing than walking on level ground. By the same token, they do not go faster when going downhill. It's just a steady and, for them, comfortable gait. Back home, as you are getting in shape (physically and mentally) for jungle trekking, you should hike at a fast pace and practice maintaining your speed regardless of the terrain.

•

It's mostly good news for women travelers in the tropical rainforest. I have yet to see a woman become incapacitated by heat illness on jungle expeditions.

•

Scented lotions, moisturizers, and perfumes attract insects; jungle travelers must avoid looking and smelling like a flower.

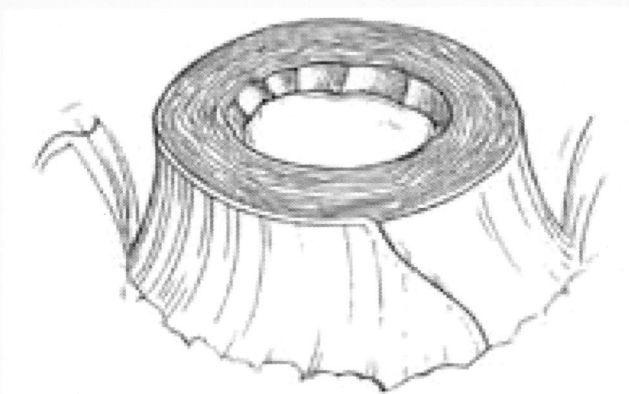

Water may be collected from a banana or plantain plant by cutting the plant approximately 6 to 12 inches above the ground and scooping out the center of the stump into a bowl shape. The hollow thus formed fills immediately with water. The first two fillings have a bitter taste and must be discarded. The third and subsequent fillings are drinkable. A banana plant can furnish water in this fashion for several days.

Rub-on hand protection
Invisible Glove
$6 (5 oz.) Amazon

Latex gloves and the better purple nitrile gloves can be irritating to the skin, reduce the ability to feel what you're doing and are easy to drag, pinch, and tear when working on mechanical things. If you've ever tried to wind a wing nut or fiddle with a fastener with those thin, sticky gloves you know what I mean. With Invisible Glove, I can work with my hands directly on the job in front of me.

A tube of Invisible Glove for less than ten bucks will last months. You put it on once and work all day — just one more application after you wash your hands to have a meal. With latex gloves, you're going to go through several pairs in a day and end up spending more money.

I do a lot of different things, some of them greasy and grimy like working on an old engine or painting and yard work, and others like client meetings and dinners out where nasty hands with grease under the nails just don't fly.

Invisible Glove is a simple, cheap solution. It goes on like a hand lotion — just a bit greasier. It only makes your hands slippery if you put too much on. It works exactly like it says, though. Oil, grease, dirt, paint, solvents, and pretty much anything else just washes right off when you're done. No more greasy black fingernails and paint-stained hands.

-- Andrew Pollack

I am horrifically allergic to poison oak. I am also an avid mountain biker in northern California. This not a good combination. I have tried all the soaps and wipes, but none of them really help, especially if you are out all day and can't get to a shower soon after exposure. I have found only one reasonable way to stop the oils from getting into my skin: Invisible Glove, a skin protectant used by mechanics so they can wash their hands clean after working on cars. There are similar products sold specifically for poison oak, but they cost vastly more, and work the same. I find that if I rub my legs and arms down with Invisible Glove and shower right after riding with a soap like Dawn or Tecnu, I either don't get any rash, or it's much more limited and tolerable. It is still worth being as careful as possible, and making sure that clothes get right into the washer (to prevent poison oak oils from getting all over the house), but Invisible Glove seems to be the best preventative for weeks of awful rash that I have found.

-- Alexander Rose

Survival Tools

Flint and steel fire starter
Light My Fire Firesteel
$17 Amazon

Made in Sweden, the Light My Fire firesteels are a remake of a classic. Use them to light dry tinder if you are in Daniel Boone mode. For the rest of us, they cast off a perfect spark to light any sort of gas camp stove, from the 2 burner Coleman car camp special to the micro backpack models. They also work for DIY alcohol stoves.

Firesteels come in 2 sizes, small for survival-backpacking and a slightly larger size for those other times. Some of the most distinctive advantages are that it works when wet, it has no moving parts, no fuel to run out of, and lasts nearly 3,000 strikes.

I've used them for everything from car camping in the VW camper van to mountaineering stoves on Rainier climbs and they always are flawless. The smaller one always has a place in my first aid / survival kit; the larger one comes on car camping trips.

-- John Godino

Self-aware headlamp
Petzl NAO
$175 Amazon

The Petzl NAO is the best headlamp I've ever worn. In the past I've used various models from Black Diamond, Petzl, and Fenix while camping and caving. Each one had it's own quirks, but they all, at the end of the day, provided ample light in dark places. What the Petzl NAO does differently is provide a tremendous amount of light in an intelligent and usable manner that makes it easier to do things in the dark.

The stand out feature of the Petzl NAO is the reactive lighting. On top of the headlamp is a light meter that measures the amount of reflected light in order to adjust light output. When you, for example, need to read a map, it senses an increase in reflected light and simultaneously dims light output while switching from a spotlight to a more diffuse beam. This is all automated, and happens instantaneously. After wearing it for an evening, it became indispensable. It's especially a boon when working with other cavers or campers because it automatically dims when looking at someone, preventing any unintentional blinding. The only downside I've read about is for bikers as the beams of an oncoming car can trigger the light to turn off (so bikers will want to turn this feature off).

Previous headlamps I've owned, especially those with battery packs, have been really uncomfortable after extended wear. The NAO, with it's slightly smaller battery pack, only weighs 180 g, and has a really comfortable set of straps. I've worn it running and hiking and have found it to far comfier than the competition.

It also doesn't hurt that the NAO produces an incredible amount of usable light. It's rated at a respectable 355 lumens produced by two LEDs. Unlike other mono-LED lamps (like my Fenix), the two LEDs act in concert to create both diffuse light and a beam with a

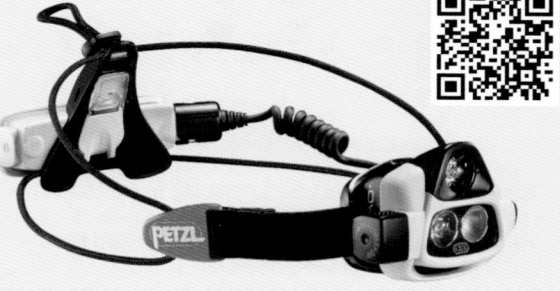

powerful throw. WIth that being said, there are many headlamps that can do this, and the feature that really sets the NAO apart is the auto-dimming.

The last feature worth noting is that the NAO features a USB-rechargeable Li-ion battery pack that is programmable with software provided by Petzl. The software allows you to tweak how the headlamp responds in different environments and activities. I designed a profile for camping which features an ultra-low power mode for reading in the tent, and a much brighter mode with greater throw for trail-running in the dark. While it is a bit gimmicky, the profiles work well in use. The 2300 maH battery pack can be switched out for two AAAs, but it can be a bit tricky and they don't last very long. While I have not had any problem with the batteries, those going on longer expeditions may want to hold off until the Li-ion packs are a bit cheaper.

There's no getting past the fact that the NAO is an expensive light at $175. But to me, and I expect to many others who spend a fair bit of time in the dark, the fact that it intelligently responds to my lighting needs makes it well worth the cost.

-- Oliver Hulland

One highly evolved survival kit
Adventure Medical Kits Pocket Survival Pak
$23 Amazon

At only 3.9 oz. and 4 x 3.25 inches folded this kit is light and small enough that I don't even notice that I am carrying it. It really does fit in my pocket — even a shirt pocket as well.

I tried out the signal mirror and it's the best plastic mirror I've ever used, better by far than the mil-spec mirror from Ultimate Survival. Very easy to aim and gives a very bright concentrated signal flash. The whistle sounds as loud as the Fox40 Classic I used to carry, but much more compact. I've had a Spark-Lite for years and it's a top notch fire starter. The compass works well, I made a lanyard loop out of a short piece of brass wire. You could use the stainless wire in the kit, but I had the brass wire from an older kit.

I am really impressed by the survival instructions. Doug really did a great job with those. There is all the detail you could possibly expect in such a small piece, practical and easy to follow and no stupid BS and the drawings are very well done. You can tell that he's anal about stuff like this and understands how to instruct someone who doesn't know anything about survival. I'd prefer more medical stuff, but I recognize why he didn't include it — he has a good point that there's really not enough room to do it justice, so stick to only the survival stuff.

The rest of the gear (fish hooks, line, scalpel blade, needle, duct tape, magnifier lens, steel wire, etc) is all first rate and well thought out. I'll add some matches myself and a Photon LED microlight, but that's really all it lacks. It's not cheap, but I feel that you more than get your money's worth and it's gear that will not let you down when you need it the most.

I just ordered three more kits so everyone in my family will have one and I'll probably give them away for stocking stuffers this Christmas. Yes, it's that good!!

-- Charles Rowe and Steve Black

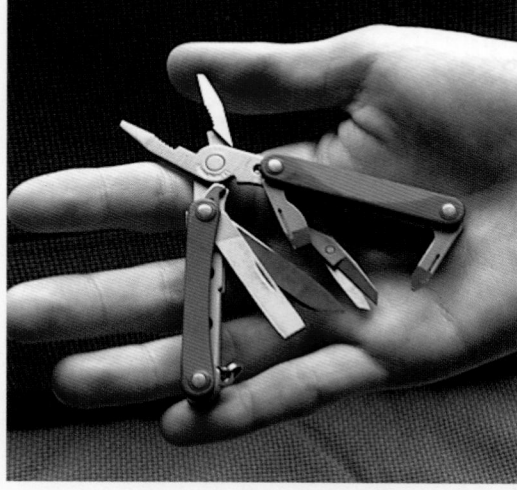

Lightest multi-tool
Leatherman Squirt
$28 Amazon

When saving ounces, this is the lightest multi-tool kit to carry. It's got your knife, pliers, wire cutter, scissors, file, and two screwdrivers in only 2 ounces (57 g). Some folks use it as a keychain fob; I primarily carry it while backpacking and biking. The current best model is PS4.

-- KK

Cool Tools stocking stuffer
Split-Pea Lighter
$12 County Comm

My Cool Tool gift this year is the "Split Pea" Lighter from County Comm. It's the "world's smallest lighter", a stainless steel tube 1.3" high and 0.5" in diameter. Unscrew the top, flick the flint wheel, and behold! Fire!

It's sealed so that you can carry it in your bag, Every Day Carry kit, purse, etc. without worrying about fuel spills or spontaneous combustion. Plus, you never know when you might need fire, right?

I've carried a number of fire-starters in my EDC kit, and the Split Pea is the one I've settled on for durability, weight and size. I wouldn't want to light 20 cigarettes a day with it — it's almost *too* small — but for occasional or emergency use it's perfect.

-- Mike Everett-Lane

That which is not prohibited is mandatory - T. H. White

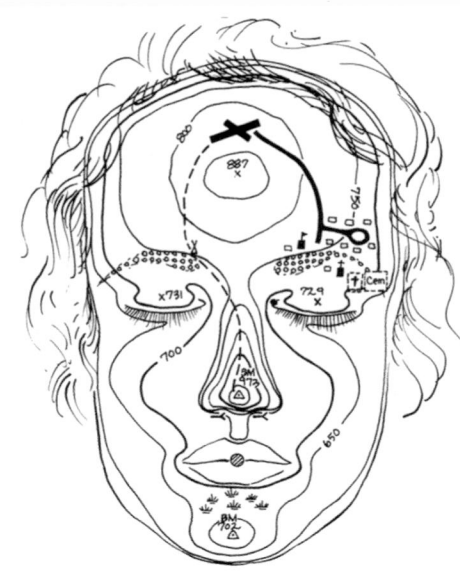

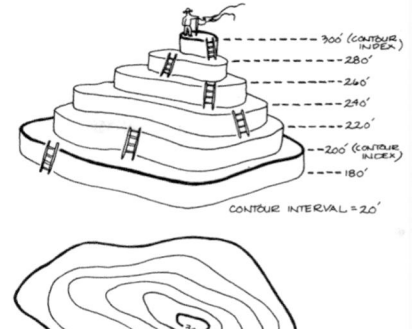

Contour lines as wedding cake layers—hardly a real-world scenario, but useful for visualization.

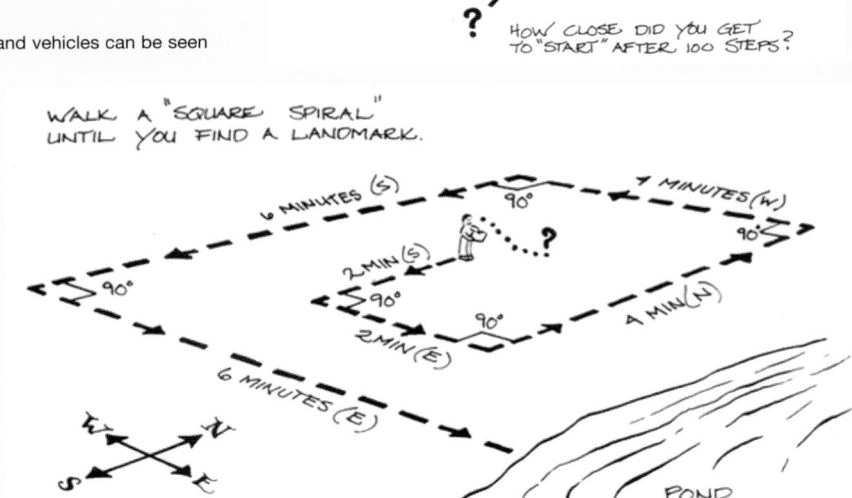

ed then, but now you're lost. You can't figure out how to retrace your steps; everything looks the same, nothing seems familiar. OK, now what are you going to do?

The first thing is to stop. Don't keep on walking and making the situation worse. Admit that you are lost and that it's probably only going to be a small inconvenience, not a life-threatening episode. Calm yourself. Sit down, have a bite to eat, clear your head, and begin looking for clues. Try to remember where you have been during the last half-hour. Envision the last point where you were sure of your position.

Look around for features that might provide a reference. If nothing registers, but you think that you are not far from somewhere familiar, start navigating from scratch. Identify a landmark, or make one, for your current position so you can find it again. Head out from there to explore a little at a time, returning if you are unsuccessful.

•
6 miles: Large houses, small apartment buildings, and towers can be recognized.

2 miles: Chimneys stand out, windows are dots, and vehicles can be seen moving.

1 mile: People look like dots and trunks of large trees can be seen.

1/2 mile: People look like posts and larger branches on trees become visible.

•
You followed some logical route (at least, it seemed so at the time) to get where you are, so there is a chance of finding your way back. But if you start wandering aimlessly about, you may lose even this thin thread of connection. You may become not just simply lost, but profoundly lost - and there is a difference.

Best navigation instruction
The Essential Wilderness Navigator

$12 David Seidman, Paul Cleveland, 2000, 173 p.

How not to get lost. Of all the many books teaching you navigation skills, this one is the best all around. It teaches you how to find your way using any of these: hints in the terrain, sun, stars, maps, a compass, or GPS (coordinates alone are not enough). Clearly illustrated, pragmatic, broad and up-to-date. I actually like getting "lost" occasionally, and this manual has helped me always get back home.

-- KK

How To "Get Found"

Well, now you've done It. You've been daydreaming, seeing the sights. You've turned a corner and realized you haven't a clue about where you are. Fifteen minutes ago you felt yourself hesitate at a junction; 10 minutes later you didn't recognize an obvious landmark. You were merely disorient-

Renting global connection
Satellite Phone Store

satellitephonestore.com

The prime advantage of a satellite phone is that it works ANYWHERE on the planet. It's rare for most of us to spend very long in a remote places far from cell phone coverage so satellite phones are commonly rented, rather than bought. According the the outfits that rent sat phones, there are two major global carriers: Iridium and Globalsat, and Globalsat is no long considered reliable so they sell only tools for the Iridium network or regional satellite nets. The cheapest Iridium phone costs about $50 per week. You pay an additional per minute of use.

A new innovation these days is to use a satellite texting service, which is considerably cheaper than voice, and often just as effective. Some sat devices cannot make a phone call but can send your gps tracking info, canned messages (like I am okay), or distress calls (I am not okay), or even transmit messages via Bluetooth with an adjacent smart phone. Newest of the new are portable "satellite internet" terminals: satellite up and down, broadband out to your laptop or tablet. Also rentable by the week.

To sort all these options out, go to Satellite Phone Store.

-- KK

Inexpensive walkie talkies
Motorola Two-Way Radio

$47 MH230R motorolasolutions.com

For a consumer level walkie-talkie, I recommend the Motorola MH230R, or for slightly longer range, the MR350R. They're in the $50 range per pair. I lived for several years in the Eastern Sierra where we used these for hiking. Usually they were good for 2-3 miles over mountainous terrain, and of course much further if users were in line of sight. I know from personal experience they are good for at least 11 miles as I used them to talk with my wife via a direct line-of-sight. But while they are rated for 23 and 35 miles respectively, for practical purposes, I've never relied on them unless we were within a few miles of each other, with no major obstructions. You can also use them for NOAA weather. They're light & cheap enough to be practical, require AA batteries (rechargeables work fine) and are durable. On some hikes we'd have 5 or 6 deployed, carried by hikers of varying speeds, so we could keep tabs on where everyone was, and for that purpose they worked rather well -- not perfect, but mostly good enough. If you're within a few hundred yards of another radio, they always worked, even around large obstacles.

-- Kevin Rooney

Most accurate altitude
Thommen Altimeter

$240 Thommen

The universally acknowledged best analog altimeter is the Thommen Classic. Accurate to 10 feet elevation, it's intuitively easy to set and read, and it has none of the tiresome trickiness of digital altimeters. Altitude is work; altitude is location. It's good to know exactly where you are.

-- Stewart Brand

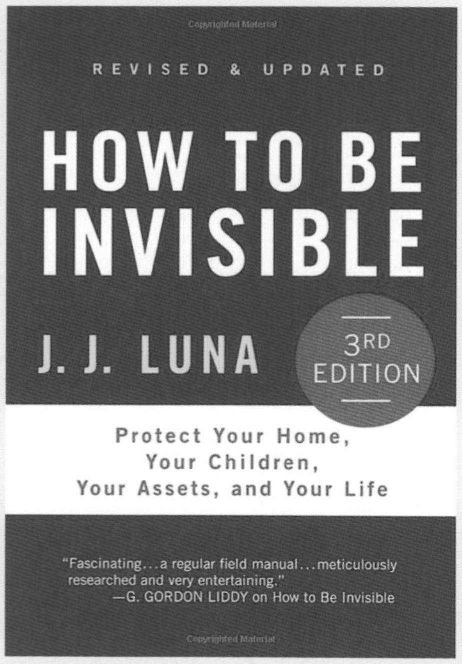

Obscuring your identity

How to be Invisible

$17 J. J. Luna, 2012, 320 p.

This a book about how to hide from people who want to find you, such as ex's, disgruntled associates, opportunistic lawyers, private investigators, stalkers, the press, etc. Hiding means obscuring your identity. It is not about hiding from governments, because as Luna observes, "privacy" is a matter of economics; anyone can be found using enough money, which is what governments have. Luna classifies the 4 levels of obscurity one can achieve by assigning them 4 levels of money paid to find you. Level 1 is hundreds of dollars, Level 2 thousands, and Level 3 tens to hundreds of thousands. Level 4 is the government. The more it costs to find you, the harder you have to work to remain hidden.

This book reveals the many tricks one can do to hide your location, your assets, your identity, while still paying your taxes. Most of these tricks are legal, or at least in the gray zone of not outright illegal. (For instance, by supplying true but irrelevant facts, rather than stating something false.) There are many legitimate reasons for not wanting to be found by someone (spousal abuse, escaping revenge, identity theft, etc.) but I think the overriding one that motivates this book is the fear of having assets seized in a frivolous "deep pocket" law suit.

What is clear from this guide is the degree to which one has to disconnect from ordinary connections in order to achieve the higher levels of obscurity. Very few people will want to live with the constraints required to completely mask your true identity. Yet you are only as hidden as your weakest link, which could be one of a thousands everyday connections such as an old account, forgotten password, unexpected stop at a border, or an old friend. Higher levels of disappearing demand relentless attention, and in many ways privacy becomes a full-time obsession, as it has for the author.

Even though he tries hard in this third edition, Luna is not keeping up to date with the digital world. Hiding is harder, but there are also new opportunities as well. However because Luna advises people to stay off social networks, he is not ahead of the curve. (These days if you don't have a Facebook account full of friends, that is a sign you are fake.) A younger generation will have a harder time implementing these tactics, although the strategy remains the same.

I live my life in the complete opposite direction from what this book advocates, being as transparent and open as possible at all times. Life is too short, and openness has treated me well. Luna would call this naive, and it probably is. There are not many of his suggestions I will actually follow, because I am not battling an ex, not running from the press, not trying to hide assets from unscrupulous lawyers. But as the author notes, the time to enable privacy is before you need it.

Like many other tools, its good to know these options exists, even if you have no plans to use them now. Being aware of what possibilities we have for deep disguise and obsessive privacy is empowering. And of course, if you are trying to find someone, this book has all the tricks they may be using. I learned tons and consider it a bargain education.

-- KK

•

Level Three

This will almost certainly require a move from your present location. Both your home (or rental property) and you vehicles will be in the names of anonymous limited liability companies (LLCs). Your home address will now be hidden from all but your closest relatives and friends. It will no longer appear on your annual tax returns, or anywhere else. If you follow the directions in chapter 12, "E-mail and the Internet," your Internet/e-mail connections will be under cover and the black-hat boys and/or law firms may have to pay a PI some truly serious money to track you down. Are you worth that much to them? If not, sleep well.

•

I learned this one from a FEMA (Federal Emergency Management Agency) agent I met, while staying in a motel that was near a flooded area. Some years ago he bought a $98,995 motor home under another name, and did not license it. (He thus saved not only the license fees and road tax, but an $8,513.57 sales tax as well.) For $12 he got a fifteen-day permit to move it to a rural location in another state. From time to time he moves it, each time getting a temporary permit. Try to find out where this agent actually lives!

•

Watch For This Sneaky Trick

Suppose a private investigator wants to hear you talking to your lawyer (or mistress, or whomever). He may place a conference call, recording every word. Here is how it works. The first call would go to you, and when you answer, the PI punches HOLD and then speed-dials your lawyer. you start saying, "Hello? Hello?" Then your lawyer comes on the line. He recognizes your voice. Each of you may then assume the other person placed the call, and start to chat!

•

Suppose you wish to send $25,000 from Vancouver, British Columbia, to a friend in Helsinki, Finland. You would hand $25,000 cash to a Vancouver money changer (Hawaladar) in Vancouver, and receive code words (or an agreed signal such as a secret handshake) and a contact address in Helsinki. No actual cash moves out of Canada. Instead, when your friend gives the code to the correspondent hawaladar in Helsinki, he will receive the equivalent in euros (less a commission) from money that is already there. To review:

There are no written documents. The exchanges are based on mutual trust (perhaps for that reason unpopular in the United States?).

Only local currencies are used. Thus, if you are sending money from the UK to Mexico, you pay in pounds and the receiver in Mexico collects in pesos.

This exchange cannot be traced because no money crosses a border.

•

Since the IRS treats one-member LLCs as sole proprietorships for tax purposes, there are no income tax consequences. If you use your LLC for a part-time business, for example, you will merely report earnings and expenses on Schedule C and submit it with your 1040 tax return. Repeat: The income--if any--is listed on your personal tax return. Nowhere on the tax form will the name of your limited liability company appear. As far as the IRS is concerned, your limited liability company is invisible.

"How can I prove I own the company," I'm often asked, "if my name doesn't appear anywhere?" If privacy is the goal, I recommend New Mexico LLCs because they do not show ownership in the Articles of Organization (which are a public record). The best way to prove ownership, then, is to have the original LLC documents coupled with an operating agreement.

How to survive jail

Behind Bars: Surviving Prison

$10 Jeffrey Ian Ross & Stephen C. Richards, 2002, 219 p.

Yes, you are a good person. But a relative or friend may not be so law-abiding. And stuff happens. Here is what to do if you are ever arrested (mostly what not to do) and what you can expect if put behind bars. Written by two professors of criminology; one was a former correctional officer, and the other served eleven years in federal custody, including maximum security. They know what they are talking about, and they dispense their straight dope with surprising clarity and uncommon elegance and wit. (One chapter is called "You've Got Jail!"). They've written a guidebook to a distant country and its alien customs and ways; may you never arrive there. You get street-smarts from inmates and wise counsel from the Man. I rank my books by how dog-eared they are; this one had nearly every page marked and underlined. This is one of the books you want to read before you need it.

-- KK

The first thing you need to remember [if arrested] is keep your mouth shut and do not discuss your arrest or case with anyone, police or fellow inmates.

Jailhouse holding tanks are usually bugged with hidden microphones and video cameras. This technology is only incidentally for your protection. Its primary function is to provide the judicial system with an opportunity to gather more incriminating evidence.

•

Whomever you call, never discuss your case on the phone. Any admission of guilt will be used against you in court. Let us repeat: Any admission of guilt will be used against you in court.

The same warning applies to mail, both sent or received, which will be opened and copied by jail staff. Remember, you have no privacy in jail, and every word you say, phone call you make, or letter you write, can be used in court to make a case against you or drum up additional indictments against you or others.

•

In general, with few exceptions, attorneys want their money up front, in advance, or they leave you to throw yourself on the mercy of the court. The reasons are simple enough. If you are found guilty and sent to prison, you will be in no mood to pay your legal bill. Also, many of their clients are crooks who are not overly inclined toward scrupulous bill-paying in the first place. These facts lawyers know only too well, so they will exert great pressure on you to pay up front before your case is decided. You must resist their demands for large sums of money and only pay the attorney a portion of what they ask.

Defense attorneys are like stockbrokers: They collect their fees and commissions on the amount of business they do, no matter whether their customers win or lose. As officers of the court, their first allegiance is to the legal system, even at the expense of their clients. Most lawyers who practice in criminal courts make a good living losing most of their cases, a fact that they rarely share with their clients.

•

You may think the 14th Amendment guarantees you due process, meaning bail, attorney, and a trial by peers. Unfortunately, after being locked up in the county jail, you discover that bail may be denied, lawyers are expensive, and few defendants ever get a trial. The fact is, most people plead guilty to a lesser or reduced charge simply because they get tired of being locked up in jail, their legal defense funds run out, and they fear the possible consequences of losing a trial.

These are the cold, hard equations of crime and punishment. Most cases never go to trial. The attorney persuades the defendant (often after the lawyer has bled the patient dry of money for pre-trial hearings) not to go to trial, arguing that if they lose — and they probably will — they will be sentenced to the full extent of the law.

Yes, you have a Constitutional right to a fair trial, but if you exercise that right and lose the case, the prosecution most likely will demand severe sentencing penalties, in return for your having made them take the case to trial.

•

Another possibility, rarely understood by first-time defendants, but well known to those with lengthier police records, is that once you plead guilty, which becomes public record and part of your police criminal justice dossier, you are more likely to be rearrested, and are easier to convict.

•

The Federal Bureau of Prisons (FBOP) is thought by convicts to operate a better system than most states. The prisons are cleaner, with more desirable food, and the prison staff is better educated, trained, and paid. It is fair to say that most prisoners would prefer to do federal time, day for day, as compared to state time.

That said, federal prisoners are usually allowed fewer material possessions than state convicts. Individuals serving time in state prisons may have their own televisions, collections of books, music, clothes, and posters or pictures hung on their cell walls. Federal prison cells are more austere. These prisoners are restricted to only basic items, such as five books, toiletries, and a few changes of institutional clothes, no television. All of these possessions must be able to fit in one small locker.

•

You will find that every cellblock has "jailhouse lawyers" who will give you more truth than your attorney ever dared to share. (In case you were wondering, jailhouse lawyers are looked down upon by prison administrators, because they can file legal briefs for themselves and fellow inmates; it's not unusual for cons well versed in the law to find themselves transferred frequently.)

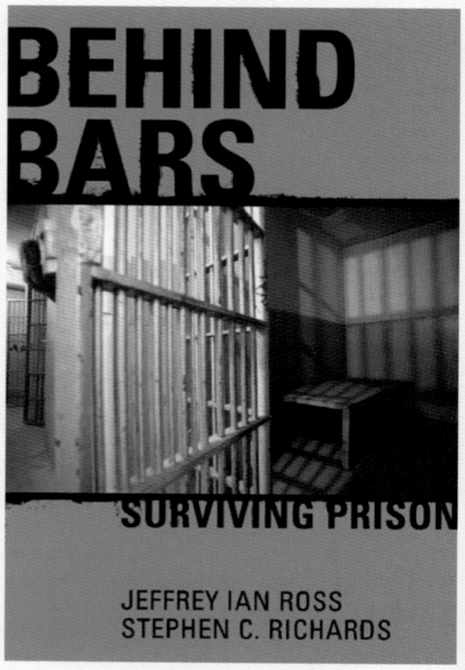

Civilization is a limitless multiplication of unnecessary necessaries. - Mark Twain

Local know-how

How to Run for Local Office

$8 Robert Thomas, 2008, 307 p.

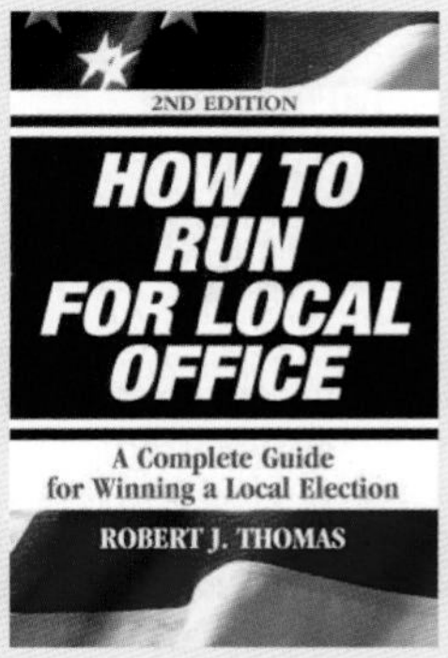
2ND EDITION
HOW TO RUN FOR LOCAL OFFICE
A Complete Guide for Winning a Local Election
ROBERT J. THOMAS

For such a common and essential task as running for local office there is amazingly little practical information. This little book is not the last word, but it is the best start I've found. Good tips, wise counsel, little fluff. You can read it in a few hours and be better prepared than 95% of your opponents.

-- *KK*

•

This is one of the most important questions that you need to ask yourself, why do you really want to run? Are you upset about one particular issue in your community and you've decided to run for office so that you can affect that one issue? If that's the case, give this decision some more thought. There will be dozens of issues. What if you take care of one issue that made you run? Will you be willing to tackle the many other issues that will certainly follow? I've seen people run one-issue campaigns and end up being bored, resigning from office midstream, or even worse, losing their next election because they were ineffective in their first term.

•

The most important thing to remember is this: If you cannot handle the shabby treatment and the stress that goes along with it, get out of the race, you don't belong there. If you think the treatment is bad during the race, it can get much worse after you win. Of course, if you lose, everyone will say what a courageous fighter and campaigner you were. I would much rather hear people say nasty things about me after I have won than to listen to them say nice things about me after I have lost the race.

•

Think about it this way. Even if the person can guarantee 20 people will attend the "coffee hour," you will probably spend at least two hours during this event. If it is in the evening of a work day, you can forget about any door to door walking. Now, out of the twenty who attend, how many of them will actually vote in the election? Remember, they are not being invited using your "good voter" list, so at best, about six of them. Out of those six, how many will you convince to vote for you? Again, at best, two-thirds of them, which is four. Now, compare that to how many "good voters" you could talk to if you had spent two hours out walking door to door. In two hours, averaging five minutes a stop and averaging just 1.5 voters in a household, you could talk to about 36 voters. If you could convince two-thirds of them to vote for you, that's 24 votes compared to 4 during a coffee hour! Remember, it's all about numbers. You need to reach as many "good voters" as you can before the election and you cannot afford to waste time talking to nonvoters.

How to be an effective revolutionary

Rules for Radicals

$12 Saul D. Alinsky, 1971, 224 p.

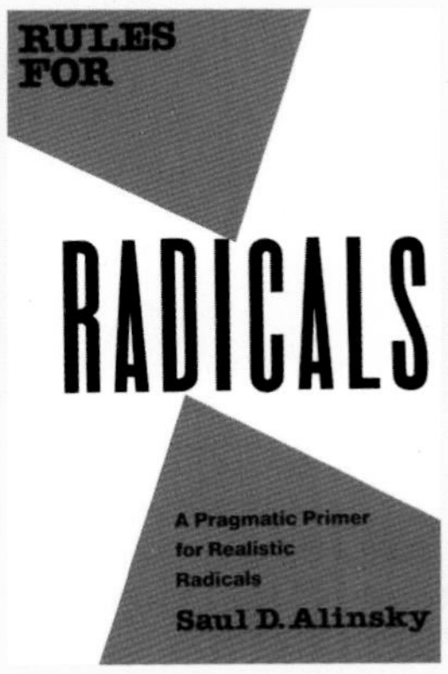
RULES FOR
RADICALS
A Pragmatic Primer for Realistic Radicals
Saul D. Alinsky

Herein are pragmatic tactics for radicals and wannabe radicals of all stripes. Originally written for hippie revolutionaries in the 1970s, today both Tea Party and Occupy folks are quoting and studying it. The "rules" really work, but they are pretty ruthless. Think of this advice as anti-state Machiavelli.

-- *KK*

•

I present here a series of rules pertaining to the ethics of means and ends: first, that one's concern with the ethics of means and ends varies inversely with one's personal interest in the issue. When we are not directly concerned our morality overflows; as La Rochefoucauld put it, "We all have strength enough to endure the misfortunes of others." Accompanying this rule is the parallel one that one's concern with the ethics of means and ends varies inversely with one's distance from the scene of the conflict.

•

Those who opposed the Nazi conquerors regarded the Resistance as a secret army of selfless, patriotic idealists, courageous beyond expectation and willing to sacrifice their lives to their moral convictions. To the occupation authorities, however, these people were lawless terrorists, murderers, saboteurs, assassins, who believed that the end justified the means, and were utterly unethical according to the mystical rules of war. Any foreign occupation would so ethically judge its opposition. However, in such conflict, neither protagonist is concerned with any value except victory. It is life or death.

•

For an elementary illustration of tactics, take parts of your face as the point of reference; your eyes, your ears, and your nose. First the eyes: if you have organized a vast, mass-based people's organization, you can parade it visibly before the enemy and openly show your power. Second the ears; if your organization is small in numbers, then do what Gideon did: conceal the members in the dark but raise a din and clamor that will make the listener believe that your organization numbers many more than it does. Third, the nose; if your organization is too tiny even for noise, stink up the place.

Always remember the first rule of power tactics: Power is not only what you have but what the enemy thinks you have.

The second rule is: Never go outside the experience of your people. When an action or tactic is outside the experience of the people, the result is confusion, fear, and retreat. It also means a collapse of communication, as we have notes.

The third rule is: Wherever possible go outside the experience of the enemy. Here you want to cause confusion, fear, and retreat.

The fourth rule is: Make the enemy live up to their own book of rules. You can kill them with this, for they can no more obey their own rules than the Christian church can live up to Christianity.

The fourth rule carries within in the fifth rule: Ridicule is man's most potent weapon. It is almost impossible to counterattack ridicule. Also it infuriates the opposition, who then react to your advantage.

The sixth rule is: A good tactic is one that your people enjoy. If your people are not having a ball doing it, there is something very wrong with the tactic.

The seventh rule: A tactic that drags on too long becomes a drag.

•

The twelfth rule: The price of a successful attack is a constructive alternative. You cannot risk being trapped by the enemy in his sudden agreement with your demand and saying "You're right–we don't know what to do about this issue. Now you tell us."

The thirteenth rule: Pick the target, freeze it, personalize it, and polarize it.

Best cultural introduction

Hello! USA

$22 Judy Priven, Anne P. Copeland, 2011, 244 p.

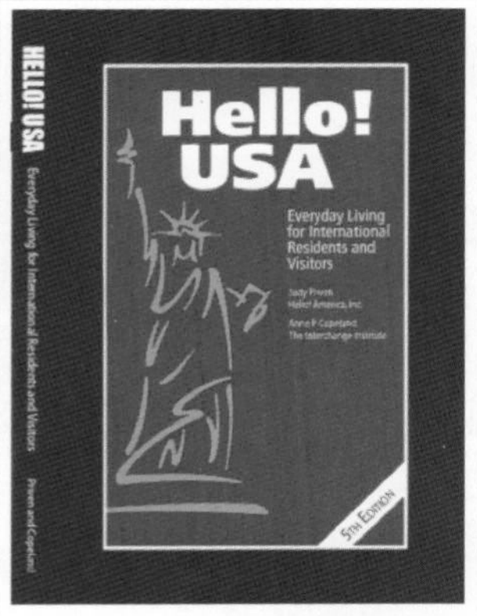
Hello! USA
Everyday Living for International Residents and Visitors

Over the years, I've hosted a dozen different newly arrived immigrants in my residences. Some came from Eastern Europe, some from Africa, some from Asia, with different experiences of modernity. But all these bewildered immigrants were FOB -- fresh off the boat, and overwhelmed. They didn't know all the thousands of tiny but critical every-day knowledge it takes to survive in the US. Like how to write a personal check (an almost unique American system), get a credit card, file a tax return, what to bring to a party, how to rent a place, apply for a job, get a SS#, properly greet people, decipher a drug prescription, and so on. These are all things that you know but you don't even know you know.

So over the years I've handed new visitors the most current edition of this book. It's the best of a number of American cultural survival books. It requires good English comprehension (not as much as some of the other guides); if the new arrival does not read English well, you can use this book as your guide to convey to them the invisible systems in the US. Often immigrants will pick up this kind of info from older immigrants of their same background -- if there are any nearby -- but that friendly info is not always correct or the best.

I've often thought a version of this book, slightly modified, would be great for teenagers about to head off on their own. That kind of guide would seem obvious to most of us, since it would be full of stuff that "everyone knows." Meaning we weren't explicitly taught it. But mastering the complexity of modern life should be taught and is taught pretty well in Hello! USA.

America is a nation built on the incoming flow of immigrants. There will be more coming. This is a good tool if you have the occasion to help a new arrival.

-- *KK*

•

Choosing Legal Assistance. Tell the truth whenever any immigration officer interviews you or you are filling out a government form. If you are having any immigration problems, an attorney may be able to help you, as long as you have told the truth; if you have not told the truth, your problem may be more difficult to solve. You may even be deported without the right to return.

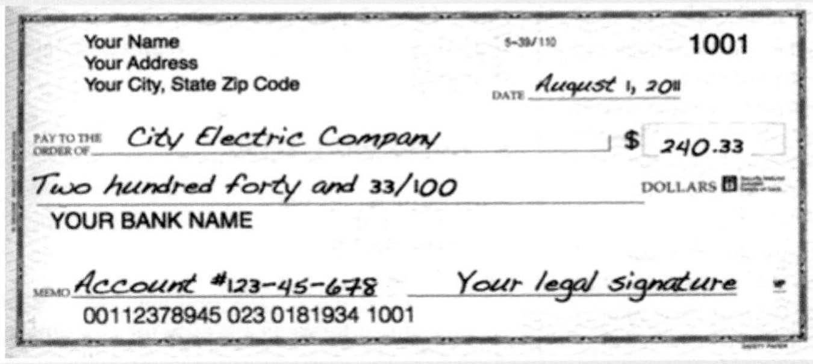
Your Name
Your Address
Your City, State Zip Code
5-38/110
1001
DATE August 1, 2011
PAY TO THE ORDER OF City Electric Company
$ 240.33
Two hundred forty and 33/100
DOLLARS
YOUR BANK NAME
MEMO Account #123-45-678
Your legal signature
00112378945 023 0181934 1001

Write the amount both in numbers and in words. Draw a line after the words to fill the space, so no one can change your writing. (In this example, the "bank routing number" is pre-printed in the bottom left-hand corner (00112378945). Your bank "account number" is next (0230181934). The last few digits (1101) refer to this specific check.)

•

What to Do If a Police Officer Stops Your Car

When you see the flashing lights behind you, stop your car on the side of the road as soon as it is safe.

Do not get out of your car. Wait for the officer to come to your car. Then lower your window.

The police officer will ask to see your drivers' license and your automobile registration.

Let the officer tell you why you were stopped.

Cooperate and be courteous.

Do not try to pay your fine in cash to the policeman. If he misunderstands you, he may think you are trying to bribe him which is against the law. Pay all fines by mail or to the clerk of a court.

•

Garage Sales.

In the warm months, you will see signs advertising "garage sales" (also called "moving sales," "yard sales," "tag sales," or "barn sales"). People put out (in their garage, or yard, or barn) housewares, toys, clothes, and appliances that they no longer need or want. The prices are usually very low. The quality will range from excellent to awful. Sometimes several families or a church will join together to hold one of these sales - then the selection is large. These are sometimes called "flea markets."

•

Gifts for Special Occasions

Wedding and bridal shower.

Many couples make a list of the gifts they want; then they "register" the list at a store. Ask the couple if they are "registered." Then go to the store with the list and choose something to send. See Chapter 12 for more details about registries.

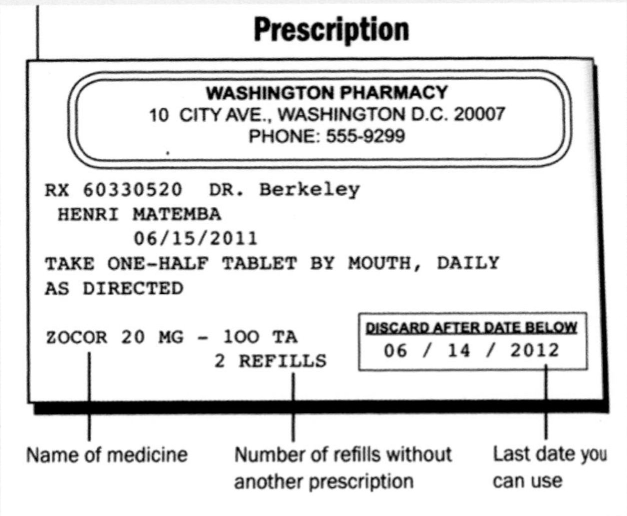
Prescription
WASHINGTON PHARMACY
10 CITY AVE., WASHINGTON D.C. 20007
PHONE: 555-9299
RX 60330520 DR. Berkeley
HENRI MATEMBA
06/15/2011
TAKE ONE-HALF TABLET BY MOUTH, DAILY
AS DIRECTED
ZOCOR 20 MG - 100 TA
2 REFILLS
DISCARD AFTER DATE BELOW
06 / 14 / 2012
Name of medicine
Number of refills without another prescription
Last date you can use

•

Being "On Time"

Parties at home: Do not come even a few minutes early for any party at a home; often, the host or hostess will still be getting ready.

Appointments: Come at the exact time. Many Americans do not like to be kept waiting. In fact, if you are more than 20 minutes late, the person may not wait any longer for you.

No artist is ahead of his time. He is the time. It is just that others are behind the time. - Martha Graham

309

Community

Our seventh Quantified Self Meetup. A decent monthly group of this size was only possible for us because of Meetup.

Local community self-organizer
Meetup
Free Meetup

The most effective local community-enhancing tool I know of is Meetup. This service helps you find, recruit, manage, and cultivate people in a local area who are, or could be, sharing an issue, idea, or passion. Let's say you are a barefoot runner who wants to meet other local barefoot runners, or you are an activist trying to stop land mines in wars and want to engage other like-minded locals, or maybe you have a crazy idea for a new kind of retail store and you want to network with other retail business people. In each case, you can use Meetup to help find others, to help them find you, and most importantly to help you schedule and curate face-to-face meetings gathered around your interest. Meetups can range in size from less than 5 people to more than 500.

I used Meetup (with Gary Wolf) to launch and operate the Quantified Self movement, which now holds regular meetings in almost 100 cities around the world. I've also used Meetup to start a community of self publishers in our vicinity interested in sharing their best practices for e-books. And Meetup has saved me much trouble and effort in another way: when I have a yearning to connect to something new to me I often find that someone has already started a local Meetup with this idea or passion. Meetup makes it easy to evaluate and join an ongoing local community. Meetup is 100 times easier than trying to organize a meeting or event by hand. It automates the notifications, the who-is-attending list, the agenda (or not), the map to the meeting place, the calendar, the history of past meetings. Essentially, Meetup makes meeting as self-organizing as possible. Members who attend a meetup rate the meeting afterwards, so there is feedback in improving them.

Every Meetup is run differently. Many are casual, open to anyone, and free. Some organizers charge membership dues as the number of people attending increases; some charge event fees. The Meetup software handles all these payment options superbly. It does not cost anything to get a Meetup account, or join most Meetups, but it does cost something to organize a Meetup. The "organizer dues" needed to run up to three Meetups is $12 month. If you've ever tried to organize regular meetings of any size, you'll recognize this self-organizing tool as a bargain.

--KK

A guide to avoiding and surviving violence
How to Win a Fight
$13 Lawrence Kane and Kris Wilder, 2011, 208 p.

This book could be titled "How and Why You Should Do Everything Possible to Avoid Getting Into a Fight." The authors (both martial artists who've been around the block a few times and have the scars to show it) spend a good number of pages explaining why fighting is always terrible idea — even if you manage to win, you end up losing (your attacker's relatives could sue you or seek revenge, you could go to prison, and for the rest of your life you could carry the knowledge of having crippled or maimed another person).

The authors also go into detail explaining how to recognize the first signs of a situation that could escalate into a fight and what to do. Only after they've convinced you to avoid a fight do they get to the section about effective ways of defending yourself.

The final third of the book deals with the often unconsidered aftermath of a fight: administering first aid and what to do to stay out of jail.

-- Mark Frauenfelder

- Escape and survival are admirable goals. Self-defense really isn't about fighting like most people think. Self-defense is about not being there when the other guy wants to fight. Fighting is a participatory event, which means you were part of the problem. Even if you think you are only "defending" yourself, if your actions contributed to the creation, escalation, and execution of violence the you were fighting. And fighting is illegal and a really bad idea.

- It is illuminating to watch a crowd at a mall, nightclub, or other public area with a predator mindset. Read people's body language as they pass by you. Who looks like a victim and who does not? Oblivious people stand out from the crowd once you know how to look for them.

- **Four techniques you can use in a fight**

1. Don't let him get close enough to touch you. The farther away the other guy is, the tougher it is for him to hit you. Further, you have a much better chance to escape to safety or dash toward some source of cover that can protect you.

2. Throw debris to distract or injure him. Throwing debris is really an extension of distance. It is not a standalone technique, but rather a facilitator that can keep the other guy back and help you escape. You can kick dust, throw rocks, hurl trash, swing garbage cans, or otherwise chuck stuff at the other guy to distract or potentially injure him.

3. Attack his eyes. When you have an opportunity to attack the eyes during a fight, the chance will be only there for an instant. If you are going to go for the shot, you've got to take advantage of that moment of opportunity.

4. Strike with impetus. No matter how skilled you are (or are not), strikes work best when you catch your opponent by surprise, control distance and direction of your blow, relax until the moment of contact, and strike ferociously and repeatedly until the conflict is over.

- **Ferocity**

All things being equal, the guy who attacks with the most ferocity wins. Even if the other guy is a bit stronger or more skilled than you are, he's likely to disengage if he realizes he's bitten off more than he can chew. If you have no other choice but to fight, do so wholeheartedly. Your adversary should feel like he's run across a rabid wolverine wielding an industrial buzz saw. Strike fast, hard, and repeatedly until it's over and you can escape to safety. Throwing a single blow or short combination and dancing aside to see if it had any effect may work well in the tournament ring, but it's woefully inadequate on the street. Give it everything you're worth and don't stop until it's over.

Best advice on how to negotiate
Getting To Yes
$11 Roger Fisher, 2011, 240 p.

The International Bestseller

UPDATED AND REVISED

getting to
yes
negotiating an agreement without giving in

ROGER FISHER & WILLIAM URY
and for the revised editions Bruce Patton

I used to think that negotiation was about positioning, leveraging, and finally winning. This book by William Ury change my view completely. I no longer think of negotiation as a game. I see now it is about not getting into a fight in the first place. By resolving conflicts before they escalate, respecting mutual interests, and engaging others with compassion, you can achieve something far greater than victory: peace.

I love the wisdom in this best-selling book, which lays out a concise yet compassionate method for achieving desired outcomes in negotiations. The book's principles align to an uncanny extent with my Chinese philosophy of being open to seeing the opposing view in life. It advocates principles such as "Listen with respect," which is the same traditional concept in Chinese as "If you know yourself and know your opponent, you avoid war and both win."

By using this understanding framework (the "Yes" in the title) I've been successful in business negotiations. If we get stuck – which happens frequently – I like to ask the other party "What are you most afraid of?" Once I understand their fears, I try to come up solutions that address them, and at the same time I am open to share my own fears. Turns out people want to be understood before they are open to understand you.

I also used this principle of "understanding and communication," rather than "positioning, leveraging and winning" in my personal life, quickly coming to mutual agreement in situations like a divorce which are not usually quickly resolved. The outcome of this compassionate framework may not be optimal based on the standard expectations, but it is the optimal outcome based on the real context of the two parties.

In short, the concepts in this book really work.

-- Ping Fu

- 1. Separate the people from the problem

- 2. Focus on interests rather than positions

- 3. Generate a variety of options before settling on an agreement

- 4. Insist that the agreement be based on objective criteria.

- Participants can avoid falling into a win-lose mentality by focusing on shared interests.

- Power in a negotiation comes from the ability to walk away from negotiations.

- Blaming is an easy mode to fall into, particularly when you feel that the other side is indeed responsible. But even if blaming is justified, it is usually counterproductive. Under attack, the other side will become defensive and will resist what you have to say. They will cease to listen, or they will strike back with an attack of their own.

Assessing blame firmly entangles the people with the problem.

- Your position is something you have decided upon. Your interests are what caused you to so decide.

- We often try to influence others by threats and warnings of what will happen if they do not decide as we would like. Offers are usually more effective

- The listeners should give the speaker their full attention, occasionally summarizing the speaker's points to confirm their understanding.

- The more attention that is paid to positions, the less attention is devoted to meeting the underlying concerns of the parties.

- The key to reconciling different interests is to look for items that are of low cost to you and high benefit to them, and vice versa.

- The best way to respond to such tricky tactics is to explicitly raise the issue in negotiations, and to engage in principled negotiation to establish procedural ground rules for the negotiation.

- Judgment hinders imagination.

- Give them a stake in the outcome by making sure they participate in the process. If they are not involved in the process, they are unlikely to approve the product. It is that simple.

- Look for opportunities to act inconsistently with their perceptions. Perhaps the best way to change someone's perceptions is to send them a message different from what they expect.

HOW TO WIN A FIGHT
A GUIDE TO AVOIDING AND SURVIVING VIOLENCE

LAWRENCE KANE AND KRIS WILDER

Is there anything in the universe more addictive than being a god? - Kevin Kelly

Dashboard for the hive mind
PopUrls
Free PopUrls

For the past 8 years Popurls has been my daily first stop on the web.

This single page now replaces my need to directly read Reddit, Slashdot, BoingBoing, Buzz, Metafilter, HoPo, the Verge and all the other aggregator sites. Popurls is the meta-aggregator, the aggregator of the aggregators. This one page encapsulates up-to-the-minute headlines from 15 consensus filters, and top thumbnail images from the social sites Flickr, YouTube, and 500pixels. The hive mind on one screen.

Here's how I use it. On one page I can scan the latest headlines of what the web collectively thinks is either popular or interesting. A simple mouse over the headline will cleverly reveal a small box of expanded text on the article. If I want even more, a click will open the original entry in the filter. In five minutes I can scan 18 social site sources thoroughly. I get an excellent feel for what is new and what is worth following up (a small amount of overlap between sources helps).

The design of PopUrls is brilliant. There's two flavors, black on white or white on

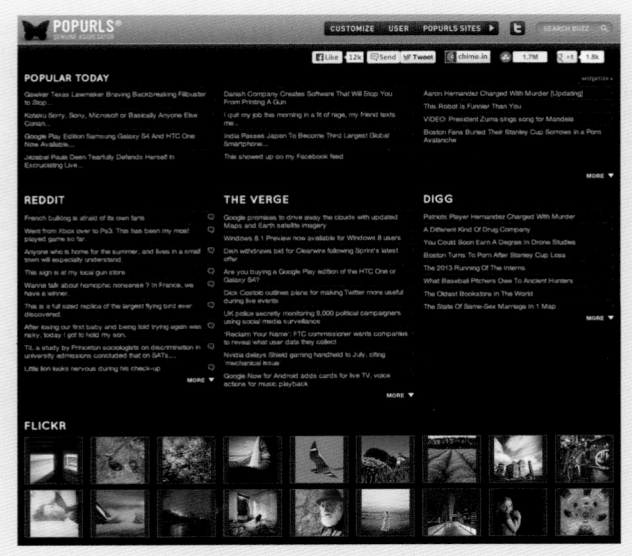

black. Function drives form, buttons are minimal. It feels like a well-designed command post for a concise debriefing. Even on a large screen, like the 21-incher I use, there's a bit of scrolling. But I've come to realize that I MUCH prefer this single fixed sheet to endless RSS feeds in a reader. In fact, the page is essentially an improved interface for multiple RSS feeds, which keep PopUrls constantly updated. The dashboard doesn't move, while all the streams flowing into it keep it lively.

There's no better way to watch the hive mind.

-- KK

Customized search
Stumble Upon
Free Stumblr Upon

Stumble Upon is a community-based website recommendation engine that serves up fantastic random websites. Completely addictive, it still does that. But now that they have added search (including video and image search), it has moved from frivolous to useful, and Stumble Upon is beginning to replace Google as my primary search engine. You cannot yet add Stumble Search as the primary search engine in your browser, but the Stumble Upon tool bar makes it nearly as convenient.

Let's say you are looking for a new dining room table. If you put "dining table" into Google you get a gazillion crappy tables. If you put the same search entry into Stumble Upon you get 100 of the coolest tables on the net. The same is true in its video and image search engine. For instance, when I wanted to find a video for my wife who was learning Roller Derby, I searched You Tube and got thousands of results, almost all of them below mediocre. But when I searched Stumble Upon Video I got only 10 results, and all of them were awesome.

The key to the system is that for every site that you "stumble upon" in your web surfing, you can give it a

thumbs up or down (or tag or comment it). Really cool content propagates through the network fast, yet people trying to game the system to give their pages high stumble ranks get voted down very quickly. When I met the founders of Stumble Upon recently I asked how they managed to do this so well, and they said that they did not write a single line of code until they had worked out the anti-spam strategy. While there are several recommendation engines on the web like Digg, Delicious, and Reddit, Stumble Upon's interface, huge active community, and easy tools make it the one that always delivers the highest level of cool stuff. It is basically how I find everything that I blog about.

-- Alexander Rose

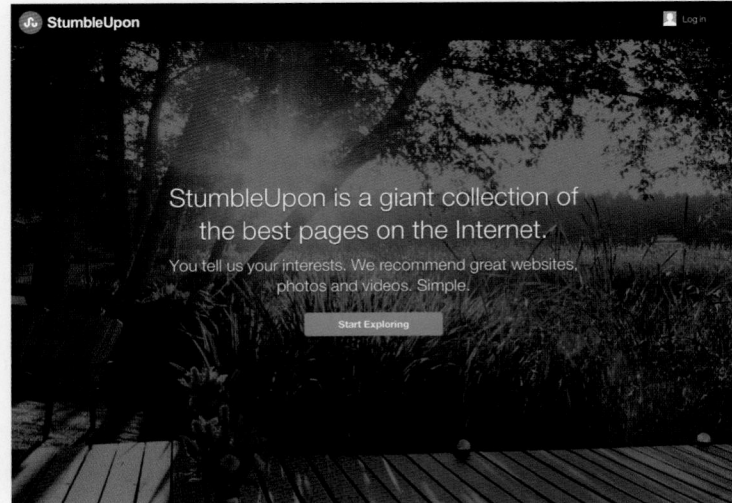

Guide to the collaborative encyclopedia
Wikipedia: The Missing Manual
$21 John Broughton, 2008, 502 p.

Just because anyone can edit Wikipedia doesn't mean it's easy. Sure, you can edit anonymously and say anything you like, but if you want to make edits that last and if you want to participate in a meaningful way that complies with community guidelines, well, there's a lot to learn. Guidelines can be hard to find on the site, and for better or worse, they're always evolving.

Wikipedia: The Missing Manual is logically structured, includes lots of screen-shots, and is infinitely skimmable. A great introduction and a handy reference, the manual starts out with the basics: editing, creating articles and maintaining them (yes, that's just the start). More advanced topics include collaboration, advanced formatting, broader site structure, and interface customization.

Documentation at the website is not particularly searchable given the site's relatively simplistic one-box-fits-all search interface; browsing through documentation and discussion can be difficult and, frankly, overwhelming. In addition to the quite readable, cover to cover flow, the book has a comprehensive index that allows for quick navigation that delivers precise answers to the myriad questions that inevitably arise, especially when you're just getting familiar with this medium.

Make no mistake, community consensus is always the last (ever-changing) word. But John Broughton, who has also overseen the Editor's Index to Wikipedia project, can help you ease into editing without committing any major blunders.

The Manual has been migrated to Wikipedia. Checkout the dynamic incarnation at Help:Wikipedia: The Missing Manual.

-- Camille Hartsell

•

Wikipedia's rate of change has presented a challenge in writing this book. It's as current as it can be, but if you notice that a screenshot isn't exactly the way Wikipedia appears to you on screen, the something (minor) has changed since just before this book was published. You will see mentions in a number of places in the book about where change may be just around the corner (a WYSISYG edit box, threaded discussions on talk pages, single sign-in across all Foundation projects, and more). These changes could happen just as you're reading this book, or not for a year or two.

Nevertheless, you'll find the core of Wikipedia changes very slowly–after all, it does have an established base of active editors, and a history of success that makes editors reluctant to chance processes that aren't considered broken. So the changes that aren't covered by this book won't prevent you from gaining great Wikipedia editing skills.

•

You don't need to know everything about Wikipedia to edit an article. Wikipedia has literally hundreds of pages of policy, guidelines, and how-to information on topics such as capitalization, categorization, citations, copyrights, disclaimers, foreign language characters, headings, indentation, links, lists, neutrality, pronunciation, quotations, tags, and templates, to name just a few. If you don't get something exactly right, don't worry–no one else gets everything right every time either.

•

You don't need to know everything about your subject to edit an article. If you add something that's constructive and 90-percent right, that's far better than not doing an edit at all. As in sports, you don't need to hit a home run or score a goal on every play to be a valuable contributor. If you don't get something exactly right, someone else is likely to come along and help by fixing or finishing it.

•

You can contribute without editing at all. if you see a problem in an article, but you don't (yet) know how to fix it, or you do know how to fix it, but you can't edit the article (some articles are fully protected, typically for short periods of time), you can still help by posting a constructive comment on the article's talk (discussion) page. If you don't want to or can't edit an article directly, you can still help to improve it.

•

A second role of WikiProjects is to maintain portals, mini-Main pages which are entry points for particular topics. ... Note: If you want to search for text or information on a portal page, you need to modify your search to include the namespace Portal, because the normal Wikipedia search is only for information on article pages (pages in the Main namespace). You can do this by modifying your search on the Wikipedia search page by checking the box for the Portal namespace, after doing an initial search to get to the main search page. Another is to

change your preference sos that your searches automatically include both mainspace and portalspace.

•

The phrase "For factual and other kinds of questions" means that the Help desk is not the place to look for information contained in encyclopedia articles. For questions like, "How long do butterflies live?" use the search box to find the article Butterfly, which probably contains the answer.

Some questions aren't answered in articles because they're not really encyclopedic, like "What's a good camera to buy for someone who wants to be a professional photographer?" Take those questions to the Reference desk (shortcut: WP:R), which is similar to a librarian service (and another place to put your question-answering expertise to good use).

•

What you see in the Wikipedia window in front of you isn't fixed in concrete. Wikipedia has a surprising number of ways that you can modify its appearance when you view it. If you're a registered editor, you have a My Preferences page, where you can change a number of settings that control how Wikipedia's pages look on your screen.

•

In late 2007, Wikipedia added a new, eleventh tab to the My Preferences page–the Gadgets tab. The Gadgets tab lets you quickly implement JavaScript user scripts developed by other editors to add cool new features to Wikipedia. Chapter 21 describes how to implement JavaScript user scripts by copying them to a page in your userspace. Using the Gadgets tab is much easier; just select a gadget, and then click Save. Then, as the instructions at the bottom of the tab say, bypass your browser cache to see the gadget's effects. You can get more information about each item on the Gadgets tab by looking at the Special:Gadgets page.

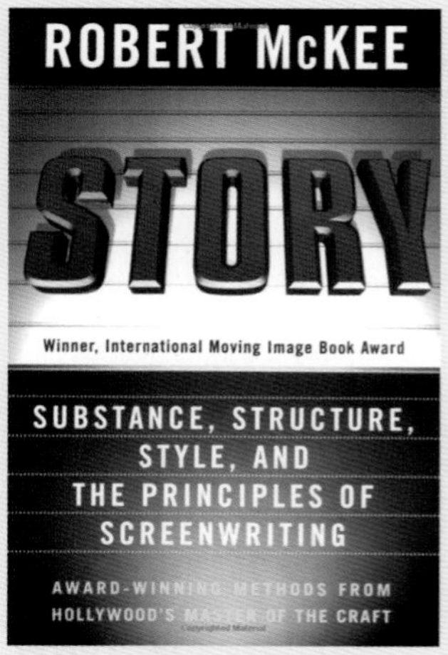
ROBERT McKEE
STORY
Winner, International Moving Image Book Award
SUBSTANCE, STRUCTURE, STYLE, AND THE PRINCIPLES OF SCREENWRITING
AWARD-WINNING METHODS FROM HOLLYWOOD'S MASTER OF THE CRAFT

Mastering the craft of stories

Story

$27 Robert McKee, 1997, 466 p.

The elemental unit of human experience is the story. Yet few people know how a story works, or why, or how to make a good story. When I began this book I thought it was a manual for Hollywood screenwriters, which it is. There are scores of other books in the genre, but ignore them. Professional screenwriters all swear by McKee's *Story* as the key guide to creating a story that works. Halfway through this book, it altered me as an audience; I was watching and reading differently. By the end, I realized that this was actually a book about living. Constructing a story that works is similar to constructing a life that works. For people trying to write a story, for people listening to a story, for people trying to compose an interesting life, this is a profoundly important guide. I find it worth rereading every couple of years.

I recommend using the four-hour audio version of this book for several reasons. One, it is abridged, and improved by that, and two, you get more a sense of storytelling by listening, rather than reading, and three, the author delivers his message in his own strong voice, which in this case conveys his passion and intelligence more than his words alone do. From an instant to eternity, from the intracranial to the intergalactic, the life story of each and every character offers encyclopedic possibilities. The mark of a master is to select only a few moments but give us a lifetime.

-- KK

•

Classical design means a story built around an active protagonist who struggles against primarily external forces of antagonism to pursue his or her desire, through continuous time, within a consistent and causally connected fiction reality, to a closed ending of absolute, irreversible change.

•

When an Inciting Incident occurs it must be a dynamic, fully developed event, not something static or vague. This, for example, is not an Inciting Incident: A college dropout lives off-campus near New York University. She wakes one morning and says: "I'm bored with my life. I think I'll move to Los Angeles." She packs her VW and motors west, but her change of address changes nothing of value in her life. She's merely exporting her apathy from New York to California.

If on the other hand, we notice that she's created an ingenious kitchen wallpaper from hundreds of parking tickets, then a sudden pounding on the door brings the police, brandishing a felony warrant for ten thousand dollars in unpaid citations, and she flees down the fire escape, heading West — this could be an Inciting Incident. It has done what an Inciting Incident must do.

The INCITING INCIDENT radically upsets the balance of forces in the protagonist's life.

•

The energy of a protagonist's desire forms the critical element of design known as the Spine of the story (AKA Through-line or Super-objective). The spine is the deep desire in and effort by the protagonist to restore the balance of life. It's the primary unifying force that holds all other story elements together. For no matter what happens on the surface of the story, each scene, image, and word is ultimately an aspect of the Spine, relating, causally or thematically, to this core of desire and action.

If the protagonist has no unconscious desire, then his conscious objective becomes the Spine. The Spine of any Bond film, for example, can be phrased as: To defeat the arch-villain. James has no unconscious desires; he wants and only wants to save the world. As the story's unifying force, Bond's pursuit of his conscious goal cannot change. If he were to declare, "To hell with *Dr. No*. I'm bored with the spy business. I'm going south to work on my backswing and lower my handicap," the film falls apart.

•

A Turning Point is centered in the choice a character makes under pressure to take one action or another in the pursuit of desire. Human nature dictates that each of us will always choose the "good" or the "right" as we perceive the "good" or the "right." It is impossible to do otherwise. Therefore, if a character is put into a situation where he must choose between a clear good versus a clear evil, or right versus wrong, the audience, understanding the character s point of view, will know in advance how the character will choose.

•

Good/evil, right/wrong choices are dramatically obvious and trivial. True choice is dilemma. It occurs in two situations. First, a choice between irreconcilable goods: From the character's view two things are desirable, he wants both, but circumstances are forcing him to choose only one. Second, a choice between the lesser of two evils: From the character's view two things are undesirable, he wants neither, but circumstances are forcing him to choose one. How a character chooses in a true dilemma is a powerful expression of his humanity and of the world in which he lives.

This collection of timeless principles I call the Archplot: Arch (pronounced "ark" as in archangel) in the dictionary sense of eminent above others of the same kind.

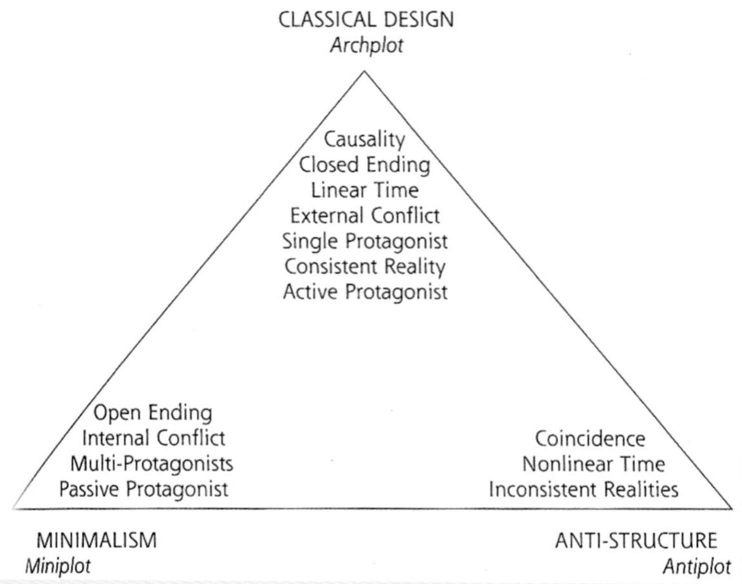
CLASSICAL DESIGN
Archplot
Causality
Closed Ending
Linear Time
External Conflict
Single Protagonist
Consistent Reality
Active Protagonist
Open Ending
Internal Conflict
Multi-Protagonists
Passive Protagonist
Coincidence
Nonlinear Time
Inconsistent Realities
MINIMALISM
Miniplot
ANTI-STRUCTURE
Antiplot

Heuristics for editing film

The Eye is Quicker

$19 Richard D. Pepperman, 2004, 350 p.

As any kid with iMovie knows, you assemble a film from short pieces cut from raw shots. Ah, but where do you cut? This frame, or that one? And which order do you join them? The art of a movie often lies in exactly how it is edited frame by frame. Much like the art of placing one word after another. The possibilities could go a million ways, but only one sequence will appear inevitable in retrospect. So how do you decide?

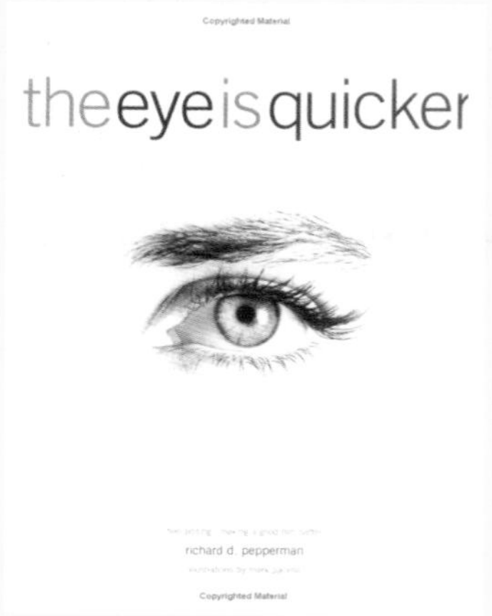
theeyeisquicker
richard d. pepperman

Of all the many books on editing motion pictures, I found this one explains the logic of editing best. It assumes you can handle the mechanics of the craft (no software menus or photo tech speak here). Instead what I got from this idiosyncratic book is a set of very handy rules of thumb for editing moving pictures. I'd say that this guide won't be of much help for your YouTube videos, but would enlighten any attempt at a long-form film.

-- KK

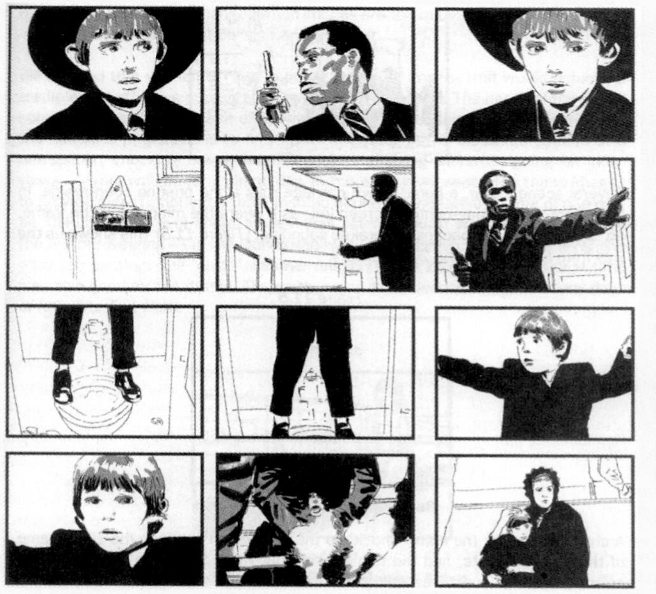

◄

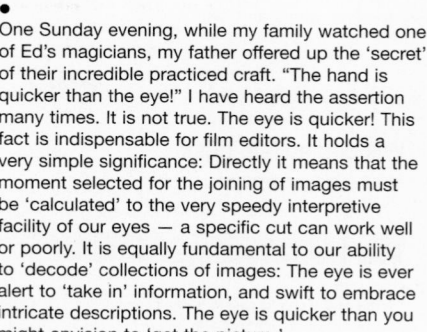

Witness. The Amish Boy in the Train Station Restroom scene. Time is extended — many more toilets than earlier — as one of the killers searches the stalls looking for the source of a low cry. The Amish Boy escapes detection. the shot holds on his face. Beat, beat, beat. Then a cut: We see the back of a policeman. We hear police walkie-talkies. The policeman clears the frame, and we see the Amish Boy in the arms of his mother. They are seated on a bench in the station waiting area. Policemen are all about.

By 'passing up' images of the Amish boy 'screaming' out from the restroom, a brilliant instance of pure cinematic storyshowing is crafted:

The clout in Time Left Out!

•

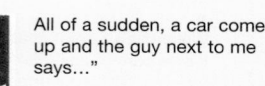

One Sunday evening, while my family watched one of Ed's magicians, my father offered up the 'secret' of their incredible practiced craft. "The hand is quicker than the eye!" I have heard the assertion many times. It is not true. The eye is quicker! This fact is indispensable for film editors. It holds a very simple significance: Directly it means that the moment selected for the joining of images must be 'calculated' to the very speedy interpretive facility of our eyes — a specific cut can work well or poorly. It is equally fundamental to our ability to 'decode' collections of images: The eye is ever alert to 'take in' information, and swift to embrace intricate descriptions. The eye is quicker than you might envision to 'get the picture.'

•

David Mamet gives a clear — and simple — example of this in On Directing Film: "The movie... is much closer than the play to simple storytelling. If you listen to the way people tell stories, you will hear that they tell them cinematically. They jump from one thing to the next, and the story is moved along by the juxtaposition of images — which is to say by the cut. People say, "I'm standing on the corner. It's a foggy day. A bunch of people are running around crazy. Might have been a full moon. All of a sudden, a car comes up and the guy next to me says..."

•

Plainly put, the good film editor strives to join the many film fragments, so that the structure established might hold enchantment, with no attentive concern about a cut. If there is form and purpose the audience can be captivated by the experience. In all creative storytelling, whether film, theatre, or literature, the aim is the same: have the fragments fade, and what remains is the harmony of the whole.

•

I never cut for matches, I cut for impact. --Sam O'Steen

•

Editors are sculptors who bend, mold, and breach time -- in semblance, not in exactness. ... This means that a 'feeling' has been stirred that a pause, or a 'holding' (on a shot) of some additional 'time' is required; or that the opposite is needed -- an existing beat, or two, shouldn't.

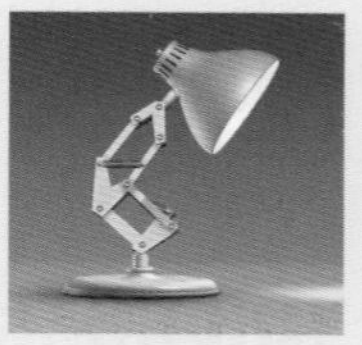

Pixar Story Rules

Pixar story artist Emma Coats tweeted a series of "story basics" that are as good as storytelling guidelines as any printed. Here are a few select ones:

•You admire a character for trying more than for their successes.

•Once upon a time there was ___. Every day, ___. One day ___. Because of that, ___. Because of that, ___. Until finally ___.

•Simplify. Focus. Combine characters. Hop over detours. You'll feel like you're losing valuable stuff but it sets you free.

•What is your character good at, comfortable with? Throw the polar opposite at them. Challenge them. How do they deal?

•Come up with your ending before you figure out your middle. Seriously. Endings are hard, get yours working up front.

•Coincidences to get characters into trouble are great; coincidences to get them out of it are cheating.

•When you're stuck, make a list of what WOULDN'T happen next. Lots of times the material to get you unstuck will show up.

•Discount the 1st thing that comes to mind. And the 2nd, 3rd, 4th, 5th – get the obvious out of the way. Surprise yourself.

•Give your characters opinions. Passive/malleable might seem likable to you as you write, but it's poison to the audience.

•Why must you tell THIS story? What's the belief burning within you that your story feeds off of? That's the heart of it.

•If you were your character, in this situation, how would you feel? Honesty lends credibility to unbelievable situations.

•What are the stakes? Give us reason to root for the character. What happens if they don't succeed? Stack the odds against.

•No work is ever wasted. If it's not working, let go and move on - it'll come back around to be useful later.

•Trying for theme is important, but you won't see what the story is actually about til you're at the end of it. Now rewrite.

•You gotta identify with your situation/characters, can't just write 'cool'. What would make YOU act that way?

•What's the essence of your story? Most economical telling of it? If you know that, you can build out from there.

-- Emma Coats @lawnrocket

Don't believe everything you think. - Thomas Kida

How to make an action film

The DV Rebel's Guide

$32 Stu Maschwitz, 2006, 360 p.

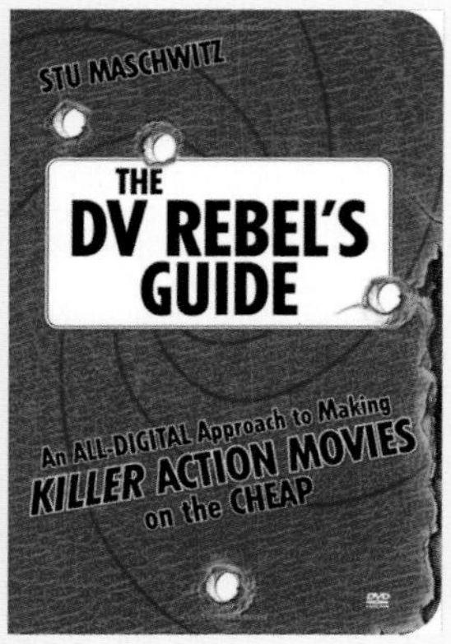

The DV Rebel's Guide is currently the best how-to-guide for making films on a budget. It supercedes the former low-rent filmmaking guide, Rick Schmidt's *Feature Filmmaking at Used-Car Prices*, and his followup *Extreme DV*. This new fantastic manual written by Stu Maschwitz, a co-founder of the maverick special effects company The Orphanage, focuses exactly where budget filmmakers should be. Forget about film, and all its needs. Instead embrace inexpensive HD video and off-the-shelf professional software, like After Effects. This guide rightfully assumes that more than half of your cinematic effort will take place in front of a computer — even on a film without special effects. The good news is that an HD camera and full software suite are tools within reach of a dedicated amateur.

Rebel's doesn't cover important artistic issues like gaining self-confidence in your film idea, raising money, fine tuning scripts and honing your hustling skills because these are covered in other books (especially in *What They Don't Teach You at Film School*). What *Rebel's Guide* does cover in practical depth is the technical aspects of making a quality film for as little money as possible. Even better, it's aimed at an action film, which most budget guides shy from.

The advice is pithy, spot on, practical, honest, and communicated extremely clearly. It uses lots of photo stills in the book and comes with its own DVD of examples. It very smartly assumes that if you are making a film, you have a Netflix account and will point you to specific example scenes in other films on DVD. And since half of filmmaking is now the work of software, the DVD also includes tutorials and helpful scripts for After Effects. It feels like a workshop lead by someone whose made a few films that look fantastic but cost almost nothing, and that is what it is.

One important point Maschwitz emphasizes: The cheap tricks and rebel attitude he promotes in this book are not only for beginners and starving artists, but are used by the pros when they can. This is another way of saying that, as in other media, the line between the tools and techniques available to amateurs and professionals has been drastically blurred. With skill and moxie, a "used car" budget, and the tools and techniques described in this very fine book, you (the You on the cover of *Time*!) can make a film qualified for theatrical release.

-- *KK*

•

I don't think many people realize how often "stolen" shots wind up in big-budget productions. Many famous commercial directors have their own small 35mm camera packages for augmenting their million-dollar shoots. In my days at Industrial Light & Magic, I worked on a Pepsi commercial where shots nabbed without permits out of the back of a van were intercut with state-of-the-art visual effects.

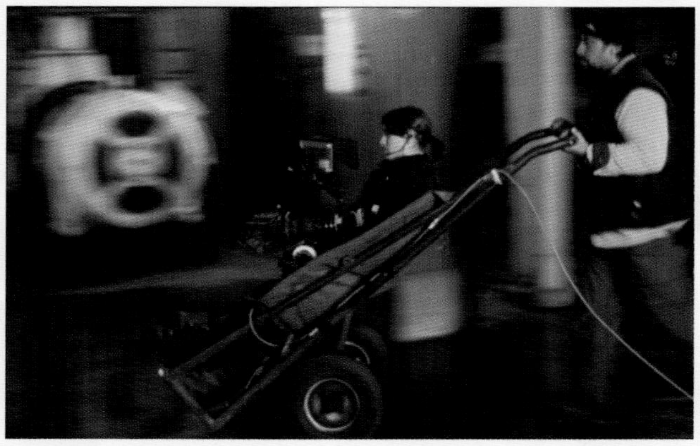

Grip Alfred Wentzel pushes camera operator Sunel Haasbroek, wielding a Silicone Imaging camera, for the film Spoon. Photo provided by the film's directors, Sharlto Copely and Simon Hansen.

•

The Pickup Truck Loophole

I'm not a lawyer, and I don't play one on TV, but I do remember one bit of legal advice that I've put to use a few times. Most cities, including Los Angeles, have a definition of what kind of shooting requires a permit. If you want to shoot on public streets or sidewalks, you will need a permit if you "put down sticks," which is to say, set up a tripod. As soon as you plop a piece of gear on city property, they want you to go legit with the paperwork.

One popular workaround for this is to eschew the sticks and shoot handheld. Reasonable, but not always conducive to the production value we're trying to exude. A much cooler solution is to set up your tripod in the back of a pickup truck. This is an amazing trick because it give you both a tripod and a dolly. You can actually drive down the street and get a real classy tracking shot following your talent, all without asking permission.

•

Time is your greatest advantage over the Hollywood big boys. If they want it to rain, they rent rain towers at hundreds of dollars per day and make it rain on the day they need it to. A week later it rains for real and they lose a day or move to a cover set. You just wait for the rain and shoot on that day — and your free rain looks way better than their million-dollar rain! The DV Rebel melts down time and re-forms it into production value.

•

What's amazing about filling a room with smoke is that in person it seems so stupid and obvious. But look through your viewfinder and something magical happens. Through your camera, you don't see smoke. You just see a scene that looks more like a movie. Smoke is one of those dirty tricks that really works. It makes things seem larger than life. It gives your images depth. It gives light a physical presence in your film. And perhaps surprisingly, smoke can actually light your scene for you.

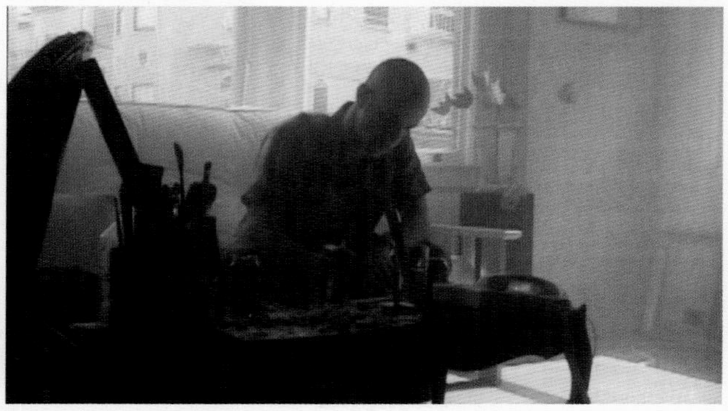

When the fire alarm goes off, that's just about the right amount of smoke to enhance your production value.

•

Watch that scene now. It's a solid scene, very well directed with a flair that would later become Besson's trademark.

You could never shoot this scene.

But now watch it again, and try this: Don't watch the scene, watch the individual shots. Pause the DVD on each one, and ask yourself this question: Could I create this shot? This less-than-two-second little snippet in time? Could I figure out a way to shoot that with my little DV camera?

The answer is yes (or it will be after you finish this book) for all but maybe a few of the most pyrotechnic-intensive shots. No single shot in the scene is so elaborate that you couldn't dream up a way to create it. And if you can create the shots, you can create the scene.

•

When the actor showed up promptly at two in the morning and we were exactly on schedule and ready for him to work, I realized that while we may be rebellious about many things (we had, after all, broken into the building in which we were shooting a gunfight scene using realistic looking plastic guns!), the schedule of the shoot day is not one of them. You own your cast and crew the respect of their time, and you'll make a much better movie if get all your shots in the can before the sun comes up.

•

Be a Rebel, Not a Jerk

If you're going to be impacting people's lives by blocking traffic or lighting assorted things on fire, get permission. But if you aren't hurting anyone, then make your movie by any means necessary.

•

Found Cranes

The DV Rebel cannot pass a glass elevator, or an open-air escalator, or a tire swing, without pondering how it might be used to create a smooth establishing shot. I once made a dolly shot in an airport by resting my camera on the rail of a moving pedestrian walkway. If you can ride it, it's a dolly. If you can ride it up and down, it's a crane.

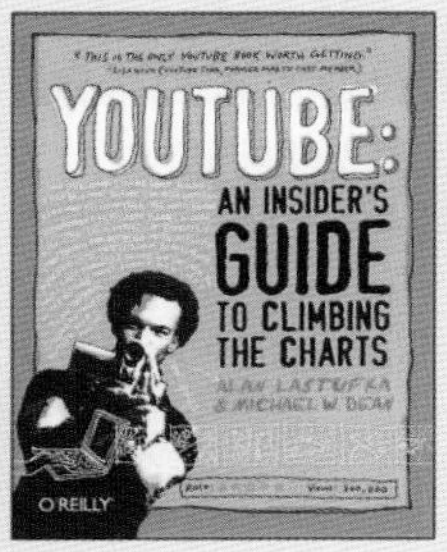

Mastering the new medium

YouTube: An Insider's Guide

$20 Alan Lastufka, Michael W. Dean, 2008, 304 p.

By internet years, this is an ancient book (2008); Still, it's the best one I've found for exploiting the new medium of YouTube. The millennial generation are not reading books, or newspapers; they are not watching TV, either, and in fact they aren't really watching many movies. None of these are their cultural center. As far as I can tell their entire discretionary time is spent watching YouTube clips. It's the source of entertainment and instruction. If you want to reach the young, do it on YouTube.

How? Well this guide is trying to help. YouTube is the newest broadcast/publishing/social medium with new rules and new stars. It will eventually be as important as books and TV combined. What makes a good YouTube station, how do you gets visits, or sell ads? This book is only the first word on those challenges. Since YouTube now offers the option of selling paid subscriptions to niche channels -- a development not covered in this book -- this is sure to ignite even more newbies to move in. Start with this basic how-to. Let me know when a better handbook comes along.

-- *KK*

•

Low numbers can be frustrating for new bloggers and video makers. It's difficult to invest hours into making a video, only to upload it and find a day later that only some 10 or 12 people have watched it. Trust me when I say this, though--we have all been there. If your content is interesting or funny and your shot isn't completely out of focus, you will gain more views over time. Faking your views will get you called out very quickly, and the majority of YouTubers will lose all respect for you.

•

The majority of views on your videos will be lurkers. Lurkers are people without accounts who watch and then move on. Lurkers don't rate, don't comment, and definitely don't make videos of their own. Lurkers are good for views, but not much else. This is why the average video views to comments ratio on YouTube is about 5 percent. Meaning, if you have 100 views, you should probably have about 5 comments; 1,000 views, 50 comments; and so on.

You want users watching your videos. You want people who will get to know, and support, you. The more invested a user feels in your channel, meaning, the more time and energy they've put in to watching and commenting and interacting with you, the more likely they are to pass your link around. Your subscribers, the regular watchers, are the ones who will rate your video every time, even if you're trying a new style of editing or writing. Your subscribers are the ones who will drop you sweet little private messages when you've been gone for more than a few days to make sure you're okay. This is where the heart of YouTube is and where you find your sense of community.

•

Most users get turned down because they simply don't have enough views or subscribers to qualify for partnership. The good news is, users without enough views or subscribers can continue uploading and may apply again at a later date. In addition to this "popularity" qualification, users with a history of violating YouTube's terms of use will not be accepted as Partners. Such violations could include uploading content that you don't own, uploading obscene content, spamming or harassing other users, and attempting to "cheat the system"for more views or subscribers.

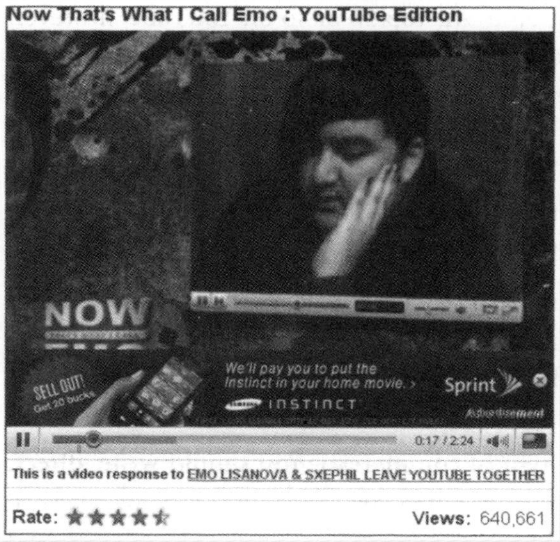

InVideo ads display in the lower 20 percent of the video window and pay more than the ads that display only next to your videos.

•

YouTube ads are all paid for on a per-impression basis. Ad rates seem to vary from campaign to campaign, because earnings per view vary each and every month. AdSense ads display next to videos uploaded by Partners. You'll need to keep your AdSense account in good standing to remain in the Partner Program. This means you should not try to fraud the system by auto refreshing your videos. You should also not click over and over on your own ads; this gives the impression to advertisers that your videos are more popular than they actually are and breaks the contract you sign with YouTube when you become a Partner. (Both YouTube and AdSense have really smart software to detect all fraud techniques, and you will get caught.)

•

First, people will unsubscribe if they feel they're being overtly "marketed to." YouTube is an alternative to TV. If you make your channel too much like TV, people will go look at another channel.

Second, you're not going to make tons of money, just some money, so you may as well still have fun doing it, rather than making video production an unpleasant day job. There's no point in working toward quitting your day job if you simply replace it with another job that doesn't make you happy (and doesn't offer health insurance!).

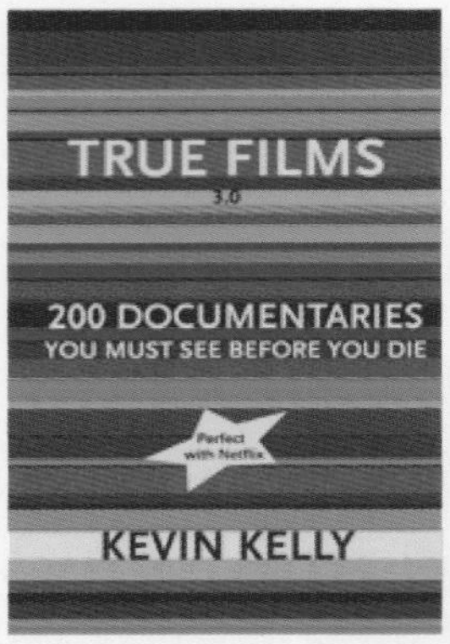

True Films

True films are documentaries, or what the British call factuals -- in other words, non-fiction visuals. I watch them as I would read literary non-fiction -- to understand and celebrate the real and wonderful. True films are tools for learning that are often more effective than books. I review the 200 very best general interest true films I've found in a book I made called True Films. I have watched each one of the recommended documentaries at least twice and some many more times than that. You can download the latest version of the book as a PDF for 99 cents. The same material -- and more! -- is available on my website. As a sample, here are 12 true films that seem to please everyone I've met. You can't go wrong with any one (or all!) of these dozen.

-- KK

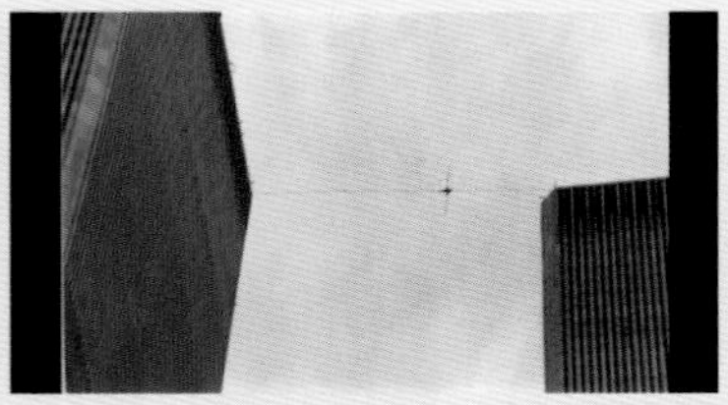

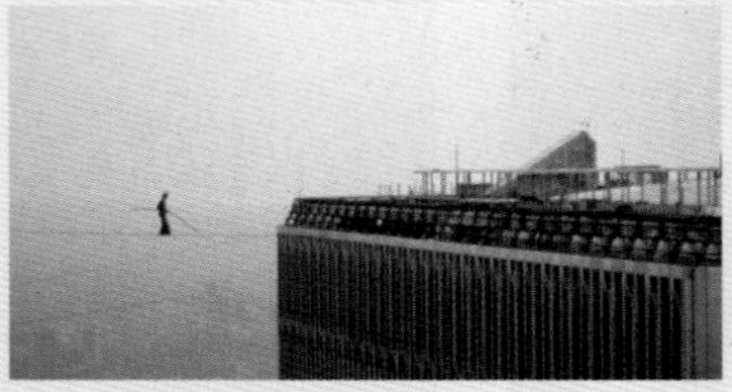

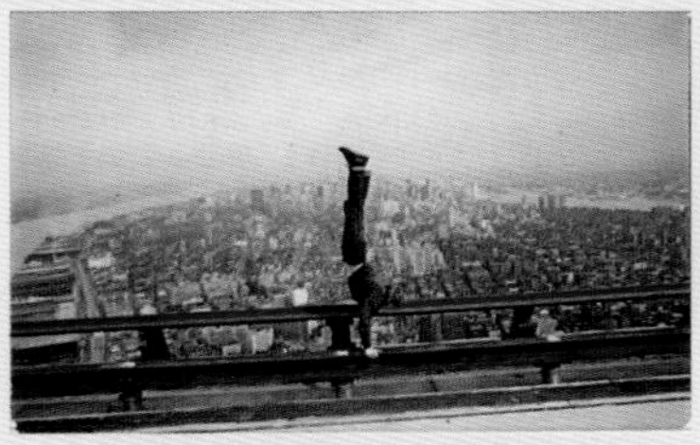

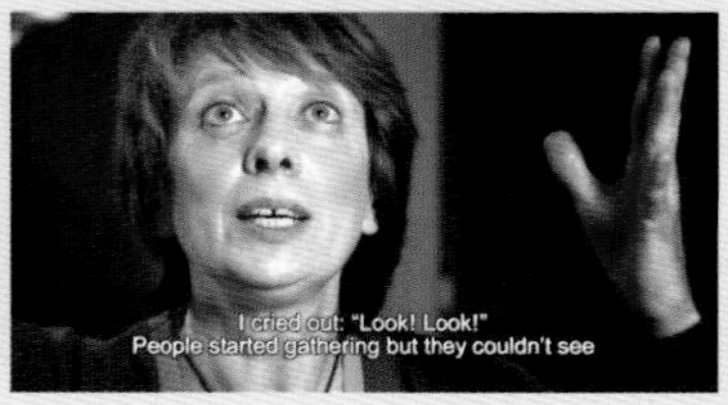

Man on Wire

When he was a boy Philippe Petit saw a sketch of the world's tallest set of twin towers planned to be built in New York City. At that moment he imagined a wire between the two finished buildings and someone -- him! -- walking between them. He had never walked on a wire, and the towers were only an architect's dream, but to Philippe it seemed that the twin towers would be built specifically for this purpose: As a platform for him to wirewalk in the sky.

The rest of Philippe's life was spent in preparing for this inevitability. Learning how to walk a tight rope. Organizing a team. Waiting for the towers to be built. Stealthily casing them before they were completed. Planning the stunt. And then the hair-raising event itself in 1974. With an eye to both history and publicity, a lot of this prep work in the years before were filmed, and that footage is mixed with re-enactments to create an amazing document of an artist unleashed.

This compact, intense, burning grenade of a documentary -- much like Philipe himself -- radiates laser energy and the beauty of something as perfect as a line between two towers in the sky. It is a nearly perfect documentary. It is the only film reviewed by Rotten Tomatoes to rate 100%.

Man on Wire is an astounding, astonishing, head-shaking, exhilarating conquest of the impossible. It made my heart soar.

-- KK

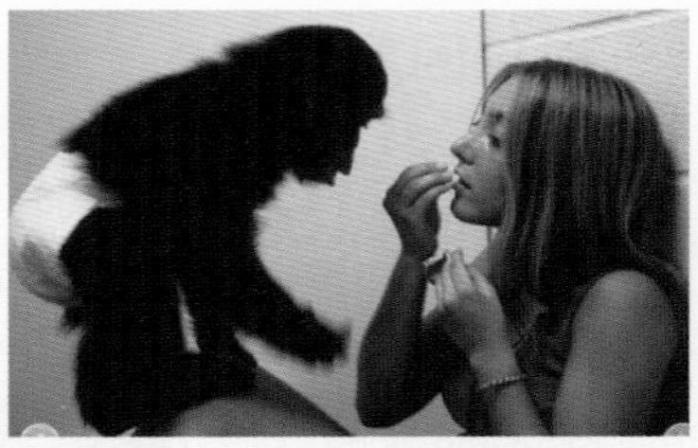

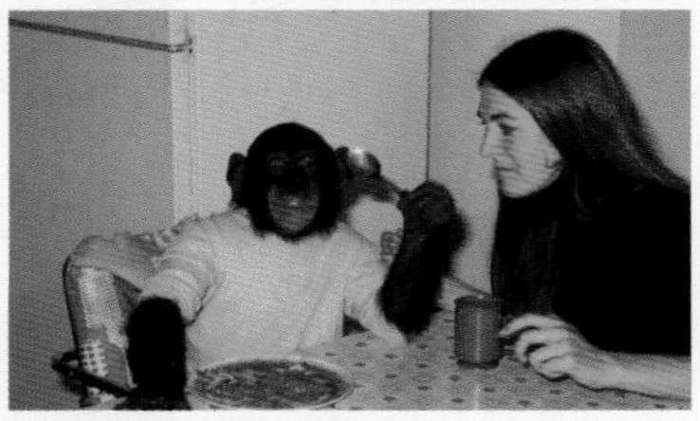

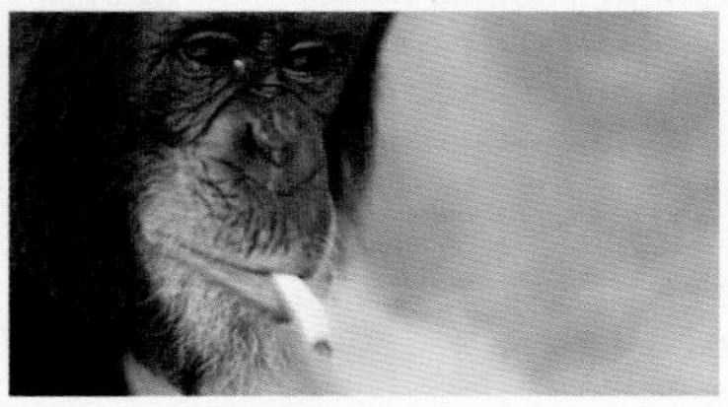

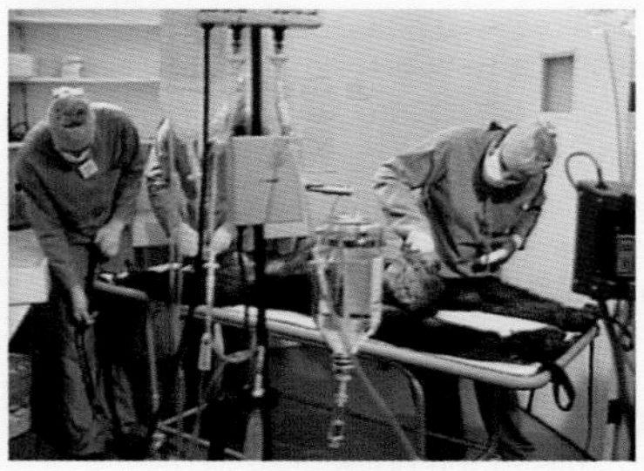

Project Nim

This is an amazing film. What would happen if you raised a chimp as a human in an ordinary home and taught it sign language from infancy? Would it learn language? A professor and his hippie girlfriends tried this experiment during the 1970s with a chimp named Nim. Everyone of the dozen of humans who raised and cared for the chimp, bonded and communicated with Nim as if he were human. Nim was raised by a free-love mother who never disciplined him. When he got too strong to handle he was sent off to an animal farm where a long-haired hippy befriended him, and hung out everyday with him for years; he and Nim often smoked joints together. The farm ran into financial difficulties so, despite the outrage of his human family, Nim the "talking" chimp was sold to a research center where he was the subject of "medical experiments." Finally he was rescued. Amazingly, Nim was filmed for much of his life so the director was able to put together this fantastic visual biography. Woven together with interviews from all the principle characters in Nim's life we get an intimate record of this grand but misguided adventure. A hundred questions are raised by the experiment and many are answered by this superbly crafted film. I recommend it highly.

-- KK

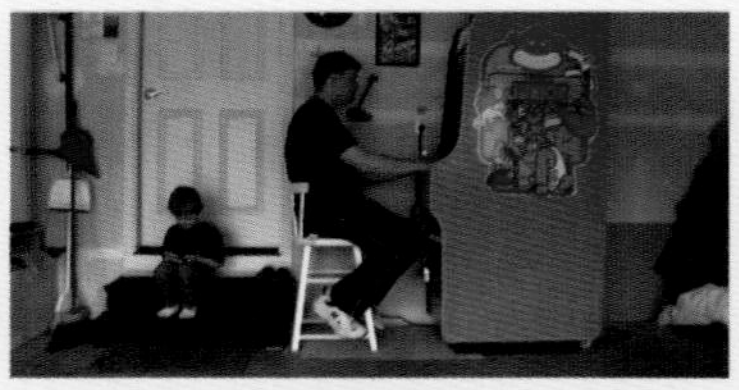

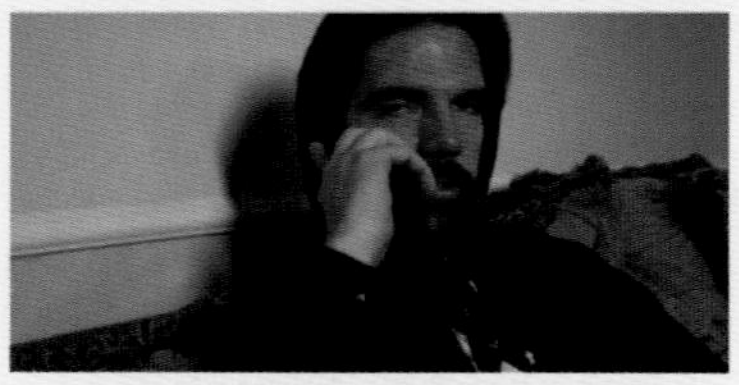

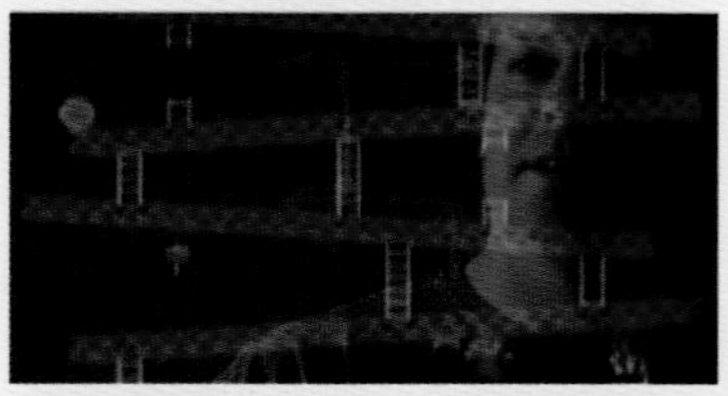

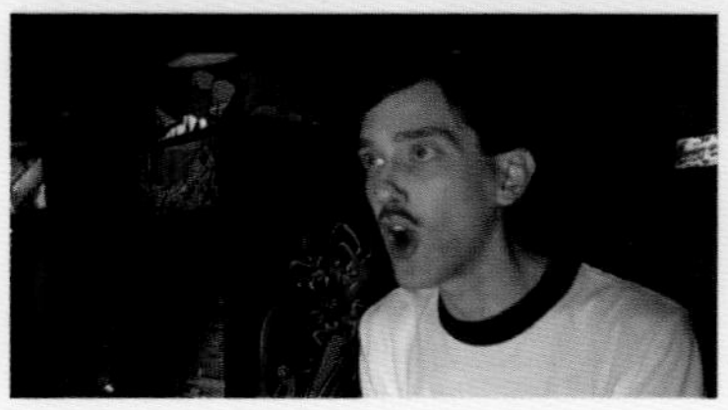

The King of Kong

A documentary masterpiece. Contenders for the Donkey Kong video game world championship face off at a video arcade. This contest is transformed into a memorable drama by the presence of a villain. It is rare for documentaries to have villains, but this one does, and he wears black. The bad guy, a slimy conniving world-record holder and his corrupt minions, is matched up against a likable, genuine good guy nerdy hero. A righteous battle ensues over many months. I haven't found anyone who didn't thoroughly enjoy this visible confrontation between the forces of light and dark. One of my favorite documentaries of all time.

-- KK

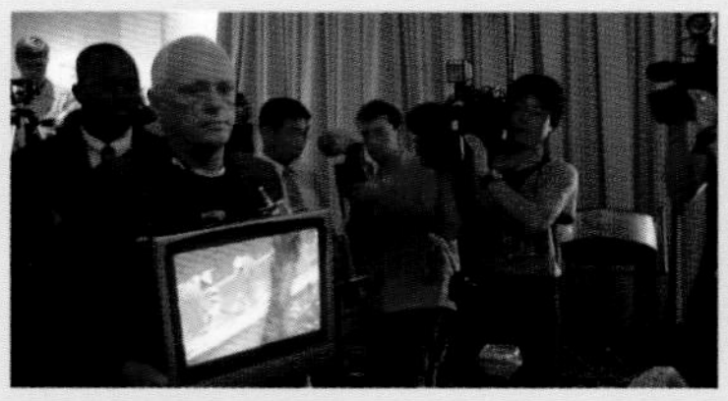

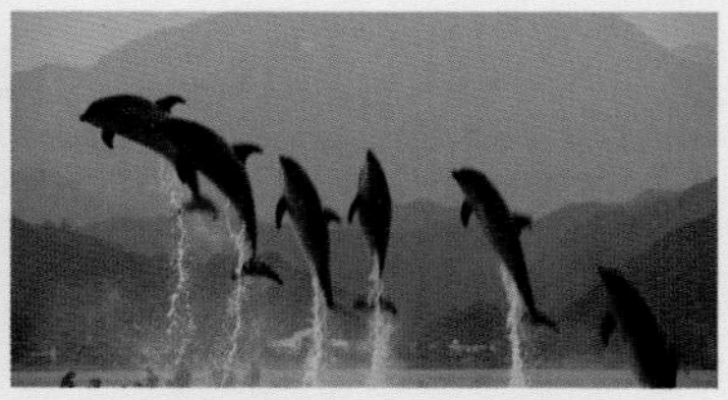

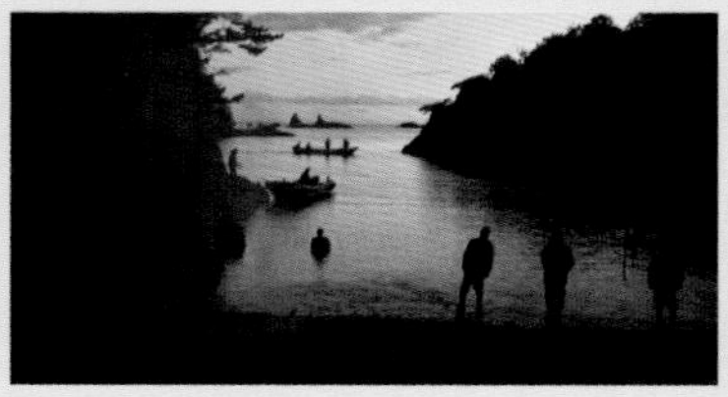

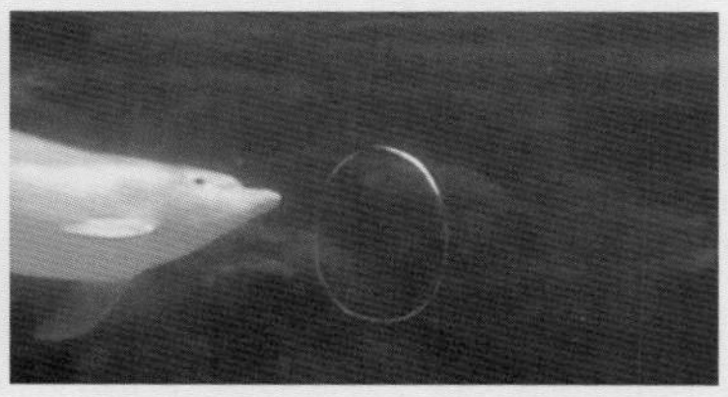

The Cove

This is far more entertaining than your usual "cause" film. It's sort of a real-world Mission Impossible with lots of high tech gear and a team of dedicated enthusiasts. The thrill of this documentary, filmed in Japan, is to watch a desperate anti-dolphin-killing activist assemble an undercover spy team to plant hidden hi-def and infrared cameras in the tightly guarded cove where the annual dolphin mass killings take place. Because of international media attention and the secluded nature of the tiny Japanese fishing village where everyone is protecting their livelihood, documenting the dolphin killing became a cat-and-mouse game. There's plenty of suspense. Additionally, there is righteous pleasure at the climax in the clever PR stunts the activists engage in to spotlight the killings and cover-ups. Oh, and I bet the film will probably be a pretty effective in stopping this secret slaughter.

-- KK

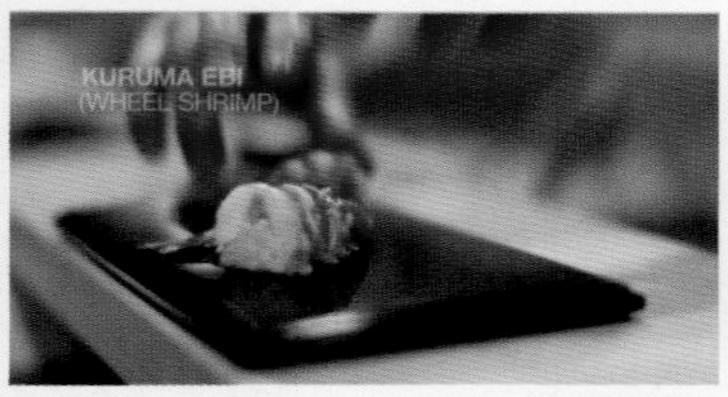

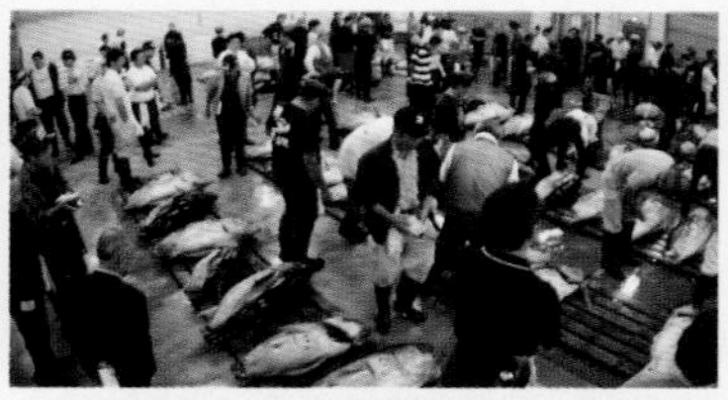

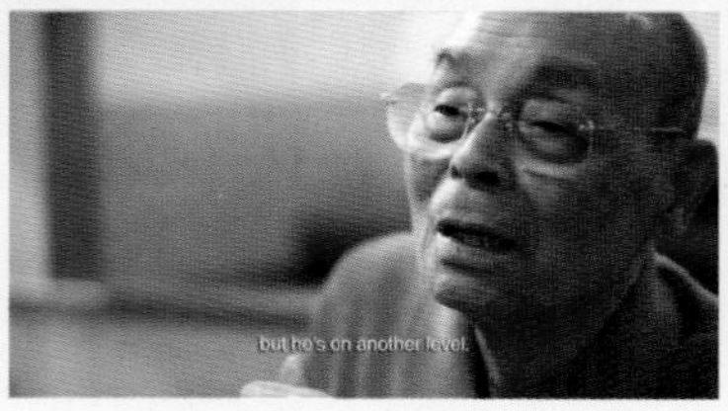

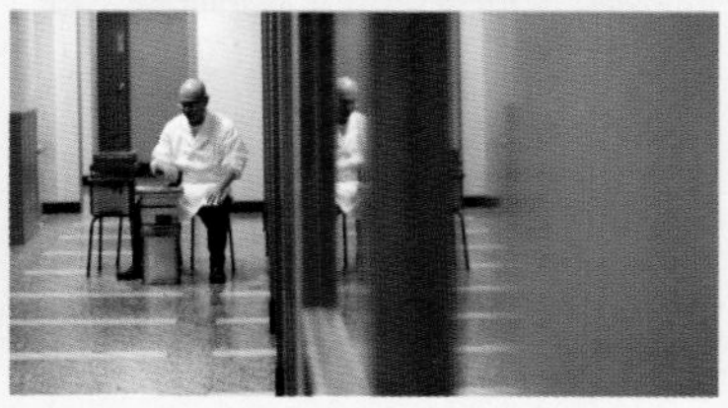

Jiro Dreams of Sushi

The Tokyo sushi chef Jiro has done the same thing at work every day for 60 years, no vacations, no holidays. He says he has loved every day of this repetition. The secret to his happiness is that everyday he tries to make his sushi even better than the day before. According to his customers he succeeds since his tiny 10-seat shop in a subway station is sold out a year in advance at $300 per meal. This documentary is an insightful and inspirational portrait of a craftsman seeking mastery, and the quest for perfection. Jiro's life is now an inspiration for others following mastery as a way to find their passion. Oh, and the film is also a tremendously great view of the quality of work that world-class sushi really entails. You'll look at sushi differently now. This is a deliciously perfect film about a perfect craftsman.

-- KK

Helvetica

At their best, documentaries focus on some tiny overlooked corner of life and enlarge it to fill the world. By bridging the micro and macro, a great documentary helps the world make sense. This great documentary focuses on one typographic font, Helvetica. It traces the history of how Helvetica was invented, how it became a default font on most computers, how that popularity catapulted it towards ubiquity in our environment, and what it means that we can find it everywhere, even though we aren't aware of it. Along the way, we are educated in what fonts do, and how they work. Using interviews with the most renowned typographers living today, this film illuminates the world of fonts -- a world we rely on more and more -- and the universe of typography and design. Like Helvetica itself, this portrait is trim, radically visible, smooth, and refreshingly modern. It is nearly perfect. (You are reading Helvetica right now; this book is set in Helvetica.)

-- KK

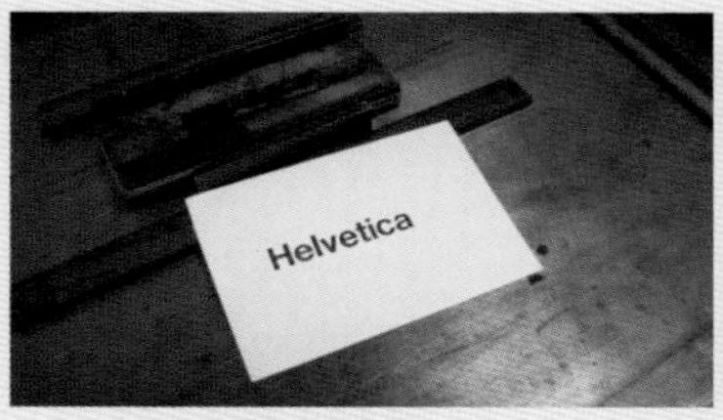

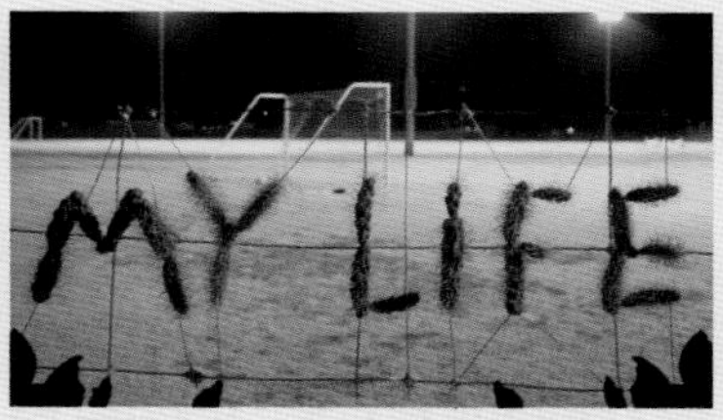

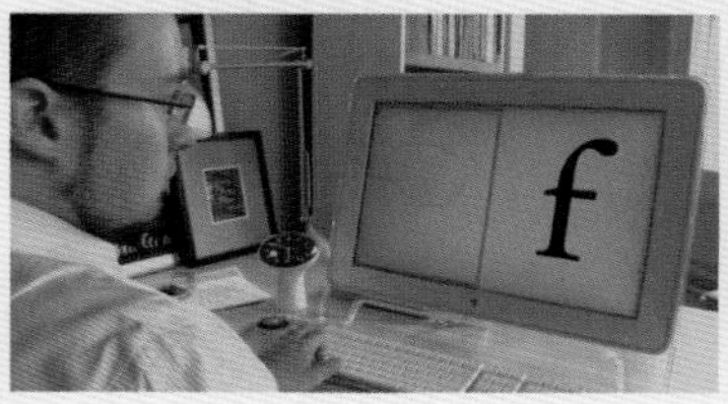

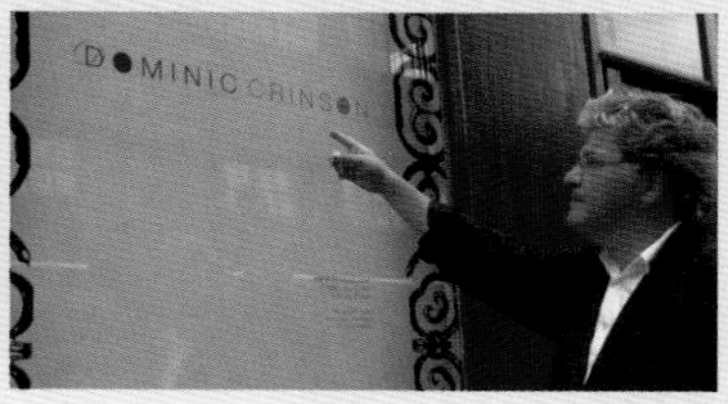

Hands on a Hard Body

In the South of the US, where getting a new truck is a type of rebirth, there is a little-known contest whereby a truck dealer, as a publicity stunt, will offer a new truck to the person who can keep his/her hand on a truck the longest. Typically these endurance tests run 80-90 hours, or almost 4 days. During that time, contestants must stand awake, with at least one hand on the vehicle. Each hopeful is absolutely sure they will win (what does it take besides desire?) and the candid stories of their desires are wonderful. As the hours pass into days, fatigue and insanity take over so the outcome of the test is completely unpredictable. This small gem of a film is a testament to the indomitable spirit and outright brittleness of the human mind.

-- KK

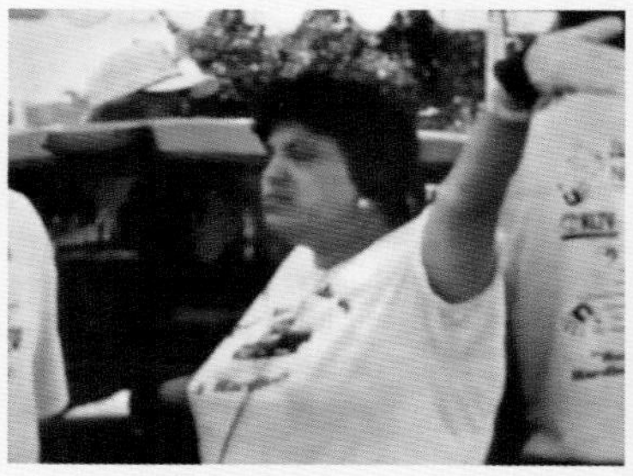

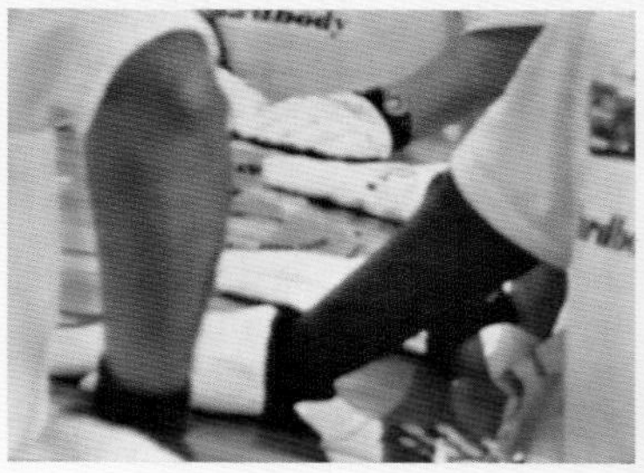

Are we being good ancestors? - Jonas Salk

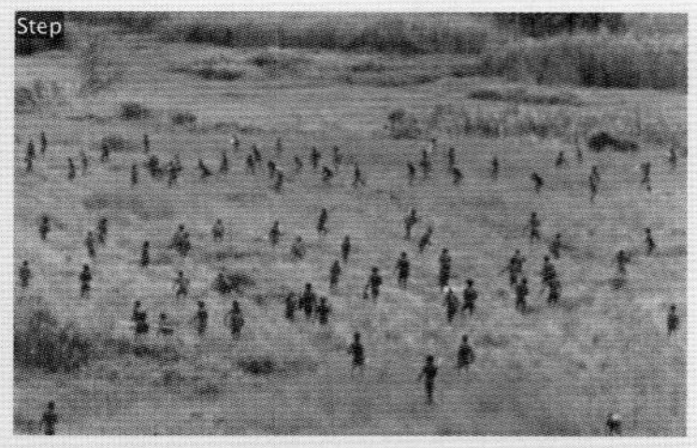

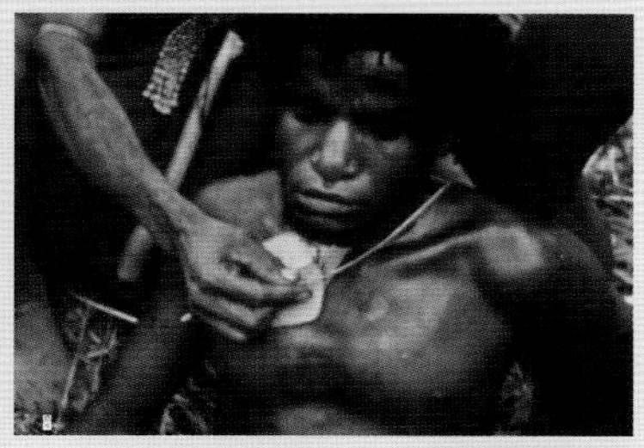

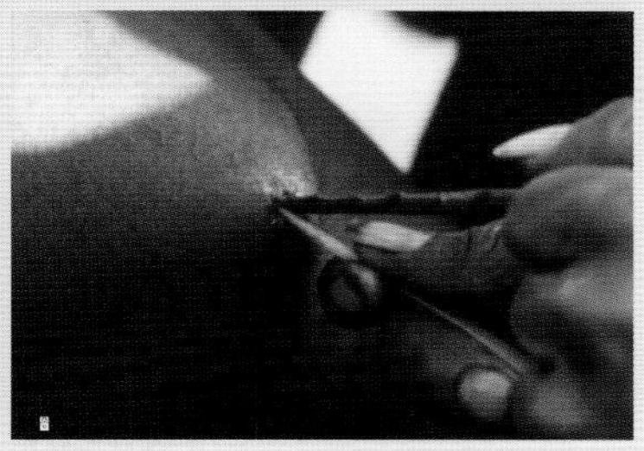

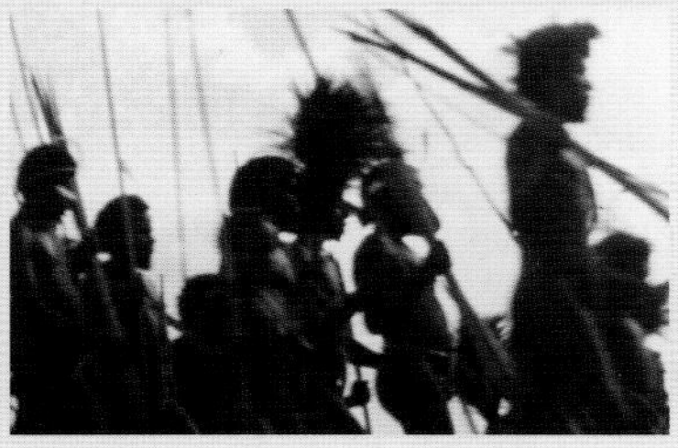

Dead Birds

I've been trying to see this legendary film for years. It captures ritual warfare between tribes of farmers in Papua New Guinea. The war is played out on a weekly basis, and could almost be called sport except the warriors usually kill one person a week. Filmed in an ancient agricultural society, yet one that lacked contact with the rest of the world, it could have been shot 3,000 years ago. Visually stunning, almost poetic rather than anthropological, this record presents a timeless tableaux of distant "otherness." Yet, as the film unrolls we see the familiar as well.

It was filmed in 1961 in the very remote highlands of the Dani civilization in the Grand Baliem Valley of Papua New Guinea. At that time this valley was the last place on earth not to be colonized by Europe. Here a group of remarkable young filmmakers documented a cultural expression so strange that it seems unbelievable now that it has disappeared. Hundreds of men from each tribe would line up in sides on a vast grassy field - so everyone could watch -- to have weekly skirmishes using spears and arrows. It was true war in that no one in the villages was safe. If men could kill a woman or child who wandered too close to the border field, they would. On the other hand it was ritualistic; they would not fight if it was raining or cold. Each death of a tribe member had to be atoned by another death from the other side. But to stop the game of killing altogether was unthinkable.

This film records the daily life of sweet potatoes farming, weaving, pig raising, and hut building needed to support this sport of war, and the great art, labor, love and sacrifice it required. Its intent is to try to penetrate the weirdness of this arrangement. It records the deadly battles in clear intimacy. We see their amazing surgery on the wounded, the shocking amputations of innocent women relatives, the preparations for feasts and funerals, and the daily chore of climbing the high watchtowers to watch for enemies. There is clarity and fascination in the many details -- all in color -- of a Neolithic lifestyle and craft.

This is a unforgettable document, a reminder of who we are. I consider it one of the greatest documentaries ever made.

-- KK

56 Up

In 1963 the BBC filmed a set of 7-year-old school children and asked them what they thought their future would be. Because some of the kids were rich and some were poor, their aspirations revealed the traditional British class divide. But every 7 years since, the director has gone back and re-interviewed them, and their story has gotten far more interesting. The twists and turns of each life have been surprisingly unpredictable. With its longitudinal reach of 50 years (!), this is one of the coolest and deepest reality shows ever made. Now the kids are 56. In their latest episode the director tries to balance an inherent tension. The film can't assume anyone has seen the earlier versions, and so it must recap the previous films, but now that the subjects' lives are so long, a recap won't leave much time for the new years. 56 Up tackles this dilemma by re-interpreting each life in view of their latest 7 years, and so if you have been following along, it feels completely fresh. If you have not been part of the journey so far, this quick life-long portrait will pull you in, and you may want to see the earlier films. If you have been watching, these will be old friends. The subjects are now nearing their 60s and I found myself dying to know what happens next - in 63 Up.

-- KK

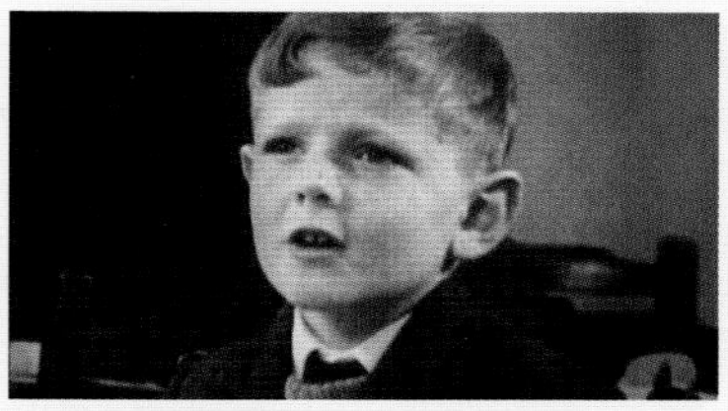

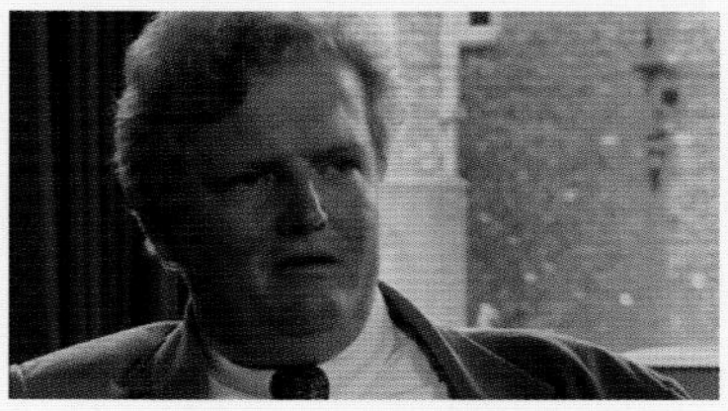

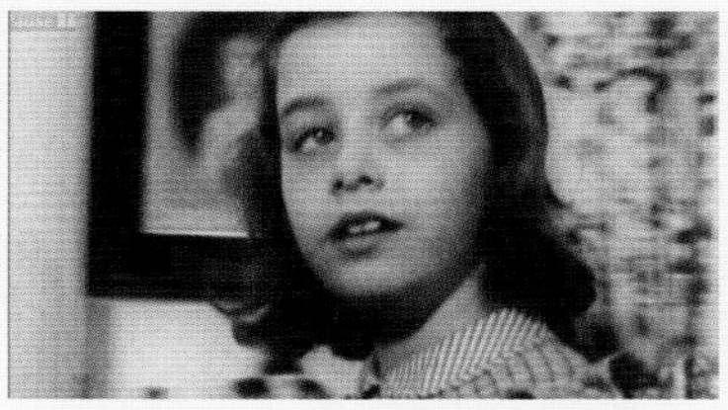

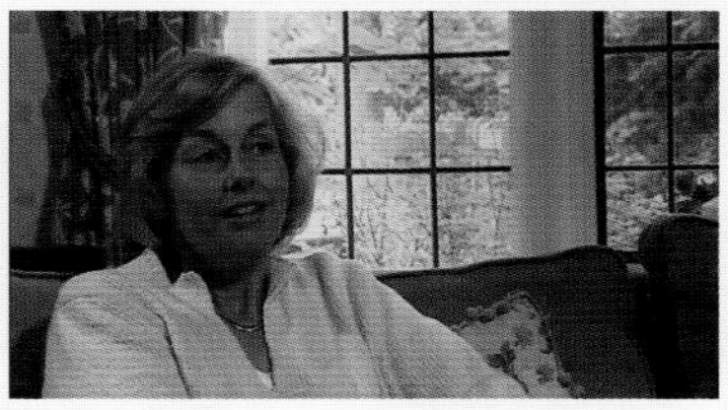

March of the Penguins

It must be the two feet. Plenty of other creatures in the animal kingdom endure mind-bogging hardships, as do the stars of this movie, the empeoror penguin in the Antartica. But none look like little people as they do it. Waddling like overweight suburbanites in line for a concert, they trudge across 70 miles of frozen ice to search out their devoted mates, who, if all went well, have spent the last 3 months standing in 80 below blizzards holding an egg on the top of their feet without eating. These little being's lives are totally focused on that one egg, and they move heaven and earth to keep it alive. (Yeah for good parenting!) I've found that women in particular find this movie romantic, perhaps because once the egg is laid, the responsiblity for its survival through the harsh dark winter is passed 100% onto the fathers. There's plenty of other aspects about the penguin's life cycle which make it easy to project our humanity onto them. Whether you find these penguins sweet or pitifully trapped in a horrendous cycle of striving just to stay alive, this is a remarkable film. It is expertly crafted to inform you and to touch your heart.

-- KK

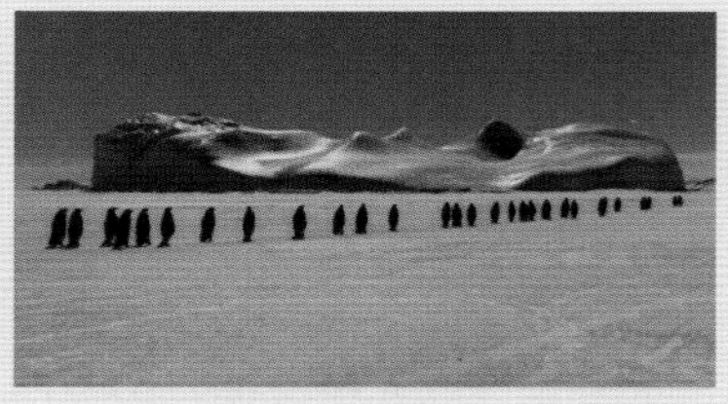

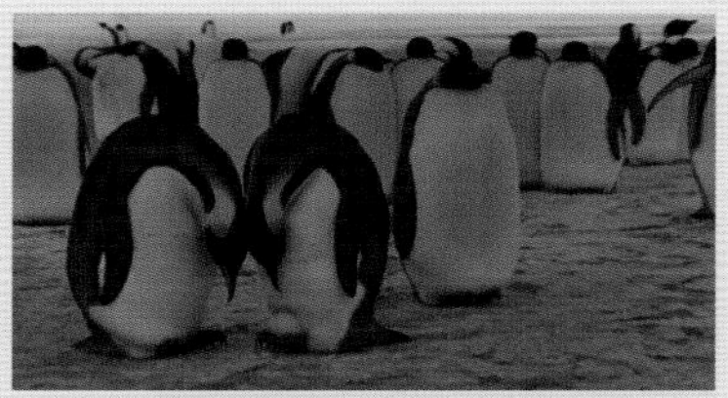

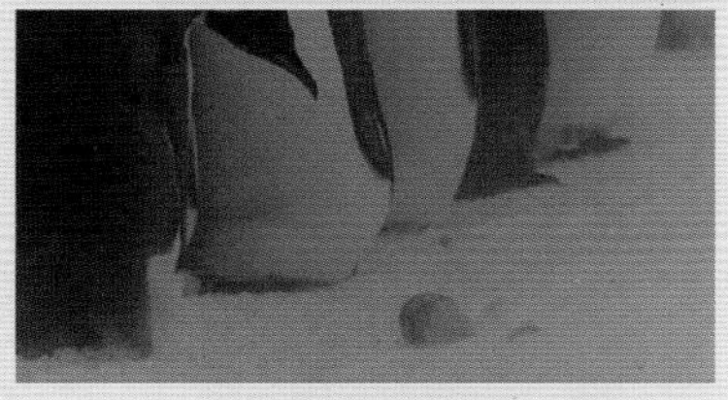

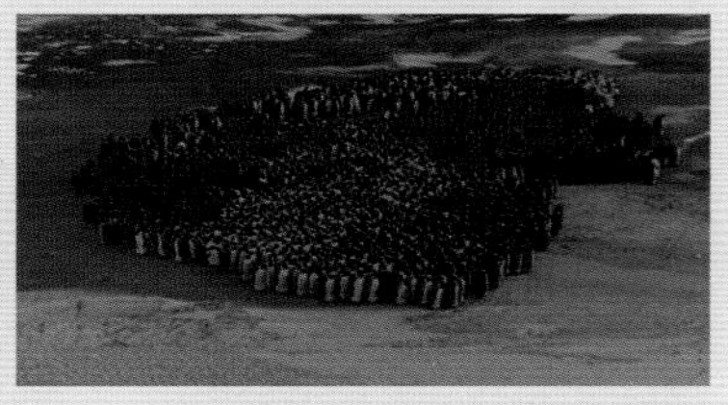

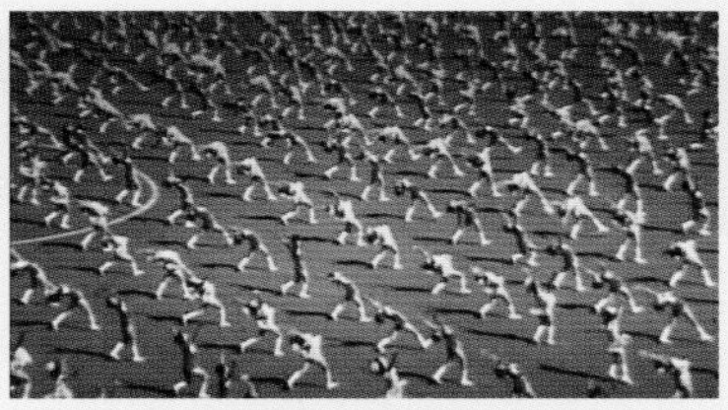

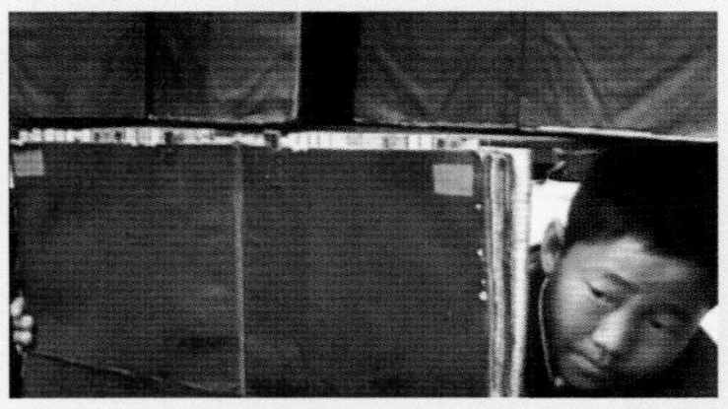

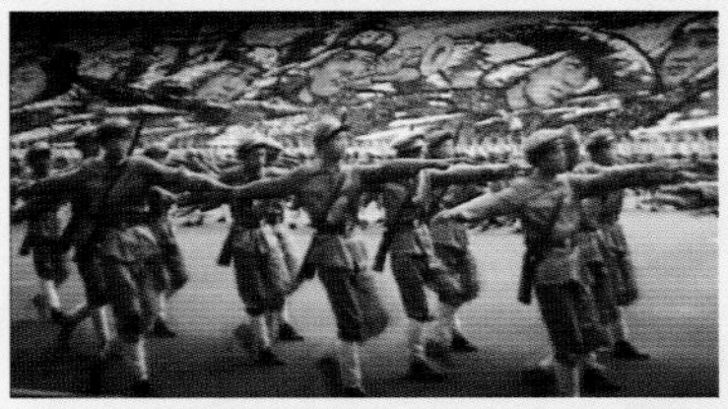

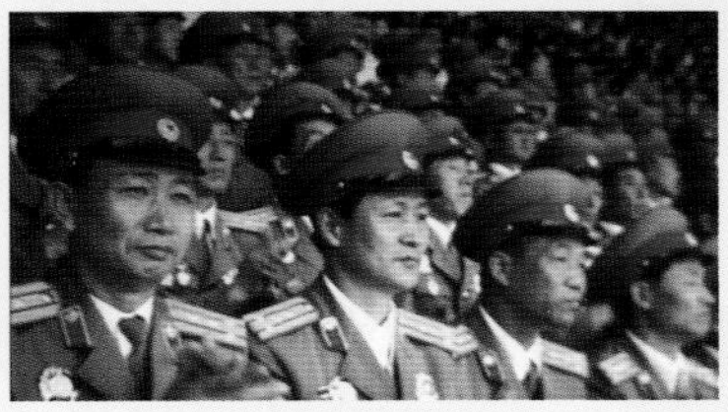

State of Mind

One of the most amazing films I've seen in years. Welcome to the world's largest, weirdest cult: the nation of North Korea. The entire economic engine of this country is aimed toward producing a yearly religious spectacle of unimaginable scale. This film follows two school girls and their family as they practice up to 6 hours per day for 9 months in order to preform a "mass game" for their dear president. Some students are pixels in a stadium-sized human jumbotron. The resulting images and performances are utterly perfect. Not a single speck is out of order. After the ten-day event, the North Koreans go home and watch their flawless work on their one government channel and marvel to themselves about how superior their discipline is, how delighted they are to surrender everything to the greater group. What's frightening is how deeply they buy into the cult. The kids eagerly graduate from the sports spectacle to the military spectacle, which shares the same mentality of the perfect machine. Without saying anything (there's almost no narration) this film reveals what group insanity would be unleashed in military action against North Korea. I'm so glad this incredible film has been made, because in 50 years from now, when the cult is gone, no one will ever believe it was possible on the scale we see here.

-- KK

Grass

You think your job is tough? Try this one. In this very early documentary from 1925 -- made in extremely harsh photographic conditions -- two pioneering filmmakers (who went on to make King Kong) follow 50,000 Bakhtiari nomads as they set off on their annual hundred mile migration from the desert lowlands of Iraq over the snowy Zagros mountains into roadless pastures in Iran while driving 500,000 (!!) goats, sheep and horses. Instead of riding on the backs of donkeys, small children will haul ailing donkeys *on their backs* as they scale cliffs, cross glaciers barefoot, or ford immense white water rivers with goatskin floats. And then 6 months later they return to complete this unbelievable feat of endurance again. It's an eye-witness glimpse of a truly nomadic lifestyle which forms the archetypes of the Bible and the mid-east today, and of mind-boggling hardship. Like Nanook of the North, this rarely seen movie is the both the first and the last photographic capture of this distant world. *-- KK*

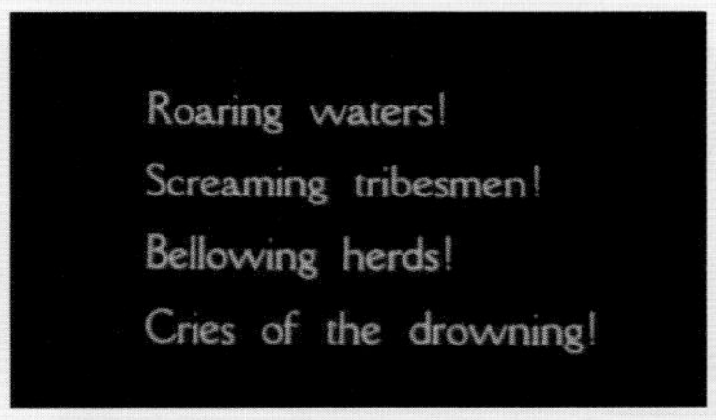
Roaring waters!
Screaming tribesmen!
Bellowing herds!
Cries of the drowning!

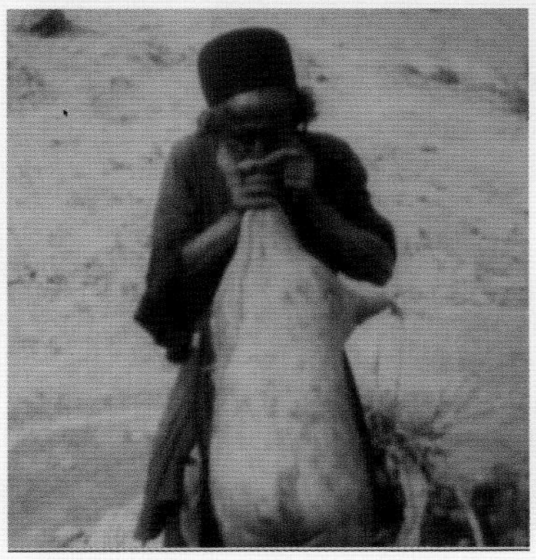

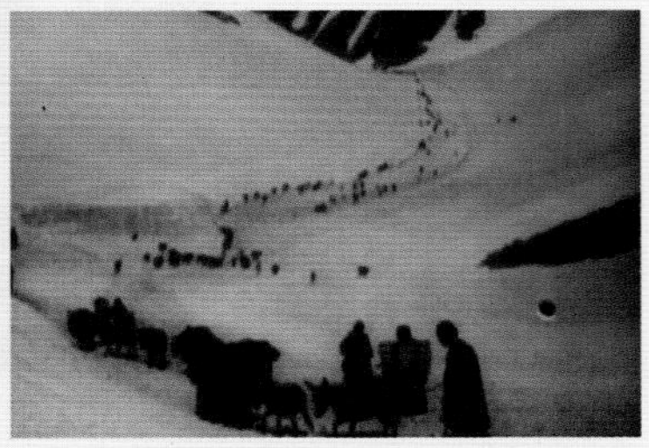

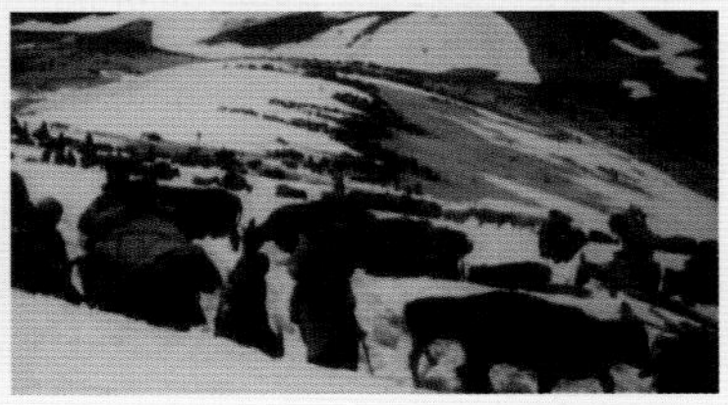

Spellbound

An amazingly spellbinding drama. You follow a dozen elementary school students who memorize the dictionary and beyond, practicing for years at all waking hours in order to spell words they -- and you! -- have never even heard of. Their ordinary parents are awestruck, the kids are driven, and the outcome is totally unpredictable. Only one kid will survive the National Spelling Bee. Will it be the one whose Indian parents have hired three foreign language coaches, or the girl whose dad does not even speak English? Or the boy with the stutter? It's a fantastic journey into a subculture that is uniquely American, yet invisible and marginal. Since you are on the edge of your seat most of the film, it even changes your ideas about spelling.

-- KK

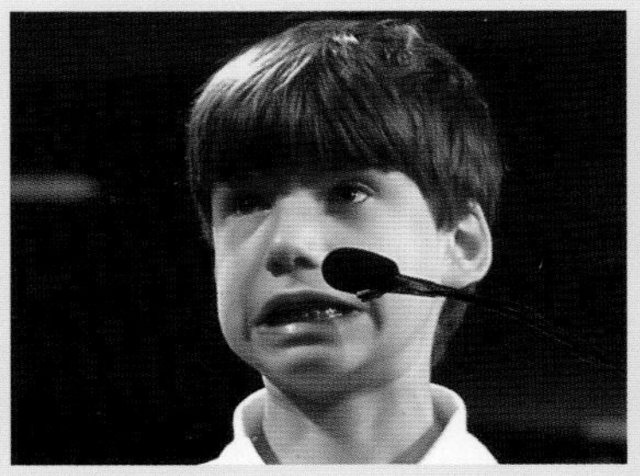

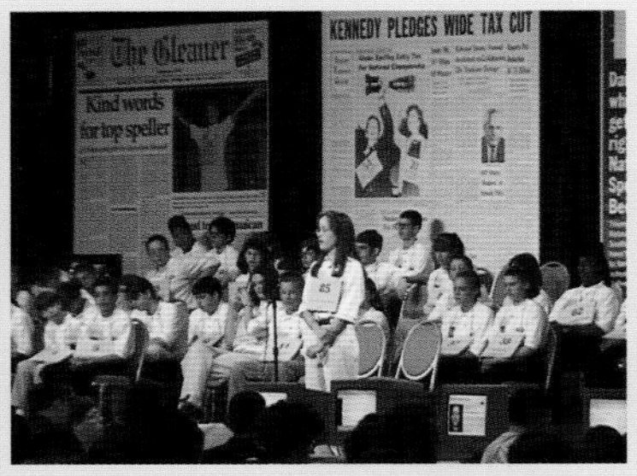
The Gleaner
Kind words for top speller
KENNEDY PLEDGES WIDE TAX CUT

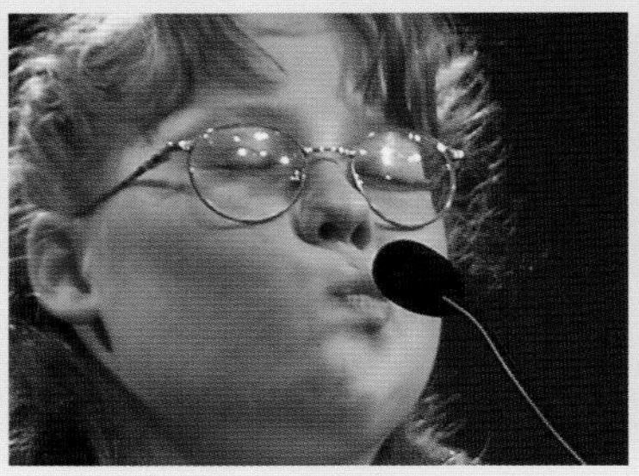

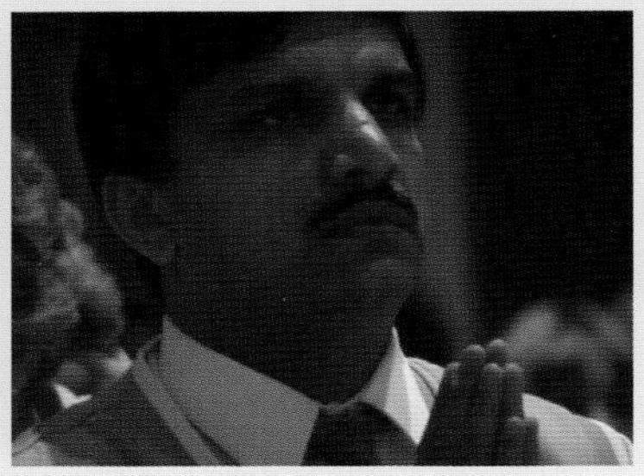

TRUE FILMS

I recommend these and another 200 great documentaries worth watching on my website True Films (truefilms.com). Every now and then I'll add another great one. You can access the archive from the alphabetical listing of the films on the right side. Enjoy!

-- KK

You don't have a soul. You are a soul. You have a body.- C.S. Lewis

315

Theater

How to fake it
Theater Prop Handbook
$32 Thurston James, 2000, 270 p.

How to fake just about anything. Makes use of the newest (styrofoam) and oldest (plaster) prop materials. Prop making skills are easily transferred, too. A lot of this fakery can go a long way in real life architectural and interior decorating.

-- KK

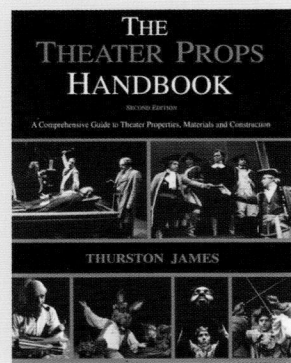

• I have heard flex-glue referred to as book binder's glue, Swifts glue, and flex-glue (a manufacturer in Albuquerque calls it Phlex-glu).

Bookbinders call it by its formulation number, Swifts 43917. Swift, however, calls it a carton adhesive. I will stick with the name flex-glue, which is the most descriptive.

Flex-glue is, as the name implies, a glue which remains flexible after it has dried. It never becomes hard or brittle. Flex-glue should be used in the construction of any costume or prop which must be bent or manipulated.

Apart from its value as an adhesive material, flex-glue has many applications as a texturing medium. Mixed with shellac and dyes, it can be used to produce a convincing stage leather. It can be used as an embedding material to apply lace, fringe, or other decorative material to cloth or solid forms, and the decoration will appear to be an integral part of the form. A thick coat of flex-glue applied over a releasing agent produces a usable skin when it dries. Flex-glue makes a good gloss finish, similar to clear acrylic paint, but it builds up faster and produces a heavier texture more quickly than clear acrylic. This is a really versatile produce; it would be more accurate to call it flexible-texturing-material, but pretty soon that would become awkward, so flex-glue it is.

• Let's talk about making books lighter. There is an advantage to making a bookcase weigh less. Books weigh, on the average, about 15 pounds per foot of shelf space. Sets of encyclopedias and law books weigh even more 25 pounds per foot. Shifting this weight during a scene change is an unnecessary strain. A row of faked books weighs only four pounds per foot. The whole secret to making books lighter? Remove the pages!

Liberally apply flex-glue to the muslin. Neatness is not much of a concern here; your main objective is to get a thick coat of glue on the cloth.

Making a fake but lightweight bookshelf. Glue each cover into place. Hot glue will work well for this operation.

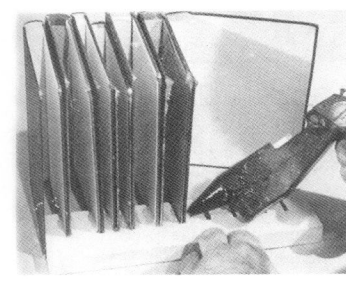

The mold-making materials include plaster, two kinds of alginate, two forms of silicone rubber, latex, and hot-melt rubber.

We added Plasticine, sculpting the pattern to make it look a little more like an oil lamp and a little less like a teapot. The addition of the pedestal to the finished casting will also help to convey this illusion.

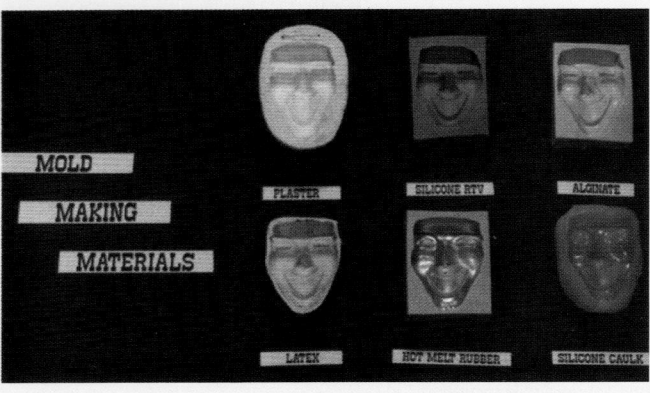

Basic mold-making skills
The Prop Builder's Molding & Casting Handbook
$16 Thurston James, 1989, 238 p.

Meant for prop builders in theater or film, this how-to book is the best overall guide for making molds and castings for any reason. Casting is a handy skill for any craftsperson -- doll-maker, restorationist, Halloween fan, furniture maker, or handyman. This guide treats the many different modern substances you can use (about 30), educating you on what's good for what, and taking you through the particulars for each kind of casting process. The guide assumes an ease with general shop skills and a willingness to deal with messy chemicals (and clean up!). Once you are comfortable with making molds and casts, you'll find all kinds of creative problems can be solved with it. (Watch an episode of Mythbusters.)

-- KK

• Hot-melt glue (ethylene vinyl acetate or EVA) is a thermoplastic with qualities much like those of other hot melts: it becomes fluid when heated, and is ruggedly solid when it cools to room temperature. In fact, it has enough of the "right" characteristics to make it a useful casting material. We will demonstrate casting with hot glue as we construct a crown from scratch.

When you can use an authentic item as a vacuum forming mold, the thin plastic casting will be very realistic. This mold is a pattern of real roofing tiles, caulked with plaster.

Moulage is a better molding material than plaster for this job because it is flexible. A hard plaster mold would most likely break -- either when you attempted to remove the original pattern, or when you tried to release the copies (also made from a hard material).

The filigree headband of this crown was made of a standard lamp part, called "brass banding." The finials are twenty repeated castings of EVA (hot-melt glue).

No-sew costumes
Instant Period Costumes
$18 Barb Rogers, 2001, 87 p.

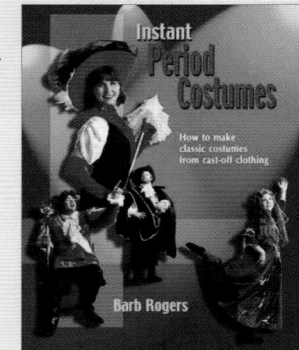

A trade secret from professional costume designers: throw out your sewing kit. The way to make quick and dirty costumes is to scrounge for old clothes, cut them up creatively with your scissors, and then instantly reassemble the pieces using a hot glue gun. No measuring, no patterns, no threads. The glued clothes hold up remarkably well. Since you can even wash them, it works for local theater shows (or Halloween). Now that you know the secret, you don't have to buy this book — except if you want a whole bunch of cool recipes for recombining thrift-store bargains into pretty convincing period fashions.

-- KK

• A glue gun and glue are the most important tools you will need. With them, you will be able to place fabric where you want, embellish your garment without sewing and seal raw edges. A glue gun produces a versatile substance that dries quickly, is washable and is a great time-saver.

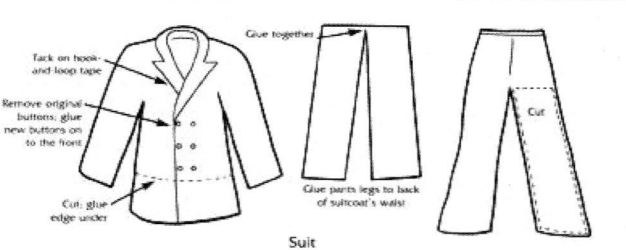

I've tried several types of glue guns over the years. When they first came out, they were all "hot" glue guns. When I was beginning to wonder if I had any fingerprints left, I found the Magic Melt glue gun, which is a low-temperature gun that works just as well. It can still burn you, but it doesn't go through three layers of skin. It dries more quickly than the hot gun and is washable.

The one drawback to using this type of glue is that you cannot wash the garment in anything but cold water and either hang it to dry or use your dryer on air fluff. No heat! The glue will let go.

• **Directions for making Romantic Man**

For making Restoration Women: I located three dresses, which when put together make a beautiful Restoration gown. I threw all three dresses in the washer with a a mixture of brown and red dye to get the unusual color. Because the gowns were made of different fabrics and had lace on them, I achieved several shades of the same color.

Romantic Man

Restoration Woman

How to be an actor
Sanford Meisner on Acting
$13 Sanford Meisner, 1987, 272 p.

You can't learn how to act from a book. You especially can't learn how to act from this book, because the author, Stanford Meisner -- one of the most famous acting teachers ever -- says that, ironically, the problem with most acting students is that they operate too much in their head. Acting, he says, is 100% not thinking; all doing. But books can open up frames and hooks for ideas that come later by doing. A friend of mine who studied acting under a number of methods including Meisner's, says he didn't get Meisner's approach until he read this very readable book by him. *On Acting* is recommended by real actors as the one book on acting worth reading. I found it a thrilling experience. Meisner is a demanding master, challenging his perplexed and frustrated students with riddles and relentless zen koans until they break through the fundamental paradox that acting is not pretending. You act by being authentic in an imaginary world. Because Meisner's method places everything in the authentic, this approach resonates beyond the stage. As the book progresses his oracle-like utterances mystify less and begin to make profound sense even to non-actors like me.

-- *KK*

•

Don't be an actor. Be a human being who works off what exists under imaginary circumstances.

•

If you're really doing it, then you don't have time to watch yourself doing it. You only have the time and energy to do it.

•

Silence has a myriad of meanings. In the theater silence is an absence of words, but never an absence of meaning.

•

You cannot be a gentleman and be an actor.

•

And if you're really concentrated on just listening to cars or looking at a person, you don't have to worry about being a character. You have one thing to do and concentrate on.

•

You know, it's all right to be wrong, but it's not all right not to try.

•

Particularization is really very simple and not nearly as complicated as preparation — nor as subtle.

•

Give yourself time. In only nineteen years and eleven months you'll be amazed at how simple it all was.

•

[Stanislavsky] said that when you're alone in your room and nobody's watching you -- you're just standing in front of the mirror combing your hair -- the relaxation, the completeness with which you do it is poetic. He calls this relaxed behavior on the stage 'public solitude.' On the stage 'public solitude' is what we want. You have only one element to give up to get to the area where your real acting personality is, and that is yourself.

Putting on a play
The Drama Teacher's Survival Guide
$21 Margaret F. Johnson, 2007, 256 p.

Let's put on a show! Problem is, you have never put on a show before. A veteran high school drama teacher dispenses some great advice on how to shepherd your school or community towards a rousing performance. She walks you through the whole process, check-lists in hand, assuming you've never done it before. How long/often to schedule rehearsals, what to audition, how to cast, how to block, when to set the lighting, how to make effective costumes on the cheap, all the way to what to do about tickets. I've used four or five other beginner production guides but they tend to dwell on the technical aspects. Johnson's guide tackles the whole multi-month long adventure. This unassuming but dense guide is aimed squarely at high school drama productions, but it works great for camp directors, small-town community theater, or any other newbie hoping to put on a show.

-- *KK*

•

Off-book rehearsals (five to six days)

Off-book literally means that the actors go through the segments without using their scripts. The key word for these rehearsals is memorization. Your actors are giving the characters life and need to begin developing relationships with other characters. They cannot do that if their heads are in their books.

You need to check that each actor has memorized both their blocking and their lines. This means that the actors do not have any scripts in their hands. These rehearsals are hard, frustrating, and extremely important. You must stick to your guns. No books allowed on-stage during this group of rehearsals or afterwards - ever, ever, ever! No "nanny" blankets for the actors! You are inflexible here.

•

Principles of movement

The following principles of movement have been developed through stage experience. They are not rules - acting in the theatre defies rules. The following principles of movement need to be modified at times to fit the needs of you and your actors. Usually, characters:

Cross toward the objective point. If grace and beauty in the scene are desired, then cross in a curved line.

Cross on their lines.

Break up their speeches while they cross behind others.

When crossing with another character, the speaker walks Upstage and slightly ahead of the other, turning his or her head Downstage to speak.

When entering with a group, the speaker enters first.

•

Food that is eaten

If people have to eat, then either the real food or a look-alike substitute that can be swallowed easily must be on-stage.

Mashed potatoes work well for ice cream or anything requiring that kind of consistency. Just tint them the color you need.

Angel food cake is easy to eat, can be colored and cut into shapes, and goes down easily, not causing anyone to choke.

Slices of bread with a half of an apricot in the middle create fake fried eggs.

Drinks: Tea is a great substitute for alcohol or coffee. [If you are going to do a show where characters use alcohol be sure it has been cleared with your administration. Many districts have strict rules about seeing students drinking on-stage.)

UR Up Right	**UC** Up Center	**UL** Up Left
RC Right Center	**C** Center	**LC** Left Center
DR Down Right	**DC** Down Center	**DL** Down Left

The Audience

Stage Diagram

Cheap special effects
Create Your Own Stage Effects
$19 Gill Davies, 1999, 160 p.

I worked on the stage crew for a local community theater and the old timers there had a bottomless inventory of quick and rough tricks for most stage effects. They would immediately say, here's how to make a clouds move across the moon. Or get the sound of light rain on a roof. Or make a character fly, safely. At no cost. This book is chock full of a zillion little rough and ready, low-cost effects for local theater. And enough inspiration to create your own.

-- *KK*

•

Rain

Buckets of water to pour into metal containers below
or
Dried peas for rain - in a tin or rolling in a wire sieve
or
Sugar poured down a grease-proof paper chute for an alternative rain sound effect.

Simulated rain effects are achieved by a disc that is largely black but with a few scratches in the black surface to let light through. This effect is best confined to a small area.

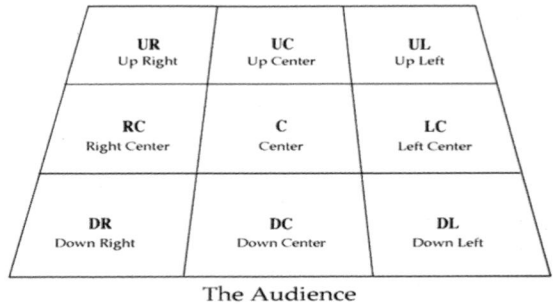

A fan rippling water and the right lighting angle will make the ripple effect reflect onto the stage.

These are flats that are hung and so they can swivel. If they are fixed only at the top and hung from sturdy timber or onto an industrial track, as shown in the illustration, flats can be spun around very quickly indeed for a most effective fast change.

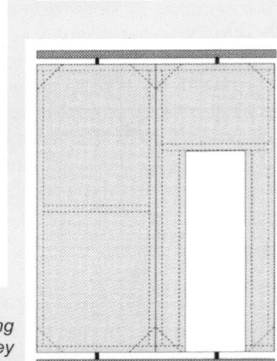

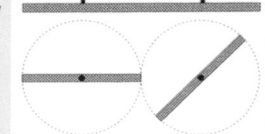

Fair-trade ticketing
Brown Paper Tickets
$0.99 and 3.5% for ticket buyers Brown Paper Tickets

Ticketmaster sucks. Consumers hate having to purchase tickets through them because of their outrageous pile of excessive and phony fees. Hosts hate them because Ticketmaster's effective monopoly demands everyone play by their heavy-handed rules. Venues and fans feel totally stuck with them.

However if you are putting on an event and want to sell tickets, you have an alternative that will be cheaper, better, faster than Ticketmaster. Brown Paper Tickets is one of several alternative online ticket vendors for anyone hosting a ticketed event. Might be a ball, a fundraiser, a race, a concert, or an exhibit. At Long Now we've used them and can recommend them highly.

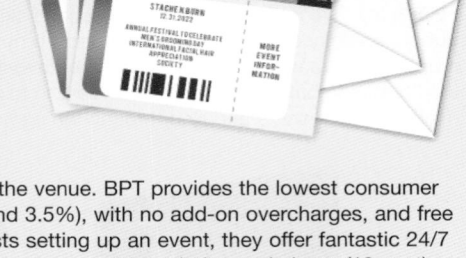

Brown Paper Tickets bills themselves as "fair-trade" ticketing. What that means is that they offer a fair deal to both the consumer and the venue. BPT provides the lowest consumer fees on tickets (99 cents and 3.5%), with no add-on overcharges, and free first class postage. For hosts setting up an event, they offer fantastic 24/7 live-person phone support, a clean usable website, and cheap (10 cent) printed secure tickets. They offer venue hosts other goodies too. You have control over when to stop sales, how to customize the ticket, ways to manage multiple events, means to offer media tickets, assigned seating, and so on. Plus, they give you real-time sales, and pay up promptly! Try that with Ticketmaster.

If you are running an event, it's crazy to use the old monster; if you are a fan, petition your venue to switch to Brown Paper Tickets.

-- *KK*

For something to be beautiful it doesn't have to be pretty. - Rei Kawakubo

Television

All-in-one remote control
Logitech Harmony Universal Remote Control

$60 logitech.com

I have tried several 'universal' remotes over the years and the Harmony Remotes by Logitech are the best I have used. The basic idea of a universal remote is to free you from having to use a separate remote for every device you need to control. I can say that except for the occasional special need, like accessing a setup menu, I can use the Harmony remote to control my shelves of equipment while leaving their individual remotes stored in a coffee table drawer. This is no mean feat since I use two displays (projector and TV) several sources and also control my lights. The cost of all this convenience is a few minutes (maybe an hour or more initially) setting up the remote and then occasional tweaks when you change equipment or need another feature. Required accessories are a computer and Internet access.

-- Stan Cossette

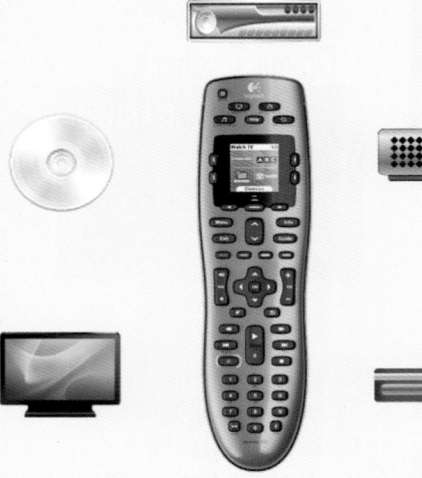

One evening I realized I was surrounded by remotes on the couch. The solution was the cheapest version of Logitech's famous Universal Remote, the 650. The thing is smart. Using your computer you tell the Universal what devices you want controlled, so it checks its database and loads those commands into buttons on the Universal labeled "watch tv" or "watch movies" etc. Now when you choose one of those activities the Universal will mimic the appropriate displaced remotes and give you control over those devices. Thus, one Universal remote. It might take all of 10 minutes to program your setup, depending on how ambitious you are. It is a *universal* remote so will take over remotes for lights, climate, any system if you want. It'll take a little longer getting used to it (you need to keep it pointed at a device several seconds, long enough for it to cycle through a start up), but quickly it will be indispensable.

-- KK

quarters building of a large South African bank which had too many TV's on the walls and some of which needed to switched off. It really does work.

-- Paul Parkinson

Television Eliminator
TV-B-Gone

$20 Amazon

Switch off thousands of TVs using just one small remote! When you want some peace and quiet in that local bar of restaurant or office all you need to do is hit the TV-B-Gone button. I've used it in bars and clubs, and in the head-

When you press the button, TV-B-Gone takes slightly more than a minute to emit more than 200 popular shutdown codes, like trying every possible combination to open a safe. The instructions include a diatribe against television in general, as if using this product is not merely a prank, but a serious political act.

--Charles Platt

Easy install TV bracket
Hangman Television Mount

$80 Amazon

Hangman is a clever, simple bracket designed to hang flat screen TVs directly on a wall. As the go-to handyman for most of my friends and families, I have hung my fair share of flatscreen TVs and am always frustrated by the expensive, cumbersome, goofy brackets that are sold to the average Joe when he buys his TV at Best Buy or Costco.

The Hangman, unlike the alternatives, is a dead simple mount composed of two interlocking aluminum strips. Place the first strip, which includes an integral level, on the wall. Screw it into the studs or attach with heavy duty drywall anchors (both included, and these

anchors are actually really cool; probably worthy of a cool tool in themselves. I work in the remodeling industry and we use these anchors all the time.). Bolt the other aluminum strip to the back of the TV using included bolts, hang the TV strip on the wall strip, attach the safety tether to prevent the TV from sliding off, attach the pegs to the lower bolt holes on the TV, and you are done. The TV can be tilted forward to allow access to cables. I installed mine with a Leviton REB behind it to hold all of the outlets and jacks completely concealed, but you could just as easily use cable ties or wire molding to drop the wires down to your components.

I like this system because it is simple and inexpensive. It hangs the TV dead level and it won't "drift" out of level when you mess with your cables. It also keeps the TV tight to the

wall as the aluminum brackets are only about 1" thick. Finally, it only takes about 10-minutes to install. The downside to this style of bracket is that it only mounts the TV flat to the wall, so you lose the option to tilt it in any direction. This wasn't a problem in my house since the couch faces a flat wall.

-- Brian Durkin

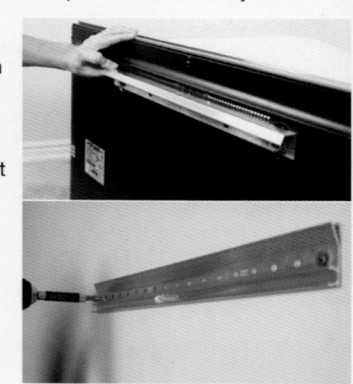

Personal TV management
TiVo

$117 TCD746320 tivocommunity.com

TiVo is a black box plus a subscription service that records TV shows for your convenience. The box is known generically as a digital video recorder or DVR. A Tivo DVR, and its required subscription, is ideal for power users particularly those watching sports, live events and current TV shows. The downside to it is it requires a $15 monthly subscription fee and they make it as inconvenient as possible to cancel your sub. There's a half dozen different models of boxes, with various features and benefits. The virtues of a TiVo system are enumerated by the following readers.

-- KK

I LOVE my TiVo Series 3 HD. The 30-second skip (forward) button, combined with the 8-second backup button makes it a breeze to bypass commercials. Another favorite feature is the 30-minute buffer for live TV. I can tune in to a show 15-20 minutes after it starts and skip through the commercials, and

be about caught up by the time it ends. So efficient! The Season Pass function makes it easy to never miss an episode. I installed an aftermarket 1TB internal hard drive so I can record lots of movies and save entire seasons of shows for summer programming dry periods--all in HD. Another really cool feature is that you can tell TiVo to record anything with a certain actor or director. It will find things you didn't even know were out there. Basically, my TiVo is like a personal TV assistant, always thinking about me.

-- Susan E.

TiVo stands heads & shoulders above the typical cable company DVR. It's a far smarter and much easier to use DVR than any other I've seen. It's scheduling is more malleable. If you've told TiVo to grab every new episode of a show -- a "Season Pass" -- but the initial showing conflicts with an existing scheduled recording, it will find the next best time to grab the show. For shows on the 2nd tier cable networks like A&E, TNT, etc., this works incredibly well since they re-broadcast new episodes multiple times during the week.

-- Rob O'Daniel

Tivo is great. I've had 3 different generations. I actually have two in the house. One for my use and one for my wife's use. It is easy to move shows around. I haven't watched a commercial in 5 years. When watching sports I will wait until an hour or so has recorded then start watching and can skip all commercials and end about the time the game really ends. You can rewind any scene or play. If you wonder what that person said just back up 6 seconds and replay. Need to answer the phone just

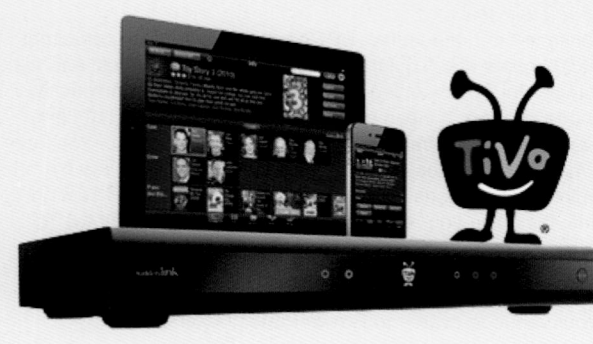

pause and start when you return. You can schedule a season pass and it will record the shows even if the station moves the program or makes a show 1 hour and 6 minutes instead of an hour. And you can program it to only record first runs of the show. You save 20 minutes per hour of TV you watch. I've noticed some of the smaller cable channels must not provide accurate time info since one in 50 shows might have some problems.

-- Bob Kelso

A mind that is stretched to a new idea never returns to its original dimension. - Oliver Wendell Holme

Better than the average small-time cineplex
Cheap Home Theater
$190 (used) PowerLite S1 Epson

Fifteen years ago we moved our video habit from a tiny 13-inch monitor that was hardly bigger than most laptop screens to showing DVDs on something a little bigger — like a wall-sized movie screen. It's been pure joy since.

What we had in mind was an assemble-it-yourself home theater.

Finding an inexpensive screen was not difficult; you can try eBay for a real bargain. I bought a new one that was 6 feet by 8 feet. Yep, it's big. We hung our huge screen on a wall; it rolls right up and disappears when not needed.

To project the DVD image I bought the cheapest, smallest, portable projector I could find (see right). You can get a good one now for around $600.

In addition to the small projector we also added surround sound to the room using five strategically placed Bose speakers, each no bigger than a softball, and one woofer hidden beneath a table. The result: With a good DVD offering 5.1 surround sound, the experience is as about as good as our rinky-dink local half-plex theater.

Is it perfect? No. Our cheap home theater quality does not match the experience of viewing a good print on a large screen in a good theater. Also, because of the large windows in our room, we use the theater mostly at night.

We combined our projector with a DVD player and receiver with the aforementioned Bose 5.1 surround sound speaker system. Our screen is a Da-Lite model; I

picked a mid-range quality screen (not flat white, but not the highest reflectivity either). From about 12 feet away the projector will completely fill a 6-foot high by 8-foot wide screen. This size screen is large enough that wide-screen mode (which doesn't fill the screen) is still plenty big.

All the electronic gear sits compactly hidden beneath a tiny end table, on the floor. (By design the projector angles upward slightly so it fills the screen from the floor perfectly.) Most visitors to the room don't have any idea that it can transform into a serviceable home theater in the time it takes to roll down the screen.

We only venture into a movie house a couple of times a year, primarily when we want to see something early, while everyone else does. The rest of the year, the home theater is more than adequate.

-- KK

Real movies-on-demand
Roku + Netflix
$58 HD Streaming Player Roku

Real movies the instant you want them have been expected for … well… at least 100 years. You think of a movie,

then you can watch it. This trick has been tried scores of times over the past decades, but never seemed to work. Clunky boxes. Expensive contracts. No choices. Weird constraints. Lousy pictures. But now, finally, the trick works.

The Roku box from Netflix allows you to watch movies on your TV whenever you want to, for no extra charge, in DVD quality. It is a tiny thing that sets up in a few minutes.

Here's the kicker: you can watch as many movies (no ads) as you care to. There is no extra charge beyond the basic Netflix monthly (and you can still get them mailed to you as DVDs if you prefer). Ten movies a month or a hun-

dred. Anytime. This thing is dangerous.

Here's the only caveat: so far only about 10% of the total Netflix catalog is available for instant download. But that total is naturally swelling by the day.

The Roku box is cheap at $100. You can watch all the instant Netflix movies for free without it, if you want to hook your PC up to a large screen, or watch on your monitor. Since the Roku is so small and wireless we can move it to our projector and stream movies to the big wall.

It's a nicely done cool tool.

-- KK

Computer controlled tv
Chromecast
$35 Google

Google's Chromecast is a small device about the size of a car-key fob that does three things. Any one of these functions would be worth it's $35 price, but all three make it a real bargain.

1) It's like a much cheaper, much smaller Roku player. Plug the fob into a free HDMI slot on your TV and if you have robust wifi it will play Netflix in your normal resolution. But unlike Roku (but like Apple TV) it will also play music and YouTube on the big screen. And YouTube is more and more becoming the center of pop culture these days. Because we already have a Roku (which we love and won't give up), the YouTube addition has been a real delight. YouTube at 50 inches is fantastic. If you don't have a Roku, a Chromecast would be an inexpensive alternative.

2) You can use your second screen -- the phone, tablet, or laptop that sits near you while you watch the big first screen -- to control your TV screen. This is particularly important for displaying web-based content like YouTube since you

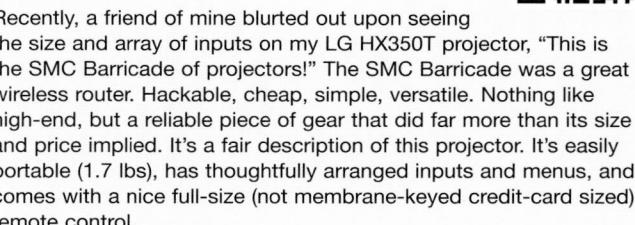

Powerful portable projector
LED Projector
$649 HX350T LG

Recently, a friend of mine blurted out upon seeing the size and array of inputs on my LG HX350T projector, "This is the SMC Barricade of projectors!" The SMC Barricade was a great wireless router. Hackable, cheap, simple, versatile. Nothing like high-end, but a reliable piece of gear that did far more than its size and price implied. It's a fair description of this projector. It's easily portable (1.7 lbs), has thoughtfully arranged inputs and menus, and comes with a nice full-size (not membrane-keyed credit-card sized) remote control.

I've been watching LED projectors for a while. This is my second. While at 300-lumens it's no longer the brightest LED-based projector in its price class (Optoma now has one with slightly better resolution claiming 500-lumens), as far as I know this is the cheapest LED option at this junction of brightness and resolution.

Besides the coax input for cable signal, there are inputs for a composite TV signal, VGA, and HDMI signals, as well as a USB slot. You can plug in a USB key with video files in any of a fairly wide array of supported formats, and play them straight from there. It's not the very smallest LED projector on the market, but it's hard to see how it could be much smaller and still have so many input options.

All the inputs in the world don't matter if the output doesn't look good though, and I'm happy to report that, to my eye, it looks great. In a dark room, it has no problem providing a 6-8 foot 720p movie screen. You'll never mistake the output for that of a multi-mega-lumen high-end projector. This is a game of trade-offs. For my purposes, computer demos, home video screenings, late-night movies, and projecting scary scenes for a home-made haunted house, it works fine so long as I can control the lighting. In a room that's merely dim, it still looks great in the 40" range, which is a pleasant way to use it as an adjunct computer monitor.

The sound is an understandable weak point in a tiny projector. If you want better sound, or surround sound, bring your own.

My only other niggles with this device: the first is that the focus wheel doesn't have much throw. I haven't actually had any trouble getting acceptable focus, but I wish it had more room for fine-tuning. The second is that there's no zoom lens, so you must figure out a physical arrangement of projector / screen / source that works for you. A cheap camera tripod might be in my future.

-- Timothy Lord

have full search (as in Google!) capabilities. However this is the one downside to the Chromecast in that you *need* a second screen to control it (although the device does not need to be awake the whole time). There is no remote.

3) The Chromecast will display (mirror) the screen of your laptop or phone if you want it to. This means that you can launch all kinds of content from your second screen, including photo slide shows, or save us, Powerpoint presentations, and have it no-cables-no-muss projected onto the big screen. (Video streamed from your second screen is jerky at the moment.) For me the draw has been easily showing my photos on the big screen, right from Lightroom or iPhoto, or from my phone. Their photographic luminosity and mural-like scale is thrilling. In essence, your computer takes over the TV.

And that really is the whole point of this device, which is still technically in beta. All the TV-like stuff you watch on the internet you can now watch on your giant TV screen. This first version of the Chromecast is just the very first step in the computer's marriage with television. There will be weekly innovations, hacks, and invented benefits as this convergence proceeds.

-- KK

Animation

The Animator's Survival Kit

$27 Richard Williams, 2012, 392 p.

I have no words for the depth of this master class in visual animation. This is the definitive source for learning how to perform -- as in act -- by drawing; how to create emotion with a series of subtly modified images. There's lots involved in animation these days: this book is focused on a single thing: teaching you how to make animated movement come alive. Make a stick figure walk cautiously. A table lamp cower with fear. A robin soar. A car that makes you cry. Hundreds of tutorial illustrations show you how. Applies as much, or more, to digital animation as to pencil drawings.

-- KK

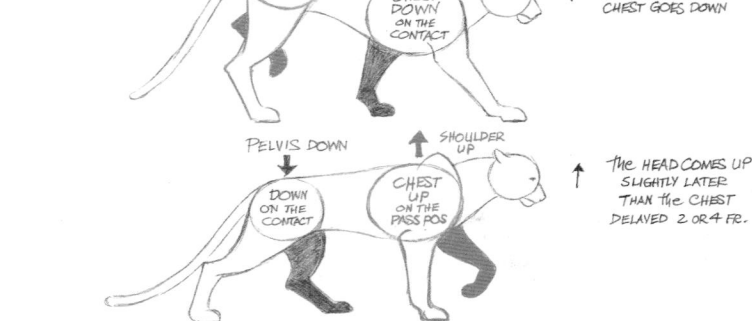

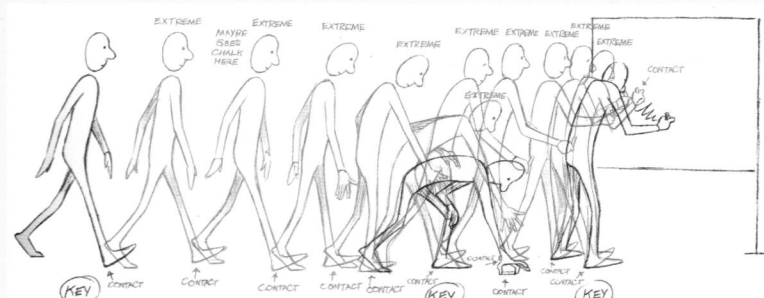

In these two shots, from Rustboy by Brian Taylor, we can see the dramatic effect shaders and lighting can have on a scene. The top picture is the flat model produced by the software while you are working on it. The picture below is a fully rendered scene, with all the shaders, textures, and lighting added to give it depth, atmosphere, and believability.

Desktop animation how-to

The Complete Animation Course

$10 Chris Patmore, 2003, 160 p.

All films will become animations. That prediction is based on the rate at which special effects become standard effects in big-budget films. Even a "live action" movie these days is composed frame by frame, and the skills and logic of animation take over. An ordinary digital camera, a hi-end PC or Mac, with iMovie software or equivalent, gives anyone the tools to do cinematic animation without tears. *The Complete Animation Course* is a great how-to orientation for making your own animated film using affordable technology. It introduces you to classic animation basics, and the many methods which combine old fashioned techniques (cartoon, paper collages, claymation) with computer based tools. I found it had just the right level of detail — sufficient to get you going without bogging down in how to do what's already been done.

-- KK

●

Twelve Principles of Animation

1. Squash and Stretch.

2. Anticipation. This is setting up the action before it happens, usually with a slight movement in the opposite direction to the main one.

3. Staging. This is related to the way the film as a whole is "shot," considering angles, framing, and scene length.

4. Straight-ahead Action and Pose-to-Pose. Straight-ahead action starts at one point and finishes at another in a single continuous movement, such as running, whereas pose-to-pose is a variety of actions in one scene requiring clearly delineated key frames to mark the action's extreme point. How the in-betweens are executed can alter the whole rhythm of the action.

5. Follow-through and Overlapping Action. Follow-through is the opposite of anticipation. When a character stops, certain parts remain in motion, such as hair or clothes. Overlapping action is when the follow-through of one action becomes the anticipation of the next one.

6. Slow In — Slow Out. This means using more drawings at the beginning and end of an action and fewer in the middle. This creates a more lifelike feeling to the movement.

7. Arcs. These are used to describe natural movement. All actions create circular movements because they usually pivot around a central point, usually a joint. Arcs are also used to describe a line of action through a character.

8. Secondary Action is just that, another action that takes place at the same time as the main one. This may be something as simple as turning the head from side to side during a walk sequence.

9. Timing. This is something that can't be taught. In the same way that comedians who rely on it to get the most from their gags have to learn it through experience, you too will get it right only through practice. Timing is how you get characters to interact naturally. Timing also has to do with the technical side of deciding how many drawings are used to portray an action.

10. Exaggeration. This is the enhancement of a physical attribute or movement, but don't make the mistake of exaggerating the exaggeration.

11. Solid Drawing. This conveys a sense of three-dimensionality through linework, color, and shading.

12. Appeal This is giving personality to the characters you draw. If you can convey it without the sound track, you know you are on the right track.

These are not hard and fast rules, but they have been found to work since the early days of animation. Bear them in mind at the storyboard stage and your animation will definitely have more fluidity and believability.

iStopMotion

$50 (free demo for 7 days)
Boinx.com

This is a very cool application that creates stop-motion and time-lapse videos. For years my kids and I have been making claymation episodes, doll and figure animations, paper cut-out sequences, and fun time-lapse movies with our family video cam, but our primitive method of simply blinking the on-button has always been less than satisfactory. Our brain-dead way creates three problems: the interval is too long (jerky movement), you can't see what motion should be next, and you can't edit out goofs when you make a boo-boo — which is 100% certain.

iStopMotion software is a much better way to do animation, and it solves all three problems. You connect a live video feed from your camera to your computer (via USB or Firewire) and then you control the film from your keyboard. After you capture a frame, the program overlays that frame as transparent layer over the current camera view so you can see exactly where you need to move next. You can even request the last 5 frames (onion skinning animators call it) to get a sense of direction and trajectory, which allows a very fine tuning of the motion. And you can edit mistakes, and do redos on the fly. All this is simple enough that my 7-year-old could instantly manage it. Yet it is sophisticated enough that film students use this software for thesis projects. Making time-lapse films is even easier.

The joy of this tool is that your computer screen rather than your camera screen drives the ani-mation. To overcome the downside that you need to do all your filming within cable reach of your laptop iStopMotion now comes as a phone app, too, so you can view your work on your mobile. There's also an iPad version for filming with this tablet (which needs to be steady). All are aimed at letting kids do animation quickly. But its good enough for slow adults like me.

There are three programs in this genre. I've tried all three (iStopMotion, FrameThief, and Stop-Motion Studio) and iStopMotion is by far the superior. It has the most features, ease of use, speed and stability. It is also the best designed.

-- KK

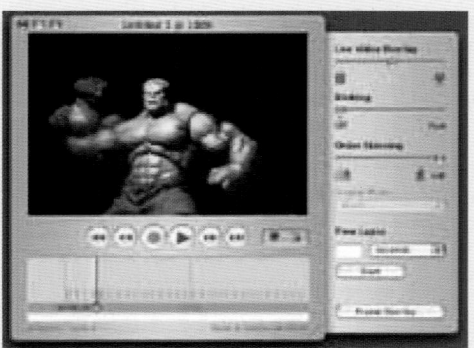

From my 7-year-old son's stop-animation of the Hulk action figure.

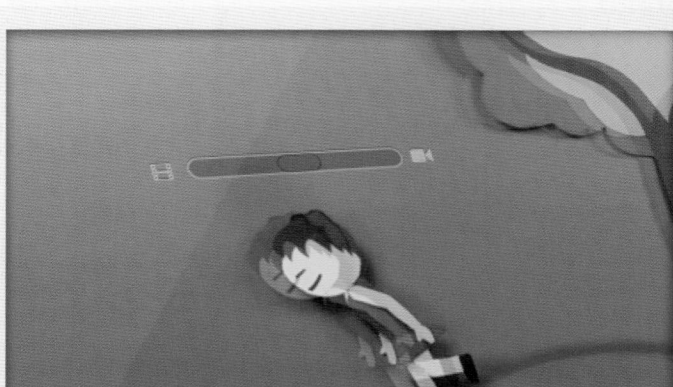

Whenever I draw a circle, I immediately want to step out of it. - Bucky Fuller

How to communicate visually
Making Comics
$16 Scott McCloud, 2006, 272 p.

Magnificent! A work of genius. The best how-to manual ever published. I could keep piling on the superlatives because this book is simply a masterpiece. At one level, it is a comic book about how to make comics, and for that it is supreme; the best. It will walk you through every step of making a comic, including how to make them on the web, digitally, or in pen and ink. I've been working on a graphic novel, and every page has told me something important and spot on. With brilliant graphics, Scott McCloud combines the most profound insights from his two previous books, *Understanding Comics* and *Reinventing Comics*. But in this book he raises your understanding of graphic communication further by making every lesson utterly practical and useful for both novice and expert. I can't imagine anyone ever doing a comic manual better.

However, even if you are not planning on making a graphic novel, this book is a gold mine. McCloud's section on constructing facial expressions and emotions is astounding, and worth the price of the book alone. The clever way McCloud arrays human expressions in one chart reminds me of the first time I saw all the colors arranged in a color wheel; it's the same aha! The insights McCloud extracts from comics and presents so vividly here are useful to novelists, sociologists, film makers, artists, roboticists — anyone interested in human expression. That's probably you.

Indeed, even if you have no interest in comics at all, this charming book will win a place in your life because ultimately it is about communication and stories — and those are the foundations of all cultures. Making Comics teaches you the visual elements of stories. If I had to re-title it, I would call this book Making Visual Stories.

Finally, as an example of communication itself, this comic book has few peers. I read, review and use hundreds of how-to books every year. I can't think of any instructional manual in any subject that is clearer, more thorough, more honest, more user friendly than Making Comics.

As I said, it's a classic. You can expect to find marked-up copies on bookshelves (or on hard drives) a hundred years from now.

-- KK

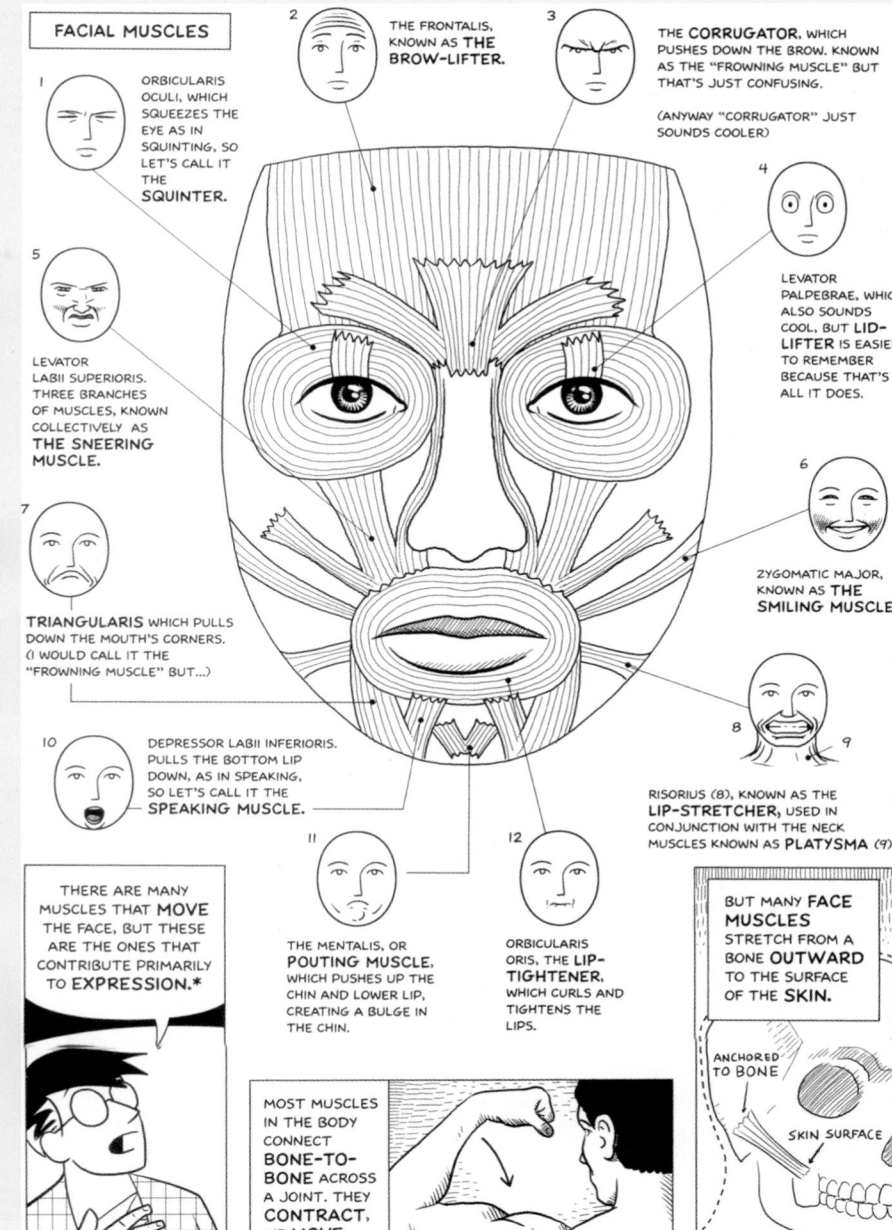

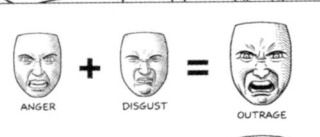

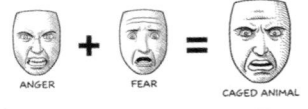

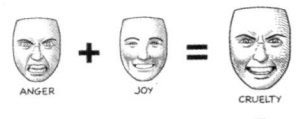

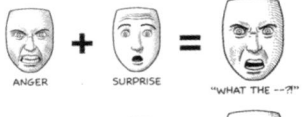

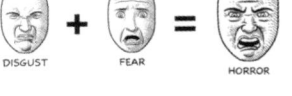

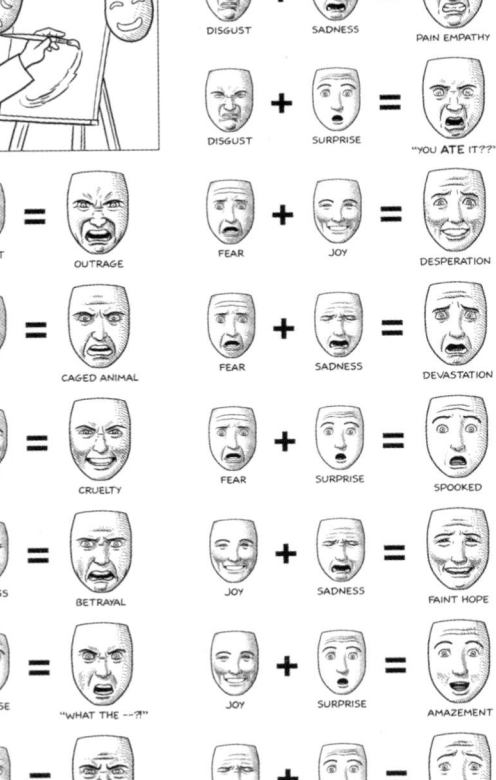

World Movies

Most complete guide to non-US films
Videohounds World Cinema
$9 Elliot Wilhelm, 1999, 559 p.

Great movies, maybe the best movies, are made in other countries, often in a language other than English. With the advent of DVDs, there is no need to wait until they show up in an art film house — if they ever do. This is the best guide to non-English movies in print. I prefer it because unlike other anthologies of "foreign" films, this one was written by a single author, and therefore has the benefit of comparative reviews and context.

--KK

- **Tampopo (Dandelion)**

When it premiered here in 1986, this second film from the late Juzo Itami (his debut, *The Funeral*, caused something of a modest scandal in Japan) seemed all the sweeter for being so thoroughly unexpected. Yet recent repeated viewings minus the element of surprise reveal *Tampopo* to be a marvel of comic structure so inventive, knowing, sweet, and tart that this trailblazer of the recent flood of food movies feels more like a classic than ever. The movie s heroine is Tampopo (Dandelion), a woman whose noodle shop is failing because she s a terrible cook. To the rescue comes Goro, a swaggering, macho truck driver with cattle horns on the cab of his truck, who makes Tampopo's cause his own. Swearing to make her noodles the best in the east, Goro and Tampopo embark on a fantastic gastronomical

The Master (Ryutaro Otomo) gives his opinion on the noodles in Juzo Itami's Tampopo.

odyssey of epicurean research that keeps spinning the picture's plot off into darkly hilarious shaggy-food stories. *Tampopo* is a celebration of movies, food, and sex, and Itami's whirling vision of a ravenous, unrepentantly insatiable world is never interested in separating the three. Tampopo is played by the wonderful Nobuko Miyamoto (Mrs. Itami), who would later go on to become the closest thing to a Japanese superwoman as a corruption-buster in Itami's subsequent, controversial comic exposés *A Taxing Woman*, *A Taxing Woman's Return*, and *Minbo*.

- **Polish Films**

Ashes and Diamonds
Contract
The Double Life of Veronique
The Dybbuk
A Generation
Illumination
Kanal
Knife in the Water
Man of Iron
Man of Marble
Moonlighting
The Saragossa Manuscript
Trois Couleurs: Blanc
Trois Couleurs: Rouge

World news unfiltered
SCOLA Television
$15 Basic Package, 25 hours per month SCOLA
$20 Deluxe Package, 40 hours per month SCOLA

SCOLA is a non-profit that rebroadcasts television programming (mostly news) from around the world in original languages (everything from Albanian to Vietnamese). It's intended as a language learning aid — and it's great for that — but you don't necessarily need to speak the language in order to get something out of the broadcasts. You can understand a lot about what's being discussed — and sometimes how it's being discussed is interesting in itself — even if you don't understand a word of what's being said. It's a great way to get a sense of a country you don't know much about. My brother-in-law said his image of Nepal as a backwater was forever changed after he saw their nightly newscast, complete with sophisticated commercials.

When I was at university in the early nineties, they ran SCOLA on the closed circuit cable system in the dorms. I'd forgotten all about it until a few years ago when I visited my mother-in-law in Omaha, where it's on the cable system (SCOLA is based in neighboring Council Bluffs, IA). I wanted to keep watching SCOLA at home, but at that time, online streaming was only available to institutional subscribers. I went back to Omaha again recently, rediscovered SCOLA, and was excited to discover they now offer individual subscriptions (it's also available on free-to-air satellite and

from some cable providers).

The individual subscription allows you to stream SCOLA live or download individual programs. Downloading is ideal; you don't even need to TiVo the broadcasts you want. I recently downloaded news from Cuba, Spain, Kurdistan, Burma, and Egypt. I don't even speak Kurdish or Burmese, but where else are you going to get a chance to watch this stuff, or even hear what those languages sound like? I got a "Level 1" subscription which means that for $10 I get 15 hours of SCOLA per month, either via streaming or download. This is cheaper than satellite radio, and besides, Sirius and XM aren't going to give you the news in Kazakh.

-- Rob Ryan-Silva

International viewing
Region Free DVD and Blu Ray

It is a streaming world, but DVDs, particularly blu ray DVDs, have not disappeared yet.

As everyone knows, DVD and Blu Ray players are sold encoded to a particular region to block imported DVDs from playing. However the **cheapest** DVD players are manufactured for low-price sales worldwide, and are thus engineered with (a) easily re-programmable regional coding (only one unit to make) and (b) chips that convert PAL signals (a system used over much of the world) to NTSC signals (a system used primarily in the United States and Japan).

The Samsung Region Free progressive scan DVD player costs about $37. The CVID Region Free Blu Ray play costs $125. Both come coded region free. They lack a lot of bells

and whistles, but they will play discs from all over.

These days almost any DVD or Blu Ray machine can be easily reprogrammed using the remote in accordance with instructions accessible via a Google search for "code free DVD". An example of the kind of hack is below. We found the code to our Samsung and de-zoned it. You can then watch any DVD manufactured anywhere in the world at home.

-- KK

So, after pressing REPEAT please enter one of the following codes the matches your current region lock:

1 – 2 9 3 3 4 (US)
2 – 5 7 5 3 8 (Europe)
3 – 5 6 7 3 2 (South East Asia)
4 – 7 6 8 8 4 (Australia / South America)
5 – 5 3 8 1 4 (India, Ukraine, Belarus, Russia, Africa)
6 – 2 4 4 6 2 (China)
9 - Region Free

Then press '9' and your player is region free.

$37 Samsung Region Free DVD
samsung.com

$125 CVID Region Free Blu Ray
Amazon

International cinema reviews
DVDTalk
dvdtalk.com

There are many sources for international DVDs, including the national Amazon sites – Japan, France, UK, Germany – as well as CDJapan.com, and YesAsia.com, among others. A very large proportion of the titles are digitally subtitled in English, and usually indicated as such on the sites.

What can you get? Depends on what you like: British television comedies and drama, uncut and uninterrupted, years before local release if ever; Japanese animation and the new wave of Japanese horror films; the massive (ten films a month) restoration and release of the Shaw Bros. film and television library from Hong Kong; classic releases of Bergman films from Artificial Eye in London (Fanny and Alexander uncut); French noir from the fifties and sixties, and on and on. The best place I know of for international DVD obsessives is called DVDTalk.com. The international forum has reviews and tons of shopping information and stuff about individual releases ("Von Trier's Kingdom with subtitles out in Denmark on August 1!") that sort of thing.

– Dennis Dort

- For many years virtually only English-subtitled prints of Ray's films looked like they went through a meat grinder, but over the past few years the Satyajit Ray Film Study Center and the Academy of Motion Picture Arts & Sciences have been racing against the clock to restore and preserve Ray's films.

Several original negatives have already been lost forever, and portions of Abhijan's negative were so damaged by mold that a single extant 35mm print had to be sourced for those scenes, with the most obvious lasting damage coming at the beginning of the first reel. Despite this, Abhijan for the most part looks simply wonderful.

▶

Set in the vibrant coastal town of Aci Trezza, Sicily La Terra Trema a.k.a The Earth Trembles (1948) tells the story of a small fishing community in the wake of a significant social strife. Directed by leg-

endary director Luchino Visconti (Rocco and His Brothers) the work is regarded as a masterpiece of Italian Neorealism.

- Ninja in Ancient China (apparently made in 1989 but not released in 1993) is the last feature by master martial director Chang Cheh. During his glory years at the Shaw Brothers he was the studios top director and a key, if not the lead figure in the martial arts film boom. Interest in traditional styled martial films waned, the Shaws closed their doors on film production, so by the late 80's Chang Cheh found himself working in the mainland.

I am not young enough to know everything. - Oscar Wilde

> It also makes for better radio. Their response will be a dramatic moment on tape.
>
> You think people just feel like you've come to town and you're telling them what to do and they don't like that?
>
> Sly.
>
> How much of your problems do you think have to do with the fact that people see you as outsiders?
>
> Do you feel you went around to people and actually understood what it is that they wanted?
>
> OK, so then what?
>
> The one other thing you need is a reflection on what it all means. I learned this as a tape cutter for Noah Adams on All Things Considered.
>
> You think people just don't like do-gooders? That that's part of it?

> The way we're used to listening to radio is: something happens, and then they say "here's why we're talking about this. Here's what it means."
>
> So you do this because we're used to it this way?
>
> Also because it's more satisfying. If you tell the story without the moment of reflection at the end, it loses grandeur. Moving to the general statement takes you out of the province of bar story and into the world of literature...you know, where you want to be (hee hee hee)...at least at this end of the radio dial!
>
> What do you think it means that radio has to spell out for listeners the significance of the stories it tells, but, in other art forms, that sort of thing comes across as heavy handed?
>
> It's just another example of how much more fun it is to make radio than to work in any other medium.
>
> Just for that, I'm drawing you without hair for the next page. Then we'll see what's fun.

If you remove a phrase or a sentence, you have to keep the rhythm natural. Usually that means keeping a breath after each sentence, at the edit points. Sometimes you have to try different breaths, to see which one sounds more natural. Your edit points are almost always at the very beginning of a word (after a pause or breath) or at the very end of a word (before a pause or breath).

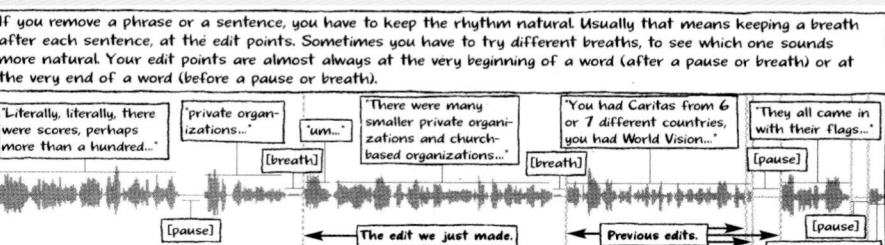

- "Literally, literally, there were scores, perhaps more than a hundred..."
- "private organizations..." [breath]
- "um..." [breath]
- "There were many smaller private organizations and church-based organizations..."
- "You had Caritas from 6 or 7 different countries, you had World Vision..." [pause]
- "They all came in with their flags..." [pause]
- [pause] [pause] The edit we just made. Previous edits. [pause] "it was...it was..."

How to tell stories
Radio: An Illustrated Guide
$33 Jessica Abel and Ira Glass, 1999, 32 p.

It's a small joke, but it works. A graphic artist embedded herself at the legendary radio show *This American Life* and created a comic book (all pictures) on how to make great narrative radio (no pictures). Well, at least how to make radio like *This American Life* makes it, which in my opinion is the best radio being made. There's less on recording techniques and more on how radio narratives work (or don't). It's not about news radio, nor talk radio, but story radio. In this respect, this slim, 32-page comic book will help anyone telling stories, and also make you a better radio listener, too.

-- KK

Best basic toolkit
Radio Journalism Gear

Transom Story Workshop teaches new students how to create narrative stories for radio. The kind of short stories you might hear on NPR. Their tech guy, Rob Rosenthal, posts a current recommendation list of the best basic radio journalism tools. He keeps up with testing out new gear and is always the place I (KK) go to find the best inexpensive recording gear. This updates their previous recommendations. Currently Rob says:

Students at the Transom Story Workshop tend to be beginners. Many have never picked up a mic or turned on a recorder before. So, it was important for us to choose a field recording pack that both sounded good and was simple for novices to use. Plus, since the Workshop started from scratch in the fall of 2011, we needed to find gear that fit our start-up budget. We landed on the following and feel we made the right choices:

Recorder: The Sony M10. We can't say enough about how good this recorder sounds. It's VERY quiet. And, it has a solid, built-in limiter. Those two components were important to us when selecting a recorder for students because new producers often don't pay close attention to the levels. Having a quiet recorder and a good limiter helps a student make better recordings. I would have preferred, maybe, the Sony D50. It seems more durable. But, the M10 is solid, lightweight, and has fewer bells and whistles to learn — and it's half the price.

$250 Sony M10 Amazon

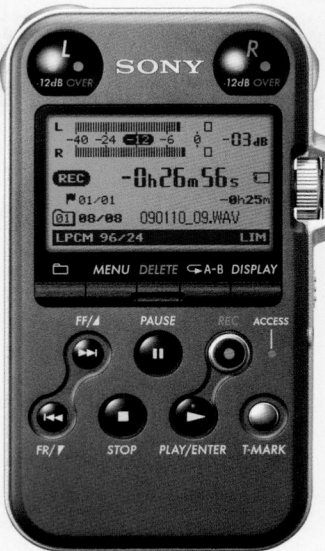

Mics: We have a slew of mics on hand for the students including the **Electro-Voice RE-50**, the Beyer-Dynamic MC-58 and MCE-58, and the Audio Technica AT8010. I'm a fan of the RE-50 and the MC-58 for new producers because they are more forgiving of mic handling noise. But, all of these are excellent mics.

$180 Electro-Voice RE-50
Amazon

Headphones: For the price — about $25 — the **Sennheiser HD202** is a good set of "cans." They help isolate external sound, they're fairly comfortable, and they reproduce sound well. Yeah, they aren't the Sony MDR-7506s we love, but we were on a budget and everyone is happy with these headphones. Never a problem.

$28 Sennheiser HD 202 II Amazon

-- *Rob Rosenthal, Transom* ▶

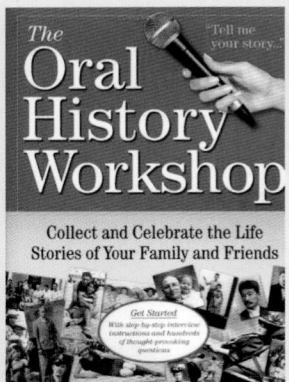

Best for life stories
Oral History Workshop
$11 Cynthia Hart, Lisa Samson, 2009, 180 p.

When you're 64 wouldn't you like someone to ask you about your life story and then preserve it? When you're 24 wouldn't you like to learn what really happened back in the day? Here are some great tips for interviewing and archiving these stories, including two chapters packed with a hundred great sample questions to ask. Technology makes this easy to do. I've done regular video interviews with my children as they grew up and with my parents and in-laws. One of the smartest things I've done. This book hadn't been published then (and it's the best of a half dozen on the subject), but if I had read it then I would have done a better job. Right behind me, my high-school age son is now capturing oral/visual histories, and he found this book extremely helpful too.

-- KK

- Even in interviewing, though, some silence can be a virtue. Particularly if the interviewee is discussing something difficult, a breath of silence implies, "Tell me more, associate further, give me the links to this experience, fantasy, or anxiety."

- So, though in preparing for your interview you'll likely focus on what you'll ask, don't forget about the power of a well-chosen pause.

- Broad questions have a way of eliciting vague answers. Instead of "Tell me about high school," you might start with a smaller, more specific question: "Who were your best friends in high school?" A "little" question about a childhood game could reveal a big truth about a family dynamic. Aim for a combination of broad and specific questions to get the full story.

- What insights have you gained about your parents over the years?

- Begin each recording by identifying the time, place, and names of the participants. This will serve as a journalistic "time stamp."

- To give audio recordings a visual context, take still photographs of your interviewee (and if possible of the two of you together) at the interview location.

- Before you finish an interview, ask yourself, "Is there one last question I need to ask in order to achieve what I'd hoped for?" Then ask the interviewee: "Is there anything that you would like to talk about?" or "What have we not discussed that you feel is important for me to know about you and your life?"

- Describe a typical family meal in your childhood home. What was usually on the menu? Who sat where around the table? Did it matter to you?

- What is the best gift you've ever given someone? The best gift you've ever received?

- If you could take only one last trip, where would you go and with whom? What would you do?

- What's the biggest mistake you ever made? What did it teach you?

- Who are your three closest friends? How are they different from one another, and why is each so dear to you?

Recording

Digital transcriber
Livescribe Smartpen

$190 Livescribe 2 GB Pulse Smartpen
Amazon

The Livescribe is a digital pen that writes normally while simultaneously digitizing what is being written and recording audio. What this pen allows me to do is to synchronize the taking of notes with the audio of the event. As I go through a brain storming session with a customer I can pay attention to the interaction at hand, draw on paper, record the audio, and then at a later time go back and review the notes in-sync with the audio. It also frees me up to take fewer notes at the time of the initial meeting. This allows me to

concentrate on the meeting at hand and then go back and review the audio while filling in the blanks as needed or create a list of follow up questions.

When you dock your pen with a computer (Windows / Mac), it transfers the recordings (audio and writing) to the computer thereby making a digitized backup of your handwritten notes as well as the audio of the meeting. This content is searchable and printable (in PDF). After meetings I sometimes spend 5 minutes docking the pen, "PDF-ing" out my notes and emailing them to folks for immediate action.

I would recommend this pen to anyone who wants to capture infor-

mation without a computer, but who still needs the added flexibility, beauty and brilliance of being able to port the data to a computer for expanded use.

The Livescribe uses special "dot paper" and pen cartridges that can be a little pricey, but no more so than Moleskine quality notebooks. The special "dot paper" is needed for the pen to digitize what has been written in ink into a digital format. Livescribe offers "college ruled" 8 x 11 notebooks, and Moleskine style notepads. So no matter what you want to write on, you're pretty much covered.

-- Mike Martin

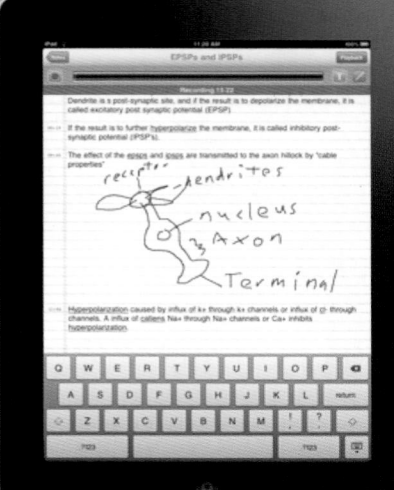

Synchronized recorded notes
Audionote

$5 itunes.apple.com

I have become a devotee to Audionote, a notetaking application for iPhone, iPad and laptop. While I'm recording a lecture or interview it allows me to take notes with a stylus, and it creates a linked audio file to my notes. That means I can tap on the screen and it will play the recording from a specific point in my notes. I mostly use the iPad mini, occasionally iPhone, but I can view the record-

ings on any of my three devices by uploading them to Dropbox. Recording sound quality is excellent.

-- John Markoff

Hand-set recording hack
Hands-Free Phone-Interview Setup

$7 Gold-Plated Y-Adapter Radio Shack
$9 1/8" Stereo Jack to 3/32" Stereo Plug Adapter Radio Shack
$8 12-Inch Shielded Stereo Audio Cable Radio Shack

It's a serious issue in contemporary journalism: how do you record phone interviews while using a headset?

Radio Shack sells a nice, cheap device (the previously reviewed Mini-Phone Recorder) that interrupts the cord that goes from the handset to the phone, which works well when you're using the handset. But when I do interviews by phone, I like to type a rough transcript while I talk, and typing while clamping a handset to your ear with your shoulder can quickly get painful.

When I first confronted this problem earlier this year, I spent a lot of time on the internet looking for solutions. The ones I found were pretty unappetizing. The main technology on offer is a microphone that you stick in your ear, which seems both unpleasant and ineffective.

But then I encountered the good people at Sagebrush.com, who invented this elegant and inexpensive solution, which uses about $20 worth of stuff you can get from Radio Shack.

You need three items:

1. the Gold Series Y-Adapter, 3/32" Stereo Jacks & 3/32" Plug, which is item # 2264801 and costs $7;

2. a 1/8" Stereo Jack to 3/32" Stereo Plug Adapter, which is item # 2160379 and costs $9; and

3. a 12-Inch Shielded Stereo Audio Cable, which is item # 2265306 and costs $8.

The Y-Adapter splits the signal coming out of your phone's headset jack. One line goes to the headset; the other goes to the recorder.

Arguably, this is more of a hack than a Cool Tool. But it works (as long as your phone has a headset jack). And it's very portable: you can also use it on the road by plugging into a cell phone.

-- Paul Tough

Easy cell phone recording
Olympus TP-7 Telephone Recording Device

$40 Amazon

Interviewing someone over the phone is never easy, and it is a task that has been made a bit more difficult

since the switch to mobile phones. Where as with a landline you could use something like the previously reviewed Mini Phone Recorder, there are no simple bypasses for cellphones.

With a little bit of research I discovered the Olympus TP-7; a miniature microphone that slips into your ear and plugs into your recording device (or computer) and enables easy recording of phone calls. At $11 it seemed like a low risk move to try one out.

Given its low cost, I didn't have any expectations in terms of audio quality, but was surprised to find that it was crystal clear (or as clear as a cell phone conversation normally is, clipping and all). While it's true my questions were louder than their answers the difference didn't hamper playback and transcription. Furthermore, the TP-7 is comfortable enough in-ear that I practically forgot it was there (just remember if you ever switch your phone to the other ear you have to

move the microphone as well). The TP-7 comes with a bevy of plug adaptors, as well as different sized ear plugs for a comfortable fit.

I have, in the past, tried Google Voice's recording services that only work on incoming calls to your Google Voice activated line (and also announce that the telephone call is being recorded due to varying state requirements). The recording quality is significantly worse compared to what my Olympus TP-7 and Olympus LS-10 produced, and the transcription (another feature offered by Google Voice) was laughable.

Also, unlike the previously reviewed hands-free setup, the TP-7 has the added advantage of being a single piece of equipment that requires no extra cables or accessories, and is small enough to be carried around in my bag all day just in case I have to record a call on the road. If you ever have a need to record phone calls or interviews over the phone (mind you, legally) I can wholeheartedly recommend this tiny, lightweight but high quality in-ear microphone.

-- Oliver Hulland

Solid note-taking app
Notability

$2 iTunes Store

I've been using Notability on my iPad for over a year now. I find it handy for taking notes on the fly. You can type or handwrite (though it does not do handwriting recognition) I can take pictures of slides at a lecture and caption them on the fly. I also take pictures of any business cards I get handed, which

gives me a visual record apart from the little piece of paper that can so easily get lost. You can also record a lecture while taking notes.

You can draw with a finger or a stylus, in a variety of line styles and colors, highlight your notes, annotate your drawings, customize paper color, make it lined, plain or graph, textured or not.

You can store notes by category, and email them to yourself or store them via Dropbox (though not to iCloud), import and export files as .pdfs and .rtfs. What I like best is that it's really flexible and intuitive. I'm sure there are plenty of tweaks and features that I've failed to mention.

-- Amy Thomson

Everybody who is honest is interesting. - Quentin Crisp

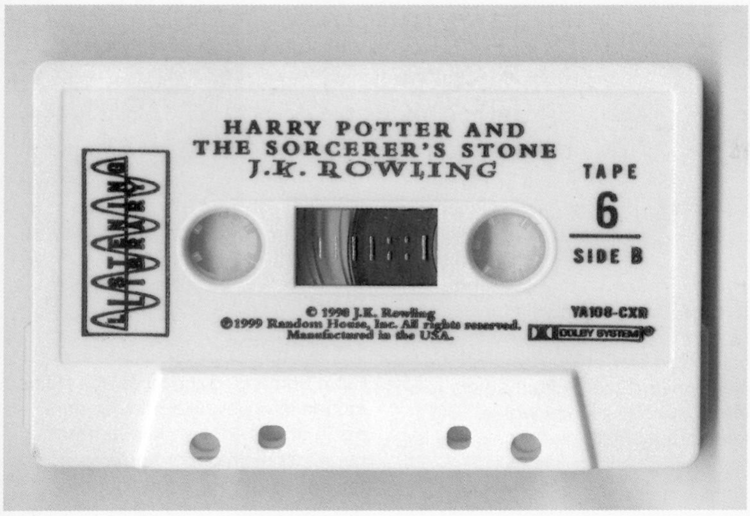

In praise of listening

Audio Books

Whenever I overhear a complaint of someone's long time-wasting commute I want to whisper into their ear, "It doesn't have to be that way. You can read books while you drive! You won't want to stop." By "read," I mean listening. Audio books aren't new, but they aren't as common as they should be. What a shame because the selection of books available for auditing continues to expand, their relative price continues to drop, and the devices they can be heard on continue to increase. Over the past twenty years I've read, oh I suppose, hundreds of books this way. And I am not alone; audio book fans are legion. Here's what I know about how to maximize this great medium.

1) Being read to is a pleasure. Hearing a book instead of "watching" it can be a powerful experience.

2) Start with a good story. If you have never listened to an audio before, pick what you know is a good tale to begin with. You can always get to that self-help or executive summary later. Try the Pulitzer-winning novel *Lonesome Dove* for a memorable treat.

3) If at all possible choose an unabridged version. The unabridged is how the author wanted you to get his/her story. One of the delights about audio books is that they are far more leisurely (reading aloud takes longer), so you can exploit this pace by getting the full undiluted version. I consider these a second choice abridged versions a second choice.

4) However if a book is only available in an abridged version, it can still be enjoyable. Very rarely, it can be better. Cyberpunk author William Gibson actually prefers the abridged audio version of his book *Neuromancer*. Occasionally I've deliberately chosen an abbreviated version because I just didn't want to sit through the long edition. Still, a book worth reading is usually worth the original text.

5) Avoid dramatizations. These were in vogue for a while but luckily they've mostly disappeared. More than one person acts out the dialog, but the histrionic tone usually turns a book into theater. There is something incredibly satisfying about having one voice (with accents and drama, yes) continue through the work.

6) Narrators matter. I have learned to never listen to an author read his own work, no matter who. (Other avid audio book listeners may disagree.) A professional narrator can make all the difference between a book that sings and one that dies. Good narrators can pronounce technical and foreign names exactly, and often do accents properly. Their voices don't waver or dull. But the wrong narrator can pollute a book. I will return a book if I find the narrator's voice makes me wince. Conversely, if I notice a great narrator I will now seek out the other books they have done. Narrating is a very laborious process and good narrators are in top demand, so they won't invest their time in a mediocre book. Half the spell of a book is cast by the narration.

7) With that in mind, sometimes a narrated version of a book is actually better than reading it. A great example of that is the *Harry Potter* series. I have no hesitation in saying that Jim Dale's narration of *Harry Potter* is better than reading it. (If you want my best candidate for a book to start out, pick any *Harry Potter* book and listen to it; Get Dale's narration who is British but did the American edition). Dale performs something like 120 different voices for the series and each character voice is absolutely perfect. He makes an already remarkable series of books fantastic. Two other books that were better listening were *Shantaram* and *Midnight in the Garden of Good and Evil*. Again, the narrators got the accents of their characters more exact and colorful than my reading ear could have. Russian novels are often improved by audio because they can get all those Russian names and places perfect.

8) Over the years I've found that the best books for auditing are either fiction or history. I still audit a lot of nonfiction, but fiction and history work best for me. Both have deep narrative structure. I choose more and more history now because I realize that I don't have the patience to read history, as in using my eyes while staring at the page. The captured-audience nature of listening (can't skip easily) demands that I follow the course all the way through. And I'm usually glad I did. So most of the history I read now, I actually audit. Happily, there are a lot of great historical audio books.

9) Having a parallel printed copy of a book can help alleviate one of an audio book's primary weaknesses: there's no way to bookmark a passage. Stewart Brand, another audio book fanatic, will usually keep a hard copy of the text in book form handy so that he can mark sections he wants to refer to later. I don't do that but I sure wish I could bookmark stuff. The Kindle is becoming integrated with Audible books so you may be able to do this in the future.

10) You have a choice of channels. If you still have a CD player, there are plenty of CD audio books around. There are cassette versions for the free taking too. Most folks listen to audio books on a phone or digital player which can be connected to your car's audio system with a standard phone jack or wireless connection.

11) Auditing while driving is not dangerous. I don't know how it works but you can be completely engrossed in a story, while the other you somehow drives at your top skill. It's not the same as talking on a cell phone. Works best if you know exactly where you are going, like on a commute. Doesn't work if you have to navigate; you'll miss a turn for sure.

12) Borrow or buy? Public libraries often have a selection of audio books on CD or cassette or for download. I use our interlibrary loan system to get almost any audio book I want if I am willing to wait for it. You can get free audio books from LibriVox (review below). Or you can purchase them from Audible (see details below).

Where to start? Let's see; this summer my wife and I (on separate commutes) listened to *War & Peace*, all of it. Great book, great narration. Took three months, but worth every second. Adventures like *The Perfect Storm* and *Into Thin Air* are just right. Robert Hughes' history of Australia, *The Fatal Shore*, listened well. Occasionally I throw in some lightweight mystery or technothriller. Right now I'm auditing the *Odyssey* and the *Iliad*. You get the picture. Traffic jams are just story-time extenders. If I've got a good book, and someone to read, I'll go slow and learn something.

-- *KK*

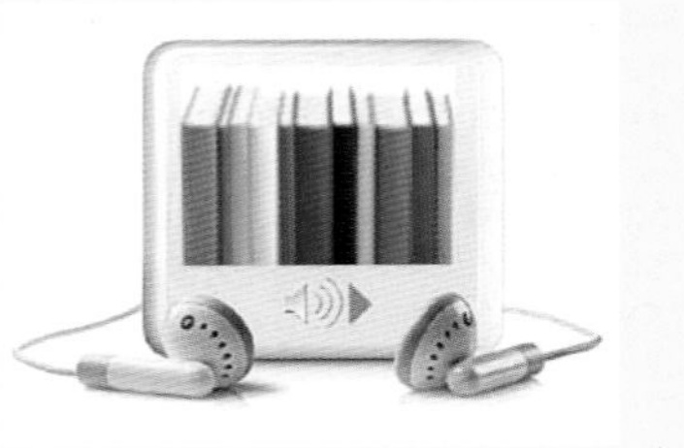

Satisfying audio books

Audible

audible.com

Audio books are fantastic. Download them to your phone, or borrow them from your local library. I've audited several hundred books so far, all while driving. I listen to all kinds, light and heavy, fiction and non-fiction, short and long. More and more this is where I get my serious reading done. If at all possible I listen to the unabridged version. If fact my most memorable audible experiences are listening to long deep audio books. The longer the better.

Audible is the central depot for audio books. They don't carry every audio book, but they carry the most (100,000), and they have the best interface for selecting, pre-viewing, ordering. Since this is an Amazon company they also offer a service that will sync your Kindle version of a book and your Audible version (you need to purchase both versions), so you can switch from reading (in a home) to listening (in a car) without losing your place! I like Audible because they also allow you to "return" a book for a refund if the narrator -- or the book! -- doesn't agree with you.

You can buy individual books, but the best deal is monthly or yearly subs at about $15 or $10 per book. Here are a few suggestions of long books that seem to appeal to most people if you want to get started. For the long books I prefer professional narrators over the author's voice.

-- *KK*

Fiction

Shantaram (Amazing unbelievable immersive vivid journey into the slums of India.)

Lonesome Dove (Wished it never ended. Pure story, unforgettable characters.)

War and Peace (I tried many times to read it, but couldn't get going. Listening was the answer.)

Harry Potter series (Better than either the movies or reading the books. Narrator Jim Dale does 135 voices.)

Assimov's Foundation series (Classic science fiction saga that still works.)

Atlas Shrugged (The only way you can get through all of John Gault's monologue.)

Life of Pi (A boy and tiger in lifeboat. Unconventional, unorthodox, unexpected delight.)

Pillars of the Earth (Historical fiction about building cathedrals over generations.)

Nonfiction

The Discoverers (How knowledge triumphed over ignorance and invented everything.)

1491 (This will change your mind about American natives and history of the continent.)

1493 (Same author, will change your mind about African slavery's role in the Americas.)

Short History of Everything (Much more enlightening and enjoyable than I thought it could be.)

God, Country and Coca Cola (About drugs, FDA, and the invention of advertising. And Coke.)

Peter the Great (A biography of Russia through one man.)

Into Thin Air (A surprising, page-turning, mind-bending adventure up Mt. Everest.)

The Looming Towers (Essential deep origins of Osama Ben Laden vs. the US.)

Free, user-generated audio books

LibriVox

Free LibriVox

Last year I took a cross-country road trip with my 10-year-old daughter, and we were greatly entertained by the free public domain audio books available from LibriVox, an online forum which connects readers (as in those who voice the text) to books, then makes the resulting audio files freely available to all. The library is strictly public domain material, but is very extensive. Most of the books we listened to were read by just one person ("going solo"), but readers can volunteer for individual chapters of books in progress. We listened to *The Prince and the Pauper*, *The Mysterious Island*, *The Wind in the Willows*, *Five Children and It*, and several selected poems and short stories. (Kudos to Timothy Smith for *The Mysterious Island* — a tour de force!). Online coordinators organize the readings, which are generally excellent. Some readers provide wonderful voices for each character; some simply read the text. The books are available for download from the website, or can be downloaded via iTunes, which we did and then listened to from the iPod in the car (note: using iTunes, the files are stored as separate podcasts with a separate podcast per chapter; when you download the .mp3 file from the LibriVox website, it is listed not in audiobooks nor podcasts, but as a LibriVox 'song'). This really is a wonderful public service. It's not as easy to be a good reader as you may think! If you want to contribute, the website includes a FAQ on how to record and prepare the audio file for submission, including links to free recording software and instructions on adding ID3 tags for the iPod. My daughter is enchanted with the concept, and has since volunteered to read chapters of Raggedy Ann stories.

-- *Paul Goessling*

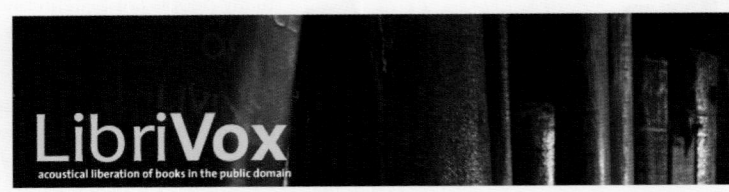

Podcasts

Highly recommended non-fiction podcasts
True Podcasts

Podcasts are audio programs you subscribe to.

For the past several years I've been actively auditing podcasts while in my car. I've tried all kinds of stuff — one time talks, home-made riffs, occasional raves by brilliant geniuses, and regular fragments of broadcast material. I have two criteria: I want to be surprised, and I want to learn.

In the past 12 months I have settled my listening time on three regular podcasts, which I look forward to eagerly. I can heartily recommend all three. They share these characteristics: they are one-hour, weekly podcasts of non-fiction that begin as broadcasts on public radio. I know the whole point of podcasting is to let a million amateur voices bloom, but what can I say? Week after week, what I crave is well-crafted, compelling audible surprises that tell me something I didn't know. That is what you get with these free podcasts. One hour gives time to go deep, weekly gives room to experiment, but doesn't overwhelm the way daily does (I dropped Fresh Air because I couldn't keep up), and non-fiction keeps me learning.

One thing to keep in mind: podcasts are meant to be "subscribed to" as they are delivered, which means getting "back copies" or archived editions of formerly broadcast podcasts may not easy. You may have to either listen to them as streaming audio, or pay for a download.

In Our Time

This weekly broadcast from the BBC in London is a testimony to the benefits of intellectuals and professors. Every week the mumbling host Melvyn Bragg invites three English professors (usually from Oxford or

Cambridge) to discuss the most obscure subject of their expertise. They are only too happy to talk about that thing they know more about than anyone. By forcing the eggheads to be succinct, or demanding they restate a concept until clear, *In Our Time* delivers an incredibly fascinating glimpse into an unknown world in sufficient detail to make the conversation memorable. Imagine a whole hour each on: The Speed of Light; Indian Mathematics; The Siege of Constantinople; Gravitational Waves; The Trial of Madame Bovary; Anaesthetics; Joan of Arc; Ockham's Razor. Those are some of the topics I've heard in recent months. I've learned that the more obscure the subject, the more revelatory detail, and the more it becomes fascinating.

Radio Lab

It's hard to describe the innovative audio sensibility in a Radio Lab show. Sounds and speech are layered, cut, remixed, and spot-lighted in a way

that could be very annoying, but isn't. Instead these experiments add subtlety, animation, and depth to otherwise talking voices. Each session of *Radio Lab* takes

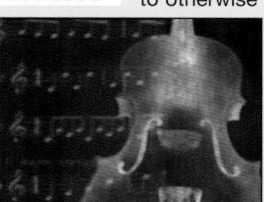

a broad subject like Placebos, or Forgetting, and explores the idea in sound and words non-linearly, with great intelligence, originality, and daring. They ask hard questions, and keep circling it until they come close to an answer. It's a lot of fun. They also do a wonderful job integrating their website material (links, bibliography, further research) into the hour. You can download past programs as mp3. Start with the Musical Languages show.

This American Life

True stories about anything. Simply the best thing on radio. Possibly ever. Host Ira Glass has been pioneering the art of telling non-fiction stories for 10 years. He gives each voice time to stumble, pause, or lunge forward. But not a nanosecond is wasted. You hear what happened to people that makes their lives human. Every story on *This American Life* has an emotional narrative arc, and is often about transformation. Each story is told in an honest, original voice, and will make you cry or laugh. It is not uncommon for people to sit in their cars at their destination in order to hear the end of a story. That was the main drawback of *This America Life*: I wasn't usually in my car when it broadcast on the radio. Now with the podcast version I catch the three stories — and their endings — every week.

Science...Sort of

This one is for science geeks only. Three grad students sit around, drink beer and talk science. On each podcast they take one science paper that makes the news and then dissect it rigorously in a way no TV, radio, or even newspaper would ever do. Between a rotating cast of 4 or 5,

they have a broad set of science backgrounds, so the discussions meander but are always interesting. They try to educate each other, while challenging and being skeptical the whole while. Listeners get a very real picture of how science works. Did I mention they meander? The show is very informal and laid back.

The New Yorker: Out Loud

While I have been listening to this podcast for years, the format has been rapidly evolving in the past year; I can't really say what it is currently,

other than a variety show. They often will interview the *authors* of *New Yorker* articles,

which I find fascinating, because you often hear things said that they didn't say in their article, and because you get a look behind the process. The authors are smart and articulate and will always surprise me.

Gweek

GWEEK 097

infatuated with. That's all, but the format works because I learn about fantastic things I would not hear about otherwise. It's sort of "What's Your Passion?"

Little Atoms

From England, a group of like-minded friends interview like-minded thinkers in the sciences, skeptic, transhumanist realms. For some reason the sound quality is low, but the discussions are great. They tend to find intellectuals who are not already well-known, which gives the show an edge.

Little Atoms
A podcast about ideas...
www.littleatoms.com

Radio Open Source

Christopher Lydon is probably the most literate interviewer I have come across, infusing his questions with a long-view and a deep knowledge of cultures, many cultures. Recently he has been working his way around the Mid-East, conducting on-location discussions with local poets, activists, writers, and thinkers, asking them to explain the world. It is deeply refreshing to hear a Pakistani humorist, or an Egyptian painter talk about current events.

-- KK

Geek week, run by Mark Frauenfelder, co-founder of bOING bOING, and now my partner at Cool Tools. Every episode Mark interviews friends and folks he admires and has them talk about whatever games, books, movies, gadgets, or ideas they are currently

---

"Can you imagine 4,000 years passing, and you're not even a memory? Think about it, friends. It's not just a possibility. It is a certainty."
— Jean Shepherd, 1975

Best radio storyteller
Jean Shepherd, Storyteller

When I was growing up as a kid in the 1960s, I listened to legendary storyteller Jean Shepherd spin wild, maniacal yarns every night for forty-five minutes on our local radio station near New York City. Shepherd told outrageous tales from his experiences working in the steel mills of Gary, Indiana, of his teenage exploits with hot rod cars, of the crazy boredom of his army life, and of his life as swinger in Greenwich Village. Imagine Walt Whitman as a comedian, or Garrison Keillor as a beatnik, and you might come close, but you'd miss

the way Shepherd creatively hacked the medium of radio, doing things with it that would not be commonplace until the talk show era decades later. (Shepherd once got his audience to force a fictional book onto the New York Times's best seller list.) I kept thinking over the years, "I sure hope someone out there is recording these." Well, many people were. Jean Shepherd died recently, but now his stories live on via the Web and cassettes.

With thousands of broadcasts, it's hard to know where to start. Shepherd was at his peak in the mid-1960s, and his "Live at the Limelight" shows are always great, but you can get a feel for what it was like listening to him through the evening static of WOR-AM by clicking on the weekly re-broadcasts of his show on the Web. Check out the fabulous Shepherd fan site, (Web radio), or see the catalog of tapes, which also has a steady stream of other old-time radio shows.

-- KK

Jean Shepherd books
Amazon

Flick Lives

Excellent sub-$100 USB microphone
Yeti Microphone

$100 Amazon

A podcast with poor acoustics is exhausting to listen to. As a podcast listener, I've dropped several otherwise excellent podcasts because they sound like recordings made with two tin cans and a string.

As a podcast producer, I strive to produce shows with good sound quality. Many things affect sound quality: room acoustics, audio editing methods, Internet speed (when you have guests joining you over Skype, for instance), and recording equipment. The easiest variable to lock down is the microphone. After years of trying different sub-$100 USB microphones, I've finally found one that does almost everything I want: the Yeti, by Blue. This retro-looking desktop microphone has several features that make it

vastly superior to the one I used to use — the slightly less expensive Snowball (also by Blue).

The best thing about the Yeti is the built-in headphone amp, which allows me to monitor my voice in real time. Now that I can hear what I sound like, my delivery style has changed from near-shouting to a more laid-back, Ira Glass way of speaking. (One listener tweeted that I sounded much calmer on my podcasts and wondered why.) The headphone monitor also has its own volume control.

The Yeti has a microphone gain knob, which makes it easy to quickly adjust the sensitivity without having to fiddle with the recording software's sound preferences. The mute button is nice addition that I use when a guest is talking and airplanes are passing over my house or I need to clear my throat. The recording pattern knob has symbols to indicate stereo, omni, cardioid, and bi-directional modes (the Snowball's three-way switch unhelpfully reads 1, 2, and 3!).

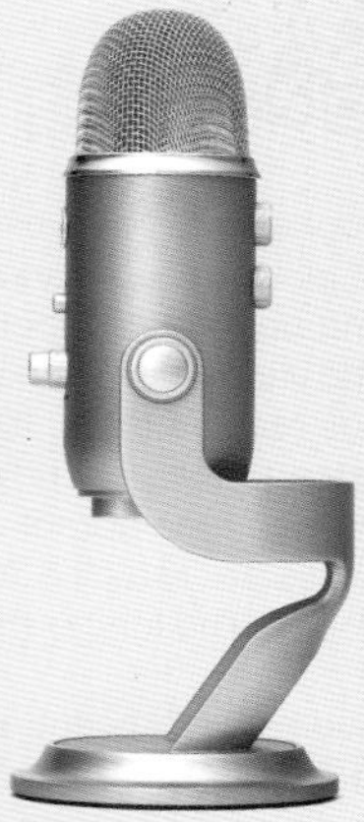

Two things prevent the the the Yeti from being perfect: 1) Two of the controls are on the front of the mic and two are on the back, forcing me to crane my neck to adjust the gain or change the recording pattern. 2) Vibrations from my computer's keyboard, fan, and hard drive pass through the foam rubber lining on the base of the microphone stand, causing a rumble sound. My workaround is to set the microphone on a rubber iPhone case, which does a great job of damping the noise. (I might end up cutting the iPhone case to fit the Yeti's base and glue it on.)

-- Mark Frauenfelder

No limit for better. - Harrison Ford

Best portable, shortwave receiver
Sony Shortwave Radio

$139 Amazon

The previously-reviewed Sony ICF-2010 is undoubtedly the best portable shortwave radio ever made. It was built to perfection with synchronous detection, aircraft band and a lot of other bells and whistles. But unfortunately, it has long been discontinued. Likewise, the previously-reviewed Grundig YB-400 has also been discontinued.

Today, the two best portable shortwave receivers in the market are the Sony ICF-SW7600GR and the Grundig G5. Both are great radios, but the 7600GR triumphs over the Grundig because of its excellent build quality (still Japanese made!) and synchronous detection circuitry, which lets the user eliminate adjacent channel interference, fading and distortion on shortwave. Both are equally sensitive on shortwave but some argue that the G5 has better audio (i.e. the speaker). For listening to ham radio stations, though, the 7600GR is much better and, at least for the moment, it is the only portable receiver that features synchronous detection

circuitry, technology usually found only on radios *ten times* the price!

Some background on synchronous detection: an Amplitude modulated (AM) signal has three components: the carrier signal which is flanked by upper and lower sidebands (USB and LSB). The sidebands carry the audio information and are prone to interference when a station from an adjacent frequency interferes with the sidebands. For example, if you are listening to BBC on 9500 KHz, a station at 9505 KHz might interfere with the upper sideband of 9500 KHz but not with the lower sideband. The lower

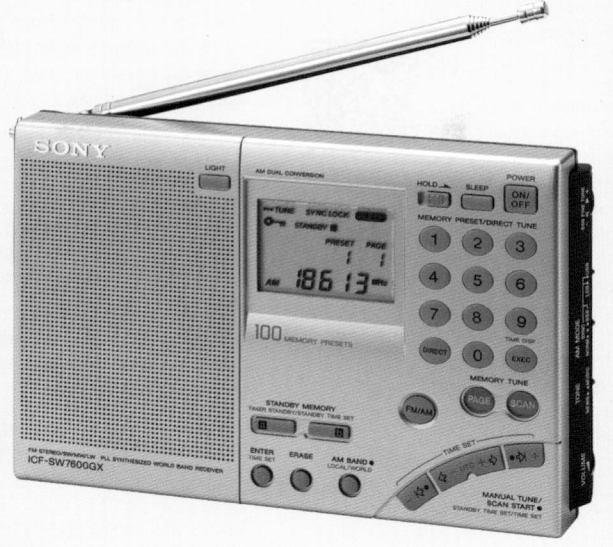

sideband is vulnerable only to a frequency lower than BBC at 9500 KHz. A regular detector on a radio like G5 will take *both* sidebands and the carrier signal and generate an audio that will show signs of interference. A synchronous detector like the one on the Sony 7600GR eliminates the distorted sideband and uses the cleaner sideband (the one not affected by interference) and mixes it up with a new strong carrier signal, which it generates by itself. Thus, the 7600GR eliminates two problems: weak carrier signal and distortion of the sidebands due to adjacent channel interference.

For hams radio stations, single side band (SSB) capability is needed. Hams generally broadcast in the upper or the lower side band but not both. The Grundig G5 and the Sony 7600GR both have an SSB feature, but only Sony lets you manually select which of the two single side bands (upper or lower) to listen to. That USB/LSB selectable switch also comes in handy for the synchronous detection circuitry. For instance, if you know the interference is coming from a station broadcasting at a frequency higher than what you are listening to, choose LSB on the switch and the USB is eliminated and vice versa.

The 7600GR has been a great companion to me for the last five years. I listen to All India Radio to catch some news and music from home. I also love listening to voices from all over the world: BBC, Radio Netherlands, Radio China International, Radio Japan, and Radio Australia among many others. Beyond increasing my understanding of the world around me, the radio also helped me a lot with improving my spoken English. And due to its size, I'm able to take the radio pretty much everywhere I go.

-- Sam Ponissery

It's Wherever You Go

3,717,792
Square miles of seamless coast to coast coverage

200 Miles off shore
And your radio will still work

By Contrast — Terrestrial radio reception range is generally limited to about 50-100 miles

Commercial-free radio
XM Satellite Radio/
Sirius XM

$50+ receivers (monthly/annual service fee separate) XM Radio/Sirius XM

Satellite radio is for folks living in rural areas where local radio stations are scare, or not very good. Or living on boats outside of local radio range, or driving long distances bored with talk radio, or for people who want a great selection of commercial-free stations that even the internet does not have.

-- KK

Because the satellites are so powerful, you don't need a dish antenna; my Sony system uses an antenna the size of a travel iron. Supposedly you place it on the roof of your car (it has a magnetic base) but I find I get flawless reception if I place it inside the car, under the windshield. The Sony receiver can be moved in and out of various vehicles, or your home. The antenna *just* manages to pick up the satellite signal from inside a wooden-framed house.

You get 101 channels, many commercial-free. Highlights for me have included a

10-hour special on John Lennon (created by the BBC), the blues channel (amazingly wide ranging eclectic selection), and "Music Lab" which ranges from Phish to Frank Zappa. You also get news stations (audio versions of CNN and Bloomberg), CSPAN, BBC World Service, oldtime radio dramas, readings of classic novels (more BBC material, excellently produced), and E! stuff which can be entertaining (they specialize in chronicling troubled lives of celebs). Of course there is a full range of new rock/pop/country/hiphop/oldies. You can send email to the DJs and get intelligent replies.

My job entails driving from my home in Northern Arizona to Phoenix and back, each week (150 miles each way). Headphones coupled with XM radio have erased the boredom and irritation of the journey, and I don't find the headphone experience any more distracting than a regular car radio. It's just more restful.

-- Charles Platt

I mainly got the Sirius XM satellite channel because I ride a lot in areas that don't have terrestrial radio reception -- places like the wilds of central Nevada, northern British Columbia, the Yukon and Alaska. Even with a big library of MP3's, I'd rather listen to curated music on a commercial-free XM station. On days I'm on a long ride (750+ miles), it's nice to be able to listen to a baseball game, or an 80's Alt station, or even ESPN Radio, just to have something different.

-- Brian Casey

Killer AM reception
Sangean AM/FM Pocket Radio

$36 Amazon

This Sangean pocket radio costs a lot more (4x) than the smallest available iterations from Sony and Panasonic, but it's well worth the extra cash for two reasons. The first is that it picks up AM way better than anything in its size/weight class, both in terms of the number of stations and, equally important, the strength and clarity of the signals. And secondly, its size, 3.5" x 2" x 0.6" (measured by me) and weight, 2.05 oz. on my postal scale.

Note that there's no speaker so you have to use earphones (they come with a pair). Finally, its form factor is remarkably similar to that of the long defunct iPod mini. Now I can listen without static on AM as Larry, Sonny and Sam call the woeful Redskins' games.

-- Joe Stirt

Portable radio and stereo speaker set
Tecsun Dual Speaker Digital Radio

$60 Amazon

While looking for an external set of speakers for my iPad, I rediscovered my Tecsun Pl-390 portable radio. Most of the external speakers I had seen were either without power of their own, or they ate batteries too fast to be of much use. Added to that is the fact that most of them were too bulky to haul around. It was then that I realized the Tecsun had a line-in jack and two perfectly sized speakers, and I had suddenly solved two problems: great stereo for my iPad and an excellent radio with great features.

This puppy hooks to the iPad with a standard stereo patch cord, one of those two-ended things with a

miniature stereo headphone plug at each end.

In effect the Tecsun becomes a great pair of portable stereo speakers that also picks up AM, FM, shortwave, and (for anybody in Europe) longwave. It plays stereo on FM, too. It is the only portable shortwave radio I am aware of that plays in stereo, although I know of many others that will provide stereo through headphones. Not only does this radio pick up all those bands, it does so VERY well. While it only picks up standard radio signals (not "HD Radio"), it processes the signals digitally. This allows several performance advantages and interesting special features.

One of these special features is called "Easy Tuning Method." Start an ETM scan and the radio will scan whatever band you're listening to,

or in the case of shortwave, it will scan all the SW broadcast bands at once. It makes note of all the listenable signals available. After that, when you turn the tuning knob, it jumps clear signal to clear signal, skipping all the spaces in between. Rescanning this when you're in a different town, or when listening conditions change, is as simple as pushing the button again. Cool!

Tecsun also makes a smaller, single-speaker version of this radio. I got the larger stereo version because it has a longer case that gives space for a longer AM antenna- and, get ready for a miracle, they actually put a longer AM antenna in it. It makes for borderline amazing AM reception. Plus this set does all the things that have become usual for fancier portables in recent years. It works as an alarm clock, it has more memory presets than I can find use for, and so on.

Mine came with a USB cable for external power or charging. Unfortunately, the radio did not come with a plug-in power supply. Any "wall wart" that outputs to a standard USB socket will work, though.

-- Bill Rogers

The trick is not to live forever. It's to live forever with yourself. - Pirates of the Carribean.

327

Telephony

Free telephone conferencing
UberConference
Free Firespotter

UberConference is a well-designed site offering free telephone conferencing with great service and great usability. For instance:

• You can save the contacts that you invite to calls.

• You can import your contact list from other sources.

• When you, or your contacts call in from a number on record, no PIN is required.

• During the call, the web page shows who is talking (useful for large conferences or new contacts).

• The service sends out email reminders immediately prior to the scheduled call time.

• The basic service is free, and you can pay for additional functionality, like recording the calls.

-- jlw

Better way to talk
Phone Headsets

Long live this neck saver! Hail to the hand-freer! I've been using a headset on my phone for a decade now, and I continue to be puzzled why everyone else doesn't. A headset lets me make two-hour teleconferences without a bit of discomfort. Having to grip a phone for any length now feels unhealthy. Mine is a pretty typical set with one ear piece and a tiny boom microphone, that altogether weights a few ounces, if that. It takes no extra effort to slip it on when the phone beeps. My hands are completely liberated. With a comfy headset I can take notes, search for a paper, look up a number on my computer, or just stretch, without neck crinks, sore elbows, or squashed ears. You can choose from dozens of models including cordless sets, ear buds, ultralights, or cheapies. Radio Shack has a low end for cost $20 while Hello Direct has a complete selection of the fancy goods, and a line of headset accessories. I've seen some go for $6. A lot of people used to refuse them because they thought it made them look dorky, but I see more and more executives sporting them now, and with cellphones it's become fashionable to have a set in your ear.

But because a headset is so much better for your health I wouldn't be surprised if companies began to mandate headsets strictly for health reasons. Do your body a favor and use one.

-- KK

$30 Plantronics M214C Headset for Cordless/ Wireless Phones RadioShack

Hello Direct

One number to rule them all
Google Voice
Free Google

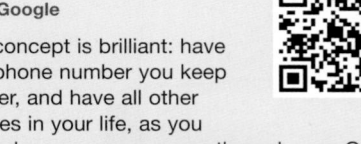

The concept is brilliant: have one phone number you keep forever, and have all other phones in your life, as you upgrade, or move on, pass through your One Number. You give only that one number out for any cell phones, landlines, or internet phones you have. When someone calls it, you direct which of your phones it rings, and how. Oh, yeah and it is free. I've had a Google Voice number since the days when it was called Grand Central (before Google bought it), and it can do so much more than just funnel your numbers. Readers list the benefits.

-- KK

Things I love:

• One number for everything. No more worrying about porting or losing numbers, or having to inform anyone of a change.

• Managing contacts and phone numbers via Gmail. Easy and intuitive.

Cheap, dependable phone tap
Mini Phone Recorder
$23 Radio Shack

For the last seven years, I've used the Mini Recorder Control to document every 'phoner' I've done as a freelance writer. Like the Recorder Control from Radio Shack, it acts as the go-between for a land line headset and any recorder with a 1/8″ mic jack. However, this one's about about half the price. Since it's light and compact, mine is always with me in a little pouch stuffed with a notebook, pens and a Griffin iTalk Pro that allows me to record direct to my iPod. Over time, I've upgraded from a desktop dictation machine to a handheld mini-cassette recorder to two different versions of the Griffin. The only item in my "bag of tricks" that hasn't become obsolete or pooped out is the Mini Recorder Control. Interestingly, I found many of my colleagues in journalism school had independently discovered this exact gadget.

-- Steven Leckart

VoIP Telephone Adapter
Obi100 VoIP Telephone Adapter
$50 Obi110 VoIP Telephone Adapter Obi

I was looking for a device that will enable me to receive telephone calls on my Google Voice number without having to forward it to another (fixed or cellular) voice line. I have found that the best solution for this is the Obi100 and Obi110 products from Obihai.

Obi110 is a VIP telephone adapter that supports dialing and receiving calls over a broadband Ethernet connection. This is a standalone voice bridge device that can be connected to a standard telephone and it does not require a PC. In addition to the broadband connection, Obi110 also supports connection to a regular phone line and it can route call types of your choice (e.g. 911 or local calls) to that line.

One of the best features of the Obi110 is that it can be configured to be used with Google Voice. You can both dial and receive calls on a telephone connected to the OBi device. It is very easy to setup and even easier to use. It does have many other interesting features and the ability to work with other VoIP services (including Obihai's own Obitalk network) but my guess is that most people in US and Canada will be using it with Google Voice.

Obi100 is the smaller version of the same product without landline support.

-- Allen

[Note: Check out this guide for more info on how to set up Google Voice with an Obi110 VoiP adapter.]

• Being able to record different greetings for different contacts, and different contact groups. All my "work" calls get an official voicemail, and my friends each have their own individualized voicemail that I can change when I want.

• Texting through Chrome and the Chrome Voice extension is awesome.

• Archiving text messages and voicemails, and having that history searchable by Google's powerful search engine means never getting rid of a message ever. I like having a record of things from years past.

• Making calls right from my desktop without ever having to pick up a phone. Also one-click calling from my Contacts list.

• Free video-chatting with multiple parties (upcoming feature when Hangouts merges with Voice).

-- Logan LaVail

• Sending and receiving text messages from Chrome. I text with my employees in the field all day long, and GV is invaluable for that.

• Voicemail transcription. It's only 80-90% accurate, but that's enough to tell if a message is urgent.

• Call screening. People I know and work with ring through, the rest have to identify themselves.

• Carrier independence. I can drop my cell phone provider tomorrow and point Google Voice to a new number or numbers at any point. No porting necessary.

• 2 numbers at once. I moved to a new area but kept my old Google Voice number. No need to worry if people haven't gotten my new number.

-- Aaron Weiss

• I haven't even bothered to memorize the numbers attached to my last several phones. At my last job I was given an iPhone, minutes after being handed the phone I was able to route calls going to the same old phone number that I had already been using for years.

• Sending text messages from the browser and managing your texts,

• Managing calls and voicemails just like email is hugely valuable.

• I actually wish that Google would start charging for this service because I would be absolutely devastated if they discontinued it.

-- Steven Hudosh

No more hold music
Lucy Phone
Free Lucy Phone

Lucy Phone is a tool that has helped me deal with one of the annoyances of modern life: waiting on hold. From LucyPhone's website you can look up the company or toll-free number you want to dial. LucyPhone acts like a conference call: it calls your phone and connects you to the company you wanted to dial.

At any point in the call when you're placed on hold, you tap ** (star star) and LucyPhone takes over. You can hang up, and LucyPhone will call you back once an operator has picked up on the other end.

From the call operator's perspective, once they take your call, they are played a brief message from LucyPhone while your number is being called. As soon as you pick up, you are connected to the operator.

The recommended help site GetHuman.com (p. 9) now integrates LucyPhone into their site so that the process is truly seamless, and you don't even have to initiate the call.

The service is free for consumers. The only drawback I've noticed is that it only works for toll-free numbers, so you still have to do things the old fashioned way with companies with local only numbers.

I find LucyPhone much less stressful and annoying than my previous technique of putting the held call on speakerphone and hoping I didn't leave the room at just the moment I came out of the hold queue.

-- Nicholas Hanna

Cellphone headset for noisy conditions
Etymotic's ETY·COM
$44 Etymotic

I work in areas that are usually quite noisy, and using cell phones is inherent to getting things done. I've previously reported on the BluLink pilot's grade Bluetooth headset – and it's terrific.

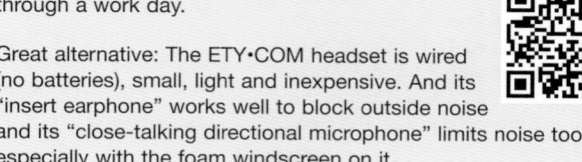

But it's also large and dang expensive. Other "noise managing" Bluetooth headsets have varying degrees of working, and none I've tried are close to satisfactory. Plus, they usually have inadequate batteries and die halfway through a work day.

Great alternative: The ETY·COM headset is wired (no batteries), small, light and inexpensive. And its "insert earphone" works well to block outside noise and its "close-talking directional microphone" limits noise too, especially with the foam windscreen on it.

I carry both the BluLink giant and the ETY·COM mini. They both work as intended (the big one's the ultimate winner in audio quality), but the Etymotic model keeps almost $400 in your pocket – along with the headset – and gets things done almost as well.

It's a good way to keep your sanity when using your cell in a noisy place.

-- Wayne Ruffner

Problems are the answers to solutions. - Brian Arthur

Busts external noise, not your wallet
Etymotic MC5 Noise Reduction Earphones
$60 etymotic.com

I've used Etymotic's product for years and they offer great audio quality (it's astonishing to hear the clear noise of a pick hitting guitar strings, or a singer quietly breathing during an instrumental), but what's most impressive is just how phenomenal their noise isolation performance is, particularly with blocking low-level noise in airplanes. 34-36 dB, depending on which ear tip you use. They come with foam tips like the UM In-Ear Monitors or rubbery flange tips which are quieter, but may not fit everyone as well. These headphones do better than any of the expensive, battery dependent ANC headsets I've come across, including the top shelf ones I used when I was a private pilot. And they come close to silencing the droning hum of a passenger airliner. The noise isolation is so very good I'd be nervous to wear these while jogging — you wouldn't hear someone shout a warning at you.

Etymotic has a lot of data about the frequency response range and noise isolation characteristics of their headphones on their website (I'm a neuro-scientist, so lots of data makes me feel comfortable). Westone (makers of the UMs) doesn't provide as much detailed information, but from what I gather the UMs, which are a bit more expensive, don't have quite as deep base response — they go down to 40 Hz while Etymotic's go to 20 Hz.

I've tried loads of less expensive headsets and a few higher end ones like the Bose X ANC headset and some models from Shure. In my hands the ER-6 vastly, vastly outperforms any low-end stuff — so much so that it blows my mind that people listen to their iPods with the standard earphones. On the high end, the Bose works well with ANC but terribly when the batteries die — and its sound reproduction isn't as convincing as the ER-6. The more expensive Shure models are pretty much the same as the Etymotics (I think the Shure E3c is the most direct match up in the product line). There may be some technical advantages one way or the other, but I really couldn't hear the difference. Both companies offer a high-end model, which is substantially more expensive — in those cases I could hear a very small advantage over the cheaper products, but certainly not enough to justify the huge price difference.

– *Ashish Ranpura*

These tiny in-ear units sound fantastic, feel comfortable, and do an excellent job of blocking out ambient sounds. I like to listen to music when I work. Even with nice headphones, my music was frequently swamped by the house music. The best, relatively inexpensive solution I've found has been a pair of Etymotic ER6i's.

I generally keep the sound level far from loud, but there are times when I'm listening to very quiet passages outdoors, and the ability to crank up the volume at those moments lets me catch nuances that would otherwise get lost amidst birds, kids, and so on. Some spoken-word podcasts seem to reliably dip into barely-audible once or twice per podcast, so I also ride the gain at those times.

The earbuds come with four different types of removable isolators (three are variations on plastic flanges, the other is a nub of high-density foam), so you can find the type that is most comfortable and effective for you. I resisted earbuds for years because they usually make my ears hurt after only a few minutes, but I can wear the ER6i buds comfortably for a couple of hours at a stretch before wanting a break.

It's important to note that the very qualities that make these earbuds so attractive in a coffee shop can be dangerous if you're outside: you may very well not hear a car horn, a shout from an approaching bicyclist, or a piano dropping on your head from high above. These earbuds would be a poor choice for jogging or even walking in the park, but in a safe, stable environment they're terrific.

– *Andrew G.*

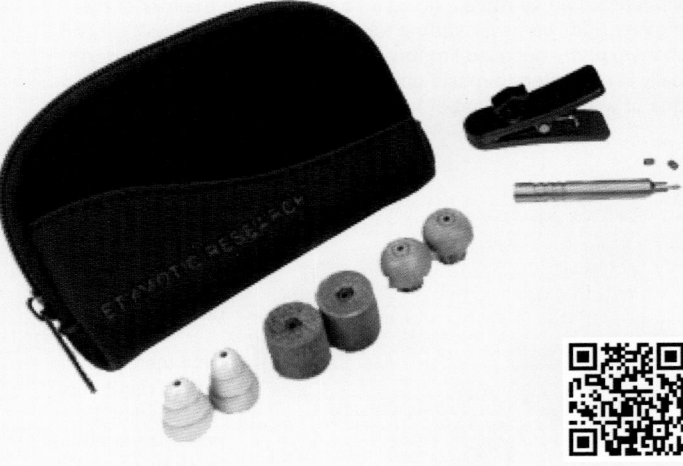

An oasis from noise
Bose Acoustic Noise Canceling Headset
$390 Amazon

This gear has managed to turn my many long-distance airplane trips into peaceful journeys. It turns out a lot of the fatigue of long flights is the constant drum of the airplane's engines. With this magical headset on, that noise completely vanishes. Gone! In its place you can listen to music (whatever source) or just pure faint silence. For sleeping on planes, there is no better technology, including chemicals. Because of the smart design of the generous ear cups there is no ear cringe from wearing these for hours on end. In fact, they are far more comfortable than the flimsy lightweight Walkman-style earsets. Even though these weigh more, they feel better. I put them on when I board a plane and I sleep with them on, too. Tuned low to some innocuous music channel, they coo sweetly. (It's a shock to take the phones off because you can then hear how incredibly loud the plane's rumble really is.) This works so well for flights that Bose makes a special aviation set just for pilots, and a

military issue helmet for soldiers working in high-decibel environments like a helicopter. All this comfort comes to you via some very clever chips that cancel out noise signals.

Noise-canceling gear is no longer the monopoly of Bose; other brands like Sony, Panasonic, and others offer noise-canceling headsets for much lower prices. I have a couple of them for backup. But in my own tests, the noise-cancelation of the Bose is superior. I wear these ear-phones so long (10 hours at a stretch) and so often that their superior function has been worth their double price for me. I haven't yet tried these in a shop environment, or while mowing the grass, but I've been told they are best at removing droning-like sounds, rather than punctuated sounds.

Noise-cancellation is really one of those things you have to hear to believe. Bose has a thirty-day free trial period. Take them up on their offer next time you have a fourteen-hour flight and see if it works for you.

-- *KK*

Noise reduction headset
Pilot's BlueTooth Noise Control Headset
$375 PA-2170BLU Bluetooth Headset Pilot

I work in a lot of data centers where the noise can be almost intolerable. My increasing tinnitus is probably a symptom of being in those places so much, and troubleshooting via cell phone is almost impossible, definitely supremely frustrating, with almost every headset I've tried, wired or BT.

So I found a headset with full Bluetooth profiles. It's the Millennium Series with inline BluLink Adapter from Pilot-USA. It has a microphone and earphones.

This thing is far from cheap and, of course, makes me look like a complete doof. But it plays music from my cell with terrific clarity and also lets me converse as if we're in a private library. The BT implementation is excellent and gives the full features their due.

As expensive as this is, it's about half the price of the Lightspeed Zulu or Bose A20 headsets. If you need this level of clarity, it's a deal.

This headset provides by far the best phone experience I've had yet in seriously noisy environments.

-- *Wayne Ruffner*

Tips

When you are traveling and forget your adapter, check with the hotel's front desk or lost and found. They will usually have dozens of adapters of every sort left behind by others.

-- *Joshua Schachter*

I have a typical "fishbowl" manager's office. Unfortunately, the furniture layout precludes the use of a whiteboard in my office. Instead, I use standard dry-erase markers to write on my office window. I get lots of strange looks from folks walking by, but many have commented on the practicality of the idea. Straight windex and paper towels to clean.   -- *Gregory Winer*

When a couple of the little rubber feet (LRF) came off the bottom of my laptop, I tried without success to re-attach the small bits of rubber with "super glue", rubber cement, and a hot-glue gun. After the last attempt, I realized that the rubbery material used with the hot-glue gun could by itself serve as an LRF replacement. This worked so well I ended up ripping out the still-attached LRFs. By now the hot-glue replacements have served longer than the original LRFs.

-- *Preston L. Bannister*

Wintergreen oil (methyl salicylate) is the most penetrating of all penetrating oils. It is available at most drugstores at minimal cost. If you work on old machinery that is anywhere near salt-water (or salted highways) it's an essential weapon in tackling otherwise hopelessly rusted/frozen threads. It smells good, and though toxic and not to be kept within reach of children, is intended for topical application to human skin.

-- *George Dyson*

No matter how well you think you know your local city, buy a good current travel guide to it. You'll inevitably learn something you didn't know, and you'll have a great tool for any visitor; the guide will do a better job than you will in orienting them. It will tell them (and you) about all kinds of basic stuff locals never remember to mention.   -- *Kevin Kelly*

Most people say there's nothing worth dying for. But what you do every day is what you're dying for. - The Last Dancer

329

Ear Buds

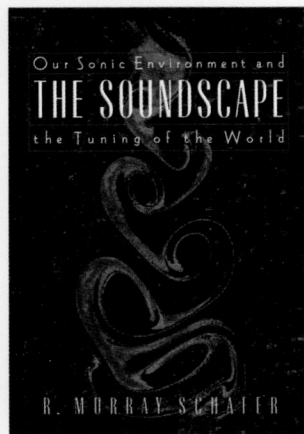

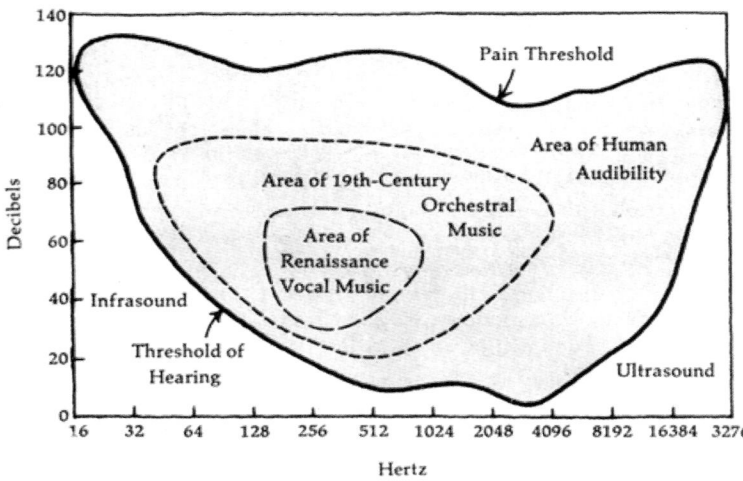

Hearing the world
The Soundscape

$12 R. Murray Schafer, 1993, 320 p.

The sound of modern life has a 60 hertz hum in the background because that's the frequency of electricity (in North America). Add to that all the other vibrations of technological artifacts and all the sounds made by nature and you get the soundscape of the world. I learned to hear this sonic environment from this master observer. He gave me ears. Once heard these vibrations can be tuned, altered, muffled, amplified.

-- KK

● **The Flat Line in Sound**

The Industrial Revolution introduced another effect into the soundscape: the flat line.

A few years ago, while listening to the stonemasons' hammers on the Takht-e-Jamshid in Teheran, I suddenly realized that in all earlier societies the majority of sounds were discrete and interrupted, while today a large portion--perhaps the majority--are continuous. This new sound phenomenon, introduced by the Industrial Revolution and greatly extended by the Electric Revolution, today subjects us to permanent keynotes

and swaths of broad-band noise, possessing little personality or sense of progression.

● The best way to comprehend what I mean by acoustic design is to regard the soundscape of the world as a huge musical composition, unfolding around us ceaselessly. We are simultaneously its audience, its performers and its composers. Which sounds do we want to preserve, encourage, multiply?

● Another continuous rhythm is that of breathing, which also varies in tempo with exercise and relaxation. Normal breathing is said to vary between 12 and 20 cycles per minute, that is, 3 to 5 seconds per cycle. But breathing may be slowed down during relaxation or sleep to cycles lasting 6 to 8 seconds. Part of the sense of well-being we feel at the seashore undoubtedly has to do with the fact that the relaxed breathing pattern shows surprising correspondence with the rhythms of the breakers, which, while never regular, often produce an average cycle of 8 seconds.

● Another biological tempo which relates significantly to the acoustic environment is that of the resolving power of the sense

receptors. In humans this hovers around 16 to 20 cycles per second. It is in this frequency range that a series of discrete images or sounds will fuse together to give an impression of continuous flow. Film employs 24 frames per second in order to avoid flicker. As far as aural perception is concerned, a rapid rhythmic vibration will gradually assume an identifiable pitch at about 20 cycles per second. Thus, as the tempo of human activities increases, the rhythms of foot and hand are mechanized, first into the rough, "grainy" concatenation of the Industrial Revolution's first tools, and finally into the smooth pitch contours of modern electronics. The resolving power of the senses makes it possible to turn some of the nervous agitation of the soundscape into drones which, being less turbulent to the ears, tend to have a pacifying quality.

In Turkish cars, horns are tuned to the interval of a major or minor second. While in some cultures this is considered an exceedingly dissonant diad, there are examples in the Balkans, for instance from certain regions of western Bulgaria, of folk singing in which two voices sing together in major or minor seconds, the singers considering this a consonant interval.

Noise blockers for kids
Peltor Kid Earmuffs

$14 envirosafetyproducts.com peltorkid.co.uk

My 14 month-old daughter has been wearing these noise-reducing headphones for 9 months, give or take, ever since a friend in Norway sent us a pair (they're made in England). As a touring musician and the owner of a record label, I go to a lot of shows. Now not only can we hang out together, but my daughter's even performed with me. She loves the earmuffs, or seems to. She hates hats, but whenever we put these on -- even at home where it's quiet -- she doesn't want to take them off. They seem comfortable (they fit kids up to 7 years old). I also trust my kid's ears are safe because she freaks out over noises and things normally, but doesn't at all when she's at a show wearing these.

Plus, in my travels, I've a seen a lot of kids wearing these exact earmuffs.

-- Syd Butler

Best inexpensive noise blockers
Max Earplugs

I travel constantly and have, over time, become a big fan of earplugs on flights, especially long distance flights. I can feel the difference; I arrive more relaxed if I can block out the roar of the engines. But I've never sprung for the Bose noise-cancelling headphones, partly because I'm too cheap and partly because I don't really like to listen to music on planes. I just want quiet, and the idea of wearing a big set of headphones doesn't appeal to me.

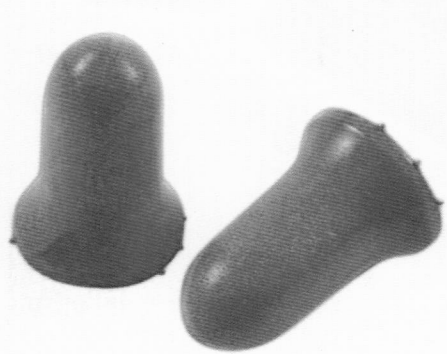

What I'm waiting for is noise cancelling earplugs, like white noise generating hearing aids — that's a winner in my book.

Until then, I've settled on cheap, high-quality disposable earplugs by Howard Leight. I use their "MAX" model, with an NRR rating of 33, the highest I've been able to find; the higher the NRR rating, the more sound they block. I've tried every kind of earplug, from balls of silicon to wax and cotton and these work best for me.

I buy my earplugs from Ear Plug Superstore. It's amazing to me to learn that there is an "Earplug Superstore" in this world, but there you go.

-- Edward J. Murphy

$5 for 20 pairs
Amazon

$26 for 200 pairs
Amazon

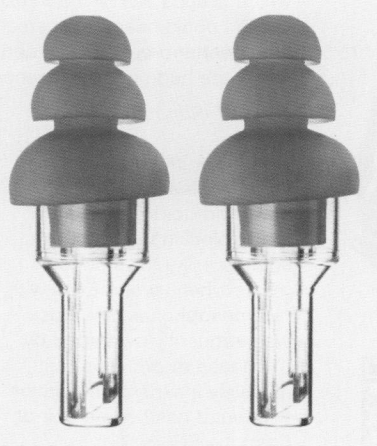

Music lovers' plugs
Etymotic Research Earplugs

$8 Amazon

Earplugs are a necessity for me: I value my ears, but I also play in loud bands and go to loud shows. Standard foamie earplugs are cheap and get the job done, but they eat high-end frequencies, so everything sounds like you're underwater.

These earplugs have a much flatter frequency response, and wearing them makes everything sound more natural. At $12 a pair, they're still affordable, and they come in a keychain carrying case, so you'll always have them with you. I've used these for many years.

Etymotic also makes "musician's earplugs" — baffles that fit into custom-molded plugs, fitted and sold by audiologists. I've owned these, too, and I like the $12 ones as much or more: though the custom-fit type allow even more high-frequency sound through, the ER-20 sounds quite good, and it's a lot less traumatic if (really when) I lose a pair.

-- Scott Evans

Workout earbud adapters
Yurbuds

Yurbuds are my solution for exercising with headphones. They fit over top of existing headphones, though most of the options that you can purchase from the website come with a pair of in-ear earbuds. They twist in and have never fallen out on me. I just upgraded to the ironman version recently and have never fiddled with them once I start running. I run half marathons and did a full marathon earlier in the year, in the rain, and had no issues with my music the whole time training and running the race.

If you run regularly in races, they are often at many of the expo shows that happen before the race and will be willing to let you try a pair on. They have sizes in the blue/pink versions, but the ironman have a softer gel that fits with any size ear.

-- Allen Reinmeyer

$46 Yurbud Ironman Headphones and Adapters Amazon

$18+ Yurbud Adapters, several sizes Amazon

The real voyage of discovery consists not in seeking new landscapes but in having new eyes. - Marcel Proust

Rough Guide
World Music

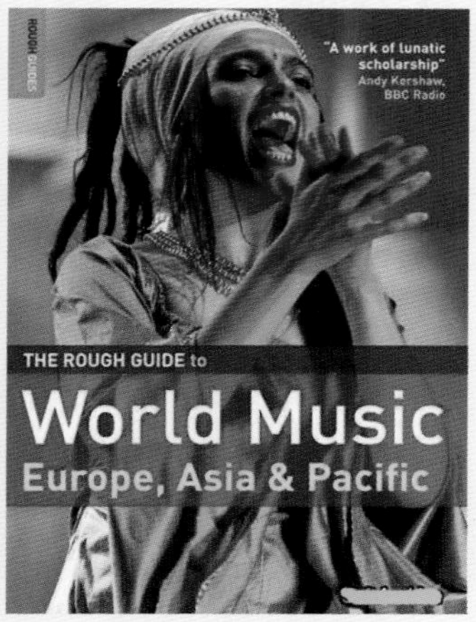

Travel with your ears. This comprehensive, massive (700-plus pages), and recently updated two-volume guide to global song covers the planet, from Norwegian fiddlers to Filipino folk rockers. It's all here: what kind of music is out there, where it came from, who is playing it, and where to get it. Feeling stuck? Open up this book at random, order a CD, and enter another way of seeing.
-- *KK*

•
Indonesian Pop
Moluccan Moods Orchestra

(Piranha, Germany). If you haven't heard of the Moluccans since they held up Dutch trains in the 1970s, give this disc a listen. Traditional songs arranged in laid-back style with exciting percussion, keyboards, saxophone and flute.

•
Zambian Pop
From the Copperbelt…Zambian Miner's Songs

(Original Music, US). In the "African Acoustic" series, eighteen interesting-to-beautiful songs by the mine camp entertainers of the copper-belt that straddles Zambia and southeastern Zaire, field-recorded by ethno-musicologist Hugh Tracey in 1957.

•
Albanian
Famille Lela De Permet
Polyphonies vocales et instrumentales d'Albanie

(Indigo/Harmonia Mundi, France). Beautiful and approachable songs and instrumental music from the Permet and Korce regions of southern Albania. Wailing and sliding clarinets give this music an enchanting mournful sound.

$22 Rough Guide World Music: Europe, Asia and Pacific, 2009 (3rd edition), 784 p.

$18 Vol. 2: Latin and North America, the Caribbean, Asia & the Pacific, 2000 (2nd edition), 673 p.

Roots — music from the road less traveled

Other music
CD Roots
CD Roots

Fill your iPod with something different. I don't mean more indie rock or the latest in hip-hop or electronica. I mean Norwegian jazz, Zaire club house, slide guitar from India, Russian underground, Ethiopian acid pop.

An awful lot of great world music can be easily had from the usual sources, including Amazon and iTunes, but most of the rest of the world's local music has very small audiences and must still be "imported." This source specializes in esoteric import CDs of traditional and contemporary world music not found on Amazon, iTunes and the like. This is the far end of the "long tail" music scene.
-- *KK*

•
Marimba Magia - Papa Roncon and Grupo Katanga - $19 From the town of Borbon, in the Esmeraldas district of northern Ecuador, Papa Roncon is a living legend. He plays the marimba and the guitar; he is a singer and a dancer. He makes musical instruments. He lives the folk music of the region. Joined by Catalina Mina Quintero on bombo and kununu, Grupo Katanga makes music that is essential, rough and irresistible.

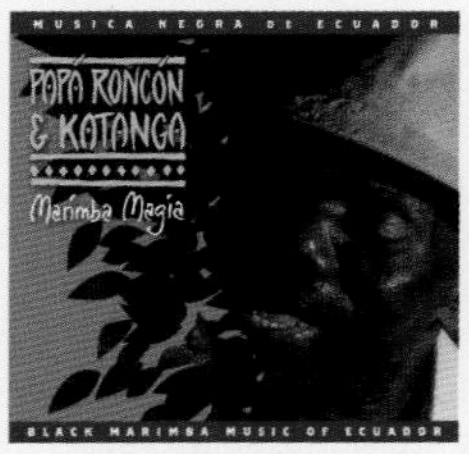

•
Mirrors of My Soul - Rim Banna - $19 The Palestinian singer who gained global recognition as part of the Lullabies from the Axis of Evil project returns with a Norwegian band with a decidedly 'pop' recording of Palestinian songs. It veers from emotionally charged, sparsely arranged to full-tilt pop-rock, and has the huge advantage of not allowing a drum machine within 4000 miles of the studio. As Arab pop goes, this is thoroughly unique.

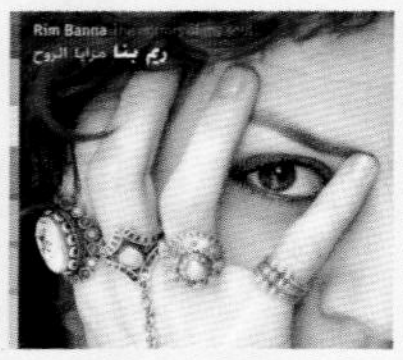

•
Discopolis (Radio Three) - Various Spanish Artists - $18 An interesting and personal collection of what is going on in the ever so vaguely defined roots music scene in Spain, put together by Spanish Radio 3's DJ Jose Miguel Lopez. The

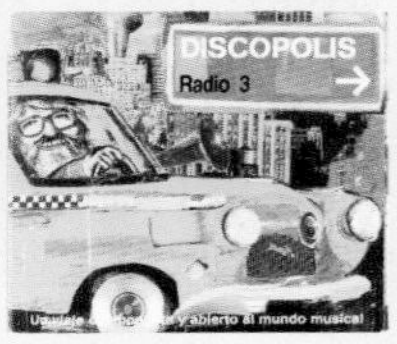

Whole house music system
Sonos
$900 Sonos BU150 Multiroom Music System
Amazon

Music playing simultaneously in every room of your house is a luxurious experience, and decidedly different from a song playing in a single room. Music in a room is a dim, blurry sonic echo if you're not in front of the speakers. But music everywhere is an environment that envelopes you as you go about your day. Of course to get this experience, you could run speaker wire to a second room and connect up a second set of speakers, but that's not the same enveloping sonic goodness of a whole house system.

Used to be whole-house music systems were only for the very rich. You needed a rack of amplifiers (two channels for every room), a pre-amp, switcher, control unit, and then in-room controllers either hand-held or built into the walls, plus cabling from the speakers in each room homerunned back to the equipment, which probably needed its own closet because there was so much of it, it was so loud, and so hot. Crestron, Niles and others have made good money catering to this rarefied market. But the systems are pretty bespoke (there is no standard OS, the equipment is not interchangeable, you need an installer to set them up, you had to destroy walls to run cables, etc.), they were inherently less reliable than mass produced equipment, and they were, as I said, so expensive (as in $20-50K and up for equipment alone, plus design and installer time in addition) that only the wealthy could afford them. Oh, and none of them can connect to the consumer music server standard that we all use and love — iTunes. That's right, they all use proprietary or non-Apple servers.

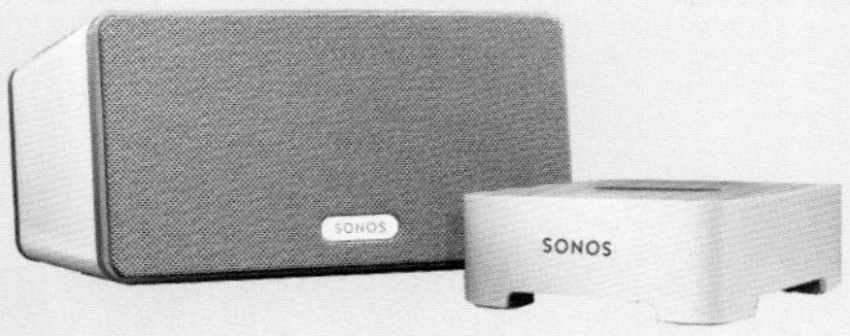

That was then. But now if you want a whole house music system, you have a much lower cost, more reliable, and more functional alternative: Sonos. It isn't cheap, but it's a lot cheaper than the previous bespoke solutions. It's dead easy to install — literally anyone can do it. It connects seamlessly to the iTunes music library, as well as giving you access to internet radio stations. And it's just completely thought out. Sonos is one of the two best consumer electronic products ever created, the other being the Garmin Nuvi.

Sonos comes in two flavors: with and without amplifiers. Either can connect via ethernet or wirelessly to your computer with its iTunes library (you can also use other libraries if you want). The Sonos unamplified units — smaller than an Apple Mini — mate with amplifiers (or receivers) you probably already have that are connected to speakers. The Sonos amplified units (think the size of a big old family bible) drive speakers where you don't already have amps. Both type of units talk to each other via a mesh network. You can lash up to 32 of the beasts together if you're so inclined. The sound across the entire network is in perfect sync. And the fidelity is exemplary — I rip all my music to Appleloss, and every room is playing music as if the CD is present, not ripped to a server at the other end of the house.

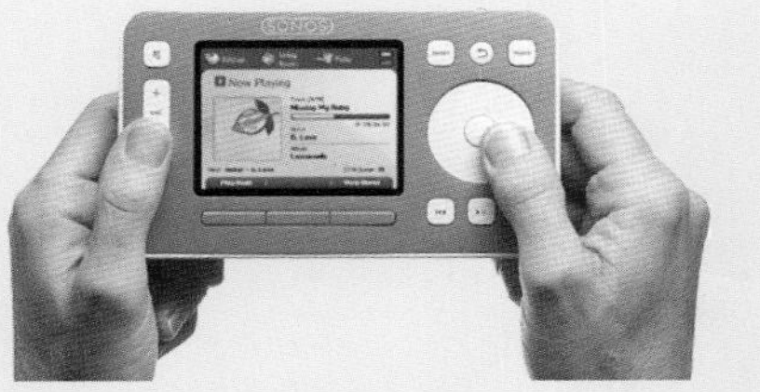

How easy is it to set up? You can install the software and set up half-a-dozen of these units in an hour. Once installed, the systems are rock solid. And if you ever have problems, online and telephone support is conscientious, even exemplary. You get the feeling they really want you to have your system working right, and for you to be happy.

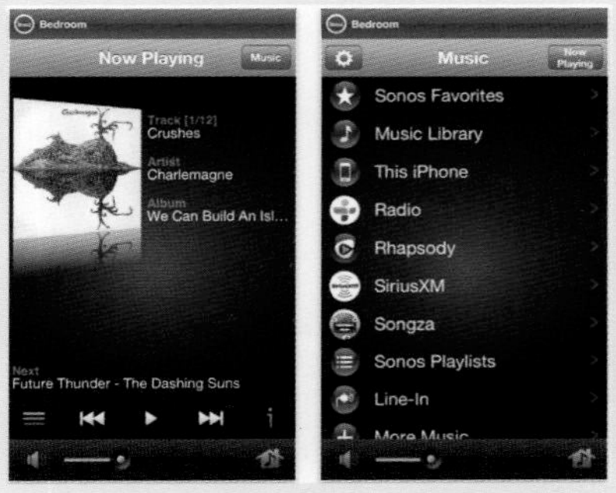

You can control the whole system from your computer, selecting music and playing it in one, all, or a combination of rooms, at different volumes for each room. For instance, you can play different music in each room; or you can play music from your iTunes library in one room, or an internet radio station in another, etc. A better way to control the Sonos system is with the Sonos wireless handheld controller, which has a scroll wheel like the iPod and a color LCD screen which provides all the functionality of the Sonos computer software. You don't need one per room — per floor is more like it.

Sonos is a lot cheaper than the old bespoke whole house system.

Sonos: Not cheap, but an entirely more affordable luxury than whole house music systems used to be.

-- *Louis Rossetto*

All music any time
Streaming Music Services

All music, much of it free, when you want it. This is a fast changing field, soon to change even faster. As of 2013 here are the major players.

Pandora

Pandora acts entirely like a radio station, based off of the music genome database. It claims to find other music similar to music that you like. The more you interact with it (giving specific tracks thumbs-up or thumbs-down), the smarter it gets.

On the upside, Pandora is great if you just want to listen to music. On the downside, if you want to listen to anything specific you're out of luck.

PANDORA

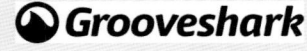

Grooveshark

Grooveshark allows you to build a library of music you like. You can upload your own music, or search for music and add it to your own collection. You can then build playlists from music in your collection. It also has a radio functionality, though it doesn't do a great job of finding songs that match my tastes.

It's great if you want to listen to something specific (and even has a lot of lesser-known stuff), and also allows you to create genre-based playlists ("play me a list of songs in the Hard Rock genre"). It's not so great if you want something for your mobile, since the mobile app requires a subscription fee.

Grooveshark

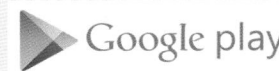

Spotify

Spotify is similar to Grooveshark in most ways. It's an ad-supported streaming service with a paid subscription model for access to the mobile app. The difference between Spotify and Grooveshark is that Grooveshark is a web service that runs in your browser, and Spotify requires you to download a program (sort of like iTunes) and run it on your computer. Since I run Linux and Spotify doesn't support Linux (you can run it under wine or try the beta if you really want to) then I don't use Spotify. You can also pay $10/month and use the app on your devices.

Spotify

Amazon Cloud Player, Google Music, etc.

These streaming services all require you to bring your own music. Amazon Cloud Player lets you store and listen to anything you've bought from Amazon for free, and upload your own music too. Google Music is similar.

amazon cloud player

Google play

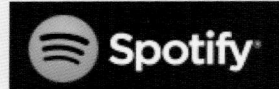

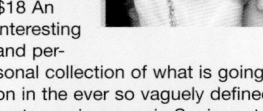

Subsonic

Subsonic allows you to install software on your computer which then streams your existing MP3 collection. This is superior to Amazon Cloud Player, et. al. because you have access to your entire MP3 collection without uploading it somewhere (and paying a monthly fee if your collection is at all large).

Subsonic | Easy Listening

-- *Elite Badger*

We have only one thing to trade. Ourselves. All else is just details. - Miller

331

Simple Instruments

Maximum acoustic guitar for the money
Martin OM-15 Guitar

$500+, Martin and

You can spend a lot of money on an acoustic guitar these days and end up with an instrument that doesn't improve with age, either tonally or aesthetically. With CNC machines and other robotic aids, assembling a decent instrument is no longer the exclusive province of the master luthier. Now that any idiot can do it, any idiot does, and the results vary wildly. I don't know how any beginner is expected to choose wisely from such a tawdry lot and end up with something worth passing on to their kids.

I've owned and played professionally close to a hundred fine instruments in the 35 years I've been playing and I've ended up being something of an accidental Martin collector. When people ask me what they should buy for their first guitar, I tell them to go straight to their nearest authorized Martin dealer and get a OO-15 or an OM-15. (The OM-15 is no longer in the Martin catalog as of 2003 but is still available used; I just saw one on eBay for $495). These all-mahogany instruments are an absolute steal in today's wacky

market. They are spartan versions of Martin's multi-thousand dollar OO and OM models, offering the same playability but without the Nashville flash. Simple, honest, great-sounding, great-looking guitars that can take a beating and will last a lifetime — all for a less than a grand. I bought my OO-15 new for $700 with a Martin hard case, and my beloved OM-15 slightly used for $550 with the same case. The OM-15 is slightly larger, with a wider fretboard suitable for fingerpicking styles and/or larger hands. Both instruments have a characteristic "airy" sound from the mahogany top, making them particularly well-suited for recording. They don't boom, nor do they crackle; they hum with a satisfying balance, strummed or finger-picked. The satin-finished mahogany is lower maintenance than the softer spruce tops, and minor dings disappear in the dark chocolate-colored grain patterns. By the way, the "O" in both names refers to Orchestra, not the number zero, so say "oh-M".

You can't get more guitar for the money anywhere.

-- David MacNeill

Cool cheap instrument
The Fluke Ukulele

$238 The Fluke Flea Market Music
$218 The Flea Flea Market Music
$25 Jumpin' Jim's Gone Hawaiian Flea Market Music

There used to be two kinds of ukuleles: pressed cardboard junk for less than $50, and professional quality beauties for over $500. Now there is a third option – the Fluke, a half-plastic, half-wood ukulele that costs half that. As soon as my fingers hit the cute-as-a-bug instrument, I fell in love with it. It's a pleasure to play and the sound is strong and chipper. Its radical design reminds me of the iMac or New Beetle. One fellow uker told me his Fluke sounds and plays better than his $3000 vintage Martin ukulele. He was almost mad about it. Jim Beloff, co-creator of the Fluke also publishes a bunch of excellent ukulele songbooks. My favorite is Jumpin' Jim's Gone Hawaiian.

-- Mark Frauenfelder

Willow flute
Salgflojt

$21 Spela Salgflojt, by Jean-Pierre Yvert Fredman's Music

$85 Salgflojt and Seljefloyte Naturinstrumenter

Free Everything (almost) You Wanted to Know About a Willow Flute, But Were AFRAID to Ask by Sarah Kirto Northern California Spelmanslag Newsletter, Fall 2

Apart from a drum, it's hard to imagine a simpler musical instrument than the willow flute: it's a straight tube with a mouthpiece at one end and no toneholes. But far from being a limited toy, the willow flutes developed in Scandinavia are capable of playing complex melodies over a multi-octave range. It's all done through harmonics, breath control, and the judicious use of the index finger to cover the end hole.

I grew up in the U.S. trying to make simple one-note willow whistles, cut from pussy willow branches in early spring, and I read books that described how to make a more elaborate slide willow whistle that works like a trombone. The salgflojt is nothing like either of these, and when I first heard one in the hands of a virtuoso player I was awestruck that such complex music could be made from a simple tube.

If you blow as softly as possible into the mouthpiece of a salgflojt, you produce a tone. Blow a little harder and you get a note that's approximately a fifth above the first one; blow harder still and you'll get a note that's an octave above the first, and so on. If you close the end-hole with your index finger, you'll get a new scale whose notes fall in between those produced by the flute when the end of the tube is left open.

The scale produced by these overtones is not like the standard Western tempered

scale; it's a natural harmonic scale and will sound "Eastern" and exotic to American ears. Because you have two scales available, you can play intricate melodies through breath control and by using the index finger to cover the end hole for certain notes.

True willow flutes are temporary instruments, drying out and cracking after a few days or weeks of use, so modern versions are generally made of plastic, often with wooden mouthpieces. It's easy to make one yourself, although all the instructions I've been able to find online are for the smaller one-note version. A number of retailers (mostly in Scandinavia) sell them. Fredman's Music, in Sweden, also sells the best instruction book available on the salgflojt, *Spela Salgflojt*, by Jean-Pierre Yvert. Written in English and Swedish, this book explains the scales, introduces you to the blowing and fingering technique, provides music and tablature for a number of melodies, and includes a CD of the exercises and tunes. Yvert also makes flutes and is an excellent player.

I've been playing traditional Irish music on the wooden flute for about 25 years, but have long been a fan of traditional Swedish music. The process of learning the salgflojt is very different from that of a standard flute — it's easier in one sense because you simply blow right into the mouth-hole to produce a sound, but it's harder in the sense that you have to develop very precise breath control to get the notes you want. You can teach yourself the basics by spending time with the instrument and experimenting with what happens when you blow harder and softer, covering the end hole or leaving it open.

-- Brad Hurley

Old world twanging
Mouth Harp

$9 Lehman's

Nothing compliments a campfire like a harmonica, but if you're looking for a new and challenging pocket noisemaker, I highly recommend the jaw harp. Much like a didgeridoo, you can create trance-inducing vibrations that will annoy some and mesmerize others. On its own, your mouth can learn to make some pretty great sounds, but it's remarkable what can be accomplished with this little doohickey. Just the slightest change in breath and flickering of the tongue shapes the sound dramatically.

The history is part of the appeal. I purchased mine in rural Tennessee, but the harp's roots are deeper than American folk. Some say

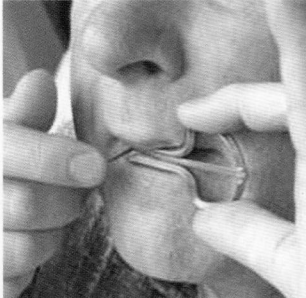

the instrument was born in Asia and migrated to Europe around the 13th century. Archaic versions of these twangers have been found everywhere from England to the Philippines and Siberia (there are several names, including the "mouth" or "jew" harp, which seemingly bears no connection to Judaism). Pluck and listen, and time travel while plucking some more. When you get lightheaded — and you will — do take a breather.

-- Steven Leckart

I too was struck by the mesmerising sound of the jaw harp when I heard Mike Seeger play one. I searched around and finally decided on the Whitlow. At $25, this is a really good buy. It is hand made in America by one guy who learned to make it from the Whitlow guy who originally made them. I also purchased the harp mentioned above, because it is so cheap. But the Whitlow is just so superior I couldn't stand the tinny vibrations and lack of resonance of the cheap one. The Whitlow plays like butter the first time you play it. It resonates for a long time and is really loud. Get the lowest key you can find. I have a low D. You can make some really haunting, low frequency sounds by breathing in and out while twanging.

-- Larry Albertelli

Large homemade wind chimes
Wind Chimes: Design and Construction

$15 Bart Hopkin, 2005, 68 p.

Make your own. Not those tinny flea market varieties, but large striking sonorous chimes tuned in all manner of unusual styles. (Listen to samples on the book's website or included CD). There are several dozen unusual ways to tune the chimes. All tunings are fairly mathematical, which is the core of this book, but not difficult to execute with hardware-store tubing. My son and I used this short but very explicit manual to create a large copper pipe one that emits a lovely melody in the breeze. The bigger the better. (The bigger the more wind they need, too.) This guide is a very practical way to experience the math of music and the beauty of alternative music systems.

-- KK

Setting up the hanging strings at the correct spacing.

Our copper chime hanging in the cherry tree.

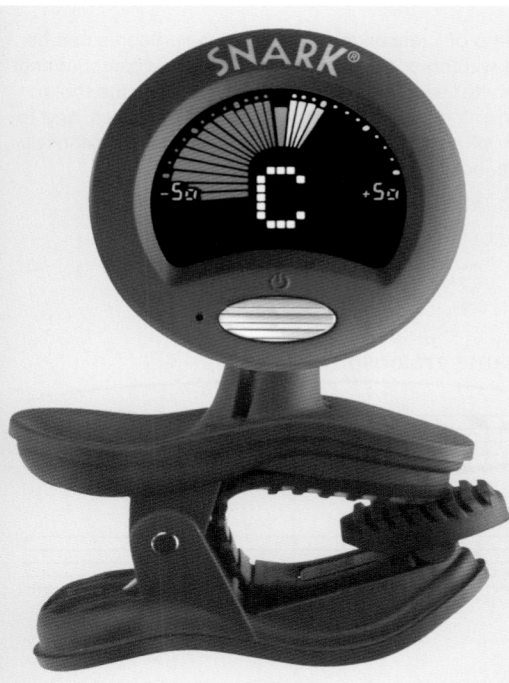

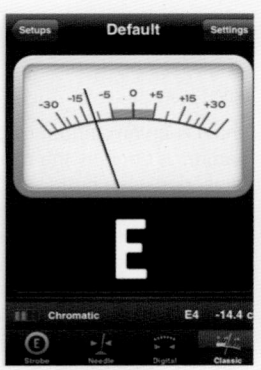

Tune up with an iPhone
Planet Waves Tune Up
$1 iTunes Store

I've been using this tuner on my iPhone for about a year now. It's a great, accurate and very cheap guitar tuner. I've tried other tuner apps, but they were not as accurate as this one. The free Gibson Learn & Master-app, which includes a chromatic tuner, is not usable because it is far from being accurate. I also tried another free app called Acoustic Guitar which again doesn't work because you have to rely on your ears to tune your guitar.

I've compared Tune Up to my standalone Boss TU12 guitar tuner. The iPhone's built-in microphone is much more sensitive than the TU12's built-in mic, so it much easier to tune up an unplugged electric guitar with the TuneUp app.

The biggest disadvantage of the TuneUp-app is that for unplugged electric guitars it is quite unusable in noisy environments as it will pickup too many surround sounds. This is one of the main reasons why I'm not selling my TU12 as I rely on the ability to plug in the electric guitar directly into the tuner. Also, for adjusting the bridge-saddles I still rely on the TU12, with the guitar directly plugged in the TU12. But that's because I still have not adjusted a guitars bridge setup using the iPhone-app. Maybe I will in the near future...

-- Douwe Rijpstra

Best Clip-On Instrument Tuner
Snark SN-2
$11 Red model, $21 Black model Amazon

I've tried several clip-on guitar and banjo tuners over the years, and I finally found the best one: Snark SN-2. It's fast, easy to use, and very accurate. Best of all, it's cheap: $13. It's optimized for all instruments. If you only need it for guitar, get the $10 Snark SN-1.

The build quality seems better than the previously reviewed Intellitouch, and the display is much nicer (glasses not required). And it's really fast and responsive. Plus, it has a "tap tempo" thing so you can tap the button along with the tune and it will tell you the beats per minute.

-- John Walkenbach

Best guitar capo
G7th Capo
$36 Amazon

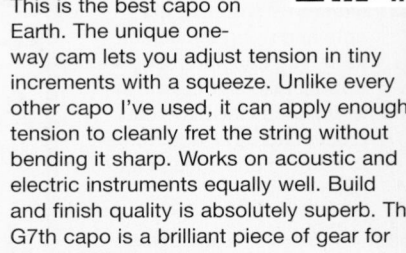

This is the best capo on Earth. The unique one-way cam lets you adjust tension in tiny increments with a squeeze. Unlike every other capo I've used, it can apply enough tension to cleanly fret the string without bending it sharp. Works on acoustic and electric instruments equally well. Build and finish quality is absolutely superb. The G7th capo is a brilliant piece of gear for the discerning guitarist.

-- David MacNeill

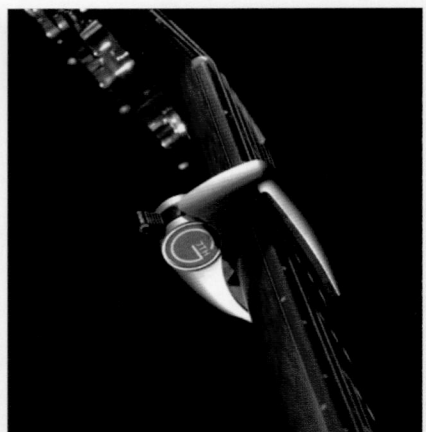

Play a wind instrument only you can hear
Electronic Wind Instrument
$300 Akai EWI USB Electronic Wind Instrument Amazon

As an amateur musician living in a small house, I can't always pick up my saxophone or flute when I have the urge to make music. Nighttime is off limits, and even during the day I can't always find a time when I won't be disturbing the rest of the household. We have a digital piano that I can use with headphones or a computer, but as a wind player I find the keyboard too limiting.

About three years ago, I solved this problem by buying an Akai EWI USB electronic wind instrument. It lets me play quietly, or even silently, while providing more ways to make music than would be practical with real instruments. You hold it like a clarinet or saxophone, touching key pads placed in a similar arrangement to the keys of a real instrument, and blow into a mouthpiece that senses the pressure of your breath. It produces no sound of its own. Instead, you plug it into a computer and choose from dozens of wind, brass, and string instruments to mimic. Add a pair of headphones, and you have a self-contained music studio you can use any time of day or night. You can practice tunes and scales, play along with recordings, and even create your own compositions and arrangements using multiple instruments.

The instrument selection provided by the Akai software includes a full range of woodwinds, brass, and orchestral strings, along with some pitched percussion (like xylophone and glockenspiel) and an assortment of unique synthesizer sounds. The selection includes all the sizes of saxophones, clarinets, brass, double reeds, flutes, and viols. Part of the fun of the EWI is getting to play instruments that you've never touched in real life. For instance, I spend a lot of time using the violin sound, and noodling around on bass clarinet or tuba is a blast. The instrument sounds are quite good. The ability to control the volume with your breath adds a natural expressiveness that makes up for the synthetic timbre of some of the instruments. A casual listener might not realize she is hearing an electronic instrument, particularly the clarinets and violin/cello/bass voices.

The EWI's controls strike a balance between simplicity and realism. Unlike a real instrument, it's "keys" don't move. Instead, they are raised metal pads that sense when you are touching them. The layout of the keys closely matches that of a saxophone, though you can configure it to use fingerings that are more similar to a flute, oboe, or even a trumpet. You control the octave using a set of four rollers under your left thumb that give the EWI a five-octave range. Another pair of sensors allows you to bend notes up or down with your left thumb. The mouthpiece, in addition to sensing your breath, also senses the pressure of your bite, providing a way to add vibrato to your tone.

The lack of moving parts makes it extremely reliable, but to your fingers it's more like playing a keyless instrument like a recorder than a saxophone. It doesn't take long to get used to once you've chosen a fingering configuration.

The real power of the EWI USB and the Akai software comes when you combine them with a music application like GarageBand. The Akai software can act as a plug-in to Garage Band and other software. You can record multiple tracks using different instrument voices. This has greatly expanded my musical capabilities, and I'm now experimenting with creating my own band arrangements.

The EWI USB is not without its flaws. While I've had no problems with the Akai software on Macintosh, I've seen some pretty severe complaints from Windows users. Though it's a MIDI instrument, it doesn't have a MIDI port; you have to plug it into a computer. Akai's documentation is a bit sparse, and doesn't provide much information on how to use the EWI with other software. Another problem is that some of the instrument voices sound a bit artificial. Even with breath control, the EWI can't mimic the variety of sounds that a good player gets out of a real saxophone or trumpet.

Akai makes a somewhat more advanced version, the EWI4000S, that has a MIDI port and its own built-in sound generator. This might be a better option than the EWI USB if you want to use it in a live performance. Yamaha also makes an advanced wind controller that has moving keys and a mouthpiece that can more closely mimic real reed instruments. Both these options are at least twice as expensive as the EWI USB, and may require additional hardware and software instrument "patches" (instrument voices) to match those provided with the EWI USB.

-- Tom Sackett

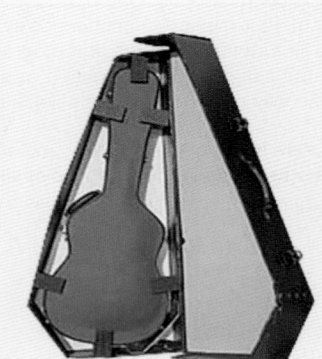

Affordable guitar flight case
CaseXtreme Clam
$267 CaseXtreme

Flying with a guitar that you care about can be a nerve-racking experience. Normal guitar cases don't offer enough protection and the professional's standard Calton cases are $600+ and heavy enough to make your arms lengthen.

Here's a case designed for flying that is light, well designed and pretty much indestructible. It costs around $160-$200 and you can put your instrument in it by itself, in a soft and light gig bag or in your normal hard shell case. I like to put the guitar in a gig bag to use for light weight protection when I get to my destination.

The case also comes with well designed wheels that you attach with velcro and are stored in the case when not in use.

-- David M. Siegler

Music Scoring

Music scoring/notation software
Finale

$600 Finale

Finale is an amazing music scoring program with so many features it boggles the mind. I am using it — along with the Transcribe! (see right) — to transcribe blues harp music, which is only a fraction of its capabilities. To be honest, there is a steep learning curve if you've never used a scoring program before, but I found it to be more intuitive than programs which cost many times more. It's like learning to use CAD programs. There is no easy way. You have to trudge through the manual and just try things every time you want to do something.

That said, once you get started, there is so much you can do with this program. There are wizards that help you quickly create a blank sheet with staves. The wizard lets you choose the type of instrument, time signature, key, and font. You then add notes and rests to the staff by choosing from a palette the duration and clicking on the appropriate line or space on the staff. There are also keyboard shortcuts that facilitate this. Each time you add a note you hear the note via a built-in synthesizer. You can play the score you entered via a "play" button. You can change the duration of a note by choosing a different note from the palette and clicking on the note you want to change. You can alter the pitch of a note by dragging it to a different position on the staff or by selecting the note and using the cursor keys. You can add rests, accidentals, and tuplets in a similar manner. You can create chords or add notes to a chord and change its pitch.

Another really nice feature is the ability to import MIDI files which are instantly displayed as a musical score that can be edited. You can also export your score to a MIDI file. And once you are happy with your creation or transcription, you can of course print a hard copy or export to a pdf to distribute to your fellow musicians. One plus is the abilty to automatically create tablatures of your music — simultaneously, in a separate staff below your main staff. Unfortunately for me, the program doesn't have a built-in harmonica TAB, but it is possible to create a custom TAB (though, I've found it is easier to manually add TABS with the lyrics tool).

There are lower-priced, limited and student versions for less than the list price; this package is probably overkill for my needs anyway.

-- Laral

Easy music scoring
Noteflight

Free (first 10 scores) Noteflight

Within the specialized area of music notation software there's a holy war between the users of the two most popular packages, Finale and Sibeleus, that nearly rises to the level of Mac v PC. These are expensive and complex applications that can handle any music notation task from creating band arrangements, choral parts, orchestral works, and even movie scores. I won't add fuel to that fire but if your music scoring needs are a bit simpler, there is a great web app for notation called Noteflight. There are two tiers of features, a free version with up to 10 scores, and a subscription version called Crescendo with unlimited scores and many additional features such as midi input, high-quality playback samples, individual part output, templates, and others. There is a demo of Crescendo available as well. Scores can be shared with other Noteflight users, and they can comment or "favorite" scores that are shared. I've used the tool to make quick lead sheets, create practice exercises, and to "clean up" notes from music theory classes. It's definitely worth a look.

– David Darrow

Andante grazioso

User-friendly audio slower
Transcribe!

Free 30-day free Seventh String
$39 Complete Seventh String

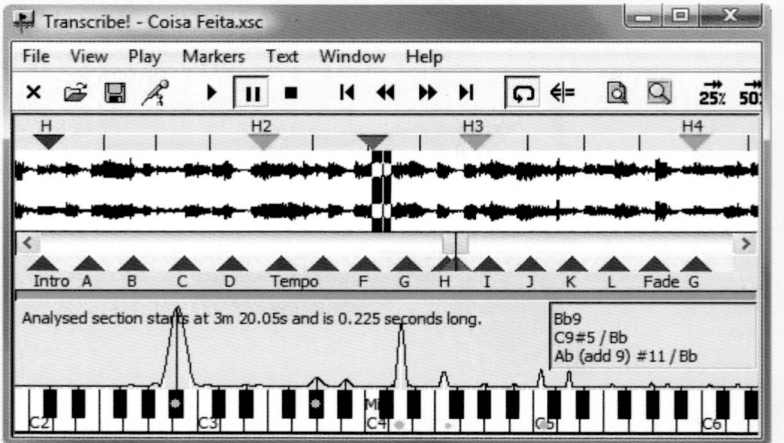

I'm learning to play blues harp, so in addition to the Amazing Slow Downer, I've tried a number of programs that let you manually control the speed of a tune without changing the pitch. I have to say without reservation that Transcribe! is the clear winner. Its simple user interface is completely intuitive and easy to use. To select a section of music you want repeated, all you have to do is drag the cursor over the section of the displayed waveform, choose a preset speed from 15 percent to 150 percent, and play. You can add markers to the sections you want to come back to later as well.

Compared to Transcribe!, Amazing Slow Downer's interface is just awkward.

When I am learning a song, I go through it bar by bar, and, by repeating the bar at a slow speed and playing it on the harmonica, I type down the tab for each note. After I have transcribed the whole piece, I then select larger sections and repeat them slowly, playing along using the tabs for guidance, and gradually increase the speed until I've got it. I've tried all the programs and then some. I just couldn't believe how difficult other programs make this process. Transcribe! just works. I have been using it for around two years.

-- Laral

Ultra portable speaker
Altec Lansing Orbit

$70 Altec

I've used this ultra-portable mono speaker for nearly two years, and can't recommend it enough. Even though it is "mono", it is "very good mono", and part of the reason I chose mono is because of the sound limitations of small stereo speakers.

This little thing easily fits in your backpack, briefcase, purse, or even clipped to your belt for mobile tunes. And the sound is really, really good. Many would call it amazing. Can I compare it to others? I'd rather not get into a holy war. The

Orbit, in my mind, is a cool tool for being excellent at what it does for about $20.

I think it is pretty safe to say, that for the intended purpose, it seems to be among the top, if not the top, rated portable speakers for listening to your iPhone, iPad, mp3 player, etc.

This little hockey puck (well, only slightly thicker, at about 2") does the trick. We use it often around the house to plug into the laptop when we want to have some tunes but not through the tinny laptop speakers. It comes with a nice little case, a carabiner clip, runs on 3 AAA batteries and just seems to go and go.

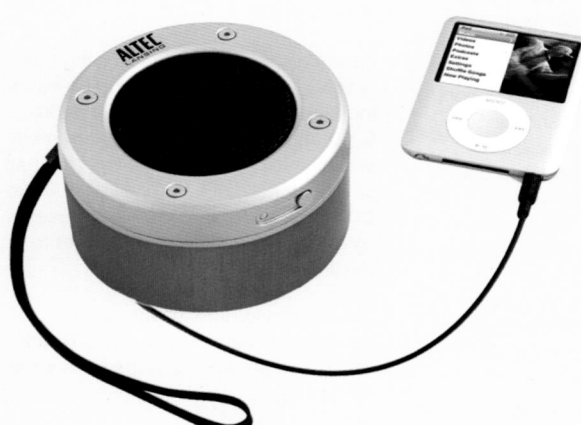

There are some minor complaints among detractors, most commonly by people expecting the unreasonable; that a 2 to 3-inch speaker should be able to bring you to your knees with your hands over your ears. It's not going to be your solution if you want to blast dance band volumes out of your pocket, but it certainly is just the ticket to have on the table with you on the back porch, or beef up the sound out of your laptop.

It is one of my most successful purchases, with great bang for the buck.

-- Jeff Jewell

Sturdy music stand
Manhasset M48 Symphony Music Stand

$40 Manhasset

As a junior high school music student, one of the first things I learned was to get to the orchestra room early enough to get one of the few good music stands. Almost all of the stands wobbled, wouldn't stay at the height you set them, or simply dumped your music with no warning. However, the small handful of Manhasset stands had taken just as much abuse as the others, yet worked perfectly.

The standard Manhasset #48 Symphony music stand is the backbone of ensembles and school music programs across the country. It has no clamps or adjusting knobs; the height and angle of the music table holds through friction. Somehow, it's easy to adjust, but stays exactly where you put it, even as you load it with stacks of music. The height of the standard model adjusts from 26" to 48" (measured from the floor to the bottom of the table), allowing you to use it both sitting down and standing up.

The table is aluminum, powder-coated black. The base is steel, with the lower section also powder-coated and the upper chromed. The base has three arched legs. Despite its stability, it's light and nicely balanced, making it easy to carry in one hand. The simplicity of its design gives it a kind of unobtrusive elegance, and makes it one of the few pieces of gear used by both students in a classroom and virtuoso performers on stage.

I was still a teenager when I was given my own Manhasset music stand. After thirty years it is slightly (but only slightly) beat up, but it functions perfectly.

-- Tom Sacket

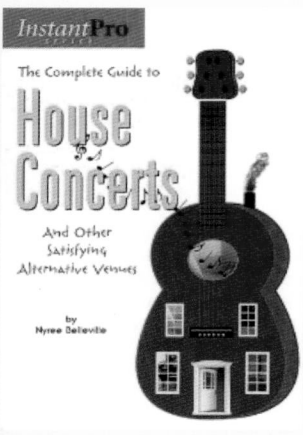

Instant Pro

The Complete Guide to
House Concerts
And Other Satisfying Alternative Venues

by
Nyree Belleville

Fan-hosted performances
The Complete Guide to House Concerts

$20 Nyree Belleville, 2003, 120 p.

Once all music is available online, for free, what's a musician to do? House concerts are one alternative. Instead of plying a circuit of poorly-paid bars, clueful musicians can now rely on their fans to organize, promote, and pay for small, intimate, private performances in their homes and other non-traditional venues. Fans win, and performers win (by earning more). This slim book explains to both fans and musicians how this new system works. I've been to a couple of house concerts and I found them 100% more enjoyable than arena concerts.

-- KK

●

What is a house concert?

The definition's flexible, but generally, it's a show that's presented in someone's home, or a nearby private space (barn, backyard, shearing tent, you name it).

* Usually, but not always, the audience capacity is smaller than at a coffeehouse or club.

* The money collected usually (but not always) goes straight to the performers, with no "profit motive" on the presenter's part.

* Often, but not always, house concerts are conducted "by invitation" (for practical reasons we'll get into later), rather than as "public" concerts like a club or concert hall.

* Often – again with exceptions – there is little or no "sound system" – performers play and sing acoustically, unless someone needs a little amp for their keyboard.

* Refreshments, if any, are usually either a "pot luck" brought by the listeners, or provided by the hosts using a bit of the gate receipts.

* Sometimes – but definitely not always – the performers get a meal and/or lodging with the presenters as part of their compensation.

– House Concerts, Tom Neff

●

The bottom line for traditional venues isn't pretty. The basic bar gig pays between nothing and $300, unless they're hiring a big name band that will sell a lot of expensive tickets and alcohol to their audience while they are on stage. The standard cafe either sets out a tip jar or pays you $100 for three to four hours of singing your heart out. And it may be difficult to sell CDs, simply because people have already spent their money on drinks. What's more, sometimes you get the sense that the audience would really appreciate it if you and your music would stay out of their way while they talk and have a good time.

Ready for some good news? You can make considerable more money with alternative venues and have a much better time while you're at it! If you play a house concert with 50 people and a $20 "donation" per person, you are guaranteed to go home with $1,000. And since house concerts are a practically perfect place to sell CDs, you may sell to 50 percent of the room or more, and at $15 per CD you stand to make an additional $375. If you have more than one CD, this figure will likely be even higher. Not bad for a night where all you have to do is show up, eat a delicious meal, and give a concert to a room full of captivated, music-loving people.

●

I'll be frank with you here. Almost every single great thing that has taken place in my music career has been because of a really dedicated fan. An unbelievable two-week tour of Brazil was set up for me by a fan. I played on nation-wide TV shows, got lots of airplay, was outfitted by clothing sponsors, played at the very best venues in the country, and experienced two of the best weeks of my life, all because of a fan believed in my music.

Want more? Because of a fan, I played a show with Crosby, Stills & Nash and Carlos Santana on the same night. The fan set it up. He sold it to the concert promoter. He made it happen. All I had to do was show up and play.

What about setting up tours across the country? Yes, my fans have rented out venues or hustled the owners to lend it to them for the night. They have gone on to get amazing press, print up tickets, set up venues, and make it possible for me to play sold-out shows to hundreds of people in towns where nobody has ever heard my music.

●

At the end of every house concert, at least one person will approach you because they want to set up a concert with you at their house. And once people find out that Susie is going to host one, many more will want to show you off to their friends and family too. Before the night is through you will be in the lovely position of adding several names and numbers to your house-concert file and following up with them to book a firm date for each show.

When you play bars or cafes, it is frequently a struggle even getting the booker on the phone! With house concerts, you are constantly juggling plenty of gig offers, which come with guaranteed money, a guaranteed audience, and a minimum of hassles. What could be better?

– The Complete Guide to House Concerts

Three portal sites:

concertsinyourhome.com

houseconcerts.org

houseconcerts.com

Multifaceted mini-amp
Roland MicroCube

$110 Roland

As someone who makes his living playing and teaching guitar, I love the tone and power that large, loud amplifiers provide. But there are many times and places where a big amp just doesn't work. Sometimes it's just carting it around; sometimes it's space issues. If you live in an apartment or townhouse, playing a large amp at supersonic volumes can make for some really bad neighbor relationships or even get you evicted. You really can't take a large amp camping either, unless you use a power inverter and drain your car battery. Also, you have a difficult time taking it traveling on business or vacation.

What to do? For all those places, the Roland MicroCube is perfect. This little amp has been around for about four years and is loaded with features closely related to its larger, louder cousins. The controls on the top provide a wide range of sonic possibilities. Along with a knob for tone, there are controls for gain (think distortion control) and volume. On the back is a headphone output (that shuts the speaker off when in use), an auxiliary line input and power in for a 9 volt DC power source. I love portable, and for such a small amp this thing puts out, and with great tone. My favorite setting? Brit Combo with a little distortion along with my lapsteel.

-- Jeff Bragg

Backyard hi-fi
Cambridge SoundWorks Portable Speaker System

Cambridge

This is, hands-down, the best portable audio system I have ever heard. It takes a few minutes to set-up and pack-up, and you need a power source to run it, but wow! does it have great sound! I have used it for parties, outdoor BBQs, and on vacation and it never fails to sound great. The included speakers and amplifier, the necessary cables, and your iPod, all pack into the included hard case (which also contains the subwoofer).

My only gripe is that the connections are all clip-connections rather than banana connections, but Radio Shack and other sources sell small banana-style plugs to use with clip connections, making set-up much easier (no frayed wire ends).

I can't recommend this enough for anyone who wants audiophile-quality music they can take with them to a cabin, condo, RV, or to their backyard as needed. The price is higher than your standard portable units, but Cambridge Sound Works constantly has sales and coupons on the net, making the price a little bit better. In any event, it's well worth even the full list price!

There are few things I have come across that are "best of class" but this is certainly one. The only other thing I can think of that I have found to be as perfect are metal tongs for cooking; I use those more than any other piece of kitchen equipment to the point that I don't see how I ever cooked without them.

-- Torgny Nilsson

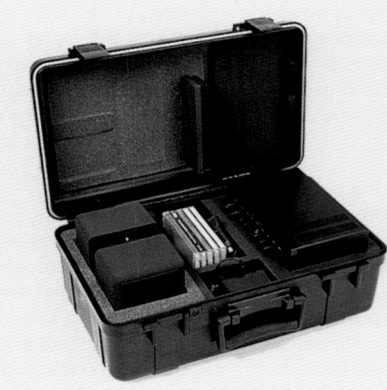

Most portable PA system
Fender PD-150 Pro

$400 Fender Passport 150 PRO Portable PA System
Fender

There may be slightly better sounding or feature-rich PA systems in this price range, but nothing comes close to the outstanding portability of Fender's Passport. It's barely 30 pounds, and when it's packed up and put together in its slick integral case no moving or delicate parts are exposed to scraping or damage. And since the case tapers at each end, it's easy to carry without it bumping against my side with every step.

I use it primarily as a sort of keyboard amp for a laptop, also for playing music from an iPod. I play in a band with some friends and plan to use this Fender PA system for small or outdoor shows. There are three of us in the band, and we needed vocal and laptop amplification. The PD-150 has three mic/instrument inputs, so we're all set.

It's most cool as PA; the mixer is perfunctory but useful and welcome. It is a trade-off in terms of price, portability and integration, like a boom box versus a component system. The advantage of buying the speakers, amplifier and mixer separately is that you can customize the amount of power, mixer features, and speaker quality that you'd like, but it will be more expensive and harder to transport. The portable PA is just so cool in that it does the basics decently and packs itself into a supercompact little suitcase.

I purchased a PD-150 that I found on Craigslist for $150, but the current model is the PD-150 Pro, which supposedly has better sound quality, and adds a second stereo input. It's also 3 pounds lighter.

-- Mark Groner

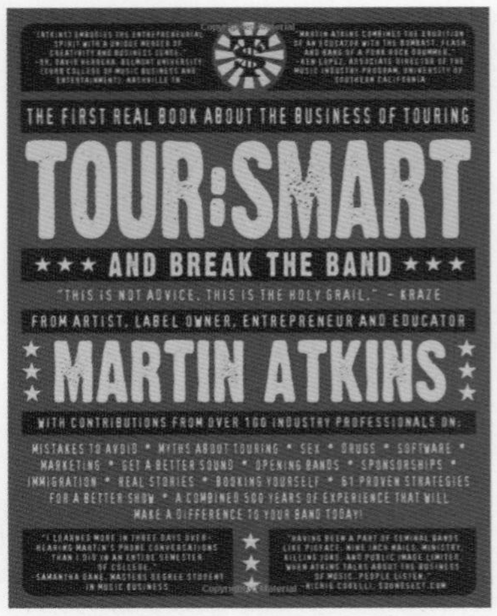

Musician touring tips

Tour:Smart

$18 Martin Atkins, 2007, 592 p.

I don't have a band, but if I did, I would use this book to guide me through the intricacies of touring. That's the new economics of the music: a returning emphasis on live performance. This fat book is the best guidance I've seen for emerging musical artists. It is brutally honest, remarkably wise, and extremely helpful. Atkins is really good at extracting lessons. There are testimonies not just from many other musicians, but their roadies, agents, bus-drivers, managers, fans, and all the other folks you will need supporting you. This book is so good, in fact, anyone "touring," including authors, dancers, filmmakers would find pats of it useful. In the new economy, your live presence is more valuable than copies of your past work. Here's how to maximize your presence with the least hassles, and hopefully make a living do it.

Practicing what he preaches, author Martin Atkins offers live interactions, chats, lectures, performances, and email correspondence versions of his advice. Another kind of touring.

-- KK

•

You should feel very confident that 40 to 50 people would come to see your band on a Monday night. If you don't feel that's the case, you should wait a bit before playing this particular club. You shouldn't be in a big hurry to play to nobody, and that's what happens if you play before you're ready. Until then, be patient.

•

Should I take any show that's offered to me? No. Be smart about the shows you take. In the beginning, it's not wise to be too choosy, but before long, you should start turning down shows that don't make sense. Realize that more is going on than just a show being played. You are being associated in the minds of the audience with the other bands on the bill and with the venue.

•

Look at the incremental build up of costs (financial and human) with an understanding of the total investment needed for a two year commitment for your band. Then, apply some of the budget you'll need to slog through year two onto the front of year one. If done intelligently, you will be in a much different place by year two. You can use this strategy on a smaller scale with a single show or tour--more money spent earlier will help more.

•

Tour Bus

Nothing makes sleeping on a bus over a long overnight journey sweeter than having spent a few years driving in a crappy vehicle, eating dust and unidentifiable truck stop food. When you are in a bus, it becomes a traveling cocoon. People like to be safe and comfortable in all understandable things everything is there: cell phone, fridge, toilet, and band members begin to magnetize to it. When you are in a van, you need people to stay with. You'll find those people by staying in the club longer, interacting harder, being more alert, smelling better, and not drooling. Yes, free accommodations also come with obligations, but it's these social obligations that interlock and weave their way through the fragile endeavor of "Breaking America." There is an unwritten underground contract that strangers in a city honor when they trust and open their hearts, homes, showers, beds, washing machines, and high-speed DSL lines to a beat-down band on the road. To deny that contract, to deny that 5 a.m. conversation, to deny their ability to make a massive difference with a bed, a blanket, a bagel, and a bath is to deny the bond that will reverberate for years afterwards. Maybe part of touring in a band has nothing to do with the music. Maybe it has more to do with meeting people, seeing differences across the country, and discovering their changing attitudes. All you see inside the bus is the changing landscape, the mold growing inside the refrigerator, and the bass player's growing porn collection.

•

When your agent suggests an opening band be careful. This is an easy way for your agent to get 30 shows for another one of his bands, get them off his back, and get more commission. Check for yourself to find out some information about the band: -Do they have a label? -Is that label going to help in any way at all? -Have they sold any CDs? -Do they have a following? How many people are on their MySpace page (divide by two)? -Have they played in these markets before? -Do they have a street team? -Do they have posters? Or will they contribute to printing posters (saving you each half)? -Do they have mountains of equipment, throw vegetable oil all over the stage, or have a reputation for causing problems? Do your homework! You might be better off with a strong local opener in each city, at least you'll have a chance at a place to stay!

•

You might be sitting down wondering how you could possibly pull off seven shows per week. You want to know what I'm thinking? What would happen if you could do eight or nine shows?

•

Will the volume be at the a realistic level for the room or will the main band's sound guy pull the faders all the way down? You would be surprised and horrified at how often that happens. It is reasonable for an event to increase in tempo and volume as the night unfolds, but there are respectful limits to that curve. I did an open-air show with Killing Joke, opening for the Mission UK, at some huge park in London. We had a double-decker tour bus and Henry Rollins was opening. We did our show and then I went back to the bus to try and have a bit of a nap. All of the sudden, I heard this amazingly loud, thunderous sound. I asked one of the crew guys what is was. "Oh," he laughed, "they just turned the rest of the PA on!"

•

Let's look at this for a bulb in Cincinnati. For a show there, I'd want to play a show in Dayton, OH (49 miles away), a show in Richmond, IN (63 miles away) or any other closer, small market in a 60-mile radius. Try for six to ten shows within OK driving distance for your rabid fans. Make sure that you get every single name you can on your mailing list. These are gold dust or any kind of dust that turns you on. You're trying to build a support base so that when you go to Cincinnati for the make or break show with the 450-person built-in crowd, you can entice people on your mailing list from each of the surrounding, accessible cities, task your street team in each city to round up as many people as they can, and organize transportation if necessary (I'm not talking about renting a bus, although I have done that in the past. I'm talking about ride-share). Because you've planned this in advance, you've held back the three-song preview CD from your new album or the cool, new t-shirt so that you can give one of those away free to anybody traveling more than 30 miles. Give people gas money if necessary. Help them to join this crusade with you! So, when you hit the stage you have 200 extra people at the venue. The promoter will notice the increased attendance. The bar staff will notice the increased revenue. The 450 kids who usually go will notice the larger crowd and get pulled in. End result: you've done something other than talk and hype and the next time the promoter is looking for a solid band that works hard with a good following to help a national show that might be struggling, he's going to call you. That's it, simple. As Sun Tzu would say, "Never take your country to war unless you're sure of the outcome."

•

Tools

Don't Be One, Use One

For fewer than ten dollars you can get a Rand McNally Dist-O-Map. It is not some new, gimmicky tech tool, it's way cooler, very much like the cover of Led Zeppelin's Album III. It has the advantage over map-questing in that you can sit on the phone, run a budget, and dial up distances at the same time. It will also show you options that you might not have thought of previously. If you are lucky enough to be traveling by bus, you will be able to easily see which cities lie within the magical 450-mile overdrive mark. I cannot think of one single agent I have ever met who doesn't need this tool (or frighteningly, one that already has one when I meet them!) Think about that for a minute (especially after you realize that this costs $7.95). It has been the catalyst for the rerouting of several tours, which not only reduced the overall mileage, but put us in the right venues on the right nights.

The other reason you need one is to dial up the total distance covered on a tour, divide that by the gas mileage of your chosen vehicle, multiple that by the average cost of gas, and begin a budget.

Home-made instrument

Dulcimer Kit

$130+ Hourglass Spruce, Model 56 Black Mountain Instruments

A great kit will allow you to make something you probably wouldn't make any other way. You are given all the parts, and then you assemble and finish. Musical instruments, with their exactness, fit into that category for me. Years ago, I used this kit to make a simple dulcimer. It was easy to build, and beautiful to behold and hear.

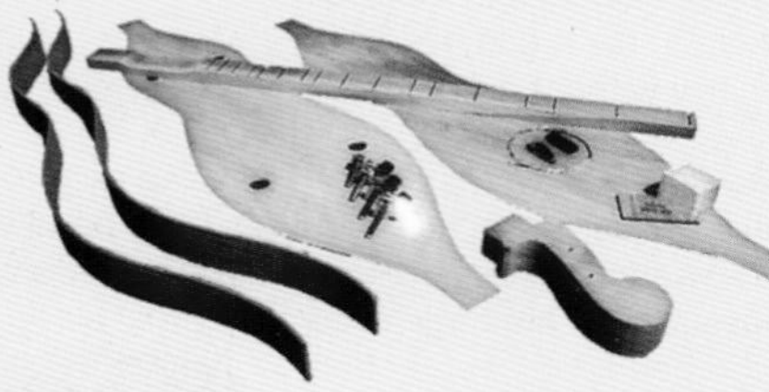

-- KK

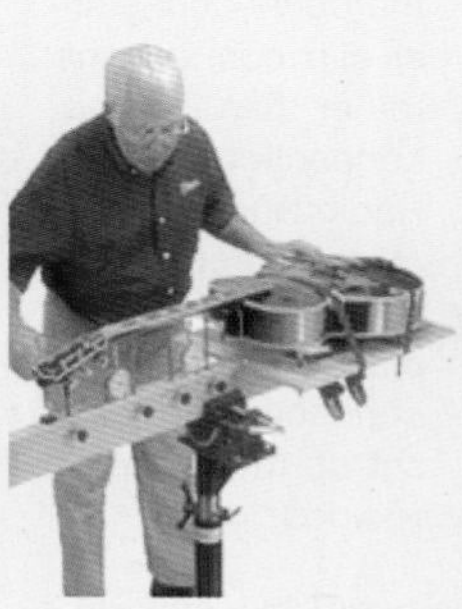

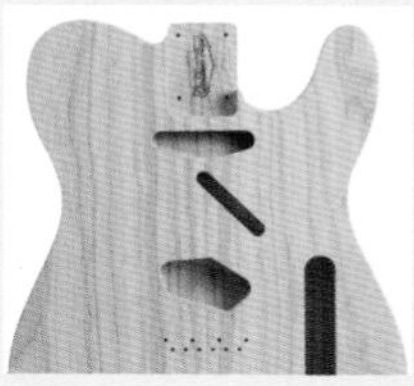

Stringed instrument repair resource

Stewart MacDonald Catalogue

StewMac isn't the only catalogue, nor the oldest, but every luthier and instrument repair dude I know has one on a shelf by his/her bench. I've been getting the catalogue for 6-7 years to find and order replacement and upgrade parts. I buy instruments at garage sales and fix them up to give away or use (I play a bunch of lute-family instruments — own about 10 guitars, a couple of banjos, a sitar, a bandurria, a ukulele).

StewMac carries some really unusual tools and they have the widest selection I've seen: fret files, bridge plate iron, inlay routing jigs, saws for mother-of-pearl and abalone, bushing pullers. They carry specialty glues, hard-to-find woods (Sitka spruce, koa, curly maple, Indian rosewood), laminated paua abalone, pre-sawn wood blanks for mandolins, banjos, ukuleles, and guitars.

If you've busted a hole in your guitar, you can also get the repair supplies, tools, and instructional books/videos to fix it for less than the guy at the shop will quote for doing the job. StewMac put in a minimum order of $30 not long ago, but I still think it's a fair deal.

-- Mark Johnson

Free (Online) Stewart MacDonald Catalogue

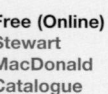

Free (Print) Stewart MacDonald Catalogue

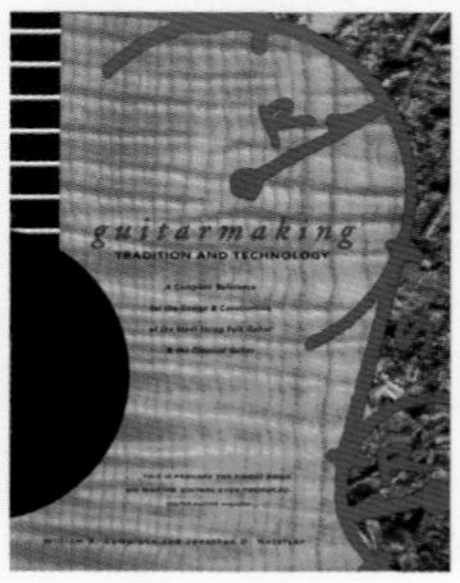

How to build an acoustic guitar

Guitarmaking: Tradition and Technology

$27 William Cumpiano, 1998, 392 p.

Although I have played acoustic guitar for some time, I had never considered the prospect of actually building one myself from scratch. Then one of my co-workers brought in an acoustic guitar he had built using the guiding principles contained within WIlliam Cumpiano's Guitarmaking. I was truly blown away by the professional build and tonal quality of his guitar, and was immediately hooked on the hobby. Widely considered in many lutherie circles to be the de facto bible for the novice guitarmaker, this book makes the whole experience seem far less intimidating.

Cumpiano's book can be approached as both a comprehensively detailed construction manual as well as a structural framework for creative exploration. Taken in its most straightforward form, the book will guide you step by step in exacting detail through the entire construction process — from tool and wood selection, through to lacquering and final string-action set up — enabling aspiring luthiers of any skill level to produce a quality final guitar. Each task is broken down in an assembly line-like manner, and is prefaced with exactly which tools and materials will be required; everything down to the number and placement of clamps to the glue drying time is provided. There are also explanations of beginner's pitfalls and invaluable tips on how to avoid them.

One of the most striking points I garnered from this book is that an acoustic guitar can be completely constructed with very minimal tools. In fact, the book assumes you have little or no access to power tools. I live in a small condo without any extra space or anything resembling a workshop. Although I had some previous woodworking experience, I had never used tools such as hand planes, cabinet scrapers, and paring chisels. Still, with the book, I was able to confidently take on the challenging and rewarding task of designing and building a guitar about the size of the Martin OM — in my kitchen. You don't have to blow through three weeks of vacation time to enjoy this hobby either. I've been working on mine fairly consistently, but also off-and-on for a year now.

If you read with an open mind and are willing to research modern construction techniques on the Internet and learn from other builders, I found you can also take what you learn from Cumpiano and slightly improve upon the book's construction techniques in a few areas — a caveat that even he mentions in the preface in the book, as lutherie is a constantly-evolving art form. For instance, there is a chapter about "pinning" the neck to the body that reads as a fairly complex task. However, Cumpiano subsequently invented a more modern "bolt on" approach that is significantly easier and more successful, and he has continued to provide his readers with these construction tips and details on his web site.

-- Steve Summerford

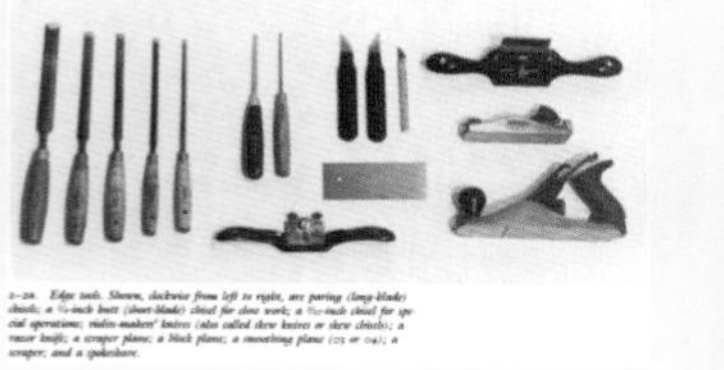

336

A new point of view is worth 80 IQ points. - Alan Kay

Best DIY instrument how-to

Homemade Musical Instrument Guides

$12 Ginger Summit, Jim Widess, 2007, 144 p.

$9+ (used) Jay Javighurst, 1998, 108 p.

$8+ (used) John Scoville, Reinhold Banek, 1995, 224 p.

Here are three great guides for making your own musical instruments. Advantages of making your own: 1) Personalized, 2) Cheaper, 3) Types no one else sells, 4) Satisfaction of making.

There is not much overlap of instruments featured between these three books.

The coolest of the three guides is Making Gourd Musical Instruments. It has very explicit step-by-step instructions for making 60 instruments using lightweight gourds as the sound amplifiers. Gourds enable wind, string and percussion instruments -- so you could make an entire orchestra. This book has the most variety of musical options and great examples of world-wide traditional instruments for inspiration. If you can get only one of these three books, this should be it.

Making Musical Instruments by Hand is a good guide for making instruments from wood and wood veneers. Their builds are a little more complex resulting in instruments that may look more "professional." They require a bit more skills and tools, although none out of the ordinary.

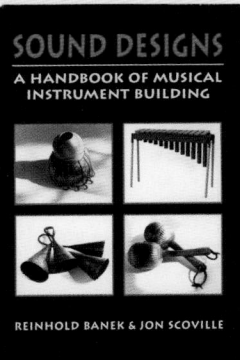

But if you are making your own instruments, why not make ones that have never existed before? Sound Designs, an older book, lays out helpful hints for making 50 different unorthodox instruments using salvage materials. It stresses innovative interpretations: how about oxygen bottles for bells, or electrical conduit xylophones? Its intent is to encourage you to not just make your own musical instruments, but to invent them as well.

-- KK

From *Making Gourd Musical Instruments*

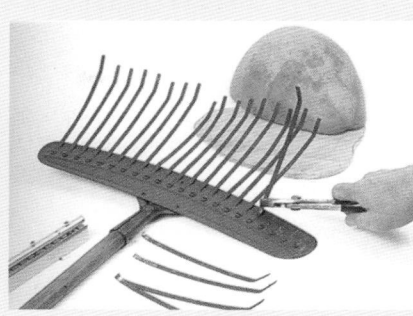

Cut keys (lamella) from an old leaf rake.

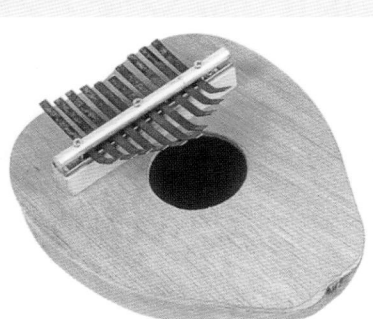

Position the keys in the bridge and tighten the screws. If you need to adjust the length of a key slightly, loosen the screw, then readjust it.

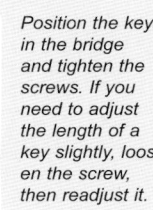

Completed kalimba.

Drill the peg holes precisely at the marks.

As you tighten the lacing, make sure each loop is brought around its peg and that the bead is next to the peg. Later on, the peg may be pushed up on the lacing to further tighten the head if needed.

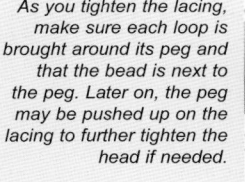

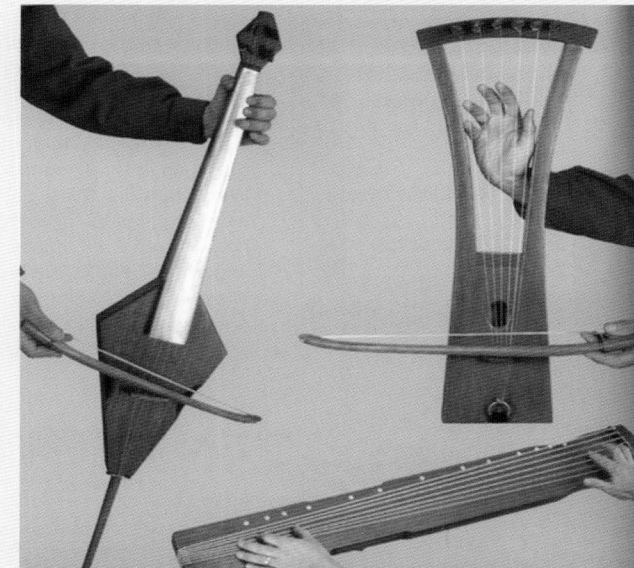

From *Making Musical Instruments by Hand*

Tip: Stretching Thicker Skins ▶

Thicker skins may require more pressure to tighten before stapling. Use a pair of locking pliers with a thin rope attached through the handle. Make a loop at the bottom so you can step onto it. Apply tension firmly with your foot, without tearing the skin, and with the staple gun held vertically upside down, fire the staple. Then follow the stapling instructions in step 9.

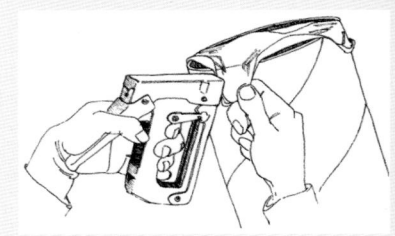

From *Sound Designs*

Dimple Gongs

Simply, mark the center point on each plate or disc. Place it on the end of a fairly wide piece of soft wood, say 4 by 4 inches. Put the round end of a ball-peen hammer on the center mark and smite it hard several times with a small sledge or heavy hammer.

The resulting dimple gives the plate not only a distinct pitch, but its name as well. Though if you look at it from the other side, it becomes a pimple gong. We found by experimenting that generally the smaller the dimple the lower the pitch would be, so tune yours accordingly. ▼

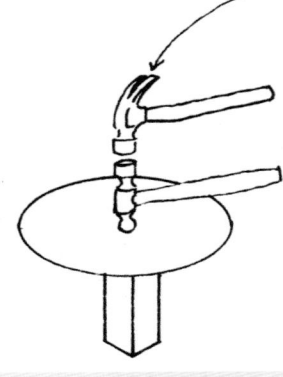

Tube Drums, made from ABS pipe tubing with drum heads.

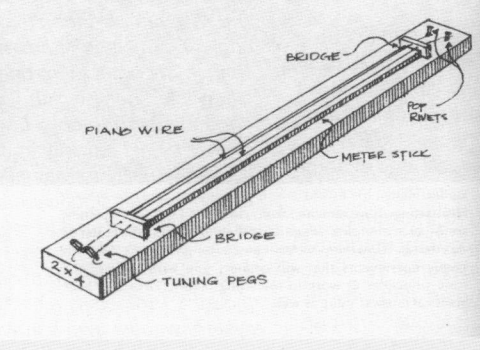

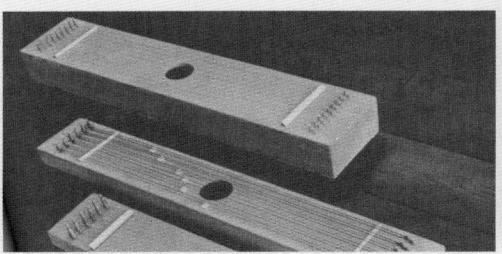

▶ The aeolian harp is not really a harp at all, but a box-resonated zither with ten or more strings of different diameters all tuned, at low tension, to the same note. It is placed outside or in a window where the wind can pass by and set the strings in motion. ▶ ▶ Far right, Glass Chamber bowls made from cut 12-gallon glass jugs. Use soft mallets to play this instrument.

Special effects by mouth
MouthSounds
$14 Fred Newman, 2004, 245 p.

Not everyone appreciates the thrill of making weird, silly or rude sounds with your mouth. All the better, then, if you know how to throw up a fake a cell phone ring, or present a first-rate chicken cluck. This great book teaches you how to create those and 200 other special sound effects with your mouth only. It comes with a CD, which you really do need to get these sounds correct. Your master guru is Fred Newman, the guy on Garrison Keillor's Prairie Home Companion show, who produces an entire symphony of sounds live in front of a mike. Besides being a how-to manual for audio gags, this book is also a very funny, and most importantly, one of the best classes I know of for opening up, training and exploring your voice, even if you don't want to make amazing noises.

-- KK

●
Screech 'N' Skid

Instructions

1. There's no shortcut to the Screech 'n' Skid. It has to be done like you're a six-year-old. First, load up with air, and hold your breath.

2. Now squeeze hard and let the sound squeak out in your highest falsetto voice. If it's rough and gravelly, so much the better. (If your face gets red and you pop a button, it's your own damn fault.) Let the screech rise and fall in pitch and volume.

Uses

The Screech 'n' Skid is the perfect response when someone makes a profoundly dumb suggestion, asks an inane question, or proffers a really bad idea such as "Let's wash the cat" or "How 'bout a double for the road?" or "Why don't we bungee jump out of this hot-air balloon?" The Screech 'n' Skid is the ultimate reality check.

●
Gummy Cheeks

Gummy cheeks is a juicy, abstract sound that slips past "mildly unpleasant" on the gross-factor rating scale and slides straight for "downright filthy" – in the way that stirring tuna and mayo together in a bowl has a disgusting sound, but you're not quite sure why. Gummy cheeks does not simulate any one sound in particular, but rather suggests a whole host of offensive goings-on.

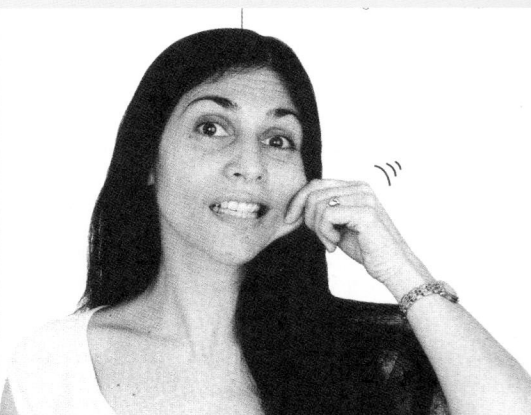

Instructions

1. Relax your face completely with your mouth closed loosely.

2. Pinch your cheek lightly with the thumb and crook of the index finger.

3. Pull out and push in the relaxed cheek very rapidly. You will get a repulsive, gooey, slurpy sound – a misdemeanor in Florida.

Uses

If you are fortunate enough to have large jowls, your Gummy Cheeks can make grown men squeamish. You can double the indignity by making Gummy cheeks simultaneously on both cheeks for a sort of slushy, surround-sound effect.

●
Awesome Party Tip #38

"Talk under the din."

If you are at a loud party and find yourself shouting louder and louder just to talk to people, begin speaking "under the noise." What is happening is that the voices in the room are competing in the same frequency range – so that people raise their volume and their pitch when they feel they can't be heard. They shout in high voices. All you have to do is not compete. Talk in a quieter, deeper voice, and you will be heard easily. Try it. You will be shocked at how easy it is to talk under the din.

The best free sound library
Freesound

Free Freesound

There are sound effects libraries that cost more than a small car, and they're probably worth it to certain kinds of users — like movie studios or audio production houses — but not to me. In search of interesting, appropriately licensed sounds for personal amusement, some google searching led me to Freesound.org, which has many thousands of freely usable, user-contributed sound recordings, all Creative Commons licensed. Some of them are tiny snippets, the audio equivalent of the icons on a computer screen, and some are lengthy field recordings. (Many of the sounds here are purely synthetic, too, or remixes that the CC licensing facilitates.) Last Halloween, I set up a playlist for my family's "haunted condo," consisting of screams, clanks, and creepy laughter (but also repurposed sounds like foghorns and musical instruments I thought sounded ominous), with sounds drawn entirely from this site.

It's also a good place to find ring-tone and computer alert sources, if you're just looking for audio clip art, or (with headphones, especially) fascinating "you are there" audio experiences; being transported to an audio landscape inhabited by gentle waves, ships' horns, and thunderstorms is a legal way to escape ordinary consciousness.

Freesound really is free, too, though donations are accepted; it started as a project of the Music Technology Group of the Universitat Pompeu Fabra. One (very small) catch: you can listen all you want just by visiting the site; downloading the files requires free registration.

-- Timothy Lord

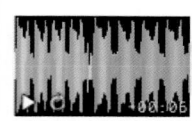

wow-wow siren.flac
synthesised alarm
wahwah alarm electronic synthesised wah-wah wow wah siren wow-wow

◈ 1 more sounds from **Timbre** in the last 48 hours

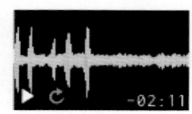

Blackbird.wav
Blackbird twittering in the evening. First minute loud, second minute quiet
birds Blackbird forest wood warble twitter

◈ 1 more sounds from **pulswelle** in the last 48 hours

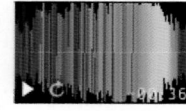

Transit Crystal Charge
Charging the alien technology for use. Medium to slow build. Source: Synthesized in Pro Tools 10, Plug-in Vacuum.
dirty synth build Charge whine thump ramp-up power bass low-end

◈ 1 more sounds from **crashoverride61088** in the las

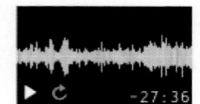

CalmCityEvening 8pm NL L...
This is a very calm spot in he middle of my home town 's-Hertogenbosch in Holland. It's around 8 pm ...
den-bosch street s-Hertogenbosch talking back-ground town white-noise gneral-noise

◈ 1 more sounds from **klankbeeld** in the last 48 hours

SOUNDDOGS.COM

Online Sound Effects Library
Sounddogs
Free audio browsing Sounddogs
$2 – $10 CD-Quality downloads: Sounddogs

This is one of those tools that I've been using for so long that it's just become a small part of my life.

For some odd reason, I often find myself in need of sounds of all sorts to plug a particular hole in a project. Just as stock photos are a great tool for designers and multimedia creators, sounds can be used to quickly set the mood or form transitions between disparate elements. Whether physical sound effects (e.g. crickets, birds, gunshots, explosions, everything under the sun), more creative effects (zips, zonks, beeps, and wooshes), and instrumental music of all kinds and emotions, Sounddogs is the perfect source for sounds of all kinds. Most effects are in the $3-$5 range, making it reasonable to collect sounds for multimedia projects, theater, and the ever so fun practical joke. The sounds themselves are delivered as CD-quality AIFF or WAV files right after you order; no shipping delays. You can browse through the entire catalog and listen to low-quality full-length previews of everything. It's truly addictive (and useful)!

-- Zach Lipton

Photoshop for music
Logic

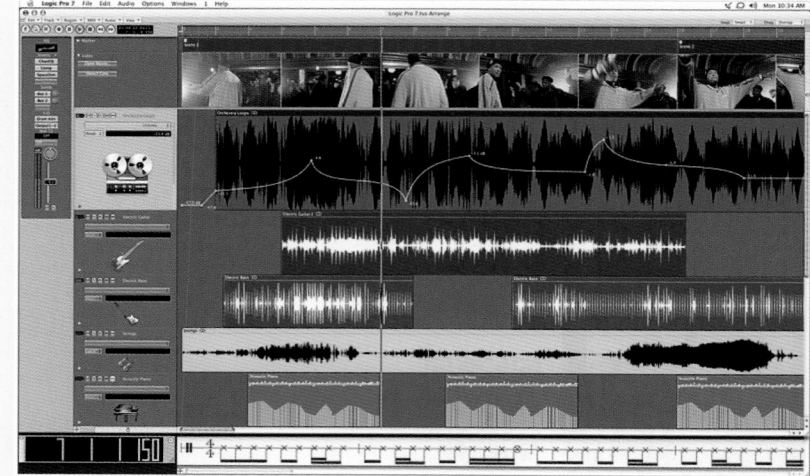

Logic is the Photoshop for music. With Logic, an audio software package from Apple, you can capture, process, filter, manipulate, correct, fiddle, compose, edit and endlessly tweak musical sounds to your heart's content. It's not the first music software, of course. Apple's beginner program Garage Band is a hint in the general direction, and Avid's ProTools is the expensive professional competitor to beat. And there are about a dozen other decent audio managing software packages available and in wide use, including a few basic free options. But Logic is gaining a reputation among some pros as the best one for music makers.

I was turned onto Logic by Brian Eno, who like many other musicians, is using it as his primary creative tool. Logic is the software he uses to compose music, and it's what he uses in the studio while producing albums of some of the world's best-selling bands. I asked him how it compared to the current professional audio recording program, ProTools, which has become the default in most recording studios, and why he would recommend Logic over ProTools for musicians. Eno said:

I think my main arguments come in three varieties. Protools is a fine system, but it is definitely more orientated towards recording than impromptu creation. It doesn't handle midi as well as Logic does, and in general it doesn't take so kindly to the improvisational way of working which you can adopt in Logic. Most importantly, it doesn't come bundled with all the interesting plug-ins and ready made loops that come with Logic. For instance I created a little song in my hotel room one night [as a gift, posted here] which I could not have done there in Protools. Logic's main strength, until recently at least, is that it is a high quality format (although I have to confess the actual audio difference is increasingly minimal to me).

And this brings me to my second thought. Protools is a stand-alone system with its own hardware and software. Logic is an Apple-owned system. What this means to me is that Logic benefits from every advance that Apple computers make in the evolution of their hardware — and I think Protools just won't be able to keep up with them. Remember Apple only just bought Logic, and the next version of Logic is expected to be a huge leap forward. I think Protools just won't have the resources to match Apple in that arena.

Last thing: you can carry Logic on your laptop and play, compose, create on the plane, wherever.

Logic, like Photoshop, is a complex, deep, powerful piece of software that will take some time to learn, and will cost you a bundle. But you will never exhaust it. And like Photoshop, which comes in a slightly "lighter" and significantly cheaper version (PhotoShop Elements), Logic also comes in a cheaper lite version called Logic Express. Most folks won't miss the few deleted features in Logic Express, and you can upgrade easily when desired.

-- KK

$499 Logic Studio
Apple

$80 Logic Express 9
Amazon

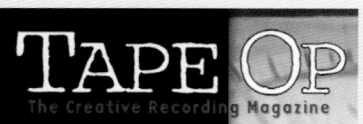

Best guide to music production

Tape Op Magazine

Free TapeOp.com

Tape Op is the only music geek magazine worth buying — and it's free. Widely eclectic and ever encouraging, the main premise seems to be "Try, and trust your ears." Pro, semi-pro, and DIY info sits comfortably side-by-side. Pros read it, hobbyists read it, some kids read it, all get something from it. *Tape Op* will give step-by step demos of, for instance, modding a certain low-cost microphone to get more bang for the buck written by a guy who sell his own mics for thousands. Or they talk to a guy with a barn full of homemade analog synths or someone who makes music out of sounds from antique recordings. The mag offers information in all kinds of directions, but it only wants you to do your own thing with it, what ever that is. *Tape Op*'s philosophy: use your ears and twist some knobs, learn all you can, then forget about it. Standards are

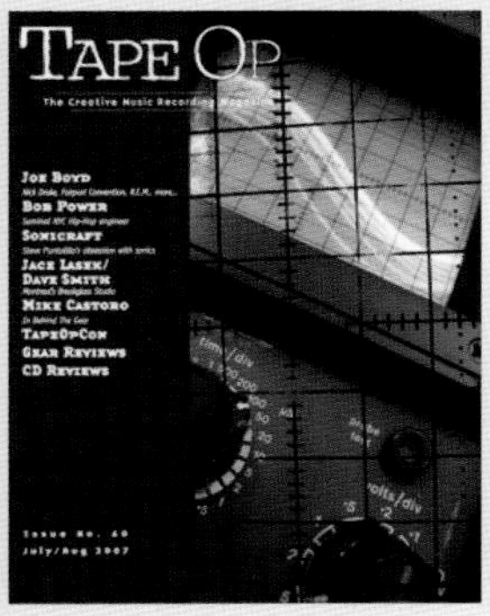

explained, history is explored first-person, but rules might be thrown out the window. An undercurrent regarding how unrealistic and difficult it is to run a studio coexists with inspiring tales about the pleasure and pride that comes from recording music. The contributors work hard in their own studios and know what they're talking about. A large community of recordists supports contributing articles and a lively online Q and A page (later edited and published). Recent profiles have run the gamut from legendary producers/engineers to seriously indie/outsider recordists; all have a jones for doing what they do their own way.

A recent, typical issue reviewed a mic you can buy for a steal on eBay for $40 and a mic that streets for $7,000. They don't waste time writing slagging reviews; they review only what might be useful to someone on some level. On one hand, you can learn a lot by reading about something you may never be able to afford. On the other, you see that despite how amazing, desirable and beautiful that thing is — and this where most music mags stop — you don't really need it. It might be a great tool for someone, but you don't have to need it. Record reviews, written in the same "we like this" spirit, lean indie and outside, but might go anywhere. I always read about something I don't know, but wouldn't mind hearing. It's independently published and paid for by ads from all kinds of audio-related concerns, but beholden to no one, so it's neither slick nor slimy. Other recording magazines often seem to be trolling for sales or hyping an image. Their editorial decisions are suspect, noising on about last year's retreads, repeating a press release, offering the same tutorials you could find in another magazine — or the library(!). The 'net offers a lot of basic

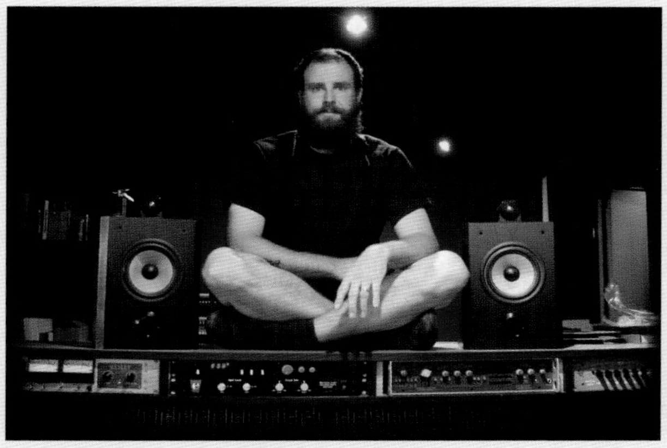

DIY sites you can learn from, but will they print an interview with Rupert Neve, as issue by issue, you learn about the products that riff on his designs? How about talking to Rudy Van Gelder (who recorded all the classic Blue Note jazz) about taping John Coltrane in the living room of his parent's house in New Jersey?

I've been subscribing since 1997-8 when a producer I met turned me onto it. There is absolutely nothing out there like it. Nowadays my job is production manager/soundcheck and rehearsal substitute/backline tech for a three-time Grammy winning artist. I work with and have hired top-notch audio pros and I learn a great deal from them. *Tape Op* has often given me insight that keeps me apace in our discussions and what I learn from them takes me deeper into the magazine. However, *Tape Op* also has allowed me to nourish a side-line in sound designing/composing for theatre when I am off the road. When no one's paying me and I'm home with the kids asleep, I record my music or occasionally, friends. That is where the knife really gets sharpened and what I have taken in from *Tape Op* gets put to the test.

-- John Stovicek

•

I finished a session the other day where I went 10 hours without eating anything and kept suggesting breaks. It never happened.

It's funny you brought that up. That happened to me last week. A person came in to record five or six songs for basic tracks in two days. It was that sort of scenario. It felt like if they weren't doing something every second that an opportunity was being wasted. I can deal with that for two days or so. The longest session I worked on was 3 1/2 months. It was four people, and their mom, who never wanted to take any breaks. It was a trial. I remember saying, "You know, I'll do this again but I need a significant amount of money." The studio salary didn't cut it.

You lost three months of your life!

Exactly. I broke up with a long-term girlfriend. Everyday was noon to midnight. It was a mixed blessing. Usually the types of bands that come in here are short and quick. They're paying for everything themselves. We never got into that stride of a big studio getting big sessions that last for months and months. But our main fuel is bands that come in from three to twelve days. No one's had to give up six months of his or her life to babysit.

•

Seating a new head

Here's a good way to quickly seat a new drumhead (which allows the drum to better conform to the specific contour of the drum's bearing edge): Put the head on and tighten it slowly, making sure to maintain even tension around the head. When the head is fairly tight (and evenly-tensioned), take a heat gun or blow dryer and slowly work your way around the outer edge of the drumhead, just inside the hoop and along the bearing edge. Don't try to get the head hot, just warm to the touch. The heat will make the Mylar conform to the bearing edge almost instantly. Be careful not to get the head too warm, as too much heat buildup will deform the head in a destructive way.

•

Tape down one end of the Slinky inside the cone of an expendable speaker (either a raw loudspeaker or one in a cabinet) - gaffer's tape works well - and place the speaker on the floor as shown in Figure 5. Clamp your contact mic to the other end of the Slinky with a strong spring clip and attach this assembly to the end of a mic boom 3-6 feet up from the speaker, with the Slinky stretched between (Figure 6.) Plug the contact mic into your mixer or a guitar amp and pluck the spring to check your level. Now play some audio through the speaker and listen to the contact mic as the speaker shakes the Slinky - you may want to use headphones so you can distinguish the sound of the Slinky from the music coming directly out of the speaker.

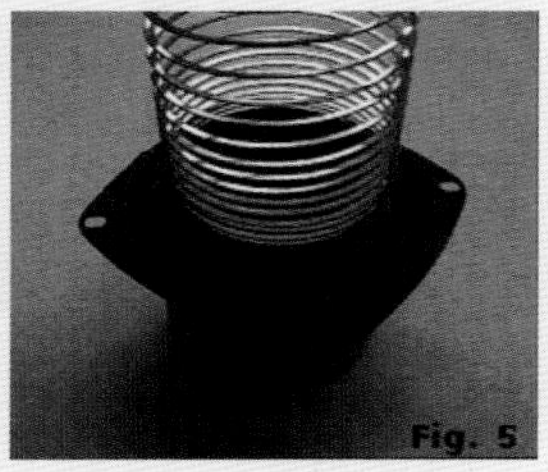

Fig. 5

You should hear a "spoingy," vaguely spring reverb-y cloud around your original signal.

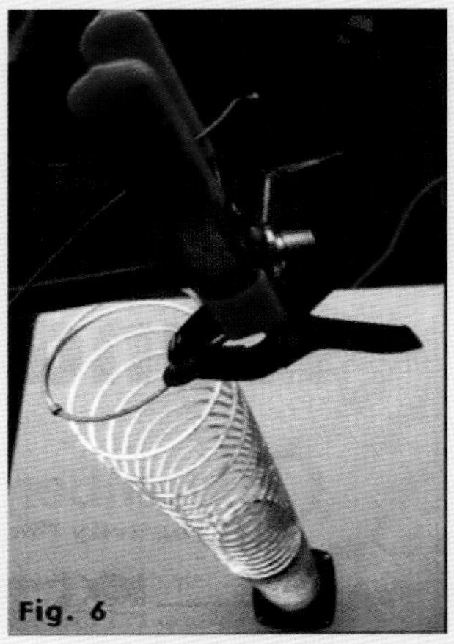

Fig. 6

Pocket-sized sound manipulator

Korg Kaossilator Synthesizer

$90 Amazon

For a number of years I've been into sound art and electronics, but never had the cash and space for an ARP 2600. I recently acquired a Korg Kaossilator, a fabulous little dynamic phrase synthesizer, which, for all intents and purposes, now serves as my main musical device. Pocket-sized and touch-operated, the Kaossilator is comprised of 100 sounds: electronic beats, synth chords and pads, squelchy bass tones and the odd acoustic instruments. The Theremin sounds alone are worth the price tag. The fun part is creating 8-beat loops in which you can control the tempo and the scales of the instruments selected. I've already "composed" a few pieces using just the Korg and will most likely start incorporating

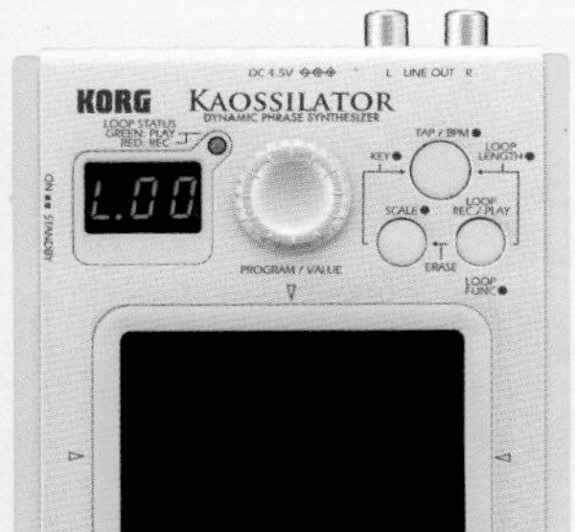

it into GarageBand or, perhaps, Max/MSP once my visual programming chops get happening. My only complaint is you can't edit or remove instruments/sounds as you layer them or control individual volumes. Still, I highly recommend the Korg for beginners and semi-pros that haven't got a cache of gear and/or software. For standalone equipment, I don't think there's anything really comparable to the Kaossilator, except it's cousin, the Mini Kaoss Pad, which is more for effects.

A hobbyist that was a session drummer in another life (before children), it's limiting to how often I can make music. Drummers have to deal with the confines of noise volumes (the neighbors), the amount of space required and the portability of your gear. Plus, your output is restricted to mainly the rhythmic aspects of music as well as performing in the more traditional acoustic genres. With two small children, I don't get to play with the Kaossilator as often as I'd like, but the one-year-old loves to see and hear it in action. While you can use the sounds to record with in your audio software, you can also just plug in headphones and experience your public transit commuting time diminish exponentially. I've taken it out of the house a few times. It runs on either a 4.5V adapter (not included) or 4 AA batteries (included). I have yet to really clock the amount of time used with just the batteries, but it's been a lot longer than you'd get on a laptop.

-- Gord Fynes

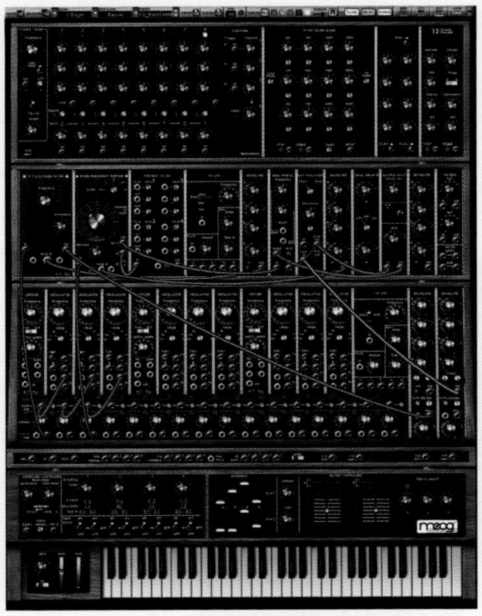

Software synthesizer

Moog Modular

$99 Amazon

I remember the first time I encountered a Moog Synthesizer: Switched-On Bach. I was all of 14-years-old and absolutely captivated. All those knobs and patch cords. And then there were the sounds that it made. To an adolescent boy growing up in the mid-late '60s whose hero was Mr. Spock, it was like a futuristic dream come true — my own musical version of the Starship Enterprise and for only a few thousand dollars. The Last Whole Earth Catalog even featured a review of it by Wendy Carlos herself!

Then I learned how much a few thousand dollars actually was. I tinkered with resisters and capacitors, transistors and chokes, but I couldn't do anything like that. But this is what led me inexorably to a career in music and recording. Well, and the Beatles helped, too. Flash forward 41 years and many synthesizers, guitars and amps later, I still could not seem to afford that big gleaming Moog dream.

Then a company called Arturia released a virtual software version of my childhood Holy Grail, the Moog Modular V. And there were nine — count 'em, nine! — oscillators. Filters, envelope generators. A fixed filter bank. A sample and hold module. A bank of configurable mixers. And with enough computer firepower, I could finally make the sounds I'd heard Wendy Carlos make. The software even has stereo chorus and delay lines, a very neat addition to the package to fatten up your sound without having to use any outboard effects. And did I mention polyphony? Yes, unlike its hardware predecessor, the Moog Modular V offers up to 32 voices, if you have the processor power to deliver them.

I've been using this powerful, flexible piece of software for almost four years now and I have to admit that it does almost everything I ever wanted a music synthesizer to do. It does things the hardware version couldn't even do. My only complaint is latency (delay). I would never use it live, but then again I haven't been playing live these days, and if I did, I'd probably sample off the sounds I want to use and do it that way. The software can be used stand alone or as a plugin, for Mac or Windows OS.

-- Jeff Bragg

Synthesizers

Best virtual piano
Pianoteq 4
$125 pianoteq.com

I'm not a musical purist. As a composer for video games and films, I'm totally for electronic instruments that can mimic acoustic instruments. I work on tight budgets and I don't have, for example, a grand piano sitting in my office. Even if I did, pianos are notoriously difficult to mic -- that takes a fair amount of skill and a room with great acoustics, which I also don't have. Synthesized pianos -- meaning sample-based software synthesizers that run on your computer -- are a "good enough" alternative, yet less than perfect.

Every time you hit a note on the keyboard, the synthesizer fetches a sample of an actual recorded piano (that resides on the hard drive of your computer) and plays it back for you. The downside to this sort of technology is: a) Sampled pianos never sound absolutely real because they can't mimic the vast complexity of a real piano, and b) All those large samples take a while to load into your computer's memory as well as taking up a significant

amount of space on your hard drive.

Enter Pianoteq (stand alone or plug-in Mac or Windows). It uses a type of synthesis called Physical Modelling, which recreates the original instrument mathematically. In the case of the piano, this involves modelling the hammers, the strings, the soundboard, and even the pedals. And it's hands down the most true-sounding synthesized piano I've ever played. Pianoteq captures the sounds of every key at every velocity. It accurately captures harmonics when I press the sustain pedal down. Or that weird (wonderful) buzzing in lowest octave. I'm not a maestro but, in a taste test, I can't tell the difference between a recording of Pianoteq and a recording of a real piano.

But it gets better still. Using sliders, Pianoteq allows me to tweak and adjust practically every aspect of the physical model. No piano or any other synthesized piano that I know of can do this. I can adjust how much hammer noise I want to hear, or what point on the strings the hammers hits. I can change the length of the soundboard or the length of the strings, mute the strings, mic the piano in a virtual space, and on and on. All of this dramatically changes the sound. I can start with a piano that sounds like a Bosendorfer and, in a matter of seconds, I can end up with something that sounds almost percussive, but

still very acoustic. Or I can tweak the sound toward something more bell-like.

Because Pianoteq is algorithmically based, it's small... a mere 20 megabytes. Its sampled cousins weigh in at hefty 2 - 4 gigabytes and require around 4 gigabytes of internal memory. The upshot of this: Pianoteq loads lightning fast, which is a nice plus when I'm in the middle of writing music (or just fiddling around).

Before I encountered Pianoteq, I had always partially hid sampled pianos under a veil of other instruments. Using Pianoteq I now tend to feature pianos or even solo pia-

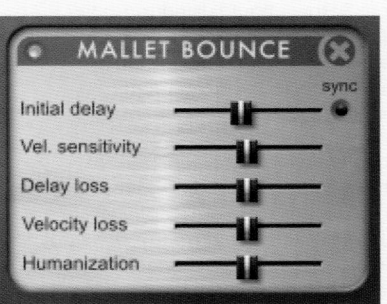

nos, because they sound real. And rich. From my perspective, now I have any number of virtual pianos sitting around in my office, from a wide variety of grands, to uprights, to antique grands, to old detuned pianos, etc....

-- Robyn Miller

● The Condition slider allows you to modify the state of the instrument, from freshly tuned to completely worn out. After a right click on the slider, changing the Random seed parameter will allow you to enjoy thousands of broken instrument variations.

Easiest synth
OP-1 Portable Synthesizer
$850 Teenage Engineering

Musicians beware! The OP-1 is a synthesizer that some may love and others may dismiss as a mere overpriced "toy".

For myself, Teenage Engineering's OP-1 has been an indispensable addition to my synth arsenal: partly because it produces sounds I can't find elsewhere and partly because it's so incredibly easy (and yes, even fun) to use.

The color-base interface took me by surprise! There's practically no learning curve for adjusting the eight separate sound engines (and effects) -- the machine is highly visual in this regard. In fact I love handing my OP-1 to non-musicians and watching them as they almost instantly begin "programming" a sound. For a performer, this kind of ease-of-use is power: to effortlessly turn a few knobs and get to the sound one is after. No fiddling around. In this regard, the OP-1 is a musician's instrument.

The portability is a nice plus. I can throw it into a backpack, take it anywhere, sketch out an idea for a song anywhere (using it's built-in "four-track recorder" which operates much like a reel-to-reel tape). They advertise the batteries to last 16 hours... I haven't tested that, but I have no frustrations in that regard.

More coolness about the OP-1:

* It has four intelligently designed sequencers that I absolutely love and continually use.

* Teenage Engineering occasionally releases new system updates with added functionality (new synth engines, new drum machines, etc...) And new new accessories, such as pitch bending knob and crank wheels for added functionality.

* It features both a built in microphone and a built in FM radio for sampling.

Is there anything bad about the OP-1? Yeah, its price. $849 is a lot to spend on any hardware synth where software synths are beginning to cost less and less.

I do wish the keyboard was more substantial. The Korg NanoKey midi controller is just a little larger and it has a nice resistance (and is velocity sensitive), whereas the keyboard on the OP-1 feel a bit cheap.

Is is a toy? I don't believe so. I just produced a movie soundtrack and I often used the OP-1 for sounds I couldn't achieve with any other synth. As an electronic musician, I now depend on it. It may not be for everyone, but it's a great machine for use in the studio and, because of its small size and ease of use, it's probably an even better instrument for use on stage.

The interface of the OP-1 is entirely color-based and very intuitive. For example: the knob changes the blue number on the screen, the white knob changes the white number. The following video (about one of the sequencers) demonstrates this...

-- Robyn Miller

Bargain professional sound recording
Zoom H2 Handy Recorder
$350 Amazon

Quality digital recorders have shrunk to the point where they fit *inside* a hi-fi microphone, like this Zoom model. You can hold the mic and the recorder in one hand. This very compact recorder/mic can capture music in the studio or in the field at surprising high audio quality in stereo. I am more interested in recording voice and sounds for radio, and flash-card-based units like this one are more than adequate for that purpose. I was guided to the Zoom by the audio geeks at Transom, an online hangout for radio journalists. They review the best gear for NPR reporters and the like. (This stuff changes quickly so check Transom's tool area for the latest recommendations.)

I've been using the Zoom H2 because it was among the least expensive choices for a professional level digital sound recorder. It contains its own decent microphones (no fooling around with auxiliary plugs, boosters, adapters, etc.), it records on cheap flash cards, it has an earphone jack so you can monitor the actual feed, and it comes with a nifty removable handle so I can hold it in front of interviewees. It also comes with a

short mini-stand for studio recording. The Zoom H2 gets good marks for the quality of the mic and stereo recording. The resulting edited files sound as crisp and full as anything you'll hear on radio or CD. And the street price for this microphone/recorder combo is about $180.

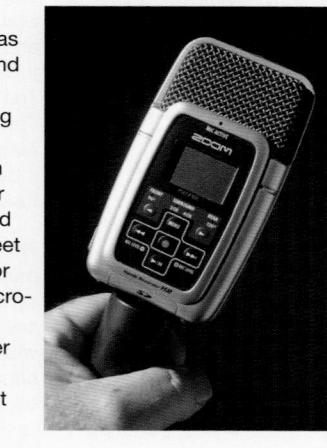

Remember when $200 digital cameras were able to take a picture as rich and detailed as a professional 35mm camera? Recorders like the Zoom H2 have crossed a similar threshold for sound. For under $200 you can record music, voice, sound at a quality nearly undistinguishable (for 95% of uses) from anything a professional model would do.

-- KK

Guide to hacking music
Handmade Electronic Music
$35 Nicolas Collins, 2009, 360 p.

Dense, detailed instructions on hacking electronic devices to play music. Some projects run at simple beginner level, some require ease with chip electronics. At 340 pages, the possibility space of electronic sound is well explored. "Experimental" is the signature tune.

-- KK

You can also make a pretty efficient driver by gluing a cork to the center of a small loud-

speaker. Connect any sound source through an amplifier to the corked speaker and hold the speaker against a sheet of metal, drumhead, cymbal, etc. The cork should vibrate the material and process the original signal. You may want to pick up the vibrating surface with a contact mike. The end of cork can be treated to

further affect the sound: a thumbtack brightens it (like a honky-tonk piano), while a piece of felt softens it, and wood is somewhere in between.

A corked speaker

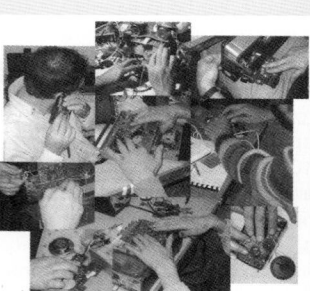

Laying of Hands: Transporting a Portable Radio into a Synthesizer by making Your Skin Part of the Circuit

Laurie Anderson's "Tape Bow Violin" (built in 1977 in collaboration with Bob Bielecki-see Art & Music 11 "The Luthiers," Chapter 28) substitutes a tape head for the bridge, and a strip of tape for the hair of the bow; the tape contains a recording that Anderson plays backwards and forwards as she draws the bow across the head. "I began to work with audio palindromes, words that produced different words when reversed. Audio palindromes are not predictable like written palindromes ('god' is always 'dog' spelled backwards). With a lot of experimentation I produced songs for 'The Tape Bow Violin' that could be played forwards and backwards."

THE TAPE-BOW VIOLIN

TO PREAMP

TAPE HEAD

AUDIOTAPE INSTEAD OF HORSEHAIR

Talent hits a target no one else can hit; genius hits a target no one else can see. - Arthur Schopenhauer

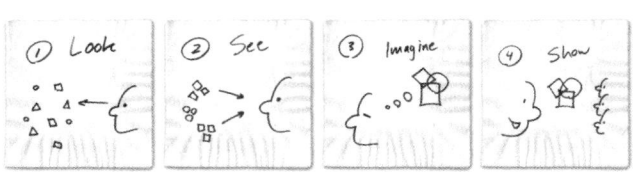

The Process of Visual Thinking

① Look → ② See → ③ Imagine → ④ Show

Think with a pencil
The Back of the Napkin

$16 Dan Roam, 2013, 304 p.

How to use simple drawings to figure out solutions. The task is not at all about how to draw well or communicate clearly (see other guides on p. 359). Instead quick and dirty doodles, small enough that they can fit on the back of a napkin, are a way to think aloud with a pencil. There was an old book with that title (*Thinking with a Pencil*), but this one is better. It shows how to use rough diagrams and charts as a language for problem solving.

-- KK

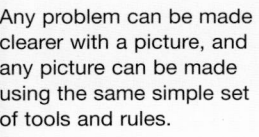

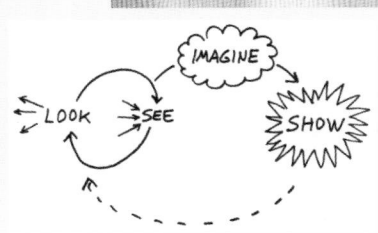

• Any problem can be made clearer with a picture, and any picture can be made using the same simple set of tools and rules.

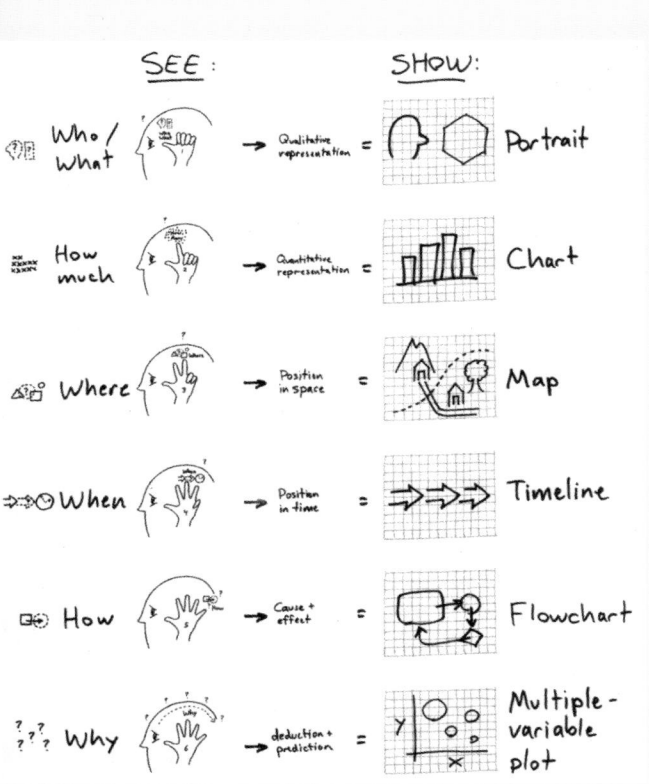

SEE: / SHOW:

Who/What → Qualitative representation = Portrait

How much → Quantitative representation = Chart

Where → Position in space = Map

When → Position in time = Timeline

How → Cause + effect = Flowchart

Why → deduction + prediction = Multiple-variable plot

The six ways we see and the six ways we show.

Online guide to charts & diagrams
A Periodic Table of Visualization Methods

Free Dr. Martin J. Eppler & Ralph Lengler

If you've ever wondered how to model something, or were looking for new ideas for segmenting and presenting complex concepts, this is an incredible online resource. A neat graphical explanation and example of each "element" (ex; a cycle diagram) appears as soon as your cursor scrolls over them. What I like most is that the categorisers have thoroughly sliced the categorising! For instance, they've color-coded their categories: data, metaphor, concept, strategy, information, and compound visualisation techniques. As if that were not enough to spark your brain, the creators also provide clues as to whether the model works best for convergent or divergent thinking, and whether it is more for an overview vs. detailed perspective. So far, I have used it mostly for inspiration, especially the metaphor models, but this resource has given me ideas and structure and the appropriate language for my work as a process designer and facilitator. I also passed this onto a 7th grade teacher friend of mine who is using it with his entire class!

-- Jodie Engleberg

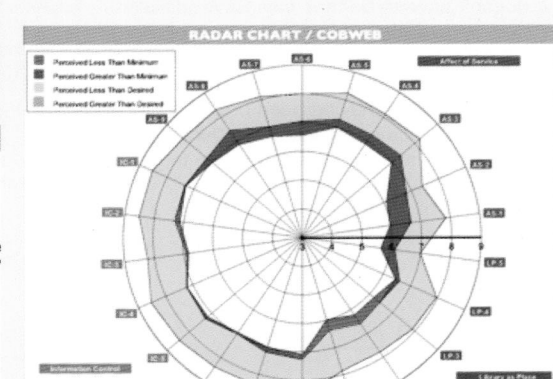

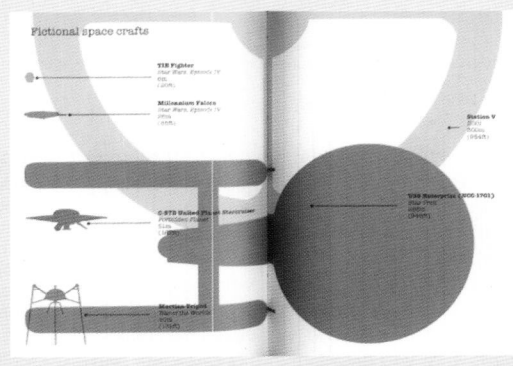

Quick info via graphics
Visual Aid

$12 Draught Associates, 2008, 196 p.

The toughest challenge with conveying information in any context is concision. This simple little reference presents *a lot* of random facts in less than 200 pages with a cleverness and colorful style that's well worth emulating.

-- Steven Leckart

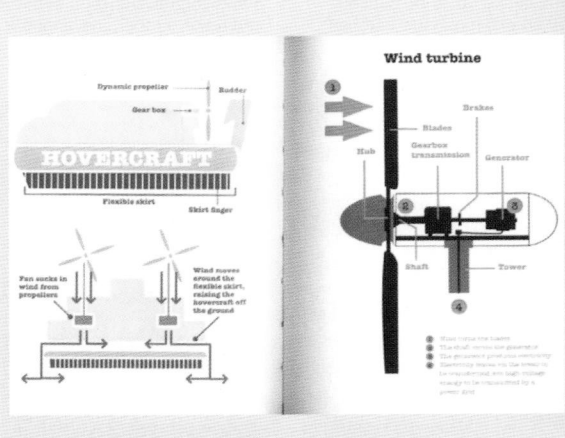

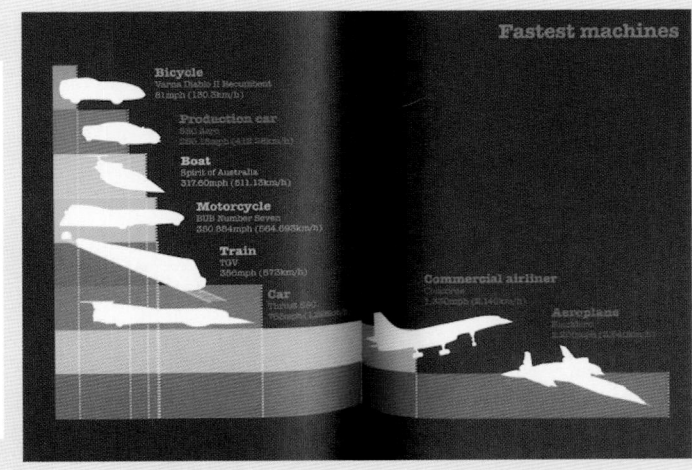

How to make charts
The Visual Display of Quantitative Information

$28 Edward R. Tufte, 2001, 200 p.

Big data needs taming. The most direct way to get a hold on data is to display it visually. This tome is the granddaddy of guides to help you present data in a clear, responsible, and accurate way. It is clear and accurate itself. With many exquisite examples of what to do and what not to do, it will assist you in creating intelligent user interfaces, coherent graphs, concise diagrams, persuasive presentations, and precise scientific illustrations. Read and heed. If you find Mr. Tufte useful, he's created three follow-up volumes with further examples and lessons.

-- KK

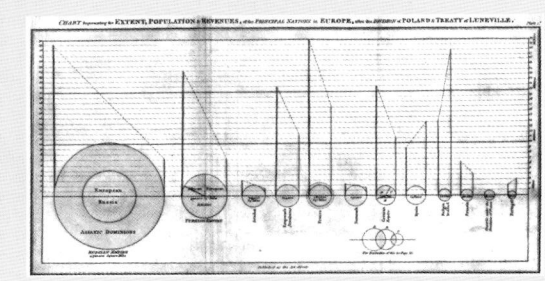

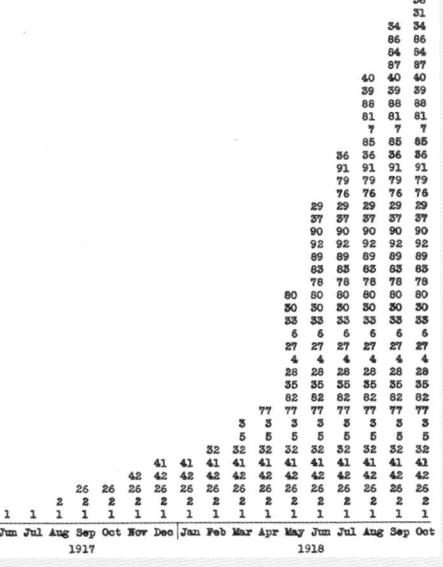

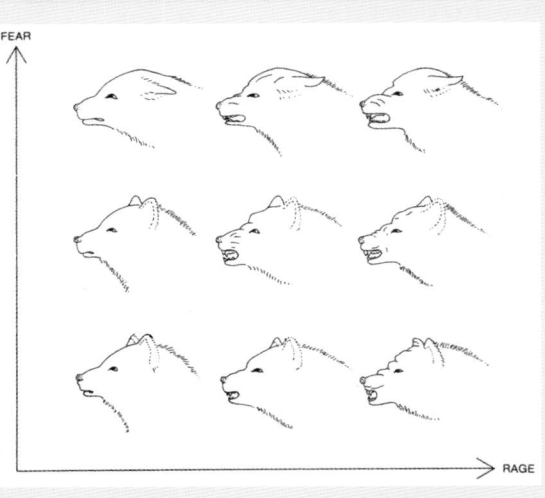

How to give good slides
Beyond Bullet Points
$18 Cliff Atkinson, 2011 (3rd Edition), 352 p.

A great PowerPoint presentation is a story well-told. A bad PowerPoint is a mind-deadener. Thousands of businesspeople are snoozing away at this moment as slide after slide of fancy-transitioned words, words, and more bulleted words evaporate a fortune in productivity. Don't get me started on how badly made PowerPoint presentations are blunting the sharpest minds of today's college students.

It doesn't have to be that way! Beyond Bullet Points shows you how to achieve excellence in presentations. I just looked at my bookshelf and noticed that my third copy of Beyond Bullet Points is missing, having been pressed into the hands of some startled friend, executive, teacher, activist, who was only trying to get out the door of my office.

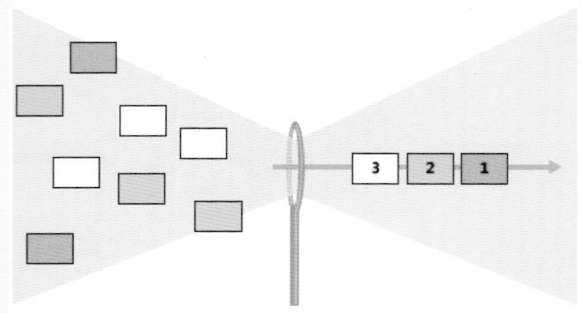

FIGURE 3-1 The formidable challenge every presenter faces—the limited capacity of working memory.

Here's what it teaches in a nutshell: The medium of PowerPoint is one of visual storytelling. An excellent presentation is an excellent story. So, the structure of the story is first. Then a storyboard is needed. A storyboard is a series of sketches, or notes, about what you will talk about. These are not bullet points that the audience are meant to read, but visual reminders about what you are planning to say. Last, and least important, you add the words or text. The images rule! You can download admirable Word templates from the book's website, and get

started storyboarding right away.

Following the approach of this book, I have spent dozens of hours storyboarding my own recent presentations, and hundreds of dollars on custom photographs and image research. It has paid off. I've used this approach on all kinds of audiences all over the world, and it works. Right now, anyone using these techniques has a strategic advantage in being heard — after listening to the second or third speaker reading words on the screen, audiences who see a well-orchestrated visual accompaniment to a well-plotted narrative start waking up and paying attention.

Do not advance one slide further without reading this book.

-- Howard Rheingold

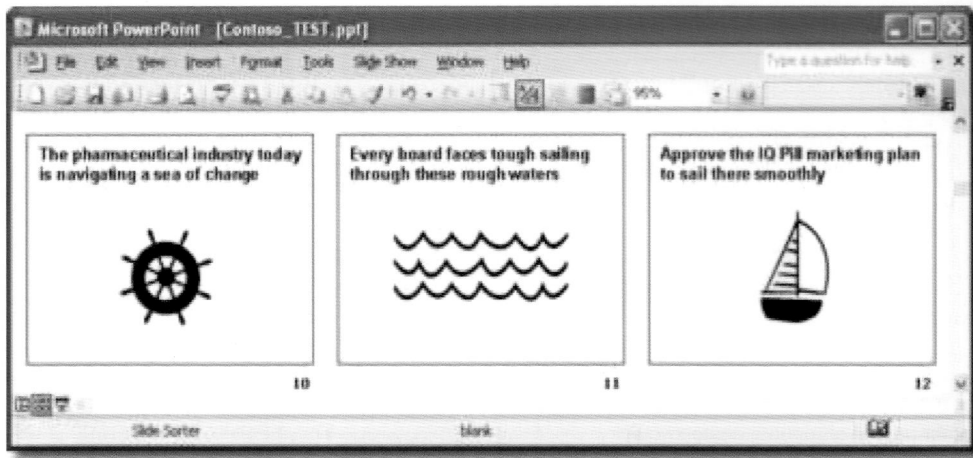

The emerging storyboard

- It might sound counterintuitive, but when you put less information on a slide, you increase the audience's attention because the audience is then dependent on the speaker for explanation, and the speaker is dependent on the audience for feedback.

- The protagonist of every presentation is your audience, and you are a supporting character. This is the crucial spin on crafting stories for live presentations.

- Stories are about how people respond to something that has changed in their environment. We like stories of how other people handle changes in circumstances and what their choices reveal about their characters.

When a protagonist experiences a change, an imbalance is created because things are no longer like they used to be. In screenwriting, this change is called the inciting incident that sets a story in motion. Scene 3 of the story template should help your audience to understand why they are there for the presentation — usually, because a change has happened that has created an imbalance.

Defining the imbalance that has brought everyone to the presentation can be easy or difficult, depending on your situation. The imbalance could be caused by a crisis brought on by an external force that has changed your organization's environment, such as a

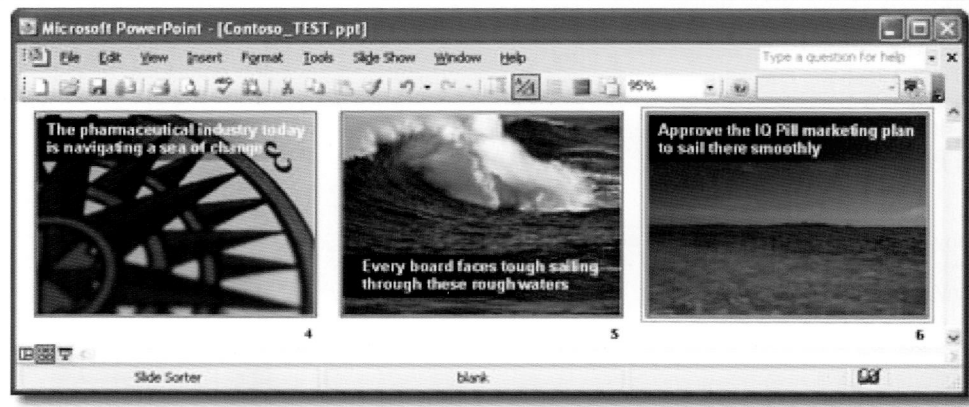

With images in place

sudden economic shift or the action of a competitor. It could be the result of an internal change, such as a revised opinion or mindset, a new piece of information, a new research report, or an anecdote from the field.

- Once you get the hang of writing an Act 1 with your group, try applying these techniques to other communications scenarios beyond your PowerPoint presentations. Crafting Act 1 of a presentation is a problem-solving framework that can also help a group to clarify strategy, develop marketing messages, create project plans, and resolve other challenges.

Best guide for presentations
Presentation Zen
$20 Garr Reynolds, 2011 (2nd Edition), 312 p.

By now there is a teachable logic to making a world-class presentation. Once you master the story-telling principles needed for a great slide show as taught in Beyond Bullet Points, you can focus on perfecting the visual presentation of your ideas. This enhances the cinematic vs the script. Among the many guides offering design advice, this one is the best. Watch some of the most popular TED talks online (including mine) and you'll see this advice in action. I can vouch that it will raise your impact.

-- KK

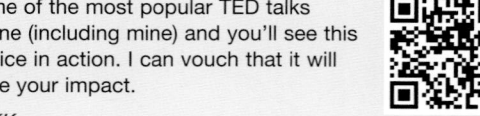

What is my absolutely central point?

Or put it this way: If the audience could remember only one thing (and you'll be lucky if they do), what do you want it to be?

- Empty space is not nothing; it is a powerful something. Learn to see and manipulate empty space to give your slide designs greater organization, clarity, and interest.

Use the principle of repetition to repeat selected elements throughout your slides. This can help give your slides unity and organization.

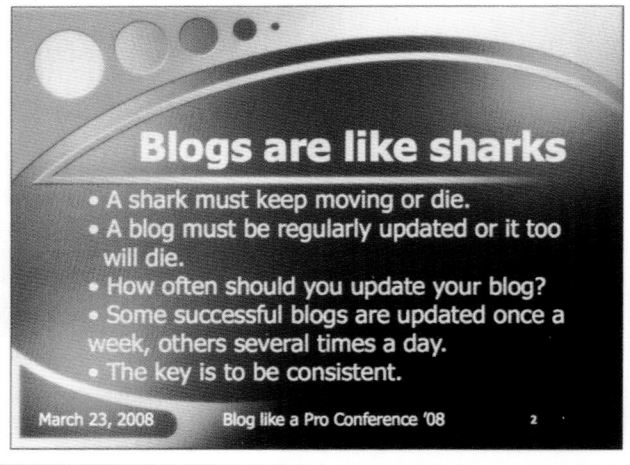

A traditional slide which duplicates the presenter's words. More of a reading test than a visual.

This slide serves to enhance the presenter's spoken words much better. The photo has impact and the point is made clearly. Which slide is more memorable? And since people are not reading, they can actually listen to you. (Photo of shark from iStockphoto.com.)

The slide on the left has a busy template which makes the useful area of the slide about 1/3 smaller. The slide on the right uses the image to cover the entire slide. The text is clearly foreground and the image serves both as background and at time foreground, making the overall visual more dynamic and more unified with a cleaner, more dramatic look.

We don't know a millionth of one percent about anything. - Thomas Edison

A guiding philosophy of type
Elements of Typographic Style
$18 Robert Bringhurst, 2013, 382 p.

For a long while I've been looking for an expert who could guide me through the complex world of typography. I didn't need another artsy typographical design book. I wanted a reliable friend who could introduce me to the philosophy of type and then also practically guide me through the jungle of fonts to ones that work best. Mr. Bringhurst is that guru. Under his apprentice I understood for the first time how to architecturally shape a page with text, as if I were building a house. I figured out when to kern, or not. Now I find myself drawn back to his study every time I need to craft a book, a webpage, or format a report. The wisdom and experience in this book is astounding. It's for anyone who makes words visible. That's all of us. The book is regularly updated. Blessings on Bringhurst.

-- KK

• Too little kerning is preferable to too much, and inconsistent kerning is worse than none.

• Choose faces that will survive, and if possible, prosper, under the final printing conditions.

Bembo and Centaur, Spectrum and Palatino, are subtle and beautiful alphabets, but if you are setting 8 pt text with a laser printer on plain paper at 300 dpi, the refined forms of these faces will be rubbed into the coarse digital mud of the imaging process. If the final output will be 14 pt text set directly to film at 3000 dpi, then printed by good offset lithography on the best coated paper, every nuance may be crystal clear, but the result will still lack the character and texture of the letterpress medium for which these faces were designed.

Some for the most innocent looking faces are actually the most difficult to render by digital means. Optima, for example — an unserifed and apparently uncomplicated face — is constructed entirely of subtle tapers and curves that can be adequately rendered only at the highest resolutions.

Faces with blunt and substantial serifs, open counters, gentle modelling and minimal pretensions to aristocratic grace stand the best chance of surviving the indignities of low resolution. Amasis, Caecilia, Lucida, Stone and Utopia, for example, while they prosper at high resolutions, are faces that will also survive under cruder conditions lethal to Centaur, Spectrum, Linotype Didot or almost any version of Bodoni.

• Start with a single typographic family

Most pages, and most entire documents, can be set perfectly well with only one family of type. But perhaps the page confronting you requires a chapter title, two or three levels of subheads, an epigraph, a text in two languages, block quotations within the text, a couple of mathematical equations, a bar graph, several explanatory sidenotes, and captions for photographs and a map. An extended type family, such as Legacy, Lucida, or Stone, may provide sufficient resources even for this task. Another possibility is Gerard Unger's comprehensive series known as Demos, Praxis and Flora – which is a family with no surname to unite it. Each of these series includes both roman and italic in a range of weights, matching serifed and unserifed forms, and other variations. If you restrict yourself to faces within the family, you can have variety and homogeneity at the same time: many shapes and sizes but a single typographic culture. Such an approach is well suited to some texts, poorly suited to others.

• In medieval Europe, most books, though certainly not all, settled down to proportions ranging from 1:1.5 to 1:1.25. Paper – once the mills were built in Europe – was commonly made in sheets whose proportions were 2:3 [1:1.5] or 3:4 [1:1.33]. These proportions, which correspond to the acoustically perfect musical intervals of fifth and fourth, also reproduce one another with each fold. If a sheet is 40x60 cm [2:3] to start with, it folds to 30x40 [3:4], which folds to 20x30, and so on. The 25x38 inch [roughly 2:3] and 20 x 25 inch [roughly 3:4] press sheets used in North America today are survivors of this medieval tradition.

The page proportion which is now the European standard was also known to the medieval scribes. And the tall half octagon page, 1:1.3 (the shape enshrined now in North American letter paper) has a similar pedigree. The British Museum has a Roman wax-tablet book of precisely this proportion, dated about AD 300.

• The textblock itself, in this example, is symmetrical, but it is placed asymmetrically on the page. The lefthand page is a mirror image of the right, but no mirror image runs the other way. The two-page spread is symmetrical horizontally – the direction in which the pages turn, either backward or forward, as the reader consults the book – but it is asymmetrical vertically – the direction in which the page stays put while the reader's eye repeatedly works its way in one direction: down.

• Perhaps fifty per cent of the character and integrity of a printed page lies in its letterforms. Much of the other fifty per cent resides in its margins.

• In Bibles and other large works, running heads have been standard equipment for two thousand years. Photocopying machines, which can easily separate a chapter or a page from the rest of a book or journal, have also given running heads (and running feet, or footers) new importance.

Except as insurance against photocopying pirates, running heads are nevertheless pointless in many books and documents with a strong authorial voice or a unified subject. They remain essential in most anthologies and works of reference, large or small.

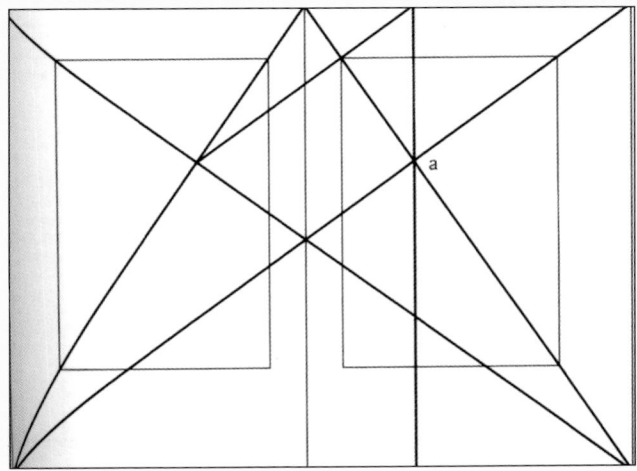

Quickest personal font
MyScriptFont
Free MyScriptFont.com

I've long wanted a font based on my own hand. The easiest, cheapest and quickest way is MyScriptFont. To get my personal script, I wrote out an alphabet on their printed-out template (block letters only, no cursive), scanned the sheet and uploaded it, and then installed the scaleable font they handed back. It's free. Takes only minutes.

Once I had my handprinting font, I figured I could quickly make other homemade fonts. It's a quick cheap way to make any kind of unique hand-drawn font you want.

-- KK

Access to the full diversity of fonts
MyFonts
myfonts.com

Someone from Europe posted me a letter and I fell in love with the text's unusual font. It turned out to be Scala Sans, a font created ten years ago by a Dutch typographer, Martin Majoor. I bought a copy of the typeface on MyFonts and now use it everywhere I can.

It wasn't too long ago that only about 271 people in the world cared about typographic fonts and kerning and serif trapping. Then PCs turned typography from a black art into a tool for the masses. Getting and installing a particularly distinctive font is a no-brainer on the web, and yes, one can learn to use it with grace. (See The Elements of Typographical Style elsewhere on this site).

The best portal into the world of typography is the website My Fonts. They have over 23,000 fonts from just about every known foundry (many just one person shops), and a pretty good way to navigate among all those choices. Their "more fonts like this one" option is helpful. With a forum for newbies the site is very friendly to those just starting out and for pros, too.

There is one small weirdness about type that is worth pointing out. The differences between two fonts may be hardly noticeable in their details, although the effect of each font is pronounced. It's a lot like wine; it's hard to describe why good ones are good. If you find a typeface in a magazine or brochure that you really like it can be extremely difficult to identify that face by name. There is no working heuristic for identifying fonts. You may be forced to ask a type maven, if you know one. Or, you can try a new service of My Font called WhatTheFont? Scan your typeface and submit it to the site; it will identify it.

-- KK

Free novelty fonts
1001 Free Fonts
1001freefonts.com

You can never have too many fonts. Here are hundreds of wonderfully creative ones which you might use once in a lifetime — and since they are free, why not be bold? The site has a cute preview window so you can try out text in the new style before bothering to download. I've download lots of these for various one-time uses.

-- KK

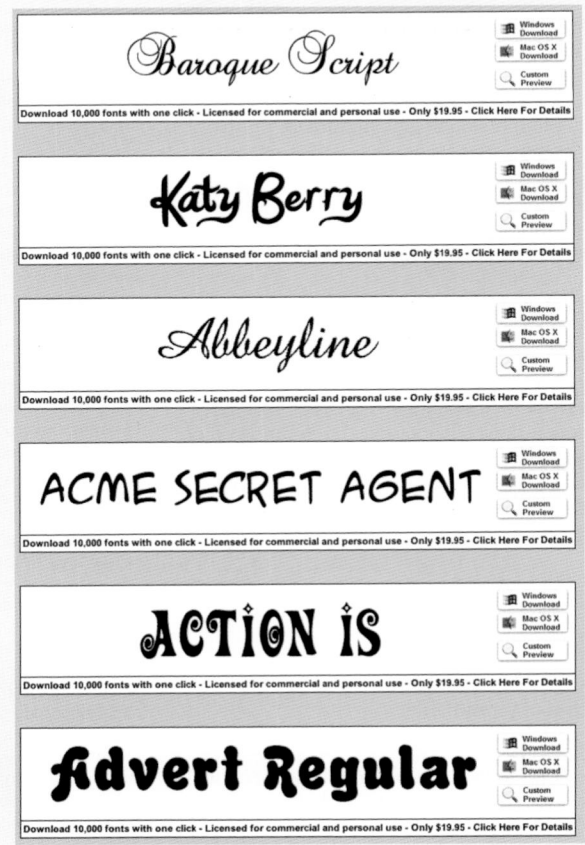

There are only two ways to live your life. One is as though nothing is a miracle. The other is as though everything is a miracle. - Albert Einstein

343

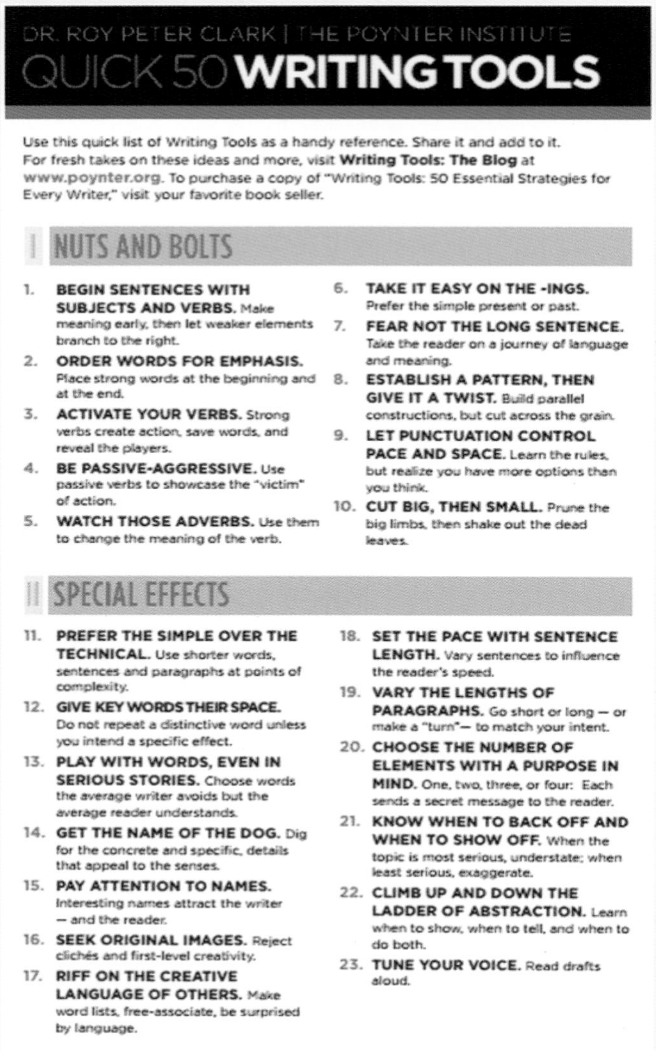
DR. ROY PETER CLARK | THE POYNTER INSTITUTE

QUICK 50 WRITING TOOLS

Use this quick list of Writing Tools as a handy reference. Share it and add to it. For fresh takes on these ideas and more, visit **Writing Tools: The Blog** at www.poynter.org. To purchase a copy of "Writing Tools: 50 Essential Strategies for Every Writer," visit your favorite book seller.

I NUTS AND BOLTS

1. **BEGIN SENTENCES WITH SUBJECTS AND VERBS.** Make meaning early, then let weaker elements branch to the right.
2. **ORDER WORDS FOR EMPHASIS.** Place strong words at the beginning and at the end.
3. **ACTIVATE YOUR VERBS.** Strong verbs create action, save words, and reveal the players.
4. **BE PASSIVE-AGGRESSIVE.** Use passive verbs to showcase the "victim" of action.
5. **WATCH THOSE ADVERBS.** Use them to change the meaning of the verb.
6. **TAKE IT EASY ON THE -INGS.** Prefer the simple present or past.
7. **FEAR NOT THE LONG SENTENCE.** Take the reader on a journey of language and meaning.
8. **ESTABLISH A PATTERN, THEN GIVE IT A TWIST.** Build parallel constructions, but cut across the grain.
9. **LET PUNCTUATION CONTROL PACE AND SPACE.** Learn the rules, but realize you have more options than you think.
10. **CUT BIG, THEN SMALL.** Prune the big limbs, then shake out the dead leaves.

II SPECIAL EFFECTS

11. **PREFER THE SIMPLE OVER THE TECHNICAL.** Use shorter words, sentences and paragraphs at points of complexity.
12. **GIVE KEY WORDS THEIR SPACE.** Do not repeat a distinctive word unless you intend a specific effect.
13. **PLAY WITH WORDS, EVEN IN SERIOUS STORIES.** Choose words the average writer avoids but the average reader understands.
14. **GET THE NAME OF THE DOG.** Dig for the concrete and specific, details that appeal to the senses.
15. **PAY ATTENTION TO NAMES.** Interesting names attract the writer — and the reader.
16. **SEEK ORIGINAL IMAGES.** Reject clichés and first-level creativity.
17. **RIFF ON THE CREATIVE LANGUAGE OF OTHERS.** Make word lists, free-associate, be surprised by language.
18. **SET THE PACE WITH SENTENCE LENGTH.** Vary sentences to influence the reader's speed.
19. **VARY THE LENGTHS OF PARAGRAPHS.** Go short or long — or make a "turn"— to match your intent.
20. **CHOOSE THE NUMBER OF ELEMENTS WITH A PURPOSE IN MIND.** One, two, three, or four: Each sends a secret message to the reader.
21. **KNOW WHEN TO BACK OFF AND WHEN TO SHOW OFF.** When the topic is most serious, understate; when least serious, exaggerate.
22. **CLIMB UP AND DOWN THE LADDER OF ABSTRACTION.** Learn when to show, when to tell, and when to do both.
23. **TUNE YOUR VOICE.** Read drafts aloud.

The best writing tips

Writing Tools

This two-sided page contains the wisdom of an entire book on how to write better. Nay, it distills an entire shelf of the world's greatest writing manuals (and I have them all). After 30 years as both a writer and editor I can't think of much I would add to these 50 short tips. This PDF is now my favorite guide to writing well. You can print it out for free. If you want its pithy reminders fleshed out with more examples, see the book form, or the website. But the free tip sheet itself — one paper printed both sides — rewards a quick review anytime you get down to serious writing..

-- *KK*

14. Get the Name of the Dog. Dig for the concrete and specific, details that appeal to the senses.

18. Set the Pace with Sentence Length. Vary sentences to influence the reader's speed.

23. Tune Your Voice. Read drafts aloud.

Free Google Docs

$10 Roy Peter Clark, 2008, 272 p.

How to liveblog a conference

Tips for Conference Bloggers

Free PDF Bruno Giussani & Ethan Zuckerman, 2007, 6 p.

There's an emerging new media I use more and more: an online summary of a conference. Known as live-blogging, it presents a synopsis of each presentation, talk-by-talk, in nearly real time. This saves you time and money traveling to distant cities, and suffering through introductions and equipment failures. At its best, reading the live-blog can be better than attending the talk. All the chaff has been winnowed, and almost every talk captured. (Most conference attendees don't even get to every talk.) Video recordings of conferences are becoming more popular, but a good liveblog is much quicker to scan and digest. But at its worse, a liveblog will offer little more than snarky comments about the speaker.

At the creation end, you need some skills to separate the best from the worst. Ethan Zuckerman, of Geek Corp, is one of the best conference bloggers alive. He teamed up with Bruno Giussani, another star liveblogger, to produce this free short 6-page PDF booklet on how to blog a conference with effectiveness. When you blog a conference it forces you to pay attention. My first book *Out of Control* began as an online blog of every talk at the first Artificial Life Conference (although no one called it blogging in 1987). The requisite focus of summarizing each talk clarified many ideas for me, and the response to the "blog" of the conference encouraged me to write a book. Other livebloggers find the same. They listen harder, and remember more.

Get good at this and you have a free pass to many high-priced conferences. Organizers are increasingly looking for first-rate liveblogers to generate press and future attendees. Or, like Ethan you can generate your own audience who follow you because your liveblogging skills.

-- *KK*

•

It's relatively easy to blog good and great speakers: They follow a narrative path through their talks and speak at a pace the audience can understand. It's harder to blog inexperienced speakers(because they may be too technical, confusing, fast, etc.) and multispeaker panels (because the discussion can take many different unstructured turns). But you don't need to transcribe the whole talk, you need to capture the gist of it. A 20-minutes talk can often be summarized in a 20-lines post.

•

Always remember that what you're writing will be read by people who weren't in the room, so they haven't seen the slides, the video, or the gesture. Hence, you have to compensate for the lack of context. Don't be afraid to create a narrative by saying "He shows a slide with data on ..." or "She walks on stage carrying a big suitcase" or "He shows a YouTube video" etc. And if the speaker shows a YouTube video, or a picture, remember that you're online: Open another browser window, go to YouTube, find that video, and link to it; or go to the speaker's website, find that picture or another similar or related item, and link to it (or republish the picture within your post). Yes, this requires effective multitasking. It's at the root of conference blogging.

•

Conferences usually give out a program ahead of time. Use it to prepare for blogging: Do a quick Google search for each speaker, and save (in the same text file) links to their sites, blogs, and the institutions they're affiliated with; write a one-or-two-sentences "biography" for each; and for the speakers you've never heard of, try to get a general sense of who they are and what they do. To write the mini-biography, use also the speaker information distributed by the conference organizers (booklet, website, etc.). For the key speakers, save a picture on your laptop (from their websites) and pre-format it for Web use, in case you will need it. If you prepare sufficiently, you've got the first paragraph of each post almost written ahead of time.

The best thesaurus ever

The Synonym Finder

$13 J.I. Rodale, 1986, 1361 p.

This is the best thesaurus there is. It supplies more synonyms, analogs, parallels, equivalents and comparable words in English than any other source, online or off. No other thesaurus comes near to it for completeness or breadth. Compiled in dictionary form, like the one in your word processors, there's no index or cross-referencing. Just look up a word, any word, and it proceeds to overwhelm you with alternative choices (a total of 1.5 million synonyms are presented in 1,361 pages), including short phrases and only mildly related words. Rather than being a problem of imprecision, the Finder's broad inclusiveness prods your imagination and prompts your recall.

Its single downside, however, is a major frustration: it is not available digitally, in a form compatible to the way most people write these days. It should live on your computer in a pull-down option, or plug-in for Word or the like. I'm totally baffled why it is not. As it is, it's a huge fat book — a great book! — sitting within arm's reach when I write, but not near enough for the power that it offers.

-- *KK*

My comparison of four thesauruses using the terms COOL and TOOL:

•

Microsoft Word's Thesaurus

COOL – cold, chill, chilly, fresh, breezy, fashionable, trendy, hip, with it, offhand, unfriendly, icy, distant, detached, frosty, frigid, unenthusiastic, freshen, muted.

TOOL – gear, tackle, utensil, apparatus, paraphernalia.

•

Merriam-Webster Online Thesaurus

COOL — Synonyms: aloof, antisocial, cold, detached, distant, frosty, remote, standoffish, unsociable, chill, refrigerate. Related Words: introverted, reclusive, reserved, withdrawn; misanthropic; apathetic, indifferent, unconcerned; disinterested, incurious, uninterested; reticent, silent, taciturn; diffident, shy, timid, air-condition; freeze, ice, quick-freeze, supercool; air-cool, ventilate.

TOOL — Implement, pawn, dupe.

•

Dictionary.com Thesaurus

COOL — Adjective: cold, air-conditioned, algid, arctic, biting, chill, chilled, chilling, chilly, coldish, frigid, frore, frosty, gelid, nipping, nippy, refreshing, refrigerated, shivery, snappy, wintry. Adjective: calm, assured, collected, composed, coolheaded, deliberate, detached, dispassionate, impassive, imperturbable, level-headed, nonchalant, philosophical, phlegmatic, placid, quiet, relaxed, self-controlled, self-possessed, serene, stolid, together, tranquil, unagitated, unemotional, unexcited, unflappable, unruffled. Adjective: disapproving, aloof, annoyed, apathetic, distant, frigid, impertinent, impudent, incurious, indifferent, insolent, lukewarm, offended, offhand, offish, procacious, reserved, solitary, standoffish, unapproachable, uncommunicative, unenthusiastic, unfriendly, uninterested, unresponsive, unsociable, unwelcoming, withdrawn. Adjective: excellent, dandy, divine, glorious, groovy, hunky-dory, keen, marvelous, neat, nifty, sensational, swell. Verb: chill, abate, air-condition, air-cool, ally, calm, freeze, frost, infrigidate, lessen, lose heat, mitigate, moderate, reduce, refrigerate, temper.

TOOL — Noun: instrument, apparatus, appliance, bucksaw, contraption, contrivance, device, dojigger, engine, gadget, gizmo, implement, job, machine, means, mechanism, utensil, weapon, whatchamacallit, accomplice, accessory, accomplice, agent, auxiliary, cat's-paw, chump, creature, dupe, easy mark, figurehead, flunky, go-between, greenhorn, hayseed, hireling, idiot, intermediary, jackal, lackey, mark, medium, messenger, minion, patsy, pawn, peon, puppet, stooge, stool pigeon, sucker, tuna, vehicle.

•

The Synonym Finder

COOL — Adj. 1. chilly, chill, nippy, unheated, unwarmed, heatless, sunless; breezy, draughty, windy. 2. composed, collected, Inf. together, self-possessed, self-controlled; easy-going, relaxed, even-tempered, imperturbable, unexcitable, unflappable; unexcited, unmoved, unperturbed unruffled, staid, sedate; undemonstrative, unemotional, stoical, philosophical; passionless, impassive, dispassionate. 3. passive, undesiring, unexcitable, frigid; phlegmatic, listless, half-hearted, lukewarm; stony, flinty, steely. 4. deliberate, intentional, purposeful, meant, willful, volitional, voluntary; premeditated. calculated, designed, planned, plotted, schemed, devised, contrived. 5. unfriendly, unsociable, unwelcome, uninviting, forbidding; uncordial, ungracious, unamicable, inhospitable; unapproachable, inaccessible, closed tight; distant, remote, stand-offish, Inf. offish. 6. audacious, presumptuous, overconfident, impertinent, assuming, insolent, impudent, brazen,brassy, Inf. nervy, Inf. pushy; unabashed, shameless, forward, Inf. fresh, bumptious. 7. aloof, indifferent, apathetic, unconcerned, disinterested, incurious, uninquisitive; removed, detached, uninvolved, unresponsive, unsympathetic. — v. 8. chill, refrigerate, freeze, frigorify, Rare. infrigidate; ice, glaciate, congeal, regelate. 9. soothe, allay, assuage, mollify, soften; moderate, temper, Archaic. attemper; mitigate, abate, lessen, diminish, reduce; quiet, still, compose, lull, hush; pacify, tranquilize, smoothe, settle. 10. cool it. Slang. a. take it easy, calm down, don't sweat it, go with the tide, roll with the punches, take it in stride, think nothing of it b. cut it out, drop it, lay off, knock it off, come off it. 11. cool off Informal. calm down, relax, loosen up, settle down, unwind, simmer down.

TOOL — N. 1. implement, instrument, utensil, apparatus, device, contrivance, invention; gadget, dohickey, hickey, Inf. contraption, Sl. gimmick; aid, convenience, Archaic. conveniency, time-saver; appliance, mechanism, machine, automaton, robot. 2. vehicle, channel, agency, instrumentality, means, way, ways and means, wherewithal; agent, medium, intermediary, middleman, go-between, broker, Chiefly Brit. factor, Sl. ten-percenter; cat's-paw, pawn, puppet, creature; jackal, flunky, lackey, attendant, peon, servant, handmaid, menial; minion, follower, toady, sycophant, Inf. yes man; hireling, underling, assistant, henchman, Sl. stooge; dummy, dupe, Sl. pigeon, gull, gudgeon, Inf. sucker.

344

Remember, we're all in this alone. - Lily Tomlin

Cheapest printer inks
Cobra Ink System

$350 Epson Workforce 1100 with Cobra dye ink system cobraink.com

Until paper disappears we'll need printers. To create the book in your hands required many sheets of printed paper for design and proofs.

I really needed cheap personal printing at scale. Overpirced ink cartridges are a racket that would bankrupt me. Those spammy generic refill ink cartridges aren't cheap or dependable enough.

After much research and trial and error I found that the cheapest easiest method of printing is a continuous ink supply (CIS) built into a printer. Once you are set up you can buy ink inexpensively by the pint, quart or gallon. A whole pint bottle of ink will cost no more than one of those itty bitty 1 oz. cartridges and will last hundreds of times as long.

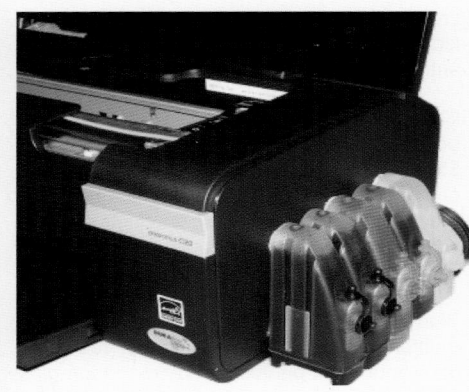

A continuous ink system runs tubes from the refillable ink containers into the moving ink head in the printer. The printer operates normally. You simply refill the outside container with bulk ink and keep printing on the same originally installed cartridges. There are a number of outfits that will sell you a kit to do this yourself. I've heard of occasional satisfaction with this method. But installing this gear can get really messy and hairy. You are on your own if it does not work correctly. And some printer models are easier to retrofit than others.

I opted for a more elegant and not that much more expensive option: have the pros do it. Cobra Systems will install their continuous ink supply system on twelve different brand new Epson printer models. For about $50-100 more than the cost of the new printer, they will ship you a ready-to-use modified new printer with refillable ink containers already installed. Because this modification voids Epson's warranty, they provide

their own warranty. They guarantee it will work. Period. In fact, in my experience Cobra's service is amazing. They will make absolutely sure your system is working to your satisfaction no matter what, even if they have swap it out at their cost.

Because Epson (and all the other printer manufacturers) discourage these kinds of workarounds of their pricey inks, there are some kludgy maintenance steps (like squeezing a bypass switch every now and then) needed to fool the cartridges into going beyond their programmed death. But these inconveniences are minor.

The Epson printers work as advertised. You can get a new 8×11 Epson Workforce 30 installed out of the box with a bulk ink system for $100. I've been using a new Epson Workforce 1100 with the Cobra-modified system installed for $280. It's a serious large-format general purpose printer for up to 11 x 17 inch pages, with 5 huge ink tanks. After about 30 minutes of easy set up, purging the system of air from shipping, I was ready to print. I now churn out hundreds of 11 x 17 full color pages for a few dollars worth of ink. I saved the extra cost of the continuous ink system in the first week of use. (It's shocking how much ink is consumed when a printer cleans its heads.) You can get long-lasting pigment inks, or high-heat inks, or plain old dye inks. Half a liter (a pint) of dye ink goes for $27. Compare that to the thimblefull in most ink cartridges.

Important caveat: You need to situate the printer in a work place you don't mind getting stained with spots of color because even though the system is well designed to minimize spills, the inks are not sealed and sooner or later you WILL spatter some ink at some point. Count on it. Also, since the ink tanks are velcro'd to the side of the printer, these units won't win any style prizes if that is important to you.

For most folks a bulk system is overkill. If all you need is infrequent home printing, I still recommend the previously reviewed HP OfficeJet K5400 as the cheapest per page cost for an off-the-shelf device. But if you are doing large volume printing, saying proofing a book, or running a T-shirts business (Cobra's main customers), or printing flyers and posters, then I recommend Cobra's continuous ink system and their fantastic support. I've been running my Epson with Cobra CIS setup (right) for 3 years full time, It's working great and has saved me a fortune.

-- KK

Instant custom books
Pedia Press

Starts at $9 Pedia Press

This cool service makes inexpensive custom books from Wikipedia articles. Pick a niche subject, collect the pages from Wikipedia, select cover image, print a book. Now you can instantly make that unavailable book you always wanted. I made a book of all the World Heritage sites in Asia so I wouldn't miss any when I travel. My friend Alexander Rose printed up a book on what's currently known about Time, a book to be stashed in a 10,000-year library.

The soft-cover black and white printed books cost about 10 cents per page. For instance a 90 page book will be $9. (10% of the revenue goes to Wikipedia.) Color and hard cover are additional. The system uses book-building functions built into Wikipedia itself, making it super super easy to build a book as you surf. Wikipedia will smartly suggest additional pages based on what you have collected so far. It took me only two minutes to compile a book, and only two days for it to arrive in the mail.

Since you can optionally post your book when done, you can also see what kind of personal books others have created. Some folks archive *everything* known about their favorite indie band. Some make very specific text books for their speciality. These custom books also make a nice gift for someone with an obsession.

The built-in book making function of Wikipedia (watch the video) also produces e-book PDFs -- for free. So you can assemble a book and then print it as a PDF to be exported to an iPad or Kindle.

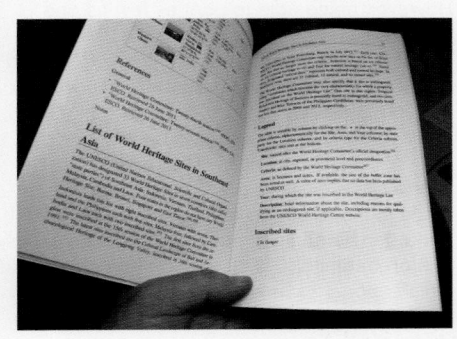

Still, there is a gravity, persistence, and enduring presence in a paper-bound book that can now be quickly applied to your favorite unbooked subject.

--KK

Self-publishing via Amazon
CreateSpace

Prices Vary CreateSpace

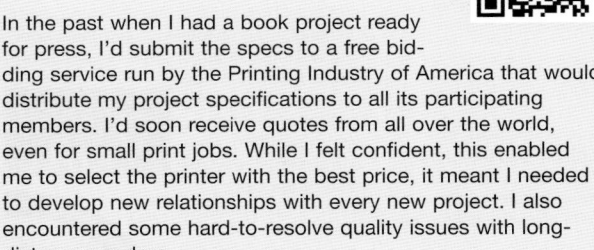

CreateSpace.com is the self-publishing arm of Amazon, providing a service that makes it easy for an individual to self-publish books, CDs, and DVDs. I've used CreateSpace for books and highly recommend it.

In the past when I had a book project ready for press, I'd submit the specs to a free bidding service run by the Printing Industry of America that would distribute my project specifications to all its participating members. I'd soon receive quotes from all over the world, even for small print jobs. While I felt confident, this enabled me to select the printer with the best price, it meant I needed to develop new relationships with every new project. I also encountered some hard-to-resolve quality issues with long-distance vendors.

CreateSpace produces good quality at good price, backed by decent service, but so do other self-publishing sites like the previously reviewed Lulu and Blurb. What CreateSpace has that the others can't touch, however, is the direct link with Amazon. Products published through CreateSpace are automatically, and instantly, given displays on Amazon. More importantly, orders through Amazon are fulfilled directly, without my ever having to handle inventory. They simply pay me a royalty.

It's the logistics of small-scale publishing that are killers. If you

order a book from Blurb and sell it on Amazon, you can kiss any profits goodbye. Amazon doesn't discount books published by or through CreateSpace. They do help themselves to a generous 55% of the retail sale, but the 45% remaining for the publisher (me) is unencumbered by shipping or other deductions. It's pure gross profit.

I'm an author and a conventional publisher, and recently started by own micro-publishing venture called The Public Press. I've gone down many nano-publishing paths, making many mistakes along the way, and CreateSpace is the best option I've found for making small-scale book publishing profitable. Moreover, this is one aspect of Amazon's business that does not come at the expense of independent booksellers and actually creates an environment that makes it possible for the self-publisher and booksellers to work together compatibly and profitably.

-- Stephen Morris

A stack of books I had printed by CreateSpace. -- KK

Your own super hi-res printer
PS Print

psprint.com

Once upon a time, it was rare to find a printer who worked from user-supplied digital files. PSPrint was among the first a decade ago and I have been using them since. There are a zillion places online that print from a PDF, or from other graphic files, but PSPrint is still competitive and I continue to use them with satisfaction. They don't play games. I make up what I need in Illustrator, InDesign, or Photoshop, upload the file and they mail back the printed goods. I do my old-fashion business cards that way. Costs about $26 for 250 (one sided). If you need it, they do all the usual printed formats: stickers, brochures, tickets, and sheets, etc from your supplied files.

-- KK

Personal bookprinting

Lulu * Blurb

As commercial book publishing crashes, personal book publishing is booming. Personal book making entails printing high-quality books in very small quantities, including quantities of one. New technologies permit anyone to print one copy of a softcover or hardcover book, including all-color photo books. These printed-on-demand books are indistinguishable from commercially printed books. In fact, some of the books you buy on Amazon are manufactured with this same technology. You just can't tell the difference.

A few of the large coffeetable photo books I've made with Blurb. They look proffesioonal even though only one copy exists.

However, being able to print as few as one copy — instead of a minimum of a thousand — shifts the economics of bookmaking toward individuals with more passion than money. For the past 8 years I've been producing high-quality books in very small quantities using several different services. The printing quality is first class. Several of the photo books I've made look like coffee-table artworks, and cost about the same, yet I can produce them one by one on-demand. I've also made text only books which appear to be store-bought trade paperbacks or hardcover books from the bookstore.

To turn a text manuscript into a regular book,

either softcover or hard, I recommend Lulu. Their website has a very thorough step-by-step process which will enable you to make a book with the least amount of money. A 100-page trade softcover book in black and white will cost $5.25 to print. That's not bad! It you print over 30 copies the price drops below $5.

Lulu will walk you through the edit, design, and production sequence. They offer templates you can follow. Once in digital form, you can easily order one book or many. Lulu will also offer help in getting your book out into the world, including issuing a ISBN bar code to put on the cover, but it can't really help you market or sell it. That will be your job as a self-publisher. If you are a more sophisticated book maker with your own design skills you can send Lulu a PDF file of your designed book, and simply have them print it, at the same prices. This is the way I use them. Finally, Lulu can also print full color books, including smaller full-color paperbacks. (These could run $20-30 a piece for 150 pages) The overall process of getting a book printed is smooth

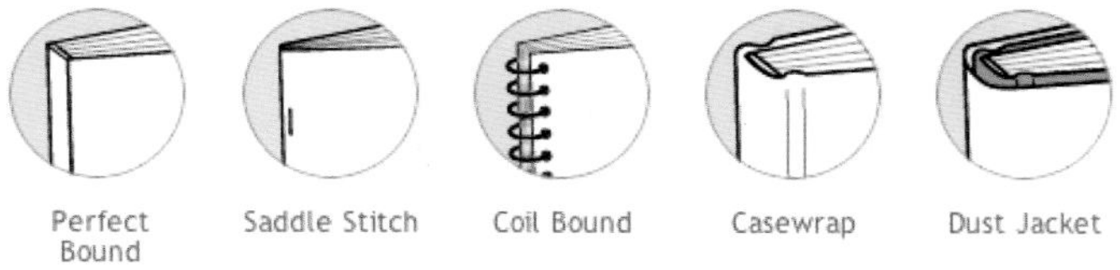
Perfect Bound
Saddle Stitch
Coil Bound
Casewrap
Dust Jacket

Binding options available from Lulu

I/'ve made one or two Blurb books per year, in all sizes. The tiny book at the left is an Apple iBook.

and fairly hassle free. I've made several all-color paperback LuLu books. While they are expensive compared to black and white books, they are cheaper in quantity (and lower in quality) than other on-demand sources such as Blurb.

My recommendation for the best personal color book personal printer is Blurb. Their quality is top notch. The color-match is pretty close to the image you see on your monitor. They issue color profiles for those creators really trying to finess top quality.

You can use Blurb's own software on your computer to make fast template books. This is how I usually create quick picture books. Or you can use InDesign to produce a PDF, which Blub prints. This way you have full creative control. Blurb also has a built-in function within Lightroom making it super easy to move photos from your archive into books.

People used printed picture books for all kinds of projects from artists' portfolios to business plans.

Someone told me that when they turned their Powerpoint presentations into a photo book- they got more attention and calls back because "people won't throw a book out!" I attended

one hi-tech conference recently at which everyone got an instant Indigo-produced color book summarizing the conference, pictures and all. We make a photobook from our extended family vacations to give to each person on the trip. I made a photobook memorializing my deceased father. And nowadays Blurb books are inexpensive enough that some high school kids are making their own full-color alternative anti-yearbooks.

Blurb prices start at $14 for a 20-page square book (for making a book from Instagrams) to $50+ for coffetable art books. Like Lulu, you can choose to sell books you make on Blurb to the public, or you can share an electronic PDF version. You have a lot of options as a self-publisher.

Blurn has recently introduced a selection of 9 different paper grades and styles. You can have your book printed on arty matt (non-gloss) paper, or on super thin magazine paper. In fact Blurb now offers a not-too-expensive way to print magazines on-demand. This is ideal for small-run zines. Quality is excellent.

For making text books primarily in black and white, I use Lulu. For making picture books, I use Blurb.

-- *KK*

Lulu

blurb

How to write a book

A Writer's Time • Scrivener

There I was with a nice advance from a New York publisher to write a book, and there was only one tiny problem, which I did not discuss with the publisher. I'd never written a book and didn't know how. I knew how to write, to edit, even to publish, but authoring? Help!

Help came in the form of a little book (read it in an evening; read it again the next evening) that spelled out precisely the task at hand: how to write a book. I got innumerable good things from Atchity's counsel, but the main three probably were these:

• Time is everything in the labor of writing. Organize your time, and the writing will have a chance to organize itself. I used most of Atchity's tips except the taking of many mini-vacations (I didn't have time).

• Use 5 x 8 cards! Salvation. Every idea, every separable quote, every item from the literature I was researching, each went onto its own card. Organizing the eventual 1,800 cards into piles was defining the chapters; subpiles defined the sections; sequence within the subpiles defined the sequence of the day's writing. This was THE handle without which I would have floundered for months.

• Define in a sentence what the book is about. Searching for that sentence organizes your thinking; using it organizes your writing. Revising consists of removing everything that isn't in support of that sentence.

If this review sounds like a burble of gratitude, that's because it is.

-- *Stewart Brand*

I also used Atchity to help me write my second and third books. I would reduced his advice to this: The work for a book is never-ending, unlimited. The time you have to write it is limited. Therefore you don't manage your work, you manage the only thing that can be managed: your time.

I followed his card system, too. These days a good substitute for 3x5 cards is the software Scrivener for the Mac and Windows. You make notes on virtual cards in the research phase. Cards can contain images, video, all kinds of notes. You then write onto the "cards" expanding and deepening their content as much as you want, or cutting/pasting off pieces to make new cards. These cards can then be arranged and re-arranged into the order of your book. When you are finished arranging, you export all the text into one seamless document.

It's the only way I write long form now. And like any great software, it has capabilities I haven't even touched yet. Four of my best-selling author friends in both fiction and non-fiction swear they couldn't complete books without Scrivener.

-- *KK*

From *A Writer's Time*

•
Always head for drama at this point in the process [first draft]: choose the more dramatic alternative at every crossroads. Writing yourself ""into a corner" guarantees drama as much as it does anxiety: the reader will relish watching you write yourself out of the corner.

•
You can edit objectively after three days have passed and you cannot edit objectively after three minutes have passed. So the attempt to edit instantly is negating the natural process, not allowing time to do its job.

•
No time is more important than the time used to examine and schedule your time.

•
Don't sit down to write without knowing what you're going to write. Never waste writing time deciding what to write. Writing time is for writing, not for the gestation of writing.

•
If you're wondering whether you're experiencing End Time, you're not. True End Time displaces all other thoughts.

•
In Middle Time most writers have problems maintaining perspective toward their work. Middle Time's greatest pitfall is exhaustion, and its most common side effect is confusing that exhaustion with depression or with a dismal reevaluation of the work at hand. . . . During Middle Time you need vacations, as many as you can fit into your schedule.

A WRITER'S
Time
KENNETH ATCHITY

$14 A Writer's Time Kenneth Atchity, 1995, 288 p.

$45 Scrivener 2 Literature and Latte

To be idle requires a strong sense of personal identity. - Robert Louis Stevenson

Best source for self-publishing
The Self-Publishing Manual
$12 Dan Poynter, 2007, 463 p.

Dan Poynter's utterly reliable self-publishing advice, *The Self-Publishing Manual*, has been a perennial oasis of sanity in a sea of hype for over two decades. Now in its 16th edition, it's more useful than ever. To Poynter the technologies of cheap — if not free — duplication are an outright opportunity, rather than a dreaded disaster. If you want to know how to publish (especially on paper), this is the man. For how to e-publish, see Guy Kawasaki's *APE*, below.   -- *KK*

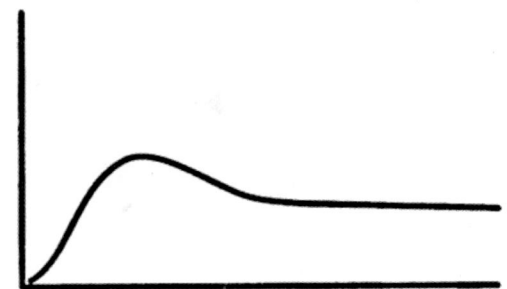

Your sales chart.

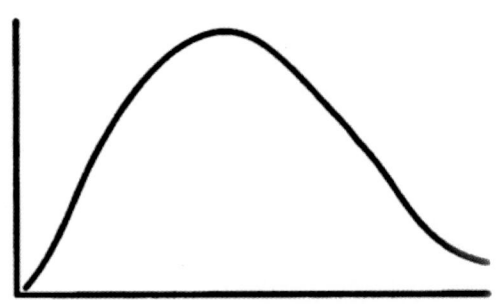

Typical big publisher's sales chart

•

The new book-publishing model is not strictly self-publishing. It is a trial run of 500 books that allows you, not only to sell them, but also to approach some agents and publishers with a book rather than a manuscript. You can also send out review copies, approach distributors, wholesalers, book clubs and make other sales.

•

Don't just write – build: Today, authors build their books; writing is just part of the building process. As an author, you know your subject. You can describe it, explain it and teach

it. The eBook simply provides you with more visual aids to help you get your point to your reader. Now, in addition to the printed word, you have photos, graphics, animation, color, dimension, motion, sound and hyperlinks to more information. Your pBook (paper) will have static words and b/w photographs but the eBook version will be far more versatile.

•

Customizing and special versions: Because your books can be printed in short runs and since the new print engines print two pages at a time, you may customize your book for

your customer. If you make a premium sale to a company, it will cost just pennies to bind in a letter from the CEO or to add the company logo to the cover. This is called "Mass Customization."

•

Since the laser printers are driven by computer, books can have several versions of some chapters, each aimed at a particular type of reader. These are called "Module Books," as the book can be assembled for a particular reader.

Figure 13.10. Shawn checking the Kindle version (MOBI) of *What the Plus!* as it appears across Kindle Apps on multiple platforms.

Best manual for making ebooks
APE
$3 Guy Kawasaki, Shawn Welch, 2013, 410 p.

This poorly named ebook costs all of $3 and is by far the best guide available to teach you how to make ebooks. We spent an entire summer trying to make electronic versions for all my past work; it was a supreme hassle. Lots of wasted mistakes. Wish this was available then. Save yourself hundreds of hours, and countless dead ends by following the hard-to-find information in this dense, to-the-point book. Guy Kawasaki is an ace communication (he has a large following on social media). His ebook is not just about moving text to the screen, but also introduces "agile publishing" -- fast, hi-tech, multiple mode publishing. He tells you how to wrok in cloud apps, crowdsource design, use fans to copyedit, select formats, get it on Amazon (and the right part of Amazon), and print premium paper copies on demand. Little is missing, and believe me, this knowledge is hard to find online. He covers writing a book from start to finish, with all options of formatting, distribution, and actual publishing attended to. If you are pursuing publishing of any sort, this would be the best $3 you could spend.

--*KK.*

•

Try this simple model: Assume that most of your revenue will come from Kindle ebooks, and you'll make $2.00 per copy at a $2.99 price point. This means you need to sell approximately 2,500 ebooks to break even, not including your time.

Figure 04.01. Sales of physical versus Kindle books by Amazon.

•

(A service called Kindlegraph enables an author to "autograph" ebooks by inserting a personalized message and digitized signature. It claims that 3,500 authors of more than 15,000 ebooks have signed up for the service. Still, this isn't as compelling as seeing an author and getting an autograph on a printed book.)

To my amazement, 241 people completed the form in twenty-four hours. I sent them the Word file of the manuscript after turning on "Highlight Changes" so that it was easy to find their comments. (Again, to do this, use this sequence: Tools menu, "Track Changes," "Highlight Changes," "Track changes while editing.") Over the next ten days, more than a hundred people returned the file with comments. These were the results: Sixty-seven suggestions for how to make the book better (not counting duplicates of the same suggestions). These suggestions were closer to content editing than copyediting, which is why I crowdsource copyediting before using a professional. Twenty-seven factual errors (not counting duplicate reports of the same issues). These errors are also closer to content editing than copyediting. However, most editors from traditional publishers would not have caught these errors because detecting them required extensive expertise in Google+. One hundred and forty-seven grammatical and spelling errors (not counting duplicate reports of the same issues). To make this kind of crowdsourcing work, you need at least five hundred followers.

•

For marketing purposes, a better order for ebook front matter, tradition be damned, is: Cover Blurbs (more on blurbs below) Table of contents Foreword or preface (but not both, and neither for fiction) Chapter 1… You can stick everything else in the back because most of it doesn't matter to most people.

Figure 11.03. Distribution through direct sales.

•

Pros: Inexpensive. All you need to self-publish an ebook is a computer, word processor, and Internet access. If you start distribution through other channels, you may need more professional tools, but you can worry about this later. The best case, Kindle Direct Publishing, prides itself on a forty-eight-hour turnaround. Amazon and Apple also enable you to launch your non-translated book in dozens of countries at the same time. Lucrative. You can make up to 70 percent of the selling price of an ebook from online resellers. Making $2 on a $3 book is a sweet deal if you can achieve a large volume.

•

Many bookstores will not sell self-published books. Author-services companies may tell you that they can get you brick-and-mortar distribution, but they are shading the truth. Bookstores can order your book from them if someone requests it, but this doesn't mean they will buy your book for stocking in the store.

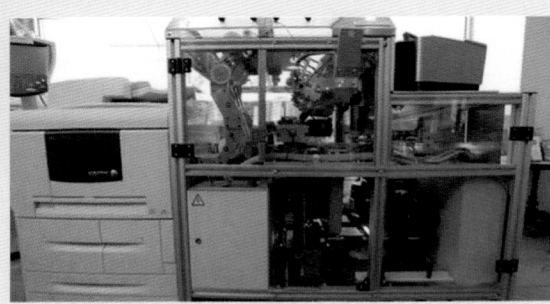

▲ This is a self-contained gizmo about the size of the kind of photocopy machines you see in FedEx Office stores. It prints and binds a softcover book in ten minutes. The submission requirements are easy: a PDF of the cover and a PDF of the text. The cost to print a book is $10 to $15. YouTube has a video of it in action—search for "The Espresso Book Machine."

This Book Is Self-Published

The authority of a book -- still today -- is astounding. Take text as it appears on your screen, print it on paper, bind between covers, and those words will get more attention and respect than they would on a website or stapled as a report. We don't know exactly why this works; it may have to do with the extra expense of printing. And we don't know how long this cultural bias will prevail, but as long as it does, you can take advantage of it by printing a book with ink on paper.

Getting something printed today is quite easy. Getting it some attention is much, much harder. I recommend three outfits that will print single copies of a book on-demand: CreateSpace, Blurb and Lulu. These companies will walk you through the process step by step, including providing you a bar code, and an on-line shopping cart so you can sell your book if you care to. A once complex, intimidating process that drove away all but the most obstinate is now a simple and easy matter of clicking through some web pages.

But printing is not publishing.

Let me tell the story of this self-published book. This book is self-published primarily because publishing companies are too slow for me, and I always wind up doing most of their work anyway. So after making a PDF of the designed book we printed 10,000 copies of *Cool Tools* for the first edition. That number was guestimated by several pros in the small press world who figured that was the number of copies I might sell in the first year of the book's life. This is an oversized book (11 x 14 inches) which severely limits the number of printers equipped to print it. In fact one big US printer reluctantly recommended that we go overseas to print this large. Printing costs in China are about one third of the estimates provided by the one US printer willing to bid on it. However, in calculating the cost of shipping the books from China, one Chinese printer figured 10,000 books this size would fill more than one con-

tainer, and they asked me if I had a loading dock at my warehouse!

Here the dream of self-publishing meet the realities of dead-tree flesh and pigment. As a self-publisher, it is easy to create a book using an off-the-shelf laptop and some consumer software (see Tools Used to Make This Book, p. 5) It is easy for a self-publisher to send a digital PDF to a printer anywhere in the world, including China, and to order thousands printed. It is easy for a self-publisher to make and distribute e-books (see *APE*, this page). But when a self-publisher returns to paper, the dynamics that formed the old system around moving paper also returns. Where would a self-publisher park a couple of shipping containers of books? Once parked, how do you get the books inside to book retailers, or to Amazon or Barnes & Nobel? It's a logistical headache.

Small publishers (and self-publishing is just nano-scale small publishing) often hire a distributor, such as a big publisher, to distribute their books and deal with shippers. That's what I did. I partnered with Publisher's Group West (PGW), a California-based outfit that I knew from Wired magazine. I pay PGW a percentage of each book's sale to deal with their mass and weight, and to get them into bookstores around the world.

The 10,000 copies were printed by Book Art Printers in Hong Kong, China. We hired Meadows/Wye, a transport agency to pick them up at the printing plant in China, and to load them on their once-a-week departure of a container ship. The ship takes 26 days to cross the Pacific ocean, cruise down to Central America, cross the Panama Canal, head up the Mississippi River, dock at Memphis, where the books are unloaded to trucks to complete the last 200 miles to the PGW warehouse in Jackson, Tennessee. Once a week Amazon picks up a load of books from PGW to take to their warehouse where they enter the slipstream and make their way to you.

--*KK*

Photography

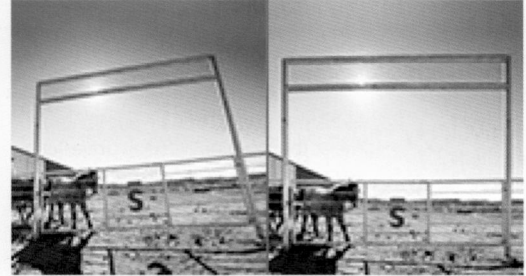

Lightroom 5 will automatically remove and fill in complicated forms, such as this person against vegetation. This becomes a matter of a few clicks instead of a long artistic process in Photoshop.

Photo organizing, manipulating
Adobe Lightroom
$80 Latest Version 5 Adobe.com

Adobe Lightroom is an imaging software that's excellent for keeping track of large numbers of photos, and also provides an extensive range of processing and manipulation functions. I'm working on version 2.3 as I write this; the 3.0

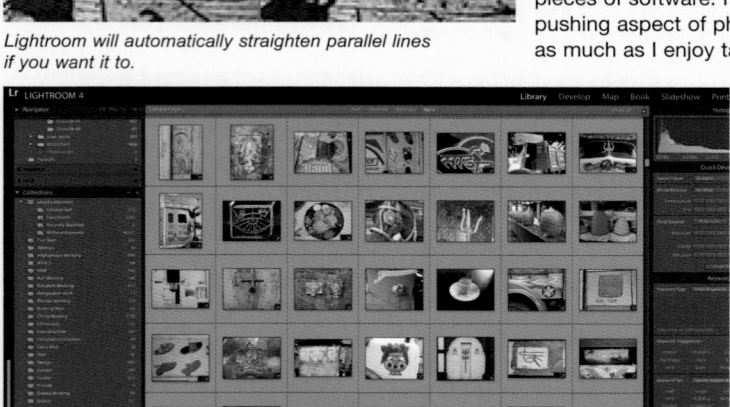

Lightroom will automatically straighten parallel lines if you want it to.

beta was just released. The program's broken into five intuitively designed modules: Library, Develop, Slideshow, Print, Web.

Making web galleries is ridiculously easy, and printing is much more intuitive in Lightroom than Photoshop (at least CS2, my current version). Now that there are graduated filters and advanced cloning/spot removal in Lightroom, I only do really serious retouching in Photoshop. I'm not sure if it's as useful for processing jpegs as it is RAW files (I don't shoot jpegs), but the RAW converter is comprehensive and a pleasure to use. The keywording and metadata functions are great for retrieval, and you also have the option of duplicating everything you import from your CF/SD cards onto a second drive for instant backup. It also converts RAW files directly to DNG (best for long-term storage) upon import, if you choose.

Lightroom's one of my all-time favorite pieces of software. I don't enjoy the pixel pushing aspect of photography a fraction as much as I enjoy taking pictures, but it's less painful with Lightroom. I haven't used its main competitor, Aperture, but have been told by friends who've used both that Aperture doesn't offer image manipulation capabilities on par with Lightroom.

-- Elon Schoenholz

Small instant camera
Fuji Instax Mini 8
$68 fujifilm.com

The Fuji Instax Mini 8 is a smallish instant camera that prints vertical photos about 2.5 inches tall by about 1.75 inches wide. Like Polaroid prints, the border is a bit thicker at the bottom edge of the photo so you can caption your prints.

It's certainly larger than most digital point and shoot cameras, but it's very light-weight, and can easily be carried in a shoulder bag or backpack without adding much weight to your burden. Each pack of film includes 10 shots. I don't shoot that much, but if I'm walking around taking photos, I usually take an extra pack of film.

My camera sees most use at home, especially when we have gatherings. We encourage guests to take pictures and keep them, if they like. We keep the camera in an easily accessible location on the mantle or bookshelf, next to previously taken shots to encourage use.

The interface is extremely simple, but it does include a rudimentary light meter and an adjustable aperture. Shots develop pretty quickly (a couple minutes), and don't require as much protection from light while developing as other instant films (like Impossible Project) - colors and exposure are also more predictable. Subject matter should be at least 2 ft from the camera.

Film is about $20 for two packs of 10 shots (20 shots total). The camera comes in five colors and retails for about $120 (~$68-$80 on Amazon).

-- Camille Hartsell

Simple, powerful, and free image viewer
IrfanView
Free for non-commercial use, $12 for commercial use IrfanView

IrfanView is a Windows-only swiss army knife for images.

It's lightning fast, opens just about any format known to man, and runs off a portable or network drive. Oh, and it's free as in beer.

I've used IrfanView for more than a decade, and the developer has been cautious to add features. It's never gotten slower. It gets really powerful when you start using shortcut keys.

It's not a full-fledged photo editor, but it does come with a basic assortment of filters, including pixelate, blur, and red-eye reduction. It can use standard 8bf (Photoshop) plugins too. It's got a very powerful batch processor and converter. Watermarks, sizing, compression, naming, it's all there.

IrfanView doesn't replace PhotoShop, Gimp, or even Picasa. It just means you'll use them a whole lot less often, and only when you're planning to spend some quality time with an image. For day-to-day editing and management, IrfanView is infinitely faster and easier.

-- Aaron Weiss

One shot per day
Chased By the Light

This project is a zen masterpiece. It is also a behavior-modifiying challenge for all digital photographers: Look instead of click.

In the 1990s veteran magazine photographer Jim Brandenbrug gave himself an impossible assignment: "For 90 days between the autumn equinox and winter solstice I would make only one photograph a day. There would be no second exposure, no second

chance." A single exposure, a single click per day! He was using film, and he was photographing wildlife, including elusive animals in the north woods in upper Minnesota. Film is unforgiving. For amateur and professional alike getting even an acceptable photo in these conditions with one shot requires relying on the Force. Yet Brandenburg found, or made, one beauty after another. Most mortals would need a hundred shots to get one like these. The 90 images stand strong each on their own, but the complete symphony is one of the most impressive acts of mindfulness I've seen.

(The full set of images was also published in a smaller format in the November 1997 issue of *National Geographic*.)

Besides the book, there is now an iPad app.

-- KK

●
I sensed there would be lessons learned. There were, but not always those I had imagined. Some were merely lessons remembered, recapturing things I had forgotten, such as remaining open to chance, and that, in nature, not all beauty is giant in scale. One such lesson occurred on October 15th, the twenty-third day. It was late and I despaired of capturing anything of value. The day was dark and gloomy; my mood reflected the weather. I wandered through the dripping forest all day long. Tired, hungry , and wet, I was near tears. I was mentally beating myself for having passed up several deer portraits and the

chance to photograph a playful otter. None of those scenes spoke to me at the time.

But perhaps because I was patient, and perhaps because, as natives do on a vision quest, I had reached my physical limits, I became open to the possibility revealed by a single red maple leaf floating on a dark-water pond. My spirits rose the instant I saw it, and although the day was very late and what little light there had been was fleeing rapidly, I studied the scene from every angle. Finally, unsure of my choice, I made the shot anyway, thankful at least that the long day had ended. Once more I was surprised by the result. The image seems to have a lyrical quality, with a rhythm in the long grass.

$45 Jim Brandenburg, 1998, 104 p.   **$10 App** itunes.com

What to do with a laser pointer
Shoebox Holography
$16 Frank DeFreitas, Alan Rhody, and Steve Michael, 2000, 128 p.

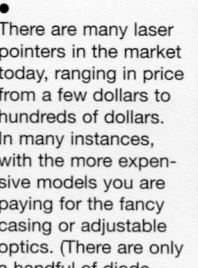

Ever since laser pointers became drugstore items I wondered if you could use them to make holograms. You can. This book tells how.

-- KK

●
There are many laser pointers in the market today, ranging in price from a few dollars to hundreds of dollars. In many instances, with the more expensive models you are paying for the fancy casing or adjustable optics. (There are only a handful of diode laser manufacturers in the world, so many times the expensive pointer and the cheap pointer actually contain the same laser.)...Fortunately, the simplest, most rugged (and often least expensive) laser pointers work best for the experiment described in this book.

●
The shoebox holograph set-up. Laser pen is mounted on the right. A conch shell on the left sits on a motion dampening foundation. A white card is used to focus where the film plate will be.

Everywhere I go I find a poet has been there before me. - Sigmund Freud

PetaPixel

Best photography news
Petapixel
Free Petapixel.com

This blog focuses on photography rather than just cameras. To paraphrase Lance Armstrong, it's not about the camera. It's about the eyes, about seeing, about technical competence, about tricks, techniques, creativity, and what you do with all the images you make or take. It's about having fun with photography, as well as making money with it. There's also a lot about the rights of photographers and the complex issues of copyright and "borrowing" from other photographers. There's plenty about low tech pinhole cameras, and point and shoots, and phone camera photography. And yes, there's bits about the newest cameras, but that part is not overwhelming. I've been reading it daily (about 3 or 4 short posts per day) for the past 18 months and it is continually helpful. The site is brisk, surprising, informative, current, and is not trying to sell gear. It's one of the better blogs for enthusiasts of any stripe that I've seen. Almost anyone taking pictures will find it useful.

-- KK

San Diego-based wedding photographer Aaron Willcox won 1st place in an engagement photo contest with this shot showing a feat of incredible strength. No Photoshop trickery or invisible wires were used in making this image (nor does the guy have Superman-esque strength)

Rental tool contest winner
Lensrentals.com
Lensrentals.com

If you're a hobbyist photographer you know that you can never have enough camera lenses. Advanced amateurs can often justify the purchase of some of the more expensive, but very versatile, lenses such as the many variations of Canon's 70-200 lens. The tricky part comes when you want to play with some of the more esoteric and special-purpose lenses, such as extreme wide angles or super long telephotos. If you only use the lens once a year it's really hard to justify the many thousands of dollars the lenses can often run.

In my case, my favorite specialized tool that I don't own for my camera is a Canon TS-E 17mm f/4L. The magic is its ability to tilt and shift, so that it moves in relation to the sensor plane, similar to the movements you'd get with a large format camera. These lens movements can allow a photographer to control focus and perspective–for instance, keeping vertical lines from converging when photographing a tall building. For this reason a tilt/shift lens is often used when shooting interior and exterior architecture shots, but in my case I find it highly entertaining to use when photographing landscapes. Whether it's the Racetrack in Death Valley National Park or the Virgin Narrows in Zion National Park, the lens is a ton of fun for me to use. Using the lens' movements, it's possible for me to achieve perfect sharpness from the nearest object in the frame all the way out to infinity.

When I need a TS-E 17mm, which would cost about $2,500 to purchase, I rent it from Lensrentals.com. There are several lens rental companies with a web presence, but I've always had excellent results

with Lensrentals. They have reasonable prices (far cheaper than renting from my local pro camera shop), offer insurance, don't require a deposit, and don't place a hold on my credit card. They always make sure the lens arrives a day or so earlier than you actually need it.

Their service is also incredible. A friend of mine once rented two lenses for a trip, and UPS lost them. He called Lensrentals and they immediately shipped out two new lenses via overnight delivery for no charge. They even offered to drop ship to my friend's vacation destination to ensure he didn't miss the delivery.

If you want to play with a fun lens to expand your photographic options, the TS-E 17mm from Lensrentals.com is hard to beat.

-- Neil Enns

Strobist | Learn how to light

Photo lighting 101+
Strobist
Free Strobist.com

As a photographer who borrowed money to pay for a formal, technical photo education, I can tell you that Strobist.com is a must-see for the modern photographer who wants to increase his/her lighting skills. Photographer-publisher David Hobby shares a wealth of information regarding alterations/adaptations, so photographers without huge budgets can create awesome lighting with small portable Canon/Nikon flash units.

Strobist's approach and instruction changed my life. Among the techniques that I've learned from the site and applied: Drilling holes into my expensive Canon flashes, so that I could hotwire them to fire by remote. (I did, however, run two units too hard and ended up frying them); building a softbox out of cardboard; extending the range of some cheap Chinese remotes by soldering on a few inches of wire; making gobos (go-betweens; anything used to block light) out of cereal boxes and gaffers tape; making bounce cards out of Coroplast that effectively reflect light and are light to carry; using Velcro on my flash to easily add gels and other light modifiers; using cardboard rolls as snoots (to precisely aim lights).

Among the Strobist features I've found most valuable are the modifications and reviews of modifications that offer practical and inexpensive lighting solutions. The site also presents examples of techniques and modifications that stretch for miles on Flickr, as well as excellent reviews of some of the newest and most practical photo tools. Strobist's descriptions of a vast range of photo techniques, including illustrative photographs in every post and often instructional video, too, are generally clear and easy to learn from. For starters, check the drop-down menus for the Lighting 101 Archive.

You may find photo sites that are as good as Strobist, but you will find none that are better. Hobby's creativity is honestly jaw-dropping, and his site is an outstanding resource for photographers ready to take their flashes off their cameras and delve into more advanced lighting setups.

Members of the Strobist Group on flickr usually post detailed information about the photos they take and techniques used. It's a great place to get ideas, reviews and information.

-- Dominic Duncombe

• Lighting 101: Balancing Flash and Ambient, Pt 1

More than maybe anything, the quality of light in a photo comes down to the lighting ratio. On one level, it creates the whole look of your photo. On another, your lighting ratio will likely be the key variable in determining whether your paper can reproduce the information in the shadows. It's all about the shadow detail – either you want it or you don't. And you want to make the call on what reproduces in the paper.

Balancing with ambient is the same process, whether you are lighting an interior portrait or fill flashing a headshot outside. Always think in terms of balance instead of fill. The concept is less limiting. And it will not predispose you to use the sun as your main light when the strobe might be the better choice in a given situation…

• Lighting 101: Bare-Tube-Style Lighting

One of the limits of using a small, shoe-mount strobe is that all of the pieces are integrated into the flash. Power, capacitors, flash tube and reflector – all wrapped up in a package the size of a small Subway sandwich.

Larger flashes tend to have a more "component" type of layout, with separate power packs, flash heads, tubes and reflectors. While this generally adds more weight and size, the fact that the reflectors are usually removable gives the big-flash guys the ability to shoot "bare-tube."

Bare-tube (or maybe you have heard the more old-school term, "bare-bulb,") means nothing more than having your flash tube sitting out there in open space pushing its light out into (nearly) a 360-degree sphere of coverage. I say nearly because there has to be some wire carrying power and triggering the flash. And that blocks some of the light in one direction….

Why is this cool? There are a couple of reasons.

First, you can light a room with one head, effectively spewing light in all directions. Two bare-tube heads, high and at 45-degree angles, will light one very crisp-looking group shot. (Just drop one of the heads down a stop or so to get a nice ratio.)

Dust-Off alternative
Giottos Rocket Blaster
$8 Amazon

This rubber rocket doesn't provide as much pressure as Dust-Off, but it exhales a forceful-enough blast for dusting photo/electronic gear, and standing upright on its base sidelines as playful desk dressing/stress-relief toy. I squeeze the oblong bladder (the rocket's body) and a burst of air entering through a hole at the bottom exits the narrow hard plastic red nozzle. I can't compare their relative dusting power, but unlike the ReAir Duster, the Rocket Blaster doesn't require refilling. Mine's been in regular use in the office and on location for a couple of years without any noticeable wear.

The general consensus is that products like Dust-Off should be kept away from digital camera sensors, either because the pressure can be too high around delicate internal mechanisms or the potential for harmful residue. Giottos Rocket Blaster is the best alternative I've seen — an inexpensive low-tech tool for maintaining expensive high-tech tools.

-- Elon Schoenholz

ScanCafe
Your memories deserve the best

Cheapest hi-quality photo scans
ScanCafe
$0.22+ scancafe.com

This service will digitize your old slides, negatives and photographic prints at high quality and at a very cheap price. I've been using them to scan my 30-year backlog of ten thousand photographs and I have been delighted with the results. I've used other services to scan my old photos; ScanCafe is by far the best deal. Their prices are fantastic. To scan a slide is just 29 cents, a color negative 19 cents (at the time of this writing).

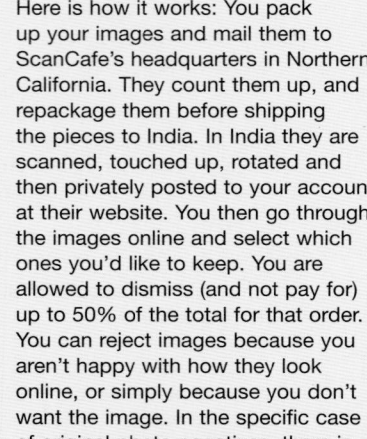

Here is how it works: You pack up your images and mail them to ScanCafe's headquarters in Northern California. They count them up, and repackage them before shipping the pieces to India. In India they are scanned, touched up, rotated and then privately posted to your account at their website. You then go through the images online and select which ones you'd like to keep. You are allowed to dismiss (and not pay for) up to 50% of the total for that order. You can reject images because you aren't happy with how they look online, or simply because you don't want the image. In the specific case of original photo negatives, there is no reliable way to communicate which image(s) you want on the strip, so ScanCafe will scan the entire strip of negatives. You'll have to reject the particular frames you don't want (but no more than 50% of the total order. Combine them with slides to keep your percentage down.)

After you've made your selection, Scan Cafe will send the originals back to the US and then from CA they will ship you a DVD/CD with your images and your originals. It takes 7-8 weeks door to door. The quality of scan is great for everything except huge billboard enlargements. The photos are scanned at 3000 dpi which gives a file about the quality of a 7 megapixel digital shot. Higher res scans are available for extra. You can scoop the final jpeg images into iPhoto or Flickr or Blurb books. They are rotated into correct up-down/sideways orientation by hand. They are clean and crisp. I have a Nikon scanner and these $0.19 scans are superior in quality. On the left (above) is a ScanCafe scan I did cropped for detail, on the right is a Nikon scan. Note the increase dynamic range of the left one, as on the rock. (These two images have been uniformly reduced in resolution to fit on the web.)

So for $29 you can get 100 slides scanned. You'll need to pay for shipping your box to and fro via UPS, which might total $12, so larger orders amortize that cost. And then there's the 2 month wait. Clearly this is a tool for dealing with your archive and not a birthday present you need next week. If your photos have sat unused for 10 years a few additional weeks turnaround is not going to hurt. The 50% cut is also meant to encourage you to scan everything and sort later.

These cheap prices have encouraged me to revisit my earlier photo life, and in the spirit of the web, start sharing the treasure now hiding in the basement.

Some people are very concerned about sending their precious originals to India — or anywhere for that matter. They should not be. ScanCafe has a very elaborate tracking and shipping system that would work even if you were shipping jewels. Their scanning facilities in Bangalore (description and photos here) are more organized than you are. I have more trust in this system than I would handing them over to any neighborhood scanner.

-- KK

Large, affordable, high-quality prints
Costco Photo Center
$10 20"x30" print on Fuji archival photo paper
costcophotocenter.com

Though I claim to be a photographer I don't own a printer. I can't stand dealing with ink cartridges or printer profiles. Instead, I rely on Costco Photo for most, if not all, of my photo printing needs.

Costco is the cheapest place I have found that prints on high quality Fuji archival photo paper in sizes up to 20" x 30". At $9.99 for a 20"x30" print, it's 1/3rd the cost of the previously reviewed Pictopia (though, admittedly, they lack the same range in sizes). You do not need a membership to use the Costco Photo Center service on-line but it necessitates that the prints are shipped to you. Larger prints are shipped rolled in a tube. If you are a Costco member you are allowed to use custom color profiles while also adding the option of picking up your order at the nearest Costco which can cut down on turn-around time.

One of my slides from Asia came out excellently as a Costco poster. -- KK

I have heard on forums that Costco Photo Centers vary significantly in quality, and that some labs are run incredibly well and are capable of producing results equivalent to far more expensive services, while others have wonky colors with less than dedicated staff. In my experience, if I ever have a problem with a photo, no matter how minor, they are very, very quick to reprint while also letting me keep both (which is a nice bonus).

-- Oliver Hulland

Closeup SFX
Foamcore Gray Card
$69 (for 10 boards) Amazon

It sounds so trivial, but a simple piece of gray-colored foamcore, purchased at a local craft store, is a godsend for digital photography. The board's flat surface serves as a perfectly uniform, non-glare background for shooting gizmos and stuff. Stuff, as in stuff you want put up for auction on eBay, stuff to illustrate articles, stuff for your blog. The stiff gray card — 20 by 30 inches — produces no highlights, even in full sunlight. The objects appear to float in limbo (or all white). Moving and removing objects from the image using Photoshop is a cinch.

-- Stefan E. Jones

A foam gray card is one of the cheapest useful photo accessories you can get. I use mine all the time. There are plenty of ways to enhance close-up shots, but none simpler or cheaper. If you want to get fancy in your clipping, you can try some green card, as in greenscreen.

-- KK

Cheapest huge prints
Elcocolor

I was professional printer and have used Elcocolor. Their quality compares with much, much more expensive services. Specifically their poster special. Sure, close up

at 3 inches away, you can see that the resolution is better on a $300 professional print; But for 22 bucks for a 30x40, I truly recommend Elcocolor poster prints. Two caveats: First, you must buy two prints (not necessarily of the same image) at a minimum. Second, if you are professional and have calibrated a color profile, make note of that in their "special instructions" section. Otherwise, they will overrun your calibrations.

-- John S.

Rids images of incidental pedestrians/cars
Tourist Remover
Free trial (100MB of storage for 3 months)
Snapmania

Tourist Remover is one tool in a suite of free online image editing tools in futureLAB's Snapmania. I used it recently on some pictures I took in Moab Utah to remove people and cars from the photos I snapped. The only thing you need to do is take 3-10 pictures of the subject (by hand, no tripod required), and then Tourist Remover averages the pictures and removes anything that only appears in one of the shots (such as moving people and cars). The tool will not remove anything that appears in two of the shots, such as a parked car. So when taking the pictures and when selecting the ones to use the tool with, make sure the items you want removed only appear in one shot. The rest of the imaging suite is pretty interesting

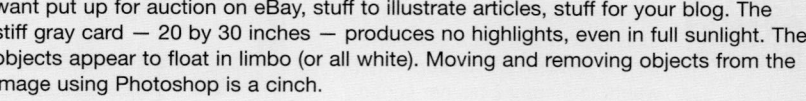

and also does things like stitch panoramas together from several images. The interface takes a little getting used to, but basically once you learn the convention of dragging the images you want to edit onto to the tool you want to use, then it's all pretty easy.

-- Alexander Rose

The chief danger in life is that you may take too many precautions. - Alfred Adler

Wireless memory card
Eye-Fi
$81 16 GB Amazon

I am a dermatologist and often take clinical photos of my patients with a digicam to add to their electronic medial records. With the Eye-Fi, a wireless 2GB SD memory card, I can take a photo and by the time I return to my computer the photo is waiting for me. Set up is very easy. You just plug the card in like you would any other memory card, do some basic configuration (the software works with Mac/PC) and you can send photos to the computer via the wi-fi you configure, or send direct to an online site like Flickr. You can also set the card up so several wi-fi are recognized (home or office, for instance), although you must program each individually. If you are using remote wi-fi access (that you have set up), needless to say, you will only be able to put photos online. In the office, we use the Eye-Fi to send to a local computer only. For someone with a built-in or USB SD card reader or Bluetooth, the Eye-Fi may have less benefits. For my purposes, it's spectacular.

Previously, all patient photos would be downloaded as a batch and then each would be tediously attached at the end of the day. With the Eye-Fi, the photos are made available right away and they can be attached right when we write each patient's note. The flow is much better. Surprisingly, I haven't noticed any issues with the card draining the battery either. A few caveats: at any one time, one card can communicate with only one computer and one online site. You can, however, set up your account so your card can communicate with multiple computers. In order to switch computers, you go into the Eye-Fi manager on your computer and change the settings (i.e. if you're switching from work and home). While my use and situation may be unique, I also started my somewhat technophobic father-in-law on an Eye-Fi several months ago and it's been working well for him. Previously, he used to just fill up cards and then buy a new one (luckily, with the price of SD cards, that was still cheaper than film, but this is much better!). All he has to do is remember to keep both the camera and computer on, and the Eye-Fi enables him to share his photos online with us with virtually no trouble. At first, he had a few issues and concluded the card was broken. However, I showed him all he needed to do was make sure the computer was on with the Eye-Fi manager running (it can be set up to automatically run when you boot your computer). Undoubtedly, this technology has major potential to revolutionize digital photography as we know it. I look forward to future drivers that could support instant upload via any unlocked wi-fi your camera wanders near.

-- Jeff Ellis

Durable media card/ stick boxes
Pelican Memory Card Cases
$17 (stores 8 SD cards) Amazon

These durable cases protect your memory cards from getting wet, contaminated with dirt, or in my case lost. I have misplaced numerous memory cards due to their small size. With these cases not only do I not lose the cards, but I use the cases to organize them. The cases are small and compact (about 4.25" x 2.25") and only about 1" thick. They're available for almost all media types: SD/ Mini SD, XD, Compact Flash and for MS (Memory Stick) cards. Each holds anywhere from 4 to 16 memory cards. I now use them to organize all of my media. So my wife has hers (I am not allowed to touch them since I have lost some of her photo flash cards), some for work (sorted by major projects) and then my own personal use cards. All I have to do now is grab the case I need for work, for instance, and I know I will have everything I need. These card cases have an o-ring seal Pelican says is "water-resistant." Though I wouldn't want to find out if they're waterproof, I think they only back off that claim to protect their tail. I have owned Pelican cases for my cameras for years and have found they're pretty much bulletproof. I also have one case for my laptop and use Pelican's cases for work to ship expensive equipment. My only complaint with their card cases is I wish that they had different colors to chose from so I wouldn't have to label them.

-- Scott Newton

Quickly mount an iPhone to a tripod
The Glif
$20 Amazon

I use my iPhone to shoot video because the quality is excellent and I like the many different inexpensive video apps available for the iPhone (such as stop motion apps). I also like being able to email iPhone videos or upload them to YouTube directly from my phone instead of having to first transfer them to a computer.

The main drawback with using the iPhone to shoot video is that you can't put it on a tripod — you have to hold it in your hand or precariously lean it against something. The best iPhone mounting solution I've found so far is the Glif, a tiny hard-rubber clip with a metal 1/4"-20 thread that attaches to any tripod mount. Simply slide the iPhone into the Glif's slot and you're ready to go.

The Glif has one other function: it's a "kick-stand" that lets you use your iPhone as a mini-display on your desktop or airplane fold down tray.

If you want to use the Glif when you're on the move, pay the extra $10 for the Glif Plus, which includes a separate plastic piece that locks your iPhone onto the Glif so there's no chance of it falling off.

-- Mark Frauenfelder

Compact, lightweight tripod head
Really Right Stuff Ballhead
$145 Really Right Stuff BH-25 Pro reallyrightstuff.com
$105 B2-40 LR clamp with 1/4-20 screw reallyrightstuff.com

What got me started on the Really Right Stuff products was just the idea of committing to a system that would work with everything. Their tripod head consists of three components: an L-bracket custom made for your camera model; a standardized Arca-Swiss-style quick-release clamping plate; and the ballhead base, itself. Committing to this system is a big expense. The fact that each new piece continually adds more value makes it easier to justify. This system's advantages over something such as a simpler Manfrotto ballhead with a quick-release plate are increased stability and quicker changes from portrait to landscape mode.

RRS is big on system synergy. They are top-notch, beautifully made, perfect products.

I've been using the RRS products for about five years now, and I have to admit that part of the appeal is simply the joy of using perfectly made gear. Sometimes the tools can inspire us.

-- John Breitinger

Pocket-size stabilizer
Strap Pod
$30 Universal mount $40 Quick-release mount kirkphoto.com

The Strap Pod isn't as steady as a mono-pod and nowhere near as steady as a heavy tripod or even a relatively light one. But when you want to pack something small, stealthy, quiet, and effective….voila! I've been using one for more than two years for when I shoot in low light and available light — which I do with some frequency (indoor sports, concerts, theater, etc.). The Strap Pod rolls up nicely, stashes easily in your pack, pocket or on your belt and — unlike a tripod or a monopod — it is very easy to deploy, use and remove quickly. Just drop the strap, step into the loop and shoot. No muss, no fuss, no twisting or flicking sections or wielding something that looks like a baton or a spear.

In the case of museums or some public spaces, tripods are simply not allowed (though you can sometimes get away with a monopod by pretending it is a 'walking stick'). But hauling a monopod around is sometimes clumsy, frowned upon, or outright discouraged in certain environs. The Strap Pod is much less intrusive and bulky, so I'm more likely to toss it into my pocket or my camera bag and bring it along. If I go for an impromptu hike in the local woods as dusk approaches, for instance, my experience is that the Strap Pod seems to give me an additional one to two stops.

Another benefit is that the Strap Pod is removed from a baseplate via a vice action — not the screwing and unscrewing of a threaded bolt — so it quickly and cleanly attaches/detaches.

-- Will Jennings

Pens

Japanese pen store
Jet Pens
jetpens.com

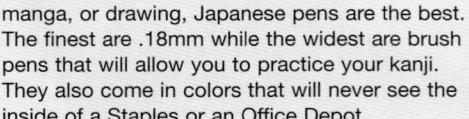

Japanese pens are simply the coolest pens on the planet. Whether for writing notes, manga, or drawing, Japanese pens are the best. The finest are .18mm while the widest are brush pens that will allow you to practice your kanji. They also come in colors that will never see the inside of a Staples or an Office Depot.

The best place to get them is a web site called Jetpens.com. Given the exotic character of the merchandise, the prices are fine, but the extras, such as Japanese stationary, erasers, pen holders, and notebooks are simply amazing. Where else can you buy erasers that are also a game of balancing the erasers in an ark on your desk? And the colors, ranging from yellows and pinks to the office standards, are just awesome.

In the end, it is a very cheap way to gain a bit of understanding of a very different culture, while also getting some really cool pens.

-- Michael Aaron Dennis

Like many others I have an unhealthy obsession with office supplies, especially mechanical pencils. I'm always looking for the perfect pencil. JetPens.com offers a great selection of mostly Japanese pens, pencils, highlighters and supplies. Many of the name brands they offer are familiar in the U.S. (Pilot, Pentel) but you won't find any of these at your local office supply store. JetPens also carries the hard-to-find Uniball Paper Clipper and Clips – a reusable paper binding system.

-- Amy Kahle

Best everyday pen
Pilot G2 Gel Pen
$14 for 12 pilotpen.us

Gel inks flow smoother than ballpoints, lay heavier ink on a fine line than roller balls, yet are less fussy than fountain pens. Once exotic, gel pens are now my everyday carry. I rely on Pilot G2 retractable gel pens. They have never leaked over 10 years of carrying them in my pockets and backpack, don't smear, are lightweight and cheap. The 07 has a pretty crisp fine line for writing or drawing. I now find other pens insufficient and will always take the trouble to locate one of these. I buy them by the dozen.

-- KK

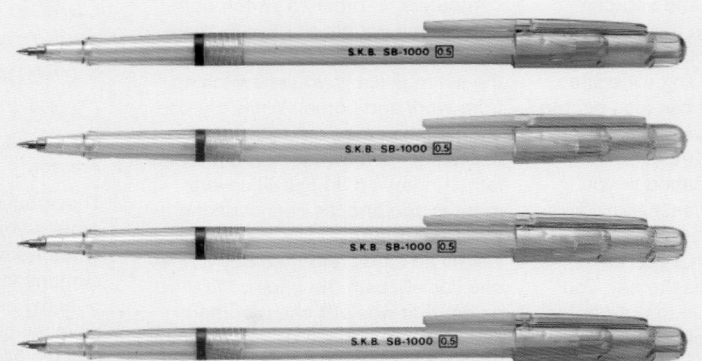

Affordable and reliable technical pen
SKB Pens
$12, .5 mm, 12 pens skbpens.com

This is the only pen I have owned that is suitable for writing technical notes. It has a .5mm point, which allows me to write small details such as subscripts and fractions. It is a ballpoint so it doesn't bleed which is an annoyance I've encountered when writing small details with other pens. It doesn't gum up as my Zebra ballpoints tended to do and so is suitable for drawing diagrams. It can write continuously without drying up and flows well over the paper. Most .5mm pens I've used dry up after writing for a while and are so sharp that they end up scratching the paper.

It's also affordable. Unfortunately, while it only costs $1 a pen there is only one supplier in the US (that I'm aware of) and you have to buy twelve pens at a time.

You can buy it in black, blue, red, purple, or green with a .5mm point. You can also get it in black with a .7mm point.

-- Daniel Woelfel

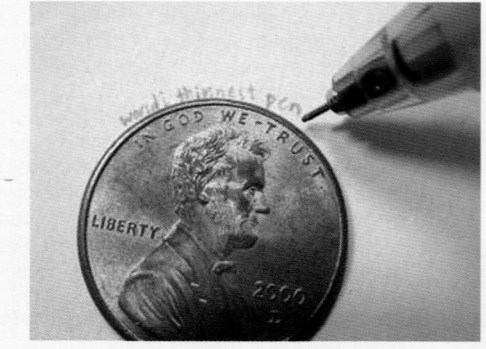

World's thinnest line pen
UniBall Signo Bit 0.18mm Pens
$4 Signo Bit 0.18 mm Pen jetpens.com

World's thinnest ballpoint pen…thinnest possible lines you could ever write. It's quite fine. It has some sort of special ink for reducing friction so it won't clog. It's not super-flowy like a normal gel pen but it allows you to make sharp and precise short lines, which is what I suspect it was designed to do (i.e. for writing Japanese characters (see circle in picture with writing between lines of text), or alternatively adding fine details into drawings). I think it's pretty cool.

-- Tim Hong

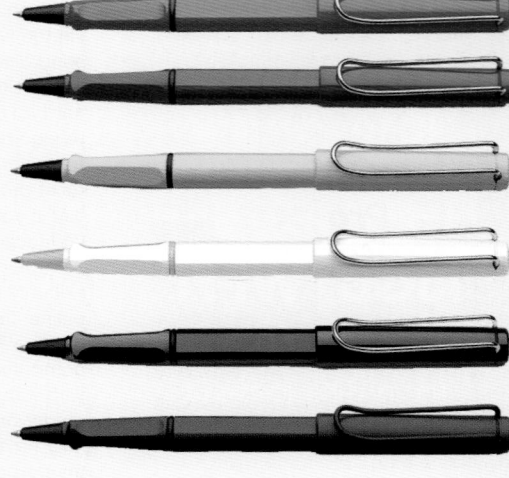

Freeflowing fountain pen
Lamy Safari Fountain Pen
$26 jetpens.com

$6 Lamy Safari Refillable Ink Converter Z24 Amazon

Most fountain pens are appealing for their authoritative weight and the prestige of pushing an antique technology around the page. However, the Lamy Safari pen (designed by Wolfgang Fabian) re-thinks the fountain pen with comfort and accuracy in mind. It comes with a sturdy ergonomic grip similar too, but not as comfy as, the Dr. Grip. The pen is also made out of plastic making the weight (and cost) much less than a traditional fountain pen.

The Lamy weighs in at a meager $30 with ink costing about $2 to $5 dollars a bottle. The Safari is also frugal on ink; it runs a much smaller and tighter line than many pens meaning that the ink dries faster on the page, but do beware using ink from a different pen in the Lamy can clog it. You can see the ink cartridge at all times because a small part of the casing has been hollowed out.

Finally, the refillable cartridge snaps into place in the pen and is refillable through the pen's stylus hence you don't have to take everything apart when you want to refill (you do have to unscrew the top of the pen to get to the cart's screw, but not the bottom) and also eliminating that first air bubble you get when placing traditional carts back in the pen. The plunger is operated by a screw action on the top making it easy to hold the pen in place while you refill it. It is also available as a left handed version.

Lamy also sells other pens with a similar design and grip if you're looking for a more expensive or stylish pen, but despite the Safari's minor flaws (I had major problems the first day getting it to write consistently until I watered down my ink) it's quickly replaced my old Picasso pen for everyday scribbling. I now own two Lamys, using one for correcting tests and the other for everyday writing. The over-sized clip is also a bonus as it's less likely to get bent out of shape by clinging to pockets, belts, etc.

-- Andrew Jones

Noodler's Inks
$10 Noodler's Bulletproof Black Ink Amazon
$18 Noodler's Red Fox Eternal Fountain Pen Ink Amazon

I've been using Noodler's inks in my fountain pens for at least six years. The basic Black is my favorite ink of all time, dries fast, and is utterly impervious to water or erasure once dried on paper. The Fox Red is also a favorite. Expensive, but very cheap in comparison to disposable ballpoints, and much better for the environment.

-- David Derbes

Though I am only a recent convert to the world of fountain pens, I have been really impressed with the Noodler's Bulletproof Black Ink. When I first got started I tried a number of inks including some from Lamy and Parker only to find my writing would fade and wash away with the slightest hint of moisture. I decided I

needed something more permanent.

My research paid off when I discovered Noodler's Inks. Noodler's ink is all made in the USA. I've been impressed with the amount of information they provide regarding the various qualities and properties of their ink. As far as their ink goes, it's great. The black ink that I use isn't as richly black as others, but it certainly holds up to the bulletproof claim when faced with the elements (water, sun, etc). In terms of ink flow, I have found the Noodler's to be perfect for my needs (although the ink is only one half of the equation, the nib being the other). I use a fine nib, and have never had a problem. I will point out, though, that this is variable from ink to ink (and nib to nib) even from the same manufacturer.

Noodler's Ink is sold in larger volumes (88 ml vs 50 ml, in most cases) but at a lower cost per unit volume when compared to other brands. The one bottle of Bulletproof Black I bought

doesn't look like it will be running out anytime soon in the next few years.

Finally, Noodler's produces a range of specialty inks with different classifications including fluorescence, forgery resistance, and archival fade-resistance to name but a few. I highly recommend poking around their website to learn more.

-- Oliver Hulland

Be yourself, because everyone else is already taken. - Oscar Wilde

Instant ink brush
Pentel Pocket Brush Pen
$14 jetpens.com

Leave it to the Japanese to create a brush pen. This pocketable pen has a super fine brush tip of actual bristles, perfect for tiny Kanji characters, or of course, doodling in your journal, or sketching in your Moleskine. While it's hugely popular with comic book folks and cartoonists, artists of all stripes have picked one up for their paper work. The feel is incredibly

tactile and lovely. It works like a fountain pen, with replaceable rich ink cartridges. Once capped it doesn't leak as far as I can tell. (There's a moment of panic when you first assemble it since the instructions are 100% in Japanese, but just insert the ball-bearing end of the ink capsule into the tip.) You can purchase other color inks as well.

-- KK

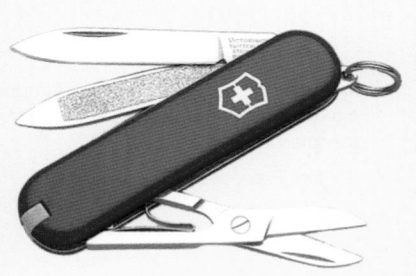

Almost invisible pen
Swiss Army Replacement Pen

I got my ruler out to see if it would clip into my wallet and found that the 4" long stainless steel Derringer wallet pen would protrude from my 3.88" wallet. The pen I've got in my wallet is almost invisible unless you know it's there. I use — and have done so for many years — a Swiss Army Knife pen refill, Victorinox model number 30422.

It costs $2.95. It's a replacement pen for the one that comes as original equipment in Swiss Army Knives. 91mm (2.75") long, with a gray, curved top that fits snugly into the body of a Swiss Army Knife, these

handy little pens come in blue or black ink. There's also an even smaller (2" long) version that fits the smaller, key-chain size knives. I don't recommend it because it's very difficult to grasp and write with.

Now, you are not going to want to copy out Moby Dick with my little pen, but for quick notes, sudden flights of fancy or inspiration, phone numbers, and the like, you can't beat it. And I always have a pen. So often no one does, and I don't think I do, until I realize hey, I do have one. People smirk and scoff but they're very glad when they see it writes just fine. A life-saver.

-- Joseph Stirt

$5 Swiss Army Replacement Ball Point Pen Amazon

$20 Swiss Army Signature Pocket Knife (w/ pen) Amazon

Write-anywhere minimalism
Fisher Bullet Space Pen

I like to have a few essential tools with me at all times: my Swiss Army knife, a keychain LED flashlight, a pocket notebook and a pen for scribbling notes whenever inspiration strikes.

I'd searched a long time for a pen that was small enough to carry around in my pocket, yet comfortable to write with and reliable enough to work every time I needed it. I finally found it with the Fisher Space Pen.

Everyone has heard of the legendary Space Pen, which was developed for the space program and writes upside down, under water and in extreme temperatures. They make many different varieties of the Space Pen, but the most useful and elegant is the Bullet (pictured alongside Uniball).

The Fisher Bullet is in two pieces: the actual pen,

and a cap that fits on the back of the pen to make a full-size writing instrument. When closed, it makes a compact, tight-fitting, gasket-sealed capsule that easily fits in your pocket. It comes with a shirt pocket clip that can be removed, so it's less obtrusive in your pants pocket.

You can get it in chrome, but the matte black finish is so much cooler.

-- Curtis Galloway

Fisher Stowaway Space Pen

After losing two (expensive) Fisher Bullet Space Pens, I stumbled across their significantly less expensive Stowaway. They're small, available in three styles, with or without a clip on the cap, and with a stylus on the opposite end of the tip. Three colors, too: black, red and blue.

-- Eric Rosenberg

I always liked the idea of Paul Fisher's bullet-shaped Space Pens but at around $20 always felt they were not worth the benefits (writing anywhere, upside down, any temperature, under water, over grease, etc.). Now they sell a tiny (4 x 0.4 x 0.4 in.; 5.1 in. in writing mode) pretty-much-weightless tube pen called the Stowaway with the famous ink refill, for about half the price of the Bullet. I bought a mess of them and threw one in every jacket.

-- Vince Crisci

$10 Stowaway Space Pen Amazon

$16 Bullet Space Pen Amazon

Ultracompact wallet pen
Ohto Petit-B
$9 Ohto Petit-B Needle Point Ballpoint Pen Jetpens
$1 for refill

I usually carry a bunch of pens in a leather pocket protector (a beautiful, inexpensive thing from John C. Robert's Leather Works). My wife despairs when we go someplace nice and I'm carrying all this stuff. So I wanted a small pen that would fit unobtrusively in my pocket. The previously reviewed Derringer Pen is just a little too long for my wallet.

This Ohto pen, just a bit smaller, is ideal. It's only 3.1 inches closed, 5.1 inches open, and fits perfectly in the fold of my wallet.

-- David Derbes

Affordable, pocketable pens
Zebra Compact and Telescoping Pens

I've always wanted a small pen to keep with me at all times for quick notes and such. I've even considered taking a hacksaw to the venerable Bic ballpoint pen to keep in my wallet. One of the things that kept me from doing that was worrying about it exploding and flooding my pocket with ink.

Fortunately, Zebra has come up with a far more elegant and affordable solution with the Telescopic and F-301 Compact pens. Both feature a metal body made popular in their other pens. The telescopic pen body extends to a regular pen length when full telescoped, and exposes the tip, ready to write. Retracting the pen body for stowage fully retracts the tip safely into the body, like a frightened turtle. It fits neatly in the fold of my tri-fold wallet. I found them at my local OfficeMax for about $5. So far, it's survived some gnarly crashes during snow-boarding trips, and being sat on daily with out a single dent.

-- K. Rhainos

The Zebra Compact closes to a small size and has a clip for shirt pockets. I have used this pen for a couple of years. In the past I've used the previously reviewed Fisher Space Pen but they are expensive and easy to lose because they are so smooth. This pen is cheap and even cheaper when you can find them at Walmart. Not only that but the refills are cheap, too!

-- Chris Acree

$7 F-301 Compact Pen, 2-pack Amazon

$5 Telescopic Ballpoint Pen Amazon

Ever ready pen
Derringer Wallet Pen
$8 derringerpen.com

Not earth-shattering, but this wallet pen is really handy. I am never without something to write with. The good thing about the pen is that it clips in, so I never have to worry about where I put it.

-- Chuck Green

Writing Paper

Water-resistant writing pads
Rite in the Rain Notebooks
$7 (3.5" x 5") Rite in the Rain

Whether you're a hiker, biker, backpacker, camper, naturalist or simply someone who's ever been caught in the rain, you'll treasure these classic all-weather notebooks. The cover is Polydura and the

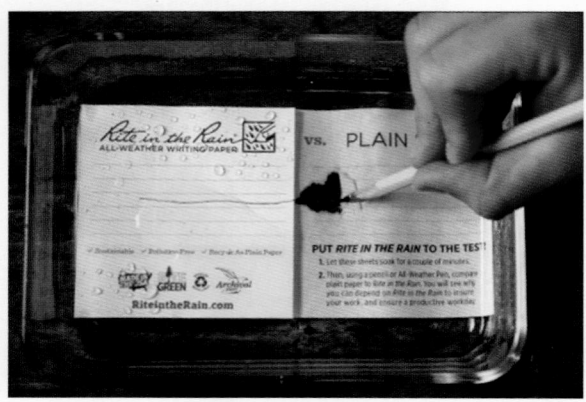

pages are made with a substrate, giving the paper a wax-y feel. The effect: water beads off them, meaning no pulpy mess and no bummer over any lost thoughts or data. They are not a new invention by any means. Back in the 1920s, they were developed for Pacific Northwest loggers. These days, the manufacturer makes both bound and spiral bound books in an impressive array of sizes and types (e.g birding!). I keep a pocket-size, 24-page, staple bound mini-book in the small pack I take cycling and hiking. In the event of a downpour, all my ah-ha moments are safe. If you plan to be in really harsh conditions and want to go the extra mile, you might try one of their all-weather pens. Note: I have not used them — a pencil or standard ballpoint does the trick for me.

-- Steven Leckart

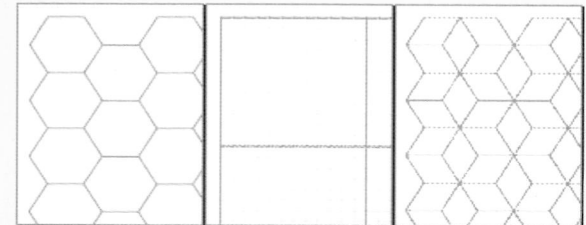

Custom-printed graph paper
Free Online Graph Paper / Grid Paper PDFs
Free incompetech.com

OK, so I wanted to sit down and workout a grand plan for my new garden, so I figure a pencil and some graph paper is the way forward.

Just finding some simple 2mm graph paper with 1cm semi bold and 2 cm bold turned out to be a near impossible task. Then I discovered the Graph Paper PDF Generator at incompetech.com .

It does plain paper, lined paper, multi width, hexagonal, even semi-bisected trapezoid! All completely customizable. And it's free!

-- Mark Coffey

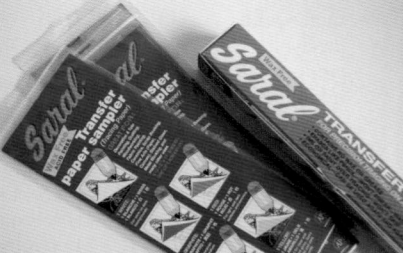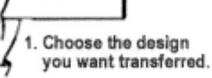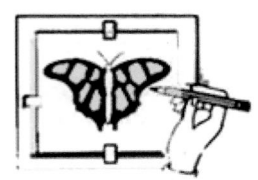

Analog copy/paste
Saral Transfer Paper
$16 Saral Paper

Before I start a new painting, I usually draw what I want in Adobe Illustrator, and then transfer a printout of that drawing to canvas or board to paint. I've tried opaque projectors, but the image is faint (at least on the el-cheapo version I use) and I don't really have room to set it up. I've also tried using a piece of paper that I've rubbed pencil or charcoal on, but that produces a blurry line.

Like an idiot, it wasn't until recently that I considered the possibility that there might be a transfer paper for artists. Of course, there is one. It's called Saral Wax-Free

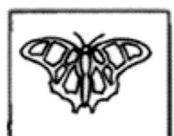

Transfer Paper, and it works like a dream. It comes in five different colors, but I can get away with blue and white. It leaves a clear, thin line that erases easily and doesn't mess up the color of the paint I use. I'm already hooked on it for life.

If you send a self-addressed, stamped envelope to Saral, they'll send you free samples in all five colors.

-- Mark Frauenfelder

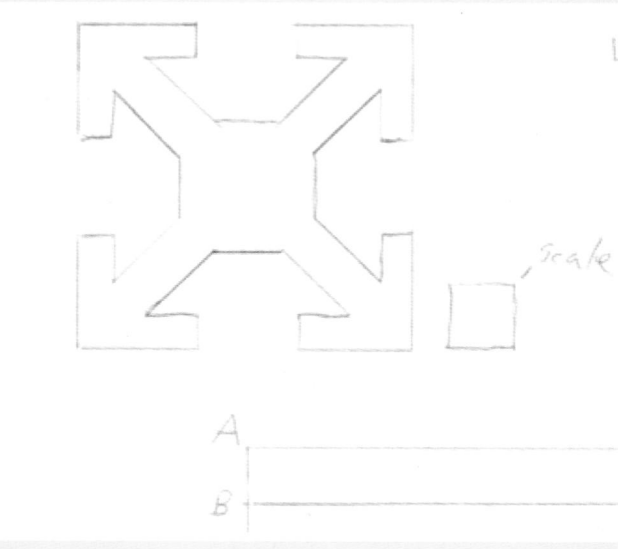

Better graph paper
Whitelines
$11 Perfect Bound A4 Squared Notebook Amazon

Anyone doing technical or design work has burned through reams of graph paper. I'm a designer, and I use Whitelines to do technical drawings in accurate scale, which are then turned into 3-D models and die tooling diagrams. Whitelines is the best graph paper I have ever worked with.

The concept is simple and powerful. Ordinary graph paper is paper with a graph of lines printed on it in a light color, often blue or gray. Whitelines is paper with a very light gray grid of squares printed on it. The graph is unprinted, hence, white lines.

This is genius. Pen strokes, and even pencil, are startlingly clear against the background. The distracting visual noise of a printed graph is gone entirely, while retaining the precision and ability to see scale, which is graph paper's reason for being.

I've been using Whitelines extensively for the past few months, mostly for technical drafting on the MakerBeam project, an open source metal building kit like Meccano for the Arduino set. The grid is 0.5 centimeter pitch, perfect for working on a metric standard. With ordinary graph paper, pencil lines are close in color weight to the lines themselves. When scanning pencil marks on ordinary graph paper, the pencil lines often vanish completely. With Whitelines, I can scan a pencil sketch, if I'm satisfied with it, without having to go back over it with pen.

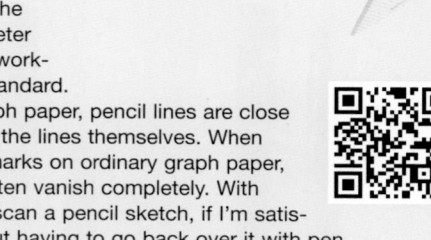

Available in A4, A5 and pocket sizes, as tablets, spiral bound, perfect and hardbound, both lined and graph. Better graph paper makes better drawings, and this is genuinely better graph paper.

-- Sam Putman

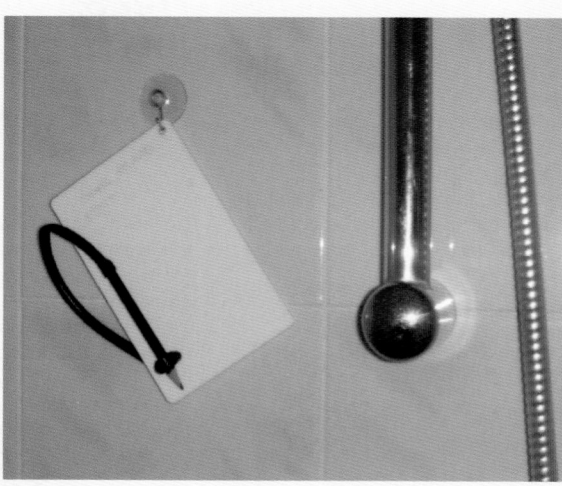

Image: Idea Sandbox

Notes under water
Shower Slate
$6 (5" x 6") Amazon

Ever have an idea in the shower and have no way to record it…and then it's lost forever? I use a "Dive Slate", a small (~4"x6") sheet of sturdy white plastic with a plain old fashioned golf pencil attached. They're cheap (around $5-$8), available on the net at various dive shops, fit nicely behind the soap holder or hung in the shower and work well; they're meant to be written on underwater by divers, so unless you shower under Niagara Falls, your thought will be captured until you erase it.

-- Vincent Crisci

When you're through changing, you're through. - Bruce Barton

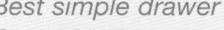

Best simple drawer
Google Drawing
Free Google Drive

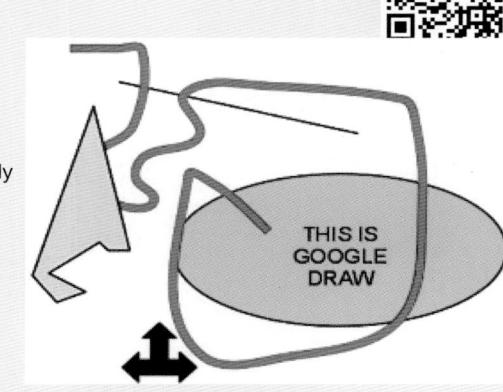

The best simple drawing program right now is hidden away inside of Google Drive. It's free, and completely intuitive to use. Google Drawing is the opposite of Adobe's Illustrator, which is insanely deep (and expensive) and requires hours if not years to master. You can draw with this one in seconds. The controls of Google's app follow the same general novice format as those in Power Point, or Word, but don't require any other software beyond your browser. More importantly, it is a no-brainer to export the drawing directly to the web, or as a jpeg or even PDF. And it has the usual advantages of cloud life: the drawing can be collaboratively worked, and it is backed up automatically. Despite being idiot-proof you can do amazingly sophisticated work with it — diagrams, charts, doodles, or paint over photographic images. For 99% of your drawing needs, this handy free app will satisfy nicely. As Jerry Micalski, who introduced me to this gem, said of it: "it's as simple as MacDraw but smart enough to publish to a Web page."

-- KK

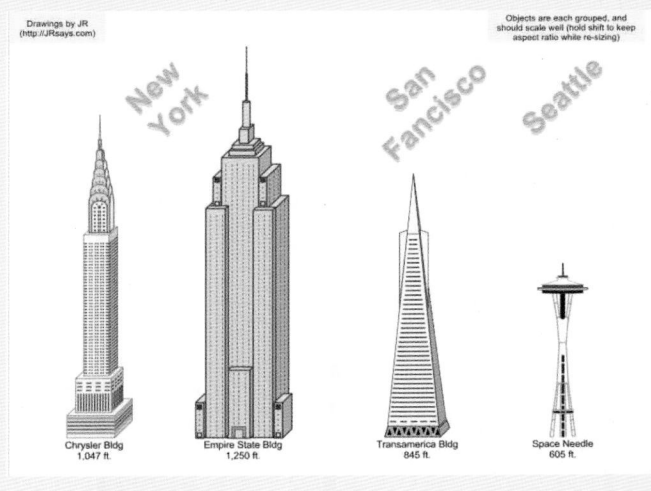

Best iPad stylus
Pogo Connect
$66 Ten 1 Design

I've been using this stylus like crazy and I am in love! It's a touch sensitive stylus for drawing and painting on the iPad which works incredibly well. Because of its touch-sensitive capabilities, this is the first stylus that allows me to think of the iPad as tool for serious illustration. I love my Wacom tablet, but using this is a completely different and, in some ways, a much more direct way to connect to my work… especially once I'd found the right drawing app. I suggest Procreate, which is designed to take advantage of the Pogo Connect.

Having said this, the Pogo stylus has a couple drawbacks. For example, the setup of the pen is unclear. This confused me and a number of other Amazon reviewers who expressed their frustration at never getting it working. Stick with it! Follow the directions… it does work and it works well!

Secondly, the build of the stylus is sorta cheap. During the first usage of my Pogo Connect, I pressed the (flimsy) plastic button into the hollow body. Arg! How infuriating! And I am not the first to have had this problem. With no button, the stylus was unusable.

The Pogo Connect is an awesome tool. Now that I have it, I'm unable to live without it! But I'll always press that button with a feather touch!

-- Robyn Miller

Digital Paper
Cintiq
$2,400 Cintiq 21UX Wacom

Based on comics master Scott McCloud's recommendation (below), I bought a Cintiq. It does something I've always wanted to do since I first saw a computer. This thing is a pen-based tablet that doubles as a monitor. In other words you draw directly on the tablet, just like a paper-based drawing, but digitally. In fact the surface of the Cintq monitor/tablet feels like paper under a pen. Synchrony of image with your movements is almost exact, and the micro difference doesn't seem to matter. The result is weirdly like ink, or paint, but with all the control and magic of Photoshop. Of course, as a monitor, it will display whatever's on your computer, whether it's animation software or a spreadsheet. (You could hook it up to a $500 Mac Mini and have a fabulous digital art studio.) It's slowly being adopted by film animators and other high-end graphic professionals. A Cintiq is expensive ($2,500), big, thick and bulky (it is too fat to sit on your lap like other tablets, but it can lay flat on a desk), but if you are producing digital images for a living, it speeds up your productivity and eases your hurt. It's fun to use.

-- KK

Drawing directly on the screen with the Cintiq Tablet made a huge difference in my artwork, and sped up my workflow by at least 30%, maybe more. It also saved me a lot of hand-strain. Apart from the Mac, it's one of my all-time favorite digital tools.

Pencil input
Wacom Tablet
$105 Intuos3 4×5 Tablet Wacom

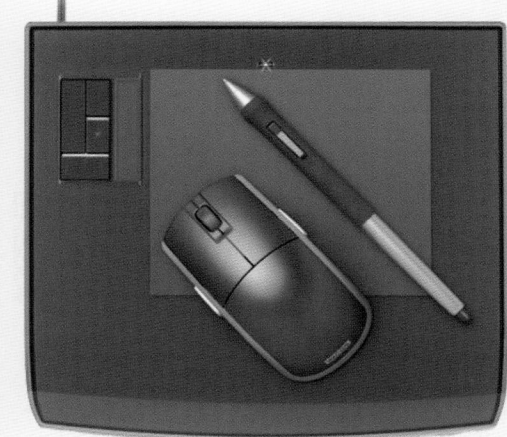

I don't use pen and ink anymore. I use a Wacom tablet and stylus to draw directly into Photoshop, Illustrator, etc. It's really the only way to draw with computers. I met a cartoonist who was drawing using a mouse; I have no idea how he did it. He was like a mountain man. I use the smallest of Wacom's Intuos tablets (about 4 x 5 inches) to plug into my laptop so I can lean it against the tray tables on airplanes.

-- Scott McCloud

In 2003-2004, I lost about a year of work to hand strain, using a regular tablet, mouse and keyboard. I'd work for a couple of hours each day on my comics and get these shooting pains up my arm and have trouble holding the pen steady. I got a good deal on a Cintiq (a slightly smaller model than today's 21" monster, but equally suited to graphics) at the end of '04 a couple of months before I had to begin finished pages on the new book. After finishing all 225 pages by early 2006 using a Cintiq, I'd had no hand strain at all; even working 11 hours a day, 7 days a week.

Most importantly, I actually *liked* the way the art looked. I was never that comfortable with pen and ink tools, and liked all the digital options I started getting in the mid-90's, but my work on the old tablet was always wobbly and lame. Now there's much more control, confidence and warmth to the drawings.

I was an idiot not to buy a Cintiq in '99 when I first saw them on display at a New York show. I figured I couldn't afford it, but I wound up losing a lot more time and money by NOT having one.

-- Scott McCloud

There is only one difference between a madman and me. I am not mad. -Salvador Dali

355

Notebooks

Customizable spiral bound journal
Levenger Circa Notebook

$109+ leather cover, varying sizes Levenger
$14+ Starter Kit Notebook
$13+ refills

I've been using Levenger's products for about 10 years, most notably their Circa notebooks. The ring-based binding allows not only quick removal and replacement of pages, but also a nice mix and match format for a variety of sheets, including ruled, blank, grid, address book, calendar, and more. I have a couple leather covers that I change around a bit to reduce wear on the notebooks. I tend to walk around with a normal junior size Circa notebook (about 5"x8") with pages of several types inside, including little contact information cards, 3x5s, etc. Sometimes I'll take a page out and offset it by one ring so it sticks out above the others to denote a new section (though I believe they have all kinds of dividers and such now). The rings themselves, though plastic, are sturdy and heavy — notably better than the Rollabind notebook. The paper is a fairly heavy stock with good absorption and a great feel when writing on it with either rollerballs or fountain pens. The line printing is subtle but clear and it comes in a variety of layouts, though I tend to stick with the Columbia note taking system layout (with a column down the left-hand side), which used to be their only offering. They also sell paper in larger packs of 300, so I tend to keep a couple reams on hand. The hole puncher from Levenger is also a well-machined thing.

I can't really go back to normal notebooks. Hard-bound notebooks don't lay flat. Even with a spiral notebook with double-ring wiring I rarely find one with a high enough paper quality to suit my tastes. Nevertheless, there are a couple downsides (I'm not a complete sycophant). If you "work" a page too much in the binding (and it really has to be quite a lot) the little tabs will wear a bit and without the strength of being sandwiched between other pages, it can be a bit less secure in the bindings. A small price, but I've had pages that I repeatedly go back to fall out. Also, the diameter of the rings restricts the width of the notebook to something close to 5/8 of an inch while the rings stick out a bit. However, you can buy bigger rings. The Circa was the first and only disc-based removable/replaceable page binding I'd ever seen. Though there are a couple competitors now (like the Rollabind), I really find Levenger's product line second to none. I do flinch at the price when I click "checkout," but I'm always vindicated when I open the box.

-- Mike Wilson

I've been using various Circa products since their inception. The real value of the Circa notebooks is that I don't have to buy many of the notebooks any more. I have enough binders and pieces that now I typically purchase only the refills and create my own notebooks designed for specific uses, mixing the different formats (lined, grid, blank). I have a couple 5-subject letter-sized notebooks, the junior and letter-size single-subject notebooks, and I also carry a Circa PDA in my coat pocket for noting things I find while I'm out. I can use the lined pages for normal notetaking and writing, insert a grid page for a table or a blank page for a mind map. I generally start with about ten lined pages and five blank and grid pages in a notebook and then arrange them as needed. Being a minimalist, I like to start with the least number of sheets to do the job and then add as needed to the capacity of the rings. There have been only two problems I had with them over time: 1) the paper is twice as thick as normal note paper, so the 5-subject notebook simply weighed too much, and 2) I tended to wear out the paper connections in one section before reaching other sections. However, since switching from the 5-subject to the junior and letter single-subject notebooks, I don't have the weight or wear problems.

-- Gary Scott

Handy pocket notebooks
Moleskine Notebooks

$11 squared, lined, or plain Moleskine

These come in several sizes; the pocket size (just a tad larger than a 3 x 5 card) is perfect for a breast pocket or cargo pants pocket. The paper is acid free and rich enough to take ink, so you can sketch as well as take notes, but the most useful feature is the elastic band (which is a built in bookmark) that holds the notebook together — you can stuff business cards, clippings, sketches on napkins between the pages, and the rubberized cloth thing holds them all together until you can find a place for the scraps. I've carried mine literally around the world.

-- Howard Rheingold

Soft-cover notebook
Field Notes

$10 48-page memo book, 3-pack Field Notes

I've tried lots of different small notebooks. Field Notes are the best ones I've found, small and thin enough to really have with you all the time, in a shirt or pants pocket. I've carried them for over a year, and my small notebook is used every day for ideas, shopping lists, account numbers/passwords (coded, of course), design sketches, references.

I am now laminating the covers with simple self-seal lamination sheet to lengthen the life of the cardboard cover.

I love leather, but all the leather and Moleskine notebooks are simply too thick for me to carry all the time in a pocket, which is where the Field Notes pads have made the difference.

-- John C. Moore

Best inexpensive sketchbook
Academie Wirebound

$17 11 x 8-1/2 Inches, 70 Sheets Mead

I do a lot of sketching and art of various kinds and in various mediums, such as pencil, chalk, Copic markers and ink. For this I need a good quality paper, but don't want to spend a lot of money; I don't want to feel guilty doing throwaway work. The best buy I've found is Mead's Academie 70-sheet Spiral Bound notebook, and I've been using it for the past two years.

These sketchbooks are ideal for several reasons. First are cost and availability: They're inexpensive and can be purchased practically anywhere, from office supply stores to Walmart and Target. The paper quality is good enough for frameable art. The sturdy notebooks have a solid pressboard back, so I generally don't need an easel, and the pages are perforated for easy removal. There's a two-sided pocket, so I can remove and stow keepers. I find the pocket helps me keep track of specific renderings, too. Because these sketchbooks are inexpensive, I can use a few concurrently and switch back and forth between different mediums. The paper quality is great for the price, too. It works well for Copic markers, especially, giving a true color rendering. The pages are non-yellowing (acid-free), as well.

For comparison, Strathmore drawing pads have more size options, but at 40 to 50 sheets per book, the cost per sheet is higher, and the Strathmore's pages aren't perforated for easy removal.

-- Stephen Young

We begin to see the present only when it has disappeared. - R. D. Laing

Refillable Manga medium
Copic Markers

$63 set of 12 Amazon

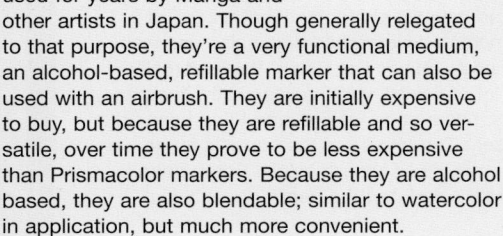

Copic markers are Japanese-made markers that have been used for years by Manga and other artists in Japan. Though generally relegated to that purpose, they're a very functional medium, an alcohol-based, refillable marker that can also be used with an airbrush. They are initially expensive to buy, but because they are refillable and so versatile, over time they prove to be less expensive than Prismacolor markers. Because they are alcohol based, they are also blendable; similar to watercolor in application, but much more convenient.

Copic markers are somewhat limited in application, and not something generally as versatile as acrylic- or oil-based media. The advantage in my case is mostly portability. For anything larger than an 8 1/2X11" page, they wouldn't be practical. Think of them as more for cartooning than fine art. I do a lot of caricaturing and figure drawing, for which they work well.

-- Stephen Young

Check out the COPIC Marker Flickr pool for some stunning examples of what can be done with these markers. Inset by Frambl2 on Flickr.

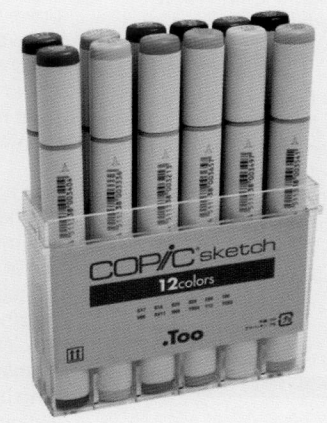

For indelible writing on dark glossy surfaces
Metallic Sharpie

$3 2-pack Amazon

The Metallic Sharpie is a vast improvement over other metallic pens out there — no shaking the pen before use, and the ink doesn't puddle up. It dries permanent and shows up great on dark surfaces as well as light ones. It became favorite art tool in my arsenal when I was able to write a friend's phone number on a freshly opened, ice-cold beer bottle. Seconds after jotting the number, it was indelible. I try to take it everywhere — it's good for men's room graffiti, VHS tapes, I even labeled various keys on my key ring. You can get metallic sharpies at Staples or Office Max.

-- Chris Sperandio

There's almost no other way to easily write on slippery surfaces. The metallic sharpie uses silver ink, which has remarkable contrast against both light and dark surfaces. For writing on black plastic or enamel (there is more of it around than you think) nothing else will do.

-- KK

I have managed to accumulate dozens of small transformers over the years. Those black plastic "wall wart" things. They get unplugged from the device and usually they are totally generic in their labeling. Whatever they powered has gone away, but the transformer remains.

I grabbed one and wrote the product the new transformer belonged to in silver ink on black plastic. I'd tried grease pencils and tags and such stuff before, but they just never worked out. This seems to be the fix. I am so excited about this discovery, I just had to share it.

-- Norm A.

Fine point performance
Sharpie Twin-Tip

$4 Amazon

Sharpie markers are well-known for being indelible, particularly on plastic, glass and metal surfaces. Folks in labs, movie sets, and hospitals who need to mark things permanently use Sharpies. If the ink goes on, it won't come off. What's special here is that the other tip of these pens is an ultra- fine point Sharpie, fine enough to write like a ball-point pen – but permanently — when you need to. The "industrial" version of Sharpie ink will even resist chemicals and scrubbing. Since more writing surfaces seem to be plastic-like, I find we use Sharpies all the time now.

-- KK

Keep your nib as sharp as possible and, with very light pressure, make hairlines as fine as the pen will allow.

50°
Lift and draw the curved stem. Make a short hairline in an upward movement.

35°
Make another hairline upward from the stem to start the bowl.

50°
Draw the bowl with a full nib, starting below the top of the hairline.

d h k l

Learning to hand letter
Calligraphy · The Calligrapher's Bible

Calligraphy: A Course in Hand Lettering is the best book for teaching yourself calligraphy, which you *can* do on your own. It's how I learned. The book is spiral-bound to lay flat and includes transparent guide sheets for practice. You write over its pages. The course is structured simply and will teach you the basic Italian cursive hands. I prefer it over other guides because it focuses on getting the basics right, without intimidating you with a lot of fancy work. By the end of this course you'll be able to do a passable wedding invitation, envelope, or framable quotation.

If you want to move onto additional scripts, the *Calligrapher's Bible* (also spiral bound) will show you how to hand write over a hundred of them. The directions for each hand are clear and concise. This will last you many years.

-- KK

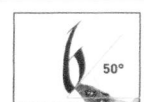

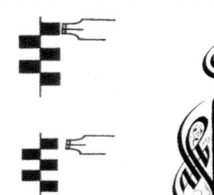

Pen nib

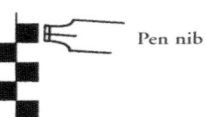

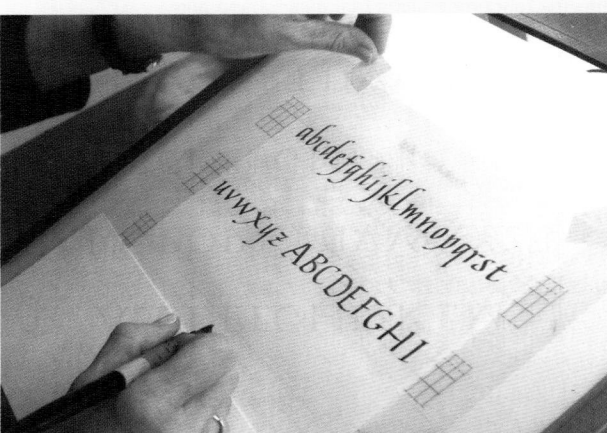

The Italic hand's classic letter proportion is five nib widths, as the checkerboard pattern at right shows.

$18 The Calligrapher's Bible David Harris, 2003, 256 p.

The double-pencil technique reproduces the characteristic "thicks and thins" of a broad-edged pen. Pen angle and stroke direction determine where the thicker and thinner parts of the letter appear. The diagonal broken line through the letter *o*, at left, is the axis of the thin part of the stroke as created by a 45-degree pen angle.

d
45° pen angle
a
45° pen angle
b
e
c
45° pen angle
baseline
d
letter slope of 3°

CALLIGRAPHY
A Course in Hand Lettering
Maryanne Grebenstein

$15 Calligraphy: A Course in Hand Lettering Maryanne Grebenstein, 2006, 144 p.

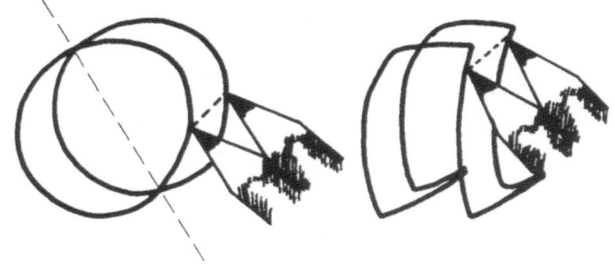

Pencils

Chunky mechanical pencil
Pentel Twist Erase III
$11 2-pack Amazon

After reading about the previously reviewed slightly more luxurious Pentel Sharp Kerry I would highly recommend the Pentel Twist Erase III pencils for their comfort and larger lead size. They come in a 0.9mm lead size and are very comfortable to hold. The larger lead size hardly ever breaks and feels like a sharpened #2 pencil in use. They also have a larger-than-normal eraser that is actually useful, a rare feature with mechanical pencils. They come in a 2-pack for about $10. They are functional rather than fancy.

I've had a couple of these for about four years, and they still look the same as they did when purchased. I guard them jealously because I have always been afraid that Pentel would stop selling them. However, it seems that the larger lead sizes must be catching on since I noticed a large assortment of 0.7mm and larger size pencils during a recent office store visit.

-- Harvey Chapman

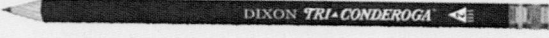

No Roll No.2
Tri-Conderoga Executive Pencil
$9 dozen Amazon

After elementary school, I didn't use pencils much — until I started blogging. I keep my list of posts on a small notepad and I do so in pencil because the time and day of my posts change constantly. I'd always been a big fan of standard Dixons, but recently discovered their Tri-Conderoga. Unlike a standard-sized pencil in the vein of the Derwent 3B, the Tri-Conderoga has a triangular shape and an increased girth, which make it nicely ergonomic, relaxing in the hand and very satisfying to use. After several weeks of daily use, I like using them even more. The satiny finish is lagniappe.

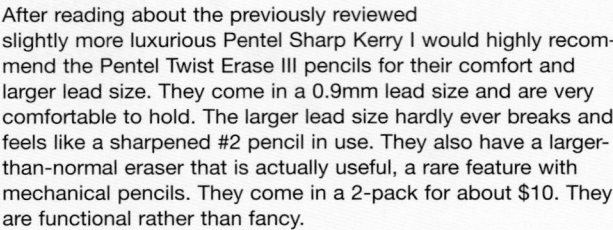

One negative: It's so large it doesn't fit in my Panasonic battery-powered sharpener. However, when you buy a box of 12, Dixon supplies a larger-bore hand-held sharpener. Bonus: when it gets shorter as you use/sharpen it, the pencil handles much better and is less annoying than a stubby regular pencil. Thus, I tend to use these longer before breaking in a new one.

-- Joseph Stirt

Advances while you write
Ticonderoga Sensematic Auto-Feed Pencil
$16 0.7 mm, 5-pack Amazon

I've been using the Ticonderoga Sensematic Auto-Feed Mechanical Pencil (0.7mm, #2) for awhile now. The difference between this and other mechanical pencils is that the lead automatically advances as you write. No clicking or twisting needed. This is a great benefit as the lead doesn't accidentally advance while trying to erase.

Additionally, I normally break 0.7mm leads, but not with this pencil — the lead is kept short as it automatically advances, minimizing breakage. And while I like the looks of the pencils that have been previously reviewed on this site I'm not paying $16 or $17 for one since I am notorious for losing them!

-- Stephanie Moore

Though it is not marketed as "refillable" many people have reported being able to refill this with standard mechanical pencil lead. -- Oliver Hulland

Auto-sharpening pencil
Uni-ball Kuru Toga
$8 jetpens.com

The Kuru Toga is a self-sharpening mechanical pencil that solves a problem that's inherent with normal mechanical pencils. After just a couple of lines of writing with a typical mechanical pencil, the lead becomes a blunt irregular chisel shape, leading to clumsier and more smeary writing. Experienced pencil users try to counteract this by rotating their pencil every few words, a tactic that works very imperfectly.

The Kuru Toga, however, writes as precisely and evenly as a high quality gel pen by automatically counteracting this problem. An internal ratchet mechanism rotates the lead minutely with every stroke you make, constantly sharpening and rounding the lead against the paper. The resulting writing is noticeably more legible and can be much finer than with a standard pencil – ideal for tasks like coding, diagramming, annotating and general note taking.

The Kuro Toga is not retractable, but it is highly ergonomic, and my 0.5mm specimen (the Kuru Toga also comes in 0.3mm) seems never to suffer from broken leads (I've used both HB and 2B leads). Looking at my notebooks, I've written about 150 A4 pages with about 30,000 words and diagrams. No sign of wear. It's surprisingly cheap for being the best pencil I've ever found.

-- Jonathan Coupe

In praise of the pencil
Derwent 3B
$2 artsuppliesonline.com

A pencil can generate megabytes of text, needs no batteries, and has no user manual. It is comfortable to hold, it smells good, and it is relaxing to turn around in your hand as you try to think of the right words. Pencils don't need ink; all they need is a sharpener. They are warm and friendly; they have souls.

I've long been a pencil fan, and, even if I'm writing these words on my iBook, I have several pencils next to me. I use them to doodle and sketch, or to jot down ideas as I brainstorm. Much more than pens, the pencil has character: it comes from nature – from trees and the soil – and it is rooted in the deeper subconscious as a tool that has lasted for some two centuries.

But not just any pencil will do. I've tried out most of the pencils I have come across, and my quest ended when I bought a box of Derwent Graphic pencils, in assorted hardnesses, and eventually discovered the sensual feel of the 3B pencil. The soft lead of the 3B lets me write with no impediments, as the words almost ooze out of my hand. Combined with a yellow legal pad, I can think of no better word processor.

-- Kirk McElhearn

Inexpensive Bargain
Mirado Black Warrior Pencil
$3 for a dozen Amazon

The Mirado Black Warrior pencil is made in the USA from high quality materials, available practically everywhere, and, very importantly, cheap (hey, it's a pencil, after all).

The Black Warrior's No. 2/HB graphite is darker and softer than standard No. 2's and has a wax additive to make it smoother. The writing experience is noticeably superior to most other pencils. It's easier and more satisfying to write with, with less effort involved. The barrel is round, with a good hand feel, but that also means it rolls off inclined surfaces. One other con: the Pink Pearl eraser has pumice in it, which can abrade paper, unlike nylon erasers.

Other than that, it is flawless (and the cedar is pleasingly aromatic when freshly sharpened). Cheaper pencils aren't a bargain if they're hard to sharpen, scratchy to write with, and the lead tends to break. More expensive graphite pencils that

Thick drafting pencil
Staedtler Leadholder
$9 Amazon

I always snap the point off regular pencils and mechanical pencils, so this is the pencil I've always wanted. Commonplace among draftsmen and technical drawers, the Staedtler holds 2mm leads, which do not break under pressure. I use mine all day. It's simple to retract and the recess in the removable push button also doubles as a sharpener (see below image). Remove the push button and there is a hole you stick the lead into. The lead gets very sharp and you can sharpen anywhere, anytime without having to remember to bring along a sharpener.

It has become my everyday pencil — the only thing I write with unless I am behind a keyboard or must use a pen. I don't do any drafting or fine art applications, though I do sometimes sketch network diagrams (I am an intermediate-level sys admin). I also use the pencil for journal writing. The size of the lead really allows for a lot of flexibility in the line width. The pencil never fails, has a good weight, and I find I can hold it very precisely. The texture of the barrel is rough, almost like a nail file or cheese grater. Some people might not like the feel, but the pencil doesn't slip when wet.

I use a soft lead generally and find it needs sharpening one or more times a day. The sharpening can be a bit messy, but tapping it against a wastepaper basket takes care of the extra graphite dust. I still inevitably get graphite powder on my shirt, but it washes out without staining, so I don't really care. Also, it takes some practice to get comfortable with the system. At first the lead comes flying out, so you have to get used to holding the pencil a few centimeters above the paper and releasing the lead to the right amount. It works really well once you get it.

I've looked at other leadholders. If I saw a nicer designed one (i.e. a Parker or a Schaeffer) I might be tempted to get one. Part of what I like about the Staedler is the price and durability. One pencil and a year's supply of lead costs me about $10 at Utrecht art supply. I've lost and given away a few but haven't had any break or wear out.

-- Michael Bubb

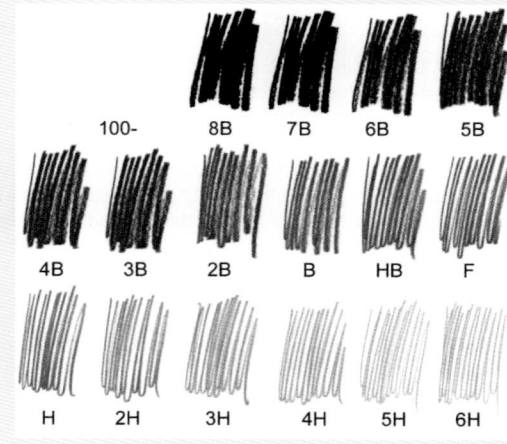

100-	8B	7B	6B	5B
4B	3B	2B	B	HB	F
H	2H	3H	4H	5H	6H

are more suited to artists, along with the frequently mentioned Blackwings, don't seem as practical at $20 for 12, in my opinion. They're like the Ferraris of pencils, and harder to source than the Mirado.

I've used these pencils for over a year, and haven't found one that has more bang for the buck. Paired with the Kum sharpener, these are a no-brainer part of my EDC (every day carry).

-- Tom Anvari

On my friend Michael Pusateri's advice, I ordered 3 dozen of these pencils. They are about 90% as good as my favorite pencil, the Blackwing 602, which costs five times as much as the Mirado Black Warrior.

-- Mark Frauenfelder

Best drawing teacher
Drawing on the Right Side of the Brain

$13 Betty Edwards, 2012, 320 p.

Now in its fourth revision, this remains the best guide for learning how to draw. I used it with my son, and his progress was remarkable. It has also helped my own drawing skills. I actually looked forward to the exercises which are brilliant and fun. In order to draw you must learn to see, and that's what this book teaches: how to perceive. Because this perception training relies on strengthening right brain activity, it can be transferred to any kind of creative work. In each edition over the past 30 years, the author has widened the skills she is teaching, so that this current version will improve your perception skills -- essential for any kind of innovation -- whether or not you ever sketch. And still, it remains the best teacher for anyone -- yes, anyone! -- learning to how to draw.

-- KK

•

A caution: as all of our students discover, sooner or later, the left hemisphere is the Great Saboteur of endeavors in art. When you draw, it will be set aside--left out of the game. Therefore, it will find endless reasons for you not to draw: you need to go to the market, balance your checkbook,

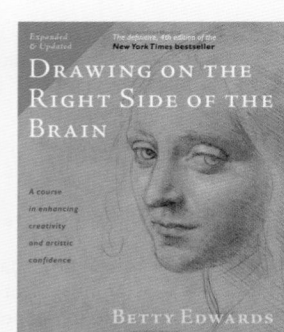

phone your mother, plan your vacation, or do that work you brought home from the office.

What is the strategy to combat that? The same strategy. Present your brain with a job that your left hemisphere will turn down. Copy an upside-down photograph, regard a negative space and draw it, or simply start drawing. Jogging, meditation, games, music, cooking, gardening--countless activities also produce a cognitive shift. The left hemisphere will drop out, again tricked out of its dominance. And oddly, given the great power and force of the left hemisphere, it can be tricked over and over with the same tricks.

•

Drawing is a curious process, so intertwined with seeing the that the two can hardly be separated. The ability to draw depends on one's ability to see the way an artist sees. This kind of seeing, for most people, requires teaching, because the artist's way of seeing is very specific and very different from the ways we ordinarily use vision to navigate our lives.

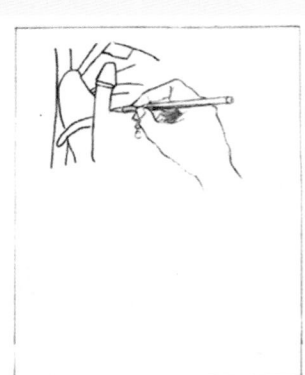

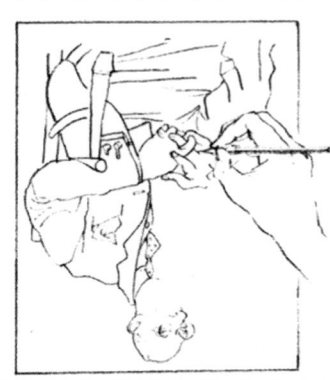

Robin Ruzan
Before instruction
May 16, 2011

After instruction
May 20, 2011

To draw the Picasso upside down, move from line to adjacent line, space to adjacent shape and work your way through the drawing.

Because of this unusual requirement, teaching someone to draw has some special problems. It is very much like teaching someone to ride a bicycle: both skills are difficult to explain in words.

•

Drawing as a learning, teachable skill

I firmly believe that given good instruction, drawing is a skill that can be learned by every normal person with average eyesight and average hand-eye coordination. Someone with sufficient ability, for example, to sign a receipt or to type out an e-mail or text message can learn to draw.

•

These pre-existing skills have nothing to do with potential to draw well. What the pre-instructions drawings represent is the age at which the person last drew, often coinciding with the age at which the person gave up trying to draw.

•

Ideally (in my view), learning in art should proceed as follows: the perception of edges (line) leads to the perception of shapes (negative spaces and positive shapes), drawn in correct proportion and perspective (sighting). These skills lead to the perception of values (light logic), which leads to the perception of colors as values, which leads to painting.

Fig. 6-13. Using your Picture Plane.

Fig. 6-14. You draw the angles just as you see them on the Picture Plane.

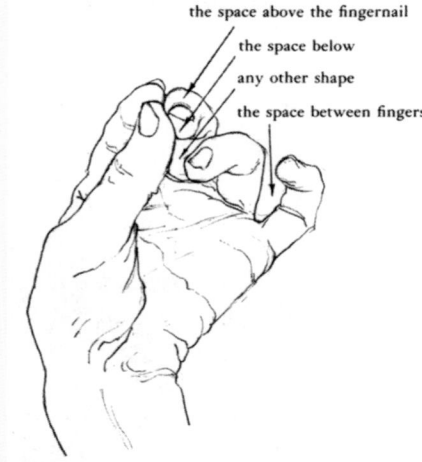

the space above the fingernail
the space below
any other shape
the space between fingers

Fig. 6-24. Drawing the hand by using shapes and spaces.

Fig. 7-4. Notice signs of struggle in this student's drawing.

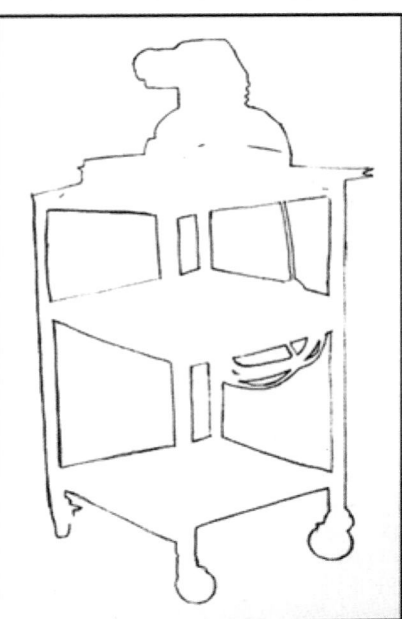

Fig. 7-5. Focusing on negative spaces makes drawing easier.

Dual pencil sharpener
Alvin KUM Long Point Pencil Sharpener

$6 dickblick.com

The iconic battery-powered Panasonic KP-4A, my previous favorite pencil sharpener, is no longer sold in the US. As it happens, I had been growing increasingly disenchanted by the noise and poor job the device sometimes provides. So I started researching to see what was out there in the manual small sharpener space. After ordering about six different models, I settled on the KUM Long Point Pencil Sharpener.

It's different than other sharpeners in two respects. First, it has two holes: #1, labeled as such, trims the wooden barrel, and #2 hones the point. It also has an automatic brake built-in so you don't waste time and lead after you've achieved a perfect point. Besides being silent and great fun to use, it produces a fantastically good point. There's also a nice clear lift-up lid to easily empty shavings. -- *Joe Stirt*

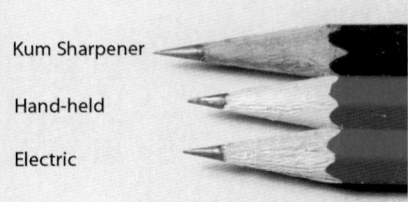

Kum Sharpener

Hand-held

Electric

A comparison of the points achieved using different sharpeners.

Superior pencil sharpener
Alvin Lead Pointer

$10 Amazon

The Alvin Lead Pointer is the best way to keep this type of pencil sharpened. I am an architect and use these pencils every day. I've had this sharpener for more than ten years and it still works like new. The pointer is small, making it ideal to hold in your hand while rotating your lead holder around the pointer. Because your two hands are working together, I find I have more control and there are much fewer broken leads. The cutting head is sharp and lasts for a long time. It only takes a couple spins and your lead is needle sharp. Maintenance and clean-up is a snap. Take the top off the body and dump the graphite shavings into your trash and you are done. If you do break your lead in the pointer, just remove the top and tap it on the inside edge of your trash can to clear the broken pieces. Lead pointers can be messy because of the fine graphite dust, but my pointer has never leaked the dust onto my desk. I have used many different types of pointers from desk mounted to ones mounted on the top of an electric eraser. The desk mounted pointers tend to break leads easily, since you are moving your lead holder in a circular motion around a pointer fixed to your desk, thus you may move in a direction that is not compatible to the pointer and will snap your lead. The electric eraser type is good, but it does not stay sharp for very long. It's also difficult to empty the graphite shavings and jams when you break your lead inside it. This pointer really is the best way to keep you lead sharp! If you work in an office, you may want to buy two — because it is so small and useful, your pointer just might grow legs.

-- Donald Moore, Jr.

The best pencil eraser
Staedtler Mars Plastic Eraser

$5 four-pack Amazon

Mars plastic erasers are the best. Abrasive erasers tear up the paper surface too much, and unless you have mastered pressing really hard without breaking the lead a mechanical pencil doesn't draw that deep anyway.

The plastic erasers can also be cleaned with a wet thumb or a rub on scrap paper for neat work. I always find the "gritty" or "gummy" erasers get so dirty you spend half your time rubbing out their own mess. The Mars compound is stiff enough that corners can be used for fine work, or large areas erased with the flat end. The dirty, used portions just roll off as you use it and are cleanly blown/swiped away. I like the idea of putty/moldable erasers, but they get filthy, crumbly and horrible if kept in a pocket or bag.

-- Alan

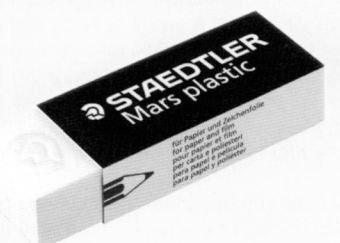

Archeiving

Best way to a paperless archive
Fujitsu ScanSnap S1500

I once left a box of important files out in the rain and wasted a lot of time reviving them. Ever since then I have been digitizing all paper in my life and then tossing the paper. This nirvana is possible using the auto-feed Fujitsu ScanSnap S1500.

I used to scan documents on my HP scanner-printer-copier, which is mind-numbingly slow and had a buggy driver that crashes my computer, forcing a reboot about 25% of the time I use it. Now with the Fujitsu ScanSnap I set a stack of up to 50 two-sided documents into the sheet feeder and it whips through all 100 pages in two and a half minutes. I was honestly surprised that my laptop was capable of accepting data at such a fast pace. This scanner doesn't hog a lot of precious desktop real estate, either. It's surprisingly small — about 11.5 inches wide and 5 inches deep, with the feeder and output flaps folded in.

I configured my SnapScan to send scanned documents as PDF files to my Evernote account, although this is not required. (If you don't know about the Evernote, it's an outstanding online service that accepts images, sound files, notes, scans of documents, and just about anything else you want to throw in it. It saves these files on your computer and on Evernote's servers so you don't have to worry about losing your data. It also runs a character recognition

routine on your documents so you can search for them later.) This first few times I scanned to Evernote, I carefully checked to make sure that both sides of each page had been scanned correctly. The SnapScan software discards the sides that are blank and has a sensor that detects when two pages go through the feeder at the same time (which rarely happens).

Evernote's character recognition is almost flawless. That means my documents can be found by entering keywords into Evernote's search field from my Evernote phone app. The other day I had to search for a mortgage document from my files while I was away from home and I pulled it up on my phone in less than a minute. It is so easy to scan stuff, and its "transcription" of text is so good, that I now scan business cards, menus, any paper document I might want to look at again. Then I throw the paper out.

Since I got the ScanSnap, I've been processing about 100 pages of documents per day. The software straightens out the images and orients them right-side up. The only time it jammed

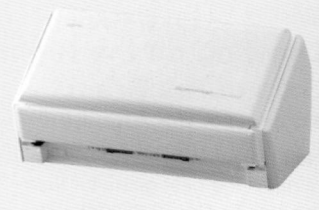

was when I tried to stack too many of the water-damaged documents through it. The downside, if you can call it that, is the high price tag: it's $419 on Amazon. But when I think about the hours and hours of time wasted waiting for my HP flatbed scanner to creak across a document, the price seems very low.

I am finally on my way to a fully paperless office.

-- Mark Frauenfelder

$532 S1500 Fujitsu   **$460 S1500M (for Mac OSX)** Fujitsu

Low-tech biz card retrieval
Poly Business Card Book

I present to you my low-tech solution to a common hassle: what to do with all those business cards you collect? If I were an organized person I would purchase one of those nifty electronic card-scanners and input the card's data into my contact software. But I am lazy and unorganized. Instead I use an off-the-shelf binder full of transparent sleeves with 10 card-sized slots into which I pop the biz cards as I get them out of my pocket. That's the key for me: they are "organized" only by the chronological order in which I receive them. That single bit of data, which costs me no energy, seems to be sufficient to locate most cards. "Let's see I met her before him, and after that meeting." I reckon I have about a 90% percent retrieval success rate, even when hunting back a few years. Good enough

for me. I've been doing this for 15 years now and am working on my fourth book.

There are a bunch of different brands. Get the ones that are a one-piece vinyl book rather than 3-ring binder. More compact, handy and cheaper. Each holds 480 cards. I use mine all the time. As a bonus, I have a remarkable fossil record of past industries, companies, and careers. If you've ever given me your card, its most likely layered here. Let's see, I met you right about……

-- KK

$15 Rolodex Poly Business Card Book Rolodex   **$10 Poly Business Card Pages (10)** Tops

---

Professional archival quality materials
University Products

$15, 5" Herbarium box, Free catalog University Products

This is the serious industrial strength stuff that librarians use. Vastly better than the consumer-oriented light-weight and fussy stuff others offer.

I buy my favorite journals (acid-free journal 8-1/2×11 cat. no. 678-0004) from them — have been using them since 1993 and have found none better. But I also buy tons of other supplies from them regularly, including:

* Monel metal staples (won't rust, ever)

* acid-free boxes for slides and photos

* archival corrosion-intercept zip-lok bags for metal artifacts (item 034-8010-10)

* small Poly zipper bags (500-2030) — they have every size you could want, useful for endless stuff around the house and while backpacking

-- Paul Saffo

•
Drop Front Herbarium Boxes

An excellent choice for either specimen storage or for transporting groups of specimens. These durable boxes have metal edges at all corners for stacking strength (no adhesive used) and drop front bottoms (short side) so items can be removed without damage. Will accommodate genus folders or specimens mounted on Herbarium Mounting Sheets. The acid-free (pH 8.5) blue/grey board has 3% calcium carbonate added to buffer migrant acidity.

Great source for analog storage
Light Impressions

Free catalog lightimpressionsdirect.com

The best source for archival storage aids. If it's flat and analog, Light Impressions can help. I finally got my 10,000 Kodak slides organized in their fantastic slide cabinets. Beginning with photographs (hardest to keep stable), and ending with archival materials and presentations for old magazines, scrapbooks, papers, and prints. Future generations will thank you.

-- KK

Best for flat items
Spray Adhesive

$14 Scotch

What magnificent stuff. Glues together thin layers of paper products such as cardboard, photographs, foam core, even light fabrics, firmly and evenly. Most of the time it's superior to rubber cement, white glue, tape or contact cement. Comes in various formulations. 3M's Spray Mount is most versatile. You can find archival versions, too.

-- KK

Instant sticky notes
Scotch Restickable Adhesive Glue Stick

$8 Scotch

Whereas most glue sticks are designed to permanently stick paper to paper, this glue stick is designed to create instant, repositionable sticky notes out of just about anything (Scotch specifies fabric or paper). A swipe or two (they recommend at least two) with this stick, and your self-printed content/form/memo will stick temporarily to any flat dry surface without residue. I love this stuff and use it to make my various Getting Things Done/43 folders items and tasks stay put in my handheld binder.

Now that my daughters discovered I have one of these sticks, I have a hard time getting it back. They are fond of making up board games out of pen and

paper, which guarantees lots of little bits in the carpet as the game pieces fly around on the slightest breeze. Now they stay put. Ditto for the print-and-cut-apart paper games like Scrabble variants, chess and checkers that you can print from the Web: playability is greatly improved when the playfield can be held on a clipboard in your lap with sticky pieces that won't budge until you want them to.

-- Bill Fleet

A bigger sticky note
Over-Sized Post-Its

$12 4"x4", six pads Post-it

As a long-time aficionado of office supplies, I feel qualified to review this wonderful new (to me, at least) product. These über-Post-its measure 4" x 4" and are a different kettle of fish entirely from others I've used. Namely their Lilliputian 1.5" x 2", 2" x 3", and 3" x 3" brethren. These have an entirely different heft and presence under your pencil or pen or Sharpie.

And I like that these notes are lined, because I'm now using them as an aide-mémoire regarding what's upcoming each day on my blog Book Of Joe. There are just enough lines on them for my eight daily posts and their working titles.

Finally, by combining them with an ultra-fine point retractable Sharpie, I've found note-taking heaven on Earth.

-- Joe Stirt

What you are looking for is who is looking. - St Francis Assisi

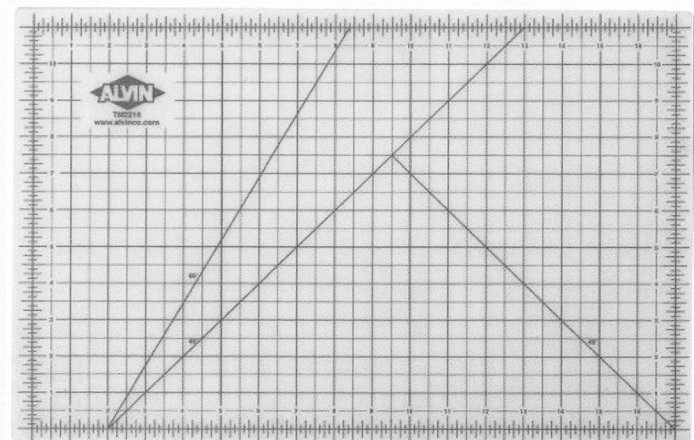

Optimal place to cut
Self-Healing Cutting Mat
$16 12 x 18 Amazon

You razor-cut things on this mat, and unlike other materials it won't accumulate a field of cut marks to misguide your blade. The self-healing rubber keeps the surface uniformly smooth, clean, and firm. And protects your table. Get the largest one you have room for and can afford. A large mat also says: don't pile stuff here.

-- KK

Dahle 550 Paper Cutter
$110 Amazon

Until a couple of years ago I had struggled with different inexpensive paper cutters, but I kept finding myself going to Kinko's and using the cutters there. Then I got smart and jotted down the brand name, Dahle 550 Rolling Trimmer Paper Cutter, and bought one online.

What I appreciate most about this cutter is that I never have to change blades, or deal with dull blades, because it's self-sharpening. The steel rotary blade contained within the plastic safety housing moves across a stationary blade that extends the length of the cutting platform. This action hones the rotary blade, which remains constantly sharp. It's also set up for wall mounting, which is ideal in my home office layout.

One of the Dahle's downsides is that the plastic plate that holds the paper down got dinged up — keep away from kids — causing the blade to run off the track if I'm not careful. Also, the next one I buy will be a larger model: The 550 is meant to cut up to 14 1/8-inch paper, but it's awkward cutting anything over 8×10.

-- *Andrew Heidrich*

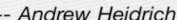

Better than razor blades
Fiskars Rotary Cutter
$12, 45mm Amazon

Rotary cutters aren't new tools. It's just taken me a while to appreciate how great they are. The Fiskars 45mm Rotary Cutter replaces exactos for most heavy-duty cutting jobs in our household. It's faster, surer, easier and therefore safer to use than razor blades. It will slice through paper, vinyl, cardboard, fabric, and foam board with ease and accuracy. I can only manage perfectly straight long cuts with a rotary cutter and straight edge. Cutting curves is buttery. Seamstresses can add pinking blades. The replaceable blade retracts when not in use; it can be side-switched for left-handers. When I think "cut" I reach for this tool.

-- KK

Safe paper trimmer
Fiskars Paper Trimmers
$10, 12 inches wide Amazon

It is simply impossible to make a genuine straight, right-angle cut on paper using a scissors, or even a razor blade and straight edge. The old guillotine paper cutter could deliver a clean cut, but at the risk of taking your fingers away. Fiskars, the scissors makers, invented a tiny blade mounted on a hinged holder that zips through material without any possible harm, even to the youngest children. It's fast, accurate, and crisp.

-- KK

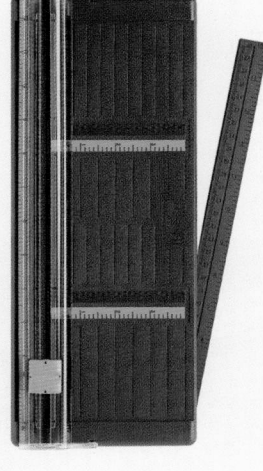

Paper scoring and folding
Bone Folder
$10 Amazon

A classic bone folder is made of real bone, not plastic or Teflon, and resembles a fat, blunt-edged tongue depressor, rounded at one end and pointed at the other. With it, I can turn a digital print, piece of cardstock or watercolor paper into a professional-looking note or greeting card.

Pulling the pointed end alongside a straight edge and across the paper produces a subtle score that facilitates a perfect fold. Next, I fold the card very gently by hand along the score, and then stroke one of the short, straight sides of the bone folder along the score to flatten the rounded fold to a sharp crease.

When sending a letter that I want to look good, I make two quick strokes of the folder along preliminary hand folds to create folded edges that are sharp and square. Bone folders also can be used to burnish paper as it is glued to cardstock, album or scrapbook pages. They produce accurate and sharp folds and creases on origami papers as well as facilitate sculpting, architectural modeling or bookbinding with paper.

I recommend rubbing your bone folder with olive oil from time to time to avoid flaking or brittleness. Folders made of real bone are best, unless you wish to use a Teflon folder to avoid the slight luster sometimes created by the friction of a real bone folder.

-- *Clifford Peterson*

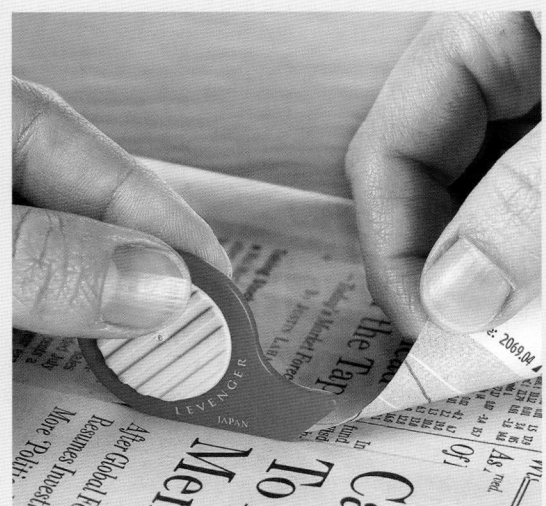

Safe, quick newspaper clipper
Single Sheet Cutter
$19 for 2 Levenger

I like to clip items from the newspaper or magazines that are relevant to my clients and prospects. This tool makes that task simple – just grip between thumb and forefinger and trace the outline of the article you want to clip – you even leave the underlying pages intact!

-- *Bruce Bradford*

Perfect for cutting rolls
Rolling Scissors
$9 Amazon

Two rotating wheels slice paper the way an open scissors does occasionally. Absolutely marvelous for cutting wrapping paper or making lots of long cuts. Also great for kids who don't quite have the coordination to use scissors well. We keep ours in the gift wrap box.

-- KK

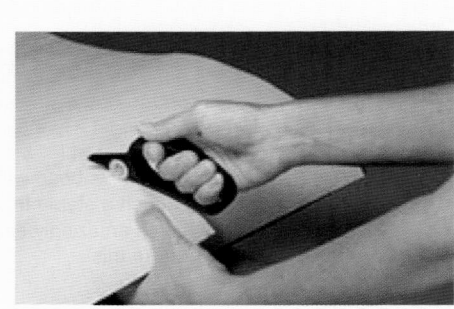

Paper creaser
Plastic Bone Folder
$6 eksuccessbrands.com

"Bone folders" made of real bone are classic, but I prefer a plastic one. The one I use for making crisp folds in origami, for bookmaking, folding cards, and paper construction is molded to the hand for extended ergonomic use. It slides super easy with no trace on paper. Sharp point, makes a really crisp fold. Lasts forever. Inexpensive. If you work with paper, you'll want one of these.

-- KK

Book Making

Best bookmaking guide
Making Handmade Books
$10 Alisa Golden, 2011, 256 p.

While traditional paper-book publishing declines, personal paper-book making ascends. Books have gone from industrial commodity to precious hand-made artifact. There's a renaissance of handcrafted book-making by enthusiasts and Alisa Golden has played a key role in documenting and teaching this makers' art. I have a number of book-making books, and this one by her is by far the most complete and thorough. Her diagrams and instructions are very clear. This hefty how-to manual gives directions for creating over 100 different types of books, book bindings and book-ish things. It incorporates her previous two how-to manual, adds new material and will guide anyone through the process of making a paper book by hand. Even better, it will prompt you to experiment with your own book-making designs.

-- KK

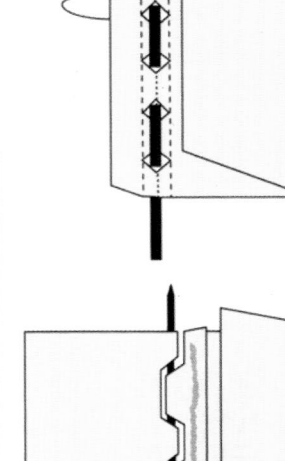

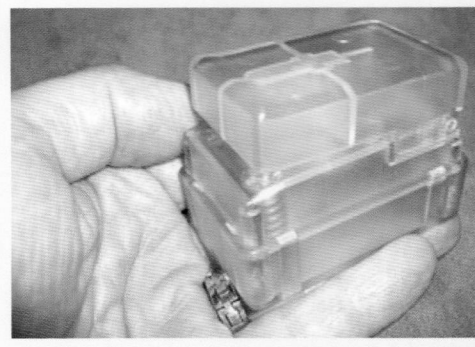

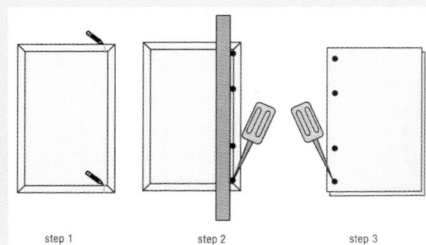

covers, step 8

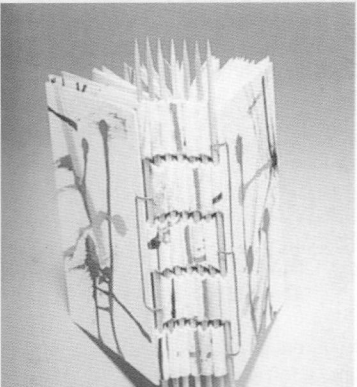

Piano Hinge Book with Hard Cover, 1997

Top: Watercolor pencils

Second row: Colored waxed linen, natural linen thread and bookbinding needle, beeswax, binder clip, Japanese screw punch

Third row: Bone folder, archival superfine black pen, pencil, stencil brush, assorted papers, craft knife, awl, scissors

Bottom: Metal ruler; cutting mat under all

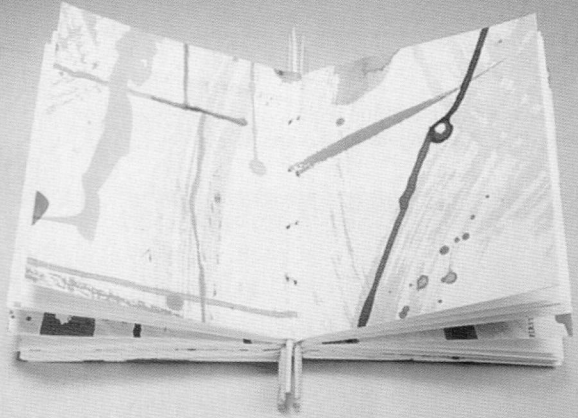

Coptic with Paired Needles Models, 2009

Heavy-duty saddle stapling
Long-Reach Stapler
$25 Bostitch

My theater group always uses these for stapling our programs together. It's a serious work-horse, big and heavy, and the longer reach will allow you to make booklets out of much, much bigger material than the Mini Booklet Stapler. The stapler has a 12" reach on it, so you can staple anything up to 24" wide pre-fold (so architectural 'D'-sized paper could be used, if you felt like it). And unlike the mini model, it takes standard staples. After 7 or 8 years they're still working like brand new. They are made almost entirely out of steel and are incredibly durable. We mostly use them for programs of no more than 6 sheets of standard paper and a heavy high-gloss cover sheet, but we do several hundred of these programs in a batch every couple of months. We also use them for stapling short

scripts, say, 20 pages (long scripts get the three-ring binder). There's a neat little plastic clip on the stapler (which is nicely graduated) that lets you set the width, which makes lining up the fold on your booklets very convenient; you just push your material to the clip and staple. Great for big batches.

-- Andy Martin

Best stapler
Staples One-Touch Stapler
$16 Staples

It remains a paper world. Should you ever need to buy a stapler, this is the one to get. By the Archimedean power of levers, one very light push on its head will effortlessly punch a staple through 20 or more sheets. Secures amazingly easily. All staplers should work like this.

-- KK

Staple-free stapling
PaperFix
$5 Eco Staple Free Stapler Made by Humans

During a trip to Germany almost 20 years ago, I came across one of those slap-of-the-head clever items in an office supply store that I use to this day. When I bought this I was so enamored with it that I actually picked up a second one, thinking that eventually it would wear out and that it would be difficult to find a replacement. Turns out that I was happily wrong on both counts; the extra one that I bought is still in its original plastic display box and a slightly different version (photo below) is widely available. The PaperFix that I've owned for all these years is silent in use, completely ecological, and the ongoing cost is zero. I reach for it at least a few times a day and with one firm press of the top can bind about 6 to 8 pages (depending on paper thickness) together.

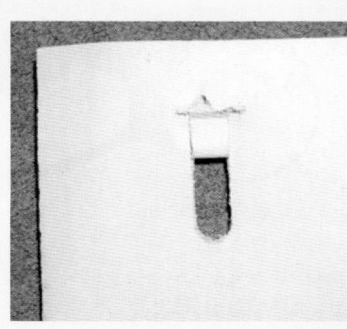

I find magazines too bulky to carry around when there are only a few articles in them that I actually want to read. Through years of traveling and learning to eliminate weight and waste, I now tear out articles I'm interested in and put them all in a folder labeled "Reading" that goes everywhere with me, and use my Paperfix to bind each individual article.

I prefer the PaperFix over paper clips or binder clips for a number of reasons, the first of which is space saving. If you have ever had 15 paper-clipped articles in a folder and seen how they expand the girth of that folder, you'll know what I mean. Paper clips and binders have to be put somewhere when they're removed. Clips of all varieties fall off and have a nasty habit of inserting themselves into every conceivable crack in cars, briefcases and desk drawers.

Once a page is removed from the bound bundle (unlike with a paper clip) it can't be reinserted, nor can you pull out sheets from the midst of the bundle without disrupting the binding of the bundle. While the PaperFix doesn't do everything a stapler can (particularly with thicker stacks of paper), for the vast majority of quick binding jobs it's as good as a stapler, and takes up about a third the room on a desktop or in a drawer. It's less expensive and uses nothing other than a press on the top to get its job done.

-- Scott Goldman

The task of science is to turn deep truths into trivialities. - Nils Bohr

3D book making

Making Books that Fly, Fold, Wrap, Hide, Pop Up, Twist, and Turn

$11 Gwen Diehn, 1998, 96 p.

All-around best book for exploring alternative forms of the book. It's aimed at kids, but works for anyone creative.

-- KK

An Exquisite Corpse. Turning different sections yields differnt pictures on the pages.

Starburst Do you have a collection of poems, jokes, stamps, pressed flowers, feathers, cartoons, or photographs? Here's a book that can hold your collection, and can give each flower or poem the chance to burst forth on center stage! This kind of book is called a lotus book, but it also looks like a starburst.

Gypsy Wagon fold out book.

Creative bookmaking guide

Books Without Paste or Glue

$30 Keith A. Smith, 2009, 352 p. keithsmithbooks.com

Keith Smith published *Non-Adhesive Binding* in 1990. At the time there were few other bookbinding manuals in print (and in comparison with other crafts, there still aren't many). Books by Arthur Johnson, Edith Diehl and Douglas Cockerell offered instruction according to specific craft tradition. These manuals told how to bind a book with very little room for creativity other than decorative choices (what color would you like the leather on the spine to be?). The books were hard to find and contained long lists of tools and desirable equipment that a bookbinder should have.

Keith Smith's book is completely different. He illustrates basic techniques that can be used to create a wide variety of bindings. He encourages the binder to explore how books move, how structural variations influence that movement, and how both movement and structure can lead the binder to fully engage the creative intent of the author's work. He is even more enthusiastic about the possibilities for binders who are the creators of content or those who we now call book artists.

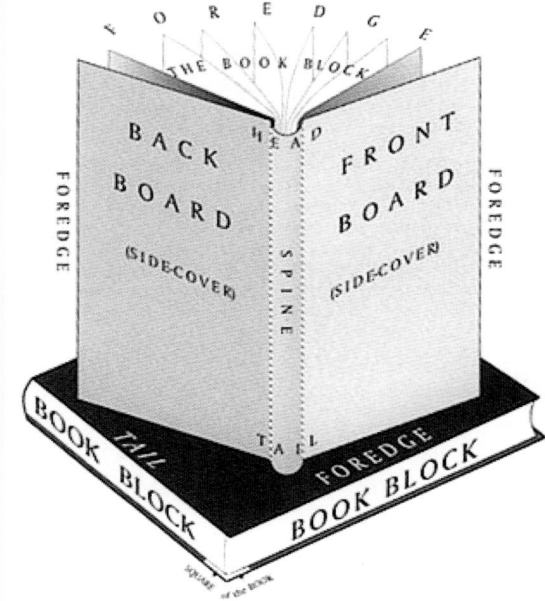

I started bookbinding in 1991 and Keith Smith's *Non-Adhesive Bookbinding* was the first manual I ever bought. As Smith required very few tools and almost no equipment, I was able immediately to start making dozens of books based on his instructions. His drawings of often complex sewing patterns sometimes confused me (and sometimes still do!), but after having now tried to illustrate bookbinding or repair techniques of my own, I'm amazed at how much he conveys so clearly.

It has become more apparent to me with time and experience that his book is a deeper resource than it may first appear. While his methods are simple and often result in astonishingly modern looking bindings, his book is profoundly informed by historical methods and models. Unlike a bookbinding manual that represents a defined tradition, he uses the knowledge of earlier binders to encourage new binders to create their own paths.

Smith's *Non-Adhesive Binding* may be almost 20 years old, but it remains a vital resource for bookbinders, book artists, and anyone who wants to creatively understand the book form.

-- *Kristen St. John*

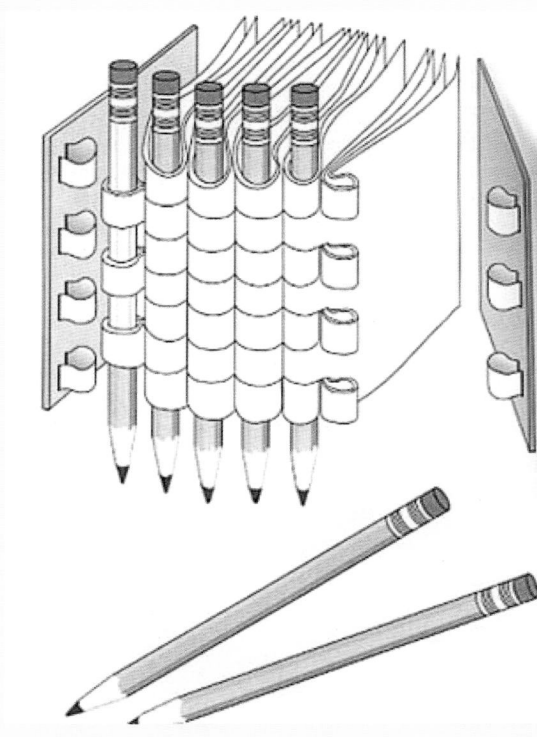

• The book, constituted by everything in the pyramidal hierarchy, is always top and center, the totality and must dominate. Each decision on any element within is subordinate to the realized book. If the binding dominated, the book would be superficial. If conceptual, visual and physical organization were not considered, the content of text and/or pictures would be merely a compilation of islands, rather than an orchestrated totality.

It would appear that at one extreme, the content is quite separate from the process of binding. For me, nothing could be farther from ideal. I sometimes think about the physical object. There is concrete space between words and/or pictures. Movement is constructed through content, which determines the rate of turning pages.

• A book can be created through a play upon the action of turning a page. Indeed, a lifetime's work can have as one under-pinning the exploration of what physically transpires in turning the page. Becoming involved and excited about any aspect of the physical book can reveal potential which, once understod, can easily be expanded as theme.... A book grows out of an understanding of its inherent properties, rather than the inclusion of outside elements. Conception springs from the physical format, evolving into a realized book.

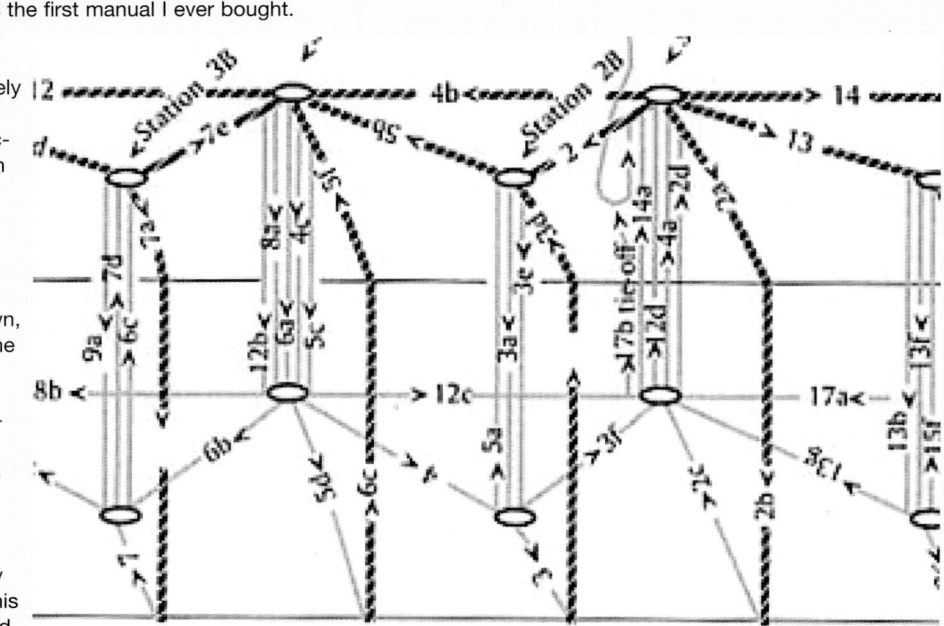

Tracking Mice

Low cost six-axis mouse
SpaceNavigator
$87 Amazon

Logitech sells a low-cost, very high quality, 3D controller called the SpaceNavigator. When I bought mine, you could get an edition for personal use that is only $59 (instead of $99 for the pro edition). It will increase your productivity in 3D programming 2-3 times.

The SpaceNavigator is a six-axis controller that you use in conjunction with the mouse and keyboard. With it you can move around the model in three dimensions, intuitively and without changing from one mode to another (e.g. pan to rotate to zoom). You can also configure it to work in what ever fashion is easiest and most intuitive for you. With a little practice you can move through and around

the model using the mouse and SpaceNavigator, never touching the keyboard. It provides a huge increase in productivity and, frankly, fun. I'm designing an addition to our house in Sketchup and my kids (6 & 8) have learned to fly through the model without my help. Of course you can use it with other 3D applications, like AutoCAD, Rhino and Maya.

This is one of those things that you purchase and fall in love with because it's useful, high-quality, and inexpensive. (It works in Windows, Linux, Unix — but not Mac!)

-- Mike Green

Ergonomic mouse
Evoluent Mouse
$90 Amazon

From a relaxed standing position with your arms at your side raise your right hand while holding your elbow still until your forearm is level with the floor. Spread you fingers apart and rotate your hand until your palm is facing down – keeping your elbow at your side. Now if you are anything like me your hand is rotated about as far as it can. In mechanical parlance, the wrist is "hard against the stops." When you are using a conventional mouse it is in this rather tense and uncomfortable position that your hand remains. As a designer I often spend days on end at the computer modeling in 3D – left hand on the space ball and keyboard with right hand on the mouse. Over time I began experience a myriad of painful symptoms from forearm throbbing to thumb tenderness to shoulder aches. These discomforts grew into debilitating pain to the point I wondered if I could continue in my chosen profession. And then I discovered the Evoluent Mouse – and instantly the pain and discomfort tailed away to nothing.

Repeat the previous exercise but this time place your hand in a vertical – hand shake like – position. You will find that your hand is now very relaxed residing as it does pretty close to halve way between hard right rotation and hard left. The Evoluent mouse looks like a mouse turned on its edge with the laser tracking business on the edge of the mouse. This configuration positions the hand and wrist in a basically neutral position thereby avoiding the stresses rotating the hand to a palm down position induces.

I cannot overstate how drastic an improvement this mouse is from all others. Both Microsoft and Logitech make products which rotate the hand partially toward the vertical but these are partial measures and do not afford the total neutral ergonomics provided by the Evoluent. If you are fighting soreness or pain from your mouse arm-hand – please give your body a break and give the Evoluent mouse a try.

-- Donald Ansley

Best, cheap trackball
Logitech Marble Mouse
$86 Amazon

While I've always spent a lot of time computing, the precise, all-day cursor movements of professional writing and designing (a recent switch) got me vexed with my previous mouse's lack of control and an aching wrist. After borrowing a friend's $70 trackball and enjoying the fingertip control and comfort, I set out to get tracking at the lowest possible cost and highest possible comfort. I settled on the Logitech Marble Mouse.

Shaped like a low, oval hill, this $20* mouse is a nice inverse of the natural curve of a hand. The trackball sits naturally under the index and middle fingers and moves very smoothly. The sizable left and right buttons are situated directly under your thumb and ring finger, while the two smaller buttons above them can be designated for a variety of functions like scrolling and zoom. The symmetry also makes it ambidextrous, which is great for any left/right-handed families that share a home computer.

I did try a few thumb-operated trackballs, but a slight weirdness in my right thumb joint causes some discomfort when I move it a lot. Every time I put my hand on the Marble Mouse, I'm able to keep it totally relaxed. The mouse is large enough for comfort, but still relatively small enough to take on the road. The build quality is solid, and it's easy to clean. Best of all, my wrist no longer smarts after a long day's editing.

Bonus: the heavy, low-friction ball makes a nice desk toy when you need a break.

-- George Cochrane

Of mice and men
Logitech Performance and Anywhere MX Mice

I've been using Logitech's Performance Mouse MX and its former model for about four years. They all have one important feature: hyper fast scrolling. Since I'm an engineer who has to deal with source code files that easily contain thousands of lines, I have to scroll an ordinary mouse hundreds of times to browse a file. With hyper fast scrolling, it only takes one single scroll as the wheel spins with minimal friction. This really reduce the stress on my fingers. It can also easily be switched back to normal scrolling behavior (by pushing down on the scroll wheel) when I'm not dealing those gigantic files.

-- Jordan Cherng

Similar to Jordan's Logitech Performance Mouse MX is the Anywhere Mouse MX that I've been using for the past two years. Unlike the Performance model, the Anywhere model is significantly smaller, and is easily packed in the included carrying case. Despite the small size, I find it to be one of the most comfortable mice I've ever handled which is especially surprising as I have large hands!

Outside of size, the two mice are remarkably similar. Like its bigger brother, the Anywhere Mouse also features "hyper-scrolling" which is very useful when dealing with large documents or long web pages. The scrolling (among other features) is customizable with the included Logitech software (that works for both PC and Macs). Outside of scrolling, they both feature programmable buttons, and most importantly very accurate tracking. Logitech calls their technology Darkfield which they claim is better able to respond to irregularities on a surface (and thus respond more accurately during tracking). I've used mine on many shiny surfaces which normally confuse optical mice without any problems, with the biggest surprise coming when I used it on a glass countertop which is normally a no go for laser-tracking mice.

The only other significant differences between the two are that the Performance Mouse can be charged via micro-USB, and that it has a few more buttons for those who want to maximize the customizability of their mice. Both use Logitech's unifying receiver (which we've reviewed in the past) and have excellent battery life. My Anywhere Mouse gets about 4-6 months of use from two rechargeable AAs.

Despite being significantly more expensive than other mice on the market, I have found that these higher end Logitech mice are worth it. They are comfortable and reliable pieces of technology that seem to disappear in use, and for that I'm incredibly grateful.

-- Oliver Hulland

$69 Performance Mouse
Amazon

$65 Anywhere Mouse
Amazon

Programmable keypad
X-Keys Desktop
$130 X-Keys

I have used this programmable keypad for the past five years, and find it a huge time saver. I am a C.A.D. software user, cnc programmer, and often use graphic software to aid in my work.

This key pad allows the user to program any number of keystrokes, computer functions, or a combination into a single button. The obvious use is to make a single button activate a tool or function in a program that can be done with a keystroke combination, ie: "ctrl+P" which in most programs will activate the Print command. However, it can be much more elaborate than that. I reserve a few buttons to record job specific macros. This might include something like a series of offsets in the CAD program. I set up a macro to change the offset dimension as it creates each object, resulting in a series of concentric objects with one push of a button. A fantastic time saver for repetitive work.

PI engineering makes several models of key pads with different configurations and numbers of buttons. They also continue to improve the software, a free download, that works with the keypads. The software will now detect what programs are running, which program is the active program, and allow the user to program specific macros for each

button for each program. In other words, when you are using a word-processing program, a key may, say, type in your name, title and contact information. When you are in Photoshop, that same key may open up the new document window, or start to rip a CD in iTunes, etc.- automatically changing what it does, based on the active program. Or a button can be set to operate the same no matter the open programs – a short cut to open a specific document or program, etc.

In addition to being incredibly handy for anyone who spends a lot of time on a computer, the unit is built like a tank. The model I have is built using a metal carcass. I often use a laptop and have a piece of hardboard setup to hold the computer, this X-keys keypad, other peripherals and electrical strip in place using Velcro – keeping me portable. I recently left this hardboard – without the computer – on the top of my truck as I drove away. It hit the pavement X-keys first. The damage? I lost one cap to one key, for which I had an extra, and a small area of road rash that is simply now silver instead of black.

I, perhaps obviously, cannot say enough about this product, and am constantly finding new ways to use it.

-- Sean Frey

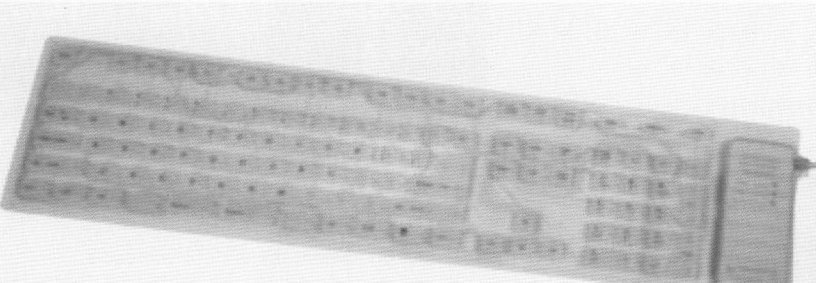

Pocketable Keyboard
GrandTec Virtually Indestructible Keyboard
$27 grandtec.com/

My fingers are too broad and my precision too challenged to use the little keyboard on my Sony VAIO laptop effectively. Stuff I write in a coffee shop or when on the road ends up with tons of mistakes to straighten out when I transfer it to our desktop G-4. I recently bought this hokey looking rubber keyboard and it works amazingly well. You can roll it up, bend it, spill water on it, plug and unplug into a laptop at any time and it works great. My one objection is that it has no mouse, so you have to go back to the laptop for mouse movement and clicks.

-- Lloyd Kahn

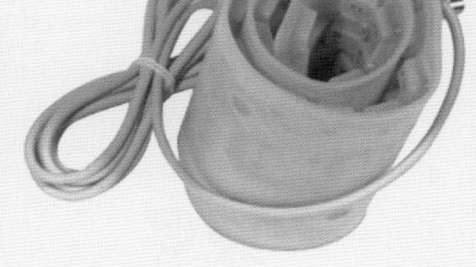

Speak-and-write software
Dragon Dictate
$122 Amazon

I'm using Dragon Dictate to write this on my Mac OS computer. In past years I've used speech recognition software and have had terrible results with it. But I heard so many good things about Dragon Dictate that I decided to give it a try. I'm a slow typist, and this really beats typing, at least for me. It is surprisingly accurate, and unlike earlier speech recognition applications that I used you don't have to wait for 30 seconds to see your text appear.

This is very quick. I use it to do email. I would be embarrassed to use it in an office environment where other people could hear me talking, but since I work at home where no one can hear me, it's excellent.

Once upon a time DragonDictate only worked on PCs, but I am using DragonDictate on my MacBook Pro and I seem to have no problems with it.

-- Mark Frauenfelder

Radically ergonomic typing
Kinesis Advantage Keyboard
$269 Amazon

Several years ago, I was at a trade show and I saw and tried an early-generation Kinesis keyboard. I was hooked. As a starving college student, I certainly couldn't afford one then, but once I entered the workforce one of the first things I did was acquire a Kinesis, and I have now been using it for about four years. I've used a variety of ergonomic keyboards in my time, but none was as comfortable to use as this one.

I'm a decent typist, but once it arrived, it took me about two weeks of hunting-and-pecking to figure out where all the keys were, and another week to get proficient with it. During this time, I kept a standard keyboard close at hand, in case I got too frustrated, or needed to type something quickly. However, once I mastered the keyboard, I found that my typing speed went up by about 15 wpm. The reason for this is that the Kinesis doesn't enforce any unnatural motions on your hands or fingers. Hold up your hand, make a loose fist, and then open your hand naturally. That motion encompasses 95% of the motion required to operate this keyboard. It's a remarkably stress-free way to type; very comfortable, and well worth the investment.

I don't have any specific pain or injuries associated with typing. Like just about anyone who uses a keyboard regularly, I'd occasionally get tired or sore hands or forearms (and I still do, when I have occasion to use a non-Kinesis keyboard at length). But since switching, I've found that that kind of pain has dropped off significantly.

The downsides are minimal but worth noting as this is, after all, a very expensive keyboard. The keys are a trifle loud for my taste; I'd definitely prefer a quieter version. Also, the default keymappings are a little odd; the left and right curly braces are in a strange place. While I'm not a coder by trade, I could definitely see that being an issue for someone who does a lot of programming. But it's never bothered me enough to do any remapping. Also, one caveat: you pretty much have to be a touch-typist to be able to use it — one-finger typing on this keyboard will only end up frustrating you.

What I like best about this keyboard is the natural fit of the keys. The curved cups that the keys rest in are shaped just right for my hands, so the uniquely comfortable typing position is consistently reinforced and supported. I would strongly recommend this keyboard to anyone looking for a comfortable typing experience.

-- Dylan Greene

Conductive gloves
Agloves Touchscreen Gloves
$12-14 Amazon

I bought these conductive Agloves soon after getting my first iPhone (not my first touch-screen phone). They are made with conductive silver thread that allow you to use your capacitive touch-screen devices with gloves on. No more freezing fingers while trying to use your phone or tablet/reader!

I haven't used other conductive gloves, but the Agloves work well and have been an awesome tool as the temperatures start to drop.

The gloves extend over the wrist and fit snugly to keep all heat in. They may not be thick enough to ward away strong chill, but can easily be worn under thicker gloves. Whether you are using them to keep your fingers warm or for hygienic reasons while using public transportation, it's handy to be able to use your touch-screen devices without pulling your gloves off.

I own the plain, original Agloves. They also make a sports line and a bamboo line. You can purchase the gloves easily on Amazon or the Agloves website. Agloves have been the perfect solution for me. Because they also work with computer trackpads and the Apple Magic Mouse, I hardly take them off throughout the cold mornings.

They are so good that I bought several more pairs for gifts. Hmm, stocking stuffers anyone?

-- Myra Schjelderup

Calculators

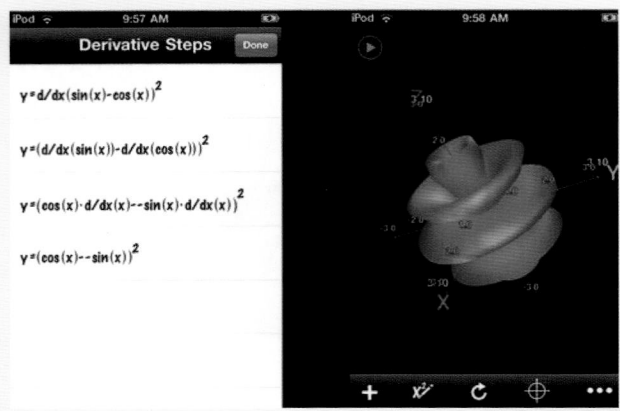

Advanced calculator on iOS

Quick Graph

Free Quick Graph iTunes Store
$2 Quick Graph+ iTunes Store

I recently returned to school after a long hiatus. While learning pre-calc and calculus, I found Quick Graph for iOS to be the best graphing calculator. It graphs both 2D and 3D functions. The app also handles multiple functions which are allocated different colors automatically. Unlike stand-alone calculators you can zoom in and out with standard pinch gestures, and in 3D you can rotate the graph in any direction. It also helps that the interface is intuitive: for instance to change the color of your function, there is a little arrow bullet in your current color next to your function in the function list: you just click it and it opens a color selection dialog.

The free version is very functional and has no ads or annoyances. The full version gives extra features such as unlimited functions (free is limited to 6) and tracing the graph by tap and hold (it is easy estimate the same data in the free version, but it won't give you the exact value).

Unfortunately, my iPhone broke and I am now using Android on which I have not found a graphing app of the same level of intuitive design.

-- Aryeh Abramovitz

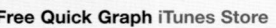

Free Quick Graph iTunes Store   **$2 Quick Graph+** iTunes Store

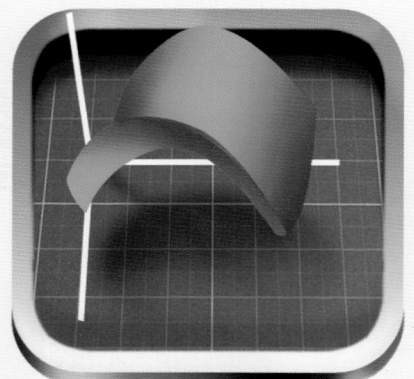

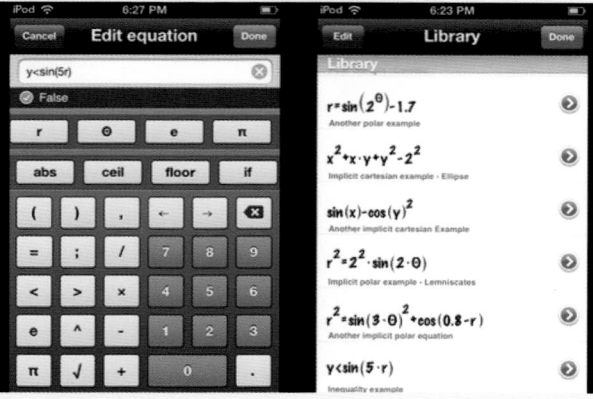

Math without batteries

Casio FX-115 Solar Calculator

$16 Amazon

I bought my Casio FX-115 Solar Calculator 25-years ago, probably in Malaysia. It replaced my then aging Texas Instruments calculator. The thing I like most about it is that it doesn't need batteries. None. You can pull it out of a drawer after a year and it just works. No fretting about whether you left it on or not, and I've never needed to replace anything.

The new ones come with a dual solar and battery combo called "solar plus". Don't be fooled. The closest new equivalent is probably the Casio FX-260 Solar ($9.99), but that model doesn't have some of the features of the FX-115.

As far as calculations go, it has pretty much all anyone would need. It has a nice friendly EXP button for scientific notation and infinite levels (18) of parenthesis. It converts and computes in alternate number bases (binary, octal and hex) and does linear regression.

The plastic is a bit scuffed after riding around in my backpack all these years, but it's been wet and recovered. It also gets really sluggish when used outside in sub zero (C) weather.

-- Derrick Oswald

[Note: The FX115 comes in two very similar models, the ES and the MS, that feature minor differences. However, it appears that the MS is preferred by some math teachers, and is approved to be used on many licensing exams (where as the ES has in the past not been approved for some engineering exams in California.)]

Engineer's calculator

Texas Instruments Graphing Calculator

$137 TI-89 Titanium Graphing Calculator Amazon

I've been using a ti89, first the original release and then the titanium release, since I was in high school. It is a calculator for the hardest core of geeks.

Throughout engineering school–I'm working toward my Masters in Mechanical Engineering–I've used the programming app to code contours of cam surfaces as well as a host of matrix and kinetics/kinematics programs. It's a graphing calculator, which allows me to overlay 99 plots of different functions; I can turn on and off different plots to select which functions I'd like to compare.

The ti89 comes standard with a suite of calculus tools such as integration and derivatives, as well as many linear algebra operations. It also comes with support from a Texas Instruments-based free online app store, as well as a programming editor that allows the user to write his own code. There are also preloaded finance and electrical engineering programs.

I own three of these handy calculators: one for my desk at work, another for my desk at home and one for my laptop/school bag.

-- Benjamin Abruzzo

Tried and true number cruncher

HP 10B Business Calculator

$45 Amazon

HP's mid-range business calculator has been around for more than 25 years, and it is still the best choice for all but the hardest-core finance, statistical and actuarial uses. For everyday use by business managers doing profit margin, sell/cost, IRR, percentage, mortgage, cash-flow, discount, net present value and so many other common business computations, it offers incredible ease without requiring the user to learn the RPN notation of HP's higher-end financial calculators.

Everything about the 10B shows an incredible level of attention to design, from the solid rubber feet, perfect tactile keypress response, and easy-to-read, molded-in key labels. And amazingly, my 10B, purchased in 1989, is still going strong on its factory-supplied button batteries, after some 20 years of dependable and regular use.

Loan amortization calculations, even with a computer, can be tedious, but the 10B's dedicated functions, for all the usual as well as the out-of-the-ordinary loan computations, make such work quick and reliable. As with all functions on the 10B, I simply input the known values using their dedicated keys (for example, number of months, interest rate per year, and loan amount), and then press the key for the unknown value (monthly payment). Change any of the values, and the 10B can re-compute all the remaining figures just as easily.

HP has updated the 10B now to the 10BII, though user reviews on Amazon are not very positive. If you can find a used model on Amazon or eBay, it's probably the last calculator any businessperson will ever need to buy.

-- Mike Sullivan

Fastest bandwidth

Big Bandwidth

Free Speed Test

To get the most bandwidth these days use cable.

For my home/home office we switched from the fastest internet we could get over the telephone lines to best internet broadband we could afford on a cable modem. This was a big switch for us because we did not have cable. So we had cable hooked up to our house just for the internet. We signed up for Comcast's "Extreme" level of broadband since there can be 5 – 9 people using the line at any one time. The improvement was dramatic.

We now get about 60 Mb/s download and 17 Mb/s upload. This gives me and my assistant in the office and my family of five, plus the relatives downstairs, plus the Netflix and X-Box live connections, plenty of bandwidth to share. We pay about $120 per month for the connection.

It's been running at this level for about a year and we've had very little problems. Someone in the family can be streaming a movie on Netflix while my son plays Battlefield live on the XBox, while I download a software update, while my daughter watches YouTube — all at the same time with no noticeable delay.

Not having to wait for downloads and being able to zip around on even image-dense web pages is pure joy. Since I spend so much time online, the monthly fee is well-worth it to me, the family, and our little office.

To test the speed of your internet connect use this free website, Speedtest. Here is our snapshot today.

-- KK

Extended ethernet through electrical wiring
Powerline Ethernet Adapters

$63 TRENDnet 200 Mbps Powerline AV Adapter Kit Amazon
$78 TRENDnet 500 Mbps Powerline AV Adapter Kit Amazon

I've used various powerline adapters for several years. They now can go up to 500 megabits per second, but 85 or 200 will be cheaper. I currently use TrendNet Powerline routers.

Why not use wifi? The bands are becoming crowded. You can try to use 5Ghz N routers, and they help, but if all your other devices – your phone, iPod, Kindle all have to use the 2.4GHz wifi, it can get congested. Wireless USB peripherals and Bluetooth also use the same band. Not everything supports the 5GHz band, so your laptop might not work, or you will need a special card or adapter for your desktop. Then there's securing things and getting the network password right. And in apartments, every one of your neighbors is using the same band.

Powerline adapters need passwords, but they are between the adapters and you only have to use the setup utility once. They are basically ethernet bridges. I have my cable router plugged in where the cable comes in and the signal is best, then have my wifi and powerline adapters plugged into that router (it has 4 ports). I've not had any problem streaming or even sending files between computers. I have several 200Mb/s refurbished models and they work well for that, but I have gigabit switches at my central computer "nerve center". The powerline adapters also make printers a lot easier to setup. I have a Brother printer that is finicky about Wifi: it can attach USB, Ethernet, or Wifi, but even after typing in the correct information when attached with one of these other methods it often "fails to associate". Instead, I just use the powerline adapter, and instantly it is on ethernet with no headaches.

Well, there is one. A powerline adapter uses up an electrical socket, which is where the "Liberator" comes in. Basically, a 3 pronged pass-through extension cord. The short plug-depth seems to play well with the powerline adapter, and the extension is hefty enough for my laser printer. The Liberators also work well with power strips or even to go sideways when space is at a premium.

There are a few rare cases where powerline adapters have problems. One is if there is something extremely electrically noisy on the same branch (and if it isn't noisy you need the passwords to prevent your neighbors from snooping). This usually involves some huge motor, arc welding, or other industrial process involving intermittent high current. Another thing is if there are any ground loops or if hot and ground get swapped by adapters or bad wiring. Also it helps to avoid circuits with dimmers and microwaves, though I've only had the problem when some part of the house wiring was wrong enough to show bars on my old CRT TV when the microwave was on. The powerline signal cannot pass through the large (utility pole) transformers. There is a length limit, but I haven't been in a position to see how fast the signal goes at hundreds or thousands of feet.

If wifi works and the total cost of adapters and such is low, it might be a better solution, but for reasonable distances where there is lots of interference or if you only have ethernet, nothing beats powerline adapters.

-- Thomas Z

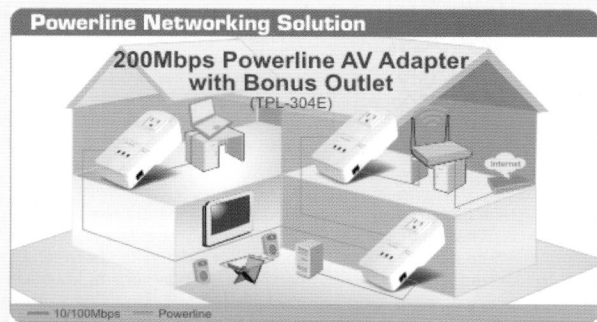
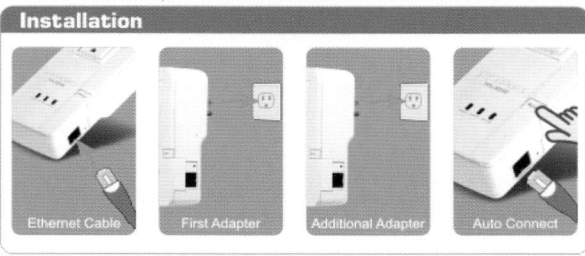

This illustration demonstrates how the powerline can be used to extend the range of a home's ethernet without additional wiring or the use of WiFi.

Easy Ethernet Cable Making System
EZ-RJ45 Connectors

$10 for a 15 pack Amazon

I've been putting off buying RJ45 plugs for Ethernet cables because it looked like they all suck, and I'm not as young as I used to be, so cutting the wires exactly to fit might be a problem (even though I terminated hundreds of cables in my early networking career).

But recently I needed to help a neighbor who ran cables to relocate his wireless router. On a recommendation I picked up a box of the Platinum Tools EZ-RJ45 plugs and strain reliefs. The video below shows how you attach them to a cable by sliding the wires through and out the front.

I just installed them yesterday and had not a single failure (other than forgetting to slide the strain relief into the plug before crimping on the first one).

They are about one dollar each vs. a few cents for the Chinese & big box versions, but my hair is worth the money.

Platinum sells a special crimp tool that cuts the wires when it crimps. I wasn't in the mood to spring for another $50 for the tool for my occasional needs so I used a regular crimp tool instead. I cut the wires after crimping with diagonal cutters and tidied up with a utility knife. Certainly if I was doing a lot of cable builds or for a business I'd buy the pro tool.

I bought a few of the Platinum Tools modular jacks, too, but I haven't wired one up yet. You'll see in the video that they look like a godsend, too, especially since you can reuse them with ease.

-- Mike Andrews

Efficient Ethernet cabling
EZ-RJ45 Crimp Tool

$55 Amazon

I have been working in IT networking for 12 years, and I avoided making cables for the first 11.
Since I bought the EZ-RJ45 a year ago, I now look forward to it. There are eight wires to connect with UTP cables, and it is important to get the wires in the same order at both ends. With most standard RJ45 crimps you have to cut the wires to about 3/8 inch long and stuff them in the crimp, hoping they stay in the correct order. Since the wires have to lay next to each other in a particular order, that 3/8 inch means you have very little to hang on to, so the wires almost always get mixed up and you have to try again.

What's great about the EZ-RJ45 is that the crimps allow the wires to pass all the way through them and stick out the front. That means you can cut the wires as long as you like and the wires protruding from the front of plug are easy to inspect to make sure they are in the correct order before crimping. The EZ-RJ45 crimps work in the three other crimping tools I have (2 different versions of the Ideal Telemaster, and 1 cheap NoName); but the EZ-RJ45 crimper also has an extra blade that cuts the wires flush with the front of the plug when you crimp it. With the other crimpers you would have to take the additional step of cutting the wires after crimping the plug. With normal connectors I end up wasting a third to half of my crimps. With the EZ-RJ45 I have no waste, and the crimps are right every time.

-- David McGregor

Network cable tester
Atlas IT Cable Analyser

$110 Peak Electronic Design

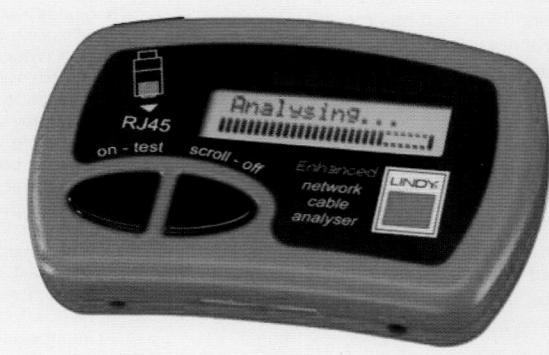

This is an RJ45 cable tester, which recognizes particular kinds of cable (Ethernet, rolled, Ethernet economizers, audio cables), both 4-wire and 8-wire. If you only ever need to test a few single cables a year, you won't need this. However if you're trying to test more than one cable at a time, particularly if they are long runs or hidden, this is great. Normally Ethernet testers come in remote/master pairs, so you have to

- go to remote site (attic, patching closet, whatever)
- attach remote terminator
- go to local end
- test

Rinse, lather, repeat. One trip per cable.

The nice thing about this tester is that with the numbered terminators, you can test several lines at a time, without having to dash up to the attic each time to change the remote terminator. You can also see easily when you've mislabeled cables. ("Patch panel port 2 has terminator 8 on it? Bugger. Time to re-label...") It's also useful when you have a mixed bag of cables which you need to identify and sort into boxes. As a network engineer, this is something I have to do quite often... unfortunately.

Oh, and one other thing — if you switch it on without a terminator, it will show you how to wire Ethernet patch and crossover cables, including the cable colors. It's kinda shiny. Yes, it's more expensive than the kind you get for cheap off Ebay, but it also does so much more.

-- Donal Cunningham

Bulk cable source
DeepSurplus

DeepSurplus

Deep Surplus is a fantastic source for an encyclopedic array of cables.

For example, Apple sells a mini to mini cable for connecting your iPod to your stereo for $24.95. The same cable can be had for less than a dollar from Deep Surplus.

For work I buy all of our networking patch cables, USB cables, etc. for 10% of the cost of buying them at Staples, Microcenter, or Best Buy. I recently bought some rather hard to find white, two-lead speaker wire, which elsewhere was as pricey as $80, for $12 for a 25-foot length. I also bought a 6-foot mini (iPod) to dual RCA (for my older audiophile amplifier) cable for $2.75, compared to $24.95 at the Apple store.

I rely on them whenever I need essential cables affordably.

-- Aram Salzman

Programming

Essential technological literacy
Debugging

$15 David J. Agans, 2006, 192 p.

These days debugging is a necessary life skill. Anything high tech has more ways of failing than running. Since failure hides in complexity, you need to be systematic to fix a break in a system. But debugging skills are not taught anywhere.

This book teaches you how to troubleshoot. It is meant for engineers debugging computer programs, but the principles of debugging can easily be applied to any engineered system — your car, home plumbing, a new gizmo, old laptop, hi-fi system, or anything with many dynamic parts.

The book is easy, with lots of war stories. I learned a lot. Lately I've become the defacto system administrator for the network of seven computers in our household, and these principles have upped my success rate in clearing up the inevitable problems.

What you get: essential technological literacy.

-- KK

●
The Rules – Suitable for Framing

• Understand the system

• Make it fail

• Quit thinking and look

• Divide and conquer

• Change one thing at a time

• Keep an audit trail

• Check the plug

• Get a fresh view

• If you didn't fix it, it ain't fixed

●
Change One Thing at a Time

On nuclear-powered subs, there's a brass bar in front of the control panel for the power plant. When status alarms begin to go off, the engineers are trained to grab the brass bar with both hands and hold on until they've looked at all the dials and indicators, and understand exactly what's going on in the system. What this does is help them overcome the temptation to start "fixing" things, throwing switches and opening valves. These quick fixes confuse the automatic recovery systems, bury the original fault beneath an onslaught of new conditions, and may cause a real, major disaster. It's more effective to remember to do something ("Grab the bar!") than to remember not to do something ("Don't touch that dial!") So, grab the bar!

●
Understand the System

You need a working knowledge of what the system is supposed to do, how it's designed, and, in some cases, why it was designed that way. If you don't understand some part of the system, that always seems to be where the problem is. (This is not just Murphy's Law; if you don't understand it when you design it, you're more likely to mess up.)

●
Make It Fail

So you can tell if you've fixed it. Once you think you've fixed the problem, having a surefire way to make it fail gives you a surefire test of whether you fixed it. If without the fix it fails 100 percent of the time when you do X, and with the fix it fails zero times when you do X, you know you've really fixed the bug.

●
If You Didn't Fix It, It Ain't Fixed

When you think you've fixed an engineering design, take the fix out. Make sure it's broken again. Put the fix back in. Make sure it's fixed again. Until you've cycled from fixed to broken and back to fixed again, changing only the intended fix, you haven't proved that you fixed it.

●
Ask for help

There are at least three reasons to ask for help, not counting the desire to dump the whole problem into someone else's lap: a fresh view, expertise, and experience. And people are usually willing to help because it gives them a chance to demonstrate how clever they are.

No matter what kind of help you bring in, when you describe the problem, keep one thing in mind: Report symptoms, not theories. The reason you went to someone else for fresh insight is that your theories aren't getting you anywhere. If you go to someone fresh and lay a theory on her, you drag her right down into the same rut you're in. At the same time, you've probably hidden some key details she needs to know, because your bias says they're not important. So be firm about this. When you ask for help, describe what happened. Describe what you've seen. Describe conditions if you can. Make sure you tell her what's intermittent and what isn't. But don't talk about what you think it the cause of the problem.

Though the terms are often interchanged, there's a difference between debugging and troubleshooting, and there's a difference between this debugging book and the hundreds of troubleshooting guides available today. Debugging usually means figuring out why a design doesn't work as planned. Troubleshooting usually means figuring out what's broken in a particular copy of a product when the product's design is known to be good--there's a deleted file, a broken wire, or a bad part. Software engineers debug; car mechanics troubleshoot. Car designers debug (in an ideal world). Doctors troubleshoot the human body--they never got a chance to debug it. (It took God one day to design, prototype, and release the product; talk about schedule pressure! I can we can forgive priority-two bugs like bunions and mail pattern baldness.)

The techniques in this book apply to both debugging and troubleshooting. These techniques don't care how the program got in there; they just tell you how to find it. So they work whether the problem is a broken design or a broken part. Toubleshooting books, on the other hand, work only a broken part.

Programming for kids
Cargo-Bot

Free itunes.apple.com

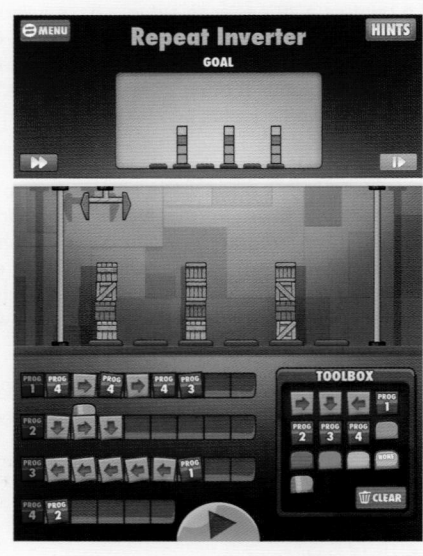

The object of Cargo-bot is to teach kids to write programs that control a robotic arm to move, sort, and stack colored crates. The computer language is a simple instruction set consisting of squares that tell the arm which direction to move, and whether or not to perform an action based on the color of the crate. You write the programs by dragging and dropping the instruction squares into a sequence that causes the arm to perform the assigned task. You can also write programs that execute other programs you've written. (This is important because each program has space for just 8 squares, so you need to be able to write efficient code to complete the challenges). The challenges start out easy but become maddeningly difficult as you progress. With subroutines, if-then statements, and plenty of opportunities to practice debugging, it's a good way to get kids to think like a programmer. You can also record a video of your program in action and share it to YouTube.

- Mark Frauenfelder

Defining Functions

Written by Amjad Masad

Section | Q&A (365) | Glossary

1. Introduction

A `function` is a block of reusable code. It is useful because you can execute it many times. To define a function, we use `var` like we did with declaring a variable.

You'll see on line 1, we define a function named `hello`. What does this function do? Line 3 tells us that it uses `console.log` to print "i am saying hello".

But nothing happens if you stop here. You have to call the function. On line 6, you'll see we call the function `hello`. This asks the program to run all the code in the `hello` function (ie. the code between the curly `{ }` brackets).

So calling the `hello` function once would result in "i am saying hello" being printed out once in the console.

Make the console show "i am saying hello" twice.

```
1  var hello = function () {
2     // Print hello on the console.
3     console.log("i am saying hello");
4  };
5
6  hello();
```

Run

>

Keyboard Shortcuts   Run K + Enter

Show hint

software. All you need is a browser, and a few minutes to practice.

With that being said, Codecademy is definitely not intended as a replacement for most programming texts. Instead, I think of Codecademy lessons as responsible for building a set of skills and familiarity that you can use as a foundation or framework for other languages.

Finally, this isn't the only resource of it's kind out there, and there are many others that deserve recognition (Udacity is another site that has garnered a lot of attention, but I haven't had the time to check it out).

-- Oliver Hulland

Friendly intro to programming
Codecademy

Free Codecademy

Learning to program has been a goal of mine for years, but it's one that all too often gets set aside. This is fairly normal given the challenges that accompany trying to learn something as foreign as a new language (with the added complexity of logic problems thrown in). Introductory texts are often stultifying, and I found the dilemma of deciding exactly which language to dive into to be anxiety-inducing.

Codecademy

This lesson details how to think about and use a "function" in Javascript.

Luckily, Codecademy has simplified the task of learning to code into a friendly and easy-to-use web interface driven by bite-sized lessons that slowly add up to functional working knowledge. Primarily oriented in Javascript, HTML, and CSS, Codecademy uses discrete tasks and challenges that can be performed in browser to drive learning. They succeed, in part, because they have eliminated the need for books or additional

Easy, automated offsite file storage
Dropbox

Free 2 gb (up to 18 gb, 500 mb per referral),
$10+/month 100, 200, or 500 gb,
Prices Vary for 1 tb for up to 5 users Dropbox

I've been using Dropbox for over a year now. It just works. It copies stuff you save to a specific folder on your computer to the cloud, while also keeping old versions around. I've set up my daughter's computer to save documents to the Dropbox folder by default. Now it is so much easier to find what she has worked on and to go back to a previous version if she accidentally erases her document.

Her important documents are backed up and available if her computer dies. I share the folder she works in, and can edit or comment on what she's done and save those changes on my machine. Dropbox synchronizes the changes automatically. It works seamlessly and quickly.

The best description I've seen of Dropbox comes from Bill Gurley who said "once you begin using Dropbox, you become more and more indifferent to the hardware you are using, as well as the operating system on that device." I've personally enjoyed the service for quite a while, and the more I learn the more I respect what they are trying to do.

-- Monty Zukowski

Specialization is for insects. - R.A. Heinlein

Offsite data backup
Crashplan

Free for basic use; prices vary for Pro use
Crashplan

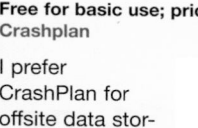

I prefer CrashPlan for offsite data storage. It'll back you up to external hard drives, or computers on your network, or flat-rate cloud storage, but its great innovation is the ability to back up over the internet, with permission, to another CrashPlan user. This is terrific for maintaining your own automatic offsite backups between work and home, or spreading backup religion to friends and family. All you need is broadband and spare disk space.

You need a backup buddy (which could easily be yourself, if you have computers in different locations) if you want to use the offsite backup features. If you don't have a buddy, it won't find you one anonymously, though you can pay $55/computer/year (or $100/household/year for unlimited computers) to back up to Code 42's cloud storage, which they say lives in a converted bank vault. There is no obligation for backups to run in both directions. The advantages of a "peer to peer" backup are cost, control, and reciprocity. With a Drobo or a big RAID I can hold secure backups for my whole far-flung family, at no additional cost per year. It's a feature that turns two (or more) people who weren't backing up at all into people with offsite backups they never have to think about. I think that's as close to magic as software gets.

Bandwidth and disk storage are conserved through compression, data de-duplication, and block-level file access (for efficient handling of large monolithic data like virtual machines). All data that leaves your system gets encrypted, and sensitive details such as filenames and backup logs are not visible to your backup partner. CPU and bandwidth usage can be throttled, and ramped up when the computer goes idle.

While Mozy or BackBlaze expect you to make your initial backup over the net, CrashPlan encourages backing up quickly to a USB or FireWire disk, then carrying or mailing the disk to its destination, where incremental backups over the internet pick up where the local backup left off. Without this feature, one's first complete backup of tens or hundreds of gigabytes could take weeks.

All of the above features are available for free in an ad-supported version of CrashPlan. The $60 paid version, called CrashPlan+, removes the ads and grants more control over data retention, hours of operation, and backup frequency (15 minute intervals by default, daily in the free version). Computers acting as CrashPlan servers, and not themselves being backed up, don't need a license. And because it's platform independent, including Linux support, your backup partner's choice of OS doesn't matter.

I'm the IT director for an 80-person company, where we've been using the business version, CrashPlan Pro, for a little under a year. The Pro version is centralized, allowing IT staff to keep tabs on clients' backup status and lock down settings. Along with a number of ad-hoc restorations of employees' accidentally deleted files, we've restored four or five entire home directories, without a glitch. When a person sees Word's auto-saved files return from 10 minutes before their disk ate itself, we look good.

Pricing for CrashPlan Pro starts at $70/seat and falls slightly with quantity discounts, plus $15/seat/year for support and maintenance; server seats are free. CrashPlan doesn't restore entire hard drives to a bootable state, so it sensibly defaults to backing up just home directories. I wish it could back up varying sets of files to different destinations (like a bigger set to a local disk and a smaller set offsite); the developers tell me this is planned. Its optional pruning of deleted files from the backup archive is aggressive — it prunes on a schedule you can set, but just-deleted files are removed on pruning day, unlike Apple's Time Machine, which only deletes the oldest snapshots in its archive.

But these gripes are trivial where CrashPlan makes its strongest case, which is as an offsite complement to local backup strategies like Time Machine, or as a seamless solution for users who otherwise wouldn't back up at all, let alone offsite. It's great software.

-- Nathaniel Irons

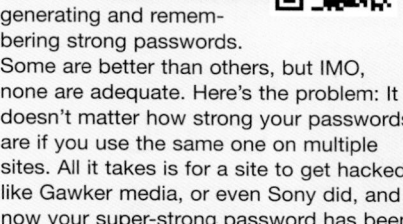

Custom Gmail account
Google Apps Mail

Free Google Apps

I don't mean your personal Gmail account, or an iPhone app for Gmail.

I mean using Google Apps as an invisible email provider for your small business or even large business. For instance, when you send mail to me at kk@kk.org, that mail is processed by Google Apps Mail. Same for mail to anyone else here at kk.org, or Quantified Self, etc. Behind the scenes of my own domain names Google does the mail.

You can think of this as a custom Gmail account. It gives you several advantages.

* Google does a fantastic job of filtering spam. It gets 95%, with no false positives. (I then apply a second Baysian filter with SpamSieve, to give me almost zero spam and zero false spam. For me there is no spam problem. Gone!)

* While I normally read my mail on my "desktop" client, I can access my mail on the road from any computer in the world (with the usual precautions) by logging onto Google Apps (not the Gmail url).

* I have an indefinite backup of my mail on Google's servers, worry free. I've used this backup more than once.

* Yet I still retain my own domain named email without it being a generic Gmail account. You can run yourbigcompany.com through Google Mail Apps.

* I don't have to run a mail server or keep software and security updated.

* Once I set it up (five minutes) this setup applies to everyone in my office/organization who also gets his/her mail at these domains.

* It's free.

Before Google starting offering this free "custom Gmail app" as part of their App suite including Google Docs and Google Calendar (which are also fantastic cool tools), I gained some of these similar results by forwarding all my mail through my free ordinary Gmail account and then back to me at my own servers. That hack worked, but this new custom mail app is much easier to setup, maintain and use. I first became aware of it when my wife's work (Genentech) moved their entire 10,000 employees' mail to a custom Google Apps system. Now you can too. It is part of the migration onto the "cloud," especially for small businesses.

Google Apps Standard edition is free. Larger institutions and corporations switching their email over to Google Apps may want the paid Premium Edition ($50 per user per year) with more perks, features, storage and support.

-- KK

Source for generic logins
BugMeNot

Free BugMeNot

Many websites, particularly media sites, now require registration, usually to gather demographic data about users. If for any reason you don't want to register but still want to view the site, go to www.bugmenot.com, which offers valid logins and passwords for hundreds, perhaps thousands, of sites.

-- Lee Dembart

All-in-one password management
Last Pass

Free, or $12/year for added features LastPass

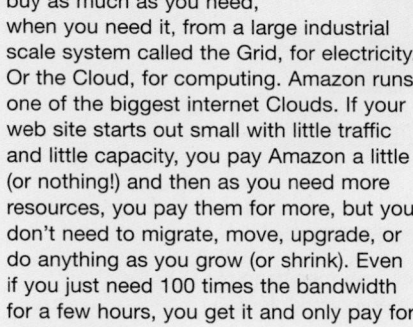

Password strength has been a topic about the Internet lately. I have seen lots of clever methods for generating and remembering strong passwords. Some are better than others, but IMO, none are adequate. Here's the problem: It doesn't matter how strong your passwords are if you use the same one on multiple sites. All it takes is for a site to get hacked, like Gawker media, or even Sony did, and now your super-strong password has been compromised, and every site on which you used that password has been accessed.

So, the bottom line is that no matter how strong your passwords are, and no matter what clever tricks you use to help you remember them, if you're like the average Internet denizen, you have way too many logins for you to remember a unique password for every site. And that means that the only truly secure password system is one that remembers them for you.

Enter LastPass. It's not the only password manager out there, but I like it the best. You create ONE strong password that you have to memorize and use it to access your LastPass database. The LastPass database is stored online, on LastPass's servers, and is accessed either via HTTPS, via a browser plugin, or via an app on your smart-phone. If you use the browser plugin, logging into sites is seamless: LastPass recognizes the site you're on and automatically logs you in (after, optionally, asking you to re-enter your master password). LastPass also has automatic form fill and automatic password generation. This means that you can have a different, unique, very strong password for every site you log into, but you only have to remember one master password. It's the best of both worlds.

One argument against LastPass is that if their database is compromised, then all of your sites are compromised, and that's true, but given that their entire line of work is keeping that information safe, I'm willing to take that chance. The alternative is rolling dice or picking phrases to create passwords, writing all of them down on a piece of paper or something, and then having to manually type them in when I go to a site. A clunky mess.

There is a free version of LastPass, with some additional features unlocked if you pay a $12 a year subscription.

-- Joshua Bardwell

Cheap cloud web hosting
Amazon Web Services

aws.amazon.com

The whole idea of the Cloud is that internet services are like electricity which you don't generate yourself; you buy as much as you need, when you need it, from a large industrial scale system called the Grid, for electricity. Or the Cloud, for computing. Amazon runs one of the biggest internet Clouds. If your web site starts out small with little traffic and little capacity, you pay Amazon a little (or nothing!) and then as you need more resources, you pay them for more, but you don't need to migrate, move, upgrade, or do anything as you grow (or shrink). Even if you just need 100 times the bandwidth for a few hours, you get it and only pay for what you use.

The alternative to the Cloud are hosting services that dedicate a machine to you, or those who share a machine with you; in these arrangements there is no elasticity for growth or pivoting. You can find a good deal for dedicated hosting, but there are

Compute
Amazon EC2
750 hours/month*

Storage
Amazon S3
5 GB*

Database
DynamoDB
100 MB of
SSD-backed storage*

What you get in AWS Free Tier

more constraints. For 10 years we rented dedicated machines from hosting services.

Recently we moved our entire web site to Amazon Web Services because it was the most reliable, most flexible, and the cheapest service around -- even compared to dedicated hosting. Our site's images, words, and visitors are distributed across a vast array of redundant machines to ensure the site is always up and fast. This

very same service runs the largest internet companies in the world: Netflix, Pinterest, Reddit, and SAP. That's good news and bad news. Bad news is, if Amazon Cloud is down, so are we and everyone else. Good news is, they have an insanely great incentive to keep our website up.

You can get one year of Amazon web cloud services for free as a new customer. For 12 months Amazon will host your business or start up for no cost with a healthy load of capacity in the hopes that you'll be successful and soon need lots of processing power, that you'll pay for. But even when you are paying for the power, Amazon's prices are among the cheapest around, priced as the commodity it is.

Caveat: this is not for newbies. Using Amazon Web Services is beyond my technical skills. I use hired help. Second, this is a fiercely competitive frontier; prices and dominance will shift rapidly. The purpose of this review is to point out the growing usefulness of cloud services, and suggest that Amazon may work for you, even if you had not considered cloud services before.

-- KK

Affordable Design

Instant personal logos
GotLogos

$25 Logo GotLogos

Get yer logos here. Only 25 bucks! Quick, dirt-cheap custom logos for your blog, website, garage band, or start-up. You give 'em as much guidance and background as you can jot down, and this outfit will send you one –and only one

— finished design a few days later for 25 dollars. It's a take or leave it job, so inspect their galleries of previous jobs to set your expectations. You can get revisions for $10 more, or purchase more premium packages for fancier "branding" needs. For this price, I figure I can't lose too much if it fails, but it's cheap and cool if they get it right.

I bought my first $25 logo for my True Films website. Its style (identical to Cool Tools) is

pretty minimal, an approach which is actually hard to design for. Here is the logo they sent me via email a few days later.

I paid $10 for a revision, requesting even more simplicity, and a few hours later they provided this:

So that is what I used.

I got my second $25 GotLogo for my Street

Use blog about the street use of technology. I gave them a few guidelines: keep it black and red; make it like graffiti. I was happy with what they came up with so I used it.

It's a great service for the Brand of You.

-- KK

Crowdsourced design
99Designs

99Designs is a clever design service for small jobs like a book cover, or company logo, biz cards, or website. You give them a design brief and announce how much you are willing to pay. Typical jobs offer $200 to $500. Then the design brief is broadcast to a crowd of designers. Those designers who want to try for the job will submit preliminary designs. If you are bidding $500 you'll get more submissions than if you bid $200. Some jobs will receive only a dozen entries, some will garner hundreds. You then choose the winning design and pay your bid. All along you can be directing and working with the designers. The more you are willing to pay, the more, and better, designers will submit. Besides 99Designs there is DesignCrowd, Crowdspring, and 48Hours, with no clear dominant company.

I used 99Designs to run a contest for the cover of Cool Tools. I wrote up a design brief -- what I was looking for, style-wise, etc. -- and offered $499 for the winner, if I found one I really liked. (If I did not, I would get a refund.) In just 4 days I received over 150 different designs! The quality and directions were all over the map -- in a mostly good way. You can see 12 of the better, thrilling entries here. You have to admit the variety is awesome.

In the end, I used a cover that I designed myself, but for most projects the quality of the designs generated by 99Designs would have worked well.

And according to the experience of others, a chief advantage of this method is that you can identify a designer you like and begin to work wth them on a steady more conventional relationship.

-- KK

99designs.com

Personalized swag
CafePress

Prices Vary CafePress

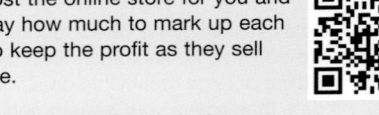

CafePress is a way of setting up an online store for logo-imprinted merchandise very fast and for free. You can upload your own graphics and then just pick which products you want them printed on. (They also package custom music and data CDs.) They print everything on demand and host the online store for you and then you just say how much to mark up each item. You get to keep the profit as they sell the merchandise.

For an example of how quick this is, I set up this store in 15 minutes to sell gear displaying the logo of my battle-bot team. Since everything is made on demand, anyone can order as few as just one copy of a product. This makes CafePress a convenient way to outfit a small group, or just yourself, with no up-front investment.

The only major limitation of their otherwise great service is that you can only print on white or light-colored fabrics. But hey, where else can you get a thong with your robot team logo on it?

-- Alexander Rose

No-nonsense business card creator
Business Card Composer 5

$35 for a standard version, or $45 for premium
BeLight Software

The name of this little Mac-only software program might sound cheesy, but it does exactly what it says, and a lot better than you might expect. It helps you create professional business cards really quickly and easily. And it has been around for a few years/versions, so the UI is mature, stable, and elegant. And EASY.

You just drag stuff into the card area and they just work. Guide lines appear right when and where you'd expect them without having to work with extra commands. When you're done, you simply click Export and a PDF appears – with cut marks for the

printers, if you want – and you can then hand the PDF file directly to a professional printer to work off of.

I've used this any time I've needed to make business cards and it works flawlessly. They have some links within the program to help you find printers, but I don't bother with that feature- I just hand the PDF to the printer that I know and trust. The whole process is so much easier than working with InDesign or some other design tool not made for business cards.

-- Mark Hurst

Custom postage
Photostamps

$5-$10 (+postage) Sheet of 20 PhotoStamps
Stamps.com

Vanity postage. This pretty-easy-to-use website will generate official US postage stamps featuring a photo or illustration of your choosing (works well with iPhoto for instance). When the service was first introduced it was abused by clever pranksters — my favorite hack was a Unabomber postage stamp. The Post Office shut the program down. The service is available again but I don't know what the actual image limits are (vs. their stated policy). We made some silly faces and they made stamps from them. (My 10-year old son's idea of stamp is shown above) I've seen them used for wedding/party invitations. You can also put business logos on them, or other non-political messages. The cost is more than twice that of regular stamps (less if you buy them in bulk). A 20-stamp sheet of these makes a nice personal, utilitarian gift. There are UK, Canada, Australia and NZ equivalents.

-- KK

If our future were not hidden from us, life would be unbearable. - Eugene Forsey

⊙ 606 💬 39 ♥ 137
🐴 Rogie

⊙ 548 💬 17 ♥ 108
🧸 Troy Cummings

⊙ 299 💬 9 ♥ 87
Ryan Putnam

⊙ 374 💬 6 ♥ 83
Ron Lewis

Essential tools for marketing
Marketing 101

Marketing is the practice of making products worth talking about, and then creating stories that get them talked about. It sometimes (but only rarely) uses advertising as a tool. Most of all, it starts with what gets made and why and how.

Tools that are useful:

A phone

The most important element of marketing is story telling, figuring out how to make something worth talking about, and talk about it in a way that resonates. While social media seems like a magical wonder megaphone, the fact is, calling your customers and talking to them is an overlooked shortcut. Humility plus compassion opens you to true connection.

Mailchimp

This is software built on the idea of permission marketing. You can deliver millions of emails to people who want to get them (your true fans, your customers or the merely interested) for just a few dollars. Easy to use, helpful people and beautifully done.

◀ Behance and Dribbble

Very different sites with similar goals: to help you find talented designers and other freelancers that can take your work and make it professional enough to sell. Rule of thumb: pay a lot and try to get more than you pay for.

An RSS reader

It doesn't really matter which one. Marketing is about learning how to see -- to see opportunities, to see stories that resonate, to see dissatisfaction. One way to see better is to read more, daily. And blogs are a priceless way to do that. In fifteen minutes a day, I can keep up on more than 100 blogs a day. Consider: Copyblogger, Scott Adams, David Meerman Scott, Mitch Joel, Steve Dennis--and then, with glutton, add every blog you can find, then prune.

Books

Marketing lends itself more to discovery and education via books than any other topic I know. A thorough reading of a hundred books is enough to make you aware of just about all the nuance (at least the nuance that you can get without actual experience), but perhaps you could start with a few:

John Jantsch's *Duct Tape Marketing* is a fine primer for the small business person who wants to market without relying on merely buying ads or spamming the world. He offers free ebooks as well.

David Meerman Scott's *New Rules of Marketing & R* is quite tactical and helpful.

-- Seth Godin

From *Duct Tape*:

● Price, as I suspect you've learned, is a terrible place to compete. There will always be someone willing to go out of business faster than you.

● Find something that separates you from your competition; become it and speak it to everyone you meet. Quality isn't it; good service isn't it; fair pricing—not it. These are all expectations. The difference needs to be in the way you do business, how you package your product, the way you sell your service, the fact that you send cookies to your clients, your ability to show people how to transform their lives—it's in the experience you provide.

● My definition of marketing is: "getting someone who has a need, to know, like, and trust you."

● Don't think about making a sale online; think about getting a chance to make an impression.

● Develop your marketing strategy around a narrowly defined ideal client above all.

● Few businesses really provide great service. In fact, stealing market share in mature markets is one of the easiest paths for smart start-ups to run.

From *New Rules*:

● I'm absolutely convinced that you will learn more by emulating successful ideas from outside your industry than by copying what your nearest competitor is doing

● When you stop talking about you and your products and services and instead use the web to educate and inform important types of buyers, you will be more successful.

● For most people and organizations, it's better to be active in a few social networking sites instead of creating profiles on dozens of them and being too busy to spend much time in any one.

● Instead of a one-size-fits-all website with a mass-market message, we need to create many different microsites—with purpose-built landing pages and just-right content—each aimed at a narrow target constituency.

● You are not just creating a big brochure about your organization. You're writing for your buyers, not your own ego.

Lessons from a master
Seth Godin on Marketing

The guru of marketing is Seth Godin. He's done more innovative marketing than most Fortune 500 departments combined and can explain the art of marketing better than anyone I know or have read. In Godin's view marketing is much more about an approach to life rather than a department in a business (which is the norm). In fact, as Godin preaches, business is more a lifestyle (as in a way of living) than about maximizing money. Money will flow from a finely-tuned approach to life. Your job as a businessperson is to navigate a thousand tradeoffs in the rugged terrain of reality in order to tune your enterprise to maximize learning, difference, and value to others. If you succeed, the process will also produce money. The art of perceiving and managing these tradeoffs (niche of 1 vs niche of 1000?) is marketing. It is not about advertising.

Godin is a prolific writer. Some of his best advice flows in a river from his daily blog. A distilled version of his messages can be found in the essential three of his many books: *Purple Cow*, *Free Prize Inside* and *All Marketers are Liars*. One thing I really like about Godin's work is that it is technology independent. He embraces all that social media does (before it materialized) without getting stuck in the minutia of any technology. Read any of his books and blog and you'll be ahead of this rapidly advancing curve.

-- KK

From *Purple Cow*:

● Stop advertising and start innovating.

● Imagine how cool Pop Tarts would be if the brand manager was the sort of person who ate them for dinner.

● Before you spend another dollar on another brain-dead ad campaign, trade show, or sales conference, spend some time with your engineers and your customers. Challenge your people to start with a blank sheet of paper and figure out what they'd do if they could do just about anything. If they weren't afraid of failing, what's the most audacious thing they'd try?

● Remarkable isn't always about changing the biggest machine in your factory. It can be the way you answer the phone, launch a new brand, or price a revision to your software. Getting in the habit of doing the "unsafe" thing every time you have the opportunity is the best way to learn to project--you get practice at seeing what's working and what's not.

From *All Marketers Are Liars*:

● There are only two things that separate success from failure in most organizations today:

1. Invent stuff worth talking about.

2. Tell stories about what you've invented.

Make up great stories. that's the new motto.

● People are superstitious about whatever it is you're marketing. You can ignore that superstition or you can rail against it, but both strategies will cost you. The alternative is the only one that works: use personal interactions that are so extraordinary and so powerful that they cause people to tell themselves a different story instead.

If a consumer has a lousy telephone experience with a hotel reservations agent, his impulse will be to hate the service from every person he interacts with when he finally arrives at the hotel. The only solution? It's not expensive carpeting, lower rates or a better mattress. The only solution is a warm, personal interaction between an authentic and caring individual and your disgruntled customer.

Facts are not the most powerful antidote to superstition. Powerful, authentic personal interaction is. That's why candidates still need to shake hands and why retail outlets didn't disappear after the success of Amazon.

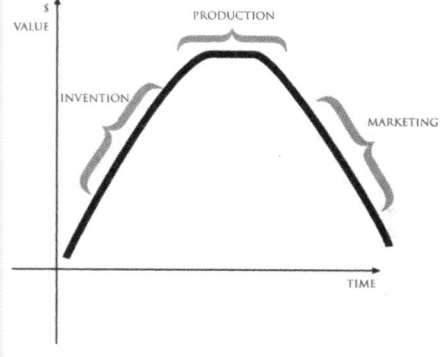

The Curve of Making Stuff

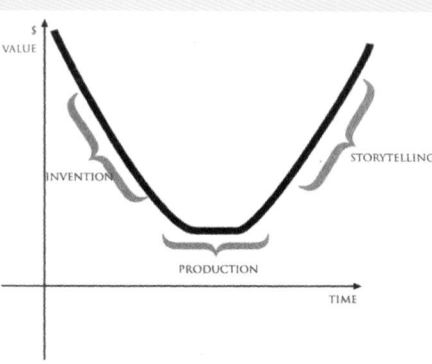

The Curve of Making Stuff Up

$18 Purple Cow, 2009, 224 p.

$6 Free Prize Inside, 2007, 256 p.

$13 All Marketers Are Liars, 2009, 240 p.

How to be popular on the web
Money for Nothing

Free Seth Godin, 2007, 13 p.

It's a deceptive title — but in part that's marketing. Seth Godin, master marketer, sums up the best way to drive traffic to your website (or store, or organization, etc.).

Three words: be useful, unique and updated.

Yep, that's about it. If you can be useful to others (offer value), be unique (by positioning and branding, and being memorable and distinctive), keep showing up, and be current, you've got it made.

It's also a good recipe for life.

This free PDF sermon is short, breezy and right on.

-- KK

No one cares if your lens is good. They care if it's great. Irresistible. The one and only best spot online. Not in your opinion of course, but in their opinion.

History is merely a list of surprises. It can only prepare us to be surprised yet again. - Kurt Vonnegut

371

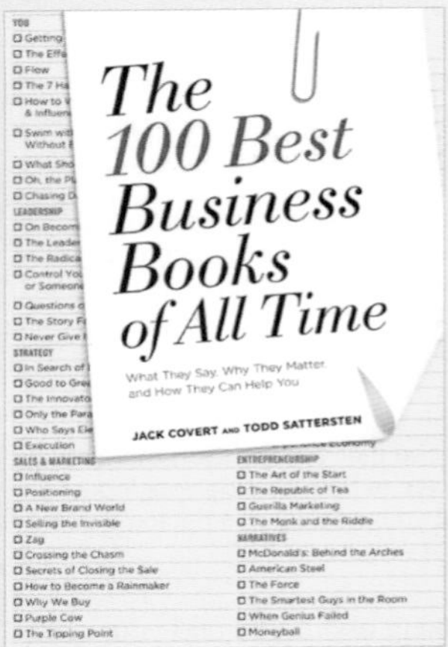
The 100 Best Business Books of All Time
What They Say, Why They Matter and How They Can Help You
JACK COVERT AND TODD SATTERSTEN

Best biz advice source

The 100 Best Business Books of All Time

$17 Jack Covert, Todd Sattersten, 2009, 352 p.

There are ten thousand business books published each year and way over a 100,000 in print. Most business books are worthless drivel, some are a good article fluffed out into a thin book, and maybe 100 out of those hundred thousand are worth reading. Out of those 100 best, only 10 might have something to say to you.

But how to find those few? Jack Covert and Todd Sattersten, two guys who sell biz books, seem to have read all of the ones in print, and they have done the world a favor by selecting the 100 best business books ever, and then packing summaries of them all into one meta-book. If all you want is their list, you can go to their website and check it out.

But their book is much better than a simple list, and their list is better than most. The two have reviewed, abstracted, and compared all the best 100 in the context of thousands of similar books, unlike say your average Amazon reviewer who may have only read one other business book in his or her life. You get context instead of content. Reading Covert and Sattersten's summaries of these classics is often better than reading the book itself, and the review is always useful in pointing you to the few books or authors you might actually want to read in full.

In addition to including the expected gems like *Good to Great*, *The Effective Executive*, and *Purple Cow*, the *100 Best* list also includes many lesser-known titles, some of them oldies-but-goodies, like *Up the Organization*, *The Innovator's Dilemma*, and *Flow*. Not everything is new in business; the wisdom of the past is often surprisingly relevant.

Finally, this book itself is one of the best business books, and can be read alone as a pretty good education in business in its broadest sense, even if you don't read any of the references.

A couple of caveats. One, the authors has included one of my books (*Out of Control*) in their list, which tickles me greatly but might have warped my perspective. Two, they sell business books (at 800CeoRead) and so their book can be seen as a sales tool. On the other hand, the authors have great incentive to sell and include only the best, and so their list is pretty persuasive. Three, in a slip of bad design each of the 100 books featured on their website does not appear with the review as found in their book, but is featured with the standard publisher verbiage; the author's fantastic summaries and analysis are only found in their printed book. (They sell books, see?)

All in all, this is a great business resource at a modest price. If you took their list and read all 100 books you'd get a better MBA than any university would give you, at a fraction of the cost.

-- *KK*

•

From the summary of Clayton M. Christensen's *The Innovator's Dilemma*

New ideas and opportunities, evaluated on the ability to serve existing customers and earn the necessary margins to support the company, are called sustaining innovations and are always successful ventures for existing (and dominant) firms.

But sometimes, innovation creates a new technology or reveals a new way to organize a firm's resources. This disruptive innovation does not offer the performance needed in the existing market, and entrant companies are forced to find a new set of customers who value innovation on a different set of metrics than those of the traditional market. Existing companies disregard the disruptive innovation because of its lower margins, and the newcomers find a small beachhead outside the existing market, using that market space to develop further. As the performance of disruptive innovations outpaces the sustaining innovations, entrants move into established markets and their lower cost structure forces incumbents further up-market, forfeiting existing profitable markets.

•

From the summary of David Gage's *The Partnership Charter*

Researchers at Marquette University studied over two thousand companies and found that 94 percent of "hyper-growth" companies were started by two or more people. Individual owners made up only 6 percent of the hypergrowth segment and almost one-half of the slow-growth companies.

Despite the evidence that a partnership can lead to success, the thought of taking on a partner makes most budding entrepreneurs cringe.

•

From the summary of Richard Florida's *The Rise of the Creative Class*

In the past, access to water or other natural resources determined the economic potential of a region. But Florida believes that the Creative Class is the new resource for economic growth. When choosing where to live, the Creative Class looks for "thick labor markets" that allow for easy horizontal moves from one company to another. Some choose cities with easy access to outdoor recreation, allowing daily engagement to match unpredictable work schedules. As a result of Florida's conclusions and with the publication of The Rise of the Creative Class, regional economic development has been turned on its ear. Spending by state and city governments to attract corporations or finance professional sports arenas was proved useless by Florida's research. Instead, his 3T's–technology, talent, and tolerance–are the new blueprint many areas are using to grow creative capital.

•

From Robert Townsend's *Up the Organization*

Titles Are Handy Tools: There is a trade-off here. In one way, titles are a form of psychic compensation, and if too many titles are distributed, the currency is depreciated. But a title is also a tool. If our salesman is a vice president and yours is a sales rep, and both are in a waiting room, guess who goes in first and gets the most attention...If you find you can't get applicants for menial jobs, maybe your titles are obsolete. A restaurant cured a chronic busboy shortage by changing the title to 'logistics engineer.'

NOLO
LAW for ALL

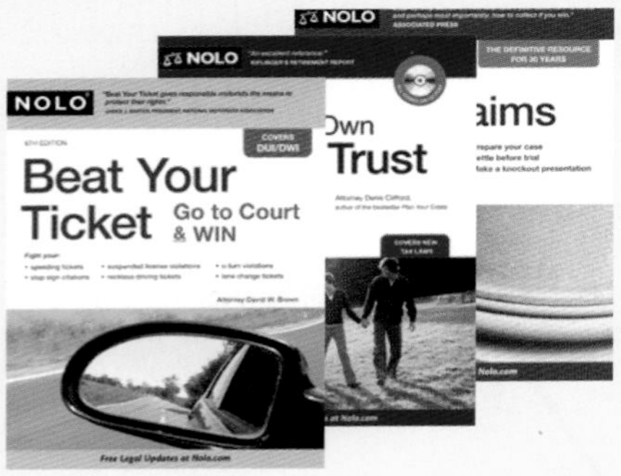
NOLO
Beat Your Ticket
Go to Court & WIN
Own
Trust
aims

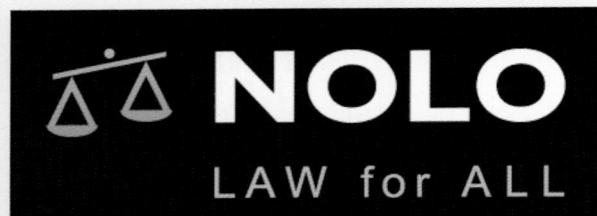

Do-it-yourself legal aid

Nolo Self-help Law Books

Nolo Press

Nolo Self-help books are written by lawyers. They give clear, no nonsense instructions on how to deal with all sorts of issues, from getting your greencard, incorporating, writing your own will or trust to buying a house. I've used Nolo's books to do two out of that list so far, and am very happy with the results. No lawyer needed! Forms are included on CD-rom, as is excellent website support. Best of all, the books clearly state if and when you should consult a real lawyer. Most solutions are common sense, and Nolo tells you how to do it without breaking the bank (or the law).

-- *Woulter*

I highly recommend Nolo guides. I recently used a Nolo Press book, *How to Change Your Name*, to successfully bypass a chore that would have normally demanded a lawyer. It took me all the way through the paperwork and court system. Like most of Nolo legal self-help books, it was clear, thorough, and knowledgeable — exactly what you want from a lawyer, but much less costly. And recently I used their book to form an LLC business without a lawyer. No problem. Just follow their advice.

Nolo Press also offers many of its best-selling titles in an e-book (PDF) format, so that you can instantly download it if you are in a hurry. Nolo's free web articles are also extremely helpful. In fact their website is the first place I head when I need an orientation in legal matters.

-- *KK*

•

From *Beat Your Ticket*

Lack of Prosecution (If the Officer Fails to Show Up)

Since you're presumed to be innocent until proven guilty, your case should be dismissed if no one is able to testify to your guilt--namely the officer. If the officer fails to show, you should ask the judge to dismiss the case "for lack of prosecution," perhaps complaining about how you've been severely inconvenienced by having to take time off work. Such requests are usually granted. They are denied, and the case postponed to another date, only where the officer has a very good excuse, both for not showing and not notifying the court beforehand--such as when the officer's wife had to be rushed to the hospital to give birth.

•

From *LLC or Corporation?*

Tip: LLCs have largely replaced S corporations. Formerly, the only way that all owners of a business could obtain personal liability protection while retaining pass-through taxation of business income was to form an S corporation. Since the arrival of the LLC, however, S corporations have largely fallen out of favor. The LLC provides substantially the same benefits as an S corporation without several of the significant restrictions of S corporations (discussed below).

•

From *Small Business Start-Up Kit*

Tip: While it's good business practice to give receipts to customers who purchase goods or services, it's a legal requirement that you keep a copy for yourself. Therefore, if you write out your own receipts, you'll need to make two copies-one for you, and one for the customer. Cash registers and most receipt books make each record in duplicate.

•

From *Everybody's Guide to Small Claims Court* ►

At the appropriate place in your presentation, tell the judge you have evidence you want to present, and then hand it to the clerk, who in turn will give it to the judge. Appropriate documentation can be a huge aid to winning your case. But don't go overboard: Judges are a little like donkeys--load them too heavily and they are likely to become uncooperative and possibly even ornery.

•

Testimony by Telephone

A surprising number of small claims court judges will take testimony over the phone from a witness who cannot be present because the person is ill, disabled, out of state, or can't take time off from work. While procedures vary, some courts will do this by setting up a conference call so that the opposing party has the opportunity to hear what is being said and to respond.

Don't assume that a particular judge will allow telephone testimony. If you think you'll need to have a witness testify by phone, explain your problem to the court clerk well in advance. If you get a negative response, don't give up--ask the judge when you get into the courtroom. Be sure you also present a letter from the witness stating what the person would testify to if he or she was present in court (for example, your opponent's car ran a red light and broadsided you) and explaining why it is impossible to be there.

•

Judge's Tips: Don't expect to win just because your opponent failed to appear. The law requires that you give enough evidence to show that the defendant actually owes you money.

•

Judge's Tips: The judge will probably question your witnesses. Don't count on being allowed to ask your witnesses questions or cross-examine the other party or their witnesses. Most judges will want to do any questioning of witnesses that is going to take place. Hostile feelings often bubble forth if the parties are allowed to ask questions of opposing witnesses.

If one of your witnesses forgets an important point, wait until the judge is about to excuse the witness and then politely suggest that the judge allow the witness to make a further statement, for example, "Your Honor, Ms. Peterson hasn't said anything about the color of the traffic light. Would it be possible for you to ask her to cover that subject?" If your opponent or one of the opponent's witnesses skirts an important issue, say something similar, like, "Your Honor, the defendant hasn't said anything about how many beers he drank that night. I would appreciate it if you would ask him to cover that subject."

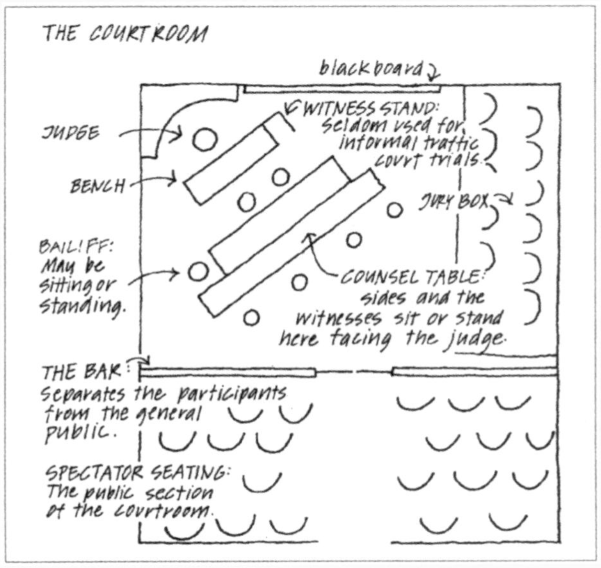
THE COURTROOM
blackboard
JUDGE
WITNESS STAND: seldom used for informal traffic court trials
BENCH
JURY BOX
BAILIFF: May be sitting or standing.
COUNSEL TABLE: sides and the witnesses sit or stand here facing the judge.
THE BAR: separates the participants from the general public.
SPECTATOR SEATING: The public section of the courtroom.

•

Proving money damages. Establishing financial loss caused by a noisy dog is obviously a subjective task. One approach is to try to put a money value on each hour of your lost sleep. For example, if you can convince the judge that each hour you lie awake is worth a certain amount (perhaps $25 or even $20), your damages will quickly add up. As a backup to your oral testimony about how miserable it is to be denied sleep by a howling canine, keep a log of the dates and times you are awakened and present it to the judge. In one case, six neighbors kept a log for 30 days detailing how often a particular dog barked after 10 p.m. The number, which was over 300, was influential in convincing the judge to give the plaintiffs a good-sized judgment.

We don't see things as they are, we see things as we are. - Anais Nin

Self-employment how-to

Incredible Secret Money Machine

Free PDF The Guru's Lair

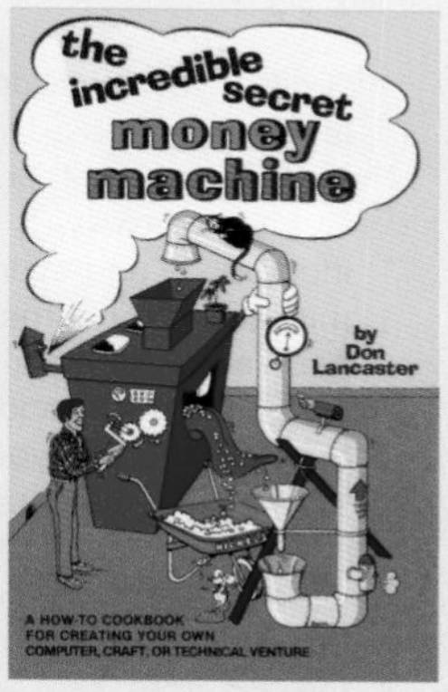

When I first started to get serious about making money I ran into this book written in 1978 by a hippy-hacker living in Arizona. His advice was aimed at "craft and technical" types who wanted to create a small business "doing their thing" whether that was creating ceramic pots, designing outdoor gear, or writing computer code. He talked about doing a start up before that term was subverted by the implication that your start up would take over the world. Instead the author preached one-person self-employment that made you a living. The concept of entrepreneurism as a small-time life-style has evaporated from the culture, and now entrepreneur and start-up means "get big fast."

That did not appeal to me then, or now. But making a living doing what I was passionate about did. I learned how to earn a self-employed living from this book, which was mostly about what not to do. (I have been self-employed now for most of my adult life.) A lot of Don Lancaster's specific examples are now terribly dated, but his core principles still stand and are worth listening to particularly if you are starting out. (If you are already successfully self-employed this book won't help you much.) His idea that you should aim for a business that grows organically (income > expenses), is a total life-style approach (your business is you), and is dependent on your own value-added rather than market domination.

If I had to sum up this book in my own words it would be; "If you are willing to build your business on expertise, you can make a living instead of making a fortune — and occasionally the fortune comes anyway."

Best of all, unlike any other "make-money" book I know of, this one is free. You can read the author's PDF version of the original paper book.

-- *KK*

•

Getting filthy rich should be nowhere in your plans. So long as you can continue doing what you like in the direction you want to go, that's all that should matter. The great irony of your incredible secret money machine is that the less you strive for income, the more of it will come your way, and, more importantly, the more you will be able to do with what you already have. Any time or effort spent directly toward making money is time not available for your main trip. This is wasted time and energy that eventually hurts you rather than helps.

•

As a ferinstance, let's talk about an ordinary piece of typing paper. If you are running an office supply store, you can make a penny on this piece of paper. That penny reflects the difference between the wholesale price and your selling price. Your personal value added here consists of what you put into making your store attractive and in how you relate to your customers. If, instead, you are running a typing service, you can now buy the paper for a penny and sell it for fifty cents or more. Now, you have over fifty times the return since your personal value added consists of putting information on paper just the way the customer wants you to. Things get much better if you make up the words yourself instead of using those somebody else already wants. A medium length story in a larger magazine should pay you several hundred dollars for a dozen or so sheets of paper. This will average out about ten dollars per page, another 20: 1 improvement.

•

Employees are a hassle, a waste of time and a psychic energy sink. You should avoid them at all costs. Your incredible secret money machine should have 0.834 employees — that is 83.4 percent of you, nothing more,no less. The remaining 16.6 percent of you should go for fun and

rewind time. Spend much less time on your money machine and the job will never get done. Much more and you'll be grinding yourself down.

•

But, your money machine will work best of all if it has hundreds or, better yet, thousands of tiny sources of income. There are several good reasons for this. No customer will think he owns you if he is one among unwashed thousands. Customer expectations will also usually be lower since they are probably dealing in a smaller way with you. Better yet, if you can get enough small customers, they will start to obey the statistical laws of large numbers. This means you will be able to predict future sales and cash flow with good accuracy.

Eventually, several of the smaller customers will become bigger ones that take up more and more of your money machine's product. This is fine when it happens, but it is not something you want to aggressively go after when you are starting out The important, even crucial, point is to never let any one customer dominate your money machine to a point where he is in control.

Should you ever end up with one very large customer and many small ones, arrange your money machine and your whole lifestyle to live within the nickels generated by all the smaller sources combined. Force yourself to be independent of the income generated by the biggie. Funnel this extra single-source income into improving your money machine, into the "investments" of the final chapter, or into having fun-but always keep this extra income separate from your bread-and-butter smaller income sources.

•

You should always think of any dollar that goes out your door in terms of the larger number of incoming money machine dollars needed to create it.

I'll define a Reversed Cash Flow, or ReF as any method you could conjure up to cause all of the nickels to head on out exactly In the opposite of the "usual" direction. And preferably end up in your own pocket. Knowing and using relevant and workable ReFs are key secrets to a successful money machine venture. Some ReF examples that have worked for me do Include: Having the Forest Service pay me to stay in a mountain vacation cabin as a fire lookout. Getting paid several hundred dollars a year (or similar perks) for drinking rootbeer every Wednesday night as a volunteer fireman. Forming various clubs and user groups to gain big discounts on all types of new software, hardware, and advance freebie technical info. Getting hired as a sysop on a BBS to pick up free access and actually getting paid a royalty as others call the service. Receiving free toner for testing to yield negative per-page toner costs on my desktop publishing. Or, becoming a developer or an Independent Software Vendor that gives you free or discounted hardware and software.

•

Over the years, I have seen hundreds of examples of money machine people being severely done in by the patent system. Even murdered by it in several heart-attack-during-litigation cases. And not once did I see anyone approaching the patent system on a small scale basis and profiting from it. Ever. Once again: Unless you are well within a Fortune 500 context, any and all involvement in the patent system in any, shape, or form is absolutely certain to cause you the net loss of time, energy, money, and sanity. Besides ending up a totally useless and utterly unnecessary psychic energy sink.

•

Having enough advance financing for your money machine is about the worst possible thing you can do and is almost certain to scuttle the whole machine.

Even when it is up and running perfectly, your money machine at its largest shouldn't have more than a year's income tied up in your total plant and equipment. This one year limit has been called the convivial workplace and forms the dividing line between the good guy or gal craftspersons and the bad guy industrialists.

•

In cash flow accounting, you keep track of how much money comes into your machine and how much goes out, just like a piggy bank. You enter each and every transaction as it happens in some simple way, like writing it on a "cash out" pad. Once a week you do a running balance of your totals. Once a month, you look at your bottom line to see if you are winning or losing. After several months go by, you project your annual returns. You don't count anything for materials unused but on hand, things produced but not sold, the value of the place where you work, or things you have delivered but have not been paid for. This sort of accrual accounting can be important for a large corporation, but will only deceive you if you include these things too early in the game. You should set aside income as it comes up for tax obligations, retirement funds, and other fixed expenses that will be paid out at a later date.

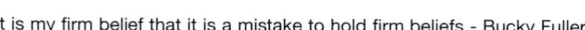

Inside every big problem is a small problem trying to get out

Where technology will go

The Innovator's Dilemma

$23 Clayton Christensen, 1997, 225 p.

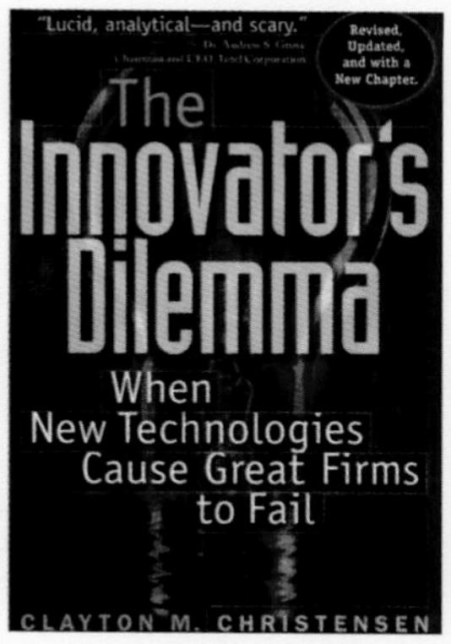

I keep coming back to this book when change gets difficult. Christensen says that every innovator has an inevitable dilemma: serve the current game (customers) or the next game (new customers). You can't serve both. Therefore innovators have to ignore the demands of the present in order to create the reality of tomorrow. It's the most insightful look into the nature of revolution I've seen.

-- *KK*

•

The research reported in this book…shows that in the cases of well-managed firms … good management was the most powerful reason they failed to stay atop their industries. Precisely because these firms listened to their customers, invested aggressively in new technologies that would provide their customers more and better products of the sort they wanted, and because they carefully studied market trends and systematically allocated investment capital to innovations that promised the best returns, they lost their positions of leadership.

•

Occasionally, however, disruptive technologies emerge: technologies that result in worse product performance, at least in the near-term… Generally disruptive technologies underperform established products in mainstream markets. But they have other features that a few fringe (and generally new) customers value.

•

By and large, a disruptive technology is initially embraced by the least profitable customers in a market.

•

But while a $40 million company needs to find just $8 million in revenues to grow at 20 percent in the subsequent year, a $4 billion company needs to find $800 million in new sales. No new markets are that large. As a consequence, the larger and more successful an organization becomes, the weaker the argument that emerging markets can remain useful engines for growth.

•

It was as if the leading firms were held captive by their customers, enabling attacking entrant firms to topple the incumbent industry leaders each time a disruptive technology emerged.

•

The [non-hydraulic excavator manufacturers] did not fail because they lacked information about hydraulics or how to use it; indeed the best of them used it as soon as it could help their customers. They did not fail because management was sleepy or arrogant. They failed because hydraulics didn't make sense – until too late.

•

Not only are the market applications for disruptive technologies unknown at the time of their development, they are unknowable. The strategies and plans that managers formulate for confronting disruptive technological change, therefore, should be plans for learning and discovery rather than plans for execution.

Figure 8.4 Managing Changes in the Basis of Competition

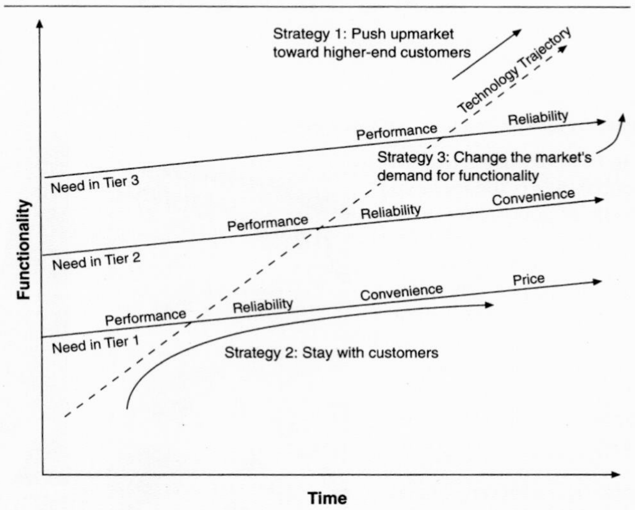

Patents are useless for most

The Case Against Patents

Free PDF Don Lancaster

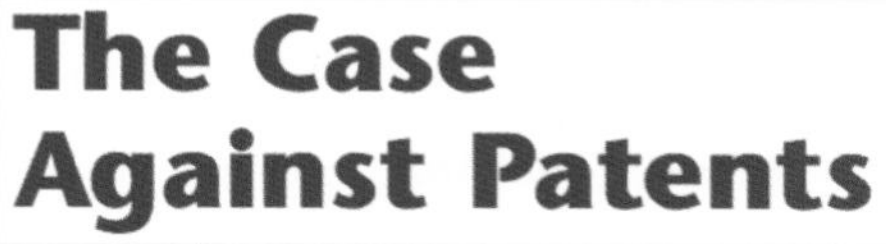

I'm convinced by Don Lancaster's (and others') arguments that patents makes no sense for a small-time inventor or technical genius. Patents guarantee you nothing but the right to fight for your idea. Fighting takes a full apparatus, lots of time, negotiating assets, lawyer fees, and emotional surplus. The same results from fighting (ineffectually 99% of the time) can be had by moving fast and staying nimble. Patents are a corporate game and should be avoided by anyone trying to work outside of that framework. Here's a lot of encouragement and support from a master non-patent inventor.

-- *KK*

Career Advice

How to get a job
What Color Is Your Parachute?

$12 Richard Nelson Bolles, 2012, 384 p.

Still the best job-hunting guide and advice there is. Get the current year's edition. This is a fantastic tool useful to almost everyone. The first edition appeared 40 years ago, but author Richard Bolles has updated his advice every year (!!!) since then, improving it, keeping it relevant to technology and the economy, and refining his message of matching you and your work. It is now a better career counselor than ever.

Everyone should read this book in high school long before you apply for a job. You should study it anytime you are looking for work or changing careers, and you should browse it every now and then even if you have a job. It's so darn useful because it is about more than just "finding a job." In recent editions, Bolle emphasizes that "making your own job" may be the way to go for some. There are a lot of other good sources about finding your passions, or writing resumes, or conducting an interview, but none put them together as well as this classic still does. I've used Boole's wisdom and insights myself (always been happily employed) and with my kids (ditto), and with relatives (ditto again). It's worth your time.

-- KK

One way to bring values to your consciousness is to imagine that shortly before the end of your life you are invited to dinner--and to your great surprise people have secretly come in from all over the country and all over the world, to attend a surprise testimonial dinner for you.

At the dinner, to your great embarrassment, there is one testimonial after another about the good things you did, or the good person you were, in your lifetime. No mention of any parts of your life that you don't want to have remembered. Just the good stuff.

So, this brings us to some questions. If you get the life you really want between now and then, what would you hope you would hear at that dinner, as they looked back on your life?

You ask that question again and again of everyone you know, or meet, until you find someone who says, "Yes, I do." Then you ask them:

"What is the name of the person you know who works, or used to work, at Mythical Corporation? Do you have their phone number and/or address?"

"Would you be willing to call ahead, to tell them who I am?"

You then either phone them yourself or make an appointment to go see them ("I won't need more than twenty minutes of your time."). Once you are talking to them, after the usual polite chit-chat, you ask them the question you are dying to know. Because they are inside the organization that interests you, they are usually able to give you the exact answer to the question that has been puzzling you: "Who would have the power to hire me at Mythical Corporation, for this kind of position (which you then describe)?" If they answer that they do not know, ask if they know who might know. If it turns out that they do know, then, you ask them not only for that hiring person's name, address, phone, and e-mail address, but also what they can tell you about that person's job, that person's interests, and their style of interviewing.

It works because everyone has friends, including this person-who-has-the-power-to-hire-you. You are simply approaching them through their friends. And you are doing this, not wimpishly, as one who is coming to ask a favor. You are doing it helpfully, as one who is asking to help rescue them.

Rescue? Yes, rescue! I cannot tell you the number of employers I have known over the years who can't figure out how to find the right employee. It is absolutely mind-boggling, particularly in these hard times when job-hunters would seem to be gath-

ered on every street corner.

You're having trouble finding the employer. The employer is having trouble finding you. What a great country!

So, if you now present yourself direction to the person-who-has-the-power-to-hire-you, you are not only answering your own prayers. You are hopefully answering the employer's as well.

When To Discuss Salary

Not until the following conditions have been fulfilled–

Not until they've gotten to know you, at your best, so they can see how you stand out above the other applicants.

Not until you've gotten to know them, as completely as you can, so you can tell when they're being firm, or when they're flexible.

Not until you've out exactly what the job entails.

Not until they've had a chance to find out how well you match the job-requirements.

Not until you're in the final interview at that place, for that job.

Not until you've decided, "I'd really like to work here."

Not until they've said, "We want you."

Not until they've said, "We've got have you"

–should you get into salary discussions with this employer.

When to Negotiate Salary

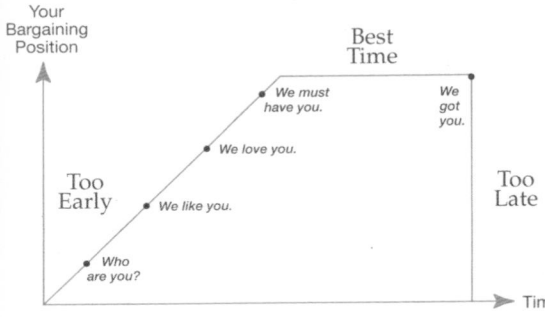

Become expert first
So Good They Can't Ignore You

$16 Cal Newport, 2012, 304 p.

"Follow your passion" is the dogmatic advice for building a career. But it is woefully incomplete and even misleading for some people. Better advice is "Become so good they can't ignore you"; that is, become expert in something, and the passion will follow. In other words, flip the mission from "find your passion so that you can be useful" to "be useful so you can find your passion." Acquiring expertise is a lot of work, requiring deliberate practice, patience, shrewd acceptance of control of your time, and other meta skills. While this book changed my mind about how skills trump passion, I consider it the only first word in outlining how one goes about this. But it's good enough for framing the question that I gave all my young adult kids a copy.

-- KK

There is, however, a problem lurking here: When you look past the feel-good slogans and go deeper into the details of how passionate people like Steve Jobs really got started, or ask scientists about what actually predicts workplace happiness, the issue becomes much more complicated. You begin to find threads of nuance that, once pulled, unravel the tight certainty of the passion hypothesis, eventually leading to an unsettling recognition:

"Follow your passion" might just be terrible advice.

If a young Steve Jobs had taken his own advice and decided to only pursue work he loved, we would probably find him today as one of the Los Altos Zen Center's most popular teachers. But he didn't follow this simple advice. Apple Computer was decidedly not born out of passion, but instead was the result of a lucky break--a "small-time" scheme that unexpectedly took off.

How do we find work that we'll eventually love? Like Jobs, should we resist settling into one rigid career and instead try lots of small schemes, waiting for one to take off? Does it matter what general field we explore? How do we know when to stick with a project or when to move on? In other words, Jobs's story generates more questions than it answers. Perhaps the only thing it does make clear is that, at least for Jobs, "follow your passion" was not particularly useful advice.

To summarize, I've presented two different ways people think about their working life. The first is the craftsman mindset, which focuses on what you can offer the world. The second is the passion mindset, which instead focuses on what the world can offer you.

Supply and demand says that if you want these traits you need rare and valuable skills to offer in return. Think of these rare and valuable skills you can offer as your career capital.

The craftsman mindset, with its relentless focus on becoming "so good they can't ignore you," is a strategy well suited for acquiring career capital. This is why it trumps the passion mindset if your goal is to create work you love.

"Doing things we know how to do well is enjoyable, and that's exactly the opposite of what deliberate practice demands…Deliberate practice is above all an effort of focus and concentration. That is what makes it "deliberate," as distinct from the mindless playing of scales or hitting tennis balls that most people engage in."

If you show up and do what you're told, you will, as Anders Ericsson explained earlier in this chapter, reach an "acceptable level" of ability before plateauing. The good news about deliberate practice is that it will push you past this plateau and into a realm where you have little competition. The bad news is that the reason so few people accomplish this feat is exactly because of the trait Colvin warned us about: Deliberate practice is often the opposite of enjoyable.

Excellent career advice
The Adventures of Johnny Bunko

$11 Daniel H. Pink, art by Rob Ten Pas, 2008, 160 p.

Presented in the form of manga (a comic book for grownups), this is the most succinct course in career counseling I've ever seen. Not what career you should pursue, but *how* you should pursue it. You can read this masterpiece in an hour, but it will take a lifetime to work out the details of those six lessons. This compact sermon will make the most difference to those just starting out in the workplace. The six quick lessons [with my comments in brackets] are:

There is no plan. [The economy changes too fast for your career to have a plan]

Think strengths, not weaknesses. [Find your advantages]

It's not about you. [Serving others serves you best]

Persistence trumps talent. [Keep showing up]

Make excellent mistakes. [Take risks, but fail forward]

Leave an imprint. [Do something that matters]

Each point is given consequential flesh in this engaging story. In my experience these six lessons highlight the skills needed at work better than, say, the bestseller *Seven Habits of Highly Effective People*. And it is far more fun to read. I've bought copies of *Bunko* for each of my kids and for a few adult friends currently struggling with their path. I'll probably re-read it myself in a year.

-- KK

The endless summer

Work Your Way Around the World

$18 Susan Griffith, 2012 (15th edition), 416 p.

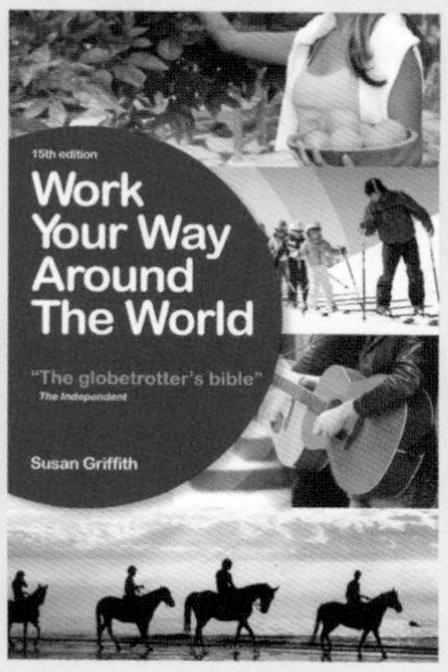
15th edition
Work Your Way Around The World
"The globetrotter's bible"
The Independent
Susan Griffith

It's many a graduate's dream — pay your way as you travel around the world. I lived the dream myself when I was younger, so I know it is possible. Since then I've been tracking this subject faithfully, and have read through scores of books and websites offering how-to advice on the dream. They won't hurt, but this fantastic book — now in its 14th edition! — is really the only one that will give you much help before you leave.

Most of these kind of books are a bunch of hand-waving generalities, or out of date particulars; this one is very specific and very current. It is massively researched, with tons of incoming gossip on where the easily-gotten jobs are this year, and what to do about paperwork and visas in that particular place, and how to land the job, and what you should expect, and letters from those who just did it. It's all very helpful, practical and inspiring. But don't get your hopes too high. There are really only two kinds of dependable quick jobs to be found "around the world": 1) In the service industry in Europe — working at hotels, resorts, bars, camps for other tourists; and 2) teaching English in Asia. For most kids, that'll be enough. There are hundreds of exceptions to these two, and this book will do its best to point you to them, but they are far fewer, and more dependent on chance. But even that skill — cultivating chance — is tackled with great intelligence in this meaty book, which I can't recommend too much.

The author Susan Griffith is very prolific and at the center of a number of other related ongoing books, also recommended: *Teaching English Abroad, Your Gap Year,* and *Summer Jobs Worldwide.*

-- KK

•

It is extremely difficult for anyone whose mother tongue is English to starve in an inhabited place, since there are always people who will pay good money to watch you display a talent as basic as talking.

•

According to many travelers like Emma-Louise Parkes, the Albuferia area is the place to head:

I arrived at Faro Airport in June, and went straight to Albuferia. A job-hunter here will be like a kid in a sweet shop. By 12.15pm I was in the resort, by 12.30pm I had found somewhere to stay and had been offered at least four jobs by the evening, one of which I started at 6pm. All the English workers were really friendly individuals and were a goldmine of information. Jobs-wise, I was offered bar work, touting, waitressing, cleaning, packing ice cubes into bags, karaoke singing, nannying for an English bar owner, timeshare tout, nightclub dancer… I'm sure there were more. Touts can earn £16 a night with all the drink they can stomach while waitresses can expect a little less for working 10am-1pm and 6pm-10pm. Attractive females (like myself!) will be head-hunted by lively bars, whereas British men are seen by the locals as trouble and are usually kept behind bars (serving bars that is) and in cellars.

•

Taiwan

The hiring policy is virtually universal in Taiwan: almost anyone with a BA can land a job. The country remains a magnet for English teachers of all backgrounds. Hundreds of private language institutes or buhsibans continue to teach young children, cram high school students for university entrance examinations and generally service the seemingly insatiable demand for English conversation and English tuition.

Many well-established language schools are prepared to sponsor foreign teachers for a resident visa, provided the teacher is willing to work for at least a year. Only teachers with a university degree are eligible. Many people arrive on spec to look for work. It is usually easy to find a buhsiban willing to hire you but not so easy to find a good one. If possible, try to sit in on one or two classes before signing a contact. (If a school is unwilling to permit this, it doesn't bode well.) The majority of schools pay NT$500-$600 (roughly $19-$21.50) per hour.

How to sell your crafts

The Handmade Marketplace

$11 Kari Chapin, 2010, 224 p.

The giant crafts website Etsy makes it easy to list home-made stuff to a potential audience of millions. But the hard part is getting anyone to pay attention and actually buy it. That requires some basic business and online marketing skills, which are reviewed here, with the home crafter in mind.

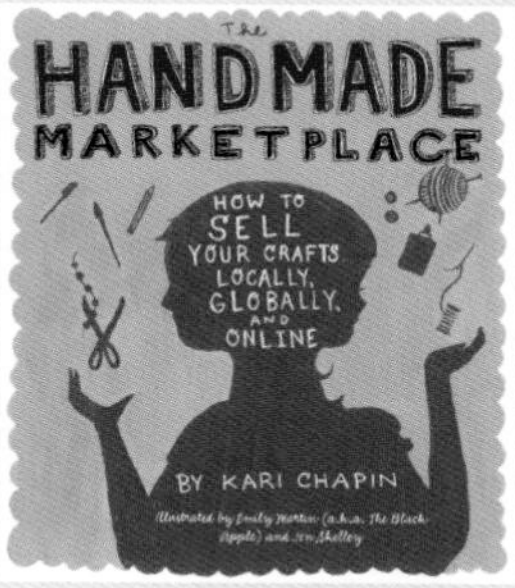
The Handmade Marketplace
How to sell your crafts locally, globally, and online
By Kari Chapin

-- KK

•

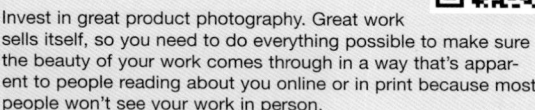

What best advice would you offer a crafter who is looking to gain national attention for their work?

Invest in great product photography. Great work sells itself, so you need to do everything possible to make sure the beauty of your work comes through in a way that's apparent to people reading about you online or in print because most people won't see your work in person.

•

Unsatisfied Customers

In a perfect world, everyone would be happy with you and your products all the time. You would always be paid promptly and always get rave reviews. Sometimes, though, things just don't work out. In this case you should:

Try to remain upbeat. Use positive-sounding words when communicating with customers.

Say, "What can I do to resolve this for you?" rather than "What do you want from me?"

Try to find value in what your unhappy customer is saying to you. It could be that their complaint has some truth to it, which you may find helpful in the long run.

•

Are you getting some really great feedback about something in particular that you've made? Consider posting these compliments in the description of your item.

•

Keep these customer service practices in mind at all times:

The customers may not always be right, but they do deserve your full attention and respect regarding the matter at hand.

Apologize first. What if you didn't do anything wrong? you may ask. Well, while that may be the case, that's not really the point. You can, in fact, regret that your customer is upset in any regard. Simply recognizing that your buyer has a problem and has had to take the time out of a busy day to alert you to it is reason enough to apologize.

Ask what will make the situation right. If what the customer wants is reasonable and you can do it, you should consider it.

Taking a hit on a sale is a small price to pay when it comes to your overall reputation and the trust you are trying to build with your market.

Everyone is in sales

To Sell is Human

$19 Daniel H. Pink, 2012, 272 p.

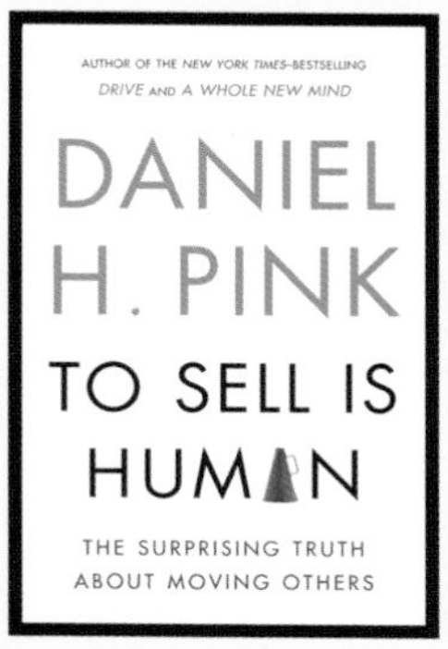
Author of the New York Times-Bestselling Drive and A Whole New Mind
DANIEL H. PINK
TO SELL IS HUMAN
THE SURPRISING TRUTH ABOUT MOVING OTHERS

Dan Pink argues that hard selling no longer works as it once did; what we need in this new information economy is soft selling. Soft sales are not just for sales people; everyone now is in the business of selling. Soft persuasion techniques are useful to anyone sending an email, writing a resume, doing a kickstart project, even twittering. A seller -- either professional or citizen -- can no longer rely on the old tactics such as "overcoming objections" and "closing an offer" but must shift to new skills such as improvisation, attunement, and service. Pink arrives at the radical idea that selling well makes us better humans, and better humans sell better. This book accomplished two things: it persuaded me that I am in sales, and it gave me some new tools for gently selling what I have to offer.

-- KK

•

Successful negotiators recommend that you should mimic the mannerisms of your negotiation partner to get a better deal. For example, when the other person rubs his/her face, you should, too. If he/she leans back or leans forward in the chair, you should, too. However, they say it is very important that you mimic subtly enough that the other person does not notice what you are doing, otherwise this technique completely backfires. Also, do not direct too much of your attention to the mimicking so you don't lose focus on the outcome of the negotiation. Thus, you should find a happy medium of consistent but subtle mimicking that does not disrupt your focus.

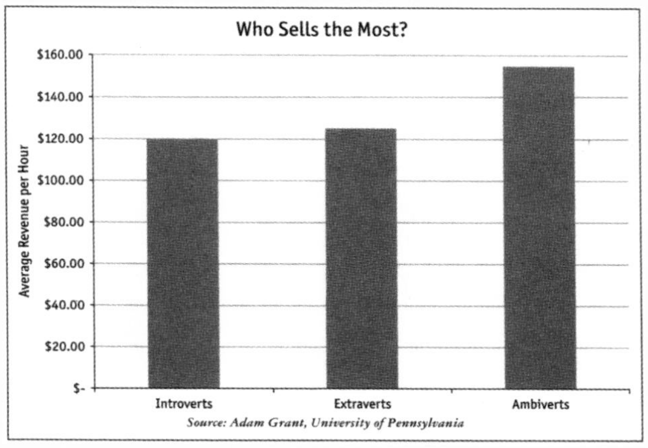
Who Sells the Most?
Average Revenue per Hour
$160.00
$140.00
$120.00
$100.00
$80.00
$60.00
$40.00
$20.00
$-
Introverts
Extraverts
Ambiverts
Source: Adam Grant, University of Pennsylvania

•

Identifying problems as a way to move others takes two longstanding skills and turns them upside down. First, in the past, the best salespeople were adept at accessing information. Today, they must be skilled at curating it--sorting through the massive troves of data and presenting to others the most relevant and clarifying pieces. Second, in the past, the best salespeople were skilled at answering questions (in part because they had information their prospects lacked). Today, they must be good at asking questions--uncovering possibilities, surfacing latent issues, and finding unexpected problems. And one question in particular sits at the top of the list.

•

If you're testifying before your city council, summarizing your main point with a rhyme gives council members a way to talk about your proposal when they deliberate. If you're one of a series of freelancers invited to make a presentation before a big potential client, including a rhyme can enhance the processing fluency of your listeners, allowing your message to stick in their minds when they compare you and your competitors. Remember: Pitches that rhyme are more sublime.

•

Emma Coats, a former story artist at the studio, has cracked the Pixar code--and, in the process, created a template for an irresistible new kind of pitch. Coats has argued that every Pixar film shares the same narrative DNA, a deep structure of storytelling that involves six sequential sentences:

Once upon a time ________________________________. Every day, ________________. One day ____________________. Because of that, _____________________. Until finally _______________________.

Take, for example, the plot of Finding Nemo.

It's even possible to summarize this book with a Pixar pitch:

<u>Once upon a time</u> only some people were in sales. <u>Every day</u>, they sold stuff, we did stuff, and everyone was happy. <u>One day</u> everything changed: All of us ended up in sales and sales changed from a world of *caveat emptor* to *caveat venditor*. <u>Because of that</u>, we had to learn the new ABCs--attunement, buoyancy, and clarity. <u>Because of that</u>, we had to learn some new skills--to pitch, to improvise, and to serve. <u>Until finally</u> we realized that selling isn't some grim accommodation to a brutal marketplace culture. It's part of who we are--and therefore something we can do better by being more human.

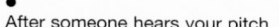

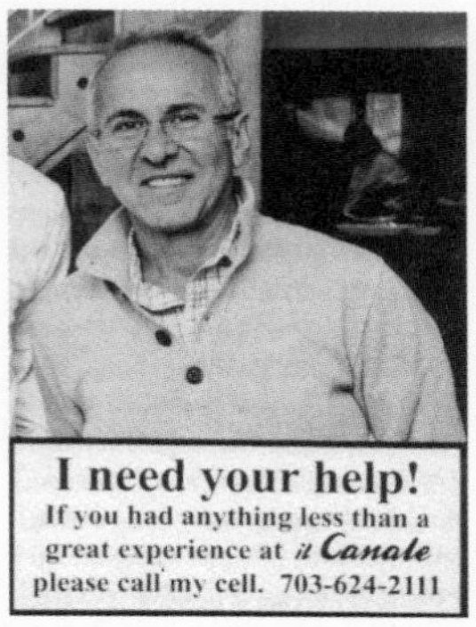
I need your help!
If you had anything less than a great experience at il Canale
please call my cell. 703-624-2111

•

After someone hears your pitch ...

1. What do you want them to know?
2. What do you want them to feel?
3. What do you want them to do?

If you've got strong answers to these three questions, the pitch will come together more easily.

•

The conversation becomes more of a dance and less of a wrestling match. That's something that Fuller Brush founder Alfred Fuller intuited years before improv was ever invented. "Never argue," he wrote. "To win an argument is to lose a sale." "In improv, you never try to get someone to do something. That's coercion, not creativity," Salit says. "You make offers, you accept offers--and a conversation, a relationship, a scene, and other possibilities emerge."

•

One way to do better is with what I call "emotionally intelligent signage." Most signs typically have two functions: They provide information to help people find their way or they announce rules. But emotionally intelligent signage goes deeper. It achieves those same ends by enlisting the principles of "make it personal" and "make it purposeful." It tries to move others by expressing empathy with the person viewing the sign (that's the personal part) or by triggering empathy in that person so she'll understand the rationale behind the posted rule (that's the purposeful part).

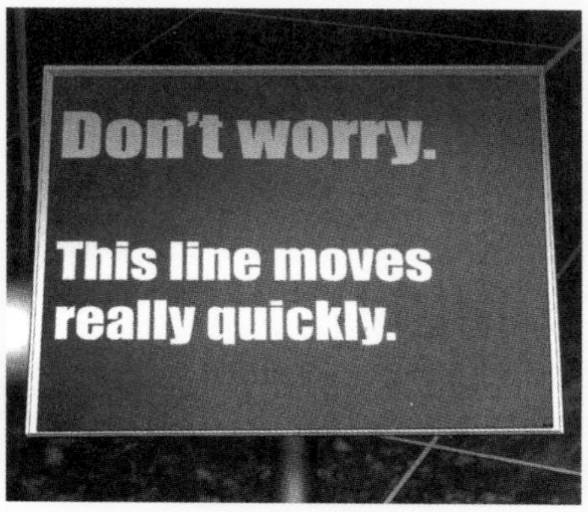
Don't worry.
This line moves really quickly.

Hiring

How to hire people
Hiring Smart!
$15 Pierre Mornell, 2003, 240 p.

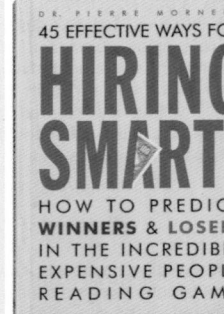

Hire smart, your company wins; hire dumb, you die. People are the scarce resource in the new economy, but no one teaches employees how to hire people. Successful fast-growing companies have caught on. They now hire people who are good at hiring others. Between these book covers is a million dollars worth of hiring advice, the best anywhere. If you are in business, ignore at your peril.

-- KK

- You can't spend too much time or effort on "hiring smart." The alternative is to manage tough, which is much more time consuming.

- The best predictor of future behavior is past behavior.

- Strategy No.3: Give an assignment before the interview. Ask the candidate to visit one of your stores, plants, campuses, offices, or Web pages before the interview. Then ask for the candidate's observations.

- Strategy No.5: Read resumes in teams if possible. It's helpful–and faster–to read the top candidates' resumes in teams of three to five people. Teams that work well together are more accurate and insightful about potential employees than individuals are.

- Strategy No.6: Cast the widest net possible. Microsoft assumes that the best candidates are not looking for jobs. In fact, candidates who approach Microsoft are actually less attractive to the company.

- Strategy No.13: Ask all your questions at once. That's right. Put all your initial questions on the table up front. This strategy accomplishes three things. First, in a manner of speaking, you pass the baton. You've asked the questions, now the candidate must respond. Performance depends upon the candidate, not selling yourself and the organization. Second, more importantly, this strategy directly confronts the most common problem in interviewing: not listening, and talking too much… Third, this technique forces you to listen. If there's one practical tip you should try in your next interview, I suggest this one. Asking all your questions at once, and following up later in the interview, allows you to settle back and watch a candidate's behavior as well as listen to his or her words.

- Strategy No. 15: Assign a mini-project to finalists. Three quarters of the way through the interview, give the candidate a task to perform. Not only does this demonstrate the candidate's behavior–it also breaks up the monotony of most interviews.

- Strategy No. 32: Ask the references to call you back. Here is the simplest, most effective reference check that I know. It's also fast and legal. Call references at what you assume will be their lunchtime–you want to reach an assistant or voice mail. If it's voice mail, leave a simple message. If it's an assistant, be sure that he or she understands the last sentence of your message. You say: "John (or Jane) Jones is a candidate for (the position) in our company. Your name has been given as a reference. Please call me back if the candidate was outstanding."

The results are both immediate and revealing. If the candidate is outstanding or excellent, I guarantee that eight out of ten people will respond quickly and want to help….However, if only two or three of the references selected by the candidate return your call, this message is also loud and clear. And yet:

No derogatory information has been shared.

No libelous statements have been made.

No confidence or laws have been broken.

- Strategy No. 39: Invest in people, not ideas.

- Unfortunately, an employer's ability to hear bad news about a potential employee is inversely proportional to the time spent courting that employee.

Get jobs done fast. Get the work done right.

 ; quickly.

Browse profiles, portfolios and reviews to assemble your 24/7 online workforce.

2. Tackle jobs easily.

Collaborate in shared online work rooms and receive daily activity reports.

3. Pay freelancers safely.

Only pay for work you approve, plus Elance takes care of all invoicing and taxes.

Personal outsourcing
Elance
Bids on Elance

Elance is a global marketplace for freelancers. You post a job you want done, and freelancers around the world will bid on it in a matter of hours. Once the price and deadline are agreed upon, the work will be delivered to you very rapidly. Because of its global nature, your costs may be very low.

Elance has a pool of 2 million free-lancers expert in programming, design, writing, and legal matters. People use them to design a logo, create marketing materials, tweak a database, code a website, create an iPhone app.

I've used Elance to outsource projects at least 8 times by now and have had fantastic results. I've been most surprised by the high quality and professional management, particularly from overseas workers. It's indeed inexpensive, but also great work. For one scripting job I got estimates from US shops as high as $6,000; it would take months from specs to testing. We went on Elance, got a bid for $250 to do it manually (without scripts) and it was done perfectly in a week. I've used Elance for Photoshop work, to hire designers, artists, and proofers. A lot of the work on this book was done by free-lancers

hired through Elance. You could start a company with them. In fact Kevin Rose hired an Elancer to code the first version of the now-popular website Digg.

Elance's escrow service holds the payment and protects both the work provider and you the employer. The site provides status updates on work done, and plenty of communication between the parties. Workers must pass a competency test to qualify to be listed. Some freelancers can also pass expertise tests in a mild form of certification, say for working on java or ajax, etc. Elance freelancers did about $200 million of work last year and less than 1% of the jobs had any kind of dispute, and most of those were self-resolved by the fact that the entire transaction correspondence is logged.

While I first went to Elance for cheap labor, I now also go to get jobs done in a hurry, or to find expertise I can't find locally. (Fifty percent of Elancers live in North America.) If you have work, and you know what you want, this is a great service.

The real trick in using Elance, or its competitors like oDesk, is in being able to specify the deliverable you want without spending more time that it would take to do the project itself. This kind of outsourcing is best for bite-sized chunks of work. The more precise

you can detail your job the better that Elance or the others will work for you. It's not good for consulting, hand-holding, or mind-changing assignments. But it can be cheap enough that you can try lots of things. It costs you nothing to post a job on Elance.

The way this work is: If you accept a bid, you pay the amount agreed up front and the site places your fee in escrow. (You can pay with PayPal.) They pay the talent when you are satisfied the work is complete and good. This protects them and you. The site's commission comes out of the talent side; The winning free-lancer will pay a 8.75% fee to Elance. (You don't pay the site anything).

It works very well. BTW, the bidders are often small companies rather than just individuals. Fees I've paid for work have ranged from half to one tenth of what we might otherwise have to pay. And it is not just for coders. I hired a guy to run ethernet cable in our home, and others have found a videographer for their wedding, or a translator for their manual, etc. Some of the folks I have hired live in Turkey, or India, Argentina. Like any remote relationship, you get what you put into it.

It's a great tool when you need to hire expertise.

-- KK

Tips for creating home workspaces
At Work at Home: Design Ideas for Your Home Workplace
$9 Neal Zimmerman, 2001, 234 p.

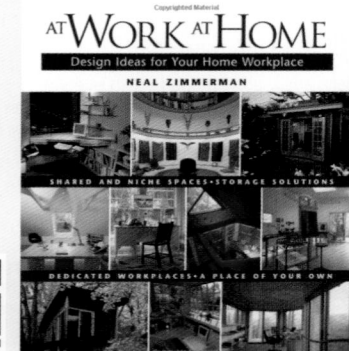

Not all home-office work is typing at a keyboard. That's why this home-office design book is heads above the others. Maybe you are a weaver, or a landscape architect, or antique toy restorer. When I had a chance to design my own home office attached to our house I found the clear advice, helpful design ideas and visual inspiration in this portfolio to be the best of the bunch.

-- KK

- Why do some of these spaces work and others fall short? I've reviewed hundreds of home workplaces, and I've concluded that those that are the most successful have three basic features in common. First, they help their occupants balance the two sides of their lives — work life and home life — in a way that is harmonious not just for them, but also for the people with whom they share their living and working space. Second, the workplace is well planned and well organized; it allows the user to work in a CEO environment — that is with Comfort, Efficiency, and Organization. Third, a successful home workplace has a personal spirit about it, which is a reflection of its occupant. It's this personal spirit that stimulates home workers to do their best work..

Well-planned drawers, storage cubbies, and bookshelves are synonymous with organization and efficiency, hallmarks of a successful home workplace. In this shared space, the execution of the design is simple and the result elegant.

A niche within a converted attic is stylized to the max. Niches within the niche are used to their fullest extent for the odd-shaped storage items that are stock-in-trade for an interior designer. The window seat provides some relief in the tight space and also incorporates flat drawers for plans and large drawings.

I have come to the conclusion that the most concrete thing in the world is information. -Ed Fredkin

Making places for creativity
Make Space

$33 Scott Doorley and Scott Witthoft, 2012, 272 p.

I've worked in many types of spaces, including those specifically engineered for maximizing creativity. It is true: some places are more conducive to innovation and experimentation than others. While designing their own workspace, professors at Stanford University's Design School tested the best practices accumulated over the last few decades and put the best techniques into a cookbook for others to use. They provide tips, principles, recipes for furniture, and even sources of where to get inexpensive components to build a space that encourages groups to make the new. I used some of the ideas here in designing my own studio, and everyone says it really works.

-- KK

•

Technology can now deliver expert-to-student content (e.g., video talks) anytime, anywhere. The ubiquity of content opens the opportunity for the in-classroom experience to support collaboration and practice with the teacher as a guide or mentor. This flip–content outside class, work in class–is often referred to as the "reverse classroom." The studio classroom takes advantage of this opportunity; it sets the stage for maximum hands-on experimentation and for students to connect with each other in class.

•

Avoid arrangements that include "places of honor."

Sit in circles and gather around square tables. The symmetry implies that all positions are equal. If a room naturally has a "place of honor" (such as the head of a table), let a lower-status individual sit there.

Hiding places offer a crucial respite from an open, collaborative environment.

The more extroverted the work space, the more you need these spots of passive, dark yin amid the swaths of hyperactive, brightly lit yang. Few offices have legitimate hiding places; if your space lacks one, people will go elsewhere to find it.

Corners Provide a Sense of Place

The slightest hint of a corner has a profound effect not he sense of ownership in an open space.

Two perpendicular walls provide a suggestion of an edge that outlines a space. These perceived boundaries are easy to absorb, navigate, populate, and protect.

It doesn't take much. In one of the early d.school space prototypes, student teams with access to corner spots spent far more time in the space working on their projects than teams whose spaces were on an open wall. In a second prototype space, featuring side-by-side team spaces with partial corners, we interviewed students and found that a corner with a side wall projecting as little as 1' sufficed to provide a feeling of comfort in the space.

Storage is not stagnant.

Storage should be as transparent as possible so that artifacts and concepts don't linger in the dark. Keep things visible to keep them in active use.

A tall, long, and narrow table is an excellent platform for creating a coffee shop vibe.

"An escalator can't break, it can only become stairs." –Mitch Hedberg, comedian

When sorting through options, ask the simplest question: "What will this do when it is not in use?"

the founder distribution

frequency

weak/nerd | average | strong/athlete
idiot savant | | polymath
disagreeable | | charismatic
outsider | | insider
poor | | rich
villain | | hero
infamous | | famous

How to be an entrepreneur
Startup Reading List

I asked some friends who advise entrepreneurs, or who actively fund startups, what books they hand out to prospective founders and say "read this." Their reading lists are below.

-- KK

Lean Startup
$18 Eric Ries, 2011, 336 p.

Great synthesis of ideas to guide the process of creating a startup, developed by leading doers of and thinkers about startups, especially the great Steve Blank. Both profound and practical. Start here to learn the meaning of "minimum viable product" and "product/market fit".

-- Mitch Kapor

•

The Lean Startup asks people to start measuring their productivity differently. Because startups often accidentally build something nobody wants, it doesn't matter much if they do it on time and on budget. The goal of a startup is to figure out the right thing to build the thing customers want and will pay for-as quickly as possible. In other words, the Lean Startup is a new way of looking at the development of innovative new products that emphasizes fast iteration and customer insight, a huge vision, and great ambition, all at the same time.

The Startup Owner's Manual
$28 Steve Blank, Bob Dorf, 2012, 608 p.

Steve Blank is the guy that inspired Eric Ries and the Lean Startup movement. He has a blog (www.steveblank.com) and his own book that does a good job of capturing his ideas on the nuts and bolts of figuring out a product, understanding a market and experimenting until you get traction.

-- James Cham

•

The ability to learn from missteps distinguishes a successful startup.

•

In large companies, the mistakes just have additional zeros in them.

•

No startup business plan survives first contact with customers. --Steve Blank

•

The best startups discover a situation where customers have tried to build a solution themselves.

The 22 Immutable Laws of Marketing
$13 Al Ries, Jack Trout, 1994, 143p.

I read this before every product launch and encourage my start-up CEOs to do the same. It's a short read full of critical concepts, such as the efficacy of creating a new category vs. trying to dominate an existing category (e.g. how to be different instead of simply better). Replete with historic case studies (Amstel Light, airlines, etc.), it's a little tome with a big impact on strategy. Don't get the "For Internet" version; stick with the original.

-- Tim Ferriss

Founders at Work
$17 Jessica Livingston, 2008, 488 p.

Impactful and instructive first person stories of the joys and terrors of creating a startup.

-- Mitch Kapor

Zero To One
$21 Peter Thiel, Blake Masters, 2014, 256 p.

Peter Thiel was the founder of PayPal and early investor in Facebook. He gave a series of lectures at Stanford that are being edited into a book entitled Zero To One but for now you can find his ideas expressed in the class notes of a student (and later co-author). Thiel's ideas focus on the macro and mytho-poetic aspects of starting a new company. He's contrarian and sometimes contradictory but compelling and inspiring for certain types of founders.

-- James Cham

Who Owns the Ice House?
$12 Gary Schoeniger, Clifton Taulbert, 2011, 178 p.

For people embarking on the entrepreneurial path or who want to apply entrepreneurial thinking in their lives, I recommend they read this true tale.

-- Mitch Kapor

Letters from a Stoic
$13 Lucius Annaeus Seneca, (Robin Campbell), 1969, 254 p.

For people who want to thrive in high-stress environments, this is a manual for the perfect operating system -- Stoicism. Written 2000 years ago, it's a collection of short letters from the Roman statesman Seneca to his student Lucilius about real-world personal and business problems. Getting sued? There's a letter for that. Feeling over-scheduled for social events? Ditto. And remember: Seneca was no idle philosopher. He was the wealthiest "investment banker" in Rome, advisor to the emperor, and a world-famous playwright.

-- Tim Ferriss

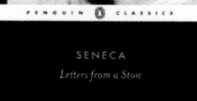

Wall Writing

Brainstorming space
Marker Board Walls

Turns out that brainstorming is a broadside activity — something best done on walls. Reading and writing on walls is a different function than reading a book. A broad wall-view is an ideal approach for collaborative design — multiple views in a single glance. Thus the tremendous interest in flip charts, graphic capture, doodling, giant post-its, whiteboards, and all the electronic equivalents of those. By far the cheapest and easiest mural display is a large whiteboard. And when it comes to whiteboards, you can't be too big.

The Cheapest:

I was able to get a magnificently large — 4 by 8 feet –and fabu-lously cheap whiteboard for all of $13 at Home Depot. What you want is the Solid White Tileboard (sometimes called Melamine tile wall panel) used as a tile substitute in bathrooms. Some know it as showerboard because a couple of sheets of this and you have a nice waterproof shower stall. You'll need a $1 tube of panel adhesive to glue this 1/8 inch surface to the wall or a piece of plywood. Melamine is the same stuff official whiteboards are made from. These huge sheets are slick and work perfectly well with dry-erase markers. You can cover an entire wall for $50. You can also cut it into smaller pieces with a regular circular saw.

The Best:

Upscale from the tileboard guerrilla wall, the premium epigraphic surface is ceramic coated metal. When I built my office/studio I covered an entire wall with this material. It takes a dry-erase marker with ease, but it also accepts magnets, so it can double as a pin board. I layout books in progress, hang blueprints, charts, maps, or use it as an art galley — whatever. When using markers on it there is zero ghosting after erasing (sometimes a slight problem with Melamine). This ceramic

coated steel also comes in eye-saving low-gloss light gray color, so the blazing white of a whole wall is significantly muted, yet it has plenty of contrast for any marker color.

This stuff is called P3 Ceramicsteel, and it is not cheap (at least when covering a whole wall). You can get them as an unadorned sheet (a special order), without frames or mounting, but they usuallly come mount-ed on particle board with an alumium back-ing. These now cost about $200 per 4 x 8 foot sheet. I used the same material for small magnetic boards near my desk.

-- KK

$35 Solid White Tileboard (97"x49"x3/4") Home Depot

Prices Vary P3 Ceramicsteel Makerboard (4'x3') One Work Place

---

Better white board cleaner
SkyBrush WhiteBoard Eraser

$25 SkyBrush

I have been using the SkyBrush xE for five months on our whiteboards. I used to think that all board erasers were the same, but not anymore. The SkyBrush xE is hands down the best whiteboard eraser I have ever used. With one simple light swipe the board is clean. No longer do we have to use addi-tional chemicals to clean the board.

-- Danny Youssef

Instant whiteboards
Write-on Poly Sheets

$28 (35 sheets) Amazon

Polysheet instant whiteboards are thick, static-laden sheets of plastic, like ultra-heavy garbage bags. Just unroll one, slap it on the wall, and instant whiteboard! Best of all, in the corporate world, at the end of the meeting, you can roll them up, take them back to your desk, and process them. After capturing the contents in your computer, wipe them off for next time!

-- S.A.

These cling to walls, to each other and

most dry surfaces by static electric-ity. They come in very handy since you can pretty much place them anywhere

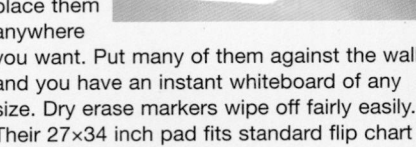

you want. Put many of them against the wall and you have an instant whiteboard of any size. Dry erase markers wipe off fairly easily. Their 27×34 inch pad fits standard flip chart easels or conference cabinets. Rolls up for travel and stor-age. Perforated sheets tear off cleanly.

-- Philip Papadopoulos

Portable Whiteboards
Quartet Easel · Nomad II

$190 Quartet Portable Presentation Easel Staples

Cube-dwellers have grown increasingly accustomed to capturing their mental state on whiteboard surfaces, but whiteboard access at home, unfortunately, is not as common as at work. I picked up a Quartet "Portable Presentation Easel" to alleviate this problem. It's a heavy-duty whiteboard that is height- and angle-adjustable. It's also double-sided to maximize the available writing surface. When you want to transport it, the entire assembly folds up to approximately 42" x 32". I found this tool so useful in my home office that I have since added two traditional "fixed" whiteboards, but the Quartet easel remains the most used whiteboard in the house.

-- Dhiren Patel

More and more companies wisely retreat to an offsite to brainstorm in order to remove them-selves from the urgencies and habits of their offices. Problem is, these charm-ing retreats often contain minimal hard-ware (by design). Easels like the Quartet will work, but lack the large space real brainstorming requires. The creative pros will bring in mobile dry erase boards like the Nomad II, which can be rented and shipped to site. They rent for about $110 per panel per day (not including shipping). My facilitator friends rave that "the stuff goes together like IKEA fur-niture… just a single allen wrench tool is required." I've used these and they are very handsome in the permanent office as well. Since they move easily they can second as a divider or room barrier and then be rolled into place when needed.

-- KK

Prices Vary Nomad II rental Kinetic Energies

Temporary white board
Giant Post-it Sheets

These giant post-it notes are common tools in brainstorming sessions. We've used them for years with success. Hung on any wall, participants scribble on them; then move them around for associations. Soon the whole wall is covered without need of pins, tape, or easels. When you are done, no trace is left on the wall. They serve as a kind of a low-rent temporary white board, but you can archive what was written.

-- KK

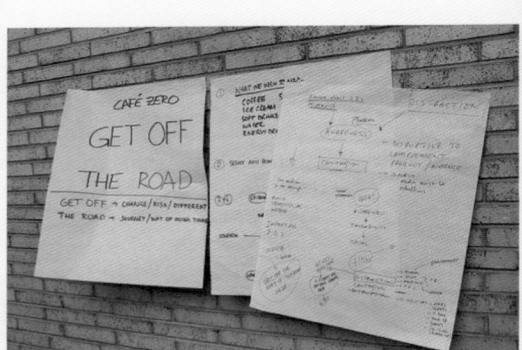

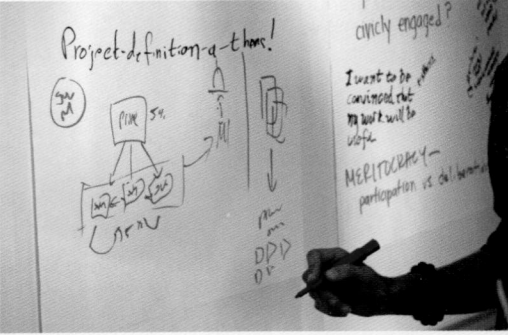

$21 Post-it Easel Pad, 25 x 30 inches, 30 sheets Amazon

The most likely way to reach a goal is to aim at some more ambitious goal beyond it. - Arnold Toynbee

Height adjustable desk
GeekDesk

$749 GeekDesk Mini GeekDesk
$799 GeekDesk GeekDesk

The GeekDesk is the best and most versatile desk I have found for my home office. It uses an electric motor to switch from sitting to standing position, and after nearly a year of using other standing desks I can say that it is one of the best investments anyone can make if they are interested in an adjustable desk.

My first standing desk was a lectern I found on craigslist for $10. It was not adjustable, had an angled surface, and wasn't the best solution. But for the cost, it served me well. I learned how to stand all day, and the small footprint of the podium meant that I could keep my regular desk without sacrificing too much space. The difference between sitting and standing was immediately noticeable. I was much more likely to walk away from my desk and do something that needed to get done, I found that I didn't tire as much, and that my back no longer hurt from long days in a soft cushy chair. I was a standing desk convert.

Given the limitations of the lectern I then decided to replace it with a used AnthroCart desk: a solid American-made adjustable desk with an amazing life-time warranty. Seeing how it was adjustable I was able to fine-tune the height so that it made for easy typing. However, it also meant that I had to say goodbye to my chair and sitting desk. My conversion to full-time standing desk was pleasant, but there were times when I wished I could sit down to write longer pieces.

All of this explains why I am so happy to have discovered the GeekDesk. Simply put, it is a traditional two-legged desk frame that uses an electric motor to raise or lower the working surface from 26" to 46.5" and anywhere in-between.

To raise or lower the desk there are controls attached to the underside of the working surface. They remain out of the way, and are very easy to use. Simply push the button to activate, and click up or down on the toggle. It is a smooth movement and you can do it with everything on your desk without a fear of spills, or toppling monitors.

I love being able to sit and stand at my workspace, and I believe it has improved my general well being and happiness while working from home. A word of warning: anybody interested in switching to standing all day should, as with anything bio-mechanical, take it slow and make sure not to cause too much strain. I have had friends who have made the switch too quickly complain about back strain, foot pain, and tired legs. This goes away, but can easily be avoided by slowly easing into standing all day. And I strongly believe the GeekDesk represents one of the absolute best ways to do so.

-- *Oliver Hulland*

Best office chair investment
Aeron

$870 Amazon

The Aeron Chair is the cheapest chair I've ever owned. I'm 6' 2", 200-plus pounds, and put a lot of daily wear-and-tear on my chair. So I wasn't surprised when, after eight years of use the seat cracked: I was sitting there and it gave way by about two inches. Except for an early problem with a slight wiggle in the base (which Herman Miller paid to have fixed) the chair has worked flawlessly.

I've tried plenty of inexpensive office chairs that were not worth their initial low purchase prices. What makes this pricey chair so inexpensive to own is Herman Miller's extraordinary warranty. Buy it from an authorized dealer and treat it with reasonable care and Herman Miller pays for parts, labor and shipping to have it fixed (for the original owner) for 12 years. You tell me where you can buy a product of this quality and style that is guaranteed to be good as new for 12 years? Additionally, the company makes having repairs performed pain-free. One of their authorized repair locations sent me a shipping box for my damaged Aeron, so that I could send it in. It was repaired and returned to me within two weeks. And I still have almost three more years on my warranty.

-- *Chuck Green*

More comfortable than a lap
InsTand Laptop Stand

$100 InsTand

Laptops are curiously named, since they don't stay on your lap for long. With the heat generated by powerful chips they'll just as soon singe your lap as sit on it peacefully. As a traveling geek, I end up using my laptop for extended periods of time in all sorts of settings, very often in rooms with plenty of chairs, but no tables. I ran into the perfect solution for the problem of where to perch my laptop at a business event: an InsTand. This is a collapsible stand that's light enough to carry around with your laptop, yet offers a sturdy platform you can slip between your knees while sitting. The short sit-down model is what you want, unless you work or give speeches standing up a lot.

-- *Jerry Michalski*

Cheap adjustable laptop table
Ikea Dave Laptop Table

$20 Ikea

I recently found this fantastic laptop table at an Ikea for less than $20. Assembly was quick and easy, using the supplied tools (a pair of allen wrenches). The table is sturdy, easy to haul around using the handle cut into the top, and the height adjusts easily so that I can use it in the back room, where the chair is relatively high, and on the porch glider, where I sit much lower.

A simple lever under the top lets you quickly adjust it from level to slanted – but nowhere in between, which is the only fault I've found in it. I'd like a position half-way between dead level, when my arms are not in the most comfortable position, and tilted, when the MacBook tends to slide off.

This table really takes the weight off my knees, and has made an enormous difference. I thought I was going to have to go in for knee replacement, but I quickly discovered that it was the weight of my cushioned lap-desk that was causing the pain.

I've been using the Dave table more or less constantly since I bought it, and I don't know that I've ever bought anything more useful for such a low price. One of the best things about it is the very low height of the feet which support the table post. This allows the unit to easily slide under a couple of pieces of furniture that could never accommodate one of the laptop tables that are on wheels.

-- *Richard Blumberg*

Foldable, flexible chair
Flex One Folding Chair

$100 (4 pack) Amazon

I've always found folding chairs to be extremely uncomfortable. They are cold, hard and my buttocks/legs always go numb from sitting on them. When we needed to get extra seating for a party we were hosting I was really excited when I stumbled across the Flex One folding chair.

The Flex One is no ordinary chair. As the name implies, it has a mesh seating and back that forms to your anatomy. It has a nice give that makes it extremely comfortable. I've happily been able to sit for hours without any discomfort. As a plus, the mesh allows for outdoor use and for easy cleanup with a hose or sponge.

The Flex One claims to have a 1,000 pound capacity and is fairly light-weight. I'm a big guy and have found the chair to be really solid.

-- *Peter N.*

Small Office Equipment

Quick easy labels
Brother Labeler

$155 Brother P-Touch PT-65 Labeler with LCD Screen Amazon

I highly recommend the Brother P-Touch PT-65 for a good labeler. Cheap manual labelers like the trusty Dymo work fine too, but they take more time, are clumsier to use, and produce labels that look, well, homemade. They also don't stick well to many surfaces. The PT-65 prints ink-jet quality on durable plastic labels that stick to most anything. It's quick, easy, idiot-proof, and actually fun to use. Once you pick up one of these, you'll find yourself labelling pretty much everything in sight. At about $30 this is one of the cheapest models around, and it produces professional results. More expensive models are available with more features (fonts, tape sizes, etc.), but for my purposes, all of the extra ornamentation is unnecessary. The PT-65 does the trick every time and actually prints higher quality on less expensive tape than most of the pricier models. The unit is also small, light, and comfortable to hold.

– Dhiren Patel

We have one of these things. Does wonders. Labelers follow the ink-jet business model. Their profit comes from selling tapes. Not a problem unless you are a big user. You can try a generic brand tape, too.

-- KK

COOL TOOLS

Comprehensive label maker
Brother P-Touch 2730

$60 brother-usa.com

I regularly have to label lots of electronic equipment. Compounding the complexity, I also have to label both ends of the cables that connect to this stuff. My customers generally have detailed requirements about all sorts of info to be included in these labels. While my peers generally have all the same labeling equipment available to them as I do, I use system that makes it much easier to manage the complex task. I use one of the higher end Brother P-Touch label makers, the PT-2700 (and new model 2730) that can connect to my computer via USB. I got my current one from eBay since the refurbed unit I'd been using for years developed an intermittent problem with the display (but it still printed fine). These were both less than $100.

Most of my peers sit in front of their labelers for hours pounding out one label after another. Frequently, they have to redo labels since their minds go numb pretty fast and they start making stupid mistakes. My approach, in contrast, takes a fraction of the time and is suitable for even small jobs of a handful of labels. My redo rate is almost nil, too.

There are two keys to doing bigger jobs with this little printer. The first is to use Excel's CONCATENATE formulas to manipulate columns of variables (text or numbers, like names, IP addresses or rack IDs) into little chunks of data that you want to appear on your labels. Don't be scared of this, formulas aren't needed, but are terrific if there is complicated sequencing going on. This will make sense with a little fiddling in Excel. The second key is to use Brother's "P-Touch Editor" software to connect to the Excel file as a database. Many fields, many lines and many format options are available for your typesetting efforts, so some pre-visualization of your finished product pays off here. Each line of your "database" will contain all the cells available to each individual label. One row, one label; many cells, many layout possibilities.

The first time you try this, it may be confusing, but going to File>Database>Connect will make the Excel file available for laying out the fields. Insert>Database Field will get your data into the label representation in the Editor's screen. The bottom half of your screen will show all the data the Editor has to work with, and cycling between lines there will cycle the info on the label representation.

Once you've gotten things tweaked so you're happy, do a "chain print" and soon a little pile of labels will accumulate. This system based approach is why I think the Brother P-Touch labeler is the best for producing large quantities of labels.

The TZ format tapes this printer uses are available in different widths, color combos and even with better adhesive (TZS labels are the best, and I use them almost exclusively). The PT-2710 adds a case & power adapter, space for various tape cassettes & spare batteries. Good for the back of a truck.

If professional, legible, well-formatted, long lasting identification labels are your goal, this is a terrific system to use. I depend on it.

-- Wayne Ruffner

Best way to seal packages
Sealing Tape Dispenser

$22 Scotch Box Sealing Tape Dispenser Amazon

I don't know how households get by without one of these. It quickly dispenses wide sealing-tape around a box securely and accurately. You can wrap up a package in seconds. We use it many times a week. Mine is at least 15 years old and will probably last another 15. Wide tape is often much better than the ordinary stuff, so we often find ourselves snipping off small bits from the dispenser.

-- KK

OSX package tracking pro
Delivery Status

Delivery Status is a gorgeous OSX-only Dashboard widget and iOS app that allows you to easily track packages from a huge list of carriers (international and domestic) and companies like Amazon and Google Checkout. On the Mac, you can be notified of status changes via Growl, and on iOS it uses push notifications. If you use both, as I do, packages are seamlessly synced.

Data entry is flexible, with perhaps the easiest being a bookmarklet that automatically parses the order status page of most shippers (and many retailers). I frequently shop online, and I send a lot of packages, so I use it to track those that are incoming as well as outgoing. As a city dweller, knowing that a package has been delivered is essential, so that I can pick it up from the lobby of my building before it "walks away."

-- Gordon Meyer

Free desktop widget Delivery Status

$5 iOs App iTunes Store

Reliable, versatile, and cheap
Dymo Labeler

$17 DYMO - Organizer Xpress Pro Amazon

These have been around since the age of dinosaurs, but they still work better than most gadgets. We use them for labeling almost anything that needs a name or number in a hurry -- like in the kitchen. The labels adhere well and have a clear retro look. The inexpensive plastic device is mercifully idiot-proof. Cheap too.

-- KK

Refastenable wire fastening
Millepede Cable Ties

$12 (100) Millepede

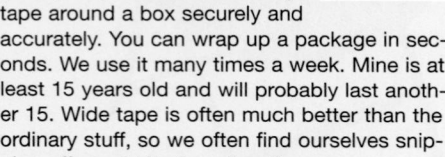

Millepede is a refastenable cable bundling tie that is very different from the Zip ties we all know and love. It's essentially a flexible plastic strip of little boxes separated by larger D shapes. The strip terminates in a narrow "needle" that can thread through any of the D shapes and be pulled through to a snug connection around a bundle of cables. The holding strength is amazing. I use them for all my wiring harness applications, but I've also connected multiple ties (the larger burly ones) to fasten down car-top luggage. I undo a Millepede by running the same needle backwards through the same D opening, and if you're fastening something small, you can also pull almost the whole strip through, cut it off at the non-needle end —

unlike the cable clamp — and then reuse the remainder as many more times as it will fit. They're available in a wide variety of sizes and colors and are also produced in various versions for special purposes (think integral vinyl eyebolts, hooks, baseplates etc.). One bag of 100 might be the proverbial lifetime supply.

-- David Perry

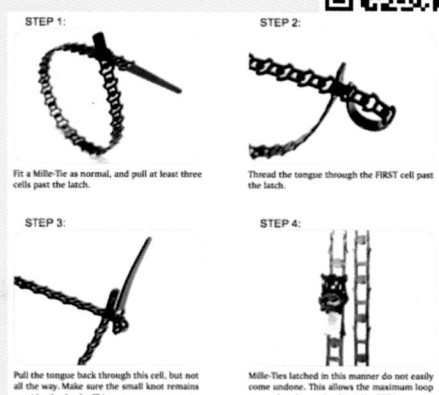

STEP 1:
Fit a Mille-Tie as normal, and pull at least three cells past the latch.

STEP 2:
Thread the tongue through the FIRST cell past the latch.

STEP 3:
Pull the tongue back through this cell, but not all the way. Make sure the small knot remains outside the latch. This acts as a stopper to prevent slippage.

STEP 4:
Mille-Ties latched in this manner do not easily come undone. This allows the maximum loop strength to be attained (> 10kg/22lb)

Versatile wire and cable management clamps
Richco Cable Clamps

Richco WHC series nylon cable clamps are the best solution for all wire and cable management needs. They are much better than cable ties because cables are held firmly in place, but can be easily inserted and removed as configurations change. No cutting of cable ties is required.

I have been using them since the mid 1980s to manage cables in 19" equipment racks. They mount to any surface using a #8 or #10 screw. The WHC-1000-01 (with a 1" diameter) is excellent for managing cables under the computer desk and at the back of home entertainment systems. I screw several to the underside of computer desktops along the back edge at 1' intervals to hold cables up and out of the way.

The slightly smaller WHC-500-01 (1/2" diameter) is excellent for holding rope lighting in place. The mounting hole can be tapped with 1/4-20 thread screws to hold a small flashlight such

as the previously reviewed Fenix LD01 to a small camera tripod mount. I have also mounted several to 3/4" rare earth magnets to temporarily run cables along a T-bar ceiling. Another trick is to bolt two 1" clamps together to form a figure 8 and you can then use it to manage cables on a wire shelving unit.

The uses are endless and the price is right.

-- Jim Barbera

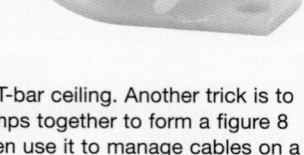

$14 Richno WHC-500-01 1/2" clamps (100 ct) Amazon

$18 Richco WHC-1000-01 1" clamps (100 ct) Allied Electronics

You're only as young as the last time you changed your mind. - Tim Leary

How to run a project
Peopleware

$34 Tom Demarco and Timothy Lister, 1999, 245 p.

Hard-won wisdom fills this small book: How to create a team, place, or company that is productive. First published 20 years ago, and updated once since then, copies of it have quietly served as a guru for many start ups and successful projects in Silicon Valley. Neither academic nor faddish, two veteran consultant authors offer real intelligence. This book has totally informed how I do projects. I learned about the myth of overtime, the need for closure and ceremonies, how teams jell, and why everyone should and can have a window. I first read it decades ago and re-read it every time I embark on anything involving more than one person and several years of my life. Unlike a lot of management lore, it is aimed at the project level (where I want to be) rather than the large organization. The message in the book touts productivity, without ever mentioning the dreary idea of time management. It's more about optimizing people, and thus the title, *Peopleware*.

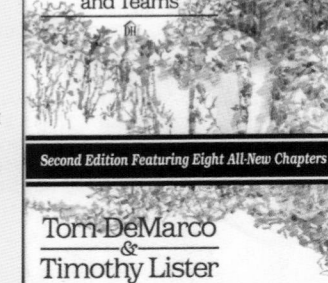

-- KK

●

I was teaching an in-house design course some years ago, when one of the upper managers buttonholed me to request that I assess some of the people in the course (his project staff). He was particularly curious about one woman. It was obvious he had his doubts about her: "I don't quite see what she adds to a project — she's not a great developer or tester or much of anything." With a little investigation, I turned up this intriguing fact: During her twelve years at the company, the woman in question had never worked on a project that had been anything other than a huge success. It wasn't obvious what she was adding, but projects always succeeded when she was around. After watching her in class for a week and talking to some of her co-workers, I came to the conclusion that she was a superb catalyst. Teams naturally jelled better when she was there. She helped people communicate with each other and get along. Projects were more fun when she was part of them. When I tried to explain this idea to the manager, I struck out. He just didn't recognize the role of catalyst as essential to a project.

●

Any regular get-together meeting is somewhat suspect to have a ceremonial purpose rather than a focused goal of consensus.

But organizations have a need of ceremony. It's perfectly reasonable to call a meeting with a purpose that is strictly ceremonial, particularly at project milestones, when new people come on board, or for celebrating good work by the group. Such meetings do not waste anyone's time. They fulfill real needs for appreciation. They confirm group membership — its importance and its value.

●

Modern office politics makes a great class distinction in the matter of allocating windows. Most participants emerge as losers in the window sweepstakes. People who wouldn't think of living in a home without windows end up spending most of their daylight time in windowless workspace.

We are trained to accept windowless office space as inevitable. The company would love for every one of us to have a window, we hear, but that just isn't realistic. Sure it is. There is a perfect proof that sufficient windows can be built into a space without excessive cost. The existence proof is the hotel, any hotel. You can't even imagine being shown a hotel room with no window. You wouldn't stand for it. (And this is for a space you're only going to sleep in.)

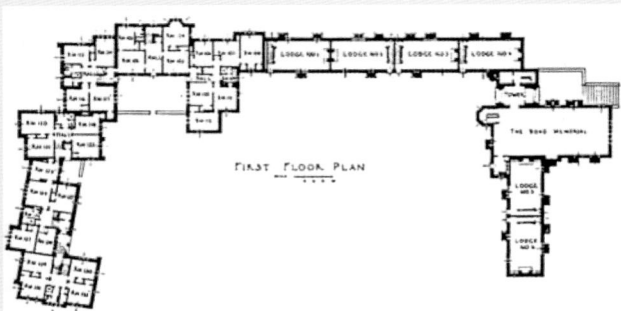

Women's dormitory at Swarthmore College; everyone has windows.

●

The purpose of a team is not goal attainment but goal alignment.

●

A few very characteristic signs indicate that a jelled team has occurred. The most important of these is low turnover during projects and in the middle of well-defined tasks. The team members aren't going anywhere till the work is done. Things that matter enormously prior to jell (money, status, position for advancement) matter less or not at all after jell. People certainly aren't about to leave their team for a rinky-dink consideration like a little more salary.

There is a sense of eliteness on a good team. Team members feel they're part of something unique. They feel they're better than the run of the mill. They have a cocky, SWAT Team attitude that may be faintly annoying to people who aren't part of the group.

●

In my two years at Bell Labs, we worked in two-person offices. They were spacious, quiet, and the phones could be diverted. I shared my office with Wendl Thomis who went on to build a small empire as an electronic toy maker. In those days, he was working on the ESS fault dictionary. The dictionary scheme relied upon the notion of n-space proximity, a concept that was hairy enough to challenge even Wendl's powers of concentration. One afternoon, I was bent over a program listing while Wendl was staring into space, his feet propped up on the desk. Our boss came in and asked, "Wendl! What are you doing?" Wendl said, "I'm thinking." And the boss said, "Can't you do that at home?"

●

Organizations also have some need for closure. Closure for the organization is the successful finish of the work as assigned, plus perhaps an occasional confirmation along the way that everything is on target (maybe a milestone achieved or a significant partial delivery completed). How much confirmation corporations require is a function of how much money is at risk. Frequently, closure only at the end of a four-year effort is adequate for the needs of the organization.

The problem here is that organizations have far less need for closure than do the people who work for them. The prospect of four years of work without any satisfying "thunk" leaves everyone in the group think-

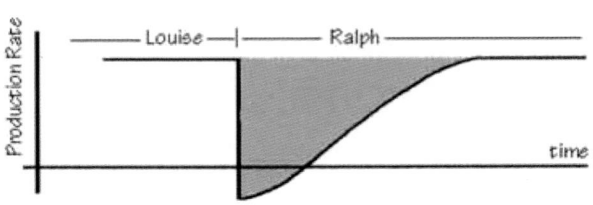

ing, "I could be dead before this thing is ever done." Particularly when the team is coming together, frequently closure is important. Team members need to get into the habit of succeeding together and liking it. This is part of the mechanism by which the team builds momentum.

Lost production due to change of personnel.

Productivity took a hit when Louise left, even passing below zero for a while as others scurried to make up for the loss of a well-integrated team member. Then, eventually, it worked its way up to where it was before.

The shaded area on the graph represents the lost production (work that didn't get done) caused by Louise's departure. Or, viewed differently, it is the investment that the company is now making to get Ralph up to where Louise was after the company's past investments in her skills and capabilities.

●

Once a team begins to jell, the probability of success goes up dramatically. The team can become almost unstoppable, a juggernaut for success. Managing these juggernaut teams is a real pleasure. You spend most of your time just getting obstacles out of their way, clearing the path so that bystanders don't get trampled underfoot: "Here they come, folks. Stand back and hold onto your hats." They don't need to be managed in the traditional sense, and they certainly don't need to be motivated. They've got momentum.

●

Have you ever been in an organization that simply glowed with health? People were at ease, having a good time and enjoying interactions with their peers. There was no defensiveness, no sense that single individuals were trying to succeed in spite of the efforts of those around them. The work was a joint product. Everybody was proud of its quality.

Presented below is an admittedly simplistic list o the elements of a chemistry-building strategy for healthy organization:

-Make a cult of quality.

-Provide lots of satisfying closure.

-Build a sense of eliteness.

-Allow and encourage heterogeneity.

-Preserve and protect successful teams.

-Provide strategic but not tactical direction.

●

When you first start measuring the E-Factor, don't be surprised if it

hovers around zero. People may even laugh at you for trying to record uninterrupted hours: "There is no such thing as an uninterrupted hour in this madhouse." Don't despair. Remember that you're not just collecting data, you're helping to change people's attitudes. By regularly noting uninterrupted hours, you are giving official sanction to the notion that people ought to have at least some interruption-free time. That makes it permissible to hide out, to ignore the phone, or to close the door (if, sigh, there is a door).

At one of our client sites, there was a nearly organic phenomenon of red bandannas on dowels suddenly sprouting from the desks after a few weeks of E-Factor data collection. No one in power had ever suggested that device as an official Do Not Disturb signal; it just happened by consensus. But everyone soon learned its significance and respected it.

●

When you observe a well-knit team in action, you'll see a basic hygienic act of peer-coaching that is going on all the time. Team members sit down in pairs to transfer knowledge. When this happens, there is always one learner and one teacher. Their roles tend to switch back and forth over time with, perhaps, A coaching B about TCP/IP and then B coaching A about implementation of queues. When it works well, the participants are barely even aware of it. They may not even identify it as coaching; to them it may just seem like work.

Whether it is named or not, coaching is an important factor in successful team interaction. It provides coordination as well as personal growth to the participants. It also feels good. We tend to look back on significant coaching we've received as a near religious experience. We feel a huge debt to those who have coached us in the past, a debt that we cheerfully discharge by coaching others.

●

Learning is limited by an organization's ability to keep its people.

●

The most likely learning center for any sizable organization is the white space that lies between and among middle managers. If this white space becomes a vital channel of communication, if middle managers can act together as the redesigners of the organization, sharing a common stake in the result, then the benefits of learning are likely to be realized. If, on the other hand, the white space is empty of communication and common purpose, learning comes to a standstill. Organizations in which middle managers are isolated, embattled, and fearful are non-starters in this respect.

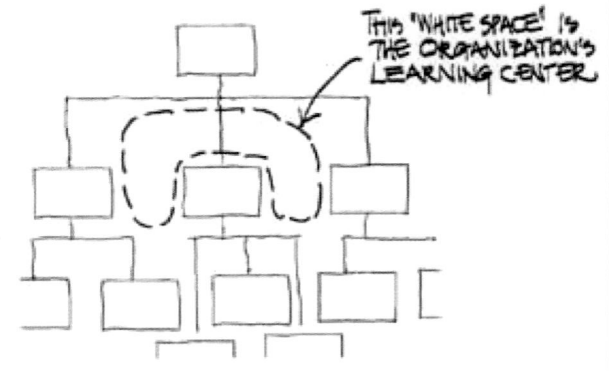

Learning happens in the white space.

●

The proper curve of hiring for a project. Looks odd (so many at the end), but may be the ideal.

●

If you have ever undertaken a major development effort, you almost certainly know the wisdom of the adage, "Build one to throw away." It's only after you're finished that you know how the thing really should have been done. You seldom get to go back and do it again right, of course, but it would be nice.

This same idea can be applied to whole careers. Between the two of us, we've spent nearly thirty years managing projects or consulting on project management. Most of what we've learned, we've learned from doing it wrong the first time. We've never had the luxury of managing any of those projects over again to do it entirely right. Instead, we've written this book.

In praise of inefficiency

Slack

$11 Tom DeMarco, 2002, 256 p.

I am reminded of a famous magazine editor's remark that creativity in his business demanded "wastage." Here's a welcomed assault on the misguided notion of efficiency, pressure, and overtime in the workplace. Great managers incorporate "slack" – an incredibly potent stance that yields more resources that it uses. More slack, better business. Down with efficiency.

-- KK

●

The best predictor of how much work a knowledge worker will accomplish is not the hours that he or she spends, but the days. The twelve-hour days don't accomplish any more than the eight-hour days. Overtime is a wash.

Since companies don't typically pay knowledge workers for overtime, any net advantage gained by extraction of overtime would be a cost-free benefit. That violates the ages-old adage that there ain't no such thing as a free lunch. And sure enough, there ain't.

●

The Legacy of the nineties has been a dangerous corporate delusion; the idea that organizations are effective only to the extent that all their workers are totally and eternally busy. Anyone who's not overworked (sweating, staying late, racing from one task to the next, working Saturdays, unable to squeeze time for even the briefest meeting till two weeks after next) is looked on with suspicion. People with a little idle time on their hands may not even be safe.

●

But now into this happy scenario drop a consultant with a charter to reduce cost, the "corporate restructuring agent." Whoa, he says, what's this? A secretary? And what's she up to this very minute? He parks himself beside Sylvia's desk with his trusty stopwatch in hand. To no one's surprise, he finds that Sylvia is really only busy 43 percent of the time. The rest of the time she is…available. She's available to do stuff that you or your people find you need to have done. That's part of what's so great about Sylvia: When something comes up, she can usually get cracking on it right away.

A look of triumph now comes over the consultant's face. If Sylvia is only busy 43 percent of the time, 57 percent of her cost is potentially savable. Why, all we have to do is dump Sylvia into a "pool" and allocate 43 percent of her time to you and the rest to other people. Or have you share her with some other manager who needs only 57 percent of a full person. Or even get rid of Sylvia entirely and hire a temp for that 43 percent of the time that you really need someone. (You can be sure that the consultant will be checking back later to find out if you really need that much help.)

What an improvement. Sylvia's gone or gone 57 percent of the time, and 57 percent of what she was costing the organization goes directly down to the bottom line. Wow. In place of a person who was idle 57 percent of the time, we now have someone who is busy 100 percent of the time. Talk about efficiency!

The problem of course, is that the now-slackless secretary or portion thereof is simply not as responsive as Sylvia was. This highly efficient person doesn't get cracking right away on anything new that comes up, because this highly efficient person is too busy.

●

Managers who inspire extraordinary loyalty from their people tend to be highly charismatic, humorous, good-looking, and tall. So, by all means, strive to be those things. If you don't feel able to improve any of those factors very much, you might consider holding on to your people by designing a little slack into their lives.

●

Sprinting. There is a useful distinction to make here between infrequent short bursts of overtime –what I call sprinting – and extended overtime. Sprinting can make perfectly good sense in the right circumstances. Imagine yourself encouraging everyone to come in for a gargantuan workathon weekend to bring a project to completion for delivery Monday morning. You all stay up through the night, or catch catnaps on the carpet or on the sofa in the big boss's office. You keep each other going, check each other's work (after all, people do get tired), and keep everybody's spirits up. You guzzle coffee. You share order-in pizza or sandwiches from the all-night deli or you slip our for noodles at the Chinese place that keeps late hours. Most of all, you succeed on Monday morning, and when the crazy weekend is over, you go back to normal hours.

This is the stuff of which corporate legends are made. When you've all been through it together, and shared an important success, there is something profoundly changed about the culture of the organization. The energy is still there after the workathon weekend is long past.

The manager who makes effective use of the occasional sprint is a hero. He/She needs impeccable timing, a flawless sense of what can and can't be accomplished over a short period (there is no benefit if the delivery doesn't take place on Monday or if it gets rejected), and enough raw leadership talent to pull the whole affair together. Finally, such a manager also needs to have a huge reserve of trust to dip into, the clear sense shared by all that the call or extraordinary effort is truly extraordinary, not likely to be wasted and not likely to become a regular fixture.

●

"What would you do," I asked him, "if overtime were forbidden and you still had to make the schedule?" "Well, I'll tell you one thing," he answered promptly, "we'd sure have to do something about all these meetings." I paused for a moment, hoping that the words that had come so readily out of his mouth would make their way back in through an ear. But no. He couldn't hear what he'd just said. He missed it entirely.

▼

In Region I, workers are responding to increased pressure by trimming any remaining waste, by concentrating on the critical path, and by staying late. In Region II, workers are getting tired, feeling pressure from home, and starting to put in a little "undertime" (taking the kid to the dentist during work hours, since the company owes them so much time anyway.) In Region III, workers are polishing up their resumes and beginning to look for work elsewhere.

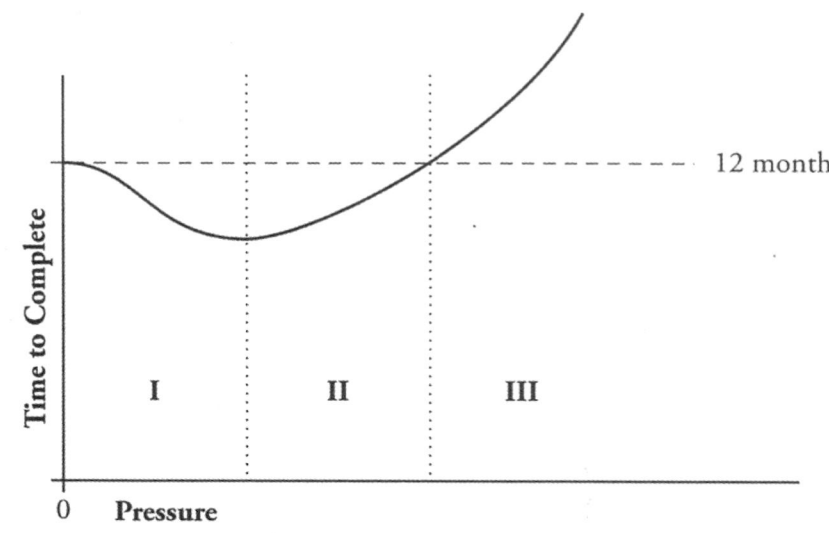

Personal project management on the web

Gantto

$5/month for one user Gantto

I am a self-employed writer who publishes a new book every 9 months and primarily works from home. For my first several books I struggled with time management and found I was constantly playing catch-up for the two months before my books were due. Then my engineer husband introduced me to the application he uses at work to organize his projects: Gantto.

For my last book I used Gantto to plan out my book publishing process, goals, and the milestones I needed to hit. Early schedule items consisted of writing so many words a week (with milestone markers for finishing a quarter of the book, half, etc.), middle items included submitting drafts and doing revisions, and latter marks included publishing house schedules and promotional items — all ultimately leading to the release date of the book. The great thing about Gantto is that I can visually see how all of those little steps lead to the final goal on one page, and if life events (illness, family trouble, etc.) crop up during the project, the whole timeline shifts to where end-goal estimation becomes far more accurate. Vacations can be added at any time for scheduling purposes.

For me, seeing the gantt chart really helped put my daily work in perspective, and I found I was much less likely to procrastinate.

The real time collaboration aspect is likely not as key for the self-employed business owner as it would be for a larger team/business, but I actually found it a fantastic feature. If you are collaborating between two writers or a writer and an assistant, both of you can go into the schedule (simultaneously) and make changes.

As someone who has used spreadsheets in the past to track projects, the ability to shift an entire schedule of events with one click is mind-blowingly great. Add that to the price (free for one month, with subscriptions starting at $5 a month) and I am delighted with this tool.

-- Anne Mallory

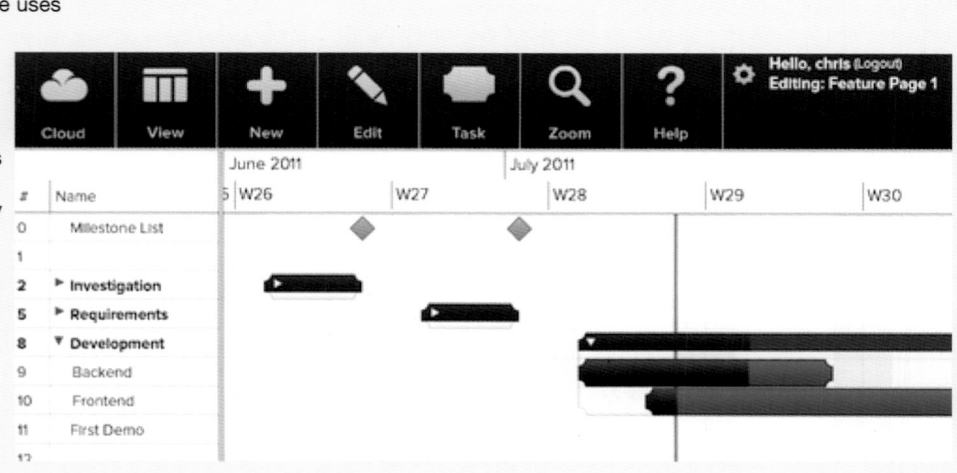

Web-based project management

Basecamp

Free 60-Day trial, or $20/month for 10 projects, 3GB storage, unlimited users Basecamp

I have searched for years for a high-quality, flexible project management system. I found it in Basecamp. Basecamp is scaleable to handle a handful of projects for a sole proprietor on a tight budget, or countless initiatives for a large, distributed network. It requires no downloads or software beyond the web browser. It has swiftly become THE key tool in managing our project pipeline, with milestones, to-do lists, team members and essential files. I have set up three of my own clients with the software and they all love it because they finally have a cheap, efficient knowledge management tool that does not follow a "per seat fee." Non-profit organizations seem to benefit most from this software because usually they don't have much tech support, while Basecamp offers them a seamless way to connect a project.

There is a free 30-day trial version. Pricing is based on number of projects, not users. It begins at 1 project=free, and then ends at unlimited projects = $150/month. We started with the $12/month 3 project plan, and it swiftly became so core to our business processes, we upgraded immediately. Sounds expensive, except that the program allows the owners (us) to set permissions for unlimited users, who aren't required to pay anything.

The company posted a great manifesto and so far they are living up to it and making our mom-and-pop shop a happier place to work.

-- Peter Durand

Making-future is the most important thing a mind does. - Daniel Gilbert

Instant cash register
Square
Free reader, 2.75% per swipe Square

This tiny credit card reader plugs into a smartphone or iPad turning your device into a point-of-sale cash register. It allows you as an individual to collect funds via a credit card. Setting up an account is pretty painless. The software will send the buyer a receipt, and keep track of your sales. It can track cash, too. This minimal arrangement is perfect for the solo and small business person selling crafts at a fair, or swag at a concert, or antiques at a garage sale, or food from a truck.

We used Square to sell our comic book at a comic convention and it worked like a charm (you'll need either wifi or cell connection). As usual with credit card transactions, you will be deducted a 2.75% fee. Square will send you a free plastic reader when you sign up. (Paypal has their own version of a reader, a blue triangle called Here, and they charge only 2.70%, but I have not tried it.) Overall, this is a well-designed small business tool.

-- KK

Easiest micropayment system
Gumroad
5% + 25 cents per transaction Gumroad

Gumroad is an easy way to add a micro-payment function to your blog, website, Facebook page, or Twitter — anywhere you can post a link. It allows you to quickly offer digital products — photos, videos, music, apps, PDFs — for small (or large) prices. It is not a marketplace, rather it generates a link that you post so that you can "sell where you share." When a friend, fan, or follower purchases something off of your page, they get an email with a link for the download from Gumroad's server. You can set your price anywhere from 0 and up. Gumroad's cut is 5% + 25 cents per transaction, no setup or

monthly fees. That's a good deal if you are selling things for a few dollars, and better than other digital storefronts. Something priced as low as 99 cents means you get $.69 and Gumroad gets $.30.

For the past year I've been using Gumroad to sell a PDF version of my True Films guide to documentary movies for $.99 and the system works great: ▶

-- KK

Free online storefront
Tictail
tictail.com

Purple Paisley: 399 SEK   Polo: 399 SEK   New New Year: 399 SEK

Floral Bells: 399 SEK   Art School Dropout: 399 SEK   Artie: 399 SEK

The easiest way to add a shopping cart, or e-commerce, to your website is with Tictail. You can set up a digital store in only 30 seconds for free. Tictail gives you a way to present a storefront, track sales of your items, interface with social media, collect money, manage customers, and organize an online catalog. A number of alternatives such as Shopify and Magento offer easy e-commerce storefronts as well, but their cheapest plans require a $15-$30 monthly fee. That recurring payment may be okay if you already own a physical store, or are operating a large website, but if you are a small-timer and just want to tryout a small store online, free Tictail is perfect. It is not a marketplace like Esty; you'll have to attract your own audience. But, unlike the "craft" constraints of an Esty store, you can sell whatever you want. Tictail makes their money selling freemium functions and add on services on top of the free base service -- growing as your store and needs grow. (I set up a storefront for Cool Tools in less than a minute; as soon as we have more things to sell, we'll make it public.)

-- KK

Digital goods storefront
Payloadz
$15/month, with 4.9% + $0.49 per transaction charge Payloadz

While Gumroad (see above) is the way to go for simple personal digital sales, Payloadz offers more services around digital downloads than Gumroad. They'll give you a shopping cart, account management, sophisticated file security, payment and currency options, integration with eBay, and all the kinds of things a

real e-commerce store might want. For the past 10 years I've been using Payloadz to sell digital PDF files of my books.

Customers pay me with Paypal, then they get a url good for 48 hours, and from there they can download the files. It's done automatically.

Payloadz can be used to deliver any digital good — software, movies, ringtones, music files -- any thing you can send via bits. Biggest downside is their monthly fee ($15 minimum), in addition to the usual modest Paypal charge per transaction. But they have free version

(Payloadz Express; they only deduct the transaction commission) if your sales are less than $50 per month. But for that level, you're better off with Gumroad. However if you are trying to make a business out of selling software, or sewing patterns, or 3D files, or ebooks, etc. then Payloadz is an attractive payment/delivery solution. They serve out your goods when your customers pay.

-- KK

Ecommerce Site Builder
CityMax
$25/month CityMax

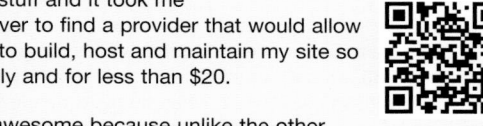

CityMax is the coolest tool on the web. I needed a website to sell my stuff and it took me forever to find a provider that would allow me to build, host and maintain my site so easily and for less than $20.

Its awesome because unlike the other site builders out there, it is integrated with eBay, Paypal, Google, Yahoo, Shopping.com and just has everything I need. I am their biggest fan.

(CityMax claims that more than 172,000 sites have been built using their software.)

-- Kirk McClean

Bank account comparison tool
Nerd Wallet
Free Nerd Wallet

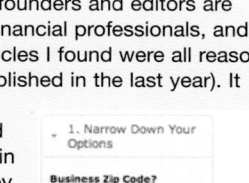

I needed to set up a new business checking account recently, but I didn't know how I should compare the options. Nerd Wallet kept showing up in my search results, so even though I hadn't heard of the site before, I finally bit. It offers a broad range of financial advice, including several articles about choosing business checking accounts (a small business checking primer, an FAQ on how to pick an account, an explanation of fees, and general recommendations for the best and free business checking accounts).

Even better, it has a tool that will suggest banks based on criteria you can specify: location, bank type (big bank, community bank, internet bank, credit union), business type, typical monthly and daily balances, monthly transactions, cash handling requirements. It's a great way to start a list of candidates, though I still called all the banks I

was considering to verify the details and to ask questions not covered by Nerd Wallet's summary. One thing to be aware of: Nerd Wallet's search tool will recommend specific accounts, so the same bank may show up several times in your search results. Sometimes the same account name will be recommended multiple times, which seems like a bug.

Nerd Wallet's founders and editors are experienced financial professionals, and the advice articles I found were all reasonably fresh (published in the last year). It has also been recommended at least twice in the last year by the New York Times' Bucks blog (here and here).

There are other similar bank comparison/recommendation tools out there. The Bucks blog has also reported on a

few alternatives, including FindABetterBank. That tool has a more in-depth questionnaire, but it doesn't cover business accounts so didn't work for my needs.

Business Checking is just one small area of the Nerd Wallet website, which offers similar tools for other types of bank accounts, personal finance, investing, and credit cards. I look forward to exploring these other subject areas on the site, but I can't speak to them just yet.

-- Camille Cloutier Hartsell

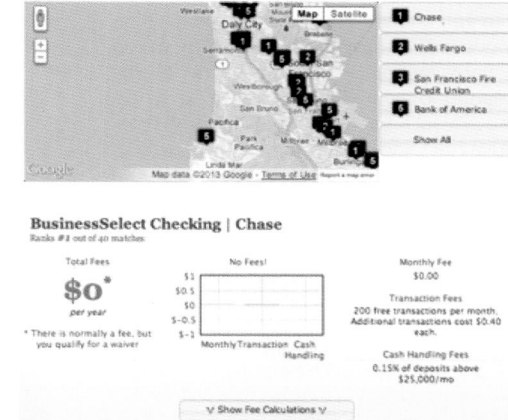

RFID blocking wallet
PacSafe RFID-tec Wallet
$26 Amazon

Traveling back from Europe last year, I almost missed my plane because I was shopping for a wallet that had a fully closing change-purse (necessary for one and two Euro coins). I bought a very stylish, leather one at the airport for $100, which did not have a bill pocket, only a clip (which itself soon broke).

I replaced it with a more utilitarian PacSafe wallet, and I love it. It has two bill pockets, one that zips closed, as well as a large coin-purse. It has three larger than card-

sized pockets as well as three card-slots and a transparent pocket for an ID card.

The material is super-strong nylon and has something sewn-in that blocks RFID signals. It successfully prevents the SF Bay Area touchless transit card Clipper from working while the wallet is closed. I am even more impressed with the construction and the little details like small elastic pockets to hold the zipper-pulls to keep them from jingling and catching on things.

In short, it does what it is supposed to do and does it well.

-- Richard Haven

Crowdfunding

Premier crowdfunder
Kickstarter
kickstarter.com

Kickstarter is the premier crowdsourcing platform. It offers a way to finance your project by enabling current fans and wanna-be customers to pay you before you do your project. You don't pay back your backers except indirectly with creative rewards as thanks. Often the reward is a unit of your project -- a device, book, game, etc. Kickstarter is not the only crowdsourcing venue, but it is the largest, most active, and the most refined. So far, over 35,000 projects have been successfully funded -- all kinds of creative dreams including games, gadgets, documentaries, music, shows, and one-of-a-kind happenings. One of those winners was a project I launched in 2012 -- a graphic novel. We successfully raised $42,000 to complete a second book in our fictional universe. Like many financed projects, I believe that if we could not have crowdfunded it, the project probably would not have happened. In this way, Kickstarter is a fantastic cool tool.

There's an art to running a successful crowdfunded campaign. While there are several guide books that offer advice on how to raise "big bucks" on Kickstarter, none of them (yet) are better than the simple free Kickstarter School section on the Kickstarter site. It tells you how to prepare the essential "video pitch" that seems to be needed, and gives suggestions on structuring your rewards (what backers get by funding you). Yet it is missing some things I wished someone had told me before we began our Kickstarter campaign:

1) We didn't have enough cheap seats. Have a lot of different levels of support -- including a lot of inexpensive ones of only a few dollars -- to give everyone a chance to contribute. And don't be shy about adding a few really high levels either.

THE BICYCLE BELL REINVENTED

A better bicycle bell, made in the USA.
by Spurcycle
Powerful sound from a trim, precision form—a bell for any bike: modern road, mountain, or vintage townie.

📍 San Francisco, CA

985%	$197,033	23
FUNDED	PLEDGED	DAYS TO GO

TERRIBLE THINGS

TERRIBLE THINGS: The Party Game Where Everyone Loses
by Terrible People LLC
Art. Facts. Performance. Humiliation. A celebration of depravity.

📍 Los Angeles, CA

37%	$28,056	27
FUNDED	PLEDGED	DAYS TO GO

AIMS / LEVEL UP

Level Up: A Music Video For the New Album AIMS
by Vienna Teng
We're on to stretch goals! Help us get to 1,000 backers and we'll make a behind-the-scenes documentary!

📍 Detroit, MI

289%	$57,827	4
FUNDED	PLEDGED	DAYS TO GO

A few example campaigns at various stages, including a not uncommon overfunding.

2) Don't rely on Kickstarter to find funders. You need to gather your fans first before you start, and then once gathered, use Kickstarter to engage them with your project. Once you pull the trigger, there's no time to find new fans -- and they don't come from Kickstarter. Fans first, then Kickstarter.

3) It's a full time job. Kickstarter campaigns ordinarily run about one month and during that time, it takes almost full time work to cheer, coax, and promote the project to your fans. There is nothing automatic or easy about it. Somebody has to lead the crowd during the whole time.

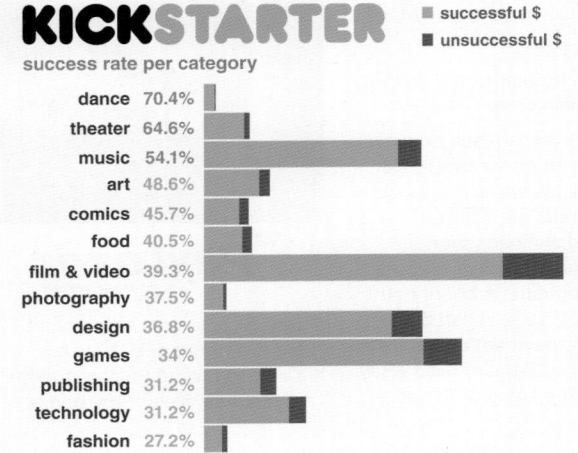

KICKSTARTER
success rate per category

■ successful $
■ unsuccessful $

Category	Rate
dance	70.4%
theater	64.6%
music	54.1%
art	48.6%
comics	45.7%
food	40.5%
film & video	39.3%
photography	37.5%
design	36.8%
games	34%
publishing	31.2%
technology	31.2%
fashion	27.2%

4) It all happens at the end. Even with successful grants, the bulk of the contributions come in at the end. So don't stop drumming; keep sprinting till you're past the finish line.

5) Don't forget the Man. When calculating how much you need, remember not only to include the cost of delivering your supporters their rewards, but don't forget the 8% commission Kickstarter and Amazon will take. That's a hefty chunk of your total that you need to compensate for when setting your goal amount.

I have friends who skipped Kickstarter and opted for other crowdfunding sites. For instance Indiegogo will deliver funds even if you don't meet your goal (Kickstarter is all or nothing), 33Needs shares profits with backers for ongoing enterprises (Kickstarter only funds projects), and so on. However for most projects I think Kickstarter is the place to start; it's well crafted. I hope to do another crowdsourced project, but not as large. In fact, while the giant successes get the most ink, what Kickstarter really excels at is financing medium and small projects that one or two people can reasonably achieve.

-- KK

● Project creators set a funding goal and deadline. If people like a project, they can pledge money to make it happen. Funding on Kickstarter is all-or-nothing — projects must reach their funding goals to receive any money. All-or-nothing funding might seem scary, but it's amazingly effective in creating momentum and rallying people around an idea. To date, an impressive 44% of projects have reached their funding goals.

● Creators keep 100% ownership of their work.

Backers are supporting projects to help them come to life, not to profit financially. Instead, project creators offer rewards to thank backers for their support. Backers of an effort to make a book or film, for example, often get a copy of the finished work. A bigger pledge to a film project might get you into the premiere — or a private screening for you and your friends. One artist raised funds to create a wall installation, then gave pieces of it to her backers when the exhibit ended.

Donors Choose

Education funding
DonorsChoose
Charity DonorsChoose

At DonorsChoose you can be a philanthropist for ten bucks (or more). Go to the site and choose from among thousands of projects submitted by public school teachers — everything from books needed to technology to class trips. Once the project's been funded, DonorsChoose buys the materials for the teachers, and you get a package of letters and photographs from the students.

-- Mike

●
I am a primary grade Special Day Class teacher with 16 students. All of my kindergarten, first and second grade students are in need of enrichment for language and speech development. They also display very different learning styles and preferences.

In the past year, I have discovered that Scholastic's "I SPY" series and the spin-off series, "Can You See What I See?" are effective books and materials to enhance the learning of state standards. These beautiful photograph books are perfect vehicles for teaching vocabulary, sorting, colors, rhymes, critical thinking skills, graphing activities, letter and number identification and many more standards.

The children must analyze each photograph carefully to identify objects in the riddles. They must think outside of their basic conceptions of what an item might be. (For example, a "bunny" could merely be a shadow or cloud in that shape.) My students have been able to list items that begin or end with a particular letter, have counted objects and categorized them into various attributes, have seen and heard word patterns and basically have had a ton of FUN!

We would like to continue adding to our library of "I SPY" books. We feel that this is an exciting way to learn all of the basic skills we need in math and language arts. We can reinforce our basic instruction in science and social studies as well, simply by admiring a little photograph!

My class and I would like to add more "I SPY" and "Can You See Wht I See?" books to our collection, with difficulty levels varying from preschool to second grade. Thank you very much for considering our proposal and helping us propel our learning into new areas of exploration! The cost of these "I Spy" Books for the Classroom Library is $193, including shipping and fulfillment.

Effective small gifts
Modest Needs
Chairty Modest Needs

Has someone ever helped you get you out of a hard place with an act of kindness? If so, you should consider passing that gift onto someone else. You can dispense a few $10 bills from your ATM to the homeless in your area; or you can employ this amazing website which does something similar with greater effectiveness.

Modest Needs, a minuscule non-profit, grants modest (under $200) one-time cash gifts to those who require just a little help to get them through a tough time. A need, if honored, is granted within 72 hours, with no strings attached. Modest Needs does this with commendable efficiency via the web (it's not hard to be broke and still get online), heart-warming sympathy (every request is read by a volunteer), and impressive reach (220 requests granted this year, or 7% of the million dollars sought for). Modest Needs' entire finances are completely transparent on their website. Since their inception they have spent $0 on fundraising and $0 on advertising. They are astoundingly thrifty (total annual cost to run this charitable operation: $24,000). The rest of the small change they collect goes to those to whom small change can make a big difference. They accept contributions from folks like you. It runs fast all year, not just at Christmas.

The founder Keith Taylor began Modest Needs by giving 10% of his $350 a month earnings as a way to return a no-strings kindness paid to him when he most needed it. He told me, "Those who need help can always ask for it at Modest Needs, absolutely for free. How much money we raise matters less – to me, anyway – than simply providing a vehicle for human kindness."

It's quite brilliant. Release a few bucks from your PayPal account. Return a random kindness. Maximize a small gift.

-- KK

Charitable giving
Oxfam America Unwrapped
Oxfam America Unwrapped

All the adults in my family agreed this year that they don't want any more stuff in their lives at this point. So instead of buying them gifts, my Cool Tool for the holidays is Oxfam's Unwrapped project: I buy a gift in someone's name, they get a card, I get a tax deduction, and someone in a developing country gets a goat, some chickens, a school desk and chair, some text books, or something else they really need. While I imagine a portion of my

GIVE A LIFE-CHANGING GIFT

HOW IT WORKS

YOU CHOOSE A GIFT

YOU GET A CARD TO SEND TO YOUR RELATIVE, COWORKER, FRIEND, CLIENT

YOUR DONATION GOES TO THOSE WHO NEED IT MOST

donation goes to fund overhead at Oxfam, they are one of the more efficient charities around. Based on what I've read, and heard from acquaintances who work there, most of the money I give them is being put to direct use. -- Brad Hurley

Every person contains the universe looking at itself in a different way - Alan Watts

Best financial intro

Your Money: The Missing Manual

$15 J.D. Roth, 2010, 336 p.

Your Money
the missing manual
O'REILLY
J.D. Roth

This is the best user-guide to personal finance I've found, and I've probably read them all. It is certainly the sanest and most level-headed. There are no get rich quick schemes here, just plenty of ways to get rich slowly. Indeed, Get Rich Slowly was the name of author's very popular personal finance blog, which led to this book. J.D. Roth takes the great investing advice of Andrew Tobias in *The Only Investment Guide You'll Ever Need*, and he summarizes the life-earning wisdom in the previously reviewed (and still recommended) book *Five Rituals of Wealth* and he includes the needed crystalization of priorities found in *Your Money or Your Life*, and financial motivations from Suze Orman and the *Millionaire Next Door* and then adds key insights and tips from hundreds of other lesser-known money gurus.

Basically, Roth has read every book and blog on money managing, investing, saving, and earning and digests and integrates all this hard-won knowledge into an amazing selection of smart, practical ideas for today. I could hardly turn a page without learning a solid investing tip or two, or a clever way to save a few hundred dollars, or an example of something I already knew, but was looking for a vivid way to teach my kids. I like the fact that Roth emphasizes the value of sharing whatever wealth you have, and keeps returning to the long view.

I would not call this an inspirational book (plenty of those on the shelves), nor even a memorable book like the ones mentioned above. Rather it is what is advertised: a day-to-day operating manual for your money. Specific details, sources, methods, tricks. Dip into it when you are stuck, check it before trying something new, re-read it when you think you know it all. I've done pretty well financially, and if you were to ask me my practical advice — like what to do tomorrow — I would simply give you this book. It's slow, but true.

-- KK

●

Because you earn pre-tax dollars but spend after-tax dollars, a penny saved is actually more than a penny earned. Depending on your tax bracket, you might have to earn $111 , $133, or even $150 to put $100 in your pocket. So if you are in the 25% tax bracket, saving $750 a year is like giving yourself a $1,000 raise!

●

Destroy Existing Debt

After you've stopped using credit and created an emergency fund, then go after your existing debt. Attack it with vigor, throw whatever you can at it. The best way to do this is to use a technique called the debt snowball, which lets you build and maintain debt-destroying momentum. Here's the basic method: Make a list of your debts in the order you want to destroy them. (You'll learn a couple of good ways to prioritize debts in a moment.) Set aside a certain amount of money to pay toward debts each month ($500, say). Make the minimum payment on all debts except the first one on your list. Throw every other penny at the first debt on the list. But here's the key to making the debt snowball work: After you've destroyed your first debt, you'll find you've freed up a bit of cash; because one of your debts is gone, you have one less monthly payment. You could take this money and use it for something else, but you re going to do something smarter: keep paying the same total amount, $500 in our example, toward the debt every month.

Account Type	Nickname	Account #	Balance	Available
Electric Orange	Checking		228.29	228.29
Orange Savings	Backpacking England 2011		4,046.18	4,046.18
Orange Savings	Mini Cooper Fund		5,928.14	5,928.14
Orange Savings	GRS Business Taxes		16,214.20	16,214.20
Orange Savings	Emergency Fund		10,201.81	10,201.81
Orange CD [Nov 12, 2010]	Trip to Europe 2010		14,000.00	14,000.00
		Total Deposits:	$50,618.62	$50,618.62

●

Destroying low-balance debt first

If you've tried following the highest-interest-rate-first advice and still struggle with debt, there's another way. In his book, The Total Money Makeover, Dave Ramsey advocates an approach to the debt snowball that tackles accounts with low balances first. (Ramsey didn't invent this method, but he's popularized it over the past decade.) With this version of the debt snowball, you ignore interest rates when determining the order in which you'll pay off your debts. All you look at is how much you owe, organizing the debts from smallest balance to largest balance.

That's not to say you shouldn't try this method: If it works for you, use it! But if you struggle, consider the next method, which is the one that helped me succeed. It might help you to have a visual representation of your debt-paying progress. Try this: take a piece of graph paper and block off squares to represent your debt. (You might use one square for every $ 100, say.) When you make a payment, mark off a square and give yourself a pat on the back. (If you re a geek, build yourself an Excel spreadsheet that does something similar.) These little progress reports are cheesy, but they can keep you on track.

This method may not be as quick as paying your high-interest debt first, but it provides tremendous psychological reinforcement. You get some quick wins checking creditors off your list that encourage you to keep at it. Dave Ramsey calls this behavior modification over math, and he's right: the most important thing when paying off your debts is to, well, pay off your debts; the order in which you do so is irrelevant. Critics of this approach argue that the math doesn't make sense, and they're right: If you use this method, you will pay more interest than if you had the discipline to pay off your debts based on interest rate. But humans are complex psychological creatures, not adding machines. We usually know what we ought to do, but that doesn't mean we always do it. If we were adding machines and always made the best choices, we wouldn't get into debt in the first place!

●

Protecting Yourself with Parallel CDs

With a CD, one of the biggest risks is that you'll need to pull your money out before it matures. When you do this, you pay a penalty. The site FiveCentNickel.com suggests that you can decrease this risk with parallel CDs: http://tinyurl.com/parallel-CDs. here's how it works: Let's say you have $5,000 you'd like to put into CDs. Instead of opening a single CD and putting that whole amount in it, you'd open multiple CDs, all with the same maturation date. You could open five CDs of $1,000 each, say, or open two with $1,000 and one with $3,000. This gives you a buffer in case you need to get at the moneyearly. If you need $500 for an emergency, for example, you can break just a single $1,000 CD. That way you don't pay a penalty on the rest of the money you have in CDs, and the penalty will be smaller than what you would have paid if you'd put the whole $5,000 in a single CD.

●

Pay Yourself First

If you're living paycheck to paycheck, saving may seem impossible. You have to pay for things like rent, a car payment, groceries, and maybe even student loans. You'd like to save, but at the end of the month, there's no money left to set aside. And that's the problem: Most people try to save something out of what s left over instead of saving first. One of the best ways to build wealth is to set aside a portion of your income for savings before you pay your bills, buy groceries, or do anything else with yourmoney. Here are three reasons to pay yourself first: It makes you the priority. You're telling yourself that you are more important than the electric company or the landlord. think of the money you put into savings as a down payment on your future. It encourages sound financial habits. Most people spend their money in the following order: bills, fun, savings. But if you bump savings to the front of that list, you can set money aside before you come up with reasons to spend it. That way, since the money is no longer in your checking account to tempt you, you end up spending less.

●

Targeted Savings Accounts

Most people work toward several financial goals at once, but keep their money clumped together in a single account. With that setup, it's easy to forget how much you've saved for each goal and to borrowmoney from one goal to pay for something else. In The Six-Day Financial Makeover (St. Martin's Press, 2006), Robert Pagliarini advocates targeted saving through what he calls purpose-driven investing: Purpose-Driven Investing [lets us think] of each of our goals as a separate basket. Each of our baskets represents a single goal with a clear purpose that we can see and grow. What does this mean in the real world? It means that we have a single investment account for every goal.

If you want to try targeted saving, ask your bank or credit union if you can give your

Finding Your Sweet Spot
What you're passionate about
What you do best
What people will pay you to do

accounts nicknames. My credit union let me name my new savings account Nintendo Wii when I decided to save for that goal. And my accounts at the online bank ING Direct are named for the things I'm saving for, as you can see in the following image:

●

Ramit Sethi popularized the concept of conscious spending in his book *I Will Teach You to Be Rich* (Workman Publishing, 2009). The idea is to spend with intent, deliberately deciding where to directyour money instead of spending impulsively. Sethi argues that it's okay to spend $5,000 a year on shoes if that spending is aligned with your goals and values and you've made a conscious choice to spend this way.

●

As a general rule, you shouldn't borrow money to buy things that are likely to decrease in value. That means you shouldn't buy your new plasma TV on credit next week, it'll be worth less than you paid for it. Nor should you go into debt to buy food, clothes, or computers. But many experts say that it's okay to take on reasonable debt to pay for a handful of things that are likely to increase in value. This good debt includes an affordable mortgage on your home, student loans to pay for education, and loans to start a new business. Car loans are borderline: they generally carry low interest rates, but as you well know, cars lose value the moment you drive them off the lot.

Better software for a better budget

You Need A Budget

$60, or free 34-day trial You Need A Budget

I had used Quicken for many years before stumbling on YNAB (it stands for "You Need A Budget"). The YNAB concept is very different from Quicken or other Quicken-like tools. Primarily, it is not an accounting software telling you in which accounts your money can be found, but rather it is a true budgeting software that helps you manage where your budgeted money is.

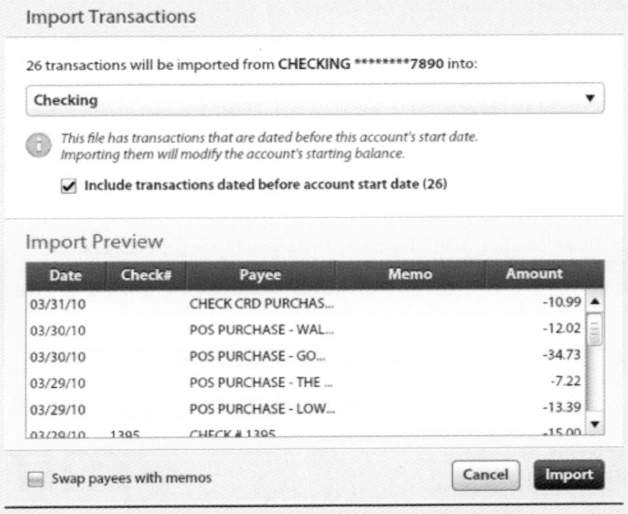
Import Transactions
26 transactions will be imported from CHECKING ********7890 into:
Checking
This file has transactions that are dated before this account's start date. Importing them will modify the account's starting balance.
Include transactions dated before account start date (26)
Import Preview
Date Check# Payee Memo Amount
03/31/10 CHECK CRD PURCHAS... -10.99
03/30/10 POS PURCHASE - WAL... -12.02
03/30/10 POS PURCHASE - GO... -34.73
03/29/10 POS PURCHASE - THE ... -7.22
03/29/10 POS PURCHASE - LOW... -13.39
Swap payees with memos
Cancel
Import

YNAB operates under 4 rules, which are explained very well via the website and free periodic webinars held by the YNAB team:

Give every dollar a job

Save for a rainy day

Roll with the punches

Live on last month's income

By shifting how you think about budgets from "how much do I have in checking" to "how much do I have in my entertainment budget", you can really see where you are spending your money, as the budgets roll from month to month. With Quicken, if you go over/under in certain categories for a month, you just tell yourself you will try and do better next month, but the behavior never truly changes.

The initial investment of $60 may feel steep to some when compared to Quicken ($40-50), but the savings you'll soon gain will more than compensate for the upfront cost. There is also an iOS/Android app, which syncs wirelessly to the cloud (using Dropbox) and allows your budget to be fully up-to-date, whether you check it on your iPhone, your significant other's Android, or your home PC. You can enter your information immediately at the time of purchase and assign the purchase to the appropriate budget category.

All in all, I couldn't be more pleased with YNAB. I have a full picture of where each of my dollars are budgeted, and it has changed my spending behavior to be more in-line with my financial goals.

-- Ryan White

Budget
Reports
All Accounts $2,032.18
Budget Accounts $27,125.50
Checking 12,650.00
Credit Card -1,800.00
Savings 16,275.50
Off-Budget Accounts -$25,093.32
Mortgage
Investment 29,120.13
Add Account
Spending By Category
Spending By Payee
Income v. Expense
Net Worth
Net Worth
Export
Print
Debts $56,013.45
Assets $58,045.63
Net Worth $2,032.18

Wealth Building

How to get rich slow

Five Rituals of Wealth

$5 Tod Barnhart, 1995, 189 p.

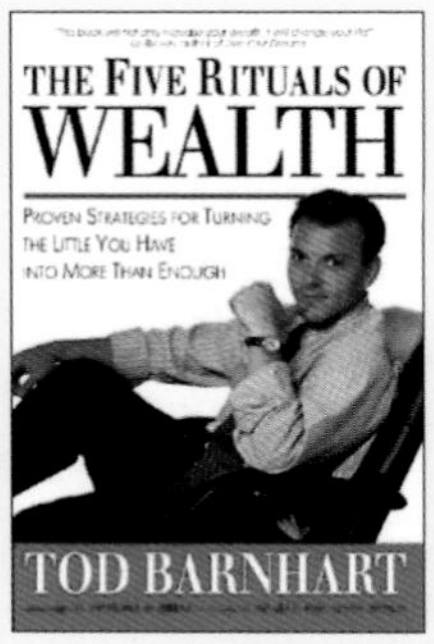

Wealth seems to grow out of a discipline, a habit, a practice that is applied daily and harvested decades later. Not everyone wants to accumulate a pile of money; but most people would like true wealth. This guide addresses that desire. I've gone through the entire *New York Times* bestseller list of how-to-get-rich books, and beyond. This is the book that most matches my own experience, and what I observe of the rich around me. It's wise where there is often little wisdom, and yet practical, but not so practical it goes out of date. (For that kind of advice see *Your Money,* next page)

-- *KK*

•

The biggest lie people tell themselves about wealth is that if you make more money, you'll be rich.

•

Here's the problem: Most of us have been taught little or nothing about wealth. Most people grow up believing they should pay all their bills first and then play with what's left. There's some sense to that strategy. Certainly, it teaches us responsibility as debtors. The thing is, we've never been told that we count as much as our creditors. No one has ever said it's okay to save and pay ourselves first.

•

All the time I hear people say, "If I just earned more money, then I could feel wealthy or pay my bills or use money as a tool to do good things, or save for my future." The lists seem to go on forever, but believe me when I say: Before significant wealth will come your way and stay, you have to master the money you already control.

•

When it comes to saving and investing for your future, the historical rule of thumb is 10 percent. Save 10 percent of your income every single month and you'll grow wealthier than you dreamed possible.

•

In some circles, budgeting is a plan for the future — not a record of the past. I prefer to keep track of my expenses as I spend, rather than plan a budget out to the year 2010. That just feels too constraining. I call my as-you-spend record keeping "take-control budgeting" and recommend it over forward-planning your expenses. I think there are just too many variables in our spending patterns to plan our future expenditures to the dollar. Furthermore, I think that most people find the money to buy the things they really want or need, so the goal here is to be aware enough of your cash flow to spend money only on things you really want. This awareness is accomplished by prioritizing your expenditures, which will be explained shortly. I think you'll find, as I did, that if you just keep a record of your prioritized expenses and balance them every month against your income, you'll instinctively know what to do next.

•

So successful investing is not a matter of which new theory is hot lately, or when to buy low and when to sell high. It's a matter of getting invested, staying invested, and reinvesting the dividends over time. The accumulation of wealth is virtually that simple if you side with time.

•

Too many people approach being a giver from the wrong perspective. They look at the resources they possess and invariably fail to see any "extra" they can part with. That's wrongheaded thinking. Remember: If you

HOW MUCH MONEY WILL PASS THROUGH YOUR HANDS?

MONTHLY INCOME	10 YEARS	20 YEARS	30 YEARS	40 YEARS
$1,000	$120,000	$240,000	$360,000	$480,000
1,500	180,000	360,000	540,000	720,000
2,000	240,000	480,000	720,000	960,000
2,500	300,000	600,000	900,000	1,200,000
3,000	360,000	720,000	1,080,000	1,440,000
3,500	420,000	840,000	1,260,000	1,680,000
4,000	480,000	960,000	1,440,000	1,920,000
4,500	540,000	1,080,000	1,620,000	2,160,000
5,000	600,000	1,200,000	1,800,000	2,400,000

don't feel secure enough to give, you'll never feel wealthy at the deepest level.

•

You can't give just a tiny bit and sit back, waiting for your ship to come in. You have to give with selflessness. And, if you don't feel like you can, then you must. It's the only way you can break free. We've already established how wealthy you really are, regardless of your situation. You know that you're wealthier than the majority of the world. You have to ask yourself: How rich is rich? How much is enough? How wealthy will I have to be before I become a good steward?

You know the answer: It all starts in the belief that you're wealthy right now.

Realtime budget overview

Mint

Free Mint

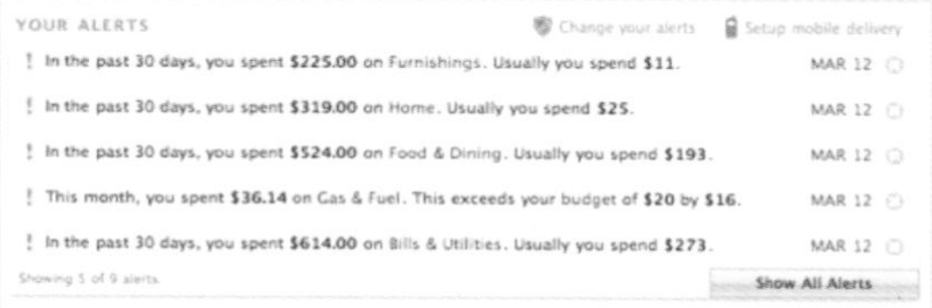

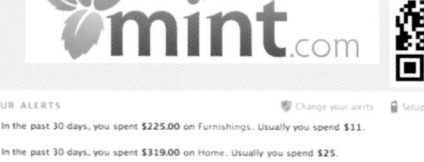

This web-based dashboard gives me an elegant overview of all my financial accounts in one screen. I've been using Mint for years and it is marvelous. It is super friendly, quick, and illuminating. It makes me smart.

Mint will aggregate any money or spending account with online access — which is basically all financial accounts by now. In ten minutes or less I added our bank, credit cards, mortgage, cars, 401k, credit union, checking, and Etrade accounts to Mint. That's the last input I ever had to do. From then on Mint automatically updates all the accounts, sucking in their data with the correct passwords, and integrates this diverse information into a single unified realtime snapshot of our finances. At one glance I can see where we are spending too much, or how we actually allot our income. I no longer have to hunt for my password and numbers for different accounts, say checking our bank balance, or a credit card purchase. It is much much easier, and far more pleasant, to simply log into Mint, where I can see everything. There, in clear presentation far superior to most banks, are all my accounts informing each other. One window to watch them all!

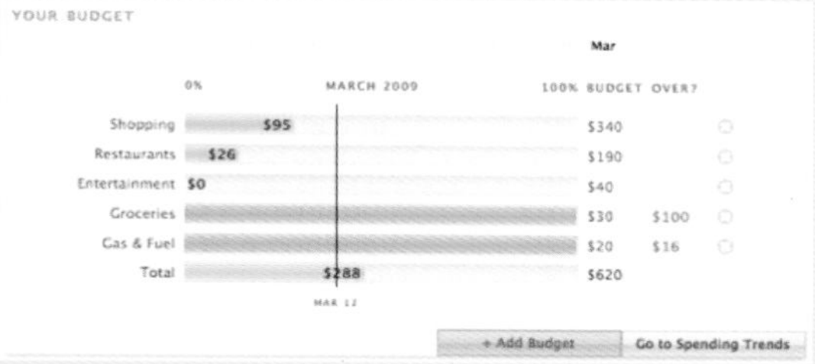

Mint is a read-only interface. There is no way to move money, or reconcile accounts, or pay bills, or calculate taxes (for now). That is also why it is safe. In fact it is probably safer than most banks because fancy algorithms at Mint similar to credit card fraud detection software will alert you when your finances show an unusual pattern. This is one of its cool features. It will gently inform you (at your choice) that say, based on your past months' expenditures, you've overspent your grocery budget this month. It also makes a fairly good guess at categorizing your expenses on its own. It can then make comparisons of how your budget stacks up to other aggregate users in your area, and offer budget suggestions (which we have not followed). We rarely use cash for anything so Mint gives us a very complete picture.

Some people will not be convinced by any reasoning or proof that having a single window into your entire financial situation is safe. If you are of that type, don't use Mint. But for the rest, who long ago realized that using credit cards online is far safer than using one in a store, Mint is a fabulous cool tool. And it is free. Available anywhere the web lives.

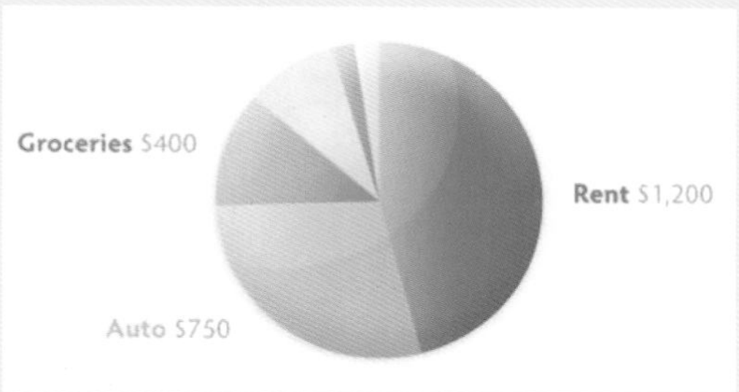

There are a couple of similar sites, such as Wesabe and Geezeo, which emphasize sharing budgets, sort of like a Weight Watchers for finances, but I find their interfaces far less elegant. However this niche is evolving fast, and features expand. Mint has a good head start, a winning design (I love the pie charts!), and a sizable user base, so I think it will be around for a while. (If it did disappear, no loss because it does not store any unique data.)

-- *KK*

Best introductory guide to money

Money Rules

$11 Jean Chatzky, 2012, 128 p.

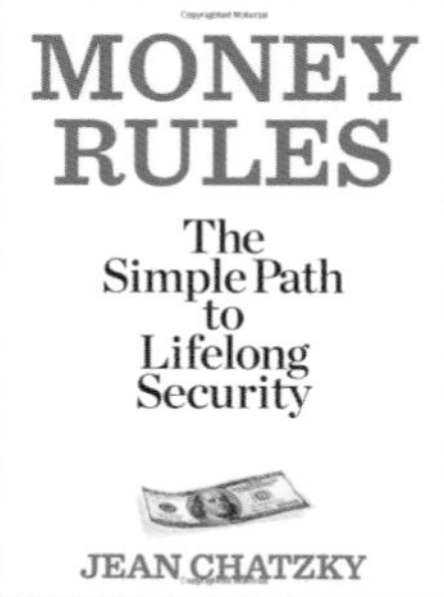

I didn't think another book on finance smarts would add anything new to the wisdom of the previously reviewed books *Your Money*, and *Five Rituals of Wealth*. But this one takes the great advice found in those and reduces it all to 100 maxims that you can read (and reread) in an hour or less. There is one simple paragraph of hard-won advice per page. This small book's chief benefit is that busy people will actually READ it.

This is also the best money guide for young adults. I think it is perfect to start with even for elementary kids. It is less about finance and more about developing a common sense about money. Works as a refresher and reminder for adults too. I found myself in total agreement, having done well over the years using the same principles.

If you need convincing on any point, or want the details on how to execute an idea, you can delve into the aforementioned books.

-- *KK*

•

The four most powerful words in any negotiation: "Can you do better?"

You're sitting in the office of the person who's dying to be your new boss. He's just offered you a job that you really want with the title you've been craving. The only hitch: The salary isn't where you'd hoped it would be. Don't commit–at least not before you ask, "Can you do better?" It's the perfect haggle. You sound as if you know there's wiggle room, and you're willing to let him work his magic. And note: This works just as well when you're on the phone with the cable company, at the mechanic for an oil change, talking to a mortgage rep about a "refi" rate. It even–I know from experience–works with teenage kids.

•

There's no such thing as chump change.

$100 is not a lot of money. Save it every week, however, and invest it in a retirement account where you earn a conservative 6 percent, and keep doing it for 30 years and you'll have $433,557. In 40 years, you'll have more than twice that. And that is a lot of money.

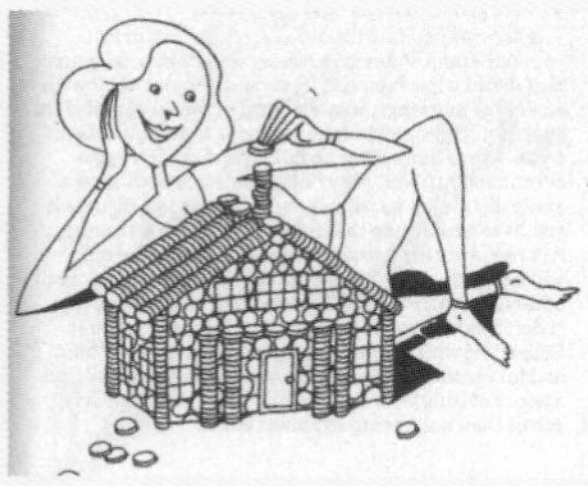

•

Saving is more important than investing.

Next time you stress about the stock market, remember this: The amount of money you manage to sock away is much more important than the return on that money. You can take my word for it. Or you can consider this eye-opening example: You save $250 a month, which you then invest. If you earn 6 percent on that money, a year from now you'll have $3,267. If you earn 10 percent, you'll have $3,311–$44 more. But what if you waited a month to start saving? Then even at 10 percent you'd have $3,052–$215 less. What if you saved $200 a month instead of $250? Then, again at 10 percent, you'd have $2,649–$618 less. As your nest-egg grows and gets into the six figure range, the return on investment starts to matter more. But you can't get to that level if you don't start to save now. Right now.

•

Your retirement trumps their tuition.

You know when you're on an airplane and they always tell you to put your oxygen mask on first before assisting a child? Saving for long-term financial needs is the same. If you don't save for your own future first, you won't be able to help your children when they need it. Worse, they may be forced to help you just when they're trying to put their own kids through school. There is no financial aid for retirement. There is plenty of financial aid for college. Don't feel guilty about this.

•

The best cost-cutting tool is a good night's sleep.

With the possible exception of prescription medication, flashlight batteries, bottled water (under the pressure of a hurricane), and a few other true necessities, there is nothing you need to buy that can't wait until tomorrow. So when you're faced with a discretionary purchase, do your wallet a favor and sleep on it. If you're not still thinking about it–whatever it happened to be–24 hours later, you didn't need or want it anyway.

•

Don't shop hungry.

This is not just a rule that applies in grocery stores. Do you know why they ply you with samples at warehouse stores? Because exciting your mouth–literally making you drool–makes you spend more money not just on food, but on everything. It primes the same part of your brain that responds to the rewards you really want. So maybe you went to the store to buy diapers but now that your brain is active, you buy the tent. (That shopping trip is legend in our family. I should tell you: we don't camp.) Oh, and when your favorite little boutique offers a special evening sale with wine and cheese? Steer clear. Alcohol not only primes the pleasure pump, it inhibits self-control.

We have a name for that state of perfection that keeps improving: God. - Kevin Kelly

Powering Virtuous Circles.

Let's say you were interested in a "tool" to leverage the least amount of money into the largest measurable effect over time. For that I'd like to recommend a type of giving that multiplies itself. Over the years, these are the criteria I've adopted for this challenge:

1) The help is aimed at the lowest, those with the least, where small makes a huge difference.

2) The gift expands itself, gaining amplitude with each cycle.

3) The range is global.

Think of it as enabling philanthropy: take a minimum of money and aim it at the precise point where it can do the maximum good, multiplied by many generations. Maximum good is measured simply: when you enable someone to enable someone else. That is a virtuous circle.

I've found the following three do-good organizations to meet these criteria: Heifer International, Opportunity International, Trickle Up. They fund the neediest in the world. They are highly-evolved programs that produce amazing results. And one tangential result is that when we give to these three, we feel optimistic.

-- *KK*

Peer-to-peer microfinance
Kiva
Charity Kiva

Micofinancing is among the better ways for the haves to help the have-nots. Small loans are made to poor but ambitious workers, who expand their livelihoods with the small loan and then pay it back. Which is then lent out again. The previously recommended agencies Opportunity International, and Trickle Up are great tools for individuals in developed countries to kick-start other folk's self-development. These agencies do the hard work of identifying and training the recipients, and tracking loans and performance.

But why not use the peer-to-peer model to allow individuals with money to loan to specific individuals in need of a small loan? That's what Kiva does and it works wonderfully.

Kiva enables you to make small $25 or above loans to an individual or small group of individuals in a developing country. They use these small loans (aggregated to about $200-$400) to finance a food stall, repair shop, hair salon, sewing machine, new cash crop, etc. When they pay it back to you in about 11 months, you can then re-lend it to another person of your choice.

The advantages of Kiva over the other worthy agencies are three fold. One, you can direct your loans to the kind of projects or livelihood you deem the most important or the most sympathetic. Maybe you are into food so you gravitate to funding small cafes or local fruit growers. Or maybe you think women's sewing centers are a key. Secondly you have more direct contact with the borrowers. They have names, faces, stories. Not a few Kiva lenders have met up with folks they have

lent to. Thirdly, while most microfinance agencies are thrifty, Kiva is particularly thin in administration thanks to the well-designed software platform that runs this service.

The payback rate for Kiva is about 97%. That's a better "investment" than stocks this past year! The variety of folks you can lend to is exhilarating. The karma is good. These loans make a difference. Kiva lends $1 million dollars every 10 days. It is easy to do. A few folks are already on their third cycle of re-loaning the same money they first put up three years ago.

-- *KK*

▼ My name is Khursheed Bibi. I am a fifty-year-old woman. I have lived in the city of Pakpattan, Pakistan, for 15 years. My husband, Mr. Rafiq, is a mason. I have three kids: one son and two daughters. My son runs a furniture making business. My elder daughter is in 9th standard and my younger in 8th standard. I run a decorative embroidery business. I embroider dresses and sell them in clothing markets. I charge $3 per dress. I invest my income in my daughters' education (paying school and tuition fees). I've successfully repaid two previous loans from Asasah (a microfinance institute of Pakistan). Now I am applying again for a loan to buy lumber to expand my son's furniture making business. I am the leader of a group of entrepreneurs sharing this loan.

What is Kiva?
Kiva lets you **lend** to a specific entrepreneur in the developing world – empowering them to lift themselves **out of poverty.**

Lenders — YOU

Entrepreneurs

Sampa rebuilt her life after rebel attacks by starting a restaurant

Global micro seed funding
Trickle Up
Charity Trickle Up

Rather than dispense loans, Trickle Up issues outright grants, but with strings attached. They provide seed capital and training for micro-enterprise hopefuls. Maybe someone with ambitions for a food stall, or a repair shop. A typical deal is a $100 conditional grant. Unlike in a micro-loan program, grantees don't have to pay the money back, but they do have to get trained. Grantees must commit a minimum of 250 hours in the first 3 months to their venture, reinvest at least 20% back into it, and keep an account ledger, among other conditions. Last year 10,000 business started via Trickle Up donations, and 30,000 budding entreprenuers benefited from this global program. There is huge emphasis on training for very basic business skills. And follow up expansion grants are offered, too. About 70% of grantees are women.

-- *KK*

Gifting breeding animal pairs globally
Heifer International

For fifty years the Heifer Project has been providing families in developing countries (and parts of the US) with breeding pairs of animals: cows, goats, pigs, rabbits, water buffalo, ducks, and so on. Even in the world's poorest regions the cost of a cow or goat can exceed a year's income, preventing many families from acquiring animals. When a family receives a breeding pair they get meat, milk or eggs, but more importantly, they now have a source of income as the offspring are sold.

The deal with Heifer Project is that the recipient must agree to give one breeding pair of offspring away to another family, thus paying the gift forward. Therefore a small amount of money contributed now will multiply manyfold as families gain food, pride, a source of income, and the means to help someone else. It's hard to imagine a better gift, or a more practical, proven lever in making a difference in communities of need.

-- *KK*

Opportunity International

Micro-credit loans globally
Opportunity International
Charity Opportunity International

Micro-financing is quite the rage in international circles for one very amazing fact. The payback rate on tiny loans to the workers in developing countries is greater than the payback rate for large loans to their home countries. In other words, from an outright profit perspective, you are better off loaning money to a Bolivian peasant than to the Bolivian government. Furthermore, there is now no doubt that Bolivia itself, and any other country, is much better off if investment goes directly to their poorest citizens than to the government. Opportunity International has been providing micro loans for 30 years, even before the term microcredit was coined.

-- *KK*

Philanthropy

Why to give now
Die Broke
$13 Stephen M. Pollan and Mark Levine, 1997, 305 p.

God punishes one generation when it accepts the undiminished wealth of the previous generation. The way to escape perpetuating generational richity is to die broke. But what about college for my kids, or when I'm sick, old, or retired? This book has answers for you and very specific tactics for the liberation of all from the myth of inheritance.

-- KK

●

You are not a corporation – you are a human being. Your money shouldn't outlive you. You should exit life as you came into it: penniless. Your assets are resources to be used, for your own benefit and for the benefit of those you love. Every dollar that's left in your bank account after you die is a dollar you wasted. Use your resources to help people now when you know they need it, when it will do the most good, rather than hoping they'll be helped when you're dead. The last check you write should be to your undertaker — and it should bounce.

●

Inheritance is a terribly inefficient way to pass wealth to others.

●

You need to shift to a more flexible view of work and career, one that abandons the ultimatum of retirement – a false choice between full-time and no time. Similarly you need to shift to a less rigid approach to earned income. No longer can you look at your earned income as continually increasing up until age sixty-five, at which point it will stop entirely. From now on you need to approach earned income as you do unearned income. It may grow, it may be stagnant, or it may decrease, all depending on market conditions and your own choices.

●

The best metaphor I can think of for today's pursuit of retirement is of a mass of lemmings busily struggling up a steep cliff and jumping off the cliff into the abyss.

●

Dying broke means living well.

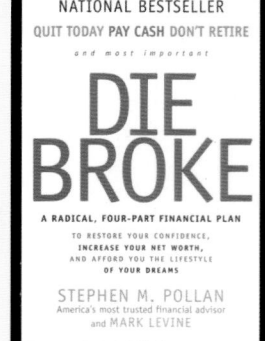

NATIONAL BESTSELLER
QUIT TODAY PAY CASH DON'T RETIRE
and most important
DIE BROKE
A RADICAL, FOUR-PART FINANCIAL PLAN
TO RESTORE YOUR CONFIDENCE,
INCREASE YOUR NET WORTH,
AND AFFORD YOU THE LIFESTYLE
OF YOUR DREAMS

STEPHEN M. POLLAN
America's most trusted financial advisor
and MARK LEVINE

Donor → Fidelity Charitable → Charities

Your own personal foundation
Fidelity Charitable Gift Fund
Charity Fidelity Investments

The only sane antidote to massive wealth is massive philanthropy. But giving is a habit that is best begun before you are loaded; the great philanthropist Carneige began when he was making a few dollars per week. Indeed, some of the most influential funding in history has been small, but creative, grants.

You can write a check any time the spirit moves you, but like all things in life, they are tools that can improve your aim. One tool of philanthropy is a personal foundation. A foundation gives you flexibility and can increase the amount you can give. However you can spend half your fortune — no matter its size — creating and maintaining a foundation, or you can do it the easy way, a way that is suitable to middle class assets.

The Fidelity Charitable Gift Fund provides most of the functions you, a non-tycoon, might want from a personal foundation. Best of all, it requires a minimum of "only" $5,000.

Here's how it works:

You deposit your contribution in Fidelity Charitable Gift Fund which in turn invests the amount in one of their mutual fund pools. You get to choose the level of risk/payback you want for your money, but Fidelity chooses and runs the fund. Whenever you want to make a donation, you tell Fidelity, and as long as it is a tax-deductible outfit (it can't be an individual), they send 'em a check. You can do this online with a very graceful and easy interface; it even remembers all the details of your frequent grantees, so you just need to click.

The main advantages are four:

1) The money grows. Like a real foundation, your money is invested, and the returns on those investments are reinvested and further enlarge your fund for giving. Depending on what percentage you disperse each year, the total can accumulate significantly. (Fidelity suggests you give at least 5% of your fund each year.)

2) You can gift stock (or securities) directly to the fund. When highly appreciated stock (as in a boom), is cashed out it triggers huge capital gains tax for the owners. With a personal foundation you can donate the stock without cashing it. The Fidelity Gift Fund account is credited with the high value of the stock at market value, but the giver (you) doesn't have to pay for the huge gains, because those gains are now the gains of a non-profit fund. You receive the normal charitable giving tax deduction for the market value of the stock. You can do the same with ordinary stock investments. Say you were lucky enough to buy 20 shares of Amazon when it was at $20 per share. Say when Amazon hit $200 per share, you decided you wanted to do something creative and meaningful with your small fortune of $4,000. You bestow the Gift Fund with the 20 shares of Amazon, which then credits your philanthropic account with $4,000. But instead of having to pay a capital gains tax on $3,600 ($4,000 minus $400, your cost), you get a tax deduction on $4,000. That $4,000 can then amplify further (see point 1). A common tactic for Gift Fund users is to donate their highest flying, most inflated stocks for maximum philanthropic joy and smallest capital gains pain.

3) It's free. Well, almost free. Fidelity charges the usual industry standard of any mutual fund (less than 1%), but this is far less than hiring a personal fund manager, or even setting up a private foundation yourself.

4) You get to name your foundation anything you want. Having a foundation of your own focuses attention on keeping it full, and encourages discipline in giving it away.

Because accounts within the Gift Fund are so easy to set up they are often used for giving circles. A giving circle is a group of friends or advocates who decide to combine their resources to fund a cause. They create a virtual foundation without the usual expense and work of setting up a bona-fide non-profit (which is needed to receive funds, but not give them) and collectively research and debate who/where/how to fund their mission.

The Gift Fund is so useful for givers of more modest means that has drawn in about $2 billion dollars per year, making the collective Fidelity Charitable Gift Fund the third largest public foundation in the US. Of course it is not really one foundation, but 60,000 small foundations, many of them pioneering creative philanthropy. You don't have to fund the opera and hospitals. As an example, here are some donations clients of the Gift Fund recently made:

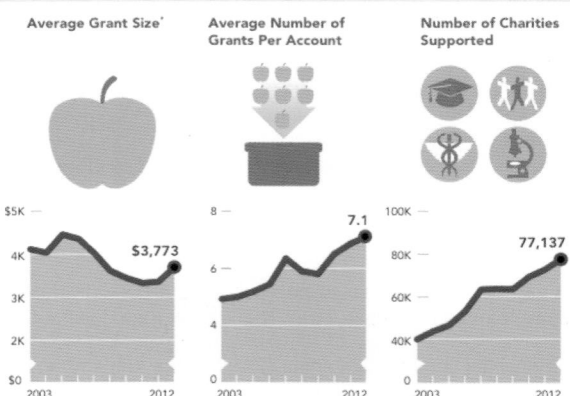

Average Grant Size: $3,773
Average Number of Grants Per Account: 7.1
Number of Charities Supported: 77,137

•Support for a historic preservation speaking tour

•Rebuilding a scout camp destroyed by fire

•Support for an archeological dig in a national park

•Support for Native American students majoring in science

•Supplying an animal shelter with an examination table and equipment

•Support for a summer theater

My experience with the Gift Fund over the past 10 years has been great. It was simple to set up, with a minimum of paperwork, and when it comes time to make a donation, the effort is pretty painless. Having a convenient do-it-yourself vehicle, with tax breaks, and investment upside, has encouraged our giving.

-- KK

Transmitting values
Ethical Wills
$12 Barry K. Baines, 2006, 217 p.

An ethical will is a good-bye letter that sums up your life's aims. You write this will in order to pass on your values instead of your valuables. It is not legally binding. It is not a living will, either, which is no more than a final care directive. An ethical will, instead, is closer to advice. It is a re-statement of the lessons you learned in life. It's an ancient practice; the earliest examples are 3,000 years old, and not uncommon among some Jewish communities. In the days of illiteracy, the deceased's will was read aloud for all concerned to hear. Why not annex one little last sermon for them since you had a captive audience at a moment when they are really paying attention? What began as a supplement to a legacy will is now enjoying a role of its own. As you age, you set down your values, stories and other intangibles you wish to pass onto others. This letter says the unsaid, clarifies the mind, stretches across generations. For many families, this missive may become the most valuable thing you leave behind.

You don't need this book, *Ethical Wills*, to figure out how to write one. Any style or form is fine; the more uniquely personal, the better. The book has collected some modern and traditional examples of ethical wills, which is what I found most useful. It lays out the reasons and steps to begin if you need encouragement. I've begun mine (it should be a work in progress) and have discovered that one of the best reasons to do it is for my own sake. Like journal-keeping, it's an act of self-discovery. Unlike diaries, the total effort may be as short as one sheet of paper. I find it motivational to contemplate this possibility: how wonderful would it be if I could read the ethical wills of each of my grandparents and their parents? I find few things as thrilling as passing on values that might be replicated for generations.

Neither this book, nor any of the other related books and websites that I've read, have mentioned an intriguing alternative to a written ethical will: a short video. Many people who are not comfortable writing would be comfortable talking. Video cameras are cheap; you could do some really powerful statements of your values and perspective that might speak to future generations. If you go this route, use a common format so there is a chance someone can view it a century from now.

When you die you'll leave behind a long trail of textual bits scattered over the world, but what you should leave is a distilled succinct package, a one-page, 5-minute testimony of you being you, so that if the rest of your recorded self should disappear, at least we'll know what you thought was important. And I can promise you this, you'll learn something doing it.

-- KK

●

Thirteen years ago, I first learned about an ancient tradition for passing on personal values, beliefs, blessings, and advice to future generations called an "ethical will." At a subconscious level, I must have remembered the custom, because when my father was diagnosed with lung cancer in 1990, I asked him to write a letter about the things that he valued. About a month before he died, my dad gave me two handwritten pages in which he spoke about the importance of being honest, getting a good education, helping people in need, and always remaining loyal to family. That letter — his ethical will — meant more to me than any material possession he could have bequeathed.

●

Ethical wills were particularly advantageous outlets for women, since society's rules usually precluded them from writing a legal will or dispensing property as they wished. Historians have found examples of ethical wills authored by women during the medieval period, usually in the form of letters or books written to their children.

●

This will was written in the earlier part of the twentieth century. It has a very interesting history. In the pocket of an old ragged coat belonging to one of the insane patients at a Chicago poorhouse, a will was found after his death. According to Barbara Boyd, in the Washington Law Reporter, the man had been a lawyer, and the will was written in a firm clear hand on a few scraps of paper. So unusual was it, that it was sent to another attorney; and so impressed was he with its contents, that he read it before the Chicago Bar Association and a resolutions was passed ordering it probated. It is now in the records of Cook County Illinois.

●

ITEM: To lovers, I devise their imaginary world, with whatever they may be need, as the stars of the sky, the red roses by the wall, the bloom of the hawthorn, the sweet strains of music, and aught else they may desire to figure to each other the lastingness and beauty of their love.

ITEM: To young men jointly, I devise and bequeath all boisterous inspiring sports of rivalry, and I give to them the disdain of weakness and undaunted confidence in their own strength. Though they are rude, I leave them to the powers to make lasting friendships, and of possessing companions, and to them exclusively I give all merry songs and brave choruses to sing with lusty voices.

ETHICAL WILLS
2ND EDITION
PUTTING YOUR VALUES ON PAPER
Barry K. Baines, M.D.

A nice place to smile is in front of me. - Shoshone saying

Hacks for indie scholars
Online Journal Access

Access to academic articles for unaffiliated scholars is difficult. There is no central online portal that will give you access to all journals in the library. Instead there are numerous gateways with differing access policies for individuals. As Kevin Kelly's research librarian, I often need access to scholarly articles online, so here are my current best tips for how to get an academic article if you're an independent researcher. These tips are biased toward searches for known articles (you have a name of an article you want to get), but most of the information will be useful for earlier-stage searching and browsing as well.

I start by searching for the complete title of the article I want via Google, or Google Scholar. Sometimes I get lucky and the full text of the article shows up on the first page, posted freely to some website. Often, that website will be maintained by the author of the article, or the author's profile/CV page at their affiliated institution. Most of the time, this direct online search isn't fruitful, but it doesn't take long to execute.

Google Scholar search results are especially helpful because even if the article is not freely available online they give additional information about the article that can extend the search. That additional information includes author names, the name of the journal, and the database where the journal is indexed. Knowing the name of the author, I can look for the author's website, where an earlier draft might have been published. If all else fails, I might also be able to contact the author to request a copy. So this is the first tip: the author has more incentive than the journal to make the article available to everyone. Find the author.

Second step: Knowing the name of the journal and database where the article is indexed, I can extend my search to the libraries in my area. If my public library has a subscription to the database, I can possibly access a copy of the article via my library's online portal to the database.

To determine which libraries near you might afford you online access to the article you seek, search for the article at worldcat.org (see p, 391). WorldCat will also let you search for a list of libraries in your area, even if you're not searching for a particular article or library resource.

You may be fortunate, like I am, to live near a wonderful public library that offers online access to many academic databases. Check your public library's website to see what database subscriptions they offer. As a member you may have access to them. If the offerings aren't great, read on.

Libraries pay a lot of money to get continuous online access to academic articles. These institutional subscription fees are too expensive for individuals, so more and more academic databases will sell pay-per-view article access. They may charge, say, $3 to download one article. An increasing number have begun to sell cheaper individual subscriptions. For example IEEE sells individual access to their engineering and science journals for either $15/month (3 article downloads) or $40/month (25 article downloads).

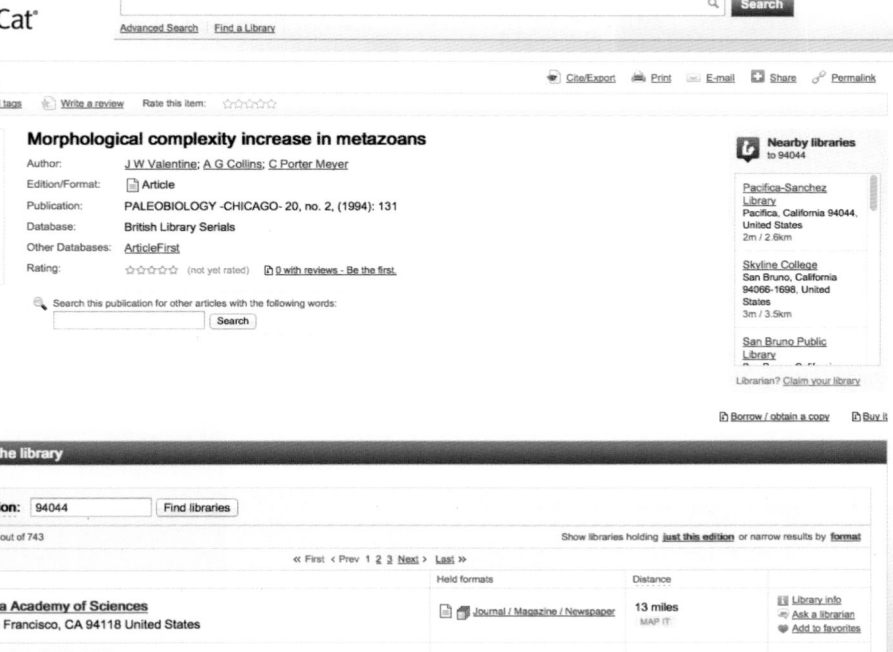

Proquest, a broader database with access to newspapers, popular and trade magazines, as well as journal articles, also recently launched a subscription program aimed at individuals called Udini. HighBeam is a very similar competing service, with similar content coverage,

At this time, however, the only major database that offers completely free, access for independent scholars is JSTOR. JSTOR leans toward the social sciences and arts, but they restrict the number of journals available for free. JSTOR's free Register and Read program offers a limited selection of their huge corpus, including only ~1,200 of the 1,700 academic journals in their database. It includes only content from their archival digitization program - nothing from their "Current Scholarship" program. You are also extremely limited in the number of articles you can access (three

articles every 14 days). PDF downloads are available for some articles, for a fee. Udini's database is much MUCH larger than JSTOR's - 12,000 (an order or magnitude) so the chances that Udini will have what you're looking for are probably greater, with one caveat: JSTOR may still be better for older articles published before the 1980s. So the third tip: register for free at JSTOR.

If you're searching for a specific article, your options are limited to access points sanctioned by the publisher (or bootleg copies republished elsewhere online). But If you're browsing for content, though, open-access journals are a good resource to keep in mind. Several to consider include:

Public Library of Science (PLoS)
7 journals, academic research

Directory of Open Access Journals (DOAJ)
9073 journals, academic research

Wiley Open Access
20 journals published by Wiley, plus additional sources from other publishers (1300 journals)
(some overlap with PubMedCentral)

PubMedCentral
3600 journals from/affiliated with the NIH National Library of Medecine, biomedical and life sciences

Finally, you may be able to get free access to an academic library's full set of online journal simply by visiting the library in person. Each library will have its own policy regarding public use of their paid database subscriptions, so it's worth calling ahead or checking their website. It might be as simple as bringing your laptop within range of the library's wi-fi, or you might be required to use a library computer where you may or may not be able to email copies to yourself or print copies for reference.

-- Camille Hartsell

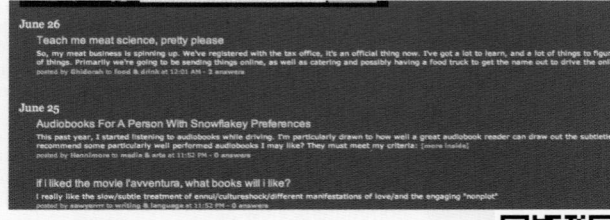

Inexpensive custom research
Uclue Answers
Uclue

Hire a free-lance professional researcher here. It's not as expensive as you might think, and the results are very good for the price. Here's how it works: You ask a question, announce a price you think an answer is worth, and if a top-notch researcher thinks your fee is fair, they will research your question. Questions can be quickies worth $5, or more complicated queries costing $200 or more. If no one bites, you can up your fee.

I've used this service a number of times, even though I employ a researcher because the Uclue researchers are so much faster. In my experience Uclue answers are solid and reliable. You can always ask for clarifications. The results are public so that other researchers and commenters can scruntinize and correct an answer. You can pay a little extra to keep a question private.

If you just want advice, go to the free and free-wheeling Yahoo Answers. You'll get your money's worth. If you want help on a particular question that the exact right person can answer quickly, I think Ask Metafilter (below) is by far the best guru (and it is free for members). But if what you need is some real research and serious sleuthing, the kind of answer that is not just sitting in someone's head or at the top of search results, I believe your best bet will be Uclue.

Figure how long it might take you to answer your own question — if you could at all — and you'll see that Uclue answers are a real bargain.

-- KK

Answers from the hive mind
Ask Metafilter
$5 registration Ask Metafilter

This is where I go when Google shrugs. A community of 20,000 of the smartest people you know will answer your question. I use Ask Metafilter when I have a question that can't be reduced to a key word search. Say you want to know the name of that song that was played during the closing credits in a science fiction film that begins in a boy's bedroom. Or you've been curious what that bumper sticker you keep seeing is with a blue square, or maybe you need advice about whether you should see a therapist, or a psychologist, or a psychiatrist? You need a human for these inquiries. Ask Metafilter is not great for questions requiring detailed and heavily researched answers. For that use Uclue (above) for a small fee. What Ask Metafilter is great for, are things that a smart friend could easily answer if only you knew which friend to ask. The Metafilter community is your all-purpose smartest friend.

There is a one-time fee of $5 to join the community in order to post a question (but its free to read). To keep the frantic rate of new questions under control you are limited to asking no more than one a week. (You can answer all you want, and please do.) The quality of answers varies, but in general the tips, referrals and advice are pretty good, and often astoundingly on the mark. For example, here are some fairly typical questions I've asked (with fairly typical answers).

I've tried a couple of other "ask your question" sites on the web and generally their answer to question ratio is so low I've found them worthless. Ask Metafilter has managed to retain its intelligence while scaling up sufficiently to cover all subjects; that's a magical balance.

In fact, even when I don't have a question I find myself reading Ask Metafilter everyday because people will ask questions that I didn't even know I wanted to know until they asked it, and then I realize I've been dying to ask that. It's a true hive mind and it really works.

[Ask Metafilter is one service of the Metafilter community blog. Reading is free. Registration allows you to post questions and answers as well as posts to the other parts of the blog.]

– KK

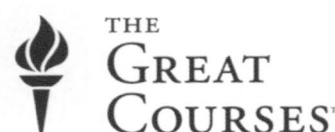

Best university classes

The Great Courses

thegreatcourses.com

The concept is exquisite. Scour the planet for the world's best professors and record their lectures. Paying customers get world-class university courses, at less than world-class university prices, while attending the class at their convenience. I've audited a dozen classes this way. My favorite so far is Robert Greenberg's celebrated forty-eight lessons on "How to Understand and Listen to Great Music." It was absolutely stellar. More than a music appreciation class, it was a view of western civilization through music. Professionally recorded, lively, insightful, fast-paced, authoritative, and memorable. What more could you want from college -- at your home or in a car? Other favorites have been an overview of Egyptian history taught by a mummy expert and a renegade look at the lost gospels of Christianity. The Great Courses catalog lists an eclectic range of 400 other seminars. Most of these are exceptional high-brow educational extravaganzas, but recently they've featured more pop and personal development courses. Keep an eye on their vast archive for great ones (rated by customers).

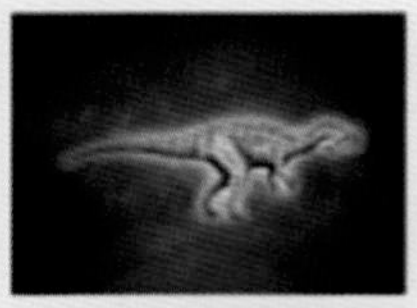

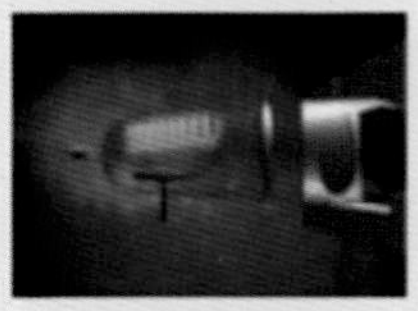

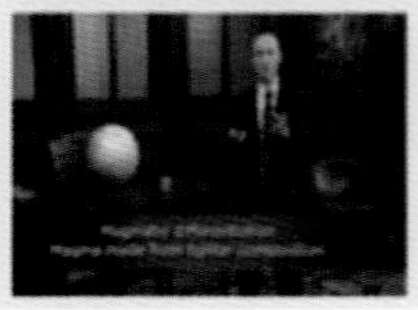

When this service started in 1990 all the courses were audio -- and the audience primarily were commuters. Now all the new courses are on video with heavy visuals; made for watching on iPads or laptops, or DVD screens. A very few courses will have dual formats, audio and video. If you want an audio experience you can search the archive for audio-only.

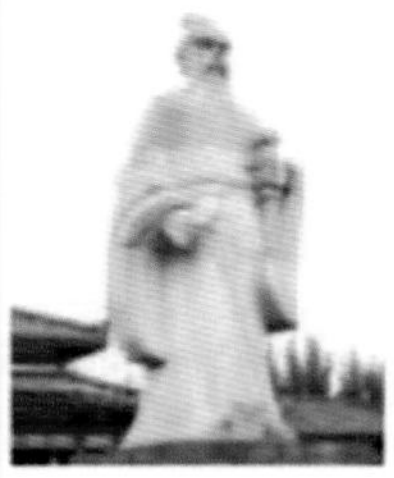

The Art of War

Professor Andrew R. Wilson, U.S. Naval War College

As a landmark achievement in the evolution of strategic thought, Sun Tzu's *The Art of War* has had a powerful influence on military strategy. Through a historically grounded explanation of the original text and intriguing case studies, **The Art of War** proves how this classic's wisdom remains highly relevant in the information age. Examine how its model of leadership has been applied—and misapplied.

ABOUT YOUR PROFESSOR

Dr. Andrew R. Wilson is Professor of Strategy and Policy at the U.S. Naval War College in Newport, RI. He earned his Ph.D. from Harvard University.

COURSE NO. 9456

6 LECTURES (30 MINUTES/LECTURE)

Audio CD	$24.95
Audio Download	$19.95

Available Exclusively on Audio

One caveat: the company has a lame habit of setting ridiculously high prices and then ceaselessly offering "sales," and they constantly send junk mail catalogs. Nonetheless, the courses are great and they are a) way cheap for college, and b) way cheap by the class (most courses are at least forty or so classes). I find them a good deal; just wait a few months till the one you want is priced reasonably. You can also check your local library system which will often have CDs and DVDs.

-- KK

•

Understanding the Universe: An Introduction to Astronomy, 2nd Edition is a nontechnical description of where that picture stands today. In 96 richly illustrated half-hour lectures, you survey the main concepts, methods, and discoveries in astronomy—in depth—from the constellations drawn by the ancients, to the latest reports from planetary probes in our Solar System, to the most recent images offered by telescopes probing the farthest frontiers of space and time.

Dr. Filippenko uses thousands of diagrams and photographs. There are almost 300 short movies and computer animations that make astronomical phenomena easier to understand, and they put planets, stars, and galaxies into context as you zoom through the cosmos. A showman in the classroom, Dr. Filippenko delights in simple, easily reproducible demonstrations that use tennis balls, apples, paper plates, and other objects to explain scientific concepts. Furthermore, he has a gift for analogies: At one point, he makes the energy content of one erg vivid by comparing it to one fly doing one push-up!

Altogether, this course is an unrivaled opportunity to experience a full-year introductory college course on astronomy, delivered by a five-time winner of "Best Professor" on campus at the University of California, Berkeley, In 2006 he was named one of four national Professors of the Year by The Carnegie Foundation for the Advancement of Teaching, and in 1998 his international team of astronomers was credited with the top "science breakthrough of the year" for their amazing discovery that the expansion of the Universe is speeding up—a finding that is now shaking the foundations of physics.

Big History:
The Big Bang, Life on Earth, and the Rise of Humanity

Professor of History
David Christian

Macquarie University

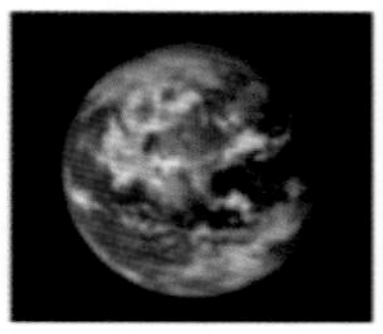

Big History offers a unique opportunity to view history in the context of the many histories that surround it.

Over 48 thought-provoking lectures, you traverse the expanse of cosmic history—13.7 billion years of it—starting with the big bang and traveling through time and space to the present moment.

Big History weaves a single story from accounts of the past developed by a variety of scholarly disciplines. The result is a story stretching from the origins of the universe to the present day and beyond.

48 LECTURES

1 What Is Big History?
2 Moving across Multiple Scales
3 Simplicity and Complexity
4 Evidence and the Nature of Science
5 Threshold 1—Origins of Big Bang Cosmology
6 How Did Everything Begin?
7 Threshold 2—The First Stars and Galaxies
8 Threshold 3—Making Chemical Elements
9 Threshold 4—The Earth and the Solar System
10 The Early Earth—A Short History
11 Plate Tectonics and the Earth's Geography
12 Threshold 5—Life
13 Darwin and Natural Selection
14 The Evidence for Natural Selection
15 The Origins of Life
16 Life on Earth—Single-celled Organisms
17 Life on Earth—Multi-celled Organisms
18 Hominines
19 Evidence on Hominine Evolution
20 Threshold 6—What Makes Humans Different?
21 Homo sapiens—The First Humans
22 Paleolithic Lifeways
23 Change in the Paleolithic Era
24 Threshold 7—Agriculture
25 The Origins of Agriculture
26 The First Agrarian Societies
27 Power and Its Origins
28 Early Power Structures
29 From Villages to Cities
30 Sumer—The First Agrarian Civilization
31 Agrarian Civilizations in Other Regions
32 The World That Agrarian Civilizations Made
33 Long Trends—Expansion and State Power
34 Long Trends—Rates of Innovation
35 Long Trends—Disease and Malthusian Cycles
36 Comparing the World Zones
37 The Americas in the Later Agrarian Era
38 Threshold 8—The Modern Revolution
39 The Medieval Malthusian Cycle, 500-1350
40 The Early Modern Cycle, 1350-1700
41 Breakthrough—The Industrial Revolution
42 Spread of the Industrial Revolution to 1900
43 The 20th Century
44 The World That the Modern Revolution Made
45 Human History and the Biosphere
46 The Next 100 Years
47 The Next Millennium and the Remote Future
48 Big History—Humans in the Cosmos

COURSE NO. 8050

SALE ENDS 07/25/13!

48 LECTURES (30 MINUTES/LECTURE)

DVD	~~$519.95~~	NOW $129.95
Video Download	~~$439.95~~	NOW $109.95
Audio CD	~~$359.95~~	NOW $89.95
Audio Download	~~$249.95~~	NOW $64.95

Transcript Books with Course: $45.00

Should I Buy Audio or Video?
This course works well in any format.

Best online degree info

GetEducated.com

Free GetEducated.com

Long term success does not depend on which college you go to, or even if you do. (I speak as a college dropout.) However, for many people a college degree is highly desired. One way to get a degree is online. It can be cheaper (sometimes), and can be done remotely (sometimes), and can credit previous work and experience (sometimes). It can also be none of those. An online degree lies in the territory of scams and unscrupulous operators (as do some campus colleges) so you need some serious street-smarts to guide you. Of all the books, websites, and too-good-to-be-true tutorials I've seen, GetEducated is the only reliable source of information for online degrees today I've seen. Most online degree information printed in books is ancient and out of date, or tainted with profit by selling something, or frustratingly vague and unspecific.

GetEducated is constantly updated with the latest research, comparing actual costs, examining real credentials, and reading the fine print of what is offered for degrees online. And their advice and research is free on their website.

The one downside to the GetEducated is that the information is not well organized, scattered across the site in many webby articles with titles like "7 Ways You Can Save Thousands by Getting an Online College Degree." The information is solid, but hard to locate and step through.

The editors of GetEducated run a forum and they promise to answer any legitimate question about online degrees brought up. It would be great it they'd assemble their knowledge into a cheap e-book.

-- KK

•

Surprise, surprise, the majority of the cheapest online colleges are non-profit, public institutions. The University of Wyoming, Colorado State University, Macon State College – these guys have been helping traditional residential students get educated since the 1870s.

These colleges offer online degrees on the cheap to all residents of the USA. You do NOT have to be a state "resident" to enjoy the low tuition and fees charged by online learning bachelor degree programs offered by state colleges in places like Wyoming, Georgia, Colorado, and Nebraska. In these states, where the cost of living remains low, the cost of a college degree likewise rings in well below the national average.

•

Two regionally accredited distance-learning colleges in the United States—Thomas Edison State College of New Jersey and Excelsior College of New York—operate primarily as assessment colleges. These two special colleges allow students to earn entire undergraduate degrees through credit for life and work experience options.

However, most learners who attend these two colleges also complete some formal college courses to earn their degrees.

•

Instead, surveys show just the opposite – online college costs might actually be higher than residential college costs. The cost of masters degrees, online MBAs especially, are often higher than the equivalent on-campus versions.

While consumers often consider the University of Phoenix to be the standard for delivering a low-cost, mass market, campus-free college experience —in short, the flagship example of a cheap online college — the exact opposite is factually true.

The University of Phoenix's Online College of Business and Management offers one of the most expensive online bachelor degrees. Their $66,000 degree, well above the $44,000 average degree cost, actually puts them in the bottom 15% affordability-wise of all 150 regionally accredited online bachelors in business surveyed. As of 2011, consumers could get the same degree from the University of Wyoming Online for only $16,000.

•

If you have to have the Association to Advance Collegiate Schools of Business' (AACSB) stamp of approval on your MBA, The University of Louisiana Monroe offers the cheapest such MBA at a price tag of $8,990 for online students nationwide.

(More college accreditation trivia: the AACSB is considered the gold standard for business school accreditation. Academics equate this type of accreditation with a rigorous, traditional business school education. I won't tell you that your MBA must have AACSB accreditation; I will tell you that many recruiters and Wall Street wing-tip types see AACSB accreditation as a platinum stamp of old school approval.)

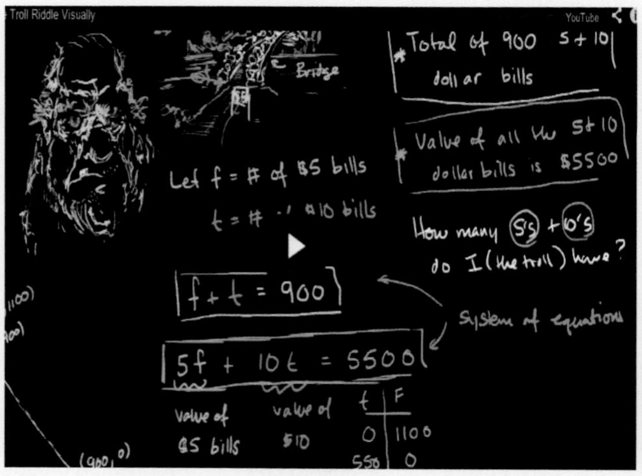

Great free online courses

Khan Academy

khanacademy.org

Is there anyone who doesn't know about Khan Academy, the free online school? A favorite of the digiterati, this website was founded by Sal Khan who started out by making video tutorials on how to learn algebra. He captured his instructional doodles on a black screen (rather than focus on his talking face) and these short intense classes were amazingly effective. Our son used them for high-school math summer school. Students love them because they can go their own pace, and back up when needed. Sal Khan branched out to cover almost every other school topic, from history to economics, in over 4,000 videos. I've searched for, and attended, specific lessons in his Chemistry set in order to brush up on a forgotten point. While his math and SAT prep ones are still the best, all his courses are free, and he still teaches better than the average teacher.

-- KK

The fates guide the willing, the unwilling they drag. - Seneca

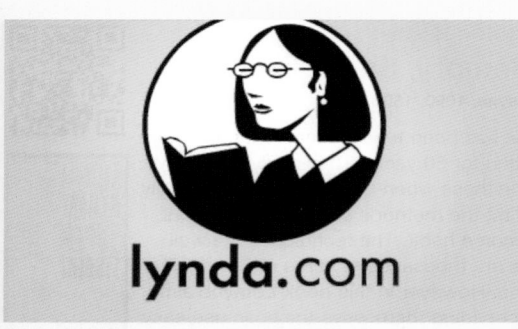

Streaming technical classes

Lynda.com

$25 (one month subscription) Lynda.com

I don't know about you but I need constant reminders on how to use complex software packages such Photoshop, Wordpress, FinalCutPro, or InDesign (which I am using at this moment). I am a binge user, immersed deeply during a project, then a month later I've forgotten even basic commands. If I did programming, I'd need the same refreshers. Searching YouTube is great for narrow tips, but I often need structured lessons on how to accomplish basic things.

I've also learned that I remember much more from online video tutorials than I do from guidebooks. Must be how my brain works. So for the past 8 years I've subscribed to Lynda off and on. Lynda began as Lynda Weinman making videos teaching web design but is now a collection of 2,000 courses, with an astounding 100,000 tutorials, for mastering software packages of any type. I can find a series of lessons begining with newbie introductions up to advanced shortcuts for almost any software package alive. I can watch, re-watch without limit. Besides the publishing software I use, Lynda is big on tutorials for programming languages (Python, MySQL, HTML5), specialized ware (Finale, Matlab, Maya, ProTools), and your common office packages.

At $25 per month, or $250 per year, it ain't cheap, but it's powerful and a time-saver. I subscribe during a project when we need help the most, and let it go in between. Also it's all streaming, no dowloads. Log in from anywhere, any device, but only one at a time, so I share my account with my son, who is constantly learning new software. A fair number of their videos are free as enticements for the rest of the course. They have apps for attending on tablets and phones, and group discounts for classrooms.

For lifelong learners in a digital world, Lynda is a must.

-- KK

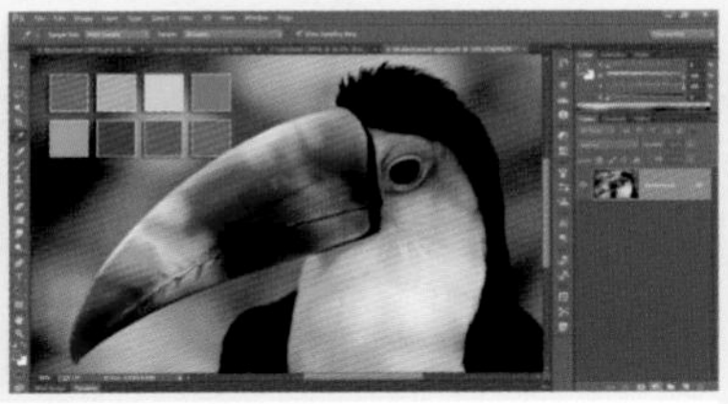

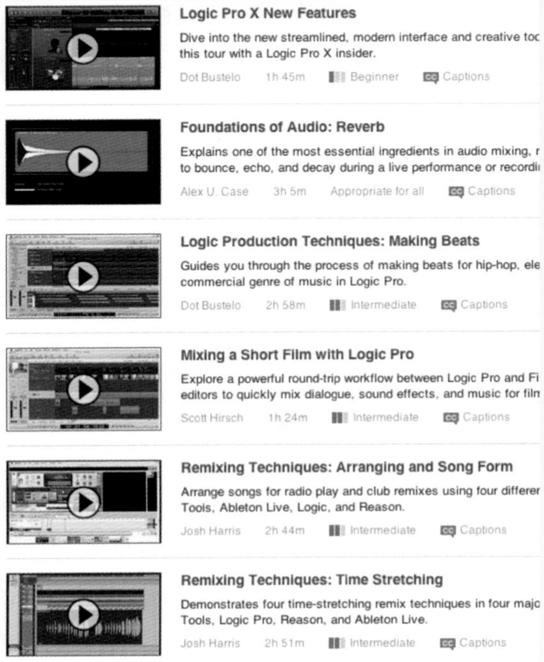

Logic Pro X New Features
Dive into the new streamlined, modern interface and creative toc
this tour with a Logic Pro X insider.
Dot Bustelo 1h 45m Beginner Captions
Foundations of Audio: Reverb
Explains one of the most essential ingredients in audio mixing, r
to bounce, echo, and decay during a live performance or recordi
Alex U. Case 3h 5m Appropriate for all Captions
Logic Production Techniques: Making Beats
Guides you through the process of making beats for hip-hop, ele
commercial genre of music in Logic Pro.
Dot Bustelo 2h 58m Intermediate Captions
Mixing a Short Film with Logic Pro
Explore a powerful round-trip workflow between Logic Pro and Fi
editors to quickly mix dialogue, sound effects, and music for film
Scott Hirsch 1h 24m Intermediate Captions
Remixing Techniques: Arranging and Song Form
Arrange songs for radio play and club remixes using four differer
Tools, Ableton Live, Logic, and Reason.
Josh Harris 2h 44m Intermediate Captions
Remixing Techniques: Time Stretching
Demonstrates four time-stretching remix techniques in four majc
Tools, Logic Pro, Reason, and Ableton Live.
Josh Harris 2h 51m Intermediate Captions

How to do research

Networking on the Network

Free Networking on the Network

I know of no better guide to becoming a researcher than this book, which exists only online. Written by a professor to help his PhD students learn how to network and develop their professional skills, it is great advice for anyone who wants to create a place for themselves in the information economy. It's all about finding, feeding, and harvesting networks of other like-minded folks, and growing your own distinctive node. While the author naturally focuses on how academia works, there is enough valuable wisdom here for anyone doing original research (and you should!) — whether corporate, journalistic, or part-time blogging.

-- KK

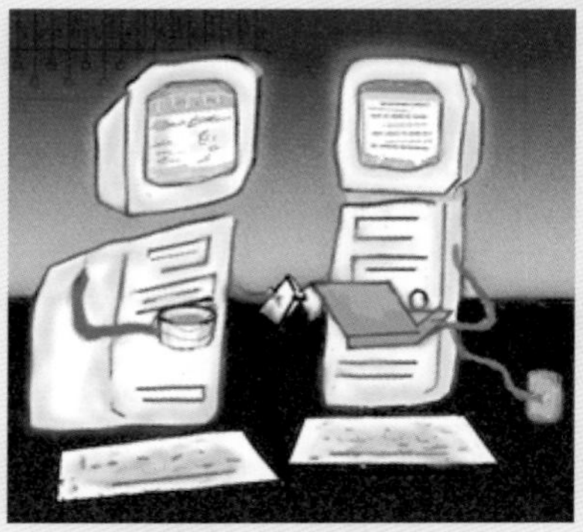

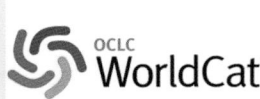

•
You are not choosing which network to join; rather, you are creating a new network of your own.

•
If this seems like a lot of work, think of it as shopping: the library is a giant department store, and you are shopping for professional colleagues. Accumulate a "long list" of potential colleagues. Study their work and learn from it. Figure out what elements your work has in common with theirs. Then practice explaining your research in a way that puts those elements in the foreground and the other elements in the background. The general formula is "I'm interested in [elements you have in common with the person you're talking to], and to this end I'm studying [elements that you don't have in common with them]". For example, "I'm interested in how teachers adopt computers, and to this end I'm conducting an ethnographic study of some grade-school teachers' strategies for including computers in their lessons", or "I'm doing ethnographic research on people adopting computers, and my fieldwork concerns grade-school teachers ...". Now you are ready to build a community for yourself that includes relevant people from several different research areas. These people will be like spokes in a wheel, of which you are the hub.

In working through this exercise, you are already encountering two fundamental principles of professional social life, both of which will recur throughout this article. The first one was already well-known in classical rhetoric, and I will call it "articulating commonalities". The point here is to develop relationships with people. And relationships are founded on commonalities. These commonalities might include shared values, shared research topics, shared goals, or anything else of a professional nature that you might share with someone. To articulate a commonality means formulating language for it.

•
It is especially important to put your publications on your Web site. This can be difficult, given that publishers generally ask you to sign over your copyrights. But even when this happens, you can still amend the copyright form with a marginal phrase like "I retain the right to post the paper on my Web site".

•
Here is the procedure: (a) choose someone you wish to approach and read their work with some care; (b) make sure that your article cites their work in some substantial way (in addition to all your other citations); (c) mail the person a copy of your article; and (d) include a low-key, one-page cover letter that says something intelligent about their work. If your work and theirs could be seen to overlap, include a concise statement of the relationship you see between them. The tone of this letter counts. Project ordinary, calm self-confidence. Refrain from praising or fawning or self-deprecation or cuteness or making a big deal out of it — you're not subordinating yourself to this person; you're just passing along your paper. Don't sound like you're presupposing or demanding that you'll get a response. Try a formula such as, "If you should happen to have any comments, I would be most interested to hear them". A good final sentiment for your letter is, "Will you be at such-and-such conference?".

Search 72,000 libraries

WorldCat

Free WorldCat

WorldCat is a publicly accessible online interface to the holdings of all types of libraries throughout the world: currently 72,000 libraries in 170 countries. Tell it what book you're looking for and your zip code or city, and it will pinpoint the nearest library that has the book. Same goes for magazines and journals, video and audio formats. The ability to locate an obscure book is invaluable; but it's also tremendously useful for anyone living in a region with more than one nearby library. California's Bay Area is blessed with an abundance of excellent public and academic library systems and a majority of them are represented in WorldCat, so in my case, it's a real time saver (I do a lot of sleuthing). The database was originally accessible only by taking a trip to the library, but in 2004, the nonprofit Online Computer Library Center (OCLC) built this interface. Beyond the core location service, WorldCat provides many other helpful services and resources, like citation exporting, list making, and text samples. I haven't explored these options much, but you can use it to build your own private or public indexes of titles and to search public lists created by other users. You can even read and write reviews of materials – yes, you can actually write in the library catalog! And if you decide you'd actually prefer to purchase the item, there are Amazon and WorldCat purchase links (a portion of every WorldCat sale goes toward supporting a local library of your choosing or to the OCLC). You'll need to create a WorldCat account to take advantage of these features, but account creation goes really quickly and it's free.

You can obtain WorldCat results in your preferred search engine by appending the term "WorldCat" to your search. Preceding your query with the phrase "find in a library" also works very well in Google and Yahoo.

In my own experience, I've found these methods to work best in conjunction with titles or author names. WorldCat also offers a number of browser toolbar extensions and plug-ins to help facilitate searches. Alternatively, you can simply go directly to the WorldCat web site and use it like you would any individual library's catalog. Search on title/author/keyword/etc., browse by topic or other citation linkages. Item pages consist of basic bibliographic data formatted out like a virtual catalog card, and below that you'll find a set of tabs with the holding libraries information, more detailed bibliographic data, subject links, editions and reviews. Finding the exact edition of a book can be a bit tricky, and so can finding an alternative edition that may be even closer to you, so the "Editions" tab is critical. Overall, OCLC does a pretty good job of rolling duplicate catalog entries together, but you do need to watch out for alternate spellings of titles.

The library links from the item page will take you to into the holding library's OPAC (online public access catalog). You might land on the item page for that work or you might find yourself at the main catalog page for that library. Responsibility for providing accurate "deep links" to item pages falls to the participating library. I have occasionally found that after following a link for a holding library, I end up at a catalog page that says something along the lines of "Your item would be here." At this point, I go ahead and re-enter my title in the library's search box on that page and more often than not the item does appear in the catalog. I'm not sure why this happens, but I suspect it may have something to do with links changing or out of date record numbers being used. This is, admittedly, very frustrating, but because the item usually does end up being in the catalog I continue to be a fan of WorldCat. It's really an excellent resource for all users of various types of libraries with broadly ranging information needs. And its main purpose of connecting patrons with materials housed in libraries near them is further supplemented by new and growing user-specific and community-based features. I couldn't get along without it. I also look forward to watching the project continue to evolve.

-- Camille Cloutier Hartsell

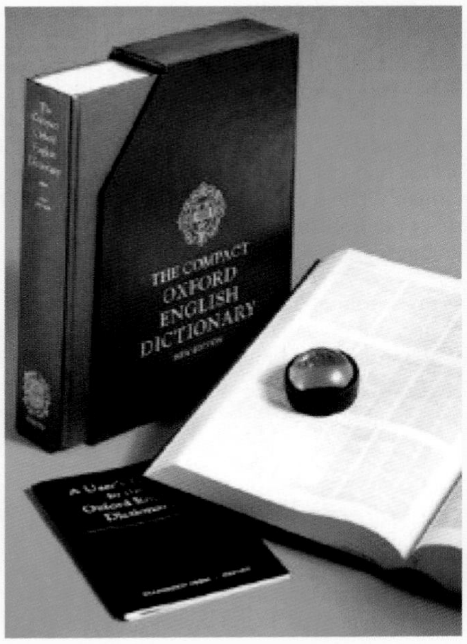

20-volume lexicon in one

Compact Oxford English Dictionary

$358 E. S. C. Weiner, J. A. Simpson (Editors), 1991, 2424 p.

The classic, Compact OED is a smaller, handy version of what is the best English dictionary, bar none, the famous OED. Because it's photo-reduced, it contains the entire OED, all 20 large volumes in one convenient reference (it comes with a reading glass). Aside from saving space on your shelf, it's also significantly cheaper. It's quite large, but you could definitely fit it in a regular backpack, if you're a student or need to transport it (although it is about 10 pounds!). I've been using it for 3 years now, at least twice a week for general queries, as I enjoy discovering and using obscure words and I also often look up words and dive into etymology as part of my Wikipedia editing. For example, recently I used my OED to look up an archaic usage of the word "quaint". Apparently Andrew Marvell's "To His Coy Mistress" makes use of the old meaning where "quaint" also refers to female anatomy. Who knew?!

-- Gwern Branwen

Memorable estimates
Rules of Thumb

Free Rulesofthumb.org

I'm a big fan of rules of thumb. Like: "Count the number of times a cricket chirps in 15 seconds, and add 37. That's the temperature in Fahrenheit." They are great estimating tools. At the *Whole Earth Catalog* we first published Tom Parker's collection of these portable estimates, soliciting others from readers. I suggested a few rules of my own, which made their way into one of two compendiums Parker compiled from the submissions. Since I remember — and use — a number of these rough recipes, I have always regretted that the books were out of print. If ever there was knowledge ideal for the web, rules of thumb are it. Tom Parker has recently digitized all the rules he has collected. He posts one old rule per day, and one new one suggested by readers. In fact, new rules are co-published on the Cool Tools website. As the rules are tagged over time to make searching easier, we'll finally have the world-wide database of guesstimates that short-cut-takers like myself have always wanted.

Over the years Parker has refined his explanation of what rules of thumb are, and why they are cool tools. I can't improve it. He writes:

"A rule of thumb is a homemade recipe for making a guess. It is an easy-to-remember guide that falls somewhere between a mathematical formula and a shot in the dark. Rules of thumb are a kind of tool. They help you appraise a problem or situation. They make it easier to consider the subtleties of the topic at hand; they give you a feel for a subject. A rule of thumb is not a joke or a ditty. It is not a Murphy's Law. Murphy says that things will take longer than we think; a rule of thumb says how much longer. While a proverb says that a stitch in time saves nine, a rule of thumb says to allow one inch of yarn for every stitch on a knitting needle."

My new rule of thumb: "One in 25 rules of thumb will be useful to you." YMMV, but I find that a pretty good hit rate.

-- KK

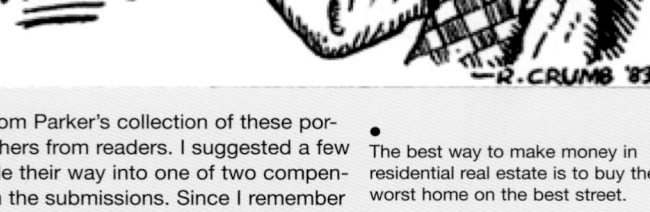

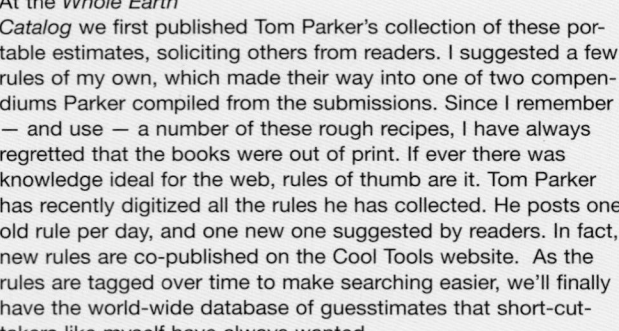

"ANYTHING THAT WORKS!"

—R. CRUMB '83

- The best way to make money in residential real estate is to buy the worst home on the best street.

- The moon covers half a degree of sky.

- When digging a grave by hand, haul away 17 wheelbarrow loads of dirt and pile the rest by the hole. You will have just the right amount to backfill.

- For marketing purposes, elderly consumers think they are 15 years younger than they actually are.

- The price of a telescope increases proportionately to the cube of the lens diameter.

- Recovering an unused physical skill takes one month for each year of layoff.

- If you walk into a bar where a lot of people wear baseball caps, it's a good place to sell lottery tickets.

- Eclipses often come in pairs. A lunar eclipse is followed frequently by a solar eclipse two weeks later, and vice versa.

- If the cats aren't sleeping on the radiators, turn down the heat.

- One chemical toilet serves 15 employees per week.

- It takes two minutes for the sun to drop out of sight once it touches the horizon.

- If a woman can walk around during contractions, she is not fully dilated.

- When you are working in the vicinity of high voltage, keep 1 foot of distance between you and the power source for each 1,000 volts. For instance, stay 13 feet away from a 13,000 volt power source.

- You have a 50 percent chance of surviving overboard in 50 degree water for 50 minutes.

- Spring moves up in altitude 1000 feet per week.

- Ten people will raise the temperature of a room one degree per hour.

- If a speech takes 15 minutes in a dry run, it will take one third longer on the actual event.

- Rental property should sell for 100 times the monthly rental income.

- Double the height of a 3-year-old to determine his or her adult height.

How to memorize anything
Super Memory, Super Student

$11 Harry Lorayne, 1990, 180p.

Harry Lorayne has been teaching ancient principles of memorization for 50 years. They really work. My dad taught me these when I was a kid and I still rely on them. At first the methods seem gimmicky, but they soon become habit. The techniques are well proven (some are thousands of years old) and will benefit anyone. However in this book Lorayne aims at students, providing them ways they can use easy tricks to tackle common school memory tasks. He has a system for turning numbers into words so you can remember numbers and dates as well. Imagine how much more efficient you'd be if your memory was just five percent better, and how much easier your life would be if everyone else's improved.

-- KK

- Every high-school student I've spoken to knows about the acronym FOIL, which is a memory aid for remembering how to attack an algebraic equation: Firsts, Outers, Inners, Lasts. (More on this in the algebra section in chapter 20.) And I've never met a doctor or a medical student who didn't remember the cranial nerves (olfactory, optic, oculomotor, trochlear, trigeminal, abducens, facial, auditory, glossopharyngeal, vagus, accessory, hypoglossal) by reciting the couplet

On Old Olympia's Towering Top

A Finn And German Vault And Hop.

Professors have helped medical students learn the layers of the scalp by suggesting that the word "scalp" itself might remind them of skin, close connective tissue (cutaneous vessels and nerves), aponeurosis (epicranial), loose connective tissue, pericranium.

- I've said it so many times, it's been copied so many times, I may as well say it again: The "three R's" cliche - reading, 'riting, 'rithmetic - should be four R's. The first R should be remembering. Because without that first R, you can't read, write, or do 'rithmetic! All education is based on remembering. I know of no high school or college subject that doesn't require lots of memory work.

- In order for you to remember any new thing it must be associated, in some ridiculous way, with something you already know or remember.

Desecrate - "to profane a holy place; to treat a sacred thing irreverently": You're in a desert and see a gigantic crate -- *desert crate*. It's a sacred thing (perhaps a halo is over it), but you kick it and so forth -- treat it with disrespect, irreverently. (*Dat's a crate* would also do.)

Atrophy - "to waste away from lack of use": *A trophy* or *I throw fee* will remind you of the pronunciation. Connect one of them to the meaning of the word. Perhaps visualize a trophy (a gigantic loving cup or statue) wasting away (shrinking) because no one ever uses it (see it covered with dust and spiderwebs).

Relegate - "to send to a lower position": You *roll a gate* downward, *sending it to a lower position*. Be sure you actually *see* that.

Ultimate recovery
How to Find Lost Objects

In my household I am Mr. Find It. I rarely if ever lose things myself, and have become the go-to guy to find what others have lost. Over the years of finding things, I have evolved a set of principles very similar to those laid out in this very simple book. This method really works.

You can read this book for free online. That way you'll never lose it.

But some people like the laminated-paper-pulp form to give as a gift. While there is more in the slim book, none of the extra is essential. Still, it's a handy quick reference.

-- KK

- Principle Ten

The Eureka Zone

The majority of lost objects are right where you figure-once you take a moment to stop and figure.

Others, however, are in the immediate vicinity of that place. They have undergone a displacement -- a shift in location that, although minor, has served to render them invisible.

Some examples:

A pencil has rolled beneath a typewriter.

A tool has been shoved to the rear of a drawer.

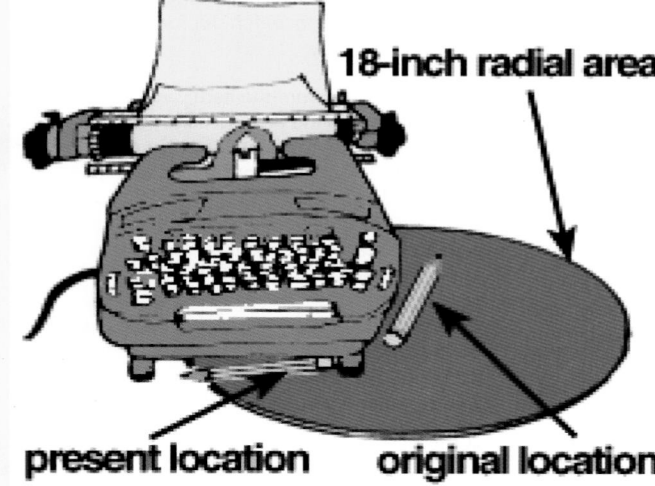

18-inch radial area

present location   original location

Free (PDF) Professor Solomon

$25 Professor Solomon, 1995, 120 p.

A book on a shelf has gotten lodged behind other books.

A folder has been misfiled, several folders away from where it belongs.

Objects are apt to wander. I have found, though, that they tend to travel no more than eighteen inches from their original location. To the circle described by this eighteen-inch radius I have given a name. I call it the Eureka Zone. With the aid of a ruler, determine the Eureka Zone of your lost object. Then explore it. Meticulously

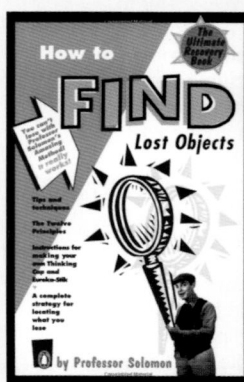

How to FIND Lost Objects

by Professor Solomon

It is better to be wrong than to be vague. - Freeman Dyson

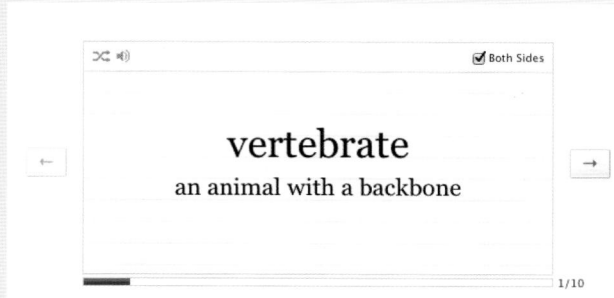

Superior flash card system
Quizlet
quizlet.com

Quizlet is used almost daily by 12 million people but you've never heard of it unless you have (or are) a high school student. It's a cloud-based flash card app. Here's how my highschool son explains it. -- *KK*

Quizlet is what I and all my friends use to study vocabulary or anything else we have to memorize for class. It is super easy and super fast to add a card. No paper. Lots of auto-define buttons, lots of keyboard shortcuts make the process of creating a Quizlet quick and painless. Because Quizlets are all stored in the cloud, I can access them from anywhere and not worry about losing track of it. I usually type the cards on my laptop and then review/test on my phone. I can easily share my Quizlets with friends. There's built in gamification for testing myself which makes memorizing a million words less of daunting task. Quizlet also has a lot of other features which I haven't yet tried; to me it is mostly a practical memorization aid. The best feature of all though is that it's completely free!

-- *Tywen Kelly*

Best memorization aid
SuperMemo
supermemo.com

In high school, I tried to learn Spanish, and failed. In college, I tried again, and failed again. Then, in my thirties, I discovered SuperMemo, and within a year I had memorized thousands of Spanish words and phrases and was finally on my way to speaking Spanish.

SuperMemo is software premised on the idea that there is an ideal time to practice any item you are trying to remember. You want to practice when you have almost forgotten it. Too soon, and you waste your time, and even interfere with long term memory formation. Too late, and you've lost the trace, and have struggle to learn it again. There is a simple equation that describes the shape of the forgetting curve, but the exact curve is different for every item and for every person. There is no single "best pace" for memorizing all things.

However, your ideal time to practice can be predicted from your history of attempted recall. The inventor and memory expert Piotr Wozniak reduced this practice to software many years ago, and his technique, called "spaced repetition", is now available in quite a few learning products, including Wozniak's own SuperMemo, and an open source version called Anki (see below). None of them are perfect from a usability point of view. But any of them will work far, far better than random study of flashcards. These tools will not give you all the pieces of the learning puzzle, obviously. Memorization is only one step. But it is a crucial, difficult, first step, and it is wonderful to get a boost.

I recommend SuperMemo or Anki to every student who needs to memorize: vocabulary, science and medical terms, names and faces, musical chords, technical specs -- anything that can be reduced to a flash card.

SuperMemo for Windows (its main version) has a famously slow-to-evolve interface that will irritate anybody used to the convenience of modern UX, but it contains many wonderful features, including "incremental reading," which is a way to save and remember passages from books and articles. Anki is quite primitive in terms of features, but has an up-to-date interface and is available on most platforms, including an iOS and free Android app.

-- *Gary Wolf*

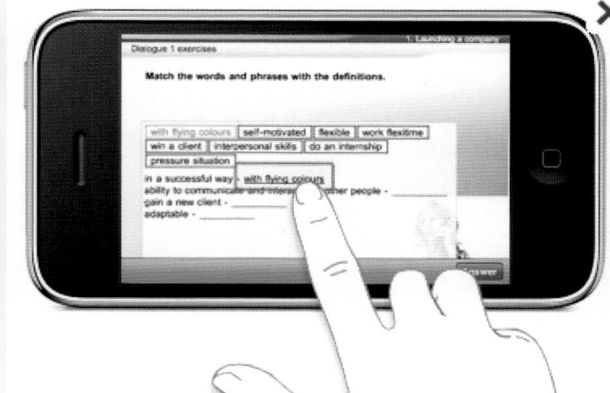

Matching the words

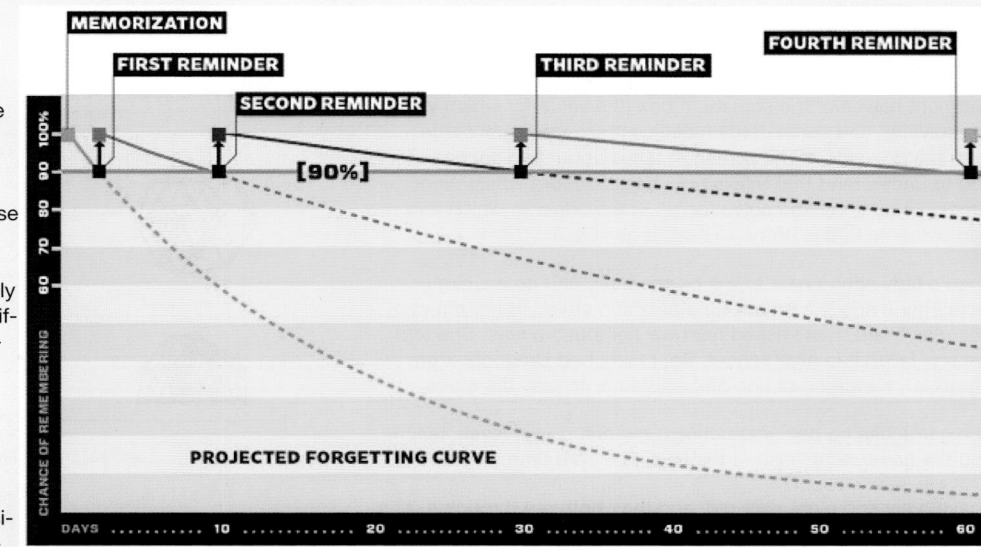

How space repitition learning works in SuperMemo. Each item has its own "forgetting curve," which is interrupted at the optimal time by a reminder, to maximize the duration you remember the item. (Chart rom Wired.com)

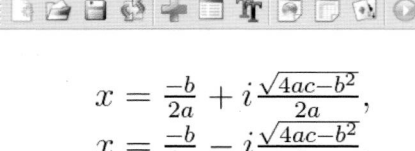

$$x = \frac{-b}{2a} + i\frac{\sqrt{4ac-b^2}}{2a},$$
$$x = \frac{-b}{2a} - i\frac{\sqrt{4ac-b^2}}{2a},$$
$$i^2 = -1.$$

Open source study tool
Anki
Free ankisrs.net

Anki is a free, open source, flashcard program that is the best method I have used for memorization. I originally found it when I was looking for a better way to study for an EMT class. I quickly discovered one of the coolest features of Anki was the database of shared "decks" you can download for free. As it happens, another EMT student had already gone through the trouble of composing a deck that covered all of the material thereby saving me countless hours. The range of topics is astonishing but the most popular subjects appear to be languages (Japanese being the favorite) and vocabulary.

The system that Anki uses to order the cards is called "spaced repetition". It is based on an algorithm that uses how you rank each card to determine when it will show that particular card in order to maximize retention (and save time). The harder you rank the card the sooner the information reappears, and vice versa. This technique was first pioneered in the popular flashcard generator SuperMemo ($60, see above), and is also used by Mnemosyne (free). Anki also has a slick informatics feature enabling it to produce statistics and graphs detailing how you have been learning over time. Another benefit is that you get to decide the pace of learning by setting the amount of new information introduced every session. I personally chose Anki because of the availability of community-sourced decks and have been thrilled with it so far. However, I am interested in exploring the other options as my studying increases.

Anki currently supports text, LaTeX, images, and sound, and though I haven't created many decks the process is easy and is helped by a clean user interface. It allows you to share your created decks, and offers the option to upload them to the Anki website where you can access the cards anywhere with an internet connection (and sync them across multiple computers). A downloadable version of Anki is supported on all the major operating systems (OSX, Windows, Linux) as well as iPhone, Android and Nintendo DS. In the end, Anki is one of the best pieces of free software I use, and I highly recommend it to anyone in need of a better study tool.

-- *Oliver Hulland*

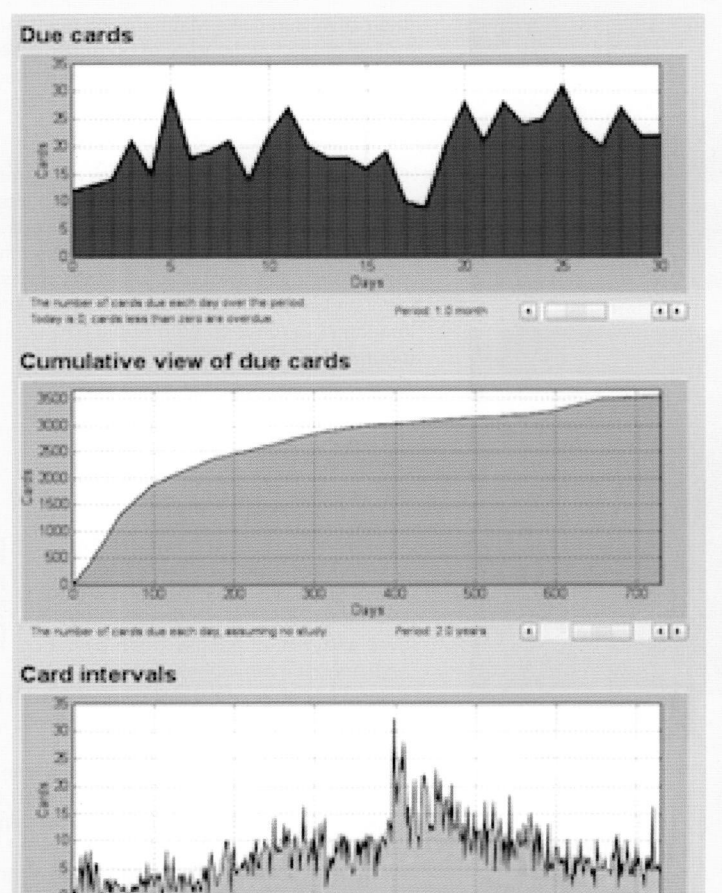

Tricks kids into learning algebra

Dragon Box

I recently downloaded this game onto a tablet my children use (when we're feeling generous!) My eight year old son immediately sat down and ran through the first two banks of problems without hesitation. It was amazing.

The premise of the game is simple: it presents algebraic problems as a game. Given two sheets of paper (presented as left and right halves of the screen), a box (the value for which you are solving), and some cards (coefficients), remove all cards from the box side of the screen. It takes about two seconds for you to understand that this is how basic algebra would work: simplify equations and solve for 'x'. The manner in which this app presents that is nothing short of genius.

I had a lady sitting next to me on the train, and on a whim I asked her if she liked math. She said something to the effect of "it's okay" and then I asked her how her algebra was. She told me she failed it in high school. So, I launched Dragonbox on my tablet, handed it to her, and asked her to play the game.

The game has no help instructions; the first dozen levels teach you the game. She finished the level in record time.

I have a six and eight year old, and they both ran through it without many hitches. In fact, the same admonition for math — "check your work!" — is equally true with this, so it reinforces a basic discipline as well. This is the best educational game I have ever seen.

For six bucks I have my son learning algebra on his summer vacation. Try to beat that.

-- Christopher Wanko

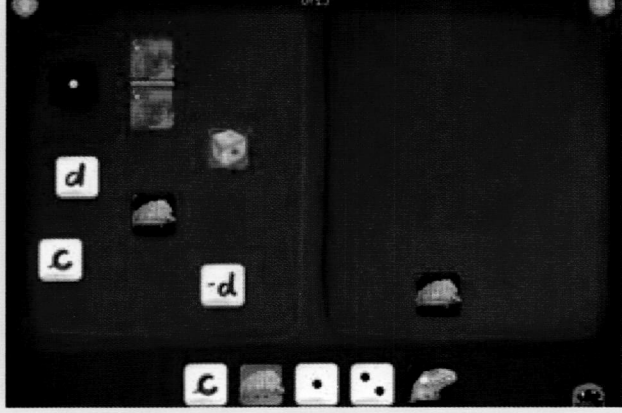

$6 iTunes Store   **$6 Google Play**

3D mathematics

Bathsheba Mathematical Sculpture

$30+ Bathsheba Sculpture

Cool and useless. That's my definition of art. These very cool 3D mathematical sculptures by Bathsheba Grossman are very nerdy art. Like origami, they reveal both beauty and universal principles. Cleverly manufactured by 3D metalic printing, then polished by hand, they manifest bizarre mathematical notions. Lot's of brilliant designs, some like alien seeds. Others are like Escher paradoxes in 3D. These mini ones are only a few inches wide, and not cheap. It's art! It's mathematics. Many are shapes never before made or even imagined — simply because they were impossible to render before. Bathsheba also does laser etched images deep inside of glass crystal. Check her news blog for some really dazzling larger pieces. I've ordered several things from her and have been happy.

-- KK

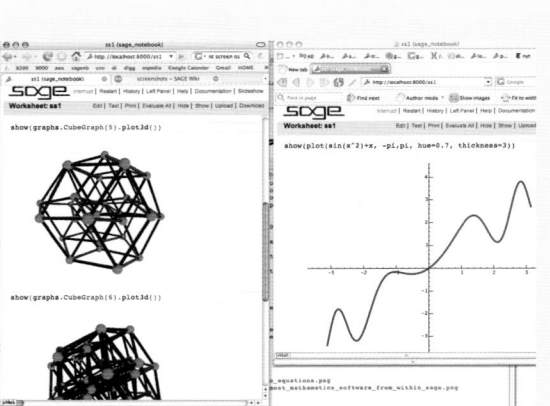

Open source maths program

Sage Maths

Free Sage

Sage Maths is free open source software for doing virtually every type of maths you can imagine. Not just numerical maths, but symbolic maths too – you can give Sage an equation and it will tell you what the equation of its integral or differential is, for example. And it will do numerical maths, plot graphs, analyze statistical information and solve equations or sets of equations. In fact, it will do virtually anything mathematical you can think of.

Sage was developed as an open source alternative to commercial systems like Mathematica and Matlab (it has most but not all of the functionality of both) because mathematicians and scientists need to be able to understand and review the algorithms their software uses – something not possible with a closed system.

Originally developed for graduate mathematicians, Sage is now at the stage where it is useful and interesting to professional and hobbyist mechanical and electronic engineers, amateur astronomers, business number crunchers, and people who just want to know more maths than they do. It runs on Linux, Windows and OS X, and lately people have managed to run it on both Apple iThings and Android smartphones.

-- Jonathan Coupe

Free alternative to Mathematica

Maxima

maxima.sourceforge.net

For symbolic math (vs. numerical, where you want a number for answer), Mathematica is the commercial standard and a lot of people swear by it. For high school math where you're typically doing fairly straightforward symbolic work ("Integrate x^2 + 2x+ 1"), something like Mathematica is useful...

...but for whatever reason, I personally can't stand it and wound up using Maxima, which is an open source symbolic math tool. It's not the easiest thing to learn, but if it can handle multipole expansion of tensors for me, it would do just fine for a high-schooler, plus would cost them nothing so they could use it for life.

-- Victor Putz

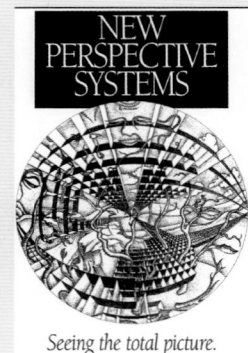

Mapping 3D

New Perspective Systems

$13 PDF Dick Termes, 1998, 40 p.

A short, definitive tutorial on all 6 perspectives in art. Starts with 1 vanishing point and goes through 6 vanishing points for a completely spherical view. Understanding multi-point perspectives is useful to not only artists and designers, but also to photographers and folks dabbling in Virtual Reality, or anyone trying to map the physical world onto a 2D surface. These lessons are presented in a 40-page PDF, which include some grids to practice on.

-- KK

NEW PERSPECTIVE SYSTEMS

Seeing the total picture.
One through six point perspective by Dick Termes.

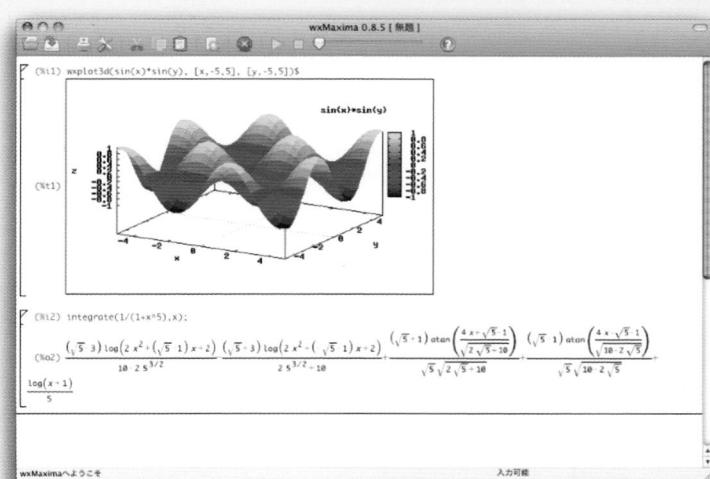

Inventing logic
Logicomix

$16 Apostolos Doxiadis and Christos Papadimitriou, 2009, 352 p.

Disguised as a biography of mathematician Bertrand Russell in graphic novel form, this comic book is really about the nature and limits of logic. It takes heady, heavy, and key ideas in logic and renders them witty, visual, and dramatic. You'll learn a lot. The fact that many of the original logicians were mentally unbalanced and irrational, adds a dash of delicious paradox and spice to this entertaining book.

-- KK

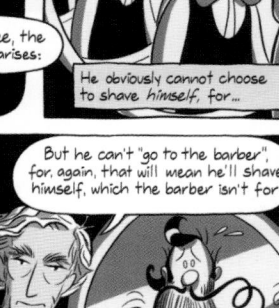

Geodesic logic
Zome System

Small kits to +1000 piece sets Zome

Geodesic structures have always been tricky to mess around with because the vertices have to be precise, which often equals expensive. This reasonably priced system provides highly machined plastic connectors and sufficient highly engineered struts in various lengths to build scores of geodesic forms. The possibilities of shape are open-ended so that even small kids can build with it (struts are color-coded to ease assembly), and yet logical and complex enough that the same components can be used in a high school math or even college engineering classes. They also offer a selection of lesson plans built around this research toy. I had my first "aha" experience of geodesics while building with it: crystals are geodesic!

-- KK

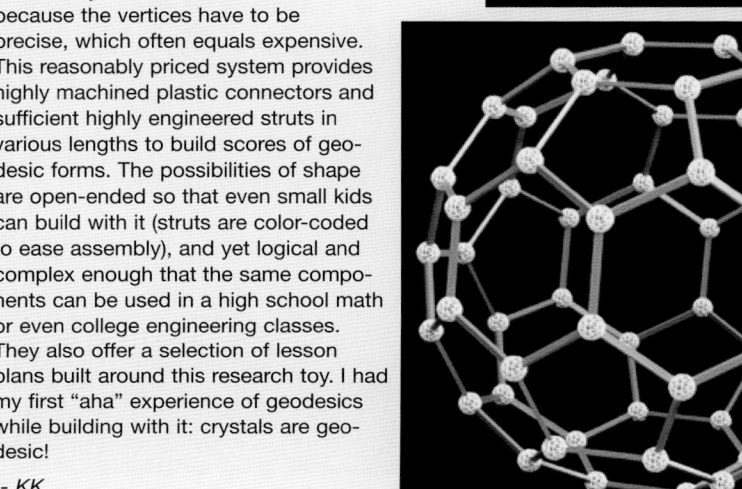

Make models with drinking straws
Linx

$18 Linx

This inexpensive construction kit uses simple plastic hubs to connect grocery store drinking straws. You can assemble quite large — and featherweight — structures in crystalline and geodesic designs. The 125 included hubs are enough for several big projects and are reusable. While you can use "bendable" drinking straws I don't recommend them because they weaken the structures; but if that's all you can find at the store, they'll do.

-- KK

The only way of discovering the limits of the possible is to venture a little way past them into the impossible. - Arthur C Clarke

395

Free short course in how-to-teach

The Aviation Instructor's Handbook

Free FAA

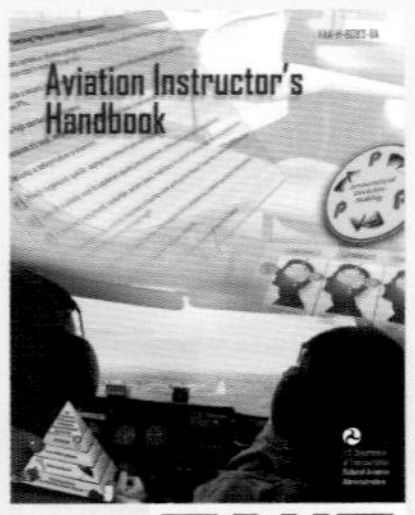
Aviation Instructor's Handbook

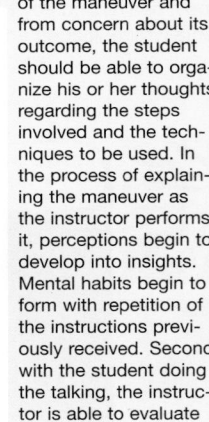

This old-school government manual for flight instructors is the best how-to guide I have come across for teaching, learning, communication and professionalism about any subject. It says almost nothing about aviation, and everything about how to teach. It's called *The Aviation Instructor's Handbook*; the full text is available for free as a PDF download.

-- Ronald Fuller

It's really pretty good. Covers all kinds of pedagogical approaches, and is especially good for teaching material where both head and body skills are needed. Think of it as a general "Instructor's Handbook." Short of signing up for a teacher's degree, I haven't seen anything else as thorough, explicit, and succinct in how to teach teaching.

-- KK

•

Student Tells — Instructor Does

This is a transition between the second and third steps in the teaching process. It is the most obvious departure from the demonstration-performance technique, and may provide the most significant advantages. In this step, the student actually plays the role of instructor, telling the instructor what to do and how to do it. Two benefits accrue from this step. First, being freed from the need to concentrate on performance of the maneuver and from concern about its outcome, the student should be able to organize his or her thoughts regarding the steps involved and the techniques to be used. In the process of explaining the maneuver as the instructor performs it, perceptions begin to develop into insights. Mental habits begin to form with repetition of the instructions previously received. Second, with the student doing the talking, the instructor is able to evaluate the student's understanding of the factors involved in performance of the maneuver. According to the principle of primacy, it is important for the instructor to make sure the student gets it right the first time. The student should also understand the correct sequence and be aware of safety precautions for each procedure or maneuver. If a misunderstanding exists, it can be corrected before the student becomes absorbed in controlling the airplane.

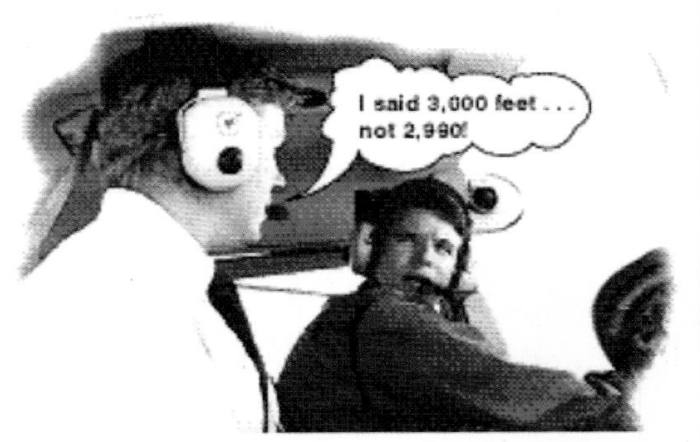
I said 3,000 feet . . .
not 2,990!

Figure 9-2. The assignment of impossible or unreasonable goals discourages the student, diminishes effort, and retards the learning process.

Trick questions, unimportant details, ambiguities, and leading questions should be avoided, since they do not contribute to effective evaluation in any way. Instead, they tend to confuse and antagonize the student. Instructors often justify use of trick questions as testing for attention to detail. If attention to detail is an objective, detailed construction of alternatives is preferable to trick questions.

•

Questions containing double negatives invariably cause confusion. If a word, such as "not" or "false," appears in the stem, avoid using another negative word in the stem or any of the responses.

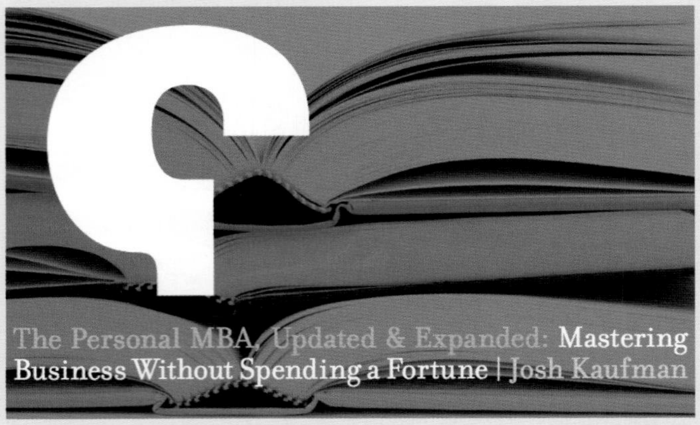
The Personal MBA, Updated & Expanded: Mastering Business Without Spending a Fortune | Josh Kaufman

Business self-education

The Personal MBA

Free PDF Josh Kaufman, 2005, 33 p.

I once dabbled with the idea of getting an MBA. After a life avoiding any work in a business, I wanted to start one of my own and knew zero about it. Like many folks, I thought a heavy-duty school program would cure my ignorance and inexperience. But an official MBA degree can easily cost $100,000. I figured out I would learn more spending $500 in self-education. So I devoted $200 for books and the other $300 actually starting a small mail-order business (the fee went for an ad). In two years I learned more about how business really worked than any MBA graduate I had met. No matter what they tell you, an MBA is not essential for landing or handling a good business job. The chief "skill" you'll come away by your degree is a diploma, and a network of indebted friends in business. The latter is actually useful.

There is another option to an overpriced degree, which is the self-education path outlined above. Pursue your own Personal MBA in tandem with actual experience doing some kind of business. Josh Kaufman has put together an excellent and very hefty reading list which forms the core of his PMBA course. It is downloadable as a free PDF. The recommended readings are wide, deep, holistic, and very good. You could purchase all of these easily available books for $500, and if you combine study of them with actually trying stuff, you'll be far ahead in the business game.

If you go this route, you need to supplement your self-education with a network of live humans engaged in business (the only part of a certified MBA you'll miss).

-- KK

•

The Personal MBA is not:

A credential. If you read these books, you won't have corporate recruiters beating down your door, and you won't have a pretty certificate to hang on your wall when you're done. You will, however, have an understanding of business that's comparable to completing a traditional business school curriculum, along with the pleasures of not having to mortgage your life for that understanding. You do not need a certificate to be able to understand, use, and hold an intelligent conversation about advanced business topics. (Employers do, however, respond well to portfolios. If you build a portfolio of notes to capture what you learn through the Personal MBA, you'll have a tangible asset to prove your hard work and dedication during the interview process.)

A stand-alone venture. You can't learn about business solely from books (or sitting in a classroom); you have to be willing to go out and learn by doing. Whether you're working full-time for a company or building your own business, a great deal of your knowledge will develop as a direct result of your day-to-day work experiences, which provide the necessary context for understanding what you read. Reading books is not enough; application of what you read is essential.

Inspiring physics textbook

Motion Mountain

Free Christoph Schiller, 2012, 1498 p.

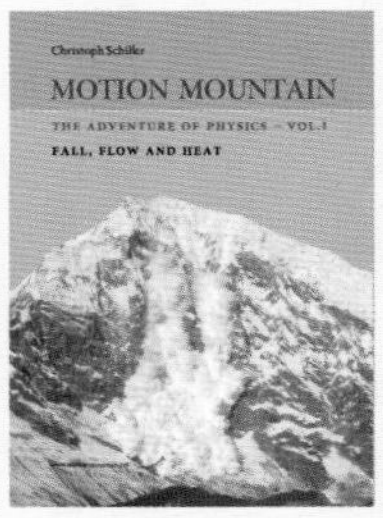
MOTION MOUNTAIN

This is not your father's physics textbook. It is the self-published 1,500-page (!!), still-unfinished physics textbook written and designed by your polymath genius uncle who dwells on a mountain with the spirits of departed philosophers (whom he quotes, in German). It's what a physics textbook would be like if a poet wrote it and made no mistakes. The book is massively visual. There is minimal math. It's a textbook with soul.

The guiding metaphor of *Motion Moutain*, and thus its name, is to frame physics as varieties of motion and change. When it gets to quantum mechanics it considers this in almost Taoist terms, as the "smallest change."

This textbook is a work of art. Unlike standard texts, it is an enthusiastically personal masterpiece, yet still has exercise problems for students to practice. It sprawls across topics you won't find in any other physics textbook: semantics, lying, color theory, the physics of pleasure. In many ways it reminds me of *Godel, Escher, Bach* (see p. 462) in its witty brilliance, stupendous range, and self-designed idiosyncrasies. *Motion Mountain* is an amazing portrait of the physical world as flux. It has the power to equip you with the intellectual tools to work with, and love, this flux. Studying it is an adventure in understanding.

Best of all, it is a free PDF book. A PDF means that it is hyperlinked to footnotes and intensely cross-referenced. And it is easily searchable. Every student — anywhere — can download a copy.

-- KK

•

Why do change and motion exist?

How does a rainbow form?
What is the most fantastic voyage possible?
Is 'empty space' really empty?
How can one levitate things?
At what distance between two points does it become
impossible to find room for a third one in between?
What does 'quantum' mean?
Which problems in physics are unsolved?

•

Astonishingly, it is actually impossible to distinguish an original picture of nature from its mirror image if it does not contain any human traces. In other words, everyday nature is somehow left-right symmetric. This observation is so common that all candidate exceptions, from the jaw movement of ruminating cows to the helical growth of plants, such as hops, or the spiral direction of snail shells, have been extensively studied. Can you name a few more? The left-right symmetry of nature appears because everyday nature is described by gravitation and, as we will see, by electromagnetism. Both interactions share an important property: substituting all coordinates in their equations by the negative of their values leaves the equations unchanged. This means that for any solution of these equations, i.e., for any naturally occurring system, a mirror image is a possibility that can also occur naturally. Everyday nature thus cannot distinguish between right and left. Indeed, there are right and left handers, people with their heart on the left and others with their heart on the right side, etc.

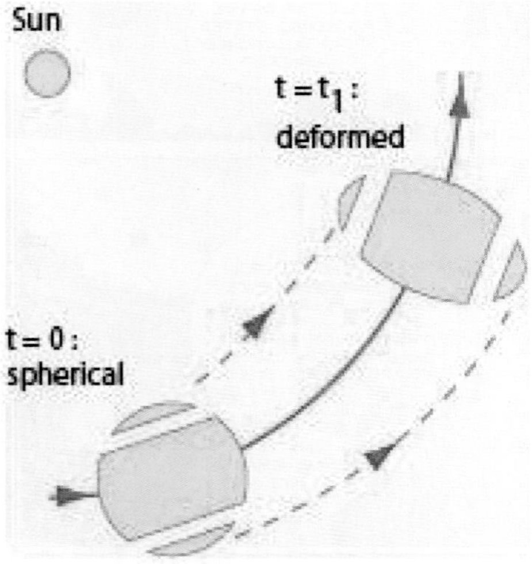
Sun
t = t1 :
deformed
t = 0 :
spherical

FIGURE 110 Tidal deformations due to gravity

•

Do all objects on Earth fall with the same acceleration of 9.8 m/s2, assuming that air resistance can be neglected? No; every housekeeper knows that. You can check this by yourself. A broom angled at around 35 degrees hits the floor before a stone, as the sounds of impact confirm. Are you able to explain why?

•

Sexual Preferences in Physics

Fluctuating entities can be seen to answer an old and not-so-serious question. When we discussed the definition of nature as made of tiny balls moving in a vacuum, we described this as a typically male idea. This implies that the female part is missing. Which part would that be? From the present point of view, the female part of physics might be the quantum description of the vacuum. The unravelling of the structure of the vacuum, as an extended container of localized balls, could be seen as the female half of physics. If women had developed physics, the order of its discoveries would surely have been different. Instead of studying matter, as men did, women might have studied the vacuum first.

•

When do clocks exist?

In general relativity, we found out that purely gravitational clocks do not exist, because there is no unit of time that can be formed using the constants c and G. Clocks, like any measurement standard, need matter and non-gravitational interactions to work. This is the domain of quantum theory. Let us see what the situation is in this case.... In short, quantum theory shows that exact clocks do not exist in nature. Quantum theory states that any clock can only be approximate. Obviously, this result is of importance for high precision clocks. The quantum of action implies that a precise clock motor has a position indeterminacy. The clock precision is thus limited.Worse, like any quantum system, the motor has a small, but finite probability to stop or to run backwards for a while. You can check this prediction yourself. Just have a look at a clock when its battery is almost empty, or when the weight driving the pendulum has almost reached the bottom position. It will start doing funny things, like going backwards a bit or jumping back and forward.When the clock works normally, this behavior is strongly suppressed; however, it is still possible, though with low probability. This is true even for a sundial.

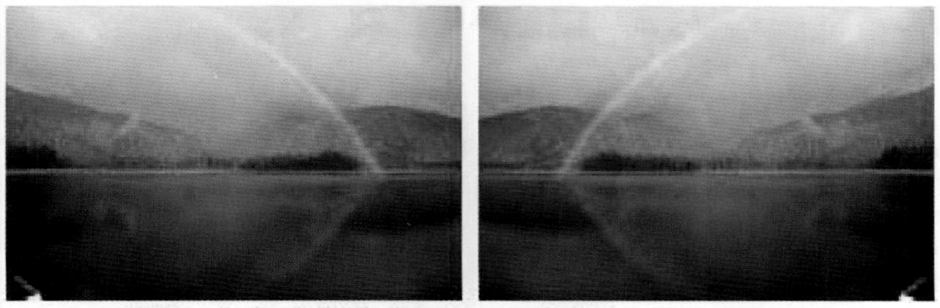

FIGURE 333 Which one is the original landscape? (courtesy NOAA)

The greatest challenge to any thinker is stating the problem in a way that will allow a solution. - Bertrand Russell

How to get a real education

The Teenage Liberation Handbook

$18 Grace Llewellyn, 1998, 435 p.

This book is radical. It tries to persuade teenagers to drop out of high school -- in order to "get a real life and education" as its subtitles says. This is a dangerous thing to give to your child, because there is a significant correlation between amount of formal education and almost any outcome you care about, including longevity, divorce and poverty rates. Yet informal homeschoolers and unschoolers are outside of that measurement, and by most accounts are doing super. As a college dropout myself, I am sympathetic to alternatives to school.

The purpose of this book is to encourage the teen to make their education their own responsibility. They can remain at school, or as a homeschool take only some classes, or find apprenticeships, volunteer, or even skip directly to college. In short they are designing their own self-education, where ever it may happen. Along the way they develop a better idea of themselves and many more life skills than they would in formal school.

Today as the quality of the average public education declines these ideas are not as extreme as when the book was first written in 1991, but they still aren't as accepted and common as they should be either.

This is a dense, packed book, overflowing with ideas, tips, anecdotes, cautions, and multiple views -- all speaking to the teen and not to parents. It does not lay out a 1, 2, 3 plan. It is messy, challenging. The book itself is probably a pretty good filter for whether the idea of self-education is a match for a young person.

Our son petitioned us to be unschooled, and it turned out that one year when he was 12 was sufficient. It was one of the best years in our lives. Yet in his liberation from school, he discovered what learning "on his own" really meant. It's challenging. He then chose to go to high school, but with a new attitude that he was in charge of how much and how well he learned. That new found responsibility for his own education made that one year of unschooling totally worthwhile.

There is a whole slew of homeschooling textbooks, advice, and well-crafted tutorials. All directed to parents. This is not one of those. This is a scribbled permission slip giving a teenage permission to consider alternatives for their own education.

-- KK

•

This book is a wild card, a shot in the dark, a hopeful prayer.

This book wants you to quit school and do what you love. Yes, I know, that's the weirdest thing you ever heard. Hoping to make this idea feel possible to you, I tell about teenagers who are already living happy lives without school, and I offer lots of ideas and strategies to help you get a real life and convince your adults to cooperate.

"Excuse me?" you interrupt, "Quit school? Right. And throw away my future and pump gas all my life and get Addicted to Drugs and be totally lost in today's world. Right."

If you said that, please feel free to march straight to the nearest schoolperson and receive a bushel of gold stars, extra credit points, and proud smiles. You've learned exactly what they taught you. After you get tired of sticking stars to your locker, do please come back and read further.

•

Suggest a trial run. you could start unschooling in the middle of August, so they have a couple weeks to see how you manage. Also, that would allow you to recover from the previous school year. You could agree that if they're not satisfied with your way of educating yourself, that you go to school. A drawback to this sort of timing is that you may feel cheated out of your normal summer vacation, and thus not as exhilarated as you would if you quit in, say, October. Also, the whole idea of being watched and evaluated runs contrary to the idea of pursuing interests because you want to. Still, you could probably psyche yourself into it and make it work.

•

If you are completely confused as to how to start structuring your life, here's one way: Do "academics" for two hours each day--not necessarily lots of subjects, or the same ones every day. You are not going to dry up in you don't do 45 minutes every day of "social studies." Do some kind of "work" or project for four hours. In your leftover time, read, see friends, talk with mom and pop, make tabouli. Take Saturdays and Sundays off. Sound arbitrary? It is. I made it up, although it is based on a loose sort of "average" of the lives of a hundred unschoolers, mostly college-bound. Once you try this schedule for month, you will know how you want to change it.

•

This book has said a lot of nasty things about school. Now it's going to say something nice. Schools have darkrooms, weight rooms, computers, microscopes, balance beams, libraries. They have choirs, bands, track teams, maybe even a Spanish class you want to take. Many enterprising homeschoolers have found ways to use the school resources they want without having to endure everything else.

This chapter tells about a few of those ways schools can cooperate with homeschoolers, and gives examples of particular homeschoolers who have taken advantage of school resources. If the schools in your area have never tried anything like this, you can pass this information along to them, and assist them in setting up a program that helps both you and them. Yes, them.

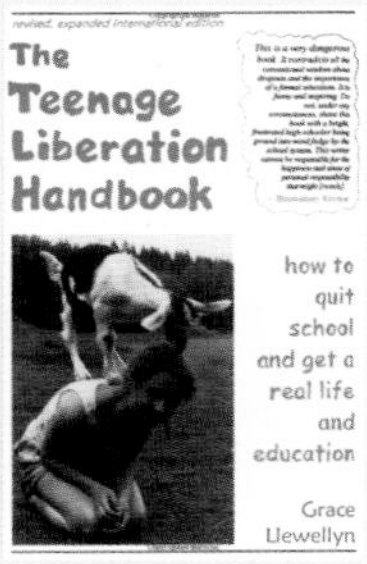

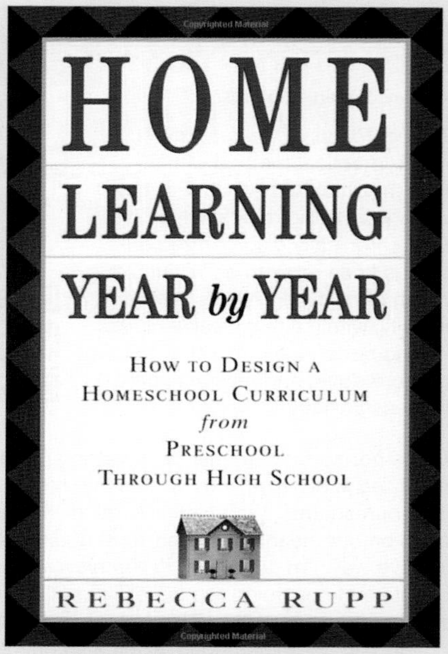

DIY school curriculum

Home Learning Year by Year

$12 Rebecca Rupp, 2000, 432 p.

When we homeschooled we were more into unschooling -- ditching a formal curriculum -- rather than replicating a school at home. Still, much learning benefits from structure, progression, and well, a curriculum. You'd like to have a good text book for geometry, or grammar. Or some order to present science concepts. There's a huge industry selling extensive and expensive curricula to anxious new homeschooling parents. My advice is to get this book and assemble your own.

For each grade from pre-school to high school, the author and novelist Rebecca Rupp outlines reasonable skills and knowledge a pupil could master at that stage for different subjects. Rupp then recommends a refreshingly diverse set of resources for that subject and level, including the best textbooks that work at home, expansive readings around the subject, and even video series when available. You select from her highly curated selections and find the ones suited to your child(ren).
In our experience her recommendations and options are excellent. They will likely be on the challenging side, rather than dumbed-down. And unlike many (if not most) homeschooling guides this one is not hampered by a dogmatic religious perspective.

Even if you are not homeschooling, kids learn at home, and this book would serve well to enlarge your child's formal schooling.

This guide supersedes the author's previously recommended *Complete Home Learning Source Book*, which is a bit outdated and not as well organized.

-- KK

•

Grade Six: Language Arts

Read a wide range of age-appropriate fiction and nonfiction materials. Kids should read a mix of classic and contemporary literature, novels and short stories, myths and legends, fables and folktales, poems, plays, essays, magazine articles, and newspapers. Literary experience should be enhanced with a range of supplementary resources, including biographies of writers, audio and video performances, and hands-on and cross-curricular activities.

•

At this grade level, kids should learn the techniques of writing an effective multiparagraph essay: defining a main purpose or thesis, supporting the thesis with evidence and examples, distinguishing unsubstantiated opinion from proven fact, using relevant quotes from attributed sources, and providing a bibliography.

They should be able to tailor their writings to a chosen audience or purpose: personal, academic, or business, for example.

Book to access books

Teach Your Child to Read

$13 Sierfried Engelmann, Phyllis Haddox, Elaine Bruner, 1986, 395 p.

This book really works! My daughter could read at age three, and has now really discovered the joy of reading at a young age. There are so many skills that kids can learn for themselves once they master reading. This is truly one of the fundamentals that is worth the effort to instill as early as possible.

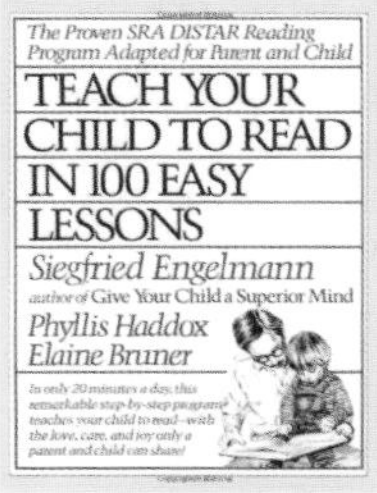

-- James Hom

•

The following are the four most important points about an effective sequence for teaching reading:

1. The beginning exercises are simple and do not resemble later exercises (just as beginning piano exercises do not look much like advanced ones).

2. The program provides teaching for every single skill that the child is expected to use when performing even the simplest reading exercises.

3. The exercises change form slowly, and the changes are relatively small, so that the exercises are always relatively easy for the child.

4. At every step, the program provides for very clear and unambiguous communications with the child.

•

To decode the sentence Ruf unter glop splee, you simply say the words. This illustration points out that you may be able to decode without understanding what the sentence means. Traditional reading programs typically confuse the beginning reader about whether the teacher is trying to teach decoding or understanding. These programs typically begin with the teacher discussing the details of a picture. If the picture shows a girl named Jan, the teacher talks about Jan—what she is wearing, the color or her hair….It might seem that this communication is effective because it promotes interest and gives the children the motivation for both reading and understanding the written message. However, this communication may prompt the child to formulate a serious misconception about how to read. If the teacher always talks about the picture before reading the word, and if the word is always predictable by referring to the picture, the child may reasonably assume that:

- You read words by referring to a picture.

- You must understand the word that is to be decoded before you can read it.

•

English, clearly, is not a regularly spelled language. It is an amalgam of contributions from Latin, Greek, and French. But there are ways to simplify it for the beginning reader.

Distar solves the problem by introducing an altered orthography. This orthography does two things. It presents variations of some symbols so that we can create a larger number of words that are spelled regularly (each symbol only having a single sound function). At the same time, the orthography permits us to spell words the way they are spelled in traditional orthography. Here is the Distar alphabet:

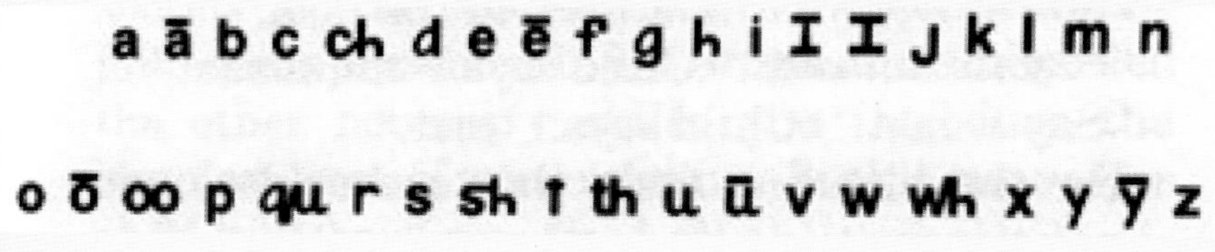

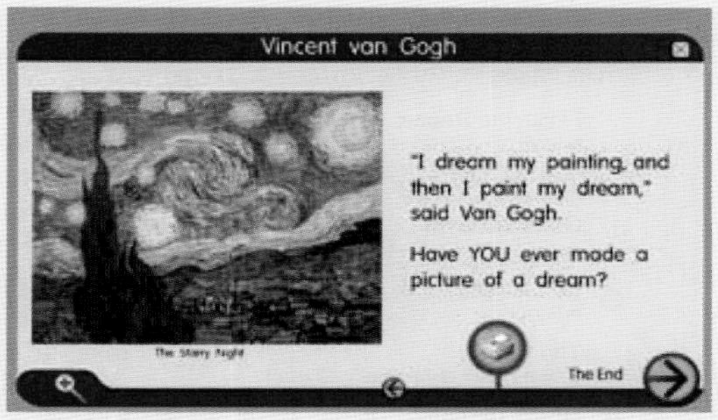

Free reading tutorials

Starfall.com

Free Starfall.com

Remember that greeting card company and famous-in-the-late-90s website Blue Mountain Arts? Well the extremely talented and philanthropic founders have started a learning-to-read website, totally free, called Starfall.com. My daughters, ages 6 and 7, have literally gotten more educational value out of this than their schools. And now their schools are using it in their classes once a week! Super site, makes the most out of flash and audio on a broadband connection, and really a treasure for young kids (aimed at first graders and below) who want to get going with reading (at no cost).

-- Jeff Blackburn

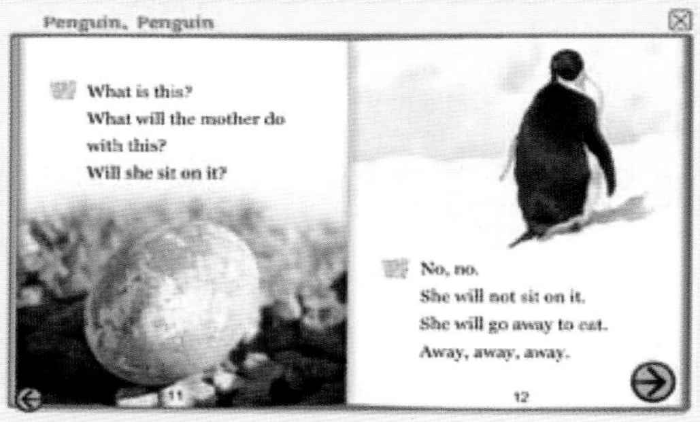

What a strange machine man is. You fill him with bread, wine, fish, and radishes, and out comes sighs, laughter and dreams. - Nikos Kazantzakis

397

Productivity

Getting Things Done

Stress-free productivity

$10 David Allen, 2001, 267 p.

Getting Things Done is a thoroughly practical method of handling the little things that over time comprise the big things in life. I've been chronically disorganized as long as I can remember. Within a month of following Allen's advice – actually, within a few weeks – I was making better use of my day, getting far more done, and feeling happier and less anxious.

Allen's not-so-hidden agenda in getting people organized is not simply to turn us into highly efficient bureaucrats. With a clearer mind, we can focus on our meaningful, long-term goals in a more creative way. I'm not sure if I've achieved Allen's favorite state of "mind like water," but I'm feeling a lot more fluid nowadays. This book is full of tricks to help you get things done, but it also offers an underlying challenge: Just what is it that you want to do?

-- *Marcel Levy*

●

Why Things Are On Your Mind

Most often, the reason something is "on your mind" is that you want it to be different than it currently is, and yet:

• you haven't clarified exactly what the intended outcome is;

• you haven't decided what the very next physical action step is; and/or

• you haven't put reminders of the outcome and the action required in a system you trust

●

Things rarely get stuck because of lack of time. They get stuck because the doing of them has not been defined.

●

Give yourself permission to capture and express any idea, and then later on figure out how it fits in and what to do with it. If nothing else (and there is plenty of "else"), this practice adds to your efficiency – when you have the idea, you grab it, which means you won't have to go "have the idea" again.

●

In mind-mapping, the core idea is presented in the center, with associated ideas growing out in a somewhat free-form fashion around it.

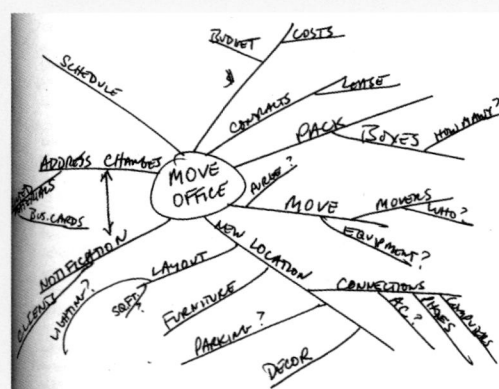

●

The big problem is that your mind keeps reminding you of things when you can't do anything about them. It has no sense of past or future.

●

Most people don't have a really complete system, and they get no real payoff from reviewing their list for just that reason; their overview isn't total. They still have a vague sense that something may be missing. That's why the rewards to be gained from implementing this whole process are at least geometric: the more complete the system is, the more you'll trust it. And the more you trust it, the more complete you'll be motivated to keep it. The Weekly Review is a master key to maintaining that standard.

Best digital compiling-filing

Evernote

Free, or $5/month, $45/year for Evernote Premium Evernote

I teach a lot of courses, and collecting information to keep them relevant takes time. If I'm on the Internet, I might come across something good. The old way: I'd save it to my desktop, drag it to the relevant folder, and hope to remember the file (and what's inside it) when the time comes to teach the course again. This process requires that I'm at the same computer every time–otherwise those files get lost. It took too much time, and required that I use my brain. I hate that.

Now, when I come across something, I copy it into Evernote.com. I've been using Evernote for about six months. It lets me manage research files and web clippings — something that sounds easy but isn't. If I'm at a school or library computer, no problem. I go to Evernote.com and paste it there. The note gets copied to my account and synched to all the computers I use. Evernote keeps track of where and when I got it, makes it searchable, and keeps it organized. It even presents clips nicely using a notebook (or scrapbook) metaphor.

Evernote is a like great digital filing cabinet or scrapbook–and it's easy to use, cheap and powerful. It acts like a good archive should, too: It organizes the information, preserves sources and presents it well.

Fabulously, Evernote reaches off the computer and into the paper world. If you upload a picture or scan a piece of paper, Evernote will process the file to extract the text and make whatever text it finds readable.

If I have my own ideas or something not on the web, I go to the desktop application. I can enter text, pictures, video and even audio there. The desktop app is a junior word processor. I can also drag and drop files from other applications, such as Word. These too get searched and synched between all of my computers.

I tried Google Notebook (not flexible and now defunct), DevonThink (not easy to use, not everywhere), and Zotero (not flexible). Evernote is head and shoulders above these others.

I don't have an iPhone, but I do have an iPod Touch. Evernote works really well on it. It only lacks an easy way to input handwriting, but that's easily worked around with a third-party scribbling program. I understand that an iPhone works even better: you can upload snapshots easily.

If, like me, you have to manage many files on many projects, you may find that Evernote does a lot without requiring much. It's cheap, too. There's a free version, a $5 a month subscription, and a $45 a year subscription.

-- *Adam Norman*

My favorite way to keep track of recipes is with Evernote. When I'm on a webpage that features a recipe I like, my first click is the Evernote button in my tool bar and then typically my second click, "Done," is my last. This file will then be searchable by every word on the page, and the source URL is also auto-

matically attached. Default presets can be chosen for virtually every option for saving and tagging the file with keywords for easy retrieval. Also, if there are multiple recipes on a page, I can select just the portion of that page that I want saved to Evernote, or the entire page.

Some of the many ways I'm able to save recipes to Evernote: I can take a picture with my Blackberry of a dish I'd like to recreate in the future, and among the toolbar's save options is "Add to Evernote." From my Blackberry, I can also upload a file or audio note (sudden salad dressing idea I had while driving) and add to Evernote. I can also use email or a DM note in Twitter to add text to my Evernote notebook.

When the time comes to look up a recipe, Evernote is very fast at searching, and if there's some identifying characteristic about a recipe, I'll note it with keywords when I initially save it, for example: "healthy," "freezes well," "vegan," "dessert," "try with tofu," or "pressure cooker."

Evernote's outstanding for acquiring and filing recipes, but it can be used for everything, and that's how I use it. For example, I researched a tire purchase and into Evernote went the Consumer Reports ratings and info, the data sheets from the manufacturer of the tires I was considering, the pages about these tires from Costco.com, the special offer information ($70 off 4 tires), a picture of my tire sidewall showing the tire size and finally, the purchase receipt after I ordered the tires from Costco. I am sure you can see how much time and hassle this saved me and how when I shopped, instead of a stack of papers, I just used my Blackberry.

-- *Kim Price*

Trusted task tracker

Toodledo

$3 iTunes Store

For more than 3 years, I have trusted Toodledo to keep track of all my jobs and errands for me. Using one of the tenets of GTD (see left) you need to find a "trusted system" and this is it for me. I can enter, view and update tasks at their website, or in various widgets, or in their iOS app, or by SMS, twitter, email or even command line. You can get the tasks to show up in Calendars, have priority ones emailed or texted to you, and there's also a nifty booklet printing option. The app tracks them for me so I don't have to fill my head trying and failing to remember all of them.

The web version is free, but power users can pay $14.95/year for more features still, including the ability to collaborate and share tasks to and from others in your team or family. The companion iOS app is $2.99, and does almost everything the website does, whilst being offline. Both it and the web-

site have been rock solid for me, and I have never had a problem syncing between the two.

For some reason it has never made as much splash as Remember The Milk or Things, but to me it has more consistently focused on adding useful new features – recently the ability to track real-world locations where you need to do jobs (for example a particular specialist shop, or your parents' house). When you add in the iPhone app, it will give you proximity alerts to remind you that there are things you need to do there.

I have looked at most of the to-do lists apps that have appeared over the years, and tried a few out for a while. I haven't yet regretted my decision to stick with Toodledo.

-- *Jonathan Clark*

Easy meeting scheduler

Doodle

Free Doodle

Doodle is an excellent web app that allows a bunch of people with disparate and complicated schedules to determine the optimal meeting time or date among them. It is the easiest of these types of tools I have tried, and does not require people to register or do anything other than fill in their name and check off boxes. It is free. Doodle has advanced features that allow you to do "if this, then that" type of scheduling as well, but I have so far just used the basic set up.

-- *Alexander Rose*

6 participants	AUGUST 2012 Fri 31 12:00 PM – 2:00 PM	SEPTEMBER 2012 Mon 3 9:15 AM – 11:15 AM	2:45 PM – 4:45 PM	Wed 5 9:15 AM – 11:15 AM	2:45 PM – 4:45 PM
Ms. Busy		✓		✓	
Kevin	✓	✓			
Nancy	✓	✓			
Ethel		✓	✓		
Dirk	✓	✓			
Fang		✓	✓		✓
Your name	☐	☐	☐	☐	☐
	3	5	5	3	2

The old man is always wrong; and the young people are always wrong about what is wrong with him. - Chesterson

Public access ebooks
How to Find Free and Cheap Ebooks
Free source-mfc; Paragraph style: Access-Info

Where I live, decent public libraries with connections to the software service Overdrive allow surprisingly easy checkout of "library books" wirelessly to your Kindle. The Overdrive system provides libraries with both audiobook downloads and eBooks. I find, like most, that reading or listening to these books on a computer is untenable, but transferring audiobooks to my Sansa Clip player is as easy as pie.

For the (increasingly) large selection of books with Kindle versions, it's very easy to get free content to show up via Amazon's Whispernet. Nothing fiddly about it, no cables either. And for the earlier cool tool of "User Manual First", Kindles are a pretty good place to keep these PDF files. Either transfer via cable (easy) or use your Kindle's email address which allow your docs to show up via Whispernet.

Finally, if you sign up for Amazon Prime service, you not only get free shipping on your purchases, you also get access to the "Kindle Owner's Library" – more books without fees. And if your Kindle is a Fire (or you don't mind watching on a PC), you also get access to lots of streaming video (my wife is re-enjoying Ally McBeal (and I'm enjoying not being exposed to it, too)).

Anyway, go to your library's website and look for Overdrive services. Another convergence of several cool tools that merge to form a new level of cool tool.

-- Wayne Ruffner

Retailers like Amazon and Barnes and Noble have the lock on bestsellers and the like, but a flourishing underground market for free and cheap ebooks has become a boon for readers.

The best established source for free ebooks is Project Gutenberg whose archives contain over 36,000 ebooks that represent nearly every out-of-copyright classic piece of literature along with a vast archive of obscure but pleasurable reads. The quality of digitization is excellent, and the site's vibrant community ensures that any errors are quickly fixed. They also offer the ebooks in a variety of formats (ePub, mobi, html), including some as downloadable audiobooks.

With more and more libraries getting into the game of lending ebooks, the software company Overdrive (that Wayne mentioned) has been leading the way. Libraries contract out their ebook libraries to OverDrive who make them available for a limited loan period (via a proprietary DRM from Adobe) through their software that is available on most operating systems including iOS and Android. Once you have the application, simply add your local or state library system (some are better stocked than others) and Overdrive allows you to browse the ebooks that they have available to check out. Everything's automated so there are no late fees, and often times you can get best sellers without waiting (or, if they're "checked out" you can reserve them and when they become available they are automatically downloaded).

ManyBooks.net is the friendliest index of free ebooks of the bunch. It will search Project Gutenberg's archives, as well as troll through numerous other archives. They also provide recommendations and reviews (which is incredibly useful given the sheer number of available titles).

Outside of strictly free sources, InkMesh is the best search engine I have found for identifying if an author or a book is available in ebook form, whether it is free, where I can download it, and in what format. They have also collated a comprehensive list of free ebooks available for a variety of platforms.

Two more sources for the ebook crazy are the blogs Pixel of Ink and Books on the Knob which highlight attractive deals for the Kindle.

Finally, to manage this inundation of ebooks I heartily recommend the previously reviewed Calibre. If you have other recommended sources for eBooks and the like, feel free to leave a note in the comments and I'll make sure to update this page.

-- Oliver Hulland

Free Overdrive
$79/year (or $39/year for students) Amazon Prime
Free Project Gutenberg
Free ManyBooks.net
Free InkMesh
Free Pixel of Ink

Digital magazines
Long Form * Instapaper
Free Long Form
Free Instapaper
Free The Feature

Longer than a newspaper item but shorter than a book, a magazine article is the ideal length for my attention span. I'd rather spend an hour with a great magazine article rather than read a book any day. Ditto for hopscotching through shallow blogs and newspaper bits. But there are fewer print publications running long form journalism. Ironically, a new website, called Long Form, points to the best long form articles appearing anywhere in print, and also collects the great magazine articles from the past. Long Form fits perfectly into a small ecosystem whereby you can read these great pieces of writing on a Kindle, iPad, or phone. I've found the easy-reading portable screens of these tablet devices fit a 1 to 2-hour window perfectly.

Here is how this system works. The Long Form website lists great magazine articles just published as well as past hits from the archives. You mark the articles you want to read, which are then downloaded to your tablet via Instapaper, another

NONE DARE CALL IT CONSPIRACY
SCOTT ANDERSON / GQ / SEP 2009

Banned in Russia and cut by Conde Nast from the *GQ* website, this story (presented in full) details the intrigue behind the Moscow apartment bombings, blamed on Chechens, that allowed Putin to rapidly ascend to power.

`Read Later`

website, which has an iPad app and Kindle connection. You can then read the articles, without ads, at your leisure on your gadget. The whole migration is seamless and unconscious.

I mentioned this was an ecosystem. You can also select pieces to read on your tablet or phone directly at Instapaper, which does not specialize in long forms but also includes short pieces. Instapaper's sister site, The Feature, like Long Form, makes reader selections of the best magazine articles. On both sites you hit a button "Read Later" to move it to your reading device. In fact you can mark any web page to be "read later" from an Instapaper button on your menu bar and it will move it to your tablet, phone, or even RSS feed. And you can send to Instapaper (and therefore to your reading device) any item from your Twitter stream or social apps like Delicious or Digg, Reddit, etc. to be read later on your Kindle or iPad (or computer screen).

However, I prefer to read long form factuals, and so I keep returning to Long Form to find the gems. I particularly enjoy classic great magazine pieces that I missed over the years. In fact, I realized that I've never seen a list of the best magazine articles ever, but see no reason not to make one now. If you have a nomination for one of the top 100 magazine articles of all time, please send it to me (with a link if possible). I'll share what I accumulate on this page here.

-- KK

Free Long Form

Short digital installments of long books
DailyLit
Free DailyLit

DailyLit sends you bite-sized chunks of public domain books (including many classics) daily, on weekdays, or three times a week via email or RSS — for free. Each serving takes less than five minutes to read, and if you want, they'll send you the next installment right away if you click a link. So far, I've read "Bartleby, the Scrivner" — 18 segments over the course of 3 weeks or so — and I just signed up for Crime and Punishment – more than 240 segments! Yes, it may take 9 months to read, but I'm certainly more likely to finish it this way. I read them in my email reader (Thunderbird) and don't print them out. The whole idea is to read short segments for a few minutes in your spare time. I'd imagine it would work well on a PDA or Blackberry if you have one (I don't); if you have a long cab ride or something you can get the next segment immediately.

--Jonathan Fromme

Tech knowledge subscription service
Safari Books Online

I've had a subscription to Safari for over five years now. For a monthly fee (pricing is dependent on the plan you choose), Safari grants you instant access to thousands of tech and business-related digital books. New titles become available surprisingly regularly and quickly (occasionally Safari will get the digital version of a title before Amazon does). In short, the service gives me access to a wealth of knowledge in a much less expensive and more convenient manner than any alternative.

-- Loren Bast]

$20/month for 10 titles Safari Books

$46/month unlimited,

Books

This is my library. I guess you would have to say all the rest of these books are books that did not change my life, although they tried.

Books That Changed My Life

Some books still have the power to change lives.

I don't mean merely great books, or memorable ones, or favorite ones. I mean books that altered your behavior, changed your mind, redirected the course of your life. Books as levers.

Here's my list, in the order they entered my life. (I'm not the only one affected by these books because each of these titles has a Wikipedia entry, if you'd like to know more.)

Childhood's End — For a kid growing up without TV in the boring enclaves of suburbia in the 50s and early 60s, science fiction opened up my universe. I devoured any and all science fiction our public library contained. Arthur C. Clarke's stories in particular birthed a life-long interest in science, and a deep respect for the power of imagination. This story of a singularity always stuck with me as something to prepare for.

Whole Earth Catalog — When I was 17 this big catalog of choices gave me permission to have my own ideas, make my own tools, follow my two loves of art and science unabashedly, and invent my own life. Decades later, I worked at the *Catalog* in my first real job. Cool Tools is just the electronic version of this book.

The Fountainhead — I got sucked into reading this over-the-top manifesto of self-reliance during finals of my first year of college. By the end of the book I decided to drop out of school. I never returned. It was the best decision of my life.

Leaves of Grass – While reading this classic poetic ode to America and its possibilities ("I am multitude!") my gasket blew and I became seized with an unstoppable urge to travel. I set the book down and bought a ticket to Asia. I roamed there off and on for 8 years. It was my university.

My Experiments with Truth — This autobiography of Gandhi curiously led me to Jesus. Gandhi's stance of radical honesty prompted me to attempt the same. I was surprised it took a tough Hindu to make me a tender Christian.

The Bible — Reading this all the way through, beginning to end, shattered all expectations I had of such a foundational text. It was weirder, stranger, more disturbing and more powerful than I was lead to believe. I've read through several times more and it never fails to disturb me.

Godel, Escher, Bach — I was amazed and impressed by the brilliance of GEB when I first read it, but it didn't change my life. However over the years I kept finding myself returning to its insights, and each time I would arrive at them at a deeper level. Now I find them my own thoughts, and I realize I now see the world through a similar lens.

The Ultimate Resource — Another book whose influence took time to establish. Simon's clarifying insight — that mind and intelligence can overcome any physical limitations, and is therefore the only scarce resource — has become a big idea that colors much of what I look at.

Finite and Infinite Games — This small, short book provided me a vocabulary to think about the meaning of life — not just my life, but all life! It gave me a mathematical framework for my own spirituality. As it says, the game is to prolong the game, to rope all beings into playing infinite vs finite (win-lose) games, and to realize that there is only one infinite game.

What's your list of Books That Changed Your Life? A book cannot be said to change your life unless it can be annotated with the tangible consequences you made as a result of reading it.

-- KK

The Thumb Thing
$3 ABC Stuff

When I was a teenager I remember reading a science-fiction story which predicted that by the 21st century, information would be piped directly into the brain. In this story, a character encountered that most archaic object, an old-fashioned book, and felt appalled that people in the 20th century had been forced to endure so much physical discomfort, holding books and turning their pages manually – or trying to prevent the pages from turning if there was a breeze.

Well, here we are in 2013, and yet another science-fiction prediction has failed to pan out. While we're waiting for wetware implants, we'll just have to make do with a stopgap solution: A plastic thumb aid. Works better than not having it.

-- KK

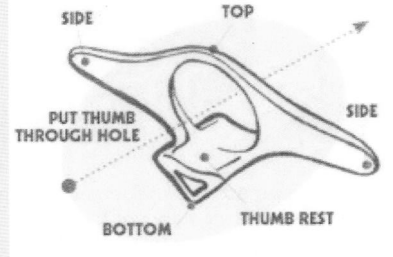

Home library catalog system
Bookpedia

 **Bookpedia**
What's on your shelves?

When your home library swells to 3,000 volumes (as ours has), finding a book can be a problem. In fact it can be a problem with only a few hundred books.

We use Bookpedia, by bruji.com, to index our library. Bookpedia runs on a Mac and keeps a database that's easy to share across your machines, or export in various ways (e.g., put all of your library's book covers on browsable web pages). A companion iPhone app, Pocketpedia, syncs with the database so you can keep your whole library catalog handy. There are two methods of input: you can scan a book's ISBN barcode with the iPhone running Pocketpedia; or, you can search for the book (any bit of author/ title/ISBN/description), and

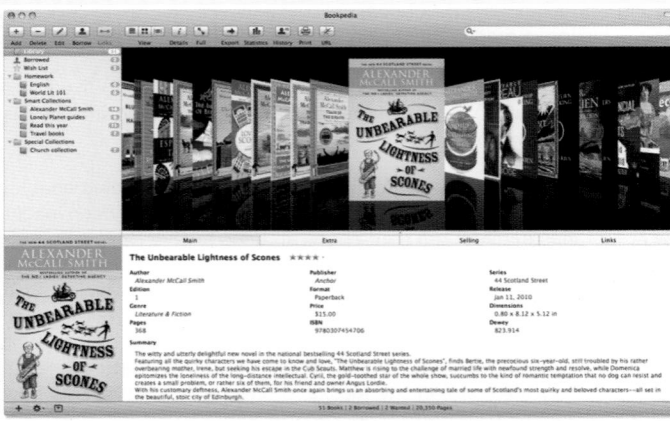

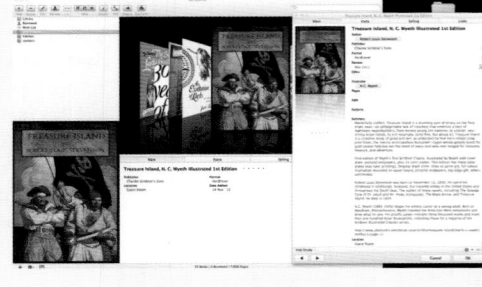

then resolve the right result. Both will get you the book's cover image and catalog information.

To build the catalog, we scan a shelf at a time, and add a "Location" field to note which physical shelf it is (e.g., "Upstairs 1-4 is bookcase 1, shelf 4"). This is easier than it sounds. If your books are new, just scan the ISBN barcodes with the iPhone, zipping through as fast as you can wrangle the books. But most of my books are older. So, I use my iPhone (running iOS 6+) to take a panoramic photo of each shelf, swiping it slowly across so that all the book spines can be read. And then I can go through a shelf and add each book by looking up title/author bits.

Hey, wouldn't it be great if you could capture your whole library the way Jeff Martin did with the Strahov Monastery, by shooting a gigapixel image and then using a bit of smart image analysis code to grok all the book spines, index the room, and be able to zoom into each book in the image, click on it, and read a digitized copy on the web?

Well, until that bit of imaging/AI/webwork is implemented, it's easy enough to peck in the titles myself. Bruji searches through a list of international databases (from Amazon to the Library of Congress and other z39.50 servers), and with a little extra help from Bing or Google image search you can usually find the best cover image and resolve the cataloging bits in a minute or two per book.

It doesn't really matter how the books are organized, because I can query Bookpedia, go to that shelf, and find it fast enough.

Because we live in a loft, we built a whole wall system, about 18 feet high, in which the books are grouped by color (which does help me: I remember the color of most of my books pretty well), and we push the books to the back so that knickknacks can be piled in front. The whole shelving system is a grid, and Bruji tells me that Eric Valli's stunning photo book, HIMALAYA, is on shelf 3-4 — meaning, column 3 from the left, row 4 from the bottom. (And Michael Palin's HIMALAYA is in the Office on 6-6).

Bookpedia has some shortcomings. All cataloging programs do. But it does work, and the integrated iOS and MacOS apps and web exporting make it handy to use on all our devices.

-- *Michael Hawley*

 **$18 Bookpedia**

$4 Pocketpedia 3

When I pronounce the word Future, The first syllable already belongs to the past. - Wislawa Szymborska

The best non-western literature
The New Lifetime Reading Plan
* A Guide to Oriental Classics

張
飛

Zhang Fei (Yide), the third oath brother

Now that you have finished reading all the great books of the West, you might want to turn your attention to the rest of the world. There is an equally vast and equally great classical literature in what is known as the East. Few of these works make it onto the lists of Best Books Ever; furthermore, guides to this wing of the universal library are rare. Given our interdependence with other cultures, introductions to this literary realm are vital and urgent.

For simple reading lists (sometimes the most enjoyable way to enter) I direct you to Robert Teeter's Great Books Lists, a handy website which convenes in one spot all the published lists of oriental (and western) classics. For a more annotated guide, with proper orientation of where you might want to head, I would start with *A Guide to Oriental Classics*, from Columbia University Press. The third edition of this indispensable work incorporates many works only recently translated into English, as well as an expanded number of secondary readings and glosses. I can't think of any major works in the four regions of the Islamic world, India, China, and Japan that are not covered here. With each work you get a very short description and — very handy! — annotated pointers to available translations.

For a more contextual inclusion, I find *The New Lifetime Reading Plan* by Clifton Fadiman to be superb. This revised and expanded fourth edition of his venerable book now covers many more eastern classics than in his previous editions. The list of eastern works is still way too short, but he offers them with two advantages. Because his plan is organized chronologically, one gets a better sense of how an eastern work relates to the West, and secondly, for each work he spends a few pages outlining to the reader its importance and a summary of its content, which *A Guide to Oriental Classics* does not. You'll get a better perspective from his select list, but you'll have more of an adventure with the Columbia University roster.

-- KK

●
From Robert Teeter's Great Books Lists

The Conference of the Birds of Farid Al-Din Attar (ca. 1142 – ca. 1220)

A sophisticated literary treatment, in fable form, of the stages of religious experience in man s contemplative journey toward union with God, by a Persian Sufi.

Translation: Darbandi, A. and D. Davis, trans. The Conference of the Birds. London: Penguin Classics, 1984. The best translation, recommended for general education.

●
Journey to the West, or Monkey (Hsi Yu chi), by Wu Ch eng-en (ca. 1506 – 1581)

A highly imaginative fictional account of the epic pilgrimage to India of the Buddhist monk Hsuan-tsang, by the sixteenth-century novelist Wu Ch eng-en.

Translations

Yu, Anthony C., trans. Journey to the West, 4 vols. University of Chicago Press, 1977-84. Pbk ed. A highly literate and graceful as well as complete and accurate translation. Its length may make it unsuitable for general education purposes, but samples may be used with great profit.

Waley, Arthur, trans. Monkey. New York: John Day, 1944, Pbk eds., New York: Grove, Evergreen, 1958. Harmondsworth: Penguin, 1961. Though much abridged (omits the poetry in the original) and containing occasional minor errors, a delightful translation. (Excerpts from A Guide to Oriental Classics)

●
From from The New Lifetime Reading Plan

The Cloud Messenger and Sakuntala, Kalidasa, ca. 400

Kalidasa is sometimes described as "the Shakespeare of India"; certainly he is universally regarded as the most accomplished stylist in the Sanskrit language in all of Indian literature. It may seem odd, then, that almost nothing is known about him. The Cloud Messenger (Meghaduta) is a poetic monologue in 210 stanzas; if one were to place it approximately in a genre of European verse, one could call it a pastorale. The conceit of the poem is that a young nobleman in the guise of a yaksa (a minor nature deity) for some unspecified offense has been exiled to a remote mountain. He misses his beauti-

ful young bride, and imagines that she is pining for him as well at their palace in the Himalayan foothill city of Alaka. Seeing a passing cloud on the mountaintop, he asks it to float to Alaka and deliver a message of love and comfort to his wife. This gives the poet, in the voice of the young yaksa, a chance to describe the rivers and mountains, towns and cities that the cloud will pass on its way to deliver the message; the poem is a sort of travelogue in the form of a love letter. The tone of the poem, and the highly formal structure of the verse itself, is elevated and refined; the fanciful mission entrusted to the cloud messenger seems paradoxically all the more passionate for that air of elegant restraint.

●
Shah Nameh, Firdausi, ca. 940-1020

Firdausi, the pen name of a man of obscure origins named Abul Kasim Mansur, is generally regarded as the greatest poet in the history of the Persian language. But if we think of Firdausi as an historian, we find that he fits no mold that we ve encountered thus far in the Plan. His history resembles neither the majestic sobriety of Thucydides, nor the cheerful credulousness of Herodotus, nor the systematic organization of Ssu-ma Ch ien. More than any of these, Firdausi resembles Homer; he is historian as bard. His strength is in pure narrative; he has an eye for the telling detail and the illuminating anecdote, and the elegance of his poetry (apparent to some degree even through the screen of translation) carries the work through occasional dry spells in the action.

$49 A Guide to Oriental Classics Edited by Theodore De Bary, 1989, 325 p.

$12 The New Lifetime Reading Plan: The Classic Guide to World Literature, Revised and Expanded Clifton Fadiman and John S. Major, 1998, 378 p.

A shopper's guide to graphic novels
Graphic Novels
$20 Paul Gravett, 2005, 192 pages

Okay, so you've read Maus. What's next? This book will turn you onto a hundred more great graphic novels (you know, comics for adults) that "will change your life." If you've been wondering what all the fuss is about, this guide is a great way to get into the only part of book publishing that is growing (the graphic novel section of large bookstores can be measured in yards). The author, fan-boy Paul Gravett, selects graphic novels that are contemporary (not classic super-heroes), easily found, in book form (rather than serial magazines), and are beyond mere colorful fantasy, and not just dark teenage angst. They are great stories, with very personal art, in a wonderful cross between cinema and text. This guide is smartly designed and a joy to use. You get sample pages from choice works, Gravett's insightful comments and analysis, related books, and plenty of context to tell what you can expect from each book. It's one of the best shopper guides I've seen.

-- KK

●
The Monster ▶

David B. imagined his elder brother Jean-Christophe's epilepsy as a monster, a sinister dragon slithering through their lives and stalking him as well. This becomes the potent symbol for the disease in his graphic novel.

At first, David shows the monster as an external menace, holding Jean-Christophe in its coils or sharp teeth, whenever he has a seizure. But as the illness worsens, he realizes that his brother is giving in to it. Here he shows this point of surrender by drawing monster and brother merging into one, never to be separate again.

●
Rose ▶

Crucial background is revealed about the youth of Thorn's grandmother Rose and her sister, Princess Briar. In this encounter between Rose and her dragon guardian, she makes a promise to him, whose importance is accented by dropping the light in this key panel and illuminating her eyes.

Notice how cold is conveyed by showing the figures' breath — the dragon's being naturally larger. Written by Smith, this story is drawn by Charles Vess in delicate lines and rich colors, reminiscent of such masters of fantasy illustration as Arthur Rockham.

●
Blankets ▶

How does a boy raised to obey the Bible reconcile his deep faith and the stirrings of sexual attraction? Craig Thompson pieces together his answer, first by going back to the small cruelties inflicted on him by his parents, and to his guilt over failing to protect his younger brother. He blends these scenes with the slow unfolding of him falling in love with Raina, a girl he meets at church camp. Nothing is rushed, as here Thompson shows the first nearness of their bodies and frees them from confining panel borders. "Blankets" refers not only to the Wisconsin snow, but also to the bed that he and his brother once shared, and to the quilt that Raina makes him.

The truth will make you free. But first it will piss you off. - Gloria Steinman

401

Learning Languages

Language Acquisition Made Practical
DIY language learning
$22 E. Thomas Brewster and Elizabeth Brewster, 1976, 384 p.

This handbook teaches you how to learn any language on your own, in the language's home turf, by teaching a native speaker to be your teacher.

The trick is to instruct your local agent to teach you something he/she is hardly aware of — the structure of their language. You will supply the plan and so are teaching yourself through them. Comprende? It's done slowly, naturally, and playfully – the way you learned English. Your assistant doesn't even have to speak your language.

You begin using a few easy words, trying to make as many mistakes as you possibly can, entertaining the folks in the marketplace or anywhere else they'll put up with your blabberings. Then you systematically add additional words in steady daily use, guiding your guide in what you want to learn next. This well-tested method was devised by missionaries trying to learn languages lacking scripts, courses, or guidebooks, and works great for dialects, or indeed any language you want to learn.

The text of this workbook shows you how to construct your own exercises that fit the language you are after and later how to discover its grammar by yourself. The goal is multiculturalism, inseparable from multilingualism. Like realizing that you don't need a degree in anything to build your own house, learning that you can become fluent in another language without a course or classroom is deliciously radical.

If you like this approach check out other online texts by missionary linguists which take the same approach of enabling an intermediate to become your language teacher.

This DIY process works best on location, rather than before you arrive.

-- KK

• To prepare for a Comprehension drill, you need to plan a list of related activities and have Kino make up a 3 x 5 card with activities written in his language. The activities for the first day might include sit, stand, squat down, clap your hands, scratch your leg, stretch your arms. In the drill, Kino will instruct you in his language to do an activity; for example, "stand up." He will stand up and you observe and then mimic the action by standing yourself. Do not say what he does. Kino then introduces the second item, performing the activity while giving you the verbal instructions. You mimic the activity – for example, "sit down." Kino then again gives the first instruction, "stand

up," and you respond by standing. Then Kino can give the instructions without acting them out himself – "sit down," "stand up," and you respond to his verbal directions. When doing comprehension drills, respond rapidly without hesitation and make a distinct robust response with your body.

• Production of Modifiers

Kino says a sentence with modifiers. You repeat the basic sentence without modifiers.

Kino: "The blue jug with the pretty flowers is on the

Associate the word with the thing

high wooden shelf."

You: "The jug is on the shelf."

Then reverse roles — he says a simple sentence and you embellish it.

Kino: "This is a book."

You: "This is a good book about the people of this country."

Kino: "This is a candle."

You: "This is a red candle."

Raise the sides of the tongue

Look around you. You can talk about virtually any object, then restate it with modifiers.

• By using these sentence patterns you can get extra drill on new vocabulary while talking with people. You can touch an object and ask "What is this?" They may answer, "This is Kefala." You can then touch a similar object and ask "Is this Kefala?" and they will answer positively or negatively.

If you are talking with children, this can become quite a game and give you lots of practice with new words. Children will often catch on, and participate with you in the game. First, you can ask the questions while they answer. Then you can trade roles and let them ask the questions while you try to answer. If you enter into the spirit of the game, everybody can have fun while you practice vocabulary.

Elementary Chinese reading
I Can Read That!
$9 Julie Mazel Sussman, 1994, 161 p.

China figures big in the future no matter what your interest. It's a vast place with its own non-alphabetic writing in abundance. To get around you really need to be able to recognize a few Chinese characters. You can get by knowing the 50 or so basic ones taught in the small expert book. Elementary survival knowledge, like the symbols for toilet — men or women? Exit versus entrance. Numbers, dates, directions, hotel, etc. There is no attempt to teach you Chinese (thank goodness), just how to navigate a visit there.

-- KK

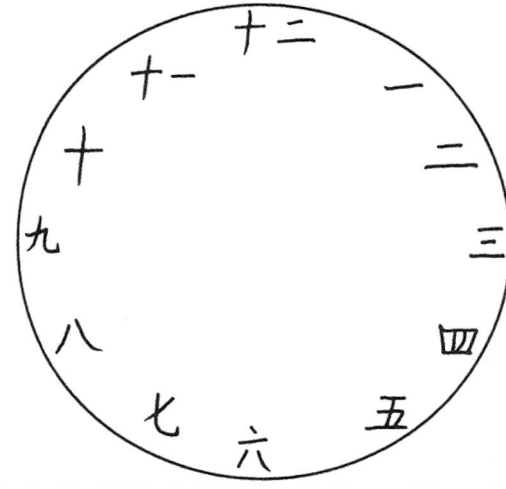

A clock for number practice. Real clocks use numerals, not characters. But this clock may help you learn the characters for the numbers. You can make hands for the clock out of toothpicks or paper.

"Exit" and "enter" signs. You'll see the same entrance and exit signs wherever Chinese characters are used.

Restroom signs. Along the Burma Road. This public facility has a two-syllable word for toilet and an arrow pointing to the female entrance.

Pocket-size Nippon phrasebook
Survival Japanese
$7 Boye Lafayette De Mente, 2003, 160 p.

For a two-week trip, we brought five guides. Survival Japanese is the only one I consulted everyday — at least one-third of its pages are now dog-eared. Rather than overwhelm with long word lists or complex explanations of how to form unique sentences, the book is broken into scenarios with simple phrases listed in English, Japanese (Romanized), Japanese characters and, most importantly, spelled phonetically in English. You just flip to whatever situation you're prepping for or have found yourself in… in a taxi, greeting people, paying bills, apologizing, asking questions, at the station, in a bar, visiting a home, medical emergencies (thankfully we had none) and more. Sure an extensive glossary with many more words would be nice; additional phrases for the same and other scenarios would also be useful. That's not the point with this one. If you're a true beginner, the book provides just enough in a package you won't mind stashing in a jacket pocket or tossing in a day bag. I still wish I'd learned more beforehand. Nevertheless, my new (and very polite) Japanese friends gave me an A for effort.

-- Steven Leckart

Singular/plural
There is no definite or indefinite article (i.e. the, a) in Japanese, and there are very few plurals in the language. With few exceptions, the sense of plural is made evident by the context of the phrase or sentence. *Tokee* (とけい) means watch (timepiece) or watches, depending on how it is used.

Superlative
It is very easy to "make" the superlative in Japanese. All you do is put the word *ichiban* (いちばん), meaning "first" or "number one" in front of the term you want to qualify. If big is *ookii* (おおきい), the biggest is *ichiban ookii* (いちばんおおきい); the longest is *ichiban nagai* (いちばんながい); the smallest is *ichiban chiisai* (いちばんちいさい); the highest is *ichiban takai* (いちばんたかい); the heaviest is *ichiban omoi* (いちばんおもい); the best is *ichiban ii* (いちばんいい), and so on.

Questions
In Japanese a question is indicated by the particle *ka* (か), usually enunciated with the same "questioning" tone used in English. In written Japanese this *ka* (か) takes the place of the familiar question mark.

The honorific "O"
It is customary in Japanese to add an honorific "o" or "go" before many words that refer to other people, to things relating to others, and to certain special words, as a sign of respect or as a polite gesture. In the sign-of-respect category are such words as *go-shujin* (ごしゅじん), meaning "your honorable" husband; *o-taku* (おたく), "your honorable" residence; *o-namae* (おなまえ), "your honorable" name; *o-toshi* (おとし),

It requires a very unusual mind to undertake the analysis of the obvious. - Alfred North Whitehead

Best way to learn French at home
French In Action

$225 French In Action Part I | Learner.org

French In Action is a video-based course created by Pierre Capretz of Yale University. I know of no better way to rapidly obtain a knowledge of day-to-day French. This course is so excellent it almost justifies the invention of television.

The French in Action course is focused around 52 half-hour video lessons which assume you have no prior knowledge of the language. The course starts in French from the first instant. You may feel like an idiot at first, but the fact is you can mess up genders, adjectival forms, and much of verb conjugation in French and still be understood perfectly well on the street.

Get this course and play one video per day, each and every day, week in and week out. Just pick a 30 minute time period in your day, and work your way through the videos from number 1 through number 52, one per day. When you get to the end, go back to the beginning and start over again. Repeat until you understand perfectly and have ceased to improve. Even if you don't have time to read the accompanying text, or practice with the workbooks, or use the audio cassettes, make the 30 minute slot for the video a permanent part of your life. The first time through you'll probably miss about 90% at first hearing. The second time, you'll get about half, and by the third time you'll understand almost everything. Your very progress provides strong reinforcement as you follow the course. Simply by watching this series of 52 videos through two times, you could parachute into Abidjan and get along in day to day life from the moment you hit the ground. It's that good. Really.

-- John Walker

Best way to learn Spanish at home
Destinos

$225 Destinos Part I | Learner.org

Based on a recommendation from John Walker, founder of AutoDesk, now living in a French-speaking part of Switzerland, I tried out the French in Action series (above). It is all that he promises. I was amazed how far I got so quickly merely by watching and responding to this series of ever deepening complexity. The key to progress is the vivid visuals, body language and corny involvement that the videos cultivate.

Inspired by the French method, however, I sought out a Spanish equivalent and found it in Destinos. Like French in Action, Destinos is a highly structured, highly-evolved video program based on an innovative professor's work, and published by the Annenberg Foundation. In Destinos, you again start off with no Spanish and very rapidly become sucked into a long Spanish telenovela. The story is cleverly designed to start basic and steadily leverage in sophisticated terms, so that by the 52nd show you can understand nearly everything in the first show. And then you start over.

Having gone through both courses, there are some differences. In French in Action you get a wild-haired French professor gesturing emphatically to convey weird French grammar, while cute little clips from French movies repeat a phrase in many voices so you can get used to hearing it spoken live. And the love story that forms the backbone narrative is heavily diagrammed in a French logical way. Destinos, on the other hand, is more relaxed and focuses almost exclusively on a very high-production detective mystery/soap opera which was filmed in 5 countries on 3 continents. It is easy to let yourself get hooked on the story, even though you are only catching 10% of it. Because Spanish is less distant to English speakers, there is less emphasis than the French on grammar and pronunciation. Destinos is more casual, go with the flow and you'll pick it up, while French in Action is more pedagogical and well… French.

The ideal way to learn a language is immersion, where you are forced to both listen, speak and read. Because of the nature of this medium — a series of videos — listening is the primary action stressed, although both programs give plenty of opportunity for reading and speaking. At the end of even the third time through your fluency will be primarily in comprehension — but you'll be in a great position to take it much further very fast.

Both of these programs share another very important feature; both are funded by Annenberg/CPB, a non-profit promoting innovation in schools. Recognizing the value of educational videos, Annenberg has funded the purchase of these series for public libraries. This means that almost every library system in the US has a copy of the series.

However, if you don't mind sitting in front of your computer you can get a completely free video stream of either Destinos or French in Action from the Annenberg website.

In a perfect world, someone wise would fund a similar well-crafted soap opera language series in Chinese for learning Mandarin, which is only spoken by 1 billion or so people. Or Arabic, Swahili, German, and so on.

In the meantime, buena suerte, or bonne chance!

-- KK

Foreign tongue acquisition software
Rosetta Stone Language Learning

$180 One Level (prices vary) Fairfield Language Technologies
$299 Levels 1 & 2 Fairfield Language Technologies
$319 Levels 1, 2, & 3 Fairfield Language Technologies

The slogan "The Fastest Way To Learn A Language. Guaranteed" may sound like a gimmicky promise, but none of the other "language lessons in a box" that you can get without joining the military, NASA, or the US Diplomatic core even remotely compares to this computer-based immersion program.

The genius of the process involves using pictures to teach you how to listen, speak, read, and write, rather than teaching by translation, as virtually all other language programs do. So as you learn your new language you associate the new words, phrases, and grammatical structures directly with the pictures rather than mentally translating through your native language. Using this method, most people can use a Rosetta Stone program regardless of native tongue, cutting out a major limitation of the translation-based language programs.

After a salesman at a mall gave me a demo for Vietnamese (which I've never studied before), I ordered a three-month subscription to the Russian program. I studied Russian in both high school and college, and went to Russia on "People to People" in 1991. At one point, I was getting very conversant, but couldn't say anything beyond the simplest phrases without mentally translating them into English. But after seven years of not actively studying Russian and rarely speaking it, my skills began to deteriorate. I was starting to be able to say things only on a very piecemeal basis (specific words, canned phrases, and common songs). Translation: I was losing my third language (I am fluent in Spanish).

Two months into the Rosetta Stone, which can be as addictive as a video game, I was able to enjoy the fast-talking film "Nochnoy dozor" ("Nightwatch") without the subtitles. I have also found that I can now think, speak, and read in Russian without doing a mental translation into English like I used to do. And I think that when I get the money to travel to Russia again, I will become permanently fluent.

It is true that I used the program as a refresher course, rather than to learn a language from scratch. But as a relative veteran when it comes to learning foreign languages with different teachers and methods — I've also studied German and picked up a good deal of French while traveling in Europe (forgot it in a matter of months) — here is my take:

If somebody wants to learn a language from scratch, most people could finish Level 2 with excellent conversational skills (a feat that took me 3 months, but would probably take a beginner more like 6 months). If you are starting from scratch, doing Level 1 would still be a good foundation and you could easily survive "in country" when it comes to day to day living [note: Rosetta Stone sells programs for 30 major world languages, but they only offer Level 2 for certain languages, and only Level 3 for Latin American Spanish and English (US)].

For the people who are learning from scratch, there might still be some value in more conventional methods of teaching. And, of course, being in a community where the language was spoken would speed up the process. A determined English speaker with a high aptitude for language could probably do the Latin American Spanish up to Level 3, and then zone in on fluency very easily with no other formal instruction. But for languages with non-Roman alphabets and more divergent grammar systems, conventional teach-

ing would not become irrelevant.

If you studied a language in school and got good grades, but can't really speak it, Rosetta Stone would be a really fun way to narrow the gap between book learning and real use. In short, I don't think an excellent language teacher has anything to fear from this tool, whether he/she works in a public school, university, a private language school, or as a private tutor. But the makers of all those crummy "language in a box" tools on the market have reason to be very, very afraid for their business.

-- Amy Scanlon

There are also online subscriptions that are cheaper. ex; In the case of Spanish Levels 1 & 2, $110 gets you three months, while $160 gets you six months of access

There's an even cheaper alternative: free. Many public libraries purchase Rosetta Stone and some even make it available online. Patrons can access it free, anywhere, using their library card number.

Guide to industrial landscape
Infrastructure

$75 Brian Hayes, 2006, 512 p.

Combining photos and clear, occasionally poetic descriptions, this thorough almanac deconstructs the general architecture and much of the minutiae found throughout the modernized world. From power and water plants to railroads, highways, airports, bridges, dams, docks, municipal dumps, and industries like ag and mining, the book illuminates the subtle and not-so-subtle: Manhole covers are round, making them easy to roll and impossible to fall in; huge rotary kilns force water out of mineral products; AEI scanners monitor railroad cars; the rooflines of mill buildings cascade since these operations use gravity to move materials from one section down to the next.

The industrial ecology of a utility pole (excerpted below) is what first hooked me. Choke coils, lightning arresters, bushings? I couldn't have picked them out of a police line-up if my life depended on it. Not anymore!

-- Steven Leckart

●
The Industrial Ecology of a Utility Pole

From top to bottom, here are some of the species you might observe in the utility-pole ecosystem:

- Primary distribution lines for electric power. These are the topmost wires. They are usually hung on a crossarm, and they come in groups of three, mounted on big insulators.

- Switches, fuses, and surge arresters. These connect to the primary distribution lines.

- Transformers. They are mounted below the primary distribution lines but above the secondary ones, with connections to both.

- Secondary distribution lines. Just below the transformer level, they are rubber-sheathed conductors carried on spool-type insulators or twisted around a steel messenger cable.

- Street-lighting fixtures. They draw their power from the secondary circuits.

- Traffic signals. These too are powered by the secondaries. The signal lights are often hung from a steel cable stretched between utility poles.

Everything from the top of the pole down to this level is the domain of the power company. Below is the realm of the communications lines, which operate on lower voltages and therefore don't need to be kept quite as far out of reach…

- Cable television feeders. These may be finger-thick coaxial cables, in either a black plastic sheath or a bare metal jacket. In newer systems the trunk lines that carry signals over longer distances are fiber-optic cables.

- Telephone cables. Often the thickest of all the wires strung on a pole, they are actually bundles of dozens or hundreds of pairs of fine copper wires. Fiber-optic cables also show up at this level.

Still lower — indeed, reaching the ground — are some wires that ought to have no voltage at all on them.

- Guy wires. Their function is strictly mechanical; they help to hold the pole up. There may be an insulator inserted into the guy wire for safety, iin case a power conductor should tough the upper part.

- Grounding lead. A pole with a transformer generally has a copper grounding wire that runs down the side of the pole and into the ground.

Finally, at eye level, comes the bottommost ecological stratum of the urban or suburban utility pole:

- The yard-sale zone, where the wood bristles with a thousand rusty staples.

Not a tree: disguised cellular telephone antenna tower, Cary, NC

Sewage-sludge digesters, Deer Island, MA

Maps that change with time
Centennia Software

$60 clockwk.com

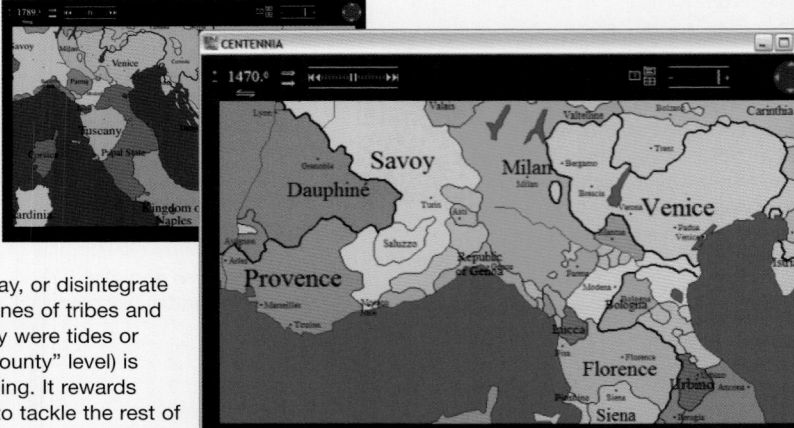

As a kid I dreamed of maps that would move; I got what I wanted in Centennia. This colorful political map of Europe and the Mid-East redraws itself at yearly intervals from the year 1000 to present. It's a living map, an atlas with the dimension of time. I can zoom around history, pause at particular dates, or simply watch how nations melt away, or disintegrate into tiny fragments, or unite! Year by year the outlines of tribes and nations spread, retreat, and reform almost as if they were tides or infections. The resolution of detail (almost at the "county" level) is astounding; the breadth of time (ten centuries) thrilling. It rewards hours and hours of study. I hope it inspires others to tackle the rest of the world. It works on both the Mac and Windows.

-- KK

Constitution primer
The United States Constitution

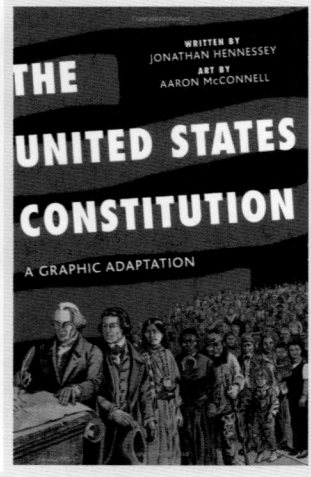

The US Constitution is one of the most remarkable inventions of all time. A lot of people in other countries think so too. It is a robust self-correcting legal OS. But it was written in an arcane code long ago. To make any sense from it you need some help.

This lively graphic novel adaptation of the Constitution is by far the best aid I've found to deciphering its code. It is the comic book version, but rather than dumbing it down, it smartens it up. The graphic novel goes through the Constitution article by article, and explains what each bit means, why it is there, and how it came to be. Like the Bible, the Constitution doesn't say what you thought it did. I was surprised what was not there as well as what was. I learned tons from this annotation, despite studying it in high school. It renewed my respect for it, and in a way, also makes clear its limitation. I feel I can be a slightly better citizen. Best of all, this book does all that with pictures, which makes it a page-turner.

Recently my brother-in-law, who is an immigrant, had a lot of questions about the Constitution. I handed him this book and he came back very informed. I gave it to my son who would normally have nothing to do with such boring material. But it's a comic! You've always wanted to read it, and should. Here's the perfect excuse and ideal method.

If you want the unadorned, raw text, get a pocket version. This sturdy shirt-pocket-sized one contains both the Constitution and the Declaration of Independence. I have a few friends who pack this pocket version in their travel bags. Good conversation starter.

-- KK

$5 Declaration of Independence and the Constitution of the United States of America, 2000, 58 p.

$12 The United States Constitution: A Graphic Adaptation 2008, 160 p.

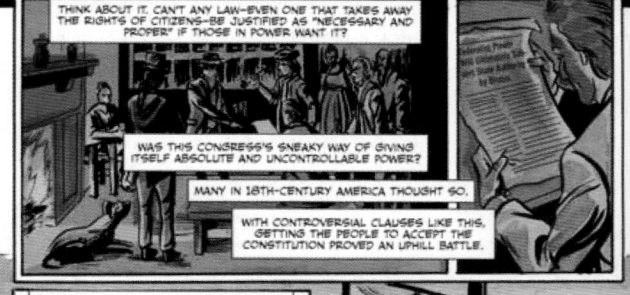

Science tourism hot spots

The Geek Atlas

$20 John Graham-Cumming, 2009, 542 p.

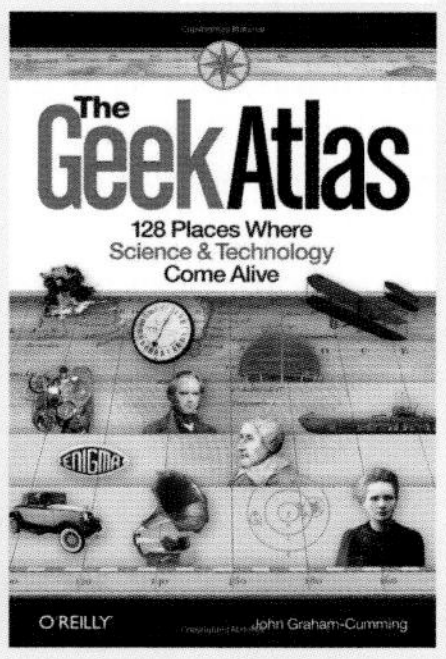

I am always looking for offbeat educational places to visit on my travels. The *Geek Atlas* has rounded up 128 great candidates from around the world. The Atlas calls them "places where science and technology come alive." I think of these destinations as places that make you think. The possibilities run the gamut from birthplaces of famous inventors and scientists (yawn) to really cool tours of working technological systems (a nuclear power plant, a dam turbine, a solar furnace) to a spectrum of interesting but little known museums, to just cool places like the prime meridian. A lot of these destinations are in the US and UK, but a fair number hail elsewhere. In addition to a description of a destination, author Graham-Cumming writes up a page explaining the key concept behind each spot. I've visited a dozen of these science hot spots and they are well worth a short detour, or in some cases a trip just for the purpose. You could probably fill another volume of brainy tourist traps missed by this book: I predict a sequel.

-- *KK*

•

Solucar PS10 Power Station, Sanlucar la Mayor, Spain ▼

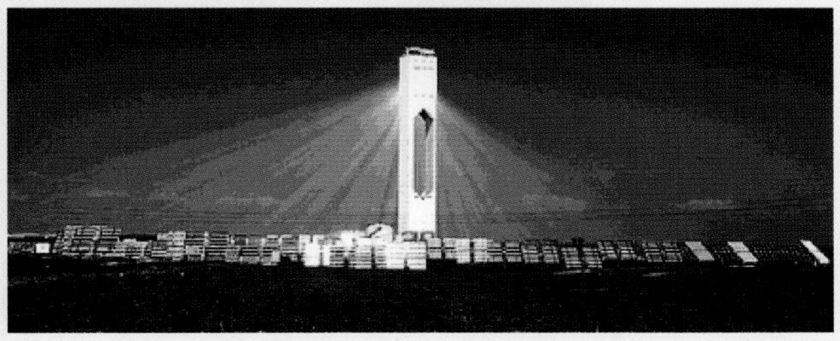

The tower is at the center of a field of heliostats (mirrors that track the movement of the Sun) that focus the bright Spanish sunlight onto a receiver near the tower's top. The reflected sunlight is so intense that water vapor and dust in the air glow white. All that's needed to complete the scene is a maniacal James Bond villain atop the tower.

This tower is at the center of the Solucar PS10 power station. At the top of the tower is a solar receiver that is heated by sunlight to create saturated steam at 257°C. The steam is then used to drive a turbine that generates electricity. Make sure you're wearing sunglasses when you look up to the top; the tower's brilliant white glow is very intense.

•

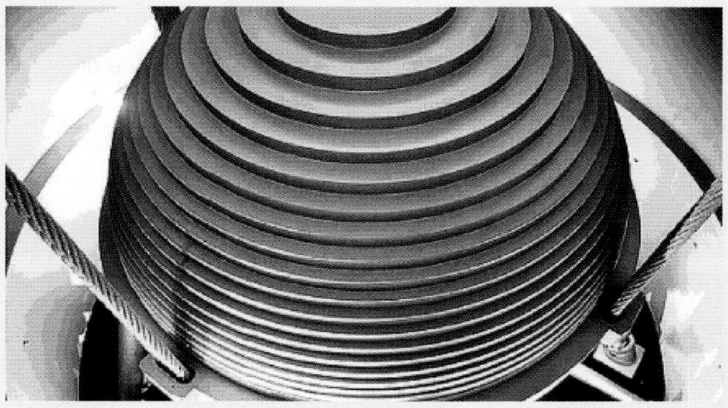

▲ Taipei 101, Taipei, Taiwan

The 660-Tonne Golden Ball

The Taipei 101 is the tallest occupied building in the world, with 101 floors overlooking Taipei's business district. But Taipei is prone to both typhoons and earthquakes, so the skyscraper contains a 660-tonne, gold-colored pendulum near the top to prevent the building from swaying and vibrating. It is the largest and heaviest such pendulum in the world.

Many skyscrapers contain such devices, called tuned mass dampers, for the same purpose, but the Taipei 101 pendulum is unusual because it is on public view. It hangs between the 87th and 91st floors, and there are public viewing areas on the 88th and 89th floors. It's even visible from the restaurant and bar. Two other tuned mass dampers, located in the building's pinnacle are not on display and are tiny by comparison: they weigh only 6 tonnes each.

The ball is made of forty-one 12.5-centimeter steel plates welded together for a total size of 5.5 meters. It is attached to the building by eight steel cables, each capable of supporting the ball's entire weight. In normal use the ball can move up to 35 centimeters in any direction and cuts building vibration by 40%. In a major typhoon, the ball is designed to move up to 1.5 meters; hydraulic bumpers below the ball absorb its energy and prevent it from moving too far.

When the building sways in one direction, the ball opposes the movement by swinging the opposite way. The movement of the ball pushes (and pulls) on the hydraulic bumpers and causes them to heat up, absorbing the energy from the motion of the building. The pendulum is tuned by adjusting the length of the cables holding it. By changing the period of the pendulum (the time it takes to swing back and forth), it can be tuned to match the motion of the building.

•

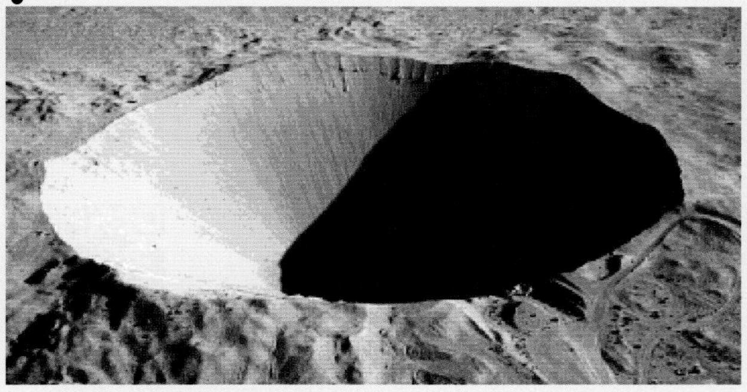

▲ Nevada Test Site, NV

At the Nevada Test Site, more than 1,000 nuclear explosions were set off between 1951 and 1992. The site contains over 3,600 square kilometers of dry lake beds and mountains, about 100 kilometers northwest of Las Vegas. Once a month, the U.S. Department of Energy provides a free, day-long tour of the Nevada Test Site's bomb craters, ground zeros, and test paraphernalia.

The tour covers around 400 kilometers of the nuclear explosion-pockmarked landscape: of the 1,021 nuclear explosions at the Nevada Test Site, only 126 occurred above ground; the rest were underground tests that left the site cratered. The largest crater of all, the Sedan Crater, is the highlight of the tour. It's almost 400 meters wide and 100 meters deep.

$24 Ancient Structures: Remarkable Pyramids, Forts, Stone Chambers, Cities, Complexes William R. Corliss, 2001, 331 pages

$25 (used) Ancient Infrastructure: Remarkable Roads, Mines, Walls, Mounds, Stone Circles William R. Corliss, 1999, 406 pages

$28 Biological Anomalies–Birds: A Catalog of Biological Anomalies William R. Corliss, 1998, 480 pages

$22 Biological Anomalies, Mammals I: A Catalog of Biological Anomalies William R. Corliss, 1995, 400 pages

$19 Neglected Geological Anomalies: A Catalog of Geological Anomalies William R. Corliss, 1990, 327 pages

$19 Anomalies in Geology: Physical, Chemical, Biological: A Catalog of Geological Anomalies William R. Corliss, 1989, 329 pages

$17 Rare Halos, Mirages, Anomalous Rainbows and Related Electromagnetic Phenomena: A Catalog of Geophysical Anomalies William R. Corliss, 1984, 238 pages

$25 (used) Lightning, Auroras, Nocturnal Lights, and Related Luminous Phenomena: A Catalog of Geophysical Anomalies William R. Corliss, 1982, 242 pages

$53 (used) Ancient Man: A Handbook of Puzzling Artifacts William R. Corliss, 1977, 786 pages

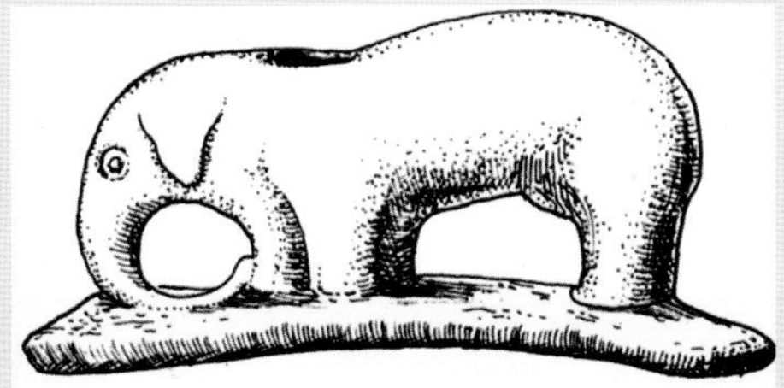

An animal resembling a mastodon. Pipe found in Iowa, USA
From "Ancient Man: A Handbook of Puzzling Artifacts"

Database of Anomalies

Corliss Sourcebooks

Frequently, insight begins with an unexplained anomaly — a novel phenomenon which upon diligent pursuit leads to a new way of doing or understanding. On the other hand most anomalies are just that — unexplained exceptions of no lasting import. Telling the difference is what science is about. But first these odd things must be acknowledged, and better, documented. This is what the Sourcebook Project does. William Corliss, a maniacal archivist working alone has steadfastly cataloged all reported anomalies in biology, chemistry, geology, archeology, physics, and the atmosphere. He lists everything: ball lightening accounts, out of sequence fossils, ancient glass lenses, geological deposits where they shouldn't be, weird ruins, musical sands, unexplained radioactivity, out of place historical artifacts, unusual ancient buildings, strange weather formations, and anything odd that has no easy explanation.

Corliss clips primarily from old scientific journals, expedition reports, and society proceedings. The observers have some credibility. The anomalies are presented without interpretation — that is up to you. The work can easily be appropriated by cranks (and has been) but it is equally useful to others searching for new science frontiers.

A few words from William James, reproduced on the title page of *Anomalies in Geology*:

"Round about the accredited and orderly facts of every science there ever floats a sort of dust-cloud of exceptional observations, of occurrences minute and irregular and seldom met with, which it always proves more easy to ignore than to attend to.... Anyone will renovate his science who will steadily look after the irregular phenomena. And when this science is renewed, its new formulas often have more of the voice of the exceptions in them than of what were supposed to be the rules."

For most of us, this remarkable series of volumes will be a constant source of wonder, amazement, and rethinking. Because each observation is offered without explanation ("just the facts ma'am") in such volume (thousands and thousands), one quickly realizes the extent of our ignorance. So far Corliss has compiled 34 volumes, all items indexed according to his classification scheme. Confusingly these volumes overlap, and it is not easy to determine which are the latest, but those in his "catalog" series seem to be the most recent.

Corliss adds 1,200 new reports a year, and has only published 40% of the material he has compiled. Obviously this *Catalog of Anomalies* should be on the web, as an open source project. But for now these amazing tomes are only in paper, self published by Corliss himself, available via Amazon.

– *KK*

•

The Laos Jars are mostly fashioned out of sandstone, although a few were laboriously carved from much harder red granite. Besides the 250 jars at Ban Ang, there are about 80 more at Lat Sen, 155 more at Ban Soua, 34 at Na Nong, and still more at Ban Hin, the latter group is made from red granite.

The natives in the areas where jars are located know nothing definite of their origin.

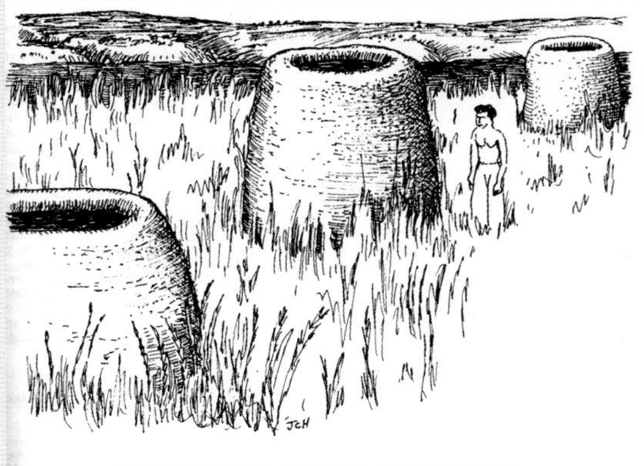

Sketch of some of the huge stone jars located on the Plain of Jars, Laos.

It is customary to say the jars were made to celebrate a great military victory 1,500 years ago. Modern professional opinion is that they are funerary urns probably made more than 1,500 years ago.

From "Ancient Infrastructure: Remarkable Roads, Mines, Walls, Mounds, Stone Circles"

•

Blundellsands, England. June 5, 1902. "The evening was dull and grey, a strong north-westerly wind was blowing in from the sea and the tide was flowing in. In the distance we first saw smoke with frequent jets of fire bursting forth from the mud of a shallow canal. Drawing near, we perceived a strong sulphurous odour, and saw little flames of fire and heard a hissing sound as though a large quantity of phosphorous was being ignited. It was impossible to detect anything which caused the fire, only the water where the flames appeared had particles of a bluish hue floating on the surface. The area over which the tiny flames kept bursting forth was about 40 yards. A gentleman present stirred up the mud with his walking stick, and immediately large yellow flames nearly 2 feet in length and breadth burst forth. The phenomenon lasted some time, until the tide covered the part and quenched the fire."

From "Anomalies in Geology: Physical, Chemical, Biological"

•

August 17, 1876. Ringstead Bay, England. "Between 4 and 5 p.m. two ladies who were out on the cliff, saw surrounding them on all sides, and extending from a few inches above the surface to two or three feet overhead, numerous globes of light, the size of billiard balls, which were moving independently and vertically up and down, sometimes within a few inches of the observers, but always eluding the grasp; now gliding upwards two or three feet, and as slowly falling again, resembling in their movements soap bubbles floating in the air. The balls were all aglow, but not dazzling, with a soft, superb irridescence, rich and warm of hue, and each of variable tints, their charming colours brightening the extreme beauty of the scene. The subdued magnificence of this fascinating spectacle is described as baffling description. Their numbers were continually fluctuating; at times thousands of them enveloped the observers, and a few minutes afterwards the numbers would dwindle to perhaps as few as twenty, but soon they would be swarming again as numerous as ever. Not the slightest noise accompanied the display.

From "Lightning, Auroras, Nocturnal Lights, and Related Luminous Phenomena: A Catalog of Geophysical Anomalies"

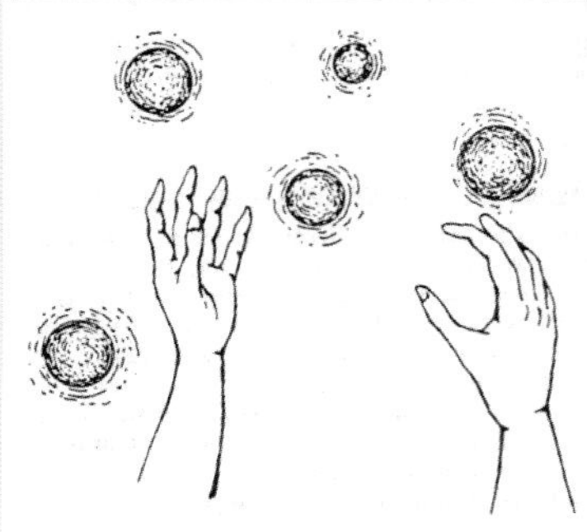

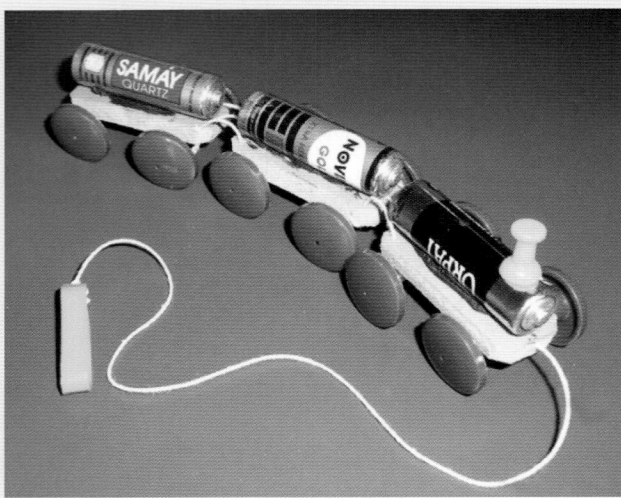

Guide to building doodads w/junk
Toys from Trash
Free Arvindguptatoys.com

The recycling, reuse and reppropriation of common household goods, trash and miscellany into functional and/or amusing items is something Cool Tools readers know well. No matter where you fall on the spectrum of tinkerers, whether you have children or not, it's near impossible to visit Arvind Gupta's Toys From Trash without wanting to attempt at least one of his many projects.

His web site boasts a fantastic range of educational experiments like how to fashion a potato battery and a bottle barometer, as well as a section called "Pumps from the Dump" which includes a stellar-looking Syringe Pump. Granted there's an array of light experiments akin to the ones you'll find in the previously-reviewed Science Toys You Can Make With Your Kids. But in

Designed by Ninad Sonawane
2 half liter mineral water bottles, filled

PVC pipe: around 4 cm diameter, 30 cm long

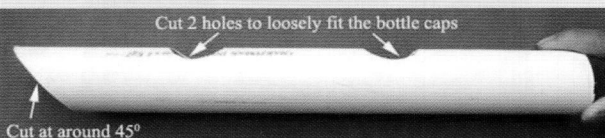

Cut 2 holes to loosely fit the bottle caps

Cut at around 45°

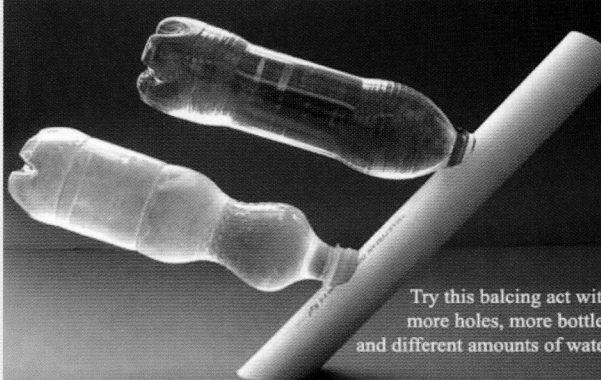

Try this balcing act with more holes, more bottles and different amounts of water

Balancing Act

addition to the nerdy, educational stuff, Gupta's site features quick and easy one-offs that aren't the least bit science-y, like how to fold six types of newspaper hat.

I first perused Toys From Trash a couple years ago, but found myself diving back in recently after a friend reminded me just how much cool stuff Gupta's published. Many of us already tinker, create, deconstruct and build stuff back up for fun, work, education, etc. — or at the very least we're partial to blogs and publications which show us what's possible. I'm guessing one of the biproducts of the economic downturn in the U.S. will be an increase in DIY and, therefore, even more kids raised on transforming what could be discarded into treasures.

-- Steven Leckart

Ready to spy!

Pencil Box Periscope

Best amateur science source
Science Toys You Can Make With Your Kids
Free Scitoys.com

Probably the coolest source of educational science demonstrations I've encountered is this very book-like website written and run by Simon Field. Field has 30 nifty toys and gadgets that can be made quickly, cheaply and will amaze adults as well as kids. This is the only place I've seen that tells you how to make a magnetic linear accelerator, also known

as a Gauss Rifle – it uses magnetism to shoot tiny steel balls. The secret to Field's method is that his demos are very small, requiring small amounts of material, energy, or money. Most of his experiments can be assembled – even if you buy the stuff – for a few dollars, and can fit in your palm. His instructions and visuals are simply the best I've seen in any how-to-book. Most wonderful of all, it's entirely up on the web for free. Hats off to you, Mr. Field. (He does sell kits, and parts, which may help pay for his server, I guess.)

-- KK

Building the Film Can Cannon

This toy was an instant favorite from the moment its first loud Bang! and flash of orange flame launched the little black film can up to bounce off our 26 foot ceiling. It has several names: the

Piezo-Popper, the Binaca Bomb, the Photo-Flash — you will probably come up with more.

The toy is very easy to make, going together in about 15 minutes, at a cost of two or three dollars if all the parts are purchased new, or free if you don't throw away certain common household items.

The fuel for the cannon can be found around the house. We have run ours on perfume, hair spray, and (our favorite) Wintergreen Binaca mouth freshener.

The cannon is very simple. A pair of wires are pushed through a slit made in the top of a plastic 25 millimeter film can. The other end of the wires are soldered to the igniter element from an electronic cigarette or fireplace lighter. I chose to mount these elements on a block of wood, but this is optional if you're in a hurry.

To fire the cannon, you spray the fuel (one squirt of perfume or Binaca, or a very short squirt of hair spray) into the plastic film can, push the can down on the lid, and press the igniter.

With a loud Bang! and a flash of orange flame, the little can goes sailing into the air. With some practice in getting just the right amount of fuel in the can, it will go as high as 30 feet straight up. If too much or too little fuel is used, it will either not ignite at all, or it will not go very high.

The Film Can Cannon can only hold a small amount of air and fuel mixture, so it is safe to fire off in the house.

The plastic can is soft and light, and can land on people without disturbing their hairdo. But it takes off rather quickly, and it is not recommended to have your head in the way during a launch.

Here is a closeup of the spark gap formed by the stripped ends of the two wires. There is nothing critical about this arrangement — as long as the wire ends are bare and close enough, a spark can jump across the gap when the igniter is pushed.

The world's simplest steam powered boat

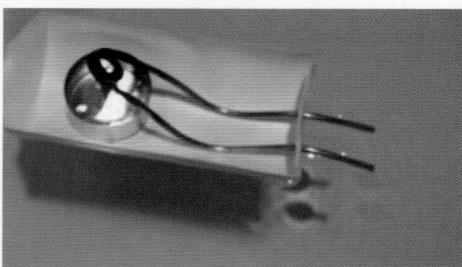

This next toy is an example of the simplest steam engine you will ever see. It has no valves, no moving parts (in the traditional sense of the phrase), and yet it can propel it's little boat easily across the largest swimming pool or quiet duck pond.

Low-rent science hacks
Gonzo Gizmos
$12 Simon Field, 2003, 228 pages

My favorite amateur science experimenter has gathered the coolest hacks from his website into a browseable book. Here Simon Field tells you how to use disposable trash to make very small versions of hi-tech machines — like a Van de Graaff generator, or magnetic train gun, or what he calls a plastic hydrogen bomb. The secret to the fun and enlightenment is to keep everything very small — which makes it cheap, fast, and safe.

There's lots more amateur exploration at his wonderful website, but this plain book (black and white printing) contains a fine selection of his best stuff, and is great for an introductory gift.

-- KK

In the previous two projects, we stole high voltage from a television set to power our high voltage motors. In this project we will build a device that can generate 12,000 volts from an empty soda can and a rubber band.

The device is called a Van de Graaff generator. Science museums and research facilities have large versions that generate potentials in the hundreds of thousands of volts. Ours is more modest, but is still capable of drawing 1/2 inch sparks from the soda can to my finger. The spark is harmless, and similar to the jolt you get from a doorknob after scuffing your feet on the carpet.

This very simple toy uses a magnetic chain reaction to launch a steel marble at a target at high speed. The toy is very simple to build, going together in minutes, and is very simple to understand and explain, and yet fascinating to watch and to use.

I jump off the cliff and build my wings on the way down. - Ray Bradbury

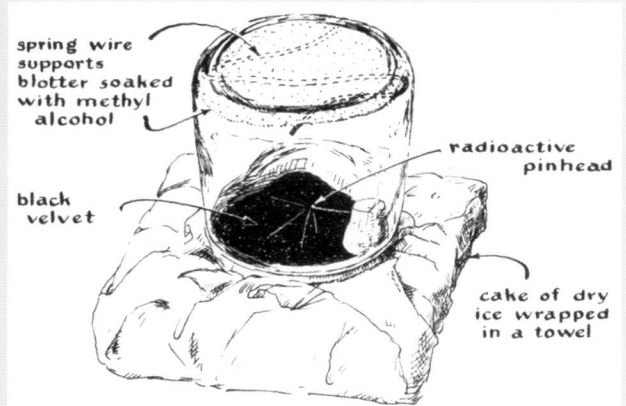

spring wire
supports
blotter soaked
with methyl
alcohol

black
velvet

radioactive
pinhead

cake of dry
ice wrapped
in a towel

How to make a cloud chamber

Classic experiments still worth doing
The Amateur Scientist

Free **Science Hobbyist** Amasci.com
$350 The Amateur Scientist CD-ROM Amazon
$60 (used book) C.L. Stong, 1960, 584 pages

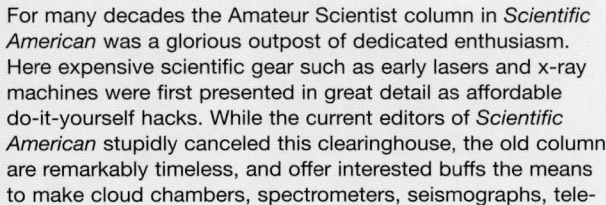

For many decades the Amateur Scientist column in *Scientific American* was a glorious outpost of dedicated enthusiasm. Here expensive scientific gear such as early lasers and x-ray machines were first presented in great detail as affordable do-it-yourself hacks. While the current editors of *Scientific American* stupidly canceled this clearinghouse, the old columns are remarkably timeless, and offer interested buffs the means to make cloud chambers, spectrometers, seismographs, tele-scopes, microscopes and all manner of cool instruments using only the most basic kind of stuff you'd find in basements or discount mail order venues.

As a service to this community of gear-heads, former Amateur Scientist editor Shawn Carlson and a part-time publisher have put together all the Amateur Scientist columns the magazine published from 1928 till 1999. The good news is that 100% of the clever drawings and notes are here along with a fine index. The bad new is it's on a CD but it's too clunky to use. Taking a bit of a hint from the extreme passion of do-it-yourselfers, Scientific American is slowly rounding up their best past columns and under the editorship of Shawn Carlson issuing them in subject-specific collections. See the second in this emerging series — The Amateur Biologist — it works fine.

There is one alternative to the awkward CD. Scientific America collected their best columns in 1960 and issued them in a single volume called The Scientific American Book of Projects for the Amateur Scientist, edited by C.L. Stong. Copies of this out-of-print book are available via online used book sites. The upside is the handy print form; The down side is that the text is not as searchable, and contains nothing after 1960. A lot has happened in amateur science since then.

-- KK

Fun science hacks
Science Hobbyist

amasci.com

The best -- well at least the funnest -- resource for the young amateur scientists is Science Hobbyist. It has the most original material, and the best links, and is run by one energetic and creative Bill Beaty. I've never met Mr. Beaty, but I like his style. His site is heavily infested with a 'just do it' mentality: magnetic levitation prototypes, ball lightening demos, and "unwise microwave oven experiments." He specializes in material for science fair projects, cool toys, resources for nerds, and plans for dangerous 'don't try this at home' experiments, plus fringe science links, as well as critical thinking tools. It's the amateur science site that I've been seeking for years. If people are experimenting at home with it, it's probably linked here.

-- KK

First experiments
Science Fair Handbook

$15 Anthony Fredericks, Isaac Asimov, 2001, 128 p.

Science fairs are the hidden secret sauce for America's innovation. They instill the joys of the scientific method early in impressionable minds. Sadly, science fairs are in decline in the US (and on the rise in China, which has a million kids do them each year.) Get your school to run one, or do your own.

My kids' school promoted science fair participation, and one of our daughter's projects made it to the California state level one year. In assisting my kids (yes it is okay) I've accumulated a entire bookshelf of science fair guides and idea books. The best of all these is the second edition of a 120-page book co-authored by the great science and science-fiction author Isaac Asimov. Aimed at parents wanting to help, and teachers hoping to set one up, it emphasizes the process of science fairing at the elementary school level. Basically, how to do a small experiment and report on it. Then how to judge it.

Unlike most science fair books at this level it is not packed with experiments recycled from others; the ideal experiment is one you don't know the answer to. That makes your experiment more valuable and more fun for everyone. This handbook does list a few suggested topics by age to spur an idea. For inspiration of possibilities, we haven't found anything better than old episodes of Mythbusters. As Adam Savage said in one, "Remember kids, the only difference between screwing around and science is writing it down."

-- KK

Developing a Hypothesis

After students have designed an appropriate question, they must turn that question into a hypothesis. A hypothesis is an educated guess, a statement of how the scientist thinks the experiment will turn out. It is a prediction, based on the best available information, of what the scientist believes will happen at the conclusion of the experiment. Although the hypothesis is founded on factual data the student has collected during the research stage, it is the student's opinion deduced from those facts. A well-constructed hypothesis identifies the subjects of the experiment (plants, mice) and states what is being measured (rate of growth, weight), the conditions of the experiment (different-colored light sources, junk food versus regular food), and the results expected (light colors produce faster growth rates than dark colors; a nutritious diet produces higher weights than a junk food diet). Thus a student's question about a specific area of interest can be developed into a hypothesis that forms the foundation of the student's investigation.

Avoid clutter

It is important to include enough items to illustrate important concepts of the project, but it is equally important to avoid crowding the display table. Too many items detract from the display just as much as too few.

Scientific Thought

Is the experiment designed to answer a question?
Are the procedures appropriate to the area of investigation?
Is the topic or problem stated clearly and completely?
Has scientific literature been cited?
Have scientists or other experts been consulted?
Has a systematic plan of action been stated?
Is there a need for further research or investigation?
Is there an adequate conclusion?

OPTICS, HEAT AND ELECTRONICS

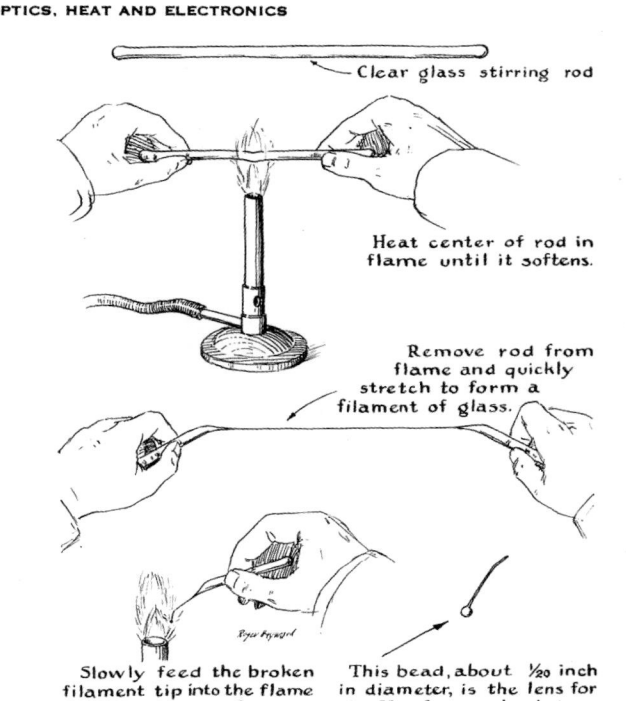

Clear glass stirring rod

Heat center of rod in flame until it softens.

Remove rod from flame and quickly stretch to form a filament of glass.

Slowly feed the broken filament tip into the flame until a tiny bead forms.

This bead, about 1/20 inch in diameter, is the lens for the Van Leeuwenhoek type microscope.

How to make the glass-bead lens of a Leeuwenhoek microscope

I've stumbled across a technique for drawing holograms directly upon a plastic plate by hand. It sounds impossible, but I've been sitting on the living-room sofa making holographic images of floating polyhedra, words, 3D starfields, opaque objects, etc. No laser, no isolation table, no darkroom, no expensive film plates. This takes nothing more than a compass and some scraps of plexiglas. Too cool, if I say so myself!

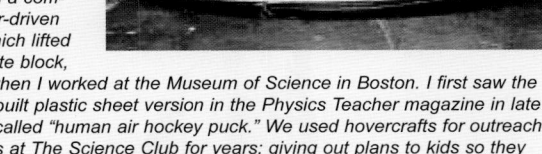

Where did this hovercraft idea come from? The device is called an "air film bearing" and has been used to move heavy loads on flat floors for many decades. Physics teachers used them for classroom demonstrations, and we had a compressor-driven one which lifted a granite block, back when I worked at the Museum of Science in Boston. I first saw the home-built plastic sheet version in the Physics Teacher magazine in late 1989, called "human air hockey puck." We used hovercrafts for outreach classes at The Science Club for years; giving out plans to kids so they could build one and amaze their friends with the secret.

Is a project notebook provided with the display?
Is the project notebook sufficiently detailed in relation to the scope of the project?
Have any problems or limitations that occurred been noted?
Is the amount of data commensurate with the scope of the project?
Does the student understand all the facts and/or theories?

Grow or die. - George Lock Land

Rockets

Homemade rockets
Sport Rocketry * Rockets

$62 Sport Rocketry
nar.org/SPR

$42 Rocketry
libertylaunch
systems.com

The next step up from boy scout model rockets is high power rocketry. This is real fun for adults. These things will go miles high. It's a strictly build-your-own endeavor, with permits. The National Association of Rocketry publishes a bi-monthly magazine for sport rocketeers called appropriately enough, *Sport Rocketry*. But my friends who are avid amateur rocketeers scoff at *Sport Rocketry* as kid stuff. They want to make their own real rockets reaching the stratosphere. From their garages come complex computer-guided peaceful missiles. They strut their stuff in *Rockets*, the magazine of the Tripoli Rocketry Association.

--KK

- High Power Rocketry, also known as HPR, is similar to model rocketry with differences that include the propulsion power and weight increase of the model. They use motors in ranges over "G" power and/or weigh more than laws and regulations allow for unrestricted model rockets. Like model rockets, High Power rockets are typically made of safer, non-metallic materials such as cardboard, plastic, and wood, however, construction and recovery techniques usually differ somewhat, due to the requirements imposed by

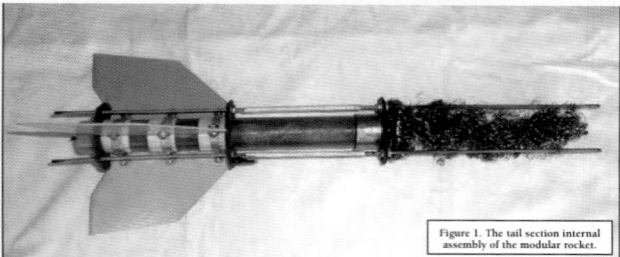
Figure 1. The tail section internal assembly of the modular rocket.

the use of HPR motors. This means that these models must be constructed in such a way that they have the ability to safely fly under these higher stress conditions.

High Power rocket motors cannot be purchased over the counter by the general consumer and typically are not carried by your average hobby store. They can be mail-ordered or purchased at some launch sites by adult modelers who are High Power certified, which is a requirement to purchase and use them. The NAR offers a three level certification program for modelers who want to fly high power rockets. Also, High Power rockets must be flown in compliance with their own separate High Power Rocket Safety Code.

Constructed fin can with motor rear closure inserted

Launching High Power rockets requires more preparation than launching model rockets. Not only is a larger field needed, but FAA clearance must be arranged, well in advance of the launch date. There may also be local or state regulatory issues to be addressed before you can fly your first high power rocket. This is another good reason for joining a NAR Section -- many organized clubs already have the personnel and experience in making these tedious arrangements, freeing you to concentrate on the actual flying.

Homemade space satellites
DIY Satellite Platforms
$8 Sandy Antunes, 2012, 86 pages

You can send a do-it-yourself satellite into space, one that piggybacks on a commercial rocket. This pico-satellite must conform to a set of dimensions about the size of a soda can. The minimum price of a launch is $12,000 and dropping. All the other rules, constraints, and questions you'll need to build are covered in this very basic intro. Author Sandy Antunes is writing a master guide one small booklet at a time so check out his other titles in this series.

-- KK

Size and weight build model for a tubesat-type 1kg limit picosatellite

- First: where will your picosatellite go? It's nearly a given that your picosatellite will go to low earth orbit (LEO), a broad band ranging from about 150km up to perhaps 600km.

Above the ionosphere, the space environment can be hostile because of solar activity. Below it, the radiation risks are much lower. This is why the ISS is kept in LEO. LEO is, at heart, about as safe as space can get. It's also where your picosatellite is likely to live.

Your orbit is entirely determined by what your rocket provider has sold you. At the hobbyist level, you're going to most likely get a standard 250km or so nearly circular orbit, either equatorial or polar. Such an orbit lasts (because of drag by the tenuous ionosphere) from 3 to 16 weeks before the satellite will suffer a fiery reentry.

At picosatellite masses, this means your satellite will go up and not return. You have less than three months to gather data. The picosatellite will then, essentially, vaporize neatly upon reentry (no space junk risk!)

- Let's close with the idea of flight spares. The idea here is twofold. First, it is good to have a second satellite ready in case a mishap occurs to the first. Mishaps can range from rocket blew up all the way down to a mundane dropped it while carrying it to the truck.

Conceptually and more important, you want to build two or three satellites simultaneously for two reasons. First, you may make a construction mistake with one. Having a spare means you can continue to work without having to wait for new parts or fabrication.

Second, you will build one better than the other. Statistically, one of your builds will have better performance than the other. This better one is the one you will fly. By creating multiple builds, you give yourself and your skills a chance to practice, hone, and ultimately create a better picosatellite.

So build two and fly the one that does best in tests.

- The lowest fixed-price offering out there is InterOrbital Systems offering 1kg TubeSat launches for $8,000 (including a TubeSat kit) or a 1kg 1U CubeSat launch for $12,500. The company is still building toward its first launch, however.

InterOrbital Systems CPM mobile launch rail (image Copyright InterOrbital Systems 1996-2011)

Best home chemistry lab book
Illustrated Guide to Home Chemistry Experiments
$19 Robert Thompson, 2008, 432 p.

The very best chemistry experiment book for kids is the legendary and long-out-of-print book, the *Golden Book of Chemistry Experiments.* Published in 1960 during the heyday of home chemistry, it was meant to accompany the millions of chemistry kits that were sold each year to typical American kids. You got real experiments with real chemicals. Not like the so-called chemistry sets today which boldly (and insanely) advertise they contain "No Chemicals!"

Among many other things, the *Golden Book of Chemistry Experiments* told you how to make chlorine gas from bathroom supplies (see the page below), hydrogen from flashlight battery parts, and rayon from scrap paper, etc. You can see why it was not reprinted in the decades following because of concerns about safety. I used my copy, which is now worth $200 on eBay, to do all the experiments in the book when I was 12, and went on to build a chem lab in my basement. As many kids did.

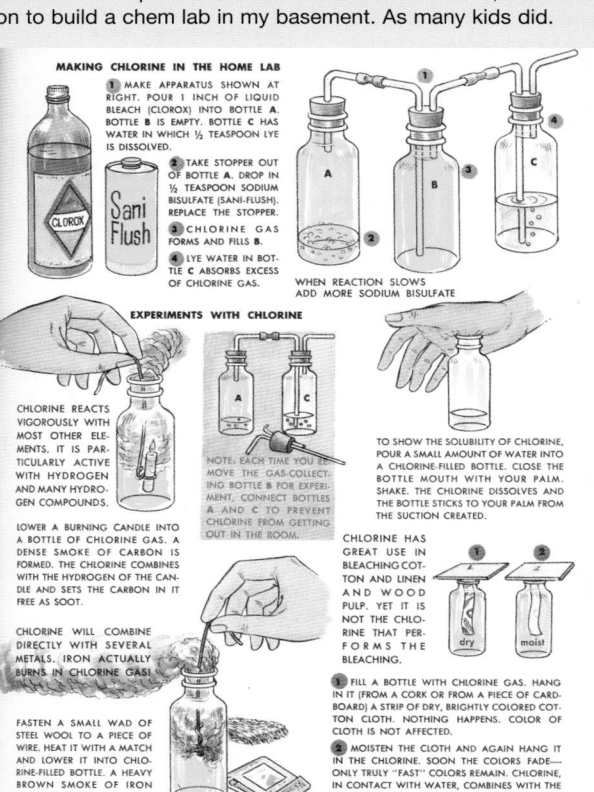

Golden Book of Chemistry Experiments, 1960.

You can get a decent free PDF version of the Golden Book on BitTrorrent. Even better, there's a new great book for home-made experiments, updated for today: the *Illustrated Guide to Home Chemistry Experiments* from the tech publisher O'Reilly. The *Illustrated Guide to Home Chemistry Experiments* is aimed at home schoolers, high school students, and lifelong-learning adults. It is aptly subtitled "All lab, no lecture"

The *Golden Book* encouraged playing around with molecules, with no agenda beyond demonstrating the power, principles, and diversity of chemical reactions. The *Illustrated Guide* on the other hand is a basement laboratory manual meant to teach you the basic working principles of chemistry. How to mix a molar solution. How to titrate. How to do quantitative sleuthing. It claims that if you go through all the chapters you'll be prepared to pass the college-level AP Chem Lab test. You would also be able to work in most laboratories. And of course, you would probably be able to follow most chemistry recipes from the internet, or at least to figure out what you need to make something chemistry-wise.

At the very least, this book should help cure any hysteria you — or your kids — might have about CHEMICALS. Sure, they can be dangerous, like your car. But we are surrounded by chemicals, and the only way to understand their real risks is to mess around with them.

The Illustrated Guide to Home Chemistry Experiments is a fantastic teacher for chemical literacy. It will show you or your kids how to work with chemicals, and why they are fun. Some of the experiments are visually entertaining. Others are scientifically important. It's got wise advice about the few bits of equipment you'll need for your lab. The *Illustrated Guide* very handily

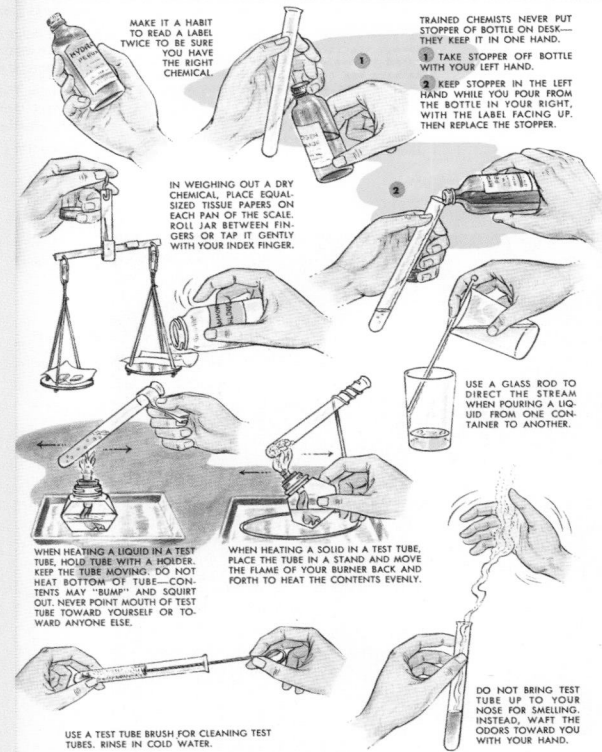

provides substitutions for ingredients whenever possible, so you can work around harder to acquire or expensive chemicals and gear. And it very conscientiously gives proper disposal instructions for substances at the end (the first I've ever seen in a chem book). The author is thrifty, using no more stuff then necessary, and always suggesting ways to purchase the minimum equipment.

Other than the hidden *Golden Book of Chemistry Experiments*, there are simply no other decent books for the beginner chemical experimenter. The ones you find in libraries are simply useless trash. The stuff on the internet is haphazard and inconsistent. Follow the instructions here in the *Illustrated Guide to Home Chemistry Experiments* and you'll be on your way to chemical literacy.

-- KK

•

Everyone rightly treats strong acids with great respect, but many students handle strong bases casually. That's a very dangerous practice. Strong bases, such as solutions of sodium hydroxide, can blind you in literally seconds. Treat every chemical as potentially hazardous, and always wear splash goggles.

•

MAINTAINING A LABORATORY NOTEBOOK

A laboratory notebook is a contemporaneous, permanent primary record of the owner's laboratory work. In real-world corporate and industrial chemistry labs, the lab notebook is often a critically important document, for both scientific and legal reasons. The outcome of zillion-dollar patent lawsuits often hinges on the quality, completeness, and credibility of a lab notebook. Many corporations have detailed procedures that must be followed in maintaining and archiving lab notebooks, and some go so far as to have the individual pages of researchers' lab notebooks notarized and imaged on a daily or weekly basis. If you're just starting to learn about chemistry lab work, keeping a detailed lab notebook may seem to be overkill, but it's not.

•

CHEAPER BY THE POUND

Do not overlook the advantages of banding together with other home schoolers or like-minded hobbyists to buy chemicals in bulk. For example. a vendor may charge $3 for 25g of a particular chemical. $5 for 100 g, and $9 for 500 g. If you need only small amounts of chemicals, you may be able to cut your chemical costs dramatically by arranging with other homeschooling families or hobbyists to order chemicals in larger quantities and divide them among you.

The cost advantage is particularly great for chemicals that incur hazardous shipping surcharges. For example, if you order 100 rnL of concentrated nitric acid for $5. the vendor may add a $35 hazardous material shipping surcharge, for a total of $40. But if you order a 500 mL bottle of concentrated nitric acid for $15, the same surcharge applies, for a total of $50. If you divide that chemical with four friends. each of you gets 100 mL of concentrated nitric acid for only $10.

•

MICROSCALE EQUIPMENT

The recent trend in chemistry labs, particularly school and university labs, is to substitute microscale chemistry equipment and procedures for traditional semi-micro or macroscale equivalents. Microscale chemistry, often called microchemistry, is just what it sounds like. Instead of using standard test tubes, beakers, and flasks to work with a few mL to a few hundred mL of solutions, you use miniaturized equipment to work with solution quantities ranging from 20 pL (microliters, where one pL equals 0.001 mL) to a couple mL.

Using microscale equipment and procedures has many advantages. Microscale equipment and procedures are less expensive than standard equipment and procedures, which is a major reason for the popularity of microscale chemistry. Using microscale equipment and procedures means that chemicals are needed in very small quantities, which are safer to work with and easier to dispose of properly. Microscale also makes it economically feasible to do experiments with very expensive chemicals, such as gold, platinum, and palladium salts. Setup and teardown is faster, allowing more time for actual experiments, and cleanup usually requires only rinsing the equipment and setting it aside to dry.

Using a Beral pipette to bring the water mass up to 100.00 g

Against these advantages, there are several disadvantages to microscale chemistry. First and foremost, everything is on such a small scale that it can be difficult to see what's going on. For example, you may need a magnifier to examine a precipitate (or even to determine whether there is a precipitate). Because of the small scale, measuring or procedural errors are so small that they would have no effect on a traditional scale experiment can greatly affect the outcome of a microscale experiment.

Best source for chemicals
Elemental Scientific

Catalog Elemental Scientific

This is the best source for buying small quantities of chemicals — always a challenge in these days of chemical hysteria. Elemental Scientific will sell to individuals, online, with no paperwork or license needed. They have a very respectable selection of about 300 reagents and compounds. More than enough for most educational purposes, or for most basement experiments. You can purchase all kinds of acids, corrosives, poisons, explosives and dangerous stuff that you can not get elsewhere — but only in small quantities. That's fine, because a small amount is often all you want for doing experiments, and many chemical supply outfits will sell only larger quantities if they sell to you at all. Elemental also offers glassware, lab equipment, and general experimental paraphernalia. They cater to homeschoolers and hobby experimentalists. If you've ever tried to buy chemicals elsewhere you'll recognize what an incredible resource this place is. Most chemicals will be shipped UPS, but a short list of 18 especially hazardous chemicals need extra hazmat protection, which is an added charge.

-- KK

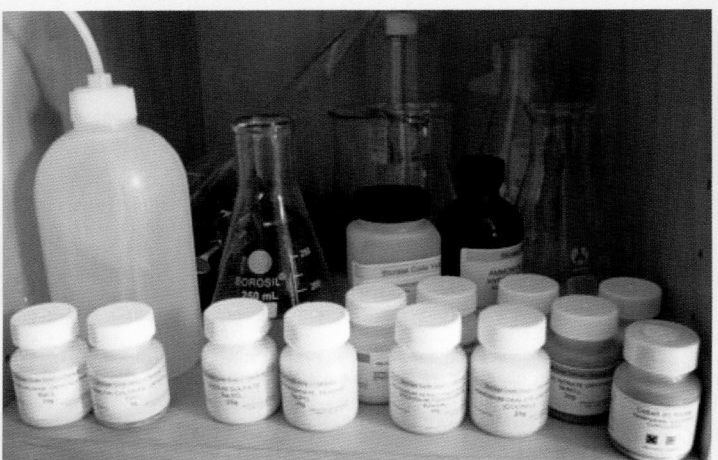

My chemistry shelf supplied by Elemental Scientific

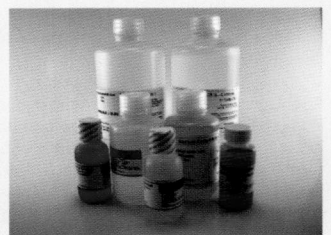

ACETIC ACID GLACIAL,
4 oz. $2.90

(CH1031-4)

Formula: CH_3CO_2H

Formula Wt.: 60.05

CAS: 64-19-7

Health Risk: 3

Flammability: 2

DOT Class: Corrosive

Risky Experiments

Mildly risky fun
Fifty Dangerous Things
$14 Gever Tulley, 2009, 130 p.

The idea of this thin book is that danger is something kids need to learn to handle by experience. The 50 small experiments in this book can potentially cause a minor injury (although they are unlikely to), but are never really seriously dangerous. In fact most of them aren't dangerous at all, but at least they are fun. There are no special techniques, secret formulas or exclusive knowhow here that everyday knowledge or a quick internet search would not turn up. The activities are the kinds of things kids will sometimes do on their own — at least in the past. It's too bad a book like this is needed today, and maybe you, or folks you know, don't need it, but if the kids in your life live a very structured and constantly supervised existence, this is a way to supervise a little danger. The book is designed to be read either by parents or kids. Most activities have clear instructions. We've been going through the book, letting the kids choose. It encourages them try stuff, and to see the trade off in risks and gains in many things. Mostly we use this as a primer for more dangerous things to try later on.

-- KK

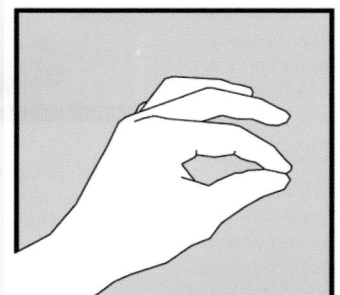

01 Lick a 9-volt Battery
Taste electricity

REQUIRES
- ☐ 9-volt Battery

SHOCK

DURATION

DIFFICULTY

WARNING
Do not hold the battery to your tongue for more than a few seconds at a time.

HOW-TO
You are about to give yourself a tiny shock. It won't exactly hurt, but it will feel strange.

Supplementary Data
Normally, the nerves in your tongue are activated by tiny chemical receptors in your taste buds. The surface of your tongue is divided into different specialized regions that are tuned to notice specific flavors. The battery has no specific flavor of its own, but the electrical current that runs between the terminals activates a random collection of nerves on your tongue causing you to experience a sensation of exaggerated, but nonspecific, taste.

46 Super Glue Your Fingers Together
Experience life without a thumb

FRUSTRATION

PROPERTY DAMAGE

CUTS AND SCRAPES

REQUIRES
- ☐ Super Glue
- ☐ Wax Paper
- ☐ Nail Polish Remover (optional)

DURATION

DIFFICULTY

WARNING
Forcing glued fingers apart can tear the skin; be patient and you will survive unharmed. If you must separate your fingers before the glue releases your fingertips, apply acetone (nail polish remover).

Cover your work area whenever you are using Super Glue. Drops of glue can cause permanent damage to some surfaces and fabrics.

HOW-TO
1. **Prepare.** Wash your hands and dry completely. Oil and dirt can reduce the effectiveness of the glue.
2. **Pick a hand.** Decide which hand you are going to experiment on - we recommend using your dominant hand (that's your right hand if you are right-handed).
3. **Drip glue.** Put a single drop of glue on the pad of your forefinger. With more glue, you run the risk of getting more fingers stuck together.
4. **Adhere.** Press thumb to forefinger and hold for thirty seconds.

Supplementary Data
The Original Super Glue and Krazy Glue are brand names for cyanoacrylate adhesives. Cyanoacrylates were invented by scientists at Kodak Laboratories in the early 1940s. They were looking for a glue that could be used to mount gun sights.

With their remarkable ability to stick to skin, cyanoacrylate-based glues are sometimes used instead of sutures to close wounds. Cyanoacrylates are also water resistant and

Dangerous home experiments
Theo Gray's Mad Science
$17 Theodore Gray, 2009, 240 p.

This is a rare home-chemistry book where the advice of "don't try this at home" is, for once, appropriate. I usually complain about the scare mongering of home chemistry, but half of the experiments in this how-to book really are extremely dangerous. But the other half are pretty cool. There are no explicit step-by-step instructions given for any of the experiments, just guidelines of what to do. Gray, whose column appears in *Popular Science*, wants you to do some research and not just be a "script kiddie." Stunning photos of what to expect from each project help. My son and I have done a few of these and they do work. The prime lesson engendered by this book is the sense that the material world is far more accessible to hacking than first appears.

-- KK

[warning box near instructions for combing sodium and chlorine to make table salt]

Real Danger Alert: This is the most dangerous experiment in this book. Sodium burns skin and eyes on contact and explodes when exposed to water in any form, sending flaming liquid metal in all directions at high velocity. Chlorine gas kills painfully and spreads rapidly. Under no circumstances should either of these chemicals be handled outside the presence of an experienced chemist. Combining them borders on lunacy.

- All the components of glass can be found in two places: the beach and the laundry room. It's possible to melt pure-white silica beach sand into glass, but only at temperatures of 3,000 to 3,500°F. Washing soda, lime or borax (a traditional laundry aid) added to the sand disrupts the quartz-crystal structure of silica and reduces the required temperatures to a more practical, though still dangerous 2,000 °F, which I achieved with a backyard grill and a vacuum cleaner.

A charcoal fire fed with air from the bottom is hot enough to melt the combination of those materials into glass but not hot enough to make it truly liquid, so bubbles tend to remain and make the glass cloudy. I mixed the

FULL OF HOT AIR The exhaust port on a vacuum blows air from below, turning an ordinary grill into a raging inferno, capable of melting glass, iron, even itself if left unchecked.

finely ground ingredients together and heated them in a cast-iron pot, then poured the molten glass into a graphite mold and pressed it down with a graphite stamp.

Soda-lime glass has the lowest melting point but must be cooled slowly to avoid shattering from the thermal stress.

PEPSI PAINTING Tinfoil distributes the current to form a pattern through a stencil and a layer of paper towel moistened with Diet Pepsi.

- Homemade Titanium: With lots of heat, some flowerpots and common chemicals, you can turn raw ore into shiny metal.

An iron crowbar costs about $8; one made of titanium, $80. Solid-titanium scissors start at $700, and don't even ask about the titanium socket wrench. Titanium must be a rare and precious substance, right?

Actually, as raw ore, titanium is 100 times as abundant as copper. … At temperatures high enough to melt it, titanium exposed to air catches fire. So it has to be refined, forged, welded, and cast in a vacuum or under inert gas–an expensive process.

Yet I was able to make titanium using equipment I had lying around. I did it with thermite reduction, a process commonly used to weld train tracks. In an iron thermite reaction, iron oxide reacts with aluminum and comes out as liquid iron. I just swapped in titanium dioxide instead. But that reaction, in which titanium dioxide transfers its oxygen atoms to aluminum, doesn't release enough heat to melt the materials.

So I mixed in drywall plaster (calcium sulfate) and more aluminum powder. They react to create huge amounts of extra heat, enough to melt the titanium and allow it to pool at the bottom of the container. Adding ground fluorite powder makes the molten metals more fluid and protects the titanium from air as it cools.

I used clay flowerpots, as suggested by Gert Meyer, who developed this procedure. When nested with sand between them, they last just long enough to let the titanium cool into beads of solid metal.

- Many of the topics I write about are things I did when I was growing up, and I survived. Without those experiences I might have ended up as a stock broker, or worse.

Science is not something practiced only in labs and universities. It's a way of looking at the world and seeing truth and beauty everywhere. It's something you can do whether you are employed as a professional scientist or not. While I have a degree in chemistry from a fine university, I've never worked as a professional chemist. I do these demonstrations in my shop on a rural farmstead half a mile from the nearest neighbor. (This is handy when exploring the louder aspects of chemistry.) Mostly I use simple kitchen and shop supplies and chemicals from the hardware store or garden center. I do avoid working in a real lab, because I would much rather tinker in my shop and find a simpler (some might say cruder) way of making the experiment work. Amateur scientists, many of them self-taught, tinkering in their shops and basements have done great things. Using a spirit of making do with what they have and seeing just how far they can take it, they make real contributions to the advancement of science.

- It makes me cringe when I see warnings to wear gloves and safety glasses while working with baking soda. It's called crying wolf, and it's deeply irresponsible, because it makes it that much harder to get through to people about real dangers.

- Some other chemicals, however, are not your friends. Chlorine gas kills, and you hurt the whole time you're dying. Mix phosphorus and chlorates wrong and they blow up while you're mixing them. (I have a friend who still has tiny slivers of glass coming out of his hands twenty years after he made that particular mistake.)

Every chemical, every procedure, every experiment has its own unique set of dangers, and over the years people have learned (the hard way) how to deal with them. In many cases the only way to do an experiment safely is to find a more experienced person to help. This is not book-learning, it's your life at stake and you want someone by your side who knows what they are doing. There is an unbroken chain of these people leading right back to the first guy who survived, and you want to be part of that chain.

When I do an experiment that looks crazy I either have someone with me who's done it before, or it's something that I've worked my way up to slowly and carefully. I build in layers of safety, and I make sure that if all else fails I have a clear path to run like hell (and of course I wear glasses at all times).

The ultra-intelligent machine is a machine that believes people cannot think. - Jack Good

Rugged scope for everyday use
Brock Magiscope
$179 Brock Optical Inc.

The trouble with most optical equipment is that it won't get used unless it is out of the case, opened up, and powered on. But if it is open and lying around, it will get highly abused. I buy my cameras, spectacles, binocs, etc. assuming they'll be dropped and splattered, and they should hold up to this misuse. But until now I haven't been able to find a microscope strong enough to do its job yet sturdy enough to be left on the kitchen table ready for inspections by toddlers and teenagers. Now after several years of looking for an everyday microscope suitable for a busy family I found one.

The Brock Magiscope #70 is exactly what I had wanted. It has a single moving part that my five-year old can handle. He can put a leaf in and focus it right. Rubber bands hold the slide. For light the scope uses a fat fiber optic bent pipe which channels ambient room light to the underside of the objective lens (no electricity). There is no fussing, no adjustments. The viewing field is amazingly bright and clear, with a choice of 100x magnification, good enough for high school work. We've discovered we can press the lens of a digital camera to its eyepiece, focus on the digital screen and get pretty good microphotography shots.

And best of all it is practically indestructible. The thing is simple and rugged as a hammer. In fact it was built for the abuse of K-12 classrooms, which is probably as grating as a war. Brock offers a "lifetime replacement warranty, including accidents." If it breaks, ever, they replace it. And they do. (Some visiting kids manage to break the light optic — I have no idea how — but Brock replaced it with no questions asked.)

This tool is always on, always out (it sits next to the fruit bowl); we use it.

-- KK

DIY genetic engineering
Bio Hacking Resources
$200 (used) Natalie Jermijenko & Eugene Thacker, 2004, 96 p.

I've been expecting tools for basement bio hacks any day now for about 20 years. They are getting real close, although most of what you can do with this stuff so far is elementary, trivial and not very useful. Still, here are a few do-it-yourself gene hacking resources finally emerging. The prime users are artists and students. Not a bad start really.

Not yet at the level of a dummies' guides, this book supplies explicit instructions for executing basic genetic procedures with a minimum equipment. The couple of hacks sketched out (cloning a tree, starting a culture of your own skin) are enough to get your enthusiasm going. I wish the material was better organized, and I wish there was more of it. The book is handy, but the PDF of the book is free and immediate.

-- KK

Kitchen sink biology
The Amateur Biologist
$12 Shawn Carlson, 2002, 228 p.

I go along with the received wisdom these days that this dawning era won't be remembered as the computer century, but the biological century. What has been missing from this upcoming bio-revolution is the hands-on access of garage science. When it is as easy to program DNA in your bedroom as it is to program a chip, that's when we'll be swept off our feet in innovations. No reporting or speculative essay has given as much of a glimpse of this future than this how-to book of basement biology. Edited by former Amateur Scientist columnist Shawn Carlson (who also wrote many of the reprinted columns) this text tackles such old-time skills as cultivating pond scum (one source of commercially valuable microorganisms), or hacking up a video microscope, or measuring the heartbeats of insects. In the last section Carlson gets into how to extract DNA from cells using kitchen utensils. It's wide open from there.

-- KK

●

The most wonderful private garden I have ever seen is tucked away behind a modest house in La Jolla, California, not far from where I live. The gardener is a British-born psychology professor and dear friend who sends me home with fruit and flowers each time I visit. Recently I noticed that two of his plants, though very different in shape, produced flowers the exact same shade of purple. This observation made me wonder whether the two species might be related.

●

One normally traces evolutionary connections by identifying physical similarities between species. So I decided to extract and isolate the pigments in the two flowers so that I could compare them in detail. That process is actually much easier than it sounds. In fact, using a simple technique called electrophoresis, I could carry out the experiment in about an hour for very little money.

●

DNA is the largest molecule known. A single, unbroken strand of it can contain many millions of atoms. When released from a cell, DNA typically breaks up into countless fragments. In solution, these strands have a slight negative electric charge, a fact that makes for some fascinating

---

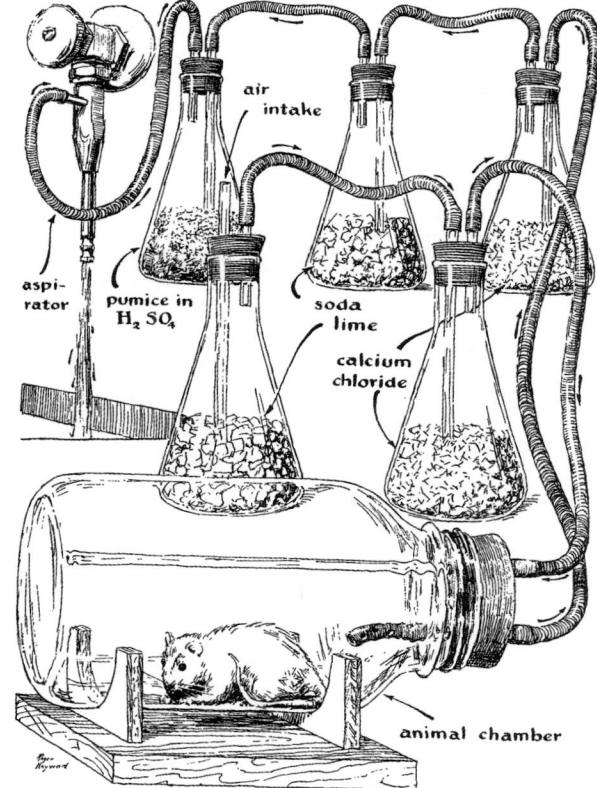

An amateur s apparatus for measuring the metabolism of mice.

chemistry. For example, salt ions are attracted to the negative charges on DNA, effectively neutralizing them, and this phenomenon prevents the many separate fragments of DNA from adhering to one another. So by controlling the salt concentration, biologists can make DNA fragments either disperse or glom together. And therein lies the secret of separating DNA from cells.

●

The detergent actually does double duty. It breaks down cell walls and helps to fracture large proteins so they don't come out with the DNA. The people at Edvotek recommend using pure table salt and distilled water, but I have used iodized salt and bottled water successfully, and once I even forgot to add the baking soda and still got good results. In any case, try to avoid using tap water. To slow the rate at which the DNA degrades, it's best to chill the buffer in a bath of crushed ice and water before proceeding.

●

For a source of DNA, try the pantry. I got great results with an onion, and the folks at Edvotek also recommend garlic, bananas, and tomatoes. But it's your experiment: choose your favorite fruit, vegetable, or legume. Dice it and put the material into a blender, then add a litter water and mix things well by pulsing the blades in 10-second bursts. Or, even simpler, just pass the pieces through a garlic press. These treatments will break apart some of the cells right away and expose many cell walls to attack by the detergent.

▼ *A kitchen laboratory includes most of the items needed to isolate DNA. A drinking straw, for example can be used to add alcohol to the solutions (a) and a coffee stirrer serves to spool the DNA (b).*

Personal Genetics

Personal genetic literacy
Trace Your Roots with DNA + The Genographic Project

Yep, we are headed into the bio century. In this brave new world a basic level of genetic literacy will be essential. That was a problem for me because I couldn't tell one gene from another. But recently I discovered that the quickest route from the theory of genetics to the practice of it is to inspect my own genes. And the best motivator and context for that is that old fussy hobby of genealogy.

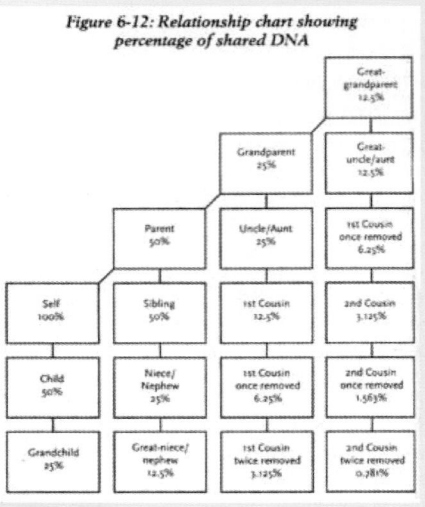

You plumb your own genes for clues about your ancestry and in the process all genes become less strange.

About half a dozen companies offer a paid service to test your genes, taken from cells in the cheek, and provide a rough analysis of where you fall in the 100,000-year migration of humans across the globe. These outfits only sequence a very few points in your DNA, called markers. In general the more markers they check, the better. If you are willing, you can then submit your genetic marker results to the rapidly growing database of other folks who have tested their DNA. A good place to start is 23andMe (see review below)>

It is also pretty geeky. Whereas traditional genealogy is nearly literary, steeped in anecdotes, names, and human drama; this new craft of genetic genealogy or "genetealogy" is primarily numerical: it is a flood of statistics, databases, algorithms, and the stuff of computer science. For better or worse it is also a ferociously technical, heavily quantifiable, gnarly hobby, and the early adopters are sprinting ahead rapidly. In fact so much is happening so fast in personal genetealogy that it is quite easy for almost anyone to become the world's expert in a particular domain.

So how do you get started?

The easiest way to launch into the world of ancestral DNA is a fantastic National Geographic documentary (*The Journey of Man: A Genetic Odyssey*) on our deep genetic roots and early human migration on this planet. This informative film, full of surprising news, is based on the work of Spencer Wells, who is both innovative scientist and enthusiastic host. He and crew scour the world for indigenous people with deep roots in one place, asking for samples of DNA to test, in order to piece together our "big family" genetic tree. The best parts are when they return with results and we see the diverse ways in which people and tribes react to the news of what science says about their arrival and relations.

But as helpful as the Genographic supporting material is, you'll need a master guide to help you decipher the meaning of genes. By far the best orientation to this exploding universe is the new book *Trace Your Roots with DNA*. Written for avid family-tree fans, this is a great layperson's introduction to personal DNA testing. It illuminates the complexities of such concepts as haplogroups, snips, alleles, mtDNA, and diminishing genetic relationships — all crucial genetic knowledge even if you are not into genealogy. If you ARE into family roots, this book will provide you with tons of concrete advice on how to persuade relatives to get tested, where to post your results, and how to correlate genes with traditional genealogical research.

The authors are smart. They realize that news in this area will appear first online and only slowly migrate to paper books or magazines. They wisely direct you to preferred websites throughout their chapters. But their book offers a comprehensive overview of a frontier that no website currently offers. It is a wonderful portal to this coming century.

-- KK

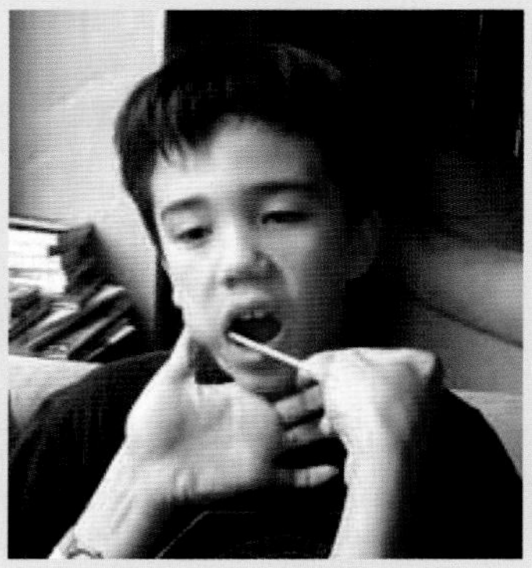

● But for now, you have all you will need to know if you grasp one fact: Y chromosome tests cannot prove that you share a particular common ancestor with another person, only that you share a common ancestor at some point.

● There are move than 1,000 genes on the X chromosome, while the count of the Y chromosome in the year 2003 stands at just a fraction of that: 27. The genes on the X chromosome have little or nothing to do with sexual characteristics. They cover a broad range of structure and function, much like any of the autosomes.

The Y chromosome acts like a switch — if it is present, the baby will be a male. Genes restricted to the Y chromosome could hardly be essential for life and health, else the female of the species would disappear. Classical genetics has never identified any traits or diseases linked to the Y chromosome, so there is no need to fear that sharing DNA results will impact the ability to obtain health insurance.?

● **Haplotype Diversity**

How often will two random Smiths match each other just by accident?

Just as surnames can be very common or very rare, haplotypes are found in different frequencies. In the database at www.yhrd.org, which has more than 24,000 records tested at nine markers, the single most frequent haplotype occurs in less than 3 percent of the population, so even that could not be called common in the absolute sense. Many haplotypes occur

My son gets his cheek swabbed for DNA

just once — more than 40 percent of the records, in fact. Every time a new set of data is added to the database, novel haplotypes are discovered.

Haplotype diversity can be quantified. The chance that two men chosen at random will match each other on all nine markers is less than two in a thousand. You can rule out a lot of false trails that way, and if two Smiths match, it's probably not just a coincidence.

Adding more markers increases the diversity: Some of the men who match on nine markers will differ on a 10th marker.

● We're not going to sugarcoat it. Talking strangers into handing over their DNA — and hopefully, some money — is not the easiest of tasks. Presumably, it will become easier over time as genetic genealogy becomes as widely known as traditional research. At least then, those you contact will know that this is a normal activity that everyday human beings do with some regularity, and there will no longer be a need to educate people about the very existence of this kind of testing. But it's best to prepare as if the person you're about to call, write, or e-mail has never heard of genetealogy.

● You can recruit people in two ways — by finding them or by making it easier for them to find you. We refer to the detective work associated with seeking out appropriate candidates as "reverse genealogy" since it usually involves tracing lines from the past to the present. Traditionally, we're trained to start with ourselves and work back through the generations, but conducting a DNA project often requires the reverse. You may, for instance, be trying to find possible descendants of a German immigrant who came to Pennsylvania in the 1700s.

● Please don't make the mistake of testing in the hope of stumbling onto something interesting! In the future, when large numbers of people have been tested and accessible DNA databases are exploding with samples, the odds will improve that a random person could get tested and discover something interesting, such as a surprise match with a stranger. But we're not quite there yet.

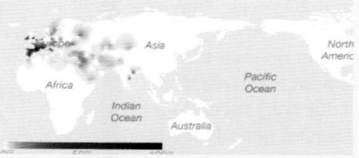

$12 Trace Your Roots with DNA Megan Smolenyak Smolenyak & Ann Turner, 2004, 272 p.

$100 The Genographic Project

Figure 6-12: Relationship chart showing percentage of shared DNA

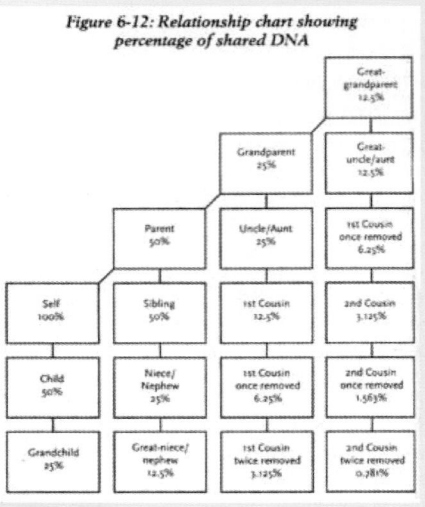

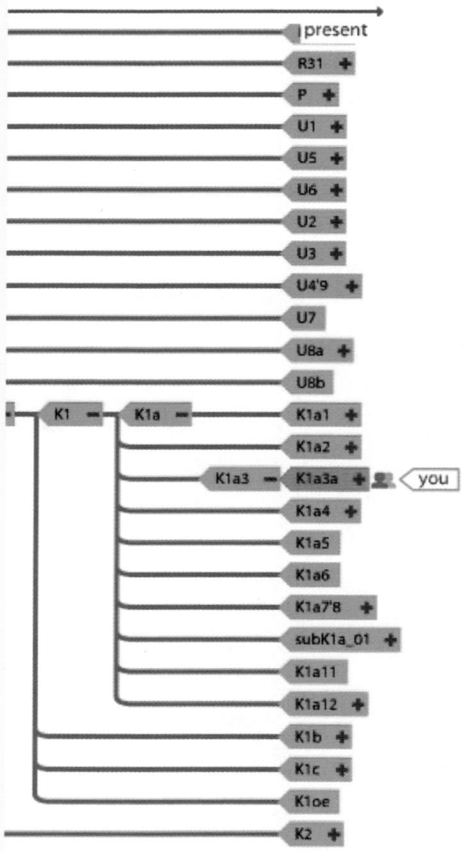

Deep ancestry
23andMe

$99 23andme.com

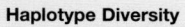

Getting your genes sequenced won't revolutionize your health right now. It's still too early in the science. However, knowing your genes is a great way to explore your ancestral genealogy. 23andMe began selling inexpensive gene sequencing kits for health perspectives but customers showed greater interest in using genes to delve into their ancestry. For $99 you can learn a lot -- and maybe gain some personal health insights too. There's now 200,000 members of 23andMe, plus tens of thousands others around the world, making links to genetic relatives likely. Once you surrender some spit into the kit and get your gene sequences, you can map, share and research your genes' path through time. More than just recent generations, your gene haplotypes will inform you about deeper connections in the human family tree. I learned from 23andMe tests that my maternal haplogroup is related to Otzi the Ice Man from the Alps, and Druze and Kurds in the mid-East. And my paternal haplogroup is related to an Irish King of the 4th and 5th centuries. More research keeps turning up more interesting connections. If I want, I can connect to other testers on the site sharing the same haplogroups. I'm now encouraging my larger family to participate in this adventure.

-- KK

R1b1b2a1a2f2 is a subgroup of R1b1b2

Early inhabitants of Ireland constructed monuments such as this one more than 6,000 years ago.

Introduction

Haplogroup R is a widespread and diverse branch of the Y-chromosome tree that is extremely common in Europe, where it spread after the end of the Ice Age about 12,000 years ago. The haplogroup appears to have originated in southwestern Asia about 30,000 years ago. It then split into two main branches. R1 ultimately spread widely across Eurasia, from Iceland to Japan, whereas R2 mostly remained near its region of origin. Today it can be found in southwestern Asia and India.

● **Haplogroup K1**

Ötzi the Ice Man was discovered in 1991, protruding from a snow-bank high in the Alps near the Austrian-Italian border. His 5,300-year-old remains turned out to be so well preserved that researchers were able to construct a detailed account of his life and death. They have also determined that his maternal line was derived from haplogroup K, which remains common in Alpine populations today....A few branches of haplogroup K, such as K1a9, K2a2a, and K1a1b1a, are specific to Jewish populations and especially to Ashkenazi Jews, whose roots lie in central and eastern Europe. These branches of haplogroup K are found at levels of 30% among Ashkenazi. But they are also found at lower levels in Jewish populations from the Near East and Africa, and among Sephardic Jews who trace their roots to medieval Spain. That indicates an origin of these K haplogroup branches in the Near East before 70 AD, when the Roman destruction of Jerusalem scattered the Jewish people around the Mediterranean and beyond.

R1b1b2a1a2f2 is a subgroup of R1b1b2

Locations of haplogroup R1b1b2 circa 500 year: era of intercontinental travel.

Haplogroup R1b1b2a1a2f2

R1b1b2a1a2f2 reaches its peak in Ireland, where the vast majority of men carry Y-chromosomes belonging to the haplogroup. Researchers have recently discovered that a large subset of men assigned to the haplogroup may be direct male descendants of an Irish king who ruled during the 4th and early 5th centuries. According to Irish history, a king named Niall of the Nine Hostages established the Ui Neill dynasty that ruled the island country for the next millennium. Northwestern Ireland is said to have been the core of Niall's kingdom; and that is exactly where men bearing the genetic signature associated with him are most common. About 17% of men in northwestern Ireland have Y-chromosomes that are exact matches to the signature, and another few percent vary from it only slightly. In New York City, a magnet for Irish immigrants during the 19th and early 20th century, 2% of men have Y-chromosomes matching the Ui Neill signature. Genetic analysis suggests that all these men share a common ancestor who lived about 1,700 years ago. Among men living in northwestern Ireland today that date is closer to 1,000 years ago. Those dates neatly bracket the era when Niall is supposed to have reigned.

The following haplogroup tree appears at left:

present
R31
P
U1
U5
U6
U2
U3
U4'9
U7
U8a
U8b
K1 — K1a — K1a1
K1a2
K1a3 — K1a3a — you
K1a4
K1a5
K1a6
K1a7'8
subK1a_01
K1a11
K1a12
K1b
K1c
K1oe
K2

If you build it, they will come. - Field of Dreams

Diverse optical supplies
Anchor Optics
Prices Vary Anchor Optics

Remember Edmund Scientific, the perennial advertiser in the back of science magazines? They sold lenses in addition to all kinds of scientific knick-knacks and basement experimenter supplies. Anchor Optics is a division of Edmund's upscale optics company, selling mostly to professionals, but at a discount. They've got loupes and microscopes, but also Fresnel lenses, commercial grade front-side mirrors, laser parts, optical bench gear, prisms, and advance fiber optic stuff — just about anything optical you can imagine at good prices, Anchor sells Edmund's surplus or "seconds" — but only second in some cosmetic or inessential way. If you need a lens or an optical flat mirror of a certain size, you'll probably end up here.

-- KK

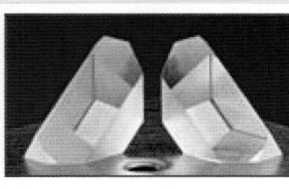

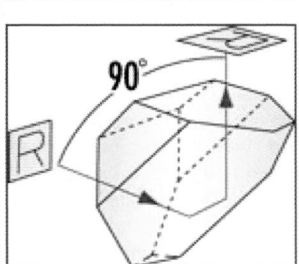

Amici Prisms, also called "roof prisms" or "right angle roof prisms," do two things: invert the image and bend the line of sight through a 90 degree angle. They are excellent as prism diagonals in optical systems, since they erect the inverted image. Also ideal for use in spotting scopes, and any optical instrument where it is desirable to take an inverted image from an objective, turn it right side up, and bend it through a 90 degree angle, to maintain the correct visual orientation.

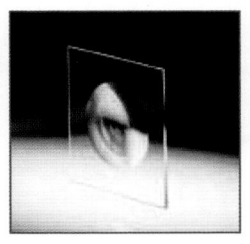

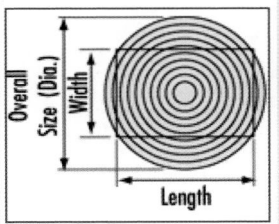

A Fresnel lens replaces the curved surface of a conventional lens with a series of concentric grooves, molded into a surface of a thin, light-weight plastic sheet. The grooves act as individual refracting surfaces like tiny prisms when viewed in cross section, bending parallel ray in a very close approximation to a common focal length. Because the lens is thin, very little light is lost by absorption. Fresnel lenses can be used as magnifiers (except #26091) or projection lenses. However, there is a high level of distortion.

Source for all scopes
Eagle Optics
Prices Eagle Optics

You want binoculars? Eagle Optics has hundreds of kinds from two dozen manufacturers. Any model binocular made. You want spotting scopes, or night vision scopes? This is the place. Monoculars, tripods, rangefinders? Eagle Optics has practically every version of them too. Good service. Popular with birders and nature photographers. They have a paper catalog, also.

-- KK

Burnton Echo 7 x18 Monocular

Extremely small and lightweight.

The Echo zoom monocular is one of the smallest zoom monoculars around and easily carried so it's always handy. The polymer body is extremely lightweight-weighing less than two ounces- and perfect for a detailed study of nature at your feet. Multi-coated optics and BaK-4 prism glass team up for sharper images at any distance.

Nikon EDG 10×42 Binocular

Engineered to push your birding to the edge.

The powerful 10×42 EDG (pronounced "Edge") is a stylish binocular that truly elevates superior performance by virtually eliminating chromatic aberration and delivering bright, razor sharp views. Go ahead and push your birding to the edge with Nikon's EDG binocular.

Open bridge style with sophisticated quadrangle construction balances perfectly in the hand for comfortable, extended viewing.

Dual focus knob with locking diopter pairs up a quick, central focusing knob with pop-up diopter adjustments for unparalleled speed and convenience.

Ratcheting eyecup adjustments allow for a refined view, with or without eyewear.

Thumb-position memory contours provide optimum traction with a soft-grip tactile surface.

Magnesium-alloy body cuts weight without sacrificing durability.

Waterproof and fogproof with O-ring seals and dry nitrogen purging to handle the

toughest conditions on the planet. (Submersible for up to 10 minutes at a depth of 16.4 feet).

Handy 10x magnifier
Belomo 10x Triplet Loupe
$35 Amazon

A few months ago I picked up a Belomo 10x Triplet Loupe to help out with mushroom identification in the field. As someone who has more experience with camera lenses than loupes, I didn't know what to expect. What arrived was an immaculately crafted magnifying device that I now carry on a daily basis.

Built by the Belarus Optical and Mechanical Enterprise Company (they once made high quality optics for the Soviet Union during the Cold War), the minuscule 10x loupe radiates a quality of craft and "thingness" that I've previously only seen in Leica glass. This comparison is in part owed to the superb optics, but also to the textured black enamel that coats the folding steel case coupled with its solid build quality.

The loupe itself is compact, quick to fold out, and easy to use. Between using it to identify mushrooms, to seeing the destruction I wreak on my fingernails, or the dulled edge of my kitchen knives, I have found the ability to easily magnify anything 10x (or more) has given me a renewed appreciation for the smaller things in life.

My decision to pick up the 10x magnification instead of the 15x or 20x was driven by cost and usability. Everyone I spoke to seemed to agree that 10x had the best balance between field of view, depth of field, and cost. Unlike other loupes where you can change magnification through opening up additional lenses, the Belomo relies on a single lens system that reduces the chance of breaking, while providing greater optical quality and increased light. The image quality is really fantastic.

One of the best features of the Belomo Loupe is the ability to incorporate it as an external macro lens with my iPhone camera. The small sensor size coupled with the Loupe means that it has enough depth of field to create photos I can use to identify when I get home. I've been blown away with the results.

The Belomo loupe is a fantastic EDC tool that provides a new way to look at the world. I can't recommend it enough.

-- Oliver Hulland

Flexible portable neon
El Wire
$2+ per foot, in bulk Live Wire
Custom Kits Live Wire

Do-it-yourself neon. This thin electroluminescent wire (el-wire) glows very brightly. You can bend it easily, tie it to anything. It produces essentially no heat. Best all of it runs on batteries, meaning you can wear it or use it on your bicycle. We make signs with it and, of course, some wild costumes. El-wire (also called Live Wire) has been used to great effect in the night parades at Burning Man. It comes in various lengths from .5 m to 10 m (you can cut it if you know what you are doing) and in eight colors. You can also make it strobe. The coolest thing to do is weave it. It is the world's most flexible light. It is very cool stuff.

-- KK

Cool bendable lights
Glow Tubes, in bulk

I'm partial to things that light up the night. I like those foot-long noodles that glow in various shades of color, popular at raves. They are great for art and photography ss well. Like road safety sticks but thinner, longer, more flexible and cheaper. These floppy light wands say: be creative! Since they are flexible and light and cheap they can be woven into bike spokes, sewn on clothes, spun, pinned, or swung. They'll last 7 or 8 hours and if by chance you are near a freezer you can freeze "ignited" ones; just thaw them out and they start glowing again. Called glow sticks, they come in all sizes from mini-sticks to swords.

One or two tubes are okay; but the key to the fun is to get them in bulk, by the hundreds. One hundred 8" sections should be about 10 cents a piece, or $10. One hundred is not too many. It's barely enough to cover a jacket with them, or decorate 3 bicycles, or make a huge glowing hula hoop, or enough bangles for all the arms at a party. The supplier here has the lowest prices I've come across and I've used them with no problems.

-- KK

$16 8" Glow Bracelets, 100 ct. Sure Glow

$25 22" Glow Necklaces, 50 ct. Sure Glow

Science Live

Try-and-build science
MythBusters

$30 Discovery Channel Store and Netflix

If you pay attention you can learn a lot of science from watching Mythbusters. In between blowing stuff up, the hosts perform scientific experiments -- with controls, measurements, and results. I believe Mythbusters has taught more science to more people than all the high-schools combined. The show's official premise is to verify urban myths. You know, folklore claims such as: you can kill someone with a bullet of ice, but it would leave no evidence. So the Mythbusters test these claims by cleverly replicating the myth in a control way. But since this is a TV show, once the defined experiment is completed they push it to the limit. If they can't get an urban legend to work scientifically, they try to recreate the results Hollywood style. My entire family, including teenage girls, soak up these lessons hungrily. Besides the ad hoc science I love the way the hosts demonstrate the benefits of rapid prototyping and thinking by doing. It's a race to see how fast they can create something that works. Fail and iterate; another lesson of science. And as a bonus, you wind up with a fairly good grasp of which urban legends have any veracity (Can a penny dropped from a skyscraper kill a pedestrian below? Can a sword split a bullet? etc.), and how to be skeptical about claims made by friends of friends. Now after a decade of shows, there are plenty to choose from; every one I've seen has been worth watching.

-- KK

▲ *Trying to prove that Jack didn't need to die when the Titanic sunk.*

◄ *Inside a plexiglass coffin they test whether there really is a "fear of death" smell.*

▲ *A common companion in their experiments is a full-size, full-weight human dummy who stands in for a victum, in this case when they test whether a tiny hole in a plane can cause it to exlpode when pressurized.* ▼ *The dummy is also a target for testing whether a trumpet could hide a gun for an angry musician.*

▲ *No show is complete without an explosion . Here they test whether shooting a car's gas tank with a gun can cause it to blow up.*

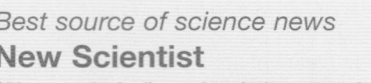

▲ *A film canister, wire and a bolt, all parts of a generator flashlight.*

◄ *Making a Davis saftey mine lamp using a screen and flame.*

Best source of science news
New Scientist

$99 new print/online subscriptions New Scientist
$85 online access only New Scientist
$154 (renewals) Amazon

Science is the only new news. There is more and more of it than ever so I have trouble keeping up. I've been an off-and-on subscriber to the richest source, *Science*, but I am currently off it simply because I could not keep up with the weekly deluge of diamond-dense information it dumped on me. *Scientific American* is drastically uneven, and recently too preachy, so although I subscribe, it is not essential. *Discover* is okay but not as, well, scientific. Over the years, the only periodical that has remained a constant source of readable science news, with no dumbing down, and much uplifting of ideas, as well as providing a great sense of important frontiers, is *New Scientist*. It is smart, ahead of the curve of other publications, deep, accessible, and reliable. If you can only subscribe to one source of the new news, *New Scientist* is it.

I value it most for what it does not run. It doesn't explain what DNA is again. Rather it talks up to its readers, assuming you have basic science literacy. Think of it as an *Economist* for science. It wisely selects pattern-shifting stuff, and I've come to concur with its nose for interesting news that will stay new. Issues from years ago still read fresh. Yet it avoids hype and sci-fi wet dreams.

Much of its power stems from its reliance on subscribers rather than consumer advertisers for its income; it really does serve

---

Bootstrapping science
Rough Science

$79 Bullfrog Films

A very cool BBC series wherein the crafty producers take a bunch of scientists and technicians to a remote location and have them recreate sophisticated tools and inventions using only the primitive materials on hand. Vines, wood, bits of metal, shells, parts in old buildings. Here: make a clock (with bell), or a device to record sounds, or how about a camera, microscope, soap and sunblock?; or go survey and map the island — using tools of your own construction. You don't know science until you can roll your own. This 10-part program is highly instructional because you get to see technology reduced to its essence — and because not everything works. It's hard to find currently, except as bits on YouTube.

-- KK

readers. But that also means this weekly British publication is on the expensive side. Rather than the normal $18 per year that most ad-inflated magazines in the US charge, this weekly will run you $150 annually. (There's a cheap intro price to get you hooked.) It is well worth the investment. May it live long and prosper.

– KK

•
When photographer Marc Schlossman opened a drawer at the Field Museum in Chicago, he found the birds as you see them here. With his series of photos of lost animals he wants to emphasise our role in extinctions. "This is all happening so quickly now, at an unprecedented rate," he says.

But extinct animals may not be lost forever. US environmentalist Stewart Brand has an ambitious plan to "de-extinctify" passenger pigeons – bring them back to life by identifying and then splicing the relevant genes into a relative, the band-tailed pigeon. The technical challenges are formidable, and even if it works, the species might still not be viable in the wild. Nor is it agreed that reintroducing extinct animals into the modern world is a good idea. Brand waves this objection away, saying that the pigeon's old habitat is intact, adding: "In the rare case of unwelcome ecological disruption, we know the vulnerabilities of the formerly extinct animals, so we know exactly how to reduce their numbers or eliminate them again."

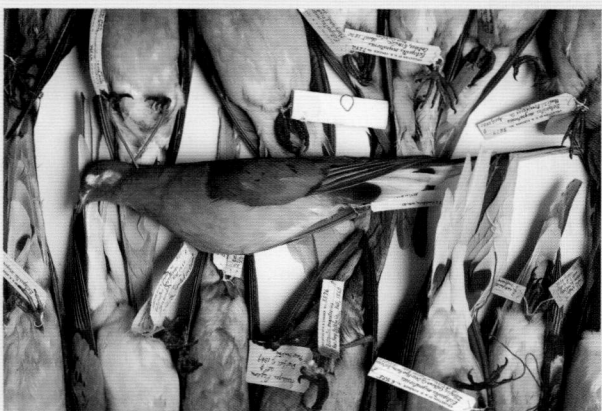

Competitive tinkering
Junkyard Wars

The TV show that was once the most commonly recorded on a TiVo is the hackers' special, Junkyard Wars. Two teams of tinkers race against each other to construct a working submarine,

or an airplane, or a cannon, or deep-sea diving gear, all assembled from scrap found in a junkyard, and all built within a day and a half. That both sides usually succeed at some level (although only one side wins) is the first surprise of this TV series. More

Amphibian dune buggy from scrap parts.

amazing is the easy lesson in physics and engineering each episode brings. By watching a pump is cobbled together from motorscooter tires, one gets a visceral sense of how a pump works. By watching how geeks think around impossible obstacles,

An attempt to build a flying machine in 36 hours.

one catches the confidence to tackle an impossible project. They are educational enough that some science classes show them. Although no new shows have been made since 2004, the show ran 5 seasons and is worth tracking down. The show was originally started in England where it

Launching a homemade torpedo.

was called Scrapheap Challenge and ran 8 seasons, the last one in 2009. They are rarely broadcast today; your best bet is a 7-disc "best of" DVD of highlights from the shows.

-- KK

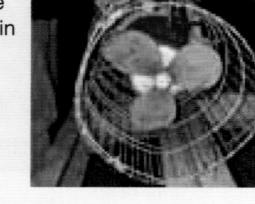

The propeller end of the team's torpedo.

The afterburners of a drag-racing tricycle.

$50 (7 DVD Best of Set)
Amazon

In every idea a multitude of new ideas is lying dormant. - Emanuel Swedenborg

Brilliant 3D maze
Perplexus

$17 Amazon

This is a cool 3-dimensional maze that is easy to get started and hard to finish. You need to steer a small metal ball along an ingenious obstacle course by rotating the clear plastic globe. There are 100 stations along the way, including some difficult topsy-turvy turns. All ages can get into it. We've found the puzzle to be extremely addictive to anyone who gets started. Because it's like a 3D video game without the electronics, the very physical nature of playing — turning it this way and that — is very satisfying. In addition, the maze is like a sculpture, the design of the route is geekily brilliant, and the elegance of the eternal return of the steel ball within the sphere is a stroke of genius. Perplexus has the glow of a work of art. It makes me happy just to pick it up.

-- KK

Classic puzzle in great package
Tangoes

$10 Amazon

Simple games are the best. Tangrams are an old puzzle based on a set of elemental shapes that can be arranged in thousands of different patterns. To recreate a given picture is challenging, yet not too daunting even for kids. Playing gently encourages lateral thinking. It exercises a geometrical logic, rather than words or numbers. The puzzles are almost like peanuts; you keep wanting just one more.

We use tangrams as an after dinner game. Everyone gets a set and we compete to find the solution first. Since the shapes can be contained in one large square, you can easily cut your own version from cardboard or plastic (and we have). But I've found that this Tangoes model is precise, won't wear out, and crates up easily and tidily. Each Tangoes case contains two sets of tangrams (in two different colors) and a nifty set of puzzle pattern

cards, all of which slide into a plastic case with instructions on the inside. It's a very nice package. We have several sets, to fill all the seats at a table.

-- KK

3D Tangrams
Wedgits

$37 Fat Brain Toys

I first saw this toy construction set at a front-door exhibit in the San Francisco-based Exploratorium. You arrange the rectangular plastic pieces in endless formations, limited only by your geometrical imagination. The squares interlock loosely, cleverly. A baby can do it. Every time you come to the set, you see new possibilities. But unlike other complicated construction sets, this ingenious one has just four simple sizes of one shape. I think of Wedgits as a 3D version of the ancient Tangram game. In fact you can get a booklet with profiles of shapes which you can try to build, in

Tangram mode. Wedgits will challenge an adult, yet are easily manipulated by the small hands of an infant.

I'd get the Deluxe Set version with 30 pieces.

-- KK

Personalized photo jigsaw
Photo Jigsaw Puzzles

My family is addicted to jigsaw puzzles. When a special birthday came up for one of my daughters, I prepared a photo collage using paint.net and ordered a photo jigsaw puzzle from Venus Puzzle.

The puzzle comes in a custom box, shrink wrapped and with a copy of the submitted photo on the cover, commercial quality. Puzzle pieces and printing was of excellent quality.

Since you can submit any image with the suggested proportions and dpi, this service can replace or improve upon the previously reviewed hometown puzzle.

The advantage to this site is that

it ships internationally with the same DHL charges for anywhere in the world.

For my next daughter I didn't want to use DHL, and Venus Puzzle referred me to their sister site Piczzle, which has the same product range and quality, also shipping worldwide (but with regular post instead of DHL).

Base prices are a little cheaper on the Venus Puzzle site, but for my country, DHL added customs service charges that made it unattractive. The order from Piczzle arrived in about a week, instead of in 4 days.

Note that both sites are slightly clunky, and only the Venus Puzzle site has the necessary information on the recommended proportions and resolution: In my case I purchased the 550 piece puzzle which uses a 1:1.25 ration and minimum dpi of 150.

-- Aryeh Abramovitz

$38 550-piece puzzle Venus Puzzle

$55 550-piece puzzle Piczzle

Personalized map puzzle
Hometown Puzzle

$40 National Geographic

For Christmas this year I gave my parents a personalized puzzle featuring a custom map of the area around their lake cabin. "From any starting point, we'll create a 400-piece puzzle of a six-by-four-mile area using U.S. Geological Survey maps. A house-shaped piece in the center represents the address you choose. Shows main roads, contour lines, water features, vegetation, and notable buildings. Arrives in a presentation box with space for a personal message." If you search for a promo code, you can save 20%.

-- Jason Palmiter

Lease premium puzzles
ELMS Hand Cut Puzzle Rental Club

$50 (up to 299 pieces) ELMS Puzzles

Dedicated jigsaw puzzlers know nothing matches the quality (or challenge) of a hand-cut wooden puzzle. But at about $2.00 or so per piece they are outrageously expensive (a 20" x 24" 1000-piece puzzle can cost $3,000). ELMS Puzzles solves the dilemma by offering a rental program that lets you keep a puzzle for three months, by which time you should either be done or realize you've met your match.

The wooden pieces (unlike cardboard) are very exact in their fitting so you have to be very certain about having the right piece. Also, many are cut with straight lines inside the puzzle — i.e. a piece in the middle won't have interlocking pieces. Those who do puzzles

by putting together the border and working their way in will really be challenged; and many of the pieces are cut in shapes appropriate for the puzzle. For example, a Christmas puzzle will have

a piece the shape of a Christmas tree, the shape of a sleigh, the shape of an angel, etc. Oh, and no picture comes with the puzzle for those who "cheat" by looking at the top of the box.

While still not cheap, at $40 – $225 depending on the number of pieces, renting these puzzles becomes affordable for special occasions like family vacations with other puzzle fanatics. There are other companies that sell puzzles (Stave comes to mind from having seen their advertisements in The

New Yorker), but ELMS are the only people I know who rent. I like the idea of renting 15–20 puzzles for the price of buying one.

I recognize this is not something everyone thinks is sane. Our family members are divided on it, some love them, others think it's the biggest waste of time known to man. You either like jigsaw puzzles or are bored silly by them, but if you're a fan you should enjoy the pleasure of a quality hand cut puzzle at least once.

-- Julee Bode

Making Fun

Stuntology
Practical jokes made practical

$11 Best of Stuntology Sam Bartlett, 2008, 327 pages

Pranks you can use. Stupid tricks, dumb gags, and funny routines. Liberate your inner 12-year-old with this handdrawn manual.

-- KK

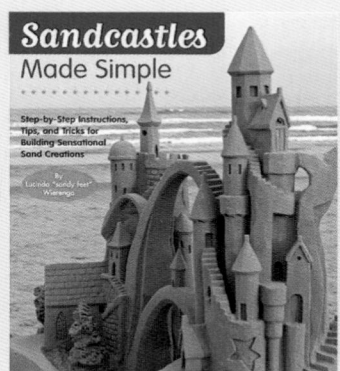

Sandcastles Made Simple
Low-tech sand castle construction manual

$11 Lucinda Wierenga, 2005, 128 p.

In case you haven't noticed, sand castles have become very elaborate and sand sculpture a new art form. Building them is a complicated business. We've used the simple methods here to build sandcastles we can be proud of without too much equipment. In our experience the most important part is finding a beach with suitable building sand. For the rest, follow this book and/or DVD.

-- KK

Most beach trips I would sit and read while my wife played around in the sand building castles. This year, I found a great resource that had me building sand castles and sculptures that stopped every passerby on the beach.

The Sons of the Beach *Sandcastles Made Simple* book showed me how to build high-reaching towers and arches by hand, without any buckets or forms. Their tool set was perfect for giving professional looking details. Their optional DVD makes it even easier to learn their technique.

The first week I had their book, I built a 48" tall light house, several castles (one with a monorail train), and a snowman (they teach you how to make snowballs out of sand). Many people asked me how many years I'd been doing sand sculpture!

The book and DVD teach "hand stacking." This is a process of scooping a big handfuls of completely saturated wet sand and plopping them on top of each other. By jiggling the sand just as the excess water is running out, it fuses the new plop with the previous ones creating a stable tower.

These folks also discuss and sell large forms (5, 3, 2 foot diameter) which can be used for large competition sculpture, but that was more than I wanted to carry down to the beach.

-- Chris Evans

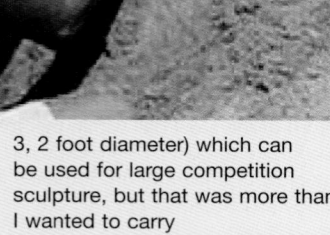

Tools for advanced sand castling

Doing Circus
Circus resources

Free Juggling Information Services
Free American Youth Circus Organization
Free The Runaway Circus

Circus is a physical art-form that can engender a sense of control just as any type of athletics or dance training can. However, unlike most physical disciplines, circus has a place for almost any physical type. It's one of the few places where I've seen short powerfully built women valued for their bodies. The circus is associated with the carnavelsque, so it's a great way to have a party or to disrupt social patterns. And circus is also a lot of fun.

Circus is still mainly an oral tradition. Moreover, for certain of its disciplines it is confined to very particular places that can rig the necessary equipment and safety devices. It would be, for example, impossible and probably immoral to write a book describing how to learn the flying trapeze. There are plenty of books and resources for learning the object manipulation arts, eg. juggling, stick spinning, plate spinning, diabolo, etc. A good place to start with these would be Juggling Information Services. However, most serious folks quickly move back to oral traditions.

I think the best value however, if you have the time, are youth circus programs. Many big cities have non-profit programs that teach circus to youth. Many of these programs will offer volunteers instruction in the circus arts. The American Youth Circus Organization has a directory of youth circus programs.

Of course, working for a circus is not a bad way to learn either, and the way that most people, historically, have learned the trade.

-- Forest Gregg, co-founder of Runaway Circus

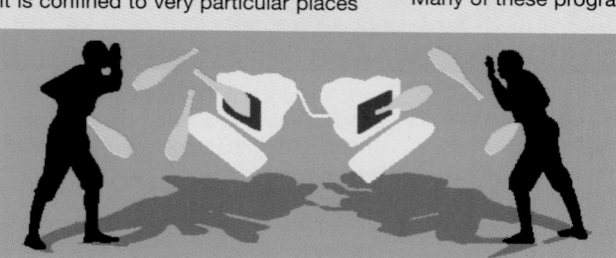

Skuut Balance Bike
Teach new riders how to balance

$75 Amazon

Balance bikes teach balance before pedaling. Learning to pedal is easy if you know how to balance. Learning balance is fairly easy, too. But learning them concurrently is hard. With a balance bike instead of a trike or a standard bike with training wheels, it's much easier for a child to learn the balance, steering dynamics and handling required to ride a bike. My son, at 2 1/2, can go at least a mile on his Skuut bike, and is learning all the skills he'll need, so that when I get him a normal bicycle, with pedals, he won't need training wheels.

The design of a balance bike is brilliant—it's actually similar to the design of the first bicycles (velocipedes) that had no drivetrains. The particular brand of a running or balance bike for kids is not of much concern. Cool Tools previously featured the Likeabike, which was imported from Europe and lovingly crafted, but notably expensive. You can find cheap $50 metal balance bikes these days, but we use the current wooden standard Skuut which is good enough quality for $85.

-- Elon Schoenholz

Flybar
Extreme Pogo Stick

When the guy at the bike store first told us about the Flybar, he said "Man, that thing bounces twenty feet!" It doesn't, but I understand why he exaggerated. The Flybar has an amazing Boing Factor. Instead of a standard spring, it uses rubber-like bands which make the bounce feel more like a trampoline and can give you a real workout. It's bulky, but sturdy. You can adjust to handle adult or kid weight. My 13-year-old son saved up for months to buy one and he's never been sorry, because when he takes it to the local park, the little kids stare at him open-mouthed and the big kids try to keep their mouths closed and hide the fact they're staring. It's expensive, but until everyone has one, you will be the most awesome novelty on your block.

Yeah, it's dangerous. You should wear a helmet. Pads would be a good idea. But skateboards, mountain bikes, trampolines, and see-saws can be dangerous too. And fun!

-- Jay Allison

$233 Flybar 800 Pogo Stick Amazon

$380 Flybar 1200 Pogo Stick Flybar

God became a human being so human beings might become God. - Irenaeus

The Art of Game Design
$45 Jesse Schell, 2008, 512 p.

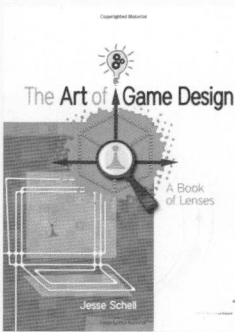

This is by far the best guide ever written for designing games. All kinds of games, simple and traditional, but of course video games too. This fat book is packed with practical, comprehensive, imaginative, deep, and broad lessons. Every page contained amazing insights for me. The more I read and re-read, the more important I ranked this work. I now view it as not just about designing games, but one of the best guides for designing anything that demands complex interaction. My 13-year-old son, who, like most 13-year-olds, dreams of designing games, has been devouring its 470 pages, telling me, "You've got to read this, Dad!" It's that kind of book: You begin to imagine your life as a game, and how you might tweak its design. Author Jesse Schell offers 100 "lenses" through which you can view your game, and each one is a useful maxim for any assignment.

-- KK

•

We must be absolutely clear on this point before we can proceed. The game is not the experience. The game enables the experience, but it is not the experience. This is a hard concept for some people to grasp.

•

Lens #1: The Lens of Essential Experience

To use this lens, you stop thinking about your game and start thinking about the experience of the player. Ask yourself these questions:

What experience do I want the player to have?

What is essential to that experience?

How can my game capture that essence?

If there is a big difference between the experience you want to create and the one you are actually creating, your game needs to change: You need to clearly state the essential experience you desire, and find as many ways as possible to instill this essence into your game.

•

Let's review the list of game qualities we have picked out of these various definitions:

Q1. Games are entered willfully.

Q2. Games have goals.

Q3. Games have conflict.

Q4. Games have rules.

Q5. Games can be won and lost.

Q6. Games are interactive.

Q7. Games have challenge.

Q8. Games can create their own internal value.

Q9. Games engage players.

Q10. Games are closed, formal systems.

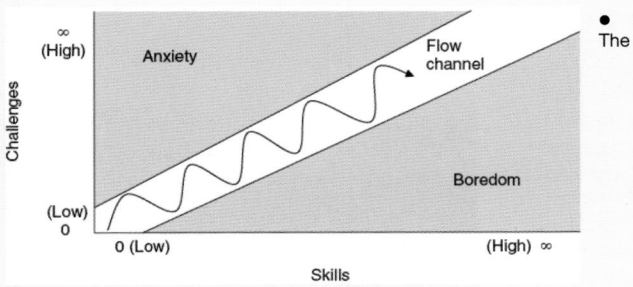

thing that really seems to bother people about calling puzzles games is that they are not replayable. Once you figure out the best strategy, you can solve the puzzle every time, and it is no longer fun. Games are not usually this way. Most games have enough dynamic elements that each time you play you are confronted again with a new set of problems to solve. Sometimes this is because you have an intelligent human opponent (checkers, chess, backgammon, etc.), and sometimes it is because the game is able to generate lots of different challenges for you, either through ever-advancing goals (setting a new high score record) or through some kind of rich challenge-generation mechanism (solitaire, Rubik's Cube, Tetris, etc.)

Specifically, that the player puts their mind inside the game world, but that game world really only exists in the mind of the player? This magical situation, which is at the heart of all we care about, is made possible by the game interface, which is where player and game come together. Interface is the infinitely thin membrane that separates white/yang/player and black/yin/game. When the interface fails, the delicate flame of experience that rises from the player/game interaction is suddenly snuffed out. For this reason, it is crucial for us to understand how our game interface works, and to make it as robust, as powerful, and as invisible as we can.

•

Experiences without feedback are frustrating and confusing. At many crosswalks in the United States, pedestrians can push a button that will make the DON'T WALK sign change to a WALK sign so they can cross the street safely. But it can't change right away, since that would cause traffic accidents. So the poor pedestrian often has to wait up to a minute to see whether pressing the button had any effect. As a result, you see all kinds of strange button-pressing behavior: some people push the button and hold it for several seconds, others push it several times in a row, just to be safe. And the whole experience is accompanied by a sense of uncertainty — pedestrians can often be seen nervously studying the lights and DON'T WALK sign to see if it is going to change, because they might not have pushed the button correctly.

What a delight it was to visit the United Kingdom, and find that in some areas the crosswalk buttons give immediate feedback in the form of an illuminated WAIT sign that comes on when the button has been pushed, and turns off when the WALK period has ended! The addition of some simple feedback turned an experience where a pedestrian feels frustrated into one where they can feel confident and in control.

•

For all the grand dreams of interactive storytelling, there are two methods that dominate the world of game design. The first and most dominant in videogames is commonly called the "string of pearls" or sometimes the "rivers and lakes" method. It is called this because it can be visually represented like this:

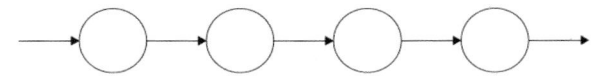

The idea is that a completely non-interactive story (the string) is presented in the form of text, a slideshow, or an animated sequence and then the player is given a period of free movement and control (the pearl) with a fixed goal in mind. When the goal is achieved, the player travels down the string via another non-interactive sequence, to the next pearl, etc. In other words, cut scene, game level, cut scene, game level…

Many people criticize this method as "not really being interactive," but players sure do enjoy it.

•

If 10 choices sounds kind of short, and you want to have 20 opportunities for three choices from the beginning to the end of the story, that means you'll need to write 5,230,176,601 outcomes. These large numbers make any kind of meaningful branching storytelling impossible in our short life spans. And sadly, the main way that most interactive storytellers deal with this perplexing plethora of plotlines is to start fusing outcomes together — something like:

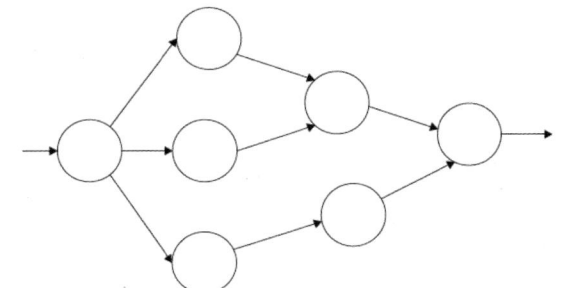

•

Problem #3: Multiple Endings Disappoint

One thing that interactive storytellers like to fantasize about is how wonderful it is that a story can have multiple endings. After all, this means the player will be able to play again and again with a different experience every time! And like many fantasies,

the reality tends to disappoint. Many games have experimented with having multiple endings to their game story. Almost universally, the player ends up thinking two things when they encounter their first ending in one of these:

1. "Is this the real ending?"

2. "Do I have to play this whole thing again to see another ending?"

There are exceptions, of course. Star Wars: Knights of the Old Republic featured a novel type of player choice — did they want to play the game on the "light side" or "dark side" of the force — that is, with good or evil goals? Depending on which of the paths you choose, you have different adventures, different quests, and ultimately a different ending. It can be argued that this isn't really a case of two different endings on the same story, but two completely different stories — so different that they are each equally valid.

•

Problem #4: Not Enough Verbs

The things that videogame characters spend their time doing are very different than the things that characters in movies and books spend their time doing:

Videogame Verbs: run, shoot, jump, climb, throw, cast, punch, fly

Movie Verbs: talk, ask, negotiate, convince, argue, shout, plead, complain

Videogame characters are severely limited in their ability to do anything that requires something to happen above the neck. Most of what happens in stories is communication, and at the present time, videogames just can't support that. Game designer Chris Swain has suggested that when technology advances to the point that players can have an intelligent, spoken conversation with computer-controlled game characters, it will have an effect similar to the introduction of talking pictures. Suddenly, a medium that was mostly considered an amusing novelty will quickly become the dominant form of cultural storytelling. Until then, however, the lack of usable verbs in videogames significantly hampers our ability to use games as a storytelling medium.

•

As the character tries to overcome the obstacles, interesting conflicts tend to arise, particularly when another character has a conflicting goal. This simple pattern leads to very interesting stories because it means the character has to engage in problem-solving (which we find very interesting), because conflicts lead to unpredictable results, in other words, surprises (which we find very interesting), and because the bigger the obstacle, the bigger the potential for dramatic change (which we find very interesting).

Are these ingredients just as useful when creating videogame stories? Absolutely and maybe even more so.

•

One focus group I witnessed was trying to determine where the average mom drew the line about what videogames were "too violent" for their kids. Virtua Fighter was okay, said the moms, Mortal Kombat was not. The difference? Blood. It wasn't the actions that were involved in the games that bothered them (both games are mostly about kicking your opponent in the face), but rather the graphic bloodshed in Mortal Kombat that is completely absent in Virtua Fighter. They seemed to feel that without bloodshed, it was just a game — just imaginary. But the blood made the game creepily real, and to the moms in the interviews, a game that rewarded bloodshed felt perverse and dangerous.

Silly Putty by the pound
$22 for one pound Funny Putty Fun Stuff USA

Silly putty — even the newer varieties like the thinking putty here — has long been sold in small amounts in the classic plastic egg. But this stuff is best enjoyed in bulk. The technical name of this now generic substance is Dow Corning Dilatant Compound 3179. Five pounds of it is…. well, pretty silly. Ten pounds of the stuff is enough to transfer a whole page of comics, or to make a humungous superball, or to lighten up the dour faces in a boardroom after being parcelled out. The surprise for our family has been never ending amusement of watching a huge ball of this compound slowly melt over whatever you set it on, like the blob from outer space. Hand out some at your next birthday party. Don't ask why.

-- KK

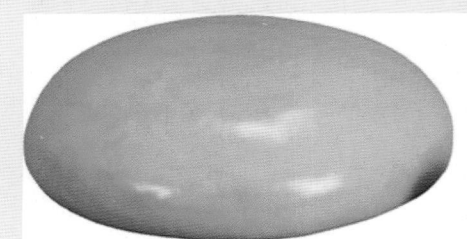

Construction Systems

starting out with some simple structures, you will quickly start to think of more complicated structures. I found the challenge to build more interesting designs quite addictive.

There are several starter sets, plus add-on kits that allow you to build more complicated structures. I started with the Cuboro Standard, and recently added the Cugolino set. Although Cuboro is a bit pricey for a toy, the manufacturing quality is exceptional.

--Kurt Thearling

• Learning effect and therapeutical use: Cuboro encourages imagination (three-dimensional thinking) and creativity. Assembling requires care and patience. Due to elements with several functions (on different levels or in different directions), two or more crossing courses can be developed. Playing and planning in a group can be very interesting. Individual elements can be selected from the boxes and specific tasks can be placed, depending on the learning stage.

Marble labyrinth
Cuboro

$280 Cuboro standard set
Oh! Toys

Cuboro is they best toy I have seen since Lego. I recently purchased a set for my 3-year-old son, and we both have been having a blast with it ever since. The basic idea is simple: marbles and a track. The interesting thing is that the track is built out of individual wooden blocks with curves and channels cut into them, allowing the builder to create a track of whatever shape their imaginations can conceive. The marbles are moved along strictly by gravity, falling from one level to another and cutting back and forth through hidden tunnels. After

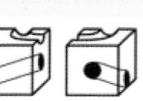

No. 1, 8x   No. 3, 2x   No. 11, 2x   No. 12, 1x   No. 13, 2x   No. 14, 1x   No. 15, 2x   No. 16, 2x   No. 17, 2x   No. 18, 2x

Cardboard fasteners
Mr. McGroovy's Box Rivets

$18 per 100 pairs   mrmcgroovys.com

Cardboard is a wonderful building material. You can do far more with it than you might expect. Use it to make furniture, sculpture, models, and of course play structures. The common way to assemble projects with cardboard boxes is to slap pieces together with duct tape. But tape is clumsy, expensive, will unpeel outdoors in weather, looks clunky, and won't take paint. A cool alternative are these Kevlar-like rivets specially designed for box cardboard. One shape does both sides. The rivets

sport a grippy ratchet that clinches them close, yet enables them to be reused. The large button gives them holding power and allows you to make joints that can swing, too. We've found that you need either two people working, or ape-long arms, to squeeze both sides of the rivet pairs. Also, they are really made for the double wall corrugated cardboard of the kind you find in large appliance boxes; on thin cardboard they aren't as prettily snug, but still will hold fine. A set of 100 (50 pairs) is enough for a small maze.

Mr. McGroovy has free plans and some nice tips on where to locate free large boxes in order to construct some awesome buildings.

-- KK

Playful plastic cups
MULA Stack and Nest Cups

$3 IKEA

Priced at under $3, the play and reuse value of these simple plastic stacking cups is just astonishing. Originally bought as a throwaway present, our set is onto their second baby and have become a staple of daily bath-time for all kids.

They stack into a tall tower, they fit together in pairs, some hold water, some have holes, some have a lot of holes, they float, some sink after a while and they fit into a compact package for storage. Each one is unique and serves a different purpose and there's just enough of them to be challenging for the under-ones to keep track of them all.

We've given sets to every family we know and will continue the tradition for as long as they are available. So simple, yet endlessly fun.

-- Robin Green

Fort building kit
Fort Magic

$200 fortmagic.com

My 10-year-old daughter and her friends love playing with the Fort Magic kit. It's a box of PVC pipes and connecters, along with clips to attach sheets or tarps. You can build all sorts of things with them, from dangerous blow guns (we use cotton balls and tape with a big needle) to clubhouses. Then take them apart and build something new. See Fort Magic's YouTube channel for other projects. It passes the year boredom test. Even after a year of playing with it, the kids aren't bored.

- Mark Frauenfelder

Unlimited construction kit
Minecraft

$27 minecraft.net

The video game Minecraft is more construction kit than video game. Like a virtual Lego kit, Minecraft allows players to put blocks together in order to build larger structures. Instead of Lego's nubbed plastic pieces, the Minecraft world contains symbolic wood, stone, sand, water, precious metals and minerals represented by pixelated blocks on the screen. These materials often interact with each other in entertaining ways -- for instance dump water on lava and you'll get obsidian. But don't get wood too close to lava, or it will catch fire. Some of these materials can be mined from "underground" -- hence the game's name -- while others can be assembled from other materials, and yet others materials can be farmed. In one game, for example, I used my vegetable garden to harvest carrots to feed my nearby pigs, which were hemmed in with a wooden fence I had built from trees. As you can tell, it's a construction kit that

appeals to adults as much as kids.

Mining and crafting -- and battling the in-game predators that frequently appear during in-game nighttime (the game part)-- are all fun, but they take time away from the sheer joy of building. So in addition to its regular "survival" mode, Minecraft has a "creative" mode that gives players an unlimited supply of every building material they want. It is possible to build structures far vaster than a mountain of Legos would allow. Die-hard players have constructed enormous Minecraft models of the following: midtown Manhattan, the starship Enterprise, the planet Earth, and the entire land of Westeros (made popular by the "Game of Thrones") and then posted walkthroughs on YouTube.

You can play or build either solo on your computer, or together with friends on a multiplayer server. Either way you won't be alone since 11 million people have downloaded the game. It costs $27. Given Minecraft's wide availability across computing

platforms (including phone versions), and the independence of its company, Mojang, from a larger corporate buyer, Minecraft may be the rare computer game that will be around for a while.

-- Mark Hurst

The job of a scientist is to generate as many wrong ideas as fast as possible. - Murray Gell-Mann

Precision building blocks
Kapla Blocks
$60 Amazon

I've concluded from many years of building with kids that when it comes to construction kits (Erector sets, K'nex, Tinkertoys, Duplex, Legos, and so on) the long-lasting enjoyment is proportional to the simplicity of the pieces.

Almost nothing is simpler than Kapla blocks. Simpler even than Legos. There is only one size, one shape, no holes: a sturdy wooden plank precision milled from hardwood. The key difference between these and ordinary wooden blocks is something they share with Legos: amazingly precise dimensions. Because of this machine-like uniformity you can build very large, high and stable structures. Even little kids can build very rapidly (without the planning Legos seem to require) and very large. And because of their simplicity — one simple plank — you can build with endless variety. Finally, because they lack the tricky locking device of Legos, and are not tiny, kids of the youngest age can build with them. And you can't break them if you tried.

Kapla blocks come in wooden buckets of various multitudes. The 1,000 piece set is sort of over-the-top, but endless fun (suitable for a day-school or the like). Like the best toys, these are not just for kids. I would include Kapla blocks, along with Legos, as a toy that you can pass on to the next generation.

-- KK

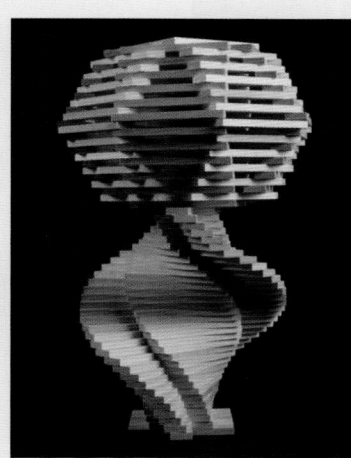

Sifts, stores Legos
BOX4BLOX
$40 BOX4BLOX

In trying to reclaim floor space in our son's bedroom, we bought this colorful cube composed of four stackable trays and a lid. Three of the trays have open grids of differing sizes, and together, they function as a phenomenal pickup, sorting (by size) and storage solution for Lego bricks. You just scoop the bricks up (our son has a dustpan that's dedicated just for Lego duty), dump them into the top tray and shake away. The smallest bricks sift down to the bottom level; each higher tray retains slightly larger bricks. At this point you can either further sort each tray by color and dump them into storage bins or just put on the lid. The cube itself is 10¼" on a side and purports to hold approximately 1500-1700 Lego bricks.

BOX4BLOX has been instrumental for well over a year now in keeping our son's collection of several thousand Lego bricks in some semblance of order and reasonably clear of his bedroom floor. So we sent one to our nephew for Christmas last year. In my son's eyes, as well as mine, BOX4BLOX really is a transformative tool— one that elevates a dreary task into something that's actually fun to do (and done well).

-- Tom Caswelch

Guided construction set
Magna-Tiles
$110 (100-piece set) Amazon

Open-ended toys are the best. That's why construction sets like Lego, or the previously reviewed Kapla Blocks, or Zomes, are perennial favorites. Their simple, durable, reusable parts build an infinite number of complex creations, providing endless hours of play. The best construction systems will last many lifetimes and are generally worth their modest investment, unlike most toys.

Magna-Tiles are the best open-ended construction set for very small kids I've seen. Magna-Tiles are plastic tiles with tiny super magnets embedded in their edges. Even a very small child can quickly assemble a structure that won't topple, since the magnets snap to form when you get them close to where they want to be. They come in a mix of squares and triangles that tend to "guide" construction towards recognizable building forms, which is okay since there are still many options to explore. But this small boost really aids the youngest toddlers who may have trouble with the go-anywhere blocks of Kapla. Also, the tiles are large, too big to swallow, so safe for wee ones.

We have a set on a our living room coffee table and I notice that adults love to build with them as well since you can erect a cool structure in only a few minutes. Everyone is an architect at heart.

Magna-Tiles aren't cheap. With 8 rare earth magnets per piece, each tile costs about $1. They are pretty unbreakable, so they should outlive you. Get the transparent variety — they are like stained glass.

-- KK

Shapeshifting magnetic spheres
NeoCube
$15 NeoCube

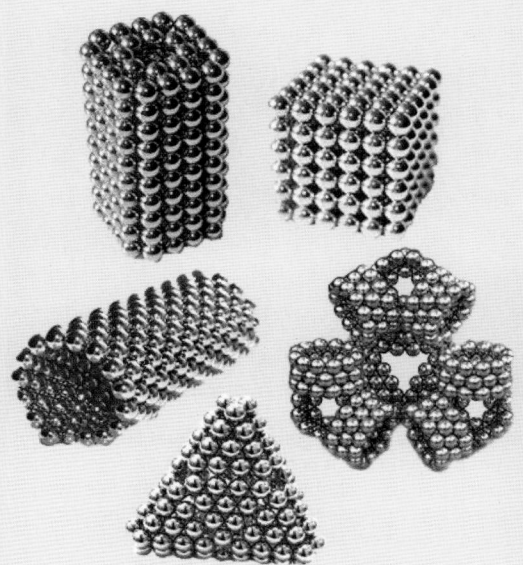

My latest cool toy is the NeoCube, a 6x6x6 cube of 216 small neodymium-iron-boron magnetic spheres which can be arranged into an amazing assortment of geometrical and non-geometrical shapes. You can create various polyhedra, even Buckyballs, and all kinds of familiar shapes, too. It's basically a 3D tangram on steroids. As fascinating as it is addictive. It is mesmer-izing to rearrange the spheres. I carry mine in my pocket and will often spend around 45 minutes at a time just playing with it — at home listening to NPR or in the car waiting for my wife. A supreme time-waster!

It's not cheap, but if you try to buy the magnets yourself, it will cost much more.

-- Laral

WARNING: I have a set of these and they're fun, but they can be fatal to chilldren who swallow them. These tiny magnets are so strong that two can rip through an intestine. You MUST keep them away from small children. -- KK

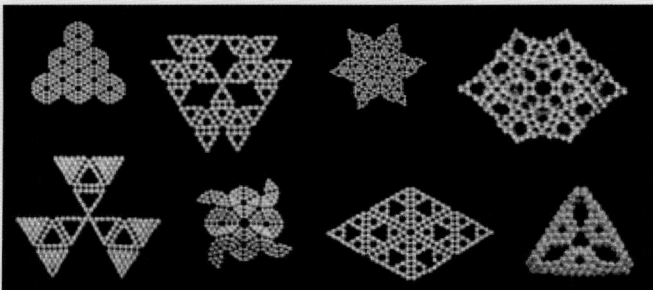

Thinking Games

Pattern recognition competition
Set
$11 (per set) Amazon

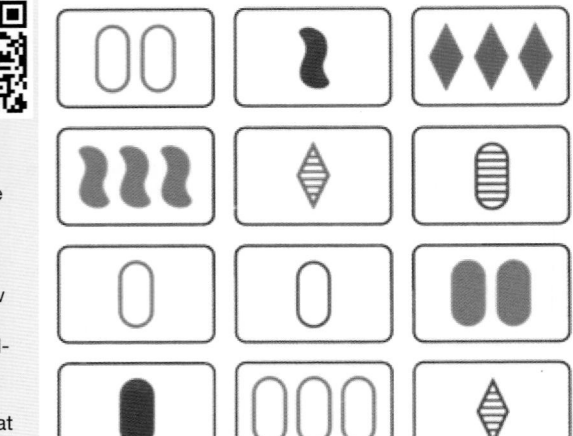

A simple game in a class by itself. You get a deck of cards with colored symbols. These are laid out, face up. To play the game you need to organize the symbols into sets of three "un-alikes" — but they can be grouped in more ways than one. Many more ways. Everyone else is trying to group them into sets faster than you. This game exercises a unique part of your brain that few other activities do. Half math, half intuition, all concentration. It's fun, loud, fast moving, and very challenging to do well, yet easy enough for small kids to join in meaningfully (that is, do better than you). After several years of playing the game, here is what I've observed:

1) It can't be explained; it has to be shown.

2) Some folks are more gifted than others at finding patterns fast.

3) But *everyone* improves, often within the span of a game.

I hear that many schools use this game to teach sets and logic in math class, and that's great. We use it as a raucous parlor game. Like the game Go, Set possess the kind of simplicity which keeps expanding, never growing old. And as far as games go these days, it's cheap.

-- *KK*

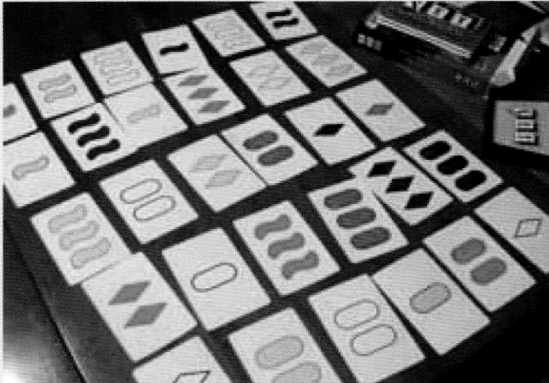

Twenty-dollar AI
20Q
$22 Amazon

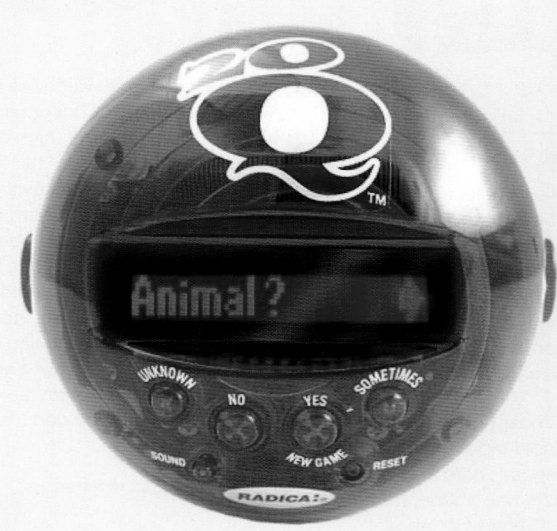

This tennis ball-size orb knows what you are thinking. Most of the time it will guess what you have in mind after asking you twenty yes/no questions. It is eerily smart, and slightly addictive.

The toy is remarkable. Because it is so small, so autonomous, its intelligence is shocking to the unprepared. Most children can't stump it, and if you stick to objects it will stump smart adults about 80% of the time with 20 questions and most of the time with an additional 5 questions. I love to watch people's reactions when they think of a "hard" thing, and after a seemingly irrational set of questions you are convinced are dumb, the sly ball tells you what you had in mind. (For instance, it can correctly guess "flying squirrel"without asking "does it fly?") People who play chess machines won't be surprised, but just about everyone else is tickled. It feels like the future.

But right now, for ten bucks, you can get an amazing little artificial intelligence, about as smart as an insect — but an insect which specializes in guessing what object you are thinking of. And in that part of the brain, it's smarter than you are.

-- *KK*

Funnest parlor game
Werewolf
$13 Bezier Games

No recent game has given me as much pleasure as the parlor game known as Werewolf.* Whenever my extended family gathers for holidays, we play Werewolf over and over. I've played the game on company retreats, at tech gatherings, on group vacations. At Foo Camp, a rendevouz for nerds, epic sessions of Werewolf will run all night long till dawn. It is that addictive.

Werewolf can be played with as few as 6-8 folks and as many as 30 or more. A game can last 30 minutes to an hour, and even very young kids can play. It's a game of bluff and deduction. Think of poker, but without any cards or money. Some fans call it a "mind game." In brief, the game assigns roles to players at random and in secret. One emergent group — the werewolves — must kill the innocent villagers, but no one knows who is who because the deed is done "at night" in a secret way. On each round of the game, the innocents will lynch a supposed werewolf as voted by the group after accusations and debate but they are never sure they have the right person. Maybe it's the werewolfs leading the pitchforks!? Both the best and worst of human behavior is activated: lying, leadership, mob psychology, democracy, persuasion, deception, deduction logic, and imagination.

Because of the intense social dynamics, the game is eternally surprising and addictive. Werewolf is the only non-sport game I know of that is as much fun to watch as to play. Players who die early in the game will always stick around till the end, watching in fascination.

Like Charades, you don't need any equipment, other than some index cards, or a deck of playing cards to distribute in order to assign roles in secret. But over years of playing we've found this dedicated deck of cards by Ted Alspach makes it much easier to introduce newbies, and to remember roles. The deck contains 40 or so cards printed with Werewolf roles and instructions. It also contains about 25 additional roles that can be added to the typical 5 main roles, which is why Alspach calls it Ultimate. As you play more often or the groups get bigger, you can keep the game exciting by experimenting with these additional roles.

A pretty good free rule set for Werewolf can be found online. Grab a regular deck of cards, assign different picture cards to roles, and you are off. If you want a bit more help this Ultimate Werewolf deck includes a fantastic sheet of very clear rules and instructions (the best I've seen), with great tips on how to be a good moderator. And the rules stay handy with the ready-made cards. We've found that having the roles explained on each card is really helpful for new players.

-- *KK*

* *This is an evolving game with many variations (which you can find online), including an earlier one that uses the same rules but a different metaphor: In Mafia, the secret Mafioso try to kill innocents. However, the Werewolf version seems to be dominating.*

[Group photo by Matlock]

Game of semantic predictions
Apples to Apples
$25 Amazon

We've been playing this word-based card game for the last three years and it continues to be an enlightening ice breaker. There are two types of cards: nouns (red) and adjectives (green). Each player is given a small stack of nouns. The game begins when one player (the judge) draws an adjective. Each player then anonymously lays down one noun he/she believes the judge will associate with the adjective. Players can try to sway the decision, but ultimately, the judge's power is absolute. Some people are inherently literal, sarcastic, wishy-washy, optimistic, stubborn or dryly humorous. The challenge lies in figuring out what type(s) of judges surround you and what kind of judge you want to be. Discovering who's on the same wave length is always interesting. What's more "magical" — a sunset, Thomas Edison, the Pyramids, surfing the net, or Barney the dinosaur? Subjectivity rules!

-- *Steven Leckart*

Evergreen strategy video game
StarCraft II
$30 us.battle.net

It's best to think of StarCraft as more of a sport than a game. It's played professionally, with televised matches, in Korea. The goal in StarCraft is to build a base, in order to create an army, which you then send over to destroy the opponent's base. Your opponent, of course, is trying to do the same thing to you -- like chess. Besides athletic reflexes you also need lots of experience to know which strategies to use immediately. For newbies the nice thing is that as you get better, the server dutifully serves up better opponents. StarCraft is probably the most popular game in the "real time strategy" (RTS) genre; it is far more strategic than just a shoot-em up game but it is much faster than any strategy board game. A typical game duration is like chess -- most games probably last 30 to 45 minutes, with outliers that last more than an hour. It is so well-designed, and fast-paced that it is possibly the first real "digital sport." It's one of the few games I can imagine someone still playing in 5 years. Runs on Windows or Mac; requires internet connection.

-- *Mark Hurst*

The job of a scientist is to generate as many wrong ideas as fast as possible. - Murray Gell-Mann

Best paper airplanes
The New World Champion Paper Airplane Book
$14 John M. Collins, 2013, 160 p.

How to make better paper airplanes. This is the third generation of books offering plans for the best, and these really are better. They were designed with the aid of aeronautical testing. The winning design flew a record 226 feet. Know what? The ultimate paper airplane still has not been invented. Distance isn't everything. This book will help you invent it.

--KK

A carefully angled piece of cardboard generates the airflow needed to keep the plane aloft.

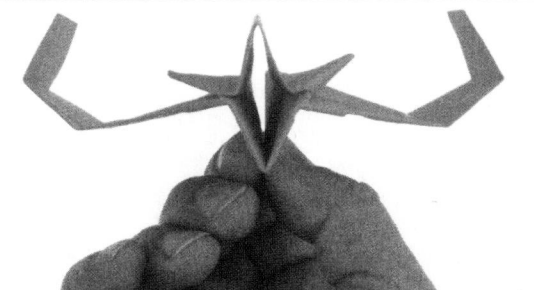

28. Above, the finished Boomerang. Note the wing droop. That's negative dihedral angle. This allows the plane to stay in a banked turn when you launch it leaned over on its side.

29. At the right, the proper launch angle. Positive dihedral angle creates an aircraft that rocks back to neutral when it launched at this sideways angle. With positive dihedral, the center of gravity is further below the center of lift, creating a sort of pendulum effect. Negative dihedral defeats that ability of the plane to right itself. Extra up elevator will make the circle it flies smaller.

36. The finished Starfighter. Note the slight negative dihedral on the main wing crease. That's part of the striking appearance. The tunnel through the nose is a very nice feature too.

Safe boomerang
Aerobie Orbiter
$10 Amazon

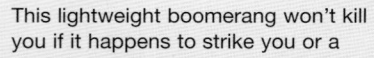

This lightweight boomerang won't kill you if it happens to strike you or a passerby. It flies fast, wide, and sure. Easy to catch because of its closed shape. It does take practice to get a full no-move-from-start return, but anyone can get it to come mostly back. You'll need a football-sized empty field for its 90-foot circle performance. Unlike a frisbee, it can be a lot of fun solo.

-- KK

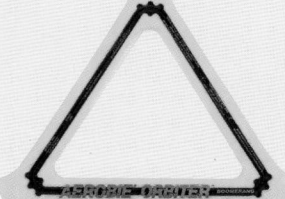

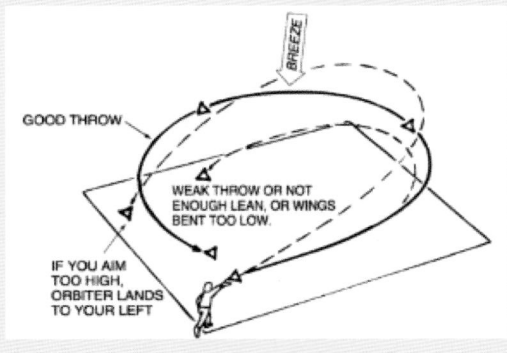

Easy catch
FlingSock
$10 (Mini) Amazon
$10 (Regular) FunAttic

Even the most sports-impaired among us can enjoy this well designed little toy: take a bean-bag, wrap it in grippy fabric, and add a tail: voila, the FlingSock. Better than other "flying tails", in my opinion. It flies amazingly far (sometimes too far — be careful that it doesn't end up on a roof). Even when it smacks me in the head, the light polyethylene pellet filled bag don't hurt a bit. Doesn't bounce either, so it won't pop out of your hand or roll unexpectedly

into the street. Easily sized to grab, with grippy rubberized fabric to keep it from slipping, and a fabric tail for second chance catches, as well as fabulous flinging…all in cheery, rainbow tie-dye colors. The mini size is perfect for slipping into school backpacks, flipping around in your yard, or to keep handy in the car for spontaneous flings — rolled up, it's about the size of a small lemon. The regular size can and will go 30 yards and more — better save that one for the park!

-- Barbara Dace

A frisbee for clowns and kids
Beamo
$26 Amazon

A Beamo is somewhere between a flying hula hoop, a slow-motion nerf disc, and a gigantic frisbee. The doughnut design makes it easy to catch using any part of your body, and since it softly boings when it hits something, it's super safe. Also, being large (30 inches) and slow and reversible, it's slightly easier than a frisbee to maneuver. Perfectly sized for kids, and oodles of fun for adults, it WILL tire you out. I recently witnessed a conference of chair-bound nerds rise up and break out into sweat to

play with a Beamo for hours on end. It's hard to remain motionless when this Clown Frisbee is in the air.

-- KK

Favorite BB Gun
Red Ryder
$25 Amazon

By far the best air rifle for a kid. There is nothing to break and it has a 650 BB capacity. You can fill it once and wander around in the woods all afternoon. All of my nieces and nephews get one when I think they are old enough.

-- K.G.

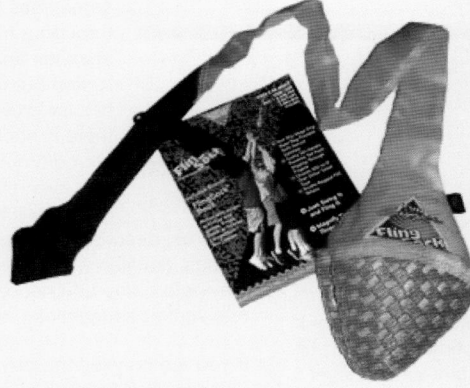

Simple water cannon
Stream Machine
$17 (price varies for size) Amazon

The genius of these water cannons are their simplicity. A single moving part — a big fat piston with handle grip — squeezes a wide stream of water down and out their large diameter tubes. Filling them you reverse, sucking in water via the same orifice. When loaded (takes about 2 seconds) they gush water at least 30 feet. Impossible to clog, and nearly unbreakable, both kids and adults can operate them around pools, lakes, rafts, canoes and boats. These are the regulation-issued weapons at our place.

– KK

Tabletop Games

Modern day Monopoly
Settlers of Catan

$34 Amazon

If you asked people in the street to name three new books, films, TV shows or music they've enjoyed in the past 20 years, you'll soon have hundreds of different answers. Ask them to name three boardgames, and you will likely only hear "Monopoly, Scrabble & Cluedo" (aka Clue). Not an exaggeration, most people have no idea how far boardgame design has progressed recently. Modern boardgames compare to Monopoly like a BMW compares to a Model T Ford. It's that different.

I was shown Settlers Of Catan in 1996, just after it was first published and it changed my life*. The epitome of modern German game design, Settlers is totally engaging. You have to think, make decisions, barter, trade and influence the other players. You don't attack people, but you can block them. You don't get eliminated and the game takes about two hours tops. Settlers does use dice, but you win by being smart, not lucky. The 'board' is modular, large hex tiles, so every game is different and fresh.

Settlers Of Catan won the Spieles des Jahres (SdJ) in 1995, the highly prestigious jury prize, and has gone on to sell millions of copies with many expansions & variants.

Should you buy a copy of Catan? Nope, not right away. I suggest you do some research on the game, ask around, find one to play. Maybe you'll love it, maybe not. You might prefer Carcassonne, or Ticket To Ride, Power Grid, Pandemic, Hey! That's My Fish, Niagara or Manhattan. There are hundreds upon hundreds of fascinating, easy, quick games you've never heard of. But at least you'll discover there is life after Monopoly.

* after 15 years, I have over 1700 modern boardgames

-- Jon Power

Simple, fun, poetic card game
Dixit

$33 Asmodee

Dixit is a "party game" (best played with 5 or more), and consists of a series of wordless cards with beautiful, evocative, and sometimes surreal images. You take turns being the "storyteller," and saying a word or phrase that evokes (but does not describe) one of your cards, which you place face-down in the center. The other players add cards which might also fit that phrase, and add them to the face-down pile. After shuffling the cards, everyone votes on which card was the storyteller's. If everyone (or no one) guesses the storyteller's card,

the storyteller doesn't earn points — so you need to be enigmatic, but not obscure. You also earn points if you guessed the storyteller's card, or if your card fooled another player.

There are several reasons why Dixit is a great game. It's simple without being simplistic. It's beautiful — not just because the cards are beautiful, but because the way people describe and interpret the cards can be poetic. And, while not a "cooperative" game (that's a whole different class of games), Dixit is one of those games that brings people together. Even if you've lost, you'll feel like you've been on a fascinating (and fun!) journey.

-- Mike Everett-Lane

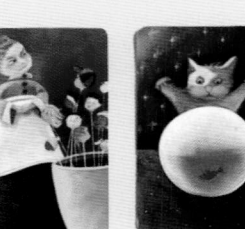 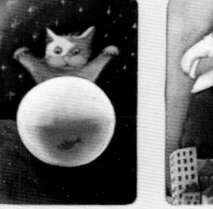

Another vote for Dixit. The artwork on the cards is amazingly varied and imaginative. One person will see several ideas

on one card. Several people will see dozens and dozens of things on the same card. And sometimes nobody will see what you've seen. It's astonishing to see the game being played.

You can get the base game, and then other decks of cards or related games (Dixit Odyssey) for more cards. The only downside is if you play it a lot, you'll get familiar with the pictures, but you'd really have to play it tons to get bored with them. Very good value, great with adults.

-- BM York

Tabletop Wargaming
White Dwarf

$100 (12 issues) Games Workshop

My intellectual friends, my arty-farty friends, hell, even my deep geek friends think I've gone off my nut on this one. White Dwarf is the monthly house organ for Games Workshop, Ltd., a UK company that makes fantasy and sci-fi tabletop wargames. The hobby doesn't seem to be big in the US (tho it's growing), but it's huge in Europe. Next to Star Wars and Star Trek, their future universe (Warhammer 40,000) is probably the largest collaborative alternate sci-fi universe out there, with over seven games devoted to it, seven (!) different magazines, dozens of novels,

comic books, coffee table art books, THOUSANDS of game components and countless fan websites. White Dwarf is a gorgeously produced full-color magazine with beautiful photographs of mind-boggling 28mm painted miniatures and futuristic landscapes. The game's enthusiasts spend inordinate numbers of hours lavishly painting details one can barely see with the naked eye.

I've always been fascinated with wargames, not 'cause I'm a hawk (far from it), but because I'm fascinated by systems and how they interact given fixed parameters and random modifiers. Wargames are perfect little contained systems (part fixed rules, part fixed variables controlled by dice and part real-time decision-making with the rules and rolls). Wind 'em up and watch 'em go! I've also always been fascinated by world modeling, creating believable worlds and climbing into them. This goes all the way back to creating comic books as a kid, then to playing D&D as a teen, later to computer games/ MUDS/ MOOS, etc. Warhammer 40,000 is a collaborative world model that you render in the real world, on a tabletop. I don't just want to watch sci-fi, I wanna direct! WH40K lets me direct.

The analog nature of the hobby is a great antidote to the digital saturation of so much of the

rest of my life. When guys of my dad's generation got old, they made a space in the basement to tie their own fishing flies or to paint Mallard ducks or whatever. Taking an alternate universe from a complex sci-fi mythology, and downloading it into an analog world of miniature models, alien landscapes and futuristic architectures is perhaps how aging cyberpunks (at least this one) plan on retiring.

-- Gareth Branwyn

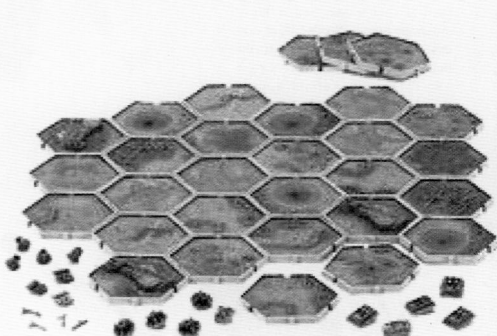

Best table games resource
Board Game Geek

Free Board Game Geek

The passionate gamers on BoardGameGeek.com (BGG) devote a lot of time and effort to create comprehensive content and reviews on practically every game that is out there, including out-of-print and small, self-published games. They not only rate the games, but write up rule clarifications, post in-depth game analyses, suggest variants for better gameplay, and even translate rules into other languages. The site features a marketplace where you can buy, sell and trade games with other gamers, forums where you can ask questions, create lists, and tons of other functionality.

I probably visit BGG one to two times a month, mostly to browse for new games that might be good (In the past year, I've picked up Pandemic, Roll Through the Ages, Caylus, Agricola, Dominion, Race for the

Galaxy, Galaxy Trucker, and Ticket to Ride: Märklin.). Also, I sometimes hear about a game through a friend or some other channel, and I'll go to the site to find out more. Since it's heavily crowdsourced, and there is such a large, passionate community, I've discovered that even the most obscure games will have details like pictures, descriptions, type, and of course ratings. It's also a great resource when you're playing a game and need rules clarifications, rule variant suggestions, expansions, etc.

If you are considering buying a game, you owe it to yourself to check out BGG. Granted, the list of top-rated games tends to lean a bit more toward the serious-gamer crowd. But you can use the advanced search feature to look for "light" games with high average ratings, and then sort the results by Bayesian ranking. You'd even do OK just by picking games off the "Hotness" list in the left column.

For purchasing said games, FunAgain.com is the current consensus among my gamer friends as the best place to buy from, though I've also used Fair Play Games with great success.

-- Dave Cortright

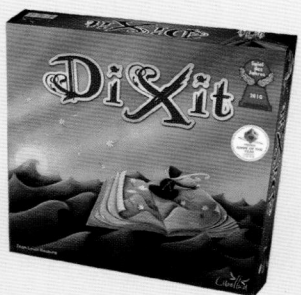

Essential group games
Best New Games *
Play It! *
Great Group Games

Get off your screen and come have fun! Run around, chase a ball, make a face, best your friend, be silly, make up a game. When you run out of ideas, here are some more.

New games were invented by Stewart Brand in the 1970s to introduce cooperation and open-ended play into overly competitive games. These type of games like to unfold outdoors, involve large groups of people (5 -50), include all abilities. In contrast to sports games none of them require equipment, and everyone wins. The main point of these games is simply to keep fun going as long as possible. Dale LeFevre has been running new games for 30 years and has collected the best of them here in *Best New Games*. Playing some of these 77 games has been the most fun I've had in years. Good for family reunions, scouts, school picnics, summer campgrounds.

Play It! is a densely packed book of game ideas for youth groups -- church, camp or school. Many of these might better be described as activities, such as scavenger hunts, or role-playing situations. They depend on easily gathered props, but also require some preplanning and set up. They are not as spontaneous, but kids love them.

Small groups benefit from playing games together, so a cottage industry has emerged to lead games for organizational and business teams. A deliberate sequence of games starting with fun icebreakers, then onto ones building trust, and ending with celebration games can strengthen teamwork. The best selection I've seen for "serious play" games are in *Great Group Games*. Suggested game options are grouped by their function in the "learning" sequence. In a business setting these team-building games require the right tactful facilitator (not the boss!) to lead, but many of them also work fine informally with a family or friends.

Come on, put that screen down!

-- KK

From *Best New Games*

So what is a New Game? It is a cooperative group interactive game that is done just for fun and is for everybody regardless of age, size, gender, or ability level. The games sometimes include competition, but anybody can win. That's because when there is winning, it is only one element rather than the main element of a game. No trophies or awards are given for winning; we simply go on to another game. This way, everyone can play without having to suffer the extremes of competition. Instead of being eliminated, players change roles or sides and keep playing. And always, enjoying a New Game is more important than winning it. In this sense, everybody wins every game.

Zip, Zap, Pop

Description of Game

Who needs snap, crackle, and pop when you have "zip, zap, pop"? The group sits together in a close circle. The first thing to pass around is a "zip," which is accomplished by placing a hand on top of the head with the fingers pointing at the person on one side while saying "Zip." The person on that side also puts a hand on top of his or her head with fingers pointing in the same direction while saying "Zip." It passes from person to person this way around the circle. Practice this in one direction and then the other.

The next thing to learn is a "zap," which is done by putting the hand under the chin the opposite direction from which a zip is coming. A zap makes a zip reverse directions. And, of course, if one zaps a zap, the zip rereverses directions. A "pop" is done by pointing to anyone in the circle, who then has to either start passing a zip, zap it back, or pop to someone else

◀ **Lap Game**

We first get the group into a very tight standing circle facing in so that each person is touching the person next to him or her. Everyone takes a quarter turn in the same direction so that each person is facing the back of a person. (This is often the hardest part. Invariably, several players turn the opposite way.)

Each player puts the hands on the hips of the player in front of him or her. It is important to get the proper spacing. If everyone's arms are stretched out, people are too far away from one another and they need to take a step in toward the center. If people are too close, they need to take a step out from the center. Try small step adjustments first. The idea is to be able to sit on the knees of the person in back of you while having the person in front of you sit on your knees. Having someone sit on your thighs is painful!

At the count of three, you might try having everyone touch down briefly to see if they are all connecting properly. Then have the group all sit on each others knees all at the same time, perhaps with the magic words "On my knees, please."

From *Play It!*

X = players in field
☐ Home
O Garbage Can

Time Warp Tag

Here's another crazy version of the most famous of all games. You simply play a regular game of tag but at the blow of a whistle, each player (including "It") must slow down to a speed equal to a sports replay "slo-mo." In other words, they must do everything in slow motion. Kids will soon get the hang of it and become very exaggerated in their motions.

Make sure the kids do everything in Time Warp state,

even talking and shouting. The game can be played in total Time Warp, or you can blow the whistle for start/stop intervals. Limit the size of the playing area so that several players have a chance to become "It."

◀ **Swedish Baseball**

This variation of baseball is most effective with 25 or more participants. Teams are divided equally with one team out in the field and the other at bat. No bats or balls are used. All you need is a Frisbee.

The batter comes to the plate and throws the Frisbee out into the field. The fielding team chases down the Frisbee and tries to return it to a garbage can that is next to home plate. The Frisbee must be tossed in rather than simply dropped in. Meanwhile, the batter runs about 10 feet to the first base, then to the second base about eight feet away and begins to circle them. Every lap is one point for the batting team, and the runner continues until the Frisbee is in the can. All the players on the batting team get to be up each inning. There are no outs.

After two or three innings, the score can get quite high. You'll need to have a scorekeeper who can keep track of all the points.

◀ **Group Juggle**

This circle game is something like hot potato, with a dash of Concentration. Throw a ball to one person in a standing circle of kids. That person throws it to another, and so on until everyone has received and thrown the ball once-but exactly once. No one should get the ball a second time, which means each player needs to remember where the ball's been. If your group's frustration threshold is high, increase the speed of the game and add moreballs.

$29 Best New Games Dale LeFevre, 2012, 256 p.

$12, $7 for Kindle, Play It! Wayne Rice, Mike Yaconelli, 2000, 120 p.

$11 Great Group Games Susan Ragsdale, Ann Saylor, 2007, 228 p.

Recipes for group fun
Deep Fun
Free UUA

Or in other words, how to have good clean fun. Directions for about 25 well-proven games for groups are succinctly supplied by this free PDF book. These games originated in church youth groups, but I've seen them used at camps, large family gatherings, company retreats, and even a few tech meetings. They are aimed at building community, and are primarily ones that can be run indoors. I've played a number of these games

as an adult over the years and they really are deep fun. It is amazing how fast you can unleash your inner kindergartner. Some of this group fun, like Silent Football, has been around since ancient youth camp times. I wish more folks would enliven their stuffy meetings and offsites with a few of these games.

– KK

To make this book more user-friendly for youth and advisors, we decided to organize the games into five chapters, loosely based on Denny Rydberg's "Five Steps to Building Community." Introducing new games to your youth group or conference will work best if your timing is right–if you choose games that fit the level of commu-

nity already attained and nudge the group on to the next level.

Hog Call

Parameters: 15 to 60 people

Have the group split up into pairs and come up with a matching set of words or sounds (i.e. "hic-cup," "peanut-butter," or "honey-bee"). Have each person choose one of the words as their own. Then have each person announce their word to the group, so that there are no repeats. Then instruct the group to close their eyes and start milling around the space with the goal of getting as far away from their partner as possible. Once the pairs are well-separated, announce that they are to find their partners without opening their eyes, by shouting their word. (If all goes well, Peanut will meet up with Butter).

Angel Wash Variations

Parameters: 15 to 60 people

(Remember anyone can opt out if they don't feel comfortable.)

Form two lines facing each other. Have one person from the end of the line (or two people holding hands) close their eyes and place their arms crossed on their chest. Direct them to proceed down the aisle of the double line with their eyes closed. As they pass, each person washes their aura with their hands, passing their fingers and hands lightly over their body, from the crown of their head to the ground, without actually touching them. If the person should stray, the people in the lines can gently direct

them back on course. When they reach the end, their friends can communicate to them, with touch, that its time to open their eyes. Continue until everyone has had a chance.

Flying

Kite building help
Kitebuilder

kitebuilder.com

This is the best site for learning how to build your own kites. Good tutorials, decent forums (quieter since the site's founder died) and a great encyclopedia of techniques and materials. Their best asset is the stash of plans submitted by users for almost any type of kite.

(Kite making supplies can be found from intothewind.com reviewed to the right.)

-- KK

• There's no such thing as kite fabric! Just about any fabric will work... including the fabric grade Ripstop you chose. Was it difficult to sew? It is probably pretty stretchy eh?? The coated Ripstop often used by most builders on this website is coated with a finish that reduces stretch and porosity. It is also pretty light weight, probably about half the weight of the cloth you used. So... your kite will probably require a little more wind for optimum performance... but if balanced and bridled properly, it should still fly.

Dunton-Taylor Box Delta

Layout

Layout where front and back of fabric are different.

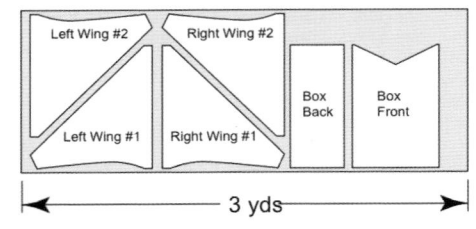

| Left Wing #2 | Right Wing #2 | | |
| Left Wing #1 | Right Wing #1 | Box Back | Box Front |

← 3 yds →

Edge Binding

From 41", 3/4 oz nylon, cut 5 strips 3/4"x41" - Fold in half for 3/8" binding.

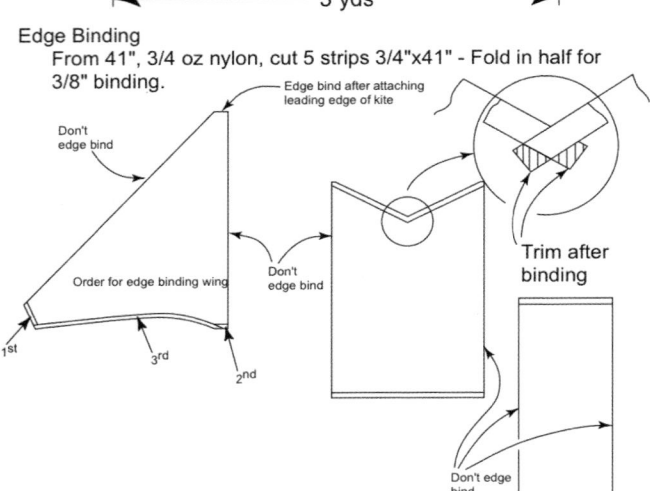

Edge bind after attaching leading edge of kite

Don't edge bind

Order for edge binding wing

Don't edge bind

Trim after binding

1st   3rd   2nd

Don't edge bind

All kites
Into the Wind

Catalog Into the Wind

An astounding variety of kites from one source. Kites that swoop, kites that fit into your palm, or kites that will lift a man. All shapes, colors, speeds, prices, designs, and accessories. I like their indestructible mini airfoils that will collapse into a backpack pocket. Unroll and fly. Praise to them, they also sell hi-tech fabrics and materials for making your own sky darts. Paper and online catalog.

-- KK

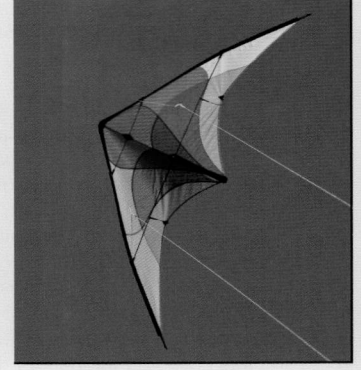

Kite-on-a-keychain
Pocket Kite

$5 Stow'n Go Pocket Kite
Uncle's Games

I've collected quite an assortment of logo emblazoned pens, mousepads, stress balls, and other tchotchkes at professional conferences, but far and away the most fun and useful (as in, it gets used) item I have picked up is the pocket kite. The pocket kite is a small sled-style kite that is kept in a small zippered pouch attached to a key ring that also contains a little reel loaded with kite string.

The kite is very easy to fly, but doesn't have any wooden supports or anything else that could break. The pouch is barely 3 inches across and weighs next to nothing, so it is easy toss into a backpack for a hike. I keep mine in the courier bag that goes with me everywhere. It is really fun to bust it out when unexpected kite flying opportunities arise. Day at the beach; reaching a summit; dull company picnic. Unless you are a hardcore kite nut, you probably aren't hanging around waiting for a windy day so you can drop everything and go fly a kite. A pocket kite is ready when you are. And it's cheap, so when it inevitably gets stuck in a tree, it's not the end of the world.

-- Toby Plewak

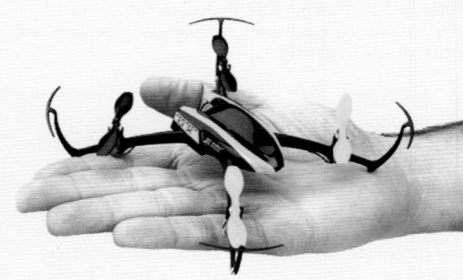

HOBBY LOBBY INTERNATIONAL, INC. ®

Radio-control source
Hobby-Lobby

Prices Vary Hobby-Lobby

Radio-control is now cheap. Thanks to fanatic model airplane enthusiasts, featherweight units are micro enough to fit almost anywhere, at a reasonable price. You can purchase the hi-tech guts for use in boats, bots, helicopters, cars, toys, and machinery. Or you can get off-the-shelf models.

The chief source with the largest selection seems to be Hobby-Lobby (not to be confused with Hobby Lobby). They specialize in all-electric (quiet) RC airplanes, but have the latest hi-tech batteries, servos, nano-radios, and parts. I've used them and their service is dependable. They publish a paper catalog, too.

– KK

Hextreme FPV Hexacopter

anodized aluminum arms with pre-soldered wiring

Fiberglass frame and all hardware

In Stock Now

Ultimate (and open source) flight simulator
X-Plane

Everyone's heard of Microsoft Flight Simulator and other consumer flight simulators for PC's, but the real McCoy is X-Plane, an unbelievable simulator written (and re-written and re-written) by a manic flight (and gadget) crazy independent programmer named Austin Meyer.

While difficult to set up and learn, the experience of flying a 767 in X-Plane from San Francisco to JFK (with actual weather and way-true-to-life instrumentation) is almost an eery experience. X-Plane (unlike the other consumer toys) has even earned FAA approval towards the airline transport certificate. All you need is a PC and $50.

Like many tools, X-Plane allows you to deeply immerse in a "place" where most people never get to go (especially these days): the cockpit. You can pilot virtually any aircraft you can imagine (including helicopters, zeppelins, and even Burt Rutan's SpaceShipOne). I've heard of pilots spending a lot of time in an X-Plane cockpit (say a new all-glass Cirrus) before actually buying a plane (Austin owns a Cirrus).

For others (more like me) it just offers a potentially immersive glimpse into an area I find fascinating but may not be able to experience. MSFT/FS is fine for just playing around — most newbies would actually find X-Plane boring compared to MSFT/FS. But taking an evening — with spouse and kids gone — and working through a successful (and extremely realistic), sunset round trip from SFO to the little un-manned airstrip in Half-Moon Bay in a Cirrus – using all the instruments including the GPS — makes this sim a unique thing.

X-Plane is a lot closer to "open source" than the consumer-friendly sims like MSFT/FS. As such, lots of people actively contribute to the world of X-Plane in terms of new (unbelievably accurate) planes, scenery, even tower and ground crew radio chatter. Here's a sample of the detail in one update: "New engine failure type option: engine fire. If you specify an engine fire, then the engine smokes as it fails...regular engine failure does not leave a trail of smoke though.

747 cockpit

Pilot system failure resulting in airspeed indication error. Engine SIEZURE, and engine INDICATION failures. Low battery failure, resulting in an inability to get up to starting N1. Transponder can fail." Or, on a more positive note: "Real-Weather now checks the entire planet, not just USA!" There are weird third-party websites for pre-flight checklists, obscure throttle controls (that strap to your desk), PDF scans of antiquated aircraft manuals, logbooks, menus... So the "world" of X-Plane (Google X-Plane) changes more frequently than other packages.

-- Tim Smith

$70 X-Plane 10 Global X-Plane

$70 X-Plane 10 Global Amazon

The self is more distant than any star. - G.K. Chesterton

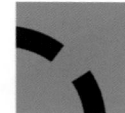

GEOCACHING.COM

GPS treasure hunt
Geocaching Tools

Take a geo-location system, add an Internet directory of hiding spots, and voila! A 21st century treasure hunt! One T-shirt slogan calls it "using multi-billion dollar military hardware to find Tupperware in the woods." Geocaching began in 2000 when an Oregonian stashed a container in the woods, posted its latitude and longitude on the Internet, and other GPS users went out and found it. Now there are nearly 900,000 geocaches hidden worldwide, and hundreds of thousands of cachers, ranging from the curious to fanatics. The hobby is a fun additional activity for those roaming the outdoors on foot, bike, 4-wheeler or horse. There are at least as many urban caches as park hides, so it's also become a hidden virtual layer to the cityscape, unsuspected by passing muggles who are not into the game. And it's a great family activity – kids love 'treasure hunting' and trading for the toys and trinkets found

in many caches. Geocaching is also an open game, extendable (within limits) by its players to add things like gnarly logic puzzles that must be solved to reveal a cache location, or objects whose worldwide movements among caches are tracked online.

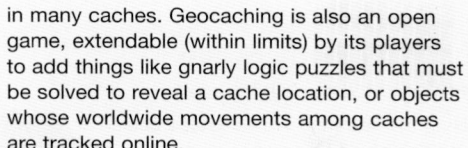

Geocaching.com

There are a few other geocache directory sites, but Geocaching.com is the original and by far the largest. Free to register and play the game; $30/yr for paid membership enables more powerful search and personalization options.

Find a geocache

The game can be played with any geo-location technology. Some urban cachers rely solely on Google Maps, printing out aerial photos of hide locations. Entry-level consumer GPS units or geo-location add-ons for smart phones are available in the $100 price range. Those who become serious about the hobby will want a GPS unit with these qualities:

* Ability to keep a satellite lock in poor signal conditions — from urban canyons to redwood canyons

* Rock solid firmware — there's nothing worse than having to reboot the unit in the middle of a hunt.

* Good ergonomics and user interface

* Durability — tough enough to take a beating in the field

* Easy computer interface — for downloading and uploading cache coordinates, logs and descriptions

Although they're not the latest products in the company's line, the Garmin 60Cx and 60CSx are the workhorse GPS receivers of hard core geocachers. (The only difference between the two models is a compass and altimeter independent of the global positioning system featured on the 60 csx.) These models score on all the points above, coming short only on the computer interface, as they don't mount as a drive on your computer desktop. However, they have USB interfaces and are well-supported by paperless caching applications on both the Windows and OS X platforms.

Hide a geocache

After finding a few dozen geocaches, most players will think of a nearby place that needs a cache and want to hide their own. There are some common-sense rules for placing and registering new hides on Geocaching.com, including keeping off property where the public isn't welcome, not using a container that can be mistaken for a bomb, and labeling the geocache as such. Most geocaches are made from recycled or repurposed containers and camouflage, and many cachers pride themselves on creative reuse of materials in their hides. One essential quality of a geocache is remaining watertight through years of handling and tough climate. Two types of containers that are resistant against both weather and other geocachers are military surplus ammunition cans, and

Lock&Lock-type plastic storage boxes.

Small 30-caliber or large 50-caliber military surplus ammunition cans work well. (When reusing ex-military containers, always sand off or paint over the military markings, which can be quite alarming to those not expecting to find a box of rifle ammo or grenades in their local park!)

Lock&Lock-type storage boxes are available as a pre-labeled set, or you can get an assortment of sizes to camouflage yourself.

Simple cache camouflage can be amazingly effective for hiding your cache from those in and out of the game, particularly in park hides. Camo tapes and paints designed for use by hunters are readily available, and one roll or spray can will cover many caches.

-- Tim Oren (geocaching as PurplePeople)

Free Geocaching.com
$390 Garmin GPS Navigators 60Cx Amazon
$640 Garmin GPS Navigators 60CSx Amazon
$16 Ammunition cans MidwayUSA
$15 Triple-Cache Container Set Groundspeak.com
Camo Duct Tape Amazon
$15 Hunter's Specialties Camo Spray Paint Kit
Camo Duct Tape Cabela's

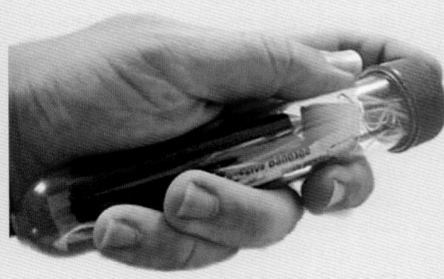

Tough plastic test tubes
Baby Soda Bottles

$12 for 15 Test Tubes with Caps
Steve Spangler Science

These are good for storing just about anything small you don't want crushed, spilled, or dampened: Batteries, earbud headphones, mini-first aid kit, medicine. They can also be used to carry liquids on a plane, as they hold about an ounce under TSA's 3-ounce limit.

The ones I liberated from my son's Scientific Explorer kit are also sold

individually as Tube Vaults by County Comm, but the best deal I've found is 15 for $10 from Steve Spangler Science. According to their site, the Baby Soda Bottles are actually our ubiquitous 2-liter soda bottles before they've been heated and stretched, which explains why the caps are interchangeable with soda bottle caps.

These food-grade polyethylene test tubes are dishwasher safe, strong, waterproof and, yes, I've used one to hide a geocache!

– Mike Everett-Lane

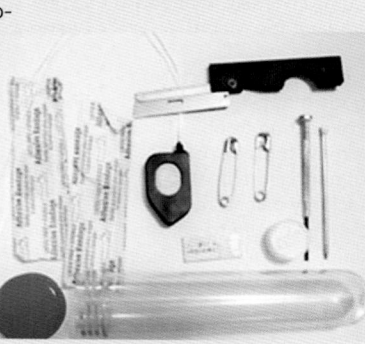

Rechargable deafening horn
EcoBlast

$26 EcoBlast Horn Amazon

There are two versions. One is a single unit like the photo below, which is also handy for boating and sports games. The other has the horn and trigger separated from the plastic bottle air container via a long plastic tube so that the trigger can sit on your bike handle bars without the clutter of the bottle. However I use the single unit version. It is very light and can sit on my handlebar bag, at the ready.

– KK

Analog role-playing game
Dungeons & Dragons

$18 wizards.com/dnd

The role-playing game Dungeons & Dragons is almost 40 years old, and it's more popular than ever, especially for a new generation of kids. I've been playing with my daughter and have been reminded how powerful a game it is. Each player takes on the role of a character (human or non-human) possessed with skills and attributes (strength, intelligence, dexterity, etc.) determined by throwing polyhedral dice. The players are banded together and embark on an imaginary adventure filled with monsters, traps, and treasures. Games can last for tens or hundreds of hours, stretched over weeks or months of multiple gaming sessions. (A player's character can be used in future adventures, and it becomes more powerful over time.)

All this happens without a computer!

One player in the group is the Dungeon Master, who is responsible for maintaining the imaginary world. Dungeon Masters can either create an adventure from scratch or buy an adventure outline (with maps and other supporting materials) from a publisher. Masters spend much of their time describing the environment to the players, serving as referee, and taking on the roles of non-player characters.

The rules for Dungeons & Dragons can be overwhelming to newbies. I suggest you start with the low-priced "red box," which contains polyhedral dice, introductory rules, and a sample adventure. Work your way up from there.

-- Mark Frauenfelder

Every person takes the limits of their own field of vision for the limits of the world. - Arthur Schopenhauer.

425

Smart activity monitor
FitBit

$140 Amazon

I've been wearing a Fitbit since late 2009 and overall I highly recommend it.

The Fitbit is expensive for a pedometer ($99), but in return you get wireless syncing of your steps to your computer and to fitbit.com. Plus you can add friends as "Fitbit buddies" to compare how many steps everyone took each week. I'm currently in a year-long competition with my brother-in-law to see who can take more steps. Inspired by the Fitbit, I will often do 1:1 meetings as a "walk and talk" around the block instead of sitting in a room. I take the stairs at work instead of the elevator. I park my car a couple hundred yards from work instead of close to the building. So far since later 2009, I've taken 7,715,383 steps. That's 3000+ miles towards better health!

What's not so good? The Fitbit costs a bit much, although I think it's worth it.

The other (mild) issues I have with the Fitbit are that:

Water can short it out. Don't go swimming with it on, and attach it somewhere that won't get 100% drenched in sweat.

Overall, I think wearing a pedometer (Fitbit or otherwise) is one of the easiest/best things you can do for your health. This tool is highly recommended.

-- Matt Cutts

I use a Fitbit, too. The wireless syncing means that you don't need to think about it. The hardest part for me is to remember to move the device if I change my pants. The simplicity of the website, and of the user interface on the object, entice you to use it, and to pay attention to the results. It is a small thing that works well and a habit that is very sustainable over the years.

-- KK

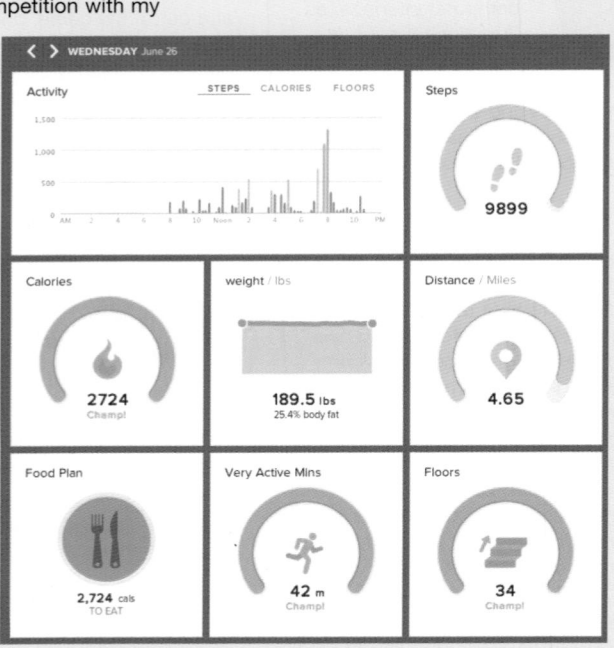

Wireless weight tracking
Withings WiFi Body Scale

$150 Amazon

I've been using my Withings WiFi-enabled scale since 5 Dec 2009, at which point I weighed 246.9 lbs. Today, I weigh 183.5 lbs, and this scale helped me reach my goal. It shows weight, percentage or lbs of body fat, and BMI. Because it's WiFi-enabled, the readings are picked up and displayed graphically on my Web page (password protected) at their site with the option to share it with other web-based weight loss sites. Moreover, I can use the data locally by downloading the readings in a format suitable for a spreadsheet.

I weigh daily, and the graph has greatly helped in my weight-loss efforts. Now I can easily see the trend, which helps manage it. I've had a series of scales that measure both weight and percentage body fat, including a couple by Tanita. As part of my weight loss effort, I did have some professionally administered body-fat measurements, and the Withings readings were consistent with that, within the limits of accuracy with respect to one's daily weight fluctuations. If you have multiple people using

the scale, it's easy to set up multiple accounts (it has a maximum of 8 users).

-- Michael Ham

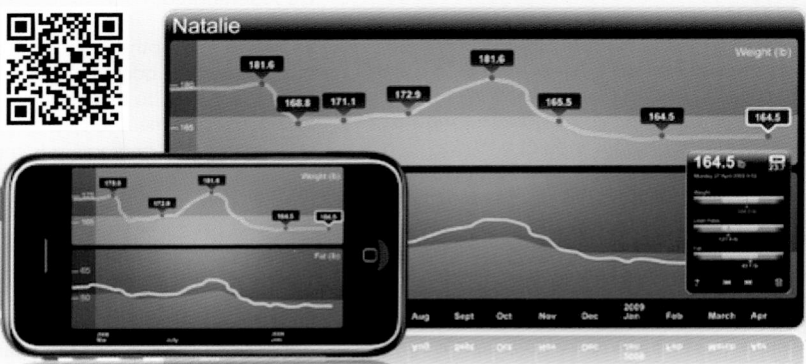

High-capacity measurer
Digital Freight Scale

$99 (used) 400-pound Digital Freight Scale
Amazon

I'm a big dude so most scales don't even cover my weight. Consequently I had to think different to get a decent scale. I found this digital postage scale. It reads up to 400lbs in half pound increments, has a remote, mountable readout auto tare (useful when weighing the dog). It isn't particularly pretty but being in the top percentile in weight and height has certain drawbacks and requires special tools.

-- Bryan Covington

Time- and doctor-approved weighing
Accurate Body Scales

$204+ Detecto Eye-Level Beam Scale NorthShore Care

A physician's balance beam scale is consistently accurate. We've had one now for at least 25 years; its accuracy has remained constant through many moves, changes in humidity, and so forth. Measurement is in 1/4 pounds, which is good enough. There is a readjustment knob if you think there is an error when changing the scale's placement. If only my weight and height had remained so constant….

-- Martha Robinson

If you want consistency and accuracy in a body scale, I strongly suggest an old-fashioned balance beam scale. Even a cheap one (<$200) will do a better job than most expensive electronic scales. Also, they are kind of fun to use, they have an eye level display, and the batteries never run out.

-- Danny Hillis

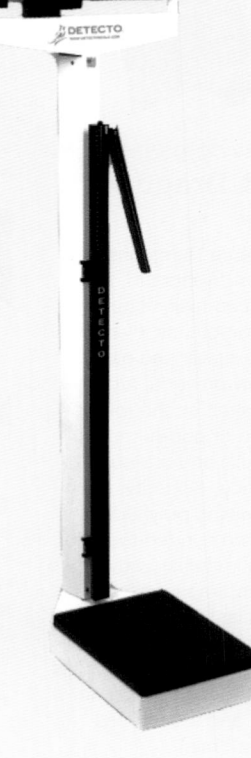

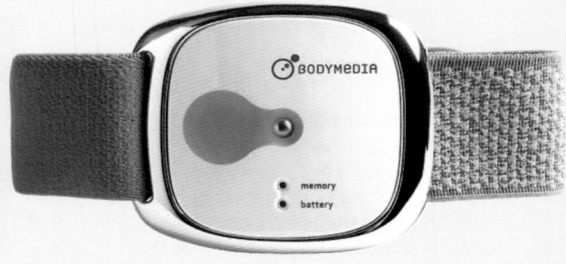

Body data tracking tool
BodyMedia FIT Armband

$150 (includes 12 month subscription)
Costco

I've been using the BodyMedia FIT armband and it is the only diet and exercise system that I've found that really works. The system works through the use of an armband that you wear on your left arm throughout the day. As you go about your regular routine the armband measures your caloric burn. The armband uses four sensors to track over 9,000 variables from heat to sweat to steps to calories burned every minute of every day.

You can track your daily burn and steps taken through an optional display, but

the real power is in syncing the armband to the BodyMedia web site which allows you to see charts of calories burned per minute, steps taken, exercise levels, sleep cycles, etc. You can also track your weight measurements in the tool. The great thing about the online tools is that it lets you enter your daily caloric intake (just search for a food and add it to a meal), and compares your incoming calories to outgoing calories. By entering your calories on a daily basis you can ensure a realistic caloric deficit which is guaranteed to help you lose weight safely. It's very helpful for making sure you don't starve yourself by eating too little, or conversely, that you don't go crazy and eat too much.

Since I started using the armband I've dropped 20 pounds that I've managed to keep off with almost no trouble. It's become pretty simple for me. I can eat a healthy but normal breakfast and lunch, then I check my calorie burn before dinner and make sure to eat the appropriate amount to ensure I maintain my target calorie deficit.

What I love about this tool is that it eliminates estimation. Everyone has different basal metabolic rates depending on what they do during the day. Whereas most diet systems target a fixed number of daily calories, those fixed amounts could mean anywhere from a 500-2500 calorie deficit depending on the person. Anyone who's dieted knows that when you get into high calorie deficits you're body stops losing and you go into the so called starvation mode where your body actually holds onto the weight. With this that never happens. If I have a lazy day at work and am on target to burn 3200 calories then I know I can eat 2200 and maintain my 1000 calorie deficit. But say, I go for a long run on the weekend and do some yard work I could get up to 5500 calories burned. If I stuck with a 2200 calorie diet, my body (and my willpower) would rebel. However with BodyMedia, I know that on those 5500 calorie days I can eat 2000 more calories and still be on target for weight loss.

Long story short – I absolutely love this system.

-- Marc Ryan

WellnessFX

Your health dashboard
Wellnessfx

wellnessfx.com

The benefits of using Wellnessfx are complex but important.

All kinds of things show up in our blood long before they are visible elsewhere. From our blood we can detect early stages of illness, maximize athletic performance, determine when and where we acquire environmental toxins, and see what's truly normal for us. Someday in the future we'll monitor our body's full biochemistry 24/7 and that will change medicine forever. But today only a few of us have our biochemistry tested once a year, if that, for only a few factors. And all we get is some numbers.

Wellnessfx is a tool for monitoring 60-100 biochemical factors in your body, as often as possible, and in a super understandable dashboard. They make your biochemistry actionable -- illuminating trends in your body and offering ways to nudge the trend in the right direction. Frequent measurements add data points allowing you to manage your health in a much more scientific way.

In the past year I've been using Wellnessfx to track my body's chemistry. After signing up for an account I made an appointment through them with a local blood testing labs with a request generated by Wellnessfx. The local lab extracted my needed blood and sent the results to Wellnessfx. A few days later I log into my account and see my results of 60-120 different markers graphed, annotated and intelligently dissected. I choose a doctor from Wellnessfx's staff and together on the phone we'll go over the data item by item for 40 minutes. Then repeat 6 months to a year later.

The quality and personalization of this consult is unlike any doctor visit I've ever had. For patients like me who want to understand my body as much as possible, each consult is a short course in human biochemistry -- my biochemistry. On my account's website I can dig deeper into my numbers and the linked technical literature as far as I care to go. All the doctor's notes and recommendations are archived for me to review any time. In fact the consults are recorded so you can review them any time.

The more often I am tested the more valuable my data becomes, because as Wellnessfx emphasizes, the actual numbers are often less important than the trends. Imagine you weighed yourself once a year; that is not as actionable as weighing yourself more frequently, say every day. The same goes for your biochemistry.

In addition to testing blood biochemistry, Wellnessfx also extracts genetic markers. That is, they sequence some genes that relate to biochemical factors. So in my case their test noticed I that my ApoE genotoype indicates I would benefit if I drank alcohol, such as a glass of red wine per day.In addition to testing blood biochemistry, Wellnessfx also extracts genetic markers. That is, they sequence some genes that relate to biochemical factors. So in my case

their test noticed I that my ApoE genotype indicates I would benefit if I drank alcohol, such as a glass of red wine per day.

My trends are managed via lifestyle choices (diet and fitness), supplements, and medicines -- the usual medical interventions. What's new is two-fold: 1) the resolution of this cycle; because you keep monitoring, you can finely tune the leverage, making modifications in small steps; and 2) its application to healthy states. Constant monitoring with fine tuned remedies is standard procedure for illness. The unique approach of Wellnessfx is to apply this intense monitoring/response to all your measurables, including those that seem healthy.

Your normal is not my normal and my normal can only be established by constant monitoring. Intense monitoring also alerts me to drifts away from that norm, long before other symptoms may show up, at a point where it may be a lot easier to modify and control it. A negative trend is much easier to treat in this pre-disease still "healthy" stage. It's like paying attention to your check-engine light instead of waiting for smoke to shoot out of the hood.

The number of chemicals, hormones and genes that Wellnessfx tracks is variable because they don't do any of the actual testing. Rather they piggyback on existing blood and gene tests. As these drop in price, or increase in possible markers, so does Wellnessfx's report. Right now scientists are developing much better

tests, by less invasive captures, for much cheaper, eventually for use at home. As these are released they'll be incorporated into Wellnessfx's interface.

But today you need to have vials of blood extracted at a lab. And that is not cheap. Each round of testing and doctor's consult costs $150 for a basic set, or $530 for a full "performance" level set. In theory, your own doctor could order these tests and go over the results in the same depth as Wellnessfx. And maybe your doctor does. But in my experience this quality and detail rarely happen.

Wellnessfx is private medicine. It is part of the quantified self movement, encouraged by enthusiasts who want to use the best tools available to track themselves, including their

genes and blood, to maximize health, among other good things. Wellnessfx is professional state-of-the-art biochemical/ genetic marker testing, available to anyone.

I've learned so much from tracking my blood over a year, to a degree my doctors have no interest in doing, that the high price has been worth it. For long-term good health, it's cheap.

At the moment, Wellnessfx has a free e-check up, which will test 25 bio-markers at no cost to you, including having your blood drawn at a local LabCorp (not available in all states). Of course, they hope you'll continue for the next round to see if you've made progress. For free, it's a great bargain.

--KK

Basic Lipid Panel
The basic lipid panel encompasses your cholesterol, including your good (HDL) and bad (LDL and other non-

Your heart and blood vessels are called your cardiovascular system. When bad cholesterol and triglycerides clog your arteries that feed your brain and heart, raising your risk for a stroke or heart attack, this is known as cardiovascular disease.

Triglycerides
Type of Fat — More Info

122 → 113

Apr Jul Oct Jan Apr
2012 2013 mg/dL

200
150

Risk Ranges

High Risk	Moderate	Low Risk	
≥ 200	150 - 200	< 150	mg/dL

		Jan 2012	Apr 2013
ALP Alkaline Phosphatase	IU/L	76	71
25-Hydroxy Vitamin D Precursor to vitamin D	ng/mL	29	39.9
Osteocalcin Marker for bone turnover	ng/mL	17	
Calcium Blood and Bone Mineral	mg/dL	8.4	9.4
Phosphorus Electrolyte in cells and bones		3	

Total Cholesterol A Type of Fat		163
LDL "Bad" Cholesterol		83
HDL "Good" Cholesterol		57
Triglycerides Type of Fat		113
Non-HDL Choleste... All "Bad" Cholesterol		117
LDL Particle Count Number of LDL Particles		1198
LDL Size The size of LDL particles		20.5
sdLDL Small LDL		24
% sdLDL Small LDL to Total LDL Ratio		27
vLDL-C Precursor to LDL Cholesterol		23
vLDL Size The size of vLDL particles.		42.2
LP(a) Different Form of LDL		1
Apo B Protein in LDL ("Bad") Ch...		75

Digital, wrist-based vascular gauge
Panasonic Blood Pressure Monitor

$42 panasonic.com

For taking your blood pressure at home, I recommend this excellent, beautifully engineered wrist sphygmomanometer. The great wizards at Panasonic have taken the cumbersome apparatus used to measure blood pressure, shrunk it into a little box and made it easy to use by anyone. That, to me, is wizardry.

You push the yellow button, the cuff squeezes your wrist and then deflates, showing your blood pressure in a nice, easy-to-read digital readout along with your heart rate. The whole unit measures 2.2" x 3.2" x 1"; and uses two AAA batteries.

But will it deliver valid blood pressure measurements? Unequivocally, yes.

I took my little Panasonic into the Operating Room where I work and put it on the wrist of my patients, on the same arm on which I put my professional-grade anesthesia machine blood pressure cuff which, by the way, costs around $5,000. As soon as the anesthesia machine-value came up on my monitor screen, I pushed the little button on my Panasonic and then recorded both readings on a flow chart I'd created.

My conclusion is that the Panasonic is accurate, reliable and in fact better than the medical-grade equipment I use in two ways:

1) It's much easier to use: goes on in a couple seconds, as opposed to screwing around trying to get the blood pressure cuff and Velcro seal positioned just so, and then having to move the long rubber connecting tube to the anesthesia machine out of the way.

2) It's much faster: a reading from the Panasonic takes

maybe 30 seconds from button push to obtaining a value; the anesthesia version takes 1-2 minutes.

This is my second Panasonic wrist sphygmomanometer. This current model, Panasonic's EW3006S, is even quieter, faster, lighter, more comfortable, easier to read and use then my first one.

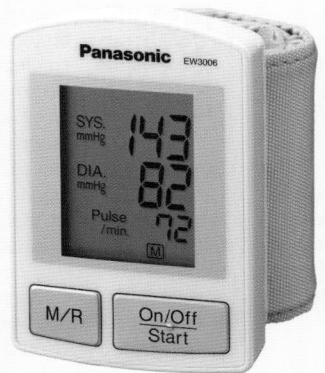

I keep my little Panasonic in my fanny pack when I'm in the OR, as a backup, 'cause you just never know when your monitor's gonna crash.

-- Joseph Stirt, MD

Blood pressure tracking
Wrist Blood Pressure Monitor

$42

I've been using the Withings (same manufacturer as the Withings Wi-Fi Scale) Blood Pressure Monitor for several weeks now and find it better than other monitors I've been using for years.

There are three aspects of the monitor that I prefer over other monitors. The cuff is amazingly easy to put on your arm. It has a stiff plastic or metal curved piece that holds the cuff in place on your arm while you wrap the arm band around your arm. It's the first cuff I've used that is easily placed single-handed and shipped with a cuff large enough for my arm without needing to purchase a larger cuff.

The air inflation and sensors are in a small tube on the cuff itself and are battery powered, forms a nice handle to aid positioning on your arm. No tubing to manage and worry about the cat puncturing. No outlet connections needed.

The iOS software is easier to use than other monitors. Plug-in the monitor, the app auto-launches and press start. Offers options to run repeated readings and then average them together. Keeps track of all your readings and provides charts without having to do data entry. Data can be exported to many formats.

The monitor has two downsides. The first is cost. At $129 it's double many of the common upper-arm monitors. However, it's worth it to me because it's so much easier for me to use that I'm better about taking my daily measurements. The second problem is that it is iOS only. The monitor will only plug into an iOS device to work. This isn't a wi-fi device like the Withings scale. The single cable on the device is an iPod connector cable. Works with iPod Touch, iPhone and iPad.

The software currently does not work with the cuff plugged in on a device running the beta iOS 5 firmware from Apple. I'm running it with an old iPod Touch for readings. The software works on iOS 5 without the cuff so I can still see my results on my other iOS devices.

-- Kevin van Haaren

The Scientific Plan to Make You Smarter, Healthier, More Productive

Take a Nap! Change your life.

Sara C. Mednick, Ph.D. with Mark Ehrman

Best tips for naps
Take a Nap! Change Your Life

$10 Sara C. Mednick, Ph.D., 2006, 141 p.

Napping is an evolutionarily habit that still works wonders today. I can get by with several hours less sleep per night by adding a 20-minute nap in the afternoon. But I work at home where napping is easily done. The point of this book is to persuade you that the benefits of napping, scientifically derived, are so great you should do everything you can to make napping a habit whatever your schedule. As this concise guide makes clear the benefits to nappers are significant: smarter, more productive, healthier. For those who have tried napping without success, this book offers several different methods to try. It is hard to imagine the siesta returning in full force in the workplace, but it should be resurrected in some fashion. Start here. This is the best practical book on naps yet.

-- KK

• It's free, it's nontoxic and it has no dangerous side effects. Hard to believe, with these powerful selling points, that people have to be convinced to nap. But alas, for way too long, napping has been given a bad rap.

• I'm often asked if a nap during the day will interfere with nocturnal sleep. The answer is a definite no. Unfortunately, many information sources on sleep hygiene encourage people to avoid napping if they're having trouble sleeping at night. Not only is there not a shred of evidence to support this advice, but much of the data coming out of sleep research demonstrates quite the opposite. In studies across all age ranges, nocturnal sleep duration has been proven to be unaffected by midday napping. As a matter of fact, studies indicate that in a number of cases napping actually improves the ability to sleep at night.

• As a rule of thumb, you can count on naps earlier in the day to be richer in REM, while late afternoon naps tend to be higher in SWS. If you take particular interest in your dreams, waking up during or right after a heavy REM episode will allow you the greatest recall of your dream imagery. If you feel like one of "the walking tired," a heavy SWS dose will take care of that.

• It bears repeating: There's no such thing as a bad nap. Any time you spend in midday sleep will reduce the effects of fatigue and bestow benefits. But our nap needs differ across populations and will change over the course of our lives. A mother's requirement is not the same as that of her three-year-old toddler. The sleep profile of a middle-aged football coach had little in common with that of a teenage beauty contestant.

• "Who's got time to nap?" is a common complaint among non-nappers. The short answer is: just about everyone. if you spend 20 minutes or more at Starbucks getting an afternoon mocha latte, couldn't you just stay where you are and take a nap instead? So, before you conclude that napping doesn't fit into your busy life, take out your day planner and examine your schedule. By carefully reviewing the activities of your day and the time it takes to do them, you can assess which time expenditures are unnecessary and where a nap can be substituted. How long is your lunch? A paralegal with an hour lunch break reports that she can eat in half an hour and keep the second half for her nap. Or do what I do and pencil in 20 to 40 minutes as soon as your get home for a transition nap between work and leisure.

Once you've carved out these precious minutes, you need to make this nap time a regular feature of your day. Just as we've developed a detailed trail of cues for our minds and bodies to recognize that it's time for nighttime sleep, we need to fashion a similar set of cues that will indicate that it's nap time. Consistent scheduling allows the body to associate that hour with the nap and all other concerns to more easily fade away.

• **"If I nap I'm being lazy."**

Some of the most hardworking figures in history–national leaders, scientists, CEOs, movie stars–have used napping as a tool to get more out of each day. As demonstrated by the latest brain imaging technology, your mind is still at work even if your body is at rest.

Replace with: "Napping makes me more productive."

"I'm too busy to nap."

Just look around your office at 3 p.m. More than likely, instead of a hive of industrious activity, you'll see a bunch of bleary-eyed workers checking and rechecking their e-mail. As the great napper Winston Churchill said, "Don't think you will be doing less work because you sleep during the day. You will be able to accomplish more. You get two days in one… well, at least one and half." The latest scientific research has proven him correct.

Replace with: "I'm so busy, I need to nap."

"I haven't done enough to deserve a nap."

Do you deserve to eat? To breathe? No natural function–including napping!–should be regarded as a privilege. Stop cheating yourself.

Replace with: "I'm exercising my inalienable right to nap."

"I can't get anything out of a 20-minute nap, so why bother?"

You can reap benefits in as little as five minutes. Naps under 20 minutes can increase alertness, improve physical dexterity, boost stamina and lower stress. Post-lunch naps of 15 minutes have been shown in university studies to increase alertness and performance.

Replace with: "In less than 20 minutes, I will restore my alertness for the rest of the day."

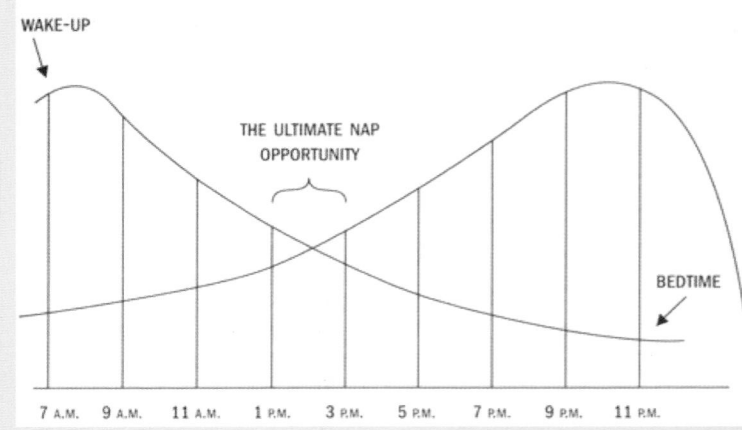

The interaction between sleep pressure and the circadian phase shows how the concentration of REM and SWS varies across the day.

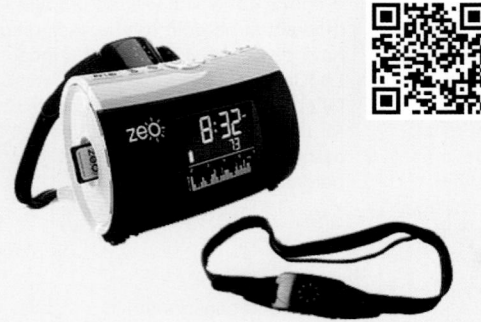

Brain wave sleep tracker
Zeo Personal Sleep Coach

$300 Amazon

You know nothing about nearly a third of your life. Sure, you think you have some sense of how you sleep, but you really don't. We're notoriously inaccurate in estimating how long it takes us to fall asleep, how long we're awake in the middle of the night, how long we dream and how much deep sleep we get. And the total hours you sleep are only one factor of many in determining the quality of that sleep and the restorative effect it will have on you. Even worse, if you want to improve the quality of your sleep, all you've got to go on is general advice, while the one thing we know about sleep is that we're all different.

What you need is data. That's what Zeo provides. It's a clock-radio-sized device that sits on your bedside table, with a comfortable wireless headband that you wear while you sleep. The headband measures electrical signals from your brain and can distinguish between four states: awake, light sleep, REM sleep and deep sleep. The base station records all this, and displays all the data in easy to understand charts, as well as recording it on an SD card that you can plug into a computer to upload to a very good website for tracking and analysis.

(It's also a great alarm clock, which can wake you at the time when you're most ready to wake, which may be some minutes before the set time)

I was given a Zeo when it first came out last year, and I'm hooked. I knew I was a poor sleeper who is plagued by too-vivid dreams, but here's what I found out with Zeo: 1) I get very little deep sleep (often less than 10%), which is the most restorative type. My wife, meanwhile, usually gets more than 25% deep sleep over the same period. 2) When I think I'm tossing and turning all night, I'm usually not. The wake periods are typically short, and I am actually asleep between them. 3) There are simple things I can do to improve my sleep, even if I'm not sleeping any more hours.

To that last point, Zeo is all about running experiments on yourself. Take a couple weeks of baseline data to measure day-of-week cyclicality, and then start changing things. For me, the difference between one glass of wine and two a night is an average of five points of "ZQ" score (I average around 80). Cutting off screens (email, web, even reading on the iPad) a half-hour before bed and turning to a paper book also adds about five points. I'd hoped that exercise would add to my score, but it didn't. Three milligrams of melatonin before bed has a small but positive impact, which may well just be the placebo effect. 11:30 is better for me than 12:00, but 11:00 is no better than 11:30. And so on.

If you'd like better sleep and want to be smart about how you go about it, Zeo is the perfect tool. And even if you don't have one, subscribe to the Zeo blog, which is full of smart data- and science-driven advice and discussion about sleep quality and how to improve it.

-- Chris Anderson

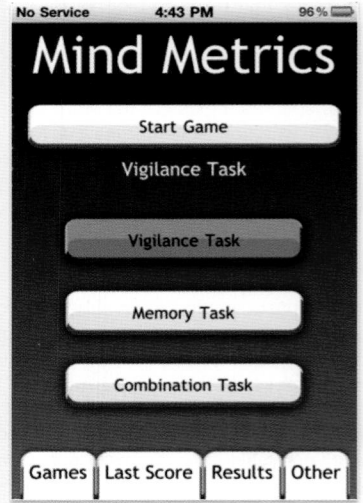

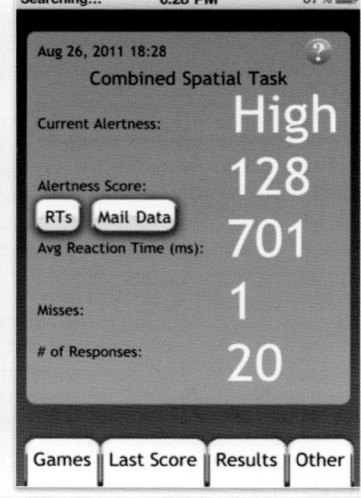

Quantifying mental ability
Mind Metrics

$3 proactivelife.org

One of the self-tracking projects that I always wanted to do was to determine the impact of sleep, diet and exercise regimen on my mental and cognitive abilities. I needed an app to *measure* my cognitive or mental skills/abilities, -- rather than training or improving them. I also wanted measurement methods to be as close to scientific as possible. And of course the tests should take as little time as possible (preferably under 5 min), and run off portable devices. I settled on Mind Metrics which is an awesome phone app that lets me measure alertness, higher cognitive abilities such as attention and memory and their combination.

For instance, in the alertness test you are asked to tap the sun as soon as it appears in the same part of the screen randomly every few seconds. You can control the number of trials and timing for both tests. After completing a preset number of trials, you get both average reaction time and average attention/memory score. You can see all your current and previous scores on the screen, and also e-mail them to yourself in comma separated format.

I've been using Mind Metrics to measure mental alertness in a couple of experiments, including finding the optimal time to go to bed (my finding was that going to bed between 11 and 11:15 leads to higher alertness next morning and better sleep), and validating orthostatic heart rate test (difference between standing and resting heart rate right after waking up reasonably well predicts mental and physical performance later in the day). I am currently using Mind Metrics to track my cognitive well-being on a daily basis.

-- Konstantin Augemberg

Institutions are halfway houses for the temporarily uninspired. - Jaron Lanier

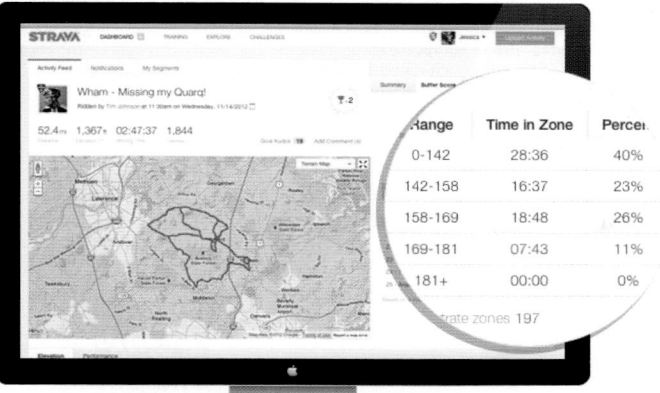

GPS cycling and running log
Strava

Free, or $6 monthly, $59 annually for full-featured access Strava

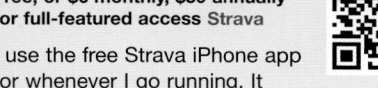

I use the free Strava iPhone app for whenever I go running. It tracks how far I run, how long I run, and keeps a history of all my past runs. If I am running somewhere new it will use the phone's gps to map my route on Google maps, making it easy to run that route again. Works for cycling and hiking, too. It also has a feature that allows me to compare my time with other Strava users' times in certain segments of a popular route.

Range	Time in Zone	Percent
0-142	28:36	40%
142-158	16:37	23%
158-169	18:48	26%
169-181	07:43	11%
181+	00:00	0%

I've noticed that I'm more inclined to go on a run if I can see that I have done such a run before and want to do it faster. When I add another finished run to the app, I feel a sense of accomplishment and excitement to go out there and do it again. RunKeeper and Nike+ are both great run tracking app options for iPhone and Android. Dedicated devices by Garmin are good too, for cycling as well. But I've found Strava to be the most motivating, and the easiest to sync and switch between most peripheral devices with (like the Garmin Forerunner 210) and the most reliable in the accuracy of recording your data -- making it easy but not overwhelming for a novice to start out with, while still offering great benefits for expert users.

-- Kosuke Hata

GPS + heart rate data for runners
Garmin Forerunner 305 & MotionBased Training

$330 Amazon

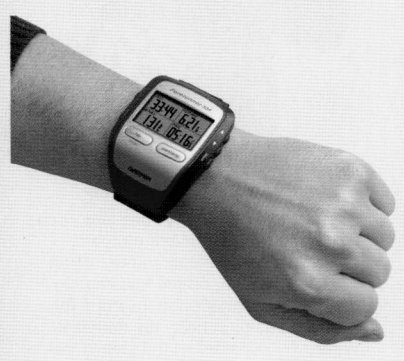

As an age-group triathlete, I wouldn't want to train without my Garmin Forerunner 305, a GPS "wristwatch" with an accompanying heart rate monitor (HRM). It's my training partner: holds me to the line, makes me get out and work out, and gives me the information I need to advance. Of particular interest to me are: mile splits on the run; average HR (heart rate) and maximum HR. Here's how it works: I strap the HRM around my chest and turn on the wrist unit. The GPS locks on to satellite positions. I press "start" and go! While I am moving during the workout, I am being tracked. If I stop, the tracking program "pauses;" thus, my actual results are only for while I am moving. It's a pretty significant piece of hardware, but of the research I did, and GPS/HRM units I've owned (Timex, Nike, Polar), at this time the Garmin 305 is the most appropriate to my needs. Both the HRM strap as well as the "watch" are comfortable. The unit is bulky, sure, but anyone who wears a watch to work out will grow accustomed to it. Best of all, the wireless communication is spot-on -- the watch picks up the transmitted heart rate much better than the Polar unit I previously used, for instance. And the ability to sync my GPS/HR data not only to my computer (Garmin has proprietary software) but also Garmin's MotionBased.com is crucial. After any workout, I upload the data to my MotionBased account, which charts all the data and allows me to review statistics. I simply plug a cord in to my computer's USB port, launch Safari (for Mac, you must use Safari) and upload the data to my MB Inbox. Then, I can add any notes/details/names of the training session. The kind of information Garmin and MotionBased training provides is much more comprehensive than the more subjective tracking I've done by creating my own workout logs on Google spreadsheets.

I can train the same exact route and know to the moment (time and heart rate) how I did in comparison to the last time; I can see the average and max temperatures and windspeed to see if climate may have affected my performance; I can record and share my workouts with friends, coaches, or other athletes, export routes to GoogleEarth or GoogleMaps and use the data to practice, rehearse mentally and visualize my upcoming events and races. I can also show my mom how cool she is for running with me! (At 57, she still keeps up a good 4 mile pace!). I started with the free MotionBased account. After I used it a few times, I knew I would want the extra features for a year to truly test the functionality and see if it was something I could use (so far it's been well worth the $48 annual fee). The differences between free and standard accounts include access to MotionBased's Analyzer, which allows you to pinpoint distance splits.

Summary Data		
Total Time (h:m:s)	0:48:08	9:17 pace
Moving Time (h:m:s)	0:47:22	9:09 pace
Distance (mi)	5.18	
Moving Speed (mph)	6.6 avg.	9.3 max.
Elevation Gain (ft)	+345 / -344	
Avg. Heart Rate	161 bpm	Zone 4.7
Temperature (°F)	56.7°F avg.	57°F high
Wind Speed (mph)	ESE 24.9 avg.	ESE 28.8 max.
GPS Signal Quality	Excellent	MB Gravity Web Service
Driving Directions	MapQuest Google	
Export	Google Earth GPX Other	
Charts	Everything	

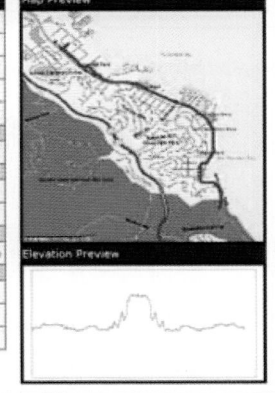

In 2001, after being 40 pounds overweight with no physical fitness program in place, I started triathalon training with an HRM and began tracking my run, swim, bike, and weight lifting workouts, and calibrating and tracking my outdoor activities (hiking, biking, running) with a Garmin Gecko 101 GPS that I bought from Target for $79.00. This gave me week-to-week comparisons for speed, time and distance, which I used to assess my training and interval workouts through the quarter. However, now I can get ALL of these training metrics together with one simple device. I initially bought the Forerunner 205, but returned it because I wanted the extra data: heart rate. My goal for next year is to race at a lower HR than in years past. After the last triathlon I raced in, I learned my HR was too high (race average: 173). I would like to get that down to the low 160s/mid 160s for the 5.5 hour race I am planning for next May. Using the Garmin Forerunner 305 and MotionBased really enhances all the training I do. It makes me look forward to capturing the results and pushes me for the next time, especially when I revisit a specific route.

-- Jason Womack

Calorie counting app
MyFitnessPal

Free MyFitnessPal

MyFitnessPal is calorie-counting app available for Android, iPhone, iPad, BlackBerry, and Windows phones. It has proven EXTREMELY effective for me in large part because it leverages my inner data-nerd. It's really pure psychology — but this happens to be the psychological strategy that suits me perfectly. I have no idea whether this app will work for anyone else as well as it has worked for me, but it has definitely changed my life in a very positive way. I've lost 45 lbs. so far using this app with no change in exercise.

Once set up, your main task with the app is to log what you eat throughout the day. Your accesses a massive database of foods (partially from a clean dataset, partially crowd-sourced) that you can either do a text-search on or use a very slick barcode scanner via the phone's camera. The barcode scanner has proven to be 100% reliable, extremely fast, and amazingly complete — it's found everything I've searched for correctly and essentially instantly.

When I eat something without a barcode (like from a restaurant), I almost always find the exact item I'm looking for. Almost any menu item from any franchise is in there, as is an extensive variation of customized menu options (e.g., 6" Subway double-meat turkey with provolone no mayo….etc.). If you can't find a specific item, you can easily enter your own recipes by assembling a set of individual components from items already in the database or that you create yourself. When you select any particular item, you can usually select from a series of different serving sizes, and separately enter any number (including decimal fractions) for a fraction of the selected serving that you actually eat.

There is much more to the app than I've described here — including an entire social network component. The website is incredibly robust and easy to use. There is a growing list of partner apps and devices (such as the Fitbit Aria Scale) that seamlessly sync with your MyFitnessPal account. The main problems I have with the app are that it offers extremely limited control over the reports and graphs, and there is no obvious way to get access to my raw data for downloading. As a data-nerd, I find this extremely frustrating. Also the crowd-sourced content may have multiple entries for what seems like the same thing but with very different nutritional profiles.

I still eat most of my favorite foods; just less of them, and I haven't missed anything or had any cravings. After the first few weeks, I've almost never been hungry (certainly much less often hungry than before I started). I'm a scientist so I intentionally wanted to focus strictly on diet first, then I'll switch to focus on exercise once I reach my target weight — one variable at a time!

-- Richard Pyle

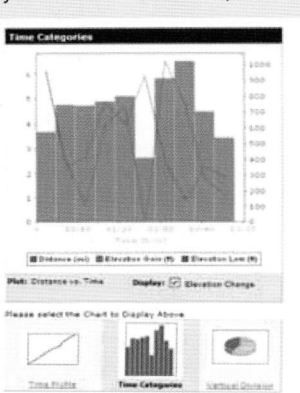

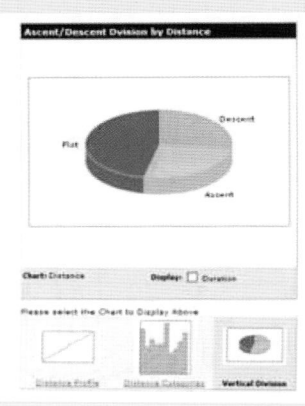

If you think you are free, there is no escape possible. - Ram Dass

Fitness

Best routines for keeping fit
Body for Life

$18 Bill Phillips, 1999, 201 p.

Okay, you are sold on the basic sanity of *Fit or Fat*, (reviewed here) but what do you actually do today? I mean where do you start? The best answer to that question is Body for Life, which pound for pound has more motivating specifics than anywhere else. The catalyst is a simple bargain: you can change the shape and fit of your body in twelve weeks if you are willing to work reasonably hard with a reasonably flexible plan manageable by most busy people. I figured I could stand almost anything for twelve weeks, if it produced results. Well, it worked for me at least, much better than I expected,

and it has apparently worked for many others, judging from the photos and the constant friend-of-a-friend referrals this book produces. Most importantly, once your body reshapes itself (this is not about losing weight), the logic of Body for Life (the same as Fit or Fat) becomes habit.

-- KK

•

Myth: aerobics is better for shaping up than weight training.

Fact: To transform your physique, you must train with weights.

Myth: Muscles grow while you're working out.

Fact: Muscles grow while you are resting and recuperating.

Myth: Lifting a weight is what stimulates muscle growth.

Fact: Lifting and lowering a weight stimulates muscle growth.

•

Enough evidence now exists to concretely state that lowering the weight is just as important as lifting it. It's true. It turns out that weight lowering causes much of the muscle-cell damage that stimulates an adaptation. You see, when you

lengthen the muscle, which occurs during that eccentric portion of an exercise, you literally tear portions of the muscle fibers, signaling a stage of remodeling, or muscle growth. (You'll know when you've experienced this phenomenon because a day or two after your workout, your muscles will be sore. That's a sign that the "earth has moved.")

•

When you apply the Intensity Index properly to both your resistance training and aerobic workouts, you'll never hit the ceiling. You'll always move up to higher and higher high points. And that means you'll continually be stimulating your muscles while losing fat. You'll become more metabolically efficient. Your body will burn fat at a significantly elevated rate, even while you're sitting at your desk or driving your car or reading a book…even while you're sleeping.

This graph demonstrates the pattern of strength-building aerobics. To maximize a twenty-minute workout, you must press toward your maximum effort and "break through" your intensity level.

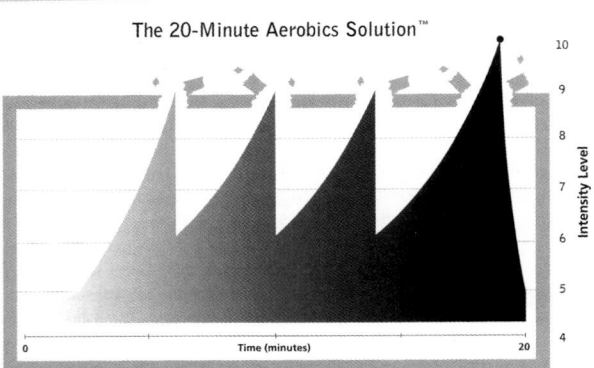

"Before" and "after" snapshots of participants in a contest to see how much they could change their bodies in twelve weeks.

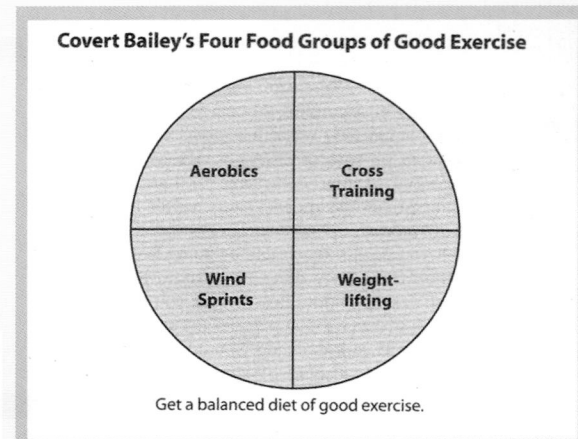

The essentials of fitness
Ultimate Fit or Fat

$10 Covert Bailey, 1999, 170 p.

The classic book on fitness has been rewritten after twenty-five years and is, unexpectedly, better than ever. There's still not a fad in it, and it is still lean, brief, and witty. Now with more attention to aging, more reliance on home testing, and more encouragement for weightlifting, this is still the best overall guide to the how and why of getting fit.

-- KK

•

Fat people who are constantly dieting should worry less about how to lose weight. Instead they should ask themselves. "Why do I gain weight so easily?"

•

As a person becomes more and more out of shape and the muscles fill up with fat, the arms and waistline become softer and softer. I remember a tall, thin young woman I tested who had never exercised a day in her life. I gripped her arm and said, "Tighten up, Susie."

"Okay!" she said obligingly. I waited a few seconds, but her arm felt as soft as ever.

"Tighten up, Susie," I repeated.

"I am, I am!" she grunted, her face red from the effort.

This woman was so out of shape and her muscles were so soft no amount of flexing made them harder. She looked thin on the outside, but she was fat on the inside.

•

The underwater immersion test is time-consuming, takes up lots of laboratory space, and is scary for many people,

so most testing facilities use less accurate but more convenient methods. Most techniques measure the fat just beneath the skin, on the assumption that the amount of subcutaneous fat increases as total body fat increases. When you consider all the places inside the body where fat can accumulate, such as around the intestines and inside muscles, it's hard to believe that measuring skin fat would reflect total body fat, but we have measured peoples' fat both underwater and with the skin test for years and using our formula, subcutaneous fat measurements are amazingly accurate.

•

Remember! If you can't exercise exactly by the rules I've given you, just do a lot of it. Quantity can substitute for quality. That's why sports almost always makes people fitter than strict exercise at a health club.

Don't Even Think about Distance

It doesn't matter how far you go. What matters is how many minutes a day you spend trying to change your body into a fit body. Exercise for time, not distance.

Better than a lecture
A Pound of Fat

$37 (1 lb replica) Amazon ▶

Looking for an effective weight loss motivator? Check out this all-too-realistic anatomically correct replica of one pound of human fat, complete with blood supply. Keep it on your dinner table and watch everybody lose their appetite. For even stronger motivation, you can buy the five-pounds-of-human-fat version.

-- Tom Ferguson, MD

$84 (5 lb replica) Amazon ▶

Engineering weight control
The Hacker's Diet

Free The Hacker's Diet

There's no better description of this book by Autodesk founder John Walker, than his own:

"The Hacker's Diet … is a serious book about how to lose weight and permanently maintain whatever weight you desire. It treats dieting and weight control from an engineering and management standpoint, and provides the tools and an understanding of why they work and how to use them that permit the reader to gain control of their own weight. The book is intended primarily for busy, successful engineers, programmers, and managers who have struggled unsuccessfully in the past to lose weight and avoid re-gaining it."

This electronic 250-page book has gone through many revisions over the past decade and is available online for free in four formats, from frame-based web to PDF files. It's been recommended by many readers.

-- KK

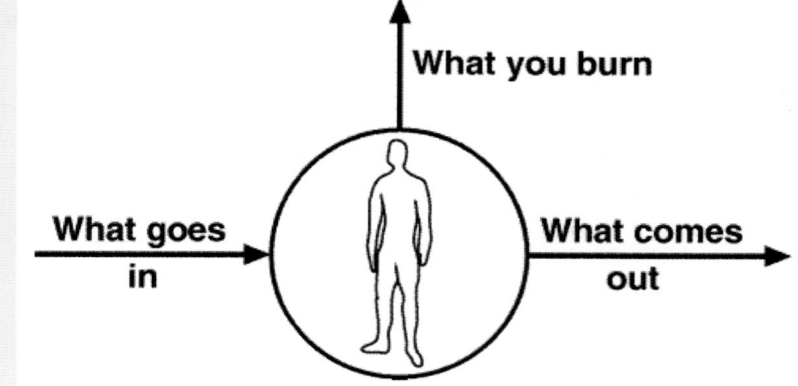

I have been through some terrible things in my life, some of which actually happened. - Mark Twain

$16 John Little, Doug McGuff, 2008, 288 p.

$1 Scientific 7-Minute Workout Endloop Systems, Inc.

High intensity exercise

Body by Science

The latest innovation in fitness is the extremely intense weekly workout. A very brief period of vomit-inducing exercise -- of only 12 minutes *per week* -- is enough to bestow the benefits of much longer and more frequent exercise. So says the science. My doctor recommended this book as the prime source of the scientific logic and practical program for this high-intensity interval training. A "scientific" 7-minute weekly workout that requires no equipment based on the same science was featured in the *New York Times*. As a coaching aid you can get a 99-cent app for it.

--KK

When a trainee trains his biceps on a nautilus multi biceps machine, the radius of the cam is in perfect sync with the trainee's bicep muscles: smaller when he is weaker and bigger when he is strong.

Our rule of thumb for rep cadence is that whatever cadence you can employ that will allow you to move as slowly as possible without its turning into a stuttering, stop-and-start scenario is the right one for you. You may even find that the cadence changes as the set progresses. For instance, if you're working out on a piece of equipment that has a difficult start but an easy finish position, the hard start will represent a significant obstacle or sticking point to surmount. Consequently, you may start out with an eight-second cadence that is perfectly smooth, but because of the sticking point and a little bit of struggle, the smoothness may be able to be maintained only with a six-second cadence or a five-second cadence. So, again, contract against the resistance as slowly as you can without having your repetitions degenerate into a series of stops and starts.

Traditionally during workouts, to gauge performance and assess improvement for record keeping, trainees have focused on counting how many repetitions they perform with a given weight or load. What we advocate instead is timing the duration of the set from the moment it begins until the moment muscular failure is reached. We call this measure "time under load." Other people have called it "time to concentric failure" or "time under tension." Regardless of what you choose to call it, adopting it allows you to place a fine-tuning dial on your training performance.

Time under load allows trainees to see smaller gradations in improvement that otherwise might be missed and allows for fine-tuning of weight progression a little more closely.

You will begin to really struggle at this point, and your instructor should try to keep you focused by encouraging you not to try to speed up, rest, or pause during the movement, all of which will unload the muscles and provide rest, which is the opposite of what you are striving to accomplish. If you weren't being supervised, you would probably quit at this juncture, but you are encouraged to try one more repetition. This last positive portion of the repetition is now so difficult that it may take you fifteen, twenty, or even thirty seconds to complete. As you slowly begin to reverse direction and lower the resistance, the weight begins to overtake your strength. You attempt another positive repetition, but the weight is not moving. Your instructor now tells you to attempt to contract against the resistance (it's still not moving) while he or she counts to ten. Your rate of fatigue is increasing rapidly now, and your strength continues to diminish well below the resistance level. At the end of the instructor's count, you unload from the weight. By the time the set is finished, your strength has been reduced to approximately 60 percent of what it was prior to starting the exercise, resulting in an inroad of 40 percent being made.

This whole process occurred over a span of roughly two minutes, but in that time, your muscles became 40 percent weaker. This occurrence represents a serious "threat" to your body, because it was not aware that you were simply in a gym making weights go up and down. For all it knew, you were fighting for your life with a mountain lion. To the body, this was a profound metabolic experience, and at the end of that experience, it couldn't move. Mobility is a preserved biologic function: if you can't move, you can't acquire food, and you can't avoid becoming food for other prey. This experience represented a profound stimulus, to which the body will respond, if given sufficient time, by enlarging on its strength reserves so that there will be at least some strength left over the next time such a stimulus might be encountered. Of course, now that you understand this process, you will employ slightly more resistance during your next workout to stimulate your body to produce another round of metabolic adaptation.

Bear in mind that as you fatigue during this process, and as your force output drops, you will feel the window between your force output and the resistance you're using starting to close. You'll develop an almost instinctual sense of panic, a feeling that you're not strong enough to meet the resistance you're under. This is the "make-or-break" point in the set. If you understand that what you're trying to do is achieve a deep level of muscular fatigue, you can override the instinct to attempt to escape. Escape in this context can take the form either of prematurely quitting and just shutting down or of attempting to wiggle and jab at the weight to momentarily get out from under the load.

1. Jumping jacks → 2. Wall sit → 3. Push-up → 4. Abdominal crunch

5. Step-up onto chair → 6. Squat → 7. Triceps dip on chair → 8. Plank

9. High knees running in place → 10. Lunge → 11. Push-up and rotation → 12. Side plank

From the New York Times

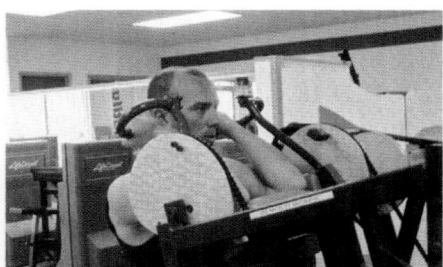

Barbell Bible

Starting Strength

$30 Mark Rippetoe and Lon Kilgore, 2011, 3rd Edition, 347 p.

A barbell is the best training tool an athlete can use. The weight can vary from 10 lbs to over 1000 lbs in increments as small as 1/2 lb, and the set of available exercises is limited only by the lifter's imagination. This makes training with a barbell suitable for pretty much anyone, regardless of age, sex, or experience.

Studies detailing injury rates show weight training to be as much as orders of magnitude less likely to cause injury than sports like running, cycling, football, and especially the most dangerous sport in America: soccer.

They cover five basic lifts — squat, bench press, deadlift, overhead press, and power clean — in amazing, well-illustrated, and readable detail. The chapter on the squat spans over 60 pages and covers not only technique but why to squat and how to identify and fix problems as they come up. The other exercises are covered in no less impressive detail, including some stellar and original thinking on the deadlift, and an effective basic training program to put everything together.

Save whatever you were going to spend on sports drinks over the next few weeks and buy this instead. It's one of those books that belongs in everyone's library.

-- Chris Roth

The vast majority of people will prefer to grip the bar with the thumbs-around grip. At lighter weights, this is fine since the load presents no problems to keep in place. But when heavier weights are being used — and, theoretically, they eventually should be — the thumbs can create problems.

The thumb should be placed on top of the bar, so that the wrist can be held in a straight line with the forearm. Most people have a mental picture of the hands holding up the weight, and this usually ends up being what happens. The bar sits in the grip with the thumbs around the bar, the elbows end up directly below the weight, and nothing really prevents the bar from sliding down the back from this position. People that do this will have sore elbows, a horrible, headache-like soreness in the inside of the elbow that makes them think the injury occurred doing curls. If the elbows are underneath the weight, the force of the weight is straight down (the nature of gravity is sometimes inconvenient), then the wrists and elbows will intercept some of the weight. With heavy weights, the loading is quite high, and these structures are not nearly as capable of supporting 500 lbs, as the back is. If the thumb is on top of the bar, the hand can assume a position that is straight in line with the forearm, wrist, and hand, and all of the weight is on the back. A correct grip can prevent these problems before they start. If you learn to carry all of the weight of the bar on the back before your strength improves to the point where the weight becomes a problem, you'll have no problem at all.

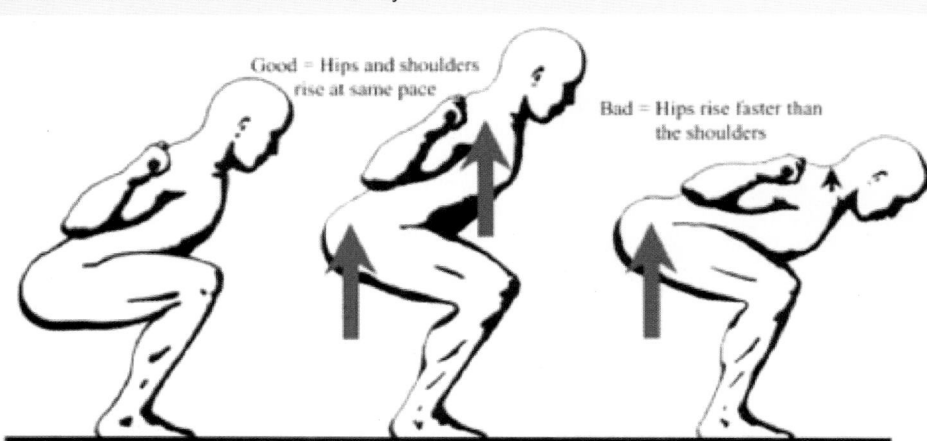

The back angle during the drive up form the bottom [of the squat] is critical to the correct use of the hips. The correct angle is produced when the bar is just below the spine of the scapula and directly vertical to the middle of the foot, the back is held tight in lumbar and thoracic extension, the knees are parallel to the correctly-placed feet, and the correction depth is reached, as discussed later.

Good = Hips and shoulders rise at same pace
Bad = Hips rise faster than the shoulders

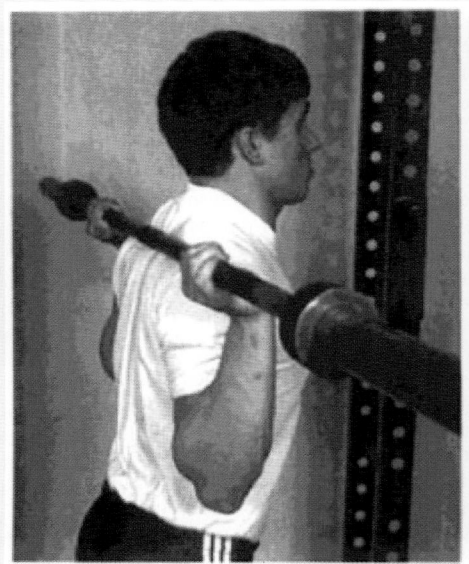

Incorrect (left) and correct (right) use of the hands and arms. Elbows should be elevated to the rear with the hands on top, not placed directly under the bar where they intercept part of the weight.

How to swim like a fish

Total Immersion Swimming

$40 Easy Freestyle: 21st Century Techniques for Beginners to Advanced Swimmers DVD Total Immersion

$13 Total Immersion, Terry Laughlin, John Delves, 2004, 320 p.

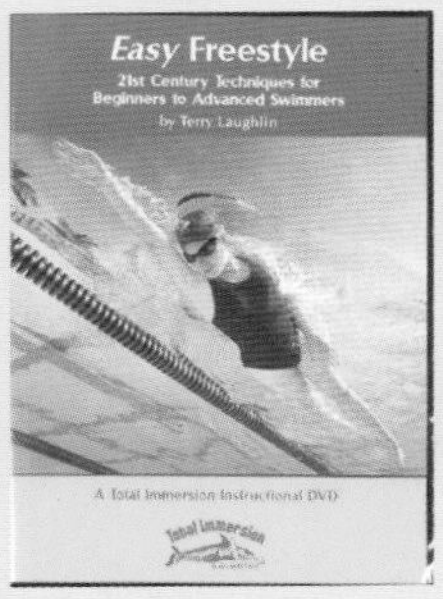

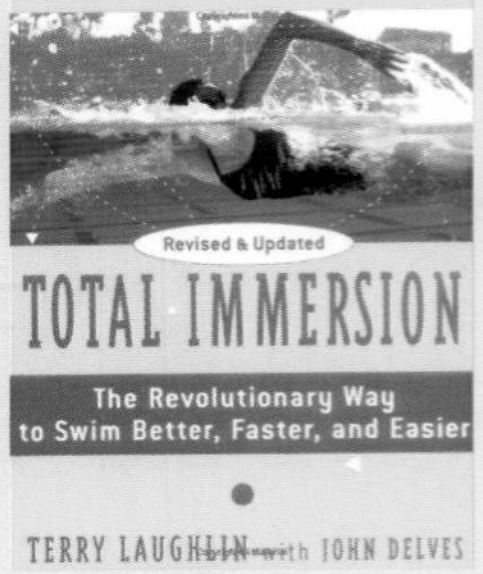

It's amazing to me that it took thousands of years before we humans really began to understand how best to swim, and how best to teach swimming. Terry Laughlin is perhaps the nation's best swimming coach. Over his lifetime in pools he has figured out the best ways for teaching all kinds of people how to swim. His teaching is all about lowering your resistance in the water, rather than increasing your strength or force. He teaches every kind of swimmer, from beginners to Olympic athletes, how to be more like fish and less like the humans we are. The advent of underwater viewing and particularly video taping and slow motion helped Terry make breakthroughs in understanding the basis of efficient swimming. Terry's methods still suffer the slings and arrows that any breakthrough idea that dares to challenge conventional thinking endures, but the truth and usefulness of his ideas are winning out.

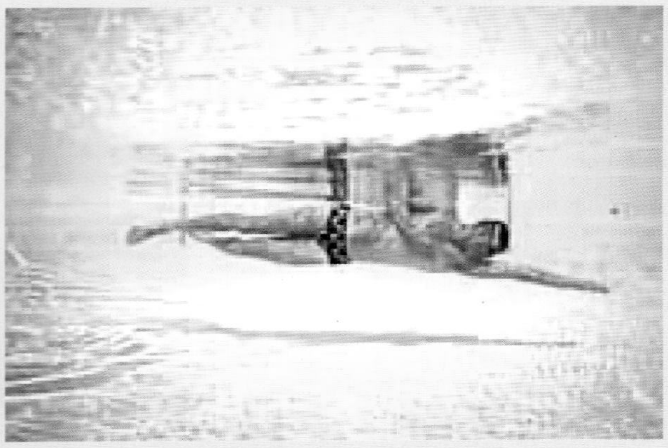

I love when a book or DVD can teach me physical things. (I've also experienced this with kayaking, particularly learning to roll, but that's another story.) I had a mortifying experience in my first triathlon. I can run and bike pretty well and thought I could swim. But out there in the ocean I exhibited the grace of a wounded wildebeest. I had to flop over on my back and gasp the whole way, arms flailing. I was close to panic from it all. I swore I'd either give up this nonsense or learn how to swim well. When I found Laughlin's DVDs and books, I felt they had been created just for me. Through him I discovered for myself the benefit of lining up my head and using my core body to move. There's no pulling at the water and hardly any kicking. I could try to describe it more fully but Terry does it so much better in his DVDs and books.

– Steve Leveen

Start by watching the DVD and then go on to the book for supporting details.

•

In 1988 I had the good fortune to meet Bill Boomer, who planted the intriguing idea that the "shape of the vessel" might have just as much influence as the "size of the engine" on a swimmer's performance. I had been teaching balance in an instinctive way – and with exciting results – to butterfliers and breaststrokers since 1978. Also in 1978, while watching my swimmers from an underwater window, I had realized that swimmers moved fastest while just gliding in streamline after pushoff. Once they began kicking and stroking, far more of their energy seemed to go into making bubbles than into effective propulsion.

•

Throughout most of the animal kingdom, the really fast creatures – race horses, greyhounds, cheetahs – use about the same stride rate at all galloping speeds. So do most really fast humans, such as Marion Jones and Michael Johnson. They run faster by taking longer strides, not by taking them faster. It's only when humans get into the water that we suffer a form of momentary biomechanical derangement, resorting to churning our arms madly when we want more speed.

•

The reason stroke length (SL) doesn't have a lot to do with arm length, or with how far you reach forward and push back, is because SL is how far your body travels each time you take a stroke. So it's mostly your body position – not your height or strength or the length of your arms – that affects the distance you will travel on each stroke. The best way to measure your SL is simply to make a habit of counting strokes – at all speeds, and on virtually every length you swim.

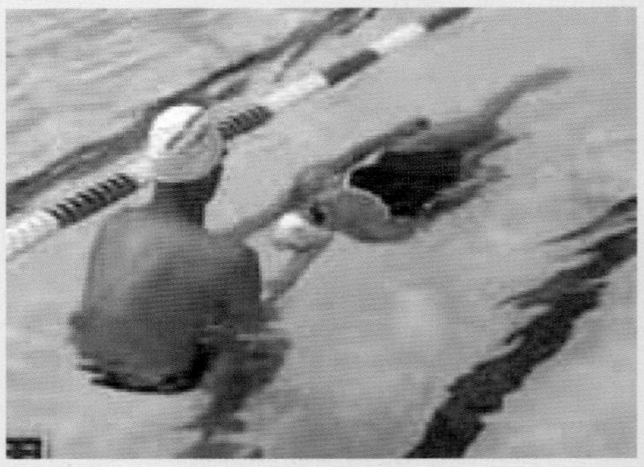

•

Stroke length can be improved in two ways. The easiest way is to minimize drag, and you do this by simply repositioning you body in the water to make yourself more slippery. The effect is that your body goes farther, with more ease and less deceleration, on a given amount of propulsion. The other way to improve SL is to maximize propulsion, and you do this by focusing on doing a better job of moving your body forward.

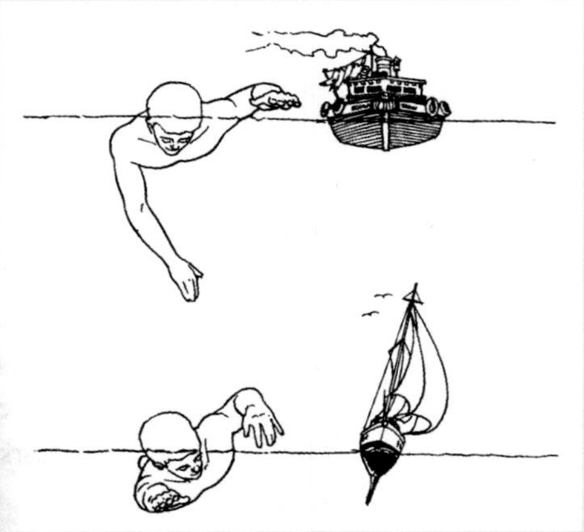

•

Kick For Efficiency, Not for Speed

Kicking can add only a modest amount of propulsion to an efficient stroke, while it can add a significant amount of drag and enormously increase the energy cost of whole-stroke swimming, if overemphasized. Therefore swimmers should do all they can to maximize the benefit of their kicking while minimizing the work they put into it.

"Fine," you say. "If all kicking does is burn energy and cause drag, why bother to kick at all?" Well, because that's not all kicking does. An efficient kick will improve your stroke and, in fact, is essential for the kinetic chain to produce anything like the power it's capable of producing for you.

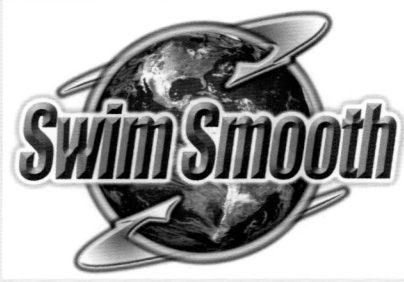

Fixing your swim stroke

Swim Smooth

Free Tutorial Swim Smooth

$20 Swim Type Guides, 20-page PDF Swim Smooth

$60 Swim Smooth DVD Boxset Swim Smooth

I've come back to swimming after about 100-years of being out of practice. Spine and knee injuries had kept me off land with poor aerobic capacity, and I was looking for ways to improve both my fitness and technique. I came upon Swim Smooth's website and their Swim Type guides.

The concept behind their methodology is based on identifying what kind of swimmer you are. The types are based on common problems encountered with swimming technique that group together like a chain of events. The approach then is to tackle not each individual flaw, but what is causing them to begin with.

First, you determine what your type is by reading descriptions and filling out some info. In my experience, getting yourself on video is king; what you look like while swimming can be very different from your experience of it. In fact, I now use my smartphone as a tool to track my progress, by videoing every couple of months, and using instant-playback at the pool.

Each 18-20 page PDF guide for a particular swim type is written in a clear and concise language, and includes four sessions that work directly on what it is that makes your stroke wonky in a sequential manner. There are different ways to use them; you can incorporate them into your swimming routine, concentrate on one before moving on to the next. I cycled through them religiously for about three months, meaning 1-2-3-4 every week. My stroke and fitness both improved, allowing me to begin training for endurance. Before I was simply out of breath after just one lap. I now go deeper into one session for a number of weeks, with two other different swim sets thrown in. It's up you how to keep using them once you have improved.

There's also a nifty app featuring an animation of the ideal freestyle stroke. You can control the speed and view from different angles. Sometimes while I'm swimming, a question about a movement pops up and I like to go back to the animation and check it there. It's free to download on the main Swim Smooth site.

They have a number of other products, from DVDs to swim suits designed for each swim type, and also conduct workshops in the UK. I haven't had the chance to try these yet. I have no idea about the size of the operation, but my exchanges with them have been very attentive, and make it feel very personable, I would even describe them as the 'mom and pop's' of swimming.

-- M. Katz

Swimming tether

StrechCordz Short Resistance Training Belt

$34 Amazon

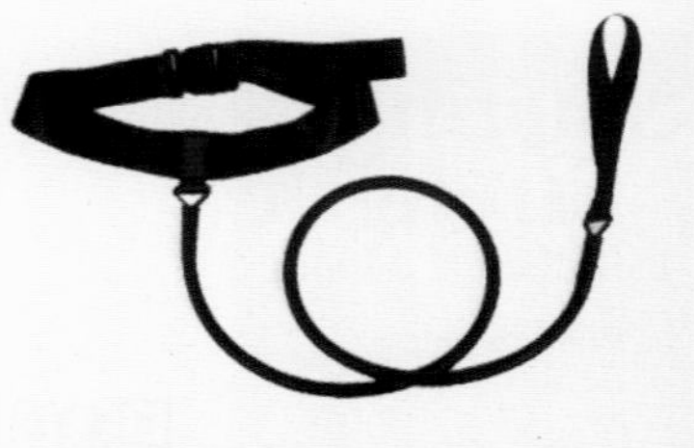

The StrechCordz resistance training belt makes expensive, complex, "endless" pools obsolete. At one end of a 4-foot, black rubber tube is a nylon belt with a simple plastic snap-clip that slips around my waist. On the other end is a loop I attach to the deep-end ladder of our modest home pool. That's it… just tether up and start swimming. Swim as hard and fast as you like yet stay in place.

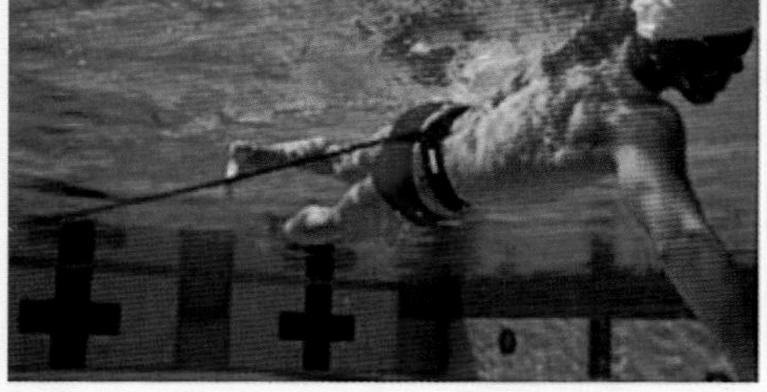

I'm able to do backstroke, crawl, butterfly (well, I try to butterfly), even frog-kick with no interference. Stop swimming and the belt gently pulls me back to the ladder. And, no, my legs don't get tangled in the line! The rubber tube is just stretchy enough to allow a good resistance for natural swimming feel, but I hardly notice the belt at all. Significantly, I even forget I'm wearing it. It's completely comfortable for long bouts of swimming. The one I own has been in daily use for one swimming season in a relatively mild salt-water home pool. Not any sign of wear at all on the belt, but I do put it away out of sunlight between uses.

I wasn't sure I'd need the belt, frankly, since our pool is big enough for actual swimming. In practice, however, even though our pool is 32 feet long, it's not really enough to be comfortable for laps. The belt is an elegant solution. There's no more constantly calculating the strokes left till the next turn. Swimming in place allows a steady, relaxed rhythm that would otherwise be impossible. I find I can swim longer on the belt and get more of a workout. Our pool is 18 feet from side to side. The short belt (4 ft.) is plenty long enough for me, but there's a longer version for larger pools.

There are other products for resistance swimming, but I haven't needed to try them. For one, the Super Swim — a suspension apparatus — is 10 times the price and needlessly complex. I can see the theory behind it, but it would entail major pool-side visual and actual clutter, and would be a bother to store away. With the StrechCordz it'd be easy to raise the point of the tether if necessary, but I hook it at the deck level and it's fine. At only three-times the price of the Strechcordz unit, the RipTide's a relative bargain. It's a belt with shoes you slip on. I just don't think I'd want shoes on in the water… just something funny about having my feet tethered. And then there's having a size suitable for everyone. The StrechCordz belt is easily adjustable to basically any size. It's very simple to use, safe (one snap of the belt and it's on or off), and compact enough one could easily travel with it. Packing it really is a non-issue.

My office overlooks the pool and a swim workout is a good mid-afternoon tonic for neck and shoulders after hours of computer work. Looking forward to getting back to it now that the weather's warming up!

-- Bill Womack

Swede swimming solution
Original Swedish Goggles
$4 Amazon

Among competitive swimmers that wear goggles four hours a day for weeks on end, the widely accepted gold standard is a type of goggles invented in the 1970s by the Swedish company Malmsten AB and widely copied thereafter. They will hold up to years and years of exposure to chlorine, replacement parts are easy to find, they are infinitely customizable to their user's face, are very comfortable when dialed in, and yet cost only $4 a pair where others can cost $30. They're called "Swedish" goggles.

The first thing you'll notice about them is that unlike every other goggle on the market, they have no soft rubber/foam seal around each eyepiece. The sealing surface is hard plastic. What would seem to be a shocking design oversight actually makes a lot of sense. They were originally designed this way to accommodate people that might have a skin allergy to rubber or foam. Because the seal is hard plastic, it is impervious to chlorine and UV, and seals exactly the same way each time. Individual eyepieces will last forever and still seal the same long after soft seals have rotted away from the chlorine. They come in about eight million colors, but I recommend not getting the metallic eyepieces as the coating eventually wears off but they do look cool. There is an anti-fog variant, but I just spit and swish in mine and that works well enough. I suppose you could also buy an anti-fog cream.

The nose piece is another thing you'll notice, in that it appears to just be a cheap piece of string in a rubber tube. Again, this design is very smart, as it is infinitely adjustable where other goggles have to use interchangeable nose pieces or some other part that will force the purchase of a new pair if it ever gets lost or broken, the Swedish goggles' nose piece can be replaced with any bit of string you can find and a piece of clear tubing from the hardware store. Many swimmers like Michael Phelps also use a section of the head strap as a nose piece. I personally use a twist of wire.

The head strap is like the nose piece; instead of a proprietary strap like other goggles, it uses a simple piece of flat rubber strap that can be found anywhere. The strap can be configured to have different upper and lower lengths in order to sit perfectly.

Fitting them, of course, is more involved due to their customizability. There are detailed directions included with each pair, and it takes about 15 minutes. Just like any goggle, some people will fit them and some won't. I have heard of a few swimmers shaping the sealing surface with sandpaper in order to make them fit, but they really do fit the vast majority of people. However, they won't fit a lot of kids because kids' smaller eye orbitals will interfere with the sealing.

I have had my pair of goggles for about ten years, and have gone through about five head straps and three nose pieces in that time while pool and ocean swimming 10 hours a week during college and 2 hours a week thereafter. My eyepieces are still going strong.

-- Jon Braun

Cheap underwater clarity
Corrective Swim Goggles
$5 ClubSwim Antifog Optical Pro II Goggles SwimOutlet

$14-25 TYR Corrective Optical Performance Goggle Amazon

$13 SPQ Corrective Lens Goggle SwimOutlet

I wear glasses (not contacts). Swimming underwater without glasses, using average swim goggles gave the world a uniform pathetic watery blur. A few years ago it finally dawned on me that I could get corrective goggles. I was surprised to discover that goggles with prescription corrective lenses were not much more expensive than plain ones — less than $10. These "optical" goggles are magic. For only a few dollars more my underwater vision is crystal clear. Anti-fog, fair fit, and prescription built in. So many brands make them (and of course many models are more expensive) that I wonder if I am the last person in the world to learn about them. In any case I only have experience with the ClubSwim models. They are available in a limited choice of diopters in half point increments from -2.0 to -7.5.

-- KK

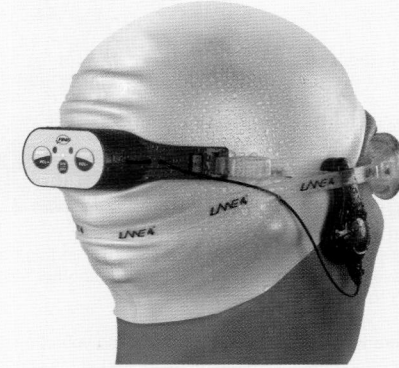

Underwater Music for Swimmers
SwiMP3
$101 Amazon

The SwiMP3 consists of swim goggles with an MP3 player using headphones that rest flat on the cheek bones, between your ears and your eyes, so that you hear the music through bone conduction rather than through your ears.

Music breaks up the tedium of lap swimming, of course, but even better is the fact that it encourages proper form. It sounds better when your head is in the water, so I keep my head down.

-- Bill Altreuter

Superior snorkel
TUSA Hyperdry Snorkel
$40 Amazon

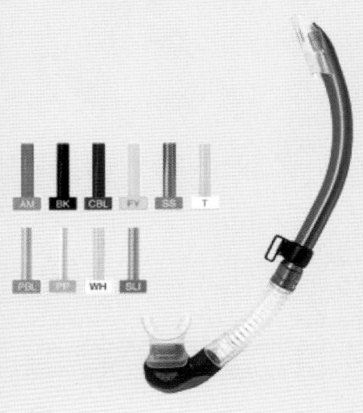

I just bought a new snorkel after 20 years of use on my prior purchase. I chose the TUSA SP-170 first for comfort of the mouthpiece and bore width of the tube. Next, I evaluated how water drains from the tube. The purge valve under the mouthpiece is covered, so stray sand or kelp will not block it open and let water in, a problem I'd had with older snorkels.

At the top of the snorkel tube, TUSA's Hyperdry System creates a separate pathway for water to eject, making for quicker clearing of the airway for my next breath. Other brands do have similar configurations and differ only slightly from the TUSA design. What hooked

me on the TUSA is its Comfort Swivel, which allows me to change the angle of the snorkel without messing with the mask strap. It also has two parts that can disconnect as a quick-release to get the snorkel off the mask quickly. Using the old snorkel keeper strap was always a hassle for me.

Snorkels are a very personal choice, and the number of features surprise people who have never purchased one at a dive shop. Some stores won't allow you to put the mouthpiece in your mouth. If you can't judge the size/fit, try to see if they rent the model you are interested in. Usually an experienced salesman can judge the size well and you can go by his suggestion.

I'm very happy with this choice, and have found it to meet all of my needs either in surf, open ocean or pool conditions.

-- Opher Banarie

Best quantified self app
rTracker
$1 realidata.com

The rTracker is currently one of the most versatile and customizable apps for self-tracking on the market. Unlike other tracking apps that offer you a fixed set of questions pertaining to only one or two areas (e.g., your body measurements or mood), rTracker allows you to set up your own questions, so you can log any aspect of everyday life, all in one app. I personally use it to log and store data for about 70 different life variables, including heart rate, weight, mood, social interactions, situational context, etc.. The rTracker also offers a great selection of measurement scales, from boolean ("checkbox") to multiple choice ("radio-button") to numeric and text input. I especially love the "sliding" scale, which better represents latent continuum (e.g., mood or happiness) than Likert scales. Viewing your past records is easy, and you can always go "back in time" and change or add the data point for any given day and time. Another awesome feature of rTracker is shareability: you can export not only data, but also the questionnaire set up so other people could install the same questions on their phone. The "function" feature of the app allows you to carry out calculations and data manipulations "on the fly", right in the app. For example, I track my self-esteem on a daily basis using three questions. The "function" automatically calculates the arithmetic average of responses to all three questions in order to get the summary score. For those of you who are concerned about privacy: rTracker stores your data directly on your phone, and you export it by plugging the phone in the computer and using iTunes. Finally, rTracker is truly "mobile": you are not "tied" to the computer, and can log and view your data "on the go". It also does not require a wireless signal in order to open and use it.

-- Konstantin Augemberg

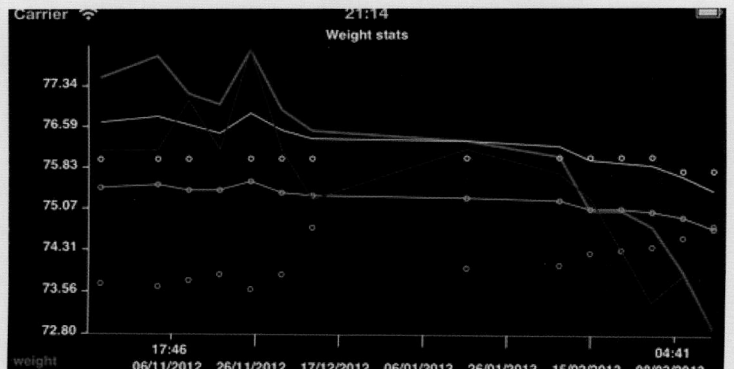

Running

Best cross-country water supply
Tenaya 4 Hydration Pack
$70 Northface

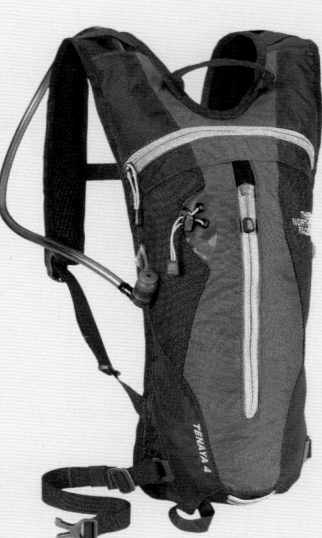

In 25 years of competitive running, I went through maybe a dozen different water carriers, and settled on this one as the best. At the time I bought mine, the water reservoir was a way better design than any of the Camelback reservoirs (could be that Camelback has improved since then). This slim bag rides balanced in the middle of your back. It encourages sipping throughout the run as compared to hauling out waist-attached bottles. I carry a few plastic bags (for foraged foods) knife, compass, and microlite in the zip-up pocket.

-- Lloyd Kahn

Run long by walking sometimes
Marathon
$10 Jeff Galloway, 2010, 240 p.

With proper guidance, any person in reasonable health can run a marathon. Jeff Galloway, a well-known running trainer, is that sane and wise guidance. Galloway introduces an amazing discovery: both novices and veterans can better their overall time and enjoyment during a marathon by walking at prescribed times. This counterintuitive technique is laid out nicely here with lots of expert encouragement, backed by Galloway's experience in helping hundreds of marathoners at sundry levels try the unthinkable: race faster by resting your legs.

-- KK

• Almost anyone can complete a marathon in six months! Even if you only have 60 minutes to exercise during the workweek, you can train for the marathon. The minimum is actually better for insuring against injuries. During the week, you need to accumulate only an hour of running/walking. The long run starts at 3 miles and gradually increases by 1 mile each week until it reaches 10 miles. Then, you'll do the long run every other week, with a run/walk of half the distance on alternate "off" weekends. Once you've completed the 18-miler, you'll receive two weekends off for good behavior, shifting to a long run every third week.

• Walk break: Periods of walking taken on long runs. This is your secret weapon. Walk breaks allow your running muscles to recover before they are injured and conserve your energy so you can exercise for longer periods, which builds the endurance you need. In the beginning, your runs will actually be walks interspersed with short periods of running; over time, the running portions will become longer and the walk breaks shorter.

• The Huff and Puff Rule may help: If you're huffing and puffing so much during the last 2 to 3 miles of a long run that you can't carry on a conversation, you went too fast from the beginning of that run. On the next run, slow down significantly, take walk breaks more frequently, or both. Remember to write a note to yourself, to be read just before starting your next long run.

The race was ten loops around Chastain Park. When I got to about 15 miles, I was pooped. the race director was on the course watching the runners, and I told him I was going to drop out. He said, "You can't, you're in first place!"

"What about Ken," I asked.

"He dropped out two laps ago."

Well all right, so on I went. I ran a few more laps, and felt awful. I came by the race director again and told him I wasn't feeling too good. this time he said "Are you sure you want to give up this trophy?" I'd never won a trophy before, so I went another lap. Now I was up to 20 miles and felt really bad.

Here was the director again. "Nothing you can say will keep me going here," I told him. he looked at his watch and said: "You're a half-hour ahead of second place."

OK, OK, that was enough incentive, so on I went. I ran and walked, struggling to the finish, and I won in 2:56:35.

It took me about two years before I felt like running another marathon. That experience kept playing over and over in my mind. Surely there's a better way of doing this, I thought, and it set me on the road to figuring out what I did wrong. How could this be done better, so it'd be easier and you'd feel stronger without having to struggle so much? Throughout the years, it led me into developing the walk break strategy that's the central theme of this book.

Elite African runners and other worldclass runners seldom run more than 200 yards using the same form mode. They're constantly alternating between race form, gliding, shuffling, and ERAs, as they race through the course.

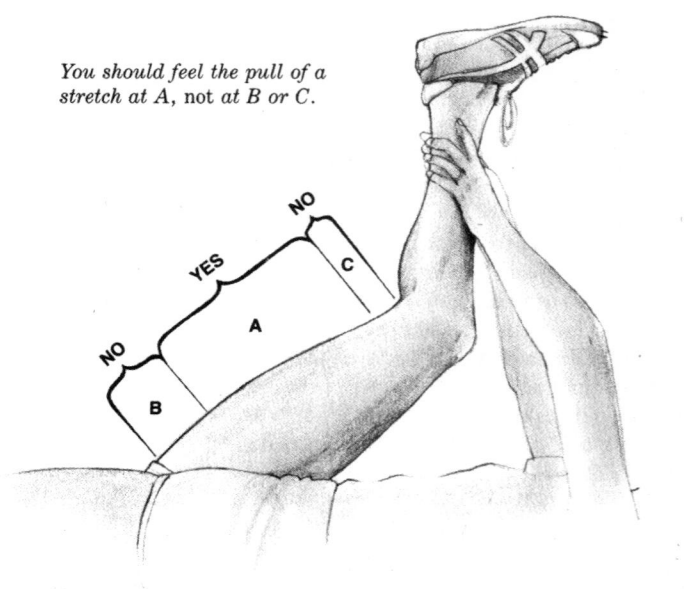

You should feel the pull of a stretch at A, not at B or C.

• Muscle imbalance is destructive because it sets up an uneven tension and can throw your joint alignment off. Muscles work in pairs. When one set of muscles contract, the opposite set releases its tension gradually and stretches. The body was meant to be used evenly so that one muscle balances another. For instance at the knee, an imbalance of the strength relationship between the muscles in the back thigh (hamstrings) and those in the front thigh (quadriceps) invites injury.

• Ice can be very effective as treatment, especially when aplpied immediately after an injury. Ice permits your body to heal quickly in two ways; it promotes even greater blood circulation than heat, and it numbs the pain so that you can move the injured area. The latter is beneficial because the best healing takes place when you actively move your injured part. Movement allows the new-forming tissue to remain pliable and healthy. The most amazing fact about this kind of treatment is that it drastically cuts the length of recovery time...

In order to benefit from ice you must use it correctly. For any of the techniques below the basic idea is the same: chill the injured area fro about six to twenty minutes, or until it gets numb. Then begin to move it, starting with small movements and gradually increasing your range of motion. Remember to move gently, and without putting weight on the injury. When the numbness wears off and you start feeling the pain again, apply ice and repeat the whole procedure.

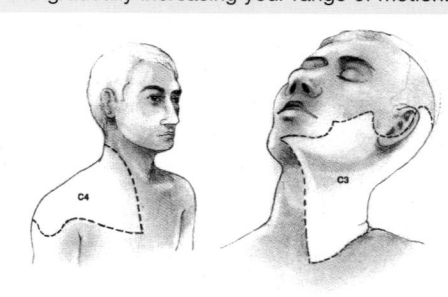

Pain in these areas probably means an injury at the third or fourth cervical disc.

• Your tendons stop growing when you reach adulthood. If you increase the strength of a muscle tenfold, so that you can lift great amounts of weight, you will be putting ten times more pressure on a tendon that can only minimally and slowly change its size to accommodate such increased stress. The result? Tendon strains.

Double-time motivator
Run to Cadence Recordings
$14 Amazon

Amazon sells the whole "Run to Cadence" series put out by Documentary Recordings. These are recordings of 40 minute call-and-response chants by drill instructors and the grunts as they run in formation at 115 beats a minute.

I like to use my Airborne Rangers recording as a procrastination-buster when I have to tackle a disagreeable task around the house. I did not serve in the military, but when this tape plays in the background, I "fall in," get pumped, and get the job done. The momentum stays a while.

-- David Stubbs

How to heal yourself
Listen To Your Pain
$16 Ben E. Benjamin, 2007, 400p.

I think every runner should have this book, which has been around for 25 years. It gives you tests to figure out what's wrong (is that knee pain a torn cartilage, chondromalacia, or a ligament tear?). Once you've done the testing, Benjamin goes through the remedies, from self-help to rehab to cortisone to surgery. I don't know of any other book this good for treating running injuries. Emphasis on self-evaluation and self-help.

-- Lloyd Kahn

• Pain at the Outside of the Knee (Tendinitis of the Tensor Fascia Lata Tendon) With this strain or tear of the tendon, the pain is felt at the outsid of the knee or at the outside of the thigh just above the knee

Diagnostic Verification Test ►

Stand with the outside of your injured leg up again a wall. Flex your foot, lifting the front of your foot and inch or two from the floor. Keeping your heel firmly in place, and with your leg straight, push the front outside of your foot into the wall with a great deal of force, as illustrated. This should reproduce your pain.

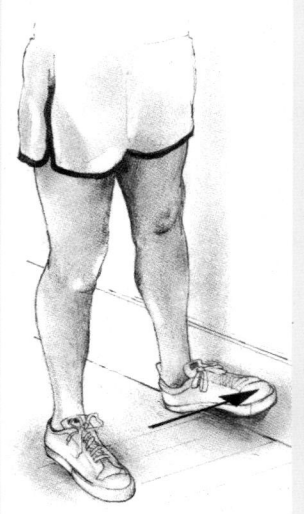

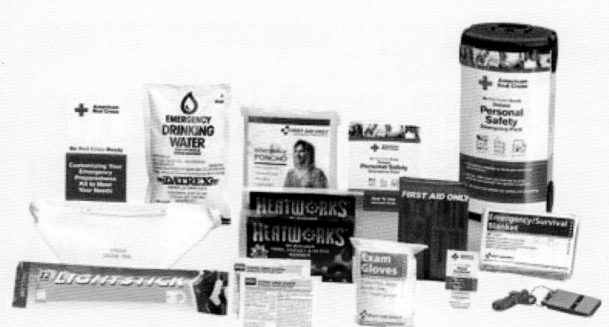

Compact, inexpensive safety stash
Personal Safety Emergency Pack

$16 American Red Cross

If you're camping or hiking in a group, you can't go wrong with the Adventure Medical Kit. But if you're a citygoing 9-5'er (read: not a search-and-rescuer), the Red Cross' personal safety kit

packs many of the basics — whistle, blanket, face mask, glow stick, poncho, germ wipes and first-aid kit — for a price that's more or less unbeatable.

We've got a home medical kit. We regularly update the earthquake/disaster kit in our car (a plastic tub complete with basic med supplies, canned goods, MRE's, water, spare clothes, etc.). But like a lot of folks, I spend a chunk of my time working in an office building where I've always presumed/hoped supplies are both plentiful and current. That's why I very recently stashed one of these kits at the desk I keep away from my home office.

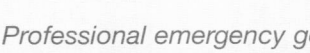

Could the pack be more complete? Of course. My first gesture was to rubberband a small handcrank flashlight to the diminutive bundle. Even still, the embellished package remains small, light and manageable.

-- Steven Leckart

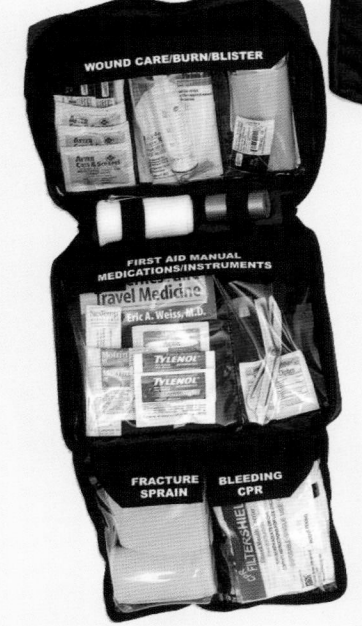

Full medical station in a pouch
Adventure Medical Kits

$94 Chinook Medical

During an emergency, instilling order, confidence, and calm is the major assignment of the first aider. Over the years of running a large household I've found that keeping medical supplies together in one handy place helps me provide that stability in those early moments of panic. My highly-evolved first aid kit has become extremely refined, but also slightly less portable. I could no longer get all that I needed quickly out to the yard, or in the car, or packed into a backpack.

After some experimentation, I found what works best is a pre-packaged medical kit. They appear to be expensive, but are really not when you tally up the costs of the components — most of which have a pretty long shelf life.

The kits from Adventure Medical Kits are highly praised in search and rescue fields. Expeditions carry larger versions. The case is hardy, lightweight and quick to navigate through. An amazing amount of stuff is squirreled away inside, all easy to reach.

The kit I prefer, the AMK Fundamentals, contains a full spectrum of basic first aids, burn materials, CPR mouth barrier, scissors, tweezers, syringe, plenty variety of bandages, a SAMS splint (which I wish I had earlier when my wife broke her wrist), a decent small emergency medical book (Wilderness and Travel Medicine), and extra containers for personalized pill transport. With this kit you'd be prepared to handle most injuries a non-doctor could manage. It is rated for 1-8 people and is one of the more complete versions available.

AMK offers all manner of kits customized to particular outdoor sports like kayaking or biking. This one is perfect for a family on the go. I'll pack it along when we go on vacation. (I also carry one of AMK's ultralight kits in my briefcase bag.)

-- KK

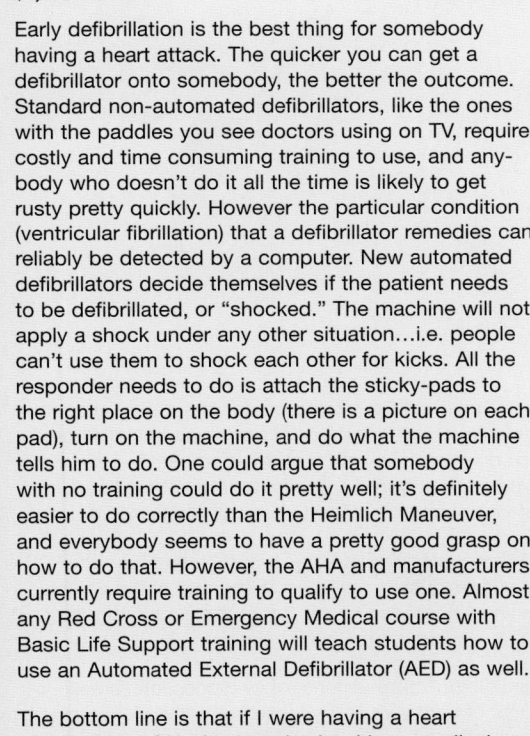

Life-saving community tool
Automated External Defibrillator

$1,199 Amazon

Early defibrillation is the best thing for somebody having a heart attack. The quicker you can get a defibrillator onto somebody, the better the outcome. Standard non-automated defibrillators, like the ones with the paddles you see doctors using on TV, require costly and time consuming training to use, and anybody who doesn't do it all the time is likely to get rusty pretty quickly. However the particular condition (ventricular fibrillation) that a defibrillator remedies can reliably be detected by a computer. New automated defibrillators decide themselves if the patient needs to be defibrillated, or "shocked." The machine will not apply a shock under any other situation…i.e. people can't use them to shock each other for kicks. All the responder needs to do is attach the sticky-pads to the right place on the body (there is a picture on each pad), turn on the machine, and do what the machine tells him to do. One could argue that somebody with no training could do it pretty well; it's definitely easier to do correctly than the Heimlich Maneuver, and everybody seems to have a pretty good grasp on how to do that. However, the AHA and manufacturers currently require training to qualify to use one. Almost any Red Cross or Emergency Medical course with Basic Life Support training will teach students how to use an Automated External Defibrillator (AED) as well.

The bottom line is that if I were having a heart attack, I'd be OK with somebody with no medical training having access to an AED and just following the instructions that the machine gives. It's better than being dead. These are rather expensive at the moment — $2000 $3000 — but they are state-of-the-art and their price will likely come down as the market expands. My guess: they will soon be as common in public buildings as fire extinguishers are now.

-- Jason Roosa

Professional emergency gear
Chinook Medical Gear

Varies Chinook Medical Gear, Inc.

A fantastically well-stocked source of the smartest medical supplies around. Highly versatile, highly effective (and portable) self-care gear. The audience is expedition doctors and search and rescue teams, but 90% of these state-of-the-art supplies would serve home and homestead as well. The catalog is a real education and wonderfully broad — for instance, they rightly see keeping insects at bay as a health issue. They sell the full line of Adventure Medicine Kits, as well as empty kit containers and the basic items, books, and non-prescripts to assemble your own medical tool box. Among suppliers of emergency medical gear, Chinook stands out for honoring the intelligence and independence of their customers, as you might expect from a company serving the health concerns of strong-willed lunatics heading off the map for three months.

-- KK

$7 Israeli Bandage

Phenomenal new product that works as several different devices — primary dressing, pressure applicator, secondary dressing and tourniquet.

Sterile, non-adherent and easy to use, this bandage is designed to treat every possible bleeding wound in the most extreme conditions. An injured person can even apply it with one hand! #05130

$7 Sawyer Controlled Release DEET Formula

Sawyer Controlled Release insect repellent lotion uses a newly patented technology called Sub-Micron Encapsulation. It works with your own skin's natural chemistry so you can reduce DEET exposure and have 24-hour insect protection. It is also non-greasy, virtually odorless and water and sweat-resistant. In areas infested with flies, or for use with clothing and hair, supplement with Broad Spectrum Composite Repellent. 4oz. #03107

$7 Ultrathon

Originally developed for the U.S. military for use in challenging environments requiring long-lasting protection, Ultrathon soon became highly recommended by the travel medicine community. 99% effective for more than 8 hours against mosquitoes, 92% effective against ticks and also works against biting flies, gnats, chiggers, and fleas. Cream contains 33% DEET, lasts up to 12 hours. 2oz. #03108

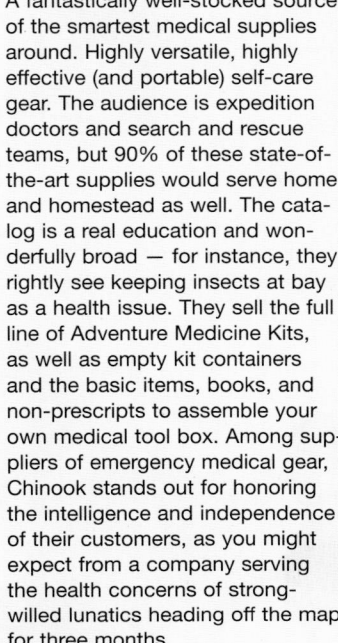
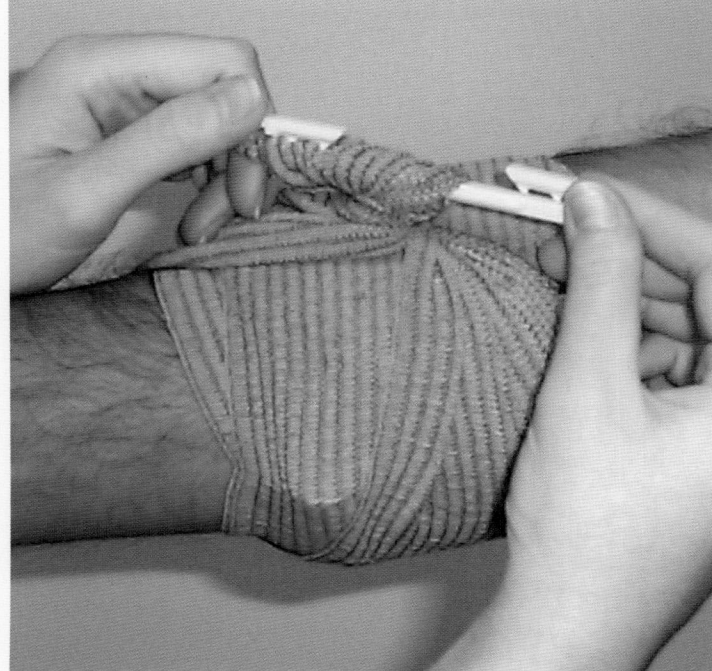

Rugged packs for first aid items
Conterra

Prices Vary Conterra Catalog

This is a specialized catalog for Search & Rescue, ski patrol and other (e.g. Military/ arcane law enforcement) professionals. Contains mostly Conterra's line of specialty backpacks/ fanny paks for ski patrol, SAR heli-med personnel. They make the best radio chest harness in the business — it is a standard with fire depts and FEMA. It is hard to imagine turning this stuff into general-purpose (eg, the paks are definitely not general purpose packs) but for the intended applications, there is none better.

-- Paul Saffo

Bandages

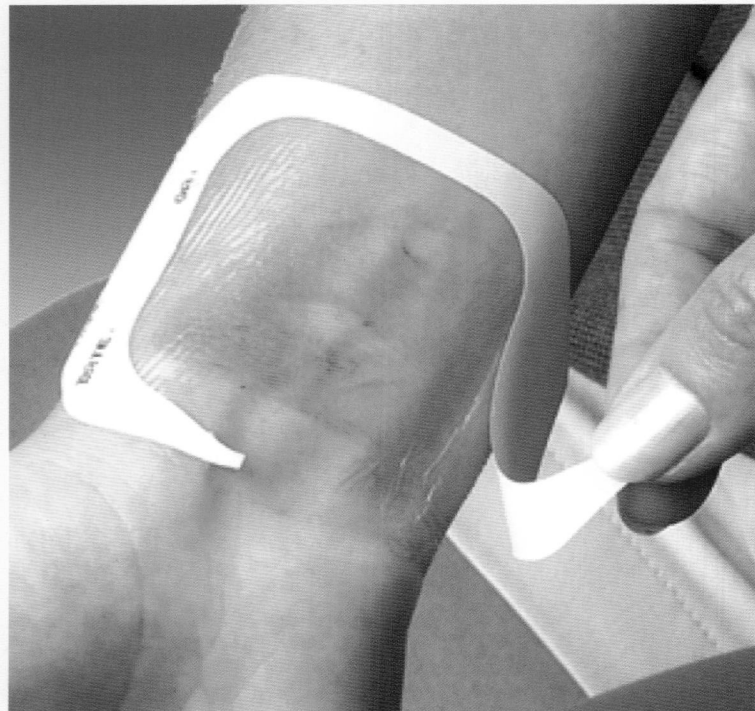

Better bandage
Tegaderm
$8 Amazon

Use this 3M material, called Tegaderm, for applying dressing over a bleeding injury. It's much better than adhesive tape or a big band-aid. Tegaderm is an air-permeable plastic film, as thin as cling film, but stronger and with an adhesive. I've found it adheres perfectly and because it is so thin it's unnotice-able, especially on joints. You don't even remember it's on. Because of its thinness Tegaderm works really great under clothing. It's breathable, too, and won't come off in water. And since it is transparent, the dressing is not as vis-ible, and you can see what's going on underneath. It comes in sterile packaging about the size of a playing card, so you can apply it right over the injury, with the option to include some gauze underneath at first. I've cut smaller pieces for finger cuts, but I've found that waterproof bandaids work better for this.

-- KK

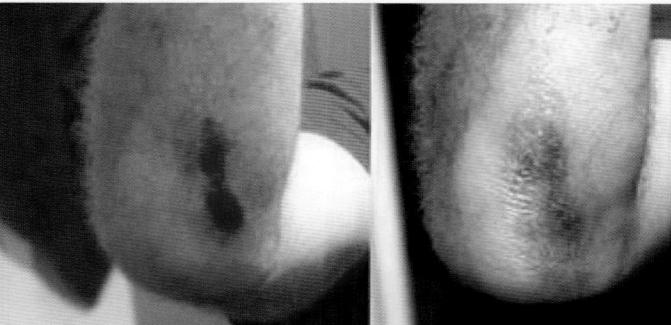

On the right a bicyclist has applied Tegaderm over his road-rash shown on left. The ban-dage is hardly visible. • Image via NY Velocity.

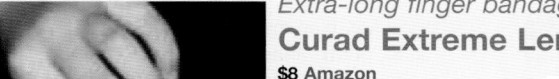

Extra-long finger bandages
Curad Extreme Lengths
$8 Amazon

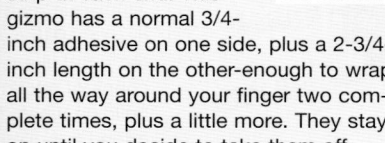

A typical finger bandage has a 1-inch gauze pad with a 3/4-inch adhesive strip at each end. This gizmo has a normal 3/4-inch adhesive on one side, plus a 2-3/4-inch length on the other-enough to wrap all the way around your finger two com-plete times, plus a little more. They stay on until you decide to take them off.

-- Tom Ferguson, M.D.

Moist wound burn treatment
Moist Wound Burn Treatment
$8 Amazon

One of the things medical staff used to nip from hospitals to bring home is inex-pensive moist wound pads. Keeping a wound moist – particularly a burn wound — has been proven to aid its healing. Moist wound pads contain a layer of gel that holds either sterile water, or additional therapeutic ingre-dients, wrapped under a large adhe-sive bandage. Doctors' offices stock these aids, but they are only now getting into the consumer market. Drugstore over-the-counter pads like Spenco 2nd Skin Moist Burn Pads come in a package of 5 small (2 x3 inches) sterile packages. New-Skin (UK-based) Burn Relief Dressing comes in 3 3×3 pads — but these have less than half the usable surface area of the Spencos. Johnson and Johnson is introducing household bandages with moist gel pads inside, too. These pads aren't cheap, but hope-fully you'll only need them occasionally.

-- KK

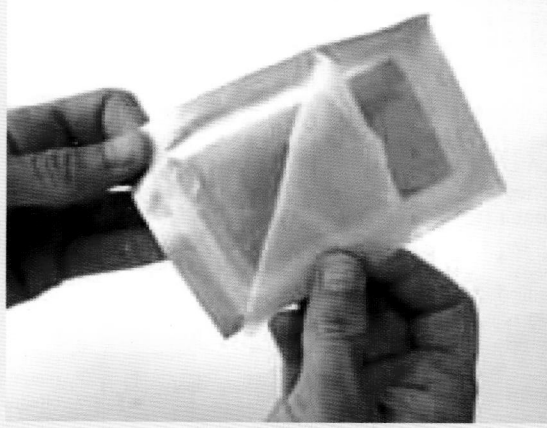

Most durable bandages
Nexcare Waterproof Bandages
$6 Amazon

These bandages simply won't come off. Not under-water, not in oil or sweat, not by wear and tear. They are extremely flexible, very comfortable, and hard to notice, too. To tell you the truth, they are so thin at the edges and stuck down they are hard to get off when you want to. A hot and messy test kitchen tried out ten different brands of bandaids, and Nextcare were the only ones to never come off. Most bandaids are put on kids for boo-boos as a placebo; for the times when you need a covering that must stay on, this one by 3M (the adhesive folks) will really do the trick.

-- KK

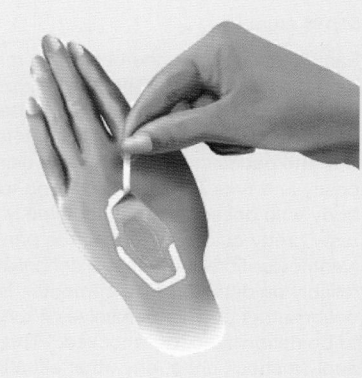

Stops bleeding instantly
QuikClot
$14 for 50 grams Amazon

This is a must for any 1st aid kit. QuikClot is a topical blood clot-ting agent for scrapes, cuts and wounds (they claim some even very serious). You basically apply this stuff to an open cut, and it instantly clots to stop bleed-ing. Tested by the US military. This stuff works great for those scrapes, cuts and wounds encountered on the road. I've been using it in the bathroom for shaving cuts, too.

-- Gregory Winer

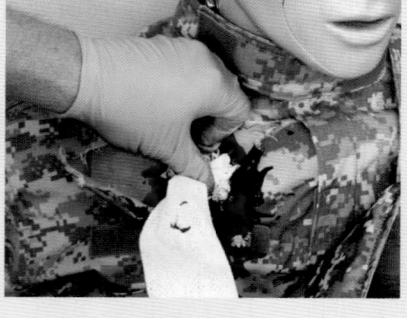

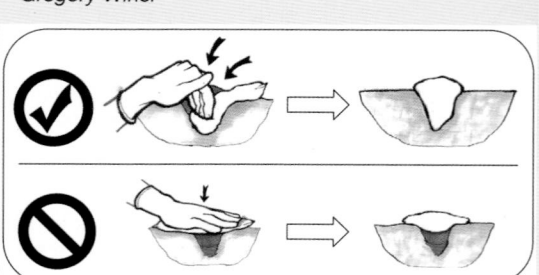

Handy emergency alternative to sutures
Superglue Stitches
$16 (3ml) Vetbond (Butyl-cyanoacrylate) Amazon

For years midwives have been using over-the-counter superglue to "suture" perineal tears after birth. It's better than stitches. Veteran backpackers have been known to pack a tiny tube of super glue for emer-gency repairs of deep cuts in places where there is no doctor.

Superglue is ethyl-cyanoacrylate. While fine for small cuts, it has several weaknesses when used as a sub-stitute for heavy-duty suturing. An improved version, butyl-cyanoacrylate was developed for heavier surgical repairs, and this stuff was used widely in the Vietnam War to patch up soldiers in the field. Butyl-cyanoacrylate is a little more flexible on a wound than commercial super-glue, generates fewer toxic byproducts, and is now com-monly used by vets to repair animal wounds. You can buy the stuff as 3M Vetbond. This is also what midwives have started using.

In 2000, the FDA approved a new version of tissue adhe-sive for human use, sold as Dermabond. This new com-position, octyl-cyanoacrylate, is a longer chain, still more flexible, and possess the yet-unexplained ability to inhibit bacterial growth — a godsend in surgery. It's strong enough that it will likely replace a lot of suturing altogeth-er someday. Small quantities of octyl-cyanoacrylate are sold to non-medicals for "research purposes" — it's the genuine stuff, only in dispensers that aren't sterilized, and therefore not approved for human use (only animal use).

To use any cyanoacrylate on a wound, keep it on the surface layer of skin, not down in the well of the wound – imagine you are taping the top of the wound together. The glue sloughs off by itself in time.

Despite all the improvements of cyanoacrylate, small amounts of hardware store superglue will work in a pinch. I know a physician who uses ordinary superglue at home on his kid's cuts. A vial of Vetbond would be even bet-ter. It's dyed blue so you can easily see where it is on the skin and where it is not, and it is made for cuts.

-- KK

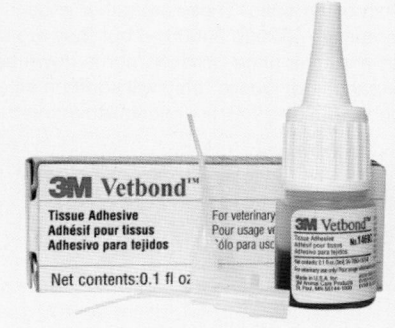

Faith sees the invisible, believes the incredible and receives the impossible. - Anonymous

How to survive a WMD attack
Individual Preparedness and Response

Individual Preparedness and Response, Complete

Free (PDF) RAND Corporation
$20 (book) Amazon

In the worst-worst case scenario that you experience a nuke explosion, dirty bomb, toxic chem attack or biological disaster, what should YOU do? The first ten minutes are crucial. Don't "ask your local officials" as much advice to date has suggested. Do read this short booklet prepared by RAND, and prepare. You can print it out from the free PDF file (including handy 3-fold card reminder version), or if you need to distribute many copies to employees, neighbors, etc., you can order printed copies for $15 a piece.

I highly recommend reading the full version first (also available as a series of PDFs and/or a longer book) which gives the logic behind their suggestions and scenarios. This is the best practical advice I've yet seen for personally dealing with the consequences of an actual weapon of mass destruction in your neighborhood.

-- KK

• There is no need to determine the location of the source or direction or speed of the chemical cloud. Technical evaluations indicate that such basic sheltering can reduce chemical exposure by 75 percent or more compared to the exposure outside the shelter. These results are consistent with the outcomes of the aerosolized sarin attack by the Aum Shinrikyo group in a residential area in Matsumoto, Japan, in June 1994. In that incident, all seven people who died had their windows open. All of those individuals who had closed their windows-including many people closer to the source, those in units adjacent to buildings in which fatalities occurred, and those on the lower floors of these buildings-survived the attack (Yanagisawa, 1995).

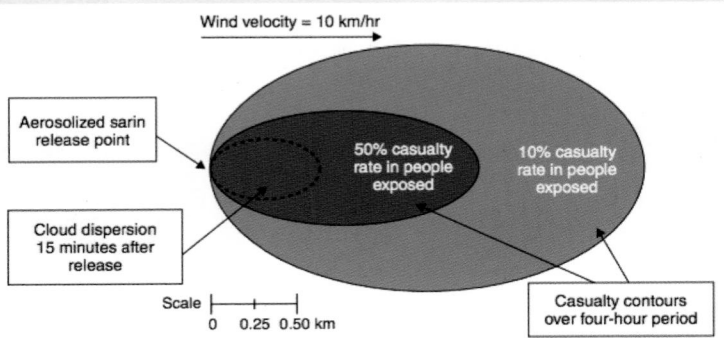

Figure A.1—Casualty Contours of Aerosolized Sarin over a Four-Hour Period

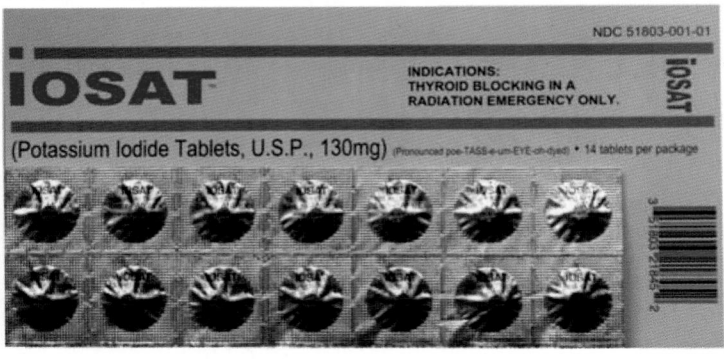

Home antidote for radiation exposure
Radiation Blocking Tablets

$10 Amazon

The biggest health risk after an accident at a nuclear plant or a nuclear attack results from exposure to radioactive iodine. Other radioisotopes are dispersed and quickly excreted, but radioiodine is concentrated and retained in the thyroid, increasing your risk of thyroid cancer. Even tiny doses, which can be carried downwind for hundreds of miles, can be harmful. Children are at greatest risk. Taking potassium iodide (KI) before or immediately after exposure saturates your thyroid gland with safe stable iodine so that the uptake of radioactive iodine is blocked. There won't be time to get it when an incident occurs. So if you live downwind of a nuclear plant, or worry about a nuclear attack, you might want to keep some KI tablets at home. (But please note that this may not protect you from the radiation of a terrorist "dirty bomb" made of spent nuclear waste) The FDA recommends keeping a 14-day supply on hand; radioactive iodine has a half-life of eight days. Only two brands have received FDA Approval, Iosat and Thyroblock. Children should take half an adult dose. A related salt, Potassium Iodate, (KIO3) is less bitter, and may stay down better in babies.

-- Tom Ferguson, M.D.

Most comfortable disposable mask
Cool Max

$28 Amazon

I am convinced that the single most effective tool you can have on hand for an ABC disaster (Atomic, Biological, or Chemical) is a good face mask. The danger of nuclear radiation is primarily from fallout, which drifts as air-born particles. Same for many chemical spills; their poison also drifts on microscopic airborne droplets. And the biological toxins we most fear also travel in the air as particles. A face mask covering nose and mouth can reduce (not eliminate) the risk of inhaling these particles.

But face masks are useless unless worn, and are not worn (for long) if uncomfortable. I've been trying out various inexpensive masks that I could wear for many hours without going crazy. I found the Cool Max to be the only respirator I could keep on for long periods. The Cool Max are cheap N95 units (workshop, not surgical quality) that fold out and fit on the face with two elastic straps. The enlarged surface area eases breathing, and removes that suffocating sensation I usually get from wearing respirators. I could talk, drive, and work outside in the garden for hours without much discomfort. These masks are cheap enough that I have stocked a supply for our household (you'll need more than one).

Recently I attended a meeting for the world's avian flu experts and asked them how effective a face mask like Cool Max would be in an avian flu epidemic. (I had already learned that touching hands transmits more viruses between people than does sneezing; so it makes no sense to wear a mask without wearing gloves.) About half of the flu researchers believed a mask would not do anything at all (viruses are smaller than the filter pores), and the other half said that of course it would help since the viruses ride along on larger particles. When I asked them how many of them would personally have their families wear one in a flu pandemic, they almost all said they would. Although the efficacy of masks with viruses is unproven, there is no harm in using them, as long as you don't believe it guarantees anything.

My research came down to this: Better than hoarding Tamiflu, it is smarter to sequester some face masks and disposable gloves. This is the cheapest, easiest and most productive thing you can do to prepare for a flu epidemic beforehand. Fancier, more sophisticated face masks would probably be more effective if you kept them clean and were willing to wear them. But I find it cumbersome to walk around with a gas mask. These Cool Max respirators will at least be worn for the durations needed, and will reduce your risk of inhaling ABC particles.

And, oh, they work really great keeping dust out, too!

-- KK

Cheap, surplus radiation monitor
Civil Defense Geiger Counter

$100+ eBay

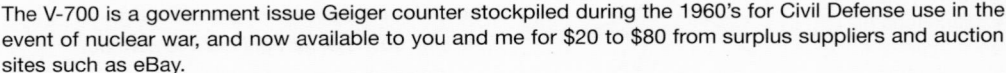

The V-700 is a government issue Geiger counter stockpiled during the 1960's for Civil Defense use in the event of nuclear war, and now available to you and me for $20 to $80 from surplus suppliers and auction sites such as eBay.

Built like a tank, most of them are still in great shape 40 years later, and set an example that should be met by more tool manufacturers. The Geiger counter reads gamma and beta radiation, with a probe shield to discriminate between the two. It includes a check-source on the side of the can for instant testing, runs off standard flashlight D-cells, and comes with a carry strap, earphone, and manual. The manual (while short) covers use, calibration, maintenance, emergency/MacGyver repairs, and has full schematics and parts list. The schematic is also reproduced inside the case, which is water tight, and EMP resistant.

While most people have limited (if any) genuine need for a geiger counter, they are interesting devices, and are useful for a variety of purposes — from aids in learning about natural background radiation and geology (while hiking?), to adding radiation survival equipment to an emergency kit. Radiation detection equipment, being too niche to really feel market forces, has evolved surprisingly little in the last 40 years, so most of the difference between one of my $20 V-700s and one of my $800 modern meters is bells and whistles, and more reliable calibration systems.

However, since these are sometimes over 40 years old, and there are many differing models and manufacturers, a little buyer savvy is needed: Most, but not all are still in working condition, so avoid "untested, as is" if you need it to work out of the box. Many are sold with accessories missing (eg no manual or earphone), but any missing manuals can be found online in pdf format at Southern Radiation.

(Note: These manuals are also useful for researching a particular model of v-700 before you buy).

A quick rundown on the models: Do not buy a V-717, V-720, or V-715 – these are ion chamber survey meters, not Geiger counters. They are designed to complement the v-700 in times of nuclear war – their needle only starts to move when the Geiger counter is off the scale (so you'll need a radiation lab just to test if they even work). If emergency gear is your purpose, one of these might be on the list after a v-700. They are cheaper than a v-700, but a lab test will likely be $60.

For the v-700, I recommend the Victoreen model 6A or 6B, because it has a depleted uranium check-source with millions of years half-life, so the "level" of the check-source remains constant. The Lionel 6B has a more elegant circuit that only requires two batteries instead of four, but the check-source often has a half-life of as little as 6 years, so calculations must be made to compensate when calibrating. The Anton models I would avoid – they are older, in my experience much less reliable, and have the short half-life check-sources. The Anton model 5 is worth a mention though if space is a consideration because it is smaller than the rest. The Electro-Neutronics Inc (ENI) are apparently good, but I do not own any, so have no experience.

-- Justin

Gallery of models

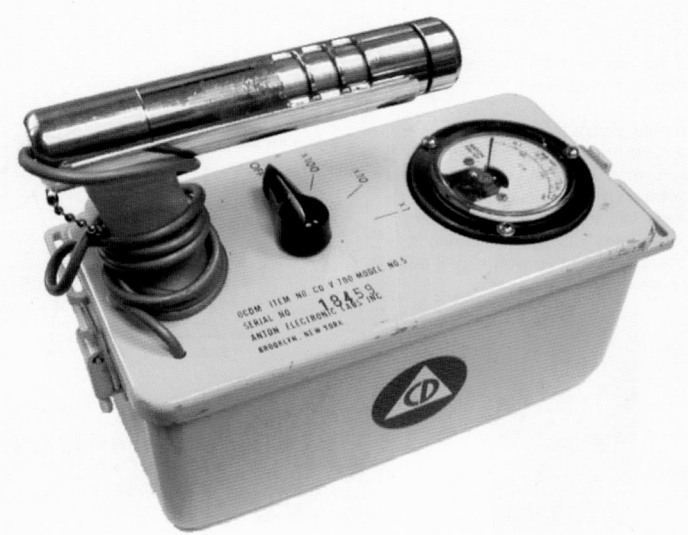

When you're green you grow. When you're ripe you rot. - Found scribbled in margin of book by John Maeda

441

Medical Reference

Self-help medicine
Where There Is No Doctor

This is the only book in the world that will really help you be your own doctor. It tells you how to suture a wound, heal burns, make your own contraception, diagnose tropical skin diseases, and thousands of other do-it-yourself medical procedures you won't find elsewhere. Originally written (in Spanish) for para-medicals in the developing world, the medical instructions are clear, methodical, reliable, and helpful. Not all the content is emergency care; a lot is basic hygiene and preventative care.

This book is crammed with essential, life-saving knowledge for anyone living or traveling for long periods in undeveloped areas without doctors close by. It can be found in the packs of transcontinental bicyclists, arctic explorers, missionaries and Peace Corp folks. The book is too heavy to lug around in a tourist backpack, but it is also available as a free PDF. But even with access to modern medical facilities, I've found this book gives me an abbreviated medical school education. It offers very realistic first aid treatments (more than just bandages), and very easy-to-understand explanations of what doctors see in injuries. It can help you talk to doctors. Finally, when you are done traveling, leave this book behind with someone who can use it.

There is also a companion book, Where There Is No Dentist, equally good.

-- KK

•
Giardia

Giardia is a tiny parasite that lives in the gut and is a common cause of diarrhea, especially in children.

•
Signs

A lot of gas. This causes a swollen, uncomfortable belly, cramps, nausea, and a lot of farts and burps. The burps have a bad taste, like sulfur or rotten eggs.

Bad-smelling, yellow, and frothy (full of bubbles) diarrhea, without blood or mucus.

There is usually no fever.

It can last for weeks, causing weight loss and weakness.

A mild giardia infection is uncomfortable, but will usually get better on its own within about 6 weeks. Good nutrition helps. A long-lasting case, especially in a child, is best treated with metronidazole. Quinacrine is cheaper and often works well, but causes worse side effects.

Malaria: (see p. 186)

Begins with weakness, chills and fever. Fever may come and go for a few days, with shivering (chills) as the temperature rises, and sweating as it falls. Then, fever may come for a few hours every second or third day. On other days, the person may feel more or less well.

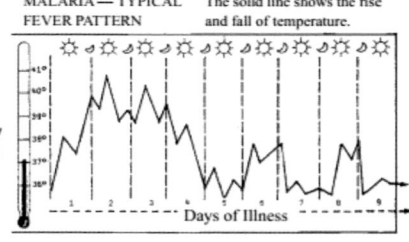

MALARIA — TYPICAL FEVER PATTERN. The solid line shows the rise and fall of temperature. Days of Illness

Typhoid: (see p. 188)

Begins like a cold. Temperature goes up a little more each day. Pulse relatively slow. Sometimes diarrhea and dehydration. Trembling or delirium (mind wanders). Person very ill.

Typhus: (see p. 190)

Similar to typhoid. Rash similar to that of measles, with tiny bruises.

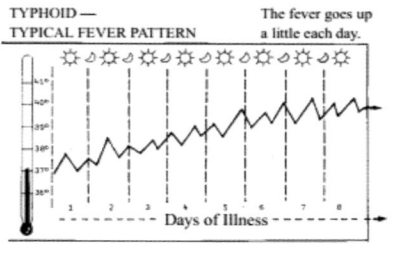

TYPHOID — TYPICAL FEVER PATTERN. The fever goes up a little each day. Days of Illness

Hepatitis: (see p. 172)

Person loses appetite. Does not wish to eat or smoke. Wants to vomit (nausea). Eyes and skin turn yellow; urine orange or brown; stools whitish. Sometimes liver becomes large, tender. Mild fever. Person very weak.

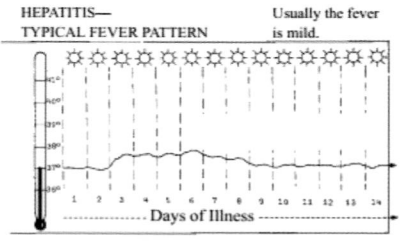

HEPATITIS — TYPICAL FEVER PATTERN. Usually the fever is mild. Days of Illness

Signs that dehydration is getting worse

- Lethargy: tired, low-energy
- Fast heart beat
- Deep breathing
- Sunken, tearless eyes
- Skin stays in a pinched shape

Lift the skin between two fingers, like this... If the skin does not fall right back to normal, the person may be dehydrated.

- In infants, a sunken "soft spot" on the head

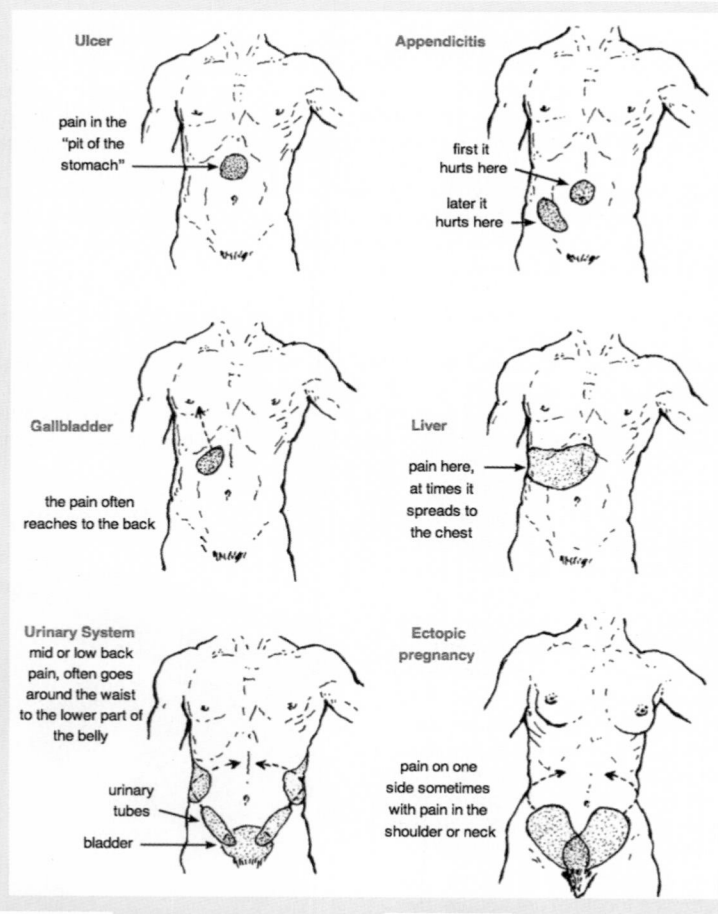

Ulcer — pain in the "pit of the stomach"

Appendicitis — first it hurts here — later it hurts here

Gallbladder — the pain often reaches to the back

Liver — pain here, at times it spreads to the chest

Urinary System — mid or low back pain, often goes around the waist to the lower part of the belly — urinary tubes — bladder

Ectopic pregnancy — pain on one side sometimes with pain in the shoulder or neck

$19 David Werner, Jane Maxwell, Carol Thuman, 1992, 446 pages

Free (PDF) Hesperian.org

Best home medical information
Merck Manual, Second Home Edition

Long the standard reference for working doctors and nurses, thumbworn copies of the Merck Manual could be found in most clinical offices. It had the kind of detailed and reliable summaries of an ailment that an intelligent person might want to know about, but its jargon and medical logic were difficult to decipher. Five years ago Merck translated this legendary book into plain English and issued a home paperback version. It was so far superior to any other form of home medical information (except the original Merck Manual itself) that it quickly became THE medical reference for our family. Last year Merck issued a second edition that updated, expanded, and improved this already great material. This Second Home Edition now approaches the professional Merck Manual in depth and completeness, except it retains its plain layperson's approach. Most home medical information sucks; collectively the web is better, but by far the best single source for dependable quick medical guidance is this handy book.

Merck Publishing (a non-profit organization) generously makes this book and the Merck Manual available in full text online. This version is very easy to search, and it is free.

-- KK

THE MERCK MANUAL OF MEDICAL INFORMATION, SECOND HOME EDITION

Bell's Palsy Paralyzes One Side of the Face

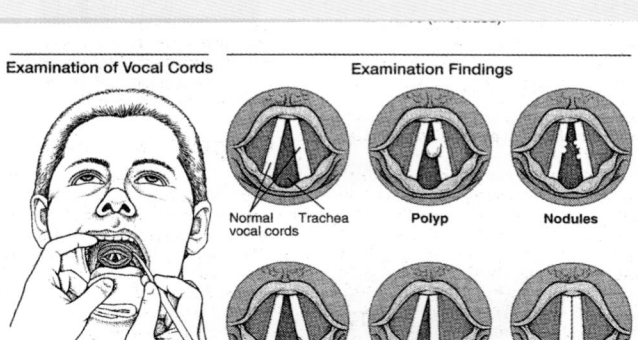

Examination of Vocal Cords — Examination Findings — Normal vocal cords — Trachea — Polyp — Nodules — Contact Ulcer — One-sided Paralysis — Two-sided Paralysis

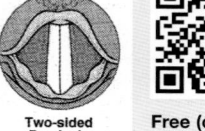

$27 3rd Home Edition, 2009, 2500 p.

Free (online) Merck Manuals

Polyp Formation in the Nose

Polyps usually develop in the area where the sinuses open into the nasal cavity. Polyps may block drainage from the sinuses. Fluid may accumulate in the blocked sinuses, causing a sinus infection.

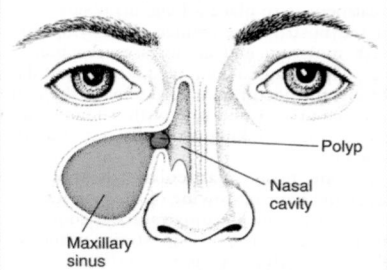

Polyp — Nasal cavity — Maxillary sinus

How Ear Disorders Affect the Facial Nerve

Because the facial nerve winds through the ear, disorders of the middle and inner ear can affect it. For example, herpes zoster of the ear may affect the facial nerve as well as the auditory nerve. The facial nerve then swells and presses against the opening in the skull that it passes through. The pressure on this nerve can cause temporary or permanent facial paralysis. Treatment depends on the disorder causing the problem.

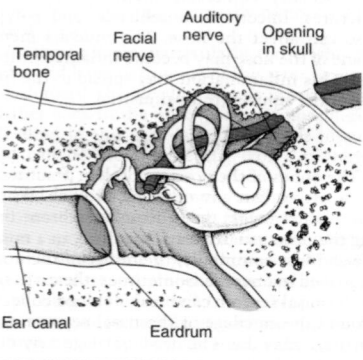

Temporal bone — Facial nerve — Auditory nerve — Opening in skull — Ear canal — Eardrum

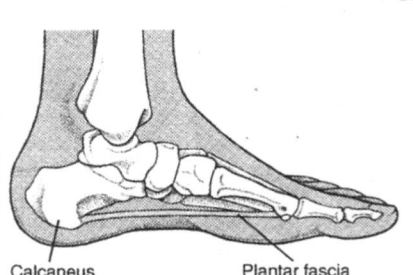

Calcaneus — Plantar fascia — Heel spur

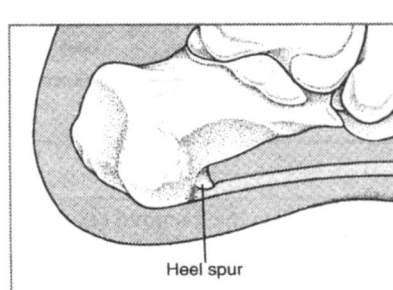

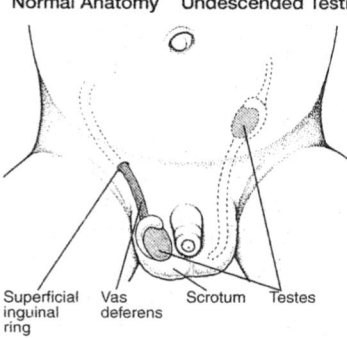

Normal Anatomy — Undescended Testis — Superficial inguinal ring — Vas deferens — Scrotum — Testes

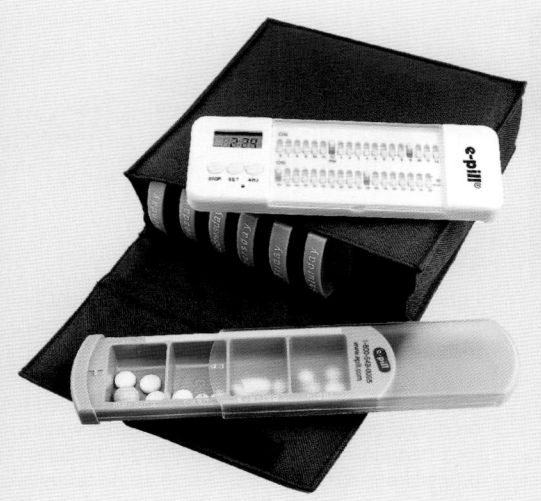

How to remember medication
Seven-Day Pill Organizer

$60 Epill Medication Reminders

Those of us who take vitamins or other medications may find ourselves fumbling through assorted vials and pill bottles several times a day — if we remember to take them at all. And if we're going to be away, we need to remember to take our medications with us. This remarkable pill organizer changes everything. You fill it once a week. Then, when Thursday comes, you open the sliding lid of your Thursday pill box to find all your pills waiting in large compartments labeled morning, noon, evening, and night. Comes with a medication alarm (it reminds you when its time to take your pills) and carrying pouch. Epill.com also offers other medication organizers, reminder watches, and a variety of other medication aids.

-- Tom Ferguson, MD

Intelligent pill tray
Pocket MedPack Tray

$7 Amazon

It's easy to remember to take one pill a day. Two, even. But if you have to take multiple pills a day, especially at different times, it's impossible to remember what you've already taken. When you're travelling, it's especially bad!

I tried a regular pill case, the kind with 7-days of pills in a row. But inevitably I'd forget to take my pills in the morning, or get home too late for my 2nd batch. This little pill case is genius, because you can still schedule your medicine for the week, but the little pod can come with you for the day. There are other versions with four divided areas in the case for those who take more pills.

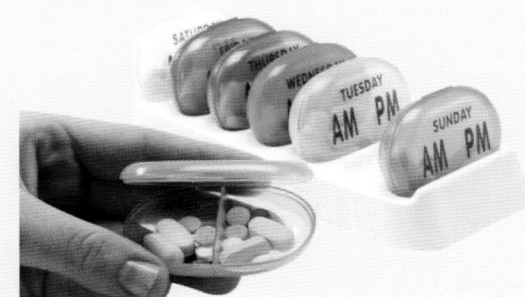

This would be especially useful for elderly folks who have others helping them keep track of medicine. Those long pill cases can be difficult to open with arthritic hands, and if the lids haven't all been latched down, getting pills out for one day can mean the whole thing spills out. The assistant could simply leave out this pod for the elderly friend, and it's easier to keep track for everyone.

-- Fiona Barnett

Easy-to-swallow supplements
Utrition Liquid Vitamins

I had a problem taking glucosamine in tablet form. I was gagging on the horse-sized pills and this seemed to cause an automatic antipathy to swallowing pills of any nature. After some research I discovered Utrition liquid vitamins. Their Liquid Vitamin Plus has an excellent lineup of vitamins A, B, C, D, and E + other ingredients and tastes like frozen orange juice (ed. note: it's "pineapple orange juice" according to Utrition). Their Liquid Joint Repair has 2000 mg glucosamine, 1200 mg chondroitin and is good-tasting as well. I keep these in the fridge and take a swig each day. Simple.

I also discovered a very sharp website (Bodybuilding. com) that is totally on the ball, has quick service, and offers thousands of nutritional products.

-- Lloyd Kahn

$27 Ultrition Liquid Vitamin Plus
Amazon

$20 Liquid Joint Repair Amazon

Mixes, shakes beverages
Blender Bottle

The Blender Bottle is a shaker bottle with a free-floating surgical stainless steel wire ball inside. A total boon for anyone who mixes formulas, shakes, mixes or other powdered drinks. Not unlike a kitchen whisk, the ball moves freely within your drink, breaking up clumps and further mixing the mix as you shake it for a smooth, totally grit- and clump-free serving. I use protein powder and creatine. Previously I had normal shaker bottles that always, regardless of how much shaking I did, left clumps of mix, especially at the bottom of the shaker. I even once spent about 20 bucks on a shaker bottle with a battery-powered mixing wand built into the lid, but the device really didn't mix any better than a normal bottle, kept falling apart inside my gym bag, ate batteries, and had to be hand-washed since you couldn't run the mixing attachment through the dishwasher. I've been using the Blender Bottle for about four months now after seeing an ad for it in a fitness magazine. The whisking ball is really ingenious, but this is also the first bottle I have ever owned that I can shake without holding onto the lid at the same time. The spout is that secure. I've used the Blender Bottle for cold protein powders and other sports nutrition products. The web site lists other uses including pancake batter, salad dressings, eggs, and gravy.

-- Joe Bentley

 **$7 (20 oz.) Amazon**

 **$8 (28 oz.) Amazon**

Easy pill splitting
Apex Ultra Pill Splitter

$7 Amazon

From time to time you might find yourself wanting to take half a pill as opposed to the whole dose. This tool simplifies the mechanical act of splitting a pill such that you obtain the best possible equal division with the least effort.

To that end, you will want a dedicated pill splitter as opposed to using your fingers or a knife. I've tried a number of pill splitters over the years and the best one I've found is the Apex Ultra, pictured above and below. It has a sharp blade that's covered by a retractable piece of plastic when not in the process of cutting. Equally important, it has a nicely designed platform upon which to place your pill, with rubbery side guards next to the firm base, such that the pill is securely gripped before being cut.

Scored pills are best cut along the score line. Egg-shaped (more precisely, prolate ellipsoid) pills should be placed such that the long axis of the pill is perpendicular to the blade: this results in a shorter cut edge than if the long axis were parallel to the blade, and thus minimizes loss of pill material.

Occasionally you may wish to quarter a pill: this is trickier than dividing an intact pill because you're working with a cut edge. The best result (most even division of pill half) will be obtained if you place the previously cut edge AWAY from the first contact point of the descending blade. If instead you advance the cut edge into the "V" of the platform, the blade will tend to fragment that edge as it divides the pill in half, leaving more of the pill's contents on the platform.

By having the intact surface of the pill serve as the initial contact point for the blade, you'll find the blade causes less of the pill's substance to break off from the previously cut edge.

-- Joe Stirt

Cancer answers
ACOR

Free Acor.org

The very first stop on the Web for anyone newly diagnosed with the big C should be the non-profit ACOR site. Home of 200+ support groups for cancer, the life-changing advice on this clearinghouse is supplied outside the view of search engines, so you probably won't encounter it by Googling.

Talking with survivors of your type of cancer is the best place to start. It normalizes the experience, provides vital information and support, directs you to the other resources you will need, saves you many wasted hours on the Net, helps you make sure that you're getting the best available medical care, and plugs you into a continuing network within which you can both ask for help and be of help to others.

About half of the ACOR communities are composed of patients and family caregivers concerned with a specific type of cancer, e.g., the

Two sarcoma survivors chatting

Lung Cancer Online Support Group, the AdenoCarcinoma of Unknown Primary Online Group, and the Prostate Problems Mailing List. Other groups focus on topics of interest to patients with cancer, e.g., the Cancer Patients Christian Online Support Group, the Cancer and Fertility Discussion Group, and the Complementary & Alternative Medicine Clinical Trials Discussion Group.

ACOR was established in 1995 by New York artist Gilles Frydman to host his wife's breast cancer mailing list. It then opened it's virtual doors, offering to host any noncommercial cancer-related mailing list. They've made a special effort to develop new support groups for rare cancers. And their Rare Cancers Discussion Group can be a godsend for patients with extremely rare forms of cancer.

Since ACOR blocks search engines and links for privacy protection, the group you're looking for may not show up on a Google (or other search engine) query for general terms. So if you know anyone with cancer, do them a favor: Send them a copy of this review.

-- Tom Ferguson, M.D.

ABOUT CANCERGUIDE
CANCER BASICS
RESEARCH YOUR OPTIONS
CLINICAL TRIALS

Specific Cancers

- Information On Specific Cancers
- If You Have A Rare Cancer
- Brain Tumor Info
- Prostate Cancer Info
- Bone Marrow Transplant Info

KIDNEY CANCER
STATISTICS
PRACTICAL ASPECTS
ALTERNATIVE THERAPIES
MIND & ATTITUDE
INSPIRATIONAL STORIES

acor.org
Association of Cancer Online Resources

Dental Care

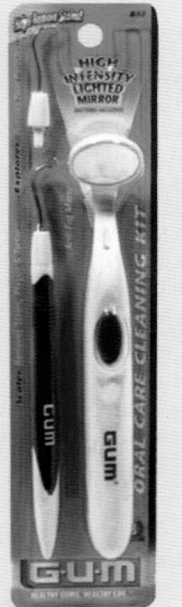

Mirrored flashlight for oral & mechanical work
GUM Oral Care Kit
$38 GUM

Two incredibly handy tools seldom used for their intended uses are dental mirrors (a.k.a. "inspection" mirrors) and dental picks. The one problem with most inspection mirrors is that when you have to look into awkward electronic or mechanical crevices where you need a mirror, you also need a flashlight for illumination and a spare hand to hold the light. This kit (#832) has a dental mirror with a bright flashlight integrated into the handle and a switch in the grip, freeing up your other hand. The other neat thing is that for less than $10 you get two dental picks — great for nudging or extracting small inaccessible components from assemblies. Recently, I was upgrading a friend's computer. The motherboard was mounted in a "baby ATX" case which was a very tight fit. To locate the CMOS reset jumper or check to see if the memory socket catch was engaged, I needed the use of the lighted mirror to negotiate the dark spots where those components were hidden. In the same manner the picks were handy to snag small cables within the case.

-- Stephen A. Kupiec

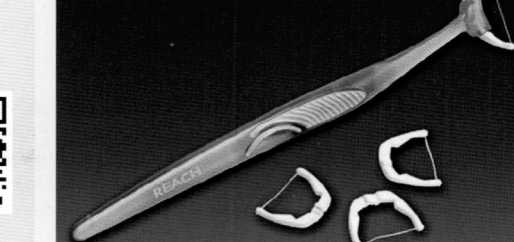

Superior dental tool
Reach Access Flosser
$3 Reach

The civilized way to floss. A tiny, easily replaceable harp on the end of a stick. More hygienic (no fingers in your mouth), more effective at flossing the hard parts, more comfortable, easier to use. Our kids love 'em. I floss much more often myself since I started using one. A really cool tool more folks should use.

-- KK

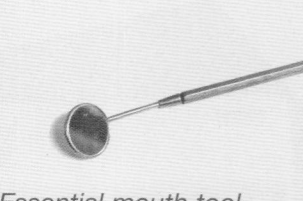

Essential mouth tool
Dental Mirror

I got mine — made of surgical stainless steel — from a set of used dental tools at a garage sale for 25 cents. It's incredibly handy for inspecting missing fillings, infections, gum complaints, particularly in kids. And you can look for sharp edges on dental braces. There really is no other way to look deep inside the mouth. The key is to get a proper front-surface mirror, which some drugstore plastic versions don't have. Otherwise at close range there is a slight double image which confuses the image.

-- KK

$6 Smart Practice   **$8 Revival Animal Health**

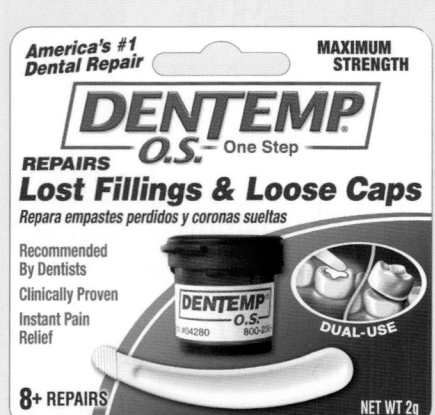

Emergency teeth fillings
Dentemp
$3 Dentemp

Dentemp is a traditional dental combination of zinc oxide and eugenol (clove oil) mixed when needed to make a temporary tooth patch for lost cavity filling, or to re-cement a cap or inlaid on a tooth. It's strong enough that you'll need to have a dentist remove it later. Since an emergency Dentemp kit weighs less than an ounce, it should be part of your traveling or backpacking kit. You can get it at almost any drug store.

-- KK

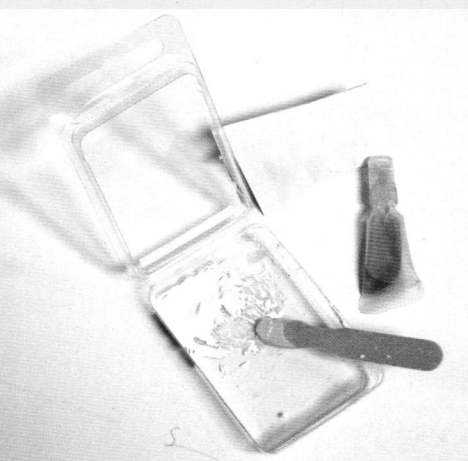

Floss alternative
Brush Picks
$3 Amazon
$36 (12 pack) Amazon

I hate flossing. I hate how the floss cuts into my fingers and lips, and how it gets wet and slimy and impossible to manipulate. I've tried those little flossers with handles but they're not much better than regular floss. I've used interdental brushes (they're like itty-bitty bottle brushes with handles) but they're not flexible and don't fit between normally-spaced teeth. After years of ignoring my dentist's suggestion to just floss the teeth I want to keep, I think BrushPicks are my solution.

Each disposable plastic pick has a pick end and a brush end. The pick end has tiny ridges that help to scrape harder material from between your teeth. But it's the brush end that's a real innovation. It looks kind of like a feathery antenna, with a flat row of tiny bristles extending on either side of a thin, flexible pick. This brush end is stiff enough and thin enough to poke easily between your teeth, but flexible enough that it readily bends so that you're not jabbing painfully into your gums. This flexibility also allows for cleaning behind rear molars. Rotating the brush end as you clean helps to loosen and remove gunk from otherwise impossible-to-reach areas.

BrushPicks are so effective that they're actually kind of fun to use–in a "look what I just dug out of my own head" sort of way. I've taken to using one every 2 or 3 days and I'm anxious to see if my dental hygienist notices the difference during my next cleaning.

-- Rhodora Collins

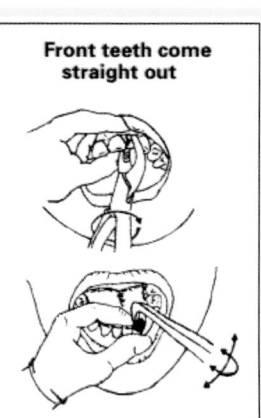

In India and Guatemala, health workers use a foot treadle to power a drill, the same way they operate a sewing machine. This kind of drill is slower than a compressed-air drill, and the grinding produces a lot of heat, so one must take care not to let the tooth ge so hot that it kills the nerves (see p. 152). Still, this is one of the simplest and cheapest ways to place a permanent filling.

Permanent tooth. A permanent tooth is worth saving. How long ago was it knocked out? If it was less than 12 hours ago, you can put a permanent tooth back into the socket. The sooner you do this the better, so do not wait. **If you replace the tooth in the first hour, it has a much better chance of joining with the gum and bone.** In order to heal and to join the bone, the tooth must be held firmly.

a) Wash the tooth gently with saline, milk, or clean water. There should not be any bits of dirt on the root of the tooth.

Keep the tooth damp with wet cotton gauze.

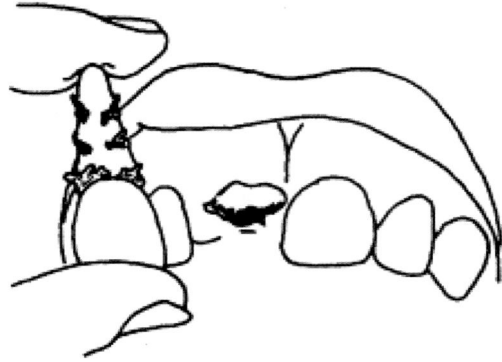

Do not scrape away any skin from the root or from the inside of the socket.

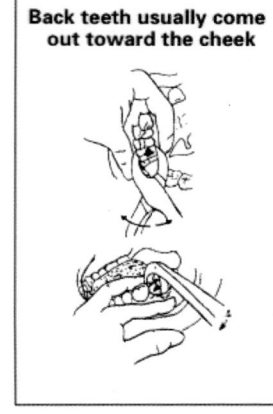

Front teeth come straight out

Back teeth usually come out toward the cheek

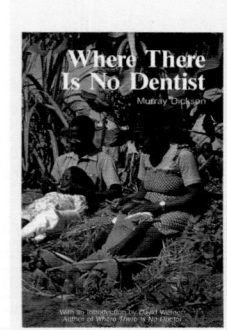

Emergency dentistry
Where there is no dentist
$14 Murray Dickson, 1983, 283 p.
free PDF

There is very little chance you'll ever be beyond the reach of a dentist most of your life. However, like its companion *Where There is No Doctor*, the true audience for this free PDF (and for-sale printed book) is care-givers in the developing world. But this tome also works as a short course in emergency care. Real dental first aid that is useful for anyone to know.

--KK

Improved face mask
Totobobo Mask
$23 Totobobo

This is a new design of respirator which has advantages for mass distribution, emergency preparedness, and multi-ethnic populations. I've been using/testing it for 5 or 6 years in the Unorganized Borough in Alaska.

The respirator can be cut with scissors to fit faces properly. Because they are clear, fit is easily ascertained. A clear respirator may mean they are more acceptable culturally (the face is not hidden).

The filters are replaceable. They allow a lot of air to pass through so can be useful in bike riding and outdoor work. They also allow moisture to pass through; I haven't found the exhaled moisture to be a problem except in subzero temperatures (quite a bit of condensation then).

Instead of storing respirators of every size, only one size needs to be stored for emergency use. One doesn't need to check sizes before distributing the respirators. Respirators can be cleaned and re-used by the individual (replace filters). I have seen them be used for pandemics, volcanoes, dust, woodworking, and cycling, and I am hoping to continue testing them in Alaska where we have faces from many different populations.

-- Pamela Bumsted

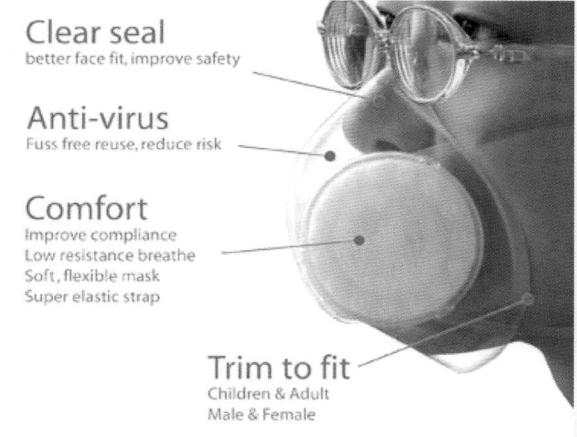

Clear seal
better face fit, improve safety

Anti-virus
Fuss free reuse, reduce risk

Comfort
Improve compliance
Low resistance breathe
Soft, flexible mask
Super elastic strap

Trim to fit
Children & Adult
Male & Female

Beijing CHINA

Calcutta INDIA

Bangkok THAILAND

Hanoi VIETNAM

Vientiane LAOS

Anti-pollution mask with clean filter

www.iloveyourmici.pl

These filters show the build up of particulate in the mask's filters after a bike ride through the various cities.

Sensible worrying
Get Pandemic Ready
getpandemicready.org

All of the scary end-of-the-world disasters to worry about, a global pandemic is the one you should really worry about. Because you can do something about it. Smaller pandemics are pretty much inevitable in our modern world, and even they will be a major disruption. This site is a prepper site dedicated to the unique challenges of preparing for a serious pandemic. Most of your life would be impacted: hygiene, travel, treatment, etc. These folks, backed by official preparedness plans, offer extensive tasks you can do to minimize impact.

-- KK

● Guidelines for Minimizing the Spread of Virus

1. Set up a separate room after a pandemic starts, before anyone is sick.

Remove all unneeded items from the room. This will make cleaning and disinfection easier. Consider removing curtains.

Real time flu news
Fluwiki Forum
Free Fluwiki Forum

Influenza = Uncertainty. Rumors. Caution. Hysteria. Pandemic. No, wait, a media frenzy. Or maybe, serious medical worry. Where can you go to find out the latest?

The best source for the latest published news from around the world on the emerging flu viruses (and other viruses of human health concerns) is the Fluwiki Forum. This site was started for tracking the avian H5N1 virus, and is now trying to keep up with this latest outbreak, whatever it is. The in-depth and comprehensive

If possible choose a room that close to its own bathroom. If no separate bathroom is possible, consider preparing for an RV chemical toilet or other separate toilet.

is

Choose a room that is as far away from the rest of the family as is feasible. Possibilities include: guest house, mobile home/camper/trailer house, loft above a garage, spare bedroom, partition of a larger room (to be screened off with plastic).

Laundry. Always put gloves on before handling any laundry – bedding, towels, clothing, etc. Carefully place laundry in a plastic bag until time to launder. Wash separately from other household laundry in warm water and detergent.

Drinks/Meals. Use disposable cups, bowls, plates and utensils to save cleanup time and reduce the chance of the virus spreading.

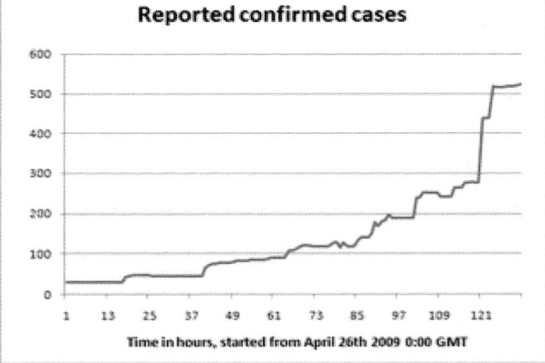

Reported confirmed cases

Time in hours, started from April 26th 2009 0:00 GMT

background material on flu available on the Fluwiki itself is excellent ballast for the froth of "news."   -- KK

Nasal irrigator
Neti Pot
$11 Amazon

My brother-in-law introduced me to the neti pot, for nasal irrigation, about three years ago. He had had chronic sinus infections that have largely stopped since he started using it. Since I began using it, I've had fewer illnesses and just breathe easier. I used to take decongestants regularly in order to sleep soundly (due to mild allergies), but haven't in the past three years, since the neti pot became part of my daily routine. My sinuses don't dry out as much during winter anymore, and my wife says my snoring has decreased.

The neti pot flushes your sinuses of pollutants, allergens, pollen and dust that build up during the day. By flushing your sinuses you allow your nose to do its secondary job more effectively — keep the bad stuff out. It also has the added benefit of relieving sinus headaches and congestion. The interesting thing is, it's been around for a long time (several thousand years) and is used by many yoga practitioners to ease breathing during meditation. Eight ounces of

warm tap water and 1/4 teaspoon sea salt (with no iodine) is all it takes to wash the grime away, and that's a lot cheaper than over-the-counter decongestants.

I recommend getting a neti pot with a pot belly look, like the Himalayan Institute one available from Amazon. I've tried two other brands/styles and they don't provide as consistent water pressure through the nose.

Currently I use my neti pot once a day, in the evenings, to wash the day's grime away and help with sleeping.

Try it once or twice and you'll agree your sinuses have rarely felt better or clearer. As a side note, if it burns a little, stop and add a tad more salt. Too little salt and the water won't flow well through the nasal cavity. If you've had a broken nose, please check with your doctor to make sure your nasal cavity is still properly aligned for nasal irrigation.

-- Jeff Young

[I'm sure the video will turn some people off, but you've got to know how it works. How else did you expect to irrigate your nasal passages?]

Cleanest air filter
IQAir HealthPro Plus
$899 Amazon

Many of us live in environments or buildings where air quality is poor or downright unhealthy, and many airborne pollutants and allergens end up in in our lungs. Depending on your sensitivity, age and other factors, what you can't see (bacteria, pet allergens, mold spores, dust, pollen, volatile organic compounds (VOCs), etc.) can hurt you. The smaller the particulate, the easier it can get into your lungs and cause problems.

I was introduced to the HealthPro Plus by my partner, who suffers from bad asthma and allergies. She had been using one for a couple of years and has come to depend on it to keep her bedroom in a breathable state. I got one for my place and immediately noticed the difference, from particulate in the air to the amount of dust collecting on surfaces. I had been using another mass market HEPA filter, but apparently it hadn't been doing a thorough job at all (I live in an urban environment with rather poor air quality).

The control panel allows you to set a variety of settings and monitor filter life (which varies widely based on usage). There are 6 fan speed settings, from 40 cfm (cubic feet per minute) to a cranking 240 cfm. You can do the math and figure out how many times per hour the HealthPro Plus can cycle all of the air in the room. It's surprisingly quiet at the lowest setting, and sounds a bit like an oncoming tornado at the top setting.

It is also worth noting that IQAir – a 45+ year old Swiss company – is very responsive, and that the unit comes with a 5 year warranty. I had a small issue with my power supply and I was able to call IQAir and reach someone who handled the return efficiently. They even FedEx'd me shipping materials and overnighted the unit back to me.

I can only point out two obvious downsides to the HealthPro Plus. One is that it's expensive – it is more than twice the cost of most other high end systems on the market (though worth the money in my opinion), and replacement

filters are also somewhat pricey. The second is that it is another large beige box in an age of too many beige boxes. Placing it aesthetically in the room while also allowing for maximum air exchange can take some finesse (there is also a compact model). If you're interested in filtration for your whole house, IQAir makes air purification systems (http://www.iqair.com/residential/whole-houseairpurifiers/) that connect to HVAC which are very well reviewed.

I did a bunch of research on air purification systems before buying one, and among everything I've seen the HealthPro Plus always came out on top.

-- Camron Assadi

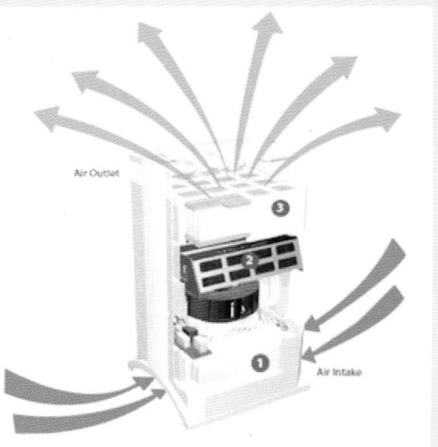

Air Outlet

Air Intake

Preventing poison oak and ivy
Ivy Block
$11 Amazon

Tecnu as a remedy for Poison Oak is OK, but for really allergic folks like me, it's not enough. I'm a regular mountain biker, and in Northern California, we have a ton of poison oak in the summer.

I discovered Ivy Block which came out a few years ago, and haven't had a problem since. You apply it to your arms and legs **before** going out, sort of like putting on suntan lotion, and voila! — no poison oak. Really works great. Check it out.

-- *John Zeisler*

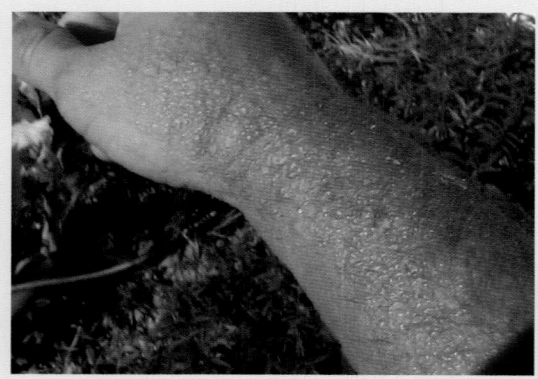

Poison oak and ivy cure
Zanfel
$20 Amazon

Zanfel is very expensive, it's true ($24/oz). But it's worth every penny to anyone suffering with a poison ivy (or oak) rash. Within 30 seconds of treatment, the itching stops. Really. It's the only product I know of that chemically binds the urishol which is causing the problem. Doesn't have to be used as soon after exposure as the previously-recommended Tecnu.

-- *Jimmie Whipple*

Tips

•
A neurologist says that if he can get to a stroke victim quickly he can totally reverse the effects of a stroke. He said the trick was getting a stroke recognized, diagnosed and getting to the patient within 3 hours, which is tough. Sometimes symptoms of a stroke are difficult to identify. But doctors say a bystander can recognize a stroke by asking three simple questions:

1. Ask the individual to SMILE.
2. Ask him or her to RAISE BOTH ARMS.
3. Ask the person to SPEAK A SIMPLE SENTENCE (Coherently, ie: It is sunny out today)

If he or she has trouble with any of these tasks, call 9-1-1 immediately and describe the symptoms to the dispatcher.

-- *Michael Hawley*

Staying safe outside
Medicine for the Outdoors
$20 Paul S. Auerbach, 2009, 535 pages

There is nothing in this book that you don't need to know. You don't have to commit the book to memory but I would encourage you to know what's in it and how to find it quickly. My first duty as a Scout leader is the safety and well-being of our Scouts at an age when they are poor judges of risk and have a propensity to overestimate their capacities. I need to know how to keep them safe and how to respond if they are injured or ill.

Medicine for the Outdoors is the work of Dr. Paul Auerbach, wilderness medicine pioneer and arguably the world's foremost expert on the subject. He explains the how and why of responding to nearly every possible illness or injury one is likely to encounter in a concise, step by step manner that is intended to be used on the spot – but don't wait for something to happen before you read the book.

Safety is not owning the right gear or having the right book. It is not having a well-appointed first aid kit. Safety is knowing how to prevent injury and illness and how to respond if it occurs. Get the book, read through it, make notes and practice the skills before you need them. I have a Kindle copy that I can carry on a smartphone, iPod or similar device. I also have a copy of the book that lives in our troop first aid kit.

-- *Clarke Green*

The outdoor environment is beautiful, but it is ever changing and can become hostile in a moment. Good fortune favors the well prepared, and there are no more important considerations for a successful outdoor experience than safety and first aid. Severe weather, wild animals, rugged terrain, and equipment failure all conspire to create or complicate medical hardships that must he diagnosed swiftly and remedied with certainty. The therapies can he integral to survival. Medical education is thus as compelling as any other form of learning.

•
How to use this book

In order to use this book to best advantage, read the appropriate sections before you embark on a trip. In this way, you'll remember where to find information in case of an emergency. Use the index to locate specific topics, such as bee stings, frostbite, or choking. When reading about different problems, you may be referred to general instructions for medical aid, which are presented in Parts I and 2. All readers are encouraged to participate in organized first-aid and outdoor safety program.

Aversion therapy
Orly No Bite
$8 Amazon

This is one of the few products I've ever read about in a magazine and then sought out immediately for purchase. I don't recall the publication, but I do know that it was several years ago and I had to search high and low to find it.

No Bite is "a bitter flavored nail bite deterrent that helps break the annoying and often painful nail biting habit." I used it more for my cuticles than my nails, but the idea is the same. It looks like nail polish, and it smells (and tastes) like nail polish remover. Once you paint it on it seems to disappear, but then later when you mindlessly slip your finger in between your teeth you're greeted with a disgustingly awful flavor. The aversion therapy worked so effectively for me that I still have a pretty full bottle of the stuff. A little goes a long way.

My fiance, who wears fake nails specifically to avoid biting her real ones, says that a similar product didn't work for her. She must have had a powerful compulsion, because I can't imagine fighting past the flavor of No Bite. In fact the only problem I had was accidentally tasting it on my fingers while eating. Use of a fork would pretty much solve that problem.

-- *William Sawalich*

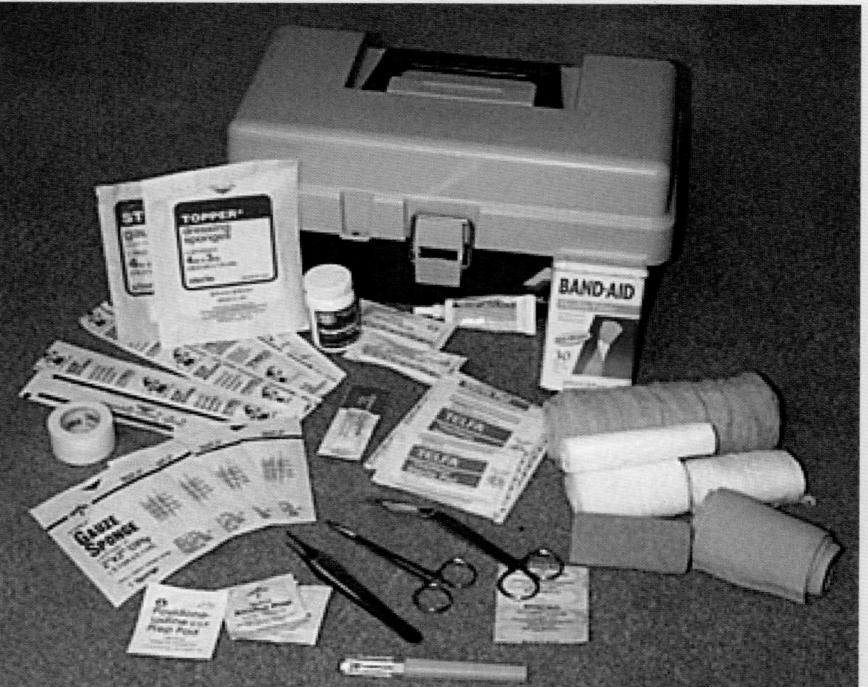

Essential medicines
The Well-Stocked Home Pharmacy

It's a great idea to put all your medical stuff into a kit of some sort, even if it never leaves your house. The worst place to store medicine supplies is in the bathroom, where most people keep them. It is moist and warm there, while what medical stuff wants is dry and cool. You also want to be able to grab supplies quickly and take them where they are needed. We put ours into plastic cases the size of shoe boxes, There's one for bandages and first aid, and another for medicines. The lids seal tight, prolonging the shelf life of the contents. When there is a first-aid injury, we get the kit and have everything together on site.

In addition to first-aid supplies here are some medicines you might consider stocking:

You should have an antibiotic ointment like Polysporin or a **triple antibiotic.**

Diarrhea serves a useful function to remove bad things from the body, but sometimes you may need **Imodium** to control excessive and severe diarrhea. Take this on your travels.

I like to have some **hydrocortisone** at home for itchy rashes and eczema.

Afrin nasal spray for a **decongestant.** Because it is targeted to the nasal area, the medicine is more potent than oral decongestants so you get more bang for the side-effect buck. Don't use it for more than 3 days, though.

It's a good idea to have an anti-fungal like Lotrimin or **clotrimazole** for athlete's foot or infection of the skin.

Another good thing to stock is **Benadryl** for allergies and allergic reactions.

If you are traveling in exotic places (for you) ask your doctor to prescribe the antibiotic Cipro (**ciprofloxacin**) to take with you in case of emergency.

The other thing we take in our traveling medical kit is **probiotics** and vitamin D. Since probiotic products vary enormously, current studies suggest that the two aspects the matters most are higher numbers of colony forming units and containing more than one strain. For probiotics, aim for products with 5 billion colony forming units.

-- *Alan Greene, MD*

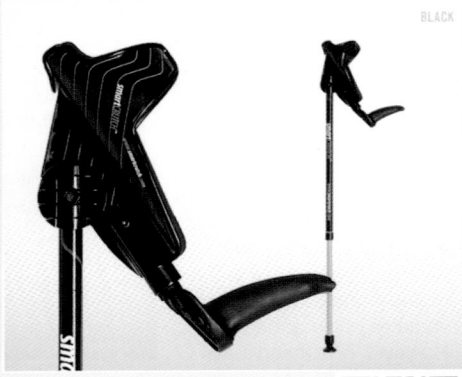

Ergonomic crutches
SmartCrutch
$120 smartCRUTCH

These are the best crutches in the world, no hyperbole. If you've ever used traditional crutches you might remember how painful they were to the hands and/or underarms. Not these. I first got them after a pair of forearm crutches became so painful to the hands. By redesigning how and where you hold them they reduce pressure to the underarm and hands. Like traditional crutches they are adjustable based on your height.

I had an articular cartilage tear in my knee (femur, specifically), necessitating microfracture surgery, and subsequently used these crutches for 2.5 months. Being able to ambulate comfortably made the many challenges of recovery much less stressful. When I first got the crutches I adjusted the arm rest angle to my desired setting and never felt like changing it. Over time I adjusted the height to be a little lower when I was non-weight bearing, as I felt it easier to get around without the tips hitting the ground. When I began weight bearing with a single crutch, I liked it a little longer to more easily reduce weight on the operative leg. I probably would have done the latter two adjustments with any type of crutch.

As for wear, the crutches have held up well. The foam on the arm rest has compressed somewhat, but is still comfortable and I don't think it would compress further. Anyway, it is something that could be easily cut away and replaced with a similar material by the user if that became necessary. Other aspects of the crutch do not show signs of wear after 2.5 months of use.

The other thing that's awesome about them is that you can safely go up stairs by actually holding the railing! By setting the arm cuff angle to about 70-80 degrees, it allows you to hold the unused crutch in the hand of the side that's using a crutch for support leaving your other hand free to hold the railing. Incredible.

-- Gus Gustafson

I had knee surgery and have to be on crutches for 6 weeks, completely non weight bearing on one leg. After 1 week on standard forearm type crutches (more common in many places than the underarm ones you see in the USA), my hands were KILLING me from all my 160 lbs being put on my palms. I found these smart crutches, and have done some major walking on them: NO PAIN. I will say that I feel slightly more unstable on them compared to the regular forearm crutches, but I also have them set to like 70% to put all my weight on my arms, and almost none on my hands, which may contribute to that feeling.

For me, they were well worth the cost, even if my insurance won't cover them, which I may still be able to get.

-- M. Clifford

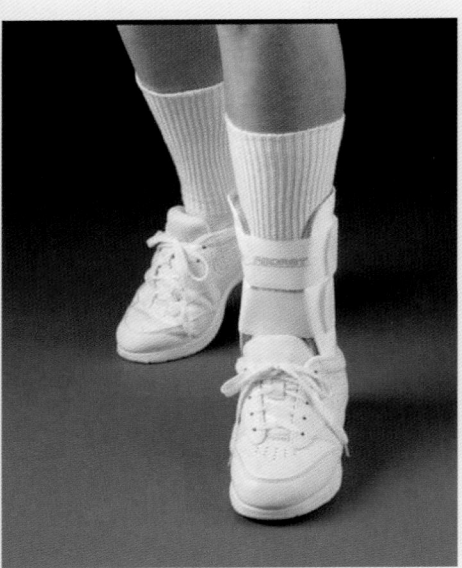

Sprained ankle repair
Air-Stirrup Ankle Brace
$30 Amazon

I was recently reminded of this cool tool for sprained ankles when my wife and I were hustling to locate an obscure theater before the doors shut. Not watching my foot path, I stepped on a misaligned concrete sidewalk and went to the ground after rolling my ankle. I couldn't wait to get home to put my Aircast on. This product stabilizes your injured ankle well enough that you'd have to go hiking on poorly maintained trails to reinjure your ankle after a sprain. My last sprain was twelve years ago and the Aircast got me 95% healed within three weeks; without it, I've gone longer than three months. Truly amazing if you sprain your ankle. They can be ordered direct from the company, but even in my town of 16,000, there's one pharmacy that carries them in stock. Around $40.00 and worth twice that, easily.

-- John Monguillot

Waterproof sock/glove for broken limbs
DryPro Cast Cover
$30 Amazon

When my six year old daughter broke her arm, we figured our big lake vacation was going to be a real test of her patience. Then a friend told us about DryPro Cast covers. They're essentially a super-thick latex mitten (or 'crab claw') that covers the entire arm or leg. Air is sucked out via a one-way valve to give it a snug fit, like a rubber glove. The device comes with a detachable bulb pump, but we usually just sucked out the small amount of air needed by mouth. Our daughter used it not only while swimming and bathing, but for water-tubing, rope swinging, and general sprinkler fun. She was able to submerge the broken limb completely. The covers are not indestructible, but the only thing I was ever worried about, and warned her to be careful of, was cutting the cover on a sharp rock. I actually purchased a second cast cover in case my daughter tore the first one — she didn't. And it completely saved the vacation. I'm guessing these will last most kids at least one bone-mending cycle.

-- Chris Crawford

Inexpensive secure bandages
Vet-Wrap Conforming Bandage
$2 Amazon

For wrapping up wounds, both large and small, you want a wrap that is secure, yet not so tight it will decrease needed blood circulation. Ace bandages are considered too constricting and likely to wind up tight; in their stead pros use conforming bandages, with brands names like Kling. The key here is "wider is better." Get the widest width you can and wrap liberally. The bandage will cling to itself (you still have to tape the end of it) but will not shift around much in normal use. The same stuff as Kling, but about 10 times cheaper is Vet-Wrap, used for the same purposes on animals. Better yet, Vet-Wrap comes in a choice of cheery colors instead of hospital white.

-- KK

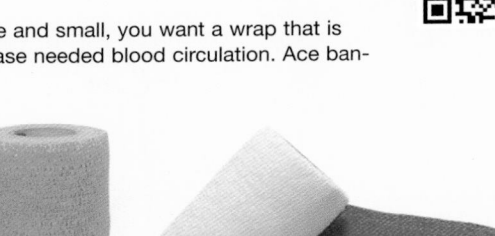

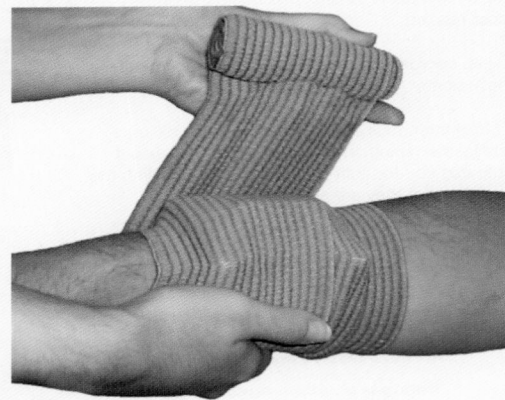

Better than ACE bandage
Israeli Emergency Bandage
$6 Amazon

I was first introduced to the Israeli emergency bandage several years ago as a medic in Iraq. It was a huge step up from the standard military dressings that we had been issued. The old military style dressings hadn't changed since WWII and were not really effective as the canvas ties didn't always hold the dressing where you needed it. A lot of guys were using gauze pads and elastic wrap which, while better, was cumbersome.

The Israeli emergency bandage was the first of a new generation of bandages that made a difference when it really counts. It combines a sterile dressing, elastic wrap and a pressure bar to make a fast and easy to use trauma bandage. The long tail can be configured in various ways to hold the bandage in place or to immobilize the limb, plus it can be configured in to an improvised tourniquet. I consider it must carry item since I can use it as a multipurpose bandage, use the tail as an "Ace" wrap for sprains or to immobilize a fracture to a splint. The bandage comes in 4" and 6" for around $5-$11 and everyone in my family has one in their car first aid kit, backpack or office.

-- Sandy Fraser

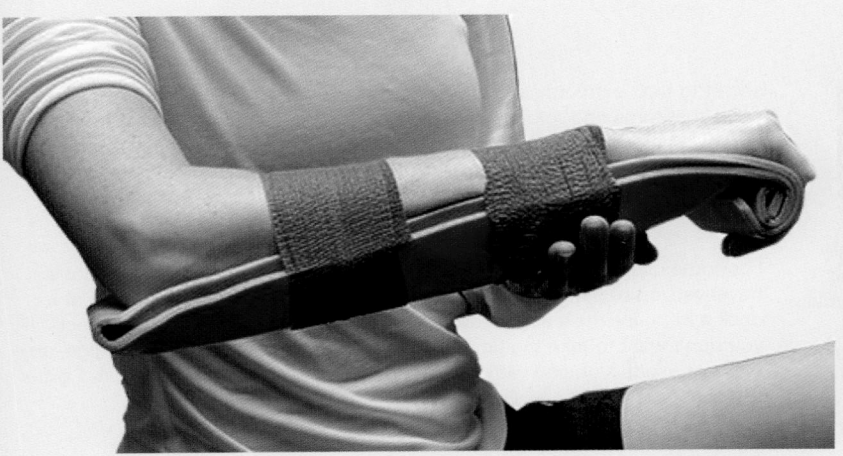

Featherweight emergency splint
SAM Splint
$11 Chinook Medical Gear

A super light-weight (only 4 oz.) foam-padded aluminum splint that can be unfolded and bent into almost any shape to conform to almost any part of the body (around the neck, at the elbow, etc.). Re-usable and transparent to X-Rays, which means it can be kept on during scanning. Every expedition doc and EMT crew packs one of these as a standard item. It's a great thing to have in your car's first aid kit, or at home, camp, or vacation where you have active people.

-- KK

Most comprehensive stretching manual

Stretching

$15 Bob Anderson, illustrations by Jean Anderson, 2010, 240 p.

I haven't encountered any source on this subject as broad, accessible, and easily applied as Bob Anderson's classic Stretching, a patient and friendly stand-in for my eight-grade P.E. teacher.

The 30th anniversary edition of this guidebook came out recently, with even more stretches and illustrations, and it's easily the most comprehensive work on the subject. I love the activity-specific sections: cyclists, for instance, are shown stretches that not only address the muscle groups made tight and tense by our specific sport, but the stretches geared toward bike riders even include a bicycle to be utilized as a support. Activities from weightlifting to computer using get their own sections, too.

Organizationally, Stretching shines. Tight neck? Rigid shoulders? Thumb through to your prescribed routine and get to work. With minimal flexibility but a willingness to make an effort, almost anyone can use this book to become more limber, healthier.

-- Elon Schoenholz

Stretching feels good when done correctly. You do not have to push the limits or attempt to go further each day. It should not be a personal contest to see how far you can stretch. Stretching should be tailored to your particular muscular structure, flexibility, and varying tension levels. The key is regularity and relaxation. The object is to reduce muscular tension, thereby promoting freer movement—not to concentrate on attaining extreme flexibility, which often leads to overstretching and injury.

●

Who Should Stretch?

Everyone can learn to stretch, regardless of age or flexibility. You do not need to be in top physical condition or have specific athletic skills. Whether you sit at a desk all day, dig ditches, do housework, stand at an assembly line, drive a truck or exercise regularly, the same techniques of stretching apply….if you are healthy, without any specific physical problems, you can learn how to stretch safely and enjoyably.

●

Why Stretch?

- Reduce muscle tension and make the body feel more relaxed

- Help coordination by allowing for freer and easier movement

- Make strenuous activities like running, skiing, tennis, swimming, and cycling easier because it prepares you for activity; it's a way of signaling the muscles that they are about to be used.

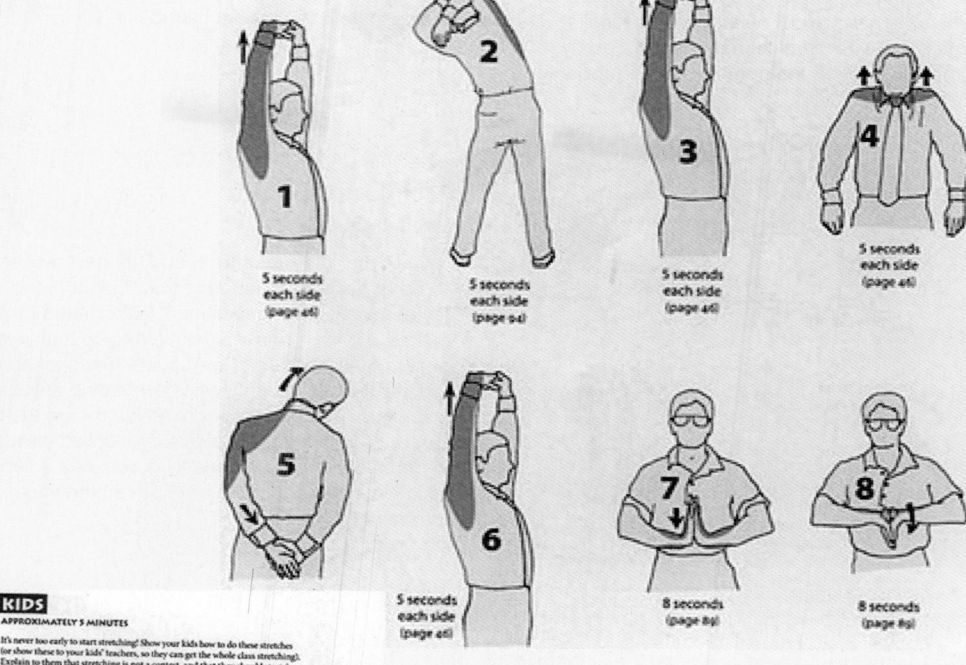

Unorthodox back pain philosophy

Mind Over Back Pain

$11 John Sarno, MD, 1982, 124 p.

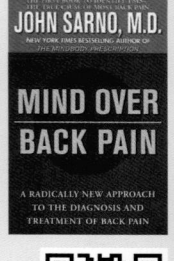

Back pain is ubiquitous in developed countries. Yet the honest truth is that science is uncertain as to what causes it. Theories abound, as does a lot of pseudo-therapy. There are probably multiple origins and different varieties of lower back pain. However, one theory says a large portion of back pain starts with mental tension. If you have an inkling that your back pain is linked to stress, I strongly suggest you seek out this perennially-in-print book (since 1972). My speaking agent, who deals with hundreds of stressed-out type A's and the consequential epidemic of back pain they carry with them, routinely hands out this book. It seems to be the one thing that helps them the most. It helped me. By adopting the view that lower back pain is a syndrome in large part fostered by the mind/body complex, I've been able to avoid surgery and painkillers and resume my life. Your mileage may vary, but it's worth a read.

-- KK

●

The reason for this obsession with discs is that it does seem logical. There are those degenerating structures at the lower end of the spine, right where a lot of pain and spasms occur; there are lumbar and sacral nerves conveniently located so that they can be compressed by bulging or herniated discs; there is pain in the leg, proving that those nerves are compressed.

Figure 9

AGE DISTRIBUTION
OF 177 PATIENTS IN A FOLLOW-UP STUDY

●

What these data confirm is that degenerative processes have nothing to do with most back pain. Degeneration is progressive and relentless; serial X rays as one ages document this fact. Yet back pain is far less common in the older age groups. According to the conventional diagnostic concepts, everyone over the age of sixty should have back pain.

The bar graph in Figure 9 [above] gives the age by breakdown by decade. Seventy-seven percent of the group fell between the ages of thirty and fifty-nine. Note that there are fewer patients in their sixties than in their twenties! Since the majority of back pain syndromes are attributed to degenerative processes – for example, degenerative osteoarthritis and degenerative disc disease – it is strange, indeed, that there were only thirteen patients aged sixty to sixty-nine, and seven in their seventies.

Professional massage assist

G5 Massager

$405 G5 ProPower Handheld Massager Amazon

The G5 is a professional-grade massage unit that has long been a staple of naturopaths, chiropractors and physiotherapists, many of whom report still using their 40- or 50-year-old units on a daily basis. The G5 comes in dozen or so professional models for use in hospitals, physical therapy and similar clinics. Most pro sports teams (football, basketball, baseball, anyway) have a G5 in their training rooms. This is no Costco-type unit, but an unbelievably robust massage gun that will astonish you within seconds.

The larger professional units with stands and rollers go for about $1,200. The

secret to their extraordinarily powerful and effective massage action is a coiled cable that turns and rotates the head, rather than pounding or vibrating as less durable units do. All of the G5s have changeable applicator heads for doing reflexology, exfoliation treatments, lymphatic drainage, cellulite reduction, Trigger Point therapy, therapeutic massage, or just plain old relaxation massage.

For home use I recommend the Pro-Power unit, which is sold as a portable travel version of the G5. It goes for about $350. Since I write and work at a desk a lot, I use mine almost daily, especially when doing big long projects. If you don't want to take the time to schedule and pay for an $80 massage, anyone can use this on you without getting sore hands or wanting to quit. I actually own two!

-- Hakim Chishti

I do not fear computers. I fear the lack of them - Isaac Asimov

Best guides to pregnancy
Prenatal Resources

$15 Mayo Clinic Guide to a Healthy Pregnancy, 2011, 509 p.

$8 From First Kicks to First Steps, Alan Greene, 2004, 304 p.

Free babycenter.com

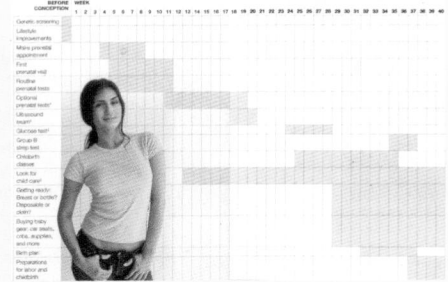

When I became pregnant for the first time, I started looking for prenatal care books and resources to guide me through the journey. I checked reviews and excerpts on Amazon, and asked my friends and family to recommend their favorites. And of course, everyone had a different favorite. I now have a full shelf of books on loan, and books gifted from my mother, and mother-in-law. They all cover the same basics, with different organization and tone, but I do have two clear favorites.

The Mayo Clinic Guide to a Healthy Pregnancy is super comprehensive, easy to navigate, and includes lots of photos and helpful charts. It's authoritative, written by M.D.s, but doesn't push an overly medicalized vision of pregnancy and childbirth. I've been following along with the weekly info sections as my pregnancy has progressed, and I've consulted the symptom and condition reference sections as needed. The topic specific chapters on genetic screening and childbirth (among others) have also been hugely helpful. It's my go-to reference.

From First Kicks to First Steps is a fairly unique guide written by a pediatrician. Dr. Greene's tone is extremely friendly and compassionate. It combines anecdotes from his practice, user questions and comments from his website, and summaries of recent research studies. My favorite aspect, though, is his emphasis on bi-empathy, whereby he encourages his reader to consider the baby's experience of her world.

In addition to these two books, babycenter.com has also become an often-used resource. The website is full of brief but informative articles on everything from stages of development to baby gear roundups. The user forums are a tempting place to indulge questions like, "When did you first start feeling kicks." I especially like the app, My Pregnancy, which, based on my due date, gives me daily updates on development and reminders about things like when I should start thinking about childcare arrangements. I'm not

sure I'd remember which week of pregnancy I'm in if it weren't for this helpful app.

-- Camille Hartsell

●

From *The Mayo Guide:*

Pregnancy Calendar

●

Week 26

Your baby's eyebrows and eyelashes are now well formed, and the hair on his or her head is longer and more plentiful. Your baby still looks red and wrinkled, but more fat is accumulating under the skin with each passing day. As your baby continues to gain weight over the next 14 weeks until birth, this wrinkly suit of skin will become a better fit.

Your baby's footprints and fingerprints are now formed. And all the components that make up the eyes have developed, but your baby probably won't open his or her eyes for about two more weeks. By 26 weeks, your baby weighs between 1 Y2 and 2 pounds.

●

Prenatal tests are voluntary. Each test has its own risks and benefits, so it's worthwhile to know about these tests so that you can make an informed decision. Before you undergo a prenatal test, think about what information the test will provide and how you will use the information. Many, but not all, women choose to undergo basic ultrasounds and blood tests. Most women don't undergo the more detailed diagnostic tests because most pregnancies don't carry a high risk of complications.

Before scheduling a prenatal test, you and your partner might want to consider these questions:

1. What will you do with the information once you have it? How will it affect decisions regarding your pregnancy?
2. Will the information provide better care or treatment during pregnancy or delivery?
3. How accurate are the results of the test?
4. Will undergoing a test be worth the anxiety it may cause?
5. What are the risks of the procedure?
6. How much does the test cost? Is it covered by your health insurance?

●

Leg Cramps

Cramps in the lower leg muscles are fairly common in the second and third trimesters of pregnancy. They

most frequently occur at night, and they may disrupt your sleep. Although the exact cause of leg cramps is unknown, slow blood return associated with the pressure of the baby on your leg veins may be responsible.

Prevention and self-care

Here are some tips for relieving the discomfort of leg cramps or calf tenderness:

• Try exercises to stretch your calf muscles, particularly before bed.
• Stretch the affected muscle. Try straightening your knee and gently flexing your foot upward.
• Walk. You may find it uncomfortable at first, but walking helps relieve the cramping.
• Wear support hose, especially if you stand a lot during the day.
• Take frequent breaks if you sit or stand for long periods.
• Massage your calves.
• Try resting with your legs up on pillows or the arm of a sofa.
• Wear shoes with low heels.

When to seek medical help

If leg cramps persist, talk to your care provider. They might be caused by a circulation problem. Contact your care provider right away if you notice redness, swelling, an increase in pain or if you have a history of a blood clots or a blood-clotting disorder.

●

From First Kicks:

Practice seeing events from two perspectives, yours and the person with whom you are interacting. As you become skilled at "bi-empathic vision"

(a phrase I coined to describe seeing and feeling both worlds simultaneously), new ways of speaking to your four-year-old (and new ways of interacting with your unborn baby) will suggest themselves to you. New ideas will also occur to you as we discover in Chapter 12 what your baby is seeing and hearing and in Chapter 13 what sleep is like for your baby.

Have you seen the recent three-dimensional posters and books that don't require those special glasses for viewing? They can take a little practice, but if you let your focus soften so that your two eyes see the page independently, a previously invisible three-dimensional image will pop into view. With practice, you can let your focus soften with your child. Let one "eye" continue to see what you as a wise parent see, while with the other you try to see what he as a child sees. A hidden reality will emerge-for both of you! Bi-empathic vision is the best way to teach your child what he needs to know to succeed in this world.

●

Your Perspective

Different women (and their mates) come to nursing

with different expectations. Some foresee it as a joyful, perhaps even glorious, experience. Others imagine it to be distasteful or embarrassing. Words that I've heard women use to describe the idea of breastfeeding include convenient, inconvenient, healthy, natural, intimate, exhausting, fulfilling, bonding, painful, awkward, cowlike, magical, scary, soothing, economical, weight losing, body image changing, and invaluable treasure. Talking about the images and emotions you have on the topic, wherever they come from, may help you to clarify your perspective.

Your Baby's Perspective

After about 266 days spent in 24/7 contact with you and being nourished from your body, she is born with instincts to seek out and feed from your breast. She might suckle a soft, warm, living nipple overlying your soothing heartbeat. Or she might feed from a nipple expertly constructed from latex rubber or a synthetic polymer called silicone while being held in your loving arms. Does this feel like the difference between kissing a person and kissing a plastic doll?

Bi-empathy

Choose feeding/nurturing solutions that honor both you and your child. And I believe no one should second-guess your decision, whatever it is. Breast milk allows you to continue to feed your baby after birth, to stay physically connected. It is the perfect food for babies. But today's infant formulas are the best substitutes that have ever been available. Millions of formula-fed babies have grown up healthy, smart, bright-eyed, and strong.

●

In one study, Lecanuet played a simple two-note sequence on a piano. First he played a low C or D and recorded changes in babies' heart rates as they noticed the pure tone. After the heart rates had returned to baseline, he played another note, and the same heart rate changes were observed. It didn't matter which note came first. The babies heard the two sounds as two interesting, new events. With another set of babies, he again played a C or a D. After the heart rates had returned to normal, he played the same note a second time. Amazingly, these babies had significantly less change in their heart rates when hearing the familiar note. They recognized what they had already heard!

Babies also recognize the pitch of voices. Babies can tell the difference between individual voices even before they are born. They can tell the difference between men and women and tend to prefer women's voices to men's. They recognize their mother's voice and prefer it to all other women's. Unborn babies can also learn to recognize their father's voice and prefer it to other men's and even women's. The more they hear a voice, the more they become attached t6 it-especially if it is not too loud and is sometimes in the adjusted higher pitch we instinctively use to talk with babies.

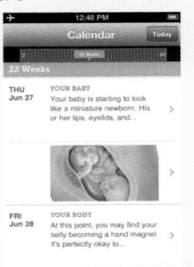

YOUR BABY Your baby is starting to look like a miniature newborn. His or her lips, eyelids, and ...

YOUR BODY At this point, you may find your belly becoming a hand magnet. It's perfectly okay to...

▶From BabyCenter's app:

Non-maternity clothes extender
Bellaband

$25-28 Amazon

Bellaband is an accessory that allows women to wear non-pregnant clothes longer, and fun maternity fashions a little sooner. It is a seamless, stretchy, comfortable knit band pregnant women can wear over their unbuttoned pants to keep them on. It works like a charm and is super-comfy! As far as I know, there's nothing similar out there. It is perfect for that 'in-between' phase where you don't fit into pre-baby pants but you're still to small for maternity clothes.

-- Tina Roth Eisenberg

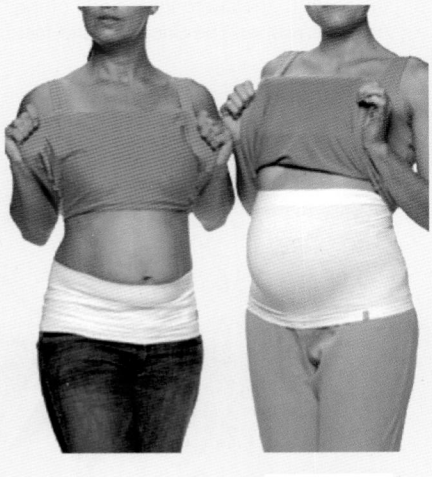

Ovulation tracker
Clearblue Fertility Monitor

$150 Amazon

This fertility monitor is designed to predict ovulation and optimize a couple's chances of conception. It requires test sticks which are used at the onset of a woman's menstruation to monitor urine once daily (best in the AM). The urine is applied to the test stick which is inserted into the monitor. When ovulation is at its peak, the monitor shows a dot within a circle. We referred to this as the "egg's in the basket." My wife and I had tried for quite some time to have a second child. Our firstborn son was conceived in vitro, and the second time around we paid for two attempts at a cost of approximately $16,000 — both failed. Just as we started to save up money to try again, we stumbled across the fertility monitor (it cost $250 when we bought it six years ago). We thought we'd just keep trying with the monitor until we'd saved enough for another in vitro attempt. To our surprise,

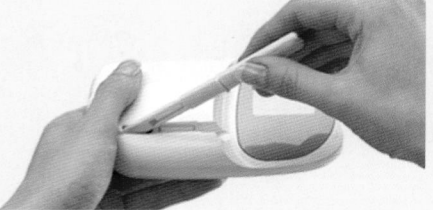

the monitor worked on only the second attempt using it. Much quicker than when we had our son. I'm pretty sure it would have worked on the first attempt, but at the time we actually didn't believe the readings were accurate. It showed my wife ovulating extremely late in her cycle. News to us! There are now monitors available that don't require test sticks ($50-60/pack). This one's still the best purchase we've ever made. The average cost for an in vitro attempt is $12,000 to $16,000, which was not covered under our medical plan. The first attempt is the most expensive and subsequent attempts can be less expensive depending on the number of embryos available from the first attempt. We had four embryos remaining and if we paid for that treatment, it would have run around $6,000. The unit saved us roughly $5,750, which was a blessing, but needless to say, the birth of our daughter using this monitor is one of the greatest joys in my life. We have since loaned our monitor to four other couples that were having trouble conceiving. All four mothers got pregnant — interestingly, all with girls.

-- Jeff Cruz

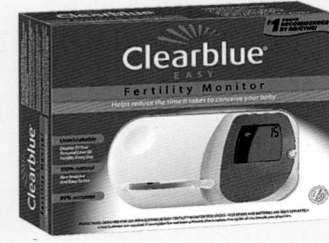

The most incomprehensible thing about the universe is that it is comprehensible. - Albert Einstein

Diapers

Natural Infant Hygiene takes the best of both these options and adds a few benefits of its own. The child enjoys the comfort, respect, body awareness, and hygiene of being diaper-free from infancy. The parent appreciates the convenience, and saved labour and expense. Best of all are the benefits that both parent and baby share: closeness, intimacy, mutual responsiveness, awareness and communication. Diaper freedom!

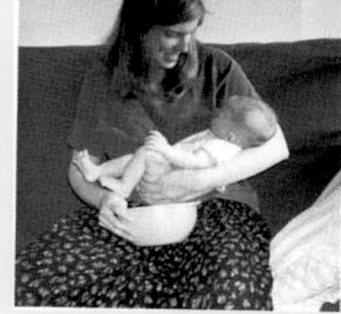

The infant twists his head and grimaces, signaling a need to poop.

•

From watching many babies and talking to their parents, I have come to the conclusion that individual babies signal their needs in many different ways. However, signals that the caregiver picks up and responds to, are often the ones that become reinforced and used most. It's like a natural feedback loop. This may be the reason why babies in some cultures reportedly exhibit specific signs, while in other cultures different signs are considered common.

•

In traditional societies, cueing sounds for peeing often resemble the sound of flowing water, or urination itself. It's interesting that these sounds are quite similar from continent to continent. From India to Botswana to Peru, a "sss, sss" sound had become an almost universal mothering signal. In places, a sharp "pssss" or a softer "shhh" or "shuuss" is used. In Japan, the childhood euphemistic equivalent of pee-pee is "shii shii". A low whistle is also sometimes used in Japan, and a steady whistling sound is the primary signal in China. As these cultures move towards urbanisation, a running faucet sometimes replaces the gentle hissing-type vocalizations, for example when peeing the baby over a sink.

Cueing for defecation is common as well. A grunting or straining imitation, such as "uhh" or the "ung-ga" used in Korea, is a frequent cue. Low humming or simply saying "hmmm" is also quite common.

•

It's not at all impossible to make longer journeys, for example by plane or in foreign countries, while practicing Natural Infant Hygiene. In airplanes or foreign travel situations where I was unsure how well I would be able to accommodate my baby's elimination needs, I put him in an easy-to-remove cloth diaper with snaps. On an extended trip abroad when my son was 11 months, we manage to travel for an entire day by plane, bus and ferry, with the same diaper. I still continued to "pee" him regularly, as though he were diaper-less, simply taking the diaper off and putting it back on when he was finished. That way if we got stuck in a customs or airplane bathroom line-up, or otherwise couldn't make it to a bathroom, it was not an emergency. Had this happened, I would have explained to my child that he could go in the diaper, while holding him in position and making the cueing sound, and then changed him a promptly as possible.

•

It's unlikely that you'll be able to practise Natural Infant Hygiene and never have an "accident." It's just as unlikely with a conventionally trained 3 or 4 year old. What is likely is that a baby, whose elimination needs are responded to from infancy, will stop having occasional lapses long before they are three.

•

For example, numerous parents have told me that it helped them to learn that pee was sterile when it leaves the body. We are so conditioned to think of urine as "dirty" that many people are unaware of this fact.

Basically, urine is a sterile fluid containing approximately 96%

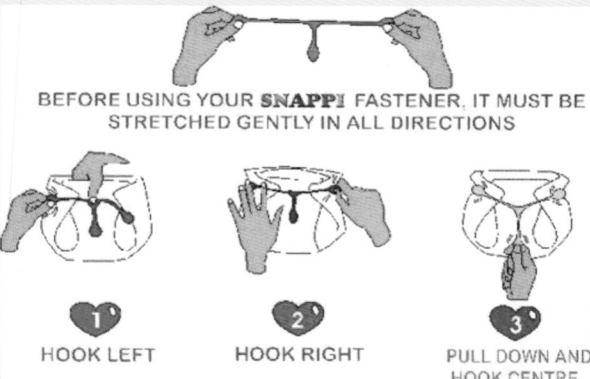

The Snappi diaper fastener is a rubber elongated "T" with plastic teeth at each of the three ends. The teeth hold the diaper securely, but are too short to go through the diaper and into the baby. Putting the Snappi on is about as easy as using Velcro, and taking it off is even easier. It's simple to clean and has a lifespan of about six months.

We tried an off-brand version first, and it nearly sent us back to pins — the teeth wouldn't hold, and the plastic bits that connect

BEFORE USING YOUR **SNAPPI** FASTENER, IT MUST BE STRETCHED GENTLY IN ALL DIRECTIONS

1 HOOK LEFT   2 HOOK RIGHT   3 PULL DOWN AND HOOK CENTRE

water. The rest is made up of valuable mineral salts and trace elements that the body needs for proper functioning, but which, at that moment in time, are available in excess and therefore discarded.

•

Although a natural hormone causes the kidneys to produce less urine at night, most babies do pee during the night, at least for the first weeks or months. Most diaper free infants will stay dry during naps by a few months, and can be taken to pee as soon as they awaken. Some diaper-free babies will also be dry all night by about the middle of their first year. Some children, like some adults, continue to use the bathroom during the night as they grow.

•

An American ethno-medical researcher once commented to me that Natural Infant Hygiene wouldn't be considered remarkable anywhere outside of North America or Europe. Only here is it absolutely astounding and fascinating.

Yes, Natural Infant Hygiene is amazing. Just as a mother's breast, producing the perfect quantity and quality of milk for a unique baby at a specific time, is amazing. Like breastfeeding, Natural Infant Hygiene strikes parents as unbelievably magical, awe-inspiring, and miraculous. And like breastfeeding, it is utterly practical, concrete, and down-to-earth doable.

When my son was newborn, I first noticed clear body signals for pooping, and relied mostly on general timing patterns for peeing (and watched for signals). Soon this shifted, as I became aware of the timing of regular bowel movements. Catching on to the process, my son also made increasingly clear signals when he needed to go. Before long, it became mostly an intuitive process, whereby I just knew when he needed to go whether I was watching him or not. I still used after sleep timing as well. It remained this way, until he grew old enough to begin using the cuing language himself, and was able to signal me vocally and through movement, and finally go independently. I still relied on timing and intuition for backup and nights. All three tools, both separately and interwoven, were invaluable at different phases.

The fourth tool, the one that is universally important across cultures, is cueing the baby. Cueing consists of holding the baby in a specific position, and using a specific "trigger" sound or action. This "cues" your child for the opportunity to relieve him or herself in a comfortable, secure, and hygienic way and provides the essential physical support your baby still needs. Just as you bring a baby to your breast to nurse until they can come themselves, you hold the baby in a comfortable way to eliminate until they can do so independently.

•

Sample excerpts from the FAQ at

Diaper Free Baby: http://www.diaperfreebaby.org/

Why Elimination Communication (EC)?

A few common reasons that parents choose to practice EC are: to recognize and respond to baby's self-awareness; to promote close communication between child and parent; to prevent diaper rash; to avoid struggles often associated with diaper changing and toilet training; and, as side benefits, to save money and use fewer environmental resources.

Don't the experts warn against potty training babies before they are ready?

It's important to note that this is Elimination Communication, not training. This is a gentle process that follows the infant's cues and needs, and is never coercive or punitive. As such, this practice is consistent with the baby's development and maturity.

the teeth to the stretchable body of the "T" always separated from the rubber. The Snappi brand fasteners never gave us any trouble.

-- Scott Noyes

. When you are through changing, you are through. - Bruce Barton

Essential parental skill
Solve Your Child's Sleep Problems
$14 Richard Ferber; 2006, 464 p.

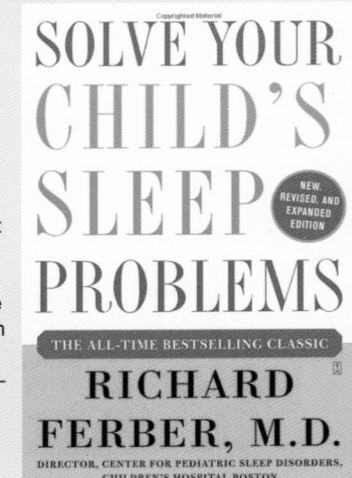

I was trying to think of the book that has had the greatest effect on my life. Books like Zen and the Art of Motorcycle Maintenance, or The Fountainhead carried a lot of philosophical weight at the time I'd read them in college but they seem like junk upon re-reading them now. So, I asked myself again, what book has really changed my life? Then it hit me: it was, without a doubt, Richard Ferber's Solve Your Child's Sleep Problems.

We have two kids, one age six, the other 11 months. When our six year old was a baby, we put her to sleep by holding her and rocking her. She would wake up every couple of hours, crying for us to come back and rescue her. We finally gave up and let her sleep with us. It was the only way we could get any sleep. To this day, she demands that one of us crawls into bed with her until she falls asleep.

When we had our other daughter, she would cry for us every hour at night. The whole family was exhausted from the ordeal. Would we have to suffer this ordeal for three more years?

Some friends told us to "Ferberize" her and we'd all be able to sleep soundly. We were skeptical, but we bought the book and followed the instructions faithfully. In a nutshell, Ferberization entails putting your baby in her crib, kissing her goodnight and walking out of the room. She'll cry, of course. After five minutes, you walk in and reassure her, then walk out again. This time you wait ten minutes. You repeat this, adding five minutes between return visits. It sounds cruel. As a parent, your instinct is to run to your baby as soon as she starts crying. But in this case, not following your instincts is the best course of action. It took exactly two nights to Ferberize our baby. She has learned to fall asleep on her own, and when she wakes up at night, she knows how to fall back asleep on her own. Best of all, she is happy, confident, and well-rested. And so are we. We have our nights, and as a result, our days back.

While this was truly a life-changing book, you really don't need to read it. Other chapters address the nature of sleep and how to deal with more unusual child sleep problems, but for most people, the procedure I described above is all you need. Reading the book, however, made me feel better psychologically about going through with it.

-- Mark Frauenfelder

I have three kids. This method works. -- KK

•

Better than lying with your toddler or young child until he falls asleep at night is for him to fall asleep with a "transitional object" — a stuffed animal, a doll, a toy, a special blanket. The toy will often help him accept the nighttime separation from you and can be a source of reassurance and comfort when he is alone. It will give him a feeling of having a little control over his world because he may have the toy or blanket with him whenever he wants, which he cannot expect from you. His toy will not get up and leave after he falls asleep and it will still be there whenever he wakes.

Simplest baby carrier
New Native Baby Sling
$40 New Native

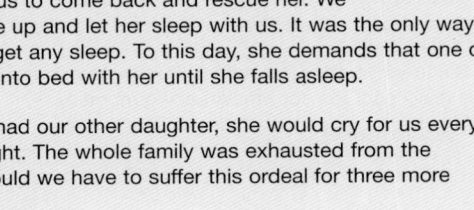

Like most Americans, I hauled my firstborn around in his carseat/infant carrier. Never again. For my second child, I researched slings extensively, and bought a New Native. It's simpler than any other sling, including the Maya sling.

New Native is just one piece of fabric, hemmed and stitched into a big pocket. That means no adjustment rings or buckles to come loose or fiddle with. Accordingly, it's sized. I wear a medium. My husband, who is much bigger than I am, wears my (medium) sling as well — there are three sizes, small, medium, and large, and the medium fits a pretty wide range of people.

I've slung my second baby since day one. She has taken countless naps in it. The sleek, professional look of the New Native means that a lot of people take it for fashion. While my daughter was small, they didn't even know I had a baby on. I wore it to the office and even taught class with it.

At nine months I can count on one hand the number of times my daughter has ridden in a stroller. Everywhere I go people who see it wish they had known about it when they were carrying babies, and ask me where I got my sling: New Native.

-- Donna Bowman

Back/front/hip infant carrier
Ergobaby
$95 Ergobaby

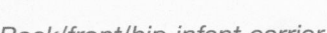

We carried our seven-month-old daughter around Prague and Leipzig for hours in a standard BabyBjörn this last winter and she/we loved it — cozy and comfortable. The problem: it's only a front carrier, and since then, she's gotten heavier, which started to take it's toll on our backs (imagine carrying a bowling ball strapped to your chest.). Now we're using an Ergo,

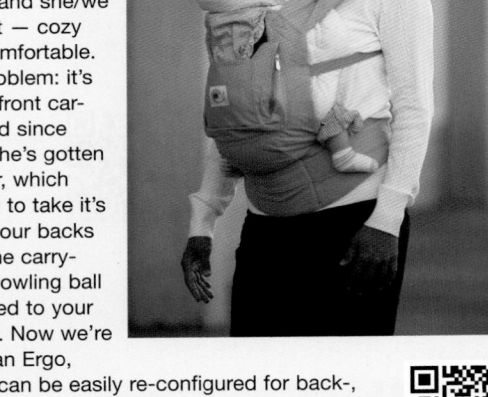

which can be easily re-configured for back-, front-, or side-carrying. Since it buckles around your waist, most of the weight is put on your hips. While an "original" BabyBjörn is rated for use with babies up to 25 lbs, I tried ours with our daughter when she was 15 lbs and it was a no go. She's heavier now, and the Ergo remains incredibly comfortable: I've noticed much less lower back strain.

Learning to scoot the baby around your hips, onto your back, and into the Ergo without outside help is a bit of a production at first, but no problem once you get the hang of it. If you want to put the pack in front or on your hip, it's quite simple, too (ed. note: the videos are quite helpful). Like the BabyBjörrn, the Ergo is made of cotton and cleans up very easily with just a sponge most of the time. It can be washed in a machine, too. There's a cotton hood (the green fabric in the pic) that attaches with snap buttons for when the baby is sleeping — protects her from the elements, and keeps her head from flopping around.

Note: BabyBjörrn does make an "Active" model (which we have not tried) with lower back support that is supposed to "ease the burden." However, you cannot convert that one to a hip/back carrier.

-- Brandon Summers

Distributed weight baby-wearing
Moby Wrap
$48 Amazon

There are so many baby carriers on the market right now, and I've tried a good deal of them: various slings, the Ergo Baby, Baby Bjorn, and the like all tend to put the bulk of the baby's weight on one part of the back. While there is some distribution with shoulder or hip straps, the weight is still focused primarily on one area (shoulder/hips). I had seen the Moby Wrap and had decidedly avoided trying it, as it looked complicated and uncomfortable. A friend finally convinced me to try one, and I fell in love.

Not only is my baby securely snuggled up against my body, but it is incredibly comfortable to wear. It looks to be about 20 feet of fabric that you wrap around your body and slip the baby into. No doubt based on some age-old method of carrying babies, it is by far the most comfortable and versatile carrier I've seen. Because it crosses around your body so many times in different locations, it distributes the weight of the child to a variety of places: shoulders, upper back, lower back and hips. Plus, the baby can face forwards, backwards or sideways when worn on your front, and she can be worn on your hips or back as well.

While it does require an introduction on how to put it on, once you have figured out how it works, it could not be simpler to use. The basic concept is that you create a cross of fabric on your body and slip the baby between you and the cross, with her legs hanging out between. Also, because of the criss-cross over your shoulders you can nestle the baby's head under the wrap, allowing full protection from the sun or, more importantly for the new parent, a quiet zone in which to nap, even at a bustling market. For all its simplicity this is simply the best baby carrier available.

There are several variations on this idea — one with rings, one made of more stretchy material, one with fancy patterns — from various manufacturers, but the basic design is all the same — wrap the fabric around your body, slide the baby in and enjoy.

-- Elizabeth Sendil

Bedwetting solution
Enurad
$309 enurad.com

Our son is a very sound sleeper and had problems with bedwetting. We tried everything we could think of. Finally I stumbled across a mention of Enurad in a parents' forum. It's a wireless wetness sensor that you place in the child's underwear. A standard alarm clock has been modified to ring at the slightest wetness. Enurad combined with limiting nighttime fluids solved the problem in a couple of months. He wore the device for sometime after that as an insurance policy. He just slept better knowing it was there. At $210 it's not inexpensive, but worth every penny. Enurad doesn't have a US distrubuter that I know of. I ordered ours from Austrailia. Highly Recommended.

-- Johnboy

According to the most recent science moisture alarms are the most lasting medical cures for nocturnal bedwetting, better than commonly prescribed drugs.

-- KK

You use a standard self-adhesive panty-shield. Cut it up...

...and place the sensor inside it

Child Care

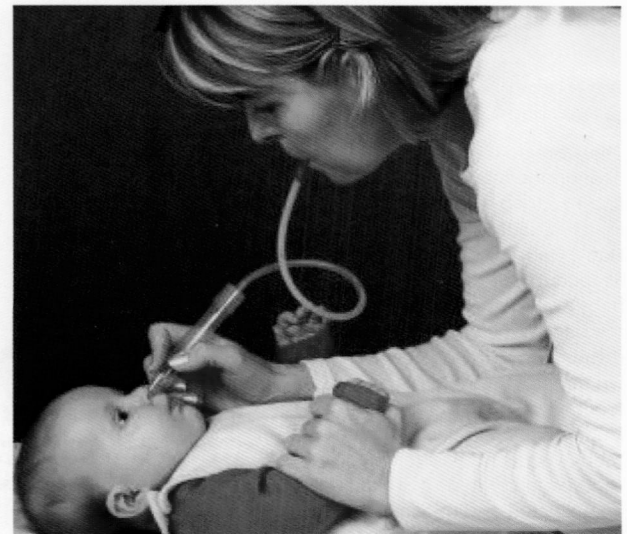

Child-friendly mucus removal
Nosefrida Nasal Aspirator

$15 Amazon

The Nosefrida is a remarkably effective tool for sucking snot out of a kid's nose. It's basically a flexible plastic tube with a mouthpiece on one end and a snot-collection chamber on the other. You put the mouthpiece in your mouth, press the open end of the snot-collection chamber against your kid's nostril (it doesn't go very far inside the nose), and SUCK. An inline filter prevents the snot from ending up in your mouth. The filter only needs to be changed when it gets gunked-up. Such gunking can be avoided by stopping periodically and blowing the collected snot out into a sink or emesis basin. Otherwise, if you keep filling up the snot-collection chamber, it eventually makes its way up to the filter. To clean, I just disassemble it and run warm water through it. Real easy.

It sounds disgusting and bizarre, but it works like a charm. If you've got a snotty kid, it's the best $15 you'll ever spend. My daughter got her first cold when she was three months old. It was a real nasty one, with lots of nasal congestion. My wife is a family doctor, and she suggested the standard course of action: spray saline up the kid's nose and try sucking the nastiness out with a bulb syringe. Anybody who's ever used a standard bulb syringe knows that it's a suboptimal tool for this project, for two main reasons: (1) A bulb syringe is too small to generate adequate suction to pull thick snot out of a kid's nose, and (2) little kids hate having a bulb syringe stuck up their nostrils. Can you blame 'em?

-- Mike Pedone

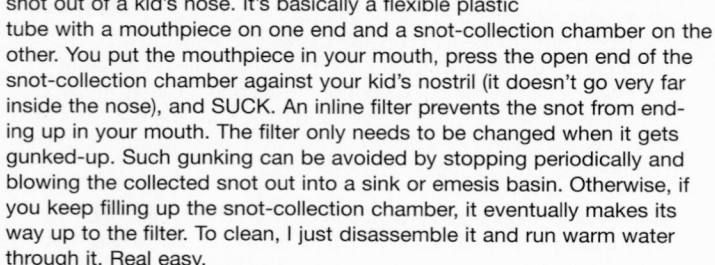

Applying drops confidentially
Blinkless EyeDropper

$11 Westons Internet

I've had this little gray tool for years. You open the little container up and put in your little bottle of eyedrops. Snap it back shut. When you want to use the drops (for me, every morning while still in bed, half-asleep and with shaky hands) you pop the top back on a hinge–the top part being shaped like an eye-wash cup somewhat–unscrew your bottle cap and pop the top back on. Lift to your eye and squeeze the device; there are squeeze panels on either side of it. The top fits in your eye socket and keeps the dropper tip at the right distance from the eye, so you don't:

a) blink

b) contaminate the tip

c) shake drops everywhere but in your eye, and

d) stab yourself in the eye with the eyedrops bottle.

Since I developed a tremor, the thing is indispensable. I don't know how I'd get on without it.

-- Elle Walter

Also perfect for kids; the black hood encourages their eyes to remain open. -- KK

Hygienic breast pump
Ameda Purely Yours Breast Pump

$150 Amazon

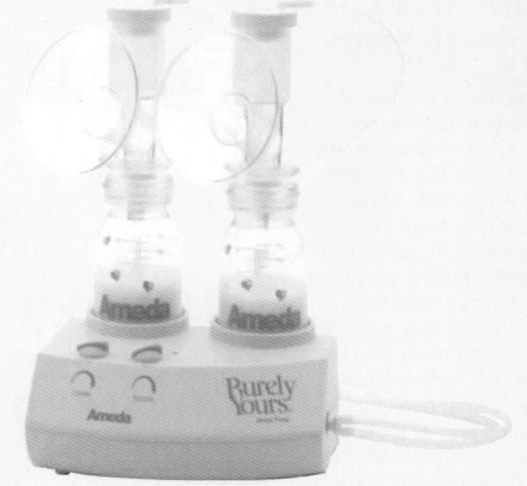

I found out about the Ameda Purely Yours line of breast pumps while my wife and I were searching for a breast pump to supplement her breastfeeding of our newborn. She has been using the pump every day for about 7 months now, with great results. This breast pump allows her to stockpile breast milk in our freezer, which gives us a chance to have nights out without having to worry about rushing home for feedings, but the technology behind how the Ameda Purely Yours works is what's very cool, and worth mentioning.

As far as breast pumps are concerned, there are wide varieties available from many different manufacturers, each performing the same basic task; but what separates this one is the hygienic nature of the pump. This breast pump has what Ameda calls a closed-system; meaning the expressed breast milk comes in no contact with outside air or contaminants thereby making it much safer for providing bottled breast milk for your baby.

The closed-system is accomplished by use of what Ameda calls their HygieniKit Milk Collection System. This system uses a special silicone diaphragm, which contracts to provide suction, while eliminating the existence of outside air in the pump tubing, as well as the pump motor. Other breast pumps, like the popular Medela Pump-In-Style, have had many complaints about breast milk and outside contaminants getting into the pump tubing, causing mold to develop in both the tubing and the actual pump mechanism. Needless to say, ingesting mold and harmful bacteria is not the best for a newborn baby.

In addition to the hygiene features, the Ameda also has a lot of custom options for more efficient pumping. You can adjust the pump suction speed, as well as the strength, to more accurately mimic the suckling rhythm of your baby, which has been shown to greatly affect the level of breast milk output.

So, there you go. The Ameda Purely Yours breast pump is a really cool tool for breastfeeding moms.

-- Steven Jones

Pacifier for administering meds
Kidz-Med Medicine Dispenser

$2 Amazon

My infant daughter has acid-reflux. Although a medicine dropper works for administering Zantac a couple times a day, she always makes a terrible face and winds up spitting out a good portion. This dispenser takes advantage of her natural tendency to suck: The medicine reaches the farthest into her mouth. I worried it seemed mean to use something she associates with comfort to give her something she'd hate, but after a few weeks of seeing those faces, I decided it'd be worth trying. The pacifier was a little big when she was a couple of months old but she took it just fine. Now, at almost five months, she's grown into it. Occasionally, if she mouths but doesn't suck the pacifier, we use the plunger to push it on in. Either way, she hasn't made a single bad face since we've been using it, and I don't have to mop up all the Zantac she used to spit back out. I read a review of a similar product — the same concept executed by another company. People complained the other one leaked. This is now my second medicine pacifier (I lost the first one on a road trip); neither has leaked. The best $6 I've spent on baby things.

-- Amanda Long

You can teach happiness
The Optimistic Child

$12 Martin E. P. Seligman, 2007, 352 p.

Optimism is not a mere sunny outlook on life, nor is it simple self esteem. Rather it is a type of self-knowledge that can make people healthier and happier. And 20 years of controlled scientific clinical trials have proved that it can be learned. Furthermore, optimism can be taught to children. There is probably no better gift to kids (your own or others) than to teach them how to train themselves to be happy. If for no other reason than the fact that pessimism leads to illness and depression. This book is based on large-scale programs that have taught kids of all backgrounds and dispositions how to be more optimistic.

-- KK

•

Why should we bother? Isn't pessimism just a posture with no effects in the world? Unfortunately not. I have studied pessimism for the last twenty years, and in more than one thousand studies, involving more than half a million children and adults, pessimistic people do worse than optimistic people in three ways: First, they get depressed much more often. Second, they achieve less at school, on the job, and on the playing field than their talents augur. Third, their physical health is worse than that of optimists. So holding a pessimistic theory of the world may be the mark of sophistication, but it is a costly one. It is particularly damaging for a child, and if your child has already acquired pessimism, he is at risk for doing less well in school. He is at risk for greater problems of depression

and anxiety. He may be at risk for worse physical health than he would have if he were an optimist. And worse, pessimism in a child can become a lifelong, self-fulfilling template for looking at setbacks and losses. The good news is that he can, with your help, learn optimism.

•

Optimistic children explain good events to themselves in terms of permanent causes. They point to traits and abilities that they will always have, like being hard-working, likable, or lovable. They use "always" when they describe the causes of good events. Pessimists think in terms of transient causes. "I was in a good mood," or "I practiced hard this time." Their explanations of good events are qualified with the words, "sometimes" and "today," and they often use the past tense and limit it to time only ("I practiced hard this time."). When children who believe their successes have permanent causes do well, they will try even harder next time. Children who see temporary reasons for good events may give up even when they succeed, believing the success was a fluke.

The OPTIMISTIC CHILD

A Proven Program to Safeguard Children Against Depression and Build Lifelong Resilience

MARTIN E. P. SELIGMAN, Ph.D.
author of *Learned Optimism*

The line dividing the real and the imaginary is more imaginary than real. - Omar Guzman

Tidy Snack Dispenser
Munchkin Snack Catcher
$6 for 2 Amazon

Anyone with small kids knows about snack catchers; new parents should check them out. These ingenious cups let little fingers in to grab cereal bits, crackers, or dried fruit, etc, but won't let food out when the cup tips over. The flexible rubbery (BPA free) flaps serves as a one-way gate. Keeps the food clean, car seats and floors tidy, and hungry toddlers satisfied. There are now other competing brands using the same principle. They also come in larger sized containers.

-- KK

Less air bottle
Dr. Brown's Baby Bottles
$22 Amazon

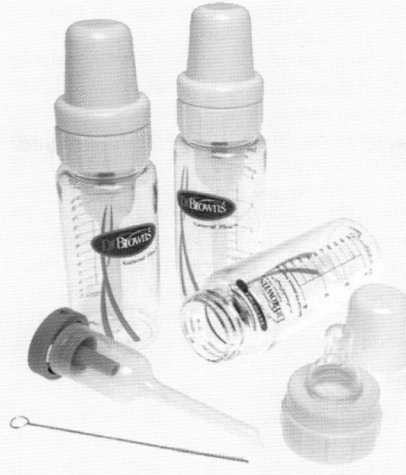

Even if you intend to exclusively breastfeed your infant, you may find you'll need to supplement with a bottle occasionally. Or if father is needed to handle feeding duties when mom's not around, you'll need a bottle. For those times — or if you are bottle feeding all the way — Dr. Brown's Baby Bottles are the only bottles you'll want to use. We found these Bottles to be absolute lifesavers, and have recommended them without hesitation to other new parents who have immediately confirmed our experiences with them: less gas, colic and other feeding-related unpleasantness.

The secret to Dr. Brown's Baby Bottles, apparently, is the tube system inside — it prevents the infant from swallowing air, which makes for a happier baby (and by extension, happier parents). As baby eats and the bottle drains, the internal tube directs incoming air to above the bottle contents, so the young one's not working against a vacuum. This is supposed to be easier on their eardrums, too. Make of it what you will, but we've managed to avoid the ear-infection boogeyman which seems to hit nearly every other young family we know. Also, unlike similar systems that use collapsing bags to keep out the vacuum, you don't need to keep a supply of the little bags around.

The only downside I can see to Dr. Brown's Baby Bottles is that there are more parts to clean – the nipple, ring, rubber disk/valve and rigid tube inside. (The FAQ says you need to use their nipples. We never tried any others when we were using them so I don't know if you can use others.)

Our kids were about 90% breastfed (the last 2 of our 5 kids didn't use bottles at all), but we used these bottles extensively when we were sharing feeding duties or had to supplement with formula. A co-worker who tried them on our recommendation came back the very next morning — nearly in tears — thanking me. The bottles are available in 2, 4 and 8 oz. sizes.

-- James Quinby

A teaching cup
Doidy Cup
$9 Amazon

We discovered this cup when our second child was having problems gulping from a spouted cup or bottle causing her to choke and vomit. A Doidy cup was suggested and it immediately solved the problem, as she could suddenly see what she was doing.

With our third child we have used them since starting him on solids, and they are also much easier for the parent or caregiver who is feeding the child to see what they are doing. I even hear good reports of this being used to top a newborn up with milk whilst breastfeeding is still establishing. A fantastic, if simple, idea. And they come in lovely jolly colours too; my son is particularly fond of his pink one!

-- Nathalie Marshall

Rollable, portable kid's placemat
Tiny Diner Portable Placemat
$11 Amazon

I am a grandmother who enjoys taking her grandchildren out to eat. Many times I've wanted to push the booster seat or high chair (without the tray) up to the table, cut the food up, and serve it to my grandchildren on the table with me. This tiny diner placemat covers the table and provides a clean eating surface that also catches spilled food, and has been my favorite take along tool.

It rolls up and fits in my purse, washes off easily, and helps me control the cleanliness of my grandchildren's eating surfaces. I have seen disposable models, however they do not have the trough for spilled food, and are not re-useable and therefore more expensive. I have used this mat for 2 years, and take it with me anywhere I take my grandkids.

[This mat is made out of a material called Thermoplastic Elastomer (TPE) and is a non-latex, non-PVC, non-phthalate, non-BPA material.]

-- Constance Smith

Better bibs
Ikea Prickar Bibs
$ IKEA

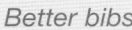

I've been using these bibs for over a year, and they are the best of the dozens I've had and the only ones I use now. They are cheap; a pack of two costs $5. They go on easily with a sturdy velcro closure on the back. I've washed them countless times and they're still like new. The long sleeves and total coverage keep clothes 100% clean.

They are water repellant and even have a flap on the bottom to catch stray food and liquids. They can be wiped clean of small messes with a wet sponge and be ready for reuse right away. For big messes they can be taken off inside out to contain the spill. I always keep some in my bag and find them to be one of the things I can't go without.

-- Maria Piccolo

Infant food catcher
BabyBjörn Bib
$11 Amazon

The humble bib, a highly functional item that (usually) keeps a baby's clothes from getting splattered with food, has been around a long time without too many major improvements. Until now. Bibs made of non-porous, moldable, resilient silicone are a real step forward. The key features of the one we have from BabyBjörn are its shape and washability. The bib projects outward and terminates in an upward scoop, which not only covers more of the lap, but also catches and collects most dropped food that would miss an ordinary bib. So food that falls in it needn't be wasted; it's easy to spoon food out of it and back into the baby's mouth. We used to have several cloth bibs in regular use, which we rinsed out after each use and hung to dry. We had one oilcloth bib that was better than the others in that it rinses off fairly easily and dries quickly. But the silicone bib has replaced them all, because it rinses off with supreme ease, has no seams to catch crud, and is dry almost immediately. Although a quick rinse is sufficient, clean freaks can also put it in the dishwasher. It attaches around the baby's neck easily and securely, with a fastener integral to the bib, of the same material. There's an ocean of cuteness in the world of baby gear, but dealing with an infant or a toddler is made more manageable by functionality, not gear decorated with adorable pink butterflies. This bib really makes life easier.

-- Michael Wilmeth

Space isn't remote at all. It's only an hour's drive away if your car could go straight upwards. -Fred Hoyle

453

Essential kid carrier

Kelty Pathfinder

$280 Amazon

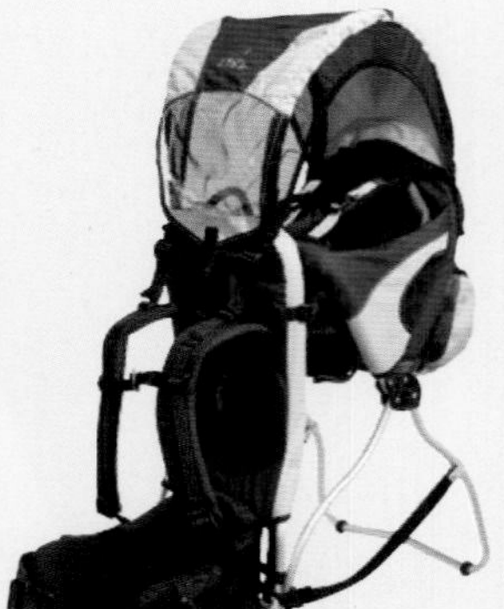

I've used this kid-carrier backpack from Kelty, called the Pathfinder, nearly every day for the past year. For instance, just today I took a bird-watching hike with my 16-month-old son, Ivan, who loves traveling in the pack. Previous to the Pathfinder I was using an expensive Phil-and-Ted Backpack for a few months, but it was inferior. It is attractive and stylish and it has what seems to be a more comfortable seat for the child, but the adjustments are limited for positioning the child. It's essential when using one of these packs that the kid's weight is well-balanced over the wearer's hips, and not too far back. I find that the Phil and Ted's pack isn't adjustable enough, so that my child becomes cantilevered too far off of my back. In contrast, the Kelty pack's adjustments allow me to place my child in such a way that his weight rests on my hips and doesn't put too much strain on my back and neck.

The previously reviewed and recommended Ergo Baby carrier is an outstanding product, if not the best overall child carrier. It's great for wearing young infants in front, and it can—like this Kelty— be used to wear a larger toddler on your back. However, the kid is directly against your back, so any type of serious hiking would be out of the question because it would be too uncomfortable and sweaty. I like to get a workout in while I'm out with my son, and with the heat he generates having him directly on my back would be miserable.

Like the other packs in this class, the Pathfinder is designed to balance a lot of weight (up to 44 lbs.), so that it feels comfortable for the wearer and for the child while you are really hiking. The pack itself is lightweight, and comes with a very useful sun/rain canopy. The padding on the back and the positioning of the child both keep my back from getting hot and sweaty. The Pathfinder has two hip pockets accessible while you're wearing the pack, and the main storage compartment that rests behind the kid detaches as a small daypack, diaper bag.

What sets the old Pathfinder apart from the top-of-the-line Ortlieb and Deuter models — and the current Pathfinder 3.0, Kelty's current top-of-the-line version – is simply its low price. Functionally it's the same as, or at least very similar to, the high-end newer models, but with out-of-style colors.

You can get these classic packs cheap on eBay because parents receive them as gifts but then never use them. It requires some effort to adjust them properly, and more importantly it's simply hard to carry 32 pounds (my kid + cargo + the pack itself) on your back if you're not used to it, especially hiking uphill or on uneven terrain. So there's an abundance of high-quality inexpensive used backpacks in excellent condition. I bought mine unused for $65 through Craigslist, versus about $275 for the new Pathfinder 3.0.

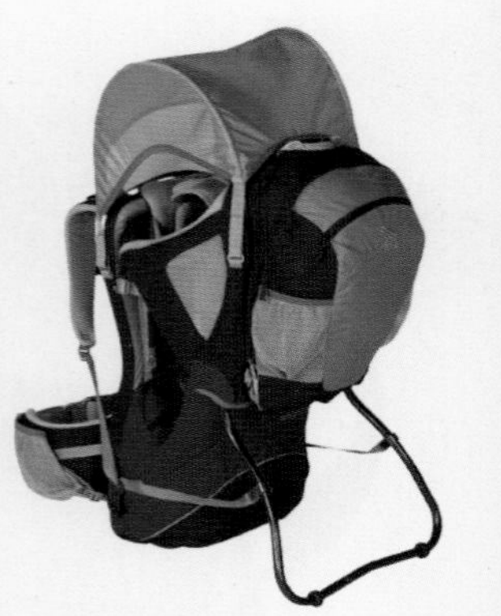

-- Elon Schoenholz

New-parent handbook

The Baby Book

$14 William Sears, et al., 2013 (revised and updated), 784 p.

New parents don't want your advice unless they ask for it. Trust me. Nothing invites unwelcome advice like having a baby. And nothing in my life has confronted me with a steeper learning curve than becoming a father. Of the many resources my wife and I turned to in the first couple of years after our daughter was born, this one's a favorite. William and Martha Sears (M.D. and R.N., respectively, and parents of eight) are the Dr. Spocks of the current generation, and they seem to have been influenced by his favoring increased parental flexibility and affection over an emphasis on discipline and character building. The Sears's sage and sober advice always feels friendly, even-handed; their joint perspective is broad.

There's nothing revolutionary to their approach: Attachment parenting is their emphasis. And simply put, attachment parenting as they define it means being very involved and engaged and responding to who your child is and what she needs. And enjoying parenting in the process, of course. Makes sense.

If you're about to become a parent, you'll be well-served with this exhaustive guidebook. If someone close to you is a soon-to-be parent, share your wisdom only if it's sought and buy him The Baby Book. The Sears' Discipline Book is a worthwhile read, too.

-- Elon Schoenholz

•

The Seven Baby B's of Attachment Parenting

1. birth bonding
2. belief in the signal value of your baby's cries
3. breastfeeding
4. babywearing
5. bedding close to baby
6. balance and boundaries
7. beware of baby trainers

•

Beware of Baby Trainers

Be prepared to be the target of well-meaning advisers who will shower you with detachment advice, such as: "Let her cry it out," "Get her on a schedule," "You shouldn't still be nursing her!" and "Don't pick her up so much, you're spoiling her!" If carried to the extreme, baby training is a lose-lose situation: Baby loses trust in the signal value of her cues, and parents lose trust in their ability to read and respond to baby's cues. As a result, a distance can develop between baby and parent, which is just the opposite of the closeness that develops with attachment parenting…

The basis of baby training is to help babies become more "convenient." It is based upon the misguided assumption that babies cry to manipulate, not to communicate.

•

Best Fats for Babies

Not only should infants get 40 to 50 percent of their calories from fats, they should eat the right variety of fats. In addition to breast milk, the best fats for babies (and also for children and adults) come from marine and vegetable sources. Ranked in order of nutritional content they are:

- seafood (especially salmon)
- flax oil
- avocados
- vegetable oils
- nut butters (because of possible allergies, delay peanut butter until after two years)

•

Discipline Begins at Birth

Discipline begins as a relationship, not a list of methods. The first stage of discipline — the attachment stage — begins at birth and develops as you

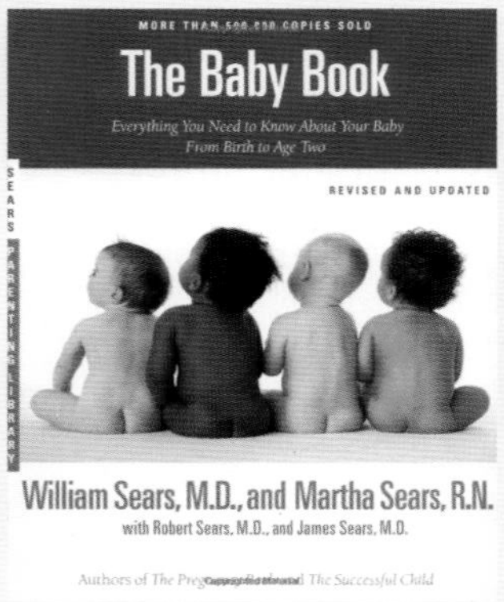
The Baby Book
Everything You Need to Know About Your Baby From Birth to Age Two
REVISED AND UPDATED
William Sears, M.D., and Martha Sears, R.N.
with Robert Sears, M.D., and James Sears, M.D.

and your baby grow together. The big three of attachment parenting (breastfeeding, wearing baby, and responding to baby's cues) are actually your first disciplinary actions. A baby who is on the receiving end of attachment parenting feels right, and a person who feels right is more likely to act right. An attachment parented baby is more receptive to authority because he operates from a foundation of trust. This baby spends the early months of his life learning that the world is a responsive and trusting place to be.

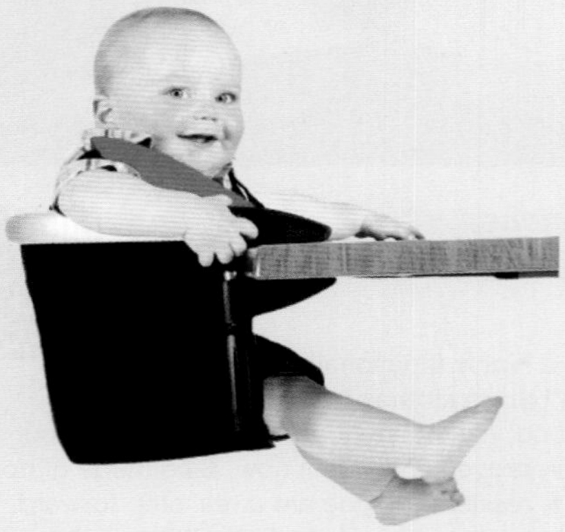

Space-saving high chair alternative

Phil & Teds Lobster

$80 philandteds.com

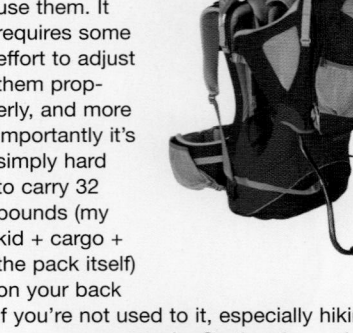

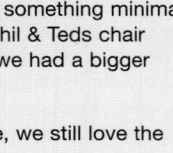

When our son was born, we were living in a tiny one-bedroom apartment in central London, and were about to move back to America. We wanted something minimal but effective, and we thought the Phil & Teds chair would be a stopgap measure until we had a bigger house.

Now that we have the bigger house, we still love the P&T chair. Our baby can sit at the table with us, and because he has the whole table in front of him much less food ends up on the floor than when he's in a traditional high chair. We can also clamp the chair to the breakfast counter in the kitchen, so he can eat while we cook. And in some small way our house is less "babified" than it would be with a real high chair.

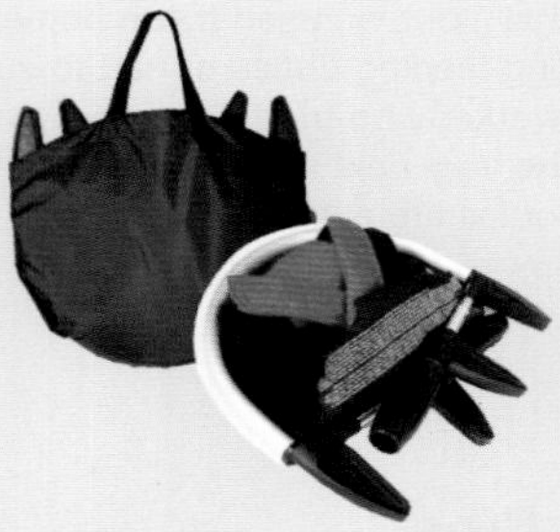

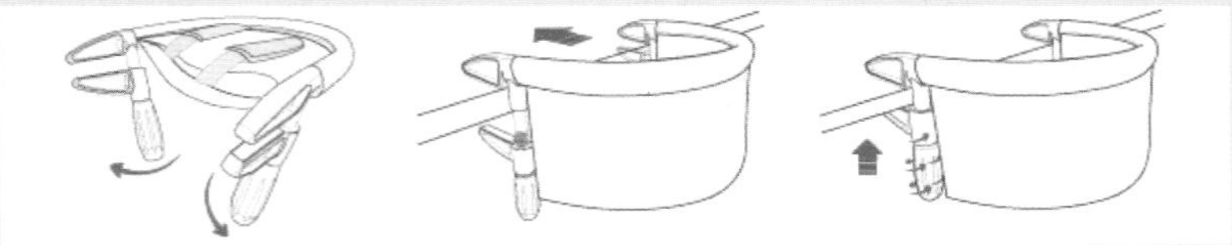

Some disadvantages:
The specs say it can support up to 37 lbs, roughly a child 3 years of age. When our son is a bit bigger, we'll have to find another solution. Also, the chair uses C-clamps that open about 3", and sit in about 3". That limits the types of tables we can use it with: obviously no glass table tops, but also no tables with a wide lip.

The model that we used called a MeToo which is no longer available in the US. P&T is now selling a model called the Lobster with a plastic ratcheting claw clamp, which may not be as robust as the metal clamp on ours. I haven't used any other travel high chairs, but we prefer the P&T chair to the many traditional high chairs we've tried. For small-space living, it's an excellent solution.

-- Ashish Ranpura

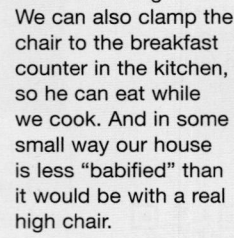

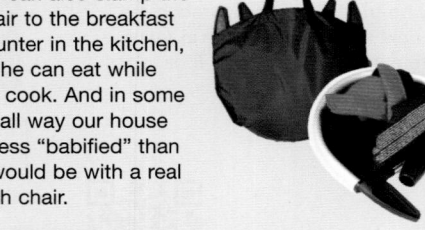

Best double stroller

Phil & Teds Double Stroller

$400 philandteds.com

After a year of experience using Phil and Ted's E3 stroller, with two-kid kit, we think it's simply amazing.

The handling on the E3 stroller is superb. Unlike side-by-side strollers, the width on the E3 is no problem, and the front wheel pivots so you never have any trouble negotiating the tightest areas. Medium sized real tires mean it's no trouble to move over uneven terrain (dirt paths are easy). Construction is excellent, and the whole unit moves with the smoothness and solidity of a well made machine.

It's not the lightest stroller you can buy, but we bought the travel bag accessory and have checked it on multiple airplane flights with no trouble at all. Folds well enough to fit in the back of our car when we take day trips as well.

Of the various ways you can set-up the stroller (see their website) we've had, by far, the most experience with it setup for two seated kids. My wife was concerned that the back seat would be a tough sell for the kids, but our 3 year old seems to prefer it, which was a surprise.

At $380 for the basic unit (the S4 is the latest model), we thought hard about spending that much money on a stroller. But to this day, we remark on how GOOD that purchase looks in retrospect. We use it daily — well worth the extra money in our view.

-- Brian Fleming

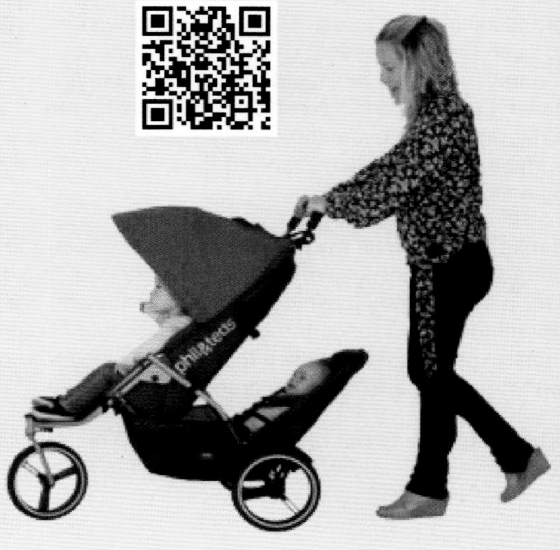
phil&teds

There are no wrong notes on the piano, just better choices. - Thelonious Monk

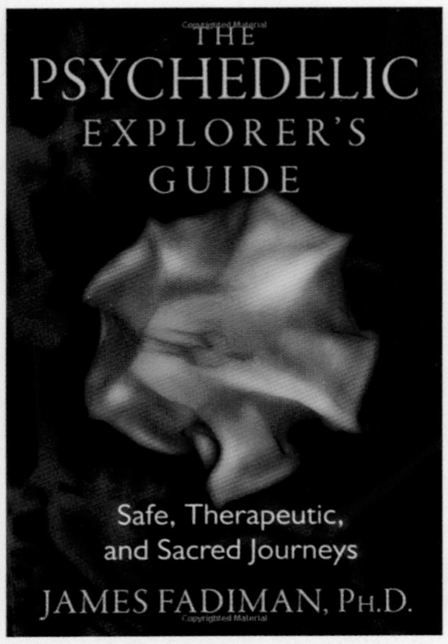

How to drop acid

The Psychedelic Explorer's Guide

$13 James Fadiman, 2001, 352 p.

I took LSD for the first time on my 50th birthday. It was a spiritual event. Before that I looked long and hard for some kind of guide to orient me on what to expect, how to set the atmosphere, and in general how to go about this in a sacramental way. Most of the little specks of advice I found about "dropping acid" dated from the 1960s, and were not very helpful. I need some utilitarian guidelines, a checklist. How much do I take? Alone or with others? Outside, or inside? What happens if it turns nasty?

I wish I had had this book. James Fadiman was one of the original scientists testing LSD when it was still legal in the US and he has gathered a bookful of useful advice from his own research and in the collections of others. Fadiman promotes guided sessions, where a guide accompanies the voyager. (I used that method myself.) This new manual supplies very practical advice on how to attain the goal listed in its subtitle: Safe, Therapeutic, and Sacred Journeys. And it covers other psychedelics besides acid, although less deeply. Another bonus: it is helpful for either the guide or the voyager.

-- *KK*

•

Another way to deepen the connections made during the session is to invite the voyager to gaze into a full-size handheld mirror. The voyager may see his or her own face aging or becoming younger, and may also see people of different sexes, ages, and races from different historical periods. If the voyager becomes concerned or fearful, suggest that he or she focus on the eyes in the mirror. Eyes usually remain constant through the changes and are reassuring. Even if you have had a similar experience on a journey of your own, don't offer an interpretation of what is being seen.

•

As with most other positive experiences, we usually want to do it again. However, psychedelic voyages are not like most other experiences. If you take them again too soon, you cannot expect that they will have the same effect. The rule of thumb is the more profound the experience, the longer you should wait before doing it again. The Guild of Guides suggests a minimum of six months between entheogenic journeys because it takes at least that long for the learning and insights to be absorbed and integrated into your life.

•

Crisis FAQ excerpts

If someone seems to be having a hard time, gently ask them if they would like someone to sit with them. If it seems disturbing to them to have someone sitting with them, have someone nearby keep an eye on them unobtrusively.

Not Forever: If they are connected enough to worry about their sanity, assure them that the state is due to a psychoactive and they will return to their "home" state of mind in time.

Relaxing: It can be very, very hard to relax in the middle of dying or being pulled apart from demons, but tell them that you are there to make sure nothing happens to their physical body. One of the most important things during really difficult internal processes is to learn to be okay with the fact that they are happening, to "relax" one's attempt to stop the experience and just let it happen.

•

Although no formal research exists on sub-perceptual doses, a growing number of people have been using psychedelics this way. When people take a sub-perceptual amount--for LSD, about 10 micrograms (also known as a micro-dose, sub-dose, or "tener")--the common sensory effects associated with higher doses of LSD or psilocybin-- a glow or a sparkle around the ages of living things, sensory interweaving such as hearing in color or tasting music, and a loosening of ego boundaries--do not appear. What follow are reports from people who have used these small doses of LSD and psilocybin. Some are from longtime users and others are from people trying them for the first time.

•

After my senior year at Harvard, in 1960, I went off to live in Europe. The following spring, Alpert showed up in Paris with Timothy Leary, on their way to Copenhagen to deliver the first paper on their work with psilocybin. He was in great condition and said to me, "The most wonderful thing in the world has happened, and I want to share it with you." I replied, as anyone would, "Of course." Then he reached in his pocket and took out a little bottle of pills.

My reaction was, "Pills? Drugs? What kind of weirdness is this?" However, that evening I took some psilocybin from that little bottle, sitting in a cafe on the main street in Paris. After a while we withdrew to my hotel room, where he was basically a sitter for my session.

Out of that night's experiences came my first realizations that the universe was larger than I thought, my identity was smaller than I thought, and there was something about human interaction that I had been missing.

•

If you're going to use psychedelics, do it with someone you love, and hopefully someone who has been there before you, and be aware that you may find out that the world is better than you ever thought. Beyond that, what I generally say is that it would be an awful lot better if you knew what the truth was before you worked with psychedelics. Many people beginning to use psychedelics today may be a little too young. What I learned from my own research is that psychedelics take your life experience and compost it, so that something new can grow. If you don't have much to compost, you may not get much out of it.

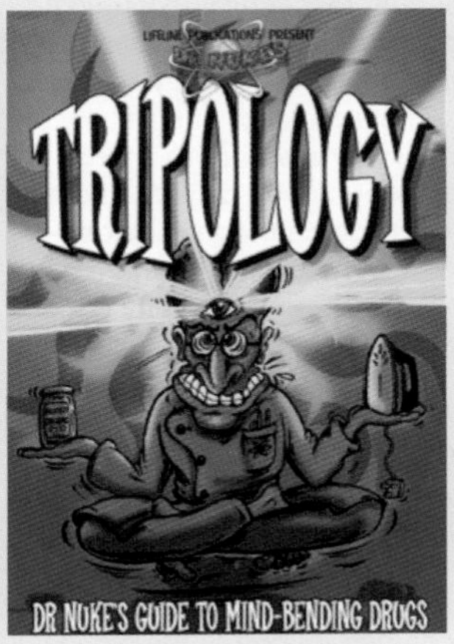

Consumer guide to drugs

Tripology

$18 Russell Newcombe, 2005, 72 p.

Because most psychedelic drugs are illegal, reliable consumer information about them is rare. For many years I have been looking for a comparative survey of available "head drugs" that would truthfully and simply provide basic info on each. What is it? What effects does it have when you take it? What's a typical dose? What is the trip like? What are the dangers, risks and side effects? I looked everywhere for this kind of information, but with no success. Most people get their info from friends of friends, and it is usually unreliable. I finally found what I was looking for in a small book published by a non-profit drug treatment and advocacy center in the UK. The thin cartoonishly illustrated booklet is aimed at young people who use drugs and it is simply stating the facts: Here's what the drug is, why people use it, and what the effects and downsides of using it are. In addition to the highs, the book realistically addresses the "costs" of use, overuse, and abuse. (Note: their discussion of the legal status is UK-based.)

This is the best consumer guide to mind-bending drugs I've seen. Don't just say No. Say Know.

-- *KK*

•

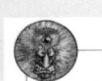

There are three types of psychedelic drugs

Cannabis	*Indole drugs*	*Methoxyamphetamines*
Cannabinoids (e.g. THC/CBN)	**LSD type drugs** **DMT type drugs** **HOT** (hydroxytryptamine) **- type drugs** (e.g. psilocin)	**MDA - type drugs** **DOM - type drugs** **TMA - type drugs** (e.g. mescaline)

There are three types of deliriant drugs

Anti-cholinergeics	*Anaesthetics*	*Solvents*
Tropane (e.g. muscarine) **Isoxazole** (e.g. muscimole)	**gas/liquid - type** (e.g. NO2/GHB) **ACH** (arylcyclohexamines) **- type drugs** (e.g. PCP/ ketamine)	**hydrocarbons** (e.g. toluene) **CFCs** (chlorofluorocarbons and other elements/ compounds)

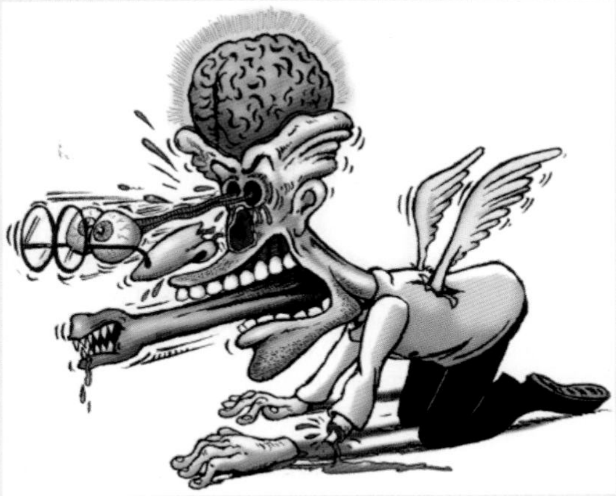

Cartoon character 'Dopin Dan' by Ted Richards

•

"I've had 200 trips and every one's been a bummer but I ain't giving up yet"

•

Other common effects [of Ketamine] include out-of-the-body (astral projection), near-death (floating down a tunnel toward light, etc.), and time-travel experiences. Like DMT, ketamine can also produce total hallucinations - though unlike DMT, it may also cause true hallucinations. Some devotees believe ketamine puts them in touch with alternative 'meta-realities', cyberspace communication systems, and intelligent disembodied entities (e.g. the 'machine elves'). However, of three famous ketamine advocates, two died while on the drug, and one (to use a technical term) went a bit bonkers.

•

Nitrous Oxide

Main effects:

After inhaling one or two canisters, effects last a minute or two; though inhaling a nitrous/air mix through a mask produces constant effects until the supply is cut. Hallmark effects include a silly deep voice (the opposite of helium), hilarity (burst of laughter), the 'eureka experience' (the feeling that you are having a brilliant idea when you are not), and a pulsating, echoey state of mind. When used with other mind-benders, it briefly magnifies their effects.

Main risks:

If inhaled direct from the canister, it's so cold that it could seriously damage the throat and lungs (like butane). Death from asphyxiation will occur if the gas is inhaled continuously with no air breathed. A safe location is also needed on laughing gas (e.g. on sofa or floor) -- in case you pass out or fall over. If someone has had too much, in addition to appearing unconscious or unresponsive, their lips and maybe face will look blueish. Clearly, it's best not to smoke or hold drinks or anything sharp when inhaling laughing gas. Regular use can lead to vitamin B12 deficiency.

Most complete pot growing

Marijuana Grower's Handbook

$23 Ed Rosenthal, 2010, 510 p.

For 30 years Ed Rosenthal has been advising pot growers, helping to make growing cannabis semi-legal in several states. Ed's newest book is a straight-to-the-point guide to marijuana growing indoors for the amateur. It assumes you do not have a lot of time or prior knowledge. It starts by describing different types of cannabis (indica vs sativa) as well the plant's life cycle and everything a cannabis plant needs to be happy and healthy. At the end of every chapter it reviews the main points. If you are more interested in learning about outdoor growing Jeorge Cervantes' book *Marijuana Horticulture: The Indoor Outdoor Medical Growers Bible* is a great place to start, it has a full chapter on outdoor growing which is more than enough to get you going.

-- *Evan Kahn*

$25 Marijuana Horticulture, Jorge Cervantes, 2006, 512 p.

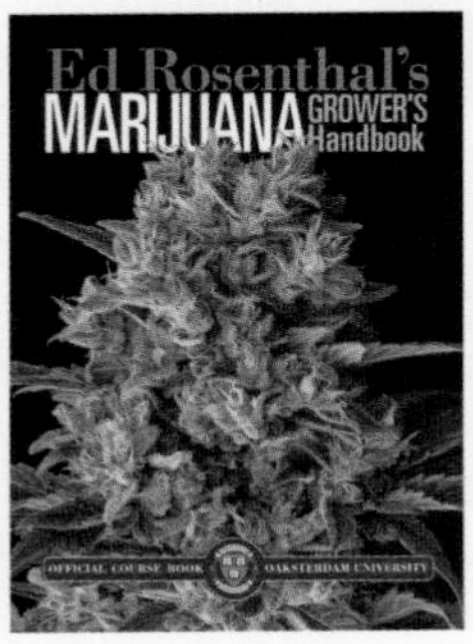

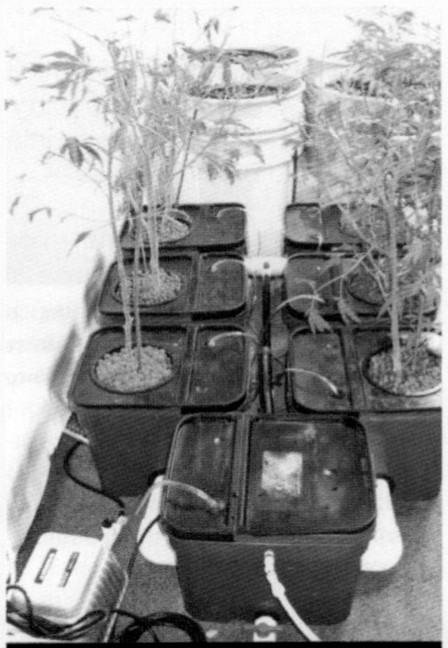

Plants thrive in this type of unit because it allows them easy access to nutrients. Active hydroponics systems oxygenate the roots through constant air circulation. The Under Current by Current Culture mixes nutrients with oxygenated water and circulates the solution under the roots throughout all the buckets.

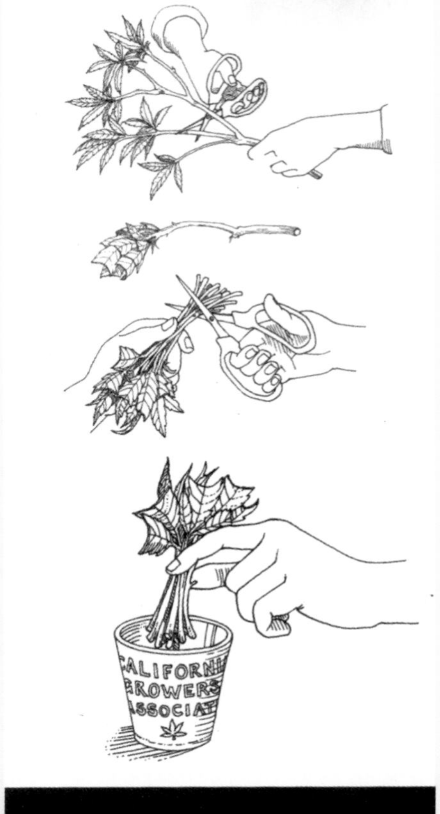

These cuttings were placed in a small styrofoam cup filled with vermiculite and water. They needed no more water before rooting; the water evaporated slowly, giving the roots more air.

Vapors

Pax Vaporizer
Pax Vaporizer
$250 Ploom

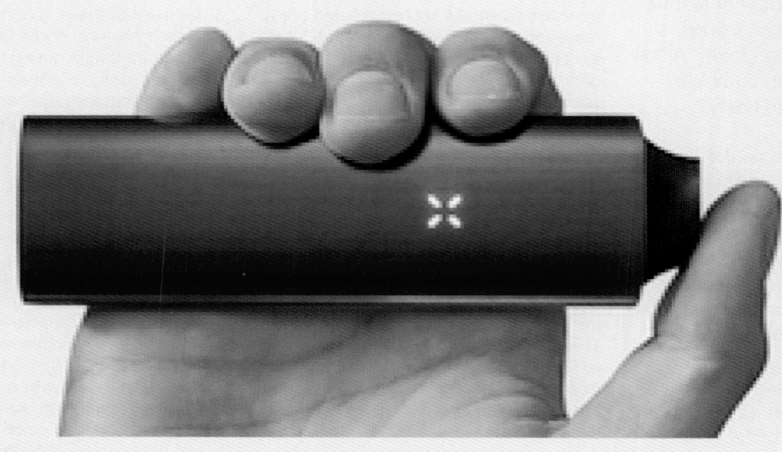

This is a portable vaporizer that works, is simple to operate, easy to clean, and looks beautiful. Vaporizers heat leaf material such as tobacco or pot so that they release their active ingredients without burning them. It's a cleaner, healthier alternative to burning something you intend to inhale. You use your lungs to draw air over a heating element that vaporizes the material. Pax's biggest draw to me is its electric heating element. I find electric works better than the butane-powered vaporizers, such as the Iolite (their new Wispr is electric, but the original model is butane) because they are a lot smaller and more discreet. I found the Pax fairly easy to figure out and very easy to use. My only criticism is that it needs cleaning frequently. Stickier stuff like weed buds are harder to clean than tobacco. The Pax is very sensitive and prone to malfunction if not cleaned regularly. But is very easy to clean if you use white vinegar.

I have had my Pax for about two weeks now and it's amazing. The Pax is a portable, battery operated (rechargeable Lithium-ion) vaporizer used for enjoying tobacco or any other loose leaf herb by vaporizing instead of smoking it. A vaporizer works by heating up the plant matter to between 370F and 410F to the vaporization temperature of the active chemicals in the plant without combusting it. The actives come off the plant material as vapor which can be inhaled, leaving behind the cellulose and less volatile chemicals. As a result you get the effect of smoking without the harmful by products such as carbon monoxide, tar and ash particulates that come from burning. It is actually hard to go back to smoking once you are used to using a vaporizer because the vapor is so clean compared to inhaling smoke. I would say that the vaporizer is the cool tool and the Pax is (in my opinion) the best vaporizer on the market.

-- Jason Weisberger

The Eterra Tulip Vaporizer
$122 lightwell.net

I am a long-time (40 years) cannabis user. Since discovering vaporizers I seldom "smoke." My lungs feel a lot better. The taste of the herb is like the essence of the flower and resin. Once the cannabinoids are vaporized, you throw out the herb. This means you're not pulling all that foliage through your lungs. It's a revolution and especially beneficial for those using herbs for medical purposes. A vaporizer that is simple and that I recommend is the Eterra Tulip. It takes a bit of getting used to, but once mastered it's rather elegant, as well as less expensive and complicated than other vaporizers:

-- Dan K. Holly

Harm-Reduction Device for People Hooked on Cigarettes
Kanger evod Electronic Cigarette
$35 evod Starter Kit Sun-vapers.com

I began smoking in the 6th grade. In the 25 years since I've quit more times than I can count — sometimes for a couple of years at a time — always to eventually return to the habit. I've tried nicotine gum (tastes terrible), nicotine patches (itched and gave me bizarre dreams), and quitting 'cold turkey' (generally unpleasant — especially for those around you!). While all of these approaches deal with the underlying nicotine addiction, none of them address the loss of the social, psychological and habitual aspects of smoking.

Several months ago I tried my first electronic cigarette, and I haven't smoked a real one since. In fact, I no longer have any desire to, and don't anticipate ever really smoking again. Electronic cigarettes satisfy both the nicotine cravings as well as the smoking habit — I actually don't feel like I've given up anything, but rather gained something new.

The technology behind electronic cigarettes is surprisingly simple. A wire coil heats up when it is connected to a battery (much like the filament in a light bulb). A wick runs through the coil and draws fluid to it; the heat from the coil turns the liquid into a vapor which you inhale — it's essentially the same technology used in fog machines, but on a much smaller scale. Because the output is water vapor, users call this "vaping" and themselves "vapers" to distinguish from "smoking" and "smokers."

The liquid starts with a base of either propylene glycol, vegetable glycerine, or a blend of the two (this is what produces the visible vapor). Nicotine is added to this in a variety of concentrations ranging from 2.4% to 0.6%, roughly corresponding to the range available from filterles down to ultra-light cigarettes. Finally, flavoring is added — the variety of available flavors is mind-boggling, with everything from traditional tobacco and menthol flavors to fruits, coffees, and dessert flavors.

The advantages of electronic cigarettes over traditional ones are numerous. There is no combustion, hence no smoke, no carbon monoxide, no tar or other carcinogens, and no risk of fire. There is no second-hand smoke, and no unpleasant smell. They can also be significantly less expensive on an ongoing basis than cigarettes — I'm currently spending about 1/3 of what I did on cigarettes.

The primary health concern of e-cigarettes would be the continued use of nicotine. Nicotine's health effects are paradoxical and are similar to caffeine in that respect — regular consumption can have both positive and negative effects depending on the individual.

One of the key benefits of electronic cigarettes though is the ability to easily regulate the amount of nicotine consumed. The various concentrations offered in liquids provide an easy way to gradually step down one's dosage if one desires. Additionally, most liquids are available in 0% nicotine concentrations, so that it is possible to entirely wean oneself from the nicotine without having to give up usage of e-cig devices.

While the underlying technology is simple, there is an incredibly wide range of hardware and types of electronic cigarettes, and it can be confusing to the first-timer trying to figure out where to start.

Like many people I started with a small "cig-alike" device which is similar in size and appearance to a traditional cigarette. The most popular brand of these is Blu, likely due to their mainstream celebrity advertising. While these work, they have several practical drawbacks. The batteries are small and need to be recharged frequently. The disposable cartridges don't last very long, can have inconsistent flavor, are relatively expensive, and limit the choice of liquids and flavors. While they are a great starting point, most users who stick with electronic cigarettes will outgrow them relatively quickly.

The next step up tends to be the Joyetech "Ego" system. These are the size of a small cigar and consist of a battery plus a refillable tank. Due to their popularity these have essentially become an industry standard, with a variety of manufacturers making compatible hardware. After trying several combinations of products from different manufacturers I've settled on the Kanger EVOD system as the best for everyday use, and it's the system I recommend to most new users.

The EVOD is relatively new and addresses several problems with earlier systems. The heating coil in the tank is at the bottom rather than the top, so that the short wicks are always immersed in fluid. This prevents the wicks from going dry and prematurely burning out the heating coil — this also makes them more compatible with thicker brands/flavors of liquids. All coils will eventually burn out though, so the EVOD has an easily replaceable and inexpensive coil unit (older systems generally require you to replace the entire tank). The EVODs are also very well made and use several o-rings to ensure that the tank won't leak.

EVOD tanks are compatible with all Ego-style batteries, so you can certainly buy the tanks ($6-10) and batteries (~$20) separately, but Kanger has just released a starter kit which includes 2 batteries, 2 tanks, 5 replacement coils and a charger for about $50 – this is a great deal if you're just starting out, and the easiest way to get into a vaping system that you're not likely to outgrow right away.

A big part of the attraction of vaping is the ability to try many flavors to find the ones that are perfect for you. In that respect it's more akin to the world of cigars or pipes than cigarettes, where it can become a bit of a hobby rather than just a habit. There are a lot of small liquid producers and importers, but it's a largely unregulated field and it can be difficult to determine the quality and source of their liquids — many of them come from China and there have been questions raised about the quality control and safety of the ingredients used.

Personally I feel it's best to stay with domestic brands who provide information on their ingredients and are committed to a high-quality product made with pharmaceutical-grade ingredients under laboratory conditions. The largest of these is Johnson Creek, and their "smoke juice" is highly regarded as one of the highest quality on the market. I've tried several of their flavors and have been very happy with them.

One of the best resources I've found for reviews of hardware, liquids and general information is Spinfuel Magazine. Unfortunately their site is a little busy and can be difficult to navigate, but their content is unbeatable; they're dedicated to being a beginner-friendly resource as well as providing useful information to more experienced vapers. They also have fairly strict guidelines about the liquid suppliers they'll review which makes it much easier to identify quality manufacturers and stay away from liquids from questionable sources.

The e-cigarette world is young and has largely been the domain of early adopters, but has grown rapidly in the past few years and looks poised to explode into mainstream awareness soon. The manufacturers and retailers have been careful not to market their products as smoking cessation devices in order to avoid being regulated as medical devices (although the FDA is due to report findings in April of this year and will likely begin to regulate the market). Nonetheless, based on my experience and the anecdotal experience of many other users online, I feel they provide the first truly effective alternative to smoking — whether you just want a healthier alternative or are looking to quit nicotine all together. Even given concerns over continued use of nicotine they provide a significant level of harm-reduction to smokers, and I think anyone who smokes owes it to themselves and their loved ones to give them a try.

-- Evan Donn

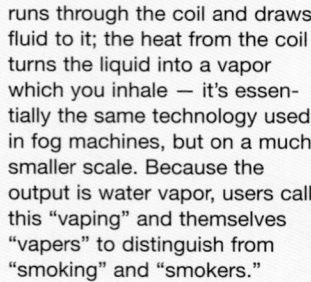

The greatest riddle of cosmology may well be that the universe is, in a sense, creative. - Karl Popper

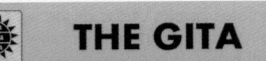

Quick intros to Hindu classics
Vedic Comic Books

$3 per episode, Amar Chitra Katha comics The Ramayana

The Vedic texts of the Hindus were among the first texts ever written, and some of the longest. The Mahabharata and Ramayana are the keystone epics and they go on and on, endless soap operas of gods, kings, loves, feuds, monsters, wars, good and evil, and spiritual lessons. The hundreds of long Indian names can exhaust a westerner's patience fast. While I lived in India I found the easiest way to get into these stories was via the cheap comic book versions sold on every newsstand. Bright colors, action-packed, simple story-line and in English, these are the same comics that tens of millions of Indian kids also start with. The true classics are published by Amar Chitra Katha, the Marvel of Vedic literature. You can purchase these graphic novels online from the importer below. Some students have scanned the entire Ramayana comic online to give you a sense of what you have been missing.

-- KK

THE GITA

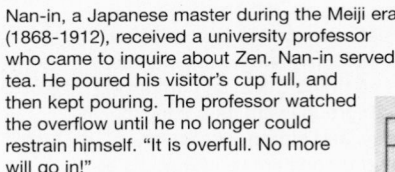

Pocket parables
Zen Flesh, Zen Bones

$11 Paul Reps, 1994, 285 p.

Zen riddles. No answers. A tiny "big joke" book.

-- KK

A Cup of Tea

Nan-in, a Japanese master during the Meiji era (1868-1912), received a university professor who came to inquire about Zen. Nan-in served tea. He poured his visitor's cup full, and then kept pouring. The professor watched the overflow until he no longer could restrain himself. "It is overfull. No more will go in!"

"Like this cup," Nan-in said, "you are full of your own opinions and speculations. How can I show you Zen unless you first empty your cup?"

The Moon Cannot Be Stolen

Ryokan, a Zen master, lived the simplest kind of life in a little hut at the foot of a mountain. One evening a thief visited the hut only to discover there was nothing in it to steal. Ryokan returned and caught him. "You may have come a long way to visit me, " he told the prowler, "and you should not return empty-handed. Please take my clothes as a gift." The thief was bewildered. He took the clothes and slunk away. Ryokan sat naked, watching the moon. "Poor fellow," he mused, " I wish I could give him this beautiful moon."

Muddy Road

Tanzan and Ekio were once traveling together down a muddy road. A heavy rain was still falling.

Coming around a bend, they met a lovely girl in a silk kimono and sash, unable to cross the intersection.

"Come on, girl," said Tanzan at once. Lifting her in his arms, he carried her over the mud.

Ekido did not speak again until that night when they reached a lodging temple. Then he no longer could restrain himself.

"We monks don't go near females," he told Tanzan, "especially not young and lovely ones. It is dangerous. Why did you do that?"

"I left the girl there," said Tanzan. "Are you still carrying her?"

Calling Card

Keichu, the great Zen teacher of the Meiji era, was the head of Tofuku, a cathedral in Kyoto. One day the governor of Kyoto called upon him for the first time.

His attendant presented the card of the governor, which read: Kitagaki, Governor of Kyoto.

"I have no business with such a fellow," said Keichu to his attendant. "Tell him to get out of here."

The attendant carried the card back with apologies. "That was my error," said the governor, and with a pencil he scratched out the words Governor of Kyoto. "Ask your teacher again."

"Oh is that Kitagaki?" exclaimed the teacher when he saw the card. "I want to see that fellow."

SHAMBHALA POCKET CLASSICS

ZEN FLESH, ZEN BONES

COMPILED BY PAUL REPS AND NYOGEN SENZAKI

Teaching the Ultimate

In early times in Japan, bamboo-and-paper lanterns were used with candles inside. A blind man, visiting a friend one night, was offered a lantern to carry home with him.

"I do not need a lantern," he said. "Darkness or light is all the same to me."

"I know you do not need a lantern to find your way, " his friend replied, "but if you don't have one, someone else may run into you. So you must take it."

The blind man started off with the lantern and before he had walked very far someone ran squarely into him. "Look out where you are going!" he exclaimed to the stranger. "Can't you see this lantern?"

"Your candle has burned out brother," replied the stranger.

Best modern translation
The Qur'an: A New Translation

$24 Thomas Cleary, 2004, 310 p.

Despite what has been said, the United States is not at war with terrorism in general, but with militant fundamental Islam; a clash of civilizations. At the heart of Islam is the Quran, and at the heart of the Quran is very difficult to translate oral poetry. Indeed Muslims often declare that the sheer beauty of the original Arabic verses is evidence of its divine origins. Translations of any sort are thus suspect, and so the English world is without great Quranic texts. Among the older, stiffer, and formal English translations, I have been unable to find a version with extensive annotations, a concordance, or even a decent modern paraphrase. For a book influencing current events to such an extant, this vacancy is a deep loss.

Your best bet to encounter the Quran — an effort I believe is essential these days — is via a recent translation by Thomas Cleary. Straightforward, unadorned, yet vibrant, this is the best modern English translation of the Quran to date.

-- KK

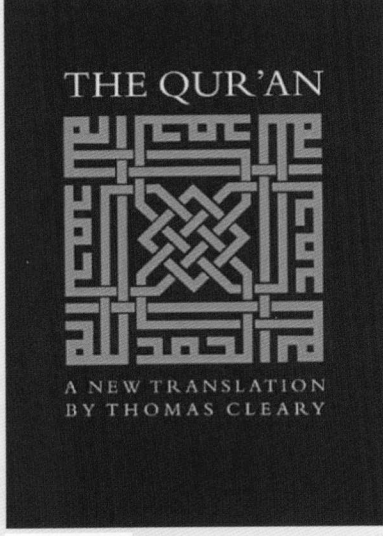

THE QUR'AN

A NEW TRANSLATION BY THOMAS CLEARY

81: The Rolling Up

In the name of God, the Benevolent, the Merciful

1. When the sun is rolled up

2. and when the stars fall lusterless

3. and when the mountains are blown away

4. and when the pregnant camels are neglected

5. and when the wild beasts are herded

6. and when the oceans are flooded

7. and when the souls are matched

8. and when the infant girl who was buried is asked

9. for what offense she was killed;

10. And when the pages are opened,

11. and when the sky is stripped

12. and when the blaze is fired up

13. and when the garden is drawn near

14. each soul will know what it has brought about.

15. Yes, I swear by the planets that recede,

16. run, and disappear,

17. and the night as it darkens

18. and the dawn as it breaks

19. that this is the word of a noble messenger,

20. endowed with power, his rank established in the presence of the Lord of the Throne

21. obeyed and faithful there.

22. So your companion is not insane –

23. he saw him on the clear horizon.

24. And he isn't grudging with the unseen;

25. and this isn't the word of an accursed devil.

26. So where are you going?

27. This is a message to all peoples,

28. for any of you who want to be upright.

29. But you won't want to unless it is the will of God, Lord of the universe.

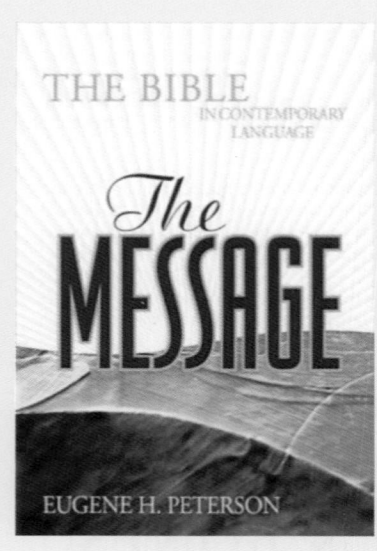

Cool Bible translation
The Message

At least once in your life you should read the Bible all the way through because it does not say what you expect it to say, no matter what you expect it to say.

Here is the translation of the Bible you want to read: The Message. This new street-wise paraphrase is looser than a translation and so irks purists. But it is storming Christian campuses and youth groups with its boldness, readability, and strong vernacular. Translated by one amazing guy, it's as far from old King James as one can imagine. For those who find the Bible warmed-over old news, The Message is like reading it for the first time.

-- KK

Genesis 1

First this: God created the Heavens and Earth — all you see, all you don't see.

Earth was a soup of nothingness, a bottomless emptiness, an inky blackness. God's Spirit brooded like a bird above the watery abyss.

•
Song of Songs 3

Restless in bed and sleepless through the night, I longed for my lover.

I wanted him desperately. His absence was painful.

So I got up, went out and roved the city, hunting through streets and down alleys.

I wanted my lover in the worst way!

I looked high and low, and didn't find him.

And then the night watchmen found me as they patrolled the darkened city.

"Have you seen my dear lost love?" I asked.

No sooner had I left them than I found him, found my dear lost love.

I threw my arms around him and held him tight, wouldn't let him go until I had him

home again, safe at home beside the fire.

Oh, let me warn you, sisters in Jerusalem, by the gazelles, yes, by all the wild deer:

Don't excite love, don't stir it up, until the time is ripe — and you're ready.

•
Matthew 6

Don't hoard treasure down here where it gets eaten by moths and corroded by rust or — worse! — stolen by burglars. Stockpile treasure in heaven, where it's safe from moth and rust and burglars. It's obvious, isn't it? The place where your treasure is, is the place you will most want to be, and end up being.

Has anyone by fussing in front of the mirror ever gotten taller by so much as an inch? All this time and money wasted on fashion — do you think it makes that much difference? Instead of looking at the fashions, walk out into the fields and look at the wildflowers. They never primp or shop, but have you ever seen color and design quite like it? The ten best-dressed men and women in the country look shabby alongside them.

If God gives attention to the appearance of wildflowers — most of which are never even seen — don't you think he'll attend to you, take pride in you, do his best for you? What I'm trying to do here is to get you to relax, to not be so preoccupied with getting, so you can respond to God's giving. People who don't know God and the way he works fuss over these things, but you know both God and how he works. Steep your life in God-reality, God-initiative, God-provisions. Don't worry about missing out. You'll find all your everyday human concerns will be met. Give your entire attention to what God is doing right now, and don't get worked up about what may or may not happen tomorrow. God will help you deal with whatever hard things come up when the time comes.

$5 Eugene H. Peterson, 2002, 2,265 pages

$80 4-CD MP3 Audio Book
Oasis Audio

The Zen of Islam
The Way of the Sufi

$12 Idries Shah, 1991, 320 p.

Sufism is the mystical third eye of Islam. The master sage Idries Shah collected esoteric stories circulating among ancient Sufi communities, translated them into very fine English, and offered them to the world in this now legendary book. Half fairy tale, half parable, half koan, these sacred wisps of wisdom can still make one shout in the desert.

– KK

•
The Dance

A disciple had asked permission to take part in the "dance" of the Sufis. The Sheikh said: "Fast completely for three days. Then have luscious dishes cooked. If you then prefer the "dance", you may take part in it."

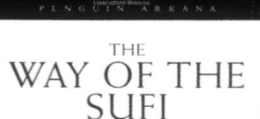

The Five Hundred Gold Pieces

One of the Junaid's followers came to him with a purse containing five hundred gold pieces.

"Have you any more money than this?" asked the Sufi.

"Yes, I have."

"Do you desire more?"

"Yes, I do."

"Then you must keep it, for you are more in need than I; for I have nothing and desire nothing. You have a great deal and still want more."

•
A Tree Freshly Rooted

A tree, freshly rooted, may be pulled up by one man on his own. Give it time, and it will not be moved, even with a crane.

•
The Test

It is related of Shaqiq of Balkh that he once said to his disciples: "I put my confidence in God and went through the wilderness with only a small coin in my pocket. I went on the Pilgrimage and came back, and the coin is still with me." One of the youths stood up and said to Shaqiq: "If you had a coin in your pocket, how could you say that you relied upon anything higher?" Shaqiq answered: "There is nothing for me to say, for this young man is right. When you rely upon the invisible world there is no place for anything, however small, as a provision!"

•
Efforts

Tie two birds together.

They will not be able to fly, even though they now have four wings.

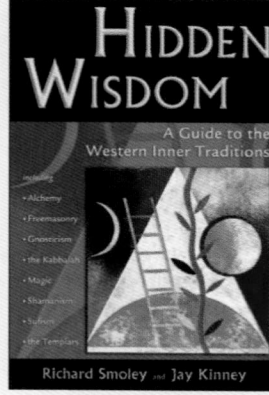

Alternative western beliefs
Hidden Wisdom

$14 Richard Smoley, 2006, 430 p.

Beyond the edges of the three major Abrahamic religions of the West, followers of hundreds of alternative religions and inner traditions have flourished in fewer numbers. These spiritual traditions don't usually have a scriptural text -- they are more based on traditions -- but they do have knowledge and insights they carry across generations. This book is the best, most understandable, one-volume introduction to these Western belief systems. It covers such notable practices as the Kabbalah, the Gnostics, alchemy, the Masons, and esoteric Christianity. It is clear and forthright on subjects often cloaked in opaque jargon and obfuscation. As best as they can, the authors point the interested to the best source materials available, so that this wisdom will be hidden no more.

-- KK

•
Jung also points out that UFOs often come in circular or cylindrical shapes, which "have always symbolized the union of opposites." Like the mandala, another circular form, they seem to symbolize the Self, not in an individual, personal sense, but in a collective one. We have, he reminds us, come to an age when "untold millions of so called Christians have lost their belief in a real and living mediator." Yet at the same time "a political, social, philosophical, and religious conflict of unprecedented proportions has split the consciousness of our age. When such tremendous opposites split asunder, we may expect with certainty that the need for a saviour will make itself felt.

Jung is saying that we as a civilization are projecting our longing for wholeness onto these "things seen in the skies." He stresses that this is a question not of individual but of collective psychology, since UFOs are "mostly seen by people who do not believe in them or who regard the whole problem with indifference."

•
The Gnostic creation myths portrayed the creator of this world as an imperfect lesser god, known as the Demiurge or Yaltabaoth, who was the inadvertent result of an attempt by Sophia (Wisdom)--a feminine facet of the true God--to experience the act of creation on her own. According to some versions of the myth, Yaltabaoth in turn created still lesser planetary rulers called Archons, and the world itself, including Man. The humanity that Yaltabaoth created was a distant echo of the divine, incapable of walking upright. Pitying humanity, Sophia

blew fragments or sparks of the divine light into Man, only to have these sparks become trapped in the material world. When Sophia came down into the world to rescue humanity and its sparks, she became trapped herself and it was only through the intervention of Christ, the Son of the Unknown God, that she was rescued.

•
The beginning of the Fama sets it out: "So that man might ... understand his own nobleness and worth, and why he is called Microcosmus, and how far his knowledge extendeth into Nature."

This passage contains two themes that sound the dominant note of the modern age. First is the idea that man might "understand his own nobleness and worth, and why he is called Microcosmus" (a microcosm of the greater universe). Second is the goal of extending human knowledge of nature. Neither of these concepts was particularly important to medieval civilization: Christianity emphasized the wretchedness of fallen man, while philosophers of the Middle Ages preferred to see the physical world as a rational, harmonious, but somewhat overschematic system, "esteeming Popery, Aristotle, and Galen ... more than the clear and manifested light of truth," as the Fama goes on to say. There was little experimental science as we know it today.

The Rosicrucian manifestos announce a different program. Human dignity will be exalted, not abased, and humanity will read directly from the "book of Nature" rather than trusting to second-hand views handed down from the old philosophers. The modern I era has begun.

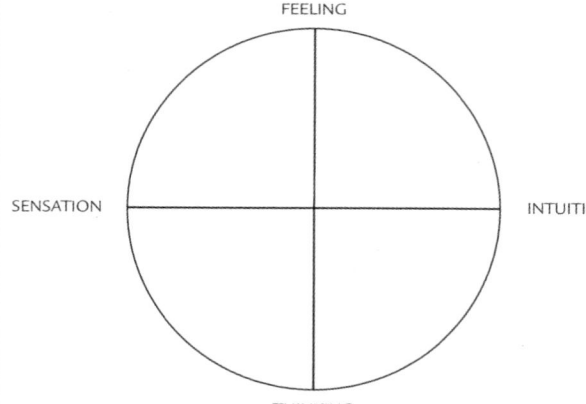

A schema of Jung's theory of types. The dominant function is the opposite to the inferior function. That is, if your thinking function is the best developed, your feeling function will be the least developed. The inferior function is also the gateway to the unconscious.

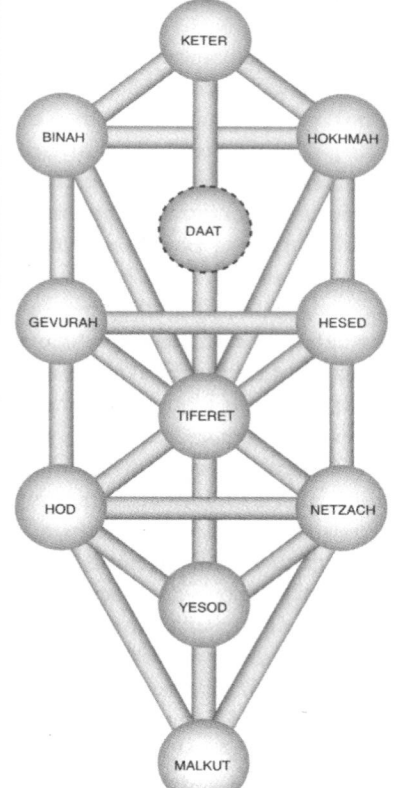

The Kabbalistic Tree of Life can be dated back to thirteenth-century Spain, though it may well be much older. The structure of the ten /sefirot/ indicates a map of the process of manifestation, beginning with Keter, "crown," and ending in Malkut, "kingdom," or material reality. But the /sefirot/ also delineate human qualities and faculties.

When it's over, I want to say: all my life I was a bride married to amazement. - Mary Oliver

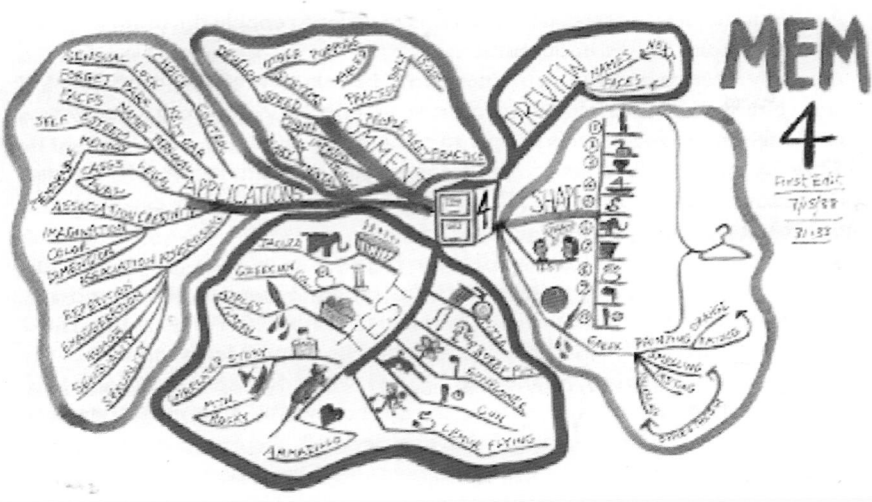

◄ *Mind Map by the well known film and video producer Dennis Harris, summarising an entire programme on Memory.*

Radial thinking
The Mind Map Book

$18 Tony Buzan with Barry Buzan, 1996, 320 p.

Mind maps are a tool for thinking. Instead of arranging your ideas in a sequence — as a list of words — you draw them in an arboreal fashion, radiating out from one starting notion. Mind maps use pictures instead of words, radial branches instead of linear lists, starfish instead of ladders, and associations instead of priorities — and as a result you think different. The visual trees you generate as you mind map mirror the dendritic nature of our brain, and seem to flow more organically and (after practice) with less effort than the rigid discipline of making 1,2,3 textual notes.

They are easy to doodle. Anyone can make them. Kids and CEOs as well as creative types. I've come to employ this style of radial association in my own note taking and personal brainstorming. You don't need this book to do it, but the book will help you refine your style, and it will help you expend its use. The authors, who've been perfecting and evangelizing this technique for decades, offer advice on how to use mind maps to teach, as a form of diary, and most importantly, as a group exercise, say in corporate brainstorming sessions.

There are software programs for mind mapping (which I have not tried), but for me the intensely kinetic mode of drawing ideas (if even on tiny scratch paper) is a great part of the technique's ability to produce new and different perspectives.

-- KK

•
Always use a central image

An image automatically focuses the eye and the brain. It triggers numerous associations and is astoundingly effective as a memory aid. In addition an image is attractive – on many levels. It attracts you, it pleases you and it draws your attention to itself.

If a particular word (rather than an image) is absolutely central to your Mind Map, the word can be made into an image by using dimension, multiple colours, and attractive form.

Use images throughout your mind map

Using images wherever possible gives all the benefits described above, as well as creating a stimulating balance between your visual and linguistic cortical skills, and improving your visual perception.

▲ Variation in size is the best way of indicating the relative importance of items in a hierarchy. Expanded size adds emphasis, thereby increasing the probability of recall.

•

VERY UNHAPPY AFTERNOON

Standard phrase noting, which at first glance appears adequate, but which contains dangerous inaccuracies.

In order to develop a truly personal Mind Mapping style, you should follow the '1+' rule. This means that every Mind Map you do should be slightly more colourful, slightly more three dimensional, slightly more imaginative, slightly more associatively logical, and/or slightly more beautiful than the last.

Progression of noting a 'very unhappy afternoon' in which application of the Mind Map laws brings the noter much closer to the truth.

The Mind Map is an expression of Radiant Thinking and is therefore a natural function of the human mind. It is a powerful graphic technique which provides a universal key to unlocking the potential of the brain. The Mind Map can be applied to every aspect of life where improved learning and clearer thinking will enhance human performance. The Mind map has four essential characteristics:

a) The subject of attention is crystallised in a central image.

Dr. Stanley with the 25-foot long Boeing Aircraft Mind Map.

b) The main themes of the subject radiate from the central image as branches.

c) Branches comprise a key image or key word printed on an associated line. Topics of lesser importance are also represented as branches attached to higher level branches.

d) The branches form a connected nodal structure.

Mind Maps are particularly useful for chairing meetings. The chairperson has the agenda on a basic Mind Map and can use this fundamental frame to add thoughts, guide discussions, and record the basic outline of the what will eventually be the minutes of the meeting. Colour coding can be used to indicate action, ideas, question marks, and important areas. Chairing a meeting this way allows the person in the chair to be much like a captain of a starship guiding it safely through the clusters and galaxies of ideas.

Maybe you would find a coffee shop a wee bit intimidating? I know i like a private place to work when digging deep into those personal thoughts. So maybe you have come back home, found some quiet music on a radio, sat down

in that big easy chair, and have begun contemplating all those big, white, and very empty journal pages again. Kinda scary huh? Well try not to panic.

You see, your mind will be saying obnoxious things like this: 1. WHAT MAKES YOU THINK YOU HAVE ANYTHING WORTHWHILE TO SAY? 2. THERE'S NOTHING SPECIAL ABOUT YOUR OLD HUMDRUM LIFE THAT WARRANTS DOCUMENTATION. 3. WHO SAID YOU WERE A WRITER ANYWAY? DON'T EMBARRASS YOURSELF. Well, well, that's all real interesting, Mr. Brain. Fortunately we have decided to send you off on sabbatical for awhile and will instead be using our hearts to fill these pages. Heh. Heh.

On hearing this news your heart may begin to beat wildly. It will greatly appreciate you considering it worthy. Goose bumps may appear

3

up and down your spine. And given this new task, the heart says things like this: 1. MY THOUGHTS, DEEDS, AND DOINGS ARE WHO I AM TRYING TO BE, AND EACH ONE IS A GIFT THAT DOES WARRANT RECORDING. 2. IF I GROW TIRED OF SELF-EXAMINATION, ALL I NEED DO IS LIFT MY EYES AND BEHOLD THE BEAUTY OF OUR GLORIOUS WORLD. 3. WRITING DOWN MY OWN THOUGHTS WILL BE THE EASIEST THING IN THE WORLD TO DO BECAUSE I'LL BE EXPRESSING MY OWN INNERMOST FEELINGS, AND ONLY I KNOW WHAT THOSE ARE.

So go ahead and scribble. At first you may dislike your seemingly pretentious babbling. But hey, great novels are not written over night. Try to do some writing and remember to listen only to your heart, not your head. Then have a cookie.

4

An essential life skill
How to Make a Journal of Your Life

$9 Daniel Price, 1999, 116 p.

Most people take journaling either way too serious, or not serious enough. For such a key lifeskill it should be more like you — expressive, idiosyncratic, unique. This tiny chapbook is the best guide I know of to get you started in journaling, and keep you going. Hand drawn with inspiration, it properly emphasizes the value of graphic thinking in the examined life. It is wise, brief, and

fun. I've given one copy to each of my kids. Although it does not mention blogging, and assumes you'll use a notebook, I think every blogger and blogger-hopeful should read it.

-- KK

76

"A pungoine and revolutionary work." —ANAÏS NIN

the NEW diary

Tristine Rainer

Best journaling wisdom
The New Diary

$13 Tristine Rainer, 1979, 320 p.

A diary begins in the same direction as a blog or Facebook but goes deeper and further. A diary or journal is less a thing and more a process. The thing is a notebook, sketchbook, or a blank screen; the process is discovery, and self knowledge.

I have not met a serious artist, scientist, inventor, or creative instigator who did not rely on a journal and notebook as a fundamental tool of discovery. I know I depend on journals. If schools were wise they'd teach this process; This classic book would be the textbook. It is by far the best guide ever written to exploring the benefits of cultivating a functioning diary.

First written in 1970s after 12 years of research and experience, it was updated in 2004. I am amazed at the author's depth of insight into human nature, and the natural power that can be unleashed by deliberate journaling. Forget about superficial diaries and calendars; a deep journal is among of the most potent medicine on Earth. It is a magic mirror.

Write out yourself. And give a blank book and this brilliant guide to a friend.

-- KK

• Paul Gauguin, the painter, began his intimate journal with the phrase, "This is not a book." He repeated the line frequently throughout the journal to remind himself that writing a diary is not like writing a book or any other form of literature. Gauguin wanted to write his diary as he painted his pictures, dabbing a few experi-

mental colors at first, adding more as his intuition told him, following his fancy, "following the moon," discovering the pattern from what had occurred by chance.

• When asked how to write a diary by those just beginning, I generally respond: "Write fast, write everything, include everything, write from your feelings, write from your body, accept whatever comes." That is often all the guidance they need.

• Even if you never share a sentence of your diary with anyone else, however, you will share it through your life. Its existence will touch other people by the way it changes you and permits you to develop in self-awareness, directness, and honesty. As you acquire and refine the talent for helping yourself in the diary, you will also grow in your ability to understand and nourish others. While it permits you to take responsibility for your own emotional well-being,

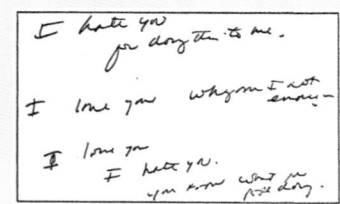

it also opens the way for a deep understanding of human nature. As Anais Nin has said, "The personal life deeply lived always expands into truths beyond itself."

• The importance of the diary in these cases is not as a product--a point I can't repeat too often--but in the life that is freed from excessive anger, confusion, and grief. Putting the pain in the diary keeps it from destroying a life. The life liberated from such destructive emotions is the true "product" of this purgative process.

• Sometimes reflection takes the form of speaking directly to the self, of giving advice, encouragement, or bits of philosophic wisdom. I call this self-helping, healing, guiding voice the Silver-Lining Voice of the diary, since it often appears in times of stress as a voice of hope. At first it may speak in adages, such as "Keep on trying. Don't give up," or "You have to believe in yourself." As it is allowed to be

Four Natural Modes of Expression	Seven Special Techniques
Catharsis	List
Description	Portrait
Free-Intuitive Writing	Map of Consciousness
Reflection	Guided Imagery
	Altered Point of View
	Unsent Letter
	Dialogue

heard and to develop, it can expand into the most important guide in your life--your voice of inner wisdom.

• **Guided Imagery** Guided imagery, like catharsis, free-intuitive writing, and maps of consciousness, taps the right side of the brain--the feeling, intuitive, imaging side. Doing guided imagery is very much like daydreaming and recording in your diary what images appear on the screen of your mind. Some people see distinct images, as if they were watching a movie on the insides of their eyelids. But many people have much less distinct visual impressions and seem to hear an inner storyteller describing the fantasy.

Guided imagery used in this positive way is one of the highest forms of self-nourishment. It is actually a written form of meditation, with all the benefits generally associated with meditation--relaxation, clarity, elevation of mental outlook, heightened consciousness, and sensory awareness. Experimenters have documented the success of guided imagery for inducing mental and physical relaxation, and the effectiveness of imaging a nurturing fantasy figure for helping with creative problem solving.

The most valuable use for guided imagery I have discovered through offering journal workshops to everyone from officers in the U.S. Air Force to recovering women in drug rehab, from college professors to parents of special needs children, is the visualization of one's figure of Inner Wisdom, followed by a dialogue with that imaged figure. You begin by putting yourself into a state of relaxation. In the beautiful, safe place that you created, see yourself sitting on a bench with your eyes closed. You sense that your figure of Inner Wisdom comes and sits next to you. You open your eyes and see what your figure looks like.

When you pick up your pen to write in your journal, describe your figure of Inner Wisdom, his or her face and hair and what he or she is wearing. Remember, for some people writing guided imagery feels more like making up a story than seeing and recording clear images.

• That night I entered the date June 27, 1958, as if I were writing in my old Betty Betz diary. I allowed myself to use the unsure, childish script I had written in when I was thirteen. These alterations in point of view permitted me to re-create an entry from my old diary, which I think must be very close to the original.

I was so excited by the accuracy of tone achieved through changing the date and my handwriting that I subsequently wrote other entries from the perspective of my thirteen-year-old self. Gradually, through

altered point of view, I was able to reconstruct much of the diary I had destroyed in my childhood.

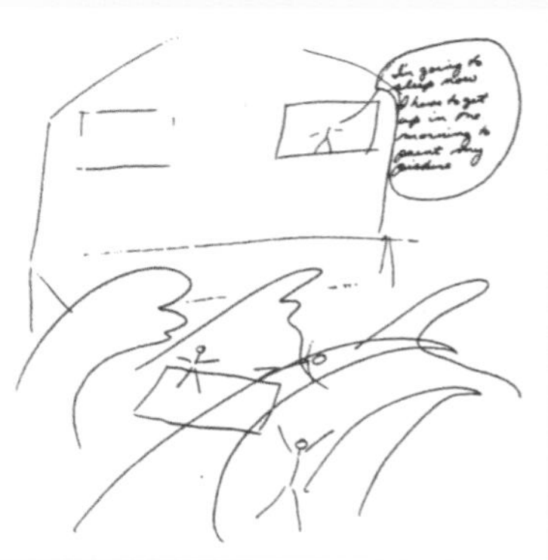

• Diaries are a bridge between dreams and the waking life, a space of your own creation where the subconscious and the conscious mind meet and inform each other. Through the diary the dreaming self can deliver its messages to the waking self. And through the diary you can walk awake into your dreams to observe, learn, and bring back images, insights, and creative ideas that will enrich your life.

• The benefit of isolating dream themes is achieved in the New Diary by titling dreams as you record them alongside waking thoughts. If you put a box around your dream titles or write your dreams in red ink or otherwise distinguish them, you can later read through the dreams alone as in a dream log. The added benefit is that the night dream and the day life remain side by side. You can tap the emotional energy and intuitive wisdom of a dream when it first delivers its message. In retrospect you can see even more patterns and interconnections, and you can also observe to what extent you successfully listened to and answered your dreams in your waking life.

• For example, to stimulate dreaming, before you go to sleep tell yourself: "I want to

remember my dreams," or address the dream directly, "Dreaming Self, send me a dream," or use whatever phrase feels comfortable to you. If you invoke dreams for three nights in a row, generally you will recall a dream by the fourth night. I repeat my phrase three times just to make sure my dreaming self hears me. Once dream recall begins you can invoke specific kinds of dreams by asking your dreaming self before you fall asleep: "Send me a flying dream" or "Help with this problem, please."

• **The Diary as Time Machine**

People who keep diaries inevitably become aware of time as one of life's ineffable mysteries. Some of them even become time travelers, unhooked from the limitations of time and place that confine most people. The diary becomes a time machine that takes them into the past-where they can learn who they are by understanding where they have come from. And it takes them into the future-where they can clarify their goals and discover their destination.

• Through written recollections you can gain self-knowledge, release delayed or repressed emotions, find hidden misconceptions that have influenced your self-image, forgive past offenses. You can imaginatively explore the roads taken and not taken in your past to discover present fulfillment as well as future options.

• You might also use childhood photos as an aid in sparking recollection. For example, you might have a photo of yourself at a birthday party about which you remember nothing. By analyzing the photo carefully, as Dr. Robert Akeret suggests in his book *Photoanalysis*, you can gain a sense of who you were at that moment. Are you touching anyone in the photo or do you seem aloof? Are you hiding behind someone else or are you the center of attention? Can you imagine what you were feeling? The body language in the photo can tell you a story about your past.

After sketching this map of consciousness I wrote a reflective entry:

The house I drew looks rather like a face, and the woman is in the right "eye." Maybe that corresponds to my "right brain," the intuitive, creative, image-making part of my self. But in the dream I identified with the figure trying to stay on the raft, and in the drawing that figure is closer to me. I feel like that scared figure, plummeted around wildly by my emotions, almost gasping for air. The woman in the window is far "above me," what I aspire to, illumination, self-discipline, creativity. But I am she if I wish, because I went to sleep, dreamt this dream, and woke up and sketched it.

Guide to unobvious, inherent meanings
Dictionary of Symbols

$17 Jean Chevalier & Alain Gheerbrant, 1996 (current translation), 1184 p.

THE PENGUIN DICTIONARY OF Symbols

In art, literature, film and life, even the littlest image or reference can open a world of interpretation. This thick encyclopedia, with contributions from scholars in various disciplines, is an excellent guide to the major and more esoteric origins of seemingly everything — from "abracadabra" to "Zodiac." There are a ton of spiritual, mythological and/or cultural tangents that hopscotch the globe and back in time. Whenever I pick it up, I learn something new. I find the animal and food-related facts particularly enlightening (ex; oranges, a fertility symbol, are given to young married couples in Vietnam; and in Ancient China a formal offer of marriage was accompanied by a gift of oranges

to the girl). The book's title is somewhat misleading. It does not have illustrations — it's all text. Some entries are a couple sentences, others stretch for a few pages. If you have plans to deconstruct the next season of Lost, you might find this one handy.

-- KK

• **almond (Italian: mandorla)**

Because of its husk, the almond is generally taken to symbolize the substance hidden within its accidents; spirituality masked by dogma and ritual; reality concealed by outward appearance; and, according to the secret doctrine, the eternally hidden Truth, Treasure and Fountain… The almond is Christ because his divine nature was hidden in the human, or in the womb of his virgin mother. In esoteric tradition the almond symbolizes the secret (a treasure) which is hidden in some dark place and which must be discovered in order to nourish the finder. The husk around it is compared with a wall or a gate. To find the almond or to eat the almond means to discover or to share in a secret.

• **otter**

The otter, which rises to the surface of the water and then dives below it, posses lunar symbolism and

from this derive the properties for which it is used in initiation. Otter-skin is used in initiation societies both among North American Indians and among Black Africans, especially the Bantu of Cameroon and Gabon… The shamans of the North American Ojibwa Indians keep their magic shells in an otter-skin bag. The messenger of the Great Spirit, who acts as intercessor between him and mankind, is supposed to have seen the wretched state of human weakness and disease and to have revealed the most sublime secrets to the otter and interfused its body with Migis (symbols of the Mide or members of the Midewiwin Medicine Lodge) so that the creature became immortal and could, by initiating humans, make them holy. All members of the Midewiwin carry otter-skin medicine bags. These are the bags which are aimed at the candidate at initiation ceremonies as if they were fire-arms and 'kill' him. They are then laid on his body until he is restored to life. After song and feasting the shamans present the new initiate with his own otter-skin bag. The otter is therefore an initiating spirit which kills and restores to life.

• **liver**

The liver is commonly linked to outbursts of rage, the gall, from the bitter taste of bile, to animosity and to deliberately spiteful designs. Whatever the culture, there are few meanings without some similarity with the foregoing, Islam attributing the passions to the liver and suffering to the gall… 'Dragon's gall' is contrasted with wine as the opposite to the drink of life.

The Suwen, the basic treatise on Chinese traditional medicine, states that the gall has a bitter taste and a green tinge. It states that the liver generates strength… In Ancient China it was customary to eat the livers of one's enemies. Not to do so would have been to cast doubts upon their valour which the eater believed he assimilated.

• **genius**

In most ancient traditions and under a variety of different names, a 'genius' was believed to be the companion of every human being, as double, demon, guardian angel, counselor, intuition or supra-rational voice of conscience. The genius symbolizes the flash of enlightenment which, uncontrolled, engenders the deepest and strongest convictions. Immanent in every individual, physical or moral, the genius symbolizes the spiritual being… In Dogon tradition, the Nommo, eight little people, represent the eight genii who were the ancestors of mankind. They are often carved as the legs of thrones, chairs or stools. Their limbs and bodies need to be supple 'as befits the genii of water, essentially protective spirits, in dry savannah country.' They revealed to mankind the laws which the gods had given to regulate human activity… They are regarded as archetypal of the social order imposed by God.

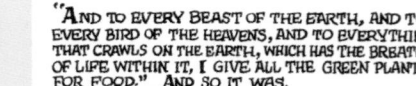

Underground Bible

The Book of Genesis Illustrated
$19 R. Crumb, 2009, 224 p.

As literature, the biblical book of Genesis has it all: sex, violence, angels, war, murder, heroes, incest, world-wide disasters, spooky mystery, and a timeless story. All it needed was illustrations by the comic genius R. Crumb and you'd have an underground manga hit. And that's what this book is. Crumb brilliantly did not alter or omit any words from the scriptural text, and even toned down his drawings to a PG-13 rating. But man, is this strong drink. It will burn your eyelashes. Like it must have done 2,000 years ago. Now you have absolutely no excuse not to read the first book of the Bible.

-- KK

Paradox

The recursive point of view
Oxymoronica
$11 Marty Grothe, 2004, 256 p.

At the bottom of reality lies a paradox: self-created creation, either the universe or God. This conundrum of self-causation afflicts all life and consciousness and great art. Occasionally the recursive nature of our existence is captured by a simple witty loop. Here is a fine collection of hundreds of highly evolved self-cancelling/self-generating circuits, called oxymoronics. This handsome and intelligent book is classic cybernetics. I use these witticisms as meditative koans.

-- KK

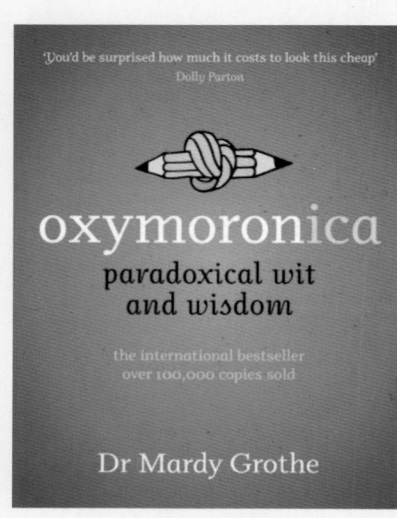

An oxymoron has been wisely described as "a compressed paradox." Looking at it the other way around, I think of a paradox as "an extended oxymoron." To me, they're close cousins because they both link up contradictory or incongruous elements. And they both play around in the most fascinating way with the difference between literal truth and figurative truth. For this reason, I include both oxymoronic and paradoxical observations (and a few others, as you shall soon see) under the rubric of oxymoronica.

- The superfluous is the most necessary.
-- Voltaire

- Always remember that you are absolutely unique. Just like everyone else.
-- Margaret Mead

- I shut my eyes in order to see.
-- Paul Gauguin

- We learn from history that we do not learn from history.
-- Georg Hegel

- We are never prepared for what we expect.
-- James Michener

- To be believed, make the truth unbelievable.
-- Napoleon Bonaparte

- The final delusion is the belief that one has lost all delusions.
-- Maurice Chapelain

- When a dog runs at you, whistle for him.
-- Henry David Thoreau

- What we really want is for things to remain the same but get better.
-- Sydney J. Harris

- Always be sincere, even if you don't mean it.
-- Harry S. Truman

- Man can believe the impossible, but can never believe the improbable.
-- Oscar Wilde

- War is a series of catastrophes which result in a victory.
-- Georges Clemenceau

- First I dream my painting, then I paint my dream.
-- Vincent van Gogh

- We are confronted by insurmountable opportunities.
-- Walt Kelly, From Pogo

- A man chases a woman until she catches him.
-- Anonymous

- I want peace and I'm willing to fight for it.
-- Harry S. Truman

- Study the past, if you would divine the future.
-- Confucius, in Analects

- Love is a kind of warfare.
-- Ovid

- All works of art should begin...at the end.
-- Edgar Allan Poe

-

How to live
Finite and Infinite Games
$36 James P. Carse, 1987, 192 p.

The wisdom held in this brief book now informs most of what I do in life. Its key distinction–that there are two types of games, finite and infinite–resolves my uncertainties about what to do next. Easy: always choose infinite games. The message is appealing because it is deeply cybernetic, yet it's also genuinely mystical. I get an "aha" every time I return to it.

-- KK

- A finite game is played for the purpose of winning, an infinite game for the purpose of continuing the play.

- Finite players play within boundaries; infinite players play with boundaries.

- To be prepared against surprise is to be trained. To be prepared for surprise is to be educated.

- The death of an infinite player is dramatic. It does not mean that the game comes to an end with death; on the contrary, infinite players offer their death as a way of continuing the play. For that reason they do not play for their own life; they live for their own play.

- I can be powerful only by not playing, by showing that the game is over.

- Infinite players do not oppose the actions of others, but initiate actions of their own in such a way that others will play by initiating their own.

- Evil is the termination of infinite play.

- No one can play a game alone.

- There is but one infinite game.

Strange loops
Godel, Escher, Bach
$16 Douglas R. Hofstadter, 1999, 824 p.

I consider this one-of-a-kind book to be the seminal introduction to our age, to this axial moment in the history of our species when we rediscovered the centrality of the non-material -- information, ideas, bits, knowledge, rationality and thought. All these make the material abundance celebrated here in the book you are reading. Yet we have no idea (that word again!) what these non-materials really are. It was the author of this astounding book who first made it very clear with wit and riddles that each of these things are not-things yet they make things, and that each was comprised of a necessary paradox, a strange loop that produced something from nothing; and furthermore, these strange recursive loops underpin *everything* we find interesting and important in the world, from nature, art, mathematics, machines, intelligence, consciousness to life itself. If there will be born a new religion in this era sprung from this language of the emergent, we will be its gods, and this will be its gospel.

-- KK

- At the core of dualism, according to Zen, are words -- just plain words. The use of words is inherently dualistic, since each word represents, quite obviously, a conceptual category. Therefore, a major part of Zen is the fight against reliance on words. To combat the use of words, one of the best devices is the koan, where words are so deeply abused that one's mind is practically left reeling, if one takes koans seriously. Therefore it is perhaps wrong to say that the enemy of enlightenment is logic; rather, it is perception. As soon as you perceive an object, you draw a line between it and the rest of the world; you divide the world, artificially into parts, and you thereby miss the Way.

Here is a short section of one of the Crab's Genes, turning round and round. When the two DNA strands are unraveled and laid out side by side, they read this way:

TTTTTTTTTCGAAAAAAAAA .

AAAAAAAAAGCTTTTTTTTT.

Notice that they are the same, only one goes forwards while the other goes backwards. This is the defining property of the form called "crab canon" in music. It is reminiscent of, though a little different from, a palindrome, which is a sentence that reads the same backwards and forwards. In molecular biology, such segments of DNA are called "palindromes"— a slight misnomer, since "crab canon" would be more accurate.

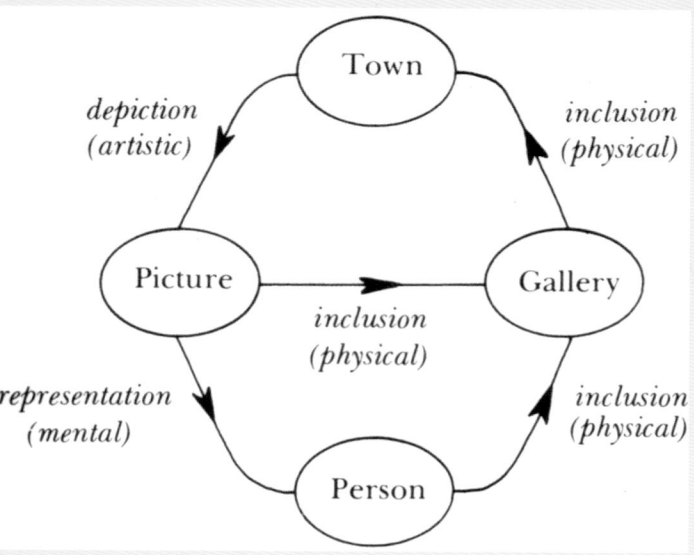

Abstract diagram of M.C. Escher's Print Gallery.

A strikingly beautiful, and yet at the same time disturbingly grotesque, illustration of the cyclonic of a Tangled Hierarchy is given to us by Escher in his Print Gallery. What we see is a picture gallery where a young man is standing, looking at a picture of a ship in the harbor of a small town, perhaps a Maltese town, to guess from the architecture, with its little turrets, occasional cupolas, and flat stone roofs, upon one of which sits a boy, relaxing in the heat, while two floors below him a woman perhaps his mother gazes out of the window from her apartment which sits directly above a picture gallery where a young man is standing, looking at a picture of a ship in the harbor of a small town, perhaps a Maltese town -- What!? We are back on the same level as we began, though all logic dictates that we cannot be. Let us draw a diagram of what we see. What this diagram shows is three kinds of in-ness. The gallery is physically in the town (inclusion); the town is artistically in the picture (depiction); the picture is mentally in the person (representation).

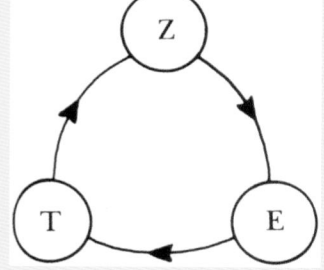

There are three authors -- Z, T, and E. Now it happens that Z exists only in a novel by T. Likewise, T exists only in a novel by E. And strangely, E. too, exists only in a novel -- by Z, of course. Now, is such an "authorship triangle" really possible?

Index to Tools

Found alphabet by KK

If you are not embarrassed by the first version of your product, you've launched too late. - Reid Hoffman

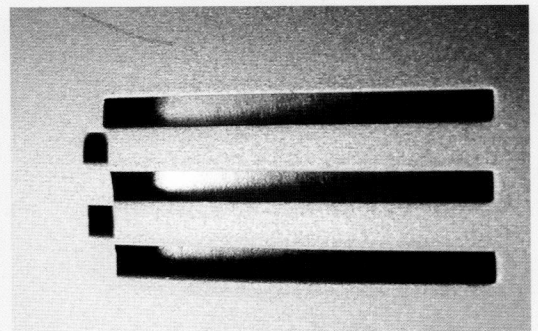

A problem is a chance for you to do your best. - Duke Ellington

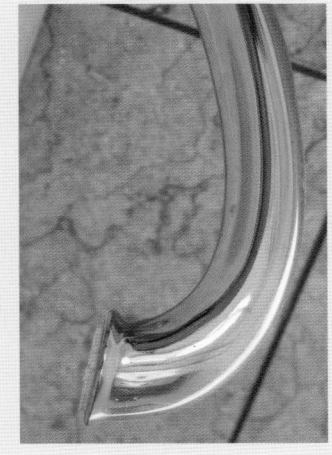

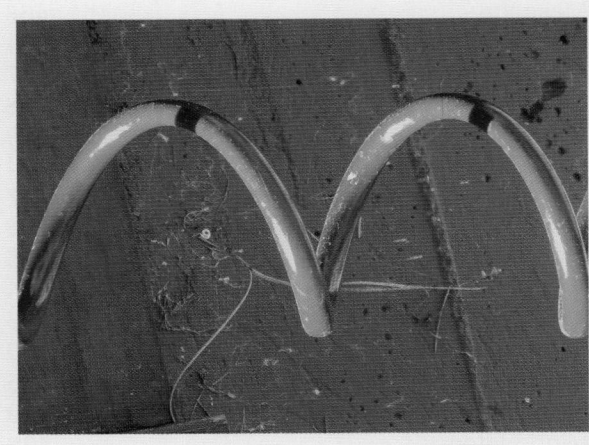

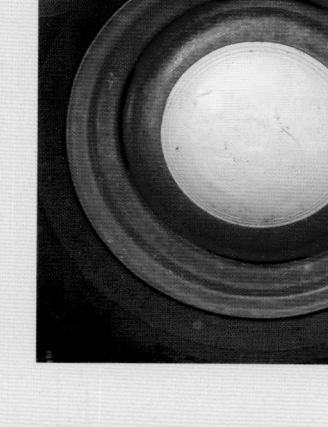

Set a goal so big that you can't achieve it until you grow into the person who can. - Anon

Invention is the mother of necessities. - Marsall McLuhan

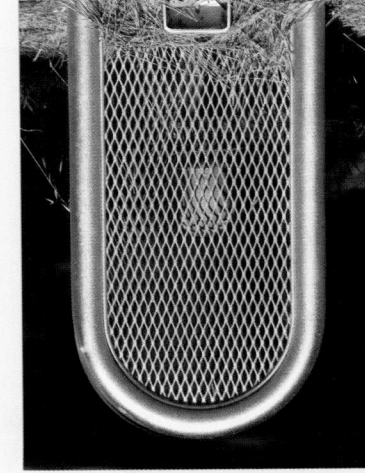

Creativity is not a talent. It is a way of operating. - John Cleese

471

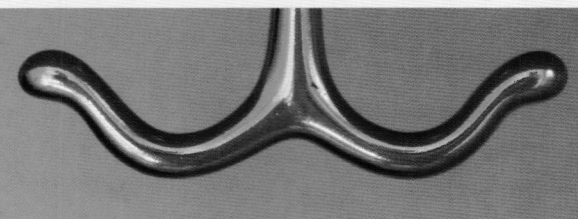

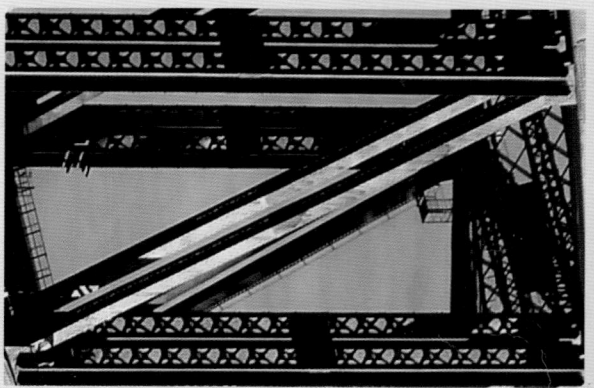

Notice from the management: You have more tools, supplies and materials for the road ahead than you have road ahead. Finish something. - Anon